# THE NEW
## INTERNATIONAL
# WEBSTER'S
# POCKET
# DICTIONARY
## OF THE ENGLISH LANGUAGE

━━━━━━━ ◆◆◆ ━━━━━━━

TRIDENT
PRESS
INTERNATIONAL

Published by

Trident Press International

1998 EDITION

Cover Design Copyright © Trident Press International
Copyright © 1997 Ferguson Publishing Company, Entries taken from
WEBSTER CONTEMPORARY DICTIONARY, ILLUSTRATED EDITION, Copyright © 1992
Compiled by Eileen Bailey 1997

ISBN 1-888-777-15-X Deluxe Edition
ISBN1-888-777-25-7 Hardcover Edition
ISBN1-888-777-33-8 Paperback Edition

Printed in Slovenia by DELO Tiskarna d.d.

# A

**ab·a·cus** (ab′ə·kəs) *n. pl.* **cus·es** or **·ci** (-sī) **1** A calculating device with counters sliding on wires or in grooves. **2** *Archit.* A slab forming the top of a capital. [L<Gk. *abax* counting table]

**a·ban·don** (ə·ban′dən) *v.t.* **1** To desert; forsake. **2** To surrender or give up. **3** To yield (oneself) without restraint, as to a feeling or pastime. —*n.* Utter surrender to one's feelings or natural impulses. [< OF *a bandon* under one's own control]. —**a·ban′don·er**, **a·ban′don·ment** *n.*

**a·base** (ə·bās′) *v.t.* **a·based**, **a·bas·ing** To humiliate, humble, or degrade. [< L *ad-* to + LL *bassus* low] —**a·bas·ed·ly** (ə·bā′sid·lē) *adv.* —**a·bas′ed·ness**, **a·base′ment**, **a·bas′er** *n.*

**a·bate** (ə·bāt′) *v.* **a·bat·ed**, **a·bat·ing** *v.t.* **1** To make less; reduce in quantity, degree, force, etc. **2** To deduct. **3** *Law* **a** To put an end to. **b** To annul. —*v.i.* **4** To become less, as in strength, degree, force, etc.: After six hours, the storm *abated*. [<L *ad-* to + *batuere* to beat] —**a·bat′a·ble** *adj.* —**a·bate′ment**, **a·bat′er** *n.*

**ab·at·toir** (ab′ə·twär′) *n.* A slaughterhouse. [F]

**ab·bey** (ab′ē) *n. pl.* **ab·beys 1** A monastery under the jurisdiction of an abbot or a convent under an abbess. **2** The church or buildings of an abbey.

**ab·bot** (ab′ət) *n.* The superior of a community of monks. [< LGk. *abbas* < Aramaic *abba* father] —**ab′bot·cy**, **ab′bot·ship** *n.*

**ab·bre·vi·ate** (ə·brē′vē·āt) *v.t.* **·at·ed**, **·at·ing 1** To condense or make briefer. **2** To shorten, as a word or expression, esp. by omission or contraction. [< L *ad-* to + *breviare* shorten] —**ab·bre′vi·a′tor** *n.*

**ab·bre·vi·a·tion** (ə·brē′vē·ā′shən) *n.* **1** A shortened form or contraction, as of a word or phrase. **2** A making shorter, or the state of being shortened. **3** *Music* A notation indicating repeated notes, chords, etc., by a single symbol.

**ab·di·cate** (ab′də·kāt) *v.* **·cat·ed**, **·cat·ing** *v.t.* **1** To give up formally; renounce, as a throne, power, or rights. —*v.i.* **2** To surrender or relinquish a throne, a right, responsibility, etc. [< L *ab-* away + *dicare* proclaim] —**ab·di·ca·ble** (ab′di·kə·bəl), **ab′di·ca′tive** *adj.* —**ab′di·ca′tion**, **ab′di·ca′tor** *n.*

**ab·do·men** (ab′də·mən, ab·dō′mən) *n.* **1** In mammals, the visceral cavity between the diaphragm and the pelvic floor; the belly. **2** In vertebrates other than mammals, the region or cavity that contains the viscera. **3** In insects, crabs, etc., the hindmost part of the body. [< L] —**ab·dom·i·nal** (ab·dom′ə·nəl) *adj.* —**ab·dom′i·nal·ly** *adv.*

**ab·duct** (ab·dukt′) *v.t.* **1** To carry away wrongfully, as by force or fraud; kidnap. **2** To draw (a part of the body) away from the median axis of the body or from a neighboring part. [< L *ab-* away + *ducere* lead] —**ab·duc′tion**, **ab·duc′tor** *n.*

**ab·er·ra·tion** (ab′ə·rā′shən) *n.* **1** Deviation from a right, customary, prescribed, or natural course or condition. **2** Partial mental derangement.

**a·bey·ance** (ə·bā′əns) *n.* Suspension or temporary inaction. Also **a·bey′an·cy**. [< OF *abaer* to gape at, yearn for]. —**a·bey′ant** *adj.*

**ab·hor** (ab·hôr′) *v.t.* **ab·horred**, **ab·hor·ring** To regard with repugnance, horror, or disgust. [< L *ab-* from + *horrere* shrink] —**ab·hor′rer** *n.* —**Syn.** loathe, detest, despise, abominate.

**a·bide** (ə·bīd′) *v.* **a·bode** or **a·bid·ed**, **a·bid·ing** *v.i.* **1** To continue, last, or endure. **2** To continue in a place; stay; dwell; reside. —*v.t.* **3** To look for; wait for. **4** To endure; put up with. —**abide by 1** To behave in accordance with, as a promise or rule. **2** To accept the consequences of; submit to. [< OE *abidan*] —**a·bid′ance**, **a·bid′er** *n.* —**a·bid′ing** *adj.* —**a·bid′ing·ly** *adv.*

**a·bil·i·ty** (ə·bil′ə·tē) *n. pl.* **·ties 1** The condition or power of being able. **2** Talent or skill. [< L *habilitas*]

1

**ab·ject** (ab′jekt, ab·jekt′) *adj.* 1 Of the lowest kind or degree; wretched. 2 Servile; cringing. [< L *ab-* away + *jacere* throw] —**ab·jec′tive** *adj.* —**ab′ject·ly** *adv.* —**ab′ject·ness, ab·jec′tion** *n.*

**ab·jure** (ab·jŏŏr′) *v.t.* **ab·jured, ab·jur·ing** 1 to renounce under oath; forswear. 2 To retract or recant, as an opinion. [< L *abjurare* deny on oath] —**ab·jur·a·to·ry** (ab·jŏŏr′a·tôr′ē, -tō′rē) *adj.* —**ab′ju·ra′tion, ab·jur′er** *n.*

**ab·lu·tion** (ab·lōō′shən) *n.* 1 A washing or cleansing of the body; a bath. 2 *Eccl.* **a** A washing of the priest's hands or of the chalice during the Mass. **b** The liquid used to do this. [< L *abluere* wash away] —**ab·lu′tion·ar′y** *adj.*

**ab·ne·gate** (ab′nə·gāt) *v.t.* **·gat·ed, ·gat·ing.** To renounce or give up, as a right or privilege. [< L *ab-* away + *negare* deny] —**ab′ne·ga′tion, ab′ne·ga′tor** *n.*

**ab·nor·mal** (ab·nôr′məl) *adj.* Not according to what is normal, usual, or average; unnatural; irregular. [< Gk. *anōmalos* irregular] —**ab·nor′mal·ly** *adv.*

**a·bode** (ə·bōd′) *p.t.* & *pp.* of ABIDE. —*n.* 1 A place of abiding; dwelling; home. 2 A sojourn; stay. [< ME *abiden* to abide]

**a·bol·ish** (ə·bol′ish) *v.t.* To do away with; put an end to. [< L *abolere* destroy] —**a·bol′ish·a·ble** *adj.* —**a·bol′ish·er, a·bol′ish·ment** *n.* —Syn. destroy, eradicate, annul, end.

**a·bom·i·na·ble** (ə·bom′ə·nə·bəl) *adj.* 1 Very hateful; loathsome. 2 Very bad or unpleasant. —**a·bom′i·na·bly** *adv.*

**ab·o·rig·i·nal** (ab′ə·rij′ə·nəl) *adj.* 1 Of or pertaining to aborigines. 2 Existing from the beginning; indigenous; primitive. —*n. pl.* **·nes** (-nēz) An aborigine. —**ab′o·rig′i·nal·ly** *adv.*

**ab·o·rig·i·ne** (ab′ə·rij′ə·nē) *n.* 1 One of the original native inhabitants of a country. 2 *pl.* Flora and fauna indigenous to a geographical area. [<L *ab origine* from the beginning]

**a·bor·tion** (ə·bôr′shən) *n.* 1 The expulsion of a fetus prematurely; miscarriage. 2 The defective result of a premature birth; a monstrosity. 3 A person or thing that fails to progress or develop normally or as expected. —**a·bor′tion·al** *adj.* —**a·bor′tion·ist** *n.*

**a·bound** (ə·bound′) *v.t.* 1 To be in abundance; be plentiful. 2 To have plenty of; be rich; with *in.* 3 To be full of; teem; with *with.* [< L *abundare* overflow]

**a·brade** (ə·brād′) *v.t.* **a·brad·ed, a·brad·ing** To rub or wear off; scrape away. [< L *ab-* away + *radere* scrape] —**a·bra′dant** *adj., n.* —**a·brad′er** *n.*

**a·bridge** (ə·brij′) *v.t.* **a·bridged, a·bridg·ing** 1 To give the substance of in fewer words; condense. 2 To shorten, as in time. 3 To curtail or lessen, as rights. [< L *abbreviare.* See ABBREVIATE.] —**a·bridg′a·ble, a·bridge′a·ble** *adj.*

**a·broad** (ə·brôd′) *adv.* 1 Out of one's home; outdoors. 2 Out of one's own country; in or to foreign lands. 3 Broadly; widely. 4 At large; in circulation. —**from abroad** From a foreign country or countries.

**ab·ro·gate** (ab′rə·gāt) *v.t.* **·gat·ed, ·gat·ing** To annul by authority, as a law. [< L *ab-* away + *rogare* ask, propose] —**ab·ro·ga·ble** (ab′rə·gə·bəl), **ab′ro·ga′tive** *adj.* —**ab′ro·ga′tion, ab′ro·ga′tor** *n.* —Syn. abolish, repeal, cancel, nullify.

**a·brupt** (ə·brupt′) *adj.* 1 Beginning, ending, or happening suddenly. 2 Brusque or curt, as in speech. 3 Changing subject suddenly; unconnected, as style. 4 Steep, as a cliff. [< L *ab-* off + *rumpere* break] —**a·brupt′ly** *adv.* —**a·brupt′ness** *n.* —Syn. 1 sudden, unexpected. 4 sheer, precipitous.

**ab·scond** (ab·skond′) *v.i.* To depart suddenly and secretly, esp. to hide oneself. [< L *ab-* away + *condere* store] —**ab·scond′er** *n.*

**ab·sence** (ab′səns) *n.* 1 The state, fact, or time of being absent. 2 Lack; want.

**ab·sent** (ab′sənt) *adj.* 1 Not present. 2 Nonexistent; missing. 3 Inattentive; absentminded. —*v.t.* (ab·sent′) To take or keep (oneself) away; not be present. [<L *ab-* away + *esse* be] —**ab·sent′er, ab′sent·ness** *n.* —**ab′sent·ly** *adv.*

**ab·sen·tee** (ab′sən·tē′) *n.* One who is absent, as from a job. —*adj.* 1 Designating or for a person qualified to vote by mail. 2 Nonresident. —**ab′sen·tee′ism** *n.*

**ab·so·lute** (ab′sə·lōōt) *adj.* 1 Free from restriction; unlimited; unconditional. 2 Complete or perfect. 3 Unadulterated; pure. 4 Positive; unquestionable. 5 Not dependent on or relative to anything else; independent. 6 Relating to or describing a form of government in which the power of the ruler is complete and unchecked, as by any constitutional restraint: *absolute* monarchy. 7 *Gram.* **a** Free from the usual relations of syntax, as *It being late* in *It being late, we started home.* **b** Of a transitive verb, having no object expressed but implied, as *She is* *one who really gives.* c Of an adjective or pronoun, standing alone with the noun understood, as *Ours is first.* 8 *Physics* a Not dependent on any arbitrary standard. b Of, pertaining to, or measured on the absolute temperature scale. —*n.* That which is absolute or perfect. —**the Absolute** The ultimate basis of all being. [<L *absolvere.* See ABSOLVE.] —**ab′so·lute·ly** *adv.* —**ab′so·lute′ness** *n.*

**ab·solve** (ab·solv′, -zolv′) *v.t.* **ab·solved, ab·solv·ing** 1 To pronounce free from the penalties or consequences of an action. 2 To release from an obligation, liability, or promise. 3 *Eccl.* To grant a remission of sin. [<L *ab-* from + *solvere* loosen] —**ab·solv′a·ble** *adj.* —**ab·sol′vent** *adj., n.* —**ab·solv′er** *n.*

**ab·sorb** (ab·sôrb′, -zôrb′) *v.t.* 1 To drink in or suck up, as through or into pores. 2 To engross completely; occupy wholly. 3 *Physics* To take up or in with no reflection or transmission. 4 To take in and incorporate; assimilate. 5 To assume or defray (costs). 6 To receive the force or action of; intercept. [<L *ab-* from + *sorbere* suck in] —**ab·sorb′a·bil′i·ty, ab·sorb′er** *n.* —**ab·sorb′a·ble, ab·sorb′ing** *adj.* —**ab·sorb′ing·ly** *adv.*

**ab·stain** (ab·stān′) *v.i.* To refrain voluntarily; with *from.* [< L *ab-* from + *tenere* hold] —**ab·stain′er** *n.*

**ab·ste·mi·ous** (ab·stē′mē·əs) *adj.* 1 Eating and drinking sparingly. 2 Characterized by abstinence. [< L *abstemius* temperate] —**ab·ste′mi·ous·ly** *adv.* —**ab·ste′mi·ous·ness** *n.*

**ab·sti·nence** (ab′stə·nəns) *n.* The act or practice of abstaining, as from alcoholic beverages, food, pleasure, etc. —**ab′sti·nent** *adj.* —**ab′sti·nent·ly** *adv.* —**Syn.** continence, self-denial, temperance, fasting.

**ab·stract** (ab·strakt′, ab′strakt) *adj.* 1 Considered apart from particular examples or concrete objects; general, as opposed to particular. 2 Theoretical; ideal, as opposed to practical. 3 Expressing a quality or relation that is thought of apart from any specific object or particular instance: Redness is an *abstract* noun. 4 Difficult to understand; abstruse. 5 Designating art that uses as subject matter the relationship of formal elements rather than the depiction or representation of recognizable objects. —*n.* (ab′strakt) 1 A summary or epitome, as of an article, book, report, etc. 2 Something abstract. —**in the abstract** Apart from actual, concrete examples or experience. —*v.t.* (ab·strakt′) 1 To take away; remove. 2 To take away secretly or dishonestly; steal. 3 To withdraw or disengage (the attention, interest, etc.). 4 To consider apart from particular or material instances. 5 (ab′strakt) To make an abstract of, as a book or treatise; summarize. [< L *ab-* away + *trahere* draw] —**ab·stract′er, ab·stract′ness** *n.* —**ab·stract′ly** *adv.*

**ab·struse** (ab·stroos′) *adj.* Hard to understand. [< L *ab- strudere* to hide] —**ab·struse′ly** *adv.* —**ab·struse′ness** *n.*

**ab·surd** (ab·sûrd′, -zûrd′) *adj.* 1 Irrational; preposterous; ridiculous. 2 Of or pertaining to the absurd. —*n.* The state of man's existence in what appears to be an unreasonable, meaningless universe: a thesis dealing with the literature of the *absurd.* [< L *absurdus* out of tune, incongruous] —**ab·surd′ism, ab·surd′ness** *n.* —**ab·surd′ist** *adj., n.* —**ab·surd′ly** *adv.*

**a·bun·dance** (ə·bun′dəns) *n.* 1 A plentiful supply. 2 Affluence; wealth.

**a·buse** (ə·byooz′) *v.t.* **a·bused, a·bus·ing** 1 To use improperly or injuriously; misuse. 2 To hurt by treating wrongly; injure. 3 To speak in coarse or bad terms of or to; revile; malign. —*n.* (ə·byoos) 1 Improper or injurious use; misuse. 2 Ill-treatment; injury. 3 An immoral or dishonest practice or act. 4 Harsh, abusive language. [< L *abuti* misuse] —**a·bus′er** *n.*

**a·bys·mal** (ə·biz′məl) *adj.* 1 Bottomless. 2 Immeasurably great or terrible: *abysmal* ignorance. —**a·bys′mal·ly** *adv.*

**a·byss** (ə·bis′) *n.* 1 A deep chasm or gulf. 2 Any bottomless void or depth: the *abyss* of infinity. 3 The lowest depths of the sea. [< Gk. *a-* without + *byssos* bottom] —**a·bys′sal** *adj.*

**ac·a·dem·ic** (ak′ə·dem′ik) *adj.* 1 Pertaining to an academy, college, or university. 2 In education, classical and literary rather than technical or vocational. 3 Theoretical rather than practical: What he might have done is *academic.* 4 Scholarly; pedantic. 5 Conventional; traditional. Also **ac′a·dem′i·cal.** —*n.* A college or university teacher or student. —**ac′a·dem′i·cal·ly** *adv.*

**a·cad·e·my** (ə·kad′ə·mē) *n. pl.* **·mies** 1 A secondary school, usu. private. 2 A school for special studies, as in art or music. 3 A learned society for the advancement of arts or sciences. [< Gk. *Akadēmeia,* name of the grove in Athens where Plato taught]

**ac·cede** (ak·sēd′) *v.i.* **ac·ced·ed, ac·ced·ing** **1** To give one's consent or adherence; agree; assent: with *to*. **2** To come into or enter upon an office or dignity: with *to*. [< L *ad-* to + *cedere* yield, go]

**ac·cel·er·ate** (ak·sel′ə·rāt) *v.* **·at·ed, ·at·ing** *v.t.* **1** To cause to act or move faster; increase the speed of. **2** *Physics* To increase or change the velocity of. **3** To hasten the natural or usual course of: to *accelerate* a schedule. **4** To cause to happen ahead of time. —*v.i.* **5** To move or become faster: The car suddenly *accelerated*. [< L *ad-* to + *celerare* hasten] —**ac·cel′er·a′tive** *adj.*

**ac·cel·er·a·tor** (ak·sel′ə·rā′tər) *n.* **1** One who or that which accelerates. **2** The throttle control of an automobile, etc. **3** *Physics* Any of several devices for accelerating various subatomic particles, as a cyclotron.

**ac·cent** (ak′sent) *n.* **1** A vocal stress or emphasis given to a word. **2** A mark used to indicate such stress: the *primary accent* (′), noting the chief stress, and the *secondary accent* (′), noting a weaker stress. **3** In certain languages, a mark used to indicate the quality of a vowel or diphthong, as in French, the acute (′), grave (`), and circumflex (ˆ) accents. **4** *Music* **a** Rhythmic prominence, as of a tone. **b** A characteristic, esp. greater loudness, that causes this. **5** A modulation of the voice. **6** A particular manner of speech or pronunciation: a British *accent*. **7** *pl. Archaic* Speech. **8** In prosody, the stress determining the rhythm of poetry. **9** A distinguishing feature or characteristic. **10** An object, color, etc., that provides interest or contrast. **11** Special emphasis: He put an *accent* on clarity. — *v.t.* (ak′sent, ak·sent′) **1** To speak, pronounce, or produce with an accent; stress. **2** To write or print with a mark indicating accent or stress. **3** To call attention to; emphasize. [< L *accentus*, lit., song added to speech]

**ac·cen·tu·ate** (ak·sen′chōō·āt) *v.t.* **·at·ed, ·at·ing** **1** To strengthen or heighten the effect of; emphasize. **2** To speak or pronounce with an accent. [< L *accentus*. See ACCENT.] —**ac·cen′tu·a′tion** *n.*

**ac·cept** (ak·sept′) *v.t.* **1** To receive with favor or willingness, as a gift. **2** To give an affirmative answer to. **3** To agree to; admit: to *accept* an apology. **4** To take with good grace; submit to: to *accept* the inevitable. **5** To agree to pay, as a draft. **6** To believe in. —*v.i.* **7** To agree or promise to fulfill an en-

gagement; receive favorably. [< L *ad-* to + *capere* take] —**ac·cept′er** *n.*

**ac·cept·a·ble** (ak·sep′tə·bəl) *adj.* Worthy or capable of being accepted. —**ac·cept′a·ble·ness, ac·cept′a·bil′i·ty** *n.* —**ac·cept′a·bly** *adv.* —Syn. adequate, satisfactory, agreeable.

**ac·cess** (ak′ses) *n.* **1** The act of approaching; approach. **2** A means of approaching, using, knowing, etc. **3** The right to approach, use, etc. **4** Increase. **5** An attack; onset, as of a disease. **6** An outburst. [< L *accedere*. See ACCEDE.]

**ac·ces·si·ble** (ak·ses′ə·bəl) *adj.* **1** Capable of being approached or reached. **2** Easy to approach or reach. **3** That can be obtained or used: *accessible* funds. **4** Open to the influence of: with *to*: *accessible* to pity. — **ac·ces′si·bil′i·ty** *n.* —**ac·ces′si·bly** *adv.*

**ac·ces·so·ry** (ak·ses′ər·ē) *n. pl.* **·ries 1** Something added as an aid, convenience, decorative item, etc. **2** *Law* A person who, even if not present during the perpetration of a felony, knowingly instigates or assists the felony beforehand (**accessory before the fact**) or assists or conceals the felon afterwards (**accessory after the fact**). —*adj.* **1** Aiding the principal design, or assisting subordinately the chief agent, as in the commission of a crime. **2** Supplemental; additional. Also, esp. in law, **ac·ces′sa·ry.** [< L *accessus* access] —**ac·ces′so·ri·ly** *adv.* —**ac·ces′so·ri·ness** *n.*

**ac·ci·dent** (ak′sə·dənt) *n.* **1** Anything that happens unexpectedly, undesignedly, or without known cause. **2** Any unpleasant or unfortunate occurrence involving injury, loss, suffering, or death. **3** Chance; fortune. **4** Any nonessential circumstance or attribute. [< L *ad-* upon + *cadere* fall]

**ac·claim** (ə·klām′) *v.t.* **1** To proclaim or receive with approval; hail. **2** To show enthusiasm for; welcome with applause or praise. **3** *Can.* To elect by acclamation. —*v.i.* **4** To applaud or shout approval. —*n.* Great approval, demonstrated by applause, shouting, etc. [< L *ad-* to + *clamare* shout] — **ac·claim′a·ble** *adj.* —**ac·claim′er** *n.*

**ac·cla·ma·tion** (ak′lə·mā′shən) *n.* **1** An expression of approval, as by applause, shouting, etc. **2** An enthusiastic vocal vote. **3** *Can.* An election in which the candidate has no opposition. —**ac·clam·a·to·ry** (ə·klam′ə·tôr′ē, -tō′rē) *adj.*

**ac·cli·mate** (ak′lə·māt, ə·klī′mit) *v.t. & v.i.* **·mat·ed, ·mat·ing** To adapt or become adapted to a different climate, environment, or situation. [< F à to + climat climate] —ac·cli·ma·ta·ble (ə·klī′mə·tə·bəl) adj. —ac·cli·ma·tion (ak′lə·mā′shən), ac·cli·ma·tion (ə·klī′mə·tā′shən) n.

ac·cliv·i·ty (ə·kliv′ə·tē) n. pl. ·ties An upward slope. [< L acclivitas steepness] —ac·cliv′i·tous, ac·cli·vous (ə·klī′vəs) adj.

ac·com·mo·date (ə·kom′ə·dāt) v. ·dat·ed, ·dat·ing v.t. 1 To do a favor for; oblige; help. 2 To provide for; give lodging to. 3 To be suitable or have space for. 4 To adapt or modify; adjust. 5 To reconcile or settle, as conflicting opinions. —v.i. 6 To be or become adjusted or conformed, as the eye to distance. [< L ad- to + commodare make fit, suit] —ac·com′mo·da′tive adj. —ac·com′mo·da′tive·ness n.

ac·com·pa·ny (ə·kum′pə·nē) v.t. ·nied, ·ny·ing 1 To go with; attend; escort. 2 To be or occur with; coexist with: Weakness often accompanies disease. 3 To supplement with. 4 Music a To provide with an accompaniment. b To be the accompaniment to or for. [< LL ad- to + companio companion] —ac·com′pa·ni·er n.

ac·com·plice (ə·kom′plis) n. An associate in wrong or crime, whether as principal or accessory. [< a, indefinite article + LL complex accomplice]

ac·com·plish (ə·kom′plish) v.t. To do, perform, effect, or finish. [< L ad- to + complere fill up, complete] —ac·com′plish·a·ble adj. —ac·com′plish·er n.

ac·cord (ə·kôrd′) v.t. 1 To render as due; grant; concede. 2 To bring into agreement, as opinions. —v.i. 3 To agree; harmonize. —n. 1 Harmony, agreement, or conformity. 2 An agreement between governments. —of one's own accord By one's own choice; voluntarily. [< LL accordare be of one mind, agree] —ac·cord′a·ble adj. —ac·cord′er n.

ac·count (ə·kount′) v.t. 1 To hold to be; consider; estimate. —v.i. 2 To provide a reckoning, as of funds paid or received: with to or with (someone) for (something). 3 To give a rational explanation: with for. 4 To be responsible; answer: with for. 5 To cause death, capture, or incapacitation: with for. —n. 1 An explanation, statement, report, or description. 2 Importance; value. 3 A reckoning or calculation. 4 A record of financial transactions, as of debits, credits, etc. 5 A bank account. 6 A charge account. 7 A customer or client. —give a good account of oneself To do well. —on account 1 On

credit. 2 As partial payment. —on account of Because of; for the sake of. —on no account Under no circumstances. —take into account To take into consideration. [< L ad- to + computare count]

ac·count·ing (ə·koun′ting) n. The occupation or system of recording, classifying, and interpreting financial accounts; also, an item so recorded, classified, etc.

ac·cre·tion (ə·krē′shən) n. 1 Growth or increase in size, as by external additions. 2 The result of such growth or increase; also, that which is added to effect such a result. 3 An accumulation, as of soil on a seashore. [< L accrescere to grow to] —ac·cre′tive adj.

ac·crue (ə·krōō′) v.i. ·crued, ·cru·ing 1 To come as a natural result or increment, as by growth: with to. 2 To accumulate, as the interest on money: with from. [< L accrescere to grow to] —ac·cru′al, ac·crue′ment n.

ac·cu·mu·late (ə·kyōōm′yə·lāt) v.t. & v.i. To gather; collect; heap or pile up. [< L < ad- to + cumulare heap] —ac·cu·mu·la·ble (ə·kyōōm′yə·lə·bəl) adj.

ac·cu·ra·cy (ak′yər·ə·sē) n. The quality or condition of being accurate. —Syn. correctness, precision, exactness

ac·cu·rate (ak′yər·it) adj. 1 Conforming exactly to truth or to a standard; without error: an accurate measurement. 2 Careful; precise. [< L accurare take care of] —ac′cu·rate·ly adv. —ac′cu·rate·ness n.

ac·cuse (ə·kyōōz′) v.t. ac·cused, ac·cus·ing 1 To charge with fault or error; blame. 2 To bring charges against, as of a crime or an offense: with of. [< L accusare call to account] —ac·cus′er n. —ac·cus′ing·ly adv.

a·cerb·ic (ə·sûr′bik) adj. 1 Sour and astringent to the taste, as unripe fruit. 2 Harsh or sharp in tone: an acerbic rejoinder. Also a·cerb (ə·sûrb′). [< L acerbus sharp] —a·cer′bi·ty n.

ac·e·tate (as′ə·tāt) n. A salt or ester of acetic acid.

a·cet·y·lene (ə·set′ə·lēn) n. A colorless hydrocarbon gas, used as an illuminant and for welding. [< ACET- + -YL + -ENE]

a·chieve (ə·chēv′) v. a·chieved, a·chiev·ing v.t. 1 To accomplish; do successfully. 2 To win or attain, as by effort or skill. —v.i. 3 To accomplish something; to attain an object. [< LL ad caput (venire) (come) to a head] —a·chiev′a·ble adj. —a·chiev′er n.

ac·id (as′id) adj. 1 Sharp and biting to the taste, as vinegar; sour. 2 Chem. Having

5

properties of or pertaining to an acid. 3 Sharp; biting; sarcastic. —*n.* 1 *Chem.* A compound which in aqueous solution produces hydrogen ions which have a sour taste, turn blue litmus red, and may be replaced by another positive ion to form a salt. 2 Any sour substance. 3 *Slang* LSD. [< L *acidus* sour] —**ac′id·ly** *adv.* —**ac′id·ness** *n.*

**ac·knowl·edge** (ak·nol′ij) *v.t.* **·edged, ·edg·ing** 1 To own or admit as true; confess. 2 To declare or admit the validity of, as a claim or right. 3 To show appreciation of; thank for. 4 To recognize and respond to, as a greeting. 5 To respond to the arrival of: to *acknowledge* a letter. [< OE *oncnāwan* recognize] —**ac·knowl′edge·a·ble** *adj.* —**ac·knowl′edg·er** *n.*

**ac·me** (ak′mē) *n.* The highest point or summit. [< Gk. *akmē* point]

**ac·o·lyte** (ak′ə·līt) *n.* 1 An attendant or assistant. 2 ALTAR BOY. 3 In the Roman Catholic Church, a member of the highest of the four minor orders. [< Gk. *akolouthos* follower, attendant]

**a·cous·tic** (ə·kōōs′tik) *adj.* 1 Pertaining to the act or sense of hearing, sound, or the science of sound. 2 Adapted for modifying sound or hearing. Also **a·cous′ti·cal.** [< Gk. *akoustikos* < *akouein* hear] —**a·cous′ti·cal·ly** *adv.*

**ac·quaint** (ə·kwānt′) *v.t.* 1 To make familiar or conversant; inform: with *with: Acquaint* yourself with the court routine. 2 To cause to know, esp. socially. [< LL *adcognitare* make known]

**ac·qui·esce** (ak′wē·es′) *v.i.* **·esced** (-est′), **·esc·ing** To consent or concur quietly or passively; comply: usu. with *in:* The candidate *acquiesced* in all his party's plans. [< L *acquiescere* to remain at rest] —**ac′qui·es′cence** *n.* —**ac′qui·es′cent** *adj.* —**ac′qui·es′cent·ly** *adv.*

**ac·quire** (ə·kwīr′) *v.t.* **·quired, ·quir·ing** 1 To obtain by one's own endeavor or purchase. 2 To gain or possess as one's own. [< L *ad*- to + *quaerere* seek] —**ac·quir′a·ble** *adj.* —**ac·quir′er** *n.*

**ac·qui·si·tion** (ak′wə·zish′ən) *n.* 1 The act of acquiring. 2 Anything acquired, as by purchase or trade.

**ac·quis·i·tive** (ə·kwiz′ə·tiv) *adj.* Eager or inclined to acquire; greedy. —**ac·quis′i·tive·ly** *adv.* —**ac·quis′i·tive·ness** *n.*

**ac·quit** (ə·kwit′) *v.t.* **ac·quit·ted, ac·quit·ting** 1 To free or clear, as from an accusation. 2

To relieve, as of an obligation. 3 To conduct (oneself): He *acquitted* himself nobly. [< L *ad*- to + *quietare* settle, quiet] —**ac·quit′ter** *n.*

**a·cre** (ā′kər) *n.* 1 A measure of area equal to 4,840 square yards. 2 *pl.* Lands. 3 *pl. Informal* A great many; lots. [< OE *æcer* field]

**ac·rid** (ak′rid) *adj.* 1 Sharp, burning, or bitter to the taste or smell. 2 Bitterly sarcastic or satirical. [< L *acer*] —**a·crid·i·ty** (ə·krid′ə·tē), **ac′rid·ness** *n.* —**ac′rid·ly** *adv.*

**ac·ri·mo·ny** (ak′rə·mō′nē) *n.* Sharpness or bitterness of speech or temper. [< L *acrimonia* < *acer* sharp] —**Syn.** acridity, acerbity, sharpness, tartness.

**ac·ro·bat** (ak′rə·bat) *n.* One who is skilled in feats requiring muscular coordination, as in tightrope walking, tumbling, trapeze performing, etc.; a gymnast. [< Gk. *akrobatos* walking on tiptoe] —**ac′ro·bat′ic** or **·i·cal** *adj.* —**ac′ro·bat′i·cal·ly** *adv.*

**a·cryl·ic** (ə·kril′ik) *adj.* Pertaining to or derived from an organic acid that polymerizes to form various commercially important transparent resins and plastics. —*n.* 1 Any of a class of clear, transparent resins and plastics derived from acrylic acid, as lucite, plexiglass, etc. 2 A substance derived from an acrylic resin, as a paint medium, a fiber, etc. 3 A painting done in such a medium. [< ACR(ID) + OLE(IN) + -YL + -IC]

**ACTH** A pituitary hormone that stimulates hormone production in the cortical area of the adrenal glands; adrenocorticotropic hormone.

**ac·tion** (ak′shən) *n.* 1 The doing of something by the use of power, movement, energy, etc. 2 The thing done; deed. 3 *pl.* Behavior; conduct. 4 Energy, initiative, and decisiveness: a man of *action.* 5 The result or effect of something: the medicine's *action.* 6 The movement or manner of movement of a body organ, mechanism, etc.: the *action* of the heart. 7 The parts that move in a mechanism, as in a gun, piano, etc. 8 An event or series of events in a novel, play, etc. 9 *Law* A lawsuit. 10 A military conflict or encounter. 11 *Slang* Lively or exciting social activity; excitement: to find out where the *action* is. [< L *actio* < *agere* do]

**ac·ti·vate** (ak′tə·vāt) *v.t.* **·vat·ed, ·vat·ing** 1 To make active. 2 To put into action, as a military unit. 3 To make radioactive. 4 To promote chemical reaction in. 5 To make pure by aeration, as sewage. —**ac′ti·va′tion, ac′ti·va′tor** *n.*

**ac·tive** (ak'tiv) *adj.* 1 Abounding in action; busy. 2 Being in or capable of action, movement, performance, etc.: an *active* volcano. 3 Causing or promoting action, change, movement etc. 4 Agile; lively; quick. 5 Characterized by actual participation, contribution, etc.: an *active* member. 6 Producing profit or bearing interest: *active* funds. 7 *Gram.* a Designating a voice of the verb which indicates that the subject of the sentence is performing the action. b Describing verbs expressing action as distinguished from being and state, as *run, hit, jump.* —*n. Gram.* The active voice. [< L *activus* < *agere* do] —**ac'tive·ly** *adv.* —**ac'tive·ness** *n.*

**ac·tor** (ak'tər) *n.* 1 A performer on the stage, in motion pictures, etc. 2 Any person who actively participates in something.

**ac·tu·al** (ak'chōō·əl) *adj.* 1 Existing in fact; real. 2 Being in existence or action now; existent; present. [< LL *actualis* < L *actus* a doing. See ACT.]

**ac·tu·ar·y** (ak'chōō·er'ē) *n. pl.* **·ar·ies** One who specializes in the mathematics of insurance; esp., an official statistician of an insurance company. [< L *actuarius* clerk < *actus.* See ACT.] —**ac·tu·ar·i·al** (ak'chōō·âr'ē·əl) *adj.* —**ac'tu·ar'i·al·ly** *adv.*

**ac·tu·ate** (ak'chōō·āt) *v.t.* **·at·ed, ·at·ing** 1 To set into action or motion. 2 To incite or influence to action: [< Med.L *actuare* < L *actus* a doing. See ACT.] —**ac'tu·a'tion, ac'tu·a'tor** *n.*

**a·cu·men** (ə·kyōō'mən, ak'yōō·mən) *n.* Quickness of insight or discernment; keenness of intellect. [< L, sharpness (of the mind) < *acuere* sharpen] —**Syn.** acuteness, cleverness, keenness, insight.

**a·cute** (ə·kyōōt') *adj.* 1 Keenly discerning or sensitive. 2 Affecting keenly; poignant; intense. 3 Critical; crucial: an *acute* lack of power. 4 Coming to a crisis quickly: *acute* appendicitis. 5 Shrill; of high pitch. 6 Less than 90° in measure: an *acute* angle. 7 Sharply pointed; not blunt. [<L *acuere* sharpen] —**a·cute'ly** *adv.* —**a·cute'ness** *n.* • See ANGLE.

**ad·age** (ad'ij) *n.* A saying or proverb. [<L *adagium*]

**ad·a·mant** (ad'ə·mant, ·mənt) *n.* In legends, a very hard but imaginary mineral. —*adj.* 1 Very hard. 2 Immovable and unyielding, as in purpose. [<Gk *adamas* the hardest metal (hence, unyielding)] —**ad·a·man·tine** (ad'a·man'tin, ·tēn, ·tīn) *adj.*

**a·dapt** (ə·dapt') *v.t.* 1 To make suitable, as by changing: to *adapt* a novel for the theater. 2 To modify (oneself) to conform to a situation or environment. —*v.i.* 3 To become adjusted to a circumstance or environment. [<L *ad·* to + *aptare* fit]

**ad·dict** (ə·dikt') *v.t.* 1 To give or devote (oneself) persistently or habitually: usu. used in the passive voice with *to:* He is *addicted* to drugs. 2 To cause to pursue or practice continuously: with *to:* This task *addicted* him to obscure research. —*n.* (ad'ikt) One who is addicted to some habit, esp. to the use of narcotic drugs. [<L *addicere* assign, devote to] —**ad·dict'ed·ness** *n.*

**ad·di·tion** (ə·dish'ən) *n.* 1 The act of adding. 2 That which is added, esp. a room, annex, etc. 3 *Math.* An operation defined for every pair of elements or numbers of a set, whereby each pair is associated with a unique element of the same set called the sum. —**ad·di'tion·al** *adj.* —**ad·di'tion·al·ly** *adv.*

**ad·dress** (ə·dres') *v.t.* **ad·dressed, ad·dress·ing** 1 To speak to. 2 To deliver a set discourse to. 3 To direct, as spoken or written words, to the attention of: with *to:* He *addressed* his prayers to his God. 4 To direct the attention, energy, or force of (oneself): with *to:* He *addressed* himself to the task. 5 To mark with a destination, as a letter. 6 To consign, as a cargo to a merchant. 7 To aim or direct the club at (a golf ball). —*n.* (ə·dres', *esp. for defs.* 3 & 4 ad'res) 1 The act of addressing or speaking to a person or persons. 2 A formal speech. 3 The writing on an envelope, etc., directing something to a person or place. 4 The name, place, residence, etc., of a person. 5 Consignment, as of a vessel or cargo. 6 Conversational manner or delivery. 7 *Usu. pl.* Any courteous or devoted attention; wooing. 8 Adroitness; tact. 9 In the memory or storage element of a computer, a particular location or its designation. [<L *ad·* to + *directus* straight] —**ad·dress'er, ad·dres'sor** *n.*

**ad·duce** (ə·dyōōs') *v.t.* **ad·duced, ad·duc·ing** To bring forward for proof or consideration, as an example. [<L *ad·* to + *ducere* lead] —**ad·duce'a·ble, ad·duc'i·ble** *adj.* —**Syn.** cite, allege, advance.

**ad·e·noid** (ad'ə·noid) *adj.* Of or like a gland; glandular: **also ad'e·noi'dal.** —*n. Usu. pl.*

7

An enlarged lymphoid growth behind the pharynx. [<Gk. *adēn* gland + -OID]

**a·dept** (ə-dept´) *adj.* Highly skillful; proficient. —**ad·ept** (ad´ept, ə-dept´) *n.* One fully skilled in any art; an expert. [<L. *adeptus* pp. of *adipisci* attain] —**a·dept´ly** *adv.* —**a·dept´ness** *n.*

**ad·e·quate** (ad´ə-kwit) *adj.* 1 Equal to what is required; suitable; sufficient. 2 Barely acceptable or sufficient. [<L *ad-* to + *aequus* equal] —**ad·e·qua·cy** (ad´ə-kwə-sē), **ad´e·quate·ness** *n.* —**ad´e·quate·ly** *adv.*

**ad·here** (ad-hir´) *v.i.* **ad·hered, ad·her·ing** 1 To stick fast or together. 2 To be attached or devoted, as to a party or faith. 3 To follow closely or without deviation. [< L *ad-* to + *haerere* stick] —**ad·her´ence** *n.*

**ad·he·sion** (ad-hē´zhən) *n.* 1 The act of sticking together or the state of being stuck together. 2 Assent; concurrence. 3 Close connection, as of ideas. 4 *Physics* The force of attraction between molecules or unlike substances in contact. 5 *Med.* Abnormal surface union of dissimilar tissues as a result of inflammation, etc. [< L *adhaerere*. See ADHERE.]

**a·dieu** (ə-dyōō´; *Fr.* à·dyæ´) *n. pl.* **a·dieus**, *Fr.* **a·dieux** (à·dyæ´) A farewell. —*interj.* Goodby; farewell: literally, "to God (I commend you)." [< F < à to + *dieu* God]

**ad·ja·cent** (ə-jā´sənt) *adj.* Lying near or close at hand. [< L *ad-* near + *jacere* lie] —**ad·ja´cence, ad·ja´cen·cy,** *n.* —**ad·ja´cent·ly** *adv.* —**Syn.** adjoining, contiguous, abutting, bordering.

**ad·jec·tive** (aj´ik-tiv) *n.* 1 *Gram.* A word used to limit or qualify a noun or other substantive. 2 A phrase or clause used similarly. —*adj.* Of, pertaining to, or functioning as an adjective. [< L *adjectivus* that is added < *adjicere* add to] —**ad´jec·tive·ly** *adv.*

**ad·join** (ə-join´) *v.t.* 1 To be next to; border upon. 2 To join to; append; unite: with *to.* —*v.i.* 3 To lie close together; be in contact. [< L *ad-* to + *jungere* join]

**ad·journ** (ə-jûrn´) *v.t.* 1 To put off to another day or place, as a meeting or session; postpone. —*v.i.* 2 To postpone or suspend proceedings for a special time. 3 *Informal* To move or go to another place. [< LL *adjurnare* set a day] —**ad·journ´ment** *n.*

**ad·junct** (aj´ungkt) *n.* 1 Something connected to another thing but in a subordinate position. 2 A person associated with another person in an auxiliary or subordinate rela-

tion; an associate; assistant. 3 *Gram.* A modifier. 4 Any nonessential quality or property. —*adj.* Joined subordinately; auxiliary. [<L *adjungere*. See ADJOIN.] —**ad·junc·tive** (ə-jungk´tiv) *adj.* —**ad·junc´tive·ly** *adv.*

**ad·jure** (ə-jōōr´) *v.t.* **ad·jured, ad·jur·ing** 1 To charge or entreat solemnly, as under oath or penalty. 2 To appeal to earnestly. [<L *ad-* to + *jurare* swear] —**ad·ju·ra·tion** (aj´ōō-rā´shən), **ad·jur´er, ad·ju´ror** *n.* —**ad·jur·a·to·ry** (ə-jōōr´ə-tor´ē, -tō´rē) *adj.*

**ad·just** (ə-just´) *v.t.* 1 To arrange or regulate so as to produce a desired accuracy, condition, fit, etc. 2 To harmonize or compose, as differences. 3 To arrange in order; systematize. 4 To determine an amount to be paid, as in settling an insurance claim. —*v.i.* 5 To adapt oneself; conform, as to a new environment: to *adjust* to civilian life. [< L *ad-* to + *juxta* near] —**ad·just´a·ble** *adj.* —**ad·just´er, ad·jus´tor** *n.* —**ad·jus´tive** *adj.*

**ad·ju·tant** (aj´ə-tənt) *n.* 1 *Mil.* A staff officer who assists and issues the administrative orders of a commanding officer. 2 A large stork of India and Africa. [< L *adjutare* to assist] —**ad´ju·tan·cy, ad´ju·tant·ship** *n.*

**ad·lib** (ad´lib´) *Informal v.t. & v.i.* **-libbed, -lib·bing** To improvise, as words, gestures, or music not called for in the original script or score. —*n.* An instance of this. [< AD LIBITUM]

**ad·min·is·ter** (ad-min´is-tər) *v.t.* 1 To have the charge or direction of; manage. 2 To provide with; apply, as medicine or treatment. 3 To inflict; dispense, as punishment. 4 *Law* To act as executor of, as an estate. 5 To tender, as an oath. —*v.i.* 6 To be helpful; minister: with *to.* 7 To carry out the functions of an administrator. [< L *administrare* minister to] —**ad·min·is·te·ri·al** (-min´is·tir´ē-əl), **ad·min·is·tra·ble** (-min´is·trə-bəl) *adj.* —**ad·min´is·trant** *adj., n.*

**ad·min·is·tra·tion** (ad-min´is·trā´shən) *n.* 1 The act of administering, or the state of being administered. 2 a The executive department of a government, school, etc. b Their policies. c Their term of office.

**ad·min·is·tra·tor** (ad-min´is·trā´tər) *n.* 1 One who administers something; an executive. 2 *Law* One commissioned by a competent court to administer the personal property of a deceased or incompetent person. —**ad·min´is·tra´tor·ship** *n.* —**ad·min·is·tra·trix** (ad-min´is·trā´triks) *n. Fem.* ( *pl.* ·tra·trix·es or ·tra·tri·ces)

**ad·mi·ra·ble** (ad′mər·ə·bəl) *adj.* Worthy of admiration or praise; excellent. [< L *admirari.* See ADMIRE.] —**ad′mi·ra·bil′i·ty, ad′mi·ra·ble·ness** *n.* —**ad′mi·ra·bly** *adv.*

**ad·mi·ral** (ad′mər·əl) *n.* See GRADE. [< Ar. *amīr-al* commander of the]

**ad·mire** (ad·mīr′) *v.* **ad·mired, ad·mir·ing** *v.t.* **1** To regard with wonder, pleasure, and approval. **2** To have respect or esteem for. — *v.i.* **3** To feel or express admiration. [< L *ad-* at + *mirari* wonder] —**ad·mir′er** *n.* —**ad·mir′ing** *adj.* —**ad·mir′ing·ly** *adv.* —Syn. **1** approve, applaud, enjoy. **2** honor, revere.

**ad·mis·si·ble** (ad·mis′ə·bəl) *adj.* **1** Such as may be admitted; allowable. **2** Worthy of being considered. —**ad·mis′si·bil′i·ty** *n.* —**ad·mis′si·bly** *adv.*

**ad·mis·sion** (ad·mish′ən) *n.* **1** The act of admitting, or the state of being admitted. **2** A right to enter. **3** An entrance fee. **4** An acknowledging or confessing. **5** That which is acknowledged or confessed. —**ad·mis′sive** *adj.*

**ad·mit** (ad·mit′) *v.* **ad·mit·ted, ad·mit·ting** *v.t.* **1** To grant entrance to. **2** To be the means or channel of admission to; let in: This key will *admit* you. **3** To have room for; contain. **4** To leave room for; permit: His impatience *admits* no delay. **5** To concede or grant. **6** To acknowledge or avow. **7** To allow to join. —*v.i.* **8** To give scope or warrant: with *of:* This problem *admits* of several solutions. **9** To afford entrance; open on: with *to.* [< L *ad-* to + *mittere* send, let go]

**ad·mon·ish** (ad·mon′ish) *v.t.* **1** To scold or reprove gently. **2** To caution against danger or error; warn. **3** To exhort; urge. [< L *ad-* to + *monere* warn] —**ad·mon′ish·er** *n.* —Syn. **1** rebuke, reprimand, censure. **2** counsel, advise.

**ad·mo·ni·tion** (ad′mə·nish′ən) *n.* **1** The act of admonishing. **2** A gentle reproof. Also **ad·mon′ish·ment.**

**a·dopt** (ə·dopt′) *v.t.* **1** To take into a new relationship, esp. to take legally and raise as one's own child. **2** To take (a course of action) and follow as one's own. **3** To use as one's own, as a phrase, practice, etc. **4** To vote to accept. [< L *ad-* to + *optare* choose] —**a·dopt′a·ble** *adj.* —**a·dopt′er, a·dop·tion** (ə·dop′shən) *n.*

**a·dor·a·ble** (ə·dôr′ə·bəl, ə·dōr′-) *adj. Informal* Attractive; pretty; charming. —**a·dor′a·bil′i·ty, a·dor′a·ble·ness.** *n.* —**a·dor′a·bly** *adv.*

**a·dore** (ə·dôr′, ə·dōr′) *v.t.* **a·dored, a·dor·ing** **1** To worship as divine. **2** To love or honor

with intense devotion. **3** *Informal* To like very much. [< L *ad-* to + *orare* speak, pray] —**a·dor′er** *n.*

**a·dorn** (ə·dôrn′) *v.t.* **1** To be an ornament to; increase the beauty of. **2** To decorate with ornaments. [< L *ad-* to + *ornare* furnish] — **a·dorn′er, a·dorn′ment** *n.*

**Ad·ren·a·lin** (ə·dren′ə·lin) *n.* EPINEPHRINE: a trade name. Also **ad·ren′a·lin, ad·ren′a·line.**

**a·droit** (ə·droit′) *adj.* Skillful; dexterous; expert. [< F *à* to + *droit* right] —**a·droit′ly** *adv.* —**a·droit′ness** *n.* —Syn. clever, deft, apt, handy.

**ad·u·late** (aj′ə·lāt) *v.t.* **·lat·ed, ·lat·ing** To flatter or praise extravagantly. [< L *adulari* to fawn] —**ad′u·la′tion, ad′u·la′tor** *n.* — **ad·u·la·to·ry** (aj′ə·lə·tôr′ē, -tō′rē) *adj.*

**a·dult** (ə·dult′, ad′ult) *n.* **1** A person who has attained the age of maturity or legal majority. **2** *Biol.* A fully developed animal or plant. —*adj.* **1** Pertaining to mature life; full-grown. **2** Of or for adults. [< L *adolescere* grow up] —**a·dult′hood, a·dul′t′ness** *n.*

**a·dul·ter·ate** (ə·dul′tər·āt) *v.t.* **·at·ed, ·at·ing** To make impure or inferior by adding other or baser ingredients; corrupt. —*adj.* (ə·dul′tər·it) **1** Adulterated; corrupted. **2** Adulterous. [< L *adulterare* corrupt < *ad-* to + *alter* other, different] —**a·dul′ter·a′tion, a·dul′ter·a′tor** *n.*

**a·dul·ter·y** (ə·dul′tər·ē) *n. pl.* **·ter·ies** The voluntary sexual intercourse of two persons, either or both of whom are married but not to each other. [< L *adulterare* to adulterate] —**a·dul′ter·er** *n.* —**a·dul′ter·ess** *n. Fem.*

**ad·vance** (ad·vans′, -väns′) *v.* **ad·vanced, ad·vanc·ing** *v.t.* **1** To move forward in position or place. **2** To put in a better or more advantageous situation. **3** To further; promote. **4** To make occur earlier; accelerate. **5** To offer; propose. **6** To raise in rate or price. **7** To pay (money) before due. **8** To lend. —*v.i.* **9** To move or go forward: The armies *advance* on all fronts. **10** To make progress; rise or improve. —*adj.* Being ahead or before in time or place. —*n.* **1** The act of advancing. **2** Progress; improvement. **3** An increase or rise, as of prices. **4** Anything paid beforehand; also, a loan. **5** An overture; proposal: His *advances* were rejected. —**in advance 1** In front. **2** Before due; beforehand. [< L *ab-* away + *ante* before] —**ad·vanc′er** *n.*

**ad·van·tage** (ad·van′tij, -vän′-) *n.* **1** Anything

favorable to success. 2 Superiority, as of position, rank, etc. 3 Gain or benefit. 4 In tennis, the first point scored after deuce. — **take advantage of** 1 To use so as to benefit. 2 To use or impose upon for selfish purposes. —**to advantage** So as to bring about the best results. —*v.t.* **·taged, ·tag·ing** To be a benefit or service to. [< OF *avant* before < L *ab ante* from before]

**ad·ven·ture** (ad·ven′chər) *n.* 1 a A hazardous or exciting experience. b A daring feat. 2 A commercial venture; a speculation. —*v.i.* **·tured, ·tur·ing** To run risks. [<L *adventura (res)* (a thing) about to happen <*advenire* to come to]

**ad·verb** (ad′vûrb) *n.* Any of a class of words used to modify the meaning of a verb, adjective, or other adverb, in regard to time, place, manner, means, cause, degree, etc. [<L *ad-* to + *verbum* verb] —**ad·ver·bi·al** (ad·vûr′bē·əl) *adj.* —**ad·ver′bi·al·ly** *adv.*

**ad·ver·sar·y** (ad′vər·ser′ē) *n. pl.* **·sar·ies** An opponent or enemy. [<L *adversarius*, lit., one turned towards]

**ad·verse** (ad·vûrs′, ad′vûrs) *adj.* 1 Opposing or opposed. 2 Unfriendly. 3 Harmful; detrimental. 4 Opposite. [<L *ad-* to + *vertere* turn] —**ad·verse′ly** *adv.* —**ad·verse′ness** *n.*

**ad·ver·tise** (ad′vər·tīz, ad′vər·tīz′) *v.* **·tised, ·tis·ing** *v.t.* 1 To proclaim the qualities of, as by publication or broadcasting, generally in order to sell. 2 To call attention to. —*v.i.* 3 To inquire by public notice, as in a newspaper: with *for:* to *advertise* for a house. 4 To distribute or publish advertisements. [<MF *advertir* warn, give notice to <L *advertere*. See ADVERT.] —**ad′ver·tis′er** *n.*

**ad·vice** (ad·vīs′) *n.* 1 Counsel or a suggestion as to a course of action. 2 *Often pl.* Information; notification. [<L *ad-* to + *visum*, p.p. of *videre* see]

**ad·vis·a·ble** (ad·vī′zə·bəl) *adj.* Recommended; expedient. —**ad·vis′a·bil′i·ty, ad·vis′a·ble·ness** *n.* —**ad·vis′a·bly** *adv.*

**ad·vise** (ad·vīz′) *v.* **ad·vised, ad·vis·ing** *v.t.* 1 To give advice to; counsel. 2 To recommend: to *advise* a course of action. 3 To notify; inform, as of a transaction: with *of.* —*v.i.* 4 To take counsel: with *with:* He *advised* with his lawyer. 5 To give advice. —**ad·vis′er, ad·vis′or** *n.*

**ad·vo·cate** (ad′və·kāt) *v.t.* **·cat·ed, ·cat·ing** To speak or write in favor of. —*n.* (ad′və·kit, -kāt) One who defends or supports some-

thing or someone. [<L *advocatus* one summoned to another] —**ad′vo·ca′tor** *n.* —**ad·voc·a·to·ry** (ad·vok′ə·tôr′ē, -tō′rē) *adj.*

**aer·i·al** (âr′ē·əl, ā·ir′ē·əl) *adj.* 1 Of, in, or by the air. 2 Like air; atmospheric. 3 Growing in the air: an *aerial* root. 4 Not real; imaginary; unsubstantial. 5 Existing or performed in the air. 6 Of, by, or for aircraft: *aerial* bombardment. —*n.* (âr′ē·əl) ANTENNA (def. 2). [<L *aer* air] —**aer′i·al·ly** *adv.* • See AIRPLANE.

**aer·o·dy·nam·ics** (âr′ō·dī·nam′iks, â′ər·ō-) *n.pl. (construed as sing.)* The branch of physics that deals with the motion of gases, esp. with the effects of bodies moving through the atmosphere. —**aer′o·dy·na·m′ic** *adj.*

**aer·o·nau·tics** (âr′ə·nô′tiks, â′ər·ə-) *n.pl. (construed as sing.)* The science and technology that deal with the design, construction, and operation of aircraft. —**aer′o·nau′tic** or **·ti·cal** *adj.*

**aer·o·sol** (âr′ə·sôl, -sol, â′ər·ə-) *n.* A colloidal dispersion of a solid or liquid in a gas. —*adj.* 1 Pertaining to a method of packaging a product under pressure in a valved container so that on release of the valve the contents escape in a spray or foam. 2 Describing a product so packaged: an *aerosol* disinfectant. [< AERO- + SOL(UTION)]

**aer·o·space** (âr′ō·spās, â′ər·ō-) *n.* 1 The earth's atmosphere and the space beyond it. 2 The science and technology of aeronautics and space flight.

**aes·thet·ic** (es·thet′ik) *adj.* 1 Of aesthetics. 2 Of, pertaining to, or appreciating beauty and art. 3 Having or characterized by fine taste. [<Gk. *aisthētikos* of sense perception] Also **aes·thet′i·cal.** —**aes·thet′i·cal·ly** *adv.*

**af·fa·ble** (af′ə·bəl) *adj.* Easy and courteous in manner; friendly; approachable. [< L *affabilis*, lit., able to be spoken to] —**af′fa·bil′i·ty, af′fa·ble·ness** *n.* —**af′fa·bly** *adv.* —Syn. amicable, cordial, genial, sociable, kind.

**af·fair** (ə·fâr′) *n.* 1 Anything done or to be done; business. 2 *pl.* Matters of business or concern. 3 Any matter, event, or thing. 4 A social event. 5 An object or device. 6 A romantic and usu. sexual relationship between two people not married to each other.

**af·fect** (ə·fekt′) *v.t.* 1 To act upon or have an effect upon. 2 To touch or move emotionally. —*n.* (af·ekt) *Psychol.* Emotion, as distinguished from thought or perception. [<L

*afficere* influence, attack < *ad-* to + *facere* do] • **affect, effect** To *effect* means to produce, accomplish, or bring about a definite, specific result, whereas to *affect* means merely to influence or act upon: The disease *affected* the patient's eyesight until her doctor *effected* a cure.

**af·fec·tion** (ə·fek′shən) *n.* 1 Good, kind, or loving feelings, as towards another. 2 A particular mental state or disposition. 3 A disease. 4 A property or attribute. [<L *afficere* to influence, affect]

**af·fi·da·vit** (af′ə·dā′vit) *n.* A sworn declaration, in writing, made before an official authority. [< Med.L, he has stated on oath]

**af·fil·i·ate** (ə·fil′ē·āt) *v.* **·at·ed, ·at·ing** *v.t.* 1 To associate or unite, as a member or branch: with *to* or *with*. 2 To join or associate (oneself): with *with*. 3 To determine the origins of. —*v.i.* 4 To associate or ally oneself: with *with*. —*n.* (ə·fil′ē·it) An affiliated person or thing. [< L *affiliare* adopt] —**af·fil′i·a′tion** *n.*

**af·fin·i·ty** (ə·fin′ə·tē) *n. pl.* **·ties** 1 Any natural liking or inclination. 2 Likenesses indicating a common origin. 3 Physical or chemical attraction. 4 Connection through certain relations formed, as by marriage. 5 An attraction held to exist between certain persons. [< L *affinis* adjacent, related]

**af·firm** (ə·fûrm′) *v.t.* 1 To declare positively; assert to be true. 2 To confirm or ratify, as a judgment or law. —*v.i.* 3 *Law* To make a formal judicial declaration, but not under oath. [< L *ad-* to + *firmare* make firm] —**af·firm′a·ble** *adj.* —**af·firm′a·bly** *adv.* —**af·firm′ant** *adj., n.* —**af·firm′er** *n.* —**Syn.** 1 maintain, propound, avow, advance, insist.

**af·firm·a·tive** (ə·fûr′mə·tiv) *adj.* 1 Asserting or confirming that something is so. 2 Positive. Also **af·firm·a·to·ry** (ə·fûr′mə·tôr′ē, ·tō′re). —*n.* 1 A word or expression of affirmation or assent. 2 That side in a debate which affirms the proposition debated. —**af·firm′a·tive·ly** *adv.*

**af·flict** (ə·flikt′) *v.t.* To distress with continued suffering; trouble. [< L *affligere* dash against, strike down] —**af·flict′er** *n.* —**af·flic′tive·ly** *adv.*

**af·flu·ent** (af′lōō·ənt, ə·flōō′-) *adj.* 1 Abounding; abundant. 2 Wealthy; opulent. —*n.* A stream that flows into another. [< L *ad-* to + *fluere* flow] —**af′flu·ent·ly** *adv.*

**af·ford** (ə·fôrd′, ə·fōrd′) *v.t.* 1 To have sufficient means for: usu. preceded by *can* or *be able to.* 2 To be able to do, say, etc., without detriment: usu. preceded by *can:* He

can *afford* to laugh now. 3 To provide or furnish: It *affords* me great delight. [< OE *geforthian* further, promote] —**af·ford′a·ble** *adj.*

**af·front** (ə·frunt′) *v.t.* 1 To insult openly; offend by word or act. 2 To confront in defiance; accost. —*n.* An open insult or indignity. [< OF *afronter* strike on the forehead] —**af·front′er** *n.* —**af·fron′tive** *adj.* —**Syn.** 1 aggravate, annoy, provoke, irritate, vex.

**a·fraid** (ə·frād′) *adj.* Filled with fear or apprehension. [<ME *affrayen* to fear <OF *esfrei* affray]

**Af·ro** (af′rō) *n. pl.* **Af·ros** A hair style in which bushy hair is shaped into a full, rounded mass. —*adj.* Of, pertaining to, or influenced by African culture, style, etc. Also **af′ro**.

**Af·ro-Amer·i·can** (af′rō·ə·mer′ə·kən) *adj.* Of or pertaining to Americans of black African descent. —*n.* An Afro-American person.

**af·ter·burn·er** (af′tər·bûr′nər, âf′-) *n. Aeron.* A device that injects extra fuel into the exhaust of a jet engine to increase its thrust.

**age·ism** (ā′jiz·əm) *n.* Discrimination or prejudice, esp. as directed against elderly people. —**age′ist** *n., adj.*

**a·gen·cy** (ā′jən·sē) *n. pl.* **·cies** 1 Active power or force. 2 Means; instrumentality. 3 Any establishment where business is done for others. 4 The office or offices of such an establishment. 5 A specific division of governmental administration. [< L *agere* do]

**a·gen·da** (ə·jen′də) *n. pl.* **·das** A list or program of things to be done, as at a meeting. [< L < *agere* to do]

**a·gent** (ā′jənt) *n.* 1 One who acts or has power to act. 2 Any force or substance having power to cause change: a chemical *agent.* 3 A person, business, etc., who represents or acts for another: an actor's *agent.* 4 A means by which something is done. 5 *Informal* A traveling salesman. [< L *agere* do] —**a·gen·tial** (ā·gen′shəl) *adj.* —**Syn.** 1 actor, doer, operator, mover. 3 representative, proxy, deputy. 4 factor, cause, instrument.

**ag·glom·er·ate** (ə·glom′ə·rāt) *v.t. & v.i.* **·at·ed, ·at·ing** To gather, form, or grow into a ball or rounded mass. —*adj.* (ə·glom′ər·it, ·ə·rāt) Gathered into a mass or heap; clustered densely. —*n.* (ə·glom′ər·it, ·ə·rāt) A heap or mass of things thrown together indiscriminately. [< L *ad-* to + *glomerare* gather into a ball] —**ag·glom′er·a′tion** *n.*

**ag·gran·dize** (ə·gran′dīz, ag′rən·dīz) *v.t.* **·dized, ·diz·ing** 1 To make great or greater.

2 To make appear greater; exalt. [< L *ad-* to + *grandire* make great or large] —**ag·gran′dize·ment**, **ag·gran′diz·er** *n.*

**ag·gra·vate** (ag′rə·vāt) *v.t.* **·vat·ed**, **·vat·ing** 1 To make worse. 2 To make heavier or more burdensome, as a duty. 3 *Informal* To provoke or exasperate. [< L *ad-* to + *gravare* make heavy] —**ag′gra·vat′ing**, **ag′gra·va′tive** *adj.* —**ag′gra·vat′ing·ly** *adv.* —**ag′gra·va′tion** *n.*

**ag·gre·gate** (ag′rə·gāt) *v.t.* **·gat·ed**, **·gat·ing** 1 To bring or gather together, as into a mass, sum, or body. 2 To amount to; form a total of. —*adj.* (ag′rə·git) Collected into a sum, mass, or total; gathered into a whole. —*n.* (ag′rə·git) 1 The entire number, sum, mass, or quantity of something; amount; total. 2 Material, as sand or pebbles, used in making concrete. —**in the aggregate** Collectively; as a whole. [< L *aggregare*, lit. bring to the flock] —**ag′gre·ga′tive** *adj.* —**ag′gre·ga′tion**, **ag′gre·ga′tor** *n.*

**ag·gres·sion** (ə·gresh′ən) *n.* 1 An unprovoked attack. 2 Aggressive action or practices.

**a·ghast** (ə·gast′, ə·gäst′) *adj.* Struck with horror or amazement; shocked. [< ᴀ-² + *gōestan* terrify]

**ag·ile** (aj′əl, aj′īl) *adj.* 1 Able to move quickly and easily; nimble. 2 Alert; lively: an *agile* mind. [< L *agilis* < *agere* do, move] —**ag′ile·ly** *adv.* —**ag′ile·ness**, **a·gil·i·ty** (ə·jil′ə·tē) *n.*

**ag·i·tate** (aj′ə·tāt) *v.* **·tat·ed**, **·tat·ing** *v.t.* 1 To shake or move irregularly. 2 To set or keep moving, as a fan. 3 To excite or endeavor to excite, as a crowd. 4 To discuss publicly and incessantly, as a controversial question. —*v.i.* 5 To excite public interest in a cause by continuous discussion, writing, etc. [< L *agitare* set in motion, freq. of *agere* do, move] —**ag′i·ta′tion** *n.*

**ag·o·ny** (ag′ə·nē) *n. pl.* **·nies** 1 Intense suffering of body or mind. 2 Any violent emotion. 3 Violent striving or effort. 4 The struggle that sometimes precedes death. [<Gk. *agōnia* <*agon* contest]

**a·gree** (ə·grē′) *v.* **a·greed**, **a·gree·ing** *v.i.* 1 To give consent; accede: with *to.* 2 To be in harmony or in accord. 3 To be of one mind; concur: with *with.* 4 To come to terms, as in the details of a transaction: with *about* or *on.* 5 To be acceptable; suit: with *with.* 6 *Gram.* To correspond in person, number, case, or gender. —*v.t.* 7 To grant as a concession: with a noun clause: I *agree* that it

is difficult. [<L *ad* to + *gratus* pleasing] —**Syn.** 1 acquiesce, assent. 2 coincide, harmonize. 3 approve, accept.

**ag·ri·cul·ture** (ag′rə·kul′chər) *n.* The act or science of cultivating the soil and of raising food crops and livestock; farming. [<L *ager* field + *cultura* cultivation] —**ag′ri·cul′tur·al** *adj.* —**ag′ri·cul′tur·al·ly** *adv.*

**aid** (ād) *v.t.* & *v.i.* To render assistance (to). —*n.* 1 Help; assistance. 2 A person or thing that helps. 3 An aide. [< L *adjuvare* give help to] —**aid′er** *n.*

**AIDS** (ādz) *n.* An infectious disease that attacks the human immune system, caused by a retrovirus, spread by transfer of infected blood or by sexual contact, usually fatal. [<ᴀ(ᴄǫᴜɪʀᴇᴅ) ɪ(ᴍᴍᴜɴᴏ) ᴅ(ᴇғɪᴄɪᴇɴᴄʏ) ꜱ(ʏɴᴅʀᴏᴍᴇ)]

**ail** (āl) *v.t.* 1 To cause uneasiness or pain to; trouble; make ill. —*v.i.* 2 To be somewhat ill; feel pain. [<OE *eglan*] —**ail′ing** *adj.*

**aim** (ām) *v.t.* 1 To direct, as a missile, blow, weapon, word, or act, toward or against some thing or person. —*v.i.* 2 To have a purpose; endeavor; with an infinitive: to *aim* to please. 3 To direct a missile, weapon, etc. —*n.* 1 The act of aiming. 2 The line or direction of anything aimed. 3 Design; purpose; intention. [<L *ad-* to + *aestimare* estimate] —**Syn.** *n.* 3 goal, end, aspiration, endeavor, intent.

**air** (âr) *n.* 1 The gaseous envelope of the earth, consisting chiefly of nitrogen and oxygen; the atmosphere. 2 The open space around and above the earth. 3 A wind; breeze. 4 Utterance or publicity: to give *air* to one's opinions. 5 Peculiar or characteristic appearance or impression: an *air* of mystery. 6 *pl.* Artificial manners or affectations: to put on *airs.* 7 Travel or transportation by aircraft. 8 *Music* A melody or tune. —**in the air** 1 Prevalent; abroad, as gossip. 2 Not finally decided or settled: **also up in the air.** —*v.t.* 1 To expose to the air, so as to dry, ventilate, etc. 2 To make public; display; exhibit. [<Gk. *aēr* air, mist] —**Syn.** *n.* 5 demeanor, look, mien, manner, way.

**air·borne** (âr′bôrn′, -bōrn′) *adj.* 1 Transported through the air, esp. in aircraft. 2 Not on the ground; aloft.

**air brake** A brake operated by compressed air.

**air conditioning** A system for controlling the temperature, purity, and humidity of air in buildings, cars, etc.

**air·craft** (âr′kraft′, -kräft′) *n.* Any form of

craft designed for flight through the air, as airplanes, dirigibles, etc.

**aircraft carrier** A large ship designed to carry aircraft, with a level upper flight deck usu. extending beyond the bow and stern.

**air·lift** (âr′lift′) n. The operation of transporting foodstuffs, other commodities, and personnel by airplane during land blockade. —v.t. & v.i. To transport (food and supplies) by airplane.

**air·mail** (âr′māl′) n. 1 Mail carried by airplane. 2 A postal system of carrying mail by airplane. —v.t. To send by airmail.

**air·plane** (âr′plān′) n. A heavier-than-air flying craft, supported by aerodynamic forces and propelled by an engine or engines.

**air·port** (âr′pôrt′, -pōrt′) n. An area for aircraft takeoffs and landings, together with buildings for maintenance, storage, and passenger service.

**air·space** (âr′spās′) n. The part of the atmosphere over a designated geographical area that is subject to territorial jurisdiction or international law in respect to use by aircraft, rockets, etc.

**aisle** (īl) n. 1 A passageway to or between rows of seats. 2 A similar passageway, as between trees. 3 An interior division of a church, alongside the main part or nave. [<OF *aile, ele* wing (of a building)] —aisled (īld) adj.

**al·a·bas·ter** (al′ə·bas′tər, -bäs′-) n. 1 A white or delicately tinted fine-grained gypsum. 2 A banded variety of calcite. —adj. 1 Made of or like alabaster. 2 Smooth and white. [<Gk. *alabast(r)os*] —al′a·bas′trine (-trin) adj.

**à la carte** (ä′lə kärt′) According to the menu: said of meals, menus, etc., in which each item of food has a separate price. [F, lit., by the bill of fare]

**a·lac·ri·ty** (ə·lak′rə·tē) n. 1 Cheerful willingness: She accepted the challenging assignment with *alacrity.* 2 Prompt and lively action: to respond to the taunt with *alacrity.* [< L *alacer* lively] —a·lac′ri·tous adj.

**à la mode** (ä′ lə mōd′, al′ə mōd′) 1 According to the mode; in the fashion. 2 Served with ice cream: pie *à la mode.* 3 Cooked in a rich sauce with vegetables: beef *à la mode.* [F, lit., in the fashion]

**a·larm** (ə·lärm′) n. 1 Sudden fear or apprehension. 2 Any sound or signal to warn of danger or arouse from sleep. 3 A mechanism, as of a clock, giving such a signal. —v.t. 1 To strike with sudden fear. 2 To

arouse to a sense of danger; give warning to. [< Ital. *all′ arme* to arms]

**al·ba·tross** (al′bə·trôs, -tros) n. pl. **·tros·ses** or **·tross** A large, web-footed sea bird with long narrow wings and a hooked beak. [< Pg. *alcatraz* pelican]

**al·bu·men** (al·byōō′mən) n. 1 The white of an egg. 2 The nutritive material surrounding the embryo in a seed. 3 ALBUMIN. [< L< *albus* white]

**al·cove** (al′kōv) n. 1 A recess connected with or at the side of a larger room. 2 Any embowered or secluded spot. 3 A niche in the face of a cliff or the wall of a building. [< Ar. *al-qobbah* the vaulted chamber]

**a·lert** (ə·lûrt′) adj. 1 Keenly watchful; vigilant. 2 Lively; nimble. 3 Intelligent. —n. 1 A warning or warning signal against sudden attack or danger. 2 The time such a warning is in effect. —on the alert On the lookout; ready. —v.t. To warn, as of a threatened attack or danger. [< Ital. *all′erta* on the watch] —a·lert′ly adv. —a·lert′ness n. —Syn. adj. 1 prepared, ready. 2 quick, brisk. 3 active, quick, perceptive, responsive.

**al·ga** (al′gə) n. pl. **·gae** (-jē) Any of a large variety of primitive chlorophyll-bearing plants widely distributed in aquatic and moist habitats, and including the seaweeds, kelps, diatoms, etc. [< L, seaweed] —al′gal (al′gəl) adj.

**al·ge·bra** (al′jə·brə) n. 1 A generalized arithmetic in which symbols representing any of a set of numbers are used in calculations. 2 A defined set of elements with various operations defined on the set. [< Ital. < Ar. *al-jebr* the reunion of broken parts, bone-setting] —al′ge·bra′ic (-brā′ik) adj. —al′ge·bra′i·cal·ly adv. —al′ge·bra′ist n.

**a·li·as** (ā′lē·əs) n. pl. **a·li·as·es** An assumed name: She used an *alias* to cash the stolen checks. —adv. Called by the assumed name of: Horace Jones, *alias* Howard Smith. [L, at another time or place]

**al·i·bi** (al′ə·bī) n. pl. **·bis** 1 A form of defense by which the accused undertakes to show that he was elsewhere when the crime was committed. 2 *Informal* Any excuse. —v.i. **·bied, ·bi·ing** *Informal* To make excuses for oneself. [< L, elsewhere]

**al·i·en** (āl′lē·ən, āl′yən) adj. 1 Of another country or people; foreign. 2 Opposed; contrary; inconsistent: with *to*: actions *alien* to his character. —n. 1 A foreign-born person who is not a citizen of the country in which he resides. 2 A person of another race,

13

country, religion, etc. **3** One excluded; an outsider. [< L *alienus*] —**Syn.** *adj.* 2 contradictory, foreign, unlike.

**al·ien·ate** (āl′yən·āt, ā′lē·ən-) *v.t.* ·**at·ed,** ·**at·ing 1** To make indifferent or unfriendly; estrange. **2** To cause to feel estranged or withdrawn from society. **3** To transfer, as property, to the ownership of another. —**al′ien·a′tion, al′ien·a′tor** *n.*

**a·light** (ə·līt′) *adj. & adv.* Lighted; on fire. [ME *alihten* light up]

**a·lign** (ə·līn′) *v.t.* **1** To place or bring into a straight line. **2** To bring (oneself, a group, etc.) to the support of an idea, cause, etc. —*v.i.* **3** To come into line. [< F *a-* to + *ligne* line] —**a·lign′ment** *n.*

**al·i·ment** (al′ə·mənt) *n.* Nourishment; food. [< L *alimentum* < *alere* nourish] —**al·i·men·tal** (al′ə·men′təl) *adj.* —**al′i·men′tal·ly** *adv.*

**al·ka·li** (al′kə·lī) *n. pl.* ·**lis** or ·**lies 1** Any of various highly reactive compounds that dissolve readily in water to form hydroxyl ions, neutralize acids, saponify fats, and turn red litmus blue. **2** Any compound that will neutralize an acid, as sodium carbonate, magnesia, etc. **3** Mineral matter found in soil and natural water and capable of neutralizing acid. [< Ar. *al-qaliy* the ashes of saltwort] —**al·ka·line** (al′kə·lin, -lin) *adj.* — **al′ka·lin′i·ty** (-lin′ə·tē) *n.*

**al·lay** (ə·lā′) *v.t.* **1** To lessen the violence or reduce the intensity of. **2** To lay to rest, as fears; pacify; calm. [< OE *ā-* away + *lecgan* lay] —**al·lay′er** *n.*

**al·le·ga·tion** (al′ə·gā′shən) *n.* **1** The act of alleging. **2** That which is alleged. **3** Something alleged without proof. **4** *Law* The assertion that a party to a suit undertakes to prove.

**al·lege** (ə·lej′) *v.t.* **al·leged, al·leg·ing 1** To assert to be true without proving; affirm. **2** To plead as an excuse, in support of or in opposition to a claim or accusation. [?< L *allegare* to send on a mission, dispatch] —**al·lege′a·ble** *adj.* —**al·leg′er** *n.*

**al·le·giance** (ə·lē′jəns) *n.* Loyalty, as the obligation of loyalty, to a government, a superior, a cause, etc. [< OF *ligeance* < *liege*. See LIEGE.]

**al·le·go·ry** (al′ə·gôr′ē, -gō′rē) *n. pl.* ·**ries 1** A story or narrative that teaches a moral or truth by using people, animals, events, etc., as symbols of that moral or truth. **2** Any symbolic representation in literature or art. [< Gk. *allēgoria*, lit., a speaking otherwise] —**al′le·go′rist** (-gôr′ist, -gō′rist, -gər·ist) *n.*

**al·ler·gy** (al′ər·jē) *n. pl.* ·**gies** A condition of heightened susceptibility to a substance, as smoke or pollen. [< G *Allergie*, lit., altered reaction]

**al·le·vi·ate** (ə·lē′vē·āt) *v.t.* ·**at·ed,** ·**at·ing** To make lighter or easier to bear; relieve. [< L *alleviare* < *ad-* to + *levis* light] —**al·le′vi·a′ tion, al·le′vi·a′tor** *n.* —**al·le·vi·a·tive** (a·lē′ vē·ā′tiv, ə·lē′vē·ə·tiv) *adj.* —**Syn.** allay, assuage, lessen, mitigate.

**al·ley** (al′ē) *n. pl.* ·**leys 1** A narrow passageway, esp. one behind or between city buildings. **2** A walk or lane bordered by trees, flowers, etc. **3** A bowling lane. [< OF *alee* a going, passage < *aler* go]

**al·li·ance** (ə·lī′əns) *n.* **1** A formal treaty or agreement between countries, states, parties, etc; also, those involved in such an agreement. **2** Any union or relationship, as by blood, marriage, interests, etc. **3** Any similarity or affinity. [< L *alligantia* < *alligare*. See ALLY.]

**al·li·ga·tor** (al′ə·gā′tər) *n.* **1** A large crocodilian reptile, found only in the southern U.S. and in China, having a shorter, blunter snout than the crocodile. **2** Leather made from the skin of the alligator. [< Sp. *el lagarto* the lizard < L *lacertus*]

**al·lit·er·a·tion** (ə·lit′ə·rā′shən) *n.* The use or repetition of a succession of words with the same initial letter or sound, as in "The river running round the rock." —**al·lit·er·a·tive** (ə·lit′ər·ə·tiv, ə·rā′tiv) *adj.* —**al·lit′er·a·tive·ly** *adv.*

**al·lo·cate** (al′ə·kāt) *v.t.* ·**cat·ed,** ·**cat·ing 1** To set apart for a special purpose, as funds. **2** To apportion; assign, as a share or in shares. **3** To locate or localize, as a person or event. [< L *ad-* to + *locare* to place] — **al′lo·ca′tion** *n.*

**al·lot** (ə·lot′) *v.t.* **al·lot·ted, al·lot·ting 1** To assign or distribute by lot. **2** To apportion or assign: with *to*. [< OF *a-* to + *lot* a portion, lot]

**all-out** (ôl′out′) *adj.* Done with maximum effort; unrestrained. —*adv.* Without stint; with maximum effort.

**al·low** (ə·lou′) *v.t.* **1** To permit to occur, do, have, enter, etc. **2** To admit; acknowledge as true or valid. **3** To make provision for: *Allow* one yard for waste. **4** To grant; allot, as a share or portion. **5** *Regional* To maintain; declare. —**allow for** To make provision for; bear in mind: *Allow for* traffic. —**allow of** To permit or be subject to: Your remark *allows of* several interpretations. [< OF *alouer* place, use, assign < Med.L *allocare* to allocate and OF *alouer, aloer* approve < L *allaudare* extol] —**al·lowed'** *adj.*

**al·loy** (al'oi, ə·loi') *n.* 1 A substance having metallic properties and consisting of a metal and at least one other element, usu. another metal. 2 Anything that reduces purity. —*v.t.* (ə·loi') 1 To reduce the purity of, as a metal, by mixing with an alloy. 2 To mix (metals) so as to form into an alloy. 3 To modify or debase, as by mixture with something inferior. [< L *alligare* to bind to]

**all-time** (ôl'tim') *adj.* Of or for all time.

**al·lude** (ə·lōōd') *v.i.* **al·lud·ed, al·lud·ing** To make indirect or casual reference: with *to.* [< L *alludere* play with, joke] —**Syn.** hint, imply, insinuate, intimate, suggest.

**al·lure** (ə·lōōr') *v.t. & v.i.* **al·lured, al·lur·ing** To attract attention and interest; entice. —*n.* The ability to attract or fascinate. [< OF *a-* to + *leurre* a lure] —**al·lur'er, al·lure'ment** *n.*

**al·lu·sion** (ə·lōō'zhən) *n.* 1 The act of alluding. 2 An indirect reference or mention. [< L *allusus*, p.p. of *alludere.* See **ALLUDE.**]

**al·lu·vi·um** (ə·lōō'vē·əm) *n. pl.* **·vi·a** (-vē·ə) or **·vi·ums** *Geol.* Any deposit, as of sand or mud, transported and left by flowing water. [< L]

**al·ly** (ə·lī') *v.* **al·lied, al·ly·ing** *v.t.* 1 To unite or combine by some relationship: usu. used in the passive or reflexively. —*v.i.* 2 To enter into alliance; become allied. —*n.* (al'ī, ə·lī') *pl.* **al·lies** 1 A country, sovereign, group, etc., leagued with another or others, as by treaty. 2 Any friend, associate, or helper. [< L *ad-* to + *ligare* bind]

**al·ma·nac** (ôl'mə·nak) *n.* 1 A yearly calendar giving weather forecasts, astronomical information, times of high and low tides, and other data. 2 An annual book containing facts and statistics on a large variety of subjects. [< Ar. *al-manākh*]

**al·mond** (ä'mənd, am'ənd) *n.* 1 A small tree related to the plum, cultivated in warm regions. 2 The edible, nutlike kernel of the fruit of this tree. [< Gk. *amygdalē*]

**alms** (ämz) *n. sing. & pl.* Money or gifts for the poor. [< Gk. *eleēmosynē* < *eleos* pity]

**a·loof** (ə·lōōf') *adj.* Distant or reserved, as in manner, interest, etc. —*adv.* At a distance. [<A-¹ + earlier *loof* luff] —**a·loof'ly** *adv.* —**a·loof'ness** *n.*

**al·pha·bet** (al'fə·bet) *n.* 1 The letters that form the elements of written language, in an order as fixed by usage. 2 Any system of characters or symbols representing the sounds of speech. 3 The simplest elements of anything. [< Gk. *alpha* alpha + *bēta* beta]

**alpha ray** *Physics* A stream of alpha particles.

**al·tar** (ôl'tər) *n.* 1 Any raised place or structure on which sacrifices may be offered or incense burned as an act of worship. 2 *Eccl.* The structure of wood or stone on which the elements are consecrated in the Eucharist. —**lead to the altar** To marry. [< L *altare*]

**al·ter** (ôl'tər) *v.t.* 1 To cause to be different; change; modify. 2 To fit (a garment) by recutting, resewing, etc. 3 To castrate. —*v.i.* 4 To change, as in character or appearance. [<Med.L *alterare* < L *alter* other] —**al'ter·a·ble** *adj.* —**al'ter·a·bly** *adv.*

**al·ter·cate** (ôl'tər·kāt, al'-) *v.i.* **·cat·ed, ·cat·ing** To dispute vehemently; wrangle. [< L *altercari* to dispute with one another < *alter* other]

**al·ter·nate** (ôl'tər·nāt, al'-) *v.* **·nat·ed, ·nat·ing.** *v.t.* 1 To arrange, use, or perform by turns. 2 To cause to follow in turns. —*v.i.* 3 To occur or appear in turns. 4 To take turns: to *alternate* on a job. 5 To pass repeatedly back and forth from one thing or condition to another —*adj.* (ôl'tər·nit, al'-) 1 Existing, occurring, or following by turns; reciprocal. 2 Referring to every second or every other (of a series). 3 Alternative: an *alternate* method. 4 *Bot.* **a** Placed singly at intervals on either side of the stem, as leaves. **b** Disposed at intervals between other parts. —*n.* (ôl'tər·nit, al'-) A substitute or second. [< L *alternare* < *alternus* every second one < *alter* other] —**al'ter·nate·ly** *adv.* —**al'ter·nate·ness** *n.*

**al·ter·na·tive** (ôl·tûr'nə·tiv, al-) *adj.* Being or affording a choice between two or, loosely, more than two things. —*n.* 1 A choice between two things or, loosely, more than two. 2 One of the things to be chosen. 3 Something still to be chosen or decided: What is the *alternative* to war? —**al·ter'na·tive·ly** *adv.* —**al·ter'na·tive·ness** *n.*

**al·tim·e·ter** (al·tim'ə·tər, al'tə·mē'tər) *n.* Any of various instruments for measuring altitude, esp. of aircraft.

**al·ti·tude** (al'tə·t'ōōd) *n.* 1 Vertical elevation above any given reference point, esp. above mean sea level; height. 2 *Astron.* Angular elevation above the horizon. 3 *Geom.* The vertical distance from the base of a figure to its highest point. 4 A high or the highest point. [< L *altus* high] —al'ti·tu'di·nal (-də·nəl) *adj.*

al·to (al'tō) *adj.* Having a range immediately below the highest or between soprano and tenor: an *alto* saxaphone. —*n. pl.* ·tos 1 The lowest female voice; contralto. 2 The highest male voice; countertenor. 3 An alto singer, instrument, or part. [< Ital. < L *altus* high]

al·to·geth·er (ôl'tə·geth'ər, ôl'tə·geth'ər) *adv.* 1 Completely; wholly; entirely. 2 With everything included; all told. —*n.* A whole.

al·tru·ism (al'trōō·iz'əm) *n.* Unselfish devotion to the welfare of others. [< L *alter* other] —al'tru·ist *n.* —al'tru·is'tic *adj.* —al'tru·is'ti·cal·ly *adv.*

a·lu·mi·num (ə·lōō'mə·nəm) *n.* A lightweight, silvery, metallic element (symbol Al) very abundant in minerals in the earth's crust and having countless technological uses, esp. as a structural and packaging material. *Brit. sp.* al·u·min·i·um (al'yə·min'ē·əm). [< L *alumen* alum] —a·lu'mi·nous *adj.*

a·lum·nus (ə·lum'nəs) *n. pl.* ·ni (-nī) A person, esp. a male, who has attended or graduated from a college or school. [< L, foster son < *alere* nourish] • In referring to graduates or former students of a coeducational school, the plural form *alumni* often is used to include both men and women.

AM, A.M., a.m., a·m, amplitude modulation.

a·mal·gam (ə·mal'gəm) *n.* 1 An alloy of mercury with another metal. 2 Any mixture or combination. [< Med.L *amalgama*]

a·man·u·en·sis (ə·man'yōō·en'sis) *n. pl.* ·ses (-sēz) One who copies manuscript or takes dictation; a secretary. [< L *ab-* from, by + *manus* hand]

am·a·ranth (am'ə·ranth) *n.* 1 Any of various plants with dry flowers that do not readily fade. 2 An imaginary, never-fading flower. 3 A purplish red. [< Gk. *amarantos*, lit., unfading] —am·a·ran·thine (am'ə·ran'thin) *adj.*

am·a·teur (am'ə·chōōr, -'tŏōr, -tər, am'ə·tûr') *n.* 1 One who practices an art, science, skill, etc., for his own pleasure and not as a paid professional. 2 An athlete who has not used any athletic skill or fame as a means of profit. 3 One who does something without professional skill or ease. —*adj.* 1 Of, pertaining to, or done by an amateur or amateurs. 2 Not expert. [< L *amator* lover < *amare* love] —am'a·teur·ism *n.*

a·maze (ə·māz') *v.t.* a·mazed, a·maz·ing To overwhelm, as by wonder or surprise; astonish greatly: explorers *amazed* to discover a flourishing civilization. [< OE *āmasian*] —a·maz·ed·ly (ə·mā'zid·lē), a·maz'ing·ly *adv.*

am·bas·sa·dor (am·bas'ə·dər, -dôr) *n.* 1 An accredited diplomatic agent of the highest rank, appointed as the representative of one government to another. 2 Any personal representative or messenger. 3 A person considered as a representative, as of his homeland: visiting athletes serving as *ambassadors* of good will. [< Ital. *ambasciatore*] —am·bas·sa·do·ri·al (am·bas'ə·dôr'ē·əl, -dô'rē-) *adj.* —am·bas'sa·dor·ship *n.* —am·bas'sa·dress (-drəs) *n. Fem.*

am·ber·gris (am'bər·grēs, -gris) *n.* An opaque, gray, waxy secretion from the intestines of the sperm whale, used in certain perfumes. [< F *ambre gris* gray amber]

am·bi·dex·trous (am'bə·dek'strəs) *adj.* 1 Able to use both hands equally well. 2 Very dexterous or skillful. 3 Dissembling; double-dealing. —am'bi·dex'trous·ly *adv.* —am'bi·dex'trous·ness *n.*

am·big·u·ous (am·big'yōō·əs) *adj.* 1 Capable of being understood in more senses than one. 2 Doubtful or uncertain. [< L *ambigere* wander about] —am·big'u·ous·ly *adv.* —am·big'u·ous·ness *n.*

am·bi·tion (am·bish'ən) *n.* 1 A strong desire to achieve something, as success, power, wealth, etc. 2 An object so desired or striven for. 3 A desire to work, or energy for work. [< L *ambitio* a going about (to solicit votes) < *ambire* to go about]

am·bu·lance (am'byə·ləns) *n.* A vehicle for conveying the sick and wounded. [< F (*hôpital) ambulant* walking (hospital)]

am·bu·la·to·ry (am'byə·lə·tôr'ē, -tō'rē) *adj.* 1 Of or for walking or walkers. 2 Able to walk, as an invalid. 3 Shifting; not fixed or stationary.

am·bus·cade (am'bəs·kād', am'bəs·kād') *n.* AMBUSH. —*v.t. & v.i.* ·cad·ed, ·cad·ing AMBUSH. [< Ital. *imboscata* an ambush]

am·bush (am'boosh) *n.* 1 The act of lying in wait to surprise or attack an enemy. 2 The hiding place or the persons hidden. Also am'bush·ment. —*v.t. & v.i.* To hide in or attack from ambush. [< Ital. *imboscare* place in a bush, set an ambush] —am'bush·er *n.*

a·mel·io·rate (ə·mēl'yə·rāt) *v.t. & v.i.* ·rat·ed, ·rat·ing To make or become better; improve. [< L *ad-* to + *miliorare* to better] —a·mel'io·rant (-rənt), a·mel'io·ra'tion *n.* —a·mel'io·ra·tive (ə·mēl'yə·rā'tiv, -rə·tiv) *adj.*

**a·me·na·ble** (ə-mē′nə-bəl, ə-men′ə-) *adj.* 1 Agreeable; tractable. 2 Accountable or responsible, as to authority. 3 Capable of being tested by rule or law. [< L *ad-* to + *minare* drive (with threats)] —**a·me′na·bil′i·ty, a·me′na·ble·ness** *n.* —**me′na·bly** *adv.*

**a·mend** (ə-mend′) *v. t.* 1 To change for the better; improve. 2 To free from faults. 3 To change or alter by authority; to *amend* a bill. —*v.i.* 4 To become better in conduct. [< L *emendare* to free from faults] —**a·mend′a·ble, a·mend′a·to′ry** *adj.* —**a·mend′a·ble·ness, a·mend′er** *n.* —**Syn.** 1 ameliorate, better, mitigate. 2 correct, rectify, reform, repair, restore.

**a·men·i·ty** (ə-men′ə-tē, ə-mēn′-) *n. pl.* **·ties** 1 Agreeableness; pleasantness. 2 *Usu. pl.* Any of the pleasant acts and courtesies of polite behavior. [< L *amoenus* pleasant]

**am·e·thyst** (am′ə-thist) *n.* 1 Quartz with purple or violet color; a semiprecious stone. 2 A purple variety of sapphire or corundum used as a gem. 3 A purplish violet color. [< Gk. *amethystos* not intoxicated, from the ancient belief that the stone prevented intoxication]

**a·mi·a·ble** (ā′mē-ə-bəl) *adj.* Friendly and good-natured. [< L *amicus* friend.] —**a′mi·a·bil′i·ty, a′mi·a·ble·ness** *n.* —**a′mi·a·bly** *adv.* —**Syn.** agreeable, kind, pleasant, pleasing.

**am·i·ca·ble** (am′i·kə-bəl) *adj.* Friendly; peaceable. [<L *amicus* friend] —**am·i·ca·bil·i·ty** (am·i·kə-bil′ə-tē), **am′i·ca·ble·ness** *n.* —**am′i·ca·bly** *adv.*

**amino acid** Any of a group of amines having both acidic and basic properties and forming the constituents of protein molecules.

**a·miss** (ə-mis′) *adj.* Out of order; wrong; improper: used predicatively: Something is *amiss.* —*adv.* In a wrong, improper, or defective way or manner. —**take amiss** To take offense at. [< ME *a-* at + *missen* miss]

**am·i·ty** (am′ə-tē) *n. pl.* **·ties** Peaceful relations; friendship. [< L *amicus* friend]

**am·me·ter** (am′mē′tər) *n. Electr.* An instrument for measuring an electric current. [< AM(PERE) + -METER]

**am·mo·nia** (ə-mōn′yə, ə-mō′nē-ə) *n.* 1 A colorless, pungent, suffocating gas composed of nitrogen and hydrogen. 2 A solution of this gas in water: **also ammonia water.** [< SAL AMMONIAC] —**am·mo′ni·ac, am·mo·ni·a·cal** (am′ə-nī′ə-kəl) *adj.*

**am·mu·ni·tion** (am′yə-nish′ən) *n.* 1 Any one of various articles used in the discharge of firearms and ordnance, as cartridges, shells, rockets, grenades, etc. 2 Any resources for attack or defense. [< L *munitio* < *munire* fortify]

**am·ne·sia** (am·nē′zhə, -zhē·ə) *n.* Loss or impairment of memory. [< Gk. *amnēsia* forgetfulness] —**am·ne′si·ac** (-zhē-ak′, -zē-) *adj., n.* —**am·ne′sic** (-sik, -zik), **am·nes′tic** (-nes′tik) *adj.*

**am·nes·ty** (am′nəs-tē) *n. pl.* **·ties** An act of pardon on the part of a government or authority, absolving offenders or groups of offenders. —*v.t.* **·tied, ·ty·ing** To grant amnesty to. [< Gk. *amnēstia* < *a-* not + *mnasthai* remember]

**a·mount** (ə-mount′) *n.* 1 A sum of two or more quantities; total. 2 The principle sum with the interest included, as in a loan. 3 The entire significance, value, or effect. 4 Quantity: a considerable *amount* of discussion. —*v.i.* 1 To total or add up: with *to*: to *amount* to ten dollars. 2 To be equivalent in effect or importance: with *to*: Their actions *amounted* to nothing. [< OF *amont* upward < *a mont* to the mountain]

**am·pere** (am′pir, am·pir′) *n.* A unit of electric current, defined as the steady current that produces a force of $2 \times 10^{-7}$ newtons per meter of length when flowing through parallel wires of negligible cross section and infinite length one meter apart in free space. [< A. M. *Ampère*, 1775–1836, French physicist]

**am·phib·i·ous** (am-fib′ē-əs) *adj.* 1 Living or adapted to life both on land and in water. 2 Capable of operating on or from land or water, as a vehicle or aircraft. 3 Of a mixed nature. [< Gk. *amphibios* having a double life] —**am·phib′i·ous·ly** *adv.* —**am·phib′i·ous·ness** *n.*

**am·phi·the·a·ter** (am′fə-thē′ə-tər) *n.* 1 A round or oval structure consisting of tiers of seats rising upward from a central open space or arena. 2 Any structure of similar shape. 3 Any arena or place of contest.

**am·ple** (am′pəl) *adj.* 1 Large in size, capacity, amount, etc. 2 More than enough; abundant. 3 Sufficient to meet all needs or requirements; adequate. [<L *amplus* large, abundant] —**am′ple·ness** *n.*

**am·pli·fi·er** (am′plə·fī′ər) *n.* 1 One who or that which amplifies or increases. 2 Any device that increases the power of a signal, esp. an electric signal.

17

**am·pli·fy** (am′plə·fī) *v.* **·fied**, **·fy·ing** *v.t.* 1 To enlarge or increase in scope, significance, or power. 2 To add to so as to make more complete, as by examples, data, etc. 3 To exaggerate; magnify. 4 To increase the power of a signal, esp. an electric signal. — *v.i.* 5 To make additional remarks; expatiate. [<L *amplus* large + *facere* make] — **am·pli·fi·ca·tive** (am′plə·fi·kā′tiv, am·plif′i·kə·tiv), **am·plif·i·ca·to·ry** (am·plif′i·kə·tôr′ē, -tō′rē) *adj.*

**am·pu·tate** (am′pyŏō·tāt) *v.t.* **·tat·ed**, **·tat·ing** To remove by cutting, as a limb. [<L < *ambi-* around + *putare* trim, prune] —**am′pu·ta′tion**, **am′pu·ta′tor** *n.*

**Am·trak** (am′trak) *n.* A private corporation, administered by the Federal Government, that manages passenger service on selected U.S. railroads.

**am·u·let** (am′yə·lit) *n.* Anything worn about one's person to protect from accident or ill luck; a charm. [<L *amuletum* charm]

**a·muse** (ə·myŏōz′) *v.t.* **a·mused**, **a·mus·ing** 1 To occupy pleasingly; entertain; divert. 2 To cause to laugh or smile. [< OF *a* to + *muser* to muse] —**a·mus′er** *n.*

**a·nach·ro·nism** (ə·nak′rə·niz′əm) *n.* 1 The representation of something existing or occurring out of its proper time. 2 Anything placed out of its proper time. [< Gk. *anachronizein* refer to a wrong time] — **a·nach′ro·nis′tic**, **a·nach′ro·nis′ti·cal**, **a·nach′ro·nous** *adj.*

**an·a·gram** (an′ə·gram) *n.* 1 A word or phrase formed by transposing the letters of another word or phrase. 2 *pl.* (*construed as sing.*) A game in which the players make words by transposing or adding letters. [< ANA- back + Gk. *gramma* a letter] — **an·a·gram·mat·ic** (an′ə·grə·mat′ik) or **·i·cal** *adj.* —**an′a·gram·mat′i·cal·ly** *adv.*

**a·nal·o·gy** (ə·nal′ə·jē) *n. pl.* **·gies** 1 A similarity or resemblance between things not otherwise identical. 2 *Biol.* A similarity in function but not in origin or structure. 3 *Logic* The assumption that things similar in some respects are probably similar in others.

**a·nal·y·sis** (ə·nal′ə·sis) *n. pl.* **·ses** (-sēz) 1 The separation of a whole into its parts or elements. 2 A statement of the results of this. 3 A method of determining or describing the nature of a thing by separating it into its parts. 4 *Chem.* The identification of some or all constituents forming a compound or

substance. 5 PSYCHOANALYSIS. [<Gk. *analysis* a releasing]

**an·ar·chy** (an′ər·kē) *n. pl.* **·chies** 1 Absence of government. 2 Lawless confusion and political disorder. 3 General disorder. [<Gk. *an-* without + *archos* leader] —**an·ar·chic** (an·är′kik), **an·ar′chi·cal** *adj.* —**an·ar′chi·cal·ly** *adv.*

**a·nat·o·my** (ə·nat′ə·mē) *n. pl.* **·mies** 1 The structure of a plant or animal. 2 The science of the structure of organisms. 3 The art or practice of dissection in order to investigate structure. 4 The human body. [<Gk. *anatomē* dissection]

**an·ces·tor** (an′ses·tər) *n.* 1 One from whom a person is descended; progenitor; forebear. 2 Anything regarded as an earlier model or forerunner. 3 An earlier organism from which later organisms have been derived. [<L *ante-* before + *cedere* go] —**an·ces·tress** (an′ses·tris) *n. Fem.*

**an·chor** (ang′kər) *n.* 1 A heavy implement, usu. metal, attached to a chain or cable and used, when lowered into the water, to hold a ship or boat in place by its weight or its hooks or flukes that grip the bottom. 2 Anything or anyone giving support or security. —**at anchor** Anchored, as a ship. —**cast** (or **drop**) **anchor** To put down the anchor in order to hold fast a vessel. —**ride at anchor** To be anchored, as a ship. —**weigh anchor** To take up the anchor so as to sail away. *v.t.* 1 To secure or make secure by an anchor. 2 To fix firmly. —*v.i.* 3 To lie at anchor, as a ship. 4 To be or become fixed. [<Gk. *ankyra*]

**an·cho·vy** (an′chō·vē, -chə·vē, an·chō′vē) *n. pl.* **·vies** Any of several small, herringlike fish found in warm seas, used as food. [<Sp., Pg. *anchova*,? <Basque *anchua*]

**an·cient** (ān′shənt) *adj.* 1 Existing or occurring in times long gone by, esp. before the fall of the Roman Empire. 2 Having existed a long time; of great age. —*n.* 1 One who lived in ancient times. 2 A very old person. —**an′cient·ly** *adv.*

**an·drog·y·nous** (an·droj′ə·nəs) *adj.* 1 Uniting the characteristics of both sexes; hermaphrodite. 2 Having male and female flowers on the same spike. Also **an·drog′y·nal**, **an·dro·gyn·ic** (an′drə·jin′ik). [<Gk. <ANDRO- + *gynē* woman] —**an·drog′y·ny** (-ə·nē) *n.*

**an·ec·dote** (an′ik·dōt) *n.* A short narrative of an interesting or entertaining nature. [<Gk. *anekdotos* unpublished] —**an′ec·dot′ic** (-

dot′ik) or ·i·cal *adj.* —an′ec·dot′ist (-dō′tist) *n.*

**a·ne·mi·a** (ə-nē′mē-ə) *n.* A deficiency in the amount or quality of red blood corpuscles or of hemoglobin in the blood. [<Gk. *an*-without + *haima* blood] —a·ne′mic *adj.*

**a·nem·o·ne** (ə-nem′ə-nē) *n.* 1 Any of various small herbs related to buttercups, having flowers with no petals but showy sepals. 2 SEA ANEMONE. [<Gk. *anemos* wind]

**an·es·the·sia** (an′is-thē′zhə, -zhē-ə) *n.* 1 Partial or total loss of physical sensation, due to disease. 2 Local insensibility to pain or general unconsciousness induced by an anesthetic. Also **an·es·the·sis** (an′is-thē′sis). [<Gk. *an*- without + *aisthēsis* sensation]

**an·es·the·tist** (ə-nes′thə-tist) *n.* A person trained to administer anesthetics.

**an·gel** (ān′jəl) *n.* 1 *Theol.* **a** One of an order of spiritual beings attendant upon the Deity; a heavenly messenger. **b** A fallen spiritual being. 2 A conventional representation of an angel, usu. a youthful winged human figure in white robes with a halo. 3 A person thought of as being angelically beautiful, pure, kind, etc. 4 A guardian spirit or attendant. 5 *Informal* The financial backer of a play or of any enterprise. [<Gk. *angelos* messenger]

**an·ger** (ang′gər) *n.* Violent and strong displeasure, as a result of opposition, mistreatment, etc.; wrath; ire. —*v.t.* 1 To make angry; enrage. —*v.i.* 2 To become angry. [<ON *ON* grief]

**an·gi·na** (an·ji′nə, an′jə-nə) *n.* 1 Inflammation of the throat characterized by spasmodic suffocation, as quinsy, croup, etc. 2 Angina pectoris. [<L, quinsy]

**an·gle** (ang′gəl) *n.* 1 *Geom.* **a** The figure formed by the intersection of two lines or of two planes. **b** The inclination of either of these lines or planes with respect to the other. 2 A corner or sharp bend. 3 A position from which something may be regarded; viewpoint. —*v.t.* & *v.i.* **an·gled, an·gling** 1 To move or turn at an angle or by angles. 2 To present with or show a particular bias or interpretation, as a story or report. [<L *angulus* a corner, angle] —an′gled *adj.*

**an·gry** (ang′grē) *adj.* **an·gri·er, an·gri·est** 1 Feeling, showing, or excited by anger. 2 Appearing to threaten: *angry* skies. 3 Badly inflamed: an *angry* sore. —**an·gri·ly** (ang′grə-lē) *adv.* —**an·gri·ness** *n.* —Syn. 1 furious, enraged, irate, wrathful. 2 stormy, turbulent. 3 sore, painful, burning.

**an·guish** (ang′gwish) *n.* Severe mental or physical distress. [<L *angustus* narrow, tight] —**an·guished** *adj.* —Syn. agony, torment, torture, suffering.

**an·gu·lar** (ang′gyə-lər) *adj.* 1 Of, having, or forming an angle or angles. 2 Measured by an angle: *angular* motion. 3 Bony; gaunt. 4 Awkwardly stiff: *angular* gestures. —**an′gu·lar·ly** *adv.*

**an·i·line** (an′ə-lin, -līn) *n.* A colorless oily compound derived from benzene, used in the production of many dyes, resins, and varnishes. —*adj.* Of, derived from, or pertaining to aniline. Also **an·i·lin** (an′ə-lin). [<ANIL + -INE]

**an·i·mal** (an′ə-məl) *n.* 1 Any member of a primary subdivision of organisms distinguished from plants by inability to produce nutrients by photosynthesis and by various other characteristics. 2 Any such creature as distinguished from man, esp. a mammal. 3 A bestial human being. —*adj.* 1 Of or pertaining to animals. 2 Like an animal; bestial. [<L *animalis* living < *animus* breath]

**an·i·mate** (an′ə-māt) *v.t.* ·mat·ed, ·mat·ing 1 To impart life to; make alive. 2 To make lively, energetic, vivacious, etc. 3 To move to action; incite; inspire. 4 To impart lifelike motion to. —*adj.* (an′ə-mit) 1 Possessing animal life; living. 2 Animated. [<L *animare* to fill with breath, make alive] —an′i·ma′tor, an′i·ma′ter *n.*

**an·i·mos·i·ty** (an′ə-mos′ə-tē) *n. pl.* ·ties Active, intense enmity or hostility. [<L *animositas* high spirit, boldness < *animus* soul, spirit]

**an·ise** (an′is) *n.* 1 A plant related to parsley, having small white or yellow flowers and seeds with a flavor like licorice. 2 Aniseed. [<Gk. *anison*]

**an·kle** (ang′kəl) *n.* 1 The joint connecting the foot and the leg. 2 The part of the leg between the foot and the calf near the ankle joint. [<OE *anclēow*]

**an·nals** (an′əlz) *n. pl.* 1 A year-by-year record of events in chronological order. 2 History or records in general. 3 A periodical publication of discoveries, transactions, etc. [<L *annales* (*libri*) yearly (record)] —an′nal·ist *n.*

**an·nex** (ə-neks′) *v.t.* 1 To add or append, esp. to something larger. 2 To incorporate as territory. 3 To attach, as an attribute, condition, etc. —n. (an′eks) 1 An addition to a building, or a nearby auxiliary building. 2 An addition to a document. *Brit. sp.* annexe *(n.)* [<L *annectere* tie together] —**an·nex′a·ble, an·nex′ive** *adj.*

**an·ni·hi·late** (ə·nī′ə·lāt) *v.t.* **·lat·ed, ·lat·ing** To destroy absolutely. [<L *ad-* to + *nihil* nothing] —**an·ni·hi·la·ble** (ə·nī′ə·lə·bəl) *adj.* —**an·ni′hi·la′tion, an·ni′hi·la′tor** *n.* —Syn. demolish, wipe out, exterminate.

**an·ni·ver·sa·ry** (an′ə·vûr′sər·ē) *n. pl.* **·ries** 1 A day or occasion recurring on the same date each year as a past event. 2 An observance or celebration on such a day. —*adj.* 1 Recurring on the same date every year. 2 Of or marking an anniversary. [<L *annus* year + *versus*, p.p. of *vertere* turn]

**an·no·tate** (an′ō·tāt) *v.t. & v.i.* **·tat·ed, ·tat·ing** To make explanatory or critical notes on or provide a commentary for (a text, etc.). [<L *ad-* to + *notare* note, mark<*nota* a mark] —**an′no·ta′tion, an′no·ta′tor** *n.* —**an′no·ta′tive** *adj.*

**an·nounce** (ə·nouns′) *v.t.* **an·nounced, an·nounc·ing** 1 To make known publicly or officially. 2 To give notice of the approach or appearance of, as by a signal. 3 To serve as the announcer for, as a radio program [<L<*ad-* to + *nuntiare* report]

**an·noy** (ə·noi′) *v.t.* To be troublesome to; bother; vex. [<LL *inodiare* to make odious] —**an·noy′er** *n.* —Syn. irk, irritate, harass, pester, bedevil, plague.

**an·nu·al** (an′yōō·əl) *adj.* 1 Returning, performed, or occurring every year. 2 Of or for a year; reckoned by the year. 3 *Bot.* Lasting or living only one year. —*n.* 1 A book or pamphlet issued once a year. 2 *Bot.* A plant living for a single year or season. [<L *annus* year] —**an′nu·al·ly** *adv.*

**an·nu·i·ty** (ə·n′yōō′ə·tē) *n. pl.* **·ties** 1 a An annual allowance or income. b The right to receive such an allowance. c The duty to pay it. 2 The return from an investment of capital, in a series of yearly payments. [<L *annus* year]

**an·nul** (ə·nul′) *v.t.* **an·nulled, an·nul·ling** To make or declare void or invalid, as a law or marriage. [<L *ad-* to + *nullus* none] —**an·nul′la·ble** *adj.* —**an·nul′ment** *n.*

**an·ode** (an′ōd) *n.* 1 The electrode of a polarized device through which current enters. 2 In an electrolytic cell, the positive pole at which oxidation of anions occurs. [<Gk. *anodos* a way up] —**an·od·ic** (an·od′ik) *adj.*

**an·o·dyne** (an′ə·dīn) *adj.* Having power to allay pain; soothing. ⌐—*n.* Anything that relieves pain or soothes. [<Gk. *an-* without + *odynē* pain]

**a·noint** (ə·noint′) *v.t.* 1 To rub with oil, ointment, etc. 2 To put oil on as a sign of consecration. [<L *inungere*<*in-* on + *ungere* smear] —**a·noint′er, a·noint′ment** *n.*

**a·nom·a·ly** (ə·nom′ə·lē) *n. pl.* **·lies** 1 Deviation from rule, type, or form; irregularity; abnormality. 2 Something anomalous. [<Gk. *anōmalos* uneven] —**a·nom′a·lism** *n.* —**a·nom·a·lis·tic** (ə·nom′ə·lis′tik) or **·ti·cal** *adj.*

**a·non·y·mous** (ə·non′ə·məs) *adj.* 1 Of unknown authorship or agency. 2 Bearing no name. [<Gk. *an-* without + *onoma, onyma* name] —**an·o·nym·i·ty** (an′ə·nim′ə·tē), **a·non′y·mous·ness** *n.* —**a·non′y·mous·ly** *adv.*

**an·swer** (an′sər, än′-) *v.t.* 1 To reply or respond, as by words or actions. 2 To prove successful. 3 To be accountable: with *for:* I will *answer* for his honesty. 4 To correspond or match, as in appearance: with *to:* He *answers* to your description. —*v.t.* 5 To speak, write, or act in response or reply to: to *answer* a letter. 6 To be sufficient for; fulfill: This rod *answers* the purpose. 7 To conform or correspond to: to *answer* a description. —**answer back** To talk back, as in contradiction. —*n.* A reply, as to a question, message, request, etc. 2 Any action in return or in kind; retaliation. 3 The result or solution, as of a problem in mathematics. 4 *Music* The restatement of a musical theme or phrase by a different voice or instrument. [<OE *andswaru* an answer] —**an′swer·er** *n.* —Syn. *v.* reply, respond, react. *n.* 1 response, rejoinder, acknowledgment. 2 reaction.

**an·tag·o·nism** (an·tag′ə·niz′əm) *n.* Mutual opposition or hostility.

**Ant·arc·tic** (ant·ärk′tik, -är′tik) *n.* 1 The region south of the Antarctic Circle: used with *the.* 2 The Antarctic Ocean. —*adj.* Of, in, or pertaining to the Antarctic or the Antarctic Ocean. [<Gk. *antarktikos* southern <*anti-* opposite + *arktos* the Bear (a northern constellation), the north]

**an·te·ce·dent** (an′tə·sēd′ənt) *adj.* Going before; prior in time, place, or order. —*n.* 1 One who or that which precedes or goes before. 2. *pl.* One's ancestry or past background. 3 *Gram.* The word, phrase, or clause referred to by a pronoun. 4 *Math.* The first term of a ratio; numerator. —**an′te·ce′dent·ly** *adv.*

**an·te·lope** (an'tə·lōp) *n. pl.* **·lope** or **·lopes 1** Any of various swift-running, long-horned bovines, including the gazelle, chamois, gnu, etc. **2** Leather made from the hide of such an animal. **3** PRONGHORN. [<LGk. *antholops*]

**an·te me·rid·i·em** (an'tē mə·rid'ē·em) *Latin* Before noon.

**an·ten·na** (an·ten'ə) *n. pl.* **·ten·nae** (-ten'ē) *for def. 1,* **·ten'nas** *for def. 2.* **1** One of the paired, movable, sensory appendages on the head of an insect or other arthropod; a feeler. **2** Any of various devices designed to project or receive electromagnetic waves, as in television or radio. [<L, a yard on which a sail is spread] • See INSECT.

**an·te·ri·or** (an·tir'ē·ər) *adj.* **1** In front or forward. **2** Preceding in time; earlier. [<L, compar. of *ante* before] **—an·te'ri·or·ly** *adv.* **—Syn. 1** front, fore, forward, foremost. **2** prior, preceding, antecedent.

**an·ther** (an'thər) *n.* The pollen-bearing part of a stamen. [<Gk. *anthēros* flowery <*anthos* flower] • See STAMEN.

**an·thra·cite** (an'thrə·sīt) *n.* Coal that burns with much heat and little flame; hard coal. [<Gk. *anthrax* coal] **—an·thra·cit·ic** (an'thrə·sit'ik) *adj.*

**an·thro·pog·e·ny** (an'thrə·poj'ə·nē) *n.* The branch of anthropology that deals with the origin and development of human beings. Also **an·thro·po·gen·e·sis** (an'thrə·pō·jen'ə·sis).

**an·thro·pol·o·gy** (an'thrə·pol'ə·jē) *n.* The scientific study of human beings and their physical, social, material, and cultural development. **—an·thro·po·log·i·cal** (an'thrə·pə·loj'i·kəl) or **·log'ic** *adj.* **—an·thro·po·log'i·cal·ly** *adv.* **—an·thro·pol'o·gist** *n.*

**an·ti·air·craft** (an'tē·âr'kraft', -âr'kräft') *adj.* Used defensively against aircraft.

**an·ti·bi·ot·ic** (an'ti·bī·ot'ik) *n.* Any of certain substances, as penicillin and streptomycin, produced by various fungi, bacteria, etc., that destroy or arrest the growth of other microorganisms, used in the treatment of infectious diseases. **—adj.** Of or acting as an antibiotic. [< ANTI- + Gk. *bios* mode of life]

**an·ti·bod·y** (an'ti·bod'ē) *n. pl.* **·bod·ies** A protein in the blood serum formed in response to a specific foreign protein and conferring immunity to that foreign protein.

**an·tic** (an'tik) *n.* A ludicrous or clownish action; a prank; caper. **—adj.** Odd; ludicrous; incongruous. **—v.i.** **an·ticked, an·tick·ing**

To perform antics. [<Ital. *antico* old, grotesque]

**an·tic·i·pate** (an·tis'ə·pāt) *v.t.* **·pat·ed, ·pat·ing 1** To count on in advance; expect; foresee. **2** To be in advance of or earlier than. **3** To act so as to prevent; forestall. **4** To foresee and act on beforehand. **5** To take or make use of beforehand, as income not yet available. [<L *ante-* before + *capere* take] **—an·tic'i·pa'tor** *n.* **—an·tic·i·pa·to·ry** (-tis'ə·pə·tôr'ē, -tō'rē) *adj.*

**an·ti·cli·max** (an'ti·klī'maks) *n.* **1** A sudden shift from the serious, lofty, etc., to the trivial or ludicrous. **2** Any sudden and disappointingly contrasting shift. **—an'ti·cli·mac'tic** (-klī·mak'tik) *adj.* **—an'ti·cli·mac'ti·cal·ly** *adv.*

**an·ti·dote** (an'ti·dōt) *n.* **1** Anything that neutralizes or counteracts the effects of a poison. **2** Something that counteracts a harmful effect. [<Gk. *antidotos* given against] **—an'ti·do'tal** *adj.* **—an'ti·do'tal·ly** *adv.*

**an·ti·his·ta·mine** (an'ti·his'tə·mēn, -min) *n.* Any of certain drugs that neutralize the action of histamine in allergic conditions and colds. **—an'ti·his'ta·min'ic** (-min'ik) *adj.*

**an·ti·knock** (an'ti·nok') *adj.* Preventing detonation in an engine. **—n.** An agent, as tetraethyl lead, that prevents knock or detonation when added to the fuel of an internal-combustion engine.

**an·ti·mat·ter** (an'ti·mat'ər) *n.* A theoretical form of matter composed of antiparticles.

**an·tip·a·thy** (an·tip'ə·thē) *n. pl.* **·thies 1** A feeling of aversion or dislike. **2** The cause of such feeling. [<Gk. *anti-* against + *pathein* feel, suffer] **—Syn.** repugnance, abhorrence, antagonism, hostility.

**an·ti·quat·ed** (an'ti·kwā'tid) *adj.* **1** Out of date; obsolete. **2** Ancient. **—Syn.** old-fashioned, passé, superannuated, archaic.

**an·tique** (an·tēk') *adj.* **1** Of or pertaining to ancient times, esp. ancient Greece or Rome. **2** Of or in the style of an earlier time. **3** Old; ancient. **—n. 1** An object, esp. a work of art or handicraft, valued because of its age. **2** The style of ancient art. **—v.t.** **an·tiqued, an·ti·quing** To cause to resemble an antique. [<L *antiquus* ancient] **—an·tique'ly** *adv.* **—an·tique'ness** *n.*

**an·tiq·ui·ty** (an·tik'wə·tē) *n. pl.* **·ties 1** The condition of being ancient; great age. **2** Ancient times. **3** *Usu. pl.* A relic of ancient times.

**an·ti·sep·tic** (an'tə·sep'tik) *adj.* **1** Of, pertaining to, or used in antisepsis. **2** Destructive of organisms causing infection, fermentation, or putrefaction. **Also** **an′ti·sep′ti·cal.** —*n.* An antiseptic substance. —**an′ti·sep′ti·cal·ly** *adv.*

**an·tith·e·sis** (an-tith′ə-sis) *n. pl.* **·ses** (-sēz) 1 The balancing of contrasted words, ideas, etc., against each other. 2 The direct contrary or opposite. [<Gk. *antitithenai* oppose] —**an·ti·thet·i·cal** (an′tə-thet′i-kəl), **an′ti·thet′ic** *adj.* —**an′ti·thet′i·cal·ly** *adv.*

**an·ti·tox·in** (an′ti-tok′sin) *n.* 1 An antibody formed in response to a specific toxin. 2 A preparation of a serum containing an antitoxin, used in treating certain diseases. —**an′ti·tox′ic** *adj.*

**a·nus** (ā′nəs) *n.* The opening at the lower end of the alimentary canal. [<L, orig. a ring]

**anx·ious** (angk′shəs, ang′-) *adj.* 1 Troubled in mind; uneasy; worried. 2 Fraught with or causing anxiety: an *anxious* wait. 3 Intently eager or desirous: *anxious* to succeed. [<L *anxius < angere* choke, distress] —**anx′ious·ly** *adv.* —**anx′ious·ness** *n.*

**a·part·heid** (ə-pärt′hīt, -hāt) *n.* The racial segregation decreed by law in the Republic of South Africa. [Afrikaans, apartness]

**a·part·ment** (ə-pärt′mənt) *n.* One of several rooms or suites of rooms in one building, equipped for housekeeping. [<Ital. *appartamento*]

**ap·a·thy** (ap′ə-thē) *n.* 1 Lack of emotion, motivation, etc. 2 Lack of concern; indifference. [<Gk. *a-* without + *pathos* feeling]

**ape** (āp) *n.* 1 A large, tailless primate, as a gorilla or chimpanzee. 2 Loosely, any monkey. 3 A mimic. —*v.t.* **aped, ap·ing** To imitate; mimic. [<OE *apa*]

**ap·er·ture** (ap′ər-chŏŏr, -chər) *n.* 1 An opening; hole. 2 An opening through which radiation is captured, as by a lens or antenna. [<L *apertus,* pp. of *aperire* open] —**ap′er·tur·al** *adj.* —**ap′er·tured** *adj.*

**a·pex** (ā′peks) *n. pl.* **a·pex·es** or **ap·i·ces** (ap′ə-sēz, ā′pə-) 1 The highest point; tip; top. 2 The vertex of an angle. 3 Climax. [<L]

**a·pha·sia** (ə-fā′zhə, -zhē-ə) *n.* Partial or total loss of the power to use language, due to brain injury or disease. [<Gk. *aphatos* speechless] —**a·pha·sic** (ə-fā′zik, -sik), **a·pha·si·ac** (ə-fā′zē-ak) *adj., n.*

**a·pi·ar·y** (ā′pē-er′ē) *n. pl.* **·ar·ies** A place where bees are kept. [<L *apis* bee]

**A·poc·a·lypse** (ə-pok′ə-lips) *n.* The book of Revelation, the last book of the New Testament.

**a·poc·ry·phal** (ə-pok′rə-fəl) *adj.* Of doubtful authenticity. —**a·poc′ry·phal·ly** *adv.*

**a·pol·o·get·ic** (ə-pol′ə-jet′ik) *adj.* 1 Making or implying an apology. 2 Defending or explaining. **Also a·pol′o·get′i·cal.** [<Gk. *apologia* a speech in defense] —**a·pol′o·get′i·cal·ly** *adv.*

**a·pol·o·gist** (ə-pol′ə-jist) *n.* One who argues in defense of a person or cause.

**a·pol·o·gy** (ə-pol′ə-jē) *n. pl.* **·gies** 1 A formal expression of regret for an offense, incivility, etc. 2 A poor substitute. [<Gk. *apologia* a speech in defense < *apo-* from + *logos* speech]

**ap·o·plex·y** (ap′ə-plek′sē) *n.* Sudden loss of sensation and voluntary motion, due to hemorrhage or impaired circulation in the brain; a stroke. [<Gk. *apoplēxia < apoplēssein* disable by a stroke]

**a·pos·ta·sy** (ə-pos′tə-sē) *n. pl.* **·sies** Desertion of one's religious faith, party, or principles, etc. [<Gk. *apostasia* a standing off, desertion]

**a·pos·tle** (ə-pos′əl) *n.* 1 *Often cap.* One of the twelve disciples originally chosen by Christ to preach the gospel. 2 A missionary or preacher in the early Christian church. 3 A Christian missionary who first evangelizes a nation or place. 4 An early or chief advocate of a cause. [<Gk. *apostolos* one sent forth, a messenger] —**a·pos′tle·ship, a·pos·to·late** (ə-pos′tə-lit, -lāt) *n.*

**a·pos·tro·phe** (ə-pos′trə-fē) *n.* A symbol (′) shown above the line, to indicate the omission of a letter or letters, the possessive case, or certain plurals, esp. of numbers *(4′s)* or letters *(i′s).* [<Gk. *(prosōidia) apostrophos* (accent) of turning away] —**ap·os·troph·ic** (ap′ə-strof′ik) *adj.*

**ap·o·thegm** (ap′ə-them) *n.* A terse, instructive, practical saying; a maxim. [<Gk. *apophthegma* a thing uttered] —**ap·o·theg·mat·ic** (ap′ə-theg-mat′ik) or **·i·cal** *adj.*

**ap·pall** (ə-pôl′) *v.t.* **ap·palled, ap·pal·ling** To fill with dismay or horror; horrify; shock. **Also ap·pal** (ap·palled, ap·pal·ling). [<OF *apallir* become or make pale]

**ap·pa·ra·tus** (ap·ə-rā′təs, -rat′əs) *n. pl.* **·tus** or **·tus·es** 1 A complex device or machine for a particular purpose. 2 An assembly of devices designed to achieve a specified result. 3 The organs and parts of the body involved in a specific function. 4 The organization or bureaucratic formula for accomplishing a political purpose, as maintaining a party in power. [L, preparation]

**ap·par·el** (ə·par′əl) *n.* Garments; clothing. — *v.t.* **·eled** or **·elled**, **·el·ing** or **·el·ling** To clothe; dress. [< OF *apareiller* prepare] — **Syn.** *n.* dress, attire, raiment, garb.

**ap·par·ent** (ə·par′ənt, ə·pâr′) *adj.* **1** Evident; obvious. **2** Seeming rather than actual. [< OF *aparoir* appear] —**ap·par′ent·ly** *adv.* —**ap·par′ent·ness** *n.*

**ap·pa·ri·tion** (ap′ə·rish′ən) *n.* **1** A specter; phantom; ghost. **2** An eerie or startlingly unusual sight. **3** An appearance. [< L *apparere* to appear] —**ap′pa·ri′tion·al** *adj.*

**ap·peal** (ə·pēl′) *n.* **1** An earnest entreaty for aid, sympathy, etc. **2** A quality or manner that attracts. **3** A resort to some higher power or final means. **4** *Law* **a** The carrying of a cause from a lower to a higher tribunal for a rehearing. **b** The right or request to do this. **c** A case so carried. —*v.i.* **1** To make an earnest supplication or request. **2** To be interesting or attractive. **3** To resort to or have recourse: to *appeal* to reason. **4** To request that a case be moved to a higher court. — *v.t.* **5** To refer or transfer (a case) to a higher court. [< L *appellare* call upon] —**ap·peal′a·ble** *adj.* —**ap·peal′er** *n.* —**ap·peal′ing·ly** *adv.*

**ap·pear** (ə·pir′) *v.i.* **1** To become visible; come into view. **2** To seem: He *appeared* tired and out of sorts. **3** To be on public view. **4** To be published or issued, as a book. **5** To present oneself formally in a law court. [< L *ad-* to + *parere* come forth, appear]

**ap·pease** (ə·pēz′) *v.t.* **ap·peased**, **ap·peas·ing** **1** To placate or pacify, as by yielding to demands. **2** To satisfy; allay. [< OF *a-* to + *pais* peace] —**ap·peas′a·ble** *adj.* —**ap·peas′a·bly**, **ap·peas′ing·ly** *adv.* —**ap·peas′er** *n.* — **Syn.** **1** calm, soothe, mollify, propitiate. **2** relieve, assuage, alleviate, quench.

**ap·pease·ment** (ə·pēz′mənt) *n.* **1** An appeasing or being appeased. **2** The policy of making concessions to a potential aggressor in order to maintain peace.

**ap·pel·lant** (ə·pel′ənt) *adj.* *Law* Of or pertaining to an appeal. —*n.* One who appeals.

**ap·pel·la·tion** (ap′ə·lā′shən) *n.* **1** A name or title. **2** The act of calling or naming.

**ap·pend** (ə·pend′) *v.t.* **1** To add, as something supplemental. **2** To attach; affix. [< L *ad-* to + *pendere* hang]

**ap·pen·di·ci·tis** (ə·pen′də·sī′tis) *n.* Inflammation of the vermiform appendix.

**ap·per·tain** (ap′ər·tān′) *v.i.* To relate or be relevant; pertain; belong: with *to*. [< L *ad-* to + *pertinere* pertain]

**ap·pe·tite** (ap′ə·tīt) *n.* **1** A desire for food or drink. **2** Any strong liking or desire. [< L *appetitus* < *appetere* strive for] —**ap·pe·ti·tive** (ap′ə·tī′tiv, ə·pet′ə·tiv) *adj.*

**ap·plaud** (ə·plôd′) *v.t. & v.i.* **1** To express approval (of) by clapping the hands. **2** To commend; praise. [< L *ad-* to + *plaudere* clap hands, strike] —**ap·plaud′a·ble** *adj.* —**ap·plaud′a·bly**, **ap·plaud′ing·ly** *adv.* —**ap·plaud′er** *n.*

**ap·pli·ance** (ə·plī′əns) *n.* A machine or device, esp. one used in the home. [< APPLY]

**ap·pli·ca·ble** (ap′li·kə·bəl, ə·plik′ə-) *adj.* Capable of or suitable for application; relevant; fitting. —**ap′pli·ca·bil′i·ty, ap′pli·ca·ble·ness** *n.* —**ap′pli·ca·bly** *adv.*

**ap·pli·cant** (ap′li·kənt) *n.* One who applies, as for employment or admission.

**ap·pli·ca·tion** (ap′li·kā′shən) *n.* **1** The act of applying. **2** That which is applied, as a medical remedy. **3** That by which one applies, as a written request or form. **4** Appropriation or relevance to a particular use. **5** Close and continuous attention. —**ap·pli·ca·tive** (ap′li·kā′tiv), **ap′pli·ca·to′ry** *adj.*

**ap·ply** (ə·plī′) *v.* **ap·plied**, **ap·ply·ing** *v.t.* **1** To put or spread on: to *apply* paint. **2** To put to a particular use: to *apply* steam to navigation. **3** To connect, as an epithet, with a person or thing. **4** To devote (oneself): to *apply* oneself to study. —*v.i.* **5** To make a formal request, as for employment or admission. **6** To be relevant or appropriate. [< L *applicare* join to < *ad-* to + *plicare* fold]

**ap·point** (ə·point′) *v.t.* **1** To designate or select, as a person for a position. **2** To name or decide upon, as a time or place for a meeting. **3** To ordain; decree. **4** To fit out; equip: a *well-appointed* office. [< OF *apointer* arrange, lit., bring to a point]

**ap·por·tion** (ə·pôr′shən, ə·pōr′-) *v.t.* To divide and assign proportionally; allot. [< L *ad-* to + *portio* position[ —**ap·por′tion·ment** *n.*

**ap·praise** (ə·prāz′) *v.t.* **ap·praised**, **ap·prais·ing** **1** To make an official valuation of. **2** To estimate the amount, quality, or worth of; judge. [< AD- + PRAISE] —**ap·prais′er** *n.*

**ap·pre·ci·a·ble** (ə·prē′shē·ə·bəl, -shə·bəl) *adj.* Sufficient to be noticed and evaluated. — **ap·pre′ci·a·bly** *adv.*

**ap·pre·ci·ate** (ə·prē′shē·āt) *v.* **·at·ed**, **·at·ing** *v.t.* **1** To be fully aware of the worth of; regard or value highly. **2** To be keenly sensitive to. **3** To enjoy deeply or fully. **4** To be grateful for. **5** To raise the price or value of.

—*v.i.* 6 To rise in value. [<L *appretiare* appraise] —ap·pre′ci·a′tor *n.* —Syn. 1 value, esteem, prize, treasure.

ap·pre·hend (ap′ri·hend′) *v.t.* 1 To seize; arrest. 2 To grasp mentally; understand. 3 To expect with fear or anxiety. [<L *ad-* to + *prehendere* seize] —ap′pre·hend′er *n.*

ap·pren·tice (ə·pren′tis) *n.* 1 One who is legally bound to serve another in order to learn a trade or business. 2 Any learner or beginner. —*v.t.* ·ticed, ·tic·ing To place as an apprentice. [<OF *aprendre* teach <L *apprehendere* comprehend] —ap·pren′tice·ship *n.*

ap·prise (ə·prīz′) *v.t.* ap·prised, ap·pris·ing To notify, as of an event; inform. [<F *apprendre* teach, inform] —ap·prise′ment, ap·pris′er *n.*

ap·proach (ə·prōch′) *v.i.* 1 To draw near or nearer. —*v.t.* 2 To draw near or nearer to. 3 To come close to; approximate. 4 To begin to treat or deal with: to *approach* a new subject. 5 To make a proposal, advances, etc., to. —*n.* 1 The act of approaching. 2 Nearness; approximation. 3 A way of approaching; access. 4 A way of treating or dealing with something: Try a new *approach.* 5 A golf stroke made toward the putting green after teeing off. [<LL *appropiare* < L *ad-* to + *prope* near]

ap·pro·ba·tion (ap′rə·bā′shən) *n.* 1 Approval; commendation. 2 Official approval; sanction. [<L *approbare* approve] —ap·pro·ba·tive (ap′rə·bā·tiv), ap·pro′ba·to·ry (ə·prō′bə·tôr′ē) *adj.*

ap·pro·pri·ate (ə·prō′prē·it) *adj.* Suitable; fitting; proper; relevant. —*v.t.* (ə·prō′prē·āt) ·at·ed, ·at·ing 1 To set apart for a particular use. 2 To take for one's own use. [<L *appropriare* to make one's own] —ap·pro′pri·ate·ly *adv.* —ap·pro′pri·ate·ness, ap·pro′pri·a′tor *n.* —ap·pro′pri·a′tive *adj.*

ap·prov·al (ə·prōō′vəl) *n.* 1 An approving or being approved; approbation. 2 Official consent; sanction. 3 Favorable opinion; praise. —on approval For a customer's examination without obligation to purchase.

ap·prove (ə·prōōv′) *v.* ap·proved, ap·prov·ing *v.t.* 1 To regard as worthy, proper, or right. 2 To confirm formally or authoritatively. 3 To show or state approval: often with *of.* [<L *ad-* to + *probare* approve, prove] —ap·prov′er *n.* —ap·prov′ing·ly *adv.*

ap·prox·i·mate (ə·prok′sə·mit) *adj.* Nearly exact, accurate, complete, etc. —*v.* (ə·prok′sə·māt) ·mat·ed, ·mat·ing —*v.t.* 1 To be almost the same as or very close to. 2 To bring close to or cause to approach closely. 3 *Math.* To calculate an approximation of. —*v.i.* 4 To come close; be similar. [<L *approximare* come near] —ap·prox′i·mate·ly *adv.*

ap·pur·te·nance (ə·pûr′tə·nəns) *n.* 1 Something added or attached as an accessory or adjunct. 2 *pl.* Accessory equipment, fittings, etc. [<L *appertinere* to pertain to]

ap·ro·pos (ap′rə·pō′) *adj.* Suited to the time, place, or occasion; pertinent. —*adv.* 1 With reference or regard; with *of.* 2 Pertinently; appropriately. 3 By the way; incidentally. [<F *à* to + *propos* purpose]

apt (apt) *adj.* 1 Likely; liable; 2 Quick to learn. 3 Pertinent; appropriate. [<L *aptus* fitted, suited] —apt′ly *adv.* —apt′ness *n.*

Aq·ua·lung (ak′wə·lung′) *n.* An underwater breathing apparatus or scuba: a trade name. Also aq′ua·lung′.

a·quar·i·um (ə·kwâr′ē·əm) *n., pl.* ·i·ums or ·i·a (-ē·ə) 1 A tank, pond, etc., for the exhibition or study of aquatic animals or plants. 2 A public building containing such an exhibition. [<L *aquarius* pertaining to water]

aq·ue·duct (ak′wə·dukt) *n.* 1 A water conduit, esp. one for supplying a community from a distance. 2 A structure supporting such a conduit across a river or over low ground. 3 *Anat.* Any of several canals through which body liquids are conducted. [<L *aqua* water + *ductus,* p.p. of *ducere* lead]

a·que·ous (ā′kwē·əs, ak′wē-) *adj.* Of, resembling, or containing water. [<L *aqua* water]

Ar·a·bic (ar′ə·bik) *adj.* Of or pertaining to Arabia, the Arabs, their language, culture, etc. —*n.* The Semitic language of the Arabians.

ar·bi·ter (är′bə·tər) *n.* 1 A person chosen to settle a dispute. 2 One who is authorized to judge or decide or whose decisions are considered final. [<L, one who goes to see, a witness] —Syn. 1 judge, referee, umpire, moderator. 2 authority, expert, master, specialist.

ar·bi·trar·y (är′bə·trer′ē) *adj.* 1 Based on mere opinion or prejudice; capricious. 2 Absolute; despotic. [<L *arbiter.* See ARBITER.] —ar′bi·trar′i·ly *adv.* —ar′bi·trar′i·ness *n.*

ar·bi·trate (är′bə·trāt) *v.t. & v.i.* ·trat·ed, ·trat·ing 1 To submit (a dispute) to or have (a dispute) settled by an arbiter. 2 To act as arbiter in (a dispute). [<L *arbiter.* See ARBITER.] —ar·bi·tra·ble (är′bə·trə·bəl), ar′bi·tra′tive *adj.*

ar·bor (är′bər) *n.* A bower, as of latticework,

supporting vines or trees; a place shaded by trees. [<L *herbarium* a collection of herbs]

**arc** (ärk) *n.* 1 Anything in the shape of an arch, of a curve, or of a part of a circle. 2 A part of any curve, esp. of a circle, 3 *Electr.* The light caused by an electric discharge in a gas. —*v.i.* **arcked** or **arced** (ärkt), **arck·ing** or **arc·ing** (är′king) *Electr.* To form an arc. [<L *arcus* bow, arch]

**ar·cade** (är·kād′) *n.* 1 A series of arches with their supporting columns or piers. 2 An arched or covered passageway or street, esp. one having shops, etc. opening from it. —*v.t.* **·cad·ed**, **·cad·ing** To furnish with or form into an arcade. [<L *arcus*, arch]

**arch** (ärch) *n.* 1 A curved structure spanning an opening, formed of wedge-shaped parts resting on supports at the two extremities. 2 Anything similarly shaped structure, object, or part: the dental *arch*. 3 The form of an arch; a bowlike curve. —*v.t.* 1 To cause to form into an arch. 2 To furnish with an arch or arches. —*v.i.* 3 To form an arch or arches. [<L *arcus* bow, arch]

**ar·cha·ic** (är·kā′ik) *adj.* 1 Belonging to a former period; ancient or antiquated. 2 Characterizing a verbal form or phrase no longer in current use except for special purposes, as poetry, the law, and church ritual. Also **ar·cha′i·cal.** [<Gk. *archaios* ancient]

**ar·che·ol·o·gy** (är′kē·ol′ə·jē) *n.* ARCHAEOLOGY. —**ar·che·o·log·i·cal** (är′kē·ə·loj′i·kəl) or **·log′ic** *adj.* —**ar′che·ol′o·gist** (-jist) *n.*

**ar·chi·pel·a·go** (är′kə·pel′ə·gō) *n. pl.* **·goes** or **·gos** A sea studded with many islands, or the islands collectively. [<ARCHI- + *pelagos* sea] —**ar·chi·pe·lag·ic** (är′kə·pə·laj′ik) *adj.*

**ar·chi·tect** (är′kə·tekt) *n.* 1 One whose profession is to design and draw up the plans for buildings, etc., and supervise their construction. 2 A planner; creator; designer. [<Gk. *archi-* chief + *tektōn* worker]

**ar·chives** (är′kīvz) *n. pl.* 1 A place where public records and historical documents are kept. 2 The records and documents themselves. [<Gk. *archeion* a public office <*archēgovernment*] —**ar·chi′val** *adj.* —**ar′chi·vist** (-kə·vist) *n.*

**Arc·tic** (ärk′tik, är′tik) *n.* 1 The region north of the Arctic Circle: used with *the.* 2 The Arctic Ocean. —*adj.* Of, in, or pertaining to the Arctic or the Arctic Ocean. [<Gk. *artikos* of the Bear (the northern constellation *Ursa Major*) < *arktos* bear]

**ar·dent** (är′dənt) *adj.* 1 Passionate; zealous;

intense. 2 Red; glowing; flashing. 3 Fiery; burning. [<L *ardere* burn] —**ar′den·cy** *n.* —**ar′dent·ly** *adv.*

**ar·dor** (är′dər) *n.* 1 Warmth or intensity of feeling; eagerness; zeal. 2 Great heat, as of fire, sun, or fever. *Brit. sp.* **ar′dour.** [<L, a flame, fire]

**ar·du·ous** (är′jŏō·əs) *adj.* 1 Involving great labor or hardship; difficult. 2 Toiling strenuously; energetic. 3 Steep. [<L *arduus* steep] —**ar′du·ous·ly** *adv.* —**ar′du·ous·ness** *n.*

**ar·e·a** (âr′ē·ə) 1 An open space, often devoted to a special purpose. 2 A tract or portion of the earth's surface; region; section. 3 The measure of a surface. 4 A yard of a building; areaway. 5 Extent; scope. [<L, an open space of level ground] —**ar′e·al** *adj.*

**a·re·na** (ə·rē′nə) *n.* 1 The central space for contestants in a Roman amphitheater. 2 Any place like this: the boxing *arena*. 3 A sphere of action or contest. [<L, sand, sandy place]

**ar·gue** (är′gyŏō) *v.* **ar·gued**, **ar·gu·ing** *v.i.* 1 To give reasons to support or contest a measure or opinion. 2 To dispute or quarrel. —*v.t.* 3 To give reasons for or against; discuss. 4 To contend or maintain. 5 To prove or indicate, as from evidence. 6 To influence or convince, as by argument. [<L *arguere* make clear, prove] —**ar′gu·a·ble** *adj.* —**ar′gu·er** *n.*

**ar·gu·ment** (är′gyə·mənt) *n.* 1 A reason offered for or against something. 2 The act of reasoning to establish or refute a position. 3 A disagreement, dispute, or quarrel. 4 A summary or synopsis of a plot, subject, etc. [<L *arguere* make clear, prove]

**ar·id** (ar′id) *adj.* 1 Lacking enough moisture to support vegetation; barren. 2 Without interest; dull. [<L *arere* be dry] —**a·rid·i·ty** (ə·rid′ə·tē), **ar′id·ness** *n.* —**ar′id·ly** *adv.*

**a·rise** (ə·rīz′) *v.i.* **a·rose** (ə·rōz′), **a·ris·en** (ə·riz′ən), **a·ris·ing** 1 To get up, as from a prone position. 2 To rise; ascend. 3 To come into being; originate. 4 To result or proceed: with *from.* [OE *ā-* up + *rīsan* rise]

**ar·is·toc·ra·cy** (ar′is·tok′rə·sē) *n. pl.* **·cies** 1 A hereditary nobility or privileged class. 2 Government by a privileged upper class. 3 A country having such a government. 4 Any group made up of the best: an *aristocracy* of musicians. [<Gk. *aristos* best + -CRACY]

**a·ris·to·crat** (ə·ris′tə·krat, ar′is·tə·krat′) *n.* 1 A member of an aristocracy. 2 A person who has the tastes, ideas, manners, etc., associated with the aristocracy. —a·ris·/to·crat'ic or ·i·cal adj. —a·ris'to·crat'i·cal·ly adv.

a·rith·me·tic (ə·rith'mə·tik) n. The use and study of integers under the operations of addition, subtraction, multiplication, division. [<Gk. (hē) arithmetikē (technē) (the) counting (art)] —ar·ith·met·ic (ar'ith·met'ik) or ·i·cal adj. —ar'ith·met'i·cal·ly adv.

arm (ärm) n. 1 The upper limb of the human body, from the shoulder to the hand or wrist. 2 The fore limb of vertebrates other than man. 3 An armlike part or appendage. 4 The part in contact with or covering the human arm: arm of a chair. 5 Anything branching out like an arm, usu. considered as a distinct part or branch: an arm of the sea. 6 Strength; might: the arm of the law. —at arm's length At a distance, so as to preclude intimacy. [<OE arm, earm]

ar·ma·da (är·mä'də, -mä'-) n. A fleet of war vessels or war planes. —the Armada The fleet sent against England by Spain in 1588 and defeated by the English navy: also Spanish Armada. [<L< armare to arm]

Ar·ma·ged·don (är'mə·ged'n) n. 1 In the Bible, the scene of a great battle between the forces of good and evil, to occur at the end of the world. Rev. 16:16. 2 Any great or decisive conflict. [<Heb. Megiddon the plain of Megiddo, a battlefield]

ar·mi·stice (är'mə·stis) n. A temporary cessation, by mutual agreement, of hostilities; a truce. [<L arma arms + -stitium a stoppage]

ar·mor (är'mər) n. 1 A defensive covering, as of mail for a warrior, or of metallic plates for a war vessel, a tank, etc. 2 Biol. Any protective covering on a plant or animal. —v.t. & v.i. To furnish with or put on armor. Brit. sp. ar'mour. [<L armatura < armare to arm] • See MAIL².

ar·my (är'mē) n. pl. ar·mies 1 A large organized body of men armed for military service on land. 2 The whole of the military land forces of a country. [<L armata < armare to arm]

a·ro·ma (ə·rō'mə) n. 1 Fragrance, as from plants; agreeable odor. 2 Characteristic quality or style. [< Gk. arōma spice]

a·rouse (ə·rouz') v. a·roused, a·rousing v.t. 1 To stir from or as if from sleep. 2 To excite, as to a state of high emotion. —v.i. 3 To become aroused from or as if from sleep.

[<ROUSE, on analogy with arise] —a·rous'al, a·rous'er n. —Syn. 1, 3 wake, waken, awake, awaken. 2 incite, provoke, stimulate, stir up.

ar·raign (ə·rān') v.t. 1 To call into court to answer to an indictment. 2 To call upon for an answer; accuse. [<LL arrationare call to account] —ar·raign'ment n.

ar·range (ə·rānj') v. ar·ranged, ar·rang·ing v.t. 1 To put in definite or proper order. 2 To adjust, as a conflict or dispute; settle. 3 To make plans or prepare for. 4 To change or adapt, as a musical composition, for performers other than those originally intended. —v.i. 5 To come to an agreement or understanding: often with with. 6 To see about the details; make plans. [<OF a- to + rangier put in order]

ar·ray (ə·rā') n. 1 Regular or proper order, esp. of troops. 2 A military force. 3 Clothing; fine dress. 4 An impressive gathering or arrangement, as of people or things. —v.t. 1 To draw up in order of battle, as troops. 2 To adorn; dress, as for display. [<OF <a- to + rei order]

ar·rest (ə·rest') v.t. 1 To stop suddenly; check, as the course, movement, or development of. 2 To take into custody by legal authority. 3 To attract and fix, as the attention; engage. —n. 1 An arresting or being arrested. 2 A device for arresting motion, as in a machine. [<L ad- to + restare stop, remain] —ar·rest'er, ar·res'tor n.

ar·rive (ə·rīv') v.i. ar·rived, ar·riv·ing 1 To reach or come to a destination or place. 2 To come at length, by any stage or process; often with at: to arrive at an idea. 3 To attain worldly success or fame. [<LL arripare come to shore <L ad- to + ripa shore]

ar·ro·gant (ar'ə·gənt) adj. Full of or characterized by excessive pride or self-esteem; overbearing; haughty. [<L arrogare. See ARROGATE.] —ar'ro·gant·ly adv.

ar·ro·gate (ar'ə·gāt) v.t. ·gat·ed, ·gat·ing 1 To claim, demand, or take presumptuously; assume; usurp. 2 To attribute or ascribe without reason. [<L arrogare claim for oneself] —ar'ro·ga'tion n.

ar·row (ar'ō) n. 1 A straight, slender shaft, usu. feathered at one end and with a pointed head at the other, to be shot from a bow. 2 Anything resembling an arrow in shape, speed, etc. 3 A sign or figure in the shape of an arrow, used to indicate directions. [<OE earh, arwe] —ar'row·y adj.

**ar·se·nal** (är′sə·nəl) *n.* 1 A place for making or storing arms and munitions. 2 Any supply or stock. [<Ar. *där aşinä′ah* **workshop**]

**ar·se·nic** (är′sə·nik) *n.* 1 An element (symbol As) chemically similar to phosphorus, used chiefly to make insecticides. 2 The highly poisonous, white, crystalline trioxide of arsenic. —**ar·sen·ic** (är·sen′ik) *adj.* Of or containing arsenic: also **ar·sen′i·cal.** [<L *arsenicum*]

**ar·son** (är′sən) *n.* The crime of deliberately setting fire to another's building, property, etc., or to one's own, esp. for a criminal or fraudulent purpose. [<L *arsus*, pp. of *ardere* burn] —**ar′son·ist** *n.*

**art** (ärt) *n.* 1 The ability of man to arrange or adapt natural things or conditions to his own uses. 2 The creation of works that are, in form, content, and execution, esthetically pleasing and meaningful, as in music, painting, sculpture, literature, architecture, dance, etc. 3 The principles and techniques governing the creation of such works. 4 The works so created, esp. paintings, drawings, and sculpture. 5 Skilled workmanship; craft. 6 Any specific skill, craft, trade, or profession: the *art* of cooking; a teacher's *art.* 7 *Printing* Any illustrative or decorative material that accompanies the text. 8 *Usu. pl.* The liberal arts. 9 Craft; cunning. 10 *Usu. pl.* A trick, stratagem, or wile. —*adj.* Of or for artists or their works. [<L *ars* skill]

**ar·te·ri·o·scle·ro·sis** (är·tir′ē·ō·sklə·rō′sis) *n.* Thickening and loss of elasticity of the walls of an artery, as in old age. —**ar·te′ri·o·scle·rot′ic** (-rot′ik) *adj.*

**ar·ter·y** (är′tər·ē) *n. pl.* **·ter·ies** 1 Any of the numerous muscular vessels and their branches that convey blood from the heart to every part of the body. ♦ See HEART. 2 Any main channel or route. [<L *arteria* artery, windpipe]

**ar·ti·choke** (är′tə·chōk) *n.* 1 A thistlelike garden plant. 2 Its succulent flower head, used as a vegetable. 3 The Jerusalem artichoke. [<Ar. *al-kharshūf*]

**ar·ti·cle** (är′ti·kəl) *n.* 1 A particular object or thing. 2 A member of a class of things. 3 A composition written for or appearing in a newspaper, magazine, etc. 4 A distinct proposition, statement, or stipulation in a series of such, as in a constitution, treaty, etc. 5 A complete item of religious belief; a point of doctrine. 6 *Gram.* One of the three words *a, an* (**indefinite articles**) or *the* (**def-**

inite **article**), used as modifiers. —*v.* ·cied, ·cling *v.t.* 1 To bind to service by a written contract. 2 To specify. 3 To accuse by formal articles. —*v.i.* 4 To make accusations: with *against.* [<L *articulus,* dim. of *artus* a joint]

**ar·tic·u·late** (är·tik′yə·lit) *adj.* 1 Jointed; segmented: also **ar·tic′u·lat′ed** (-lā′tid). 2 Able to speak. 3 Able to speak clearly, easily, and effectively. 4 Divided into syllables or words so as to be intelligible. 5 Clear and logically coherent. —*v.* (är·tik′yə·lāt) ·lat·ed, ·lat·ing *v.t.* 1 To utter distinctly; enunciate. 2 To express clearly in words. 3 *Phonet.* To produce, as a speech sound, by the movement of the organs of speech. 4 To unite by joints. —*v.i.* 5 To speak distinctly. 6 *Phonet.* To produce a speech sound. 7 *Anat.* To form a joint: used with *with.* [<L *articulare* divide into joints, utter distinctly] —**ar·tic′u·late·ly** *adv.* —**ar·tic′u·late·ness,** **ar·tic′u·lat·or** *n.* —**ar·tic′u·la′tive** *adj.*

**ar·ti·fact** (är′tə·fakt) *n.* Anything made by human work or art. Also **ar′te·fact.** [<L *ars* art, skill + *factus,* p.p. of *facere* make]

**ar·ti·fice** (är′tə·fis) *n.* 1 Subtle or deceptive craft; trickery. 2 Skill; ingenuity. 3 An ingenious expedient; stratagem. [<L *artificium* handicraft, skill]

**ar·ti·fi·cial** (är′tə·fish′əl) *adj.* 1 Produced by human art rather than by nature. 2 Made in imitation of or as a substitute for something natural. 3 Not genuine or natural; affected. [See ARTIFICE.] —**ar′ti·fi′ci·al′i·ty,** **ar′ti·fi′cial·ness** *n.* —**ar′ti·fi′cial·ly** *adv.*

**ar·til·ler·y** (är·til′ə·rē) *n.* 1 Guns of larger caliber than machine guns. 2 Military units armed with such guns. 3 Branches of the U.S. Army composed of such units. 4 *Informal* Any small firearm. 5 The science of gunnery. [<OF *artiller* fortify] —**ar·til′ler·y·man** *n.* ( *pl.* **·men**).

**ar·ti·san** (är′tə·zən) *n.* A trained or skilled workman. [<L *ars* art]

**art·ist** (är′tist) *n.* 1 One who is skilled in or who makes a profession of any of the fine arts or the performing arts. 2 One who does anything with artistry. [<L *ars* art]

**Ar·y·an** (âr′ē·ən, ar′-, är′yən) *n.* 1 A member or descendant of a prehistoric people who spoke Indo-European. 2 In Nazi ideology, a Caucasian gentile, esp. one of Nordic stock. —*adj.* Of or pertaining to Aryans. [<Skt. *ārya* noble]

**as·bes·tos** (as·bes′təs, az-) *n.* A white or gray mineral silicate of calcium and magnesium which may be woven or shaped into acid-resisting, nonconducting, and fireproof articles. —*adj.* Of asbestos. [<Gk., unquenchable]

**as·cend** (ə·send′) *v.i.* 1 To go or move upward; rise. 2 To go from a lower to a higher degree, pitch, etc. 3 To slope upward. —*v.t.* 4 To move or climb upward on. 5 To succeed to (a throne). [<L *ad-* to + *scandere* climb] —**as·cend′a·ble** or **·i·ble** *adj.* —**as·cen′der** *n.*

**as·cer·tain** (as′ər·tān′) *v.t.* To learn with certainty about; find out. [<OF *a-* to + *certain* certain] —**as′cer·tain′a·ble** *adj.* —**as′cer·tain′a·bly** *adv.* —**as′cer·tain′ment** *n.*

**as·cet·ic** (ə·set′ik) *n.* 1 A religious hermit or recluse. 2 One who leads a very austere and self-denying life. —*adj.* Given to or involving severe self-denial and austerity: also **as·cet′i·cal.** [<Gk. *askētēs* one who exercises (self-denial), a monk] —**as·cet′i·cal·ly** *adv.*

**as·cribe** (ə·skrīb′) *v.t.* **as·cribed, as·crib·ing** 1 To attribute, as to a cause, source, author, etc. 2 To assign as a quality or attribute. [<L *ad-* to + *scribere* write] —**as·crib·a·ble** (ə·skrī′bə·bəl) *adj.*

**a·sep·sis** (ā·sep′sis, ā-) *n.* 1 An aseptic condition. 2 The prevention of infection by maintaining sterile conditions. [A- (not) + SEPSIS]

**a·skance** (ə·skans′) *adv.* 1 With a side glance; sidewise. 2 Disdainfully; distrustfully. Also **a·skant′.** [?]

**a·skew** (ə·skyoō) *adj.* Oblique. —*adv.* In an oblique position or manner; to one side. [<A- on + SKEW]

**as·par·a·gus** (ə·spar′ə·gəs) *n.* 1 The edible shoots of a cultivated plant of the lily family. 2 Any plant of this genus. [<Gk. *asparagos, aspharogos*]

**as·pect** (as′pekt) *n.* 1 The look a person has; expression of countenance. 2 Appearance presented to the eye by something; look. 3 Appearance presented to the mind by circumstances, etc.; interpretation. 4 A facing in a given direction. 5 The side or surface facing in a certain direction. 6 In astrology, the configuration of the planets in relation to each other or to the observer, as a supposed influence on human affairs. [<L *aspicere* to look at]

**as·per·i·ty** (as·per′ə·tē) *n. pl.* **·ties** 1 Roughness or harshness, as of surface, sound, weather, etc. 2 Bitterness or sharpness of temper [<L *asper* rough]

**as·perse** (ə·spûrs′) *v.t.* **as·persed** (ə·spûrst′),

**as·pers·ing** To spread false charges against; slander. [<L *aspergere* sprinkle on] —**as·pers′er, as·per′sor** *n.*

**as·phalt** (as′fôlt) *n.* 1 A dark brown, semisolid, bituminous substance obtained from natural deposits or as a residue in refining petroleum; mineral pitch. 2 A mixture of this with sand or gravel, used for paving, etc. Also **as·phal′tum** (as·fôl′təm). —*v.t.* To pave or cover with asphalt. [<Gk. *asphaltos*] —**as·phal·tic** (as·fôl′tik) *adj.* [<F]

**as·phyx·i·a** (as·fik′sē·ə) *n.* Loss of consciousness, usu. resulting from suffocation caused by too little oxygen and too much carbon dioxide in the blood. [<Gk. *asphyxia* stopping of the pulse] —**as·phyx′i·ant** *adj.,*

**as·pic** (as′pik) *n.* A savory jelly of meat or vegetable juices, served as a relish or mold for meat, vegetables, etc. [<F]

**as·pi·rant** (as′pər·ənt, ə·spīr′ənt) *n.* One who aspires after something. —*adj.* Aspiring.

**as·pi·ra·tion** (as′pə·rā′shən) *n.* 1 Exalted desire; high ambition. 2 The act of breathing. 3 The use of an aspirator. 4 *Phonet.* **a** The pronunciation of a consonant with an aspirate. **b** An aspirate.

**as·pire** (ə·spīr′) *v.i.* **as·pired, as·pir·ing** 1 To have an earnest desire or ambition: with *to.* 2 To long for: with *after.* [<L *aspirare* breathe on, attempt to reach] —**as·pir′er** *n.*

**as·pi·rin** (as′pər·in) *n.* A white crystalline synthetic compound, used to allay pain and fever and to treat rheumatism. [<A(CETYL) + spir(aeic acid)* former name of salicylic acid + -IN]

**as·sail** (ə·sāl′) *v.t.* To attack violently, as by force, argument, or censure; assault. [<LL *assalire* leap upon] —**as·sail′a·ble** *adj.* —**as·sail′a·ble·ness, as·sail′er** *n.*

**as·sas·sin** (ə·sas′in) *n.* A murderer, esp. one who murders a politically prominent person. [<Ar. *hashshāshīn* hashish-eaters, from hashish-eating Muslims who murdered Christians during the Crusades]

**as·sault** (ə·sôlt′) *n.* 1 Any violent physical or verbal attack. 2 *Law* An unlawful attempt or offer to do bodily injury to another. 3 A rape. 4 *Mil.* A violent attack by troops, as upon a fortified place. *v.t. & v.i.* To make an assault (upon). [<L *ad-* to + *salire* leap] —**as·sault′er** *n.*

**as·say** (ə·sā′, as′ā) *n.* 1 The analysis of an alloy, etc., to ascertain the ingredients and their proportions. 2 The substance to be so examined. 3 The result of such a test. 4 Any

28

examination or testing. —v.t. (ə·sā´) 1 To make an assay of. 2 To test. —v.i. 3 To show by analysis a certain value or proportion, as of a precious metal. [< L *exagium* a weighing < *exigere* prove] —as·say´er n.

as·sem·ble (ə·sem´bəl) v.t. & v.i. ·bled, ·bling 1 To collect or convene; congregate. 2 To fit together, as the parts of a mechanism. [< L *assimulare* < *ad-* to + *simul* together] —as·sem´bler n.

as·sent (ə·sent´) v.i. To express agreement; concur: usu. with *to*. —n. Concurrence or agreement. [< L *assentire* < *ad-* to + *sentire* feel] —as´sen·ta´tion, as·sent´er n.

as·sert (ə·sûrt´) v.t. 1 To state positively; affirm. 2 To maintain as a right or claim. — assert oneself To state and defend firmly one's rights, opinions, etc. [< L *asserere* bind to, claim] —as·sert´er, as·ser´tor n.

as·sess (ə·ses´) v.t. 1 To charge with a tax, fine, etc., as a person or property. 2 To determine the amount of, as a tax or fine, on a person or property. 3 To put a value on, as property, for taxation. 4 To take stock of; evaluate. [< LL *assessare* fix a tax] —as·ses´s a·ble adj.

as·set (as´et) n. 1 An item of property. 2 A person, thing, or quality regarded as useful or valuable to have. 3 pl. In accounting, the entries in a balance sheet showing all the property or resources of a person or business, as cash, accounts receivable, equipment, etc. 4 pl. Law a The property of a deceased person which can be used to pay debts or legacies. b All the property, real or personal, of a person or corporation. [< L *ad-* to + *satis* enough]

as·sid·u·ous (ə·sij´ŏō·əs) adj. Carefully attentive and diligent. [< L *assidere* sit by] — as·sid´u·ous·ly adv. —as·sid´u·ous·ness n.

as·sign (ə·sīn´) v.t. 1 To set apart, as for a particular function; designate. 2 To appoint, as to a post. 3 To give out or allot, as a lesson. 4 To ascribe or attribute, as a motive. 5 Law To make over or transfer, as personal property, to another. —n. Law Usu. pl. Assignee. [< L *ad-* to + *signare* make a sign] —as·sign´a·bil´i·ty, as·sign´er, Law as·sign´or n. —as·sign´a·ble adj.

as·sign·ment (ə·sīn´mənt) n. 1 An assigning or being assigned. 2 Anything assigned, as a lesson or task. 3 Law a The transfer of a claim, right, or property or the instrument or writing of transfer. b The claim, right, or property transferred.

as·sim·i·late (ə·sim´ə·lāt) v. ·lat·ed, ·lat·ing v.t. 1 To absorb and incorporate (food) into the body. 2 To make part of one's own thinking. 3 To absorb (a different culture, group, etc.) into the main social or cultural body. 4 To make alike; cause to resemble. —v.i. 5 To become alike or similar. 6 To become absorbed or assimilated. [< L *ad-* to + *similare* make like] —as·sim´i·la´tion n. — as·sim´i·la´tive, as·sim·i·la·to·ry (ə·sim´ə·lə·tôr´ē, -tō´rē) adj.

as·sist (ə·sist´) v.t. 1 To give succor or support to; help; relieve. 2 To act as an assistant to. —v.i. 3 To give help or support. 4 In baseball, to aid a teammate or partner in a play. —assist at To be present at (a ceremony, etc.). —n. 1 An act of helping. 2 In baseball, a play that helps to put out a runner. [< L *ad-* to + *sistere* cause to stand] —as·sist´er n.

as·so·ci·ate (ə·sō´shē·it, -āt, -sē-) n. 1 A companion. 2 A co-worker; colleague. 3 Anything that accompanies or is associated with something else; a concomitant. 4 One admitted to partial membership in an association, society, etc. —adj. 1 Joined with another or others; united; allied. 2 Having subordinate or secondary status: an *associate* professor. —v. (ə·sō´shē·āt) ·at·ed, ·at·ing v.t. 1 To bring into company or relation; combine together. 2 To unite (oneself) with another or others, as in friendship. 3 To connect mentally: to *associate* poetry with madness. —v.i. 4 To join or be in company or relation: with *with*. 5 To unite, as nations. [< L *associare* join to]

as·sort (ə·sôrt´) v.t. 1 To distribute into groups or classes according to kinds; classify. 2 To furnish, as a warehouse, with a variety of goods, etc. —v.i. 3 To fall into groups or classes of the same kind. 4 To associate; consort: with *with*. [< OF *a-* to + *sorte* sort, kind] —as·sort·a·tive (ə·sôr´tə·tiv) adj.

as·suage (ə·swāj´) v. as·suaged, as·suag·ing v.t. 1 To lessen or reduce the intensity of. 2 To reduce to a quiet or peaceful state. 3 To end by satisfying. [< L *ad-* to + *suavis* sweet] —as·suage´ment n. —Syn. 1 ease, alloy, mitigate. 2 calm, pacify, mollify. 3 appease, slake, quench.

as·sume (ə·sōōm´) v.t. as·sumed, as·sum·ing 1 To take up or adopt, as a style of dress, aspect, or character. 2 To undertake, as an office or duty. 3 To arrogate to oneself; usurp, as powers of state. 4 To take for granted; suppose to be true. 5 To affect; pretend to have. [<L *assumere* to take up, adopt] —**as·sum·a·ble** (ə-sōō′mə-bəl) *adj.*

**as·sump·tion** (ə-sump′shən) *n.* 1 The act of assuming. 2 Something taken for granted; supposition. 3 Presumption; arrogance. —**the Assumption** 1 The doctrine that the Virgin Mary was bodily taken up into heaven at her death. 2 A church feast, observed on August 15, commemorating this event. —**as·sump′tive** *adj.*

**as·sure** (ə-shōōr′) *v.t.* **as·sured, as·sur·ing** 1 To make sure or secure; establish. 2 To give confidence to; convince. 3 To guarantee, as something risky. 4 To promise confidently. 5 *Brit.* To insure. [<L *ad-* to + *securus* safe] —**as·sur′a·ble** *adj.*

**as·ter** (as′tər) *n.* Any of a large group of related plants having composite flowers with white, purple, or blue rays and yellow disk. [<Gk. *astēr* star]

**as·ter·isk** (as′tər·isk) *n.* A starlike figure (*) used to indicate omissions, footnotes, references, etc. —*v.t.* To mark with an asterisk. [<Gk. *astēr* star]

**asth·ma** (az′mə, as′-) *n.* A chronic disorder characterized by recurrent breathing difficulty and bronchial spasms. [<Gk. *azein* breathe hard] —**asth·mat·ic** (az·mat′ik, as) *adj., n.* —**asth·mat′i·cal** *adj.* —**asth·mat′i·cal·ly** *adv.*

**a·stig·ma·tism** (ə-stig′mə·tiz′əm) *n.* A defect of the eye or a lens such that the rays of light from an object do not converge to a perfect focus. [<A-⁴ without + Gk. *stigma* mark] —**as·tig·mat·ic** (as′tig·mat′ik) *adj.*

**a·ston·ish** (ə-ston′ish) *v.t.* To affect with wonder and surprise; amaze; confound. [<L *ex-* out + *tonare* thunder] —**a·ston′ish·ing** *adj.* —**a·ston′ish·ing·ly** *adv.*

**as·tral** (as′trəl) *adj.* 1 Of, coming from, or like the stars. 2 In theosophy, pertaining to or consisting of a supersensible substance supposed to pervade all space. [<Gk. *astron* star] —**as′tral·ly** *adv.*

**as·trol·o·gy** (ə-strol′ə·jē) *n.* 1 Originally, the practical application of astronomy to human uses. 2 The study professing to interpret the influence of the heavenly bodies upon the destinies and behavior of men. [<Gk. < ASTRO- + -LOGY] —**as·trol′o·ger** *n.* —**as·tro·log·ic** (as′trə·loj′ik), **as·tro·log·i·cal** *adj.* —**as′tro·log′i·cal·ly** *adv.*

**as·tro·naut** (as′trə·nôt) *n.* One who travels in space. [<ASTRO- + Gk. *nautēs* sailor]

**as·tron·o·my** (ə-stron′ə·mē) *n.* The science

that studies stars, planets, and other bodies in space and the phenomena that involve them. [<Gk. *astronomia* < *astron* star + *nomos* law]

**as·tro·phys·ics** (as′trō·fiz′iks) *n. pl. (construed as sing.)* The branch of astronomy that deals with the physical constitution and properties of bodies in space. —**as′tro·phys′i·cal** *adj.* —**as·tro·phys·i·cist** (as-′trō·fiz′ə·sist) *n.*

**as·tute** (ə·st′ōōt′) *adj.* Having or showing keen intelligence or shrewdness: an *astute* businessman. [<L *astus* cunning] —**as·tute′ly** *adv.* —**as·tute′ness** *n.* —**Syn.** acute, sagacious, cunning, crafty.

**a·sy·lum** (ə·sī′ləm) *n.* 1 An institution for the care of the aged, the mentally disturbed, the poor, etc. 2 A place of refuge. 3 An inviolable shelter from arrest or punishment, as a temple or church in ancient times. 4 The protection afforded by a sanctuary or refuge. [<Gk. *a-* without + *sylon* right of seizure]

**a·the·ism** (ā′thē·iz′əm) *n.* The belief that there is no God. [<Gk. *a-* without + *theos* god] —**a′the·ist** *n.* —**a′the·is′tic** or **·ti·cal** *adj.* —**a′the·is′ti·cal·ly** *adv.*

**ath·lete** (ath′lēt) *n.* A person trained or skilled in acts or games requiring physical strength, agility, speed, etc. [<Gk. *athlētēs* a contestant in the games]

**at·las** (at′ləs) *n.* 1 A book of maps. 2 A collection of charts, tables, etc. illustrating any subject.

**at·mos·phere** (at′məs·fir) *n.* 1 The envelope of gases that surrounds the earth or any body in space. 2 The particular climatic condition of any place or region regarded as dependent on the air. 3 Any surrounding or pervasive element or influence: an *atmosphere* of gloom. 4 *Physics* A unit of pressure equal to 14.69 pounds per square inch or $1.01325 \times 10^5$ newtons per square meter. [<Gk. *atmos* vapor + *sphaira* sphere]

**at·om** (at′əm) *n.* 1 The smallest unit of an element capable of existing, consisting of the electrically neutral combination of a nucleus and its complement of electrons. 2 An exceedingly small quantity or particle; iota. [<Gk. *atomos* indivisible]

**atomic bomb** A bomb whose explosive power is derived from nuclear fission.

**atomic energy** The energy released from an atom, as by nuclear fission or nuclear fusion.

**at·om·ize** (at′əm·īz) *v.t.* **·ized, ·iz·ing** 1 To reduce to or separate into atoms; pulverize. 2 To reduce to a spray.

**a·tone** (ə·tōn′) v. **a·toned**, **a·ton·ing** v.i. To make amends, as for sin. [< earlier *at one* in accord, short for *to set at one*, reconcile] —**a·ton′a·ble**, **a·tone′a·ble** adj. —**a·ton′er** n.

**a·tro·cious** (ə·trō′shəs) adj. 1 Outrageously wicked, criminal, cruel, etc. 2 *Informal.* Very bad or in bad taste: an *atrocious* remark. [< L *atrox* harsh, cruel < *ater* black] —**a·tro′cious·ly** adv. —**a·tro′cious·ness** n.

**at·ro·phy** (at′rə·fē) n. pl. **·phies** 1 A wasting away of the body or any of its parts. 2 A stoppage of growth or development, as of a part. —v. **·phied**, **·phy·ing** v.t. 1 To affect with atrophy. —v.i. 2 To waste away; wither. [< Gk. *atrophas* poorly nourished] —**a·troph·ic** (ə·trof′ik).

**at·tach** (ə·tach′) v.t. 1 To make fast to something; fasten on. 2 To connect, join on, or bind: He *attached* himself to the expedition. 3 To add or append, as a word or signature. 4 To attribute; ascribe: to *attach* great importance to the outcome of an event. 5 *Law* To secure for legal jurisdiction; seize or arrest by legal process: to *attach* an employee's salary. 6 *Mil.* To order to serve temporarily or as a nonintegral part: The regiment *attached* a medical officer. —v.i. 7 To belong, as a quality or circumstance; be incidental: with *to*: Much interest *attaches* to this opinion. [< OF *attachier* < a- to + *tache* nail] —**at·tach′a·ble** adj.

**at·tack** (ə·tak′) v.t. 1 To set upon suddenly; assault or begin conflict with. 2 To assail with hostile words; criticize, censure. 3 To begin work on, esp. with vigor. 4 To begin to affect seriously or injuriously: Acid *attacks* metal; Disease *attacks* a person. —v.i. 5 To make an attack. —n. 1 The act of attacking. 2 The first movement toward any undertaking. 3 Any hostile, offensive movement or action, as with troops. 4 A seizure, as by disease. [< Ital. *attaccare*]

**at·tain** (ə·tān′) v.t. 1 To achieve, accomplish or gain. 2 To come to; arrive at. —**attain to** To arrive at with effort; succeed in reaching. [< L *attingere* reach] —**at·tain′a·bil′i·ty**, **at·tain′a·ble·ness** n. —**at·tain′a·ble** adj.

**at·tempt** (ə·tempt′) v.t. To make an effort to perform, get, etc.; endeavor; try. —n. 1 A putting forth of effort; trial; endeavor; essay. 2 An attack. [< L *attemptare* try] —**at·tempt′a·bil′i·ty** n. —**at·tempt′a·ble** adj.

**at·tend** (ə·tend′) v.t. 1 To wait upon; minister to; visit or care for professionally. 2 To be present at or in, as a meeting. 3 To follow as a result. 4 To accompany. 5 *Archaic* To give heed; listen. [< L *attendere* give heed to, consider]

**at·ten·tion** (ə·ten′shən) n. 1 The act or faculty of concentrating on something. 2 Observation; notice: to get someone's *attention*. 3 *Usu. pl.* An act of courtesy, gallantry, or devotion. 4 Practical or thoughtful consideration or care. 5 *Mil.* a The prescribed position of readiness to obey orders. b The order to assume this position. [< L *attendere* to attend]

**at·ten·tive** (ə·ten′tiv) adj. 1 Giving or showing attention; observant. 2 Courteous; gallant; polite. —**at·ten′tive·ly** adv. —**at·ten′tive·ness** n.

**at·ten·u·ate** (ə·ten′yōō·āt) v. **·at·ed**, **·at·ing** v.t. 1 To make thin, small, or fine. 2 To reduce in value, quantity, severity, strength, etc.; weaken. 3 To reduce in density; rarefy, as a liquid or gas. 4 To weaken the virulence of a microorganism. —v.i. 5 To become thin, weak, rarefied, etc. —adj. (ə·ten′yōō·it) Attenuated. [< L *ad-* + *tenuare* make thin] —**at·ten′u·a·ble** adj. —**at·ten′u·a′tion** n.

**at·test** (ə·test′) v.t. 1 To confirm as accurate, true, or genuine; vouch for. 2 To certify, as by signature or oath. 3 To be proof of. 4 To put upon oath. —v.i. 5 To bear witness; testify: with *to*. [< L *ad-* to + *testari* bear witness]

**at·tire** (ə·tīr′) v.t. **at·tired**, **at·tir·ing** To dress; array; adorn. —n. Dress or clothing. [< OF *atirer* arrange, adorn]

**at·ti·tude** (at′ə·t'ōōd) n. 1 Position of the body, as suggesting some thought, feeling, or action. 2 State of mind, behavior, or conduct, as indicating one's feelings, opinion, or purpose. [< LL *aptitudo* fitness, aptitude] —**at·ti·tu·di·nal** (at′ə·t'ōō′də·nəl) adj.

**at·tor·ney** (ə·tûr′nē) n. pl. **·neys** A person empowered by another to act in his stead, esp. a lawyer. —**by attorney** By proxy. —**power of attorney** Legal written authority to transact business for another. [< OF *atorner* turn to; assign] —**at·tor′ney·ship** n.

**at·tract** (ə·trakt′) v.t. 1 To draw to or cause to come near by some physical force, without apparent mechanical connection. 2 To draw the admiration, attention, etc. of. [< L *ad-* toward + *trahere* draw, drag] —**at·trac′t′a·ble** adj. —**at·tract′a·ble·ness**, **at·tract′a·bil′i·ty**, **at·tract′er**, **at·trac′tor** n.

**at·trib·ute** (ə·trib′yŏŏt) *v.t.* ·ut·ed, ·ut·ing To ascribe as belonging to, resulting from, or created or caused by. —**at·tri·bute** (at′rə·byŏŏt) *n.* 1 A quality or characteristic. 2 *Gram.* An adjective or its equivalent. 3 In art and mythology, a distinctive mark or symbol. [< L *ad-* to + *tribuere* allot, give over] —**at·trib′u·ta·ble** *adj.* —**Syn.** *v.* assign, impute, associate. *n.* 1 property, trait, feature, peculiarity.

**at·tri·bu·tion** (at′rə·byŏŏ′shən) *n.* 1 An attributing or being attributed. 2 An ascribed characteristic or quality; attribute.

**au·burn** (ô′bûrn) *adj.* & *n.* Reddish brown. [< LL *alburnus* whitish]

**auc·tion** (ôk′shən) *n.* 1 A public sale in which the price offered for individual items is increased by bids, until the highest bidder becomes the purchaser. 2 The bidding in bridge. —*v.t.* To sell by or at auction: usu. with *off.* [< L *auctio* an increase, a public sale (with increasing bids)]

**au·da·cious** (ô·dā′shəs) *adj.* 1 Fearless; bold. 2 Defiant of convention, decorum, etc.; brazen; insolent. [< L *audax* bold] —**au·da′cious·ly** *adv.* —**au·da′cious·ness** *n.*

**au·di·ble** (ô′də·bəl) *adj.* Perceptible by the ear. [< L *audire* hear] —**au′di·ble·ness** *n.* —**au′di·bly** *adv.*

**au·di·ence** (ô′dē·əns) *n.* 1 An assembly gathered to hear and see, as at a concert. 2 Those who are reached by a book, television program, etc. 3 A formal hearing, interview, or conference. 4 Opportunity to be heard. [< L *audientia* a hearing]

**au·di·o·vis·u·al** (ô′dē·ō·vizh′ŏŏ·əl) *adj.* 1 Relating to both hearing and sight. 2 Pertaining to instructional materials other than books, as filmstrips, motion pictures, television, and recordings.

**au·dit** (ô′dit) *v.t.* 1 To examine, adjust, and certify, as accounts. 2 To attend (a college course) as a listener only without receiving credit. —*n.* 1 An examination of financial accounts to establish their correctness. 2 A prepared statement concerning such an examination. 3 An adjustment and settlement of accounts. [< L *auditus* a hearing]

**au·di·to·ri·um** (ô′də·tôr′ē·əm, -tō′rē·əm) *n. pl.* ·to·ri·ums or ·to·ri·a (-tôr′ē·ə, -tō′rē·ə) 1 The room or part of a building, as a church, theater, etc., occupied by the audience. 2 A building for concerts, public meetings, etc. [< L, lecture room, courtroom]

**aug·ment** (ôg·ment′) *v.t.* & *v.i.* To make or become greater, as in size, number, or amount. [< L *augere* to increase] —**aug·men·t′a·ble** *adj.* —**aug·ment′er** *n.* —**Syn.** enlarge, intensify, increase, expand.

**au·gur** (ô′gər) *n.* A prophet; soothsayer. —*v.t.* 1 To be an omen of. —*v.i.* 2 To be an augury or omen. [< L]

**au·gust** (ô·gust′) *adj.* Majestic; grand; imposing. [< L *augere* increase, exalt] —**au·gust′ly** *adv.* —**au·gust′ness** *n.*

**au·ral** (ôr′əl) *adj.* Pertaining to the ear or the sense of hearing. [< L *auris* ear + -AL]

**Au·re·o·my·cin** (ôr′ē·ō·mī′sin) *n.* An antibiotic effective against bacteria and certain viruses: a trade name.

**aus·pice** (ôs′pis) *n. pl.* **aus·pi·ces** (ôs′pə·sēz) 1 *Usu. pl.* Patronage; sponsorship: under the *auspices* of the alumni association. 2 An omen or sign. [< L *auspex* a bird augur]

**aus·pi·cious** (ôs·pish′əs) *adj.* 1 Favoring or conducive to future success. 2 Attended by good fortune; fortunate; successful. —**aus·pi′cious·ly** *adv.* —**aus·pi′cious·ness** *n.* —**Syn.** 1 propitious, favorable, hopeful, promising.

**aus·tere** (ô·stir′) *adj.* 1 Severe, grave, or stern, as in look or conduct. 2 Abstemious; ascetic. 3 Severely simple; unadorned. [< Gk. *austēros* harsh, bitter] —**aus·tere′ly** *adv.*

**au·then·tic** (ô·then′tik) *adj.* 1 Authoritative; trustworthy; reliable. 2 Genuine; real. 3 *Law* Duly executed before the proper officer. Also **au·then′ti·cal.** [< Gk. *authentikos*] —**au·then′ti·cal·ly** *adv.*

**au·thor** (ô′thər) *n.* 1 The writer of a book, article, etc. 2 A person who writes as a profession. 3 A person who originates or creates something. —*v.t. Informal* To be the author of. [< L *auctor* originator, producer] —**au′thor·ess** *n. Fem.* —**au·tho·ri·al** (ô·thôr′ē·əl, ô·thō′rē-) *adj.*

**au·thor·i·ty** (ə·thôr′ə·tē, ə·thôr′-, ô-) *n. pl.* ·ties 1 The right to command, enforce obedience, make decisions, etc. 2 Such a right given to another; authorization. 3 *pl.* Persons having the right to command and govern. 4 Personal power or expertness that commands influence, respect, or confidence. 5 That which may be appealed to in support of action or belief, as an author, volume, etc. 6 One who has special skill, knowledge, etc.; expert. 7 An authoritative opinion, decision, or precedent. [< L *auctoritas* power, authority < *augere* increase]

**au·thor·ize** (ô′thər·īz) *v.t.* ·ized, ·iz·ing 1 To confer authority upon; empower; commission. 2 To warrant; justify. 3 To sanction;

approve. —au′thor·i·za′tion, au′thor·iz′er n.

au·to·crat (ô′tə·krat) n. 1 A supreme ruler of unrestricted power. 2 An arrogant, dictatorial person. [< Gk. *autokratēs* self-ruling, independent] —au′to·crat′ic or ·i·cal *adj.* —au′to·crat′i·cal·ly *adv.*

au·to·graph (ô′tə·graf, -gräf) n. 1 A person's own handwriting or signature. 2 Something written in a person's own handwriting, as a manuscript. —*v.t.* 1 To write one's name in or affix one's signature to. 2 To write in one's own handwriting. —*adj.* Written by one's own hand, as a will. [<Gk. *autographos* written with one's own hand] —au′to·graph′ic or ·i·cal *adj.* —au′to·graph′i·cal·ly *adv.*

au·to·mat (ô′tə·mat) n. U.S. A restaurant in which certain foods are automatically made available from a receptacle when money is deposited in a slot alongside.

au·to·ma·tion (ô′tə·mā′shən) n. 1 The automatic performance or control of an operation, system, device, etc. 2 The equipment or devices used to accomplish this. 3 The design and installation of such devices. [<AUTOM(ATIC) + (OPER)ATION] —au′to·ma′tive *adj.*

au·to·mo·bile (ô′tə·mə·bēl′, ô′tə·mə·bēl′, ô′tə·mō′bēl) n. A usu. four-wheeled vehicle for a small number of passengers, driven by an engine or motor and independent of rails or tracks; a motorcar. —*adj.* (ô′tə·mō ′bil) Of or for automobiles. [<AUTO-¹ + MO-BILE]

au·ton·o·my (ô·ton′ə·mē) n. pl. ·mies 1 The condition or quality of being autonomous; esp., the power or right of self-government. 2 A self-governing state, community, or group. —au·ton′o·mist n. —Syn. 1 independence, freedom, self-rule, self-determination.

au·top·sy (ô′top·sē, ô′təp-) n. pl. ·sies Postmortem examination of a human body, esp. to determine the cause of death. [<Gk. *autopsia* a seeing for oneself]

au·tumn (ô′təm) n. 1 The season between summer and winter; fall. 2 A time of maturity and incipient decline. —*adj.* Of, in, or like autumn. [<L *autumnus*] —au·tum·nal (ô·tum′nəl) *adj.* —au·tum′nal·ly *adv.*

aux·il·ia·ry (ôg·zil′yər·ē, -zil′ər-) *adj.* 1 Giving or furnishing aid. 2 Subsidiary; subordinate. 3 Supplementary; additional. —n. pl. ·ries 1 An auxiliary person, group, ship, etc. 2 pl. Foreign troops helping those of a

nation at war. 3 AUXILIARY VERB. [<L *auxilium* a help]

a·vail (ə·vāl′) n. 1 Use or advantage; benefit; good. 2 pl. Proceeds. —*v.t.* 1 To assist or aid; profit. —*v.i.* 2 To be of value or advantage; suffice. —avail oneself of To take advantage of; utilize. [<L *ad-* to + *valere* be strong] —a·vail′ing *adj.* —a·vail′ing·ly *adv.*

av·a·lanche (av′ə·lanch, -länch) n. 1 A large mass of snow, ice, rocks, etc., sliding down a mountain slope. 2 Something like an avalanche, as in power, destructiveness, etc. —*v.* ·lanched, ·lanch·ing —*v.i.* 1 To fall or slide like an avalanche. —*v.t.* 2 To fall or come down upon like an avalanche. [F]

av·a·rice (av′ə·ris) n. Passion for riches; covetousness; greed. [<L *avarus* greedy] —av·a·ri·cious (av′ə·rish′əs) *adj.* —av′a·ri′cious·ly *adv.* —av′a·ri′cious·ness n.

a·venge (ə·venj′) *v.t.* a·venged, a·veng·ing 1 To take vengeance or exact punishment for (a crime, insult, etc.) or on behalf of (a person or persons). —*v.i.* 2 To take vengeance. [<L *ad-* to + *vindicare* avenge] —a·veng′er n.

a·ver (ə·vûr′) *v.t.* a·verred, a·ver·ring 1 To declare confidently as fact; affirm. 2 Law To assert formally; prove or justify (a plea). [<L *ad-* to + *verus* true] —a·ver′ment n. —a·ver′ra·ble *adj.*

av·er·age (av′rij, av′ər·ij) n. 1 Math. A number representing a set of numbers of which it is a function, esp. an arithmetic mean. 2 A symbol, ratio, etc., representing such a number: a B *average.* 3 The normal or ordinary quality, amount, kind, degree, etc.: This meal is above *average.* 4 In marine law: a The loss arising by damage to a ship or cargo. b The proportion of such loss falling to a single person in an equitable distribution among those interested. —*adj.* 1 Obtained by calculating the mean of several. 2 Normal; ordinary. —*v.* ·aged, ·ag·ing *v.t.* 1 To fix or calculate as the mean. 2 To amount to or obtain an average of: He *averages* three dollars profit every hour. 3 To apportion on the average. —*v.i.* 4 To be or amount to an average. 5 To sell or purchase more of something so as to increase the average price. [<OF *avarie* damage to a ship or its cargo] —av′er·age·ly *adv.*

a·verse (ə·vûrs′) *adj.* Opposed; unfavorable; reluctant: with *to.* [<L *avertere* turn aside] —a·verse′ly *adv.* —a·verse′ness n.

a·vert (ə·vûrt′) *v.t.* 1 To turn or direct away: to *avert* one's eyes. 2 To prevent or ward off, as a danger. [< L *avertere* turn aside] —**a·vert'ed·ly** *adv.* —**a·vert'i·ble, a·vert'a·ble** *adj.*

**a·vi·ar·y** (ā'vē·er'ē) *n. pl.* **-ar·ies** An enclosure or large cage for birds. [< L *avis* bird] —**a·vi·ar·ist** (ā'vē·er'ist, -ər·ist) *n.*

**a·vi·a·tion** (ā'vē·ā'shən, av'ē-) *n.* The operation or production of heavier-than-air aircraft. [< L *avis* bird]

**av·o·ca·tion** (av'ə·kā'shən) *n.* An occupation or hobby that one has in addition to one's regular work or profession. [< L *ab-* away + *vocare* to call]

**a·void** (ə·void') *v.t.* 1 To keep away or at a distance from; shun; evade. 2 *Law* To make void. [< L *ex-* out + *viduare* empty, deprive] —**a·void'a·ble** *adj.* —**a·void'a·bly** *adv.* — **a·void'ance, a·void'er** *n.*

**a·vow** (ə·vou') *v.t.* To declare openly, as facts; own; acknowledge. [< L *advocare* summon] —**a·vow'a·ble** *adj.* —**a·vow'a·bly** *adv.* — **a·vow'er** *n.*

**a·wake** (ə·wāk') *adj.* 1 Not asleep. 2 Alert; vigilant. —*v.* **a·woke** (or **a·waked**), **a·waked** (or **a·woke** or **a·wok·en**), **a·wak·ing** *v.t.* 1 To arouse from sleep. 2 To stir up; excite. — *v.i.* 1 To cease to sleep; become awake. 4 To become alert or aroused. 5 To become aware of something: with *to*. [< OE ā- A-² + *wacian* watch]

**a·ward** (ə·wôrd') *v.t.* 1 To adjudge as due, as by legal decisions. 2 To bestow as the result of a contest or examination, as a prize. — *n.* 1 A decision, as by a judge or arbitrator. 2 That which is awarded. [< OF *es-* out + *guarder* watch] —**a·ward'a·ble** *adj.* —**a·ward'er** *n.*

**a·ware** (ə·wâr') *adj.* Knowing or conscious of something; cognizant. [< OE *gewǣr* watchful] —**a·ware'ness** *n.*

**awe** (ô) *n.* 1 Wonder and veneration somewhat mixed with fear. 2 Overwhelming admiration or appreciation. —*v.t.* awed, aw·ing or awe·ing to fill with awe. [< ON *agi* fear]

**awk·ward** (ôk'wərd) *adj.* 1 Ungraceful in bearing. 2 Unskillful in action; bungling. 3 Embarrassing or perplexing. 4 Difficult or dangerous to deal with, as an opponent. 5 Inconvenient for use; uncomfortable. [< ON *afug* turned the wrong way + -WARD] —**awk'ward·ly** *adv.* —**awk'ward·ness** *n.* — Syn. 1 ungainly, gawky. 2 clumsy, inept.

**awn·ing** (ô'ning) *n.* A rooflike cover, as of canvas, for protection from sun or rain. [?]

**AWOL** (*as an acronym pronounced* ā'wôl) *Mil.* Absent or absence without leave. **Also awol, A.W.O.L., a.w.o.l.**

**a·wry** (ə·rī') *adj. & adv.* 1 Toward one side; crooked; askew. 2 Out of the right course; erroneously [<A- (on) + WRY]

**ax** (aks) *n. pl.* **ax·es** A tool with a bladed head mounted on a handle, used for chopping, hewing, etc. —**get the ax** *Informal* 1 To be beheaded. 2 To be fired from one's job. — **have an ax to grind** *Informal* To have a private purpose or interest to promote. —*v.t.* 1 To cut or shape with an ax. 2 *Informal* To dismiss or delete. **Also axe.** [OE *æx, eax*]

**ax·i·om** (ak'sē·əm) *n.* 1 A self-evident or universally recognized truth. 2 An established principle or rule. 3 *Logic & Math.* A proposition assumed to be true. [< Gk. *axiōma* a thing thought worthy]

**ax·is** (ak'sis) *n. pl.* **ax·es** (ak'sēz) 1 A line around which a turning body rotates or may be supposed to rotate. 2 *Geom.* a A straight line through the center of a figure, esp. one with respect to which the figure is symmetrical. b A line along which distances are measured or to which positions are referred. 3 A real or imaginary central line about which things or parts are symmetrically arranged. 4 An affiliation or coalition of two or more nations to promote mutual interest, cooperation, etc. —**the Axis** In World War II, the coalition between Germany, Italy, and later Japan and other countries that opposed the United Nations. [<L, axis, axle]

**ax·le** (ak'səl) *n.* 1 A shaft or spindle on which a wheel is mounted and on or with which it turns. 2 AXLETREE. [<ON *ŏxull*] —**ax'led** *adj.*

**a·zal·ea** (ə·zāl'yə) *n.* Any of various usu. deciduous shrubs with showy flowers, related to rhododendrons. [<Gk. *azein* parch, from its preference for dry soil]

**az·ure** (azh'ər, ā'zhər) *adj.* Sky-blue. —*n.* 1 A clear sky-blue color or pigment. 2 The sky. [<Ar. *al-lāzward* lapis lazuli]

# B

**bab·ble** (bab'əl) *n.* 1 A murmuring sound, as of a stream. 2 Prattle, as of an infant. 3 A confusion of sounds, as of a crowd. —*v.* **bab·bled, bab·bling** —*v.t.* 1 To utter unintelligibly. 2 To blurt out thoughtlessly —*v.i.* 3 To utter inarticulate or meaningless noises. 4 To murmur, as a brook. 5 To talk unwisely or foolishly. [ME *babelen*] —**bab'bler** *n.*

**Ba·bel** (bā'bəl, bab'əl) *n.* In the Bible, an ancient city now thought to be Babylon. — **Tower of Babel** A tower built in Babel and intended to reach to heaven. God punished such presumption by preventing the workers from understanding each other and from completing the tower. *Gen.* 11;1–9.

**ba·boon** (ba·bōōn′) *n.* A large, terrestrial monkey of Africa and Asia having large bare callosities on the buttocks, and usu. a short tail. [<OF *babuin*] —**ba·boon′ish** *adj*

**ba·bush·ka** (bə·bŏŏsh′kə) *n.* A woman's scarf for the head. [<Russ., grandmother]

**ba·by-sit** (bā′bē·sit′) *v.* -**sat**, **sit**·**ting** To act as a baby sitter.

**bac·ca·lau·re·ate** (bak′ə·lôr′ē·it) *n.* 1 The degree of bachelor of arts, bachelor of science, etc. 2 An address to a graduating class at commencement; *also* baccalaureate sermon. [<Med. L *baccalaurius* a squire]

**bach·e·lor** (bach′ələr, bach′lər) *n.* 1 An unmarried man. 2 One who has a baccalaureate degree. —*adj.* Of or for a bachelor. [<Med. L *baccalaurius* a squire] —**bach′e·lor·hood′**, **bach′e·lor·ship′** *n.*

**ba·cil·lus** (bə·sil′əs) *n. pl.* **ba·cil·li** (-sil′ī) 1 Any of a genus of aerobic, rod-shaped, spore-forming bacteria often growing linked together. 2 Any rod-shaped bacterium. [<L *baculum* rod] —**ba·cil·lar**, **bac·il·lar·y** (bas′ə·ler′ē) *adj.* • See BACTERIUM.

**back·bite** (bak′bīt) *v.t. & v.i.* **-bit**, **-bit·ten** (or *Informal* **-bit**), **-bit·ing** To revile behind one's back; slander. —**back′bit′er**, **back′bit′ing** *n.*

**back·lash** (bak′lash′) *n.* 1 A sudden, usu. violent backward movement. 2 *In* angling, a snarl or tangle of the line on a reel. 3 A sudden, violent reaction, as of public opinion.

**back·log** (bak′lôg, -log′) *n. U.S.* 1 A large log at the back of a fireplace. 2 Any reserve or accumulation, as of funds, business orders, etc.

**ba·con** (bā′kən) *n.* The salted and dried or smoked back and sides of the hog. —**bring home the bacon** *Informal* 1 To provide a living. 2 To succeed. [< OF]

**bac·te·ri·a** (bak·tir′ē·ə) Plural of BACTERIUM.

**badge** (baj) *n.* 1 A token, decoration, or emblem of office, rank, attainment, etc. 2 Any distinguishing mark or symbol. —*v.t.* **badged**, **badg·ing** To decorate or provide with a badge. [ME *bagge*]

**badg·er** (baj′ər) *n.* 1 A small, burrowing, nocturnal, carnivorous mammal, with a broad body, short legs, and long clawed forefeet.

2 The fur of a badger. —*v.t.* To worry persistently; nag. [?]

**bad·i·nage** (bad′ə·näzh′, bad′ə·nij) *n.* Playful raillery; banter. —*v.t.* **·naged**, **·nag·ing** To tease with badinage. [< F *badin* silly, jesting]

**baf·fle** (baf′əl) *v.* **baf·fled**, **baf·fling** *v.t.* 1 To confuse or perplex. 2 To thwart or frustrate; defeat. 3 To block with or as with a baffle. —*v.i.* 4 To struggle to no avail. —*n.* A plate or partition acting as a barrier to sound, motion of a fluid, etc. —**baf′fling** *adj.* —**baf′fling·ly** *adv.* —**baf′fle·ment**, **baf′fler** *n.*

**bag·a·telle** (bag′ə·tel′) *n.* 1 A trifle. 2 A game similar to billiards. [< Ital. *bagatella*]

**bag·gage** (bag′ij) *n.* 1 The trunks, packages, etc., of a traveler. 2 *Archaic* A prostitute. [< OF *bague* bundle]

**bag·pipe** (bag′pīp′) *n. Often pl.* A reed musical instrument in which the several drone pipes and the melody pipe with its finger stops are supplied with air from a windbag filled by the player's breath. —**bag′pip′er** *n.*

**bail**[1] (bāl) *n.* In cricket, one of the crosspieces of the wicket. [< OF *baile* barrier]

**bail**[2] (bāl) *Law n.* 1 Money or security given to a court to secure the release of an arrested person on the proviso that the person will be present later to stand trial. 2 Such a release. 3 The person or persons who give such money or security. —*v.t.* 1 To release (an arrested person) on bail: often with *out*. 2 To obtain the release of (an arrested person) on bail: usu. with *out*. 3 To help out of any difficulty: usu. with *out*. —**go (or stand) bail for** To provide bail for. [< OF *baillier* guard, carry] —**bail′a·ble** *adj.*

**bait** (bāt) *n.* 1 Food or other lure in a trap, on a hook, etc. 2 Any allurement or enticement. —*v.t.* 1 To put food or some other lure on or in. 2 To torment, as by setting dogs upon, for sport: to *bait* a bear. 3 To harass; heckle. 4 To lure; entice. [< ON *beita* food] —**bait′er** *n.*

**bal·ance** (bal′əns) *n.* 1 An instrument for measuring weights, often a bar pivoted on a central point with matched pans at either end; scales. 2 The imaginary scales of destiny; a symbol of justice. 3 The power to decide fate, value, etc., as by a balance. 4 A state of equilibrium or equality, as in value, importance, etc. 5 Equilibrium of the body. 6 Mental or emotional stability; sanity. 7 Harmonious proportion, as in the design or arrangement of parts. 8 Something used to produce an equilibrium; counteracting influence; counterpoise. 9 The act of balancing. 10 a Equality between the credit and debit totals of an account. b A difference between such totals; the excess on either the debit or credit side. 11 *Informal* Whatever is left over; remainder: the *balance* of the week. 12 A balance wheel. —**in the balance** Being judged; not yet settled. —**strike a balance** To compromise. —*v.* ·anced, ·anc·ing *v.t.* 1 To bring into or keep in equilibrium; poise. 2 To weigh in a balance. 3 To compare or weigh in the mind. 4 To offset or counteract. 5 To bring into harmony, proportion, etc. 6 To be equal to. 7 To compute the difference between the debit and credit sides of (an account). 8 To reconcile, as by making certain entries, the debit and credit sides of (an account). 9 To adjust (an account) by paying what is owed. —*v.i.* 10 To be or come into equilibrium. 11 To be equal. 12 To hesitate or waver; tilt: to *balance* on the edge of a chasm. [< L *bilanx* having two plates or scales < *bis* two + *lanx* plate] —**bal·ance·a·ble** *adj.* —**bal·an·cer** *n.*

**bal·co·ny** (bal′kə·nē) *n. pl.* ·nies 1 A platform with balustrade or railing projecting from a wall of a building. • See BALUSTRADE. 2 A projecting gallery inside a theater, auditorium, etc. [< Ital. *balco* a beam]

**bald** (bôld) *adj.* 1 Without hair on the head. 2 Without natural growth, as a mountain. 3 Unadorned; without embellishments; plain. 4 Without disguise: *bald* jealousy. 5 Having white feathers or fur on the head: the *bald* eagle. [ME *ballede*] —**bald′ly** *adv.* —**bald′ness** *n.*

**bale·ful** (bāl′fəl) *adj.* Hurtful; malignant; 2 Sorrowful: a *baleful* look. [< OE *bealu* evil + -FUL] —**bale′fu·ly** *adv.* —**bale′ful·ness** *n.*

**balk** (bôk) *v.t.* 1 To render unsuccessful; thwart; frustrate. —*v.i.* 2 To stop short and refuse to proceed. 3 To refuse to consider or act upon: with *at*: He *balked* at every idea. 4 In baseball, to make a balk. —*n.* 1 a hindrance, disappointment, defeat, etc. 2 An error; blunder. 3 In baseball, an illegal, uncompleted motion by a pitcher when there are men on base. 4 A ridge left unplowed between furrows. 5 A squared beam or timber. [< OE *balca* bank, ridge]

**ball** (bôl) *n.* 1 A large, formal gathering for dancing. 2 *Slang* A very good time. —*v.i. Slang* To have a very good time. [< LL *ballare* dance]

**bal·lad** (bal′əd) *n.* 1 A narrative poem or song

of popular origin in short stanzas, often with a refrain. 2 A popular song, usu. slow in tempo and sentimental in nature. [< OF *ballade* dancing song] —**bal·lad·eer** (bal′ə·dir′), **bal′lad·ry** *n.*

**bal·last** (bal′əst) *n.* 1 Any heavy substance carried in a vessel or vehicle to stablize it or, in a balloon, to control altitude. 2 Gravel or broken stone laid down as a railroad bed. 3 That which gives stability to character, morality, etc. —*v.t.* 1 To provide with ballast. 2 To stabilize. [< Odan. *barlast* bare load]

**ball bearing** *Mech.* 1 A bearing in which the shaft rests upon small metal balls that turn freely as it revolves. 2 Any of the metal balls in such a bearing.

**bal·let** (bal′ā, ba·lā′) *n.* 1 An elaborate group dance using conventionalized movements, often for narrative effects. 2 This style of dancing. 3 Music for a ballet. 4 A company of ballet dancers. [<LL *ballare* to dance] —**bal·let·ic** (ba·let′ik) *adj.*

**bal·lis·tic** (bə·lis′tik) *adj.* Pertaining to projectiles or to ballistics.

**ballistic missile** A missile that is powered and guided at launch and through the early part of its trajectory, and in free fall thereafter.

**bal·lis·tics** (bə·lis′tiks) *n. pl.* (*construed as sing.*) The science that deals with the motion of projectiles. —**bal·lis·ti·cian** (bal′ə·stish′ən) *n.*

**bal·loon** (bə·lōōn′) *n.* 1 A large, airtight bag, inflated with gas lighter than air, designed to rise and float in the atmosphere, often carrying passengers, instruments, etc. 2 A small inflatable rubber bag, used as a toy. 3 In comic strips, the outline containing the dialogue. —*v.i.* 1 To increase quickly in scope or magnitude; expand. 2 To swell out like a balloon. 3 To ascend in a balloon. —*v.t.* 4 To inflate or swell with air. [< Ital. *balla* ball, sphere] —**bal·loon′ist** *n.*

**bal·lot** (bal′ət) *n.* 1 A written or printed slip or ticket used in secret voting. 2 The total number of votes cast in an election. 3 The act or system of voting secretly by ballots or by voting machines. 4 The list of candidates in an election. —*v.* **bal·lot·ed, bal·lot·ing** —*v.i.* 1 To vote or decide by ballot. —*v.t.* 2 To vote for or decide on by means of a ballot: to *ballot* the players in selecting a captain. [< Ital. *ballotta*, dim. of *balla* ball]

**ball-point pen** (bôl′point′) A pen having for a

point a ball bearing that rolls against an ink cartridge. Also **ball′point′, ball point.**

**balm** (bäm) *n.* 1 An aromatic gum resin from various trees or shrubs. 2 Any of a genus of fragrant herbs. 3 Any oil or resin used as ointment, esp. if fragrant. 4 Anything that soothes or heals. [< L *balsamum* balsam]

**bam·boo** (bam·bōō′) *n.* 1 A tall shrubby grass of tropical and semi-tropical regions. 2 The tough, hollow, jointed stem of this plant. [< Malay *bambu*]

**ban** (ban) *v.t.* To forbid or prohibit, esp. officially. —*n.* 1 An official prohibition. 2 Disapproval or prohibition, as by public opinion. 3 An ecclesiastical edict of excommunication or interdiction. [< ME *bannen* to summon & OF *ban* a summoning]

**ba·nan·a** (bə·nan′ə) *n.* 1 A large, tropical, tree-like plant cultivated for its fruit. 2 The edible, pulpy fruit of this plant. [< native w African name]

**band·age** (ban′dij) *n.* A strip, usu. of soft cloth, used in dressing wounds, etc. —*v.t.* **·aged, ·ag·ing** To bind or cover with a bandage. [< F *bande* band]

**ban·dit** (ban′dit) *n. pl.* **ban·dits** or **ban·dit·ti** (ban·dit′ē) 1 A robber. 2 Any outlaw. [<Ital. *bandire* to join together in a band] —**ban′dit·ry** *n.*

**bane** (bān) *n.* 1 Anything destructive or ruinous. 2 A deadly poison. [< OE *bana* murderer, destruction]

**bang** (bang) *n.* 1 A sudden or noisy blow, thump, whack, or explosion. 2 *Informal* A sudden spurt of energy, activity, etc. 3 *Slang* Thrill; excitement. —*v.t.* 1 To beat, slam, or strike loudly. —*v.i.* 2 To make a heavy, loud sound. 3 To strike noisily. —*adv.* 1 Loudly and with force. 2 Suddenly. [< ON *banga* hammer, beat]

**ban·gle** (bang′gəl) *n.* A decorative bracelet or anklet. [<Hind. *bangrī* glass bracelet]

**ban·ish** (ban′ish) *v.t.* 1 To compel to leave a country by political decree; exile. 2 To expel; drive away; dismiss, as a thought from one's mind. [< LL *banire*] —**ban′ish·er, ban′ish·ment** *n.*

**ban·jo** (ban′jō) *n. pl.* **·jos** A long-necked, stringed musical instrument having a circular body covered on top with stretched skin and played by plucking. [Alter. of *mbanza*, a similar instrument of Africa] —**ban′jo·ist** *n.*

**bank** (bangk) *n.* 1 Any moundlike formation or mass, as of ground, clouds, etc. 2 A steep rising, as of ground. 3 The slope of land at the edge of a body of water. 4 A large, raised portion of the bed of an ocean; also, a shallow; sandbar; shoal. 5 An upward lateral slope, as on the curve of a race track. 6 The cushioned edge of a billiard table. 7 *Aeron.* The sidewise inclination of an airplane in making a turn. —*v.t.* 1 To enclose, cover, or protect by a bank, dike, or border; embank. 2 To heap up into a bank or mound. 3 To cover (a fire) with fuel, ashes, etc., to keep it alive but burning low. 4 To give an upward lateral slope to, as the curve of a road. 5 To incline (an airplane) laterally. 6 In billiards and pool, to cause (a ball) to rebound at an angle from a cushion. —*v.i.* 7 To form or lie in banks. 8 To incline an airplane laterally. [ME *banke*]

**bank·rupt** (bangk′rupt) *n.* 1 A person unable to pay his debts. 2 *Law* One judicially declared insolvent, whose property is administered for and divided among his creditors. 3 A person who has failed in or totally lacks something. —*adj.* 1 Being a bankrupt; insolvent. 2 Destitute or depleted: spiritually *bankrupt.* 3 Utterly ruined. —*v.t.* To make bankrupt. [< Ital. *banca rotta* bankruptcy, lit., broken counter] —**bank′rupt·cy** *n.* (*pl.* **·cies**)

**ban·ner** (ban′ər) *n.* 1 A piece of cloth, often long, bearing a design, motto, advertisement, etc. 2 Any flag or standard. 3 In journalism, a headline extending across a newspaper page. —*v.t.* To furnish with a banner. —*adj.* Leading; foremost; outstanding. [< LL *bandum* banner]

**bap·tism** (bap′tiz·əm) *n.* 1 The act of baptizing or of being baptized. 2 Any initiatory or purifying experience. [< Gk. *baptismos* immersion] —**bap·tis·mal** (bap·tiz′məl) *adj.* —**bap·tis′mal·ly** *adv.*

**bar** (bär) *n.* 1 A piece of solid material, evenly shaped and long in proportion to its width and thickness. 2 Any barrier or obstruction. 3 Any hindrance. 4 A sandbar. 5 The enclosed place in court occupied by counsel; also, the place where a prisoner stands to plead. 6 A court or any place of justice. 7 Lawyers collectively or the legal profession. 8 A room, establishment, or a counter where liquors or refreshments are dispensed. 9 A stripe; a band, as of color. 10 *Mil.* Small metal or cloth strips showing rank. 11 *Music* a Any of the vertical lines that mark off measures. b A double bar. c The unit of music between two bars; measure. 12 A handrail for certain ballet exer-

37

cises; also, the exercises done at a bar. —
*v.t.* **barred, bar·ring 1** To fasten, lock, or secure with or as with a bar. **2** To confine or
shut out with or as with bars. **3** To obstruct
or hinder. **4** To exclude or except. **5** To mark
with bars. —*prep.* Excluding; excepting:
*bar* none. [<LL *barra* bar] —**Syn.** *v.* **3** block,
impede, thwart, check. **4** prohibit, reject,
prevent, boycott.

**bar.** barometer; barometric; barrel; barrister.

**barb** (bärb) *n.* **1** A backward-projecting point
on a sharp weapon, as on an arrow, fish
hook, etc. **2** A beard, as in certain grains
and grasses; awn. **3** One of the threadlike
outgrowths from the shaft of a feather. **4** A
cutting remark. **5** Sting: the *barb* of his wit.
—*v.t.* To provide with a barb or barbs. [<L
*barba* beard] —**barbed, bar′bate** *adj.*

**bar·bar·i·an** (bär·bâr′ē·ən, -bar′-) *n.* **1** A member of a tribe or race thought of as uncivilized. **2** Any rude, brutal, or coarse person.
**3** A person lacking culture. **4** Originally, a
non-Greek, non-Roman, or non-Christian.
—*adj.* **1** Uncivilized; cruel; barbarous. **2**
Foreign; alien.

**bar·be·cue** (bär′bə·kyōō) *n.* **1** An outdoor meal
for which the food is roasted over an open
fire. **2** Any meat roasted over an open fire.
—*v.t.* **·cued, ·cu·ing 1** To roast (meat, fowl,
etc.) over an open fire or in a trench. **2** To
cook (meat) with a highly seasoned sauce.
[<Taino *barbacoa* framework of sticks]

**bar·bit·u·rate** (bär·bich′ər·it, bär′bə·t′ŏŏr′it)
*n.* Any of various derivatives of barbituric
acid used in medicine to induce sedation or
sleep.

**bare** (bâr) Obsolete *p.t.* of BEAR.

**bar·gain** (bär′gən) *n.* **1** An agreement between
persons, esp. one to buy or sell goods. **2**
That which is agreed upon or the terms of
the agreement. **3** The agreement as it affects one of the parties: a bad *bargain*. **4** An
article bought or offered at a price favorable
to the buyer. —*v.i.* **1** To discuss terms for
selling or buying. **2** To make a bargain;
reach an agreement. —*v.t.* **3** To barter or
sell by bargaining. —**bargain for** (or **on**) To
expect; count on: usu. in the negative: We
didn't *bargain on* getting twins. [< OF *bar-
gaine*]

**barge** (bärj) *n.* **1** A flat-bottomed freight boat
for harbors and inland waters. **2** A large
boat, for pleasure, state occasions, etc. —
*v.* **barged, barg·ing** *v.t.* **1** To transport by
barge. —*v.i.* **2** To move clumsily and slowly.
**3** *Informal* To collide with: with *into*. **4** *In-*

*formal* To intrude; enter rudely: with *in* or
*into*. [< OF! - -**barge′man** *n.*

**bar·i·tone** (bar′ə·tōn) *n.* **1** A male voice higher
than bass and lower than tenor. **2** One having such a voice. **3** A small tuba, used
chiefly in military bands. —*adj.* **1** Of, like,
or pertaining to a baritone. **2** Having the
range of a baritone. [< Gk. *barytonos* deep-
sounding]

**bark**[1] (bärk) *n.* **1** The short, explosive sound
made by a dog. **2** Any sound like this. —*v.i.*
**1** To utter a bark, as a dog, or to make a
sound like a bark. **2** *Informal* To cough. **3**
To speak loudly and sharply. **4** *Slang* To announce the attractions of a show at its entrance. —*v.t.* **5** To say roughly and curtly.
[< OE *beorcan* to bark]

**bark**[2] (bärk) *n.* The covering of the stems,
branches, and roots of a woody plant. —*v.t.*
**1** To remove the bark from. **2** To rub off the
skin of. **3** To tan or treat with an infusion
of bark. [< Scand.]

**bar·ley** (bär′lē) *n.* **1** A hardy, bearded cereal
grass. **2** Its grain. [< OE *bœrlic*]

**bar·na·cle** (bär′nə·kəl) *n.* **1** A marine shellfish
that attaches itself firmly to rocks, ship
bottoms, etc. **2** Something or someone that
clings tenaciously. [ME *bernacle*] —**bar′-
na·cled** *adj.*

**ba·rom·e·ter** (bə·rom′ə·tər) *n.* **1** An instrument for measuring atmospheric pressure.
**2** Anything that indicates changes. —
**bar·o·met·ric** (bar′ə·met′rik) or **·ri·cal** *adj.*
—**bar′o·met′ri·cal·ly** *adv.* —**ba·rom′e·try**
*n.*

**bar·on** (bar′ən) *n.* **1** A member of the lowest
order of hereditary nobility in Great
Britain, Japan, and several European
countries; also, the dignity or rank itself. **2**
One who has great power in a commercial
field: a coal *baron*. [<LL *baro*] —**ba·ro·ni·al**
(bə·rō′nē·əl) *adj.*

**bar·rack** (bar′ək) *n.* **1** *pl.* A structure or group
of structures for the housing of soldiers. **2**
*pl.* A temporary or rough shelter for a gang
of laborers, etc. —*v.t.* & *v.i.* To house in
barracks. [<Ital. *baracca* soldiers' tent]

**bar·rage** (bə·räzh′) *n.* **1** A curtain of artillery
fire designed to prevent enemy advance-
ment, protect one's own advancing troops,
etc. **2** Any overwhelming attack, as of words
or blows. —*v.t.* & *v.i.* **·raged, ·rag·ing** To lay
down a barrage (against) or subject to a
barrage. [<F *(tir de) barrage* barrage (fire)]

**bar·rel** (bar′əl) *n.* **1** A large, round, wooden
vessel, made with staves and hoops, hav-

ing a flat base and top and slightly bulging sides. 2 As much as a barrel will hold; in liquid measure varying from 31 to 42 U.S. gallons. 3 Something resembling a barrel, as the rotating drum of a windlass, capstan, etc. 4 In firearms, the tube through which the projectile is discharged. • See REVOLVER. —v. ·reled or ·relled, ·rel·ing or ·rel·ling —v.t. 1 To put or pack in a barrel. —v.i. 2 Slang To move at high speed. [<OF baril]

**bar·ren** (bar'ən) adj. 1 Incapable of producing; sterile. 2 Not producing crops, fruit, etc. 3 Unprofitable, as an enterprise. 4 Lacking in interest or attractiveness; dull. 5 Devoid; lacking: barren of any new ideas. —n. Usu. pl. A tract of level, usu. sandy, barren land. [<OF baraigne] —bar'ren·ly adv. —bar'ren·ness n.

**bar·ri·cade** (bar'ə·kād, bar'ə·kād') n. 1 A barrier hastily built for obstruction or for defense. 2 Any obstruction or barrier closing a passage. —v.t. ·cad·ed, ·cad·ing To enclose, obstruct, or defend with a barricade. [<Sp. barricada barrier < barrica barrel]

**bar·ri·er** (bar'ē·ər) n. 1 Something that prevents entrance, obstructs passage, etc., as a fence. 2 Anything that tends to separate or retard progress: a language barrier. 3 A boundary or limit. [<OF barre bar]

**bar·tend·er** (bär'ten'dər) n. One who serves liquors over a bar.

**bar·ter** (bär'tər) v.i. 1 To exchange goods or services without use of money. —v.t. 2 To trade (one thing) for another of equal value. —n. 1 The act of bartering. 2 Something bartered. [<OF barater exchange] —bar'ter·er n.

**base¹** (bās) n. 1 The lowest or supporting part of anything; bottom; foundation. 2 The essential or main part or element of anything: the base of our plan. 3 The essential ingredient or bottom layer of something: a tar base. 4 Any point, line, or quantity from which a measurement, inference, or conclusion is made; basis. 5 In certain games, a starting point or goal; esp. in baseball, any one of the four points of the diamond. 6 A place from which operations proceed, supplies are stored, etc.: a military base. 7 The point of attachment of a bodily organ. 8 Archit. The lowest part of a column, wall, etc. 9 Chem. a A compound capable of reacting with an acid to form a salt. b Any molecule or radical that takes up positive ions. 10 Geom. The side or face of a figure

on which it appears to rest. 11 Math. A number whose powers are used as the various orders of units in a numeration system. 12 Ling. The form of a word used in making derivatives, as by adding prefixes or suffixes; root. 13 Her. The lower part of a shield. —off base 1 In baseball, not on the base one should be on. 2 Informal In error. —v.t. based, bas·ing 1 To put on a logical basis, as an argument, decision, or theory: with on or upon. 2 To make or form a base for. 3 To assign to a base: with in or at. —adj. Serving as a base. [<Gk. basis step, pedestal]

**base²** (bās) adj. 1 Vile; low; contemptible: base conduct. 2 Menial; degrading: base employment. 3 Inferior, as in quality. 4 Debased or counterfeit, as money. 5 Having comparatively little value: said of metals. [<LL bassus low] —base'ly adv. —base'ness n. —Syn. 1 ignoble, infamous, mean, sordid, despicable. 2 miserable, wretched.

**base·ball** (bās'bôl') n. 1 A game played with a wooden bat and a hard ball by two teams of nine players each, one team being at bat and the other in the field, alternately, for a minimum of nine innings. The game is played on a field having four bases in a diamond formation. 2 The ball used in this game.

**base·ment** (bās'mənt) n. 1 The lowest floor of a building, usu. underground. 2 The substructure of any building, structure, or member.

**bash·ful** (bash'fəl) adj. Shy; timid; modest. [<ABASH + -FUL] —bash'ful·ly adv. —bash'ful·ness n.

**ba·sin** (bā'sən) n. 1 A round, wide, shallow vessel for holding liquids. 2 The amount that a basin will hold. 3 A sink or wash bowl. 4 A depression in the earth's surface, as a valley. 5 The region drained by a river. 6 A partially enclosed harbor or bay. 7 A bowllike depression in the floor of the ocean. [<LL bacca] —ba'sined adj.

**ba·sis** (bā'sis) n. pl. ba·ses (bā'sēz) 1 That on which anything rests; support; foundation. 2 Fundamental principle. 3 The main component of a thing. [<Gk., base, pedestal] —Syn. 1 base, groundwork. 2 theory, premise.

**bask** (bask, bäsk) v.i. 1 To lie in and enjoy a pleasant warmth, as of the sun. 2 To enjoy a pleasing circumstance: to bask in the affection of a friend. [<Scand.]

**bas·ket** (bas'kit, bäs'-) n. 1 A container made

of interwoven twigs, rushes, strips, etc. 2 Something resembling a basket, as the structure under a balloon for carrying passengers or ballast. 3 The amount a basket will hold. 4 In basketball, either of the goals, consisting of a cord net suspended from a metal ring; also, the point or points made by throwing the ball through the basket. [ME]

**bas·ket·ball** (bas′kit·bôl′, băs′-) n. 1 A game played by two teams of five players each, in which the object is to throw the ball through the elevated goal (basket) at the opponent's end of a zoned, oblong court. 2 The inflated ball used in this game.

**bass** (bās) n. 1 The lowest-pitched male singing voice. 2 A deep, low sound, as of this voice or of low-pitched instruments. 3 The lowest of two or more musical parts. 4 A low-pitched musical instrument, esp. a double bass. —*adj.* 1 Low in pitch or range. 2 Pertaining to, for, or able to play bass. [<OF *bas* low, base]

**bas·soon** (ba·sōōn′, bǝ-) n. A large, double-reed woodwind instrument with a long, curved mouthpiece. [<F *bas* low]

**baste**[1] (bāst) v.t. **bast·ed, bast·ing** To sew together with long, temporary stitches. [<OF *bastir*]

**baste**[2] (bāst) v.t. **bast·ed, bast·ing** To moisten (meat or fish) with drippings, butter, etc., while cooking. [?]

**batch** (bach) n. 1 The quantity of bread, etc., baked at one time. 2 The amount of material required for one operation. 3 The amount produced at one operation. 4 Persons or things in a group; lot. [<OE *bacan* to bake]

**bath** (bath, băth) n. pl. **baths** (bathz, băthz; baths, băths) 1 The act of washing or immersing something, esp. the body, in water or other liquid. 2 The liquid used for this. 3 The container for such a liquid, as a bathtub. 4 A bathroom. 5 *Often pl.* A set of rooms or a building for bathing. 6 *Often pl.* A resort where bathing is part of a medical treatment. —v.t. Brit. To bathe. [<OE *bæth*]

**bathe** (bāth) v. **bathed, bath·ing** v.t. 1 To place in liquid; immerse. 2 To wash; wet. 3 To apply liquid to, as for comfort or healing. 4 To cover or suffuse as with liquid: The hill was *bathed* in light. —v.i. 5 To take a bath. 6 To go into or remain in water so as to swim or cool off. 7 To be covered or suffused as if with liquid: to *bathe* photographic prints in a fixer solution. —n. Brit.

The act of bathing, as in the sea. [<OE *bathian*] —**bath′er** n.

**bath·y·scaph** (bath′ǝ·skaf) n. A self-propelled diving ship for deep-sea exploration. Also **bath·y·scaphe** (-skaf, -skäf). [<BATHY- + Gk. *skaphē* bowl]

**bat·tal·ion** (bǝ·tal′yǝn) n. 1 *Mil.* a A regimental unit, consisting of a headquarters and two or more companies, batteries, or comparable units. b A body of troops. 2 *Usu. pl.* A large group or number. [<Ital. *battaglione*]

**bat·ter** (bat′ǝr) v.t. 1 To strike with repeated, violent blows. 2 To break or injure with or as with such blows. —v.i. 3 To beat with blow after blow. [<L *battuere* beat]

**bat·ter·y** (bat′ǝr·ē) n. pl. ·ter·ies 1 Any group or array of similar things used or connected together to serve a common end or purpose. 2 *Electr.* a An array of similar parts or devices, esp. primary or secondary cells, connected together. b A primary cell: a flashlight *battery*. 3 *Mil.* a A unit of an artillery regiment equivalent to an infantry company. b A group of heavy artillery, as guns, missiles, etc. 4 *Law* The illegal beating or touching of another person. 5 In baseball, the pitcher and catcher together. 6 *Music* The percussion instruments of an orchestra. [<F *battre* beat]

**bat·tle** (bat′l) n. 1 An extensive combat between hostile armies or fleets. 2 Any fighting, dispute, or conflict. —v. **bat·tled, bat·tling** —v.i. 1 To contend in or as in battle; struggle. —v.t. 2 To fight. [<LL *battuere* beat] —**bat′tler** n. —**Syn.** n. 1 engagement, encounter. v. 1 vie.

**baux·ite** (bôk′sīt, bō′zīt) n. A claylike mineral of varying composition, the principal ore of aluminum. [<Les *Baux*, town in southern France]

**bay·o·net** (bā′ǝ·nit, -net′, bā′ǝ·net′) n. A daggerlike weapon attachable to the muzzle of a rifle, for close fighting. —v.t. ·net·ed, ·net·ing To stab or pierce with a bayonet. [< *Bayonne*, France, where first made]

**ba·zaar** (bǝ·zär′) n. 1 An Oriental market place or range of shops. 2 A shop or store for the sale of miscellaneous wares. 3 A sale of miscellaneous articles, as for charity. Also **ba·zar′**. [<Pers. *bāzār* market]

**ba·zoo·ka** (bǝ·zōō′kǝ) n. *Mil.* A long, tubular launcher which fires an explosive rocket at short range. [< the *bazooka,* a comical musical instrument]

**beach** (bēch) n. 1 The shore of a body of water, as of a lake or sea, esp. when covered with sand or pebbles. 2 Loose pebbles on the shore; shingle. —*v.t.* & *v.i.* To drive or haul up (a boat or ship) on a beach; strand. [?]

**beach·head** (bēch′hed′) *n. Mil.* A landing position on a hostile shore established by an advance invasion force.

**bea·con** (bē′kən) *n.* 1 A signal fire or light on a hill, tower, or the like. 2 A lighthouse or other warning signal on a coast or shoreline. 3 Something that serves as a conspicuous warning or a guide. 4 *Aeron.* A radio device used to establish and plot flight courses. —*v.t.* 1 To furnish with a beacon. —*v.i.* 2 To shine or serve as a beacon. [< OE *bēacen* sign, signal]

**beak** (bēk) *n.* 1 The horny projecting mouth parts of birds; the bill. 2 A beaklike part or organ, as the horny jaws of turtles. 3 *Slang* The nose of a person. 4 Something shaped like a beak, as the spout of a pitcher. [<L *beccus*] —**beaked** (bēkt, bē′kid) *adj.*

**beak·er** (bē′kər) *n.* 1 A large, wide-mouthed cup or goblet. 2 A cylindrical, flat-bottomed vessel with a pouring lip, used in laboratories. 3 The contents or capacity of a beaker. [< ON *bikarr*]

**beam** (bēm) *n.* 1 A long, horizontal piece of material forming part of a structure. 2 *Naut.* a One of the heavy pieces of timber or iron set transversely across a vessel. b The greatest width of a vessel. 3 The widest part of anything. 4 The bar of a balance; also, the balance. 5 *Slang* The hips. 6 A ray or a group of nearly parallel rays of light or other radiant energy. 7 A radiant smile. 8 *Aeron.* A continuous radio signal used as a beacon: **also radio beam.** —**off the beam** 1 *Aeron.* Not following the radio beam. 2 *Informal* On the wrong track; wrong. —**on the beam** 1 *Aeron.* Following the radio beam. 2 *Informal* a Functioning well or quickly. b In the right direction; correct. —*v.t.* 1 To send out in or as in beams or rays. 2 *Telecom.* To aim or transmit (a signal) in a specific direction. 3 *Aeron.* To guide (an airplane) by a radio beam. —*v.i.* 4 To emit light. 5 To smile or grin radiantly. [< OE *bēam* tree]

**bear¹** (bâr) *v.* bore (*Archaic* bare), borne or born, bear·ing *v.t.* 1 To support; hold up. 2 To carry; convey. 3 To show visibly; carry: to *bear* a scar. 4 To conduct or guide. 5 To spread: to *bear* tales. 6 To hold in the mind: to *bear* a grudge. 7 To suffer or endure; undergo. 8 To accept or assume, as responsibility. 9 To give birth to (see note below). 10

To conduct or comport (oneself). 11 To manage or carry (oneself or a part of oneself). 12 To render; give: to *bear* witness. 13 To be able to withstand; allow: His story will not *bear* investigation. 14 To have or stand (in comparison or relation): with *to:* What relation does this *bear* to the other? 15 To possess as a right or power: to *bear* title. —*v.i.* 16 To carry burdens; convey. 17 To rest heavily; lean; press. 18 To endure patiently; suffer: often with *with.* 19 To produce fruit or young. 20 To move, point, or lie in a certain direction: Later, we *bore* west. 21 To be relevant; have reference: with *on* or *upon.* —**bear down** upon To approach. 2 To put pressure on. —**bear out** To confirm; justify. [< OE *beran*] • In def. 9, meaning *to give birth to,* borne is the participle used when speaking of the mother or when followed by *by:* She has *borne* twins; The twins were *borne* by her. When speaking of the offspring, born is used: He was *born* today. In all other meanings, the participle *borne* is the only one used: They have *borne* their troubles well; *air-borne* bacteria.

**bear²** (bâr) *n.* 1 Any of various large carnivorous or omnivorous mammals with massive thick-furred body and short tail. 2 An ill-mannered, grumpy, or clumsy person. 3 A speculator who sells shares of stock, etc., in the belief that prices will decline and he can buy later at a profit. —*adj.* Of or favorable to bears (def. 3). [< OE *bera*]

**Bear** (bâr) *n.* Either of two constellations, the Great Bear or the Little Bear.

**beard** (bird) *n.* 1 The hair on a man's face, esp. on the chin. 2 The long hair on the chin of some animals, as the goat. 3 Any similar growth or appendage. 4 *Bot.* A tuft of hairlike processes; an awn. • See WHEAT. —*v.t.* 1 To defy courageously. 2 To furnish with a beard. [<OE] —**beard′ed** *adj.*

**beast** (bēst) *n.* 1 Any animal except man. 2 Any large quadruped. 3 Animal characteristics or animal nature. 4 A cruel, rude, or filthy person. [<L *bestia* beast]

**beat** (bēt) *v.* beat, beat·en (*Informal* beat), beat·ing *v.t.* 1 To strike repeatedly; pound. 2 To punish in this way; thrash. 3 To dash or strike against. 4 To make, as a path, by repeated walking, blows, pushing, etc. 5 To forge or shape by hammering. 6 To walk on for a long time. 7 To defeat or outdo. 8 To flap; flutter, as wings. 9 *Music* To mark (time or rhythm) with or as with a baton. 10

To hunt over; search. 11 To sound (a signal) as on a drum. 12 To whip (ingredients) so as to make lighter or frothier. 13 *Informal* To baffle; perplex: It *beats* me. 14 *Slang* To defraud; swindle. —*v.i.* 15 To strike repeated blows. 16 To strike or pound as with blows. 17 To throb; pulsate. 18 To give forth sound, as when struck. 19 To sound a signal, as on a drum. 20 *Physics* To fluctuate periodically in intensity. 21 To be adaptable to beating: The yolk *beats* well. 22 To hunt through underbrush, etc., as for game. 23 To win a victory or contest. —**beat around the bush** To be evasive. —**beat it** *Slang* To go hastily. —**beat up** *Informal* To thrash thoroughly. —*n.* 1 A stroke or blow. 2 A pulsation or throb, as of the pulse. 3 *Physics* A periodic reinforcement and cancellation that results when waves of slightly different frequencies interact. 4 *Naut.* A tack. 5 *Music* a One of a series of pulses used to mark time in music. b The gesture or symbol for this. 6 A round, line, or district regularly traversed, as by a sentry or a policeman. 7 *Slang* A scoop for a newspaper. 8 *Slang* A deadbeat. 9 *Informal* A beatnik. —*adj.* 1 *Informal* Fatigued; worn out. 2 Of or pertaining to the Beat Generation. [< OE *bēatan*]

**be·at·i·tude** (bē·at′ə·t'ōod) *n.* Supreme blessedness. —**the Beatitudes** The declarations of special blessedness in the Sermon on the Mount. *Matt.* 5:3–11. [<L *beatitudo* blessedness]

**beat·nik** (bēt′nik) *n.* A member of the Beat Generation. [< BEAT, *adj.* def. 2 + -NIK]

**beau·ti·fy** (byōō′tə·fī) *v.t.* & *v.i.* ·fied, ·fy·ing To make or grow beautiful; embellish; adorn. —**beau′ti·fi·ca′tion**, **beau′ti·fi′er** *n.*

**beau·ty** (byōō′tē) *n. pl.* ·ties 1 Any of those attributes of form, sound, color, execution, character, behavior, etc., which give pleasure and gratification to the senses or to the mind. 2 A person or thing that is beautiful, esp. a woman. 3 Physical attractiveness. 4 Any special or compelling feature. [<OF *beaute* < L *bellus* handsome, fine, pretty]

**bea·ver** (bē′vər) *n.* 1 An aquatic rodent with a scaly, broad tail and webbed hind feet, noted for skill in damming shallow streams. 2 The fur of the beaver. 3 A high silk hat, originally made of this fur. [<OE *beofor*]

**beck·on** (bek′ən) *v.t.* & *v.i.* 1 To signal, direct, or summon by sign or gesture. 2 To entice or lure. —*n.* A summoning gesture; beck. [<OE *biecnan*, *beacnian* to make signs]

**be·come** (bi·kum′) *v.* **be·came**, **be·come**, **be·com·ing** *v.i.* 1 To grow to be: The chick *becomes* the chicken. 2 To come to be: The land *became* dry. —*v.t.* 3 To suit or befit. 4 To show to advantage: Your dress *becomes* you. —**become of** To be the fate of: What *became of* him? [<OE *becuman* happen, come about]

**bed·lam** (bed′ləm) *n.* 1 An excited crowd. 2 An incoherent uproar. 3 A lunatic asylum. [<*Bedlam*, a former London asylum]

**Bed·ou·in** (bed′ōō·in, -ēn) *n.* 1 One of the nomadic Arabs of Syria, Arabia, etc. 2 Any nomad or vagabond. —*adj.* 1 Of or pertaining to the Bedouins. 2 Roving; nomadic. [<Ar. *badāwī* desert dweller]

**beef** (bēf) *n. pl.* **beeves** (bēvz) or **beefs** *for def. 2*; **beefs** *for def. 4* 1 The flesh of a slaughtered adult bovine animal. 2 Any adult bovine animal, as an ox, cow, steer, bull, etc., fattened for the butcher. 3 *Informal* Muscular power; brawn. 4 *Slang* A complaint. —*v.i.* *Slang* To complain. —**beef up** *Slang* To strengthen. [<L *bos*, *bovis* ox]

**bee·tle** (bēt′l) *n.* 1 A heavy wooden hammer or mallet. 2 A pestle or mallet for pounding, mashing, etc. —*v.t.* ·**tled**, ·**tling** To beat or stamp with or as with a beetle. [<OE *bietel* mallet]

**be·fall** (bi·fôl′) *v.* **be·fell**, **be·fall·en**, **be·fall·ing** *v.i.* 1 To come about; happen. —*v.t.* 2 To happen to. [<OE *bef(e)allan* fall]

**beg** (beg) *v.* **begged**, **beg·ging** *v.t.* 1 To ask for or solicit in charity. 2 To entreat of; beseech. —*v.i.* 3 To ask alms or charity. 4 To entreat politely or humbly. —**beg off** To ask to be excused from. —**beg the question** 1 To take for granted the matter in dispute. 2 To avoid the question or issue; equivocate. [?] —Syn. 2 implore, plead, supplicate.

**beg·gar** (beg′ər) *n.* 1 One who asks alms, esp. one who lives by begging. 2 An impoverished person. 3 A fellow; rogue. —*v.t.* 1 To impoverish. 2 To exhaust the resources of: It *beggars* analysis. —**beg′gar·dom**, **beg′gar·hood** *n.*

**be·gin** (bi·gin′) *v.* **be·gan**, **be·gun**, **be·gin·ning** *v.i.* 1 To take a first step in doing something; start. 2 To come into being; arise. 3 To have the essentials or the ability: It doesn't *begin* to compare with the original painting. —v.t. 4 To enter upon; commence. 5 To give origin to; start. [<OE *beginnan*]

**be·grudge** (bi·gruj′) v.t. **be·grudged, be·grudg·ing** 1 To envy one the possession of (something). 2 To give or grant reluctantly. —**be·grudg′ing·ly** adv.

**be·guile** (bi·gīl′) v.t. **be·guiled, be·guil·ing** 1 To deceive; mislead by guile. 2 To cheat; defraud: with *of* or *out of*. 3 To while away pleasantly, as time. 4 To charm; divert. —**be·guile′ment, be·guil′er** n. —**be·guil′ing·ly** adv.

**be·have** (bi·hāv′) v. **be·haved, be·hav·ing** v.i. 1 To comport oneself properly. 2 To conduct oneself or itself: The car *behaves* well. 3 To react to stimuli or environment. —v.t. 4 To conduct (oneself) properly or suitably. [ME *be*-thoroughly + *haven* hold oneself, have]

**be·hold** (bi·hōld′) v.t. **be·held, be·hold·ing** To look at or upon. —*interj.* Look! See! [<OE *beh(e)aldan* hold] —**be·hold′er** n.

**belch** (belch) v.t. & v.i. 1 To eject forcibly or violently. 2 To eject (gas) noisily from the stomach through the mouth. —n. The act of belching or the thing belched. [<OE *bealcian*] —**belch′er** n.

**bel·fry** (bel′frē) n. pl. **·fries** 1 A tower in which a bell is hung. 2 The part of such a tower containing the bell. [<OF *berfrei*] —**bel′fried** adj.

**be·lie** (bi·lī′) v.t. **be·lied, be·ly·ing** 1 To misrepresent; disguise. 2 To contradict: Her actions *belied* her words. 3 To fail to fulfill: to *belie* hopes. 4 To slander. [<OE *belē-ogan*] —**be·li′er** n.

**be·lief** (bi·lēf′) n. 1 The acceptance of something as true or actual. 2 That which is believed true, as a creed. 3 Religious faith. 4 Confidence; trust. 5 An opinion.

**be·lieve** (bi·lēv′) v. **be·lieved, be·liev·ing** v.t. 1 To accept as true or real. 2 To accept the word of (someone). 3 To think; assume: with a clause as object. —v.i. 4 To accept the truth, existence, worth, etc., of something: with *in*. 5 To have confidence: with *in*: The country *believes* in you. 6 To have religious faith. [<OE *gelēfen* believe] —**be·liev′a·ble** adj. —**be·liev′a·bly** adv. —**be·liev′er** n.

**belle** (bel) n. 1 A beautiful woman or girl. 2 The reigning beauty of a city, social function, etc. [F, beautiful]

**bel·li·cose** (bel′ə·kōs) adj. Pugnacious; warlike. [<L *bellum* war] —**bel′li·cose′ly** adv. —**bel′li·cos′i·ty** (-kos′ə·tē) n.

**bel·lig·er·ent** (bə·lij′ər·ənt) adj. 1 Warlike. 2 Engaged in or pertaining to war. 3 Aggressively quarrelsome. —n. A belligerent nation or person. [<L *belligare* wage war] —**bel·lig′er·ence, bel·lig′er·en·cy,** n. —**bel·lig′er·ent·ly** adv.

**bel·low** (bel′ō) v.i. 1 To utter a loud, hollow sound; roar, as a bull. 2 To roar, usu. with anger. —v.t. 3 To utter with a loud, roaring voice. —n. A loud, hollow cry or roar. [ME *belwen*] —**bel′low·er** n.

**bel·lows** (bel′ōz, *earlier* bel′əs) n. 1 An instrument with flexible sides, for drawing in air and expelling it under pressure through a tube. 2 The expansible portion of a camera. 3 *Informal* The lungs. [< OE *belg, belig* bag]

**be·long** (bi·lông′, -long′) v.i. 1 To be in the possession of someone: with *to*. 2 To be a part of or an appurtenance to something: with *to*: The screw *belongs* to this fan. 3 To be suitable: That lamp *belongs* in this room. 4 To have relation or be a member: with *to*. [<ME *be*- completely + *longen* to suit, go along with]

**be·lov·ed** (bi·luv′id, -luvd′) adj. Greatly loved; dear to the heart. —n. One greatly loved.

**bench** (bench) n. 1 A long, wooden seat, with or without a back. 2 A stout worktable. 3 The judges' seat in court. 4 The judge or the judges collectively; also, the court. 5 The office or status of a judge. 6 In sports: a The seat or seats for the players not playing. b Such players collectively. —**on the bench** 1 Presiding, as a judge. 2 In sports, not playing, as a substitute player. —v.t. 1 To furnish with benches. 2 To seat on a bench. 3 In sports, to remove (a player) from a game. [<OE *benc*]

**bend** (bend) v. **bent** (*Archaic* **bend·ed**), **bend·ing** v.t. 1 To make curved or different in shape. 2 To direct or turn, as one's course, in a certain direction. 3 To subdue; cause to yield, as to one's will. 4 To direct or concentrate, as the mind. 5 To resolve: used in the passive: with *on*: They were *bent* on winning. 6 *Naut.* To tie; make fast. —v.i. 7 To take or assume a new or different shape. 8 To take a new or different direction; swerve. 9 To bend over; stoop. 10 To yield or conform. —n. 1 A curve or crook. 2 A bending or being bent. 3 Any of various knots used to fasten a rope to something. [<OE *bendan*]

**ben·e·dic·tion** (ben′ə·dik′shən) n. 1 The act of blessing. 2 The invocation of divine favor upon a person. 3 Any of various formal ecclesiastical ceremonies of blessing. [<L *benedicere* bless} —**ben′e·dic′tive, ben′e·dic′to·ry** *adj.*

**ben·e·fac·tion** (ben′ə·fak′shən) *n.* 1 The act of giving or doing something for charitable reasons. 2 That which is given or done. [<L *benefacere* do well]

**ben·e·fac·tor** (ben′ə·fak′tər, ben′ə·fak′-) *n.* A friendly and generous helper; a patron. —**ben′e·fac′tress** *n. Fem.*

**ben·e·fice** (ben′ə·fis) *n.* 1 A church office, as for a rector, parson, etc., endowed with funds or property. 2 The revenue from such funds or property. —*v.t.* ·ficed, ·fic·ing To invest with a benefice. [<L *beneficium* favor] —**ben′e·ficed** *adj.*

**be·nef·i·cence** (bə·nef′ə·səns) *n.* 1 The quality of being charitable and good. 2 A charitable act or gift. [<L *beneficus* generous] —**be·nef′i·cent** *adj.* —**be·nef′i·cent·ly** *adv.*

**ben·e·fi·cial** (ben′ə·fish′əl) *adj.* Benefiting or tending to benefit; advantageous; helpful; useful; salutary. [<L *beneficium* favor] —**ben′e·fi′cial·ly** *adv.*

**ben·e·fi·ci·ar·y** (ben′ə·fish′ē·er′ē, -fish′ər·ē) *n. pl.* ·ar·ies 1 One who receives benefit. 2 The holder of a benefice or church living. 3 The person designated to receive the income from an insurance policy, annuity, inheritance, etc. [<L *beneficium* favor]

**ben·e·fit** (ben′ə·fit) *n.* 1 Something helpful; profit; advantage. 2 A special public event, as a performance, bazaar, etc., the proceeds of which are donated to a charitable cause. 3 *Usu. pl.* Payments made by a government, employer, insurance company, etc., to the aged, unemployed, sick, etc. — *v.* ·fit·ed, ·fit·ing *v.t.* 1 To be helpful or useful to. —*v.i.* 2 To profit; gain advantage. [<L *benefacere* do well] —**Syn.** *v.* 1 help, serve, assist, profit, improve, aid, better.

**be·nev·o·lence** (bə·nev′ə·ləns) *n.* 1 Good will; charitableness. 2 Any act of kindness or charity.

**be·nign** (bi·nīn′) *adj.* 1 Kindly; genial. 2 Mild; temperate. 3 Beneficial; favorable. 4 *Pathol.* Not likely to worsen; harmless: a *benign* tumor. [<L *benignus* kindly] —**be·nign′ly** *adv.* —**Syn.** 1 kind, gentle, gracious, amiable, affable. 3 Salutary, salubrious, wholesome.

**bent** (bent) *p.t.* & *p.p.* of BEND. —*adj.* 1 Not straight; crooked. 2 Set; determined: *bent* on having her own way. —*n.* Inclination; tendency; penchant: following one's nat-

ural *bent*. —**to** (or **at**) **the top of one's bent** To the limit of capacity or endurance.

**ben·zene** (ben′zēn, ben·zēn′) *n.* A flammable liquid hydrocarbon obtained from coal tar and used in the manufacture of various synthetic chemicals. [< BENZOIN]

**ben·zine** (ben′zēn, ben·zēn′) *n.* A mixture of hydrocarbons derived from petroleum by fractional distillation and used as a solvent and fuel. [< BENZOIN]

**be·queath** (bi·kwēth′, -kwēth′) *v.t.* 1 *Law* To give (personal property) by will. 2 To hand down, as to posterity. [< OE *becwethan*] —**be·queath′al, be·queath′ment** *n.*

**be·quest** (bi·kwest′) *n.* 1 The act of bequeathing. 2 Something bequeathed. [ME *biqueste*]

**be·reave** (bi·rēv′) *v.t.* ·reaved or ·reft (bi·reft′), ·reav·ing 1 To leave saddened by someone's death. 2 To deprive, as of hope or happiness. [<OE *berēafian*] —**be·reave′ment** *n.*

**ber·i·ber·i** (ber′ē·ber′ē) *n.* A disease affecting the nervous system and due to a deficiency of thiamine in the diet. [<Singhalese *beri* weakness]

**ber·ry** (ber′ē) *n. pl.* ber·ries 1 Any small, succulent fruit, as the blackberry or strawberry. 2 *Bot.* A fruit with seeds in a juicy pulp, as the grape or tomato. 3 A dry seed or kernel of various plants, as the coffee bean. —*v.i.* ·ried, ·ry·ing 1 To form or bear berries. 2 To gather berries. [<OE *berie*]

**berth** (bûrth) *n.* 1 A bunk or bed in a ship, sleeping car, etc. 2 A place where a ship may anchor or dock. 3 A job; employment. —**give a wide berth to** To keep out of the way of. —*v.t.* 1 To bring (a ship) to a berth. 2 To provide with a berth. —*v.i.* 3 To come to or occupy a berth. [?]

**be·siege** (bi·sēj′) *v.t.* ·sieged, be·sieg·ing 1 To lay siege to, as a castle or city. 2 To crowd around; block. 3 To overwhelm, as with requests. —**be·siege′ment, be·sieg′er** *n.*

**be·smirch** (bi·smûrch′) *v.t.* 1 To soil; stain. 2 To sully; dishonor. —**be·smirch′er, be·smirch′ment** *n.*

**be·stir** (bi·stûr′) *v.t.* ·stirred, ·stir·ring To rouse to activity.

**be·stow** (bi·stō′) *v.t.* 1 To present as a gift or honor; confer: with *on* or *upon*. 2 To expend; apply. 3 To give in marriage. [ME *bito*, *upon* + *stowen* place] —**be·stow′al, be·stow′ment** *n.*

**bet** (bet) *n.* 1 An offer or agreement to risk winning or losing money or something of value on an uncertain outcome. 2 The wager thus risked. 3 A contestant, event, etc. on which a bet is made. 4 Anything to be risked or chanced. —*v.* **bet** or **bet·ted**, **bet·ting** *v.t.* 1 To stake or pledge (money, etc.) in a bet. 2 To declare as in a bet: I'll *bet* he doesn't come. —*v.i.* 3 To place a wager. —**you bet** *Informal* Certainly. [?]

**beta rays** A stream of high-energy electrons, esp. as emitted by radioactive substances.

**be·ta·tron** (bā'tə·tron) *n.* An accelerator designed to operate on electrons, raising them to high velocities. [<BETA (RAY) + (ELEC)TRON]

**be·tray** (bi·trā') *v.t.* 1 To commit treason against; be a traitor to. 2 To be faithless or disloyal to. 3 To disclose, as secret information. 4 To reveal unwittingly. 5 To seduce and desert; wrong. 6 To indicate; show. [<ME *bi* over, to + OF *trair* <L *tradere* deliver, give up] —**be·tray'al**, **be·tray'er** *n.*

**be·troth** (bi·trōth', -trôth') *v.t.* 1 To engage to marry. 2 To contract to give in marriage. [<ME *bi* to + *treuthe* truth]

**bev·er·age** (bev'rij, bev'ər·ij) *n.* Any kind of drink. [<L *bibere* to drink]

**bev·y** (bev'ē) *n. pl.* **·ies** 1 A flock of quail, grouse, etc. 2 A small group, usu. of girls or women. [ME]

**be·wail** (bi·wāl') *v.t. & v.i.* To lament.

**be·ware** (bi·wâr') *v.t. & v.i.* To be wary (of); look out (for): used in the imperative and infinitive. [ME *be ware* be on guard, be wary]

**be·wil·der** (bi·wil'dər) *v.t.* To confuse utterly; perplex. [<BE- + archaic English *wilder*] —**be·wil'dered·ly**, **be·wil'der·ing·ly** *adv.* —**be·wil'der·ment** *n.*

**be·witch** (bi·wich') *v.t.* 1 To gain power over by witchcraft. 2 To charm; fascinate. —**be·witch'ment**, **be·witch'er·y** *n.* —**Syn.** 2 captivate, entrance, enchant, beguile.

**bi·an·nu·al** (bī·an'yōō·əl) *adj.* Occurring twice a year; semiannual. —**bi·an'nu·al·ly** *adv.*

**bi·as** (bī'əs) *n. pl.* **bi·as·es** 1 A line crossing the weave of a fabric obliquely: sewn on the *bias*. 2 A personal inclination, esp. one based on fixed attitudes unresponsive to persuasion or influence. 3 A personal preference. 4 A fixed or steady force, voltage, current, etc., impressed on a device or system to set its conditions of operation. —*adj.* Diagonal; slanting: *bias* seams. —*adv.* Diagonally. —*v.t.* **bi·ased** or **bi·assed**, **bi·as·ing** or **bi·as·sing** 1 To influence unduly or unfairly; prejudice. 2 To impose a

fixed condition of operation on. [<F *biais* oblique]

**Bi·ble** (bī'bəl) *n.* 1 The sacred writings of Christianity; the Old Testament and the New Testament. 2 The Holy Scriptures of Judaism; the Old Testament. 3 The sacred text or writings of any religion. [<Gk. *biblion* book]

**bick·er** (bik'ər) *v.i.* 1 To dispute petulantly; wrangle. 2 To flow noisily, as a brook. —*n.* A petulant dispute; a petty squabble. [ME *bikeren*] —**bick'er·er** *n.* '

**bi·cy·cle** (bī'sik·əl) *n.* A two-wheeled vehicle with the wheels in tandem, a seat or seats, a steering handle, and propelled by pedals or a motor. —*v.i.* **·cled**, **·cling** To ride a bicycle. [<BI- + Gk. *kyklos* wheel] —**bi'cy·cler**, **bi'cy·clist** *n.* • See TANDEM.

**bid** (bid) *v.* **bade** (bad, bād) *for defs.* 1,2,3 or **bid** *for defs.* 4,5,6 **bid·den** (bid'ən), **bid·ding** *v.t.* 1 To command; order. 2 To invite. 3 To say (to) in greeting or farewell. 4 To offer (a price), as in an auction. 5 In card games, to declare (the number of tricks one intends to make in a specified trump suit). —*v.i.* 6 To make a bid, as in cards or at an auction. —**bid fair** To seem probable. —**bid up** To increase the price of by offering higher bids. —*n.* 1 a An offer to pay or accept a price. b The amount offered. 2 a In card games, the number of tricks or points that a player engages to make. b A player's turn to bid. 3 An effort to win or attain. 4 An invitation to join. [Fusion of OE *biddan* ask, demand and *bēodan* proclaim, command] —**bid'der** *n.*

**bi·en·ni·al** (bī·en'ē·əl) *adj.* 1 Occurring every second year. 2 Lasting or living for two years. —*n.* 1 A plant that normally dies after two seasons of growth. 2 An event occurring once in two years. [<L *bi-* two + *annus* year] —**bi·en'ni·al·ly** *adv.*

**bi·fo·cal** (bī·fō'kəl) *adj.* Having two foci: said of a lens ground for both near and far vision. [<BI- + FOCAL] —**bi·fo'cals** *n. pl.* A pair of glasses having bifocal lenses. [<BI- + L *focus* hearth, focus of a lens]

**big·a·my** (big'ə·mē) *n.* The crime of marrying another person while still legally married. [<BI- + Gk. *gamos* wedding] —**big'a·mist** *n.* —**big'a·mous** *adj.* —**big'a·mous·ly** *adv.*

**big·ot** (big'ət) *n.* One intolerant of or prejudiced against those of differing religious beliefs, political opinions, etc. [<F] —**big'ot·ed** *adj.* —**big'ot·ed·ly** *adv.* —**big'ot·ry** *n.*

**bi·ki·ni** (bi·kē'nē) *n. pl.* **·nis** A very scanty two-piece bathing suit for women. [<*Bikini* atoll in the Pacific]

**bile** (bīl) *n.* 1 A bitter, golden brown or greenish digestive fluid secreted by the liver. 2 Anger; peevishness. [< *bilis* bile, anger] — **bil·i·ar·y** (bil′ē·er′ē) *adj.*

**bilge** (bilj) *n.* 1 The lower, rounded part of a ship's bottom. 2 The foul water that collects there: **also bilge water.** 3 The bulge of a barrel. 4 *Slang* Stupid nonsense. —*v.t. & v.i.* **bilged, bilg·ing** To leak or cause to leak in the bilge. [Var. of BULGE] —**bilg′y** *adj.* (·i·er, ·i·est)

**bill¹** (bil) *n.* 1 A statement of payment due for goods or services. 2 A piece of paper money. 3 A list of items: a *bill* of fare. 4 The draft of a proposed law. 5 An advertising poster. 6 A theater program. 7 *Law* A formal statement of a case, charge, etc. —**fill the bill** *Informal* To meet the needs. —**foot the bill** *Informal* To pay the costs. —*v.t.* 1 To enter in a bill; charge. 2 To present a bill to. 3 To advertise by bills or placards. [< L *bulla* document, seal] —**bill′er** *n.*

**bill²** (bil) *n.* A beak, as of a bird. —*v.i.* To join bills, as birds. —**bill and coo** To kiss and murmur lovingly. [< OE *bile*]

**bill³** (bil) *n.* 1 A hook-shaped gardening instrument: **also bill′hook.**. 2 A weapon with a hook-shaped blade. [< OE *bill* sword, ax]

**bil·let** (bil′it) *n.* 1 A lodging for soldiers in a household or nonmilitary building. 2 A requisition for such lodging. 3 A job; position. —*v.t. & v.i.* To lodge (soldiers) in a private household or other billet. [< L *bulla* seal, document] —**bil′let·er** *n.*

**bil·liards** (bil′yərdz) *n.* A game played with a cue and hard balls (**billiard balls**) on an oblong, cloth-covered table with cushioned edges. [< OF *bille* log] —**bil′liard·ist** *n.*

**bil·lion** (bil′yən) *n.* See NUMBER. [< F] —**bil·li·onth** (bil′yənth) *adj., n.*

**bil·low** (bil′ō) *n.* 1 A great wave or surge of the sea. 2 A swell or surge, as of sound. —*v.i.* To form billows; surge. [< ON *bylgja*] —**bil′low·y** *adj.* —**bil′low·i·ness** *n.*

**bin** (bin) *n.* An enclosed place for holding foods, coal, etc. —*v.t.* **binned, bin·ning** To store or deposit in a bin. [< OE *binn* basket, crib]

**bind** (bīnd) *v.* **bound, bind·ing** *v.t.* 1 To tie together; make fast by tying; secure. 2 To encircle, as with a belt. 3 To bandage. 4 To cause to cohere or adhere. 5 To strengthen or ornament at the edge, as in sewing. 6 To fasten together within a cover, as a book. 7 To make irrevocable, as a bargain. 8 To oblige, as by moral or legal authority. 9 To make constipated. —*v.i.* 10 To tie up anything. 11 To cohere; stick together. 12 To have binding force; be obligatory. 13 To become stiff, hard, or tight. —**bind over** *Law* To hold under bond for appearance at a future time. —*n.* 1 *Informal* A difficult or constraining situation. 2 That which fastens, ties, or binds. [< OE *bindan*]

**bin·oc·u·lar** (bə·nok′yə·lər, bī-) *adj.* Of, for, or using eyes at once. —*n.* *Often pl.* A telescope, opera glass, etc., adapted for use by both eyes at once. [< BI + OCULAR] —**bin·oc′u·lar′i·ty** (-lar′ə·tē) *n.* —**bin·oc′u·lar·ly** *adv.*

**bi·o·chem·is·try** (bī′ō·kem′is·trē) *n.* The branch of chemistry relating to life processes, their mode of action, and their products. —**bi′o·chem′i·cal** *adj.* —**bi′o·chem′i·cal·ly** *adv.* —**bi′o·chem′ist** *n.*

**bi·o·de·grad·a·ble** (bī′ō·di·grā′də·bəl) *adj.* Capable of being broken down by natural processes, such as bacterial action, etc. [< BIO + DEGRADABLE]

**bi·og·ra·phy** (bī·og′rə·fē, bē-) *n. pl.* ·**phies** 1 A written account of a person's life. 2 Such writing as a literary form or practice. [< Gk. *bios* life + *graphein* write] —**bi·og′raph·er** *n.* —**bi·o·graph·ic** (bī′ə·graf′ik) or ·**i·cal** *adj.* —**bi′o·graph′i·cal·ly** *adv.*

**bi·ol·o·gy** (bī·ol′ə·jē) *n.* The science of life and the origin, structure, reproduction, growth, and development of living organisms. [< BIO + -LOGY] —**bi·ol′o·gist** *n.*

**bi·par·ti·san** (bī·pär′tə·zən) *adj.* Of or supported by two political parties. —**bi·par′ti·san·ship** *n.*

**bi·ped** (bī′ped) *n.* A two-footed animal. —*adj.* Two-footed: **also bi·pe·dal** (bī·ped′əl, bī′pə·dəl). [< L *bipes* two-footed]

**birch** (bûrch) *n.* 1 Any of a genus of hardy trees and shrubs usu. having the outer bark separable in thin layers. 2 A rod from such a tree, used as a whip. 3 The tough, close-grained wood of the birch. —*v.t.* To whip with a birch rod. [< OE *birce*] —**birch·en** (bûr′chən) *adj.*

**bird** (bûrd) *n.* 1 Any of a class of warm-blooded, feathered, egg-laying vertebrates having the forelimbs modified as wings. 2 GAME BIRD. 3 A shuttlecock used in the game of badminton. 4 CLAY PIGEON. 5 *Slang* A peculiar or remarkable person. 6 *Slang* A derisive sound of disapproval. —**for the birds** *Slang* Worthless. —*v.i.* 1 To be a bird watcher. 2 To trap or shoot birds. [< OE *bridd*]

**birth** (bûrth) *n.* 1 The act or fact of being born.

2 The bringing forth of offspring; parturition. 3 Beginning; origin. 4 Ancestry or descent. 5 Inborn or inherent tendency. —give birth to 1 To bear as offspring. 2 To give rise to. [<ON *byrth*]

**bis·cuit** (bis′kit) *n.* 1 Bread in the form of a small cake leavened with baking powder or soda. 2 *Brit.* A cracker or cooky. 3 Fired, unglazed pottery. 4 A pale brown. [<L *bis* twice + *coquere* to cook]

**bi·sect** (bī′sekt, bī·sekt′) *v.t.* 1 To cut into two parts; halve. 2 *Geom.* To divide into two equal parts. —*v.i.* 3 To fork, as a road. [<BI- + L *sectus* cut] —**bi·sec′tion, bi·sec′tor** *n.* —**bi·sec′tion·al** *adj.* —**bi·sec′tion·al·ly** *adv.*

**bi·sex·u·al** (bī·sek′shōō·əl) *adj.* 1 Pertaining to both sexes. 2 Having both male and female organs; hermaphroditic. 3 Attracted sexually by both sexes. —**bi·sex′u·al·ism, bi·sex′u·al′i·ty** (-shōō·al′ə·tē) *n.* —**bi·sex′u·al·ly** *adv.*

**bish·op** (bish′əp) *n.* 1 In various Christian churches, a clergyman of the highest order, usu. head of a diocese. 2 A chessman which may be moved only diagonally. [<LL *episcopus*]

**bi·son** (bī′sən, -zən) *n. pl.* **bi·son** 1 A bovine mammal of western North America, having a dark, shaggy mane; buffalo. 2 A similar European animal. [<L *bison* wild ox]

**bit** (bit) *n.* 1 A small piece, amount, etc. 2 A short time: Wait a *bit*. 3 A very small part, as in a play. 4 *Informal* An amount worth 12 1/2 cents: now used mostly in the expression *two bits*. —**a bit of** To some degree; somewhat: *a bit of* a nuisance. —**do one's bit** To contribute one's share of work, money, etc. [<OE *bita* piece bitten off] —**Syn.** 1 morsel, fragment, scrap, mite, iota.

**bitch** (bich) *n.* 1 A female dog, coyote, etc. 2 *Slang* A woman regarded as hateful, sluttish, mean, etc. 3 *Slang* Something difficult or troublesome to accomplish. —*v.i. Slang* To complain. —**bitch up** *Slang* To botch. [<OE *bicce*]

**bite** (bīt) *v.* **bit, bit·ten** (bit′n) *or* **bit, bit·ing** *v.t.* 1 To seize, cut, tear, or wound with the teeth. 2 To cut, tear, etc., as if with teeth. 3 To pierce with a sting, fangs, etc. 4 To cause to smart; sting. 5 To corrode, as acid. 6 To grip or hold, as by traction. —*v.i.* 7 To seize or cut into something with or as if with the teeth. 8 To have a stinging effect. 9 To take firm hold. 10 To take bait, as fish. 11 To be taken in by a trick. —**bite the dust** To fall

dead or wounded, as in battle. —*n.* 1 The act of biting. 2 An injury inflicted by biting. 3 A smarting sensation or effect. 4 An amount taken by or as by biting. 5 A quick, light meal; snack. 6 A grip or hold, as of a tool. 7 The way in which the jaws meet. [<OE *bitan*] —**bit′a·ble, bite′a·ble** *adj.* —**bit′er** *n.*

**bit·ter** (bit′ər) *adj.* 1 Having an acrid, usu. unpleasant taste. 2 Causing acute physical discomfort or mental anguish. 3 Feeling or showing resentment, animosity, etc. 4 Hard to bear or accept. —*v.t. & v.i.* To make or become bitter. [<OE *biter*] —**bit′ter·ly** *adv.* —**bit′ter·ness** *n.*

**bi·tu·men** (bi·t′ōō′mən, bich′ōō·mən) *n.* A mixture of solid and semisolid hydrocarbons, as naphtha or asphalt. [<L] —**bi·tu·mi·noid** (bi·t′ōō′mə·noid), **bi·tu′mi·nous** *adj.*

**bituminous coal** Coal containing volatile hydrocarbons and burning with a smoky flame.

**bi·valve** (bī′valv′) *n.* A mollusk having a shell of two hinged valves. —*adj.* Having two valves, as a mollusk: *also* **bi′valved′, bi·val·vous** (bī·val′vəs), **bi·val·vu·lar** (bī·val′vyə·lər). —**bit′ter·ness** *n.*

**biv·ou·ac** (biv′ōō·ak, biv′wak) *n.* A temporary field encampment with little or no shelter, esp. for soldiers. —*v.i.* **biv·ou·acked, biv·ou·ack·ing** To encamp in a bivouac. [<G *Beiwacht* guard]

**bi·zarre** (bi·zär′) *adj.* Startingly odd. [F] —**bi·zarre′ly** *adv.* —**bi·zarre′ness** *n.* —**Syn.** outré, outlandish, fantastic, grotesque, freakish.

**black** (blak) *adj.* 1 Reflecting little or no light; of the darkest color, as of coal or jet. 2 Without light; very dark. 3 a Belonging to a dark-skinned ethnic group; esp., Negroid. b Of or relating to members of such a group: *black* power; *black* studies. 4 Soiled; stained. 5 Gloomy; dismal. 6 Disastrous; unlucky. 7 Indicating or deserving disgrace, censure, etc. 8 Evil; wicked. 9 Angry; scowling. 10 Dressed in black clothing. 11 Without cream or milk: *black* coffee. —*n.* 1 The darkest of all colors. 2 Something black, esp. black clothing. 3 A dark-skinned person, esp. a Negro. —**in the black** Ahead in business or finance; prospering. —*v.t. & v.i.* 1 To make or become black. 2 To polish with blacking. —**black out** 1 To extinguish or screen all light. 2 To become temporarily unconscious. 3 To delete by scoring through. [< OE *blǣc*] —**black'ish** *adj.* — **black'ly** *adv.* —**black'ness** *n.*

**black·ball** (blak'bôl') *v.t.* 1 To vote against and ban from membership. 2 To exclude or ostracize. —*n.* 1 A negative vote resulting in the rejection of an application for membership. 2 A willful act of ostracism. [< BLACK + BALL, a black ball to signify a negative vote during balloting] —**black'ball'er** *n.*

**black·board** (blak'bôrd', -bōrd') *n.* A slate or black surface on which chalk is used to write or draw.

**black·mail** (blak'māl') *n.* 1 The extortion of payment by threats of public exposure. 2 Money, etc. obtained by such extortion. — *v.t.* 1 To subject to blackmail. 2 To coerce, as by threats. [< BLACK + obs. *mail* tribute] —**black'mail'er** *n.*

**black market** A place or business in which merchandise is sold in amounts or at prices contrary to legal restrictions. — **black mar·ket·eer** (mar'kə·tir')

**Black Muslim** A member of a U.S. Negro sect (the **Nation of Islam**) which follows the practices of Islam and rejects integration with whites.

**black·out** (blak'out') *n.* 1 The hiding or extinguishing of all lights, esp. as a precautionary measure against air attack. 2 A temporary loss of consciousness or vision. 3 The sudden darkening of the stage in a theatrical performance. 4 A ban or suppression, as of news, a television broadcast, etc.

**blad·der** (blad'ər) *n.* 1 A distensible sac for the temporary retention of urine. 2 Any similar part or organ for retaining fluid or gas. 3 An air vessel or float in some seaweeds. [<OE *blǣdre*] —**blad'der·y** *adj.*

**blade** (blād) *n.* 1 The flat cutting part of an edged tool or weapon. 2 A thin, flat part, as of an oar, propeller, plow, etc. 3 a The expanded part of a leaf. b A narrow leaf having no petiole: a *blade* of grass. 4 a A sword. b A swordsman. 5 A rakish young man. [< OE *blǣd* blade of a leaf] —**blad'ed** *adj.*

**blanch** (blanch, blänch) *v.t.* 1 To remove the color from; bleach. 2 To cause to turn pale. 3 To plunge (food) briefly into boiling water, as to remove the skin or in preparation for freezing. —*v.i.* 4 To turn or become white or pale. [< F *blanc* white] —**blanch'er** *n.*

**bland** (bland) *adj.* 1 Smooth; suave; unctuous. 2 Mild; gentle; temperate. 3 Not stimulating or irritating. 4 Insipid; flat. [<L *blandus* mild] —**bland'ly** *adv.* —**bland'ness** *n.*

**blan·ket** (blang'kit) *n.* 1 A large cloth covering used esp. for warmth, as on a bed. 2 Any thick, extensive covering: a *blanket* of snow. —*adj.* Covering a wide range of conditions, needs, items, etc.: a *blanket* injunction. —*v.t.* 1 To cover with or as with a blanket. 2 To have uniform application to. 3 To obscure or suppress as with a blanket. [<OF *blankete*, dim. of *blanc* white]

**blare** (blâr) *v.t.* & *v.i.* **blared, blar·ing** 1 To sound loudly and harshly, as a trumpet. 2 To exclaim loudly and stridently. —*n.* 1 A loud, brazen sound. 2 Brightness or glare, as of color. [Prob. imit.]

**blar·ney** (blär'nē) *n.* Coaxing flattery. —*v.t.* & *v.i.* To flatter or cajole. [<BLARNEY STONE]

**blas·phe·my** (blas'fə·mē) *n. pl.* **·mies** 1 Words or action showing impious irreverence toward God or sacred things. 2 Any irreverent act or utterance. —**blas'phe·mous** *adj.* —**blas'phe·mous·ly** *adv.*

**blast** (blast, bläst) *v.t.* 1 To shatter, destroy, etc., by or as by explosion. 2 To cause to wither or fail to mature. 3 To attack or criticize with intense force. —*v.i.* 4 To make a loud, harsh sound. —**blast off** To begin a flight with explosive force, as a rocket. —*n.* 1 A strong or sudden wind. 2 The strong jet of air in a blast furnace. 3 The discharge of an explosive, or its effect. 4 A loud, sudden sound, as of a trumpet. 5 A blight or blighting influence —**at full blast** At maximum speed or capacity. [< OE *blǣst* a blowing] —**blast'er** *n.*

**blast·off** (blast'ôf', -of) *n.* The launching of a rocket, space vehicle, etc.

**bla·tant** (blā'tənt) *adj.* 1 Offensively loud or clamorous. 2 Obtrusively obvious; glaring: a *blatant* lie. [? <L *blatire* babble] — **bla'tan·cy** *n.* —**bla'tant·ly** *adv.*

**blaze** (blāz) *v.i.* **blazed, blaz·ing** 1 To burn brightly. 2 To burn as with emotion: to *blaze* with anger. 3 To shine; be resplendent. —**blaze away** 1 To keep on firing. 2 To attack persistently. —*n.* 1 A brightly burning fire. 2 Intense light or glare. 3 A brilliant display. 4 A burst, as of emotion. 5 *pl.* Hell: a euphemism in oaths. [<OE *blǣse* firebrand] —**blaz'ing·ly** *adv.*

**bleach** (blēch) *v.t.* & *v.i.* To make or become colorless, pale, or white. —*n.* 1 An act of bleaching. 2 A fluid or powder used as a bleaching agent. [<OE *blǣcean*]

**bleak** (blēk) *adj.* 1 Exposed to wind and weather; bare. 2 Cold; cutting. 3 Dreary; gloomy. [< ON *bleikja* pale] —**bleak′ly** *adv.* —**bleak′ness** *n.* —**Syn.** 1 barren, unsheltered, windswept, withered. 3 melancholy, miserable.

**bleed** (blēd) *v.* **bled, bleed·ing** *v.i* 1 To lose or shed blood. 2 To exude sap or other fluid. 3 To suffer wounds or die, as in battle. 4 To feel grief or sympathy. —*v.t.* 5 To draw blood from. 6 To exude (sap, blood, etc.). 7 To draw sap or other fluid from. 8 *Informal* To extort money from. —**bleed white** To deplete of all resources, as if by draining of blood. [< OE *blēdan*]

**blem·ish** (blem′ish) *v.t.* To mar the perfection of; sully. —*n.* 1 A spot or surface defect, as on the skin. 2 A fault or shortcoming. [< OF *blemir* make livid] —**blem′ish·er** *n.*

**blend** (blend) *v.* **blend·ed** or **blent, blend·ing** *v.t.* 1 To mix or combine so as to obtain a product of a desired quality, taste, color, or consistency. —*v.i.* 2 To mix; intermingle. 3 To pass or shade imperceptibly into each other, as colors. 4 To harmonize. —*n.* The act or result of blending. [< ON *blanda* mingle]

**bless** (bles) *v.t.* **blessed** or **blest, bless·ing** 1 To consecrate; make holy by religious rite. 2 To glorify. 3 To make the sign of the cross over or upon. 4 To invoke divine favor upon (a person or thing). 5 To make happy. 6 To endow, as with a gift: She was *blessed* with a beautiful face. 7 To guard; protect: *Bless* me! [< OE *blētsian* consecrate (with blood)] —**bless′er** *n.*

**blight** (blīt) *n.* 1 Any of a number of destructive plant diseases, as rust, smut, etc. 2 An environmental factor injurious to a specific group or groups of plants or animals. 3 A person or thing that withers hopes, destroys prospects, etc. 4 A blighted condition. —*v.t.* 1 To cause to decay. 2 To ruin; frustrate. —*v.i.* 3 To suffer blight. [?]

**blind** (blīnd) *adj.* 1 Without the power of seeing. 2 Of or for blind persons. 3 Lacking in perception, sound judgment, or logic. 4 Done without preparation, plan, or control: a *blind* effort. 5 Impossible to control or foresee: *blind* fate. 6 Having no opening or outlet: a *blind* ditch. 7 Open at one end only: a *blind* alley. 8 Hard to see; hidden: a *blind* driveway. 9 Using instruments only: *blind* flying. —*n.* 1 Something that obstructs vision or shuts off light, as a window shade. 2 A person or thing meant to deceive; decoy. 3 A hiding place, esp. for hunters. —**the blind** Blind people. —*v.t.* 1 To make blind. 2 To dazzle. 3 To deprive of judgment. 4 To darken; obscure. 5 To outshine; eclipse. —*adv.* 1 By using instruments only. 2 So as to be insensible. [< OE] —**blind′ly** *adv.* —**blind′ness** *n.*

**blink** (blingk) *v.i* 1 To wink rapidly. 2 To squint, as in sunlight. 3 To twinkle; glimmer; also, to flash on and off. 4 To ignore or disregard something: He *blinked* at the corruption in politics. —*v.t.* 5 To cause to wink. 6 To shut the eyes to; evade. 7 To send (a message) by a flashing light. —*n.* 1 A blinking of the eye. 2 A gleam of light. —**on the blink** *Informal* Out of order; not working. [ME *blinken*]

**bliss** (blis) *n.* 1 Superlative happiness and joy. 2 A cause of delight. [< OE *blīths*] —**bliss′ful** *adj.* —**bliss′ful·ly** *adv.*

**blis·ter** (blis′tər) *n.* 1 A raised sac under the epidermis, containing watery matter, as from a burn or irritation. 2 Something that resembles a blister, as on a plant, on a painted surface, etc. —*v.t.* 1 To produce a blister or blisters upon. 2 To rebuke harshly. —*v.i.* 3 To become blistered. [OF *blestre*] —**blis′ter·y** *adj.*

**blithe** (blīth) *adj.* Joyous; gay; carefree. [<OE] —**blithe′ly** *adv.* —**blithe′ness** *n.*

**blitz·krieg** (blits′krēg) *n.* A sudden, overwhelming attack. [G, lit., lightning war]

**bliz·zard** (bliz′ərd) *n.* 1 A severe storm with heavy snow. 2 Anything resembling a blizzard, as in the swirl or rush of great numbers of things. [?]

**bloat** (blōt) *v.t.* 1 To cause to swell, as with fluid or gas. 2 To make proud or vain. —*v.i.* 3 To swell; become puffed up. [<ME *blout* swollen]

**block** (blok) *n.* 1 A solid piece of wood, stone, etc., usu. with flat surfaces. 2 An obstacle, obstruction, or hindrance. 3 The act of obstructing or the condition of being obstructed. 4 A wooden log or cube on which chopping is done: a butcher's *block*; a headsman's *block*. 5 In sports, an interference with an opponent's movements. 6 An auctioneer's stand. 7 The mold on which something is shaped: a hat *block*. 8 A pulley, or set of pulleys, in a frame or shell. 9 A toy building cube, usu. of wood. 10 A piece of wood, linoleum, etc., for engraving a design to be printed. 11 A city square bounded by streets; also, the distance along any of such streets. 12 A large group

49

of adjacent buildings. 13 A group acting or considered as a unit: a *block* of theater seats; the Asian *block* of nations. 14 A section of a railroad track controlled by signals. 15 An interruption of normal physical or mental functioning: a nerve *block*; a memory *block*. 16 *Austral.* An area of farming land. —*v.t.* 1 To obstruct; impede the progress of. 2 To fill (an area or space) so as to prevent movement into or through. 3 In sports: a To hinder the movements of (an opposing player). b To stop (a ball, etc.) with the body. 4 To shape on a block, as a hat. 5 To put up on blocks. —*v.i.* 6 To act so as to hinder. —**block out** 1 To obscure from view. 2 To plan broadly without details: to *block out* a design. [< OF *bloc*] —**block′age, block′er** *n.*

**block·ade** (blo·kād′) *n.* 1 A military or naval closing of an enemy port, coast, etc., to traffic or communication. 2 The forces that set up a blockade. 3 Any hindrance or obstruction to action or traffic. —**run the blockade** To elude a blockade. —*v.t.* ·ad·ed, ·ad·ing To subject to a blockade. [< F *bloquer* obstruct]

**block·head** (blok′hed′) *n.* A stupid person. —Syn. ass, dolt, dunce, fool.

**blond** (blond) *adj.* 1 Having flaxen or yellowish brown hair, fair skin and light eyes. 2 Flaxen, golden, or yellowish brown: said of hair. 3 Light-colored. —*n.* A blond person. [<Med.L *blondus*]

**blonde** (blond) *adj.* (*feminine only*) BLOND (def. 1). —*n.* A blond woman or girl. • In modern usage the final *-e* is usu. kept in the noun when it refers to a fair-haired woman or girl and in the adjective describing such a woman or girl.

**blood** (blud) *n.* 1 The usu. red fluid that circulates throughout the bodies of vertebrates, delivering oxygen and nutrients to the cells and tissues and removing waste products. 2 A fluid resembling blood, as in certain invertebrates. 3 The shedding of blood, esp. murder. 4 Temperament; disposition: cool *blood*. 5 Vitality; life; lifeblood. 6 Relationship by descent from a common ancestor; kinship. 7 Ancestry; lineage. 8 Royal or noble lineage. —**in cold blood** Without passion or mercy; deliberately. —**make one's blood boil** To make one very angry. —**make one's blood run cold** To terrify one. [< OE *blōd*]

**blood bank** A reserve of processed blood from various donors for clinical use.

**bloom** (bloom) *n.* 1 A flower; blossom. 2 Flowers collectively. 3 The state of being in flower. 4 A time of freshness, vigor, and health; prime. 5 A fresh flush or glow, as on the cheeks. 6 A whitish, powdery coating on certain fruits and leaves. —*v.i.* 1 To bear flowers; blossom. 2 To glow with health and vigor. 3 To flourish; be in a prime condition. —*v.t.* 4 To bring into bloom; cause to flourish. [<ON *blōm* flower, blossom] —**bloom′er** *n.*

**blos·som** (blos′əm) *n.* 1 A flower, esp. one of a plant yielding edible fruit. 2 The state or period of flowering; bloom. —*v.i.* 1 To come into blossom; bloom. 2 To prosper; thrive. [OE *blōstma*] —**blos′som·y** *adj.*

**blot** (blot) *n.* 1 A spot or stain, as of ink. 2 A moral fault or disgrace. 3 Something unattractive; blemish. —*v.* **blot·ted, blot·ting** *v.t.* 1 To spot, as with ink; stain. 2 To disgrace; sully. 3 To obliterate, as a memory, etc.: often with *out*. 4 To dry with blotting paper. 5 To obscure; darken: usu. with *out*. —*v.i.* 6 To spread in a blot or blots, as ink. 7 To become blotted; acquire spots. 8 To absorb: This paper *blots* well. [ME *blotte*]

**blotch** (bloch) *n.* 1 A spot or blot. 2 An eruption on the skin. —*v.t.* To mark or cover with blotches. [Blend of BLOT and BOTCH] —**blotch′y** *adj.* (·i·er, ·i·est)

**blouse** (blous, blouz) *n.* 1 A loose garment extending from the neck to the waist or below, worn by women and children. 2 A loose, knee-length shirt usu. belted at the waist, worn chiefly by French workmen. 3 A U.S. Army service coat. —*v.t. & v.i.* **bloused** (bloust, blouzd), **blous·ing** To drape at the waistline. [F]

**blow¹** (blō) *v.* **blew, blown, blow·ing** *v.t.* 1 To move by a current of air. 2 To cause air to be released from (a bellows, etc.). 3 To emit, as air or smoke, from the mouth. 4 To force air upon, as for cooling, drying, warming, etc. 5 To empty or clear by forcing air through, as pipes. 6 To cause to sound, as a bugle or horn. 7 To sound (a signal) by blowing. 8 To form or shape, as by inflating: to *blow* glass. 9 To put out of breath, as a horse. 10 To shatter or destroy by or as by explosion: usu. with *up, down, out, through,* etc.: to *blow* a hole through a wall; to *blow* up a house. 11 To melt (a fuse). 12 To lay eggs in, as flies in meat. 13 *Informal* To spend (money) lavishly; also, to treat or entertain: I'll *blow* you to a meal. 14 *Informal* To forget (one's lines) in a play, etc. 15

*Slang* To leave; go out of. 16 *Slang* To handle badly; bungle. —*v.i.* 17 To be in motion, usu. with some force: said of wind or air. 18 To move in a current of air; be carried by the wind. 19 To emit a current or jet of air, water, steam, etc. 20 To sound by being blown: The bugle *blew* at dawn. 21 To fail or become useless, as by melting: The fuse *blew.* 22 To explode: usu. with *up, down, to,* etc. 23 To pant; gasp for breath. 24 *Informal* To talk boastfully. 25 *Slang* To leave; go. —**blow hot and cold** *Informal* To vacillate. —**blow off** 1 To let off steam, as from a boiler. 2 *Informal* To speak in anger, as to relieve pent-up emotion. —**blow out** 1 To extinguish (a fire or flame) by blowing. 2 To be extinguished by air or wind. 3 To explode, as a tire. 4 To subside: The storm will *blow* itself *out.* —**blow over** 1 To overturn by blowing. 2 To be forgotten. 3 To pass, as a storm; subside. —**blow up** 1 To inflate. 2 To enlarge, as a photographic print. 3 To explode. 4 *Informal* To lose self-control; become enraged. 5 To arise, as a storm. 6 To exaggerate (an incident, etc.). —*n.* 1 The act of blowing. 2 A gale. 3 *Slang* Boastfulness. 4 *Slang* A braggart. [<OE *blāwan*]

**blow²** (blō) *n.* 1 A hard hit or punch, as with the fist or a weapon. 2 A sudden misfortune. 3 A hostile or combative act. —**come to blows** To start fighting. [<ME *blaw*]

**blub·ber** (blub′ər) *n.* The layer of fat beneath the skin of whales and other sea mammals. [ME *bluber*] —**blub′ber·y** *adj.*

**bludg·eon** (bluj′ən) *n.* A short club, commonly loaded at one end, used as a weapon. —*v.t.* 1 To strike with or as with a bludgeon. 2 To coerce; bully. [?]

**blue** (blōō) *adj.* **blu·er, blu·est** 1 Having the color of the clear, daytime sky. 2 Livid: said of the skin. 3 Sad; melancholy. 4 Depressing; discouraging. 5 Puritanic; strict: *blue* laws. 6 *Informal* Risqué. 7 *Can.* BLEU. —*n.* 1 The color of the clear, daytime sky; azure. 2 Any blue coloring matter or pigment. 3 BLUING. 4 *Often pl.* Blue clothing. 5 *Sometimes cap.* A person who wears a blue uniform. 6 *pl.* See BLUES. 7 *Can.* BLEU. —**out of the blue** From an unsuspected source; completely unforeseen. —*v.t.* **blued, blu·ing** 1 To make blue. 2 To treat with bluing. [<OF *bleu*] —**blue′ly** *adv.* —**blue′ness** *n.*

**bluff** (bluf) *n.* A high, steep cliff or bank. —*adj.* 1 Blunt, frank, and hearty. 2 Having an upright, broad, flattened front. [?<Du. *blaf* flat, as in *blaf aensicht* broad flat face] —

**bluff′ly** *adv.* —**bluff′ness** *n.* —Syn. 1 abrupt, brusque, open, plain-spoken.

**blun·der** (blun′dər) *n.* A stupid mistake. —*v.t.* 1 To move carelessly or awkwardly. 2 To make a stupid and awkward mistake. —*v.t.* 3 To say clumsily or thoughtlessly: often with *out.* 4 To bungle. [ME *blondren* mix up, confuse] —**blun′der·er** *n.* —**blun′der·ing·ly** *adv.*

**blunt** (blunt) *adj.* 1 Having a thick or dull end or edge. 2 Abrupt and plain-spoken in manner. 3 Slow of wit; dull. —*v.t.* & *v.i.* 1 To make or become blunt or dull. 2 To make or become less keen or poignant. [ME *blunt;* origin unknown] —**blunt′ly** *adv.* —**blunt′ness** *n.*

**blur** (blûr) *n.* 1 A smeared or indistinct marking. 2 Something vague or indistinct to the sight or mind. —*v.t.* & *v.i.* **blurred, blur·ring** *v.t.* 1 To stain, smear, or smudge. 2 To make or become obscure or indistinct in outline. 3 To make or become dim or cloudy. [?] —**blur′ry** *adj.* (·ri·er, ·ri·est)

**blurt** (blûrt) *v.t.* To utter abruptly, as if on impulse: usu. with *out.* [?]

**blush** (blush) *v.i.* 1 To redden in the face, as from embarrassment. 2 To be or become red or rosy. 3 To feel shame or regret: usu. with *at* or *for.* —*v.t.* 4 To make red. —*n.* 1 A reddening of the face, as from modesty, etc. 2 A red or rosy tint; flush. [<OE *blyscan* redden] —**blush′er** *n.* —**blush′ful** *adj.*

**blus·ter** (blus′tər) *n.* 1 Boisterous talk or swagger. 2 A noisy blowing of the wind. —*v.i.* 1 To blow gustily, as the wind. 2 To act or speak noisily and aggressively. —*v.t.* 3 To utter noisily and boisterously. 4 To force or bully by blustering. [ME *blusteren*] —**blus′ter·er** *n.* —**blus′ter·y, blus′ter·ous** *adj.*

**bo·a** (bō′ə) *n. pl.* **bo·as** 1 Any of several nonvenomous serpents that crush their prey, as the anaconda, python, and esp. the **boa constrictor.** 2 A long feather or fur neckpiece for women. [<L]

**boar** (bôr, bōr) *n. pl.* **boars** or **boar** 1 An uncastrated male hog. 2 The wild hog of Europe, North Africa, and Asia. [<OE *bār*]

**board** (bôrd, bōrd) *n.* 1 A flat piece of sawed wood whose length is much greater than its width. 2 A slab of wood or other material prepared for a specific purpose: a diving *board.* 3 Pasteboard or other material, often used for book covers. 4 A table, spread for serving food. 5 Meals regularly furnished for pay. 6 An organized official body: a *board* of directors. **7** A table around which meetings are held. —**on board** On or in a vessel or other conveyance. —**tread the boards** To appear as an actor. —*v.t.* **1** To cover or enclose with boards: often with *up.* **2** To furnish with meals or meals and lodging for pay. **3** To place (someone) where meals are provided, as in a boarding school. **4** *Naut.* To come alongside or go on board of (a ship). **5** To enter, as a ship or train. —*v.i.* **6** To take meals or meals and lodging for pay. [<OE *bord*]

**boast** (bōst) *v.i.* **1** To extol the deeds or abilities of oneself or of another; brag. **2** To be excessively proud: with *of.* —*v.t.* **3** To brag about. **4** To be proud to possess; take pride in. —*n.* **1** A boastful speech. **2** A source of pride. [ME *bosten*] —**boast′er** *n.* —**Syn.** *v.* **1** crow, flaunt, swagger, vaunt.

**boat** (bōt) *n.* **1** A small, open watercraft propelled by oars, sails, or an engine. **2** A large, seagoing vessel; ship: a nautically incorrect usage. **3** A dish resembling a boat. —**be in the same boat** To be in the same situation. —*v.i.* **1** To travel by boat. **2** To go boating for pleasure. —*v.t.* **3** To transport or place in a boat. [<OE *bāt*]

**bob** (bob) *n.* **1** In fishing: **a** A cork or float on a line. **b** A ball-shaped bait of anglえworms, rags, etc. **2** A small, pendent object or weight: a plumb *bob.* **3** A jerky bow or curtsy. **4** Any short, jerky movement. **5** A short style of haircut. **6** The docked tail of a horse. —*v.* **bobbed, bob·bing** *v.t.* **1** To move up and down: to *bob* the head. **2** To cut short, as hair. —*v.i.* **3** To move up and down with an irregular motion. **4** To curtsy. **5** To fish with a bob. —**bob up** To appear or emerge suddenly. [ME *bobbe* a hanging cluster] —**bob′ber** *n.*

**bob·bin** (bob′in) *n.* A spool or reel to hold weft or thread in spinning, weaving, or in machine sewing. [F *bobine*]

**bobby pin** A metal hairpin so shaped as to hold the hair tightly. **Also bobbie pin.**

**bobby socks** *Informal* Ankle-length socks worn by girls.

**bob·by·sox·er** (bob′ē·sok′sər) *n. Informal* An adolescent girl, esp. in the 1940's.

**bod·y** (bod′ē) *n. pl.* **bod·ies 1** The entire physical structure of a person, animal, or plant. **2** A corpse. **3** The trunk of a person or animal. **4** *Informal* A person. **5** A collection of persons or things considered as a unit. **6** The principal part or mass of anything. **7** Any mass of matter: a celestial *body;* a

*body* of water. **8** Density or substance: a fabric with *body.* **9** Fullness and richness, as of a wine. —*v.t.* **bod·ied, bod·y·ing** To give shape or form to; embody; represent: usu. with *forth.* [<OE *bodig*]

**bog** (bog, bôg) *n.* Wet and spongy ground; marsh; morass. —*v.t. & v.i.* **bogged, bog·ging** To sink or stick in or as in a bog: often with *down.* [<Ir., soft] —**bog′gish** *adj.*

**bo·gus** (bō′gəs) *adj.* Counterfeit; spurious; fake. [?]

**boil** (boil) *n.* A pussy and painful swelling in the skin, of bacterial origin. [<OE *bȳl, bȳle*]

**bois·ter·ous** (bois′tər·əs) *adj.* **1** Noisy; rowdy; unrestrained. **2** Violent; turbulent. [ME *boistous*] —**bois′ter·ous·ly** *adv.* —**bois′ter·ous·ness** *n.*

**bold** (bōld) *adj.* **1** Possessing courage; fearless. **2** Showing or requiring courage. **3** Shameless; forward; brazen. **4** Striking; vigorous, as language. **5** Clear; prominent: *bold* outlines. **6** Abrupt; steep, as a cliff. —**make bold** To take the liberty; venture. [<OE *bald*] —**bold′ly** *adv.* —**bold′ness** *n.* —**Syn.** **1** audacious, brave, daring, valiant. **3** brassy, immodest, impudent.

**bo·lo** (bō′lō) *n. pl.* **-los** (-lōz) A heavy, single-edged weapon used in the Philippine Islands. [Sp.]

**Bol·she·vik** (bōl′shə·vik, bol′-) *n. pl.* **Bol·she·viks** or **Bol·she·vi·ki** (bōl′shə·vē′kē, bol′-) **1** A member of the dominant branch of the Russian Social Democratic Party or, since the 1917 Revolution, of the Russian Communist Party. **2** A Communist. **3** Loosely, any radical. **Also bol′she·vik.** [Russ., a member of the majority (group in the party)]

**bol·ster** (bōl′stər) *n.* **1** A long, narrow pillow as wide as a bed. **2** A pad used as a support or for protection. **3** Anything shaped like or used as a bolster. —*v.t.* To prop up, as something ready to fall. [<OE] —**bol′ster·er** *n.*

**bolt** (bōlt) *n.* **1** A sliding bar or piece for fastening a door, etc. **2** In a lock, the movable bar or piece that is operated by the key. **3** A metal pin or rod usu. threaded and having a head at one end, used with a nut for holding anything in its place. **4** A sliding bar that closes the breech in certain firearms. **5** An arrow for a crossbow. **6** A lightning flash. **7** A sudden start or departure. **8** A roll of cloth, wall paper, etc. —**bolt from the blue** A sudden and wholly unexpected event. —*v.i.* **1** To move, go, or spring suddenly: usu. with *out* or *from*: He *bolted* from the room. 2 *U.S.* To break away, as from a political party. —*v.i.* 3 To fasten with or as with bolts. 4 *U.S.* To break away from, as a political party. 5 To gulp, as food. 6 To blurt out. —*adv.* Rigidly; erectly; to sit *bolt* upright. [<OE, arrow for a crossbow]

**bomb** (bom) *n.* 1 A hollow projectile containing explosive, incendiary, or chemical material to be discharged by concussion or by a time fuse. 2 An unexpected occurrence. 3 *Slang* A flop; failure; dud. 4 *Informal* In football, a long forward pass. —*v.t.* 1 To attack or destroy with or as with bombs. —*v.i.* 2 *Slang* To fail utterly. [<L *bombus* loud sound]

**bom·bard** (bom-bärd′) *v.t.* 1 To attack with bombs or shells. 2 To attack or press as with bombs: to *bombard* with questions. 3 To expose to the effect of radiation or to the impact of high-energy atomic particles. [<MF *bombarde* a cannon] —**bom·bard′er**, **bom·bard′ment** *n.*

**bom·bast** (bom′bast) *n.* Pompous, high-flown language. [<OF *bombace* cotton padding] —**bom·bas′tic**, **bom·bas′ti·cal** *adj.* —**bom·bas′ti·cal·ly** *adv.* —**Syn.** grandiloquence, prolixity, verbosity, wordiness.

**bomb·er** (bom′ər) *n.* 1 One who attacks with bombs. 2 An airplane employed in bombing.

**bo·nan·za** (bə-nan′zə) *n.* 1 A rich mine, vein, or find of ore. 2 Any profitable operation. [Sp., success]

**bond** (bond) *n.* 1 Something that binds, holds, or fastens. 2 The union thus formed. 3 A tie, link, or union: a family *bond.* 4 An obligation, promise, or agreement. 5 *pl.* a Fetters. b Captivity. 6 An interest-bearing certificate sold by a government or business to raise money and carrying the promise to repay the purchaser by a specified date. 7 An insurance policy covering losses suffered through the acts of an employee. 8 The condition of goods stored in a warehouse until duties are paid. 9 *Law* a An obligation in writing under seal. b One who furnishes bail. c Bail. 10 *Chem.* A force that holds together the atoms of a molecule. —**bottled in bond** Bottled after storage in a bonded warehouse for a specified amount of time, as some whiskies. —*v.t.* 1 To put a certified debt upon; mortgage. 2 To furnish bond for; be surety for (someone). 3 To place, as goods or an employee, under bond. 4 To unite or bind tightly together. —

*v.i.* 5 To hold or cohere with or as with a bond. [<ON *band*]

**bone** (bōn) *n.* 1 A separate piece of the skeleton of a vertebrate animal. 2 The hard tissue of which a skeleton is composed. 3 One of various objects made of bone or similar material, as a corset stay. 4 A material resembling bone, as whalebone. 5 *pl. Slang* Dice. —**feel in (one's) bones** To have an intuition of. —**have a bone to pick** To have grounds for complaint or dispute. —**make no bones about** To be totally frank or honest about. —*v.* **boned**, **bon·ing** *v.t.* 1 To remove the bones from. 2 To stiffen with whalebone. —*v.i.* 3 *Slang* To study intensely: often with *up*. [<OE *bān*]

**bon·fire** (bon′fīr′) *n.* A large fire in the open air. [<BONE + FIRE; formerly a fire for calcining bones]

**bon·net** (bon′it) *n.* 1 An outdoor headdress for women and children, usu. tied under the chin. 2 A brimless cap for men and boys, worn esp. in Scotland. 3 An American Indian headdress of feathers. 4 Any of various metal hoods protecting machinery, etc. 5 *Brit.* The hood of an automobile. —*v.t.* To cover with or as with a bonnet. [<OF *bonet*]

**bo·nus** (bō′nəs) *n. pl.* **bo·nus·es** Something given, as a sum of money, over and above what is usual, current, or stipulated. [L, good]

**book** (bŏŏk) *n.* 1 A number of printed or written sheets of paper bound together, usu. between covers. 2 A literary or other written composition or treatise so bound and usu. of some length. 3 A subdivision of a literary composition or treatise: one of the *books* of the Bible. 4 A business record or ledger. 5 LIBRETTO. 6 A script for a play, musical comedy, etc. 7 A booklike pack of matches, etc. 8 A list of bets made. —**by the book** According to rule. —**like a book** Thoroughly. —**the Book** The Bible. —*v.t.* 1 To enter or list in a book. 2 To arrange for beforehand, as accommodations or seats. 3 To engage, as actors or a play, for performance. 4 To make a record of charges against (someone) on a police blotter. [<OE *bōc*]

**boom**[1] (bŏŏm) *n.* 1 A spar used to extend or support the foot of a sail. 2 A chain of logs to intercept or retard the advance of a vessel, to confine timbers, sawlogs, etc. 3 A long mobile beam projecting upward from the foot of a derrick to carry or guide a load suspended from its outer end. 4 A long, mobile arm with a microphone attached at one end. [<Du. *boom* tree, beam]

**boom²** (bōōm) *v.i.* 1 To emit a deep, resonant sound, as cannon. 2 To grow rapidly; flourish. —*v.t.* 3 To utter or sound in a deep, resonant tone. 4 To praise or advertise vigorously. —*n.* 1 A deep, reverberating sound, as of a cannon. 2 Any sudden or rapid growth or popularity. [Imit.] —**Syn.** *v.* 1 resound, reverberate, roar. 2 increase, prosper, succeed, thrive.

**boor** (bōōr) *n.* A rude, coarse, or unpleasant person. [<Du. *boer* farmer, rustic] — **boor′ish** *adj.* —**boor′ish·ly** *adv.* —**boor′ish·ness** *n.*

**boost** (bōōst) *v.t.* 1 To raise by or as by pushing from beneath or behind. 2 To speak in praise of; help by speaking well of. 3 To increase: to *boost* prices. —*n.* 1 A lift; help. 2 An increase. [?]

**boot** (bōōt) *n.* 1 A shoelike covering, as of leather, rubber, etc., for the foot and all or part of the leg. 2 A shoe reaching to or above the ankle. 3 An overshoe. 4 A medieval instrument of torture for crushing the foot and leg. 5 A kick. 6 *Informal* In the U.S. Navy or Marine Corps, a new recruit. —**die with one's boots on** To die fighting or working. —**get the boot** *Slang* To be discharged. —*v.t.* 1 To put boots on. 2 To kick; also, in football, to punt. 3 *Slang* To dismiss; fire. —*v.i.* To load a program into a computer. [<OF *bote*]

**booth** (bōōth, bōōth) *n.* 1 A stall at a fair, market, etc. 2 A small compartment or enclosure: a voting *booth.* 3 A stationary table and seating compartment, as in a restaurant. [<Scand.]

**boot·leg** (bōōt′leg′) *v.t. & v.i.* **·legged, ·leg·ging** To make, sell, or carry for sale (liquor, etc.) illegally; smuggle. —*adj.* Unlawful: *bootleg* whisky. —*n.* 1 The part of a boot above the instep. 2 Something bootlegged, esp. liquor. [With ref. to the smuggling of liquor in bootlegs] —**boot′leg′ger, boot′leg′ging** *n.*

**bor·der** (bôr′dər) *n.* 1 A margin or edge. 2 The peripheral line or district of a country or state; a boundary or frontier. 3 A surrounding or enclosing strip or edge. 4 A decorative edge or margin. —*adj.* Of, on, forming, or pertaining to a border. —*v.t.* 1 To put a border or edging on. 2 To lie next to; form a boundary to. —**border on** (or **upon**) 1 To resemble; have the appearance of: That *borders on* piracy. 2 To touch or abut. [<OF *bord* edge] —**bor′der·er** *n.*

**bore** (bôr, bōr) *v.* **bored, bor·ing** *v.t.* 1 To make a hole in or through, as with a drill. 2 To make (a tunnel, hole, well, etc.) by or as by drilling. 3 To advance or force (one's way). 4 To weary by monotony, dullness, etc. — *v.i.* 5 To make a hole, etc., by or as by drilling. 6 To admit of being drilled: This wood *bores* easily. 7 To force one's way. — *n.* 1 A hole made by or as if by boring. 2 The interior diameter of a firearm or cylinder. 3 A tiresome person or thing. [<OE *borian*]

**boric acid** A white crystalline compound of hydrogen, boron, and oxygen, used as a mild antiseptic.

**bor·ough** (bûr′ō) *n.* 1 An incorporated village or town. 2 One of the five administrative divisions of New York, N.Y. 3 *Brit.* **a** A town having a municipal corporation endowed by royal charter with certain privileges. **b** A town, whether corporate or not, entitled to representation in Parliament. [<OE *burg, burh* fort, town]

**bor·row** (bôr′ō, bor′ō) *v.t. & v.i.* 1 To take or obtain (something) on a promise to return it or its equivalent. 2 To adopt for one's own use: to *borrow* an idea. 3 *Math.* In subtraction, to perform the operation inverse of carrying, in addition. [<OE *borgian* give a pledge, borrow] —**bor′row·er** *n.*

**bos·om** (bōōz′əm, bōō′zəm) *n.* 1 The breast of a human being, esp. of a woman. 2 That portion of a garment covering the breast, as a shirt front. 3 The breast thought of as the seat of emotion or thought. 4 The central part; midst. —*adj.* Close; intimate; cherished: a *bosom* friend. —*v.t.* 1 To have or cherish in the bosom; embrace. 2 To hide; conceal. [<OE *bōsm*]

**boss¹** (bôs, bos) *n.* 1 A person who employs workers or supervises their work. 2 One who controls a political party or organization. —*v.t.* 1 To control or supervise. 2 *Informal* To order or control in a domineering manner: often with *around.* —*adj.* 1 *Informal* Chief. 2 *Slang* Great; excellent. [<Du. *baas* master]

**boss²** (bôs, bos) *n.* 1 A circular prominence; a knob. 2 A raised ornament on a surface. 3 *Mech.* An enlargement of a shaft to couple with a wheel or another shaft. —*v.t.* To ornament with bosses. [<OF *boce* bump, knob]

**bot·a·ny** (bot′ə·nē) *n. pl.* **·nies** 1 That division of biology which treats of plants with reference to their structure, functions, classification, etc. 2 The plant life of a region. 3 The common characteristics of a group of plants: the *botany* of orchids.

**botch** (boch) *v.t.* 1 To patch or mend clumsily. 2 To do ineptly; bungle. —*n.* A bungled piece of work. [ME *bocchen*] —**botch′er** *n.* —**botch′er·y** *n.*

**bot·tle** (bot′l) *n.* 1 A vessel for holding, carrying, and pouring liquids, having a relatively narrow neck and mouth. 2 As much as a bottle will hold: also **bot′tle·ful.** —**hit the bottle** *Slang* To drink alcoholic beverages to excess. —*v.t.* **·tled, ·tling** 1 To put into a bottle or bottles. 2 To restrain; shut in: with *up.* [<LL *buticula* flask, dim. of *butis* vat, vessel] —**bot′tler** *n.*

**bot·tle·neck** (bot′l·nek′) *n.* 1 A narrow or congested way. 2 Any condition that retards progress.

**bot·tom** (bot′əm) *n.* 1 The lowest part of anything. 2 The undersurface or base of something. 3 The last or lowest place. 4 The seat of a chair. 5 The ground beneath a body of water. 6 *Often pl.* BOTTOM LAND. 7 The real meaning, cause, or source of something. 8 The part of a ship's hull below the water line. 9 *Informal* The buttocks. 10 Endurance; stamina; grit. —**at bottom** Basically; fundamentally. —*adj.* Lowest; fundamental; basal. —*v.t.* 1 To provide with a bottom. 2 To base or found: with *on* or *upon.* 3 To fathom; comprehend. —*v.i.* 4 To be founded; rest. 5 To touch or rest upon the bottom. [<OE *botm*]

**bough** (bou) *n.* A limb of a tree. [<OE *bog* shoulder, bough]

**boul·der** (bōl′dər) *n.* A large stone moved, as by a glacier, from its original location. [< Scand.]

**boul·e·vard** (bool′ə·värd, boo′lə-) *n.* A broad avenue, often planted with trees. [<MHG *bolwerc* bulwark]

**bounce** (bouns) *v.* **bounced, bounc·ing** *v.t.* 1 To cause to bound or rebound. 2 *Slang* To eject forcibly. 3 *Slang* To discharge from employment. —*v.i.* 4 To bound or rebound. 5 To move suddenly and violently; jump or spring. 6 *Informal* To be returned because of insufficient funds: said of a check. —*n.* 1 A sudden spring or leap. 2 A bounding or elastic motion; rebound. [ME *bunsen*]

**bound¹** (bound) *p.t. & p.p.* of BIND. —*adj.* 1 Made fast; tied. 2 Obligated legally or morally. 3 Connected; related. 4 Certain:

*bound* to fail. 5 Having a cover or binding. 6 *Informal* Determined; resolved.

**bound²** (bound) *adj.* Having one's course directed; on the way: with *for* or *to.* [<ON *būinn* < *būa* prepare]

**bound·a·ry** (boun′də·rē, -drē) *n. pl.* **·ries** Anything forming or serving to indicate a limit or end. —*Syn.* border, confines, edge, margin.

**boun·te·ous** (boun′tē·əs) *adj.* 1 Bountiful; generous. 2 Plentiful. —**boun′te·ous·ly** *adv.* —**boun′te·ous·ness** *n.*

**boun·ty** (boun′tē) *n. pl.* **·ties** 1 Liberality in giving. 2 Gifts or favors generously bestowed. 3 A reward paid by a government for the killing of predatory animals, raising certain crops, etc. [<L *bonitas* goodness]

**bou·quet** (bō·kā′, boo·kā′ *for def.* 1; boo·kā′ *for def.* 2) *n.* 1 A bunch of flowers. 2 The distinctive aroma of a wine. [< OF *boschet*, dim. of *bosc* wood]

**bout** (bout) *n.* 1 A contest or match, as in boxing. 2 An active period; spell: a *bout* of illness [Var. of ME *bought* bending, turn]

**bow¹** (bou) *v.i.* 1 To bend the body or head, as in greeting, reverence, assent, etc. 2 To bend or incline downward. 3 To submit; yield. —*v.t.* 4 To bend (the head, knee, etc.) in reverence, assent, etc. 5 To express by bowing. 6 To escort or direct while bowing. 7 To cause to bend, stoop, etc., as by weighting down. 8 To cause to yield or submit. —**bow out** To withdraw or resign. —*n.* 1 A bending of the body or head, as in greeting. 2 An indication of polite acknowledgment. [< OE *bugan* bow, bend, flee] —*Syn.* *v.* 3 capitulate, surrender, acquiesce. *n.* 1 obeisance, curtsey, salaam.

**bow²** (bō) *n.* 1 A weapon for shooting arrows, made from a flexible strip of wood, etc., strung from end to end with a cord. 2 A rod with hairs stretched between the ends, used to vibrate the strings of a violin, cello, etc., by friction. 3 A knot tied with a loop or loops. 4 Something bent or curved. 5 A rainbow. —*adj.* Bent; curved. —*v.t. & v.i.* 1 To bend into the shape of a bow. 2 To play (a stringed instrument) with a bow. [<OE *boga*]

**bowl** (bōl) *v.i.* 1 To engage in the game of bowling. 2 To roll a ball or similar object in or as in this game. 3 To move swiftly and smoothly. —*v.t.* 4 To throw (a ball) with a rolling motion. —**bowl over** 1 To knock down. 2 To dumbfound; astound. —*n.* 1 A large ball used for bowling or similar games. 2 A throw of the ball in or as in bowling. [<F *boule* ball]

**boy·cott** (boi'kot) *v.t.* 1 To combine together in refusing to deal or associate with, so as to punish or coerce. 2 To refuse to use or buy. —*n.* An act or instance of boycotting. [< Capt. C. *Boycott*, 1832–1897, Irish landlord's agent]

**bra** (brä) *n.* A brassiere.

**brace** (brās) *v.* **braced**, **brac·ing** *v.t.* 1 To make firm or steady; strengthen with or as with a prop or support. 2 To make ready to withstand pressure, impact, assault, etc. 3 To stimulate; enliven. —*v.i.* 4 To strain against pressure. —**brace up** *Informal* To rouse one's courage or resolution. —*n.* 1 A support, as of wood or metal, to hold something firmly in place. 2 A clasp or clamp used for connecting, fastening, etc. 3 A cranklike handle for turning a bit or other boring tool. 4 *Often pl.* A wire device attached to the teeth to correct malformation. 5 A pair: a *brace* of ducks. 6 A doubly curved line, (or), used to connect printed or written lines, staves of music, etc. 7 *pl. Brit.* Suspenders. [< *brachia*, pl. of *brachium* arm] —**Syn.** *v.* 1 support, prop, shore, buttress.

**brace·let** (brās'lit) *n.* 1 An ornamental band worn around the wrist or arm. 2 *Informal* A handcuff. [< *brachium* arm]

**brack·et** (brak'it) *n.* 1 A piece projecting from a wall to support a shelf or other weight. 2 A projecting fixture, as for a lamp. 3 A brace used to strengthen an angle. 4 One of two marks, [ ], used to enclose part of a text. 5 A part within a graded grouping or category: the high-income *bracket.* —*v.t.* 1 To provide or support with a bracket. 2 To enclose within brackets. 3 To group or categorize together. [< L *bracae*, pl., breeches]

**brack·ish** (brak'ish) *adj.* 1 Somewhat saline; briny. 2 Unpleasant to taste. [<Du. *brak* salty] —**brack'ish·ness** *n.*

**brag** (brag) *v.* **bragged**, **brag·ging** *v.t. & v.i.* To say or talk boastfully. —*n.* 1 Boastfulness; boastful language. 2 Something bragged of. 3 A person who brags. [<ME *braggen*] —**brag'ger** *n.*

**braid** (brād) *v.t.* 1 To interweave or intertwine several strands of; plait. 2 To form by braiding: to *braid* a mat. 3 To ornament with braid. —*n.* 1 Anything braided or plaited: a *braid* of hair. 2 A flat tape or strip for binding or ornamenting fabrics. [<OE *bregdan* brandish, weave, braid] —**braid'er, braid'ing** *n.*

**brain** (brān) *n.* 1 The mass of nerve tissue contained within the cranium of vertebrates and continuous with the spinal cord. 2 The chief focal area of the nervous system in any animal. 3 *Often pl.* Mind; intellect. 4 *Informal* A notably intelligent person. —**have on the brain** To be obsessed by —*v.t.* 1 To dash out the brains of. 2 *Slang* To strike on the head. [<OE *brǣgen*]

**brain·wash** (brān'wosh', -wôsh') *v.t.* To alter the convictions, beliefs, etc., of by systematic indoctrination. —**brain'wash·ing** *n.*

**braise** (brāz) *v.t.* **braised**, **brais·ing** To cook by browning quickly and then simmering in a covered pan. [<F *braise* charcoal]

**brake** (brāk) *n.* 1 A device for retarding or arresting the motion of a vehicle, a wheel, etc. 2 *Often pl.* Anything that checks or slows an action or process. 3 An instrument for separating the fiber of flax, hemp, etc., by bruising. —*v.* **braked**, **brak·ing** *v.t.* 1 To apply a brake to. 2 To bruise and crush, as flax. —*v.i.* 3 To operate a brake or brakes. 4 To be retarded or stopped by a brake. [<MDu. *braeke* brake for flax]

**branch** (branch, bränch) *n.* 1 A secondary stem growing from the trunk or main limb of a tree, shrub, etc. 2 A similar division or part, as of a deer's antler. 3 A part or subdivision of a comprehensive whole. 4 A separate unit, department, etc., as of a business organization or institution. 5 A division of a family, tribe, etc. 6 A subdivision of a linguistic family. 7 A tributary of a river or main stream. 8 A small stream or creek. —*v.i.* 1 To put forth branches. 2 To divide into branches or subdivisions; diverge. —*v.t.* 3 To separate into branches. —**branch out** To extend or diversify, as one's business or interests. [<LL *branca* paw]

**brand** (brand) *n.* 1 A name or trademark used to identify a product. 2 A product so identified: a popular *brand* of toothpaste. 3 A distinctive type or kind. 4 A mark burned with a hot iron, as on cattle for identification. 5 A mark of disgrace or shame. 6 A burning stick of wood. —*v.t.* 1 To mark with or as with a hot iron. 2 To mark or label, as with disgrace; stigmatize: to *brand* someone a traitor. [<OE, torch, sword] —**brand'er** *n.*

**bran·dish** (bran'dish) *v.t.* To wave or flourish triumphantly, menacingly, etc. —*n.* A flourish, as with a weapon. [<OF *brand* sword] —**brand'ish·er** *n.*

**brass** (bras, bräs) *n.* 1 A yellow alloy of copper and zinc. 2 *Sometimes pl.* Brass ornaments, utensils, etc. 3 The brass wind instruments of an orchestra or band, collectively. 4 *Informal* Impudence; effrontery. 5 *Slang* High-ranking military officers, executives, etc. —*adj.* Made of brass. [<OE *brǣs*]

**bra·va·do** (brə·vä′dō) *n. pl.* **·dos** or **·does** 1 Affectation of reckless bravery; bluster. 2 A show of false courage or daring. [<Sp. *bravo* brave]

**brave** (brāv) *adj.* **brav·er, brav·est** 1 Having or showing courage. 2 Showy; splendid. —*v.t.* —**braved, brav·ing** 1 To face with courage and fortitude. 2 To defy; challenge. —*n.* A North American Indian warrior. [<L *barbarus* wild, fierce] —**brave′ly** *adv.* —**brave′ness** *n.* —**Syn.** *adj.* 1 courageous, fearless, bold, intrepid, valorous.

**brawl** (brôl) *n.* 1 A noisy quarrel or fight; a row. 2 *Slang* A noisy celebration. —*v.i.* 1 To quarrel or fight noisily. 2 To move noisily, as water. [<ME *braulen*] —**brawl′er** *n.*

**brawn** (brôn) *n.* 1 Strong, well-developed muscles. 2 Muscular strength; physical power. [<OF *braon* slice of flesh] —**brawn′y** *adj.* (**·i·er, ·i·est**) —**brawn′i·ness** *n.*

**bra·zen** (brā′zən) *adj.* 1 Made of or resembling brass. 2 Trumpetlike; blaring. 3 Bold and shameless. —*v.t.* To face with bold or defiant self-assurance: with *out.* —**bra′zen·ly** *adv.* —**bra′zen·ness** *n.*

**bra·zier** (brā′zhər) *n.* An open pan for holding burning coals. [<F *braise* hot coals]

**breach** (brēch) *n.* 1 Violation or infraction of a law, legal obligation, promise, etc. 2 A gap or break, as in a wall. 3 A break in friendly relations; an estrangement. —*v.t.* To make a breach in; break through. [<OE *bryce* a breaking]

**breadth** (bredth, bretth) *n.* 1 Measure or distance from side to side; width. 2 A piece of something, as cloth, of full or standard width. 3 Comprehensive range or scope. 4 Freedom from bias or restriction. [<OE < *brad* broad]

**break** (brāk) *v.* **broke** (*Archaic* **brake**), **bro·ken** (*Archaic* **broke**), **break·ing** *v.t.* 1 To separate into pieces by or as by force, a blow, etc. 2 To crack; fracture. 3 To pierce or part the surface of. 4 To cause to burst. 5 To make useless or inoperative. 6 To make a way through by force. 7 To escape from: to *break* jail. 8 To end by force or opposition: to *break* a strike. 9 To destroy the order, continuity, or completeness of: to *break* step; to *break* the silence. 10 To diminish the force of; moderate: to *break* a fall. 11 To interrupt (an electric circuit, a journey, etc.). 12 To violate: to *break* a law. 13 a To discontinue (a habit). b To cause to discontinue a habit. 14 To train or tame, as a horse. 15 To demote in rank. 16 To subdue or destroy; crush. 17 To surpass; excel: to *break* a record. 18 To make known, as news. 19 To exchange for smaller units: to *break* a dollar. 20 To invalidate (a will) by court action. 21 To solve or decipher. 22 To bankrupt. 23 To overwhelm with grief: It *broke* his heart. —*v.i.* 24 To become separated into pieces or fragments; come or fall apart. 25 To burst. 26 To become unusable or inoperative. 27 To move apart or away; disperse: The crowd *broke.* 28 To move or escape suddenly: He *broke* from the crowd. 29 To come into being or evidence: Dawn *broke.* 30 To collapse or crash. 31 To diminish or fall abruptly: The fever *broke.* 32 To change suddenly, as the voice. 33 To be overwhelmed with grief: Her heart *broke.* 34 In baseball, to curve near the plate, as a pitched ball. —**break down** 1 To become inoperative. 2 To have a physical or nervous collapse. 3 To give way, as to grief. 4 To decompose. 5 To analyze. —**break in** 1 To enter by force. 2 To interrupt. 3 To train. 4 To adapt to use or wear. —**break off** 1 To stop suddenly, as in speaking. 2 To sever relations. —**break out** 1 To start suddenly. 2 To develop a rash, pimples, etc. —**break up** 1 To disperse. 2 To bring or come to an end. 3 *Informal* To overwhelm or be overwhelmed, as with distress or laughter. —**break with** To sever connection with. —*n.* 1 An instance or result of breaking; a fracture, crack, etc. 2 An opening, rift, gap, etc. 3 A breach or interruption of continuity. 4 A pause or interval. 5 A beginning; start: the *break* of day. 6 A dash or run, esp. to escape. 7 A severing of connection or friendly relations. 8 A sudden change or decline. 9 *Informal* An opportunity or piece of luck. 10 A point where there is a change of register of a voice or instrument. [<OE *brecan*] —**break′a·ble** *adj.* —**Syn.** *v.* 1 shatter, smash, fragment, shiver, disintegrate, splinter, dash.

**break·fast** (brek′fəst) *n.* The first meal of the day. —*v.i.* To eat breakfast. —**break′fast·er** *n.*

**break·through** (brāk′thrōō′) *n.* 1 A decisive or dramatic advance, as in research, knowledge, etc. 2 An attack that penetrates an enemy's defensive system.

**breast** (brest) *n.* 1 The front of the body from the neck to the abdomen. 2 One of the two milk-secreting organs on the upper front part of a woman's torso. 3 A similar organ in any mammal. 4 The part of a garment that covers the breast. 5 The seat of the emotions. 6 Anything likened to the human breast. —**make a clean breast of** To confess. —*v.t.* To face or advance against boldly or resolutely. [<OE *brēost*]

**breath** (breth) *n.* 1 Air inhaled or exhaled in respiration. 2 An act of respiration, esp. an inhalation. 3 Ability to breathe or breathe freely. 4 The moisture of exhaled air condensed by cooling. 5 The time of a single respiration; an instant. 6 A slight breeze or motion of air. 7 A slight indication, suggestion, etc. 8 A whisper. —**hold one's breath** To prevent oneself from breathing temporarily. —**in the same breath** At the same moment. —**out of breath** Panting, as from exertion. —**take one's breath away** To awe, astonish, etc. —**under one's breath** In a whisper. [<OE *brǣth* vapor]

**breathe** (brēth) *v.* **breathed** (brēthd), **breath·ing** *v.i.* 1 To inhale and exhale air. 2 To be alive; live. 3 To pause for breath. 4 To move gently, as a breeze. 5 To allow air to penetrate: said of a fabric or garment. —*v.t.* 6 To inhale and exhale, as air. 7 To take in or emit by inhaling or exhaling. 8 To infuse or impart, as by breathing. 9 To evince; manifest. 10 To utter; whisper. 11 To allow to rest. [<ME *brethren*< *breth* breath] —**breath'a·ble** *adj.*

**breech·es** (brich'iz) *n. pl.* 1 Trousers, usu. close-fitting, that reach to or just below the knee. 2 *Informal* Trousers. [<OE *brec*]

**breed** (brēd) *v.* **bred**, **breed·ing** *v.t.* 1 To produce (offspring). 2 To control the reproduction of (animals or plants), often to develop new strains in. 3 To cause; give rise to. 4 To bring up; train. —*v.i.* 5 To procreate. 6 To originate or be caused. —*n.* 1 A strain or type, esp. of an animal, produced by selective mating. 2 A sort or kind. [<OE *brēdan*] —**breed'er** *n.*

**breeze** (brēz) *n.* 1 A moderate current of air; a gentle wind. 2 *Informal* An easily accomplished thing or action. —*v.i.* **breezed**, **breez·ing** *Informal* To go quickly and blithely. [<Sp. and Pg. *brisa, briza* northeast wind]

**brev·i·ty** (brev'ə·tē) *n.* 1 Shortness of duration

or time. 2 Condensation of language; conciseness. [<L *brevis* short]

**brew** (brōō) *v.t.* 1 To make, as beer or ale, by steeping, boiling, and fermentation of malt, hops, etc. 2 To make (a beverage) by boiling, steeping, etc. 3 To concoct; devise. —*v.i.* 4 To make ale, beer, etc. 5 To be imminent. —*n.* A beverage, etc., made by brewing. [<OE *brēowan*] —**brew'er** *n.*

**bribe** (brīb) *n.* 1 Something of value given or offered as an inducement to do something wrong. 2 Anything that seduces or allures. —*v.* **bribed**, **brib·ing** *v.t.* 1 To offer or give a bribe to. 2 To gain or influence by means of bribery. —*v.i.* 3 To give bribes. [<OF, piece of bread given a beggar] —**brib'a·ble** *adj.* —**brib'er** *n.*

**brib·er·y** (brī'bər·ē) *n. pl.* ·**er·ies** The giving, offering, or accepting of a bribe.

**bric-a-brac** (brik'ə·brak) *n.* Small objects displayed as ornaments; knickknacks. Also **bric-à-brac.** [F]

**brick** (brik) *n.* 1 A molded block of baked or fired clay, used for building, paving, etc. 2 Bricks collectively. 3 An object shaped like a brick. 4 *Informal* An admirable fellow. —*v.t.* 1 To build or line with bricks. 2 To cover or close with bricks: with *up* or *in.* [<OF *brique* fragment, bit]

**bri·dal** (brīd'l) *adj.* Of a bride or a wedding; nuptial. —*n.* A wedding. [<OE *brȳdeala* wedding feast]

**bride** (brīd) *n.* A woman newly married or about to be married. [<OE *brȳd*]

**bridge** (brij) *n.* 1 A structure built to span and afford passage across a waterway, railroad, ravine, etc. 2 Something that spans or connects in the manner of a bridge. 3 An observation platform across and above a ship's deck for the use of the officers, the pilot, etc. 4 The bony upper portion of the nose. 5 The part of a pair of eyeglasses resting on this part of the nose. 6 A block for raising the strings of a musical instrument, as a violin or guitar. • See VIOLIN. 7 A mounting for holding false teeth, attached to adjoining teeth on each side. 8 *Music* A transitional passage. —**burn one's bridges (behind one)** To cut off all possibility of retreat. —*v.t.* **bridged**, **bridg·ing** 1 To construct a bridge over. 2 To span or connect as by a bridge. [<OE *brycg*] —**bridge'a·ble** *adj.*

**bridge·head** (brij'hed') *n.* An advance military position on or near a river bank, pass, etc., in enemy territory.

**bri·dle** (brīd′l) *n.* 1 The head harness of a horse, including bit and reins. 2 Anything that restrains or checks. —*v.* **bri·dled, bri·dling** *v.t.* 1 To put a bridle on. 2 To check or control with or as with a bridle. —*v.i.* 3 To raise the head and draw in the chin, as in resentment, pride, etc. [<OE *brīdel*] —**bri′dler** *n.*

**brief** (brēf) *adj.* 1 Short in duration or extent. 2 Of few words; concise. 3 Curt; abrupt. —*n.* 1 A concise statement or summary. 2 A written summary of the relevant facts, points of law, etc., in a legal case. 3 *pl.* Short, close-fitting underpants. —**in brief** Briefly; in short. —**hold a brief for** To champion. —*v.t.* 1 To make a summary of. 2 To instruct or advise in advance. [<L *brevis* short] —**brief′ly** *adv.* —**brief′ness** *n.* —Syn. *adj.* 2 condensed, succinct, terse, laconic.

**brig** (brig) *n.* 1 A prison on shipboard. 2 *Slang* A guardhouse. [?<BRIG¹]

**bri·gade** (bri-gād′) *n.* 1 A U.S. Army unit of varying size, together with its headquarters and supporting units. 2 Any of various large military units. 3 A group of persons organized to work together: a fire *brigade.* —*v.t.* **·gad·ed, ·gad·ing** To form into a brigade. [<Ital. *brigata* crew < *brigare* to brawl]

**brigadier general** See GRADE.

**bright** (brīt) *adj.* 1 Emitting or reflecting much light; shining. 2 Full of light. 3 Brilliant, as in color or tone; vivid. 4 Intelligent; quick-witted. 5 Cheerful; gay. 6 Promising; auspicious. —*adv.* In a bright manner. [<OE *beorht, briht*] —**bright′ly** *adv.* —**bright′ness** *n.* —Syn. 1 Radiant, luminous, glowing, gleaming, effulgent.

**bril·liant** (bril′yənt) *adj.* 1 Very bright or vivid: a *brilliant* light. 2 Splendid; dazzling: a *brilliant* performance. 3 Strikingly intelligent or extraordinarily able or talented. —*n.* A diamond cut with many facets. [<MF *briller* to sparkle] —**bril′liance, bril′lian·cy** *n.* —**bril′liant·ly** *adv.*

**brim** (brim) *n.* 1 The rim or uppermost edge of a cup, bowl, etc. 2 A projecting rim, as of a hat. —*v.t.* & *v.i.* **brimmed, brim·ming** To fill or be filled to the brim. —**brim over** To overflow. [ME *brimme*]

**brine** (brīn) *n.* 1 Water saturated with salt. 2 The sea; the ocean. —*v.t.* **brined, brin·ing** To steep in brine. [<OE *brȳne*] —**brin′i·ness** *n.* —**brin′y** *adj.* (**·i·er, ·i·est**)

**bring** (bring) *v.t.* **brought, bring·ing** 1 To convey or cause (a person or thing) to come

with oneself to or toward a place. 2 To cause to come about; result in. 3 To cause to appear, come to mind, etc. 4 To persuade or induce, as to a course of action. 5 To sell for: The house *brought* a good price. 6 To institute (a lawsuit, charge, etc.). —**bring about** 1 To cause to happen. 2 *Naut.* To turn, as a ship. —**bring around** (or **round**) 1 To cause to adopt an opinion, course of action, etc. 2 To restore to consciousness. —**bring down** 1 To cause to fall. 2 To fell. —**bring forth** 1 To give birth to. 2 To produce. —**bring in** 1 To render or submit (a verdict). 2 To yield or produce, as profits. —**bring off** To do successfully. —**bring on** To cause; lead to. —**bring out** 1 To reveal; cause to be evident. 2 To publish or produce. 3 To introduce, as a young girl to society. —**bring to** 1 To restore to consciousness. 2 *Naut.* To cause (a ship) to lie to. —**bring up** 1 To raise and train during childhood; rear. 2 To mention or introduce, as a subject. 3 To cough or vomit up. [<OE *bringan*] —**bring′er** *n.* • In strict usage, *bring* (def. 1) means to convey or accompany to a place, while *take* means to remove or go with from a place: *Take* the books from the shelf and *bring* them to the office.

**brink** (bringk) *n.* 1 The upper edge of a steep place. 2 The edge; verge: the *brink* of despair. [<Scand.]

**brisk** (brisk) *adj.* 1 Quick; energetic; spirited. 2 Zestful; stimulating. 3 Active: *brisk* sales. [? <F *brusque* abrupt, sudden] —**brisk′ly** *adv.* —**brisk′ness** *n.*

**bris·tle** (bris′əl) *n.* A short, stiff hair or similar part. —*v.* **·tled, ·tling** *v.i.* 1 To erect the bristles. 2 To stand up stiffly, as bristles. 3 To be thickly set as if with bristles. 4 To show anger, irritation, etc. —*v.t.* 5 To erect as or like bristles. [<OE *byrst*] —**bris·tli·ness** (bris′lē·nis) *n.* —**bris·tly** (bris′lē) *adj.* (**·i·er, ·i·est**)

**brit·tle** (brit′l) *adj.* 1 Likely to break or snap; fragile. 2 Stiff or tense in manner. —*n.* A crisp candy made with sugar and nuts. [ME *britel*] —**brit′tle·ness** *n.*

**broach** (brōch) *v.t.* 1 To introduce or mention for the first time, as a subject. 2 To pierce (a cask, etc.) to draw off liquid. —*n.* A pointed, tapering tool for boring or reaming. [<OF *broche* a spit] —**broach′er** *n.*

**broad** (brôd) *adj.* 1 Extended in lateral dimensions; wide. 2 Extensive; spacious. 3 Clear; full: *broad* daylight. 4 Wide in scope or range; comprehensive. 5 Liberal; tolerant. 6 Obvious; plain: a *broad* hint. 7 Not detailed or specific; general. 8 Coarse; ribald. 9 Strongly dialectal. 10 *Phonet.* Formed with the oral passage wide open and the tongue low and flat, as the *a* in *calm.* —*n.* 1 The broad part of anything. 2 *Slang* A woman: a disparaging term. —*adv.* Completely; fully. [<OE *brād*] —**broad′ly** *adv.* —**broad′ness** *n.*

**broad·cast** (brôd′kast′, -käst′) *v.* **·cast** or **·casted**, **·cast·ing** *v.t.* 1 To transmit over an area by radio or television. 2 To make known; disseminate. 3 To scatter, as seed, over a wide area. —*v.i.* 4 To transmit or take part in a broadcast program. —*adj.* 1 Of or for transmission by broadcasting. 2 Scattered widely, as seed. —*n.* 1 The transmitting of a radio or television program. 2 A program so transmitted. —*adv.* Over an extended area. —**broad′cast′er** *n.*

**broad·cloth** (brôd′klôth′, -kloth′) *n.* 1 A fine, smooth-surfaced wool cloth. 2 A closely woven fabric of silk, cotton, etc.

**bro·cade** (brō·kād′) *n.* A rich fabric with a raised interwoven design. —*v.t.* **·cad·ed**, **·cad·ing** To weave (cloth) with a raised design. [<Med. L *broccare* embroider]

**bro·chure** (brō·shŏor′) *n.* A pamphlet. [<F *brocher* to stitch]

**brogue**[1] (brōg) *n.* A dialectal accent, esp. an Irish accent, in speaking English. [? <BROGUE[2]]

**brogue**[2] (brōg) *n.* 1 A heavy oxford shoe with decorative perforations. 2 A shoe of untanned hide formerly worn in Ireland and Scotland. [<Ir. *brōg* brogue (def. 2)]

**broil** (broil) *v.t.* 1 To cook, as meat, by subjecting to direct heat. 2 To expose to great heat. —*v.i.* 3 To become cooked by broiling. 4 To be exposed to great heat. —*n.* 1 Something broiled. 2 A broiling heat. [<OF *bruller*]

**bro·ken** (brō′kən) *p.p.* of BREAK. —*adj.* 1 Shattered; fractured. 2 Not working; out of order. 3 Violated; disregarded: *broken* oaths. 4 Not continuous; interrupted. 5 Incomplete: a *broken* set. 6 Disordered; disrupted. 7 Rough or irregular. 8 Crushed, as in spirit. 9 Weakened; infirm. 10 Tamed; trained. 11 Imperfectly spoken: *broken* English. —**bro′ken·ly** *adv.* —**bro′ken·ness** *n.*

**bro·ker** (brō′kər) *n.* One who acts as a commissioned agent in negotiating contracts, buying and selling stocks, real estate, etc. [ME, peddler]

**bron·chi·tis** (brong·kī′tis) *n.* Inflammation of

the bronchial tubes, or, loosely, of the bronchi or trachea. [<Gk. *bronchos* windpipe + -ITIS] —**bron·chit·ic** (brong·kit′ik) *adj.*

**bron·co** (brong′kō) *n. pl.* **·cos** A small, wild, or partly broken horse of the w U.S. **Also bron′cho.** [<Sp., rough]

**bronze** (bronz) *n.* 1 A reddish brown alloy of copper, esp. with tin. 2 The color of bronze. 3 A sculpture cast in bronze. —*v.* **bronzed**, **bronz·ing** *v.t.* 1 To color like or cover with bronze. —*v.i.* 2 To become brown or tan. [<Ital. *bronzo*] —**bronz′y** *adj.* (·i·er, ·i·est)

**brooch** (brōch, brōōch) *n.* An ornamental pin fastened with a clasp. [Var. of BROACH, *n.*]

**brood** (brōōd) *n.* 1 All the young birds of a single hatching. 2 The children of a household. —*v.t.* 1 To sit upon or incubate (eggs). 2 To protect (young) by or as by covering with the wings. —*v.i.* 3 To sit on eggs; incubate. 4 To think about gloomily and persistently; ponder moodily. —*adj.* Kept for breeding: a *brood* mare. [<OE *brod*]

**brook**[1] (brŏŏk) *n.* A small, natural stream. [<OE *brōc*]

**brook**[2] (brŏŏk) *v.t.* To put up with; tolerate: He will *brook* no disobedience. [<OE *brūcan* use, enjoy]

**broom** (brōōm, brŏŏm) *n.* 1 A brush with a long handle, used for sweeping. 2 Any of various leguminous shrubs with flexible shoots and usu. yellow flowers. —*v.t.* To sweep with a broom. [<OE *brōm*]

**broth** (brôth, broth) *n.* Thin soup consisting of the water in which meat, vegetables, etc., have been boiled. [<OE]

**brow** (brou) *n.* 1 The forehead. 2 An eyebrow. 3 The countenance in general. 4 The upper edge of a cliff, precipice, etc. [<OE *brū*]

**browse** (brouz) *v.* **browsed**, **brows·ing** *v.i.* 1 To feed on leaves, twigs, etc. 2 To read or inspect casually. —*v.t.* 3 To nibble at (leaves, twigs, etc.). —*n.* Leaves, twigs, etc., eaten by animals. [<MF *broust* bud, sprout] —**brows′er** *n.*

**bruise** (brōōz) *v.* **bruised**, **bruis·ing** *v.t.* 1 To injure, as by a blow, without breaking the surface of the skin. 2 To dent or mar the surface of. 3 To hurt or offend slightly, as feelings. 4 To crush, as with a mortar and pestle. —*v.i.* 5 To become discolored as the result of a blow. —*n.* A surface injury, usu. with discoloration of the skin. [Fusion of OE *brȳsan* crush and OF *bruisier* break, shatter]

**brunch** (brunch) *n.* A meal combining breakfast and lunch. [Blend of BREAKFAST and LUNCH]

bru·nette (broō·net′) *adj.* BRUNET. —*n.* A woman or girl with dark hair, complexion, etc. [<F *brun* brown]

brunt (brunt) *n.* The main force or impact of a blow, attack, etc. [?]

brush (brush) *n.* 1 An implement having bristles, hair, wires, etc., fixed in a handle or a back, and used for applying paint, removing dirt, grooming the hair, etc. 2 The act of brushing. 3 A light, grazing touch. 4 A short, brisk fight; skirmish. 5 Something resembling a brush, as the bushy tail of a fox. 6 An electrical conductor bearing on the commutator of a dynamo or motor. —*v.t.* 1 To sweep, polish, smooth, paint, etc., with a brush. 2 To remove with or as with a brush. 3 To touch lightly in passing. 4 To refuse to consider; dismiss: used with *aside, away,* or *off.* —*v.i.* 5 To move with a slight contact: to *brush* past someone. —**brush up** To refresh one's knowledge or skill. [<OF *brosse*]

brusque (brusk, *esp. Brit.* broōsk) *adj.* Blunt or gruff, esp. so as to cause offense; rudely abrupt. **Also brusk.** [<Ital. *brusco* rough, rude] —**brusque′ly** *adv.* —**brusque′ness** *n.* —**Syn.** curt, short, bluff.

bru·tal (broōt′l) *adj.* 1 Of or typical of a brute; savagely cruel; unfeeling. 2 Harsh; insufferable; punishing: *brutal* weather; He maintained a *brutal* pace. [<L *brutus* stupid] —**bru′tal·ly** *adv.* —**Syn.** bestial, barbarous, inhuman, savage.

brute (broōt) *n.* 1 An animal as distinguished from a human being. 2 A brutal person. —*adj.* 1 Of or typical of a brute; animal. 2 Merely physical: *brute* force. [<L *brutus* stupid]

bub·ble (bub′əl) *n.* 1 A rounded film of cohesive liquid filled with air or other gas. 2 A globule of air or other gas confined in a liquid or solid. 3 A usu. transparent glass or plastic dome. 4 Something insubstantial or delusive. 5 The process or sound of bubbling. —*v.* ·bled, ·bling *v.i.* 1 To form or rise in bubbles. 2 To move or flow with a gurgling sound. 3 To behave in a lively, irrepressible manner. —*v.t.* 4 To cause to bubble. 5 To utter as by bubbling. [ME *buble*] —**bub′bly** *adj.* (·i·er, ·i·est)

buck (buk) *n.* 1 A male deer, rabbit, etc. 2 A sudden upward leap, as of a horse. 3 A dashing young fellow. —*v.i.* 1 To leap upward suddenly, as a horse trying to dis-

lodge a rider. 2 To charge with the head down. 3 To move with jerks and jolts. —*v.t.* 4 To throw by bucking. 5 To butt with the head. 6 To resist stubbornly; struggle against. 7 To charge into (the opposing line in football). —**buck for** *Slang* To strive for (a raise, promotion, etc.). —**buck up** *Informal* To cheer up. —*adj.* Being of the lowest grade within a class: *buck* sergeant. [Fusion of OE *buc* he-goat and *bucca* male deer] —**buck′er** *n.*

buck·et (buk′it) *n.* 1 A cylindrical container with a curved handle at the top; a pail. 2 As much as a bucket will hold: also **buck·′et·ful′.** 3 A scooplike part, as of a steam shovel. —*v.t.* 1 To draw or carry in a bucket. —*v.i.* 2 To move along rapidly. —**kick the bucket** *Slang* To die. [<OF *buket* kind of tub]

buck·le (buk′əl) *n.* 1 A metal clasp for fastening together ends of a strap, belt, etc. 2 An ornament resembling this, as on a shoe. —*v.t. & v.i.* ·led, ·ling To fasten or be fastened with a buckle. —**buckle down** To apply oneself vigorously or industriously. [<F *boucle* cheek strap, boss of a shield]

budge (buj) *v.t. & v.i.* budged, budg·ing 1 To move or stir slightly. 2 To give in or cause to give in. [<F *bouger* stir, move]

budg·et (buj′it) *n.* 1 A statement of probable revenue and expenditure and of financial proposals for the ensuing year. 2 A summary of probable income for a given period, with approximate allowances for certain expenditures. 3 A collection or stock of items. —*v.t.* 1 To determine in advance the expenditure of (time, money, etc.) over a period of time. 2 To put on or into a budget. —*v.i.* 3 To make a budget. [<L *bulga* leather bag] —**budg·et·ar·y** (buj′ə·ter′ē) *adj.* —**budg′et·er** *n.*

buf·fa·lo (buf′ə·lō) *n. pl.* ·loes or ·los or ·lo 1 Any of several wild or domesticated oxlike mammals, as the water buffalo, etc. 2 The North American bison. —*v.t.* *Slang* To overawe; hoodwink. [<Gk. *boubalos* buffalo]

buf·fet (buf′it) *n.* 1 To strike or cuff, as with the hand. 2 To strike again and again; knock about, as if by blows: *buffeted* by high winds. 3 To force (a way) by pushing or striking. —*v.i.* 4 To struggle. 5 To force a way. —*n.* A blow; cuff. [<OF *buffe* blow, slap] —**buf′fet·er** *n.*

buf·foon (bu·foōn′, bə-) *n.* 1 One given to jokes, coarse pranks, etc.; a clown. 2 A loutish or inept person. [<Ital. *buffone* clown] —buf·foon′er·y *n.* —buf·foon′ish *adj.*

bug (bug) *n.* 1 Any of a large variety of insects with piercing and sucking mouth parts. 2 Loosely, any insect. 3 *Informal* A pathogenic microorganism. 4 *Informal* Any small but troublesome defect in a motor, machine, etc. 5 *Slang* An enthusiast. 6 *Informal* A miniature electronic microphone, used in wiretapping, etc. —*v.* bugged, bug·ging *v.i.* 1 To stare; stick out: said of eyes. —*v.t.* 2 *Informal* To fix an electronic eavesdropping device in (a room, etc.) or to (a wire, etc.). 3 *Slang* To annoy or anger; also to bewilder or puzzle. —bug off *Slang* Go away! Get lost! —bug out *Slang* To quit, esp. hastily or ignominiously. [?]

bug·gy¹ (bug′ē) *n. pl.* ·gies 1 A light, horse-drawn vehicle. 2 A baby carriage. [?]

bug·gy² (bug′ē) *adj.* ·gi·er, ·gi·est 1 Infested with bugs. 2 *Slang* Crazy. —bug′gi·ness *n.*

bu·gle (byōō′gəl) *n.* A brass, trumpetlike instrument, usu. without keys or valves. — *v.t. & v.i.* bu·gled, bu·gling 1 To summon with a bugle. 2 To sound a bugle. [<L *buculus,* dim. of *bos* ox; because first made from the horns of oxen] —bu′gler *n.*

build (bild) *v.* built (*Archaic* build·ed), build·ing *v.t.* 1 To construct, erect, or make by assembling separate parts or materials. 2 To establish and increase: often with *up:* to *build* up a business. 3 To make a basis for; found: immigrants who *built* a new life. —*v.i.* 4 To construct a house, building, etc. 5 To be in the business of building. 6 To grow in intensity, force, etc.: often with *up.* 7 To base or form an idea, theory, etc.: with *on* or *upon.* —build up 1 To renew or strengthen, as health. 2 To fill, as an area, with houses. —*n.* The manner in which a person or thing is shaped or formed; form; figure: a good *build;* a slight or husky *build.* [<OE *byldan*]

bulb (bulb) *n.* 1 An underground plant stem having a cluster of thickened leaves above and sending down roots, as in the onion, lily, etc. 2 An underground stem resembling a bulb, as a corm, tuber, or rhizome. 3 An enlargement resembling a plant bulb, as the end of a thermometer tube. 4 An incandescent electric lamp. [<Gk. *bolbos* bulbous root] —bul·ba·ceous (bul·bā′shəs), bul′bar, bul′bous *adj.* • See INCANDESCENT.

bulge (bulj) *v.t. & v.i.* bulged, bulg·ing To swell out; make or be protuberant. —*n.*

Something that swells out or protrudes. [<OF *boulge*] —bulg′y *adj.* —bulg′i·ness *n.*

bulk (bulk) *n.* 1 Mass, volume, or size, esp. if large or great. 2 A large body, esp. a human body. 3 The largest or principal part. —In bulk Loose; not boxed or packaged. —*v.i.* 1 To have an appearance of largeness or weight. 2 To be of importance: to *bulk* large in his thought. —*v.t.* 3 To cause to expand or grow large. [<ON *būlki* heap, cargo]

bull¹ (bŏŏl) *n.* 1 The male of cattle or of some other animals, as of the elephant, moose, giraffe, whale, seal, etc. 2 A dealer who seeks or expects higher prices, and buys stocks or bonds accordingly. 3 One whose actions or looks suggest a bull. 4 *Slang* A policeman. 5 *Slang* Exaggerated or non-sensical talk. —*v.t.* 1 To attempt to raise the price of or in. 2 To push or force (a way). — *v.i.* 3 To go up in price: said of stocks, etc. —*adj.* 1 Male. 2 Large; bull-like. 3 Going up or advancing: a *bull* market. [OE *bola*]

bull² (bŏŏl) *n.* An official edict or decree issued by the Pope. [<L *bulla* edict, seal]

bull·doz·er (bŏŏl′dō′zər) *n.* 1 A powerful tractor with a heavy plowing blade, used for moving soil, cleaning debris, etc. 2 *Slang* One who bulldozes.

bul·let (bŏŏl′it) *n.* 1 A small projectile for a firearm. 2 Any small ball. [<F *boule* ball]

bul·le·tin (bŏŏl′ə·tən) *n.* 1 A brief news item, usu. of special or immediate interest. 2 A periodical publication, as of the proceedings of a society. —*v.t.* To make public by bulletin. [<L *bulla* edict] —bul′le·tin·ist *n.*

bull·frog (bŏŏl′frog′, -frôg′) *n.* A large frog with a deep hoarse voice.

bul·lion (bŏŏl′yən) *n.* Gold or silver uncoined or in mass, as in ingots. [<AF *bullion*]

bul·ly¹ (bŏŏl′ē) *n. pl.* bul·lies A person who likes to hurt or intimidate those weaker than himself. —*adj.* bul·li·er, bul·li·est 1 *Informal* Excellent, admirable. 2 Jolly; dashing; gallant. —*interj.* Well done! —*v.* bul·lied, bul·ly·ing *v.t.* 1 To coerce by threats; intimidate. —*v.i.* 2 To be quarrelsome and blustering. [?]

bul·ly² (bŏŏl′ē) *n.* Canned or pickled beef. Also bul′ly·beef′ (-bēf′). [?<F *bouillir* boil]

bul·wark (bŏŏl′wərk) *n.* 1 A defensive wall or rampart. 2 A person or thing considered as a strong support or defense. 3 *Usu. pl.* The raised side of a ship, above the upper deck. —*v.t.* To fortify with, or as with, a bulwark. [<MHG *bolwerc*]

bum (bum) *n. Informal* 1 A shiftless, often

drunken loafer or beggar. 2 A hobo; tramp.
3 An irresponsible devotee: a ski *bum*. —
*adj.* **bum·mer, bum·mest** *Slang* 1 Bad; inferior. 2 Ailing. —*v.* **bum·med, bum·ming** *Informal v.i.* 1 To live by sponging from others. 2 To loaf. —*v.t.* 3 To get by begging. [Short for *bummer*, alter. of G *bummler* loafer, dawdler] —**bum′mer** *n.*

**bum·ble·bee** (bum′bəl·bē′) *n.* Any of certain large, hairy, social bees.

**bump** (bump) *v.t.* 1 To come into contact with; knock into. 2 To cause to knock into or against. 3 *Informal* To displace, as from a position or seat. —*v.i.* 4 To come into contact; collide. 5 To move with jerks and jolts. 6 *Slang* To do a bump (def. 3). —*n.* 1 An impact or collision; a jolt. 2 A swelling, protuberance, or rough part. 3 *Slang* A sharp forward movement of the pelvis, as in a striptease. [Imit.]

**bump·er** (bum′pər) *n.* A guard on the front or rear of an automobile to absorb the shock of collision.

**bun** (bun) *n.* 1 A small bread roll, usu. sweetened or spiced. 2 A roll of hair worn at the nape of the neck. [ME *bunne*]

**bunch** (bunch) *n.* 1 A group of usu. like objects growing or fastened together. 2 *Informal* A group or cluster, as of people. —*v.t. & v.i.* 1 To make into or form bunches or groups. 2 To gather, as in pleats or folds. [ME *bonche, bunche*]

**bun·dle** (bun′dəl) *n.* 1 A number of things or a quantity of anything bound together. 2 A parcel or package. 3 A group; collection. 4 *Slang* A large sum of money. —*v.* **·dled, ·dling** *v.t.* 1 To tie, roll, or otherwise secure in a bundle. 2 To send away in haste: with *away, off, out,* or *into.* —*v.i.* 3 To leave or move hastily. 4 To practice bundling. — **bundle up** To dress warmly for outdoors. [<MDu. *bond* group] —**bun′dler** *n.*

**bun·ga·low** (bung′gə·lō) *n.* 1 In India, a one-storied house with wide verandas. 2 A small house or cottage. [<Hind. *banglā* Bengalese]

**bun·gle** (bung′gəl) *v.t. & v.i.* **·gled, ·gling** To do (something) badly; botch. —*n.* An imperfect job or performance; botch. —**bun′gler** *n.* [? < Scand.]

**bun·ion** (bun′yən) *n.* A painful swelling of the bursa at the base of the great toe. [? < OF *bugne* swelling]

**bunk**[1] (bungk) *n.* 1 A small compartment, shelf, or recess, used as a sleeping place. 2 *Informal* Any bed, esp. a small one. —*v.i.* 1

To sleep in a bunk or bed. 2 *Informal* To sleep overnight, esp. in makeshift accommodations. —*v.t.* 3 To provide with a bunk or place to sleep. [?]

**bunk**[2] (bungk) *n.* *Slang* Inflated or empty speech; balderdash. [Short for BUNCOMBE]

**buoy** (boi, boo′e) *n.* 1 A float moored near a dangerous rock or shoal or at the edge of a channel, as a guide to ·navigators. 2 LIFE BUOY. —*v.t.* 1 To keep from sinking in a liquid; keep afloat. 2 To sustain the courage or heart of; encourage: usu. with *up.* 3 To mark, as a channel, with buoys. [<MDu. *boeie*]

**bur·den** (bûr′dən) *n.* 1 Something carried; a load. 2 Something difficult to bear, as a worry, responsibility, etc. 3 The carrying of loads: beasts of *burden.* 4 *Naut.* a The carrying capacity of a vessel. b The weight of the cargo. —*v.t.* 1 To load or overload. 2 To oppress, as with care. [<OE *byrthen* load]

**bu·reau** (byoor′ō) *n. pl.* **bu·reaus** or **bu·reaux** (byoor′ōz) 1 A chest of drawers for clothing. 2 A government department or subdivision of a department. 3 Any agency providing specialized information and services: travel *bureau.* [<F, cloth-covered desk]

**bur·glar** (bûr′glər) *n.* One who commits a burglary. [<Med.L *burglator*]

**bur·i·al** (ber′ē·əl) *n.* The burying of a dead body. [<OE *byrgels* tomb]

**bur·lap** (bûr′lap) *n.* A coarse fabric made of jute or hemp, used for wrapping, bagging, etc. [?]

**bur·lesque** (bər·lesk′) *n.* 1 Broad, satirical imitation or caricature; parody. 2 A product of such imitation, as a literary work. 3 A theatrical entertainment marked by low comedy, striptease, etc. —*v.* **·lesqued, ·lesquing** *v.t.* 1 To imitate or parody by using burlesque. —*v.i.* 2 To use burlesque. [<Ital. *burla* joke] —**bur·les′quer** *n.*

**bur·ly** (bûr′lē) *adj.* **bur·li·er, bur·li·est** 1 Large and muscular of body; stout. 2 Rough and lusty in manner. [ME *borlich*] —**bur′li·ly** *adv.* —**bur′li·ness** *n.*

**burn** (bûrn) *v.* **burned** or **burnt, burn·ing** *v.t.* 1 To destroy or consume by fire. 2 To set afire; ignite. 3 To injure or kill by fire. 4 To injure or damage by friction, heat, steam, etc.; scald; wither. 5 To produce by fire, as a hole in a suit. 6 To brand; also, to cauterize. 7 To finish or harden by intense heat; fire. 8 To use or employ so as to give off light, heat, etc. 9 To cause a feeling of heat in. 10 To sunburn. 11 To transform into energy, as fat in body tissues. 12 *Slang* To electrocute. 13 *Slang* To cheat. —*v.i.* 14 To be on fire; blaze. 15 To be destroyed, damaged, or changed by fire. 16 To give off light, heat, etc.; shine. 17 To die by fire. 18 To appear or feel hot. 19 To be eager, excited, or inflamed. 20 To oxidize; undergo combustion. 21 *Slang* To be electrocuted. — **burn out** 1 To become extinguished through lack of fuel. 2 To destroy or wear out by heat, friction, etc. —**burn up** 1 To consume by fire. 2 *Slang* To make or become irritated or enraged. —*n.* 1 An effect or injury from burning; a burnt place. 2 The process or result of burning. 3 *Aerospace* A single firing of a space rocket. [Fusion of OE *beornan* be on fire and OE *bærnan* set afire]

**bur·nish** (bûr′nish) *v.t. & v.i.* To polish by friction; make or become brilliant or shiny. —*n.* Polish; luster. [< OF *burnir* polish] —**bur′nish·er, bur′nish·ment** *n.*

**bur·ro** (bûr′ō, bŏŏr′ō) *n. pl.* ·ros A small donkey, used as a pack animal. [Sp.]

**bur·row** (bûr′ō) *n.* A hole or tunnel made in the ground, as by an animal, for shelter, etc. —*v.t.* 1 To make by burrowing. 2 To perforate with burrows. —*v.i.* 3 To live or hide in or as in a burrow. 4 To make a burrow. [ME *borow*] —**bur′row·er** *n.*

**burst** (bûrst) *v.* **burst, burst·ing** *v.i.* 1 To break open or come apart suddenly and violently; explode, as from internal force. 2 To be full of something to the breaking point. 3 To issue forth or enter suddenly or violently. 4 To appear or begin; become audible or evident, etc. 5 To give sudden expression to passion, grief, etc. —*v.t.* 6 To cause to break open suddenly or violently; puncture. 7 To fill or cause to swell to the point of breaking open. —*n.* 1 The act or result of bursting. 2 A sudden eruption, as of feeling. 3 A sudden effort; spurt. 4 A series of shots fired. [< OE *berstan*] —**burst′er** *n.* —**Syn.** *v.* 1, 6 rupture, shatter, tear, rip, rend.

**bury** (ber′ē) *v.t.* **bur·ied, bur·y·ing** 1 To put (a dead body) in a grave, etc.; inter. 2 To conceal in the ground. 3 To cover, as for concealment. 4 To sink or embed. 5 To end; put out of mind; to *bury* a quarrel. 6 To occupy deeply; engross: He *buried* himself in study. [< OE *byrgan*]

**bush¹** (bŏŏsh) *n.* 1 A low, thickly branching shrub. 2 A thick growth of shrubs. 3 Land that is unsettled, remote, often arid, and

covered with a scrubby undergrowth, esp. such land in Australia: with *the*. 4 A bushy tail. —*v.i.* 1 To grow or branch like a bush. —*v.t.* 2 To protect or support with bushes. —*adj. Slang* Bush-league; small-time. [ME *bussche*]

**bush·el** (bŏŏsh′əl) *n.* 1 A measure of capacity; four pecks, 35.238 liters, or 2150.42 cubic inches. 2 A vessel holding that amount. 3 *Informal* A large amount. [< OF *boissel*]

**bust** (bust) *Slang v.t.* 1 To burst. 2 To tame; train, as a horse. 3 To make bankrupt or short of funds. 4 To reduce in rank; demote. 5 To arrest. 6 To hit; strike. —*v.i.* 7 To burst. 8 To become bankrupt or short of funds. —*n.* 1 Failure; bankruptcy. 2 A spree. 3 An arrest. [Alter. of BURST]

**bus·tle** (bus′əl) *n.* Excited activity; noisy stir; fuss. —*v.t. & v.i.* ·**tled,** ·**tling** To hurry noisily; make a stir or fuss. [?]

**bus·y** (biz′ē) *adj.* **bus·i·er, bus·i·est** 1 Intensely active; constantly occupied. 2 Temporarily engaged; not at leisure. 3 Prying; meddling. 4 In use, as a telephone. 5 Full of varied designs, colors, etc., usu. excessively so. —*v.t.* **bus·ied, bus·y·ing** To make or be busy. [<OE *bysig* active]

**butch·er** (bŏŏch′ər) *n.* 1 One who slaughters animals or deals in meats for food. 2 A bloody or cruel murderer. 3 A vendor of candy, cigarettes, etc., on trains, in theaters, etc. —*v.t.* 1 To slaughter or dress (animals) for market. 2 To kill (people or game) barbarously or brutally. 3 *Slang* To botch. [<OF *bouchier*<*boc* buck, he-goat]

**but·ler** (but′lər) *n.* The chief male servant in a household, usu. in charge of the dining room, wine, plate, etc. [<OF *bouteillier* bottle-bearer<Med. L] —**but′ler·ship** *n.*

**but·ter** (but′ər) *n.* 1 The fatty constituent of milk, separated by churning into a soft, whitish yellow solid, processed for cooking and table use. 2 A substance like butter — *v.t.* 1 To put butter on. 2 *Informal* To flatter: usu. with *up*. [<OE *butere*, ult.<Gk. *boutyron* lit. cow cheese]

**but·ter·fly** (but′ər·flī′) *n. pl.* ·**flies** 1 A diurnal lepidopterous insect with large, often brightly colored wings, knobbed antennae, and slender body. 2 One who lives frivolously. [<OE *buttor flēoge*]

**but·ter·milk** (but′ər·milk′) *n.* The sour liquid left after the butterfat has been separated from milk or cream.

**but·ton** (but′n) *n.* 1 A knob or disk, as of

bone, metal, leather, etc., used as an ornament or fastening. 2 Anything like a button. 3 A knob or protuberance, as for operating an electric switch, etc. 4 *Slang* The point of the jaw. —*v.t.* 1 To fasten with or as with a button or buttons. 2 To provide with buttons. —*v.i.* 3 To admit of being buttoned. [<OF *boton* button, bud] —**but′ton·er** *n.*

**bux·om** (buk′səm) *adj.* 1 Attractively plump and well-proportioned: said of women. 2 Having a large bosom. [<OE *būhsum* pliant] —**bux′om·ly** *adv.* —**bux′om·ness** *n.*

**buy** (bī) *v.* **bought, buy·ing** *v.t.* 2 To obtain for a price; purchase. 2 To be a price for. 3 To obtain by an exchange or sacrifice: to *buy* wisdom with experience. 4 To bribe; corrupt. 5 *Slang* To accept as true, possible, etc. —*v.i.* 6 To make purchases; be a purchaser. —**buy off** To bribe. —**buy out** To purchase the stock, interests, etc., of, as in a business. —*n. Informal* 1 A purchase. 2 A bargain. [<OE *bycgan*] —**buy′a·ble** *adj.* —**buy′er** *n.*

**buzz** (buz) *v.i.* 1 To make a vibrating hum, as a bee. 2 To discuss or gossip excitedly. 3 To bustle about. —*v.t.* 4 To utter or gossip about in a buzzing manner. 5 To cause to buzz, as wings. 6 To fly an airplane low over. 7 To summon with a buzzer. 8 *Informal* To telephone. —*n.* 1 A low vibrating hum, as of bees, of talk, or of distant sounds. 2 Rumor; gossip. 3 Activity; bustle. 4 The sound of a buzzer. 5 *Informal* A telephone call. [Imit.]

**buzz·ard** (buz′ərd) *n.* 1 One of several large, slow-flying hawks. 2 TURKEY BUZZARD. [<OF *busart* <L *buteo* hawk]

**by** (bī) *prep.* 1 Next to; near: the house *by* the road. 2 Toward: west *by* north. 3 Past or beyond: The train flashed *by* us. 4 In the course of; during: birds flying *by* night. 5 Not later than: Be here *by* four tomorrow. 6 For the period of; according to: They work *by* the day. 7 As a result of the effort, means, or action of: a play written *by* Shakespeare. 8 With the perception of: a loss felt *by* all. 9 By means of: leading a child *by* the hand. 10 In consequence of: a case won *by* default. 11 As a means of conveyance; via: Mail your letters *by* air. 12 To the extent or amount of: insects *by* the thousands. 13 On the basis of: four miles long *by* actual measurement. 14 Considered according to: advancing step *by* step; reading word *by* word. 15 With reference to:

to do well *by* one's friends. 16 And; and in another dimension: used in numerical measurements and processes: to divide 9 *by* 3; a room ten *by* twelve. 17 In the name of: swearing *by* all that is sacred. —*adv.* 1 At hand; near: to keep one's sword *by.* 2 Up to and beyond something; past: the train roared *by.* 3 Apart; aside: to lay something *by.* 4 At or into a person's house, store, etc.: to stop *by.* —*adj. & n.* BYE. [<OE *bī* near, about]

**by·pass** (bī′pas′, -päs′) *n.* Any road, channel, duct, or route that is auxiliary to the one normally used; a detour. —*v.t.* 1 To go around (an obstacle). 2 To provide with a bypass. 3 To pay no attention to.

**by·prod·uct** (bī′prod′əkt) *n.* 1 Any material or product produced in the making of something else. 2 A secondary result or effect.

**by·word** (bī′wûrd′) *n.* 1 A proverb, common saying, etc. 2 Something that has become an object of derision. [<OE *biword* proverb]

# C

**cab** (kab) *n.* 1 TAXICAB. 2 A one-horse public carriage. 3 The part of a locomotive, truck, crane, etc., where the controls are operated. [Short form of CABRIOLET]

**ca·bal** (kə·bal′) *n.* 1 A number of persons secretly united, as in a plot or conspiracy. 2 Intrigue; conspiracy. —*v.i.* **ca·balled, ca·bal·ling** To form a cabal; plot. [<Med. L *cabala* cabala]

**ca·ba·na** (kə·bä′nə, -ban′ə) *n.* 1 A small cabin. 2 A small bathhouse, as on a beach. Also **ca·ba′ña** (-bän′yə, -ban′yə). [<Sp.]

**cab·in** (kab′in) *n.* 1 A small, crudely built house; hut. 2 A compartment in a vessel, aircraft, etc., for crew or passengers. —*v.t. & v.i.* To shut up or dwell in or as in a cabin. [<LL *capanna*]

**cab·i·net** (kab′ə·nit) *n.* 1 A piece of furniture, case, etc., with shelves, drawers, or compartments. 2 *Often cap.* The body of official advisers of a chief of state. 3 A private council room or study. —*adj.* Of or suitable for a cabinet. [<OF *cabine*]

**ca·ble** (kā′bəl) *n.* 1 A heavy rope of wire strands, hemp, etc. 2 A unit of nautical measure, 720 feet in the U.S. and 608 feet in England. Also **cable length, cable's length.** 3 An insulated electrical conductor or group of conductors protected by an outer covering. 4 CABLEGRAM. —*v.* ·**bled,**

·**bling** v.t. 1 To send a cablegram to. 2 To fasten with a cable. —v.i. 3 To send a cablegram. [<LL *capulum* rope]

**cack·le** (kak′əl) v. ·**led**, ·**ling** v.i. 1 To make a shrill cry, as a hen that has laid an egg. 2 To laugh or talk with a sound resembling this. —v.i. 3 To utter in a cackling manner. —n. 1 The shrill, broken cry made by a hen after laying an egg. 2 A laugh or sound resembling this. 3 Idle talk. [Imit.] —**cack′ler** n.

**cac·tus** (kak′təs) n. pl. ·**tus·es** or ·**ti** (-tī) Any of a family of plants native to arid regions of America, having fleshy, usu. leafless and spiny stems and often showy flowers. [<Gk. *kaktos* a prickly plant]

**ca·dav·er** (kə·dav′ər, -dā′vər) n. A dead body, esp. a human corpse intended for dissection. [<L]

**cad·die** (kad′ē) n. One paid to carry clubs for golf players. —v.i. ·**died**, ·**dy·ing** To act as a caddie. [<CADET]

**ca·dence** (kād′ns) n. 1 Rhythmic flow, as of poetry. 2 Rhythmic beat or measure, as of marching. 3 Modulation or inflection, as of the voice. 4 A formula for ending a phrase, section, etc. Also **ca′den·cy**. [<LL *cadentia* a falling]

**ca·det** (kə·det′) n. 1 A student at a military or naval school who is training for commissioning as an officer. 2 A younger son or brother. [F, ult. < dim. of L *caput* head, chief] —**ca·det′ship** n.

**ca·fé** (kə·fā′, ka-) n. 1 A coffee house, restaurant, barroom, etc. 2 Coffee. Also **ca·fé.** [F]

**ca·fé au lait** (kà·fā′ ō lā′) French 1 Coffee with scalded milk. 2 A light brown.

**caf·e·te·ri·a** (kaf′ə·tir′ē·ə) n. A restaurant where the patrons wait upon themselves. [<Am. Sp., coffee store]

**cage** (kāj) n. 1 A structure enclosed with bars or wires, for confining birds, animals, etc. 2 A structure or enclosure resembling this. 3 In baseball, a backstop used for batting practice. 4 In hockey, the frame and network forming the goal. 5 In basketball, the basket. —v.t. **caged**, **cag·ing** To confine in or as in a cage. [<L *cavea* an enclosure < *cavus* empty, hollow]

**ca·jole** (kə·jōl′) v.t. & v.i. ·**joled**, ·**jol·ing** To persuade or coax with flattery; wheedle. [<F *cajoler*] —**ca·jole′ment**, **ca·jol′er**, **ca·jol′er·y** n. —**ca·jol′ing·ly** adv.

**ca·lam·i·ty** (kə·lam′ə·tē) n. pl. ·**ties** 1 An event causing great suffering, grief, or misery;

disaster. 2 A state or time of affliction, distress, etc. [<L *calamitas*]

**cal·cu·late** (kal′kyə·lāt) v. ·**lat·ed**, ·**lat·ing** v.t. 1 To determine by arithmetical means. 2 To ascertain beforehand; determine by estimation. 3 To adapt to a purpose; intend: used chiefly in the passive: *calculated* to carry a two-ton load. 4 *Regional* To suppose; believe. —v.i. 5 To compute. 6 *Informal* To rely; depend. [<LL *calculatus*, pp. of *calculare* reckon < *calculus* a pebble used in reckoning] —**Syn.** 1 compute, figure, reckon. 2 estimate, surmise, presume, conjecture.

**cal·dron** (kôl′drən) n. A large kettle or boiler. [<L *caldaria* kettle <*calidus* hot]

**cal·en·dar** (kal′ən·dər) n. 1 A systematic arrangement of subdivisions of time, as years, months, days, weeks, etc. 2 A table showing such subdivisions, esp. of a single year. 3 A schedule or list: a *calendar* of events. —v.t. To register in a calendar or list. [<L *calendae* calends]

**calf** (kaf, käf) n. pl. **calves** (kavz, kävz) 1 The young of cattle. 2 The young of certain mammals, as the elephant, whale, etc. 3 Leather made from the skin of a calf. 4 *Informal* An awkward young fellow. [<OE *cealf*]

**cal·i·ber** (kal′ə·bər) n. 1 The internal diameter of a tube or of the barrel of a gun, cannon, etc. 2 The diameter of a bullet, shell, etc. 3 Degree of personal ability or quality. Also **cal′i·bre.** [<Ar. *qālib* mold, form]

**cal·i·co** (kal′i·kō) n. pl. ·**coes** or ·**cos** A cotton cloth printed in bright colors. —adj. 1 Made of calico. 2 Resembling calico; dappled or spotted: a *calico* cat. [<*Calicut*, India]

**cal·i·per** (kal′ə·pər) n. Usu. pl. Any of various instruments for making precise measurements of dimensions. —v.t. & v.i. To measure by using calipers. [Var. of CALIBER.]

**cal·is·then·ics** (kal′is·then′iks) n. pl. 1 Light gymnastic exercises to promote physical fitness. 2 (construed as sing.) The art of practice of such exercises. [<Gk. *kallos* beauty + *sthenos* strength] —**cal′is·then′ic** adj.

**Cal·li·o·pe** (kə·lī′ə·pē) Gk. Myth. The Muse of eloquence and epic poetry.

**cal·lous** (kal′əs) adj. 1. Thickened and hardened, as the skin by friction or pressure. 2 Coldly or cruelly unfeeling. —v.t. & v.i. To make or become callous. [<L *callus* hard skin] —**cal′lous·ly** adv. —**cal′lous·ness** n.

—**Syn.** 2 insensitive, thick-skinned, hard, heartless, hardhearted.

**calm** (kām) *adj.* 1 Free from agitation; unruffled; composed. 2 Not turbulent; quiet; still. —*n.* 1 Lack of turbulence, wind, or motion. 2 Serenity; peacefulness. —*v.t.* & *v.i.* To make or become calm. [<LL *cauma* heat of the day, rest at midday] —**calm′ly** *adv.* —**calm′ness** *n.* —**Syn.** *adj.* 1 tranquil, serene, placid, peaceful, untroubled.

**cal·o·rie** (kal′ə·rē) *n.* 1 One of two units of heat. The **great, large,** or **kilogram calorie** is the amount of heat required to raise the temperature of one kilogram of water 1°C. The **small** or **gram calorie** is the amount of heat required to raise one gram of water 1°C. 2 The large calorie, used as a measure of the energy value of foods or the heat output of organisms. [<F *calorie* <L *calor* heat]

**cal·um·ny** (kal′əm·nē) *n.* *pl.* **·nies** 1 A false accusation or report made with malicious or injurious intent. 2 The making of such statements; defamation. [<L *calumnia* slander]

**ca·lyp·so** (kə·lip′sō) *n.* *pl.* **·sos** A type of improvised, often topical song that originated in Trinidad. [<Calypso]

**cam·bric** (kām′brik) *n.* A fine white linen or cotton fabric. [<Flemish *Kameryk* Cambrai, city in France]

**cam·el** (kam′əl) *n.* Either of two species of domesticated ruminants used as beasts of burden in arid regions of Africa and Asia: the **Arabian camel,** or dromedary, having one hump on the back, and the **Bactrian camel,** having two. [<Gk. *kamēlos* <Semitic]

**cam·e·o** (kam′ē·ō) *n.* *pl.* **·e·os** 1 A gem of onyx, agate, shell, etc., carved in relief with design and background of different colors. 2 A small part, as in a movie or TV show, played by a well-known performer. [<Ital. *cammeo*]

**cam·er·a** (kam′ər·ə, kam′rə) *n.* *pl.* **·er·as** *for defs.* 1 & 2, **·er·ae** *for def.* 3 1 A device for exposing a sensitized plate or film to light that forms an image thereon. 2 A device that converts optical images into electrical impulses for television transmission. 3 *Law* A judge's private room. —**in camera** *Law* Not in public court; privately. [<Gk. *kamara* vault]

**cam·ou·flage** (kam′ə·fläzh) *n.* 1 A protective disguise that matches, blends in with, or imitates natural surroundings. 2 Any disguise or pretense. —*v.t.* **·flaged, ·flag·ing** To

hide or obscure with or as with camouflage. [<F *camoufler* disguise] —**cam′ou·flag′er** *n.*

**cam·paign** (kam·pān′) *n.* 1 A series of military operations conducted for a particular objective. 2 A series of related political or other activities designed to bring about a result. —*v.i.* To conduct or take part in a campaign. [<L *campus* open field] —**cam·paign′er** *n.*

**cam·phor** (kam′fər) *n.* A crystalline compound with a penetrating odor and pungent taste, obtained synthetically or from the wood of an Asian tree, and used as a moth repellant, in medicine, etc. [<Ar. *kāfūr* <Malay *kāpūr*] —**cam·phor·ic** (kam·fôr′ik, -for′-) *adj.*

**cam·pus** (kam′pəs) *n.* The grounds of a school, college, etc. [L. field, plain]

**ca·nal** (kə·nal′) *n.* 1 An artificial waterway for navigation, irrigation, etc. 2 *Anat.* A duct, tube, or groove. 3 One of the faint lines visible on the planet Mars. 3 *Zool.* A groove. —*v.t.* **ca·nalled** or **ca·naled, ca·nal·ling** or **ca·nal·ing** To make a canal in or through. [<L *canalis* groove.]

**ca·nard** (kə·närd′, *Fr.* kà·når′) *n.* A false or baseless story or rumor. [F, lit., duck]

**ca·nar·y** (kə·nâr′ē) *n.* *pl.* **·nar·ies** 1 A small, usu. yellow songbird native to the Canary Islands, popular as a cage bird. 2 A bright yellow color: also **canary yellow.** 3 A sweet, white wine from the Canary Islands. [<L *Canaria* (*Insula*) Dog (Island) < the dogs found there]

**ca·nas·ta** (kə·nas′tə) *n.* A card game similar to rummy, using two decks. [<Sp., basket]

**can·cel** (kan′səl) *v.t.* **can·celed** or **·celled, can·cel·ing** or **·cel·ling** 1 To strike out, as by marking lines through; cross off. 2 To countermand or call off. 3 To stamp or mark, as a postage stamp, to prevent reuse. 4 To make up for; counterbalance. 5 *Math.* To eliminate (a common factor) by dividing the numerator and denominator of a fraction, or both sides of an equation. —*v.i.* 6 To be canceled or counterbalanced: with *out.* —*n.* A cancellation. [<L *cancellare* cross out] —**can′cel·a·ble, can′cel·la·ble** *adj.* —**can′cel·er, can′cel·ler** *n.* —**Syn.** 1 delete, expunge, obliterate. 2 repeal, annul, abrogate.

**can·cer** (kan′sər) *n.* 1 A malignant neoplasm, as carcinoma, sarcoma, etc. 2 Any baneful and spreading evil. [<L, crab, ulcer] —**can′cer·ous** *adj.*

**can·did** (kan′did) *adj.* 1 Frank, open, and sincere. 2 Impartial; fair. 3 Unposed; natural or informal: a *candid* snapshot. [<L *candidus* white, pure] —**can′did·ly** *adv.* —**can′did·ness** *n.* —**Syn.** 1 straightforward, outspoken, ingenuous, guileless.

**can·di·date** (kan′də·dāt, -dit) *n.* One seeking or considered for an elective office, position, honor, etc. [<L *candidatus* wearing white < the white togas of Roman candidates] —**can·di·da·cy** (kan′də·də·sē), **can·di·da·ture** (kan′də·də·chŏŏr, -dă′chər) *n.*

**can·dle** (kan′dəl) *n.* 1 A usu. cylindrical stick of wax, tallow, etc., containing a wick ignited to give light. 2 Something resembling this. 3 CANDELA. —**burn the candle at both ends** To expend one's energy or resources excessively. —**hold a candle to** To compare with favorably: usu. used in the negative. —*v.t.* **·dled, ·dling** To test (eggs) for freshness by holding between the eye and a light. [<L *candela* < *candere* shine, gleam] —**can′dler** *n.*

**can·dor** (kan′dər) *n.* 1 Openness; frankness. 2 Freedom from prejudice; impartiality; fairness. *Brit. sp.* **can′dour.** [<L, sincerity, purity, whiteness]

**cane** (kān) *n.* 1 A stick carried or used as an aid in walking. 2 A similar rod, esp. one used for flogging. 3 A plant, as bamboo, rattan, or sugar cane, having jointed, woody stems. 4 The stem of certain of these plants, often split and woven, as for furniture. 5 The woody stem of a raspberry, blackberry, rose, etc. —*v.t.* **caned, can·ing** 1 To strike or beat with a cane. 2 To weave or repair with cane, as a chair seat. [<Gk. *kanna* reed < Semitic] —**can′er** *n.*

**ca·nine** (kā′nīn) *adj.* Of, resembling, or characteristic of a dog or related animal. —*n.* 1 A dog or related animal, as a wolf, coyote, etc. 2 Any of the four conical teeth adjoining the incisors at the front of the upper and lower jaws: also **canine tooth.** [<L < *canis* dog] • See TOOTH.

**can·is·ter** (kan′is·tər) *n.* 1 A usu. metal container, as for tea, coffee, or spices. 2 A metal cylinder containing shot, etc., that shatters when fired, as from a cannon. [<L *canistrum* basket]

**can·ker** (kang′kər) *n.* 1 An ulcerous sore in the mouth. 2 A plant disease marked by dead tissue. 3 Any secret or spreading evil. —*v.t.* 1 To infect with canker. 2 To decay or corrupt. —*v.i.* 3 To be affected by a canker. [<L *cancer* crab, ulcer] —**can′ker·ous** *adj.*

**can·ni·bal** (kan′ə·bəl) *n.* 1 A human being

who eats human flesh. 2 An animal that devours members of its own species. [<Sp. *Canibales*, var. of *Caribes* Caribs] —**can′ni·bal·ism** *n.* —**can′ni·bal·is′tic** *adj.* —**can′ni·bal·is′ti·cal·ly** *adv.*

**can·non** (kan′ən) *n. pl.* **·nons** or **·non** 1 A large, usu. mounted tubular weapon for discharging a heavy projectile. 2 The large bone between the fetlock and knee of a horse or related animal: also **cannon bone.** 3 *Brit.* CAROM. —*v.t. & v.i.* 1 To fire or attack with cannon. 2 *Brit.* To carom or cause to carom.

**ca·noe** (kə·nŏŏ′) *n.* A light, narrow boat, pointed at both ends and propelled by paddles. —*v.t. & v.i.* To travel or convey by canoe. [<Sp. *canoa* boat] —**ca·noe′ist** *n.*

**can·on** (kan′ən) *n.* 1 A law, rule, or body of rules of a church. 2 An established rule or principle; standard; criterion. 3 Writings, as books of the Bible, considered holy or authoritative by a church, sect, etc. 4 An official list or catalogue. 5 *Often cap.* A portion of the Mass following the Sanctus. 6 *Music* A composition in which each voice or part in turn takes up the melody and all combine in counterpoint. [<Gk. *kanōn* rule, straight rod]

**can·o·py** (kan′ə·pē) *n. pl.* **·pies** 1 A covering or shelter suspended or supported over a throne, bed, entrance, etc. 2 Any similar overhead covering. —*v.t.* **·pied, ·py·ing** To cover with or as with a canopy. [<Gk. *kō nōpeion* bed with mosquito net < *kōnōps* mosquito]

**cant** (kant) *n.* 1 Hypocritically pious talk. 2 Any specialized or esoteric jargon or vocabulary: thieves' *cant*; legal *cant*. 3 Whining speech, as of beggars. —*v.i.* To use or speak in cant. [<L *cantus* song] —**cant′er** *n.*

**can·ta·loupe** (kan′tə·lōp) *n.* A variety of muskmelon with a hard, rough rind and orange flesh. Also **can′ta·loup.** [< *Cantalupo*, a villa near Rome]

**can·ta·ta** (kən·tä′tə) *n.* A vocal composition in several movements. [Ital. < *cantare* to sing]

**can·teen** (kan·tēn′) *n.* 1 A usu. metal flask for carrying drinking water, etc. 2 A shop at a military base where soldiers buy provisions, refreshments, etc. 3 A cafeteria, recreation center, etc., usu. operated by an institution. [< Ital. *cantina* cellar]

**can·ter** (kan′tər) *n.* A moderate, easy gallop. —*v.t. & v.i.* To ride or go at a canter. [<Short

for *Canterbury gallop;* with ref. to the pace of pilgrims riding to Canterbury]

**can·to** (kan′tō) *n. pl.* **-tos** A division of an extended poem. [< L *cantus* song]

**can·vas** (kan′vəs) *n.* 1 Strong, close-woven cloth of cotton, flax, or hemp, used for sails, tents, etc. 2 A piece of such cloth used for a painting. 3 A painting on such cloth. 4 A sail or sails. —**under canvas** 1 With sails set. 2 In tents. [< L *cannabis* hemp]

**can·vass** (kan′vəs) *v.t.* 1 To go about (an area) or to (persons) to solicit opinions, votes, orders, etc. 2 To examine or discuss thoroughly. —*v.i.* 3 To go about seeking votes, information, etc. —*n.* 1 A survey, poll, etc., as to ascertain opinion or solicit votes. 2 A detailed examination or discussion. [< CANVAS] —**can′vass·er** *n.*

**can·yon** (kan′yən) *n.* A deep gorge or narrow valley with high, steep sides. [< Sp. *cañon*]

**ca·pa·ble** (kā′pə-bəl) *adj.* Having suitable ability; competent. —**capable of** 1 Having the required ability or capacity for. 2 Open to; susceptible of. [< LL *capabilis* < L *capere* take, receive] —**ca′pa·ble·ness** *n.* —**ca′pa·bly** *adv.*

**ca·pac·i·ty** (kə-pas′ə-tē) *n. pl.* **-ties** 1 Ability to receive or contain. 2 A measure of the ability to receive or contain; volume. 3 Maximum ability to contain, perform, etc. 4 Ability to do something; power. 5 Specific position, role, etc. 6 Legal qualification. 7 *Electr.* **a** CAPACITANCE. **b** The maximum output of an electric generator. [< L *capax* able to hold]

**cape** (kāp) *n.* A point of land extending into the sea or other body of water. [< L *caput* head]

**ca·per** (kā′pər) *v.i.* To leap or skip playfully; frisk. —*n.* 1 A playful skip or jump. 2 A prank; antic. —**cut a caper** (or capers) To caper; frolic. [Short for CAPRIOLE] —**ca′per·er** *n.* —**Syn.** *v.* gambol, frolic, prance, cavort.

**cap·il·lar·y** (kap′ə·ler′ē) *n. pl.* **-lar·ies** 1 Any of the microscopic blood vessels connecting the arterial and venous systems. 2 Any tube with a fine, hairlike bore. —*adj.* 1 Of or resembling a hair; fine; slender. 2 Having a slender, hairlike opening, as a tube or vessel. 3 Of capillarity. [< L *capillus* hair]

**cap·i·tal** (kap′ə·təl) *n.* 1 A city that is the seat of government of a country, state, etc. 2 CAPITAL LETTER. 3 Wealth or property assets available for producing more wealth, as through investment. 4 The assets of a busi-

ness after deduction of liabilities. 5 Capitalists or wealthy people as a class. 6 A quality, resource, etc., that can be used to advantage. —*adj.* 1 Chief; principal; foremost. 2 Serving as the seat of government. 3 Excellent; first-rate. 4 Of or pertaining to financial capital. 5 Involving or punishable by the death penalty. [< MF < L *caput* head]

**Cap·i·tol** (kap′ə·təl) *n.* 1 The official building of the U.S. Congress in Washington. 2 The temple of Jupiter in ancient Rome. [< L *Capitolium*]

**ca·pit·u·late** (kə·pich′ŏŏ·lāt) *v.i.* **·lat·ed, ·lat·ing** 1 To surrender on stipulated conditions. 2 To give in; yield. [< L *capitulare* draw up in chapters, arrange terms] —**ca·pit′u·la′tor** *n.* —**ca·pit′u·la·to′ry** *adj.*

**ca·price** (kə·prēs′) *n.* 1 A sudden, unreasonable impulse or change of mind; a whim. 2 A tendency to such acts or impulses. 3 *Music* CAPRICCIO. [< Ital. *capriccio*]

**cap·size** (kap′sīz, kap·sīz′) *v.t. & v.i.* **·sized, ·siz·ing** To upset or overturn. [?]

**cap·sule** (kap′səl, -syŏŏl) *n.* 1 A small gelatinous case for containing a dose of a drug. 2 *Bot.* A dry seed vessel or spore case, esp. one that splits open when ripe. 3 A membrane enclosing an organ or structure. 4 The cargo or passenger container of a space vehicle. [< L *capsula,* dim. of *capsa* box] —**cap′su·lar** *adj.*

**cap·tain** (kap′tən, -tin) *n.* 1 One at the head of or in command; chief; leader. 2 The master or commander of a vessel. 3 See GRADE. —*v.t.* To be captain of; command. [< LL *capitaneus* < L *caput* head] —**cap′tain·cy** (-sē), **cap′tain·ship** *n.*

**cap·tion** (kap′shən) *n.* 1 A heading of a chapter, section, document, etc. 2 The title and explanatory material accompanying an illustration. 3 A subtitle in a motion picture. —*v.t.* To provide a caption for. [< L *captio* deception, sophism < *capere* take]

**cap·tious** (kap′shəs) *adj.* 1 Apt to find fault. 2 Intended to confuse or trip up: *captious questions.* [< L *captiosus* fallacious] —**cap′tious·ly** *adj.* —**cap′tious·ness** *n.* —**Syn.** 1 critical, carping, caviling.

**cap·ti·vate** (kap′tə·vāt) *v.t.* **·vat·ed, ·vat·ing** To charm; fascinate. [< L *captivus.* See CAPTIVE.] —**cap′ti·vat′ing·ly** *adv.* —**cap′ti·va′tion, cap′ti·va′tor** *n.*

**cap·tive** (kap′tiv) *n.* 1 One captured and held; a prisoner. 2 One who is captivated or enthralled. —*adj.* 1 Taken or held as a prisoner. 2 Held under constraint or control. 3

Unable to avoid being present or listening: a *captive* audience. **4** Captivated; enthralled. [<L *captivus* < *capere* take]

**cap·ture** (kap′chər) *v.t.* **·tured, ·tur·ing** **1** To seize and hold, as by force, skill, etc. **2** To win possession of; gain. **3** To succeed in preserving an impression or image of. —*n.* **1** The act of capturing or of being captured. **2** One who or that which is captured. [<L *captura* < *capere* take]

**car** (kär) *n.* **1** An automobile. **2** A wheeled vehicle that moves on rails. **3** An enclosure for passengers, as of an elevator. **4** A chariot. [<L *carrus* wagon]

**car·a·mel** (kar′ə·məl, -mel, kär′məl) *n.* **1** A chewy candy made with butter, sugar, etc. **2** A brown syrup made by heating sugar, used to flavor and color foods. [Prob. <L *calamus* reed]

**car·at** (kar′ət) *n.* **1** A unit of weight for gems, equal to 200 milligrams, or 3.086 grains. **2** Loosely, a karat. [<Ar. *qīrāt* weight of 4 grains < Gk. *keration* seed, small weight]

**car·a·van** (kar′ə·van) *n.* **1** A company of people traveling together, as across a desert. **2** A group of vehicles traveling together. **3** *Brit.* TRAILER (def. 3). [< Pers. *kārwān* caravan]

**car·bo·hy·drate** (kär′bō·hī′drāt) *n.* Any of a group of compounds synthesized by plants from carbon dioxide and water, including sugars, starches, and cellulose.

**car·bon** (kär′bən) *n.* **1** A nonmetallic element (symbol C) that occurs in three allotropic forms and as a constituent of all organisms and in many inorganic minerals and in atmospheric gases. **2** *Electr.* A rod of carbon, used as an electrode in an arc light. **3** A piece of carbon paper. **4** CARBON COPY. —*adj.* **1** Of, pertaining to, or like carbon. **2** Treated with carbon. [<L *carbo* coal]

**car·bun·cle** (kär′bung·kəl) *n.* **1** A skin eruption resembling a boil but larger and more painful. **2** A garnet or other red gemstone cut without facets. [<L *carbunculus*, dim. of *carbo* coal] —**car·bun·cu·lar** (kär·bung′kyə·lər) *adj.*

**car·cass** (kär′kəs) *n.* **1** The dead body of an animal. **2** The human body: a contemptuous use. **3** Something lifeless or worthless. **4** A framework or skeleton. Also **car′case.** [<MF *carcasse* a corpse]

**car·di·ac** (kär′dē·ak) *adj.* **1** Of or pertaining to the heart. **2** Of or designating the upper part of the stomach. —*n.* **1** One suffering from a heart disease. **2** A cardiac stimulant. [<Gk. *kardia* heart]

**car·di·nal** (kär′də·nəl) *adj.* **1** Of prime importance. **2** Of a deep scarlet color. —*n.* **1** In the Roman Catholic Church, a member of the Sacred College whose members elect and advise the Pope. **2** A North American, bright red, crested finch. **3** A deep scarlet. **4** CARDINAL NUMBER. [<L *cardinalis* important < *cardo* hinge] —**car′di·nal·ly** *adv.*

**ca·reen** (kə·rēn′) *v.i.* **1** To lurch or twist from side to side. **2** To lean sideways. —*v.t.* **3** To cause (a ship) to turn over to one side, as for repairing. **4** To clean, repair, or calk (a careened ship). **5** To tilt; tip. —*n.* A careening. [<L *carina* keel of a ship]

**ca·reer** (kə·rir′) *n.* **1** One's lifework or employment. **2** The course or progress of one's life or lifework. **3** A swift course or run. —*adj.* Pursuing the (stated) occupation as a lifework: a *career* diplomat. —*v.i.* To move with a swift, free, and headlong motion. [<LL *carraria (via)* road for carriages] —**ca·reer′er** *n.*

**ca·ress** (kə·res′) *n.* An expression of affection by patting, embracing, or stroking. —*v.t.* To touch or handle lovingly. [<L *carus* dear] —**ca·ress′er** *n.* —**ca·ress′ive** *adj.* —**Syn.** *v.* fondle, embrace, pet, cuddle.

**car·et** (kar′ət) *n.* A sign (‸) placed below a line to denote an omission. [<L, it is missing]

**car·go** (kär′gō) *n. pl.* **·goes** or **·gos** Goods and merchandise taken on board a vessel, aircraft, etc. [<LL *carricum* load]

**car·i·bou** (kar′ə·bōō) *n.* Any of several large North American deer having antlers projecting forward in both sexes. [<Algon.]

**car·i·ca·ture** (kar′i·kə·chŏŏr, -chər) *n.* **1** A picture or description using gross exaggeration or distortion, as for humorous effect or in ridicule. **2** The act or art of caricaturing. **3** A poor imitation. —*v.t.* **·tured, ·tur·ing** To represent so as to make ridiculous; travesty. [<Ital. *caricatura*, lit., an overloading] —**car′i·ca·tur′al** *adj.* —**car′i·ca·tur′ist** *n.*

**car·nage** (kär′nij) *n.* Extensive and bloody slaughter; massacre. [<L *caro* flesh, meat]

**car·nal** (kär′nəl) *adj.* **1** Pertaining to bodily appetites; not spiritual. **2** Sensual; sexual. [<L *caro, carnis* flesh] —**car′nal·ist,** **car·nal·i·ty** (kär·nal′ə·tē) *n.* —**car′nal·ly** *adv.*

**car·na·tion** (kär·nā′shən) *n.* **1** Any of many cultivated varieties of plants related to the pink, having fragrant, usu. double, flowers.

2 A light pink, bright rose, or scarlet color. [< L *carnatio* fleshiness < *caro* flesh]

**car·ni·val** (kär′nə·vəl) *n.* 1 A period of festival and gaiety immediately preceding Lent. 2 Any gay festival, esp. one featuring sports contests or other amusements. 3 A traveling amusement show. [< Ital. *carnivale*, lit., the putting away of flesh]

**car·niv·o·rous** (kär·niv′ə·rəs) *adj.* Eating or living on flesh. [< L *caro* flesh + *vorare* eat, devour] —**car·niv′o·rous·ly** *adv.* —**car·niv′o·rous·ness** *n.*

**car·ol** (kar′əl) *v.* ·oled or ·olled, ·ol·ing or ·ol·ling *v.t.* 1 To sing, as a carol. 2 To celebrate in song. —*v.i.* 3 To sing, esp. in a joyous strain. —*n.* A song of joy; esp., a Christmas song. [< L *choraules* a flutist] —**car′o·ler, car′ol·er** *n.*

**ca·rouse** (kə·rouz′) *v.i.* ca·roused, ca·rous·ing To drink heavily and boisterously with others. —*n.* CAROUSAL. [< G *gar aus (trinken)* (drink) all out] —**ca·rous′er** *n.*

**carp** (kärp) *v.i.* To nag or find fault excessively. [< ON *karpa* boast] —**carp′er** *n.*

**car·pen·ter** (kär′pən·tər) *n.* One who builds or repairs houses, ships, etc., with timber or wood. —*v.t.* 1 To make by carpentry. —*v.i.* 2 To work with wood. [< LL *carpentarius* carpenter, wagon-maker] —**car′pen·try** (-trē) *n.*

**car·riage** (kar′ij) *n.* 1 A wheeled, usu. horse-drawn vehicle for carrying persons. 2 BABY CARRIAGE. 3 A wheeled or moving mechanical part for supporting or carrying something. 4 One's physical posture; bearing. 5 The act or cost of transporting something. [< AF *carier* to carry]

**car·ri·on** (kar′ē·ən) *n.* Dead and putrefying flesh. —*adj.* 1 Feeding on carrion. 2 Like or pertaining to carrion; putrefying. [< L *caro* flesh]

**car·rot** (kar′ət) *n.* 1 A widely cultivated plant related to parsley. 2 Its reddish yellow edible root. [< L *carota* < Gk. *karōton*]

**car·ry** (kar′ē) *v.* ·ried, ·ry·ing *v.t.* 1 To bear from one place to another; transport; convey. 2 To have or bear upon or about one's person or in one's mind. 3 To serve as a means of conveyance or transportation: The wind *carries* sounds. 4 To lead; urge; move; influence: Love for art *carried* him abroad. 5 To have or bear as a feature, quality, consequence, etc. 6 To bear up; hold in position. 7 To conduct (oneself) or move or hold (oneself) in a specified manner. 8 To transfer, as a number or figure, to

the column of next highest order, as in adding. 9 To keep on the account books. 10 To have or keep on hand: We *carry* a full stock. 11 To have as part of its program, contents, etc.: This radio station does not *carry* the news. 12 To win, as an election; also, to win the majority of votes in (a state, city, etc.). 13 To win the support of (a group, audience, etc.). 14 To gain the acceptance or adoption of (a cause, law, etc.). 15 To support or sustain, esp. financially. 16 To be pregnant with. 17 To extend or continue: to *carry* a joke too far. 18 *Music* To sing or play (a melody or part). —*v.i.* 19 To act as bearer or carrier. 20 To have a specified range, propelling power, etc.: The sound *carried* nearly a mile. 21 To gain acceptance or adoption. —**carry off** 1 To cause to die. 2 To win, as a prize or honor. 3 To face or handle (an embarrassment, etc.) well. —**carry on** 1 To keep going; continue. 2 To behave in a free, frolicsome manner. 3 To continue, as a tradition. —**carry out** To accomplish; bring to completion. —**carry through** 1 To carry to completion or success. 2 To sustain or support to the end. —*n. pl.* ·ries 1 The act or manner of carrying. 2 A portage, as between navigable steams. 3 The range of, or the distance covered by, a gun, projectile, golf ball, etc. [< LL *carricare* L *carrus* cart] —**Syn.** *v.* 1 move, transfer, haul, ship. 4 impel. 5 show, display, harbor.

**car·tel** (kär·tel′, kär′təl) *n.* 1 An association of businesses aiming at monopolistic control of the market. 2 A written official agreement between governments at war, as for the exchange of prisoners. [< Ital. *carta* paper]

**car·ton** (kär′tən) *n.* 1 A pasteboard box. 2 A heavyweight paper container for liquids. [< L *charta* paper]

**car·toon** (kär·tōōn′) *n.* 1 A humorously critical or satirical drawing or caricature, as in a periodical. 2 A sketch for a fresco or mosaic. 3 COMIC STRIP. 4 ANIMATED CARTOON. —*v.t.* 1 To make a caricature or cartoon of; satirize pictorially. —*v.i.* 2 To make cartoons. [< Ital. *cartone* pasteboard < *carta* card] —**car·toon′ist** *n.*

**car·tridge** (kär′trij) *n.* 1 An explosive charge for a small arm, consisting of primer, gunpowder, cardboard or metal case, and projectile or projectiles. 2 *Phot.* A roll of protected sensitized films. 3 A small case attached to the arm of a phonograph and containing the stylus and pickup. 4 CAS-SETTE. [<F *cartouche*]

**carve** (kärv) *v.* **carved, carv·ing** *v.t.* 1 To cut figures or designs upon. 2 To make by cutting or chiseling. 3 To cut up, as cooked meat. —*v.i.* 4 To make carved work or figures. 5 To cut up meat. [<OE *ceorfan*] —**carv′er, carv′ing** *n.*

**cas·cade** (kas·kād′) *n.* 1 A fall of water over steeply slanting rocks, or one of a series of such falls. 2 Anything resembling a waterfall. —*v.t.* **cad·ed, ·cad·ing** To fall in the form of a waterfall; form cascades. [<Ital. *cascare* to fall]

**case·ment** (kās′mənt) *n.* 1 A window arranged to open on hinges at the side. 2 A case; covering. [<OF *encassement*] —**case′ment·ed** *adj.*

**cash·ier** (ka·shir′) *v.t.* 1 To dismiss in disgrace, as a military officer. 2 To discard. [<L *quassare* destroy]

**cask** (kask, käsk) *n.* 1 A barrel made of staves, used for liquids, nails, etc. 2 The quantity a cask will hold. [<Sp. *casco* skull, cask]

**cas·ket** (kas′kit, käs′-) *n.* 1 A coffin. 2 A small box or chest. —*v.t.* To enclose in or as in a casket. [<F *casse* chest]

**cas·sette** (kə·set′, ka-) *n.* 1 A lightproof, quick-loading case for holding film in a camera. 2 A small cartridge containing magnetic tape for use in a tape recorder. [F, lit., small box]

**cast** (kast, käst) *v.* **cast, cast·ing** *v.t.* 1 To throw with force; fling; hurl. 2 To place with violence or force, as by the sea. 3 To throw up, as with a shovel. 4 To put into some form or system; formulate. 5 To deposit; give: He *cast* his vote. 6 To draw by chance; throw, as dice. 7 To cause to fall upon or over; direct: to *cast* a shadow. 8 To throw out or forth; get rid of. 9 To let down; put out; let drop: to *cast* anchor. 10 To discard or shed, as in the process of growth. 11 To give birth to, esp. prematurely; drop. 12 *Metall.* To shape in a mold; make a cast of; found. 13 *Printing* To stereotype or electroplate. 14 To assign roles, as in a play; assign to a part. 15 To add; total, as a column of figures. 16 To calculate (a horoscope, tides, etc.). 17 *Naut.* To veer. —*v.i.* 18 To throw or throw out something, as dice or a fishing line. 19 To calculate a horoscope, tides, etc. 20 To take shape in a mold. 21 To add up a column of figures. 22 *Naut.* To veer; tack. —**cast about** 1 To consider ways

and means; scheme. 2 To search for. —**cast away** To discard; reject. —**cast down** 1 To overthrow; destroy. 2 To discourage; depress. —**cast off** 1 To reject or discard. 2 To let go, as a ship from a dock. —*n.* 1 The act of throwing or casting. 2 The manner of casting; also the distance thrown or cast. 3 A throw of dice; also, the number or total thrown. 4 Anything thrown out or off, as an insect's skin. 5 The material run into molds at one operation. 6 An object formed in a mold; also, the mold. 7 An impression taken of something and usu. forming a mold. 8 An electrotype plate. 9 A hardened plaster support for a broken limb. 10 An appearance or type: a man of his *cast*. 11 Shade; tinge: a bluish *cast*. 12 A twisting of the eye to one side. 13 A glance; look. 14 The actors in a play, movie, etc. [<ON *kasta* throw]

**cas·ta·net** (kas′tə·net′) *n.* One of a pair of small concave disks of wood or ivory, clapped together with the fingers, as an accompaniment to song or dance. [<L *tanea* chestnut]

**caste** (kast, käst) *n.* 1 One of the hereditary classes into which Hindu society is traditionally divided in India. 2 Any rigidly exclusive social class. 3 Any system of such class distinctions. 4 Social standing or prestige. [<L *castus* pure]

**cas·ti·gate** (kas′tə·gāt) *v.t.* **·gat·ed, ·gat·ing** To punish or scold severely; chastise. [< L *castigare* chasten] —**cas′ti·ga′tion, cas′ti·ga′tor** *n.* —**cas·ti·ga·to·ry** (kas′ti·gə·tôr′ē, -tō′rē) *adj.*

**cas·tle** (kas′əl, käs′-) *n.* 1 The fortified dwelling of a feudal noble. 2 Any massive or imposing dwelling. 3 Any place of security or refuge. 4 In chess, a rook. —*v.t. & v.i.* **·tled, ·tling** In chess, to move (the king) two squares to the right or left, at the same time bringing the rook to the square over which the king has passed. [< L *castellum,* dim. of *castrum* camp, fort]

**cas·u·al** (kazh′o͞o·əl) *adj.* 1 Occurring by chance; not planned; accidental. 2 Irregular; occasional. 3 Nonchalant. 4 Careless; haphazard. 5 Slight: a *casual* acquaintance. 6 Informal: *casual* clothes. —*n.* 1 A casual laborer. 2 *pl.* Informal clothes and accessories. [< L *casus* accident < *cadere* fall] —**cas′u·al·ly** *adv.* —**cas′u·al·ness** *n.* —Syn. *adj.* 1 random; incidental. 2 haphazard, cursory. 3 dispassionate, unconcerned, offhand. 4 negligent, slovenly.

**cas·u·al·ty** (kazh′ōō·əl·tē) *n. pl.* **·ties** 1 A fatal or serious accident. 2 A person killed or severely injured in an accident. 3 Any person or thing badly harmed or damaged. 4 *Mil.* a A soldier missing in action or removed from active duty by death, wounds, or capture. b *pl.* Losses arising from death, etc.

**cat** (kat) *n.* 1 A small, domesticated, carnivorous mammal with retractile claws. 2 Any animal of the cat family, as a lion, tiger, lynx, ocelot, etc. 3 *Informal* A spiteful woman given to gossip. 4 CAT-O′-NINE-TAILS. 5 *Slang* CATERPILLAR. 6 *Slang* a A person, esp. a man. b A jazz musician or devotee. 7 *Naut.* A device used for hoisting an anchor. [< OE]

**cat·a·clysm** (kat′ə·kliz′əm) *n.* 1 An overwhelming flood. 2 Any violent change or upheaval, as a war or earthquake. [< Gk. *kataklysmos* flood] —**cat·a·clys·mal** (kat′ə·kliz′məl), **cat′a·clys′mic** *adj.*

**cat·a·comb** (kat′ə·kōm) *n. Usu. pl.* A long underground gallery with excavations in its sides for tombs or human remains. [< LL *catacumbas*]

**cat·a·log** (kat′ə·lôg, -log) *n.* 1 A systematic list or enumeration of names, persons, or things, bound in book form, printed on cards, etc. 2 A publication listing wares for sale by a commercial establishment. —*v.* **·loged, ·log·ing** *v.t.* 1 To make a catalog of. —*v.i.* 2 To work on or make a catalog. [< Gk. *kata-* down + *legein* select, choose] —**cat′a·log′er, cat′a·log′ist** *n.*

**cat·a·ma·ran** (kat′ə·mə·ran′) *n. Naut.* 1 A boat having twin hulls. 2 A long, narrow raft of logs, often with an outrigger. [< Tamil *kattamaram* tied wood]

**cat·a·ract** (kat′ə·rakt) *n.* 1 A waterfall. 2 *Pathol.* Opacity of the crystalline lens of the eye. 3 A deluge; downpour. [< Gk. *kata-* down + *arassein* fall headlong]

**ca·tas·tro·phe** (kə·tas′trə·fē) *n.* 1 Any great and sudden misfortune; disaster. 2 A sudden, violent change. 3 A ruinous failure. [< Gk. *kata-* over, down + *strephein* turn] —**cat·a·stroph·ic** (kat′ə·strof′ik) *adj.* —**Syn.** 1 calamity, mishap, débacle. 2 cataclysm, convulsion, upheaval.

**catch·er** (kach′ər) *n.* 1 One who or that which catches. 2 In baseball, the player stationed behind home plate to catch balls that pass the batter.

**cat·e·go·ry** (kat′ə·gôr′ē, -gō′rē) *n. pl.* **·ries** A class, division, or group in any system of classification. [< Gk. < *katēgoreein* allege, predicate]

**ca·ter** (kā′tər) *v.i.* 1 To furnish food or entertainment. 2 To provide for the gratification of any need or taste. —*v.t.* 3 To furnish food for. [< LL *acceptare* buy, procure, accept] —**ca′ter·er** *n.*

**cat·er·pil·lar** (kat′ər·pil′ər) *n.* The larva of certain insects, esp. of a butterfly or moth. [< L *catta* cat + *pilum* hair]

**ca·the·dral** (kə·thē′drəl) *n.* 1 The church containing the official chair of the bishop. 2 Any large or important church. —*adj.* Of, pertaining to, or like a cathedral. [< Gk. *kata-* down + *hedra* seat]

**cath·ode** (kath′ōd) *n. Electr.* The electrode through which negative charges leave a nonmetallic conductor and toward which positive ions flow from the anode. [< Gk. *kata-* down + *hodos* road, way]

**cath·o·lic** (kath′ə·lik, kath′lik) *adj.* 1 Broadminded, as in belief, tastes, or views; liberal; comprehensive. 2 Universal in reach; general. [<Gk. *katholikos* universal] —**ca·thol·i·cal·ly** (kə·thol′ik·lē) *adv.* —**cath·o·lic·i·ty** (kath′ə·lis′ə·tē) *n.*

**Cath·o·lic** (kath′ə·lik, kath′lik) *adj.* 1 Of or pertaining to the Roman Catholic Church. 2 Of or pertaining to the ancient, undivided Christian Church or its later divisions, as the Anglican or Eastern Orthodox. —*n.* A member of any Catholic Church. —**Cath·o·lic·i·ty** (kath′ə·lis′ə·tē) *n.*

**cat·sup** (kat′səp, kech′əp) *n.* KETCHUP.

**cat·tle** (kat′l) *n.* 1 Domesticated cows, bulls, steers, and oxen. 2 Formerly, all livestock. 3 Human beings: a contemptuous term. [< L *capitale* capital, wealth]

**Cau·ca·sian** (kô·kā′zhən) *n.* 1 A Caucasoid person. 2 A native of the Caucasus region. —*adj.* 1 Of the Caucasus region, its inhabitants, or their languages. 2 CAUCASOID. Also **Cau·cas·ic** (kô·kas′ik). [< *Caucasus*, the region where the "white" race was once thought to have originated]

**cau·cus** (kô′kəs) *n.* A meeting of members of a political party to select candidates or plan a campaign. —*v.i.* **cau·cused** or **·cussed, ·cus·ing** or **·cus·sing** To meet in or hold a caucus. [< Algon.]

**cau·li·flow·er** (kô′lə·flou′ər, kol′i-) *n.* 1 A vegetable consisting of the dense, white, flower head of a plant related to cabbage. 2 The plant bearing this. [< NL *cauliflora* flowering cabbage]

**cau·sa·tion** (kô·zā′shən) *n.* 1 The act of causing. 2 That which causes an effect. 3 CAUSAL-
ITY.

**caus·tic** (kôs′tik) *adj.* 1 Capable of corroding
or eating away tissue. 2 Stinging; biting;
sarcastic. —*n.* A caustic substance. [< Gk.
*kausos* burning < *kaiein* to burn] —**caus′-
ti·cal·ly** *adv.* —**caus·tic′i·ty** (-tis′ə·tē) *n.*

**cau·ter·ize** (kô′tər·īz) *v.t.* ·ized, ·iz·ing To destroy dead or abnormal tissue by applying
a caustic, intense heat or cold, etc. [< L
*cauterium* branding iron] —**cau′ter·i·za′-
tion** *n.*

**cau·tion** (kô′shən) *n.* 1 Care to avoid injury
or misfortune; prudence; wariness. 2 An
admonition or warning. 3 *Informal* A person
or thing that alarms, astonishes, provokes,
etc. —*v.t.* To advise to be prudent; warn. [<
L *cautio* < *cavere* beware, take heed]

**cav·al·cade** (kav′əl·kād, kav′əl·kād′) *n.* 1 A
procession or parade, esp. of horsemen. 2
A series or procession of events. [< Ital. *cav-
alcare* to ride on horseback]

**cav·a·lier** (kav′ə·lir′) *n.* 1 A horseman; knight.
2 GALLANT. —*adj.* 1 Free and easy; offhand.
2 Haughty; supercilious. —**cav′a·lier′ly**
*adj., adv.*

**cav·al·ry** (kav′əl·rē) *n. pl.* ·ries Mobile ground
troops, originally mounted on horses, but
now using mechanized or motorized units.
[< LL *caballarius* horseman < L *caballus*
horse] —**cav′al·ry·man** *n.*

**cav·ern** (kav′ərn) *n.* A large cave.

**cav·il** (kav′əl) *v.i.* **cav·iled** or **·illed, cav·il·ing**
or **·il·ling** To pick flaws or raise trivial objections; quibble; with *at* or *about.* —*n.* A
trivial objection. [< L *cavilla* a jeering, a
scoffing] —**cav′il·er, cav′il·ler** *n.*

**cav·i·ty** (kav′ə·tē) *n. pl.* ·ties 1 A hollow or depression. 2 A natural hollow in the body. 3
A hollow place in a tooth, esp. one caused
by decay. [< L *cavus* hollow, empty]

**cease** (sēs) *v.* **ceased, ceas·ing** *v.t.* 1 To leave
off or discontinue. —*v.i.* 2 To come to an
end; stop; desist. —**Without cease** Without
end. [< L *cessare* stop < *cedere* withdraw,
yield] —**cease′less** *adj.* —**cease′less·ly**
*adv.* —**cease′less·ness** *n.* —Syn. *v.* 1 conclude, end, finish, terminate, quit, stop,
break off.

**ce·dar** (sē′dər) *n.* 1 Any of a genus of large,
Old World conifers, having needlelike
leaves and fragrant wood. 2 Any of a large
variety of similar evergreen trees. 3 The

wood of any of these trees. —*adj.* Pertaining to or made of cedar. [<Gk *kedros*]

**cede** (sēd) *v.t.* **ced·ed, ced·ing** 1 To yield or
give up: to *cede* disputed territory to avoid
war. 2 To surrender title to; transfer. [<L
*cedere* withdraw, yield]

**ceil·ing** (sē′ling) *n.* 1 The overhead covering
of a room. 2 The top limit or maximum, as
of prices, wages, etc. 3 *Aeron.* a The maximum height attainable by a given aircraft.
b The upward limit of visibility for flying.
[ME *celing*]

**cel·e·brate** (sel′ə·brāt) *v.* **·brat·ed, ·brat·ing**
*v.t.* 1 To observe, as a festival or occasion:
to *celebrate* an anniversary. 2 To make
known or famous; extol. 3 To perform a
ceremony publicly and as ordained: to *celebrate* the mass. —*v.i.* 4 To observe or commemorate a day or event. 5 *Informal* To
have a lively and happy time. [<L *celebrare*
<*celeber* famous] —**cel′e·brat′er** or **·bra′-
tor** *n.* —Syn. *v.* 1 commemorate, keep. 2
glorify, exalt, commend. 3 solemnize. 5 rejoice, make merry.

**ce·leb·ri·ty** (sə·leb′rə·tē) *n. pl.* **·ties** 1 A famous or much publicized person. 2 Fame;
renown.

**cel·er·y** (sel′ər·ē) *n.* An herb related to parsley, having long, crisp, edible leafstocks.
[<Gk *selinon* parsley]

**ce·les·tial** (sə·les′chəl) *adj.* 1 Of or pertaining
to the sky or heavens. 2 Heavenly; divine.
[<L *caelum* sky, heaven] —**ce·les′tial·ly**
*adv.*

**cel·i·ba·cy** (sel′ə·bə·sē) *n.* 1 The state of being
unmarried, esp. in accordance with religious vows. 2 Abstinence from sexual intercourse. [<L *caelebs* unmarried]

**cell** (sel) *n.* 1 A small room, as in a prison or
monastery. 2 Any small area or space, as a
chamber in a seedcase, a single compartment in a honeycomb, an area bounded by
veins on an insect's wing. 3 *Biol* One of the
fundamental structural units of which all
living tissue is composed, typically consisting of a cell membrane enclosing a mass
of cytoplasm that contains a nucleus and
various ultramicroscopic structures. 4
*Electr.* A device consisting of electrodes in
contact with an electrolyte. 5 A body of persons forming a single unit in an organization of similar groups. —**dry cell** A voltaic
cell with its electrolyte in the form of a
paste. [<L *cella*]

**cel·lar** (sel′ər) *n.* 1 An underground room
usu. under a building. 2 A room for storing

74

wines. 3 The wines so stored. —*v.t.* To put or keep in or as in a cellar. [<L *cellarium* pantry <*cella* cell, small room]

**cel·lo·phane** (sel′ə·fān) *n.* A specially treated cellulose in transparent sheets, used as a wrapping. [<CELL(ULOSE) + -PHANE]

**Cel·lu·loid** (sel′yə·loid) *n.* A flammable synthetic solid derived from cellulose: a trade name.

**cel·lu·lose** (sel′yə·lōs) *n.* A complex carbohydrate forming the cell walls of plants and the principal component of wood, paper, cotton, etc. [<L *cella* cell]

**ce·ment** (si·ment′) *n.* 1 A powdery substance, usu. of burned lime and clay, that when mixed with water or with water, sand, and gravel produces mortar or concrete. 2 Any gluelike substance. 3 A dental filling for cavities. • See TOOTH. 4 Any bond or union, as between persons. —*v.t.* 1 To unite or join with or as with cement. 2 To cover or coat with cement. —*v.t.* 3 To become united by cement; cohere. [<L *caementum* rough stone, stone chip <*caedere* cut] —**ce·men·ta·tion** (sē′mən·tā′shən, sem′ən-), **ce·men·t′er** *n.* • *Cement* is often used as a synonym for *concrete.* This is technically incorrect, since cement is only one, although the principal, ingredient of concrete.

**cem·e·ter·y** (sem′ə·ter′ē) *n. pl.* **·ter·ies** A place for the burial of the dead. [<Gk. *koimaein* put to sleep]

**cen·ser** (sen′sər) *n.* A vessel for burning incense. [<Med. L *incensum* incense]

**cen·sor** (sen′sər) *n.* 1 An official examiner of manuscripts, plays, movies, etc., empowered to delete or suppress whatever is considered offensive or objectionable. 2 An official who deletes from letters, dispatches, etc., any secret or forbidden information. 3 Anyone who censures or criticizes. 4 In Ancient Rome, one of two magistrates who took the census and supervised public morals. —*v.t.* To act as censor of. [<L *censere* judge] —**cen·so·ri·al** (sen·sôr′ē·əl, -sō′rē-) *adj.*

**cen·so·ri·ous** (sen·sôr′ē·əs, -sō′rē-) *adj.* Given to or expressing censure; critical. —**cen·so′ri·ous·ly** *adv.* —**cen·so′ri·ous·ness** *n.*

**cen·sure** (sen′shər) *n.* Condemnation or blame; disapproval. —*v.t.* **·sured, ·sur·ing** To express disapproval of; condemn. [<L *censere* judge] —**cen′sur·er** *n.*

**cen·sus** (sen′səs) *n. pl.* **cen·sus·es** An official count of the people of a country or district,

including age, sex, employment, etc. [<L *censere* assess]

**cen·ten·ni·al** (sen·ten′ē·əl) *adj.* Of a hundred or a hundredth anniversary. —*n.* A hundredth anniversary. [<L *centum* hundred + *annus* a year] —**cen·ten′ni·al·ly** *adv.*

**cen·ter** (sen′tər) *n.* 1 *Geom.* The point within a circle or sphere equally distant from any point on the circumference or surface. 2 The middle: the *center* of the town. 3 The point, object, person, or place about which things cluster or revolve or from which they emanate: a *center* of interest. 4 Any hub of a specified activity: a manufacturing *center.* 5 *Mech.* A point on or by which an object is secured or rotated. 6 The person who takes the middle position in certain games, as football, basketball, etc. 7 *Often cap.* a The moderate position of a political group neither conservative nor liberal but sharing some views with both. b Such a group. —*v.t.* 1 To place in or at the center. 2 To supply with a center. 3 To draw to or direct toward one place; concentrate. —*v.i.* 4 To be in or at the center. 5 To have a focal point; concentrate. —*adj.* Central; middle. [<Gk. *kentron* point (i.e., around which a circle is described)]

**cen·ti·grade** (sen′tə·grād) *adj.* 1 Graduated to a scale of a hundred. 2 CELSIUS. [<L *centum* hundred + *gradus* step, degree]

**cen·ti·me·ter** (sen′tə·mē′tər) *n.* The hundredth part of a meter.

**cen·ti·pede** (sen·tə·pēd) *n.* Any of a class of elongated anthropods having a pair of legs to each segment. [<L *centum* hundred + *pes, pedis* foot]

**cen·trif·u·gal** (sen·trif′yə·gəl, -ə·gəl) *adj.* 1 Directed or tending away from a center; radiating. 2 Employing centrifugal force: a *centrifugal* pump. [<L *centrum* center + *fugere* flee] —**cen·trif′u·gal·ly** *adv.*

**cen·trip·e·tal** (sen·trip′ə·təl) *adj.* 1 Directed, tending, or drawing toward a center. 2 Employing centripetal force: a *centripetal* pump. [<L *centrum* center + *petere* seek]

**cen·tu·ry** (sen′chə·rē) *n. pl.* **·ries** 1 A period of 100 years in any system of chronology, esp. in reckoning from the first year of the Christian era. 2 A body of Roman foot soldiers (at one time 100 men). [<L *centum* hundred]

**ce·ram·ic** (sə·ram′ik) *adj.* Of or pertaining to earthenware, pottery, porcelain, etc., or to their manufacture. —*n.* An article of ceramic manufacture. [<Gk. *keramos* potters' clay]

**ce·re·al** (sir′ē·əl) *n.* 1 The grain of certain grasses used as food, as rice, wheat, etc. 2 Any of the plants yielding such grains. 3 A breakfast food made from a cereal —*adj.* Pertaining to edible grain. [< Ceres]

**cer·e·bel·lum** (ser′ə·bel′əm) *n. pl.* **·bel·lums** or **·bel·la** (-bel′ə) The part of the brain that acts as the coordination center of voluntary movement, posture, and equilibrium. [< L *cerebrum* brain] —**cer′e·bel′lar** *adj.*

**cer·e·bral** (ser′ə·brəl, sə·rē′-) *adj.* 1 Of or pertaining to the cerebrum or the brain. 2 Appealing to or requiring the intellect; intellectual.

**cere·ment** (sir′mənt) *n. Usu. pl.* shroud.

**cer·e·mo·ny** (ser′ə·mō′nē) *n. pl.* **·nies** 1 A formal act, or a series of them, as on religious and state occasions. 2 The performance of such acts. 3 Mere outward form. 4 Formal civility; formality. [< L *caerimonia* awe, veneration]

**cer·tain** (sûr′tən) *adj.* 1 Established as fact or truth; beyond doubt or question; true. 2 Absolutely sure; convinced. 3 Definitely settled; fixed; determined. 4 Inevitable: Death is *certain.* 5 Sure in its workings or results; reliable. 6 Appreciable; limited: to a *certain* extent. 7 Indefinite, but assumed to be determinable: a *certain* man. —**for certain** Without doubt. [< L *certus,* p.p. of *cernere* determine] —**Syn.** 1 undeniable, indisputable, incontestable, irrefutable. 2 positive. 3 assured, decided. 4 unavoidable.

**cer·tif·i·cate** (sər·tif′ə·kit) *n.* A document or written statement declaring something to be true, genuine, or legally valid. —*v.t.* (-kāt) **·cat·ed, ·cat·ing** To furnish with or attest by a certificate. [< Med.L *certificare* certify]

**cer·ti·fi·ca·tion** (sûr′tə·fi·kā′shən) *n.* 1 The act of certifying. 2 The state of being certified. 3 A certified statement.

**cer·ti·fy** (sûr′tə·fī) *v.t.* **·fied, ·fy·ing** 1 To guarantee (something) to be true, genuine, etc., usu. in a formal, written statement. 2 To issue a certificate to. 3 To give assurance of; vouch for. 4 To declare to be legally insane. [< L *certus* certain + *facere* make] —**cer′ti·fi′a·ble** *adj.* —**cer′ti·fi′er** *n.*

**chaff** (chaf, châf) *n.* 1 The husks of grain. 2 Worthless matter; refuse. [OE *ceaf*] —**chaff′y** *adj.*

**chaf·ing dish** (chā′fing) *n.* A vessel with a heating apparatus beneath, to cook or keep hot its contents at table.

**cha·grin** (shə·grin′) *n.* Distress or embarrassment caused by disappointment, failure, etc.; mortification. —*v.t.* To humiliate; mortify. [F. sad] —**Syn.** *n.* confusion, dismay, humiliation, vexation.

**chain** (chān) *n.* 1 A series of connected rings or links, serving to bind, drag, hold, or ornament. 2 *pl.* Shackles; bonds. 3 *pl.* Bondage; captivity. 4 Any connected series: a *chain* of events. 5 A range of mountains. 6 A unit of linear measure equal to 66 or 100 feet. 7 *Chem.* A series of atoms linked together. 8 A series of associated stores, banks, etc. —*v.t.* 1 To fasten, as with a chain. 2 To bring into or hold in subjection. [< L *catena*]

**chain reaction** A series of reactions each of which develops from the energy or products released by its predecessor.

**chaise longue** (shāz′ lông′, *Fr.* shez lông′) *n.* A chair having a backrest at one end and the seat prolonged to support the sitter's outstretched legs. [F, lit., long chair]

**chalk** (chôk) *n.* 1 A soft, grayish white or yellowish limestone, largely composed of minute sea shells. 2 A piece of chalk or chalklike material used for marking or drawing. 3 A score or reckoning, as one recorded with chalk. —*v.t.* 1 To mark or draw with chalk. 2 To put chalk on or in. 3 To make pale. —**chalk up** 1 To score. 2 To give credit. —*adj.* Made with chalk. [< OE *cealc* < L *calx* limestone] —**chalk′i·ness** *n.* —**chalk′y** *adj.* (·i·er, ·i·est)

**chal·lenge** (chal′ənj) *v.* **·lenged, ·leng·ing** *v.t.* 1 To dare or invite to a duel, contest, etc. 2 To stop and demand identification. 3 To call in question; object to: to *challenge* a decision, voter, juror, etc. 4 To stimulate: to *challenge* the imagination. 5 To call for; claim as due. —*v.i.* 6 To utter or make a challenge. —*n.* 1 A call or dare to fight, esp. to fight a duel. 2 A formal objection or exception to a person or thing. 3 A sentry's call, requiring one to halt and give identification. 4 Something that stimulates a person or persons to greater effort, dedication, etc. [< LL *calumniare* accuse falsely < *calumnia* slander] —**Syn.** *v.* 3 dispute, query, contest, doubt. 4 excite, arouse, animate, spur, stir. —**chal′lenge·a·ble** *adj.* —**chal′leng·er** *n.*

**cham·ber** (chām′bər) *n.* 1 A room in a house, esp. a bedroom. 2 *pl.* A suite of rooms or offices for the use of one person, as a judge's office. 3 a A hall where an assembly or council meets. **b** The council or assembly itself. **4** An enclosed space, as one of the cavities in the cartridge cylinder of a revolver. **5** *Anat.* A cavity or compartment, as in the heart, eyeball, etc. —*v.t.* To make chambers in, as a gun. [< L *camera* vaulted room < Gk. *kamara*]

**cha·me·le·on** (kə·mē′lē·ən, -mēl′yən) *n.* **1** Any of various lizards having the power to change its color. **2** A person of changeable character or habits. [< Gk. < *chamai* on the ground + *leōn* lion] —**cha·me·le·on·ic** (kə·mē′lē·on′ik) *adj.*

**cham·pi·on** (cham′pē·ən) *n.* **1** The victor in a contest. **2** One who defends a person, principle, etc. —*adj.* Acknowledged superior to all competitors; holding the first prize. —*v.t.* To stand up for the rights of; defend. [< LL *campio* fighter < L *campus* field]

**chan·cel·lor** (chan′sə·lər, chän′-, chans′lər, chäns′-) *n.* **1** In certain universities, the president. **2** In certain countries, the head of state or prime minister. **3** A judicial officer sitting in a court of chancery or equity. [< LL *cancellarius* one who stands at the bar in a court < *cancelli,* pl., railing] —**chan′cel·lor·ship′** *n.*

**chan·cer·y** (chan′sər·ē, chän′-) *n. pl.* **·cer·ies 1** In the U.S., a court of equity. **2** In Great Britain, one of the five divisions of the High Court of Justice. **3** A court of records; archives. **4** CHANCELLERY (def. 3). —**in chancery 1** Pending in a court of chancery. **2** In a hopeless predicament. [< LL *cancellarius.* See CHANCELLOR.]

**chan·de·lier** (shan′də·lir′) *n.* A branched light fixture. [< L *candela* candle]

**change** (chānj) *v.* **changed, chang·ing** *v.t.* **1** To make different; alter. **2** To exchange; interchange: to *change* places. **3** To replace, substitute, or abandon (something) for another thing: to *change* plans. **4** To give or get the equivalent of, as money. **5** To put other garments, coverings, etc., on: to *change* the bed. —*v.i.* **6** To become different; vary. **7** To make an exchange. **8** To transfer from one train to another. **9** To put on other garments. —*n.* **1** The act or result of changing. **2** A substitution or something used in substitution: a *change* of clothes. **3** Something different or varied. **4** The money returned to a purchaser who has given a bill or coin of greater value than his purchase. **5** Money of smaller denomination given in exchange for money of larger denomination. **6** Small coins. **7** An exchange

for the transaction of business: also **'change.** —**ring the changes 1** To operate a chime of bells so as to produce a variety of tuneful combinations. **2** To repeat something with much variation. [< LL *cambiare* exchange] —**change′ful** *adj.* —**change′ful·ly** *adv.* —**chang′er, change′ful·ness** *n.* — Syn. *v.* **1** transmute, transform, vary, modify.

**chan·nel** (chan′əl) *n.* **1** The bed of a stream. **2** A wide strait: the English *Channel.* **3** The deep part of a river, harbor, strait, etc. **4** A groove or tubular passage, as for liquids. **5** *pl.* A usu. official course or route through which communications, requests, etc., are handled or transmitted. **6** *Telecom.* **a** A path for the transmission of telegraph, telephone, and radio communications. **b** A wave band of specified frequency over which radio and television programs are transmitted. —*v.t.* **chan·neled** or **·nelled, chan·nel·ing** or **·nel·ling 1** To cut or wear channels in. **2** To convey through or as through a channel. [< L *canalis* groove]

**chant** (chant, chänt) *n.* **1** A vocal melody sung in free rhythm, usu. unaccompanied, and with a series of words sung at a single pitch. **2** A psalm or canticle so recited. **3** A song; melody. **4** Any measured monotonous singing or speaking. —*v.t.* **1** To sing to a chant. **2** To celebrate in song. **3** To say repetitiously and monotonously. —*v.i.* **4** To sing chants. **5** To sing. **6** To talk monotonously and continuously. [< L *cantare,* freq. of *canere* sing] —**chant′er** *n.*

**cha·os** (kā′os) *n.* **1** A condition of utter disorder and confusion. **2** *Often cap.* The primal, formless condition said to have existed before the creation of the universe. [< Gk., abyss < *chainein* gape, yawn]

**chap·el** (chap′əl) *n.* **1** A building for Christian worship, but smaller than a church. **2** A room for worship, as in a hospital, etc. **3** A building for religious services on a campus; also, the services. **4** A compartment or recess in a church where independent services may be held. [< Med. L *cappa* cloak; orig., a sanctuary where the cloak of St. Martin was kept as a relic]

**chap·er·on** (shap′ə·rōn) *n.* **1** A woman who acts as attendant to a young unmarried woman in public. **2** An older person who attends a social function to maintain its decorum and propriety. —*v.t.* To act as chaperon to. **Also chap′er·one.** [F < *chape* cape; because she protects her charges from harm] —**chap·er·on·age** (shap'ə·rō' nij) n.

**chap·lain** (chap'lin) n. A clergyman authorized to conduct religious services in a legislative assembly, in a regiment, on board a ship, at court, etc. [< Med. L *cappella* CHAPEL] —**chap'lain·cy, chap'lain·ship** n.

**chap·ter** (chap'tər) n. 1 A division of a book or treatise, usu. marked by a number and heading. 2 Any period or a sequence of episodes. 3 The canons of a cathedral or other collegiate church. 4 A meeting of such canons or of monks or nuns. 5 A branch of a club, fraternity, etc. —v.t. To divide into chapters, as a book. [< L *caput* head, capital, chapter]

**char** (chär) n. *Brit.* A chore; an odd job. —v.i. **charred, char·ring** To clean and scrub for pay. [OE *cerr* turn of work]

**char·ac·ter** (kar'ik·tər) n. 1 The combination of qualities or traits distinguishing any person or class of persons. 2 Any distinguishing or essential quality or property. 3 Moral excellence. 4 A good reputation. 5 Position; status. 6 A person in a novel, play, etc. 7 A person of note. 8 Any person. 9 A humorous or eccentric person. 10 A written or printed figure, as a letter, mark, sign, etc. 11 *Genetics* A structural or functional trait in a plant or animal. v.t. 1 To write or print. 2 To describe. [<Gk. *charaktēr* stamp, mark < *charassein* engrave]

**cha·rade** (shə·rād') n. A guessing game in which a word or each syllable of a word is acted in pantomime. [< Prov. *charrado* chatter]

**char·coal** (chär'kōl') n. 1 An impure carbon obtained by driving off volatile compounds of organic matter, as of wood, used as a fuel, a filter, etc. 2 A drawing pencil or crayon of charcoal. 3 A drawing made in charcoal. —v.t. To write, draw, or mark with charcoal. [ME *charcole*]

**charge** (chärj) v. **charged, charg·ing** v.t. 1 To lay or impose a load, burden, responsibility, etc. upon. 2 To put something into or upon. 3 To put carbon dioxide into (water, etc.). 4 *Electr.* To replenish, as a storage battery. 5 To load (a firearm, etc.). 6 To command or instruct authoritatively: to *charge* a jury. 7 To accuse: with *with.* 8 To make an onset against or attack upon, as a fort. 9 To set or state, as a price. 10 To set down or record, as a debt to be paid later; also, to purchase (something) by this method. —v.i. 11 To demand or fix a price.

12 To make an onset: *Charge!* —**charge off** To regard or write off as a loss. —n. 1 The quantity of gunpowder, fuel, etc., put or to be put into a firearm, a furnace etc. 2 A quantity of electricity, as in a storage battery or carried by an atomic particle. 3 Care, custody, responsibility, etc. 4 The person or thing for which one is responsible. 5 Instruction or command: the *charge* to a jury. 6 An accusation. 7 A price or cost. 8 A debt; expense. 9 An entry in an account of indebtedness. 10 A charge account. 11 An attack or onslaught; also, the signal for it. [< LL *carricare* carry] —**charge'a·ble** adj.

**char·i·ta·ble** (char'ə·tə·bəl) adj. 1 Of or characterized by charity. 2 Generous in giving gifts to the poor. 3 Tolerant; benevolent; kindly. —**char'i·ta·ble·ness** n. —**char'i·ta·bly** adv.

**char·i·ty** (char'ə·tē) n. pl. **·ties** 1 The giving of aid to the poor. 2 The aid given. 3 An institution, organization, or fund for the help of the needy. 4 A feeling of good will or kindness towards others. 5 An act of good will or kindness. 6 Tolerance; leniency. [< L *caritas* love < *carus* dear]

**char·la·tan** (shär'lə·tən) n. A person who claims to possess a knowledge or skill he does not have; a fake; quack. —**char'la·tan·ry, char'la·tan·ism** n. [< Ital. *ciarlatano* babbler]

**charm** (chärm) v.t. 1 To attract irresistibly; delight; enchant. 2 To influence as by magic power. 3 To protect as by a spell: a *charmed* life. —v.i. 4 To be pleasing or fascinating. 5 To act as a charm; work as a spell. —n. 1 The power to allure or delight; fascination. 2 Something that delights or fascinates. 3 A small ornament worn on a bracelet, etc. 4 Something worn or used to avert evil or bring good luck. [< L *carmen* song, incantation] —**charm'er** n. —**Syn.** v. 1 bewitch, captivate, entrance, fascinate.

**char·nel house** (chär'nəl) A room or building where bones or bodies of the dead are placed. [< L *caro, carnis* flesh]

**chart** (chärt) n. 1 A map; esp., one for the use of navigators, aviators, and meteorologists. 2 A sheet showing facts graphically or in tabular form. —v.t. To map out; lay out on a chart. [< Gk. *chartē* leaf of paper]

**char·ter** (chär'tər) n. 1 A document, given by a ruler or government, granting special rights or privileges to a person, institution, etc. 2 *Usu. cap.* A document outlining the aims or purposes of a group: *Charter* of the

United Nations. 3 A permit to establish a branch or chapter of a society. 4 The leasing or renting of a vessel, airplane, bus, etc. —*v.t.* 1 To hire or rent. 2 To give a charter to. [< L *charta* paper] —**char′ter·er** *n.*

**char·y** (châr′ē) *adj.* **char·i·er, char·i·est** 1 Cautious; wary. 2 Slow to give; sparing. [< OE *cearig* sorrowful, sad]

**chase** (chās) *v.* **chased, chas·ing** *v.t.* 1 To pursue with intent to catch, capture, or molest. 2 To drive away; dispel: often with *away, out* or *off.* 3 To hunt, as deer. —*v.i.* 4 To follow in pursuit. 5 *Informal* To rush; go hurriedly. —*n.* 1 Earnest pursuit. 2 That which is pursued. 3 The sport of hunting: usu. with *the.* [< LL *captiare,* freq. of *capere* take, hold]

**chasm** (kaz′əm) *n.* 1 A deep gorge. 2 A gap or void. 3 A difference, as of opinions, feelings, etc. [< Gk. *chasma* < *chainein* gape] —**chas·mal** (kaz′məl) *adj.*

**chaste** (chāst) *adj.* 1 Free from unlawful sexual activity; virtuous. 2 Sexually abstinent. 3 Pure and modest, as in conduct. 4 Pure and simple in style; not ornate. [< L *castus* pure] —**chaste′ly** *adv.* —**chaste′ness** *n.*

**chast·en** (chās′sən) *v.t.* 1 To discipline by punishment or affliction; chastise. 2 To moderate; soften; temper. [< L *castigare* castigate] —**chast′en·er** *n.* —**chast′en·ing** *n.*

**chas·tise** (chas·tīz′) *v.t.* **·tised, ·tis·ing** 1 To punish, esp. by whipping. 2 To scold sharply. [< L *castigare* castigate] —**chas·tise·ment** (chas′tiz·mənt, chas·tīz′-), chas·tis′er *n.*

**chas·ti·ty** (chas′tə·tē) *n.* The state or quality of being chaste. [< L *castus* pure]

**chat·tel** (chat′l) *n.* An article of personal property that is movable, such as furniture, livestock, etc. [< L *capitale* property < *caput* head]

**chat·ter** (chat′ər) *v.i.* 1 To click together rapidly, as the teeth in shivering. 2 To talk rapidly and trivially. 3 To make rapid and indistinct sounds, as a monkey or squirrel. —*v.t.* 4 To utter in a trivial or chattering manner. —*n.* 1 Idle prattle. 2 Jabbering, as of a monkey. [Imit.] —**chat′ter·er** *n.*

**chauf·feur** (shō′fər, shō·fûr′) *n.* One employed to drive an automobile for someone else. —*v.t.* To serve as a chauffeur for. [F< *chauffer* warm]

**cheap** (chēp) *adj.* 1 Low in price; inexpensive. 2 Lower in price than the going rate or the real value. 3 Demanding little effort: a *cheap* victory. 4 Of little value. 5 Inferior in quality. 6 Low; vulgar; contemptible. 7 Stingy; tight. 8 Embarrassed; sheepish. 9 *Econ.* Obtainable at a low interest rate; also, depreciated: said of money. —*adv.* 1 At a low cost. 2 In a cheap manner. [Earlier *good cheap* a bargain < OE *ceap* business, trade] —**cheap′ly** *adv.* —**cheap′ness** *n.*

**cheat** (chēt) *v.t.* 1 To deceive or defraud. 2 To delude; trick. 3 To elude or escape; foil: to *cheat* the hangman. —*v.i.* 4 To practice fraud or act dishonestly. —**cheat on** *Slang* To be sexually unfaithful to. —*n.* 1 An act of cheating. 2 One who cheats. [ME *chete,* short for *achete* escheat] —**cheat′er** *n.* —**cheat′ing·ly** *adv.*

**check·ers** (chek′ərz) *n. pl. (construed as sing.)* A game played by two persons with 24 pieces on a checkerboard.

**cheer** (chir) *n.* 1 A shout of approval or encouragement. 2 Cheerfulness; gaiety. 3 Something that promotes cheerfulness. 4 Food or drink. —*v.t.* 1 To make cheerful; comfort: often with *up.* 2 To applaud or salute with cheers. 3 To encourage; incite: often with *on.* —*v.i.* 4 To become cheerful, happy or glad: with *up.* 5 To utter cheers. [<OF *chere* face, countenance <LL *cara*] —**cheer′er** *n.*

**cheese** (chēz) *n.* 1 The pressed curd of milk, variously prepared and flavored. 2 A cake or mass of this substance. [<L *caseus* cheese]

**chef** (shef) *n.* 1 A head cook. 2 Any cook. [< OF *chef* chief]

**chem·i·cal** (kem′i·kəl) *adj.* 1 Of or pertaining to chemistry. 2 Obtained by or used in chemistry. —*n.* A substance obtained by or used in a chemical process. —**chem′i·cal·ly** *adv.*

**che·mise** (shə·mēz′) *n.* 1 A woman's undergarment resembling a short slip. 2 A dress that hangs straight from the shoulders. [< LL *camisia* shirt]

**chem·is·try** (kem′is·trē) *n.* 1 That science which treats of the structure, composition, and properties of substances and of the transformations which they undergo. 2 Chemical composition or processes.

**chem·ur·gy** (kem′ər·jē) *n.* The utilization of organic raw materials, esp. agricultural products, in the development of new products. —**chem·ur·gic** (kem·ûr′jik) or **·gi·cal** *adj.*

**cher·ish** (cher′ish) *v.t.* 1 To care for kindly. 2 To hold dear. 3 To entertain fondly, as a

79

hope or an idea. [< F *cher* dear < L *carus*] — **cher′ish·er** *n.*

**cher·ry** (cher′ē) *n. pl.* **·ries** 1 Any of various trees related to the plum and bearing small, round or heart-shaped drupes enclosing a smooth pit. 2 The wood or fruit of a cherry tree. 3 A bright red color: also **cherry red.** —*adj.* 1 Bright red. 2 Made of cherry wood. 3 Made with or from cherries. 4 Having a cherrylike flavor. [< Gk. *kerasos* cherry tree]

**cher·ub** (cher′əb) *n. pl.* **cher·ubs** *for defs. 1 & 2,* **cher·u·bim** (cher′′ə·bim) *for def. 3.* 1 In art, the representation of a beautiful winged child. 2 Any beautiful child or infant. 3 One of an order of angelic beings ranking second to the seraphim. [< Heb. *kerūbh,* an angelic being.] —**che·ru·bic** (chə·rōō′bik) *adj.* —**che·ru′bi·cal·ly** *adv.*

**chess** (ches) *n.* A game played by two persons on a checkered board, with 16 pieces on each side, the object being to checkmate an opponent's king. [< OF *eschec* check (at chess)]

**chew** (chōō) *v.t. & v.i.* 1 To cut or grind with the teeth. 2 To consider carefully. —**chew out** *Slang* To scold or reprimand severely. —*n.* 1 The act of chewing. 2 Something chewed or made for chewing. [< OE *cēowan*] —**chew′er** *n.*

**Chi·ca·no** (chi·kä′nō) *n. pl.* **·nos** A Mexican-American.

**chick·en** (chik′ən) *n.* 1 The young of the common domestic fowl. 2 Loosely, a fowl of any age. 3 Its flesh used as food. 4 *Informal* A young or inexperienced person. —*adj.* 1 Of chicken. 2 Small. 3 *Slang* Cowardly. [< OE *cÿcen*]

**chide** (chīd) *v.t. & v.i.* **chid·ed** or **chid** (chid), **chid·ed** or **chid·den** (chid′n), **chid·ing** To scold or reprove. [< OE *cīdan*] —**chid′er** *n.* —**chid′ing·ly** *adv.*

**chief** (chēf) *n.* 1 A ruler, leader, head, etc., of an organization, group, or establishment. 2 *Usu. cap. Naut.* **a** A chief petty officer. **b** A chief engineer. 3 *Slang* A boss. —*adj.* 1 Highest in rank or authority. 2 Principal, most important, or most eminent. [< L *caput* head]

**chif·fon** (shi·fon′) *n.* A sheer fabric of silk, nylon, etc. [F < *chiffe* rag]

**chill** (chil) *n.* 1 A sensation of cold, often with shivering or shaking. 2 A disagreeable feeling of coldness, as from fear. 3 A dampening of enthusiasm, joy, etc. 4 A distant or unfriendly manner. —*v.t.* 1 To reduce to a low or lower temperature. 2 To make chilly; seize with a chill. 3 To discourage; dampen, as joy. —*v.i.* 4 To become cold. 5 To be stricken with a chill. —*adj. chilly.* [< OE *ciele, cyle*] —**chill′er, chill′ness** *n.* —**chill′ing·ly** *adv.*

**chime** (chīm) *n.* 1 *Often pl.* A set of bells tuned to a scale. 2 A single bell, as in a clock. 3 *Often pl.* The sounds produced by a chime or chimes. 4 Accord; harmony. —*v.* **chimed, chim·ing** *v.t.* 1 To cause to ring musically, as by striking. 2 To announce, as the hour, by the sound of bells. 3 To summon, welcome, or send by chiming. 4 To recite in unison or cadence. —*v.i.* 5 To ring musically, as bells. 6 To harmonize; agree: with *with.* 7 To recite or intone in cadence. [< L *cymbalum* cymbal] —**chim′er** *n.*

**chi·me·ra** (kə·mir′ə, kī-) *n.* 1 An impractically fanciful or absurd hope, plan, or conception. 2 Any fabulous creature composed of incongruous parts 3 *Biol.* An organism or mass of living cells incorporating diverse genetic patterns. Also **chi·mae′ra.** [See CHIMERA.]

**chim·ney** (chim′nē) *n. pl.* **·neys** 1 A pipe or tube for the escape of smoke or gases from a fire. 2 A structure containing such a pipe or tube, often extending above a roof. 3 A tube for enclosing a flame, as of a lamp. 4 *Geol.* A rock formation or a volcano vent resembling a chimney. [< Gk. *kaminos* furnace]

**chim·pan·zee** (chim′pan·zē′, chim·pan′zē) *n.* An African anthropoid ape with large ears and black hair, smaller than the gorilla. [< native w African name]

**chin·chil·la** (chin·chil′ə) *n.* 1 A small South American rodent having soft pearl-gray fur. 2 Its highly valued fur. 3 A heavy wool fabric with a nubbed surface, used esp. for overcoats. [<Sp.]

**Chi·nese** (chī·nēz′, -nēs′) *n. pl.* **·nese** 1 A native or citizen of China. 2 A person whose ancestry is Chinese. 3 Any of a group of related languages spoken in China, esp. the official language. —*adj.* Of or pertaining to China, its peoples, or any of their languages.

**chintz** (chints) *n.* A usu. glazed, brightly printed cotton fabric. [<Skt. *chitra* variegated]

**chip·munk** (chip′mungk) *n.* Any of various squirrellike striped North American rodents. [<N.Am. Ind.]

80

**chi·rog·ra·phy** (kī·rog′rə·fē) *n.* Handwriting; penmanship. —**chi·rog′ra·pher** *n.*

**chi·rop·o·dy** (kə·rop′ə·dē, kī-) *n.* PODIATRY. [<CHIRO- + Gk. *pous, podos* foot] —**chi·rop′o·dist** *n.*

**chi·ro·prac·tic** (kī′rə·prak′tik) *n.* Therapeutic treatment involving manipulation of the body, esp. the spine. [<CHIRO + Gk. *praktikos* effective<*prattein* do, act] —**chi′ro·prac′tor** *n.*

**chis·el** (chiz′əl) *n.* A tool with a sharp, beveled edge, used for cutting or shaping metal, stone, or wood. —*v.t.* & *v.i.* **chis·eled** or ·**elled, chis·el·ing** or ·**el·ling** 1 To cut, engrave, or carve with or as with a chisel. 2 *Informal.* To cheat; swindle. [<L *caesus* pp. of *caedere* cut] —**chis′el·er** or **chis′el·ler** *n.*

**chiv·al·ry** (shiv′əl·rē) *n.* 1 The system or spirit of medieval knighthood. 2 The idealized qualities of knighthood, as courtesy, magnanimity, bravery, etc. 3 An instance of such qualities. [<LL *caballarius* cavalier]

**chlo·ro·form** (klôr′ə·fôrm, klō′rə-) *n.* A colorless, volatile, sweetish liquid compound, used as an anesthetic and a solvent. —*v.t.* To anesthetize or kill with chloroform. [<CHLORO- + FORM(YL)]

**choc·o·late** (chôk′lit, chôk′ə·lit, chok′-) *n.* 1 Roasted and ground cacao seeds, often sweetened or flavored. 2 A beverage or confection made from this. 3 A dark brown. —*adj.* 1 Flavored or made with chocolate. 2 Dark brown. [< Nah. *chocólatl*]

**choice** (chois) *n.* 1 The act of choosing; selection. 2 The right or power to choose; option. 3 Something or someone chosen. 4 A number or variety from which to choose. 5 An alternative. 6 The best or preferred part. —*adj.* **choic·er, choic·est** 1 Of special quality; excellent. 2 Carefully selected. [< OF *choisir* choose] —**choice′ly** *adv.* —**choice′ness** *n.*

**choir** (kwīr) *n.* 1 A body of trained singers, esp. in a church. 2 The part of a church used by such a group. 3 A group of musicians, as instrumentalists. —*v.t.* & *v.i.* To sing in a choir or chorus. [< L *chorus* chorus]

**choke** (chōk) *v.* **choked, chok·ing** *v.t.* 1 To stop or obstruct the breathing of; strangle. 2 To keep back; suppress. 3 To obstruct or close up by filling. 4 To retard the progress, growth, or action of. 5 To lessen the air intake in order to enrich the fuel mixture of (a gasoline engine). —*v.i.* 6 To become suffocated or stifled. 7 To have difficulty in breathing. 8 To be so affected by emotion, fright, etc., that one's behavior is noticeably constrained or one's speech faltering: usu. with *up.* 9 To become clogged or obstructed. —*n.* 1 The act or sound of choking. 2 A device to control the supply of air to a gasoline engine. [< OE *acēocian*]

**chol·er·a** (kol′ər·ə) *n.* An acute, infectious, epidemic disease, characterized by serious intestinal disorders. [< Gk. < *cholē* bile, gall]

**cho·les·ter·ol** (kə·les′tə·rōl, -rōl) *n.* A fat-soluble, solid alcohol found in the blood, brain and nerve tissue, etc., and in deposits constricting blood vessels in arteriosclerosis. [< Gk. *cholē* bile + *stereos* solid + -OL]

**choose** (chōōz) *v.* **chose, cho·sen, choos·ing** *v.t.* 1 To select among others or as an alternative. 2 To desire or prefer (to do something). —*v.i.* 3 To make a selection or decision. [< OE *cēosan*] —**choos′er** *n.*

**chop** (chop) *v.* **chopped, chop·ping** *v.t.* 1 To cut or make by strokes of a sharp tool; hew. 2 To cut up in small pieces; mince. 3 To utter jerkily. —*v.i.* 4 To make cutting strokes, as with an ax. 5 To move with a sudden, jerky motion. —*n.* 1 A small cut of meat, usu. containing a rib. 2 The act of chopping. 3 A short, swift blow. 4 A sudden choppy motion, as of a wave. [ME *choppen* var. of *chappen* to chap]

**chord** (kôrd) *n.* A combination of three or more musical tones sounded together. [Earlier *cord,* short for ACCORD]

**chore** (chôr, chōr) *n.* 1 A small or routine task. 2 An unpleasant or hard task. [Var. of CHAR[1]]

**cho·re·og·ra·phy** (kôr′ē·og′rə·fē, kō′rē-) *n.* 1 The art of devising ballets and dances. 2 The art of dancing, esp. for theatrical performance. 3 The written representation of figures and steps of dancing. [< Gk. *choreia* dance + -GRAPHY] —**cho·re·o·graph·ic** (kôr′ē·ə·graf′ik, kō′rē) *adj.*

**cho·rus** (kôr′əs, kō′rəs) *n.* 1 A group of singers who perform together. 2 A musical composition or section for such a group. 3 A group of dancers and singers who perform together in singing roles in musical comedy, etc. 4 Any group uttering something simultaneously. 5 Something uttered by such a group. 6 A repeated section of a song; refrain. 7 In Greek drama, a body of actors who comment upon and sometimes take part in the main action of a play. —**in chorus** All together; in unison. —*v.t.* & *v.i.* **cho·rused** or ·**russed, ·rus·ing** or ·**rus·sing**

To sing or utter in chorus. [< L < Gk. *choros* dance]

**chris·ten** (kris'ən) *v.t.* 1 To name in baptism. 2 To baptize. 3 To give a name to in some ceremony: to *christen* a ship. 4 *Informal* To use for the first time. [< OE *cristnian* < *cristen* Christian]

**chro·mat·ic** (krō·mat'ik) *adj.* 1 Of color or colors. 2 *Music* Using or proceeding by semitones. —**chro·mat'i·cal·ly** *adv.*

**chro·mo·some** (krō'mə·sōm) *n.* One of the rodlike bodies formed from chromatin in the nucleus during cell division, acting as a carrier of the genes or units of heredity. [< CHROMO- + Gk. *sōma* body]

**chron·ic** (kron'ik) *adj.* 1 Continuing for a long period, as a disease. 2 Inveterate; habitual: a *chronic* complainer. [< Gk. *chronos* time] —**chron'i·cal·ly** *adv.*

**chron·i·cle** (kron'i·kəl) *n.* A record of events chronologically arranged. —*v.t.* ·**cled**, ·**cling** To record in or as a chronicle. [< Gk. *chronikos* of time] —**chron'i·cler** *n.*

**chro·nol·o·gy** (krə·nol'ə·jē) *n. pl.* ·**gies** 1 The science that treats of the measurement of time or the order of events. 2 An arrangement of events in the order of the time of their occurrence. 3 A table or list so arranged. [< CHRONO- + -LOGY] —**chro·nol'o·ger**, **chro·nol'o·gist** *n.*

**chro·nom·e·ter** (krə·nom'ə·tər) *n.* A timekeeping instrument of high precision and accuracy. [< CHRONO- + -METER] —**chron·o·met·ric** (kron'ə·met'rik) or ·**ri·cal** *adj.* —**chron'o·met'ri·cal·ly** *adv.*

**chrys·a·lis** (kris'ə·lis) *n. pl.* **chrys·a·lis·es** or **chry·sal·i·des** (kri·sal'ə·dēz) 1 The capsule-enclosed pupal stage of a butterfly or moth, from which the winged adult emerges. 2 Anything in an undeveloped stage. [< Gk. *chrysallis* < *chrysos* gold]

**chrys·an·the·mum** (kri·san'thə·məm) *n.* 1 Any of several varieties of plants cultivated for their showy, composite flowers. 2 The flower. [< Gk. *chrysanthemon*, lit., golden flower]

**chub·by** (chub'ē) *adj.* ·**bi·er**, ·**bi·est** Plump. [< CHUB] —**chub'bi·ness** *n.*

**chuck·le** (chuk'əl) *v.i.* ·**led**, ·**ling** 1 To laugh quietly, as to oneself. 2 To cluck, as a hen. —*n.* A low, quiet laugh. [? Imit.] —**chuck'ler** *n.*

**chunk** (chungk) *n.* 1 A thick piece, lump, etc. 2 A goodly amount. [Var. of CHUCK²]

**churl** (chûrl) *n.* 1 A surly, boorish fellow. 2 A

peasant, esp. in medieval England. [< OE *ceorl*] —**churl'ish** *adj.* —**churl'ish·ly** *adv.* —**churl'ish·ness** *n.*

**churn** (chûrn) *n.* A vessel in which milk or cream is agitated to produce butter. —*v.t.* 1 To stir or agitate (cream or milk) in or as in a churn. 2 To make (butter) in a churn. 3 To agitate violently. —*v.i.* 4 To use a churn. 5 To be in violent agitation. [< OE *cyrin*] —**churn'er** *n.*

**chute** (shōōt) *n.* 1 An inclined trough, slide, or passageway, as for grain, ore, coal, etc. 2 A waterfall or a rapid in a river. 3 *Informal* A parachute.

**ci·der** (sī'dər) *n.* The juice of apples, used to make vinegar and as a beverage before fermentation (**sweet cider**) or after fermentation (**hard cider**). [< OF *sidre* < LL *sicera* strong drink < Heb. *shēkār*]

**ci·gar** (si·gär') *n.* A small roll of tobacco leaves prepared for smoking. [< Sp. *cigarro*]

**cig·a·rette** (sig'ə·ret', sig'ə·ret) *n.* A small roll of finely cut tobacco in thin paper, used for smoking. Also **cig'a·ret'**. [< F *cigare* cigar]

**cin·na·mon** (sin'ə·mən) *n.* 1 The aromatic inner bark of any of several tropical trees of the laurel family, used as a spice. 2 Any tree that yields cinnamon. 3 A light reddish brown. —*adj.* 1 Made with cinnamon. 2 Light reddish brown. [< Gk. *kinnamōmon* < Heb. *qinnāmōn*]

**cir·cle** (sûr'kəl) *n.* 1 A plane figure bounded by a curved line everywhere equally distant from a fixed point. 2 Something having the form of such a figure, as a ring, round object or enclosure, etc. 3 A course, cycle, series, etc., that ends at the starting point. 4 A group of persons sharing a common interest, occupation, or other tie. 5 A sphere or area of influence. 6 A tier of seats in a theater. —*v.* ·**cled**, ·**cling** *v.t.* 1 To enclose with or as with a circle. 2 To move around, or over, as in a circle. —*v.i.* 3 To move in a circle. [< L *circulus*, dim. of *circus* ring] —**cir'cler** *n.* —**Syn.** *n.* 4 set, crowd, coterie, clique.

**cir·cuit** (sûr'kit) *n.* 1 A more or less circular route, course, etc.; a round. 2 A journey from place to place through such a course, as by a judge or clergyman. 3 A district visited by or within the jurisdiction of one having such a route, esp. a judge. 4 An association, as of theaters or teams, in which performances, contests, etc., take place in turn. 5 A curve forming a closed circumference. 6 **a** The entire course traversed by an electric current. **b** An assembly of parts and components that function together in an electric or electronic device or system. 7 A radio transmission and reception system. —*v.t. & v.i.* To go or move through in a circuit. [< F < L *circuitus,* pp of < *circumire* go around]

**cir·cu·lar** (sûr′kyə·lər) *adj.* 1 Shaped like a circle; round. 2 Of, forming, or moving in a circle. 3 Ending at the point of beginning. 4 Circuitous; indirect. —*n.* A communication or notice for general circulation. [< L *circulus* CIRCLE] —**cir·cu·lar·i·ty** (sûr′kyə·lar′ə·tē) *n.* —**cir′cu·lar·ly** *adv.*

**cir·cu·late** (sûr′kyə·lāt) *v.* **·lat·ed, ·lat·ing** —*v.i.* 1 To move in a closed course. 2 To move or travel about. 3 To move or flow freely, as air. —*v.t.* 4 To cause to circulate. [< L *circulari*] —**cir′cu·la′tive,** **cir·cu·la·to·ry** (sûr′kyə·lə·tôr′ē, ‑tō′rē) *adj.* —**cir′cu·la′tor** *n.*

**cir·cum·fer·ence** (sər·kum′fər·əns) *n.* 1 The boundary line of a circle. 2 Distance or measurement around something. [< L *circumferentia* < *circum-* around + *ferre* bear] —**cir·cum·fer·en·tial** (sər·kum′fər·en′shəl) *adj.*

**cir·cum·flex** (sûr′kəm·fleks) *n.* A mark (û) used over a vowel to indicate a pronunciation. —*adj.* 1 Pronounced or marked with the circumflex accent. 2 Bent or curved. —*v.t.* To mark with a circumflex. [< L *circum-* around + *flectere* bend]

**cir·cum·lo·cu·tion** (sûr′kəm·lō·kyōō′shən) *n.* A long, roundabout way of saying or expressing something. [< L *circum-* around + *loqui* speak] —**cir·cum·loc·u·tory** (sûr′kəm·lok′yə·tôr′ē, ‑tō′rē) *adj.*

**cir·cum·nav·i·gate** (sûr′kəm·nav′ə·gāt) *v.t.* **·gat·ed, ·gat·ing** To sail around. —**cir′cum·nav′i·ga′tion,** **cir′cum·nav′i·ga′tor** *n.*

**cir·cum·scribe** (sûr′kəm·skrīb′) *v.t.* **·scribed, ·scrib·ing** 1 To draw a line around; encircle. 2 To confine within bounds; restrict. 3 *Geom.* **a** To surround with a figure that coincides at every possible point: to *circumscribe* a triangle with a circle. **b** To cause to surround a figure thus: to *circumscribe* a circle about a triangle. [< L *circum-* around + *scribere* write] —**cir′cum·scrib′er,** **cir·cum·scrip·tion** (sûr′·kəm·skrip′shen) *n.*

**cir·cum·spect** (sûr′kəm·spekt) *adj.* Attentive to all possibilities; cautious. [< L *circum-* around + *specere* look] —**cir′cum·spec′tion,** **cir′cum·spect′ness** *n.* —**cir′cum·spec′tive** *adj.* —**cir′cum·spect′ly** *adv.* —Syn. prudent, wary.

**cir·cum·stance** (sûr′kəm·stans) *n.* 1 A related or concomitant condition, fact, occurrence, etc. 2 Any condition, fact, etc. 3 *pl.* The situation a person is in relative to certain conditions, esp. financial conditions. 4 Formal display; ceremony; pomp and *circumstance.* —**under no circumstances** Never; under no conditions. —**under the circumstances** Such being the case or conditions. [< L *circum-* around + *stare* stand] —**cir′cum·stanced** *adj.*

**cir·cum·vent** (sûr′kəm·vent′) *v.t.* 1 To avoid by or as by going around; bypass. 2 To get the better of by strategy or craft; outwit. [< L *circum-* around + *venire* come] —**cir′·cum·vent′er, cir′cum·vent′or, cir′cum·ve·n′tion** *n.* —**cir′cum·ven′tive** *adj.*

**cir·cus** (sûr′kəs) *n.* 1 A show in which acrobats, trained animals, clowns, etc., perform. 2 The circular, often tented enclosure in which such a show is held. 3 The members of such a show. 4 A large arena with tiers of seats around it, used in ancient Rome for contests or public spectacles. 5 *Brit.* A circular intersection of several streets. 6 *Informal* Something uproariously entertaining. [< L, a ring, racecourse]

**cit·ron** (sit′rən) *n.* 1 A fruit like a lemon, but larger and less acid. 2 The tree producing this fruit. 3 A variety of watermelon with hard-fleshed fruit: **also citron melon.** 4 The candied rind of either of these fruits. [< L *citrus* citron tree]

**cit·rus** (sit′rəs) *adj.* Of or pertaining to a genus of fruit-bearing trees or shrubs including the orange, lemon, lime, grapefruit, etc. **Also cit′rous.** —*n. pl.* **·rus·es** A citrus tree or fruit. [< L, citron tree]

**civ·ic** (siv′ik) *adj.* Of or pertaining to a city, citizens, or citizenship. [< L *civis* citizen]

**civ·il** (siv′əl) *adj.* 1 Of or pertaining to citizens, esp. in relation to the state. 2 Of or pertaining to general public life as distinguished from military or ecclesiastical activities. 3 Of or involving internal relationships and affairs of a country. 4 Socially acceptable; polite. [< L *civis* citizen] —**civ′il·ly** *adv.* —Syn. 4 courteous, well-bred, civilized, proper, well-mannered, attentive.

**civil defense** A civilian program of action by civilians for general protection and maintenance of essential services in case of enemy attack or widespread disaster.

**ci·vil·ian** (sə·vil′yən) *n.* One who is not a member of the armed forces. —*adj.* Of civilians or civil life.

**ci·vil·i·ty** (sə·vil′ə·tē) *n. pl.* **·ties** 1 Courtesy; politeness. 2 A courteous act, expression, etc.

**claim** (klām) *v.t.* 1 To demand as a right; assert ownership or title to. 2 To hold to be true. 3 To require or deserve. —*n.* 1 A demand for something due; assertion of a right. 2 The basis for such a demand or assertion. 3 An assertion, as of a fact. 4 Something claimed, as a piece of land for use by a settler or miner. [< L *clamare* declare] — **claim′a·ble** *adj.* —**claim′er** *n.*

**clam** (klam) *n.* 1 Any of numerous often edible bivalve mollusks. 2 *Informal* An uncommunicative person. —*v.i.* **clammed, clam·ming** To hunt for or dig clams. —**clam up** *Slang* To become silent. [< OE *clamm* a clamp]

**clam·ber** (klam′bər) *v.t. & v.i.* To climb clumsily or laboriously as by using the hands and feet. —*n.* A difficult climb. [< ON *klimbra* to grip] —**clam′ber·er** *n.*

**clam·or** (klam′ər) *n.* 1 A loud, persistent outcry or noise. 2 A vehement general demand or protest. —*v.i.* 1 To make a clamor. —*v.t.* 2 To utter with loud outcry. *Brit. sp.* **clam′our.** [< L *clamare* cry out] —**clam′or·er** *n.* —**Syn.** *n.* 1 din, uproar, hubbub, racket.

**clamp** (klamp) *n.* A device for holding or pressing together two or more parts. —*v.t.* To join or press with or as with a clamp. [< MDu. *klampe*]

**clan** (klan) *n.* 1 A group of families having a common ancestor, as in the Scottish Highlands. 2 A group of related or closely associated persons. [< Scot. Gael. *clānn*]

**clan·des·tine** (klan·des′tin) *adj.* Kept secret; surreptitious. [< L *clandestinus* < *clam* in secret] —**clan·des′tine·ly** *adv.* —**clan·de·s′tine·ness** *n.*

**clang** (klang) *v.t. & v.i.* 1 To make or cause to make a loud, ringing, metallic sound. 2 To strike together with such a sound. —*n.* A loud, ringing sound, as of metal struck. [< L *clangere*]

**clar·i·fy** (klar′ə·fī) *v.* **·fied, ·fy·ing** *v.t.* 1 To make clear or understandable. 2 To free from impurities, as fats. —*v.i.* 3 To become clear. [< L *clarus* clear + *facere* make] — **clar·i·fi·ca·tion** (klar′ə·fə·kā′shən) *n.* — **clar′i·fi′er** *n.*

**clar·i·net** (klar′ə·net′) *n.* A cylindrical woodwind instrument with a bell mouth, having a single reed mouthpiece, finger holes, and keys. [< F *clarine* bell < L *clarus* clear] — **clar′i·net′ist** or **clar′i·net′tist** *n.*

**clash** (klash) *v.i.* 1 To collide with a harsh, metallic sound. 2 To be in opposition; conflict. —*v.t.* 3 To strike together with a harsh, metallic sound. —*n.* 1 A loud, harsh sound, as of metal objects striking. 2 A marked conflict. [Imit.]

**clasp** (klasp, kläsp) *n.* 1 A fastener by which things are held together. 2 A firm grasp or embrace. —*v.t.* 1 To fasten with or as with a clasp. 2 To embrace. 3 To grasp firmly in or with the hand. [ME *claspe*] —**clasp′er** *n.*

**clas·sic** (klas′ik) *adj.* 1 Regarded as best or exemplary of its kind. 2 Of or pertaining to the art, literature, etc., of ancient Greece and Rome. 3 Considered typical of such art or literature; formal; regular. 4 Founded or celebrated in tradition. 5 Fashionable because of the simplicity of its style: said of wearing apparel, furniture, etc. —*n.* 1 An author, artist, or creative work generally regarded as of the highest excellence. 2 A traditional event, as in sports. 3 Something that is classic (def. 5). —**the classics** Ancient Greek and Roman literature. [< L *classicus* of the first rank < *classis* order, class]

**clas·si·fi·ca·tion** (klas′ə·fə·kā′shən) *n.* 1 The act, process, or result of classifying. 2 A category; class. 3 TAXONOMY. —**clas·si·fi·ca·to·ry** (klas′ə·fə·kə·tôr′ē, -tō′rē, klas′ə·fə·kā′tər·ē, klə·sif′ə·kə·tôr′ē, -tō′rē) *adj.*

**clas·si·fy** (klas′ə·fī) *v.t.* **·fied, ·fy·ing** 1 To arrange systematically on the basis of class or category. 2 To restrict as to circulation or use, a specially designated document or item of information. [< L *classis* class + -FY] —**clas′si·fi′a·ble** *adj.* —**clas′si·fi′er** *n.*

**clat·ter** (klat′ər) *v.i.* 1 To make or move with a rattling noise. 2 To chatter noisily. —*v.t.* 3 To cause to make a rattling noise. —*n.* 1 A rattling noise. 2 Noisy chatter. [< OE *clatrung* a clattering noise] —**clat′ter·er** *n.*

**clause** (klôz) *n.* 1 *Gram.* A group of words containing a subject and predicate and usu. forming part of a compound or complex sentence. 2 A separate statement or proviso in a legal document, treaty, etc. [< L *clausus*, pp. of *claudere* close] —**claus′al** *adj.*

**clef** (klef) *n. Music* A symbol placed upon the staff to determine the pitch of the notes, namely, the treble or G clef, bass or F clef, and the C clef. [< L *clavis* key]

**cleft** (kleft) *v.* A *p.t.* & *p.p.* of CLEAVE[1]. —*adj.* Divided partially or completely. —*n.* A fissure; crevice; crack.

**clem·en·cy** (klem′ən·sē) *n. pl.* **·cies** 1 Leniency; mercy. **2** An act of leniency. **3** Mildness, as of weather. [< L *clemens* mild]

**cler·gy** (klûr′jē) *n. pl.* **·gies** The group of people ordained for service in a Christian church. [< OF *clerc* clerk, cleric < LL *clericus*]

**cler·i·cal** (kler′i·kəl) *adj.* **1** Of, pertaining to, or characteristic of a clergyman or the clergy. **2** Of or pertaining to workers or clerks in an office or to their work. —*n.* **1** A clergyman. **2** *pl.* The garb of a clergyman. —**cler′i·cal·ly** *adv.*

**clerk** (klûrk, *Brit.* klärk) *n.* **1** A person employed in an office to take care of records, filing, correspondence, etc. **2** An employee of a court, legislative body, etc. who has charge of records and accounts. **3** A salesperson in a store. **4** A hotel employee who assigns guests to their rooms. —*v.i.* To work or act as clerk. [< Gk. *klērikos* < *klēros* lot, portion] —**clerk′li·ness** *n.* —**clerk′ly** *adj.*

**clev·er** (klev′ər) *adj.* **1** Physically skillful; dexterous; adroit. **2** Mentally quick and intelligent; bright; keen; able. **3** Marked by ingenuity and originality. [? < Scand.] —**clev′er·ly** *adv.* —**clev′er·ness** *n.* —**Syn. 1** adept, expert, handy, deft. **2** sharp, shrewd, knowing, smart, talented. **3** inventive, ingenious, felicitous.

**cli·ché** (klē·shā′) *n.* A trite saying, idea, etc. —*adj.* Being a cliché. [< F *clicher* to stereotype]

**click** (klik) *n.* **1** A short, sharp, metallic sound, as that made by the latch of a door. **2** *Phonet.* A speech sound occurring in certain African languages, produced by the sudden withdrawal of the tip of the tongue from the teeth or palate. —*v.i.* **1** To cause to make a click or clicks. —*v.i.* **2** To produce a click or clicks. **3** *Slang* To succeed. **4** *Slang* To agree or be in accord. [Imit.] —**click′er** *n.*

**cli·ent** (klī′ənt) *n.* **1** One in whose interest a lawyer acts. **2** One who engages the services of any professional adviser. **3** A customer. [< L *cliens* follower] —**cli·en·tal** (klī·en′təl, klī′ən·təl) *adj.*

**cliff** (klif) *n.* A high steep face of rock; a precipice. [< OE *clif*]

**cli·mate** (klī′mit) *n.* **1** The weather and other meteorological conditions characteristic of a locality or region over an extended period of time. **2** A region as characterized by such conditions. **3** A prevailing or dominant trend in social affairs: *climate* of opinion. [< Gk. *klima* region, zone] —**cli·mat·ic** (klī·mat′ik) or **·i·cal** *adj.* —**cli·mat′i·cal·ly** *adv.*

**cli·max** (klī′maks) *n.* **1** The highest point of intensity, interest, activity, etc.; culmination. **2** ORGASM. —*v.t.* & *v.i.* To reach or bring to a climax. [< Gk. *klimax* ladder]

**climb** (klīm) *v.t.* **1** To ascend or descend (something), esp. by means of the hands and feet. —*v.i.* **2** To mount, rise, or go up, esp. by using the hands and feet. **3** To rise, as in position or status; to *climb* to the top of one's profession. **4** To incline or slope upward. **5** To rise during growth, as certain vines, by clinging to a support. —*n.* **1** The act or process of climbing. **2** A place ascended by climbing. [< OE *climban*] —**climb′a·ble** *adj.* —**climb′er** *n.*

**cling** (kling) *v.i.* **clung, cling·ing** **1** To hold on to something firmly, as by grasping, embracing, or winding round. **2** To resist separation: with *together*. **3** To stick to tenaciously, as in the memory. [< OE *clingan*] —**cling′er** *n.* —**cling′y** *adj.* (**·i·er, ·i·est**)

**clip** (klip) *v.t.* **clipped, clip·ping** **1** To cut or trim with shears or scissors, as hair. **2** To cut short; curtail; to *clip* the ends of words. **3** *Informal* To strike with a sharp blow. **4** *Slang* To cheat or defraud. —*v.i.* **5** To cut or trim. **6** *Informal* To run or move swiftly. —*n.* **1** The act of clipping, or that which is clipped. **2** The wool yielded at one shearing or season. **3** *Informal* A blow with the hand or fist. **4** *Informal* A quick pace. [< ON *klippa*]

**clique** (klēk, klik) *n.* An exclusive or clannish group of people; coterie. —*v.i.* **cliqued, cli·quing** To unite in a clique; act clannishly. [< F *cliquer* click, clap]

**cloak** (klōk) *n.* **1** A loose outer garment. **2** Something that covers or hides; a pretext; disguise. —*v.t.* **1** To cover with a cloak. **2** To disguise; conceal. [< OF *cloque*, bell, cape]

**clod** (klod) *n.* **1** A lump of earth, clay, etc. **2** A dull, stupid fellow. [< OE *clott* lump, clot] —**clod′dish, clod′dy** *adj.*

**clog** (klog) *n.* **1** Anything that impedes motion, as a block attached to an animal or a vehicle. **2** An obstruction or hindrance. **3** A wooden-soled shoe. **4** CLOG DANCE. —*v.* **clogged, clog·ging** —*v.t.* **1** To choke up or obstruct. **2** To hinder. **3** To fasten a clog to; hobble. —*v.i.* **4** To become choked up. **5** To adhere in a mass; coagulate. **6** To perform a clog dance. [ME *clogge* block of wood] —**clog′gi·ness** *n.*

**clois·ter** (klois′tər) *n.* 1 A covered walk along the inside walls of buildings enclosing a courtyard, as in a monastery or college. 2 A monastery or convent. 3 Monastic life. —*v.t.* 1 To seclude; confine, as in a cloister. 2 To provide with cloisters. [< L *claustrum* enclosed place] —**clois′ter·ed, clois′tral** *adj.*

**close** (klōs) *adj.* **clos·er, clos·est** 1 Near or near together in space, time, order, etc. 2 Compact; dense: a *close* weave. 3 Tight: a *close* fit. 4 Near to the surface; very short. 5 Affectionately associated; intimate: a *close* friend. 6 Near to the original; exact; literal: a *close* copy. 7 Thorough; strict: a *close* search. 8 Accurate. 9 Nearly even or equal in score, performance, etc.: said of contests or contestants. 10 Shut in or about. 11 Confined or encompassed by limits, walls, etc.: *close* quarters. 12 Carefully watched or guarded: *close* custody. 13 Secretive; reticent. 14 Not liberal; stingy. 15 Ill-ventilated; warm; stifling. 16 Difficult to obtain; tight; said of money, credit, etc. 17 Not open or free; restricted. 18 *Phonet.* Describing those vowels pronounced with a part of the tongue relatively near to the palate, as the (ē) in *seat*. —*v.* (klōz) closed, **clos·ing** *v.t.* 1 To shut, as a door. 2 To fill or obstruct, as an opening or passage. 3 To bring together; unite; join. 4 To bring to an end; terminate. 5 To shut in; enclose. —*v.i.* 6 To become shut or closed. 7 To come to an end. 8 To come to close quarters. 9 To join; coalesce; unite. 10 To come to an agreement. 11 To be worth at the end of a business day: Stocks closed three points higher. —*n.* (klōz) 1 The act of closing. 2 An end; conclusion. 3 (klōs) *Chiefly Brit.* Any place shut in or enclosed, esp. such a place adjoining a cathedral or abbey. —*adv.* (klōs) In a close manner or position. [< L *claudere* to close] —**close′ly** (klōs′lē) *adv.* —**close′ness** (klōs′nis) *n.* —**clos·er** (klō′zər) *n.*

**clot** (klot) *n.* A thickened or coagulated mass, as of blood. —*v.t. & v.i.* **clot·ted, clot·ting** To form clots; coagulate. [< OE *clott* lump, mass] —**clot′ty, clot′ted** *adj.*

**cloth** (klôth, kloth) *n. pl.* **cloths** (klôthz, klothz, klôths, kloths) 1 A woven, knitted, or felted fabric of wool, cotton, rayon, etc. 2 A piece of cloth for a special use, as a tablecloth. —**the cloth** Clerical attire; also, the clergy. [< OE *clath*]

**clothe** (klōth) *v.t.* **clothed** or **clad, cloth·ing** 1 To cover or provide with clothes. 2 To cover as if with clothing; invest. [< OE *clathian*]

**clo·ver·leaf** (klō′vər·lēf′) *n.* A highway intersection with curving ramps in the form of a four-leaf clover, designed to route traffic in four directions without interference.

**clown** (kloun) *n.* 1 A professional buffoon in a play or circus who entertains by antics, jokes, tricks, etc. 2 A person who behaves like a clown. —*v.i.* To behave like a clown. [? < Scand.] —**clown′er·y, clown′ish·ness** *n.* —**clown′ish** *adj.* —**clown′ish·ly** *adv.*

**club·foot** (klub′fŏŏt′) *n. pl.* **·feet** 1 Congenital distortion of the foot; talipes. 2 A foot so affected. —**club′foot′ed** *adj.*

**cluck** (kluk) *v.i.* 1 To make the noise of a hen calling her chicks. 2 To make any sound similar to a cluck. —*v.t.* 3 To call by clucking. 4 To express by clucking: to *cluck* disapproval. —*n.* The sound of clucking. [Imit.]

**clump** (klump) *n.* 1 A thick cluster. 2 A heavy sound, as of tramping. 3 A lump or mass. —*v.t.* 1 To place or plant in a cluster or group. —*v.i.* 2 To walk clumsily and noisily. 3 To form clumps. [< LG] —**clump′y** (·i·er, ·i·est), **clump′ish** *adj.*

**clum·sy** (klum′zē) *adj.* **·si·er, ·si·est** 1 Lacking physical dexterity, ease, or grace; awkward. 2 Badly constructed; unwieldy. 3 Awkwardly worded, delivered, etc.; inept. [< ME *clumsen* be numb (with cold) < Scand.] —**clum′si·ly** *adv.* —**clum′si·ness** *n.* —**Syn.** 1 ungainly, unhandy, maladroit. 2 heavy, cumbersome, ungainly. 3 Bungling, heavy-handed, gauche.

**clus·ter** (klus′tər) *n.* 1 A group or bunch of objects or things joined together. 2 A group or assembly of persons or things close together. —*v.t. & v.i.* To be, form, or grow in a cluster or clusters. [< OE *clyster*] —**clus′tered** *adj.*

**clutch**[1] (kluch) *v.t.* 1 To snatch, as with hands or talons. 2 To grasp and hold firmly. —*v.i.* 3 To attempt to seize, snatch, or reach: with *at.* —*n.* 1 The act of clutching. 2 A tight, powerful grasp. 3 *pl.* Control; power: to fall into the *clutches* of an enemy. 4 *Mech.* a Any of various devices for coupling two working parts. b A pedal or lever for operating such a device. 5 A device for seizing and holding. 6 *Informal* A crisis or emergency. [< OE *clyccan* to grasp]

**clutch**[2] (kluch) *n.* 1 A nest of eggs. 2 A brood of chickens. 3 A tightly bunched group or cluster: a *clutch* of reporters. —*v.t.* To hatch.

**clut·ter** (klut′ər) *n.* A disordered state or collection; litter. —*v.t.* 1 To make disordered; litter: often with *up*. —*v.i.* 2 To run or move with bustle. [ME *clotteren* to clot]

**coach** (kōch) *n.* 1 A large four-wheeled closed carriage; stagecoach. 2 A passenger bus. 3 The lowest-priced accommodations on a passenger train or airplane. 4 A trainer or director, as of athletes, singers, actors, etc. 5 A private tutor. —*v.t.* 1 To train or direct (athletes, singers, etc.). —*v.i.* 2 To study with or be trained by a coach. 3 To act as coach. [< *Kocs*, a Hungarian village where first used] —**coach′er** *n.*

**co·ag·u·late** (kō·ag′yə·lāt) *v.t.* & *v.i.* ·lat·ed, ·lat·ing To change from a liquid state into a clot or jelly, as blood. [< L *coagulare* curdle] —**co·ag′u·la′tion, co·ag′u·la′tor** *n.* —**co·ag′u·la·ble, co·ag′u·la′tive** *adj.*

**co·a·lesce** (kō′ə·les′) *v.i.* ·lesced, ·lesc·ing To grow or come together into one; fuse; blend. [< L *coalescere* unite] —**co′a·les′cence** *n.* —**co′a·les′cent** *adj.*

**co·a·li·tion** (kō′ə·lish′ən) *n.* 1 An alliance, often temporary, of persons, parties, or states, usu. for a specific purpose. 2 A fusion or union. [< L *coalitio* < *coalescere* to coalesce] —**co′a·li′tion·ist** *n.*

**coarse** (kôrs, kōrs) *adj.* coars·er, coars·est 1 Composed of somewhat large or rough parts or particles. 2 Not fine or delicate in form, texture, etc. 3 Vulgar; indelicate; crude. [Adjectival use of COURSE, *n.*, def. 2] —**coarse′ly** *adv.* —**coarse′ness** *n.*

**coast** (kōst) *n.* 1 The land next to the sea; the seashore. 2 A slope suitable for sliding, as on a sled; also, a slide down it. —**the Coast** That part of the United States bordering on the Pacific Ocean. —*v.t.* 1 To sail or travel along, as a coast or border. —*v.i.* 2 To slide or ride down a slope by force of gravity alone, as on a sled. 3 To continue moving on momentum after the source of power has been stopped. 4 To move or behave aimlessly. [< L *costa* rib, flank] —**coast′al** *adj.*

**coaxial cable** An electric cable consisting of two insulated conductors, one of which surrounds the other.

**cob·bler** (kob′lər) *n.* 1 A shoemaker. 2 A clumsy workman. [< COBBLE²]

**co·bra** (kō′brə) *n.* Any of various poisonous snakes of Asia and Africa that when ex-

cited dilate the loose skin at their necks into a hood. [< L *colubra* snake]

**cob·web** (kob′web′) *n.* 1 The network of fine thread spun by a spider; also, a single thread of this. 2 Anything finespun or ensnaring. —*v.t.* **cob·webbed, cob·web·bing** To cover with or as with cobwebs. [< ME *coppe* spider + WEB] —**cob′web′by** *adj.*

**co·caine** (kō·kān′, kō′kān) *n.* A white, bitter, crystalline alkaloid, obtained from coca and used as a local anesthetic and as a narcotic. Also **co·cain′.** [< COCA]

**cock** (kok) *n.* 1 A full-grown male of the domestic fowl. 2 Any male bird. 3 A leader; champion. 4 WEATHERCOCK. 5 A faucet, often with the nozzle bent downward. 6 In a firearm, the hammer; also, its position when ready to fire. 7 A jaunty, upward turn or position, as of a hat brim, the ears, eyes, etc. —*v.t.* 1 To raise the cock or hammer of (a firearm) preparatory to firing. 2 To turn up or to one side alertly, jauntily, or inquiringly, as the head, eye, ears, etc. —*v.i.* 3 To raise the hammer of a firearm. 4 To stick up; be prominent. —*adj.* Male. [< OE *cocc*]

**cock·le** (kok′əl) *n.* 1 An edible European bivalve mollusk. 2 COCKLESHELL. 3 A wrinkle; pucker. —*v.t.* & *v.i.* **cock·led, cock·ling** To wrinkle; pucker. [< L *conchylium* shell]

**cock·roach** (kok′rōch′) *n.* Any of a large group of swift-running, chiefly nocturnal insects having long feelers and flat, oval bodies, several species of which are household pests. [< Sp. *cucaracha*]

**cock·tail** (kok′tāl′) *n.* 1 Any of various mixed alcoholic drinks. 2 Any of various appetizers, as diced fruits, fruit juices, sea food, etc. [?]

**co·coa** (kō′kō) *n.* 1 A powder made from the roasted, husked seed kernels of the cacao. 2 A beverage made from it. 3 A reddish brown color. [Alter. of CACAO]

**co·coon** (kə·kōōn′) *n.* The envelope spun by the larvae of certain insects in which they are enclosed during the pupa stage. [< F *coque* shell]

**C.O.D., c.o.d.** cash on delivery; collect on delivery.

**code** (kōd) *n.* 1 A systematized body of law. 2 Any system of rules or regulations. 3 A system of signals, characters, or symbols used in communication. 4 A set of prearranged symbols used for purposes of secrecy or brevity in transmitting messages. —*v.t.* **cod·ed, cod·ing** 1 To systematize as laws;

make a digest of. 2 To put into the symbols of a code. [< L *codex* writing tablet]

**cod·i·fy** (kod'ə·fī, kō'də-) *v.t.* **·fied, ·fy·ing** To systematize, as laws. —**cod'i·fi·ca'tion, cod'i·fi'er** *n.*

**co·ed** (kō'ed') *Informal n.* A young woman being educated at a coeducational institution. —*adj.* Of, pertaining to, or devoted to coeducation. Also **co'-ed'.**

**co·erce** (kō·ûrs') *v.t.* **co·erced, co·erc·ing** 1 To constrain or force to do something. 2 To bring under control by force; repress. 3 To bring about by coercion; to *coerce* obedience. [< L *co-* together + *arcere* shut up, restrain] —**co·er'cer** *n.* —**co·er'ci·ble** *adj.*

**cof·fin** (kôf'in, kof'-) *n.* The case or chest in which a corpse is buried. —*v.t.* To put into or as into a coffin. [< Gk. *kophinos* basket]

**cog** (kog) *n.* 1 A tooth or one of a series of teeth projecting from the surface of a wheel or gear to impart or receive motion. 2 COG-WHEEL. 3 A person regarded as making a minor contribution to a large organization or process. [< Scand.]

**co·gent** (kō'jənt) *adj.* Compelling belief, assent, or action; forcible; convincing. [< L *cogere* compel] —**Syn.** forceful, persuasive, weighty, compelling, trenchant.

**cog·i·tate** (koj'ə·tāt) *v.t.* & *v.i.* **·tat·ed, ·tat·ing** To think carefully (about); ponder. [< L *co-* together + *agitare* consider] —**cog'i·ta·ble** (koj'ə·tə·bəl) *adj.* —**cog'i·ta'tor** *n.*

**cog·i·ta·tion** (koj'ə·tā'shən) *n.* Consideration; reflection; thought. —**cog'i·ta'tive** *adj.* —**cog'i·ta'tive·ly** *adv.* —**cog'i·ta'tive·ness** *n.*

**cog·nate** (kog'nāt) *adj.* 1 Allied by blood; kindred. 2 Belonging to the same stock or root: English *cold* and Latin *gelidus* are *cognate* words. 3 Having the same nature or quality. —*n.* A cognate person or thing. [< L *co-* together + *(g)natus,* pp. of *(g)nasci* be born] —**cog·na'tion** *n.*

**cog·ni·tion** (kog·nish'ən) *n.* 1 The act or faculty of apprehending, knowing, or perceiving. 2 Something known or perceived; a perception. [< L *co-* together + *(g)noscere* know] —**cog·ni'tion·al, cog·ni·tive** (kog'nə·tiv) *adj.*

**cog·ni·zance** (kog'nə·zəns) *n.* 1 Knowledge; perception; awareness. 2 *Law* a The hearing of a case in court. b Jurisdiction. [< L *cognoscere* to know]

**cog·no·men** (kog·nō'mən, kog'nə-) *n.* pl. **·no·mens** or **·nom·i·na** (-nom'ə·nə) 1 One's family name; surname. 2 Any name or

nickname. [< L *co-* together + *(g)nomen* name] —**cog·nom·i·nal** (kog·nom'ə·nəl) *adj.*

**co·here** (kō·hir') *v.i.* **co·hered, co·her·ing** 1 To stick or hold firmly together. 2 To be logically consistent or connected, as a piece of writing. [< L *co-* together + *haerere* stick]

**co·her·ence** (kō·hir'əns) *n.* 1 A sticking together; union; cohesion. 2 The quality of being consistent and intelligible, as in logic, thought, etc. 3 *Physics* That relation between two sets of waves, as light or sound waves, in which the phase of either can be determined from the other. Also **co·her'en·cy.**

**co·her·ent** (kō·hir'ənt) *adj.* 1 Cleaving or sticking together. 2 Logical, intelligible, or articulate, as in thought, speech, etc. 3 *Physics* Exhibiting coherence. —**co·her'ent·ly** *adv.*

**coif·feur** (kwà·fœr') *n.* A male hairdresser. [F] —**coif·feuse** (kwà·fœz') *n.* Fem.

**coin** (koin) *n.* 1 A piece of metal stamped by government authority, for use as money. 2 Metal currency, collectively. 3 A corner; quoin. —*v.t.* 1 To stamp or mint (coins) from metal. 2 To make into coins, as metal. 3 To originate or invent, as a word or phrase. [< F, wedge, die < L *cuneus* wedge] —**coin'a·ble** *adj.* —**coin'er** *n.*

**co·in·cide** (kō'in·sīd') *v.i.* **·cid·ed, ·cid·ing** 1 To be alike in parts, shape, space occupied, or position. 2 To agree exactly, as in opinions, interests, etc. 3 To occur at the same time. [< L *co-* together + *incidere* to happen]

**co·in·ci·dence** (kō·in'sə·dəns) *n.* 1 The fact or condition of coinciding; correspondence. 2 A remarkable occurrence of events, ideas, etc., at the same time or in the same way, apparently by mere accident.

**co·in·ci·dent** (kō·in'sə·dənt) *adj.* 1 Occurring at the same time. 2 Having the same shape, position, etc. 3 Exactly corresponding; identical. —**co·in'ci·dent·ly** *adv.*

**co·i·tus** (kō'i·təs, kō·ēt'əs) *n.* Sexual intercourse. Also **co·i·tion** (kō·ish'ən). [< L *co-* together + *ire* go] —**co'i·tal** *adj.*

**cold war** Intense rivalry between nations in diplomacy, economic strategy, etc., falling just short of armed conflict.

**col·i·se·um** (kol'ə·sē'əm) *n.* A large building or stadium for sports events, exhibitions, etc.

**col·lab·o·rate** (kə·lab'ə·rāt) *v.i.* **·rat·ed, ·rat·ing** 1 To labor or cooperate with another, esp. in literary or scientific pursuits. 2 To be a collaborationist. [< L *com-* with + *laborare* work] —col·lab'o·ra'tion, col·lab'o·ra'tor *n.* —col·lab'o·ra'tive *adj.*

col·lapse (kə·laps') *v.* ·lapsed, ·laps·ing *v.i.* 1 To give way; cave in. 2 To fail utterly. 3 To become compact by the folding in of parts. 4 To lose health, strength, value, etc., suddenly and completely. —*v.t.* 5 To cause to collapse. —*n.* 1 The act of collapsing. 2 Extreme prostration. 3 Utter failure; ruin. [< L *collapsus*, pp. of *collabi* fall together] —col·laps'i·ble or ·a·ble *adj.* —col·laps'i·bil'i·ty *n.*

col·lar (kol'ər) *n.* 1 The part of a garment that circles the neck. 2 An article worn about the neck. 3 A band, part of a harness, etc., for the neck of an animal. 4 A growth of fur or ring of color about the neck of an animal. 5 *Mech.* Any of various cylindrical or ring-shaped devices used to limit or control motion. —*v.t.* 1 To grasp by the collar. 2 To provide with a collar. 3 *Informal* To detain or to capture. [< L *collum* neck]

col·lat·er·al (kə·lat'ər·əl) *adj.* 1 Subordinate; secondary. 2 Corroborating; confirmatory. 3 Being or lying alongside; parallel. 4 Descended from the same ancestor but in a different line. 5 Guaranteed by property, as stocks or bonds, deposited as security: a *collateral* loan. —*n.* 1 Property, stocks, bonds, etc. deposited as security for a loan or the like. 2 A collateral relative. [< L *com-* together + *latus*, *-eris* side] —col·lat'er·al·ly *adv.*

col·la·tion (kə·lā'shən, ko-, kō-) *n.* 1 The act or process of collating. 2 A light meal.

col·league (kol'ēg) *n.* A fellow worker, as in an office, or a fellow member of the same profession, etc. [< L *collega* one chosen simultaneously with another]

col·lect (kə·lekt') *v.t.* 1 To gather together; assemble. 2 To bring together as for a hobby. 3 To gather or obtain (payments of money). 4 To regain control of: to *collect* one's wits. —*v.i.* 5 To assemble or congregate, as people. 6 To accumulate, as dust. 7 To gather payments or donations. —*adj.* To be paid for by the receiver. —*adv.* So that the receiver pays. [< L *com-* together + *legere* gather] —col·lect'a·ble or ·i·ble *adj.*

col·lec·tiv·ism (kə·lek'tiv·iz'əm) *n.* An economic theory or system in which the people as a whole own or control the material and means of production and distribution. —col·lec'tiv·ist *adj.*, *n.* —col·lec'tiv·is'tic *adj.*

col·lege (kol'ij) *n.* 1 A school of higher learning, as an undergraduate school at a university, that offers a four-year course of study leading to a bachelor's degree. 2 A school, often a graduate school in a university, offering instruction in a specialized course of study: a *college* of medicine. 3 A building or buildings used by a college. 4 A body of associates or colleagues engaged in some definite work or duty: electoral *college*. [<L *collegium* body of associates] — col·le·gi·al (kə·lē'jē·əl) *adj.*

col·lide (kə·līd') *v.i.* ·lid·ed, ·lid·ing 1 To come together with violent impact; crash. 2 To come into conflict; clash. [< L *com-* together + *laedere* strike]

col·lie (kol'ē) *n.* A breed of shepherd dogs which originated in Scotland, characterized by a long, narrow head and an abundant long-haired coat. [Prob. < Scot. Gael. *cuilean* puppy]

col·li·sion (kə·lizh'ən) *n.* 1 A violent impact or crash. 2 A conflict, as of views, interests, etc. [< L *collidere* to collide]

col·lo·qui·al (kə·lō'kwē·əl) *adj.* 1 Characteristic of or suitable to the informal language of ordinary conversation or writing. 2 Of or pertaining to conversation; conversational. —col·lo'qui·al·ly *adv.* —col·lo'qui·al·ness *n.*

col·lo·qui·al·ism (kə·lō'kwē·əl·iz'əm) *n.* A colloquial style, usage, word, or expression.

col·lo·quy (kol'ə·kwē) *n. pl.* ·quies A more or less formal conversation or conference. [< L *colloquium* conversation] —col'lo·quist *n.*

co·logne (kə·lōn') *n.* A toilet water consisting of alcohol scented with aromatic oils. Also Cologne water. [< *Cologne*, Germany]

co·lon[1] (kō'lən) *n.* A punctuation mark (:) used to introduce a series or catalog of things, a speech, quotation, example, etc., and after the salutation in a formal letter. [<Gk. *kōlon* member, limb, clause]

co·lon[2] (kō'lən) *n. pl.* co·lons or co·la (kō'lə) The large intestine between the cecum and the rectum. [< Gk. *kolon*] —co·lon·ic (kə·lon'ik) *adj.* • See INTESTINE.

colo·nel (kûr'nəl) *n.* See GRADE. [<Ital. *colonna* column of soldiers] —colo'nel·cy, colo'nel·ship *n.*

col·o·nist (kol'ə·nist) *n.* 1 A member or inhabitant of a colony. 2 A founder of a colony.

col·o·ny (kol'ə·nē) *n. pl.* ·nies 1 A body of emigrants who settle in a remote region but remain under the control of a parent country. 2 The region thus settled. 3 Any group of people having common ethnic backgrounds, interests, etc., and living in a particular area or region: the movie *colony*. 4 The area or region in which they live. 5 A discrete group of microorganisms growing in a culture medium. 6 A group of related plants or animals living or growing together. —**the Colonies** The British colonies that became the original thirteen states of the U.S.: Va., N.Y., Mass., Conn., R.I., N.H., Md., N.J., N.C., S.C., Pa., Del., and Ga. [< L *colonus* farmer]

**col·los·sal** (kə·los′əl) *adj.* 1 Enormous; huge. 2 *Informal* Unbelievable; extraordinary: a *colossal* bore. —**co·los′sal·ly** *adv.*

**col·umn** (kol′əm) *n.* 1 A vertical shaft or pillar, usu. having a base and a capital, and used as a support or as ornamentation. 2 Any object or structure resembling a column: the spinal *column*. 3 A vertical, usu. narrow section of printed matter separated from similar sections by a rule or a blank space. 4 A unit of troops, vehicles, ships, etc., arranged in single file or several abreast. 5 An article by a special writer or on a specific subject that appears regularly in a newspaper or periodical. [<L *columna*] —**co·lum·nar** (kə·lum′nər), **col·umned** (ko·l′əmd) *adj.*

**col·um·nist** (kol′əm·nist, -əm·ist) *n.* A person who writes or conducts a special column for a newspaper or periodical.

**co·ma** (kō′mə) *n. pl.* **co·mas** 1 A state of deep, prolonged unconsciousness caused by disease, injury, etc. 2 Stupor; lethargy. [< Gk. *kōma* deep sleep] —**co′ma·tose** (-tōs) *adj.* —**co′ma·tos′ly** *adv.* —**co′ma·tose′ness** *n.*

**com·bat** (kom′bat, kum′-) *n.* A battle or fight; struggle. —*v.* (kəm·bat′) **·bat·ed** or **·bat·ted**, **·bat·ing** or **·bat·ting** *v.t.* 1 To fight or contend with. 2 To resist. —*v.i.* 3 To do battle; struggle: with *with* or *against*. [< L *com-* with + *battuere* fight, beat] —**com·bat′a·ble** *adj.* —**com·bat′er** *n.*

**com·bine** (kəm·bīn′) *v.t. & v.i.* **·bined**, **·bin·ing** 1 To bring or come into a close union; join; unite. 2 To unite chemically to form a compound. —*n.* (kom′bīn) 1 An association of persons united for political or business control, often by dishonest means. 2 A farm machine which combines the heading, threshing, and cleaning of grain while harvesting it. [< LL *com-* together + *bini* two by two] —**com·bin′a·ble** *adj.* —**com·bin′er** *n.*

**com·bo** (kom′bō) *n. pl.* **·bos** *Informal* 1 A small group of jazz musicians performing together. 2 A combination.

**com·bus·ti·ble** (kəm·bus′tə·bəl) *adj.* 1 That burns easily. 2 Excitable; fiery. —*n.* Any substance that burns easily. —**com·bus′ti·ble·ness, com·bus′ti·bil′i·ty** *n.*

**com·bus·tion** (kəm·bus′chən) *n.* 1 The action or operation of burning. 2 The rapid combination of a substance with oxygen, accompanied by heat and usu. light. 3 Slow oxidation, as of food in the body. 4 Disturbance; tumult. [< LL *comburere* burn up] —**com·bus′tive** *adj.*

**com·e·dy** (kom′ə·dē) *n. pl.* **·dies** 1 Originally, a literary work with a nontragic view of life and a happy ending. 2 A play, motion picture, etc., characterized by a humorous treatment of characters, situation, etc., and having a happy ending. 3 Comedies collectively, esp. as a branch of the drama. 4 Any comic or ludicrous incident or series of incidents. [< Gk. *kōmos* revel + *aeidein* sing]

**come·ly** (kum′lē, kōm′lē) *adj.* **·li·er, ·li·est** Pleasing in appearance; attractive. [< OE *cymlic*] —**come′li·ness** *n.*

**com·fort** (kum′fərt) *n.* 1 Freedom from pain, annoyance, want, etc. 2 Anything that contributes to such relief. 3 Relief from sorrow or distress. 4 One who or that which helps relieve sorrow or distress. 5 A bed comforter. —*v.t.* To give cheer or ease to; console; solace. [< LL *confortare* strengthen] —**com′fort·ing** *adj.* —**com′fort·ing·ly** *adv.*

**com·ic** (kom′ik) *adj.* 1 Of, like, or connected with comedy. 2 Amusing, funny, ludicrous, etc. 3 Acting in or composing comedy. —*n.* 1 A comedian. 2 A comic book or comic strip. 3 The humorous side of art, life, etc. 4 *pl.* A newspaper section devoted to comic strips. [< Gk. *kōmos* revelry]

**com·ma** (kom′ə) *n.* 1 A punctuation mark (,) indicating a slight separation in ideas or construction within a sentence. 2 Any pause or separation. [< Gk. *komma* short phrase < *koptein* cut]

**com·mand** (kə·mand′, -mänd′) *v.t.* 1 To order, require or enjoin with authority. 2 To control or direct; rule. 3 To have at one's disposal or use. 4 To overlook, as from a height. 5 To exact as being due or proper. —*v.i.* 6 To be in authority; rule. 7 To overlook, as from a height. —*n.* 1 The right to command; authority. 2 An order. 3 The troops or district under the command of one person. 4 Dominating power; control. 5

Mastery. 6 Range of view. [< L *com-* thoroughly + *mandare* order, charge]

com·mem·o·rate (kə·mem'ə·rāt) *v.t.* ·rat·ed, ·rat·ing To celebrate the memory of, as with a ceremony. [< L *com-* together + *memorare* remember] —com·mem·o·ra·ble (kə·mem'ə·rə·bəl), com·mem'o·ra'tive, com·mem·o·ra·to·ry (kə·mem'ə·rə·tôr'ē, -tō'rē) *adj.* —com·mem'o·ra'tion *n.*

com·mence (kə·mens') *v.t.* & *v.i.* ·menced, ·menc·ing To begin; initiate; start. [< L *com-* together + *initiare* begin]

com·mend (kə·mend') *v.t.* 1 To express a favorable opinion of; praise. 2 To recommend. 3 To present the regards of. 4 To entrust. [< L *com-* thoroughly + *mandare* order, charge] —com·mend'a·ble *adj.* —com·mend'a·bly *adv.*

com·men·su·rate (kə·men'shə·rit, -sə·rit) *adj.* 1 In proper proportion; proportionate. 2 COMMENSURABLE. 3 Equal in size or extent. [< LL *com-* together + *mensurare* measure] —com·men'su·rate·ly *adv.* —com·men'su·rate·ness, com·men'su·ra'tion *n.*

com·ment (kom'ent) *n.* 1 A note in explanation or criticism. 2 A remark made in observation or criticism. 3 Talk; conversation; gossip. —*v.i.* To make a comment or comments: with *on* or *upon*. [< L *comminisci* contrive]

com·merce (kom'ərs) *n.* 1 Exchange of goods, products, or property, as between states or nations. 2 Social intercourse. 3 SEXUAL INTERCOURSE. [< L *com-* together + *merx, mercis* wares]

com·mer·cial (kə·mûr'shəl) *adj.* 1 Of or belonging to trade or commerce; mercantile. 2 Made in large quantities for the market. 3 Having financial gain or popular appeal as an object: a *commercial* novel. —*n.* In radio and television, a paid advertisement. —com·mer'cial·ly *adv.*

com·mis·er·ate (kə·miz'ə·rāt) *v.* ·at·ed, ·at·ing *v.t.* 1 To feel or manifest pity for; sympathize. —*v.i.* 2 To condole: with *with*. [< L *com-* with + *miserari* feel pity] —com·mis·er·a·tive *adj.* —com·mis'er·a'tive·ly *adv.* —com·mis'er·a'tion, com·mis'er·a'tor *n.*

com·mis·sion (kə·mish'ən) *n.* 1 The act of entrusting or giving authority to perform certain acts or duties. 2 The acts or duties so entrusted. 3 An authorization or order to do something; also, a document conferring this. 4 *Mil.* a A document conferring rank and authority. b The rank or authority so conferred. 5 A body of persons authorized to perform certain duties. 6 The fee given an agent or salesperson for his or her services. 7 The act of committing or perpetrating, as a crime. —*v.t.* 1 To give rank or authority to, as an officer. 2 To put into active service, as a ship of war. 3 To give a commission to. 4 To appoint; delegate. 5 To order to be done: to *commission* a painting. [< L *committere*. See COMMIT.]

com·mit (kə·mit') *v.t.* ·mit·ted, ·mit·ting 1 To do; perpetrate. 2 To place in an institution or prison. 3 To entrust or consign to any person, place, or use. 4 To devote or pledge (oneself) to the doing of something. 5 To consign for future reference, preservation, etc.: to *commit* a speech to memory. 6 To refer, as to a committee, for consideration or report. [< L *com-* together + *mittere* send]

com·mit·tee (kə·mit'ē) *n.* A group of persons organized or appointed to act upon some matter. [< COMMIT]

com·mod·i·ty (kə·mod'ə·tē) *n.* *pl.* ·ties 1 Something bought and sold. 2 Something useful. [< L *commoditas* convenience]

**Common Market** EUROPEAN ECONOMIC COMMUNITY.

com·mo·tion (kə·mō'shən) *n.* 1 A disturbance; fuss. 2 Violent agitation; tumult. [< L *com-* thoroughly + *movere* move]

com·mune (kə·myōōn') *v.i.* ·muned, ·mun·ing 1 To converse or confer intimately. 2 To partake of the Eucharist. —*n.* (kom'yōōn) Intimate conversation. [< OF *comun* common]

com·mu·ni·cate (kə·myōō'nə·kāt) *v.* ·cat·ed, ·cat·ing *v.t.* 1 To impart; transmit, as news, a disease, or an idea. —*v.i.* 2 To make or hold communication. 3 To be connected, as rooms. 4 To partake of the Eucharist. [< L *communicare* share < *communis* common] —com·mu'ni·ca'tor *n.*

com·mu·ni·ca·tion (kə·myōō'nə·kā'shən) *n.* 1 The act of communicating; exchange of ideas, conveyance of information, etc. 2 That which is communicated, as a letter or message. 3 *pl.* Means of communicating, as a highway, telephone, radio, television, etc.

com·mu·nism (kom'yə·niz'əm) *n.* 1 A social system in which there are no classes and no private ownership of the means of production. 2 The theory of social change on which such a system is based. 3 *Often cap.* The system based on this theory in force in any state.

Com·mu·nist (kom'yə·nist) *n.* 1 A member of the Communist party. 2 Any person who endorses, supports, or advocates communism: **also communist.** —com′mu·nis′tic adj.

**com·mu·ni·ty** (kə·myōō′nə·tē) n. pl. ·ties 1 The people who reside in one locality and are subject to the same laws, have the same interests, etc. 2 The locality of such a group. 3 The public; society at large. 4 A group of plants and animals mutually reacting to create common habitat. 5 Common sharing, participation, or ownership. 6 Similarity or likeness: community of interest. [< L communis common]

**com·mute** (kə·myōōt′) v. ·mut·ed, ·mut·ing v.t. 1 To exchange reciprocally for something else. 2 To change to something less severe: to commute a sentence. —v.i. 3 To serve as or be a substitute. 4 To travel as a commuter. —n. Informal A commuter's trip, or its duration or distance: a two-hour commute. [<L commutare. See COMMUTATION] —com·mut′a·ble adj. —com·mut′a·ble·ness, com·mut′a·bil′i·ty n.

**com·pact** (kəm·pakt′, kom′pakt) adj. 1 Closely and firmly united, pressed together; solid; dense. 2 Condensed; brief; terse. 3 Composed; made up: with of. 4 Relatively small: a compact car. —v.t. (kəm·pakt′) To pack or press closely; condense. —n. (kom′pakt) 1 A small, hinged box for face powder and sometimes rouge. 2 A compact car. [<L compactus, pp. of compangere fasten together] —com·pact′ly adv. —com·pact′ness n.

**compact disc** A small digital disc on which recorded sound has been encoded so as to be replayed on an electronic device that utilizes a laser beam to reproduce the original sound with a very high level of fidelity.

**com·pan·ion** (kəm·pan′yən) n. 1 One who or that which accompanies; a comrade; associate. 2 One hired to live or travel with another. 3 A mate; one of a pair. —v.t. To be a companion to; accompany. [<LL companio <L com- together + panis bread] —com·pan′ion·ship n.

**com·pa·ny** (kum′pə·nē) n. pl. ·nies 1 The society or presence of another or others. 2 One or more guests or visitors. 3 A business firm or corporation. 4 A number of persons associated for some common purpose. 5 The person or persons with whom one often associates: keeping bad company. 6 A body of soldiers, usu. a unit made up of two or more platoons and a headquarters. 7 A ship's crew, including officers. 8 A group of performers who work together: a ballet

company. [<OF compagnon companion] — **Syn.** n. 1 companionship, fellowship. 2 assembly, group. 3 troupe.

**com·pa·ra·ble** (kom′pər·ə·bəl, kəm·par′-) adj. 1 Capable of being compared. 2 Worthy of comparison. —com′pa·ra·ble·ness, com′pa·ra·bil′i·ty n. —com′pa·ra·bly adv.

**com·par·a·tive** (kəm·par′ə·tiv) adj. 1 Of, using, or resulting from comparison. 2 Not total or absolute; relative. 3 Gram. Expressing a degree of an adjective or adverb higher than the positive and lower than the superlative: "Better" is the comparative form of "good." —n. Gram. The comparative degree. —com·par′a·tive·ly adv.

**com·pare** (kəm·pâr′) v. ·pared, ·par·ing v.t. 1 To represent or speak of as similar, analogous, or equal: with to. 2 To examine so as to perceive and note similarity or dissimilarity: with with. 3 Gram. To form the degrees of comparison of (an adjective or adverb). —v.i. 4 To be worthy of comparison: with with. —n. Comparison: usu. in the phrase beyond compare. [<L comparare < com- together + par equal] • **compare to; compare with** Formal usage requires that one use compare to when noting a striking similarity between two things: The industrial potential of Japan compares to that of many larger nations. If the things being compared are similar in some aspects but dissimilar in others, compare with is preferred: to compare the physical discipline demanded of a classical ballet dancer with that required of a gymnast.

**com·par·i·son** (kəm·par′ə·sən) n. 1 An estimate or statement of relative likeness or unlikeness. 2 Similarity. 3 Gram. That inflection of adjectives or adverbs which indicates the positive, comparative, and superlative degrees.

**com·part·ment** (kəm·pärt′mənt) n. 1 One of the divisions or sections into which an enclosed space is subdivided. 2 Any separate section, category, division, etc. [<L com- together + pars part]

**com·pass** (kum′pəs) n. 1 An instrument for determining direction, as from the earth's magnetic field. 2 Often pl. Any of various instruments having two legs hinged at the top, used for drawing circles, taking measurements, etc. 3 An enclosed area. 4 A boundary or circumference. 5 A range or scope, esp. the range of a voice or instrument. —v.t. 1 To go around; make a circuit of. 2 To surround; encompass. 3 To grasp mentally; comprehend. **4** To plot or scheme. **5** To attain or accomplish. [<L *com-* together + *passus* step] —**com·pass·a·ble** *adj.*

**com·pas·sion** (kəm·pash′ən) *n.* Pity for suffering, with desire to help; sympathy. [<L *com-* together + *pati* feel, suffer] —**Syn.** mercy, commiseration, empathy, clemency, charity.

**com·pat·i·ble** (kəm·pat′ə·bəl) *adj.* **1** Capable of existing or living together; congruous; congenial. **2** Describing a television system in which broadcasts in color may be received in black and white on sets not adapted for color reception. [<L *com-* together + *pati* suffer] —**com·pat′i·bil′i·ty, com·pat′i·ble·ness** *n.* —**com·pat′i·bly** *adv.*

**com·pel** (kəm·pel′) *v.t.* **·pelled, ·pel·ling 1** To drive or urge irresistibly; constrain. **2** To get or obtain by force. [<L *com-* together + *pellere* drive] —**com·pel′la·ble** *adj.* —**com·pel′la·bly** *adv.* —**com·pel′ler** *n.*

**com·pen·sate** (kom′pən·sāt) *v.* **·sat·ed, ·sat·ing** *v.t.* **1** To make suitable amends to or for; remunerate. **2** To counter-balance or make up for; offset. —*v.i.* **3** To make compensation or amends: often with *for.* [<L *com-* together + *pensare,* freq. of *pendere* weigh] —**com·pen′sa·tive** (kəm·pen′sə·tiv), **com·pen·sa·to·ry** (kəm·pen′sə·tôr′ē, ·tō′rē) *adj.* —**com′pen·sa′tor** *n.*

**com·pete** (kəm·pēt′) *v.i.* **·pet·ed, ·pet·ing** To contend with another or others for a prize, superiority, etc.; vie. [<L *com-* together + *petere* seek]

**com·pe·tence** (kom′pə·təns) *n.* **1** The state of being competent. **2** Sufficient means for comfortable living. **Also com′pe·ten·cy.**

**com·pe·ti·tion** (kom′pə·tish′ən) *n.* **1** The act of competing; rivalry, as in business, athletics, etc. **2** The quality or degree of competitiveness or opposition. **3** Those persons against whom one competes. **4** A specific contest.

**com·pile** (kəm·pīl′) *v.t.* **·piled, ·pil·ing 1** To compose (a literary work, etc.) from other works or sources. **2** To gather (facts, data, etc.) into a volume or into orderly form. [<L *com-* thoroughly + *pilare* strip, plunder] —**com·pi·la·tion** (kom′pə·lā′shən) *n.*

**com·pla·cen·cy** (kəm·plā′sən·sē) *n. pl.* **·cies 1** Satisfaction, esp. with oneself. **2** EQUANIMITY. **Also com·pla′cence.**

**com·pla·cent** (kəm·plā′sənt) *adj.* Feeling or showing complacency, esp. smugly self-satisfied. [<L *com-* thoroughly + *placere* to please] —**com·pla′cent·ly** *adv.*

**com·plain** (kəm·plān′) *v.i.* **1** To express a sense of ill-treatment or of pain, grief, etc. **2** To find fault. **3** To make a formal accusation. [<L *com-* thoroughly + *plangere* beat (the breast in grief)] —**com·plain′er** *n.* —**com·plain′ing·ly** *adv.* —**Syn. 1** murmur, whine, lament. **2** grumble, deplore, gripe.

**com·plaint** (kəm·plānt′) *n.* **1** A statement of wrong, grievance, or injury. **2** The paper setting forth the plaintiff's cause of action. **3** A grievance. **4** A physical ailment; disease.

**com·ple·ment** (kom′plə·mənt) *n.* **1** That which fills up, completes, or makes perfect. **2** The number needed to fill or make complete. **3** Either of two parts that together form a whole; a counterpart. **4** Full number: the vessel has her *complement* of men. **5** *Geom.* The amount by which an angle or arc falls short of 90 degrees. **6** *Gram.* A word or phrase used after a verb to complete the meaning of the predicate, as *happy* in *She is happy.* —*v.t.* To supply a lack in; make complete; supplement. [<L *complere* complete] —**com·ple·men·tal** (kom′plə·men′təl) *adj.* • See SUPPLEMENT.

**com·plete** (kəm·plēt′) *adj.* **·plet·er, ·plet·est 1** Having all needed or normal parts, elements, or details; lacking nothing; entire. **2** Thoroughly wrought; finished. **3** Perfect. —*v.t.* **·plet·ed, ·plet·ing 1** To make entire or whole. **2** To make perfect. **3** To finish; fulfill; end. [<L *com-* thoroughly + *plere* fill] —**com·plete′ly** *adv.* —**com·plete′ness** *n.* —**com·ple′tive** *adj.*

**com·ple·tion** (kəm·plē′shən) *n.* **1** The act of completing or the state of being completed. **2** Accomplishment; fulfillment.

**com·plex** (kəm·pleks′, kom′pleks) *adj.* **1** Consisting of various parts or elements; composite. **2** Complicated; involved; intricate. —*n.* (kom′pleks) **1** A whole made up of interrelated parts or units. **2** *Psychoanal.* A group of interrelated and usu. repressed ideas with strong emotional content which distorts patterns of thought and behavior. **3** Loosely, an extreme or exaggerated fear or dislike. [<L *complexus,* pp. of *complectere* twist together] —**com·plex′ly** *adv.* —**com·plex′ness** *n.*

**com·plex·ion** (kəm·plek′shən) *n.* **1** The color and appearance of the skin, esp. of the face. **2** General aspect; character; quality. [<L *complexio* the constitution of a body, a combination < *complectere* twist together] —**com·plex′ion·al** *adj.*

**com·pli·ance** (kəm·plī′əns) *n.* 1 The act of complying, yielding, or acting in accord. 2 The disposition or willingness to please. Also **com·pli′an·cy.**

**com·pli·cate** (kom′plə·kāt) *v.t.* & *v.i.* **·cat·ed, ·cat·ing** *v.t.* To make or become complex, difficult, or perplexing. —*adj.* (kom′plə·kit) Complicated; complex. [<L *com-* together + *plicare* to fold] —**com′pli·ca′tive** *adj.*

**com·plic·i·ty** (kəm·plis′ə·tē) *n. pl.* **·ties** The act or state of being an accomplice, as in a crime.

**com·pli·ment** (kom′plə·mənt) *n.* 1 An expression of admiration, praise, congratulation, etc. 2 *pl.* A formal greeting or remembrance. —*v.t.* (kom′plə·ment) 1 To pay a compliment to. 2 To show regard for, as by a gift or other favor. [<Sp. *cumplimiento*, lit., completion of courtesy <L *complementum* completion]

**com·ply** (kəm·plī′) *v.i.* **·plied, ·ply·ing** To act in conformity; consent; obey: with *with*. [<Sp. *cumplir* complete an act of courtesy <L *complere* to complete] —**com·pli′er** *n.*

**com·po·nent** (kəm·pō′nənt) *n.* A constituent part. —*adj.* Forming a part or ingredient. [<L *componere* to place together]

**com·port** (kəm·pôrt′, -pōrt′) *v.t.* To conduct (oneself). —*v.i.* To be compatible; agree. [<L *com-* together + *portare* carry]

**com·pose** (kəm·pōz′) *v.* **·posed, ·pos·ing** *v.t.* 1 To be the constituent elements or parts of; constitute; form. 2 To tranquilize; calm. 3 To reconcile, arrange, or settle, as differences. 4 To create artistically, as a literary or musical work. 5 To arrange (type) in lines; set. —*v.i.* 6 To engage in composition, as of a literary or musical work. 7 To set type. [<L *com-* together + *poser* to put]

**com·pos·er** (kəm·pō′zər) *n.* One who composes, esp. one who composes music.

**com·po·si·tion** (kom′pə·zish′ən) *n.* 1 The act or art of composing a literary, musical, or artistic work. 2 The work so composed or its general arrangement or style. 3 Any putting together of separate elements or parts to form a whole; also, the whole so formed. 4 The general nature or makeup of a thing or person. 5 The act or skill of setting type.

**com·pos·i·tor** (kəm·poz′ə·tər) *n.* One who sets type; typesetter.

**com·po·sure** (kəm·pō′zhər) *n.* Tranquility, as of manner; calmness; serenity.

**com·pound** (kom′pound) *n.* 1 A combination of two or more elements, ingredients, or parts. 2 *Chem.* A substance composed of two or more elements combined chemically in definite proportions by weight. —*v.* (kom·pound′, kəm-) *v.t.* 1 To make by the combination of various elements or ingredients. 2 To mix (elements or parts); combine. 3 To settle for less than the sum due: to *compound* a debt. 4 To make more serious or complicated. 5 To compute (interest) on the principal and the interest that has accrued. —*v.i.* 6 To compromise or agree. —*adj.* (kom′pound, kom·pound′) Composed of or produced by the union of two or more elements, ingredients, or parts. [< L *componere* to put together] —**com·pound′a·ble** *adj.* —**com·pound′er** *n.*

**com·pre·hend** (kom′pri·hend′) *v.t.* 1 To grasp mentally; understand fully. 2 To include, take in, or comprise. [< L *com-* together + *prehendere* seize] —**com′pre·hend′i·ble** *adj.*

**com·press** (kəm·pres′) *v.t.* To press together or into smaller space; compact. —*n.* (kom′pres) 1 A device for compressing. 2 *Med.* A soft pad for applying pressure, heat, moisture, etc. to a part of the body. [< LL *compressare*, freq. of *comprimere* press together] —**com·press′i·ble, com·press′ive** *adj.* —**com·press′i·bil′i·ty, com·press′i·ble·ness** *n.*

**com·prise** (kəm·prīz′) *v.t.* **·prised, ·pris·ing** To include and contain; consist of. [< L *comprehendere* comprehend] —**com·pris′a·ble** *adj.* —**com·pri′sal** *n.*

**com·pro·mise** (kom′prə·mīz) *n.* 1 A settlement by arbitration and mutual concession. 2 An adjustment or concession between conflicting courses, ideas, desires, etc. 3 An imperiling or surrender, as of character or reputation. —*v.* **·mised, ·mis·ing** *v.t.* 1 To adjust or settle by concessions. 2 To imperil or surrender. —*v.i.* 3 To make a compromise. [<L *com-* together + *promittere* promise] —**com′pro·mis′er** *n.*

**comp·trol·ler** (kən·trō′lər) *n.* CONTROLLER (def. 2). —**comp·trol′ler·ship** *n.*

**com·pul·sion** (kəm·pul′shən) *n.* 1 The act of compelling or the state of being compelled. 2 *Psychol.* An irresistible urge to perform some act without rational purpose. —**com·pul′sive** *adj.* —**com·pul′sive·ly** *adv.* —**com·pul′sive·ness** *n.*

**com·pul·so·ry** (kəm·pul′sər·ē) *adj.* 1 Employing compulsion; coercive. 2 Required by law or other rule. —**com·pul′so·ri·ly** *adv.* —**com·pul′so·ri·ness** *n.*

**com·punc·tion** (kəm·pungk′shən) *n.* 1 Self-reproach for wrong-doing; guilt. 2 A feeling of slight regret. [< L *com-* greatly + *pungere* to prick, sting] —**com·punc′tious** *adj.*

**com·pute** (kəm·pyo͞ot′) *v.t.* ·put·ed, ·put·ing To estimate numerically; calculate. [< L *com-* together + *putare* reckon] —**com·put′a·bil′i·ty** *n.* —**com·put′a·ble** *adj.*

**com·put·er** (kəm·pyo͞o′tər) *n.* 1 One who or that which computes. 2 An electronic machine capable of accepting data, manipulating or performing arithmetic on such data at high speed, and showing or printing the results.

**com·rade** (kom′rad, -rid) *n.* 1 A friend or close companion. 2 A fellow member, as of a political party, esp. the Communist party. [< Sp. *camarada* roommate < L *camera* room] —**com′rade·ship** *n.*

**con·cave** (kon·kāv′, kon′kāv, kong′-) *adj.* Hollow and rounded, as the interior of a sphere or circle. —*n.* (kon′kāv, kong′-) A concave surface. [< L *com-* thoroughly + *cavus* hollow] —**con·cave′ly** *adv.* • See CONVEX.

**con·ceal** (kən·sēl′) *v.t.* To keep from sight, discovery, or knowledge; hide. [< L *com-* thoroughly + *celare* hide] —**con·ceal′a·ble** *adj.* —**con·ceal′er, con·ceal′ment** *n.*

**con·cede** (kən·sēd′) *v.* ·ced·ed, ·ced·ing *v.t.* 1 To grant as a right or privilege. 2 To acknowledge as true, correct, or proper; admit. —*v.i.* 3 To make a concession. [< L *com-* thoroughly + *cedere* yield, go away] —**con·ced′er** *n.*

**con·ceit** (kən·sēt′) *n.* 1 Excessive self-esteem or vanity. 2 A fanciful or elaborate idea, expression, or metaphor. 3 Imagination. 4 A small, ingenious article or design. [< CONCEIVE]

**con·ceive** (kən·sēv′) *v.* ·ceived, ·ceiv·ing *v.t.* 1 To become pregnant with. 2 To form in the mind; think of. 3 To believe or suppose. 4 To express in words. —*v.i.* 5 To form an idea or conception: with *of.* 6 To become pregnant. [< L *com-* thoroughly + *capere* take] —**con·ceiv′a·ble** *adj.* —**con·ceiv′a·bil′i·ty, con·ceiv′a·ble·ness, con·ceiv′er** *n.* —**con·ceiv′a·bly** *adv.*

**con·cen·trate** (kon′sən·trāt) *v.* ·trat·ed, ·trat·ing *v.t.* 1 To bring or draw to a common center; focus. 2 To increase the strength or density of, as by condensation. 3 To fix or focus (one's thoughts, actions, etc.). —*v.i.* 4 To converge toward a center. 5 To fix or focus one's thoughts, actions, etc.: with *on* or *upon.* —*n.* A product of concentration.

[< L *com-* together + *centrum* center] —**con·cen·tra′tive** (kon′sən·trā′tiv, kən·sen′trə·tiv) *adj.* —**con′cen·tra′tor** *n.*

**con·cen·tric** (kən·sen′trik) *adj.* Having a common center: *concentric circles.* Also **con·cen′tri·cal.** —**con·cen′tri·cal·ly** *adv.* —**con·cen·tric·i·ty** (kon′sen·tris′ə·tē) *n.*

**con·cept** (kon′sept) *n.* An idea, thought, or opinion. [< L *conceptus* a conceiving]

**con·cern** (kən·sûrn′) *v.t.* 1 To be of interest, relevance, or importance to. 2 To cause to be anxious or troubled. —*n.* 1 That which concerns one; something affecting one's interest or welfare. 2 Interest or regard. 3 Anxiety; worry. 4 Relation; reference. 5 A business establishment. [< Med. L. *com-* thoroughly + *cernere* to see, discern]

**con·cert** (kon′sûrt) *n.* 1 A performance, as by a solo musician, an orchestra, dance group, etc. 2 Harmony; unity. —**in concert** Together. —*adj.* Of or for concerts. —*v.* (kən·sûrt′) *v.t.* & *v.i.* To arrange or contrive by mutual agreement. [< Ital. *concertare* agree]

**con·cer·to** (kən·cher′tō) *n.* *pl.* ·tos, ·ti (-tē) A composition, usu. having three movements, for performance by a solo instrument or instruments accompanied by an orchestra. [< Ital., concert]

**con·ces·sion** (kən·sesh′ən) *n.* 1 The act of conceding, or that which is conceded. 2 A privilege granted by a government, as the right to use land. 3 The right or a lease to operate a small business, as selling food, newspapers, etc., in office buildings, railroad stations, etc. 4 The space, land, etc., so leased, or the activity carried on there. [< L *concessus,* pp. of *concedere* to concede]

**con·cil·i·ate** (kən·sil′ē·āt) *v.t.* ·at·ed, ·at·ing 1 To overcome the enmity or hostility of; placate. 2 To secure or attract by reconciling measures; win. [< L *concilium* council] —**con·cil′i·a′tion, con·cil′i·a′tor** *n.* —**con·cil·i·a·to·ry** (kən·sil′ē·ə·tôr′ē, -tō′rē), **con·cil′i·a·tive** *adj.* —**con·cil′i·a·to′ri·ly** *adv.*

**con·cise** (kən·sīs′) *adj.* Expressing much in brief form; compact. [< L *concisus,* pp. of *concidere* to cut thoroughly] —**con·cise′ly** *adv.* —**con·cise′ness** *n.* —**Syn.** brief, terse, pithy, short, compact.

**con·clude** (kən·klo͞od′) *v.* ·clud·ed, ·clud·ing *v.t.* 1 To come to a decision about; decide or determine. 2 To infer or deduce as a result or effect. 3 To arrange or settle finally. 4 To terminate. —*v.i.* 5 To come to an end.

6 To come to a decision. [< L *com-* thoroughly + *claudere* close, shut off] —**con·clud′er** n.

**con·clu·sion** (kən·klōō′zhən) n. 1 The act or an instance of concluding; termination. 2 A conviction reached by reasoning, inference, etc. 3 The last or closing part of something. 4 A result or outcome.

**con·clu·sive** (kən·klōō′siv) adj. 1 Putting an end to doubt; decisive. 2 Leading to a conclusion; final. —**con·clu′sive·ly** adv. —**con·clu′sive·ness** n.

**con·coct** (kon·kokt′, kən-) v.t. 1 To make by mixing ingredients, as a drink or soup. 2 To contrive; devise. [< L *com-* together + *coquere* to cook, boil] —**con·coct′er, con·co·c′tor** n.

**con·cord** (kon′kôrd, kong′-) n. 1 Unity of feeling or interest; agreement; accord. 2 A peace treaty. 3 *Music* A harmonious combination of simultaneous tones. 4 *Gram.* AGREEMENT (def. 5). [< L *concors* agreeing < *com-* together + *cor* heart]

**con·cor·dance** (kon·kôr′dəns, kən-) n. 1 An alphabetical list of the important words in a book or books, with reference to the passages in which each word is found. 2 Concord; agreement; harmony.

**con·course** (kon′kôrs, -kōrs, kong′-) n. 1 An assembly or moving together; confluence. 2 An assembly; throng. 3 A large area for the passage of crowds, as a boulevard or a long passageway in a railroad station, subway, etc. [< L *concurrere* to run together]

**con·crete** (kon′krēt, kon·krēt′) adj. 1 Not general or abstract; specific. 2 Actually existing; real. 3 Made of concrete. 4 Joined into or being a solid mass. —n. 1 A material made of sand and gravel that is united by cement into a hardened mass, used for roads, foundations, etc. ● See CEMENT. 2 Something concrete, as an idea, circumstance, etc. —v. (kon·krēt′; *usu. for def. 2* kon′krēt) ·cret·ed, ·cret·ing v.t. 1 To unite together in one mass or body. 2 To treat or cover with concrete. —v.i. 3 To solidify. [< L *concretus*, pp. of *concrescere* to grow together] —**con·crete′ly** adv. —**con·crete′ness** n.

**con·cur** (kən·kûr′) v.i. ·curred, ·cur·ring 1 To agree, as in opinion or action: Three justices *concurred* in the finding. 2 To happen at the same time; coincide. 3 To act together: Many facts *concurred* to defeat him. [< L *com-* together + *currere* to run] —**con·cur′rence** n.

**con·cus·sion** (kən·kush′ən) n. 1 A violent shaking; shock. 2 Injury to soft tissue, esp. the brain, due to a violent shock or blow. [< L *concussus*, pp. of *concutere* to beat together] —**con·cus·sive** (kən·kus′iv) adj.

**con·demn** (kən·dem′) v.t. 1 To hold or prove to be wrong; censure. 2 To prove to be wrong or guilty, esp. to pronounce judicial sentence against. 3 To forbid the use of, commonly by official order, as something unfit. 4 To appropriate for public use by judicial decree. 5 To doom. [< L *com-* thoroughly + *damnare* condemn] —**con·dem·na·ble** (kən·dem′nə·bəl), **con·dem·na·to·ry** (kən·dem′nə·tôr′ē, -tō′rē) adj. —**con·demn·er** (kən·dem′ər) n. —Syn. 1 blame, denounce, rebuke, vilify.

**con·dense** (kən·dens′) v. ·densed, ·dens·ing v.t. 1 To compress or make dense; subject to condensation. 2 To abridge or make concise. —v.i. 3 To become condensed. [< L *condensus* thick < *com-* together + *densus* crowded, close] —**con·dens′a·ble** or **con·dens′i·ble** adj.

**con·de·scend** (kon′di·send′) v.i. 1 To come down voluntarily to equal terms with a supposed inferior so as to do something; deign. 2 To behave towards others in a patronizing manner. [< L *com-* thoroughly + *descendere* to descend] —**con′de·scen′dence** n. —**con′de·scen′ding** adj. —**con′de·scend′ing·ly** adv.

**con·de·scen·sion** (kon′di·sen′shən) n. 1 An act or instance of condescending. 2 A patronizing manner.

**con·dign** (kən·dīn′) adj. Merited; deserved: said of punishment. [< L *com-* thoroughly + *dignus* worthy]

**con·di·ment** (kon′də·mənt) n. A sauce, relish, spice, etc. [< L *condimentum*]

**con·di·tion** (kən·dish′ən) n. 1 The state or mode in which a person or thing exists. 2 State of health. 3 A sound state of health or fitness. 4 *Informal* An ailment. 5 A modifying circumstance. 6 An event, circumstance, or fact necessary to the occurrence, completion, or fulfillment of something else: Luck is often a *condition* of success. 7 *Usu. pl.* Any circumstances that affect a person or activity: good working *conditions.* 8 Rank or social position. —**on condition that** Provided that; if. —v.t. 1 To place a stipulation upon; prescribe. 2 To be the prerequisite to. 3 To specify as a requirement. 4 To render fit. 5 *Psychol.* To train to a behavior pattern or conditioned response. 6 To accustom (a person or animal) to something. —*v.i.* 7 To stipulate. [< L *com*- together + *dicere* say] —**con·di′tion·er** *n.*

**con·do·min·i·um** (kon′də·min′ē·əm) *n. U.S.* An apartment house in which the units are owned separately by individuals and not by a corporation or cooperative; also, an apartment in such a building. [< L *com*- together + *dominium* rule]

**con·done** (kən·dōn′) *v.t.* **·doned, ·don·ing** To overlook or forgive. [< L *com*- thoroughly + *donare* give] —**con·do·na·tion** (kon′dō·nā′shən), **con·don′er** *n.*

**con·du·cive** (kən·dyōō′siv) *adj.* Contributing; helping; with *to.* —**con·duc′ive·ly** *adv.* —**con·du′cive·ness** *n.*

**con·duct** (kən·dukt′) *v.t.* 1 To accompany and show the way; guide; escort. 2 To manage or control. 3 To direct and lead the performance of. 4 To serve as a medium of transmission for, as electricity. 5 To act or behave: used reflexively. —*v.i.* 6 To serve as a conductor. 7 To direct or lead. —*n.* (kon′dukt†) 1 One's course of action; behavior. 2 Direction; control. 3 The act of leading. [< L *com*- together + *ducere* lead] —**con·duct′i·bil′i·ty** *n.* —**con·duct′i·ble, con·duct′ive** *adj.*

**con·duit** (kon′dit, -dōō·it) *n.* 1 A means for conducting something, as a tube or pipe for a fluid. 2 A passage for electric wires, underground cables, gas and water pipes, etc. [< L *conducere.* See CONDUCT.]

**con·el·rad** (kon′əl·rad) *n.* A technique for arranging radio signals from separate stations so as to prevent enemy aircraft from using the signals as a navigation aid or for information. [< *con*(trol *of*) *el*(*ectromagnetic*) *rad*(*iation*)]

**con·fec·tion** (kən·fek′shən) *n.* Any sweet, such as candy. [< L *confectus,* pp. of *conficere* to prepare, make together] —**con·fec′tion·ar′y** *adj.*

**con·fed·er·a·cy** (kən·fed′ər·ə·sē) *n. pl.* **·cies** 1 A number of states or persons in league with each other; league. 2 An unlawful conspiracy. —**the Confederacy** The 11 southern States that seceded from the U.S. in 1860-61.

**con·fed·er·a·tion** (kən·fed′ə·rā′shən) *n.* 1 The act of confederating. 2 CONFEDERACY. —**the Confederation** The union of the American colonies, 1781-89, under the Articles of Confederation.

**con·fer** (kən·fûr′) *v.* **·ferred, ·fer·ring** *v.t.* 1 To give or grant; bestow. —*v.i.* 2 To hold a conference; consult. [< L *com*- together + *ferre* bring, carry] —**con·fer′ment, con·fer′rer** *n.* —**con·fer′ra·ble** *adj.*

**con·fer·ence** (kon′fər·əns, -frəns) *n.* 1 A formal meeting for counsel or discussion. 2 A discussion or consultation. 3 A league or association, as of churches, schools, athletic teams, etc. [< L *conferre* to confer]

**con·fess** (kən·fes′) *v.t.* 1 To acknowledge or admit, as a fault, guilt, or debt. 2 To acknowledge belief or faith in. 3 a To admit or make known (one's sins) to a priest, to obtain absolution. b To hear the confession of: said of a priest. 4 To concede or admit to be true. —*v.i.* 5 To make acknowledgment of, as a fault, crime, or error. 6 To make confession to a priest. [< L *confessus,* pp. of *confiteri* declare thoroughly] —**con·fes′sed·ly** *adv.*

**con·fes·sion** (kən·fesh′ən) *n.* 1 An avowal or admission, as of guilt. 2 That which is confessed or admitted. 3 *Eccl.* A contrite acknowledgment of one's sins to a priest in order to obtain absolution. 4 A formal declaration of belief or faith.

**con·fi·dant** (kon′fə·dant′, -dänt′, kon′fə·dant′, -dänt′) *n.* A person to whom secrets are entrusted. [< L *confidere* to confide] —**con′fi·dante′** *n. Fem.*

**con·fide** (kən·fīd′) *v.* **·fid·ed, ·fid·ing** *v.t.* 1 To reveal in trust or confidence. 2 To put into one's trust or keeping. —*v.i.* 3 To reveal secrets in trust: often with *in.* [< L *com*- thoroughly + *fidere* to trust] —**con·fid′er** *n.*

**con·fi·dence** (kon′fə·dəns) *n.* 1 Trust in or reliance upon something or someone. 2 Assurance. 3 Self-reliance; courage or boldness. 4 A private conversation or a secret. 5 A relationship of trust: take into one's *confidence.*

**con·fi·dent** (kon′fə·dənt) *adj.* Having or showing confidence; assured. —*n.* A confidant. —**con′fi·dent·ly** *adv.*

**con·fi·den·tial** (kon′fə·den′shəl) *adj.* 1 Trusted with secret or private information. 2 Imparted in confidence; secret: *confidential* information. 3 Of or marked by trust in others; confiding: a *confidential* manner. —**con′fi·den′tial·ly** *adv.* —**con′fi·den′tial·ness** *n.*

**con·fine** (kən·fīn′) *v.* **·fined, ·fin·ing** *v.t.* 1 To shut within an enclosure; imprison. 2 To restrain or oblige to stay within doors. 3 To keep within limits; restrict: to *confine* remarks. —*n. Usu. pl.* A boundary; limit; border. [< L *confinis* bordering < *com-* together + *finis* border] —con·fin′a·ble *adj*. —con·fi·n′er *n*.

con·firm (kən·fûrm′) *v.t.* 1 To assure by added proof; verify; make certain. 2 To strengthen. 3 To ratify, as a bill, law, etc. 4 To receive into the church by confirmation. [< L *confirmare* strengthen < *com-* thoroughly + *firmus* strong] —con·firm′a·ble, con·firm·a·tive, con·firm·a·to·ry (kən·fûr′mə·tôr′ē, -tō′rē) *adj*. —con·firm′er, con·fir·m′or *n*. —Syn. 1 corroborate, prove, settle, substantiate, establish.

con·fir·ma·tion (kon′fər·mā′shən) *n*. 1 The act of confirming. 2 That which confirms; proof. 3 A rite administered to baptized persons, confirming or strengthening their faith, and admitting them to all the privileges of the church.

con·fis·cate (kon′fis·kāt) *v.t.* ·cat·ed, ·cat·ing 1 To appropriate as forfeited to the public use or treasury, usu. as a penalty. 2 To appropriate by or as by authority. [< L *confiscare* < *com-* together + *fiscus* chest, treasury] —con′fis·ca′tion *n*. —con′fis·ca′tor *n*.

con·fla·gra·tion (kon′flə·grā′shən) *n*. A great or disastrous fire. [< L *com-* thoroughly + *flagrare* to burn]

con·flict (kon′flikt) *n*. 1 A struggle; battle. 2 A state or condition of opposition; antagonism. 3 Emotional disturbance due to opposed and contradictory impulses. —*v.i.* (kən·flikt′) 1 To come into collision; be in mutual opposition; clash. 2 To battle; struggle. [< L *com-* together + *fligere* strike] —con·flic′tion *n*. —con·flic′tive *adj*.

con·form (kən·fôrm′) *v.t.* 1 To make like or similar in form or character: with *to*. 2 To bring into agreement: often used reflexively. —*v.i.* 3 To be or act in accord; comply: with *to*. 4 To hold to or comply with the accepted modes of behavior, prevailing opinions, etc. [< L *com-* together + *formare* shape] —con·form′er *n*.

con·found (kon·found′, kən-) *v.t.* 1 To amaze, confuse, or perplex. 2 To mingle or mix up (elements, things, ideas, etc.) indistinguishably. 3 (kon′found′) To damn: used as a mild oath. [< L *confundere*. See CON-FUSE.] —con·found′er *n*.

con·front (kən·frunt′) *v.t.* 1 To stand face to face with. 2 To place or put face to face: with *with*: Confront him with the evidence. 3 To face defiantly. [< L *com-* together + *frons* face, forehead] —con·front′er *n*.

con·fuse (kən·fyōōz′) *v.t.* ·fused, ·fus·ing 1 To perplex; confound; bewilder. 2 To mix indiscriminately. 3 To mistake (a person or thing) for another. 4 DISCONCERT. [< L *confusus*, pp. of *confundere* to pour together] —con·fus·ed·ly (kən·fyōō′zid·lē) *adv*. —con·fus′ed·ness *n*. —con·fus′ing·ly *adv*.

con·fute (kən·fyōōt′) *v.t.* ·fut·ed, ·fut·ing 1 To prove to be false or invalid; refute successfully. 2 To prove (a person) to be in the wrong. [< L *confutare* check, restrain] —con′fu·ta′tion *n*. —con·fut′er *n*.

con·geal (kən·jēl′) *v.t.* 1 To solidify or thicken, as by cooling. 2 To curdle or coagulate. —*v.i.* 3 To become hard, stiff, or viscid. [< L *com-* together + *gelare* freeze < *gelum* frost] —con·geal′a·ble *adj*. —con·geal′er, con·geal′ment *n*.

con·gen·ial (kən·jēn′yəl) *adj*. 1 Having similar character or tastes. 2 Suited to one's disposition. [< CON- + GENIAL] —con·ge·ni·al·i·ty (kən·jē′nē·al′ə·tē) *n*. —con·gen′ial·ly *adv*. —Syn. 1 Sympathetic, kindred, congenial. 2 Agreeable, gratifying, pleasant.

con·gen·i·tal (kən·jen′ə·təl) *adj*. Existing at or from birth. [< L *com-* together + *genitus*, pp. of *gignere* bear, produce] —con·gen′i·tal·ly *adv*.

con·gest (kən·jest′) *v.t.* 1 To collect or crowd together; overcrowd. 2 To cause excessive accumulation of blood in (an organ or tissue). —*v.i.* 3 To become congested. [< L *congestum*, pp. of *congerere* to carry together] —con·ges′tion *n*. —con·ges′tive *adj*.

con·grat·u·late (kən·grach′ōō·lāt) *v.t.* ·lat·ed, ·lat·ing To express sympathetic pleasure in the joy, success, or good fortune of (another). [< L *com-* together + *gratulari* rejoice] —con·grat′u·lant, con·grat′u·la·to′ry *adj*. —con·grat′u·la′tor *n*.

con·gre·gate (kong′grə·gāt) *v.t. & v.i.* ·gat·ed, ·gat·ing To bring or come together into a crowd; assemble. —*adj*. (kong′grə·git) Gathered together; collected. [<L *com-* together + *gregare* crowd, collect + *grex* flock] —con′gre·ga′tive *adj*. —con′gre·ga′tor *n*.

con·gre·ga·tion (kong′grə·gā′shən) *n*. 1 The act of congregating. 2 An assemblage of people or of things. 3 A group of people gathered for worship. 4 The body of persons who regularly attend a place of worship. —con′gre·ga′tion·al *adj*.

Con·gress (kong′gris) *n*. The national legislative body of the U.S., consisting of the

Senate and the House of Representatives. —**Con·gres·sion·al** (kən·gresh′ən·ən) *adj.*

**con·gres·sion·al** (kən·gresh′ən·əl) *adj.* Of or pertaining to a congress.

**con·jec·ture** (kən·jek′chər) *v.t.* ·tured, ·tur·ing 1 To conclude or suppose from incomplete evidence; guess. —*v.i.* 2 To make a conjecture. —*n.* 1 An indecisive opinion; a guess. 2 The act of conjecturing. [< L *conjectura* < *conjicere* to throw together] —**con·jec′tur·a·ble** *adj.* —**con·jec′tur·a·bly** *adv.* —**con·jec′tur·er** *n.*

**con·ju·gal** (kon′jōō·gəl) *adj.* Of or pertaining to marriage; matrimonial. [< L *conjungere* join in marriage] —**con·ju·gal·i·ty** (kon-′jōō·gal′ə·tē) *n.* —**con′ju·gal·ly** *adv.*

**con·ju·gate** (kon′jōō·gāt), *for adj. & n., usu.* -git) *v.* ·gat·ed, ·gat·ing *v.t.* 1 To give the inflections of: said of verbs. 2 To unite or join together. —*adj.* Joined in pairs; coupled; paired. —*n.* 1 A word closely related to another or others. 2 A member of a conjugate pair. [< L *com-* together + *jugare* to yoke] —**con′ju·ga′tive** *adj.* —**con′ju·ga′tor** *n.*

**con·ju·ga·tion** (kon′jōō·gā′shən) *n.* 1 CONJUNCTION (def. 1). 2 *Gram.* The inflection of a verb or the expression of such inflection. 3 A class of verbs with a similar inflection. —**con′ju·ga′tion·al** *adj.*

**con·junc·tion** (kən·jungk′shən) *n.* 1 The act of joining or the state of being joined together. 2 *Astron.* The position of a planet when it, the earth, and the sun lie on the same straight line. 3 Simultaneous occurrence of events. 4 *Gram.* A word used to connect words, phrases, clauses, or sentences. [< L *com-* together + *jungere* join]

**con·jure** (kən·jōōr′ *for def. 1,* kon′jər, kun′- *for defs.* 2–5) *v.* ·jured, ·jur·ing *v.t.* 1 To appeal to solemnly. 2 To summon, bring, or drive away by incantation or spell, as a devil or spirit. 3 To accomplish or effect by or as by magic. —*v.i.* 4 To practice magic. 5 To summon a devil or spirit by incantation. [< L *com-* together + *jurare* swear] —**con′jur·er** *n.*

**con·nect** (kə·nekt′) *v.t.* 1 To join together, as by links; combine. 2 To associate mentally. 3 To close or complete, as an electric circuit or telephone connection. —*v.i.* 4 To unite or join; be in close relation. 5 To meet as scheduled, as buses or trains, for transference of passengers. [< L *com-* together + *nectere* bind] —**con·nect′er, con·nect′or** *n.*

**con·nec·tion** (kə·nek′shən) *n.* 1 The act of connecting or the state of being connected.

2 The means or place of connection. 3 That which connects or serves to connect. 4 *Often pl.* A relative, associate, or friend. 5 A direct transfer from one route to another, as in railway service. 6 Logical coherence or consistency. 7 *Slang* A contact for acquiring narcotics. *Brit. sp.* **con·nex′ion.**

**con·ni·vance** (kə·nī′vəns) *n.* 1 The act of conniving. 2 *Law* Knowledge of a wrongful or criminal act during its occurrence. Also **con·ni′van·cy.**

**con·nive** (kə·nīv′) *v.i.* ·nived, ·niv·ing 1 To encourage or assent to a wrong by silence or feigned ignorance: with *at.* 2 To be in collusion: with *with.* [< L *conivere* shut the eyes] —**con·niv′er** *n.*

**con·nois·seur** (kon′ə·sûr′) *n.* A competent critical judge, esp. in matters of art and taste. [F<L *cognoscere* know thoroughly] —**con′nois·seur′ship** *n.*

**con·note** (kə·nōt′) *v.t.* ·not·ed, ·not·ing To indicate or imply along with the literal meaning. [< L *com-* together + *notare* mark]

**con·nu·bi·al** (kə·n/ōō′bē·əl) *adj.* Pertaining to matrimony. [< L *com-* together + *nubere* marry] —**con·nu·bi·al·i·ty** (kə·n/ōō′bē·al′ə·tē) *n.* —**con·nu′bi·al·ly** *adv.*

**con·quer** (kong′kər) *v.t.* 1 To overcome or subdue by force, as in war. 2 To acquire or gain control of by or as by force. 3 To overcome by mental or moral force. —*v.i.* 4 To be victorious. [< L *conquirere* + *com-* thoroughly + *quaerere* seek] —**con′quer·a·ble, con′quer·ing** *adj.* —**con′quer·ing·ly** *adv.* —**con′quer·or** *n.*

**con·san·guin·e·ous** (kon′sang·gwin′ē·əs) *adj.* Descended from the same parent or ancestor; related. Also **con·san·guine** (kon·sang′gwin). [< L *com-* together + *sanguis* blood] —**con′san·guin′e·ous·ly** *adv.* —**con′san·guin′i·ty** *n.*

**con·science** (kon′shəns) *n.* The faculty by which distinctions are made between right and wrong; ethical judgment or sensibility. —**in (all) conscience** 1 In reason and honesty. 2 Certainly; assuredly. [< L *conscientia* < *com-* together + *scire* know]

**con·sci·en·tious** (kon′shē·en′shəs) *adj.* 1 Governed or dictated by conscience. 2 Characterized by or done with care and attention. —**con′sci·en′tious·ly** *adv.* —**con′sci·en′tious·ness** *n.* —**Syn.** 1 scrupulous, honest, principled, moral. 2 careful, thorough, meticulous, attentive.

**con·scious** (kon′shəs) *adj.* 1 Mentally aware of one's inner thoughts and feelings and also of things external to oneself. 2 In possession of one's mental faculties; awake. 3 Able to think, will, perceive, etc.; rational. 4 Felt or acknowledged by oneself: *conscious* guilt. 5 Self-conscious. 6 Deliberate; intentional: a *conscious* lie. —*n. Psychoanal.* That part of mental life of which an individual is aware. [< L *conscius* < *com-* together + *scire* know] —con′scious·ly *adv.*

con·se·crate (kon′sə·krāt) *v.t.* ·crat·ed, ·crat·ing 1 To set apart as sacred; dedicate to sacred uses. 2 To dedicate solemnly or devote: *consecrate* one's life to a cause. 3 To make reverend; hallow. [< L *com-* thoroughly + *sacer* holy] —con′se·cra′tion, con′se·cra′tor *n.* —con·se·cra·to·ry (kon′sə·krə·tôr′ē, -tō′rē) *adj.*

con·sec·u·tive (kən·sek′yə·tiv) *adj.* 1 Following in uninterrupted succession; successive. 2 Characterized by logical sequence. [< L *consequi* follow together] —con·sec′u·tive·ly *adv.* —con·sec′u·tive·ness *n.*

con·sen·sus (kən·sen′səs) *n.* A collective opinion; general agreement. [< L *com-* together + *sentire* feel, think]

con·sent (kən·sent′) *v.i.* To yield or accede; agree. —*n.* 1 A voluntary yielding to what is proposed or desired by another; acquiescence. 2 Agreement in opinion or sentiment. [< L *consentire*. See CONSENSUS.] —con·sent′er *n.*

con·se·quence (kon′sə·kwens, -kwəns) *n.* 1 That which naturally follows from a preceding action or condition; result. 2 A logical conclusion of an inference; deduction. 3 Distinction; note: a woman of *consequence.* 4 Significance; moment: an event of no *consequence.*

con·ser·va·tive (kən·sûr′və·tiv) *adj.* 1 Adhering to and tending to preserve the existing order of things; opposed to change. 2 *Often cap.* Of, pertaining to, or characterizing a political party or philosophy that favors the preservation of the status quo and is critical of proposals for change. 3 Conserving; preservative. 4 Moderate; cautious: a *conservative* estimate or statement. —*n.* 1 A conservative person. 2 *Often cap.* A member of a conservative political party. —con·ser′va·tive·ly *adv.* —con·ser′va·tive·ness *n.*

con·ser·va·to·ry (kən·sûr′və·tôr′ē, -tō′rē) *n., pl.* ·ries 1 A glass-enclosed room in which plants are grown and displayed. 2 A school of art, music, etc.

con·serve (kən·sûrv′) *v.t.* ·served, ·serv·ing 1 To keep from loss, decay, or depletion; supervise and protect. 2 To preserve with sugar. —*n.* (kon′sûrv, kən·sûrv′) *Often pl.* A preserve made of several fruits stewed together in sugar, often with nuts, raisins, etc. [< L *com-* thoroughly + *servare* keep, save] —con·serv′a·ble *adj.* —con·serv′er *n.*

con·sid·er (kən·sid′ər) *v.t.* 1 To think about or deliberate upon. 2 To think to be. 3 To make allowance for. 4 To take into account: *consider* the feelings of others. —*v.i.* 5 To think closely; cogitate. [< L *considerare,* lit., to observe the stars]

con·sid·er·a·ble (kən·sid′ər·ə·bəl) *adj.* 1 Somewhat large in amount, extent, etc. 2 Worthy of consideration; significant. —con·sid′er·a·bly *adv.*

con·sid·er·a·tion (kən·sid′ə·rā′shən) *n.* 1 The act of considering. 2 Something resulting from deliberation; a thought. 3 Thoughtful and kindly feeling or treatment. 4 A circumstance to be taken into account. 5 Something given in return for a service. 6 Importance; consequence.

con·sign (kən·sīn′) *v.t.* 1 To entrust or commit to the care of another. 2 To make over or relegate. 3 To forward or deliver, as merchandise, for sale or disposal. 4 To set apart, as for a specific purpose or use. [< L *com-* with + *signum* a seal] —con·sign′a·ble *adj.* —con·sign·or (kən·sī′nər, kon′sī·nôr′), con·sign′er *n.*

con·sist (kən·sist′) *v.i.* 1 To be made up or constituted: with *of.* 2 To have as substance, quality, or nature: with *in.* 3 To exist in agreement: with *with.* [< L *com-* together + *sistere* stand]

con·sis·ten·cy (kən·sis′tən·sē) *n., pl.* ·cies 1 Compatibility or harmony, as between things, acts, or statements. 2 Agreement with what has been previously done, expressed, etc. 3 Firmness, or density, as of a liquid. 4 Degree of firmness, thickness, or density. Also con·sis′tence.

con·so·la·tion (kon′sə·lā′shən) *n.* 1 The act of consoling or the state of being consoled; solace. 2 A comforting thought, person, or fact.

con·sole (kən·sōl′) *v.t.* ·soled, ·sol·ing To comfort (a person) in grief or sorrow; solace. [< L *com-* together + *solari* solace] —con·sol′a·ble *adj.* —con·sol′er *n.*

con·sol·i·date (kən·sol′ə·dāt) *v.* ·dat·ed, ·dat·ing *v.t.* 1 To make solid, firm, or coherent. 2 *Mil.* To secure and strengthen, as a newly captured position. 3 To form a union of. —*v.i.* 4 To become united, solid, or firm. [< L *com-* together + *solidus* solid] —con·sol′i·da′tion, con·sol′i·da′tor *n.*

con·so·nant (kon′sə-nənt) *adj.* 1 Being in agreement or harmony; consistent. 2 CON-SONANTAL. 3 Having the quality of musical consonance. —*n.* 1 *Phonet.* A sound produced by partial blockage of the breath stream. 2 A letter representing such a sound. [< L *com-* together + *sonare* to sound] —con′so·nant·ly *adv.*

con·sort (kon′sôrt) *n.* 1 A companion or associate. 2 A husband or wife; mate. 3 An accompanying vessel. —*v.t.* (kən-sôrt′) 1 To join; associate. —*v.i.* 2 To keep company; associate. 3 To be in agreement; harmonize. [< L *consors*, lit., one who shares the same fate]

con·spic·u·ous (kon-spik′yoō-əs) *adj.* 1 Clearly visible; prominent; obvious. 2 Unusual; striking. [< L *com-* together + *specere* look at] —con·spic′u·ous·ly *adv.* —con·spic′u·ous·ness *n.*

con·spir·a·cy (kən-spir′ə-sē) *n. pl.* ·cies 1 The act of conspiring. 2 A plot, esp. one to do something harmful, illegal, or treasonable. 3 The persons engaged in such a plot. 4 A striking concurrence, as of circumstances or tendencies. —con·spir·a·tor (kən-spir′ə-tər) *n.* —con·spir·a·to·ri·al (kən-spir′ə-tôr′ē-əl, -tō′rē-) *adj.*

con·spire (kən-spīr′) *v.* ·spired, ·spir·ing *v.i.* 1 To plot. —*v.i.* 2 To form a plot, especially secretly, for evil or unlawful purposes. 3 To concur in action or endeavor, as circumstances. [< L *com-* together + *spirare* breathe] —con·spir·ant (kən-spī′rənt) *adj.*, *n.* —con·spir′er *n.*

con·stant (kon′stənt) *adj.* 1 Steady in purpose; resolute; persevering. 2 Steady in faithfulness; loyal. 3 Continually recurring. 4 Invariable; unchanging. —*n.* 1 That which is permanent or invariable. 2 *Math.* A quantity which retains a fixed value throughout a given discussion. 3 In the sciences, any characteristic of a substance, event, or phenomenon, numerically determined, that remains always the same under specified conditions, as gravitation, the velocity of light, etc. [< L *com-* together + *stare* stand] —con′stan·cy *n.* —con′stant·ly *adv.*

con·stel·la·tion (kon′stə-lā′shən) *n.* 1 *Astron.* Any of 88 apparent clusters of stars, each named for a mythological person, an ani-

mal, or some object that it suggests; also, the area in the heavens covering such a group. 2 Any assemblage of things or persons. 3 In astrology, the position of the planets, esp. at the time of one's birth.

con·ster·na·tion (kon′stər-nā′shən) *n.* Complete confusion or dismay. [< L *consternare* to stretch out, perplex] —Syn. amazement, astonishment, shock, distraction.

con·sti·pate (kon′stə-pāt) *v.t.* ·pat·ed, ·pat·ing To cause constipation in. [< L *com-* together + *stipare* press, crowd] —con′sti·pat′ed *adj.*

con·stit·u·ent (kən-stich′oō-ənt) *adj.* 1 Serving to form or compose as a necessary part; constituting. 2 Entitled to vote for a public officer or representative. 3 Having the power to frame or modify a constitution. —*n.* 1 One represented politically; a voter. 2 An essential part; a component. [< L *constituere.* See CONSTITUTE.]

con·sti·tute (kon′stə-t′oōt) *v.t.* ·tut·ed, ·tut·ing 1 To form or be the substance of; make up. 2 To establish or found, as a school. 3 To set up or enact, as a law. 4 To depute or appoint, as to an office or function. [< L *constituere* < *com-* together + *statuere* place, station] —con′sti·tut′er *n.*

con·sti·tu·tion (kon′stə-t′oō′shən) *n.* 1 The act of constituting. 2 A system of related parts; composition, esp. bodily make-up. 3 The fundamental laws and practices that normally govern the operation of a state or association. 4 A document containing these laws. —the Constitution The document drawn up in 1787 containing the laws by which the United States of America is governed.

con·strain (kən-strān′) *v.t.* 1 To compel; oblige. 2 To confine, as by bonds. 3 To restrain. [< L *com-* together + *stringere* bind tight] —con·strain′a·ble *adj.* —con·strain′er *n.*

con·straint (kən-strānt′) *n.* 1 The act of constraining or the state of being constrained. 2 Embarrassment. 3 Anything that constrains.

con·strict (kən-strikt′) *v.t.* To compress or draw together at some point; bind. [< L *constrictus*, pp. of *constringere* to bind together] —con·stric′tive *adj.*

con·stric·tion (kən-strik′shən) *n.* .. A constricting. 2 That which constricts or is constricted. 3 A feeling of tightness, as in the chest.

con·sul (kon′səl) *n.* 1 An officer appointed to

reside in a foreign city, chiefly as a representative of his country's commercial interests. 2 Either of two chief magistrates ruling in Ancient Rome. 3 Any of the three chief magistrates of the French republic, 1799–1804. [< L] —con·su·lar adj. —con′sul·ship n.

con·su·late (kon′sə·lit) n. 1 The offices and residence of a consul. 2 The position, duties and authority of a consul. 3 A consul's term of office.

con·sult (kən·sult′) v.t. 1 To ask advice or information of. 2 To consider. —v.i. 3 To ask advice. 4 To compare views: with with. [< L consultare, freq. of consulere seek advice] —con·sult′a·ble adj. —con·sult′er n.

con·sume (kən·syoom′) v. ·sumed, ·sum·ing v.t. 1 To destroy, as by burning. 2 To eat or drink up. 3 To squander; use up, as money or time. 4 To hold the interest of; engross. —v.i. 5 To be wasted or destroyed. [< L com- thoroughly + sumere take up, use] —con·sum′a·ble adj.

con·sum·mate (kon′sə·māt) v.t. ·mat·ed, ·mat·ing 1 To bring to completion or perfection; achieve. 2 To fulfill, as a marriage by the first act of sexual intercourse. —adj. (kən·sum′it) Of the highest degree; perfect. [< L com- together + summa sum, total] —con·sum′mate·ly adv. —con′sum·ma′tion, con′sum·ma′tor n. —con′sum·ma′tive adj.

con·sump·tion (kən·sump′shən) n. 1 The act or process of consuming. 2 The amount used up. 3 The using up of goods by consumers. 4 A wasting disease; specifically, pulmonary tuberculosis.

con·tact (kon′takt) n. 1 The coming together, meeting, or touching of two bodies. 2 Electr. a The touching or joining of points or surfaces of conductors, permitting the passage or flow of a current. b One of two or more conductors that touch in this way. 3 Immediate proximity or association. 4 A useful or helpful acquaintance. —v.t. 1 To bring or place in contact; touch. 2 Informal To get or be in touch with (a person); communicate with. —v.i. 3 To be or come in contact. [< L com- together + tangere touch]

con·ta·gion (kən·tā′jən) n. 1 The communication of disease by contact, direct or indirect. 2 A disease communicated in this way. 3 The medium of transmission of a disease. 4 A poison. 5 The transmission of an emotion, idea, etc., from person to person. [< L < contingere]

con·ta·gious (kən·tā′jəs) adj. 1 Transmissible by contact, as a disease. 2 Transmitting disease; pestilential. 3 Communicable from one person to another; catching; spreading. —con·ta′gious·ly adv. —con·ta′gious·ness n.

con·tain (kən·tān′) v.t. 1 To hold or enclose. 2 To include or comprise. 3 To be able to hold. 4 To keep within bounds; restrain. 5 Math. To have as an exact factor. [< L com- together + tenere hold] —con·tain′a·ble adj. —con·tain′er n.

con·tam·i·nate (kən·tam′ə·nāt) v.t. ·nat·ed, ·nat·ing To make impure by contact or admixture. [< L com- together + tangere touch] —con·tam′i·nant, con·tam′i·na′tion, con·tam′i·na′tor n. —con·tam′i·na′tive adj. —Syn. taint, defile, pollute, debase.

con·temn (kən·tem′) v.t. To despise; scorn. [< L com- thoroughly + temnere slight, scorn] —con·temn·er (kən·tem′ər, -tem′nər), con·tem·nor (kən·tem′nər) n.

con·tem·plate (kon′təm·plāt) v. ·plat·ed, ·plat·ing v.t. 1 To look at attentively; gaze at. 2 To consider thoughtfully; ponder. 3 To intend or plan. 4 To treat as possible. —v.i. 5 To meditate; muse. [< L contemplari < com- together + templum temple; with ref. to the art of divination] —con·tem·pla·ble (kən·tem′plə·bəl) adj. —con′tem·pla′tion, con′tem·pla′tor n.

con·tem·po·rar·y (kən·tem′pə·rer′ē) adj. 1 Contemporaneous. 2 Having the same age. 3 Modern. —n. pl. ·rar·ies A person or thing that is contemporary.

con·tempt (kən·tempt′) n. 1 Disdain; scorn. 2 Law Willful disregard of authority, as of a court. 3 The state of being despised; disgrace; shame. [< L contemptus < contemnere despise, disdain. See CONTEMN.]

con·temp·tu·ous (kən·temp′chŏŏ·əs) adj. Disdainful; scornful. —con·temp′tu·ous·ly adv. —con·temp′tu·ous·ness n.

con·tend (kən·tend′) v.t. 1 To maintain or assert in argument. —v.i. 2 To debate earnestly; dispute. 3 To strive in competition: to contend for a prize. 4 To struggle or fight in opposition or combat. [< L com- together + tendere strive, strain] —con·tend′er n.

con·tent[1] (kon′tent) n. 1 Usu. pl. All that a thing contains or deals with. 2 The significance or basic meaning, as of a literary work. 3 Holding capacity; size. 4 Included area or space. 5 The quantity of a specified part: the silver *content* of a ton of ore. [< L *continere* contain]

con·tent² (kən·tent′) *adj.* Satisfied with things as they are. —*v.t.* To satisfy. —*n.* Contentment; satisfaction. [< L *continere* contain]

con·ten·tion (kən·ten′shən) *n.* 1 The act of contending; strife, conflict, struggle, dispute, argument, etc. 2 An object or point in debate or controversy.

con·ten·tious (kən·ten′shəs) *adj.* 1 Of, pertaining to, or fond of contention; quarrelsome. 2 Full of or marked by contention. —con·ten′tious·ly *adv.* —con·ten′tious·ness *n.*

con·test (kon′test) *n.* 1 A struggle to determine a winner; a competition. 2 Verbal conflict; controversy. —*v.t.* (kən·test′) 1 To fight about; contend for; strive to win, keep, or control. 2 To argue about or challenge: to *contest* an election. —*v.i.* 3 To contend, struggle, or vie: with *with* or *against.* [< L *contestari* bring legal action against] —con·test′a·ble *adj.* —con·test′er *n.*

con·text (kon′tekst) *n.* The portions of a discourse, treatise, etc., preceding and following a passage quoted or considered. [< L *com-* together + *texere* weave] —con·tex·tu·al (kən·teks′chōō·əl) *adj.* —con·tex′tu·al·ly *adv.*

con·tig·u·ous (kən·tig′yōō·əs) *adj.* 1 Touching or joining at the edge or boundary. 2 Adjacent; close. [< L *contingere* to contact] —con·tig′u·ous·ly *adv.* —con·tig′u·ous·ness *n.*

con·ti·nence (kon′tə·nəns) *n.* 1 Self-restraint; 2 Moderation, esp. in sexual passion; chastity. Also con′ti·nen·cy.

con·ti·nent (kon′tə·nənt) *n.* One of the great bodies of land on the globe, generally regarded as Africa, Antarctica, Asia, Australia, Europe, North America, and South America. —the Continent Europe, exclusive of the British Isles. —*adj.* Self-restrained; abstinent; chaste. [< L *continere* contain] —con·ti·nen·tal (kon′tə·nen′təl) *adj.* —con′ti·nent·ly *adv.*

con·tin·gent (kən·tin′jənt) *adj.* 1 Not certain to happen; possible. 2 Accidental; fortuitous. 3 Dependent upon an uncertain occurrence or condition. —*n.* A contingency. 2 A representational group: the American *contingent* at the conference. 3 A quota of troops, laborers, etc. [<L *contingere* to contact] —con·tin′gent·ly *adv.*

con·tin·ue (kən·tin′yōō) *v.* ·tin·ued, ·tin·u·ing *v.t.* 1 To extend or prolong in space or time. 2 To persist in. 3 To cause to last or remain, as in a position or office. 4 To take up again after an interruption. 5 *Law* To postpone, as a judicial proceeding. —*v.i.* 6 To last; endure. 7 To keep on or persist. 8 To remain, as in a place or position. 9 To resume after an interruption. 10 To extend. [<L *continere* hold together, contain] —con·tin′u·a·ble *adj.* —con·tin′u·er *n.*

con·ti·nu·i·ty (kon′tə·nyōō′ə·tē) *n.* 1 The state or quality of being continuous. 2 That which has or exhibits such a state or quality; an unbroken sequence or whole.

con·tin·u·ous (kən·tin′yōō·əs) *adj.* Connected, extended, prolonged, or going on without a break. —con·tin′u·ous·ly *adv.* —con·tin′u·ous·ness *n.* • See CONTINUAL.

con·tort (kən·tôrt′) *v.t.* To twist or wrench out of shape or place. [<L *com-* together + *torquere* twist] —con·tor′tion *n.* —con·tor′tive *adj.* —Syn. bend, distort, deform.

con·tour (kon′tŏor) *n.* The line bounding a figure, land, etc.; outline. —*v.t.* To make or draw in outline or contour. —*adj.* Following the contour lines of land so as to avoid erosion. [< LL *com-* together + *tornare* make round]

con·tra·band (kon′trə·band) *adj.* Forbidden or excluded, as by law or treaty. —*n.* 1 Illegal or forbidden trade. 2 Contraband goods. 3 CONTRABAND OF WAR. [< LL *contra* against + *bannum* law, proclamation] —con′tra·band′ist *n.*

con·tract (kən·trakt′ *for v. defs. 1, 3–6;* kon′trakt, kən·trakt′ *for v. def.* 2) *v.t.* 1 To reduce in size; shrink; narrow. 2 To arrange or settle by agreement; enter upon with reciprocal obligations. 3 To acquire or become affected with, as a disease or habit. 4 To shorten, as a word, by omitting or combining medial letters or sounds. —*v.i.* 5 To shrink. 6 To make a contract. —*n.* (kon′trakt) 1 An agreement between two or more parties, esp. when legally enforceable. 2 A formal document containing the terms of such an agreement. 3 The act of marriage. 4 A formal agreement of marriage; betrothal. 5 CONTRACT BRIDGE. 6 The highest bid in a hand of contract bridge. [<L *contractus,* pp. of *contrahere* pull together] —con·tract′ed *adj.* —con·tract′i·bil′i·ty *n.* con·tract′a·ble *adj.*

con·trac·tor (kon′trak·tər, kən·trak′-) *n.* 1

One of the parties to a contract. 2 One who agrees to supply labor or materials or both.

**con·tra·dict** (kon′trə·dikt′) *v.t.* 1 To maintain the opposite of (a statement); deny. 2 To be inconsistent with or opposed to. 3 To disagree with (someone). —*v.i.* 4 To dispute, deny, or maintain the opposite of something. [< L *contra-* against + *dicere* say, speak] —**con′tra·dict′a·ble**, **con′tra·dic′tive** *adj.* —**con′tra·dict′er** or **con′tra·dic′tor**, **con′tra·dic′tion** *n.*

**con·trail** (kon′trāl) *n.* The vapor trail sometimes left by an airplane flying at high altitudes, caused by the condensation of moisture from exhaust gases. [<CON(DENSATION) + TRAIL]

**con·tral·to** (kən·tral′tō) *n. pl.* **·tos** or **·ti** (-tē) 1 The lowest female voice, intermediate between soprano and tenor. 2 A part written for such a voice. 3 A singer with such a voice. —*adj.* Of or for a contralto. [< Ital.]

**con·trar·y** (kon′trer·ē; *for adj. def. 4, also* kən·trâr′ē) *adj.* 1 Totally different; opposed. 2 Adverse: *contrary* winds. 3 Opposite or other. 4 Inclined to opposition or contradiction; perverse —*n. pl.* **·trar·ies** 1 One of two opposing things. 2 The opposite. —**on the contrary** 1 On the other hand. 2 Just the opposite of what has been said. —**to the contrary** To the opposite effect. —*adv.* In a contrary manner. [< L *contra* against] —**con′trar·i·ly** *adv.* —**con′trar·i·ness** *n.*

**con·trast** (kən·trast′) *v.t.* 1 To place or set in opposition so as to show dissimilarities. —*v.i.* 2 To show dissimilarities when set in opposition. —*n.* (kon′trast) 1 The dissimilarity between two or more things or persons, as revealed by comparison. 2 A person or thing that contrasts with another. [< L *contra-* against + *stare* stand] —**con·trast′a·ble** *adj.*

**con·trib·ute** (kən·trib′yŏot) *v.* **·ut·ed**, **·ut·ing** *v.t.* 1 To give or furnish (money, ideas, etc.), as for a common purpose. 2 To furnish, as an article or story, to a magazine or other publication. —*v.i.* 3 To share in effecting a result. 4 To make or give a contribution. [< L *com-* together + *tribuere* grant, allot] —**con·trib′ut·a·ble**, **con·trib′u·tive** *adj.* —**con·trib′u·tive·ly** *adv.* —**con·trib′u·tive·ness**, **con·trib′u·tor** *n.*

**con·trite** (kən·trīt′, kon′trīt) *adj.* 1 Remorseful or guilty because of one's sins or shortcomings. 2 Proceeding from or showing remorse or guilt. [< L *contritus* bruised, pp. of *conterere* to rub together] —**con·trite′ly**

*adv.* —**con·trite′ness**, **con·tri′tion** (-trish′ən) *n.*

**con·tri·vance** (kən·trī′vəns) *n.* 1 The act or manner of contriving. 2 Something contrived, as a device, tool, etc.

**con·trol** (kən·trōl′) *v.t.* **·trolled**, **·trol·ling** 1 To exercise authority over; govern. 2 To restrain; curb. 3 To direct, guide, or regulate, as a machine. 4 To verify, as an experiment, by comparison with a parallel experiment or other standard. 5 To check, as an account, by means of a duplicate register; verify or rectify. —*n.* 1 The act of controlling. 2 The power or ability to govern, regulate, or direct. 3 The condition of being controlled: The machine was out of *control*. 4 Something that directs, guides, or regulates, as a mechanical device. 5 A standard of comparison against which to check the results of an experiment. [< Med. L *contrarotulus* a check list < L *contra-* against + *rotulus* list] —**con·trol′la·bil′i·ty**, **con·trol′la·ble·ness** *n.* —**con·trol′la·ble** *adj.*

**con·tro·ver·sy** (kon′trə·vûr′sē) *n. pl.* **·sies** 1 Debate or disputation arising from conflicting attitudes and opinions. 2 A quarrel or dispute. [< L *contra-* against + *versus*, pp. of *vertere* turn]

**con·tro·vert** (kon′trə·vûrt, kon′trə·vûrt′) *v.t.* 1 To endeavor to disprove; argue against. 2 To argue about. [< L *controversus* turned against] —**con′tro·vert′er** *n.* —**con·tro·vert′i·ble** *adj.* —**con′tro·vert′i·bly** *adv.*

**con·tu·ma·cy** (kon′t<sup>y</sup>ŏŏ·mə·sē) *n. pl.* **·cies** Contemptuous disregard of authority; insolent and stubborn disobedience. **Also con·tu·mac·i·ty** (kon′t<sup>y</sup>ŏŏ·mas′ə·tē). [< L *contumax* stubborn] —**con·tu·ma·cious** (kon′t<sup>y</sup>ŏŏ·mā′shəs) *adj.* —**con′tu·ma′cious·ly** *adv.* —**con′tu·ma′cious·ness** *n.*

**con·tu·me·ly** (kon′t<sup>y</sup>ŏŏ·mə·lē, -mē′lē; kən·t<sup>y</sup>ŏŏ′mə·lē) *n. pl.* **·lies** 1 Insulting rudeness in speech or manner; scornful insolence. 2 An example of this. [< L *contumelia* reproach] —**con·tu·me·li·ous** (kon′t<sup>y</sup>ŏŏ·mē′lē·əs) *adj.* —**con′tu·me′li·ous·ly** *adv.* —**con′tu·me′li·ous·ness** *n.*

**con·tu·sion** (kən·t<sup>y</sup>ŏŏ′zhən) *n.* A bruise.

**con·va·lesce** (kon′və·les′) *v.i.* **·lesced** **·lesc·ing** To regain health after illness. [< L *com-* thoroughly + *valere* be strong] —**con·va·les·cent** (kon′və·les′ənt) *adj.*, *n.*

**con·va·les·cence** (kon′və·les′əns) *n.* 1 Gradual recovery from illness. 2 The period of such recovery. **Also con′va·les′cen·cy.**

**con·vene** (kən·vēn′) v. **-vened, -ven·ing** v.t. **1** To cause to assemble; convoke. **2** To summon to appear, as by judicial authority. — v.i. **3** To assemble. [< L com- together + venire come] —**con·ven′a·ble** adj. —**con·ven′er** n.

**con·ven·ient** (kən·vēn′yənt) adj. **1** Conducive to comfort or ease; serviceable; handy. **2** Easy to get to; nearby. [< L convenire. See CONVENE.] —**con·ven′ient·ly** adv.

**con·vent** (kon′vent, -vənt) n. **1** A religious community, esp. of nuns. **2** The building or buildings occupied by such a body. [< L conventus meeting]

**con·ven·tion** (kən·ven′shən) n. **1** A formal meeting of delegates, esp. for political or professional purposes. **2** The delegates themselves. **3** A generally accepted social custom or mode of behavior. **4** An established rule, form, or principle, as in art. **5** A formal agreement or compact.

**con·verge** (kən·vûrj′) v. **-verged, -verg·ing** v.i. **1** To cause to tend toward one point. —v.i. **2** To move toward one point; come together by gradual approach. **3** To tend toward the same conclusion or result. [< L com- together + vergere bend]

**con·ver·sant** (kon′vər·sənt, kən·vûr′sənt) adj. Familiar, as a result of study, experience, etc.: with with [< L conversari. See CONVERSE[1]] —**con′ver·sant·ly** adv.

**con·verse[1]** (kən·vûrs′) v.i. **-versed, -vers·ing** To speak together informally; engage in conversation. —n. (kon′vûrs) **1** Conversation. **2** Close fellowship. [< L conversari, freq. of convertere to turn together] —**con·vers′a·ble** adj. —**con·vers′a·bly** adv. —**con·vers′er** n.

**con·verse[2]** (kən·vûrs′, kon′vûrs) adj. Turned about so that two parts are interchanged; transposed; reversed. —n. (kon′vûrs) That which exists in a converse relation; opposite. [< L convertere to turn around] —**con·verse·ly** (kən·vûrs′lē, kon′vûrs·lē) adv.

**con·ver·sion** (kən·vûr′zhən, -shən) n. **1** The act of converting, or the state of being converted, in any sense. **2** A change in one's opinions, way of life, etc., esp. the adoption of a religious belief. —**con·ver′sion·al** adj.

**con·vert** (kən·vûrt′) v.t. **1** To change into another state, form, or substance; transform. **2** To apply or adapt to a new or different purpose or use. **3** To change from one belief, doctrine, creed, opinion, or course of action to another. **4** To exchange for an equivalent value, as goods for money. **5** To

exchange for value of another form, as preferred for common stock. **6** Law To assume possession of illegally. —v.i. **7** To become changed in character. **8** In football, to score the extra point after touchdown, as by kicking a field goal. —n. (kon′vûrt) A person who has been converted, as from one opinion, creed, etc., to another. [< L convertere to turn around]

**con·vert·i·ble** (kən·vûr′tə·bəl) adj. Capable of being converted. —n. **1** A convertible thing. **2** An automobile with a top that can be removed or folded back. —**con·vert′i·bil′i·ty**, **con·vert′i·ble·ness** n. —**con·vert′i·bly** adv.

**con·vex** (kon·veks′, kon′veks) adj. Curving outward like a segment of a globe or of a circle viewed from outside; bulging out. — n. (kon′veks) A convex surface, body, line, etc. [< L convexus vaulted, curved] —**con·vex′i·ty, con·vex′ness** n. —**con·vex′ly** adv.

**con·vey** (kən·vā′) v.t. **1** To carry from one place to another; transport. **2** To serve as a medium or path for; transmit. **3** To make known or impart; communicate. **4** To transfer ownership of, as real estate. [< L com- together + via road, way] —**con·vey′a·ble** adj.

**con·vict** (kən·vikt′) v.t. To prove or find guilty, esp. after a judicial trial. —n. (kon′vikt) One found guilty of or undergoing punishment for crime; a criminal. [< L convictus, pp. of convincere. See CONVINCE.] —**con·vic′tive** adj.

**con·viv·i·al** (kən·viv′ē·əl) adj. Pertaining to or fond of feasting, drinking, or sociability; festive; jovial. [< L convivium a feast, banquet < com- together + vivere live] —**con·viv′i·al·ist, con·viv′i·al·i·ty** (kən·viv′-ē·al′ə·tē) n. —**con·viv′i·al·ly** adv.

**con·voke** (kən·vōk′) v.t. **-voked, -vok·ing** To call together, as for a meeting. [< L com- together + vocare summon] —**con·vok′er** n. —**Syn.** summon, assemble, gather, muster.

**con·voy** (kon′voi) n. **1** A protecting force, as for accompanying ships at sea. **2** A group of vehicles, ships, etc., traveling together for protection. **3** The act of convoying. [< MF convoi < convoyer] —v.t. (kən·voi′, kon′voi) To act as convoy to. [< L com- together + via road]

**con·vulse** (kən·vuls′) v.t. **-vulsed, -vuls·ing 1** To affect with violent movements; agitate violently. **2** To cause to laugh violently. [< L convulsus, pp. of convellere to pull together] —**con·vul·sive** (kən·vul′siv) adj. —**con·vul′sive·ly** adv. —**con·vul′sive·ness** n.

**con·vul·sion** (kən·vulʹshən) *n.* 1 A violent and abnormal muscular contraction of the body; spasm; fit. 2 An uncontrollable fit of laughter. 3 Any violent disturbance. — **con·vul·sion·ar·y** (kən·vulʹshən·erʹē) *adj., n.*

**cook·out** (kŏŏkʹoutʹ) *n. Informal* A picnic at which the meal is cooked out-of-doors; also, the meal itself.

**co·op·er·ate** (kō·opʹə·rāt) *v.i.* ·at·ed, ·at·ing To work or operate together for a common purpose, effect, etc. —**co·opʹer·aʹtor** *n.*

**co·op·er·a·tion** (kō·opʹə·rāʹshən) *n.* 1 Joint action or effort. 2 A union of laborers, farmers, small capitalists, etc., for mutual benefit. —**co·opʹer·aʹtion·ist** *n.*

**co·op·er·a·tive** (kō·opʹə·rə·tiv, -opʹrə-, -opʹə·rāʹtiv) *adj.* 1 Working together or inclined to work together. 2 Of, pertaining to, or set up as a cooperative. —*n.* An organization, store, apartment house, etc., owned in common by persons who use its services, facilities, etc. —**co·opʹer·a·tive·ly** *adv.* —**co·opʹer·a·tive·ness** *n.*

**co·or·di·nate** (kō·ôrʹdə·nit, -nāt) *adj.* 1 Of the same order, importance, or rank. 2 *Math.* Of or pertaining to coordinates. —*n.* 1 One who or that which is of the same order, rank, power, etc. 2 *Math.* Any of an ordered set of numbers that define the position of a point. —*v.* (kō·ôrʹdə·nāt) ·nat·ed, ·nat·ing *v.t.* 1 To put in the same rank, class, or order. 2 To bring into harmonious relation or action. —*v.i.* 3 To be of the same order or rank. 4 To act in harmonious or reciprocal relation. [< L *co-* together + *ordinare* set in order] —**co·orʹdi·nate·ly** *adv.* —**co·orʹdi·nate·ness, co·orʹdi·naʹtor** *n.* —**co·orʹdi·naʹtive** *adj.*

**co·or·di·na·tion** (kō·ôrʹdə·nāʹshən) *n.* 1 The act of coordinating. 2 The state of being coordinate. 3 The harmonious action of the various parts of a system.

**co·pi·ous** (kōʹpē·əs) *adj.* Ample in quantity; abundant. [< L *copia* abundance] —**coʹpi·ous·ly** *adv.* —**coʹpi·ous·ness** *n.* —**Syn.** plentiful, plenteous, profuse.

**cop·per** (kopʹər) *n.* 1 A heavy, reddish metallic element (symbol Cu) with high thermal and electrical conductivity. 2 A coin made of this metal. 3 *Brit.* A large metal vat or pot. 4 A reddish brown. —*v.t.* To coat with copper. [< L *(aes) cyprium* Cyprian (metal)] —**copʹper·y** *adj.*

**cop·y** (kopʹē) *n. pl.* **cop·ies** 1 Something made to reproduce or imitate an original. 2 A single example of a printed edition, issue, etc. 3 Manuscript or other material to be reproduced in print. 4 A newsworthy or suitable subject for writing about. —*v.* **cop·ied, cop·y·ing** *v.t.* 1 To make a copy of; reproduce. 2 To follow as a model; imitate. —*v.i.* 3 To make a copy. [< L, supply, abundance]

**cop·y·right** (kopʹē·rītʹ) *n.* The exclusive statutory right to publish and dispose of a literary, musical, artistic, or dramatic work for a specified time. —*v.t.* To secure copyright for. —**copʹy·rightʹa·ble** *adj.* —**copʹy·rightʹer** *n.*

**co·quet** (kō·ketʹ) *v.* **co·quet·ted, co·quet·ing** *v.i.* 1 To flirt; play the coquette. 2 To act in a trifling manner; dally. [< F *coq* a cock; with ref. to its strutting] —**co·quetʹry** (kōʹkə·trē, kō·ketʹrē) *n.* (*pl.* ·ries)

**co·quette** (kō·ketʹ) *n.* A woman or girl who flirts, esp. to gratify her vanity. [F< *coq* a cock] —**co·quetʹtish** *adj.* —**co·quetʹtish·ly** *adv.* —**co·quetʹtish·ness** *n.*

**cor·al** (kôrʹəl, korʹ-) *n.* 1 The calcareous skeletons secreted by various marine polyps and deposited in various forms and colors. 2 Any of numerous marine polyps that secrete coral. 3 A yellowish pink or red. —*adj.* 1 Made of coral. 2 Yellowish pink or red. [< Gk. *korallion*]

**cor·date** (kôrʹdāt) *adj.* Heart-shaped. [< L *cor, cordis* heart] —**corʹdate·ly** *adv.*

**cor·dial** (kôrʹjəl) *adj.* Warm and sincere. —*n.* 1 A liqueur. 2 A medicine, etc., that stimulates or invigorates. [< L *cor, cordis* heart] —**cor·dial·i·ty** (kôr·jalʹə·tē, -jē·alʹ-, -dē·alʹ-), **corʹdial·ness** *n.* —**corʹdial·ly** *adv.* —**Syn.** *adj.* hearty, heartfelt, genial.

**cor·don** (kôrʹdən) *n.* 1 An extended line, as of men, ships, etc., enclosing or guarding an area. 2 A cord, ribbon, etc., esp. worn as a badge of honor. [< F *corde* cord]

**cor·du·roy** (kôrʹdə·roi, kôrʹdə·roiʹ) *n.* 1 A durable usu. cotton fabric with ribs and wales of cut pile. 2 *pl.* Trousers made of corduroy. —*adj.* 1 Made of corduroy. 2 Formed from logs laid transversely; a *corduroy* road. [?]

**core** (kôr, kōr) *n.* 1 The hard or fibrous central part of certain fruits, usu. containing the seeds. 2 The innermost or most important part of something. 3 a The insulated conducting wires of an electric cable. b A ferromagnetic mass used to intensify or hold the magnetic field of a wire. —*v.t.* **cored, cor·ing** To remove the core of. [?]

**co·ri·an·der** (kôrʹē·anʹdər, kōʹrē-) *n.* 1 A plant

related to parsley, having aromatic seeds used for seasoning. 2 The seeds of this plant. [< Gk. *koriannon*]

**cork** (kôrk) *n.* 1 The light, porous, elastic outer bark of a tree, the **cork oak**, of the Mediterranean region. 2 Something, esp. a bottle stopper, made from this bark. 3 A similar stopper, as of rubber. 4 *Bot.* The outer protective layer of the stems of woody plants. —*v.t.* 1 To stop with a cork. 2 To restrain; check. 3 To blacken with burnt cork. [< OSp. *alcorque* a cork slipper] — **cork'y** *adj.* (·**i·er**, ·**i·est**)

**cor·mo·rant** (kôr'mər·ənt) *n.* 1 A web-footed diving bird with dark plumage and a hooked bill. 2 A greedy or rapacious person. [< L *corvus marinus* sea crow]

**cor·net** (kôr·net') *n.* 1 A wind instrument like the trumpet but having a more flaring tube. 2 A cone-shaped paper wrapper, pastry shell, etc. [< L *cornu* a horn] —**cor·net'tist** or **cor·net'ist** *n.*

**cor·nice** (kôr'nis) *n.* 1 A horizontal projecting molding at the top of a wall, column, etc. 2 A framework or molding to conceal curtain rods, etc. —*v.t.* ·**niced**, ·**nic·ing** To provide with a cornice. [< Gk. *korōnis* wreath, garland]

**cor·nu·co·pi·a** (kôr'nə·kō'pē·ə) *n.* 1 A stylized representation of a goat's horn filled with fruit, grain, etc., symbolizing plenty or prosperity. 2 A cone-shaped container. [< L *cornu copiae* horn of plenty] — **cor'nu·co'pi·an** *adj.*

**cor·o·ner** (kôr'ə·nər, kor'-) *n.* A public officer who seeks to determine the cause of deaths not clearly due to natural causes. [< AF *coruner* officer of the crown]

**cor·o·net** (kôr'ə·net, -nit, kor'-) *n.* 1 A small crown, denoting noble rank below that of sovereign. 2 An ornamental band, wreath, etc., worn on the head. [< L *corona* crown]

**cor·po·ral** (kôr'pər·əl) *adj.* Of or relating to the body: *corporal* punishment. [< L *corpus* body] —**cor·po·ral·i·ty** (kôr'pə·ral'ə·tē) *n.* — **cor'po·ral·ly** *adv.* —Syn. physical, bodily.

**cor·po·rate** (kôr'pər·it) *adj.* 1 Constituting a corporation; incorporated. 2 Of or belonging to a corporation. 3 Combined; collective. [< L *corporare* make into a body < *corpus* body] —**cor'po·rate·ly** *adv.*

**cor·po·ra·tion** (kôr'pə·rā'shən) *n.* 1 A group of people having a legal charter that empowers them to transact business as a single body. 2 *Informal* A protuberant abdomen. —**cor·po·ra·tive** (kôr'pə·rā'tiv,

-pər·ə·tiv') *adj.* —**cor·po·ra·tor** (kôr'pə·rā'tər) *n.*

**corps** (kôr, kōr) *n. pl.* **corps** (kôrz, kōrz) 1 *Mil.* a A special department or subdivision: the Quartermaster *Corps.* b A tactical unit consisting of two or more divisions. 2 An organized group of persons acting together. [< L *corpus* body]

**corpse** (kôrps) *n.* A dead body, esp. of a human being. [< L *corpus* body]

**cor·pu·lent** (kôr'pyə·lənt) *adj.* Having a fat body. [< L *corpulentus* < *corpus* body] — **cor'pu·lence, cor'pu·len·cy,** *n.* —**cor'pu ·lent·ly** *adv.* —Syn. fat, obese, fleshy, stout.

**cor·ral** (kə·ral') *n.* 1 An enclosed space or pen for livestock. 2 A space enclosed by wagons for protection against attack. —*v.t.* ·**ralled**, ·**ral·ling** 1 To drive into and enclose in a corral. 2 *Informal* To seize or capture; secure. [Sp.]

**cor·rect** (kə·rekt') *v.t.* 1 To remove errors from; make right. 2 To mark or indicate the errors of. 3 To rebuke or chastise. 4 To remedy or counteract, as a malfunction. 5 To make conformable to a standard: to *correct* a lens. —*adj.* 1 Free from fault or mistake. 2 True; right; accurate. 3 Proper; acceptable. [< L *com-* together + *regere* make straight] —**cor·rect'a·ble** or ·**i·ble** *adj.* — **cor·rect'ly** *adv.* —**cor·rect'ness, cor·rec' tor** *n.* —Syn. *v.* 1 rectify, right, redress. 5 adjust, regulate.

**cor·re·late** (kôr'ə·lāt, kor'-) *v.* ·**lat·ed**, ·**lat·ing** *v.t.* 1 To place or put in reciprocal relation. —*v.i.* 2 To be mutually or reciprocally related. —*adj.* Having mutual or reciprocal relations. —*n.* **CORRELATIVE** (def. 1). [< COM- + RELATE]

**cor·re·la·tion** (kôr'ə·lā'shən, kor'-) *n.* 1 Mutual or reciprocal relation. 2 The act or process of correlating. —**cor're·la'tion·al** *adj.*

**cor·rel·a·tive** (kə·rel'ə·tiv) *adj.* 1 Having a corresponding or reciprocal relationship. 2 Used together and indicating a grammatical or logical relationship, as the conjunctions *either* and *or.* —*n.* 1 Either of two things in correlation. 2 A correlative term, as in grammar. —**cor·rel'a·tive·ly** *adv.* — **cor·rel'a·tive·ness, cor·rel'a·tiv'i·ty** *n.*

**cor·re·spond** (kôr'ə·spond', kor'-) *v.i.* 1 To be in agreement, or conformity. 2 To be similar, equivalent, or analogous. 3 To communicate by letters. [< Med. L *com-* together + *respondere* to answer]

**cor·ri·dor** (kôr'ə·dər, -dôr, kor'-) *n.* 1 A hallway or passageway usu. having rooms opening on it. 2 A strip of land belonging to one country crossing the territory of another. 3 A densely populated strip of territory including major cities. [< Ital. *corridore* < *correre* to run]

cor·rob·o·rate (kə·rob′ə·rāt) *v.t.* ·rat·ed, ·rat·ing To confirm or support (evidence, a statement, etc.) [< L *com-* together + *robur* strength] —cor·rob′o·ra′tor, cor·rob′o·ra′tion *n.* —cor·rob′o·ra·tive (kə·rob′ə·rā·tiv, -rob′ər·ə·tiv), cor·rob·o·ra·to·ry (kə·rob′ər·ə·tôr′ē, -tō′rē) *adj.* —cor·rob′o·ra′tive·ly *adv.*

cor·rode (kə·rōd′) *v.t. & v.i.* ·rod·ed, ·rod·ing To wear away gradually, esp. by chemical action such as rusting. [< L *com-* thoroughly + *rodere* gnaw] —cor·rod′i·ble, cor·ro·si·ble (kə·rō′sə·bəl) *adj.*

cor·ru·gate (kôr′ə·gāt, kor′-) *v.t. & v.i.* ·gat·ed, ·gat·ing To form into alternating ridges and furrows. [< L *com-* together + *ruga* a wrinkle] —cor′ru·ga′tion *n.*

cor·rupt (kə·rupt′) *adj.* 1 Viciously immoral; depraved. 2 Capable of being bribed, improperly influenced, etc.; dishonest. 3 Altered or debased by errors, changes, etc., as a text. 4 Rotten; putrid. —*v.t. & v.i.* To make or become corrupt. [< L *com-* thoroughly + *rumpere* to break] —cor·rupt′er, cor·rup′tor, cor·rupt′ness *n.* —cor·rupt′ly *adv.* —cor·rup′tive *adj.*

cor·tege (kôr·tezh′, -tāzh′) *n.* 1 A train of attendants. 2 A ceremonial procession. **Also** cor·tège′. [< Ital. *corte* court]

cor·ti·sone (kôr′tə·sōn, -zōn) *n.* A hormone secreted by the cortex of the adrenal gland and also made synthetically. [Short for *corticosterone* < L *cortex, -icis* cortex + STER(OID) + (HORM)ONE]

cor·us·cate (kôr′ə·skāt, kor′-) *v.i.* ·cat·ed, ·cat·ing To sparkle; glitter; flash. [< L *coruscare* to glitter] —cor′us·ca′tion *n.*

cosmic rays High-energy radiation that reaches the earth from space.

cos·mol·o·gy (koz·mol′ə·jē) *n. pl.* ·gies The general science or philosophy of the universe. —cos·mo·log·ic (koz′mə·loj′ik) or ·i·cal *adj.* —cos·mol′o·gist *n.*

cos·mo·pol·i·tan (koz′mə·pol′ə·tən) *adj.* 1 Common to all the world; not local or limited. 2 At home in all parts of the world. 3 *Biol.* Widely distributed, as a plant or animal. —*n.* A cosmopolitan person. —cos·′mo·pol′i·tan·ism *n.*

cos·tume (kos·t′ōōm) *n.* 1 Clothing or style of

dress characteristic of a particular country, period, etc. 2 Such clothing, or other distinctive dress, worn by a theatrical performer, to a masquerade, etc. 3 A set of clothing; ensemble; outfit. —*v.t.* (kos·t′ōōm′) ·tumed, ·tum·ing To furnish with costumes. [< Ital. *costuma* fashion, guise < L *consuetudo* custom]

co·te·rie (kō′tə·rē) *n.* A closely knit group of persons with shared interests. [< OF, group of landholding peasants < *cote* hut]

co·til·lion (kō·til′yən, kə-) *n.* 1 A ballroom dance with many different figures. 2 A formal ball, esp. for debutantes. **Also** co·til·lon (kō·til′yən, kə-; *Fr.* kô·tē·yôn′). [< OF *cotillon* petticoat.]

couch (kouch) *n.* 1 A long, usu. upholstered piece of furniture on which one may sit or lie. 2 Any place for repose. —*v.t.* 1 To cause to recline. 2 To put into words; phrase. 3 To hold in readiness for use, as a spear. —*v.i.* 4 To lie down; recline. [< F *coucher* put to bed < L *collocare* to set, place] —couch′er *n.*

cou·gar (kōō′gər) *n.* MOUNTAIN LION. [< Tupian]

cough (kôf, kof) *v.i.* 1 To expel air from the lungs in a noisy or spasmodic manner. —*v.t.* 2 To expel by coughing. —cough up 1 To expel (phlegm, etc.) by coughing. 2 *Slang* To hand over, as money. —*n.* 1 A sudden, harsh expulsion of breath. 2 An illness characterized by much coughing. [ME *coughen*] —cough′er *n.*

coun·cil (koun′səl) *n.* 1 An assembly of persons convened for consultation or deliberation. 2 A body of persons elected or appointed to assist in the administration of government. 3 Deliberation or consultation among the members of a council. [< L *concilium*] • See COUNSEL.

coun·sel (koun′səl) *n.* 1 Consultation for exchange of advice, opinions, etc. 2 Advice; opinion. 3 A lawyer or lawyers engaged for legal advice. —keep one's (own) counsel To keep one's ideas, plans, etc., to oneself. —*v.* ·seled or ·selled, ·sel·ing or ·sel·ling *v.t.* 1 To advise; give advice to. 2 To advise in favor of; recommend. —*v.i.* 3 To confer; deliberate. [< L *consilium*] • The nouns *counsel* (def. 2) and *council* (def. 1) have related meanings, but are not interchangeable. *Council* in this sense is used chiefly in the phrase *in council*, while *counsel* is used in such expressions as *take counsel, heed someone's counsel*, etc.

count·down (kount′doun′) *n.* A specified interval of time before an intended action, measured in descending units to zero.

**coun·te·nance** (koun'tə-nəns) *n.* 1 The face or features. 2 Expression; appearance. 3 Approval; support. 4 Composure; aplomb — **out of countenance** Disconcerted; abashed. —*v.t.* ·nanced, ·nanc·ing To approve; give sanction to. [< L *continentia* behavior < *continere* to contain] —**coun'te·nanc·er** *n.* —Syn. *v.* condone, sanction, favor, abet.

**coun·ter** (koun'tər) *adv.* In a contrary manner or direction. —*adj.* Opposing; opposite; contrary. —*v.t.* 1 To act so as to oppose or offset. 2 To return or parry, as a blow. —*v.i.* 3 To make an opposing or offsetting move or action. —*n.* 1 That which counters or opposes. 2 A parrying blow. 3 An outer piece of shoe leather that stiffens the heel. [< L *contra* against]

**coun·ter·act** (koun'tər·akt') *v.t.* To act in opposition to; have an offsetting effect on. —**coun'ter·ac'tion** *n.* —**coun'ter·ac'tive** *adj.* —**coun'ter·ac'tive·ly** *adv.*

**coun·ter·feit** (koun'tər·fit) *v.t.* 1 To make a copy or imitation of (money, etc.) with intent to defraud. 2 To pretend; feign. 3 To imitate; resemble closely. —*v.i.* 4 To practice deception; dissemble. 5 To make counterfeits. —*n.* 1 A copy or imitation fraudulently intended to pass as genuine. 2 An imitation or close resemblance. —*adj.* 1 Fraudulently made to resemble something genuine. 2 Pretended; feigned. [< L *contra-* against + *facere* make] —**coun'ter·feit'er** *n.* —Syn. *adj.* false, spurious, fake, bogus.

**coun·ter·mand** (koun'tər·mand', ·mänd', koun'tər·mand, ·mänd) *v.t.* 1 To cancel or revoke (an order, command, etc.). 2 To recall by a contradictory order. —*n.* (koun'tər·mand, ·mänd) An order contrary to or revoking a previous one. [< L *contra-* against + *mandare* to order]

**coun·ter·part** (koun'tər·pärt') *n.* One having a close resemblance or corresponding relationship to another.

**coun·ter·poise** (koun'tər·poiz') *v.t.* ·poised, ·pois·ing To balance by opposing with an equal weight or force; counterbalance. —*n.* (koun'tər·poiz) 1 A counterbalancing weight. 2 A force, influence, etc., that offsets another. 3 A state of equilibrium. [< L *contra-* against + *pensare* weight]

**coun·ter·sign** (koun'tər·sīn') *v.t.* To add one's signature to (a signed document) as authentication. —*n.* A password or secret signal to be given, as to a sentry. —**coun·ter·sig·na·ture** (koun'tər·sig'nə·chər) *n.*

**coun·ty** (koun'tē) *n. pl.* ·ties 1 A civil division of a nation or territory. 2 In most of the U.S., an administrative division of a state. 3 The inhabitants of a county. [< L *comes* count, companion]

**cou·pé** (kōō·pā') *n.* 1 A small, closed, two-door automobile: also **coupe** (kōōp) 2 A closed carriage with two passenger seats and an outside seat. [< F *couper* to cut]

**cou·ple** (kup'əl) *n.* 1 Two of a kind; a pair. 2 Two persons of opposite sex, married or otherwise paired. 3 *Informal* A few. —*v.* **coup'led, coup·ling** *v.t.* 1 To join, as one thing to another; link. 2 *Electr.* **a** To connect (two circuits). **b** To transfer (electricity), as by such connection. —*v.i.* 3 To copulate. 4 To form a pair or pairs. [< L *copula* a band, a bond]

**cou·pon** (k'yōō'pon) *n.* 1 One of a number of dated certificates attached to a bond, representing interest payable at stated periods. 2 A certificate, detachable form, etc., entitling one to something in exchange. [< F *couper* to cut]

**cour·age** (kûr'ij) *n.* The capacity to meet danger or difficulty with firmness; bravery. [< L *cor* heart]

**cou·ra·geous** (kə·rā'jəs) *adj.* Possessing or characterized by courage. —**cou·ra'geous·ly** *adv.* —**cou·ra'geous·ness** *n.* —Syn. brave, fearless, intrepid, valorous, valiant.

**cou·ri·er** (kōōr'ē·ər, kûr'-) *n.* 1 A messenger, esp. one of official business. 2 An attendant who makes arrangements for travelers. [<Ital. *corriere* < *corre* to run]

**cour·te·ous** (kûr'tē·əs) *adj.* Showing courtesy; polite. —**cour'te·ous·ly** *adv.* —**cour'te·ous·ness** *n.*

**cour·te·sy** (kûr'tə·sē) *n. pl.* ·sies 1 Gracious or considerate behavior; habitual politeness. 2 A courteous act. 3 Custom or indulgence rather than strict usage: He was called "Colonel" by *courtesy*. [<OF *corteisie*]

**court·ly** (kôrt'lē, kört'-) *adj.* ·li·er, ·li·est 1 Of or befitting a royal court. 2 Ceremonious and polite. —*adv.* In a courtly manner. —**court'li·ness** *n.*

**court-mar·tial** (kôrt'mär'shəl, kört'-) *n. pl.* **courts-mar·tial** 1 A military court convened to try persons subject to military law. 2 A trial by such a court. —*v.t.* ·mar·tialed or

·tialled. —mar·tial·ing or ·tial·ling To try by court-martial.

**cove**[1] (kōv) n. 1 A small, sheltered bay or inlet. 2 A recess or sheltered place. [OE *cofa* chamber, cave]

**cove**[2] (kōv) n. *Brit. Slang* A man; fellow. [<Romany *covo* that man]

**cov·e·nant** (kuv′ə·nənt) n. 1 A formal and binding agreement entered into by two or more persons or parties; a compact. 2 God's promises to mankind as set forth in the Bible. —*v.t. & v.i.* To promise by or in a covenant. [<L *convenire* meet together, agree] —**cov′e·nant·er** n.

**cov·ert** (kuv′ərt, kō′vərt) adj. 1 Concealed; secret. 2 Sheltered. —n. 1 A place of shelter or concealment, as for hunters or game. 2 Any of the feathers overlying the bases of the quills of a bird's wings and tail. 3 A closely woven twilled cloth used for suits, coats, etc: also **covert cloth.** [<OF *couvrir* to cover] —**cov′ert·ly** adv. —**cov′ert·ness** n.

**cov·et** (kuv′it) *v.t. & v.i.* To have an inordinate desire for (esp. something belonging to another). [<: *cupere* to desire] —**cov′et·a·ble** adj. —**cov′et·er** n.

**cow·ard** (kou′ərd) n. One lacking in courage; esp., one who gives in ignobly to fear. —adj. Cowardly. [< L *cauda* tail; with ref. to a dog with its tail between its legs]

**cow·er** (kou′ər) *v.i.* To crouch or draw back tremblingly as in fear. [(Prob. < Scand.] —**Syn.** cringe, quail, shrink, grovel.

**cow·hide** (kou′hīd′) n. 1 The hide of a cow. 2 Leather made from this. 3 A heavy, flexible leather whip. —*v.t.* ·hid·ed, ·hid·ing To whip with or as with a cowhide.

**cowl** (koul) n. 1 A monk's hood or similar hooded garment. 2 A hood-shaped top for a chimney. 3 *Aeron.* COWLING. 4 The part of an automobile body to which the windshield, dash board, and the rear of the hood are attached. —*v.t.* To cover with or as with a cowl. [<L *cucullus* hood]

**cox·comb** (koks′kōm′) n. 1 A vain, pretentious fellow; fop. 2 COCKSCOMB. [Var. of *cockscomb*] —**cox·comb·i·cal** (koks·kom′i·kəl, -kō′mi-) adj.

**coy** (koi) adj. 1 Shy; diffident. 2 Pretending shyness or reluctance. [<L *quietus* quiet] —**coy′ly** adv. —**coy′ness** n.

**coy·o·te** (kī·ō′tē, kī′ōt) n. A wolflike North American animal common in the w U.S. [<Nah.]

**coz·en** (kuz′ən) *v.t. & v.i.* To cheat in a petty way. [F *cousiner* deceive by claiming kinship < *cousin* cousin] —**coz·en·age** (kuz′ən·ij), coz′en·er n.

**crab·bed** (krab′id) adj. 1 Sour-tempered; cross; peevish. 2 Hard to understand; abstruse. 3 Irregular in form; cramped. [<CRAB[1], n. (def. 1)] —**crab′bed·ly** adv. —**crab′bed·ness** n.

**crack** (krak) *v.t.* 1 To cause to break open partially or completely. 2 To cáuse to give forth a short, sharp sound: to *crack* a whip. 3 *Slang* To open in order to drink, read, etc.: to *crack* a bottle or book. 4 *Informal* To break into, as a safe or building, in order to rob. 5 To solve, as a puzzle, crime, or code. 6 *Slang* To tell (a joke). 7 To destroy or crush: to *crack* one's spirit. 8 To cause (the voice) to break or change register. 9 *Informal* To strike sharply or with a sharp sound: He *cracked* him on the jaw. —*v.i.* 10 To split or break, esp. with suddenness. 11 To make a sharp snapping sound, as a whip or pistol. 12 To have a break in tone or to change register suddenly: said of the voice. 13 To become impaired or broken, as the spirit or will. —**crack down** To introduce severe disciplinary or corrective action. —**crack up** 1 To crash, as an airplane. 2 *Informal* To have a breakdown, nervous or physical. 3 *Informal* To break or cause to break into laughter. —n. 1 An incomplete separation into two or more parts; a fissure. 2 A narrow space, as between two boards. 3 A sudden sharp or loud sound. 4 *Informal* A blow that resounds. 5 A mental or physical defect or flaw. 6 A break in tone or change of register in the voice. 7 *Informal* An attempt. 8 An exact instant: the *crack* of dawn. 9 *Informal* A witty or sarcastic remark. —adj. *Informal* Of superior excellence; first-class. [<OE *cracian*]

**crack·le** (krak′əl) *v.* ·led, ·ling *v.i.* 1 To crack or snap repeatedly with light, sharp noises. —*v.t.* 2 To crush with such sounds. 3 To cover, as china, with a delicate network of cracks. —n. 1 A succession of light, cracking sounds. 2 The appearance produced in china, porcelain, etc., by the cracking of the glaze in all directions. 3 Such ware: also **crack′le·ware′.** [Freq. of CRACK] —**crack′ly** adj.

**cra·dle** (krād′l) n. 1 A rocking or swinging bed for an infant. 2 A place of birth or origin. 3 A scythe with fingers that catch the grain when cut. 4 A frame or device for supporting an object or structure. 5 A support or holder for a handset telephone. —*v.* ·dled,

·dling *v.t.* 1 To rock in or as in a cradle; soothe. 2 To cut or reap, as grain, with a cradle. 3 To place or support in or as in a cradle. —*v.i.* 4 To cut or reap with a cradle. [<OE *cradol*]

-craft *combining form* Skill; trade; art of: *woodcraft.*

crag (krag) *n.* A rough, steep, or broken rock rising or jutting out prominently. [ME *cragg* < Celtic]

cramp[1] (kramp) *n.* 1 A metal bar with both ends bent into right angles, for holding together two stones, pieces of timber, etc.: also cramp iron. 2 An adjustable clamp. 3 Something that restrains or confines. —*v.t.* 1 To restrain or confine the action of; hinder. 2 To make fast; hold tightly, as with a cramp. 3 To turn (the wheels of an automobile, etc.) sharply to one side. [<MDu. *krampe* hook]

cramp[2] (kramp) *n.* 1 An involuntary, sudden, painful muscular contraction. 2 *pl.* Acute abdominal pains. —*v.t.* To affect with cramps. [<OF *crampe*]

crane (krān) *n.* 1 One of a family of large, long-necked, long-legged, heronlike birds allied to the rails. 2 Any of various similar birds, as a heron, stork, etc. 3 A hoisting machine having a movable arm for lifting, lowering, or shifting heavy weights. 4 An iron arm, swinging horizontally, attached to a fireplace, used for suspending pots or kettles. —*v.t.* & *v.i.* craned, cran·ing 1 To stretch out; elongate or be elongated. 2 To elevate or lift by or as if by a crane. [<OE *cran*]

cra·ni·um (krā′nē·əm) *n. pl.* ·ni·ums or ·ni·a (-nē·ə) The skull, esp. the part that encloses the brain. [<Gk. *kranion* skull] —cra′ni·al *adj.*

crank (krangk) *n.* 1 A device, as a handle attached at right angles to a shaft, for transmitting motion or for converting reciprocating motion into rotary motion, or vice versa. 2 *Informal* a A person given to odd notions or actions; an eccentric. b A grouchy, ill-tempered person. —*v.t.* 1 To bend into the shape of a crank. 2 To operate or start by a crank. —*v.i.* 3 To turn a crank. [<OE *cranc,* as in *crancstǽf* a weaving comb]

cran·ny (kran′ē) *n. pl.* ·nies A narrow opening, fissure. [<OF *cran, cren* notch] —cran′nied *adj.*

crash (krash) *v.t.* 1 To break in pieces noisily and with violence. 2 To proceed noisily and

with violence: He *crashed* his way through the jungle. 3 *Informal* To enter uninvited or without paying admission: to *crash* a dance. 4 To cause, as an airplane, truck, or train, to fall to the earth or strike an obstacle with force. —*v.i.* 5 To break or fall in pieces with a violent sound. 6 To make a noise of clashing or breaking. 7 To move with such a noise. 8 To fall to the earth or violently strike an obstacle, as an airplane or automobile. 9 To fail or collapse; come to ruin. —*n.* A loud noise, as of something falling and breaking. 2 A breaking, colliding, or crashing. 3 A failure or collapse; ruin. [Imit.]

crate (krāt) *n.* 1 a A large hamper or packing box for shipping or storing. b Its contents. 2 *Slang* An old or decrepit vehicle or airplane. —*v.t.* crat·ed, crat·ing To pack, store, or send in a crate. [<L *cratis* wickerwork]

cra·ter (krā′tər) *n.* 1 The bowl-shaped depression forming the outlet of a volcano or of a hot spring. 2 A pit made by an explosion or impact. 3 Any large bowl or cavity. [<Gk. *kratēr* bowl]

cra·vat (krə·vat′) *n.* 1 A neckcloth or scarf. 2 A necktie. [<F *Cravate* a Croatian, with ref. to the neckcloths worn by Croatian soldiers]

crave (krāv) *v.* craved, crav·ing *v.t.* 1 To beg for humbly and earnestly. 2 To long for; desire greatly. 3 To be in need of; require. —*v.i.* 4 To desire or long: with *for* or *after.* [< OE *crafian*] —crav′er *n.* —Syn. 1 ask, solicit, seek, request, beseech, petition. 2 yearn for, wish, wish for, want.

cra·ven (krā′vən) *adj.* Lacking in courage; cowardly. —*n.* A base coward. [<L *crepare* to break] —cra′ven·ly *adv.*

craw (krô) *n.* 1 The crop of a bird. 2 The stomach of any animal. [ME *crawe*]

craw·fish (krô′fish′) *n. pl.* ·fish or ·fish·es CRAYFISH. [Var. of CRAYFISH]

crawl (krôl) *v.i.* 1 To move by dragging the body along a surface; creep. 2 To move slowly, feebly, or cautiously. 3 To have a sensation as of crawling things upon the body. 4 To have crawling things in or on the body, as a dead body. 5 To act with servility. —*n.* 1 The act of crawling. 2 An overarm swimming stroke. [< ON *krafla*] —crawl′er *n.* —crawl′ing·ly *adv.*

cray·on (krā′ən, -on) *n.* 1 A small cylinder of colored wax, chalk, etc., used for coloring or drawing. 2 A drawing made with crayons. —*v.t.* To sketch or draw with a crayon or crayons. [<L *creta* chalk] —**cray′on·ist** *n.*

**cra·zy** (krā′zē) *adj.* **cra·zi·er, cra·zi·est** 1 Insane; mentally unbalanced. 2 Excessively emotional or disturbed as with rage. 3 *Informal* Impractical, illogical, etc.: a *crazy* plan. 4 *Informal* Inordinately eager or enthusiastic: *crazy* about jazz. —**cra′zi·ly** *adv.* —**cra′zi·ness.** *n.*

**creak** (krēk) *n.* A sharp, squeaking sound, as from friction. —*v.t.* & *v.i.* To make, or cause to make, a creak. [imit.] —**creak′i·ly** *adv.* —**creak′i·ness** *n.* —**creak′y** *adj.* (·i·er, ·i·est)

**crease** (krēs) *n.* 1 The mark of a wrinkle, fold, or the like. 2 In cricket, any of the lines limiting the position of the bowler or batsman. —*v.* **creased, creas·ing** *v.t.* 1 To make a crease or fold in; wrinkle. 2 To wound by a shot that grazes the flesh. —*v.i.* 3 To become wrinkled. [Var. of ME *creste* a crest, ridge] —**creas′er** *n.* —**creas′y** *adj.*

**cre·ate** (krē·āt′) *v.* **·at·ed, ·at·ing** *v.t.* 1 To cause to come into existence; originate. 2 To be the cause of; bring about: *create* interest. 3 To invest with a new rank, office, etc. 4 To be the first to portray, as a character in a play. [<L *creare*] —**Syn.** 1 fashion, make, form, produce, conceive, invent, build.

**cre·a·tion** (krē·ā′shən) *n.* 1 The act of creating or the fact of being created. 2 That which is created. 3 The universe or all things in it. —**the Creation** The act of God in creating the world. —**cre·a′tion·al** *adj.*

**cre·a·tor** (krē·ā′tər) *n.* One who or that which creates. —**the Creator** God.

**crea·ture** (krē′chər) *n.* 1 Anything created. 2 Something living, esp. an animal. 3 A human being. 4 An imaginary being.

**cre·dence** (krēd′ns) *n.* Confidence based upon external evidence; belief. [<L *credere* believe]

**cre·den·tial** (kri·den′shəl) *n.* 1 That which certifies one's authority, credit, or claim to confidence. 2 *pl.* Testimonials certifying a person's authority or claim to confidence or consideration.

**cred·i·ble** (kred′ə·bəl) *adj.* Capable of being believed; reliable. [<L *credibilis* < *credere* believe] —**cred′i·ble·ness** *n.* —**cred′i·bly** *adv.*

**cred·it** (kred′it) *n.* 1 Belief; trust; confidence. 2 Reputation for trustworthiness; character; repute. 3 Influence derived from trust-worthiness, good opinion of others, etc. 4 Approval; praise: Give him *credit* for telling the truth. 5 One who or that which adds honor or reputation: a *credit* to his class. 6 *Usu. pl.* Acknowledgment of work done, as in the making of a motion picture. 7 In an account, the balance in one's favor. 8 An amount made available by a bank, against which a person or business may draw. 9 In bookkeeping: **a** The entry of any amount paid by a debtor. **b** The amount so entered. **c** The righthand side of an account where such amounts are recorded. 10 Confidence in a firm's or person's solvency or ability to meet payments. 11 The time allowed for payment of a debt. 12 The amount to which a person or business may be financially trusted. 13 In education, official certification that a course of study has been finished; also, a recognized unit of school or college work. —**on credit** With a promise to pay later. —*v.t.* 1 To give credit for; accept as true. 2 To ascribe, as intelligence or honor, to: with *with.* 3 In bookkeeping, to give credit for or enter as credit to. 4 In education, to give educational credits to (a student). [<L *credere* believe, trust] —**cred′it·a·bil′i·ty, cred′it·a·ble·ness** *n.* —**cred′it·a·ble** *adj.* —**cred′it·a·bly** *adv.*

**credit card** A card issued by a business, bank, etc., giving the owner the privilege to charge bills at certain stores, restaurants, etc.

**cre·du·li·ty** (krə·dʸ̅o̅o̅′lə·tē) *n.* A disposition to believe on slight evidence. [<L *credulus* credulous]

**cred·u·lous** (krej′o̅o̅·ləs) *adj.* 1 Apt or disposed to believe on slight evidence. 2 Arising from credulity. [<L *credere* believe] —**cred′u·lous·ly** *adv.* —**cred′u·lous·ness** *n.*

**creed** (krēd) *n.* 1 A formal summary of religious belief. 2 Any statement of things believed, principles held, etc. [< L *credo* I believe]

**creep** (krēp) *v.i.* **crept, creep·ing** 1 To move with the body close to a surface; crawl. 2 To move or change imperceptibly, slowly, secretly, or stealthily. 3 To exhibit servility; cringe. 4 To feel as if covered with creeping things. 5 To grow along a surface or support: *creeping* plants. 6 To slip out of place. —*n.* 1 The act of creeping. 2 *pl.* A sensation of uneasy apprehensiveness. 3 *Slang* A distasteful or obnoxious person. [<OE *crēopan*]

**cre·mate** (krē′māt, kri·māt′) *v.t.* **·mat·ed,**

·mat·ing To burn (a dead body) to ashes. [<L *cremare* burn to ashes] —cre·ma'tion, cre'ma·tor *n.*

cres·cent (kres'ənt) *n.* 1 The visible part of the moon in its first quarter, having one concave edge and one convex edge. 2 Something crescent-shaped. —*adj.* 1 Increasing: said of the moon in its first quarter. 2 Shaped like the moon in its first quarter. [< L *crescere* to increase] • See MOON.

crest (krest) *n.* 1 A comb or tuft on the head of an animal or bird. 2 The decoration on the top of a helmet; a plume; tuft. 3 The ridge of a wave or a mountain. 4 The highest point or maximum degree of anything. 5 A heraldic device placed above the shield in a coat of arms and also used on stationery, silverware, etc. —*v.t.* 1 To serve as a crest for; cap. 2 To furnish with or as with a crest. 3 To reach the crest of. 4 To adorn with a crest. —*v.i.* 5 To come to a crest, as a wave prior to breaking. [< L *crista* tuft] —crest'ed *adj.*

cre·vasse (krə·vas') *n.* 1 A deep fissure, as in a glacier. 2 A break in a levee. —*v.t.* ·vassed, ·vass·ing To split with crevasses. [<OF *crevace* crevice] —cre·vassed' *adj.*

crev·ice (krev'is) *n.* A small fissure or crack. [<L *crepare* to crack, creak] —crev'iced *adj.*

crew (krōō) *n.* 1 All of the seamen manning a specific ship, usu. excluding officers. 2 All those manning an aircraft. 3 Any group of people organized for a particular work project. 4 A company of people in general; crowd. 5 The oarsmen and coxswain of a racing shell. [<OF *creue* an increase]

crib (krib) *n.* 1 A manger for fodder. 2 A stall for cattle. 3 A child's bed, with side railings. 4 A box, bin, or small building for grain. 5 A frame of wood or metal, used to support or retain earth, etc., as in a mine. 6 *Informal* PLAGIARISM. 7 A translation or other unauthorized aid in study. —*v.* cribbed, crib·bing *v.t.* 1 To enclose in or as in a crib; confine closely. 2 *Informal* To take and pass off as one's own, as an answer; plagiarize. 3 *Informal* To steal. 4 *Informal* To translate with a crib. —*v.i.* 5 *Informal* To use a crib in translating. [<OE *cribb*] —crib'ber *n.*

crick·et (krik'it) *n.* A leaping insect related to the grasshopper but having long antennae, the male of which makes a chirping sound by friction of the forewings. [<OF *criquet*]

crime (krīm) *n.* 1 *Law* An act that subjects the doer to legal punishment. 2 Any grave offense against morality or social order. 3 *In-*formal* Any unjust or shameful action. [<L *crimen* accusation, charge]

crim·son (krim'zən) *n.* A deep red color. —*adj.* 1 Of a deep red color. 2 Bloody. —*v.t.* & *v.i.* To make or become crimson. [<Ar. *qirmiz* kermes (insect used in making a red dye)]

cringe (krinj) *v.i.* cringed, cring·ing 1 To crouch, wince, draw back, etc., as in fear. 2 To seek favor in a servile or flattering manner. —*n.* The act of cringing. [ME *cringen, crengen*] —cring'er *n.*

crin·kle (kring'kəl) *v.t.* & *v.i.* ·kled, ·kling 1 To be or cause to be full of wrinkles or twists. 2 To make a crackling sound. —*n.* A wrinkle; ripple. [ME < *crenklen*] —crin'kly *adj.* (·kli·er, ·kli·est)

crip·ple (krip'əl) *n.* A lame person or animal or one lacking the natural use of a limb or the body. —*v.t.* ·pled, ·pling 1 To lame. 2 To impair or disable in some way. [<OE *crypel*] —crip'pler *n.*

cri·sis (krī'sis) *n. pl.* cri·ses (-sēz) 1 A decisive or crucial turning point in the progress of a series of events. 2 A dangerous or critical moment or development. 3 *Pathol.* A decisive change, favorable or unfavorable, in the course of a disease. [<Gk. *krisis* < *krinein* decide]

crisp (krisp) *adj.* 1 Firm and fresh. 2 Brittle or crumbling readily, as pastry. 3 Clean and neat. 4 Terse or pithy: a *crisp* reply. 5 Fresh and bracing. 6 Tightly curled or waved. —*v.t.* & *v.i.* To make or become crisp. [<L *crispus* curled] —crisp'er, crisp'ness *n.* —crisp'ly *adv.* —crisp'y *adj.*

cri·te·ri·on (krī·tir'ē·ən) *n. pl.* ·te·ri·a (-tir'ē·ə) or ·te·ri·ons A standard, rule, or test by which a correct judgment can be made. [<Gk. *kritēs* a judge]

crit·ic (krit'ik) *n.* 1 One who judges anything by some standard or criterion. 2 One whose profession is to judge or evaluate literary, theatrical, musical, or other artistic productions. 3 A faultfinder. —*adj.* Pertaining to criticism; critical. [<Gk. *kritēs* a judge]

crit·i·cize (krit'ə·sīz) *v.t.* & *v.i.* ·cized, ·ciz·ing 1 To examine and judge as a critic. 2 To judge severely; censure. *Brit. sp.* crit'i·cise. —crit'i·ciz'a·ble *adj.* —crit'i·ciz'er *n.*

croak (krōk) *v.i.* 1 To utter a hoarse, low-pitched cry, as a frog or raven. 2 To speak in a low, hoarse voice. 3 To forbode evil; grumble. 4 *Slang* To die. —*v.t.* 5 To utter with a croak. 6 *Slang* To kill. —*n.* A hoarse vocal sound. [Imit.] —croak'y *adj.*

**cro·chet** (krō·shā´) *v.t. & v.i.* **·cheted** (-shād´), **·chet·ing** (-shā´ing) To form or ornament (a fabric) by interlacing thread with a hooked needle. —*n.* A kind of fancywork produced by crocheting. [<F *croche* a hook]

**croc·o·dile** (krok´ə·dil) *n.* A large, lizardlike, aquatic reptile of tropical regions, having the head longer and narrower than that of an alligator. [< Gk. *krokodilos* lizard, crocodile.] —**croc·o·dil·i·an** (krok´ə·dil´ē·ən), **croc′o·dil′e·an** *adj., n.*

**cro·cus** (krō´kəs) *n. pl.* **cro·cus·es** or **cro·ci** (krō´si) 1 Any of a genus of plants related to the iris with long grasslike leaves and large flowers. 2 The flower of this plant. 3 An orange-yellow or saffron color. [<Gk. *krokos* saffron]

**cro·ny** (krō´nē) *n. pl.* **·nies** A familiar friend. [<Gk. *chronios* long-lasting]

**crook** (krŏŏk) *n.* 1 A bend or curve. 2 The curved or bent part of a thing: the *crook* of a branch. 3 An implement with a crook in it: a shepherd's *crook.* 4 *Informal* A criminal; swindler; cheat. [<ON *krōkr*]

**crop** (krop) *n.* 1 Cultivated plants, grains, fruits, etc., collectively. 2 The plant product of a particular kind, place, or season. 3 The entire yield of anything. 4 A short haircut. 5 The first stomach of a bird; craw. 6 A hunting or riding whip with a leather loop for a lash. 7 A collection of things: a *crop* of lies. —*v.* **cropped, crop·ping** *v.t.* 1 To cut or eat off the stems or ends of. 2 To pluck or reap. 3 To cut off closely, as hair; trim, as a dog's ears or tail. 4 To raise a crop or crops on; cause to bear crops. —*v.i.* 5 To appear above the surface; sprout: with *up* or *out.* 6 To develop or come up unexpectedly: with *up* or *out*: A new problem *cropped* up. [<OE *cropp*]

**cro·quet** (krō·kā´) *n.* An outdoor game played by knocking wooden balls through a series of wire arches by means of mallets. [< AF *croquet*]

**crotch·et** (kroch´it) *n.* 1 A whimsical notion; an eccentricity. 2 A small hook. [<OF *crochet* a hook]

**crouch** (krouch) *v.i.* 1 To stoop or bend low. 2 To cringe; cower. —*v.t.* 3 To bend low. —*n.* A crouching or the position taken in crouching. [<OF *croc* a hook]

**crow¹** (krō) *n.* 1 Any of various omnivorous, raucous birds with glossy black plumage. 2 Loosely, a rook or raven. [<OE *crāwe*]

**crow²** (krō) *v.i.* **crowed** or (*for def. 1) Chiefly Brit.* **crew, crowed, crow·ing** 1 To utter the cry of a rooster. 2 To exult; boast. 3 To utter sounds expressive of delight, as an infant. —*n.* A crowing sound of a rooster, infant, etc. [<OE *crāwan*]

**crown** (kroun) *n.* 1 A decorative circlet for the head, esp. as a mark of sovereign power. 2 *Often cap.* A sovereign ruler; also, sovereignty: with *the.* 3 A wreath or garland for the head. 4 A reward or prize for excellence or merit. 5 A complete or perfect state or type; acme. 6 The top or summit; crest. 7 The top of the head: a bald *crown.* 8 The head itself. 9 The upper portion of a hat. 10 *Dent.* **a** The part of a tooth exposed beyond the gum. **b** An artificial substitute for this. • See TOOTH. 11 **a** A coin stamped with a crown or crowned head. **b** Formerly, a British five-shilling piece. 12 *Naut.* The outer point of junction of the two arms of an anchor. —*v.t.* 1 To place a crown or garland on the head of. 2 To enthrone; make a monarch of. 3 To be the topmost part of. 4 To form the ultimate ornament to or aspect of. 5 To endow with honor or dignity. 6 To bring to completion; consummate. 7 *Dent.* To put a crown on (a tooth). 8 *Slang* To hit, as a person, on the head. 9 In checkers, to make into a king. [<L *corona*] —**crown′er** *n.*

**cru·cial** (krōō´shəl) *adj.* 1 Of immense and decisive importance; critical. 2 Severely difficult and trying. [< L *crux, crucis* cross, torture] —**cru′cial·ly** *adv.*

**cru·ci·ble** (krōō´sə·bəl) *n.* 1 A pot or vessel made of a substance that will stand extreme heat. 2 The hollow place in the bottom of an ore furnace. 3 A trying and purifying test. [< Med. L *crucibulum* earthen pot]

**cru·ci·fix** (krōō´sə·fiks) *n.* A cross bearing an effigy of Christ crucified. [< L *crucifixus* one hanged on a cross]

**cru·ci·fy** (krōō´sə·fi) *v.t.* **·fied, ·fy·ing** 1 To put to death by nailing or binding to a cross. 2 To torture; torment. [< L *crucifigere* fasten to a cross] —**cru′ci·fi′er** *n.*

**crude** (krōōd) *adj.* **crud·er, crud·est** 1 Not in a state ready for use; raw; unrefined: *crude* oil. 2 Lacking refinement, tact, good taste, etc. 3 Rough in workmanship, design, etc. 4 Not disguised; bare: a *crude* truth. [< L *crudus*] —**crude′ly** *adv.* —**crude′ness** *n.* — **Syn.** 2 coarse, gross, vulgar.

**cru·el** (krōō´əl) *adj.* 1 Disposed to inflict suffering, pain, etc., on others. 2 Causing suffering, distress, etc.: a *cruel* fate. [< L *crudelis* severe] —**cru′el·ly** *adv.* —**Syn.** 1

pitiless, inhuman, merciless, sadistic, ruthless.

**cruise** (krōōz) v. **cruised, cruis·ing** v.i. 1 To sail about, as for pleasure. 2 To drive about, as a taxi or police patrol car. 3 To move or proceed at a speed suitable for sustained travel. —v.t. 4 To cruise over or about. —n. The act of cruising, esp. at sea. [< Du. *kruisen*]

**crul·ler** (krul′ər) n. A small, twisted cake of sweetened fried dough. [< Du. *krullen* to curl]

**crum·ble** (krum′bəl) v.t. & v.i. **·bled, ·bling** To fall or cause to fall into small pieces; disintegrate. —n. 1 A crumb. 2 Any crumbly material. [Freq. of CRUMB, v.] —**crum′bly** adj.

**crum·ple** (krum′pəl) v.t. & v.i. **·pled, ·pling** 1 To become or cause to become wrinkled; rumple. 2 *Informal* To collapse. —n. A wrinkle, as in cloth or the earth. [Freq. of obs. *crump*, var. of CRIMP]

**crunch** (krunch) v.t. 1 To chew with a brittle, crushing sound. 2 To crush or grind noisily. —v.i. 3 To chew noisily. 4 To move or advance with a crushing sound. —n. 1 The act or sound of crunching. 2 *Slang* A critical time, as the moment of decision. [Imit.] —**crunch′y** adj. (**·i·er, ·i·est**)

**cru·sade** (krōō·sād′) n. 1 Any of the military expeditions undertaken by Christians from the 11th through the 13th century to recover the Holy Land from the Muslims. 2 Any similar expedition sanctioned by a church. 3 Any movement or cause conducted aggressively and vigorously, esp. against public evil. —v.i. **·sad·ed, ·sad·ing** To go on or engage in a crusade. [< Med. L. *cruciare* mark with a cross] —**cru·sad′er** n.

**crush** (krush) v.t. 1 To press or squeeze out of shape; mash. 2 To smash or grind into particles. 3 To obtain or extract by pressure. 4 To press upon; crowd. 5 To put down; subdue; overwhelm. 6 To oppress. —v.i. 7 To become broken or misshapen by pressure. 8 To crowd: with *into, against*, etc. —n. 1 The act of crushing. 2 A pressing or crowding together. 3 A fruit drink. 4 *Informal* An infatuation. [< OF *croissir* break] —**crush′er** n.

**crust** (krust) n. 1 A hard, thin coating over something softer. 2 **a** The outer part of bread. **b** A bit of stale, hard bread. 3 The pastry envelope of a pie or the like. 4 The cold, exterior portion of the earth. 5 *Slang*

insolence; impertinence. —v.t. & v.i. To cover with or acquire a crust. [< L *crusta*]

**crus·ta·cean** (krus·tā′shən) n. One of a class of arthropods having a hard shell, two pairs of antennae, and usu. gills, including lobsters, crabs, shrimps, etc. —adj. Of or pertaining to these animals. [< L *crusta* crust, shell]

**crypt** (kript) n. A recess or vault, esp. one under some churches, used for burial, etc. [< Gk. *kryptos* hidden]

**crys·tal** (kris′təl) n. 1 The solid form assumed by many minerals, esp. colorless transparent quartz, or rock crystal. 2 *Physics* A definite and symmetrical structure, based on a recurring unit cell, assumed by the atoms, molecules, or ions of a solid. 3 Flint glass, or any fine glass; also, tableware and decorative pieces made of such glass. 4 The transparent cover for a watch face. 5 Anything clear and transparent. —adj. 1 Composed of crystal. 2 Like crystal; extremely clear; limpid. [<Gk. *krystallos*] —**crys·tal·lic** (kris·tal′ik) adj.

**cub** (kub) n. 1 The young of the bear, fox, wolf, and certain other carnivores; a whelp. 2 An awkward youth. 3 A beginner or learner. —adj. Young; inexperienced: a *cub* reporter; *cub* pilot. [?]

**cube** (kyōōb) n. 1 *Geom.* A solid bounded by six equal squares and having all its angles right angles. 2 *Math.* The third power of a quantity; the product of three equal factors. —v.t. **cubed, cub·ing** 1 To raise (a number or quantity) to the third power. 2 To find the cubic capacity of. 3 To form or cut into cubes or cubelike shapes. [< Gk. *kybos* cube, die²]

**cuck·oo** (kōōk′ōō) n. 1 Any of a large family of slender birds with slightly curved bills, long, narrow tails, and a call like the sound of its name. 2 A cuckoo's cry. 3 An imitation of this sound. —v. **·ooed, ·oo·ing** v.t. 1 To repeat without cessation. —v.i. 2 To utter or imitate the cry of the cuckoo. —adj. (also kōō′kōō) *Slang* Slightly deranged mentally. [< OF *cucu, coucou*; imit.]

**cu·cum·ber** (kyōō′kum·bər) n. 1 The long, hard-rinded fruit of a creeping plant of the gourd family cultivated as a vegetable. 2 The plant. [< L *cucumis*]

**cud** (kud) n. Food forced up into the mouth from the first stomach of a ruminant and chewed over again. [< OE *cudu, cwidu*]

**cudg·el** (kuj′əl) n. A short, thick stick used as a club. —v.t. **·eled** or **·elled, ·el·ing** or **·el**

·ling To beat with a cudgel. [< OE *cycgel*] —
**cudg′el·er** or **cudg′el·ler** n.

**cue** (kyōō) n. 1 A long, tapering rod, used to
strike the cue ball in billiards, pool, etc. 2
A queue or line of persons. —v.t. cued,
cu·ing 1 In billiards, etc., to hit with a cue.
—v.i. 2 To form a line of persons: usu. with
up. [< F *queue* tail]

**cuff** (kuf) n. 1 A band about the wrist, as a
part of a sleeve. 2 The part of a long glove
covering the wrist. 3 A turned-up hem on a
trouser leg. 4 HANDCUFF. —**off the cuff** *Informal* Extemporaneous; unrehearsed. [ME
*cuffe*]

**cu·li·nar·y** (kyōō′lə·ner′ē, kul′ə-) adj. Of or
pertaining to cooking or the kitchen. [< L
*culina* kitchen]

**cull** (kul) v.t. culled, cull·ing 1 To pick or sort
out; collect. 2 To select and gather. —n.
Something picked or sorted out and rejected. [< L *colligere* collect] —**cull′er** n.

**cul·mi·nate** (kul′mə·nāt) v.i. ·nat·ed, ·nat·ing
1 To attain the highest point or degree. 2 To
come to a complete result; reach a final effect. [< L *culmen* top, highest point] —**cul·
l′mi·nal** adj.

**cul·pa·ble** (kul′pə·bəl) adj. Deserving of
blame or censure. [< L *culpa* fault] —
**cul′pa·bil′i·ty, cul′pa·ble·ness** n. —**cul′
pa·bly** adv.

**cult** (kult) n. 1 A system of religious observances. 2 Extravagant devotion to a person, cause, or thing. 3 The object of such
devotion. 4 A group of persons having an
excessive interest in something. [< L *cultus*,
pp. of *colere* worship]

**cul·ti·vate** (kul′tə·vāt) v.t. ·vat·ed, ·vat·ing 1 To
prepare and use (land), as by plowing, fertilizing, sowing, etc. 2 To loosen the soil
about (growing plants) with a cultivator,
hoe, etc. 3 To plant and tend. 4 To improve
or develop by study, exercise, training, etc.:
to *cultivate* the mind. 5 To study carefully;
pay special attention to: to *cultivate* philosophy. 6 To try to make friends with: to
*cultivate* one's teacher. [< L *cultus*, pp. of
*colere* care for, worship]

**cul·ti·va·tion** (kul′tə·vā′shən) n. 1 The act or
result of cultivating. 2 Refinement; culture.

**cul·ture** (kul′chər) n. 1 The sum total of the
attainments and activities of any specific
period, race, or people; civilization: the *culture* of the ancient Greeks. 2 The knowledge, good taste, refinement, etc., acquired
by training the mind and faculties. 3 Development or improvement, as of the mind

or body, by special care, training, etc.:
physical *culture*; voice *culture*. 4 *Bacteriol.* a
The proliferation of a specific microorganism in a specially prepared nutrient, or **culture medium.** b The organisms so developed. 5 The cultivation or raising of a plant
or animal. 6 Cultivation of the soil; tillage.
—v.t. ·tured, ·tur·ing 1 CULTIVATE. 2 *Bacteriol.*
To produce in a culture. [< L *cultura* < *cultus.* See CULTIVATE.]

**cul·vert** (kul′vərt) n. An artificial, covered
channel for water, as under a road. [?]

**cun·ning** (kun′ing) n. 1 Skill in deception;
guile; artifice. 2 Proficiency; skill; dexterity.
—adj. 1 Crafty; tricky; artful; guileful. 2 Appealing because of prettiness, charm,
smallness, etc. 3 Showing ingenuity, skill,
dexterity, etc. [<OE *cunnung* < *cunnan*
know] —**cun′ning·ly** adv. —**cun′ning·ness**
n.

**cu·pid·i·ty** (kyōō·pid′ə·tē) n. An inordinate
wish for possession, esp. of wealth; avarice.
[< L *cupidus* desirous]

**cu·po·la** (kyōō′pə·lə) n. 1 A dome-shaped roof
or ceiling. 2 A small structure, often with a
dome-shaped top, built on a roof. —v.t.
·laed, ·la·ing To provide with a cupola. [< L
*cupula*, dim. of *cupa* tub, cask]

**cu·rate** (kyōōr′it) n. A clergyman assisting a
parish priest, rector, or vicar. [<Med. L *cura*
care or cure (of souls)] —**cu′rate·ship** n.

**cu·ra·tor** (kyōō·rā′tər, kyōō′rā′tər) n. A person having charge, as of a museum or library; a superintendent. [<L *curare* care for
< *cura* care] —**cu·ra·to·ti·al** (kyōōr′ə·tôr′
ē·əl, -tō′rē) adj. —**cu·ra′tor·ship** n.

**curb** (kûrb) n. 1 A chain or strap to brace a
bit against a horse's lower jaw, used to
check the horse when the reins are pulled.
2 Anything that restrains or controls. 3 A
raised border or edge, as that which forms
a gutter along a street. 4 A market dealing
in securities not listed on a stock exchange.
—v.t. 1 To hold in check; control, with or as
with reins. 2 To provide with a curb. 3 To
lead (a dog) off a curb for defecation in the
street. [<OF *courbe* curved <L *curvus*] —
**Syn.** v. 1 restrain, subdue, repress, manage.

**curd** (kûrd) n. Often pl. The solids separated
from the watery whey of milk. —v.t. & v.i.
CURDLE. [Metathetic var. of CRUD] —**cur·
d′i·ness** n. —**curd′ly, curd′y** adj.

**cur·dle** (kûrd′l) v.t. & v.i. ·dled, ·dling 1 To
change or turn to curds. 2 To thicken; congeal. 3 To turn sour. [Freq. of CURD, v.]

**cure** (kyŏŏr) n. 1 A recovery from an unhealthy condition. 2 That which effects such a recovery, as a drug, treatment, etc. 3 Spiritual care: the *cure* of souls. 4 A manner of preserving something, as meat or fish. —v. **cured, cur·ing** v.t. 1 To restore to a healthy condition. 2 To remedy or eradicate, as a disease or bad habit. 3 To preserve, as by salting or smoking. 4 To vulcanize, as rubber. —v.i. 5 To bring about recovery. 6 To be preserved, as meat. [< L *cura* care]

**cu·ri·os·i·ty** (kyŏŏr′ē·os′ə·tē) n. pl. **·ties** 1 A desire for knowledge. 2 Inquisitive interest in things which are not of proper concern; nosiness. 3 A person or thing that excites interest or inquiry. [< L *curiosus*. See CURIOUS.]

**cu·ri·ous** (kyŏŏr′ē·əs) adj. 1 Eager for knowledge. 2 Too inquisitive; prying. 3 Novel; odd; strange; mysterious. [< L *curiosus* < *cura* care] —**cu′ri·ous·ly** adv. —**cu′ri·ous·ness** n. —Syn. 1 inquiring, inquisitive, questioning. 2 meddlesome, nosy, intrusive.

**curl** (kûrl) v.t. 1 To twist into ringlets or curves, as the hair. 2 To form into a curved or spiral shape. —v.i. 3 To become curved; take a spiral shape. 4 To play at the game of curling. —n. 1 Anything coiled or spiral, as a ringlet. 2 The act of curling or the condition of being curled. [<MDu. *crulle* curly]

**cur·mudg·eon** (kər·muj′ən) n. A bad-tempered, ill-mannered man. [?] —**cur·mudg′eon·ly** adj.

**cur·rant** (kûr′ənt) n. 1 A small, round, acid berry, used for making jelly. 2 Any of a genus of hardy shrubs whose fruit is the red, white, or black currant. 3 A small seedless raisin from the Levant. [< AF *(raisins de) Corauntz* (raisins from) Corinth]

**cur·ren·cy** (kûr′ən·sē) n. pl. **·cies** 1 The money in general use in any country. 2 A circulation or passing from person to person. 3 General acceptance; prevalence; use.

**cur·ry** (kûr′ē) v.t. **·ried, ·ry·ing** 1 To rub down and clean with a currycomb or other implement; groom (a horse, dog, etc). 2 To prepare (tanned hides) for use, as by soaking, beating, etc. —**curry favor** To seek favor, as by adulation and subserviency. [<OF *carreier, conreder* make ready, prepare]

**curse** (kûrs) v. **cursed** or **curst, curs·ing** v.t. 1 To invoke evil or injury upon; damn. 2 To swear at. 3 To cause evil or injury to. —v.i. 4 To utter curses; swear; blaspheme. —n.

1 A blasphemous or profane oath. 2 A calling on a god to visit trouble or evil upon some person or thing. 3 A source of trouble or evil. 4 The evil which comes as a result of a curse. 5 A person or thing that is cursed. [< OE *cursian*]

**cur·so·ry** (kûr′sər·ē) adj. Rapid and superficial; hasty, with no attention to detail. [<L *cursor* a runner < *currere* run] —**cur′so·ri·ly** adv. —**cur′so·ri·ness** n.

**curt** (kûrt) adj. 1 Concise; brief; terse. 2 Short and sharp in manner; brusque; abrupt. [<L *curtus* shortened] —**curt′ly** adv. —**curt′ness** n.

**cur·tail** (kər·tāl′) v.t. To cut off or cut short; abbreviate; lessen; reduce. [<obs. *curtal* short; infl. in form by TAIL] —**cur·tail′er, cur·tail′ment** n.

**cur·tain** (kûr′tən) n. 1 A piece of fabric, often adjustable, hung for decoration, concealment, or to shut out light, as before a wall, window, doorway, etc. 2 Something that conceals, covers, or separates like a curtain. 3 In a theater, the drapery hanging at the front of a stage, drawn up or aside to reveal the stage. 4 pl. Slang The end; death. —v.t. 1 To supply or adorn with or as with a curtain or curtains. 2 To conceal or shut off as with a curtain; cover. [<LL *cortina*]

**cur·va·ture** (kûr′və·chər) n. 1 The act of curving or the state of being curved. 2 A curve or curved part, often an abnormal one: *curvature* of the spine.

**curve** (kûrv) n. 1 A line continuously bent so that no portion of it is straight, as the arc of a circle. 2 The form, movement, or path of a curve. 3 Something having the form of a curve. 4 An instrument for drawing curves, used by draftsmen. 5 Math. A set of connected points having only length as a variable measure. 6 In baseball, a pitched ball so thrown that it veers to one side before crossing the plate. —v. **curved, curv·ing** v.t. 1 To cause to assume the form of a curve. —v.i. 2 To assume the form of a curve. 3 To move in a curve, as a projectile or ball; bend. [<L *curvus* bent]

**cush·ion** (kŏŏsh′ən) n. 1 A flexible bag or casing filled with some soft or elastic material, as feathers, air, etc. 2 Anything resembling a cushion in appearance, construction, or application, as a device to deaden the jar or impact of parts. 3 The elastic rim of a billiard table. —v.t. 1 To place, seat, or arrange on or as on a cushion. 2 To provide with a cushion. 3 To cover or hide as with a cushion. 4 To absorb the shock or effect of. [<OF *coissin*]

**cus·to·di·an** (kus·tō′dē·ən) *n.* A guardian, caretaker, or janitor. —**cus·to′di·an·ship′** *n.*

**cus·to·dy** (kus′tə·dē) *n. pl.* ·**dies** 1 A keeping; guardianship. 2 The state of being held in keeping or under guard; imprisonment. [<L *custos* guardian]   —**cus·to·di·al** (kus·tō′dē·əl) *adj.*

**cus·tom** (kus′təm) *n.* 1 An ordinary or usual manner of doing or acting. 2 The habitual practice of a community or people; common usage. 3 *Law* An old and general usage that has obtained the force of law. 4 Business support; patronage. 5 *pl.* a A tariff or duty by a government upon goods imported or exported. b The government agency which collects such tariffs or duties. —*adj.* 1 Made to order. 2 Specializing in made-to-order goods: a *custom* tailor. [<L *consuetudo*]

**cu·ta·ne·ous** (kyōō·tā′nē·əs) *adj.* Of, pertaining to, affecting, or on the skin. [<L *cutis* skin]

**cut·back** (kut′bak′) *n.* A reduction or cessation, as of production or in supply: a *cutback* in fuel.

**cute** (kyōōt) *adj.* **cut·er, cut·est** *Informal* 1 Pretty or dainty; attractive. 2 Clever or sharp. 3 Artificially striving for effect. [Var. of ACUTE] —**cute′ly** *adv.* —**cute′ness** *n.*

**cu·ti·cle** (kyōō′ti·kəl) *n.* 1 The outer layer of cells that protect the true skin; epidermis. 2 The crescent of toughened skin around the base of a fingernail or toenail. [<L *cutis* skin] —**cu·tic′u·lar** *adj.*

**cut·lass** (kut′ləs) *n.* A short, swordlike weapon, often curved, formerly used by sailors. Also **cut′las.** [<F *couteau* knife]

**cut·let** (kut′lit) *n.* 1 A thin piece of meat from the ribs or leg, for broiling or frying. 2 A flat croquette of chopped meat, fish, etc. [<F *côte* rib <L. *costa*]

**cy·ber·net·ics** (sī′bər·net′iks) *n. pl. (construed as sing.)* The study of the control processes in physical and biological systems. [<Gk. *kybernētēs* steersman] —**cy′ber·net′ic** *adj.*

**cy·cle** (sī′kəl) *n.* 1 A period of time during which one sequence of a succession of regularly recurring phenomena or events is completed. 2 A sequence of phenomena or events that recur regularly in the same order. 3 A very long period of time; eon; age. 4 All of the legends, poems, romances, etc., relating to one period, person, event, etc. 5

A series of poems, songs, etc., dealing with a single theme. 6 A bicycle, tricycle, etc. — *v.i.* **cy·cled, cy·cling** 1 To pass through or occur in cycles. 2 To ride a bicycle, tricycle, or the like. —*v.t.* 3 To put through a cycle or process. [<Gk. *kyklos* circle]

**cy·clone** (sī′klōn) *n.* 1 *Meteorol.* A storm or system of winds rotating clockwise in the southern hemisphere or counterclockwise in the northern hemisphere, about a center of low atmospheric pressure. 2 Loosely, any violent and destructive whirling windstorm. [<Gk. *kykloein* move in a circle] — **cy·clon·ic** (sī·klon′ik) or ·**i·cal** *adj.* —**cy·clon′i·cal·ly** *adv.*

**cy·clo·tron** (sī′klə·tron) *n. Physics* An apparatus for accelerating charged particles to high energies in spiral paths by means of a fluctuating magnetic field. [<CYCLO- + (ELEC)TRON]

**cyg·net** (sig′nit) *n.* A young swan. [<Gk. *kyknos*]

**cyl·in·der** (sil′in·dər) *n.* 1 *Geom.* A solid described by the circumference of a circle as its center moves along a straight line, the ends of the solid being parallel, equal circles. 2 Any object, container, etc., having this shape. 3 Any cylindrical portion of a machine, esp. one of a motor in which a piston moves. 4 The rotating chamber that holds the cartridges of a revolver. • See RE-VOLVER. [<Gk. *kylindros<kylindein* to roll]

**cy·lin·dri·cal** (si·lin′dri·kəl) *adj.* 1 Of or pertaining to a cylinder. 2 Having the form or shape of a cylinder. Also **cy·lin′dric.** — **cy·lin′dri·cal·ly** *adv.* —**cy·lin·dri·cal·i·ty** (si·lin′dri·kal′ə·tē) *n.*

**cym·bal** (sim′bəl) *n.* A platelike metallic musical instrument, played by being struck with a drumstick or brush or by striking one against another. [<Gk. *kymbē* cup, hollow of a vessel] —**cym′bal·ist** *n.*

**Cyn·ic** (sin′ik) *n.* One of a sect of ancient Greek philosophers who held that virtue was the ultimate goal of life, their doctrine gradually coming to symbolize insolent self-righteousness. —*adj.* Belonging to or like the Cynics: also **Cyn′i·cal.**

**cy·press** (sī′prəs) *n.* 1 Any of a genus of evergreen conifers growing in warm climates. 2 Any of various similar trees, as the white cedar. 3 The wood of these trees. [<Gk. *kyparissos*]

**cyst** (sist) *n.* A saclike structure in a plant or

animal containing liquid or semisolid material. [<Gk. *kystis* bladder] —**cys'tic** *adj.*

**cy·tol·o·gy** (sī·tol'ə·jē) *n.* The branch of biology concerned with the structure and functions of cells. —**cy·to·log·ic** (sī'tə·loj'ik) or **·i·cal** *adj.* —**cy'to·log'i·cal·ly** *adv.* —**cy·tol'o·gist** *n.*

**czar** (zär) *n.* 1 An emperor or absolute monarch; esp., one of the former emperors of Russia. 2 A person having great power or authority. [<Russ. *tsare*, ult. <L *Caesar* Caesar] —**czar'ism** *n.* —**czar'ist** *adj., n.*

# D

**dachs·hund** (däks'hoont', daks'hoond', dash'-) *n.* A breed of dog native to Germany, of medium size, with long, compact body and short legs, and reddish brown or black coat. [G < *Dachs* badger + *Hund* dog]

**Da·cron** (dā'kron, dak'ron) *n.* A strong synthetic fiber or washable fabric, resistant to stretching and wrinkling: a trade name. Also **da'cron**.

**daf·fo·dii** (daf'ə·dil) *n.* A species of narcissus having yellow flowers with a long, trumpet-shaped corona. Also **daf'fa·dil'ly, daf'fa·down·dil'ly** (-doun·dil'ē), **daf'fy·down·dil'ly**. [<L *asphodelus* asphodel]

**daft** (daft, däft) *adj.* 1 Silly; frolicsome. 2 Insane; crazy. [<OE *gedǣfte* mild, meek] —**daft'ly** *adv.* —**daft'ness** *n.*

**dagger** *Printing* A mark of reference (‡). —*v.t.* 1 To pierce with a dagger; stab. 2 *Printing* To mark with a dagger. [< OF *dague* dagger]

**dahl·ia** (dal'yə, däl'-, dāl'-) *n.* 1 A perennial plant having tuberous roots and large, composite flower heads of various colors. 2 Its flower or root. [< Anders *Dahl*, 18th c. Swedish botanist]

**dai·ly** (dā'lē) *adj.* Occurring, appearing, or pertaining to every day. —*n. pl.* **·lies** A daily publication. —*adv.* Day after day; on every day. [< OE *dǣg* day]

**dain·ty** (dān'tē) *adj.* **·ti·er, ·ti·est** 1 Charmingly pretty or graceful. 2 Refined or delicate in tastes, manners, etc. 3 Overly nice or fastidious. 4 Delicious; tasty. —*n. pl.* **·ties** A choice bit of food. [<L *dignitas* dignity] —**dain'ti·ly** *adv.* —**dain'ti·ness** *n.*

**dair·y** (dâr'ē) *n. pl.* **dair·ies** 1 A building or room where milk and cream are kept and made into butter and cheese. 2 A place for the sale of milk products. 3 DAIRY FARM. 4 DAIRY CATTLE. 5 DAIRYING. [< OE *dǣge* dairymaid]

**dai·sy** (dā'zē) *n. pl.* **dai·sies** Any of various small plants having composite flowers consisting of a yellow disk with white or rose-colored rays. [<OE *dǣges ēage* day's eye]

**dal·ly** (dal'ē) *v.* **dal·lied, dal·ly·ing** *v.i.* 1 To make love sportively; frolic. 2 To toy with; trifle; flirt: to *dally* with disaster. 3 To waste time. —*v.t.* 4 To waste (time): with *away*. [<OF *dalier* converse, chat] —**dal'li·er** *n.*

**dam** (dam) *n.* 1 A barrier to check the flow of a body of water. 2 The water held up by a dam. 3 Any obstruction. —*v.t.* **dammed, dam·ming** 1 To erect a dam in; obstruct by a dam. 2 To restrain: with *up* or *in*. [<MDu. *damm*]

**dam·age** (dam'ij) *n.* 1 Destruction, injury, or harm to a person or thing. 2 *pl. Law* Money recoverable for a wrong or an injury. 3 *pl. Informal* Cost. —*v.* **dam·aged, dam·ag·ing** *v.t.* 1 To cause damage to; impair the usefulness or value of. —*v.i.* 2 To be susceptible to damage. [< L *damnum* loss] —**dam'age·a·ble** *adj.* —**Syn.** *n.* 1 impairment, deterioration, loss. *v.* 1 injure, harm, ruin.

**damp** (damp) *n.* 1 Moisture; humidity; mist. 2 Foul air or gas, esp. in coal mines. 3 *Archaic* Depression of spirits. —*adj.* 1 Somewhat wet; moist. 2 Depressed in spirit. —*v.t.* 1 To moisten; make damp. 2 To check or lessen (energy, sound, flames, etc.). [<MDu., vapor, steam] —**damp'er, damp'ness.** *n.* —**damp'ly** *adv.*

**dan·de·li·on** (dan'də·lī'ən) *n.* A weed with composite yellow flower heads and deeply toothed, edible leaves. [<F *dent de lion* lion's tooth; with ref. to the shape of the leaves]

**dan·dle** (dan'dəl) *v.t.* **·dled, ·dling** 1 To move up and down lightly on the knees, as an infant. 2 To fondle; caress. [?]

**dan·druff** (dan'drəf) *n.* Dead, scaly skin shed by the scalp; scurf. [?]

**dan·dy** (dan'dē) *n. pl.* **·dies** 1 A man overly refined in dress and affected in manner; a fop. 2 *Informal* A particularly fine specimen. —*adj.* 1 Like a dandy. 2 *Informal* Excellent; very fine. [?] —**dan'dy·ish** *adj.* —**dan'dy·ism** *n.*

**dan·ger** (dān'jər) *n.* 1 Exposure to chance of evil, injury, or loss; risk. 2 A cause of peril or risk. [<OF *dangier* power] —**Syn.** 1, 2 peril, jeopardy, hazard.

**dan·gle** (dang'gəl) *v.* **·gled, ·gling** *v.i.* 1 To hang loosely; swing to-and-fro. 2 To follow someone as a suitor or hanger-on. 3 *Gram.* To lack clear connection as a modifier in sentence construction: a *dangling* participle. —*v.t.* 4 To hold so as to swing loosely. [<Scand.] —**dan′gler** *n.*

**dap·per** (dap′ər) *adj.* 1 Smartly dressed; natty. 2 Small and active. [<MDu., strong, energetic] —**dap′per·ly** *adv.* —**dap′per·ness** *n.*

**dare** (dâr) *v.* **dared** (*Archaic* **durst**), **dar·ing** *v.t.* 1 To have the courage or boldness for; venture on. 2 To challenge (someone) to do something dangerous or difficult. 3 To defy; oppose and challenge. —*v.i.* 4 To have the courage or boldness to do or attempt something; venture. —**I dare say** I am reasonably certain. —*n.* A challenge. [<OE *durran*] —**dar′er** *n.*

**dart** (därt) *n.* 1 A small, arrowlike, pointed missile, usu. thrown or shot. 2 Something resembling this. 3 A sudden and rapid motion. 4 A tapering tuck made in a garment to fit it to the figure. —*v.t.* & *v.i.* 1 To emit swiftly or suddenly. 2 To move swiftly and suddenly. [<OF]

**dash** (dash) *v.t.* 1 To strike with violence, esp. so as to break or shatter. 2 To throw, thrust, or knock suddenly and violently; usu. with *away*, *out*, *down*, etc. 3 To splash; bespatter. 4 To do, write, etc., hastily: with *off* or *down*. 5 To frustrate; confound; to *dash* hopes. 6 To daunt or discourage. 7 To put to shame; abash. 8 To adulterate; mix: with *with*. —*v.i.* 9 To strike; hit: The waves *dashed* against the shore. 10 To rush or move impetuously. —*n.* 1 A sudden advance or rush. 2 A short race. 3 A small addition or bit: a *dash* of humor. 4 Impetuosity; spirit; vigor. 5 Striking or ostentatious display. 6 A check or hindrance. 7 An impact or collision or its sound. 8 A quick stroke, as with a pen. 9 A horizontal line (—), as a mark of punctuation, etc. 10 The long element of the Morse code. 11 DASHBOARD. [<Scand.] —**dash′er** *n.*

**data processing** The preparing, storing, or otherwise handling of information for or by computers.

**date** (dāt) *n.* 1 The oblong, sweet, fleshy fruit of the date palm. 2 A lofty palm bearing this fruit: also **date palm.** [<Gk. *daktylos* finger; with ref. to its shape]

**daub** (dôb) *v.t.* & *v.i.* 1 To smear or coat (something), as with plaster, grease, mud, etc. 2 To paint without skill or taste. —*n.* 1 Any sticky application. 2 A smear or spot. 3 A coarse, amateurish painting. 4 An instance or act of daubing. [<L *dealbare* whitewash] —**daub′er** *n.*

**daunt** (dônt, dänt) *v.t.* To dishearten or intimidate; cow; abash. [< L *domitare*, freq. of *domare* tame]

**daw·dle** (dôd′l) *v.t.* & *v.i.* **·dled, ·dling** To waste (time) in slow trifling; loiter. [Prob. var. of earlier *daddle* < DIDDLE] —**daw′dler** *n.* — Syn. linger, dally, trifle.

**dawn** (dôn) *v.i.* 1 To begin to grow light at the start of day. 2 To begin to be understood: with *on* or *upon*. 3 To begin to expand or develop. —*n.* 1 DAYBREAK. 2 An awakening or beginning. [Back formation < *dawning*, earlier *dawenyng* daybreak < Scand.]

**daze** (dāz) *v.t.* **dazed, daz·ing** To stupefy or bewilder; stun. —*n.* The state of being dazed. [ME *dasen* < Scand.] —**daz′ed·ly** (dā′zid·lē) *adv.*

**daz·zle** (daz′əl) *v.* **·zled, ·zling** *v.t.* 1 To blind or dim the vision of by excess of light. 2 To bewilder or charm, as with brilliant display. —*v.i.* 3 To be blinded by lights or glare. 4 To excite admiration. —*n.* 1 The act of dazzling; dazzled condition. 2 Something that dazzles. [Freq. of DAZE] —**daz′zler** *n.* — **daz′zling·ly** *adv.*

**DDT** A highly toxic derivative of chloral, widely used as an insecticide. [< *d(ichloro)d(iphenyl-)t(richloroethane)*]

**dea·con** (dē′kən) *n.* 1 A lay church officer or subordinate minister. 2 In the Anglican, Greek, and Roman Catholic churches, a clergyman ranking next below a priest. [< Gk. *diakonos* servant, minister] —**dea′con·ry, dea′con·ship** *n.*

**dead** (ded) *adj.* 1 Having ceased to live; lifeless. 2 In a state or condition resembling death. 3 Inanimate; inorganic: *dead* rocks. 4 Without interest, effectiveness, vitality, brilliance, resonance, etc.: a *dead* color; a *dead* sound; a *dead* passage in a book. 5 Unresponsive; insensible: *dead* to feeling. 6 Motionless and unfeeling; numb: His arm felt *dead.* 7 Extinguished: *dead* cinders. 8 No longer productive or operative: *dead* capital; *dead* ground. 9 No longer used; obsolete: a *dead* language. 10 Without elasticity or resilience: These tennis balls are *dead.* 11 Unfailing; certain; sure: a *dead* shot. 12 Complete; absolute; utter: a *dead* stop; *dead* level. 13 *Informal* Exhausted; worn-out. 14 Not transmitting an electric current: a *dead* wire. 15 In sports, no longer in play: a *dead* ball. —*n.* 1 The part of most intense cold, darkness, etc.: the *dead* of night. 2 Dead persons collectively: with *the.* —*adv.* To the last degree; wholly; absolutely; exactly: *dead* right; *dead* straight. [< OE *dēad*] —**dead·ness** *n.*

**deaf** (def) *adj.* **1** Partially or entirely unable to hear. **2** Determined not to listen or be persuaded. [< OE *dēaf*] —**deaf·ly** *adv.* — **deaf·ness** *n.*

**deal** (dēl) *v.* **dealt** (delt), **deal·ing** *v.t.* **1** To distribute; mete out, as playing cards. **2** To apportion to (one person) as a share. **3** To deliver, as a blow. —*v.i.* **4** To conduct oneself; behave towards: with *with:* to *deal* with an angry child. **5** To be concerned or occupied: with *in* or *with:* I *deal* in facts. **6** To consider, discuss, or administer; take action: with *with:* The court will *deal* with him. **7** To trade; do business: with *in, with,* or *at.* **8** In card games, to distribute the cards. — *n.* **1** In card games: **a** The act of distributing cards. **b** The cards so distributed. **c** The right or turn to distribute cards. **d** A single round of play. **2** An indefinite quantity, degree, or extent: a great *deal* of trouble. **3** A transaction or agreement, often secret: a political *deal.* **4** Treatment given or received: a square *deal.* [< OE *dǣlan* to divide] —**deal′er** *n.* —**Syn.** *n.* **3** scheme, arrangement, accommodation, understanding.

**dean** (dēn) *n.* **1** The chief officer of a cathedral or of a collegiate church. **2** A college or university official having jurisdiction over a particular group of students, field of study, or acting as head of a faculty. **3** The senior or preeminent member of a group: the *dean* of American composers. [<LL *decanus* head of ten men <L *decem* ten] —**dean′ship** *n.*

**dearth** (dûrth) *n.* Scarcity; lack; famine. [ME *derthe* costliness <*dere* dear] —**Syn.** paucity, want, absence, need.

**death** (deth) *n.* **1** The permanent cessation of physical life in a person, animal, or plant. **2** The condition of being dead. **3** Extinction of anything; destruction. **4** A cause or occasion of death. **5** Something similar to dying or being dead. **6** *Usu. cap.* The personification of death, usu. a skeleton holding a scythe. **7** Slaughter; bloodshed. —**to death** Very much: He frightened me *to death.* —**put to death** To kill; execute. [< OE *dēath*]

**de·bar** (di-bär′) *v.t.* **·barred**, **·bar·ring** **1** To shut out; exclude; prevent. with *from.* **2** To prohibit; hinder. [<F *dé-* away + *barrer* to bar] —**de·bar′ment** *n.*

**de·base** (di-bās′) *v.t.* **de·based**, **de·bas·ing** To lower in character, purity, value, etc.; degrade. [<DE- + ABASE] —**de·base′ment**. **de·bas′er** *n.* —**Syn.** abase, demean, devalue, cheapen.

**de·bate** (di-bāt′) *v.* **de·bat·ed**, **de·bat·ing** *v.t.* **1** To discuss or argue about, as in a public meeting. **2** To discuss in formal argument. **3** To consider; deliberate upon in the mind. —*v.i.* **4** To argue; discuss. **5** To engage in formal argument. **6** To deliberate mentally; consider. —*n.* **1** The discussing of any question; dispute. **2** A formal argument conducted as a contest between opposing sides, usu. on a specific question. [<L *de-* down + *batuere* to strike] —**de·bat′a·ble** *adj.* —**de·bat′er** *n.*

**de·bauch** (di-bôch′) *v.t.* **1** To corrupt in morals; deprave. —*v.i.* **2** To indulge in depravity. —*n.* **1** DEBAUCHERY. **2** An act or occasion of debauchery, as an orgy. [<OF *desbaucher* to lure from work <OF *desbaucher*] —**de·bauch′ed·ly** (-id·lē) *adv.* — **de·bauch′er, de·bauch′ed·ness** *n.*

**de·bil·i·tate** (di-bil′ə-tāt) *v.t.* **·tat·ed**, **·tat·ing** To make feeble; weaken. [<L *debilis* weak] —**de·bil′i·ta′tion** *n.* —**de·bil′i·ta′tive** *adj.*

**de·bil·i·ty** (di-bil′ə-tē) *n. pl.* **·ties** Bodily weakness; feebleness. [<L *debilis* weak]

**deb·it** (deb′it) *n.* **1** Something owed; a debt. **2′** An item of debt. **3** The left-hand side of an account where debts are listed. —*v.t.* **1** To enter (a debt) in an account. **2** To charge (a customer) for goods. [<L *debitum,* p.p. of *debere* owe]

**de·bris** (də·brē′, dā′brē; *Brit.* deb′rē) *n.* **1** Accumulated fragments; rubbish; rubble. **2** An aggregation of detached fragments of rocks. *Also* **dé·bris′.** [<OF *des-* away + *brisier* to break]

**debt** (det) *n.* **1** That which one owes. **2** An obligation. **3** The condition of being indebted. **4** *Theol.* A sin. [<L *debitum.* See DEBIT.]

**debt·or** (det′ər) *n.* One who owes a debt. [<L *debitor* < *debere* owe]

**de·but** (di·byōō′, dā-, dā′byōō) *n.* **1** A first appearance, as in society or on the stage. **2** An opening or beginning. —*v.i. Informal* **1** To appear in a debut. **2** To open, as a show. *Also* **dé·but′.** [<F *débuter* begin, lead off]

**dec·ade** (dek′ād, de·kād′) *n.* **1** A period of ten years. **2** A group or set of ten. [< L *decas* a group of ten]

**dec·a·dence** (dek′ə·dəns, di·kād′ns) *n.* **1** A process of deterioration; decay. **2** A condition or period of decline, as in literature, art, morals, etc. [< L *de-* down + *cadere* to fall]

**dec·a·dent** (dek′ə-dənt, di-kād′nt) *adj.* Characterized by decadence. —*n.* A decadent person, esp. a decadent painter, writer, composer, etc. —**dec′a·dent·ly** *adv.*

**de·cal·co·ma·ni·a** (di-kal′kə-mā′nē-ə, -mān′yə) *n.* 1 A transferring of decorative pictures or designs from paper to glass, porcelain, etc. 2 DECAL. [< F *décalquer* transfer a tracing + *-manie* -MANIA]

**Dec·a·logue** (dek′ə-lôg, -log) *n.* TEN COMMANDMENTS. Also **Dec′a·log.** [< Gk. *deka* ten + *logos* word]

**de·cant** (di-kant′) *v.t.* 1 To pour off gently so as not to disturb the sediment. 2 To pour from one container into another. [< L *de-* from + *canthus* lip of a jug] —**de·can·ta·tion** (dē′kan-tā′shən) *n.*

**de·cap·i·tate** (di-kap′ə-tāt) *v.t.* **·tat·ed, ·tat·ing** To cut off the head of; behead. [< L *de-* down + *caput* head] —**de·cap′i·ta′tion, de·cap′i·ta′tor** *n.*

**de·cay** (di-kā′) *v.i.* 1 To diminish slowly in health, power, beauty, quality, etc. 2 To rot; decompose. —*v.t.* 3 To cause to decay. —*n.* 1 A slow deterioration or weakening. 2 Decomposition; rottenness. 3 *Physics* The disintegration of a radioactive element. [< L *de-* down + *cadere* to fall]

**de·cease** (di-sēs′) *v.i.* **de·ceased, de·ceas·ing** To die. —*n.* Death. [< L *decessus* < *decedere* go away]

**de·ceit** (di-sēt′) *n.* 1 The act of deceiving. 2 A lie or other dishonest action. 3 The quality of being deceptive. [< OF *deceveir* deceive]

**de·ceive** (di-sēv′) *v.* **de·ceived, de·ceiv·ing** *v.t.* 1 To mislead by or as by falsehood; delude. —*v.i.* 2 To practice deceit. [< L *decipere* < *de-* away, down + *capere* to take] —**de·ceiv′a·ble** *adj.* —**de·ceiv′a·bly** *adv.* —**de·ceiv′er** *n.*

**de·cen·cy** (dē′sən-sē) *n. pl.* **·cies** 1 Propriety in conduct, speech, dress, etc. 2 *pl.* Actions that are socially proper or seemly. 3 *pl.* Things required for a proper manner of life. [< L *decens.* See DECENT.]

**de·cent** (dē′sənt) *adj.* 1 Characterized by propriety of conduct, speech, manners, or dress; proper; respectable. 2 Modest; chaste. 3 Moderately good; satisfactory. 4 Kind; generous. 5 *Informal* Adequately clothed. [< L *decens,* pr.p. of *decere* be fitting, be proper] —**de′cent·ly** *adv.* —**de′cent·ness** *n.*

**de·cep·tion** (di-sep′shən) *n.* 1 The act of de-

ceiving. 2 The state of being deceived. 3 Anything deceptive; a delusion.

**dec·i·bel** (des′ə-bel) *n.* A logarithmic unit defined so that an increase of 1 decibel represents multiplication of sound or signal power by about 1.258, with, for sound, 0 decibels representing a pressure of 0.0002 microbar. [< L *decem* ten + E *bel,* logarithmic unit < Alexander Graham *Bell,* 1847–1922, U.S. inventor]

**de·cide** (di-sīd′) *v.* **·cid·ed, ·cid·ing** *v.t.* 1 To determine; settle, as a dispute, contest, etc.; arbitrate. 2 To cause the outcome of; settle. 3 To bring (someone) to a decision. —*v.i.* 4 To give a decision. 5 To make a decision. [< MF *décider* < L *decidere* < *de-* down, away + *caedere* cut] —**de·cid′a·ble** *adj.* —**de·cid′er** *n.*

**de·cid·u·ous** (di-sij′ōō-əs) *adj.* 1 Falling off or shed at specific seasons, as petals or leaves. 2 Characterized by such a falling off; not evergreen. [< L *de-* down, away + *cadere* to fall] —**de·cid′u·ous·ly** *adv.* —**de·cid′u·ous·ness** *n.*

**dec·i·mal** (des′ə-məl) *adj.* 1 Founded on the number 10. 2 Proceeding by powers of 10 or of one tenth. —*n.* A decimal fraction. [< L *decem* ten] —**dec′i·mal·ly** *adv.*

**de·ci·pher** (di-sī′fər) *v.t.* 1 To figure out the sense of, as hieroglyphics, a scribble, etc. 2 To translate from cipher into ordinary characters; decode. [< DE- + CIPHER] —**de·ci′pher·a·ble** *adj.* —**de·ci′pher·er, de·ci′pher·ment** *n.*

**de·ci·sion** (di-sizh′ən) *n.* 1 The act of deciding or making up one's mind. 2 The result or conclusion arrived at by deciding. 3 The quality of being positive and firm; determination. 4 In boxing, a victory determined by points rather than by a knockout.

**de·ci·sive** (di-sī′siv) *adj.* 1 Putting an end to uncertainty or debate; conclusive. 2 Prompt; positive; decided. 3 Crucially important; critical. —**de·ci′sive·ly** *adv.* —**de·ci′sive·ness** *n.*

**deck** (dek) *n.* 1 A platform covering or extending horizontally across a vessel. 2 Any similar flat surface. 3 A pack of cards. —**clear the deck** To prepare for activity. —**hit the deck** 1 *Slang* To rise from bed quickly. 2 *Slang* To prepare for activity. 3 *Slang* To drop to a prone position. —**on deck** 1 Present and available for action. 2 Next at bat in a baseball game. —*v.t.* 1 To array; adorn. 2 To put a deck on. [< MDu. *dek* roof, covering]

**de·claim** (di·klām′) *v.i.* 1 To speak loudly and in a rhetorical manner. 2 To give a recitation. 3 To condemn or attack verbally and vehemently: with *against*. —*v.t.* 4 To utter aloud in a rhetorical manner. [< L *de*- completely + *clamare* shout] —**de·clam·a·to·ry** (di·klam′ə·tôr′ē, -tō′rē) *adj.* —**de·claim′er,**

**dec·la·ma·tion** (dek′lə·mā′shən *n.*

**dec·la·ra·tion** (dek′lə·rā′shən) *n.* 1 The act of declaring. 2 That which is declared. 3 In law, a formal presentation of facts by the plaintiff. 4 A statement of goods that can be taxed. 5 In bridge: **a** A meld. **b** The final or winning bid.

**de·clare** (di·klâr′) *v.* **·clared, ·clar·ing** *v.t.* 1 To assert positively or emphatically. 2 To announce or state formally and solemnly. 3 To reveal; manifest. 4 To make full statement of, as dutiable goods. 5 In bridge, to name, as a trump suit. —*v.i.* 6 To make a declaration. 7 To proclaim a choice or decision. [< L *de*- completely + *clarare* make clear < *clarus* clear] —**de·clar′er** *n.*

**de·cline** (di·klīn′) *v.* **·clined, ·clin·ing** *v.i.* 1 To refuse to accept, comply with, or do something, esp. politely. 2 To lessen or fail, as in health. 3 To come to an end; wane. 4 To bend or incline downward or aside. 5 To degrade oneself, as to an unworthy action. —*v.t.* 6 To refuse to accept, comply with, or do, esp. politely. 7 To cause to bend or incline downward or aside. 8 To give the inflected forms of (a noun, pronoun, or adjective). —*n.* 1 The act or result of declining; deterioration; decay. 2 The period of such declining. 3 Any enfeebling disease, as tuberculosis. 4 A declivity; a slope. [< L *declinare* lean down] —**de·clin′a·ble** *adj.* —**de·clin′er** *n.*

**de·coct** (di·kokt′) *v.t.* To extract by boiling; condense. [< L *de*- down + *coquere* to cook] —**de·coc′tion** *n.*

**de·com·pose** (dē′kəm·pōz′) *v.t.* & *v.i.* **·posed, ·pos·ing** 1 To separate into constituent elements. 2 To decay. —**de′com·pos′a·ble** *adj.* —**de′com·pos′er, de′com·po·si′tion** *n.*

**dec·o·rate** (dek′ə·rāt) *v.t.* **·rat·ed, ·rat·ing** 1 To adorn; ornament. 2 To furnish, paint, refurbish (a dwelling, room, etc.). 3 To devise a décor, as for a home, and supervise its execution. 4 To confer a medal or decoration upon: *decorated* for valor. [< L *decorare* < *decus* embellishment] —**dec′o·ra′tor** *n.*

**dec·o·rous** (dek′ər·əs, di·kôr′əs, -kō′rəs) *adj.* Characterized by proper behavior and good taste. [< L *decus* grace, embellishment] —**dec′o·rous·ly** *adv.* —**dec′o·rous·ness** *n.* —**Syn.** becoming, suitable, seemly, correct.

**de·co·rum** (di·kôr′əm, -kō′rəm) *n.* 1 Propriety, as in manner, conduct, etc.; seemliness. 2 An act demanded by social custom. [< L *decorus* decorous]

**de·coy** (dē′koi, di·koi′) *n.* 1 A person or thing that lures others into danger or a snare. 2 A bird or animal, or the likeness of one, used to lure game within gunshot. 3 An enclosed place into which game may be lured. —*v.t.* & *v.i.* (dē′koi) To lure or be lured into danger, a snare, etc. [<Du. *de kooi* the cage] —**de′coy·er** *n.*

**de·crease** (di·krēs′) *v.t.* & *v.i.* **·creased, ·creas·ing** To grow or cause to grow gradually less or smaller; abate; reduce. —*n.* (*usu.* dē′krēs) 1 The act, process, or state of decreasing. 2 The amount or degree of decreasing. [< L *decrescere* < *de*- down + *crescere* grow] —**de·creas′ing·ly** *adv.*

**de·cree** (di·krē′) *n.* 1 A formal order or ordinance, as of a civil or an ecclesiastical body. 2 Anything unalterably ordained. —*v.t.* 1 To order, adjudge, ordain, or appoint by law or edict. —*v.i.* 2 To issue an edict or decree. [< L *decretum*, neut. pp. of *decernere* decide]

**de·crep·it** (di·krep′it) *adj.* Enfeebled by old age or overuse; broken down. [< L *decrepitus* < *de*- completely + *crepare* to creak] —**de·crep′it·ly** *adv.*

**de·crep·i·tude** (di·krep′ə·t′ōōd) *n.* Enfeeblement through infirmity or old age.

**ded·i·cate** (ded′ə·kāt) *v.t.* **·cat·ed, ·cat·ing** 1 To set apart for sacred uses; consecrate. 2 To set apart for any special use, duty, or purpose. 3 To devote (oneself) to some special work, action, etc. 4 To open (a new building, park, etc.) with ceremonies. 5 To preface with a dedication, as a book. —*adj.* Dedicated; devoted. [< L *de*- down + *dicare* proclaim] —**ded′i·ca′tive** *adj.* —**ded′i·ca′tor** *n.*

**ded·i·ca·tion** (ded′ə·kā′shən) *n.* 1 A dedicating or being dedicated. 2 An inscription in a book, etc., as to a friend or cause.

**de·duce** (di·d′ōōs′) *v.t.* **·duced, ·duc·ing** 1 To derive as a conclusion; infer. 2 To trace, as derivation or origin. [< L *deducere* < *de*- down + *ducere* to lead] —**de·duc′i·ble** *adj.*

**de·duct** (di·dukt′) *v.t.* To subtract; take away. [< L *deductus*, pp. of *deducere*. See DEDUCE.]

**deed** (dēd) *n.* 1 Anything done; an act. 2 A notable achievement or action. 3 Action performed, as opposed to words. 4 *Law* A written instrument under seal, whether a bond, agreement, or contract, but most frequently used in the conveyance of real estate. —**in deed** In fact; actually. —*v.t.* To convey or transfer by deed. [< OE *dǣd*]

**deem** (dēm) *v.t. & v.i.* To judge; think; regard; believe. [< OE *dēman* judge]

**deep-freeze** (dēp′frēz′) *v.t.* -froze or -freezed, -fro·zen or -freezed, -freez·ing To freeze (foods) quickly to preserve natural flavor.

**de·face** (di·fās′) *v.t.* ·faced, ·fac·ing To mar or disfigure the surface of. [< OF *des-* down, away + *face* face] —**de·face′a·ble** *adj.* —**de·face′ment,** **de·fac′er** *n.*

**de·fame** (di·fām′) *v.t.* ·famed, ·fam·ing To attack the good name or reputation of. [< L *dis-* away, from + *fama* a report, reputation] —**def·a·ma·tion** (def′ə·mā′shən), **de·fam′er** *n.* —**de·fam·a·to·ry** (di·fam′ə·tôr′ē) *adj.* — Syn. revile, besmirch, slander, libel.

**de·fault** (di·fôlt′) *n.* A failure to fulfill an obligation or duty; failure to appear, as in a contest or a legal suit. —**in default of** Owing to lack or failure of. —*v.i.* 1 To fail or neglect to fulfill or do a duty, obligation, etc. 2 To fail to meet financial obligations. 3 *Law* To fail to appear in court. 4 In sports, to fail to compete or complete a game, etc. —*v.t.* 5 To fail to perform or pay. 6 In sports, to fail to compete in, as a game; also, to forfeit by default. [< L *de-* down + *fallere* deceive] —**de·fault′er** *n.*

**de·feat** (di·fēt′) *v.t.* 1 To overcome in any contest; vanquish. 2 To thwart or frustrate, as plans. 3 *Law* To make void; annul. —*n.* 1 The act of defeating. 2 A failure to win or succeed. [< OF *defaire* undo]

**de·fect** (di·fekt′, dē′fekt) *n.* 1 Lack or absence of something essential; deficiency. 2 An imperfection; failing; fault. —*v.i.* (di·fekt′) To desert; go over to the enemy or opposition. [< L *deficere* fail] —**de·fec′tor** *n.* —Syn. *n.* 2 blemish, flaw, drawback.

**de·fend** (di·fend′) *v.t.* 1 To shield from attack; protect. 2 To justify or vindicate; support. 3 *Law* a To act in behalf of (an accused). b To contest, as a claim, charge, or suit. 4 In sports, to try to keep one's opponent from scoring at (a goal, etc.). —*v.i.* 5 To make a defense. [< L *de-* down, away + *fendere* to strike] —**de·fend′a·ble** *adj.* —**de·fend′er** *n.*

**de·fense** (di·fens′) *n.* 1 The act of defending or guarding. 2 The state of being defended. 3 Anything that defends. 4 A plea or statement that supports or justifies something.

5 *Law* a The arguments brought forth by a defendant or his legal counsel. b A defendant and his lawyer or lawyers. 6 Protection of oneself, as in boxing, or of one's goal, as in team sports. 7 Any group that is defending, as in sports. *Brit. sp.* **de·fence.** —**de·fense′less** *adj.* —**de·fense′less·ly** *adv.* —**de·fense′less·ness** *n.*

**de·fen·si·ble** (di·fen′sə·bəl) *adj.* Capable of being defended or justified. —**de·fen′si·bil′i·ty,** **de·fen′si·ble·ness** *n.* —**de·fen′si·bly** *adv.*

**de·fer** (di·fûr′) *v.t. & v.i.* ·ferred, ·fer·ring To delay; put off to some other time; postpone. [< L *differre* to distract] —**de·fer′ra·ble** *adj.* —**de·fer′ment** *n.*

**def·er·ence** (def′ər·əns) *n.* 1 Respectful yielding. 2 Polite respect; regard. —**def′er·ent** *adj.*

**def·er·en·tial** (def′ə·ren′shəl) *adj.* Marked by deference; respectful; courteous. —**def′er·en′tial·ly** *adv.*

**de·fi·ance** (di·fi′əns) *n.* 1 Bold opposition; disposition to oppose or resist. 2 The act of defying.

**de·fi·ant** (di·fi′ənt) *adj.* Showing or characterized by defiance; resisting boldly. [< OF, pr.p. of *defier.* See DEFY.] —**de·fi′ant·ly** *adv.*

**de·fi·cien·cy** (di·fish′ən·sē) *n. pl.* ·cies 1 The state of being deficient. 2 A lack; insufficiency. Also **de·fi′cience.**

**de·fi·cient** (di·fish′ənt) *adj.* 1 Lacking an adequate or proper supply; insufficient. 2 Lacking some essential; incomplete. [< L *deficere* to lack] —**de·fi′cient·ly** *adv.*

**def·i·cit** (def′ə·sit) *n.* The amount of money lacking in a required or expected sum. [L, it is lacking]

**de·file** (di·fīl′) *v.t.* ·filed, ·fil·ing 1 To make foul or dirty; pollute. 2 To corrupt the purity of. 3 To sully; profane (a name, reputation, etc.). 4 To render ceremonially unclean. [< OF *de-* down + *fouler* trample] —**de·file′ment,** **de·fil′er** *n.*

**de·fine** (di·fīn′) *v.t.* ·fined, ·fin·ing 1 To state the meaning of (a word, etc.). 2 To describe or give the characteristics of. 3 To determine and specify the limits of. 4 To determine and fix the boundaries of. 5 To show or bring out the form or outline of. [< L *de-* down + *finire* finish] —**de·fin′a·ble** *adj.* —**de·fin′er** *n.*

**def·i·nite** (def′ə·nit) *adj.* 1 Having precise limits. 2 Precise; clear, as in meaning. 3 Certain; sure. 4 *Gram.* Limiting; particulariz-

ing: The *definite* article in English is "the".
—**def′i·nite·ly** *adv.* —**def′i·nite·ness** *n.*

**def·i·ni·tion** (def′ə·nish′ən) *n.* 1 A defining or being defined. 2 A statement of the meaning of a word, phrase, etc. 3 A statement describing or making clear an object, process, etc. 4 The state of being clear, definite, etc. 5 The determining of the outline, character, or limits of anything. 6 *Optics* The power of a lens to give a distinct image at whatever magnification. 7 In television and radio, the clarity of detail in the transmitted images or sounds.

**de·fla·tion** (di·flā′shən) *n.* 1 The act of deflating or the condition of being deflated. 2 A decrease in the amount of currency in circulation in a country, resulting in a decline in prices. —**de·fla·tion·ar·y** (di·flā′shən·er′ē) *adj.*

**de·flect** (di·flekt′) *v.t.* & *v.i.* To turn aside; swerve or cause to swerve from a course. [< L *de-* down + *flectere* bend] —**de·flec′tion, de·flec′tor** *n.* —**de·flec′tive** *adj.*

**de·fo·li·ate** (dē·fō′lē·āt) *v.t.* ·at·ed, ·at·ing To deprive or strip of leaves. [< L *de-* down + *folium* leaf] —**de·fo′li·a′tion, de·fo′li·a′tor** *n.*

**de·form** (di·fôrm′) *v.t.* 1 To distort the form or shape of. 2 To make ugly or dishonorable. —*v.i.* 3 To become deformed or disfigured. —**def·or·ma·tion** (def′ər·mā′shən) *n.*

**de·fraud** (di·frôd′) *v.t.* To take or withhold property, etc., from by fraud; cheat. —**de·fraud·a·tion** (dē′frô·dā′shən), **de·fraud′er** *n.*

**de·fray** (di·frā′) *v.t.* To pay for; bear the expense of. [< OF *de-* away + *frai* cost, charge] —**de·fray′a·ble** *adj.* —**de·fray′al, de·fray′ment, de·fray′er** *n.*

**de·frost** (dē·frôst′, ·frost′) *v.t.* 1 To remove ice or frost from. —*v.i.* 2 To be rid of ice or frost.

**deft** (deft) *adj.* Skillful; adroit; dexterous. [< OE *gedǣfte* meek, gentle] —**deft′ly** *adv.* —**deft′ness** *n.*

**de·funct** (di·fungkt′) *adj.* Having passed out of existence or life; no longer functioning or alive: a *defunct* publication. [< L *de-* not + *fungi* perform]

**de·fy** (di·fī′) *v.t.* ·fied, ·fy·ing 1 To resist openly or boldly. 2 To challenge; dare: to *defy* a rival politician to make public his tax returns. 3 To resist successfully; baffle; obstruct: to *defy* definition. [< OF *defier* < Med. L *dis-* not + *fidare* be faithful]

**de·gen·er·ate** (di·jen′ə·rāt) *v.i.* ·at·ed, ·at ing

To become worse or inferior. 2 *Biol.* To revert to a lower type; deteriorate. —*adj.* (di·jen′ər·it) 1 Having become worse or inferior; deteriorated. 2 Morally depraved or perverted. —*n.* (·it) 1 A deteriorated or degraded animal or human. 2 A morally depraved or perverted person. [< L *de-* down, away + *generare* create] —**de·gen′er·ate·ly** *adv.* —**de·gen′er·a′tive** *adj.* —**de·gen′er·ate·ness** *n.*

**de·grade** (di·grād′) *v.* ·grad·ed, ·grad·ing *v.t.* 1 To reduce in rank, status, quality, etc. 2 To debase or lower in character, morals, etc. 3 To bring into contempt; dishonor. 4 *Geol.* To reduce the height of by erosion. 5 *Chem.* To break down (an organic compound) into simpler parts. —*v.i.* 6 To degenerate; become of a lower type. [< L *de-* down + *gradus* position, step]

**de·gree** (di·grē′) *n.* 1 One of a succession of steps, grades, or stages. 2 Relative rank, position, or dignity: an executive of high *degree.* 3 Relative extent, amount, or intensity: burns of the first *degree.* 4 Relative manner, condition, ability, etc. 5 *Gram.* One of the forms in which an adjective or adverb is compared: "Worst" is the superlative *degree* of "bad." 6 An academic rank or title conferred by an institution of learning. 7 One remove in the direct line of descent. 8 A subdivision or unit on a scale, as for temperature. 9 The 360th part of a circle. 10 *Math.* The power to which an algebraic quantity is raised. 11 *Music* a A line or space of a staff. b The interval between two such lines or spaces. 12 *Law* A grade of seriousness: murder in the first *degree.* —**by degrees** Little by little; gradually. —**to a degree** 1 Extremely. 2 Somewhat. [< L *de-* down + *gradus* a step]

**de·hisce** (di·his′) *v.i.* ·hisced, ·hisc·ing *Biol.* To burst open, as a cocoon or a seed pod. [< L *de-* down + *hiscere* to gape, yawn] —**de·his′cence** *n.* —**de·his′cent** *adj.*

**de·hy·drate** (dē·hī′drāt) *v.* ·drat·ed, ·drat·ing *v.t.* 1 To deprive of water. 2 To remove water from. —*v.i.* 3 To suffer loss of water. —**de′hy·dra′tion, de·hy′dra·tor** *n.*

**de·ice** (dē·īs′) *v.t.* & *v.i.* ·iced, ·ic·ing 1 To remove ice from. 2 To prevent ice forming on. —**de·ic′er** *n.*

**de·i·fy** (dē′ə·fī) *v.t.* ·fied, ·fy·ing 1 To make a god of; rank as a deity. 2 To regard or worship as a god. [< L *deus* god + *facere* make] —**de·if′ic** (·if′ik) *adj.* —**de·i·fi·ca·tion** (dē′ə·fə·kā′shən), **de′i·fi′er** *n.*

**deign** (dān) *v.i.* 1 To think it befitting or suitable (to do something). —*v.t.* 2 To condescend to grant or allow. [< L *dignari* to deem worthy]

**de·i·ty** (dē′ə·tē) *n. pl.* ·ties 1 A god, goddess, or divine person. 2 Divine nature or status; godhead; divinity. —**the Deity** God. [< L *deus* a god]

**de·ject** (di·jekt′) *v.t.* To depress in spirit; make unhappy. [< L *de-* down + *jacere* throw] —**de·jec′tion** *n.*

**de·lay** (di·lā′) *v.t.* 1 To put off to a later time; postpone; defer. 2 To cause to be late; detain. —*v.i.* 3 To linger; procrastinate. —*n.* 1 The act of delaying or the condition of being delayed. 2 The period of time during which a thing or person is delayed. [< L *de-* off + *laxare* to slacken] —**de·lay′er** *n.* —**Syn.** *n.* 1 deferment, postponement, stop, stay.

**de·lec·ta·ble** (di·lek′tə·bəl) *adj.* Giving pleasure; delightful; charming. [< L *delectare* to please] —**de·lec′ta·bil′i·ty, de·lec′ta·ble·ness** *n.* —**de·lec′ta·bly** *adv.*

**de·lec·ta·tion** (dē′lek·tā′shən) *n.* 1 Delight; enjoyment. 2 Amusement; entertainment.

**del·e·gate** (del′ə·gāt, ·git) *n.* 1 A person empowered to act for others; deputy; representative. 2 *U.S.* A nonvoting participant representing a Territory in the House of Representatives. 3 A member of the House of Delegates. —*v.t.* (·gāt) ·gat·ed, ·gat·ing 1 To send as a representative, with authority to act; depute. 2 To commit or entrust (powers, authority, etc.) to another. —*adj.* (·gāt, ·git) Sent as a deputy. [< L *de-* down + *legare* send]

**del·e·ga·tion** (del′ə·gā′shən) *n.* 1 The act of delegating. 2 A group of delegates; also, delegates collectively.

**del·e·te·ri·ous** (del′ə·tir′ē·əs) *adj.* Causing moral or physical injury. [< Gk. *dēlētērios* harmful] —**del′e·te′re·ous·ly** *adv.* —**del′ e·te′ri·ous·ness** *n.*

**de·lib·er·ate** (di·lib′ər·āt) *v.* ·at·ed, ·at·ing *v.i.* 1 To consider carefully and at length. 2 To consider reasons or arguments so as to reach a decision. —*v.t.* 3 To think about or consider carefully; weigh. —*adj.* (di·lib′ər·it) 1 Acting with or characterized by deliberation; not hasty. 2 Done after deliberation; intentional. 3 Slow and careful, as in movement. [< L *de-* completely + *librare* weigh] —**de·lib′er·ate·ly** *adv.* —**de·lib′er ·ate·ness** *n.* —**Syn.** *adj.* 1 careful, thoughtful. 2 studied. 3 measured, unhurried.

**del·i·ca·cy** (del′ə·kə·sē) *n. pl.* ·cies 1 The qual-

ity of being delicate. 2 Fragility or frailty, as of health. 3 Need for careful or subtle treatment: a question of great *delicacy*. 4 Refinement of feeling, appreciation, etc. 5 Sensitiveness of touch, response, performance, etc. 6 A fine consideration for others. 7 A choice bit of food.

**del·i·cate** (del′ə·kit) *adj.* 1 Nicely light, mild, subtle, etc., as in flavor or color. 2 Exceedingly fine in quality, construction, texture, etc. 3 Very subtle: a *delicate* distinction. 4 Frail; fragile. 5 Easily injured or disordered: a *delicate* stomach. 6 Requiring cautious or subtle handling or treatment. 7 Nicely sensitive in feeling, appreciating, discriminating, etc: a *delicate* ear for music. 8 Extremely accurate or sensitive, as an instrument. 9 Finely skillful in touch or technique. 10 Tactful and considerate of others. [< L *delicatus* pleasing] —**del′i· cate·ly** *adv.* —**del′i·cate·ness** *n.*

**de·li·cious** (di·lish′əs) *adj.* Extremely pleasant or enjoyable, esp. to the taste. [< L *delicia* a delight] —**de·li′cious·ly** *adv.* —**de·li′ cious·ness** *n.*

**de·light·ful** (di·līt′fəl) *adj.* Affording delight; very pleasing; charming. —**de·light′ful·ly** *adv.* —**de·light′ful·ness** *n.*

**de·lin·e·ate** (di·lin′ē·āt) *v.t.* ·at·ed, ·at·ing 1 To draw in outline; trace out. 2 To portray pictorially. 3 To describe verbally. [< L *de-* completely + *linea* a line] —**de·lin′e·a′tion, de·lin′e·a′tor** *n.* —**de·lin′e·a′tive** *adj.*

**de·lin·quen·cy** (di·ling′kwən·sē) *n. pl.* ·cies 1 Neglect of duty. 2 A fault; offense. 3 Illegal or antisocial behavior of a juvenile.

**de·lin·quent** (di·ling′kwənt) *adj.* 1 Neglectful of or failing in duty or obligation; faulty. 2 Due and unpaid, as taxes. —*n.* A person who is delinquent, esp. a young person who engages in illegal or antisocial behavior. [< L *de-* down, away + *linquere* leave] —**de·lin′quent·ly** *adv.*

**de·lir·i·ous** (di·lir′ē·əs) *adj.* 1 Suffering from delirium. 2 Pertaining to or caused by delirium. 3 Extremely excited. —**de·lir′i·ous·ly** *adv.* —**de·lir′i·ous·ness** *n.*

**de·lir·i·um** (di·lir′ē·əm) *n.* 1 A temporary mental disturbance associated with fever, intoxication, etc., and marked by agitation, hallucinations, and incoherence. 2 Intense excitement; frenzy. [< L *delirare* to deviate from a straight line]

**de·liv·er** (di·liv′ər) *v.t.* 1 To hand over; transfer possession of. 2 To carry and distribute: to *deliver* mail. 3 To utter; say: to *deliver* a

speech. **4** To assist (a female) in the birth of (a child). **5** To free from evil, danger, etc.; rescue. **6** To send forth; discharge; emit. **7** To give; strike, as a blow. **8** To throw or pitch, as a ball. **9** *Informal* To bring (votes, etc.) to the support of a political candidate. —*v.i.* **10** *Informal* To achieve good or proper results; perform well. [< L *de-* down, away + *liberare* set free] —de·liv′er·a·ble *adj.* —de·liv′er·er *n.*

**del·ta** (del′tə) *n.* **1** The fourth letter in the Greek alphabet. (Δ, δ). **2** An alluvial silt deposit, usu. triangular, at or in the mouth of a river. —del·ta·ic (del·tā′ik) *adj.*

**de·lude** (di·lōōd′) *v.t.* ·lud·ed, ·lud·ing To mislead the mind or judgment of; deceive. [< L *de-* down, away + *ludere* to play] —de·lud′er *n.*

**del·uge** (del′yōōj) *v.t.* ·uged, ·ug·ing **1** To flood with water; inundate. **2** To overwhelm: He *deluged* her with compliments. —*n.* **1** A great flood; inundation. **2** Anything that comes like a flood. —the Deluge The flood in the time of Noah. *Gen.* 7. [< L *diluere* wash away]

**de·lu·sion** (di·lōō′zhən) *n.* **1** The act of deluding or the state of being deluded. **2** A false, irrational, and persistent belief. —de·lu′sion·al *adj.*

**de·lu·sive** (di·lōō′siv) *adj.* Tending to deluce; misleading; deceptive. Also **de·lu·so·ry** (di·lōō′sər·ē) —de·lu′sive·ly *adv.* —de·lu′sive·ness *n.*

**delve** (delv) *v.* delved, delv·ing *v.i.* To make careful investigation for facts, knowledge, etc.: to *delve* into a crime. [< OE *delfan*] —delv′er *n.*

**de·mand** (di·mand′, ·mänd′) *v.t.* **1** To ask for boldly; insist upon. **2** To claim as due; ask for authoritatively. **3** To ask to know; inquire formally. **4** To have need for; require. **5** *Law* **a** To summon to court. **b** To make formal claim to (property). —*v.i.* **6** To make a demand. —*n.* **1** The act of demanding, or that which is demanded. **2** A requirement; claim; need. **3** *Econ.* **a** The desire to possess combined with the ability to purchase. **b** The amount of a given commodity people will buy at a certain price. —in demand Desired; sought after. —on demand On presentation: a note payable *on demand.* [< L *de-* down, away + *mandare* to command; order] —de·mand′a·ble *adj.* —de·mand′er *n.*

**de·mean** (di·mēn′) *v.t.* To lower in character

or reputation; degrade; debase. [< MEAN²]

**de·ment·ed** (di·men′tid) *adj.* Depriv[...] son; insane. —de·ment′ed·ly [...] de·ment′ed·ness *n.*

**dementia prae·cox** (prē′koks) *Obs* PHRENIA. [NL, premature dementia] mentia prae′cox.

**de·mer·it** (di·mer′it) *n.* **1** In school mark for failure or misconduc[...] surable conduct. [< L *demerere* d[...]

**de·mil·i·ta·rize** (dē·mil′ə·tə·rīz′) *v.* ·riz·ing **1** To remove the military [...] free from militarism. **2** To remov[...] equipment and troops from an[...] neutral, as an area or zone. —[...] ta·ri·za′tion *n.*

**de·mise** (di·mīz′) *n.* **1** Death. **2** *Law* fer or conveyance of rights or es[...] ·mised, ·mis·ing *v.t.* **1** To bestow [...] power) by death or abdication. [...] lease (an estate) for life or for [...] years. —*v.i.* **3** To pass by will or in[...] [< OF *demettre* send away] —de[...] *adj.*

**de·moc·ra·cy** (di·mok′rə·sē) *n.* pl. ·c[...] ernment in which political contro[...] by all the people, either directly [...] resentatives whom they elect. **2** [...] governed. **3** Political, legal, or soc[...] ity. [< Gk. *dēmos* people + *kratee*[...]

**Dem·o·crat** (dem′ə·krat) *n.* A mem[...] Democratic party in the U.S.

**de·mog·ra·phy** (di·mog′rə·fē) *n.* T[...] dealing with vital and social sta[...] Gk. *dēmos* people + -GRAPHY] [...] ′ra·pher, de·mog′ra·phist *n.* [...] graph·ic (dem′ə·graf′ik) or ·i·c[...] dem′o·graph′i·cal·ly *adv.*

**de·mol·ish** (di·mol′ish) *v.t.* **1** To t[...] raze, as a building. **2** To destro[...] ruin. [< L *de-* down + *moliri* build[...] l′ish·er, de·mol′ish·ment *n.*

**dem·o·li·tion** (dem′ə·lish′ən) *n.* Th[...] sult of demolishing; destruction. li′tion·ist *n.*

**de·mon** (dē′mən) *n.* **1** An evil spirit [...] wicked or cruel person. **3** A perso[...] energy, skill, etc. [< Gk *daimōn*] [...] ·ic (di·mon′ik) *adj.* —de·mon′i·c[...]

**dem·on·strate** (dem′ən·strāt) *v.* [...] ·strat·ing *v.t.* **1** To explain or d[...] use of experiments, examples, et[...] plain or show the operation or u[...] prove or show by logic; make evi[...] exhibit; make clear, as emotions.[...]

ake part in a public demonstration. 6 To make a show of military force. [< L de- completely + *monstrare* show, point out]

on·stra·tion (dem'ən·strā'shən) n. 1 The ct of making known. 2 Cogent proof by he use of facts, principles, and arguments. A presentation of how something operates is done. 4 An organized public exhibition welcome, approval, or condemnation, as y a mass meeting or procession. 5 A show military force or invincibility. —Syn. 2 evence, testimony, substantiation.

mor·al·ize (di·môr'əl·īz, -mor'-, dē'-) v.t. sed, ·iz·ing 1 To undermine the morale of. To throw into disorder. —de·mor'al·i·za·ion, de·mor'al·iz'er n.

ur (di·mûr') v.i. ·murred, ·mur·ring 1 To fer objections. 2 To delay; hesitate. 3 Law interpose a demurrer. —n. 1 A delay. 2 objection. [< L de- completely + *morari* delay]

ure (di·myŏŏr') adj. 1 Sedate; modest. 2 ffecting modesty; coy. [< OF *demore*] —:·mure'ly adv. —de·mure'ness n.

i·al (di·nī'əl) n. 1 A refusal to grant a reuest. 2 A declaration that a statement is ntrue; contradiction. 3 A disowning or dis-owal; rejection. 4 A refusal to agree with believe in a doctrine, proposal, etc. —n. 1 declining, rebuff. 3 repudiation, reunciation.

i·zen (den'ə·zən) n. 1 A resident; inhabnt. 2 A person who frequents a place. 3 person, animal, or thing at home in a reon, although not a native. —v.t. Brit. NAT-RALIZE. [< AF *deinz* inside] —den'i·zen·a'on n.

om·i·na·tion (di·nom'ə·nā'shən) n. 1 The t of naming. 2 The name or designation a class of things. 3 A specific unit of lue: coins of all *denominations*. 4 A reli-ous sect or group having a specific name. —de·nom'i·na'tion·al adj. —de·nom'i·na'-on·al·ism, de·nom'i·na'tion·al·ist n. —·nom'i·na'tion·al·ly adv.

ounce (di·nouns') v.t. ·nounced, ·nounc-g 1 To condemn openly and vehemently; veigh against. 2 To inform against; ac-se. 3 To give formal notice of the termi-ation of (a treaty, truce, etc.). [< L de-wn + *nuntiare* proclaim, announce] —·nounce'ment, de·nounc'er n. —Syn. 1 cry, charge, attack, censure, curse.

se (dens) adj. dens·er, dens·est 1 Having parts crowded closely together; com-pact; 2 Hard to penetrate. 3 Stupid; dull-

witted. [< L *densus*] —dense'ly adv. —dense'ness n.

den·si·ty (den'sə·tē) n. pl. ·ties 1 The state or quality of being dense; compactness. 2 Stupidity. 3 Physics The mass of a substance per unit of its volume. 4 The number of units, as persons, families, etc., per specified area.

den·tal (den'təl) adj. 1 Of or pertaining to the teeth. 2 Of or pertaining to dentistry. 3 Phonet. Produced with the tip of the tongue against or near the upper front teeth. —n. Phonet. A dental consonant. [< L dens, dentis a tooth]

den·tist (den'tist) n. One who practices dentistry. [< F dent a tooth]

den·ture (den'chər) n. A block or set of teeth, esp. artificial ones. [< F dent tooth] —den'tur·al adj.

de·nude (di·nŏŏd') v.t. ·nud·ed, ·nud·ing 1 To strip the covering from. 2 Geol. To wear away and expose by erosion. [< L de- down, completely + *nudare* to strip] —den·u·da·tion (den'yŏŏ·dā'shən, dē'nyŏŏ-) n.

de·nun·ci·a·tion (di·nun'sē·ā'shən) n. 1 The act of denouncing, esp. a vehement and public condemnation. —de·nun'ci·a'tive adj. —de·nun'ci·a'tive·ly adv.

de·ny (di·nī') v.t. ·nied, ·ny·ing 1 To declare to be untrue; contradict. 2 To reject (a doctrine, etc.) as false or not real. 3 To refuse to give; withhold. 4 To refuse (someone) a request. 5 To refuse to acknowledge; disown; repudiate. 6 To refuse access to. — deny oneself To refuse oneself a gratification. [< L de- completely + *negare* refuse]

de·o·dor·ant (dē·ō'dər·ənt) adj. Destroying, absorbing, or disguising bad odors. —n. A deodorant substance, as a cream, spray, etc. [< DE- + L *odorare* have an odor]

de·o·dor·ize (dē·ō'dər·īz) v.t. ·ized, ·iz·ing To modify, destroy, or disguise the odor of. — de·o'dor·i·za'tion, de·o'dor·iz'er n.

de·ox·i·dize (dē·ok'sə·dīz) v.t. ·dized, ·diz·ing To remove oxygen, esp. chemically combined oxygen, from. —de·ox'i·di·za'tion, de·ox'i·diz'er n.

de·part (di·pärt') v.i. 1 To go away; leave. 2 To deviate; differ; vary: with from. 3 To die. — v.t. 4 To leave: to depart this life. [< OF de- away + *partir* divide]

de·part·ment (di·pärt'mənt) n. 1 A separate and distinct part, branch, division, or subdivision of a government, business, school, etc.: the accounting department; French depart-ment. 2 A special area of activity, skill, etc.:

Cooking is my *department*. 3 In France, a government administrative district. [< OF *departir* divide] —de·part·men·tal (dē′pärt ·men′təl) *adj.* —de′part·men′tal·ly *adv.* — de′part·men′tal·ism *n.*

de·par·ture (di·pär′chər) *n.* 1 The act of departing or leaving. 2 The act of deviating from a method, set of ideas, etc.: with *from*. 3 A starting out, as on a new venture.

de·pend (di·pend′) *v.i.* 1 To trust; have full reliance: with *on* or *upon*. 2 To be determined by or contingent on something else: with *on* or *upon*. 3 To rely for maintenance, support, etc.: with *on* or *upon*. 4 To hang down: with *from*. [< L *de-* down + *pendere* hang]

de·pict (di·pikt′) *v.t.* 1 To portray or represent by drawing, sculpturing, painting, etc. 2 To describe verbally. [< L *depictus*, pp. of *depingere* to paint] —de·pic′ter, de·pic′tion *n.*

de·plete (di·plēt′) *v.t.* ·plet·ed, ·plet·ing 1 To reduce or lessen, as by use, exhaustion, or waste. 2 To empty wholly or partially. [< L *de-* not + *plere* to fill] —de·ple′tion *n.* — de·ple′tive *adj.*

de·plore (di·plôr′, -plōr′) *v.t.* ·plored, ·plor·ing To feel or express deep regret or concern for; lament. [< L *de-* completely + *plorare* bewail]

de·pop·u·late (dē·pop′yə·lāt) *v.t.* ·lat·ed, ·lat·ing To remove the inhabitants from, by massacre, famine, etc. [< L *de-* away + *populus* people] —de·pop′u·la′tion, de·pop′u·la′tor *n.*

de·port (di·pôrt′, -pōrt′) *v.t.* 1 To banish or expel from a country. 2 To behave or conduct (oneself). [< L *de-* away + *portare* carry] —de′por·ta′tion *n.*

de·pose (di·pōz′) *v.* ·posed, ·pos·ing *v.t.* 1 To deprive of official rank or office; oust, as a king. 2 To state on oath. —*v.i.* 3 To bear witness. [< OF *de-* down + *poser* put] —de·pos′a·ble *adj.* —de·pos′al *n.*

de·pos·it (di·poz′it) *v.t.* 1 To give in trust or for safekeeping. 2 To give as part payment or as security. 3 To set down; put. 4 To cause, as sediment, to form a layer. —*n.* 1 Money deposited, as in a bank. 2 Something, as money, given as security or first payment. 3 The act of depositing. 4 In Canada, money put up as evidence of good faith by a candidate for Parliament or a Legislature. 5 A depositary. 6 Something, as sediment, deposited. 7 An accumulated mass of iron, oil, salt, etc. —on deposit Placed for safekeeping. [< L *deponere* lay aside]

de·pos·i·tar·y (di·poz′ə·ter′ē) *n. pl.* ·tar·ies 1 A

person entrusted with anything for safekeeping; a trustee. 2 A place where things are stored; depository.

de·pot (dē′pō, *Mil. & Brit.* dep′ō) *n.* 1 A warehouse or storehouse. 2 A railroad or bus station. 3 *Mil.* A storehouse or collecting station for personnel or materiel. [< L *depositum* a pledge, deposit]

de·prave (di·prāv′) *v.t.* ·praved, ·prav·ing To render bad or worse, esp. in morals; corrupt; pervert. [< L *de-* completely + *pravus* corrupt, wicked] —de·praved′ *adj.* —de·prav′er, dep·ra·va·tion (dep′rə·vā′shən) *n.*

dep·re·cate (dep′rə·kāt) *v.t.* ·cat·ed, ·cat·ing 1 To express disapproval of or regret for. 2 To belittle; depreciate. [< L *de-* away + *precari* pray] —dep′re·cat′ing·ly *adv.* —dep′re·ca′tion, dep′re·ca′tor *n.* • The use of deprecate as a synonym for depreciate is regarded as incorrect by many, but it is increasingly common: While not wishing to deprecate their motives, he did question their judgement.

dep·re·ca·to·ry (dep′rə·kə·tôr′ē, -tō′rē) *adj.* 1 Belittling; apologetic. 2 Tending to deprecate; disparaging. Also dep′re·ca′tive (-kā′tiv) *adj.*

dep·re·date (dep′rə·dāt) *v.t. & v.i.* ·dat·ed, ·dat·ing To prey upon; pillage; plunder. [< L *de-* completely + *praeda* booty, prey] — dep′re·da′tion, dep′re·da′tor *n.*

de·press (di·pres′) *v.t.* 1 To lower the spirits of; sadden. 2 To lessen in vigor, force, or energy. 3 To lessen the price or value of. 4 To press or push down. [< L *de-* down + *primere* to press] —de·press′ing *adj.* — de·press′ing·ly *adv.* —de·pres′sor (-ər) *n.*

de·pres·sion (di·presh′ən) *n.* 1 The act of depressing, or the state of being depressed. 2 Low spirits or vitality. 3 A low or hollow place. 4 A period marked by a severe decline in business or trade, unemployment, etc. 5 Low atmospheric pressure; also, a region of low atmospheric pressure. 6 *Psychiatry* A profound, immobilizing dejection and despair. —de·pres′sive *adj.* —de·pres′sive·ly *adv.*

dep·ri·va·tion (dep′rə·vā′shən) *n.* 1 The act of depriving, or the state of being deprived. 2 Loss; want.

de·prive (di·prīv′) *v.t.* ·prived, ·priv·ing 1 To take something away from; divest. 2 To keep from acquiring, using, or enjoying. [< L *de-* completely + *privare* strip, remove] — de·priv′a·ble *adj.*

depth (depth) *n.* 1 The state or quality of being

deep. 2 Extent or distance downward, inward, or backward. 3 *Usu. pl.* The deepest part. 4 *Usu. pl.* The innermost part. 5 *Usu. pl.* The part of greatest intensity: the *depths* of despair. 6 Profundity of thought or feeling. 7 Intensity of color or shade. 8 Lowness of pitch. —**in depth** In a thorough and extensive manner. [ME *depthe*]

**dep·u·ta·tion** (dep′yə·tā′shən) *n.* 1 A person or persons acting for another; a delegation. 2 The act of deputing, or the state of being deputed.

**dep·u·ty** (dep′yə·tē) *n. pl.* **·ties** 1 One appointed to act for another; representative agent. 2 A member of a legislative assembly in certain countries. [<OF *deputer* depute]

**de·range** (di·rānj′) *v.t.* **·ranged,** **·rang·ing** 1 To disturb the arrangement of; disorder. 2 To make insane. [<F *déranger*]

**der·e·lict** (der′ə·likt) *adj.* 1 Neglectful of obligation; remiss. 2 Deserted or abandoned. — *n.* 1 That which is deserted or abandoned, as a ship at sea. 2 A person considered as socially outcast; a vagrant. [<L *de-* completely + *relinquere* abandon]

**de·ride** (di·rī′) *v.t.* **·rid·ed,** **·rid·ing** To treat or laugh at with contempt; ridicule. [<L *de-* completely + *ridere* laugh, mock] —**de·ri·d′er** *n.* —**de·rid′ing·ly** *adv.*

**de·ri·sion** (di·rizh′ən) *n.* 1 The act of deriding; ridicule; scorn. 2 An object of ridicule or scorn.

**de·ri·sive** (di·rī′siv) *adj.* Expressive of or characterized by derision. **Also de·ri·so·ry** (di·rī′sər·ē). —**de·ri′sive·ly** *adv.* —**de·ri′sive·ness** *n.*

**der·i·va·tion** (der′ə·vā′shən) *n.* 1 The act of deriving, or the condition of being derived. 2 Something derived; a derivative. 3 Origin; source. 4 The tracing of a word from its origins; also, a statement of this. 5 The formation of a word from another word, as by the addition of a prefix or suffix. —**der′i·va′tion·al** *adj.*

**de·riv·a·tive** (di·riv′ə·tiv) *adj.* Derived; not original or basic. —*n.* 1 That which is derived. 2 A word developed from a basic word, as by the addition of a prefix or suffix. 3 *Chem.* A compound formed or regarded as being formed from another. —**de·riv′a·tive·ly** *adv.* —**de·riv′a·tive·ness** *n.*

**de·rive** (di·rīv′) *v.* **·rived,** **·riv·ing** *v.t.* 1 To draw or receive, as from a source, principle, or root; be descended from. 2 To deduce; draw, as a conclusion. 3 To trace the de-

rivation of (a word). 4 *Chem.* To obtain (a compound) from another. —*v.i.* 5 To have derivation; originate. [<L *de-* from + *rivus* stream] —**de·riv′a·ble** *adj.* —**de·riv′er** *n.*

**de·rog·a·to·ry** (di·rog′ə·tôr′ē, -tō′rē) *adj.* Harmful to the reputation or esteem of a person or thing; disparaging. —**de·rog′a·to′ri·ly** *adv.*

**der·rick** (der′ik) *n.* 1 An apparatus with a hinged boom for hoisting heavy objects into place. 2 The framework over the mouth of an oil well or similar drill hole. [<*Derrick*, 17th c. London hangman]

**de·scend** (di·send′) *v.i.* 1 To move from a higher to a lower point. 2 To slope or incline downward. 3 To stoop; lower oneself. 4 To come down by inheritance; be inherited. 5 To be derived by heredity: with *from.* 6 To come overwhelmingly, as in an attack or visit: with *on* or *upon.* 7 To pass, as from the general to the particular. 8 *Astron.* To move southward or toward the horizon, as a star. —*v.t.* 9 To move from an upper to a lower part of; go down. [<L *de-* down + *scandere* climb] —**de·scend′er** *n.*

**de·scent** (di·sent′) *n.* 1 The act of descending. 2 Decline; deterioration. 3 A declivity; slope. 4 Lineage; ancestry. 5 A genealogical generation. 6 A hostile raid or invasion. 7 The transmission of an estate by inheritance.

**de·scribe** (di·skrīb′) *v.t.* **·scribed,** **·scrib·ing** 1 To give an account of; represent with spoken or written words. 2 To draw the figure of; trace; outline. [<L *de-* down + *scribere* write] —**de·scrib′a·ble** *adj.* —**de·scrib′er** *n.* —**Syn.** 1 narrate, relate, recount, portray, characterize.

**de·scrip·tion** (di·skrip′shən) *n.* 1 The act of describing. 2 An account, statement, or report that describes. 3 A drawing or tracing. 4 Sort; kind; nature.

**de·scrip·tive** (di·skrip′tiv) *adj.* Characterized by or containing description; serving to describe. —**de·scrip′tive·ly** *adv.* —**de·scrip′tive·ness** *n.*

**de·scry** (di·skrī′) *v.t.* **·scried,** **·scry·ing** 1 To discover with the eye; discern; detect. 2 To discover by observation. [< OF *des-* away + *crier* to cry] —**de·scri′er** *n.*

**des·e·crate** (des′ə·krāt) *v.t.* **·crat·ed,** **·crat·ing** To divert from a sacred to a common use; profane. [< DE- + L *sacrare* make holy] —**des′e·crat′er** or **des′e·cra′tor, des′e·cra′tion** *n.*

**de·seg·re·gate** (dē·seg′rə·gāt) *v.t.* **·gat·ed,**

130

·gat·ing To eliminate racial segregation in. —de′seg·re·ga′tion *n.*

de·sert[1] (di·zûrt′) *n.* 1 The state of deserving reward or punishment. 2 *Often pl.* That which is deserved or merited. [< OF *deservir* deserve]

de·sert[2] (di·zûrt′) *v.t.* 1 To forsake or abandon. 2 To forsake in violation of one's oath or orders. —*v.i.* 3 To abandon one's post, duty, etc. [< L *deserere* abandon] —de·sert′er, de·ser′tion *n.*

de·serve (di·zûrv′) *v.* ·served, serv·ing *v.t.* 1 To be entitled to or worthy of. —*v.i.* 2 To be worthy. [< L *de-* completely + *servire* serve] —de·serv′er *n.*

des·ha·bille (dez′ə·bēl′) *n.* DISHABILLE.

des·ic·cate (des′ə·kāt) *v.* ·cat·ed, ·cat·ing *v.t.* 1 To remove the moisture from, as for preserving. 2 To dry thoroughly. —*v.i.* 3 To become dry. [< L *de-* completely + *siccare* dry out] —des′ic·ca′tion, des′ic·ca′tor *n.* —des′ic·ca′tive *adj., n.*

de·sid·er·a·tum (di·sid′ə·rā′təm, -zid′-, -rä′təm) *n. pl.* ·ta (-tə) Something desirable. [< L *desiderare* to desire]

de·sign (di·zīn′) *v.t.* 1 To make, draw, or prepare preliminary plans or sketches of. 2 To plan and make with art or skill. 3 To form or make (plans, schemes, etc.) in the mind; invent. 4 To intend; purpose. —*v.i.* 5 To make drawings or plans; be a designer. 6 To plan mentally; conceive. —*n.* 1 A plan, sketch or pattern for making something. 2 A decorative or artistic arrangement of forms, colors, etc.: a floral *design.* 3 Any arrangement of parts, shapes, etc., that forms a complete and functioning unit: the new car *designs.* 4 The act or art of designing. 5 A purpose or pattern: to seek a *design* in the chaos of history. 6 *Often pl.* A plot, scheme, or intention, usu. secret or sinister: with *on, upon,* or *against.* 7 Any plan, undertaking, or objective: a *design* to achieve better living conditions. [< L *designare* designate] —de·sign′a·ble *adj.*

des·ig·nate (dez′ig·nāt) *v.t.* ·nat·ed, ·nat·ing 1 To indicate by some mark, sign, or name. 2 To name; characterize. 3 To select or appoint for a specific purpose, duty, office, etc. —*adj.* (dez′ig·nit, -nāt) Designated; selected. [< L *de-* completely + *signare* to mark] —des′ig·na′tor *n.*

de·sire (di·zīr′) *v.t.* ·sired, ·sir·ing 1 To wish or long for; crave. 2 To ask for; request. —*n.* 1 A longing; craving; yearning. 2 A request; wish. 3 Something desired. 4 Sexual appetite; passion. [< L *desiderare*] —de·sir′er *n.* —**Syn.** *v.* 1 want, covet, thirst after, yearn for, aspire after.

de·sist (di·zist′) *v.i.* To cease; stop: often with *from.* [< L *de-* from + *sistere* stop, cease] —de·sis′tance *n.*

des·o·late (des′ə·lit) *adj.* 1 Uninhabited; deserted. 2 Laid waste; devastated. 3 Lonely; solitary. 4 Without friends; forlorn; sorrowful. —*v.t.* (des′ə·lāt) ·lat·ed, ·lat·ing 1 To deprive of inhabitants. 2 To lay waste; devastate. 3 To make sorrowful or forlorn. 4 To abandon. [< L *de-* completely + *solus* alone] —des′o·late·ly *adv.* —des′o·late·ness, des′o·lat′er, des′o·la′tor *n.*

des·o·la·tion (des′ə·lā′shən) *n.* 1 Loneliness; dreariness. 2 Sadness; grief. 3 A laying waste; devastation. 4 A desolate condition or place.

de·spair (di·spâr′) *v.t.* To lose or abandon hope: with *of.* —*n.* 1 Utter hopelessness and discouragement. 2 That which causes despair or which is despaired of. [< L *de-* away + *sperare* to hope] —de·spair′ing *adj.* —de·spair′ing·ly *adv.*

des·per·a·do (des′pə·rä′dō, -rā′dō) *n. pl.* ·does or ·dos A desperate, dangerous outlaw or criminal.

des·per·ate (des′pər·it) *adj.* 1 Without care for danger; reckless, as from despair. 2 Resorted to in a last extremity; drastic. 3 In frantic need, desire, etc.: *desperate* for money. 4 Hopelessly bad or critical: in *desperate* circumstances. [< L *desperare.* See DESPAIR.] —des′per·ate·ly *adv.* —des′per·ate·ness *n.* —**Syn.** 1 rash, foolhardy, imprudent, risky. 2 extreme, severe.

des·per·a·tion (des′pə·rā′shən) *n.* 1 The state of being desperate. 2 The recklessness of despair.

des·pi·ca·ble (des′pi·kə·bəl, di·spik′ə·bəl) *adj.* Despised; contemptible; mean; vile. [< L *despicari* despise] —des′pi·ca·bil′i·ty, des·pi·ca·ble·ness *n.* —des′pi·ca·bly *adv.*

de·spise (di·spīz′) *v.t.* ·spised, ·spis·ing To regard as contemptible or worthless; scorn. [< L *de-* down + *specere* look at] —de·spis′er *n.*

de·spoil (di·spoil′) *v.t.* To deprive of something by force; plunder. [< L *de-* completely + *spoliare* rob] —de·spoil′er, de·spoil′ment, de·spo·li·a·tion (di·spō′lē·ā′shən) *n.*

de·spond (di·spond′) *v.i.* To lose spirit, courage, or hope; be depressed. —*n. Archaic* DESPONDENCY. [< L *de-* away + *spondere* to promise] —de·spond′ing·ly *adv.*

**des·pot** (des′pət, -pot) *n.* 1 An absolute monarch; autocrat. 2 A hard master; tyrant. [< Gk. *despotēs* a master]

**des·sert** (di·zûrt′) *n.* Something served at the close of a meal, as pastry, pudding, fruit, cheese, etc. [< F *desservir* clear a table]

**des·tine** (des′tin) *v.t.* **·tined**, **·tin·ing** 1 To design or set apart for a distinct purpose or end. 2 To determine the future of, as by destiny or fate. —**destined for** 1 Bound for; directed toward. 2 Fated or set apart for. [< L *destinare* make fast]

**des·ti·ny** (des′tə·nē) *n. pl.* **·nies** 1 That to which any person or thing is destined. 2 Inevitable necessity; fate.

**des·ti·tute** (des′tə·t′ōōt) *adj.* 1 Entirely lacking: with *of.* 2 Being in want; extremely poor. [< L *destituere* abandon] —**des′ti·tu′tion** *n.*

**de·stroy** (di·stroi′) *v.t.* 1 To ruin utterly; consume. 2 To demolish; tear down. 3 To put an end to; do away with. 4 To kill. 5 To make ineffective; counteract. [< L *de-* down + *struere* build]

**de·struc·tion** (di·struk′shən) *n.* 1 The act of destroying, or state of being destroyed. 2 That which destroys. [< L *destruere* destroy]

**des·ul·to·ry** (des′əl·tôr′ē, -tō′rē) *adj.* 1 Aimless; changeable; unmethodical. 2 Not connected or relevant; random. [< L *de-* down + *salire* to leap, jump] —**des′ul·to′ri·ly** *adv.* —**des′ul·to′ri·ness** *n.*

**de·tach** (di·tach′) *v.t.* 1 To unfasten and make separate; disconnect. 2 To send off for a special service, duty, etc., as a regiment or a ship. [< F *détacher*] —**de·tach′a·bil′i·ty** *n.* —**de·tach′a·ble** *adj.*

**de·tail** (di·tāl′, dē′tāl) *n.* 1 A small part, item, or particular of a whole. 2 A dealing with or attending to such items or particulars: to go into too much *detail.* 3 *Mil.* **a** A small detachment assigned to some particular task. **b** The person or persons assigned. 4 In art and architecture, a minor but essential component of the finished work. —**in detail** Item by item. —*v.t.* (di·tāl′) 1 To report minutely; give the details of. 2 (*often* dē′tāl) To select for a special service, duty, etc. [< F *dé-* completely + *tailler* cut up]

**de·tain** (di·tān′) *v.t.* 1 To restrain from going; stop; delay. 2 To keep back; withhold. 3 To hold in custody. [< L *de-* away + *tenere* hold] —**de·tain′er**, **de·tain′ment** *n.*

**de·tect** (di·tekt′) *v.t.* 1 To discover. 2 To expose or uncover, as a crime, fault, or a criminal.

3 *Telecom.* DEMODULATE. [< L *de-* away + *tegere* to cover] —**de·tect′a·ble** or **·i·ble** *adj.* —**de·tect′er** *n.* —**Syn.** 1 perceive, find, discern. 2 reveal, disclose, unearth.

**de·tec·tion** (di·tek′shən) *n.* 1 The act of detecting or the condition of being detected. 2 *Telecom.* Any method of demodulation.

**de·tec·tive** (di·tek′tiv) *n.* A person, often a policeman, whose work is to investigate crimes, discover evidence, etc. —*adj.* 1 Of or pertaining to detectives or their work. 2 Of or for detection.

**dé·tente** (dā·tänt′) *n.* An easing, as of discord between nations. [F]

**de·ten·tion** (di·ten′shən) *n.* 1 The act of detaining or keeping in custody. 2 The state of being detained. —**de·ten′tive** *adj.*

**de·ter** (di·tûr′) *v.t.* **·terred**, **·ter·ring** To prevent or restrain (someone) from acting or proceeding, as by reminding of difficulties, dangers, etc. [< L *de-* away + *terrere* frighten] —**de·ter′ment** *n.*

**de·ter·gent** (di·tûr′jənt) *adj.* Having cleansing qualities. —*n.* A cleansing substance, esp. a synthetic substitute for soap. —**de·ter′gence, de·ter′gen·cy** *n.*

**de·te·ri·o·rate** (di·tir′ē·ə·rāt′) *v.t. & v.i.* **·rat·ed, ·rat·ing** To make or become worse; reduce in quality, value, etc. [< L *deterior* worse] —**de·te′ri·o·ra′tion** *n.* —**de·te′ri·o·ra′tive** *adj.* —**Syn.** decline, degenerate, ebb, fall off, wane.

**de·ter·mi·na·tion** (di·tûr′mə·nā′shən) *n.* 1 The act of determining or the condition of being determined. 2 A firm resolve or intention. 3 The quality of being firmly resolute. 4 The fixing of the size, quality, amount, etc., of anything; also, the result of this.

**de·ter·mine** (di·tûr′min) *v.* **·mined, ·min·ing** *v.t.* 1 To settle or decide, as an argument or question. 2 To ascertain or fix, as after investigation or observation. 3 To cause to reach a decision. 4 To influence or affect: Demand *determines* supply. 5 To give purpose or direction to. 6 To set bounds to; limit. 7 *Law* To limit; terminate. —*v.i.* 8 To decide; resolve. 9 *Law* To come to an end. [< L *de-* completely + *terminare* to end] —**de·ter′min·er** *n.*

**de·test** (di·test′) *v.t.* To hate; abhor. [< L *detestari* denounce] —**de·test′er** *n.* —**Syn.** despise, dislike, abominate.

**det·o·nate** (det′ə·nāt) *v.t. & v.i.* **·nat·ed, ·nat·ing** To explode or cause to explode suddenly and with violence. [< L *de-* down + *tonare* to thunder] —**det′o·na′tion, det′o·na′tor** *n.*

**de·tour** (dē′tŏŏr, dĭ·tŏŏr′) *n.* 1 A roundabout way or deviation from a direct route or course of action. 2 A road substituted for part of a main road temporarily impassable. —*v.t. & v.i.* To go or cause to go by a detour. [< F *dé-* away + *tourner* to turn]

**de·tract** (dĭ·trakt′) *v.t.* 1 To take away; withdraw. —*v.i.* 2 To take away a part, as from a reputation, enjoyment, etc.: with *from*. [< L *de-* away + *trahere* draw, pull] —**de·trac′tion, de·trac′tor** *n.* —**de·trac′tive** *adj.*

**det·ri·ment** (det′rə·mənt) *n.* 1 Something that impairs, injures, or causes loss. 2 Injury or loss. [< L *deterere* rub away] —**det′ri·men′tal** *adj.* —**det′ri·men′tal·ly** *adv.*

**de·val·ue** (dē·val′yōō) *v.t.* **·val·ued, ·val·u·ing** 1 To reduce or annul the value of. 2 To fix the value of (a currency) at a point below par. Also **de·val′u·ate** (-yōō·āt). —**de·val′u·a′tion** *n.*

**dev·as·tate** (dev′ə·stāt) *v.t.* **·tat·ed, ·tat·ing** 1 To lay waste, as by war, fire, etc. 2 To crush; overwhelm. [< L *de-* completely + *vastare* lay waste] —**dev′as·tat′ing·ly** *adv.* —**dev′as·ta′tion, dev′as·ta′tor** *n.*

**de·vel·op** (dĭ·vel′əp) *v.t.* 1 To expand or bring out the potentialities, capabilities, etc., of. 2 To expand; enlarge upon; work out, as a plot or idea. 3 To increase the strength, effectiveness, etc., of: to *develop* one's body. 4 To make more extensive or productive, as atomic power. 5 *Phot.* a To bring (a picture) to view by subjecting an exposed photographic film or plate to a developer. b To subject (a plate or film) to a developer. 6 *Music* To elaborate on (a theme). —*v.i.* 7 To increase in capabilities, maturity, etc. 8 To advance from a lower to a higher state; grow; evolve. 9 To disclose itself; become apparent: The plot of a novel *develops.* [< OF *de-* + *voluper* to fold] —**de·vel′op·a·ble** *adj.*

**de·vi·ate** (dē′vē·āt) *v.* **·at·ed, ·at·ing** *v.i.* 1 To turn aside from a course or a norm; diverge. 2 To differ, as in thought or belief. —*v.t.* 3 To cause to turn aside. —*n.* (dē′vē·ĭt) One who deviates, esp. in sexual behavior: also **de·vi·ant** (dē′vē·ənt). [< L *de-* from + *via* a road] —**de′vi·a′tion, de′vi·a′tor** *n.*

**de·vice** (dĭ·vīs′) *n.* 1 Something invented and constructed for special use; contrivance. 2 A plan or scheme, esp. a sly or tricky one. 3 A means to obtain an artistic effect. 4 A

fanciful design or pattern, as in ornamentation. 5 A motto or emblem, as on a shield. —**leave to one's own devices** To allow (a person) to follow his own wishes, without help, guidance, etc. [< OF *devis* intention, will]

**de·vi·ous** (dē′vē·əs) *adj.* 1 Winding or deviating from a straight course; rambling. 2 Straying from the proper or usual way. 3 Not straightforward or honest. [< L *de-* from + *via* way] —**de′vi·ous·ly** *adv.* —**de′vi·ous·ness** *n.*

**de·vise** (dĭ·vīz′) *v.* **·vised, ·vis·ing** *v.t.* 1 To form in the mind; invent; contrive. 2 *Law* To transmit (real estate) by will. —*v.i.* 3 To form a plan. —*n. Law* 1 A gift of lands by will. 2 The act of bequeathing lands. 3 A will, or a clause in a will, conveying real estate. [< OF *deviser* divide, distinguish, contrive] —**de·vis′a·ble** *adj.* —**de·vis′er** *n.* —Syn. *v.* 1 produce, plan, fashion, concoct.

**de·vote** (dĭ·vōt′) *v.t.* **·vot·ed, ·vot·ing** 1 To give or apply (attention, time, or oneself) completely to a purpose, activity, another person, etc. 2 To set apart; dedicate; consecrate. [< L *de-* away + *vovere* vow]

**dev·o·tee** (dev′ə·tē′, -tā′, dĭ·vō′tē′) *n.* 1 One intensely devoted to something or someone. 2 A religious zealot.

**de·vo·tion** (dĭ·vō′shən) *n.* 1 The quality or condition of being devoted. 2 Strong attachment or affection. 3 *Usu. pl.* An act of worship; prayer. 4 Piety. 5 The act of devoting. —**de·vo′tion·al** *adj.* —**de·vo′tion·al·ly** *adv.*

**de·vour** (dĭ·vour′) *v.t.* 1 To eat up greedily. 2 To destroy; lay waste to. 3 To take in greedily with the mind or senses: He *devoured* the book. 4 To engross the attention of. 5 To engulf; absorb. [< L *de-* down + *vorare* to gulp, swallow] —**de·vour′er** *n.*

**de·vout** (dĭ·vout′) *adj.* 1 Earnestly religious; pious. 2 Heartfelt; sincere. 3 Containing or expressing devotion. [< L *devovere* devote] —**de·vout′ly** *adv.* —**de·vout′ness** *n.*

**dex·ter·i·ty** (dek·ster′ə·tē) *n.* 1 Manual skill; adroitness. 2 Mental quickness or skill. [< L *dexteritas* skill < *dexter* on the right]

**dex·ter·ous** (dek′strəs, -stər·əs) *adj.* 1 Possessing dexterity; adroit. 2 Done with dexterity. Also **dex·trous** (dek′strəs). —**dex′ter·ous·ly, dex′trous·ly** *adv.* —**dex′ter·ous·ness, dex′trous·ness** *n.*

**di·a·bol·ic** (dī′ə·bol′ik) *adj.* 1 Of, pertaining to, or coming from the devil; satanic. 2 Fiendishly wicked or cruel. Also **di′a·bol′**

i·cal. [< Gk. *diabolos* devil] —di'a·bol'i·cal·ly *adv.* —di·ab·o·lism (dī·ab'ə·liz'əm) *n.* —Syn. 2 malevolent, infernal, demoniacal.

di·a·crit·ic (dī'ə·krit'ik) *n.* DIACRITICAL MARK. *adj.* DIACRITICAL. [< Gk. *dia-* between + *krinein* distinguish]

di·a·dem (dī'ə·dem) *n.* 1 A crown worn as a symbol of royalty. 2 Regal power; sovereignty. [< Gk. *diadēma*]

di·ag·no·sis (dī'əg·nō'sis) *n.* 1 The art or act of identifying diseases, disorders, etc., by their characteristic symptoms. 2 An examination of the facts in any situation in order to understand its nature: a *diagnosis* of city traffic. 3 The conclusions reached by diagnosing. [< Gk. *diagignōskein* discern] —di·ag·nos·tic (dī'əg·nos'tik) *adj.* —di·ag·nos'ti·cal·ly *adv.*

di·ag·o·nal (dī·ag'ə·nəl) *adj.* 1 Crossing or moving obliquely; slanting. 2 Marked by oblique lines or the like. 3 *Geom.* a Joining two nonadjacent vertices of a figure. b Joining two nonadjacent edges of a solid. —*n.* 1 *Geom.* A diagonal line or plane. 2 Anything running diagonally. [< L *dia-* across + *gonia* angle] —di·ag'o·nal·ly *adv.*

di·a·gram (dī'ə·gram) *n.* 1 A drawing, plan, or outline that illustrates or explains an object, area, concept, etc. 2 A figure drawn to demonstrate a geometrical proposition or relationship. 3 A graph or chart. —*v.t.* ·gramed or ·grammed, ·gram·ing or ·gram·ming To represent or illustrate by a diagram. [< Gk. *dia-* across + *graphein* write] —di·a·gram·mat·ic (dī'ə·grə·mat'ik) or ·i·cal *adj.* —di'a·gram·mat'i·cal·ly *adv.*

di·al (dī'əl, dīl) *n.* 1 A graduated circular plate or face on which an amount, a direction, or degree are indicated by a moving pointer. 2 The face of a watch or clock. 3 A disk or knob used to indicate and change frequencies in a radio or television set. 4 A rotating disk, as on a telephone, used to indicate a number. 5 SUNDIAL. —*v.t.* & *v.i.* di·aled or di·ailed, di·al·ing or di·al·ling 1 To measure or survey with a dial. 2 To indicate on a dial. 3 To telephone by means of a dial. 4 To adjust a radio or television set to (a station, program, etc.). [< Med. L *dialis* daily] —di'al·er, di'al·ler *n.*

di·a·lect (dī'ə·lekt) *n.* 1 The aggregate variations from standard language of the speech peculiar to a local region: the Southern *dialect* of American English. 2 Loosely, the speech adopted by a particular class, trade,

or profession; jargon. 3 An imperfect use of the standard language by those to whom another language is native. 4 A language or group of languages with distinguishing characteristics but related in their origins: The Romance languages are *dialects* of Latin. —*adj.* Of or in a dialect. [< Gk. *dialektos* discourse, way of speaking]

di·a·logue (dī'ə·lôg, -log) *n.* 1 A conversation. 2 A literary work in which the characters are represented as conversing. 3 An open exchange of different points of view for the purpose of mutual understanding. 4 Those sections of a play, story, etc., devoted to conversation. —*v.* ·logued, ·logu·ing *v.t.* 1 To express in dialogue form. —*v.i.* 2 To carry on a dialogue. Also di'a·log. [< Gk. *dialegesthai* converse] —di'a·log'ic (dī'ə·loj'ik) or ·i·cal *adj.* —di·al·o·gist (dī·al'ə·jist, dī'ə·lôg'ist, -log'-) *n.*

di·am·e·ter (dī·am'ə·tər) *n.* 1 A straight line passing through the center of a circle, sphere, figure, etc., and reaching from one boundary to the other. 2 The length of such a line. 3 The width or thickness of an object as measured by such a line. [<Gk. *dia-* through + *metron* measure]

dia·mond (dī'mənd, dī'ə-) *n.* 1 A colorless, crystalline, extremely hard form of carbon, valued as a gem and as an abrasive or cutting tool. 2 *Geom.* A plane figure bounded by four equal straight lines, and having two of the angles acute and two obtuse; a lozenge or rhombus. 3 In card games: a A lozenge-shaped, red spot on a playing card. b A card having such a mark. c *pl.* A suit so marked. 4 The square enclosed by the lines between the bases on a baseball field; also, loosely, the field itself. —*adj.* Of or like diamonds. —*v.t.* To adorn with or as with diamonds. [< LL *daimas*]

di·a·per (dī'pər, dī'ə-) *n.* 1 A soft, absorbent cloth or other material, folded and placed between a baby's legs and fastened around the waist. 2 A repeated, usu. geometric design. —*v.t.* 1 To put a diaper on (an infant). 2 To decorate with a repeated design. [< Med. Gk. *dia-* completely + *aspros* white]

di·a·phragm (dī'ə·fram) *n.* 1 The muscular partition between the thoracic and abdominal cavities; the midriff. 2 Any dividing membrane or partition. 3 Something resembling a diaphragm in shape or elasticity, as the thin, vibrating disk of a telephone. 4 A perforated mechanism which regulates the amount of light entering the lens of a camera, telescope, etc. **5** A contraceptive device consisting of a flexible rubber cap inserted in the vagina to cover the uterine cervix. —*v.t.* To act upon or furnish with a diaphragm. [< Gk. *dia-* across + *phragma* a fence] —**di·a·phrag·mat·ic** (dī′ə·frag·mat′ik) *adj.* —**di′a·phrag·mat′i·cal·ly** *adv.*

**di·ar·rhe·a** (dī′ə·rē′ə) *n.* Abnormally frequent and fluid evacuation of the bowels. Also **dī′ar·rhoe′a.** [< Gk. *dia-* through + *rheein* to flow] —**di′ar·rhe′al** or **·rhoe′al, di′ar·rhe′ic** or **rhoe′ic, di′ar·rhet′ic** or **·rhoet′ic** (-ret′ik) *adj.*

**di·a·ry** (dī′ə·rē) *n. pl.* **·ries 1** A written, daily record of the writer's experiences, feelings, activities, etc. **2** A book for keeping such a record. [< LL *diarium* < L *dies* a day]

**di·as·to·le** (dī·as′tə·lē) *n.* **1** The rhythmic relaxation and dilation of the heart between contractions. **2** In classical prosody, the lengthening of a syllable naturally short. [< Gk. *diastolē* a separation, lengthening] —**di·as·tol·ic** (dī′ə·stol′ik) *adj.*

**di·a·ther·my** (dī′ə·thûr′mē) *n.* Medical treatment by means of heat generated in the body by high-frequency radiation. [< Gk. *dia-* through + *thermē* heat] —**di′a·ther′mic** *adj.*

**dice** (dīs) *n. pl.* of **die 1** Small cubes of bone, ivory, plastic, etc., having the sides marked with spots from one to six. **2** A game of chance played with such cubes. **3** Any small cubes. —*v.* **diced, dic·ing** *v.t.* **1** To cut into small cubes. **2** To gamble away or win with dice. —*v.i.* **3** To play at dice. —**dic′er** *n.*

**dick·er** (dik′ər) *v.t. & v.i.* To trade, haggle, or barter, esp. on a small scale. —*n.* The act of dickering. [ME *dyker*]

**dick·ey** (dik′ē) *n.* **1** A detachable shirt or blouse front. **2** A detachable collar. **3** A bib or pinafore. **4** A small bird: also **dickey bird. 5** An outside seat on a carriage, as for the driver. Also **dick′y.** [< *Dicky,* dim. of the name *Richard*]

**Dic·ta·phone** (dik′tə·fōn) *n.* A type of instrument that records and reproduces spoken words, as for transcription by a stenographer: a trade name.

**dic·tate** (dik′tāt, dik·tāt′) *v.* **·tat·ed, ·tat·ing** *v.t.* **1** To utter or read aloud (something) to be recorded by another. **2** To prescribe authoritatively, as commands, terms, rules, etc. —*v.i.* **3** To utter aloud something to be recorded by another. **4** To give orders. —*n.*

(dik′tāt) **1** An authoritative suggestion, rule, or command. **2** A precept or prompting. [< L *dictare,* freq. of *dicere* say, speak]

**dic·ta·tion** (dik·tā′shən) *n.* **1** The act of dictating. **2** The matter or material dictated. —**dic·ta′tion·al** *adj.*

**dic·tion** (dik′shən) *n.* **1** The use, choice and arrangement of words and modes of expression. **2** The manner of enunciating words in speaking or singing. [< L *dicere* say]

**dic·tion·ar·y** (dik′shən·er′ē) *n. pl.* **·ar·ies 1** A book containing the words of a language arranged alphabetically, usu. with their syllabication, pronunciation, definition, and etymology. **2** A similar work having definitions or equivalents in another language. **3** Any list of specialized words or terms arranged alphabetically and defined. [<Med. L *dictionarium* a collection of words and phrases]

**die¹** (dī) *v.i.* **died, dy·ing 1** To suffer death; expire. **2** To suffer the pains of death: The coward *dies* a thousand deaths. **3** To lose energy, force, importance, etc.: with *away, down,* or *out.* **4** To fade away: The smile *died* on his lips. **5** To become extinct: with *out* or *off.* **6** To become indifferent or insensible: with *to:* to *die* to the world. **7** *Informal* To desire exceedingly, as if to death: He's *dying* to meet her. **8** To stop functioning, as an engine. **9** To faint or swoon. [<ON *deyja*]

**die²** (dī) *n. pl.* **dice** *for defs. 1 and 2,* **dies** *for def. 3* **1** A small cube used in games. See **DICE. 2** A cast, as in playing dice; stake; hazard. **3** Any of various tools, mechanisms, patterns, etc., for cutting, molding, shaping, or stamping. —**the die is cast** The irrevocable choice has been made. —*v.t.* To cut or stamp with or as with a die. [< L *datum* something given]

**di·et** (dī′ət) *n.* **1** Limited or prescribed food and drink, as for losing weight, for controlling disease, etc. **2** One's daily or normal food and drink. —*v.t.* **1** To regulate or restrict the food and drink of. —*v.i.* **2** To take food and drink according to a regimen. [<Gk. *diaita* a way of living] —**di′et·er** *n.*

**dif·fer** (dif′ər) *v.i.* **1** To be dissimilar; be distinct, as in kind or appearance: often with *from.* **2** To hold contrary or unlike views; disagree: often with *with.* [< L *dis-* apart + *ferre* carry] —**Syn. 1** vary, contrast. **2** dissent, clash.

**dif·fer·ence** (dif′ər·əns, dif′rəns) *n.* **1** The

state, quality, or an instance of being different. 2 The way in which persons or things are different. 3 A distinguishing characteristic. 4 A disagreement, controversy, or quarrel. 5 Distinction; discrimination. 6 *Math.* The result obtained by subtraction. —**make a difference** 1 To change or have an effect on something. 2 To distinguish or discriminate: with *between.* — *v.t.* **·enced, ·enc·ing** To make or mark as different; distinguish.

**dif·fi·cult** (dif′ə·kult, -kəlt) *adj.* 1 Hard to do or be done; arduous. 2 Hard to understand; perplexing. 3 Hard to persuade or overcome; stubborn. 4 Hard to please, deal with, or satisfy. —**dif′fi·cult·ly** *adv.* —**Syn.** 1 onerous, irksome, laborious. 2 troublesome, complicated. 4 trying, perverse.

**dif·fi·dent** (dif′ə·dənt) *adj.* Showing or characterized by a lack of self-confidence; timid; shy. [< L *dis-* away + *fīdere* to trust] —**dif′fi·dence** *n.* —**dif′fi·dent·ly** *adv.*

**dif·fuse** (di·fyo̅o̅z′) *v.t. & v.i.* **·fused, ·fus·ing** 1 To pour or send out so as to spread in all directions; permeate. 2 To subject to or spread by diffusion. —*adj.* (di·fyo̅o̅s′) 1 Excessively wordy. 2 Widely spread out. [< L *dis-* away, from + *fundere* pour] —**dif·fuse′ly** (-fyo̅o̅s′-) *adv.* —**dif·fuse′ness, dif·fus·er** or **dif·fus·or** (di·fyo̅o̅′zər) *n.* —**dif·fus′i·ble** *adj.*

**di·gest** (di·jest′, dī-) *v.t.* 1 To convert (food) into forms that can be assimilated by the body. 2 To take in or assimilate mentally. 3 To arrange in systematic form, usu. by condensing. 4 To tolerate patiently; endure. 5 *Chem.* To soften or decompose by subjecting to heat or moisture. —*v.i.* 6 To be assimilated, as food. 7 To assimilate food. 8 To be subjected to heat, moisture, chemical agents, etc. —*n.* (dī′jest) A systematic, classified, and abridged collection of writings, as of news, scientific material, legal statutes, etc. [< L *dis-* away + *gerere* carry] —**di·gest′er** *n.*

**di·ges·tion** (di·jes′chən, dī-) *n.* 1 The process of digesting food. 2 The power to digest food. 3 The reception and assimilation of ideas.

**dig·it** (dij′it) *n.* 1 A finger or toe. 2 Any one of the ten Arabic numeral symbols, 0 to 9. [< L *digitus* finger]

**dig·ni·fy** (dig′nə·fī) *v.t.* **·fied, ·fy·ing** 1 To impart or add dignity to. 2 To give a high-sounding name to. [< L *dignus* worthy + *facere* make]

**dig·ni·tar·y** (dig′nə·ter′ē) *n. pl.* **·tar·ies** One having an important position or office.

**dig·ni·ty** (dig′nə·tē) *n. pl.* **·ties** 1 A grave or lofty stateliness, as of manner or language. 2 High rank, title, or position. 3 The state or quality of being excellent, worthy, or honorable: the *dignity* of work. 4 Pride or self-respect: beneath one's *dignity.* [< L *dignus* worthy]

**di·gress** (di·gres′, dī-) *v.i.* To turn aside from the main subject in speaking or writing; ramble; wander. [< L *di-* away, apart + *gradi* go, step] —**di·gres′sion** *n.*

**di·lap·i·date** (di·lap′ə·dāt) *v.t. & v.i.* **·dat·ed, ·dat·ing** To fall or cause to fall into partial ruin or decay. [< L *dis-* away + *lapidare* throw stones] —**di·lap′i·da′tion** *n.*

**di·late** (di·lāt′, dī-) *v.* **·lat·ed, ·lat·ing** *v.t.* 1 To make wider, larger or expanded. —*v.i.* 2 To expand; become larger or wider. 3 To speak or write diffusely; enlarge; expatiate: with *on* or *upon.* [< L *dis-* apart + *latus* wide] —**di·lat′a·bil′i·ty** *n.* —**di·lat′a·bly** *adv.* —**di·la′tive** *adj.*

**dil·a·to·ry** (dil′ə·tôr′ē, -tō′rē) *adj.* 1 Given to or characterized by delay; tardy; slow. 2 Causing delay. —**dil′a·to′ri·ly** *adv.* —**dil′a·to′ri·ness** *n.*

**di·lem·ma** (di·lem′ə) *n.* 1 A necessary choice between equally undesirable alternatives. 2 A situation requiring a choice but apparently lacking a satisfactory resolution. 3 *Logic* An argument presenting two (or more) alternatives, equally conclusive against the antagonist. —**the horns of a dilemma** The equally undesirable alternatives between which a choice must be made. [< Gk. *di-* two + *lēmma* a premise] —**dil·em·mat·ic** (dil′ə·mat′ik) *adj.* —**Syn.** 2 predicament, quandary.

**dil·i·gence** (dil′ə·jəns) *n.* 1 Assiduous application; industry. 2 Meticulous care or attention.

**di·lute** (di·lo̅o̅t′, dī-) *v.t.* **·lut·ed, ·lut·ing** 1 To make weaker or less concentrated by admixture. 2 To reduce the intensity, strength, or purity of (a color, drug, etc.) by admixture. —*adj.* Weak; diluted. [< L *dis-* away + *luere* wash] —**di·lute′ness** *n.*

**di·men·sion** (di·men′shən) *n.* 1 Any measurable extent or magnitude, as length, breadth, or thickness. 2 *pl.* Actual measurements, as of length or breadth. 3 *Often pl.* Scope; importance; magnitude. [< L *dimensio*] —**di·men′sion·al** *adj.* —**di·men′sion·al·ly** *adv.*

**di·min·ish** (di·min′ish) *v.t.* 1 To make smaller or less; decrease, as in size, rank, importance, etc. 2 *Music* To lessen (an interval) by a half-step. —*v.i.* 3 To become smaller or less; dwindle; decrease. [< OF *diminuer* < OF *menusier* make smaller] —**di·min′ish·a·ble** *adj.* —**di·min′ish·ment** *n.*

**dim·i·nu·tion** (dim′ə·nyōō′shən) *n.* The act of diminishing, or the condition of being diminished.

**di·min·u·tive** (di·min′yə·tiv) *adj.* 1 Of relatively small size; tiny; little. 2 Expressing diminished size: said of certain suffixes. —*n.* 1 A word formed from another to express diminished size, or familiarity, affection, etc., as: *Johnny, piglet, babykin.* 2 A very small variety or form of anything.

**di·o·cese** (dī′ə·sēs, -sis) *n.* The territory or the churches under a bishop's jurisdiction. [< Gk. *dioikēsis,* orig. management of a house] —**di·oc·e·san** (dī·os′ə·sən, dī′ə·sē′sən) *adj.*

**diph·the·ri·a** (dif·thir′ē·ə, dip-) *n.* An acute contagious disease caused by a bacillus and characterized by the formation of a false membrane in the upper air passages. [< Gk. *diphthera* leather, membrane] —**diph·the·rit·ic** (dif′thə·rit′ik, dip′-), **diph·the·ri·al,** **diph·ther′ic** *adj.*

**diph·thong** (dif′thông, -thong, dip′-) *n.* A combination of two vowel sounds in one syllable, as *oi* in *coil* and *ou* in *doubt,* or as *i* in *fine* and *a* in *name.* [< Gk. *di-* two + *phthongos* sound] —**diph·thon′gal** *adj.*

**di·plo·ma** (di·plō′mə) *n.* 1 A certificate bestowed by a school, college, or university on those who have completed a course of study or have earned a degree. 2 A certificate bestowing some honor or privilege. [< Gk. *diplōma* paper folded double, a letter]

**di·plo·ma·cy** (di·plō′mə·sē) *n. pl.* **·cies** 1 The art, science, or practice of conducting negotiations between nations. 2 Tact or skill in dealing with people.

**dip·lo·mat** (dip′lə·mat) *n.* 1 A person who represents his country in its official relations with other countries. 2 A person who is skilled and tactful in dealing with others. Also **di·plo·ma·tist** (di·plō′mə·tist). [< L *diploma* a document]

**dip·lo·mat·ic** (dip′lə·mat′ik) *adj.* 1 Of or pertaining to diplomats or to diplomacy. 2 Skillful and tactful in dealing with people. —**dip′lo·mat′i·cal·ly** *adv.*

**dip·so·ma·ni·a** (dip′sə·mā′nē·ə) *n.* An uncon-

trollable craving for alcoholic drink. [< Gk. *dipsa* thirst + -MANIA] —**dip′so·ma′ni·ac** [-ak) *n.* —**dip·so·ma·ni·a·cal** (dip′sə·mə·nī′ə·kəl) *adj.*

**di·rect** (di·rekt′, dī-) *v.t.* 1 To control or conduct the affairs of; manage; govern. 2 To order or instruct with authority; command. 3 *Music* To lead as a conductor. 4 To tell (someone) the way. 5 To cause to move, face, or go in a desired direction; aim: He *directed* his gaze toward her. 6 To indicate the destination of, as a letter. 7 To intend, as remarks to be heard by a person; address: Did you *direct* that remark at me? 8 a To supervise the filming or staging of (a play, motion picture, etc.). b To supervise the performance of (actors, etc.). —*v.i.* 9 To give commands or guidance. 10 To supervise the production of a play, motion picture, etc. —*adj.* 1 Having or being the straightest course; shortest; nearest. 2 Free from intervening agencies or conditions; immediate; first-hand. 3 Unbroken in the line of descent; lineal. 4 Complete; total: the *direct* opposite. 5 Straightforward; candid; plain. 6 *Electr.* Flowing in one direction only: *direct* current. —*adv.* In a direct manner; directly. [< L *dis-* apart + *regere* set straight] —**di·rect′ness** *n.* —**Syn.** 1 supervise, run, guide, oversee.

**di·rec·tion** (di·rek′shən, dī-) *n.* 1 The act of directing; supervision. 2 *Usu. pl.* Information or instructions for doing something, going somewhere, etc. 3 An order or command. 4 The position or course of movement of a point or object in its spatial relationship to something else: to go in a northerly *direction.* 5 Trend, tendency, way, etc.: a new *direction* in medicine. 6 The art or act of directing actors, musicians, films, plays, etc.

**di·rec·tor** (di·rek′tər, dī-) *n.* 1 One who or that which directs. 2 A member of a governing body, as of a club or corporation. 3 A conductor of an orchestra. 4 One who directs or stages a film, play, etc. —**di·rec′tor·ship′** *n.* —**di·rec′tress** *n. Fem.*

**di·rec·to·ry** (di·rek′tər·ē, dī-) *n. pl.* **·ries** 1 An alphabetical or classified list, as of the names and addresses of the inhabitants of a city. 2 A book of rules. 3 A body of directors; directorate. —*adj.* Containing directions.

**dirge** (dûrj) *n.* 1 A song or melody expressing grief and mourning. 2 A funeral hymn. [< L *dirige* direct (imperative), the first word of the antiphon (*Psalms* 5:8) of matins in the Latin burial office]

**dir·i·gi·ble** (dir'ə·jə·bəl) *n.* A lighter-than-air aircraft equipped with means for propulsion and steering. —*adj.* That may be directed or controlled. [< L *dirigere* to direct + -IBLE]

**dis·a·bil·i·ty** (dis'ə·bil'ə·tē) *n. pl.* **·ties** 1 That which disables; an infirmity or handicap. 2 Lack of ability; inability. 3 Legal incapacity or inability to act.

**dis·a·ble** (dis·ā'bəl) *v.t.* **·a·bled**, **·a·bling** 1 To render incapable or unable; cripple. 2 To render legally incapable, as of inheriting property, etc. —**dis·a'ble·ment** *n.*

**dis·ad·van·tage** (dis'əd·van'tij, -vän'-) *n.* 1 An unfavorable condition, element, or circumstance; drawback; hindrance. 2 Loss; detriment. —*v.t.* **·taged**, **·tag·ing** To injure the interest of; prejudice; hinder.

**dis·a·gree** (dis'ə·grē') *v.i.* **·a·greed**, **·a·gree·ing** 1 To vary in opinion; differ; dissent. 2 To quarrel. 3 To fail to agree or harmonize, as facts. 4 To produce an unfavorable effect, as food or climate: with *with*.

**dis·al·low** (dis'ə·lou') *v.t.* 1 To refuse to allow or permit. 2 To reject as untrue or invalid. —**dis'al·low'ance** *n.*

**dis·ap·pear** (dis'ə·pir') *v.i.* 1 To pass from sight or view; fade away; vanish. 2 To cease to exist: His anger *disappeared*. —**dis·ap·pear'ance** *n.*

**dis·ap·point** (dis'ə·point') *v.t.* 1 To fail to fulfill the expectation, hope, or desire of. 2 To prevent the fulfillment of (a hope or plan); frustrate. [< OF *des-* away + *appointer* arrange, appoint] —**dis'ap·point'ing·ly** *adv.*

**dis·ap·prove** (dis'ə·prōōv') *v.* **·proved**, **·prov·ing** *v.t.* 1 To regard with disfavor or censure; condemn. 2 To refuse assent to; decline to approve. —*v.i.* 3 To have or express an unfavorable opinion: often with *of.* —**dis'ap·prov'al** *n.* —**dis'ap·prov'ing·ly** *adv.* —**Syn.** 1 dislike, object to, frown upon, denounce, disparage.

**dis·arm** (dis·ärm') *v.t.* 1 To deprive of weapons. 2 To render harmless. 3 To allay or reduce suspicion, aloofness, or hostility. —*v.i.* 4 To lay down arms. 5 To reduce or restrict the size of armed forces.

**dis·ar·ma·ment** (dis·är'mə·mənt) *n.* 1 The act of disarming. 2 The reduction or limitation of armed forces or of certain types of weapons.

**dis·ar·range** (dis'ə·rānj') *v.t.* **·ranged**, **·rang**

·ing To disturb the arrangement of. —**dis·'ar·range'ment** *n.*

**dis·as·ter** (di·zas'tər, -zäs'-) *n.* Any sudden event that causes great damage; a great misfortune or calamity. [< MF *des-* away + *astre* a star]

**dis·as·trous** (di·zas'trəs, -zäs'-) *adj.* Causing or accompanied by disaster; calamitous. —**dis·as'trous·ly** *adv.* —**dis·as'trous·ness** *n.*

**dis·a·vow** (dis'ə·vou') *v.t.* To disclaim responsibility for or approval of; repudiate. —**dis'a·vow'al**, **dis·a·vow'er** *n.*

**dis·band** (dis·band') *v.t.* 1 To break up (an organization, etc.). 2 To remove from military service. —*v.i.* 3 To cease to be an organization. —**dis·band'ment** *n.*

**dis·be·lief** (dis'bi·lēf') *n.* A lack of belief.

**dis·be·lieve** (dis'bi·lēv') *v.t. & v.i.* **·lieved**, **·liev·ing** To refuse to believe; deem false. —**dis'be·liev'er** *n.*

**dis·burse** (dis·bûrs') *v.t.* **·bursed**, **·burs·ing** To pay out; expend. [< OF *des-* away + *bourse* a purse] —**dis·burs'a·ble** *adj.* —**dis·burse'ment**, **dis·burs'er** *n.*

**disc** (disk) *n.* 1 A phonograph record. 2 DISK. [Var. of DISK]

**dis·card** (dis·kärd') *v.t.* 1 To cast aside as useless or undesirable; reject. 2 In card games, to throw out (a card or cards) from one's hand; also, to play (a card, other than a trump, of a different suit from the suit led). —*v.i.* 3 In card games, to throw out a card or cards from one's hand. —*n.* (dis'kärd) 1 The act of discarding. 2 A card or cards discarded. 3 A person or thing cast off.

**dis·charge** (dis·chärj') *v.* **·charged**, **·charg·ing** *v.t.* 1 To unload; remove the contents of: to *discharge* a ship. 2 To remove or send forth: to *discharge* passengers. 3 To send forth; emit (fluid). 4 To shoot or fire, as a gun, bow, shot, or arrow. 5 To dismiss from office; fire. 6 To release, as a prisoner, soldier, or patient. 7 To relieve of duty: to *discharge* a jury. 8 To perform or fulfill the functions and duties of (a trust, office, etc.). 9 To pay (a debt) or meet (an obligation or duty). 10 *Electr.* To free of an electrical charge. —*v.i.* 11 To get rid of a load, burden, etc. 12 To go off, as a cannon. 13 To give or send forth contents. 14 *Electr.* To lose a charge of electricity. —*n.* (*also* dis'chärj) 1 The act of discharging or the state or condition of being discharged. 2 That which discharges, as a certificate releasing one from military service. 3 That which is discharged, as blood from a wound. 4 *Electr.* a The equalization of potential between terminals of a charged capacitor when connected by a conductor. b A disruptive flow of current through a dielectric, esp. through a gas. —**dis·charge/ a·ble** *adj.* —**dis·charg/er** *n.*

**dis·ci·ple** (di·sī/pəl) *n.* 1 A student or follower of a teacher or a doctrine. 2 One of the 12 chosen companions and apostles of Jesus. [< L *discipulus*] —**dis·ci/ple·ship** *n.*

**dis·ci·pline** (dis/ə·plin) *n.* 1 Systematic and rigorous training of the mental, moral, and physical powers by instruction and exercise. 2 The result of this. 3 Self-control. 4 Control over others, as by enforcing obedience. 5 Orderly conduct, etc., resulting from such control. 6 Punishment; chastisement. 7 A specific branch of learning or knowledge. 8 A system of rules, as of a church. 9 A small, penitential whip or scourge. —*v.t.* **·plined, ·plin·ing** 1 To train to obedience or subjection. 2 To drill; educate. 3 To punish or chastise. [< L *disciplina* instruction < *discipulus* disciple] —**dis/ci·plin·er** *n.*

**disc jockey** A person who conducts and announces a radio or television program that presents recorded music, usu. interspersed with comments and commercials.

**dis·claim** (dis·klām/) *v.t.* 1 To deny; repudiate; disavow. 2 To renounce a right or claim to.

**dis·close** (dis·klōz/) *v.t.* **·closed, ·clos·ing** 1 To lay bare; uncover. 2 To make known; divulge. —**dis·clos/er** *n.*

**dis·com·fit** (dis·kum/fit) *v.t.* 1 To defeat the plans or purposes of; frustrate. 2 To embarrass. 3 To vanquish. [< OF *des-* away + *confire* prepare] —**dis·com/fi·ture** *n.*

**dis·com·pose** (dis/kəm·pōz/) *v.t.* **·posed, ·pos·ing** 1 To disturb the composure of; make uneasy. 2 To disorder or disarrange.

**dis·com·po·sure** (dis/kəm·pō/zhər) *n.* The state of being discomposed.

**dis·con·cert** (dis/kən·sûrt/) *v.t.* 1 To cause to lose one's composure or confidence; confuse; upset. 2 To frustrate, as a plan. [< MF *dis-* apart + *concerter* agree] —**dis/con·cert/ing** *adj.* —**dis/con·cert/ing·ly** *adv.*

**dis·con·nect** (dis/kə·nekt/) *v.t.* To undo or break the connection of; detach; separate.

**dis·con·so·late** (dis·kon/sə·lit) *adj.* 1 Without consolation; inconsolable; sad. 2 Gloomy; cheerless. [< L *dis-* not + *consolari* console] —**dis·con/so·late·ly** *adv.* —**dis·con/so·late ·ness, dis·con/so·la/tion** *n.*

**dis·con·tent** (dis/kən·tent/) *n.* Lack of contentment; dissatisfaction: also **dis/con ·tent/ment.** —*v.t.* To made discontented.

**dis·con·tin·ue** (dis/kən·tin/yōō) *v.* **·tin·ued, ·tin·u·ing** *v.t.* 1 To break off or cease from; stop. 2 To cease using, receiving, etc. —*v.i.* 3 To come to an end; stop. —**dis/con·tin/ u·ance, dis/con·tin/u·a/tion** *n.*

**dis·cord** (dis/kôrd) *n.* 1 Lack of agreement; contention; strife. 2 *Music* A dissonant combination of tones; dissonance. 3 Harsh or disagreeable noises. —*v.i.* To be out of accord or harmony; clash. [< L *dis-* away + *cor, cordis* heart]

**dis·cor·dant** (dis·kôr/dənt) *adj.* 1 Contradictory; inconsistent. 2 Quarrelsome. 3 Not harmonious; dissonant. —**dis·cor/dance, dis·cor/dan·cy,** *n.* —**dis·cor/dant·ly** *adv.*

**dis·co·thèque** (dis/kə·tek, dis/kə·tek/) *n.* A night club or other public place offering recorded music for dancing. [F, lit., record library]

**dis·count** (dis/kount) *n.* 1 An amount deducted from a sum to be paid. 2 In lending money, the interest deducted in advance. 3 The act of discounting. 4 The rate of discount. —**at a discount** At less than the face value or amount regularly charged. —*v.t.* (dis/kount, dis·kount/) 1 To deduct, as a portion of an amount owed. 2 To buy or sell (a bill or note) for face value less interest. 3 To fail to heed; disregard. 4 To believe only part of. 5 To take into account beforehand so as to lessen value, effect, enjoyment, etc. —*v.i.* 6 To lend money, deducting the interest beforehand. [< L *dis-* away + *computare* compute] —**dis/count·a·ble** *adj.* —**dis/count·er** *n.*

**dis·coun·te·nance** (dis·koun/tə·nəns) *v.t.* **·nanced, ·nanc·ing** 1 To look upon with disfavor. 2 To abash; disconcert. [< MF *des-* away + *contenancer* to favor]

**dis·cour·age** (dis·kûr/ij) *v.t.* **·aged, ·ag·ing** 1 To deprive of courage; dispirit; dishearten. 2 To deter or dissuade: with *from.* 3 To obstruct; hinder. 4 To attempt to prevent by disapproval. —**dis·cour/age·ment, dis· cour/ag·er** *n.* —**dis·cour/ag·ing** *adj.* —**dis· cour/ag·ing·ly** *adv.*

**dis·course** (dis/kôrs, dis·kôrs/) *n.* 1 Familiar conversation; talk. 2 Formal expression of thought, oral or written. —*v.i.* (dis·kôrs/) **·coursed, ·cours·ing** 1 To set forth one's thoughts and conclusions concerning a subject: with *on* or *upon.* 2 To converse; confer. [< L *dis-* apart + *cursus* a running] —**dis·cours/er** *n.*

139

**dis·cour·te·ous** (dis·kûr'tē·əs) *adj.* Showing discourtesy; rude. —**dis·cour'te·ous·ly** *adv.* —**dis·cour'te·ous·ness** *n.*

**dis·cov·er** (dis·kuv'ər) *v.t.* To come upon, find out, make known, or realize, esp. for the first time. [< OF *des-* away + *covrir* to cover] —**dis·cov'er·a·ble** *adj.* —**dis·cov'er·er** *n.*

**dis·cred·it** (dis·kred'it) *v.t.* 1 To disbelieve. 2 To injure the credit or reputation of. 3 To show to be unworthy of belief or confidence. —*n.* 1 Distrust or disbelief. 2 Dishonor or disgrace. 3 Something that causes distrust or disgrace. —**dis·cred'it·a·ble** *adj.* —**dis·cred'it·a·bly** *adv.*

**dis·creet** (dis·krēt') *adj.* Showing consideration of the privacy or trust of others, as by suppressing curious inquiry; prudent; circumspect. [< LL *discretus* pp. of *discernere* discern] —**dis·creet'ly** *adv.* —**dis·creet'ness** *n.*

**dis·crep·an·cy** (dis·krep'ən·sē) *n. pl.* **·cies** 1 Disagreement or difference; inconsistency. 2 An example of this. [< L < *dis-* away + *crepare* creak] —**dis·crep'ant** *adj.* —**dis·crep'ant·ly** *adv.*

**dis·crete** (dis·krēt') *adj.* 1 Distinct or separate. 2 Made up of distinct parts or separate units. [< LL *discretus*. See DISCREET.] —**dis·crete'ly** *adv.* —**dis·crete'ness** *n.*

**dis·cre·tion** (dis·kresh'ən) *n.* 1 The quality of being discreet; prudence; caution. 2 Liberty of action; freedom in the exercise of judgment. —**at one's discretion** According to one's own judgment.

**dis·crim·i·nate** (dis·krim'ə·nāt) *v.* **·nat·ed** **·nat·ing** *v.i.* 1 To act with partiality. 2 To observe a difference. —*v.t.* 3 To discern the difference in or between. 4 To make or constitute a difference in or between. —*adj.* (-nit) Noting or involving differences. [< L *dis-* apart + *crimen* a judgment] —**dis·crim'i·nat'ing** *adj.* —**dis·crim'i·nat'ing·ly** *adv.* —**dis·crim'i·nat'or** *n.*

**dis·crim·i·na·tion** (dis·krim'ə·nā'shən) *n.* 1 The act of discriminating or the ability to discriminate. 2 Biased or unfair judgments or treatment.

**dis·cuss** (dis·kus') *v.t.* To treat of in conversation or in writing. [< L *discutere*] —**dis·cuss'er** *n.* —**dis·cuss'i·ble** *adj.* —**Syn.** argue, debate, deliberate, examine.

**dis·cus·sion** (dis·kush'ən) *n.* The act of discussing.

**dis·dain** (dis·dān') *v.t.* To consider unworthy of one's regard or notice; scorn. —*n.* A feeling of superiority and dislike; proud contempt. [< OF *des-* away + *deignier* deign] —**dis·dain'ful** *adj.* —**dis·dain'ful·ly** *adv.*

**dis·ease** (di·zēz') *n.* 1 Any disturbed or abnormal condition in the living organism. 2 A specific ailment or illness. 3 Any disturbed or harmful condition. *v.t.* **eased,** **·eas·ing** To cause disease in; disorder; derange. [< OF *des-* away + *aise* ease] —**dis·eased'** *adj.*

**dis·em·bark** (dis'im·bärk') *v.t. & v.i.* 1 To put or go ashore from a ship. 2 To get off or land: to *disembark* from an airplane at San Francisco. —**dis·em'bar·ka'tion,** **dis·'em·bark'ment** *n.*

**dis·en·chant** (dis'in·chant', -chänt') *v.t.* To free from enchantment or illusion. —**dis·'en·chant'ment** *n.*

**dis·en·gage** (dis'in·gāj') *v.t. & v.i.* **gaged,** **·gag·ing** To set free or be free, as from engagement, attachment, etc. —**dis'en·gage'ment** *n.*

**dis·fa·vor** (dis·fā'vər) *n.* 1 Lack of favor; disapproval; dislike. 2 The state of being disliked or opposed. 3 An unkind act. —*v.t.* To treat or regard without favor.

**dis·fig·ure** (dis·fig'yər) *v.t.* **·ured,** **·ur·ing** To mar or destroy the figure or beauty of; render unsightly; deform. —**dis·fig'ure·ment,** **dis·fig'u·ra'tion** *n.*

**dis·gorge** (dis·gôrj') *v.t. & v.i.* **gorged,** **·gorg·ing** 1 To throw out, as from the throat or stomach; eject; vomit. 2 To give up unwillingly. [< OF *des-* from + *gorge* throat]

**dis·grace** (dis·grās') *v.t.* **graced,** **·grac·ing** 1 To bring reproach or shame upon. 2 To put out of favor. —*n.* 1 The state of a person who has lost respect or favor. 2 Loss of respect or favor. 3 That which disgraces. [< Ital. < *dis-* away + *grazia* favor] —**dis·gra'c'er** *n.*

**dis·guise** (dis·gīz') *v.t.* **·guised,** **·guis·ing** 1 To hide or change the appearance of. 2 To misrepresent or cover up the actual nature or character of. —*n.* 1 The act of disguising, or the state of being disguised. 2 Something that disguises. [< OF *des-* down + *guise* guise] —**dis·guis'ed·ly** (-id·lē) *adv.* —**dis·guis'er** *n.*

**dis·gust** (dis·gust') *v.t.* 1 To offend the senses of. 2 To affect with loathing or aversion. —*n.* Strong aversion or repugnance. [<MF *des-* away + *gouster* to taste] —**dis·gust'ed** *adj.* —**dis·gust'ed·ly** *adv.*

**dis·heart·en** (dis·här'ten) *v.t.* To weaken the spirit or courage of; discourage. —**dis·**

**heart′en·ing** *adj.* —**dis·heart′en·ing·ly**
*adv.* —**dis·heart′en·ment** *n.*

**di·shev·el** (di·shev′əl) *v.t.* ·**eled** or ·**elled,**
·**el·ling** or ·**el·ling** 1 To disarrange, as hair
or clothing. 2 To disarrange the hair, clothing, etc. of (a person). [<MF *des-* away +
*chevel* hair]

**dis·hon·est** (dis·on′ist) *adj.* 1 Lacking in honesty; untrustworthy. 2 Characterized by
fraudulence. —**dis·hon′es·ty** *n.* —**dis·hon′**
**est·ly** *adv.*

**dis·hon·or** (dis·on′ər) *v.t.* 1 To disgrace or insult. 2 To seduce. 3 To decline or fail to pay,
as a note. —*n.* 1 Lack or loss of honor or respect. 2 Something that causes such a lack
or loss. 3 Refusal or failure to pay a note,
etc., when due. *Brit. sp.* ·**our.**

**dis·in·cline** (dis′in·klīn′) *v.t. & v.i.* ·**clined,**
·**clin·ing** To make or be unwilling or averse.

**dis·in·fect** (dis′in·fekt′) *v.t.* 1 To free from infection, harmful bacteria, etc. 2 To clean
with a disinfectant. —**dis′in·fec′tion** *n.*

**dis·in·gen·u·ous** (dis′in·jen′yŏŏ·əs) *adj.* Not
sincere or candid; artful; deceitful. —**dis-**
**′in·gen′u·ous·ly** *adv.*

**dis·in·her·it** (dis′in·her′it) *v.t.* To deprive of
an inheritance or of a right or privilege. —
**dis′in·her′i·tance** *n.*

**dis·in·te·grate** (dis·in′tə·grāt, di·zin′-) *v.t. &*
*v.i.* ·**grat·ed,** ·**grat·ing** To reduce or become
reduced into parts or particles. —
**dis·in′te·gra·ble** (-grə·bəl) *adj.* —**dis·in′**
**te·gra′tion** *n.*

**dis·in·ter·est·ed** (dis·in′tər·is·tid, -tris·tid, -
tə·res′-) *adj.* 1 Free from self-interest or
bias. 2 Lacking interest; uninterested. —
**dis·in′ter·est·ed·ly** *adv.* —**dis·in′ter·est·**
**ed·ness** *n.* —**Syn.** 1 unselfish, impartial,
detached, 2 apathetic, unconcerned, indifferent. • **disinterested, uninterested** *Disinterested* and *uninterested* are widely used
interchangeably, but in precise usage *disinterested* refers to a lack of special or personal interest (the arbiter's *disinterested*
decision) and *uninterested* to a lack of any
interest whatsoever (an *uninterested* spectator, nodding through the performance).

**disk** (disk) *n.* 1 A flat, more or less circular
plate of any material. 2 Any surface that is
flat and circular. 3 A quoit or discus. 4 A
phonograph record. 5 A round, flat,
magnetically-coated plate on which computer data and programs may be stored.

**dis·like** (dis·līk′) *v.t.* ·**liked,** ·**lik·ing** To regard
with aversion or antipathy. —*n.* Distaste;

repugnance; aversion. —**dis·lik′a·ble,** dis·
like′a·ble *adj.* —**dis·lik′er** *n.*

**dis·lo·cate** (dis′lō·kāt, dis·lō′kāt) *v.t.* ·**cat·ed,**
·**cat·ing** 1 To put out of joint, as a bone. 2
To put out of proper place or order. —**dis-**
′**lo·ca′tion** *n.*

**dis·lodge** (dis·loj′) *v.* ·**lodged,** ·**lodg·ing** *v.t.*
To remove or drive out, as from an abode.
—*v.i.* 2 To leave a place of abode; move. —
**dis·lodg′ment,** *n.*

**dis·loy·al** (dis·loi′əl) *adj.* False to one's allegiance; faithless. —**dis·loy′al·ly** *adv.*

**dis·mal** (diz′məl) *adj.* 1 Gloomy; cheerless;
mournful. 2 Calamitous; horrible. [< L *dies
mali* evil or unpropitious days] —**dis′mal·ly**
*adv.* —**dis′mal·ness** *n.*

**dis·man·tle** (dis·man′təl) *v.t.* ·**tled,** ·**tling** 1 To
strip of furniture, equipment, clothing, etc.
2 To take apart; reduce to pieces. [< ME
*des-* away + *manteller* cover with a cloak] —
**dis·man′tle·ment** *n.*

**dis·may** (dis·mā′) *v.t.* To put at a loss, as from
surprise, fear, or disappointment; cause to
lose spirit or confidence. —*n.* A state of
being dismayed. [< ME *dismayen*]

**dis·miss** (dis·mis′) *v.t.* 1 To put out of office
or service; discharge. 2 To cause or allow to
depart. 3 To put aside; reject. [< L *dis-* away
+ *mittere* send] —**dis·mis′sal** *n.* —**dis·mis-**
**s′i·ble** *adj.*

**dis·o·be·di·ent** (dis′ə·bē′dē·ənt) *adj.* Neglecting or refusing to obey; refractory. —
**dis′o·be′di·ence** *n.* —**dis′o·be′di·ent·ly**
*adv.*

**dis·o·bey** (dis′ə·bā′) *v.t. & v.i.* To refuse or fail
to obey. —**dis′o·bey′er** *n.*

**dis·or·der** (dis·ôr′dər) *n.* 1 The state of being
disarranged. 2 Disregard or neglect of orderliness. 3 A disturbance of the peace;
breach of public order. 4 A derangement of
bodily or mental function; illness. —*v.t.* 1
To throw out of order; disarrange. 2 To disturb the natural functions of, as body or
mind.

**dis·own** (dis·ōn′) *v.t.* To refuse to acknowledge responsibility for or ownership of; repudiate.

**dis·par·age** (dis·par′ij) *v.t.* ·**aged,** ·**ag·ing** 1 To
speak of slightingly; undervalue. 2 To bring
discredit or dishonor upon. [< OF *des-*
down, away + *parage* equality, rank] —
**dis·par′age·ment, dis·par′ag·er** *n.* —**dis·**
**par′ag·ing·ly** *adv.* —**Syn.** 1 belittle, depreciate, decry, discredit.

**dis·par·i·ty** (dis·par′ə·tē) *n. pl.* ·**ties** The state of being dissimilar; difference. [< L *dis-* apart + *paritas* equality]

**dis·pas·sion·ate** (dis·pash′ən·it) *adj.* Free from passion, prejudice, or personal interest; detached. —**dis·pas′sion·ate·ly** *adv.* —**dis·pas′sion·ate·ness** *n.*

**dis·patch** (dis·pach′) *v.t.* 1 To send off, esp. on official business. 2 To transact with promptness. 3 To kill summarily. —*n.* 1 The act of dispatching. 2 A message, news story, etc., sent with haste. 3 Speed; promptness; expedition. 4 The act of killing. [< Ital. *dispacciare*]

**dis·pel** (dis·pel′) *v.t.* **·pelled**, **·pel·ling** To scatter; drive away; disperse. [< L *dis-* away + *pellere* to drive]

**dis·pen·sa·tion** (dis′pən·sā′shən) *n.* 1 A dealing out; distribution. 2 Something dealt out or distributed. 3 Special exemption granted from the requirements of a law, rule, or obligation. 4 *Theol.* Any of the systems in which God has revealed his mind and will to man. —**dis′pen·sa′tion·al** *adj.* —**dis′pen·sa′tor** *n.*

**dis·pense** (dis·pens′) *v.* **·pensed**, **·pens·ing** *v.t.* 1 To give or deal out in portions; distribute. 2 To compound and give out (medicines). 3 To administer, as laws. 4 To relieve or excuse; absolve. —*v.i.* 5 To grant exemption or dispensation. —**dispense with** To do without; relinquish; forgo. [< L *dis-* away + *pendere* weigh] —**dis·pens′er** *n.*

**dis·per·sion** (dis·pûr′zhən, -shən) *n.* 1 The act of dispersing or the state of being dispersed. 2 The separation of light rays of different colors by the action of a prism or lens.

**dis·place** (dis·plās′) *v.t.* **·placed**, **·plac·ing** 1 To move from the proper place. 2 To take the place of; supplant. 3 To remove from a position or office; discharge.

**dis·play** (dis·plā′) *v.t.* 1 To show; make apparent to the eye or the mind. 2 To reveal, as ignorance. —*n.* 1 The act of displaying. 2 The thing or things displayed. 3 Ostentatious show. [< LL *displicare* scatter]

**dis·please** (dis·plēz′) *v.t. & v.i.* **·pleased**, **·pleas·ing** To annoy, vex, or offend.

**dis·port** (dis·pôrt′, -pōrt′) *v.i.* 1 To play; gambol. —*v.t.* 2 To amuse (oneself). [< L *dis-* away + *portare* carry]

**dis·pose** (dis·pōz′) *v.* **·posed**, **·pos·ing** *v.t.* 1 To put in order; arrange properly. 2 To incline or influence the mind of. 3 To put or set in a particular place or location. 4 To settle (affairs). —*v.i.* 5 To arrange or settle some-

thing. —**dispose of** 1 To settle; finish. 2 To throw away. 3 To get rid of by selling or giving. [< OF *dis-* apart + *poser* put, pose] —**dis·pos′er** *n.*

**dis·po·si·tion** (dis′pə·zish′ən) *n.* 1 The act of disposing; arrangement, as of troops. 2 Final settlement or management. 3 Control; power. 4 Natural tendency or temperament; bent; propensity. 5 A selling or giving away.

**dis·pos·sess** (dis′pə·zes′) *v.t.* To deprive (someone) of possession, as of a house or land. —**dis′pos·ses′sion, dis′pos·ses′sor** *n.*

**dis·pro·por·tion** (dis′prə·pôr′shən, -pōr′-) *n.* Lack of proportion or symmetry. —*v.t.* To make disproportionate. —**dis′pro·por′tion·al** *adj.* —**dis′pro·por′tion·al·ly** *adv.*

**dis·prove** (dis·prōōv′) *v.t.* **·proved**, **·prov·ing** To prove to be false or erroneous; refute. —**dis·prov′a·ble** *adj.*

**dis·pute** (dis·pyōōt′) *v.* **·put·ed**, **·put·ing** *v.t.* 1 To argue about; discuss. 2 To question the validity, genuineness, etc., of. 3 To strive for, as a prize. 4 To resist; oppose. —*v.i.* 5 To argue. 6 To quarrel; wrangle. —*n.* 1 A controversial discussion. 2 A wrangle; quarrel. [< L *dis-* away + *putare* think] —**dis·put′er** *n.*

**dis·qual·i·fy** (dis·kwol′ə·fī) *v.t.* **·fied**, **·fy·ing** 1 To render unqualified or unfit; incapacitate; disable. 2 To pronounce unqualified or ineligible, esp. in sports.

**dis·qui·et** (dis·kwī′ət) *n.* Restlessness; uneasiness. Also **dis·qui′e·tude** (-kwī′ə·t′ōōd). —*v.t.* To make anxious or uneasy.

**dis·qui·si·tion** (dis′kwi·zish′ən) *n.* A systematic treatise or discourse. [< L *dis-* from + *quaerere* seek, ask]

**dis·re·gard** (dis′ri·gärd′) *v.t.* 1 To pay no attention to; ignore. 2 To treat without respect or attention; slight. —*n.* Want of regard; neglect; slight. —**dis′re·gard′ful** *adj.*

**dis·rep·u·ta·ble** (dis·rep′yə·tə·bəl) *adj.* Being in or causing ill repute; disgraceful. —**dis·rep′u·ta·ble·ness** *n.* —**dis·rep′u·ta·bly** *adv.*

**dis·re·pute** (dis′ri·pyōōt′) *n.* Lack or loss of reputation; ill repute.

**dis·re·spect** (dis′ri·spekt′) *n.* Lack of respect; discourtesy. —*v.t.* To treat or regard with lack of respect. —**dis′re·spect′ful** *adj.* —**dis′re·spect′ful·ly** *adv.* —**dis′re·spect′ful·ness** *n.*

**dis·rupt** (dis·rupt′) *v.t. & v.i.* 1 To burst or break asunder. 2 To act to interrupt the normal or proper course of (a meeting, etc.). [< L *dis-* apart + *rumpere* burst] —**dis·rup'ter** or **dis·rup'tor, dis·rup'tion** *n.*

**dis·sat·is·fac·tion** (dis'sat·is·fak'shən) *n.* 1 A dissatisfied state or feeling; discontent. 2 Something that dissatisfies.

**dis·sat·is·fy** (dis·sat'is·fī) *v.t.* ·fied, ·fy·ing To fail to satisfy; disappoint; displease.

**dis·sect** (di·sekt', dī-) *v.t.* 1 To separate the disparate tissues of (an organism.) 2 To analyze critically; examine. [< L < *dis-* apart + *secare* to cut] —**dis·sec'tion, dis·sec'tor** *n.*

**dis·sem·ble** (di·sem'bəl) *v.* ·bled, ·bling *v.t.* 1 To conceal the true nature of (intentions, feelings, etc.) so as to deceive. 2 To pretend to feel; to *dissemble* shock. —*v.i.* 3 To conceal one's true nature, intentions, etc.; act hypocritically. [< OF *dis-* not, away + *sembler* seem] —**dis·sem'blance, dis·sem'bler** *n.*

**dis·sem·i·nate** (di·sem'ə·nāt) *v.t.* ·nat·ed, ·nat·ing To spread about; scatter; promulgate. [< L *dis-* away + *seminare* to sow] —**dis·sem'i·na'tion, dis·sem'i·na'tor** *n.*

**dis·sen·sion** (di·sen'shən) *n.* Angry or violent difference of opinion. —**Syn.** discord, strife, conflict, disagreement.

**dis·sent** (di·sent') *v.i.* 1 To differ in thought or opinion; disagree. 2 To refuse adherence to an established church. —*n.* The act or state of dissenting. [< L *dis-* apart + *sentire* think, feel] —**dis·sent'er** *n.*

**dis·ser·ta·tion** (dis'ər·tā'shən) *n.* An extended treatise or discourse; thesis. [< L *dissertare* examine, discuss]

**dis·sim·i·lar** (di·sim'ə·lər) *adj.* Unlike; different. —**dis·sim'i·lar'i·ty** *n.* —**dis·sim'i·lar·ly** *adv.*

**dis·sim·i·la·tion** (di·sim'ə·lā'shən) *n.* The act or process of becoming dissimilar.

**dis·si·pate** (dis'ə·pāt) *v.* ·pat·ed, ·pat·ing *v.t.* 1 To disperse or drive away. 2 To disintegrate or dissolve utterly. 3 To squander; to *dissipate* a fortune. —*v.i.* 4 To become dispersed; scatter. 5 To engage in excessive or dissolute pleasures. [< L *dissipare*]

**dis·si·pa·tion** (dis'ə·pā'shən). *n.* 1 The act of dissipating or the state of being dissipated. 2 Excessive indulgence, esp. in pleasures. 3 Idle distraction or amusement.

**dis·so·lute** (dis'ə·lōōt) *adj.* Dissipated; immoral; profligate. [< L *dissolutus*, loose, pp. of *dissolvere* dissolve] —**dis'so·lute·ly** *adv.* —**dis'so·lute·ness** *n.*

**dis·so·lu·tion** (dis'ə·lōō'shən) *n.* 1 The act or

state of dissolving or breaking up into parts; disintegration. 2 An ending or breaking up, as of an assembly, business, or partnership. 3 Death.

**dis·solve** (di·zolv') *v.t. & v.i.* ·solved, ·solv·ing 1 To change or make change from a solid to a fluid condition. 2 To pass or cause to pass into or combine with a solution. 3 To end or conclude; terminate, as a meeting or marriage. 4 To fade or cause to fade into or out of view, as a motion-picture or television scene. 5 To vanish or make vanish. —*n.* In films and television, the slow emergence of one scene out of another. [< L *dis-* apart + *solvere* loosen] —**dis·solv'a·ble** *adj.* —**dis·sol'vent** *adj., n.* —**dis·solv'er** *n.*

**dis·so·nance** (dis'ə·nəns) *n.* 1 A discordant mingling of sounds. 2 *Music* A combination of tones that give a harsh or unpleasant effect when sounded together. 3 Harsh disagreement. Also **dis'so·nan·cy.**

**dis·so·nant** (dis'ə·nənt) *adj.* 1 Having the quality of dissonance. 2 Naturally hostile; incongruous. 3 [< L *dis-* away + *sonare* to sound] —**dis'so·nant·ly** *adv.*

**dis·suade** (di·swād') *v.t.* ·suad·ed, ·suad·ing To change the plans of (a person) by persuasion or advice; with *from*. [< L *dis-* away + *suadere* persuade] —**dis·suad'er, dis·sua'sion** (-swā'zhən) *n.* —**dis·sua'sive** (-swā'siv) *adj.*

**dis·tance** (dis'təns) *n.* 1 The space or interval separating two objects, points, or places. 2 The length of a line segment connecting two points. 3 The period between two points of time. 4 The state of being separated in space or time. 5 A distant place or point. 6 Reserve; haughtiness; coldness. 7 *Music* The interval between two tones. —*v.t.* ·tanced, ·tanc·ing To leave behind, as in a race; outstrip; excel.

**dis·tant** (dis'tənt) *adj.* 1 Separated in space or time; far apart. 2 Not closely related in qualities, relationship, or in position; remote. 3 Reserved or unapproachable; formal. 4 Indistinct; faint. 5 Not obvious or plain; indirect. [< L *dis-* apart + *stare* to stand] —**dis'tant·ly** *adv.*

**dis·taste** (dis·tāst') *n.* Aversion; dislike.

**dis·tend** (dis·tend') *v.t. & v.i.* To expand; swell; dilate, as by pressure from within. [< L < *dis-* apart + *tendere* to stretch] —**dis·ten'si·ble** *adj.* —**dis·ten'sion, dis·ten'tion** *n.*

**dis·till** (dis·til') *v.* ·tilled, ·til·ling *v.t.* 1 To subject to or as to distillation. 2 To extract or produce by distillation: to *distill* whiskey. 3 To give forth —*v.i.* 4 To undergo distillation. 5 To exude in drops. Also **dis·til′**. [< L *de-* down + *stillare* to drop, trickle] —**dis·til′la·ble** *adj.*

**dis·tinct** (dis·tingkt′) *adj.* 1 Clear to the senses or mind; plain; unmistakable; definite. 2 Clearly standing apart from other objects; unconnected; separate. 3 Decidedly different; not alike. [< L *distinctus*, pp. of *distinguere* distinguish] —**dis·tinct′ly** *adv.* —**dis·tinct′ness** *n.*

**dis·tinc·tion** (dis·tingk′shən) *n.* 1 A distinguishing mark or quality; a characteristic difference. 2 The act of distinguishing; discrimination. 3 Fame; eminent reputation. 4 Excellence; superiority. 5 A mark of honor or regard.

**dis·tin·guish** (di·sting′gwish) *v.t.* 1 To indicate or constitute the differences of or between. 2 To recognize as separate or distinct; discriminate. 3 To divide into classes; classify. 4 To bring fame or credit upon. 5 To perceive by one of the physical senses. —*v.i.* 6 To make or discern differences. [< L *distinguere* to separate] —**dis·tin′guish·a·ble** *adj.* —**dis·tin′guish·a·bly** *adv.*

**dis·tort** (dis·tôrt′) *v.t.* 1 To twist or bend out of shape. 2 To twist the meaning of; misrepresent. [< L *dis-* apart + *torquere* to twist] —**dis·tort′er, dis·tort′ed·ness** *n.* —**Syn.** 2 misconstrue, mislead, falsify, misquote.

**dis·tract** (dis·trakt′) *v.t.* 1 To divert (the mind, etc.) in a different direction. 2 To bewilder; confuse. 3 To make frantic; craze. [< L *dis-* away + *trahere* to draw] —**dis·tract′er** *n.* —**dis·tract′i·ble, dis·tract′ing, dis·trac′tive** *adj.*

**dis·trac·tion** (dis·trak′shən) *n.* 1 A drawing off or diversion of the mind. 2 Confusion; perplexity. 3 Strong agitation, distress, or grief. 4 Mental aberration; madness. 5 Anything that distracts or diverts.

**dis·tress** (dis·tres′) *v.t.* 1 To cause to be anxious or worry. 2 To inflict suffering upon; subject to pain or agony. —*n.* 1 The state of being distressed; pain, trouble, worry, etc. 2 Anything causing such a condition. 3 A condition requiring immediate help: a ship in *distress.* 4 *Law* a DISTRAINT. b Goods taken by distraint. [< OF < L *distringere* draw asunder] —**dis·tress′ful** *adj.* —**dis·tress′ful·ly** *adv.* —**dis·tress′ful·ness** *n.*

**dis·trib·ute** (dis·trib′yo͞ot) *v.t.* ·ut·ed, ·ut·ing 1 To divide and deal out in shares. 2 To classify; categorize. 3 To scatter, as in an area

or over a surface. 4 To put or arrange into distinctive parts or places. [< L *dis-* away + *tribuere* give, allot] —**dis·trib′ut·a·ble** *adj.*

**dis·tri·bu·tion** (dis′trə·byo͞o′shən) *n.* 1 The act of distributing. 2 That which is distributed. 3 The arrangement in number and place of a set of things: the *distribution* of doctors throughout the U.S. 4 In commerce, all the steps involved in the delivery of goods from producer to consumer.

**dis·trict** (dis′trikt) *n.* 1 A division of territory specially defined, as for judicial, political, educational, or other purposes. 2 Any region of space; a tract. —*v.t.* To divide into districts. [< Med. L *districtus* jurisdiction]

**dis·trust** (dis·trust′) *v.t.* To feel no trust for or confidence in. —*n.* A lack of trust or confidence. —**dis·trust′ful** *adj.* —**dis·trust′ful·ly** *adv.* —**Syn.** *v.* suspect, mistrust, doubt. *n.* doubt, suspicion, disbelief.

**dis·turb** (dis·tûrb′) *v.t.* 1 To interfere with or destroy the peace or quiet of. 2 To trouble mentally or emotionally; ruffle or annoy. 3 To upset the order or system of. 4 To interrupt. 5 To cause inconvenience to. [< L *dis-* completely + *turbare* to disorder] —**dis·tur·b′er** *n.*

**di·u·ret·ic** (dī′yo͝o·ret′ik) *adj.* Stimulating the secretion of urine. —*n.* A diuretic medicine. [< Gk. *dia-* thoroughly + *ourēsis* urination]

**di·ur·nal** (dī·ûr′nəl) *adj.* 1 Happening every day; daily. 2 Done in or pertaining to the daytime. [< L *diurnus* daily] —**di·ur′nal·ly** *adv.*

**div·er** (dī′vər) *n.* 1 One whose work is to explore or gather objects under water. 2 A bird that dives.

**di·verge** (di·vûrj′, dī-) *v.i.* ·verged, ·verg·ing 1 To extend or lie in different directions from the same point. 2 To vary from a typical form; differ. 3 *Math.* To approach no finite limit. [< L *dis-* apart + *vergere* to incline] —**di·ver′gence, di·ver′gen·cy** *n.* —**di·ver′gent** *adj.* —**di·ver′gent·ly** *adv.*

**di·verse** (di·vûrs′, dī-, dī′vûrs) *adj.* 1 Differing one from another; distinct. 2 Varied. [< L *diversus*, pp. of *divertere* divert] —**di·verse′ly** *adv.* —**di·verse′ness** *n.*

**di·ver·si·fy** (di·vûr′sə·fī, dī-) *v.t.* ·fied, ·fy·ing To make diverse; impart variety to; vary. —**di·ver′si·fi·ca′tion** *n.*

**di·ver·sion** (di·vûr′zhən, -shən, dī-) *n.* 1 The act of diverting or turning aside. 2 *Mil.* An attack or feint intended to divert enemy troops from the point where a full scale attack is to be made. 3 That which diverts;

amusement; recreation. —di·ver′sion·ar·y adj.

di·ver·si·ty (di·vûr′sə·tē, dī-) n. pl. ·ties 1 The state of being diverse; dissimilitude. 2 Variety: a diversity of interests.

di·vert (di·vûrt′, dī-) v.t. 1 To turn aside; deflect, as in direction, interest, or purpose. 2 To amuse; entertain. [< L dis- apart + vertere turn] —di·vert′er n. —di·vert′ing adj. —di·vert′ing·ly adv.

di·vest (di·vest′, dī-) v.t. 1 To strip, as of clothes. 2 To deprive, as of office, rights, or honors. [< L dis- apart + vestire clothe]

di·vide (di·vīd′) v. ·vid·ed, ·vid·ing v.t. 1 To cut or separate into parts. 2 To distribute in shares; portion out. 3 To separate into classes; categorize. 4 To separate; keep apart. 5 To form the boundary between. 6 To graduate with lines; calibrate. 7 Math. a To subject to division. b To be an exact divisor of. 8 To cause to disagree. —v.i. 9 To be or come apart; separate. 10 To disagree. 11 To vote in two groups, one for and one against a measure. 12 To share. —n. Geol. A ridge of land separating one drainage system from another. [< L dividere separate] —di·vid′a·ble adj. —di·vid′er n.

di·vid·ed (di·vī′did) adj. 1 Parted; disunited. 2 Bot. Having deep incisions.

di·vine (di·vīn′) adj. 1 Pertaining to, proceeding from, or of the nature of God or of a god; sacred. 2 Addressed or offered up to God. 3 Altogether excellent or admirable. —n. A theologian or clergyman. —v. ·vined, ·vin·ing v.t. 1 To foretell or prophesy. 2 To surmise; guess. —v.i. 3 To practice divination. [< L divinus] —di·vine′ly adv. —di·vine′ness, di·vin′er n.

di·vin·i·ty (di·vin′ə·tē) n. pl. ·ties 1 The quality or character of being divine. 2 A divine being; deity. 3 Theology. 4 A divine attribute, virtue, or quality. —the Divinity The Deity; God.

di·vi·sion (di·vizh′ən) n. 1 The act of dividing. 2 A part, section, or particular category. 3 A disagreement; discord. 4 That which separates, divides, or makes different. 5 The act of sharing; distribution. 6 Math. The operation of finding the factor by which a divisor must be multiplied to produce a given dividend. 7 Mil. A major tactical and administrative unit that can function independently, in the army commanded by a major general. 8 A separation into opposing groups of voters in a legislative body. —di·vi′sion·al adj.

di·vorce (di·vôrs′, -vōrs′) n. 1 The legal dissolution of a marriage. 2 Severance; separation. —v. ·vorced, ·vorc·ing v.t. 1 To free legally from a marriage relationship. 2 To sunder; sever; separate. 3 To obtain a legal divorce from. —v.i. 4 To get a divorce. [< L divortium < divertere separate, divert] —di·vorce′ment n.

di·vulge (di·vulj′, dī-) v.t. ·vulged, ·vulg·ing To tell, as a secret; disclose; reveal. [< L dis- away + vulgare make public] —di·vulge′ment, di·vul′gence (-jəns), di·vulg′er n.

DNA deoxyribonucleic acid.

doc·ile (dos′əl, Brit. dō′sīl) adj. 1 Easy to train; teachable. 2 Easy to manage or handle. [< L docilis able to be taught] —do·c′ile·ly adv. —do·cil·i·ty (do·sil′ə·tē, dō-) n. —Syn. 2 tractable, complaint, obedient, pliant.

doc·trine (dok′trin) n. That which is set forth for acceptance or belief, esp., in religion, a belief or precept; dogma. [< L doctrina teaching]

doc·u·ment (dok′yə·mənt) n. Written or printed matter conveying authoritative information, records, or evidence. —v.t. 1 To prove by documentary evidence. 2 To supply with notes and references to authoritative material; to document a text. [< L documentum a lesson] —doc′u·men·ta′tion n.

doc·u·men·ta·ry (dok′yə·men′tər·ē) adj. 1 Of, pertaining to, supported by, or based upon documents: also doc′u·men′tal. 2 Of, pertaining to, or of the nature of a presentation, as in a film, that purports to record with little or no fictionalization the action displayed. —n. pl. ·ries A documentary film, television show, etc.

dog·ger·el (dôg′ər·əl, dog′-) n. Trivial, awkwardly written verse. —adj. Of or composed of such verse. Also dog′grel. [ME]

do·gie (dō′gē) n. In the w U.S., a stray or motherless calf. [?]

dog·ma (dôg′mə, dog′-) n. pl. ·mas or ·ma·ta (-mə·tə) 1 Theol. A system of teachings of religious truth as maintained by the Christian church or any portion of it. 2 Any doctrine asserted and adopted on authority. 3 Any accepted principle, maxim, or tenet. [< Gk. dogma opinion]

dog·mat·ic (dôg·mat′ik, dog-) adj. 1 Stating opinions without evidence. 2 Overly positive or arrogant. 3 Of, like, or pertaining to dogma. Also dog·mat′i·cal. —dog·mat′i·cal·ly adv. —dog·mat′i·cal·ness n. —Syn.

2 opinionated, overbearing, dictatorial. 3 doctrinal.

**dole** (dōl) *n.* 1 Something given to the needy, as food or money. 2 A sum of money officially paid to an unemployed person for sustenance. 3 Something given out in small portions. —*v.t.* doled, dol·ing To dispense in small quantities; distribute; usu. with *out.* [< OE *dāl*]

**dole·ful** (dōl′fəl) *adj.* Melancholy; mournful. Also **dole′some** (-səm). [< LL *dolium* grief] —**Syn.** dismal, sad, sorrowful, woeful. — **dole′ful·ly** *adv.* —**dole′ful·ness** *n.*

**dol·phin** (dol′fin) *n.* 1 Any of various members of the whale family, having beaklike snouts. 2 *Naut.* A spar or buoy for mooring boats. [< Gk. *delphis*]

**do·main** (dō·mān′) *n.* 1 A territory over which dominion is exercised. 2 A department, as of knowledge. 3 Land owned by one person; estate. [< L < *dominus* lord]

**dome** (dōm) *n.* 1 A vaulted, hemispherical roof; a cupola. 2 Any cuplike top or covering. —*v.* domed, dom·ing *v.t.* 1 To furnish or cover with a dome. 2 To shape like a dome. —*v.i.* 3 To rise or swell upward like a dome. [< Ital. *duomo* cupola]

**do·mes·tic** (də·mes′tik) *adj.* 1 Belonging to the family, house, or household. 2 Fond of family life, duties, or housekeeping. 3 Domesticated; tame. 4 Produced in one's own country. —*n.* A household servant. [< L *domus* house] —**do·mes′ti·cal·ly** *adv.*

**do·mes·ti·cate** (də·mes′tə·kāt) *v.* ·cat·ed, ·cat·ing *v.t.* 1 To train for domestic use; tame. 2 To make domestic. —*v.i.* 3 To become domestic. —**do·mes′ti·ca′tion** *n.*

**do·mes·tic·i·ty** (dō′mes·tis′ə·tē) *n. pl.* ·ties 1 Fondness of home and family. 2 A household.

**dom·i·cile** (dom′ə·səl, -sīl) *n.* A home, house, or dwelling. —*v.t. & v.i.* ·ciled, ·cil·ing *v.t.* To settle in a domicile. Also **dom′i·cil.** [< L *domus* house]

**dom·i·nate** (dom′ə·nāt) *v.* ·nat·ed, ·nat·ing *v.t.* 1 To control; govern. 2 To have supreme or masterful power or influence over. 3 To tower above; loom over: The city *dominates* the plain. —*v.i.* 4 To have control; hold sway. [< L *dominare* rule, dominate] — **dom′i·na′tion, dom′i·na′tor** *n.*

**do·min·ion** (də·min′yən) *n.* 1 Sovereign authority; sway. 2 A country under a particular government. 3 Formerly, a self- governing member of the Commonwealth of Nations. [< L *dominus* lord]

**do·nate** (dō′nāt, dō·nāt′) *v.t.* ·nat·ed, ·nat·ing To bestow as a gift, esp. to a cause; present; contribute. [< L *donare* give < *donum* a gift] —**do′na·tor** *n.*

**do·na·tion** (dō·nā′shən) *n.* 1 The act of donating. 2 That which is donated; a gift.

**don·key** (dong′kē, dung′-) *n.* 1 Any of a domesticated species of the ass. 2 A stupid or stubborn person. [?]

**do·nor** (dō′nər) *n.* 1 A giver; donator. 2 One from whom blood is taken for transfusion or from whom tissue, an organ, etc., is obtained for another. [< L *donare* give]

**doo·dle** (dōōd′l) *v.i. Informal* To draw pictures, symbols, etc., while the mind is otherwise occupied. —*n.* A drawing so made. [dial. E *doodle* be idle]

**dor·mant** (dôr′mənt) *adj.* 1 Sleeping. 2 Quiet; motionless. 3 Sleeping or resting, as certain animals and plants in winter. 4 Not erupting: said of a volcano. 5 Inactive; unused. [< L *dormire* to sleep] —**dor′man·cy** *n.*

**dor·mer** (dôr′mər) *n. Archit.* 1 A vertical window in a small gable rising from a sloping roof: also **dormer window.** 2 The gable in which this window is set. [< OF *dormeor* < *dormir* to sleep]

**dor·mi·to·ry** (dôr′mə·tôr′ē, -tō′rē) *n. pl.* ·ries 1 A large room in which many persons sleep. 2 A building providing sleeping and living accommodations, esp. at a school or college. [< L *dormire* to sleep]

**dose** (dōs) *n.* 1 The quantity of medicine prescribed to be taken at one time; also, the degree of exposure to X-rays or other radiation in a certain period of time. 2 Anything disagreeable given as a prescription or infliction. —*v.* dosed, dos·ing *v.t.* 1 To give medicine to in a dose. 2 To give, as medicine or drugs, in doses. —*v.i.* 3 To take medicines. [< L *dosis* < Gk., orig., a giving] —**dos′er** *n.*

**dot** (dot) *n.* 1 A minute, round, or nearly round mark. 2 *Music* A point, written after a note or rest, which lengthens its value by half; also, a staccato mark. 3 A precise moment of time: on the *dot.* 4 A signal of shorter duration than the dash, used in the transmission of messages. —*v.* dot·ted, dot·ting *v.t.* 1 To mark with a dot or dots. 2 To spread or scatter like dots. 3 To cover with dots. —*v.i.* 4 To make a dot or dots. [< OE *dott* head of a boil] —**Syn.** *n.* 1 flake, fleck, speck, spot.

**do·tage** (dō′tij) n. 1 Feebleness of mind, as a result of old age; senility. 2 Foolish and extravagant affection. [< DOTE + -AGE]

**do·tard** (dō′tərd) n. A senile old person.

**dote** (dōt) v.t. **dot·ed, dot·ing** 1 To lavish extreme fondness: with on or upon. 2 To be in one's dotage. [< MDu. doten be silly] — **dot′er** n. —**dot′ing·ly** adv.

**doub·le** (dub′əl) adj. 1 Having two of a sort together; being in pairs; coupled. 2 Twice as large, much, strong, heavy, valuable, or many. 3 Consisting of two unlike parts: a double standard. 4 Ambiguous, deceitful, or two-faced. 5 Doubled; folded. 6 Bot. Having the petals increased in number. —n. 1 Something that is twice as much. 2 A fold or plait. 3 A person or thing that closely resembles another. 4 An apparition or wraith. 5 A turning about or shift in direction. 6 A stand-in for an actor. 7 pl. A tennis game between two pairs of players; also, two successive faults in tennis. 8 In baseball, a two-base hit. 9 In card playing, the act of doubling. See DOUBLE (v. def. 7). —**on (or at) the double** In double-time: a military command. —v. **doub·led, doub·ling** v.t. 1 To make twice as great in number, size, value, force, etc. 2 To fold or bend one part of upon another: usually with over, up, back, etc. 3 To do over again; repeat. 4 To be twice the quantity or number of. 5 To act or be the double of. 6 Naut. To sail around: to double a cape. 7 In bridge, to increase the value of (an opponent's bid) if the contract is fulfilled, or to increase the penalty if the contract is not fulfilled. —v.i. 8 To become double. 9 To turn and go back on a course: often with back. 10 To act or perform in two capacities. 11 In baseball, to hit a double. 12 In bridge, to double a bid. —**double up** 1 To bend over or cause to bend over, as from pain or laughter. 2 To share one's quarters, bed, etc., with another. 3 In baseball, to complete a double play upon. — adv. 1 Twice. 2 In twice the quantity. Also **doub′ly** (dub′lē) adv. [< L duplus double] — **doub′ler** n.

**doub·le-deck·er** (dub′əl·dek′ər) n. 1 Any structure, vehicle, or vessel having two decks or levels. 2 A sandwich made with three slices of bread and two layers of filling.

**double feature** A program of two full-length motion pictures.

**doubt** (dout) v.t. 1 To hesitate to believe; question. 2 To hold as uncertain. —v.i. 3 To be uncertain or unconvinced. 4 To be mistrustful. —n. 1 Lack of certain knowledge; uncertainty. 2 A matter or case of indecision. 3 A question, objection, or difficulty. [< L dubitare] —**doubt′a·ble** adj. —**doubt′er** n. —**doubt′ing·ly** adv. —Syn. v. 1 distrust, mistrust, suspect. n. 1 hesitancy, misgiving.

**dough** (dō) n. 1 A soft mass of flour, liquid, and other ingredients mixed for baking into bread, cake, etc. 2 Any soft pasty mass. 3 Slang Money. [< OE dāh] —**dough′y** adj.

**douse** (dous) v. **doused, dous·ing** v.t. 1 To plunge into liquid. 2 To drench with water or other liquid. 3 To put out quickly: to douse a light. —v.i. 4 To become drenched or immersed. —n. A ducking or drenching. [?]

**dove·tail** (duv′tāl′) n. 1 A manner of joining boards, timbers, etc., by interlocking wedge-shaped tenons and spaces. 2 The joint so made. —v.t. & v.i. 1 To join by means of a dovetail or dovetails. 2 To fit in closely or aptly.

**dow·el** (dou′əl) n. A pin or peg that fits into a corresponding hole, used for joining together two adjacent pieces. —v.t. ·**eled** or ·**elled, ·el·ing** or ·**el·ling** To fasten with dowels. [< MLG dovel plug]

**dow·ry** (dou′rē) n. pl. ·**ries** 1 The property a wife brings to her husband in marriage. 2 Any endowment or gift. [< L dos, dotis]

**dox·ol·o·gy** (dok·sol′ə·jē) n. pl. ·**gies** A hymn of praise to God, esp. the one beginning "Praise God, from whom all blessings flow." —**greater doxology** The Gloria in Excelsis. —**lesser doxology** The Gloria Patri. [< Gk. doxa praise + legein speak]

**doze** (dōz) v. **dozed, doz·ing** v.i. 1 To sleep lightly; nap. —v.t. 2 To spend (time) napping. —**doze off** To drift into a light sleep. —n. A light, unsound sleep. [< Scand.]

**doz·en** (duz′ən) n. pl. **doz·ens** or **doz·en** 1 A group or set of 12. 2 A large unspecific number: dozens of errands. [< L < duo two + decem ten] —**doz′enth** adj.

**drab** (drab) n. A slattern; a slut. [< Celtic]

**draft** (draft, dräft) n. 1 A current of air. 2 The act of drinking or breathing; also, that which is so taken in, as water or air. 3 Naut. The depth to which a vessel sinks in the water. 4 The act of drawing a load, etc.; also, that which is drawn. 5 A plan, outline or sketch, as of a piece of writing, work to be done, etc. 6 A written order for money drawn by one person, bank, etc., and payable to another.

7 A device for controlling the airflow in a furnace, stove, etc. 8 A military or naval conscription; also, those so conscripted. 9 A drain or lessening: a *draft* on one's time. —**on draft** Ready to be drawn, as beer, etc., from a cask or the like. —*v.t.* 1 To outline in writing; sketch; delineate. 2 To select and draw off, as for military service; conscript. 3 To draw off or away. —*adj.* 1 Suitable or used for pulling heavy loads: a *draft* animal. 2 Drawn from a cask, as beer. [< OE *dragan* to draw] —**draft′er, draft′i·ness** *n.*

**drafts·man** (drafts′mən, dräfts′-) *n. pl.* **·men** (-mən) 1 One who prepares drawings, plans, etc., as in architecture and engineering. 2 One who plans and draws up legal documents, speeches, etc. —**drafts′man·ship** *n.*

**drag** (drag) *v.* **dragged, drag·ging** *v.t.* 1 To pull along by main force. 2 To sweep or search the bottom of, as with a net; dredge. 3 To catch or recover, as with a net. 4 To pull along heavily and wearily. 5 To harrow (land). 6 To continue tediously: often with *on* or *out.* —*v.i.* 7 To be pulled along the ground. 8 To move heavily or slowly. 9 To pass slowly, as time. 10 To operate a dredge. —*n.* 1 The act of dragging. 2 That which drags or is dragged, as a grapple, a dredge, a dragnet. 3 A heavy four-wheeled carriage. 4 Something that impedes motion, as the brake on a wagon wheel. 5 A slow or difficult movement: to walk with a *drag.* 6 *Slang* Influence; pull. 7 *Slang* A puff of a cigarette. 8 *Slang* A dull, boring person or thing. 9 *Slang* Women's clothing worn by a man. [< OE *dragan*]

**drag·on** (drag′ən) *n.* 1 A mythical, serpentlike, winged monster. 2 A fierce or overbearing person. [<Gk. *drakōn* serpent.]

**drain** (drān) *v.t.* 1 To draw off gradually, as a fluid. 2 To draw water or fluid from: to *drain* a swamp. 3 To empty. 4 To exhaust; use up. —*v.i.* 5 To flow off or leak away gradually. 6 To become empty. —*n.* 1 The act of draining. 2 Continuous strain, leak, or outflow. 3 A pipe, trench, tube, etc., for draining. [< OE *drēahnian* strain out] —**drain′er** *n.*

**drake** (drāk) *n.* A male duck. [ME]

**dra·ma** (drä′mə, dram′ə) *n.* 1 A literary composition to be performed upon the stage; a play. 2 The art or profession of writing, acting, or producing plays: often with *the.* 3 A series of striking actions or events like those in a play. [Gk., a deed, an action]

**dra·mat·ic** (drə·mat′ik) *adj.* 1 Of, connected with, or like the drama. 2 Vivid, intense, etc. —**dra·mat′i·cal·ly** *adv.*

**dram·a·tist** (dram′ə·tist) *n.* One who writes plays.

**dram·a·tize** (dram′ə·tīz) *v.t.* **·tized, ·tiz·ing** 1 To convert for stage use. 2 To tell, represent, or interpret (events, one's personality, etc.) in a theatrical manner. *Brit. sp.* **·tise.** —**dram′a·ti·za′tion** (-ə·tə·zā′shən) *n.*

**drape** (drāp) *v.* **draped, drap·ing** *v.t.* 1 To cover or adorn in a graceful fashion, as with drapery or clothing. 2 To arrange in graceful folds. —*v.i.* 3 To hang in folds. —*n.* 1 *Usu. pl.* Drapery; curtain. 2 The way in which cloth hangs, as in clothing. [< OF *draper* to weave <*drap* cloth]

**dras·tic** (dras′tik) *adj.* 1 Acting vigorously. 2 Extreme; severe. [<Gk. *drastikos* effective] —**dras′ti·cal·ly** *adv.*

**draught** (draft, dräft) *n., v., & adj. Chiefly Brit.* DRAFT.

**draw** (drô) *v.* **drew, drawn, draw·ing** *v.t.* 1 To cause to move to or with the mover; pull; haul. 2 To acquire or obtain: to *draw* water. 3 To cause to flow forth: to *draw* blood. 4 To induce: to *draw* praise. 5 To take off, on, or out, as gloves or a sword. 6 To earn, as a salary or interest. 7 To remove, as money from a bank. 8 To deduce; formulate: to *draw* a conclusion. 9 To attract; allure. 10 To close, as curtains, a bag, etc. 11 To elicit; bring out, as truth. 12 To stretch out tightly; also, to manufacture by stretching or hammering, as wire. 13 DISEMBOWEL: to *draw* a chicken. 14 To take in; inhale, as breath. 15 To drain of contents, as a pond. 16 To win or obtain, as by chance. 17 *Naut.* To require (a specified depth) to float: said of vessels. 18 To depict or sketch; delineate, as with lines or words. 19 To write out as a check or deed: often with *up.* 20 To leave undecided, as a game or contest. —*v.i.* 21 To exert a pulling force. 22 To come or go: to *draw* near. 23 To exercise an attracting influence. 24 To pull out a weapon. 25 To shrink; become contracted, as a wound. 26 To cause pus or blood to gather in one spot, as a poultice. 27 To obtain money, supplies, etc., from some source. 28 To produce a current of air: The fire *draws* well. 29 To end a contest without decision; tie. 30 *Naut.* To fill or swell out with wind. 31 To sketch; delineate: he *draws* well. 32 To steep, as tea. —**draw down** To reduce or deplete by using; expend. —**draw on** 1 To rely upon: He *drew on* his reputation. 2 To

lure or entice. 3 To approach its end. —
**draw out** 1 To protract; prolong. 2 To cause (someone) to give information or express opinions. —**draw the line** To fix the limit. —**draw up** 1 To put in required legal form, as a will. 2 To bring or come to a halt. 3 To straighten (oneself); stiffen, as in anger. —*n.* 1 An act of drawing or state of being drawn; also, that which is drawn. 2 A tie game. 3 Anything that draws or attracts. 4 A drawn chance or ticket. [<OE *dragan*]

**draw·back** (drô'bak') *n.* 1 Anything that checks or hinders progress, success, etc. 2 REBATE.

**drawl** (drôl) *v.t. & v.i.* To speak or pronounce slowly, esp. vowels. —*n.* The act of drawling. [?] —**drawl'er** *n.* —**drawl'ing·ly** *adv.* —**drawl'y** *adj.*

**dread** (dred) *v.t. & v.i.* To anticipate with great fear or anxiety. —*adj.* 1 Causing great fear; terrible. 2 Exciting awe. —*n.* 1 Unconquerable fright or terror. 2 Fear joined to awe. [<OE *drǣdan* to fear]

**dream** (drēm) *n.* 1 A train of thoughts or images passing through the mind in sleep. 2 A mental condition similar to that of one sleeping; daydreaming. 3 A visionary idea or fancy. 4 Something so beautiful, pleasant, etc., as to seem possible only in a dream. —*v.* **dreamed** or **dreamt** (dremt), **dream·ing** *v.t.* 1 To see or imagine in a dream. 2 To imagine as in a dream. 3 To while away, as in idle reverie. —*v.i.* 1 To have a dream or dreams. 5 To have a vague idea or conception of something. —**dream up** *Informal.* To concoct or create. [< OE *drēam*] —**dream'er** *n.* —**dream'ful** *adj.* —**dream'ful·ly** *adv.* —**Syn.** *n.* 2 fancy, fantasy, reverie. *v.* 2 muse, meditate, reflect.

**dredge** (drej) *n.* A device for bringing up mud, silt, etc., from under water. —*v.* **dredged**, **dredg·ing** *v.t.* 1 To clear or widen by means of a dredge. 2 To remove, catch, or gather by a dredge. —*v.i.* 3 To use a dredge. [?] —**dredg'er** *n.*

**dregs** (dregz) *n. pl.* 1 The sediment of liquids. 2 The worthless or coarse part: the *dregs* of society.

**drench** (drench) *v.t.* 1 To wet thoroughly; soak. 2 In veterinary science, to force (an animal) to swallow, as medicine. —*n.* 1 A liquid medicine, administered to an animal. 2 A water solution for soaking. 3 The act of drenching. [< OE *drencan* cause to drink] —**drench'er** *n.*

**dress** (dres) *v.t.* 1 To clothe; supply with

clothing. 2 To trim or decorate; adorn. 3 To treat medicinally, as a wound. 4 To comb and arrange (hair). 5 To prepare (stone, timber, leather, etc.) for use or sale. 6 To clean (fowl, game, fish, etc.) for cooking. 7 To till, trim, or prune. 8 To put in proper alignment, as troops. 9 *Informal.* To scold: usu. with *down.* —*v.i.* 10 To put on or wear clothing, esp. formal clothing. 11 To come into proper alignment. —**dress up** To put on or wear clothing more elaborate than that usually worn. —*n.* 1 Clothes; apparel. 2 A gown or frock of a woman or child. 3 Formal attire. 4 External appearance; guise. —*adj.* 1 Of, pertaining to, or suitable for making dresses: *dress* goods. 2 To be worn on formal occasions: a *dress* suit. [< OF *dresser* arrange]

**drib·ble** (drib'əl) *v.t. & v.i.* ·**bled**, ·**bling** 1 To fall or let fall in drops; drip. 2 To drool; slobber. 3 In certain games, to propel (the ball) by bouncing or kicking. —*n.* 1 A dripping or trickle of liquid. 2 In basketball and soccer, the act of dribbling. [Freq. of earlier *drib* < DRIP] —**drib'bler** *n.*

**drift** (drift) *n.* 1 That which is carried onward by a current: a *drift* of clouds. 2 A heap of any matter piled up by wind or sea. 3 A tendency, trend, or meaning: the *drift* of a discourse. 4 A number of objects moving onward by one force, as logs in a river. 5 The distance a ship or airplane is driven from its course by wind, etc. 6 An ocean current. 7 *Geol.* Material transported by moving masses of ice or by running water. 8 *Mining* A horizontal passage in a mine. —*v.t.* 1 To carry along, as on a current. 2 To cause to pile up in heaps, as snow, or sand. —*v.i.* 3 To float or be carried along, as by a current. 4 To wander aimlessly. 5 To accumulate in heaps. [< OE *drīfan* to drive]

**drill** (dril) *n.* 1 A tool for boring metal or other hard substance. 2 The art or action of training in military exercises. 3 Thorough and regular exercises in any branch of knowledge, activity, or industry. 4 A snail that feeds on oysters through holes it drills in their shells. —*v.t.* 1 To bore a hole in. 2 To bore (a hole). 3 To train or teach by methodical exercises. —*v.i.* 4 To use a drill. 5 To engage in an exercise or exercises. [Du. *dril* < *drillen* to bore] —**drill'er** *n.*

**drink** (dringk) *v.* **drank** (*Archaic* **drunk**), **drunk** (*Archaic* **drunk·en**), **drink·ing** *v.t.* 1 To swallow, as water. 2 To absorb (a liquid or moisture). 3 To take in eagerly through the senses or the mind: with *in.* **4** To make a toast. **5** To swallow the contents of. —*v.i.* **6** To swallow a liquid. **7** To consume alcoholic liquors, esp. to excess. **8** To drink a toast: with *to.* —*n.* **1** Any beverage. **2** Alcoholic liquor. **3** The practice of drinking to excess. [< OE *drincan*] —**drink′a·ble** *adj.* —**drink′er** *n.*

**drip** (drip) *n.* **1** A falling in drops. **2** That which drips. **3** *Slang* A person regarded as socially inept. —*v.t. & v.i.* **dripped, drip·ping** To fall or let fall in drops. [< OE *dryppan* to drip]

**drip-dry** (drip′drī) *v.t.* **-dried, -dry·ing** To dry after being hung while dripping wet, as fabrics requiring little or no ironing. —*adj.* Designed to be drip-dried, as a fabric or garment.

**drive** (drīv) *v.* **drove, driv·en, driv·ing** *v.t.* **1** To propel onward or forward. **2** To force to act or work. **3** To bring to a state or condition. **4** To cause to penetrate: often with *in:* to *drive* in a nail. **5** To form by penetrating or passing through: to *drive* a well. **6** To control the movements of: to *drive* an automobile. **7** To transport in a vehicle. **8** To carry on or complete (trade, a bargain, etc.) with energy. **9** In sports, to strike and propel (a ball) with force. **10** *Mech.* To provide power for. —*v.i.* **11** To move forward rapidly or with force. **12** To operate or travel in a vehicle. **13** To have an object or intention: with *at:* What are you *driving* at? **14** To aim a blow: with *at.* —**let drive at** To aim or discharge a blow, missile, etc. —*n.* **1** The act of driving. **2** A road for driving. **3** A journey in a vehicle. **4** A basic need, longing, or pressure. **5** Energy; vitality. **6** A hunt or roundup, as of cattle. **7** An organized campaign to achieve a certain goal. **8** A hard, swift stroke or thrust. **9** *Mech.* A system for transmitting mechanical power. **10** A mass of floating logs. [< OE *drīfan*] —**Syn.** *v.* **1** impel, push, press, thrust.

**drive-in** (drīv′in′) *n.* A restaurant, motion-picture theater, etc., serving patrons in their automobiles. —*adj.* So constructed as to be a drive-in.

**droll** (drōl) *adj.* Odd in a humorous or quaint way. —*n.* A droll person. [MF *drôle* jester] —**droll′ly** *adv.*

**drom·e·dar·y** (drom′ə·der′ē) *n. pl.* **·dar·ies** The one-humped Arabian camel trained for riding. [< LL < Gk. *dromas, dromad-* a dromedary, a running]

**drone** (drōn) *v.* **droned, dron·ing** *v.i.* **1** To make a dull, humming sound; hum. **2** To speak in a slow, dull tone. —*v.t.* **3** To say in a slow, dull tone. —*n.* **1** A dull, humming sound, as of a bee. **2** One of the pipes of the bagpipe that plays a single tone. **3** BAGPIPE. [< ME *drone* a male bee]

**droop** (drōop) *v.i.* **1** To sink down. **2** To lose vigor or vitality. **3** To become dejected. —*v.t.* **4** To allow to hang or sink down. —*n.* A hanging down. [< ON *drūpa*] —**droop′ing** *adj.* —**droop′ing·ly** *adv.*

**drop** (drop) *n.* **1** A globule of liquid. **2** A very small quantity of anything, as of a liquid. **3** Anything that resembles a drop of liquid. **4** A fall, or the distance fallen. **5** A sudden change of level. **6** Any of various contrivances that drop or hang, as a drop curtain in a theater. **7** A trap door. **8** *pl.* Any liquid medicine given by the drop. **9** A slot for letters. **10** A fall in prices. —*v.* **dropped, drop·ping** *v.t.* **1** To let fall in drops. **2** To let fall in any way. **3** To give birth to: said of animals. **4** To say in a casual way. **5** To write (a note, etc.) **6** To bring down or cause to fall. **7** To stop, have done with, or give up. **8** To leave at a specific place. **9** To omit (a syllable, letter, or word) **10** *Slang* To lose (money), as in gambling. **11** To discharge or dismiss. —*v.i.* **12** To fall in drops. **13** To fall rapidly; come down. **14** To fall down exhausted, injured, or dead. **15** To crouch, as a hunting dog at sight of game. **16** To come to an end; cease; stop. **17** To fall into some state or condition. **18** To fall behind: often with *behind* or *back.* —**drop in** To pay an unexpected call. —**drop out** To leave; withdraw from. [< OE *dropa*]

**drop·out** (drop′out′) *n.* **1** A student who leaves school or college before graduation. **2** One who abandons any undertaking before completing it.

**dross** (drôs, dros) *n.* **1** Refuse or impurity in melted metal. **2** Waste matter; refuse. [< OE *drōs*] —**dross′i·ness** *n.* —**dross′y** *adj.* —**Syn.** **2** debris, junk, remains, rubbish.

**drought** (drout) *n.* Long-continued dry weather; want of rain. **Also drouth** (drouth). [< OE *drūgoth*] —**drought′y** *adj.*

**drove** (drōv) *n.* **1** A number of animals driven or herded for driving. **2** A moving crowd of human beings. —*v.t.* **·droved, drov·ing** To drive (cattle, etc.) for some distance. [< OE *drāf*] —**drov′er** *n.*

**drown** (droun) *v.t.* **1** To kill by suffocation in water or other liquid. **2** To flood; deluge. **3** To overwhelm; overpower; extinguish. —

*v.i.* 4 To die by suffocation in water or other liquid. [< Scand.]

**drowse** (drouz) *v.* drowsed, drows·ing *v.i.* 1 To be sleepy; doze. —*v.t.* 2 To make sleepy. 3 To pass (time) in drowsing. —*n.* The state of being half asleep. [< OE *drūsian* become sluggish]

**drub** (drub) *v.t.* drubbed, drub·bing 1 To beat, as with a stick. 2 To vanquish; overcome. —*n.* A blow; thump. [< Ar. *darb* a beating] —drub′ber *n.*

**drudge** (druj) *v.i.* drudged, drudg·ing To toil; work hard at menial tasks. —*n.* One who toils at menial tasks. [ME *druggen*]

**drug** (drug) *n.* 1 Any substance used in or as a medicine. 2 Any narcotic. 3 An over-abundant commodity: a *drug* on the market. —*v.t.* drugged, drug·ging 1 To mix drugs with (food, drink, etc.). 2 To administer drugs to. 3 To stupefy or poison with or as with drugs. [< MF *drogue*]

**drum** (drum) *n.* 1 A percussion instrument consisting of a hollow, usu. cylindrical object with skin or vellum stretched over each end, played by beating with drumsticks or the hands. 2 The sound produced by beating this instrument. 3 Anything resembling a drum in shape, as a cylindrical receptacle. 4 Any mechanical device shaped like a drum. 5 TYMPANIC MEMBRANE —*v.* drummed, drum·ming *v.t.* 1 To perform on or as on a drum. 2 To expel in disgrace: usu. with *out*. 3 To summon by beating a drum. 4 To force upon the attention by constant repetition. —*v.i.* 5 To beat a drum. 6 To beat on anything continuously. —drum up To seek: to *drum up* trade. [Prob. < MDu. *tromme*]

**drunk·ard** (drungk′ərd) *n.* One who habitually drinks to intoxication; a sot.

**dry** (drī) *adj.* dri·er, dri·est 1 Lacking moisture; not wet or damp. 2 Not covered by water: *dry* land. 3 Not green, as wood. 4 Having little or no rain: the *dry* season. 5 Lacking lubrication, as bearings. 6 Thirsty. 7 Lacking interest; lifeless; dull. 8 Slyly shrewd, as wit. 9 Free from sweetness: said of wines. 10 Subject to or in favor of a prohibitory liquor law: a *dry* town. 11 Not giving milk: a *dry* cow. 12 Not liquid; solid: said of merchandise, etc. 13 Tearless: said of the eyes. 14 Characterized by absence of bloodshed. 15 Without butter: said of toast. 16 Wanting in cordiality; not genial. —*v.t.* & *v.i.* dried, dry·ing To make or become dry. —dry up 1 To cease or cause to cease flowing. 2 *Informal* To stop talking. —*n.* *pl.* dries

The state or condition of being dry. [< OE *dryge*] dry′a·ble *adj.* —dry′ly, dri′ly *adv.* —dry′ness *n.*

**du·al** (d<sup>y</sup>ōō′əl) *adj.* 1 Of or pertaining to two. 2 Composed of two. [< L *duo* two] —du·al·i·ty (d<sup>y</sup>ōō·al′ə·tē) *n.* —du′al·ly *adv.*

**dub** (dub) *v.t.* dubbed, dub·bing 1 To confer knighthood upon by tapping on the shoulder with a sword. 2 To call or honor by a title, description, epithet, etc. [< OE *dubbian*] —**Syn.** 2 name, nickname, term, style.

**du·bi·ous** (d<sup>y</sup>ōō′bē·əs) *adj.* 1 In a state of doubt; doubtful. 2 Causing doubt. 3 Of uncertain result. 4 Questionable; suspect: a *dubious* person. [<L *dubium* doubt] —du′bi·ous·ly *adv.* —du′bi·ous·ness *n.*

**duck** (duk) *n.* 1 A web-footed, short-legged, broad-billed water bird. 2 The female of this bird. 3 The flesh of this bird; 4 *Informal* A dear; darling. 5 *Slang* A person; a fellow. [< OE *dūce*, lit. diver]

**duct** (dukt) *n.* 1 Any tube or passage by which a fluid is conveyed. 2 *Anat.* A tubular passage for fluid: the bile *duct*. 3 *Electr.* A tubular channel for carrying wires or cables. [L *ductus* a leading < *ducere* to lead]

**duc·tile** (duk′til, -tīl′) *adj.* 1 Capable of being hammered thin or drawn out, as certain metals. 2 Easily led; tractable. [<L *ducere* lead] —duc·til′i·ty, duc′tile·ness *n.*

**duct·less gland** (dukt′lis) Any of several hormone-producing glands whose secretions are released directly into the blood or lymph.

**dude** (d<sup>y</sup>ōōd) *n.* 1 A fop; dandy. 2 In the w U.S., a city person, esp. one from the E U.S. who is vacationing on a ranch. 3 *Slang* A man; fellow. [?] —dud′ish *adj.*

**due** (d<sup>y</sup>ōō) *adj.* 1 Owing and demandable; payable. 2 That should be given; appropriate. 3 Suitable; sufficient: *due* cause for alarm. 4 Appointed or expected to arrive. 5 Ascribable; owing: with *to*: The delay was *due* to rain. —*n.* 1 That which is due. 2 *pl.* Fee: club *dues*. —*adv.* Directly; exactly: *due* east. [< OF *deu*, pp. of *devoir* owe] • *Due to* as a preposition, though widely used, is still questioned by some, who would substitute for it *because of* or *on account of*: *Because of* (*not due to*) rain, we were delayed.

**du·el** (d<sup>y</sup>ōō′əl) *n.* 1 A prearranged combat between two persons, usu. fought with deadly weapons. 2 A struggle between two parties. —*v.t.* & *v.i.* du·eled or ·elled, du·el·ing or ·el·ling To fight or fight with, in a duel. [<L

*duellum,* var. of *bellum* war] —**du′el·er** or **du′el·ler, du′el·ist** or **du′el·list** *n.*

**du·et** (dyŏo·et′) *n.* 1 A musical composition for two voices or instrumentalists. 2 The performance of such a composition; also, the two persons who perform. [<L *duo* two]

**duke** (dyŏok) *n.* 1 An English peer of the highest rank, below a prince or an archbishop. 2 A Continental noble of corresponding rank. 3 A prince ruling over a duchy or a small state. [<L *dux* leader]

**dul·cet** (dul′sit) *adj.* Pleasant to the ear. [<L *dulcis* sweet] —**Syn.** sweet, soothing, agreeable, melodious.

**dull** (dul) *adj.* 1 Having a blunt edge or point. 2 Not acute or intense: *dull* pain. 3 Not quick, as in thought. 4 Lacking perception or sensibility. 5 Depressed; sad. 6 Boring: a *dull* affair. 7 Not brisk or active; sluggish. 8 Not bright or vivid, as colors. 9 Cloudy; overcast; a *dull* day. 10 Muffled; indistinct, as sounds. —*v.t.* & *v.i.* To make or become dull. [<ME *dul* < MLG] —**dull′ish** *adj.* —**dul·l′ly** *adv.* —**dull′ness** or **dul′ness** *n.*

**du·ly** (dyŏo′lē) *adv.* 1 In accordance with what is due; fitly. 2 In due time or manner. 3 When due.

**dumb** (dum) *adj.* 1 Having no power of speech. 2 Not using words or sounds; silent. 3 *Informal* Stupid. [OE] —**dumb′ly** *adv.* —**dumb′ness** *n.*

**dumb·found** (dum′found′) *v.t.* To strike dumb with amazement. Also **dum′found.** [Blend of DUMB and CONFOUND] —**Syn.** confuse, confound, amaze, astonish.

**dump** (dump) *v.t.* 1 To drop or throw down abruptly. 2 To empty out, as from a container. 3 To empty (a container), as by overturning. 4 To throw (goods) on a market in quantity and at low prices. 5 To get rid of. —*v.i.* 6 To fall or drop. 7 To unload commodities. 8 To unload refuse. —*n.* 1 A dumping ground, as for refuse. 2 That which is dumped. 3 A place where ammunition, supplies, etc. are held for rapid distribution. 4 *Slang* A poor, ill-kept dwelling or place. [<Scand.] —**dump′er** *n.*

**dump·y** (dump′ē) *adj.* **dump·i·er, dump·i·est** Short and thick; stocky. —**dump′i·ly** *adv.* —**dump′i·ness** *n.*

**dun**[1] (dun) *v.t.* & *v.i.* **dunned, dun·ning** To press (a debtor) for payment. —*n.* 1 One who duns. 2 A demand for payment. [?]

**dun**[2] (dun) *adj.* Grayish or reddish brown. —

*n.* Dun color. —*v.t.* **dunned, dun·ning** To make dun-colored. [<OE *dunn*]

**dunce** (duns) *n.* A stupid or ignorant person. [<Johannes *Duns* Scotus, 13th-century theologian]

**dune** (dyŏon) *n.* A hill of loose sand heaped up by the wind. [<MDu. *dūne*]

**dun·ga·ree** (dung′gə·rē′) *n.* 1 A coarse cotton cloth, used for working clothes, tents, sails, etc. 2 *pl.* Working clothes made of this fabric. [<Hind. *dungrī*]

**dun·geon** (dun′jən) *n.* 1 A dark underground prison. 2 DONJON. [<OF *donjon*]

**du·o·dec·i·mal** (dyŏo′ō·des′ə·məl) *adj.* Of, pertaining to, or based on twelve. —*n.* A twelfth. [<L *duodecim* twelve]

**du·o·de·num** (dyŏo′ə·dē′nəm, dyŏo·od′ə·nəm) *n. pl.* **·na** (-nə) or **·nums** That part of the small intestine next to the stomach. [<Med. L *duodenum* (*digitorum*) of twelve (fingers): with ref. to its length] —**du′o·de′nal** *adj.* • See INTESTINE.

**du·pli·cate** (dyŏo′plə·kit) *adj.* 1 Made or done exactly like an original. 2 Double. 3 Designating a way of playing a card game in which, for purposes of comparing scores, the same hands are played by different players. —*n.* 1 An exact copy of an original. 2 A double or counterpart. 3 A duplicate game of cards. —*v.t.* (dyŏo′plə·kāt) **·cat·ed, ·cat·ing** 1 To make an exact copy of. 2 To double; make twofold. 3 To repeat, as an effort. [<L *duplicare* to double] —**du′pli·cate·ly** *adv.* —**du′pli·ca′tion** *n.* —**du′pli·ca′tive** *adj.*

**du·plic·i·ty** (dyŏo·plis′ə·tē) *n. pl.* **·ties** Deception in speech or conduct. [<L *duplex* twofold] —**Syn.** deceitfulness, double-dealing, dissimulation, hypocrisy.

**du·ra·ble** (dyŏor′ə·bəl) *adj.* Able to continue long in the same state. [<L *durus* hard] —**du′ra·bil′i·ty, du′ra·ble·ness** *n.* —**du′ra·bly** *adv.* —**Syn.** lasting, strong, enduring, stable.

**du·ra·tion** (dyŏo·rā′shən) *n.* 1 The period of time during which anything lasts. 2 Continuance in time. [<L *durare* endure]

**du·ress** (dyŏo·res′, dyŏor′is) *n.* 1 Compulsion by force or fear. 2 Restraint, as by confinement in prison. [<OF *duresse* hardness, constraint <L *durus* hard]

**dusk** (dusk) *n.* 1 The dark period of twilight. 2 Partial darkness; semidarkness. —*adj.* Dusky. —*v.t.* & *v.i.* To make or grow dim. [<OE *dox* dark]

**du·te·ous** (dʸōō′tē·əs) *adj.* Obedient; dutiful. —**du′te·ous·ly** *adv.* —**du′te·ous·ness** *n.*

**du·ti·ful** (dʸōō′ti·fəl) *adj.* 1 Submissive; obedient. 2 Showing respect or a sense of duty; respectful. —**du′ti·ful·ly** *adv.* —**du′ti·ful ·ness** *n.*

**du·ty** (dʸōō′tē) *n. pl.* **·ties** 1 Something which one is legally or morally bound to pay, do, or perform. 2 A specific obligatory service or function: to do sea *duty*. 3 A moral obligation; right action; also, a sense of this: *duty* calls. 4 Respectful or obedient conduct, as to one's parents. 5 A tax, as upon goods imported, exported, or consumed. [<OF *deu* DUE]

**dwarf** (dwôrf) *n.* A person, animal, or plant that is unusually small. —*v.t.* 1 To stunt development of. 2 To cause to appear small by comparison. —*v.i.* 3 To become stunted. —*adj.* Smaller than others of its kind; stunted. [<OE *dweorh*] —**dwarf′ish** *adj.* —**dwarf′ish·ly** *adv.* —**dwarf′ish·ness** *n.*

**dwell** (dwel) *v.i.* **dwelt** or **dwelled, dwell·ing** 1 To have a fixed abode; reside. 2 To linger, as on a subject: with *on* or *upon.* [<OE *dwellan* hinder, stay] —**dwell′er** *n.*

**dwin·dle** (dwin′dəl) *v.t. & v.i.* **·dled, ·dling** To make or become smaller or less; diminish; decline. [<OE *dwinan* waste away]

**dye** (dī) *v.* **dyed, dye·ing** *v.t.* 1 To fix a color in (fabric, hair, etc.) by soaking in liquid coloring matter. 2 To stain; color; tint. —*v.i.* 3 To take or give color by dyeing. —*n.* A fluid or coloring matter used for dyeing; also, the color or hue produced by dyeing. [<OE *deag* dye, color] —**dy′er** *n.*

**dy·nam·ic** (dī·nam′ik) *adj.* 1 Of or pertaining to motion or unbalanced forces. 2 Of or pertaining to dynamics. 3 Mentally or spiritually energetic, forceful, or powerful: a *dynamic* leader. Also **dy·nam′i·cal.** [<Gk. *dynamis* power] —**dy·nam′i·cal·ly** *adv.*

**dy·nam·ics** (dī·nam′iks) *n. pl.* (construed as *sing.* in *defs. 1* and *3*) 1 The branch of physics that treats of the motion or equilibrium of bodies or of the forces that produce such motion or equilibrium. 2 The forces producing or governing activity or movement of any kind: spiritual *dynamics.* 3 *Music* The production of varying degrees of loudness; also, the words, symbols, etc., indicating this.

**dy·na·mo** (dī′nə·mō) *n. pl.* **·mos** 1 A machine for changing mechanical energy into electrical energy by electromagnetic induction.

2 A vital, energetic person. [Short for DYNAMOELECTRIC machine]

**dy·nas·ty** (dī′nəs·tē, *esp. Brit.* din′ə·stē) *n. pl.* **·ties** 1 A succession of sovereigns in one line of family descent. 2 The length of time during which one family is in power. —**dy·nas·tic** (dī·nas′tik) or **·ti·cal** *adj.* —**dy·nas′ti·cal·ly** *adv.*

**dys·en·ter·y** (dis′ən·ter′ē) *n.* A severe inflammation of the large intestine, marked by bloody evacuations. [<Gk. *dys-* bad + *enteron* intestine] —**dys′en·ter′ic** or **·i·cal** *adj.*

**dys·pep·sia** (dis·pep′shə, -sē·ə) *n.* Difficult or painful digestion. [<Gk. *dys-* hard + *peptein* cook, digest]

**dys·pep·tic** (dis·pep′tik) *adj.* 1 Relating to or suffering from dyspepsia. 2 Gloomy; cross. Also **dys·pep′ti·cal.** —*n.* A dyspeptic person. —**dys·pep′ti·cal·ly** *adv.*

# E

**ea·ger** (ē′gər) *adj.* Having or showing an intense desire for something. [<L *acer* sharp] —**ea′ger·ly** *adv.* —**ea′ger·ness** *n.* —Syn. avid, desirous, keen, zealous.

**ea·gle** (ē′gəl) *n.* 1 A large diurnal bird of prey with powerful wings and keen eyesight. 2 A former gold coin of the United States, value $10. 3 A picture or design of an eagle, used as an emblem on a seal, flag, etc. 4 In golf, two strokes less than par in playing a hole. [<L *aquila*]

**ear** (ir) *n.* The grain-bearing part of a cereal plant. —*v.i.* To form ears, as grain. [< OE *ēar*]

**earl** (ûrl) *n.* A member of the British nobility ranking below a marquess and above a viscount. [<OE *eorl* nobleman] —**earl′dom, earl′ship** *n.*

**earn** (ûrn) *v.t.* 1 To receive, as salary or wages, for labor. 2 To merit as a result, reward, or punishment. 3 To bring in (interest, etc.) as gain or profit. [<OE *earnian*] —**earn′er** *n.*

**ear·nest** (ûr′nist) *adj.* 1 Intent and direct in purpose; zealous. 2 Marked by deep feeling or conviction; heartfelt. 3 Serious; important. —*n.* Seriousness. —**in earnest** With full and serious intent. [<OE *eorneste*] —**ear′nest·ly** *adv.* —**ear′nest·ness** *n.*

**ear·ring** (ir′ring′) *n.* An ear ornament.

**earth** (ûrth) *n.* 1 *Often cap.* The planet on which man lives; the planet of the solar system third in distance from the sun. • See PLANET. 2 The people who inhabit this planet. 3 The abode of man, considered as distinct from heaven and hell. 4 The dry land portion of the surface of the globe. 5 Soil; dirt; ground. 6 The hole of a burrowing animal. 7 Worldly interests and pursuits. —**down to earth** Realistic. —**run to earth** To hunt down and find, as a fox. — v.t. 1 To protect with earth. 2 To chase, as a fox, into a burrow or hole. —v.i. 3 To burrow or hide in the earth, as a fox. [<OE eorthe]

**earth·quake** (ûrth′kwāk′) n. A tremor of a portion of the earth's crust, caused by volcanic or other disturbances below the earth's surface.

**earth·worm** (ûrth′wûrm′) n. A burrowing worm that lives in and enriches the soil.

**ease** (ēz) n. 1 Freedom from pain, agitation, or worry; comfort. 2 Freedom from or absence of apparent effort; facility. 3 Freedom from affectation, formality, etc.; naturalness. —v. **eased, eas·ing** v.t. 1 To relieve the mental or physical pain or oppression of; comfort. 2 To make less painful or oppressive. 3 To lessen the pressure, weight, tension, etc., of. 4 To move, lower, or put in place carefully. —v.i. 5 To diminish in severity, speed, etc.: often with *up* or *off*. [<OF *aise* < LL *adjacens, -entis* neighboring] —**ease′ful** adj. —**ease′ful·ly** adv. —**ease′ ful·ness, eas′er** n. —**Syn.** n. 1 rest, luxury, repose, content. 2 expertness.

**ea·sel** (ē′zəl) n. A folding frame for supporting a picture, panel, etc. [<Du. *ezel* easel, orig., an ass]

**east** (ēst) n. 1 The general direction in which the sun appears at sunrise. 2 The point of the compass at 90°, directly opposite west. 3 Any direction, region, or part of the horizon near that point. —**the East** 1 Asia, esp. China, Japan, and the other countries of ᴇ Asia. 2 In the U.S., the region east of the Allegheny Mountains and north of Maryland. —adj. 1 To, toward, facing, or in the east. 2 Coming from the east. —adv. In or toward the east; in an easterly direction. [< OE *ēast*]

**eat** (ēt) v. **ate** (āt or Brit. et) or Regional **eat** (et), **eat·en, eat·ing** v.t. 1 To take (food) into the mouth and swallow. 2 To consume or destroy as if by eating: to *eat* away one's savings. 3 To wear into or away; corrode; rust. 4 To make (a way or hole) by or as by gnawing or chewing. —v.i. 5 To take in food; have a meal. —**eat one's words** To retract what one has said. [<OE *etan*] —**eat′a·ble** n., adj. —**eat′er** n.

**eaves** (ēvz) n. pl. The projecting edge of a roof. [< OE *efes* edge]

**ebb** (eb) v.i. 1 To recede, as the tide. 2 To decline; fail. —n. 1 The flowing away of tidewater to the ocean; low tide: **also ebb tide.** 2 A condition or period of decline. [<OE *ebbian*]

**eb·on·y** (eb′ən·ē) n. pl. **·on·ies** 1 A hard, heavy wood, usu. black, used for cabinetwork, etc. 2 A hardwood tree of Ceylon and s India. —adj. 1 Made of ebony. 2 Black. [<Gk. *ebenos* ebony < Egyptian *hebni*]

**ec·cen·tric** (ek·sen′trik) adj. 1 Not having the same center: *eccentric* circles. 2 Not having the axis or support exactly in the center: an *eccentric* wheel. 3 Deviating from a circular form or path: *eccentric* orbit. 4 Erratic; odd; unconventional: *eccentric* behavior. —n. 1 A person characterized by unusual or erratic behavior. 2 Mech. A disk mounted out of center on a driving shaft in order to produce reciprocating motion. [<Gk. *ek-* out, away + *kentron* center] —**ec·cen′tri·cal·ly** adv. —**Syn.** adj. 4 peculiar, strange, bizarre, singular.

**ec·cen·tric·i·ty** (ek′sen·tris′ə·tē) n. pl. **·ties** 1 An odd or capricious act. 2 The state or quality of being eccentric.

**ec·cle·si·as·tic** (i·klē′zē·as′tik) adj. Ecclesiastical. —n. A cleric; churchman. [<Gk. *ekklēsia* assembly]

**ech·o** (ek′ō) n. pl. **·oes** 1 The sound or repetition of sound produced by the reflection of sound waves from an opposing surface. 2 A close imitation of another's views or thoughts. 3 A response or reaction, esp. sympathetic. 4 A suggestion or trace; reminder: an *echo* of the past. —v.t. 1 To repeat or send back (sound) by echo. 2 To repeat the words, opinions, etc., of. 3 To repeat (words, opinions, etc.) in imitation of another. —v.i. 4 To resound or reverberate by or as by echo. [<Gk. *ēchō*] —**ech′o·er** n.

**ec·lec·tic** (ek·lek′tik, ik-) adj. 1 Selecting from various sources. 2 Composed of selections from various sources. —n. One who uses an eclectic method. [<Gk. *ek-* out + *legein* select] —**ec·lec′ti·cal·ly** adv. —**ec·lec′ti· cism** (-tə·siz′əm) n.

**e·clipse** (i·klips′) n. 1 Astron. The dimming or elimination of light reaching an observer from a heavenly body. A **lunar eclipse** is caused by the passage of the moon through the earth's shadow; a **solar eclipse** by the passage of the moon between the sun and the observer. 2 Any dimming or passing into obscurity, as of fame. —*v.t.* **e·clipsed,** **e·clips·ing** 1 To cause an eclipse of; darken. 2 To dim or obscure: *Age eclipsed* her beauty. 3 To outshine; surpass. [< Gk *ek-* out + *leipein* leave] —**Syn.** *v.* 1 obscure, hide, conceal. 3 overshadow.

**e·clip·tic** (i·klip′tik, ē-) *n. Astron.* 1 That plane, passing through the center of the sun, which contains the orbit of the earth: **also plane of the ecliptic.** 2 The great circle in which this plane intersects the celestial sphere. —*adj.* Pertaining to eclipses or to the ecliptic. —**e·clip′ti·cal** *adj.* —**e·clip′ti·cal·ly** *adv.* • See ZONE.

**e·col·o·gy** (i·kol′ə·jē) *n.* 1 That division of biology which treats of the relations between organisms and their environment. 2 The system of relationships between organisms and their environments. [<Gk. *oikos* home + -LOGY] —**ec′o·log′ic** (ek′ə·loj′ik) or -i·cal *adj.* —**ec′o·log′i·cal·ly** *adv.* —**e·col′o·gist** *n.*

**ec·o·nom·ic** (ek′ə·nom′ik, ē′kə-) *adj.* 1 Of or relating to the production, distribution, or management of wealth. 2 Of or pertaining to the financial matters of a country, household, etc. 3 Of or pertaining to the science of economics. 4 Of practical utility: *economic* botany. [<Gk. *oikonomia.* See ECONOMY.]

**ec·o·nom·i·cal** (ek′ə·nom′i·kəl, ē′kə-) *adj.* 1 Careful in management; frugal; saving. 2 Not exaggerated or excessive: an *economical* style of writing. 3 ECONOMIC. —**ec′o·nom′i·cal·ly** *adv.*

**ec·o·nom·ics** (ek′ə·nom′iks, ē′kə-) *n. pl.* (construed as sing.) 1 The science that treats of the production, distribution, and consumption of wealth. 2 Financial matters.

**e·con·o·mize** (i·kon′ə·mīz) *v.* **·mized, ·miz·ing** *v.t.* 1 To use thriftily. —*v.i.* 2 To be frugal. —**e·con′o·miz′er** *n.*

**e·con·o·my** (i·kon′ə·mē) *n. pl.* **·mies** 1 The management of the financial and other resources of a country, community, etc. 2 Care and frugality in the use of money, time, resources, etc.; also, an instance of this. 3 A particular system of producing or managing material resources: an industrial *economy.* 4 Any practical organization of parts in a system. [<Gk. *oikonomia < oikos* house + *nemein* manage]

**ec·sta·sy** (ek′stə·sē) *n. pl.* **·sies** 1 The state of being beside oneself through overpowering emotion or mental exaltation. 2 Intense joy; rapture. 3 A state of trance. [<Gk. *ekstasis* distraction] —**Syn.** 1 Frenzy, transport. 2 bliss.

**ec·stat·ic** (ek·stat′ik) *adj.* Of, pertaining to, like, or in a state of ecstasy. —*n.* A person subject to ecstasies or trances. —**ec·stat′i·cal·ly** *adv.*

**ec·u·men·i·cal** (ek′yōō·men′i·kəl) *adj.* 1 General; universal. 2 Of or pertaining to ecumenism. 3 Belonging to or accepted by the Christian church everywhere. [<Gk. oikoumenē (*gē*) the inhabited (world) < *oikein* dwell] —**ec′u·men′i·cal·ly** *adv.*

**ec·ze·ma** (ek′sə·mə, eg′zə·mə, eg·zē′mə) *n.* An inflammatory skin disease often attended by itching, watery discharge, and lesions. [<Gk. *ek-* out + *zeein* to boil]

**ed·dy** (ed′ē) *n. pl.* **·dies** A circling current of water, air, or other fluid. —*v.t. & v.i.* **·died, ·dy·ing** To move, or cause to move, in or as in an eddy. [< ON *idha*]

**ed·i·ble** (ed′ə·bəl) *adj.* Fit to eat. —*n. Usu. pl.* Something suitable for food. [<L *edere* eat] —**ed′i·bil′i·ty** *n.*

**e·dict** (ē′dikt) *n.* An official proclamation or decree. [<L < *ex-* out + *dicere* say]

**ed·i·fice** (ed′ə·fis) *n.* A building or other structure, esp. if large or imposing. [<L *aedes* building + *facere* make]

**ed·i·fy** (ed′ə·fī) *v.t.* **fied, fy·ing** To strengthen morally; enlighten. [<L *aedes* building + *facere* make] —**ed′i·fi·ca′tion, ed′i·fi′er** *n.* —**ed′i·fy′ing** *adj.* —**ed′i·fy′ing·ly** *adv.*

**edit.** edited; edition; editor.

**e·di·tion** (i·dish′ən) *n.* 1 A published form of a literary work, or a copy of the form so published. 2 The total number of copies of a book, magazine, etc., issued at one time.

**ed·i·tor** (ed′i·tər) *n.* 1 One who prepares manuscripts, copy, etc., for publication. 2 One who writes editorials. —**ed′i·tor·ship′** *n.*

**ed·u·cate** (ej′ōō·kāt) *v.t.* **·cat·ed, ·cat·ing** 1 To develop or train the mind, capabilities, and character of by or as by formal schooling or instruction; teach. 2 To train for some special purpose. 3 To develop and train (taste, special ability, etc.). 4 To provide schooling for. [< L *educare* bring up] —**ed′u·ca′tor** *n.*

**ed·u·ca·tion** (ej′ōō·kā′shən) *n.* 1 The development and training of one's mind, character, skills, etc., as by instruction, study, or example. 2 Instruction and training in an institution of learning. 3 The knowledge and skills resulting from such instruction and training. 4 Teaching as a system, science, or art; pedagogy. **—ed′u·ca′tion·al** *adj.* **—ed′u·ca′tion·al·ly** *adv.*

**e·duce** (i·d′o̅o̅s′) *v.t.* **e·duced, e·duc·ing** 1 To call forth; draw out; evoke. 2 To develop or formulate, as from data. [< L *ex-* out + *ducere* to lead] **—e·duc′i·ble** *adj.* **—e·duc·tion** (i·duk′shən), **e·duc′tor** *n.*

**ef·face** (i·fās′) *v.t.* **·faced, ·fac·ing** 1 To rub out, as written characters; erase; cancel. 2 To obliterate or destroy. 3 To make (oneself) inconspicuous or insignificant. [< L *ex-* out + *facies* face] **—ef·face′a·ble** *adj.* **—ef·face′ment, ef·fac′er** *n.*

**ef·fect** (i·fekt′) *n.* 1 A result or consequence of some cause or agency. 2 The power or capacity to produce a result; efficacy. 3 The condition of being in actual operation: When does the ruling go into *effect?* 4 Actual meaning: usu. with *to:* They wrote to this *effect.* 5 An impression or reaction resulting from something seen, done, or experienced: the *effect* of a play. 6 Something causing a particular impression or reaction: many weird *effects.* 7 *pl.* Movable goods or property; belongings. **—in effect** 1 In fact; actually. 2 In essence; virtually. 3 In operation or force. **—take effect** To begin to show results; become operative. *—v.t.* 1 To bring about; cause. 2 To achieve; accomplish. [< L *ex-* out + *facere* do, make] **—ef·fect′er** *n.* **—Syn.** *n.* 1 upshot, outcome, conclusion. • See AFFECT[1].

**ef·fec·tive** (i·fek′tiv) *adj.* 1 Producing a desired effect or result. 2 Impressive; striking. 3 In force, as a law. 4 Ready, as an army. *—n.* A soldier or military unit ready for active duty. **—ef·fec′tive·ly** *adv.* **—ef·fec′tive·ness** *n.*

**ef·fec·tu·al** (i·fek′cho̅o̅·əl) *adj.* 1 Possessing or exercising power to produce a desired effect. 2 In force; legal. **—ef·fec′tu·al′i·ty** (-al′ə·tē) *n.* **—ef·fec′tu·al·ly** *adv.*

**ef·fem·i·nate** (i·fem′ə·nit) *adj.* 1 Having womanish traits or qualities inappropriate to a man; unmanly. 2 Characterized by weakness, a lack of dynamism, overrefinement, etc.: an *effeminate* culture. [< L *ex-* out + *femina* a woman] **—ef·fem′i·na·cy** (-nə·sē) *n.* **—ef·fem′i·nate·ly** *adv.*

**ef·fer·vesce** (ef′ər·ves′) *v.i.* **·vesced, ·vesc·ing** 1 To give off bubbles of gas, as carbonated water. 2 To issue forth in bubbles, as a gas. 3 To show exhilaration or lively spirits. [< L *ex-* out + *fervescere* to boil.] **—ef′fer·ves′cence, ef′fer·ves′cen·cy** *n.* **—ef′fer·ves′cent** *adj.* **—ef′fer·ves′cent·ly** *adv.*

**ef·fete** (i·fēt′) *adj.* 1 Incapable of further production; exhausted; barren. 2 Characterized by weakness, self-indulgence, decadence, etc. [< L *ex-* out + *fetus* a breeding] **—ef·fete′ness** *n.*

**ef·fi·ca·cy** (ef′ə·kə·sē) *n.* *pl.* **·cies** Power to produce a desired result or effect.

**ef·fi·cient** (i·fish′ənt) *adj.* 1 Acting or operating effectively with little waste of energy, effort, or material. 2 Productive of effects or results; causative. [< L *efficere* to effect] **—ef·fi′cient·ly** *adv.* **—Syn.** 1 skillful, competent. 2 operative, effectual.

**ef·fi·gy** (ef′ə·jē) *n.* *pl.* **·gies** 1 A figure representing a person, as in sculpture or numismatics. 2 A representation of a despised person. **—burn (or hang) in effigy** To burn or hang publicly an image of a person who is hated. [< L *effigies* image]

**ef·fort** (ef′ərt) *n.* 1 A voluntary exertion of mental or physical power in order to accomplish something. 2 An endeavor; attempt. 3 A result or display of power; an achievement. [< L *ex-* out + *fortis* strong] **—Syn.** 1 strain, stress, exertion.

**ef·front·er·y** (i·frun′tər·ē) *n.* *pl.* **·er·ies** Insolent assurance; audacity; impudence. [< L *ex-* out + *frons, frontis* forehead, face]

**ef·ful·gence** (i·ful′jəns) *n.* A shining forth brilliantly; beaming brightness; radiance. [< L *ex-* out + *fulgere* to shine] **—ef·ful′gent** *adj.* **—ef·ful′gent·ly** *adv.*

**ef·fuse** *v.* (i·fyo̅o̅z′) **·fused, ·fus·ing** *v.t.* 1 To pour forth; shed. *—v.i.* 2 To emanate; exude. *—adj.* (i·fyo̅o̅s′) 1 *Bot.* Spread loosely or flat. 2 *Zool.* Having the lips separated, as a shell. [< L *effusus,* pp. of *effundere* to pour out]

**egg·head** (eg′hed′) *n.* *Slang* An intellectual; a highbrow: usu. slightly derisive.

**e·go** (ē′go, eg′ō) *n.* *pl.* **e·gos** 1 The conscious self. 2 *Psychoanal.* The superficial conscious part of the psyche, developed in response to environment. 3 Self-centeredness; egotism; conceit. [L, I]

**e·go·tism** (ē′gə·tiz′əm, eg′ə-) *n.* 1 The excessive and habitual practice of talking only about oneself or one's concerns. 2 CONCEIT. 3 EGOISM. **—e′go·tist** *n.* **—e′go·tis′tic** or **·ti·cal** *adj.* **—e′go·tis′ti·cal·ly** *adv.* • *Egoism* and *egotism* are often used interchangeably. However, *egoism* is felt by many to manifest itself more in self-centered thought and inner concern, whereas *egotism* is outwardly revealed in speech and actions.

e·gre·gious (i·grē′jəs, -jē·əs) *adj.* Unusually or conspicuously bad; flagrant. [<L *ex-* out + *grex, gregis* the herd] —e·gre′gious·ly *adv.* —e·gre′gious·ness *n.*

e·jac·u·late (i·jak′yə·lāt) *v.* ·lat·ed, ·lat·ing *v.t.* 1 To utter suddenly. 2 To eject suddenly, as semen. —*v.i.* 3 To eject semen. [<L *ex-* out + *jaculari* to throw] —e·jac′u·la′tion, e·jac′u·la′tor *n.* —e·jac′u·la·to′ry *adj.*

e·ject (i·jekt′) *v.t.* 1 To throw or drive out by sudden force; expel. 2 EVICT. [< L *ex-* out + *jacere* to throw] —e·jec′tion, e·ject′ment *n.* —e·jec′tive *adj.* —e·jec′tive·ly *adv.* —Syn. 1 banish, oust, exile, deport.

e·lab·o·rate (i·lab′ə·rāt) *v.* ·rat·ed, ·rat·ing *v.t.* 1 To create and work out with care and in detail. 2 To produce by labor; make. —*v.i.* 3 To speak or write so as to embellish a matter, subject, etc., with additional details: with *on* or *upon.* —*adj.* (-ər·it) 1 Developed in detail and with care: an *elaborate* plan. 2 Ornate; complicated, as a design. 3 PAINSTAKING. [< L *ex-* out + *laborare* to work] —e·lab′o·rate·ly *adv.* —e·lab′o·rate·ness, e·lab′o·ra′tion *n.* —e·lab′o·ra′tive *adj.* —Syn. *v.* 1 develop, devise. 2 execute. —*adj.* 2 showy, extravagant, fancy.

e·lapse (i·laps′) *v.i.* e·lapsed, e·laps·ing To slip by; pass away: said of time. [< L *elapsus,* pp. of *elabi* glide away]

e·las·tic (i·las′tik) *adj.* 1 Spontaneously returning to a former size, shape, etc., after being altered from it. 2 Capable of quick recovery, as from misfortune. 3 Changing or adapting readily in response to new circumstances or demands. —*n.* 1 A stretchable fabric having rubber or rubberlike threads woven therein. 2 A garter, suspender, etc., made of this fabric. 3 RUBBER BAND. [< Gk. *elastikos* driving] —e·las′ti·cal·ly *adv.*

e·lect (i·lekt′) *v.t.* 1 To choose for an office by vote. 2 To take by choice or selection. 3 *Theol.* To choose or set aside for eternal life. —*v.i.* 4 To make a choice. —*adj.* 1 Elected to office, but not yet in charge: used in compounds, as president-*elect.* 2 *Theol.* Chosen of God for salvation. 3 Selected; chosen; picked out. —*n.* An elect person. [< L *ex-* out + *legere* choose]

e·lec·tion (i·lek′shən) *n.* 1 The selecting of a person or persons for office, as by ballot. 2 Any choice or act of choosing. 3 In Calvinism, the predestination of some individuals to be saved by God.

e·lec·tric (i·lek′trik) *adj.* 1 Relating to, derived

from, produced, or operated by electricity. 2 Containing, producing, or carrying electricity. 3 Dynamic; exciting; electrifying; also, tense, as if electrified. —*n.* A street car, train, or other vehicle run by electricity. [< Gk. *ēlektron* amber: in ref. to static charge produced when amber is rubbed.]

e·lec·tri·cal (i·lek′tri·kəl) *adj.* 1 ELECTRIC. 2 Of or skilled in the use or science of electricity. —e·lec′tri·cal·ly *adv.*

electric eye PHOTOELECTRIC CELL.

e·lec·tric·i·ty (i·lek′tris′ə·tē, ē′lek-) *n.* 1 A property of matter associated with atomic particles that are capable of attracting and repelling each other over relatively long distances, and which can be made to perform work. 2 A flow of such particles, usu. electrons, used as a source of power or energy. 3 The science dealing with electricity.

e·lec·tro·car·di·o·graph (i·lek′trō·kär′dē·ə·graf′, -gräf′) *n.* An instrument for recording the electrical activity of the heart, used in the diagnosis of heart diseases. —e·lec·tro·car·di·og·ra·phy (i·lek′trō·kär′dē·og′rə·fē) *n.*

e·lec·tro·cute (i·lek′trə·kyōōt) *v.t.* ·cut·ed, ·cut·ing 1 To kill by electricity. 2 To execute in an electric chair. [<ELECTRO- + (EXE)CUTE] —e·lec′tro·cu′tion *n.*

e·lec·trode (i·lek′trōd) *n.* *Electr.* A conducting element through which an electric charge leaves or enters an electrolytic cell, vacuum tube, electric arc, furnace, etc.

e·lec·tro·en·ceph·a·lo·graph (i·lek′trō·en·sef′ə·lə·graf′) *n.* A device for recording electric activity in the brain.

e·lec·tron (i·lek′tron) *n.* An atomic particle having a negative electric charge equal to $1.602 \times 10^{-19}$ coulomb and a mass equal to 1/1837 that of a proton. [<Gk. *ēlektron* amber. See ELECTRIC.]

e·lec·tron·ics (i·lek′tron′iks, ē′lek-) *n. pl.* *(construed as sing.)* The study of the properties and behavior of electrons and other carriers of electric charge, esp. with reference to technical and industrial applications.

electron microscope A microscope which uses high-energy streams of electrons in order to magnify objects too small to reflect the relatively large wavelengths of visible light.

el·e·gance (el′ə·gəns) *n.* 1 The state or quality of being elegant or refined. 2 Anything elegant. Also el′e·gan·cy.

el·e·gant (el′ə·gənt) *adj.* 1 Characterized by a

tasteful luxuriousness and grace of style, design, content, etc. **2** Possessing or exhibiting a refined taste and gracefulness of manner, dress, etc. **3** *Informal* Excellent; capital. **4** Marked by appropriateness and simplicity: an *elegant* solution. [< L *elegans* fastidious] —**el′e·gant·ly** *adv.* —**Syn.** 2 refined, polished.

**el·e·gy** (el′ə·jē) *n. pl.* **·gies 1** A meditative poem with sorrowful theme. **2** A classical poem written in elegiac verse. **3** A musical composition of a sad or meditative character. [< Gk. *elegos* a song]

**el·e·ment** (el′ə·mənt) *n.* **1** A component or essential part, esp. of anything complex. **2** *pl.* First principles or fundamental ideas; rudiments. **3** One of the four substances (earth, air, fire, and water) anciently supposed to make up all things. **4** *pl.* Atmospheric conditions or powers, as rain, wind, etc. **5** An essential or determining factor. **6** A group or class having certain characteristics in common: the *rowdy* element in the crowd. **7** The natural or appropriate sphere or environment for a person or thing. **8** *Eccl.* The bread and wine of the Lord's Supper. **9** Any of a number of substances composed entirely of atoms having identical nuclear charges, as gold, carbon, sodium, etc. **10** One of the primary parts of an organism; a cell. **11** *Geom.* One of the forms or data which together compose a figure, as a line, a point, a plane, a space. **12 a** Any one of the members of a set. **b** A term in an algebraic expression. [< L *elementum* first principle]

**el·e·men·tal** (el′ə·men′təl) *adj.* **1** Of or pertaining to an element or elements. **2** Having to do with rudiments or first principles; basic. **3** Of or like the basic, powerful forces or drives in man or nature. —**el′e·men′tal·ly** *adv.*

**el·e·men·ta·ry** (el′ə·men′tər·ē) *adj.* **1** ELEMENTAL. **2** Rudimentary; basic; fundamental. **3** Simple. —**el′e·men′ta·ri·ly** *adv.* —**el′e·men′ta·ri·ness** *n.*

**el·e·phant** (el′ə·fənt) *n.* A massively built, almost hairless mammal of Asia or Africa having a flexible trunk and tusks valued as the chief source of ivory. [< Gk. *elephas*] —**el′e·phan′tine** (-fan′tēn, -tīn, -tĭn) *adj.*

**el·e·vate** (el′ə·vāt) *v.t.* **·vat·ed, ·vat·ing 1** To raise; lift up. **2** To raise in rank, status, position, etc. **3** To raise the spirits of; inspire. **4** To raise the moral or intellectual level of. [< L *ex-* out, up + *levare* lighten] —**Syn.** 1

heighten. **2** promote, advance. **3** exalt, cheer.

**el·e·va·tion** (el′ə·vā′shən) *n.* **1** The act of elevating or the condition of being elevated. **2** An elevated place. **3** Height above sea level or the earth's surface. **4** *Astron.* The angular distance of a celestial body above the horizon. **5** In dancing, the ability to perform leaps. **6** *Eccl.* The raising of the eucharistic elements: also **elevation of the Host.**

**el·e·va·tor** (el′ə·vā′tər) *n.* **1** One who or that which elevates. **2** A hoisting mechanism for grain. **3** A warehouse where grain is elevated, stored, and distributed. **4** A movable platform or cage for carrying freight or passengers up or down, as in a building. **5** *Aeron.* A movable airfoil used to control an aircraft's ascent or descent. • See AIRPLANE.

**e·lic·it** (i·lis′it) *v.t.* To draw out or forth, as by some attraction or inducement; bring to light. [< L *ex-* out + *lacere* entice] —**e·lic′i·ta′tion, e·lic′i·tor** *n.*

**el·i·gi·ble** (el′ə·jə·bəl) *adj.* **1** Capable of being chosen or elected. **2** Worthy of acceptance. —*n.* One who is eligible. [< L *eligere* to select, elect] —**el′i·gi·bil′i·ty** *n.* —**el′i·gi·bly** *adv.* —**Syn.** 1 qualified, fitted. 2 suitable, desirable.

**e·lim·i·nate** (i·lim′ə·nāt) *v.t.* **·nat·ed, ·nat·ing 1** To get rid of. **2** To disregard as irrelevant or incorrect; ignore. **3** *Physiol.* To void; excrete. [< L *ex-* out + *limen* a threshold] —**e·lim′i·na′tion, e·lim′i·na′tor** *n.* —**e·lim′i·na′tive** *adj.*

**e·li·sion** (i·lizh′ən) *n.* The eliding or striking out of a part of a word, as in "o'er" for "over."

**el·lipse** (i·lips′) *n. Geom.* A plane curve such that the sum of the distances from any point of the curve to two fixed points is a constant. [< ELLIPSIS]

**el·lip·sis** (i·lip′sis) *n. pl.* **·ses** [-sēz] **1** The omission of a word or words necessary to complete a sentence or expression. **2** A sudden jump from one thought or subject to another without the inclusion of logical connectives. **3** Marks indicating omission, as . . . or ✱ ✱ ✱. [< Gk. *elleipsis* a falling short]

**el·o·cu·tion** (el′ə·kyōō′shən) *n.* **1** The art of speaking or reading in public. **2** Manner of utterance. [< L *ex-* + *loqui* speak] —**el′o·cu′tion·ar′y** *adj.* —**el′o·cu′tion·ist** *n.*

**e·lon·gate** (i·lông′gāt, i·long′-) *v.t. & v.i.* **·gat·ed, ·gat·ing** To make or grow longer; lengthen. —*adj.* **1** Made longer; lengthened. **2** Long and slender. —**e′lon·ga′tion** *n.*

**e·lope** (i·lōp′) *v.i.* **e·loped, e·lop·ing** To run away, esp. to get married in secret. [<ME *alepen* run away] —**e·lope′ment, e·lop′er** *n.*

**el·o·quence** (el′ə·kwəns) *n.* **1** Graceful, articulate, and convincing expression; also, the art or forcefulness of such expression. **2** The quality of being forceful or persuasive.

**el·o·quent** (el′ə·kwənt) *adj.* **1** Having or exhibiting eloquence. **2** Expressive; affecting: an *eloquent* glance. [<L < *ex*- out + *loqui* speak] —**el′o·quent·ly** *adv.*

**e·lude** (i·lōōd′) *v.t.* **e·lud·ed, e·lud·ing** **1** To avoid or escape from by swiftness or cleverness. **2** To escape the notice or understanding of. [<L *ex*- out + *ludere* to play] —**e·lud′i·ble** *adj.* —**e·lu·sion** (i·lōō′zhən) *n.*

**e·lu·sive** (i·lōō′siv) *adj.* **1** Tending to elude. **2** Difficult to understand. —**e·lu′sive·ly** *adv.* —**e·lu′sive·ness** *n.*

**e·ma·ci·ate** (i·mā′shē·āt) *v.t.* **·at·ed, ·at·ing** To make abnormally thin, as from starvation. [<L *emaciare* waste away] —**e·ma′ci·a′tion** *n.*

**em·a·nate** (em′ə·nāt) *v.i.* **·nat·ed, ·nat·ing** To come or flow forth, as from a source. [<L *ex*- out + *manare* to flow]

**em·a·na·tion** (em′ə·nā′shən) *n.* **1** The act of emanating. **2** That which flows from an origin or source. —**em′a·na′tive** *adj.* —**em′a·na′tive·ly** *adv.*

**e·man·ci·pate** (i·man′sə·pāt) *v.t.* **·pat·ed, ·pat·ing** **1** To release from bondage or slavery. **2** To release from any oppression or restraint. [<L *ex*- out + *manus* hand + *capere* take] —**e·man′ci·pa′tion, e·man′ci·pa′tor** *n.* —**e·man′ci·pa·to′ry** (-pə·tôr′ē, -tō′rē) *adj.*

**em·balm** (im·bäm′) *v.t.* **1** To treat (a dead body) so as to preserve from quick decay. **2** To perfume. **3** To preserve the memory of. [< OF < *em*- in + *basme* balm] —**em·balm′er, em·balm′ment** *n.*

**em·bar·go** (im·bär′gō) *n. pl.* **·goes** **1** A prohibition by a government temporarily restraining vessels from leaving or entering its ports. **2** Authoritative stoppage of any commerce. **3** Any imposed impediment or hindrance. —*v.t.* **·goed, ·go·ing** To lay an embargo upon. [<Sp. *embargar* to restrain]

**em·bark** (im·bärk′) *v.i.* **1** To go aboard a ship, airplane, etc., as for a voyage. **2** To get started, as with a venture: usu. with *on* or *upon.* —*v.t.* **1** To put or take aboard a ship, airplane, etc. **2** To invest (money) or involve (a person) in a venture. [<LL *in*- in + *barca* boat] —**em′bar·ka′tion, em·bark′ment** *n.*

**em·bar·rass** (im·bar′əs) *v.t.* **1** To make ill at ease, self-conscious, and uncomfortable. **2** To involve in difficulties, esp. in business. **3** To hamper; encumber. **4** To render difficult; complicate. [<F *embarrasser*] —**em·bar′rass·ing** *adj.* —**em·bar′rass·ing·ly** *adv.* —**em·bar′rass·ment** *n.* —Syn. **1** abash, discomfit, disconcert, rattle.

**em·bas·sy** (em′bə·sē) *n. pl.* **·sies** **1** The mission or office of an envoy or ambassador. **2** The official residence of an ambassador and his staff. **3** An ambassador and his associates. [< Med. L *ambactia* service]

**em·bel·lish** (im·bel′ish) *v.t.* **1** To add ornamental features to. **2** To heighten the interest of, as a story, by adding details that are often fictitious. [< OF *embellir* beautify] —**em·bel′lish·ment** *n.*

**em·bez·zle** (im·bez′əl) *v.t.* **·zied, ·zling** To appropriate fraudulently for one's own use; steal. [< AF *embesiler*] —**em·bez′zle·ment, em·bez′zler** *n.*

**em·blem** (em′bləm) *n.* **1** A figurative representation or symbol of an idea, organization, or object. **2** A distinctive badge. [<L *emblema* inlaid work]

**em·brace** (im·brās′) *v.* **·braced, ·brac·ing** *v.t.* **1** To put one's arms around in greeting or affection. **2** To accept willingly; adopt. **3** To avail oneself of: to *embrace* an offer. **4** To encircle. **5** To include; contain. **6** To take in visually or mentally. —*v.i.* **7** To hug each other. —*n.* The act of embracing; a clasping in the arms. [<L *in*- in + *bracchia* arm] —**em·brace′a·ble** *adj.* —**em·brace′ment, em·brac′er** *n.* —Syn. **1** hug, caress, hold. **2** espouse, endorse.

**em·broi·der** (im·broi′dər) *v.t.* **1** To ornament with designs in needlework. **2** To execute in needlework. **3** To exaggerate, as a narrative, with usu. fictitious details. —*v.i.* **4** To make embroidery. [<EN-[1] + obs. *broider* < MF *brouder* to stitch] —**em·broi′der·er** *n.*

**em·broil** (em·broil′) *v.t.* **1** To involve in dissension or conflict. **2** To throw into uproar or confusion. [< OF *em*- in + *brouiller* confuse] —**em·broil′ment** *n.*

**em·bry·o** (em′brē·ō) *n. pl.* **·os** **1** An animal in the early stages of development of the fertilized ovum. **2** The fertilized human ovum during two months following implantation in the uterus. **3** A rudimentary plant within the seed. **4** Anything in process of developing its distinctive form. —**in embryo** In an

159

undeveloped or incipient stage. —*adj.* Pertaining to an embryo; rudimentary: also **em′bry·al.** [< Gk. *en-* in + *bryein* to swell]

**em·bry·on·ic** (em′brē·on′ik) *adj.* 1 Of, pertaining to, or like an embryo. 2 Undeveloped. Also **em·bry·o·nal** (em′brē·ə·nəl, em·brī′-).

**em·cee** (em′sē′) *Informal n.* Master of ceremonies. —*v.i.* & *v.t.* **em·ceed, em·cee·ing** To act or direct as master of ceremonies. [< *m(aster of) c(eremonies)*]

**e·men·da·tion** (ē′men·dā′shən, em′ən-) *n.* 1 A correction or alteration. 2 The act of emending. —**e′men·da′tor** *n.* —**e·mend·a·to·ry** (i·men′də·tôr′ē, -tō′rē) *adj.*

**em·er·ald** (em′ər·əld, em′rəld) *n.* A bright green precious stone, a variety of beryl. —*adj.* 1 Of or like the emerald. 2 Of a rich green color. [< OF *emeraude, esmeraldus*]

**e·merge** (i·murj′) *v.i.* **e·merged, e·merg·ing** 1 To come forth into view or existence. 2 To become noticeable or apparent: The truth *emerged.* [< L *ex-* out + *mergere* to dip] — **e·mer·gent** (i·mûr′jənt) *adj.* —**e·mer′gence** *n.*

**e·mer·gen·cy** (i·mûr′jən·sē) *n. pl.* **·cies** A sudden, unexpected state of affairs calling for immediate action.

**e·mer·i·tus** (i·mer′ə·təs) *adj.* Retired from active service but retained in an honorary position. [< L *emereri* earn, deserve]

**e·met·ic** (i·met′ik) *adj.* Causing vomiting. —*n.* A medicine used to induce vomiting. [< Gk. *emeein* to vomit]

**em·i·grate** (em′ə·grāt) *v.i.* **·grat·ed, ·grat·ing** To go from one country, or section of a country, to settle in another. [< L *ex-* out + *migrare* to move] —**em·i·gra′tion** *n.*

**em·i·nence** (em′ə·nəns) *n.* 1 An outstanding rank or degree. 2 A lofty place, as a hill. 3 *Usu. cap.* A title of honor applied to cardinals of the Roman Catholic Church. Also **em′i·nen·cy.**

**em·i·nent** (em′ə·nənt) *adj.* 1 Standing out from others by achievement or station; outstanding. 2 Rising above other things: an *eminent* tower. [< L *eminere* stand out, project] —**em′i·nent·ly** *adv.* —Syn. 1 distinguished, prominent.

**em·is·sar·y** (em′ə·ser′ē) *n. pl.* **·sar·ies** 1 A person sent on a special mission, often as a representative of a government. 2 A secret agent. [< L *emittere* send out]

**e·mis·sion** (i·mish′ən) *n.* 1 Something emitted. 2 The act of emitting. 3 *Electronics* The ejection of electrons from a surface. — **e·mis′sive** *adj.*

**e·mit** (i·mit′) *v.t.* **e·mit·ted, e·mit·ting** 1 To send or give out; discharge. 2 To utter (cries, etc.). 3 To put into circulation, as money. [< L *ex-* out + *mittere* send] —**e·mit′ter** *n.*

**e·mo·tion** (i·mō′shən) *n.* 1 Any feeling, esp. a strong or intense feeling, as of love, joy, fear, etc., often accompanied by complex physiological changes. 2 Such feelings collectively, or the power of experiencing them. [< L *ex-* out + *movere* to stir, move]

**em·per·or** (em′pər·ər) *n.* The ruler of an empire. [< L *imperare* to order]

**em·pha·sis** (em′fə·sis) *n. pl.* **·ses** (-sēz) 1 Special attention, importance, or stress: to place *emphasis* on discipline. 2 Forceful expression. 3 A stress laid upon some spoken or written words. [< Gk. *en-* in + *phainein* to show]

**em·pha·size** (em′fə·sīz) *v.t.* **·sized, ·siz·ing** To make especially distinct or prominent.

**em·phat·ic** (im·fat′ik) *adj.* 1 Conveying or expressing emphasis. 2 Forceful and decisive. —**em·phat′i·cal·ly** *adv.*

**em·pire** (em′pīr) *n.* 1 A state, or union of states, governed by an emperor. 2 Any vast organization or enterprise under unified control. [< L *imperium* rule]

**em·ploy** (im·ploi′) *v.t.* 1 To engage the services of; hire. 2 To provide work and livelihood for. 3 To make use of: to *employ* cunning. 4 To devote or apply: to *employ* all one's energies. —*n.* The state of being employed. [< L *implicare* involve, fold in]

**em·press** (em′pris) *n.* 1 A woman who rules an empire. 2 The wife or widow of an emperor.

**em·u·late** (em′yə·lāt) *v.t.* **·lat·ed, ·lat·ing** 1 To try to equal or surpass, esp. by imitating or copying. 2 To rival with some success. [< L *aemulari* to rival < *aemulus* jealous] — **em′u·la′tion, em′u·la′tor** *n.* —**em′u·la′tive** *adj.*

**e·mul·sion** (i·mul′shən) *n.* 1 A liquid mixture in which a substance is suspended in minute globules, as butterfat in milk. 2 *Phot.* A substance sensitive to light, used to coat films. [< L *emulgere* to drain out] — **e·mul′sive** *adj.*

**en·act** (in·akt′, en-) *v.t.* 1 To make into a law. 2 To represent in or as in a play.

**en·am·el** (in·am′əl) *n.* 1 A vitreous material fused to metals, porcelain, and other materials for protection or decoration. 2 A work executed in such material. 3 A glossy lacquer or varnish used for leather, paper, etc. 4 Any hard, glossy coating. 5 The layer of hard, glossy material forming the exposed outer covering of the teeth. • See TOOTH. —v.t. ·eled or ·elled, ·el·ing or ·el·ling 1 To cover or inlay with enamel. 2 To surface with or as with enamel. 3 To adorn with different colors, as if with enamel. [< AF en- on + OF esmail enamel] —en·am'el·er, en·am'el·ler, en·am'el·ist, en·am'el·list, e·nam'el·work n.

en·chant (in·chant', -chänt', en-) v.t. 1 To put a magic spell upon. 2 To delight or charm completely. [<L in- in + cantare sing] —en·chant'er, en·chant'ment n. —en·chant'ress (-tris) n. Fem.

en·cir·cle (in·sûr'kəl, en-) v.t. ·cled, ·cling 1 To form a circle around. 2 To go around; make a circuit of. —en·cir'cle·ment n.

en·co·mi·um (in·kō'mē·əm, en-) n. pl. ·mi·ums or ·mi·a (-mē·ə) A formal expression of praise; eulogy. [< Gk. enkōmion eulogy]

en·com·pass (in·kum'pəs, -kom'-, en-) v.t. 1 To form a circle around; encircle. 2 To surround; hem in. 3 To include; embrace. —en·com'pass·ment n.

en·core (äng'kôr, -kōr, än'-) n. 1 A request by an audience for the repetition of a performance, usu. indicated by sustained applause. 2 The performance given in response to the audience. —v.t. ·cored, ·cor·ing To call for an encore by (a performer) or of (a performance). [<F, again]

en·coun·ter (in·koun'tər, en-) n. 1 A coming together, esp. when casual or unexpected. 2 A hostile meeting; contest. —v.t. 1 To meet accidentally; come upon. 2 To meet in conflict; face in battle. 3 To be faced with (opposition, difficulties, etc.). —v.i. 4 To meet accidentally or in battle. [<L in- in + contra against]

en·cour·age (in·kûr'ij, en-) v.t. ·aged, ·ag·ing 1 To inspire with courage, hope, or confidence. 2 To help or be favorable toward. [<OF en- in + corage courage] —en·cour'ag·er n. —Syn. 1 hearten, embolden, rally. 2 foster, abet.

en·croach (in·krōch', en-) v.i. 1 To intrude upon the possessions or rights of another, esp. by stealth: with on or upon. 2 To make inroads beyond the proper or usual limits. [< OF encrochier to seize with a hook] —en·croach'er, en·croach'ment n.

en·cum·ber (in·kum'bər, en-) v.t. 1 To obstruct or hinder in action or movement, as with a burden. 2 To make hard to use;

block. 3 To weigh down or burden, as with duties. [< OF encombrer]

en·cum·brance (in·kum'brəns, en-) n. 1 That which encumbers. 2 Law Any lien or liability attached to real property.

-ency suffix Var. of -ENCE: urgency.

en·cy·clo·pe·di·a (in·sī'klə·pē'dē·ə, en-) n. A work containing information on all subjects, or exhaustive of one subject. Also en·cy·clo·pae'di·a. [< Gk. enkyklios paideia a general education] —en·cy·clo·pe'dic, en·cy·clo·pae'dic adj.

en·deav·or (in·dev'ər, en-) n. An earnest attempt or effort to do or accomplish a desired end. —v.t. 1 To make an effort to do or bring about; try: usu. used with an infinitive. —v.i. 2 To make an effort; strive. Brit. sp. en·deav·our. ME endeveren to exert oneself] —en·deav'or·er n.

en·do·crine (en'dō·krin, -krīn, -krēn) adj. 1 Denoting an organ or gland that produces one or more hormones that pass directly into the blood. 2 Pertaining to a hormonal secretion. —n. The secretion of a ductless gland. [< ENDO- + Gk. krinein separate] —en'do·cri'nal (-krī'nəl) adj.

en·dorse (in·dôrs', en-) v.t. ·dorsed, ·dors·ing 1 To write, esp. one's name, on the back of, as a check or other document. 2 To support: to endorse a policy or candidate. [< L in- on + dorsum back] —en·dors'a·ble adj.

en·dow (in·dou', en-) v.t. To provide with a permanent fund or income. 2 To furnish or equip, as with talents or natural gifts: usu. with with. [< OF en- in + douer to provide with a dowry]

en·dure (in·d'ŏŏr', en-) v. ·dured, ·dur·ing v.t. 1 To bear or undergo, as pain, grief, or injury, esp. without yielding. 2 To tolerate; put up with. —v.i. 3 To last; continue to be. 4 To suffer without yielding; hold out. [< L in- in + durare harden] —en·dur'a·ble adj.

en·e·my (en'ə·mē) n. pl. ·mies 1 One who hates or bears ill will toward another; foe. 2 One hostile to an organization, idea, etc. 3 A hostile nation or military force; also, a member of a hostile nation or force. —adj. Of a hostile army or power. [< L in- not + amicus friend]

en·er·gy (en'ər·jē) n. pl. ·gies 1 The power by which anything acts effectively. 2 The power to be physically or mentally active, often without the normal attendant fatigue. 3 Force or power in activity: His singing lacks energy. 4 Physics The ability to do work. See also ATOMIC ENERGY, CHEMICAL EN-

ERGY, ELECTRICAL ENERGY, GEOTHERMAL ENERGY, KINETIC ENERGY, MECHANICAL ENERGY, POTENTIAL ENERGY, SOLAR ENERGY. **5** The motive power essential to modern technology, derived from various natural sources. —*adj.* Of, for, caused by, or relating to energy or the lack of it: the *energy* crisis; *energy* needs. [< Gk. *en-* on, at + *ergon* work]

**en·er·vate** (en′ər-vāt) *v.t.* **·vat·ed**, **·vat·ing** To deprive of energy or strength; weaken. —*adj.* (i·nûr′vit) Enervated. [< L *enervare* weaken] —**en·er·va′tion**, **en′er·va′tor** *n.*

**en·gage** (in·gāj′, en-) *v.* **·gaged**, **·gag·ing** *v.t.* **1** To bind by a promise, pledge, etc. **2** To promise to marry: usu. in the passive. **3** To hire, as a lawyer, or his services; secure the use of, as a room. **4** To hold the interest or attention of. **5** To hold (interest or attention); occupy. **6** To begin a battle with. **7** To mesh or interlock, as gears. —*v.i.* **8** To bind oneself by a promise, pledge, etc. **9** To devote or occupy oneself: to *engage* in research. **10** To begin a battle. **11** To mesh, as gears. [< OF *en-* in + *gager* to pledge]

**en·gen·der** (in·jen′dər, en-) *v.t.* To cause to exist; produce. [<L *ingenerare* to generate in]

**en·gine** (en′jin) *n.* **1** A machine that uses energy, esp. energy from a fuel, to perform work. **2** A railroad locomotive. **3** Any apparatus: the *engines* of war. [<L *ingenium* talent, skill]

**en·gi·neer** (en′jə·nir′) *n.* **1** One practicing any branch of engineering. **2** One who runs or manages an engine. **3** A manager; inventor; plotter. **4** A member of the division of an army which constructs bridges, clears and builds roads and airfields, etc. —*v.t.* **1** To put through or manage by contrivance: to *engineer* a scheme. **2** To plan and superintend as an engineer.

**en·gi·neer·ing** (en′jə·nir′ing) *n.* The application of scientific knowledge to the solution of practical problems, as in designing structures and apparatus.

**en·grave** (in·grāv′, en-) *v.t.* **·graved**, **·grav·ing** **1** To carve or etch figures, letters, etc., into (a surface). **2** To impress deeply. **3** To cut (pictures, lettering, etc.) into metal, stone, or wood, for printing. **4** To print from plates made by such a process. [< EN-¹ + GRAVE³] —**en·grav′er** *n.*

**en·grav·ing** (in·grā′ving, en-) *n.* **1** The act or art of cutting designs on a plate. **2** An engraved design on a plate. **3** A picture or design printed from an engraved plate.

**en·gross** (in·grōs′, en-) *v.t.* **1** To occupy completely; absorb. **2** To copy in large writing; make a formal transcript of. **3** To monopolize, as the supply of a product. [<LL *ingrossare* write large] —**en·gross′er**, **en·gross′ment** *n.* —**en·gross′ing** *adj.*

**en·hance** (in·hans′, -häns′, en-) *v.t.* **·hanced**, **·hanc·ing** To make higher or greater, as in reputation, cost, beauty, quality, etc. [<L *in-* in + *altus* high] —**en·hance′ment** *n.* —**Syn.** heighten, intensify, strengthen, improve.

**e·nig·ma** (i·nig′mə) *n.* **1** An obscure or ambiguous saying; a riddle. **2** A baffling or inexplicable circumstance, person, etc. [<Gk. *ainissesthai* speak in riddles]

**en·joy** (in·joi′, en-) *v.t.* **1** To experience joy or pleasure in; receive pleasure from the possession or use of. **2** To have the use or benefit of. [< L *in-* + *gaudere* rejoice] —**en·joy′a·ble** *adj.* —**en·joy′a·ble·ness** *n.* —**en·joy′a·bly** *adv.*

**en·light·en** (in·līt′n, en-) *v.t.* **1** To impart knowledge to; cause to know or understand; teach. **2** To convey information to; inform. —**en·light′en·er** *n.*

**en·mi·ty** (en′mə·tē) *n. pl.* **·ties 1** The spirit of an enemy; hostility. **2** The state of being an enemy; a hostile condition. [<L *inimicus* hostile]

**e·nor·mi·ty** (i·nôr′mə·tē) *n. pl.* **·ties 1** The state of being outrageous or extremely wicked. **2** A flagrant instance of depravity; an atrocity. **3** Great size or extent; enormousness. • Traditionally, *enormity* refers to great wickedness, not to great size or extent, whereas *enormousness* means greatness in any sense. One speaks of the *enormity* of a crime but the *enormousness* of an Olympic stadium. However, *enormity* (def. 3) is now often used, esp. to express great extent, complexity, difficulty, etc.: The *enormity* of the task filled him with awe.

**e·nor·mous** (i·nôr′məs) *adj.* **1** Excessive or extraordinary in size, amount, or degree. **2** Wicked above measure; atrocious. [<L *enormis* immense] —**e·nor′mous·ly** *adv.* —**e·nor′mous·ness** *n.* • See ENORMITY.

**en·sign** (en′sən, -sīn) *n.* **1** A flag or banner, esp. a national standard or naval flag. **2** (en′sən) See GRADE. **3** In the British Army, until 1871, a commissioned officer who carried the flag of his regiment or company. **4** A badge or symbol, as of office. [<L *insignia* insignia]

**en·sue** (in·s⁽ʸ⁾ōō′, en-) *v.i.* **·sued**, **·su·ing 1** To occur afterward or subsequently; follow. **2**

To follow as a consequence; result. [<L *in-on*, in + *sequi* follow]

**en·tan·gle** (in·tang'gəl, en-) *v.t.* **·gled**, **·gling** **1** To catch in or as in a snare; hamper. **2** To make tangled; complicate. **3** To involve in difficulties. —**en·tang'le·ment, en·tang'ler** *n.*

**en·ter·prise** (en'tər·prīz) *n.* **1** Any projected task or work; esp., a risky or bold undertaking. **2** Boldness, energy, and invention in practical affairs. [<F *entre-* between + *prendre* take]

**en·ter·pris·ing** (en'tər·prī'zing) *adj.* Energetic and adventuresome; showing initiative. —**en'ter·pris'ing·ly** *adv.*

**en·ter·tain** (en'tər·tān') *v.t.* **1** To hold the attention of; amuse; divert. **2** To extend hospitality to; receive as a guest. **3** To take into consideration, as a proposal. **4** To keep or bear in mind: to *entertain* a grudge. —*v.i.* **5** To receive and care for guests. [<OF *entretenir* to hold between] —**en'ter·tain'er** *n.*

**en·thu·si·asm** (in·thoō'zē·az'əm, en-) *n.* **1** Earnest and intense feeling; zeal. **2** A source or cause of such feeling. [<Gk. *enthusiasmos* inspiration]

**en·thu·si·as·tic** (in·thoō'zē·as'tik, en-) *adj.* Characterized by or showing enthusiasm; ardent; zealous. —**en·thu'si·as'ti·cal·ly** *adv.*

**en·tice** (in·tīs', en-) *v.t.* **·ticed**, **·tic·ing** To lead on or attract by arousing hope of pleasure, profit, etc. [<OF *enticier* arouse] —**en·tice'ment, en·tic'er** *n.* —**en·tic'ing·ly** *adv.*

**en·tire** (in·tīr', en-) *adj.* **1** Complete in all its parts; whole. **2** Consisting of only one piece; not broken or divided. **3** Pure; unalloyed. **4** Uncastrated: an *entire* horse. **5** *Bot.* Having a smooth margin, as a leaf. [<L *integer* whole, intact] —**en·tire'ly** *adv.* —**en·tire'ness** *n.* —**Syn.** **2** intact, of a piece, undivided.

**en·to·mol·o·gy** (en'tə·mol'ə·jē) *n.* The branch of zoology dealing with insects. [< Gk. *entomon* insect] —**en·to·mo·log·i·cal** (en'tə·mə·loj'i·kəl) or **·log'ic** *adj.* —**en'to·mol'i·cal·ly** *adv.* —**en·to·mol'o·gist** *n.*

**en·trance¹** (en'trəns) *n.* **1** The act of entering. **2** A passage into a house or other enclosed space. **3** The right or power of entering; entrée. [<OF *entrer* enter]

**en·trance²** (in·trans', -träns', en-) *v.t.* **·tranced**, **·tranc·ing** **1** To fill with rapture or wonder; delight; charm. **2** To put into a trance. —**en·trance'ment** *n.* —**en·tranc'ing** *adj.* —**en·tranc'ing·ly** *adv.*

**en·treat** (in·trēt', en-) *v.t. & v.i.* To ask earnestly or abjectly; beseech; implore. [<OF *entraiter* to deal with, treat] —**en·treat'ment** *n.*

**en·trée** (än'trā, än·trā') *n.* **1** The act or privilege of entering; access. **2** The principal course at a dinner or luncheon. **Also en·tree'.** [F]

**en·try** (en'trē) *n. pl.* **·tries** **1** The act of coming or going in; entrance. **2** A place of entrance; a small hallway. **3** The act of entering an item in a register or list. **4** An item entered in such a list. **5** The reporting at a customhouse of a ship's arrival and the nature of her cargo. **6** *Law* The act of assuming actual possession of property by entering upon it. **7** A contestant entered in a race or competition. [< F *entrer* to enter]

**e·nu·mer·ate** (i·n'yoō'mə·rāt) *v.t.* **·at·ed**, **·at·ing** **1** To name one by one; list. **2** To count or ascertain the number of. [<L *ex-* out + *numerare* count] —**e·nu'mer·a'tion, e·nu'mer·a'tor** *n.* —**e·nu'mer·a'tive** *adj.*

**e·nun·ci·ate** (i·nun'sē·āt, -shē-) *v.* **·at·ed**, **·at·ing** *v.t.* **1** To pronounce or articulate (words), esp. clearly and distinctly. **2** To state with exactness, as a theory. **3** To announce or proclaim. —*v.i.* **4** To utter or pronounce words. [<L *ex-* out + *nunciare* announce] —**e·nun'ci·a'tion, e·nun'ci·a'tor** *n.* —**e·nun'ci·a'tive** *adj.*

**en·vel·op** (in·vel'əp) *v.t.* **·oped**, **·op·ing** **1** To wrap or enclose completely. **2** To hide or obscure, as by enclosing: to *envelop* in fog. **3** To surround. [<OF *en-* in + *voluper* to wrap, fold] —**en·vel'op·er, en·vel'op·ment** *n.*

**en·ve·lope** (en'və·lōp, än'-) *n.* **1** A folded wrapper of paper, usu. with gummed edges, for enclosing a letter or the like. **2** Anything that encloses completely or wraps around. [<OF *enveloper* to envelop]

**en·vi·ron·ment** (in·vī'rən·mənt, -ərn-, en-) *n.* **1** The aggregate of all conditions affecting the existence, growth, and welfare of an organism or group of organisms. **2** Surroundings or external circumstances. —**en·vi'ron·men'tal** *adj.* —**en·vi'ron·men'tal·ly** *adv.*

**en·vi·rons** (in·vī'rəns, en-) *n. pl.* The surrounding region; outskirts; suburbs.

**en·voy** (en'voi, än'-) *n.* **1** A diplomatic agent of a government, ranking next below an ambassador. 2 One sent on a mission. [<F < OF *envoier* to send on the way]

**en·vy** (en′vē) *n.* 1 A feeling of resentment and jealousy over the possessions, achievements, etc., of another. 2 Desire for something belonging to another. 3 An object of envy. —*v.t.* **vied, ·vy·ing** 1 To regard with envy. 2 To feel envy because of. [<L *invidia*] —**en′vi·er** *n.* —**en′vy·ing·ly** *adv.* —Syn. *n.* 2 greed, covetousness, cupidity.

**en·zyme** (en′zīm, -zim) *n.* A proteinlike substance produced by cells and having the power to initiate or accelerate specific biochemical reactions in an organism. [<Gk. < *en-* in + *zymē* leaven] —**en·zy·mat·ic** (en′zī·mat′ik, -zi-) *adj.*

**ep·au·let** (ep′ə·let) *n.* A shoulder ornament, as on uniforms. Also **ep′au·lette.** [F, dim. of *épaule* shoulder]

**e·phem·er·al** (i·fem′ər·əl) *adj.* 1 Living one day only, as certain insects. 2 Short-lived; transitory. —*n.* Anything lasting for a very short time. [Gk. *ephēmeros* < *epi-* on + *hēmera* day] —**e·phem′er·al·ly** *adv.* —**e·phem′er·al·ness** *n.* —Syn. *adj.* 2 transient, passing, temporal, temporary.

**ep·ic** (ep′ik) *n.* 1 A long, narrative poem, celebrating in stately, formal verse heroic or grandiose events or achievements. 2 Any novel, play, historical event, etc., having a heroic or grandiose quality or theme. —*adj.* 1 Of, pertaining to, or like an epic. 2 Grand, noble, legendary, or heroic: also·**ep′i·cal.** [<Gk. < *epos* song, word]

**ep·i·cure** (ep′ə·kyŏor) *n.* A person who enjoys and is knowledgeable about good food and drink; gourmet. [<*Epicurus*, 342?–370 B.C., Greek philosopher] —**ep′i·cu·re′an** (-kyŏo·rē′ən) *adj., n.* —**ep′i·cu·re′an·ism, ep′i·cur·ism** *n.*

**ep·i·dem·ic** (ep′ə·dem′ik) *adj.* Affecting many in a large area or community at once: also **ep′i·dem′i·cal.** —*n.* 1 A disease temporarily prevalent in a community or throughout a large area. 2 A circumstance that suddenly becomes widespread: an *epidemic* of business failures. [< Gk. *epi-* upon + *dēmos* people] —**ep′i·dem′i·cal·ly** *adv.*

**ep·i·der·mis** (ep′ə·dûr′mis) *n.* The outer covering of the skin; the cuticle. [<Gk. *epi-* upon + *derma* skin] —**ep′i·der′mal, ep′i·der′mic** *adj.*

**ep·i·glot·tis** (ep′ə·glot′is) *n.* The leaf-shaped piece of cartilate, at the base of the tongue, that closes the trachea, or windpipe, during the act of swallowing. [< NL < Gk. *epi-* upon + *glōtta* tongue] —**ep′i·glot′tal** *adj.*

**ep·i·gram** (ep′ə·gram) *n.* 1 A pithy, caustic, or thought-provoking saying. 2 A short, witty, usu. satiric poem. [< Gk. *epigramma* an inscription] —**ep′i·gram·mat′ic** or ·**i·cal** *adj.* —**ep′i·gram·mat′i·cal·ly** *adv.* —**ep′i·gra·m′ma·tist** *n.*

**E·pis·co·pal** (i·pis′kə·pəl) *adj.* Belonging or pertaining to the Protestant Episcopal Church, or to any church in the Anglican communion.

**e·pis·co·pa·li·an** (i·pis′kə·pā′lē·ən, -pāl′yən) *n.* An advocate of episcopacy.· —*adj.* Pertaining to or favoring episcopal government.

**ep·i·sode** (ep′ə·sōd) *n.* 1 An incident or story in a literary work, separable from, yet related to it. 2 A notable incident or action occurring as a break in the regular course of events. 3 An installment of a serial. [<Gk. *epi-* upon + *eisodos* entrance] —**ep′i·sod′ic** (-sod′ik) or ·**i·cal, ep′i·so′dal** or ·**di·al** *adj.* —**ep′i·sod′i·cal·ly** *adv.*

**e·pis·tle** (i·pis′əl) *n.* 1 A letter; esp., a long, formal letter that instructs. 2 *Usu. cap.* One of the letters of an apostle. 3 *Usu. cap.* A selection from an apostle's letter, read in certain church services. [< Gk. *epi-* on + *stellein* send]

**ep·i·taph** (ep′ə·taf, -tãf) *n.* An inscription on a tomb or monument in honor or in memory of the dead. [<Gk. *epi-* upon, at + *taphos* a tomb] —**ep′i·taph′ic** (-taf′ik) *adj.*

**ep·i·thet** (ep′ə·thet) *n.* A word or phrase, often disparaging, used to describe or to substitute for the name of a person or thing. [< L < Gk. < *epi-* upon + *tithenai* place] —**ep′i·thet′ic** or ·**i·cal** *adj.*

**e·pit·o·me** (i·pit′ə·mē) *n.* 1 A typical example; essence; embodiment: the *epitome* of arrogance. 2 A concise summary; abridgement. [< Gk. *epitomē*] —**ep·i·tom·ic** (ep′ə·tom′ik) or ·**i·cal** *adj.* —**e·pit′o·mist, e·pit′o·miz′er** *n.*

**ep·och** (ep′ək, *Brit.* ē′pok) *n.* 1 A point in time which marks the beginning of some new development, condition, discovery, etc. 2 An interval of time regarded in terms of extraordinary events and far-reaching results. 3 *Geol.* A time interval shorter than a period. 4 *Astron.* An arbitrarily chosen moment of time, used as a reference point. [< Gk. *epochē* a stoppage, point of time] —**ep′och·al** *adj.*

**e·pox·y** (i·pok′sē) *adj.* Designating an oxygen-carbon bond characteristic of certain durable resins used for varnishes and adhesives. [< EP(I) + OXY-]

e·qual (ē′kwəl) *adj.* 1 Of the same size, quantity, intensity, value, etc. 2 Having the same rank, rights, importance, etc. 3 Fair; impartial; just: *equal laws.* 4 Having the strength, ability, requirements, etc., that are needed: with to. 5 Balanced; level; even. —*v.t.* e·qualed or e·qualled, e·qual·ing or e·qual·ling 1 To be or become equal to. 2 To do or produce something equal to. —*n.* A person or thing equal to another. [< L *aequus* even] —e′qual·ly *adv.* —e′qual·ness *n.*

e·qual·i·ty (i·kwol′ə·tē) *n. pl.* ·ties 1 The state or an instance of being equal. 2 An equation.

e·qua·nim·i·ty (ē′kwə·nim′ə·tē, ek′wə-) *n.* Evenness of mind or temper; composure; calmness. [< L *aequus* even + *animus* mind] —**Syn.** repose, serenity, self-possession, poise, tranquility.

e·qua·tion (i·kwā′zhən, -shən) *n.* 1 The process or act of making equal. 2 The state of being equal. 3 A complex of interrelated and variable elements or factors: the human *equation.* 4 A mathematical statement expressing the equality of two quantities. 5 *Chem.* A quantitative, symbolic representation of a chemical reaction. —e·qua′tion·al *adj.* —e·qua′tion·al·ly *adv.*

e·qua·tor (i·kwā′tər) *n.* 1 A circle around the earth, at right angles to its axis and equidistant from the poles. 2 Any similar circle, as of the sun, a planet, etc. 3 CELESTIAL EQUATOR. [< LL *(circulus) aequator* equalizer (circle)]

e·ques·tri·an (i·kwes′trē·ən) *adj.* 1 Pertaining to horses or horsemanship. 2 On horseback. —*n.* One skilled in horsemanship. [< L *equus* a horse] —e·ques′tri·enne′ (-en′) *n. Fem.*

e·qui·lat·er·al (ē′kwə·lat′ər·əl) *adj.* Having all the sides equal. —e′qui·lat′er·al·ly *adv.*

e·qui·lib·ri·um (ē′kwə·lib′rē·əm) *n.* 1 A state of balance produced by the counteraction of two or more forces or influences in a system. 2 Bodily balance. 3 Mental or emotional balance or poise. Also e′qui·lib′ri·ty. [< L *aequus* equal + *libra* a balance]

e·quine (ē′kwīn, ek′wīn) *adj.* Of, pertaining to, or like a horse. —*n.* A horse. [< L *equus* horse]

e·qui·nox (ē′kwə·noks) *n.* 1 One of the two times in each year when the sun crosses

the celestial equator, making day and night of equal length all over the earth. The vernal or spring equinox takes place about Mar. 21. the autumnal equinox about Sept. 21. 2 Either of two opposite points at which the sun crosses the celestial equator on these dates. [< L *aequus* equal + *nox* night]

e·quip (i·kwip′) *v.t.* e·quipped, e·quip·ping 1 To furnish or prepare with whatever is needed for any purpose or undertaking. 2 To dress or attire; array. [< OF *equiper*]

eq·ui·ta·ble (ek′wə·tə·bəl) *adj.* 1 Characterized by equity, or fairness and just dealing, impartial. 2 *Law* Of, pertaining to, or valid in equity, as distinguished from common law or statute law. —eq′ui·ta·ble·ness *n.* —eq′ui·ta·bly *adv.*

eq·ui·ty (ek′wə·tē) *n. pl.* ·ties 1 Fairness or impartiality; justness. 2 Something that is fair or equitable. 3 *Law* a Justice based on natural reason or ethical judgment. b That field of jurisprudence superseding statute law and common law when these are considered inadequate or inflexible for the purposes of justice. 4 The value of property in excess of mortgage or other liens. [< L *aequus* equal]

e·quiv·a·lent (i·kwiv′ə·lənt) *adj.* 1 Equal in value, force, meaning, etc. 2 *Chem.* Having the same valence or the same combining weight. —*n.* 1 That which is equivalent; something equal in value, power, effect, etc. 2 *Chem.* The weight of an element which combines with or displaces eight grams of oxygen or one gram of hydrogen. [< L *aequus* equal + *valere* be worth] —e·quiv′a·lent·ly *adv.* —**Syn.** *adj.* 1 alike, analogous, reciprocal, tantamount, same.

e·quiv·o·cate (i·kwiv′ə·kāt) *v.i.* ·cat·ed, ·cat·ing To use ambiguous language with intent to deceive. —e·quiv′o·ca′tion, e·quiv′o·ca′tor *n.*

e·ra (ir′ə, ē′rə) *n.* 1 A system of chronological notation reckoned from some fixed point of time. 2 A period of time dating from an important date, occurrence, etc. 3 A period of time characterized by certain social, intellectual, or physical conditions, etc. 4 A date or event from which time is reckoned: the Christian *era.* 5 Any of the major divisions of geological time. [< L *aera* counters for reckoning]

e·rad·i·cate (i·rad′ə·kāt) *v.t.* ·cat·ed, ·cat·ing 1 To pull up by the roots; root out. 2 To destroy utterly. [< L *e-* out + *radix* a root] —e·rad′i·ca·ble (-ə·kə·bəl) *adj.* —e·rad′i·ca′

tion, e·rad′i·ca′tor n. —Syn. 2 abolish, extirpate, blot out, erase, eliminate. —e·rad′i·ca′tive adj.

e·rase (i·rās′) v.t. e·rased, e·ras·ing 1 To remove or wipe out. 2 To remove all signs or traces of; obliterate. 3 To remove (recorded matter) from (a tape). 4 Slang To kill. [< L e- out + radere scrape] —e·ras′a·ble adj.

e·rect (i·rekt′) v.t. 1 To construct, as a house; build. 2 To assemble the parts of; set up. 3 To set upright; lift up: to erect a flagpole. 4 To construct or formulate, as a theory. 5 To establish or cause to exist. —adj. 1 Upright in position, form, or posture; vertical. 2 Sticking upward or outward; bristling. [< L e- out + regere make straight] —e·rect′ly adv. —e·rect′ness n.

er·mine (ûr′min) n. 1 A weasel of the N hemisphere, having brown fur that in winter turns white with a black tip on the tail. 2 Its fur, used in Europe for the facings of official robes, as of judges. 3 The position, rank, or functions of a judge. [< OF ermine] —er′mined adj.

err (ûr) v.i. erred, err·ing 1 To make a mistake; be wrong. 2 To go astray morally; sin. [< L errare wander]

er·rand (er′ənd) n. 1 A trip made to carry a message, to purchase something, to attend to personal business, etc. 2 The reason for such a trip. [< OE ærende message, news]

er·rat·ic (i·rat′ik) adj. 1 Not conforming to rules or standards; queer; eccentric. 2 Irregular, as in course or direction; wandering; straying. —n. An erratic person or thing. Also er·rat′i·cal. [< L errare wander] —er·rat′i·cal·ly adv. —Syn. 1 odd, peculiar, capricious, abnormal, unpredictable, whimsical, changeable.

er·ro·ne·ous (ə·rō′nē·əs, e·rō′-) adj. Marked by error; incorrect; mistaken. —er·ro′ne·ous·ly adv. —er·ro′ne·ous·ness n.

er·ror (er′ər) n. 1 The condition of being incorrect, esp. in matters of opinion or belief. 2 Something done, said, or believed wrongly; inaccuracy; mistake. 3 Any misplay in baseball which prolongs the batter's time at bat or permits a base runner to make one or more bases. 4 A wrongdoing; transgression; sin. [< L < errare wander]

er·satz (er·zäts′) n. A substitute or replacement, usu. inferior to the original. —adj. Substitute. [< G ersetzen replace]

er·u·dite (er′yōō·dīt) adj. Very learned; scholarly. [< L erudire instruct] —er′u·dite·ly adv. —er′u·dite·ness n.

e·rupt (i·rupt′) v.i. 1 To cast forth smoke, lava, etc., suddenly and with violence: The volcano erupted. 2 To burst forth: Steam is erupting from the volcano. 3 To break through a gum, as a tooth. 4 To become covered with a rash or pimples. —v.t. 5 To cause to burst forth. [< L e- out + rumpere burst]

es·ca·late (es′kə·lāt) v.t. & v.i. ·lat·ed, ·lat·ing 1 To increase or be increased: to escalate a war. 2 To ascend or carry up, as on an escalator. [Back formation from ESCALATOR] —es′ca·la′tion n.

es·ca·la·tor (es′kə·lā′tər) n. A moving stairway, built on an endless loop of chain. [< Escalator, a trade name]

escalator clause A clause in a contract stipulating an increase or decrease in wages, prices, etc., under certain specified conditions.

es·ca·pade (es′kə·pād) n. 1 A reckless adventure or mischievous prank. 2 An escape from restraint. [< Sp. escapar to escape]

es·cape (ə·skāp′, e·skāp′) v. es·caped, es·cap·ing v.t. 1 To get away from; flee from, as guards or prison. 2 To avoid, as harm or evil. 3 To slip or come from involuntarily: No cry escaped him. 4 To slip away from or elude (notice or recollection). —v.i. 5 To get free from or avoid arrest, custody, danger, etc. 6 To fade or slip away; disappear; vanish. 7 To come forth; emerge; leak: Gas is escaping from the stove. —n. 1 The act of escaping. 2 The fact or state of having escaped. 3 A means of escape. 4 Mental relief from monotony, anxiety, etc.: literature of escape. 5 Flow, as of a fluid; leakage. [< L ex- out + cappa a cloak] —es·cap′a·ble adj. —es·cap′er n.

es·chew (es·chōō′) v.t. To shun, as something unworthy or injurious. [< OF eschiver] —es·chew′al n.

es·cort (es·kôrt′) v.t. To accompany; go with, as from courtesy or to protect. —n. (es′kôrt) 1 One or more persons accompanying another person or persons, an object, etc., for protection or as a mark of respect. 2 One or more ships, planes, etc. accompanying another to furnish protection, guidance, etc. 3 A male who accompanies a woman on a date. [< Ital. scorgere lead]

Es·ki·mo (es′kə·mō) n. pl. ·mos 1 A member of a Mongoloid people indigenous to the Arctic coasts of North America, Greenland,

and NE Siberia. 2 The language of the Eskimos. —**Es′ki·mo′an** *adj.*

**e·soph·a·gus** (i·sŏf′ə·gəs) *n. pl.* **·gi** (-gī, -jī) The tube through which food passes from the mouth to the stomach; gullet. [< Gk. *oisophagos*] —**e·so·phag·e·al** (ē′sō·faj′ē·əl, i·sŏf′ə·jē′əl), **e·soph′a·gal** (-ə·gəl) *adj.* • See LIVER.

**ESP** extrasensory perception.

**es·pou·sal** (es·pou′zəl) *adj.* Of or pertaining to a betrothal or marriage. —*n.* 1 Betrothal. 2 Marriage. 3 The act of taking up or supporting, as a cause or principle.

**es·pouse** (es·pouz′) *v.t.* **·poused, ·pous·ing** 1 To take as a spouse; marry. 2 To take up or support, as a cause or doctrine. [< *spondere* promise] —**es·pous′er** *n.*

**es·quire** (es′kwīr, es·kwīr′) *n.* 1 *Usu. cap.* A title of courtesy, usu. abbreviated after a man's surname. 2 In England, a member of the gentry ranking next below a knight. 3 A candidate for knighthood serving as an attendant to a knight. [< LL *scutarius* shield-bearer]

**es·say** (e·sā′) *v.t.* To try to do or accomplish; attempt. —*n.* 1 (es′ā) A literary composition, esp. one dealing with a single subject from a personal point of view. 2 (e·sā′) An endeavor; effort. [< OF *essai* a trial] —**es·say′er** *n.*

**es·sence** (es′əns) *n.* 1 The intrinsic nature or characteristic quality of anything; that which makes a thing what it is. 2 Something that is; an existent being or entity. 3 A substance considered to have, in concentrated form, the special qualities (as flavor, scent, etc.) of the plant, food, drug, etc. from which it was taken. 4 An alcoholic solution of such a substance. 5 Perfume; scent. [< L *esse* be] —**Syn.** 1 substance, gist, quintessence, reality, kernel, pith, core.

**es·sen·tial** (ə·sen′shəl) *adj.* 1 Of or pertaining to the essence or intrinsic nature of anything; substantial; basic. 2 Indispensable, necessary, or highly important. —*n.* That which is fundamental, basic, or indispensable. —**es·sen′ti·al′i·ty** (-shē·al′ə·tē) *n.* —**es·sen′tial·ly** *adv.*

**es·tab·lish** (es·tab′lish) *v.t.* 1 To settle or fix firmly; make stable or permanent. 2 To set up; found, as an institution or business. 3 To set up; install (oneself or someone else) in business, a position, etc. 4 To cause to be recognized or accepted. 5 To put into effect permanently; ordain, as laws. 6 To gain acceptance for; prove, as a theory or argument. 7 To appoint (a church) as a national institution. [< L *stabilire* to make firm or stable] —**es·tab′lish·er** *n.*

**es·tate** (es·tāt′) *n.* 1 One's entire property, possessions, and wealth. 2 Landed property, esp. a large tract of land with an elaborate residence, etc. 3 Condition or state: man's *estate*. 4 A class or order of persons in a state. 5 *Law* The degree, nature, and amount of one's lawful interest in any property. [< L *status* state]

**es·teem** (es·tēm′) *n.* Favorable opinion or estimation; respect; regard. —*v.t.* 1 To value highly. 2 To think to be; deem; consider: to *esteem* one fortunate. [< L *aestimare* to value]

**es·ti·ma·ble** (es′tə·mə·bəl) *adj.* 1 Deserving of esteem. 2 That may be estimated or calculated. —**es′ti·ma·ble·ness** *n.* —**es′ti·ma·bly** *adv.*

**es·ti·mate** (es′tə·māt) *v.* **·mat·ed, ·mat·ing** *v.t.* 1 To form an approximate opinion of (size, amount, number, etc.); calculate roughly. 2 To form an opinion about; judge, as character. —*v.i.* 3 To make or submit an estimate. —*n.* (es′tə·mit) 1 A rough calculation. 2 A statement, as by a builder, in regard to the cost of certain work. 3 A judgment; opinion; evaluation. [< L *aestimare* to value] —**es′ti·ma·tive** *adj.* —**es′ti·ma′tor** *n.*

**es·ti·ma·tion** (es′tə·mā′shən) *n.* 1 The act of estimating. 2 Opinion; estimate. 3 Esteem; regard.

**es·trange** (es·trānj′) *v.t.* **·tranged, ·trang·ing** 1 To make (someone previously friendly or affectionate) indifferent or hostile; alienate. 2 To remove or dissociate (oneself, etc.): to *estrange* oneself from society. [< L *extraneus* foreign] —**es·trange′ment** *n.*

**es·tu·ar·y** (es′chōō·er′ē) *n. pl.* **·ar·ies** 1 The wide mouth of a river where it is met by and mixes with the sea. 2 An arm or inlet of a sea. [< L *aestus* tide]

**etch** (ech) *v.t.* 1 To produce (a design, drawing, etc.) on glass, metal, etc. by the corrosive action of an acid. 2 To engrave (metal, glass, etc.) in this manner. 3 To impress deeply and clearly. —*v.i.* 4 To make etchings. [< G *ätzen*] —**etch′er** *n.*

**etch·ing** (ech′ing) *n.* 1 The act, art, or process of making designs on metal, glass, etc., by the corrosive action of acid. 2 A figure or design formed by etching. 3 An impression or print made from an etched plate.

167

**e·ter·nal** (i·tûr′nəl) *adj.* 1 Having neither beginning nor end of existence; infinite in duration. 2 Having no end; everlasting. 3 Continued without interruption; perpetual. 4 Independent of time or its conditions; timeless; unchangeable; immutable. 5 Of or pertaining to eternity. 6 Appearing interminable; incessant: Vaughn and his *eternal* jokes. —the Eternal God. [< L *aeternus*] —**e·ter′nal·ly** *adv.* —**e·ter′nal·ness** *n.*

**e·ter·ni·ty** (i·tûr′nə·tē) *n. pl.* **·ties** 1 The fact, state, or quality of being eternal. 2 Infinite duration or existence. 3 A seemingly endless or limitless time. 4 Immortality.

**e·ther** (ē′thər) *n.* 1 *Chem* a A colorless, flammable, volatile, liquid organic compound, used as an anesthetic and solvent. b Any of a group of organic compounds in which an oxygen atom is joined with two organic radicals. 2 A perfectly elastic medium formerly assumed to pervade all of space. 3 The upper air. [< L *aether* sky]

**e·the·re·al** (i·thir′ē·əl) *adj.* 1 Having the nature of ether or air. 2 Light; airy; fine; subtle; exquisite. 3 Existing in or belonging to the ether or upper air; aerial; heavenly. 4 Of or ·pertaining to ether. —**e·the′re·al′i·ty**, **e·the′re·al·ness** *n.* —**e·the′re·al·ly** *adv.*

**eth·ics** (eth′iks) *n.pl.* (*construed as sing. in defs.* 1 & 3) 1 The study and philosophy of human conduct, with emphasis on the determination of right and wrong. 2 The basic principles of right action, esp. with reference to a particular person, profession, etc. 3 A work or treatise on morals.

**eth·nic** (eth′nik) *adj.* 1 Of, pertaining to, or belonging to groups of mankind who are of the same race or nationality and who share a common language, culture, etc. 2 Pertaining to peoples neither Jewish nor Christian. —*n. Informal* A member of a minority ethnic group, esp., in the U.S., a nonblack minority. Also **eth′ni·cal.** [< Gk. *ethnos* nation] —**eth′ni·cal·ly** *adv.* —**eth′nic·i·ty** (eth·nis′ə·tē) *n.*

**eth·nol·o·gy** (eth·nol′ə·jē) *n.* The science of the subdivisions and families of men, their origins, characteristics, distribution, and physical and linguistic classification. —**eth·no·log·i·cal** (eth′nō·loj′i·kəl) or **eth′no·log′ic** *adj.* —**eth′no·log′i·cal·ly** *adv.*

**et·i·quette** (et′ə·ket, ·kət) *n.* The rules and customs for polite social or professional behavior. [< OF *estiquette* routine, ticket]

**et·y·mol·o·gy** (et′ə·mol′ə·jē) *n. pl.* **·gies** 1 The history of a word, prefix, suffix, etc., tracing it back to its earliest known form or root. 2 The branch of linguistics dealing with the origin and development of words, prefixes, etc. [< Gk. *etymon* original meaning + -LOGY]

**Eu·char·ist** (yōō′kə·rist) *n.* 1 A Christian sacrament in which bread and wine are consecrated, distributed, and consumed in commemoration of the passion and death of Christ. 2 The consecrated bread and wine of this sacrament. [< Gk. *eu-* well + *charizesthai* give thanks] —**eu′cha·ris′tic** or **·ti·cal** *adj.*

**eu·gen·ics** (yōō·jen′iks) *n. pl.* (*construed as sing.*) The science and art of improving a race or breed by mating individuals with desired characteristics.

**eu·lo·gize** (yōō′lə·jīz) *v.t.* **·gized**, **·giz·ing** 1 To speak or write a eulogy about. 2 To praise highly. *Brit. sp.* **eu′lo·gise.** —**eu·lo·gis·tic** (yōō′lə·jis′tik) or **·ti·cal** *adj.* —**eu′lo·gis′ti·cal·ly** *adv.* **Meu′lo·giz′er** *n.* —Syn. 2 laud, extol, glorify.

**eu·lo·gy** (y′′lə·jē) *n. pl.* **·gies** 1 A spoken or written composition in praise of a person's life or character. 2 High praise. Also **eu′lo·gism**, **eu·lo·gi·um** (yōō·lō′jē·əm). [< Gk. *eu-* well + *legein* speak] —**eu·log·ic** (yōō·loj′ik) *adj.*

**eu·pho·ni·ous** (yōō·fō′nē·əs) *adj.* Pleasant in sound, as a word; characterized by euphony. —**eu·pho′ni·ous·ly** *adv.* —**eu·pho′ni·ous·ness** *n.*

**eu·pho·ny** (yōō′fə·nē) *n. pl.* **·nies** 1 Agreeableness of sound. 2 Pleasant-sounding combination or arrangement of words. [< Gk. *eu-* good + *phone* sound]

**eu·tha·na·si·a** (yōō′thə·nā′zhē·ə, ·zhə) *n.* 1 Painless, peaceful death. 2 The deliberate putting to death of a person suffering from a painful and incurable disease; mercy killing. [< Gk. *eu-* good + *thanatos* death]

**e·vac·u·ate** (i·vak′yōō·āt) *v.* **·at·ed**, **·at·ing** *v.t.* 1 *Mil.* a To give up or abandon possession of; withdraw from, as a fortress or city. b To withdraw (troops, inhabitants, etc.) from a threatened area or place. 2 To depart from; vacate. 3 To produce a near vacuum in. 4 *Physiol.* To discharge or eject, as from the bowels. —*v.i.* 5 To withdraw, as from a threatened area or place. [< L*<e-* out + *vacuare* make empty] —**e·vac′u·a′tion** *n.* —**e·vac′u·a′tive** *adj.*

**e·vade** (i·vād′) *v.* **e·vad·ed**, **e·vad·ing** *v.t.* 1 To escape or get away from by tricks or cleverness. 2 To avoid or get out of. —*v.i.* 3 To avoid doing something by clever or deceitful means. [< L e- out + *vadere* go] — **e·vad′a·ble** *adj.* —**e·vad′er** *n.* —**Syn.** 1 elude. 2 dodge, neglect, foil, shun.

**ev·a·nes·cent** (ev′ə·nes′ənt) *adj.* Passing away, or liable to pass away, gradually or imperceptibly. —**ev′a·nes′cence** *n.* —**ev′a·nes′cent·ly** *adv.*

**e·van·gel·i·cal** (ē′van·jel′i·kəl, ev′ən-) *adj.* 1 In or agreeing with the four Gospels or the teachings of the New Testament. 2 Of, pertaining to, or believing in the authority of Scripture and salvation through Christ. 3 EVANGELISTIC. —*n.* A member of an evangelical church, or of an evangelical party within a church. Also **e′van·gel′ic.** —**e′van·gel′i·cal·ism, e′van·gel′i·cism** *n.* —**e′van·gel′i·cal·ly** *adv.*

**e·van·gel·ist** (i·van′jə·list) *n.* 1 *Usu. cap.* One of the four writers of the New Testament Gospels; Matthew, Mark, Luke, or John. 2 An itinerant or missionary preacher; a revivalist.

**e·vap·o·rate** (i·vap′ə·rāt) *v.* ·rat·ed, ·rat·ing *v.t.* 1 To convert into vapor. 2 To remove moisture from. —*v.i.* 3 To become vapor. 4 To yield vapor. 5 To vanish; disappear. [< L e- out, away + *vapor* vapor] —**e·vap′o·ra′tive** *adj.* —**e·vap′o·ra′tion, e·vap′o·ra·tor** *n.*

**e·va·sion** (i·vā′zhən) *n.* 1 The act of evading. 2 A means or an instance of doing this; subterfuge.

**e·va·sive** (i·vā′siv) *adj.* 1 Not direct, open or straight-forward: an *evasive* answer. 2 Tending to elude; elusive. —**e·va′sive·ly** *adv.* —**e·va′sive·ness** *n.*

**e·vent** (i·vent′) *n.* 1 Anything that happens or comes to pass. 2 The result or outcome of any action. 3 One of the items making up a program of sports. [< L e- out + *ventre* come] —**Syn.** 1 occurrence, happening, episode, incident.

**e·ven·tu·al** (i·ven′chōō·əl) *adj.* Taking place after a period of time or as a result of a succession of events; subsequent. [< EVENT] —**e·ven′tu·al·ly** *adv.*

**e·vict** (i·vikt′) *v.t.* To expel (a tenant) by legal process; dispossess; put out. [< L e- out + *vincere* conquer] —**e·vic′tion, e·vic′tor** *n.*

**ev·i·dence** (ev′ə·dəns) *n.* 1 That which makes evident or clear; an outward sign or indication. 2 That which serves to prove. 3 *Law* That which is submitted to a court to establish the truth or falsehood of something alleged or presumed. 4 *Law* A witness. —**in evidence** In plain view; visible. —*v.t.*

·denced, ·denc·ing 1 To make evident; show clearly; display. 2 To support by one's testimony; attest.

**e·vince** (i·vins′) *v.t.* **e·vinced, e·vinc·ing** To show plainly or certainly; make evident; display. [< L *evincere* to conquer] — **e·vin′ci·ble** *adj.* —**e·vin′ci·bly** *adv.*

**e·voke** (i·vōk′) *v.t.* **e·voked, e·vok·ing** 1 To call or summon forth; elicit, as an emotion or reply. 2 To summon up (spirits) by or as by spells. [< L e- out + *vocare* call] —**ev·o·ca·ble** (ev′ə·kə·bəl, i·vok′ə-) **ev·o·ca·tive** (i·vok′ə·tiv) *adj.* —**ev·o·ca·tion** (ev′ə·kā′shən, ē′vō-) *n.*

**ev·o·lu·tion** (ev′ə·lōō′shən, ēv′ə-) *n.* 1 The process of unfolding; development or growth. 2 Anything evolved. 3 *Biol.* a The theory that all forms of life originated by descent, with gradual or abrupt modifications, from preexisting forms which themselves trace backward in a continuing series to the most rudimentary organisms. b The series of changes by which a given type of organism has acquired the physiological and structural characteristics differentiating it from other types. 4 *Math.* The operation of extracting a root. 5 A move or maneuver, as of troops. 6 A movement forming one of a series of complex motions. 7 The emission or setting free, as of gas, energy, etc. [< L *evolvere* to evolve] —**ev′o·lu′tion·al, ev′o·lu′tion·ar·y,** *adj.* —**ev′o·lu′tion·al·ly** *adv.* —**ev′o·lu′tion·ism** *n.* —**ev′o·lu′tion·ist** *n., adj.*

**e·volve** (i·volv′) *v.* **e·volved, e·volv·ing** *v.t.* 1 To work out or develop gradually: to *evolve* a plan. 2 *Biol.* To develop, as by a differentiation of parts or functions, to a more highly organized condition. 3 To give or throw off (vapor, heat, etc.); emit. —*v.i.* 4 To undergo the process of evolution. 5 To open out; develop. [< L *evolvere* < e- out + *volvere* roll] —**e·volv′a·ble** *adj.* —**e·volv′ent** *adj., n.* — **e·volve′ment** *n.*

**ewe** (yōō, *Regional* yō) *n.* A female sheep. [< OE *eowu*]

**ew·er** (yōō′ər) *n.* A wide-mouthed pitcher, sometimes with a lid. [< OF *evier*]

**ex·ac·er·bate** (ig·zas′ər·bāt) *v.t.* ·bat·ed, ·bat·ing To make more intense or severe. [< L ex- completely + *acerbus* bitter, harsh] — **ex·ac′er·ba′tion** *n.*

**ex·act** (ig·zakt′) *adj.* 1 Clear and complete; definite; precise: *exact* instructions. 2 Absolutely accurate: *exact* answers. 3 Specified or required: an *exact* amount. 4 Rigor-

169

ous; demanding; strict: an *exact* teacher. —*v.t.* 1 To compel the yielding or payment of; extort. 2 To demand; insist upon as a right. 3 To require; call for: The task will *exact* great effort. [< L *exigere* determine] —**ex·act′a·ble** *adj.* —**ex·act′er, ex·ac′tor** *n.*

**ex·ag·ger·ate** (ig·zaj′ə·rāt) *v.* ·**at·ed, ·at·ing** *v.t.* 1 To describe or think about as greater than is actually the case. 2 To increase or enlarge beyond what is normal or expected. —*v.i.* 3 To describe or think about something in exaggerated terms. [< L *ex-* out + *agger* mound, heap] —**ex·ag′ger·at′ed·ly, ex·ag′ger·at′ing·ly** *adv.* —**ex·ag′ger·a′tion, ex·ag′ger·a′tor** *n.*

**ex·alt** (ig·zôlt′) *v.t.* 1 To raise high; lift up; elevate. 2 To raise in rank, character, honor, etc. 3 To glorify or praise; pay honor to. 4 To fill with delight, pride, etc. 5 To increase the force or intensity of, as colors. [< L *ex-* out + *altus* high] —**ex·alt′er** *n.*

**ex·al·ta·tion** (eg′zôl·tā′shən) *n.* 1 The act of exalting. 2 The state of being exalted. 3 An extreme or sometimes exaggerated sense of well-being, importance, or power.

**ex·am** (ig·zam′) *n. Informal* An examination.

**ex·am·i·na·tion** (ig·zam′ə·nā′shən) *n.* 1 The act or process of examining or the state of being examined. 2 A testing of knowledge, progress, skill, qualifications, etc.; also, the questions used in such testing. 3 *Law* A formal interrogation. —**ex·am′i·na′tion·al** *adj.*

**ex·am·ple** (ig·zam′pəl, -zäm′-) *n.* 1 Something that belongs to and typifies a group of things, and that is singled out as a sample of the group. 2 A thing or person suitable to be used as a model. 3 A case serving or designed to serve as a warning. 4 A problem or exercise, as in mathematics, that is worked out or designed to be worked out to illustrate a method or principle. —*v.t.* ·**pled, ·pling** To exemplify: now used only in the passive. [< L *exemplum* something taken out]

**ex·as·per·ate** (ig·zas′pə·rāt) *v.t.* ·**at·ed, ·at·ing** 1 To irritate or annoy exceedingly; infuriate. 2 To make worse; intensify; inflame. [< L *ex-asperare* make rough] —**ex·as′per·at′er, ex·as′per·a′tion** *n.* —**ex·as′per·at′ing** *adj.* —**ex·as′per·at′ing·ly** *adv.*

**ex·ca·vate** (eks′kə·vāt) *v.t.* ·**vat·ed, ·vat·ing** 1 To make a hole or cavity in. 2 To form or make (a tunnel, etc.) by digging out or scooping. 3 To remove by digging or scooping out, as soil. 4 To uncover by digging, as

ruins. [< L *ex-* out + *cavus* hollow] —**ex′ca·va′tion, ex′ca·va′tor** *n.*

**ex·ceed** (ik·sēd′) *v.t.* 1 To surpass, as in quantity, quality, measure, or value. 2 To go beyond the limit or extent of: to *exceed* one's income. —*v.i.* 3 To be superior; surpass others. [< L *ex-* out, beyond + *cedere* go]

**ex·cel** (ik·sel′) *v.t. & v.i.* ·**celled, ·cel·ling** To go beyond or above; outdo; surpass (another or others). [< L *excellere* rise]

**ex·cel·lence** (ek′sə·ləns) *n.* 1 The state or quality of excelling; superiority. 2 That in which a person or thing excels or is superior. Also **ex′cel·len·cy.**

**ex·cess** (ik·ses′) *n.* 1 The condition of exceeding what is ordinary, reasonable, or required. 2 An amount greater than is necessary; overabundance. 3 The amount by which one thing is greater than another; surplus. 4 Overindulgence; intemperance. —**to excess** To an unnecessary or extreme degree or extent. —*adj.* (*also* ek′ses) Being above a stipulated amount; extra. [< L *ex-cedere* go beyond]

**ex·ces·sive** (ik·ses′iv) *adj.* Being in, tending to, marked by excess; immoderate; extreme. —**ex·ces′sive·ly** *adv.* —**ex·ces′sive ·ness** *n.*

**ex·change** (iks·chānj′) *n.* 1 The act of giving or receiving one thing as an equivalent for another; bartering. 2 Interchange: an *exchange* of wit, remarks, etc. 3 A substituting of one thing for another. 4 Something given or substituted for another. 5 A place where merchants, brokers, etc., buy, sell, or trade: a stock *exchange.* 6 A central telephone office. 7 A system of paying debts without transfer of actual money but by means of credits, drafts, etc.; also, the fee charged for this. 8 BILL OF EXCHANGE. 9 The value of one currency in terms of another currency. 10 The difference in value between two currencies. 11 *pl.* Checks, drafts, etc., presented to a clearing-house for settlement. —*v.* ·**changed, ·chang·ing** 1 To give or part with for something regarded as of equal value, etc.: to *exchange* francs for dollars. 2 To give and receive in turn; reciprocate. 3 To replace by or give up for something else: to *exchange* poverty for wealth. —*v.i.* 4 To be given or taken in exchange. 5 To make an exchange. [< L *ex-* out + *cambiare* exchange] —**ex·change′a·bil′i·ty** *n.* —**ex·change′a·ble** *adj.* —**ex·change′a·bly** *adv.*

**ex·cise¹** (ek′sīz, ek′sīs) *n.* 1 An indirect tax on commodities manufactured, produced,

sold, used, or transported within a country.
2 A license fee for various sports, trades, or
occupations. —*v.t.* ·cised, ·cis·ing To levy
an excise upon. [< L *ad-* to + *census* a tax]

**ex·cise²** (ik·sīz′) *v.t.* ·cised, ·cis·ing To cut out
or cut off, as in a surgical operation: to *excise* a cyst. [< L *ex-* out + *caedere* cut] —
**ex·ci·sion** (ik·sizh′ən) *n.*

**ex·cit·a·ble** (ik·sī′tə·bəl) *adj.* 1 Easily excited;
high-strung. 2 Susceptible to stimuli. —
**ex·cit′a·bil′i·ty, ex·cit′a·ble·ness** *n.* —
**ex·cit′a·bly** *adv.*

**ex·cite** (ik·sīt′) *v.t.* ·cit·ed, ·cit·ing 1 To arouse
(a feeling, interest, etc.) into being or activity; evoke. 2 To arouse feeling in; stimulate
the emotions of. 3 To cause action in; stir
to activity or motion. 4 To bring about; stir
up: to *excite* a riot. 5 *Physics* To give increased energy to. [< L *ex-* out + *ciere*
arouse, stir up] —**ex·cit′ed** *adj.* —
**ex·cit′ed·ly** *adv.* —**ex·cit′er** *n.* —Syn. 1, 2,
3 awaken, stir, inspire, provoke, kindle,
evoke. 4 foment, incite.

**ex·claim** (iks·klām′) *v.t. & v.i.* To say or cry
out abruptly, as in surprise or anger. [< L
*ex-* out + *clamare* cry] —**ex·claim′er** *n.*

**ex·cla·ma·tion** (eks′klə·mā′shən) *n.* 1 The act
of exclaiming. 2 An abrupt or emphatic expression, outcry, etc. —**ex·clam·a·to·ry**
(iks·klam′ə·tôr′ē, -tō′rē) *adj.*

**ex·clude** (iks·klood′) *v.t.* ·clud·ed, ·clud·ing 1
To keep from entering; shut out; bar. 2 To
refuse to notice or consider. 3 To put out;
eject. [< L *ex-* out + *claudere* close] —**ex·clu-
d′a·ble** *adj.* —**ex·clud′er, ex·clu′sion** *n.*

**ex·com·mu·ni·cate** (eks′kə·myoo′nə·kāt) *v.t.*
·cat·ed, ·cat·ing 1 To punish by an ecclesiastical sentence of exclusion from the
sacraments and communion of the church.
2 To expel in disgrace from any organization. —*adj.* Excommunicated. —*n.* An excommunicated person [< LL *excommuni-
care* to put out of the community]
—**ex′com·mu′ni·ca′tion,
ex′com·mu′ni·ca′tor** *n.*

**ex·cres·cence** (iks·kres′əns) *n.* 1 An unnatural or disfiguring outgrowth, as a wart. 2
Any unnatural addition or development. 3
A natural outgrowth, as hair. [< L *ex-* out +
*crescere* grow] —**ex·cres′cent** *adj.*

**ex·crete** (iks·krēt′) *v.t.* ·cret·ed, ·cret·ing To
eliminate, as waste matter, by normal discharge. [< L *excretus,* pp. of *excernere* separate out] —**ex·cre′tion** *n.* —**ex·cre′tive,
ex′cre·to′ry** *adj.*

**ex·cul·pate** (eks′kəl·pāt, ik·skul′-) *v.t.* ·pat-

ed, ·pat·ing To declare free from blame;
prove innocent. [< EX-¹ + L *culpare* blame.
—**ex′cul·pa′tion** *n.* —**ex·cul′pa·to′ry** *adj.*

**ex·cur·sion** (ik·skûr′zhən, -shən) *n.* 1 A short
journey, usu. for pleasure. 2 A boat or train
trip at reduced rates, accommodating passengers in groups. 3 Such passengers collectively. 4 A digression; deviation. 5
*Physics* Half the amplitude of a vibration or
oscillation. [< L *excursio < excurrere* to run
out] —**ex·cur′sion·ist** *n.*

**ex·cur·sive** (ik·skûr′siv) *adj.* Digressive; rambling; wandering; desultory. —**ex·cur′
sive·ly** *adv.* —**ex·cur′sive·ness** *n.*

**ex·cuse** (ik·skyooz′) *v.t.* ·cused, ·cus·ing 1 To
pardon and overlook (a fault, offense, etc.).
2 To try to free (someone) from blame; seek
to remove blame from. 3 To offer a reason
or apology for (an error, fault, etc.); try to
obtain pardon for or minimize. 4 To serve
as a reason for; justify. 5 To release or dismiss, as from attendance. 6 To refrain from
exacting or enforcing, as a demand or
claim. —*n.* (ik·skyoos′) 1 A plea or reason
given to justify an offense, neglect, failure,
etc. 2 Something that excuses, as from attendance. 3 One who or that which is a bad
or inferior example: a poor *excuse* for a
statesman. [< L *ex-* out, away + *causa*
charge, accusation] —**ex·cus′a·ble** *adj.* —
**ex·cus′a·bly** *adv.* —**ex·cus′er** *n.*

**ex·e·crate** (ek′sə·krāt) *v.* ·crat·ed, ·crat·ing *v.t.*
1 To curse, or call down evil upon. 2 To de-
test; abhor. —*v.i.* 3 To utter curses. [< L *ex-
ecrari* to curse] —**ex′e·cra′tion, ex′e·
cra′tor** *n.* —**ex′e·cra′tive** *adj.*

**ex·e·cute** (ek′sə·kyoot) *v.t.* ·cut·ed, ·cut·ing 1
To do or carry out fully. 2 To put in force;
administer, as a law. 3 To put to death by
legal sentence. 4 *Law* To make (a will, deed,
etc.) legal or valid. 5 To perform, as a maneuver or a musical work. 6 To produce or
create. [< L *ex-* out + *sequi* follow] —
**ex′e·cut′a·ble** *adj.* —**ex′e·cut′er** *n.* —Syn.
1 perform, fulfill, effect. 2 enforce.

**ex·e·cu·tion** (ek′sə·kyoo′shən) *n.* 1 The act of
doing, putting into force, etc. 2 A putting to
death, as by legal decree. 3 The manner,
style, or skill with which something is done.
4 *Law* A judicial writ, as for the seizure of
goods, etc.

**ex·ec·u·tive** (ig·zek′yə·tiv) *adj.* 1 Having the
function or skill of executing or performing.
2 Having ability or aptitude for directing or
controlling. 3 Of or pertaining to direction
or control; administrative, as distinguished

from *judicial* and *legislative*. —*n.* 1 An official or body of officials charged with the administration of the laws and affairs of a nation or state. 2 A person or group having administrative control, as of a business or other organization.

**ex·em·pla·ry** (ig·zem'plər·ē) *adj.* 1 Serving as a model or example worthy of imitation; commendable. 2 Serving as a warning example: *exemplary* damages. 3 Serving to exemplify; illustrative. —**ex·em'pla·ri·ly** *adv.* —**ex·em'pla·ri·ness** *n.*

**ex·em·pli·fy** (ig·zem'plə·fī) *v.t.* ·**fied**, ·**fy·ing** 1 To show by example; illustrate. 2 *Law* To make an authenticated transcript from, as a public record. [L *exemplum* example + *facere* make] —**ex·em'pli·fi·ca'tion** *n.* —**ex·em'pli·fi·ca'tive** *adj.*

**ex·empt** (ig·zempt') *v.t.* To free or excuse from some obligation to which others are subject; grant immunity to. —*adj.* Free, clear, or excused, as from some duty. —*n.* A person who is exempted, as from military service. [< L *ex-* out + *emere* buy, take] —**ex·empt'i·ble** *adj.* —**ex·emp'tion** *n.* —Syn. *v.* release, remit, discharge, let off, spare.

**ex·er·cise** (ek'sər·sīz) *v.* ·**cised**, ·**cis·ing** *v.t.* 1 To subject to drills, systematic movements, etc., so as to train or develop (troops, muscles, the mind, etc.). 2 To make use of; employ. 3 To perform or execute, as duties. 4 To wield; exert, as influence or authority. 5 To make a habit of: used reflexively or in the passive: to be *exercised* in good works. 6 To occupy the mind of; esp. to make anxious. —*v.i.* 7 To take exercise. 8 To undergo training. —*n.* 1 A putting into use or practice. 2 A specific bodily activity or movement for developing strength, agility, etc. 3 Something played or practiced to develop a specific skill or technique: a violin *exercise*. 4 A problem or lesson to be worked out. 5 *pl.* A program or ceremony: graduation *exercises.* [< L *exercere* to practice] —**ex'er·cis'a·ble** *adj.*

**ex·ert** (ig·zûrt') *v.t.* To put forth or put in action, as strength, force, or faculty; bring into strong or vigorous action. —**exert one·self** To put forth effort. [< L *exertus* < *exserere* thrust out] —**ex·er'tive** *adj.*

**ex·er·tion** (ig·zûr'shən) *n.* 1 The act of exerting some power, faculty, etc. 2 Vigorous action or effort.

**ex·hale** (eks·hāl', ig·zāl') *v.* ·**haled**, ·**hal·ing** *v.i.* 1 To expel air or vapor; breathe out. 2 To pass off or rise as a vapor; evaporate. —

*v.t.* 3 To breathe forth or give off. 4 To draw off; cause to evaporate. [< L *ex-* out + *halare* breathe] —**ex·hal'a·ble** *adj.* —**ex·ha·la·tion** (eks'hə·lā'shən, eg'zə-) *n.*

**ex·haust** (ig·zôst') *v.t.* 1 To make tired; wear out completely. 2 To drain of resources, strength, etc.; use up. 3 To draw off, as gas, steam, etc., from or as from a container. 4 To empty (a container) or contents; drain. 5 To study, treat of, or develop thoroughly and completely: to *exhaust* a subject. —*v.i.* 6 To pass out as the exhaust: The steam *exhausts* from the pipe. —*n.* 1 a Waste gases or vapor discharged from an engine. b The system by which these are vented. 2 The discharge of any waste gas, as by a fan. [< L *ex-* out + *haurire* draw] —**ex·haust'er, ex·haust'i·bil'i·ty** *n.* —**ex·haust'i·ble** *adj.*

**ex·haus·tion** (ig·zôs'chən) *n.* 1 Extreme fatigue or weakness. 2 The condition of being entirely used up or spent.

**ex·haus·tive** (ig·zôs'tiv) *adj.* 1 Having the effect or tendency to exhaust. 2 Complete and totally comprehensive: an *exhaustive* study. —**ex·haus'tive·ly** *adv.* —**ex·haus'tive·ness** *n.*

**ex·hib·it** (ig·zib'it) *v.t.* 1 To present to view; display. 2 To show or reveal. 3 To present for public inspection or entertainment. —*v.i.* 4 To place something on display. —*n.* 1 A public showing or display. 2 Any object or objects exhibited. 3 *Law* A document or object marked for use as evidence. [< L *ex-* out + *habere* hold, have] —**ex·hib'i·tive, ex·hib'i·to'ry** *adj.* —**ex·hib'i·tor, ex·hib'it·er** *n.*

**ex·hi·bi·tion** (ek'sə·bish'ən) *n.* 1 The act of exhibiting; display. 2 Anything exhibited. 3 A public showing, as of works of art, etc.

**ex·hil·a·rate** (ig·zil'ə·rāt) *v.t.* ·**rat·ed**, ·**rat·ing** To induce a lively or enlivening feeling in; enliven; cheer; stimulate. [< L *ex-* completely + *hilaris* glad] —**ex·hil'a·ra'tion** *n.* —Syn. elate, exalt, animate, gladden, invigorate.

**ex·hort** (ig·zôrt') *v.t.* To urge by earnest appeal or argument; advise or caution strongly. [< L *ex-* completely + *hortari* urge] —**ex·hor·ta·tion** (eg'zôr·tā'shən, ek'sər-), **ex·hort'er** *n.*

**ex·hume** (ig·zyōōm', iks·hyōōm') *v.t.* ·**humed**, ·**hum·ing** 1 To dig out of the earth, as a dead body. 2 To disclose; reveal. [< L *ex-* out + *humus* ground] —**ex·hu·ma·tion** (eks'hyōō·mā'shən) *n.*

**ex·i·gen·cy** (ek'sə·jən·sē, ig·zij'ən-) *n. pl.* ·**cies**

172

1 The state of being urgent or exigent. 2 A condition requiring immediate attention. 3 *Usu. pl.* Urgent needs or demands. Also **ex′i·gence.**

**ex·i·gent** (ek′sə·jənt) *adj.* 1 Urgent; pressing. 2 Very demanding or exacting. [< L *exigere* to demand]

**ex·ig·u·ous** (ig·zig′yŏŏ·əs, ik·sig′-) *adj.* Scanty; meager. [< L *exiguus* scantly] — **ex·i·gu·i·ty** (ek′sə·gyŏŏ′ə·tē), **ex·ig′u·ous·ness** *n.*

**ex·ile** (eg′zil, ek′sil) *n.* 1 Separation, either enforced or by choice, from one's home or native land. 2 One separated from his native country or home; an expatriate. —*v.t.* **ex·iled, ex·il·ing** To expel from and forbid to return to a native land or home; banish. [< L *exsilium*]

**ex·ist** (ig·zist′) *v.i.* 1 To have actual being or reality; be. 2 To continue to live or be. 3 To be present; occur. [< L *existere*] —**ex·is′tent** *adj.*

**ex·is·ten·tial·ism** (eg′zis·ten′shəl·iz′əm) *n.* A philosophical doctrine holding that existence takes precedence over essence, and that man, being totally free in an indifferent and purposeless universe, is responsible only to himself for the actions he takes in the development of his self. —**ex′is·ten′tial·ist** *adj., n.*

**ex·it** (eg′zit, ek′sit) *n.* 1 A way or passage out; egress. 2 The departure of an actor from the stage. 3 Any departure. —*v.i.* To go out. [< L *exitus* < *exire* go out]

**ex·o·dus** (ek′sə·dəs) *n.* A going forth, or departure. —**the Exodus** The departure of the Israelites from Egypt under the guidance of Moses, described in Exodus, the second book of the Old Testament. [< Gk. *ex-* out + *hodos* way]

**ex·on·er·ate** (ig·zon′ə·rāt) *v.t.* **·at·ed, ·at·ing** 1 To free from accusation or blame; acquit. 2 To relieve or free from a responsibility. [< L *ex-* out, away + *onus, oneris* burden] — **ex·on·er·a′tion** *n.* —**ex·on′er·a′tive** *adj.*

**ex·or·bi·tant** (ig·zôr′bə·tənt) *adj.* Going beyond usual and proper limits; excessive; extravagant. [< LL *exorbitare* go astray] — **ex·or′bi·tance, ex·or′bi·tan·cy** *n.* — **ex·or′bi·tant·ly** *adv.*

**ex·or·cise** (ek′sôr·siz) *v.t.* **·cised, ·cis·ing** 1 To cast out (an evil spirit) by prayers or incantations. 2 To free of an evil spirit. Also **ex′or·cize.** [< Gk. *exorkizein*] —**ex′or·cism′, ex′or·cist** *n.*

**ex·ot·ic** (ig·zot′ik) *adj.* 1 Belonging by nature or origin to another part of the world; for-

eign. 2 Unusually strange or different; fascinating. —*n.* Something exotic. [< Gk. *exōtikos* foreign < *exō* outside] —**ex·ot′i·cal·ly** *adv.* —**ex·ot′i·cism** *n.*

**ex·pand** (ik·spand′) *v.t.* 1 To increase the range, scope, volume, size, etc., of. 2 To spread out by unfolding or extending; open. 3 To write or develop in full the details or form of. —*v.i.* 4 To grow larger, wider, etc.; unfold; increase. [< L *ex-* out + *pandere* spread] —**ex·pand′er** *n.*

**ex·panse** (ik·spans′) *n.* 1 A vast continuous area or stretch. 2 Expansion.

**ex·pan·sion** (ik·span′shən) *n.* 1 The act of expanding or the state of being expanded. 2 The amount of increase in size, scope, volume, etc. 3 That which is expanded.

**ex·pan·sive** (ik·span′siv) *adj.* 1 Able or tending to expand. 2 Characterized by expansion; broad; extensive; comprehensive. 3 Amiable and effusive; outgoing. —**ex·pan′sive·ly** *adv.* —**ex·pan′sive·ness** *n.*

**ex·pa·ti·ate** (ik·spā′shē·āt) *v.i.* **·at·ed, ·at·ing** To speak or write in a lengthy manner; elaborate: with *on* or *upon.* [< L *ex(s)patiari* to spread out] —**ex·pa′ti·a′tion, ex·pa′ti·a′tor** *n.* —**ex·pa′ti·a·to·ry** (-tôr′ē, -tō′rē) *adj.*

**ex·pect** (ik·spekt′) *v.t.* 1 To look forward to as certain or probable; anticipate in thought. 2 To look for as right, proper, or necessary; require. 3 *Informal* To presume; suppose. [< L *ex-* out + *spectare* look at] —**ex·pect′a·ble** *adj.*

**ex·pec·ta·tion** (ek′spek·tā′shən) *n.* 1 The act of expecting something; also, the mental attitude of one who expects something. 2 *Often pl.* A prospect or hope of good to come. 3 Something expected.

**ex·pec·to·rate** (ik·spek′tə·rāt) *v.t. & v.i.* **·rat·ed, ·rat·ing** 1 To discharge, as mucus, by coughing up and spitting. 2 To spit. [< L *ex-* out + *pectus, -oris* breast] —**ex·pec′to·ra′tion** *n.*

**ex·pe·di·en·cy** (ik·spē′dē·ən·sē) *n. pl.* **·cies** 1 The state or quality of being expedient. 2 That which is expedient. 3 The doing of what is politic or advantageous, regardless of justice or right. Also **ex·pe′di·ence.**

**ex·pe·di·ent** (ik·spē′dē·ənt) *adj.* 1 Serving to promote a desired end; suitable; useful; advisable. 2 Pertaining to or based on utility or advantage rather than what is just or right. —*n.* 1 That which furthers or promotes an end. 2 A device; shift. [< L *expedire* make ready] —**ex·pe′di·ent·ly** *adv.*

**ex·pe·dite** (ek′spə·dīt) *v.t.* **·dit·ed, ·dit·ing** 1 To speed up the process or progress of; facilitate. 2 To do quickly. [< L *expedire* make ready] —**ex′pe·dit′er** *n.*

**ex·pe·di·tion** (ek′spə·dish′ən) *n.* 1 A journey, march or voyage for a definite purpose. 2 The body of persons engaged in such a journey, together with their equipment. 3 Speed; dispatch. [< L *expedire* make ready, extricate]

**ex·pel** (ik·spel′) *v.t.* **·pelled, ·pel·ling** 1 To drive out by force or authority; force out. 2 To dismiss, as a pupil from a school; eject. [< L *ex-* out + *pellere* drive, thrust] —**ex·pel′la·ble** *adj.* —**Syn.** 1 Remove, dispel, evict, oust, banish, exile.

**ex·pend** (ik·spend′) *v.t.* To pay out or spend; use up. [< L *ex-* out + *pendere* weigh]

**ex·pense** (ik·spens′) *n.* 1 *pl.* a Costs or charges of something: the *expenses* of a trip. b Money to pay for such costs or charges. 2 Anything requiring the outlay of money: A boat is an *expense*. 3 Any cost, sacrifice, or loss: at the *expense* of his health.

**ex·pen·sive** (ik·spen′siv) *adj.* Causing or involving much expense; costly. —**ex·pen′sive·ly** *adv.* —**ex·pen′sive·ness** *n.*

**ex·pe·ri·ence** (ik·spir′ē·əns) *n.* 1 The act of undergoing or being involved in an event, situation, etc. 2 Something lived through or undergone: an amazing *experience*. 3 The sum total of one's knowledge, observations, perceptions, etc.: It is outside my *experience*. 4 The duration of one's involvement with a particular activity, occupation, etc. 5 The skill or knowledge acquired from such involvement. —*v.t.* **·enced, ·enc·ing** To undergo or be involved in personally. [< L *experiri* try out] —**Syn.** *v.* know, understand, feel, realize, have, apprehend.

**ex·per·i·ment** (ik·sper′ə·mənt) *n.* 1 A procedure or test meant to yield or illustrate a principle, effect, or fact. 2 The conducting of such procedures or tests. —*v.i.* (-ment) To make experiments. [< L *experimentum* < *experiri* try out] —**ex·per′i·ment′er** *n.*

**ex·pert** (ek′spûrt) *n.* One who has special skill or knowledge; a specialist. —*adj.* (*also* ik·spûrt′) 1 Skillful as the result of practice; dexterous. 2 Of or from an expert. [< L *expertus*, pp. of *experiri* try out] —**ex·pert′ly** *adv.* —**ex·pert′ness** *n.*

**ex·pi·ate** (ek′spē·āt) *v.t.* **·at·ed, ·at·ing** To atone for; make amends for. [< L *ex-* completely + *piare* appease] —**ex′pi·a′tion**, **ex′pi·a′tor** *n.* —**ex′pi·a·to′ry** *adj.*

**ex·pire** (ik·spir′) *v.* **·pired, ·pir·ing** *v.i.* 1 To exhale one's last breath; die. 2 To breathe out. 3 To die out, as embers. 4 To come to an end; terminate. —*v.t.* 5 To breathe out. [< L *ex-* out + *spirare* breathe] —**ex·pir′er** *n.*

**ex·plain** (ik·splān′) *v.t.* 1 To make plain or clear; make understandable. 2 To give a meaning to; interpret. 3 To give reasons for; state the cause or purpose of. —*v.i.* 4 To give an explanation. [< L *ex-* out + *planare* make level] —**ex·plain′a·ble** *adj.*

**ex·pla·na·tion** (ek′splə·nā′shən) *n.* 1 The act of explaining. 2 Something, as a statement, that explains. 3 Meaning; significance; sense.

**ex·plic·it** (ik·splis′it) *adj.* 1 Plainly stated; clearly expressed. 2 Having no disguised meaning or reservation; definite; open. [< L *explicare* unfold, explicate. See EXPLICATE.] —**ex·plic′it·ly** *adv.* —**ex·plic′it·ness** *n.*

**ex·plode** (ik·splōd′) *v.* **·plod·ed, ·plod·ing** *v.t.* 1 To cause to expand violently or pass suddenly from a solid to a gaseous state. 2 To cause to burst or blow up violently and with noise. 3 To disprove utterly; refute. —*v.i.* 4 To be exploded or blow up. 5 To burst forth noisily or violently: to *explode* with laughter. 6 To become greater very quickly. [< L *explodere*, orig., drive off the stage, hiss < *ex-* out + *plaudere* clap] —**ex·plod′er** *n.*

**ex·ploit** (eks′ploit, ik·sploit′) *n.* A deed or act, esp. one marked by heroism, daring, skill, or brilliancy. —*v.t.* (ik·sploit′) 1 To use for one's own advantage; take advantage of. 2 To put to use; make use of. [< OF] —**ex·ploit′a·ble** *adj.* —**ex′ploi·ta′tion, ex·ploi′ter** *n.*

**ex·plore** (ik·splôr′, -splōr′) *v.* **·plored, ·plor·ing** *v.t.* 1 To search through or travel in or over, as new lands, for discovery. 2 To look into or examine carefully; scrutinize. —*v.i.* 3 To make explorations. [< L *explorare* investigate < *ex-* out + *plorare* cry out] —**ex′plo·ra′tion, ex·plor′er** *n.* —**ex·plor·a·to·ry** (ik·splôr′ə·tôr′ē), **ex·plor′a·tive** *adj.*

**ex·plo·sion** (ik·splō′zhən) *n.* 1 The act of exploding; rapid release of energy, usu. causing a loud noise. 2 A sudden and violent outbreak, as of physical or emotional forces. 3 A sudden and large increase.

**ex·plo·sive** (ik·splō′siv) *adj.* 1 Pertaining to or characterized by explosion. 2 Liable to explode, become violent, or cause turmoil: *explosive* news. —*n.* A material that can explode or cause an explosion. —**ex·plo′sive·ly** *adv.* —**ex·plo′sive·ness** *n.*

**ex·po·nent** (ik·spō′nənt) *n.* 1 One who explains or expounds. 2 *Math.* A number or symbol placed as a superscript to the right of a quantity to indicate a power, reciprocal, or root. 3 Any person or thing that symbolizes or exemplifies something. [< L *exponere* indicate] —**ex·po·nen·tial** (ek′spə·nen′shəl) *adj.* —**ex′po·nen′tial·ly** *adv.*

**ex·port** (ik·spôrt′, -spôrt′, eks′pôrt, -pôrt) *v.t.* To carry or send, as goods or raw materials, to other countries for sale or trade. — *n.* (eks′pôrt, -pôrt) 1 The act of exporting; exportation. 2 That which is exported; esp. merchandise. —*adj.* (eks′pôrt, -pôrt) Of or pertaining to exports or exportation. [< L *exout* + *portare* carry] —**ex·port′a·ble** *adj.* —**ex′por·ta′tion, ex·port′er** *n.*

**ex·pose** (ik·spōz′) *v.t.* ·posed, ·pos·ing 1 To lay open, as to harm, ridicule, etc. 2 To leave open to the action of a force or influence. 3 To present to view; show; display. 4 To cause to be known; make public, as a crime. 5 To lay open or make known the crimes, faults, etc., of (a person). 6 To abandon so as to cause the death of: to *expose* an unwanted child. 7 *Phot.* To admit light to (a sensitized film or plate). [< MF *exposer* < L *exponere*] —**ex·pos′er** *n.*

**ex·po·sé** (ek′spō·zā′) *n.* A disclosure or exposure of something corrupt, evil, etc. [F]

**ex·po·si·tion** (eks′pə·zish′ən) *n.* 1 A large, comprehensive, public exhibition, as a world's fair. 2 A detailed explanation or commentary. 3 Any detailed presentation of a topic, either written or oral. 4 The part of a play that tells something about the characters, what has happened before, etc. [< L *expositio* < *exponere* to expose] —**ex·pos′i·tor** *n.* —**ex·pos′i·to′ry** *adj.*

**ex·pos·tu·late** (ik·spos′chə·lāt) *v.i.* ·lat·ed, ·lat·ing To reason earnestly with a person, against some action: usu. with *with.* [< L *exout* + *postulare* demand] —**ex·pos′tu·la′tion** *n.* —**ex·pos′tu·la′tive, ex·pos′tu·la·to′ry** *adj.*

**ex·po·sure** (ik·spō′zhər) *n.* 1 The act or process of exposing, or the state of being exposed in any sense. 2 Situation in relation to the sun, elements, or points of the compass: The house had a southern *exposure.* 3 *Phot.* a The act of subjecting a sensitized film or plate to light rays or other radiation. b The time necessary for this. c An amount of film necessary for one picture.

**ex·press** (ik·spres′) *v.t.* 1 To put (thought or opinion) into spoken or written words. 2 To make apparent; reveal. 3 To represent in symbols, as in art or mathematics. 4 To send by express. 5 To press out; squeeze out, as juice or moisture. 6 To force out by or as by pressure. —**express oneself** To make known one's thoughts, feelings, or creative impulses. —*adj.* 1 Set forth distinctly; explicit; direct. 2 Specially prepared; adapted to a specific purpose. 3 Traveling at high speeds. 4 Designed for fast driving. 5 Making few stops: an *express* elevator. 6 Exact: an *express* likeness. — *adv.* By fast delivery. —*n.* 1 A system of transporting goods rapidly. 2 The goods so sent. 3 A message, money, etc. sent with speed. 4 Any means of rapid transmission. 5 An express train, elevator, etc. [< L *exout* + *pressare* to press] —**ex·press′er** *n.* —**ex·press′i·ble** *adj.*

**ex·pres·sion** (ik·spresh′ən) *n.* 1 The act of representing or expressing something by using words, gestures, art, music, etc. 2 Any means by which some truth or idea is conveyed: the *expression* of pleasure. 3 The manner of expressing or doing something, esp. an effective or eloquent manner. 4 A phrase or saying. 5 A gesture, tone, facial aspect, etc., that conveys a thought or feeling. 6 A pressing out, as of juice. 7 *Math.* A meaningful group of characters, numbers, etc.

**ex·pres·sive** (ik·spres′iv) *adj.* 1 Of or characterized by expression. 2 Expressing or indicating: a look *expressive* of hate. 3 Meaningful; significant: an *expressive* glance. —**ex·pres′sive·ly** *adv.* —**ex·pres′sive·ness** *n.*

**ex·pul·sion** (ik·spul′shən) *n.* 1 The act of expelling; forcible ejection. 2 The state of being expelled. —**ex·pul′sive** *adj.*

**ex·punge** (ik·spunj′) *v.t.* ·punged, ·pung·ing To blot or scratch out, as from a record or list; obliterate. [< L *exout* + *pungere* prick] —**ex·pung′er** *n.*

**ex·qui·site** (eks′kwi·zit, ik·skwiz′it) *adj.* 1 Skillfully and delicately made or designed: an *exquisite* silk fan. 2 Delicately beautiful: an *exquisite* child. 3 Unusually refined and sensitive, as in perception or judgment: *exquisite* taste. 4 Extremely fine; consummate: an *exquisite* interpretation. 5 Intense; extreme: *exquisite* pain or pleasure. —*n.* One overly sensitive or fastidiously elegant in taste, manners, perceptions, etc. [< L *exout* + *quarere* seek] —**ex′qui·site·ly** *adv.* —**ex′qui·site·ness** *n.*

**ex·tant** (ek′stənt, ik·stant′) *adj.* Still existing and known; not lost or extinct. [< L *ex*- out + *stare* stand]

**ex·tem·po·ra·ne·ous** (ik·stem′pə·rā′nē·əs) *adj.* 1 Done or made with no preparation; unpremeditated. 2 Somewhat prepared but not memorized, rehearsed, etc., as a speech. 3 Made with what is at hand; improvised. [< L *ex*- out + *tempus, temporis* time] —**ex·tem′po·ra′ne·ous·ly** *adv.* —**ex·tem′po·ra′ne·ous·ness** *n.*

**ex·tem·po·rar·y** (ik·stem′pə·rer′ē) *adj.* EXTEMPORANEOUS. —**ex·tem′po·rar′i·ly** *adv.* —**ex·tem′po·rar′i·ness** *n.*

**ex·tend** (ik·stend′) *v.t.* 1 To open or stretch to full length. 2 To make longer. 3 To cause to last or continue until or for a specified time. 4 To widen or enlarge the range, scope, meaning, etc., of: to *extend* the duties of an office. 5 To hold out or put forth, as the hand. 6 To give or offer to give: to *extend* hospitality. 7 To straighten, as a leg or arm. —*v.t.* 8 To be extended; stretch. 9 To reach, as in a specified direction: This road *extends* west. —**extend oneself** To put forth great effort. [< L *ex*- out + *tendere* stretch] —**ex·tend′i·bil′i·ty** *n.* —**ex·tend′i·ble** *adj.*

**ex·ten·sion** (ik·sten′shən) *n.* 1 The act of extending or the condition of being extended. 2 Something extended or additional, as an annex to a building, a second telephone in a home, a branch of a school or university, an extended time limit for a debt, etc. 3 The straightening of a flexed limb. —*adj.* Capable of extending or being extended. —**ex·ten′sion·al** *adj.*

**ex·ten·sive** (ik·sten′siv) *adj.* 1 Great in area. 2 Broad or wide in scope, range, influence, etc. 3 Large in amount, extent, etc.; considerable: *extensive* damage. —**ex·ten′sive·ly** *adv.* —**ex·ten′sive·ness** *n.*

**ex·tent** (ik·stent′) *n.* 1 The dimension, amount, or degree to which anything is extended; reach; size. 2 Range, scope, or limits of something: the *extent* of his power. 3 A large area or space: an *extent* of pastureland.

**ex·ten·u·ate** (ik·sten′yōō·āt) *v.t.* ·at·ed, ·at·ing 1 To represent as less blameworthy; make excuses for. 2 To cause to seem less serious or blameworthy: *extenuating* circumstances. [< L *extenuare* weaken < *ex*- out + *tenuis* thin] —**ex·ten′u·a′tion, ex·ten′u·a′tor** *n.*

**ex·te·ri·or** (ik·stir′ē·ər) *adj.* 1 Of, on, or for the outside. 2 Acting or coming from outside. —*n.* 1 Something located outside; an outside part or surface. 2 External features or qualities. [< L compar. of *exterus* outside] —**ex·te′ri·or·ly** *adv.*

**ex·ter·mi·nate** (ik·stûr′mə·nāt) *v.t.* ·nat·ed, ·nat·ing To destroy entirely; annihilate. [< L *exterminare* to drive out] —**ex·ter′min·a′tion** *n.* —**ex·ter′mi·na′tive, ex·ter′mi·na·to′ry** (-tôr′ē, -tō′rē) *adj.* —**Syn.** demolish, eradicate, remove, root out, abolish.

**ex·ter·nal** (ik·stûr′nəl) *adj.* 1 Of, pertaining to, or situated on the outside; exterior. 2 On, of, or for the outside of the body: an *external* medicine. 3 Visible from the outside. 4 Having existence separate from one's perceptions. 5 Coming or acting from outside. 6 Merely for outward appearance; superficial: *external* show. —*n.* 1 An exterior or outer part. 2 *Usu. pl.* Outward and often superficial appearances, circumstances, etc. [< L *externus* outer < *exterus* outside] —**ex·ter·nal′i·ty** *n.* —**ex·ter′nal·ly** *adv.*

**ex·tinct** (ik·stingkt′) *adj.* 1 No longer active or burning: an *extinct* volcano. 2 No longer existing: an *extinct* animal. 3 Void; lapsed: an *extinct* title. [< L *ex(s)tinguere* extinguish]

**ex·tinc·tion** (ik·stingk′shən) *n.* 1 The act of extinguishing, or the state of being extinguished; extinguishment. 2 A dying out or becoming extinct. 3 The act of destroying, or the state of being destroyed.

**ex·tin·guish** (ik·sting′gwish) *v.t.* 1 To put out; quench, as a fire. 2 To make extinct; wipe out. 3 To obscure or throw into the shade; eclipse. [< L *ex*- completely + *stinguere* quench] —**ex·tin′guish·a·ble** *adj.* —**ex·tin′guish·er, ex·tin′guish·ment** *n.*

**ex·tir·pate** (ek′stər·pāt) *v.t.* ·pat·ed, ·pat·ing To root out or up; eradicate; destroy wholly. [< L *ex*- out + *stirps* stem, root] —**ex′tir·pa′tion** *n.* —**ex′tir·pa·tive** *adj.*

**ex·tol** (ik·stōl′) *v.t.* ·tolled, ·tol·ling To praise in the highest terms; magnify. Also **ex·toll′**. [< L *ex*- out, up + *tollere* raise] —**ex·tol′ler, ex·tol′ment** or **ex·toll′ment** *n.*

**ex·tort** (ik·stôrt′) *v.t.* To obtain from a person by violence, threat, oppression, or abuse of authority; wring; wrest. [< L *ex*- out + *torquere* twist] —**ex·tort′er** *n.* —**ex·tor′tive** *adj.*

**ex·tract** (ik·strakt′) *v.t.* 1 To draw or pull out by force. 2 To obtain (pleasure, benefit, etc.) from some action, circumstance, or source. 3 To obtain by force, extortion, pressure, etc.: to *extract* money. 4 To obtain (a concentrate, juice, etc.) by pressing, chemical action, etc. 5 To copy out; select for quotation. 6 *Math.* To calculate (the root of a number). —*n.* (eks′trakt) Something extracted or drawn out, as: a A concentrate or essence of a food, flavoring, etc.: vanilla *extract.* b A selection or passage from written or spoken matter. [< L *ex-* out + *trahere* draw, pull] —**ex·tract′a·ble** or **ex·tract′i·ble** *adj.* —**ex·trac′tive** *adj., n.* —**ex·tract′or** *n.*

**ex·tra·cur·ric·u·lar** (eks′trə·kə·rik′yə·lər) *adj.* Of or pertaining to activities outside a school's regular curriculum, as clubs, school publications, etc.

**ex·tra·dite** (eks′trə·dīt) *v.t.* ·**dit·ed**, ·**dit·ing** 1 To deliver up (an accused person, prisoner, etc.) as to another state or nation. 2 To obtain the extradition of. —**ex′tra·dit′a·ble** *adj.*

**ex·tra·ne·ous** (ik·strā′nē·əs) *adj.* Not intrinsic, relevant, or essential to matter under consideration. [< L *extraneus* foreign] —**ex·tra′ne·ous·ly** *adv.* —**ex·tra′ne·ous·ness** *n.*

**ex·traor·di·nar·y** (ik·strôr′də·ner′ē; *esp. for def. 3,* eks′trə·ôr′də·ner′ē) *adj.* 1 Beyond or out of the common order, course, or method. 2 Exceeding the ordinary or usual; exceptional; remarkable. 3 Employed for a special purpose or occasion; special: an envoy *extraordinary.* —**ex·traor′di·nar′i·ly** *adv.* —**Syn.** 1,2 amazing, marvelous, uncommon, unusual, unprecedented, odd, rare.

**ex·trap·o·late** (ik·strap′ə·lāt) *v.t. & v.i.* ·**lat·ed**, ·**lat·ing** 1 *Math.* To estimate (a function) beyond the range of known values. 2 To infer (a possibility) beyond the strict evidence of a series of facts, events, observations, etc. [< EXTRA- + (INTER)POLATE] —**ex·trap′o·la′tion** *n.*

**ex·tra·sen·so·ry** (eks′trə·sen′sər·ē) *adj.* Outside of or beyond normal sensory perception.

**ex·trav·a·gance** (ik·strav′ə·gəns) *n.* 1 Excessive expenditure of money. 2 Exaggerated or unreasonable conduct or speech. 3 An instance of excessive or immoderate conduct, speech, or spending. Also **ex·trav′a·gan·cy.**

**ex·trav·a·gant** (ik·strav′ə·gənt) *adj.* 1 Excessively free or lavish in expenditure. 2 Immoderate; fantastic; unrestrained: *extravagant* behavior. 3 Unusually ornate or fanciful: an *extravagant* costume. 4 Exorbitant. [< L *extra-* outside + *vagari* wander] —**ex·trav′a·gant·ly** *adv.* —**ex·trav′a·gant·ness** *n.*

**ex·treme** (ik·strēm′) *adj.* 1 At or to the far-

thest limit or point; outermost. 2 In the utmost degree; very great: *extreme* joy. 3 Far from the normal, average, or usual. 4 Immoderate; radical; *extreme* opinions. 5 Drastic: *extreme* measures. 6 Last; final: *extreme* unction. —*n.* 1 The utmost or highest degree, limit, etc.: the *extreme* of cruelty. 2 Either of the two ends or limits of a series, range, etc.: *extremes* of temperature. 3 An act or condition that is extreme or drastic. —**go to extremes** To be excessive or immoderate in action, thought, etc. [< L *extremus,* superl. of *exterus* outside] —**ex·treme′ly** *adv.* —**ex·treme′ness** *n.*

**ex·trem·i·ty** (ik·strem′ə·tē) *n. pl.* ·**ties** 1 The utmost or farthest point; termination, end, or edge. 2 The greatest degree. 3 Desperate distress or need. 4 *pl.* Extreme measures. 5 *Usu. pl.* The end part of a limb or appendage.

**ex·tri·cate** (eks′trə·kāt) *v.t.* ·**cat·ed**, ·**cat·ing** To free from hindrance, difficulties, etc.; disentangle. [< L *ex-* out + *tricae* troubles] —**ex·tri·ca·ble** (eks′tri·kə·bəl) *adj.* —**ex′tri·ca·bly** *adv.* —**ex·tri·ca′tion** *n.*

**ex·tro·vert** (eks′trō·vûrt) *n.* One whose attention and interest are directed chiefly towards other people and the external world rather than towards himself. [< EXTRA- + L *vertere* turn] —**ex′tro·ver′sion** *n.*

**ex·u·ber·ance** (ig·zōō′bər·əns) *n.* 1 The state or quality of being exuberant. 2 An instance of this. Also **ex·u′ber·an·cy.**

**ex·u·ber·ant** (ig·zōō′bər·ənt) *adj.* 1 Characterized by high spirits, enthusiasm, and vitality. 2 Effusive; overflowing; lavish. 3 Marked by plentifulness; producing copiously. [< L *ex-* completely + *uberare* be fruitful] —**ex·u′ber·ant·ly** *adv.*

**ex·ult** (ig·zult′) *v.i.* To rejoice in or as in triumph; take great delight. [< L *ex-* out + *salire* leap] —**ex·ul·ta·tion** (ig′zul·tā′shən, ek′sul-) *n.* —**ex·ult′ing·ly** *adv.*

**ex·ur·ban·ite** (eks·ûr′bən·īt) *n.* One living outside a city in a residential area beyond the suburbs, who commutes to work in the city, and who is sometimes considered above a suburbanite in economic and social status. [< EX(TRA-) + (SUB)URBANITE]

# F

**fa·ble** (fā′bəl) *n.* 1 A brief story embodying a moral, often with animals as the characters. 2 A myth or legend. 3 A falsehood; lie. —*v.t. & v.i.* **fa·bled**, **fa·bling** To invent or tell (fables, lies, etc.). [< L *fabula* < *fari* say, speak]

**fab·ric** (fab′rik) *n.* 1 Any woven, felted, or knitted cloth. 2 Something that has been fabricated, constructed, or put together. 3 The manner of construction; workmanship. [< L *fabrica* a workshop]

**fab·ri·cate** (fab′rə·kāt) *v.t.* **·cat·ed, ·cat·ing** 1 To make, assemble, or manufacture. 2 To invent, as lies or reasons; concoct. [< L *fabricare* to construct] —**fab′ri·ca′tion, fab′ri·ca′tor** *n.*

**fab·u·lous** (fab′yə·ləs) *adj.* 1 Fictitious; mythical. 2 Unbelievable; incredible. [< L *fabula* FABLE] —**fab′u·lous·ly** *adv.* —**fab′u·lous·ness** *n.*

**fac·et** (fas′it) *n.* 1 Any of the flat surfaces on a gem or similar object. 2 One side or aspect of a person's mind or character. —*v.t.* **fac·et·ed** or **·et·ted, fac·et·ing** or **·et·ting** To cut or work facets upon. [< F *facette*, lit., small face]

**fa·ce·tious** (fə·sē′shəs) *adj.* Indulging in or marked by wit or humor; jocular. [< L *facetia* wit + -OUS] —**fa·ce′tious·ly** *adv.* —**fa·ce′tious·ness** *n.* —**Syn.** clever, droll, funny, pungent, waggish.

**fac·ile** (fas′il) *adj.* 1 Easy to do or master. 2 Easily moved or persuaded; pliant. 3 Ready or quick in performance; dexterous. [< L *facilis* easy to do < *facere* do] —**fac′ile·ly** *adv.* —**fac′ile·ness** *n.* • *Facile* means *easy* but implies that little effort is expended and that the result is not worth much. A *facile* style of violin playing is superficial and lacking in depth. An *easy* style is relaxed but has both depth and precision.

**fa·cil·i·tate** (fə·sil′ə·tāt) *v.t.* **·tat·ed, ·tat·ing** To make easier or more convenient.

**fa·cil·i·ty** (fə·sil′ə·tē) *n. pl.* **·ties** 1 Ease or readiness in doing; dexterity. 2 Readiness of compliance; pliancy. 3 *Often pl.* Any means, aid, or convenience; dining *facilities*. 4 A place or office equipped to fulfill a special function: a government *facility*. [< L *facilitas* ability < *facere* do]

**fac·sim·i·le** (fak·sim′ə·lē) *n.* 1 An exact copy or reproduction. 2 *Telecom.* A method of transmitting graphic information, as an electrical signal. —*adj.* Of or like a facsimile. [< L *fac simile* make like]

**fact** (fakt) *n.* 1 Anything that is done or happens. 2 Anything actually existent. 3 Any statement strictly true; truth; reality. [< L *factum* < *facere* do]

**fac·tion** (fak′shən) *n.* 1 A number of persons

combined for a common purpose, esp. a dissenting group within a larger group; clique. 2 Violent opposition, as to a government; dissension. [< L *factio* < *facere* do.] —**fac′tion·al** *adj.* —**fac′tion·al·ism** *n.*

**fac·tious** (fak′shəs) *adj.* Given to, characterized by, or promoting faction; turbulent; partisan. —**fac′tious·ly** *adj.* —**fac′tious·ness** *n.*

**fac·ti·tious** (fak·tish′əs) *adj.* Artificial; affected; unnatural. [< L *factitius* < *facere* do] —**fac·ti′tious·ly** *adv.* —**fac·ti′tious·ness** *n.*

**fac·tor** (fak′tər) *n.* 1 *Math.* One of two or more quantities that when multiplied make a given product. 2 One of several elements or causes that produce a result. 3 An agent who transacts business for another, usu. on commission. 4 *Biol.* A gene. —*v.t. Math.* To express as a product of factors. [< L *facere* make]

**fac·to·ry** (fak′tər·ē) *n. pl.* **·ries** A building or buildings used for manufacturing. [< L *factor* < *facere* make]

**fac·ul·ty** (fak′əl·tē) *n. pl.* **·ties** 1 Any natural endowment or acquired power: the *faculty* of seeing, feeling, reasoning. 2 Any special skill or unusual ability; knack. 3 The members of any one of the learned professions, collectively. 4 The body of instructors in a school, university, or college. 5 A department of learning or instruction: the history *faculty*. [< L *facultas*]

**fade** (fād) *v.* **fad·ed, fad·ing** *v.i.* 1 To lose brightness or clearness; become indistinct. 2 To lose freshness, vigor, youth, etc. —*v.t.* 3 To cause to fade. —**fade in** In motion pictures, etc., to come into view gradually. — **fade out** In motion pictures, etc., to disappear gradually. [< OF *fade* pale, insipid] —**Syn.** 1 dim, pale. 2 age, decline, wane, wither.

**fail** (fāl) *v.i.* 1 To be unsuccessful. 2 To be deficient or wanting, as in ability, faithfulness, etc. 3 To give out, break, or stop working. 4 To fade away; disappear. The light *failed* rapidly. 5 To weaken gradually, as in illness or death. 6 To go bankrupt. 7 To receive a failing grade. —*v.t.* 8 To prove to be inadequate or of no help to. 9 To leave undone or unfulfilled; neglect: He *failed* to carry out orders. 10 In education: **a** To receive a failing grade in. **b** To assign a failing grade to (a pupil). —*n.* Failure: now only in the phrase **without fail.** [< L *fallere* to deceive]

**faint** (fānt) *v.i.* To lose consciousness temporarily; swoon. —*adj.* 1 Lacking in purpose or courage; timid. 2 Ready to faint; weak. 3 Weak and feeble, as in effort. 4 Indistinct; dim. —*n.* A swoon: also **faint′ing.** [< OF *faindre* to feign] —**faint′ly** *adv.* —**faint′ness** *n.*

**fair** (fâr) *n.* 1 An exhibit and sale of things, often for charity. 2 An exhibit of agricultural products, manufactures, or other articles of value or interest: a county *fair*, an industrial *fair.* 3 A regular gathering of buyers and sellers. [< L *feria* a holiday]

**fair·y** (fâr′ē) *n. pl.* **fair·ies** 1 An imaginary being of small and graceful human form. 2 *Slang* A male homosexual. —*adj.* 1 Of or pertaining to fairies. 2 Like a fairy; dainty; graceful. [< OF *faerie* enchantment]

**faith** (fāth) *n.* 1 Belief without evidence. 2 Confidence; trust. 3 Belief in God, the Bible, etc. 4 A specific religion. 5 Anything given adherence or credence: a man's political *faith.* 6 Allegiance; faithfulness. —**bad faith** Deceit; dishonesty. —**in faith** Indeed; truly. —**in good faith** Honestly.

**fal·con** (fal′kən, fô′-, fôl′-) *n.* 1 Any of various fast-flying birds of prey, having a large head and long tail. 2 Any of various hawks used in sport, esp. the peregrine falcon, with long, pointed wings. [< LL *falco*]

**fall** (fôl) *v.* **fell, fall·en, fall·ing** *v.i.* 1 To drop by force of gravity from a higher to a lower place or position. 2 To drop from an erect position: He *fell* to his knees. 3 To collapse: The bridge *fell.* 4 To become less in measure, number, etc. 5 To descend or become less in rank, estimation, importance, etc. 6 To be wounded or slain, as in battle. 7 To be overthrown, as a government. 8 To be taken or captured: The fort *fell.* 9 To yield to temptation; sin. 10 To hit; land: The bombs *fell* short. 11 To slope downward. 12 To hang down; droop. 13 To begin and continue: Night *fell.* 14 To pass into a state or condition: to *fall* asleep. 15 To experience or show dejection: His face *fell.* 16 To come or happen by chance: Suspicion *fell* on him. 17 To happen; occur: Hallowe'en *falls* on Tuesday. 18 To be directed: His glance *fell* on me. 19 To happen or come at a specific place: The accent *falls* on the last syllable. 20 To be classified or divided: with *into.* —**fall away** 1 To become lean or emaciated. 2 To die; decline. —**fall away from** To renounce allegiance to. —**fall back** To recede; retreat. —**fall back on** (or **upon**) 1 *Mil.* To retreat to. 2 To resort to; have recourse to. —

**fall flat** To fail to produce the intended effect or result. —**fall for** *Informal* 1 To be deceived by. 2 To fall in love with. —**fall in with** 1 To meet and accompany. 2 To agree with; conform to. —**fall off** 1 To drop. 2 To become less. —**fall on** (or **upon**) 1 To attack; assail. 2 To find; discover. —**fall out** 1 To quarrel. 2 To happen; result. —**fall short** 1 To be inadequate. 2 To fail to reach something, as a target, goal, or standard. —**fall through** To come to nothing; fail. —*adj.* *Often cap.* 1 Of, for, or pertaining to autumn. 2 *Slang* Easily duped: a *fall* guy. — *n.* 1 The act, process, or result of falling. 2 *Usu. pl.* A waterfall; cascade. 3 That which falls or is caused to fall; also, the amount of descent. 4 *Often cap.* Autumn. 5 In wrestling, the throwing of an opponent, so that his back hits the floor. —**the Fall** The disobedience of Adam and Eve. [< OE *feallan*]

**fal·la·cious** (fə·lā′shəs) *adj.* Of, pertaining to, or involving a fallacy. —**fal·la′cious·ly** *adv.* —**fal·la′cious·ness** *n.* —**Syn.** deceptive, erroneous, illusory, misleading.

**fal·la·cy** (fal′ə·sē) *n. pl.* **·cies** 1 Something false or deceptive, as an idea or opinion. 2 The quality of being false or misleading. 3 Any reasoning, argument, etc., that contains an error of logic. [< L *fallere* deceive]

**fal·li·ble** (fal′ə·bəl) *adj.* 1 Liable to error or mistake. 2 Liable to be erroneous or false. [< L *fallere* deceive] —**fal′li·bly** *adv.* —**fal-′li·bil′i·ty, fal′li·ble·ness** *n.*

**fall·out** (fôl′out′) *n.* 1 The descent of minute particles of radioactive material resulting from a nuclear explosion. 2 The particles themselves. 3 Any incidental result; unplanned or unpredictable consequences. Also **fall′-out′.**

**false** (fôls) *adj.* 1 Contrary to truth or fact. 2 Not real or genuine; artificial. 3 Added only for decoration, deception, etc.: a *false* door. 4 Lying; dishonest. 5 Faithless; treacherous. 6 Out of tune. 7 Not correctly named: *false* foxglove. [< L *falsus*, pp. of *fallere* deceive] —**false′ly** *adv.* —**false′ness** *n.*

**fal·si·fy** (fôl′sə·fī) *v.* **·fied, ·fy·ing** *v.t.* 1 To misrepresent; tell lies about. 2 To prove to be false; disprove. 3 To tamper fraudulently with, as a document. —*v.i.* 4 To tell falsehoods; lie. —**fal′si·fi·ca′tion, fal′si·fi′er** *n.*

**fa·mil·iar** (fə·mil′yər) *adj.* 1 Well acquainted; thoroughly versed; followed by *with.* 2 Intimate; close, as in friendship. 3 Informal: *familiar* verse. 4 Exercising undue intimacy; forward; bold. 5 Well known; common; frequent; customary. —*n.* 1 An intimate friend. 2 A spirit supposed to attend a witch or sorcerer. [< L *familia* family] —**fa·mil′iar·ly** *adv.*

**fa·mil·i·ar·i·ty** (fə·mil′ē·ar′ə·tē, -mil′yar′-) *n. pl.* **·ties** 1 The state or condition of being familiar. 2 Intimate knowledge, as of a subject. 3 Conduct implying familiar intimacy. 4 *Often pl.* Offensively familiar conduct.

**fa·mil·iar·ize** (fə·mil′yə·rīz) *v.t.* **·ized, ·iz·ing** 1 To make (oneself or someone) accustomed or familiar. 2 To cause to be well known or familiar. —**fa·mil′iar·i·za′tion** *n.*

**fam·i·ly** (fam′ə·lē, fam′lē) *n. pl.* **·lies** 1 A group of persons, consisting of parents and their children. 2 The children as distinguished from the parents. 3 A group of persons forming a household. 4 A succession of persons connected by blood, name, etc. 5 Distinguished or ancient lineage. 6 *Biol.* A taxonomic category higher than a genus. 7 Any class of like or related things, as a group of languages. —*adj.* Of, belonging to, or suitable for a family. [< L *familia* < *famulus* servant]

**fam·ine** (fam′in) *n.* 1 A widespread scarcity of food. 2 A great scarcity of anything. 3 Starvation. [< L *fames* hunger]

**fa·mous** (fā′məs) *adj.* 1 Having fame or celebrity; renowned. 2 *Informal* Admirable, excellent. —**fa′mous·ly** *adv.* —**fa′mous·ness** *n.*

**fa·nat·ic** (fə·nat′ik) *adj.* Inordinately and unreasonably enthusiastic: also **fa·nat′i·cal.** —*n.* One who is fanatic about something. [< L *fanum* a temple] —**fa·nat′i·cal·ly** *adv.* —**fa·nat·i·cism** (fə·nat′ə·siz′əm) *n.* —**Syn.** *n.* enthusiast, monomaniac, zealot. *adj.* extreme, irrational, zealous.

**fan·cy** (fan′sē) *n. pl.* **·cies** 1 Imagination, esp., if whimsical or odd. 2 Any imaginary notion, representation, or image. 3 A notion or whim. 4 A liking or fondness, resulting from caprice. 5 A pet pursuit; hobby; fad. 6 Taste exhibited in artistic invention or design. —*adj.* **·ci·er, ·ci·est** 1 Ornamental; decorative; elaborate: *fancy* embroidery. 2 Evolved from the fancy; imaginary. 3 Capricious; whimsical. 4 In commerce, of higher grade than the average: *fancy* fruits. 5 Extravagant; exorbitant: *fancy* prices. 6 Selectively bred to a type, as an animal. 7 Performed with grace and skill: the *fancy* bowing of a violinist. —*v.t.* **·cied, ·cy·ing** 1 To imagine; picture. 2 To take a fancy to; like. 3 To be-

lieve without proof or conviction; suppose. [Short for FANTASY]

**fang** (fang) *n.* 1 A long pointed tooth or tusk by which an animal seizes or tears its prey. 2 One of the long, curved, hollow or grooved teeth with which a serpent injects its poison into its victim. 3 Any of various pointed objects, organs, or devices. [< OE] —**fanged** (fangd) *adj.*

**fan·tas·tic** (fan·tas′tik) *adj.* 1 Of an odd appearance; grotesque. 2 Capricious; whimsical: a *fantastic* imagination. 3 Unreal; fanciful; illusory. 4 Unbelievably good; incredible. —*n.* One who is fantastic in conduct or appearance. Also **fan·tas′ti·cal.** [< Gk. *phantazein* to present to the mind] —**fan·tas′ti·cal·ly** *adv.* —**fan·tas′ti·cal′i·ty** (-kal′ə·tē), **fan·tas′ti·cal·ness** *n.*

**farce** (färs) *n.* 1 A short comedy with exaggerated effects and incidents. 2 A ridiculous proceeding; an absurd failure. —*v.t.* **farced, farc·ing** To fill out with witticisms, jibes, etc., as a play. [< L *farcire* to stuff] —**far·cial** (fär′shəl) *adj.*

**fare** (fâr) *v.i.* **fared, far·ing** 1 To be in a specified state; get on. 2 To turn out; happen. 3 To eat; be supplied with food. —*n.* 1 Money or its equivalent paid for transportation of a passenger. 2 A passenger carried for hire. 3 Food and drink. [< OE *faran* go, travel]

**far·ther** (fär′thər) Comparative of FAR. —*adj.* More distant in space; more advanced. — *adv.* 1 To or at a more distant point in space. 2 More fully or completely.

**fas·ci·nate** (fas′ə·nāt) *v.* **·nat·ed, ·nat·ing** *v.t.* 1 To attract irresistibly, as by beauty or other qualities; captivate. 2 To hold spellbound, as by terror. —*v.i.* 3 To be fascinating. [< L *fascinare* to charm] —**fas′ci·nat′ing·ly** *adv.* —**fas′ci·na′tor** *n.*

**fas·ci·na·tion** (fas′ə·nā′shən) *n.* 1 The act of fascinating. 2 The state of being fascinated. 3 Enchantment; charm.

**Fas·cism** (fash′iz·əm) *n.* The system of one-party government developed by the Fascist in Italy. —**Fas′cist** *n.*

**fash·ion** (fash′ən) *n.* 1 The prevailing style or mode, esp. in dress. 2 A manner of doing a thing; method; way. 3 The make or shape of a thing. 4 Common practice or custom; usage. 5 Something fashionable. —*v.t.* 1 To give shape or form to. 2 To conform; accommodate; fit. [< L *facere* to make] —**fash′ion·er** *n.*

**fast·en** (fas′ən, fäs′-) *v.t.* 1 To attach or secure; connect. 2 To make fast; secure: to *fasten* a door. **3** To direct, as attention or the eyes, steadily. **4** To cause to be attributed: to *fasten* blame. —*v.i.* **5** To take fast hold; cling: usually with *on.* **6** To become firm or attached. [<OE *fæst* fixed] —**fas·t′en·er** *n.*

**fas·tid·i·ous** (fas·tid′ē·əs) *adj.* **1** Hard to please. **2** Overly delicate or sensitive; squeamish. [<L *fastidium* disgust] —**fas·tid′i·ous·ly** *adv.* —**fas·tid′i·ous·ness** *n.*

**fa·tal** (fāt′l) *adj.* **1** Causing death. **2** Bringing ruin; destructive. **3** Portentous; ominous. **4** Determining fate or destiny; fateful. [<L *fatum* fate] —**fa′tal·ly** *adv.*

**fate** (fāt) *n.* **1** That power which is thought to determine one's future, success or failure, etc. **2** Destiny; fortune; lot. **3** Evil destiny; doom. **4** Outcome; final result. —*v.t.* **fat·ed, fat·ing** To predestine: obsolete except in passive: They were *fated* to meet again. [<L *fatum* < *fari* speak]

**fath·om** (fath′əm) *n.* *pl.* **·oms** or **·om** A measure equal to six feet, used mainly for depths. —*v.t.* **1** To find the depth of; sound. **2** To get to the bottom of; understand; interpret. [<OE *fæthm* the span of two arms outstretched] —**fath′om·a·ble** *adj.* —**fath′om·less** *adj.*

**fa·tigue** (fə·tēg′) *n.* **1** Exhaustion of physical or mental strength. **2** *Metall.* The failure of metals under prolonged or repeated stress. **3** FATIGUE DUTY. **4** *pl.* Clothes worn on fatigue duty. —*v.t.* & *v.i.* **·tigued, ·ti·guing** To make or become weak or weary from physical or mental effort; tire out. [<L *fatigare*] —**fa·ti′guing·ly** *adv.*

**fa·tu·i·ty** (fə·t′oo′ə·tē) *n. pl.* **·ties** **1** Something idiotic or stupid. **2** Imbecility; idiocy. [<L *fatus* foolish]

**fat·u·ous** (fach′oo·əs) *adj.* Stubbornly or complacently stupid. [<L *fatuus* foolish] —**fat′u·ous·ly** *adv.* —**fat′u·ous·ness** *n.*

**fau·cet** (fô′sit) *n.* A spout fitted with a valve, for drawing liquids through a pipe. [<OF *fausser* break into, damage]

**fault** (fôlt) *n.* **1** A slight offense; misdeed. **2** Whatever impairs excellence; an imperfection or defect. **3** Responsibility for an error or misdeed. **4** *Geol.* A fracture in a rock formation that causes strata to shift along the line of fracture. **5** In tennis, etc., an error in serving. —**at fault 1** In the wrong. **2** Worthy of blame. —**to a fault** Excessively: *excessively: generous to a fault.* —*v.t.* **1** To find fault with; blame. **2** *Geol.* To cause a fault in. —*v.i.* **3** *Geol.* To fracture so as to

produce a fault. [<L *fallere* deceive] —**fault′ful·ly** *adv.* —**fault′ful·ness** *n.*

**faux pas** (fō pä′) *pl.* **faux pas** (fō päz′) A social error; a breach of tact or manners. [F, lit., false step]

**fa·vor** (fā′vər) *n.* **1** A kind or helpful act. **2** The state or condition of being approved. **3** Favoritism; bias; partiality. **4** Something given as a small gift or souvenir. —**in favor of 1** On the side of. **2** To the benefit of; payable to. —*v.t.* **1** To look upon with favor or kindness; like. **2** To treat with partiality. **3** To make easier; facilitate. **4** To be in favor of; support; help. **5** To do a favor for; oblige. **6** To use carefully; spare, as an injured foot. **7** *Informal* To resemble. *Brit. sp.* **fa′vour.** [<L *favere* to favor] —**fa′vor·er** *n.*

**fawn** (fôn) *v.i.* **1** To show cringing fondness, as a dog: often with *on* or *upon.* **2** To seek favor by or as by cringing. [<OE *fægnian* rejoice] —**fawn′er** *n.* —**fawn′ing·ly** *adv.*

**faze** (fāz) *v.t.* **fazed, faz·ing** *Informal* To worry; disturb; disconcert. [<OE *fēsian* frighten]

**fear** (fir) *n.* **1** An emotion excited by danger, evil, or pain; apprehension; dread. **2** Uneasiness about a thing; anxiety. **3** That which causes fear. **4** Reverence or awe. —*v.t.* **1** To be afraid of; be fearful of. **2** To look upon with awe or reverence. **3** To be anxious about; be apprehensive about. —*v.i.* **4** To be afraid; feel fear. **5** To be anxious or doubtful. [<OE *fær* peril, sudden attack] —**fear′less** *adj.* —**fear′less·ly** *adv.* —**fear′less·ness** *n.*

**fea·si·ble** (fē′zə·bəl) *adj.* **1** That may be done; practicable. **2** Capable of being successfully used. **3** Reasonable; probable. [<OF *faisable* < *faire* do] —**fea′si·bil′i·ty, fea′si·ble·ness** *n.* —**fea′si·bly** *adv.*

**feast** (fēst) *n.* **1** A sumptuous meal. **2** Anything affording great pleasure or enjoyment. **3** A festival. —*v.t.* **1** To give a feast for; entertain lavishly. **2** To delight; gratify: He *feasted* his eyes on her beauty. —*v.i.* **3** To partake of a feast. [<L *festus* joyful] —**feast′er** *n.*

**feat** (fēt) *n.* A notable act or performance, as one displaying skill, endurance, or daring. [<L *factum* a deed]

**feath·er** (feth′ər) *n.* **1** One of the elongated structures which cover the body and wings of a bird. **2** Something resembling a feather. **3** Kind; class or species: birds of a *feather.* **4** In rowing, the act of feathering. **5** *pl.* Plumage. **6** Dress or attire. —**a feather in one's cap** An achievement to be proud of. —*v.t.* **1** To fit with a feather, as an arrow. **2**

To cover or adorn with feathers. 3 To join by a tongue and groove. 4 In rowing, to turn (the oar blade) horizontally as it comes from the water, thereby lessening resistance. 5 *Aeron.* To turn one edge of (a propeller blade) windward to cut drag. —*v.i.* 6 To grow or become covered with feathers. 7 To move, spread, or expand like feathers. —**feather one's nest** To provide well for one's future. [<OE *fether*] —**feath′ered** *adj.*

**fea·ture** (fē′chǝr) *n.* 1 Any part of the human face. 2 *pl.* The whole face. 3 A distinguishing part or characteristic; salient point. 4 A magazine or newspaper article or story on a special subject. 5 A full-length motion picture. 6 Something or someone outstanding or special. —*v.t.* **fea·tured, fea·tur·ing** 1 To make a feature of, as in a newspaper story. 2 To be a feature of. 3 To portray or outline the features of. 4 *Slang* To imagine; fancy. [<L *factura* a making <*facere* do] —**fea′ture·less** *adj.*

**Feb·ru·ar·y** (feb′rōō·er′ē) *n. pl.* **·ar·ies** or **·ar·ys** The second month of the year, having twenty-eight or, in leap years, twenty-nine days. [<L *februa,* a Roman purificatory festival, celebrated on Feb. 15]

**fe·ces** (fē′sēz) *n. pl.* Human or animal excrement. [<L *faex* sediment] —**fe·cal** (fē′kǝl) *adj.*

**Fed·er·al** (fed′ǝr·ǝl, -rǝl) *adj.* 1 Of, pertaining to, or representing the United States. 2 Supporting the Union cause in the American Civil War. —*n.* One who favored or fought for the Union cause in the American Civil War.

**fed·er·ate** (fed′ǝ·rāt) *v.t. & v.i.* **·at·ed, ·at·ing** To unite in a federation. —*adj.* United in a federation. [<L *foedus* a league]

**fee** (fē) *n.* 1 A payment, as for professional service. 2 A charge for a privilege, as a license, membership, etc. 3 A gratuity; tip. 4 *Law* An estate of inheritance in land. 5 In feudal law, a fief. [<OF *fé, fief* fief, property money]

**fee·ble** (fē′bǝl) *adj.* **fee·bler, fee·blest** 1 Lacking muscular strength; weak; frail. 2 Lacking force or effectiveness; inadequate: a *feeble* argument. [<L *flebilis* tearful] —**fee′ble·ness** *n.* —**fee′bly** *adv.*

**feed** (fēd) *n.* 1 Food; esp. food for domestic animals; fodder. 2 The amount of fodder given at one time. 3 The motion that carries material into a machine. 4 The machinery supplying this motion. 5 The material supplied to a machine. 6 *Informal* A meal. —*v.* **fed,**

**feed·ing** *v.t.* 1 To give food to; supply with food. 2 To give as food. 3 To furnish with what is necessary for the continuance, growth, or operation of: to *feed* a furnace; to *feed* steel to a factory. 4 To enlarge; increase: Compliments *feed* his vanity. —*v.i.* 5 To take food; eat: said of animals. 6 To subsist; depend: usu. with *on:* to *feed* on hopes. [<OE *fēdan*] —**feed′er** *n.*

**feed·back** (fēd′bak′) *n.* 1 The transfer of energy from the output of an electronic or other system to the input, usu. causing major changes in the system characteristics. 2 A process whereby the results of action serve continually to modify further action.

**feel** (fēl) *v.* **felt, feel·ing** *v.t.* 1 To examine by touching. 2 To perceive by the senses: to *feel* pain. 3 To experience emotionally: to *feel* joy. 4 To be affected by: to *feel* a snub. 5 To be convinced of: to *feel* the need for reform. —*v.i.* 6 To seem; appear. The air *feels* humid. 7 To have a sensation of: to *feel* cold. 8 To have the emotions or opinions stirred: to *feel* strongly about something. 9 To have compassion for: to *feel* for a sick friend. 10 To be in a specific frame of mind: to *feel* scared. 11 To examine by touching; grope: to *feel* around a wall. —**feel like** *Informal* To have a desire or inclination for. —**feel out** 1 To examine the possibilities of (a situation). 2 To talk to (a person) so as to determine opinions, ideas, etc. —**feel up to** To feel able to do. —*n.* 1 The act of feeling. 2 The sense of touch. 3 A sensation: a *feel* of spring in the air. 4 The quality of a thing perceived by touch: Fur has a soft *feel.* [<OE *fēlan*]

**feign** (fān) *v.t.* 1 To simulate; pretend. 2 To invent deceptively, as excuses. 3 To make up or imagine, as stories. —*v.i.* 4 To pretend. [<L *fingere* to shape] —**feign′ed·ly** (fā′nid·lē), **feign′ing·ly** *adv.* —**feign′er** *n.*

**feint** (fānt) *n.* 1 A ruse or pretense. 2 In boxing, fencing, war, etc., an apparent or pretended blow or attack meant to divert an opponent's attention. —*v.i.* To make a feint. [<F *feindre* to feign]

**fe·lic·i·tate** (fǝ·lis′ǝ·tāt) *v.t.* **·tat·ed, ·tat·ing** To wish joy or happiness to; congratulate. [<L *felix* happy] —**fe·lic′i·ta′tion** *n.*

**fe·lic·i·ty** (fǝ·lis′ǝ·tē) *n. pl.* **·ties** 1 Happiness, comfort, and content. 2 Something causing happiness. 3 A pleasing faculty for expression, as in art, writing, etc. 4 A clever or apt expression. [< L *felix* happy]

**fe·line** (fē'lin) *adj.* 1 Of or pertaining to cats or catlike animals. 2 Catlike; sly. —*n.* One of the cat family. [< L *felis* cats] —**fe'line·ly** *adv.* —**fe·lin·i·ty** (fə·lin'ə·tē) *n.*

**fel·low** (fel'ō) *n.* 1 A man; boy. 2 A person or individual. 3 A companion. 4 An equal. 5 One of a pair; mate. 6 A trustee in some educational institutions. 7 A member of a scholarly society. 8 A graduate student of a university holding a fellowship or stipend. 9 *Informal* A girl's beau. —*adj.* Joined or associated in some way: a *fellow* student. [< OE *fēolaga* business partner]

**fel·on** (fel'ən) *n.* One who has committed a felony. —*adj.* Wicked; criminal; treacherous. [<Med. L *fello*]

**fe·lo·ni·ous** (fə·lō'nē·əs) *adj.* 1 Malicious; villainous. 2 Like or involving legal felony. —**fe·lo'ni·ous·ly** *adv.* —**fe·lo'ni·ous·ness** *n.* —**Syn.** 2 Criminal, illegal, unlawful.

**fel·o·ny** (fel'ə·nē) *Law n. pl.* **·nies** One of the gravest of crimes, as treason, murder, rape, etc., and punishable by imprisonment or death.

**felt** (felt) *n.* 1 A fabric made by compacting wool, fur, or hair, by pressure, chemical action, moisture, and heat. 2 An article made of felt. —*adj.* Made of felt. —*v.t.* 1 To make into felt. 2 To overlay with felt. [< OE]

**fe·male** (fē'māl) *adj.* 1 Of or pertaining to the sex that brings forth young or produces ova. 2 Of, pertaining to, or like this sex; feminine. 3 Designating a plant or flower which has a pistil but no stamen. 4 *Mech.* Denoting a part having a hollow or bore into which a matching part fits. —*n.* A female person, animal, or plant. [<L *femina* woman] —**fe'male·ness** *n.*

**fem·i·nine** (fem'ə·nin) *adj.* 1 Of or pertaining to the female sex. 2 Belonging to or characteristic of womankind; womanly. 3 Lacking in manly qualities; effeminate. 4 *Gram.* Applicable to females only or to objects classified as female. —*n. Gram.* A word belonging to the feminine gender. [<L *femina* a woman] —**fem'i·nine·ly** *adv.* —**fem'i·nine·ness, fem·i·nin·i·ty** (fem'ə·nin'ə·tē) *n.*

**fem·i·nism** (fem'ə·niz'əm) *n.* 1 The doctrine which declares that social, political, and economic rights for women be the same as those for men. 2 A movement advocating this doctrine. —**fem'i·nist** *n.* —**fem'i·nis'tic** *adj.*

**fe·mur** (fē'mər) *n. pl.* **fe·murs** or **fem·o·ra** (fe-

m'ər·ə) *Anat.* The long bone that forms the chief support of the thigh; thighbone. [<L, thigh] —**fem·o·ral** (fem'ər·əl) *adj.*

**fence** (fens) *n.* 1 An enclosing structure or barrier of rails, pickets, wires, or the like. 2 The art of fencing. 3 Skill in repartee or debate. 4 A receiver of stolen goods, or the place where such goods are received. —**on the fence** Undecided or noncommittal. —*v.* **fenced, fenc·ing** *v.t.* 1 To enclose with or as with a fence. 2 To separate with or as with a fence. —*v.i.* 3 To engage in the art of fencing. 4 To avoid giving direct answers; parry. 5 To deal in stolen goods. [Var. of DEFENSE] —**fenc'er** *n.*

**fend** (fend) *v.t.* 1 To ward off; parry: usu. with *off*. —*v.i.* 2 To offer resistance; parry. 3 To provide or get along: with *for*: to *fend* for oneself. [Short for DEFEND]

**fend·er** (fen'dər) *n.* 1 One who or that which fends or wards off. 2 The part of a frame of a motor vehicle that covers each wheel. 3 A metal guard before an open fire. 4 A device at the front of a locomotive or streetcar, used to push aside objects on the tracks.

**fer·ment** (fər·ment') *v.t.* 1 To produce fermentation in. 2 To stir with anger; agitate. —*v.i.* 3 To undergo fermentation; work. 4 To be agitated, as by emotion. —*n.* (fûr'ment) 1 A substance productive of fermentation, as yeast. 2 FERMENTATION. 3 Excitement or agitation. [<L *fermentum* < *fervere* to boil] —**fer·ment'a·ble** or **·i·ble** *adj.* —**fer·ment'a·bil'i·ty** *n.*

**fe·ro·cious** (fə·rō'shəs) *adj.* 1 Savage; bloodthirsty; rapacious. 2 *Informal* Very great: *ferocious* heat. [<L *ferus* wild] —**fe·ro'cious·ly** *adv.* —**fe·ro'cious·ness** *n.*

**fer·ry** (fer'ē) *v.* **fer·ried, fer·ry·ing** *v.t.* 1 To carry across a relatively narrow body of water in a boat. 2 To cross (a river, bay, etc.) in a boat. 3 To bring or take (an airplane or vehicle) to a point of delivery. —*v.i.* 4 To cross a body of water in a boat or by ferry. —*n. pl.* **·ries** 1 FERRYBOAT. 2 The place of crossing a river, bay, or the like, by boat. 3 The legal right to operate a service that transports people or goods across waterways. [<OE *ferian* carry]

**fer·tile** (fûr'təl) *adj.* 1 Producing or capable of producing abundantly. 2 Reproducing or capable of reproducing. 3 Capable of growth or development; said of seeds or eggs. 4 Productive; prolific; inventive: a *fertile* imagination. [<L *fertilis* < *ferre* to bear] —**fer'tile·ly** *adv.* —**fer'tile·ness** *n.*

**fer·vid** (fûr′vid) *adj.* 1 Fervent; zealous. 2 Hot; glowing; fiery. [<L *fervere* be hot] —**fer·vid′i·ty**, **fer′vid·ness** *n.* —**fer′vid·ly** *adv.*

**fer·vor** (fûr′vər) *n.* 1 Great intensity of feeling; ardor; zeal. 2 Heat; warmth. *Brit. sp.* **fer′vour.** [<L *fervere* be hot] —**Syn.** 1 enthusiasm, passion, intenseness, gusto, zest.

**fes·ter** (fes′tər) *v.i.* 1 To generate pus. 2 To become embittered; rankle. 3 To decay; rot. —*v.t.* 4 To cause to fester or rankle. —*n.* An ulcerous sore. [<L *fistula* ulcer]

**fes·ti·val** (fes′tə·vəl) *n.* 1 A period of feasting or celebration. 2 A season devoted periodically to some form of entertainment. 3 A series of performances, art exhibits, etc.: a jazz *festival.* —*adj.* FESTIVE. [<L *festivus* festive]

**fes·tive** (fes′tiv) *adj.* Pertaining or suited to a feast or festival; gay; joyful. [<L *festum* feast] —**fes′tive·ly** *adv.* —**fes′tive·ness** *n.*

**fes·tiv·i·ty** (fes·tiv′ə·tē) *n. pl.* **·ties** 1 FESTIVAL (def. 1). 2 Gaiety; merrymaking. 3 A social activity or celebration.

**fes·toon** (fes·tōōn′) *n.* 1 A decorative garland hanging in a curve between two points. 2 An ornamental carving resembling such a garland. —*v.t.* 1 To decorate with festoons. 2 To fashion into festoons. 3 To link together by festoons. [<F <Ital. *festa* a feast] —**fes·toon′ery** *n.*

**fete** (fāt) *n.* A festival; holiday. —*v.t.* **fet·ed**, **fet·ing** To honor with festivities. Also **fête.** [F < OF *feste* feast]

**fet·id** (fet′id, fē′tid) *adj.* Emitting an offensive odor. [<L *fetere* stink] —**fet′id·ly** *adv.* —**fet′id·ness** *n.*

**fet·ish** (fet′ish, fē′tish) *n.* 1 A natural object believed to be endowed with magical powers. 2 Any object of excessive devotion. 3 *Psychiatry* An object, usu. nonsexual in nature, that arouses sexual feelings. Also **fet′ich.** [<Pg. *feitiço* a charm <L *factitius* artificial]

**fet·ish·ism** (fet′ish·iz′əm, fē′tish-) *n.* 1 The belief in or worship of fetishes. 2 *Psychiatry* Sexual pleasure or excitement derived from an object not normally associated with sex. Also **fet′ich·ism.** —**fet′ish·ist** *n.* —**fet′ish·is′tic** *adj.*

**fet·ter** (fet′ər) *n.* 1 A shackle for the ankles. 2 Anything that restricts or confines. —*v.t.* 1 To fasten fetters upon; shackle. 2 To prevent the activity of; restrain. [<OE *feter, fetor*]

**fe·tus** (fē′təs) *n. pl.* **fe·tus·es** The young in the womb of animals, esp. in the later stages of development. [L]

**feud** (fyōōd) *n.* 1 Vindictive strife or hostility between families or clans, often hereditary. 2 Any quarrel or conflict. —*v.i.* To engage in a feud; quarrel bitterly. [<OHG *fehida* hatred, revenge] —**feud′er, feud′ist** *n.*

**fe·ver** (fē′vər) *n.* 1 Body temperature above the normal. 2 A disorder or illness marked by high temperature. 3 Emotional excitement or enthusiasm. —*v.t.* To affect with fever. [<L *febris*]

**fez** (fez) *n. pl.* **fez·zes** A brimless, tapering, felt hat, usu. red with a black tassel, worn esp. by men in Egypt and elsewhere. [<Turkish *fes*, after *Fez*, a city in Morocco]

**fi·an·ceé** (fē′än·sā′, fē·än′sā) *n.* A woman engaged to be married. [F < OF < *fier* to trust]

**fi·as·co** (fē·as′kō) *n. pl.* **·cos** or **·coes** A complete or humiliating failure. [Ital.]

**fi·at** (fē′at, -at) *n.* An authoritative command that something be done; an order or decree. [L, let it be done]

**fi·ber** (fī′bər) *n.* 1 A fine filament. 2 A threadlike component of a substance, as of wood, cotton, spun glass, etc. 3 A material composed of filaments. 4 The texture of anything. 5 Character; nature; make-up: a woman of strong *fiber.* Also **fi′bre.** [<L *fibra* fiber] —**fi′bered, fi′ber·less** *adj.*

**fi·ber·glass** (fī′bər·glas′, -gläs′) *n.* A flexible, nonflammable material made of glass spun into filaments, used for textiles, insulators, etc. Also **fiber glass.**

**fick·le** (fik′əl) *adj.* Inconstant in feeling or purpose; capricious. [<OE *ficol* crafty] —**fick′le·ness** *n.* —**Syn.** changeable, unsteady, erratic, irresolute, mercurial.

**fic·tion** (fik′shən) *n.* 1 Literature made up of imaginary events and characters, as novels, short stories, plays, etc.; also, such works collectively. 2 The act of feigning or imagining that which does not exist or is not actual. 3 That which is feigned or imagined. [<L *fictio* < *fingere* to form] —**fic′tion·al** *adj.* —**fic′tion·al·ly** *adv.* —**fic′tive** (fik′tiv) *adj.*

**fic·ti·tious** (fik·tish′əs) *adj.* 1 Of or like fiction; imaginary. 2 Not real; counterfeit; false: a *fictitious* name. —**fic·ti′tious·ly** *adv.* —**fic·ti′tious·ness** *n.*

**fi·del·i·ty** (fə·del′ə·tē, fī-) *n. pl.* **·ties** 1 Faithfulness in honoring an obligation, vow, duty, etc. 2 Strict adherence to truth or fact. 3 Exactness in the reproduction of something. 4 *Electronics* The accuracy with which an amplifier or other system reproduces the important characteristics of its input signal at the output. [< L *fides* faith] —**Syn.** 1 constancy, loyalty, allegiance. 2 honesty, integrity.

**fi·du·ci·ar·y** (fĭ-dy͞oo′shē-ĕr′ē, -shə-rē) *adj.* 1 Of or pertaining to a trustee or guardian. 2 Relying on the confidence of the public, as for paper currency or value. 3 Held in trust. —*n. pl.* ·**ar·ies** *Law* A person who holds a thing in trust. [< L *fiducia* trust]

**field** (fēld) *n.* 1 A relatively large area of open land. 2 A piece of cleared land set apart and enclosed for tillage or pasture. 3 A region of the countryside considered as yielding some natural product: a coal *field*. 4 Any wide or open expanse: an ice *field*. 5 An airport. 6 *Mil.* An area of action or operations. 7 In sports or contests: **a** The area on which the game is played. **b** An area usu. enclosed by a running track where contests in hurling, throwing, and leaping are held in track-and-field meets. **c** In baseball, the outfield. **d** The contestants, as in a race or other contest. **e** The players actually playing on a field. 8 A sphere or area of study, knowledge, or practice: the *field* of physics. 9 In business or research, an area of work away from the main office, laboratory, etc. 10 *Physics* A region of space throughout which a physical effect, as gravitational force, can be detected. 11 The background area of a painting, coin, flag, heraldic shield, etc. 12 *Optics* The space or apparent surface within which objects are seen in an optical instrument. —**play the field** *Informal* To be interested or active in all or many aspects of something. —**take (or leave) the field** To begin (or cease) an activity, military contest, etc. —*adj.* 1 Of, pertaining to, or found in the fields. 2 Used in, or for use in, the fields. 3 Played on a field. —*v.t.* 1 To catch and return (a ball in play), as in baseball. 2 To put (a player or team) on the field. —*v.i.* 3 In baseball, cricket, etc., to play as a fielder. [< OE *feld*]

**fiend** (fēnd) *n.* 1 An evil spirit; a devil; demon. 2 An intensely malicious or wicked person. 3 *Informal* One exceptionally interested or skilled in a certain subject or activity. 4 *Informal* One addicted to some harmful habit. —**the Fiend** Satan; the devil. [< OE *fēond* devil]

**fierce** (fîrst) *adj.* **fierc·er, fierc·est** 1 Having a violent and cruel nature or temper; savage; ferocious. 2 Violent in action; furious. 3 Ve-

hement; passionate; extreme. 4 *Informal* Very bad, difficult, disagreeable, etc. [< L *ferus* wild] —**fierce′ly** *adv.* —**fierce′ness** *n.*

**fier·y** (fī′ər-ē, fīr′ē) *adj.* **fier·i·er, fier·i·est** 1 Of, like, or containing fire. 2 Blazing; glowing. 3 Passionate; spirited; ardent. 4 Easily aroused, as to anger. 5 Inflamed, as a sore. —**fier′i·ly** *adv.* —**fier′i·ness** *n.*

**fifth column** A group, within a city or country, of civilian sympathizers with an enemy. —**fifth columnist**

**fight** (fīt) *v.* **fought, fight·ing** *v.t.* 1 To struggle against in battle or physical combat. 2 To box with in a boxing match. 3 To struggle against in any manner. 4 To carry on or engage in (a battle, duel, court action, etc.). 5 To make (one's way) by struggling. 6 To cause to fight, as dogs or gamecocks. —*v.i.* 7 To take part in battle or physical combat. 8 To box, esp. professionally. 9 To struggle in any manner. —**fight shy of** To avoid meeting or facing. —*n.* 1 Conflict or struggle between adversaries. 2 An effort to attain an object in spite of opposition. 3 Power or disposition to fight; pugnacity. [< OE *feohtan*]

**fig·ur·a·tive** (fĭg′yər-ə-tĭv) *adj.* 1 Of, using, or like a figure or figures of speech; not literal; metaphorical. 2 Of or pertaining to the representation of form or figure. 3 Representing by means of a form or figure; emblematic. —**fig′ur·a·tive·ly** *adv.* —**fig′ur·a·tive·ness** *n.*

**fig·ure** (fĭg′yər, *Brit.* fĭg′ər) *n.* 1 The visible form or outline of something. 2 The human form. 3 A person, esp. if active or prominent in some specific way: a *figure* in world affairs. 4 A representation or likeness of a person or thing. 5 The impression made by a person's appearance or conduct: a sorry *figure*. 6 An illustration, diagram, or drawing. 7 A pattern or design, as in a fabric. 8 **a** A number or the numeral that represents it. **b** An amount represented by a number. **c** *pl. Mathematical calculations:* a head for *figures*. 9 In dancing or skating, a movement or pattern of movements. 10 *Geom.* A surface or space enclosed by lines or planes. 11 *Music* Any short succession of tones or chords that produces a single, complete impression. —*v.* **fig·ured, fig·ur·ing** *v.t.* 1 To make an image, picture, or other representation of; depict. 2 To form an idea or mental image of; imagine. 3 To ornament or mark with a design. 4 To compute numerically;

calculate. 5 To express metaphorically; symbolize. 6 *Informal* To think; believe; predict. 7 *Music* To embellish; ornament —*v.i.* 8 To be conspicuous; appear prominently. 9 To make computations; do arithmetic. —**figure in** To include or add in. —**figure on** (or **upon**) 1 To think over; consider. 2 To plan; expect. —**figure out** 1 To reckon; to ascertain. 2 To solve; understand. —**figure up** To total. [< L *figura* form < *fingere* to form] —**fig′ur·er** *n.*

**fil·a·ment** (fil′ə-mənt) *n.* 1 A fine thread or fiber. 2 Any threadlike structure or appendage. 3 *Bot.* The part of the stamen supporting the anther. • See STAMEN. 4 *Electr.* The slender wire in a lamp bulb that is heated to incandescence by an electric current. • See INCANDESCENT. [< LL *filare* spin < L *filum* a thread] —**fil·a·men·ta·ry** (fil′ə-men′tə-rē), **fil′a·men′tous** *adj.*

**file** (fil) *n.* 1 Any device to keep papers in order for reference. 2 A collection of papers, documents, or data arranged for reference. 3 Any orderly succession or line of men or things. —**on file** In or as in a file for reference. —*v.* **filed, fil·ing** *v.t.* 1 To put on file for reference. 2 To send (a news item or story) to a newspaper. 3 To submit (a job application, etc.) for consideration. 4 To institute (a legal action, divorce proceeding, etc.). —*v.i.* 5 To march in file, as soldiers. 6 To make an application, as for a job. [< L *filum* a thread] —**fil′er** *n.*

**fil·i·al** (fil′ē-əl, fil′yəl) *adj.* 1 Of, pertaining to, or befitting a son or daughter. 2 *Genetics* Pertaining to a generation following the parental. [< L *filius* a son] —**fil′i·al·ly** *adv.*

**fil·i·gree** (fil′ə-grē) *n.* 1 Delicate ornamental work formed of intertwisted gold or silver wire. 2 Anything fanciful and delicate, but purely ornate. —*adj.* Made of or adorned with filigree. —*v.t.* **·greed, ·gree·ing** To adorn with filigree. Also **fil′la·gree.** [< L *filum* thread + *granum* a grain]

**Fil·i·pi·no** (fil′ə-pē′nō) *n.* *pl.* **·nos** A native or citizen of the Philippines. —*adj.* Of or pertaining to the Philippines.

**fill** (fil) *v.t.* 1 To make full; put as much in as possible. 2 To occupy or be diffused through the whole of. 3 To abound in. 4 To stop up or plug: to *fill* a tooth. 5 To supply with what is necessary or ordered: to *fill* a prescription. 6 To occupy (an office or position). 7 To put someone into (an office or position). 8 To feed to fullness. 9 To build up or make full, as an embankment or a ravine, by adding fill. —*v.i.* 10 To become full. —**fill in** 1 To fill completely, as an excavation. 2 To insert (something), as into a blank space. 3 To insert something into (a blank space). 4 To be a substitute. —**fill (someone) in** *Informal* To bring (someone) up to date on additional details or facts. —**fill out** 1 To become fuller or more rounded. 2 To make complete, as an application. —**fill the bill** *Informal* To do or be what is wanted or needed. —*n.* 1 That which fills or is sufficient to fill or satisfy: to have one's *fill* of adventure. 2 An embankment built up by filling in with stone, gravel, etc. 3 Something, as stone, gravel, etc., used to fill in a hole, depression, etc. [< OE *fyllan* fill]

**fil·ly** (fil′ē) *n.* *pl.* **fil·lies** 1 A young mare. 2 *Informal* A sprightly girl. [< ON *fylja*]

**film** (film) *n.* 1 A thin coating, layer, or membrane. 2 A haze or blur. 3 A flexible roll or sheet of cellulose material coated with light-sensitive emulsion, used for making photographs. 4 a A sequence of pictures, each slightly different from the last, photographed on a single strip of film (def. 3) for projection on a screen, giving the optical illusion of continuous, ordered movement. b Such films, collectively; the movies. c The art of making such films. —*v.t.* 1 To cover or obscure by or as by a film. 2 To photograph, esp. with a motion-picture camera. 3 To record on motion-picture film, as a story or event. —*v.i.* 4 To become covered or obscured by a film. 5 To take motion-picture films. [< OE *filmen* membrane]

**film·strip** (film′strip′) *n.* A length of film containing frames of still pictures projected on a screen, usu. as a visual aid in lectures.

**fil·ter** (fil′tər) *n.* 1 Any device used to strain solid particles or remove impurities from a liquid, air, etc. 2 Any of various devices that on the basis of frequency selectivity block part of a flow of energy, as light, electricity, sound, etc. —*v.t.* 1 To pass (liquids, air, etc.) through a filter. 2 To separate (solid matter, impurities, etc.) from a liquid, air, etc., by a filter. 3 To act as a filter for. —*v.i.* 4 To pass through or as if through a filter. 5 To leak out, as news. [< Med. L *filtrum*] —**fil′ter·er** *n.*

**filth** (filth) *n.* 1 Anything that soils or makes foul. 2 A foul or dirty condition. 3 Moral defilement; obscenity. [< OE *fylth*]

**fil·trate** (fil′trāt) *v.t.* **·trat·ed, ·trat·ing** FILTER.

—*n.* The liquid or other substance that has passed through a filter. [< Med. L *filtrum* a filter] —**fil·tra′tion** *n.*

**fin** (fin) *n.* **1** A membranous extension from the body of a fish or other aquatic animal, serving to propel, balance, or steer it. **2** Any finlike or projecting part, appendage, or attachment. **3** FLIPPER (def. 2). **4** *Slang* The hand. —*v.* **finned, fin·ning** *v.t.* **1** To cut up or trim off the fins of (a fish). —*v.i.* **2** To beat the water with the fins, as a whale when dying. [< OE *finn*]

**fi·nal** (fī′nəl) *adj.* **1** Being, pertaining to, or coming at the end; ultimate; last. **2** Making further action or controversy unnecessary; conclusive. **3** Relating to or consisting of the end or purpose aimed at: a *final* cause. —*n.* **1** Something that is terminal or last. **2** *Usu. pl.* The last match in a series of games. **3** The last examination of a term in a school or college. [< L *finis* end] —**fi′nal·ly** *adv.*

**fi·nance** (fī·nans′, fī′nans) *n.* **1** The management or science of monetary affairs. **2** *pl.* The monetary resources, as of a country, business, or individual. —*v.t.* **·nanced, ·nanc·ing** **1** To manage the finances of. **2** To supply the money for. [< OF *finer* settle < *fin* end]

**fi·nan·cial** (fī·nan′shəl, fī-) *adj.* **1** Of or pertaining to finance; monetary. **2** Of or pertaining to those dealing professionally with money and credit. —**fi·nan′cial·ly** *adv.*

**fin·an·cier** (fin′ən·sir′) *n.* One skilled in or occupied with financial affairs. —*v.i.* To manage financial operations, esp. unscrupulously.

**find** (fīnd) *v.* **found, find·ing** *v.t.* **1** To come upon unexpectedly. **2** To perceive or discover, as by search, experience, or examination. **3** To recover (something lost). **4** To reach; arrive at. **5** To give a judicial decision upon. **6** To gain or recover the use of. **7** To consider or think: I *found* the play a bore. —*v.i.* **8** To arrive at and express a judicial decision: to *find* for the plaintiff. —**find oneself** To become aware of one's special ability or vocation. —**find out** To detect or discover. —**find out about** To learn the truth concerning. —*n.* A thing found or discovered. [< OE *findan*]

**fine** (fīn) *adj.* **fin·er, fin·est** **1** Excellent in quality; admirable; superior. **2** Enjoyable; pleasant. **3** Light and delicate, as in texture, etc. **4** Made up of very small particles: *fine* dirt. **5** Thin or narrow: *fine* wire. **6** Very small: *fine* print. **7** Very sharp: a *fine* cut-

ting edge. **8** Cloudless; sunny: *fine* weather. **9** Subtle; acute: a *fine* point. **10** Elegant; cultivated; polished. **11** Overly elegant; pretentious; showy. **12** Refined; pure, as syrup. **13** Containing a specified proportion of pure metal: said of gold or silver. —*adv. Informal* Very much; well. —*v.t.* & *v.i.* **fined, fin·ing** To make or become fine or finer. [< L *finire* to complete < *finis* end] —**fine′ly** *adv.* —**fine′ness** *n.*

**fin·ger** (fing′gər) *n.* **1** One of the digits of the hand, esp. excluding the thumb. **2** That part of a glove which covers a finger. **3** Any small projecting piece or part, like a finger. **4** A unit of measure, roughly equal to either the width of a finger or the length of the middle finger. —**burn one's fingers** To suffer the consequences of meddling or interfering. —**have a finger in the pie** **1** To take part in some matter. **2** To meddle. —**have at one's finger tips** To have ready and available knowledge of or access to. —**put one's finger on** To identify or indicate correctly. —**put the finger on** *Slang* **1** To betray to the police. **2** To indicate (the victim) of a planned crime. —**twist around one's (little) finger** To be able to influence or manage with ease. —*v.t.* **1** To touch or handle with the fingers; toy with. **2** To steal; purloin. **3** *Music* **a** To play (an instrument) with the fingers. **b** To mark the notes of (music) showing which fingers are to be used. **4** *Slang* To betray. —*v.i.* **5** To touch or feel anything with the fingers. [< OE] —**fi·n′ger·er** *n.*

**fi·nis** (fin′is, fī′nis) *n. pl.* **fi·nis·es** The end. — **write finis to** To end. [L]

**fin·ish** (fin′ish) *v.t.* **1** To complete or bring to an end. **2** To come to or reach the end of: to *finish* a trip. **3** To use up entirely. **4** To kill or destroy. **5** To defeat; make powerless. **6** To bring the surface of (wood, leather, etc.) to a desired condition. —*v.i.* **7** To reach or come to an end; stop. —*n.* **1** The conclusion or last stage of anything. **2** Something that finishes or completes. **3** Completeness; perfection. **4** Refinement and poise in manners, speech, etc. **5** The surface quality or texture, as on wood, cloth, etc. **6** A material used to finish a surface, as wax, varnish, etc. **7** Downfall or defeat; also, the cause. [< L *finire* < *finis* end] —**fin′ish·er** *n.* —**Syn.** *v.* 1,2 terminate, conclude, close. — *n.* 1 end, close, termination, cessation, completion.

**fi·nite** (fī′nīt) *adj.* **1** Having boundaries or limits; not infinite. 2 Subject to natural limitations: man's *finite* powers. 3 *Gram.* Limited by number, person, tense, and mood: said of verb forms that can serve as predicates in sentences. —*n.* Finite things collectively, or that which is finite: usu. with *the.* [< L *finitus* limited, pp. of *finire* to end] —fi′nite·ly *adv.* —fi′nite·ness *n.*

**fiord** (fyôrd, fyōrd) *n.* A long, narrow inlet of the sea, with high rocky banks. [Norw.]

**fir** (fûr) *n.* 1 An evergreen tree of the pine family, cone-bearing and resinous. 2 Its wood. [< OE *fyrh*]

**fire** (fīr) *n.* 1 The state or form of combustion that is manifested in light, flame, and heat. 2 Something burning: the *fire* in the furnace. 3 A destructive burning: a brush *fire*. 4 Something resembling fire in its brilliance, heat, etc. 5 Intense feeling or enthusiasm; ardor. 6 An intense suffering, severe trial, or ordeal. 7 Torture or death by fire. 8 Vividness, as of imagination. 9 Fever. 10 A discharge of firearms. 11 Any rapid burst or volley: a *fire* of questions. —**between two fires** Exposed to attack, criticism, etc., from both sides. —**catch (on) fire** To ignite. —**hang fire** 1 To fail or delay to discharge. 2 To be delayed, as a decision. —**miss fire** 1 To fail to discharge. 2 To be ineffective; fail. —**on fire** 1 Burning; ablaze. 2 Ardent; zealous. —**open fire** 1 To begin to shoot. 2 To begin; commence. —**set on fire** or **set fire to** 1 To ignite. 2 To excite, as passions. —**take fire** 1 To begin to burn. 2 To begin to respond or be excited. —**under fire** 1 Exposed to gunshot or artillery fire. 2 Exposed to critical or other attack. —*v.* **fired, fir·ing** *v.t.* 1 To set on fire. 2 To tend the fire of: to *fire* a furnace. 3 To bake or expose to heat. 4 To cause to glow or shine. 5 To inflame the emotions or passions of; excite. 6 To discharge, as a gun or bullet. 7 To hurl, as with force: to *fire* questions. 8 To discharge from employment. —*v.i.* 9 To become ignited. 10 To discharge firearms. 11 To discharge a missile. 12 To become inflamed or excited. 13 To tend a fire. —**fire away** To begin, esp. in asking questions. [< OE *fýr*] —fir′er *n.fire·pow·er* (fīr′pou′ər) *n. Mil.* 1 Capacity for delivering fire, as from the guns of a ship. 2 The total amount of fire delivered by a given weapon or unit.

**fire·proof** (fīr′prōōf′) *adj.* Resistant to fire; not easily burned. —*v.t.* To make resistant to fire.

**firm** (fûrm) *adj.* 1 Not yielding readily to touch

or pressure; solidly composed; compact. 2 Difficult to move; stable. 3 Enduring; steadfast; constant: a *firm* loyalty. 4 Having or showing strength, determination, etc.: a *firm* voice. 5 Not fluctuating widely, as prices. —*v.t.* & *v.i.* To make or become firm, solid, or compact. —*adv.* Solidly; resolutely; fixedly. [< L *firmus*] —firm′ly *adv.* —firm′ness *n.* —**Syn.** *adj.* 3 resolute, steady, immovable, true, stout.

**fir·ma·ment** (fûr′mə·mənt) *n.* The expanse of the heavens; sky. [< L *firmamentum* a support] —fir′ma·men′tal *adj.*

**fis·cal** (fis′kəl) *adj.* 1 Of or pertaining to the treasury or finances of a government. 2 Financial. [< L *fiscus* a purse]

**fis·sion** (fish′ən) *n.* 1 The act of splitting or breaking apart. 2 *Biol.* The splitting of a unicellular organism into two daughter cells as a mode of asexual reproduction. 3 *Physics* The splitting of an atomic nucleus into particles and smaller nuclei with the release of energy. [< L *fissus*, pp. of *findere* to split] —fis′sion·a·ble *adj.*

**fis·sure** (fish′ər) *n.* 1 A narrow opening, cleft, or crevice. 2 A splitting apart or break; cleavage. —*v.t.* & *v.i.* **fis·sured, fis·sur·ing** To crack; split; cleave. [< L *fissus*, pp. of *findere* to split]

**fist** (fist) *n.* 1 The hand closed tightly, as for striking. 2 *Informal* **a** The hand. **b** Handwriting. 3 *Printing* An index mark (☞). —*v.t.* To strike with the fist. [< OE *fýst*]

**fit** (fit) *adj.* **fit·ter, fit·test** 1 Adapted or suited to an end, purpose, situation, etc. 2 Proper; suitable; appropriate. 3 *Informal* Ready: *fit* to be tied. 4 In good physical condition. —*v.* **fit·ted** or **fit, fit·ting** *v.t.* 1 To be suitable for. 2 To be of the right size and shape for. 3 To make or alter to the proper size: to *fit* a suit. 4 To provide with what is suitable or necessary. 5 To put in place carefully or exactly. —*v.i.* 6 To be suitable or proper. 7 To be of the proper size, shape, etc. —*n.* 1 The condition or manner of fitting. 2 The act of fitting. 3 Something that fits. [ME] —fit′ness, fit′ter *n.* —**Syn.** *adj.* 1 apt, pertinent, applicable, relevant, germane, apropos. 2 meet, becoming.

**fit·ting** (fit′ing) *adj.* Fit or suitable for the intended purpose. —*n.* 1 The act of adjusting, measuring, etc., for a proper fit. 2 A mechanical fixture or part. 3 *pl.* Furnishings or accessories for a house, boat, etc. —fit′ting·ly *adv.* —fit′ting·ness *n.*

**fix** (fiks) *v.t.* 1 To make firm or secure; attach

securely. 2 To set or direct (attention, gaze, etc.) steadily. 3 To look at steadily or piercingly: He *fixed* her with his eyes. 4 To attract and hold, as attention or regard. 5 To decide definitely; settle. 6 To decide or agree on; determine: We *fixed* a date. 7 To place firmly in the mind. 8 To lay, as blame or responsibility, on. 9 To repair, mend, tend to, heal, etc. 10 To arrange or put in order; adjust, as hair. 11 To make ready and cook (food or a meal). 12 *Informal* To arrange or influence the outcome, decision, etc., of (a race, game, jury, etc.) by bribery or collusion. 13 *Informal* To chastise or get even with. 14 To prepare (specimens) for microscopic study. 15 *Chem.* To cause to form a stable compound. 16 *Phot.* To bathe (exposed film) in chemicals which prevent further reaction to light. 17 To regulate or stabilize (wages, prices, etc.). —*v.i.* 18 To become firm or fixed. 19 *Informal* To intend or prepare: I'm *fixing* to go. —**fix on** (or **upon**) To decide upon; choose. —**fix up** *Informal* 1 To repair. 2 To arrange or put in order. 3 To supply the needs of. —*n.* 1 *Informal* A position of embarrassment; dilemma. 2 An observed or calculated position of a ship, aircraft, etc. 3 *Slang* A contest, decision, etc., that has been influenced by bribery or corruption. 4 *Slang* A single shot of an addictive drug. [< L *fixus*, pp. of *figere* fasten] —**fix'a·ble** *adj.* —**fix'er** *n.*

**fix·a·tion** (fik·sā'shən) *n.* 1 The act of fixing, or the state of being fixed. 2 An obsession. 3 *Psychoanal.* An early-occurring and excessive concentration of the libido on a particular object or person.

**fix·ture** (fiks'chər) *n.* 1 Anything fixed firmly in its place. 2 Any permanently attached device or apparatus in a house, store, etc.: a light *fixture.* 3 One so long associated with something as to be considered permanently fixed.

**flab·by** (flab'ē) *adj.* ·bi·er, ·bi·est 1 Lacking muscle tone; flaccid. 2 Lacking vigor; feeble. [< FLAP] —**flab'bi·ness** *n.*

**flac·cid** (flak'sid) *adj.* Lacking firmness or elasticity; flabby. [< L *flaccidus* < *flaccus* limp] —**flac'cid·ly** *adv.* —**flac·cid'i·ty**, **fla·c'cid·ness** *n.*

**flag** (flag) *n.* 1 A piece of cloth commonly bearing a device or colors and used as a standard, symbol, or signal. 2 The bushy part of the tail of a dog, as that of a setter. 3 The tail of a deer. 4 *pl. Ornithol.* The long feathers on the leg of a hawk or other bird of prey. 5 *Music* Any of the flag-shaped lines extending from the stem of certain notes to indicate their value. —*v.t.* **flagged, flag·ging** 1 To mark out or adorn with flags. 2 To signal with a flag. —**flag down** To cause to stop, as a train, by signaling. [?] —**flag'ger** *n.*

**fla·gi·tious** (flə·jish'əs) *adj.* Flagrantly wicked; atrocious; heinous. [< L *flagitium* disgraceful act] —**fla·gi'tious·ly** *adv.* —**fla·gi'tious·ness** *n.*

**fla·grant** (flā'grənt) *adj.* Openly scandalous; notorious. [< L *flagrare* to blaze, burn] —**fla'grance, fla'gran·cy** *n.* —**fla'grant·ly** *adv.* —**Syn.** glaring, outrageous, shocking.

**flake** (flāk) *v.* **flaked, flak·ing** *Slang v.i.* 1 To retire or go to sleep, as from exhaustion: usu. with *out.* —*v.t.* 2 To fatigue; exhaust: usu. with *out.*

**flame** (flām) *n.* 1 The burning, luminous gas of a fire; blaze. 2 A state of luminous burning. 3 Excitement or passion. 4 *Slang* A sweetheart. —*v.* **flamed, flam·ing** *v.i.* 1 To give out flame; blaze; burn. 2 To light up or burn as if on fire; flash. 3 To become enraged or excited. —**flame up** To erupt in or as in flames. [< L *flamma*] —**flam'er** *n.* —**flam'ing·ly** *adv.*

**flame·out** (flām'out') *n.* The sudden loss of the flame in a jet engine.

**flange** (flanj) *n.* A projecting rim or edge, as on a car wheel, etc., used for guidance, strength, or attachment to another object. —*v.* **flanged, flang·ing** *v.t.* To supply with a flange. [?<OF *flangir* to bend]

**flank** (flangk) *n.* 1 The hind part of an animal's side, between the ribs and the hip. • See HORSE. 2 A cut of meat from this part. 3 The side of anything. 4 The side, right or left, of a military force or marching column. —*v.t.* 1 To be on one or both sides of. 2 *Mil.* a To get around in and back of (an enemy position or unit). b To attack the flank of. —*adj.* Of, on, or from the flank or side. [<OF *flanc*] —**flank'er** *n.*

**flap** (flap) *n.* 1 A broad, thin, and loosely hanging part or attachment. 2 The motion of such a part. 3 A movable control surface along the rear edge of a wing of an airplane. 4 *Slang* An agitated or tempestuous reaction. —*v.* **flapped, flap·ping** *v.t.* 1 To move by beating: to *flap* the wings. 2 To move with a flapping sound. 3 To strike with something flat and flexible. —*v.i.* 4 To move by beating the wings. 5 To move as if blown by the wind. **6** *Slang* To lose one's composure. [Imit.]

**flare** (flâr) *v.* **flared, flar·ing** *v.i.* **1** To blaze or burn with a brilliant, wavering light. **2** To break out in sudden emotion: often with *up* or *out*. **3** To open or spread outward. —*v.t.* **4** To cause to flare. —*n.* **1** A large, bright, but unsteady light. **2** A signaling device that makes a clear, bright flame. **3** A widening or spreading outward, as of the sides of a funnel; also, the part that widens or spreads out. [?] —**flar′ing·ly** *adv.* —**Syn.** *v.* 1, *n.* 1 flash, flicker, glare, shine.

**flash** (flash) *v.i.* **1** To break forth with light or fire suddenly and briefly. **2** To gleam; glisten. **3** To move very quickly. **4** To be known or perceived in an instant. —*v.t.* **5** To send forth (fire, light, etc.) in brief flashes. **6** To send or communicate with great speed. **7** *Informal* To display briefly or ostentatiously: to *flash* a badge. —*n.* **1** A sudden gleam of light. **2** A sudden outburst, as of anger. **3** A moment; instant. **4** Display; esp., a vulgar, showy display. **5** A brief news dispatch. —*adj.* **1** Obtained by flashlight, as a photograph. **2** Flashy; smart; sporty. [ME *flaschen*] —**flash′er** *n.*, **flash′ing·ly** *adv.*

**flash·back** (flash′bak′) *n.* **1** In fiction, motion pictures, etc., a break in continuity made by the presentation of a scene or event occurring earlier. **2** Such a scene or event.

**flask** (flask, fläsk) *n.* **1** Any of variously shaped receptacles, usu. of glass, used in laboratory work. **2** A small container, often of metal, for carrying liquids or liquor on the person. [<Med. L *flasco*]

**flat** (flat) *adj.* **flat·ter, flat·test 1** Having a plane, usu. horizontal surface. **2** Broad, level, and thin: a *flat* board. **3** Having full contact with another surface. **4** Lying prone upon the ground; prostrate. **5** Positive; absolute: a *flat* refusal. **6** Having little flavor or sparkle: a *flat* drink. **7** Without air: a *flat* tire. **8** Having little activity; slow: a *flat* market. **9** Not varying; uniform: a *flat* rate. **10** *Music* **a** Below the true or right pitch. **b** Lowered by a semitone. **c** Having flats in the signature. **11** Without gloss, as a painted surface. **12** In painting: **a** Uniform in tint. **b** Lacking contrast and perspective: *flat* figures. —*adv.* **1** In a flat state or position. **2** In a flat manner. **3** *Music* Below the true pitch. **4** Exactly; precisely: It weighed ten pounds *flat*. —**flat out** *Informal* **1** With maximum effort; all-out. **2** Openly: to say *flat out* that he's a liar. —*n.* **1** A flat surface. **2**

A strip of level land, esp. low meadowland over which the tide flows. **3** *Usu. pl.* Shoal. **4** Anything that is flat. **5** *Music* **a** A tone a half step lower than a tone from which it is named, identified by the character ♭. **b** The character ♭. **6** A wooden frame covered with canvas, used as stage scenery. **7** A deflated pneumatic tire. **8** A shallow, earth-filled tray for seed germination. —*v.t.* & *v.i.* **flat·ted, flat·ting** To make or become flat. [< ON *flatr*] —**flat′tish** *adj.* —**flat′ly** *adv.* —**flat′ness** *n.*

**flat·ter** (flat′ər) *v.t.* **1** To praise unduly or insincerely. **2** To try to win over by flattery. **3** To please or gratify. **4** To represent too favorably: The picture *flatters* her. **5** To display to advantage. —*v.i.* **6** To use flattery. —**flatter oneself** To believe: I *flatter* myself that my gifts are acceptable. [< OF *flater* fawn, caress] —**flat′ter·er** *n.* —**flat′ter·ing·ly** *adv.*

**flaunt** (flônt) *v.i.* **1** To make an ostentatious display. **2** To wave or flutter freely. —*v.t.* **3** To display in an ostentatious or impudent manner. —*n.* **1** The act of flaunting. **2** A boast; vaunt. [?< Scand.] —**flaunt′y** *adj.* (·ier, ·i·est) —**flaunt′ing·ly** *adv.* —**flaunt′er** *n.* • *Flaunt* and *flout* should not be confused. To *flaunt* is to wave or make an ostentatious display. To *flout* is to regard with contempt: to *flout* convention.

**fla·vor** (flā′vər) *n.* **1** The quality of a thing that affects the sense of taste. **2** Odor; scent. **3** Distinctive quality. **4** Flavoring. —*v.t.* To give flavor or any distinguishing quality to. *Brit. sp.*, **fla′vour.** [< OF *flaor*] —**fla′vor·less, fla′vor·ous, fla′vor·y** *adj.*

**flaw** (flô) *n.* **1** An inherent defect, as in construction. **2** A crack; fissure. **3** A fault or error. —*v.t.* & *v.i.* To make or become defective or faulty. [< ON *flaga* slab of stone] —**flaw′less** *adj.* —**flaw′less·ly** *adv.* —**flaw′less·ness** *n.*

**flay** (flā) *v.t.* **1** To strip off the skin from. **2** To attack with scathing criticism. **3** To pillage; rob. [< OE *flēan*] —**flay′er** *n.*

**flea** (flē) *n.* A jumping, wingless insect that feeds upon the blood of mammals or birds. [< OE *flēa*]

**fleck** (flek) *n.* **1** A dot or speck. **2** A particle; flake. —*v.t.* To mark with flecks. [? ON *flekkr* spot]

**flee** (flē) *v.* **fled, flee·ing** *v.i.* **1** To run away, as from danger. **2** To move away quickly; disappear. **3** To leave abruptly. —*v.t.* **4** To run away from. [< OE *fléon*] —**fle′er** n. —**Syn.** 3 decamp, depart, escape, fly.

**fleece** (flēs) n. 1 The wool coat of a sheep. 2 The wool sheared from a sheep at one time. 3 Anything like fleece. 4 A textile fabric with a soft, silky pile. —v.t. fleeced, fleec·ing 1 To shear the fleece from. 2 To defraud; cheat. [< OE *fléos*] —**fleec′er** n.

**fleet** (flēt) adj. Moving swiftly; rapid. —v.i. To move swiftly. [< OE *fléotan* to float] —**fleet′ly** adv. —**fleet′ness** n.

**flesh** (flesh) n. 1 The soft tissues of a human or animal body, esp. the muscular portions. 2 Meat, esp. that of mammals. 3 The human body as opposed to the spirit. 4 Mankind. 5 All creatures. 6 The sensual side of human nature. 7 The color of a white person's skin. 8 The soft, edible parts of fruits and vegetables. —**in the flesh** 1 In person. 2 Alive. —**own flesh and blood** One's family; relatives. —v.t. 1 To initiate, as troops, in a first battle experience. 2 To incite, as hawks, for hunting by feeding with meat. 3 To make fat. —**flesh out** To give substance to: to *flesh out* an idea. [< OE *flæsc*] —**flesh′less** adj.

**flex·i·ble** (flek′sə-bəl) adj. 1 Capable of being bent without breaking; pliant. 2 Tractable; yielding; compliant. Also **flex·ile** (flek′sil). —**flex′i·bil′i·ty, flex′i·ble·ness** n. —**flex′i·bly** adv.

**flight** (flīt) n. 1 The act, process, or power of flying. 2 The distance flown. 3 A group or flock flying through the air together. 4 A single trip of an airplane. 5 In the U.S. Air Force, a tactical unit of two or more aircraft. 6 A soaring and sustained effort or utterance. 7 A continuous series of stairs or steps. 8 The act of fleeing. —**put to flight** To cause to flee or run; rout. [< OE *flyht*] —**flight′less** adj.

**flim·sy** (flim′zē) adj. ·si·er, ·si·est 1 Not substantial or solid: a *flimsy* chair. 2 Ineffective; trivial: a *flimsy* reason. —n. pl. **flim·sies** A thin paper used for carbon copies. [? < FILM] —**flim′si·ly** adv. —**flim′si·ness** n.

**flinch** (flinch) v.i. To shrink back, as from pain or danger; wince. —n. Any act of flinching. [< OF *flenchir, flechier* to bend] —**flinch′er** n. —**flinch′ing·ly** adv.

**fling** (fling) v. **flung, fling·ing** v.t. 1 To throw with violence; hurl. 2 To cast off. 3 To put abruptly or violently. 4 To hurl (oneself) into something completely. 5 To overthrow, as

in wrestling. 6 To emit, as a fragrance. —v.i. 7 To move or rush, as with anger. —n. 1 The act of flinging. 2 A try; attempt. 3 A time of lively action or indulgence. 4 A lively Scottish dance. [< Scand.] —**fling′er** n.

**flint** (flint) n. 1 A very hard, dull-colored variety of quartz which produces a spark when struck with steel. 2 A piece of material from which sparks are easily struck. 3 Anything very hard or cruel. [< OE]

**flip·pant** (flip′ənt) adj. Marked by a lack of concern or respect; impertinent; disrespectful. [< FLIP¹] —**flip′pan·cy, flip′pant·ness** n. —**flip′pant·ly** adv.

**flirt** (flûrt) v.i. 1 To play at courtship by trying to attract attention or admiration. 2 To trifle; toy: to *flirt* with danger. 3 To move with sudden jerk motions. —v.t. 4 To toss or throw with a jerk. —n. 1 A person who flirts. 2 A flirting motion; fling. [?] —**flir·ta′tion, flirt′er** n. —**flirt′y** adj.

**flir·ta·tious** (flər·tā′shəs) adj. Inclined to flirt. —**flir·ta′tious·ly** adv. —**flir·ta′tious·ness** n.

**float** (flōt) v.i. 1 To rest on the surface of a liquid. 2 To drift on the surface of a liquid, in air, etc. 3 To move or drift without purpose. 4 To hover; stay vaguely: The image *floated* in his mind. —v.t. 5 To cause to rest on the surface of a liquid. 6 To put in circulation; place on sale: to *float* a loan. 7 To irrigate; flood. —n. 1 An object that floats, as a cork on a bait line or a hollow ball in a tank. 2 A truck or wheeled platform, decorated for display in a pageant. [< OE *flotian* float] —**float′a·ble** adj.

**flock** (flok) n. 1 A company or collection of animals, as sheep, goats, or birds. 2 The members of a church. 3 A company of persons; a crowd. —v.i. To assemble or go in flocks, crowds, etc.; congregate. [< OE *flocc*] —**Syn.** n. 1 bevy, drove, flock, herd.

**flog** (flog, flôg) v.t. **flogged, flog·ging** 1 To beat with a whip, rod, etc. 2 To work to a punishing degree: to *flog* one's memory. 3 *Brit. Informal* To sell, esp. fraudulently or illegally. [?< L *flagellare*] —**flog′ger** n.

**flood** (flud) n. 1 An unusually large overflow of water onto land. 2 The coming in of the tide. 3 A copious flow or stream, as of sunlight, lava, etc. 4 A stage light that throws a broad beam. —v.t. 1 To cover with a flood; deluge. 2 To fill or overwhelm as with a flood. —v.i. 3 To overflow. 4 To flow in a flood; gush. [< OE *flōd*] —**flood′er** n.

**floor** (flôr, flōr) n. 1 The surface in a room upon which one walks. 2 A level of a building; story. 3 Any similar bottom surface: the *floor* of a bridge. 4 In any parliamentary body, the part of the hall occupied by its members. 5 The right to address an assembly: to have the *floor.* 6 The main business hall of an exchange. 7 The lowest price charged for a given thing. —*v.t.* 1 To cover or provide with a floor. 2 To throw down. 3 *Informal* To defeat. 4 *Informal* To baffle. [<OE *flōr*] —**floor′er** *n.*

**flo·ra** (flôr′ə, flō′rə) *n. pl.* **·ras** or **·rae** (-ē) Plants collectively, esp. the species represented in a given area or period. [<L *Flora* < *flos, floris* flower]

**flor·id** (flôr′id, flor′-) *adj.* 1 Having a lively reddish hue. 2 Extremely ornate. [<L *flos, floris* a flower] —**flo·rid·i·ty** (flə-rid′ə-tē), **flor′id·ness** *n.* —**flor′id·ly** *adv.* —**Syn.** 1 rosy, rubicund, ruddy. 2 gaudy, ornate.

**flo·rist** (flôr′ist, flō′rist, flor′ist) *n.* A grower of or dealer in flowers. [<L *flos, floris* flower]

**floss** (flôs, flos) *n.* 1 FLOSS SILK. 2 The silk of some plants, as corn. 3 The stray silk on silkworm cocoons. 4 A flossy surface; fluff. [?<OF *flosche*]

**flo·til·la** (flō-til′ə) *n.* 1 A small fleet. 2 In the U.S. Navy, an organized group of destroyers. [<Sp. *flota* a fleet]

**floun·der** (floun′dər) *v.i.* 1 To struggle clumsily as if mired or injured. 2 To speak or act in a clumsy or confused manner. —*n.* A stumbling or struggling motion. [? Blend of FLOUNCE² and FOUNDER] —**floun′der·ing·ly** *adv.*

**flour** (flour) *n.* 1 The ground and bolted substance of wheat. 2 The finely ground particles of any cereal. 3 Any finely powdered substance. —*v.t.* 1 To make into flour. 2 To cover with flour. [Var. of FLOWER] —**flour′y** *adj.*

**flour·ish** (flûr′ish) *v.i.* 1 To grow or fare well; thrive. 2 To be at the peak of success or development. 3 To move with sweeping motions. 4 To write with ornamental strokes. —*v.t.* 5 To brandish; wave. —*n.* 1 An ornamental mark or design, as in writing. 2 Anything done for display alone. 3 The act of brandishing or waving. 4 *Music* A short, elaborate passage; fanfare. [<L *florere* to bloom] —**flour′ish·er** *n.* —**flour′ish·ing·ly** *adv.*

**flout** (flout) *v.t.* To show contempt for; scoff at. —*v.i.* To mock; jeer. —*n.* A gibe; scoff. [?<ME *flouten* play the flute] —**flout′er** *n.* —**flout′ing·ly** *adv.* • See FLAUNT.

**flow** (flō) *v.i.* 1 To move along in a stream, as

a liquid or gas. 2 To move like water. 3 To stream forth; proceed from a source. 4 To move with continuity and pleasing rhythm, as music. 5 To fall in waves, as garments or hair. 6 To be full or too full; abound. 7 To come in or rise, as the tide. —*v.t.* 8 To flood; inundate. —*n.* 1 The act of flowing. 2 That which flows; something flowing. 3 The incoming of the tide. 4 The quantity or rate of flow. [< OE *flōwan*]

**flow·er** (flou′ər, flour) *n.* 1 *Bot.* The organ of reproduction in a plant; blossom. 2 A blooming plant. 3 The brightest, choicest part, period, or specimen of anything. 4 *pl. Chem.* A fine powder obtained by sublimation: *flowers* of sulfur. —*v.i.* 1 To put forth blossoms; bloom. 2 To come to full development. —*v.t.* 3 To decorate with flowers or a floral pattern. [<OF *flour, flor* < L *flos, floris* a flower] —**flow′er·y** *adj.* (·i·er, ·i·est) —**flow′er·i·ly** *adv.* —**flow′er·i·ness** *n.*

**fluc·tu·ate** (fluk′chōō·āt) *v.* **·at·ed, ·at·ing** *v.i.* 1 To change or vary often and in an irregular manner. 2 To move with successive rise and fall; undulate. —*v.t.* 3 To cause to fluctuate. [<L *fluctus* a wave] —**fluc′tu·ant** *adj.* —**fluc′tu·a′tion** *n.* —**Syn.** 1 alternate, vacillate, waver, oscillate.

**flue** (flōō) *n.* 1 A channel or passage for smoke, air, or gases, as in a chimney. 2 An air channel in a wind instrument. [?]

**flu·ent** (flōō′ənt) *adj.* 1 Smooth and effortless, as in speaking or writing; facile. 2 Flowing freely and easily; smooth. [<L *fluere* to flow] —**flu′en·cy** (-sē) *n.* —**flu′ent·ly** *adv.*

**flu·id** (flōō′id) *adj.* 1 Capable of flowing, as a liquid or gas. 2 Of or pertaining to liquid. 3 Capable of changing; not fixed: a *fluid* policy. 4 Smooth: a *fluid* style. —*n.* A substance that flows, as a liquid or gas. [<L *fluere* to flow] —**flu·id·ic** (flōō·id′ik) *adj.* —**flu·id′i·ty, flu′id·ness** *n.* —**flu′id·ly** *adv.*

**fluke** (flōōk) *n.* 1 A lucky stroke, as in pool. 2 Any lucky stroke. [?] —**fluk′ey** or **fluk′y,** (·i·er, ·i·est) *adj.*

**flunk** (flungk) *Informal v.t.* 1 To fail in, as an examination. 2 To give a failing grade to. —*v.i.* 3 To fail, as in an examination. 4 To give up. —**flunk out** To leave or cause to leave a school because of failure in studies. —*n.* A complete failure. [?]

**flu·o·res·cence** (flōō′ə·res′əns) *n. Physics* 1 The property by which certain substances absorb radiation and emit light of a different, usu. longer wavelength. 2 The light so produced. [<FLUOR + -ESCENCE] —flu'o·res' cent adj.

**fluorescent lamp** A lamp, usu. tubular, containing a vapor that radiates on the passing of an electric current and energizes a fluorescent coating in the tube.

**fluor·i·date** (floor'ə·dāt, floo'ə·ri·dāt) v.t. ·dat·ed, ·dat·ing To add a fluoride to (drinking water), esp. as a means of preventing tooth decay. —fluor'i·da'tion n.

**flush** (flush) v.i. 1 To become red in the face; blush. 2 To flow suddenly; rush. 3 To be washed out or cleansed by a sudden flow of water. 4 To glow. 5 To rise from cover, as game birds. —v.t. 6 To cause to blush. 7 To encourage; excite: flushed with victory. 8 To wash out by a flow of water. 9 To startle (birds) from cover. 10 To make level or straight. —n. 1 A warm glow; blush. 2 Sudden elation or excitement. 3 A sudden growth; bloom: the first flush of manhood. 4 A sudden gush of water. 5 A sudden sensation of heat. —adj. 1 Full of life; vigorous. 2 Powerful and direct, as a blow. 3 Having the surfaces in the same plane; level. 4 Full; copious. 5 Well supplied with money. — adv. 1 So as to be level, straight, or even. 2 In a direct manner; squarely: a punch flush in the jaw. [ME flusschen] —flush'er n.

**flus·ter** (flus'tər) v.t. & v.i. To make or become confused, agitated, or befuddled. —n. Confusion of mind. [? < Scand.]

**flute** (floot) n. 1 A tubular wind instrument of small diameter with holes and usu. keys along the side and a mouthpiece on the side near one end. 2 A groove, usu. semicircular, as in a column or drill. 3 A groovelike pleat in fabric. —v. flut·ed, flut·ing v.i. 1 To play on a flute. 2 To produce a high, clear sound. —v.t. 3 To sing or utter like a flute. 4 To make flutes in, as a column. [< OF flaute] —flute'like', flut'y adj.

**flut·ter** (flut'ər) v.i. 1 To wave rapidly and irregularly, as in the wind. 2 To flap the wings rapidly. 3 To move or proceed with irregular motion. 4 To move about lightly and quickly; flit. 5 To be excited or nervous. — v.t. 6 To cause to flutter. 7 To excite; fluster. —n. 1 The act of fluttering. 2 Agitation or confusion. 3 A rapid, unwanted vibration in a device. [< OE flotorian] —flut'ter·er n. —flut'ter·y adj. —Syn. v. 1 agitate flap, oscillate, vibrate.

**flux** (fluks) n. 1 A flowing; esp., the flowing in of the tide. 2 A constant changing; fluctuation. 3 An abnormal discharge of body fluids. 4 Metall. A substance that promotes the fusing of minerals or metals, as borax. 5 Physics The rate of flow of water, heat, electricity, etc., over a surface. —bloody flux DYSENTERY. —v.t. 1 To make fluid; melt; fuse. 2 To treat, as metal, with a flux. [<L fluxus < fluere to flow] —flux·a'tion n.

**fly** (flī) v. flew or flied (def. 7), flown, fly·ing v.i. 1 To move through the air by using wings, as a bird. 2 To travel by aircraft; also, to operate an aircraft. 3 To move through the air with speed, as an arrow or bullet. 4 To wave or move in the air, as a flag. 5 To pass swiftly: The years flew by. 6 To move swiftly. 7 In baseball, to bat a ball high into the air. 8 To flee. —v.t. 9 To cause to wave or float in the air. 10 To operate (an aircraft). 11 To pass over in an aircraft: to fly the Atlantic. 12 To transport by aircraft. 13 To flee from. —fly at To attack. —fly in the face of To defy openly. —n. pl. flies 1 A strip on a garment to cover buttons, zippers, etc. 2 The flap at the entrance of a tent. 3 The length of an extended flag. 4 A baseball batted high into the air. 5 A light passenger carriage. 6 pl. In a theater, the space above the stage and behind the proscenium. —on the fly 1 While flying. 2 Informal While in great haste. [<OE flēogan]

**fly·er** (flī'ər) n. FLIER.

**FM** frequency modulation.

**foam** (fōm) n. 1 A collection of minute bubbles forming a frothy mass. 2 Frothy saliva or sweat. 3 The white crest of a breaking wave. —v.i. 1 To gather or form foam; froth. —v.t. 2 To cause to foam. [<OE fām] —foam'less adj.

**fo·cus** (fō'kəs) n. pl. ·cus·es or ·ci (-sī) 1 Optics a The point where light rays converge after passage through a lens or after reflection from a mirror. b The point from which such rays appear to diverge. 2 a Adjustment so as to form a clear image: to be out of focus. b The relative clarity of an image. 3 Physics The meeting point of any system of rays, beams, or waves. 4 Any central point of activity, attraction, etc.: the focus of an earthquake. —v.t. fo·cused or fo·cussed, fo·cus·ing or fo·cus·sing 1 To adjust the focus of. 2 To bring to a focus. 3 To concentrate. —v.i. 4 To come to a focus. [L, hearth] —fo'cus·er n.

**foe** (fō) n. An enemy; adversary. [Fusion of OE fah hostile and gefāh an enemy] —Syn. antagonist, competitor, opponent, rival.

**fog** (fog, fôg) n. 1 Condensed water vapor suspended in the atmosphere at or near the earth's surface. 2 Any hazy condition of the atmosphere, or the material causing it. 3 Bewilderment; confusion. 4 A blur obscuring a developed photographic image. —v. fogged, fog·ging v.t. 1 To surround with or as with fog. 2 To confuse; bewilder. 3 *Phot.* To cloud with a fog. —v.i. 4 To become foggy. [? < Scand.]

foi·ble (foi'bəl) n. A slight fault or weakness in one's character. [<F < *faible* feeble]

foil (foil) v.t. To prevent the success of; frustrate. [<OF *fouler, fuler* crush, trample down]

foist (foist) v.t. 1 To put in or introduce slyly. 2 To pass off (something spurious) as genuine. [? <dial. Du. *vuisten* hold in the hand]

fold (fōld) v.t. 1 To turn back (something) upon itself one or more times. 2 To close; collapse: to *fold* an umbrella. 3 To place together and interlock: to *fold* one's hands. 4 To wrap up; enclose. 5 To embrace; enfold. —v.i. 6 To come together in folds. 7 *Slang* To fail; close: often with *up.* —n. 1 The act of folding. 2 Something folded. 3 The crease made by folding. 4 *Geol.* A smooth bend or flexure in a layer of rock. [< OE *fealdan*]

fo·li·age (fō'lē·ij) n. 1 Leaves collectively. 2 A representation of leaves, flowers, and branches, used in architectural ornamentation. [< F < L *folium* a leaf] —fo'li·aged adj.

fo·li·o (fō'lē·ō, fōl'yō) n. pl. ·li·os 1 A sheet of paper folded once, thereby forming two leaves or four pages of a book, etc. 2 A book of the largest size, usu. more than 11 inches high, composed of such sheets. 3 A page of a book with a number on one side only. 4 The number of a page. —adj. Consisting of a sheet or sheets folded once. —v.t. To number the pages of (a book or manuscript) consecutively. [< L *folium* a leaf]

folk (fōk) n. pl. folk or folks 1 A people; nation; race. 2 Usu. pl. People of a particular group or class: old *folks.* 3 pl. *Informal* People in general. 4 pl. *Informal* One's family. —adj. 1 Of, pertaining to, originating among, or characteristic of the common people of a district or country. 2 Of, pertaining to, or being music written by or characteristic of such common people, and handed down by them. 3 Of, pertaining to, or being music written in imitation of genuine folk music. [<OE *folc*]*Folk,* in the adjectival use, may appear as the first element in two-word phrases; as in:

| folk art | folk literature | folk song |
| folk custom | folk music | folk tale |
| folk dance | folk singer | folk tune |

folk·lore (fōk'lôr', -lōr') n. 1 The traditions, beliefs, customs, sayings, stories, etc., preserved among the common people. 2 The study of folk cultures. —folk'lor·ist n.

fol·li·cle (fol'i·kəl) n. 1 *Anat.* A small cavity or saclike structure: a hair *follicle.* 2 *Bot.* A dry seed vessel of one carpel. [<L *follis* bag] —fol·lic·u·lar (fə·lik'yə·lər) adj.

fol·low (fol'ō) v.t. 1 To go or come after. 2 To seek to overtake. 3 To accompany; attend. 4 To hold to the course of: to *follow* a path. 5 To conform to. 6 To be under the leadership of. 7 To work at as a livelihood. 8 To come after as a result. 9 To take as a model; imitate. 10 To watch or observe closely: to *follow* sports. 11 To understand the meaning of. —v.i. 12 To happen or come after something in time, sequence, or motion. 13 To understand. 14 To come after as a result. —follow out To carry out, as instructions. —follow through To perform fully; complete, as a stroke or action. —follow up 1 To pursue closely. 2 To achieve more by acting upon what has already been done. —n. The act of following. [< OE *folgian*] —Syn. 2 chase, pursue. 11 comprehend, grasp, see.

fol·low·ing (fol'ō·ing) adj. Next in order; succeeding or ensuing. —n. A body of adherents, attendants, or disciples.

fol·ly (fol'ē) n. pl. ·lies 1 The condition of being foolish or deficient in understanding. 2 Any foolish act, idea, or undertaking. 3 Immoral conduct. [<F *fol* fool]

fo·ment (fō·ment') v.t. 1 To stir up or incite, as rebellion or discord. 2 To treat with warm water or medicated lotions. [<L *fomentum* a poultice] —fo'men·ta'tion, fo·ment'er n.

fond (fond) adj. 1 Liking: with *of: fond* of music. 2 Cherished: *fond* hopes. 3 Loving or affectionate; devoted: a *fond* glance. 4 *Archaic* Silly. [<ME *fon* be foolish] —fond'ly adv. —fond'ness n.

fon·dle (fon'dəl) v. ·dled, ·dling v.t. To handle lovingly; caress. [<FOND] —fon'dler n.

font¹ (font) n. 1 A receptacle for the water used in baptizing. 2 A receptacle for holy water. 3 A fountain. 4 Origin; source. [<L *fons, fontis* a fountain]

font² (font) n. A full assortment of printing type of a particular face and size. [<F *fondre* melt]

**fool** (fo͞ol) *n.* 1 A person lacking in understanding, judgment, or common sense. 2 A jester, formerly kept at court and in great households. 3 A dupe; butt. —*v.i.* 1 To act like a fool. —*v.t.* 2 To make a fool of; deceive. —**fool around** *Informal* 1 To waste time on trifles. 2 To hang about idly. —**fool away** *Informal* To spend foolishly; squander. —**fool with** 1 To meddle with. 2 To joke with. 3 To play with. [< L *follis* a bellows; later, a windbag]

**fool·ish** (fo͞o′lĭsh) *adj.* 1 Showing or resulting from folly or stupidity; unwise. 2 Ridiculous; absurd. —**fool′ish·ly** *adv.* —**fool′ish·ness** *n.*

**foot** (fo͝ot) *n. pl.* **feet** 1 The terminal part of the leg, upon which a person or animal stands or moves. 2 Anything corresponding to the foot: the *foot* of a chair; the *foot* of a stocking. 3 The lowest part; bottom: the *foot* of a ladder. 4 The part or end opposite the head: the *foot* of a bed. 5 A unit of length equal to 12 inches or 0.3048 meter. 6 A unit of poetic meter consisting of a fixed group of stressed and unstressed syllables. 7 *Brit.* Infantry. —**on foot.** 1 Walking. 2 Happening; going on. —**put one's foot down.** To be decisive. —**put one's foot in it** To get into an embarrassing scrape. —**under foot.** 1 In the way. 2 On the ground. —*v.i.* 1 To walk. 2 To dance. —*v.t.* 3 To move on or through by walking or dancing. 4 To furnish with a foot, as a stocking. 5 To add, as a column of figures. 6 *Informal* To pay, as a bill. —**foot it** To walk, run, or dance. [< OE *fōt*]

**foot·ball** (fo͝ot′bôl′) *n.* 1 A game played between two teams on a field with goals at each end, points being scored by running or passing an oval ball across the opponent's goal line, or kicking it between the goal posts. 2 The ball itself. 3 *Brit.* a Soccer. b Rugby.

**fop** (fŏp) *n.* A man affectedly fastidious in dress or deportment; a dandy. [ME] —**fop′pish** *adj.* —**fop′pish·ly** *adv.* —**fop′per·y**, **fop′pish·ness** *n.*

**for·age** (fôr′ĭj, fŏr′-) *n.* 1 Any food suitable for horses or cattle. 2 The act of seeking food. —*v.* **for·aged**, **for·ag·ing** *v.t.* 1 To search through for food or supplies. 2 To provide with forage. 3 To obtain by foraging. —*v.i.* 4 To search for food or supplies. 5 To search: usu. with *about* or *for.* 6 To make a foray. [< OF *feurre* fodder] —**for′ag·er** *n.*

**for·ay** (fôr′ā, fŏr′ā) *v.i.* 1 To venture out, as to raid or explore. —*v.t.* 2 *Archaic* To pillage.

—*n.* 1 A raid, esp. on a military mission: a *foray* behind enemy lines. 2 A venturing out, as into unfamiliar surroundings. [< OF *feurre* forage] —**for′ay·er** *n.*

**for·bear** (fôr·bâr′, fər-) *v.* **·bore**, **·borne**, **·bear·ing** *v.t.* 1 To refrain from (an action) voluntarily. —*v.i.* 2 To abstain or refrain. 3 To be patient or act patiently. [< OE *for·beran*] —**for·bear′ing·ly** *adv.* —**for·bear′er** *n.*

**for·bear·ance** (fôr·bâr′əns, fər-) *n.* 1 The act of forbearing; the patient endurance of offenses. 2 A refraining from retaliation or retribution.

**for·bid** (fər·bĭd′, fôr-) *v.t.* **for·bade** or **for·bad**, **for·bid·den** or **for·bid**, **for·bid·ding** 1 To command not to do, use, enter, etc. 2 To prohibit the use or doing of. 3 To make impossible. [< OE *forbēodan*] —**for·bid′dance**, **for·bid′der** *n.*

**force** (fôrs, fōrs) *n.* 1 Power and energy, esp. when used to constrain or coerce. 2 *Physics* That which is capable of accelerating a body that has mass. 3 The capacity to convince or move. 4 Binding effect; efficacy: a rule still in *force.* 5 An organized body of individuals engaged in some activity: a police *force.* 6 A military or naval unit. 7 The total military power, as of a nation. 8 A person or group wielding power effectively. —*v.t.* **forced**, **forc·ing** 1 To compel to do something by or as by force. 2 To get or obtain by or as by force: to *force* an answer. 3 To bring forth by or as by effort: to *force* a smile. 4 To break open, as a door or lock. 5 To make, as a passage or way, by force. 6 To press or impose upon someone as by force. 7 To strain, as the voice. 8 To hasten the growth of, as plants in a hothouse. 9 To rape. 10 In baseball: a To put out (a base runner) who has been compelled by another base runner to leave one base for the next. b To allow (a run) in such a manner when the bases are full. 11 In card games: a To compel (a player) to play a trump card. b To compel a player to play (a particular card). 12 To stimulate the growth of artificially, as plants in a hothouse. [< L *fortis* brave, strong] —**force′a·ble** *adj.* —**forc′er** *n.*

**for·ci·ble** (fôr′sə·bəl) *adj.* Accomplished by or having force. —**for′ci·ble·ness** *n.* —**for′ci·bly** *adv.*

**fore·arm** (fôr·ärm′, fōr-) *v.t.* 1 To arm beforehand. 2 To prepare in advance.

**fore·arm** (fôr·ärm′, fōr-) *v.t. & v.i.* **·bod·ed**,

·bod·ing 1 To have a premonition of (evil or harm) 2 To portend; predict. [< FORE- + BODE] —fore·bod′er n.

fore·bod·ing (fôr·bōd′ing, fōr-) n. Apprehension of coming misfortune. —fore·bod′ing·ly adv.

fore·cast (fôr′kast′, -kȧst′, fōr′-) v.t. ·cast, ·cast·ing 1 To calculate or plan beforehand. 2 To predict; foresee. 3 To foreshadow. —n. 1 Meteorol. A prediction of weather conditions on the basis of charted data. 2 A prophecy or prediction. —fore′cast·er n. — Syn. v. 2 augur, foretell, prophesy, prognosticate. n. 2 foresight, foreknowledge.

fore·close (fôr·klōz′, fōr-) v. ·closed, ·clos·ing v.t. 1 Law a To deprive (a mortgager in default) of the right to redeem mortgaged property. b To take away the power to redeem (a mortgage or pledge). 2 To shut out; exclude. —v.i. 3 To foreclose a mortgage. [<OF for- outside + clore to close] — fore·clos′a·ble adj. —fore·clo′sure (-klō′zhər) n.

fore·fa·ther (fôr′fä′thər, fōr′-) n. An ancestor.

fore·fin·ger (fôr′fing′gər, fōr′-) n. The finger next to the thumb; index finger.

fore·go¹ (fôr·gō′, fōr-) v. FORGO.

fore·go² (fôr·gō′, fōr-) v.t. & v.i. fore·went, fore·gone, fore·go·ing To go before or precede in time, place, etc.

fore·head (fôr′id, fōr′-, -hed) n. 1 The part of the face above the eyes. 2 The front part of a thing.

for·eign (fôr′in, for′-) adj. 1 Situated outside one's own country or locale. 2 Belonging to, characteristic of, or derived from another country; not native. 3 Not usual or characteristic of: something foreign to one's nature. 4 Occurring where not normally found: a foreign object in the eye. 5 Not pertinent; irrelevant. [<LL forānus located on the outside] —for′eign·ness n.

fore·man (fôr′mən, fōr′-) n. pl. ·men (-mən) 1 The overseer of a body of workers, as in a factory. 2 The spokesman of a jury. —fore′man·ship n.

fo·ren·sic (fə·ren′sik) adj. 1 Of, pertaining to, or appropriate for courts of justice or public debate. 2 Argumentative; rhetorical. [<L forum market place, forum] —fo·ren′si·cal·ly adv.

fore·run·ner (fôr′run′ər, fōr′-) n. 1 A person sent before to give news, a warning, etc. 2 A sign or portent of something to come. 3 A predecessor; ancestor.

fore·see (fôr·sē′, fōr-) v.t. fore·saw, fore·seen,

fore·see·ing To know beforehand; anticipate. —fore·see′a·ble adj. —fore·se′er n.

fore·sight (fôr′sīt′, fōr′-) n. 1 Thoughtful care for the future. 2 The act or capacity of foreseeing. —fore′sight′ed adj. —fore′sight′ed·ness n.

for·est (fôr′ist, for′-) n. 1 A large tract of land covered with trees and underbrush. 2 Such trees. —adj. Of or inhabiting a forest. —v.t. To plant with trees; make a forest of. [<Med. L (silva) foresta an unenclosed (wood)]

fore·tell (fôr·tel′, fōr-) v.t. & v.i. ·told, ·tell·ing To tell or declare in advance; predict; prophesy. —fore·tell′er n.

for·ev·er (fôr·ev′ər, fər-) adv. 1 To the end of time. 2 At all times; incessantly.

for·feit (fôr′fit) v.t. To incur the loss of through some fault, omission, error, or offense. —adj. Lost by way of a penalty. —n. 1 A thing lost by way of penalty for some default. 2 FORFEITURE. [<OF forfait a misdeed <L foris outside + factum deed] —for′feit·a·ble adj. —for′feit·er n.

for·fei·ture (fôr′fi·chər) n. 1 The act of forfeiting. 2 That which is forfeited.

forge (fôrj, fōrj) n. 1 A furnace for heating metal ready for hammering or shaping. 2 A shop or factory having such a furnace. 3 A place where metal is refined, as in producing wrought iron. —v. forged, forg·ing v.t. 1 To shape (metal) by heating and hammering. 2 To fashion or form in any way. 3 To make, alter, or imitate with intent to defraud. —v.i. 4 To commit forgery. 5 To work as a smith. [<OF, ult. <L fabrica smithy] —forg′er n.

for·ger·y (fôr′jərē, fōr′-) n. pl. ·ger·ies 1 The illegal act of falsely making or altering something, as money, a signature, etc. 2 Anything forged.

for·get (fər·get′, fôr-) v. for·got, for·got·ten or for·got, for·get·ting v.t. 1 To be unable to recall (something previously known) to the mind. 2 To fail (to do something) unintentionally; neglect. 3 To lose interest in or regard for: I will never forget you. —v.i. 4 To lose remembrance of something. —forget oneself 1 To be unselfish. 2 To act in an unbecoming manner. [<OE forgietan] — for·get′ter n.

for·give (fər·giv′, fôr-) v. for·gave, for·giv·en, for·giv·ing v.t. 1 To grant pardon for or remission of (something). 2 To cease to blame or feel resentment against. 3 To remit, as a debt. —v.i. 4 To show forgiveness. [<OE forgiefan] —for·giv′a·ble adj. —for·giv′er n.

—**Syn.** 1 absolve, exculpate, excuse, exonerate.

**fork** (fôrk) *n.* 1 An implement having a handle and two or more tines or prongs, used for handling food. 2 A pronged agricultural or mechanical implement: a *pitchfork.* 3 The point at which a road, stream, tree trunk, or bough branches off. 4 Each of the branches so formed. —*v.t.* 1 To make forkshaped. 2 To pierce, pitch, or dig with a fork. —*v.i.* 3 To branch; bifurcate: The trail *forked.* —**fork out** (or **over** or **up**) *Slang* To pay or hand over. [<OE *forca* < L *furca*]

**for·lorn** (fər·lôrn´, fôr-) *adj.* 1 Left in distress; deserted. 2 Miserable; pitiable. 3 All but hopeless, as an effort. [<OE *forlēosan* lose, abandon] —**for·lorn´ly** *adv.* —**for·lorn´-ness** *n.*

**for·mal** (fôr´məl) *adj.* 1 Of, pertaining to, made, or based on established forms, methods, rules, etc. 2 Marked by or demanding elaborate dress, ceremony, etc.: a *formal* banquet. 3 Correct for elaborate or ceremonious occasions: *formal* attire. 4 Regular or symmetrical in form, design, etc.: a *formal* garden. 5 Stiff; punctilious: a *formal* manner. 6 Made or done in accordance with social customs and etiquette: a *formal* invitation. 7 Of or pertaining to external appearance or form: the *formal* elements of a painting. 8 Of or designating language of a more elaborate vocabulary and construction than that of everyday speech or writing. 9 Of or pertaining to the characteristic composition of anything. —**for´mal·ly** *adv.* —**for´mal·ness** *n.*

**for·mal·i·ty** (fôr·mal´ə·tē) *n. pl.* **·ties** 1 The state or character of being formal. 2 Adherence to standards and rules. 3 A proper order of procedure. 4 A formal act, method, or ceremony.

**for·ma·tion** (fôr·mā´shən) *n.* 1 The act or process of forming or developing. 2 Manner in which anything is shaped or composed; structure. 3 Anything that is formed. 4 The disposition of military troops, ships, persons, etc., as in a column, line, or square. 5 *Geol.* A series of associated rocks, having similar conditions of origin.

**for·mer** (fôr´mər) *adj.* Going before in time; previously mentioned; preceding. —**the former** The first of two mentioned persons or things. [<OE *forma* first]

**For·mi·ca** (fôr·mī´kə, fər-) *n.* A plastic used in sheets as table tops, paneling, etc.: a trade name.

**for·mi·da·ble** (fôr´mi·də·bəl, fôr·mid´ə-) *adj.* 1 Exciting fear or awe; impressive. 2 Difficult to accomplish. [<L *formidare* to fear] —**for´mi·da·ble·ness** *n.* —**for´mi·da·bly** *adv.* —**Syn.** 1 dire, dreadful, fearful, redoubtable. 2 insurmountable, overwhelming.

**for·mu·la** (fôr´myə·lə) *n. pl.* **·las** or **·lae** (-lē) 1 A fixed form of words, esp. a conventional expression or statement. 2 Any set method for doing something. 3 A medical prescription. 4 A prescription for a baby's liquid food. 5 Any recipe. 6 *Math.* A rule or combination expressed in algebraic or symbolic form. 7 *Chem.* A symbolic representation of the composition and structure of a chemical compound. [L, dim. of *forma* form]

**for·mu·late** (fôr´myə·lāt) *v.t.* **·lat·ed, ·lat·ing** 1 To express in a formula, or as a formula. 2 To put or state in exact, concise form. —**for´mu·la´tion, for´mu·la´tor.** *n.*

**for·ni·cate** (fôr´nə·kāt) *v.i.* **·cat·ed, ·cat·ing** To commit fornication. [<L *fornix* brothel, vault] —**for´ni·ca´tor** *n.*

**for·ni·ca·tion** (fôr´nə·kā´shən) *n.* Sexual intercourse between unmarried persons.

**for·sake** (fər·sāk´, fôr-) *v.t.* **for·sook** (-sook´), **for·sak·en** (-sā´kən), **for·sak·ing** 1 To give up; renounce. 2 To abandon; desert. [<OE *forsacan*]

**for·sooth** (fər·sooth´, fôr-) *adv.* In truth; certainly: chiefly ironical. [<OE *forsōth*]

**fort** (fôrt, fōrt) *n.* A military enclosure armed and equipped against enemy attack; fortification. [<L *fortis* strong]

**forte** (fôrt) *n.* That which one does most readily or excellently: Dancing is her *forte.* [<OF *fort* strong]

**for·ti·fi·ca·tion** (fôr´tə·fə·kā´shən) *n.* 1 A fortified structure or place, as a fort. 2 A strengthening or enriching. 3 The act or science of fortifying.

**for·ti·fy** (fôr´tə·fī) *v.* **·fied, ·fy·ing** *v.t.* 1 To provide with defensive works against attack. 2 To confirm; corroborate. 3 To strengthen the structure of; reinforce. 4 To give physical or moral strength to. 5 To strengthen, as wine, by adding brandy. 6 To enrich (food) by adding minerals, vitamins, etc. —*v.i.* 7 To raise defensive works. [<L *fortis* strong + *facere* make] —**for´ti·fi´a·ble** *adj.* —**for´ti·fi´er** *n.*

**for·tis·si·mo** (fôr·tis´ə·mō, *Ital.* fôr·tēs´sē·mō) *adj. & adv. Music* Very loud. [Ital., superl. of *forte* strong]

**for·ti·tude** (fôr´tə·t'ood) *n.* Patient and constant courage to endure pain, adversity, or peril. [<L *fortis* strong]

**fort·night** (fôrt′nīt′, -nit′) *n.* A period of two weeks; fourteen days. [<OE *fēowertēne* fourteen + *niht* night]

**for·tress** (fôr′tris) *n.* A large permanent fort; a stronghold. —*v.t.* To furnish or strengthen with a fortress. [<L *fortis* strong]

**for·tu·i·tous** (fôr·t′yōō′ə·təs) *adj.* 1 Occurring by chance; accidental: a *fortuitous* circumstance. 2 Fortunate; lucky. [<L *fortuitus* < *fors* chance] —**for·tu′i·tous·ly** *adv.* —**for·tu′i·tous·ness** *n.* • Although traditionally the use of *fortuitous* in the sense of fortunate has been deplored, such use is now widespread in all but the most formal written contexts. [L]

**for·tu·nate** (fôr′chə·nit) *adj.* 1 Happening by a favorable chance; lucky. 2 Having good fortune. —**for′tu·nate·ly** *adv.* —**for′tu·nate·ness** *n.* • See FORTUITOUS.

**for·tune** (fôr′chən) *n.* 1 Chance or luck as the cause of good or bad in human affairs: often personified. 2 That which befalls one as his lot, whether good or bad. 3 Future destiny: to tell *fortunes.* 4 Good luck; success. 5 A large amount of money or possessions; wealth. [<L *fortuna* < *fors* chance]

**fo·rum** (fôr′əm, fō′rəm) *n. pl.* **·rums** or **·ra** (-rə) 1 The public market place of an ancient Roman city, where most legal and political business was transacted. 2 A tribunal; a court. 3 An assembly for discussion of public affairs. [L]

**fos·sil** (fos′əl, fôs′-) *n.* 1 A remnant or trace of an organism of a past geological age, preserved in the earth's crust. 2 *Informal* A person or thing that is behind the times, or out of date. —*adj.* 1 Dug out of the earth; petrified. 2 Of or like a fossil. 3 Outworn; antiquated. [<L *fossilis* dug up]

**fos·ter** (fôs′tər, fos′-) *v.t.* 1 To rear; bring up, as a child. 2 To promote the growth of; forward; help: to *foster* genius. 3 To keep; cherish; nurse: to *foster* a grudge. —*adj.* Having the relation of being a specific family member, but unrelated by blood: a *foster* child. [<OE *fōstrian* nourish]

**foul** (foul) *adj.* 1 Offensive or disgusting to the senses. 2 Dirty; filthy. 3 Clogged or choked with foreign matter: a *foul* pipe line. 4 Spoiled, as food. 5 Entangled; encumbered: a *foul* anchor. 6 Stormy or unpleasant: *foul* weather. 7 Obscene; profane: *foul* language. 8 Wicked; detestable. 9 Not according to justice or rule; unfair. 10 In baseball, of or pertaining to a foul ball or foul line. —*n.* 1 An act of fouling, colliding, or becoming entangled. 2 A breach of rule in various sports and games. 3 In baseball, a foul ball. —*v.t.* 1 To make foul or dirty. 2 To clog or choke, as a drain. 3 To entangle; snarl, as a rope in a pulley. 4 *Naut.* To cover or encumber (a ship's bottom) with barnacles, seaweed, etc. 5 To collide with. 6 To dishonor; disgrace. 7 In sports, to commit a foul against. 8 In baseball, to bat (the ball) outside of the foul lines. —*v.i.* 9 To be or become foul or fouled. 10 In sports, to violate a rule. 11 In baseball: a To bat a foul ball. b To be retired by batting a foul ball which is caught before it strikes the ground: usually with *out.* —**foul up** *Slang* To bungle: make a mess (of). [<OE *fūl*] —**foul′ly** *adv.* —**foul′ness** *n.*

**found** (found) *p.t. & p.p.* of FIND.

**foun·da·tion** (foun·dā′shən) *n.* 1 The act of founding or establishing. 2 That on which anything is founded; basis. 3 A fund or endowment for the permanent maintenance of an institution. 4 An endowed institution. 5 A base or supporting structure upon which a building, wall, machine, etc., is erected. 6 A cosmetic application underlying other makeup. —**foun·da′tion·al** *adj.*

**found·ling** (found′ling) *n.* A deserted infant of unknown parentage. [<ME *foundlen,* pp. of *finden* find]

**foun·dry** (foun′drē) *n. pl.* **·dries** 1 A place in which articles are cast from metal. 2 The operation of founding. Also **foun′der·y** (-dər·ē).

**foun·tain** (foun′tən) *n.* 1 A spring or jet of water issuing from the earth. 2 The origin or source of anything. 3 An artificial jet or spray of water, as for drinking, cooling the air, or display. 4 A structure designed for such a jet to rise and fall in. 5 A container for holding oil, ink, etc. 6 SODA FOUNTAIN. [<L *fons, fontis*]

**four·score** (fôr′skôr′, fōr′skōr′) *adj. & n.* Four times twenty; eighty.

**fowl** (foul) *n. pl.* **fowl** or **fowls** 1 Any of the common domestic birds used as food, as the chicken, turkey, duck, etc. 2 The flesh of fowls. 3 Poultry in general. 4 Birds collectively: *wildfowl.* —*v.i.* To catch or hunt wildfowl. [< OE *fugol*] —**fowl′er** *n.*

**fox** (foks) *n.* 1 A wild, carnivorous animal of the dog family, having a pointed muzzle and long bushy tail, commonly reddish brown in color, noted for its cunning. 2 The fur of the fox. 3 A sly, crafty person. —*v.t.*

1 To trick; outwit. 2 To stain, as paper or timber, with a reddish color. —*v.i.* 3 To become reddish in color. [< OE]

**fox·hole** (foks′hōl′) *n.* A shallow pit dug by a soldier as cover against enemy fire.

**fox·y** (fok′sē) *adj.* **fox·i·er, fox·i·est** 1 Of or like a fox; crafty. 2 Discolored; foxed. 3 Denoting a wild flavor found in wine made from some American grapes. —**fox′i·ness** *n.*

**fra·cas** (frā′kəs) *n.* A noisy fight; brawl. [< Ital. *fracassare* shatter]

**frac·tion** (frak′shən) *n.* 1 A disconnected part; fragment. 2 A tiny bit. 3 *Math.* A number expressed as a quotient of two other numbers, esp. a pair of integers with the divisor greater than the dividend, as 7/10. 4 *Chem.* A component separated from a mixture by crystallization, distillation, etc. —*v.t.* To separate into fractions. [< L *fractus,* pp. of *frangere* to break] —**frac′tion·al** *adj.* —**frac′tion·al·ly** *adv.*

**frac·tious** (frak′shəs) *adj.* 1 Disposed to rebel; unruly. 2 Peevish; cross. —**frac′tious·ly** *adv.* —**frac′tious·ness** *n.*

**frac·ture** (frak′chər) *n.* 1 The act of breaking, or the state of being broken. 2 A break or crack. 3 A break in a bone or cartilage. —*v.t.* & *v.i.* **·tured, ·tur·ing** To break or be broken; crack. [< L *fractus,* pp. of *frangere* to break] —**frac′tur·al** *adj.*

**frag·ile** (fraj′əl, -īl) *adj.* Easily broken; frail; delicate. [< L *frangere* to break] —**frag′ile·ly** *adv.* —**fra·gil·i·ty** (frə-jil′ə-tē), **frag′ile·ness** *n.*

**frag·ment** (frag′mənt) *n.* 1 A part broken off; a detached portion. 2 An unfinished or incomplete part: *fragments* of a novel. [< L *fragmentum*]

**frag·men·tar·y** (frag′mən·ter′ē) *adj.* Composed of fragments; broken; incomplete: also **frag·men′tal.** —**frag′men·tar′i·ly** *adv.* —**frag′men·tar′i·ness** *n.*

**fra·grance** (frā′grəns) *n.* The state or quality of being fragrant; a sweet odor. **Also fra′gran·cy.**

**fra·grant** (frā′grənt) *adj.* Having an agreeable or sweet smell. [< L *fragrare* smell sweet] —**fra′grant·ly** *adv.*

**frail** (frāl) *adj.* 1 Easily broken or destroyed. 2 Slender; delicate. 3 Easily tempted; liable to be led astray. [< L *fragilis* fragile] —**frail′ly** *adv.* —**frail′ness** *n.*

**frame** (frām) *v.* **framed, fram·ing** *v.t.* 1 To surround with or put in a frame. 2 To put together; build, as a house. 3 To put in words; utter: to *frame* a reply. 4 To draw up: to

*frame* a law. 5 To think out; conceive, as a plan. 6 *Informal* To incriminate (an innocent person) by false charges. —*n.* 1 Something composed or constructed of parts united to one another in a system; a framework. 2 The general arrangement or constitution of a thing. 3 Structure or build, as of a person. 4 A machine characterized by a wooden framework or structure: a silk *frame.* 5 A case or border made to enclose or surround a thing, as a window, door, picture, etc. 6 A mental state or condition; mood. 7 In tenpins and bowling, a division of the game during which a player bowls at one setting of the pins. 8 The triangular rack in which the balls in a pool game are bunched ready for the break. 9 One of the individual exposures in a roll of motion-picture film. 10 In television, a single complete scanning of the field of view. [< OE *framian* to benefit] —**fram′er** *n.*

**fran·chise** (fran′chīz) *n.* 1 A political or constitutional right reserved to or vested in the people, as the right of suffrage. 2 *Law* A right to do something, as run a railroad, a bus line, etc. 3 The territory or boundary of a special privilege or immunity. 4 Authorization granted by a manufacturer to sell his products. [< OF *franc, franche* free] —**fran′chised** *adj.* —**fran′chise·ment** *n.*

**fran·gi·ble** (fran′jə·bəl) *adj.* Easily broken; fragile. [< L *frangere* to break] —**fran′gi·bil′i·ty, fran′gi·ble·ness** *n.* —**Syn.** breakable, brittle, delicate, frail.

**frank** (frangk) *adj.* 1 Candid and open; honest. 2 Not concealed or disguised; evident. —*v.t.* 1 To mark, as a letter or package, so as to be sent free of charge. 2 To send, as a letter, free of charge. —*n.* 1 The right to send mail free. 2 The mail so sent. 3 The signature that authenticates it. [< OF *franc* frank, free] —**frank′ly** *adv.* —**frank′ness** *n.*

**fran·tic** (fran′tik) *adj.* Excessively excited by fear, worry, grief, etc.; frenzied. [< OF *frenetique* frenetic] —**fran′ti·cal·ly, fran′tic·ly** *adv.* —**fran′tic·ness** *n.*

**fra·ter·nal** (frə·tûr′nəl) *adj.* 1 Of or befitting a brother; brotherly. 2 Of or pertaining to a fraternal order or association. 3 Derived from separately fertilized ova: said of twins who are not identical. [< L *frater* brother] —**fra·ter′nal·ism** *n.* —**fra·ter′nal·ly** *adv.*

**fra·ter·ni·ty** (frə·tûr′nə·tē) *n. pl.* **·ties** 1 The condition or relation of brotherhood; brotherliness. 2 A social or service organization, usu. having Greek letter names, and consisting of men students of American colleges. 3 A group of men of the same profession, interests, etc.: the medical *fraternity*.

**frat·er·nize** (frat'ər·nīz) v. ·nized, ·niz·ing v.i. 1 To be friendly or fraternal. 2 To be friendly with the enemy or with the people of an occupied or conquered territory. —**frat'er·ni·za'tion, frat'er·niz'er** n.

**fraud** (frôd) n. 1 Deception; trickery; guile. 2 *Law* Any artifice or deception practiced to cause one to surrender something of value or a legal right. 3 One who acts fraudulently; a cheat. 4 A deceptive or spurious thing. [< L *fraus, fraudis* deceit]

**fraud·u·lent** (frô'jə·lənt) adj. Proceeding from, characterized by, or practicing fraud. —**fraud'u·lence, fraud'u·len·cy** n. —**fraud'u·lent·ly** adv.

**fray** (frā) v.t. & v.i. To wear, rub, or become worn, as by friction; ravel. [< L *fricare* to rub]

**freak** (frēk) n. 1 A sudden change of mind; a whim. 2 One who or that which is malformed or abnormal; monstrosity. 3 *Slang* One who is given to the use of drugs, esp. illegal drugs. 4 *Slang* One who is very unconventional by society's standards. 5 *Slang* One who is very interested in or enthusiastic about something: an opera *freak.* —adj. Very different; strange; abnormal. —**freak out** *Slang* 1 To experience, often in an unpleasant way, the effects of certain drugs, esp. psychedelic drugs. 2 To behave, without the use of such drugs, in ways similar to those of persons who do use them: to *freak out* over a rock concert. [?] —**freak'ish, freak'y** (·i·er, ·i·est) adj. —**freak'ish·ly** adv. —**freak'ish·ness** n.

**freck·le** (frek'əl) n. A small mark on the skin produced by exposure to the sun. —v. **freck·led, freck·ling** v.t. 1 To mark with freckles. —v.i. 2 To become marked with freckles. [< ON *freknur* freckles]

**free** (frē) adj. fre·er, fre·est 1 Having liberty of action or thought; independent. 2 Not confined, imprisoned, or enslaved. 3 Not subject to despotic or arbitrary rule. 4 Not subject to certain regulations or impositions: *free* trade. 5 Not encumbered or burdened: *free* from debt. 6 Without charge or cost: *free* samples. 7 Available to all; open: a *free* port. 8 Acquitted, as from a legal charge. 9 Not occupied or busy: I am *free* all day. 10 Not limited by strict rules or conventions: *free* verse. 11 Not literal or precise: a *free* trans-

lation. 12 Not formal or conventional. 13 Frank; candid. 14 Impertinent; forward. 15 Not constrained; easy. 16 Not attached or fixed: the *free* end of a rope. 17 Not combined chemically: *free* oxygen. 18 Unobstructed; open: a *free* road. 19 Generous; liberal. —**set free** To let go; release. —**make free with** To use freely. —adv. 1 Without cost or charge. 2 In a free manner. —v.t. **freed, free·ing** 1 To make free; release from bondage, obligation, worry, etc. 2 To clear or rid of obstruction. [< OE *frēo*] —**free'ly** adv. —**free'ness** n.

**freeze** (frēz) v. **froze, fro·zen, freez·ing** v.i. 1 To become converted from a fluid to a solid state by loss of heat. 2 To become stiff or hard with cold, as wet clothes. 3 To be very cold: It's *freezing* in here! 4 To become covered or obstructed with ice. 5 To adhere by freezing. 6 To be damaged or killed by freezing or frost. 7 To become motionless, as if frozen, through fear, awe, etc. 8 To become formal or unyielding in manner. —v.t. 9 To change into ice. 10 To make stiff or hard by freezing the moisture of. 11 To cover or obstruct with ice. 12 To damage or kill by freezing or frost. 13 To make or hold motionless or in position, through fear, awe, etc. 14 To fix or stabilize (prices, stocks, wages, etc.) so as to prevent change, as by government order. —**freeze out** *Informal* To exclude or drive away, as by unfriendliness or severe competition. —n. 1 The act of freezing or the state of being frozen. 2 A spell of freezing weather. 3 The fixing of prices, labor, etc. [< OE *frēosan*]

**freeze-dry** (frēz'drī') v.t. **-dried, -dry·ing** To freeze (foods, bone tissue, etc.) and remove their water content in a near-vacuum.

**freez·er** (frē'zər) n. 1 A refrigerator for freezing foods or keeping frozen foods. 2 An apparatus for making ice-cream.

**freight** (frāt) n. 1 a The service of transporting commodities by land, air, or water. b The commodities so transported. 2 The price paid for the transportation of commodities. 3 FREIGHT TRAIN. —v.t. 1 To load with commodities for transportation. 2 To load; burden: a sentence *freighted* with adjectives. 3 To send or transport as or by freight. [< MDu. *vracht* a load]

**fren·zy** (fren'zē) n. pl. ·zies 1 Violent agitation or action. 2 A brief madness or delirium. —v.t. **·zied, ·zy·ing** To throw into frenzy; make frantic. [< Gk. *phrenitis* delirium < *phrēn* mind]

**fre·quen·cy** (frē'kwən·sē) n. pl. ·cies 1 Repeated or frequent occurrence. 2 *Physics* The number of occurrences of a periodic event, as a cycle of a wave, vibration, or oscillation, per unit of time. 3 *Stat.* The number of times a given case, value, or score occurs in a set of data. 4 *Ecol.* The relative number of plant and animal species in a given region. Also **fre′quence.**

**fre·quent** (frē′kwənt) *adj.* 1 Occurring or appearing often. 2 Habitual; persistent. —*v.t.* (*usu.* fri·kwent′) 1 To visit often. 2 To be in or at often or habitually. [< L *frequens, entis* crowded] —**fre′quen·ta′tion, fre·quent′er** *n.* —**fre′quent·ly** *adv.*

**fres·co** (fres′kō) *n. pl.* **·coes** or **·cos** 1 The art of painting on a surface of plaster, esp. while the plaster is still moist. 2 A picture so painted. —*v.t.* **fres·coed, fres·co·ing** To paint in fresco. [Ital., fresh] —**fres′co·er, fres′co·ist** *n.*

**fresh** (fresh) *adj.* 1 Newly made, obtained, received, etc.: *fresh* coffee; *fresh* footprints. 2 Additional; further: *fresh* supplies. 3 Not salted, pickled, smoked, etc. 4 Not spoiled, stale, musty, etc. 5 Not faded, worn, etc.: *fresh* colors. 6 Not salt: *fresh* water. 7 Pure; refreshing: *fresh* air. 8 Appearing healthy or youthful. 9 Not fatigued; active. 10 Inexperienced; unsophisticated. 11 *Meteorol.* Moderately rapid and strong: a *fresh* breeze. 12 Having a renewed supply of milk: said of a cow that has recently calved. [< OF *freis* < Gmc.] —**fresh′ly** *adv.* —**fresh′ness** *n.*

**fret**[1] (fret) *v.* **fret·ted, fret·ting** *v.t.* 1 To irritate; worry; annoy. 2 To wear or eat away, as by rubbing or gnawing. 3 To form by wearing away. 4 To make rough; agitate. —*v.i.* 5 To be angry, troubled, or irritated. 6 To be worn or eaten away. 7 To become rough or agitated. —*n.* 1 The act of fretting. 2 A worn spot. 3 A state of irritation, ill temper, or vexation. [< OE *fretan* devour]

**fret**[2] (fret) *n.* One of a series of ridges on the fingerboard of a musical instrument, as a guitar. —*v.t.* **fret·ted, fret·ting** To provide with frets, as of a stringed instrument. [?]

**fri·a·ble** (frī′ə·bəl) *adj.* Easily crumbled or pulverized. [< L *friare* crumble] —**fri′a·bil′i·ty, fri′a·ble·ness** *n.*

**fric·as·see** (frik′ə·sē′, frik′ə·sē′) *n.* A dish of meat cut small, stewed, and served with gravy. —*v.t.* **·seed, ·see·ing** To make into a fricassee. [< F *fraicasser* sauté]

**fric·tion** (frik′shən) *n.* 1 The rubbing of one thing against another. 2 The force that opposes relative motion of two surfaces in contact. 3 Lack of harmony; conflict. [< L *fricare* rub] —**fric′tion·al** *adj.* —**fric′tion·al·ly** *adv.* —**Syn.** 1 abrasion, chafing, wearing. 3 disagreement, discord, dissent.

**friend** (frend) *n.* 1 A person whom one knows well and cherishes. 2 An acquaintance. 3 A person who promotes or favors something: a *friend* of wildlife. 4 A person of the same nation or group as oneself; ally. [< OE *frēond*]

**frig·ate** (frig′it) *n.* A square-rigged war vessel in use until the early 19th century. [< Ital. *fregata*]

**fright** (frīt) *n.* 1 Sudden and violent alarm or fear. 2 *Informal* Anything ugly, ridiculous, or shocking in appearance. —*v.t.* FRIGHTEN. [< OE *fryhto*]

**fright·en** (frīt′n) *v.t.* 1 To throw into a state of fear or fright; terrify; scare. 2 To drive by scaring: with *away* or *off.* —*v.i.* 3 To become frightened. —**fright′en·ing·ly** *adv.*

**frig·id** (frij′id) *adj.* 1 Very cold. 2 Lacking in warmth of feeling; stiff. 3 Lacking in sexual feeling or response: said of women. [< L *frigere* be cold] —**frig′id·ly** *adv.* —**fri·gid·i·ty** (frə·jid′ə·tē), **frig′id·ness** *n.* —**Syn.** 1 bitter, freezing, glacial, icy. 2 distant, stuffy, remote, reserved.

**frill** (fril) *n.* 1 An ornamental ruffle. 2 *pl.* Affected airs or manners. 3 Any unnecessary ornament or decoration. 4 *Zool.* A ruff of feathers, hair, or membrane on certain birds or animals. —*v.t.* 1 To make into a frill. 2 To put frills on. [?] —**frill′er** *n.* —**frill′y** *adj.* (**·i·er, ·i·est**).

**fringe** (frinj) *n.* 1 An ornamental border or trimming of hanging threads or tassels. 2 Any outer edge or margin. —*v.t.* **fringed, fring·ing** 1 To ornament with a fringe. 2 To serve as a fringe or border for. [< L *fimbria* a fringe]

**frisk** (frisk) *v.t.* 1 To move briskly or playfully. 2 *Slang* To search (someone) for weapons, smuggled goods, etc., by running the hand rapidly over his clothing. 3 *Slang* To steal from in this way. —*v.i.* 4 To leap about playfully; frolic. —*n.* 1 A playful skipping about. 2 *Slang* A frisking. [< OF *frisque* lively] —**frisk′er** *n.*

**frit·ter** (frit′ər) *n.* A small fried cake, often containing corn, fruit, or pieces of meat. [< L *frigere* fry]

**friv·o·lous** (friv′ə·ləs) *adj.* 1 Petty; trivial; unimportant. 2 Lacking seriousness, sense, or reverence; trifling; silly. [< L *frivolous* silly] —**friv·o·lous·ly** *adv.* —**friv·o·lous· ness** *n.*

**frock** (frok) *n.* 1 A dress. 2 A monk's robe. 3 FROCK COAT. —*v.t.* 1 To clothe in a frock. 2 To invest with ecclesiastic office. [< OF *froc*]

**frog** (frog, frôg) *n.* 1 One of various small, tailless, web-footed amphibians. 2 The triangular, horny pad in the sole of a horse's foot. 3 A section of a railway track where rails cross or join. 4 An ornamental fastening on a cloak or a coat. —**a frog in one's throat** A slight hoarseness. [< OE *frogga*]

**frog·man** (frog′mən, -man′, frôg′-) *n. pl.* ·**men** (-mən, -men′) A swimmer or diver equipped for underwater work, as with a wet suit, flippers, and a breathing apparatus, used esp. for wartime demolition.

**frol·ic** (frol′ik) *n.* 1 A scene of gaiety. 2 A gay act; a prank. 3 A party. —*v.i.* **frol·icked, frol·ick·ing** To play merrily; gambol. —*adj.* Full of mirth or playfulness; merry. [< MDu. *vro* glad] —**frol′ick·er** *n.*

**frond** (frond) *n. Bot.* 1 A leaflike expansion, as the so-called leaf of ferns and seaweeds. 2 The leaf of a palm. [L *frons, frondis* leaf]

**front** (frunt) *n.* 1 The forward part or surface of anything. 2 The position directly ahead or before a person or thing: the steps *in front* of the church. 3 A face of a building; usu. the face on the entrance side. 4 The line of contact of opposing armies; also, a battle zone. 5 Land facing a road, body of water, etc.; frontage. 6 A coalition of diverse forces working for a common aim: a labor *front*. 7 The forehead or face. 8 Bearing or demeanor, esp. in facing a problem. 9 Outward behavior contrasted with inner feelings: a bold *front*. 10 *Informal* An outward semblance of wealth or position. 11 A person chosen for his prestige to serve as an official of an organization; a figurehead. 12 A person, group, or business serving as a cover for underhanded activities. 13 A starched shirt front, worn by men with formal clothes. 14 In hotels, the bellhop first in line. 15 *Meteorol.* The boundary between masses of cold and warm air. —*adj.* 1 Of, pertaining to or viewed from the front. 2 Situated on, at, or in the front. 3 *Phonet.* Describing those vowels produced with the front of the tongue raised toward the hard palate, as (ē) in *feed.* —*v.t.* 1 To have the front opposite to; face. 2 CONFRONT. 3 To furnish with a front. 4 To serve as a front for. —*v.i.* 5 To face in a specific direction. 6 To be or serve as a front. [< L *frons, frontis* forehead]

**fron·tier** (frun·tir′) *n.* 1 The part of a nation's territory that borders on another country.

2 That portion of a country bordering on the wilderness, newly or thinly settled by pioneer settlers. 3 Any region of thought or knowledge not yet explored: a *frontier* of science. —*adj.* Of, from, inhabiting, or characteristic of a frontier. [< OF *front* front]

**fron·tis·piece** (frun′tis·pēs′, fron′-) *n.* 1 An illustration or picture facing the title page of a book. 2 An ornamental front; a façade. [< L *frons,* forehead + *specere* look at]

**frost** (frôst, frost) *n.* 1 Frozen water vapor or dew. 2 The action of freezing. 3 A temperature below the freezing point. 4 Coldness and austerity of manner. 5 *Slang* A failure. —*v.t.* 1 To cover with frost. 2 To damage or kill by frost. 3 To apply frosting to. [< OE] —**frost′less** *adj.*

**froth** (frôth, froth) *n.* 1 A mass of bubbles; foam. 2 Something trivial or frivolous. —*v.t.* (frôth, froth) 1 To cause to foam. 2 To cover with froth. 3 To give forth in the form of foam. —*v.i.* 4 To form or give off froth; foam. [< ON *frodha*]

**fro·ward** (frō′ərd, -wərd) *adj.* Disobedient; perverse. [< FRO + -WARD] —**fro′ward·ly** *adv.* —**fro′ward·ness** *n.*

**frown** (froun) *v.i.* 1 To contract the brow, as in displeasure or concentration; scowl. 2 To show one's displeasure or disapproval: with *on* or *upon.* —*v.t.* 3 To make known (one's displeasure, disgust, etc.) by contracting one's brow. 4 To silence, rebuke, etc., by or as by a frown. —*n.* 1 A wrinkling of the brow, as in anger; a scowl. 2 Any manifestation of displeasure. [< OF *froigner*] —**frown′er** *n.* —**frown′ing·ly** *adv.*

**fruc·ti·fy** (fruk′tə·fī) *v.* ·**fied,** ·**fy·ing** —*v.t.* 1 To make fruitful; fertilize. —*v.i.* 2 To bear fruit. [< L *fructus* fruit + *facere* do, make] —**fruc·tif′er·ous** *adj.* —**fruc′ti·fi·ca′tion** *n.*

**fru·gal** (frōō′gəl) *adj.* 1 Exercising economy; saving; sparing. 2 Meager or inexpensive. [< L *frugalis*] —**fru·gal′i·ty** *n.* —**fru′gal·ly** *adv.* —**Syn.** 1 parsimonious, provident, thrifty, stinting. 2 mean, scanty.

**fruit** (frōōt) *n. pl.* **fruits** or, collectively, **fruit** 1 The seed-bearing part of a plant. 2 An edible, usu. seed-bearing plant product, esp. a sweet and succulent one. 3 *Usu. pl.* Any natural product of value to man: the *fruits* of the earth. 4 Offspring; issue. 5 A consequence, outcome, or result; the *fruits* of labor. —*v.t.* & *v.i.* To bear or make bear fruit. [< OF < L *fructus*]

**fru·i·tion** (frōō·ish′ən) *n.* 1 The bearing of fruit. 2 The yielding of natural or expected results; fulfillment. 3 Enjoyment. [< L < *frui* enjoy]

**frus·trate** (frus′trāt) *v.t.* ·trat·ed, ·trat·ing 1 To keep (someone) from doing or achieving something; defeat the efforts or hopes of. 2 To keep, as plans or schemes, from being fulfilled; thwart. [< L *frustrari* disappoint] — **Syn.** 2 defeat, foil, balk, nullify.

**frus·tra·tion** (frus·trā′shən) *n.* 1 The act of frustrating or the state of being frustrated. 2 An instance of being frustrated. 3 Something that frustrates.

**fry** (frī) *v.t.* & *v.i.* **fried, fry·ing** To cook or be cooked in hot fat, usu. over direct heat. — *n. pl.* **fries** 1 A dish of anything fried. 2 A social occasion, usu. a picnic, at which foods are fried and eaten: a fish *fry*. [< L *frigere*]

**fudge** (fuj) *n.* 1 A soft confection made of butter, sugar, chocolate, etc. 2 Humbug; nonsense. —*v.i.* **fudged, fudg·ing** 1 To violate or ignore a rule or customary practice. 2 To fail to take a stand; equivocate; hedge. — *v.t.* 3 To make, adjust, or fit together in a clumsy or dishonest manner. 4 To fail to make clear or be decisive about. [?]

**fu·el** (fyōō′əl) *n.* 1 Combustible matter burned as a source of energy. 2 An element, as plutonium, used in a nuclear reaction to provide energy. 3 Whatever feeds or sustains any expenditure, outlay, passion, or excitement. —*v.t.* & *v.i.* **fu·eled** or **fu·eiled, fu·el·ling** or **fu·el·ling** To supply with or take in fuel. [< OF *fouaille* ult. < L *focus* hearth] —**fu·el·er, fu′el·ler** *n.*

**fu·gi·tive** (fyōō′jə·tiv) *adj.* 1 Fleeing or having fled, as from pursuit, danger, arrest, etc. 2 Not fixed or lasting; transient. 3 Wandering; shifting. 4 Treating of subjects of passing interest; occasional. —*n.* One who or that which flees; a runaway or deserter. [< L *fugere* flee] —**fu′gi·tive·ly** *adv.* —**fu′gi·tive·ness** *n.*

**ful·crum** (fōol′krəm) *n. pl.* **·crums** or **·cra** (-krə·) 1 The support on or against which a lever rests. 2 Any prop or support

**ful·fill** (fōō·fil′) *v.t.* 1 To perform, as a duty or command. 2 To bring into effect or to consummation. 3 To finish; come to the end of. 4 To fill the requirements of; satisfy, as the conditions of a contract. **Also ful·fil′** [·filled, ·fill·ing]. [< OE *fulfyllan*] —**ful·fill′er** *n.* —**ful·fill′ment, ful·fill′ment** *n.*

**full·back** (fōol′bak′) *n.* In American football, one of the backfield, traditionally the player farthest from the line of scrimmage.

**ful·mi·nate** (ful′mə·nāt) *v.* ·nat·ed, ·nat·ing

*v.i.* 1 To explode or detonate violently. 2 To shout accusations, threats, etc.; denounce. —*v.t.* 3 To cause to explode violently. 4 To shout (accusations, threats, etc.). —*n. Chem.* An explosively unstable compound. [< L *fulmen, fulminis* lightning] —**ful′mi·na′tion, ful′mi·na·tor** *n.* —**ful′mi·na·to′ry** (-tôr′ē, -tō′rē) *adj.*

**ful·some** (fōol′səm, ful′-) *adj.* Offensive and distasteful because excessive: *fulsome* praise. [< FULL, *adj.* + -SOME] —**ful′some·ly** *adv.* —**ful′some·ness** *n.*

**fum·ble** (fum′bəl) *v.* **fum·bled, fum·bling** *v.i.* 1 To search for something blindly or clumsily; grope: with *for* or *after*. 2 To do something clumsily or nervously. 3 To handle or touch something nervously or awkwardly. 4 In sports, to fail to catch or hold the ball. —*v.t.* 5 To handle clumsily or awkwardly. 6 To do (something) badly or awkwardly; bungle. 7 To make (one's way) unsteadily. 8 In sports, to fumble (the ball). —*n.* The act or an instance of fumbling. [Prob. < Scand.] —**fum′bler** *n.*

**fume** (fyōōm) *n.* 1 Any poisonous, irritating, or odorous smoke or vapor. 2 Furious anger. —*v.* **fumed, fum·ing** *v.i.* 1 To give off fumes. 2 To pass off in a mist or vapor. 3 To express or show anger, irritation, etc. —*v.t.* 4 To expose to fumes. [< L *fumus* smoke] —**fum′er** *n.*

**fu·mi·gate** (fyōō′mə·gāt) *v.t.* **·gat·ed, ·gat·ing** To subject to smoke or fumes, as for killing vermin. [< L *fumus* smoke + *agere* to drive] —**fu′mi·ga′tion, fu′mi·ga′tor** *n.*

**func·tion** (fungk′shən) *n.* 1 The specific, natural, or proper action or activity of something. 2 One's appropriate or assigned duties or activities. 3 The normal action of any organ or set of organs: the respiratory *function*. 4 A public or official ceremony or entertainment. 5 *Math.* A variable whose value depends on the value of another variable. —*v.i.* 1 To perform as expected or required; operate properly. 2 To perform the role of something else. [< L *fungi* perform]

**fund** (fund) *n.* 1 A sum of money or stock of convertible wealth employed in, set aside for, or available for a business enterprise or other purpose. 2 *pl.* Money in general: out of *funds*. 3 A reserve store; an ample stock: a *fund* of humor. —*v.t.* 1 To convert into a more or less permanent debt bearing a fixed rate of interest. 2 To furnish a fund for. 3 To amass. [< L *fundus* bottom] —**fund′a·ble** *adj.*

**fun·da·men·tal** (fun′də·men′təl) *adj.* 1 Basic; indispensable; essential: *fundamental* principles. 2 Primary; chief: his *fundamental* error. 3 *Physics* Designating that component of a periodic oscillation that has the lowest frequency. —*n.* 1 Anything that serves as the foundation or basis of a system, as a truth, law, or principle. 2 *Music* The root of a chord. 3 *Physics* The fundamental component of a periodic oscillation. —**fun′da·men′tal·ly** *adv.*

**fu·ner·al** (fyōō′nər·əl) *n.* 1 The rites and ceremonies preceding and accompanying burial; obsequies. 2 A gathering or procession of persons on the occasion of a burial. —*adj.* Pertaining to, suitable for, or used at a funeral. [< L *funus, funeris*]

**fu·ne·re·al** (fyōō·nir′ē·əl) *adj.* 1 Pertaining to or suitable for a funeral. 2 Mournful; gloomy. —**fu·ne′re·al·ly** *adv.*

**fun·gus** (fung′gəs) *n. pl.* **fun·gus·es** or **fun·gi** (fun′jī, fung′gī) 1 Any of a group of plants that reproduce by spores and have no stems, leaves, roots, or chlorophyll, comprising the mushrooms, puffballs, molds, smuts, etc. 2 Anything that springs up rapidly like a fungus. —*adj.* Fungous. [< L, a mushroom]

**fun·nel** (fun′əl) *n.* 1 A wide-mouthed conical vessel, terminating in a tube, for filtering, decanting, etc. 2 A smoke pipe, chimney, or flue. 3 A smokestack on a steamship. 4 Any funnellike part or process. —*v.t. & v.i.* ·neled or ·nelled, ·nel·ing or ·nel·ling To pass or move through or as through a funnel. [< L *infundibulum* <*in-* into + *fundere* pour]

**fur·bish** (fûr′bish) *v.t.* 1 To make bright by rubbing; burnish. 2 To restore to brightness or beauty; renovate: often with *up.* [< OF *forbir*] —**fur′bish·er** *n.*

**fu·ri·ous** (fyōōr′ē·əs) *adj.* 1 Full of anger; raging. 2 Violent; fierce. 3 Very great; excessive. —**fu′ri·ous·ly** *adv.* —**fu′ri·ous·ness** *n.* — **Syn.** 1 irate, fuming, angry, wrathful, boiling. 2 wild, vehement, turbulent, frenzied, frantic, stormy.

**furl** (fûrl) *v.t.* 1 To roll up and make secure, as a sail to a spar. —*v.i.* 2 To become furled. —*n.* 1 The act of furling. 2 Something furled. [< OF *fermlier* < *ferm* close + *lier* bind]

**fur·lough** (fûr′lō) *n.* An authorized leave of absence, esp. one granted to a person in the armed forces. —*v.t.* To grant a furlough to. [< Du. *verlof*]

**fur·nace** (fûr′nis) *n.* 1 A chamber for heating, fusing, hardening, etc., usu. by heat derived from burning a fuel. 2 A chamber in which fuel is burned to heat a building. [< L *fornax*]

**fur·nish** (fûr′nish) *v.t.* 1 To equip, or fit out, as with fittings or furniture. 2 To supply; provide. [< OF *furnir*] —**fur′nish·er** *n.*

**fur·ni·ture** (fûr′nə·chər) *n.* 1 Movable household articles, such as chairs, tables, bureaus, beds, etc. 2 Necessary equipment, as for a ship, shop, etc. [< F *fourniture* < *fournir* furnish]

**fur·row** (fûr′ō) *n.* 1 A trench made in the earth by a plow. 2 One of the grooves in the face of a millstone. 3 Any groove or wrinkle. — *v.t.* 1 To make furrows in; plow. 2 To make wrinkles in, as the brow. —*v.i.* 3 To become wrinkled. [< OE *furh*] —**fur′row·er** *n.*

**fur·ther** (fûr′thər) Comparative of FAR. —*adv.* 1 At or to a more distant or remote point in space or time. 2 To a greater degree; more. 3 In addition; besides; also. —*adj.* 1 More distant or advanced in time or degree. 2 Wider or fuller; additional. 3 More distant in space; farther. —*v.t.* To help forward; promote. [< OE *furthra*] —**fur′ther·er** *n.*

**fur·tive** (fûr′tiv) *adj.* 1 Done on the sly; secret; stealthy. 2 Not direct; evasive. [< F < L *fur* a thief] —**fur′tive·ly** *adv.* —**fur′tive·ness** *n.*

**fu·ry** (fyōōr′ē) *n. pl.* ·ries 1 A state or fit of violent anger or rage. 2 Violent action or agitation; fierceness; frenzy. 3 A person of violent temper, esp. a woman. [< L *furere* rave]

**fuse**[1] (fyōōz) *n.* A treated cord, ribbon, etc., used to carry fire to explosives. 2 FUZE. [< L *fusus* a spindle]

**fuse**[2] (fyōōz) *v.t. & v.i.* **fused, fus·ing** 1 To liquefy by heat; melt. 2 To join or cause to join as if by melting together. —*n. Electr.* An enclosed length of fusible metal set in a circuit to melt and open the circuit in case of an overload. [< L *fusus,* pp. of *fundere* pour]

**fu·se·lage** (fyōō′sə·läzh, -zə-) *n. Aeron.* The part of an airplane that accomodates the crew, passengers, etc., and to which the lifting and control surfaces are fastened. [F < L *fusus* a spindle] • See AIRPLANE.

**fu·sion** (fyōō′zhən) *n.* 1 The act of blending, or the state of being blended throughout. 2 The coalescing of two political parties, or the state of coalescence: often used attributively: a *fusion* ticket. 3 The act or process of changing from a solid into a liquid by the agency of heat; melting. **4** *Physics* A nuclear reaction in which light nuclei fuse into those of a heavier element, with the release of great energy. [< L *fusus,* pp. of *fundere* pour]

**fuss** (fus) *n.* **1** Nervous agitation or excitement, esp. over trivial matters; bustle; ado. **2** A quarrel. **3** An excessive praising of something. **4** An objection or protest. —*v.i.* **1** To make a fuss. **2** To fret or fidget, as a baby. —*v.t.* **3** *Informal* To bother or perplex with trifles. [?] —**fuss′er** *n.*

**fus·tian** (fus′chən) *n.* **1** Formerly, a kind of stout cloth made of cotton and flax; now, a coarse, twilled cotton fabric, such as corduroy or velveteen. **2** Pretentious verbiage; bombast. —*adj.* **1** Made of fustian. **2** Pompous; bombastic. [< Med. L]

**fu·tile** (fyoo′təl, -til; *esp. Brit.* -tīl) *adj.* **1** Of no avail; done in vain; useless. **2** Frivolous; trivial: *futile* chatter. [< L *futilis* pouring out easily, useless] —**fu′tile·ly** *adv.* —**fu′tile·ness, fu·til′i·ty** *n.*

**fu·ture** (fyoo′chər) *n.* **1** The time yet to come. **2** That which will be or happen in time to come. **3** The condition, rank, status, etc., of a person or thing in time to come, esp. a condition of success or achievement: a business with a *future*. **4** *Usu. pl.* Any security sold or bought upon an agreement for future delivery. **5** *Gram.* **a** A verb tense denoting action that will take place at some time to come. **b** A verb in this tense. —*adj.* **1** Such as will or may be in time to come. **2** Pertaining to or expressing time to come. [< L *futurus*]

# G

**gab** (gab) *n. Informal* Idle talk; loquacity. —*v.i.* **gabbed, gab·bing** To talk much or idly; chatter. [?<ON *gabba* mock]

**gab·ble** (gab′əl) *v.* **·bled, ·bling** *v.i.* **1** To talk rapidly and incoherently; babble. **2** To utter rapid, cackling sounds, as geese. —*v.t.* **3** To utter rapidly and incoherently. —*n.* **1** Noisy and incoherent or foolish talk. **2** Cackling, as of geese. [? Freq. of GAB] —**gab′bler** *n.*

**ga·ble** (gā′bəl) *n. Archit.* **1** The upper usu. triangular part of an end wall enclosed by the sloping ends of a ridged roof. **2** The entire end wall of a building, the upper section of which is a gable. —*v.t. & v.i.* **ga·bled,**

ga·bling To build or be built with gables. [Prob.<ON *gafl*] —**ga′bled** *adj.*

**gadg·et** (gaj′it) *n.* Any small, usu. mechanical or electronic device or contrivance. [?] —**gadg′et·ry** *n.*

**gag** (gag) *n.* **1** Something placed in or across the mouth to prevent speech or crying out. **2** Any restraint on free speech or discussion. **3** An instrument for holding open the jaws during a dental operation. **4** A humorous remark or action interpolated by an actor in a play or the like. **5** A practical joke. —*v.* **gagged, gag·ging** *v.t.* **1** To keep from speaking or crying out by means of a gag. **2** To keep from speaking or discussing freely, as by force or authority. **3** To cause nausea in; cause to retch. **4** *Slang* To introduce one's own words or improvise actions into (a theatrical role): often with *up.* —*v.i.* **5** To heave with nausea; retch. **6** *Slang* To make jokes or actions of an improvised nature. [ME *gaggen*; prob. imit.] —**gag′ger** *n.*

**gai·e·ty** (gā′ə·tē) *n. pl.* **·ties** **1** Merrymaking; fun. **2** A gay, merry manner. **3** Bright and showy finery.

**gain** (gān) *v.t.* **1** To obtain by or as by effort; earn. **2** To get in competition; win. **3** To reach; arrive at. **4** To get or undergo as an increase, profit, addition, etc.: to *gain* interest or weight. —*v.i.* **5** To increase in weight or speed. **6** To make progress; increase; improve. **7** To draw nearer or farther away: He *gained* on me steadily. —*n.* **1** *Often pl.* An increase or profit, as in money. **2** An increase in size, weight, speed, etc. **3** An improvement or advantage. **4** *Electronics* The ratio of output signal power to input signal power. [< OF *gaaignier* < Gmc.] —**Syn.** *v.* **1** achieve, acquire, attain, get, master, realize, reap.

**ga·la** (gā′lə, gal′ə, gä′lə) *n.* A festive celebration. —*adj.* Festive or appropriate for a festive occasion. [< MF *gale*]

**gal·ax·y** (gal′ək·sē) *n. pl.* **·ax·ies** **1** *Astron.* Any of the very large systems of stars, nebulae, and other celestial bodies, comparable with the Milky Way. **2** *Usu. cap.* MILKY WAY. **3** Any brilliant group, as of persons. [< L *galaxias* the Milky Way <Gk. *gala* milk]

**gale** (gāl) *n.* **1** A strong wind, esp. one between 32 and 63 miles per hour. **2** An outburst: *gales* of merriment. [?]

**gall** (gôl) *n.* **1** An excrescence on plants, caused by various parasitic organisms. **2** A similar excrescence on animals. [< L *galla* the gallnut]

**gal·lant** (gal′ənt) *adj.* 1 Brave; daring; chivalrous. 2 Stately; imposing; noble. 3 Showy; gay, as in attire. 4 (ga·lant′, -länt′, gal′ənt) Polite and attentive to women; courteous. —*n.* (ga·lant′, -länt′, gal′ənt) 1 A brave and high-spirited man. 2 A man who is attentive to women; also, a man of fashion. [< OF *galer* rejoice] —**gal′lant·ly** *adv.* —**Syn.** *adj.* 1 courageous, fearless, valiant, bold. 4 mannerly, civil, gracious, cordial, affable.

**gal·lant·ry** (gal′ən·trē) *n. pl.* **·ries** 1 Courage; heroism; chivalrousness. 2 Polite or showy attention to women. 3 A gallant act.

**gal·ler·y** (gal′ər·ē) *n. pl.* **·ler·ies** 1 A long, narrow, usu. roofed balcony or other passage projecting from the inner or outer wall of a building. 2 *U.S.* In the South, a veranda. 3 A platform with seats which projects from the rear or side walls of a theater, legislative chamber, church, etc., out over the main floor; specifically, in a theater, the highest of such platforms, containing the cheapest seats. 4 The audience occupying the gallery seats; also, the spectators at a sporting event, etc. 5 The general public and its tastes. 6 A long, narrow room or corridor. 7 A room or building used for the display of works of art. 8 A collection of works of art. 9 A room suggestive of a gallery, used for business purposes: a shooting *gallery;* a photographer's *gallery.* 10 An underground passage, as in a mine. —*v.t.* **gal·ler·ied, gal·ler·y·ing** To furnish or adorn with a gallery or galleries. [< Med. L *galeria*]

**gal·ley** (gal′ē) *n. pl.* **·leys** 1 A long, low vessel used in ancient and medieval times, propelled by oars and sails or by oars alone. 2 A large rowboat. 3 The kitchen of a ship. 4 *Printing* a A long tray, for holding composed type. b GALLEY PROOF. [< Med. L *galea*]

**gal·lon** (gal′ən) *n.* 1 A unit of volume equal to 4 quarts. 2 A dry measure; one eighth of a bushel. [< OF]

**gal·lop** (gal′əp) *n.* 1 A fast, natural gait of a horse or other quadruped. 2 The act of riding, or a ride at a gallop. 3 Any speedy action. —*v.i.* 1 To ride at a gallop. 2 To go, run, or move very fast. —*v.t.* 3 To cause to run at a gallop. [< OF *galop* < Gmc.] —**gal′lop·er** *n.*

**gal·lows** (gal′ōz) *n. pl.* **·lows** or **·lows·es** A framework consisting of two or more uprights supporting a crossbeam, used for execution by hanging. **Also gallows tree.** [< OE *galga*]

**gal·va·nize** (gal′və·nīz) *v.t.* **·nized, ·niz·ing** 1 To stimulate to muscular action by electricity. 2 To rouse to action; startle; excite. 3 To protect (iron or steel) from rust with a coating of zinc. —**gal′va·ni·za′tion** *n.*

**gam·ble** (gam′bəl) *v.* **gam·bled, gam·bling** *v.i.* 1 To risk or bet something of value on the outcome of an event, a game of chance, etc. 2 To take a risk to obtain a desired result. —*v.t.* 3 To wager or bet (something of value). 4 To lose or squander by gaming: usu. with *away.* —*n.* 1 Any risky or uncertain venture. 2 A gambling transaction. [< OE *gamenian* sport, play] —**gam′bler** *n.*

**gam·bol** (gam′bəl) *v.i.* **·boled** or **·bolled, ·bol·ing** or **·bol·ling** To skip or leap about in play; frolic. —*n.* A skipping about in sport. [< Ital. *gamba* leg]

**gam·in** (gam′in; *Fr.* à·man′) *n.* 1 A neglected boy of city streets. 2 A girl with elfin charm. [F]

**gamma globulin** A component of blood serum which contains various antibodies.

**gamma rays** Electromagnetic waves having higher frequencies and energies than X-rays and, thus, greater penetrating power.

**gan·der** (gan′dər) *n.* 1 A male goose. 2 A dunce. 3 *Slang* A look; glance. [< OE *gandra*]

**gang** (gang) *n.* 1 A group of persons acting or operating together: a *gang* of workers. 2 A group of criminals operating together as a unit. 3 A neighborhood group, usu. of young people, often engaged in antisocial behavior. 4 A group of friends. 5 A set of similar tools, etc. —*v.t.* 1 To unite into or as into a gang. 2 *Informal* To attack as a group. —*v.i.* 3 To come together as a gang; form a gang. [< OE *gangan* go]

**gan·gli·on** (gang′glē·ən) *n. pl.* **·gli·ons** or **·gli·a** (glē·ə) 1 A nexus or center of nerve cells. 2 Any center of energy, activity, or strength. [< Gk., tumor] —**gan·gli·on·ic** (gang′glē·on′ik) *adj.*

**gang·ster** (gang′stər) *n.* A member of a gang of criminals. —**gang′ster·ism** *n.*

**gan·try** (gan′trē) *n. pl.* **·tries** 1 A raised, horizontal framework for supporting a traveling crane, railway signals, etc. 2 A movable tower used in servicing or assembling rockets. 3 A frame to hold a barrel horizontally. [< OF *chantier* < L *cantherius* framework]

**gape** (gāp, gap) *v.i.* **gaped, gap·ing** 1 To stare open-mouthed, as in awe or surprise. 2 To

open the mouth wide, as in yawning. 3 To
be or become open wide; present a wide
opening. —*n.* 1 The act of gaping. 2 A gap.
[< ON *gapa*] —**gap′er** *n.*

**ga·rage** (gə·räzh′, -räj′, *Brit.* gar′ij) *n.* A building in which motor vehicles are parked, ser-
viced, or repaired. —*v.t.* **ga·raged, ga·rag
·ing** To put or keep in a garage. [< OF *garer*
protect <Gmc.]

**garb** (gärb) *n.* 1 Clothes, esp. as characteristic of some office, rank, etc. 2 External appearance or manner. —*v.t.* To clothe; dress.
[< MF *garbe* gracefulness]

**gar·bage** (gär′bij) *n.* 1 Refuse matter, as waste
food, empty bottles, paper, etc. 2 Anything
worthless or disgusting. [Prob. < AF]

**gar·den** (gär′dən) *n.* 1 A place for the cultivation of flowers, vegetables, or small plants.
2 Any fertile or highly cultivated territory.
3 A piece of ground, commonly with ornamental plants or trees, used as a public
park. —*adj.* 1 Of, for, used, or grown in a
garden. 2 Ordinary; common. 3 Like a garden; ornamental: *garden* spot of the world.
—*v.t.* 1 To cultivate as a garden. —*v.i.* 2 To
till or work in a garden. [< AF *gardin*] —**ga·
r′den·er** *n.*

**gar·gle** (gär′gəl) *v.* **gar·gled, gar·gling** *v.t.* 1 To
rinse (the throat) with a liquid agitated by
air from the windpipe. —*v.i.* 2 To use a gar-
gle. 3 To make a sound as if gargling. —*n.*
A liquid for gargling. [< OF *gargouille* throat]

**gar·ish** (gâr′ish) *adj.* Bright and showy, esp.
in a gaudy or vulgar manner. [< ME *gauren*
to stare] —**gar′ish·ly** *adv.* —**gar′ish·ness** *n.*
—Syn. flashy, ornate, tawdry, cheap, ostentatious.

**gar·land** (gär′lənd) *n.* 1 A wreath of leaves,
flowers, etc., as a token of victory, joy, or
honor. 2 An anthology of short literary selections. —*v.t.* To deck with or as with a
garland. [< OF *garlande*]

**gar·lic** (gär′lik) *n.* 1 A hardy bulbous perennial of the same genus as the onion. 2 Its
pungent bulb, used in cooking. [< OE *gār*
spear + *lēac* leek] —**gar′lick·y** *adj.*

**gar·ment** (gär′mənt) *n.* 1 An article of clothing. 2 *pl. Clothes.* 3 Any covering. —*v.t.* To
clothe. [< OF *garnir* garnish]

**gar·ner** (gär′nər) *v.t.* To gather or store; collect. —*n.* 1 GRANARY. 2 Any storage place. [<
L *granarium* a granary]

**gar·net** (gär′nit) *n.* 1 One of various glassy silicate minerals, used as abrasives and
sometimes as gems. 2 Its usual color, a

deep red. [< Med. L *granatum* a pomegran-
ate]

**gar·nish** (gär′nish) *v.t.* 1 To decorate, as with
ornaments; embellish. 2 In cookery, to decorate (food) for the table. 3 *Law* To give
warning to (someone) to answer to an action; garnishee. —*n.* 1 Something placed
around food for ornamentation or a relish.
2 Anything added as an ornament; embellishment. —**gar′nish·er** *n.* [< OF *garnir* prepare < Gmc.]

**gar·ret** (gar′it) *n.* A space, room, or rooms directly under a roof. [< OF *garite* a watch-
tower]

**gar·ri·son** (gar′ə·sən) *n.* 1 The military force
defending a fort, town, etc. 2 The place
where such a force is stationed. —*v.t.* 1 To
place troops in (a fort, town, etc.) for its defense. 2 To station (troops) in a fort, town,
etc. 3 To be the garrison of. [< OF *garir* defend <Gmc.]

**gar·ru·lous** (gar′ʸə·ləs) *adj.* Given to continual and tedious talking. [< L *garrulus* talk-
ative] —**gar′ru·lous·ly** *adv.* —**gar·ru·li·ty**
(gə·rōō′lə·tē), **gar′ru·lous·ness** *n.* —Syn.
talkative, loquacious, verbose, effusive,
long-winded.

**gar·ter** (gär′tər) *n.* An elastic band or fastening device used to hold a stocking in place.
—*v.t.* To support or fasten with a garter. [<
OF *garet* bend of the knee]

**gas** (gas) *n.* 1 *Physics* That fluid form of matter which is compressible within limits, and
which diffuses readily and is capable of indefinite expansion in all directions. 2 Any
gas or vapor other than air: tear *gas*, fuel
*gas.* 3 Flatulence. 4 *Informal* a Gasoline. b
The accelerator of an automobile. 5 *Slang*
Empty boasting. 6 *Slang* def>A person or
thing that is fun, exciting, etc. —*v.* **gassed,
gas·sing** *v.t.* 1 To overcome, affect, or kill by
gas or gas fumes. 2 To treat or saturate
with gas. 3 To supply with gas or gasoline.
4 *Slang* def>To provide fun, excitement, etc.,
for. —*v.i.* 5 To give off gas. 6 *Slant* def>To
boast. [Coined by J. B. van Helmont,
1577–1644, Belgian chemist]

**gas·e·ous** (gas′ē·əs, -yəs) *adj.* 1 Having the
nature or form of gas. 2 Unsubstantial.

**gash** (gash) *v.t.* To make a long, deep cut in.
—*n.* a long, deep cut or flesh wound. [< OF
*garser* scratch]

**gas·ket** (gas′kit) *n.* 1 *Mech.* def>A ring, disk, or
plate of packing used to seal a joint against
leaks. 2 *Naut.* dèf>A rope or cord used to

confine furled sails to the yard or boom. Also **gas′kin** (-kin), **gas′king** (-king). [?]

**gas·o·line** (gas′ə·lēn, gas′ə·lēn′) *n.* A volatile, flammable liquid hydrocarbon derived from petroleum and used as a fuel and solvent. Also **gas′o·lene**. [< GAS + -OL + -INE]

**gasp** (gasp, gäsp) *v.i.* 1 To take in the breath suddenly and sharply; breathe convulsively, as from fear or exhaustion. —*v.t.* 2 To say or utter with gasps. —*n.* An act of gasping. [< ON *geispa*]

**gas·tric** (gas′trik) *adj.* Of, pertaining to, in, or near the stomach.

**gath·er** (gath′ər) *v.t.* 1 To bring together in one place or group. 2 To bring together from various places, sources, etc. 3 To bring closer to oneself: to *gather* one's skirts. 4 To pick, harvest, or collect. 5 To collect or summon up, as one's energies. 6 To increase in amount or degree: The storm *gathered* force. 7 To clasp or enfold: to *gather* someone into one's arms. 8 To conclude or infer. 9 To draw (cloth) into folds or pleats. 10 To wrinkle (the brow). —*v.i.* 11 To come together. 12 To increase. 13 To wrinkle up, as the brow. 14 To come to a head, as a boil. —*n.* A pleat. [< OE *gadrian*] —**gath′er·a·ble** *adj.* —**gath′er·er** *n.*

**gaud·y** (gô′dē) *adj.* **gaud·i·er, gaud·i·est** Obtrusively brilliant in color: garish; flashy. —**gaud′i·ly** *adv.* —**gaud′i·ness** *n.*

**gauge** (gāj) *n.* 1 An instrument for measuring, indicating, or regulating quantity, dimension, capacity, etc. 2 A standard or system of measurement or comparison. 3 The measure of something as expressed by means of such a system or standard: the *gauge* of a shotgun bore. 4 The distance between rails of a railroad track or a pair of wheels on an axis. —*v.t.* **gauged, gaug·ing** 1 To measure or regulate with or as with a gauge. 2 To estimate, appraise, or judge. 3 To bring into conformity with a standard. [< OF, a measure] —**gauge′a·ble** *adj.* —**gau·g′er** *n.*

**gaunt** (gônt) *adj.* 1 Emaciated, as from lack of food; lank; lean; meager; thin. 2 Grim; desolate. [ME] —**gaunt′ly** *adv.*

**gauze** (gôz) *n.* 1 A light, loosely woven fabric. 2 Any thin open-woven material: wire *gauze*. 3 A mist. —*adj.* Resembling or made of gauze. [< MF *gaze*] —**gauz′i·ly** *adv.* —**gauz′i·ness** *n.* —**gauz·y** (-i·er, -i·est) *adj.*

**gay** (gā) *adj.* 1 Joyous; light-spirited; merry. 2 Brilliant; showy; *gay* colors. 3 Loving or given to pleasure and amusement. 4 In-formaldef>HOMOSEXUAL. [< OF *gai*] —**gay′ness** *n.* —**gay′some** *adj.* —**Syn.** 1 cheerful, happy, merry, vivacious, lively, sunny, blithe. 2 sparkling, bright, vivid, shiny.

**gaze** (gāz) *v.i.* **gazed, gaz·ing** To look earnestly and steadily, as in scrutiny, admiration, or concern. —*n.* A continued or intense look. [< Scand.] —**gaz′er** *n.*

**ga·zelle** (gə·zel′) *n.* Any of various small antelopes with long necks and large, gentle eyes. [< Ar. *ghazāl* gazelle]

**ga·zette** (gə·zet′) *n.* 1 A newspaper. 2 *Brit.*def>Any official government journal announcing appointments, promotions, etc. —*v.t.* *Brit.* **ga·zet·ted, ga·zet·ting** To publish or announce in a gazette. [< dial. Ital. (Venetian) *gazeta* a coin, orig. the price of the paper]

**gaz·et·teer** (gaz′ə·tir′) *n.* 1 A dictionary or alphabetical list of geographical names. 2 A writer for a gazette.

**gear** (gir) *n.* 1 *Mech.* **a** A set of moving parts that transmit motion, often changing its rate or direction. **b** One of several possible arrangements of such a set of parts: low *gear.* **c** A wheel with teeth around its edge, designed to engage a part with similar teeth and transmit motion; cogwheel. **d** Any group of parts performing a specific function: the steering *gear.* 2 Any equipment, tools, etc., for some specific task or purpose, as the rigging of a ship, a repairman's tools, etc. 3 Clothes, esp. for a specific purpose: a skier's *gear.* 4 Harmonious and effective action: out of *gear.* —*v.t.* 1 **a** To equip with gears. **b** To connect by means of gears. 2 To regulate so as to match or suit something else: to *gear* production to demand. 3 To put gear on; harness; dress. —*v.i.* 4 To come into or be in gear; mesh. [< ON *gervi* equipment]

**Gei·ger counter** (gī′gər) An electronic instrument for detecting and counting ionizing particles and rays, used to measure radioactivity. [< Hans *Geiger*, 1882–1945, German physicist]

**gei·sha** (gā′shə) *n. pl.* **·sha** or **·shas** A Japanese girl trained to entertain men by singing, dancing, etc.

**gel·a·tin** (jel′ə·tin) *n.* 1 A brittle, tasteless protein produced from animal tissues, which forms a gel with water. 2 A gel made usu. with gelatin and used as a base for desserts, aspics, etc. Also **gel′a·tine.** [< L *gelare* freeze]

**gem** (jem) *n.* 1 A precious or semiprecious

208

stone, esp. when cut and polished; jewel. 2 Anything rare, delicate, and perfect, as a work of literature or art. 3 A light, muffin-like cake. —*v.t.* **gemmed, gem·ming** To adorn with or as with gems. [< L *gemma* jewel]

**gen·der** (jen′dər) *n.* 1 *Gram.*def>In many languages, a grammatical designation of nouns and pronouns governing the form assumed by the words which modify or refer to them. 2 Any one of these designations, esp. masculine, feminine, or neuter. 3 *Informal*def>Sex. [< L *genus, -eris* kind]

**gene** (jēn) *n.* A unit occupying a distinct position on a chromosome and having a crucial function in the transmission of a specific characteristic from parent to offspring. [< G *Gen*, ult. < -GEN]

**ge·ne·al·o·gy** (jē′nē·ol′ə·jē, -nē·al′-, jen′ē-) *n. pl.* **·gies** 1 A record of descent from some ancestor; a list of ancestors and their descendants. 2 Descent in a direct line; pedigree. 3 The science that treats of pedigrees. [<Gk. *genea* race + -LOGY] —**ge·ne·a·log·i·cal** (jē′nē·ə·loj′i·kəl, jen′ē-) *adj.* —**ge′ne·a·log′i·cal·ly** *adv.* —**ge·ne·al′o·gist** *n.*

**gen·er·al** (jen′ər·əl, -rəl) *adj.* 1 Pertaining to, including, or affecting all or the whole; not local or particular: a *general* election. 2 Common to or current among the majority; prevalent: the *general* opinion. 3 Not restricted in application: a *general* principle. 4 Not limited to or dealing with a particular class; unspecialized: a *general* store; a *general* practitioner. 5 Not detailed or precise: a *general* idea. 6 Usual or customary: one's *general* habit. 7 Superior in rank: attorney *general*. *n.* 1 See GRADE. 2 The chief of a religious order. 3 A general statement, fact, or principle. [< L *generalis* of a race or kind < *genus* kind]

**gen·er·ate** (jen′ə·rāt) *v.t.* **·at·ed, ·at·ing** 1 To produce or cause to be; bring into being. 2 To beget as a parent; procreate. [< L *generare* < *genus* kind]

**gen·er·a·tion** (jen′ə·rā′shən) *n.* 1 The process of begetting or procreating. 2 Production or origination by any process; creation: the *generation* of electricity. 3 A step or degree in natural descent. 4 The average time elapsing between the birth of parent and offspring, and usu. estimated for humans at 30 years. 5 A body of persons existing at the same time or having common interests, characteristics, or outlooks.

**gen·er·a·tor** (jen′ə·rā′tər) *n.* 1 One who or that

which generates or originates. 2 An apparatus in which the generation of a gas is effected. 3 A machine that changes heat or mechanical energy into electricity.

**ge·ner·ic** (ji·ner′ik) *adj.* 1 Of or pertaining to a whole group or class; general. 2 Not having proprietary status: said esp. of names for drugs. 3 *Biol.*def>Of or like a genus. [< L *genus, generis* race, kind + -IC] —**ge·ner′i·cal·ly** *adv.*

**gen·e·sis** (jen′ə·sis) *n. pl.* **·ses** (-sēz) 1 The act or mode of originating; creation. 2 Origin; beginning. [< Gk. *genēsis* origin]

**ge·net·ics** (jə·net′iks) *n. pl.* (construed as *sing.*) 1 That branch of biology which deals with the interaction of the genes in producing the similarities and differences between individuals related by descent. 2 The inherited characteristics of an organism or group of organisms. —**ge·net′i·cist** *n.*

**gen·ial** (jēn′yəl, jē′nē·əl) *adj.* 1 Kindly in disposition; cordial and pleasant in manner. 2 Imparting warmth, comfort, or life: a *genial* climate. [< L *genialis* of birth, pleasant] —**ge·ni·al·i·ty** (jē′nē·al′ə·tē) *n.* —**ge′nial·ly** *adv.* —**Syn.** 1 affable, friendly, cheerful, blithe, sunny, light-hearted, warm, good-natured.

**gen·ius** (jēn′yəs) *n. pl.* **gen·ius·es**; *for def. 6* **ge·ni·i** (jē′nē·ī). 1 Extraordinary intellectual or creative gifts. 2 Remarkable aptitude, talent, or capacity: a *genius* for oratory. 3 A person having such gifts or abilities. 4 The dominant nature or essential character of a nation, era, place, etc. 5 A representative type; embodiment. 6 In Roman antiquity: **a** A beneficient spirit or evil demon supposed to accompany one through life. **b** A guardian or tutelary spirit of a person or place. 7 A person having strong influence over another. [L, tutelary spirit]

**gen·o·cide** (jen′ə·sīd) *n.* The systematic extermination of a racial or national group. [<Gk. *genos* race + -CIDE]

**gen·tile** (jen′tīl) *n.* 1 *Often cap.*def>Any person not a Jew, esp. a Christian. 2 Formerly, among Christians, a pagan. 3 *Often cap.*def>Among Mormons, a non-Mormon. —*adj. Often cap.* Of, being, or relating to a gentile. [<L *gentilis* of a gens, foreign]

**gen·tle** (jen′təl) *adj.* 1 Mild and serene in nature or disposition. 2 Not harsh or rough; soft: a *gentle* touch. 3 Tame; docile: a *gentle* horse. 4 Not steep or abrupt: a *gentle* slope. 5 Of good birth; upper-class. 6 Refined; polite. —*v.t.* **gen·tled, gen·tling** 1 To tame, as a horse. 2 To soothe. [< L *gentilis* of good birth<*gens, gentis* race, clan] — **gen′tly** *adv.* —**gen′tle·ness** *n.*

**gen·u·flect** (jen′yə·flekt) *v.i.* To bend the knee, as in worship. [< L *genu* knee + *flectere* to bend] —**gen·u·flec′tion** *n.*

**gen·u·ine** (jen′yōō·in) *adj.* 1 Of the original stock; purebred. 2 Not spurious, false, or counterfeit; real; authentic. 3 Not affected or hypocritical; frank; sincere; true. [<L *genuinus* innate] —**gen′u·ine·ly** *adv.* —**gen′u·ine·ness** *n.*

**ge·nus** (jē′nəs) *n. pl.* **gen·e·ra** (jen′ər·ə) 1 A biological category ranking below the family or subfamily and consisting of one or more species. 2 A kind; class. [L, race, kind]

**geodesic dome** An approximately hemispherical structure formed of straight elements that make up a network of rigid polygons.

**ge·od·e·sy** (jē·od′ə·sē) *n.* The study and measurement of the size and shape of the earth. [<Gk. *geodaisia* earth division] —**ge·o·des·ic** (jē′ə·des′ik, -dē′sik) *adj.* —**ge·od′e·sist** *n.*

**ge·o·det·ic** (jē′ə·det′ik) *adj.* Of, pertaining to, determined, or effected by geodesy. Also **ge′o·det′i·cal.** —**ge′o·det′i·cal·ly** *adv.*

**ge·og·ra·phy** (jē·og′rə·fē) *n. pl.* **·phies** 1 The science that describes the surface of the earth and its associated physical, biological, economic, political, and demographic characteristics. 2 The physical aspect, features, etc., of a place or area. [<GEO- + Gk. *graphein* write, describe] —**ge·og′ra·pher** *n.* —**ge′o·graph′ic** or **·i·cal** *adj.* —**ge′o·graph′i·cal·ly** *adv.*

**ge·ol·o·gy** (jē·ol′ə·jē) *n. pl.* **·gies** 1 The science that studies the origin, history, constitution, and structure of the earth. 2 The structure of a particular part of the earth. —**ge·o·log·ic** (jē′ə·loj′ik) or **·i·cal** *adj.* —**ge′o·log′i·cal·ly** *adv.* —**ge·ol′o·gist** *n.* • See GEOLOGICAL TIME SCALE, next page.

**ge·o·met·ric** (jē′ə·met′rik) *adj.* 1 Pertaining to or according to the rules and principles of geometry. 2 Of or characterized by straight lines, regular curves, and angles: a *geometric* design. Also **ge′o·met′ri·cal.** —**ge′o·met′ri·cal·ly** *adv.*

**ge·om·e·try** (jē·om′ə·trē) *n. pl.* **·tries** The branch of mathematics that deals with the properties, relations, and measurement of points, lines, angles, surfaces, and solids. [<GEO- + Gk. *metrein* measure]

**ge·o·phys·ics** (jē′ə·fiz′iks) *n. pl.* *(construed as sing.)* The science that investigates the physical forces, influences, and phenomena associated with the earth. —**ge′o·phys′i·cal** *adj.* —**ge′o·phys′i·cist** *n.*

**ge·o·pol·i·tics** (jē′ō·pol′ə·tiks) *n. pl. (construed as sing.)* The study of the interrelationship of geography, climate, etc., and politics. —**ge′o·po·lit′i·cal** *adj.* —**ge′o·po·lit′i·cal·ly** *adv.* —**ge′o·pol′i·ti′cian** *n.*

**ger·i·at·rics** (jer′ē·at′riks) *n. pl. (construed as sing.)* The branch of medicine which deals with the diseases and physiological changes associated with aging and old people. [< Gk. *gēras* old age + *iatros* physician] —**ger·i·at·ric** *adj.*

**germ** (jûrm) *n.* 1 Any rudimentary living substance that can develop into an organism. 2 A microorganism that causes disease; microbe. 3 The primary source from which something may be developed. [< L *germen* offshoot]

**ger·mi·nate** (jûr′mə·nāt) *v.* **·nat·ed, ·nat·ing** *v.i.* 1 To begin to grow or develop; sprout. —*v.t.* 2 To cause to sprout. [<L *germinare*] —**ger′mi·na′tion, ger′mi·na′tor** *n.* —**ger′mi·na′tive** *adj.*

**ges·tic·u·late** (jes·tik′yə·lāt) *v.* **·lat·ed, ·lat·ing** *v.i.* 1 To make motions with the hands or arms, as in speaking. —*v.t.* 2 To express by gestures. [<L *gestus* bearing, gesture] —**ges·tic′u·la′tion** *n.* —**ges·tic′u·la′tive** *adj.*

**ges·ture** (jes′chər) *n.* 1 An expressive motion of the body and esp. of the hand or hands, used for emphasis or to express some idea or emotion. 2 Something said or done for mere effect or as a concession to manners, courtesy, etc. —*v.* **·tured, ·tur·ing** *v.i.* 1 To make gestures. —*v.t.* 2 To express by gestures. [<L *gestus*, pp. of *gerere* carry on, do] —**ges′tur·er** *n.*

**get** (get) *v.* **got** or *Archaic* **gat, got** or *U.S.* **got·ten, get·ting** *v.t.* 1 To come into possession of; obtain. 2 To go for and bring back: to *get* one's hat. 3 To cause to come, go, move, etc.: We *got* him to talk; I can't *get* the window up. 4 To take; carry away: *Get* your things out of this house. 5 To prepare: to *get* breakfast. 6 To bring to a state or condition: to *get* the work done. 7 To find out or obtain by calculation, experiment, etc.: to *get* the range of a gun. 8 To communicate with; contact: We can't *get* them on the phone. 9 To receive as a reward, punishment, etc.: to *get* ten years in jail. 10 To obtain, receive, or earn: to *get* permission. 11 To capture; catch. 12 To learn or master: to *get* a lesson. 13 To become sick with. 14 To board; catch, as a train. 15 To beget: said chiefly of animals. 16 *Informal*def>To come to an understanding of; comprehend; I *get* the idea. 17 *Informal*def>To possess: with *have* or *has*: He has *got* quite a temper. 18 To square accounts with: I'll *get* you yet. 19 *Informal*def>To be obliged or forced to do: with *have* or *has*: I have *got* to go home. 20 *Informal*def>To make helpless or ineffective: Drink finally *got* him. 21 *Informal*def>To strike; hit: That shot *got* him in the arm. 22 *Slang* To puzzle; baffle. 23 *Slang* To cause irritation or pleasure to: His impudence *gets* me. 24 *Slang* To notice: *Get* that dress she's wearing. —*v.i.* 25 To arrive: When does the train *get* there? 26 To come or go: *Get* in here! 27 To board; enter: to *get* on a train. 28 To become: to *get* drunk. —**get across** 1 To make or be convincing or clear. 2 To be successful, as in projecting one's personality. —**get ahead** To succeed; prosper. —**get along** 1 To leave; go. 2 To be successful or fairly successful, as in business. 3 To be friendly. 4 To proceed. 5 To grow old or older. —**get around** 1 To become known. 2 To move about. 3 To avoid; circumvent. 4 To flatter, cajole, etc., so as to obtain the favor of. —**get at** 1 To reach; arrive at: to *get at* the truth. 2 To intend; mean: I don't see what you're *getting at*. 3 To apply oneself to: to *get* at a problem. —**get away** 1 To escape. 2 To leave; go. 3 To start. —**get away with** *Slang* To do (something) without discovery, criticism, or punishment. —**get back at** *Slang* To revenge oneself on. —**get by** 1 To pass: This *got by* the censor. 2 *Informal* To manage to survive. —**get in** 1 To arrive. 2 To interject effectively, as a remark. —**get lost** 1 To lose one's way. 2 *Slang* Go away! —**get off** 1 To descend from; dismount. 2 To leave; depart. 3 To be relieved, as of duty. 4 To be released without punishment; escape penalty. 5 To utter: to *get off* a joke. 6 To take off: *Get off* your wet clothes. —**get on** 1 To mount, as a horse. 2 To get along. —**get out** 1 To depart. 2 To escape. 3 To become known, as a secret. 4 To publish; issue. —**get over** 1 To recover from, as illness or surprise. 2 To get across. —**get through** 1 To finish. 2 To survive. —**get to** 1 To start or begin. 2 To succeed, as in reaching or making clear to: also get through to. —**get together** 1 To collect, as

facts. 2 To meet; assemble. 3 *Informal* To come to an agreement. —**get up** 1 To rise, as from sleep. 2 To prepare and arrange; devise. 3 *Informal* To dress up. [<ON *geta*] —**get′ta·ble, get′a·ble** *adj.* —**get′ter** *n.* • See GOT and GOTTEN.

**gey·ser** (gī′zər) *n.* A spring from which intermittent jets of steam, hot water, or mud are ejected. [<ON *geysa* gush]

**ghast·ly** (gast′lē, gäst′-) *adj.* ·li·er, ·li·est 1 Having a haggard, deathlike appearance. 2 Terrifying or shocking. 3 *Informal* Very bad: a *ghastly* blunder. —*adv.* In a ghastly manner. [< OE *gāstlic* ghostly] —**ghast′li·ness** *n.*

**ghet·to** (get′ō) *n. pl.* ·tos 1 In Europe, a part of a city in which Jews were formerly required to live. 2 A section of a city, often rundown or overcrowded, inhabited chiefly by a minority group. 3 Any community or group separated physically or culturally from the rest of society. [Ital.]

**ghost** (gōst) *n.* 1 A disembodied spirit, esp. of a dead person and supposedly able to manifest itself to the living in various ways. 2 The soul or spirit: now only in the phrase **give up the ghost**, to die. 3 A shadow or semblance; slight trace. 4 A false, secondary image produced in an optical instrument or on a television screen. 5 *Informal* A ghost writer. —*v.t. & v.i.* 1 To haunt as a ghost. 2 *Informal* To write as a ghost writer. [< OE *gāst* spirit] —**ghost′like′** *adj.*

**GI** (jē′ī) *n. pl.* **GI's, GIs** *Informal* A soldier, esp. an enlisted man, in the U.S. Army. —*adj.* 1 Of, pertaining to, or issued by the government to U.S. military forces. 2 *Informal* Conforming to U.S. military regulations. Also **G.I.** [< G(overnment) I(ssue)]

**gi·ant** (jī′ənt) *n.* 1 Any imaginary person of gigantic size. 2 Any person or thing of great size, either physically, mentally, or figuratively. —*adj.* Gigantic. [< Gk. *gigas, gigantos*] —**gi′ant·ess** *n. Fem.*

**gib·bet** (jib′it) *n.* 1 An upright timber with a crosspiece projecting at right angles from its upper end, upon which criminals were formerly hanged. 2 GALLOWS. —*v.t.* ·bet·ed or ·bet·ted, ·bet·ing or ·bet·ting 1 To execute by hanging. 2 To hang and expose on a gibbet. 3 To hold up to public contempt. [< OF *gibe* a staff]

**gib·bous** (gib′əs, jib′-) *adj.* 1 Irregularly rounded; convex, as the moon when less than full and yet more than half full. 2 Humpbacked. Also **gib·bose** (gib′ōs, gi·bos′). [< L *gibbus* a hump] —gib′bous·ly *adv.* —gib′bous·ness *n.* • See MOON.

gibe (jīb) *v.t.* & *v.i.* gibed, gib·ing To mock; sneer; scoff. —*n.* An expression of sarcasm and ridicule. [? < OF *giber* treat roughly in play] —gib′er *n.* —Syn. *v.* derive, taunt, scorn, ridicule.

gib·let (jib′lit, gib′-) *n.* One of the edible visceral parts of a fowl, as the gizzard, heart, or liver. [< OF *gibelet*]

gift (gift) *n.* 1 That which is given; a donation; present. 2 The act, right, or power of giving. 3 A natural endowment; aptitude; talent. —*v.t.* 1 To give as a present to. 2 To make a gift of. [< OE < *gifan* give]

gi·gan·tic (jī·gan′tik) *adj.* 1 Like a giant; colossal; huge. 2 Tremendous; extraordinary. [See GIANT.]

gig·gle (gig′əl) *v.i.* gig·gled, gig·gling To laugh in a high-pitched, nervous manner; titter. —*n.* Such a laugh; titter. [Imit.] —gig′gler *n.* —gig′gly *adj.*

gild (gild) *v.t.* gild·ed or gilt, gild·ing 1 To coat with or as with gold or gold leaf. 2 To give a pleasing or attractive appearance to; gloss over. [< OE *gyldan*] —gild′er *n.*

gim·mick (gim′ik) *n. Informal* 1 Something new or ingenious, as a gadget, scheme, stunt, etc., usu. devised to win publicity or make something more attractive. 2 A secret or surprising element; twist. 3 Any object whose name cannot be recalled. 4 A secret device for controlling the movements of a prize wheel. —*v.t. Slang* To add gimmicks to: often with *up.* [?] —gim′mick·y *adj.*

gin (jin) *n.* 1 An alcoholic liquor distilled from various grains and flavored with juniper berries. 2 Such a liquor with other flavoring. [Short for Du. *jenever* juniper]

gin·ger (jin′jər) *n.* 1 The pungent, spicy rootstock of a tropical plant, used in medicine and cookery. 2 The plant itself. 3 *Informal* Liveliness; spunk. [< Gk. *zingiberis*]

ging·ham (ging′əm) *n.* A plain-weave cotton fabric, usu. in checks or stripes. [< Malay *ginggang*]

gi·raffe (jə·raf′, -räf′) *n. pl.* ·raffes or ·raffe A large spotted African ruminant, having a very long neck and limbs; the tallest of the quadrupeds. [< Ar. *zarāfah*]

gird (gûrd) *v.t.* gird·ed or girt, gird·ing 1 To surround with a belt or girdle. 2 To encircle; hem in. 3 To prepare (oneself) for action. 4 To clothe; equip. [< OE *gyrdan*]

gird·er (gûr′dər) *n.* A principal horizontal beam of a structure, receiving a vertical load.

gir·dle (gûr′dəl) *n.* 1 A belt, cord, or sash worn around the waist. 2 A woman's corsetlike, usu. elastic undergarment, reaching from the waist to below the hips. 3 Anything that encircles. 4 The edge of a cut gem. 5 An encircling cut through the bark of a branch or tree. —*v.t.* gir·dled, gir·dling 1 To fasten a girdle or belt around. 2 To encircle; encompass. 3 To make an encircling cut through the bark of (a branch or tree). [< OE *gyrdel*] —gir′dler *n.*

gist (jist) *n.* The substance, point, or main idea. [< OF *giste* place of rest < *gesir* to lie] —Syn. heart, core, essence.

give (giv) *v.* gave, giv·en, giv·ing *v.t.* 1 To turn over to another without receiving anything in exchange. 2 To transfer to the possession or control of another for a price or equal value. 3 To hand over for safekeeping, delivery, etc. 4 To offer, esp. as entertainment: to *give* a play, toast, etc. 5 To be the cause or source of: The sun *gives* light. 6 To provide or furnish; impart: to *give* the news on TV. 7 To express by word or gesture. 8 To be the agent of transfer of, as a disease. 9 To grant: to *give* permission. 10 To impose, as a punishment. 11 To emit or show, as a movement, shout, etc. 12 To administer, as medicine. 13 To deal; inflict, as a blow. 14 To concede or yield: to *give* ground. 15 To devote or sacrifice: to *give* one's life. 16 To confer, as a title. —*v.i.* 17 To make gifts. 18 To yield, as from pressure, melting, or thawing; collapse. 19 To be springy or resilient; bend. —give away 1 To bestow as a gift. 2 To bestow (the bride) upon the bridegroom. 3 To reveal or disclose. —give back To return. —give in 1 To yield. 2 To collapse, as under stress. —give off (or forth) To send forth; emit, as odors. —give out 1 To send forth; emit. 2 To distribute. 3 To make known; publish. 4 To become worn out, exhausted, etc. —give rise to To cause or result in. —give up 1 To surrender; cede; hand over. 2 To stop; cease. 3 To desist from as hopeless. 4 To lose all hope for. 5 To devote wholly. —*n.* The quality of being yielding; elasticity. [< OE *giefan*] —giv′er *n.*

gla·cial (glā′shəl) *adj.* 1 Of, pertaining to, or caused by glaciers. 2 Of or pertaining to a glacial epoch. 3 Very cold or icy. 4 Cold in manner, appearance, etc.: a *glacial* look. [< L *glacies* ice] —gla′cial·ly *adv.*

gla·cier (glā′shər) *n.* A field of ice which

moves slowly downward over slopes or through valleys until it either melts or breaks off to form icebergs. [<L *glacies* ice]

**glade** (glād) *n.* 1 An open space in a wood. 2 An everglade. [Prob. akin to *glad* in obs. sense "sunny"]

**glad·i·o·lus** (glad′ē·ō′ləs) *n. pl.* ·lus·es or ·li (-lī) A plant of the iris family with fleshy bulbs, sword-shaped leaves, and spikes of colored flowers. Also **glad·i·o·la** (glad′ē·ō′lə), **glad′i·ole** (-ōl). [< L *gladius* sword]

**glance** (glans, gläns) *v.* **glanced, glanc·ing** *v.i.* 1 To strike something at an angle and bounce off. 2 To look quickly or hurriedly. 3 To glint; flash. 4 To make passing reference; allude. —*v.t.* 5 To cause to strike something at an angle and bounce off. —*n.* 1 A quick look. 2 A momentary gleam. 3 A glancing movement or rebound. [< OF *glacier* to slip]

**gland** (gland) *n.* 1 Any of various tissues or organs that secrete substances essential to the body or for the elimination of waste products: salivary *glands;* endocrine *glands.* 2 A node of nonsecreting tissue: lymph *gland.* [< L *glandula,* dim. of *glans, glandis* acorn]

**glare** (glâr) *n.* A glassy, smooth surface, as of ice. —*adj.* Having a glassy, smooth surface. [? <GLARE¹]

**glass** (glas, gläs) *n.* 1 A hard, amorphous, brittle, usu. translucent substance of varying composition, usu. made y fusing sand with various oxides chosen according to the properties desired. 2 Any substance resembling glass. 3 An article made of glass, as a window pane, a goblet or tumbler, a mirror, telescope, barometer, etc. 4 *pl.* EYE-GLASSES. 5 *pl.* BINOCULARS. 6 The amount of something contained in a drinking glass. 7 GLASSWARE. —*v.t.* 1 To enclose with glass. 2 To reflect; mirror. 3 To give a glazed surface to. —*adj.* Made of, relating to, or like glass. [< OE *glæs*]

**glass·y** (glas′ē, gläs′ē) *adj.* **glass·i·er, glass·i·est** 1 Composed of or like glass. 2 Fixed, blank, and uncomprehending: a *glassy* stare. —**glass′i·ly** *adv.* —**glass′i·ness** *n.*

**glaze** (glāz) *v.* **glazed, glaz·ing** *v.t.* 1 To fit, as a window, with glass panes. 2 To provide (a building, etc.) with windows. 3 To coat, as pottery, with a glasslike surface applied by fusing. 4 To cover with a glaze, as meat or biscuits. 5 To make glossy, as by polishing. —*v.i.* 6 To become glassy; take on a glaze.

—*n.* 1 A smooth, shining, transparent surface. 2 A substance used to produce it, as on pottery. 3 An icy surface. 4 Transparent stock or icing applied to the surface of meat, fish, vegetables, etc. [ME *glasen*<*glas* glass] —**glaz′er, glaz′i·ness** *n.* —**glaz′y** *adj.*

**gleam** (glēm) *n.* 1 A glimmer or flash of light. 2 A small, faint light. 3 Something likened to a flash of light: a *gleam* of wit. —*v.i.* 1 To shine with a gleam. 2 To appear clearly and briefly, as a signal fire. —*v.t.* 3 To show w:th a gleam. [< OE *glǣm*] —**gleam′y** *adj.* —**Syn.** *v.* 1 flash, sparkle, glitter, glare, dazzle.

**glean** (glēn) *v.t.* & *v.i.* 1 To collect (information, facts, etc.) by patient effort. 2 To gather (the leavings) from a field after the crop has been reaped. 3 To gather the leavings from (a field, etc.). [<LL *glenare*] —**glean′er** *n.*

**glee** (glē) *n.* 1 Joy; gaiety; merriment. 2 A part song for three or more unaccompanied, usu. male voices. [< OE *glēo*] —**glee′some** (-səm) *adj.* —**Syn.** 1 mirth, exuberance, delight, hilarity, fun.

**glee club** A group organized to sing light choral music.

**glib** (glib) *adj.* **glib·ber, glib·best** 1 Speaking or writing with smooth fluency. 2 More facile than sincere; superficial: a *glib* compliment. 3 Characterized by easiness or informality. [Prob. <MLG *glibberich* slippery] —**glib′ly** *adv.* —**glib′ness** *n.*

**glide** (glīd) *v.* **glid·ed, glid·ing** *v.i.* 1 To move, slip, or flow smoothly or easily. 2 To pass unnoticed, as time. 3 *Aeron.* To descend gradually and without power; also, to operate a glider. 4 *Music & Phonet.* To produce a glide. —*v.t.* 5 To cause to glide. —*n.* 1 The act of gliding; a gliding motion. 2 *Music* An unbroken passage from tone to tone. 3 *Phonet.* A transitional sound made in passing from the position of one speech sound to that of another. [< OE *glīdan*]

**glid·er** (glī′dər) *n.* 1 One who or that which glides. 2 An aircraft similar to an airplane but without an engine, supported by currents of air. 3 A couch hung in a metal frame so as to glide back and forth.

**glim·mer** (glim′ər) *v.i.* 1 To shine with a faint, unsteady light; flicker. 2 To appear fitfully or faintly. —*n.* 1 A faint, unsteady light. 2 A momentary apprehension; glimpse: a *glimmer* of the truth. [Prob. < Scand.] —**glim′mer·ing** *n.*

**glimpse** (glimps) *n.* 1 A momentary view or look. 2 A glimmer; inkling. —*v.* **glimpsed,**

**glimps·ing** v.t. 1 To see for an instant. —v.i. 2 To look for an instant. [< Gmc.]

**glis·ten** (glis'ən) v.i. To sparkle; shine; gleam. —n. A shining. [< OE *glisnian* shine] — **glis'ten·ing·ly** adv.

**glis·ter** (glis'tər) Archaic v.i. GLISTEN. —n. GLITTER. [< MDu. *glisteren*]

**glit·ter** (glit'ər) v.i. 1 To sparkle with a gleaming light. 2 To be bright or colorful. —n. Sparkle; brilliancy. [< ON *glitra*] —**glit'ter·ing, glit'ter·y** adj.

**gloat** (glōt) v.i. 1 To look with cruel or triumphant satisfaction. 2 To think about something with exultation or avarice. [?]

**glob·al** (glō'bəl) adj. 1 Of or involving the world in its entirety: *global* war. 2 Spherical.

**globe** (glōb) n. 1 Something perfectly round; sphere. 2 The earth. 3 A spherical map of the earth or of the heavens. [< L *globus*]

**glob·ule** (glob'yōōl) n. A small globe or spherical particle. [< L *globus* ball]

**gloom** (glōōm) n. 1 Depression of the mind or spirits; melancholy. 2 Partial or total darkness. 3 A dark or gloomy place. —v.i. 1 To look sullen or dejected. 2 To be or become dark or threatening. —v.t. 3 To make dark, sad, or sullen. [< ME *glom(b)en* look sad]

**glo·ri·fy** (glôr'ə·fī, glō'rə-) v.t. ·fied, ·fy·ing 1 To honor or worship: to *glorify* God. 2 To make exalted or blessed. 3 To praise; extol. 4 To represent as better or finer than the facts warrant. [< L *gloria* glory + -FY] —**glo'ri·fi'er** n.

**glo·ri·ous** (glôr'ē·əs, glō'rē-) adj. 1 Full of glory. 2 Bestowing glory. 3 Deserving glory. 4 Extremely delightful; splendid: a *glorious* time. —**glo'ri·ous·ly** adv. —**glo'ri·ous·ness** n.

**glo·ry** (glôr'ē, glō'rē) n. pl. ·ries 1 Distinguished honor, praise, or renown. 2 Something that brings or deserves honor, praise, or renown. 3 Adoration; worshipful praise. 4 Splendor; magnificence. 5 The bliss of heaven. 6 A state of exaltation, well-being, prosperity, etc.: He was in his *glory*. 7 Radiance; brilliancy. 8 A nimbus; halo —v.i. **glo·ried, glo·ry·ing** To rejoice proudly or triumphantly; exult: with *in*. [< L *gloria*]

**gloss** (glôs, glos) n. 1 The brightness or sheen of a polished surface. 2 A deceptive or superficial appearance or show. —v.t. 1 To make smooth or lustrous, as by polishing. 2 To attempt to hide (errors, defects, etc.) by falsehood or equivocation: with *over*. — v.i. 3 To become shiny. [< Scand.] —**gloss'er** n.

**glos·sa·ry** (glos'ə·rē, glôs'-) n. pl. ·ries An explanatory list of the difficult, technical, or foreign words used in a particular work or area of knowledge. [< L *glossa* gloss²] — **glos·sar·i·al** (glo·sâr'ē·əl, glô-) adj. — **glos·sar'i·al·ly** adv. —**glos'sa·rist** n.

**glot·tis** (glot'is) n. pl. **glot·tis·es** or **glot·ti·des** (-ə·dēz) The passage between the vocal folds at the upper opening of the larynx. [< Gk. *glōtta* tongue]

**glove** (gluv) n. 1 A covering for the hand, having a separate sheath for each finger. 2 A padded, leather mitt for catching a baseball. 3 BOXING GLOVE. —v.t. **gloved, glov·ing** 1 To put gloves on. 2 To cover with or as with a glove. 3 To serve as a glove for. [< OE *glōf*]

**glow** (glō) v.i. 1 To give off light, with or without heat or flame. 2 To be bright or red, as with animation. 3 To be animated with strong emotion. 4 To be excessively hot; burn. —n. 1 Brightness or incandescence, as of a heated substance. 2 Bright color; ruddiness. 3 Strong emotion or enthusiasm. 4 Bodily warmth, as caused by exercise, etc. [< OE *glōwan*] —**glow'ing** adj. — **glow'ing·ly** adv.

**glow·er** (glou'ər) v.i. To stare with an angry frown; scowl sullenly. —n. A fierce or sullen stare. [? < Scand.] —**glow'er·ing·ly** adv.

**glue** (glōō) n. 1 A viscid cement or adhesive used to stick things together, derived from boiling animal skin, bones, and cartilage. 2 Any of a number of adhesive substances. — v.t. **glued, glu·ing** To stick together with or as with glue. [< LL *glus, glutis*] —**glue'y** adj.

**glum** (glum) adj. **glum·mer, glum·mest** Moody and silent; sullen. [Akin to GLOOM] —**glum'ly** adv. —**glum'ness** n.

**glut** (glut) v. **glut·ted, glut·ting** v.t. 1 To fill or supply to excess; satiate; gorge. 2 To furnish (the market) with an excessive quantity of goods so that supply exceeds demand. —v.i. 3 To eat gluttonously. —n. 1 An excessive supply; plethora. 2 The act of glutting, or the condition of being glutted. [< L *glutire* swallow]

**glu·ten** (glōōt'n) n. A tough, sticky, nutritious protein substance found in wheat and other grain. [L, glue] —**glu'te·nous** adj.

**glyc·er·in** (glis'ər·in) n. GLYCEROL. Also **glyc'er·ine.**

**gnash** (nash) v.t. 1 To grind (the teeth) together, as in rage or pain. 2 To bite with

214

grinding teeth. —*v.i.* 3 To grind the teeth together. [< Scand.]

**gnat** (nat) *n.* Any of various small, usu. biting, two-winged flies. [< OE *gnǣt*]

**gnaw** (nô) *v.* **gnawed, gnawed** or **gnawn** (nôn), **gnaw·ing** *v.t.* 1 To bite or eat away little by little. 2 To make by gnawing. 3 To bite on repeatedly. 4 To wear away; erode. 5 To torment or oppress with fear, pain, etc. —*v.i.* 6 To bite or chew, or corrode persistently. 7 To cause constant worry, pain, etc. [< OE *gnagan*] —**gnaw′er** *n.* —**gnaw′ing** *adj., n.* —**gnaw′ing·ly** *adv.*

**goal** (gōl) *n.* 1 A point, end, or place that one is striving to reach: the *goal* of a race; a *goal* in life. 2 In certain games, the area or object that a ball, puck, etc., must reach to score; also, the act of making such a score or the score so made. [ME *gol*]

**goat** (gōt) *n.* 1 Any of various agile, bearded, hollow-horned mammals related to the sheep and including wild and domesticated forms. 2 A lecherous man. 3 *Slang* SCAPEGOAT. —**get one's goat** *Slang* To anger or annoy by teasing, tormenting, etc. [< OE *gāt*] —**goat′ish** *adj.* —**goat′ish·ly** *adv.* —**goat′ish·ness** *n.*

**gob·ble** (gob′əl) *n.* The sound made by the male turkey. —*v.i.* **gob·bled, gob·bling** To utter a gobble. [Var. of GABBLE]

**gob·ble·dy·gook** (gob′əl·dē·gook′) *n. Informal* Involved, pedantic, and pompous talk or writing. Also **gob′ble·de·gook′.**

*Gobbledygook* usually refers to wordiness, the unnecessary use of long words, and a stuffy style often encountered in bureaucratic memoranda. "The writer is disposed to regard as contrary to efficient office procedure the utilization of government communications apparatus to conduct non-government business," for example, means "Don't use our phones to conduct your personal business."

**goi·ter** (goi′tər) *n.* A chronic enlargement of the thyroid gland, often visible as a swelling on the front part of the neck. Also **goi′tre.** [< L *guttur* throat] —**goi′trous** *adj.*

**golf** (gôlf, golf, gôf, gof) *n.* An outdoor game played on a large course with a small hard ball and a set of clubs, the object being to direct the ball into a series of holes in as few strokes as possible. —*v.i.* To play golf. [ME] —**golf′er** *n.*

**Go·mor·rah** (gə·môr′ə, -mor′ə) *n.* In the Bible, a city on the shore of the Dead Sea. Also **Go·mor′rha.** See SODOM.

**gon·or·rhe·a** (gon′ə·rē′ə) *n.* A venereal disease affecting the mucous membrane of the genital organs, usu. characterized by inflammation and a purulent discharge. Also **gon′or·rhoe′a.** [< Gk. *gonos* seed + *rheein* flow] —**gon′or·rhe′al, gon′or·rhoe′al** *adj.*

**good-by** (good′bī′) *adj., n. & interj. pl.* **-bys** (-bīz′) Farewell. Also **good-bye.** [Contraction of *God be with you*]

**goose** (gōōs) *n. pl.* **geese** 1 One of a subfamily of wild or domesticated web-footed birds larger than ducks and smaller than swans. 2 The female of the goose: distinguished from *gander.* 3 *pl.* **goos·es** A tailor's heavy pressing iron, having a curved handle. 4 A silly creature; ninny. —**cook one's goose** *Informal* To spoil one's chances. [< OE *gōs*]

**goose·ber·ry** (gōōs′ber′ē, -bər·ē, gōōz′-) *n. pl.* **·ries** 1 The tart fruit of a spiny shrub. 2 This shrub. [?GOOSE[1] + BERRY]

**go·pher** (gō′fər) *n.* 1 A burrowing North American rodent, esp. one with large cheek pouches. 2 One of various western North American ground squirrels. 3 A large, burrowing land tortoise of the s U.S. [?]

**gorge** (gôrj) *n.* 1 A deep, narrow ravine or passage. 2 A jam: an ice *gorge.* 3 The throat or gullet. 4 The act of gorging. 5 That which is gorged, as a full meal. 6 Anger, disgust, etc.: to make one's *gorge* rise. —*v.* **gorged, gorg·ing** *v.t.* 1 To stuff with food; glut. 2 To swallow gluttonously; gulp down. —*v.i.* 3 To stuff oneself with food. [< L *gurges* a whirlpool] —**gor′ger** *n.*

**gor·geous** (gôr′jəs) *adj.* 1 Resplendently beautiful, esp. as to color: a *gorgeous* sunset. 2 *Informal* Very pretty, delightful, amusing, etc. [< OF *gorgias* elegant] —**gor′geous·ly** *adv.* —**gor′geous·ness** *n.*

**go·ril·la** (gə·ril′ə) *n.* 1 An African anthropoid ape about five and a half feet tall with a massive body and limbs, long arms, and tusklike canine teeth. 2 *Slang* A tough person, esp. a gangster. [< Gk. *Gorillai,* an African tribe]

**gos·sa·mer** (gos′ə·mər) *n.* 1 A fine thread of spider's silk, usu. floating in the air. 2 A fine, transparent fabric. 3 Something fine and filmy, as gossamer. —*adj.* Thin and light as gauze; flimsy: also **gos′sa·mer·y.** [ME, Indian summer]

**gos·sip** (gos′əp) *n.* 1 Mischievous or idle talk, usu. about the affairs of others. 2 One who tattles or talks idly: also **gos′sip·er.** —*v.i.* To talk idly, usu. about the affairs of others. [< OE *god sibb* a godparent] —**gos′ sip·y** *adj.*

**gouge** (gouj) *n.* 1 A chisel having a curved, hollow blade, used for making grooves, etc. 2 A groove made, or as if made, by it. 3 *Informal* Stealing or cheating. —*v.t.* **gouged, goug·ing** 1 To cut or scoop out with or as with a gouge. 2 To scoop, force, or tear out. 3 *Informal* To cheat; also, to charge exorbitant prices to. [< LL *gulbia*] —**goug′er** *n.*

**gourd** (gôrd, gōrd, gŏōrd) *n.* 1 The fruit with a hard rind, as pumpkin or squash, of various trailing plants or vines. 2 The plant producing such fruit. 3 Any of various items made from the rinds of such fruit, as dippers, bowls, rattles, etc. [< L *cucurbita*]

**gour·mand** (gŏōr′mənd; *Fr.* gŏōr·män′) *n.* A person who takes great pleasure in eating and drinking, but without the knowledge or discrimination of a gourmet. [< OF, a glutton]

**gour·met** (gŏōr·mā′; *Fr.* gŏōr·me′) *n.* A person who has a considerable knowledge and appreciation of fine foods and wines. [F < OF, a winetaster]

**gout** (gout) *n.* 1 A disease characterized by painful inflammation of a joint, as of the great toe, and an excess of uric acid in the blood. 2 A drop; clot. [< L *gutta* a drop]

**gov·ern** (guv′ərn) *v.t.* 1 To rule or control by right or authority. 2 To control or influence morally or physically. 3 To serve as a rule or regulation for; determine: This decision *governed* the case. 4 To discipline or curb. —*v.i.* 5 To exercise authority. [< L *gubernare* to steer] —**gov′ern·a·ble** *adj.* —**gov′ern·ance** (-ər·nəns) *n.*

**gown** (goun) *n.* 1 A woman's dress, esp. when elegant or costly. 2 A long and loose outer robe worn as a distinctive or official habit, as by judges, clergymen, etc. 3 Any loose usu. long outer garment. 4 Those people associated administratively or educationally with a college or university in a town: town and *gown.* —*v.t. & v.i.* To dress in a gown. [< Med. L *gunna* a loose robe]

**grab** (grab) *v.* **grabbed, grab·bing** *v.t.* 1 To grasp or seize forcibly or suddenly. 2 To take possession of violently or dishonestly. —*v.i.* 3 To make a sudden grasp. 4 *Slang* To involve or hold emotionally; affect. —*n.* 1 The act of grabbing, or that which is grabbed. 2 An apparatus for grappling. — **up for grabs** *Slang* Available to anyone with the means or money. [< MDu. *grabben*] — **grab′ber** *n.*

**grace** (grās) *n.* 1 Beauty or harmony of form, movement, manner, mode of expression, etc. 2 Any attractive characteristic, quality, etc. 3 Social aptness or thoughtfulness. 4 An extension of time granted, as in the payment of a debt. 5 *Theol.* a The love of God toward mankind. b A state of mind or spirit that is pleasing to God. c A power coming from God that enables one to achieve such a state. d Any divine favor. 6 A short prayer before or after meals. 7 Good will; favor. 8 *Music* An ornament, as a trill or turn. —*v.t.* **graced, grac·ing** 1 To add grace and beauty to; adorn. 2 To dignify; honor. 3 *Music* To ornament with grace notes or other embellishments. [< L *gratia* favor]

**gra·cious** (grā′shəs) *adj.* 1 Kind, courteous, and affable. 2 Compassionate; lenient. 3 Pleasantly luxurious and comfortable: *gracious* living. —**gra′cious·ly** *adv.* —**gra′cious·ness** *n.* —**Syn.** 1 polite, cordial, amiable. 2 benevolent, considerate, sympathetic.

**gra·da·tion** (grā·dā′shən) *n.* 1 Orderly or continuous change by steps or degrees from one size, quality, state, etc., to another. 2 A step, degree, rank, or relative position in a graded series. 3 The act or process of arranging in grades or stages. [< L *gradatio* a going by steps <*gradus* a step] —**gra·da′tion·al** *adj.* —**gra·da′tion·al·ly** *adv.*

**grad·u·al** (graj′ŏō·əl) *adj.* Moving, changing, developing, etc., slowly and by degrees. [< L *gradus* a step] —**grad′u·al·ly** *adv.* — **grad′u·al·ness** *n.*

**grad·u·ate** (graj′ŏō·āt) *v.* **·at·ed, ·at·ing** *v.t.* 1 To grant a diploma or degree to. 2 To mark in units or degrees, as a thermometer scale; calibrate. 3 To arrange into grades or divisions, as according to size or quality. — *v.i.* 4 To receive a diploma or degree indicating completion of a course of study. 5 To change by degrees. —*n.* (graj′ŏō·it) 1 One who has completed any academic or professional course. 2 A graduated vessel used in measuring liquids, etc. —*adj.* (graj′ŏō·it) 1 Having a degree or diploma from a college, school, etc. 2 Designed for or pertaining to students working towards a degree beyond the bachelor's. [< L *gradus* step, degree] — **grad′u·a′tor** *n.*

**graft** (graft, gräft) *n.* 1 A piece of living plant or animal tissue excised and inserted in a new site in the same or a different organism. 2 The juncture between such a graft and the place where it is inserted. 3 A union resembling a graft. —*v.t.* **1** To implant (tissue) in a new site in a living organism. —*v.i.* **2** To insert grafts. **3** To be or become grafted. [< LL *graphium* stylus < Gk. *graphein* write] —**graft′age** (-ij), **graft′er** *n.*

**grain** (grān) *n.* **1** A seed or kernel, as of wheat, corn, rice, etc. **2** Any of the common cereal plants, as wheat, oats, rye, barley, etc. **3** Any minute, hard particle, as of sugar or sand. **4** Any very small amount: a *grain* of sense. **5** The arrangement or direction of particles or fibers, as of wood, stone, leather, etc. **6** The patterns produced on a surface by such arrangements or directions. **7** The smallest unit used in the systems of weights of the U.S. and Great Britain. **8** The innate quality or character of a thing. **9** Natural disposition or nature. —*v.t.* **1** To form into grains; granulate. **2** To paint or stain in imitation of the grain of wood, marble, etc. —*v.i.* **3** To form grains. [< L *granum* a seed]

**gram** (gram) *n.* A metric unit of mass or weight, equal to $10^{-3}$ (0.0001) kilogram, or about 0.035 ounce. [< Gk. *gramma* letter, small thing]

**gram·mar** (gram′ər) *n.* **1** The systematic analysis of the classes and structure of words (morphology) and of their arrangements and interrelationships in larger constructions (syntax). **2** A system of morphological and syntactical rules and principles for speaking and writing a given language. **3** A treatise or book dealing with such rules. **4** Speech or writing considered with regard to current standards of correctness. **5** The elements of any science or art, or a book or treatise dealing with them. [< Gk. *grammatikē (technē)* literary (art)]

**gram·mat·i·cal** (grə·mat′i·kəl) *adj.* **1** Conforming to the principles of standard speech or writing. **2** Of or pertaining to grammar. —**gram·mat′i·cal·ly** *adv.* —**gram·mat′i·cal·ness** *n.*

**gran·a·ry** (grā′nər·ē, gran′ər-) *n. pl. pl.* **·ries** **1** A storehouse for grain. **2** A country or region where grain grows in abundance. [< L *granum* grain]

**grand** (grand) *adj.* **1** Of imposing character or aspect; magnificent, as in size, beauty, etc. **2** Main; principal: the *grand* hall. **3** Preeminent; noble, distinguished. **4** Highest in rank or order: a *grand* duke. **5** Pretentiously haughty or arrogant. **6** Lofty; exalted: a *grand* style. **7** Complete; overall: the *grand* total. **8** *Informal* Very good, excellent, etc.: We had a *grand* time. —*n.* **1** A grand piano. **2** *Slang* One thousand dollars. [< L *grandis*] —**grand′ly** *adv.* —**grand′ness** *n.* —**Syn.** **1** great, mighty, impressive, sublime. **5** ostentatious, showy, pompous. **6** elevated, eloquent, sublime.

**gran·deur** (gran′jər, -jŏōr) *n.* The quality of being grand; magnificence; sublimity.

**gran·dil·o·quent** (gran·dil′ə·kwənt) *adj.* Speaking in or characterized by a pompous or bombastic style. [< L < *grandis* great + *loqui* speak] —**gran·dil′o·quence** *n.*

**grant** (grant, gränt) *v.t.* **1** To give or accord, as permission, a request, etc. **2** To confer or bestow, as a privilege, charter, favor, etc. **3** To admit as true, esp. something not proved, as for the sake of argument; concede. **4** To transfer (property), esp. by deed. —*n.* **1** The act of granting. **2** Something granted, as property, funds for a specific purpose, etc. [< AF *granter*, ult. < L *credere* believe] —**grant′a·ble** *adj.* —**grant′er**, *Law* **grant′or** *n.*

**gran·u·lar** (gran′yə·lər) *adj.* **1** Composed of, like, or containing grains or granules. **2** Having a grainy surface. Also **gran′u·lose** (-lōs). —**gran′u·lar′i·ty** (-lar′ə·tē) *n.*

**gran·ule** (gran′yōōl) *n.* A small grain or particle.

**grape** (grāp) *n.* **1** The smooth-skinned, edible, juicy, berrylike fruit of various species of the grapevine, from which most wines are made. **2** Any grapevine yielding this fruit. **3** Figuratively, wine. **4** A dark blue color with a slight reddish tint. [< OF, bunch of grapes, hook < Gmc.]

**graph·ic** (graf′ik) *adj.* **1** Vividly effective and detailed. **2** Of, like, or represented by graphs. **3** Of, pertaining to, or expressed in handwriting. **4** Written or expressed by means of signs, symbols, etc. **5** Of or pertaining to the graphic arts. Also **graph′i·cal.** [< Gk. *graphein* write] —**graph′i·cal·ly, graph′ic·ly** *adv.*

**graph·ite** (graf′īt) *n.* A soft, black, chemically inert, crystalline form of carbon with a metallic luster and oily feel, used as a lubricant and in the making of lead pencils. [< Gk. *graphein* write] —**gra·phit·ic** (grə·fit′ik) *adj.*

**grap·ple** (grap′əl) *v.* **grap·pled, grap·pling** *v.t.* **1** To take hold of; grasp firmly. —*v.i.* **2** To use a grapnel. **3** To seize or come to grips with another, as in wrestling. **4** To deal or contend: with *with.* —*n.* **1** A close hold, as in wrestling. 2 GRAPNEL (def. 1). [<OF *grappil* grapnel] —**grap′pler** *n.*

**grasp** (grasp, gräsp) *v.t.* 1 To lay hold of with or as with the hand; grip. 2 To seize greedily or eagerly; snatch. 3 To take hold of with the mind; understand. —*v.i.* 4 To make grasping motions. —**grasp at** 1 To try to seize. 2 To accept eagerly or desperately. —*n.* 1 The act of seizing or grasping. 2 The ability to seize and hold. 3 Power of comprehension; understanding. [ME *graspen*] —**grasp′er** *n.*

**grass** (gras, gräs) *n.* 1 The vegetation typically forming a green carpet over the ground of lawns, pastures, etc. 2 Any of a large family of monocotyledons, as wheat, oats, sugar cane, bamboo, and various forage plants. 3 Ground covered with grass; lawn or pasture. 4 Any plants resembling the true grasses, as the sedges, the rushes, etc. 5 *Slang* MARIHUANA. —*v.t.* 1 To cover with grass or turf. 2 To feed with grass; pasture. —*v.i.* 3 To graze on grass. 4 To produce grass; become covered with grass. [< OE *græs*]

**grass·hop·per** (gras′hop′ər, gräs′-) *n.* Any of several insects, including the locust and katydid, having powerful hind legs adapted for leaping.

**grate** (grāt) *n.* 1 A framework of bars to hold fuel in burning. 2 A similar framework used to prohibit entry through a window or other opening. 3 A fireplace. —*v.t.* **grat·ed, grat·ing** To fit with a grate or grates. [<L *cratis* a lattice]

**grate·ful** (grāt′fəl) *adj.* 1 Having or expressing gratitude; thankful. 2 Affording gratification; pleasurable; agreeable. [<L *gratus* pleasing + -FUL] —**grate′ful·ly** *adv.* —**grate′ful·ness** *n.* **Syn.** 1 obliged, beholden, indebted to, under obligation.

**grat·i·fi·ca·tion** (grat′ə·fə·kā′shən) *n.* 1 The act of gratifying or the state of being gratified. 2 Something that gratifies.

**grat·i·fy** (grat′ə·fī) *v.t.* **·fied, ·fy·ing** 1 To give pleasure or satisfaction to. 2 To satisfy or indulge, as a desire or need. [<L *gratus* pleasing + -FY] —**grat′i·fi′er** *n.* —**grat′i·fy′ ing** *adj.* —**grat′i·fy′ing·ly** *adv.*

**grat·i·tude** (grat′ə·t*y*ōōd) *n.* A feeling of thankfulness.

**gra·tu·i·tous** (grə·t*y*ōō′ə·təs) *adj.* Given freely without charge or conditions. 2 Without cause; uncalled for; unnecessary. [<L *gratuitus* given as a favor] —**gra·tu′i·tous·ly** *adv.* —**gra·tu′i·tous·ness** *n.*

**gra·tu·i·ty** (grə·t*y*ōō′ə·tē) *n. pl.* **·ties** 1 A present. 2 Money given in return for service, etc.; a tip.

**grave¹** (grāv) *adj.* **grav·er, grav·est** 1 Of momentous import; weighty; important. 2 Severely dangerous; critical. 3 Serious; dignified; sedate, as in manner or speech. 4 Somber in color or fashion. 5 Low in tone or pitch. —*n.* (grāv, gräv) A mark (`) used in French to indicate the open quality of *e* or in English to indicate a falling inflection or the pronunciation of a final *ed*, as in prepar*èd*: also **grave accent**. [<L *gravis* heavy] —**grave′ly** *adv.* —**grave′ness** *n.*

**grave²** (grāv) *n.* 1 A place for the burial of a dead body, usu. an excavation in the ground. 2 A tomb. —**the grave** Death. [< OE *græf*]

**grav·el** (grav′əl) *n.* 1 A mixture of small, usu. rounded, pebbles or stones. 2 *Pathol.* The formation in the kidneys of numerous granular concretions. —*v.t.* **grav·eled** or **grav·elled, grav·el·ing** or **grav·el·ling** 1 To cover or fill with gravel. 2 To bring up short, as in embarrassment or confusion. 3 *Informal* To irritate; annoy. [<OF *grave* sand] —**grav′el·ly, grav′el·y** *adj.*

**grave·yard** (grāv′yärd′) *n.* A burial place; a cemetery.

**grav·i·tate** (grav′ə·tāt) *v.i.* **·tat·ed, ·tat·ing** 1 To be attracted by force of gravity. 2 To move or be attracted as though drawn by a powerful force: with *to* or *toward.* 3 To sink or fall to the lowest level. —**grav′i·tat′er** *n.* —**grav′i·ta′tive** *adj.*

**grav·i·ta·tion** (grav′ə·tā′shən) *n.* 1 *Physics* The force whereby any two bodies attract each other in proportion to the product of their masses and inversely as the square of the distance between them. 2 The act or process of gravitating. —**grav′i·ta′tion·al** *adj.* —**grav′i·ta′tion·al·ly** *adv.*

**grav·i·ty** (grav′ə·tē) *n. pl.* **·ties** 1 The force that attracts bodies toward the center of the earth. 2 A similar force exerted on other bodies by any object in space. 3 Weight. 4 Gravitation. 5 Extreme importance; seriousness. 6 Danger; peril: the *gravity* of their plight. 7 Dignified reserve; sedateness. —*adj.* Employing gravity; worked by gravity. [< L *gravis* heavy]

**gra·vy** (grā′vē) *n. pl.* **·vies** 1 The juice that exudes from meat being cooked. 2 A sauce made from these juices. 3 *Slang* Any added, easily acquired payment or income. [ME *gravey*]

**gray** (grā) *adj.* 1 Of a color intermediate between black and white and lacking hue. 2 Having gray hair; hoary. 3 Old; aged. —*n.* 1 A color between black and white with no hue. 2 Something gray, esp. a gray animal. —*v.t.* & *v.i.* To make or become gray. [< OE *grǣg*] —**gray′ly** *adv.* —**gray′ness** *n.*

**graze**[1] (grāz) *v.* **grazed, graz·ing** *v.i.* 1 To feed upon growing grass or herbage. —*v.i.* 2 To put (cattle, etc.) to feed on growing grass or herbage. —*n.* The act of cropping or feeding upon growing grass or the like. [< OE *grasian* < *grǣs* grass] —**graz′er** *n.*

**graze**[2] (grāz) *v.* **grazed, graz·ing** *v.t.* 1 To touch or rub against lightly in passing. 2 To scrape or cut slightly in passing. —*v.i.* 3 To touch lightly in passing. 4 To scrape slightly. —*n.* 1 A light or passing touch. 2 A scrape or abrasion. [?] —**graz′er** *n.* —**graz′ing·ly** *adv.*

**grease** (grēs) *n.* 1 Animal fat, esp. when soft or melted. 2 A thick, oily substance derived from petroleum and used as a lubricant. —*v.t.* (grēs, grēz) **greased, greas·ing** 1 To apply grease to. 2 *Slang* To influence by gifts or bribes. [< L *crassus* fat] —**greas′er** *n.*

**great** (grāt) *adj.* 1 Very large in size, expanse, etc.; immense; vast. 2 Large in number, quantity, etc.: a *great* assembly. 3 Long in extent or time: a *great* distance; a *great* while. 4 Of very considerable degree, intensity, etc.: a *great* sorrow. 5 Unusually important, impressive, or remarkable: a *great* achievement. 6 Of unusual excellence; superior; eminent: a *great* dancer. 7 Noble and elevated, as in character, action, feeling, etc.: a *great* humanitarian. 8 Most important of its kind; chief; main: the *great* prize. 9 *Informal* Adept; skilled: usu. with *at*: *great* at sports. 10 *Informal* Excellent; first-rate: to have a *great* time. 11 More remote by a single generation than the relationship indicated: used in combination with a hyphen: *great*-uncle, *great*-grandson. —*adv. Informal* Very well. —*n. Usu. pl.* A person who is great, noble, distinguished, etc.: with *the:* one of the *greats.* [< OE *grēat*] —**great′ly** *adv.* —**great′ness** *n.*

**greed** (grēd) *n.* Eager and selfish desire for something. [Back formation < GREEDY]

**greet** (grēt) *v.t.* 1 To address words of friendliness, courtesy, respect, etc., to, as in speaking or writing. 2 To receive or meet in a specified manner. 3 To come into the sight or awareness of: The sea *greeted* their eyes. [< OE *grētan*] —**greet′er** *n.*

**greet·ing** (grē′ting) *n.* 1 The act or words of one who greets. 2 *Often pl.* A message of welcome or regards.

**gre·gar·i·ous** (gri-gâr′ē·əs) *adj.* 1 Habitually living in flocks, herds, or companies. 2 Of or pertaining to a flock or herd. 3 Socially outgoing and affable. [< L *grex, gregis* a flock] —**gre·gar′i·ous·ly** *adv.* —**gre·gar′i·ous·ness** *n.*

**grem·lin** (grem′lin) *n.* 1 A mischievous, invisible imp said to ride airplanes and cause mechanical trouble. 2 Any unidentified source of trouble. [?]

**gre·nade** (gri·nād′) *n.* 1 A small bomb designed to be thrown by hand or fired from a rifle or launching device. 2 A glass bottle containing a flammable mixture, tear gas, etc., that is ignited or dispersed when the bottle is broken. [F, a pomegranate]

**grey·hound** (grā′hound′) *n.* One of a breed of tall, slender dogs with a long narrow head and smooth short coat, used for hunting and racing. [<OE *grīghund*]

**grid·dle** (grid′l) *n.* A shallow pan for baking or frying pancakes. —*v.t.* **grid·dled, grid·dling** To cook on a griddle. [<L *cratis* wickerwork]

**grid·i·ron** (grid′ī′ərn) *n.* 1 A framework of metal bars for broiling or cooking foods. 2 Any object resembling a cooking gridiron. 3 A football field. [ME *gredire*]

**grief** (grēf) *n.* 1 Intense sorrow or mental suffering resulting from loss, affliction, regret, etc. 2 A cause of such sorrow. [< OF *grever* grieve] —**Syn.** 1 affliction, agony, distress, sadness, tribulation, trouble, woe.

**griev·ance** (grē′vəns) *n.* 1 Something that annoys, causes resentment, etc. 2 A written or vocal complaint against a wrong suffered.

**grieve** (grēv) *v.* **grieved, griev·ing** *v.t.* 1 To cause great sorrow or grief to; make sad. —*v.i.* 2 To feel sorrow or grief; mourn; lament. [<L *gravis* heavy] —**griev′er** *n.* —**griev′ing** *adj.* —**griev′ing·ly** *adv.*

**grill** (gril) *v.t.* 1 To cook on a gridiron; broil. 2 To torture with heat. 3 To cross-examine persistently and searchingly. —*v.i.* 4 To be cooked on a gridiron. —*n.* 1 A gridiron. 2 That which is broiled on a gridiron. 3 A grillroom. 4 A grille. [<OF *greil*]

**grim** (grim) *adj.* **grim·mer, grim·mest** 1 Stern and forbidding in aspect or nature. 2 Fierce; ferocious: a *grim* attack. 3 Unyielding; resolute: *grim* courage. **4** Unpleasant; repellent: the *grim* job of counting bodies. [< OE] —**grim′ly** *adv.* —**grim′ness** *n.*

**gri·mace** (grim′əs, gri·mās′) *n.* A distortion of the face, usu. occasioned by annoyance, disgust, contempt, etc.; a wry face. —*v.i.* ·**maced**, ·**mac·ing** To make grimaces. [< MF < Gmc.] —**gri′mac·er** *n.*

**grime** (grīm) *n.* Dirt or soot, esp. when rubbed into a surface. —*v.t.* **grimed**, **grim·ing** To make dirty; begrime. [< MDu. *grīme*]

**grin** (grin) *v.* **grinned**, **grin·ning** *v.i.* **1** To smile broadly. **2** To draw back the lips so as to show the teeth, as in pain, rage, etc. —*n.* The act or facial look of grinning. [< OE *grennian*] —**grin′ner** *n.* —**grin′ning·ly** *adv.*

**grind** (grīnd) *v.* **ground**, **grind·ing** *v.t.* **1** To sharpen, polish, or shape by friction. **2** To reduce to fine particles, as by crushing or friction. **3** To rub or press gratingly or harshly: to *grind* one's teeth. **4** To oppress; harass cruelly. **5** To operate by turning a crank, as a coffee mill. **6** To produce by or as by grinding. **7** *Informal* To teach laboriously. —*v.i.* **8** To perform the operation of grinding. **9** To undergo grinding. **10** To rub; grate. **11** *Informal* To study or work hard and steadily. —*n.* **1** The act of grinding. **2** A degree of fineness obtained by grinding. **3** *Informal* Difficult, tedious work or study. **4** *Informal* A hard-working student. [< OE *grindan*] —**grind′ing** *adj.*, *n.* —**grind′ing·ly** *adv.*

**grip** (grip) *n.* **1** The act of grasping firmly or holding fast, as with the hands, teeth, etc. **2** The manner of doing this. **3** The power or strength to do this: He lost his *grip.* **4** Ability to understand mentally. **5** Self-control; mastery. **6** Control; power: in the *grip* of circumstances. **7** A valise; gripsack. **8** That part of a thing by which it is grasped. **9** One of various mechanical grasping devices. **10** *Slang* A stagehand; a scene-shifter. —*v.* **gripped** or **gript**, **grip·ping** *v.t.* **1** To take firm hold of with or as with the hand; hold onto tightly. **2** To join or attach securely with a grip. **3** To seize or capture, as the mind or imagination of. —*v.i.* **4** To take firm hold. **5** To take hold of the attention, imagination, etc. [< OE *gripe* < *gripan* seize] —**grip′per** *n.* —**grip′ping** *adj.* —**grip′ping·ly** *adv.*

**gris·ly** (griz′lē) *adj.* ·**li·er**, ·**li·est** Terrifying; horrible. [< OE *grislic*] —**gris′li·ness** *n.*

**gris·tle** (gris′əl) *n.* Cartilage, esp. in meat. [< OE] —**gris′tly** *adj.* —**gris′tli·ness** *n.*

**Grit** (grit) *Can.* *n.* A member of the Liberal Party. —*adj.* Of or pertaining to the Liberal Party.

**groan** (grōn) *v.i.* **1** To utter a low, prolonged sound of or as of pain, sorrow, etc. **2** To be oppressed or overburdened. —*v.t.* **3** To utter or express with groans. —*n.* A low moaning sound uttered in anguish, distress, or derision. [< OE *grānian*] —**groan′er** *n.* —**groan′ing** *adj.*, *n.* —**groan′ing·ly** *adv.*

**gro·cer** (grō′sər) *n.* A retail dealer in food supplies and other household articles. [< OF *grossier*, lit., one who trades in grosses]

**groin** (groin) *n.* **1** The fleshy hollow where the thigh joins the abdomen. **2** *Archit.* The line of intersection of two vaults. • See VAULT. —*v.t.* To build with or form into groins. [? < OE *grynde* abyss, hollow]

**groom** (grōōm, grŏŏm) *n.* **1** A person who cares for horses in the stable. **2** BRIDEGROOM. —*v.t.* **1** To take care of; esp. to clean, curry, and brush (a horse). **2** To make neat, clean, and smart. **3** To prepare by training and developing, as for political or other service. [ME *grom*]

**groove** (grōōv) *n.* **1** A furrow, channel, or long hollow, esp. one cut by a tool for something to fit into or work in. **2** A fixed routine in the affairs of life. —*v.t.* **grooved**, **groov·ing** **1** To form a groove in. **2** To fix in a groove. **3** *Slang* To take satisfaction or delight in; dig. —*v.i.* **4** *Slang* To find satisfaction or delight. [< MDu. *groeve*] —**groov′er** *n.*

**grope** (grōp) *v.* **groped**, **grop·ing** *v.i.* To feel about with or as with the hands, as in the dark; feel one's way. —*v.t.* To seek out or find by or as by groping. [< OE *grāpian*.] —**grop′er** *n.* —**grop′ing** *adj.*

**gross** (grōs) *adj.* **1** Conspicuously bad; glaring; flagrant: a *gross* lie or error. **2** Excessively or repulsively large and coarse. **3** Vulgar; obscene; indelicate. **4** Lacking in perception or feeling; dull; insensitive. **5** Coarse in texture or composition. **6** Dense; thick. **7** Undiminished by deductions; total; entire: *gross* earnings. —*n.* **1** *pl.* **gross** Twelve dozen, as a unit. **2** *pl.* **gross·es** The total or entire amount. —**in the gross 1** In bulk; all together. **2** Wholesale: also **by the gross.** —*v.t.* & *v.i.* To make or earn (total profit) before deduction of expenses, taxes, etc. [< LL *grossus* thick] —**gross′ly** *adv.* —**gross′ness** *n.* —**Syn.** *adj.* **1** dreadful, deplorable, awful shocking, heinous. **2** lumpish, hulking, bulky. 3 improper, unseemly, coarse.

gro·tesque (grō·tesk´) adj. 1 Bizarre or extravagantly odd in shape, look, design, composition, etc. 2 Absurdly odd or eccentric; fantastically strange: grotesque behavior. —n. Something grotesque. [< Ital. grotta a grotto, excavation] —gro·tesque´ly adv. —gro·tesque´ness n.

ground (ground) n. 1 The firm, solid portion of the earth at or near the surface. 2 Soil; earth; dirt. 3 Any tract or portion of land, esp. one put to special use: a parade ground. 4 Often pl. Private land, esp. the lawns, gardens, etc., surrounding a home or estate. 5 A topic, discussion or subject, or any part thereof: to cover the same old ground. 6 Often pl. A sufficient cause; good reason; basis: grounds for divorce. 7 Often pl. A basic proposition or premise; foundation: grounds for an argument. 8 The background or main surface, as of a painting. 9 pl. The particles that settle at the bottom of a liquid; dregs. 10 a A point in an electric circuit considered to have zero potential and used as a reference for other voltages. b A point of this kind actually connected to the earth. —cover ground 1 To proceed rapidly or a certain distance. 2 To accomplish quickly and efficiently. —from the ground up In a detailed manner; thoroughly. —gain ground 1 To make progress. 2 To gain favor, popularity, power, etc. —get off the ground To get underway; develop. —give ground To concede; yield. —hold (or stand) one's ground To maintain one's position, opinions, etc. —lose ground 1 To slip backward; drop behind. 2 To lose in favor, popularity, power, etc. —on home (or one's own) ground 1 At home. 2 On a familiar topic, subject, etc. —adj. 1 Being on the ground or on a level with it. 2 Growing or living on or in the ground. 3 Fundamental. —v.t. 1 To put, place, or set on the ground. 2 To fix firmly on a basis; found; establish. 3 To train (someone) in first principles or elements. 4 To cause (an airplane or pilot) to stay on the ground. 5 Naut. To cause to run aground, as a ship. 6 To furnish (a surface) with a ground or background for painting, etc. 7 To connect (an electric circuit or device) to a ground. —v.i. 8 To come or fall to the ground. 9 In baseball: a To hit a grounder. b To be retired on

a grounder: usu. with out. 10 Naut. To run aground. [< OE grund]

ground zero The point on the ground directly beneath or above the detonation of a nuclear bomb.

group (grōōp) n. 1 A number of closely placed or associated persons or things regarded as a unit. 2 A number of individuals classed together because of common characteristics, interests, etc. 3 Figures or objects forming a harmonious unit of design. 4 Chem. a A number of connected atoms constituting part of a molecule. b A set of elements having similar properties. 5 In the U.S. Air Force, a unit constituting a subdivision of a wing. 6 In the U.S. Army or Marine Corps, a tactical unit consisting of two or more battalions. —v.t. 1 To place or classify in a group or groups. —v.i. 2 To form a group or groups. [< Ital. groppo knot, lump < Gmc.]

grove (grōv) n. A small wood or group of trees, esp. without underbrush. [< OE gráf]

grov·el (gruv´əl, grov´-) v.i. grov·eled or grov·elled, grov·el·ing or grov·el·ling 1 To crawl face downward or lie prostrate, as in servility or fear. 2 To act with abject humility. 3 To take pleasure in what is base or sensual. [Back formation < earlier groveling, prone < ON á grúfu face down] —grov´el·er or grov´el·er n.

grow (grō) v. grew, grown, grow·ing v.i. 1 To increase in size by assimilation of nourishment or a natural process. 2 To progress toward maturity. 3 To sprout and develop. 4 To flourish; thrive. 5 To increase in size, quantity, intensity, etc. 6 To become. 7 To come to be; develop. 8 To become fixed or attached by or as by growth. —v.t. 9 To cause to grow; raise by cultivation. 10 To produce or develop by a natural process. 11 To cover with a growth: used in the passive. —grow on To become gradually more pleasing or important to. —grow up To become an adult. [< OE grōwan] —grow´er n.

growl (groul) n. 1 A low, guttural sound, as that made by an angry animal. 2 A sound similar to this. —v.i. 1 To utter a growl. 2 To speak in a gruff, surly manner. 3 To rumble, as distant thunder. —v.t. 4 To express by growling. [ME groulen to rumble] —growl´er n.

growth (grōth) n. 1 The process of growing. 2 A stage of development or maturity reached in growing. 3 An increase in size, number, etc. 4 Something produced by or in the process of growing. 5 An abnormal formation, as a wart, tumor, etc.

**grub** (grub) v. **grubbed, grub·bing** v.i. 1 To dig in the ground. 2 To drudge; toil. 3 To make careful or plodding search; rummage. —v.t. 4 To dig up; root out. 5 To clear (ground) of roots, stumps, etc. 6 *Slang* To get by begging; mooch. —n. 1 A fat, wormlike larva, as of beetles and some other insects. 2 DRUDGE. 3 *Slang* Food. [ME *grubben*] —**grub′ber** n.

**grudge** (gruj) v.t. **grudged, grudg·ing** 1 To envy the possessions or good fortunes of (another). 2 To give or allow unwillingly and resentfully; begrudge. —n. Ill will or resentment, as for some remembered wrong. [< OF *groucher*] —**grudg′er** n. —**grudg′ing·ly** adv.

**grue·some** (grōō′səm) adj. Inspiring horror and loathing; grisly. [? < MDu. *gruwen* to shudder + -SOME] —**grue′some·ly** adv. —**grue′some·ness** n.

**gruff** (gruf) adj. 1 Rough or brusque in manner. 2 Hoarse; harsh. [< Du. *grof* rough] —**gruff′ly** adv. —**gruff′ness** n.

**grum·ble** (grum′bəl) v. **grum·bled, grum·bling** v.i. 1 To complain in a surly manner; mutter discontentedly. 2 To make growling sounds in the throat. 3 To rumble, as thunder. —v.t. 4 To say with a grumble. —n. 1 A surly complaint; discontented muttering. 2 A rumble. [? < MDu. *grommen* to growl] —**grum′bler** n. —**grum′bling·ly** adv. —**grum′bly** adj.

**grunt** (grunt) v.i. 1 To make a short, guttural sound typical of a hog. 2 To make a similar sound, as in annoyance, assent, effort, etc. —v.t. 3 To express by grunting. —n. 1 A short, guttural sound, as of a hog. 2 A chiefly tropical marine fish that makes grunting sounds. 3 *Mil. Slang* A U.S. infantryman. [< OE *grunnettan*] —**grunt′er** n.

**guar·an·tee** (gar′ən·tē′) n. 1 A pledge or formal assurance that something will meet stated specifications or that a specified act will be performed. 2 Something given as security. 3 GUARANTOR. 4 Something that assures a certain outcome. —v.t. ·teed, ·tee·ing 1 To give a guarantee for; certify or vouch for. 2 To assume responsibility for. 3 To secure against loss or damage. 4 To give assurance of; promise. [Var. of GUARANTY]

**guard** (gärd) v.t. 1 To keep protective watch over, as to shield or defend from harm or loss. 2 To maintain supervisory watch over,

as to prevent escape. 3 To keep in check; control. —v.i. 4 To take precautions: with *against*. —n. 1 One who guards, as a sentry, prison employee, etc. 2 Watchful care or supervision. 3 Protection; defense. 4 A device that protects, shields, etc. 5 A posture or attitude of defense. 6 A person or body of persons providing protection, ceremonial escort, etc. 7 In football, either of two offensive line players whose position is next to the center. 8 In basketball, either of two players covering the rear of the court. —**off (one's) guard** Unprepared for defense, protection, etc. —**on (one's) guard** On the alert; vigilant. —**stand guard** 1 To act as sentry. 2 To keep careful watch. [< OF *garder* < Gmc.] —**guard′er** n. —**Syn.** v. 1 protect, safeguard, preserve.

**guard·i·an** (gär′dē·ən) n. 1 *Law* One who guards or has protective care. 2 One legally empowered to care for the person or property of another, esp. an infant or minor. —**guard′i·an·ship** n.

**gu·ber·na·to·ri·al** (gōō′bər·nə·tôr′ē·əl, -tō′rē) adj. Of or pertaining to a governor or the office of governor. [< L *gubernare* govern]

**guer·ril·la** (gə·ril′ə) n. One of an irregular, independent band of partisan soldiers often harassing opposing troops. **Also gue·ril′la.** [< Sp. *guerra* a war] —adj. Of or carried on by guerrillas.

**guess** (ges) v.t. & v.i. 1 To form a judgment or opinion (of something) on uncertain or incomplete knowledge. 2 To judge or estimate correctly. 3 To believe; think. —n. 1 An opinion or conclusion reached by guessing. 2 The act of guessing. [Prob. < Scand.] —**guess′er** n.

**guest** (gest) n. 1 A person received or entertained by another as a visitor or recipient of hospitality. 2 One paying for lodging and services at a hotel, etc. 3 A visiting performer or participant in a program. [< ON *gestr*]

**guf·faw** (gə·fô′) n. A burst of loud, boisterous laughter. —v.i. To utter such laughter. [Imit.]

**guide** (gīd) v. **guid·ed, guid·ing** v.t. 1 To lead, accompany, direct, show the way, etc. 2 To direct the motion or action of, as a vehicle, tool, etc. 3 To lead or direct the affairs, standards, opinions, etc., of. —v.i. 4 To act as a guide. —n. 1 One who shows the way by accompanying or going in advance, as in conducting travelers, sightseers, etc. 2 One who or that which provides direction, in-

spiration, etc. 3 Something that guides or informs, as a book, sign, or set of instructions. 4 A device acting as an indicator or serving to restrict motion of a part. [< OF *guider*] —**guid′er** n.

**guided missile** An unmanned missile whose course can be altered after launch.

**guild** (gild) n. 1 In medieval times, an association of craftsmen or merchants. 2 An association of persons with kindred pursuits, interests, or aims. [< ON *gildi* payment] —**guilds′man** n. (pl. ·men)

**guile** (gīl) n. Deceitful slyness; duplicity. [< OF < Gmc.]

**guilt** (gilt) n. 1 The state or fact of having committed a crime, legal offense, or wrongdoing. 2 Responsibility for having committed a crime or wrong; culpability. 3 A feeling of blameworthiness for having committed a crime or wrong. [< OE *gylt*]

**guinea pig** 1 A domesticated rodent with short ears and no visible tail, used in biological and medical experiments. 2 Any subject of experimentation or research.

**guise** (gīz) n. 1 Outward appearance; aspect. 2 False appearance or assumed manner; pretense. 3 Garb; costume. [< OF < Gmc.]

**gui·tar** (gi·tär′) n. A musical instrument having a fretted fingerboard and usu. six strings, played by plucking. [< Gk. *kithara* lyre] —**gui·tar′ist** n.

**gulch** (gulch) n. A narrow, steep-sided ravine.

**gulf** (gulf) n. 1 A considerable area of marine water partly enclosed by an indentation of a coastline. 2 An abyss; chasm. 3 A wide separation or gap not easily bridged. —v.t. ENGULF. [< Gk. *kolpos* a bay]

**gull**[1] (gul) n. Any of various usu. gray and white aquatic birds with long wings, webbed feet, and a hooked bill. [ME]

**gull**[2] (gul) v.t. To trick; deceive; dupe. —n. One who is easily tricked or deceived; a dupe. [?]

**gul·let** (gul′it) n. 1 The passage from the mouth to the stomach; esophagus. 2 The throat. [< L *gula* throat]

**gul·ly** (gul′ē) n. pl. ·lies A channel, ravine, etc., cut in the earth by running water, as after a rainfall. —v.t. ·lied, ·ly·ing To cut or wear a gully in. [Var. of GULLET]

**gum·bo** (gum′bō) n. pl. ·bos 1 The okra or its pods. 2 A soup or stew containing okra. 3 A fine soil of the North American plains that forms a very sticky mud. [<Bantu]

**gun** (gun) n. 1 A piece of ordnance fixed in a mount, whose essential element is a metal

tube from which a projectile is launched at high velocity, usu. in a fairly flat trajectory. 2 A portable firearm, as a pistol or rifle. 3 The firing of a large gun. 4 Any device resembling a gun in form or function. 5 The throttle of an engine. —**stick to one's guns** To persist in an opinion, course of action, etc. —v. **gunned, gun·ning** v.i. 1 To go hunting with a gun. —v.t. 2 To shoot with a gun: often with *down*. 3 To open the throttle of (an engine) so as to accelerate. —**gun for** 1 To seek with intent to harm, thwart, or kill. 2 To seek eagerly. [ME *gunne*]

**gun·ner** (gun′ər) n. 1 A soldier, sailor, or member of an aircraft crew who operates a gun. 2 See GRADE. 3 One who hunts with a gun.

**gun·pow·der** (gun′pou′dər) n. An explosive mixture of potassium nitrate, charcoal, and sulfur.

**gu·ru** (gōō′rōō) n. pl. ·rus 1 One who provides instruction or spiritual leadership in Hindu mysticism. 2 A teacher or leader regarded as having special knowledge, powers, etc. [< Hind.]

**gush** (gush) v.i. 1 To flow out suddenly and in volume. 2 To produce a sudden outflow. 3 To express oneself with exaggerated sentiment or enthusiasm. —v.t. 4 To pour forth (blood, tears, etc.). —n. 1 A sudden outpouring. 2 *Informal* An exaggerated display of sentiment. [Prob. < Scand.] —**gush′ing·ly** adv. —**Syn.** spurt, spout, ⌒

**gush·er** (gush′ər) n. 1 One who or that w gushes. 2 A free-flowing oil well.

**gust** (gust) n. 1 A sudden, strong blast wind. 2 A sudden outburst of strong emo tion. —v.i. To blow in gusts.

**gus·ta·to·ry** (gus′tə·tôr′ē, -tō′rē) adj. Of or relating to the sense of taste. [< L *gustus* taste]

**gut** (gut) n. 1 The alimentary canal, esp. the intestine. 2 *Usu. pl.* The bowels. 3 CATGUT. 4 pl. *Slang* Stamina; courage; grit. —v.t. **gut·ted, gut·ting** 1 To take out the intestines of; eviscerate. 2 To destroy the interior or contents of. —adj. *Slang* 1 Central; basic; fundamental: *gut* issues. 2 Deeply felt, as though physically experienced: a *gut* conviction. [< OE *guttas* viscera]

**gut·tur·al** (gut′ər·əl) adj. 1 Pertaining to the throat. 2 Produced or formed in the throat. 3 Hoarse; harsh; rasping. 4 *Phonet.* VELAR. —n. *Phonet.* A velar sound. [< L *guttur* throat] —**gut·tur·al·i·ty** (gut′ə·ral′ə·tē), **gut′tur·al·ness** n. —**gut′tur·al·ly** adv.

**guy¹** (gī) n. A rope, cable, etc., that steadies or secures something, as a mast. —v.t. To secure with a guy. [?]

**guy²** (gī) n. 1 Informal A fellow; man. 2 Brit. A person of grotesque appearance. —v.t. To ridicule; make fun of. [< Guy Fawkes, 1570–1606, English conspirator]

**gym·na·si·um** (jim·nā′zē·əm) n. pl. ·si·ums or ·si·a (-zē·ə) 1 A building or room containing equipment for physical education activities and sports. 2 (gim·nä′zē·ŏŏm) Sometimes cap. In Germany and some other European countries, a secondary school that prepares students for universities. [L < Gk. gymnazein exercise, train naked]

**gy·ne·col·o·gy** (gī′nə·kol′ə·jē, jī′nə-, jin′ə-) n. The branch of medicine dealing with the reproductive functions and diseases of women. [< Gk. gynē, gynaikos woman + -LOGY] —gy′ne·co·log′i·cal adj. —gy′ne·col′o·gist n.

**gyp·sy** (jip′sē) n. pl. ·sies One who resembles or leads the wandering life of a Gypsy. —v.i. ·sied, sy·ing To wander from place to place in the manner of the Gypsies.

**gy·rate** (jī′rāt) v.i. ·rat·ed, ·rat·ing 1 To rotate or revolve. 2 To move in a spiral or circle. —adj. Convoluted; coiled. [< Gk. gyrus a circle] —gy·ra′tion, gy′ra·tor n. —gy·ra·to·ry (jī′rə·tôr′ē, -tō′rē) adj.

**gy·ro·scope** (jī′rə·skōp) n. An instrument consisting of a rotating mass whose axis remains fixed in space unless it is subjected to external torque. —gy′ro·scop′ic (-skop′ik) adj.

# H

**ha·bil·i·ment** (hə·bil′ə·mənt) n. 1 An article of clothing. 2 pl. Clothes; garb. [< OF habiller dress, make fit]

**hab·it** (hab′it) n. 1 A tendency toward an action or condition, which by repetition has become involuntary. 2 An action so induced. 3 Habitual condition, appearance, or temperament; physical or mental make-up. 4 Biol. A characteristic mode of growth or aspect of a plant or animal. 5 An outer garment or garments; esp., a woman's costume for horseback riding. 6 The distinctive garment of a religious order. —v.t. To furnish with a habit; clothe; dress. [< L habitus condition, dress < habere have] —Syn. n. 1 Custom, practice, routine, rule, wont.

**hab·it·a·ble** (hab′it·ə·bəl) adj. Suitable to be lived in. [< L habitare inhabit] —hab·it·a·bil·i·ty (hab′it·ə·bil′ə·tē), hab′it·a·ble·ness n. —hab′it·a·bly adv.

**hab·i·ta·tion** (hab′ə·tā′shən) n. 1 A place of residence; home. 2 The act or state of inhabiting.

**ha·bit·u·al** (hə·bich′ŏŏ·əl) adj. 1 Of, pertaining to, or constituting a habit. 2 Resulting from habit or repeated use; inveterate: a habitual liar. 3 Frequently seen, done, etc.; usual; inevitable: the habitual roar of city traffic. —ha·bit′u·al·ly adv. —ha·bit′u·al·ness n.

**ha·bit·u·ate** (hə·bich′ŏŏ·āt) v.t. ·at·ed, ·at·ing 1 To make familiar by repetition or use; accustom. 2 Informal To go to habitually; frequent. —ha·bit′u·a′tion n.

**ha·bit·u·é** (hə·bich′ŏŏ·ā′) n. A habitual visitor or frequenter of a place, such as a restaurant. [F < habituer accustom]

**hack·ney** (hak′nē) n. pl. ·neys 1 One of a breed of driving and saddle horses. 2 A horse kept for hire. 3 A coach for hire: also hackney coach. —v.t. 1 To make trite by constant use. 2 To let out or use as a hackney. —adj. Let out for hire. [ME hakeney]

**had·dock** (had′ək) n. pl. ·dock or ·docks A food fish of the North Atlantic, related to the cod. [ME]

**hag·gard** (hag′ərd) adj. Worn and gaunt in appearance. [< OF hagard wild hawk] —hag′gard·ly adv. —hag′gard·ness n. —Syn. careworn, emaciated, exhausted, wan.

**hag·gle** (hag′əl) v. hag·gled, hag·gling v.t. 1 To cut unskillfully; mangle. —v.i. 2 To argue about price or terms. —n. The act of haggling. [< ON hǫggva to cut] —hag′gler n.

**hail¹** (hāl) n. 1 Pellets of ice, sometimes fairly large, that often fall during thunderstorms. 2 Anything falling thickly and with violence: a hail of blows. —v.i. 1 To pour down hail. —v.t. 2 To hurl or pour down like hail. [< OE hægel]

**hail²** (hāl) v.t. 1 To call loudly in greeting; salute. 2 To call to so as to attract attention. 3 To name as; designate. —v.i. 4 To call out or signal so as to attract attention. —hail from To come from; have as one's original home. —n. 1 A call to attract attention; greeting. 2 The distance a shout can be heard: within hail. —interj. Salutations! [< ON heill whole, hale] —hail′er n.

**hair** (hâr) n. 1 One of the filaments of modified epidermal tissue growing from the skin of people and animals. 2 Any mass of such filaments. 3 Bot. A threadlike outgrowth on

plants. 4 An exceedingly minute space, degree, etc.: to escape by a *hair*. —*adj*. Like, made of, or for hair. —**let one's hair down** To drop one's reserve; relax. —**not turn a hair** To remain calm and unruffled. —**split hairs** To quibble; make petty distinctions. [< OE *hǣr*]

**hair·pin** (hâr′pin′) *n*. A U-shaped pin made of wire, bone, plastic, etc., for keeping the hair in place. • See PIN.

**half** (haf, häf) *n*. *pl*. **halves** (havz, hävz) One of two equal parts or a quantity equal to such a part. —**by halves** 1 Incompletely. 2 With little enthusiasm. —**go halves** To share in equal parts. —*adj*. 1 Being one of two equal parts of a thing. 2 Partial; approximately one half of, in amount or value. —*adv*. To the degree or extent of a half; partially. [< OE *hǣlf*]

**half-life** (haf′lif′, häf′-) *n*. *Physics* The time taken for half the nuclei in a sample of a radioactive isotope to disintegrate. **Also half-life period.**

**hal·i·to·sis** (hal′ə-tō′sis) *n*. Malodorous breath. [< L *halitus* breath + -OSIS]

**hall** (hôl) *n*. 1 A passage or corridor in a building. 2 A small room or enclosure at the entry of a house; a vestibule; lobby. 3 A building or room for public business, entertainments, meetings, etc. 4 In a school, university, or college, a building used as a dormitory, classroom building, laboratory, etc. 5 The meeting place or headquarters of an organization or society; also, the organization itself. 6 *Brit*. A college dining room. 7 The large main room of a castle or other great house. 8 The country residence of a baron, squire, etc. [< OE *heall*]

**Hal·low·e'en** (hal′ō-ēn′) *n*. The evening of Oct. 31, vigil of All Saints' Day, now popularly observed esp. by children by masquerading and playful solicitations for sweets, etc. [< (*All-*)*hallow*(*s*) *e*(*v*)*en*]

**hal·lu·ci·na·tion** (hə-lōō′sə-nā′shən) *n*. 1 An apparent perception without any corresponding external stimulus. 2 A sense object perceived but not present in reality. —**hal·lu·ci·na·to·ry** (hə-lōō′sə-nə-tôr′ē, -tō′rē) *adj*.

**hal·lu·ci·no·gen** (hə-lōō′sin-ə-jən) *n*. Any substance capable of inducing hallucinations. —**hal·lu′ci·no·gen′ic** *adj*.

**ha·lo** (hā′lō) *n*. *pl*. ·**los** or ·**loes** 1 A luminous circle around the sun or the moon. 2 A radiance encircling the head in portrayals of sacred personages. 3 The splendor with which imagination surrounds an object of affection or esteem. —*v*. ·**loed**, ·**lo·ing** *v.t*. 1 To enclose in a halo. —*v.i*. 2 To form a halo. [< Gk. *halōs*]

**hal·ter** (hôl′tər) *n*. 1 A strap or rope by which to hold or lead a horse or other animal. 2 A hangman's rope. 3 Execution by hanging. 4 A woman's blouse designed for exposing the back and arms to the sun, fastened around the neck and waist. —*v.t*. To secure with a halter. [< OE *hǣlftre*]

**ham** (ham) *n*. 1 The thigh of a hog, smoked, salted, etc., for food. 2 *pl*. The buttocks. 3 The space or region behind the knee joint; the hock of quadrupeds. 4 *Slang* A performer who overacts. 5 An amateur radio operator. —*v.t*. **hammed, ham·ming** *Slang* To overact; use exaggerated speech and gestures; often in the expression **ham it up**. [< OE *hamm*] —**ham′my** *adj*. (·i·**er**, ·i·**est**)

**ham·mer** (ham′ər) *n*. 1 A hand tool with a head at right angles to the handle, used for driving nails, pounding, etc. 2 A machine or part of a machine performing functions similar to those of a heavy hand hammer. 3 That part of a gunlock which strikes the cap or cartridge. • See REVOLVER. 4 A padded piece that strikes the string of a piano. 5 An auctioneer's mallet. 6 *Anat*. The malleus of the middle ear. —**under the hammer** For sale at auction. —*v.t*. 1 To strike with or as with a hammer; drive, as a nail. 2 To shape or fasten with a hammer. 3 To form or force as if with hammer blows. —*v.i*. 4 To strike blows with or as with a hammer. [< OE *hamer*] —**ham′mer·er** *n*. —**Syn**. *v*. 1 bang, beat, pound, whack.

**ham·mock** (ham′ək) *n*. A couch of canvas or netting, swung from supports at both ends. [Sp. *hamaca*]

**ham·per** (ham′pər) *n*. A large covered basket, as for food, laundry, fire, etc. [< OF *hanapier*]

**hand** (hand) *n*. 1 The part of the human forelimb that is attached to the forearm below the wrist, used for holding and grasping. 2 The corresponding segment of a limb in apes, etc. 3 Side or direction: She sat at his right *hand*. 4 A role in doing something: They all had a *hand* in it. 5 *pl*. Possession; control: It is in your *hands* now. 6 Aid; assistance: to lend a *hand*. 7 A pledge of betrothal, or a giving in marriage. 8 A manual laborer. 9 A person as the performer of an action: a book written by many *hands*. 10 A person with reference to his ability: a good *hand* with children. 11 Skill; ability;

touch. 12 A specified remove from a source: a story heard at second *hand.* 13 *pl.* The members of a group. 14 The cards held by a player at one deal; also, the player. 15 The playing of the cards at one deal. 16 Clapping of hands; applause. 17 Handwriting. 18 A person's signature. 19 The pointer of a clock or watch. 20 Four inches, the approximate width of the hand, used as a measure for the height of horses, etc. —**a great hand at** or **for** A person specially fond of or clever at. —**at first hand** At the source. —**at hand** Within reach; convenient. —**at the hand of** From the hand of; by the operation of. —**by hand** With the hands only: a dress made *by hand.* —**have one's hands full** To have all or more than one can do. —**in hand** 1 In one's possession. 2 In process of being done. 3 Entirely under control. —**off one's hands** Out of one's care or control. —**on hand** 1 In present or rightful possession. 2 In place; present. —**on one's hands** In one's care; under one's responsibility —**on the other hand** Looking at the opposed point of view. —**out of hand** 1 Unruly; lawless. 2 Immediately; without delay. —**wash one's hands of** To dismiss from consideration. —*v.t.* 1 To give, pass, or deliver with or as with the hand. 2 To lead or help with the hand. —**hand down** 1 To transmit, as to one's successors. 2 To deliver, as the decision of a court. —**hand it to** *Slang* To acknowledge the abilities, success, etc., of. —**hand on** To pass on; transmit. —**hand out** To mete out; distribute. —**hand over** To give up possession of; surrender. [< OE]

**hand·cuff** (hand′kuf′) *n.* One of two manacles connected by a chain, and designed to be locked around the wrists. —*v.t.* To put handcuffs on; manacle.

**hand·i·cap** (han′dē·kap′) *n.* 1 A condition imposed to equalize the chances of competitors in a contest. 2 A race or contest in which such conditions are imposed. 3 A disadvantage or hindrance. —*v.t.* **·capped**, **·cap·ping** 1 To impose a handicap on. 2 To be a handicap to. [< *hand in cap,* a lottery game in which winners were penalized] — **hand′i·cap′per** *n.* —**Syn.** *n.* 3 burden, encumbrance, impediment, shortcoming.

**hand·i·craft** (han′dē·kraft′, -kräft′) *n.* 1 Skill and expertness in working with the hands. 2 A trade or craft calling for such skill. [< HAND + CRAFT]

**hand·ker·chief** (hang′kər·chif) *n.* 1 A small,

square piece of soft cloth for wiping the face or nose. 2 A neckerchief.

**han·dle** (han′dəl) *v.* **han·dled**, **han·dling** *v.t.* 1 To touch, feel, etc., with the hands. 2 To manage or use with the hands. 3 To manage or direct; control. 4 To deal with: to *handle* a disagreement. 5 To trade or deal in: to *handle* cotton. 6 To act toward; treat. —*v.i.* 7 To respond to handling. —*n.* That part of an object intended to be grasped with the hand. —**fly off the handle** To be suddenly and unreasonably angry. [< OE *handlian*]

**hand·some** (han′səm) *adj.* 1 Agreeable to the eye or to good taste; of pleasing aspect. 2 Of liberal dimensions or proportions. 3 Marked by generosity or liberality. [<HAND + -SOME, orig. with sense "easy to handle"] — **hand′some·ly** *adv.* —**hand′some·ness** *n.*

**hand·work** (hand′wûrk′) *n.* Work done by hand.

**hand·y** (han′dē) *adj.* **hand·i·er**, **hand·i·est** 1 Ready at hand or convenient for use; nearby. 2 Skillful with the hands. 3 Easy to handle: said of a ship or a tool. —**hand′i·ly** *adv.* —**hand′i·ness** *n.*

**hang** (hang) *v.* **hung** or (*esp. for v. defs. 3 & 9*) **hanged**, **hang·ing** *v.t.* 1 To fasten to something above; suspend. 2 To attach, so as to allow some motion. 3 To execute on a gallows. 4 To cover or furnish by something suspended. 5 To fasten in position or at the correct angle. 6 To cause a deadlock, as in a jury's vote. —*v.i.* 7 To be suspended; dangle. 8 To be suspended without visible support; float. 9 To be put to death on the gallows. 10 To project out; overhang. 11 To droop; incline downward. 12 To be imminent or impending. 13 To be dependent or contingent. 14 To be uncertain or in doubt. 15 To attend closely: to *hang* on someone's words. 16 To be or remain in deadlock, as a jury. —**hang around** (or **about**) 1 To linger or loiter. 2 To group around. —**hang back** To be reluctant. —**hang fire** 1 To fail to fire promptly, as a firearm. 2 To be delayed. — **hang in** *Slang* To stay; persevere; hold on. —**hang out** 1 To lean out. 2 To suspend out in the open. 3 *Slang* To reside or spend one's time: usu. with *at* or *in.* —**hang together** 1 To stay together. 2 To be coherent or consistent. —**hang up** 1 To place on hooks or hangers. 2 To end a telephone call by replacing the receiver. 3 To become caught or jammed, as a machine part. 4 To delay or suspend. —*n.* 1 The way a thing hangs. 2 *Informal* Familiar knowledge; knack. 3 A bit: I don't care a *hang*. —**get the hang of** *Informal* To come to understand or be able to do. [< OE *hangian* hang down and *hon* suspend and ON *hanga*] • *Hanged* and *hung* are the two past tenses and past participles of *hang*, and each has a distinct meaning. Criminals are *hanged*. Pictures, curtains, etc., are *hung*.

**han·gar** (hang′ər, -gär) *n.* A shelter or shed, esp. for aircraft. [F]

**han·ker** (hang′kər) *v.i.* To yearn; want greatly. [<Du. *hankeren* long for] —**han′-ker·er** *n.*

**hap·haz·ard** (hap′haz′ərd) *adj.* Accidental; happening by chance. —*adv.* By chance; at random. —*n.* Mere chance; hazard. [<HAP + HAZARD] —**hap′haz′ard·ly** *adv.* —**hap′haz′-ard·ness** *n.*

**hap·pen** (hap′ən) *v.i.* 1 To take place or occur. 2 To come about or occur by chance. 3 To chance; have the fortune. 4 To come by chance: to *happen* upon the answer. 5 To come or go by chance: with *in, along, by,* etc. —**happen to** 1 To befall. 2 To become of. [<HAP]

**hap·py** (hap′ē) *adj.* ·pi·er, ·pi·est 1 Enjoying, giving, or indicating pleasure; joyous; blessed. 2 Fortunately effective; opportune; felicitous. 3 Yielding or marked by great pleasure. [<HAP] —**hap′pi·ly** *adv.* —**hap′pi-ness** *n.*

**ha·rangue** (hə·rang′) *n.* An oration; esp., a loud and vehement speech. —*v.* ·rangued, ·rangu·ing *v.t.* To address in a harangue. —*v.i.* To deliver a harangue. [< OF] —**ha·ran-gu′er** *n.*

**har·ass** (har′əs, hə·ras′) *v.t.* 1 To trouble or worry persistently. 2 *Mil.* To worry (an enemy) by repeated raids and small attacks. [<OF *harer* set dogs on] —**har′ass·er, har′ass·ment** *n.* —**Syn.** 1 annoy, bother, disturb, plague, torment.

**har·bin·ger** (här′bin·jər) *n.* A forerunner and announcer of something to come. —*v.t.* To act as a harbinger to; presage [< OF *herbergeor* provider of shelter]

**har·bor** (här′bər) *n.* 1 A port or haven that provides shelter for ships. 2 Any place of refuge or rest. —*v.t.* 1 To give refuge to; shelter; protect. 2 To entertain in the mind; cherish. —*v.i.* 3 To take shelter in a habor. *Brit. sp.* **har′bour.** [< OE *here* army + *beorg* refuge] —**har′bor·er** *n.*

**hard core** 1 The basic, central, or most im-

portant part; nucleus. 2 Unemployed or underemployed people not trained for any job.

**har·le·quin** (här′lə·kwin, -kin) *n.* A buffoon. —*adj.* 1 Comic; buffoonlike. 2 Many-colored, usu. in a diamond pattern. [< OF *Herlequin*]

**harm** (härm) *n.* 1 That which inflicts injury or loss. 2 The injury inflicted; hurt. 3 Offense against morality; wrong. —*v.t.* To damage; hurt. [< OE *hearm* insult] —**harm′er** *n.* — **Syn.** *n.* 1 blemish, detriment, impairment, abuse.

**har·mo·ni·ous** (här·mō′nē·əs) *adj.* 1 Characterized by harmony or agreement; in accord. 2 Having the parts pleasingly related; symmetrical, congruous. 3 Pleasing to the ear. —**har′mo′ni·ous·ly** *adv.* —**har·mo′ni-ous·ness** *n.*

**har·mo·ny** (här′mə·nē) *n. pl.* ·nies 1 Accord or agreement in feeling, manner, or action. 2 A state of order, agreement, or completeness in the relations of parts of a whole to each other. 3 Pleasing sounds; music. 4 *Music* a Any agreeable combination of simultaneous tones. b The constitution and succession of groups of tones that sound simultaneously in music. [< Gk. *harmonia* < *harmos* joint]

**har·ness** (här′nis) *n.* 1 The combination of traces, straps, etc., forming the gear of a draft animal and used to attach it to a vehicle or plow. 2 *Archaic* The defensive armor of a soldier or of his horse. 3 Any similar apparatus or gear. —**in harness** Engaged in one's daily work. —*v.t.* 1 To put harness on, as a horse. 2 To make use of the power of: to *harness* a waterfall. [< OF *harneis*]

**harp** (härp) *n.* 1 A musical instrument consisting of a roughly triangular frame fitted with strings of graded lengths and played by plucking. 2 Something resembling a harp. —*v.i.* 1 To play on a harp. 2 To speak or write persistently; dwell tediously: with *on* or *upon.* [< OE *hearpe*] —**harp′er, harp′-ist** *n.*

**har·ry** (har′ē) *v.* **har·ried, har·ry·ing** *v.t.* 1 To lay waste; pillage; sack. 2 To harass. —*v.i.* 3 To make raids for plunder. [< OE *hergian* ravage]

**harsh** (härsh) *adj.* 1 Grating or rough to the senses; discordant; rasping. 2 Rigorous; severe; unfeeling: a *harsh* judge. 3 Bleak in appearance: a *harsh* landscape. [ME *harsk*] —**harsh′ly** *adv.* —**harsh′ness** *n.*

**har·vest** (här′vist) *n.* 1 A crop, as of grain, vegetables, fruits, etc., ready for gathering. 2

The time or season of gathering. **3** The act of gathering in a crop. **4** The product of any toil or effort. —*v.t.* **1** To gather (a crop). **2** To gather the crop of (a field, etc.). **3** To achieve as a result of preparation and effort. —*v.i.* **4** To gather a crop. [< OE *hœrfest*]

**hasp** (hasp, hăsp) *n.* A fastening for a door, box, etc., passing over a staple and secured usu. by a padlock. [< OE *hœpse*]

**has·sock** (hăs′ək) *n.* **1** An upholstered footstool. **2** A rank tuft of coarse or boggy grass. [< OE *hassuc* coarse grass]

**haste** (hāst) *n.* **1** Speed of movement or action; dispatch. **2** Necessity for speed; urgency. **3** Hurry; precipitancy. —**in haste 1** Quickly. **2** Thoughtlessly; rashly. —**make haste** To hurry; rush. —*v.t.* & *v.i.* **hast·ed, hast·ing** *Archaic* To hasten. [< OF < Gmc.]

**hast·en** (hā′sən) *v.t.* To cause to hurry or move quickly; expedite. —*v.i.* To be quick; hurry. —**hast′en·er** *n.*

**hast·y** (hās′tē) *adj.* **hast·i·er, hast·i·est 1** Acting or done with haste. **2** Acting or done impetuously; rash. **3** Quick-tempered; irascible. —**hast′i·ly** *adv.* —**hast′i·ness** *n.*

**hatch**[1] (hach) *n.* **1** *Naut.* **a** An opening in the deck of a vessel affording passage to the hold. **b** The cover over a hatch. **2** Any similar opening in the floor or roof of a building. **3** The lid or cover for such an opening. [< OE *hœcc* grating]

**hatch**[2] (hach) *v.t.* **1** To bring forth (young) from the egg by incubation. **2** To bring forth young from (the egg). **3** To devise, as a plan. **4** To contrive secretly; plot. —*v.i.* **5** To emerge from the egg. **6** To produce young: said of eggs. —*n.* **1** The act of hatching. **2** The brood hatched at one time. [ME *hacchen*] —**hatch′er** *n.*

**hatch·et** (hach′it) *n.* A small short-handled ax, for use with one hand. —**bury the hatchet** To cease from hostilities; make peace. [< OF *hache* an ax]

**hate** (hāt) *v.* **hat·ed, hat·ing** *v.t.* **1** To regard with extreme aversion; detest. **2** To be unwilling; dislike. —*v.i.* **3** To feel hatred. —*n.* **1** Intense aversion; animosity. **2** A person or thing detested. [< OE *hatian*] —**hat′er** *n.*

**ha·tred** (hā′trid) *n.* Bitter dislike or aversion; antipathy; animosity. —**Syn.** abhorrence, detestation, enmity, hate, hostility.

**haugh·ty** (hô′tē) *adj.* **·ti·er, ·ti·est 1** Proud and disdainful; arrogant. **2** *Archaic* Lofty; exalted. [< OF *haut* high] —**haugh′ti·ly** *adv.* —**haugh′ti·ness** *n.*

**haul** (hôl) *v.t.* **1** To pull or draw with force; drag. **2** To transport as if by pulling. **3** *Naut.* To shift the course of (a ship) —*v.i.* **4** To drag or pull. **5** To shift in direction: said of the wind. **6** *Naut.* To change course, esp. so as to sail nearer the wind. —**haul off 1** To draw back the arm so as to deliver a blow. **2** *Naut.* To change course so as to move farther away from an object. —**haul up 1** To come to a stop. **2** *Naut.* To sail nearer the wind. —*n.* **1** A pulling with force. **2** That which is obtained by hauling. **3** The drawing of a fish net. **4** The amount caught in, or as in, one pull of a net. **5** The distance over which anything is hauled. [< OF *haler* < Gmc.] —**haul′er** *n.*

**haunch** (hônch, hänch) *n.* **1** The fleshy part of the hip, the buttock, and the upper thigh. **2** The combined loin and leg of an animal. [< OF *hanche* < Gmc.] —**haunched** *adj.*

**haunt** (hônt, hänt) *v.t.* **1** To visit frequently or customarily. **2** To appear to as a disembodied spirit. **3** To recur persistently to the mind or memory of. **4** To visit often; frequent, as a saloon. —*v.i.* **5** To make ghostly appearances. —*n.* **1** A place often visited. **2** *Regional* A ghost. [< OF *hanter* < Gmc.] —**haunt′er** *n.*

**have** (hav) *v.t.* Present indicative: I, you, we, they **have** (*Archaic* thou hast), he, she, it has (*Archaic* hath); past indicative had (*Archaic* thou hadst); present subjunctive have; past subjunctive had; *p.p.* had; *pr.p.* hav·ing **1** To hold as a possession; own. **2** To possess as a characteristic, attribute, etc. **3** To receive; get: I *had* a letter today. **4** To entertain, as an opinion or doubt. **5** To manifest or exercise: *Have* patience! **6** To experience; undergo. **7** To be affected with. **8** To carry on; engage in. **9** To cause to be: *Have* him here at 9 o'clock. **10** To allow or tolerate: I will *have* no interference. **11** To possess a certain relation to: to *have* the wind at one's back. **12** To be in relationship to or association with: to *have* three children. **13** To bring forth or beget (young). **14** To maintain or declare: so rumor *has* it. **15** *Informal* To baffle: He *had* me there. **16** *Informal* To trick; cheat: I've been *had*! **17** *Informal* To engage in sexual relations with.— *auxiliary* As an auxiliary *have* is used: **a** With past participles to express completed action: I *have* gone. **b** With the infinitive to express obligation: I *have* to go. —**have at** To attack. —**have done** To stop; desist. —

**have it in for** *Informal* To hold a grudge against. **—have it out** To continue a fight or discussion to a final settlement. **—have on** To be clothed in. [< OE *habban*]

**ha·ven** (hā′vən) *n.* 1 An anchorage for ships; harbor; port. 2 A refuge; shelter. *—v.t.* To shelter (a vessel, etc.). [< OE *hæfen*] **—Syn.** *n.* 2 asylum, retreat, sanctuary.

**hav·oc** (hav′ək) *n.* 1 General carnage or destruction; ruin. 2 Tumultuous disorder, confusion, or uproar. **—cry havoc** To give a signal for pillage and destruction. **—play havoc with** To bring to confusion; destroy; ruin. *—v.t.* **hav·ocked, hav·ock·ing** *Archaic* To lay waste; destroy. [< OF *havot* plunder < Gmc.] **—hav′ock·er** *n.*

**Ha·wai·ian** (hə·wī′yən) *adj.* Of or pertaining to the Hawaiian Islands, their people, or their language. *—n.* 1 A native or citizen of the Hawaiian Islands. 2 The Polynesian language of the aboriginal Hawaiians.

**hawk** (hôk) *n.* 1 Any of various birds of prey related to eagles and kites, with relatively short rounded wings, a hooked beak, and strong claws. 2 One who favors military rather than conciliation and negotiation, as in a dispute. *—v.i.* 1 To hunt game with trained hawks. *—v.t.* 2 To hunt or catch in flight, as a hawk does. [< OE *hafoc, hafuc*] **—hawk′er** *n.* **—hawk′ish** *adj.*

**haz·ard** (haz′ərd) *n.* 1 Exposure to loss or injury; risk; peril. 2 A chance result or occurrence. 3 A gambling game played with dice. 4 An obstacle on a golf course, as a bunker or sand trap. *—v.t.* 1 To expose to danger; imperil. 2 To risk; venture. [< OF *hasard*] **—Syn.** *n.* 1 danger, jeopardy. 2 gamble, risk, speculation.

**haze** (hāz) *n.* 1 Very fine suspended particles in the air, as of smoke or dust. 2 A vague or muddled mental state. [Back formation < HAZY]

**haz·y** (hā′zē) *adj.* **haz·i·er, haz·i·est** 1 Misty, smoky, etc. 2 Confused; obscure. [?] **—haz′i·ly** *adv.* **—haz′i·ness** *n.*

**H-bomb** (āch′bom′) *n.* HYDROGEN BOMB.

**head** (hed) *n.* 1 The part of the body of man and most animals that contains the brain and the ears, eyes, mouth, and nose. 2 An analogous part in other organisms. 3 A representation of a head, as in art. 4 Mind; intelligence: Use your *head.* 5 Mental aptitude: a good *head* for figures. 6 Mental poise; self-possession: He kept his *head.* 7 A person: learned *heads.* 8 (*pl.* head) An individual considered as a unit of counting:

six *head* of cattle. 9 A part or end that has a shape, position, or relationship resembling or analogous to that of a head: the *head* of a bed. 10 The source, as of a river. 11 The fore or forward part: the *head* of a column of troops. 12 A headland; cape. 13 A leader, chief; director. 14 One having topmost rank: the *head* of one's profession. 15 The top or uppermost part: the *head* of the stairs. 16 A heading, headline, etc. 17 A division of a subject, discourse, etc.: He had little to say on that *head.* 18 Culmination; climax: to come to a *head.* 19 The maturated part of a boil or abscess before breaking. 20 Advance in the face of opposition: to make *head* against the storm. 21 A compact cluster of leaves, flowers, or seeds, as of cabbage, clover, or grain. 22 The foam that rises to the surface of beer, ale, etc. 23 The measure of stored-up force or capacity, as of steam. 24 The height of a column or body of fluid above a certain point, considered as causing pressure: a *head* of water driving a turbine. 25 The striking, holding, or pushing part, as of a club, hammer, pin, etc. 26 The obverse of a coin. 27 *Naut.* A toilet. 28 The membrane stretched over a drum or tambourine. 29 The active part of a tool or device: a cutting *head;* a recording *head.* 30 HEADMASTER. 31 *Slang* One who habitually uses a drug that distorts perception, as LSD or marihuana: an acid *head;* a pot*head.* **—go to one's head** 1 To make intoxicated or lightheaded. 2 To cause to become conceited. **—out of (or off) one's head** Crazy; delirious. **—over one's head** 1 Beyond one's ability to understand. 2 To someone of higher authority. **—turn one's head** To make vain or conceited. *—v.t.* 1 To be first or foremost in or on: to *head* the list. 2 To be chief or leader of; command. 3 To turn or direct the course of: to *head* a vessel toward shore. 4 To furnish with a head. 5 To remove the head or top of, as a tree. 6 In soccer, to hit (the ball) with the head. *—v.i.* 7 To move in a specified direction or toward a specified point. 8 To come to or form a head. **—head off** To intercept the course of: We'll *head* him *off* at the pass. **—head up** *Informal* To be in charge. *—adj.* 1 Principal; chief. 2 Situated at the top or front. 3 Directed against the front: a *head* wind. [< OE *hēafod*]

**heal** (hēl) *v.t.* 1 To restore to health or soundness; make well again. 2 To cause the cure or recovery of (a wound, injury, etc.). 3 To smooth over or resolve (a breach, quarrel, etc.). 4 To free from grief, worry, etc. —*v.i.* 5 To become well or sound. 6 To perform a cure or cures. [< OE *hǣlan*] —**heal′a·ble** *adj.* —**heal′er** *n.*

**health** (helth) *n.* 1 Soundness of body or mind; well-being. 2 General condition of body or mind: poor *health*. 3 General well-being, as of a nation. 4 A toast wishing good health. [< OE *hǣlth*]

**heap** (hēp) *n.* 1 A collection of things piled up; a pile. 2 *Often pl. Informal* A large number; lot. —*v.t.* 1 To pile into a heap. 2 To fill or pile into or onto to an excessive degree. 3 To give or bestow in great quantities: to *heap* insults on someone. —*v.i.* 4 To form or rise in a heap. [< OE *hēap* a crowd]

**hear** (hir) *v.* **heard** (hûrd), **hear·ing** *v.t.* 1 To perceive (sound) by means of the ear. 2 To listen to. 3 To give heed to. 4 To learn or be informed of: I *hear* you are leaving town. 5 To listen to and review in an official capacity: to *hear* a case in court. 6 To respond to and grant: *Hear* our prayers! —*v.i.* 7 To perceive or be capable of perceiving sound by means of the ear. 8 To be informed or made aware. [< OE *hēran*] —**hear′er** *n.*

**hearse** (hûrs) *n.* A vehicle used in a funeral for carrying a dead person to the cemetery. [ME *herse* a harrow, frame]

**heart** (härt) *n.* 1 A hollow muscular structure which maintains the circulation of the blood by alternate contraction and dilation. 2 Feeling, as compassion, earnest desire, or deep emotion, regarded as emanating from the heart. 3 Love; affection: to win her *heart*. 4 Mood; spirit: a heavy *heart.* 5 Courage; resolution: to lose *heart.* 6 A person, esp. one regarded with love or affection: many brave *hearts.* 7 Innermost part; core or center. 8 Essential part; gist: the *heart* of the matter. 9 A conventionalized representation of the heart. 10 **a** A playing card marked with this symbol. **b** *pl.* The suit of cards bearing this symbol. 11 *pl.* A card game in which one tries to win none or all of the hearts. [< OE *heorte*]

**hearth** (härth) *n.* 1 The floor of a fireplace, furnace, etc. 2 The fireside; home. 3 In a blast furnace, the lowest part, through which the melted metal flows. [< OE *heorth*]

**heat** (hēt) *n.* 1 The condition or sensation of being hot. 2 Comparatively high temperature or degree of warmth. 3 Energy associated with and proportional to the random motions of the molecules of a substance or body. 4 The condition or process of maintaining a warm temperature, as in a home. 5 Hot weather or climate. 6 Intensity, as of feeling, excitement, or activity. 7 A time or instance of such activity or feeling: the *heat* of battle. 8 A recurring state of sexual activity in female mammals. 9 In sports: **a** A single bout or round. **b** A preliminary race to determine the finalists. —*v.t. & v.i.* 1 To make or become hot or warm. 2 To excite or become excited. [< OE *hǣtu*]

**heave** (hēv) *v.* **heaved** or *chiefly Naut.* **hove, heav·ing** *v.t.* 1 To raise with effort. 2 To throw with effort or force. 3 To cause to swell, rise, or move up and down. 4 To emit with a deep breath, as a sigh. 5 *Naut.* **a** To raise, haul up, or pull on (an anchor, cable, etc.). **b** To cause (a ship) to move by or as by hauling on cables or ropes. —*v.i.* 6 To rise, swell up, or move up and down repeatedly. 7 To breathe with effort; gasp. 8 To vomit or retch. 9 *Naut.* **a** To move or proceed: said of ships. **b** To haul, pull, or push. —*n.* The action, effort, or result of heaving. [< OE *hebban*] —**heav′er** *n.*

**heav·en** (hev′ən) *n.* 1 In Christian theology, the abode of God, the angels, and of deserving souls after death. 2 A similar state or concept in other religions. 3 A place or condition of supreme happiness. 4 *Often pl.* Divine providence. 5 *Usu. pl.* The region above and surrounding the earth; the sky. [< OE *heofon*] —**heav′en·ward** *adj., adv.* —**heav′en·wards** *adv.*

**heav·y** (hev′ē) *adj.* **heav·i·er, heav·i·est** 1 Of great or considerable weight; hard to lift or carry. 2 Of relatively great weight in relation to volume: a *heavy* metal. 3 Of more than the usual weight, thickness, etc.: a *heavy* fabric. 4 Laden or as if laden or weighted: air *heavy* with moisture. 5 Of or involving a great amount, volume, etc.: *heavy* trading. 6 Forceful; powerful: a *heavy* blow. 7 Concentrated; intense: *heavy* gunfire. 8 Thick, broad, and massive: *heavy* features. 9 Pervasive and often oppressive: a *heavy* odor. 10 Hard to do: *heavy* work. 11 Hard to bear; oppressive: *heavy* taxes. 12 Sorrowful; despondent: a *heavy* heart. 13 Serious; grave: a *heavy* offense. 14 Dull; ponderous: a *heavy* prose style. 15 Lacking lightness, grace, etc.: a *heavy* tread. 16 Having a dense, doughy texture. 17 Not easily digested. 18 Using or consuming something in great amounts: a *heavy* eater. 19 Of a theatrical role, intensely dramatic.

20 Pregnant: *heavy* with child. 21 Producing on a large or massive scale: *heavy* industry. 22 *Mil.* a Of great size, weight, etc.: *heavy* artillery. b Armed with such equipment; *heavy* infantry. —*adv.* Heavily. —*n. pl.* **heav·ies** 1 A heavy, dramatic theatrical role, as that of a villain; also, one who plays such a role. 2 Something heavy. [< OE *hefig*] —**heav′i·ly** *adv.* —**heav′i·ness** *n.*

**heavy water** Water composed of oxygen and deuterium.

**heav·y·weight** (hev′ē·wāt′) *n.* 1 One of more than average weight. 2 A boxer or wrestler over 175 pounds in weight. 3 *Informal* A person of considerable importance, influence, etc.

**hec·tor** (hek′tər) *v.t. & v.i.* 1 To bully; badger. 2 To tease; torment. —*n.* A bully. [< HECTOR]

**hedge** (hej) *n.* 1 A fence or barrier formed by bushes set close together. 2 The act or an instance of hedging. —*v.* **hedged, hedg·ing** *v.t.* 1 To surround or border with a hedge. 2 To guard or hem in with or as with barriers: usu. with *in.* 3 To try to compensate for possible loss from (a bet, investment, etc.) by making offsetting bets or investments. —*v.i.* 4 To make offsetting bets, investments, etc. 5 To avoid definite statement or involvement; refuse to commit oneself. [< OE *hegg*] —**hedg′er** *n.*

**heed** (hēd) *v.t.* To take special notice of; pay attention to. —*v.i.* To pay attention. —*n.* Careful attention or consideration. [< OE *hēdan*] —**heed′er** *n.*

**heel** (hēl) *n.* 1 In man, the rounded posterior part of the foot. 2 A similar or corresponding part, as of the foot of an animal or the palm of the hand where it joins the wrist. 3 The part of a sock, shoe, etc., that covers the heel. 4 The supporting part of a shoe, boot, etc., attached to the sole beneath the heel. • See SHOE. 5 Something resembling or placed like a heel, as an end of a loaf of bread. 6 *Slang* A contemptible, treacherous fellow; a cad. —*v.t.* 1 To supply with a heel. 2 To follow or pursue closely. [< OE *hēla*] —**heel′less** *adj.*

**heif·er** (hef′ər) *n.* A young cow, esp. one that has not borne a calf. [< OE *hēahfore*]

**height** (hīt) *n.* 1 Measure or distance from the lowest part or level to the top or uppermost extent; altitude, elevation, or stature. 2 The condition of being high or tall. 3 The highest or uppermost part or point. 4 Something high; an eminence. 5 The greatest or most intense degree: the *height* of stupidity. [< OE *hīehtho*]

**hei·nous** (hā′nəs) *adj.* Extremely wicked; atrocious; hateful. [< OF *haine* hatred] —**hei′nous·ly** *adv.* —**hei′nous·ness** *n.*

**heir** (âr) *n.* 1 One who inherits or is legally entitled to inherit the property, title, or rank of another. 2 One who acquires a position, distinctive quality, etc., from a predecessor as if by inheritance. [< L *heres*] —**heir′dom, heir′ship** *n.*

**heir·ess** (âr′is) *n.* A woman or girl who is an heir, esp. one of considerable wealth.

**heir·loom** (âr′lōōm) *n.* 1 Something, as a valued possession, that has been handed down within a family for generations. 2 *Law* A piece of personal property inherited by an heir. [< HEIR + obs. *loom* tool]

**hel·i·cop·ter** (hel′ə·kop′tər, hē′lə-) *n.* A type of aircraft whose lift is obtained from airfoils rotating on a vertical axis and which is capable of rising and descending vertically. [< Gk. *helix, -ikos* a spiral + *pteron* a wing]

**hel·i·port** (hel′ə·pôrt′, -pôrt′, hē′lə-) *n.* An airport for helicopters.

**he·li·um** (hē′lē·əm) *n.* An inert, odorless, nonflammable, gaseous element (symbol He), abundant on the sun and other stars. [NL < Gk. *hēlios* sun]

**hell** (hel) *n.* 1 *Sometimes cap.* a In Christianity and other religions, the abode of evil spirits after death, considered a place of eternal torment. b In certain ancient religions, the dwelling place of the spirits of the dead. 2 The powers of evil. 3 Any place, condition, or cause of extreme suffering, evil, etc. —*interj. Slang* An exclamation of anger, annoyance, disappointment, etc. —*v.i. Slang* To behave in an unrestrained or riotous manner: with *around.* [< OE *hel*]

**hel·met** (hel′mit) *n.* 1 A protective covering for the head, used in ancient and modern warfare. 2 A protective head covering, as of leather or plastic, worn by athletes, firemen, motorcyclists, etc. 3 Something resembling a helmet. [< OF, dim. of *helme* < Gmc.] —**hel′met·ed** *adj.*

**help** (help) *v.t.* 1 To give assistance to; aid. 2 To assist in some action, motion, etc.: with *on, into, out of, up, down,* etc. 3 To give support to; contribute to: to *help* a good cause. 4 To give relief to; ease: to *help* a cold. 5 To be responsible for: He can't *help* his infirmities. 6 To refrain from: I couldn't *help* giggling. 7 To serve, as with food. 8 To wait on, as a sales clerk. —*v.i.* 9 To give assistance. 10 To be useful or effective: Nothing seems to *help*. —cannot help but To be compelled to; must. —*n.* 1 Aid; assistance. 2 Support; comfort. 3 Remedy; relief. 4 a A worker hired to help. b Such workers collectively. [< OE *helpan*] —help′er *n.* —Syn. *v.* 1 succor, assist. 4 benefit, improve.

hem (hem) *n.* 1 A finished border on fabric, made by folding one edge over and sewing it down. 2 A comparable border or edge. —*v.t.* hemmed, hem·ming 1 To make a hem on. 2 To border; edge. 3 To shut in; enclose; restrict: with *in*, *about*, etc. [< OE] —hem′mer *n.*

hem·i·sphere (hem′ə·sfir) *n.* 1 Half of a sphere. 2 a A half of the terrestrial or celestial globe, esp. one of the halves of the earth, including the **Northern** and **Southern Hemispheres**, divided at the equator, and the **Eastern** and **Western Hemispheres**, divided at a meridian. The Eastern Hemisphere includes Europe, Asia, Africa, and Australia; the Western Hemisphere includes North and South America. b A map or projection of one of these. —hem·i·spher·ic (hem′ə·sfer′ik) or ·i·cal *adj.*

hem·or·rhage (hem′ər·ij, hem′rij) *n.* Discharge of blood from a ruptured blood vessel. —*v.i.* ·rhaged, ·rhag·ing To bleed copiously. [< Gk. *haima* blood + *rhēgnynai* burst] —hem·or·rhag·ic (hem′ə·raj′ik) *adj.*

hep·ta·gon (hep′tə·gon) *n.* A polygon having seven sides and seven angles. —hep·tag·o·nal (hep·tag′ə·nəl) *adj.*

her·ald (her′əld) *n.* 1 The bearer of significant news, an important message, etc. 2 A forerunner or portent of something to come; harbinger. 3 *Brit.* An official who traces and records genealogies, assigns heraldic arms, etc. —*v.t.* 1 To announce; proclaim. 2 To foretell the coming of. [< Gmc.] —he·ral·dic (hi·ral′dik) *adj.*

her·ald·ry (her′əl·drē) *n. pl.* ·ries 1 The art or occupation of establishing and devising coats of arms, tracing and recording genealogies, etc. 2 Coats of arms or similar heraldic bearings collectively. 3 Pomp or ceremony suggestive of heraldry.

herb (ûrb, hûrb) *n.* 1 A seed plant devoid of persistent woody tissue. 2 A plant used in medicine or for flavoring food. [< L *herba* grass, herbage]

her·ba·ceous (hûr·bā′shəs) *adj.* Of, pertaining to, or typical of herbs.

herb·age (ûr′bij, hûr′-) *n.* 1 Herbs or grass,

esp. used as pasturage. 2 The succulent leaves, stems, etc., of herbaceous plants.

her·biv·o·rous (hûr·biv′ər·əs) *adj.* Feeding on plants or vegetable matter. [< L *herba* grass + *vorare* devour]

herd (hûrd) *n.* 1 A group of animals, as cattle or sheep, that stay or are kept together. 2 A large, often unthinking or easily led crowd. —*v.t.* & *v.i.* To bring or keep together in or as in a herd. [< OE *heord*] —herd′er *n.*

he·red·i·tar·y (hə·red′ə·ter′ē) *adj.* 1 a Inherited or capable of being inherited legally. b Having title or right through legal inheritance: *hereditary* ruler. 2 Transmitted by biological heredity from one's parents or ancestors. 3 Passed on by or as by one's forebears: *hereditary* rights. —he·red′i·tar′i·ly *adv.* —he·red′i·tar′i·ness *n.*

he·red·i·ty (hə·red′ə·tē) *n. pl.* ·ties 1 Transmission of characteristics from parents to offspring by a code embodied in the genes in the chromosomes. 2 The tendency of an organism to develop in the likeness of its progenitors because of such transmission. 3 The sum total of an individual's genetic inheritance.

her·e·sy (her′ə·sē) *n. pl.* ·sies 1 A religious or doctrinal belief contrary to those of an established body or authority. 2 Any similar unorthodox or controversial belief. 3 Adherence to such beliefs. [< Gk. *hairesis* a sect]

her·e·tic (her′ə·tik) *n.* 1 One who maintains a heresy, esp. a religious heresy. 2 One whose views are unorthodox and controversial.

he·ret·i·cal (hə·ret′i·kəl) *adj.* Of, involving, or typical of heresy or heretics. —he·ret′i·cal·ly *adv.*

her·i·tage (her′ə·tij) *n.* 1 Something that is or can be inherited. 2 Tradition, culture, rights, etc., transmitted from generation to generation. [< OF < *heriter* inherit]

her·met·ic (hûr·met′ik) *adj.* Impervious to liquids or gases. Also her·met′i·cal. [< Gk. *Hermes (Trismegistus)*, god of alchemy] —her·met′i·cal·ly *adv.*

her·mit (hûr′mit) *n.* 1 A person who abandons society and lives alone, often for religious contemplation. 2 A spicy molasses cooky. [< Gk. *erēmos* solitary] —her·mit′ic or ·i·cal *adj.* —her·mit′i·cal·ly *adv.*

he·ro (hir′ō) *n. pl.* ·roes 1 A person of great courage, spirit, etc., esp. one who has undergone great danger or difficulty. 2 Any admirable or highly regarded man. **3** The main male character in a fictional or dramatic work. **4** In classical mythology, a man of both mortal and divine parentage, noted for outstanding courage, fortitude, etc. **5** A sandwich made from a loaf of bread or large roll split lengthwise. [< Gk. *hērōs*]

**he·ro·ic** (hi·rō′ik) *adj.* **1** Of or typical of a hero. **2** Characterized by or requiring great daring, strength, etc.: a *heroic* attempt. **3** Describing or in a style befitting the deeds of heroes: *heroic* poetry. **4** Larger than life size, as a statue. Also **he·ro′i·cal.** —*n.* **1** *pl.* Melodramatic behavior intended to display one's bravery, prowess, etc. **2** *pl.* HEROIC VERSE. —**he·ro′i·cal·ly** *adv.*

**her·o·ine** (her′ō·in) *n.* **1** A girl or woman of heroic character. **2** The chief female character in a fictional or dramatic work.

**hes·i·tan·cy** (hez′ə·tən·sē) *n. pl.* **·cies** The act or condition of hesitating. Also **hes′i·tance.**

**hes·i·tant** (hez′ə·tənt) *adj.* Hesitating or tending to hesitate; faltering, indecisive, or uncertain. —**hes′i·tant·ly** *adv.* —**Syn.** irresolute, undecided, unsure, doubtful.

**hes·i·tate** (hez′ə·tāt) *v.i.* **·tat·ed, ·tat·ing 1** To delay doubtfully or irresolutely; pause uncertainly; waver. **2** To be unwilling; have qualms. **3** To pause or falter in speaking. [< L *haesitare*, freq. of *haerere* to stick] —**hes′i·tat′er** *n.* —**hes′i·tat′ing·ly** *adv.*

**hes·i·ta·tion** (hez′ə·tā′shən) *n.* **1** The act of hesitating. **2** A state of uncertainty or doubt. **3** A pause or faltering in speech. —**hes′i·ta′tive** *adj.* —**hes′i·ta′tive·ly** *adv.*

**het·er·o·dox** (het′ər·ə·doks′) *adj.* At variance with an established or generally accepted doctrine or belief, esp. in religion; unorthodox. [< Gk. *hetero-* other + *doxa* opinion] —**het′er·o·dox′y** *n.*

**het·er·o·ge·ne·ous** (het′ər·ə·jē′nē·əs) *adj.* **1** Consisting of dissimilar elements or ingredients. **2** At variance; unlike; differing. [< Gk. *hetero-* other + *genos* kind] —**het·er·o·ge·ne·i·ty** (het′ər·ə·jə·nē′ə·tē), **het′er·o·ge′ne·ous·ness** *n.* —**het′er·o·ge′ne·ous·ly** *adv.*

**hew** (hyōō) *v.* **hewed, hewn** or **hewed, hew·ing** *v.t.* **1** To make or shape with or as with blows of an ax. **2** To hack or chop with an ax, sword, etc. **3** To fell with or as with blows of an ax. —*v.i.* **4** To make repeated cutting blows, as with an ax. **5** To keep steadfastly. [< OE *hēawan*] —**hew′er** *n.*

**hex·a·gon** (hek′sə·gon) *n.* A polygon with six

sides and six angles. [< HEXA- + Gk. *gonia* angle] —**hex·ag·o·nal** (hek·sag′ə·nəl) *adj.* —**hex·ag′on·al·ly** *adv.*

**hi·ber·nate** (hī′bər·nāt) *v.t.* **·nat·ed, ·nat·ing 1** To pass the winter, esp. in a torpid state, as certain animals. **2** To pass the time in seclusion or inactivity. [< L *hibernare*] —**hi·ber·na′tion** *n.*

**hic·cup** (hik′əp) *n.* A spasmodic contraction of the diaphragm accompanied by an involuntary sound. —*v.i.* **·cuped** or **·cupped, ·cup·ing** or **·cup·ping** To have the hiccups; make a hiccup. Also **hic·cough** (hik′əp). [Imit.]

**hid** (hid) *p.t.* & *a p.p.* of HIDE[1].

**hide**[1] (hīd) *v.* **hid, hid·den** or **hid, hid·ing** *v.t.* **1** To put or keep out of sight; conceal. **2** To keep secret; withhold from knowledge: to *hide* one's fears. **3** To block or obstruct the sight of. —*v.i.* **4** To keep oneself out of sight; remain concealed. [< OE *hȳdan*] —**hid′er** *n.* —**Syn. 1** secrete, cover, screen, bury. **2** cover up, cloak, mask, disguise, camouflage, veil, suppress.

**hide**[2] (hīd) *n.* **1** An animal skin, esp. as material for leather. **2** *Informal* The human skin. —*v.t.* **hid·ed, hid·ing 1** To whip; flog severely. **2** To remove the hide from. [< OE *hȳd*]

**hid·e·ous** (hid′ē·əs) *adj.* Shocking or dreadful; ghastly; revolting. [< OF *hisde, hide* fright] —**hid′e·ous·ly** *adv.* —**hid′e·ous·ness** *n.*

**hi·er·ar·chy** (hī′ər·är′kē) *n. pl.* **·chies 1** A system of church government by ecclesiastics graded and empowered according to rank. **2** A body of ruling clergymen. **3** A group of things, people, ideas, etc., arranged in order of importance. [< Gk. *hieros* sacred + *archos* ruler] —**hi′er·ar′chic, hi′er·ar′chi·cal, hi′er·ar′chal** *adj.*

**hi·er·o·glyph·ic** (hī′ər·ə·glif′ik, hī′rə·glif′ik) *n.* **1** *Usu. pl.* Picture writing, esp. of the ancient Egyptians. **2** A character or symbol used in such writing. **3** A symbol, word, etc., difficult to understand. **4** *pl.* Illegible handwriting. Also **hi·er·o·glyph** (hī′ər·ə·glif′, hī′rə·glif). —*adj.* Of, like, pertaining to, or written in hieroglyphics: also **hi·er·o·glyph** (hī′ər·ə·glif′, hī′rə·glif). [< Gk. *hieros* sacred + *glyphein* carve] —**hi′er·o·glyph′i·cal·ly** *adv.*

**hi-fi** (hī′fī′) *adj.* Of or having high fidelity. —*n. pl.* **-fis** A sound-reproducing system, esp. one with high fidelity.

**high-rise** (hī′rīz′) *adj.* Describing a relatively

**tall** building or structure. —*n.* A tall building, as a many-storied apartment house: **also high rise.**

**high·way** (hī'wā) *n.* 1 A public road, usu. a main road. 2 A way to some goal or objective.

**hi·jack** (hī'jak') *v.t. Informal* 1 To steal a shipment of (goods, bootleg liquor, etc.) by force. 2 To rob or steal (a truck, etc., carrying such goods). 3 To seize control of (an aircraft) while in flight by the threat or use of force and redirect it to a different destination; skyjack. 4 To rob, swindle, etc., by force or coercion. [?] —**hi'jack'er** *n.*

**hi·lar·i·ous** (hi·lâr'ē·əs, -lar'-) *adj.* Boisterously funny and gay. —**hi·lar'i·ous·ly** *adv.* —**hi·lar'i·ous·ness** *n.*

**hi·lar·i·ty** (hi·lâr'ə·tē, -lar'-, hī-) *n. pl.* **·ties** Boisterous fun and gaiety. [< Gk. *hilaros* cheerful]

**hilt** (hilt) *n.* The handle and guard of a sword or dagger. —*v.t.* To provide with a hilt. [< OE]

**hin·der** (hin'dər) *v.t.* 1 To keep back or delay; check. 2 To prevent; obstruct. —*v.i.* 3 To be an obstruction or obstacle. [< OE *hinder* behind] —**hin'der·er** *n.* —**Syn.** 1 impede, stop, stay, halt, bar, block. 2 encumber, foil, frustrate.

**hin·drance** (hin'drəns) *n.* 1 The act of hindering. 2 A person or thing that hinders or obstructs.

**hinge** (hinj) *n.* 1 A device allowing one part to turn upon another, esp. the hook or joint on which a door or shutter swings or turns. 2 A device consisting of two metal plates joined by a rod, used as to connect a lid to a box. 3 A natural joint, as in the shell of an oyster. 4 A pivotal point on which anything depends for its effect or course. —*v.* **hinged, hing·ing** *v.i.* 1 To have one's course determined by an action or eventuality; be dependent: with *on* or *upon*. —*v.t.* 2 To attach by or equip with hinges. [ME *hengen*]

**hint** (hint) *n.* 1 An indirect suggestion or implication. 2 A small amount or part: a *hint* of rain. —*v.t.* 1 To suggest indirectly; imply. —*v.i.* 2 To make hints: often with *at*. [< OF *hentan* seize, grasp] —**hint'er** *n.* —**Syn.** *n.* 1 reminder, tip, prompting, innuendo, insinuation. —*v.* 1 allude to, insinuate, remind, prompt.

**hip** (hip) *n.* 1 The lateral part of the body between the brim of the pelvis and the free part of the thigh. 2 The joint between the thigh bone and the pelvis: **also hip joint.** 3

*Archit.* The external angle in which adjacent roof slopes meet each other. —*v.t.* **hipped, hip·ping** *Archit.* To build with a hip or hips, as a roof. [< OE *hype*]

**hip·pie** (hip'ē) *n.* One of a group of young people whose alienation from conventional society is expressed by informal and eccentric clothing, a preoccupation with drugs and mysticism, and an interest in communal living. [Var. of HIPSTER]

**hip·po·pot·a·mus** (hip'ə·pot'ə·məs) *n. pl.* **·mus·es** or **·mi** (-mī) A massive, herbivorous, short-legged, thick-skinned African mammal. [< Gk. *hippos* horse + *potamos* river]

**hire** (hīr) *v.t.* **hired, hir·ing** 1 To obtain the services of (a person) or the use of (a thing) in exchange for payment; employ; rent: to *hire* a new plant manager; to *hire* a tuxedo for a formal dinner. 2 To grant the use of (a thing) or the services of (a person) for a fee; let: often with *out*. —*n.* 1 Compensation for labor, services, etc. 2 The act of hiring or the condition of being hired. [< OE *hȳran*] —**hir'a·ble, hir'a·ble** *adj.* —**hir'er** *n.*

**hire·ling** (hīr'ling) *n.* One who serves for hire, esp. such a one whose motives are primarily mercenary.

**hir·sute** (hûr'sōot, hir'-, hûr·sōot', hir-) *adj.* Hairy. [< L *hirsutus* rough] —**hir'sute·ness** *n.*

**hiss** (his) *n.* 1 The prolonged sound of *s*, as that made by escaping air. 2 Such a sound made to express disapproval, hatred, etc. —*v.i.* 1 To make or emit a hiss or hisses. 2 To express disapproval or hatred by hissing. —*v.t.* 3 To express disapproval or hatred of by hissing. 4 To express by means of a hiss or hisses. 5 To pursue, drive off, silence, etc., by hissing: usu. with *off*, *down*, etc. [< OE *hyscan* jeer at] —**hiss'er** *n.*

**his·to·ri·an** (his·tôr'ē·ən, -tō'rē-) *n.* 1 One who writes a history. 2 One versed in history.

**his·tor·i·cal** (his·tôr'i·kəl, -tor'-) *adj.* 1 Of or relating to history. 2 Serving as a record or as evidence of past events, etc.: a *historical* letter. 3 Dealing with past events, etc.: a *historical* novel. 4 Factually true or real. 5 HISTORIC (def. 1). —**his·tor'i·cal·ly** *adv.* —**his·tor'i·cal·ness** *n.* • See HISTORIC.

**his·to·ry** (his'tə·rē, his'trē) *n. pl.* **·ries** 1 A recorded narrative of past events, esp. those concerning a particular period, nation, individual, etc. 2 The branch of knowledge dealing with the events and people of the past. **3** The aggregate of events concerning a given subject, object, etc.: the *history* of their marriage. **4** Past events in general: in the course of *history*. **5** A past worthy of notice. **6** Something in the past: This is all *history* now. **7** A drama, story, etc., of past events, whether real or imaginary. [< Gk. *historia* knowledge, narrative]

**hit** (hit) *v.* **hit, hit·ting** *v.t.* **1** To come against or in contact with, usu. with impact or force. **2** To inflict (a blow, etc.). **3** To strike with a blow. **4** To cause to strike or come against with force: with *on*, *against*, etc.: I *hit* my leg on the door. **5** To strike with or as with a missile: He *hit* the robber in the leg. **6** To move or propel by striking: He *hit* the ball over the fence. **7** To reach, arrive at, or achieve: to *hit* a new low; to *hit* upon the solution. **8** To suit: The idea *hit* her fancy. **9** To affect adversely: His death *hit* her hard. **10** *Informal* To go at vigorously or to excess: to *hit* the bottle. **11** *Slang* To ask or demand of: with *for*: He *hit* me for a loan. **12** *Slang* To arrive at: We *hit* the city late. **13** In baseball, to make a (specified base) hit: to *hit* a triple. —*v.i.* **14** To deliver a blow or blows: often with *out*. **15** To strike with force; bump: often with *against*. —*n.* **1** A stroke, blow, shot, etc., that reaches its mark. **2** COLLISION. **3** A success: The play was a *hit*. **4** A piece of wit or sarcasm. **5** BASE HIT. [< ON *hitta* come upon] —**hit′ter** *n.*

**hitch** (hich) *n.* **1** A stop or sudden halt. **2** A hindrance or obstacle, as to an enterprise. **3** The act of catching or fastening, as by a rope, hook, etc.; also, a connection so made. **4** *Naut.* Any of various knots made with rope, rigging, etc. **5** A limp; hobble. **6** *Slang* A ride given in hitchhiking. **7** *Slang* A period of time spent in military service, prison, etc. —*v.t.* **1** To fasten or tie, esp. temporarily, with a knot, rope, strap, etc. **2** To secure to a vehicle: often with *up*: to *hitch* up a trailer to a car. **3** To move or shift with a jerk or jerks: He *hitched* himself around in his chair. **4** *Informal* To marry: usu. in the passive. **5** *Slang* To obtain (a ride) by hitchhiking. —*v.i.* **6** To move with jerks: to *hitch* forward. **7** To become caught or entangled. **8** *Slang* To travel by hitchhiking. [ME *hicchen*]

**hive** (hīv) *n.* **1** A structure in which bees may dwell. **2** A colony of bees. **3** A place full of activity. **4** A teeming crowd of people. —*v.* **hived, hiv·ing** *v.t.* **1** To cause (bees) to enter a hive. **2** To store (honey) in a hive. **3** To store (anything) for future use. —*v.i.* **4** To enter or dwell in or as in a hive. [< OE *hỹf*]

**hives** (hīvz) *n.* Any of various skin diseases characterized by wheals, itching, etc., esp. urticaria. [?]

**hoard** (hôrd, hōrd) *n.* An accumulation of something put away for safeguarding or for future use. —*v.t.* **1** To gather and store away or hide for future use. —*v.i.* **2** To gather and store away food, money, etc. [< OE *hord* treasure] —**hoard′er** *n.*

**hoarse** (hôrs, hōrs) *adj.* **hoars·er, hoars·est 1** Harsh and rough in sound. **2** Having the voice harsh and rough. [< OE *hā(r)s*] —**hoarse′ly** *adv.* —**hoarse′ness** *n.*

**hoar·y** (hôr′ē, hō′rē) *adj.* **hoar·i·er, hoar·i·est 1** White or grayish white, as from age, **2** Ancient. —**hoar′i·ness** *n.*

**hoax** (hōks) *n.* A deception or fraud, usu. practiced as a joke. —*v.t.* To deceive with a hoax. [< HOCUS(-POCUS)] —**hoax′er** *n.*

**hob·ble** (hob′əl) *v.* **hob·bled, hob·bling** *v.i.* **1** To walk with or as with a limp. **2** To move or proceed in an irregular or clumsy manner. —*v.t.* **3** To hamper the free movement of (a horse, etc.), as by tying the legs together. **4** To cause to move lamely or awkwardly. —*n.* **1** A limping gait. **2** A rope, strap, etc., used to fetter the forelegs of an animal. [ME *hoppeln* hobble] —**hob′bler** *n.*

**hob·by** (hob′ē) *n. pl.* **·bies** A subject or activity pursued for pleasure rather than for payment. [< *Robin*, a personal name] —**hob′by·ist** *n.*

**hob·by·horse** (hob′ē·hôrs′) *n.* **1** ROCKING HORSE. **2** A toy consisting of a stick with a wooden horse's head attached.

**hod** (hod) *n.* **1** A long-handled receptacle for holding bricks and mortar. **2** A coal scuttle. [< OF *hotte*]

**hodge-podge** (hoj′poj′) *n.* A jumbled mixture; conglomeration. [ME *hochepot*]

**hoe** (hō) *n.* A tool for digging, scraping, and tilling, having a flat, thin blade set nearly at a right angle to a long handle. —*v.t. & v.i.* **hoed, hoe·ing** To dig, scrape, or till with a hoe. [< OF *houe*] —**ho′er** *n.*

**hog** (hôg, hog) *n.* **1** A pig, esp. one that is full-grown. **2** An animal related to the pig, as the peccary. **3** *Informal* A filthy or gluttonous person. —*v.t.* **hogged, hog·ging** *Slang* To take more than one's share of; grab selfishly. [< OE *hogg*]

**hog·gish** (hôg′ish, hog′-) *adj.* **1** Of or like a

hog. 2 Greedy, selfish, dirty, etc. —**hog′g·ish·ly** adv. —**hog′gish·ness** n.

**hoist** (hoist) v.t. To raise to a higher position; lift or heave up, esp. by some mechanical means. —n. 1 A machine for hoisting; lift. 2 The act of hoisting; a boost. 3 Naut. The length of a sail between the boom and the peak or the jaws of the gaff. [?] —**hoist′er** n.

**ho·kum** (hō′kəm) n. Slang 1 Obvious and contrived comic or sentimental devices or effects in a play, novel, movie, etc. 2 Nonsense; bunk. [Alter. of HOCUS]

**hold** (hōld) v. **held, held** or in legal use **hold·en, hold·ing** v.t. 1 To take and keep in the hand, arms, etc.; grasp. 2 To prevent the movement or escape of: Hold the bus! 3 To restrain from acting or speaking: Hold your tongue! 4 To keep in a specified place, position, or state: to hold one's arm up. 5 To regard in a specified manner; consider: to hold someone dear. 6 To require to fulfill, as the conditions of a contract; obligate. 7 To support or keep in position: Ropes held the tower in position. 8 To be capable of enclosing or containing: The barrel holds ten gallons. 9 To maintain in the mind; believe: to hold an opinion. 10 To conduct or engage in; carry on: to hold court or services. 11 To have and retain ownership or control of; keep as one's own; occupy: to hold the position of chairman. 12 To get and retain possession or control of: to hold an enemy town; to hold one's attention. 13 To keep for later use, delivery, etc.: to hold a hotel room. 14 Music To prolong or sustain (a note or rest). —v.i. 15 To maintain a grip or grasp. 16 To remain firm or unbroken: if the rope holds; He held to his purpose. 17 To continue unchanged: The breeze held all day. 18 To be or remain true, valid, etc.: This decision holds. 19 To check or restrain oneself; forbear: usu. used in the imperative. —**hold down** 1 To suppress; keep under control. 2 Informal To occupy (a job, etc.) successfully. —**hold forth** To harangue; preach or speak at length. —**hold off** 1 To keep at a distance. 2 To refrain. —**hold on** 1 To maintain a grip or hold. 2 To persist; continue. 3 Informal To stop or wait: used in the imperative. —**hold one's own** To maintain one's position, as in a contest; lose no ground. —**hold out** 1 To stretch forth; offer. 2 To last to the end: Our supplies held out. 3 To continue resistance; endure; persist. 4 U.S. Slang To keep back part or all of (something). —**hold out for** Informal To insist upon as a condition of an agreement: He held out for a higher salary. —**hold up** 1 To support; prop. 2 To exhibit to view. 3 Informal To last; endure. 4 To delay; stop. 5 Informal To rob. —n. 1 The act or manner of holding, as with the hands. 2 In wrestling, a specific grip on an opponent. 3 A controlling force or influence. 4 A place to grasp. 5 A place of confinement. [< OE healdan]

**hole** (hōl) n. 1 A cavity extending into a solid body, as a pit, cave, etc. 2 An opening or aperture in anything: a hole in a dress. 3 A deep place in a stream or creek. 4 An animal's burrow or den. 5 A small, dingy room, dwelling, etc. 6 A prison cell. 7 A fault or defect: the holes in his argument. 8 Informal A dilemma or predicament. 9 In golf: a A small sunken cup into which the ball must be hit. b Any of the 9 or 18 sections of a course, from the tee to the cup inclusive. 10 Electronics An empty electron energy state in a crystal, acting as a positive charge carrier with the magnitude of an electron. —**in the hole** Informal In debt. —v. **holed, hol·ing** v.t. 1 To make a hole or holes in; perforate. 2 To drive or put into a hole, as in billiards or golf. 3 To dig (a shaft, tunnel, etc.). —v.i. 4 To make a hole or holes. —**hole up** 1 To hibernate, as in a hole. 2 To take refuge in hiding. [< OE hol]

**hol·i·day** (hol′ə·dā) n. 1 A day appointed by law or custom for the suspension of general business, usu. in commemoration of some person or event. 2 Any day of rest. 3 Often pl. A period of festivity or leisure; a vacation. —adj. Suitable for a holiday; festive. —v.i. To vacation. [< OE hālig dǣg holy day]

**ho·li·ness** (hō′lē·nis) n. The state or quality of being holy. —**His** (or **Your**) **Holiness** A title of the Pope.

**hol·low** (hol′ō) adj. 1 Having empty space or a cavity within; not solid: a hollow tree. 2 Sunken: hollow cheeks. 3 Depressed or sunk below the surface; concave. 4 Empty; vacant; insincere: hollow praise. 5 Muffled; dully reverberating: a hollow sound. 6 Hungry. —n. 1 Any depression in a body; a cavity. 2 A small valley. —v.t. & v.i. To make or become hollow. [< OE holh] —**hol′low·ly** adv. —**hol′low·ness** n.

**hol·o·caust** (hol′ə·kôst) n. 1 A sacrifice wholly consumed by fire. 2 Wholesale destruction or loss of life by fire, war, etc. [< Gk. holos

whole + *kaustos* burnt] —**hol'o·caus'tal,
hol'o·caus'tic** *adj.*

**hol·ster** (hōl'stər) *n.* A pistol case. [< Du.]

**ho·ly** (hō'lē) *adj.* **·li·er, ·li·est 1** Devoted to religious or sacred use; consecrated; hallowed. **2** Of highest spiritual purity; saintly. **3** Evoking or worthy of veneration, awe, respect, etc. **4** Religious: a *holy* war. —*n. pl.* **ho·lies** A holy thing or place. [< OE *hālig*] —**Syn.** *adj.* **1** sanctified, sacred, sacrosanct. **2** godly, pure, angelic, righteous.

**hom·age** (hom'ij, om'-) *n.* **1** Deep regard, honor, respect, or veneration, esp. as shown by some action. **2** In feudal law, formal acknowledgment of tenure by a tenant to his lord. [< LL *homo* vassal, client, man]

**home** (hōm) *n.* **1** One's dwelling place or residence. **2** The country, state, city, etc., where one lives or was reared. **3** A family thought of as a unit: a happy *home.* **4** A place regarded as a home: She found a *home* in the convent. **5** The seat or habitat of something; the place of origin: New Orleans is the *home* of jazz. **6** An establishment for the shelter and care of the needy or inform. **7** In some games, the goal that must be reached in order to win or score. —**at home 1** In one's own house, place, or country. **2** At ease, as if in familiar surroundings. **3** Prepared to receive callers. —*adj.* **1** Of or pertaining to one's home or country. **2** At the place regarded as the base of operations: the *home* office; a *home* game. **3** Going to the point; effective: a *home* thrust. —*adv.* **1** To, at, or in the direction of home. **2** To the place or point intended: to thrust the dagger *home.* **3** Deeply and intimately; to the heart: Her words struck *home.* —*v.* **homed, hom·ing** *v.t.* **1** To carry or send to a home. **2** To furnish with a home. —*v.i.* **3** To go to a home; fly home, as homing pigeons. **4** To have residence. —**home in on** To direct toward, seek, or find a destination, target, etc., esp. by radio or radar. [< OE *hām*]**home·stead** (hōm'sted) *n.* **1** A home, together with subsidiary buildings and adjacent land. **2** A tract of land occupied by a settler under the Homestead Act (1862) or its revisions. —*v.i.* *U.S.* To become a settler on a homestead under the Homestead Act. —*v.t.* *U.S.* To settle on land under the Homestead Act. —**home'stead'er** *n.*

**hom·i·cide** (hom'ə·sīd, hō'mə-) *n.* **1** The killing of one human being by another. **2** A person who has killed another. [< L *homo* man + -CIDE] —**hom'i·ci'dal** *adj.* —**hom'i·ci'dal·ly** *adv.*

**hom·i·ly** (hom'ə·lē) *n. pl.* **·lies 1** A sermon, esp. one based on the Bible. **2** A lecture on morals or conduct. [< Gk. *homilia* < *homilos* assembly] —**hom'i·let'ic** or **·i·cal** *adj.*

**hom·i·ny** (hom'ə·nē) *n.* Hulled dried corn (maize), coarsely ground and boiled for food. **Also hominy grits.** [<Algonquian *rockahominie* parched corn]

**ho·mo·ge·ne·ous** (hō'mə·jē'nē·əs, hom'ə-) *adj.* **1** Of the same composition or character throughout. **2** Of the same kind, nature, etc., as another; similar. [< Gk. *homos* the same + *genos* race] —**ho'mo·ge'ne·ous·ly** *adv.* —**ho·mo·ge·ne·i·ty** (hō'mə·jə·nē'ə·tē, hom'ə-), **ho'mo·ge'ne·ous·ness** *n.*

**ho·mog·en·ize** (hə·moj'ə·nīz) *v.t.* **·ized, ·iz·ing 1** To render homogeneous. **2 a** To distribute throughout a fluid, as tiny particles. **b** To make (milk) more uniform by emulsification of its butterfat. —**ho·mog'en·ized** *adj.* —**ho·mog'en·i·za'tion, ho·mog'en·iz'er** *n.*

**hom·o·nym** (hom'ə·nim, hō'mə-) *n.* **1** A word identical with another in pronunciation, but differing from it in meaning, origin, and usu. in spelling, as *fair* and *fare, read* and *reed.* **2** Loosely, a homograph. [< Gk. *homos* same + *onyma* name] —**hom·o·nym·ic** (hom'ə·nim'ik, hō'mə-) or **·i·cal** *adj.*

**ho·mo·sex·u·al** (hō'mə·sek'shoo·əl, hom'ə-) *adj.* Pertaining to or characterized by homosexuality. —*n.* A homosexual person.

**hon·est** (on'ist) *adj.* **1** Not given to lies, theft, cheating, etc. **2** Not false or misleading; true: an *honest* answer. **3** Free from fraud; fair; equitable: an *honest* test. **4** Earned or acquired in a just and fair manner: an *honest* living. **5** Frank; open; sincere: an *honest* face. [< L *honos* honor] —**hon'est·ly** *adv.* —**Syn. 1** trustworthy, reliable, fair, honorable, upright. **2** frank, candid, straightforward, artless, forthright. **3** just, impartial, unbiased.

**hon·ey** (hun'ē) *n.* **1** A sweet food made by bees from the nectar of flowers. **2** Sweetness or lusciousness in general. **3** Darling; dear: a term of endearment. **4** *Informal* Something considered as an excellent example of its kind: a *honey* of a boat. —*v.* **hon·eyed** or **hon·ied, hon·ey·ing** —*v.t.* **1** To talk in an endearing or flattering manner to. **2** To sweeten. —*v.i.* **3** To talk fondly or in a coaxing manner. —*adj.* Honeylike; sweet. [< OE *hunig*]

**hon·or** (on′ər) *n.* 1 High regard or respect. 2 Fame; renown; glory. 3 A cause of pride or esteem: an *honor* to be chosen. 4 A sense of what is right and just; integrity: to act with *honor.* 5 A reputation for being just, good, fair, etc.: a man of *honor.* 6 High rank or dignity: the *honor* of the office. 7 *Often pl.* An outward token or sign of respect or regard, as a decoration, ceremony, etc. 8 *pl.* a Recognition given to students for outstanding scholarship, etc. b Academic courses for advanced or exceptional students, usu. in addition to regular courses. 9 Privilege: May I have the *honor* of this dance? 10 In bridge, one of the five highest cards of any suit. 11 In golf, the privilege of playing first from the tee. —**do the honors** To act as host or hostess. —*v.t.* 1 To regard with honor or respect. 2 To treat with courtesy or respect. 3 To do or bestow something in honor of. 4 To accept or pay, as a check or draft. —*adj.* Of or showing honor or respect: an *honor* guard. *Brit. sp.* ·our. [< L] —**hon′or·er** *n.*

**hood** (hood) *n.* 1 A soft or flexible covering for the head and the back of the neck, often attached to a garment. 2 Anything of similar form or character, as a monk's cowl or an ornamental fold attached to the back of an academic gown. 3 In falconry, a cover for the entire head of a hawk. 4 A projecting cover to a hearth, ventilator, etc. 5 A movable cover, as of the engine of an automobile, etc. —*v.t.* To cover or furnish with or as with a hood. [< OE *hōd*]

**hood·lum** (hood′lom, hōod′-) *n.* 1 A rowdy or thug. 2 A criminal. [?] —**hood′lum·ism** *n.*

**hoof** (hoof, hōof) *n. pl.* **hoofs** or **hooves** 1 The horny sheath encasing the ends of the foot in the horse, swine, ox, etc. 2 An animal with hoofs. —**on the hoof** Alive; not butchered: said of cattle. —*v.t. & v.i.* 1 To trample with the hoofs. 2 *Informal* To walk or dance: usu. with *it.* [< OE *hōf*] —**hoofed** (hooft, hōoft) *adj.*

**hook** (hook) *n.* 1 A curved or bent piece serving to catch or hold another object. 2 A fishhook. 3 A cutting tool having a curved blade, as a sickle. 4 A trap or snare. 5 Something shaped like a hook as: a A sharply curved organ of an animal or plant. b A bend in a river. c A curved point of land or a cape. d A hook-shaped written character. 6 In golf, a ball that curves to the left of a right-handed player or vice versa. 7 In

baseball, a curve. 8 In boxing, a short blow delivered crosswise and with the elbow bent and rigid. —*v.t.* 1 To fasten, attach, or take hold of with or as with a hook. 2 To catch on a hook, as fish. 3 *Informal* To trick; take in: I've been *hooked.* 4 To make or bend in the shape of a hook; crook. 5 To catch on or toss with the horns, as a bull. 6 To make, as a rug, by looping thread, yarn, etc., through canvas or burlap with a hook. 7 *Slang* To steal; pilfer. 8 In baseball, to throw (a ball) with a hook. 9 In boxing, to strike with a hook. 10 In golf, to drive (the ball) in a hook. —*v.i.* 11 To curve like a hook; bend. 12 To be fastened with a hook. [< OE *hōc*]

**hoop** (hoop, hōop) *n.* 1 A circular band of metal, wood, etc., esp. one used to confine the staves of a barrel, cask, etc. 2 A child's toy in the shape of a large ring. 3 A framework made of rings of whalebone, steel, etc., used for expanding a woman's skirt. 4 The band of a finger ring. —*v.t.* 1 To surround or fasten with hoops. 2 To encircle. [< OE *hōp*]

**hoot·en·an·ny** (hoot′n·an′ē) *n. pl.* ·**nies** 1 A gathering of folk singers. 2 A gadget; thingamajig. [?]

**hop** (hop) *v.* **hopped, hop·ping** *v.i.* 1 To move in short leaps with one foot off the ground. 2 To jump about by raising both or all feet simultaneously, as a frog. 3 *Informal* To take a trip, esp. a brief one: with *up, down,* or *over.* —*v.t.* 4 To jump over, as a fence. 5 *Informal* To board or catch; get on: to *hop* a train. —*n.* 1 The act or result of hopping. 2 *Informal* A dance or dancing party. 3 *Informal* A short flight in an airplane. [< OE *hoppian*]

**hope** (hōp) *v.* **hoped, hop·ing** *v.t.* 1 To desire with expectation of fulfilment. 2 To wish; want. —*v.i.* 3 To have desire or expectation: usu. with *for*: to *hope* for the best. —*n.* 1 Desire accompanied by expectation. 2 The reason or cause of such desire. 3 The thing hoped for. 4 A person or thing about which one can be hopeful. [< OE *hopian*]

**horde** (hôrd, hōrd) *n.* 1 A multitude, pack, or swarm, as of men, animals, or insects. 2 A clan or tribe of Mongolian nomads. 3 Any nomadic group. —*v.i.* **hord·ed, hord·ing** To gather in a horde. [< Turk. *ordū* camp]

**ho·ri·zon** (ha·rī′zan) *n.* 1 The line of the apparent meeting of the sky with the earth or sea. 2 The plane passing through a position on the earth's surface at right angles to the line of gravity. 3 *Usu. pl.* The limits of one's knowledge, interests, experience, etc. [< Gk *horos* limit, bound] • See PERSPECTIVE.

**hor·i·zon·tal** (hôr′ə·zon′təl, hor′-) *adj.* 1 Parallel to the horizon; level. 2 In the plane of the horizon. 3 Of, on, or close to the horizon. 4 Equal and uniform: a *horizontal* tariff. 5 Made up of similar units; a *horizontal* trust. —*n.* A line or plane assumed to be parallel with the horizon. —**hor′i·zon′tal·ly** *adv.*

**hor·mone** (hôr′mōn) *n.* 1 An internal secretion released in minute amounts into the blood stream by a specific gland or other tissue and stimulating a specific physiological activity. 2 A similar substance in plants. [< Gk. *hormaein* excite] —**hor·mo·nal** (hôr·mō′nəl), **hor·mon·ic** (hôr·mon′ik) *adj.*

**horn** (hôrn) *n.* 1 A permanent bonelike growth projecting from the head of various hoofed animals, as oxen, sheep, etc.; also, the antler of a deer, shed annually. 2 Any natural growth that protrudes from an animal's head, as a feeler, antenna, tentacle, etc. 3 The substance of which animal horns are made. 4 A somewhat similar substance made synthetically. 5 An object formed from or shaped like a horn: a powder *horn*. 6 A wind instrument made of brass, esp. the French horn. 7 *Slang* A trumpet or other brass or wind instrument. 8 Any pointed or tapering projection. 9 One of the extremities of a crescent moon. 10 A cape or peninsula. 11 The pommel of a saddle. 12 The point of an anvil. 13 A flaring tube used to collect or project sound, as in some loudspeakers. 14 A device for sounding warning signals; an automobile *horn*. —**on the horns of a dilemma** Forced to choose between two painful alternatives. —*adj.* Of horn or horns. —*v.t.* 1 To provide with horns. 2 To shape like a horn. 3 To attack with the horns; gore. —**horn in** *Slang* To enter without invitation. [< OE] —**horned** *adj.*

**hor·net** (hôr′nit) *n.* Any of various social wasps capable of inflicting a severe sting. [< OE *hyrnet*]

**hor·ri·ble** (hôr′ə·bəl, hor′-) *adj.* 1 Arousing horror. 2 Very unpleasant or offensive. [< L *horrere* to bristle] —**hor′ri·ble·ness** *n.* —**hor′ri·bly** *adv.* —**Syn.** frightful, terrible, dreadful, hideous, ghastly.

**hor·rid** (hôr′id, hor′-) *adj.* 1 Causing horror or repugnance: dreadful. 2 Very unpleas-

ant, obnoxious, etc. [< L *horrere* to bristle] —**hor′rid·ly** *adv.* —**hor′rid·ness** *n.*

**hor·ri·fy** (hôr′ə·fī, hor′-) *v.t.* ·fied, ·fy·ing 1 To affect or fill with horror. 2 To shock; appall. —**hor′ri·fi·ca′tion** *n.*

**hor·ror** (hôr′ər, hor′-) *n.* 1 A strong feeling of fear, repugnance, terrified alarm, etc. 2 A quality, experience, etc., that arouses such feeling. 3 Intense dislike; aversion. 4 *Informal* Something very unpleasant, ugly, etc. [< L]

**horse** (hôrs) *n.* 1 A large, hoofed mammal with a long mane and tail, used since early times for riding, pulling and carrying loads, etc. 2 The adult male of this animal, as distinguished from a mare. 3 Soldiers mounted on horses; cavalry. 4 A framelike, usu. four-legged device for supporting something. 5 A padded device used for gymnastic exercises such as vaulting. —*v.* **horsed**, **hors·ing** *v.t.* 1 To furnish with a horse or horses; mount. —*v.i.* 2 *Informal* To engage in horseplay: usu. with *around*. —*adj.* Coarse or large for its kind: *horse* chestnut. [< OE *hors*]

**horse·pow·er** (hôrs′pou′ər) *n.* A unit of power equal to 550 foot-pounds per second, or about 746 watts.

**hor·ti·cul·ture** (hôr′tə·kul′chər) *n.* The art and science of growing vegetables, fruits, flowers, etc. [< L *hortus* garden + *cultura* cultivation] —**hor′ti·cul′tur·al** *adj.* —**hor′ti·cul′tur·al·ly** *adv.* —**hor′ti·cul′tur·ist** *n.*

**hose** (hōz) *n. pl.* **hose** for defs. 1 & 2, **hos·es** for def. 3 1 *pl.* Stockings or socks. 2 *Usu. pl.* A tight-fitting, trouserlike garment formerly worn by men. 3 A flexible tube or pipe for conveying water or other fluids. —*v.t.* **hosed**, **hos·ing** To water, wash, or douse with a hose. [< OE *hosa*]

**Ho·se·a** (hō·zē′ə, -zā′ə) *n.* 1 A Hebrew minor prophet of the eighth century B.C. 2 The book of the Old Testament bearing his name.

**hos·pi·ta·ble** (hos′pi·tə·bəl, hos·pit′ə·bəl) *adj.* 1 Welcoming and entertaining guests with generous kindness. 2 Characterized by hospitality. 3 Open-minded; receptive. [< L *hospitare* entertain] —**hos′pi·ta·ble·ness** *n.* —**hos′pi·ta·bly** *adv.*

**hos·pi·tal** (hos′pi·təl) *n.* An institution for the reception, care, and treatment of the sick or injured. [< L *hospes* guest]

**host** (hōst) *n.* 1 One who entertains or receives guests. 2 An innkeeper. 3 A person who introduces and interviews guests, as on certain television or radio shows. 4 An organism that supports a parasite. —*v.t. Informal* To conduct or entertain in the role of a host. [< L *hospes* guest, host]

**hos·tage** (hos′tij) *n.* A person held as a pledge or prisoner until the terms of a stipulation are met. [< OF]

**hos·tile** (hos′tal, *esp. Brit.* hos′til) *adj.* 1 Of or pertaining to an enemy. 2 Feeling, showing, or characterized by enmity, antagonism, etc. 3 Unfavorable or forbidding. [< L *hostilis*] —**hos′tile·ly** *adv.* —*Syn.* 2 unfriendly, antagonistic, malicious, unsociable. 3 adverse, untoward, opposing, contrary.

**hos·til·i·ty** (hos·til′ə·tē) *n. pl.* **·ties** 1 The state of being hostile. 2 *pl.* Warlike activities; warfare.

**hot dog** *Informal* A frankfurter, usu. served in a split roll.

**ho·tel** (hō·tel′) *n.* An establishment or building providing lodging, food, etc., for paying customers. [< OF *hostel* inn]

**hot line** A direct means of communication, esp. a telephone line kept available for emergency use.

**hot rod** *Slang* An automobile modified for increased power and speed.

**hound** (hound) *n.* 1 Any of various breeds of usu. short-haired, long-eared hunting dogs. 2 *Informal* A devotee; enthusiast. —*v.t.* 1 To hunt or pursue persistently. 2 To nag persistently. [< OE *hund*]

**hour** (our) *n.* 1 A unit of time equal to one twenty-fourth of a day; sixty minutes. 2 The point of time indicated by a chronometer, watch, or clock; the time of day. 3 A set, appointed, or definite time. 4 *pl.* Prayers to be repeated at stated times of the day. [< Gk. *hōra* time, period]

**house** (hous) *n.* 1 A building intended for human habitation. 2 A household; family. 3 A building used for any purpose: a coffee *house.* 4 The abode of a fraternity, order, etc.: a sorority *house.* 5 A dormitory or residence hall in a college or university. 6 A legislative body; also, the chamber it occupies. 7 A place of business. 8 A business firm: the *house* of Morgan. 9 The management of a business, gambling establishment, etc. 10 A theater; also, the audience in a theater. 11 *Often cap.* A line of ancestors and descendants regarded as forming a single family: the *House* of Tudor. 12 In astrology, one of the twelve divisions of the heavens, each division having special significance in casting horoscopes. —*v.* (houz)

housed, hous·ing *v.t.* 1 To take or put into a house. 2 To store in a house or building. 3 To fit into a mortise, joint, etc. —*v.i.* 4 To take shelter or lodgings; dwell. [< OE *hūs*] —**house′ful** *n.*

**hov·er** (huv′ər, hov′-) *v.i.* 1 To remain suspended in or near one place in the air. 2 To linger; be nearby, as if waiting or watching: with *around, near,* etc. 3 To remain in an uncertain or irresolute state: with *between.* —*n.* The act of hovering. [< obs. *hove* to float] —**hov′er·er** *n.*

**howl** (houl) *v.i.* 1 To utter the loud, mournful wail of a wolf or dog. 2 To utter such a cry in rage, grief, etc. 3 To make a similar sound. 4 To laugh loudly. —*v.t.* 5 To utter or express with a howl or howls. 6 To drive or effect with a howl or howls. —*n.* 1 The cry of a wolf or dog. 2 Any sound suggesting this, esp. a cry of grief or rage. 3 *Informal* Something considered hilariously funny. [Imit.]

**hoy·den** (hoid′n) *n.* A romping, boisterous girl; tomboy. —*adj.* Rude or unseemly; bold. —*v.i.* To romp rudely or indecently. [?] —**hoy′den·ish** *adj.*

**hub** (hub) *n.* 1 The central part of a wheel. 2 Any center of activity, interest, etc. [? < HOB]

**hub·bub** (hub′ub) *n.* Tumult; uproar.

**huck·ster** (huk′stər) *n.* 1 A glib and aggressive salesman, esp. one having a flamboyant manner. 2 Any peddler or hawker of small wares. 3 *Informal* A producer or writer of advertising commercials, as on radio or television. —*v.t.* 1 To peddle. 2 To promote by showy or aggressive means. [< MDu. *hoekster*] —**huck′ster·ism** *n.*

**hud·dle** (hud′l) *v.* **hud·dled, hud·dling** *v.i.* 1 To crowd closely together. 2 To draw or hunch oneself together, as from cold. 3 To come together for a conference or huddle. —*v.t.* 4 To bring together in a group. 5 To hunch (oneself) together. —*n.* 1 A confused crowd or collection of persons or things. 2 In football, the grouping of a team before each play, in which signals and instructions are given. 3 Any small, intimate conference. [?]

**hue** (hyōō) *n.* A vociferous cry; shouting. [< OF *hu* cry]

**hug** (hug) *v.* **hugged, hug·ging** *v.t.* 1 To clasp tightly within the arms, as from affection. 2 To keep fondly in the mind; cherish, as a belief or opinion. 3 To keep close to, as a shore. —*v.i.* 4 To lie close; nestle. —*n.* A close embrace. [< Scand.]

**huge** (hyōōj) *adj.* Very large in size, degree, or extent. [< OF *ahuge* high] —**huge′ly** *adv.* —**huge′ness** *n.*

**hulk** (hulk) *n.* 1 The body of a ship, esp. of one that is old or wrecked. 2 A heavy, clumsy ship. 3 An abandoned wreck or shell. 4 A bulky or unwieldly object or person. —*v.i.* To rise or loom bulkily: usu. with *up.* [< Gk. *holkas* towed vessel]

**hull** (hul) *n.* 1 An outer covering, as a husk of grain or a nutshell. 2 The calyx attached to a strawberry, tomato, etc. 3 *Naut.* The body of a ship, exclusive of the masts and rigging. 4 The outermost structures of a spacecraft, missile, etc. —*v.t.* To shell; free from the hull. [< OE *hulu* a covering] —**hul′l′er** *n.*

**hum** (hum) *v.* **hummed, hum·ming** *v.i.* 1 To make a low, continuous, buzzing sound, as a bee. 2 To sing with the lips closed. 3 To give forth a confused, indistinct sound, as of mingled voices. 4 *Informal* To be busily active. —*v.t.* 5 To sing, as a tune, with the lips closed. 6 To put into a specified state by humming: to *hum* someone to sleep. —*n.* A dull, low, continuous sound. [Imit.] —**hum′mer** *n.*

**hu·man** (hyōō′mən) *adj.* 1 Of, pertaining to, or like man or mankind. 2 Created by or belonging to man or mankind: *human* problems. 3 Characterized by or exemplifying the strengths, weaknesses, emotions, struggles, etc., typical of man and mankind: a very *human* situation. —*n.* A human being. [< L *humanus*] —**hu′man·ness** *n.*

**hu·mane** (hyōō·mān′) *adj.* 1 Having or showing kindness, tenderness, compassion, etc. 2 Tending to refine or make civilized. —**hu·mane′ly** *adv.* —**hu·mane′ness** *n.* —**Syn.** 1 charitable, merciful, sympathetic, benevolent, clement.

**hu·man·i·tar·i·an** (hyōō·man′ə·târ′ē·ən) *n.* One who seeks to promote the welfare of mankind; a philanthropist. —*adj.* 1 That aids others. 2 Of humanitarianism. —**hu·man′i·tar′i·an·ism** *n.*

**hu·man·i·ty** (hyōō·man′ə·tē) *n. pl.* **·ties** 1 Mankind collectively. 2 Human nature. 3 The state or quality of being human. 4 The state or quality of being humane. —**the hu·manities** The branches of learning including literature, language, philosophy, fine arts, etc., as distinguished from the sciences.

**hum·ble** (hum′bəl) *adj.* **·bler, ·blest** 1 Having or expressing a sense of selflessness, meekness, modesty, etc. 2 Lowly in condition, rank, etc.; unpretending. —*v.t.* **hum·bled, hum·bling** 1 To reduce the pride of; humiliate. 2 To lower in rank or dignity; abase. [< L *humus* ground] —**hum′ble·ness, hum′bler** *n.* —**hum′bly** *adv.* —**Syn.** *adj.* 1 modest, meek, selfless, unassuming, submissive.

**hum·bug** (hum′bug) *n.* 1 A deception; sham. 2 Foolish talk; nonsense. 3 An impostor. —*v.t.* **·bugged, ·bug·ging** To deceive. —*interj.* Nonsense! [?] —**hum′bug·ger, hum′bug·ger·y** *n.*

**hu·mid** (hyōō′mid) *adj.* Containing moisture; damp. [< L *humere* be moist] —**hu′mid·ly** *adv.*

**hu·mid·i·fy** (hyōō·mid′ə·fī) *v.t.* **·fied, ·fy·ing** To make moist or humid, as the atmosphere of a room. —**hu·mid′i·fi·ca′tion, hu·mid′i·fi′er** *n.*

**hu·mid·i·ty** (hyōō·mid′ə·tē) *n.* 1 Moisture; dampness, esp. of the atmosphere. 2 The measure of the water vapor in the air. • See RELATIVE HUMIDITY. **Also hu′mid·ness.**

**hu·mil·i·ate** (hyōō·mil′ē·āt) *v.t.* **·at·ed, ·at·ing** To lower or offend the pride or self-respect of; mortify; humble. [< L *humilis* lowly] —**hu·mil′i·a′tion** *n.*

**hu·mil·i·ty** (hyōō·mil′ə·tē) *n. pl.* **·ties** The state or quality of being humble. —**Syn.** modesty, meekness, unpretentiousness, docility, humbleness.

**hum·ming·bird** (hum′ing·bûrd′) *n.* Any of a family of tiny, nectar-feeding birds with brilliant plumage, long, needlelike bills, and having very rapid wing motion.

**hu·mor** (hyōō′mər) *n.* 1 A person's disposition, mood, or state of mind. 2 The quality of being amusing, comical, ludicrous, etc. 3 The capacity to perceive, appreciate, or give expression to what is amusing, comical, ludicrous, etc. 4 A sudden whim or caprice. 5 A fluid or fluidlike substance of the body. In medieval times the humors, consisting of blood, phlegm, yellow bile, and black bile, were supposed to give rise to the sanguine, phlegmatic, choleric, and melancholic temperaments, respectively. —**out of humor** Irritated; annoyed. —*v.t.* 1 To comply with the moods or caprices of. 2 To accommodate or adapt oneself to. *Brit. sp.* **hu′mour.** [L, liquid]

**hun·ger** (hung′gər) *n.* 1 A need or craving for food. 2 The discomfort or physical debility caused by lack of food. 3 Any strong desire. —*v.i.* 1 To feel hunger. 2 To have a craving or desire: with *for* or *after*: to *hunger* for a chance to return to one's homeland. [< OE]

**hun·gry** (hung′grē) *adj.* **·gri·er, ·gri·est** 1 Having or feeling hunger. 2 Indicating hunger. 3 Eagerly desiring; craving. 4 Barren: said of land. —**hun′gri·ly** *adv.* —**hun′gri·ness** *n.*

**hunt** (hunt) *v.t.* 1 To pursue (game) for the purpose of killing or catching. 2 a To search (a region) for game. b To search (a place): to *hunt* a room. 3 To search for diligently; look for. 4 To use (hounds or horses) in hunting. 5 To chase; pursue. 6 To persecute; harass. —*v.i.* 7 To pursue game or other wild animals; follow the chase. 8 To make a search; seek. —*n.* 1 The act of hunting. 2 A search. 3 The participants in a hunt. 4 A district hunted over. [< OE *huntian*]

**hurl** (hûrl) *v.t.* 1 To throw with violence; fling. 2 To throw down; overthrow. 3 To utter with vehemence. —*v.i.* 4 To throw something. 5 To move or rush violently. —*n.* The act of throwing. [ME *hurlen*] —**hurl′er** *n.*

**hur·ri·cane** (hûr′ə·kān′) *n.* A tropical cyclone having winds moving at about 75 miles per hour or more, usu. originating in the West Indies. [< Cariban]

**hur·ry** (hûr′ē) *v.* **hur·ried, hur·ry·ing** *v.i.* 1 To act or move rapidly or in haste; hasten. —*v.t.* 2 To cause or urge to act or move more rapidly. 3 To hasten the progress, completion, etc., of, often unduly: to *hurry* a decision. —*n. pl.* **hur·ries** 1 The act of hurrying. 2 Eager haste; precipitation. [?]

**hus·band** (huz′bənd) *n.* A married man; man with a wife. —*v.t.* 1 To use or spend wisely; conserve. 2 *Archaic* To be a husband to; marry. 3 *Archaic* To till; cultivate. [< OE < *hūs* house + *bonda* freeholder]

**husk** (husk) *n.* 1 The outer covering of certain fruits or seeds. 2 Any covering, esp. when comparatively worthless. —*v.t.* To remove the husk of. [ME *huske*] —**husk′er** *n.*

**husk·y** (hus′kē) *adj.* **husk·i·er, husk·i·est** 1 Abounding in husks; like husks. 2 Somewhat hoarse: said of the voice. —**husk′i·ly** *adv.* —**husk′i·ness** *n.*

**hus·tle** (hus′əl) *v.* **hus·tled, hus·tling** *v.t.* 1 To push or knock about roughly; jostle. 2 To force or push roughly and hurriedly. 3 *Informal* To cause to be done or proceed rapidly. 4 *Slang* To sell or obtain in an ag- gressive, often underhanded manner. —*v.i.* 5 To push one's way; shove; elbow. 6 *Informal* To act or work with energy and speed. 7 *Slang* a To obtain money in an aggressive, usu. underhanded manner. b To be a prostitute. —*n.* 1 The act of hustling. 2 *Informal* Energetic activity; push. [MDu. *hutselen* shake, toss] —**hus′tler** *n.*

**hy·a·cinth** (hī′ə·sinth) *n.* 1 A plant related to the lily with a spike of small, fragrant flowers. 2 The bulb or flower of this plant. 3 A gem, a brownish, reddish, or orange zircon. [< L < Gk. *hyakinthos*] —**hy′a·cin′thine** (-thin, -thīn) *adj.*

**hy·brid** (hī′brid) *n.* 1 An offspring of two animals or plants of different species, varieties, breeds, etc. 2 Anything of mixed origin or unlike parts. 3 *Ling.* A word composed of elements from more than one language. —*adj.* Of, pertaining to, or like a hybrid. [< L *hybrida*] —**hy′brid·ism** *n.*

**hy·drant** (hī′drənt) *n.* A large, upright street pipe from which water may be obtained from a water main for fighting fires, cleaning streets, etc. [< HYDR(O)- + -ANT]

**hy·drau·lic** (hī·drô′lik) *adj.* 1 Of or involving the moving of water, or force exerted by water. 2 Denoting a machine or device operated by liquid under pressure. 3 Hardening under water: *hydraulic* cement. [< Gk. *hydraulos* water organ] —**hy·drau′li·cal·ly** *adv.*

**hy·dro·e·lec·tric** (hī′drō·i·lek′trik) *adj.* Of or pertaining to electricity developed from water power. —**hy·dro·e·lec·tric·i·ty** (hī′drō·i·lek·tris′ə·tē) *n.*

**hy·dro·foil** (hī′drə·foil) *n.* 1 One of a set of fins attached to a vessel to provide a reaction force with the water at high speeds and lift the hull from the water. 2 A vessel equipped with hydrofoils.

**hy·dro·gen** (hī′drə·jən) *n.* The lightest and most abundant element (symbol H) in the universe, on earth found mainly in combination with oxygen as water. [< Gk. *hydōr* water + *-genēs* born] —**hy·drog·e·nous** (hī·droj′ə·nəs) *adj.*

**hydrogen bomb** An extremely powerful thermonuclear bomb based on the fusion of light nuclei, as of deuterium and lithium.

**hy·dro·pho·bi·a** (hī′drə·fō′bē·ə) *n.* 1 RABIES. 2 Any morbid dread of water. —**hy′dro·pho′bic** *adj.*

**hy·e·na** (hī·ē′nə) *n.* A wolflike carnivorous mammal of Africa and Asia, with very strong, large teeth, striped or spotted body, and a piercing cry. [< Gk. *hyaina* < *hys* pig]

**hy·giene** (hī′jēn, -ji·ēn) *n.* 1 The science and preservation of health. 2 Practices and conditions that promote good health. [< Gk. *hygienios* healthful]

**hymn** (him) *n.* 1 A song of praise to God. 2 Any religious song. 3 A poem of praise. —*v.* **hymned, hymn·ing** *v.t.* 1 To express or praise in hymns. —*v.i.* 2 To sing hymns or praises. [< Gk. *hymnos* a song, ode] —**hym′nic** (-nik) *adj.* —**hym′nist** *n.*

**hym·nal** (him′nəl) *n.* A book of hymns: **also hymn book.** —*adj.* Of a hymn or hymns.

**hy·per·bo·le** (hī·pûr′bə·lē) *n.* Deliberate exaggeration in writing or speaking, used to create an effect, as in *He was as tall as a mountain.* [< Gk. *hyperbolē* excess]

**hy·per·son·ic** (hī·pər·son′ik) *adj.* Of, at, or pertaining to speeds of mach 5 or greater.

**hy·per·ten·sion** (hī′pər·ten′shən) *n.* Excessively high arterial blood pressure. —**hy′per·ten′sive** *adj., n.*

**hy·phen** (hī′fən) *n.* A mark (-or -or=) used to connect the elements of certain compound words, to show division of a word at the end of a line, and to indicate a unit modifier: a *hit-and-run* driver. [< Gk. *hypo-* under + *hen* one]

**hyp·no·tism** (hip′nə·tiz′əm) *n.* 1 The act, practice, or technique of inducing hypnosis. 2 The theory of hypnosis. —**hyp′no·tist** *n.*

**hyp·no·tize** (hip′nə·tīz) *v.t.* **·tized, ·tiz·ing** 1 To produce hypnosis in. 2 To fascinate; entrance. *Brit. sp.* **hyp′no·tise.** —**hyp′no·tiz′a·ble** *adj.* —**hyp′no·ti·za′tion** (-tə·zā′shən, -tī·zā′-), **hyp′no·tiz′er** *n.*

**hy·poc·ri·sy** (hi·pok′rə·sē) *n. pl.* **·sies** A pretending to be what one is not; extreme insincerity; dissimulation. [< Gk. *hypokrisis* acting a part, feigning] —**Syn.** pretense, dissembling, affectation, sham, fakery.

**hyp·o·crite** (hip′ə·krit) *n.* One who pretends to have virtues, feelings, qualities, etc., that he does not possess. [< Gk. *hypokritēs* an actor.] —**hyp′o·crit′i·cal** *adj.* —**hyp′o·crit′i·cal·ly** *adv.* —**Syn.** deceiver, dissembler, pretender, cheat.

**hy·po·der·mic** (hī′pə·dûr′mik) *adj.* 1 Of or pertaining to the tissue just under the skin. 2 Of or pertaining to a hypodermic injection. —*n.* A hypodermic injection or syringe.

**hy·pot·e·nuse** (hī·pot′ə·nyo͞os, hi-) *n. Geom.* The side of a right triangle opposite the right angle. **Also hy·poth′e·nuse** (-poth′-). [<Gk. *hypo-* under + *teinein* to stretch]

**hy·poth·e·sis** (hī·poth′ə·sis, hi-) *n. pl.* **·ses** (-sēz) 1 A set of assumptions provisionally accepted as a basis of reasoning, experiment, or investigation. 2 An unsupported or ill-supported theory. [< Gk. *hypotithenai* put under]

**hys·te·ri·a** (his·tir′ē·ə, -ter′-) *n.* 1 A psychoneurotic condition characterized by symptoms of organic disorders, as blindness, deafness, etc. 2 Uncontrollable emotional excitement. **Also hys·ter·ics** (his-ter′iks). [<Gk. *hystera* the womb, thought to be the source of such symptoms]

# I

**ICBM** Intercontinental Ballistic Missile.

**ice** (īs) *n.* 1 The solid state of water, assumed at or below 32°F. or 0°C. 2 Something resembling ice. 3 A frozen dessert made without cream, as sherbet. 4 Icing for cake. 5 *Slang* A diamond or diamonds. —**break the ice** 1 To break through reserve or formality. 2 To make a start. —**on ice** *Slang* 1 Set aside for future action. 2 Sure; already determined. —**on thin ice** *Informal* In a difficult or dangerous situation. —*v.* **iced, ic·ing** *v.t.* 1 To cause to congeal into ice. 2 To cover with ice. 3 To chill with or as with ice. 4 To frost, as cake, with icing. 5 In ice hockey, to shoot (the puck) from one's own end of the rink past the opponent's goal line. 6 *Slang* To clinch victory in (a contest). —*v.i.* 7 To freeze. [< OE *īs*]

**ice·berg** (īs′bûrg′) *n.* 1 A thick mass of floating ice that has separated from a glacier. 2 *Informal* A cold, unemotional person. [< Du. *ijsberg* ice mountain]

**i·ci·cle** (ī′si·kəl) *n.* A hanging mass of ice formed by dripping water. [< OE is ice + *gicel* piece of ice, icicle] —**i′ci·cled** *adj.*

**ic·ing** (ī′sing) *n.* A coating for cakes and pastry, usu. made of sugar and water, flavoring, egg whites, cream, butter, etc.; frosting.

**i·con** (ī′kon) *n. pl.* **i·cons** or **i·con·es** (ī′kə·nēz) 1 In the Eastern Orthodox Church, a holy picture or mosaic of Jesus, Mary, etc. 2 An image or likeness. [< Gk. *eikon* image] —**i·con′ic, i·con′i·cal** *adj.*

**i·con·o·clast** (i·kon′ə·klast) *n.* 1 One who destroys religious images. 2 One who attacks traditional beliefs or institutions. [< Gk.

*eikōn* image + *-klastēs* breaker] **—i·con′o·clasm** n. **—i·con′o·clas′tic** adj. **—i·con′o·clas′ti·cal·ly** adv.

**id** (id) n. *Psychoanal.* The part of the psyche that is impelled towards fulfilling instinctual needs; the reservoir of libido. [< L *id* it]

**i·de·a** (ī·dē′ə) n. 1 A thought, concept, or image present in the mind. 2 A definitely formulated thought; belief; opinion. 3 A plan or project. 4 A vague thought or supposition: I had an *idea* you'd come. 5 *Informal* Meaning; aim: What's the *idea?* 6 In Platonic philosophy, the archetype or model of which all existing things are imperfect representations. [< Gk. < *ideein* see]

**i·de·al** (ī·dē′əl, ī·dēl′) adj. 1 Of, relating to, or existing in ideas, images, or concepts of the mind. 2 Existing only in imagination or notion as regards perfection, etc.; imaginary. 3 Supremely excellent or desirable; perfect: the *ideal* job. 4 In philosophy, existing as an archetypal idea or model. —n. 1 That which is taken as a standard of perfection, excellence, or beauty; model; type. 2 An ultimate aim or goal. 3 That which exists only in imagination. [< L *idealis*]

**i·de·al·ism** (ī·dē′əl·iz′əm) n. 1 The practice or habit of conceiving of things as ideal or as they should be rather than as they actually are. 2 The forming of and striving after ideals. 3 In art and literature, the treatment of persons or things according to an imaginative or preconceived idea of perfection instead of adhering strictly to facts. 4 In philosophy, any theory which holds that reality is essentially spiritual or mental and that there is no world of objects apart from a reacting mind or consciousness.

**i·de·al·ist** (ī·dē′əl·ist) n. 1 One who idealizes. 2 A visionary or a romantic. 3 An exponent of idealism in art, philosophy, or literature. **—i·de·al·is′tic** or **·ti·cal** adj. **—i·de·al·is′ti·cal·ly** adv.

**i·de·al·ize** (ī·dē′əl·īz) v. **·ized**, **·iz·ing** v.t. To represent or think of (a person, thing, etc.) as conforming to some standard, usu. unattainable, of perfection or beauty; make ideal; exalt. —v.i. To form an ideal or ideals. **—i·de·al·i·za·tion** (ī·dē′əl·ə·zā′shən, -ī·zā′-), **i·de·al·iz′er** n.

**i·den·ti·cal** (ī·den′ti·kəl) adj. 1 The very same. 2 Alike in all respects. [< L *idem*] **—i·den′ti·cal·ly** adv. **—i·den′ti·cal·ness** n.

**i·den·ti·fy** (ī·den′tə·fī) v.t. **·fied**, **·fy·ing** 1 To determine as a particular person or thing.

2 To consider or treat as the same: He *identifies* money with happiness. 3 To serve as a means of identification of. 4 To join or associate in interest, action, etc.: usu. with *with*. 5 *Psychoanal.* To unconsciously incorporate (in one's self) the identity of someone else. [< LL *identitas* identity + -FY] **—i·den′ti·fi′a·ble** adj. **—i·den′ti·fi′er** n.

**i·den·ti·ty** (ī·den′tə·tē) n. pl. **·ties** 1 The state of being identical. 2 The state of being exactly that which has been claimed, asserted, or described. 3 The distinctive character belonging to an individual; individuality. 4 A mathematical equation that is satisfied by all values of its variables for which the expressions involved have meaning. [< LL *identitas* < IDEM]

**i·de·ol·o·gy** (ī′dē·ol′ə·jē, id′ē-) n. pl. **·gies** 1 The ideas, doctrines, or way of thinking characteristic of a political or economic theory or system. 2 The science that treats of the nature and evolution of ideas. 3 Visionary or impractical thinking. [IDEO- + -LOGY] **—i·de·o·log·ic** (ī′dē·ə·loj′ik, id′ē-) or **·i·cal** adj. **—i′de·o·log′i·cal·ly** adv. **—i′de·ol′o·gist** n.

**id·i·o·cy** (id′ē·ə·sē) n. pl. **·cies** 1 An extreme degree of congenital mental deficiency. 2 A foolish utterance or act.

**id·i·om** (id′ē·əm) n. 1 An expression not readily analyzable from its grammatical construction or from the meaning of its component parts, as *to put up with* (tolerate, endure). 2 The dialect or language characteristic of a certain group, class, trade, region, etc.: legal *idiom*. 3 The distinctive form or construction of a particular language. 4 Specific character, form, or style, as in art, literature, music, etc. [< Gk. *idiōma* peculiarity, property]

**id·i·ot** (id′ē·ət) n. 1 A person having an extreme degree of congenital mental deficiency. 2 Any foolish or stupid person. [< Gk. *idiōtēs* private person]

**i·dle** (īd′l) adj. 1 Not occupied; doing nothing. 2 Not being used: *idle* factories. 3 Averse to labor; lazy. 4 Used for leisure. 5 Without effect; useless: *idle* talk. —v. **i·dled**, **i·dling** v.i. 1 To spend time in idleness. 2 To saunter or move idly. 3 To operate without a load, as an engine or motor. —v.t. 1 To pass in idleness; waste, as a day. 2 To cause to be idle, as a person or an industry. [< OE *idel* empty, useless] **—i′dle·ness**, **i′dler** n. **—i′dly** adv. **—Syn.** adj. 3 inactive, indolent, laggard, slothful. *v.* 1 dally, laze, loaf, lounge.

**i·dol** (īd′l) *n.* 1 An image of a god, esp. a heathen god, to which worship is offered. 2 In the Bible, a false god. 3 Any object of extreme or passionate devotion. 4 A source of error; a fallacy. [< Gk. *eidōlon* image, phantom]

**i·dol·a·ter** (ī·dol′ə·tər) *n.* 1 An adorer of images. 2 One who is inordinately fond of some person or thing. [< Gk. *eidōlon* an idol + *latreuein* worship] —**i·dol′a·tress** (-tris) *n. Fem.*

**i·dol·a·trous** (ī·dol′ə·trəs) *adj.* 1 Of or like idolatry. 2 Extravagant in admiration. — **i·dol′a·trous·ly** *adv.* —**i·dol′a·trous·ness** *n.*

**i·dol·a·try** (ī·dol′ə·trē) *n. pl.* **·tries** 1 The worship of idols. 2 Excessive admiration or devotion.

**i·dol·ize** (ī′dəl·īz) *v.* **·ized, ·iz·ing** *v.t.* 1 To have inordinate love for; adore. 2 To worship as an idol. —*v.i.* 3 To worship idols. —i′dol·i·za′tion, i′dol·iz′er *n.*

**i·dyll** (īd′l) *n.* 1 A short poem or prose piece depicting simple scenes of pastoral life. 2 Any event or scene suitable for such a work. 3 A romantic episode. Also i′dyl. [< Gk. *eidos* form] —i′dyl·list, i′dyl·ist *n.*

**ig·ne·ous** (ig′nē·əs) *adj.* 1 Of or like fire. 2 *Geol.* Pertaining to the heat inside the earth: said esp. of rocks formed from molten magma. [< L *ignis* fire]

**ig·ni·tion** (ig·nish′ən) *n.* 1 The act of igniting. 2 The explosion of the fuel mixture in the cylinder of an internal-combustion engine. 3 The electrical system that does this.

**ig·no·ble** (ig·nō′bəl) *adj.* Unworthy or degraded in character or quality. [< L *ignobilis* < IN-[1] + *nobilis* noble] —**ig·nob′ly** *adv.* —**ig′no·bil′i·ty, ig·no′ble·ness** *n.* —*Syn.* base, contemptible, despicable, low, mean.

**ig·no·min·i·ous** (ig′nə·min′ē·əs) *adj.* 1 Marked by or implying dishonor or disgrace. 2 Deserving ignominy; despicable. 3 Abasing; humiliating. —**ig′no·min′i·ous·ly** *adv.* —**ig′no·min′i·ous·ness** *n.*

**ig·no·min·y** (ig′nə·min′ē) *n. pl.* **·min·ies** 1 Disgrace or dishonor. 2 That which causes disgrace. [< L *in-* not + *nomen* name, reputation]

**ig·no·ra·mus** (ig′nə·rā′məs, -ram′əs) *n. pl.* **·mus·es** An ignorant person. [< L, we do not know]

**ig·no·rance** (ig′nər·əns) *n.* The state or quality of being ignorant.

**ig·no·rant** (ig′nər·ənt) *adj.* 1 Lacking education or knowledge. 2 Lacking awareness: with *of.* 3 Not informed or experienced: with *in.* 4 Manifesting or caused by ignorance. [< L *ignorare* not to know] —**ig′no·rant·ly** *adv.*

**ig·nore** (ig·nôr′, -nōr′) *v.t.* **·nored, ·nor·ing** To refuse to notice or recognize; disregard intentionally. [< L *ignorare* not to know] —**ig·nor′er** *n.*

**ill** (il) *adj.* 1 Not well; sick. 2 Evil; bad: *ill* repute. 3 Hostile; unfriendly: *ill* will. 4 Not favorable; dangerous: *ill* wind. 5 Of inferior quality; imperfect. —*n.* Anything that brings about misfortune, harm, sickness, evil, etc. —*adv.* 1 Not well; badly. 2 With difficulty; hardly. 3 Unfavorably; unkindly: to speak *ill* of someone. —**ill at ease** Uneasy; uncomfortable. [< ON *illr*]

**ill-bred** (il′bred′) *adj.* Badly taught, reared, or trained; rude. —*Syn.* boorish, discourteous, impolite, unmannerly.

**il·le·gal** (i·lē′gəl) *adj.* Contrary to the law; not legal. —**il·le·gal·i·ty** (il′ē·gal′ə·tē) *n.* (pl. ·ties) —**il·le′gal·ly** *adv.*

**il·leg·i·ble** (i·lej′ə·bəl) *adj.* not legible; undecipherable. —**il·leg′i·bly** *adv.* — **il·leg′i·bil′i·ty, il·leg′i·ble·ness** *n.*

**il·lic·it** (i·lis′it) *adj.* Not permitted; unlawful. [< L *in-* not + *licitus* licit] —**il·lic′it·ly** *adv.* —**il·lic′it·ness** *n.*

**il·lit·er·a·cy** (i·lit′ər·ə·sē) *n. pl.* **·cies** 1 The state of being illiterate. 2 A mistake in speaking or writing, usu. resulting from a lack of education.

**il·lit·er·ate** (i·lit′ər·it) *adj.* 1 Unable to read or write. 2 Having or showing little or no education. —*n.* An illiterate person, esp. one who cannot read or write. [< L *in-* not + *literatus* literate] —**il·lit′er·ate·ly** *adv.* —**il·lit′er·ate·ness** *n.*

**ill·ness** (il′nis) *n.* 1 The state of being in poor health. 2 An ailment; sickness.

**il·log·i·cal** (i·loj′i·kəl) *adj.* Not logical or reasonable. —**il·log′i·cal′i·ty, il·log′i·cal·ness** *n.* —**il·log′i·cal·ly** *adv.*

**il·lu·mi·nate** (i·lōō′mə·nāt) *v.* **·nat·ed, ·nat·ing** *v.t.* 1 To give light to; light up. 2 To explain; make clear. 3 To enlighten, as the mind. 4 To make illustrious. 5 To decorate with lights. 6 To decorate (a manuscript, letter, etc.) with ornamental borders, figures, etc., of gold or other colors. —*v.i.* 7 To light up. [< L *in-* thoroughly + *luminare* to light] —**il·lu′mi·na′tive** *adj.* —**il·lu′mi·na′ting·ly** *adv.* —**il·lu′mi·na′tor** *n.*

**il·lu·mi·na·tion** (i·lōō′mə·nā′shən) *n.* 1 The

act of illuminating or the state of being illuminated. 2 Decoration by lighting. 3 An amount of or the intensity of light. 4 Mental or spiritual enlightenment. 5 Embellishment of manuscript, with colors and gold, or a particular figure or design in such ornamentation.

il·lu·mine (i·lōō′min) *v.t.* & *v.i.* ·mined, ·min·ing To illuminate or be illuminated. —il·lu′mi·na·ble *adj.*

il·lu·sion (i·lōō′zhən) *n.* 1 An unreal image or appearance. 2 A sensory impression which misrepresents the true character of the object perceived: an optical *illusion.* 3 A false or misleading idea or concept; delusion: the *illusions* of youth. 4 A thin material resembling tulle. [< L *illusio* mocking < *illudere* make sport of] —il·lu′sion·al, il·lu′sion·ar·y (-er-ē) *adj.*

il·lu·so·ry (i·lōō′sər·ē, -zər-) *adj.* Misleading; deceptive; unreal. Also il·lu′sive (-siv). —il·lu′so·ri·ly *adv.* —il·lu′so·ri·ness *n.*

il·lus·tra·tive (i·lus′trə·tiv, il′əs·trā′tiv) *adj.* Serving to illustrate or exemplify. —il·lus′tra·tive·ly *adv.*

il·lus·tri·ous (i·lus′trē·əs) *adj.* Very famous; celebrated; renowned. [< L *in-* in + *lustrum* light] —il·lus′tri·ous·ly *adv.* —il·lus′tri·ous·ness *n.*

im·age (im′ij) *n.* 1 A representation of a person or thing, as a statue, picture, idol, etc. 2 The picture or counterpart of an object produced by a lens, mirror, etc. 3 A natural resemblance; likeness; counterpart. 4 A mental picture, impression, or idea. 5 The way in which a person or thing is popularly perceived or regarded: a politician striving to improve his *image.* 6 A metaphor or a simile. 7 A symbol; embodiment; type. —*v.t.* ·aged, ·ag·ing 1 To form a mental picture of; imagine. 2 To make a visible representation of; portray; delineate. 3 To mirror; reflect. 4 To describe vividly in speech or writing. 5 To symbolize. [< L *imago*]

im·age·ry (im′ij·rē, -ə·rē) *n. pl.* ·ries 1 The act of making images. 2 Mental images. 3 Decorative images, esp. statues. 4 Figurative description in speech or writing.

i·mag·i·nar·y (i·maj′ə·ner′ē) *adj.* 1 Existing only in imagination; unreal. 2 *Math.* Having a negative square, as $\sqrt{-1}$. —im·ag′i·nar′i·ly *adv.*

i·mag·i·na·tion (i·maj′ə·nā′shən) *n.* 1 The act or power of producing images in the mind of things not actually present to the senses. 2 The creative act or faculty of producing

mental images and concepts that are or seem to be totally new and original. 3 That which is imagined, as a mental image or fantasy. 4 An irrational notion or belief. —im·ag′i·na′tion·al *adj.*

i·mag·ine (i·maj′in) *v.* ·ined, ·in·ing *v.t.* 1 To form a mental image of; conceive or create in the mind. 2 To suppose or conjecture. —*v.i.* 3 To use the imagination. 4 To make conjectures; suppose. [< L *imago* image]

im·be·cile (im′bə·sil) *adj.* 1 Mentally deficient. 2 Stupid; foolish. —*n.* 1 A person with a marked degree of, congenital mental deficiency. 2 Any foolish or stupid person. [< L *imbecillus* weak]

im·be·cil·i·ty (im′bə·sil′ə·tē) *n. pl.* ·ties 1 The condition or quality of being imbecile. 2 Foolishness or stupidity, as of action, speech, etc.

im·bue (im·byōō′) *v.t.* ·bued, ·bu·ing 1 To wet thoroughly; saturate. 2 To impregnate with color; dye. 3 To fill, as the mind, with emotions, principles, etc. [< L *imbuere* wet]

im·i·tate (im′ə·tāt) *v.t.* ·tat·ed, ·tat·ing 1 To try to be the same as. 2 To mimic. 3 To make a copy of; duplicate. 4 To assume the appearance of; look like. [< L *imitari* imitate] —im·i·ta·ble (im′ə·tə·bəl) *adj.* —im′i·ta·bil′i·ty, im′i·ta′tor *n.*

im·i·ta·tion (im′ə·tā′shən) *n.* 1 The act of imitating. 2 That which results from imitating; likeness; copy. —*adj.* Imitating something genuine or superior: *imitation* diamonds.

im·mac·u·late (i·mak′yə·lit) *adj.* 1 Without spot or blemish; totally clean. 2 Without evil or sin; pure. 3 Faultless; flawless. [< L *in-* not + *maculatus* spotted] —im·mac′u·late·ly *adv.* —im·mac′u·late·ness *n.* —Syn. 1 impeccable, spotless, unsullied. 2 innocent, irreproachable, sinless.

im·ma·nent (im′ə·nənt) *adj.* Remaining or operating within; inherent. [< L *in-* in + *manere* stay] —im′ma·nent·ly *adv.*

im·ma·te·ri·al (im′ə·tir′ē·əl) *adj.* 1 Not made of matter; incorporeal. 2 Unimportant. —im′ma·te′ri·al·ly *adv.* —im′ma·te′ri·al·ness *n.*

im·ma·ture (im′ə·chōōr′, -t′ōōr′) *adj.* 1 Not mature or ripe; not full-grown. 2 Not complete or perfected. —im′ma·ture′ly *adv.* —im′ma·tur′i·ty *n.*

im·me·di·ate (i·mē′dē·it) *adj.* 1 Without anything intervening: the *immediate* cause of his death. 2 Not appreciably separated in space or time; closest; nearest: the *immediate* past. 3 Next or closest in rank, relationship, etc.: his *immediate* successor. **4** Present; current: our *immediate* problem. **5** Without delay; instant: his *immediate* reaction. [< Med. L *immediatus*] —**im·me′di·ate·ness** *n.*

**im·mense** (i·mens′) *adj.* **1** Very great in degree or size; vast; huge. **2** *Informal* Very good; excellent. [< L *in-* not + *mensus*, pp. of *metiri* to measure] —**im·mense′ly** *adj.*

**im·merse** (i·mûrs′) *v.t.* **·mersed, ·mers·ing 1** To plunge or dip entirely in water or other fluid. **2** To involve deeply; engross: He *immersed* himself in study. **3** To baptize by submerging in water. [< L *immergere* dip] —**im·mer′sion** *n.*

**im·mi·grant** (im′ə·grənt) *n.* A person who immigrates. —*adj.* Immigrating.

**im·mi·grate** (im′ə·grāt) *v.* **·grat·ed, ·grat·ing** *v.i.* **1** To come into a new country or region for the purpose of settling there. —*v.t.* **2** To bring in as an immigrant or settler. [< L *in-* in + *migrare* migrate] —**im′mi·gra′tion** *n.* —**im′mi·gra·to′ry** (-tôr′ē, -tō′rē) *adj.*

**im·mi·nent** (im′ə·nənt) *adj.* About to happen; impending: said esp. of danger or misfortune. [< L *imminere* lean over, impend] —**im′mi·nent·ly** *adv.*

**im·mo·bile** (i·mō′bəl, -bēl) *adj.* **1** Unmovable; stable. **2** Not moving; motionless. —**im·mo·bil·i·ty** (i′mō·bil′ə·tē) *n.*

**im·mor·al** (i·môr′əl, i·mor′-) *adj.* **1** Contrary to moral principles; not right or good. **2** Impure; lewd; licentious. —**im·mor′al·ly** *adv.* • See UNMORAL.

**im·mor·tal** (i·môr′təl) *adj.* **1** Having unending existence; deathless. **2** Lasting or enduring forever. —*n.* **1** A person considered worthy of immortality. **2** In mythology, a god. —**im·mor′tal·ly** *adv.* —**Syn.** *adj.* **1** deathless, imperishable, undying. **2** endless, infinite, permanent, perpetual.

**im·mor·tal·i·ty** (im′ôr·tal′ə·tē) *n.* **1** Exemption from death; eternal life. **2** Eternal fame.

**im·mune** (i·myōōn′) *adj.* **1** Exempt, as from a penalty, burden, duty, or taxation. **2** Protected from a communicable or allergic disease by the presence of antibodies in the blood. **3** Pertaining to immunity or immunization. [< L *in-* not + *munus* service, duty] —**im·mu·ni·ty** (i·myōō′nə·tē) *n.* (*pl.* **·ties**)

**im·mu·nol·o·gy** (im′yə·nol′ə·jē) *n.* The science which treats of the reactions of animal tissues against foreign proteins, as in viruses, allergens, tissue transplants, etc. [< IM-MUNO- + -LOGY] —**im·mu·no·log·ic**

(i·myōō′nə·loj′ik), **im·mu′no·log′i·cal** *adj.* —**im′mu·nol′o·gist** *n.*

**im·mu·ta·ble** (i·myōō′tə·bəl) *adj.* Not changing or altering; unchangeable. [< L *immutabilis*] —**im·mu·ta·bil′i·ty, im·mu′ta·ble·ness** *n.* —**im·mu′ta·bly** *adv.*

**im·pact** (im·pakt′) *v.t.* To press firmly together; pack; wedge. —*n.* (im′pakt) **1** The act of striking; collision. **2** The forcible contact of a moving body with another. **3** A powerful influence: the *impact* of science on culture. [< L *impingere* to thrust against] —**im·pac′tion** *n.*

**im·pair** (im·pâr′) *v.t.* To diminish in quality, strength, or value; injure; damage. [< LL *in-* thoroughly + *pejorare* make worse] —**im·pair′er, im·pair′ment** *n.*

**im·pal·pa·ble** (im·pal′pə·bəl) *adj.* **1** Imperceptible to the touch. **2** Not easily grasped or discerned by the mind. —**im·pal′pa·bil′i·ty** *n.* —**im·pal′pa·bly** *adv.*

**im·part** (im·pärt′) *v.t.* **1** To make known; tell; communicate. **2** To give a portion of; give. —*v.t.* **3** To give a part; share. [< L *in-* on + *partire* to share] —**im·par·ta′tion, im·part′er** *n.*

**im·par·tial** (im·pär′shəl) *adj.* Not partial; unbiased; just. —**im·par′tial·ly** *adv.* —**im·par′tial·ness** *n.*

**im·par·ti·al·i·ty** (im′pär·shē·al′ə·tē, im·pär′-) *n.* The quality or character of being impartial.

**im·pas·sive** (im·pas′iv) *adj.* **1** Insensible to suffering or pain. **2** Unmoved by or not exhibiting feeling; calm. —**im·pas′sive·ly** *adv.* —**im·pas′sive·ness, im·pas·siv·i·ty** (im′pa·siv′ə·tē) *n.*

**im·pa·tience** (im·pā′shəns) *n.* **1** Lack of patience, esp. when faced with delay, opposition, etc. **2** A restless longing or eagerness.

**im·pa·tient** (im·pā′shənt) *adj.* **1** Not possessed of patience; disturbed by or intolerant of delay, pain, opposition, etc. **2** Exhibiting or expressing impatience. —**im·pa′tient·ly** *adv.* —**im·pa′tient·ness** *n.*

**im·peach** (im·pēch′) *v.t.* **1** To bring discredit upon; challenge: to *impeach* one's honesty. **2** To charge with crime or misdemeanor, esp. to arraign (a public official) before a competent tribunal on such a charge. [< LL *impedicare* entangle] —**im·peach′a·bil′i·ty, im·peach′ment** *n.* —**im·peach′a·ble** *adj.*

**im·pede** (im·pēd′) *v.t.* **·ped·ed, ·ped·ing** To retard or hinder in progress or action; obstruct. [L *impedire*, lit., shackle the feet] —**im·ped′er** *n.*

**im·ped·i·ment** (im·ped′·ə·mənt) *n.* 1 That which hinders or impedes; an obstruction. 2 A speech defect, as a stammer. 3 *Law* Anything that prevents the contraction of a valid marriage. —im·ped′i·men′tal, im·ped′i·men′ta·ry *adj.* —Syn. 1 barrier, encumbrance, hindrance, obstacle.

**im·pel** (im·pel′) *v.t.* ·pelled, ·pel·ling 1 To drive or push (something) forward or onward. 2 To urge or force (someone) to an action, course, etc.; incite; compel. [< L *in-* on + *pellere* to drive] —im·pel′lent *adj., n.* —im·pel′ler *n.*

**im·pend** (im·pend′) *v.i.* 1 To be imminent; threaten, as something evil or destructive. 2 To be suspended; hang: with *over.* [< L *in-* on + *pendere* to hang] —im·pen′dence, im·pen′den·cy *n.*

**im·per·a·tive** (im·per′ə·tiv) *adj.* 1 Expressive of positive command; authoritative. 2 *Gram.* Designating that mood of the verb which expresses command, entreaty, or exhortation. 3 Not to be evaded or avoided; obligatory. —*n.* 1 Something imperative, as a command, rule, duty, etc. 2 *Gram.* The imperative mood; also, a verb in this mood. [< L *imperare* to command] —im·per′a·tive·ly *adv.* —im·per′a·tive·ness *n.*

**im·pe·ri·al** (im·pir′ē·əl) *adj.* 1 Of or pertaining to an empire, or to an emperor or an empress. 2 Designating the legal weights and measures of the United Kingdom. 3 Of or pertaining to a country having control over colonies or the like. 4 Majestic; regal. 5 Superior in size or quality. —*n.* 1 A pointed tuft of hair on the chin. 2 Anything of more than usual size or excellence. 3 A size of paper, 23 in. × 31 in. [< L *imperium* rule] —im·pe′ri·al·ly *adv.*

**im·per·son·ate** (im·pûr′sən·āt) *v.t.* ·at·ed, ·at·ing 1 To mimic the appearance, mannerisms, etc., of. 2 To act or play the part of. 3 To represent in human form; personify: He *impersonates* the quality of virtue. —*adj.* (-it) Embodied in a person; personified. —im·per′son·a′tion, im·per′son·a′tor *n.*

**im·per·ti·nent** (im·pûr′tə·nənt) *adj.* 1 Rude; impudent. 2 Irrelevant; not to the point. 3 Not suitable or fitting. —im·per′ti·nent·ly *adv.*

**im·per·vi·ous** (im·pûr′vē·əs) *adj.* 1 Permitting no passage of fluids, light rays, etc.; impenetrable. 2 Not influenced or affected by. [< L *in-* not + *per-* through + *via* way, road] —im·per′vi·ous·ly *adv.* —im·per′vi·ous·ness *n.*

**im·pet·u·ous** (im·pech′ŏŏ·əs) *adj.* 1 Characterized by energy or violent force: *impetuous* haste. 2 Spontaneous; impulsive. [< L *impetuosus*] —im·pet′u·os′i·ty (-os′ə·tē), im·pet′u·ous·ness *n.* —im·pet′u·ous·ly *adv.*

**im·pe·tus** (im′pə·təs) *n.* 1 The energy or momentum of a moving body. 2 Any force that begins or sets in motion; incentive. [L < *im-petere* rush upon]

**im·pinge** (im·pinj′) *v.i.* ·pinged, ·ping·ing 1 To strike; collide: with *on, upon,* or *against.* 2 To encroach; infringe: with *on* or *upon.* [< L *in-* against + *pangere* to strike] —im·pinge′ment, im·ping′er *n.*

**im·pla·ca·ble** (im·plak′ə·bəl, -plā′kə-) *adj.* 1 That cannot be placated or appeased. 2 Unalterable; inexorable. —im·pla′ca·bil′i·ty, im·pla′ca·ble·ness *n.* —im·pla′ca·bly *adv.*

**im·plant** (im·plant′, -plänt′) *v.t.* 1 To insert or graft in or onto living tissue. 2 To instill, as principles. 3 To plant, as seeds. —*n.* (im′plant′, -plänt′) *Med.* Something implanted in the body, as a tissue graft or therapeutic device. —im′plan·ta′tion, im·plant′er *n.*

**im·ple·ment** (im′plə·mənt) *n.* A thing used in work; a utensil; tool. —*v.t.* (-ment) 1 To fulfill; accomplish. 2 To provide what is needed for; supplement. 3 To furnish with implements. [< L *implementum* a filling up] —im′ple·men′tal *adj.* —im′ple·men·ta′tion *n.*

**im·pli·cate** (im′plə·kāt) *v.t.* ·cat·ed, ·cat·ing 1 To show to be involved, as in a plot or crime. 2 To imply. 3 To fold or twist together; entangle. [< L *in-* in + *plicare* to fold] —im′pli·ca′tive, im·pli·ca·to·ry (im′pli·kə·tôr′ē, -tō′rē) *adj.*

**im·pli·ca·tion** (im′plə·kā′shən) *n.* 1 The act of implicating or the state of being implicated. 2 The act of implying. 3 Something implied, esp. so as to lead to a deduction.

**im·plic·it** (im·plis′it) *adj.* 1 Implied or to be understood, but not specifically stated. 2 Absolute; unquestioning: *implicit* trust. 3 Virtually contained or involved in, though not immediately apparent or stated; inherent. [< L *implicare* involve] —im·plic′it·ly *adv.* —im·plic′it·ness *n.*

**im·plore** (im·plôr′, -plōr′) *v.* ·plored, ·plor·ing *v.t.* 1 To beseech; entreat. 2 To beg for urgently; pray for. —*v.i.* 3 To make urgent supplication. [< L *in-* thoroughly + *plorare* cry out] —im·plor′er *n.* —im·plor′ing·ly *adv.*

**im·ply** (im·plī′) *v.t.* ·plied, ·ply·ing 1 To involve necessarily as a circumstance, condition, effect, etc.: An action *implies* an agent. 2 To indicate (a meaning not expressed); hint at; intimate. [< L *implicare* involve] • See INFER.

im·port (im·pôrt′, -pōrt′, im′pôrt, -pōrt) *v.t.* 1 To bring (goods) into one country from a foreign country in commerce. 2 To bring in; introduce. 3 To mean; signify. —*v.i.* 4 To be of importance or significance; matter. —*n.* (im′pôrt, -pōrt) 1 Importation. 2 That which is imported. 3 Meaning; significance. 4 Importance. [< L *in-* in + *portare* carry] —im·port′a·ble *adj.*

im·por·tance (im·pôr′təns) *n.* The condition or quality of being important.

im·por·tant (im·pôr′tənt) *adj.* 1 Of great import, consequence, prominence, or value. 2 Pompous; pretentious. [< L *importare* bring in] —im·por′tant·ly *adv.* —Syn. 1 momentous, serious, significant, weighty.

im·por·ta·tion (im′pôr·tā′shən, -pōr-) *n.* 1 The act of importing merchandise, etc. 2 That which is imported.

im·por·tu·nate (im·pôr′chən·nit) *adj.* Urgent in requesting or demanding; insistent; pertinacious. —im·por′tu·nate·ly *adv.* —im·por′tu·nate·ness *n.*

im·por·tune (im′pôr·t<sup>y</sup>ōōn′, im·pôr′chən) *v.* ·tuned, ·tun·ing *v.t.* 1 To annoy or trouble with persistent requests or demands. —*v.i.* 2 To make persistent requests or demands. [< L *importunus* having no access, vexatious] —im′por·tun′er *n.*

im·pose (im·pōz′) *v.t.* ·posed, ·pos·ing 1 To place or lay by authority: to *impose* a tax. 2 To place by or as by force: to *impose* opinions on another. 3 To force (oneself, one's presence, etc.) upon others. 4 To palm off (something) as true or genuine; foist. 5 *Printing* To arrange in a form, as pages of type. —impose on (or upon) 1 To take advantage of; presume. 2 To cheat or deceive by trickery. [< L *imponere* put in] —im·pos′a·ble *adj.* —im·pos′er *n.*

im·po·si·tion (im′pə·zish′ən) *n.* 1 The act of imposing. 2 A severe or unjust demand, requirement, duty, etc. 3 A deception; imposture. 4 A tax, toll, or duty.

im·pos·si·bil·i·ty (im·pos′ə·bil′ə·tē) *n. pl.* ·ties 1 The fact or state of being impossible. 2 That which is impossible.

im·pos·si·ble (im·pos′ə·bəl) *adj.* 1 Not capable of existing or occurring. 2 Hopelessly difficult to do or accomplish. 3 Utterly objectionable or intolerable. —im·pos′si·bly *adv.*

im·pos·tor (im·pos′tər) *n.* One who deceives, esp. one who goes under an assumed name or identity. [< L *imponere* lay on, impose]

im·po·tent (im′pə·tənt) *adj.* 1 Lacking in physical power; week; feeble. 2 Unable to have sexual intercourse: said of the male. 3 Powerless, defenseless, or ineffectual. —im′po·tent·ly *adv.*

im·prac·ti·ca·ble (im·prak′ti·kə·bəl) *adj.* Impossible or unreasonably difficult to do or to use. —im·prac′ti·ca·bil′i·ty, im·prac′ti·ca·ble·ness *n.* —im·prac′ti·ca·bly *adv.*

im·prac·ti·cal (im·prak′ti·kəl) *adj.* Not practical. —im·prac′ti·cal′i·ty (-kal′ə·tē) *n.*

im·pre·cate (im′prə·kāt) *v.t.* ·cat·ed, ·cat·ing To invoke, as a judgment, calamity, or curse. [< L *in-* on + *precari* pray] —im′pre·ca·to′ry (-kə·tôr′ē, -tō′rē) *adj.* —im′pre·ca′tion, im′pre·ca′tor *n.*

im·preg·nate (im·preg′nāt) *v.t.* ·nat·ed, ·nat·ing 1 To make pregnant. 2 To fertilize. 3 To saturate or permeate. 4 To fill or imbue with emotion, ideas, principles, etc. —*adj.* Made pregnant. —im·preg′na·ble (-nə·bəl) *adj.* —im′preg·na′tion, im·preg′na·tor *n.*

im·press[1] (im·pres′) *v.t.* 1 To produce a marked effect upon, as the mind; influence. 2 To fix firmly in the mind. 3 To form or make (an imprint or mark) by pressure; stamp. 4 To form or make an imprint or mark upon. 5 To press: to *impress* one's hand into the mud. —*n.* (im′pres) 1 The act of impressing. 2 A mark or seal produced by pressure. 3 A stamp. 4 An impression or effect made on the mind. [< L *in-* on + *premere* to press] —im·press′er *n.*

im·press[2] (im·pres′) *v.t.* 1 To compel to enter public service by force: to *impress* seamen. 2 To seize (property) for public use. [< *in-* in + PRESS[1]] —im·press′er, im·press′ment *n.*

im·pres·sion (im·presh′ən) *n.* 1 The act of impressing. 2 A stamp, mark, figure, etc. made by pressure. 3 An effect produced on the senses, the mind, or the feelings. 4 An effect or change: Our hard work made little *impression* on the lawn. 5 A vague or indistinct remembrance; a notion. 6 *Printing* a The imprint of type, illustrations, etc., on a page or sheet. b All the copies of a book, etc., printed at one time. c One copy of a book, engraving, etching, etc. —im·pres′sion·al *adj.*

im·pres·sive (im·pres′iv) *adj.* Producing or tending to produce a strong impression on the mind, emotions, etc., esp. one of awe or admiration. —im·pres′sive·ly adv. —im·pres′sive·ness n.

im·promp·tu (im·promp′t'ōō) adj. Made, done, or uttered on the spur of the moment; extempore; offhand. —n. Anything impromptu. —adv. Without preparation. [F < L in promptu in readiness]

im·prop·er (im·prop′ər) adj. 1 Not fit or appropriate; unquitable. 2 Contrary to accepted standards of taste, conduct, speech, etc. 3 Not true or correct. —im·prop′er·ly adv. —im·prop′er·ness n.

im·prove (im·prōōv′) v. ·proved, ·prov·ing v.t. 1 To make better the quality, condition, etc., of. 2 To use to good advantage; utilize. 3 To increase the value of, as land by cultivation. —v.i. 4 To become better. 5 To make improvements: with on or upon. [< OF en- into + prou profit] —im·prov′a·bil′i·ty, im·prov′a·ble·ness, im·prov′er n. —im·prov′a·ble adj. —im·prov′a·bly adv.

im·pro·vise (im′prə·vīz) v.t. & v.i. ·vised, ·vis·ing 1 To compose, recite, sing, etc., without previous preparation; extemporize. 2 To make or devise from what is at hand. [< L in- not + provisus foreseen] —im·pro′vi·sa′tion·al adj. —im·prov·i·sa·tion (im·prov′·ə·zā′shən, im′prə·vī·zā′shən), im′pro·vis′er n.

im·pru·dent (im·prōō′dənt) adj. Not prudent; lacking discretion. —im·pru′dence n. —im·pru′dent·ly adv.

im·pugn (im·pyōōn′) v.t. 1 To attack by words or arguments. 2 To challenge or oppose as false. [< L in- against + pugnare to fight] —im·pugn′a·ble adj. —im·pug·na·tion (im′pəg·nā′shən), im·pugn′er, im·pugn′ment n.

im·pulse (im′puls) n. 1 A force, esp. one that acts for a short time and produces motion. 2 The change in momentum produced by such a force. 3 A sudden mental urge to act, caused by the feelings or by some external stimulus. 4 Any natural, unreasoned tendency or propensity: a kind impulse. 5 Physiol. The propagation of a stimulus through nerve or muscle tissue. [< L impulsus, pp. of impellere. See IMPEL.]

im·pul·sive (im·pul′siv) adj. 1 Acting on impulse: an impulsive child. 2 Resulting from impulse; unpremeditated: an impulsive act. 3 Having the power to impel or drive. —im·pul′sive·ly adv. —im·pul′sive·ness n.

im·pu·ni·ty (im·pyōō′nə·tē) n. pl. ·ties Freedom from punishment or from injurious

consequences. [< L in- not + poena punishment]

im·pu·ta·tion (im′pyōō·tā′shən) n. 1 The act of imputing. 2 Something imputed, as an accusation or insinuation. —im·pu·ta·tive (im·pyōō′tə·tiv) adj. —im·pu′ta·tive·ly adv.

im·pute (im·pyōōt′) v.t. ·put·ed, ·put·ing To attribute, as a fault or crime, to a person; ascribe. [< L in- in + putare reckon, think] —im·put′a·bil′i·ty, im·put′er n. —im·put′a·ble adj. —im·put′a·bly adv.

in·a·bil·i·ty (in′ə·bil′ə·tē) n. The state of being unable; lack of necessary power, ability, etc. —Syn. impotence, incapability, incapacity, incompetence.

in·ac·cu·ra·cy (in·ak′yər·ə·sē) n. pl. ·cies 1 The state or condition of being inaccurate. 2 Something which is inaccurate.

in·ac·cu·rate (in·ak′yər·it) adj. Not accurate, correct, or exact. —in·ac′cu·rate·ly adv. —in·ac′cu·rate·ness n.

in·ac·tion (in·ak′shən) n. Absence of action, activity, or motion; idleness.

in·ac·tive (in·ak′tiv) adj. 1 Characterized by inaction; inert. 2 Marked by absence of effort or action; indolent. 3 Mil. Not engaged in military duty. —in·ac′tive·ly adv. —in·ac·tiv′i·ty, in·ac′tive·ness n.

in·ad·e·quate (in·ad′ə·kwit) adj. Not adequate; insufficient. —in·ad′e·qua·cy, in·ad′e·quate·ness n. —in·ad′e·quate·ly adv.

in·ad·ver·tent (in′əd·vûr′tənt) adj. 1 Not careful or attentive; negligent. 2 Unintentional; not deliberate: an inadvertent omission of the translator's name. [< L in- not + advertere to turn toward] —in′ad·ver′tent·ly adv.

in·al·ien·a·ble (in·āl′yən·ə·bəl) adj. Not transferable; that cannot be rightfully taken away. —in·al′ien·a·bil′i·ty n. —in·al′ien·a·bly adv.

in·ane (in·ān′) adj. 1 Lacking sense or significance; pointless; silly: an inane remark. 2 Empty; vapid. [< L inanis empty] —in·ane′ly adv.

in·an·i·mate (in·an′ə·mit) adj. 1 Without life; not animate. 2 Not lively; dull; torpid. —in·an′i·mate·ly adv. —in·an′i·mate·ness n.

in·an·i·ty (in·an′ə·tē) n. pl. ·ties 1 The condition of being inane. 2 A frivolous or silly act, remark, etc.

in·au·gu·rate (in·ô′gʲə·rāt) v.t. ·rat·ed, ·rat·ing 1 To induct into office with formal ceremony. 2 To begin or commence upon formally. 3 To celebrate the public opening or first use of. [< L inaugurare take omens, consecrate, install] —in·au′gu·ra′tor n.

**in·au·gu·ra·tion** (in·ô´gʹə·rāʹshən) n. The act of inaugurating; esp., a ceremony of induction into office.

**in·can·desce** (in´kən·desʹ) v.t. & v.i. ·desced, ·desc·ing To be or cause to be incandescent. —**in´can·desʹcence, in´can·desʹcen·cy** n.

**in·can·des·cent** (in´kən·desʹənt) adj. 1 Made luminous or glowing with heat. 2 Extremely bright or brilliant. [< L in- in + candescere to become hot] —**in´can·desʹcent·ly** adv.

**in·can·ta·tion** (in´kan·tāʹshən) 1 The utterance of magical words for enchantment or exorcism. 2 The formula so used. [< L incantare make an incantation] —**in·can·ta·to·ry** (in·kanʹtə·tôr´ē, ·tōʹrē) adj.

**in·ca·pa·ble** (in·kāʹpə·bəl) adj. 1 Not capable; lacking power, capacity or ability: with of. 2 Without legal qualifications or eligibility. —**in·ca´pa·bilʹi·ty, in·ca´pa·ble·ness** n. —**in·ca´pa·bly** adv.

**in·ca·pac·i·tate** (in´kə·pasʹə·tāt) v.t. ·tat·ed, ·tat·ing 1 To make incapable or unfit; disable. 2 Law To disqualify. —**in´ca·pacʹi·taʹtion** n.

**in·ca·pac·i·ty** (in´kə·pasʹə·tē) n. pl. ·ties 1 Lack of capacity; incapability. 2 Law Want of competency.

**in·car·cer·ate** (in·kärʹsər·āt) v.t. ·at·ed, ·at·ing 1 To imprison; put in jail. 2 To confine. [< L in- in + carcer jail] —**in·carʹcer·aʹtion, in·carʹcer·aʹtor** n.

**in·car·nate** (in·kärʹnāt) v.t. ·nat·ed, ·nat·ing 1 To give bodily form to. 2 To give concrete shape or form to; actualize. 3 To be the embodiment of; typify. —adj. (·nit) 1 Invested with flesh. 2 Embodied; personified: a fiend incarnate. 3 Flesh-colored. [< LL incarnare embody in flesh]

**in·car·na·tion** (in´kär·nāʹshən) n. 1 The condition of being incarnate, esp. the embodiment of a god or spirit in human form, as an avatar. 2 Often cap. The assumption of human nature by Jesus Christ. 3 The embodiment of a quality, idea, principle, etc.

**in·cen·di·ar·y** (in·senʹdē·er´ē) adj. 1 Of, pertaining to, or involving a malicious setting on fire of property. 2 Generating intense heat so as to cause fire: an incendiary bomb. 3 Inciting riot, disturbance, etc. —n. pl. ·ries 1 One who maliciously sets property on fire. 2 One who incites riots, quarrels, etc. 3 An incendiary bomb or substance. [< L incendere set on fire] —**in·cenʹdi·a·rism** (·ə·riz´əm) n.

**in·cense¹** (in·sensʹ) v.t. ·censed, ·cens·ing To inflame to anger; enrage. [< L incendere set on fire] —**in·censeʹment, in·cenʹsor** n.

**in·cense²** (inʹsens) n. 1 An aromatic substance that emits perfume during burning. 2 The odor or fumes from such a substance. 3 Any agreeable odor. —v. ·censed, ·cens·ing v.t. 1 To perfume with incense. 2 To burn incense to as an act of worship. —v.i. 3 To burn incense. [< L incendere set on fire]

**in·cen·tive** (in·senʹtiv) adj. Encouraging or motivating action. —n. That which incites, or tends to incite, to action; motive; stimulus. [< L incinere set the tune] —**in·cenʹtive·ly** adv.

**in·cep·tion** (in·sepʹshən) n. A beginning or initial period; start. [< L incipere begin]

**in·cep·tive** (in·sepʹtiv) adj. 1 Beginning; initial. 2 Gram. Denoting the commencement of an action. —n. Gram. An inceptive word. [< L incipere begin] —**in·cepʹtive·ly** adv.

**in·ces·sant** (in·sesʹənt) adj. Continued or repeated without cessation. [< L in- not + cessare cease] —**in·cesʹsan·cy** (·ən·sē) n. —**in·cesʹsant·ly** adv. —Syn. ceaseless, constant, perpetual, unremitting, unending, persistent, continuous, unceasing.

**in·ci·dence** (inʹsə·dəns) n. 1 A falling upon, or the direction or manner of falling upon or affecting. 2 ANGLE OF INCIDENCE. 3 The degree of occurrence or effect of something: a high incidence of typhus.

**in·ci·dent** (inʹsə·dənt) n. 1 Anything that takes place; event; occurrence. 2 A subordinate or minor event or act. —adj. 1 Falling or striking upon: incident rays. 2 Likely to occur in connection with: the discomfort incident to surgery. [< L incidere fall upon]

**in·cin·er·ate** (in·sinʹər·āt) v.t. ·at·ed, ·at·ing To consume with fire; reduce to ashes; cremate. [< L in- in + cinis, cineris ashes] —**in·cinʹer·aʹtion** n.

**in·cin·er·a·tor** (in·sinʹə·rā´tər) n. A furnace for reducing refuse, etc., to ashes.

**in·cip·i·ent** (in·sipʹē·ənt) adj. Just beginning; in the first stages. [< L incipere begin] —**in·cipʹi·ence, in·cipʹi·en·cy** n. —**in·cipʹi·ent·ly** adv.

**in·cise** (in·sīzʹ) v.t. ·cised, ·cis·ing 1 To cut into with a sharp instrument. 2 To engrave. [< L incidere cut into]

**in·ci·sion** (in·sizhʹən) n. 1 The act of incising. 2 A cut; gash. 3 A slit or opening made with a cutting instrument, as in an operation. 4 Incisiveness; keenness.

**in·ci·sive** (in·sī'siv) *adj.* 1 Cutting; incising. 2 Acute; penetrating; sharp: *incisive* wit. —**in·ci'sive·ly** *adv.* —**in·ci'sive·ness** *n.*

**in·ci·sor** (in·sī'zər) *n.* A front or cutting tooth; in man, one of eight such teeth, four in each jaw. • See TOOTH.

**in·cite** (in·sīt') *v.t.* **·cit·ed, ·cit·ing** To urge to action; instigate; stir up. [< L *in-* thoroughly + *citare* rouse] —**in·cite'ment, in·cit'er** *n.*

**in·clem·ent** (in·klem'ənt) *adj.* 1 Rough; stormy: *inclement* weather. 2 Merciless; harsh. [< L *in-* not + *clemens* clement] —**in·clem'en·cy** *n.* —**in·clem'ent·ly** *adv.*

**in·cli·na·tion** (in'klə·nā'shən) *n.* 1 Deviation or the degree of deviation from the vertical or horizontal; slant. 2 A slope. 3 A tendency; predilection. —**in'cli·na'tion·al** *adj.*

**in·cline** (in·klīn') *v.* **·clined, ·clin·ing** *v.i.* 1 To slant; slope. 2 To have a tendency. 3 To tend in some quality or degree: purple *inclining* toward blue. 4 To bow or bend the head or body, as in courtesy. —*v.t.* 5 To cause to bend, lean, or slope. 6 To influence. 7 To bow, as the head. —**incline one's ear** To hear with favor; heed. —*n.* (in'klīn) That which inclines from the horizontal; a gradient; slope. [< L *in-* on + *clinare* to lean] —**in·clin'a·ble** *adj.*

**in·clu·sion** (in·klōō'zhən) *n.* 1 The act of including. 2 That which is included.

**in·clu·sive** (in·klōō'siv) *adj.* 1 Including the things, limits, or extremes mentioned: from A to Z *inclusive*. 2 Including or taking into account everything pertinent or applicable: an *inclusive* list of purchases. —**in·clu'sive·ly** *adv.* —**in·clu'sive·ness** *n.*

**in·cog·ni·to** (in·kog'nə·tō, in'kəg·nē'tō) *adj.* & *adv.* With one's true name or identity not revealed. —*n. pl.* **·tos** (-tōz) 1 The state or disguise of being incognito. 2 One who lives, travels, etc., incognito. [< L *in-* not + *cognoscere* know]

**in·co·her·ence** (in'kō·hir'əns) *n.* 1 Want of coherence. 2 Something incoherent. Also **in'co·her'en·cy.**

**in·co·her·ent** (in'kō·hir'ənt) *adj.* 1 Without logical order or progression; disconnected. 2 Not clear; confused; muddled, as in speech or thought. 3 Without physical coherence of parts. —**in'co·her'ent·ly** *adv.*

**in·come** (in'kum) *n.* Money, or other benefit, periodically received, as from one's labor, investments, etc. [ME, a coming in]

**in·com·pa·ra·ble** (in·kom'pər·ə·bəl) *adj.* 1 Not admitting of comparison, because of being so superior; matchless. 2 Unsuitable for comparison. —**in·com'pa·ra·bil'i·ty, in·com'pa·ra·ble·ness** *n.* —**in·com'pa·ra·bly** *adv.*

**in·com·pat·i·ble** (in'kəm·pat'ə·bəl) *adj.* 1 Incapable of living or acting together in agreement or harmony. 2 Incapable of being used in combination; mutually discordant or antagonistic. 3 In disagreement; contradictory. —*n. Usu. pl.* Incompatible persons or things. —**in'com·pat'i·bil'i·ty** *n.* —**in'com·pat'i·bly** *adv.*

**in·com·pe·tent** (in·kom'pə·tent) *adj.* 1 Not competent; unable to do what is required. 2 Not legally qualified. —*n.* An incompetent person. —**in·com'pe·tence, in·com'pe·ten·cy** *n.* —**in·com'pe·tent·ly** *adv.*

**in·com·plete** (in'kəm·plēt') *adj.* 1 Not complete or finished. 2 Lacking in certain parts. 3 Imperfect. —**in'com·plete'ly** *adv.* —**in'com·plete'ness, in'com·ple'tion** *n.*

**in·com·pre·hen·si·ble** (in'kom·pri·hen'sə·bəl, in·kom'-) *adj.* 1 Not comprehensible; not understandable. 2 *Archaic* That cannot be included or confined within limits. —**in'com·pre·hen·si·bil'i·ty, in·com'pre·hen'si·ble·ness** *n.* —**in·com'pre·hen'si·bly** *adv.*

**in·con·ceiv·a·ble** (in'kən·sē'və·bəl) *adj.* That cannot be conceived, believed, imagined, etc. —**in'con·ceiv'a·ble·ness, in'con·ceiv'a·bil'i·ty** *n.* —**in'con·ceiv'a·bly** *adv.*

**in·con·gru·i·ty** (in'kən·grōō'ə·tē) *n. pl.* **·ties** 1 The state or quality of being incongruous. 2 That which is incongruous.

**in·con·gru·ous** (in·kong'grōō·əs) *adj.* 1 Not harmonious or compatible. 2 Not fit or suitable. 3 Not consistent or corresponding; disagreeing. [< L *in-* not + *congruus* harmonious] —**in·con'gru·ous·ly** *adv.* —**in·con'gru·ous·ness** *n.*

**in·con·sid·er·ate** (in'kən·sid'ər·it) *adj.* 1 Not considerate; thoughtless. 2 Lacking sufficient consideration. —**in'con·sid'er·ate·ly** *adv.* —**in'con·sid'er·ate·ness, in'con·sid'er·a'tion** *n.*

**in·con·sis·ten·cy** (in'kən·sis'tən·sē) *n. pl.* **·cies** 1 The state or quality of being inconsistent. 2 That which is inconsistent. Also **in'con·sis'tence.**

**in·con·sis·tent** (in'kən·sis'tənt) *adj.* 1 Not in agreement or compatible with other assertions, facts, etc. 2 Self-contradictory. 3 Changeable; erratic; capricious, as in thought or behavior. —**in'con·sis'tent·ly** *adv.*

**in·con·tro·vert·i·ble** (in′kon·trə·vûr′tə·bəl) *adj.* Not admitting of dispute or controversy; undeniable. —in′con·tro·vert′i·bil′i·ty, in′con·tro·vert′i·ble·ness *n.* —in′con·tro·vert′i·bly *adv.*

**in·con·ven·ience** (in′kən·vēn′yəns) *n.* 1 The state or quality of being inconvenient. 2 Something inconvenient. —*v.t.* ·ienced, ·ienc·ing To cause inconvenience to; trouble.

**in·con·ven·ient** (in′kən·vēn′yənt) *adj.* Not convenient; causing difficulty or bother; troublesome. —in′con·ven′ient·ly *adv.*

**in·cor·po·rate** (in·kôr′pə·rāt) *v.* ·rat·ed, ·rat·ing *v.t.* 1 To take into or include as part of a whole. 2 To form into a legal corporation. 3 To combine or unite into one body or whole; blend; mix. —*v.i.* 4 To become combined or united as one body or whole. 5 To form a legal corporation. —*adj.* (-pər·it) 1 Joined or combined into one. 2 Incorporated legally. [< LL *incorporare* embody] —in·cor′po·ra′tive *adj.* —in·cor′po·ra′tor *n.*

**in·cor·po·ra·tion** (in·kôr′pə·rā′shən) *n.* 1 The act of incorporating. 2 A corporation.

**in·cor·po·re·al** (in′kôr·pôr′ē·əl, -pō′rē-) *adj.* 1 Not consisting of matter; immaterial; spiritual. 2 *Law* Having no material existence, but regarded as existing by the law; *incorporeal* rights. —in′cor·po′re·al·ly *adv.*

**in·cor·ri·gi·ble** (in·kôr′ə·jə·bəl, -kor′-) *adj.* That cannot be corrected, changed, or reformed: an *incorrigible* liar. —*n.* An incorrigible person. [< L *in-* not + *corrigere* to correct] —in·cor′ri·gi·bil′ness, in·cor′ri·gi·bil′i·ty *n.* —in·cor′ri·gi·bly *adv.*

**in·crease** (in·krēs′) *v.* ·creased, ·creas·ing *v.i.* 1 To become greater, as in amount, size, degree, etc.; grow. 2 To grow in numbers, esp. by reproduction. —*v.t.* 3 To make greater, as in amount, size, degree, etc.; augment; enlarge. —*n.* (in′krēs) 1 The act or process of increasing. 2 The result or amount of increasing. —in·creas′a·ble *adj.* —in·creas′ing·ly *adv.*

**in·cred·i·ble** (in·kred′ə·bəl) *adj.* Seeming too far-fetched or extraordinary to be believed or possible. —in·cred′i·bil′i·ty, in·cred′i·ble·ness *n.* —in·cred′i·bly *adv.*

**in·cred·u·lous** (in·krej′ə·ləs) *adj.* 1 Refusing belief; skeptical. 2 Caused by or showing doubt or disbelief. [< L *in-* not + *credulus* gullible] —in·cred′u·lous·ly *adv.*

**in·cre·ment** (in′krə·mənt) *n.* 1 The act of increasing; enlargement. 2 That which is

added; increase. [< L *increscere.* See IN-CREASE] —in′cre·men′tal (-men′təl) *adj.*

**in·crim·i·nate** (in·krim′ə·nāt) *v.t.* ·nat·ed, ·nat·ing To charge with or involve in a crime or of fault. [< L *in-* in + *criminare* accuse one of a crime] —in·crim′i·na′tion, in·crim′i·na′tor *n.* —in·crim′i·na·to′ry (-nə·tôr′ē, -tō′rē) *adj.*

**in·cu·bate** (in′kyə·bāt, ing′-) *v.* ·bat·ed, ·bat·ing *v.t.* 1 To sit upon (eggs) in order to hatch; brood. 2 To hatch (eggs) in this manner or by artificial heat. 3 To maintain under conditions favoring optimum growth or development, as bacterial cultures. —*v.i.* 4 To sit on eggs; brood. 5 To undergo incubation. [< L *in-* on + *cubare* to lie] —in′cu·ba′tive *adj.*

**in·cu·ba·tion** (in′kyə·bā′shən, ing′-) *n.* 1 The act of incubating or the condition of being incubated. 2 The period between exposure to an infectious disease and the appearance of symptoms.

**in·cu·ba·tor** (in′kyə·bā′tər, ing′-) *n.* Any of various enclosures kept at a stable temperature, as for incubating eggs or bacterial cultures, or nurturing a premature infant.

**in·cul·cate** (in·kul′kāt, in′kul-) *v.t.* ·cat·ed, ·cat·ing To impress upon the mind by frequent and emphatic repetition; instill. [< L *inculcare* tread on] —in·cul·ca′tion (in-′kul·kā′shən), in′cul·ca′tor *n.*

**in·cul·pate** (in·kul′pāt, in′kul-) *v.t.* ·pat·ed, ·pat·ing To incriminate. [< L *in-* in + *culpa* fault] —in′cul·pa′tion *n.* —in·cul′pa·to·ry (-pə·tôr′ē, -tō′rē) *adj.*

**in·cum·bent** (in·kum′bənt) *adj.* 1 Resting upon one as a duty or moral obligation; obligatory. 2 Resting, leaning, or weighing wholly or partly upon something. —*n.* One who holds an office. [< L *incumbere* recline]

**in·cur** (in·kûr′) *v.t.* ·curred, ·cur·ring To meet with or become subject to, as unpleasant consequences, esp. through one's own action; bring upon oneself. [< L *incurrere* run into]

**in·cur·a·ble** (in·kyōōr′ə·bəl) *adj.* Not able to be cured or remedied. —*n.* One having an incurable disease. —in·cur′a·bil′i·ty, in·′cur′a·ble·ness *n.* —in·cur′a·bly *adv.*

**in·cur·sion** (in·kûr′zhən, -shən) *n.* A hostile invasion; raid. [< L *incurrere* run into] —in·cur′sive *adj.*

**in·de·cen·cy** (in·dē′sən·sē) *n. pl.* ·cies 1 The quality of being indecent; offensiveness. 2 An indecent act, word, etc.

**in·de·cent** (in·dē′sənt) *adj.* 1 Offensive to decency or propriety; immodest; obscene. 2 Contrary to what is fit and proper. —**in·de′cent·ly** *adv.*

**in·de·fat·i·ga·ble** (in′də·fat′ə·gə·bəl) *adj.* Not yielding readily to fatigue; tireless. [< L *in-* not + *defatigare* to tire out] —**in′de·fat′i·ga·bil′i·ty, in′de·fat′i·ga·ble·ness** *n.* —**in′de·fat′i·ga·bly** *adv.* —**Syn.** persevering, unfaltering, unflagging, untiring.

**in·def·i·nite** (in·def′ə·nit) *adj.* 1 Not definite or precise; uncertain; vague. 2 Without fixed boundaries or limits. 3 *Gram.* Not defining or determining, as the **indefinite** articles *a* and *an*. —**in·def′i·nite·ly** *adv.* —**in·def′i·nite·ness** *n.*

**in·del·i·ble** (in·del′ə·bəl) *adj.* 1 That cannot be removed, erased, etc. 2 Making indelible marks: an *indelible* pen. [< L *in-* not + *delibilis* perishable] —**in·del′i·bil′i·ty** *n.* —**in·del′i·bly** *adv.*

**in·dem·ni·fy** (in·dem′nə·fī) *v.t.* **·fied, ·fy·ing** 1 To compensate for loss or damage sustained. 2 To make good (a loss). 3 To give security against future loss or damage to. [< L *indemnis* unhurt + -FY] —**in·dem′ni·fi·ca′tion, in·dem′ni·fi′er** *n.*

**indent**[1] (in·dent′) *v.t.* 1 To set, as the first line of a paragraph, in from the margin. 2 To cut or mark the edge of with toothlike notches; serrate. 3 To indenture, as an apprentice. —*v.i.* 4 To be notched or cut. 5 To set a line, etc., in from the margin. —*n.* (in′dent, in·dent′) 1 A cut or notch in the edge of anything. 2 An indentation. 3 An indented line or paragraph. [< L *in-* in + *dens, dentis* tooth]

**in·dent**[2] (in·dent′; *n. also* in′dent) *v.t.* 1 To make a dent in. 2 To press inward so as to form a mark, hollow, etc. —*n.* A dent.

**in·den·ta·tion** (in′den·tā′shən) *n.* 1 The act of indenting. 2 A cut or notch in an edge or border. 3 An indention, as of a line or paragraph. 4 A dent.

**in·de·pen·dence** (in′di·pen′dəns) *n.* 1 The quality or condition of being independent, esp. freedom from dependence upon or control by others. 2 An income large enough to live on without being employed.

**in·de·pen·dent** (in′di·pen′dənt) *adj.* 1 Not under the control or rule of others; self-governing. 2 Not part of or connected to another group, etc.; separate: an *independent* merchant. 3 Not identified with any political party or faction. 4 Not under the influence or guidance of others; self-reliant. 5 Of, possessing, or indicating an income that permits one to live without labor or dependence on others. —*n.* 1 One who is independent. 2 *Often cap.* One who is not an adherent of any political party. —**in′de·pen′dent·ly** *adv.*

**in-depth** (in′depth′) *adj.* Extensive and thorough; not superficial; penetrating: an *in-depth* opinion survey.

**in·de·ter·mi·nate** (in′di·tûr′mə·nit) *adj.* 1 Not definite in extent, amount, or nature. 2 Not clear or precise; vague; undefined. —**in′de·ter′mi·nate·ly** *adv.* —**in′de·ter′mi·na·cy** (-nə·sē), **in′de·ter′mi·nate·ness** *n.*

**in·dex** (in′deks) *n. pl.* **·dex·es** or **·di·ces** (-də·sēz) 1 Anything used to indicate, point out, or guide, as the hand of a clock, a pointer, etc. 2 Anything that manifests or denotes: an *index* of character. 3 An alphabetical list, usu. found at the back of a book or other publication, of the names and topics included in the work and the page numbers on which they can be found. 4 A descriptive list or catalogue: an *index* of paintings. 5 *Math.* a An exponent. b A number placed near a radical sign to indicate the order of the root. c A subscript or superscript indicating position, order, etc. 6 A number that is a function of and which represents a set of data: the air-pollution *index.* 7 A mark [☞] employed to direct attention. —*v.t.* 1 To provide with an index. 2 To enter in an index. 3 To indicate; mark. [L]

**In·dex** (in′deks) *n.* In the Roman Catholic Church, a list of books that cannot be read without special permission.

**in·di·cate** (in′də·kāt) *v.t.* **·cat·ed, ·cat·ing** 1 To be or give a sign of: Those clouds *indicate* rain. 2 To point out; direct attention to: to *indicate* the correct page. 3 To express or make known, esp. briefly or indirectly. 4 To show or suggest the need for. [< L *in-* in + *dicare* point out, proclaim] —**in′di·ca·to′ry** (-kə·tôr′ē, -tō′rē) *adj.* —**Syn.** 1 betoken, mean, signify. 2 designate. 3 imply.

**in·di·ca·tion** (in′də·kā′shən) *n.* 1 The act of indicating. 2 That which indicates. 3 A degree or reading as shown on an indicator.

**in·dic·a·tive** (in·dik′ə·tiv) *adj.* 1 Serving to indicate or signify. 2 *Gram.* Of or pertaining to a mood in which an act or condition is stated or questioned as an actual fact, rather than as a potentiality or an unrealized condition. —*n. Gram.* The indicative mood, or a verb in this mood. —in·dic′a·tive·ly adv.

in·di·ca·tor (in′də·kā′tər) n. 1 One who or that which indicates or points out. 2 Any device or apparatus that indicates the amount, condition, or position of something. 3 Chem. A substance that reveals states of acidity, oxidation, etc. by changing color under known conditions.

in·dict (in·dīt′) v.t. 1 Law To prefer an indictment against. 2 To charge with a crime. [< AF enditer make known, inform] —in·dict′a·ble adj. —indict′er, in·dict′or n.

in·dict·ment (in·dīt′mənt) n. 1 The act of indicting, or the state of being indicted. 2 A formal written charge of crime, presented by a grand jury on oath to a court.

in·dif·fer·ence (in·dif′ər·əns, -rəns) n. The state or quality of being indifferent.

in·dif·fer·ent (in·dif′ər·ənt, -rənt) adj. 1 Having no inclination, concern, or interest; apathetic. 2 Only average or ordinary in size, excellence, etc.; without distinction. 3 Without any preference; neutral. 4 Having little or no importance or value. [< L indifferens making no difference] —in·dif′fer·ent·ly adv.

in·dig·e·nous (in·dij′ə·nəs) adj. 1 Originating naturally in a (specified) place or country; native. 2 Innate; inherent. [< L indigena native] —in·dig′e·nous·ly adv. —in·dig′e·nous·ness n.

in·di·gent (in′də·jənt) adj. Needy; poor. [< L indigere to lack, want] —in′di·gence, in′di·gen·cy n. —in′di·gent·ly adv.

in·di·gest·i·ble (in′dī·jes′tə·bəl) adj. Not digestible; difficult to digest. —in′di·gest′i·bil′i·ty, in′di·gest′i·ble·ness n. —in′di·gest′i·bly adv.

in·di·ges·tion (in′dī·jes′chən) n. 1 Difficult or defective digestion of food. 2 An instance of indigestion.

in·dig·nant (in·dig′nənt) adj. Having or showing indignation. —in·dig′nant·ly adv.

in·di·go (in′di·gō) n. 1 A blue dye obtained from certain plants or synthetically produced. 2 A deep violet blue. Also indigo blue. 3 A plant yielding indigo. —adj. Deep violet blue: also in′di·go·blue′ (-blōō′). [< Gk. Indikon (pharmakon) Indian (dye)]

in·dis·creet (in′dis·krēt′) adj. Lacking discretion; imprudent. —in′dis·creet′ly adv. —in′dis·creet′ness n. —Syn. tactless, undiplomatic, blunt.

in·dis·cre·tion (in′dis·kresh′ən) n. 1 The state

of being indiscreet. 2 An indiscreet act, word, etc.

in·dis·pen·sa·ble (in′dis·pen′sə·bəl) adj. Not to be dispensed with; absolutely necessary. —n. An indispensable person or thing. —in′dis·pen′sa·bil′i·ty, in′dis·pen′sa·ble·ness n. —in′dis·pen′sa·bly adv.

in·dis·put·a·ble (in′dis·pyōō′tə·bəl, in·dis′pyōō·tə·bəl) adj. Incapable of being disputed; unquestionable. —in′dis·put′a·bil′i·ty, in′dis·put′a·ble·ness n. —in′dis·put′a·bly adv.

in·dis·tinct (in′dis·tingkt′) adj. 1 Not clearly distinguishable or separable by the senses; dim; vague. 2 Not well-defined or clear to the intellect; obscure; uncertain. —in′dis·tinct′ly adv. —in′dis·tinct′ness n. —Syn. 1 cloudy, faint, unclear, blurry, bleary. 2 abstruse, confused, undefined, vague.

in·di·vid·u·al (in′də·vij′ōō·əl) adj. 1 Existing as an entity; single; particular. 2 Designed or intended for a single person or thing. 3 Pertaining, belonging, or peculiar to one particular person or thing. 4 Having peculiar or distinctive characteristics: an individual style. —n. A single being or thing; esp., a particular human being. [< L in- not + dividuus divisible] • The use of individual as a noun to refer to one human being should be avoided except when a person is to be distinguished from others in a group: Two individuals stepped forward to volunteer. Even in such a context, people may be preferred as being less pretentious.

in·di·vid·u·al·i·ty (in′də·vij′ōō·al′ə·tē) n. pl. ·ties 1 Something that distinguishes one person or thing from others. 2 Distinctive character or personality. 3 The quality or state of existing separately. 4 An individual.

in·doc·tri·nate (in·dok′trə·nāt) v.t. ·nat·ed, ·nat·ing 1 To instruct in doctrines, principles, etc. 2 To instruct; teach. [< LL in- into + doctrinare teach] —in·doc′tri·na′tion, in·doc′tri·na′tor n.

in·do·lent (in′də·lənt) adj. Averse to exertion; habitually inactive or idle. [< L in- not + dolere feel pain] —in′do·lence n. —in′do·lent·ly adv.

in·dom·i·ta·ble (in·dom′i·tə·bəl) adj. Not easily subdued or disheartened; unconquerable. [< L in- not + domitus tamed] —in·dom′i·ta·ble·ness n. —in·dom′i·ta·bly adv.

in·du·bi·ta·ble (in·dyōō′bə·tə·bəl) adj. Not open to doubt; unquestionable; certain. [<

L *in-* not + *dubitare* to doubt] —**in·du′ bi·ta·ble·ness** *n.* —**in·du′bi·ta·bly** *adv.* —**Syn.** indisputable, manifest, sure, undeniable.

**in·duce** (in·d⁷ōōs′) *v.t.* ·**duced,** ·**duc·ing** 1 To lead on to a specific action, belief, etc.; persuade. 2 To bring on; cause: a sickness *induced* by fatigue. 3 *Electr.* To produce by a process of induction. 4 To reach as a conclusion by an inductive process of reasoning. [< L *in-* in + *ducere* to lead] —**in·duc′er** *n.* —**in·duc′i·ble** *adj.*

**in·duce·ment** (in·d⁷ōōs′mənt) *n.* 1 An incentive; motive. 2 The act of inducing.

**in·duct** (in·dukt′) *v.t.* 1 To install formally in an office, benefice, etc. 2 To introduce; initiate. 3 To bring into a military service. [< L *inducere* lead in]

**in·duc·tion** (in·duk′shən) *n.* 1 The act or process of inducting or the state of being inducted; initiation; installation. 2 The process of arriving at a general conclusion from observation of particular facts; also, the conclusion so arrived at. 3 The bringing forward of separate facts as evidence in order to prove a general statement. 4 *Electr.* The production of magnetization or electrification in a body by the mere proximity of a magnetic field or electric charge, or of an electric current in a conductor by the variation of the magnetic field in its vicinity. —**in·duc′tion·al** *adj.*

**in·duc·tive** (in·duk′tiv) *adj.* 1 Persuasive; inducing. 2 Of, using, or produced by logical induction. 3 Introductory. 4 Of or produced by electrical or magnetic induction. —**in·duc′tive·ly** *adv.* —**in·duc′tive·ness** *n.*

**in·dulge** (in·dulj′) *v.* ·**dulged,** ·**dulg·ing** *v.t.* 1 To gratify, as desires or whims. 2 To gratify the desires, whims, etc., of. —*v.i.* 3 To yield to or gratify one's desires; indulge oneself; with *in.* [< L *indulgere* be kind to, concede] —**in·dulg′er** *n.* —**in·dulg′ing·ly** *adv.*

**in·dul·gence** (in·dul′jəns) *n.* 1 The act of indulging or of being indulgent. 2 That which is indulged in. 3 A privilege or favor. 4 Permission to defer payment, as of a note. 5 In the Roman Catholic Church, remission of the temporal punishment still due to sin after sacramental absolution. **Also in·dul′gen·cy.**

**in·dus·tri·al** (in·dus′trē·əl) *adj.* 1 Of, like, or resulting from industry. 2 Engaged in industry. 3 Used specifically in industry. 4 Of or for workers in industry. —*n.* 1 One engaged in industry. 2 A stock or security issued by an established industry. —**in·dus′tri·al·ly** *adv.*

**in·dus·tri·ous** (in·dus′trē·əs) *adj.* Hardworking; diligent. —**in·dus′tri·ous·ly** *adv.* —**in·dus′tri·ous·ness** *n.* —**Syn.** assiduous, busy, occupied, persevering, sedulous.

**in·dus·try** (in′dəs·trē) *n. pl.* ·**tries** 1 Diligent or constant application to work or business. 2 Any branch of productive work or manufacture; also, the capital or workers employed in it: the steel *industry;* the farming *industry.* 3 The business or the activities of manufacturing as a whole. [< L *industrius* diligent]

**in·e·bri·ate** (in·ē′brē·āt) *v.t.* ·**at·ed,** ·**at·ing** 1 To make drunk; intoxicate. 2 To exhilarate; excite. —*n.* (·it, ·āt) A habitual drunkard. —*adj.* (·it, ·āt) Intoxicated: also **in·e′bri·at′ed.** [< L *in-* thoroughly + *ebriare* make drunk] —**in·e′bri·a′tion** *n.*

**in·el·i·gi·ble** (in·el′ə·jə·bəl) *adj.* Not eligible; disqualified; unsuitable. —*n.* An ineligible person. —**in·el′i·gi·bil′i·ty** *n.* —**in·el′i·gi·bly** *adv.*

**in·ept** (in·ept′) *adj.* 1 Not suitable or fit. 2 Absurd; foolish. 3 Clumsy; awkward. [< L *in-* not + *aptus* fit] —**in·ep′ti·tude, in·ept′ness** *n.* —**in·ept′ly** *adv.*

**in·ert** (in·ûrt′) *adj.* 1 Without any inherent power to move. 2 Very slow; sluggish. 3 Devoid of reactive properties: *inert* gas. [< L *iners*] —**in·ert′ly** *adv.* —**in·ert′ness** *n.*

**in·er·tia** (in·ûr′shə) *n.* 1 The state of being inert; sluggishness. 2 *Physics* The tendency of any material body to maintain its velocity indefinitely unless accelerated or decelerated by some force. [L, idleness] —**in·er′tial** *adj.*

**in·ev·i·ta·ble** (in·ev′ə·tə·bəl) *adj.* 1 That cannot be prevented; unavoidable. 2 Customary; usual. [< L *in-* not + *evitare* avoid] —**in·ev′i·ta·bil′i·ty, in·ev′i·ta·ble·ness** *n.* —**in·ev′i·ta·bly** *adv.*

**in·ex·o·ra·ble** (in·ek′sər·ə·bəl) *adj.* Not to be moved by entreaty; unyielding. [< L *in-* not + *exorare* move by entreaty] —**in·ex′o·ra·bil′i·ty, in·ex′o·ra·ble·ness** *n.* —**in·ex′o·ra·bly** *adv.*

**in·fal·li·ble** (in·fal′ə·bəl) *adj.* 1 Incapable of fallacy or error. 2 Not apt to fail; reliable; certain: an *infallible* cure. 3 In Roman Catholic theology, incapable of error in matters relating to faith and morals: said of the Pope speaking *ex cathedra.* —*n.* One who or that which is infallible. —**in·fal-**

'li·bil'i·ty, in·fal'i·ble·ness n. —in·fal'li·bly adv.

in·fa·mous (in'fə·məs) adj. 1 Having an odious reputation; notorious. 2 Involving or deserving infamy. [< L in- not + fama fame] —in'fa·mous·ly adv. —in'fa·mous·ness n.

in·fa·my (in'fə·mē) n. pl. ·mies 1 Total lack of honor or reputation. 2 The state of being infamous. 3 An infamous act.

in·fan·cy (in'fən·sē) n. pl. ·cies 1 The state of being an infant. 2 Law The years during which one is a minor. 3 The earliest period in the development of something.

in·fant (in'fənt) n. 1 A baby. 2 Law A minor; in most states of the U.S., a person under 21 years of age. —adj. 1 Of, for, or like infants or infancy. 2 In the earliest state. [< L in- not + fans, pr.p. of fari to talk]

in·fan·try (in'fən·trē) n. pl. ·tries Soldiers or units of an army that are trained and equipped to fight on foot. [< Ital. infante boy, page, foot soldier]

in·fat·u·ate (in·fach'ōō·āt) v.t. ·at·ed, ·at·ing 1 To make foolish or fatuous. 2 To inspire with foolish passion. [< L in- very + fatuus foolish] —in·fat'u·a'tion n.

in·fect (in·fekt') v.t. 1 To contaminate with disease-producing organisms. 2 To communicate disease to, as a person, etc. 3 To affect or influence, as with emotion, beliefs, etc., esp. harmfully; taint. [< L inficere dip into, stain] —in·fect'er, in·fec'tor n. —Syn. 3 corrupt, debauch, deprave, lead astray, pollute.

in·fer (in·fûr') v. ·ferred, ·fer·ring v.t. 1 To conclude by reasoning from evidence or premises; deduce. 2 To involve or imply as a conclusion; give evidence of. 3 To suggest; hint. —v.i. 4 To draw inferences. [< L in- in + ferre carry] —in·fer'a·ble, in·fer'ri·ble adj. —in·fer'rer n. • infer, imply To infer is to make a rational or logical conclusion based on evidence: I inferred from the absence of cutting teeth that the animal was herbivorous. Imply may refer to the drawing of a necessary conclusion, and in this sense it is interchangeable with infer: The possibility of life on other planets implies (or infers) the presence of amino acids. But more often imply means simply to suggest or hint, and in this sense the use of infer (def. 3) should be avoided because it is ambiguous. She implied that he was scared is clear, but She inferred . . . might mean that she concluded privately that he was scared because of his manner or appearance.

in·fer·ence (in'fər·əns) n. 1 The act of inferring. 2 That which is inferred, as a deduction.

in·fer·en·tial (in'fə·ren'shəl) adj. Of or deduced by inference. —in'fer·en'tial·ly adv.

in·fe·ri·or (in·fir'ē·ər) adj. 1 Poor or mediocre in quality: an inferior meal. 2 Lower in merit, importance, or rank. 3 Situated or placed lower, as certain parts of the body. 4 Astron. Between the earth and the sun: an inferior planet. —n. One who or that which is inferior. [< L inferus low]

in·fe·ri·or·i·ty (in·fir'ē·ôr'ə·tē, -or'-) n. The state or quality of being inferior.

in·fer·nal (in·fûr'nəl) adj. 1 In mythology, of the world of the dead. 2 Of hell. 3 Hellish; diabolical. 4 Informal Damned; outrageous. [< L infernus situated below] —in·fer'nal·ly adv.

in·fest (in·fest') v.t. To overrun or spread in large numbers so as to be unpleasant or unsafe. [< L infestus hostile] —in'fes·ta'tion, in·fest'er n.

in·fi·del·i·ty (in'fi·del'ə·tē) n. pl. ·ties 1 Lack of fidelity, esp. violation of the marriage vow by adultery. 2 Any disloyal act. 3 The state of being an infidel.

in·fi·nite (in'fə·nit) adj. 1 So great as to be immeasurable and unbounded; limitless. 2 All-embracing; absolute: infinite love. 3 Very great, numerous, etc.: to take infinite pains. 4 Math. a Larger than any given number or value; arbitrarily large. b Capable of being arranged in a one-to-one correspondence with a proper subset of itself, as the set of natural numbers. —n. That which is infinite. —the Infinite God. [< L in- not + finitus finite] —in'fi·nite·ly adv. —in'fi·nite·ness n.

in·fin·i·tes·i·mal (in'fin·ə·tes'ə·məl) adj. 1 Too small to be measured or calculated. 2 Math. Arbitrarily close to zero in value. —n. An infinitesimal quantity. [< L infinitus infinite + -esimus (after centesimus hundredth)] —in'fin·i·tes'i·mal·ly adv.

in·fin·i·ty (in·fin'ə·tē) n. pl. ·ties 1 The quality of being infinite. 2 Something, as space or time, regarded as boundless or endless. 3 Math. An infinite number or set. [< L infinitus infinite]

in·firm (in·fûrm') adj. 1 Feeble or weak, as from age. 2 Lacking purpose or determination of mind. 3 Not legally secure. [< L in- not + firmus strong] —in·firm'ly adv. —in·firm'ness n. —Syn. 1 ailing, fragile, frail, ill, sickly.

**in·fir·mi·ty** (in·fûr′mə·tē) *n. pl.* **·ties** 1 A physical weakness or disability. 2 A defect of personality or character. 3 An infirm condition; feebleness.

**in·flam·ma·tion** (in′flə·mā′shən) *n.* 1 *Pathol.* A localized reaction to infection, injury, etc., characterized by heat, redness, swelling, and pain. 2 The act of inflaming.

**in·flate** (in·flāt′) *v.* **·flat·ed, ·flat·ing** *v.t.* 1 To fill with gas or air so as to distend or expand; blow up. 2 To increase or puff up: to *inflate* one's pride. 3 To increase unduly, esp. so that the nominal value exceeds the real: to *inflate* currency or prices. —*v.i.* 4 To become inflated. [< L *in-* in + *flare* blow] —**in·fla′ta·ble** *adj.* —**in·fla′ter, in·fla′tor** *n.*

**in·fla·tion** (in·flā′shən) *n.* 1 The act of inflating, or the state of being inflated. 2 An increase of currency in circulation or an overissue of credit, resulting in a rise of price levels when or if demand for goods exceeds supply. 3 The resulting rise in price levels. —**in·fla′tion·ar′y** *adj.*

**in·flect** (in·flekt′) *v.t.* 1 *Gram.* To give the inflections of (a word); conjugate or decline. 2 To vary the pitch of (the voice); modulate. 3 To turn inward or aside; deflect; curve. [< L *in-* in + *flectere* to bend]

**in·flec·tion** (in·flek′shən) *n.* 1 A bending or bend; curvature; angle. 2 *Gram.* a A pattern of change undergone by words to express grammatical and syntactical relations, as of case, number, gender, person, tense, etc. b An inflectional element. c An inflected form. 3 A change in pitch or intensity in the voice. *Brit. sp.* **in·flex′ion.**

**in·flex·i·ble** (in·flek′sə·bəl) *adj.* 1 Unyielding; firm; stubborn. 2 Incapable of being physically bent; rigid. 3 That cannot be altered or varied: the *inflexible* laws of nature. —**in·flex′i·bil′i·ty, in·flex′i·ble·ness** *n.* —**in·flex′i·bly** *adv.* —**Syn.** 1 dogged, obstinate, steadfast. 2 stiff. 3 fixed, unalterable.

**·n·flict** (in·flikt′) *v.t.* 1 To cause (pain, wounds, etc.), as with a blow. 2 To impose, as punishment. 3 To impose as if by force: to *inflict* one's views on the public. [< L *in-* on + *fligere* to strike] —**in·flict′er, in·flic′tor** *n.* —**in·flic′tive** *adj.*

**in·flic·tion** (in·flik′shən) *n.* 1 The act or process of inflicting. 2 That which is inflicted.

**in·flu·ence** (in′flōō·əns) *n.* 1 The power of a person or thing to produce an effect upon others, often indirectly or intangibly. 2 The effect of such power. 3 Power arising from social, financial, moral, or similar authority. 4 A person or thing that has or exerts influence. —*v.t.* **·enced, ·enc·ing** To have or exert influence on. [< L *in-* in + *fluere* to flow] —**in′flu·enc′er** *n.*

**in·flu·en·tial** (in′flōō·en′shəl) *adj.* Having or exercising great influence or power; effective. —**in′flu·en′tial·ly** *adv.*

**in·flu·en·za** (in′flōō·en′zə) *n.* An acute, sometimes epidemic, infectious disease of varying severity caused by a virus and characterized by inflammation of the air passages, fever, and nervous and muscular prostration. [< L *influere* flow in] —**in′flu·en′zal** *adj.*

**in·flux** (in′fluks) *n.* 1 A continuous flowing or pouring in. 2 The mouth of a river. [< L *influere* flow in]

**in·form** (in·fôrm′) *v.t.* 1 To give (someone) facts or information; make something known to. 2 To give character to; animate. —*v.i.* 3 To give information, esp. to accuse or charge others, usu. for gain: with *on* or *against.* [< L *informare* give form to, describe.] —**Syn.** 1 advise, apprise, acquaint, notify.

**in·for·mal** (in·fôr′məl) *adj.* 1 Not in the usual or prescribed form; unofficial. 2 Without ceremony or formality; casual. 3 Not requiring formal clothes. 4 Describing a manner of speech or writing characteristic of familiar conversation. —**in·for′mal·ly** *adv.*

**in·for·mal·i·ty** (in′fôr·mal′ə·tē) *n. pl.* **·ties** 1 Absence of regular or official form. 2 An informal act or proceeding.

**in·fra·red** (in′frə·red′) *adj.* Designating electromagnetic waves having wavelengths exceeding those of visible red light but shorter than those of radio waves.

**in·fringe** (in·frinj′) *v.t.* **·fringed, ·fring·ing** To break or disregard the terms of requirements of, as an oath or law; violate. —**infringe on** (or **upon**) To transgress or trespass on rights or privileges. [< L *in-* in + *frangere* to break] —**in·fringe′ment, in·fring′er** *n.*

**in·fu·ri·ate** (in·fyŏŏr′ē·āt) *v.t.* **·at·ed, ·at·ing** To make furious. —*adj.* (-it) Infuriated; enraged. [< L *in-* in + *furia* rage] —**in·fu′ri·ate·ly, in·fu′ri·at′ing·ly** *adv.* —**in·fu′ri·a′tion** *n.*

**in·fuse** (in·fyŏŏz′) *v.t.* **·fused, ·fus·ing** 1 To instill or inculcate, as principles or qualities. 2 To inspire; imbue; with *with.* 3 To pour in or upon. 4 To steep or soak so as to make an extract: to *infuse* tea leaves. [< L *in*- in + *fundere* pour] —**in·fus′er** *n.*

**in·fu·sion** (in·fyōo′zhən) *n.* 1 The act of infusing, imbuing, or pouring in. 2 That which is infused. 3 The process of steeping or soaking any substance in a liquid to extract its properties without boiling. 4 The liquid extract so obtained.

**in·gen·ious** (in·jēn′yəs) *adj.* 1 Possessed of skill in making or inventing. 2 Cleverly conceived or made. [< L *ingenium* natural ability] —**in·gen′ious·ly** *adv.* —**in·gen′ious·ness** *n.* —Syn. 1 adroit, clever, creative, resourceful.

**in·ge·nu·i·ty** (in′jə·n′ōō′ə·tē) *n.* 1 Cleverness in making or originating. 2 Originality of execution or design.

**in·gen·u·ous** (in·jen′yōo·əs) *adj.* 1 Free from dissimulation; frank. 2 Innocent; artless. [< L *ingenuus* inborn, natural, frank] —**in·gen′u·ous·ly** *adv.* —**in·gen′u·ous·ness** *n.*

**in·grate** (in′grāt) *n.* One who is ungrateful. [< L *in*- not + *gratus* pleasing]

**in·gra·ti·ate** (in·grā′shē·āt) *v.t.* ·at·ed, ·at·ing To bring (oneself) into the favor or confidence of others. —**in·gra′ti·at′ing·ly** *adv.* —**in·gra′ti·a′tion** *n.* —**in·gra′ti·a·to′ry** (-ə·tòr′ē, -tō′rē) *adj.* [< L *in gratiam* in favor]

**in·gre·di·ent** (in·grē′dē·ənt) *n.* 1 Any of the things that enter into the composition of a mixture. 2 A component part of anything. [< L *in*- in + *gradi* to walk]

**in·hab·it** (in·hab′it) *v.t.* To live or dwell in (a specified region, house, etc.); occupy as a home. [< L *in*- in + *habitare* dwell] —**in·hab′it·a·bil′i·ty**, **in·hab′i·ta′tion**, **in·hab′i·ter** *n.* —**in·hab′it·a·ble** *adj.*

**in·hale** (in·hāl′) *v.* ·haled, ·hal·ing *v.t.* To draw into the lungs, as breath or fumes; breathe in. —*v.i.* To draw breath, fumes, etc., into the lungs. [< L *in*- in + *halare* breathe] —**in·ha·la′tion** (in′hə·lā′shən) *n.*

**in·her·ent** (in·hir′ənt, -her′-) *adj.* Naturally and inseparably associated with a person or thing; innate. —**in·her′ence, in·her′en·cy** ( *pl.* ·cies) *n.* —**in·her′ent·ly** *adv.* —Syn. essential, natural, characteristic, instinctual, native.

**in·her·it** (in·her′it) *v.t.* 1 To receive, as property or a title, by succession or will; fall heir to. 2 To receive (traits, qualities, etc.) by or as if by heredity: She *inherits* her mother's good looks. —*v.i.* 3 To come into or possess an inheritance. [< L *in*- in + *heres* heir] —**in·her′i·tor** *n.*

**in·hib·it** (in·hib′it) *v.t.* 1 To keep from happening or from acting; block or prevent the action of. 2 To keep from spontaneous activity, feeling, etc.; restrain. 3 To forbid or prohibit. —*v.i.* 4 To cause inhibition. [< L *in*- in + *habere* have, hold] —**in·hib′it·a·ble, in·hib′i·tive, in·hib′i·to′ry** *adj.* —**in·hib′i·tor** or **in·hib′i·ter** *n.*

**in·hi·bi·tion** (in′hi·bish′ən, in′i-) *n.* 1 The act of inhibiting or the state of being inhibited. 2 The repression of an impulse, as by a mental process. 3 The process by which an impulse is repressed.

**in·im·i·ta·ble** (in·im′ə·tə·bəl) *adj.* That cannot be imitated; matchless. —**in·im′i·ta·bil′i·ty, in·im′i·ta·ble·ness** *n.* —**in·im′i·ta·bly** *adv.*

**in·iq·ui·ty** (in·ik′wə·tē) *n. pl.* ·ties 1 Deviation from right; wickedness. 2 A wrongful or unjust act. [< L *iniquus* unequal]

**in·i·tial** (in·ish′əl) *adj.* Having to do with or standing at the beginning; first. —*n.* The first letter of a word, esp. a name. —*v.t.* ·tialed or ·tialled, ·tial·ing or ·tial·ling To mark or sign with initials. [< L *initium* beginning]

**in·i·ti·ate** (in·ish′ē·āt) *v.t.* ·at·ed, ·at·ing 1 To begin; originate. 2 To introduce, as into a club, usu. with ceremony. 3 To instruct in fundamentals or principles. —*adj.* (-it, -āt) Initiated. —*n.* (-it, -āt) 1 One who is being or has been newly initiated. 2 One who is learned in some special field. [< L *initium* beginning] —**in·i′ti·a′tor** *n.* —Syn. 1 start, commence, inaugurate, invent, create.

**in·i·ti·a·tion** (in·ish′ē·ā′shən) *n.* 1 The act of initiating. 2 Ceremonial admission, as into a society.

**in·i·ti·a·tive** (in·ish′ē·ə·tiv) *n.* 1 A first move. 2 The ability for original conception and independent action. 3 The process by which the electorate initiates or enacts legislation. 4 The process by which a group of citizens may propose by petition a legislative measure to the voters. —*adj.* Pertaining to initiation; preliminary. —**in·i′ti·a·tive·ly** *adv.*

**in·junc·tion** (in·jungk′shən) *n.* 1 The act of enjoining; a command. 2 *Law* A judicial order requiring the party enjoined to take or, usu., to refrain from some specified action. [< L *injungere* join to, enjoin]

**in·jure** (in′jər) *v.t.* ·jured, ·jur·ing 1 To do harm or hurt to. 2 To do wrong to; treat with injustice. [< L *injuria* injury] —**in′jur·er** *n.*

**in·ju·ri·ous** (in·jŏŏr′ē·əs) *adj.* 1 Hurtful or

harmful. 2 Offensive; insulting; abusive. —
in·ju′ri·ous·ly adv. —in·ju′ri·ous·ness n.
in·ju·ry (in′jər·ē) n. pl. ·ries 1 Harm or damage, esp. to the body. 2 A wrong or injustice done to another. [< L injurius unjust]
in·mate (in′māt) n. 1 One who is kept or confined in an institution, hospital, prison, etc.
2 One who lives in a place with others. [?]
in·nate (i·nāt′, in′āt) adj. Native to or original with the individual; inborn. [< L in-
+ nasci be born] —in·nate′ly adv. —in·
nate′ness n. —Syn. congenital, inherent,
natural.
in·ning (in′ing) n. 1 In baseball, the period in
which one team is at bat, completed by
three outs. 2 Often pl. The period during
which a party or person is in power. [< OE
innung, gerund of innian put in]
in·no·cent (in′ə·sənt) adj. 1 Free from evil,
guile, or wrongdoing. 2 Free from the guilt
of a specific crime or charge. 3 Free from
qualities that can harm: innocent pastimes.
4 Not maliciously intended: an innocent remark. —n. One ignorant of evil, as a young
child. [< L in- not + nocere to harm] —in′
no·cent·ly adv.
in·no·vate (in′ō·vāt, in′ə-) v. ·vat·ed, ·vat·ing
v.i. To make changes or alterations in;
bring in new ideas, methods, etc. [< L in- in
+ novare make new] —in′no·va′tive adj. —
in′no·va′tor n.
in·nu·en·do (in′yŏō·en′dō) n. pl. ·dos or ·does
An indirect suggestion, remark, etc., usu.
disparaging; insinuation. [L, by nodding at,
intimating]
in·nu·mer·a·ble (i·n′ŏŏ′mər·ə·bəl) adj. Too
numerous to be counted; myriad. —in·nu′
mer·a·bil′i·ty, in·nu′mer·a·ble·ness n. —
in·nu′mer·a·bly adv.
in·oc·u·late (in·ok′yə·lāt) v.t. ·lat·ed, ·lat·ing
1 To immunize (a person or animal) by administering a serum or vaccine to. 2 To introduce microorganisms into (a culture
medium, soil, an animal or plant, etc.). 3 To
implant ideas, opinions, etc., in the mind
of. [< L inoculare engraft an eye or bud] —
in·oc′u·la·ble, in·oc′u·la·tive adj. —in·oc′
u·la′tion, in·oc′u·la′tor n.
in·or·di·nate (in·ôr′də·nit) adj. Not restrained
by prescribed rules or bounds; immoderate. —in·or′di·na·cy (-nə-sē), in·or′di·nate·
ness n. —in·or′di·nate·ly adv. —Syn. excessive, exorbitant, extravagant, unreasonable.
in·put (in′pŏŏt) n. 1 Something put into a
system or device, as energy into a machine,

food into the body, data into a computer, or
a signal into an electronic device. 2 A place
or point of introduction, as of data into a
computer. 3 An effect or influence resulting
from contributing opinions, information,
suggestions, etc.: The staff had real input
in the directive.
in·quest (in′kwest) n. A judicial inquiry,
aided by a jury, into a matter, esp. a death
possibly resulting from a crime. [< L in-
quisita (res) (thing) inquired (into)]
in·quire (in·kwīr′) v. ·quired, ·quir·ing v.t. 1
To seek information about. —v.i. 2 To ask
questions; make inquiries. 3 To make investigation; search into carefully: with into.
—inquire after To ask about the well-being
of. [< L in- into + quaerere seek] —in·quir′er
n. —in·quir′ing·ly adv.
in·quir·y (in·kwīr′ē, in′kwə·rē) n. pl. ·quir·ies
1 The act of inquiring. 2 Investigation; research. 3 A query.
in·qui·si·tion (in′kwə·zish′ən) n. 1 An investigation. 2 The proceedings and findings of
a jury of inquest. 3 Any searching examination or questioning. [< L inquisitio] —in·
′qui·si′tion·al adj. —in′qui·si′tion·al·ly
adv.
in·quis·i·tive (in·kwiz′ə·tiv) adj. 1 Given to
questioning, esp. to satisfy curiosity. 2 Inclined to the pursuit of knowledge. —
in·quis′i·tive·ly adv. —in·quis′i·tive·ness
n.
in·road (in′rōd′) n. 1 A hostile entrance into
a country or territory; a raid. 2 Any detrimental encroachment; inroads upon one's
health.
in·sane (in·sān′) adj. 1 Foolish, extravagant,
or impractical. 2 Mentally ill; deranged. 3
Too mentally disturbed to be legally responsible. —in·sane′ly adv. —in·sane′
ness n.
in·san·i·ty (in·san′ə·tē) n. pl. ·ties 1 Irra-
tionality; extreme folly. 2 Mental illness; derangement. 3 Law Mental unsoundness to
the degree of being not responsible in various legally defined respects. • Insanity and
insane are no longer scientific terms in
medicine and psychiatry and have been replaced by more specific terms describing
various states of mental illness. However,
both words are still acceptable in legal parlance.
in·sa·tia·ble (in·sā′shə·bəl, -shē·ə·bəl) adj.
Not to be sated or satisfied; unappeasable.
Also in·sa′ti·ate (-it). —in·sa′ti·a·bil′i·ty,
in·sa′tia·ble·ness n. —in·sa′tia·bly adv.

**in·scribe** (in·skrīb′) *v.t.* ·**scribed,** ·**scrib·ing** 1 To write or engrave (signs, words, names, etc.). 2 To mark the surface of with engraved or written characters. 3 To dedicate, as a book. 4 To enter the name of on a list. 5 *Geom.* To enclose (a figure) with another so that a particular subset of the points in one figure coincides with points in the other. [< L *in-* on, in + *scribere* write] — **in·scrib′er** *n.*

**in·scrip·tion** (in·skrip′shən) *n.* 1 The act of inscribing, or that which is inscribed. 2 Incised or relief lettering on a durable object. 3 An entry in a list, roll, etc. 4 A dedication written in a book or the like. — **in·scrip′tion·al, in·scrip′tive** *adj.*

**in·sect** (in′sekt) *n.* 1 Any of a large class of arthropods having three distinct body segments, three pairs of legs, one pair of antennae, and usu. two pairs of wings. 2 Loosely, any small invertebrate resembling an insect, as spiders, centipedes, ticks, etc. [< L (*animal*) *insectum* (animal) notched] — **in·sec′te·an** (-sek′tē·ən) *adj.*

**in·sec·ti·cide** (in·sek′tə·sīd) *n.* Any substance that kills insects.

**in·sert** (in·sûrt′) *v.t.* 1 To put or place into something else. 2 To put between or among other things. — *n.* (in′sûrt) 1 That which is inserted. 2 A circular or the like placed within a newspaper or book for mailing. [< L *in-* in + *serere* place, join] — **in·sert′er** *n.*

**in·ser·tion** (in·sûr′shən) *n.* 1 The act of inserting, or the state of being inserted. 2 That which is inserted, as lace or embroidery placed between pieces of plain fabric. 3 Additional or explanatory material inserted in a written or printed page.

**in·sid·i·ous** (in·sid′ē·əs) *adj.* 1 Designed to entrap; full of wiles. 2 Doing or contriving harm. 3 Awaiting a chance to harm. 4 Causing harm by stealth, usu. imperceptible means: an *insidious* disease. [< L *insidere* sit in, lie in wait] — **in·sid′i·ous·ly** *adv.* — **in·sid′i·ous·ness** *n.*

**in·sig·ni·a** (in·sig′nē·ə) *n. sing. or pl.* 1 A badge, emblem, etc., used as a mark of office or distinction. 2 Something significant or indicative of a calling. [< L *in-* in + *signum* sign, emblem] • In Latin and formerly in English, *insignia* was the plural form of **in·sig·ne** (in·sig′nē). Now, however, *insignia* has virtually replaced *insigne* in the singular. The plural form *insignias* is well established, although *insignia* is still sometimes used in its original plural sense.

**in·sig·nif·i·cant** (in′sig·nif′ə·kənt) *adj.* 1 Not significant; without importance. 2 Meaningless. 3 Without dignity; not imposing: an *insignificant* person. — **in′sig·nif′i·cance, in′sig·nif′i·can·cy** *n.* — **in′sig·nif′i·cant·ly** *adv.* — **Syn.** 1 petty, trifling, trivial. 2 immaterial, irrelevant.

**in·sin·cere** (in′sin·sir′) *adj.* Not sincere, honest, or genuine; hypocritical. — **in′sin·cere′ly** *adv.*

**in·sin·cer·i·ty** (in′sin·ser′ə·tē) *n. pl.* ·**ties** 1 Lack of sincerity. 2 An insincere act, remark, etc.

**in·sin·u·ate** (in·sin′yōō·āt) *v.t.* ·**at·ed,** ·**at·ing** 1 To indicate slyly or deviously. 2 To infuse or instill gradually or subtly into the mind. 3 To introduce gradually, artfully, or stealthily: to *insinuate* oneself into an enviable position. [< L *insinuare* to curve] — **in·sin′u·a′ting·ly** *adv.* — **in·sin′u·a′tive** *adj.* — **in·sin′u·a′tor** *n.*

**in·sin·u·a·tion** (in·sin′yōō·ā′shən) 1 The act of insinuating. 2 An injurious suggestion or implication. 3 A subtly ingratiating act, remark, etc.

**in·sip·id** (in·sip′id) *adj.* 1 Without flavor; tasteless. 2 Unexciting; dull. [< L *in-* not + *sapidus* savory] — **in·sip′id·ly** *adv.* — **in·sip′id·ness** *n.*

**in·sist** (in·sist′) *v.i.* 1 To make emphatic or repeated assertion, demand, or request: often with *on* or *upon* — *v.t.* 2 To state or demand emphatically: He *insisted* that he was right. [< L *in-* on + *sistere* to stand] — **in·sis′tence, in·sis′ten·cy** *n.*

**in·so·lent** (in′sə·lənt) *adj.* 1 Defiantly offensive in language or manner. 2 Grossly disrespectful. [< L *insolens* unusual, haughty] — **in′so·lent·ly** *adv.*

**in·sol·u·ble** (in·sol′yə·bəl) *adj.* 1 Not capable of being dissolved, as in a liquid; not soluble. 2 That cannot be explained or solved. — **in·sol′u·bil′i·ty, in·sol′u·ble·ness** *n.* — **in·sol′u·bly** *adv.*

**in·som·ni·a** (in·som′nē·ə) *n.* Chronic inability to sleep. [< L *insomnis* sleepless] — **in·som′ni·ac′** (-nē·ak′) *n.*

**in·spect** (in·spekt′) *v.t.* 1 To look at or examine carefully. 2 To examine or review officially, as troops. [< L *in-* into + *specere* to look] — **Syn.** 1 investigate, scan, scrutinize.

**in·spec·tion** (in·spek′shən) *n.* 1 A critical viewing or investigation. 2 An official examination. — **in·spec′tion·al** *adj.*

**in·spi·ra·tion** (in′spə·rā′shən) *n.* 1 The infusion of an idea, an emotion, or mental in-

inspire

fluence. 2 That which is so infused. 3 A stimulus to creativity in thought or action. 4 The state or quality of being inspired. 5 Divine or supernatural influence. 6 A person or thing that inspires. 7 The act of drawing air into the lungs. —in·spi·ra′tion·al adj. —in·spi·ra′tion·al·ly adv.

in·spire (in·spīr′) v. ·spired, ·spir·ing v.t. 1 To stir or affect by some mental or spiritual influence: stimulate. 2 To imbue with a specified idea or feeling: to inspire survivors with hope. 3 To give rise to: Fear inspires hatred. 4 To motivate or cause by supernatural influence. 5 To draw into the lungs: inhale. 6 To prompt the saying or writing of indirectly: This rumor was inspired by my enemies. —v.i. 7 To draw in breath; inhale. 8 To give or provide inspiration. [< L inspirare breathe into] —in·spir′a·ble adj. —in·spir′er n. —in·spir′ing·ly adv.

in·stall (in·stôl′) v.t. 1 To place in office, etc., with formal ceremony. 2 To establish in a place or position. 3 To place in position for service or use. [< Med. L in- in + stallare to seat] —in·stal·la·tion (in′stə·lā′shən), in·stall′er n.

in·stance (in′stəns) n. 1 Something offered or occurring as an example; a case. 2 The act of suggesting or urging; a request. 3 A step in proceeding: in the first instance. —for instance For example. —v.t. ·stanced, ·stanc·ing 1 To refer to an illustration or example. 2 To serve as an example of; exemplify. [< L instantia a standing near]

in·stant (in′stənt) adj. 1 Immediately impending; imminent. 2 Of the current month. 3 Direct; immediate: an instant result. 4 Urgent: an instant need for help. 5 Available in premixed or soluble form for quick preparation, as pudding, coffee, etc. —n. 1 A particular point of time. 2 A very brief portion of time; moment. —the instant As soon as. [< OF < L in- upon + stare to stand]

in·stan·ta·ne·ous (in′stən·tā′nē·əs) adj. 1 Acting or done instantly. 2 Of or at a particular instant. —in′stan·ta′ne·ous·ly adv. —in′stan·ta′ne·ous·ness n.

in·sti·gate (in′stə·gāt) v.t. ·gat·ed, ·gat·ing 1 To bring about by inciting; foment. 2 To urge or incite to an action or course. [< L instigare] —in′sti·ga′tion, in′sti·ga′tor n. —in′sti·ga′tive adj.

in·still (in·stil′) v.t. ·stilled, ·still·ing 1 To put into the mind gradually, as if drop by drop.

instrument

2 To pour in by drops. Also in·stil′. [< L instillare to drop, drip] —in′stil·la′tion (in′stə·lā′shən), in·stil′ler, in·still′ment or in·stil′ment n.

in·stinct (in′stingkt) n. 1 The innate ability of animals to perform functions peculiar to each species without training. 2 A natural aptitude. —adj. (in·stingkt′) Imbued or filled with: a picture instinct with life. [< L instinguere impel]

in·stinc·tive (in·stingk′tiv) adj. Of the nature of, or prompted by, instinct; innate: also in·stinc′tu·al (-chōō·əl). —in·stinc′tive·ly adv.

in·sti·tute (in′stə·t′ōōt′) v.t. ·tut·ed, ·tut·ing 1 To establish; found. 2 To set in operation; initiate. 3 To appoint to an office, position, etc. —n. 1 An established organization or society pledged to some special purpose and work. 2 The building occupied by such an organization. 3 An established principle, rule, or order. [< L in- in, on + statuere set up, stand] —in′sti·tut′er, in′sti·tu′tor n. —Syn. v. 1 erect, install, set up. 2 begin, commence, start.

in·sti·tu·tion (in′stə·t′ōō′shən) n. 1 An established principle, law, or usage. 2 A corporate body or establishment organized for an educational, medical, charitable, or similar purpose. 3 The building occupied by such an establishment. 4 The act of instituting or establishing: the institution of an investigation. 5 Informal A well-known person or thing.

in·struct (in·strukt′) v.t. 1 To impart knowledge or skill to, esp. by systematic method. 2 To give specific orders or directions to. 3 To give information or explanation to; inform. [< L in- in + struere build]

in·struc·tion (in·struk′shən) n. 1 The act of instructing; teaching. 2 Imparted knowledge. 3 The act of giving specific directions or commands. 4 pl. The directions given. —in·struc′tion·al adj.

in·struc·tor (in·struk′tər) n. 1 One who instructs; a teacher. 2 In the U.S., a college teacher of lower rank than the lowest professorial grade. —in·struc′tor·ship n.

in·stru·ment (in′strə·mənt) n. 1 A means by which work is done; an implement or tool. 2 A device for making measurements, records, etc. 3 Any means of accomplishment. 4 A device for the production of musical sounds. 5 A person doing the will of another. 6 Law A formal document, as a contract, deed, etc. [< L *instrumentum* < *instrure* fit out]

**in·stru·men·tal** (in′strə·men′təl) *adj.* 1 Serving as a means or instrument; serviceable. 2 For or produced by musical instruments. 3 Done by or pertaining to a mechanical instrument or a tool. —**in·stru·men′tal·ly** *adv.*

**in·stru·men·tal·i·ty** (in′strə·men·tal′ə·tē) *n. pl.* ·**ties** 1 The condition of being instrumental. 2 That which is instrumental; means.

**in·sub·or·di·nate** (in′sə·bôr′də·nit) *adj.* Not obedient; not submitting to authority. —*n.* A disobedient person.

**in·sub·or·di·na·tion** (in′sə·bôr′də·nā′shən) *n.* An act of being disobedient to constituted authorities.

**in·suf·fer·a·ble** (in·suf′ər·ə·bəl, -rə·bəl) *adj.* Not to be endured; intolerable. —**in·suf′fer·a·ble·ness** *n.* —**in·suf′fer·a·bly** *adv.*

**in·su·lar** (in′sy′ə·lər) *adj.* 1 Of or pertaining to an island or its inhabitants. 2 Standing alone; isolated. 3 Not broad, liberal, or cosmopolitan: *insular* ideas. [< L *insula* island] —**in′su·lar·ism**, **in·su·lar·i·ty** (in′s′ə·lar′ə·tē) *n.*

**in·su·late** (in′sə·lāt) *v.t.* ·**lat·ed**, ·**lat·ing** 1 To place in a detached state or situation; isolate. 2 To apply (to walls, electric wiring, etc.) a nonconducting substance or device. 3 To prevent or slow the passage of heat, electricity, sound, or other energy to or from. [< L *insula* island]

**in·su·la·tion** (in′sə·lā′shən) *n.* 1 The act of insulating. 2 Any nonconducting material used in insulating.

**in·su·la·tor** (in′sə·lā′tər) *n.* 1 One who or that which insulates. 2 A nonconducting substance or device used to insulate.

**in·su·lin** (in′sə·lin) *n.* 1 A hormone essential for carbohydrate metabolism, secreted by island cells in the pancreas. 2 A preparation of this hormone made from animal pancreas and used to control diabetes. [< NL *insula* island]

**in·sult** (in·sult′) *v.t.* To treat with insolence, contempt, or rudeness. —*n.* (in′sult) Something offensive said or done; an indignity. [< L *insultare* leap at, insult] —**in·sult′er** *n.* —**in·sult′ing·ly** *adv.* —**Syn.** *v.* abuse, affront, hurt, offend.

**in·su·per·a·ble** (in·sōō′pər·ə·bəl) *adj.* That cannot be overcome; insurmountable. [< L *in-* not + *superare* overcome] —**in·su′per-**

**a·bil′i·ty**, **in·su′per·a·ble·ness** *n.* —**in·su′per·a·bly** *adv.*

**in·sup·port·a·ble** (in′sə·pôr′tə·bəl, -pôr′-) *adj.* 1 Intolerable; insufferable. 2 Without grounds; unjustifiable. —**in′sup·port′a·ble·ness** *n.* —**in′sup·port′a·bly** *adv.*

**in·sure** (in·shŏŏr′) *v.* ·**sured**, ·**sur·ing** *v.t.* 1 To contract to pay or be paid an indemnity in the event of harm to or the loss or death of. 2 ENSURE (def. 1). 3 ENSURE (def. 2). —*v.i.* 4 To issue or take out a policy of insurance. [< OF *enseurer* make sure < *en-* in + *seur* sure] —**in·sur′a·bil′i·ty** *n.* —**in·sur′a·ble** *adj.*

**in·sur·gent** (in·sur′jənt) *adj.* Rising in rebellion against an existing government. —*n.* One who takes part in active opposition to constituted authorities. [< L *in-* against + *surgere* to rise]

**in·sur·rec·tion** (in′sə·rek′shən) *n.* An organized resistance to established government. [< L *insurgere* rise up against] —**in′sur·rec′tion·al** *adj.* —**in′sur·rec′tion·ar′y** *adj.*, *n.* —**in′sur·rec′tion·ism**, **in′sur·rec′tion·ist** *n.*

**in·tact** (in·takt′) *adj.* Left complete or unimpaired. [< L *intactus* untouched] —**in·tact′ness** *n.*

**in·te·ger** (in′tə·jər) *n.* 1 Any member of the set [. . . –3, –2, –1, 0, 1, 2, 3, . . .]; a whole number. 2 A whole. [< L, whole]

**in·te·gral** (in′tə·grəl) *adj.* 1 Constituting a completed whole. 2 Constituting an essential part of a whole. 3 *Math.* Of or being an integer or integers. —*n.* An entire thing; a whole. —**in′te·gral·ly** *adv.* —**in′te·gral′i·ty** (-gral′ə·tē) *n.*

**in·te·grate** (in′tə·grāt) *v.* ·**grat·ed**, ·**grat·ing** *v.t.* 1 To make or form into a whole; unify. 2 To combine (parts) into a whole. 3 *U.S.* a To make (schools, housing, public facilities, etc.) available to people of all races and ethnic groups on an equal basis. b To remove any barriers imposing segregation upon (religious, racial, or other groups). —*v.i.* 4 To become integrated. [< L *integer* whole, intact] —**in·te·gra·tion** (in′tə·grā′shən), **in′te·gra′tion·ist** (*esp. for def.* 3), **in′te·gra′tor** *n.* —**in′te·gra′tive** *adj.*

**in·teg·ri·ty** (in·teg′rə·tē) *n.* 1 Uprightness of character; honesty. 2 Unimpaired state; soundness. 3 Undivided or unbroken state; completeness. [< L *integer* whole]

**in·tel·lect** (in′tə·lekt) *n.* 1 The power to perceive, interpret, know, and understand. 2

Great and keen intelligence. 3 A person having such intelligence.

**in·tel·lec·tu·al** (in′tə·lek′chŏŏ·əl) *adj.* 1 Of or pertaining to the intellect: *intellectual* ability. 2 Possessing or showing a high degree of intelligence and knowledge. 3 Requiring intelligence or study: *intellectual* pursuits. —*n.* A person of trained intelligence, or one whose work requires exercise of the intellect. [< L *intellectualis*] —in′tel·lec′tu·al′i·ty, in′tel·lec′tu·al·ness *n.* —in′tel·lec′tu·al·ly *adv.*

**in·tel·li·gence** (in·tel′ə·jəns) *n.* 1 The ability to exercise mental functions. 2 The ability to grasp the significant factors of a complex problem or new situation. 3 Information acquired or communicated; news. 4 The gathering of secret information, esp. of a political or military nature. 5 A group of persons assigned to gather such secret information. 6 An intelligent being.

**in·tel·li·gent** (in·tel′ə·jənt) *adj.* 1 Learning easily; of active mind. 2 Showing intelligence: an *intelligent* reply. 3 Endowed with intellect; reasoning: Man is an *intelligent* animal. [< L *intelligere* understand, perceive] —in′tel′li·gent·ly *adv.* —Syn. 2 astute, bright, clever, discerning.

**in·tel·li·gi·ble** (in·tel′ə·jə·bəl) *adj.* Capable of being understood; clear. —in·tel′li·gi·bil′i·ty, in·tel′li·gi·ble·ness *n.* —in·tel′li·gi·bly *adv.*

**in·tem·per·ance** (in·tem′pər·əns) *n.* 1 Lack of moderation or due restraint. 2 Excessive use of alcohol.

**in·tend** (in·tend′) *v.t.* 1 To have in mind to accomplish or do. 2 To make or destine for a purpose, use, etc.: a game *intended* for adults. 3 To mean: She *intended* nothing by the remark. [< L *intendere* stretch out (for)] —in·tend′er *n.*

**in·tense** (in·tens′) *adj.* ·tens·er, ·tens·est 1 Strained or exerted to a high degree; fervid: *intense* study. 2 Extreme in degree, concentration, or measure: *intense* light. 3 Putting forth strenuous effort. 4 Susceptible to or exhibiting strong emotions. [< L *intendere* stretch out (for)] —in·tense′ly *adv.* —in·tense′ness *n.*

**in·ten·si·fy** (in·ten′sə·fī) *v.t.* & *v.i.* ·fied, ·fy·ing To make or become intense or more intense; increase in degree. —in·ten′si·fi·ca′tion, in·ten′si·fi′er *n.*

**in·ten·si·ty** (in·ten′sə·tē) *n. pl.* ·ties 1 The state or quality of being intense. 2 Extreme depth or violence of feeling, activity, etc. 3 The measure of how intense a force, flow of energy, etc., is.

**in·tent** (in·tent′) *adj.* 1 Having the mind fixed; earnest: *intent* on winning. 2 Firmly or constantly directed: an *intent* gaze. ––*n.* 1 The meaning expressed by an act or words. 2 An aim or purpose. —**to all intents and purposes** In practically every aspect. [< L *intendere* stretch out (for)] in·tent′ly *adv.* —in·tent′ness *n.*

**in·ten·tion** (in·ten′shən) *n.* 1 A settled plan for doing a certain thing. 2 That upon which the mind is set; purpose. 3 *pl. Informal* Purpose with respect to a proposal of marriage.

**in·ter** (in·tûr′) *v.t.* ·terred, ·ter·ring To place in a grave or tomb; bury. [< L *in-* in + *terra* earth]

**in·ter·cede** (in′tər·sēd′) *v.i.* ·ced·ed, ·ced·ing 1 To plead in behalf of another. 2 To act as a mediator in order to resolve disagreements between or among others. [< L *inter-* between + *cedere* pass, go] —in′ter·ced′er *n.* —Syn. 2 arbitrate, intervene, moderate, referee.

**in·ter·cept** (in′tər·sept′) *v.t.* 1 To seize or stop on the way to a destination: to *intercept* contraband; to *intercept* a pass. 2 To stop, interrupt, or prevent. 3 To cut off from connection, sight, etc. 4 *Math.* To contain or include, as between two points of a curve. —*v.i.* 5 In various sports, to intercept a pass intended for an opponent. —*n.* (in′tər·sept)*Math.* A point in which a figure intersects an axis of a coordinate system. [< L *inter-* between + *capere* seize] —in′ter·cep′tion *n.* —in′ter·cep′tive *adj.*

**in·ter·ces·sion** (in′tər·sesh′ən) *n.* The act of interceding between persons; entreaty in behalf of others. —in′ter·ces′sion·al, in′ter·ces′so·ry (-ses′ə·rē) *adj.* —in′ter·ces′sor *n.*

**in·ter·course** (in′tər·kôrs, -kōrs) *n.* 1 Mutual exchange or communication. 2 The interchange of ideas. 3 SEXUAL INTERCOURSE. [< L *inter-* between + *currere* to run]

**in·ter·dict** (in′tər·dikt′) *v.t.* 1 To prohibit or restrain authoritatively. 2 In the Roman Catholic Church, to exclude from religious privileges. —*n.* 1 A prohibitive order; ban. 2 In the Roman Catholic Church, a ban excluding a person, parish, etc. from religious privileges. [< L *interdicere* forbid] —in′ter·dic′tion, in′ter·dic′tor *n.* —in′ter·dic′tive, in′ter·dic′to·ry *adj.* —in′ter·dic′tive·ly *adv.*

**in·ter·est** (in′tər·ist, -trist) *n.* 1 A feeling of attraction or curiosity about something. 2 The power to excite or hold such a feeling. 3 Something bringing about this feeling: a man of many *interests*. 4 *Often pl.* That which is of advantage or profit. 5 Payment made for the use of money; also, the money so paid, usu. a percentage of the amount borrowed. 6 Something added in repaying: to return a blow with *interest*. 7 A right or share in something, esp. a business enterprise. 8 The persons involved in an industry, cause, etc.: the oil *interest*. 9 Importance: a story of little *interest*. 10 Power to procure favor or regard; influence. —**in the interest of** In behalf of; for. —*v.t.* (*also* in′tə·rest) 1 To excite or hold the curiosity or attention of. 2 To cause to have a share or interest in; induce to participate. [< L *interesse* lie between, be important]

**in·ter·fere** (in′tər·fir′) *v.i.* ·**fered**, ·**fer·ing** 1 To come into conflict or opposition; clash. 2 To take part unasked in the concerns of others; meddle. 3 To intervene for a specific purpose. 4 *Physics* To act in opposition, as waves of light, sound, or electricity. 5 In sports, to obstruct the actions of an opponent in an illegal manner. —**interfere with** To thwart; hinder. [< L *inter-* between + *ferire* to strike] —**in′ter·fer′er** *n.* —**in′ter·fer′ing·ly** *adv.*

**in·ter·fer·ence** (in′tər·fir′əns) *n.* 1 The act of interfering; conflict; collision. 2 *Physics* The action of wave trains, as of light, sound, or electricity, that on meeting tend to cancel each other. 3 In sports, obstruction of the actions of an opponent in an illegal manner.

**in·te·ri·or** (in·tir′ē·ər) *adj.* 1 Existing, pertaining to, or occurring within something; internal. 2 Inland or far from the borders. 3 Of a private or confidential nature. —*n.* 1 The internal part; inside. 2 The inland or central region of a country. 3 The domestic affairs of a country. 4 Inner nature; basic character. [< L, compar. of *inter* within] —**in·te′ri·or′i·ty** (-ôr′ə·tē, -or′-) *n.* —**in·te′ri·or·ly** *adv.*

**in·ter·ject** (in′tər·jekt′) *v.t.* To throw between other things: introduce abruptly; interpose. [< L *inter-* between + *jacere* to throw]

**in·ter·jec·tion** (in′tər·jek′shən) *n.* 1 *Gram.* A word expressing emotion or simple exclamation, as *oh! alas! look!* 2 A sudden interposition or interruption. —**in′ter·jec′tion·al** *adj.* —**in′ter·jec′tion·al·ly** *adv.*

**in·ter·lop·er** (in′tər·lō′pər) *n.* One who thrusts himself into a space without right. [<INTER- + Du *loopen* to run] —**Syn.** interposer, intruder, meddler, trespasser.

**in·ter·lude** (in′tər·lōōd) *n.* 1 An intervening time or space. 2 An independent performance, usu. light or humorous, introduced between the acts of a play or the parts of a performance. 3 A passage of music that forms a transition. [< L *inter-* between + *ludus* a game, play]

**in·ter·me·di·ar·y** (in′tər·mē′dē·er′ē) *adj.* 1 Situated, acting, or coming between. 2 Acting as a mediator. —*n. pl.* ·**ies** An agent or mediator.

**in·ter·me·di·ate** (in′tər·mē′dē·it) *adj.* Being or occurring in a middle place or degree. —*n.* 1 Something intermediate. 2 INTERMEDIARY. —*v.i.* (-āt) ·**at·ed**, ·**at·ing** To act as an intermediary; mediate. [< L *intermedius* middle] —**in′ter·me′di·ate·ly** *adv.* —**in′ter·me′di·ate·ness** *n.*

**in·ter·ment** (in·tûr′mənt) *n.* The act of interring; burial.

**in·ter·mi·na·ble** (in·tûr′mə·nə·bəl) *adj.* Continuing, or seeming to continue, for a very long time; endless. —**in·ter′mi·na·bly** *adv.*

**in·ter·mis·sion** (in′tər·mish′ən) *n.* 1 Temporary cessation. 2 An interval, as between acts in the theater. [< L *intermittere* send between] —**in′ter·mis′sive** *adj.*

**in·ter·mit·tent** (in′tər·mit′ənt) *adj.* Alternately ceasing and beginning; not continuous. —**in′ter·mit′tent·ly** *adv.*

**in·tern**[1] (in·tûrn′) *v.t.* To confine within the limits of a country or area, as enemy aliens or prisoners of war. [<L *internus* internal] —**in·tern′ment** *n.*

**in·tern**[2] (in′tûrn) *n.* A medical doctor undergoing resident training in a hospital. —*v.i.* To serve as an intern in a hospital. [See INTERN[1].] —**in′tern·ship** *n.*

**in·ter·nal** (in·tûr′nəl) *adj.* 1 Situated in or applicable to the inside; interior. 2 Pertaining to or derived from the inside. 3 Pertaining to the inner self or the mind; subjective. 4 Pertaining to the domestic affairs of a country. —*n.* 1 *pl.* The internal bodily organs; entrails. 2 The essential quality of anything. [< L *internus* <in in] —**in·ter′nal·ly** *adv.*

**in·ter·na·tion·al** (in′tər·nash′ən·əl) *adj.* 1 Of or pertaining to the relations among nations: *international* law. 2 Carried on among nations: *international* trade. 3 Between two or more nations: an *international* treaty. —**in′ter·na′tion·al′i·ty** *n.* —**in′ter·na′tion·al·ly** *adv.*

**in·ter·plan·e·tar·y** (ĭn'tər-plăn'ə-tĕr'ē) *adj.*
Between or among planets.

**in·ter·po·late** (ĭn-tûr'pəlāt) *v.* ·**lat·ed**, ·**lat·ing**
*v.t.* 1 To alter, as a manuscript, by the insertion of new or unauthorized matter. 2 To
insert (such matter). 3 *Math.* To estimate a
value of (a function) between known values.
—*v.i.* 4 To make interpolations. [<L *inter-*
between + *polire* to polish] —**in·ter'**
**po·la'ter, in·ter'po·la'tion, in·ter'po·la'tor**
*n.* —**in·ter'po·la'tive** *adj.*

**in·ter·pose** (ĭn'tər-pōz') *v.* ·**posed**, ·**pos·ing**
*v.t.* 1 To place between other things; insert.
2 To introduce by way of intervention: He
*interposed* his authority. 3 To inject, as a
remark, into a conversation, argument, etc.
—*v.i.* 4 To come between; intervene. 5 To
put in a remark; interrupt. [<L *inter-* between + *ponere* put] —**in'ter·pos'er, in·ter·**
**po·si·tion** (ĭn·tər·pə·zĭsh'ən) *n.* —**in'ter·pos·**
**s'ing·ly** *adv.*

**in·ter·pret** (ĭn·tûr'prĭt) *v.t.* 1 To give the meaning of; make clear. 2 To derive a particular
understanding of; construe. 3 To bring out
the meaning of by artistic representation or
performance. 4 To translate. —*v.i.* 5 To act
as interpreter. 6 To explain. [<L *interpres*
agent, interpreter] —**in·ter'pret·a·bil'i·ty** *n.*
—**in·ter'pret·a·ble** *adj.* —**Syn.** 1 clarify, elu-
cidate, explain, illuminate.

**in·ter·pre·ta·tion** (ĭn·tûr'prə·tā'shən) *n.* 1 The
act or result of interpreting. 2 The performance or representation of a work of art so
as to reveal one's conception of it. [F] —
**in·ter'pre·ta'tion·al** *adj.*

**in·ter·pret·er** (ĭn·tûr'prĭt·ər) *n.* 1 One who interprets. 2 One who serves as translator
between people speaking different languages.

**in·ter·ro·gate** (ĭn·tĕr'ə·gāt) *v.* ·**gat·ed**, ·**gat·ing**
*v.t.* To put questions to; question. —*v.i.* To
ask questions. [<L *inter-* between + *rogare*
ask] —**in·ter'ro·ga'tor** *n.*

**in·ter·ro·ga·tion** (ĭn·tĕr'ə·gā'shən) *n.* 1 The
act of interrogating. 2 A question; query. 3
A formal or official questioning, as of a prisoner or witness. —**in·ter'ro·ga'tion·al** *adj.*

**in·ter·rupt** (ĭn'tə·rŭpt') *v.t.* 1 To cause a delay
or break in: to *interrupt* service. 2 To break
the continuity, course, or sameness of. 3 To
break in on (someone) talking, working, etc.
—*v.i.* 4 To break in upon an action or
speech. [<L *inter-* between + *rumpere* to
break] —**in'ter·rupt'er** *n.* —**in'ter·rup'tive**
*adj.*

**in·ter·rup·tion** (ĭn'tə·rŭp'shən) *n.* 1 The act of

interrupting. 2 A break in continuity; an interval. 3 Obstruction caused by breaking in
upon any course, progress, or motion.

**in·ter·sect** (ĭn'tər·sĕkt') *v.t.* 1 To pass across;
cut through or into so as to divide. —*v.i.* 2
To cross each other. [<L *inter-* between + *se-*
*care* to cut]

**in·ter·sec·tion** (ĭn'tər·sĕk'shən) *n.* 1 The act
of intersecting. 2 The point or line of contact between two lines, planes, etc. 3 The
area where two streets cross. —**in'ter·se·**
**c'tion·al** *adj.*

**in·ter·sperse** (ĭn'tər·spûrs') *v.t.* ·**spersed**,
·**spers·ing** 1 To scatter among other things:
set here and there. 2 To diversify or adorn
with other things scattered here and there.
[<L *inter-* among + *spargere* scatter] —
**in'ter·spers'ed·ly** *adv.* —**in'ter·sper'sion**
(-spûr'zhən) *n.*

**in·ter·state** (ĭn'tər·stāt') *adj.* Between different states, as of the U.S.: *interstate* commerce.

**in·ter·stel·lar** (ĭn'tər·stĕl'ər) *adj.* Situated or
occurring among the stars.

**in·ter·val** (ĭn'tər·vəl) *n.* 1 The time that intervenes between two events or periods. 2 An
open space between two objects; distance
between points. 3 *Music* a The difference in
pitch between two tones. b A sound composed of two tones sounded simultaneously. —**at intervals** 1 From time to time. 2
At a series of points with spaces between.
[<L *inter-* between + *vallum* rampart] —**Syn.**
1 interim, interlude, intermission, pause.

**in·ter·vene** (ĭn'tər·vēn') *v.i.* ·**vened**, ·**ven·ing** 1
To come between by action or authority; in-
terfere or mediate. 2 To occur, as something irrelevant or unexpected: I will come
if nothing *intervenes*. 3 To be located between. 4 To take place between other events
or times. [<L *inter-* between + *venire* come]
—**in'ter·ven'er** *n.* —**in'ter·ven'ient** (-vē
n'yənt) *adj., n.*

**in·ter·ven·tion** (ĭn'tər·vĕn'shən) *n.* 1 The act
of coming between. 2 Interference with the
acts of others. 3 Interference in the affairs
of one country by another. 4 An intervening time, event, or thing. —**in'ter·ven'tion·**
**al** *adj.* —**in·ter·ven·tion·ist** (ĭn'tər·vĕn'
shən·ĭst) *adj., n.*

**in·ter·view** (ĭn'tər·vyōō) *n.* 1 A meeting between two or more people, as to evaluate
qualifications or consider for employment.
2 A meeting for soliciting views or opinions,
as by reporters or investigators. 3 The report of such a meeting. —*v.t.* To have an in-

266

terview with. [<L *inter-* between + *videre* see]
—in′ter·view′er *n.*

in·tes·tate (in·tes′tāt) *adj.* 1 Not having made
a will. 2 Not legally devised or disposed of
by will. —*n.* A person who dies intestate.
[<L *in-* not + *testari* make a will] —in·tes·
ta·cy (in·tes′tə·sē) *n.*

in·tes·tine (in·tes′tin) *n.* *Usu. pl.* The part of
the alimentary canal between the stomach
and the anus, consisting of the long small
intestine and the shorter, wider large intestine including the colon and rectum. —
*adj.* Internal with regard to state or community; domestic. [<L *intestinus* internal]
—in·tes′ti·nal *adj.* —in·tes′ti·nal·ly *adv.*

in·ti·ma·cy (in′tə·mə·sē) *n.* *pl.* ·cies 1 Close or
confidential friendship. 2 An intimate act.
3 Illicit sexual connection: a euphemism.

in·ti·mate¹ (in′tə·mit) *adj.* 1 Closely connected
by friendship or association; personal; confidential. 2 Pertaining to the inmost being;
innermost. 3 Adhering closely; close. 4 Proceeding from within; internal. 5 Having illicit sexual relations (with): a euphemism.
—*n.* A close or confidential friend. [<L *in-
timus,* superl. of *intus* within] —in′ti·
mate·ly *adv.*

in·ti·mate² (in′tə·māt) *v.t.* ·mat·ed, ·mat·ing 1
To make known without direct statement;
hint; imply. 2 To make known formally; declare. [<L *intimare* announce] —in′ti·
ma′ter *n.*

in·ti·ma·tion (in′tə·mā′shən) *n.* 1 Information
communicated indirectly; a hint. 2 A declaration or notification.

in·to·na·tion (in′tō′nā′shən, in′tə-) *n.* 1 The
modulation of the voice in speaking. 2 The
act of intoning, as of the church service by
a priest. 3 *Music* Production of tones, as by
the voice, esp. in regard to precision of
pitch.

in·tone (in·tōn′) *v.* ·toned ·ton·ing *v.t.* 1 To
utter or recite in a musical monotone;
chant. 2 To give particular tones or intonation to. —*v.i.* 3 To utter a musical monotone; chant. [<L *in-* in + *tonus* tone] —in·ton′
er *n.*

in·tox·i·cate (in·tok′sə·kāt) *v.t.* ·cat·ed, ·cat·
ing 1 To make drunk; inebriate. 2 To elate
or excite to a degree of frenzy. 3 To poison,
as by toxins, drugs, etc. [<L *in-* in + *toxicum*
poison] —in·tox′i·cant *adj., n.* —in·tox′i·
ca′tion *n.* —in·tox′i·ca′tive *adj.*

in·tran·si·tive (in·tran′sə·tiv) *Gram. adj.* 1 Not
taking or requiring an object, as certain
verbs. 2 Of or pertaining to such verbs. —

*n.* An intransitive verb. —in·tran′si·tive·ly
*adv.*

in·tra·state (in′trə·stāt′) *adj.* Confined within
or pertaining to a single state, usu. of the
U.S.

in·trep·id (in·trep′id) *adj.* Unshaken in the
presence of danger; dauntless. [<L *in-* not +
*trepidus* agitated] —in·tre·pid·i·ty (in′trə·
pid′ə·tē) *n.* —in·trep′id·ly *adv.*

in·tri·ca·cy (in′tri·kə·sē) *n.* *pl.* ·cies 1 The
quality of being complicated or entangled.
2 A complication; complexity.

in·tri·cate (in′tri·kit) *adj.* 1 Exceedingly entangled, complicated, or involved. 2 Difficult to follow or understand. [<L *in-* in + *tricae* difficulties] —in′tri·cate·ly *adv.* —in′
tri·cate·ness *n.*

in·trigue (in·trēg′, in′trēg) *n.* 1 The working
for an end by secret or underhand means;
a plot or scheme. 2 An illicit love affair; liaison. —*v.* ·trigued, ·tri·guing *v.t.* 1 To
arouse and hold the interest or curiosity of;
beguile. 2 To plot for; bring on or get by secret or underhand means. —*v.i.* 3 To use
secret or underhand means; make plots. 4
To carry on a secret or illicit love affair. [<L
*in-* in + *tricae* difficulties] —in·tri′guer *n.*

in·trin·sic (in·trin′sik, -zik) *adj.* 1 Belonging
to the nature of a thing or person; inherent;
essential. 2 Contained or being within. [<L
*intrinsecus* internally] —in·trin′si·cal·ly
*adv.*

in·tro·duce (in′trə·dyōōs′) *v.t.* ·duced, ·duc·
ing 1 To bring (someone) to acquaintance
with another. 2 To present formally. 3 To
bring (someone) to acquaintance with or
knowledge of something: with *to.* 4 To bring
into notice, use, or practice. 5 To bring or
put into; insert. 6 To bring forward for consideration: to *introduce* a resolution. 7 To
begin; start: to *introduce* a new line of questioning. [<L *intro-* in + *ducere* to lead] —
in′tro·duc′er *n.* —in′tro·duc′i·ble *adj.*

in·tro·duc·tion (in′trə·duk′shən) *n.* 1 The act
of introducing. 2 The means of introducing
one person to another, as by letter, card,
etc. 3 A preface by an author or speaker in
explanation of the subject or design of his
writing or discourse. 4 An elementary treatise: an *introduction* to chemistry. 5 *Music*
A short opening passage or movement.

in·tro·duc·to·ry (in′trə·duk′tər·ē) *adj.* Serving as an introduction; preliminary. **Also**
in′tro·duc′tive. —in′tro·duc′to·ri·ly *adv.*

in·tro·vert (in′trə·vûrt) *n.* One whose attention and interest are primarily directed in-

wardly towards himself rather than towards other people or the external world. —*v.t.* To turn within; cause to take an inward direction. —*adj.* Characterized by or tending to introversion. [<L *intro-* within + *vertere* to turn]

**in·trude** (in-trōōd′) *v.* **·trud·ed, ·trud·ing** *v.t.* 1 To thrust or force in without leave or excuse. —*v.i.* 2 To come in without leave or invitation; thrust oneself in. 3 *Geol.* To enter by intrusion. [<L *in-* in + *trudere* to thrust] —**in·trud′er** *n.*

**in·tru·sion** (in-trōō′zhən) *n.* 1 The act of intruding; encroachment. 2 *Geol.* a The thrusting of molten rock into an earlier formation. b A rock thus formed within an earlier formation.

**in·tru·sive** (in-trōō′siv) *adj.* 1 Coming without warrant; intruding; obtrusive; prone to intrude. 2 *Geol.* Formed by intrusion, as certain igneous rocks. [See INTRUDE.] —**in·tru′sive·ly** *adv.* —**in·tru′sive·ness** *n.*

**in·tu·i·tion** (in′t′ōō-ish′ən) *n.* 1 Quick perception of truth or knowledge without conscious attention or reasoning. 2 That which is perceived or known intuitively. [<L *intueri* look upon] —**in′tu·i′tion·al** *adj.* —**in′tu·i′tion·al·ly** *adv.*

**in·tu·i·tive** (in-t′ōō′ə-tiv) *adj.* 1 Perceived by the mind without rigorous logic or analysis. 2 Discovering truth or reaching a just conclusion without resort to the powers of reason. —**in·tu′i·tive·ly** *adv.* —**in·tu′i·tive·ness** *n.*

**in·un·date** (in′ən-dāt) *v.t.* **·dat·ed, ·dat·ing** To cover or fill by overflowing. [<L *in-* in + *undare* overflow] —**in′un·da′tion, in′un·da′tor** *n.* —**Syn.** deluge, drown, flood, overwhelm.

**in·ure** (in-yŏŏr′) *v.* **·ured, ·ur·ing** *v.t.* 1 To harden or toughen; habituate. —*v.t.* 2 To have or take effect; be applied. [<OF *en-* (causative) + *euvre* work, use] —**in·ure′ment** *n.*

**in·vade** (in-vād′) *v.* **·vad·ed, ·vad·ing** *v.t.* 1 To enter with hostile intent, as for conquering. 2 To encroach upon; trespass on. 3 To spread over or penetrate injuriously: Disease *invaded* the lungs. —*v.i.* 4 To make an invasion. [<L *in-* in + *vadere* go] —**in·vad′er** *n.*

**in·va·lid¹** (in′və-lid) *n.* A sickly person, or one disabled, as by wounds, disease, etc. —*adj.* 1 Enfeebled by ill health. 2 Pertaining to or for the use of sick persons. —*v.t.* 1 To cause to become invalid; disable. 2 To release (a

soldier, sailor, etc.) from active service because of injury or illness. [< F < L *invalidus* not strong] —**in′va·lid·ism** *n.*

**in·val·id²** (in-val′id) *adj.* Without force, weight, or cogency; void. [< L *invalidus*] —**in·va·lid·i·ty** (in′və-lid′ə-tē) *n.* —**in·val′id·ly** *adv.*

**in·val·i·date** (in-val′ə-dāt) *v.t.* **·dat·ed, ·dat·ing** To weaken or destroy the force or validity of; annul. —**in·val′i·da′tion, in·val′i·da′tor** *n.*

**in·val·u·a·ble** (in-val′yōō-ə-bəl, -yōō-bəl) *adj.* Of a value beyond estimation; very precious. —**in·val′u·a·ble·ness** *n.* —**in·val′u·a·bly** *adv.*

**in·va·sion** (in-vā′zhən) *n.* 1 The act of invading; a military incursion for conquest, reconquest, or plunder. 2 Any attack with harmful intent or result. 3 Encroachment, as by an act of intrusion or trespass. —**in·va·sive** (in-vā′siv) *adj.*

**in·vec·tive** (in-vek′tiv) *n.* Violent, verbal denunciation or accusation; vituperation. —*adj.* Using or characterized by harsh words of abuse. [< L *invectus*, p.p. of *invehere*. See INVEIGH.] —**in·vec′tive·ly** *adv.* —**in·vec′tive·ness** *n.*

**in·veigh** (in-vā′) *v.i.* To utter vehement censure or invective: with *against.* [< L *in-* into + *vehere* carry] —**in·veigh′er** *n.*

**in·vei·gle** (in-vā′gəl, -vē′-) *v.t.* **·gled, ·gling** 1 To lead on, as by trickery or flattery; draw; entice. 2 To win over or seduce; captivate. [< OF *aveugle* blind] —**in·vei′gle·ment, in·vei′gler** *n.*

**in·vent** (in-vent′) *v.t.* 1 To create the idea, form, or existence of by original thought or effort; devise. 2 To make up, as something untrue or contrary to fact. [< L *invenire* come upon, discover] —**in·vent′i·ble** *adj.*

**in·ven·tion** (in-ven′shən) *n.* 1 The act or process of inventing (something new). 2 That which is invented. 3 Skill or ingenuity in contriving. 4 A fabrication; falsehood.

**in·ven·to·ry** (in′vən-tôr′ē, -tō′rē) *n. pl.* **·ries** 1 An itemized list of articles, with the number and value of each. 2 The items so listed or to be listed, as the stock of goods of a business. —*v.t.* **·ried, ·ry·ing** 1 To make an inventory of; to list in detail. 2 To list in an inventory. [<L *invenire* come upon, find out] —**in′ven·to′ri·al** (-tôr′ē-əl, -tō′rē-) *adj.* —**in′ven·to′ri·al·ly** *adv.*

**in·verse** (in-vûrs′, in′vûrs) *adj.* Opposite in order or effect; inverted. —*n.* That which is inverted. —*v.t.* **·versed, ·vers·ing** To invert. —**in·verse'ly** *adv.*

**in·ver·sion** (in-vûr'zhən, -shən) *n.* **1** The act of inverting. **2** The state of being inverted. **3 a** A change in the order of a set of things. **b** That which results from such a change. **4** In rhetoric or grammar, a reversal of the natural order of words in a phrase or sentence. **5** *Meteorol.* A condition in which atmospheric temperature increases with increasing altitude, often trapping pollutants near the ground. —**in·ver'sive** *adj.*

**in·vert** (in-vûrt') *v.t.* **1** To turn upside down or inside out. **2** To reverse the position, order, or sequence of. **3** To change to the opposite. **4** *Music* To interchange the tones or parts of. —*v.i.* **5** To undergo inversion. —*n.* (in'vûrt) **1** One who or that which is inverted. **2** HOMOSEXUAL. [< L *in-* in + *vertere* to turn] —**in·vert'i·ble** *adj.* —**in·ver'tor** *n.*

**in·ver·te·brate** (in-vûr'tə-brit, -brāt) *adj.* Lacking a backbone; not vertebrate. —*n.* Any animal having no backbone. —**in·ver'te·bra·cy** (-brə-sē), **in·ver'te·brate·ness** *n.*

**in·vest** (in-vest') *v.t.* **1** To use (money or capital) for the purchase of property, stocks, securities, etc., with the expectation of profit or income. **2** To spend (money, time, effort, etc.) in hopes of a return. **3** To place in office formally; install. **4** To give power, authority, or rank to. **5** To cover or surround as if with a garment: Mystery *invested* the whole affair. **6** To surround or hem in; lay siege to. —*v.i.* **7** To make an investment or investments. [< L *in-* on + *vestire* clothe] —**in·ves'tor** *n.*

**in·ves·ti·gate** (in-ves'tə-gāt) *v.* **·gat·ed, ·gat·ing** *v.t.* **1** To search or inquire into; examine in detail. —*v.i.* **2** To make an investigation. [< L *in-* in + *vestigare* to track, trace] —**in·ves'ti·ga·ble** (-tə-gə-bəl), **in·ves'ti·ga'tive** *adj.* —**in·ves'ti·ga'tor** *n.* —*Syn.* explore, inspect, review, scrutinize, study.

**in·ves·ti·ga·tion** (in-ves'tə-gā'shən) *n.* **1** The act of investigating; careful inquiry or research. **2** An inquiry by authority, as by a legislative committee, into certain facts. **3** A systematic examination of some scientific question.

**in·vet·er·ate** (in-vet'ər-it) *adj.* **1** Firmly established by long continuance; deep-rooted. **2** Confirmed in a particular character or habit. [< L *inveterare* make old] —**in·vet'er·a·cy** (*pl.* **·cies**), **in·vet'er·ate·ness** *n.* —**in·vet'er·ate·ly** *adv.*

**in·vid·i·ous** (in·vid'ē-əs) *adj.* **1** Expressing,

prompted by, or provoking envy or ill will. **2** Unjustly discriminating. [< L *invidia* envy] —**in·vid'i·ous·ly** *adv.* —**in·vid'i·ous·ness** *n.*

**in·vig·or·ate** (in·vig'ər·āt) *v.t.* **·at·ed, ·at·ing** To give energy to; animate. [< L *in-* in + *vigor* vigor + -ATE²] —**in·vig'or·at'ing·ly** *adv.* —**in·vig'or·a'tion** *n.*

**in·vi·o·la·ble** (in·vī'ə-ləbəl) *adj.* That must not or cannot be violated: an *inviolable* agreement. —**in·vi'o·la·bil'i·ty, in·vi'o·la·ble·ness** *n.* —**in·vi'o·la·bly** *adv.*

**in·vi·ta·tion** (in'və-tā'shən) *n.* **1** The act of inviting. **2** A means of inviting; a written *invitation.* **3** An act of alluring or encouraging; inducement: The unlocked door was an *invitation* to burglary.

**in·vite** (in·vīt') *v.* **·vit·ed, ·vit·ing** *v.t.* **1** To ask (someone) politely to be present in some place or to perform some action. **2** To make formal or polite request for: to *invite* suggestions. **3** To present inducement for: The situation *invites* criticism. **4** To tempt; entice. —*n.* (in'vīt) *Slang* An invitation. [< L *invitare* entertain] —**in·vit'er** *n.*

**in·vo·ca·tion** (in'və-kā'shən) *n.* **1** The act of invoking. **2** An opening prayer in a church service. **3** The act of conjuring an evil spirit. **4** The formula or incantation thus used. —**in·voc·a·to·ry** (in·vok'ə-tôr'ē, -tō'rē) *adj.*

**in·voice** (in'vois) *n.* A list of goods sent to a purchaser, etc., containing prices and charges for shipping. —*v.t.* **·voiced, ·voic·ing** To itemize; make an invoice of. [< F *envoyer* send]

**in·voke** (in·vōk') *v.t.* **·voked, ·vok·ing** **1** To call on for aid, protection, etc.; address, as in prayer. **2** To call for, as in supplication. **3** To summon or conjure by incantation, as evil spirits. [< L *in-* on + *vocare* to call] —**in·vok'er** *n.*

**in·vol·un·tar·y** (in·vol'ən·ter'ə) *adj.* **1** Contrary to one's will or wish. **2** Unintentional. **3** Independent of conscious control: *involuntary* muscles. —**in·vol'un·tar'i·ly** *adv.* —**in·vol'un·tar'i·ness** *n.*

**in·volve** (in·volv') *v.t.* **·volved, ·volv·ing** **1** To have as a necessary circumstance, condition, or outcome; entail: The study of medicine *involves* hard work. **2** To affect: The collision *involved* four cars. **3** To commit (oneself); engage, as in a productive effort: usu. in p.p.: to want to feel *involved.* **4** To draw into engangelment, trouble, etc.; implicate. **5** To make intricate or difficult; complicate. **6** To hold the attention of; engross. 7 To wrap up or conceal; envelop. 8 To wind in spirals or curves; coil. [< L *involvere* roll into or up] —**in·volve′ment** *n.*

**in·vul·ner·a·ble** (in·vul′nər·ə·bəl) *adj.* Not capable of being wounded; having no weak point. —**in·vul′ner·a·bil′i·ty, in·vul′ner·a·ble·ness** *n.* —**in·vul′ner·a·bly** *adv.* —**Syn.** indomitable, invincible, inviolable, unassailable.

**i·on** (i′ən, i′on) *n.* An atom or connected group of atoms that has an excess or deficiency of electrons and is, hence, electrically charged. [< Gk. *iōn,* p.p. of *ienai* go]

**i·on·o·sphere** (i·on′ə·sfir) *n.* A layer of the earth's atmosphere extending from about 30 miles to over 250 miles above the surface, consisting of partially ionized gases. [< ION + SPHERE]

**i·o·ta** (i·ō′tə) *n.* 1 The ninth letter and fourth vowel in the Greek alphabet (I,ι); corresponding to English I,i. 2 A small or insignificant mark or part. —**Syn.** 2 jot, particle, shred, speck, whit.

**I O U** 1 I owe you. 2 A paper having on it these letters followed by a named sum of indebtedness and the borrower's signature. Also **I.O.U.**

**i·ras·ci·ble** (i·ras′ə·bəl, i-) *adj.* 1 Easily angered; irritable. 2 Caused by anger. [< L *irasci* be angry.] —**i·ras′ci·bil′i·ty, i·ras′ci·ble·ness** *n.* —**i·ras′ci·bly** *adv.*

**IRBM** intermediate range ballistic missile.

**Ire.** Ireland.

**ir·i·des·cence** (ir′ə·des′əns) *n.* The rainbowlike appearance shown by various bodies, as oil films, mother-of-pearl, etc., when they reflect light. [< Gk. *iris, iridos* rainbow + -ESCENCE] —**ir′i·des′cent** *adj.* —**ir′i·des′cent·ly** *adv.*

**irk** (ûrk) *v.t.* To annoy or weary; irritate. [ME *irken*]

**i·ron** (i′ərn) *n.* 1 A tough, abundant, malleable, ductile, and strongly magnetic metallic element (symbol Fe) essential to animal and plant life, used in a wide range of alloys essential to industry. 2 A tool, weapon, utensil, etc., made of iron. 3 *pl.* Fetters, esp. for the feet. 4 A golf club having a metal head. • See GOLF. 5 A device with a smooth, flat surface that is heated and used to press wrinkles out of cloth. 6 A preparation of iron used as a medicine. —**in irons** Fettered or in chains. —*adj.* 1 Made of iron. 2 Resembling iron in hardness, firmness, etc.: an *iron* constitution. —*v.t.* 1 To smooth or press (cloth) with an iron. 2

To fetter. 3 To furnish or arm with iron. —*v.i.* 4 To smooth or press cloth, clothing, etc. with an iron. —**iron out** To eliminate, as difficulties. [< OE *īren*] —**i′ron·er** *n.*

**iron curtain** An impenetrable barrier of secrecy and censorship, originally used to describe the dividing line between w Europe and the Soviet Union's sphere of influence.

**i·ron·ic** (i·ron′ik) *adj.* 1 Conveying a meaning that contradicts the literal sense of the words used. 2 Being the reverse of what was expected. 3 Of the nature of or given to the use of irony. Also **i·ron′i·cal.** —**i·ron′i·cal·ly** *adv.* —**i·ron′i·cal·ness** *n.*

**iron lung** An apparatus used to maintain artificial respiration in a person enclosed in it from the neck down.

**i·ro·ny** (i′rə·nē) *n. pl.* **·nies** 1 The use of words to signify the opposite of what they usu. express, as: "When he lost his wallet, he said, 'This is my lucky day.' " 2 A condition of affairs or events exactly the reverse of what was expected or hoped for. [< Gk. *eirōneia* affected ignorance, pretense]

**ir·ra·tion·al** (i·rash′ən·əl) *adj.* 1 Not possessed of or not exercising reasoning powers. 2 *Math.* Not expressible as an integer or a quotient of integers, as √3. 3 Contrary to reason; absurd. —**ir·ra′tion·al′i·ty, ir·ra′tion·al·ness** *n.* —**ir·ra′tion·al·ly** *adv.*

**ir·rec·on·cil·a·ble** (i·rek′ən·si′lə·bəl, i·rek′ən·si′lə·bəl) *adj.* That cannot be reconciled. —*n.* One who will not agree or become reconciled. —**ir·rec′on·cil′a·bil′i·ty, ir·rec′on·cil′a·ble·ness** *n.* —**ir·rec′on·cil′a·bly** *adv.*

**ir·ref·u·ta·ble** (i·ref′yə·tə·bəl, ir′i·fyoo′tə·bəl) *adj.* Not refutable; that cannot be disproved. —**ir·ref′u·ta·bil′i·ty** *n.* —**ir·ref′u·ta·bly** *adv.*

**ir·reg·u·lar** (i·reg′yə·lər) *adj.* 1 Not regular; departing from the usual or accepted state of things: an *irregular* heartbeat. 2 Not symmetrical or even: *irregular* features. 3 Not conforming in action or character to rule, duty, discipline, etc.: *irregular* habits. 4 Not belonging to a regular military force. 5 *Gram.* Not inflected or conjugated according to the most prevalent pattern: *irregular* verbs. 6 Not according to rule; not complying with legal formalities. —*n.* An irregular person or thing. —**ir·reg′u·lar·ly** *adv.* —**Syn.** 1 abnormal, erratic. 2 asymmetrical, uneven. 3 lawless, uncontrolled.

**ir·reg·u·lar·i·ty** (i·reg′yə·lar′ə·tē) *n. pl.* **·ties** 1 The condition of being irregular; an aberration, inconsistency, etc. 2 Something in an irregular state or condition.

**ir·rel·e·vant** (i·rel'ə·vənt) *adj.* Not relevant or pertinent. —**ir·rel'e·vance, ir·rel'e·van·cy** ( *pl.* ·cies) *n.* —**ir·rel'e·vant·ly** *adv.*

**ir·re·proach·a·ble** (ir'i·prō'chə·bəl) *adj.* Not reproachable; blameless. [< F *irréprochable*] —**ir're·proach'a·bil'i·ty, ir're·proach'a·ble·ness** *n.* —**ir're·proach'a·bly** *adv.*

**ir·re·spec·tive** (ir'i·spek'tiv) *adj.* Regardless: with *of.* —**ir're·spec'tive·ly** *adv.*

**ir·rev·o·ca·ble** (i·rev'ə·kə·bəl) *adj.* Incapable of being revoked; unalterable. —**ir·rev'o·ca·bil'i·ty, ir·rev'o·ca·ble·ness** *n.* —**ir·rev'o·ca·bly** *adv.*

**ir·ri·gate** (ir'ə·gāt) *v.t.* ·gat·ed, ·gat·ing 1 To supply (land) with water by means of ditches or other artificial channels. 2 *Med.* To wash out (a wound, body cavity, etc.) with water or other fluid. [< L *irrigare* bring water to] —**ir'ri·ga·ble** (ir'ə·gə·bəl) *adj.* —**ir'ri·ga'tion, ir'ri·ga'tor** *n.*

**ir·ri·ta·ble** (ir'ə·tə·bəl) *adj.* 1 Showing impatience or ill temper on little provocation; irascible. 2 Responsive to stimuli. 3 *Pathol.* Abnormally sensitive. [< L *irritare* irritate] —**ir'ri·ta·bil'i·ty, ir'ri·ta·ble·ness** *n.* —**ir'ri·ta·bly** *adv.*

**Is·lam** (is'ləm, iz'-, is·läm') *n.* 1 The religion of the Muslims, which maintains that there is but one God, Allah, and that Mohammed is his prophet. 2 The body of Muslim believers, their culture, and the countries they inhabit. —**Is·lam'ic** *adj.* —**Is'lam·ism, Is'lam·ite** *n.*

**is·land** (ī'lənd) *n.* 1 A land mass, usu. of moderate size, surrounded by water. 2 Anything isolated or like an island. 3 A raised safety area in the middle of a wide street or at a crossing. 4 *Anat.* A group of cells differing from the surrounding tissue. —*v.t.* To make into an island or islands; insulate. [< OE *igland,* lit., island land]

**isle** (īl) *n.* A small island. —*v.* isled, isl·ing *v.t.* To make into an isle. [< L *insula* island]

**i·so·late** (ī'sə·lāt, is'ə-) *v.t.* ·lat·ed, ·lat·ing 1 To place in a detached or separate situation; set apart. 2 *Electr.* To insulate. 3 *Chem.* To obtain in a pure form, as an element or compound. 4 *Med.* To set apart from others, as a person with a communicable disease. 5 *Bacteriol.* To obtain a pure culture of (a specified virus or bacterium). —*n.* A unit or group that is set apart. [< Ital. *isolare* isolate < *isola* island < L *insula* island] —**i'so·la'tion, i'so·la'tor** *n.* —**Syn.** *v.* 1 banish, seclude, segregate. 4 quarantine.

**i·so·met·ric** (ī'sō·met'rik) *adj.* 1 Having equal measures. 2 Having a constant measure. Also **i'so·met'ri·cal.** [< ISO- + Gk. *metron* measure] —**i'so·met'ri·cal·ly** *adv.*

**i·sos·ce·les** (ī·sos'ə·lēz) *adj. Geom.* Having two sides of equal length, as a triangle. [< Gk. *isoskelēs* equal-legged]

**i·so·tope** (ī'sə·tōp) *n.* Any of two or more forms of an element having the same atomic number and similar chemical properties but differing in atomic weight. [< ISO- + Gk. *topos* place] —**i·so·top·ic** (ī'sə·top'ik, -tō'pik) *adj.* —**i·sot·o·py** (ī·sot'ə·pē) *n.*

**is·sue** (ish'ŌŌ) *v.* ·sued, ·su·ing *v.t.* 1 To give out or deliver in a public or official manner: to *issue* a magazine. 2 To deal out or distribute: to *issue* ammunition. 3 To send forth; let out. —*v.i.* 4 To come forth or flow out; emerge. 5 To come as a result or consequence; proceed. 6 To be given out or published; appear. 7 To come as profit or revenue; accrue: with *out of.* —*n.* A subject of discussion or interest; the matter at hand. 2 Result; outcome; upshot. 3 The action of giving out or supplying officially or publicly. 4 An item or amount which is issued. 5 Offspring; progeny. 6 Profits; proceeds. 7 The act of going out; outflow. 8 A place or way of egress. 9 *Law* The point in question between parties to an action. [< L *ex-* out of + *ire* go] —**at issue** Under dispute; in question. —**take issue** To disagree. —**is'su·er** *n.* —**Syn.** *v.* 1 print, publish. 2 allot, dispense. 3 discharge, emit.

**isth·mus** (is'məs) *n. pl.* ·mus·es or ·mi (-mī) A narrow body of land connecting two larger bodies. —**the Isthmus** The Isthmus of Panama. [< Gk. *isthmos* narrow passage]

**i·tal·ic** (i·tal'ik) *Printing n.* A style of type in which the letters slope, as *these:* also **i·tal'ics.** —*adj.* Designating, or printed in, italic.

**i·tal·i·cize** (i·tal'ə·sīz) *v.t. & v.i.* ·cized, ·ciz·ing 1 To print in italics. 2 To underscore (written words or phrases) with a single line to indicate italics. *Brit. sp.* ·cise.

**it·er·ate** (it'ə·rāt) *v.t.* ·at·ed, ·at·ing To utter or do again. [< L *iterum* again] —**it'er·a·ble** (it'ər·ə·bəl) *adj.* —**it'er·ance, it'er·a'tion** *n.*

**i·tin·er·ant** (ī·tin'ər·ənt, i·tin'-) *adj.* Going from place to place. —*n.* One who travels from place to place. [< L *iter, itineris* journey] —**i·tin'er·ant·ly** *adv.* —**Syn.** *adj.* nomadic, peripatetic, wandering, wayfaring.

**i·tin·er·ar·y** (ī·tin'ə·rer'ē, i·tin'-) *n. pl.* ·ar·ies 1 A detailed account or diary of a journey. 2 A plan of a proposed tour. 3 A route pursued in traveling. 4 A guidebook. —*adj.* 1 Pertaining to or done on a journey. 2 ITIN-ERANT. [< L *iter, itineris* journey, route]

**i·vo·ry** (ī′vər·ē) *n. pl.* **·ries** 1 The hard, creamy-white dentine that forms the tusks of the elephant, walrus, etc. 2 Any ivorylike substance. 3 *pl.* Things made of or similar to ivory; esp. in slang use, the teeth, dice, keys of a piano, etc. 4 The color of ivory. —*adj.* Made of or resembling ivory. [< L *ebur* ivory]

# J

**jack** (jak) *n.* 1 *Mech.* **a** One of various machines or devices used to replace a human worker: often used in combination: *bootjack*. **b** Any of various devices using the principle of a lever, screw, etc., placed under or against a load and used to lift or move it. 2 A man or ♂boy. 3 A manual laborer: often used in combination: *lumberjack*. 4 *Often cap.* A sailor. 5 A male donkey; jackass. 6 JACK RABBIT. 7 Any of various birds, as a jackdaw. 8 *Electr.* A socket equipped with a spring clip for holding a plug to make a connection. 9 A playing card with a young man's picture on it; knave. 10 One of the small, pronged metal pieces used in the game of jacks; a jackstone. 11 A ship's flag showing its nationality; union jack. 12 *Slang* Money. —*v.t.* 1 To raise or lift with or as with a jack. 2 *Informal* To advance, as a price or charge: often with *up*. [< *Jack,* a personal name]

**jack·ass** (jak′as′) *n.* 1 The male ass. 2 A stupid person; fool.

**jack·et** (jak′it) *n.* 1 A short coat, usu. not extending below the hips. 2 A close-fitting outer covering, as the paper cover for a bound book, a paper or cardboard cover for a phonograph record, the skin of a potato, the casing of a bullet, an open envelope or folder for filing letters, documents, etc. —*v.t.* To cover with or put into a jacket. [< OF *jaque* a coat] —**jack′et·ed** *adj.*

**jade** (jād) *n.* 1 A tough, hard, silicate mineral, usu. green or white, used for making jewelry. 2 The color of green jade. [< Sp. *(piedra de) ijada* (stone for) colic]

**jag·uar** (jag′wär, jag′yōō·är) *n.* A large, tawny, spotted cat of tropical America. [< Tupian *jaguara*]

**ja·lop·y** (jə·lop′ē) *n. pl.* **·lop·ies** *Informal* A decrepit automobile. [?]

**Jam.** Jamaica.

**Ja·mai·ca** (jə·mā′kə) *n.* An independent member of the Commonwealth of Nations, located on an island in the Caribbean, 4,411 sq. mi., cap. Kingston. —**Ja·mai′can** *adj., n.* • See map at CUBA.

**jamb** (jam) *n.* A side post or side of a doorway, window, etc. [< OF *jambe* leg, support]

**jam·bo·ree** (jam′bə·rē′) *n.* 1 *Informal* A boisterous frolic or spree. 2 A large, esp. international, assembly of Boy Scouts. [?]

**jam session** An informal gathering of jazz musicians performing improvisations.

**jan·i·tor** (jan′i·tər) *n.* One who has the care of a building, offices, etc. [< L *janua* door]

**jar·gon** (jär′gən) *n.* 1 Unintelligible speech; gibberish. 2 Any language thought to be meaningless or excessively confused. 3 The technical or specialized language of a particular profession, group, etc. 4 A mixture of two or more dissimilar languages; pidgin. —*v.i.* To talk in jargon; gabble. [< OF]

**jaun·dice** (jôn′dis, jän′-) *n.* 1 Abnormal yellowness of the skin, eyeballs, etc., due to bile pigments in the blood. 2 A hostile or resentful state of mind, as that caused by prejudice, envy, etc. —*v.t.* **·diced, ·dic·ing** 1 To affect with jaundice. 2 To affect with prejudice, envy, etc. [< L *galbinus* yellowish]

**jaunt** (jônt, jänt) *n.* A short journey; pleasure trip; excursion. —*v.i.* To make such a trip. [?]

**jazz** (jaz) *n.* 1 A kind of music achieving its effects by syncopated rhythms, dissonances, solo and ensemble improvisation, and, in the newer styles, by sophisticated harmonic patterns. 2 Popular dance music. 3 *Slang* Nonsense; claptrap. —*adj.* Of or pertaining to jazz. —*v.t.* 1 To play or arrange (music) as jazz. —*v.i.* 2 To dance to or play jazz. —**jazz up** *Slang* To make exciting or more exciting. [?]

**jeal·ous** (jel′əs) *adj.* 1 Suspicious and resentful of a rival or of rivalry in general. 2 Hostile or envious over the advantages, good fortune, etc., of others. 3 Earnestly vigilant in guarding or keeping something: *jealous* of our freedoms. 4 Resulting from or showing such feelings: a *jealous* rage. [< Gk. *zēlos* zeal] —**jeal′ous·ly** *adv.* —**jeal′ous·ness** *n.*

**jean** (jēn) *n.* 1 A sturdy, twilled cotton cloth, used esp. in work clothes or for casual wear. 2 *pl.* Trousers made of this fabric. 3 *pl. Informal* Trousers. [< ME *Jene, Gene* Genoa, where it was made]

**jeep** (jēp) *n.* A small, sturdy motor vehicle with four-wheel drive and a load capacity of one quarter of a ton. [Alter. of *G.P.*, for General Purpose (Vehicle), its military designation)]

**jeer** (jir) *v.i.* 1 To speak or shout in a derisive, mocking manner; scoff. —*v.t.* 2 To treat with derision or mockery; scoff at. —*n.* A derisive or taunting sound or word. [?] —**jeer′er** *n.* —**jeer′ing·ly** *adv.*

**jel·ly** (jel′ē) *n. pl.* **·lies** 1 A semisolid gelatinous food product, as fruit juice boiled with sugar or meat juice boiled down. 2 Any substance having the consistency of jelly. —*v.t. & v.i.* **·lied, ·ly·ing** To bring or turn to jelly. [< L *gelare* freeze]

**jeop·ard·ize** (jep′ər·dīz) *v.t.* **·ized, ·iz·ing** To put in jeopardy; expose to loss or injury; imperil. Also **jeop′ard.**

**jeop·ard·y** (jep′ər·dē) *n. pl.* **·ard·ies** 1 Exposure to death, loss, or injury; danger; peril. 2 The peril in which a defendant is put when placed on trial for a crime. [< OF *jeu parti* even chance]

**jerk** (jûrk) *v.t.* 1 To give a sharp, sudden pull or twist to. 2 To throw or move with a sharp, suddenly arrested motion. 3 To utter in broken or abrupt manner. —*v.i.* 4 To give a jerk or jerks. 5 To move with sharp, sudden motions; twitch. —*n.* 1 A short, sharp pull, twitch, or fling. 2 An involuntary muscular spasm. 3 *Slang* A stupid or unsophisticated person. [?] —**jerk′i·ly** *adv.* — **jerk′i·ness** *n.* —**jerk′y** *adj.* (**·i·er, ·i·est**)

**jet¹** (jet) *n.* 1 A rich black variety of hard coal, used, when highly polished, for beads, etc. 2 A deep, glossy black. —*adj.* Made of or resembling jet. [< Gk. *gagatēs*]

**jet²** (jet) *n.* 1 A flow or gush, as of gas or liquid, coming from a narrow orifice. 2 A spout or nozzle. 3 JET AIRPLANE. 4 JET ENGINE. —*v.t. & v.i.* **jet·ted, jet·ting** 1 To spurt forth or emit in a stream; spout. 2 To travel or send by jet airplane. [< F *jeter* to throw]

**jet airplane** A jet-propelled airplane. Also **jet aircraft.**

**jet propulsion** 1 Propulsion by means of a jet of gas or other fluid. 2 *Aeron.* Aircraft propulsion by means of jet engines. —**jet′-pro·pul′sion** *adj.*

**jet stream** 1 The exhaust gas or fluid expelled from a jet engine, rocket motor, etc. 2 *Meteorol.* A high-velocity, usu. westerly wind circulating near the base of the stratosphere.

**jew·el** (jōō′əl) *n.* 1 A precious stone; gem. 2 A pin, ring, etc., usu. made of precious metals set with gems, etc. 3 Any person or thing of rare excellence. 4 A bit of precious stone,

crystal, or glass used as a bearing in a watch. —*v.t.* **·eled** or **·elled, ·el·ling** or **·el·ling** To adorn with or as with jewels. [< L *jocus* a game, joke]

**jilt** (jilt) *v.t.* To cast off (a previously favored lover or sweetheart). —*n.* One who capriciously discards a lover. [?] —**jilt′er** *n.*

**jin·gle** (jing′gəl) *v.* **·gled, ·gling** *v.i.* 1 To make light, ringing sounds, as keys striking together. 2 To sound rhythmically or pleasingly on the ear. —*v.t.* 3 To cause to jingle. —*n.* 1 A tinkling or clinking sound. 2 A light, rhythmical verse; also, a short song using such verse: She is a composer of TV *jingles.* [Imit.] —**jin′gly** *adj.*

**jinx** (jingks) *n.* A person or thing supposed to bring bad luck; a hoodoo. —*v.t.* To bring bad luck to. [< Gk. *iynx* the wryneck (a bird used in witchcraft)]

**jock·ey** (jok′ē) *n. pl.* **·eys** One employed to ride horses in races. —*v.* **·eyed, ·ey·ing** *v.i.* 1 To maneuver for an advantage. 2 To be tricky; cheat. 3 To ride as a jockey. —*v.t.* 4 To maneuver or guide by skillful handling or control. 5 To trick; cheat. 6 To ride (a horse) in a race. [Dim. of *Jock*, a nickname for *John*]

**jog** (jog) *v.* **jogged, jog·ging** *v.t.* 1 To push or touch with a slight jar; shake. 2 To nudge. 3 To stimulate (one's memory). —*v.i.* 4 To move with a slow, steady pace. 5 To proceed slowly or monotonously: with *on* or *along.* —*n.* 1 A slight push or nudge. 2 A slow steady motion or pace. [?] —**jog′ger** *n.*

**joint** (joint) *n.* 1 The place, point, or line where two or more things are joined together. 2 The manner in which two things are joined together: a tight *joint.* 3 One of the components of an articulated whole. 4 *Anat.* A place of union of two bones; an articulation. 5 One of the large pieces into which a carcass is divided by a butcher. 6 *Slang* A marihuana cigarette. 7 *Slang* A somewhat disreputable bar, nightclub, etc. 8 *Slang* Any place of dwelling or gathering. —**out of joint** 1 Not fitted at the joint; dislocated. 2 Disordered; disorganized. —*adj.* 1 Produced by combined action. 2 Shared by two or more. 3 Participated in or used by two or more. —*v.t.* 1 To fasten by means of a joint or joints. 2 To form or shape into a joint or joints, as a board. 3 To separate into joints, as meat. [< L *junctus* joined]

**joist** (joist) *n.* A horizontal timber supporting a floor or ceiling. —*v.t.* To furnish with joists. [< L *jacere* to lie down]

**joke** (jōk) *n.* 1 Something said or done to cause

amusement, esp. a brief, comic story. **2** A person or thing that causes laughter, ridicule, etc. **3** Something said or done in fun or to tease. —*v.* **joked, jok·ing** *v.t.* **1** To tease; kid. —*v.i.* **2** To make jokes; jest. [< L *jocus*] —**jok′ing·ly** *adv.* —**Syn.** *n.* **1** jest, witticism, gag, crack, wisecrack, quip.

**jolt** (jōlt) *v.t.* **1** To strike or shake about, as with a blow. **2** To surprise or stun. —*v.i.* **3** To move with jolts or bumps, as over a rough road. —*n.* **1** A sudden bump or jerk. **2** A surprise or shock. [?] —**jolt′er** *n.* — **jolt′y** *adj.*

**jon·quil** (jon′kwil, jong′-) *n.* A species of narcissus having short-crowned yellow or white flowers. [< L *juncus* a rush]

**jos·tle** (jos′əl) *v.t. & v.i.* **·tled, ·tling** To push or crowd; elbow; hustle; bump. —*n.* A collision, bumping against, or slight shaking. [Freq. of JOUST] —**jos′tler** *n.*

**jot** (jot) *v.t.* **jot·ted, jot·ting** To make a hasty note of: usu. with *down.* —*n.* The least bit; an iota. [< IOTA]

**jour·nal** (jûr′nəl) *n.* **1** A record of daily occurrences, as a diary. **2** A record of the proceedings of a legislature, club, etc. **3** A daily newspaper. **4** Any periodical or magazine. **5** *Naut.* A logbook. **6** In bookkeeping: **a** DAY-BOOK. **b** In double entry, a book in which transactions of the day are entered in systematic form in order to facilitate later posting in the ledger. **7** *Mech.* The part of a shaft or axle which is held by a bearing. [< L *diurnus* daily]

**jour·nal·ist** (jûr′nəl·ist) *n.* One whose occupation is journalism. —**jour′nal·is′tic** *adj.* —**jour′nal·is′ti·cal·ly** *adv.*

**jour·ney** (jûr′nē) *n.* **1** Travel from one place to another; a trip. **2** Something that suggests such travel: one's *journey* through life. — *v.i.* To travel; go on a journey. [< OF *journee* a day's travel] —**jour′ney·er** *n.* —**Syn.** *n.* **1** excursion, tour, voyage, cruise, expedition.

**jo·vi·al** (jō′vē·əl) *adj.* Possessing or expressive of good-natured mirth or gaiety; jolly. [< LL *Jovialis* (born under the influence of Jupiter] —**jo·vi·al·i·ty** (jō′vē·al′ə·tē) *n.* — **jo′vi·al·ly** *adv.*

**jowl** (joul, jōl) *n.* The cheek or jaw. [< OE *ceafl*] —**jowled** *adj.*

**ju·bi·lant** (jōō′bə·lənt) *adj.* Filled with or showing great joy or triumph. [< L *jubilare* exult] —**ju′bi·lance** *n.* —**ju′bi·lant·ly** *adv.* —**Syn.** overjoyed, rapturous, elated, exultant, triumphant.

**ju·bi·lee** (jōō′bə·lē′, jōō′bə·lē′) *n.* **1** A special anniversary of an event, as the 50th; also, the celebration of this. **2** Any time or season of rejoicing; a commemoration or festivity. [LL < Heb. *yōbēl* ram's horn, trumpet]

**judge** (juj) *n.* **1** An official, elected or appointed, invested with authority to administer legal justice. **2** In contests, controversies, etc., one who selects the winner, evaluates the merits of contestants, etc. **3** One qualified to have opinions on the worth or value of something: a good *judge* of wines. **4** In Jewish history, one of the rulers of the Israelites from the death of Joshua to the anointing of Saul. —*v.* **judged, judg·ing** *v.t.* **1** To hear and decide in an official capacity the merits of (a case) or the guilt of (a person); try. **2** To select the winner of (a contest). **3** To settle (a controversy). **4** To appraise or evaluate: to *judge* a painting. **5** To estimate: to *judge* a distance. **6** To consider; think: We *judged* it improper. **7** To censure; criticize: *Judge* her not. —*v.i.* **8** To act as a judge; sit in judgment. **9** To form a judgment or estimate. **10** To make a decision. [< L *judex*] —**judg′er** *n.*

**judg·ment** (juj′mənt) *n.* **1** The act of judging. **2** The result or outcome of judging; as: **a** A legal decision, order, or sentence. **b** An obligation or debt resulting from a court decision. **c** A record of such a decision. **d** Any decision or opinion. **e** An evaluation or estimation. **f** Censure; criticism. **3** An ability to make decisions or evaluations that are wise, reasonable, and valid. **4** A disaster or affliction regarded as inflicted by God. Also **judge′ment.** —**judg·men′tal** *adj.*

**ju·di·cial** (jōō·dish′əl) *adj.* **1** Of, pertaining to, or resulting from the administration of justice. **2** Of, pertaining to, or connected with a court or judge. **3** Discriminating; unbiased; impartial. [< L *judex* a judge] —**ju·di·cial·ly** *adv.*

**ju·di·cious** (jōō·dish′əs) *adj.* Having, acting on, or resulting from sound judgment; wise; prudent. [< L *judicium* a judgment] —**ju·di′cious·ly** *adv.* —**ju·di′cious·ness** *n.*

**jug·gle** (jug′əl) *v.* **·gled, ·gling** *v.t.* **1** To toss (balls, plates, etc.) into the air, keeping them in continuous motion by successively catching and tossing them up again. **2** To hold or catch (a ball, etc.) awkwardly or precariously. **3** To manipulate in order to deceive. —*v.i.* **4** To perform as a juggler. **5** To practice deception or trickery. —*n.* **1** A feat of juggling. **2** A trick or deception. [< L *joculari* to jest] —**jug′gler** *n.*

**juice** (jōōs) *n.* 1 The watery matter in fruits, plants, and vegetables. 2 *Usu. pl.* The fluids of the body. 3 The essence of anything. 4 *Slang* a Electric current. b Any liquid fuel. 5 *Informal* Vital energy. [< L *jus*]

**ju·jit·su** (jōō·jit′sōō) *n.* A Japanese system of unarmed self-defense in which the strength and weight of one's opponent are used to one's own advantage. **Also ju·jut·su** (jōō·jit′sōō, -jōōt′-). [< Jap. *ju* soft + *jitsu* art]

**juke·box** (jōōk′boks′) *n.* A large automatic phonograph, usu. coin-operated and permitting selection of the records to be played. **Also juke box.** [< Gullah *juke*, orig. a brothel (of west African origin) + BOX¹]

**jump·er** (jum′pər) *n.* 1 One who or that which jumps. 2 *Electr.* A short length of connecting wire, esp. one used temporarily.

**junc·tion** (jungk′shən) *n.* 1 The act of joining, or condition of being joined. 2 A place of union or meeting, as of railroads. [< L *jungere* join] —**junc′tion·al** *adj.*

**junc·ture** (jungk′chər) *n.* 1 An act of joining; junction. 2 A point or line of joining. 3 A point in time. 4 A crisis; exigency. 5 *Ling.* A significant manner of transition between consecutive speech sounds.

**jun·gle** (jung′gəl) *n.* 1 Land, usu. in tropical regions, covered with trees and a dense thicket of high grass, vines, brush, etc. 2 Any similar tangled mass. 3 *Slang* A camp for hoboes. 4 *Slang* A place or circumstance of fierce competition for survival, success, etc. [< Skt. *jangala* dry, desert]

**jun·ior** (jōōn′yər) *adj.* 1 Younger in years or lower in rank. 2 Denoting the younger of two, and distinguishing a father from a son, usu. abbreviated *Jr.* 3 Belonging to youth or earlier life. 4 Later in date. 5 Pertaining to a junior or juniors in a high school or college. —*n.* 1 The younger of two. 2 One later or lower in service or rank. 3 A third-year student in a high school or college. [< L comp. of *juvenis* young]

**junk** (jungk) *n.* 1 Castoff materials, as metal, glass, paper etc. 2 Anything of little value or importance. 3 *Slang* A narcotic, esp. heroin. —*v.t.* To scrap, demolish, or cast aside. [< L *juncus* rush] —**junk′y** *adj.* (·i·er, ·i·est)

**jun·ket** (jung′kit) *n.* 1 A feast or picnic. 2 A pleasure trip. 3 A trip taken with all expenses paid by a government, company, etc. 4 A dessert made of milk and rennet. —*v.i.* To go on a junket. [< AF *jonquette* rush basket]

**ju·ris·dic·tion** (jŏŏr′is·dik′shən) *n.* 1 Lawful right to exercise official authority. 2 The range or scope of such authority. 3 A court, or series of courts, of justice. 4 Power, authority, or control. [< L *jus, juris* law + *dicere* declare] —**ju′ris·dic′tion·al** *adj.* —**ju′ris·dic′tion·al·ly** *adv.*

**ju·ror** (jŏŏr′ər, -ôr) *n.* One who serves on a jury or is sworn in for jury duty.

**ju·ry** (jŏŏr′ē) *n. pl.* **·ries** 1 A body of persons (usu. twelve) sworn to hear evidence in a legal proceeding and to arrive at an unprejudiced verdict on the basis of the facts as presented. 2 A committee to decide the winner or winners in a competition. [< L *jurare* swear < *jus, juris* law]

**jus·ti·fi·a·ble** (jus′tə·fī′ə·bəl, jus′tə·fī′-) *adj.* Capable of being justified. —**jus′ti·fi′a·bil′i·ty** *n.* —**jus′ti·fi′a·bly** *adv.*

**jus·ti·fi·ca·tion** (jus′tə·fə·kā′shən) *n.* 1 The act of justifying or the state of being justified. 2 The grounds of justifying; that which justifies. —**jus′ti·fi·ca′tive** *adj.*

**jus·ti·fy** (jus′tə·fī) *v.* **·fied, ·fy·ing** *v.t.* 1 To show to be just, right, or proper. 2 To declare or prove guiltless or blameless. 3 To show sufficient reason for (something done). 4 *Printing* To adjust (lines) to the proper length by spacing. —*v.i.* 5 *Law* a To show sufficient reason for something done. b To qualify as a bondsman. 6 *Printing* To be properly spaced. [< L *justus* just + *facere* make] —**jus′ti·fi′er** *n.*

**ju·ve·nile** (jōō′və·nil, -nəl) *adj.* 1 Characteristic of youth; young. 2 Adapted to or suitable for youth. —*n.* 1 A young person; child. 2 An actor who interprets youthful roles. 3 A book for children. [< L *juvenis* young]

# K

**kan·ga·roo** (kang′gə·rōō′) *n. pl.* **·roos** Any of a large family of leaping herbivorous marsupials of the Australian region, having short forelimbs, strong hind limbs, and a long, tapering tail. [native Australian name]

**kangaroo court** An unofficial court in which the law is disregarded or willfully misinterpreted or misapplied.

**ka·ra·te** (kə·rä′tē) *n.* An Oriental style of self-defense using sudden forceful blows with the side of the hand. [Jap., lit., empty-handed]

**keel** (kēl) *n.* 1 *Naut.* The lowest lengthwise member of the framework of a vessel, serving to give it stability. 2 Figuratively, a ship.

3 Anything suggesting a keel in shape or function. —on an even keel 1 In a level position. 2 Steady. —v.t. 1 To provide with a keel. 2 To upset (a vessel). —v.i. 3 To roll over. —keel over 1 To turn bottom up; capsize. 2 To fall over or be felled unexpectedly. 3 *Informal* To faint. [< ON *kjölr*]

**keen** (kēn) *adj.* 1 Very sharp, as a knife. 2 Cutting; piercing, as wit. 3 Vivid; pungent. 4 Having or exhibiting sharpness or penetration. 5 Acute: *keen* sight. 6 Exceptionally intelligent. 7 Characterized by intensity: a *keen* appetite. 8 *Informal* Impatient; eager: *keen* to be off. [< OE *cēne*] —**keen′ly** *adv.* —**keen′ness** *n.* —**Syn.** 2 acute, sharp. 6 brilliant, penetrating.

**ken·nel** (kən′əl) *n.* 1 A house for a dog or for a pack of hounds. 2 A pack of hounds. 3 *pl.* A professional establishment where dogs are bred, raised, boarded, trained, etc. —*v.* ·**neled** or ·**nelled**, ·**nel·ing** or ·**nel·ling** *v.t.* 1 To keep or confine in a kennel. —*v.i.* 2 To take shelter in a kennel. [< L *canis* a dog]

**ker·o·sene** (ker′ə·sēn, kar′-, ker·ə·sēn′, kar-) *n.* A liquid mixture of hydrocarbons, derived from petroleum and used as fuel. [< Gk. *kēros* wax + -ENE]

**ket·tle** (ket′l) *n.* 1 A metallic vessel for stewing or boiling. 2 TEAKETTLE. [< ON *ketill*] —**kettle of fish** A troublesome situation.

**ket·tle·drum** (ket′l·drum′) *n.* A drum having a brass shell and tunable parchment head.

**khak·i** (kak′ē, kä′kē) *adj.* Having a tannish brown or olive-drab color. —*n. pl.* **khak·is** 1 A tannish brown or olive-drab color. 2 A cloth of this color, used esp. for military uniforms. 3 *Usu. pl.* Trousers or a uniform of this cloth. [<Hind. *khākī* dusty]

**kib·butz** (ki·bŏŏts′) *n. pl.* **kib·butz·im** (-bŏŏt·sēm′) A collective farming settlement in Israel. [<Heb. *qibbūs*]

**kid** (kid) *n.* 1 A young goat. 2 Leather made from the skin of young goats, esp. as used in gloves, shoes, etc. 3 The meat of a young goat. 4 *Informal* A child or infant. —*adj.* 1 Made of kidskin. 2 *Informal* Younger: my *kid* brother. —*v.t. & v.i.* **kid·ded**, **kid·ding** 1 To give birth to (young): said of goats. 2 *Slang* To tease jokingly. 3 *Slang* To deceive or try to deceive (someone). [< ON *kidh*] —**kid′der** *n.*

**kid·nap** (kid′nap) *v.t.* ·**naped** or ·**napped**, ·**nap·ing** or ·**nap·ping** 1 To seize and carry off (someone) by force or fraud, usu. followed by a demand for ransom. 2 To steal (a child). [< KID + *nap*, dial. var. of NAB] —**kid′nap′er, kid′nap·per** *n.*

**kid·ney** (kid′nē) *n. pl.* ·**neys** 1 One of a pair of organs at the back of the abdominal cavity in vertebrates. They regulate the volume, acidity, and composition of body fluids by filtering the blood and excreting waste products as urine. 2 This organ of a slaughtered animal, used as food. 3 Temperament; disposition. 4 Type or kind. [?]

**kiln** (kil, kiln) *n.* An oven or furnace for baking, burning, or drying various products, as bricks, lime, enamel, pottery, etc. [< L *culina* kitchen]

**kil·o·cy·cle** (kil′ə·sī′kəl) *n.* 1 One thousand cycles. 2 KILOHERTZ.

**kil·o·gram** (kil′ə·gram) *n.* 1 The basic metric unit of mass and weight, equal to the mass of a prototype kept in Sèvres, France, and equal to approximately 2.2 pounds. 2 The weight of a one-kilogram mass at the surface of the earth. Also **kil′o·gramme.**

**kil·o·me·ter** (ki·lom′ə·tər, kil′ə·mē′tər) *n.* A metric unit of length equal to 1,000 meters or about 5/8 mile. Also **kil′o·me·tre.**

**ki·mo·no** (kə·mō′nə, ki·mō′nō) *n. pl.* ·**nos** 1 A Japanese loose robe fastened with a sash. 2 A woman's dressing gown.

**kin·der·gar·ten** (kin′dər·gär′tən) *n.* A school for children, usu. five or six years of age, to encourage socialization by group play and readiness for first-grade skills. [< G < *Kinder* children + *Garten* garden]

**kin·dle** (kin′dəl) *v.* ·**dled**, ·**dling** *v.t.* 1 To cause (a flame, fire, etc.) to burn; light. 2 To set fire to; ignite. 3 To excite or inflame, as the feelings. 4 To make bright or glowing. —*v.i.* 5 To start burning. 6 To become excited. 7 To become bright or glowing. [< ON *kynda*] —**kin′dler** *n.*

**kin·dling** (kind′ling) *n.* Small sticks of wood and other inflammable material with which a fire is kindled.

**kin·e·scope** (kin′ə·skōp) *n.* 1 A cathode-ray tube on which a television picture is displayed. 2 A film record of a television program. [KINE(TIC) + -SCOPE]

**ki·net·ic** (ki·net′ik) *adj.* 1 Producing motion; motor. 2 Consisting in or depending upon motion: *kinetic* energy. [< Gk. *kineein* to move]

**kink** (kingk) *n.* 1 An abrupt bend, twist, or tangle, as in a wire or rope. 2 A tightly twisted curl, as in hair or wool. 3 A mental quirk or prejudice. 4 A hindrance, obstruction, or difficulty. 5 A crick; cramp. —*v.t. &*

*v.i.* To form or cause to form a kink or kinks. [Du., twist, curl]

**kitch·en** (kich′ən) *n.* 1 A room set apart for cooking food. 2 A culinary department; cuisine. [< L *coquina*]

**kite** (kīt) 1 Any of certain birds of prey of the hawk family, having long, pointed wings and a forked tail. 2 A light frame, usu. of wood, covered with paper or light fabric, to be flown in the air at the end of a long string. 3 Any of several light sails for use in a very light wind. 4 In commerce: a Any negotiable paper not representing a genuine transaction but so employed as to obtain money. b A bank check drawn with insufficient funds on deposit to secure the advantage of the time period prior to collection. —*v.* **kit·ed, kit·ing** *v.i.* 1 *Informal* To soar or fly like a kite. 2 In commerce, to obtain money by the use of kites. —*v.t.* 3 In commerce, to issue as a kite. [< OE *cȳta*]

**kit·ten** (kit′n) *n.* A young cat or other feline animal. [< OF *chitoun*]

**klep·to·ma·ni·a** (klep′tə·mā′nē·ə) *n.* An uncontrollable, abnormal propensity to steal. [< Gk. *kleptein* to steal + -MANIA] —**klep′to·ma′ni·ac** (-mā′nē·ak) *n.*

**knack** (nak) *n.* 1 The trick of doing a thing readily and well. 2 Cleverness; adroitness. 3 A clever device. [ME, a sharp blow] —**Syn.** 2 aptitude, dexterity, facility.

**knap·sack** (nap′sak) *n.* A bag of leather or canvas worn across the shoulders, for carrying clothing, supplies, etc. [< Du. *knappen* to bite + *zak* a sack]

**knead** (nēd) *v.t.* 1 To mix and work, as dough or clay, into a uniform mass, usu. by pressing, turning, etc., with the hands. 2 To work upon with the hands; massage. 3 To make by or as by kneading. [< OE *cnedan*] —**knead′er** *n.*

**knee** (nē) *n.* 1 The joint of the human leg midway between the hip and the ankle. 2 A joint in the foreleg of various animals corresponding to the knee. 3 Anything like or suggesting a bent knee. 4 The part of a stocking or garment covering the knee. —**bring to one's knees** To cause to surrender. —*v.t.* To touch or strike with the knee. [< OE *cnēow*]

**kneel** (nēl) *v.i.* **knelt** or **kneeled, kneel·ing** To fall or rest on the bent knee or knees. [< OE *cnēowlian*] —**kneel′er** *n.*

**knell** (nel) *n.* 1 The tolling of a bell, as in announcing a death. 2 An omen of death, failure, etc. —*v.i.* 1 To sound a knell; toll. 2 To give a sad or warning sound. —*v.t.* 3 To proclaim or announce by a knell. [< OE *cnyllan* knock]

**knife** (nīf) *n. pl.* **knives** (nīvz) 1 A cutting instrument consisting of a sharp single-edged or double-edged blade, commonly set in a handle. 2 An edged blade forming a part of an implement or machine. 3 A weapon such as a cutlass or sword. —**go under the knife** *Informal* To undergo a surgical operation. —*v.t.* **knifed, knif·ing** 1 To stab or cut with a knife. 2 *Slang* To work against with underhand methods. —**knife in the back** *Informal* To undermine the reputation, position, etc., of. [< OE *cnīf*]

**knight** (nīt) *n.* 1 In medieval times, a gentleman admitted with special ceremonies to honorable military rank. 2 *Brit.* The holder of an honorary, nonhereditary rank next below that of baronet, giving him the title of *Sir.* 3 A champion or devoted follower, as of a cause, principle, or woman. 4 A member of any society in which the official title of knight obtains. 5 A chessman bearing a horse's head. —*v.t.* To make (someone) a knight. [< OE *cniht* boy, servant]

**knit** (nit) *v.* **knit** or **knit·ted, knit·ting** *v.i.* 1 To form (a fabric or garment) by interlocking loops of a single yarn or thread by means of needles. 2 To make into fabric by interlocking loops of thread, as on a machine, instead of by weaving. 3 To fasten or unite closely and firmly. 4 To contract (the brows). —*v.i.* 5 To make a fabric by interweaving a yarn or thread. 6 To grow together firmly, as a broken bone. —*n.* A knitted garment or fabric. [< OE *cnyttan*] —**knit′ter** *n.*

**knob** (nob) *n.* 1 A rounded protuberance. 2 A rounded handle, as of a door. 3 A rounded mountain; knoll. [< MLG *knobbe.*] —**knobbed** (nobd) *adj.*

**knock** (nok) *v.t.* 1 To give a heavy blow to; hit. 2 To strike (one thing) against another; bring into collision. 3 To drive or impel by striking: to *knock* a ball over a fence. 4 To make or cause by striking: to *knock* a hole in a wall. 5 *Slang* To find fault with; carp. at. —*v.i.* 6 To strike a blow or blows, as with the fist or a club. 7 To come into collision; bump. 8 To make a pounding noise: to *knock* on a door. 9 *Slang* To find fault; carp. —**knock about (or around)** 1 To strike repeatedly; hit from side to side. 2 To wander from place to place. 3 To treat neglectfully; abuse. —**knock down** 1 To take apart for convenience in shipping or storing. 2 In auctions, to sell to the highest bidder. — **knock off** 1 To leave off; stop, as work, talking, etc. 2 To deduct. 3 To do or make quickly or easily. 4 *Slang* To kill or defeat. —**knock out** 1 In boxing, to defeat (an opponent) by striking him to the ground. 2 To render unconscious or exhausted. —**knock together** To build or make roughly or hurriedly. —**knock up** 1 *Brit.* To rouse, as by knocking on the door. 2 *Brit. Informal* To tire out; exhaust. —*n.* 1 A sharp blow; a rap; also, a knocking. 2 *Mech.* A sharp noise indicating some malfunction, as badly timed combustion in an engine. 3 *Informal* Hostile criticism. [< OE *cnocian*] —**Syn.** *v.* 1 bang, punch, smack, smite, strike, pat, smash, clobber, rap, hammer, hit, pound, thrash, wallop.

**knock·out** (nok′out′) *adj.* Rendering insensible; overpowering. —*n.* 1 A knockout blow. 2 *Slang* An overwhelmingly attractive person or thing.

**knot** (not) *n.* 1 A fastening made by tightly intertwining one or more ropes, cords, etc. 2 A lump formed of hard tangles in a string, cord, etc. 3 An ornamental bow of silk, lace, etc. 4 A hard, gnarled portion of the trunk of a tree where a branch grows out. 5 *Bot.* A node or joint in a stem. 6 A cluster or group, as of persons. 7 *Naut.* a A division of a log line used to determine the rate of a ship's motion. b A speed of one nautical mile per hour. c One nautical mile. 8 A knob. 9 A bond or union. 10 A hard lump resembling a knot: a *knot* of muscle. 11 An intricate or complex difficulty; problem. 12 A state of being drawn taut, as from nervous tension: a stomach in *knots*. —*v.* **knot·ted, knot·ting** *v.t.* 1 To tie in a knot; form a knot or knots in. 2 To secure or fasten by a knot. 3 To form knobs, bosses, etc., in. —*v.i.* 4 To form a knot or knots. 5 To tie knots for fringe. [< OE *cnotta*]

**know** (nō) *v.* **knew, known, know·ing** *v.t.* 1 To perceive or understand clearly or with certainty: to *know* the truth. 2 To have information about: to *know* their plans. 3 To have experience of or familiarity with. 4 To distinguish between: to *know* peas from beans. 5 To have securely in the mind or memory: to *know* historical facts. 6 To have practical skill in or knowledge of: often with *how*. —*v.i.* 7 To have knowledge: often with *of*. 8 To be or become aware or cognizant. —*n.* The fact or condition of knowing;

knowledge. —**in the know** *Informal* Having full or privileged information. [< OE *cnāwan*] —**know′a·ble** *adj.* —**know′er** *n.* —**Syn.** *v.* 1 apprehend, comprehend, discern, perceive.

**know-how** (nō′hou′) *n. Informal* Knowledge of how to perform a complicated procedure; technical skill.

**knowl·edge** (nol′ij) *n.* 1 Information or understanding acquired through experience. 2 Information acquired through study. 3 The act, fact, or state of knowing. 4 The accumulated body of facts concerning a specified field of study. 5 Everything that has been learned, discovered, or perceived. —**to the best of one's knowledge** As far as one can determine. [< OE *cnawan* know]

**knuck·le** (nuk′əl) *n.* 1 One of the joints of the fingers, esp. one connecting the fingers to the rest of the hand. 2 The knee or ankle joint of certain animals, used as food. 3 *pl.* A device of metal, fitting over the knuckles, used as a weapon. —*v.i.* **knuck·led, knuck·ling** To hold the knuckles on the ground in shooting a marble. —**knuckle down** To apply oneself seriously and assiduously. —**knuckle under** To give in; yield. [< MLG *knökel*]

**KO, K.O., k.o.** knockout.

**Ko·ran** (kō·rän′, -ran′) *n.* The Muslims' sacred scripture, accepted by them as the revelations of Allah (God) to Mohammed.

**ko·sher** (kō′shər) *adj.* 1 Permitted by the Jewish ceremonial law; clean: said usu. of food. 2 Dealing in kosher food. 3 *Slang* All right; legitimate. —*n.* A shop selling kosher food; also the food sold there. —*v.t.* (kosh′ər) To make kosher. [< Heb. *kāshēr* fit, proper]

**kryp·ton** (krip′ton) *n.* A colorless, inert, gaseous element (symbol Kr) present in minute amounts in the atmosphere. [< Gk. *kryptos* hidden]

# L

**la·bel** (lā′bəl) *n.* 1 A slip, as of paper, affixed to something to indicate its character, ownership, destination, etc. 2 A brief, descriptive, written or spoken phrase designating certain characteristics of a person or group. —*v.t.* **·beled** or **·belled, ·bel·ing** or **·bel·ling** 1 To mark with a label; attach a label to. 2 To classify; designate. [< OF, a ribbon] — **la′bel·er** or **la′bel·ler** *n.*

**la·bor** (lā′bər) *n.* 1 Hard and exhausting physical or mental exertion. 2 That which requires exertion or effort; a task. 3 Wage earners collectively. 4 Workers who engage in manual work. 5 Work done by workers as a group. 6 The process of giving birth. — *v.i.* 1 To do work; toil. 2 To move with difficulty or painful exertion. 3 To be in the process of giving birth. —*v.t.* 4 To develop in too minute detail: to *labor* a point. —**labor under** To be hindered or troubled by: to *labor under* a misapprehension. *Brit. sp.* **la'bour.** [< L, toil, distress] —**la'bor·ing·ly** *adv.*

**lab·o·ra·to·ry** (lab'rə·tôr'ē, -tō'rē; *Brit.* lə·bor'ə·trē) *n. pl.* **·ries** 1 A place adapted to conducting scientific experiments, analyses, etc. 2 A department, as in a factory, for research, testing, etc. —*adj.* Pertaining to or performed in a laboratory. [< L *laborare* to labor]

**la·bo·ri·ous** (lə·bôr'ē·əs, -bō'rē-) *adj.* 1 Requiring much labor; toilsome. 2 Diligent; industrious. 3 Strained; labored. *Brit. sp.* **la·bour'ious.** —**la·bo'ri·ous·ly** *adv.* —**la·bo'ri·ous·ness** *n.* —**Syn.** 1 arduous, difficult, onerous. 2 assiduous; persevering.

**lab·y·rinth** (lab'ə·rinth) *n.* 1 A confusing, winding network of passages or paths; a maze. 2 Any perplexing combination or condition. 3 *Anat.* The winding passages of the inner ear. —**lab'y·rin'thine** (-thin, -thēn) or **·thi·an** or **·thic** or **·thi·cal** *adj.* —**lab'y·rin'thi·cal·ly** *adv.*

**lace** (lās) *n.* 1 A cord or string for fastening together the parts of a shoe, a corset, etc. 2 A delicate network of threads of linen, silk, cotton, etc., arranged in figures or patterns. 3 A dash of spirits, as in tea or coffee. —*v.* **laced, lac·ing** *v.t.* 1 To draw together by tying the lace or laces of. 2 To pass (a cord or string) through hooks, eyelets, etc., as a lace. 3 To trim with or as with lace. 4 To compress the waist of (a person) by tightening laces, as of a corset. 5 To intertwine or interlace. 6 To streak, as with color. 7 To add a dash of spirits to. 8 *Informal* To beat; thrash. —*v.i.* 9 To be fastened by means of a lace. —**lace into** 1 To attack. 2 To scold. [< L *laqueus* a noose, trap]

**lac·er·ate** (las'ər·āt) *v.t.* **·at·ed, ·at·ing** 1 To tear raggedly, as the flesh. 2 To hurt; injure, as the feelings. —*adj.* Jagged; torn. [< L *lacer* mangled] —**lac'er·a·ble, lac'er·a'tive** *adj.* —**lac'er·a'tion** *n.* —**Syn.** *v.* 1 rend, rip, rupture, split, sunder.

**lack** (lak) *v.t.* 1 To be without; have none or too little of. 2 To be short by; require: It

*lacks* two months till summer. —*v.i.* 3 To be wanting or deficient; be missing. —*n.* 1 The state of being needy or without something. 2 Want; deficiency. 3 That which is needed. [ME *lac*]

**lac·quer** (lak'ər) *n.* 1 A quick-drying varnish made from resin, nitrocellulose, and sometimes a pigment, dissolved in a volatile solvent. 2 A varnish yielding a high polish made from the resin of a tree of SE Asia. 3 Objects coated with such varnish: also **lac'quer·work'.** —*v.t.* To coat or varnish with lacquer. **Also lack'er.** [< Pg. *lacré* sealing wax]

**lac·tic** (lak'tik) *adj.* Of or derived from milk.

**lad·der** (lad'ər) *n.* 1 A device of wood, metal, etc., for climbing up and down that consists of two vertical side pieces connected by horizontal pieces. 2 A means of raising one's status or position by stages. [< OE *hlǣdder*]

**la·dle** (lād'l) *n.* 1 A cup-shaped utensil, with a long handle, for dipping out or conveying liquids. 2 A device like this in form or function. —*v.t.* **·died, ·dling** To dip up and carry in a ladle. [< OE *hladan* lade] —**la'dler** *n.*

**la·dy** (lā'dē) *n. pl.* **·dies** 1 A refined and well-bred woman. 2 A woman of good family and recognized social standing. 3 Any woman: in the plural, used as a form of address. 4 A woman who is at the head of a household: the *lady* of the house. 5 A sweetheart or wife. 6 In Great Britain: a a marchioness, countess, viscountess, or baroness. b A title given by courtesy to a daughter of a duke, marquis, or earl, or to the wife of a baronet or knight or one having the courtesy title of Lord. —*adj.* 1 Of, like or becoming to a lady. 2 Female: a *lady* carpenter. [< OE *hlǣfdige*, lit., bread-kneader] • In modern usage, *lady* in the sense of any woman is considered to be either falsely genteel or old-fashioned. Terms such as *saleslady, cleaning lady, lady doctor*, etc., are to be avoided. *Woman* is the more appropriate term for any adult female human being as well as for female persons in various occupations: a *woman* doctor, a *saleswoman*, a cleaning *woman*.

**lag** (lag) *v.i.* **lagged, lag·ging** To stay or fall behind. —*n.* 1 The act of lagging; retardation of motion, development, etc. 2 The amount of such retardation. [?] —**Syn.** *v.* dawdle, drag, linger, loiter, retard.

**la·ger** (lä'gər) *n.* Beer that has been aged for

several months before use. **Also lager beer.**
[< G *Lagerbier*, lit., storehouse beer]

**lag·gard** (lag′ərd) *n.* One who lags; a loiterer.
—*adj.* Falling behind; slow. —**lag′gard·ly**
*adv.* —**lag′gard·ness** *n.*

**la·goon** (lə·gōōn′) *n.* 1 A shallow body of salt
water separated from but connecting with
the sea, esp. one within an atoll. • See
ATOLL. 2 A shallow body of fresh water usu.
connecting with a river or lake. [< L *lacuna*
hole, pond]

**lair** (lâr) *n.* The resting place or den of a wild
animal. [< OE *leger* bed]

**la·i·ty** (lā′ə·tē) *n. pl.* **·ties** 1 People who are not
members of the clergy. 2 Those outside any
specified profession. [< LAY²]

**lamb** (lam) *n.* 1 A young sheep. 2 Its flesh consumed as food. 3 Any gentle or innocent
person. 4 An unsophisticated person; simpleton. —**like a lamb** 1 Mildly; very gently.
2 Unsuspicious; easily misled. —*v.i.* To give
birth: said of sheep. [< OE]

**lame** (lām) *adj.* 1 Crippled or disabled, esp. in
the legs. 2 Poor; halting: a *lame* apology. 3
Sore; painful: a *lame* back. —*v.t.* **lamed,**
**lam·ing** To make lame; cripple. [< OE *lama*]
—**lame′ly** *adv.* —**lame′ness** *n.*

**la·ment** (lə·ment′) *v.t.* 1 To feel or express sorrow for. —*v.i.* 2 To feel or express sorrow;
mourn. —*n.* 1 The expression of grief;
lamentation. 2 A plaintive song or melody.
[< L *lamentum* a wailing, weeping] —**la·**
**ment′er** *n.*

**lam·en·ta·ble** (lam′ən·tə·bəl, lə·men′-) *adj.* 1
Expressing sorrow; mournful. 2 Exciting
regret or dissatisfaction: a *lamentable* failure. —**lam′en·ta·bly** *adv.*

**lam·poon** (lam·pōōn′) *n.* A written satire designed to bring a person into ridicule or
contempt. —*v.t.* To abuse or satirize in a
lampoon. [< MF *lampons* let's drink] —
**lam·poon′er** or **lam·poon′ist, lam·poon′**
**er·y** *n.* —**Syn.** *v.* deride, mock, ridicule.

**lan·cet** (lan′sit, län′-) *n.* 1 A surgeon's small,
pointed knife, usu. two-edged. 2 *Archit.* a A
lancet-shaped or sharply pointed window:
also lancet window. b A sharply pointed
arch: also lancet arch. 3 A small lance. [<
F *lancette*, dim. of *lance*]

**land·mark** (land′märk′) *n.* 1 A fixed object
serving as a boundary mark to a tract of
land. 2 A prominent or memorable object in
the landscape, serving as a guide. 3 A distinguishing fact, event, etc., of a period. 4
A historic or architecturally important

building, site, etc., preserved by law for
posterity.

**land·scape** (land′skāp) *n.* 1 A stretch of country as seen from a single point. 2 A picture
representing natural scenery. —*v.* **·scaped,**
**·scap·ing** *v.t.* 1 To improve or change the
natural features or appearance of, as a
park or garden. —*v.i.* 2 To be a landscape
gardener. [<Du. *land* land + *-schap* -ship] —
**land′scap·er** *n.*

**lan·guage** (lang′gwij) *n.* 1 The expression and
communication of emotions or ideas between human beings by means of speech,
either written or spoken. 2 The vocal
sounds or their written symbol used in
such expression and communication. 3 The
means of communication among members
of a single nation or group; tongue: the
French *language*. 4 Transmission of emotions or ideas between any living creatures
by any means. 5 The vocabulary or technical expressions used in a specific business,
science, etc.; jargon. 6 One's characteristic
manner of expression or use of speech. 7
The study of a language or languages. [<L
*lingua* tongue, language]

**lan·guid** (lang′gwid) *adj.* 1 Indisposed to
physical exertion; affected by weakness. 2
Wanting in interest or animation. 3 Lacking in force or quickness of movement. [<
*languere* languish] —**lan′guid·ly** *adv.* —
**lan′guid·ness** *n.* —**Syn.** 1 drooping, fatigued, languorous, listless, weary.

**lan·guish** (lang′gwish) *v.i.* 1 To grow faint or
listless. 2 To live or be in wretched circumstances: to *languish* in a dungeon. 3 To affect a look of sentimental longing or melancholy. 4 To pine with love or desire. [<L
*languere* languish] —**lan′guish·er, lan′**
**guish·ment** *n.*

**lan·guor** (lang′gər) *n.* 1 Lassitude of body or
depression of mind. 2 Amorous dreami-
ness. 3 The absence of activity: dullness.
[<L *languere* languish] —**lan′guor·ous** *adj.*
—**lan′guor·ous·ly** *adv.* —**lan′guor·ous·**
**ness** *n.*

**lank** (langk) *adj.* 1 Long and lean. 2 Long,
straight, and thin: *lank* hair. [< OE *hlanc*
flexible] —**lank′ly** *adv.* —**lank′ness** *n.*

**lan·tern** (lan′tərn) *n.* 1 A case with transparent sides, as on a lamppost or of portable
character, for enclosing and protecting a
light. 2 *Archit.* A glassed-in or open structure on a roof or tower, open below and admitting light and air. 3 The chamber at the

top of a lighthouse housing the light. 4
MAGIC LANTERN. [<Gk. *lamptēr*]

**lap** (lap) *v.t.* & *v.i.* **lapped, lap·ping** 1 To scoop
up (a liquid) into the mouth with the
tongue: said usu. of animals. 2 To wash
against (the shore, etc.) with a slight, rippling sound: said of water. —**lap up** 1 To
scoop up (a liquid) with the tongue. 2 *Informal* To accept eagerly: to *lap up* praise.
—*n.* 1 The act of lapping; a lick. 2 The sound
of lapping. [< OE *lapian*] —**lap′per** *n.*

**lapse** (laps) *v.i.* **lapsed, laps·ing** 1 To pass
slowly or by degrees; slip: to *lapse* into a
coma. 2 To deviate from virtue or truth. 3
To pass, as time. 4 To become void, usu. by
disuse or neglect: The agreement *lapsed*. 5
*Law* To be forfeited to another because of
the negligence, failure, or death of the
holder. —*n.* 1 A gradual slipping or passing
away, as of time. 2 A minor fault or mistake.
3 A fall to a lower form or state. 4 A deviation from what is right, proper, or just: a
*lapse* in conduct. 5 *Law* The defeat of a
right or privilege through fault, failure, or
neglect. [<L *lapsus* a slip <*labi* glide, slip]
—**laps′a·ble, laps′i·ble** *adj.* —**laps′er** *n.* —
**Syn.** *v.* 1 fall, sink. 2 err, stray. 3 elapse, slip
by. *n.* 2 blunder, error.

**lar·ce·ny** (lär′sə·nē) *n. pl.* **·nies** *Law* The taking, without claim of right or without permission, or the personal goods of another;
theft. [<L *latrocinari* rob] —**lar′ce·nous** *adj.*
—**lar′ce·nous·ly** *adv.* • The distinction between *grand larceny* (more than a specified
amount) and *petty* (or *petit*) *lar·ceny* (less
than such an amount) has been dropped in
many parts of the U.S.

**lard** (lärd) *n.* The semisolid oil of hog's fat
after rendering. —*v.t.* 1 To prepare (meat or
poultry) for cooking by covering with or inserting something, as strips of fat. 2 To
cover or smear with grease. 3 To mix with
something so as to enrich or improve. [<L
*lardum*] —**lard′y** *adj.*

**lar·der** (lär′dər) *n.* 1 A room where the provisions of a household are kept. 2 Provisions.
[<L *lardum* lard]

**lar·i·at** (lar′ē·ət) *n.* 1 A rope, esp. of horsehair,
for tethering animals. 2 LASSO. —*v.t.* To fasten or catch with a lariat. [<Sp. *la* the +
*reata* rope]

**lark¹** (lärk) *n.* 1 Any of a large family of small
songbirds, as the European skylark. 2 Any
of various similar birds, as the mead-
owlark, etc. [<OE *lāferce*]

**lark²** (lärk) *n. Informal* A hilarious time; hu-

morous adventure. —*v.t.* 1 To make fun of;
tease. —*v.i.* 2 To play pranks; frolic. [< ON
*leika* to leap] —**lark′er** *n.* —**lark′some,
lark′y** *adj.* (·i·er, ·i·est)

**lar·va** (lär′və) *n. pl.* **·vae** (·vē) or **·vas** An early,
immature form of an animal that is struc-
turally unlike the adult, as the first stage
of an insect after leaving the egg, the tad-
pole of a frog, etc. [L, a ghost, a mask] —
**lar′val** *adj.*

**lar·ynx** (lar′ingks) *n. pl.* **la·ryn·ges** (lə·rin′jēz)
or **lar·ynx·es** 1 The human organ or voice,
consisting of a structure of cartilage and
muscle in the upper trachea, and containing the vocal cords whose vibrations produce sound. 2 A similar structure in most
vertebrates. [< Gk. *larynx*]

**la·ser** (lā′zər) *n.* A device in which energy supplied to an atomic or molecular system is
released as a narrow beam of coherent light
whose wavelength depends on the energy
transitions of the atoms or molecules.
[<*l(ight) a(mplification by) s(timulated) e(mission of) r(adiation)*]

**lash** (lash) *n.* 1 A thong on a whip handle; a
whip. 2 A stroke with or as with a whip. 3
A sharp, sarcastic remark. 4 An eyelash. 5
Any heavy blow, as of waves beating the
shore. —*v.t.* 1 To strike or urge forward with
or as with a whip. 2 To throw or move
quickly or suddenly, as from side to side:
to *lash* the tail. 3 To beat or dash against
with force or violence: The waves *lashed*
the pier. 4 To attack or criticize severely. 5
To arouse the emotions of, as with words.
6 To bind or tie with or as with a lashing.
—*v.i.* 7 To move quickly or violently; dash.
—**lash out** 1 To strike out violently or
wildly. 2 To break into angry or vehement
speech. [ME *lashe*] —**Syn.** *v.* 1 beat, flog,
hit, thrash, whip. 4 berate, scold, upbraid.

**las·so** (las′ō, las·ōō′) *n. pl.* **·sos** or **·soes** A
long rope or leather thong, with a running
noose, for catching horses and cattle. —
*v.t.* To catch with a lasso. [<L *laqueus* a
snare] —**las′so·er** *n.*

**last** (last, läst) *adj.* 1 Having no successor;
final. 2 Next before the present; most recent. 3 Least fit or likely; most remote. 4 Beyond or above all others; utmost. 5 Beneath
all others. —*adv.* 1 After all others in time
or order. 2 At a time next preceding the present: He was *last* seen heading west. In
conclusion. —*n.* 1 The end: a rebel to the
*last*. 2 The final appearance, experience, or
mention. 3 The element of an ordered set

that has no successor. —**at last** Finally. —**at long last** Finally. —**breathe one's last** To die. —**see the last of** Never to see again. [< OE *latost*] —**last′ly** *adv.*

**latch** (lach) *n.* A catch for fastening a door, lid, shutter, etc. —*v.t. & v.i.* To fasten by means of a latch; close. —**latch on to** *Slang* 1 To fasten (oneself) 2 To obtain; get. [< OE *lǽccan* seize]

**la·tent** (lā′tənt) *adj.* Not visible or apparent; dormant. [<L *latere* be hidden] —**la′ten·cy** *n.* —**la′tent·ly** *adv.*

**lat·er·al** (lat′ər·əl) *adj.* Pertaining to, proceeding from, or directed toward the side. —*n.* 1 A lateral protuberance or outgrowth. 2 LATERAL PASS. [<L *latus, lateris* a side] —**lat′er·al·ly** *adv.*

**la·tex** (lā′teks) *n. pl.* **lat·i·ces** (lat′ə·sēz) or **la·tex·es** 1 The viscid, milky emulsion secreted by certain plants, as the milkweed, rubber tree, etc. 2 A watery emulsion of rubber or synthetic plastic, used in making adhesives, paint, etc. [L, a liquid]

**lathe** (lāth) *n.* A machine for shaping articles on which an object is mounted and rotated, while a cutting tool is thrust against it. —*v.t.* **lathed, lath·ing** To form or shape on a lathe. [?]

**lath·er** (lath′ər) *n.* 1 Foam or froth of soapsuds. 2 Foam of profuse sweating, as of a horse. —**in a lather** *Informal* In a state of intense excitement or agitation. —*v.t.* 1 To cover with lather. 2 *Informal* To flog; thrash. —*v.i.* 3 To become covered with lather. 4 To form lather. [< OE *lēathor* washing soda] —**lath′er·y** *adj.* —**lath′er·er** *n.*

**lat·i·tude** (lat′ə·t′ood) *n.* 1 *Geog.* Distance on the earth's surface toward or away from the equator expressed as an arc of a meridian. 2 A region or place with reference to its distance north or south of the equator: *warm latitudes.* 3 Freedom from restrictions, as in action or thought. 4 Range or scope. [< L *latus* broad] —**lat′i·tu′di·nal** *adj.*

**lat·ter** (lat′ər) A comparative of LATE. —*adj.* 1 Of, relating to, or nearer the end. 2 Recent or more recent; later. —**the latter** The second of two mentioned persons or things. [< OE *lǽtra*] —**lat′ter·ly** *adv.*

**lat·tice** (lat′is) *n.* 1 Openwork of metal or wood, formed by crossing or interlacing strips or bars. 2 Anything made of such work, as a window, a blind, or a screen. 3 *Physics* An arrangement consisting of a module periodically repeated throughout a

region or space. —*v.t.* **lat·ticed, lat·tic·ing** 1 To furnish or enclose with a lattice. 2 To arrange or interlace like latticework. [< OF *latte* a lath]

**laugh** (laf, läf) *v.i.* 1 To show amusement, hilarity, derision, etc., by expressions of the face and by a series of explosive sounds made in the chest and throat. 2 To be or appear gay or lively. —*v.t.* 3 To express by laughter. 4 To move or influence by laughter or ridicule: He *laughed* himself out of his worries. —**laugh at** 1 To express amusement concerning. 2 To make light of; belittle —**laugh off** To dismiss or reject lightly or scornfully. —*n.* 1 The act or sound of laughter. 2 *Informal* Anything producing laughter. —**have the last laugh** To triumph after apparent defeat. [< OE *hlǽhhan*] —**laugh′er** *n.*

**laugh·ter** (laf′tər, läf′-) *n.* 1 The sound or action of laughing. 2 Any exclamation or expression indicating merriment or derision.

**launch** (lônch, länch) *v.t.* 1 To cause to move into water for the first time, as a newly built ship. 2 To set afloat, as a boat or log. 3 To make a beginning of: to *launch* an enterprise. 4 To start (someone) on a career, course, etc. 5 To give a start to the flight or course of, as a rocket, torpedo, or airplane. —*v.i.* 6 To put or go to sea: usu. with *out* or *forth.* 7 To start on a career, course, etc. 8 To begin something with vehemence or urgency. He *launched* into an argument. —**launch out** To start; commence, esp. something new. —*n.* 1 The act of launching. 2 The process of being launched. [< OF *lance* lance] —**launch′er** *n.*

**launching pad** The platform from which a rocket or spacecraft is launched.

**laun·dro·mat** (lôn′drə·mat, län-) *n.* An establishment, usu. self-service, where the customer brings laundry to be washed and dried in coin-operated machines. [< *Laundromat,* a trade name]

**laun·dry** (lôn′drē, län′-) *n. pl.* **·dries** 1 A room or building for laundering clothes. 2 Articles to be washed. [< OF *lavendier*] —**laun′dry·man** (-mən) *n.*

**la·va** (lä′və, lav′ə) *n.* 1 Melted rock, issuing from a volcanic crater or a fissure in the earth's surface. 2 Such rock when solidified. [< Ital., orig., a stream of rain]

**lav·a·to·ry** (lav′ə·tôr′ē, -tō′rē) *n. pl.* **·ries** 1 A room in a public or semipublic place, as in a school or hotel, provided with appliances for washing, usu. toilets, and sometimes urinals. 2 Any bathroom. 3 A basin to wash in. [< L *lavare* to wash]

**lav·ish** (lav′ish) *adj.* 1 Bestowed, expended, or existing in profusion: *lavish* gifts. 2 Spending extravagantly; prodigal. 3 Exaggerated; unrestrained: *lavish* compliments. —*v.t.* To give or bestow profusely or generously. [< OF *lavache* a downpour of rain] —**lav′ish·er, lav′ish·ness** *n.* —**lav′ish·ly** *adv.* —**Syn.** *adj.* 1 abundant, bountiful, copious, generous. *v.* indulge with, heap upon.

**law** (lô) *n.* 1 A custom or rule of conduct which a community, state, etc., considers binding upon its members, and which is enforced by compelling authority or legislation. 2 A body of such rules. 3 The condition of society when such rules are observed: to establish *law* and order. 4 The body of rules related to a specified subject: criminal *law.* 5 Statute and common law, as opposed to equity. 6 An enactment of a legislature, as opposed to a constitution. 7 The system of courts administering remedial justice: to resort to the *law.* 8 The branch of knowledge concerned with jurisprudence: to study *law.* 9 The vocation of an attorney, solicitor, etc.: to practice *law.* 10 The legal profession as a whole. 11 A rule of conduct having divine origin. 12 An imperative rule or command: His word is *law.* 13 Any rule of conduct or procedure: the *laws* of hospitality. 14 In science, a statement of the manner or order in which a defined group of natural phenomena occur under certain conditions. 15 *Math.* A rule or formula governing a function or the performance of an operation. 16 The police, personifying legal force: preceded by *the.* [< OE *lagu*] —**go to law** To take a case or complaint to court to be settled. —**lay down the law** 1 To scold thoroughly. 2 To give firm orders. —**read law** To study for a legal degree. —**the Law** 1 The first five books of the Old Testament, containing the Mosaic law. 2 The Old Testament.

**law·suit** (lô′sōōt′) *n.* A proceeding in a court of law for redress of wrongs.

**law·yer** (lô′yər) *n.* One who practices law and represents clients in lawsuits or gives legal advice.

**lax** (laks) *adj.* 1 Lacking tenseness or firmness; yielding. 2 Not stringent or energetic. 3 Wanting exactness of meaning or application. [< L *laxus* loose] —**lax′i·ty, lax′ness** *n.* —**lax′ly** *adv.*

**lay** (lā) *v.* **laid, lay·ing** *v.t.* 1 To cause to lie. 2

To put or place; *Lay* the book on the table. 3 To strike or beat down; overthrow. 4 To cause to settle or subside, as dust, a storm, etc. 5 To calm or allay, as doubts. 6 To place in regular order or proper position: to *lay* title. 7 To think out; devise: to *lay* plans. 8 To attribute or ascribe: to *lay* blame. 9 To give importance to. 10 To bring forward; advance, as a claim. 11 To bring forth from the body and deposit, as an egg. 12 To construct; build, as a foundation. 13 To make (a table) ready for a meal. 14 To bury; inter. 15 To impose, as taxes, punishment, etc. 16 To spread over a surface: to *lay* a fixative. 17 To strike with or apply, as in punishment. 18 To locate: The scene is *laid* in the boudoir. 19 To set or prepare, as a trap. 20 To place as a wager or bet: He *laid* twenty dollars on the favorite. —*v.i.* 21 To bring forth and deposit eggs. 22 To place a bet or bets. 23 To lie; recline: an incorrect use. —**lay aside** (or **by**) To store up; save. —**lay away** 1 To store up; save. 2 To bury. —**lay before** To put forward or present, as a report. —**lay down** 1 To give up (one's life). 2 To state or proclaim: to *lay down* the law. 3 To bet. —**lay for** *Informal* To wait to attack or harm. —**lay hold of** To seize or grasp. —**lay in** To procure and store. —**lay into** *Informal* To attack vigorously. —**lay it on** *Informal* To be extravagant or exorbitant, as in praise or demands. —**lay off** 1 To take off and put aside, as clothes. 2 To survey; mark off. 3 To dismiss (a worker) from a job, usu. temporarily. 4 *Informal* To take a rest; stop working. 5 *Slang* To stop annoying, teasing, etc. —**lay on** 1 To put on; apply, as color. 2 To beat or strike; attack. —**lay out** 1 To spend. 2 To prepare for burial. 3 *Slang* To strike prostrate or unconscious. 4 To set forth, as a plan. —**lay over** To stop, as for a rest on a journey. —**lay siege to** To besiege. —**lay up** 1 To make a store of. 2 To confine, as by illness or injury. —*n.* 1 The manner in which something lies or is placed; relative arrangement: the *lay* of the land. 2 *Whaling* A share in the profits. [< OE *lecgan*] • **lay, lie** Educated speaking and writing require a careful distinction between these two related verbs. *Lay (laid, laying)*, meaning to place or put, takes an object: *He lays his briefcase on the desk. Lie (lay, lain, lying)*, meaning to rest, recline, or be situated, does not take an object: *The dog lies on the rug.* The confusion occurs because the present tense of *lay* is identical with the past tense of *lie: Lay your coat over that chair; Yesterday he lay on the couch for two hours.*

**lay·er** (lā′ər) *n.* 1 One who or that which lays. 2 A single horizontal thickness, as a stratum or lamina. 3 *Bot.* A shoot or twig bent into the ground to take root without being detached from the parent plant. —*v.t. Bot.* To propagate (a plant) by means of a layer. —**lay′er·ing** *n.*

**lay·man** (lā′mən) *n. pl.* ·**men** (-mən) A man not belonging to the clergy or other profession or body of experts.

**lay·out** (lā′out′) *n.* 1 That which is laid out; a set of articles set out or provided. 2 A laying out or planning, as of a piece of work, a campaign, etc. 3 The make-up of a book, magazine, etc. Also **lay′out.**

**lead¹** (lēd) *v.* **led, lead·ing** *v.t.* 1 To go with or ahead of so as to show the way; guide. 2 To guide by or as by pulling: to *lead* a person by the hand. 3 To serve as a direction or route for: The path *led* them to a valley. 4 To cause to go in a certain direction, as wire, water, etc. 5 To direct the affairs, actions, etc., of: to *lead* an army. 6 To have the first or foremost place among: He *led* the field. 7 To influence or control the opinions, thoughts, actions, etc., of. 8 To live or experience; pass: to *lead* a happy life. 9 To begin or open: to *lead* a discussion. 10 In card games, to begin a round of play with: He *led* the ace. —*v.i.* 11 To act as guide; conduct. 12 To have leadership or command; be in control. 13 To submit to being guided: The horse *leads* easily. 14 To be first or in advance. 15 To afford a way or passage: The road *led* into a swamp. 16 In card games, to make the first play. 17 In boxing, to strike at an opponent: to *lead* with a left. —**lead off** To make a beginning; start. —**lead on** To entice or tempt. —**lead to** To result in; cause: His carelessness *led* to his downfall. —*n.* 1 Position in advance or at the head; priority. 2 The distance, time, etc., by which anything precedes. 3 Leadership; guidance. 4 A clue or hint: Have you any *leads?* 5 In cards, etc., the right to play first or the card or suit played first. 6 In drama, the principal part or the actor who performs in such a part. 7 *Electr.* A wire that joins to a circuit device. 8 In baseball, the distance from base of a runner ready to run to the next base. 9 A leash for leading a dog. 10 In journalism, the opening paragraph of a news story. —*adj.*

Acting as leader: the *lead* dog. [< OE *lœden* cause to go] —**Syn.** *v.* 1 conduct, direct, escort. 7 induce, persuade.

**lead²** (led) *n.* 1 A soft, heavy, gray metallic element (symbol Pb) forming many technologically useful alloys and compounds. 2 Any one of various articles made of lead or its alloys. 3 *Printing* A thin strip of type metal used to separate lines of type. 4 *Naut.* A weight of lead used in sounding at sea. 5 A thin rod of graphite, used in pencils. 6 WHITE LEAD. 7 Bullets. —*v.t.* 1 To cover, weight, fasten, line, or fill with lead. 2 *Printing* To separate (lines of type) with leads. —*v.i.* 3 To become filled or clogged with lead. [< OE *lēad*] —**lead′y** *adj.*

**lead·en** (led′n) *adj.* 1 Made of lead. 2 Of a dull gray color. 3 Heavy. 4 Dull or sluggish. 5 Depressed; sad. —**lead′en·ly** *adv.* —**lead′en·ness** *n.*

**leaf** (lēf) *n. pl.* **leaves** (lēvz) 1 A photosynthetic, lateral outgrowth from the stem of a plant, commonly broad, flat, thin, and green. 2 Leaves collectively; leafage. 3 Loosely, a petal. 4 A single sheet of paper, as in a book, on each side of which is a page. 5 A hinged, folding, sliding, or removable part or section, as of a table, gate, screen, or folding door. 6 A very thin sheet of metal: gold *leaf.* —**turn over a new leaf** To change one's ways or conduct for the better. —*v.i.* 1 To put forth or produce leaves. —*v.t.* 2 To turn or run through the pages of a book: often with *through.* [< OE *lēaf*]

**league** (lēg) *n.* 1 An alliance of persons or states for mutual support in a common cause. 2 In sports, an association of ball teams that play among themselves. —*v.t. & v.i.* **leagued, lea·guing** To join in a league; combine. [< Ital. < *legare* to bind] —**lea′guer** (lē′gər) *n.*

**leak** (lēk) *n.* 1 An opening that permits the unintended entrance or escape of something. 2 Anything which permits the transmission, loss, or escape of something: a *leak* in the espionage system. 3 Leakage. —*v.i.* 1 To let a liquid, etc., enter or escape undesignedly, as through a hole or crack. 2 To pass in or out accidentally: often with *in* or *out.* 3 To become known despite efforts at secrecy: usu. with *out.* —*v.t.* 4 To let (a liquid, etc.) enter or escape undesignedly. 5 To disclose (privileged information) with or without authorization. [< ON *leka* to drip] —**leak′i·ness** *n.* —**leak′y** *adj.* (·**i·er,** ·**i·est**)

**lean¹** (lēn) *v.* **leaned** or **leant** (lent), **lean·ing**
*v.i.* 1 To incline from an erect position. 2 To
incline against or rest on something for
support. 3 To depend or rely: with *on* or
*upon*: to *lean* on friendship. 4 To have a
mental inclination: to *lean* toward an opinion. —*v.t.* 5 To cause to incline from an
erect position. 6 To place (one thing)
against another for support. —*n.* A leaning;
inclination. [< OE *hleonian*]

**lean²** (lēn) *adj.* 1 Not fat or stout; thin. 2 With
little or no fat: *lean* meat. 3 Lacking in richness, productiveness, etc.: a *lean* harvest.
—*n.* Meat with little or no fat. [< OE *hlǣne*
thin] —**lean′ly** *adv.* —**lean′ness** *n.*

**leap** (lēp) *v.* **leaped** or **leapt** (lēpt or lept),
**leap·ing** *v.i.* 1 To jump with the feet in the
air; spring. 2 To move suddenly by or as by
jumping. —*v.t.* 3 To clear by jumping over.
4 To cause to leap: to *leap* a horse. —*n.* 1
The act of leaping. 2 A place to leap from or
over. 3 The space passed over in leaping. 4
A sudden change or transition. [< OE *hlēa-
pan*] —**leap′er** *n.*

**learn** (lûrn) *v.* **learned** or **learnt**, **learn·ing** *v.t.*
1 To acquire knowledge of or skill in by ob-
servation, study, instruction, etc. 2 To find
out; ascertain: to *learn* the facts. 3 To mem-
orize. 4 To acquire by or as by practice: to
*learn* good habits. —*v.i.* 5 To gain knowledge; acquire skill. 6 To be informed; hear.
[< OE *leornian*] —**learn′er** *n.*

**lease** (lēs) *v.t.* **leased**, **leas·ing** 1 To grant the
temporary possession and profits of, as
lands, buildings, etc., usu. for a specified
rent; let. 2 To hold under a lease. —*n.* 1 A
contract for leasing land, buildings, etc. 2
The duration of such leasing. [< L *laxare*
loosen] —**leas′a·ble** *adj.*

**leash** (lēsh) *n.* A line or thong, as for holding
in check a dog, etc. —*v.t.* To hold or restrain by or as by a leash. [< L *laxus* loose]

**leath·er** (leth′ər) *n.* 1 The skin or hide of an
animal, when tanned or dressed for use. 2
Something made of leather. —*v.t.* 1 To cover
or furnish with leather. 2 *Informal* To beat
with or as with a leather strap. [< OE *lether*]
—**leath′er·y** *adj.* —**leath′er·i·ness** *n.*

**leave** (lēv) *v.* **left**, **leav·ing** *v.t.* 1 To go or depart from; quit. 2 To allow to remain be-
hind: to *leave* a plow in a field. 3 To place
or deposit so as to cause to remain behind:
to *leave word.* 4 To cause to remain after
departure, cessation, healing, etc.: The war
*left* its mark. 5 To allow to continue or be
as specified: *Leave* the light on. 6 To refer

or entrust to another for doing, deciding,
etc.: I *leave* the matter to you. 7 To terminate connection, employment, etc., with:
to *leave* a job. 8 To have as a remainder:
Three minus two *leaves* one. 9 To have remaining after death: to *leave* a large family. 10 To bequeath. —*v.i.* 11 To depart or go
away. —**leave off** To cease. —**leave out** 1 To
omit from consideration. 2 To fail to include. [< OE *lǣfan*, lit., let remain] —**leav′**
**er** *n.* —**Syn.** 1 abandon, desert, forsake, relinquish. 11 withdraw, flee, set out. • The
use of *leave* as a synonym for *let* in the
sense of refraining from disturbing, bothering, etc., is only acceptable when *leave* is
followed by a noun or pronoun and also by
the word "alone." Thus, *Leave your little
brother alone* may be substituted for *Let
your little brother alone.* However, such a
substitution can result in ambiguity since
*leave alone,* in this context, may be inter-
preted to mean that the little brother is to
be left by himself.

**leav·en** (lev′ən) *n.* 1 An agent that lightens
baked goods by forming gas bubbles in it,
as yeast or baking powder. 2 A piece of
yeasty dough; sourdough. 3 Any influence
or addition that causes general change of
the whole. —*v.t.* 1 To add a leaven to; make
light. 2 To affect in character; imbue. [< L
*levare* raise] —**leav′en·ing** *n.*

**lec·ture** (lek′chər) *n.* 1 A talk delivered aloud
for instruction or entertainment. 2 A
lengthy reprimand. —*v.* **·tured**, **·tur·ing** *v.t.*
1 To deliver lectures to; instruct by lectur-
ing. 2 To rebuke authoritatively or at
length. —*v.i.* 3 To give a lecture. [< L *lectura*
an act of reading] —**lec′tur·er**, **lec′ture·**
**ship** *n.* —**Syn.** *n.* 1 address, discourse, oration, speech.

**ledge** (lej) *n.* 1 A shelf. 2 Something resembling a shelf, as a ridge of rock or a projection from a building. 3 A lode or vein. [ME
*legge*] —**ledg′y** *adj.*

**ledg·er** (lej′ər) *n.* The principal book of accounts of a business establishment, in
which all transactions are entered to show
the debits and credits of each account. [ME
*legger*]

**leer** (lir) *n.* A sly look or glance expressing
lust, malicious intent, etc. —*v.i.* To look
with a leer. [< OE *hlēor* a cheek, face] —
**leer′ing·ly** *adv.*

**lees** (lēz) *n. pl.* Sediment, esp. of wine, dregs.
[< OF *lie*]

**left¹** (left) *p.t. & p.p. of* LEAVE¹.

**left²** (left) *adj.* 1 Of, designating, for, or on that side of the body which is toward the north when one faces the rising sun. 2 Situated closer to the left hand of an observer than to his right: the *left* fork of a road. 3 Designating that side or bank of a river which is on the left when the observer faces downstream. —*n.* 1 The left side. 2 Anything on, toward, or for the left side. 3 *Often cap.* In politics, a liberal, socialistic, or radical position, or a party or group advocating such a position, so designated because of the views of the party occupying seats on the left side of the presiding officer in certain European legislative bodies: used with *the.* 4 In boxing, the left hand or a blow with the left hand. [< OE *lyft*]

**left·ist** (lef′tist) *n.* In politics, one who is a member of or sympathetic to the left. —*adj.* Liberal or radical.

**leg·a·cy** (leg′ə·sē) *n. pl.* **·cies** 1 Something left by will; a bequest. 2 Something handed down or derived from an ancestor or earlier time. [< L *legare* bequeath]

**le·gal** (lē′gəl) *adj.* 1 Created or permitted by law. 2 Of, pertaining to, or connected with law. 3 Capable of being remedied by a resort to statute law rather than to equity. 4 Of or suitable for lawyers: a *legal* approach. [< L *lex, legis* law] —**le′gal·ly** *adv.*

**le·gal·i·ty** (li·gal′ə·tē) *n. pl.* **·ties** 1 The condition or quality of being legal. 2 Something legal, as a law.

**leg·ate** (leg′it) *n.* 1 An official envoy or emissary. 2 A representative of the pope in various functions. [< L *legare* send as a deputy, bequeath] —**leg′ate·ship** *n.*

**le·ga·tion** (li·gā′shən) *n.* 1 A diplomatic mission sent to a foreign country; also, those persons composing it. 2 The official residence or place of business of such a diplomatic mission, usu. ranking below an embassy.

**leg·end** (lej′ənd) *n.* 1 An unauthenticated story from early times, preserved by tradition and popularly thought to have a basis in fact. 2 Such stories, collectively. 3 An unusually famous or notable person, thing, or event. 4 An inscription or motto on a coin or monument. 5 A key to a map or chart. 6 A title, brief explanation, etc., accompanying an illustration. [< L *legere* read]

**leg·en·dar·y** (lej′ən·der′ē) *adj.* 1 Of, based on, or known from legends. 2 Traditional.

**leg·er·de·main** (lej′ər·də·mān′) *n.* 1 Slight of hand. 2 Any artful trick or deception. [< F *léger de main,* lit., light of hand] —**leg′·er·de·main′ist** *n.*

**leg·i·ble** (lej′ə·bəl) *adj.* Capable of being deciphered or read with ease. [< L *legere* to read] —**leg′i·bil′i·ty, leg′i·ble·ness** *n.* —**leg′i·bly** *adv.*

**le·gion** (lē′jen) *n.* 1 A division of the ancient Roman army, comprising between 4,200 and 6,000 men. 2 *Usu. pl.* A large military force. 3 A great number; multitude. [< L *legere* choose, levy an army]

**leg·is·late** (lej′is·lāt) *v.* **·lat·ed, ·lat·ing** *v.i.* 1 To make a law or laws. —*v.t.* 2 To bring about or effect by legislation.

**leg·is·la·tion** (lej′is·lā′shən) *n.* 1 The making of a law or laws. 2 The law or laws made by a legislative power. [< L *lex, legis* a law + *latus* carried]

**leg·is·la·tive** (lej′is·lā′tiv) *adj.* 1 Having the power to make or enact laws. 2 Of, pertaining to, or suitable to legislation. 3 Of or pertaining to a legislature. 4 Created or enforced by legislation. —*n.* LEGISLATURE.

**leg·is·la·ture** (lej′is·lā′chər) *n.* A body of persons empowered to make laws for a country or state.

**le·git·i·mate** (lə·jit′ē·mit) *adj.* 1 Having the sanction of law, lawful. 2 Born in wedlock. 3 Genuine; valid. 4 Logically correct; reasonable. 5 Based on or resulting from strict hereditary rights: a *legitimate* heir to the throne. 6 In the theater, designating or of plays or musicals produced live on a stage, as distinguished from motion pictures, etc. —*v.t.* (lə·jit′ə·māt) **·mat·ed, ·mat·ing** 1 To make legitimate. 2 To justify. [< L *legitimus* lawful] —**le·git′i·ma·cy, le·git′i·mate·ness** *n.* —**le·git′i·mate·ly** *adv.* —**Syn.** 1 legal, licit, rightful. 3 authentic, bona fide, real.

**lei·sure** (lē′zhər, lezh′ər) *n.* Time during which one is free from the demands of work or duty. —**at leisure** 1 Free from work or duties. 2 Not employed. —**at one's leisure** When it is convenient or easy. —*adj.* 1 Free or unoccupied: *leisure* time. 2 Having leisure: the *leisure* class. [< L *licere* be permitted]

**lem·on** (lem′ən) *n.* 1 A citrus fruit with a yellow rind and very acid pulp and juice. 2 The tree that produces this fruit. 3 A bright yellow. 4 *Slang* Something or someone disappointing or unpleasant. —*adj.* 1 Flavored with or containing lemon. 2 Bright yellow. [< Pers. *līmūn*]

**lem·on·ade** (lem′ən·ād′) *n.* A drink made of lemon juice, water, and sugar.

**lend** (lend) *v.* **lent, lend·ing** *v.t.* 1 To grant the temporary use of. 2 To grant the use of (money) at interest. 3 To impart; furnish. 4 To accommodate (oneself or itself): The statement *lends* itself to misinterpretation. —*v.i.* 5 To make a loan or loans. [< OE *lǣnan*] —**lend′er** *n.*

**lend-lease** (lend′lēs′) *n.* In World War II, the furnishing of goods and services to any country whose defense was deemed vital to the defense of the U.S.

**length** (lengkth) *n.* 1 Linear extension from end to end, usu. the greatest dimension of a surface or body. 2 The state or quality of being long. 3 Duration in time. 4 Distance in space. 5 A long expanse. 6 A piece or section of something: a *length* of rope. 7 The linear extent of something specified or understood, used as a unit of measure: an arm's *length*. —**at length** 1 Finally; at last. 2 In full. —**go to great lengths** (or **any length**) To do everything that is needed. [< OE *lengthu < lang* long]

**length·en** (lengk′thən) *v.t. & v.i.* To make or become longer. —**Syn.** elongate, expand, extend, stretch.

**le·ni·en·cy** (lē′nē·ən·sē, lēn′yən-) *n. pl.* **·cies** 1 The quality of being lenient; mercifulness. 2 A lenient act. Also **le′ni·ence**.

**le·ni·ent** (lē′nē·ənt, lēn′yənt) *adj.* Not exacting full retribution; merciful or mild. [< L *lenis* soft, mild] —**le′ni·ent·ly** *adv.*

**lens** (lenz) *n.* 1 A piece of glass or other transparent substance, having one surface curved and the other plane, or both curved, by which rays of light may be made to converge or to diverge. 2 Two or more lenses used in combination. 3 Any device for concentrating or dispersing radiation. 4 A biconvex transparent body, whose function is to focus light rays upon the retina. [< L *lens* a lentil; so called from the similarity in form] • See EYE.

**lent** (lent) *p.t. & p.p.* of LEND.

**Lent** (lent) *n. Eccl.* A period of forty days (excluding Sundays), observed in Christian churches from Ash Wednesday to Easter as a season of penitence and self-denial. [< OE *lengten* the spring]

**le·o·nine** (lē′ə·nīn) *adj.* Of, pertaining to, or like a lion. [< L *leo, leonis* a lion]

**leop·ard** (lep′ərd) *n.* 1 A ferocious mammal of the cat family of Asia and Africa, having a fawn, dark-spotted coat. 2 The jaguar. [< Gk. *leōn* a lion + *pardos* a panther]

**lep·er** (lep′ər) *n.* One afflicted with leprosy. [< Gk. *lepros* scaly]

**lep·ro·sy** (lep′rə·sē) *n.* A chronic, bacterial disease characterized by skin lesions, nerve paralysis, and physical mutilation. [< L *lepra* leper]

**lep·rous** (lep′rəs) *adj.* 1 Having leprosy. 2 Of or like leprosy. Also **lep′er·ous** (-ər·əs). —**lep′rous·ly** *adv.* —**lep′rous·ness** *n.*

**les·bi·an** (lez′bē·ən) *Often cap. n.* A homosexual woman. —*adj.* Of or pertaining to lesbians. [< *Lesbos*, the home of Sappho, reputed to have been homosexual]

**less·en** (les′ən) *v.t.* 1 To make less; decrease. 2 To make little of; disparage. —*v.i.* 3 To become less. —**less′en·er** *n.* —**less′en·ing** *adj., n.* —**Syn.** 1 abate, diminish, dwindle, shrink, wane. 2 belittle, depreciate.

**les·son** (les′ən) *n.* 1 A specific assignment or division in a course of instruction. 2 *pl.* A course of instruction: painting *lessons.* 3 Knowledge gained by experience. 4 A portion of the Bible read or appointed to be read in divine service. 5 A reprimand. [< L *lectio* a reading]

**let** (let) *v.* **let, let·ting** *v.t.* 1 To allow; permit. 2 To allow to go, come, or pass: They would not *let* us on board. 3 To cause; make: She *let* him know the truth. 4 To cause to escape or be released: to *let* blood. 5 To rent (a room, house, etc.). 6 To assign, as a contract, esp. after bidding. 7 As an auxiliary verb, *let* is used to express command, suggestion, or acquiescence: *Let* it pour!; *Let* Bonnie play the lead. —*v.i.* 8 To be rented or leased. —**let alone** 1 To refrain from disturbing, bothering, etc. 2 To say nothing of; not to mention: He can't float, *let alone* swim. —**let be** 1 To leave alone. 2 To stop; cease. —**let down** 1 To lower. 2 To reduce effort or concentration. 3 To disappoint. — **let off** 1 To discharge or reduce, as pressure. 2 To excuse from an engagement, duty, or penalty; dismiss. —**let on** *Informal* 1 To pretend. 2 To reveal; allow to be known. —**let out** 1 To release. 2 To reveal; divulge. 3 To make (a garment) larger by releasing a part. 4 To rent or lease. 5 *Informal* To dismiss or be dismissed, as a school. — **let up** To slacken; abate. —**let up on** *Informal* To cease applying pressure or harsh measures to. [< OE *lǣtan*] • See LEAVE.

**le·thal** (lē′thəl) *adj.* 1 Causing death; fatal. 2

Pertaining to death. [< L *lethum, letum* death] —le**′**thal·ly *adv.*

le·thar·gic (li·thär**′**jik) *adj.* Affected by lethargy. Also le·thar**′**gi·cal. —le·thar**′**gi·cal·ly *adv.*

leth·ar·gy (leth**′**ər·jē) *n. pl.* ·gies 1 A state of abnormal drowsiness or prolonged sleep. 2 Great indifference; apathy. [< Gk. *lēthē* oblivion] —Syn. 1 coma, stupor. 2 inactivity, sluggishness.

let·ter (let**′**ər) *n.* 1 A mark or character used to represent a speech sound and usu. part of an alphabet. 2 A written or printed communication, usu. sent by mail. 3 A document granting authority, right, privilege, or the like. 4 Literal or exact meaning. 5 *pl.* Literary knowledge or erudition; also, literature in general: the domain of *letters.* 6 An emblem given in schools to athletes, etc., usu. in the form of the initial letter of the school. —*v.t.* 1 To write with letters. 2 To mark with letters. [< L *littera* a letter of the alphabet, in pl., an epistle] —let**′**ter·er *n.*

let·tuce (let**′**is) *n.* 1 A garden plant of several varieties whose crisp, edible leaves are used for salad. 2 *Slang* Paper money. [< L *lac, lactis* milk; with ref. to its milky juice]

lev·ee (lev**′**ē) *n.* 1 An embankment built beside a river to prevent overflow. 2 A steep natural bank. —*v.t.* To furnish with a levee or levees. [< L *levare* to raise]

lev·er (lev**′**ər, lē**′**vər) *n.* 1 A device consisting of a rigid structure, often a straight bar, turning freely on a fixed point (the fulcrum). A force applied at one point of the rigid structure does work at another with a mechanical advantage equal to the ratio of the distances of the points from the fulcrum. 2 Any one of various tools used for prying, as a crowbar. 3 Any means of exerting effective power. —*v.t.* & *v.i.* To move with or use a lever. [< L *levare* to raise]

lev·er·age (lev**′**ər·ij, lē**′**vər·) *n.* 1 The action of a lever. 2 The mechanical advantage of a lever. 3 Increased power or advantage.

le·vi·a·than (lə·vī**′**ə·thən) *n.* 1 A large aquatic but unidentified animal mentioned in the Bible. 2 Anything colossal in size of its kind. [< Heb. *liwyāthān*]

lev·i·ty (lev**′**ə·tē) *n. pl.* ·ties 1 Lightness or humor; lack of gravity in mood, character, or behavior. 2 Fickleness. [< L *levis* light]

lev·y (lev**′**ē) *v.* lev·ied, lev·y·ing *v.t.* 1 To impose (a tax, fine, etc.). 2 To enlist or call up (troops, etc.) for military service. 3 To prepare for or wage (war). —*v.i.* 4 To make a levy. 5 *Law* To seize property in order to fulfill a judgment: usu. with *on.* —*n. pl.* lev·ies 1 The act of levying (a tax, troops, etc.). 2 Something levied. [< L *levare* to raise] —lev**′**i·er *n.*

lex·i·cog·ra·phy (lek**′**sə·kog**′**rə·fē) *n.* The act, business, or principles of writing or compiling a dictionary. [< Gk. *lexikon* lexicon + *graphein* write] —lex**′**i·cog**′**ra·pher *n.* —lex**′**i·co·graph**′**ic (-kō·graf**′**ik) or ·i·cal *adj.* —lex**′**i·co·graph**′**i·cal·ly *adv.*

lex·i·con (lek**′**sə·kon) *n.* 1 A word list or vocabulary pertaining to a specific subject, field, author, etc. 2 DICTIONARY. [< Gk. *lexikos* pertaining to words]

li·a·ble (lī**′**ə·bəl) *adj.* 1 Justly or legally responsible, as for payment. 2 Inclined to get or have; subject to: *liable* to headaches. 3 Likely; apt: I am *liable* to see them. 4 Undesirably likely: *liable* to lose his money. [< L *ligare* to bind]

li·ai·son (lē**′**ə·zon, lē·ā**′**zon; *Fr.* lē·ā·zôn**′**) *n.* 1 A bond or close relationship; union. 2 An illicit sexual relationship. 3 Any form of intercommunication, as between military units, etc. 4 In cookery, a thickening agent. 5 In speaking French, the carrying over of a final consonant to a succeeding word beginning with a vowel or silent *h.* —*adj.* Of, bringing about, or involved in a liaison. [< L *ligare* to bind]

li·ar (lī**′**ər) *n.* One who tells lies.

li·bel (lī**′**bəl) *n. Law* 1 Anything written, drawn, etc., esp. if published or publicly circulated, that tends to damage a person's reputation. 2 The act or crime of publishing or circulating such libel. —*v.t.* ·beled or ·belled, ·bel·ing or ·bel·ling 1 To publish or circulate a libel concerning. 2 To defame or disparage in any way. [< L *libellus,* dim. of *liber* book] —li**′**bel·er, li**′**bel·ler *n.* • See SLANDER.

lib·er·al (lib**′**ər·əl, lib**′**rəl) *adj.* 1 Generous in giving; bounteous. 2 Abundant; lavish: a *liberal* reward. 3 Of or based on the liberal arts: a *liberal* education. 4 Characterized by or favoring policies of reform and progress and generally opposing conservatism or reaction. 5 Not bigoted or prejudiced; broadminded. 6 Not restricted to the literal meaning: a *liberal* interpretation of a rule. —*n.* One favoring liberal policies or doctrines, as in politics, religion, etc. Also lib**′**er·al·ist. [< L *liber* free] —lib**′**er·al·is**′**tic *adj.* —lib**′**er·al·ly *adv.*

liberal arts The course of study that includes

literature, philosophy, languages, history, etc., as distinguished from purely scientific or technical subjects; the humanities.

**lib·er·al·i·ty** (lib′ə·ral′ə·tē) *n. pl.* **·ties** 1 The quality of being liberal. 2 Generosity. 3 Broad-mindedness. 4 A gift; donation.

**lib·er·ate** (lib′ə·rāt) *v.t.* **·at·ed, ·at·ing** 1 To set free, as from bondage, foreign occupation, etc. 2 *Informal* To free from oppression or from conventions considered oppressive. 3 To release from chemical combination. [< L *liber* free] —**lib′er·a′tor** *n.*

**lib·er·a·tion** (lib′ər·ā′shən) *n.* 1 The act of liberating, or the state of being liberated. 2 A political and social movement formed to promote the interests of a group regarded as the object of unfair discrimination or bias: women's *liberation*. —**lib′er·a′tion·ist** *n.*

**lib·er·ty** (lib′ər·tē) *n. pl.* **·ties** 1 The state of being free in action or thought from the domination of others or from restricting circumstances; freedom. 2 The possession and exercise of the right of self-government. 3 A particular permission, right, or privilege. 4 In the U.S. Navy, permission to be absent from one's ship or station, usu. for less than 48 hours. 5 *Often pl.* Unusual or undue freedom or familiarity. —**at liberty** 1 Free; unconfined. 2 Having permission to do something. 3 Not in use. 4 Unemployed. [< L *libertas* < *liber* free] —*Syn.* 1 emancipation, independence, liberation, self-determination.

**li·bid·i·nous** (li·bid′ə·nəs) *adj.* Lustful; lewd. [< L *libido* lust] —**li·bid′i·nous·ly** *adv.* —**li·bid′i·nous·ness** *n.*

**li·bi·do** (li·bē′dō, -bī′-) *n.* 1 *Psychoanal.* The instinctual craving or drive behind all human activities. 2 Sexual desire or instinct. [L, lust] —**li·bid′i·nal** (-bid′ə·nəl) *adj.*

**li·brar·i·an** (lī′brâr′ē·ən) *n.* 1 A person in charge of a library. 2 A person qualified by training for library service.

**li·brar·y** (lī′brer·ē, -brə·rē) *n. pl.* **·brar·ies** 1 A collection of books, pamphlets, computer programs, etc., esp. one arranged for easy location of desired material. 2 A building, room, etc., containing such a collection. [< L *liber* book]

**li·cense** (lī′səns) *n.* 1 A legal permit to do something. 2 A written or printed certificate of a legal permit. 3 Unrestrained liberty of action; disregard of propriety. 4 Allowable deviation from an established rule, form, or

standard: poetic *license*. —*v.t.* **·censed, ·cens·ing** To grant a license to or for; authorize. Also **li′cence**. —**li′cens·a·ble** *adj.* —**li′cens·er, li′cens·er** *n.*

**li·cen·tious** (lī·sen′shəs) *adj.* Morally or sexually unrestrained; wanton; lewd. [< L *licentia* freedom] —**li·cen′tious·ly** *adv.* —**li·cen′tious·ness** *n.*

**lid** (lid) *n.* 1 A movable cover for putting on top of a pan, box, or other receptacle. 2 An eyelid. 3 *Slang* A hat. [< OE *hlid*] —**lid′ded** *adj.*

**lie¹** (lī) *v.i.* **lay, lain, ly·ing** 1 To be or place oneself in a horizontal position, as on a bed: often with *down*. 2 To be on or rest against a usu. horizontal surface: The book is *lying* on the shelf. 3 To be or continue in a specified condition or position: to *lie* in ambush. 4 To be situated: Rome *lies* in a plain. 5 To extend in some direction: Our route *lies* northward. 6 To have source or cause; exist: usu. with *in:* His trouble *lies* in his carelessness. 7 To be buried. —**lie (or lay) down on the job** *Informal* To do less than one's best. —**lie in wait (for)** To wait in ambush (for). —**lie low** *Slang* To go into hiding or remain inactive so as to conceal one's motives, plans, etc. —**lie over** To wait for attention, etc., until a later time. —*n.* The position or arrangement in which a thing lies; manner of lying; lay. [OE *licgan*] • See LAY¹.

**lie²** (lī) *n.* 1 An untrue statement intended to deceive; falsehood. 2 Anything that deceives or creates a false impression. —**give the lie to** 1 To accuse of lying. 2 To expose as false. —*v.* **lied, ly·ing** *v.i.* 1 To make untrue statements knowingly, esp. with intent to deceive. 2 To give an erroneous or misleading impression: Figures do not *lie*. —*v.t.* 3 To obtain by lying: He *lied* his way out of trouble. [< OE *licgan*] —*Syn.* 1 fabrication, falsification, fib, untruth.

**lieu** (lōō) *n.* Place; stead: now only in the phrase in lieu of. [< L *locus*]

**lieu·ten·ant** (lōō·ten′ənt, *Brit.* lef·ten′ənt) *n.* 1 See GRADE. 2 A person who fills the place of a superior, as during his absence. [< F *lieu* place + *tenant,* pr.p. of *tenir* hold] —**lieu·ten′an·cy** *n.*

**lift** (lift) *v.t.* 1 To raise to a higher position or place; hoist. 2 To hold up or support in the air. 3 To raise to a higher degree or condition; exalt. 4 To make clearly audible; shout: to *lift* a cry. 5 To subject (the face) to plastic surgery, so as to restore an appearance of youth. 6 *Informal* To take surreptitiously; steal; also, to plagiarize. 7 To pay off, as a mortgage. —*v.i.* 8 To put forth effort in order to raise something: All together now, *lift!* 9 To yield to upward pressure; rise. 10 To rise or disperse; dissipate: The fog *lifted. n.* 1 The act or an instance of lifting or rising. 2 The distance through which something rises or is raised. 3 The amount lifted. 4 A machine or device for lifting. 5 A stimulation of the mind or feelings. 6 A rise in condition; promotion. 7 Elevated carriage or position: the *lift* of her chin. 8 Any assistance. 9 A ride in a vehicle offered to a pedestrian. 10 *Brit.* An elevator. 11 A slight rise in the ground. 12 In shoemaking, any layer of material forming the heel. 13 *Aeron.* The vertical component of the aerodynamic force on an aircraft. [< ON *lypta* raise in the air] —**lift′er** *n.*

**lift·off** (lift′ôf′, -of′) *n.* The vertical ascent of a rocket or spacecraft.

**lig·a·ment** (lig′ə·mənt) *n.* ·1 A band of tough tissue binding together bones, etc., or holding organs in place. 2 A bond or connecting tie. [< L *ligare* to bind] —**lig′a·men′tal, lig′a·men′ta·ry, lig′a·men′tous** *adj.*

**lig·a·ture** (lig′ə·chər) *n.* 1 The act of tying, binding, or constricting. 2 Something used for this, esp. a thread or wire used in surgery. 3 *Printing* Two or more connected letters, as *fi, ffi, æ.* 4 *Music* A slur or the notes joined by a slur. —*v.t.* ·tured, ·tur·ing LIGATE. [< L *ligare* to bind]

**light·ning** (lit′ning) *n.* 1 A sudden discharge of electricity between clouds or between a cloud and the earth. 2 The flash made by this. —*adj.* Fast; rapid: a *lightning* movement. [< ME *lighten* to flash]

**light·weight** (lit′wāt′) *n.* 1 A boxer or wrestler weighing between 127 and 135 pounds. 2 *Slang* An unimportant, incompetent, or stupid person. —*adj.* 1 Having little weight. 2 Of or pertaining to lightweights. 3 Trivial.

**light-year** (lit′yir′) *n.* The distance that light travels in one year, 5,878 trillion miles: used as a unit of astronomical distance.

**lig·nite** (lig′nit) *n.* A brownish coal, often retaining the original woody texture, and intermediate between peat and true coal. [<L *lignum* wood] —**lig·nit′ic** (-nit′ik) *adj.*

**li·lac** (li′lak, -lək, -lok) *n.* 1 An ornamental shrub having clusters of small, fragrant, usu. purplish flowers. 2 The flower. 3 A light purple color, like that of a lilac. —*adj.* Of a light purple color. [< Pers. *lilak* bluish]

**lil·y** (lil′ē) *n. pl.* **lil·ies** 1 Any of a large genus

of bulbous plants having showy, usu. trumpetlike flowers. 2 The flower of these plants. 3 Any of numerous plants resembling the true lilies: *waterlily.* 4 The heraldic fleur-de-lis. —*adj.* Like a white lily; pure and delicate. [< L *lilium*]

**lim·ber** (lim′bər) *adj.* 1 Easily bent; flexible. 2 Lithe and agile; supple. —*v.t.* & *v.i.* To make or become limber: often with *up.* [?] —**lim′ber·ly** *adv.* —**lim′ber·ness** *n.* —**Syn.** *adj.* 1 elastic, pliable, pliant. 2 lissom, nimble.

**lime** (lim) *n.* Calcium oxide in either its dry state (**quicklime**) or combined with water (**slaked lime**), used in mortar, cement, and as a conditioner for acid soil. —*v.t.* limed, **lim·ing** To treat or mix with lime. [< OE *lim*]

**lim·it** (lim′it) *n.* 1 A boundary enclosing a specified area. 2 *pl.* An area near or enclosed by a boundary: city *limits.* 3 The utmost point, degree, or extent beyond which something no longer functions, avails, etc.: to reach the *limit* of one's patience. 4 The maximum amount permitted: a *limit* of two cans per person. 5 *Math.* A number such that the difference between it and the final term of a sequence of numbers becomes arbitrarily small as the sequence is made arbitrarily long. —**off limits** Forbidden to military personnel except on official business. —**the limit** *Slang* One who or that which is considered intolerable, exasperating, etc. —*v.t.* To keep within a limit; restrict. [< L *limes, limites*] —**lim′it·a·ble, lim·i·ta·tive** (lim′ə·tā′tiv) *adj.* —**lim′it·er** *n.* —**Syn.** *v.* check, circumscribe, restrain, restrict.

**limp** (limp) *v.i.* 1 To walk with a halting or irregular gait. 2 To proceed in a defective or irregular manner: His logic *limps.* —*n.* The step of a lame person [?] —**limp′er** *n.*

**lim·pid** (lim′pid) *adj.* 1 Characterized by liquid clearness; transparent. 2 Clear and intelligible; lucid: a *limpid* style. [< L *limpidus* clear] —**lim·pid·i·ty** (lim·pid′ə·tē), **lim′pid·ness** *n.* —**lim′pid·ly** *adv.*

**line** (lin) *n.* 1 A string, rope, or cord, as used for hanging clothes, fishing, measuring, etc. 2 A pipe, wire, cable, etc., for conveying electricity, gas, oil, etc. 3 In a telephone or telegraph system: a A wire or cable conducting communication signals between two stations. b The system as a whole. c A connection in such a system. 4 Any slender mark or stroke, as drawn with a pen, pencil, tool, etc. 5 Something resembling this, as a band or strip. 6 A furrow or wrinkle on the face or hands. **7** In art, a mark or stroke used to represent a form or forms, as distinguished from shading or color. **8** *Music* One of the parallel horizontal strokes that form a musical staff. **9** A boundary or border: the *Mason-Dixon line.* **10** Contour; outline: the shore *line.* **11** *Geog.* **a** The equator. **b** Any circle, arc, or boundary used to plot the earth's surface: the date *line.* **12** *Math.* A set of points, straight or curved, conceived of as having length without breadth or thickness. **13** A row of persons or things. **14** A row of printed or written words bounded by the margins of a page or column. **15** A single row of words forming a verse of poetry. **16** A short letter; note. **17** *pl.* The words of a play or of an actor's part. **18** Alignment. **19** Agreement; conformity: Bring him into *line.* **20** A division or demarcation between contrasting qualities, classes, etc. **21** A course of action, thought, procedure, etc.: a *line* of argument. **22** A course of movement; route: the *line* of march. **23** General plan, concept, or construction: a novel on heroic *lines.* **24** One's business, vocation, or branch of activity. **25** Extent or scope of one's talent, ability, etc.: Comedy is not in his *line.* **26** Merchandise of a particular type or quality: the cheap *line.* **27** A series of persons or things connected chronologically: the *line* of senators from Ohio. **28** Lineage; ancestry. **29** A railroad track or roadbed. **30** Any system of public transportation. **31** *Mil.* **a** A series of fortifications presenting an extended front. **b** A trench or rampart. **c** An arrangement or disposition of troops: the front *line.* **d** Combat forces, as distinguished from the staff, special services, etc. **32** In football: **a** The linemen collectively. b LINE OF SCRIMMAGE. **33** *Informal* **a** A glib manner of speech. **b** The words spoken in this manner, intended to sway or influence. —**draw the (a) line** To establish a limit. —**get a line on** *Informal* To get information about. —**hold the line** **1** To stand firm. **2** To prevent others from advancing. —**in line for** Next in succession for. —**toe the line** To obey; behave. —*v.* **lined, lin·ing** *v.t.* **1** To mark with lines. **2** To place in a line; bring into alignment or conformity: often with *up.* **3** To form a line along: Police *lined* the side of the road. **4** To place something in a line along: to *line* a wall with archers. **5** In baseball, to bat (the ball) in a line drive. —*v.i.* **6** To form a line: usu. with *up.* —**line out** In baseball, to be

retired by batting a line drive to a fielder. —**line up** **1** To form a line. **2** To bring into alignment. **3** To organize for or against some activity, issue, etc. [< L *linea* linen thread]

**lin·e·age** (lin′ē·ij) *n.* **1** Direct descent from a progenitor. **2** Ancestry; family. [< L *linea* line]

**lin·e·al** (lin′ē·əl) *adj.* **1** Of or being in a direct line of descent. **2** Based upon or derived from ancestors; hereditary. **3** Made of lines; linear. —**lin′e·al·ly** *adv.*

**lin·en** (lin′in) *n.* **1** A thread or fabric spun or woven from the fibers of flax. **2** Articles made of linen but now often of cotton: bed *linen,* table *linen.* —*adj.* Made of linen. [< OE *lin* flax]

**lin·ger** (ling′gər) *v.i.* **1** To stay on as if reluctant to leave. **2** To move slowly; saunter: to *linger* on the way. **3** To delay or be slow: often with *over:* to *linger* over a meal. **4** To continue in life. —*v.t.* **5** To pass (time) slowly or idly: with *away* or *out.* [< OE *lengen* to delay] —**lin′ger·er** *n.* —**Syn.** **1** dawdle, delay. **2** hang back, lag, loiter.

**lin·guist** (lin′gwist) *n.* **1** One who knows many languages. **2** An authority in linguistics. [< L *lingua* the tongue + -IST]

**lin·guis·tic** (ling·gwis′tik) *adj.* Of or pertaining to language or to linguistics. **Also** **lin·guis′ti·cal.** —**lin·guis′ti·cal·y** *adv.*

**link** (lingk) *n.* **1** One of the loops or rings of which a chain is made. **2** Something which connects separate things; a tie: a *link* with the past. **3** A single part or element in a whole: the weak *link* in his story. **4** A section of a chain of sausages. **5** A measure equal to 7.92 inches, used in surveying. **6** *Chem.* BOND. —*v.t.* & *v.i.* To connect by or as by links; unite. [< Scand.] —**Syn.** *v.* attach, combine, fuse, join.

**lint** (lint) *n.* **1** The soft down of raveled or scraped linen. **2** Fuzzy bits of thread, cloth, etc. [< L *linum* flax] —**lint′y** *adj.* (·i·er, ·i·est)

**lin·tel** (lin′təl) *n.* horizontal top piece, as over a doorway or window opening. [< L *limes, limites* limit]

**li·on** (lī′ən) *n.* **1** A large, tawny carnivore of the cat family, native to Africa and Asia, the adult male having a long mane. **2** An animal resembling the lion, as the cougar. **3** A person of great courage, strength, etc. **4** A prominent or notable person. [< Gk. *leōn*]

**li·on·ize** (lī′ən·īz) *v.t.* **·ized, ·iz·ing** To treat or regard as a celebrity. —**li′on·i·za′tion** *n.*

**lip·stick** (lip′stik′) *n.* A small, colored cosmetic stick of creamy texture, used to tint lips.

**liq·ue·fac·tion** (lik′wə·fak′shən) *n.* The process of liquefying or the state of being liquefied.

**liq·ue·fy** (lik′wə·fī) *v.t. & v.i.* **·fied**, **·fy·ing** To convert into or become liquid. [< L *liquere* be liquid + *facere* make]

**li·queur** (li·kûr′) *n.* A strong alcoholic beverage, usu. sweet and having various flavorings; a cordial. [< OF *licur* liquor]

**liq·uid** (lik′wid) *adj.* 1 Flowing or capable of flowing. 2 *Physics* Composed of molecules having free movement among themselves, but without a tendency to expand indefinitely like a gas. 3 Limpid; clear. 4 Smooth and flowing, as movements or sounds. 5 *Phonet.* Vowellike in production, as the consonants (l) and (r). 6 Easily converted into cash: *liquid* assets. —*n.* 1 A liquid substance. 2 *Phonet.* The consonants (l) and (r). [< L *liquere* be liquid] —**li·quid·i·ty** (li·kwid′ə·tē), **liq′uid·ness** *n.* —**liq′uid·ly** *adv.*

**liq·ui·date** (lik′wə·dāt) *v.* **·dat·ed**, **·dat·ing** *v.t.* 1 To determine and settle the liabilities of (an estate, firm, etc.) and apportion the assets. 2 To determine and settle the amount of, as indebtedness or damages. 3 To pay, as a debt. 4 To convert into cash. 5 To do away with, esp. to murder. —*v.t.* 6 To settle one's debts. [< Med. L *liquidare* make liquid or clear] —**liq′ui·da′tor** *n.*

**liq·ui·da·tion** (lik′wə·dā′shən) *n.* The act of liquidating or the state of being liquidated. —**go into liquidation** To cease from transacting business and gather in assets, settle debts, and divide surpluses, if any.

**liq·uor** (lik′ər) *n.* 1 Any alcoholic drink, esp. one that is distilled. 2 A liquid, as broth, milk, etc. —*v.t.* 1 *Slang* To ply with alcoholic liquor: often with *up.* —*v.i.* 2 *Slang* To drink alcoholic liquor, esp. in quantity: usu. with *up.* [< L *liquor*]

**lisp** (lisp) *n.* 1 A speech defect or affectation in which the sibilants (s) and (z) are pronounced like (th) in *thank* and (th) and *this.* 2 The act or habit of speaking with a lisp. 3 The sound of a lisp. —*v.t. & v.i.* 1 To pronounce or speak with a lisp. 2 To speak imperfectly or in a childlike manner. [< OE *wlispian*] —**lisp′er** *n.*

**list** (list) *n.* A series of words, numbers, names, etc.; a roll or catalogue. —*v.t.* To place on or in a list or catalogue, esp. in alphabetical or numerical order. [< OF *liste*]

**lis·ten** (lis′ən) *v.i.* 1 To make an effort to hear;

give ear. 2 To pay attention, as to warning or advice. —**listen in** 1 To overhear others talking, esp. on a telephone. 2 To hear a radio program. —*n.* The act of listening. [< OE *hlysnan*] —**lis′ten·er** *n.* —**Syn.** *v.* 1 attend, hearken. 2 heed.

**list·less** (list′lis) *adj.* Inattentive or indifferent, as from lack of energy or spirit; languid. [< OE *lust* desire + -LESS] —**list′less·ly** *adv.* —**list′less·ness** *n.*

**lit·a·ny** (lit′ə·nē) *n. pl.* **·nies** 1 A form of prayer, consisting of a series of supplications said by the clergy, to which the choir or people repeat the same response. 2 Any repetitive listing or dreary account. [< Gk. *litaneuein* pray]

**li·ter** (lē′tər) *n.* The basic metric unit of volume or capacity, equal to the volume of one kilogram of water at 4°C and 760 mm. atmospheric pressure; $10^{-3}$ (0.001) cubic meter or about 1.06 liquid quarts. [< Gk. *litra* pound]

**lit·er·al** (lit′ərəl) *adj.* 1 Strictly based on the exact, standard meanings of the words or expressions: a *literal* interpretation of the Bible. 2 Following the exact words or construction of the original: a *literal* translation. 3 Matter-of-fact; unimaginative: a *literal* person. 4 Exact as to fact or detail; not exaggerated. [< L *littera* letter] —**lit′er·al′i·ty**, **lit′er·al·ness** *n.*

**lit·er·ar·y** (lit′ə·rer′ē) *adj.* 1 Of, pertaining to, or used in literature. 2 Versed in or devoted to literature. 3 Engaged or occupied in the field of literature: a *literary* man. —**lit′er·ar′i·ly** *adv.* —**lit′er·ar′i·ness** *n.*

**lit·er·a·ture** (lit′ər·ə·chŏŏr, lit′rə·chər) *n.* 1 Written or printed works collectively, esp. those works characterized by creativeness and imagination, as poetry, fiction, essays, etc. 2 The writings that pertain to a particular epoch, country, language, or branch of learning: French *literature.* 3 The act or occupation of producing literary works. 4 *Music* The total number of compositions for a particular instrument or ensemble. 5 Any printed matter: campaign *literature.* [< L *littera* letter]

**lith·o·graph** (lith′ə·graf, -gräf) *v.t.* To produce or reproduce by lithography. —*n.* A lithographic print. [LITHO- + -GRAPH] —**li·thog·ra·pher** (li·thog′rə·fər) *n.* —**lith′o·graph′ic** or **·i·cal** *adj.* —**lith′o·graph′i·cal·ly** *adv.*

**li·thog·ra·phy** (li·thog′rə·fē) *n.* The art of producing printed matter from a stone or metal plate on which the design or matter to be printed consists of a material that accepts ink, the other parts being ink-repellent.

**lit·i·gant** (lit′ə-gənt) *adj.* Engaged in litigation. —*n.* A party to a lawsuit.

**lit·i·gate** (lit′ə-gāt) *v.* **·gat·ed, ·gat·ing** *v.t.* 1 To bring before a court of law. —*v.i.* 2 To carry on a lawsuit. [< L < *lis, litis* lawsuit + *agere* do, act] —**lit′i·ga·ble** (-gə-bəl) *adj.* —**lit′i·ga′tor** *n.*

**lit·ter** (lit′ər) *n.* 1 The offspring borne at one time by a cat, dog, or other multiparous animal. 2 A stretcher used for conveying sick or wounded. 3 A couch carried on shafts protruding at each end, and used to carry one person. 4 Straw, hay, or other similar material, used as bedding for horses, cattle, etc. 5 Things scattered about in disorder. 6 Discarded trash scattered about, as in a public park or street. —*v.t.* 1 To bring forth young: said of animals. 2 To furnish, as cattle, with litter. 3 To cover or strew with or as with litter. 4 To throw or spread about carelessly. —*v.i.* 5 To give birth to a litter of young. 6 To strew trash, garbage, etc., about. [< L *lectus* bed] —**lit′ter·y** *adj.*

**lit·ter·bug** (lit′ər·bug′) *n. Informal* A person who litters sidewalks, parks, and other public places.

**li·tur·gi·cal** (li·tûr′ji·kəl) *adj.* Of, pertaining to, or used in liturgies. Also **li·tur′gic.** — **li·tur′gi·cal·ly** *adv.*

**lit·ur·gy** (lit′ər·jē) *n. pl.* **·gies** 1 A collection of prescribed forms for public worship. 2 The Eucharistic rite. [< Gk. *leitourgia* public duty]

**live** (liv) *v.* **lived, liv·ing** *v.i.* 1 To be alive; have life. 2 To continue in life. 3 To endure or persist; last: This day will *live* in infamy. 4 To maintain life; subsist: to *live* on a pittance. 5 To depend for food; feed: with *on* or *upon:* to *live* on carrion. 6 To dwell; abide. 7 To conduct or pass one's life in a specified manner: to *live* frugally. 8 To enjoy a varied and active life. —*v.t.* 9 To pass: to *live* the life of a saint. 10 To practice in one's life: to *live* a lie. —**live down** To live in such a manner as to expiate or erase the memory of (a crime, error, shame, etc.). —**live high** To live luxuriously. —**live in** To reside, as a domestic, at one's place of employment. —**live through** To have experience of and survive. —**live up to** To fulfill the hopes, terms, or character of. [< OE *li-fian* live]

**-lived** *combining form* Having a (specified kind

of) life or life span or (a given number of) lives: *long-lived, nine-lived.* [< LIFE] • Having been formed from *life, -lived* is properly pronounced (livd). The pronunciation (livd) is based on the mistaken assumption that the verb *live* is the source of *-lived.*

**live·li·hood** (līv′lē·hŏŏd) *n.* Means of maintaining life: subsistence. [< ME < OE *līf* life + *lād* way]

**liz·ard** (liz′ərd) *n.* 1 Any of a large group of reptiles having an elongate, scaly body, a long tail, and usu. four legs, as the chameleon, iguana, gecko, etc. 2 Leather made from the skin of a lizard. [< L *lacerta*]

**lla·ma** (lä′mə) *n.* A south American wooly-haired, humpless animal related to the camel, used in the Andes as a beast of burden and as a source of wool and milk. [< Quechua]

**load** (lōd) *n.* 1 That which is laid upon or put into anything for conveyance. 2 A quantity carried or conveyed at one time: often used in combination: a *busload.* 3 The weight supported by a structure. 4 Something carried or borne with difficulty, esp. a grievous mental burden. 5 A charge for a firearm. 6 An amount of work expected from an employee. 7 *pl. Informal* A great amount; abundance: *loads* of time. 8 *Mech.* The resistance met by a motor or engine in driving its machinery. 9 *Electr.* **a** The power delivered by a generator or circuit. **b** The device to which the power is delivered. —**get a load of** *Slang* To listen to or look at. —*v.t.* 1 To put something on or into to be carried. 2 To place in or on a carrier: to *load* wood. 3 To supply with something excessively or in abundance: to *load* one with honors. 4 To weigh down or oppress; burden. 5 To charge (a firearm) with ammunition. 6 To put film into (a camera). 7 To make heavy on one side or end: to *load* dice. 8 To add a substance to for the purpose of falsifying; adulterate. —*v.i.* 9 To take on or put on a load or cargo. 10 To charge a firearm with ammunition. [< OE *lād* way, journey, act of carrying goods] —**load′er** *n.*

**loaf** (lōf) *n. pl.* **loaves** (lōvz) 1 A shaped mass of bread. 2 Any mass of food having a somewhat rectangular shape. [< OE *hlāf* bread]

**loaf·er** (lō′fər) *n.* 1 One who loafs; an idler. 2 A casual shoe resembling a moccasin. [? < G *Landläufer* an idler]

**loam** (lōm) *n.* A rich soil of sand and clay, containing organic matter. —*v.t.* To cover or

293

fill with loam. [< OE *lām*] —loam′y (·i·er,
·i·est) *adj.*

loan (lōn) *n.* 1 Something lent, esp. a sum of
money lent at interest. 2 The act of lending.
—*v.t.* & *v.i.* To lend. [< OE *lān*]

loathe (lōṯh) *v.t.* loathed, loath·ing To feel
great hatred or disgust for; abhor; detest.
[< OE *lāthian* be hateful] —loath′er *n.*

lob·by (lob′ē) *n. pl.* ·bies 1 A hall, vestibule,
or foyer on the main floor of a theater, hotel,
etc. 2 The persons or groups of persons
who lobby in the interest of a special group,
industry, etc. —*v.* ·bied, ·by·ing *v.i.* 1 To attempt to influence a legislator or legisla-
tors. —*v.t.* 2 To attempt to obtain passage
or defeat of (a bill, etc.) by such means.
[Med. L *lobia* porch] —lob′by·er *n.* —Syn.
1 entrance hall, lounge, waiting room.

lobe (lob) *n.* 1 A rounded projecting part, as
of a body organ, leaf, etc. 2 The soft lower
extension of the external ear. [< Gk. *lobos*]
—lo′bar, lobed *adj.*

lob·ster (lob′stər) *n.* 1 Any of numerous edible marine crustaceans having five pairs of
legs, the first pair forming claws, and compound eyes. 2 One of various similar crustaceans. 3 The flesh of these crustaceans,
used as food. [< L *locusta* lobster, locust]

lo·cal (lō′kəl) *adj.* 1 Of, pertaining to, or characteristic of a particular place or a limited
portion of space. 2 Pertaining to place in
general. 3 Not broad or universal: *local* customs. 4 Relating to or affecting a specific
part of the body. 5 Making every stop on its
run: a *local* train. —*n.* 1 A local subway,
bus, or train. 2 A local branch of a trade
union or fraternal organization. 3 An item
of local interest in a newspaper. [< L *locus*
place] —lo′cal·ly *adv.*

lo·cal·i·ty (lō·kal′ə·tē) *n. pl.* ·ties 1 A definite
place, location, or position. 2 The condition
of having a location.

lo·cal·ize (lō′kəl·īz) *v.t.* ·ized, ·iz·ing 1 To limit
or assign to a specific area or locality. 2 To
determine the place of origin of. —lo′cal·
i·za′tion *n.*

lo·cate (lō′kāt, lō·kāt′) *v.* ·cat·ed, ·cat·ing *v.t.*
1 To discover the position or source of; find.
2 To assign place or locality to: to *locate* a
scene in a valley. 3 To establish in a place;
situate: My office is *located* in Portland. 4 To
designate the site of, as a mining claim.
—*v.i.* 5 *Informal* To establish oneself or take
up residence; settle. [< L *locare* < *locus*
place] —lo′ca·tor *n.*

lock (lok) *n.* 1 A device to secure a door,
drawer, etc., operated by a special key or
combination. 2 Any of various mechanical
devices used to fix something in place, prevent something from working, etc. 3 A
spring mechanism for exploding the charge
of a firearm. 4 A section of a canal, etc., enclosed by gates at either end, within which
the water level may be varied to raise or
lower vessels from one level to another. 5
An interlocking or fastening together. 6 Any
of various holds in wrestling. —lock, stock,
and barrel *Informal* Totally; completely. —
*v.t.* 1 To secure or fasten by means of a
lock. 2 To shut, confine, or exclude by
means of a lock: with *in, up,* or *out.* 3 To join
or unite; link: to *lock* arms. 4 To embrace
closely. 5 To make immovable, as by jam-
ming or by a lock. 6 To move (a ship) by
means of locks. —*v.i.* 7 To become locked
or fastened. 8 To become joined or linked.
—lock out To subject (workers) to a lock-
out. —lock up 1 To fasten the doors of by
locking. 2 To put in jail. 3 To make sure that
(something specified) will turn out the way
one wants it to: enough backing to *lock up*
the nomination. [< OE *loc* fastening, enclo-
sure] —Syn. *n.* 1 bolt, catch, fastening,
latch.

lock·er (lok′ər) *n.* 1 One who or that which
locks. 2 A closet, cabinet, chest, etc., usu.
having a lock, and used for personal belongings. 3 A refrigerated cabinet for frozen
foods.

lock·jaw (lok′jô′) *n.* 1 TETANUS. 2 Abnormal
muscular contraction causing the jaws to
clench.

lock·out (lok′out′) *n.* The closing of a place
of business to force workers to accept the
employer's terms.

lo·co·mo·tion (lō′kə·mō′shən) *n.* The act or
power of moving from one place to another.
[< L *loco* from a place + *motio* movement]

lo·co·mo·tive (lō′kə·mō′tiv) *adj.* 1 Pertaining
to locomotion. 2 Moving or able to move
from one place to another. 3 Self-propelling:
said of machines. —*n.* A self-propelling
electric, diesel, or steam engine on wheels,
esp. one for use on a railway.

lode (lōd) *n.* 1 A mineral-bearing vein filling a
fissure in rock. 2 A deposit of ore between
definite boundaries of associated rock. [<
OE *lād* way, journey]

lodge (loj) *v.* lodged, lodg·ing *v.t.* 1 To furnish
with temporary living quarters; house. 2 To
rent a room or rooms to. 3 To serve as a

shelter or dwelling for. **4** To deposit for safe-keeping or storage. **5** To place or implant, as by throwing, thrusting, etc. **6** To place (a complaint, information, etc.) before proper authority. **7** To confer or invest (power, etc.). —*v.i.* **8** To take temporary shelter or quarters. **9** To live in a rented room or rooms. **10** To become fixed in some place or position. —*n.* **1** A small house, hut, or cabin. **2** A small dwelling on an estate. **3** The lair of a wild animal, esp. of beavers. **4** A local chapter of a secret or fraternal society, or its meeting place. **5** A small hut or tepee of American Indians; also, its inhabitants. [< Med. L *lobia, laubia* porch, gallery]

**loft** (lôft, loft) *n.* **1** A low space or attic directly under a roof. **2** A large, unpartitioned storeroom on an upper floor of a warehouse, etc. **3** An elevated gallery, as in a church. **4** HAYLOFT. **5** A backward slope on the face of a golf club; also, a stroke with such a club which lifts the ball high in the air. **6** A place for keeping pigeons. —*v.t.* **1** To keep or house in a loft. **2** In sports, to strike (a ball) so that it rises or travels in a high arc. —*v.i.* **3** To strike a ball so that it rises in a high arc. [< ON, upper room, air, sky]

**loft·y** (lôf′tē, lof′-) *adj.* **loft·i·er, loft·i·est 1** Very high. **2** Exalted or elevated in character, language, etc. **3** Haughty; arrogant. —**loft′i·ly** *adv.* —**loft′i·ness** *n.* —**Syn.** 1 tall. 2 grand, majestic, sublime. 3 disdainful.

**log** (lôg, log) *n.* **1** A bulky piece or length of timber cut down and cleared of branches. **2** *Naut.* **a** A device for showing the speed of a vessel. **b** A record of the daily speed and progress of a vessel. **3** Any of various records of performance, progress, etc. —*v.* **logged, log·ging** *v.t.* **1** To cut (trees) into logs. **2** To cut down the trees of (a region) for timber. **3** *Naut. & Aeron.* **a** To enter in a logbook. **b** To travel (a specified distance) as shown by a log. **c** To travel at (a specified speed). —*v.i.* **4** To cut down trees and transport logs for sawing into lumber. [? < Scand.]

**log·ic** (loj′ik) *n.* **1** The science which investigates the principles of valid reasoning and correct inference. **2** The basic principles of reasoning applicable to any field of knowledge: the *logic* of science. **3** Reasoning or argumentation in general, esp. when relevant or effective: The *logic* of his answer was unassailable. **4** The connection or interrelation of facts, events, etc., esp. when

viewed as inevitable. [< Gk. *logos* word, speech, thought]

**log·i·cal** (loj′i·kəl) *adj.* **1** Relating to or of the nature of logic. **2** Conforming to the laws of logic. **3** Capable of or characterized by clear reasoning. —**log′i·cal′i·ty** (-kal′ə·tē), **log′i·cal·ness** *n.* —**log′i·cal·ly** *adv.*

**loin** (loin) *n.* **1** The part of the body of a human being or quadruped between the lower ribs and hip bone. **2** *pl.* Loosely, the hips, thighs, and the genital region. **3** The forepart of the hindquarters of beef, lamb, veal, etc., with the flank removed. —**gird up one's loins** To prepare for action. [< L *lumbus*] • See HORSE.

**loi·ter** (loi′tər) *v.i.* **1** To pass time idly or aimlessly; loaf. **2** To linger on the way; dawdle. —*v.t.* **3** To pass (time) idly: with *away.* [ME *loyteren*] —**loi′ter·er** *n.* —**loi′ter·ing·ly** *adv.* —**Syn.** 1 laze. 2 delay, lag, procrastinate, tarry.

**loll** (lol) *v.i.* **1** To lie or lean in a relaxed or languid manner. **2** To hang loosely; droop. —*v.t.* **3** To permit to droop or hang, as the tongue. —*n.* The act of lolling. [ME *lollen*] —**loll′er** *n.*

**lon·gev·i·ty** (lon·jev′ə·tē) *n.* **1** Great age or length of life. **2** The tendency to live long. [< L *longus* long + *aevum* age]

**lon·gi·tude** (lon′ji·t⁻ood) *n.* **1** *Geog.* Distance east or west on the earth measured by the angle which the meridian through a specific place makes as it intersects with some standard meridian, as that of Greenwich, England. **2** *Astron.* The angular distance from the vernal equinox to the great circle passing through a point on the celestial sphere. [< L *longus* long]

**look** (look) *v.i.* **1** To direct the eyes toward something in order to see. **2** To direct one's attention or consideration. **3** To make examination or inquiry: to *look* through a desk. **4** To appear to be; seem. **5** To face in a specified direction; front. **6** To expect: with an infinitive. —*v.t.* **7** To direct the eyes upon: He *looked* her up and down. **8** To express by looks: to *look* one's hatred. **9** To give the appearance of being (a specified age). **10** To influence by looks: to *look* someone into silence. —**look after** To take care of. —**look down on** To regard condescendingly or contemptuously. —**look for 1** To search for. **2** To expect. —**look forward to** To anticipate pleasurably. —**look in** (or **in on**) To make a short visit to. —**look into** To examine; make inquiry. —**look like 1** To resemble. 2 To indicate the probability of: It *looks* like rain. —**look on** 1 To be a spectator. 2 To consider; regard. —**look oneself** To seem to be in good health, good spirits, etc. —**look out** To be on the watch; take care. —**look over** To examine; scrutinize. —**look to** 1 To attend to. 2 To turn to, as for help, advice, etc. —**look up** 1 To search for and find, as in a file, dictionary, etc. 2 *Informal* To discover the whereabouts of. 3 *Informal* To improve; become better. —**look up to** To have respect for. —*n.* 1 The act of looking or seeing. 2 Aspect or expression: a fiendish *look*. 3 *Usu. pl. Informal* Personal appearance, esp. when attractive. 4 Appearance in general: I do not like the *look* of the thing. [< OE *lōcian*] —**Syn.** *v.* 1 gaze, glance, regard. 3 search. 6 anticipate.

**loom**[1] (lōom) *v.i.* 1 To appear or come into view indistinctly, esp. so as to seem large or ominous. 2 To appear to the mind as threatening or portentous. [?]

**loom**[2] (lōom) *n.* A machine in which yarn or thread is woven into a fabric. [< OE *gelōma* tool]

**loop** (lōop) *n.* 1 The more or less oval-shaped bend that is created when a string, rope, etc., is crossed over on itself. 2 Something shaped like a loop, as certain ornamental fastenings. 3 A complete, vertical, circular turn made by an airplane in flight. 4 *Electr.* A closed path in an electric circuit. 5 Any of several types of intrauterine contraceptive devices. —**loop the loop** To make a vertical, circular turn, as an airplane in flight. —*v.t.* 1 To form a loop or loops in or of. 2 To fasten, connect, or encircle by means of a loop or loops. 3 To fly (an aircraft) in a loop or loops. —*v.i.* 4 To make a loop or loops. 5 To move by forming loops, as a measuring worm. [ME *loupe*]

**loop·hole** (lōop′hōl′) *n.* 1 A narrow opening, as in a wall, through which small arms are fired. 2 A means of escaping or evading something disagreeable.

**loose** (lōos) *adj.* **loos·er, loos·est** 1 Not fastened or confined; unattached. 2 Not tightly stretched; slack. 3 Not tight, as a garment. 4 Not firmly fastened or secured: a *loose* bolt. 5 Not bundled, tied, or fastened together. 6 Not dense or compact: *loose* soil. 7 Not in individual packages or containers: *loose* sugar. 8 a Not constricted: a *loose* cough. b Moving freely or too often: *loose* bowels. 9 Free from confinement, restraint, etc. 10 Not controlled or restrained: a *loose*

tongue. 11 Not chaste; lewd. 12 Not precise or exact: a *loose* translation. 13 Free and relaxed: a *loose* walk. —**on the loose** 1 Unconfined; at large. 2 *Informal* Free and unrestrained in behavior. —*adv.* 1 In a loose manner. 2 So as to become loose: The dog broke *loose*. —*v.* **loosed, loos·ing** *v.t.* 1 To set free, as from bondage, penalty, etc. 2 To untie or undo. 3 To loosen; slacken. 4 To make less strict or rigid. 5 To let fly; shoot, as arrows. —*v.i.* 6 To become loose. 7 To loose something. [< ON *lauss*] —**loose′ly** *adv.* —**loose′ness** *n.*

**loos·en** (lōo′sən) *v.t.* 1 To untie or undo, as bonds. 2 To set free; release. 3 To make less tight, firm, or compact. 4 To relax the strictness of, as discipline. —*v.i.* 5 To become loose or looser. —**loos′en·er** *n.*

**loot** (lōot) *v.t. & v.i.* To plunder. —*n.* 1 Goods taken as spoils by an enemy during war. 2 Anything unlawfully taken. 3 *Slang* Money. [< Hind. *lūt*] —**loot′er** *n.*

**lop**[1] (lop) *v.t.* **lopped, lop·ping** 1 To trim the branches, twigs, etc., from, as a tree. 2 To cut off, as branches, twigs, etc. —*n.* Something lopped off. [?] —**lop′per** *n.*

**lop**[2] (lop) *v.* **lopped, lop·ping** *v.i.* 1 To droop or hang down. 2 To move about in an awkward manner. —*v.t.* 3 To permit to droop or hang down. —*adj.* Drooping. [?]

**lop-eared** (lop′ird′) *adj.* Having drooping ears.

**lop-sid·ed** (lop′sī′did) *adj.* 1 Heavy or hanging down on one side. 2 Lacking in symmetry or balance. —**lop′sid′ed·ly** *adv.* —**lop′-sid′ed·ness** *n.*

**lo·qua·cious** (lō·kwā′shəs) *adj.* Given to continual talking. [< L *loqui* to talk] —**lo·qua′cious·ly** *adv.* —**lo·qua′cious·ness, lo·quac·i·ty** (lō·kwas′ə·tē) *n.* —**Syn.** chattering, garrulous, talkative, verbose, vociferous.

**lose** (lōoz) *v.* **lost, los·ing** *v.t.* 1 To be unable to find; mislay. 2 To fail to keep, control, or maintain: to *lose* one's footing. 3 To suffer or undergo the loss of, as by accident, death, removal, etc. 4 To fail to gain or win. 5 To fail to utilize or take advantage of; miss: to *lose* a chance. 6 To fail to see or hear: I *lost* not a word of the speech. 7 To fail to keep in sight, memory, etc. 8 To cease to have: to *lose* one's sense of duty. 9 To squander; waste, as time. 10 To wander from so as to be unable to find: to *lose* the path. 11 To outdistance or elude. 12 To cause the loss of: His rashness *lost* him his opportunity. 13 To bring to destruction or ruin: All hands were *lost.* —*v.i.* 14 To suffer loss. 15 To be defeated. —**lose oneself** 1 To lose one's way. 2 To disappear or hide. 3 To become engrossed. —**lose out** *Informal* To fail or be defeated. [< OE *lōsian* be lost] —**los′er** *n.*

**loss** (lôs, los) *n.* 1 The act of losing or the state of being lost. 2 One who or that which is lost. 3 The harm, privation, etc., caused by losing someone or something. 4 *pl.* Soldiers killed, wounded, or captured in battle. 5 In insurance, the amount owed to the insured by the insurer because of death, property damage, theft, etc. 6 *Physics* Any part of the energy of a system that cannot be made to do useful work. —**at a loss** 1 At so low a price as to result in a loss. 2 In confusion or doubt. [< OE *los*]

**lost** (lôst, lost) *adj.* 1 Not to be found or recovered; missing. 2 No longer seen, enjoyed, etc.; *lost* friends. 3 Not won or gained: a *lost* way. 4 Having wandered from the way. 5 Helpless. 6 Ruined physically or morally. 7 Wasted; squandered: a *lost* opportunity. 8 Abstracted; rapt: *lost* in thought. 9 Bewildered; perplexed. 10 No longer known or used: a *lost* art. —**be lost to** 1 To belong to no longer. 2 To be insensible or hardened to. 3 To be unavailable to. —**be lost upon** (or **on**) To have no effect upon (a person). —**Syn.** 1 mislaid, misplaced. 4 astray. 9 confused, dazed.

**lot** (lot) *n.* 1 Anything, as dice or a piece of paper, used in determining something by chance. 2 The act or the result of deciding something in this manner. 3 The share that comes to one as the result of drawing lots. 4 The part in life that comes to one without his planning; chance; fate. 5 A number of persons or things considered as a group. 6 A parcel or quantity of land. 7 *Informal* A certain kind of person: he is a bad *lot.* 8 *Often pl. Informal* A great quantity or amount: a *lot* of money, *lots* of trouble. 9 A motion-picture studio and the adjacent area. —**the lot** The entire amount or quantity. —**throw** (or **cast**) **in one's lot with** To share the fortunes of. —*adv.* Very much: a *lot* worse. —*v.* **lot·ted, lot·ting** *v.t.* 1 To divide, as land, into lots. 2 To apportion by lots; allot. —*v.i.* 3 To cast lots. [< OE *hlot*] • **lots, lots of** These words, meaning "a great deal" or "many," are common and unobjectionable in informal speech and writing: *She is lots cleverer than I; They make lots of*

*complaints.* They should be avoided, however, in formal contexts.

**lo·tion** (lō′shən) *n.* A cosmetic or medicinal liquid preparation for external use. [< L *lotio* washing]

**lot·ter·y** (lot′ər·ē) *n. pl.* **·ter·ies** 1 A method of awarding prizes involving numbered chances, the winning numbers being selected by drawing lots. 2 Any chance disposition of any matter. [< Ital. *lotto* lottery, lot]

**loud** (loud) *adj.* 1 Having great volume or intensity of sound. 2 Making a great sound or noise: a *loud* engine. 3 Pressing or urgent; clamorous: a *loud* demand. 4 *Informal* Very showy: a *loud* tie. 5 *Informal* Offensively noisy and talkative: a *loud* boor. —*adv.* With loudness; loudly. [< OE *hlūd*] —**loud′ly** *adv.* —**loud′ness** *n.*

**loud·speak·er** (loud′spē′kər) *n.* A device for converting electrical energy to sound.

**lounge** (lounj) *v.* **lounged, loung·ing** *v.i.* 1 To lie, lean, move, etc., in an idle or lazy manner. 2 To pass time indolently. —*v.t.* 3 To spend or pass indolently, as time. —*n.* 1 The act of lounging. 2 A room in a hotel, club, etc., for lounging. 3 A couch or sofa. —**loung′er** *n.* [?]

**louse** (lous) *n. pl.* **lice** (līs) 1 Any of various small, wingless, parasitic insects that suck blood and inhabit the hair, fur, or feathers of the host animal. 2 Any of various insects or arthropods externally parasitic on various animals. 3 An aphid (**plant louse**). 4 *Slang pl.* **lous·es** A contemptible person. —*v.t. & v.i. Slang* To ruin; bungle: with *up.* [< OE *lūs*]

**lous·y** (lou′zē) *adj.* **lous·i·er, lous·i·est** 1 Infested with lice. 2 *Slang* Dirty. 3 *Slang* Contemptible; mean. 4 *Slang* Inferior; poor. 5 *Slang* Having plenty (of): usu. with *with*: *lousy* with money.

**lov·a·ble** (luv′ə·bəl) *adj.* Worthy of love; amiable; also, inspiring love. **Also love′a·ble.** —**lov′a·bly** *adv.* —**lov′a·bil′i·ty, lov′a·ble·ness** *n.*

**low·er** (lō′ər) Comparative of LOW. —*adj.* 1 Inferior in position, value, rank, etc. 2 *Geol.* Older; designating strata normally beneath the newer (and upper) rock formations. —*n.* That which is beneath something above; esp., a lower berth. —*v.t.* 1 To bring to a lower position or level; let down, as a window. 2 To reduce in degree, quality, amount, etc.: to *lower* prices. 3 To bring down in estimation, rank, etc.; humble or degrade. 4 To weaken or undermine. 5 To change, as a sound, to a lower pitch or volume. —*v.i.* 6 To become lower; sink. —**Syn.** *v.* 2 decrease, diminish, lessen. 3 abase, debase. 6 fall.

**lox** (loks) *n.* Liquid oxygen. [<*l(iquid) ox(ygen)*]

**loy·al** (loi′əl) *adj.* 1 Constant and faithful in any relationship implying trust or confidence. 2 Unswerving in allegiance to constituted authority, as one's country or sovereign. 3 Characterized by or showing loyalty. [< L *legalis* legal] —**loy′al·ism** *n.* —**loy′al·ly** *adv.* —**Syn.** 1 devoted, steadfast, true, trustworthy.

**loy·al·ty** (loi′əl·tē) *n. pl.* **·ties** The state, quality, or an instance of being loyal; allegiance; fidelity.

**loz·enge** (loz′inj) *n.* A small medicated or sweetened tablet. [< OF *losenge*]

**lu·bri·cate** (lōō′brə·kāt) *v.t.* **·cat·ed, ·cat·ing** 1 To apply grease, oil, or other lubricant to so as to reduce friction and wear. 2 To make slippery or smooth. [< L *lubricus* slippery] —**lu′bri·ca′tive** *adj.* —**lu′bri·ca′tion, lu′bri·ca′tor** *n.*

**lu·cid** (lōō′sid) *adj.* 1 Easily understood; clear. 2 Mentally sound; rational. 3 Giving forth light; shining. 4 Translucent. [< L *lucere* to shine] —**lu·cid·i·ty** (lōō·sid′ə·tē), **lu′cid·ness** *n.* —**lu′cid·ly** *adv.*

**lu·cra·tive** (lōō′krə·tiv) *adj.* Productive of wealth; profitable. [< L *lucrum* wealth] —**lu′cra·tive·ly** *adv.*

**lu·di·crous** (lōō′də·krəs) *adj.* Exciting laughter because absurd, incongruous, ridiculous, etc. [< L *ludere* to play] —**lu′di·crous·ly** *adv.* —**lu′di·crous·ness** *n.*

**lug·gage** (lug′ij) *n.* Suitcases, valises, etc., used by a traveler; baggage. [< LUG²]

**lull** (lul) *v.t.* 1 To soothe to sleep. 2 To calm; allay, as suspicions. —*v.i.* 3 To become calm. —*n.* An interval of calm, quiet, or diminishing activity. [ME *lullen*] —**Syn.** *v.* 1 Hush, pacify, quiet, tranquilize. 2 Alleviate, mitigate.

**lull·a·by** (lul′ə·bī) *n. pl.* **·bies** A song to lull a child to sleep. —*v.t.* **·bied, ·by·ing** To soothe with or as with a lullaby.

**lum·bar** (lum′bər, -bär) *adj.* Pertaining to or situated near the loins. [< L *lumbus* loin]

**lum·ber** (lum′bər) *n.* 1 Timber sawed into boards, planks, etc. 2 Disused articles, as household furniture, that take up room or are stored away. —*v.t.* 1 To cut down (timber). 2 To fill or obstruct with useless articles. —*v.i.* 3 To cut down or saw timber for

marketing. [? var. of *Lombard* in obs. sense of "money-lender, pawnshop"; hence, stored articles] —**lum′ber·er** *n.*

**lump** (lump) *n.* 1 A shapeless mass. 2 A mass of things thrown together. 3 A protuberance; swelling. 4 A heavy, ungainly person, esp., one who is stupid. —**in a (or the) lump** All together; with no distinction. —*v.t.* 1 To put together in one mass, group, etc. 2 To consider or treat collectively: to *lump* facts. 3 To make lumps in or on. —*v.i.* 4 To become lumpy. [Prob. < Scand.]

**lu·na·cy** (lōō′nə·sē) *n. pl.* **·cies** 1 Insanity. 2 Wild foolishness; senseless conduct. [< LUNATIC]

**lu·nar** (lōō′nər) *adj.* 1 Of or pertaining to the moon. 2 Round or shaped like a crescent. 3 Measured by revolutions of the moon. [< L *luna* the moon]

**lu·na·tic** (lōō′nə·tik) *adj.* 1 Insane. 2 Of, pertaining to, or for the insane. 3 Irrational; wildly foolish. Also **lu·nat·i·cal** (lōō·nat′i·kəl). —*n.* 1 An insane person. 2 A very foolish person. [< L *luna* the moon] —**Syn.** *adj.* 1 demented, deranged, mad, unbalanced. 3 foolhardy, rash.

**lunch** (lunch) *n.* 1 A light meal, esp. the one between breakfast and dinner. 2 Food provided for a lunch. —*v.i.* 1 To eat lunch. —*v.t.* 2 To furnish lunch for. [?] —**lunch′er** *n.*

**lunch·eon** (lun′chən) *n.* A lunch, esp. one taken with others.

**lung** (lung) *n.* Either of the two porous organs of respiration in the thorax of vertebrates, having the function of absorbing oxygen and discharging carbon dioxide. [< OE *lungen*]

**lunge** (lunj) *n.* 1 A sudden pass or thrust, as with a sword or a bayonet. 2 A sudden forward lurch; plunge. —*v.* **lunged, lung·ing** —*v.i.* 1 To make a lunge or pass; thrust. 2 To move with a lunge. —*v.t.* 3 To thrust with or as with a lunge. [< F *allonger* prolong < L *ad* to + *longus* long] —**lung′er** *n.*

**lurch** (lûrch) *v.i.* 1 To roll suddenly to one side, as a ship at sea. 2 To move unsteadily; stagger. —*n.* A lurching or unsteady movement. [?]

**lure** (lōōr) *n.* 1 A feathered device resembling a bird, sometimes baited with food and fastened to a falconer's wrist to recall the hawk. 2 In angling, an artificial bait; also, a decoy for animals. 3 Anything that invites by the prospect of advantage or pleasure. —*v.t.* **lured, lur·ing** 1 To attract or entice.

**lu·rid** (lōōr′id) *adj.* 1 Violent; terrible; sensational: a *lurid* crime. 2 Shining or suffused with a red glow, as of flames seen through smoke or clouds. 3 Pale; sallow. [< L *luridus* sallow] —**lu′rid·ly** *adv.* —**lu′rid·ness** *n.*

**lurk** (lûrk) *v.i.* 1 To lie hidden, as in ambush. 2 To exist unnoticed or unsuspected. 3 To move secretly or furtively; slink. [ME *lurken*] —**lurk′er** *n.* —**lurk′ing·ly** *adv.*

**lus·cious** (lush′əs) *adj.* 1 Very pleasant to taste and smell; delicious. 2 Appealing to any of the senses. 3 Too sweet; cloying. [? Blend of LUSH and DELICIOUS] —**lus′cious·ly** *adv.* —**lus′cious·ness** *n.*

**lush** (lush) *adj.* 1 Full of juice or succulence; fresh and tender. 2 Of or characterized by abundant growth. 3 Elaborate, extravagant, or ornate. [? < L *laxus* loose] —**lush′ly** *adv.* —**lush′ness** *n.*

**lust** (lust) *n.* 1 A very strong craving or desire. 2 An intense sexual appetite. —*v.i.* To have an intense desire, esp. sexual desire. [< OE, pleasure]

**lus·ter** (lus′tər) *n.* 1 Sheen; gloss. 2 Radiance; brightness. 3 Brilliance or splendor, as of beauty, character, or achievement. 4 The glossy look given to certain pottery by glazing. 5 A glossy fabric of wool and cotton. —*v.* **·tered** or **·tred, ·ter·ing** or **·tring** *v.t.* 1 To give a luster or gloss to. —*v.i.* 2 To be or become lustrous. Also **lus′tre.** [< L *lustrum* purification]

**lux·u·ri·ant** (lug·zhŏŏr′ē·ənt, luk·shŏŏr′-) *adj.* 1 Exhibiting or characterized by vigor and abundance in growth. 2 Rich in nature, form, or content; extravagant, ornate, or abundant. 3 LUXURIOUS. —**lux·u′ri·ant·ly** *adv.*

**lux·u·ri·ate** (lug·zhŏŏr′ē·āt, luk·shŏŏr′-) *v.i.* **·at·ed, ·at·ing** 1 To take great pleasure; indulge oneself fully. 2 To live sumptuously. 3 To grow profusely. [< L *luxuria* luxury] —**lux·u′ri·a′tion** *n.*

**lux·u·ry** (luk′shər·ē, lug′zhər·ē) *n. pl.* **·ries** 1 A way of life characterized by great comfort or pleasure. 2 Anything that contributes to comfort or pleasure but is not necessary to life, health, subsistence, etc. [< L *luxus* extravagance]

**lye** (lī) *n.* 1 A solution leached from wood ashes, used in making soap. 2 Any strong alkali. [< OE *lēah*]

**ly·ing** (lī′ing) *n.* The practice of telling lies; untruthfulness. —*adj.* Addicted to, conveying, or constituting falsehood. —**ly′ing·ly** *adv.* —**Syn.** *n.* deceit, deception, fabrication, prevarication. *adj.* false, mendacious.

**lymph** (limf) *n.* A colorless fluid resembling plasma and containing white blood corpuscles, which moves in the lymph vessels of vertebrates and merges with the blood through certain veins. [< L *limpa* water]

**lym·phat·ic** (lim·fat′ik) *adj.* 1 Pertaining to, containing, or conveying lymph. 2 Without energy; listless. —*n.* A vessel that conveys lymph.

**lynch** (linch) *v.t.* To kill by mob action without legal sanction. [< LYNCH LAW] —**lynch′er, lynch′ing** *n.*

**lyre** (līr) *n.* A harplike stringed instrument, used by the ancient Greeks to accompany song and poetry. [< Gk.]

**lyr·ic** (lir′ik) *adj.* 1 Of poetry, expressing the poet's personal emotions. 2 Of, pertaining to, or having written such poetry. 3 Musical; singing or meant to be sung. 4 Having or suitable for a relatively light, flexible vocal quality: a *lyric* tenor; a *lyric* aria. Also **lyr′i·cal.** —*n.* 1 A lyric poem. 2 *Usu. pl.* The words of a song, esp. as distinguished from the music. [< Gk. *lyra* a lyre] —**lyr′i·cal·ly** *adv.*

# M

**mac·a·ro·ni** (mak′ə·rō′nē) *n. pl.* **·nis** or **·nies** 1 An edible paste of wheat flour made into short tubes. 2 An English dandy of the 18th century. Also **mac′ca·ro′ni.** [< Ital. *macherone*]

**mac·a·roon** (mak′ə·rōōn′) *n.* A small cooky of ground almonds or coconut, white of egg, and sugar. [< Ital. *macherone* macaroni]

**ma·chine** (mə·shēn′) *n.* 1 Any combination of parts for utilizing, modifying, applying, or transmitting energy, performing a specific function, etc. 2 An automobile or other vehicle, as a bicycle, airplane, etc. 3 One who acts in a mechanical manner; a robot. 4 The organization of the powers of any complex body: the *machine* of government. 5 An organization within a political party, controlled by politicians chiefly by the use of patronage. —*adj.* 1 Of, for, or produced by a machine or machinery. 2 Mechanical; stereotyped. —*v.t.* **·chined, ·chin·ing** To shape, make, etc., by machinery. [< L *machina* contrivance]

**ma·chin·er·y** (mə·shē′nər·ē) *n. pl.* **·er·ies** 1 The parts of a machine, or a number of machines collectively. 2 Any combination of means working together to achieve a specific action or result: the *machinery* of elections.

**mach number** (mak, māk) The ratio of the speed of an object in a fluid medium to the speed of sound in the same medium. [< Ernst *Mach*, 1838–1916, Austrian physicist]

**mac·ra·mé** (mak′rə·mā) *n.* 1 A fringe, lace, wall hanging, etc., made of coarsely knotted thread or cord. 2 The technique of making such items. [< Ar. *miqramah* a veil]

**mac·ro·bi·ot·ics** (mak′rō·bī·ot′iks) *n. pl. (construed as sing.)* A dietetic regimen advocating the use of whole-grain cereals, the avoidance of meat, etc. [< MACRO- + -BIOTIC] —**mac′ro·bi·ot′ic** *adj.* —**mac′ro·bi·ot′ic·al·ly** *adv.*

**Ma·don·na** (mə·don′ə) *n.* 1 Mary, mother of Jesus. 2 A painting or statue of her. [Ital. < *ma my* + *donna* lady]

**mael·strom** (māl′strəm) *n.* 1 A powerful, dangerous whirlpool. 2 Any violent, irresistible influence, emotion, etc. [< MDu. *malen* grind + *stroom* a stream]

**mag·a·zine** (mag′ə·zēn′, mag′ə·zēn) *n.* 1 A periodical publication containing sketches, stories, essays, etc. 2 A depot, warehouse, etc., for storage, esp. for storage of explosives, ammunition, etc. 3 A chamber in a repeating firearm which holds the supply of reserve cartridges. 4 A supply chamber in a battery, camera, or the like. [< Ar. *makhzan* a storehouse]

**mag·got** (mag′ət) *n.* A wormlike insect larva; a grub. [ME *maddock, mathek*] —**mag′got·y** *adj.*

**mag·ic** (maj′ik) *n.* 1 Any supernatural power or control over natural laws or the forces of nature, esp. by the use of charms, etc. 2 The theatrical art of performing tricks and illusions by sleight of hand, mechanical devices, etc. 3 Any mysterious or spellbinding power or enchantment: the *magic* of her voice. —*adj.* 1 Of, used in, or produced by magic. 2 Bringing forth unusual results, as if by magic. • See MAGICAL. [< Gk. *magikos* of the Magi]

**ma·gi·cian** (mə·jish′ən) *n.* 1 An expert in magic arts. 2 Any person of unusual abilities.

**mag·is·te·ri·al** (maj′is·tir′ē·əl) *adj.* 1 Of a magistrate, his duties, etc. 2 Like or befitting a master; commanding; authoritative. 3 Domineering; pompous. —**mag′is·te′ri·al·ly** *adv.*

**mag·is·trate** (maj′is·trāt, -trit) *n.* 1 One

clothed with public civil authority; an executive or judicial officer. 2 A minor public official, as a justice of the peace. [< L *magister* a master]

**mag·na·nim·i·ty** (mag′nə·nim′ə·tē) *n. pl. ·ties* 1 The quality or condition of being magnanimous. 2 A magnanimous deed.

**mag·nan·i·mous** (mag·nan′ə·məs) *adj.* Noble and generous; not petty, mean, or selfish. [< L *magnus* great + *animus* mind, soul] —**mag·nan′i·mous·ly** *adv.* —**mag·nan′i·mous·ness** *n.*

**mag·nate** (mag′nāt, -nit) *n.* A person of rank, power, or importance in any sphere. [< L *magnus* great]

**mag·net** (mag′nit) *n.* 1 Any mass of material capable of attracting bodies that are magnetized or capable of being magnetized. 2 A person or thing exercising a strong attraction. [< Gk. *Magnēs (lithos)* Magnesian (stone)]

**mag·net·ic** (mag·net′ik) *adj.* 1 Of, pertaining to, or caused or operated by a magnet or magnetism. 2 Capable of being magnetized. 3 Of the earth's magnetism. 4 Fascinatingly attractive or dynamic: a *magnetic* personality. —**mag·net′i·cal·ly** *adv.*

**magnetic tape** A thin ribbon coated with magnetized particles, usu. wound on a reel and used to preserve magnetic recordings.

**mag·net·ism** (mag′nə·tiz′əm) *n.* 1 The specific properties of a magnet, produced by the alignments of certain atoms and the movements of their electrons. 2 The science that studies magnetic phenomena. 3 The measure of the force of a magnetic field. 4 The sympathetic personal quality that attracts or interests.

**mag·net·ize** (mag′nə·tīz) *v. ·ized, ·iz·ing v.t.* 1 To produce magnetic properties in. 2 To attract by strong personal influence; captivate. —*v.i.* 3 To become magnetic. —**mag′net·iz′a·ble** *adj.* —**mag′net·i·za′tion, mag′net·iz′er** *n.*

**mag·ne·to** (mag·nē′to) *n. pl. ·tos* An electric alternator using a field produced by permanent magnets, sometimes used in ignition systems of internal-combustion engines.

**mag·ne·tom·e·ter** (mag′nə·tom′ə·tər) *n.* An instrument for measuring the intensity and direction of magnetic forces. —**mag′ne·tom′e·try** *n.*

**mag·nif·i·cence** (mag·nif′ə·səns) *n.* The state or quality of being magnificent.

**mag·nif·i·cent** (mag·nif′ə·sənt) *adj.* 1 Grandly

imposing or beautiful: a *magnificent* ruin.
2 Sublime; exalted: *magnificent* prose. 3
Lavish; sumptuous: a *magnificent* banquet.
4 Exceptionally fine; excellent: a *magnificent* physique. [< L *magnus* great + *facere* make] —**mag·nif′i·cent·ly** *adv.*

**mag·ni·fy** (mag′nə·fī) *v.t.* **·fied, ·fy·ing** 1 To increase the apparent size of, as with an optical instrument. 2 To increase the size of; enlarge. 3 To cause to seem greater; intensify. 4 To exaggerate. 5 *Archaic* To extol; exalt. [< L *magnus* great + *facere* make] —**mag′ni·fi′a·ble** *adj.* —**mag′ni·fi·ca′tion, mag′ni·fi′er** *n.*

**mag·ni·tude** (mag′nə·t⁄o͞od) *n.* 1 Great size or extent. 2 Great importance or significance. 3 *Math.* a Any of the numbers associated with individual elements of a set and by which they can be compared. b That which is measurable. 4 *Astron.* A logarithmic measure of the relative or absolute brightness of stars, with lower numbers denoting greater brightness. [< L *magnus* large]

**mag·no·li·a** (mag·nō′lē·ə, ·nōl′y·ə) *n.* 1 Any of a genus of trees or shrubs with large, fragrant flowers. 2 The flower. [< Pierre *Magnol*, 1638–1715, French botanist]

**ma·hog·a·ny** (mə·hog′ə·nē) *n.* 1 A large tropical American tree, with fine-grained, hard, reddish wood much used for cabinet work. 2 The wood itself. 3 Any of various shades of reddish brown. —*adj.* 1 Of mahogany. 2 Reddish brown. [?]

**maid** (mād) *n.* 1 An unmarried woman or young girl. 2 A virgin. 3 A female servant. [Short for MAIDEN]

**maid·en** (mād′n) *n.* 1 An unmarried woman. 2 A young girl. 3 A virgin. 4 A race horse that has never won an event. —*adj.* 1 Of or for a maiden. 2 Virgin. 3 Unmarried. 4 First; initiatory: a *maiden* voyage. [< OE *mǣgden*] —**maid′en·li·ness** *n.* —**maid′en·ly** *adj., adv.*

**mail** (māl) *n.* 1 Armor of chains, rings, or scales. 2 Any strong covering or defense, as the shell of a turtle. —*v.t.* To cover with or as with mail. [< L *macula* spot, mesh of a net]

**maim** (mām) *v.t.* To deprive of the use of a bodily part; mutilate; disable. [< OF *mahaigner*] —**maim′er** *n.*

**main·tain** (mān·tān′) *v.t.* 1 To carry on or continue; engage in, as a correspondence. 2 To keep unimpaired or in proper condition: to *maintain* roads. 3 To supply with food or livelihood; support; pay for. 4 To uphold;

claim to be true. 5 To assert or state; affirm. 6 To hold or defend, as against attack. [< L *manu tenere*, lit., hold in one's hand] —**main·tain′a·ble** *adj.* —**main·tain′er** *n.*

**ma·jes·tic** (mə·jes′tik) *adj.* Having or exhibiting majesty; stately; dignified. Also **ma·jes′ti·cal.** —**ma·jes′ti·cal·ly** *adv.* —**ma·jes′ti·cal·ness** *n.* —**Syn.** grand, impressive, awesome, grandiose, magnificent.

**maj·es·ty** (maj′is·tē) *n. pl.* **·ties** 1 Exalted dignity; stateliness; grandeur. 2 Sovereign power: the *majesty* of the law. [< L *majestas* greatness]

**ma·jor** (mā′jər) *adj.* 1 Greater in number, quantity, or extent. 2 Greater in dignity, rank, or importance; principal; leading. 3 Considerable in extent, degree, etc.: a *major* repair. 4 Serious; grave: a *major* illness. 5 In education, of or designating the specific field of study specialized in by a candidate for a degree. 6 *Music* Of or characteristic of the tone successions or chords of a major scale, esp. the triad built on the tonic. 7 *Law* Being of legal age. —*n.* 1 See GRADE. 2 *Law* One who is of legal age. 3 *Music* A major key, chord, or interval. 4 In education: a A major subject or field of study. b A student who follows a (specified) course of study: an English *major.* —*v.i.* To pursue a definite field of study: with *in*: to *major* in history. [L, greater]

**ma·jor·i·ty** (mə·jôr′ə·tē, ·jor′-) *n. pl.* **·ties** 1 More than half of a given number or group; the greater part. 2 The amount or number by which one group of things exceeds another group; excess. 3 The age at which a person becomes legally responsible. 4 The rank or commission of a major. 5 In U.S. politics, the number of votes cast for a candidate over and above the number cast for his nearest opponent; a plurality. 6 The party having the most power in a legislature. [< L *major* greater]

**make** (māk) *v.* **made, mak·ing** *v.t.* 1 To bring about the existence of by the shaping or combining of materials; produce; build; construct; fashion. 2 To bring about; cause: Don't *make* trouble. 3 To bring to some state or condition; cause to be: The wind *made* him cold. 4 To appoint or assign; elect: They *made* him captain. 5 To form or create in the mind, as a plan. 6 To compose or create, as a poem or piece of music. 7 To understand or infer to be the meaning or significance: with *of*: What do you *make* of it? 8 To put forward; advance: to *make* an offer. 9 To utter or express: to *make* a declaration. 10 To obtain for oneself; earn; accumulate. 11 To add up to: Four quarts *make* a gallon. 12 To bring the total to: That *makes* five attempts. 13 To develop into; become: He *made* a good soldier. 14 To accomplish; effect or form: to *make* an agreement. 15 To estimate to be; reckon. 16 To induce or force; compel: He *made* me do it! 17 To draw up, enact, or frame, as laws, testaments, etc. 18 To prepare for use, as a bed. 19 To afford or provide: This brandy *makes* good drinking. 20 To be the essential element or determinant of: Stone walls do not a prison *make.* 21 To cause the success of: His speech *made* him politically. 22 To traverse; cover: to *make* fifty miles before noon. 23 To travel at the rate of: to *make* fifty miles per hour. 24 To arrive at; reach: to *make* Boston. 25 To board before departure: to *make* a train. 26 To earn so as to count on a score: to *make* a touchdown. 27 *Electr.* To complete (a circuit). 28 *Informal* To win a place on: to *make* the team. 29 In bridge, to win (a bid). 30 *Slang* To seduce. —*v.i.* 31 To cause something to assume a specified condition: to *make* fast. 32 To act in a certain manner: to *make* merry. 33 To start: They *made* to go. 34 To go or extend in some direction: with *to* or *toward.* 35 To flow, as the tide; rise, as water. —**make believe** To pretend, as in play. —**make do** To get along with what is available, esp. with an inferior substitute. —**make for** 1 To go toward. 2 To attack; assail. 3 To have effect on; contribute to. —**make it** *Informal* To do or achieve something; succeed. —**make off** To run away. —**make off with** To carry away; filch; purloin. —**make out** 1 To see; discern. 2 To comprehend; understand. 3 To try to prove or imply to be: They *made* us *out* criminals. 4 To fill out, as a printed form. 5 To succeed; manage. 6 *Slang* a To neck. b To have sexual intercourse. —**make over** 1 To renovate. 2 To transfer title or possession of. —**make up** 1 To compose; compound, as a prescription. 2 To be the parts of; comprise. 3 To settle differences: to kiss and *make up.* 4 To devise; invent: to *make up* an answer. 5 To supply what is lacking in. 6 To compensate for; atone for. 7 To settle; decide: to *make up* one's mind. 8 *Printing* To arrange, as lines, into columns or pages. 9 To put cosmetics on. —**make up to** *Informal* To make a show of friendliness and affection

toward. —*n.* 1 The manner in which something is constructed. 2 Brand: a new *make* of automobile. 3 The act of making or producing. 4 The amount produced; yield. 5 The physical or mental qualities of a person. 6 The closing or completion of an electrical circuit. —**on the make** *Informal* 1 Greedy for profit, success, etc. 2 Eager for amorous conquest. [< OE *macian*]

**make·shift** (māk′shift′) *adj.* Being a temporary substitute. —*n.* A temporary substitute in any emergency.

**mal·ad·just·ed** (mal′ə·jus′tid) *adj.* Poorly adjusted, as to the circumstances of one's life. —**mal′ad·just′ment** *n.*

**mal·a·dy** (mal′ə·dē) *n. pl.* ·**dies** 1 A disease; illness. 2 Any disordered condition. [< LL *male habitus,* lit., ill kept]

**ma·lar·i·a** (mə·lâr′ē·ə) *n.* 1 An infectious disease caused by a protozoan transmitted by infected anopheles mosquitoes, and resulting in intermittent chills and fever. 2 Any foul or unwholesome air; miasma. [< Ital. *mal′aria,* lit., bad air] —**ma·lar′i·al, ma·lar′i·an, ma·lar′i·ous** *adj.*

**male** (māl) *adj.* 1 Of or pertaining to the sex that begets young. 2 Masculine. 3 Made up of men or boys. 4 *Bot.* Having stamens, but no pistil; also, adapted to fertilize, but not to produce fruit, as stamens. 5 Denoting a tool or object which fits into a corresponding hollow part. —*n.* A male person, animal, or plant. [< L *masculus*]

**mal·e·dic·tion** (mal′ə·dik′shən) *n.* 1 An invocation of evil; a curse. 2 Slander. [< L *male* ill + *dicere* speak] —**mal′e·dic′to·ry** *adj.*

**mal·e·fac·tor** (mal′ə·fak′tər) *n.* One who commits a crime. [< L *male* ill + *facere* do] —**mal′e·fac′tion** *n.*

**ma·lev·o·lent** (mə·lev′ə·lənt) *adj.* Wishing evil toward others; malicious. [< L *male* ill + *volens* wishing] —**ma·lev′o·lence** *n.* —**ma·lev′o·lent·ly** *adv.*

**mal·fea·sance** (mal·fē′zəns) *n. Law* The performance of an unlawful or wrongful act, esp. by a public official. [< OF *mal* ill + *faire* do] —**mal·fea′sant** *adj., n.*

**mal·ice** (mal′is) *n.* 1 A disposition to injure another; spite; ill will. 2 *Law* A willfully formed design to do another an injury: also **malice aforethought.** [< L *malus* bad]

**ma·li·cious** (mə·lish′əs) *adj.* Harboring or resulting from malice; ill will, or enmity; spiteful. —**ma·li′cious·ly** *adv.* —**ma·li′cious·ness** *n.* —**Syn.** hostile, malevolent, hateful, harmful, treacherous, invidious.

**ma·lign** (mə·līn′) *v.t.* To speak slander of. —
*adj.* 1 Having an evil disposition toward
others; ill-disposed; malevolent. 2 Tending
to injure; pernicious. [< L *malignare* contrive maliciously] —**ma·lign′er** *n.* —**ma·lig-
n′ly** *adv.* —**Syn.** *v.* slur, vilify, defame, depreciate, discredit, belittle, disparage.

**ma·lig·nant** (mə·lig′nənt) *adj.* 1 Having or
manifesting extreme malevolence or enmity. 2 Evil in nature, or tending to do great
harm. 3 *Pathol.* Tending to grow progres-
sively worse. —**ma·lig′nance, ma·lig′nan-
cy** *n.* —**ma·lig′nant·ly** *adv.*

**ma·lig·ni·ty** (mə·lig′nə·tē) *n. pl.* **·ties** 1 The
state or quality of being malign; violent animosity. 2 Destructive tendency; virulence.
3 *Often pl.* An evil thing or event.

**mal·le·a·ble** (mal′ē·ə·bəl) *adj.* 1 Capable of
being shaped by hammering, rolling, pressure, etc. 2 Capable of being disciplined,
trained, changed, etc. [< L *malleus* ham-
mer] —**mal′le·a·bil′i·ty, mal′le·a·ble·ness**
*n.* —**mal′le·a·bly** *adv.*

**mal·nu·tri·tion** (mal′n<sup>y</sup>ōō·trish′ən) *n.* Faulty
or inadequate nutrition.

**mam·mal** (mam′əl) *n.* Any of a class of vertebrate animals, including man, whose female suckles its young. [< L *mamma* breast]

**mam·moth** (mam′əth) *n.* Any of a genus of extinct elephants with coarse hair and enormous upward-curving tusks. —*adj.* Huge;
colossal. [< Russ. *mammot*]

**man** (man) *n. pl.* **men** (men) 1 A human being,
specifically the most highly developed of
the primates, differing from other animals
in having erect posture, extraordinary development of the brain, and the power of
articulate speech. 2 The human race. 3 An
adult male of the human kind. 4 The male
part of the race collectively. 5 A male person who is manly; also, manhood. 6 An
adult male servant, member of a team, employee, etc. 7 A piece used in playing certain games, as chess or checkers. 8 A ship
or vessel: used in composition: a *man-of-
war.* 9 A husband; lover: *man* and wife; Her
*man* is dead. 10 *Slang* Fellow: used in direct
address: Hey, *man,* look at this! —**the Man**
*Slang* A white man regarded as an agent of
power. —*v.t.* **manned, man·ning** 1 To supply with men. 2 To take stations at, on, or
in for work, defense, etc.: *Man* the pumps!
—*adj.* Male. [< OE *mann*]

**man·a·cle** (man′ə·kəl) *n.* 1 *Usu. pl.* One of a
connected pair of metallic instruments for
confining or restraining the hands; a hand-

cuff. 2 Anything that constrains or fetters.
—*v.t.* **·cled, ·cling** 1 To put manacles on. 2
To hamper; constrain. [< OF < L, dim. of
*manus* hand]

**man·age** (man′ij) *v.,* **·aged, ·ag·ing** *v.t.* 1 To direct or conduct the affairs or interests of. 2
To control the direction, operation, etc., of,
as a machine. 3 To cause to do one's bidding; handle; manipulate. 4 To bring about
or contrive: He always *manages* to win. 5 To
handle or wield, as a weapon or implement.
—*v.i.* 6 To carry on or conduct business or
affairs. 7 To contrive to get along: I'll *manage.* [< L *manus* a hand]

**man·age·a·ble** (man′ij·ə·bəl) *adj.* Capable of
being managed; tractable; docile. —**man′-
age·a·bil′i·ty, man′age·a·ble·ness** *n.* —
**man′age·a·bly** *adv.*

**man·age·ment** (man′ij·mənt) *n.* 1 The act, art,
or manner of managing, controlling, or conducting. 2 The skillful use of means to accomplish a purpose. 3 Managers or directors collectively.

**man·da·rin** (man′də·rin) *n.* 1 A high official of
the former Chinese Empire, either civil or
military. 2 A distinguished, influential, usu.
elderly person, esp. one of literary or intellectual attainment. 3 MANDARIN ORANGE. 4 A
reddish orange color. —*adj.* 1 Of a mandarin. 2 Complex and ornate, as a literary
style. [< Skt. *mantra* counsel]

**man·date** (man′dāt, -dit) *n.* 1 An authoritative
command or order. 2 A charge given to a
nation by a congress or league of nations
to develop and administer a conquered territory; also, the territory itself. 3 A judicial
command from a higher court to a subordinate court or court officer. 4 An order
from an electorate to the legislative body, or
its representative, to follow a certain course
of action. —*v.t.* (-dāt) **·dat·ed, ·dat·ing** To assign (a territory) to a specific nation under
a mandate. [< L *mandare* to command]

**man·do·lin** (man′də·lin, man′də·lin′) *n.* A
stringed musical instrument related to the
lute, having five pairs of strings. [< Ital.
*mandolino* < L *pandura* a kind of lute] —
**man′do·lin′ist** *n.*

**mane** (mān) *n.* 1 The long hair growing on and
about the neck of some animals, as the
horse, lion, etc. 2 Long human hair. [< OE
*manu*] —**maned** (mānd) *adj.*

**ma·neu·ver** (mə·n<sup>y</sup>ōō′vər) *n.* 1 a An extensive,
planned movement of troops, warships, air-
craft, etc. b *Often pl.* Such movements used
in training or practice. 2 Any physically

adroit movement or skill. 3 A controlled change in the flight path of an aircraft or spacecraft. 4 A skillful or cunning action to gain some specific end or object, often involving trickery. —v.t. 1 To put through a maneuver or maneuvers. 2 To put, bring, make, etc., by a maneuver or maneuvers. 3 To manipulate; conduct adroitly. —v.i. 4 To perform a maneuver or maneuvers. 5 To use tricks or stratagems; manage adroitly. [< L *manu operari* work with the hand] —ma·neu′ver·a·bil′i·ty, ma·neu′ver·er n. —ma·neu′ver·a·ble adj.

man·gle (mang′gǝl) v.t. ·gled, ·gling 1 To disfigure or mutilate, as by cutting, bruising, or crushing; lacerate. 2 To mar or ruin; spoil. [< AF *mangler*] —man′gler n.

man·hat·tan (mǝn·hat′ǝn, man-) n. *Often cap.* A cocktail made of whisky and vermouth, often with a dash of bitters and a cherry. [< *Manhattan*, borough of New York City]

man-hour (man′our′) n. A unit equal to the average amount of work that can be done by one person in one hour.

ma·ni·a (mā′nē·ǝ, mān′yǝ) n. 1 A psychotic state characterized by an exaggerated sense of well-being, accompanied by excessive mental and physical activity. 2 A strong, ungovernable desire; a craze. [< Gk., madness]

ma·ni·ac (mā′nē·ak) adj. Having a mania; raving. —n. A person wildly or violently insane; a madman. —ma·ni·a·cal (mǝ·nī′ǝ·kǝl) adj. —ma·ni′a·cal·ly adv.

man·i·cure (man′ǝ·kyoor′) n. The care or treatment of the hands and fingernails. —v.t. & v.i. ·cured, ·cur·ing To take care of or treat (the hands and nails). [< L *manus* hand + *cura* care] —man′i·cur′ist n.

man·i·fest (man′ǝ·fest′) adj. Clearly apparent to the understanding or the senses; palpable; obvious. —v.t. 1 To make plain to sight or understanding; reveal; display. 2 To prove; be evidence of. —v.i. 3 To appear or become evident; reveal itself. —n. A detailed listing of the cargo of a ship or plane for customs inspection. [< L *manifestus* evident, lit., struck by the hand] —man′i·fes′t′ly adv.

man·i·fes·ta·tion (man′ǝ·fǝ·stā′shǝn, -fes-) n. 1 The act of manifesting or the state of being manifested. 2 Something that manifests or reveals. 3 A public demonstration, as by a government or party, to display its power or special views. —man′i·fes′tant n.

man·i·fes·to (man′ǝ·fes′tō) n. pl. ·toes An official declaration by an organized group or government body of intentions, motives, or principles of action. [< L *manifestus* manifest]

man·i·fold (man′ǝ·fōld) adj. 1 Of great variety; numerous. 2 Manifested in many ways, or including many acts or elements; complex. 3 Existing in great abundance. —v.t. To make more than one copy of at once, as with carbon paper on a typewriter. —n. 1 A copy made by manifolding. 2 A tube or pipe with several inlets or outlets. [< OE *manigfeald* varied, numerous] —man′i·fold·ly adv. —man′i·fold·ness n.

man·i·kin (man′ǝ·kin) n. 1 A model of the human body. 2 A little man; dwarf. 3 MANNEQUIN. [< Du. *manneken*, dim. of *man* man]

ma·nip·u·late (mǝ·nip′yǝ·lāt) v.t. ·lat·ed, ·lat·ing 1 To handle, operate, or use with or as with the hands, esp. with skill. 2 To influence or control artfully or deceptively. 3 To change or alter (figures, accounts, etc.), usu. fraudulently. [< L *manipulus* a handful] —ma·nip′u·la′tion, ma·nip′u·la′tor n. —ma·nip′u·la′tive adj.

man·ne·quin (man′ǝ·kin) n. 1 A woman who models new clothes for display to potential customers. 2 A figure of the human body used by fashion designers, tailors, and display artists. [< Du. *manneken*, dim. of *man* man]

man·ner (man′ǝr) n. 1 The way in which something is done or takes place. 2 The demeanor, bearing, or behavior peculiar to a person; also, a distinguished air or bearing. 3 pl. General modes of life or conduct; esp., social behavior. 4 pl. Polite, civil, or well-bred behavior. 5 A characteristic style in art, literature, music, etc. 6 Sort or kind. 7 Character; guise. —in a manner of speaking In one way of describing; in a sense: She was, *in a manner of speaking*, a hard-nosed negotiator. [< L *manuarius* of the hand]

man·ner·ism (man′ǝr·iz′ǝm) n. 1 An action, way of behaving, speech pattern, etc., that is characteristic of a particular person. 2 An artificial or affected manner or style. —man′ner·ist n. —man′ner·is′tic adj.

man·or (man′ǝr) n. 1 *Brit.* A nobleman's or gentleman's landed estate. 2 In feudal England, a tract of land granted by the king to one as lord, with authority to exercise jurisdiction over it. 3 In colonial America, a tract of land originally granted as a manor and let by the proprietor to tenants. 4 A mansion, esp. one on an estate. [< L *manere* stay, remain] —**ma·no·ri·al** (mə·nôr′ē·əl, -nō′rē-) *adj.*

**man·sard** (man′särd) *n.* A roof with a double slope or pitch on all sides. **Also mansard roof.** [< F. *Mansard*, 1598–1666, French architect]

**man·sion** (man′shən) *n.* A large, imposing house. [< L < *mansus*, pp. of *manere* remain, dwell]

**man·slaugh·ter** (man′slô′tər) *n. Law* The unlawful killing of a person by another person but without malice.

**man·tel** (man′təl) *n.* The facing about a fireplace, including the shelf above it; also, the shelf. [< L *mantellum* cloak]

**man·tel·piece** (man′təl·pēs′) *n.* A mantel shelf.

**man·tle** (man′təl) *n.* 1 A loose cloak, usu. without sleeves, worn over other garments, often thought of figuratively as a symbol of authority, greatness, etc. 2 Anything that covers, envelops, or conceals. 3 *Zool.* A membranous flap or fold in the body wall of a mollusk. • See OYSTER. 4 A mesh supporting certain salts, used to enclose a flame and produce light when heated. 5 The layer of the earth beneath the crust and outside the core. 6 MANTEL. —*v.* ·tled, ·tling *v.t.* 1 To cover with or as with a mantle; conceal. —*v.i.* 2 To overspread or cover the surface of something. 3 To be or become covered, overspread, or suffused. [< L *mantellum*, a cloak, towel]

**man·u·al** (man′yōō·əl) *adj.* 1 Of or involving the hands. 2 Done or operated by hand. 3 Involving or using physical strength or dexterity: *manual* labor. —*n.* 1 A compact handbook of instruction or directions. 2 A keyboard, as of an organ. 3 A systematic exercise in the handling of some military weapon. [< L *manus* hand] —**man′u·al·ly** *adv.*

**man·u·fac·ture** (man′yə·fak′chər) *v.t.* ·tured, ·tur·ing 1 To make or fashion by hand or machinery, esp. in large quantities. 2 To work into useful form, as wool or steel. 3 To invent (evidence, testimony, etc.) falsely; concoct. 4 To produce in a mechanical way, as art, poetry, etc. —*n.* 1 The production of goods by hand or by industrial processes. 2 Anything made by industrial art or processes; manufactured articles collectively. 3 The making or contriving of anything. [< L *manus* hand + *factura* a making]

—**man′u·fac′tur·er** *n.* —**man′u·fac′tur·ing** *adj., n.*

**ma·nure** (mə·nyŏŏr′) *n.* Any substance, as dung, decaying animal or vegetable matter, or certain minerals, applied to fertilize soil. —*v.t.* ·nured, ·nur·ing To apply manure or other fertilizer to, as soil. [< AF *maynoverer* work with the hands] —**ma·nur′er** *n.*

**man·u·script** (man′yə·skript) *n.* 1 A piece of writing, either written or typewritten, as distinguished from printed matter; esp., an author's copy of a work to be considered for publication. 2 Matter written by hand. —*adj.* Written by hand or typed. [< L *manus* hand + *scriptus* written]

**mar** (mär) *v.t.* **marred, mar·ring** 1 To do harm to; impair or ruin. 2 To deface; disfigure. —*n.* A disfiguring mark; blemish; injury. [< OE *merran* injure] —**mar′rer** *n.*

**mar·ble** (mär′bəl) *n.* 1 A compact, partly crystallized, variously colored limestone, used for building or ornaments. 2 A sculptured or inscribed piece of this stone. 3 A small ball made of this stone, or of baked clay, glass, or porcelain. 4 *pl.* A game played with such balls. —*v.t.* ·bled, ·bling To color or vein in imitation of marble. —*adj.* 1 Made of or like marble. 2 Without feeling; cold. [< Gk. *marmaros*, lit., sparkling stone] —**mar′bly** *adj.*

**march** (märch) *n.* A region or district lying along a boundary line; frontier. [< OF *marche* < Gmc.]

**mare** (mâr) *n.* The female of the horse and other equine animals. [< OE *mēre*]

**mar·ga·rine** (mär′jə·rin, -rēn) *n.* A blend of hydrogenated vegetable oils resembling butter; also **mar′ga·rin** (-jə·rin). [F]

**mar·gin** (mär′jin) *n.* 1 A bounding line; border. 2 An allowance or reservation for contingencies or changes, as of time or money. 3 Range or scope; provision for increase or progress. 4 A sum of money deposited with a broker to protect him against loss in contracts undertaken for a buyer or seller of stocks, etc. 5 The difference between selling price and cost of production: profit *margin.* 6 The blank parts of a page that surround the printed or written text. —*v.t.* 1 To furnish with a margin; border. 2 In commerce, to deposit a margin upon. [< L *margo* edge] —**Syn.** *n.* 1 boundary, brink, edge, verge.

**mar·gi·nal** (mär′jə·nəl) *adj.* 1 Of or constituting a margin. 2 Written, printed, or placed on the margin. 3 *Econ.* Operating or furnishing goods at a rate barely meeting the costs of production. **4** Of a nature that barely qualifies as useful, productive, or necessary. —**mar′gi·nal·ly** *adv.*

**mar·i·hua·na** (mar′ə-ʰwä′nə, mär′-) *n.* **1** The hemp plant. **2** Its dried leaves and flower tops which when smoked in cigarettes or otherwise ingested can produce distorted perception and other hallucinogenic effects. Also **ma′ri·jua′na.** [Am. Sp.]

**ma·ri·na** (mə·rē′nə) *n.* A basin or safe anchorage for small vessels, esp. one at which supplies, etc., may be obtained. [< L *marinus* of the sea]

**ma·rine** (mə·rēn′) *adj.* **1** Of, native to, or produced by the sea. **2** Having to do with shipping. **3** Naval. **4** Intended for use at sea or in navigation. **5** Trained for service on shipboard. —*n.* **1** A soldier trained for service at sea and on land, esp. a member of the U.S. Marine Corps: also **Marine. 2** Shipping, or shipping interests generally: the merchant *marine.* **3** A picture of the sea. [< L *marinus* < *mare* sea]

**mar·i·o·nette** (mar′ē·ə·net′) *n.* A jointed puppet moved by strings. [F]

**mar·i·tal** (mar′ə·təl) *adj.* **1** Of or pertaining to marriage. **2** Of or pertaining to a husband. [< L *maritus* a husband] —**mar′i·tal·ly** *adv.*

**mar·i·time** (mar′ə·tīm) *adj.* **1** Situated on or near the sea: a *maritime* region. **2** Living on the borders of the sea: a *maritime* people. **3** Pertaining to the sea or matters connected with the sea. [< L < *mare* sea]

**mar·jo·ram** (mär′jər·əm) *n.* Any of several perennial herbs related to mint, esp. **sweet marjoram** and **wild marjoram** (oregano) both used for seasoning in cookery. [< Med. L *majorana*]

**mar·ket** (mär′kit) *n.* **1** An open space or large building where merchandise, esp. produce, is displayed for sale: also **market place. 2** A private store for the sale of provisions: a meat *market.* **3** The state of trade in goods, stocks, etc.; traffic: a brisk *market.* **4** A locality or country where anything can be bought or sold: the South American *markets.* **5** A gathering of people for selling and buying, esp. of a particular commodity: the wheat *market.* **6** Demand for commercial products or services. —**be in the market for** To be looking for an opportunity to buy. —**be on the market** To be for sale. —**play the market** To speculate in stocks, bonds, etc. —*v.t.* **1** To take or send to market for sale; sell. —*v.i.* **2** To deal in a market; sell or buy.

**3** To buy food. [< L *merx, mercis* merchandise] —**mar′ket·a·bil′i·ty, mar′ket·er** *n.* — **mar′ket·a·ble** *adj.*

**mar·ma·lade** (mär′mə·lād) *n.* A preserve made in part with the rind of fruits, esp. citrus fruits. [< Gk. *melimēlon,* lit., honey apple]

**ma·roon** (mə·rōōn′) *v.t.* **1** To put ashore and abandon on a desolate island or coast. **2** To abandon; leave helpless. —*n.* **1** In the West Indies and Dutch Guiana, formerly a fugitive Negro slave. **2** One of the descendants of these slaves. [< Sp. *cimarrón* wild]

**mar·quis** (mär′kwis, *Fr.* mår·kē′) *n.* The title of a nobleman next in rank below a duke. [< OF *marche* boundary, a march[2]]

**mar·riage** (mar′ij) *n.* **1** The act of marrying, or the state of being married; wedlock. **2** A wedding. **3** Any close union. [< L *maritus* a husband]

**mar·riage·a·ble** (mar′ij·ə·bəl) *adj.* Fitted by age, physical condition, etc., for marriage. —**mar′riage·a·bil′i·ty, mar′riage·a·ble·ness** *n.*

**mar·row** (mar′ō) *n.* **1** A soft vascular tissue found in the central cavities of most bones. **2** The interior substance of anything; essence. [< OE *mearg*] —**mar′row·y** *adj.*

**mar·ry** (mar′ē) *v.* **·ried, ·ry·ing** *v.t.* **1** To join as husband and wife in marriage. **2** To take in marriage. **3** To give in marriage: usu. with *off.* **4** To unite closely. —*v.i.* **5** To take a husband or wife. [< L *maritus* a husband, married] —**mar′ri·er** *n.*

**marsh** (märsh) *n.* A tract of low, wet land; swamp. [< OE *mersc*] —**marsh′i·ness** *n.* — **marsh′y** *adj.* (**·i·er, ·i·est**)

**mar·shal** (mär′shəl) *n.* **1** An officer authorized to regulate ceremonies, processions, etc. **2** A U.S. federal official appointed to a judicial district and having functions similar to those of a sheriff. **3** The head of the police force or fire department in some cities. **4** In some European countries, a military officer of high rank. —*v.t.* **·shaled** or **·shalled, ·shal·ing** or **·shal·ling 1** To arrange or dispose in order, as facts. **2** To array or draw up, as troops for battle. **3** To lead; usher. [< OHG *marah* a horse + *scalh* a servant] — **mar′shal·cy** (·sē), **mar′shal·ship** *n.*

**marsh·mal·low** (marsh′mal′ō, ·mel′ō) *n.* A soft, spongy confection made of syrup and gelatin.

**mar·su·pi·al** (mär·sōō′pē·əl) *n.* Any of an order of mammals lacking a placenta and carrying their young in a marsupium, as the kangaroo, opossum, etc. —*adj.* 1 Having a marsupium. 2 Pertaining to or like a marsupium or pouch.

**mar·tial** (mär′shəl) *adj.* 1 Pertaining to war or military life: court *martial.* 2 Suitable for war: *martial* music. 3 Fond of war; brave. [< L *Martialis* pertaining to Mars] —**mar′tial·ly** *adv.*

**mar·ti·net** (mär′tə·net′) *n.* An overly strict disciplinarian, esp. military or naval. [< General *Martinet,* 17th c. French drillmaster]

**mar·ti·ni** (mär·tē′nē) *n. pl.* **·nis** A cocktail made of gin or vodka and dry vermouth, usu. served with a green olive or a twist of lemon peel. [?< *Martini* and Rossi, a company making vermouth]

**mar·tyr** (mär′tər) *n.* 1 One who submits to death rather than forswear his faith. 2 One who dies or suffers for principles, or sacrifices all for a cause. 3 One who suffers much or long, as from ill health or misfortune. —*v.t.* 1 To put to death as a martyr. 2 To torture; persecute. [< Gk. *martyr* a witness] —**mar′tyr·dom** *n.*

**mar·vel** (mär′vəl) *v.* **·veled** or **·velled, ·vel·ing** or **·vel·ling** *v.i* 1 To be filled with wonder, surprise, etc. —*v.t.* 2 To wonder at or about: with a clause as object. —*n.* 1 That which excites wonder; a prodigy. 2 A miracle. [< L *mirari* wonder at]

**mar·vel·ous** (mär′vəl·əs) *adj.* 1 Provoking astonishment or wonder; remarkable. 2 Supernatural; miraculous. 3 *Informal* Splendid; extraordinarily good. Also **mar′vel·lous.** —**mar′vel·ous·ly** *adv.* —**mar′vel·ous·ness** *n.* —**Syn.** 1 amazing, extraordinary, prodigious, wonderful, singular.

**mar·zi·pan** (mär′zə·pan) *n.* A confection of grated almonds, sugar, and white of eggs, usu. made into a paste and molded into various shapes. [< Ital. *marzapane,* orig. a small box, a dry measure, a weight]

**mas·cot** (mas′kot, -kət) *n.* A person, animal, or thing thought to bring good luck by its presence. [< Provençal *masco* a sorcerer]

**mas·cu·line** (mas′kyə·lin) *adj.* 1 Having the distinguishing qualities of the male sex. 2 Of, pertaining to, or suitable for males; manly. 3 *Gram.* Being of the male gender. —*n. Gram.* The masculine gender or a word of this gender. [< L *masculus* male] —**mas′cu·line·ly** *adv.* —**mas′cu·lin′i·ty** *n.*

**ma·ser** (mā′zər) *n. Physics* A device similar to a laser that operates with microwaves. [<

m(icrowave) a(mplification by) s(timulated) e(mission of) r(adiation)]

**mash** (mash) *n.* 1 A pulpy mass. 2 A mixture of meal, bran, etc., and water, fed to cattle. 3 Crushed or ground grain or malt, infused in hot water to produce wort. 4 In winemaking, the crushed grapes before fermentation. —*v.t.* 1 To crush or beat into a mash. 2 To convert into mash, as malt or grain, by infusing in hot water. [< OE *māsc*]

**mask** (mask, mäsk) *n.* 1 A cover or disguise for the features. 2 A protective appliance for the face or head: a gas *mask.* 3 Anything used to disguise or dissimilate; subterfuge. 4 A likeness of a face cast in plaster, clay, etc. 5 An elaborate dramatic presentation with music, fanciful costumes, etc., and actors masked as allegorical or mythological subjects; also, the text or music for it. 6 MASQUERADE. 7 An artistic covering for the face, used esp. by Greek and Roman actors. —*v.t.* 1 To cover, shield, or protect with or as with a mask. 2 To hide or conceal with or as with a mask; disguise. —*v.i.* 3 To put on a mask; assume a disguise. [< Ar. *maskharah* a buffoon] —**mask′er** *n.*

**mas·o·chism** (mas′ə·kiz′əm) *n.* The obtaining of pleasure, esp. sexual gratification, by submitting to physical or mental cruelty. [< Leopold von Sacher-*Masoch,* 1835–95, Austrian writer] —**mas′o·chist** *n.* —**mas′o·chis′tic** *adj.* —**mas′och·is′ti·cal·ly** *adv.*

**ma·son** (mā′sən) *n.* One who lays brick and stone in building; also, a stonecutter. [< Med. L *macio*]

**mas·quer·ade** (mas′kə·rād′, mäs′-) *n.* 1 A party attended by persons masked and costumed. 2 The costumes and disguises worn on such an occasion. 3 A false show or disguise. —*v.i.* **·ad·ed, ·ad·ing** 1 To take part in a masquerade. 2 To wear a mask or disguise. 3 To disguise one's true character; assume a false appearance. [< Sp. *máscara* a mask] —**mas′quer·ad′er** *n.*

**mass** (mas, mäs) *n.* 1 An assemblage of things that collectively make one quantity. 2 A body of matter; a lump. 3 The principal part of anything. 4 Extent of volume: bulk. 5 *Physics* The measure of the degree to which a body resists acceleration by a force, used also as a measure of the matter contained in the body. —**the masses** The common people. —*adj.* 1 Of, for, or consisting of the public in general. 2 Done on a large scale: *mass* production. —*v.t. & v.i.* To form into a mass; assemble. [< Gk. *maza* barley cake, lump] —**Syn.** *n.* 1 accumulation, aggregate, heap, collection, pile, group. *v.* accumulate, amass, gather, collect, pile up.

**mas·sa·cre** (mas′ə-kər) *n.* The indiscriminate, ruthless killing of human beings or animals; slaughter. —*v.t.* **·cred** (-kərd), **·cring** To kill indiscriminately or in great numbers. [< OF *maçacre* < *mache-col* butcher] —**mas′sa·crer** (-kə-rər, -krər) *n.*

**mas·sage** (mə-säzh′) *n.* A remedial treatment of kneading, rubbing, and otherwise manipulating a part or the whole of the body. —*v.t.* **·saged**, **·sag·ing** To treat by massage. [< F *masser* to massage] —**mas·sag′er**, **mas·sag′ist** *n.*

**mas·sive** (mas′iv) *adj.* 1 Constituting a large mass; ponderous. 2 Belonging to the total mass of anything. 3 Without definite form, as a mineral; amorphous. 4 Imposing in scope or degree; having considerable magnitude. —**mas′sive·ly** *adv.* —**mas′sive·ness** *n.* —**Syn.** 1 ample, broad, capacious, extensive, spacious.

**mast** (mast, mäst) *n.* 1 *Naut.* A pole or spar, of round timber or tubular metal, set upright in a sailing vessel to sustain the yards, sails, etc. 2 The upright pole of a derrick. 3 Any large, upright pole. —**before the mast** Serving as a common sailor. —*v.t.* To furnish with a mast or masts. [< OE *mǣst*]

**mas·ter** (mas′tər, mäs′-) *n.* 1 One who has authority over others, as the principal of a school, an employer, the head of a household, the owner of a domestic animal, etc. 2 One who has control of something; an owner. 3 In the U.S. merchant marine, the captain of a vessel. 4 One who is highly skilled; esp., an expert craftsman. 5 An artist of the first rank. 6 An original or a copy made from an original, as of a phonograph record, tape recording, or film, used as a source of making usu. numerous copies, as for commercial distribution. 7 A master key, switch, or other device. 8 *Chiefly Brit.* A male schoolteacher. 9 A title of respect for a young boy: *Master* Wilson. 10 An officer of the court who assists the judges. 11 One who has disciples or followers, esp. a religious leader. 12 One who gains the victory; a victor. —**the** (or **our**) **Master** Jesus. —*v.t.* 1 To overcome or subdue. 2 To become expert in: to *master* Greek. 3 To control or govern. —*adj.* 1 Being a master; being in control; chief. 2

Being an acknowledged expert: a *master* tactician. 3 Being a master from which others are duplicated. 4 Being a device that controls or can function in place of other mechanisms or that serves as a standard: a *master* key or switch. [< L *magister* greater] —**mas′ter·dom** *n.*

**master of ceremonies** A person presiding over an entertainment or dinner and introducing the performers or speakers.

**mas·ter·piece** (mas′tər-pēs′, mäs′-) *n.* An artistic work done with consummate skill.

**mas·ter·y** (mas′tər-ē, mäs′-) *n.* 1 The condition of having power and control. 2 Great knowledge or skill. 3 Superiority in a contest; victory. —**Syn.** 1 command, dominion, sway. 2 expertness. 3 triumph.

**mas·ti·cate** (mas′tə-kāt) *v.t.* **·cat·ed**, **·cat·ing** 1 To crush or grind (food) for swallowing; chew. 2 To reduce, as rubber, to a pulp by crushing or kneading. [< Gk. *mastichaein* gnash the teeth] —**mas′ti·ca′tion**, **mas′ti·ca′tor** *n.*

**mas·tur·bate** (mas′tər-bāt) *v.* **·bat·ed**, **·bat·ing** *v.i.* 1 To excite one's genitals, as by contact, for sexual pleasure, usu. inducing orgasm. —*v.t.* 2 To induce orgasm in (another) by exciting the genitals without having sexual intercourse. [< L *masturbari*] —**mas′tur·ba′tion**, **mas′tur·ba′tor** *n.* —**mas′tur·ba·to′ry** (-bə-tôr′ē, -tō′rē) *adj.*

**match** (mach) *n.* 1 A person or thing equal to another. 2 Two or more persons or things that harmonize or are alike. 3 A contest of skill, strength, etc.: a tennis *match.* 4 A marriage or an agreement to marry. 5 A person considered as a future husband or wife. —*v.t.* 1 To be similar to or in accord with in quality, degree, etc.: His looks *match* his mood. 2 To make or select as equals or as suitable for one another: to *match* pearls. 3 To marry. 4 To adapt: *Match* your efforts to your strength. 5 To compare so as to decide superiority; test: to *match* wits. 6 To set (equal opponents) in opposition: to *match* boxers. 7 To equal: No one could *match* him. —*v.i.* 8 To be equal, similar, or corresponding; suit. 9 To get married. —**match coins** To flip or reveal coins to make a decision. [< OE *gemǣcca* companion] —**match′a·ble** *adj.* —**match′er** *n.*

**match·book** (mach′book′) *n.* A folder enclosing and usu. stapled to a set of cardboard matches.

**match·mak·er** (mach′mā′kər) *n.* 1 One who

plans or schemes to bring about marriages for others. 2 One who arranges games or contests. —**match′mak′ing** *adj., n.*

**mate** (māt) *n.* 1 An associate; comrade. 2 One that is paired with another, as in matrimony; also, an animal paired for propagation. 3 An equal in a contest; a match. 4 An officer of a merchant vessel, ranking next below the captain. 5 *Nav.* A petty officer. — *v.* **mat·ed, mat·ing** *v.t.* 1 To join as mates; marry. 2 To pair for breeding, as animals. 3 To associate; couple. —*v.i.* 4 To match; marry. 5 To pair. 6 To consort; associate. [< MLG *gemate*]

**ma·te·ri·al** (mə·tir′ē·əl) *n.* 1 That of which anything is composed or may be constructed. 2 Collected facts, impressions, ideas, etc., for use in completing a creative endeavor. 3 The tools, instruments, articles, etc., for doing something. 4 A cloth or fabric. —*adj.* 1 Pertaining to anything having a physical existence. 2 Of or pertaining to the body or the appetites. 3 More interested in worldly things than in spiritual ones. 4 Important; significant: It makes no *material* difference to me. 5 Pertaining to matter as opposed to form. [< L *materia* matter]

**ma·te·ri·al·ize** (mə·tir′ē·əl·īz′) *v.* **·ized, ·iz·ing** *v.t.* 1 To give material or actual form to; represent as material. 2 To cause (a spirit, etc.) to appear in visible form. —*v.i.* 3 To assume material or visible form; appear. 4 To take form or shape; be realized: Our plans never *materialized.* —**ma·te′ri·al·i·za′tion, ma·te′ri·al·iz′er** *n.*

**ma·ter·nal** (mə·tûr′nəl) *adj.* 1 Pertaining to a mother; motherly. 2 Connected with or inherited from one's mother. [< L *mater* a mother] —**ma·ter′nal·ly** *adv.*

**ma·ter·ni·ty** (mə·tûr′nə·tē) *n. pl.* **·ties** 1 The condition of being a mother. 2 The qualities of a mother; motherliness. —*adj.* Pertaining to pregnancy or childbirth: *maternity* dress; *maternity* hospital.

**math·e·ma·ti·cian** (math′ə·mə·tish′ən) *n.* One skilled or trained in mathematics.

**math·e·mat·ics** (math′ə·mat′iks) *n.pl. (construed as sing.)* 1 The logical study of quantity, form, arrangement, and magnitude; esp., the methods for disclosing, by the use of rigorously defined concepts and symbols, the properties of quantities and relations. 2 A particular application or use of mathematics.

**mat·i·née** (mat′ə·nā′) *n.* An entertainment or reception held in the daytime; esp. a the-

atrical or cinematic performance given in the afternoon. **Also mat′i·nee′.** [F< *matin* morning]

**mat·ri·cide** (mat′rə·sīd, mā′trə-) *n.* 1 The killing of one's mother. 2 One who kills his or her mother. [< MATRI- + -CIDE] —**mat′ri·ci′dal** *adj.*

**ma·tric·u·late** (mə·trik′yə·lāt) *v.t. & v.i.* **·lat·ed, ·lat·ing** 1 To enroll, esp. in a college or university as a candidate for a degree. 2 *Can.* To pass final high-school examinations. —*n.* A candidate for a college or university degree. [< Med. L. *matrix* womb, origin, public roll] —**ma·tric′u·lant, ma·tric′u·la′tion, ma·tric′u·la′tor** *n.*

**mat·ri·mo·ny** (mat′rə·mō′nē) *n. pl.* **·nies** 1 The union of a man and a woman in marriage; wedlock. 2 The state of being married. [< L *matrimonium*] —**mat′ri·mo′ni·al** *adj.* —**mat′ri·mo′ni·al·ly** *adv.*

**ma·trix** (mā′triks) *n. pl.* **ma·tri·ces** (mā′trə·sēz, mat′rə-) or **ma·trix·es** 1 That which contains and gives shape or form to anything. 2 A mold in which anything is cast or shaped. 3 *Printing* A papier-mâché, plaster, or other impression of a form, from which a plate for printing may be made. [L, womb, breeding animal]

**ma·tron** (mā′trən) *n.* 1 A married woman. 2 A woman of established age and dignity. 3 A housekeeper, or a female superintendent, as of an institution. [< L *mater* mother] —**ma′tron·al, ma′tron·ly** *adj.* —**ma′tron·li·ness** *n.*

**mat·ter** (mat′ər) *n.* 1 That which makes up the substance of anything; material. 2 *Physics* That which occupies space, is reciprocally convertible with energy, and from which all physical objects are made. 3 A specific substance: inorganic *matter.* 4 Importance: It's of no *matter.* 5 That which is actually stated or written, as contrasted with style or form. 6 A subject or thing: a family *matter.* 7 A subject for discussion or feeling. 8 A condition of affairs, esp. if unpleasant or unfortunate: What's the *matter?* 9 Pus. 10 Written or printed documents sent by mail. 11 Amount: a *matter* of a few dollars. —**as a matter of fact** Actually; in fact. —**for that matter** As far as that is concerned. —*v.i.* To be of concern or importance. [< L *materia* stuff]

**mat·u·rate** (mach′o͞o·rāt, mat′yo͞o-) *v.i.* **·rat·ed, ·rat·ing** 1 To ripen or mature. 2 To suppurate; form pus. [< L *maturare* ripen]

—**mat′u·ra′tion** n. —**mat·u·ra·tive** (mach′-ōō·rā′tiv, mə·chŏŏr′ə·tiv) adj.

**ma·ture** (mə·chŏŏr′, -t′ŏŏr′) adj. 1 Completely developed; full-grown. 2 Fully developed in character and powers. 3 Highly developed; complete in detail: a mature scheme. 4 Due and payable, having reached its time limit: a mature bond. —v. ·tured, ·tur·ing v.t. 1 To cause to ripen or come to maturity. 2 To perfect; complete. —v.i. 3 To come to maturity or full development; ripen. 4 To become due, as a note. [< L maturus of full age] —ma·ture′ly adv. —ma·ture′ness n. —Syn. adj. 1 adult, grown, grown-up, ripe.

**ma·tur·i·ty** (mə·chŏŏr′ə·tē, -t′ŏŏr′-) n. 1 The state or condition of being mature. 2 Full development, as of the body. 3 The time at which a thing matures: a note payable at maturity.

**ma·tu·ti·nal** (mə·t′ŏō′tə·nəl) adj. Pertaining to morning; early. [< L matutinus early in the morning < Matuta, goddess of morning] —ma·tu′ti·nal·ly adv.

**maud·lin** (môd′lin) adj. 1 Foolishly and tearfully sentimental. 2 Made foolish from drinking too much alcoholic liquor. [< OF Maudelene, (Mary) Magdalen, who was often depicted with eyes swollen from weeping]

**mau·so·le·um** (mô′sə·lē′əm) n. pl. ·le·ums or ·le·a (-lē′ə) A large, stately tomb. [< Gk. Mausōleion tomb of King Mausolus, erected at Halicarnassus about 350 B.C.] —mau′so·le′an adj.

**mauve** (mōv, môv) n. Any of various pale purple shades of color. —adj. Of any of these shades. [< L malva mallow]

**mav·er·ick** (mav′ər·ik) n. 1 An unbranded or orphaned animal, esp. a calf. 2 A person characterized by independence or nonconformity in relation to a group with which he is affiliated, as a political party. [< S. A. Maverick, 1803–70, Texas lawyer, who did not brand his cattle]

**mawk·ish** (mô′kish) adj. 1 Characterized by false or feeble sentimentality. 2 Provoking disgust; sickening. [< obs. mawk a maggot] —mawk′ish·ly adv. —mawk′ish·ness n.

**max·i** (maks′ē) n. pl. max·is A long skirt or coat, usu. reaching to the ankle.

**max·il·la** (mak·sil′ə) n. pl. ·lae (-ē) 1 The upper jawbone in vertebrates. 2 One of the pair or pairs of mouth parts behind the mandibles of an insect, crab, etc. [L, jaw] —max·il·lar·y (mak′sə·ler′ē, mak·sil′ər·ē) adj., n. (pl. ·lar·ies).

**max·im** (mak′sim) n. A brief statement of a practical principle or proposition; a saying. [< L maxima (propositio) greatest (premise)] —Syn. adage, aphorism, epigram, motto, proverb.

**max·i·mum** (mak′sə·məm) n. pl. ·mums or ·ma (-mə) The greatest quantity, amount, degree, or magnitude that is possible. —adj. 1 As large or great as possible. 2 Pertaining to or setting a maximum: maximum weight. [< L maximus greatest]

**may·hem** (mā′hem) n. 1 Law The offense of depriving a person by violence of any limb, member, or organ, or causing any mutilation of the body. 2 Egregious disorder or damage. [< OF mahaigner maim]

**may·or** (mā′ər, mâr) n. The chief magistrate of a city, borough or municipal corporation. [< L major greater] —may′or·al adj.

**maze** (māz) n. 1 An intricate network of paths or passages; a labyrinth. 2 Uncertainty; perplexity. [< AMAZE] —maz′i·ly adv. —maz′i·ness n. —maz′y (i·er, i·est) adj.

**mea·ger** (mē′gər) adj. 1 Deficient in quantity or quality; scanty. 2 Scantily supplied with fertility, strength, or richness. 3 Wanting in flesh; thin. Also mea′gre. [< L macer lean] —mea′ger·ly adv. —mea′ger·ness n. — Syn. 1 inadequate, sparse, paltry, slight, exiguous. 3 emaciated, gaunt, skinny, spare.

**meal** (mēl) n. 1 Comparatively coarsely ground and unbolted grain. 2 Any powder produced by grinding. [< OE melu]

**mean**[1] (mēn) v. meant, mean·ing v.t. 1 To have in mind as a purpose or intent: I meant to visit him. 2 To intend or design for some purpose, destination, etc.: Was that remark meant for me? 3 To denote: The Latin word "vir" means "man." 4 To portend: Those clouds mean rain. —v.i. 5 To be disposed: He means well. 6 To be of specified importance or influence: Her beauty means everything to her. [< OE mænan tell, wish, intend]

**mean**[2] (mēn) adj. 1 Poor in quality; low ingrade. 2 Of humble antecedents; lowly. 3 Having little value or importance. 4 Shabby, as in appearance. 5 Unkind or selfish. 6 Informal Ashamed; guilty: to feel mean about something. 7 Stingy; miserly. 8 Informal Sick or irritable: He feels mean in the morning. 9 Slang Excellent; skillful: to play a mean game of chess. 10 Ill-tempered; unmanageable: said of animals:

a *mean* dog. [< OE *(ge)mǣne*, common, ordinary] —**mean′ly** *adv.* —**mean′ness** *n.* — Syn. 1 inferior. 2 common, ordinary, plebeian. 5 base, contemptible, ignoble.

**mean³** (mēn) *n.* 1 The middle state between two extremes; moderation. 2 *Math.* An average, often an arithmetic mean. 3 *pl. (often construed as sing.)* The medium through which anything is done: a *means* to an end. 4 *pl.* Money or property; wealth. —**by all means** Without hesitation; certainly. —**by any means** In any manner possible; somehow. —**by means of** By the help or use of; through. —**by no means** Most certainly not. —*adj.* 1 Intermediate as to position between extremes. 2 Intermediate as to size, degree, or quality; average. 3 Of or indicating an average: the *mean* distance covered daily. [< L *medius* middle]

**me·an·der** (mē·an′dər) *v.i.* 1 To wind and turn in a course. 2 To wander aimlessly. —*n.* 1 A tortuous or winding course. 2 An aimless wandering. [< Gk. *Maiandros* a river known for its winding course] —**me·an′der·er** *n.*

**mea·sles** (mē′zəlz) *n.* Either of two distinct, contagious viral diseases characterized by small red skin eruptions: **a** RUBEOLA. **b** RUBELLA, or German measles. [ME *masel* a blister]

**meas·ure** (mezh′ər) *n.* 1 The extent or dimensions of anything. 2 A standard or unit of measurement. 3 A system of measurements • **See pp. 448–449 for tables of** MEASURES AND WEIGHTS **for metric and U.S. sytems.** 4 An instrument or utensil used in measurement. 5 The act of measuring. 6 A quantity measured. 7 Reasonable limits; moderation: reward beyond *measure.* 8 A certain proportion; relative extent. 9 *Often pl.* A specific act or course: to take drastic *measures.* 10 A legislative bill. 11 That which makes up a total. 12 Any quantity regarded as a unit and standard of comparison with other quantities. 13 *Music* **a** The division of time by which melody and rhythm are regulated. **b** The portion of music contained between two bar lines; bar. 14 In prosody, meter. 15 A slow and stately dance or dance movement. —**in a measure** Somewhat; partly. —**take one's measure** To estimate one's character. —*v.* ·**ured, ·ur·ing** *v.t.* 1 To take or ascertain the dimensions, quantity, capacity, etc., of, esp. by means of a measure. 2 To set apart, mark off, etc., by measuring: often with *off*

or *out.* 3 To estimate by comparison; judge; weigh. 4 To serve as the measure of. 5 To bring into competition or comparison. 6 To traverse as if measuring; travel over. 7 To adjust; regulate. 8 To appraise or observe carefully with the eyes: She *measured* him up and down before replying. —*v.i.* 9 To make or take measurements. 10 To yield a specified measurement: The table *measures* six by four feet. 11 To admit of measurement. —**measure one's length** To fall prostrate at full length. —**measure out** To distribute or allot by measure. —**measure up** To fulfill, as expectations: often with *to.* [< L *metiri* to measure] —**meas′ur·er** *n.*

**meat** (mēt) *n.* 1 The flesh of animals used as food: sometimes excluding fish and fowl. 2 Anything eaten for nourishment; victuals: *meat* and drink. 3 The edible part of anything. 4 The essence, gist, or pith: the *meat* of an essay. 5 *Slang* Anything one likes very much or does with special ease. [< OE *mete*] —**meat′less** *adj.*

**me·chan·ic** (mə·kan′ik) *n.* One engaged in mechanical employment, esp. in making, using, or repairing machines or tools. —*adj.* 1 Pertaining to mechanics; mechanical. 2 Involving manual labor or skill. [< Gk. *mēchanē* a machine]

**me·chan·i·cal** (mə·kan′i·kəl) *adj.* 1 Of or pertaining to mechanics or the laws of mechanics. 2 Produced by a machine. 3 Operated by mechanism. 4 Operating as if by a machine or machinery. 5 Doing or done by mere force of habit. 6 Lifeless; expressionless: a *mechanical* recitation. 7 Skilled in the use of tools and mechanisms. 8 Having to do with certain physical aspects of singing. —**me·chan′i·cal·ly** *adv.* —**me·chan′i·cal·ness** *n.*

**me·chan·ics** (mə·kan′iks) *n. (construed as sing.* defs. 1, 2; *usu. construed as pl.* def. 3) 1 The branch of physics that deals with the phenomena caused by the action of forces on material bodies. 2 The science and technology of machinery. 3 The mechanical or technical aspects of anything.

**mech·a·nism** (mek′ə·niz′əm) *n.* 1 The parts of a machine collectively. 2 The action or operation of a machine or a mechanical device. 3 Something similar to a machine in the arrangement and working of its parts, as the human body. 4 A process by which a given result is achieved: the *mechanisms* of heredity. 5 Technique; mechanical execution or action. 6 The philosophical doctrine that physical and chemical agencies alone are sufficient to explain all phenomena, including life. —**mech′a·nist** *n.* —**mech′a·nis′tic** *adj.* —**mech′a·nis′ti·cal·ly** *adv.*

**mech·a·nize** (mek′ə·nīz) *v.t.* ·**nized**, ·**niz·ing** 1 To make mechanical. 2 To convert (an industry, etc.) to machine production. 3 *Mil.* To equip with tanks, trucks, etc. —**mech′a·ni·za′tion** *n.*

**med·al** (med′l) *n.* A small piece of metal, bearing a device, usu. commemorative of some event or deed of bravery, scientific research, etc. —*v.t.* ·**aled** or ·**alled**, ·**al·ing** or ·**al·ling** To confer a medal upon. [< L *metallum* metal] —**med·al·lic** (mə·dal′ik) *adj.*

**me·dal·lion** (mə·dal′yən) *n.* 1 A large medal. 2 A decorative element, as of fabrics, shaped like a large medal.

**med·dle** (med′l) *v.i.* ·**dled**, ·**dling** To take part in or concern oneself with something that is not one's proper business; interfere: often with *in* or *with*. [< OF *medler, mesdler*] —**med·dler** (med′lər) *n.*

**me·di·al** (mē′dē·əl) *adj.* 1 Of or pertaining to the middle, in position or character or in calculation. 2 Ordinary; average. [<L *medius* middle] —**me′di·al·ly** *adv.*

**me·di·ate** (mē′dē·āt) *v.* ·**at·ed**, ·**at·ing** *v.t.* 1 To settle or reconcile by mediation, as differences. 2 To bring about or effect by mediation. 3 To serve as the medium for effecting (a result) or conveying (an object, information, etc.). —*v.i.* 4 To act between disputing parties in order to bring about a settlement, compromise, etc. 5 To occur or be in an intermediate relation or position. —*adj.* (-ĭt) 1 Acting as an intervening agency; indirect. 2 Occurring or effected as a result of indirect or median agency. 3 Intermediate. [< L *mediare* stand between] —**me′di·ate·ly** *adv.* —**me′di·a′tive** *adj.* —**me′di·a′tor** *n.*

**me·di·a·tion** (mē′dē·ā′shən) *n.* 1 The act of mediating; intercession; interposition. 2 A friendly intervention in the disputes of others, with their consent, for the purpose of adjusting differences.

**med·i·cal** (med′i·kəl) *adj.* 1 Pertaining to medicine or its practice. 2 Having curative properties. [< L *medicus* a physician] —**med′i·cal·ly** *adv.*

**Med·i·care** (med′i·kâr′) *n.* In the U.S., a health insurance program supported in part by government funds, serving esp. the aged.

**med·i·cate** (med′ə·kāt) *v.t.* ·**cat·ed**, ·**cat·ing** 1 To treat with a drug or other substance. 2 To tincture or impregnate with medicine. [< L *medicus* a physician] —**med′i·ca′tive**, **med′i·ca·to′ry** (-kə·tôr′ē, -tō′rē) *adj.*

**med·i·ca·tion** (med′ə·kā′shən) *n.* 1 Any substance used to treat disease, heal wounds, etc.; a medicine. 2 The act or process of medicating.

**me·dic·i·nal** (mə·dis′ə·nəl) *adj.* Adapted to cure or mitigate disease. —**me·dic′i·nal·ly** *adv.*

**med·i·cine** (med′ə·sin) *n.* 1 A substance used to treat disease, as a drug. 2 The science of preserving health and treating disease. 3 This science exclusive of surgery or obstetrics. 4 Among North American Indians, any agent or rite, as a medicine dance, medicine song, etc., used to invoke supernatural aid in health or disease. —**take one's medicine** To endure deserved or necessary hardship. —*v.t.* ·**cined**, ·**cin·ing** To treat with medicine. [< L *medicus* physician]

**me·di·e·val** (mē′dē·ē′vəl, med′ē-, mid′-, mē·dē′vəl) *adj.* Belonging to or descriptive or characteristic of the Middle Ages. [< L *medius* middle + *aevum* age] —**me′di·e′val·ly** *adv.*

**me·di·o·cre** (mē′dē·ō′kər, mē′dē·ō′kər) *adj.* Of only middle quality; ordinary; commonplace. [<L *medius* middle]

**me·di·oc·ri·ty** (mē′dē·ok′rə·tē) *n. pl.* ·**ties** 1 The condition of being mediocre. 2 Commonplace ability. 3 A commonplace person.

**med·i·tate** (med′ə·tāt) *v.* ·**tat·ed**, ·**tat·ing** *v.i.* 1 To engage in contemplative thought. —*v.t.* 2 To think about; consider. 3 To think about doing; intend; to *meditate* mischief. [< L *meditari* muse, ponder] —**med′i·ta′tive** *adj.* —**med′i·ta′tive·ly** *adv.* —**med′i·ta′tor** *n.* —Syn. 1 contemplate, muse, reflect, ponder, consider, weigh.

**med·i·ta·tion** (med′ə·tā′shən) *n.* The act of meditating; deep, deliberate thought; contemplation.

**me·di·um** (mē′dē·əm) *n. pl.* ·**di·ums** or **me·di·a** (-dē·ə) 1 An intermediate quality, degree, or condition; mean. 2 A surrounding or enveloping element; environment. 3 Any substance, as air, through or in which something may move or an effect be produced. 4 (*pl. usu.* **me·di·a**) An intermediate means or agency; instrument; esp., a means of communication that includes advertising: the mass *media;* Radio is the best *medium* to reach motorists. 5 (*pl.* **me·di·ums**) A person believed to be in communication with the spirits of the dead. 6 In painting, a liquid which gives fluency to the pigment. 7 Any nutritive substance adapted to the development of bacteria, viruses, and other microorganisms: also **culture medium.** —*adj.* Intermediate in quantity, quality, position, size, or degree; middle. [< L *medius* middle]

**med·ley** (med′lē) *n.* 1 A mingled and confused mass of ingredients, usu. incongruous; jumble. 2 A composition of different songs or parts of songs arranged to run as a continuous whole. —*adj.* Composed of parts that are not alike; mixed. [< OF *medlee*]

**meek** (mēk) *adj.* 1 Of gentle and long-suffering disposition. 2 Submissive; compliant. 3 Humble; lowly. —*adv.* In a meek manner. [< ON *miukr* gentle, soft] —**meek′ly** *adv.* —**meek′ness** *n.*

**meer·schaum** (mir′shəm, -shôm, -shoum) *n.* 1 A soft, light, heat-resistant magnesium silicate mineral used for tobacco pipes, cigar holders, etc. 2 A pipe made from this material. [< G *Meer* sea + *Schaum* foam]

**meet** (mēt) *v.* **met, meet·ing** *v.t.* 1 To come upon; encounter. 2 To make the acquaintance of. 3 To be at the place of arrival of: We *met* him at the station. 4 To come into contact or intersection with: where the path *meets* the road. 5 To keep an appointment with. 6 To come into the view, hearing, etc., of: A ghastly sight *met* our eyes. 7 To experience; undergo: to *meet* bad weather. 8 To oppose in battle; fight with. 9 To face or counter: to *meet* a blow with a blow. 10 To deal with; refute: to *meet* an accusation. 11 To comply with; act or result in conformity with, as expectations or wishes. 12 To pay, as a bill. —*v.i.* 13 To come together, as from different directions. 14 To come together in contact, conjunction, or intersection; join. 15 To assemble. 16 To make acquaintance or be introduced. 17 To come together in conflict or opposition; contend. 18 To agree. —**meet with** 1 To come upon; encounter. 2 To deal or confer with. 3 To experience. —*n.* A meeting or assembly for some specific activity, esp. for an athletic contest. [< OE *mētan*]

**meg·a·lo·ma·ni·a** (meg′ə·lō·mā′nē·ə, -mān′yə) *n.* A mental disorder in which the subject thinks himself great or exalted. —**meg′a·lo·ma′ni·ac** *adj., n.*

**meg·a·lop·o·lis** (meg′ə·lop′ə·lis) *n.* A densely populated urban area, usu. including one or more major cities. [< MEGALO- + Gk. *polis* city] —**meg·a·lo·pol·i·tan** (meg′ə·lō·pol′ə·tan) *adj., n.*

**meg·a·phone** (meg′ə·fōn) *n.* A funnel-shaped device for projecting or directing sound. —*v.t. & v.i.* **·phoned, ·phon·ing** To address or speak through a megaphone.

**meg·a·ton** (meg′ə·tun′) *n.* A unit of nuclear explosive power equivalent to one million tons of TNT.

**mel·an·chol·y** (mel′ən·kol′ē) *adj.* 1 Gloomy; sad. 2 Causing sadness or dejection. 3 Pensive. —*n.* 1 Low spirits; depression. 2 Pensive or sober reflection. [< Gk. *melas* black + *cholē* bile] —**mel′an·chol′ic** *adj., n.* —**mel′an·chol′i·cal·ly** *adv.* —**Syn.** *adj.* 1 dejected, depressed, downcast. *n.* 1 dejection, despondency, sadness.

**mel·lif·lu·ous** (mə·lif′loō·əs) *adj.* Sweetly or smoothly flowing; dulcet: a *mellifluous* voice. [< L *mel* honey + *fluere* flow] —**mel·lif′lu·ous·ly** *adv.* —**mel·lif′lu·ous·ness** *n.*

**mel·low** (mel′ō) *adj.* 1 Soft and sweet because of ripeness: *mellow* fruit. 2 Well-matured, as wines. 3 Full and rich; not harsh or strident: the *mellow* tones of a cello. 4 Gentle and understanding, as from age or experience. 5 Happy and relaxed, as from liquor. 6 Soft and friable, as soil. —*v.t. & v.i.* To make or become mellow. [ME *melwe*] —**mel′low·ly** *adv.* —**mel′low·ness** *n.*

**mel·o·dra·ma** (mel′ə·drä′mə, -dram′ə) *n.* 1 Originally, a drama with a romantic story or plot, sensational incidents, and usu. including some music and song. 2 Any sensational and emotional drama, usu. having a happy ending. 3 Excessively dramatic or emotional behavior or language. [< Gk. *melos* song + *drama* drama]

**mel·o·dra·mat·ic** (mel′ə·drə·mat′ik) *adj.* Of, pertaining to, or like melodrama; sensational. —**mel′o·dra·mat′i·cal·ly** *adv.*

**mel·o·dy** (mel′ə·dē) *n. pl.* **·dies** 1 Pleasing sounds or an agreeable arrangement of such sounds. 2 *Music* **a** A succession of tones constituting, in combination, a whole. **b** The chief part or voice in a composition; the air. [< Gk. *melos* song + *aoidos* singer]

**mel·on** (mel′ən) *n.* 1 Any of various trailing plants of the gourd family bearing large, many-seeded fruits with a thick rind and sweet, pulpy flesh. 2 The fruit of any of these plants, as the watermelon, cantaloupe, etc. —**cut a** (or **the**) **melon** *Slang* To divide surplus profits, as among stockholders. [< Gk. *mēlopepōn* apple-shaped melon]

**mem·ber** (mem′bər) *n.* 1 A person belonging to an incorporated or organized body, society, etc.: a *member* of a club. 2 A limb or other functional organ of an animal body or plant. 3 A part or element of a structural or composite whole. 4 *Math.* a The expression on one side or the other of an equation. b An element contained in a set. [<L *membrum* limb]

**mem·ber·ship** (mem′bər·ship) *n.* 1 The state of being a member. 2 The members of an organization, collectively. 3 The number of members.

**mem·brane** (mem′brān) *n.* A thin, pliable sheet of material, esp. animal or vegetable tissue serving as a cover, connection, or lining. [<L *membrana*, lit., limb coating]

**me·men·to** (mə·men′tō) *n. pl.* **·toes** or **·tos** A hint or reminder to awaken memory, esp. a souvenir. [<L *meminisse* remember]

**mem·oir** (mem′wär) *n.* 1 *pl.* A written account of a person's experiences, reminiscences, etc.; an autobiography. 2 A biography. 3 A monograph or report. [F <L *memoria* memory] —**mem′oir·ist** *n.*

**mem·o·ra·ble** (mem′ər·ə·bəl) *adj.* Worthy to be remembered; notable. —**mem′o·ra·bil′i·ty, mem′o·ra·ble·ness** *n.*

**mem·o·ran·dum** (mem′ə·ran′dəm) *n. pl.* **·dums** or **·da** (-də) 1 A brief note of a thing or things to be remembered. 2 An informal note or letter, usu. sent from one person to another in an office. 3 *Law* A brief written outline of the terms of a transaction. 4 A statement of goods sent from a consignor to a consignee. [L, a thing to be remembered]

**me·mo·ri·al** (mə·môr′əl, -mō′rē-) *adj.* Commemorating the memory of a deceased person or of any event. —*n.* 1 Something designed to keep in remembrance a person, event, etc. 2 A presentation of facts made to a government or an official, and usu. accompanies by a petition. [<L *memorialis*]

**mem·o·ry** (mem′ər·ē, mem′rē) *n. pl.* **·ries** 1 The act, faculty, or capacity of remembering something that is past. 2 Everything that one can remember. 3 A specific act, event, person, or thing remembered. 4 The period of time covered by the faculty of remembrance: beyond the *memory* of man. 5 The state of being remembered. 6 Commemoration or remembrance: in *memory* of

her parents. 7 The information storage unit of a computer. [<L *memor* mindful] —**Syn.** 1 recollection, remembrance, reminiscence.

**men·ace** (men′is) *v.* **·aced, ·ac·ing** *v.t.* 1 To threaten with evil or harm. —*v.i.* 2 To make threats; appear threatening. —*n.* 1 A threat. 2 A person or thing that is troublesome or dangerous. [<L *minari* threaten] —**men′ac·ing·ly** *adv.*

**me·nag·er·ie** (mə·naj′ər·ē) *n.* 1 A collection of wild animals kept for exhibition. 2 The enclosure in which they are kept. [<F]

**men·da·cious** (men·dā′shəs) *adj.* 1 Addicted to lying; deceitful. 2 Untrue; false. [<L *mendax* lying] —**men·da′cious·ly** *adv.* —**men·da′cious·ness, men·dac′i·ty** (men·das′ə·tē) *n.*

**men·di·cant** (men′də·kənt) *adj.* 1 Depending on alms for a living; begging. 2 Pertaining to or like a beggar. —*n.* 1 A beggar. 2 A begging friar. [<L *mendicus* needy]

**me·ni·al** (mē′nē·əl, mēn′yəl) *adj.* 1 Pertaining or appropriate to servants. 2 Servile; base. 3 Low; humble; esp., marked by low prestige or tedious routine: a *menial* job; *menial* tasks. —*n.* 1 A domestic servant. 2 A person of low or servile nature. [<L *mansio* house] —**me′ni·al·ly** *adv.*

**men·in·gi·tis** (men′ən·jī′tis) *n.* Inflammation of the meninges, often caused by infection. —**men′in·git′ic** (-jit′ik) *adj.*

**men·o·pause** (men′ə·pôz) *n.* Final cessation of menstruation; change of life. [<Gk. *mēn* month + PAUSE]

**men·stru·a·tion** (men′strŏō·ā′shən) *n.* A bloody flow from the uterus, resulting when an ovum is not fertilized and occurring in women at about monthly intervals.

**men·tal** (men′təl) *adj.* 1 Of or pertaining to the mind. 2 Done by or occurring in the mind, esp. without the aid of written symbols: *mental* arithmetic. 3 Affected by a disorder of the mind: a *mental* patient. 4 Psychiatric: a *mental* hospital. [< L *mens, mentis* mind] —**men′tal·ly** *adv.*

**men·tion** (men′shən) *v.t.* 1 To speak of incidentally, briefly, or in passing. 2 To cite, as for achievement. —*n.* 1 A brief or casual reference or notice. 2 A citing, as for achievement. [<L *mens, mentis* mind] —**men′tion·a·ble** *adj.* —**men′tion·er** *n.*

**men·tor** (men′tər, -tôr) *n.* A wise and trusted teacher, guide, and friend. [<*Mentor,* the wise guardian of Telemachus in the *Odyssey.*]

**mer·can·tile** (mûr′kən·til, -til) *adj.* 1 Of, pertaining to, or characteristic of merchants. 2 Of or like mercantilism. [< Ital. *mercante* merchant]

**mer·ce·nar·y** (mûr′sə·ner′ē) *adj.* 1 Influenced by desire for gain or reward; greedy. 2 Serving in a foreign army for pay or profit; hired: *mercenary* soldiers. —*n. pl.* ·nar·ies 1 A mercenary soldier. 2 Any hireling. [< L *merces* reward, pay] —**mer′ce·nar′i·ly** *adv.* — **mer′ce·nar′i·ness** *n.*

**mer·chan·dise** (mûr′chən·dīz, -dīs) *n.* Anything bought and sold for profit; wares. — *v.t. & v.i.* (-dīz) ·dised, ·dis·ing 1 To buy and sell. 2 To promote the sale of (an article) through advertising, etc. Also **mer′ chan· dize.** [See MERCHANT.] —**mer′chan·dis′er** *n.*

**mer·chant** (mûr′chənt) *n.* 1 A person who buys and sells commodities as a business or for profit. 2 A storekeeper. —*adj.* 1 Of or pertaining to merchants or merchandise. 2 Of the merchant marine. [< L *mercari* to traffic, buy <*merx* wares] —**Syn.** *n.* 1 businessman, trader, bourgeois. 2 dealer, shopkeeper, tradesman.

**mer·cu·ri·al** (mər·kyōō′rē·əl) *adj.* 1 Apt to change moods abruptly and with little cause; volatile. 2 Suggestive of the qualities associated with the god Mercury; lively, quick, and ingenious: a *mercurial* wit. 3 Of, containing, or caused by the element mercury. —*n.* A preparation containing mercury. —**mer·cu′ri·al·ly** *adv.* —**mer·cu′ri·al· ness** *n.*

**mer·cy** (mûr′sē) *n. pl.* ·cies 1 Kind or compassionate behavior shown to an enemy, offender, etc., who is in one's power. 2 Compassion or kindness towards others, esp. those in distress. 3 The power to show clemency or forgiveness. 4 A fortunate happening or circumstance. —**at the mercy of** Wholly in the power of. [< L *merces* hire, payment, reward] —**Syn.** 1 benevolence, compassion, forbearance, leniency.

**mer·e·tri·cious** (mer′ə·trish′əs) *adj.* Deceitfully or artificially attractive; tawdry. [< L *meretrix* prostitute] —**mer′e·tri′cious·ly** *adv.* —**mer′e·tri′cious·ness** *n.*

**merge** (mûrj) *v.t. & v.i.* merged, merg·ing To combine or be combined so as to lose separate identity; blend. [< L *mergere* dip, immerse]

**merg·er** (mûr′jər) *n.* 1 The act of merging. 2 A combination of two or more commercial interests or companies into one.

**me·rid·i·an** (mə·rid′ē·ən) *n.* 1 *Astron.* A great circle passing through the poles of the celestial sphere. 2 *Geog.* a A great circle of the earth, passing through both poles. b Either half of such a great circle, extending from one pole to the other. 3 The highest or culminating point of anything; the zenith. 4 In acupuncture, a pathway beneath the skin through which energy is believed to flow and along which specific acupuncture points are located. —*adj.* 1 Of or pertaining to noon. 2 Of or at the highest or culminating point. 3 Of or pertaining to a meridian. [< L *meridies* noon, south]

**me·ringue** (mə·rang′) *n.* 1 The beaten white of eggs, sweetened and usu. baked as a topping for pies or other pastry. 2 A small baked shell of meringue. [F]

**mer·it** (mer′it) *n.* 1 The quality or fact of deserving praise, reward, etc. 2 Worth, value, or excellence; quality. 3 That which deserves esteem, praise, or reward. 4 *pl.* The actual rights or wrongs of a matter: to decide a case on its *merits.* —*v.t.* To deserve. [< L *meritus,* pp. of *merere* deserve]

**mer·i·to·ri·ous** (mer′ə·tôr′ē·əs, -tō′rē-) *adj.* Deserving of reward, praise, etc. —**mer′i·toəri·ous·ly** *adv.* —**mer′i·to′ri·ous·ness** *n.*

**mer·maid** (mûr′mād′) *n.* A legendary sea creature having the head and body of a woman and the tail of a fish. Also **mer′ maid′en** (-mād′n). [< MERE[2] + MAID]

**mer·ri·ment** (mer′i·mənt) *n.* Gaiety; mirth.

**mer·ry** (mer′ē) *adj.* ·ri·er, ·ri·est 1 Given to mirth and laughter. 2 Marked by cheerfulness and gay spirits. —**make merry** To be in high spirits. [< OE *myrige* pleasant] — **mer′ri·ly** *adv.* —**mer′ri·ness** *n.* —**Syn.** 1 blithe, frolicsome, gleeful, light-hearted.

**mer·ry-go-round** (mer′ē·gō·round′, mer′i-) *n.* 1 A revolving platform fitted with wooden horses, seats, etc., on which people ride for amusement; a carousel. 2 A whirl, as of pleasure.

**mesh** (mesh) *n.* 1 One of the open spaces in a net, screen, sieve, etc. 2 *pl.* The cords or wires that form such open spaces. 3 A net or network. 4 Anything that entangles or involves. 5 *Mech.* The engagement of gear teeth. —*v.t. & v.i.* 1 To make or become entangled, as in a net. 2 To make or become engaged, as gear teeth. [< MDu. *maesche*]

**mes·mer·ism** (mes′mə·riz′əm, mez′-) *n.* HYPNOTISM. [< F. A. *Mesmer,* 1734–1815, German physician] —**mes·mer·ic** (mes·mer′ik, mez-), **mes·mer′i·cal** *adj.* —**mes·mer′i·cal·ly** *adv.* —**mes′mer·ist** *n.*

**mes·mer·ize** (mes′mə·rīz, mez′-) *v.t.* ·ized,

·iz·ing 1 HYPNOTIZE.. 2 To fascinate as if hypnotized. —mes′mer·i·za′tion, mes′mer·iz′
er n.

**mess** (mes) n. 1 A state of disorder, confusion,
or untidiness. 2 A confusing, troublesome,
or embarrassing situation. 3 A quantity of
food sufficient for one meal or for a dish. 4
A portion of soft, partly liquid food, as porridge. 5 A number of persons who habitually take their meals together, as in military
units; also, a meal taken by them. 6 MESS
HALL. 7 Unpleasant or unclean food. —v.i. 1
To make a mess: often with up. 2 To eat
with a mess (def. 5). —v.t. 3 To make a mess
of; muddle: often with up. 4 To make dirty;
befoul: often with up. 5 To provide meals
for. —mess around (or about) To busy oneself; dabble. [< L missus course at a meal]

**mes·sage** (mes′ij) n. 1 A communication sent
in any way. 2 A formal communication, as
from a chief executive to a legislative body.
3 A communication embodying a truth,
principle, or advice. 4 The carrying out of a
mission; errand. 5 A television or radio
commercial. [< L missus, pp. of mittere]

**mes·sen·ger** (mes′ən·jər) n. 1 One sent with
a message or on an errand of any kind. 2 A
forerunner; herald.

**Mes·si·ah** (mə·sī′ə) n. 1 In Judaism, the name
for the promised deliverer of the Hebrews.
2 In Christianity, Jesus. 3 Any long-awaited
liberator. [< Hebrew māshīah anointed] —
**Mes·si·an·ic** (mes′ē·an′ik) adj.

**me·tab·o·lism** (mə·tab′ə·liz′əm) n. The aggregate of physical and chemical processes
by which a living organism converts assimilated materials into living tissue, energy, and waste. [< Gk. meta- beyond +
ballein throw]

**met·al** (met′l) n. 1 Any of the elements that
tend to lose electrons and form positive
ions in chemical reactions, form bases in
combination with hydroxyl groups and are
usu. lustrous, malleable, ductile, and good
conductors of heat and electricity. 2 A combination of such elements; an alloy. 3
Molten glass. 4 Printing Type metal; also,
composed type. 5 The essential quality or
substance of a person or thing. —adj. Of,
like, or consisting of metal. —v.t. ·aled or
·alled, ·al·ing or ·al·ling To furnish or cover
with metal. [< L metallum mine, metal]

**met·al·lur·gy** (met′ə·lûr′jē) n. The technology
of extracting metals from ores and producing alloys with desired properties. [< Gk. <

metallon metal + -ergos working] —met′
al·lur′gic or ·gi·cal adj. —met′al·lur′gist
n.

**met·a·mor·phose** (met′ə·môr′fōz) v. ·phosed,
·phos·ing v.t. 1 To change the form of. —v.i.
2 To undergo metamorphism or metamorphosis.

**met·a·mor·pho·sis** (met′ə·môr′fə·sis) n. pl.
·pho·ses (-fə·sēz) 1 A passing from one form
or shape into another, esp. by means of
sorcery, etc. 2 Complete transformation of
character, purpose, circumstances, etc. 3 A
person or thing metamorphosed. 4 Biol. A
developmental change in form, structure,
or function in an organism, esp. after leaving the egg and before attaining sexual maturity. [< Gk. meta- beyond + morphē form]

**met·a·phor** (met′ə·fôr, -fər) n. A figure of
speech in which one object is likened to
another by speaking of it as if it were that
other, as in The sun was a chariot of fire. [<
Gk. meta- beyond, over + pherein to carry]
—met′a·phor′ic (-fôr′ik, -for′ik) or ·i·cal
adj. —met′a·phor′i·cal·ly adv. • Metaphors
and similes both make comparisons, but
the metaphor is distinguished from the
simile by the omission of an introductory
word such as "like" or "as." For example,
The moon is a silver coin is a metaphor; The
moon is like a silver coin is a simile.

**met·a·phys·i·cal** (met′ə·fiz′i·kəl) adj. 1 Of,
pertaining to, or like metaphysics. 2 Very
abstract or abstruse. 3 Designating certain
poets of the 17th century whose verses
were characterized by complex, intellectu-
alized imagery. —met′a·phys′i·cal·ly adv.

**met·a·phys·ics** (met′ə·fiz′iks) n.pl. (construed
as sing.) 1 The branch of philosophy that
deals with the first principles of being and
knowledge and with the essential nature of
reality. 2 All speculative philosophy. [< Med.
Gk. ta meta ta physika the (works) after the
physics; in ref. to Aristotle's Physics] —
met′a·phy·si′cian n.

**meteor., meteorol.** meteorological; meteorol-
ogy.

**me·te·or·ic** (mē′tē·ôr′ik, -or′ik) adj. 1 Of or
pertaining to meteors. 2 Pertaining to atmospheric phenomena; meteorological. 3
Like a meteor in brilliance or swiftness: a
meteoric career. —me′te·or′i·cal·ly adv.

**me·te·or·ite** (mē′tē·ə·rīt′) n. 1 A solid mass
that has fallen to the earth from space. 2
METEOROID. —me′te·or·it′ic (-ə·rit′ik) adj.

**me·te·or·ol·o·gy** (mē′tē·ə·rol′ə·jē) n. The science that deals with atmospheric phe-

neomena, esp. those that relate to weather. [< Gk. *meteōros* high in the air + -LOGY] — **me'te·or'o·log'i·cal** (-ôr'ə·loj'ə·kəl) or **·log'ic** *adj.* —**me'te·or'o·log'i·cal·ly** *adv.* —**me'te·or·ol'o·gist** *n.*

**me·ter** (mē'tər) *n.* An instrument for measuring and recording something. —*v.t.* To measure or test by means of a meter. [<METE[1]]

**meth·od** (meth'əd) *n.* 1 A systematic, established, or orderly procedure or way of doing anything. 2 System, order, or regularity in general. 3 The disciplines and techniques used in any field of knowledge, creativity, etc.: the Renaissance *methods* of painting. 4 Orderly and systematic arrangement, as of ideas and topics, etc. [< Gk. *meta-* after + *hodos* way]

**me·thod·i·cal** (mə·thod'i·kəl) *adj.* 1 Characterized by or performed with method and order. 2 Orderly; systematic: a *methodical* worker. Also **me·thod'ic.** —**me·thod'i·cal·ly** *adv.* —**me·thod'i·cal·ness** *n.*

**me·tic·u·lous** (mə·tik'yə·ləs) *adj.* Extremely or excessively careful about details; finical. [<L *meticolosus* fearful] —**me·tic'u·los'i·ty** (-los'ə·tē) *n.* —**me·tic'u·lous·ly** *adv.* —**Syn.** exacting, fastidious, finicky, particular, punctilious.

**me·ton·y·my** (mə·ton'ə·mē) *n.* **·mies** A figure of speech that employs an associated or closely connected word rather than the word itself, as "the crown prefers" for "the king prefers." [< Gk. *meta-* altered + *onyma* name] —**met·o·nym·ic** (met'ə·nim'ik), **met'o·nym'i·cal** *adj.* —**met'o·nym'i·cal·ly** *adv.*

**met·ro·nome** (met'rə·nōm) *n.* An instrument for indicating tempo in music, consisting of a mechanical or electronic oscillator producing pulses at a fixed, controllable rate. [<METRO- + Gk. *nomos* law] —**met'ro·nom'ic** (-nom'ik) *adj.*

**me·trop·o·lis** (mə·trop'ə·lis) *n.* 1 The capital or the largest or most important city of a state or country. 2 Any large city that is the center of some activity. 3 The seat of a metropolitan bishop. [< Gk. *mētēr* mother + *polis* city]

**met·ro·pol·i·tan** (met'rə·pol'ə·tən) *adj.* 1 Of, like, or constituting a metropolis (defs. 1 & 2). 2 Of or designating a metropolitan or his province. —*n.* 1 An archbishop who has authority over the bishops of his ecclesiastical province. 2 One who lives in a metropolis or has the manners and customs of a metropolis.

**met·tle** (met'l) *n.* 1 Inherent quality of character. 2 Courage; spirit. —**on one's mettle** Aroused to one's best efforts. [Var. of METAL] —**met'tled** *adj.*

**mez·za·nine** (mez'ə·nēn, mez·ə·nēn') *n.* 1 A low-ceilinged story or long, inner balcony between two main stories. Also **mezzanine floor, mezzanine story.** 2 In a theater, the first balcony or the front rows of the first balcony. [< Ital. *mezzano* middle]

**mi·as·ma** (mī·az'mə, mē-) *n. pl.* **·mas** or **·ma·ta** (-mə·tə) 1 The poisonous effluvium once supposed to rise from putrid matter, swamps, etc. 2 Any unwholesome influence or atmosphere. [< Gk., pollution] —**mi·as'mal, mi·as·mat·ic** (mī'az·mat'ik), **mi·as'mic** *adj.*

**mi·crobe** (mī'krōb) *n.* A microscopic organism, esp. a disease-producing bacterium. [< Gk. *mikro-* small + *bios* life] —**mi·cro'bi·al, mi·cro'bi·an, mi·cro'bic** *adj.*

**mi·cro·bi·ol·o·gy** (mī'krō·bī·ol'ə·jē) *n.* The branch of biology that deals with microorganisms. —**mi'cro·bi'o·log'i·cal** *adj.* —**mi'cro·bi·ol'o·gist** *n.*

**mi·cro·cosm** (mī'krə·koz'əm) *n.* 1 A little world; esp., a community or environment regarded as a small-scale version or example of the universe or of a much larger entity. 2 Man seen as the epitome of the universe. Also **mi'cro·cos'mos** (-koz'məs). [< Gk. *mikros kosmos*, lit., little world]

**mi·cro·film** (mī'krə·film) *n.* A film on which is a photographic reproduction of a printed page, document, or other object, highly reduced for ease in transmission and storage, and capable of reenlargement. —*v.t. & v.i.* To reproduce on microfilm.

**mi·cro·groove** (mī'krə·grōōv) *n.* A very fine groove cut in the surface of a long-playing phonograph record.

**mi·crom·e·ter** (mī·krom'ə·tər) *n.* 1 An instrument for measuring very small distances or dimensions as used on a microscope or telescope. 2 MICROMETER CALIPER.

**mi·cro·or·gan·ism** (mī'krō·ôr'gən·iz'əm) *n.* An organism visible only in an optical or electron microscope, as a bacterium, protozoan, or virus. Also **mi'cro·or'gan·ism.**

**mi·cro·phone** (mī'krə·fōn) *n.* A device for changing sound waves into corresponding electric signals.

**mi·cro·scope** (mī'krə·skōp) *n.* Any of various instruments for magnifying objects too small to be seen or clearly observed by the naked eye. [<MICRO- + -SCOPE]

**mi·cro·scop·ic** (mī′krə·skop′ik) *adj.* 1 So small as to be visible only with the aid of a microscope. 2 Exceedingly small or minute. 3 Of, relating to, or done with a microscope or microscopy. 4 Resembling a microscope. Also **mi′cro·scop′i·cal.** —**mi′cro·scop′i·cal·ly** *adv.*

**mi·cro·wave** (mī′krə·wāv) *n.* An electromagnetic wave having a wavelength in the range longer than red light and shorter than radio waves.

**mid·dle** (mid′l) *adj.* 1 Equally distant from the extremes of place, position, time, etc.; central. 2 Being in neither the one nor the other extreme; intermediate. 3 *Often cap.* Designating a language midway in development between an earlier (Old) and later (Modern) form. —*n.* 1 The part or point equally distant from the extremes of place, position, time, etc. 2 Something that is intermediate. 3 The middle part of the body; waist. —*v.t.* **·dled, ·dling** To place in the middle. [< OE *middel*] **Syn.** *adj.* 1 median, mid, moderate. *n.* 1 midway, center.

**middle age** The time of life between youth and old age, commonly between 40 and 60. —**mid′dle-aged′** (-ājd′) *adj.*

**mid·dle·man** (mid′l·man′) *n. pl.* **·men** (-men′) 1 One who acts as an agent or go-between; intermediary. 2 One who buys in bulk from producers and sells to retailers or directly to consumers.

**mid·dle·weight** (mid′l·wāt′) *n.* A boxer or wrestler weighing between 147 and 160 pounds. —*adj.* Of middleweights.

**midg·et** (mij′it) *n.* 1 An abnormally small person. 2 Anything very small of its kind. —*adj.* Small; diminutive. [Dim. of MIDGE]

**mid·i** (mid′ē) *n. pl.* **mid·is** A skirt, dress, or coat with a hemline at mid-calf. [< MIDDLE]

**mid·riff** (mid′rif) *n.* 1 The diaphragm. 2 The part of the body between the chest and the abdomen. [< OE *midd* mid + *hrif* belly]

**mien** (mēn) *n.* The bearing, demeanor, or expression of a person. [< DEMEAN]

**might**[1] (mit) *p.t.* of MAY[1].

**might**[2] (mit) *n.* 1 Physical strength. 2 Great power, ability, or resources of any kind. —**with might and main** With one's whole strength. [< OE *meaht, miht*] —**Syn.** 1 force, potency, puissance, vigor, power.

**might·y** (mi′tē) *adj.* **might·i·er, might·i·est** 1 Possessed of might; powerful; strong. 2 Of unusual size, consequence, etc. —*adv.* In-

*formal* Very; exceedingly. —**might′i·ly** *adv.* —**might′i·ness** *n.*

**mi·graine** (mī′grān) *n.* A recurrent, severe form of headache, temporarily disabling, usu. affecting one side of the head and often accompanied by nausea, dizziness, and sensitivity to light. [< Gk. *hēmi* half + *kranion* skull]

**mi·grate** (mī′grāt) *v.i.* **·grat·ed, ·grat·ing** 1 To move, as from one place, region, etc., to another. 2 To move periodically from one region or climate to another, as birds or fish. [< L *migrare* roam, wander] —**mi′gra·tor** *n.*

**mi·gra·tion** (mī·grā′shən) *n.* 1 The act of migrating. 2 The totality of persons or animals migrating at one time. 3 *Chem.* The shifting of one or more atoms from one position in the molecule to another. 4 *Physics* The drift or movement of ions due to the effect of an electric field. —**mi·gra′tion·al** *adj.* —**mi·gra′tion·ist** *n.*

**mi·gra·to·ry** (mī′grə·tôr′ē, -tō′rē) *adj.* 1 Of or pertaining to migration. 2 Given to migrating. 3 Roving; nomadic.

**mild** (mīld) *adj.* 1 Gentle in nature or disposition. 2 Moderate; temperate: a *mild* winter. 3 Not harsh or strong, as in flavor. [< OE *milde*] —**mild′ly** *adv.* —**mild′ness** *n.*

**mil·dew** (mil′d(y)ōō) *n.* 1 Any of various fungi that form a spotty coating on damp surfaces, as plant leaves, clothing, leather, etc. 2 Any of various plant diseases due to these fungi. —*v.t. & v.i.* To affect or be affected with mildew. [< OE *mildēaw* honeydew] —**mil′dew·y** *adj.*

**mile** (mīl) *n.* 1 A unit of length equal to 5,280 feet or 1.609 kilometers: **also statute miles.** 2 NAUTICAL MILE. 3 AIR MILE. [< L *mille* thousand]

**mile·age** (mī′lij) *n.* 1 Length or distance as measured in miles. 2 An allowance for expenses while traveling, reckoned at so much per mile. 3 Length of service, quality of performance, etc.; usefulness; advantage. Also **mil′age.**

**mil·i·tant** (mil′ə·tənt) *adj.* 1 Actively engaged in war; fighting. 2 Aggressive or combative, esp. in support of a cause. —*n.* A militant person. [< L *militare* be a soldier] —**mil′i·tan·cy** *n.* —**mil′i·tant·ly** *adv.*

**mil·i·ta·rism** (mil′ə·tə·riz′əm) *n.* A policy or system emphasizing and exalting the military spirit and stressing the need of constant preparation for war. —**mil′i·ta·rist** *n.*

—**mil·i·ta·ris′tic** adj. —**mil′i·ta·ris′ti·cal·ly** adv.

**mil·i·ta·rize** (mil′ə·tə·rīz′) v.t. ·rized, ·riz·ing 1 To imbue with militarism. 2 To prepare for war. —**mil′i·ta·ri·za′tion** n.

**mil·i·tar·y** (mil′ə·ter′ē) adj. 1 Of or relating to soldiers or to the army. 2 Made, performed, or supported by soldiers or the army. —n. 1 Armed forces; army: with the. 2 Army officials or officers: with the. [< L miles, militis soldier] —**mil′i·tar′i·ly** adv.

**mil·i·tate** (mil′ə·tāt) v.i. ·tat·ed, ·tat·ing To have influence: usu. with against. [< L militare be a soldier]

**mi·li·tia** (mə·lish′ə) n. An organized body of citizens, as the National Guard, drilled and equipped as soldiers but called to active service only in emergencies. —**mi·li′tia·man** (-mən) (pl. ·men) [L, military service]

**mill** (mil) n. 1 A machine for grinding grain into flour; also, the building in which this is done. 2 A machine for grinding or crushing hard substances of any kind: a pepper mill. 3 Any of various machines that by cutting, shaping, rolling, etc., treat or process raw material; usu. in combination: sawmill. 4 A factory. 5 Anything, as an agency or institution, that turns out products quickly and mechanically: a propaganda mill. 6 A difficult or painful experience: used chiefly in the phrase through the mill. —v.t. 1 To grind, shape, polish, roll, etc., in or with a mill. 2 To raise and ridge or corrugate the edge of (a coin). —v.i. 3 To undergo a milling process. 4 To move in a circular motion, as cattle: usu. with about. [< L mola millstone]

**mil·len·ni·um** (mi·len′ē·əm) n. pl. ·ni·a (-ē·ə) or ·ums 1 A period of a thousand years. 2 The thousand years during which Christ is to establish his kingdom on earth. Rev. 20:1–5. 3 Any period of happiness, peace, etc. [< L mille thousand + annus year] —**mil·len′ni·al** adj.

**mill·er** (mil′ər) n. 1 One who keeps or tends a mill, esp. a flour mill. 2 A milling machine. 3 Any of various moths with scales forming a fine powder on their wings.

**mil·li·gram** (mil′ə·gram) n. A metric unit of mass or weight equal to $10^{-6}$ (one millionth) kilogram or one thousandth of a gram. Chiefly Brit. sp. **mil′li·gramme**.

**mil·li·li·ter** (mil′ə·lē′tər) n. A metric unit of volume, equal to $10^{-3}$ (0.001) liter, or about 0.034 fluid ounce. Chiefly Brit. sp. **mil′li·li′tre**.

**mil·li·me·ter** (mil′ə·mē′tər) n. A metric unit of length equal to $10^{-3}$ (0.001) meter, or about 0.04 inch. Chiefly Brit. sp. **mil′li·me′ter**.

**mil·li·ner·y** (mil′ə·ner′ē, -nər·ē) n. 1 Women's hats. 2 The business of a milliner.

**mil·lion** (mil′yən) n. & adj. 1 See NUMBER. 2 An indefinitely great number. —adj. 1 Being a million. 2 Very many. [< Ital. milione, aug. of mille thousand]

**mil·lion·aire** (mil′yən·âr′, mil′yən·âr′) n. One whose wealth is valued at a million or more, as of dollars, pounds, etc.: also **mil′lion·naire′**.

**mim·e·o·graph** (mim′ē·ə·graf′, -gräf′) n. An apparatus for reproducing copies of written or typewritten matter by means of a stencil. —v.t. To reproduce by means of a mimeograph. [<Mimeograph, a trade name]

**mim·ic** (mim′ik) v.t. ·icked, ·ick·ing 1 To imitate the speech or actions of. 2 To copy closely; ape. 3 To have or assume the color, shape, etc., of. —n. One who or that which mimics. —adj. 1 Of the nature of mimicry. 2 Imitative. 3 Copying the real; simulated; mock: a mimic court. [<Gk. mimos mime] —**mim′i·cal** adj. —**mim′ick·er** n.

**mim·ic·ry** (mim′ik·rē) n. pl. ·ries 1 The act or art of mimicking or imitating. 2 Biol. A superficial resemblance of one organism to another or to its environment, resulting in concealment or protection. —Syn. 1 imitation, parody, burlesque, take off.

**min·a·ret** (min′ə·ret′) n. A high, slender tower attached to a Muslim mosque and surrounded by balconies, from which the summons to prayer is called by a muezzin. [<Ar. manārah lamp, lighthouse]

**mince** (mins) v. minced, minc·ing v.t. 1 To cut or chop into small bits, as meat. 2 To subdivide minutely. 3 To diminish the force or strength of; moderate: He didn't mince words with her. 4 To do or express with affected primness or elegance. —v.i. 5 To walk with short steps or affected daintiness 6 To speak or behave with affected primness. —n. MINCEMEAT. [<L minuere lessen, make smaller] —**minc′er** n. —**minc′ing·ly** adv.

**mince·meat** (mins′mēt′) n. A mixture of chopped apples, raisins, spices, etc., usu. without meat, used in mince pie. —**make mincemeat of** To destroy or defeat completely.

**mind** (mīnd) n. 1 The aggregate of all conscious and unconscious processes originating in and associated with the brain. 2

Memory: to bear in *mind*. 3 Opinion: to change one's *mind*. 4 Desire; inclination: to have a *mind* to leave. 5 Mental disposition, character, or temper: a cheerful *mind*. 6 Intellectual power or capacity: He has a fine *mind*. 7 An extremely intelligent person: She is one of the great *minds* of our time. 8 Sanity; reason: to lose one's *mind*. 9 Attention; concentration: to let one's *mind* wander. —a **piece of one's mind** An opinion, criticism, or rebuke very frankly or bluntly expressed. —**on one's mind** Occupying one's thoughts. —**out of one's mind** 1 Insane. 2 Deeply agitated; frantic. —**take one's mind off** To turn one's thoughts from. —*v.t.* 1 To pay attention to. 2 To be careful concerning: *Mind* your step. 3 To obey. 4 To care for; tend. 5 To object to; dislike: Do you *mind* the noise? 6 *Regional* To notice; perceive. 7 *Regional* To remember. —*v.i.* 8 To pay attention; take notice. 9 To be obedient. 10 To be concerned; care: I don't *mind*. 11 To be careful. [< OE *gemynd*] —**mind′er** *n.*

**mine** (mīn) *n.* 1 An excavation in the earth for the extraction of coal, ore, precious stones, etc. 2 Any deposit of such material suitable for extraction. 3 *Mil.* a An underground tunnel dug beneath an enemy's fortifications. b A case of explosive material buried in the earth, or floating on or beneath the surface of water. 4 Any source of supply: a *mine* of ideas. —*v.* **mined, min·ing** *v.t.* 1 To dig (coal, ores, etc.) from the earth. 2 To dig into (the earth, etc.) for coal, ores, etc. 3 To make by digging, as a tunnel. 4 To obtain information, ideas, etc., from 5 UNDERMINE. 6 To place an explosive mine or mines in or under. —*v.i.* 7 To dig in a mine for coal, ores, etc. 8 To make a tunnel, etc., by digging. 9 To place explosive mines. [< OF] —**min′er** *n.*

**min·er·al** (min′ər·əl) *n.* 1 A naturally occurring substance obtained from the earth by mining, as ore, coal, granite, etc. 2 Any of certain elements essential to life and usu. having special physiological functions, as iron, calcium, iodine, etc. 3 Any substance that is neither animal nor vegetable. —*adj.* 1 Pertaining to, consisting of, or resembling minerals. 2 Impregnated with mineral constituents. [< L *minera* a mine]

**min·er·al·o·gy** (min′ə·ral′ə·jē, -räl′-) *n.* The science that deals with minerals. —**min′er·al′o·gist** *n.*

**min·gle** (ming′gəl) *v.* **min·gled, min·gling** *v.t.*

1 To mix or unite together; blend. 2 To make or concoct by mixing. —*v.i.* 3 To be or become mixed, united, or closely joined. 4 To enter into company; mix or associate, as with a crowd. [< OE *mengan* to mix] —**min′gler** *n.*

**min·i·a·ture** (min′ē·ə·chər, min′ə·chər) *n.* 1 A portrait or painting of very small dimensions and delicate workmanship. 2 The art of painting such pictures. 3 A portrayal or copy of anything on a small scale. 4 Reduced scale, dimensions, or extent. —*adj.* Being or done on a small scale. [< L *miniare* paint red]

**min·i·a·tur·ize** (min′ē·ə·chər·īz, min′ə·chər·īz′) *v.t.* **·ized, ·iz·ing** To reduce the size of, as the parts of an instrument or machine. —**min′i·a·tur′i·za′tion** *n.*

**min·i·mize** (min′ə·mīz) *v.t.* **·mized, ·miz·ing** 1 To reduce to the smallest possible amount or degree. 2 To regard or represent as having the least possible importance, value, etc.

**min·i·mum** (min′ə·məm) *n. pl.* **·mums** or **·ma** (-mə) 1 The least possible quantity, amount, or degree. 2 The lowest degree, variation, etc., reached or recorded. —*adj.* Of, relating to, or being a minimum. [< L *minimus* smallest]

**min·is·ter** (min′is·tər) *n.* 1 One who is authorized to preach, administer the sacraments, etc. in a church; clergyman. 2 The chief of a department of a government. 3 One commissioned to represent his government in diplomatic relations with another government, esp. one ranking next below an ambassador. 4 An agent of someone or something. —*v.i.* 1 To provide for the wants or needs of someone. 2 To be conductive; contribute. —*v.t.* 3 To administer or apply (a sacrament, aid, etc.) [<L, an attendant]

**min·is·tra·tion** (min′is·trā′shən) *n.* 1 The act of serving as a minister. 2 Help; aid. —**min′is·tra′tive** *adj.*

**min·is·try** (min′is·trē) *n. pl.* **·tries** 1 The clergy. 2 The office or duties of a minister of religion. 3 *Govt.* a Ministers collectively. b The office or duties of a minister; also, the building where his work is conducted. c A department presided over by a minister. 4 Ministration; service.

**mink** (mingk) *n.* 1 A small, semiaquatic, carnivorous mammal, related to the weasel and valued for its soft, thick, usu. brown fur. 2 The fur of this mammal. [<Scand.]

**min·now** (min′ō) *n.* 1 Any of various small cyprinoid fishes, often used as bait. 2 Any very small fish. **Also min′nie** (-nē). [< OE *myne* small fish]

**mi·nor** (mī′nər) *adj.* 1 Less in number, quantity, or extent. 2 Of secondary importance or consideration. 3 Not yet of legal age. 4 In education, of or designating a course of study requiring fewer hours in class than a major field of study. 5 *Music* a Smaller than the corresponding major interval by a semitone. b Characterized by minor intervals, scales, or tones. c In a minor key. —*n.* 1 One not yet of legal age. 2 In education, a minor course of study. 3 *Music* A minor key, interval, etc. —*v.i.* In education, to study as a minor subject: with *in:* to minor in art. [L, less]

**mi·nor·i·ty** (mə·nôr′ə·tē, -nor′-, mī-) *n. pl.* **·ties** 1 The smaller in number of two parts or parties. 2 The state or period of being under legal age. 3 MINORITY GROUP.

**mint** (mint) *n.* 1 Any of several aromatic herbs, esp. spearmint and peppermint. 2 A mint-flavored candy. [< Gk. *mintha*]

**mi·nus** (mī′nəs) *prep.* 1 Lessened by; less: 10 *minus* 5. 2 *Informal* Deprived of; lacking: *minus* a hat. —*adj.* 1 Of or used in subtraction. 2 Negative: a *minus* quantity. 3 Less than in quantity or quality: a B *minus*. —*n.* 1 MINUS SIGN. 2 A negative quantity. 3 A defect; drawback. [L, neut. of *minor* less]

**min·ute** (min′it) *n.* 1 The 60th part of an hour; 60 seconds. 2 Any short period of time; moment. 3 The 60th part of a degree, indicated by the sign (′). 4 A memorandum. 5 *pl.* The official record of the proceedings of a meeting. —**up to the minute** In or having the latest style, equipment, etc. —*v.t.* **·ut·ed, ·ut·ing** To make a brief note of; record. [< L *minutus* small]

**mir·a·cle** (mir′ə·kəl) *n.* 1 An act or event that seems to transcend or contradict all known natural or scientific laws and is usu. thought to be supernatural in origin. 2 Any wonderful or amazing thing, fact, or event; a wonder. [< L *mirus* wonderful]

**mi·rac·u·lous** (mi·rak′yə·ləs) *adj.* 1 Of the nature of a miracle; supernatural. 2 Surpassingly strange; wonderful. 3 Possessing the power to work miracles. —**mi·rac′u·lous·ly** *adv.* —**mi·rac′u·lous·ness** *n.*

**mi·rage** (mi·räzh′) *n.* 1 An optical illusion, as of an oasis in the desert or ships seen in-

verted in the air, that occurs when light rays from these usu. distant objects are refracted through layers of the atmosphere having different densities. 2 Anything that appears to be real or attainable but is not. [< L *mirari* wonder at]

**mir·ror** (mir′ər) *n.* 1 Any of various reflecting surfaces, esp. glass when backed with a silver or aluminum coating. 2 Whatever reflects or clearly represents. 3 An exemplar; model. —*v.t.* To reflect or show an image of, as in a mirror. [< L *mirari* wonder at, admire]

**mirth** (mûrth) *n.* Gaiety of spirits; merriment; jollity. [< OE *myrig* pleasant, merry] —**mirth′ful** *adj.* —**mirth′ful·ly** *adv.* —**mirth′ful·ness** *n.*

**mis·an·thrope** (mis′ən·thrōp, miz′-) *n.* One who hates or distrusts his fellow men. **Also mis·an·thro·pist** (mis·an′thrə·pist). [< Gk. *misein* hate + *anthrōpos* a man] —**mis′an·throp′ic** (-throp′ik) or **·i·cal** *adj.* —**mis′an·throp′i·cal·ly** *adv.*

**mis·ap·pre·hend** (mis′ap·ri·hend′) *v.t.* To apprehend or understand wrongly.

**mis·ap·pro·pri·ate** (mis′ə·prō′prē·āt) *v.t.* **·at·ed, ·at·ing** To use or take improperly or dishonestly; misapply. —**mis′ap·pro′pri·a′tion** *n.*

**mis·be·have** (mis′bi·hāv′) *v.i.* To behave badly. —**mis′be·hav′ior** (-hāv′yər) *n.*

**mis·car·ry** (mis·kar′ē) *v.i.* **·ried, ·ry·ing** 1 To fail; go wrong. 2 To bring forth a fetus prematurely. 3 To fail to reach an expected destination, as mail.

**mis·ce·ge·na·tion** (mis′i·jə·nā′shən, mi·sej′ə-) *n.* Intermarriage or interbreeding between different races. [< L *miscere* mix + *genus* race] —**mis′ce·ge·net′ic** (-jə·net′ik) *adj.*

**mis·cel·la·ne·ous** (mis′ə·lā′nē·əs) *adj.* 1 Consisting of various things or types; varied; mixed. 2 Having various qualities, interests, or capabilities. [< L *miscellus* mixed] —**mis′cel·la′ne·ous·ly** *adv.* —**mis′cel·la′ne·ous·ness** *n.*

**mis·cel·la·ny** (mis′ə·lā′nē) *n. pl.* **·nies** 1 *Often pl.* A collection of literary compositions on various subjects. 2 Any miscellaneous collection.

**mis·chief** (mis′chif) *n.* 1 Action or conduct, often playful in intent, that annoys or vexes. 2 A disposition to tease or annoy. 3 Damage, harm, or trouble. 4 A person or thing that causes harm, annoyance, etc. [< OF *meschever* come to grief]

**mis·chie·vous** (mis′chi·vəs) *adj.* 1 Inclined to

tease, play pranks, annoy, etc. 2 Causing harm, injury, or damage. 3 Annoying; troublesome. —**mis′chie·vous·ly** adv. —**mis′chie·vous·ness** n.

**mis·con·strue** (mis′kən-strōō′) v.t. ·**strued**, ·**stru·ing** To interpret erroneously; misunderstand. —**mis′con·struc′tion** (-struk′shən) n.

**mis·cre·ant** (mis′krē-ənt) n. 1 One who does evil. 2 Archaic An unbeliever. —adj. 1 Villainous; evil. 2 Archaic Unbelieving. [< OF mescreant unbelieving]

**mis·de·mean·or** (mis′di-mē′nər) n. Law Any offense less serious than a felony.

**mi·ser** (mī′zər) n. Any stingy, grasping person, esp. one who hoards money avariciously. [< L miser wretched]

**mis·er·a·ble** (miz′ər-ə-bəl, miz′rə-) adj. 1 Wretchedly poor or unhappy. 2 Causing misery, discomfort, or unhappiness: a miserable cold. 3 Proceeding from or exhibiting misery: a bare, miserable room. 4 Of bad quality; inferior; worthless. 5 Pitiable; sorry. 6 Shameful; disgraceful. [< L miserari to pity] —**mis′er·a·ble·ness** n. —**mis′er·a·bly** adv. —Syn. 4 unsatisfactory, shoddy, second-rate.

**mis·er·y** (miz′ər·ē) n. pl. ·**er·ies** 1 Extreme distress or suffering, esp. as a result of poverty, physical or mental pain, etc. 2 A cause of such distress or suffering. [< L miser wretched]

**mis·fit** (mis·fit′) v.t. & v.i. ·**fit·ted**, ·**fit·ting** To fail to fit or make fit. —n. (mis′fit′, mis·fit′) 1 Something that fits badly. 2 (mis′fit′) A person who does not adjust well to his surroundings. 3 The act or condition of fitting less serious than a felony.

**mis·for·tune** (mis·fôr′chən) n. 1 Bad luck; trouble; adversity. 2 An unlucky occurrence; calamity.

**mis·guide** (mis·gīd′) v.t. ·**guid·ed**, ·**guid·ing** To guide wrongly in action or thought; mislead: misguided confidence. —**mis·guid′ance, mis·guid′er** n.

**mis·hap** (mis′hap, mis·hap′) n. An unfortunate accident.

**mis·in·form** (mis′in·fôrm′) v.t. To give false or erroneous information to. —**mis′in·form′ant, mis′in·for·ma′tion, mis′in·form′er** n.

**mis·in·ter·pret** (mis′in·tûr′prit) v.t. To interpret wrongly. —**mis′in·ter′pre·ta′tion, mis′in·ter′pret·er** n. —Syn. misunderstand, misconstrue, mistake, confuse.

**mis·lead** (mis·lēd′) v.t. ·**led** (led′), ·**lead·ing** 1 To direct wrongly. 2 To lead astray or into error. —**mis·lead′er** n. —**mis·lead′ing** adj. —**mis·lead′ing·ly** adv.

**mis·man·age** (mis·man′ij) v.t. & v.i. ·**aged**, ·**ag·ing** To manage badly or improperly. —**mis·man′age·ment, mis·man′ag·er** n.

**mis·no·mer** (mis·nō′mər) n. 1 A name wrongly applied. 2 The giving of a wrong name to a person in a legal document. [< OF mes- wrongly + nomer name]

**mis·og·a·my** (mis·og′ə·mē) n. Hatred of marriage. [< MISO- + -GAMY] —**mis·og′a·mist** n.

**mis·og·y·ny** (mis·oj′ə·nē) n. Hatred of women. [< MISO- + Gk. gynē woman] —**mis·og′y·nist** n. —**mis·og′y·nous** adj.

**mis·print** (mis·print′; for n. also mis′print′) v.t. To print incorrectly. —n. An error in printing.

**mis·pro·nounce** (mis′prə·nouns′) v.t. & v.i. ·**nounced**, ·**nounc·ing** To pronounce incorrectly or in a nonstandard way. —**mis·′pro·nun′ci·a′tion** (-nun′sē·ā′shən) n.

**mis·rep·re·sent** (mis′rep·ri·zent′) v.t. 1 To give an incorrect or false representation of. 2 To represent (a client, constituent, etc.) badly. —**mis′rep·re·sen·ta′tion** n. —**mis′rep·re·sen′ta·tive** adj., n.

**miss**[1] (mis) n. 1 A young girl: chiefly informal or in trade use: clothing for misses. 2 Often cap. A title used in speaking to an unmarried woman or girl: used without the name. See also MISS. [Contraction of MISTRESS]

**miss**[2] (mis) v.t. 1 To fail to hit or strike. 2 To fail to meet, catch, obtain, accomplish, see, hear, perceive, etc.: to miss the point. 3 To fail to attend, keep, perform, etc.: to miss church. 4 To overlook or fail to take advantage of, as an opportunity. 5 To discover or feel the loss or absence of. 6 To escape; avoid: He just missed being wounded. —v.i. 7 To fail to hit; strike wide of the mark. 8 To be unsuccessful; fail. —n. A failure to hit, find, attain, succeed, etc. [< OE missan]

**mis·shape** (mis·shāp′, mish·shāp′) v.t. ·**shaped**, ·**shaped** or ·**shap·en**, ·**shap·ing** To shape badly; deform. —**mis·shap′en** adj.

**mis·sile** (mis′əl, chiefly Brit. mis′īl) n. 1 Any object, esp. a weapon, intended to be thrown or discharged, as a spear, bullet, arrow, etc. 2 GUIDED MISSILE. [< L missus, pp. of mittere send]

**mis·spell** (mis·spel′) v.t. & v.i. ·**spelled** or ·**spelt**, ·**spell·ing** To spell incorrectly.

**mis·state** (mis·stāt′) v.t. ·**stat·ed**, ·**stat·ing** To state wrongly or falsely. —**mis·state′ment** n.

**mist** (mist) n. 1 An aggregation of fine drops

of water in the atmosphere, similar to but less dense than fog. **2** Any suspension or cloud of small particles, as of dust. **3** Anything that dims or obscures, esp. a watery film before one's eyes. —*v.i.* **1** To be or become dim or misty; blur. **2** To rain in very fine drops. —*v.t.* **3** To make dim or misty; blur. [< OE]

**mis·take** (mis·tāk′) *n.* An error in action, judgment, perception, impression, etc. — *v.* ·took, ·tak·en, ·tak·ing *v.t.* **1** To understand wrongly; misinterpret. **2** To take (a person or thing) to be another. —*v.i.* **3** To make a mistake. [< ON *mis-* wrongly + *taka* take]

**mis·tle·toe** (mis′əl·tō) *n.* **1** An evergreen shrub with yellowish green leaves and poisonous white berries, parasitic on various trees. **2** A sprig of this hung as a Christmas decoration. [< OE *misteltān* mistletoe twig]

**mis·tress** (mis′tris) *n.* **1** A woman in authority or control, as: **a** The head of a household, institution, or estate. **b** An employer or supervisor of servants. **c** An animal owner. **2** *Chiefly Brit.* A female schoolteacher. **3** A woman with whom a man has an unlawful but usu. a long-lasting sexual relationship. **4** *Often cap.* Something having supremacy or power and personified as feminine. **5** A woman who is well skilled in or has mastered anything. [< OF *maistre* master]

**mis·trust** (mis·trust′) *n.* Lack of trust or confidence. —*v.t.* & *v.i.* To regard (someone or something) with suspicion or doubt. —**mis·trust′ful** *adj.* —**mis·trust′ful·ly** *adv.* —**mis·trust′ful·ness** *n.* —Syn. *v.* distrust, suspect, doubt, disbelieve

**mist·y** (mis′tē) *adj.* mist·i·er, mist·i·est **1** Containing, characterized by, or like mist. **2** Dimmed or obscured by or as by mist. **3** Lacking clarity; indistinct; vague. —**mis·t′i·ly** *adv.* —**mist′i·ness** *n.*

**mis·un·der·stand** (mis′un·dər·stand′, mis·un′-) *v.t.* & *v.i.* ·stood, ·stand·ing To understand wrongly; misinterpret.

**mis·un·der·stand·ing** (mis′un·dər·stan′ding, mis·un′-) *n.* **1** A mistake as to meaning or motive. **2** A quarrel; disagreement.

**mis·use** (mis·yōōs′) *n.* **1** Wrong or improper use; misapplication. **2** Ill-treatment; abuse. —*v.t.* (mis·yōōz′) ·used, ·us·ing **1** To use or apply wrongly or improperly. **2** To abuse; maltreat. —**mis·us′er** *n.*

**mite** (mīt) *n.* Any of various minute arachnids including forms that are parasitic on man

or on specific animals or plants. [< OE *mīte*] —**mit′y** *adj.*

**mit·i·gate** (mit′ə·gāt) *v.t.* & *v.i.* ·gat·ed, ·gat·ing To make or become milder or less severe; moderate. [< L *mitis* mild + *agere* do, drive] —**mit′i·ga′tion**, **mit′i·ga′tor** *n.* —**mit′i·ga′tive**, **mit′i·ga·to′ry** (-gə·tôr′ē, -tō′rē) *adj.*

**mit·ten** (mit′n) *n.* **1** A covering for the hand, encasing the four fingers together and the thumb separately. **2** MITT (def. 1). [< MF *mitaine*]

**mix** (miks) *v.* mixed or mixt, mix·ing *v.t.* **1** To put together in one mass or composite; blend. **2** To make by combining ingredients: to *mix* dough. **3** To combine or join: to *mix* business with pleasure. **4** To cause to associate or mingle: to *mix* social classes together. **5** HYBRIDIZE. —*v.i.* **6** To be mixed or blended. **7** To associate; get along. **8** To take part; become involved. —**mix up 1** To blend thoroughly. **2** To confuse. **3** To implicate or involve. —*n.* **1** The act of mixing. **2** A mixture, esp. a commercial mixture of prepared ingredients: a cake *mix*. **3** A beverage, as soda or ginger ale, used in mixed drinks. **4** *Telecom.* The correct blending of two or more input signals into a composite signal. **5** A proportion, as of things that make up a mixture: evaluating the *mix* of black and white students in the city schools. **6** A combination of various elements; mixture: a movie providing a heady *mix* of violence, sex, and glamour. [< L *mixtus*, pp. of *miscere* mix]

**mix·ture** (miks′chər) *n.* **1** The act of mixing or the condition of being mixed. **2** Anything made or resulting from mixing things of different qualities, kinds, or types: a tea *mixture*. **3** *Chem.* A substance containing in variable proportions two or more ingredients which retain their individual properties and which may be separated without chemical change.

**mne·mon·ics** (ni·mon′iks) *n. pl. (construed as sing.)* The science of or the techniques used in memory improvement.

**moan** (mōn) *n.* **1** A low mournful sound indicative of grief or pain. **2** A similar sound. —*v.i.* **1** To utter moans of grief or pain. **2** To make a low, mournful sound, as wind in trees. —*v.t.* **3** To lament; bewail. **4** To say with a moan. [ME *mone*]

**mob** (mob) *n.* **1** A disorderly or lawless crowd. **2** Any large crowd. **3** The lowest class of people; the masses; populace. 4 *Slang* A gang, as of criminals. —*v.t.* mobbed, mob·bing 1 To attack in a mob. 2 To crowd around and annoy. 3 To crowd into, as a hall. [<L *mobile (vulgus)* movable (crowd)] —mob′ber *n.* —mob′bish *adj.* —mob′bish·ly *adv.*

mo·bile (mō′bəl, -bēl) *adj.* 1 Characterized by freedom of movement; movable. 2 Flowing freely. 3 Changing easily or quickly, as in expression, mood, etc. 4 Easily adaptable; versatile: a *mobile* intelligence. 5 Having or permitting movement or change in social status: a *mobile* society. 6 Designating a mobile. —*n.* (mō′bēl) A form of sculpture having freely moving parts, usu. suspended from rods, wires, etc. [<L *mobilis* movable] —mo·bil·i·ty (mō·bil′ə·tē) *n.*

mo·bi·lize (mō′bə·līz) *v.* ·lized, ·liz·ing *v.t.* 1 To make ready for war, as an army, industry, etc. 2 To assemble for use; organize. 3 To put into circulation, movement, or use. —*v.i.* 4 To undergo mobilization. *Brit.* sp. mo′bi·lise. —mo′bi·li·za′tion (-lə·zā′shən, -lī·zā′-) *n.*

mob·ster (mob′stər) *n. Slang* A gangster.

moc·ca·sin (mok′ə·sin) *n.* 1 A heelless foot covering made of soft leather or buckskin, formerly worn by North American Indians. 2 A shoe or slipper somewhat like a moccasin. 3 COTTONMOUTH. [< Algon.]

mock (mok) *v.t.* 1 To treat or address scornfully or derisively; hold up to ridicule. 2 To ridicule by imitation; mimic derisively. 3 To deceive; delude. 4 To defy; make futile. 5 To imitate; counterfeit. —*v.i.* 6 To express or show ridicule, scorn, or contempt; scoff. —*adj.* Imitation; sham. —*n.* 1 An act of mocking; a jeer. 2 One who or that which is mocked. 3 An imitation; counterfeit. [< OF *mocquer*] —mock′er *n.* —mock′ing·ly *adv.*

mock·ing·bird (mok′ing·bûrd′) *n.* A long-tailed, gray songbird common in the SE U.S., noted for imitating the songs of other birds.

mock·up (mok′up′) *n.* A model, usu. full-scale, as of a structure, machine, or apparatus, for purposes of study, testing, etc.

mode (mōd) *n.* 1 Manner, way, or method of acting, being, doing, etc. 2 Prevailing style or fashion of dress, behavior, etc. 3 *Gram.* MOOD. 4 *Music* Any of the seven possible permutations of the tones of a major scale in which the original order is preserved. 5 *Stat.* That value, magnitude, or score which occurs the greatest number of times in a

given series of observations; norm. [< L *modus* measure, manner]

mod·el (mod′l) *n.* 1 An object, usu. in miniature, representing accurately something already existing, or something to be made or tested. 2 One who or that which serves as an example or pattern of excellence. 3 A person who poses for painters, sculptors, etc. 4 A person employed to wear articles of clothing to display them. 5 A type, style, or design. 6 An analogue or analogy: a mathematical *model* of an atom. —*v.* ·eled or ·elled, ·el·ing or ·el·ling *v.t.* 1 To plan or fashion after a model or pattern. 2 To make a model of. 3 To fashion; make. 4 To display by wearing, as an article of clothing. —*v.i.* 5 To make a model or models. 6 To pose or serve as a model (defs. 3 and 4). 7 To assume the appearance of natural form. —*adj.* 1 Serving or used as a model. 2 Worthy or suitable to be used as a model. [< L *modus* measure, manner] —mod′el·er, mod′el·ler *n.*

mod·er·ate (mod′ər·it) *adj.* 1 Keeping or kept within reasonable limits; not extreme. 2 Not strongly partisan, radical, or excessive: said of political, social, or religious beliefs or those holding such beliefs. 3 Mild; temperate: a *moderate* climate. 4 Medium or average, as in quality, extent, effect, etc. —*n.* A person of moderate views, opinions, or practices. —*v.* (mod′ə·rāt) ·at·ed, ·at·ing *v.t.* 1 To reduce the violence, severity, etc., of; make less extreme; restrain. 2 To preside over. —*v.i.* 3 To become less intense or violent; abate. 4 To act as moderator. [< L *moderare* regulate] —mod′er·ate·ly *adv.* —mod′er·ate·ness *n.*

mod·ern (mod′ərn) *adj.* 1 Of, pertaining to, or characteristic of the present or most recent past; contemporary. 2 *Usu. cap.* Of, pertaining to, or characteristic of the present or most recent development of a language: *Modern* English. 3 Up-to-date: the most *modern* equipment. —*n.* 1 A person living in modern times or having modern views, characteristics, etc. 2 *Printing* A style of typeface characterized by contrasting heavy downstrokes and thin cross-strokes. [< LL *modernus* recent < L *modo* just now]

mod·est (mod′ist) *adj.* 1 Having a moderate or unpretentious opinion of one's worth, ability, etc. 2 Characterized by reserve, propriety, or purity in dress, actions, speech, etc. 3 Not excessive; moderate; limited: a

*modest* income. [< L *modestus* moderate] —
mod'est·ly *adv.*

mod·es·ty (mod'is·tē) *n.* 1 Freedom from vanity. 2 Propriety and decorum, as in dress or behavior. 3 Moderation.

mod·i·fy (mod'ə·fī) *v.* ·fied, ·fy·ing *v.t.* 1 To make somewhat different in form, character, etc.; vary. 2 To reduce in degree or extent; moderate. 3 *Gram.* To qualify the meaning of; restrict; limit. —*v.i.* 4 To be or become modified; change. [< L *modus* measure + *facere* make]

mo·diste (mō·dēst') *n.* A woman who makes or deals in fashionable women's clothing. [F]

mod·u·late (moj'ŏŏ·lāt) *v.* ·lat·ed, ·lat·ing *v.t.* 1 To vary the tone, inflection, or pitch of. 2 To regulate or adjust. 3 *Music* To change or cause to change to a different key. 4 To intone or sing. 5 *Electronics* To vary a parameter, as frequency or amplitude of (a carrier wave). —*v.i.* 6 *Electronics* To alter a parameter of a carrier wave. 7 *Music* To make a transition from one key to another. [< L *modulari* regulate] —mod'u·la·to'ry (-lə·tôr'ē, -tō'rē) *adj.*

mod·u·la·tion (moj'ŏŏ·lā'shən) *n.* 1 The act of modulating, or the state of being modulated. 2 A change in pitch or stress in the voice. 3 *Music* A transition from one key to another. 4 *Telecom.* a The changing of one or more of the parameters of a carrier wave. b The information transmitted by the carrier wave as a result of this.

mo·hair (mō'hâr) *n.* 1 The hair of the Angora goat. 2 A fabric made of mohair pile with a cotton or wool backing. [< Ar. *mukhayyar*]

Mo·ham·me·dan (mō·ham'ə·dən) *adj.* Of or pertaining to Mohammed or to his religion and institutions. —*n.* A follower of Mohammed or believer in Islam; a Muslim.

moi·e·ty (moi'ə·tē) *n. pl.* ·ties 1 A half. 2 An indefinite portion. [< L *medius* half]

moist (moist) *adj.* 1 Having slight wetness; damp. 2 Tearful: *moist* eyes. [< OF *moiste*] —moist'ly *adv.* —moist'ness *n.*

mois·ture (mois'chər) *n.* A small amount of liquid exuding from, diffused through, or resting on a substance; dampness. — mois'tur·ize *v.t.* (·ized, ·iz·ing)

mo·lar (mō'lər) *n.* A grinding tooth with flattened crown, situated behind the canine and incisor teeth. —*adj.* 1 Grinding, or adapted for grinding. 2 Pertaining to a molar. [< L *mola* mill] • See TOOTH.

mo·las·ses (mə·las'iz) *n.* A thick, dark-colored syrup drained from raw sugar during the refining process. [< L *mellaceus* honeylike]

mold¹ (mōld) *n.* 1 A hollow form or matrix for shaping anything that is in a fluid or plastic condition. 2 A frame on or around which something is made or shaped. 3 That which is made or shaped in or on a mold. 4 The form or shape given by a mold. 5 General form or shape. 6 Distinctive character or type. —*v.t.* 1 To work into a particular shape or form; model. 2 To shape or cast in, as in, or on a mold. 3 To influence or direct: to *mold* another's opinions. 4 In founding, to form a mold of or from. 5 To ornament with molding. [< L *modulus,* dim. of *modus* measure, limit] —mold'er *n.*

mold² (mōld) *n.* 1 Any of various fungous growths usu. forming a furry coating on decaying food or in moist, warm places. 2 Any fungus producing such growths. —*v.t.* & *v.i.* To become or cause to become moldy. [Prob. < Scand.]

mold·y (mōl'dē) *adj.* mold·i·er, mold·i·est 1 Covered with mold. 2 Musty, as from age, neglect, etc. —mold'i·ness *n.*

mole (mōl) *n.* A small permanent spot on the skin, usu. elevated slightly and pigmented. [< OE *māl*]

mo·lec·u·lar (mə·lek'yə·lər) *adj.* Of, effected by, or consisting of molecules.

mol·e·cule (mol'ə·kyōōl) *n.* 1 The smallest particle of an element or compound having all the properties of the element or compound. 2 Any small particle. [< NL *molecula,* dim. of L *moles* mass]

mo·lest (mə·lest') *v.t.* 1 To annoy or disturb. 2 To accost or interfere with sexually. [< L *molestus* troublesome] —mo·les·ta·tion (mō'les·tā'shən, mol'es-), mo·lest'er *n.*

mol·li·fy (mol'ə·fī) *v.t.* ·fied, ·fy·ing 1 To make less angry. 2 To reduce the violence or intensity of. [< L *mollis* soft + *facere* make] —mol'li·fi·ca'tion, mol'li·fi'er *n.* —mol'li·fy'ing·ly *adv.* —Syn. 1 soothe, pacify, appease, conciliate. 2 mitigate, ease, temper, allay.

mol·lusk (mol'əsk) *n.* Any of a large phylum of unsegmented, soft-bodied invertebrates, usu. having gills and a mantle which secretes a calcareous shell, and including snails, oysters, cuttlefish, slugs, octopuses, etc. Also mol'lusc. [< L *molluscus (nux)* soft, thin-shelled (nut)]

mo·ment (mō'mənt) *n.* 1 A very short period of time; an instant. 2 A definite point in time, esp. the present time. **3** Consequence or importance: something of little *moment*. **4** A time of excellence, accomplishment, enjoyment, etc.: She has her *moments*. **5** *Physics* **a** The product of a quantity and its distance to some significant related point: *moment* of inertia. **b** The measure of a force about a given point or axis; torque. [< L *momentum* movement]

**mo·men·tar·y** (mō′mən·ter′ē) *adj.* Lasting but a moment. —**mo′men·tar′i·ness** *n.*

**mo·men·tous** (mō·men′təs) *adj.* Of great importance. —**mo·men′tous·ly** *adv.* —**mo·men′tous·ness** *n.* —**Syn.** weighty, serious, outstanding, memorable.

**mo·men·tum** (mō·men′təm) *n. pl.* ·ta (-tə) or ·tums **1** *Physics* **a** The quantity of motion in a body as measured by the product of its mass and velocity. **b** A similar quantity defined with respect to angular motion. **2** Any forward or ongoing motion; impetus. [L, movement]

**mon·arch** (mon′ərk) *n.* **1** A hereditary constitutional sovereign, as a king, queen, etc. **2** One who or that which surpasses others of the same kind. **3** A large butterfly with orange-brown, black-veined wings whose larvae feed on milkweed. [< Gk. *monos* alone + *archein* rule] —**mo·nar·chal** (mə·när′kəl) *adj.* —**mo·nar′chal·ly** *adv.*

**mon·ar·chy** (mon′ər·kē) *n. pl.* ·chies **1** Government by a monarch; sovereign control. **2** A government or territory ruled by a monarch.

**mon·as·ter·y** (mon′əs·ter′ē) *n. pl.* ·ter·ies **1** A dwelling place occupied by monks, living under religious vows. **2** The monks living in such a place. [< Gk. *monastēs* a monk <*monazein* be alone]

**mo·nas·tic** (mə·nas′tik) *adj.* **1** Of, pertaining to, or like a monastery or the people who live there. **2** Ascetic. **Also mon·as·te·ri·al** (mon′əs·tir′ē·əl), **mo·nas′ti·cal.** —*n.* A monk or other religious recluse. —**mo·nas′ti·cal·ly** *adv.*

**mon·au·ral** (măn·ôr′əl) *adj.* **1** Pertaining to the perception of sound by one ear only. **2** Designating the transmission or reproduction of sound through a single channel. [<MON(O)- + AURAL]

**mon·e·tar·y** (mon′ə·ter′ē, mun′-) *adj.* **1** Of or pertaining to currency or coinage. **2** Of or pertaining to money. [< L *moneta* mint] —**mon′e·tar′i·ly** *adv.*

**mon·ey** (mun′ē) *n. pl.* **mon·eys** or **mon·ies 1** Anything that serves as a common medium of exchange, a measure of value, or as a means for the payment of debts or services rendered, esp. coins and paper currency officially issued by a government. **2** A specific form or denomination of coin or paper currency. **3** MONEY OF ACCOUNT. **4** Assets having monetary value. **5** Profit or pecuniary gain: to make *money*. **6** Wealth: That town has *money*. [< L *moneta* money, mint]

**mon·grel** (mong′grəl, mung′-) *n.* **1** A plant or animal resulting from interbreeding different types or varieties; esp., a dog of mixed breed. **2** Any incongruous mixture. —*adj.* Of mixed breed, origin, character, etc. [< OE *gemang* mixture]

**monk** (mungk) *n.* **1** A man who is a member of a monastic order and is usu. vowed to poverty, chastity, and obedience. **2** Formerly, a religious hermit. [< Gk. *monos* alone]

**mon·key** (mung′kē) *n. pl.* ·keys **1** Any of the primates except lemurs, anthropoid apes, and man, as marmosets, baboons, etc. **2** A person likened to a monkey, as a mischievous child. —*v.i. Informal* To play or trifle; meddle: often with *with* or *around with*. [?<MLG *Moneke*, name of an ape in a medieval epic]

**mo·nog·a·my** (mə·nog′ə·mē) *n.* **1** The principle or practice of marriage with but one person at a time. **2** *Zool.* The habit of having but one mate. [< Gk. *monos* single + *gamos* marriage] —**mo·nog′a·mous** *adj.* —**mo·nog′a·mist** *n.*

**mon·o·gram** (mon′ə·gram) *n.* Two or more letters interwoven into one, as the initials of one's name. —*v.t.* ·grammed, ·gram·ming To mark with a monogram. [< Gk. *monos* single + *gramma* letter] —**mon′o·gram·mat′ic** (-grə·mat′ik) *adj.*

**mon·o·graph** (mon′ə·graf, -gräf) *n.* A book, paper, or treatise written about a single topic, usu. in great detail. —**mo·nog·ra·pher** (mə·nog′rə·fər) *n.* —**mon′o·graph′ic** *adj.*

**mon·o·lith** (mon′ə·lith) *n.* **1** A single, usu. very large piece or block of stone, often in the shape of an obelisk. **2** Something like a monolith, as in size, structure, aspect, or quality.

**mon·o·logue** (mon′ə·lôg, -log) *n.* **1** A story or drama told or performed by one person. **2** A lengthy speech by one person, occurring in conversation. **3** A literary composition, or a poem, written as a soliloquy. **Also mon′o·log.** [< Gk. *monos* alone + *logos* discourse]

—**mon′o·logu′ist, mo·nol·o·gist** (mə·nol′ə·jist) *n.*

**mo·nop·o·lize** (mə·nop′ə·līz) *v.t.* **·lized, ·liz·ing** 1 To obtain or exercise a monopoly of. 2 To assume exclusive possession or control of. *Brit. sp.* **mo·nop′o·lise.** —**mo·nop′o·li·za′tion, mo·nop′o·liz′er** *n.*

**mo·nop·o·ly** (mə·nop′ə·lē) *n. pl.* **·lies** 1 The exclusive ownership or control of a specific commodity or service. 2 A person, company, etc. having a monopoly. 3 Exclusive possession or control of anything. 4 The commodity or service under the control of a monopoly. 5 *Law* An exclusive license from the government for buying, selling, making, or using anything. [< Gk. *monos* alone + *pōlein* sell] —**mo·nop′o·lism** *n.* —**mo·nop′o·list** *adj., n.* —**mo·nop′o·lis′tic** *adj.*

**mon·o·rail** (mon′ō·rāl) *n.* 1 A single rail serving as a track for railway cars. 2 A railway using such a track.

**mon·o·so·di·um glu·ta·mate** (mon′ə·sōd′ē·əm glōō′tə·māt) A white salt obtained from various vegetable sources and having the property of intensifying the sensation of taste.

**mo·not·o·nous** (mə·not′ə·nəs) *adj.* 1 Tiresomely uniform or repetitious. 2 Not varied in inflection, cadence, or pitch. [< Gk. *monotonous* having a single tone] —**mo·not′o·nous·ly** *adv.* —**mo·not′o·nous·ness** *n.* —**Syn.** 1 tedious, dull, dreary.

**mo·not·o·ny** (mə·not′ə·nē) *n.* 1 A tiresome or tedious uniformity. 2 Sameness of tone or sound.

**mon·ster** (mon′stər) *n.* 1 Any plant or animal of markedly abnormal structure and appearance. 2 A person or thing that is abhorred because of its ugliness, cruelty, wickedness, etc. 3 An abnormally huge person, animal, or thing. 4 An imaginary animal of huge or hideous form. —*adj.* Enormous; huge. [< L *monstrum* divine omen]

**mon·stros·i·ty** (mon·stros′ə·tē) *n. pl.* **·ties** 1 Anything unnaturally huge, malformed, or distorted. 2 The character or condition of being monstrous.

**mon·strous** (mon′strəs) *adj.* 1 Deviating greatly from the natural or normal. 2 Of extraordinary size; huge. 3 Hateful; hideous; intolerable. 4 Incredible; absurd. 5 Like an imaginary monster. —**mon′strous·ly** *adv.* —**mon′strous·ness** *n.*

**month** (munth) *n.* 1 One of the 12 parts into which the calendar year is divided, called a **calendar month.** 2 Loosely, thirty days or four weeks. 3 The twelfth part of a solar year, called a **solar month.** 4 The time during which the moon makes one revolution, equal on the average to 29.53 days, called a **lunar month.** [< OE *mōnath*]

**month·ly** (munth′lē) *adj.* 1 Continuing a month. 2 Payable, done, or happening once a month. —*adv.* Once a month. —*n. pl.* **·lies** 1 A periodical published once a month. 2 *pl. Informal* A menstrual period.

**mon·u·ment** (mon′yə·mənt) *n.* 1 Something, as a statue, building, plaque, etc., erected to perpetuate the memory of a person or of an event. 2 A notable work of art, heroic deed, scholarly production, etc., thought of as having enduring significance. 3 A stone boundary marker. 4 A tomb. [< L *monere* remind]

**mood** (mōōd) *n.* 1 A particular, usu. temporary state of mind; humor; disposition. 2 *pl.* Fits of morose or sullen behavior. [< OE *mōd*]

**mood·y** (mōō′dē) *adj.* **mood·i·er, mood·i·est** 1 Given to petulant, sullen, or melancholy moods. 2 Expressive of such moods. —**mood′i·ly** *adv.* —**mood′i·ness** *n.*

**moon** (mōōn) *n.* 1 A body that orbits the earth from west to east in 29.53 days. The moon has a mean diameter of 2,160 miles and a mean distance from the earth of 238,900 miles. 3 A particular phase of the moon: full *moon.* 3 A satellite revolving about any planet. 4 A month, esp. a lunar month. 5 Something resembling a moon or crescent. 6 Moonlight. —*v.i.* 1 To stare or wander about in an abstracted or listless manner. —*v.i.* 2 To pass (time) thus. [< OE *mōna*]

**moon·light** (mōōn′līt′) *n.* The light of the moon. —*adj.* Pertaining to or illuminated or done by moonlight. —*v.i. Informal* To work at a job in addition to one's regular job. —**moon′light′er, moon′light′ing** *n.*

**moon·shine** (mōōn′shīn′) *n.* 1 Moonlight. 2 Foolish talk; nonsense. 3 *Informal* Smuggled or illicitly distilled liquor.

**moose** (mōōs) *n. pl.* **moose** A very large deer of N North America having huge, palmate antlers in the male. 2 A large Old World elk. [< Algon.]

**mor·al** (môr′əl, mor′-) *adj.* 1 Of or pertaining to character and behavior from the point of view of right and wrong. 2 Good and virtuous in behavior, character, etc.; esp., sexually virtuous. 3 Concerned with the principles of right and wrong; ethical: *moral* values. 4 Capable of understanding the difference between right and wrong: a *moral* agent. 5 Coming from a sense of duty or one's conscience: a *moral* obligation. 6 Arising from one's sympathies or sense of justice but without overt action: *moral* support. 7 Probable but not yet proven objectively: a *moral* certainty. —*n.* 1 The moral point or lesson made by a story, action, etc. 2 *pl.* Conduct or behavior from the point of view of right and wrong, esp. sexual conduct. 3 A maxim. [< L *mos, moris* custom; in the pl., manners, morals] — **mor'al·ly** *adv.* • **moral, morale** *Moral,* with the stress on the first syllable, is both an adjective (meaning virtuous or ethical) and a noun (meaning a moral point or lesson): *It took moral courage to admit she was wrong; The moral is, "The weed of crime bears bitter fruit." Morale,* with the stress on the second syllable, is a noun only, and refers to a feeling of confidence or spirit, esp. within a group: *When the pay raise was canceled, morale fell sharply.*

**mo·rale** (mə·ral', -räl', mō-) *n.* State of mind with reference to confidence, courage, hope, etc. [< F *moral, moral*] • See MORAL.

**mor·al·ist** (môr'əl·ist, mor'-) *n.* 1 A teacher of morals. 2 One who leads a virtuous life. — **mor'al·is'tic** *adj.*

**mo·ral·i·ty** (mə·ral'ə·tē, mō-) *n. pl.* **·ties** 1 A doctrine or system of moral principles or conduct: Victorian *morality.* 2 Moral conduct; virtue. 3 The quality or condition of being morally right or wrong. 4 A moral lesson. 5 MORALITY PLAY.

**mor·al·ize** (môr'əl·iz, mor'-) *v.* **·ized, ·iz·ing** *v.i.* 1 To make moral reflections; talk about morality. —*v.t.* 2 To explain in a moral sense; derive a moral from. 3 To improve the morals of. *Brit. sp.* **·ise.** —**mor'al·i·za' tion, mor'al·iz'er** *n.*

**mo·rass** (mə·ras', mō-, mō-) *n.* 1 A tract of low-lying, soft, wet ground; marsh. 2 Anything that impedes or creates difficulties. [< OF *maresc*]

**mor·a·to·ri·um** (môr'ə·tôr'ē·əm, -tō'rē-, mor'-) *n. pl.* **·ri·ums** or **·ri·a** (-ē·ə) 1 A legal act authorizing a debtor or bank to suspend payments for a given period; also, the period during which it is in force. 2 Any authorized suspension of an activity. [< L *morari* to delay]

**mor·bid** (môr'bid) *adj.* 1 Of, caused by, or having a disease. 2 Abnormally intrigued by the gruesome or unwholesome. 3 Grisly;

gruesome: a *morbid* story. [< L *morbus* disease] —**mor·bid'i·ty, mor'bid·ness** *n.* — **mor'bid·ly** *adv.*

**morgue** (môrg) *n.* 1 A place where cadavers are kept awaiting identification or determination of cause of death. 2 The department of a newspaper or other periodical where reference material, back issues, etc., are filed. [F]

**mo·ron** (môr'on, mō'ron) *n.* A person with a mild degree of mental retardation. [< Gk. *mōros* dull, sluggish] —**mo·ron·ic** (mô·ron'ik, mō-) *adj.* —**mo·ron'i·cal·ly** *adv.* — **mo'ron·ism, mo·ron'i·ty** *n.*

**mo·rose** (mə·rōs') *adj.* Sullen; gloomy. [< L *mos, moris* manner, habit] —**mo·rose'ly** *adv.* —**mo·rose'ness** *n.* —Syn. sad, melancholy, surly, ill-tempered.

**mor·phol·o·gy** (môr·fol'ə·jē) *n.* 1 The branch of biology that deals with the form and structure of plants and animals. 2 The branch of linguistics that deals with the arrangement, composition, and inflection of the morphemes of a language. [< Gk. *morphē* form + -LOGY] —**mor·pho·log·ic** (môr'fə·loj'ik) or **·i·cal** *adj.* —**mor'pho·log' i·cal·ly** *adv.* —**mor·phol'o·gist** *n.*

**mor·sel** (môr'səl) *n.* 1 A bit of food; bite. 2 A small piece of anything. [< OF, dim. of *mors* bite]

**mor·tal** (môr'təl) *adj.* 1 Subject to death. 2 Causing death; fatal. 3 Of or connected with death: *mortal* agony. 4 Deadly and unrelenting: a *mortal* foe. 5 Human: *mortal* desires. 6 Very great; extreme: a *mortal* fright. 7 Very long and tedious. 8 *Theol.* Incurring eternal death unless repented of: said of grave sins. 9 *Informal* Conceivable: every *mortal* reason for not going. —*n.* A human being. —*adv. Regional* Very; exceedingly: *mortal* tired. [< L *mors, mortis* death] —**mor'tal·ly** *adv.*

**mor·tal·i·ty** (môr·tal'ə·tē) *n.* 1 The quality of being mortal. 2 Death, esp. of large numbers of people. 3 The number of deaths in a population during a specified time. 4 Humanity; mankind.

**mor·tar** (môr'tər) *n.* 1 A strong bowllike vessel in which substances are crushed or pounded with a pestle. 2 *Mil.* A muzzle-loading cannon for firing heavy shells at low muzzle velocity and great angles of elevation. [< L *mortarium*]

**mort·gage** (môr'gij) *n. Law* 1 A transfer of ownership of property to a creditor as security for a loan or debt. 2 The contract ef-

328

fecting such a transfer. —*v.t.* **·gaged, ·gag·ing 1** To make over or pledge (property) by mortgage. **2** To pledge. [< OF, lit., dead pledge]

**mor·ti·cian** (môr·tish′ən) *n.* A funeral director; undertaker. [< L *mors, mortis* death + -ICIAN]

**mor·ti·fi·ca·tion** (môr′tə·fə·kā′shən) *n.* **1** Shame or humiliation caused by a loss of self-esteem or wounded pride. **2** The cause of such humiliation or shame. **3** Necrosis; gangrene. **4** In religion, the act of subduing the passions and appetites by fasting, penance, etc.

**mor·ti·fy** (môr′tə·fī) *v.* **·fied, ·fy·ing** *v.t.* **1** To humiliate. **2** To discipline or punish (the body, passions, etc.) by fasting or other ascetic practices. **3** To cause (a part of the body) to become gangrenous. —*v.i.* **4** To practice ascetic self-discipline. **5** To become gangrenous. [< L *mors, mortis* death + *facere* make] —**mor′ti·fi′er** *n.* —**mor′ti·fy′ing·ly** *adv.*

**mor·tise** (môr′tis) *n.* A space hollowed out, as in a piece of wood, to receive a tenon or other projecting part. —*v.t.* **·tised, ·tis·ing 1** To cut or make a mortise in. **2** To join by a tenon and mortise. [< OF *mortaise*]

**mo·sa·ic** (mō·zā′ik) *n.* **1** Inlaid work composed of bits of stone, glass, etc., forming a pattern or picture. **2** The art or process of making a mosaic. **3** Anything resembling a mosaic. —*adj.* Of, pertaining to, or resembling mosaic. —*v.t.* **·icked, ·ick·ing 1** To make by or as if by combining in a mosaic. **2** To decorate with mosaic. [< Gk. *mouseios* of the Muses, artistic] —**mo·sa·i·cist** (mō·zā′ə·sist) *n.*

**Mos·lem** (moz′ləm, mos′-) *n. pl.* **·lems** or **·lem** MUSLIM. —*adj.* MUSLIM. —**Mos′lem·ism** *n.*

**mosque** (mosk) *n.* A Muslim temple of worship. [< Ar. *masjid*]

**mos·qui·to** (məs·kē′tō) *n. pl.* **·toes** or **·tos** Any of a family of small, dipterous insects having in the female mouth parts that puncture the skin of animals and suck their blood. [< Sp. *mosca* fly] —**mos·qui′tal** *adj.*

**mo·tel** (mō·tel′) *n.* A hotel for motorists, usu. comprising cabins or rooms directly accessible from parking areas. [< MO(TOR) + (HO)TEL]

**moth** (môth, moth) *n. pl.* **moths** (môthz, môths, mothz, moths) Any of various, usu. nocturnal, lepidopterous insects distinguished from butterflies by their featherlike

antennae and wings that fold flat over the abdomen. [< OE *moththe*]

**moth·er** (muth′ər) *n.* A ropy, jellylike mass of bacteria that forms in vinegar and other fermenting liquids, used to start new batches. **Also mother of vinegar.** [Special use of MOTHER[1]]

**moth·er-in-law** (muth′ər·in·lô′) *n. pl.* **moth·-ers-in-law** The mother of one's spouse.

**moth·er-of-pearl** (muth′ər·əv·pûrl′) *n.* The hard, iridescent lining of certain mollusk shells; nacre. —*adj.* Made of or ornamented with mother-of-pearl.

**mo·tif** (mō·tēf′) *n.* **1** The main idea or central theme of a literary, musical, or artistic work. **2** In the decorative arts, a distinctive element of design. **3** The shortest fragment of a musical theme in which structure is evident. [F]

**mo·tion** (mō′shən) *n.* **1** Any physical movement or spatial change in position or place. **2** A formal proposition in a deliberative assembly. **3** *Law* An application to a court to obtain an order, ruling, or direction. **4** A mental impulse or inclination. —*v.i.* **1** To make a gesture of direction or intent, as with the hand. —*v.t.* **2** To direct or guide by a gesture. [< L *motus*, p.p. of *movere* move] —**mo′tion·al, mo′tion·less** *adj.* —**mo′t·ion·less·ly** *adv.* —**mo′tion·less·ness** *n.* — **Syn.** *n.* 1 action, passage, transit.

**motion picture 1** A sequence of filmed pictures giving the illusion of continuous movement; film (def. 4). **2** A story, drama, etc., adapted for and photographed as a motion picture. —**mo′tion-pic′ture** *adj.*

**mo·ti·vate** (mō′tə·vāt) *v.t.* **·vat·ed, ·vat·ing** To provide with a motive; instigate; induce. — **mo′ti·va′tion** *n.* —**mo′ti·va′tion·al** *adj.*

**mo·tive** (mō′tiv) *n.* **1** Something, as a need or desire, that impels or incites a person to a certain course of action or behavior. **2** MOTIF. —*adj.* **1** Causing motion. **2** Relating to a motive or motives. —*v.t.* **·tived, ·tiv·ing** MOTIVATE. [< L *motus*, p.p. of *movere* move]

**mot·ley** (mot′lē) *adj.* **1** Composed of many different elements or types. **2** Variegated in color. —*n.* **1** A garment of various colors, such as was formerly worn by court jesters. **2** A many-colored, woolen fabric. **3** An incongruous mixture. [ME *motteley*]

**mo·tor** (mōtər) *n.* **1** A machine that converts electric energy into mechanical power. **2** An internal-combustion engine. **3** Anything that produces motion. **4** AUTOMOBILE. —*adj.* **1** Causing, producing, or imparting motion.

2 Driven or operated by a motor. 3 Of, pertaining to, or for vehicles operated by a motor. 4 Transmitting impulses from the nerve centers to the muscles. 5 Of or involving muscular movement. —*v.i.* To travel or ride in an automobile. [< L *motus*, p.p. of *movere*]

**mo·tor·boat** (mō′tər·bōt′) *n.* A boat propelled by a motor.

**mo·tor·cade** (mō′tər·kād) *n.* A procession of automobiles.

**mo·tor·car** (mō′tər·kär′) *n.* AUTOMOBILE.

**mo·tor·cy·cle** (mō′tər·sī′kəl) *n.* A two-wheeled vehicle propelled by an internal-combustion engine. —*v.i.* ·cled, ·cling To travel or ride on a motorcycle. —**mo′tor·cy′clist** *n.*

**mot·tled** (mot′ld) *adj.* Marked with spots of different colors or shades; variegated.

**mot·to** (mot′ō) *n. pl.* ·toes or ·tos 1 A word or phrase expressing a guiding principle or rule of conduct. 2 A phrase inscribed on something as being indicative of its qualities or uses. [Ital., word]

**mount** (mount) *v.t.* 1 To ascend by climbing; go up, as stairs. 2 To climb or get up upon: to *mount* a horse. 3 To put on horseback. 4 To furnish with a horse. 5 To set or place in an elevated position: to *mount* a plaque on a wall. 6 To place or fix in or on a support, frame, slide, etc., as for exhibition, examination, etc.: to *mount* a photograph, to *mount* a butterfly. 7 To furnish, as a play, with scenery, costumes, etc. 8 To copulate with a female: said of a male animal. 9 *Mil.* a To place in position for use, as a cannon. b To stand or post (guard). c To prepare for and begin: to *mount* an offensive. —*v.i.* 10 To rise or ascend; to up. 11 To increase. 12 To get up on or on top of something. —*n.* 1 Anything, as a support, frame, jewel setting, etc., on or in which something is mounted. 2 Something which one mounts and rides, as a horse, bicycle, etc. 3 The act or manner of mounting or riding a horse, etc. [< L *mons, montis* mountain] —**mount′er** *n.*

**moun·tain** (moun′tən) 1 A natural elevation of the earth's surface, higher than a hill and rising more or less steeply to a small summit area. 2 A large number or amount. 3 Something of great size. —*adj.* 1 Of, pertaining to, or like a mountain. 2 Living, growing, or located on a mountain. [< L *mons, montis* mountain]

**mourn** (môrn, mōrn) *v.i.* 1 To feel or express

grief or sorrow, esp. for the dead. —*v.t.* 2 To grieve or sorrow for (someone dead). 3 To grieve over or lament (misfortune, failure, etc.). [< OE *murnan*] —**mourn′er** *n.*

**mouse** (mous) *n. pl.* **mice** (mīs) 1 Any of numerous small rodents found throughout the world, esp. the common **house mouse**, which frequents human habitations. 2 *Informal* A timid person. 3 *Slang* A black eye. 4 A small, hand-held electronic device, used to control a cursor, or point to commands on a menu, instead of typing commands via the computer keyboard. —*v.* (mouz) **moused, mous·ing** *v.i.* 1 To hunt or catch mice. 2 To hunt for something cautiously and softly; prowl. [< OE *mūs*]

**mouth** (mouth) *n. pl.* **mouths** (mouthz) 1 The opening at which food is taken into the body; also, the cavity between the lips and throat. 2 The human mouth thought of in terms of eating and speaking: Shut your *mouth; mouths* to feed. 3 An opening or entrance that can be likened to a mouth: as a That part of a stream where its waters are discharged into a river, lake, etc. b The entrance to a harbor. c The entrance or opening into a mine or cave. d The opening of a jar or similar container. —**down in** (or at) **the mouth** Disconsolate; dejected. —*v.t.* (mouth) 1 To utter in a forced or affected manner; declaim. 2 To seize or take in the mouth. 3 To repeat mechanically and without understanding. 4 To form (words) as if speaking but without sound. —*v.i.* 5 To speak in a forced or affected manner. [< OE *mūth*] —**mouth′er** (mou′thər) *n.*

**mou·ton** (mōō′ton) *n.* Processed sheepskin dyed and cut to resemble beaver or seal. [F. sheep]

**mov·a·ble** (mōō′və·bəl) *adj.* 1 Capable of being moved. 2 Changing in date from year to year: *movable* holidays. —*n.* 1 Anything that can be moved. 2 *Usu. pl. Law* Personal property, as distinguished from real or fixed property. Also **move′a·ble.** —**mov′a·ble·ness,** mov′a·bil′i·ty *n.* —**mov′a·bly** *adv.*

**move** (mōōv) *v.* **moved, mov·ing** *v.i.* 1 To change place or position, esp. to go from one place to another. 2 To change one's residence. 3 To make progress; advance. 4 To live or associate; be active: to *move* in cultivated circles. 5 To operate or revolve; work: said of machines, etc. 6 To take action; begin to act. 7 To be disposed of by sale. 8 To make an application, appeal, or proposal: to *move* for adjournment. 9 To evacuate: said of the bowels. 10 In chess, checkers, etc., to change the position of a piece. 11 *Informal* To go or depart rapidly. —*v.t.* 12 To change the place or position of. 13 To set or keep in motion. 14 To rouse, influence, or urge to some action. 15 To affect with passion, sympathy, etc.; stir; excite. 16 To propose for consideration, action, etc. 17 To cause (the bowels) to evacuate. —*n.* 1 The act of moving; movement. 2 A purposeful act or maneuver in the carrying out of a plan. 3 In chess, checkers, etc., the act of moving a piece; also, one's turn to move. 4 A change of residence. —**on the move** 1 Moving about from place to place. 2 Making progress. [< L *movere*]

**mov·ie** (mōō′vē) *n.* 1 A motion-picture film. 2 A motion-picture theater. 3 *pl.* A showing of films. 4 *pl.* The film industry. —*adj.* Of, in, or for movies. [Contraction of *moving picture*]

**mow** (mō) *v.* **mowed, mowed** or **mown, mow·ing** *v.t.* 1 To cut down (grain, grass, etc.) with a scythe or machine. 2 To cut the grain or grass of (a lawn, field, etc.). 3 To cut down or kill rapidly or indiscriminately: with *down.* —*v.i.* 4 To cut down grass or grain. [< OE *māwan*] —**mow′er** *n.*

**mu·ci·lage** (myōō′sə·lij) *n.* 1 An aqueous solution of vegetable gum or similar substance, used as an adhesive. 2 Any of various gummy or gelatinous substances obtained from certain plants. [< LL *mucilago*] —**mu·ci·lag·i·nous** (myōō′si·laj′ə·nes) *adj.* —**mu′ci·lag′i·nous·ness** *n.*

**muck** (muk) *n.* 1 Any moist dirt or filth, esp. mud. 2 Moist manure. 3 Dark soil consisting largely of decaying organic matter. 4 Something, as writings, that defames or injures. —*v.t.* 1 To fertilize with manure. 2 *Informal* To make dirty; pollute. 3 To remove muck from. [< ON *mykr*] —**muck′y** *adj.* (·i·er, ·i·est)

**mu·cus** (myōō′kəs) *n.* A viscid secretion of mucous membrane, serving as a lubricant.

**mud·dle** (mud′l) *v.* **·dled, ·dling** *v.t.* 1 To mix in confusion; jumble. 2 To confuse mentally; bewilder. 3 To make muddy or turbid; roil. 4 To make a mess of; bungle. —*v.i.* 5 To act or think in a confused or ineffective manner. —*n.* A mixed or confused condition, as of the mind; a mess. [? < MUD]

**muf·fler** (muf′lər) *n.* 1 A heavy scarf worn about the neck. 2 A device to reduce noise, as from the exhaust of an internal-combustion engine. 3 Anything used for muffling.

**mug·gy** (mug′ē) *adj.* **·gi·er, ·gi·est** Warm, humid, and close. [< ON *mugga* drizzle] —**mug′gi·ness** *n.*

**mu·lat·to** (mə·lat′ō, myōō-, -lä′tō) *n.* *pl.* **·toes** 1 A person having one white and one Negro parent. 2 Anyone having mixed white and Negro ancestry. —*adj.* Of a light brown color. [< Sp. *mulato* of mixed breed < *mulo* mule]

**mulch** (mulch) *n.* Any covering, as straw, compost, etc., placed on the ground around plants to protect their roots, as from frost or drying. —*v.t.* To cover with mulch. [ME *molsh*]

**mulct** (mulkt) *v.t.* 1 To punish by a fine. 2 To deprive (a person) of something fraudulently; cheat. —*n.* A fine or similar penalty. [< L *mulcta, multa* a fine]

**mule** (myōōl) *n.* 1 A hybrid bred of the ass and horse, esp. a jackass and a mare. 2 A spinning machine that draws, stretches, and twists at one operation. 3 *Informal* A stubborn person. [< L *mulus*]

**mull** (mul) *v.t.* To heat and spice, as wine or beer. [?]

**mul·ti·form** (mul′tə·fôrm) *adj.* Having many forms, shapes, or appearances. —**mul′ti·form′i·ty** *n.*

**mul·ti·lat·er·al** (mul′ti·lat′ər·əl) *adj.* 1 Having many sides. 2 Involving more than two nations, states, or parties.

**mul·ti·par·tite** (mul′ti·pär′tīt) *adj.* 1 Divided into many parts. 2 MULTILATERAL (def. 2).

**mul·ti·ple** (mul′tə·pəl) *adj.* 1 Containing or consisting of more than one part, element, characteristic, etc.; manifold. 2 Shared by or involving many. 3 *Electr.* Of or being a circuit having two or more conductors connected in parallel. —*n.* The product of a given number and another factor. [< LL *multiplus* manifold]

**multiple sclerosis** A chronic disease of the nervous system in which hard patches develop in the brain and spinal cord.

**mul·ti·plex** (mul′tə·pleks) *adj.* 1 Multiple; manifold. 2 *Telecom.* Designating a system for the simultaneous transmission of two or more messages or signals over the same channel.

**mul·ti·pli·ca·tion** (mul′tə·plə·kā′shən) *n.* 1 The process of multiplying. 2 The process of finding the sum (the *product*) of a number (the *multiplicand*) repeated a given number of times (the *multiplier*).

**mul·ti·plic·i·ty** (mul'tə·plis'ə·tē) *n.* 1 The condition of being manifold or various. 2 A large number.

**mul·ti·ply** (mul'tə·plī) *v.* ·plied, ·ply·ing *v.t.* 1 To increase the quantity, amount, or degree of. 2 To perform the operation of multiplication upon. —*v.i.* 3 To become more in number, amount, or degree; increase. 4 To perform multiplication. [< L *multiplex* manifold] —Syn. 3 grow, enlarge, proliferate, expand.

**mul·ti·tude** (mul'tə·t'ōod) *n.* 1 A large crowd or gathering. 2 A great number. 3 The condition of being many. [< L *multus* much, many]

**mul·ti·tu·di·nous** (mul'tə·t'ōo'də·nəs) *adj.* 1 Consisting of a vast number; numerous. 2 Having many elements, parts, aspects, etc. —**mul'ti·tu'di·nous·ly** *adv.* —**mul'ti·tu'di·nous·ness** *n.*

**mum·ble** (mum'bəl) *v.t. & v.i.* ·bled, ·bling To speak or utter in low, indistinct tones; mutter. —*n.* A low, mumbling speech; mutter. [ME *momelen*] —**mum'bler** *n.*

**mum·my** (mum'ē) *n. pl.* ·mies 1 A body embalmed in the ancient Egyptian manner. 2 Any dead body which is very well preserved. 3 A person or thing that is dried up and withered. —*v.t. & v.i.* ·mied, ·my·ing MUMMIFY. [< Pers. *mūm* wax]

**mumps** (mumps) *n.pl.* (*construed as singular*) An acute, contagious, febrile disease of viral origin, characterized by swelling of the salivary glands. [pl. of obs. *mump* grimace]

**munch** (munch) *v.t. & v.i.* To chew with a crunching sound. [ME *monchen, manchen*] —**munch'er** *n.*

**mun·dane** (mun·dān', mun'dān) *adj.* 1 Characterized by being ordinary, practical, and everyday. 2 Of or pertaining to the world. [< L *mundus* world] —**mun·dane'ly** *adv.* —**mun·dane'ness** *n.*

**mu·nic·i·pal** (myōo·nis'ə·pəl) *adj.* 1 Of or pertaining to a town or city or its government. 2 Having local self-government. [< L *municeps* free citizen] —**mu·nic'i·pal·ly** *adv.*

**mu·nic·i·pal·i·ty** (myōo·nis'ə·pal'ə·tē) *n. pl.* ·ties An incorporated borough, town, or city.

**mu·nif·i·cent** (myōo·nif'ə·sənt) *adj.* Extraordinarily generous or bountiful; liberal. [< L *munus* gift + *facere* to make] —**mu·nif'i·cence** *n.* —**mu·nif'i·cent·ly** *adv.*

**mu·ni·tion** (myōo·nish'ən) *n. Usu. pl.* Ammunition and all necessary war materiel. —*v.t.*

To furnish with munitions. [< L *munire* fortify]

**mur·der** (mûr'dər) *v.t.* 1 To kill (a human being) with premeditated malice. 2 To kill in a barbarous or inhuman manner; slaughter. 3 *Informal* To spoil by bad performance, etc.; mangle; butcher. —*v.i.* 4 To commit murder. —*n.* 1 The unlawful and intentional killing of one human being by another; homicide. 2 *Informal* Something very difficult, unpleasant, or dangerous. [Fusion of OE *morthor* + OF *murdre*] —**mur'der·er** *n.* —**mur'der·ess** *n. Fem.*

**mur·der·ous** (mûr'dər·əs) *adj.* 1 Of, pertaining to, or causing murder. 2 Capable of or plotting murder. 3 Violently hostile; menacing: a *murderous* look. 4 *Informal* Very difficult, unpleasant, or dangerous. —**mur'der·ous·ly** *adv.* —**mur'der·ous·ness** *n.*

**murk·y** (mûr'kē) *adj.* murk·i·er, murk·i·est 1 Dark; obscure. 2 Hazy; misty, as with fog. 3 Lacking in clarity; confused or ambiguous. —**murk'i·ly** *adv.* —**murk'i·ness** *n.*

**mur·mur** (mûr'mər) *n.* 1 A low sound continually repeated. 2 A complaint uttered in a low, indistinct voice. 3 An abnormal sound heard in some region of the body during auscultation: a heart *murmur.* —*v.i.* 1 To make a murmur. 2 To complain in a low tone. —*v.t.* 3 To utter in a low tone. [< L] —**mur'mur·er** *n.* —**mur'mur·ous** *adj.*

**mus·cle** (mus'əl) *n.* 1 Any of the organs, composed of bundles of fibers, by whose contraction all bodily motion is effected. 2 The fibrous, elastic tissue of these organs. 3 Muscular strength. 4 *Informal* Power; force: a law with *muscle.* —*v.i.* ·cled, ·cling *Informal* To push in or ahead by sheer physical strength. [< L *musculus*, lit., little mouse] —**mus'cled** *adj.*

**muscular dystrophy** Any of various chronic diseases of undetermined cause, characterized by wasting away of muscles.

**muse** (myōoz) *n.* A source of inspiration for artists, poets, etc. [< MUSE]

**Muse** (myōoz) *Gk. Myth.* Any of the nine goddesses presiding over poetry, the arts, and the sciences.

**mu·se·um** (myōo·zē'əm) *n.* A building or place preserving and exhibiting works of nature, art, curiosities, etc.; also, any collection of such objects. [< Gk. *mouseion* temple of the Muses]

**mush** (mush) *n.* 1 Thick porridge, made by boiling cornmeal in water or milk. 2 Anything soft and pulpy. 3 *Informal* Sentimentality. [Var. of MASH] —**mush′y** adj. (-i·er, -i·est)

**mush·room** (mush′rōōm, -rŏŏm) n. 1 The fleshy, sporebearing body of any of an order of fungi, consisting of an erect stalk and a caplike expansion. 2 Any nonpoisonous mushroom used as food, esp. the **field mushroom**. —v.i. 1 To grow or spread rapidly. 2 To expand into a mushroomlike shape. —adj. 1 Pertaining to or made of mushrooms. 2 Like a mushroom in shape or rapid growth. [< OF *mouscheron*]

**mu·sic** (myōō′zik) n. 1 The art of organizing tones, esp. with respect to time, to form an aesthetic whole. 2 A composition, or mass of compositions: contemporary *music*. 3 Any pleasing succession or combination of sounds. —**face the music** To accept the consequences or punishment for one's actions. [< Gk. *mousikē (technē)* (art) of the Muses]

**mu·si·cal** (myōō′zi·kəl) adj. 1 Of, pertaining to, or characteristic of music. 2 Talented in or appreciative of music. 3 Set to music. — n. A theatrical or film production that tells a story by means of dialogue interspersed with music, songs, and dancing in a more or less popular idiom: also **musical comedy, musical play.** —**mu′si·cal·ly** adv. — **mu′si·cal′i·ty** (-kal′ə·tē), **mu′si·cal·ness** n.

**mu·si·cian** (myōō·zish′ən) n. One skilled in music, esp. a professional performer or composer. —**mu·si′cian·ly** adj. —**mu·si′cian·ship** n.

**musk** (musk) n. 1 A substance having a penetrating odor, obtained from a sac (**musk bag**) on the abdomen of the male musk deer. 2 A similar substance from certain other animals. 3 This substance, or a synthetic substitute, used to make perfumes. [< Pers. *mushk*]

**mus·lin** (muz′lin) n. Any of several varieties of plainweave cotton cloth ranging in texture from fine to heavy. [< F < Ital. *Mussolo* Mosul, city in Iraq where made]

**mus·tache** (mus′tash, məs·tash′) n. 1 The growth of hair on the upper lip. 2 The hair or bristles growing near the mouth of an animal. Also **mus·ta′chio** (-tä′shō). [< Gk. *mystax* upper lip]

**mus·tang** (mus′tang) n. The wild horse of the American plains. [< Sp. *mesteño* wild animal]

**mus·tard** (mus′tərd) n. 1 Any of various plants related to cabbage, having yellow flowers and pods of round seeds. 2 The pungent seed of certain kinds of mustard, crushed for use as a condiment. 3 A strong, dark yellow color. [< OF *moustarde*]

**must·y** (mus′tē) adj. must·i·er, must·i·est 1 Having a moldy, stale odor or taste. 2 Not original; trite; stale. 3 Dull; lifeless. [? Alter. of earlier *moisty* < MOIST] —**must′i·ly** adv. — **must′i·ness** n.

**mu·ta·ble** (myōō′tə·bəl) adj. 1 Capable of or liable to change. 2 Fickle; unstable. [< *mutare* to change] —**mu′ta·ble·ness, mu′ta·bil′i·ty** n. —**mu′ta·bly** adv.

**mu·ta·tion** (myōō·tā′shən) n. 1 The act or process of change; alteration. 2 A change or modification in form, function, etc. 3 *Biol.* A heritable characteristic not inherited from forebears but due to an alteration in a gene or genes in a germ cell. [< L *mutare* to change] —**mu·ta′tion·al, mu·ta·tive** (myōōt′ə·tiv) adj.

**mute** (myōōt) adj. 1 Uttering no word or sound; silent. 2 Lacking the power of speech; dumb. 3 Expressed without speech or sound: a *mute* refusal. 4 *Law* Refusing to plead upon arraignment. 5 *Phonet.* Not pronounced, as the *e* in *house*. —n. 1 One who refuses or is unable to speak. 2 *Music* A device to soften or muffle the tone of an instrument. 3 *Phonet.* A stop consonant. — v.t. mut·ed, mut·ing To soften or muffle the sound of (a musical instrument). [< L *mutus* dumb] —**mute′ly** adv. —**mute′ness** n.

**mu·ti·late** (myōō′tə·lāt) v.t. ·lat·ed, ·lat·ing 1 To deprive (a person, animal, etc.) of a limb or essential part; maim. 2 To damage or injure by the removal of an important part or parts: to *mutilate* a speech. [< L *mutilare* maim] —**mu′ti·la′tion, mu′ti·la′tor** n. — **mu′ti·la′tive** adj.

**mu·ti·ny** (myōō′tə·nē) n. pl. ·nies Rebellion against constituted authority; esp., a revolt of soldiers or sailors against their officers or commander. —v.i. ·nied, ·ny·ing To take part in a mutiny. [< OF *mutin* riotous]

**mut·ter** (mut′ər) v.i. 1 To speak in a low, indistinct tone. 2 To complain; grumble. 3 To make a low, rumbling sound. —v.t. 4 To say in a low, indistinct tone. —n. A low, indistinct utterance. [ME *muteren*] —**mut′ter·er** n. —**Syn.** 1 mumble, murmur, whisper.

**mut·ton** (mut′n) n. The flesh of mature sheep as food. [< OF *moton* ram] —**mut′ton·y** adj.

**mu·tu·al** (myōō′chōō·əl) adj. 1 Shared, felt, received, etc., by each of two or more; reciprocal: *mutual* trust. 2 Having similar feelings each for the other or others: *mutual* enemies. 3 Possessed in common. [< L *mutuus* lent, exchanged, mutual] —mu'tu·al'i·ty n. —mu'tu·al·ly adv.

muz·zle (muz'əl) n. 1 The projecting jaws and nose of an animal. 2 A guard or covering for an animal's snout. 3 The discharging end of a firearm. —v.t. ·zled, ·zling 1 To put a muzzle on. 2 To restrain from speaking, expressing opinions, etc. [< LL *musus* snout] —muz'zler n.

my·o·pi·a (mī·ō'pē·ə) n. 1 A defect in vision in which objects can be seen distinctly only when very near the eye; nearsightedness. 2 Lack of insight or good judgment. [< Gk. *myein* to close + *ōps* eye] —my·op'ic (-op'ik) adj.

myr·i·ad (mir'ē·əd) adj. Multitudinous; innumerable. —n. 1 A vast indefinite number. 2 Ten thousand. [< Gk. *myrios* numberless]

myrrh (mûr) n. 1 An aromatic gum resin that exudes from several trees or shrubs of Arabia and E Africa, used in perfumes, incense, etc. 2 Any shrub or tree that yields this gum. [< L < Gk. *myrrha* < Ar. *murr*]

myr·tle (mûr'təl) n. 1 An evergreen shrub with dense, glossy leaves that are fragrant when crushed, white or pink flowers, and black berries. 2 One of various other plants, as the periwinkle. [< Gk. *myrtos*]

mys·ter·y (mis'tər·ē) n. pl. ·ter·ies 1 Something that cannot be explained or comprehended. 2 Any action, affair, or event so obscure or concealed as to arouse suspense, curiosity, or fear. 3 A story, play, film, etc. dealing with such actions or affairs. 4 Secrecy or obscurity: an event wrapped in *mystery*. 5 *Theol.* A truth known only through faith or revelation and incomprehensible to human reason. 6 *Eccl.* A sacrament, esp. the Eucharist. 7 *Usu. pl.* Secret rites or practices. 8 MYSTERY PLAY. [< Gk. *mystērion* secret worship, secret thing]

mys·tic (mis'tik) adj. 1 Of or pertaining to mystics or mysticism. 2 Of or designating an occult or esoteric rite, practice, belief, etc. 3 Mysterious; enigmatic. —n. One who practices mysticism or has mystical experiences. [< Gk. *mystikos* pertaining to secret rites]

mys·ti·cal (mis'ti·kəl) adj. 1 Characteristic of, relating to, or involving mysticism or mystics. 2 Believing in or practicing mysticism. 3 Inscrutable; inexplicable.

mys·ti·cism (mis'tə·siz'əm) n. 1 Any of various disciplines, usu. involving meditation

and asceticism, by which one can supposedly attain intuitive knowledge of or direct union with God or some ultimate reality. 2 The experience of such knowledge or union. 3 Any theory or belief which states that it is possible to have immediate, intuitive experience of realities beyond man's senses or rational faculties. 4 Vague or obscure thinking.

mys·ti·fy (mis'tə·fī) v.t. ·fied, ·fy·ing 1 To confuse or perplex, esp. deliberately. 2 To make obscure or mysterious. [< L *mysterium* mystery] —mys'ti·fi·ca'tion, mys'ti·fi'er n.

myth (mith) n. 1 A traditional story, presented as historical, often purporting to explain some natural phenomenon, as the creation of life, and expressive of the character of a people, their gods, culture, heroes, religious beliefs, etc. 2 Any real or imaginary story, theme, or character that excites the interest or imagination of a people. 3 Myths collectively. 4 Any imaginary person or thing. 5 A false belief or opinion. [<Gk. *mythos* word, speech, story]

myth·i·cal (mith'i·kəl) adj. 1 Of or like a myth. 2 Existing only in a myth. 3 Imaginary; fictitious. Also myth'ic.

my·thol·o·gy (mi·thol'ə·jē) n. pl. ·gies 1 A collection of myths of a people, person, thing, event, etc. 2 The scientific collection and study of myths. —myth·o·log·i·cal (mith'ə·loj'i·kəl), myth'o·log'ic adj. —myth'o·log'i·cal·ly adv. —my·thol'o·gist n.

# N

na·bob (nā'bob) n. 1 A native governor in India under the Mogul empire. 2 A very rich and prominent man. [< Ar. *nuwwab*] —na'bob·er·y, na'bob·ism n. —na'bob·ish adj.

na·dir (nā'dər, -dir) n. 1 The point of the celestial sphere intersected by a diameter extending from the zenith. 2 The lowest possible point. [< Ar. *nadir (es·semt)* opposite (the zenith)]

nag (nag) n. 1 A pony or small horse. 2 An old or inferior horse. [ME *nagge*]

nail (nāl) n. 1 A thin, horny plate on the end of a finger or toe. 2 Claw, talon, or hoof. 3 A slender piece of metal having a point and a head, driven through or into wood, etc., as a fastener. —hit the nail on the head 1 To express something aptly. 2 To perform correctly. —on the nail *Informal* 1 Right away; immediately. 2 At the exact spot or moment. —*v.t.* 1 To fasten or fix in place with a nail or nails. 2 To close up or shut in by means of nails. 3 To secure by prompt action: to *nail* a contract. 4 To fix firmly or immovably: Terror *nailed* him to the spot. 5 To succeed in hitting or striking. 6 *Informal* To catch; intercept. 7 *Informal* To detect and expose, as a lie or liar. [< OE *nœgel*] —**nail′er** *n.*

**na·ked** (nā′kid) *adj.* 1 Having no clothes or garments on. 2 Having no covering, as an unsheathed sword. 3 Having no defense or protection; exposed. 4 Being without concealment or excuse. [< OE *nacod*] —**na′ked·ly** *adv.* —**na′ked·ness** *n.*

**name** (nām) *n.* 1 The distinctive appellation by which a person or thing is known. 2 A descriptive designation; title. 3 General reputation. 4 An abusive appellation. 5 A memorable person, character, or thing: great *names* in music. —**by the name of** Named. —**call names** To insult by using uncomplimentary terms. —**in the name of** In behalf of. —**to one's name** Belonging to one: not a cent *to her name.* —*v.t.* named, nam·ing 1 To give a name to. 2 To mention or refer to by name; cite. 3 To designate for some particular purpose or office; nominate. 4 To give the name of: *Name* the capital of Peru. 5 To set or specify, as a price or requirement. [< OE *nama*] —**nam′er** *n.*

**nap** (nap) *n.* The short fibers on the surface of certain fabrics. —*v.t.* napped, nap·ping To raise a nap on. [< MDu. *noppe*] —**napped** *adj.*

**nape** (nāp) *n.* The back of the neck. [ME]

**naph·tha** (naf′thə, nap′-) *n.* 1 A volatile, flammable mixture of hydrocarbons obtained by distilling petroleum, wood, etc. 2 Petroleum. [< Gk.]

**nar·cis·sus** (när·sis′əs) *n. pl.* ·cis·sus·es, ·cis·si (-sis′ē) 1 Any of a genus of bulbous plants having straplike leaves and flowers with a central, tubular crown, as the daffodil and jonquil. [< Gk. *narkissos*]

**nar·co·sis** (när·kō′sis) *n.* ·ses (-sēz) Stupor or unconsciousness produced by a narcotic drug. [< Gk.]

**nar·cot·ic** (när·kot′ik) *n.* 1 Any of various drugs, as opium and its derivatives, that induce sleep and relieve pain, and are usu. addictive when used repeatedly. 2 Anything that serves to soothe, calm, or make drowsy. —*adj.* 1 Causing narcosis or stupor. 2 Pertaining to addiction to drugs or to

persons addicted. 3 Causing drowsiness or dullness. [< Gk. *narkē* torpor] —**nar·cot′i·cal·ly** *adv.*

**nar·rate** (nar′āt, na·rāt′) *v.t.* ·rat·ed, ·rat·ing To tell or relate as a story; give an account of. [< L *narrare* relate] —**nar′ra·tor, nar′rat·er** *n.*

**nar·ra·tion** (na·rā′shən) *n.* 1 The act of narrating the particulars of an event or series of events. 2 That which is narrated; narrative.

**nar·ra·tive** (nar′ə·tiv) *n.* 1 An orderly, continuous account of an event or series of events. 2 The act or art of narrating. —*adj.* Pertaining to narration. —**nar′ra·tive·ly** *adv.* —**Syn.** 1 anecdote, report, story, tale.

**nar·row** (nar′ō) *adj.* 1 Having comparatively little distance from side to side. 2 Limited in extent or duration; circumscribed. 3 Illiberal; bigoted. 4 Limited in means or resources. 5 Niggardly; parsimonious. 6 Barely accomplished or sufficient: a *narrow* escape. 7 Scrutinizing closely: a *narrow* gaze. —*v.t.* & *v.i.* To make or become narrower, as in width or scope. —*n. Usu. pl.* A narrow strait or similar passage. [< OE *nearu*] —**nar′row·ly** *adv.* —**nar′row·ness** *n.*

**na·sal** (nā′zəl) *adj.* 1 Of or pertaining to the nose. 2 *Phonet.* Pronounced with the voiced breath passing through the nose, as in (m), (n) and (ng). —*n. Phonet.* A nasal sound. [< L *nasus* the nose] —**na·sal·i·ty** (nā·zal′ə·tē) *n.* —**na′sal·ly** *adv.*

**nas·cent** (nas′ənt, nā′sənt) *adj.* Beginning to exist or develop. [< L *nasci* be born] —**nas′cence, nas′cen·cy** *n.*

**na·stur·tium** (na·stûr′shəm) *n.* 1 A common garden plant having spurred flowers of varying colors and rounded leaves with a cresslike taste. 2 The flower. [L]

**na·ta·to·ri·um** (nā′tə·tôr′ē·əm, -tō′rē-) *n. pl.* ·to·ri·ums or ·to·ri·a (-tôr′ē·ə, -tō′rē·ə) A swimming pool.

**na·tion** (nā′shən) *n.* 1 A people as an organized body politic, usu. associated with a particular territory and possessing a distinctive language and way of life. 2 A race or tribe having the same ancestry, history, language, etc.; a people. [< L *natio* breed, race]

**na·tion·al·ism** (nash′ən·əl·iz′əm) *n.* 1 Devotion to the nation as a whole; patriotism. 2 A system demanding national ownership and control of all industries. 3 A demand for national independence. —**na′tion·al·ist**

*adj.*, *n.* —**na·tion·al·is·'tic** *adj.* —**na'tion·al·is·'ti·cal·ly** *adv.*

**na·tive** (nā'tĭv) *adj.* 1 Born or produced in a region or country in which one lives; indigenous. 2 Of or pertaining to one's birth or to its place or circumstances. 3 Natural rather than acquired; inborn. 4 Of or pertaining to original inhabitants: usu. applied to non-European peoples. 5 Natural to any one or any thing. 6 Plain or simple; untouched by art. 7 Occurring in nature as a free element: *native* copper. —*n.* 1 One born in, or any product of, a given country or place. 2 Plants or animals common to a country or region. [< L *natus*, pp. of *nasci* be born.] —**na'tive·ly** *adv.* —**na'tive·ness** *n.* —**Syn.** *adj.* 3 innate, inherent.

**na·tiv·i·ty** (nā·tĭv'ə·tē, nə-) *n.* *pl.* **·ties** 1 The coming into life or the world; birth. 2 A horoscope. 3 The condition of being a native. —**the Nativity** 1 The birth of Jesus. 2 Christmas Day.

**NATO** (nā'tō) North Atlantic Treaty Organization.

**nat·ty** (nāt'ē) *adj.* **·ti·er**, **·ti·est** Smart; spruce; tidy: a *natty* dresser. [?] —**nat'ti·ly** *adv.* —**nat'ti·ness** *n.*

**nat·u·ral** (nach'ər·əl, -rəl) *adj.* 1 Of or pertaining to one's nature or constitution; inborn. 2 Of or pertaining to nature: *natural* history. 3 Of or pertaining to the existing order of things: *natural* law. 4 Coming within common experience: a *natural* result. 5 Not forced or artificial. 6 Without affectation. 7 Produced by nature: a *natural* bridge. 8 Connected by ties of consanguinity; being such by birth: a *natural* brother. 9 Born out of wedlock; illegitimate. 10 *Music* Neither sharped nor flatted: G *natural.* —*n.* 1 *Music* a A note on a line or a space that is affected by neither a sharp nor a flat. b A character (♮) which cancels the effect of an earlier flat or sharp: **also natural sign.** 2 In keyboard musical instruments, a white key. 3 One lacking powers of reason or understanding; idiot. 4 *Informal* A person or thing admirably suited for some purpose or obviously destined for success. [< L *natura* nature] —**nat'u·ral·ness** *n.*

**nat·u·ral·ist** (nach'ər·əl·ist, -rəl-) *n.* 1 One versed in natural sciences, as a zoologist or botanist. 2 An adherent of naturalism.

**nat·u·ral·ize** (nach'ər·əl·īz, -rəl-) *v.* **·ized**, **·iz·ing** *v.t.* 1 To confer the rights and privileges of citizenship upon, as an alien. 2 To adopt (a foreign word, custom, etc.) into the common use of a country or area. 3 To adapt (a foreign plant, animal, etc.) to the environment of a country or area. 4 To make natural; free from conventionality. —*v.i.* 5 To become as if native; adapt. *Brit.* sp. **·ise.** —**nat'u·ral·i·za'tion, nat'u·ral·iz'er** *n.*

**na·ture** (nā'chər) *n.* 1 The qualities or essential traits of anything; essence. 2 General type or kind; behavior of a questionable *nature.* 3 The entire physical universe and its phenomena. 4 *Often cap.* The force that supposedly controls these. 5 The inherited or habitual condition and tendencies of a person; also, a specified cast of character: a gentle *nature.* 6 Man in a natural state; also, a simplified way of life resembling this state. 7 Natural scenery or the open spaces. [< L *natus*, pp. of *nasci* be born] —**Syn.** 1 substance. 2 class, sort. 3 cosmos. 5 disposition, temperament.

**naught** (nôt) *n.* 1 Not anything; nothing. 2 A cipher; zero; the character 0. —*adj.* Of no value or account. —*adv.* Not in the least. [< OE *nā* not + *wiht* thing]

**naugh·ty** (nô'tē) *adj.* **·ti·er**, **·ti·est** Perverse and disobedient; wayward. [< NAUGHT] —**naugh'ti·ly** *adv.* —**naugh'ti·ness** *n.*

**nau·sea** (nô'zhə, -zē·ə, -shə, -sē·ə) *n.* 1 A disagreeable sensation accompanied by an impulse to vomit. 2 A feeling of loathing. [< Gk. *nausia* seasickness < *naus* ship]

**nau·se·ate** (nô'zhē·āt, -zē-, -shē-, -sē-) *v.t.* & *v.i.* **·at·ed**, **·at·ing** To affect with nausea or disgust. —**nau'se·a'tion** *n.*

**nau·seous** (nô'zhəs, -shəs) *adj.* 1 Nauseating; disgusting. 2 *Informal* Affected with nausea; queasy. —**nau'seous·ly** *adv.* —**nau'seous·ness** *n.* —**Syn.** 1 offensive, repulsive, revolting, sickening. • *Nauseous* means provoking nausea or disgust: *a nauseous display of sentimentality. Nauseated* means affected with nausea or disgust: *nauseated during a boat ride; nauseated at political corruption. Nauseous* is widely used to mean *nauseated*, but especially in formal usage the distinction is observed.

**nau·ti·cal** (nô'tǐ·kəl) *adj.* Pertaining to ships, seamen, or navigation. [< Gk. *naus* ship] —**nau'ti·cal·ly** *adv*

**na·val** (nā'vəl) *adj.* 1 Pertaining to ships and a navy. 2 Having a navy: a *naval* power. [< L *navis* ship]

**nave** (nāv) *n. Archit.* The main body of a cruciform church, between the side aisles. [< L *navis* ship]

**na·vel** (nā′vəl) n. 1 The depression on the abdomen where the umbilical cord was attached. 2 A central part or point. [< OE *nafela*]

**nav·i·gate** (nav′ə-gāt) v. ·gat·ed, ·gat·ing v.t. 1 To travel over, across, or on by ship or aircraft. 2 To steer; direct the course of. —v.i. 3 To travel by means of ship or aircraft. 4 To steer or manage a ship or aircraft. 5 To plot a course for a ship or aircraft. [< L *navis* a boat + *agere* to drive]

**nav·i·ga·tion** (nav′ə-gā′shən) n. 1 The act of navigating. 2 The art of directing the course of vessels at sea or of aircraft in flight. —nav′i·ga′tion·al adj.

**nav·i·ga·tor** (nav′ə-gā′tər) n. 1 One who navigates, or directs the course of a ship, aircraft, etc. 2 A person skilled in navigation.

**na·vy** (nā′vē) n. pl. ·vies 1 The marine military force of a country, under the control of a government department. 2 The entire shipping of a country engaged in trade and commerce; the merchant marine. 3 A fleet of ships.

**Na·zi** (nä′tsē, nat′sē, na′zē) n. A member of the National Socialist German Workers' Party, founded in 1919 and dominant from 1933 to 1945 in Germany under Hitler. —adj. Of or pertaining to the Nazis or their party. [G, short for *Nationalsozialistische (Partei)*]

**neat** (nēt) adj. 1 Characterized by strict order and cleanliness. 2 Well-proportioned; shapely. 3 Clever; adroit: a *neat* move. 4 Clear of extraneous matter; undiluted. 5 Remaining after every deduction; net. [< OF *net* < L *nitidus* shining] —neat′ly adv. —neat′ness n. —Syn. 1 orderly, spruce, tidy, trig, trim. 3 deft.

**neb·u·la** (neb′yə-lə) n. pl. ·lae (-lē) or ·las Astron. A rarified, luminous or nonluminous mass of interstellar gas or dust. [L, vapor, mist] —neb′u·lar adj.

**neb·u·lous** (neb′yə-ləs) adj. 1 Having its parts confused or mixed; indistinct: a *nebulous* idea. 2 Like a nebula. —neb′u·lous·ly adv. —neb′u·lous·ness n.

**nec·es·sar·y** (nes′ə-ser′ē) adj. 1 Being such in its nature that it must exist, occur, or be true; inevitable. 2 Absolutely needed to accomplish a desired result. —n. pl. ·sar·ies That which is indispensable: usu. in the plural: the *necessaries* of life. [< L *necessarius*]

**ne·ces·si·tate** (nə-ses′ə-tāt) v.t. ·tat·ed, ·tat·ing 1 To make necessary, unavoidable, or

certain. 2 To compel. —ne·ces′si·ta′tion n. —ne·ces′si·ta′tive adj.

**ne·ces·si·ty** (nə-ses′ə-tē) n. pl. ·ties 1 The quality of being necessary: the *necessity* for sleep. 2 That which is indispensable. 3 Often pl. That which is indispensable to a desired end. 4 The condition of being in want; poverty. —of necessity Necessarily; unavoidably. [< L *necessitas*] —Syn. 1 exigency. 2 essential, requisite, requirement.

**ne·crol·o·gy** (ne-krol′ə-jē) n. pl. ·gies 1 A list of persons who have died in a certain place or time. 2 A treatise on or an account of the dead. [NECRO- + -LOGY] —nec·ro·log·ic (nek′rə-loj′ik), nec′ro·log′i·cal adj. —nec′ro·log′i·cal·ly adv. —ne·crol′o·gist n.

**nec·ro·man·cy** (nek′rə-man′sē) n. 1 Divination by means of communication with the dead. 2 Black magic; sorcery. [< L *niger* black + Gk. *mantis* prophet] —nec′ro·man′cer n. —nec′ro·man′tic adj.

**ne·crop·o·lis** (ne-krop′ə-lis) n. A cemetery, esp. one belonging to an ancient city. [< NECRO- + Gk. *polis* city]

**ne·cro·sis** (ne-krō′sis) n. pl. ·ses (-sēz) Localized death of tissue in a plant or animal. [< Gk. *nekrōsis* deadness] —ne·crot′ic (-krot′ik) adj.

**nec·tar** (nek′tər) n. 1 Gk. Myth. The drink of the gods. 2 Any sweet, delicious drink. 3 A sweet liquid secreted by cells at the base of some flowers. [< Gk. *nektar*] —nec·tar·e·an (nek·târ′ē-ən), nec·tar′e·ous adj.

**nec·tar·ine** (nek′tə-rēn′, nek′tə-rēn) n. A variety of peach having a smooth, waxy skin. [< NECTAR]

**need** (nēd) v.t. 1 To have want of; require. —v.i. 2 To be in want. 3 To be necessary: It *needs* not. 4 To be obliged or compelled: He *need* not go. —n. 1 A lack of something requisite or desirable. 2 A situation of want or peril: to be a friend in *need*. 3 The thing needed: His *need* is education. —have need to Must; should. —if need be If necessary. [< OE *nied, nēd*] —need′er n.

**need·ful** (nēd′fəl) adj. 1 Needed; necessary. 2 Needy. —need′ful·ly adv. —need′ful·ness n.

**ne·far·i·ous** (ni-fâr′ē-əs) adj. Wicked in the extreme; heinous. [< L *nefas* a crime] —ne·far′i·ous·ly adv. —ne·far′i·ous·ness n. —Syn. atrocious, flagrant, infamous, villainous.

**ne·ga·tion** (ni-gā′shən) n. 1 The act of denying. 2 Absence of anything affirmative; nullity.

**neg·a·tive** (neg'ə·tiv) *adj.* 1 Containing contradiction or expressing negation. 2 Characterized by denial or refusal: a *negative* reply. 3 Exhibiting the absence of positive or affirmative character. 4 *Phot.* Showing dark for light and light for dark: a *negative* plate or film. 5 *Math.* Less than zero. 6 *Electr.* Denoting a charge like that carried by an electron. 7 *Biol.* In a direction away from a stimulus: a *negative* response. 8 *Med.* Not showing evidence of a suspected condition: a *negative* biopsy. —*n.* 1 A proposition, word, or act expressing refusal or denial. 2 The side in an argument that denies or is against the affirmative. 3 The right to veto. 4 A photograph having the lights and shades reversed, used for printing positives. 5 *Gram.* A word or particle, such as *non-* or *not,* employing or expressing denial. 6 *Math.* A negative number or sign. —**in the negative** 1 Being on the side against the affirmative. 2 Denying or refusing. —*v.t.* **·tived, ·tiv·ing** 1 To deny; contradict. 2 To refuse to sanction or enact; veto. 3 To prove to be false; disprove. [< L *negare* deny] —**neg'a·tive·ly** *adv.* —**neg'a·tive·ness, neg'a·tiv'i·ty** *n.*

**neg·lect** (ni·glekt') *v.t.* 1 To disregard; ignore. 2 To fail to give proper attention to or take proper care of. 3 To fail to do or perform. —*n.* 1 The act of neglecting, or the state of being neglected. 2 Habitual want of attention or care. [< L *nec-* not + *legere* gather, pick up] —**neg·lect'er** *n.* —**Syn.** *v.* 1 slight. 3 overlook. *n.* 2 carelessness, heedlessness, oversight, slackness.

**neg·li·gée** (neg'li·zhā', neg'li·zhā) *n.* 1 A woman's soft, flowing dressing gown. 2 Any informal, careless, or incomplete attire. —*adj.* Careless or informal in dress. Also **neg'li·gé'.** [< F *négliger* to neglect]

**neg·li·gence** (neg'lə·jəns) *n.* 1 The act of neglecting or failing to pay proper heed to. 2 Carelessness; lack of interest.

**neg·li·gent** (neg'lə·jənt) *adj.* 1 Apt to omit what ought to be done; neglectful. 2 Inattentive; careless. [< L *negligere* neglect] —**neg'li·gent·ly** *adv.*

**ne·go·ti·a·ble** (ri·gō'shē·ə·bəl, -shə·bəl) *adj.* 1 That can be negotiated. 2 *Law* Transferable to a third person, as for the payment of debts. 3 That can be managed or successfully dealt with. —**ne·go'ti·a·bil'i·ty** *n.* —**ne·go'ti·a·bly** *adv.*

**ne·go·ti·ate** (ni·gō'shē·āt) *v.* **·at·ed, ·at·ing** *v.i.* 1 To treat or bargain with others in order to reach an agreement. —*v.t.* 2 To procure, arrange, or conclude by mutual discussion: to *negotiate* an agreement. 3 To transfer for a value received; assign, as a note or bond. 4 To surmount, cross, or cope with (some obstacle). [< L *negotium* business] —**ne·go'ti·a'tion, ne·go'ti·a'tor** *n.* —**ne·go'ti·a·to'ry** *adj.*

**neigh·bor** (nā'bər) *n.* 1 One who lives near another. 2 One who is near another. —*adj.* Close at hand; adjacent. —*v.t.* 1 To live or be near to or next to; adjoin. —*v.i.* 2 To be in proximity; lie close. *Brit. sp.* **neigh'bour.** [< OE *nēah* near + *gebūr* farmer]

**neigh·bor·hood** (nā'bər·hŏŏd) *n.* 1 The region near where one is or resides; vicinity. 2 The people collectively who dwell in the vicinity. 3 Nearness. 4 A district considered with reference to a given characteristic. —**in the neighborhood of** *Informal* About; near. *Brit. sp.* **neigh'bour·hood.**

**nei·ther** (nē'thər, nī-) *adj.* Not either. —*pron.* Not the one nor the other. —*conj.* 1 Not one nor the other: followed by correlative *nor:* He will *neither* eat nor drink. 2 Nor yet. [< OE *nā* no + *hwæther*]

**ne·ol·o·gism** (nē·ol'ə·jiz'əm) *n.* 1 A new word or phrase. 2 The use of new words or new meanings for old words. Also **ne·ol'o·gy** (*pl.* **·gies**). [< NEO- + Gk. *logos* word] —**ne·ol'o·gist** *n.* —**ne·ol'o·gis'tic, ne·ol'o·gis'ti·cal** *adj.*

**ne·on** (nē'on) *n.* A colorless, odorless, gaseous element (symbol Ne) of very low chemical activity, used in neon lamps. [< Gk. *neos* new]

**ne·o·phyte** (nē'ə·fīt) *n.* 1 A recent convert. 2 Any novice or beginner. [< Gk. *neophytos* novice]

**neph·ew** (nef'yōō, *esp. Brit.* nev'yōō) *n.* 1 The son of one's sister or brother. 2 The son of one's sister-in-law or brother-in-law. [< L *nepos*]

**nep·o·tism** (nep'ə·tiz'əm) *n.* Favoritism by those in power extended toward relatives, esp. by appointing them to desirable positions. [< L *nepos* a grandson, nephew] —**ne·pot·ic** (ni·pot'ik) *adj.* —**nep'o·tist** *n.*

**nep·tu·ni·um** (nep·t'yōō'nē·əm) *n.* An artificially produced radioactive element (symbol Np).

**nerve** (nûrv) *n.* 1 A cordlike structure, composed of delicate filaments by which impulses are transmitted between different parts and organs of the body and the central nervous system. 2 Anything likened to a nerve, as a rib or vein of a leaf or of an insect's wing. 3 *Slang* Offensive boldness; effrontery. 4 Fearlessness; intrepidity. 5 *pl.* Nervous excitability; a nervous attack. — **get on one's nerves** To try the patience of; exasperate. —*v.t.* **nerved, nerv·ing** To give strength, vigor, or courage to. [< L *nervus* sinew]

**ner·vous** (nûr′vəs) *adj.* 1 Of or pertaining to the nerves or the nervous system. 2 Having or made up of nerves. 3 Strong; forceful, as literary style: *nervous* prose. 4 Easily disturbed or agitated. 5 Fearful; timid. —**ner′vous·ly** *adv.* —**ner′vous·ness** *n.* —**Syn.** 4 excitable, high-strung, tense. 5 anxious, apprehensive.

**nes·tle** (nes′əl) *v.* **·tled, ·tling** *v.i.* 1 To lie closely or snugly; cuddle. 2 To settle down in comfort. 3 To lie as if sheltered; be half-hidden: a lake *nestled* in the valley. —*v.t.* 4 To place or press lovingly or fondly. 5 To shelter in or as in a nest. [<OE *nestlian*] —**nes′tler** *n.*

**net**[1] (net) *n.* 1 An open fabric, woven or tied with meshes, for the capture of fishes, birds, etc. 2 An openwork fabric, as lace. 3 Something constructed with meshes, as a tennis net. —*v.t.* **net·ted, net·ting** 1 To catch in or as in a net; ensnare. 2 To make into a net. 3 To cover or enclose with a net. —*adj.* Made of or resembling netting. [<OE]

**net**[2] (net) *adj.* 1 Free from everything extraneous; obtained after deducting all expenses. 2 Not subject to any discount or deduction. —*n.* A net profit, amount, weight, etc. —*v.t.* **net·ted, net·ting** To earn or yield as clear profit. [<OF, neat]

**net·work** (net′wûrk′) *n.* 1 NETTING. 2 A system of interlacing lines, tracks, or channels. 3 An interconnection of electric devices. 4 *Telecom.* A chain of broadcasting stations.

**neu·ras·the·ni·a** (nyŏŏ′əs·thē′nē·ə, -thēn′yə) *n.* A kind of neurosis marked by headaches, digestive disturbances, depression, etc. [<NEUR(o)- + Gk. *asthenia* weakness] —**neu′ras·then′ic** (-then′ik) *adj., n.*

**neu·ri·tis** (nyŏŏ·rī′tis) *n.* Inflammation of a nerve. —**neu·rit′ic** (-rit′ik) *adj.*

**neu·ron** (nyŏŏr′on) *n.* A nerve cell, consisting of a nucleated central body and two long processes. Also **neu′rone** (-ōn). [<Gk. *neuron* nerve] —**neu·ron·ic** (nyŏŏ·ron′ik), **neu′ron·al** (-rən·əl) *adj.*

**neu·ro·sis** (nyŏŏ·rō′sis) *n. pl.* **·ses** (-sēz) Any of several functional mental disorders usu.

characterized by anxiety, depression, etc. [<Gk. *neuron* nerve]

**neu·rot·ic** (nyŏŏ·rot′ik) *adj.* 1 Of, being, or suffering from neurosis. 2 Having a morbid nature or tendency. —*n.* A person afflicted with neurosis. —**neu·rot′i·cal·ly** *adv.* —**neu·rot′i·cism** *n.*

**neu·ter** (nyŏŏ′tər) *adj.* 1 *Gram.* Neither masculine nor feminine in gender. 2 *Biol.* Having functionless or imperfectly developed sex organs. 3 Taking the part of neither side; neutral. —*n.* 1 An animal of no apparent sex, as a worker bee. 2 A eunuch. 3 A castrated animal. 4 *Gram.* a The neuter gender. b A word in this gender. 5 A neutral in warfare or other conflict. —*v.t. Informal* To castrate or spay, esp. cats; alter. [<L *ne-* not + *uter* either]

**neu·tral** (nyŏŏ′trəl) *adj.* 1 Refraining from taking the part of either side in a quarrel, contest, or war. 2 Having no decided character; indefinite. 3 Having no decided color: predominantly brownish or grayish. 4 *Biol.* Neuter. 5 *Bot.* Lacking pistils or stamens. 6 *Chem.* Being neither acid nor alkaline. 7 *Electr.* Neither positive nor negative. —*n.* One who or that which is neutral. [<L *neuter* neuter] —**neu′tral·ly** *adv.*

**neu·tral·i·ty** (nyŏŏ·tral′ə·tē) *n. pl.* **·ties** 1 The state of being a neutral nation during a war. 2 The state of being neutral.

**neu·tri·no** (nyŏŏ·trē′nō) *n. pl.* **·nos** *Physics* Either of two stable subatomic particles having no electric charge and a theoretical mass of zero when at rest.

**neu·tron** (nyŏŏ′tron) *n. Physics* An electrically neutral particle of the atom, having a mass approximately equal to that of the proton. [<NEUTRAL]

**new** (nyŏŏ) *adj.* 1 Lately made: a *new* car. 2 Lately discovered or become well known: a *new* invention. 3 Beginning or recurring afresh: the *new* moon. 4 Changed in essence, constitution, etc.: I feel a *new* man. 5 Different from that heretofore known or used; unfamiliar: This game is *new* to me. 6 Up-to-date: *new* styles in clothing. 7 Unaccustomed: a horse *new* to the saddle. 8 Named for another: used to distinguish a place from its namesake: *New* Orleans. 9 Having reached a specified rank, position, etc.: a *new* governor. 10 More; additional: *new* data. —*adv.* Newly; recently. —*n.* Something new: off with the old and on with the *new*. [< OE *nēowe*] —**new′ness** *n.*

—**Syn.** *adj.* 2 fresh, novel. 4 better. 6 latest, modern. 10 further.

**news·cast** (nyo͞oz′kast′, -käst′) *n.* A radio or television news program. —*v.t.* & *v.i.* To broadcast (news). —**news′cast′er** *n.*

**news·pa·per** (nyo͞oz′pā′pər) *n.* A publication issued for general circulation at frequent, usu. regular, intervals.

**ni·a·cin** (nī′ə·sin) *n.* The antipellagra factor in the vitamin B complex. [< NI(COTINIC) AC(ID) + -IN]

**niche** (nich) *n.* 1 A recessed space or hollow, esp. one in a wall for a statue, etc. 2 Any position specially adapted to its occupant. —*v.t.* **niched, nich·ing** To put in a niche. [< L *nidus* a nest]

**nick·el** (nik′əl) *n.* 1 A hard, silver-white metallic element (symbol Ni) widely used in steel and other alloys. 2 A five-cent coin of the U.S. or of Canada. —*v.t.* To plate with nickel. [< G (*Kupfer)nickel*, lit., copper demon; because its ore looks like an ore of copper but contains none]

**nick·name** (nik′nām′) *n.* 1 A diminutive, as Tom for Thomas. 2 A descriptive or facetious name given to a person, place, or thing in derision or affection. —*v.t.* **named, ·nam·ing** 1 To give a nickname to. 2 To misname. [ME *an ekename* an additional name, taken as a *nickname*]

**nic·o·tine** (nik′ə·tēn, -tin) *n.* A poisonous alkaloid contained in the leaves of tobacco. [< J. *Nicot*, 1530–1604, French courtier, who introduced tobacco into France] —**nic·o·tin·ic** (nik′ə·tin′ik) *adj.*

**niece** (nēs) *n.* 1 The daughter of one's brother or sister. 2 The daughter of one's brother-in-law or sister-in-law. [< L *neptis* niece]

**nig·gard** (nig′ərd) *n.* A parsimonious person. —*adj.* Niggardly. [< Scand.]

**nig·gard·ly** (nig′ərd·lē) *adj.* 1 Avaricious; stingy. 2 Scanty or measly: a *niggardly* portion. —*adv.* Stingily. —**nig′gard·li·ness** *n.* —**Syn.** *adj.* 1 miserly, parsimonious, tightfisted.

**night** (nīt) *n.* 1 The period during which the sun is below the horizon from sunset to sunrise. 2 The dark. 3 A condition of gloom or misfortune. 4 Death. —**night and day** Continuously. —**nights** *Informal* At night. [< OE *niht*]

**night·in·gale** (nī′tən·gāl, nī′ting-) *n.* A small, Old World thrush noted for the melodious song of the male. [< OE *nihtegale*, lit., night-singer]

**night·mare** (nīt′mâr) *n.* 1 A terrifying dream.

2 Any oppressive or terrifying experience. [< NIGHT + OE *mare* goblin] —**night′mar·ish** *adj.*

**ni·hil·ism** (nī′əl·iz′əm, nī′hil-) *n.* 1 *Philos.* The doctrine that nothing exists or can be known. 2 The rejection of religious and moral creeds. 3 A political doctrine holding that the existing structure of society should be destroyed. [< L *nihil* nothing + -ISM] —**ni′hil·ist** *n.* —**ni′hil·is′tic** *adj.*

**Ni·ke** (nī′kē) *Gk. Myth.* The winged goddess of victory.

**nim·ble** (nim′bəl) *adj.* **·bler, ·blest** 1 Light and quick in motion or action; agile. 2 Intellectually alert or acute. [< OE *numel* quick at learning & *næmel* receptive] —**nim′ble·ness** *n.* —**nim′bly** *adv.* —**Syn.** 1 Lively, sprightly, spry.

**nim·bus** (nim′bəs) *n. pl.* **·bus·es** or **·bi** (-bī) 1 A halo or bright disk encircling the head, as of Jesus, saints, etc., in pictures, on medallions, etc. 2 A cloud of glory about a god, a person, or thing. 3 Any atmosphere or aura of fame, glamour, etc. 4 Formerly, a nimbostratus. [L, rain cloud]

**ninth** (nīnth) *adj.* & *adv.* Next in order after the eighth. —*n.* 1 The element of an ordered set that corresponds to the number nine. 2 One of nine equal parts.

**nit** (nit) *n.* 1 The egg of a louse or similar insect. 2 The immature insect itself. [< OE *hnitu*] —**nit′ty** *adj.*

**ni·trate** (nī′trāt) *v.t.* **·trat·ed, ·trat·ing** To treat with nitric acid; to change into a nitrate. —*n.* 1 A salt or ester of nitric acid: silver *nitrate*. 2 A fertilizer consisting of sodium or potassium nitrate. [< L *nitrum*, a native sodium salt] —**ni·tra′tion** *n.*

**ni·tro·gen** (nī′trə·jən) *n.* An odorless, colorless, gaseous element (symbol N) forming 78 percent of the atmosphere and forming essential compounds in all living organisms. [< NITRO- + -GEN] —**ni·trog′e·nous** (-ə·nəs) *adj.*

**ni·tro·glyc·er·in** (nī′trō·glis′ər·in) *n.* A pale yellow, oily, explosively unstable liquid, made by nitrating glycerol, used to form dynamite and in medicine. Also **ni′tro·gly·c′er·ine.**

**no·bil·i·ty** (nō·bil′ə·tē) *n. pl.* **·ties** 1 The state of being noble, as in character or rank. 2 A class composed of nobles. 3 In Great Britain, the peerage. 4 High-mindedness; magnanimity. 5 Great moral excellence. 6 Noble lineage.

**no·ble** (nō′bəl) *adj.* **·bler, ·blest** 1 Of or pertaining to an aristocracy; of lofty lineage. 2 Characterized by or indicative of virtue or magnanimity; high-minded. 3 Imposing in appearance; grand: a *noble* face. —*n.* A person having hereditary title, rank, and privileges; in Great Britain, a peer. [< L *nobilis* noble, well-known] —**no′ble·ness** *n.* — **no′bly** *adv.* —**Syn.** *adj.* 2 excellent, honorable, worthy, righteous, fine. 3 impressive, magnificent, splendid.

**no·ble·man** (nō′bəl·mən) *n. pl.* **·men** (-mən) A man of noble rank; in England, a peer. — **no′ble·wom′an** (-wŏŏm′ən) *n. Fem.*

**noc·tur·nal** (nok·tûr′nəl) *adj.* 1 Pertaining to night. 2 Occurring or active at night. 3 Seeking food by night, as animals. 4 Having blossoms that open by night. [< L *nocturnus* < *nox* night] —**noc·tur′nal·ly** *adv.*

**noc·turne** (nok′tûrn) *n.* 1 In painting, a night scene. 2 *Music* A composition evocative of night. [< L *nocturnus* nightly]

**nod** (nod) *n.* A forward and downward motion of the head, more or less quick or jerky. — *v.* **nod·ded, nod·ding** *v.i.* 1 To make a brief forward and downward movement of the head, as in agreement, invitation, etc. 2 To let the head fall forward involuntarily, as when drowsy. 3 To be inattentive or careless. 4 To incline the top or upper part as if nodding: said of trees, flowers, etc. —*v.t.* 5 To bend (the head) forward and downward briefly. 6 To express or signify by nodding: to *nod* approval. [ME *nodden*] —**nod′der** *n.*

**node** (nōd) *n.* 1 A knot or knob; swelling. 2 *Bot.* The joint or knob on the stem of a plant, from which leaves grow. 3 *Astron.* Either of the two points at which the intersection of the planes of two orbits touches the celestial sphere. 4 *Physics* A point, line, or plane in a vibrating body where the amplitude is virtually zero. [< L *nodus* knot] — **no·dal** (nōd′l) *adj.*

**nod·ule** (noj′ōōl) *n.* 1 A little knot, lump, or node. 2 *Bot.* A tubercle. —**nod·u·lar** (noj′ə·lər) *adj.*

**noise** (noiz) *n.* 1 Any annoying or undesired sound, esp. one that is random. 2 A similar electrical signal. 3 Clamor caused by raised voices and restless moving about. 4 Any sound. —*v.* **noised, nois·ing** *v.t.* 1 To spread by rumor or report; often with *about* or *abroad.* —*v.i.* 2 To make a noise. 3 To talk in a loud manner. [< OF *noyse*]

**noi·some** (noi′səm) *adj.* 1 Very offensive, particularly to the sense of smell. 2 Injurious;

harmful. [< *noy,* var. of ANNOY + -SOME] — **noi′some·ly** *adv.* —**noi′some·ness** *n.* — **Syn.** 1 fetid, foul, mephitic, stinking. 2 destructive, detrimental, hurtful, noxious.

**nois·y** (noi′zē) *adj.* **nois·i·er, nois·i·est** 1 Making a loud noise. 2 Characterized by much noise. —**nois′i·ly** *adv.* —**nois′i·ness** *n.*

**no·mad** (nō′mad, nom′ad) *adj.* Nomadic. — *n.* A rover; one of an unsettled, wandering people, tribe, or race. [< Gk. *nomein* to pasture, feed] —**no′mad·ism** *n.*

**no·mad·ic** (nō·mad′ik) *adj.* 1 Of or pertaining to nomads. 2 Wandering from one place to another; unsettled. Also **no·mad′i·cal.** — **no·mad′i·cal·ly** *adv.*

**no·men·cla·ture** (nō′mən·klā′chər) *n.* A system of names used in any art, science, or other specialized field. [L *nomenclatura* list of names]

**nom·i·nal** (nom′ə·nəl) *adj.* 1 Of or pertaining to a name or names. 2 Existing in name only; not actual: a *nominal* peace. 3 So slight as to be hardly worth naming: a *nominal* sum. [< L *nomen* name] —**nom′i·nal·ly** *adv.*

**nom·i·nate** (nom′ə·nāt) *v.t.* **·nat·ed, ·nat·ing** 1 To name as a candidate for elective office. 2 To appoint to some office or duty. —*adj.* Nominated. [< L < *nomen, nominis* a name] —**nom·i·na′tion, nom′i·na′tor** *n.*

**nom·i·nee** (nom′ə·nē′) *n.* A person who receives a nomination, esp. for an election.

**non·a·ge·nar·i·an** (non′ə·jə·nâr′ē·ən, nō′nə-) *adj.* Pertaining to the nineties in age. —*n.* One between the ages of ninety and a hundred. [< L *nonagenarius* of ninety]

**non·cha·lance** (non′shə·läns′, non′shə·ləns) *n.* Jaunty indifference or unconcern.

**non·cha·lant** (non′shə·länt′, non′shə·lənt) *adj.* Without concern; casual; indifferent. [< L *non* not + *calere* be warm] —**non′cha·lant·ly** *adv.*

**non·com·mit·tal** (non′kə·mit′l) *adj.* Not having or expressing a decided opinion. —**non′com·mit′tal·ly** *adv.*

**non·con·duc·tor** (non′kən·duk′tər) *n.* A substance or material that offers resistance to the passage of some form of energy.

**non·con·form·ist** (non′kən·fôr′mist) *n.* One who does not conform to established beliefs and procedures, esp. in religious matters. —**non′con·form′ance** (-məns), **non′con·for′mi·ty** (-fôr′mə·tē) *n.*

**non·de·script** (non′di·skript) *adj.* Not distinctive enough to be described; difficult to classify. —n. A nondescript person or thing. [< NON- + L *descriptus*]

**non·en·ti·ty** (non·en′tə·tē) n. pl. ·ties 1 A person or thing of small significance. 2 The negation of being; nonexistence.

**non·pa·reil** (non′pə·rel′) adj. Of unequaled excellence. —n. 1 Something of unequaled excellence. 2 *Printing* A name for 6-point type. [< OF *non* not + *pareil* equal]

**non·par·ti·san** (non·pär′tə·zən, -sən) adj. 1 Not partisan. 2 Not pertaining or adhering to any established political party. —n. A nonpartisan person or group.

**non·plus** (non·plus′, non′plus) v.t. ·plused or ·plussed, ·plus·ing or ·plus·sing To baffle; perplex. —n. A mental standstill; perplexity. [< L *non plus* no further] —Syn. v. confound, embarrass, mystify, puzzle.

**non·sec·tar·i·an** (non′sek·târ′ē·ən) n. Not allied formally with or restricted to any religious denomination.

**non·sense** (non′sens, -səns) n. 1 That which is without good sense; meaningless or ridiculous language. 2 Things of no importance. 3 Absurd or affected behavior. —adj. Consisting of a grouping of letters or sounds that are not intelligible but often formed on a pattern of standard words: "Glip" is a *nonsense* word. —interj. How absurd! —non·sen′si·cal adj. —non·sen′si·cal·ly adv.

**noon** (noon) n. 1 That time of day when the sun·is on the meridian; the middle of the day. 2 The highest point of any period or career. —adj. Of or taking place at noon: the *noon* meal. [< L *nona* (*hora*) ninth (hour)]

**noose** (noos) n. 1 A loop furnished with a running knot, as in a hangman's halter or a snare. 2 Anything that restricts one's freedom. —v.t. noosed, noos·ing 1 To capture or secure with a noose. 2 To make a noose in (a rope). [< L *nodus* a knot]

**norm** (nôrm) n. 1 A model, type, pattern, or value considered as representative of a specified group. 2 *Psychol.* The average or median of performance in a given function or test. [< L *norma* rule]

**nor·mal** (nôr′məl) adj. 1 Conforming to a type or standard; regular. 2 Constituting a standard; model. 3 *Math.* Perpendicular. 4 Average; mean. 5 *Chem.* Denoting a salt having no replaceable hydrogen. 6 *Psychol.* Of average intelligence or mental health. 7 In good physical health. —n. 1 A common or natural condition. 2 A usual or accepted rule or process. 3 The average or mean value of observed quantities. 4 *Math.* A straight line perpendicular to a curve or surface at a point. [< L *norma* rule] —nor′mal·cy (-sē), nor·mal·i·ty (nôr·mal′ə·tē), nor′mal·ness n. —nor′mal·ly adv. —Syn. 1 common, everyday, ordinary, typical, usual.

**north** (nôrth) n. 1 The general direction to the left of sunrise. 2 The point of the compass at 0° or 360°, directly opposite south. 3 Any region north of a given point. 4 *Sometimes cap.* The northern part of any region, country, etc. —**the North** 1 The states in the part of the U.S. north of Maryland, Missouri, and the Ohio river. 2 The states that opposed the Confederacy. —adj. 1 Lying toward or in the north. 2 Issuing from or inhabiting the north. 3 Facing or proceeding toward the north. 4 *Usu. cap.* Denoting the northern part of a country, continent, hemisphere, etc.: *North* America. —adv. Toward the north. [< OE]

**north·ern** (nôr′thərn) adj. Pertaining to the north or the North. —n. 1 A northerner. 2 A north wind. [< OE *northerne*] —north′ern·most adj.

**Nor·we·gian** (nôr·wē′jən) n. 1 A citizen or native of Norway. —adj. Of or pertaining to Norway, its people, or their language.

**nose** (nōz) n. 1 The part of the face just above the mouth, containing the nostrils and the organ of smell. 2 The power or sense of smelling. 3 Anything resembling a nose, as a ship's prow. 4 The ability to discover: a *nose* for the facts. —**lead by the nose** To control absolutely. —**look down one's nose at** *Informal* To show contempt for. —**pay through the nose** To pay an exorbitant price. —**turn up one's nose at** To reject scornfully. —**under one's (very) nose** In plain sight; obvious. —v. nosed, nos·ing v.t. 1 To perceive or discover by or as by the sense of smell. 2 To examine or touch with the nose. —v.i. 3 To smell; sniff. 4 To pry; meddle. 5 To push (one's way) slowly and carefully. —**nose out** To defeat by a small margin. [< OE *nosu*]

**nos·tal·gi·a** (nos·tal′jē·ə, -jə) n. 1 Severe homesickness. 2 Any longing for something far away or long ago. [< Gk. *nostos* a return home + *algos* a pain] —nos·tal′gic adj.

**nos·tril** (nos′trəl) n. One of the outer openings in the nose. [< OE *nosu* nose + *thyrel* a hole]

**nos·trum** (nos′trəm) n. 1 A patent medicine; quack recipe. 2 Anything savoring of quackery: political *nostrums*. [< L *noster* our own; because prepared by those selling it]

**no·ta·ble** (nō′tə·bəl) *adj.* Worthy of note; distinguished. —*n.* One who is worthy of note; a distinguished person. [< L *nota* a mark] —**no·ta·bil·i·ty** (nō′tə·bil′ə·tē), **no′ta·ble·ness** *n.* —**no′ta·bly** *adv.*

**no·ta·ry** (nō′tə·rē) *n. pl.* **·ries** An officer empowered to authenticate contracts, administer oaths, take depositions, etc. Also **notary public.** [< L *notarius* a clerk < *notare* to note] —**no·tar·i·al** (nō·târ′ē·əl) *adj.*

**no·ta·tion** (nō·tā′shən) *n.* 1 The process of designating by figures, etc. 2 Any system of signs, figures, or abbreviations used for convenience in a science or art. 3 A brief note; annotation. —**no·ta′tion·al** *adj.*

**note** (nōt) *n.* 1 A brief written record kept as a reminder. 2 *Often pl.* A written summary of a meeting, conversation, etc., to serve as a record for future reference: students taking copious *notes.* 3 A comparatively short letter. 4 An official communication in writing from one government to another. 5 A brief comment in a margin, at the bottom of a page, or at the end of a text. 6 A guarantee in writing to pay a specified sum at a certain time. 7 A government or bank certificate, usu. payable in cash upon presentation. 8 An account or bill. 9 *Music* **a** A written character used to indicate the pitch and length of a tone. **b** Any musical sound. **c** A key of a keyboard instrument. 10 A bird's song. 11 The general tone or quality of something: a *note* of anxiety. 12 High importance or repute: people of *note.* 13 Special notice or attention: He took *note* of the situation. —**compare notes** To exchange opinions; talk over. —*v.t.* **not·ed, not·ing** 1 To take notice or note of; observe. 2 To set down, as in writing; make a note of. 3 To mention specially or separately in the course of writing. 4 To set down in musical notation. [< L *nota* a mark, orig. pp. fem. of *noscere* know] —**not′er** *n.*

**no·tice** (nō′tis) *v.t.* **·ticed, ·tic·ing** 1 To pay attention to or take cognizance of. 2 To treat courteously or with favor. 3 To mention or comment on. 4 To serve with a notice; notify. —*n.* 1 The act of noticing or observing. 2 Announcement; warning. 3 Respectful treatment; civility. 4 A formal written or printed notification, instruction, or warning, as of the termination or intended termination of an agreement. 5 A public communication openly displayed. 6 A critique or review: The play closed because of bad *notices.* [< L *notus* known] —**no′tice·a·ble** *adj.* —**no′tice·a·bly** *adv.*

**no·ti·fi·ca·tion** (nō′tə·fə·kā′shən) *n.* 1 The act of notifying. 2 Notice given. 3 Written matter that gives information.

**no·ti·fy** (nō′tə·fī) *v.t.* **·fied, ·fy·ing** 1 To give notice to; inform. 2 To make known. [< L *notus* known + *facere* to make] —**no′ti·fi′er** *n.*

**no·tion** (nō′shən) *n.* 1 A thought; idea. 2 A hastily formed theory. 3 Intention; inclination. 4 *pl.* Miscellaneous small articles, such as ribbons, thread, pins, needles, etc. [< L *notus,* pp. of *noscere* know]

**no·to·ri·ous** (nō·tôr′ē·əs, -tō′rē-) *adj.* 1 Being publicly and unfavorably known and discussed. 2 Well-known. [< L *notus* known, orig. pp. of *noscere* know] —**no·to′ri·ous·ly** *adv.* —**no·to′ri·ous·ness** *n.* —**Syn.** 1 egregious, flagrant, outrageous, unsavory.

**nought** (nôt) *n., adj., adv.* NAUGHT.

**noun** (noun) *Gram. n.* A word used as the name of a thing, quality, or action existing or conceived by the mind; a substantive. —*adj.* Of or used as a noun or nouns: also **noun·al** (noun′əl). [< L *nomen* name]

**nour·ish** (nûr′ish) *v.t.* 1 To furnish material to sustain the life and promote the growth of (a living organism). 2 To support; maintain: to *nourish* illusions. [< L *nutrire* nourish] —**nour′ish·er** *n.*

**nour·ish·ment** (nûr′ish·mənt) *n.* 1 Nutriment; food. 2 The act of nourishing or the state of being nourished. 3 Anything that promotes growth and sustains life.

**no·va** (nō′və) *n. pl.* **·vas** or **·vae** (-vē) A star which suddenly increases in brightness, then fades to its former magnitude after a time. [< L *novus* new]

**nov·el** (nov′əl) *n.* A fictional prose narrative of considerable length with a plot and characters. —*adj.* New in a striking or unusual way. [Fusion of Ital. *novella* a novel and OF *novel* new] —**Syn.** *adj.* fresh, unfamiliar, unusual. *n.* 1 romance, story, tale.

**nov·el·ist** (nov′əl·ist) *n.* A writer of novels.

**nov·el·ty** (nov′əl·tē) *n. pl.* **·ties** 1 The quality of being novel. 2 *pl.* Small manufactured articles or trinkets. 3 An innovation.

**nov·ice** (nov′is) *n.* 1 A beginner in any business or occupation; tyro. 2 *Eccl.* One who enters a religious house or community on probation. [< L *novus* new] —**nov′ice·hood** (-hōōd) *n.*

**nox·ious** (nok′shəs) *adj.* Causing, or tending to cause, injury to health or morals; poisonous. [< L *nocere* to hurt] —**nox′ious·ly** *adv.* —**nox′ious·ness** *n.* —Syn. deadly, hurtful, pernicious.

**noz·zle** (noz′əl) *n.* A projecting spout from which something, esp. a fluid, issues. 2 An inlet or outlet pipe. [Dim. of NOSE]

**nuclear fission** FISSION (def. 3).

**nu·cle·us** (nyōō′klē·əs) *n. pl.* **·cle·i** (-klē·ī) 1 A central mass; kernel. 2 *Biol.* A complex, spheroidal body found in plant and animal cells and essential in the vital activities of the cell, as growth, reproduction, etc. 3 *Astron.* A bright central point as in the head of a comet or at the center of a nebula. 4 *Physics & Chem.* The central core of an atom, having a positive charge, composed mainly of protons and neutrons, and containing most of the atomic mass. [L, a kernel, dim. of *nux, nucis* a nut]

**nude** (nyōōd) *adj.* Without clothing or covering; naked. —*n.* 1 A nude figure, as in painting or sculpture. 2 The state of being nude: to appear in the *nude*. [< L *nudus* naked] —**nude′ly** *adv.* —**nude′ness** *n.*

**nug·get** (nug′it) *n.* 1 A lump. 2 A lump of precious metal, as gold. 3 A small amount of anything of value: a *nugget* of good sense. [?]

**nui·sance** (nyōō′səns) *n.* A person or thing that annoys, vexes, or harms. [< OF *nuire* to harm]

**null** (nul) *adj.* 1 Of no legal force or effect. 2 Having no existence. 3 Lacking distinction or individuality. 4 Zero. —**null and void** Having no force or effect; invalid. [< L *nullus* no, none]

**nul·li·fy** (nul′ə·fī) *v.t.* **·fied**, **·fy·ing** 1 To bring to nothing; render ineffective or valueless. 2 To deprive of legal force or effect; make void. [< L *nullus* none + *facere* make] —**nul·li·fi·ca·tion** (nul′ə·fə·kā′shən), **nul′li·fi′er** *n.*

**numb** (num) *adj.* Wholly or partially without the power of sensation or of motion. —*v.t.* To make numb. [< ME *nomen* taken, seized] —**numb′ly** *adv.* —**numb′ness** *n.* —Syn. *adj.* benumbed, deadened, frozen, insensible.

**num·ber** (num′bər) *n.* 1 An element of one of various mathematical sets, defined, often by axioms, as having certain properties, esp. with respect to certain operations, as integers, real numbers, imaginary numbers, etc. 2 A collection of units or individuals, whether large or small: a *number* of facts; large *numbers* of people. 3 *pl.* Arithmetic. 4 The character or quality of being numerous: Reliance is placed more on spirit than on *number*. 5 An element of an ordered set. 6 One of the divisions or movements of a piece of music. 7 A series of digits used for identification: a serial *number*. 8 *Often pl.* Poetic measure; rhythm. 9 *Gram.* The form of inflection of a noun, pronoun, adjective, or verb, that indicates whether one thing or more is meant. 10 *Informal* An article of merchandise: our most popular *number*. 11 A single issue, as of a periodical. 12 *Informal* A person or thing set apart: That blouse is a stylish *number*. —**a number of** More than two or three; many. —**get (or have) someone's number** *Informal* To have insight into a person's motives, character, etc. —**the numbers** NUMBERS POOL. —*v.t.* 1 To determine the total number of; count. 2 To assign a number to. 3 To include as one of a collection or group. 4 To amount to; total: We *number* fifty men. 5 To set or limit the number of: Your days are *numbered*. —*v.i.* 6 To make a count; total. 7 To be included, as in a group: He was *numbered* among the civilians. [< L *numerus*] —**num′ber·er** *n.*

**nu·mer·al** (nyōō′mər·əl) *n.* A symbol, character, letter, or word, used to express a number: Arabic *numerals*. —*adj.* 1 Used in expressing a number. 2 Denoting a number. [< L *numerus* number] —**nu′mer·al·ly** *adv.*

**nu·mer·ous** (nyōō′mə·rəs) *adj.* Consisting of a great number of units; being many. —**nu′mer·ous·ness** *n.*

**nu·mis·mat·ics** (nyōō′miz·mat′iks, -mis-) *n. pl. (construed as sing.)* The science of coins and medals. [< L *numisma* a coin] —**nu′mis·mat′ic, nu′mis·mat′i·cal** *adj.* —**nu·mis′ma·tist, nu·mis′ma·tol′o·gist** *n.*

**nun** (nun) *n.* A woman devoted to a religious life, and living under vows of poverty, chastity, and obedience, often in a convent. [< Med. L *nonna*] —**nun′nish** *adj.*

**nup·tial** (nup′shəl) *adj.* Pertaining to marriage or the marriage ceremony. —*n. pl.* A wedding; marriage ceremony. [< L *nuptus*, pp. of *nubere* marry] —**nup′tial·ly** *adv.*

**nurse** (nûrs) *n.* 1 A person who cares for the sick, esp. professionally. 2 A female servant who takes care of young children. 3 A person who fosters, protects, and promotes. —*v.* **nursed**, **nurs·ing** *v.t.* 1 To take care of, as in sickness or infirmity. 2 To feed (an infant) at the breast; suckle. 3 To feed and care for in infancy. 4 To promote the growth and development of. 5 To preserve from injury or undue strain: to *nurse* a weak wrist. 6 To try to cure, as a cold, by taking care of oneself. 7 To clasp or hold carefully or caressingly; fondle. 8 To keep in mind, as a grievance. 9 To use or consume slowly: to *nurse* a drink. —*v.i.* 10 To act or serve as a nurse. 11 To take milk from the breast. 12 To suckle an infant. [< L *nutrix* < *nutrire* nourish, foster] —**nurs′er** *n.*

**nurs·er·y** (nûr′sər·ē) *n. pl.* **·er·ies** 1 A room set apart for the use of children and babies. 2 A place where trees, shrubs, etc., are raised for sale or transplanting. 3 The place where anything is fostered, bred, or developed.

**nur·ture** (nûr′chər) *v.t.* **·tured, ·tur·ing** 1 To feed; nourish. 2 To bring up or train; educate. —*n.* 1 The act of rearing or bringing up. 2 Nourishment. [< L *nutrire* nourish] —**nur′tur·er** *n.* —**Syn.** *v.* 2 cherish, foster, raise, rear.

**nu·tri·ent** (nʸo͞o′trē·ənt) *adj.* 1 Giving nourishment. 2 Conveying nutrition. —*n.* Something that nourishes. [< L *nutrire* nourish]

**nu·tri·ment** (nʸo͞o′trə·mənt) *n.* 1 That which nourishes. 2 That which promotes development. [< L *nutrire* nourish] —**nu′tri·men′tal** *adj.* —**Syn.** 1 food, meat, nourishment, sustenance.

**nu·tri·tion** (nʸo͞o·trish′ən) *n.* 1 The aggregate of all the processes by which food is assimilated in living organisms. 2 Food. —**nu·tri′tion·al** *adj.* —**nu·tri′tion·al·ly** *adv.*

**nu·tri·tious** (nʸo͞o·trish′əs) *adj.* Nourishing; promoting nutrition. —**nu·tri′tious·ly** *adv.* —**nu·tri′tious·ness** *n.*

**nu·tri·tive** (nʸo͞o′trə·tiv) *adj.* 1 Having nutritious properties. 2 Of or relating to nutrition. —**nu′tri·tive·ly** *adv.* —**nu′tri·tive·ness** *n.*

**ny·lon** (nī′lon) *n.* 1 A synthetic substance that may be formed into fibers, bristles, sheets, etc., and characterized by extreme toughness, elasticity, and strength. 2 *pl.* Stockings made of nylon thread. [< *Nylon,* a tradename]

**nymph** (nimf) *Gk. & Rom. Myth.* A beautiful maiden inhabiting groves, forests, fountains, springs, mountains, etc. —*n.* 1 Any lovely young woman. 2 The young of certain insects which undergo incomplete metamorphosis. [< Gk. *nymphē* nymph, bride] —**nymph′al, nym·phe·an** (nim·fē′ən), **nymph′ic, nymph′i·cal** *adj.*

# O

**oak** (ōk) *n.* 1 Any of various hardwood, acorn-bearing trees and shrubs of the beech family. 2 The hard, durable wood or timber of the oak. 3 Any of various other plants having a resemblance or relation to the oak: poison *oak.* [< OE *āc*]

**oar** (ôr, ōr) *n.* 1 An implement for propelling or, occasionally, for steering a boat, consisting of a long shaft with a blade at one end. 2 An oarsman. —*v.t.* 1 To propel with or as with oars; row. 2 To make (one's way) or traverse (water) with or as with oars. —*v.i.* 3 To proceed by or as by rowing; row. [< OE *ār*]

**o·a·sis** (ō·ā′sis) *n. pl.* **·ses** (-sēz) 1 An area in a waste or desert made fertile by ground water or by surface irrigation. 2 Any place providing relief or refreshment; refuge: a small city park that provided an *oasis* of quiet amidst the street noises. [< Gk., fertile spot]

**oat** (ōt) *n. Usu. pl.* A cereal grass extensively cultivated for its edible grain. [< OE *āte*] —**oat′en** *adj.*

**oath** (ōth) *n. pl.* **oaths** (ō͟thz, ōths) 1 A solemn confirmation of a promise, course of action, etc., made by appealing to God or to some person or thing regarded as high and holy. 2 The course of action, promise, etc., so supported, or the form of words used in supporting it. 3 An irreverent or profane use of the name of the Deity or of any sacred name or object. 4 A swearword; curse. [< OE *āth*] —**Syn.** 3 blasphemy, curse, imprecation, profanity.

**ob·du·rate** (ob′dʸo͝o·rit) *adj.* 1 Unmoved by feelings of humanity or pity; hard. 2 Perversely impenitent. 3 Unyielding; stubborn. [< L *ob-* completely + *durare* harden] —**ob′du·ra·cy** (-rə·sē), **ob′du·rate·ness** *n.* —**ob′du·rate·ly** *adv.*

**o·be·di·ence** (ō·bē′dē·əns, ə·bē′-) *n.* 1 The state of being obedient; willingness to obey. 2 The act of obeying, or an instance of it.

**o·be·di·ent** (ō·bē′dē·ənt, ə·bē′-) *adj.* Complying with or submitting to a command, prohibition, law, or duty. [< L *obedire* obey] —**o·be′di·ent·ly** *adv.*

**o·bei·sance** (ō·bā′səns, ō·bē′-) *n.* 1 An act of courtesy or deference, as a bow or curtsy. 2 Reverent courtesy; deference. [< OF *obeir* obey] —**o·bei′sant** *adj.* —**o·bei′sant·ly** *adv.*

**ob·e·lisk** (ob′ə·lisk, ō′bə-) *n.* 1 A usu. monumental structure with a square, tapered shaft and a pyramidal top. 2 *Printing* The dagger sign (†) used as a mark of reference: also **ob·e·lus** (ob′ə·ləs). [< Gk. *obeliskos*, dim. of *obelos* a spit, pointed pillar]

**o·bese** (ō·bēs′) *adj.* Very fat; corpulent. [< L *ob-* completely + *edere* eat] —**o·be·si·ty** (ō·bē′sə·tē) *n.*

**o·bey** (ō·bā′, ə·bā′) *v.t.* 1 To do the bidding of; be obedient to. 2 To carry into effect; execute, as a command. 3 To act in accordance with; be guided by: to *obey* the law. —*v.i.* 4 To be obedient. [< L *obedire*] —**o·bey′er** *n.*

**o·bit·u·ar·y** (ō·bich′ōō·er′ē) *n.* *pl.* **·ar·ies** A published notice of a person's death, often including a biographical sketch. —*adj.* Of or pertaining to a death. [< L *obitus*, pp. of *obire*, die, go down]

**ob·ject¹** (əb·jekt′) *v.i.* 1 To offer arguments or opposition; dissent. 2 To feel or state disapproval or dissent. —*v.t.* 3 To offer as opposition or criticism; charge. [< L *ob-* towards, against + *jacere* to throw] —**ob·jec′tor** *n.*

**ob·ject²** (ob′jikt, -jekt) *n.* 1 Anything that lies within the cognizance of the senses; esp. anything tangible or visible; any material thing. 2 Something to which feeling or action is directed: an *object* of affection. 3 A purpose or goal; aim. 4 *Gram.* A noun or pronoun that receives the action of a verb or is governed by a preposition. [< Med. L *objectum* something thrown in the way]

**ob·jec·tion** (əb·jek′shən) *n.* 1 The act of objecting. 2 An argument, fact, etc., used in dissent or disapproval. 3 A feeling of disapproval or disinclination.

**ob·jec·tion·a·ble** (əb·jek′shən·ə·bəl) *adj.* Deserving of disapproval; offensive. —**ob·jec′tion·a·bil′i·ty, ob·jec′tion·a·ble·ness** *n.* —**ob·jec′tion·a·bly** *adv.*

**ob·jec·tive** (əb·jek′tiv) *adj.* 1 Of or belonging to an object; having the nature of an object; esp., being that which is external to the mind or perceived by the senses and subject to verification. 2 Treating of or representing facts or reality without reference to feelings or opinions: an *objective* report or test. 3 Not prejudiced; unbiased. 4 *Gram.* Denoting the case of an object of a transitive verb or preposition. —*n.* 1 A goal or purpose, as of a mission or assignment. 2 Something that is objective. 3 *Gram.* a The objective case. b A word in this case. 4 The lens or lenses of an optical instrument closest to the object observed. —**ob·jec′tive·ly** *adv.* —**ob·jec·tiv·i·ty** (ob′jek·tiv′ə·tē), ob·

**jec′tive·ness** *n.* —**Syn.** *adj.* 2 impersonal. 3 detached, disinterested, fair-minded.

**ob·la·tion** (ob·lā′shən) *n.* 1 Anything offered in worship, esp. the elements of the Eucharist. 2 Any grateful and solemn offering. [< L *oblatus*, carried toward, offered] —**ob·la′tion·al, ob·la·to·ry** (ob′lə·tôr′ē, -tō′rē) *adj.*

**ob·li·gate** (ob′lə·gāt) *v.t.* **·gat·ed, ·gat·ing** To bind or compel, as by contract, conscience, promise, etc. —*adj.* (ob′lə·git, -gāt) Bound or restricted. [< L *obligare* oblige]

**ob·li·ga·tion** (ob′lə·gā′shən) *n.* 1 The act of obligating, or state of being obligated. 2 A duty, promise, etc., by which one is bound; responsibility. 3 The constraining power of conscience or law. 4 A requirement imposed by the customs of society or the laws of propriety; what one owes in return for a service, kindness, or favor. 5 A binding legal agreement bearing a penalty. 6 The condition of being indebted for an act of kindness, a service received, etc. —**ob′li·ga′tor** *n.*

**ob·lig·a·to·ry** (ə·blig′ə·tôr′ē, -tō′rē, ob′lə·gə-) *adj.* 1 In civil or moral law, binding. 2 Of the nature of or constituting a duty or obligation; imperative.

**o·blige** (ə·blīj′) *v.t.* **o·bliged, o·blig·ing** 1 To obligate; constrain. 2 To place under an obligation, as for a favor or kindness. 3 To do a favor or service for. [< L *ob-* towards + *ligare* to bind] —**o·blig′er** *n.*

**ob·lique** (ō·blēk′, ə-, *in military usage* ə·blīk′) *adj.* 1 Neither perpendicular nor horizontal; slanting. 2 Acute or obtuse, as an angle. 3 Indirect or allusive rather than straightforward: an *oblique* reference to his uncertain paternity. —*v.i.* **·liqued, ·li·quing** 1 To deviate from the perpendicular; slant. 2 *Mil.* To march or advance in an oblique direction. [< L *ob-* against, completely + *liquis* slanting, awry] —**ob·lique′ly** *adv.* —**ob·lique′ness** *n.*

**ob·lit·er·ate** (ə·blit′ə·rāt) *v.t.* **·at·ed, ·at·ing** To destroy utterly; leave no trace of. 2 To blot or wipe out; erase, as writing. [< L *oblit-erare* blot out] —**ob·lit′er·a′tion, ob·lit′er·a′tor** *n.* —**ob·lit′er·a′tive** *adj.*

**ob·liv·i·ous** (ə·bliv′ē·əs) *adj.* 1 Taking no notice, as though unaware or indifferent: usu. with *of* or *to*: *oblivious* of the noise. 2 Distracted; forgetful: usu. with *of*. —**ob·liv′i·ous·ly** *adv.* —**ob·liv′i·ous·ness** *n.*

**ob·long** (ob′lông, -long) *adj.* Longer in one dimension than in another; esp., elongated along the horizontal axis. —*n.* An oblong figure, as a rectangle. [< L *oblongus* somewhat long]

**ob·lo·quy** (ob′lə-kwē) *n. pl.* **·quies** 1 An expression of severe censure or denunciation. 2 The state of one who is so censured; disgrace. —**Syn.** 1 reprobation, vilification, defamation, calumny, opprobrium. 2 ignominy. [< L *ob-* against + *loqui* speak]

**ob·nox·ious** (ab·nok′shəs) *adj.* Strongly offensive; disgusting; repulsive; odious. [< L *ob-* towards + *noxa* injury] —**ob·nox′ious·ly** *adv.* —**ob·nox′ious·ness** *n.*

**ob·scene** (ob·sēn′, əb-) *adj.* 1 Offensive to one's sense of modesty or propriety. 2 Intended to provoke lust; licentious; lewd. 3 Disgusting; foul. [< L *obs-*, var of *ob-* towards + *caenum* filth] —**ob·scene′ly** *adv.*

**ob·scen·i·ty** (ob·sen′ə·tē, -sē′nə-, əb-) *n. pl.* **·ties** 1 The state or quality of being obscene. 2 An obscene remark, act, representation, etc. Also **ob·scene′ness.**

**ob·scure** (ob·skyŏŏr′, əb-) *adj.* **·scur·er, ·scur·est** 1 Lacking in light; dim; dark; dusky. 2 Not clear to the mind; vague; abstruse. 3 Faintly marked; hard to discern; undefined. 4 Remote or apart; hidden from view or notice. 5 Little known; unnoticed: an *obscure* hamlet. —*v.t.* **·scured, ·scuring** 1 To darken or cloud; dim. 2 To hide from view; conceal 3 To make unintelligible; confuse. [< L *obscurus*, lit., covered over] —**ob·scure′ly** *adv.* —**ob·scu′ri·ty** (-skyŏŏr′ə-tē), **ob·scure′ness** *n.*

**ob·se·qui·ous** (ob·sē′kwē·əs, əb-) *adj.* Too eager to please; fawning; servile. [< L *ob-* towards + *sequi* follow] —**ob·se′qui·ous·ly** *adv.* —**ob·se′qui·ous·ness** *n.*

**ob·ser·vance** (əb·zûr′vəns) *n.* 1 The act of observing, as a custom or ceremony; compliance, as with law or duty. 2 Any common custom, form, rite, etc. 3 Heedful attention; observation. 4 *Eccl.* The rule or constitution of a religious order.

**ob·ser·vant** (əb·zûr′vənt) *adj.* 1 Carefully attentive; alert or watchful. 2 Having the habit of keen perception. 3 Strict in observing; heedful: usu. with *of*: *observant* of protocol. —**ob·ser′vant·ly** *adv.*

**ob·ser·va·tion** (ob′zər-vā′shən) *n.* 1 The act, faculty, or habit of observing. 2 The fact of being observed. 3 The practice of observing and recording, as for scientific study, certain data, events, etc.; also, the record so obtained, or an item within the record. 4 A

remark apparently based upon things observed. —**ob′ser·va′tion·al** *adj.*

**ob·ser·va·to·ry** (əb·zûr′və·tôr′ē, -tō′rē) *n. pl.* **·ries** 1 A building designed and equipped for the systematic observation of astronomical or other natural phenomena. 2 A tower built for obtaining a panoramic view.

**ob·serve** (əb·zûrv′) *v.* **·served, ·serv·ing** *v.t.* 1 To notice by the sense of sight; see. 2 To watch attentively; keep under surveillance. 3 To make methodical observation of, as for scientific purposes. 4 To abide by or conform to; to *observe* the law. 5 To celebrate or solemnize (an occasion), as with appropriate ritual. 6 To say as a comment or opinion; mention. —*v.i.* 7 To make a remark; comment: often with *on* or *upon.* 8 To take notice. 9 To act as an observer. [< L *ob-* towards + *servare* keep, watch] —**ob·ser′v′er** *n.* —**ob·serv′ing·ly** *adv.*

**ob·so·les·cent** (ob′sə·les′ənt) *adj.* Becoming obsolete. —**ob′so·les′cence** *n.* —**ob′so·les′cent·ly** *adv.*

**ob·so·lete** (ob′sə·lēt) *adj.* Being out of use or out of fashion, as a word or style. [< L *ob-solescere* grow old] —**ob′so·lete′ly** *adv.* —**ob′so·lete′ness** *n.*

**ob·sta·cle** (ob′stə·kəl) *n.* Something that stands in the way; a hindrance or obstruction. [< L *ob-* before, against + *stare* stand]

**ob·sti·nate** (ob′stə·nit) *adj.* 1 Persistently and unreasonably resolved in a purpose or opinion; stubborn. 2 Hard to control or cure, as a disease. [< L *obstinare* persist] —**ob′sti·na·cy** (-nə·sē), **ob′sti·nate·ness** *n.* —**ob′sti·nate·ly** *adv.* —**Syn.** 1 dogged, willful, headstrong, obdurate, unyielding.

**ob·strep·er·ous** (əb·strep′ər·əs, ob-) *adj.* 1 Making a great disturbance; clamorous; boisterous. 2 Unmanageable; unruly. [< L *ob-* against + *strepere* to roar] —**ob·strep′er·ous·ly** *adv.* —**ob·strep′er·ous·ness** *n.*

**ob·struct** (əb·strukt′) *v.t.* 1 To stop or impede movement through (a way or passage) by obstacles or barriers; choke; clog. 2 To block or retard the progress or way of. 3 To obscure from sight; to *obstruct* a view. [< L *ob-* against + *struere* pile, build] —**ob·struc′t′er, ob·struct′or, ob·struc′tive·ness** *n.* —**ob·struc′tive** *adj.* —**ob·struc′tive·ly** *adv.*

**ob·struc·tion** (əb·struk′shən) *n.* 1 Anything that obstructs; hindrance; obstacle. 2 The act of obstructing, or the state of being obstructed.

**ob·tain** (əb·tān′) *v.t.* 1 To gain possession of, esp. by effort; acquire; get. —*v.i.* 2 To be established or prevail; exist: When the play was made into a film, a different impression *obtained*. [< L *ob-* against + *tenere* hold, keep] —**ob·tain′a·ble** *adj.* —**ob·tain′er, ob·tain′ment** *n.*

**ob·trude** (əb·trōōd′) *v.* **ob·trud·ed, ob·trud·ing** *v.t.* 1 To thrust or force (oneself, an opinion, etc.) upon others without request or warrant. 2 To push forward or out; eject. —*v.i.* 3 To intrude oneself. [< L *ob-* towards, against + *trudere* to thrust] —**ob·trud′er, ob·tru′sion** *n.*

**ob·tru·sive** (əb·trōō′siv) *adj.* 1 Forcing itself to the attention; too conspicuous: *obtrusive* colors. 2 Bold or meddlesome in manner; pushing. 3 Tending to obtrude. —**ob·tru′sive·ly** *adv.* —**ob·tru′sive·ness** *n.*

**ob·tuse** (əb·t′ōōs′) *adj.* 1 Blunt or rounded. 2 Lacking alertness or sensitivity; intellectually sluggish or slow. 3 Heavy, dull, and indistinct, as a sound. 4 Having a measure between 90° and 180°: an *obtuse* angle. • See ANGLE. [< L *obtusus* blunt] —**ob·tuse′ly** *adv.* —**ob·tuse′ness** *n.*

**ob·verse** (ob·vûrs′, ob′vûrs) *adj.* 1 Turned toward or facing one. 2 Narrower at the base than at the apex. 3 Corresponding to something else as its counterpart. —*n.* (ob′vûrs) 1 The side of a coin or medal bearing the face or main device. 2 The side of any object that is meant to be seen; the front as opposed to the back. 3 A counterpart of a truth or fact. [< L *ob-* towards, against + *vertere* to turn] —**ob·verse′ly** *adv.*

**ob·vi·ate** (ob′vē·āt) *v.t.* **·at·ed, ·at·ing** To meet or provide for, as an objection or difficulty, by effective measures; make unnecessary: The burglar alarm system *obviated* the need for a guard. [< L *obviare* meet, withstand] —**ob′vi·a′tion, ob′vi·a′tor** *n.*

**ob·vi·ous** (ob′vē·əs) *adj.* Immediately evident; easily perceived; manifest. [< L *obvius* in the way, obvious] —**ob′vi·ous·ly** *adv.* —**ob′vi·ous·ness** *n.* —**Syn.** clear, apparent, plain.

**oc·ca·sion** (ə·kā′zhən) *n.* 1 A particular event or juncture of events. 2 An important event or celebration. 3 A time at which an event occurs. 4 A circumstance that presents some reason, opportunity, or cause for action: no *occasion* for haste. 5 A circumstance that precipitates an event or condition: His confusion was the *occasion* of much merriment. 6 A need or exigency. — **on occasion** Now and then; occasionally. — *v.t.* To cause or bring about; cause acci-

dentally or incidentally. [< L *occasio*, a falling toward, an opportunity]

**oc·ci·dent** (ok′sə·dənt) *n.* The west. [< OF < L *occidens, -entis* sunset, the west, orig. pr.p. of *occidere* to fall)

**oc·ci·den·tal** (ok′sə·den′təl) *adj.* Of or belonging to the west, or the countries constituting the Occident. —*n.* One born or living in a western country. **Also Oc′ci·den′tal.** —**oc′ci·den′tal·ly** *adv.*

**oc·clude** (ə·klōōd′) *v.* **·clud·ed, ·clud·ing** *v.t.* 1 To shut up or block off: to *occlude* an artery. 2 *Chem.* To absorb or adsorb. —*v.i.* 3 *Dent.* To fit together: said of the upper and lower teeth. [< L *ob-* against, upon + *claudere* to close] —**oc·clu′dent, oc·clu′sive** *adj.* —**oc·clu·sion** (ə·klōō′zhən) *n.*

**oc·cult** (ə·kult′, ok′ult) *adj.* 1 Of or designating those mystic arts involving magic, astrology, alchemy etc. 2 Not divulged; secret. 3 Beyond human understanding; mysterious. —*n.* Occult arts or sciences. —*v.t.* 1 To hide or conceal from view. 2 *Astron.* To block the light from or view of. —*v.i.* 3 To become hidden or concealed from view. [< L *occulere* cover over, hide] —**oc·cult′ism, oc·cult′ist, oc·cult′ness** *n.* —**oc·cult′ly** *adv.*

**oc·cu·pa·tion** (ok′yə·pā′shən) *n.* 1 One's regular, principal, or immediate business. 2 The state of being busy. 3 The possession and holding of land by military force. —**oc′cu·pa′tion·al** *adj.* —**oc′cu·pa′tion·al·ly** *adv.*

**oc·cu·py** (ok′yə·pī) *v.t.* **·pied, ·py·ing** 1 To take and hold possession of, as by conquest. 2 To fill or take up (space or time). 3 To inhabit; dwell in. 4 To hold; fill, as an office or position. 5 To busy; employ: to *occupy* oneself with a hobby. [< L *ob-* against + *capere* take] —**oc′cu·pi′er** *n.*

**oc·cur** (ə·kûr′) *v.i.* **·curred, ·cur·ring** 1 To happen; come about. 2 To be found or met with; appear. 3 To present itself; come to mind. [< L *ob-* towards, against + *currere* run]

**o·cean** (ō′shən) *n.* 1 The great body of salt water that covers over two thirds of the earth's surface. 2 Any one of its five main divisions: the Atlantic, Pacific, Indian, Arctic, or Antarctic Ocean. 3 Any unbounded expanse or quantity. [< Gk. *ōkeanos*] —**o·ce·an·ic** (ō′shē·an′ik) *adj.* —**o′ce·an′ic·al·ly** *adv.*

**o·ce·an·og·ra·phy** (ō′shən·og′rə·fē) *n.* The branch of physical geography that deals

with oceanic life and phenomena. —o'·
ce·an·og'ra·pher n. —o'ce·an·o·graph'ic (-
ə·graf'ik) or ·i·cal adj. —o'ce·an·o·graph'
i·cal·ly adv.

oc·ta·gon (ok'tə·gon) n. A polygon with eight
sides and eight angles. [< Gk. okta- eight +
gōnia an angle] —oc·tag·o·nal (ok·tag'ə·nəl)
adj. —oc·tag'o·nal·ly adv.

oc·tane (ok'tān) n. A hydrocarbon containing
a chain of eight carbon atoms per molecule.
[< OCTO- + -ANE]

oc·tave (ok'tiv, -tāv) n. 1 Music The interval
between any tone and another having twice
or half its frequency. 2 The eighth day from
a feast day; also, the lengthening of a festival to include eight days. 3 Any group or
series of eight. 4 In prosody, the first eight
lines in an Italian sonnet, or a stanza of
eight lines. —adj. 1 Composed of eight. 2 In
prosody, composed of eight lines. Also
oc·ta·val (ok·tā'vəl, ok'tə-) adj. [< L octo
eight]

oc·tet (ok·tet') n. 1 A musical composition for
eight parts. 2 A group of eight musical performers. 3 Any group of eight; esp., OCTAVE
(def. 4). Also oc·tette'. [< L octo eight]

oc·to·ge·nar·i·an (ok'tə·jə·nâr'ē·ən) adj.
Being eighty or from eighty to ninety years
of age: also oc·tog·e·nar·y (ok·toj'ə·ner'ē).
—n. A person between eighty and ninety
years of age. [< L octoginta eighty]

oc·to·pus (ok'tə·pəs) n. pl. ·pus·es or ·pi (-pī)
1 Any of a genus of cephalopods having a
saclike body with a mouth on the under
surface and eight tentacles covered with
suckers. 2 Any organized power with far-
reaching influence. [< Gk. okta- eight +
pous a foot]

oc·u·lar (ok'yə·lər) adj. Pertaining to, like, derived from, or connected with the eye; visual. —n. The eyepiece of an optical instrument. [< L oculus eye] —oc'u·lar·ly adv.

oc·u·list (ok'yə·list) n. OPTHALMOLOGIST. [< L
oculus eye]

odd (od) adj. 1 Not even; leaving a remainder
when divided by two. 2 Marked with an odd
number. 3 Left over after a division. 4 Plus
an additional number: 200-odd miles. 5
Occasional; casual; to work at odd jobs. 6
Peculiar; singular; queer; eccentric. 7 Single: an odd slipper. [< ON oddi a point of
land, triangle] —odd'ly adv. —odd'ness n.
—Syn. 6 bizarre, extraordinary, fantastic,
strange.

odd·i·ty (od'ə·tē) n. pl. ·ties 1 The state or

quality of being odd. 2 A person or thing
that is odd or peculiar.

odds (odz) n.pl. (sometimes construed as singular) 1 difference to the advantage of one
side over another: The odds are in my favor.
2 The amount of difference in advantage
between competing sides: to fight against
overwhelming odds. 3 The probability or
ratio of probabilities that something will
happen or be found to be the case. 4 An
equalizing allowance based on the apparent chances of success of an opponent or
contestant: to give odds. —at odds At variance; disagreeing. —by all odds Far and
away; beyond doubt.

ode (ōd) n. A lyric poem, originally intended
to be sung or chanted, typically marked by
lofty tone, dignified theme, and often in the
form of an address. [< Gk. ōidē a song] —
od·ic (ō'dik) adj.

o·di·ous (ō'dē·əs) adj. 1 Exciting hate, repugnance, or disgust. 2 Regarded with
aversion or disgust. [< L odium hatred] —
o'di·ous·ly adv. —o'di·ous·ness n.

o·di·um (ō'dē·əm) n. 1 The state of being odious; offensiveness; opprobrium. 2 A feeling
of extreme repugnance, disgust, or hate.
[L, hatred < odisse to hate]

o·dor (ō'dər) n. 1 That quality of a substance
that renders it perceptible to the sense of
smell. 2 A smell or scent. 3 A quality detected by the mind or feelings; air: an odor
of righteousness. 4 Regard or estimation: to
be in bad odor. Brit. sp. o'dour. [L] —o'
dored adj.

o·dor·ous (ō'dər·əs) adj. Having an odor; fragrant. —o'dor·ous·ly adv. —o'dor·ous·
ness n.

of·fal (ô'fəl) n. 1 Those parts of a butchered
animal that are rejected as worthless. 2
Rubbish or refuse of any kind. [< OFF + FALL]

off-col·or (ôf'kul'ər, of'-) adj. 1 Of doubtful or
offensive taste; indelicate or indecent. 2 Unsatisfactory in color, as a gem. 3 Brit.
Slightly ill; under the weather. Brit. sp. -
col·our.

of·fend (ə·fend') v.t. 1 To give displeasure or
offense to; displease; anger. 2 To affect (the
senses or sensibilities) in a way that causes
displeasure, outrage, etc. —v.i. 3 To give
displeasure or offense; be offensive. 4 To
commit an offense, sin, or crime. [< L ob-
against + fendere to hit, thrust] —of·fend'
er n.

of·fense (ə·fens') n. 1 The act of offending; a
fault, sin, or crime. 2 The act of injuring an-

other's feelings, of causing displeasure, etc.
3 That which injures the feelings, causes displeasure, etc. 4 That which affects the senses or sensibilities with displeasure, outrage, etc. 5 The state of being offended. 6 Assault or attack. 7 In sports, the team or team members attempting to score. *Brit. sp.* **of·fence.**

**of·fen·sive** (ə·fen′siv) *adj.* 1 Giving offense; disagreeable, displeasing, outrageous, etc. 2 Pertaining to or marked by attack; aggressive. —*n.* 1 Aggressive methods, operations, or attitudes: often with *the.* 2 An attack. —**of·fen′sive·ly** *adv.* —**of·fen′sive·ness** *n.*

**of·fer** (ô′fər, of′ər) *v.t.* 1 To present for acceptance or rejection. 2 To suggest for consideration or action; propose. 3 To present with solemnity or in worship. 4 To show readiness to do or attempt. 5 To attempt or to begin to do or inflict. 6 To suggest as payment; bid. 7 To present for sale. —*v.i.* 8 To present itself; appear. 9 To make an offering in worship or sacrifice. —*n.* 1 The act of offering. 2 Something offered, as a bid, proposal, etc. 3 An attempt or endeavor to do something. [< L *ob-* before + *ferre* bring] —**of′fer·er, of′fer·or** *n.*

**of·fice** (ô′fis, of′is) *n.* 1 A particular duty, charge, or trust, esp. a part of one's work. 2 A post or position held officially, esp. a position of trust or authority under a government. 3 That which is performed, assigned, or intended to be done by a particular person or thing. 4 *U.S.* A branch of the federal government, ranking next below the departments. 5 A room or building in which the affairs of a business, profession, or governmental branch are conducted; also, the people employed there. 6 *Eccl.* A prescribed religious or devotional service, esp. that for the canonical hours. 7 Any religious or social ceremony; rite. 8 *pl.* A proffered action of any kind; esp. a service: reinstated through the good *offices* of a friend. [< L *officium* a service]

**of·fi·cer** (ô′fə·sər, of′ə-) *n.* 1 One elected or appointed to office, as in a business, a society, etc. 2 One appointed to a certain military or naval rank and authority, specifically by commission. 3 On a nonnaval ship, the captain or any of the mates. 4 A policeman. —*v.t.* 1 To furnish with officers. 2 To command; direct; manage.

**of·fi·cial** (ə·fish′əl) *adj.* 1 Of, pertaining to, or holding an office or public trust. 2 Derived

from the proper office or officer; authoritative. 3 Formal; studied; ceremonious. —*n.* One holding an office or performing duties of a public nature. —**of·fi′cial·dom, of·fi′cial·ism** *n.* —**of·fi′cial·ly** *adv.*

**of·fi·ci·ate** (ə·fish′ē·āt) *v.i.* **·at·ed, ·at·ing** 1 To perform the duties or functions of an office. 2 To serve as a priest or minister; conduct a service. [< L *officium* service] —**of·fi′ci·a′tion, of·fi′ci·a′tor** *n.*

**of·fi·cious** (ə·fish′əs) *adj.* Volunteering unwanted service or advice, esp. in an unduly forward manner. [< L *officium* service] —**of·fi′cious·ly** *adv.* —**of·fi′cious·ness** *n.* —Syn. meddlesome, interfering, obtrusive, nosy.

**off·set** (ôf′set′, of′-) *n.* 1 Anything which counterbalances or compensates for something else. 2 An extension, branch, spur, or offshoot. 3 A ledge in a wall formed by a reduction in its thickness above. 4 A bend in a pipe, bar, etc. that allows it to pass an obstruction. 5 OFFSET PRINTING. 6 An impression made by the offset printing method. —*v.* (ôf′set′, of′-) **·set, ·set·ting** *v.t.* 1 To compensate for; counterbalance. 2 To print by offset printing. 3 *Archit.* To make an offset in. —*v.i.* 4 To make an offset, as in printing. 5 To branch off; project as an offset.

**off·spring** (ôf′spring′, of′-) *n.* 1 The progeny of any person, animal, or plant. 2 A result; product. [< OE *of* off + *springan* to spring]

**o·gle** (ô′gəl) *v.* **o·gled, o·gling** *v.t.* 1 To look at with amorous or impertinent glances. —*v.i.* 2 To look or stare in an amorous or impertinent manner. —*n.* An amorous or coquettish look. [Prob. < LG *oegelen* < *oege* an eye] —**o′gler** *n.*

**ohm** (ōm) *n.* The unit of electrical resistance, equal to the resistance of a conductor in which a current of one ampere is produced by a potential difference of one volt. [< G. S. *Ohm,* 1787–1854, German physicist] —**ohm′ic** *adj.*

**oil** (oil) *n.* 1 A slippery, combustible liquid of vegetable, animal, or mineral origin, insoluble in water but soluble in ether. 2 PETROLEUM. 3 An oil paint; also, an oil painting. 4 Anything of an oily consistency. 5 Fawning or flattering speech. —*v.t.* 1 To smear, lubricate, or supply with oil. 2 To bribe; flatter. —*adj.* Of, like, relating to, yielding, or producing oil. [< L *oleum* oil] —**oil′er** *n.*

**oint·ment** (oint′mənt) *n.* A medicated fat or

oil used to soothe, heal, or protect the skin. [< L *unguentum* an unguent]

**OK** (ō'kā') *interj., adj., & adv.* All correct; all right: expressing approval, agreement, etc. —*n. pl.* **OK's** An endorsement; approval. —*v.t.* (ō·kā') **OK'd, OK'ing** To endorse; approve, as by signing with an OK. **Also O.K., o'kay', o'keh'.** [Prob. < *o(ll) k(orrect)*, humorous misspelling of *all correct;* but possibly < The Democratic *O.K.* Club, organized in 1840 to support President Martin Van Buren, nicknamed *Old Kinderhook,* from *Kinderhook,* N.Y., his birthplace]

**o·kra** (ō'krə) *n.* **1** A tall annual herb cultivated for its edible, mucilaginous pods. **2** Its green pods, used in soups and as a vegetable. [< native African name]

**o·le·ag·i·nous** (ō'lē·aj'ə·nəs) *adj.* **1** Of or pertaining to oil. **2** Unctuous; oily. [< L *oleaginus* pertaining to the olive] —*o'le·ag'i·nous·ly adv.* —*o'le·ag'i·nous·ness n.*

**o·le·an·der** (ō'lē·an'dər) *n.* A poisonous shrub with leathery evergreen leaves and clusters of fragrant flowers. [< Med. L]

**o·le·o·mar·ga·rine** (ō'lē·ō·mär'jə·rin, -rēn) *n.* MARGARINE. **Also o'le·o·mar'ga·rin.**

**ol·fac·to·ry** (ol·fak'tər·ē, -trē) *adj.* Pertaining to the sense of smell. **Also ol·fac'tive.** —*n. pl.* **·ries 1** *Usu. pl.* The organ of smell. **2** The capacity to smell. [< L *olere* have a smell + *facere* make]

**ol·i·gar·chy** (ol'ə·gär'kē) *n. pl.* **·chies 1** A form of government in which supreme power is restricted to a few persons. **2** The persons who exercise such power. **3** A state governed by an oligarchy. [< Gk. *oligos* few + *archein* to rule] —*ol'i·gar'chic, ol'i·gar'chal, ol'i·gar'chi·cal adj.*

**ol·ive** (ol'iv) *n.* **1** An evergreen tree with leathery leaves. hard yellow wood, and an oily fruit. **2** The fruit of the olive tree. **3** A medium yellowish green color: also **olive green. 4** An olive branch. —*adj.* **1** Of or pertaining to the olive. **2** Having a dull yellowish green color. [< L *oliva*]

**om·buds·man** (om'boodz·mən, -budz-, om·boodz'mən) *n. pl.* **·men** (-mən) A government official appointed to receive and report grievances against the government. [Norw.]

**om·e·let** (om'ə·lit, om'lit) *n.* A dish of eggs, beaten together, cooked and then folded, often around a filling, as of cheese, jelly, etc. **Also om'e·lette.** [< OF *alemette*, lit., a thin plate]

**o·men** (ō'mən) *n.* A phenomenon or incident believed to foretell some future event. —*v.t.* To foretell as or by an omen. [L] —**Syn.** *n.* portent, sign, indication, augury, *v.* indicate, presage, augur, portend.

**om·i·nous** (om'ə·nəs) *adj.* Like or marked by an evil omen; sinister; threatening. [< L *omen, ominis* an omen] —*om'i·nous·ly adv.* —*om'i·nous·ness n.*

**o·mis·sion** (ō·mish'ən) *n.* **1** The act of omitting or state of being omitted or neglected. **2** Anything omitted or neglected.

**o·mit** (ō·mit') *v.t.* **o·mit·ted, o·mit·ting 1** To leave out; fail to include. **2** To fail to do or use; neglect. [< L *ob-* down, away + *mittere* send]

**om·ni·bus** (om'nə·bəs, -bus) *n.* **1** BUS **2** A printed anthology, either of works by a single author or of works of the same general type. —*adj.* Of, pertaining to, or including many things, classes, situations, etc. [< L, for all]

**om·nip·o·tence** (om·nip'ə·təns) *n.* **1** Unlimited and universal power. **2** *Usu. cap.* An omnipotent force, esp. God.

**om·nip·o·tent** (om·nip'ə·tənt) *adj.* Unlimited in authority or power. —**the Omnipotent** God. —*om·nip'o·tent·ly adv.* —**Syn.** mighty, almighty, powerful, authoritative.

**om·ni·pres·ence** (om'nə·prez'əns) *n.* The quality of being everywhere present at the same time; ubiquity. —*om'ni·pres'ent adj.*

**om·ni·scient** (om·nish'ənt) *adj.* Having infinite knowledge; knowing everything. —**the Omniscient** God. [< L *omni-* all + *sciens* knowing] —*om·ni·science* (om·nish'əns) *n.* —*om·ni'scient·ly adv.*

**om·niv·o·rous** (om·niv'ər·əs) *adj.* **1** Eating both animal and vegetable food. **2** Taking in everything; consuming or devouring, as with the mind. [< L *omni-* all + *vorare* devour] —*om·niv'o·rous·ly adv.* —*om·niv'o·rous·ness n.*

**on·er·ous** (on'ər·əs) *adj.* Imposing or characterized by difficulty, labor, responsibility, etc. [< L *onus, oneris* a burden] —*on' er'ous·ly adv.* —*on'er·ous·ness n.* —**Syn.** arduous, burdensome, exacting, oppressive.

**on·ion** (un'yən) *n.* **1** A plant of the lily family with a pungent, edible bulb. **2** The bulb. [< L *unio* unity, an onion]

**on·set** (on'set', ôn'-) *n.* **1** An attack; assault, as of troops. **2** A setting out; start; beginning.

**on·slaught** (on'slôt', ôn'-) *n.* a violent hostile assault. [< Du. *annslag* a striking at] —**Syn.** attack, incursion.

**o·nus** (ō′nəs) *n.* 1 A burden or obligation; duty. 2 Responsibility or blame. [L]

**on·yx** (on′iks) *n.* A variety of quartz consisting of layers of different colors. [Gk, a nail or claw, onyx]

**ooze** (ōōz) *v.* **oozed, ooz·ing** *v.i.* 1 To flow or leak out slowly or gradually, as through pores or small holes. 2 To exude moisture. 3 To escape or disappear: His courage *oozed* away. —*v.t.* 4 To emit, give off, or exude. —*n.* 1 A slow, gradual leak; gentle flow. 2 That which oozes. [< OE *wōs* sap, juice] —**ooz′i·ness** *n.* —**ooz′zy** *adj.*

**o·pac·i·ty** (ō·pas′ə·tē) *n. pl.* **·ties** 1 The condition, quality, or degree of being opaque. 2 That which is opaque.

**o·pal** (ō′pəl) *n.* A colored, translucent silica, softer and less dense than quartz, valued as a gemstone. [< Skt. *upala* a precious stone]

**o·paque** (ō·pāk′) *adj.* 1 Impervious to light or other radiation. 2 Loosely, imperfectly transparent. 3 Impervious to reason; unintelligent. 4 Having no luster; dull. 5 Unintelligible; obscure: an *opaque* style. —*n.* Something opaque. [< L *opacus* shaded, darkened] —**o·paque′ly** *adv.* —**o·paque′ness** *n.*

**op·er·a** (op′ər·ə, op′rə) *n.* 1 A musical drama made up of arias, recitatives, choruses, etc., with orchestral accompaniment, scenery, acting, and sometimes dance. 2 A particular musical drama or its music or libretto; also, its performance. 3 The theater in which operas are given: also **opera house.** [< L *opus, operis* work] —**op·er·at·ic** (op′ə·rat′ik) *adj.* —**op′er·at·i·cal·ly** *adv.*

**op·er·ate** (op′ə·rāt) *v.* **·at·ed, ·at·ing** *v.i.* 1 To act or function; work. 2 To bring about or produce the proper effect. 3 To perform a surgical operation. 4 To carry on a military or naval operation: usu. with *against.* —*v.t.* 5 To control the working or function of, as a machine. 6 To conduct the affairs of: to *operate* a business. 7 To bring about or cause. [< L *operari* to work, have an effect < *opus, operis* a work]

**op·er·a·tion** (op′ə·rā′shən) *n.* 1 The act or process of operating. 2 A method of exercising or applying force. 3 A single specific act or transaction. 4 A series of acts to effect a certain purpose; process. 5 The state of being in action. 6 *Surg.* A manipulation performed on the body to remedy a defect or disorder. 7 *Math.* A process or procedure that associates elements of a set, as numbers, with elements of the same or a different set. 8 A military or naval campaign.

**op·er·a·tive** (op′ər·ə·tiv, -ə·rā′tiv) *adj.* 1 Exerting force or influence. 2 Moving or working efficiently; effective. 3 Connected with surgical operations: *operative* technique. 4 Concerned with practical work. 5 Engaged in practical activity. —*n.* 1 A person employed as a skilled worker. 2 *Informal* A detective; one who works secretly. —**op′er·a′tive·ly** *adv.* —**op′er·a·tive′ness** *n.*

**o·ral** (ô′rəl, ō′rəl) *adj.* 1 Uttered through the mouth; spoken. 2 Pertaining to or situated at or near the mouth. 3 Of, pertaining to, or using speech. —*n.* An oral examination, as in a college. [< L *os, oris* mouth] —**o′ral·ly** *adv.* —**o′ral·ness** *n.* • *oral, verbal* Both of these words are commonly used with the sense of "spoken": an *oral* (or *verbal*) *agreement* Verbal, however, can also mean "composed of or relating to words, as distinguished from ideas or things": *verbal skills.* Oral, derived from the Latin word for *mouth,* suggests the source of expression, whereas *verbal,* from the Latin word for *word,* suggests the form of expression.

**or·ange** (ôr′inj, or′-) *n.* 1 An edible, round, juicy citrus fruit with a reddish yellow rind. 2 Any of the evergreen trees or related shrubs yielding this fruit. 3 A reddish yellow color. —*adj.* 1 Reddish yellow. 2 Of or pertaining to an orange. [< Pers. *nārang*]

**o·rang·u·tan** (ō·rang′ə·tan′) *n. pl.* **·tans** or **·tan** A large anthropoid ape of Borneo and Sumatra, having brownish red hair, small ears, a hairless face, and very long arms. Also **o·rang′, o·rang′u·tan′, o·rang′ou·tan′, o·rang′u·tang′** (-ə·tang′). [< Malay *oran̄* a man + *utan* a forest]

**o·ra·tion** (ō·rā′shən, ō·rā′-) *n.* A formal public speech delivered on a ceremonial occasion. —**Syn.** address, discourse, talk.

**or·a·tor** (ôr′ə·tər, or′-) *n.* One who delivers an oration; an eloquent public speaker.

**or·a·tor·i·cal** (ôr′ə·tôr′ə·kəl, -tō′rə-, or′-) *adj.* Of, like, or characteristic of oratory or an orator. —**or′a·tor′i·cal·ly** *adv.*

**or·a·to·ry** (ôr′ə·tôr′ē, -tō′rē, or′-) *n. pl.* **·ries** 1 The art of public speaking; eloquence. 2 Eloquent language. 3 A place for prayer; a private chapel. [< L *orator* one who speaks]

**or·bit** (ôr′bit) *n.* 1 *Astron.* The path in space along which a celestial body moves. 2 *Anat.* One of the two sockets of the eyes. 3 *Physics* The path of a body subject to a field of force, esp. that of an electron around the atomic nucleus. 4 A range of influence or action: the *orbit* of imperialism. —*v.t.* 1 To cause to move in an orbit, as an artificial satellite. —*v.i.* 2 To move in an orbit. [< L *orbis* a wheel, a circle] —or′bi·tal *adj.*

or·chard (ôr′chərd) *n.* A plantation of trees grown for their products, as fruit, nuts, oils, etc.; also, the enclosure or ground containing them. [< Med. L *ortus* a garden + OE *geard* a yard, enclosure]

or·ches·tra (ôr′kis·trə) *n.* 1 A fairly large group of musicians playing together, esp. a symphony orchestra. 2 The instruments on which they play. 3 In theaters, the place immediately before the stage, occupied by the musicians: also orchestra pit. 4 In the U.S., the main floor of a theater. [< Gk. *orchēstra*, lit., a dancing space] —or·ches′tral (ôr·kes′trəl) *adj.* —or·ches′tral·ly *adv.*

or·chid (ôr′kid) *n.* 1 Any of a widely distributed family of plants having bulbous roots and often very showy flowers. 2 The flower of any of these plants. 3 A delicate, rosy purple color. [< Gk. *orchis* a testicle: so called from the shape of its tubers]

or·dain (ôr·dān′) *v.t.* 1 To order or decree; establish. 2 To predestine; destine: said of God, fate, etc. 3 To invest with ministerial or priestly functions. [< L *ordo* an order] —or·dain′er *n.*

or·deal (ôr·dēl′, -dē′əl, ôr′dēl) *n.* 1 Any trying or painful experience. 2 An old method of trial in which the accused underwent physical ordeals, as carrying or walking over burning coals, which, if he were innocent, would supposedly leave him unharmed. [< OE *ordāl*]

or·der (ôr′dər) *n.* 1 Methodical and harmonious arrangement, as of successive things in a formation. 2 Proper or working condition. 3 A command or authoritative regulation. 4 *Law* Any direction of a court made to be entered of record in a cause, and not included in the final judgment. 5 A commission or instruction to supply, purchase, or sell something. 6 Established use or customary procedure. 7 Established or existing state of things. 8 *Sometimes cap.* A group of persons united by some common bond: the *Order* of Odd Fellows. 9 A group of persons upon whom a government has conferred an honor and who are thus entitled to affix to their names designated initials and to wear specific insignia; also, the insignia worn. 10 Social rank. 11 A class, kind, or degree: a chef of the first *order.* 12

*Usu. pl.* Any of the various grades or degrees of the Christian ministry: also holy **orders, sacred orders.** 13 *Archit.* The general character of a column and its parts as distinguishing a style of architecture: the Ionic *order.* 14 *Biol.* A taxonomic category ranking below the class and above the family. 15 *Math.* A number indicating how many times an operation is performed or implied. 16 *Gram.* The sequence of words in a sentence or construction. 17 The position of the rifle as a result of the command order arms. 18 Any one of the ancient nine grades of angels. —**call to order** To ask to be quiet in order to start, as a meeting. —**in order** 1 In accordance with rule. 2 Neat; tidy. —**in order that** So that; to the end that. —**in order to** For the purpose of; to the end that. —**in short order** Quickly; without delay. —**on order** Ordered but not yet delivered. —**on the order of** Similar to. —**take orders** 1 To enter the ministry. 2 To obey. —**to order** As specified by the buyer. —*v.t.* 1 To give a command or direction to. 2 To command to go, come, etc. 3 To give an order that (something) be done; prescribe. 4 To give an order for: to *order* a new suit. 5 To put in systematic arrangement. 6 To ordain: He was *ordered* deacon. —*v.i.* 7 To give an order or orders. [< L *ordo* a row, series, an order] —or′der·er *n.*

or·der·ly (ôr′dər·lē) *adj.* 1 Neat; systematic. 2 Peaceful and law-abiding: an *orderly* demonstration. 3 Characterized by order. —*n. pl.* ·lies 1 A soldier or noncommissioned officer detailed to carry orders for superior officers. 2 A male hospital attendant. —or′der·li·ness *n.* —Syn. *adj.* 1 clean, methodical, tidy. 2 peaceful, quiet.

or·di·nal (ôr′də·nəl) *adj.* 1 Denoting position in an order or succession. 2 Pertaining to an order, as of plants, animals, etc. —*n.* 1 ORDINAL NUMBER. 2 *Sometimes cap.* A book of forms for special church services. [< L *ordo, ordinis* an order]

or·di·nance (ôr′də·nəns) *n.* 1 An authoritative rule; decree. 2 A religious rite or ceremony. 3 A municipal statute. [< L *ordinans* ordained]

or·di·nar·i·ly (ôr′də·ner′ə·lē, ôr′də·nâr′ə·lē) *adv.* In ordinary cases; commonly; usually.

or·di·nar·y (ôr′də·ner′ē) *adj.* 1 Of common or everyday occurrence; usual. 2 According to an established order; regular. 3 Mediocre; commonplace. —*n. pl.* ·nar·ies 1 That which is usual or common. 2 *Brit.* A meal provided regularly at a fixed price. 3 *Brit.* An eating place. 4 One who exercises jurisdiction in his own right, esp. a church official. 5 A rule or book prescribing the form for saying mass. —**in ordinary** In actual and constant service. —**out of the ordinary** Very unusual. [< L *ordinarius* < *ordo* an order] —**or′di·nar′i·ness** *n.*

**or·di·na·tion** (ôr′də·nā′shən) *n.* 1 The rite of consecration to the ministry. 2 The state of being ordained.

**ord·nance** (ôrd′nəns) *n. Mil.* 1 All military weapons. 2 Cannon or artillery. [Contraction of ORDINANCE]

**ore** (ôr, ōr) *n.* A mineral or similar material from which a valuable substance, esp. a metal, can be extracted at reasonable cost. [< OE *ār* brass, copper]

**or·gan** (ôr′gən) *n.* 1 Any of various keyboard musical instruments capable of sustained tones, esp. a collection of pipes made to sound by means of compressed air; a pipe organ. 2 A musical instrument resembling the pipe organ: a barrel *organ.* 3 A structure of specialized tissue in a plant or animal performing some definite function. 4 A means of making public the opinions and ideas of a person or group, as a periodical. [< Gk. *organon* a tool, a musical instrument]

**or·gan·ic** (ôr·gan′ik) *adj.* 1 Of, pertaining to, or of the nature of animals and plants. 2 Having a physical basis in a bodily organ. 3 Serving the purpose of an organ. 4 *Chem.* Of or pertaining to carbon compounds. 5 Inherent in or pertaining to the organization or fundamental structure; structural. 6 Of or characterized by systematic coordination of parts; organized. 7 *Law* Designating the basic laws or principles of a government. 8 Pertaining to foodstuffs grown with only natural fertilizers of animal or plant origin. Also **or·gan′i·cal.** —**or·gan′i·cal·ly** *adv.*

**or·gan·ism** (ôr′gən·iz′əm) *n.* 1 An animal or plant internally organized to maintain vital activities. 2 Anything analogous in structure and function to a living thing. —**or′gan·is′mal** *adj.*

**or·gan·ist** (ôr′gən·ist) *n.* One who plays the organ.

**organization man** A member of an organization, party, company, etc., who is fully committed to its aims and methods of operation.

**or·gan·ize** (ôr′gən·īz) *v.* **·ized, ·iz·ing** *v.t.* 1 To arrange systematically; order. 2 To furnish with organic structure. 3 To enlist (workers) in a trade union. 4 To unionize the workers of (a factory, etc.). —*v.i.* 5 To form or join an organization. *Brit. sp.* **or′gan·ise.** —**or′gan·iz′er** *n.*

**or·gy** (ôr′jē) *n. pl.* **·gies** 1 Wild and drunken revelry; debauch. 2 Any immoderate indulgence in something: an *orgy* of reading. 3 *pl.* In ancient Greece and Rome, the rites honoring certain gods, as Dionysus, marked by frenzied songs and dances. [< Gk. *orgia* secret rites.] —**or′gi·as′tic** (-as′tik) *adj.* —**or′gi·as′ti·cal·ly** *adv.*

**o·ri·ent** (ôr′ē·ənt, ō′rē-) *n.* 1 The east. 2 The eastern sky. 3 The iridescent luster of a pearl. —*v.t.* 1 To cause to face or turn to the east. 2 To place or adjust, as a map, in exact relation to the points of the compass. 3 To adjust the physical position of. 4 To adjust or adapt according to first principles or recognized facts. —*adj.* 1 Resembling sunrise; bright. 2 Ascending. [< L *oriens* rising sun, east]

**or·i·fice** (ôr′ə·fis, or′-) *n.* A small opening into a cavity; an aperture. [< L *os, oris* mouth + *facere* make]

**or·i·gin** (ôr′ə·jin, or′-) *n.* 1 The commencement of the existence of anything; primary source. 2 Parentage; ancestry. 3 *Math.* The point at which the axes of a Cartesian coordinate system intersect. [< L *origo* a rise < *oriri* to rise]

**o·rig·i·nal** (ə·rij′ə·nəl) *adj.* 1 Of or belonging to the beginning. 2 Immediately produced by one's own mind; not copied. 3 Able to produce new creations; inventive. 4 Fresh; new: What an *original* idea! —*n.* 1 The first form of anything from which copies, imitations, translations, etc., are made. 2 The language in which a book is first written. 3 A person of unique character or genius; also, an eccentric. 4 Origin. —**o·rig′i·nal·ly** *adv.*

**o·rig·i·nate** (ə·rij′ə·nāt) *v.* **·nat·ed, ·nat·ing** *v.t.* 1 To bring into existence; create; initiate. —*v.i.* 2 To come into existence; have origin; arise. —**o·rig′i·na′tion, o·rig′i·na′tor** *n.* —**o·rig′i·na′tive** *adj.* —**o·rig′i·na′tive·ly** *adv.*

**or·i·son** (ôr′i·sən, or′-, -zən) *n. Usu. pl.* A devotional prayer. [< L *oratio* a prayer]

**Or·lon** (ôr′lon) *n.* A synthetic textile fiber with a high resistance to heat, light, and chemicals: a trade name.

**or·na·ment** (ôr′nə·mənt) *n.* 1 Something that contributes to the beauty or elegance of a thing. **2** Any thing or person considered as a source of honor or credit. **3** *Music* A decorative melodic tone or tones independent of the harmony. —*v.t.* (ôr′nə·ment) To adorn with ornaments. [< L *ornare* adorn] —or′na·ment′er *n.* —**Syn.** *v.* beautify, decorate, embellish.

or·na·men·tal (ôr′nə·men′təl) *adj.* Serving to adorn. —*n.* An ornamental object. —or′na·men′tal·ly *adv.*

or·na·men·ta·tion (ôr′nə·men·tā′shən, -mən-) *n.* **1** The act of adorning, or the state of being adorned. **2** Ornamental things collectively.

or·ni·thol·o·gy (ôr′nə·thol′ə·jē) *n.* The branch of zoology that deals with the study of birds. [< Gk. *ornis, ornithos* bird + -LOGY] —or′ni·tho·log′ic (-thə·loj′ik) or ·i·cal *adj.* —or′ni·tho·log′i·cal·ly *adv.* —or′ni·thol′o·gist *n.*

o·ro·tund (ôr′ə·tund, ō′rə-) *adj.* **1** Full, clear, rounded, and resonant: said of the voice. **2** Pompous; inflated, as a manner of speech. [< L *os, oris* mouth + *rotundus* round] —o′ro·tun′di·ty *n.*

or·phan (ôr′fən) *n.* A child whose parents are dead. —*adj.* **1** Having lost one or both parents: said of a child. **2** Pertaining to a child so bereaved. —*v.t.* To bereave of parents or of a parent. [< Gk. *orphanos* bereaved] —or′phan·hood (-hŏŏd) *n.*

or·phan·age (ôr′fən·ij) *n.* **1** The state of being an orphan. **2** An institution for orphans.

or·tho·don·tics (ôr′thə·don′tiks) *n. pl.* (construed as sing.) The branch of dentistry which is concerned with preventing and correcting faulty positions of the teeth. Also or·tho·don′tia (-shə, -shē·ə). [< ORTHO- + Gk. *odous, odontos* a tooth] —or′tho·don′tic (-don′tik) *adj.* —or′tho·don′tist *n.*

or·tho·dox (ôr′thə·doks) *adj.* **1** Correct or sound in doctrine. **2** Holding the commonly accepted faith, esp. in religion. **3** Approved; accepted. [< Gk. *orthos* right + *doxa* opinion] —or′tho·dox′ly *adv.* —**Syn.** **3** acknowledged, conventional, established, fixed, traditional.

or·tho·e·py (ôr·thō′ə·pē, ôr′thō·ep′ē) **1** The art of correct pronunciation. **2** Pronunciation in general. [< Gk. *orthos* right + *epos* a word] —or·tho·ep·ic (ôr′thō·ep′ik) or ·i·cal *adj.* —or·tho′e·pist *n.*

or·thog·ra·phy (ôr·thog′rə·fē) *n. pl.* **·phies 1** A mode or system of spelling, spelling correctly or according to usage. **2** The study of spelling. —or·thog′ra·pher *n.* —or·tho·

graph·ic (ôr′thə·graf′ik), or′tho·graph′i·cal *adj.*

or·tho·pe·dics (ôr′thə·pē′diks) *n.pl.* (construed as sing.) The branch of surgery concerned with treating chronic disorders of the joints, spine, bones, and muscles used in movement. Also or′tho·pae′dics. [< Gk. *orthos* right + *paideia* training of children] —or′tho·pe′dic or ·di·cal *adj.* —or′tho·pe′dist *n.*

os·cil·late (os′ə·lāt) *v.* **·lat·ed, ·lat·ing** *v.i.* **1** To go periodically through an orderly series or cycle of changes, as a pendulum or other physical system. **2** To vary undecidedly; waver. —*v.t.* **3** To cause to oscillate. [< L *oscillum* a swing] —os′cil·la′tor *n.* —os′cil·la·to′ry (-lə·tôr′ē, -tō′rē) *adj.*

os·cil·la·tion (os′ə·lā′shən) *n.* **1** The act or state of oscillating. **2** *Physics* A single cycle of an oscillating system.

os·cu·late (os′kyə·lāt) *v.t. & v.i.* **·lat·ed, ·lat·ing 1** To kiss. **2** To bring or come into close contact or union. **3** *Biol.* To have (characteristics) in common. [< L *osculari* to kiss] —os′cu·la·to′ry (-l [< tôr′ē, -tō′rē) *adj.*

os·si·fy (os′ə·fī) *v.t. & v.i.* **·fied, ·fy·ing 1** To convert or be converted into bone. **2** To make or become set, conventional, etc. [< L *os, ossis* a bone + -FY] —os·sif·ic (o·sif′ik) *adj.* —os′si·fi·ca′tion *n.*

os·ten·si·ble (os·ten′sə·bəl) *adj.* Offered as real or having the character represented; seeming; professed or pretended. [< L *ostendere* to show] —os·ten′si·bly *adv.*

os·ten·ta·tion (os′tən·tā′shən) *n.* Elaborate or pretentious display; showiness. [< L *ostendere* to show]

os·ten·ta·tious (os′tən·tā′shəs) *adj.* Marked by a showy or pretentious display. —os′ten·ta′tious·ly *adv.* —os′ten·ta′tious·ness *n.*

os·te·ol·o·gy (os′tē·ol′ə·jē) *n.* The study of the functions and structure of bones. —os′te·o·log′i·cal (-ə·loj′i·kəl) *adj.* —os′te·o·log′i·cal·ly *adv.* —os′te·ol′o·gist *n.*

os·te·op·a·thy (os′tē·op′ə·thē) *n.* Therapy based on a theory that most disorders are due to structural abnormalities that may be corrected by manipulation. —os′te·o·path′, os′te·op′a·thist *n.* —os′te·o·path·ic (-ə·path′ik) *adj.*

os·tra·cism (os′trə·siz′əm) *n.* **1** Exclusion, as from society or common privileges, by general consent. **2** In ancient Greece, banishment by popular vote.

**os·tra·cize** (os′trə·sīz) *v.t.* ·cized, ·ciz·ing To exclude, banish, etc., by ostracism. [<Gk. *ostrakon* a potsherd, shell, voting tablet] — **Syn.** reject, expatriate, expel, oust.

**os·trich** (ôs′trich, os′-) *n.* 1 A large, two-toed bird of Africa and Arabia, with aborted wings and long, powerful legs. 2 RHEA. [<L *avis* a bird + LL *struthio* an ostrich]

**ot·ter** (ot′ər) *n.* 1 A weasel-like, carnivorous, swimming mammal with webbed feet and a flattened, oarlike tail. 2 Its valuable, dark-brown fur. [< OE *oter*]

**ounce** (ouns) *n.* 1 a A unit of weight equal to .0625 pound avoirdupois. b A unit of weight equal to .0833 pound troy. 2 FLUID OUNCE. 3 A small quantity. [< L *uncia* twelfth part (of a pound or foot)]

**oust** (oust) *v.t.* To force from possession or occupancy; eject. [< L *ob-* against + *stare* stand] —**Syn** dispossess, evict, expel, turn out.

**out·cast** (out′kast′, -käst′) *n.* One who is cast out from home or country. —*adj.* Rejected as unworthy or useless.

**out·come** (out′kum′) *n.* A consequence or result.

**out·er** (ou′tər) *adj.* 1 Being on the exterior side; external. 2 Farther from a center or the inside.

**out·fit** (out′fit′) *n.* 1 A set of garments or equipment for a particular purpose, as for a camping trip. 2 A set of clothes worn together and regarded as harmonious. 3 A group of people engaged in a common undertaking: a military *outfit*. *v.t. & v.i.* ·fit·ted, ·fit·ting To provide with or acquire an outfit. —**out′fit′er** *n.*

**out·ing** (ou′ting) *n.* An excursion; short pleasure trip.

**out·land·ish** (out·lan′dish) *adj.* 1 Strange, as in appearance or behavior; bizarre; freakish. 2 Situated in an unfamiliar spot; remote. 3 *Archaic* Foreign. [<OE *ūtlandisc* of the outland] —**out·land′ish·ly** *adv.* —**out·land′ish·ness** *n.*

**out·law** (out′lô) *n.* 1 A person deprived of the benefit of the law, as for having committed a crime. 2 One who habitually breaks or defies the law. —*v.t.* 1 To declare an outlaw; proscribe. 2 To prohibit; ban. 3 To deprive of legal force or protection, as contracts or debts. [<ON *ūtlagi*] —**out′law·ry** *n.*

**out·lay** (out′lā′) *n.* 1 The act of laying out or disbursing, as money or effort. 2 That which is laid out; expenditure. —*v.t.* (out·lā′) ·laid, ·lay·ing To expend (money)

**out·let** (out′let, -lit) *n.* 1 A passage or vent for escape or discharge. 2 A means of expressing needs or desires: an *outlet* for aggression. 3 In trade or commerce, a retail or wholesale market. 4 A point in an electrical wiring system at which an appliance be connected.

**out·line** (out′līn) *n.* 1 A bordering line that defines a figure. 2 A sketch made of such lines without shading. 3 *Often pl.* A preliminary sketch showing the principal features of a thing; general plan. —*v.t.* ·lined, ·lin·ing 1 To draw the outline of; sketch. 2 To describe in general terms; give the main points of.

**out·look** (out′look′) *n.* 1 A view from a particular place. 2 A place having a view. 3 A predicted or probable course; prospect: the *outlook* for the nation's economy. 4 A mental view or position.

**out·put** (out′poot′) *n.* 1 The quantity put out or produced in a specified time; amount or rate of production. 2 a The useful energy delivered by a machine, system, etc. b The point at which this energy is available. 3 The information derived by a computer from processing a given input.

**out·rage** (out′rāj′) *n.* 1 An act of shocking violence, cruelty, immorality, or viciousness. 2 A gross insult. 3 Vehement anger or resentment. —*v.t.* ·raged, ·rag·ing 1 To commit outrage upon; wrong or abuse grossly; violate; offend. 2 To make violently angry. 3 To rape. [<OF *ultrage* <L *ultra* beyond]

**out·ra·geous** (out·rā′jəs) *adj.* 1 Of the nature of an outrage; atrocious. 2 Indifferent to or contemptuous of reasonable authority or decency; violating the limits of tolerable behavior; shocking. 3 Unrestrained; flagrant: an *outrageous* practical joker. —**out·ra′geous·ly** *adv.* —**out·ra′geous·ness** *n.*

**out·stand·ing** (out·stan′ding) *adj.* 1 Standing prominently forth; preeminent. 2 Standing out; conspicuous. 3 Unsettled; continuing. 4 Still standing, as an unpaid debt.

**out·strip** (out·strip′) *v.t.* ·stripped, ·strip·ping 1 To leave behind; outrun, as in a race. 2 To excel; surpass.

**out·weigh** (out·wā′) *v.t.* 1 To weigh more than. 2 To exceed in importance, value, etc.

**out·wit** (out·wit′) *v.t.* ·wit·ted, ·wit·ting To defeat by superior ingenuity or cunning.

**o·val** (ō′vəl) *adj.* 1 Having the shape of an egg. 2 Elliptical. —*n.* A figure or body of such form or outline. [< L *ovum* egg] —**o′val·ly** *adv.* —**o′val·ness** *n.*

**o·va·ry** (ō′və·rē) *n. pl.* **·ries 1** *Biol.* The genital organ of female animals in which are produced the eggs and usu. certain sex hormones. **2** *Bot.* In flowering plants, the enlarged portion of the pistil in which the seed develops. [< L *ovum* an egg] —**o·var′i·al, o·var′i·an** *adj.*

**o·va·tion** (ō·vā′shən) *n.* A spontaneous acclamation, as of applause, cheers, etc. [< L *ovare* rejoice, exult] —**o·va′tion·al** *adj.*

**ov·en** (uv′ən) *n.* An enclosed chamber in which substances are heated, cooked, dried, etc. [< OE *ofen*]

**o·ver·alls** (ō′vər·ôlz′) *n.pl.* Loose, coarse trousers, often with suspenders and a piece extending over the breast, worn over the clothing as protection from soiling.

**o·ver·bear·ing** (ō′vər·bâr′ing) *adj.* **1** Arrogant; dictatorial. **2** Of greatest importance; dominant. **3** Overwhelming. —**o′ver·bear′ing·ly** *adv.* —**o′ver·bear′ing·ness** *n.* —Syn. 1 haughty, arbitrary, domineering, presumptuous, dogmatic, imperious.

**o·ver·cast** (ō′vər·kast′, -käst′, ō′vər·kast′, -käst′) *v.t.* **·cast, ·cast·ing 1** To overcloud; darken. **2** To sew, as the edge of a fabric, so as to prevent raveling. —*adj.* **1** Clouded; dark; gloomy. **2** Sewn with long wrapping stitches. —*n.* A covering, esp. of clouds over the sky.

**o·ver·charge** (ō′vər·chärj′) *v.t.* **·charged, ·charg·ing 1** To charge (someone) too high a price. **2** To load or fill to excess; overburden. **3** To exaggerate. —*n.* An excessive charge.

**o·ver·coat** (ō′vər·kōt′) *n.* A warm outdoor coat worn over a suit or other clothing.

**o·ver·come** (ō′vər·kum′) *v.t.* **1** To get the better of; defeat; conquer. **2** To prevail over or surmount, as difficulties, obstacles, etc. **3** To make helpless, as by emotion, sickness, etc. —*v.i.* **4** To win. [< OE *ofercuman*] —**o′ver·com′er** *n.*

**o·ver·do** (ō′vər·dōō′) *v.* **·did, ·done, ·do·ing** *v.t.* **1** To do excessively; carry too far. **2** To overtax; exhaust. **3** To cook too much, as meat. **4** To exaggerate. —*v.i.* **5** To do too much.

**o·ver·due** (ō′vər·d′ōō′) *adj.* **1** Remaining unpaid after becoming due. **2** Past due: an *overdue* plane or train.

**o·ver·flow** (ō′vər·flō′) *v.* **·flowed, ·flown, ·flow·ing** *v.i.* **1** To flow or run over the brim or bank, as water, rivers, etc. **2** To be filled beyond capacity; spill over. **3** To be extremely full. —*v.t.* **4** To flow over the brim or bank of. **5** To flow or spread over; cover.

**6** To fill beyond capacity; cause to overflow. —*n.* (ō′vər·flō′) **1** The act of overflowing. **2** That which flows over; excess; surplus. **3** A passage or outlet for liquid. —**o′ver·flow′ing** *adj., n.* —**o′ver·flow′ing** *adj., n.* —**o′ver·flow′ing·ly** *adv.*

**o·ver·hang** (ō′vər·hang′) *v.* **hung, ·hang·ing** *v.t.* **1** To hang or project over (something); jut over. **2** To impend over; threaten. —*v.i.* **3** To hang or jut over something. —*n.* Something that projects over another thing; also, the amount or degree of such projection.

**o·ver·haul** (ō′vər·hôl′) *v.t.* **1** To examine carefully, as for needed repairs; also, to make such repairs. **2** To catch up with; gain on. —*n.* (ō′vər·hôl′) A thorough inspection and repair. Also **o′ver·haul′ing.**

**o·ver·head** (ō′vər·hed′) *adj.* **1** Situated, working, or passing above or over the head. **2** Of or pertaining to the overhead of a business. —*n.* General expenditure applicable to all departments of a business, as light, heat, taxes, etc. —*adv.* (ō′vər·hed′) Above one's head; aloft.

**o·ver·hear** (ō′vər·hir′) *v.t.* **·heard, ·hear·ing** To hear (something said or someone speaking) without the knowledge or intention of the speaker. —**o′ver·hear′er** *n.*

**o·ver·kill** (ō′vər·kil′) *n.* **1** The capacity of a nation's nuclear weapons which is considered in excess of the number needed to demolish all key enemy targets. **2** *Informal* Any action regarded as excessive or extreme.

**o·ver·lap** (ō′vər·lap′) *v.t. & v.i.* **lapped, ·lap·ping 1** To lie or extend partly over or upon (another or one another). **2** To extend in time over or into (another period of time, activity, etc.). —*n.* (ō′vər·lap′) The state, extent, or place of overlapping; also, the part that overlaps.

**o·ver·load** (ō′vər·lōd′) *v.t.* To load excessively. —*n.* (ō′vər·lōd′) An excessive load.

**o·ver·look** (ō′vər·lŏŏk′) *v.t.* **1** To fail to see or notice; miss. **2** To disregard purposely or indulgently; ignore. **3** To look over or see from a higher place. **4** To afford a view of: The castle *overlooks* the harbor. **5** To supervise; oversee. —*n.* (ō′vər·lŏŏk′) **1** An elevated place from which one may view the surroundings; also, the view from such a place. **2** Oversight; neglect.

**o·ver·night** (ō′vər·nīt′) *adj.* **1** Of, pertaining to, or caused by the previous evening: *overnight* euphoria that vanished at dawn. **2** Lasting or staying one night: an *overnight* flight; an *overnight* guest. 3 Used for a brief visit: an *overnight* bag. 4 Occurring or appearing quickly or suddenly: *overnight* fame. —*adv.* (ō′vər·nīt′) 1 During or through the night: to stay *overnight*. 2 On or during the previous evening: remembering a joke he'd heard *overnight*. 3 Quickly or suddenly: to achieve success *overnight*.

o·ver·pass (ō′vər·pas′, -päs′) *v.t.* 1 To pass across, over, or through; cross. 2 To surpass or exceed. 3 To overlook; disregard. 4 To transgress. —*n.* (ō′vər·pas′, -päs′) An elevated section of highway or a pedestrian bridge crossing other lines of travel.

o·ver·rate (ō′vər·rāt′) *v.t.* ·rat·ed, ·rat·ing To rate or value too highly.

o·ver·rule (ō′vər·rōōl′) *v.t.* ·ruled, ·rul·ing 1 To decide or rule against; nullify by superior authority; set aside; invalidate. 2 To prevail over.

o·ver·run (ō′vər·run′) *v.* ·ran, ·run, ·run·ning *v.t.* 1 To spread or swarm over, esp. harmfully, as vermin or invaders do. 2 To run or flow over so as to cover. 3 To spread rapidly across or throughout: said of fads, ideas, etc. 4 To run or extend beyond; pass the limit of. —*v.i.* 5 To run over; overflow. 6 To pass the usual or desired limit. —*n.* (ō′vər·run′) 1 The act or an instance of overrunning. 2 The amount or extent of overrunning.

o·ver·see (ō′vər·sē′) *v.t.* ·saw, ·seen, ·see·ing 1 To direct or supervise. 2 To survey; watch.

o·ver·se·er (ō′vər·sē′ər) *n.* A person who oversees; esp. one who directs the work of others.

o·ver·shoot (ō′vər·shōōt′) *v.* ·shot, ·shoot·ing *v.t.* 1 To shoot, pass, fly, etc. over or beyond. 2 To go beyond; exceed, as a limit. —*v.i.* 3 To shoot or go too far or beyond a mark.

o·ver·sight (ō′vər·sīt′) *n.* 1 An error due to inattention; an inadvertent mistake or omission. 2 Watchful supervision.

o·ver·sleep (ō′vər·slēp′) *v.i.* ·slept, ·sleep·ing To sleep beyond an intended time for waking.

o·ver·step (ō′vər·step′) *v.t.* ·stepped, ·step·ping To step over or go beyond; exceed (some limit or restriction).

o·vert (ō′vûrt, ō·vûrt′ *adj.* Open to view; outwardly manifest. [< OF, pp. of *ovrir* to open] —o·vert′ly *adv.* —**Syn.** apparent, evident, obvious, clear, patent.

o·ver·take (ō′və·tāk′)*v.t.* ·took, ·tak·en, ·tak·ing 1 To catch up with. 2 To catch up with and go past; leave behind. 3 To come upon suddenly.

o·ver·throw (ō′vər·thrō′) *v.t.* >·threw, ·thrown, ·throw·ing 1 To throw over or down; upset. 2 To bring down or remove from power by force; defeat; ruin. —*n.* (ō′vər·thrō′) 1 The act of overthrowing. 2 The condition of being overthrown.

o·ver·ture (ō′vər·chər) *n.* 1 *Music* An instrumental prelude, as to an opera or other large work. 2 An introductory proposal or offer; approach. [< L *apertura* an opening]

o·ver·turn (ō′vər·tûrn′) *v.t.* 1 To turn or throw over; capsize; upset. 2 To destroy the power of; overthrow; defeat. —*v.i.* 3 To turn over; capsize; upset. —*n.* (ō′vər·tûrn′) The act of overturning or the state of being overturned.

o·ver·view (ō′vər·vyōō′) *n.* A broad survey or review of a subject, field of activity, etc.

o·ver·ween·ing (ō′vər·wē′ning) *adj.* Presumptuous; arrogant. [< OE *ofer* over + *wēnan* think] o′ver·ween′ing·ly *adv.* —o′ver·ween′ing·ness *n.* —**Syn.** haughty, overbearing, patronizing, pompous.

o·ver·whelm (ō′vər·ʰwelm′) *v.t.* 1 To bury or submerge completely, as with a wave or flood. 2 To overcome or defeat by or as by irresistible force or numbers; crush. —o′ver·whelm′ing *adj.* —o′ver·whelm′ing·ly *adv.*

o·ver·wrought (ō′vər·rôt′) *adj.* 1 Worked up or excited excessively; strained. 2 Having the surface adorned. 3 Too elaborate; overdone.

owe (ō) *v.* owed, ow·ing *v.t.* 1 To be indebted to (a person). 2 To be obligated to pay or repay the sum of. 3 To be obligated to render or offer: to *owe* an apology. 4 To have or possess by virtue of gift, labor, etc.: with *to*: He *owes* his success to his own efforts. 5 To cherish (a certain feeling) toward another: to *owe* a grudge. —*v.i.* 6 To be in debt. [< OE *āgan*]

owl (oul) *n.* 1 Any of a large order of predatory nocturnal birds having large forward-looking eyes, a short, sharply hooked bill, long powerful claws, and a circular facial disk of radiating feathers. 2 A person having a solemn, thoughtful appearance, nocturnal habits, etc. [< OE *ūle*] —owl′ish *adj.* —owl′ish·ly *adv.* —owl′ish·ness *n.*

own (ōn) *adj.* Belonging or relating to oneself or itself: my *own* idea; under its *own* momentum. —*n.* That which belongs to oneself or itself: The success was her *own.* —

**come into one's own 1** To obtain possession of one's property. **2** To receive one's reward, as recognition or praise. —**hold one's own** To maintain one's place, position, condition, etc. —**on one's own** Entirely dependent on one's self for support or success. —*v.t.* **1** To have or hold as one's own; possess. **2** To admit or acknowledge. —*v.i.* **3** To confess: with *to.* —**own up (to)** To confess (to). [< OE *āgen,* orig. pp. of *āgan* owe, possess] —**own'a·ble** *adj.* —**own'er** *n.*

**own·er·ship** (ō'nər·ship) *n.* **1** The state of being an owner. **2** Legal title to something.

**ox** (oks) *n. pl.* **ox·en** (ok'sən) **1** An adult castrated bull, used as a draft animal or for food. **2** Any bovine mammal. [< OE *oxa*]

**ox·y·gen** (ok'sə·jin) *n.* A highly reactive element (symbol O) essential to life, occurring as an odorless gas in the atmosphere and in chemical combination in water and rocks, and comprising about 50 percent of the material in and above the earth's crust. [< OXY-[1] + -GEN]

**oys·ter** (ois'tər) *n.* Any of a family of irregularly shaped marine bivalves, including various edible species. [< Gk. *ostreon*]

**o·zone** (ō'zōn) *n.* **1** An acrid, unstable, allotropic form of oxygen having three atoms per molecule, formed by electric discharge in air and by high-energy solar radiation in the upper atmosphere. **2** *Informal* Air that is pure and refreshing. [< Gk. *ozein* to smell] —**o·zon·ic** (ō·zon'ik, ō·zō'nik), **o·zo·nous** (ō'zə·nəs) *adj.*

# P

**pace** (pās) *n.* **1** A step in walking. **2** A conventional measure of length approximating the average length of stride in walking, usu. estimated at from 30 to 40 inches. **3** The manner of movement in going on the legs; gait, esp. of a horse. **4** Rate of speed in moving on the legs: a fast *pace.* **5** Rate of movement or work, or of any process or activity. **6** A gait of a horse, etc. in which both feet on the same side are lifted and moved forward at once. —*v.* **paced, pac·ing** *v.t.* **1** To walk back and forth across. **2** To measure by paces. **3** To set or make the pace for. **4** To train to a certain gait or pace. —*v.i.* **5** To walk with slow or regular steps. **6** To move at a pace. [< L *passus* step] —**pac'er** *n.*

**pace·mak·er** (pās'mā'kər) *n.* **1** One who makes or sets the pace for another in a race.

**2** A node of muscle fibers in the heart that regulates the heartbeat. **3** Any of various devices, usu. electronic, used to regulate the heartbeat. —**pace'mak'ing** *adj., n.*

**pach·y·derm** (pak'ə·dûrm) *n.* Any of certain thick-skinned, hoofed mammals, as an elephant, hippopotamus, or rhinoceros. [< Gk. *pachys* thick + *derma* skin] —**pach'y·der'ma·tous, pach'y·der'mous** *adj.*

**pa·cif·ic** (pə·sif'ik) *adj.* **1** Pertaining to the making of peace; leading to peace. **2** Peaceable; calm. [< L < *pax, pacis* peace + *facere* make] —**pa·cif'i·cal·ly** *adv.*

**pac·i·fi·ca·tion** (pas'ə·fə·kā'shən) *n.* The act of pacifying, or the state of being pacified. —**pa·cif'i·ca'tor** *n.* —**pa·cif'i·ca·to'ry** (-kə·tôr'ē, -tō'rē) *adj.*

**pac·i·fism** (pas'ə·fiz'əm) *n.* Opposition to violence, esp. war, for any purpose, often accompanied by the refusal to bear arms by reason of conscience or religious conviction. —**pac'i·fist** *adj., n.* —**pac'i·fis'tic** *adj.*

**pac·i·fy** (pas'ə·fī) *v.t.* ·**fied,** ·**fy·ing 1** To bring peace to; end war or strife in. **2** To allay the anger or agitation of. [< L *pax, pacis* peace + *facere* make] —**Syn. 2** appease, calm, allay, tranquilize.

**pack** (pak) *n.* **1** A bundle or large package, esp. one to be carried on the back of a man or animal. **2** A full set of like or associated things handled or considered as a unit: a *pack* of cards; a *pack* of lies. **3** A group of animals, as dogs or wolves. **4** Any gang or band. **5** A large area of floating broken ice: also **ice pack. 6** A cosmetic paste spread on the skin and allowed to dry. **7** A wrapping about a patient: a wet or cold *pack.* —*v.t.* **1** To make a pack or bundle of. **2** To place compactly in a trunk, box, etc. **3** To fill compactly, as for storing or carrying. **4** To compress tightly; crowd together. **5** To fill to overflowing; cram. **6** To cover, fill, or surround so as to prevent leakage, damage, etc. **7** To load with a pack; burden. **8** To carry or transport, as on pack animals. **9** To carry habitually: to *pack* a gun. **10** To send or dispatch summarily: with *off* or *away.* **11** To treat (a patient) with a pack. **12** *Slang* To be able to inflict: He *packs* a wallop. —*v.i.* **13** To place one's clothing and belongings in trunks, boxes, etc., for storing or carrying. **14** To crowd together. **15** To settle in a hard, firm mass. **16** To leave in haste: often with *off* or *away.* —**send packing** To send away or dismiss abruptly. [ME *pakke*] —**pack'er** *n.*

**pack·age** (pak′ij) *n.* 1 Something wrapped up or bound together; a parcel. 2 A receptacle in which something is contained or packed. 3 A combination of items considered as a unit: a salary increase and fringe benefits all in one *package*. —*v.t.* ·aged, ·ag·ing 1 To bind or make into a package or bundle. 2 To offer as a package. —**pack′ag·er** *n.*

**pack·et** (pak′it) *n.* 1 A small package; parcel. 2 A boat carrying passengers, freight, and mail, esp. along a coast: also **packet boat.**

**pact** (pakt) *n.* An agreement, esp. between nations; compact. [< L *pactum* agreement]

**pad** (pad) *n.* 1 Anything stuffed and soft enough to protect from jarring, friction, etc.; cushion. 2 A launching pad. 3 A soft saddle. 4 A number of sheets of paper gummed together at the edge. 5 A floating leaf of an aquatic plant: a lily *pad.* 6 a A soft cushion of flesh under the toes of an animal. b An animal's footprint. 7 *Slang* A room or apartment; lodgings. —*v.t.* **pad·ded, pad·ding** 1 To stuff, line, or protect with pads or padding. 2 To lengthen (speech or writing) by inserting unnecessary matter. 3 To expand (an expense account) by recording nonexistent expenditures.

**pad·ding** (pad′ing) *n.* 1 The act of stuffing or forming a pad. 2 Any material used to make a pad. 3 Matter used in writing to fill space.

**pad·dle** (pad′l) *n.* 1 An implement resembling a short oar with a broad blade at one or both ends, used to propel a canoe or small boat. 2 A similarly shaped implement for inflicting bodily punishment. —*v.* ·died, ·dling *v.i.* 1 To move a canoe, etc., on or through water by means of a paddle. 2 To row gently or lightly. 3 To swim with short, downward strokes. —*v.t.* 4 To propel by means of a paddle or paddles. 5 To beat with a paddle. [ME *padell* small spade] —**pad′dler** *n.*

**pad·lock** (pad′lok′) *n.* A detachable lock with a shackle hinged at one end, and devised so as to pass through a staple or chain and lock at the other end. —*v.t.* To fasten with or as with a padlock. [ME *padlocke*]

**pae·an** (pē′ən) *n.* A song of praise, joy, thanksgiving, or exultation. [< Gk. *paian* a hymn addressed to Paian, the god Apollo]

**pa·gan** (pā′gən) *n.* 1 One who is neither a Christian, a Jew, nor a Muslim; a heathen. 2 An irreligious person. —*adj.* Pertaining to pagans; heathenish. [< L *paganus* a rural villager] —**pa′gan·dom, pa′gan·ism** *n.*

**page** (pāj) *n.* 1 One side of a leaf of a book, letter, manuscript, etc. 2 The written or printed matter on such a leaf. 3 An entire leaf of a book, magazine, etc.: to tear out a *page.* 4 Something that marks a stage, esp. a memorable one, in a process or sequence: a *page* from one's experience. 5 Any source or record of knowledge. —*v.t.* **paged, pag·ing** To mark the pages of with numbers. [< L *pagina*]

**pag·eant** (paj′ənt) *n.* 1 A public exhibition, parade, or spectacle, as of floats or other elaborate display. 2 Empty and elaborate display; ostentation. [< Med. L *pagina* a framework]

**pag·eant·ry** (paj′ən·trē) *n. pl.* ·ries 1 Pageants collectively. 2 Elaborate and colorful display; splendor. 3 Empty, ostentatious display.

**pa·go·da** (pə·gō′də) *n.* In the countries of the Far East, a tower having several stories, each of which has a roof that curves upward, built as a temple or memorial. [Pg. *pagode*]

**pail** (pāl) *n.* 1 A usu. cylindrical container for carrying liquids, etc. 2 The amount carried in this vessel: also **pail′ful′.** [< L *patella* a small pan]

**pain** (pān) *n.* 1 A feeling of distress resulting from the stimulation of certain nerve endings by some physical injury or disorder. 2 Mental suffering, as anxiety, grief, etc. 3 *pl.* Care or exertion expended on anything. 4 *pl.* The pangs of childbirth. 5 *Slang* A person or thing that irritates or annoys; nuisance. —**on** (or **upon** or **under**) **pain of** With the penalty of (some specified punishment). —*v.t.* 1 To cause pain to; hurt or grieve; disquiet. —*v.i.* 2 To cause pain. [< Gk. *poinē* a penalty] —**Syn.** *n.* 1 ache, discomfort. 2 anguish, distress, misery, wretchedness.

**paint** (pānt) *n.* 1 A color or pigment, either dry or mixed with oil, water, etc. 2 A cosmetic, as rouge. —*v.t.* 1 To make a representation of in paints or colors. 2 To make, as a picture, by applying paints or colors. 3 To cover or coat with or as with paint. 4 To describe vividly in words. 5 To apply cosmetics to. 6 To apply (medicine, etc.), as with a swab. —*v.i.* 7 To cover or coat something with paint. 8 To practice the art of painting. 9 To apply cosmetics to the face, etc. [< L *pingere* to paint]

**pair** (pâr) *n.* 1 Two things of a kind that are joined, complementary, or otherwise related, and are used together: a *pair* of socks.

**2** Something consisting of two like parts: a *pair* of eyeglasses. **3** Any two persons, animals, or things considered to share certain characteristics or circumstances, as a married couple or mated animals. **4** In legislative bodies, two opposed members who agree to abstain from voting, and so offset each other. —*v.t.* **1** To bring together or arrange in a pair or pairs; match; couple; mate. —*v.i.* **2** To come together as a couple or pair. **3** To marry or mate. —**pair off 1** To separate into couples. **2** To arrange by pairs. [< L *paria*, neut. plural of *par* equal]

**pa·ja·mas** (pə·jä′məz, -jam′əz) *n.pl.* **1** Loose trousers with jackets or blouses to match, used as nightwear. **2** Loose trousers worn by both men and women in the Orient. *Brit. sp.* **py·ja·mas.** [< Pers. *pāi* a leg + *jāmah* a garment] —**pa·ja′ma** *adj.*

**pal·ace** (pal′is) *n.* **1** A royal residence, or the official residence of some high dignitary. **2** Any splendid residence or stately building. **3** A spacious and often showy place of public entertainment. [< L *palatium*, orig., the Palatine Hill at Rome, on which stood the palace of the Caesars]

**pal·at·a·ble** (pal′it·ə·bəl) *adj.* **1** Agreeable to the taste or palate; savory. **2** Acceptable. —**pal′at·a·bly** *adv.*

**pal·ate** (pal′it) *n.* **1** The roof of the mouth, comprising the anterior bony hard palate and the posterior fleshy soft palate. • See MOUTH. **2** The sense of taste; relish: the gourmet's sensitive *palate*. **3** Intellectual taste or preference. [< L *palatum*]

**pa·la·tial** (pə·lā′shəl) *adj.* Of, like, or befitting a palace; magnificent. —**pa·la′tial·ly** *adv.*

**pa·lav·er** (pə·lav′ər) *n.* **1** A discussion or talk; conference. **2** Originally, a lengthy conference between European explorers and native Africans. —*v.i.* **1** To talk idly and at length. **2** To meet in conference. —*v.t.* **3** To flatter; cajole. [< Pg. *palavra* word, speech < LL *parabola* a story, word]

**pale** (pāl) *adj.* **1** Of a whitish or ashen appearance. **2** Of any color containing a large proportion of white; lacking in saturation. —*v.t.* & *v.i.* **paled, pal·ing** To make or turn pale; blanch. [< L *pallidus*] —**pale′ly** *adv.* —**pale′ness** *n.* —**Syn.** 1 pallid, wan, ashy, bloodless.

**pal·ette** (pal′it) *n.* **1** A thin tablet providing a surface for the mixing of colors by an artist, usu. designed to be held in the hand. **2** The colors used by an artist in his work as a whole or in a particular work. [F, dim. of *pale* shovel]

**pal·i·sade** (pal′ə·sād′) *n.* **1** A fence made of strong stakes set in the ground. **2** *pl.* A sheer cliff, usu. along a river. —*v.t.* **-sad·ed, ·sad·ing** To enclose or fortify with a palisade. [< MF *palisser* enclose with pales]

**pall** (pôl) *v.i.* **1** To become insipid or uninteresting. **2** To have a dulling or displeasing effect: with *on*. —*v.t.* **3** To satiate. [< APPALL]

**pall·bear·er** (pôl′bâr′ər) *n.* One who escorts or bears a coffin at a funeral.

**pal·let** (pal′it) *n.* A humble or makeshift bed, as a straw mattress or a blanket laid on the floor. [< L *palea* chaff]

**pal·li·ate** (pal′ē·āt) *v.t.* **·at·ed, ·at·ing 1** To cause (a crime, fault, etc.) to appear less serious or offensive. **2** To relieve the symptoms of without curing, as a disease. [< LL *palliare* to cloak] —**pal′li·a′tion, pal′li·a′tor** *n.* —**Syn.** 1 extenuate, excuse. 2 alleviate, mitigate.

**pal·li·a·tive** (pal′ē·ā′tiv, -ə·tiv) *adj.* Having a tendency to palliate. —*n.* That which serves to palliate.

**pal·lid** (pal′id) *adj.* **1** Of a pale or wan appearance. **2** Lacking in color or spirit: a *pallid* version of the original show. [< L *pallere* be pale] —**pal′lid·ly** *adv.* —**pal′lid·ness** *n.*

**pal·lor** (pal′ər) *n.* The state of being pale or pallid.

**palm** (päm) *n.* **1** The inner surface of the hand between the wrist and the base of the fingers. **2** The breadth (three or four inches) of the hand used as a rough measure. **3** That which covers the palm, as part of a glove. **4** The flattened portion of an antler, as of a moose. **5** The flat expanding end of any armlike projection, as the blade of an oar. —*v.i.* **1** To hide (cards, dice, etc.) in or about the hand, as in sleight of hand. **2** To handle or touch with the palm. —**palm off** To pass off or impose fraudulently. [< L *palma* a hand] —**pal·mar** (pal′mər) *adj.*

**pal·pa·ble** (pal′pə·bəl) *adj.* **1** That may be touched or felt. **2** Readily perceived; apparent. **3** Obvious to the mind; manifest. [< L *palpare* to touch] —**pal′pa·bil′i·ty, pal′pa·ble·ness** *n.* —**pal′pa·bly** *adv.*

**pal·pi·tate** (pal′pə·tāt) *v.i.* **·tat·ed, ·tat·ing 1** To quiver; tremble. **2** To throb, usu. at increased speed: said of the heart. [< L *palpitare* to tremble, freq. of *palpare* to touch] —**pal′pi·ta′tion** *n.*

**pal·sy** (pôl′zē) *n.* Paralysis or trembling due to impairment of nerves controlling voluntary movement. —*v.t.* **·sied, ·sy·ing** To affect with or as if with palsy. [< L *paralysis* paralysis] —**pal′sied** *adj.*

**pal·try** (pôl′trē) *adj.* **·tri·er, ·tri·est** Having little or no worth or value; trifling; trivial [< regional E *palt* a piece of coarse or dirty cloth] —**pal′tri·ly** *adv.* —**pal′tri·ness** *n.*

**pam·per** (pam′pər) *v.t.* To treat too indulgently; gratify the whims of; coddle. [ME *pamperen*] —**pam′per·er** *n.*

**pam·phlet** (pam′flit) *n.* A printed publication having relatively few pages and unbound, stapled, or stitched. [< L *Pamphilus seu de Amore,* popular 12th c. love poem]

**pan** (pan) *n.* **1** A wide, shallow vessel for holding liquids or for cooking. **2** A circular sheet-iron dish with sloping sides, in which gold is separated. **3** The powder cavity of a flintlock. **4** HARDPAN (def. 1). **5** Either of the two receptacles on a pair of scales. **6** *Informal* A severe criticism. —*v.* **panned, pan·ning** *v.t.* **1** To separate (gold) by washing gold-bearing earth in a pan. **2** To wash (earth, gravel, etc.) for this purpose. **3** *Informal* To criticize severely. —*v.i.* **4** To search for gold by washing earth, gravel, etc., in a pan. —**pan out** *Informal* To result or turn out; transpire. [< L *patina* a pan or dish]

**pan·a·ce·a** (pan′ə·sē′ə) *n.* A remedy for all diseases or ills; a cure-all. [< Gk. *panakeia* a universal remedy] —**pan′a·ce′an** *adj.*

**pan·cre·as** (pan′krē·əs, pang′-) *n.* A large gland situated behind the stomach and manufacturing fat-digesting enzymes and the hormone insulin. [< Gk. *pankreas* sweetbread] —**pan′cre·at′ic** (-at′ik) *adj.*

**pan·de·mo·ni·um** (pan′də·mō′nē·əm) *n.* A tumultuous uproar; wild disorder. —**Syn.** riot, chaos, tumult. [< Gk. *pan,* neut. of *pas* all + *daimōn* an evil spirit]

**pan·der** (pan′dər) *v.i.* To seek to satisfy another's immoral, vulgar, or uninformed tastes or desires: to *pander* to the mob. — *n.* One who panders; esp., a go-between in sexual intrigues; procurer; pimp. [< *Pandarus,* a character in the Iliad] —**pan′der·er** *n.*

**pane** (pān) *n.* **1** A piece of window glass filling one opening in a frame. **2** A piece or compartment, esp. if flat and rectangular. **3** A flat surface or side. [< L *pannus* a piece of cloth] —**paned** *adj.*

**pan·el** (pan′əl) *n.* **1** A rectangular section, as part of a fence or wall, often set in a frame and sometimes raised above or depressed below the surrounding surface. **2** A vertical section of a woman's skirt of a distinctive fabric or color. **3** A tablet of wood used as the surface for a painting; also, a painting on such a surface. **4** A set of instruments and controls displayed in an aircraft, automobile, or complex system. **5** *Law* **a** The official list of persons called for jury duty; also, the persons so called. **b** The persons composing a jury. **6** A group of people selected to act cooperatively for some purpose, as to conduct a public investigation, judge a contest, participate in a discussion, etc. —*v.t.* **·eled** or **·elled, ·el·ing** or **·el·ling** **1** To fit, furnish, or adorn with panels. **2** To divide into panels. [< L *pannus* rag]

**pang** (pang) *n.* **1** A sudden, brief, penetrating pain. **2** A sudden feeling of keen mental anguish. [?] —**Syn.** 1 stab, ache. 2 throe.

**pan·ic** (pan′ik) *n.* **1** A sudden, overpowering fear often affecting many simultaneously and compelling immediate, unreasoning action, esp. flight. **2** Any sudden fear or alarm that provokes unreasonable action, as a sudden loss of confidence in the soundness of the financial system. **3** *Slang* Something extremely funny. —*adj.* **1** Of, like, or caused by panic. **2** Of or caused by the god Pan, believed to inspire fear. —*v.* **·icked, ·ick·ing** *v.t.* **1** To affect with panic. **2** *Slang* To cause to laugh or otherwise express pleasure without restraint. —*v.i.* **3** To become affected with panic. [< Gk. *panikos* of or for the god Pan] —**pan′ick·y** *adj.*

**pan·o·ply** (pan′ə·plē) *n. pl.* **·plies** **1** The complete equipment of a warrior. **2** Any complete covering that protects or magnificently arrays. [< Gk. *panoplia* full armor] —**pan′o·plied** *adj.*

**pan·o·ram·a** (pan′ə·ram′ə, -rä′mə) *n.* **1** A complete view in every direction. **2** A complete or comprehensive view of a subject or of constantly passing events. **3** A picture unrolled before the spectator and representing a continuous scene. **4** CYCLORAMA. [< PAN- + Gk. *horama* sight] —**pan′o·ram′ic** *adj.* —**pan′o·ram′i·cal·ly** *adv.*

**pant** (pant) *v.i.* **1** To breathe rapidly or spasmodically; gasp for breath. **2** To emit smoke, steam, etc., in loud puffs. **3** To have a strong desire; yearn: with *for* or *after.* **4** To beat or pulsate rapidly; throb, as the heart. —*v.t.* **5** To breathe out or utter gaspingly. —*n.* **1** A short or labored breath. **2** A quick or violent heaving, as of the breast. [< OF *pantoisier* to gasp] —**pant′er** *n.*

**pan·to·mime** (pan′tə·mīm) n. 1 A series of gestures and postures, used without words to express ideas or convey information. 2 Any play in which the actors express themselves without speaking. 3 An ancient, classical play or part of a play in which the actors used gestures or movement only. —v.t. & v.i. **·mimed, ·mim·ing** To act or express in pantomime. [< Gk. *pantomimos* an imitator of all] —**pan′to·mim′ic** (-mim′ik) or **·i·cal** adj. —**pan′to·mi′mist** (-mī′mist) n.

**pan·try** (pan′trē) n. pl. **·tries** A room or closet for keeping provisions, dishes, table linen, etc. [< L *panis* bread]

**pants** (pants) n.pl. 1 A garment extending from the waist to the ankles or knees and divided so as to cover each leg separately; trousers. 2 Drawers or panties.

**pa·pa·cy** (pā′pə·sē) n. pl. **·cies** 1 The dignity, office, or jurisdiction of the pope of Rome. 2 The succession of popes in the Roman Catholic Church. 3 The tenure of office of the pope. [< L *papa* pope]

**pa·pal** (pā′pəl) adj. 1 Of or pertaining to the papacy or the pope. 2 Of or pertaining to the Roman Catholic Church.

**pa·per** (pā′pər) n. 1 A substance typically prepared in thin, flat sheets, made from chemically treated fibrous cellulose, usu. from wood, rags, etc., and used as a writing and printing surface, in packaging, etc. 2 A sheet of paper. 3 A printed or written document. 4 NEWSPAPER. 5 A written essay, report, or examination, as for a school assignment. 6 A scholarly study or treatise read aloud or published in a journal. 7 Written or printed pledges or promises to pay which are negotiable, as bills of exchange, notes, etc.: **also commercial paper.** 8 WALLPAPER. 9 pl. Personal or business documents, as of identification, permission, agreement, credit, etc. 10 Free tickets, as to a theater; also, the audience so admitted. —**on paper** 1 In writing or print. 2 Based upon theoretical sources or superficial evidence. —adj. 1 Of, made of, or like paper. 2 Theoretical rather than actual: *paper* profits. —v.t. 1 To put paper on; cover with wallpaper. 2 To fold or enclose in paper. 3 To issue free tickets of admission to (a place of amusement). [< L *papyrus*] —**pa′per·er** n. —**pa′per·y** adj.

**pa·pier-mâ·ché** (pā′pər·mə·shā′, Fr. pà·pyā′ mä·shā′) n. A tough material molded from paper pulp and a binding material. [F, lit., chewed paper]

**pa·pri·ka** (pa·prē′kə, pap′rə·kə) n. A condiment made from the fruit of a mild red pepper. [< Gk. *peperi* pepper]

**par** (pär) n. 1 The established value of a national monetary unit defined in monetary units of another country. 2 The value printed on a negotiable document, as a stock certificate or bond. 3 An accepted standard with which to compare variation: not feeling up to *par.* 4 Equivalent level, status, value, etc.; equal basis: on a *par.* 5 In golf, the number of strokes allotted to a round or hole on the basis of faultless play. —adj. Equal to par. [L, equal]

**par·a·ble** (par′ə·bəl) n. A short, simple tale based on familiar things, meant to convey a moral or religious lesson. [< Gk. *parabolē* a placing side by side, a comparison]

**par·a·chute** (par′ə·shŏŏt) n. An apparatus of lightweight fabric that when unfurled assumes the shape of a large umbrella and acts to retard the speed of a body moving or descending through air. —v. **·chut·ed, ·chut·ing** v.t. 1 To land (troops, materiel, etc.) by means of parachutes. —v.i. 2 To descend by parachute. [< F < PARA- + *chute* fall] —**par′a·chut·ist** n.

**pa·rade** (pə·rād′) n. 1 A marshaling and maneuvering of troops for display or official inspection. 2 A ceremonious, public procession. 3 A promenade or public walk. 4 Pompous show; ostentation. —v. **·rad·ed, ·rad·ing** v.t. 1 To walk or march through or about. 2 To display or show off ostentatiously; flaunt. 3 To cause to assemble for military parade or review. —v.i. 4 To march formally or with display. 5 To walk in public for the purpose of showing oneself. 6 To assemble in military order for inspection or review. [< LL *parare* adorn, prepare] —**pa·rad′er** n.

**par·a·dise** (par′ə·dīs) n. 1 The intermediate place or state where the souls of the saved await the resurrection. 2 Heaven. 3 Any region or state of surpassing delight. [< OPers. *pairidaēza* an enclosure, park] —**par′a·di·sa′ic** (-di·sā′ik) or **·i·cal, par′a·dis′al, par′a·dis′i·ac** (-dis′ē·ak) or **par·a·di·si·a·cal** (par′ə·di·sī′ə·kəl) adj.

**par·a·dox** (par′ə doks) n. 1 A statement that seems to contradict common belief but may nevertheless be true. 2 A self-contradictory statement or proposition. 3 A person or thing that seems to possess contradictory qualities and is thus inexplicable or inscrutable; enigma. [< Gk. *para-* contrary to + *doxa* opinion] —**par′a·dox′i·cal** *adj.* —**par′a·dox′i·cal·ly** *adv.* —**par′a·dox′i·cal·ness** *n.*

**par·af·fin** (par′ə-fin) *n.* 1 A white, water-repellent, waxy mixture of hydrocarbons, usu. derived from petroleum, used for making candles, matches, etc.: also **paraffin wax.** 2 Any of a series of saturated, open-chain hydrocarbons analogous to methane in molecular structure. 3 *Brit.* Kerosene. — *v.t.* To treat or impregnate with paraffin. Also **par′af·fine** (-fin, -fēn). [< L *parum* too little + *affinis* related to, because it has little affinity for other bodies]

**par·a·gon** (par′ə-gon) *n.* 1 A model of excellence: a *paragon* of virtue. 2 A round pearl of exceptional size. [< Gk. *para-* beside + *akonē* whetstone]

**par·a·graph** (par′ə-graf, -gräf) *n.* 1 A passage in a written work begun on a new and usu. indented line and usu. signaling a distinct thought, statement, or expression. 2 A short article, complete and unified. 3 A mark (¶) used to indicate where a paragraph is to start. —*v.t.* 1 To arrange in or into paragraphs. 2 To comment on or express in a paragraph. [< Gk. *para-* beside + *graphein* write] —**par′a·graph′er, par′a·graph′ist** *n.*

**par·al·lel** (par′ə-lel) *adj.* 1 Extending in the same direction and being equidistant at all points: *parallel* rows of seats. 2 *Geom.* Not intersecting, however far extended: said of planes or straight lines in the same plane. 3 Having parallel sides or parts. 4 Of the same kind or form functioning in like ways: *parallel* clauses. 5 Displaying the same pattern or course: *parallel* development; *parallel* careers. —*n.* 1 Something essentially similar to another; counterpart. 2 Essential likeness; correspondence. 3 A comparison tracing similarity: to draw a *parallel* between two presidents. 4 *Geom.* A line parallel to another line or to a plane. 5 An imaginary circle parallel to the equator and having all of its points the same latitude. 6 The state of being parallel. —*v.t.* ·leled, or ·lelled, ·lel·ing or ·lel·ling 1 To be, go, or extend parallel to. 2 To furnish with a parallel; equal. 3 To be a parallel to; correspond. 4 To compare; liken. 5 To make parallel. [< Gk. *para-* beside + *allēlos* one another]

**pa·ral·y·sis** (pə·ral′ə-sis) *n.* *pl.* ·ses (-sēz) 1 Partial or complete loss of sensation and the power of voluntary motion. 2 Inability to act or respond effectively. [< Gk. < *paralyein* disable]

**par·a·lyt·ic** (par′ə-lit′ik) *adj.* 1 Of, causing, or affected with paralysis. 2 Subject to paralysis. —*n.* A person subject to or suffering from paralysis.

**par·a·lyze** (par′ə-līz) *v.t.* ·lyzed, ·lyz·ing 1 To bring about paralysis in. 2 To render powerless, ineffective, or inactive. —**par′a·ly·za′tion, par′a·lyz′er** *n.*

**par·a·med·ic** (par′ə-med′ik) *n.* One trained to assist a physician.

**par·a·mount** (par′ə-mount) *adj.* Having the highest title or rank; superior to all others. —*n.* A supreme lord. [< L *per* by + *ad montem* to the hill] —**par′a·mount·ly** *adv.* —**par′a·mount·cy** *n.* —**Syn.** *adj.* chief, foremost, preeminent, supreme.

**par·a·noid** (par′ə-noid) *adj.* 1 Of, like, or suffering from paranoia: also **par′a·noi′dal.** 2 Exhibiting symptoms suggestive of paranoia; esp., suspicious without cause. —*n.* A paranoid person. Also **par′a·noi′ac** (-noi′ak, -ak).

**par·a·pher·na·li·a** (par′ə-fər-nāl′ē-ə, -nāl′yə, -fə-) *n.pl.* (construed as sing. or pl.) 1 Personal belongings. 2 Articles or accessories of equipment or adornment; furnishings; trappings. [< Gk. *para-* beside + *phernē* dower]

**par·a·phrase** (par′ə-frāz) *n.* A restatement of the meaning of a passage, work, etc. —*v.t.* & *v.i.* ·phrased, ·phras·ing To express in or make a paraphrase. [< Gk. < *paraphrazein* tell the same thing in other words] —**par′a·phras′er** *n.* —**par′a·phras′tic** (-fras′tik) *adj.* —**par′a·phras′ti·cal·ly** *adv.*

**par·a·psy·chol·o·gy** (par′ə-sī·kol′ə-jē) *n.* The investigation of psychic phenomena, as extrasensory perception, telepathy, etc.

**par·a·site** (par′ə-sīt) *n.* 1 *Biol.* An animal or plant that lives on or in another living organism from which it takes nourishment, usu. with harm to the host. 2 A person or thing that lives or survives by dependence on and at the expense of another. [< Gk. *parasitos*, lit., one who eats at another's table] —**par′a·sit′ic** (-sit′ik) or ·i·cal *adj.* —**par′a·sit′i·cal·ly** *adv.* —**par′a·sit·ism** (par′ə-sī′tiz·əm, -sə·tiz′əm) *n.*

**par·a·sol** (par′ə-sôl, -sol) *n.* A small, light umbrella used as a sunshade, esp. by women. [< Ital. *parasole*]

**par·a·troops** (par′ə-trōops) *n.pl.* A military force trained to parachute into hostile ter-

ritory from an airplane. —**par′a·troop** *adj.*
—**par′a·troop′er** *n.*

**par·cel** (pär′səl) *n.* 1 Anything wrapped up; a
package; bundle. 2 An integral part: part
and *parcel.* 3 A group or lot of merchandise
offered for sale. 4 A group or assortment, as
of people or things: a *parcel* of misfits. 5 A
distinct portion of land. 6 A separated part
of anything. —*v.t.* ·**celed** or ·**celled,** ·**cel·ing**
or ·**cel·ling** 1 To divide or distribute in parts
or shares: usu. with *out.* 2 To make up into
a parcel. [< L *particula,* dim. of *pars, partis*
part]

**parch** (pärch) *v.t.* 1 To make extremely dry;
shrivel with heat. 2 To dry (corn, peas, etc.)
by exposing to great heat; roast slightly. —
*v.i.* 3 To become extremely dry; shrivel with
heat. [< L *per-* thoroughly + *siccare* dry]

**parch·ment** (pärch′mənt) *n.* 1 Animal skin, as
of sheep, goats, etc., prepared for writing.
2 A paper resembling this. 3 A college graduation diploma. [< Gk. *Pergamon,* the ancient city of Pergamum, Asia Minor]

**par·don** (pär′dən) *v.t.* 1 To remit the penalty
of (a crime, insult, etc.). 2 To release from
punishment; forgive for an offense. 3 To
allow for; forgive. —*n.* 1 The act of pardon-
ing. 2 A waiving of the execution of the
penalties of a violated law. 3 Courteous forbearance: used in making polite excuses. 4
An indulgence. [< L *per-* through + *donare*
give] —**par′don·a·ble** *adj.* —**par′don·a·bly**
*adv.*

**pare** (pâr) *v.t.* **pared, par·ing** 1 To cut off the
covering layer or part of. 2 To cut off or trim
away (a covering layer or part): often with
*off* or *away.* 3 To reduce or diminish, esp.
gradually. [< L *parare* prepare] —**par′er** *n.*

**par·ent** (pâr′ənt) *n.* 1 A father or a mother. 2
Any organism that generates another. 3 A
source or wellspring; basis; cause. [< L
*parens* parent, orig. pr.p. of *parere* beget] —
**pa·ren·tal** (pə·ren′təl) *adj.* —**pa·ren′tal·ly**
*adv.*

**par·ent·age** (pâr′ən·tij) *n.* 1 The relation of a
parent; parenthood. 2 Descent or derivation from parents.

**pa·ren·the·sis** (pə·ren′thə·sis) *n. pl.* ·**ses** (-
sēz) 1 A word, phrase, or clause inserted in
a sentence that is grammatically complete
without it, separated usually by commas,
dashes, or upright curves. 2 Either or both
of the upright curves ( ) so used. 3 Any intervening episode or incident [< Gk. < *par-
entithenai* put in beside]

**pa·ren·the·size** (pə·ren′thə·sīz) *v.t.* ·**sized,**
·**siz·ing** 1 To insert as a parenthesis. 2 To
insert parentheses in.

**pa·ri·ah** (pə·rī′ə) *n.* 1 One of a people of low
caste in s India and Burma. 2 A social outcast. [< Tamil *paraiyar* drummer, because
drummers at festivals came from this
caste]

**par·ish** (par′ish) *n.* 1 *Eccl.* In certain
churches, a district in charge of a priest or
other clergyman. 2 *U.S.* **a** A religious congregation, comprising all those who worship at the same church. **b** The district in
which they live. 3 In Louisiana, a civil district corresponding to a county. 4 *Can.* In
Quebec and New Brunswick, a political division resembling a township. [< Gk.
*paroikia,* orig., a neighborhood]

**pa·rish·ion·er** (pə·rish′ən·ər) *n.* A member of
a parish.

**par·i·ty** (par′ə·tē) *n. pl.* ·**ties** 1 The state or
quality of being like or equal, as in rank,
value, or position; equivalence. 2 The equivalence of value of currency between two
countries, or of the prices of commodities
as expressed in a currency. 3 In the U.S., a
level for farm prices which gives to the
farmer the same purchasing power aver-
aged during a base period. [< L *pars* equal]

**par·lance** (pär′ləns) *n.* Manner of speech; language: legal *parlance.* [< OF < *parler* speak]

**par·ley** (pär′lē) *n.* An oral conference or discussion, as with an enemy. —*v.i.* To hold a
conference, esp. with an enemy. [< OF *parler* speak]

**par·lia·ment** (pär′lə·mənt) *n.* A meeting or assembly for consultation and deliberation;
esp., a national legislative body. [< OF *parler* speak]

**par·lia·men·ta·ry** (pär′lə·men′tər·ē, -men′trē)
*adj.* 1 Pertaining to, characterized by, or
enacted by a parliament. 2 According to the
rules of Parliament. 3 Admissible in a deliberative assembly. —**par′lia·men′tar′i·an**
(-men′târ′ē·ən) *adj., n.*

**pa·ro·chi·al** (pə·rō′kē·əl) *adj.* 1 Pertaining to,
supported by, or confined to a parish. 2 Restricted in scope; narrow; provincial. [< LL
*parochialis*] —**pa·ro′chi·al·ism** *n.* —**pa·ro′-
chi·al·ly** *adv.* —**Syn.** 2 limited, uninformed,
unenlightened.

**par·o·dy** (par′ə·dē) *n. pl.* ·**dies** 1 A literary
composition imitating and ridiculing some
serious work. 2 Any burlesque imitation of
something serious. 3 A poor imitation. —*v.t.*
·**died,** ·**dy·ing** To make a parody of; travesty.

[< Gk. *paroidia* a burlesque poem or song] —**pa·rod·ic** (pə·rod′ik) or ··i·cal *adj.* —**par′o·dist** *n.*

**pa·role** (pə·rōl′) *n.* 1 The conditional release of a prisoner from jail prior to the expiration of his term. 2 A pledge of honor by a prisoner of war in return for his release, as that he will not serve against his captors. —*v.t.* ·**roled,** ·**rol·ing** To release on parole. [F *parole* (*d'honneur*) word (of honor)]

**par·ox·ysm** (par′ək·siz′əm) *n.* 1 A sudden attack or worsening of a disease; a fit. 2 A sudden and violent outburst, as of anger or laughter. [< Gk. *para-* beside + *oxynein* to goad] —**par·ox·ys·mal** (par′ək·siz′məl) *adj.*

**par·quet** (pär·kā′) *n.* 1 The main-floor space of a theater; orchestra. 2 Flooring of inlaid woodwork; parquetry. —*v.t.* ·**queted** (-kād′), ·**quet·ing** (-kā′ing) To make of or ornament with parquetry. **Also par·quette** (pär·ket′). [< OF *parchet* a small compartment, dim. of *parc* park]

**par·ri·cide** (par′ə·sīd) *n.* 1 The murder of a parent, or of a close relative. 2 One who commits such a crime. [< L *paricidium* a killing of a relative] —**par′ri·ci′dal** *adj.*

**par·rot** (par′ət) *n.* 1 Any of certain birds of warm regions having a hooked bill, usu. brilliant plumage, and, in some, an ability to simulate human speech. 2 A person who repeats or imitates without understanding. —*v.t.* To repeat or imitate without understanding. [? < F *Pierrot*, dim. of *Pierre* Peter, a personal name] —**par′rot·er** *n.*

**par·ry** (par′ē) *v.* ·**ried,** ·**ry·ing** *v.t.* 1 To ward off, as a blow or a thrust in fencing. 2 To avoid, esp. by a deft evasion: to *parry* a question. —*v.i.* 3 To make a parry. 4 To avoid something, as by skillful maneuvers. —*n.* *pl.* ·**ries** 1 A defensive movement, as in fencing. 2 An evasion or diversion. [< Ital. *parare* defend] —**Syn.** *v.* 2 evade, dodge, sidestep, duck.

**par·si·mo·ni·ous** (pär′sə·mō′nē·əs) *adj.* Stingy; niggardly; miserly. —**par′si·mo′ni·ous·ly** *adv.* —**par′si·mo′ni·ous·ness** *n.*

**par·son** (pär′sən) *n.* 1 The clergyman of a parish or congregation. 2 Any minister. [< Med. L *persona* a rector]

**part** (pärt) *n.* 1 A certain portion or amount of anything; a piece. 2 One of a number of separable elements that together constitute a whole: the *parts* of a motor. 3 An essential portion of a body or an organism; a member. 4 *Usu. pl.* A portion of territory; re-

gion: in foreign *parts.* 5 An individual share, as of duty, business, or performance: to do one's *part.* 6 A side, cause, or party opposed to another. 7 The role or lines assigned to an actor. 8 *Usu. pl.* A quality of mind or character; talent: a man of *parts.* 9 *Music* **a** The series of sounds to be made by a single voice or instrument in a concerted piece. **b** The notated version of this. 10 A line formed by dividing the hair. —**for my part** As far as I am concerned. —**for the most part** On the whole; generally. —**in part** Partly. —**on the part of** So far as regards. —**part and parcel** An essential part. —**take part** To participate: usu. with *in.* —**take someone's part** To support someone's position, as in a dispute. —*v.t.* 1 To divide or break (something) into parts. 2 To sever or discontinue (a relationship or connection): to *part* company. 3 To separate by being or coming between. 4 To comb (the hair) so as to leave a dividing line. —*v.i.* 5 To become divided or broken into parts; come apart; divide. 6 To go away from each other; separate. 7 To depart; leave. —**part from** To separate from; leave. —**part with** 1 To give up; relinquish. 2 To part from. —*adj.* Of or concerning only a part; partial. —*adv.* In some degree; to some extent; partly. [< L *pars, partis* part] —**Syn.** *n.* 1 segment, section, fraction. 2 component, constituent, ingredient, module.

**par·tial** (pär′shəl) *adj.* 1 Pertaining to, constituting, or involving a part only; not complete or total. 2 Favoring one side; prejudiced; biased. 3 Having a special liking: with *to.* —**par′tial·ly** *adv.*

**par·ti·al·i·ty** (pär′shē·al′ə·tē) *n.* 1 The state of being partial. 2 Unfairness; bias. 3 A particular fondness. **Also par′tial·ness.**

**par·tic·i·pant** (pär·tis′ə·pənt) *n.* One who participates. —*adj.* Participating.

**par·tic·i·pate** (pär·tis′ə·pāt) *v.i.* ·**pat·ed,** ·**pat·ing** To take part or have a share in common with others: with *in.* [< L *pars, partis* a part + *capere* take] —**par·tic′i·pa′tion, par·tic′i·pance, par·tic′i·pa′tor** *n.* —**par·tic′i·pa·to′ry** (-pə·tôr′ē, -tō′rē) *adj.*

**par·ti·cle** (pär′ti·kəl) *n.* 1 A minute part, piece, or portion. 2 Any very small amount or slight degree: without a *particle* of truth. 3 *Physics* Any of the minute components of matter; esp., an **elementary particle,** one of the elementary constituents of an atom, thought to be irreducible, as an electron, neutron, proton, etc. 4 *Gram.* **a** A short, uninflected part of speech, as a conjunction. **b** A prefix or suffix. [< L *particula*, dim. of *pars*, *partis* a part]

**par·tic·u·lar** (pər·tik′yə·lər) *adj.* 1 Of, being, or pertaining to a single or separate thing. 2 Having a special character; distinctive: a *particular* way of doing things. 3 More than usual; especial: no *particular* hurry. 4 Comprising all details or circumstances: a *particular* description. 5 Characterized by careful attention to detail; requiring high standards of performance; exacting; fastidious. —**in particular** Especially. —*n.* 1 A specific fact or detail, as distinguished from a generalization. 2 A separate or single instance; item. —**Syn.** *adj.* 1 definite, specific. 2 individual, peculiar. [<L *particularis* concerning a part]

**par·tic·u·lar·i·ty** (pər·tik′yə·lar′ə·tē) *n. pl.* **·ties** 1 The state or quality of being particular as distinguished from general. 2 Careful attention to detail; fastidiousness. 3 Something that is particular, as a circumstance or detail.

**par·ti·san** (pär′tə·zən, -sən·) *n.* 1 One who supports or endorses a party or cause with great devotion or zeal; esp., an overzealous or fanatical devotee. 2 A member of a body of irregular troops; a guerrilla. —*adj.* Pertaining to or characteristic of a partisan. Also **par′ti·zan.** [<Ital. *parte* a part] —**par′ti·san·ship** *n.*

**par·ti·tion** (pär·tish′ən) *n.* 1 The act of parting, or the state of being parted; division; separation. 2 A wall or other barrier dividing an area, esp. an interior space. —*v.t.* 1 To divide into parts, segments, etc. 2 To separate by a partition: with *off.* 3 To divide, as property, into shares or portions. [< L *partire* divide] —**par·ti′tion·er** *n.*

**part·ner** (pärt′nər) *n.* 1 One who takes part or is associated with another or others in a business or other enterprise. 2 A husband or wife. 3 Either of two people dancing together. 4 One of two or more people comprising a side or team in a competitive game or sport. [< L *partitio* a share]

**par·ty** (pär′tē) *n. pl.* **·ties** 1 A body of persons united for some common purpose, as a political organization. 2 One who participates in or is involved with an action, proceeding, inquiry, etc.: a *party* to the investigation. 3 *Law* One of the persons named on the record in an action. 4 A social gathering: a dinner *party.* 5 A detachment of soldiers. 6 *Informal* A person. —*adj.* 1 Of or pertaining

to a political party. 2 Suitable for a social party: a *party* dress. —*v.i.* **·tied, ·ty·ing** *Informal* To attend or give social parties. [< L *pars*, *partis* a part]

**par·ve·nu** (pär′və·n¹ōō) *n.* One who has suddenly attained wealth or power but lacks the social status commensurate with it; an upstart. —*adj.* 1 Being a parvenu. 2 Like or characteristic of a parvenu. [< L *pervenire* to come through]

**pas·chal** (pas′kəl) 1 Of or pertaining to the Jewish Passover. 2 Of or pertaining to Easter. [< L *pascha* Passover]

**pass** (pas, päs) *v.t.* 1 To go by or move past and leave behind. 2 To go across, around, over, or through. 3 To permit to go unnoticed or unmentioned. 4 To undergo; experience: to *pass* a bad night. 5 To meet the requirements of. 6 To go beyond; surpass: It *passes* comprehension. 7 To cause to go or move: to *pass* one's eyes over a book. 8 To cause to go or move past: to *pass* troops in review. 9 To cause or allow to advance or proceed. 10 To spend: to *pass* the night at an inn. 11 To give approval to. 12 To enact, as a law. 13 To be approved by: The bill *passed* the senate. 14 To omit paying (a dividend). 15 To put in circulation: *Pass* the word. 16 To pronounce, esp. judicially, as judgment or sentence. 17 To discharge from the body. 18 To pledge, as one's word. 19 To perform a pass (n. def. 6) on or over. 20 In sports, to transfer (the ball, etc.) to another player on the same side. 21 *Law* To transfer or assign ownership of to another by will, deed, etc. —*v.i.* 22 To go or proceed; move. 23 To have course or direction; extend: The road *passed* under a bridge. 24 To go away; depart. 25 To come to an end; disappear. 26 To elapse or go by; be spent: The day *passed* slowly. 27 To die. 28 To go by; move past in or as in review. 29 To go from person to person; circulate. 30 To be mutually given and received, as greetings. 31 To go or change from one condition, circumstance, etc., to another. 32 To take place; happen. 33 To go unheeded or unpunished. 34 To undergo a test, examination, etc., successfully. 35 To be approved, ratified, enacted, etc. 36 To obtain or force passage. 37 To be excreted or voided. 38 *Law* **a** To give or pronounce judgment, sentence, etc.: with *on* or *upon.* **b** To be transferred or assigned to another by will, deed, etc. 39 In sports, to transfer the ball, etc., to another player on the same side. 40 In fencing, to make a thrust; lunge. 41 In card games, to decline to make a play, bid, etc. —bring to pass To cause to happen or to be realized. —come to pass To happen; come about. —pass away 1 To come to an end. 2 To die. 3 To allow (time) to elapse. —pass for To be accepted as, usu. fraudulently. —pass off 1 To come to an end. 2 To give out or circulate as genuine; palm off. —pass out 1 To distribute. 2 *Informal* To faint. —pass over To fail to notice or consider. —pass up *Informal* To fail to take advantage of, as an offer. —n. 1 The act of passing. 2 A way or opening that affords a passage, as a gap in a mountain range. 3 Permission or a permit to proceed. 4 A state of affairs; crisis. 5 The successful undergoing of an examination, test, or inspection. 6 A sleight-of-hand movement of a hand, wand, etc. 7 A movement made in attempting to stab or strike. 8 In sports, the action of passing the ball, puck, etc., in the course of play. 9 *Slang* a An attempt to caress. b Any aggressive action intended to lead to sexual familiarity. —a pretty pass *Informal* An unpleasant or difficult situation. [< L *passus* a step] —pass′er n. • *passed, past* Passed is the past tense of the verb *to pass*, but unlike many participles, its use as an adjective is restricted to a very few expressions in which the sense is that of an object physically moving by, as in the baseball term *passed ball. Past*, on the other hand, is commonly used as an adjective *(past time)*, adverb *(a bird flew past)*, noun *(in the past)*, or preposition *(ten minutes past the hour)*, and is found only in archaic contexts as the past participle of *pass.*

**pas·sage** (pas′ij) n. 1 A corridor, hall, or gallery affording access from one part, as of a building, to another. 2 A way through or over. 3 Free entrance, exit, or transit. 4 A passing: the *passage* of the days. 5 A portion of a discourse, writing, etc.: a *passage* from Shakespeare. 6 A journey, as by ship. 7 A navigable route. 8 The enactment of a legislative measure. 9 A personal encounter: a *passage* with swords. 10 Migration, esp. of birds. 11 In music, any short portion of a composition.

**pas·sé** (pa·sā′, pas′ā) adj. 1 Past the prime; faded. 2 Old-fashioned. [F, orig., pp. of *passer*]

**pas·sen·ger** (pas′ən·jər) n. A person who trav-

els in a car, train, bus, etc. [< OF *passager* < *passage*]

**pas·sim** (pas′im) adv. Here and there; in various passages: used as a bibliographic reference. [L]

**pas·sion** (pash′ən) n. 1 Fervent devotion. 2 Ardent sexual feelings and desire; love. 3 The object of such feelings. 4 A fit of intense anger; rage. 5 Any transport of excited feeling. 6 *Archaic* Suffering; agony. [< L *passus,* pp. of *pati* suffer] —pas′sion·less adj. —pas′sion·less·ly adv.

**pas·sion·ate** (pash′ən·it) adj. 1 Susceptible to strong emotion; excitable. 2 Easily moved to anger. 3 Expressing or displaying some intense feeling. 4 Ardent in expressing sexual desire. [< L *passio* suffering] —pas′sion·ate·ly adv. —pas′sion·ate·ness n.

**pas·sive** (pas′iv) adj. 1 Acted upon or receiving impressions from external agents or causes. 2 In a state of rest or quiescence; unresponsive. 3 Unresisting; submissive. 4 *Chem.* Inert; inactive. 5 *Gram.* Designating a voice of a verb which indicates that the subject is being acted upon, as *Caesar was killed by Brutus.* —n. *Gram.* 1 The passive voice. 2 A verb or construction in this voice. [< L *passus,* pp. of *pati* suffer] —pas′sive·ly adv. —pas′sive·ness, pas·siv·i·ty (pa·siv′ə·tē)

**pass·port** (pas′pôrt′, -pôrt′, pås′-) n. 1 An official warrant certifying the citizenship of the bearer when traveling abroad. 2 Anything that gives the privilege or right to enter into some place or sphere of action. [< F *passer* pass + *port* harbor]

**paste** (pāst) n. 1 An adhesive mixture used for joining or affixing paper articles and the like. 2 A mixture of flour and water, often with other materials, for cooking purposes; dough. 3 Any doughy or moist plastic substance: *toothpaste; almond paste.* 4 A vitreous composition for making imitation gems. —v.t. past·ed, past·ing 1 To stick or fasten with paste or the like. 2 *Slang* To strike, as with the fist. [< Gk. *pastē* barley porridge]

**paste·board** (pāst′bôrd′, -bōrd′) n. 1 Paper pulp compressed, or paper pasted together to form a stiff sheet. 2 *Slang* Something made of pasteboard, as a playing card. —adj. 1 Made of or resembling pasteboard. 2 Thin and flimsy.

**pas·tel** (pas·tel′) n. 1 A picture drawn with colored crayons. 2 The art of drawing such pictures. 3 A hard crayon made of pipe clay and a pigment, mixed with gum and water. 4 A soft, delicate shade of a color. —*adj.* 1 Of or pertaining to a pastel. 2 Having a delicate, soft tint. [< Ital. *pastello*] —**pas·tel′ist** or **pas·tel′list** *n.*

**pas·time** (pas′tīm′, päs′-) *n.* Something that serves to make time pass agreeably; recreation. [< PASS, *v.* + TIME]

**pas·tor** (pas′tər, päs′-) *n.* A Christian minister who has a church or congregation under his official charge. [< L *pastor* a shepherd. lit., a feeder]

**pas·tor·al** (pas′tər·əl, päs′-) *adj.* 1 Pertaining to shepherds and their work. 2 Describing the conventionalized life of shepherds and rustics: a *pastoral* poem. 3 Having the peaceful simplicity of country life; natural. 4 Pertaining to a pastor and his work. —*n.* 1 A poem, play, etc., set in rustic surroundings. 2 A picture illustrating rural scenes. 3 *Eccl.* A letter from a pastor to his congregation. —**Syn.** *adj.* 3 bucolic, rustic.

**pas·try** (pās′trē) *n. pl.* **·tries** 1 Articles of food made with a crust of shortened dough, as pies. 2 Any of various sweet baked goods, as cakes, buns, etc. [< PASTE + -RY]

**pas·ture** (pas′chər, päs′-) *n.* 1 Ground for the grazing of domestic animals. 2 Grass or herbage that grazing domestic animals eat. —*v.* **·tured**, **·tur·ing** *v.t.* 1 To lead to or put in a pasture to graze. 2 To graze on (grass, land, etc.). —*v.i.* 3 To graze. [< L *pastus*, pp. of *pascere* to feed] —**pas′tur·er** *n.*

**patch** (pach) *n.* 1 A small piece of material, used to repair a hole, tear, or worn place. 2 A piece of adhesive tape or the like, applied to the skin to hide a blemish or protect a small wound. 3 a A small piece of ground. b The plants growing on it: a *patch* of corn. 4 A piece of cloth or other material worn over an injured eye. 5 A small piece of cloth sewed on a garment, esp. a uniform, as an emblem or insignia of rank. 6 A shred or scrap. —*v.t.* 1 To put a patch or patches on. 2 To repair or put together hurriedly or crudely: often with *up* or *together.* 3 To make of patches, as a quilt. —**patch (things) up** To resolve or settle, as a quarrel. [ME *pacehe*] —**patch′er** *n.*

**pat·ent** (pat′nt, *Brit.* pāt′nt; *for adj. defs.* 2 & 3, *usu.* pāt′nt) *n.* 1 A government protection to an inventor, securing to him for a specific time exclusive rights to his invention. 2 The rights so granted. 3 Any official document securing a right. —*v.t.* To obtain a patent on (an invention). —*adj.* 1 Protected

or conferred by a patent. 2 Manifest or apparent to everybody. 3 Open; unobstructed, as a duct in the body. [< L *patens* pr.p. of *patere* lie open]

**pa·ter·nal** (pə·tûr′nəl) *adj.* 1 Pertaining to a father; fatherly. 2 Derived from one's father; hereditary. 3 Related through one's father: a *paternal* aunt. [< L *pater* a father] —**pa·ter′nal·ly** *adv*

**pa·ter·nos·ter** (pā′tər·nos′tər) *n.* 1 The Lord's Prayer, esp. in Latin: **also Pater Noster.** 2 A bead of the rosary representing one recitation of the Lord's Prayer. [< L *pater noster* our father]

**pa·thet·ic** (pə·thet′ik) *adj.* Inspiring pity; arousing compassion. **Also pa·thet′i·cal.** [< Gk. *pathētikos* sensitive] —**pa·thet′i·cal·ly** *adv.*

**pa·thol·o·gist** (pə·thol′ə·jist) *n.* A physician or other expert specializing in pathology.

**pa·thol·o·gy** (pə·thol′ə·jē) *n. pl.* **·gies** 1 The branch of medical science dealing with the causes, nature, and effects of diseases, esp. disease-induced changes in organs, tissues, and body chemistry. 2 A diseased or abnormal condition. —**path·o·log·i·cal** (path′ə·loj′i·kəl) or **path′o·log′ic** *adj.* —**path·o·log′i·cal·ly** *adv.*

**pa·thos** (pā′thos) *n.* The quality, attribute, or element, in events, speech, or art, that rouses the tender emotions, as compassion or sympathy. [Gk., suffering]

**pa·tience** (pā′shəns) *n.* 1 The quality of enduring without complaint. 2 The exercise of sustained perseverance. 3 Forbearance toward the faults or infirmities of others. 4 *Brit.* Any solitaire card game. —**Syn.** 1 endurance, fortitude, resignation. 2 steadiness. 3 leniency, tolerance.

**pa·tient** (pā′shənt) *adj.* 1 Possessing quiet, uncomplaining endurance under distress. 2 Tolerant and forbearing. 3 Capable of tranquilly awaiting events. 4 Persevering. —*n.* A person undergoing medical care. [< L *patiens*, pr.p. of *pati* suffer] —**pa′tient·ly** *adv.*

**pa·tri·arch** (pā′trē·ärk) *n.* 1 The leader of a family or tribe who rules by paternal right. 2 One of the earliest fathers of the human race, as Adam or Noah. 3 One of the fathers of the Hebrew race, Abraham, Isaac, or Jacob. 4 A venerable man; esp. the founder of a religion. 5 A prelate in the early Roman Catholic church or in the modern Greek Church. [< Gk. *patria* family, clan + *archein*

to rule] —**pa·tri·ar′chal, pa′tri·ar′chic** *adj.*
—**pa′tri·ar′chal·ly** *adv.*

**pa·tri·cian** (pə·trish′ən) *n.* 1 A member of a
nobility; aristocrat. 2 A member of the aristocracy of ancient Rome. —*adj.* 1 Of or pertaining to an aristocracy. 2 Aristocratic;
having high rank. 3 Belonging to or suitable
for an aristocrat. [< L *pater, -tris* a senator,
lit., a father]

**pat·ri·cide** (pat′rə·sīd) *n.* 1 The killing of a father. 2 One who slays a father; a parricide.
—**pat′ri·ci′dal** *adj.*

**pat·ri·mo·ny** (pat′rə·mō′nē) *n. pl.* **·nies** 1 An
inheritance from a father or an ancestor. 2
An endowment of property to a church. 3
Any heritage. [< L *pater* a father] —**pat-
′ri·mo′ni·al** *adj.* —**pat′ri·mo′ni·al·ly** *adv.*

**pa·tri·ot** (pā′trē·ət, -ot) *n.* One who loves his
country and zealously guards its welfare. [<
Gk. *patris* fatherland] —**pa′tri·ot′ic** (-ot′ik)
*adj.* —**pa′tri·ot′i·cal·ly** *adv.*

**pa·tri·ot·ism** (pā′trē·ə·tiz′əm) *n.* Devotion to
one's country.

**pa·trol** (pə·trōl′) *v.t. & v.i.* **·trolled, ·trol·ling**
To walk or go through or around (an area,
town, etc.) for the purpose of guarding or
inspecting. —*n.* 1 One or more soldiers, po-
licemen, etc., patrolling a district. 2 A reconnaissance group of ships, planes, vehicles, or men on foot sent out to observe the
enemy. 3 The act of patrolling. 4 A small
unit of Boy Scouts. [< MF *patouiller,* orig.,
paddle in mud] —**pa·trol′ler** *n.*

**pa·tron** (pā′trən) *n.* 1 One who protects, fosters, or supports some person or thing;
benefactor. 2 A regular customer. 3 A saint
regarded as one's personal guardian. 4 One
who sponsors a charitable entertainment
or a cause. [< L *patronus* protector] —**pa′-
tron·al** *adj.* —**pa′tron·ess** *n. Fem.*

**pa·tron·age** (pā′trən·ij, pat′rən-) *n.* 1 Encouragement and support given by a patron. 2 Favor or support given with a condescending manner. 3 The power to make
appointments to certain positions or offices
in public service. 4 Such positions or offices. 5 The financial support given by customers to commercial enterprises.

**pa·tron·ize** (pā′trən·īz, pat′rən-) *v.t.* **·ized,
·iz·ing** 1 To give support or protection to. 2
To treat in a condescending manner. 3 To
trade with as a regular customer. —**pa′
tron·iz′er** *n.* —**pa′tron·iz′ing·ly** *adv.*

**pat·ter** (pat′ər) *v.t. & v.i.* To speak or say
glibly or rapidly. —*n.* 1 Glib and rapid talk,
as used by comedians, etc. 2 Patois or di-

alect. [Short for PATERNOSTER; from the rapid
repetition of the prayer] —**pat′ter·er** *n.*

**pat·tern** (pat′ərn) *n.* 1 An original or model
proposed for or worthy of imitation. 2 Anything shaped or designed to serve as a
model or guide in making something else.
3 Any decorative design or figure worked on
something: a vase with a geometrical *pattern.* 4 Arrangement of natural or accidental markings. 5 The stylistic composition or
design of a work of art. 6 A complex of integrated parts functioning as a whole: *patterns* of American culture. —*v.t.* 1 To make
after a model or pattern: with *on, upon,* or
*after.* 2 To decorate or furnish with a pattern. [< L *patronus* patron]

**pau·ci·ty** (pô′sə·tē) *n.* 1 Smallness of number
or quantity. 2 Scarcity; insufficiency. [< L
*paucus* few]

**pau·per** (pô′pər) *n.* 1 Any very poor person. 2
A destitute person who receives public
charity. [L, poor]

**pau·per·ize** (pô′pər·īz) *v.t.* **·ized, ·iz·ing** To
make a pauper of.

**pause** (pôz) *v.i.* **paused, paus·ing** 1 To cease
action or utterance temporarily. 2 To dwell
or linger: with *on* or *upon:* to *pause* on a
word. —*n.* 1 A ceasing of action. 2 A holding back because of doubt or irresolution.
3 A momentary cessation in speaking or
music for emphasis. 4 A character or sign
indicating such cessation. —**give (one)
pause** To cause (one) to hesitate or be uncertain, as from trepidation. [< L *pausa* a
stop] —**paus′er** *n.*

**pave** (pāv) *v.t.* **paved, pav·ing** To cover or surface with concrete, macadam, etc., as a
road. —**pave the way (for)** To make preparation (for); lead up to. [< L *pavire* ram
down]

**pave·ment** (pāv′mənt) *n.* 1 A hard, solid surface for a road or sidewalk, usu. resting
immediately on the ground. 2 A paved road
or sidewalk. 3 The material with which a
surface is paved.

**pa·vil·ion** (pə·vil′yən) *n.* 1 A movable or open
structure for temporary shelter. 2 A related
or connected part of a principal building:
the dancing *pavilion.* 3 A canopy or tent. 4
A detached building for patients, as at a
hospital. —*v.t.* 1 To provide with a pavilion
or pavilions. 2 To shelter by a pavilion. [< L
*papilio* a butterfly, tent]

**pawn** (pôn) *n.* 1 Any of the 16 chessmen of
lowest rank. 2 Any insignificant person

used at another's will. [< OF *peon, pedon* a foot soldier]

**pawn·brok·er** (pôn′brō′kər) *n.* One engaged in the business of lending money on pledged personal property. —**pawn′ brok′ ing** *n.*

**pay** (pā) *v.* **paid, pay·ing** *v.t.* **1** To give to (someone) what is due for a debt, purchase, etc. **2** To give (money, etc.) for a purchase, service rendered, etc. **3** To discharge, as a debt, bill, etc. **4** To yield as return or recompense. **5** To afford profit or benefit to. **6** To defray, as expenses. **7** To answer in kind; requite, as for a favor or an insult. **8** To render or give, as a compliment, attention, etc. **9** To make (a call or visit). —*v.i.* **10** To make recompense or payment. **11** To afford compensation or profit: It *pays* to be honest. —**pay back** To repay. —**pay off** **1** To pay the entire amount of. **2** To pay the wages of and discharge. **3** To gain revenge upon or for. **4** *Informal* To afford full return. **5** *Slang* To bribe. **6** *Naut.* To turn or cause to turn to leeward. —**pay out** **1** To disburse or expend. **2** *Naut.* To let out by slackening, as a rope or cable. —**pay up** To make full payment of. —*n.* **1** That which is given as a recompense or to discharge a debt. **2** That act of paying or the state of being paid. **3** Whatever compensates for labor or loss. —**in the pay of** Employed by: sometimes derogatory. —*adj.* **1** Of or pertaining to payments, persons who pay, or services paid for: *pay* day. **2** Yielding enough metal to be worth mining: *pay* dirt. [< L *pacare* appease<*pax* peace]

**pay·a·ble** (pā′ə·bəl) *adj.* **1** Due to be paid; owed. **2** That may be paid: *payable* on demand. —**pay′a·bly** *adv.*

**pay·load** (pā′lōd) *n.* **1** That part of a cargo producing revenue. **2** The explosive material in the warhead of a missile. **3** The persons, instruments, etc., carried in a spacecraft that are directly related to the objective of the flight rather than to the operation of the craft.

**pay·ment** (pā′mənt) *n.* **1** The act of paying. **2** Something that is paid. **3** Something done in requital.

**pea** (pē) *n.* **1** A tendril-climbing annual leguminous herb widely cultivated for food and fodder. **2** Its edible seed or green pod. **3** Any of various other plants of the same family or their pods or seeds, as the cowpea. [<L *pisum* pea]

**peace** (pēs) *n.* **1** The absence or cessation of war. **2** General order and tranquillity. **3** A state of reconciliation after strife or enmity. **4** Freedom from mental agitation or anxiety. —**hold** (or **keep**) **one's peace** To be silent. [< L *pax, pacis*] —Syn. **1** amity, concord. **3** agreement, reconciliation. **4** content, relaxation, repose.

**peace·a·ble** (pē′sə·bəl) *adj.* **1** Inclined to peace; accommodating; not combative. **2** Peaceful; tranquil. —**peace′a·ble·ness** *n.* —**peace′a·bly** *adv.*

**Peace Corps** A U.S. agency that recruits and trains volunteers who live and work in underdeveloped countries for a period of time.

**peace·ful** (pēs′fəl) *adj.* **1** Free from war, commotion, or other disturbance. **2** Inclined to be accommodating; not combative or pugnacious: a *peaceful* disposition. **3** Of or characteristic of peace or of a time of peace. **4** Serene; still: a *peaceful* scene. **5** Inclined to or used in peace. —**peace′ful·ly** *adv.* —**peace′ful·ness** *n.*

**pea·cock** (pē′kok) *n.* **1** A male peafowl, having a crested head, long erectile tail feathers marked with eyelike spots, and iridescent greenish blue neck and breast. **2** A person of excessive vanity. [< OE *pēa, pāwa* a peacock + cock] —**pea′cock·ish** *adj.*

**peak** (pēk) *n.* **1** A projecting point or edge; an end terminating in a point: the *peak* of a roof. **2 a** A mountain with a pointed summit. **b** The summit itself. **3** The highest point in a pattern of change or development: at the *peak* of his career. **4** A point formed on the forehead by the growth or cut of the hair. —*v.i.* **1** To reach a peak; climax. —*v.t.* **2** To raise to or almost to a vertical position. [?]

**peal** (pēl) *n.* **1** A prolonged, sonorous sound, as of a bell, trumpet, or thunder. **2** A set of large bells attuned to the major scale. **3** A change rung on a chime. —*v.t.* & *v.i.* To sound with a peal or peals. [< OF *apeler* call, appeal]

**pea·nut** (pē′nut′) *n.* **1** An annual, leguminous vine that bears underground pods containing one or more oily, edible seeds. **2** The seeds of this plant, with or without the brittle pod. **3** A small or insignificant person.

**pearl** (pûrl) *n.* **1** A lustrous calcareous concretion found in the shells of various mollusks, and valued as a gem. **2** Something like or likened to such a jewel in form, luster, etc. **3** Nacre or mother-of-pearl. **4** A delicate gray color: also **pearl gray**. **5** *Printing* A size of type, smaller than agate, 5 points

—*adj.* **1** Pertaining to or made of pearl or mother-of-pearl: a *pearl* button. **2** Shaped like a pearl. —*v.i.* **1** To seek or fish for pearls. **2** To form beads like pearls. [< OF *perle*] —**pearl′i·ness** *n.* —**pearl′y** *adj.* (·i·er, ·i·est)

**peas·ant** (pez′ənt) *n.* In Europe and Asia, a small farmer or farm laborer. [<OF *païs* country]

**pe·can** (pi·kan′, -kän′, pē′kan) *n.* **1** A species of hickory with olive-shaped, thin-shelled nuts. **2** The nut borne by this tree. [< Algon.]

**pe·cu·liar** (pi·kyōōl′yər) *adj.* **1** Odd or strange; queer; singular. **2** Having a character exclusively its own. **3** Select or special. **4** Belonging exclusively to one: a talent *peculiar* to him. [< L *peculiaris* < *peculium* private property] —**pe·cul′iar·ly** *adv.*

**pe·cu·li·ar·i·ty** (pi·kyōō′lē·ar′ə·tē, -kyōōl′yar′-) *n. pl.* ·ties **1** The quality of being peculiar. **2** Something that is odd or peculiar, as a trait. **3** A distinguishing trait: The thumb is a *peculiarity* of primates. —**Syn.** **2** eccentricity, idiosyncrasy, oddity. **3** attribute, characteristic.

**pe·cu·ni·ar·y** (pi·kyōō′nē·er′ē) *adj.* Consisting of or relating to money; monetary. [< L *pecunia* money < *pecus* cattle] —**pe·cu′ni·ar′i·ly** *adv.*

**ped·a·gogue** (ped′ə·gog, -gôg) *n.* A school teacher, esp. a pedantic, narrow-minded one. Also **ped′a·gog.** [< Gk. *pais* child + *agōgos* leader]

**ped·a·go·gy** (ped′ə·gō′jē, -goj′ē) *n.* **1** The science or profession of teaching. **2** The theory or the teaching of how to teach.

**ped·al** (ped′l) *adj.* Of or relating to a foot, feet, or a footlike part. —*n.* A lever operated by the foot, as that used to control the tone of a piano, organ, etc., or to govern the rate of movement of an automobile, bicycle, or a mechanical part. —*v.t. & v.i.* ·aled or ·alled, ·al·ing or ·al·ling To move or operate by working pedals. [< L *pes, pedis* the foot]

**ped·ant** (ped′ənt) *n.* **1** A scholar who makes needless display of his learning, esp. in trifling points of scholarship. **2** A dull, narrow-minded teacher. [< Ital. *pedante*] —**pe·dan·tic** (pi·dan′tik) *adj.* —**pe·dan′ti·cal·ly** *adv.*

**ped·ant·ry** (ped′ən·trē) *n. pl.* ·ries **1** Ostentatious display of knowledge. **2** Undue and slavish adherence to forms or rules.

**ped·es·tal** (ped′is·təl) *n.* **1** A base or support for a column, statue, or vase. **2** Any foun-

dation, base, or support, either material or immaterial. —**put on a pedestal** To hold in high estimation; idolize. [< Ital. *piè, pied* foot + *di* of + *stallo* a stall, standing place]

**pe·des·tri·an** (pə·des′trē·ən) *adj.* **1** Moving on foot. **2** Commonplace, prosaic, or dull. —*n.* One who journeys or moves from place to place on foot; a walker. [< L *pedester* on foot] —**pe·des′tri·an·ism** *n.*

**pe·di·at·rics** (pē′dē·at′riks, ped′ē-) *n. pl.* (*construed as sing.*) The branch of medicine dealing with the care and treatment of children and their diseases. [< Gk. *pais, paidos* a child + *iatros* healer] —**pe′di·at′ric** *adj.* —**pe·di·a·tri·cian** (-trish′ən), **pe′di·at′rist** *n.*

**ped·i·gree** (ped′ə·grē) *n.* **1** A line of ancestors; lineage. **2** A genealogical register, esp. of an animal of pure breed. [< MF *pié de grue* a crane's foot; from a mark denoting succession in pedigrees] —**ped′i·greed** *adj.*

**peek** (pēk) *v.i.* To look furtively, slyly, or quickly. —*n.* A peep; glance. [ME *piken*]

**peel** (pēl) *n.* The skin of certain fruits, as oranges, etc. —*v.t.* **1** To strip off the bark, skin, etc., of. **2** To strip off; remove. —*v.i.* **3** To lose bark, skin, etc. **4** To come off: said of bark, skin, etc. **5** *Slang* To undress. —**keep one's eye peeled** *Informal* To keep watch; be alert. —**peel off** *Aeron.* To veer off from a flight formation. [< OF *peler* to strip off skin]

**peep** (pēp) *v.i.* **1** To utter a small, sharp cry; chirp; cheep. **2** To speak in a weak, small voice. —*n.* The cry of a small bird or of certain frogs; chirp. [ME *pepen*] —**peep′er** *n.*

**peeping Tom** (tom) One who seeks to look at others clandestinely or from concealment, usu. for sexual pleasure. [< *Peeping Tom,* a tailor in English legend, struck blind because he peeped at the naked Lady Godiva]

**peer** (pir) *n.* **1** An equal, as in natural gifts or in social rank. **2** An equal before the law. **3** A noble, as a duke, marquis, earl, viscount, or baron. —**peer of the realm** Any British peer entitled to serve in the House of Lords. [< L *par* equal]

**peer·less** (pir′lis) *adj.* Of unequaled excellence. —**peer′less·ly** *adv.* —**peer′less·ness** *n.*

**peeve** (pēv) *v.t. & v.i.* peeved, peev·ing *Informal* To make or become peevish or irritable. —*n. Informal* A complaint; grievance. [Back formation < PEEVISH]

**pee·vish** (pē′vish) *adj.* **1** Irritable or fretful; cross. **2** Showing petulant discontent and

vexation. [ME *pevische*] —**pee·vish·ly** *adv.*
—**pee·vish·ness** *n.*

**pel·i·can** (pel′i·kən) *n.* Any of a genus of large, fish-eating, web-footed birds, having a distensible, membranous pouch on the lower bill for scooping up and holding fish. [< Gk. *pelekan*]

**pel·la·gra** (pə·lā′grə, -lag′rə) *n.* A chronic disease due to deficiency of niacin in the diet, marked by gastric disturbance, skin eruptions, and mental derangement. [Ital.] —**pel·la′grous** *adj.*

**pell-mell** (pel′mel′) *adv.* 1 In a confused or disorderly manner. 2 With a headlong rush. —*adj.* Devoid of order or method. —*n.* Confusion; disorder. Also **pell′mell′.** [< OF *pesle-mesle*]

**pelt** (pelt) *n.* 1 An undressed fur skin; raw hide. 2 *Slang* The human skin. [Prob. back formation < PELTRY]

**pel·vis** (pel′vis) *n. pl.* **·vis·es** or **·ves** (-vēz) 1 A basinlike or funnel-shaped structure. 2 The part of the skeleton that forms a bony girdle joining the lower or hind limbs to the body: also **pelvic arch, pelvic girdle.** [L. *basin*] —**pel′vic** *adj.*

**pe·nal** (pē′nəl) *adj.* 1 Of, relating to, or prescribing punishment: a *penal* code; a *penal* institution. 2 Liable, or rendering liable, to punishment. [< L *poena* a penalty]

**pen·al·ty** (pen′əl·tē) *n. pl.* **·ties** 1 The consequences that follow the breaking of any law, rule, or custom. 2 Judicial punishment for crime or violation of the law. 3 A handicap imposed for a violation of rules of a game. 4 Any unpleasant consequence: the *penalties* of a misspent life. [< L *poenalis* penal]

**pen·ance** (pen′əns) *n.* 1 *Eccl.* A sacramental rite involving contrition, confession to a priest, the acceptance of penalties, and absolution. 2 A feeling of sorrow for sin or fault, evinced by some outward act; repentance. —**do penance** To perform an act or acts of penance. [< L *paenitens* penitent]

**pen·chant** (pen′chənt) *n.* A strong leaning or inclination: a *penchant* for jotting down ideas on scraps of paper. [F < L *pendere* hang]

**pen·cil** (pen′səl) *n.* 1 A long, pointed strip of graphite, colored chalk, slate, etc., often encased in wood, used for writing or drawing. 2 Any slender instrument used for similar purposes. 3 A set of rays diverging from or converging to a point. 4 A small stick of any substance having caustic or styptic

properties. —*v.t.* **·ciled** or **·cilled,** **·cil·ing** or **·cil·ling** To mark, write, or draw with or as with a pencil. [< L *penicillum* a paint brush] —**pen′cil·er** or **pen′cil·ler** *n.*

**pend** (pend) *v.i.* To await or be in process of adjustment or settlement. [< L *pendere* hang]

**pen·dant** (pen′dənt) *n.* 1 Any hanging ornament, as an earring or locket. 2 A suspended chandelier. 3 An ornament hanging from a ceiling or roof. —*adj.* PENDENT. [< OF *pendre* hang]

**pen·du·lum** (pen′jōō·ləm, pen′də-) *n.* 1 A body suspended from a fixed point, and free to swing to and fro. 2 Such a device serving to regulate the rate of a clock. [< L *pendulus* hanging]

**pen·e·trate** (pen′ə·trāt) *v.* **·trat·ed,** **·trat·ing** *v.t.* 1 To force a way into or through; pierce. 2 To spread or diffuse itself throughout; permeate. 3 To perceive the meaning of; understand. 4 To affect profoundly. —*v.i.* 5 To enter or pass through something. 6 To have effect on the mind or emotions. [< L *penetrare* put within] —**pen′e·tra′tive** *adj.* —**pen′e·tra′tive·ly** *adv.*

**pen·e·tra·tion** (pen′ə·trā′shən) *n.* 1 The act or power of penetrating physically. 2 Ability to penetrate mentally; acuteness.

**pen·guin** (pen′gwin, peng′-) *n.* Any of various webfooted, flightless, aquatic birds of the southern hemisphere, with flipperlike wings.

**pen·i·cil·lin** (pen′ə·sil′in) *n.* An antibiotic found in a species of penicillium.

**pe·nin·su·la** (pə·nin′sə·lə, -syə-) *n.* An area of land almost surrounded by water, and connected with the mainland by an isthmus. [< L *paene* almost + *insula* an island] —**pe·nin′su·lar** *adj.* —**pe·nin·su·lar·i·ty** (pən·in′sə·lar′ə·tē, -syə-) *n.*

**pen·i·tence** (pen′ə·təns) *n.* Sorrow for sin, with desire to amend and atone. [< L *paenitare* repent]

**pen·i·tent** (pen′ə·tənt) *adj.* Affected by sorrow because of one's own guilt. —*n.* 1 One who is penitent. 2 One who confesses his sins to a priest and submits himself to the penance prescribed. —**pen′i·tent·ly** *adv.* —**Syn.** *adj.* contrite, remorseful, repentant, regretful.

**pen·i·ten·tia·ry** (pen′ə·ten′shər·ē) *n. pl.* **·ries** A prison, esp. a state or federal prison for those convicted of serious crimes. —*adj.* 1 Pertaining to penance. 2 Relating to or used for the punishment and discipline of criminals. 3 Rendering the offender liable to imprisonment in a penitentiary. [< L *paenitentia*]

**pen·nant** (pen′ənt) *n.* 1 A long, narrow flag displayed on ships or used as a signal. 2 A flag symbolizing a championship in certain sports competitions, as baseball. [< PENNON; infl. by PENDANT]

**pen·ni·less** (pen′i·lis) *adj.* 1 Being without even a penny. 2 Very poor. —**pen′ni·less·ly** *adv.* —**pen′ni·less·ness** *n.*

**pen·ny** (pen′ē) *n. pl.* **pen·nies** or *Brit.* **pence** (pens) 1 In the U.S. and Canada, a cent. 2 A coin of Great Britain, Ireland, and various members of the Commonwealth. 3 In the United Kingdom, a coin equal in value to 1/100 pound. 4 A piece of money. [< OE *penning, penig*] —**a pretty penny** *Informal* A large sum of money.

**pen·sion** (pān·syôn′) *n. French* 1 Room and board. 2 A boarding house. Also *Ital.* **pen·si·on·e** (pen·sē·ō′nä).

**pen·ta·gon** (pen′tə·gon) *n.* A figure with five angles and five sides. —**the Pentagon** 1 The military establishment of the U.S. 2 A five-sided building in Arlington, Va., housing the offices of the Department of Defense and the U.S. Armed Forces. [< Gk. *pentagōnon*] —**pen·tag′o·nal** (pen·tag′ə·nəl) *adj.* —**pen·tag′o·nal·ly** *adv.*

**pent·house** (pent′hous′) *n.* An apartment or dwelling on the roof of a building. [< OF *apentis*]

**pe·nu·ri·ous** (pə·n′ōōr′ē·əs) *adj.* Excessively sparing or saving in the use of money. —**pe·nu′ri·ous·ly** *adv.* —**pe·nu′ri·ous·ness** *n.* —Syn. frugal, miserly, stingy, tight-fisted.

**pen·u·ry** (pen′yə·rē) *n.* Extreme poverty or want. [< L *penuria* want]

**peo·ple** (pē′pəl) *n. pl.* **·ple** or (*for defs. 1 and 2*) **·ples** 1 The aggregate of human beings living under the same government: the *people* of England. 2 A body of human beings belonging to the same linguistic stock and having the same culture. 3 The whole body of persons composing a common class or profession. 4 Persons collectively: Who cares what *people* say? 5 The populace; public. 6 Subjects: A ruler cares for his *people.* 7 Family; relatives: Her *people* are from Ohio. 8 Human beings in general: Most *people* are friendly. —*v.t.* **·pled, ·pling** To fill with inhabitants; populate. [< L *populus* the populace] —**peo′pler** *n.*

**pep·per** (pep′ər) *n.* 1 A spice made from the black, dried berries of an East Indian climbing shrub. 2 CAYENNE PEPPER. 3 GREEN PEPPER. 4 Any plant yielding pepper. 5 *Informal* Spiciness; pungency; raciness. —*v.t.* 1 To sprinkle or season with pepper. 2 To sprinkle like pepper. 3 To shower, as with missiles; spatter. —*v.i.* 4 To discharge missiles at something. [< Gk. *peperi*]

**pep·sin** (pep′sin) *n.* 1 A digestive enzyme that acts on proteins in the stomach. 2 A preparation obtained from the stomachs of pigs, calves, etc., used to aid digestion. Also **pep′sine.** [< Gk. *pepsis* digestion]

**pep·tic** (pep′tik) *adj.* 1 Of, pertaining to, or promotive of digestion. 2 Of, pertaining to, or producing pepsin. 3 Pertaining to or connected with the action of digestive secretions: *peptic* ulcer. —*n.* An agent that promotes digestion. [< Gk. *peptein* to digest]

**per** (pûr) *prep.* 1 By; by means of; through. 2 For each: ten cents *per* yard. 3 *Informal* According to: *per* your memo. [L, through, by]

**per·ceive** (pər·sēv′) *v.t. & v.i.* **·ceived, ·ceiv·ing** 1 To become aware of (something) through the senses. 2 To come to understand; apprehend with the mind. [< L *per-* thoroughly + *capere* take] —**per·ceiv′a·bly** *adv.* —**per·ceiv′er** *n.*

**per·cent·age** (pər·sen′tij) *n.* 1 A part considered in its quantitative relation to the whole, expressed in hundredths. 2 A proportion; part. 3 A share or portion, as an allowance, commission, duty, interest, etc., that varies in proportion to some larger sum. 4 *Informal* Advantage; profit.

**per·cep·tion** (pər·sep′shən) *n.* 1 The act, power, process, or product of perceiving. 2 Cognition of fact or truth; appreciation. 3 a Knowledge acquired through the senses. b The process of acquiring such knowledge. c The mental product so obtained; percept. 4 Insight or intuitive judgment. [< L *percipere* perceive] —**per·cep′tion·al** *adj.*

**per·co·late** (pûr′kə·lāt) *v.t. & v.i.* **·lat·ed, ·lat·ing** 1 To pass or cause to pass through fine pores or openings; filter. 2 To brew (coffee) in a percolator. —*n.* That which has percolated; a filtered liquid. [< L *per-* through + *colare* to strain] —**per′co·la′tion** *n.*

**per·cus·sion** (pər·kush′ən) *n.* 1 The impact of one body against another, as that of the hammer against the percussion cap in a firearm. 2 The impression of sound upon the ear. 3 *Med.* A tapping on the back, chest, etc., for diagnosing the condition of the organ beneath. **4** Those musical instruments, collectively, whose tone is produced by striking or hitting, as the timpani, piano, etc. [< L *per-* thoroughly + *quatere* to shake] —**per·cus′sive** (-kus′ĭv) *adj.* —**per·cus′sive·ly** *adv.* —**per·cus′sive·ness** *n.*

**per·di·tion** (pər-dish′ən) *n.* **1** *Theol.* Future misery or eternal death as the condition of the wicked; hell. **2** *Archaic* Utter destruction or ruin. [< L *perdere* destroy, lose]

**per·emp·to·ry** (pə-remp′tər-ē) *adj.* **1** *Law* Precluding or putting an end to debate or discussion; final. **2** Not admitting of debate or appeal; decisive; absolute. **3** Opinionated; dogmatic. [< L *peremptorius* destructive] —**per·emp′to·ri·ly** *adv.* —**per·emp′to·ri·ness** *n.*

**per·en·ni·al** (pə-ren′ē-əl) *adj.* **1** Continuing or enduring through the year. **2** Enduring, unceasing, or recurrent. **3** *Bot.* Lasting more than two years. —*n.* A perennial plant. [< L *per-* through + *annus* a year] —**per·en′ni·al·ly** *adv.*

**per·fect** (pûr′fĭkt) *adj.* **1** Having all the qualities or elements requisite to its nature or kind; complete. **2** Thoroughly qualified or informed; skilled: a *perfect* teacher. **3** Correct, exact, or accurate: a *perfect* replica. **4** Meeting all requirements; lacking no essential: a *perfect* antidote. **5** *Informal* Excessive in degree; very great: She has a *perfect* horror of spiders. **6** Total; utter: a *perfect* idiot. **7** *Gram.* Denoting the tense of a verb expressing action completed at the time of speaking or in the past. In English, the perfect tenses include a *present perfect*, *past perfect* (or *pluperfect*), and a *future perfect* tense. **8** *Music* Denoting a fifth containing seven semitones or a fourth containing five semitones. —*n. Gram.* The perfect tense, or a verb in this tense. —*v.t.* (pər-fekt′) **1** To bring to perfection; complete; finish. **2** To make thoroughly skilled or accomplished: to *perfect* oneself in art. [< L *per-* thoroughly + *facere* do, make] —**per·fect′i·bil′i·ty** *n.* —**per·fect′i·ble** *adj.* —**per′fect·ly** *adv.*

**per·fid·i·ous** (pər-fĭd′ē-əs) *adj.* Of or characterized by perfidy. —**per·fid′i·ous·ly** *adv.* —**per·fid′i·ous·ness** *n.*

**per·fi·dy** (pûr′fə-dē) *n. pl.* ·**dies** The deliberate violation of faith or trust. [< L *perfidia*] —Syn. treachery, disloyalty, betrayal, faithlessness.

**per·fo·rate** (pûr′fə-rāt) *v.t.* ·**rat·ed**, ·**rat·ing 1** To make a hole or holes through, by or as by stamping or drilling. **2** To pierce with holes in rows or patterns, as sheets of stamps, etc. —*adj.* (-rĭt) Pierced with a hole or a series of holes. [< L *per-* through + *forare* to bore] —**per′fo·rat′ed** *adj.* —**per′fo·ra′tor** *n.*

**per·fo·ra·tion** (pûr′fə-rā′shən) *n.* **1** A perforating or state of being perforated. **2** A hole or series of holes drilled in or stamped through something.

**per·form** (pər-fôrm′) *v.t.* **1** To execute; do: to *perform* an operation. **2** To act in accord with the requirements or obligations of; fulfill; discharge, as a duty or promise. **3** To act (a part) or give a performance of (a play, piece of music, etc.). —*v.i.* **4** To carry through to completion. **5** To give an exhibition or performance. [< OF *par-* thoroughly + *fournir* accomplish, furnish] —**per·form′er** *n.*

**per·form·ance** (pər-fôr′məns) *n.* **1** The act of performing. **2** Something performed; deed, feat, etc. **3** The ability to perform; also, the effectiveness of performance. **4** A presentation before spectators; any entertainment: two *performances* daily.

**per·fume** (pûr′fyōōm, pər-fyōōm′) *n.* **1** A pleasant odor, as from flowers; fragrance. **2** A fragrant substance, usu. a volatile liquid, prepared to emit a pleasant odor; scent. —*v.t.* (pər-fyōōm′) **·fumed**, **·fum·ing** To give a fragrant odor to; scent. [< Ital. *perfumare*, lit., impregnate with smoke]

**per·func·to·ry** (pər-fungk′tər-ē) *adj.* **1** Done mechanically or routinely; superficial. **2** Without interest or concern; apathetic. [< L *per-* through + *fungi* perform] —**per·func′to·ri·ly** *adv.* —**per·func′to·ri·ness** *n.*

**per·il** (per′əl) *n.* Exposure to the chance of injury, loss, or destruction. —*v.t.* **·iled** or **·illed**, **·il·ing** or **·il·ling** To expose to danger. [< L *periculum* trial, danger] —Syn. *n.* danger, jeopardy, risk, insecurity. *v.* imperil, endanger, jeopardize, risk.

**per·il·ous** (per′əl·əs) *adj.* Full of, involving, or attended with peril. —**per′il·ous·ly** *adv.* —**per′il·ous·ness** *n.*

**pe·rim·e·ter** (pə-rim′ə-tər) *n.* **1** *Math.* The bounding line or curve of a plane area. **2** *Math.* The measure of this line or curve. **3** A strip or boundary defining or protecting an area. [< Gk. *peri* around + *metron* a measure] —**per′i·met′ric** (per′ə-met′rik) or **·ri·cal** *adj.* —**per′i·met′ri·cal·ly** *adv.*

**pe·ri·od** (pir′ē·əd) *n.* **1** A portion of time

marked and defined by certain events or phenomena, or by the existence of a specific culture. **2** A portion of time between successive occurrences of some astronomical event. **3** A portion of time between certain events: the *period* between the two World Wars. **4** A conclusion or end, as of any sequence of years, events, acts, or phenomena. **5** A portion of time marking one of the divisions of a game, academic day, etc. **6** *Med.* The course of a disease or one of its phases. **7** MENSES. **8** *Gram.* A sentence, esp. a well-constructed complex sentence. **9** The full pause in speaking at the end of a sentence. **10** A dot (.) used in writing as a mark of punctuation after every complete declarative sentence and after most abbreviations. **11** *Geol.* A division of geologic time that may contain two or more epochs. **12** *Physics* The time between two successive similar phases of a wave or oscillation. [<Gk. *periodos* a going around.]

**pe·ri·od·ic** (pir′ē·od′ik) *adj.* **1** Of, pertaining to, or of the nature of a period. **2** Happening or recurring at regular intervals. **3** Happening now and then; intermittent. **4** Repeating exactly after a given interval, as a mathematical function, physical variable, etc. **5** Of, expressed in, or characterized by periodic sentences.

**pe·ri·od·i·cal** (pir′ē·od′i·kəl) *adj.* **1** PERIODIC (def. 2). **2** Pertaining to publications, as magazines, professional journals, etc., that are published at fixed intervals of more than one day. **3** Published at such intervals. —*n.* A publication, usu. a magazine, appearing at such fixed intervals. —**pe′ri·od′i·cal·ly** *adv.*

**pe·riph·er·y** (pə·rif′ər·ē) *n. pl.* **·er·ies 1** The outer bounds of any surface or area. **2** The surface of the body. **3** PERIMETER (def. 1). **4** A surrounding region, country, or area. [<Gk. *peripchereia* circumference]

**per·i·scope** (per′ə·skōp) *n.* An instrument capable of reflecting an image down a vertical tube. [< PERI- + -SCOPE] —**per′i·scop′ic** or **·i·cal** (-skop′i·kəl) *adj.*

**per·ish** (per′ish) *v.i.* **1** To die, esp. to suffer a violent or untimely death. **2** To be destroyed; pass from existence. [< L *per* away + *ire* go]

**per·ish·a·ble** (per′ish·ə·bəl) *adj.* **1** Liable to perish. **2** Liable to speedy decay, as fruit in transportation. —*n.pl.* Goods liable to rapid decay: used chiefly of foods in transit. —**per′ish·a·bil′i·ty, per′ish·a·ble·ness** *n.* —**per′ish·a·bly** *adv.*

**per·jure** (pûr′jər) *v.t.* **·jured, ·jur·ing** To make (oneself) guilty of perjury. [< L *per-* through, badly + *jurare* swear] —**per′jur·er** *n.*

**per·ju·ry** (pûr′jə·rē) *n. pl.* **·ries 1** *Law* The willful giving of false testimony while under lawfully administered oath. **2** The breaking of any oath, vow, or promise.

**per·ma·nence** (pûr′mə·nəns) *n.* The state of being permanent; durability; fixity.

**per·ma·nent** (pûr′mə·nənt) *adj.* Continuing or intended to continue in the same state or without essential change. —*n.* PERMANENT WAVE. [< L *per-* through + *manere* remain] —**per′ma·nent·ly** *adv.* —**Syn.** durable, stable, fixed, lasting.

**per·me·ate** (pûr′mē·āt) *v.* **·at·ed, ·at·ing** *v.t.* **1** To spread thoroughly through; pervade. **2** To pass through the pores or interstices of. —*v.i.* To spread itself through something. [< L *per-* through + *meare* to pass] —**per′me·a′tion** *n.* —**per′me·a′tive** *adj.*

**per·mis·si·ble** (pər·mis′ə·bəl) *adj.* That can be permitted; allowable. —**per·mis′si·bil′i·ty** *n.* —**per·mis′si·bly** *adv.*

**per·mis·sion** (pər·mish′ən) *n.* The act of permitting or allowing; formal authorization; consent.

**per·mis·sive** (pər·mis′iv) *adj.* **1** That permits; granting permission. **2** That is permitted; optional. **3** Tolerant; lenient; indulgent: *permissive* parents. —**per·mis′sive·ly** *adv.* —**per·mis′sive·ness** *n.*

**per·mit** (pər·mit′) *v.* **·mit·ted, ·mit·ting** *v.t.* **1** To allow the doing of; consent to. **2** To give (someone) leave or consent; authorize. **3** To afford opportunity for: His answer *permits* no misinterpretation. —*v.i.* **4** To afford possibility or opportunity. —*n.* (pûr′mit) **1** Permission or warrant. **2** A formal, written authorization to do something. [< L *per-* through + *mittere* send, let go] —**per·mit′ter** *n.*

**per·mu·ta·tion** (pûr′myōō·tā′shən) *n.* **1** The act of permuting; transformation. **2** *Math.* **a** Change in the order of the elements of a set. **b** Any one of the set of arrangements that can be produced in this way.

**per·ni·cious** (pər·nish′əs) *adj.* **1** Destructive; deadly. **2** *Archaic* Malicious; wicked. [< L *per-* thoroughly + *nex, necis* death] —**per·ni′cious·ly** *adv.* —**per·ni′cious·ness** *n.*

**per·o·ra·tion** (per′ə·rā′shən) *n.* The concluding portion of an oration; the recapitulation of an argument.

**per·pen·dic·u·lar** (pûr′pən·dik′yə·lər) *adj.* **1** Being at right angles to the plane of the horizon; upright or vertical. 2 *Math.* Meeting a given line or plane at right angles. —*n.* 1 A perpendicular line. 2 A device used to indicate the vertical line from any point. 3 A vertical line or vertical face. 4 Perpendicular position. [< L *perpendiculum* a plumb line] —**per′pen·dic′u·lar′i·ty** (-lar′ə·tē) *n.* —**per′pen·dic′u·lar·ly** *adv.*

**per·pe·trate** (pûr′pə·trāt) *v.t.* ·**trat·ed**, ·**trat·ing** To perform or commit (a crime, etc.). [< L *perpetrare* carry through] —**per′pe·tra′tion**, **per′pe·tra′tor** *n.*

**per·pet·u·al** (pər·pech′o͞o·əl) *adj.* 1 Continuing for all time. 2 Happening continually; repeated ceaselessly. [< L *per-* through + *petere* seek] —**per·pet′u·al·ly** *adv.* —**per·pet′u·al·ness** *n.*

**per·pet·u·ate** (pər·pech′o͞o·āt) *v.t.* ·**at·ed**, ·**at·ing** To make perpetual or enduring. —**per·pet′u·a′tion**, **per·pet′u·a′tor** *n.*

**per·pe·tu·i·ty** (pûr′pə·t′o͞o′ə·tē) *n.* *pl.* ·**ties** 1 The quality or state or being perpetual. 2 Something that has perpetual existence or worth, as an annuity that is to be paid for life. 3 Unending or unlimited time.

**per·plex** (pər·pleks′) *v.t.* 1 To cause to hesitate, as from doubt; confuse; puzzle. 2 To make complicated, intricate, or confusing. [< L *per* thoroughly + *plectere* to twist] —**per·plexed′** *adj.* —**per·plex′ed·ly** (-plek′sid·lē) *adv.*

**per·plex·i·ty** (pər·plek′sə·tē) *n.* *pl.* ·**ties** 1 The state of being perplexed; bewilderment; confusion, etc. 2 That which perplexes; also, an instance of bewilderment.

**per·qui·site** (pûr′kwə·zit) *n.* 1 Any incidental profit from service beyond salary or wages. 2 A privilege or benefit claimed as due. [< L *perquisitum* a thing diligently sought]

**per·se·cute** (pûr′sə·kyo͞ot) *v.t.* ·**cut·ed**, ·**cut·ing** 1 To harass with cruel or oppressive treatment, esp. because of race, religion, or opinions. 2 To annoy or harass persistently. [< L *per-* thoroughly + *sequi* follow] —**per′se·cu′tion**, **per′se·cu′tor** *n.* —**per′se·cu′tion·al**, **per′se·cu′tive** *adj.*

**per·se·ver·ance** (pûr′sə·vir′əns) *n.* 1 The act or habit of persevering. 2 Steadfastness; tenacity.

**per·se·vere** (pûr′sə·vir′) *v.i.* ·**vered**, ·**ver·ing** To persist in any purpose or enterprise; continue striving in spite of opposition, difficulty, etc. [< L *per-* thoroughly + *severus* strict] —**per′se·ver′ing·ly** *adv.* —**Syn.** endure, carry on, strive, hold out.

**per·sim·mon** (pər·sim′ən) *n.* 1 A tree related

to ebony with astringent, plumlike fruit. 2 The fruit of this tree. [< Algon.]

**per·sist** (pər·sist′, -zist′) *v.i.* 1 To continue firmly in some course, state, etc., esp. despite opposition or difficulties. 2 To be insistent, as in repeating a statement. 3 To continue to exist; endure. [< L *per-* thoroughly + *sistere* to stand]

**per·sis·tence** (pər·sis′təns, -zis′-) *n.* 1 The act of persisting. 2 The quality of being persistent; perseverance. 3 The continuance of an effect longer than the cause that first produced it.

**per·son** (pûr′sən) *n.* 1 A human being; an individual. 2 The body of a human being or its characteristic appearance and condition. 3 The personality of a human being; self. 4 *Law* Any human being, corporation, or other legal entity having legal rights and responsibilities. 5 *Gram.* a A modification of the pronoun and verb that distinguishes the speaker (**first person**), the person or thing spoken to (**second person**), and the person or thing spoken of (**third person**). b Any of the forms or inflections indicating this, as *I* or *we, you, he, she, it.* —**in person** Present in the flesh; in bodily presence. [< L *persona* mask for actors]

**per·son·age** (pûr′sən·ij) *n.* 1 A person of importance or rank. 2 Any person. 3 A character in fiction, history, etc. [< L *persona* a person]

**per·son·al** (pûr′sən·əl) *adj.* 1 Of, pertaining to, characteristic of, or affecting a person. 2 Performed by or done to the person directly concerned. 3 Carried on directly by the persons concerned. 4 Of or pertaining to the body or appearance: *personal* beauty. 5 Directly relating to a person's character, conduct, personal affairs or habits, etc. 6 Making or tending to make personal remarks or to ask personal questions, esp. of a derogatory nature. 7 *Law* Of, pertaining to, or constituting personal property. 8 *Gram.* Denoting or indicating grammatical person. —*n.* A news item or advertisement that is personal in nature.

**per·son·al·i·ty** (pûr′sən·al′ə·tē) *n.* *pl.* ·**ties** 1 The state or quality of being a person, esp. a particular person. 2 Those special characteristics that distinguish a person, a group, or a nation. 3 The sum of such characteristics as they impress or tend to impress others. 4 Excellent or distinctive traits of character, sociability, etc. 5 A person having such traits. 6 A person who is famous or notorious. 7 *Usu. pl.* A remark, esp. one that is personally disparaging.

**per·son·i·fi·ca·tion** (pər·son´ə·fə·kā´shən) *n.* 1 The endowment of inanimate objects or qualities with human attributes. 2 Striking or typical exemplification of a quality in one's person; embodiment: She was the *personification* of joy. 3 The representation of an abstract quality or idea by a human figure.

**per·son·i·fy** (pər·son´ə·fī) *v.t.* ·fied, ·fy·ing 1 To think of or represent as having life or human qualities. 2 To represent (an abstraction or inanimate object) as a person; symbolize. 3 To be the embodiment of; typify. [< L *persona* a mask, person + *facere* make] —**per·son´i·fi´er** *n.*

**per·son·nel** (pûr´sə·nel´) *n.* 1 Persons collectively. 2 The persons employed in a business or in military service. • *Personnel*, when it is construed as a unit, takes a singular verb: *The company's personnel has been cut.* When the term refers to the individuals that make up a unit, it takes a plural verb: *All personnel were requested to donate blood.*

**per·spec·tive** (pər·spek´tiv) *n.* 1 The art or theory of representing, by a drawing made on a flat or curved surface, solid objects or surfaces conceived of as not lying in that surface. 2 The art of conveying the impression of depth and distance by means of correct drawing, shading, etc. 3 The effect of distance upon the appearance of objects, by means of which the eye judges spatial relations. 4 The relative importance of facts or matters from any special point of view; also, the ability to discern this relative importance. 5 A distant view; vista; prospect. —*adj.* 1 Of or pertaining to perspective. 2 Drawn in perspective. [< L *per-* through + *specere* look] —**per·spec´tive·ly** *adv.*

**per·spi·ca·cious** (pûr´spə·kā´shəs) *adj.* Keenly discerning or understanding. [< L *perspicax* sharp-sighted] —**per´spi·ca´cious·ly** *adv.* —**per´spi·ca´cious·ness**, **per´spi·cac´i·ty** (-kas´ə·tē) *n.*

**per·spi·ra·tion** (pûr´spə·rā´shən) *n.* 1 The exuding of the saline fluid secreted by the sweat glands of the skin. 2 The saline fluid excreted; sweat. —**per·spir·a·to·ry** (pər·spī´rə·tôr´ē, -tō´rē, pûr´spə-) *adj.*

**per·spire** (pər·spīr´) *v.* ·spired, ·spir·ing *v.i.* 1 To give off perspiration through the pores of the skin; sweat. —*v.t.* 2 To give off

through pores; exude. [< L *per-* through + *spirare* breathe] —**per·spir´a·ble** *adj.*

**per·suade** (pər·swād´) *v.t.* ·suad·ed, ·suad·ing 1 To move (a person, etc.) to do something by arguments, inducements, pleas, etc. 2 To induce to a belief; convince. [< L *per-* thoroughly + *suadere* advise] —**per·suad´a·ble** *adj.* —**per·suad´er** *n.*

**per·sua·sion** (pər·swā´zhən) *n.* 1 The act of persuading. 2 The state of being persuaded; conviction. 3 The power to persuade; persuasiveness. 4 A particular sect, denomination, etc. 5 *Informal* Sort; kind: the male *persuasion.*

**per·sua·sive** (pər·swā´siv) *adj.* Having the power or tendency to persuade. —**per·sua´sive·ly** *adv.* —**per·sua´sive·ness** *n.* —**Syn.** convincing, influential, assuring, cogent.

**per·tain** (pər·tān´) *v.i.* 1 To have reference; relate. 2 To belong to as an adjunct, function, quality, etc. 3 To be fitting or appropriate. [< L *pertinere* extend]

**per·ti·na·cious** (pûr´tə·nā´shəs) *adj.* 1 Marked by a dogged or even perverse firmness, as of purpose. 2 Stubbornly tenacious; hard to get rid of. [< L *per-* thoroughly, very + *tenax* tenacious] —**per´ti·na´cious·ly** *adv.* —**per´ti·na´cious·ness**, **per´ti·nac´i·ty** (-nas´ə·tē) *n.*

**per·ti·nent** (pûr´tə·nənt) *adj.* Related to or properly bearing upon the matter in hand; relevant. [< OF *partenir* pertain] —**per´ti·nence**, **per´ti·nen·cy** *n.* —**per´ti·nent·ly** *adv.*

**per·turb** (pər·tûrb´) *v.t.* 1 To disquiet or disturb greatly; alarm; agitate. 2 To cause confusion or disorder in. [<L *per-* thoroughly + *turbare* disturb] —**per´tur·ba´tion** *n.*

**pe·ruse** (pə·rōōz´) *v.t.* ·rused, ·rus·ing 1 To read carefully or attentively. 2 To read. 3 To examine; scrutinize. [< PER- + USE, *v.*] —**pe·rus´a·ble** *adj.* —**pe·ru´sal**, **pe·rus´er** *n.*

**per·vade** (pər·vād´) *v.t.* ·vad·ed, ·vad·ing To pass or spread through every part of; be diffused throughout; permeate. [< L *per-* through + *vadere* go] —**per·va´sion** (-zhən) *n.*

**per·verse** (pər·vûrs´) *adj.* 1 Different or varying from the correct or normal. 2 Wicked; corrupt. 3 Obstinate and unreasonable in resisting what is reasonable, accepted, etc. 4 Petulant; peevish. [< L *pervertere* turn the wrong way] —**per·verse´ly** *adv.* —**per·verse´ness**, **per·ver´si·ty** *n.* —**per·ver´sive** *adj.*

**per·ver·sion** (pər·vûr´zhən, -shən) *n.* 1 The act of perverting, or the state of being per-

verted. 2 Something perverted. 3 A deviation from the normal, esp. in sexual desires or activities.

**per·vert** (pər·vûrt′) *v.t.* 1 To turn to an improper use or purpose; misapply. 2 To distort the meaning of; misconstrue. 3 To turn
from approved opinions or conduct; lead
astray; corrupt. —*n.* (pûr′vûrt) A person
who is perverted, esp. one affected with or
addicted to sexual perversion. [< L *per*-
away + *vertere* turn] —**per·vert′er** *n.* —**per·
vert′i·ble** *adj.*

**pes·si·mism** (pes′ə·miz′əm) *n.* 1 A disposition to expect the worst possible conclusion
of the course of events or of the resolution
of present uncertainties or conditions. 2
The philosophical doctrine that the world
as it exists is basically evil. 3 The belief that
the evils in life outweigh the good and the
happiness. [< L *pessimus* worst + -ISM] —
**pes′si·mist** *n.* —**pes′si·mis′tic** *adj.* —**pes′
si·mis′ti·cal·ly** *adv.*

**pes·ti·cide** (pes′tə·sīd) *n.* A chemical used to
destroy weeds or vermin. —**pes′ti·ci′dal**
*adj.*

**pes·ti·lence** (pes′tə·ləns) *n.* 1 Any widespread
infectious malady. 2 A dangerous or harmful doctrine, influence, etc. [< L *pestis* a
plague] —**pes′ti·lent, pes′ti·len′tial** (-shəl)
*adj.* —**pes′ti·lent·ly, pes′ti·len′tial·ly** *adv.*

**pes·tle** (pes′əl) *n.* 1 An implement used for
crushing or mixing substances, as in a
mortar. 2 A vertical moving bar employed in
pounding, as in a stamp mill, etc. —*v.t.* &
*v.i.* **·tled, ·tling** To pound, grind, or mix with
or as with a pestle. [< L *pistillum*]

**pet** (pet) *n.* 1 A tamed or domesticated animal
that is treated with affection. 2 Any person
who is treated with affection or to whom
great attention is paid. —*adj.* 1 Being or
treated like a pet. 2 Regarded as a favorite;
cherished: my *pet* hobby. —*v.* **pet·ted,
pet·ting** —*v.t.* 1 To pamper; indulge. 2 To
stroke or caress. —*v.i.* 3 *Informal* To kiss
and caress or fondle in making love. [?]

**pet·al** (pet′l) *n. Bot.* A division of a corolla. [<
Gk. *petalon* a thin plate, leaf] —**pet′aled** or
**pet′alled** *adj*

**pe·ti·tion** (pə·tish′ən) *n.* 1 A request, supplication, or prayer; a solemn or formal supplication. 2 A formal request, written or
printed, setting forth such a request, addressed to a person or persons in authority and often signed by a group of petition-
ers. 3 *Law* A formal application in writing
made to a court, requesting judicial action

concerning some matter therein set forth.
4 That which is requested or asked for. —
*v.t.* 1 To make a petition to; entreat. 2 To
ask for. —*v.i.* 3 To make a petition. [< L <
*petere* seek] —**pe·ti′tion·ar′y** *adj.* —**pe·ti′
tion·er** *n.*

**pet·ri·fy** (pet′rə·fī) *v.* **·fied, ·fy·ing** *v.t.* To replace (organic material) with stony miner-
als. 2 To make fixed and unyielding;
harden. 3 To immobilize with fear, surprise,
etc. —*v.i.* 4 To become stone or a stony substance. [< L *petra* a rock + *facere* make] —
**pet′ri·fac′tion** (-fak′shən), pet′ri·fi·ca′tion**
*n.* —**pet′ri·fac′tive** *adj.*

**pe·tro·le·um** (pə·trō′lē·əm) *n.* An oily, liquid
mixture of hydrocarbons found in scattered
subterranean deposits, and used as a
source of fuels, as gasoline, kerosene, etc.
and as raw material for many synthetic
products. [< L *petra* rock + *oleum* oil]

**pet·ti·coat** (pet′ē·kōt) *n.* 1 A skirt, esp. an un-
derskirt worn by young girls and women. 2
*Informal* A girl or woman. —*adj.* Of, pertaining to, or influenced by, women: *petticoat* politics. [< PETTY + COAT]

**pet·ty** (pet′ē) *adj.* **·ti·er, ·ti·est** 1 Having little
worth, importance, position, or rank. 2
Having little generosity; small-minded;
mean; spiteful. [< OF *petit* small] —**pet′ti·ly**
*adv.* —**pet′ti·ness** *n.*

**pet·u·lant** (pech′ōō·lənt) *adj.* Displaying or
characterized by bad humor, esp. over a
minor irritation. [< L *petulans* forward] —
**pet′u·lance, pet′u·lan·cy** *n.* —**pet′u·lant·ly**
*adv.* —**Syn.** fretful, peevish, grumpy, com-
plaining.

**pew** (pyōō) *n.* 1 A bench with a back for seating people in church. 2 A boxlike enclosure
with seats, for seating a family or other
group in a church. [< L *podium* balcony]

**pew·ter** (pyōō′tər) *n.* 1 An alloy of tin with
lead and other metals. 2 Tableware, etc.,
made of pewter. —*adj.* Made of pewter. [<
OF *peutre*]

**phan·tasm** (fan′taz·əm) *n.* 1 A figment of the
imagination, as a ghost or specter. 2 A deceptive likeness or appearance. —**phan·
tas′mal, phan·tas′mic,** *adj.*

**phan·tom** (fan′təm) *n.* 1 Something that exists only in appearance; illusion. 2 An apparition; specter. 3 Something dreaded or
feared. 4 The visible representative of an
abstract state or incorporeal person. —*adj.*
Of, like, or being a phantom. [< Gk. *phan-
tasma* an appearance]

**Phar·i·see** (far′ə·sē) *n.* One of an ancient, exclusive Jewish sect that paid excessive regard to tradition and ceremonies, and in so doing separated themselves from the other Jews. [< Heb. *pārūsh* separated]

**phar·ma·cy** (fär′mə·sē) n. pl. **·cies** 1 The art or business of compounding and dispensing medicines. 2 A drugstore. [< Gk. *pharmakon* a drug]

**phar·ynx** (far′ingks) n. pl. **pha·ryn·ges** (fə·rin′jēz) or **phar·ynx·es** The tract between the palate and the esophagus, serving as a passage for air and food. [Gk., throat]

**phase** (fāz) n. 1 Any one of the aspects, parts, etc., that are a distinguishable part of a cycle, development, etc. 2 *Astron.* One of the appearances or forms presented periodically by the moon and planets. 3 *Physics* a A stage in a periodic process or phenomenon, as an oscillation, wave, etc. b Any homogeneous form of a given substance that may occur alone, or exist independently as a component of a heterogeneous system, as ice in water, etc. 4 *Biol.* Any distinct stage in the reproduction, growth, development, or life pattern of a cell or organism. —**in phase** Having the same phase at a given time and place, as two waves. —v.t. **phased, phas·ing** To accomplish in planned phases. —**phase down** To reduce or lessen in planned phases. —**phase in** To introduce in planned phases. —**phase out** To terminate work on, production of, etc., step by step, according to plan. [< Gk. *phasis* an appearance] —**pha·sic** (fā′zik) adj.

**pheas·ant** (fez′ənt) n. 1 A long-tailed chicken-like bird noted for the gorgeous plumage of the male. 2 One of various other birds, as the ruffed grouse. [< Gk. *Phasianos (ornis)* (bird) of Phasis, a river in the Caucasus]

**phe·nom·e·nal** (fi·nom′ə·nəl) adj. 1 Of, pertaining to, or being a phenomenon. 2 Extraordinary or marvelous. —**phe·nom′e·nal·ly** adv.

**phe·nom·e·non** (fi·nom′ə·non) n. pl. **·na** (-nə) or, *for defs. 3 and 4,* **·nons** 1 A fact, event, etc., that can be explained on the basis of scientific principles, as a lunar eclipse. 2 Any fact, appearance, etc., as it is apprehended by the senses, in contrast with or in opposition to the thing in itself. 3 Any unusual fact, thing, occurrence, etc. 4 An unusual, exceptional, or extraordinary person; prodigy. [< Gk. *phainomenon* an appearance]

**phi·lan·thro·py** (fi·lan′thrə·pē) n. pl. **·pies** 1 The disposition or effort to promote the well-being of mankind, as by making donations to charities, working for the improvement of social conditions, etc. 2 A charitable donation, work for the improvement of social conditions, etc. 3 An organization devoted to charity, social improvement, etc. [< Gk. *phileein* love + *anthropos* man] —**phil·an·throp·ic** (fil′ən·throp′ik) or **·i·cal** adj. —**phil′an·throp′i·cal·ly** adv. —**phi·lan′thro·pist** n. —Syn. 1 benevolence, charity, generosity, munificence.

**phi·lat·e·ly** (fi·lat′ə·lē) n. The study and collection of postage stamps, stamped envelopes, wrappers, etc.; stamp collecting. [< Gk. *philos* loving + *ateleia* exemption from tax; with ref. to prepaid postage] —**phil·a·tel·ic** (fil′ə·tel′ik) or **·i·cal** adj. —**phil′a·tel′i·cal·ly** adv. —**phi·lat′e·list** n.

**phi·lol·o·gy** (fi·lol′ə·jē) n. 1 The scientific study of written records, esp. literary works, to determine their meaning, authenticity, etc. 2 LINGUISTICS. 3 Literary scholarship. [< Gk. *philos* fond + *logos* a word] —**phil·o·log·ic** (fil′ə·loj′ik) or **·i·cal** adj. —**phil′o·log′i·cal·ly** adv. —**phi·lol′o·gist** n.

**phi·los·o·pher** (fi·los′ə·fər) n. 1 A student of or a specialist in philosophy. 2 The creator of a system of philosophy. 3 A person who is reasonable, calm, patient, etc., under all circumstances.

**phi·los·o·phize** (fi·los′ə·fīz) v.i. **·phized, ·phiz·ing** To speculate like a philosopher; seek ultimate causes and principles. —**phi·los′o·phiz′er** n.

**phi·los·o·phy** (fi·los′ə·fē) n. pl. **·phies** 1 The search for knowledge of general principles; the study of the elements, powers, or causes and laws that explain facts and existences. 2 A philosophical system or treatise based on such a search or study. 3 The general laws that furnish the rational explanation of anything: the *philosophy* of banking. 4 The system of values adopted by an individual, group, etc. 5 Calm judgment and equable temper; practical wisdom; fortitude. 6 A study of human behavior, ethics, morals, character, etc. [< Gk. *philos* loving + *sophos* wise]

**phlegm** (flem) n. 1 A viscid, stringy mucus secreted in the air passages. 2 Apathy; cold, undemonstrative temper; self-possession. 3 One of the four natural humors in ancient physiology. [< Gk. *phlegma* inflammation]

**phleg·mat·ic** (fleg·mat′ik) adj. Having a sluggish or stolid temperament; not easily moved or excited. Also **phleg·mat′i·cal.** — **phleg·mat′i·cal·ly** *adv.* —**Syn.** indifferent, calm, dull, undemonstrative.

**pho·ne·mics** (fə·nē′miks) *n.pl. (construed as sing.)* The study of the phonemic system of a language.

**pho·net·ic** (fə·net′ik) *adj.* 1 Of or pertaining to phonetics, or to speech sounds and their production. 2 Representing speech or speech sounds by characters that refer to specific properties, such as place or manner of articulation. Also **pho·net′i·cal.** [< Gk. *phōnē* sound] —**pho·net′i·cal·ly** *adv.*

**pho·no·graph** (fō′nə·graf, -gräf) *n.* An apparatus for recording and reproducing sounds on and from plastic disks. —**pho′no·graph′ic** *adj.* —**pho′no·graph′i·cal·ly** *adv.*

**phos·pho·rous** (fos′fər·əs, fos·fôr′əs, -fō′rəs) *adj.* Of, pertaining to, resembling, containing, or derived from phosphorus, esp. in its lower valence.

**pho·to·cop·y** (fō′tō·kop′ē) *n. pl.* **·cop·ies** A photographic reproduction of printed or other graphic material. —*v.* **·cop·ied, ·copy·ing** *v.t.* 1 To make a photocopy of. —*v.i.* 2 To make a photocopy. —**pho′to·cop′i·er** *n.*

**pho·to·e·lec·tric** (fō′tō·i·lek′trik) *adj.* Of, pertaining to, or indicating the electric effects due to the action of light. Also **pho′to·e·lec′tri·cal.**

**photo finish** 1 The finish of a race in which the leaders are so close that only a photograph taken as they cross the finish line can determine the winner. 2 A close finish.

**pho·to·gen·ic** (fō′tō·jen′ik) *adj.* 1 Generating or producing light; phosphorescent, as fireflies. 2 Having visually interesting qualities suitable for being photographed: said esp. of a person. —**pho′to·gen′i·cal·ly** *adv.*

**pho·to·graph** (fō′tə·graf, -gräf) *n.* A picture or image taken by photography. —*v.t.* 1 To take a photograph of. —*v.i.* 2 To practice photography. 3 To undergo photographing. —**pho·tog·ra·pher** (fə·tog′rə·fər) *n.*

**pho·to·graph·ic** (fō′tə·graf′ik) *adj.* 1 Pertaining to, used in, or produced by photography. 2 Like a photograph; vividly depicted. 3 Capable of precise retention or recall. —**pho′to·graph′i·cal·ly** *adv.*

**pho·tog·ra·phy** (fə·tog′rə·fē) *n.* The art or process of forming and fixing images by the chemical action of light and other forms of radiant energy on sensitive surfaces.

**Pho·to·stat** (fō′tə·stat) *n.* A device designed to

reproduce documents, drawings, etc., directly as positives on special paper: a trade name.

**phrase** (frāz) *n.* 1 A manner or style of expression; phraseology. 2 *Gram.* A group of words denoting a single idea or forming a separate part of a sentence, but not containing a subject and predicate. 3 A concise, forceful, or colorful expression. 4 *Music* A section of a melody or composition, several measures long. —*v.t. & v.i.* **phrased, phras·ing** 1 To express or be expressed in words or phrases, esp. in a certain way: He *phrased* his objections tactfully. 2 *Music* To execute or divide (music) in or into phrases. [< Gk. *phrazein* point out, tell] —**phras′al** *adj.*

**phra·se·ol·o·gy** (frā′zē·ol′ə·jē) *n.* The choice and arrangement of words and phrases to express ideas in speech or writing; diction; style. —**phra′se·o·log′i·cal** (-ə·loj′i·kəl) *adj.* —**phra′se·ol′o·gist** *n.*

**phys·i·cal** (fiz′i·kəl) *adj.* 1 Of or relating to the material universe, the natural sciences, or to physics. 2 Of, relating to, or concerned with the human body. [< Gk. *physis* nature] —**phys′i·cal·ly** *adv.*

**phy·si·cian** (fi·zish′ən) *n.* 1 A doctor authorized to practice medicine. 2 One engaged in the general practice of medicine as distinguished from a surgeon. 3 Any healer. [< L *physica* natural medicine]

**phys·ics** (fiz′iks) *n. pl. (construed as sing.)* The science of matter and energy and their mutual interactions.

**phys·i·og·no·my** (fiz′ē·og′nə·mē) *n. pl.* **·mies** 1 The face or features as revealing character or disposition. 2 Outward appearance; external features. 3 The art or practice of reading character by the features of the face or form of the body. [< Gk. *physiognō monia* the judging of a man's nature (by his features)] —**phys′i·og·nom′ic** (-og·nom′ik) or **·i·cal** *adj.* —**phys′i·og·nom′i·cal·ly** *adv.* —**phys′i·og′no·mist** *n.*

**phys·i·ol·o·gy** (fiz′ē·ol′ə·jē) *n.* 1 The branch of biology that deals with the functions of living organisms or their parts; the science of the vital processes of animals or plants. 2 The aggregate of organic processes of an organism or a part of it: the *physiology* of the frog. [< Gk. *physis* nature + *logos* a word] —**phys′i·ol′o·gist** *n.* —**phys′i·o·log′i·cal** (fiz′ē·ə·loj′i·kəl), **phys′i·o·log′ic** *adj.* —**phys′i·o·log′i·cal·ly** *adv.*

**phy·sique** (fi·zēk′) *n.* The physical structure,

organization, appearance, strength, etc., of a person's body.

**pi·an·o** (pē·an′ō) *n. pl.* **·an·os** A musical instrument having felt-covered hammers, operated from a manual keyboard, which strike steel wires to produce the tones. [Ital., short for PIANOFORTE]

**pi·an·o·for·te** (pē·an′ə·fôr′tē, -fōr′-, -fôrt′, -fōrt′) *n.* A piano. [Ital. < *piano e forte* soft and loud]

**pi·az·za** (pē·az′ə, *Ital.* pē·at′tsä) *n.* 1 A veranda or porch. 2 In Europe, esp. in Italy, an open square. 3 A covered outer walk or gallery. [Ital. < L *platea* a broad street]

**pi·ca** (pī′kə) *n.* 1 A size of type, 12-point or about 1/6 inch. 2 A size of typewriter type equivalent to 12-point, with 10 characters to the inch. [Med. L, church book]

**pick** (pik) *v.t.* 1 To select; cull, as from a group. 2 To detach; pluck: to *pick* a flower. 3 To harvest: to *pick* cotton. 4 To prepare by removing the feathers, hulls, etc.: to *pick* a chicken. 5 To remove extraneous matter from: to *pick* the teeth. 6 To pull apart, as rags. 7 To penetrate with or as with a pointed instrument. 8 To form or make in this manner: to *pick* a hole. 9 To point out too critically: to *pick* flaws. 10 To bring on purposely; provoke: to *pick* a quarrel. 11 To remove the contents of by stealth: to *pick* a pocket. 12 To open (a lock) by a piece of wire, etc. 13 a To pluck (the strings) of a musical instrument. b To play (an instrument) in this way. —*v.i.* 14 To eat daintily; nibble. —**pick at** 1 To touch or irritate with the finger. 2 To eat without appetite. 3 *Informal* To nag at. —**pick off** 1 To remove by picking. 2 To shoot one at a time. —**pick on** *Informal* To tease; annoy. —**pick out** 1 To choose or select. 2 To distinguish (something) from its surroundings. 3 To grasp (the meaning). —**pick over** To examine one by one. —**pick up** 1 To take up, as with the hand. 2 To take up or receive into a vehicle, etc. 3 To acquire by chance. 4 To gain speed. 5 To recover spirits, health, etc. 6 *Informal* To make the acquaintance of, casually or informally. 7 To make orderly; tidy. —*n.* 1 Selection; choice. 2 The choicest part or thing. 3 The quantity of a crop picked at one time. 4 The act of picking. 5 A plectrum for a stringed instrument. [ME *piken*] —**pick′er** *n.* —**Syn.** *v.* 1 choose. 3 collect, gather. 7 pierce.

**pick·et** (pik′it) *n.* 1 A pointed stick, tent peg, bar, fence paling, or stake. 2 *Mil.* A soldier or detachment of soldiers posted to guard a camp, army, etc. 3 A person stationed by a labor union outside a place affected by a strike to attempt to keep out employees or customers. —*v.t.* 1 To fence or fortify with pickets or pointed stakes. 2 *Mil.* a To guard by means of a picket. b To post as a picket. 3 To station pickets outside of. 4 To tie to a picket, as a horse. —*v.i.* 5 To act as a picket (def. 3). [< OF *piquer* pierce] —**pick′et·er** *n.*

**pick·le** (pik′əl) *n.* 1 A liquid, as brine or vinegar, usu. spiced, for preserving meat, fish, vegetables, etc. 2 A vegetable, esp. a cucumber, preserved in a pickling solution. 3 Diluted acid used in cleaning metal castings, etc. 4 *Informal* An embarrassing condition or position. —*v.t.* **·led**, **·ling** To preserve or clean in a pickling solution. [MDu. *pekel*] —**pick′ler** *n.*

**pick·pock·et** (pik′pok′it) *n.* One who steals from people's pockets or purses.

**pick·up** (pik′up′) *n.* 1 Acceleration, as in the speed of an automobile, engine, etc. 2 A device, as that coupled to the stylus of a phonograph, that changes mechanical motion to an electrical signal. 3 *Telecom.* a In radio, the location of microphones in relation to program elements. b The system for broadcasting material gathered outside the studio. 4 *Informal* Gain; improvement: a *pickup* in the stock market. 5 *Slang* A stranger with whom a casual acquaintance is made, as for sexual purposes. 6 One of a group casually enlisted or assembled, as for a sport or game. 7 A small, usu. open, truck for light loads. 8 The act of calling for, as a parcel. 9 *Informal* Something taken to renew energy or spirits; a pick-me-up.

**pic·nic** (pik′nik) *n.* 1 An outdoor party, during which a meal is eaten. 2 *Slang* An easy or pleasant time or experience. —*v.i.* **·nicked**, **·nick·ing** To have or attend a picnic. Also **pick′nick**. [< F *pique-nique*] —**pic·nick·er** *n.*

**pic·to·ri·al** (pik·tôr′ē·əl, -tō′rē-) *adj.* 1 Pertaining to or concerned with pictures. 2 Representing in or as if in pictures; graphic. 3 Containing or illustrated by pictures. —*n.* An illustrated publication. [< L *pictor* painter] —**pic·to′ri·al·ly** *adv.*

**pic·ture** (pik′chər) *n.* 1 A surface representation of an object or scene or a design, as by a painting, drawing, engraving, or photograph. 2 A mental image. 3 A vivid or graphic description. 4 A striking resemblance: *She is the picture of her mother.* 5

TABLEAU. 6 A visual image or scene. 7 MOTION PICTURE. 8 Something beautiful or striking. 9 The sum of significant facts in an event. —*v.t.* ·tured, ·tur·ing 1 To give visible representation to; draw, paint, etc. 2 To describe graphically. 3 To form a mental image of. [< L *pictus*, p.p. of *pingere* to paint]

**Pic·ture·phone** (pik/chər·fōn/) *n.* A telephone equipped with a television screen: a trade name.

**pic·tur·esque** (pik/chə·resk/) *adj.* 1 Having pictorial quality; like or suitable for a picture. 2 Having quaintness or charm. 3 Abounding in striking or original expression or imagery; richly graphic. [< L *pictor* painter] —pic/tur·esque/ly *adv.* —pic/tur·esque/ness *n.*

**piece** (pēs) *n.* 1 A portion considered as a distinct part of a whole. 2 A thing existing as an individual entity: a *piece* of paper; a *piece* of music. 3 A single object forming one of a group: a *piece* of furniture. 4 A definite quantity or length in which an article is manufactured or sold. 5 An instance: a *piece* of luck. 6 A firearm. 7 A coin: a fifty-cent *piece.* 8 A single artistic creation, as a literary, dramatic, or musical composition; also, a painting or sculpture. 9 *Regional* A short time, space, or distance: to walk a *piece.* 10 A figure, disk, or counter used in such games as chess, checkers, backgammon, etc. —**a piece of one's mind** Criticism or censure frankly expressed. —**go to pieces** 1 To fall apart. 2 To lose self-control. —**in one piece** Unharmed; intact. —**of a piece** Of the same sort or class. —*adj.* Of, made of, or by the piece. —*v.t.* pieced, piec·ing 1 To add or attach a piece or pieces to. 2 To unite or reunite the pieces of. 3 To find meaning or coherence in by linking elements; often with *together*: to *piece* together a sequence of events from the testimony of eyewitnesses. [< OF *pece*] —piec/er *n.*

**piece·meal** (pēs/mēl/) *adj.* Made up of pieces or done one piece at a time. —*adv.* 1 Piece by piece; gradually. 2 Into pieces. [<PIECE + OE *mǣl* a measure]

**pier** (pir) *n.* 1 A plain, detached mass of masonry, usu. serving as a support: the *pier* of a bridge. 2 An upright projecting portion of a wall. 3 A jetty; projecting wharf. 4 A solid portion of a wall between window openings, etc. [< AF *pere*]

**pierce** (pirs) *v.t.* pierced, pierc·ing 1 To pass into or through; penetrate, as with a

pointed object. 2 To make an opening or hole in, into, or through. 3 To force a way into or through: to *pierce* the wilderness. 4 To affect sharply or deeply, as with emotion, pain, etc. 5 To sound suddenly and sharply, as a scream. 6 To penetrate as if seeing; understand: to *pierce* a mystery. [< OF *percer*] —pierc/er *n.* —pierc/ing·ly *adv.* —Syn. 1 perforate, puncture.

**pi·e·ty** (pī/ə·tē) *n. pl.* ·ties 1 Religious reverence; devoutness. 2 Filial honor and obedience as due to parents or country, etc. 3 A pious action or belief. [< L < *pius* dutiful]

**pig** (pig) *n.* 1 A hog or hoglike animal, esp. when small or young. 2 Pork. 3 An oblong mass of metal just run from the smelter and cast in a rough mold. 4 *Informal* A person regarded as like a pig, esp. one who is filthy, gluttonous, or grasping. [ME *pigge*]

**pig·eon** (pij/ən) *n.* 1 Any of a widely distributed family of birds with small heads; a dove. 2 *Slang* One easily swindled. [< LL *pipio* a young chirping bird]

**pig·eon·hole** (pij/ən·hōl/) *n.* 1 A hole for pigeons to nest in, esp. in a compartmented pigeon house. 2 A small compartment, as in a desk, for filing papers. —*v.t.* ·holed, ·hol·ing 1 To place in a pigeonhole; file. 2 To file away and ignore. 3 To place in categories; classify mentally.

**pig·gy·back** (pig/ē·bak/) *adv.* 1 On the back or shoulders. 2 On a railroad flatcar, as a loaded truck body. —*n.* 1 The act of carrying piggyback. 2 The transporting of loaded truck bodies on railroad flatcars. —*adj.* 1 Done up on the back or shoulders: a *piggyback* ride. 2 Of or pertaining to the transporting of loaded truck bodies on railroad flatcars. —*v.t. & v.i.* 1 To carry or be carried on the back or shoulders. 2 To transport or be transported on railroad flat cars. **Also** pig/gy·back/.

**pig·ment** (pig/mənt) *n.* 1 Any of a class of finely powdered, insoluble coloring matters suitable for making paints, enamels, oil colors, etc. 2 Any substance that imparts color to animal or vegetable tissues. [< L *pingere* to paint] —pig/men·tar/y *adj.*

**pile** (pīl) *n.* 1 A quantity of anything gathered up together; a heap. 2 A funeral pyre. 3 A large accumulation or number of something. 4 A massive building or group of buildings. 5 *Informal* A great quantity of money. 6 *Physics* A nuclear fission reactor. —**make one's pile** To amass a fortune. —*v.* piled, pil·ing *v.t.* 1 To make a heap of: often with *up.* 2 To load with a pile or piles: to *pile* a plate with food. —*v.i.* 3 To form a heap. 4 To proceed or go in a confused mass: to *pile* off a bus. —**pile up** 1 To accumulate; collect, as in a heap: The bills kept *piling up.* 2 *Informal* To reduce or become reduced to a pile or wreck. [< L *pila* a pillar]

**pil·fer** (pil′fər) *v.t.* & *v.i.* To steal in small quantities. [< OF *pelfre* plunder] —**pil′fer·age** (-ij), **pil′fer·er** *n.*

**Pil·grim** (pil′grim) *n.* One of the English Puritans who founded Plymouth Colony in 1620.

**pil·grim·age** (pil′grə·mij) *n.* 1 A journey made to a sacred place. 2 Any long journey.

**pil·lage** (pil′ij) *n.* 1 The act of pillaging; open robbery, as in war. 2 Spoil; booty. —*v.·laged, ·lag·ing* *v.t.* 1 To strip of money or property by violence, esp. in war; loot. 2 To take as loot. —*v.i.* 3 To take plunder. [< OF *piller* to plunder] —**pil′lag·er** *n.*

**pil·lar** (pil′ər) *n.* 1 A firm, slender, upright column, used to support a roof, etc. 2 A single column designed as a monument. 3 One who or that which strongly supports a work or cause. —**from pillar to post** From one thing to another; hither and thither. —**pillar of society** A person holding an important position. [< L *pila*] —**pil′lared** *adj.*

**pil·low** (pil′ō) *n.* 1 A case stuffed with feathers, batting, etc., or inflated with air, used as a support for the head, as in sleeping. 2 Any cushion. —*v.t.* 1 To rest on or as on a pillow. 2 To act as a pillow for. —*v.i.* 3 To recline as on a pillow. [< L *pulvinus* a cushion] —**pil′low·y** *adj.*

**pi·lot** (pi′lət) *n.* 1 A helmsman, esp. one qualified by training and licensed by law to conduct a ship into and out of port. 2 Any guide. 3 One who operates an aircraft or spacecraft. 4 A device for guiding the action of a part of a machine, etc. —*v.t.* 1 To act as the pilot of; steer. 2 To guide. 3 To serve as pilot on, over, or in. [< Ital. *pilota*] —**Syn.** *v.* 2 conduct, direct, lead.

**pin** (pin) *n.* 1 A short stiff piece of wire, with a sharp point and a round head, used in fastening things together. 2 An ornamental device mounted on a clasp to fasten to a garment; also, a badge. 3 A rigid peg or bar of wood used for a fastening or support. 4 Anything like a pin, as a hairpin, clothespin, rolling pin, belaying pin, etc. 5 *Usu. pl.* A wooden club turned in long, oval, or cylindrical shape, set up as a target in bowling games. 6 *pl.* Legs. 7 The merest tri-

fle. 8 A peg holding the string of a violin, guitar, or other stringed instrument. 9 A peg to keep an oar in place. —**on pins and needles** Anxious; worried. —*v.t.* pinned, pin·ning 1 To fasten with a pin or pins. 2 To transfix with a pin, spear, etc. 3 To seize and hold firmly: to *pin* an opponent against a wall. 4 To force (someone) to make a definite statement, abide by a promise, etc.: usu. with *down.* [< OE *pinn* a peg]

**pin·a·fore** (pin′ə·fôr, -fōr) *n.* A sleeveless garment worn as an apron or as a light dress. [< PIN, *v.* + AFORE]

**pin·cers** (pin′sərz, -chərz) *n.pl.* (*sometimes construed as sing.*) 1 An instrument having two handles and a pair of jaws working on a pivot, used for holding objects. 2 *Zool.* A grasping organ, as the chela of a lobster. [< OF *pincier* to pinch]

**pinch** (pinch) *v.t.* 1 To squeeze between two hard edges, or between a finger and thumb. 2 To bind or compress painfully. 3 To affect with pain or distress. 4 To contract or make thin, as from cold or hunger. 5 To limit, as for lack of something: *pinched* for time. 6 *Informal* To distress financially: usu. in the passive. 7 *Slang* To capture or arrest. 8 *Slang* To steal. —*v.i.* 9 To squeeze; hurt. 10 To be stingy. 11 To become narrow or constricted. —**pinch pennies** To be economical or stingy. —*n.* 1 The act of pinching. 2 Painful pressure of any kind. 3 A case of emergency. 4 So much of a loose substance as can be taken between the finger and thumb. 5 *Slang* A theft. 6 *Slang* An arrest or raid. [< OF *pincier*] —**pinch′er** *n.*

**pine** (pin) *n.* 1 Any of several cone-bearing trees having needle-shaped evergreen leaves growing in clusters. 2 The wood of a pine tree. [< L *pinus*]

**pine·ap·ple** (pin′ap′əl) *n.* 1 A tropical plant having spiny leaves and a large cone-shaped fruit. 2 The edible fruit of this plant. 3 *Slang* A bomb or hand grenade. [< OE *pin* a pine + *æppel* apple]

**pin·ion** (pin′yən) *n.* *Mech.* A toothed wheel meshing with a larger cogwheel. [< OF *peigne* a comb] • See RACK.

**pink** (pingk) *n.* 1 A pale hue of red. 2 Any of a genus of garden plants having pink, red, or white flowers with a clovelike scent. 3 The flower of the pink. 4 A type of excellence or perfection. 5 *Often cap.* A person who holds somewhat radical opinions: a derogatory term. —**in the pink** *Informal* In the best of health and spirits. —*adj.* 1 Pale red in color; rose. 2 Somewhat radical in opinion. [?]

**pin·na·cle** (pin′ə·kəl) *n.* 1 The topmost point; acme. 2 A small turret or tall ornament, as on a parapet. 3 A mountain peak. —*v.t.* ·cled, ·cling 1 To place on or as on a pinnacle. 2 To furnish with a pinnacle; crown. [< L *pinna* wing, pinnacle] —**Syn.** *n.* 1 apex, zenith. 3 summit.

**pin·point** (pin′point′) *n.* 1 The point of a pin. 2 Something extremely small. —*v.t.* To locate or define precisely. —*adj.* Located or aimed very precisely.

**pin-up** (pin′up′) *n. Informal* 1 A picture of an attractive girl hung on a wall or board for display. 2 A lamp fastened on a wall. —*adj.* Designating a photograph or lighting device so affixed.

**pi·o·neer** (pī′ə·nir′) *n.* 1 One of the first explorers, settlers, or colonists of a new region. 2 One of the first investigators or developers in a new field of research, enterprise, etc. 3 *Mil.* An engineer who goes before the main body building roads, bridges, etc. —*v.t.* 1 To prepare (a way, etc.). 2 To prepare the way for. 3 To be a pioneer of. —*v.i.* 4 To act as a pioneer. [< OF *paonier* a foot soldier]

**pi·ous** (pī′əs) *adj.* 1 Actuated by religious reverence; godly. 2 Dutiful, respectful, or sanctimonious. 3 Practiced in the name of religion. [< L *pius* dutiful, devout] —**pi′ous·ly** *adv.* —**pi′ous·ness** *n.*

**pipe** (pīp) *n.* 1 An apparatus, usu. a small bowl with a hollow stem, for smoking tobacco, opium, etc. 2 Enough tobacco to fill the bowl of a pipe. 3 A duct of metal, etc., for conveying a fluid. 4 A single section of such a duct. 5 Any hollow or tubular part in an animal or plant body. 6 *Music* a A wind instrument consisting of a tube or tubes. b Any of the tubular tone-producing parts used in an organ. c *pl.* The bagpipe. 7 A high-pitched voice; also, a bird's call. 8 A large cask for wine. 9 A boatswain's whistle. —*v.* **piped, pip·ing** *v.i.* 1 To play on a pipe. 2 To make a shrill sound. 3 *Naut.* To signal the crew by means of a pipe. —*v.t.* 4 To convey by or as by means of pipes, esp. to transmit (television programs) by coaxial cables or wire instead of by airwaves. 5 To provide with pipes. 6 To play, as a tune, on a pipe. 7 To utter shrilly or in a high key. 8 *Naut.* To call to order by means of a boatswain's pipe. 9 To lead, entice, or bring by piping. 10 To trim, as a dress, with pip-

ing. —**pipe down** *Slang* To become silent; stop making noise. —**pipe up** 1 To start playing or singing. 2 To speak out, esp. in a shrill voice. [< L *pipare* to cheep]

**pipe·line** (pīp′līn′) *n.* 1 A line of pipe, as for the transmission of water, oil, etc. 2 A channel for the transmission of information.

**pi·quant** (pē′kənt, -känt′) *adj.* 1 Having an agreeably pungent or tart taste. 2 Interesting; tart; racy; also, charmingly lively. [< F *piquer* sting] —**pi′quan·cy** *n.* —**pi′quant·ly** *adv.*

**pique** (pēk) *n.* A feeling of irritation or resentment. —*v.t.* **piqued, pi·quing** 1 To excite resentment in. 2 To stimulate or arouse; provoke. [< MF *piquer* to sting, prick] —**Syn.** *n.* anger, displeasure. *v.* 1 irritate, nettle, offend.

**pi·ra·cy** (pī′rə·sē) *n. pl.* ·cies 1 Robbery on the high seas. 2 The unauthorized publication, reproduction, or use of another's invention, idea, or literary creation. [< Gk. *peiratēs* a pirate]

**pi·rate** (pī′rit) *n.* 1 A rover and robber on the high seas. 2 A vessel engaged in piracy. 3 A person who appropriates without right the work of another. —*v.t. & v.i.* **rat·ed, rat·ing** 1 To practice or commit piracy (upon). 2 To publish or appropriate (the work, ideas, etc., of another) illegally; plagiarize. [< Gk. *peiraein* to attach] —**pi·rat·ic** (pī·rat′ik) or **·i·cal** *adj.* —**pi·rat′i·cal·ly** *adv.*

**pis·ta·chi·o** (pis·tä′shē·ō, -tash′ē·ō) *n. pl.* ·chi·os 1 A small tree of w Asia and the Levant. 2 Its pale green, edible seed: also **pistachio nut.** 3 The flavor of the pistachio nut. 4 A delicate shade of green. [< Gk. *pistakion*]

**pis·til** (pis′til) *n.* The seed-bearing organ of flowering plants, composed of the ovary, the stigma, and usu. a style. [< L *pistillum* a pestle] • See OVARY.

**pis·tol** (pis′tǝl) *n.* A small firearm held and fired by one hand. —*v.t.* ·toled or ·tolled, ·tol·ing or ·tol·ling To shoot with a piston. [< F *pistole*]

**pis·ton** (pis′tǝn) *n.* 1 *Mech.* A disk fitted to slide in a cylinder and connected with a rod for receiving the pressure of or exerting pressure upon a fluid in the cylinder. 2 A valve in a wind instrument for altering the pitch of tones. [< Ital. *pistone*]

**pit** (pit) *n.* 1 A cavity in the ground. 2 A pitfall for animals; snare. 3 A deep abyss. 4 Hell. 5 In Great Britain, the portion of the main floor of the auditorium of a theater under the first balcony. 6 The space just in front of and below the stage, usu. occupied by the orchestra. 7 An enclosed space in which animals engage in fighting: a *cockpit*. 8 Any natural cavity or depression in the body: the *armpit*. 9 A scar like that made by a healed smallpox pustule. 10 That part of the floor of an exchange where a special line of trading is done: the wheat *pit*. 11 A mining excavation. —*v.* **pit·ted**, **pit·ting** *v.t.* 1 To mark with dents or hollows. 2 To match as antagonists. —*v.i.* 3 To become marked with pits. [< OE *pytt*]

**pitch**[1] (pich) *n.* 1 A sticky nonvolatile residue obtained from the distillation of petroleum, coal tar, etc. 2 Asphalt. 3 A resin exuded by certain conifers. —*v.t.* To caulk, waterproof, cover, or treat with pitch. [< L *pix, picis* pitch]

**pitch**[2] (pich) *v.t.* 1 To erect or set up (a tent, camp, etc.). 2 To throw or hurl. 3 To set the level, angle degree, etc., of. 4 To put in a definite place or position. 5 In baseball, to deliver (the ball) to the batter. 6 *Music* To set the pitch or key of. —*v.i.* 7 To fall or plunge forward or headlong. 8 to lurch. 9 To rise and fall alternately at the front and back. 10 To incline downward; slope. 11 To encamp. 12 In baseball, to deliver the ball to the batter. —**pitch in** *Informan* To start vigorously. —**pitch into** To attack, assail. —*n.* 1 Point or degree of elevation or depression. 2 The degree of descent or inclination of a slope. 3 *Mech.* a The amount of advance of a screw thread in a single turn. b The distance between two corresponding points on the teeth of a gearwheel. 4 *Music* the subjective characteristic of a tone that correlates essentially with frequency. 5 In games, the act of pitching; a throw. 6 Something pitched. 7 The act of dipping or plunging downward. 8 An attempt to sell or persuade: to make a *pitch*. [ME *picchen*] —**Syn.** *v.* 2 cast, fling, heave, toss.

**pitch·er**[1] (pich′ər) *n.* One who pitches, esp., in baseball, the player who delivers the ball to the batter.

**pitch·er**[2] (pich′ər) *n.* A vessel with a spout and a handle, used for holding liquids to be poured out. [< Gk. *bikos* a wine jar]

**pit·e·ous** (pit′ē·əs) *adj.* Exciting great pity or sympathy. —**pit′e·ous·ly** *adv.* —**pit′e·ous·ness** *n.* • **piteous, pitiable, pitiful** These words all mean "causing or deserving pity," but they have different shades of meaning. *Piteous* is the strongest, connoting a heart-rending anguish that is keenly felt by the

observer: *the piteous cry of a wounded animal.* A *pitiable* thing gives rise to milder compassion mixed with understanding: *his pitiable attempts to appear respectable.* A *pitiful* thing tends to inspire stronger feeling than does a *pitiable* one: *a pitiful account of an unhappy childhood.* The pity suggested by *pitiable* and *pitiful* may be mixed with contempt or condescension.

**pith** (pith) *n.* 1 The soft, spongy tissue in the center of the stems and branches of certain plants. 2 Any soft central part, as the marrow of bones. 3 Concentrated force; substance. 4 The essential part; quintessence. —*v.t.* To remove the pith from, as a plant stem. [< OE *pitha*]

**pith·y** (pith′ē) *adj.* **pith·i·er**, **pith·i·est** 1 Consisting of or like pith. 2 Forcible; effective. —**pith′i·ly** *adv.* —**pith′i·ness** *n.*

**pit·i·a·ble** (pit′ē·ə·bəl) *adj.* 1 Arousing or meriting pity or compassion; pathetic. 2 Insignificant; contemptible. —**pit′i·a·ble·ness** *n.* —**pit′i·a·bly** *adv.* • See PITEOUS.

**pit·i·ful** (pit′i·fəl) *adj.* 1 Arousing pity or compassion. 2 Arousing contempt or scorn. 3 *Archaic* Full of pity; compassionate. —**pit′i·ful·ly** *adv.* —**pit′i·ful·ness** *n.* —**Syn.** 1 lamentable, miserable, pathetic, touching. 2 abject, contemptible, paltry. • See PITEOUS.

**pit·i·less** (pit′i·lis) *adj.* Having no pity or mercy; ruthless. —**pit′i·less·ly** *adv.* **pit′i·less·ness** *n.*

**pit·tance** (pit′əns) *n.* 1 A small allowance of money. 2 Any meager income or remuneration. [< OF *pitance*, orig. a monk's food allotment, pity]

**pit·y** (pit′ē) *n. pl.* **pit·ies** 1 The feeling of grief or pain awakened by the misfortunes of others; compassion. 2 A cause for compassion or regret: It's a *pity* that their house burned down. —*v.t.* & *v.i.* **pit·ied**, **pit·y·ing** To feel compassion or pity (for). [< LL *pietas*] —**pit′i·er** *n.* —**pit′y·ing·ly** *adv.*

**piv·ot** (piv′ət) *n.* 1 *Mech.* Something upon which a related part oscillates or rotates. 2 Something on which an important matter hinges or turns; a turning point. 3 *Mil.* In wheeling troops, the soldier, officer, or point upon which the line turns. —*v.t.* 1 To place on, attach by, or provide with a pivot or pivots. —*v.i.* 2 To turn on a pivot; swing. [F] —**piv′ot·al** *adj.* —**piv′ot·al·ly** *adj.*

**piz·za** (pēt′sə) *n.* A doughy crust overlaid and baked with a mixture of cheese, tomatoes, spices, etc. [Ital.]

386

**piz·ze·ri·a** (pēt'sə·rē'ə) n. A place where pizzas are prepared, sold, and eaten.

**plac·ard** (plak'ərd, plak'ärd) n. A printed or written notice to be publicly displayed. —v.t. (usu. plak'ärd) 1 To announce by means of placards. 2 To post placards on or in. 3 To display as a placard. [< OF plackart]

**pla·cate** (plā'kāt, plak'āt) v.t. ·cat·ed, ·cat·ing To appease the anger of; pacify. [<L placare appease] —pla'cat·er, pla·ca'tion n. —pla'ca·tive, pla'ca·to'ry (-tô'rē, -tō'rē) adj.

**place** (plās) n. 1 A particular point or portion of space; a definite locality or location. 2 An occupied situation or building; space regarded as abode or quarters. 3 An open space or square in a city; also, a court or street. 4 Position in relative order. 5 Station in life; degree; rank. 6 An office, appointment, or employment; also, rank, position, or station. 7 Room; stead: One thing gives place to another. 8 A particular passage, as in a book. 9 The second position among the first three competitors in a horse race. 10 Math The position of a digit, and hence its weight, in relation to other digits of a numeral. —in place 1 In its natural position; also, in a suitable place, position, job, etc. 2 IN SITU. —in place of Instead of. —out of place 1 Not in the appropriate place, order, or relation. 2 Inappropriate; ill-timed. —take place To happen; occur. —v. placed, plac·ing v.t. 1 To put in a particular place or position. 2 To put or arrange in a particular relation or sequence. 3 To find a situation, home, etc., for. 4 To appoint to a post or office. 5 To identify; classify: Historians place him in the time of Nero. 6 To arrange for: to place an order. 7 To bestow or entrust: I place my life in your hands. 8 To invest, as funds. 9 To adjust the tones of (the voice) consciously, as in singing. —v.i. 10 In racing, to finish among the first three contestants; esp., to finish second. [< L platea a wide street] —Syn. v. 1 lay, locate, set, situate.

**pla·ce·bo** (plə·sē'bō) n. pl. ·bos or ·boes Any inactive substance given out as medication either to humor a patient or as a control in testing the effects of other medicines. [< L placebo I shall please]

**plac·id** (plas'id) adj. Quiet; calm. [<L placere to please] —pla·cid·i·ty (plə·sid'ə·tē), plac'id·ness n. —plac'id·ly adv. —Syn. pacific, peaceful, tranquil, unruffled.

**pla·gia·rize** (plā'jə·rīz, -jē·ə-) v. ·rized, ·riz·ing v.t. 1 To appropriate as one's own the writings, ideas, etc., of another). 2 To appropriate and use passages, ideas, etc., from. —v.i. 3 To commit plagiarism. Brit. sp. pla'gia·rise. —pla'gia·riz'er n.

**plague** (plāg) n. 1 A pestilence or epidemic disease of man or animals, usu. very deadly and contagious: bubonic plague. 2 A person or thing that is troublesome and harassing. —v.t. plague, pla·guing 1 To harass or torment; annoy. 2 To afflict with plague or disaster. [<LL plaga a pestilence]

**plaid** (plad) adj. Having a tartan pattern; checkered. —n. 1 An oblong woolen scarf of tartan or checkered pattern, worn in the Scottish Highlands as a cloak fastened over one shoulder. 2 Any fabric of this pattern. [< Scot. Gaelic plaide a blanket]

**plain** (plān) adj. 1 Presenting few difficulties; easy. 2 Clear; understandable: plain English. 3 Lowly in station; humble. 4 Having no conspicuous ornamentation; unadorned. 5 Not figured or twilled: said of textiles. 6 Flat; smooth. 7 Homely. 8 Not rich, as food. —n. An expanse of level, treeless land; a prairie. [< L planus flat] —plain'ly adv. —plain'ness n.

**plain·tiff** (plān'tif) n. The person that begins an action at law. [< OF plaintif plaintive]

**plain·tive** (plān'tiv) adj. Expressing a subdued sadness; mournful. [< OF plaintif] —plain'tive·ly adv. —plain'tive·ness n.

**plait** (plāt, plat) v.t. 1 BRAID. 2 PLEAT. 3 To make by pleating or braiding. —n. 1 A braid of hair. 2 PLEAT. [< L plicitum a folded thing] —plait'er n.

**plan** (plan) n. 1 A means for the attainment of some object; a scheme. 2 A drawing showing the proportion and relation of parts, as of a building. 3 A mode of action. —v.t. planned, plan·ning 1 To form a scheme or method for doing, achieving, etc. 2 To make a plan of, as a building; design. 3 To have as an intention or purpose. [< OF, a plane (surface), a ground plan] —plan'ner n. —Syn. n. 1 design, method, arrangement, program. v. 1 contrive, devise, invent, organize.

**plane** (plān) n. 1 Geom. A surface such that a straight line joining any two of its points lies wholly within the surface. 2 Any flat or uncurved surface. 3 A grade of development; stage; level, as of thought, knowledge, rank, etc. 4 Aeron. A lifting surface of an airplane; airfoil. 5 An airplane. —adj. 1 Of or lying in a plane. 2 Having a flat surface. —*v.i.* **planed, plan·ing** 1 To glide; soar. 2 To rise partly out of the water, as a power boat at high speed. [< L *planus* flat]

**plan·et** (plan′it) *n.* 1 *Astron.* One of the large bodies that orbit the sun and shine by reflected sunlight. The major solar planets are Mercury, Venus, Earth, Mars, Jupiter, Saturn, Uranus, Neptune, and Pluto. 2 A similar body revolving around another star. 3 In ancient astronomy, one of the seven heavenly bodies (the Sun, Moon, Mercury, Venus, Mars, Jupiter, and Saturn) that have an apparent motion among the fixed stars. 4 In astrology, one of these bodies in relation to its supposed influence on human beings and their affairs. [< Gk. *planētes* wanderer]

**plan·e·tar·i·um** (plan′ə·târ′ē·əm) *n. pl.* **·tar·i·ums** or **·tar·i·a** 1 An apparatus for exhibiting the features of the heavens as they exist at any time and for any place on earth. 2 A building containing such an apparatus. [< LL *planetarius* planetary]

**plank** (plangk) *n.* 1 A broad piece of sawed timber, thicker than a board. 2 One of the principles of a political platform. —**walk the plank** To walk off a plank projecting from the side of a ship: a method used by pirates for executing prisoners. —*v.t.* 1 To cover, furnish, or lay with planks. 2 To broil or bake and serve on a plank, as fish. 3 *Informal* To put down emphatically. [< LL *planca* board]

**plant** (plant, plänt) *n.* 1 Any member of one of the two great kingdoms of organisms, usu. distinguishable from animals by various criteria, as the ability to carry on photosynthesis, the presence of cellulose cell walls, a fixed position, etc. 2 One of the smaller forms of vegetable life, as distinct from shrubs and trees. 3 A set of machines, tools, apparatus, etc., comprising a manufacturing enterprise or other business. 4 A building or buildings used for a manufacturing or industrial process: a packing *plant.* 5 The buildings and equipment needed for any institution, as a college. 6 A sapling; a slip or cutting from a tree or bush. 7 *Slang* A trick; swindle. —*v.t.* 1 To set in the ground for growing. 2 To furnish with plants or seed: to *plant* a field. 3 To place firmly; put in position. 4 To found; establish. 5 To introduce into the mind. 6 To deposit (fish or spawn) in a body of water. 7 *Slang* To deliver, as a blow. 8 *Slang* To

place (a person or thing) for purposes of deception. [< L *planta* a sprout]

**plan·ta·tion** (plan·tā′shən) *n.* 1 A farm or estate of many acres, esp. in the s U.S., planted in cotton, tobacco, rice, or sugar cane. 2 A newly settled region; a settlement; colony. 3 A grove cultivated to provide a certain product. [<L *plantare* to plant]

**plaque** (plak) *n.* 1 A plate, disk, or slab of metal, porcelain, etc., ornamented, as for wall decoration. 2 A brooch. 3 A hardened deposit of microorganisms and mucus on teeth. [<MDu. *placke* flat disk]

**plas·ma** (plaz′mə) *n.* 1 The liquid portion of blood, lymph, milk, or similar fluids containing suspended solids. 2 PROTOPLASM. 3 *Physics* An intensely ionized, electrically neutral gas. [< Gk. *plassein* to mold, form] —**plas·mat·ic** (plaz·mat′ik), **plas′mic** *adj.*

**plas·ter** (plas′tər, pläs′-) *n.* 1 A composition of lime, sand, and water for coating walls and partitions. 2 Plaster of Paris. 3 A viscid substance spread on cloth and applied to the body for healing purposes. —*v.t.* 1 To cover or overlay with plaster. 2 To apply a plaster to, as a part of the body. 3 To apply like plaster: to *plaster* posters on a fence. 4 To cause to adhere or lie flat like plaster. [< Gk. *emplastron*]

**plas·tic** (plas′tik) *adj.* 1 Giving form or fashion to matter. 2 Capable of being molded; pliable. 3 Pertaining to modeling or molding; sculptural. 4 Made of plastic. 5 *Slang* Not genuine; sham: *plastic* moral values. — *n.* Any of a class of synthetically produced organic compounds capable of being molded and hardened into any form required by commercial use. [< Gk. *platos* formed<*plassein* to form, mold] —**plas′ti·cal·ly** *adv.*

**plastic surgery** Surgery that deals with structural remodeling or restoration of lost, injured, or deformed parts of the body. — **plastic surgeon**

**plate** (plāt) *n.* 1 A shallow, usu. round dish upon which food is served. 2 A portion of food; plateful. 3 Service, dishes, food, etc., for one person: a fund-raising dinner at $25 a *plate.* 4 Household utensils covered or lined with a thin coating of silver or gold. 5 Metal in sheets. 6 A cup or other article of silver or gold offered as a prize in a contest. 7 A piece of flat metal bearing an engraved design or inscription. 8 An electrotype or stereotype, esp. a full-page illustration printed on special paper. 9 A

horizontal timber for supporting a framework. 10 *Dent.* A device fitted to the mouth
and holding one or more artificial teeth. 11
Armor made from metal plates. 12 A thin
part of the brisket of beef. 13 A sensitized
sheet of glass, metal, or the like, for taking
photographs. 14 In baseball, the home
base. 15 *Biol.* A platelike structure; a lamina or a lamella. 16 *Geol.* A section of the
earth's crust that floats on the surface of
the mantle. 17 A dish used in taking up
collections, as in churches; also, such a
collection. 18 A hinge. 19 The principal
anode in an electron tube. —*v.t.* plat·ed,
plat·ing 1 To coat with a thin layer of gold,
silver, etc. 2 To cover or sheathe with metal
plates for protection. 3 *Printing* To make an
electrotype or stereotype plate from. [< Gk.
*platys* broad, flat]

pla·teau (pla·tō′) *n. pl.* ·teaus or ·teaux (-tōz′)
1 A stretch of elevated and comparatively
level land; tableland. 2 A period of relatively
little change in circumstance. 3 A comparatively horizontal area of a graph indicating an unchanging variable. [< OF *platel* a
flat piece of metal or wood]

plat·form (plat′fôrm) *n.* 1 Any floor or flat surface raised above the adjacent level, as a
stage for public speaking. 2 An enclosed
space at the end of a railroad car, etc. 3 A
raised walk, usu. of wood, built parallel to
the tracks at a railroad station. 4 A statement of principles or objectives put forth by
a political party, etc. [<MF *plate* flat + *forme*
form]

plat·i·num (plat′ə·nəm) *n.* A heavy, whitish
metallic element (symbol Pt) that is highly
resistant to corrosion and fusion, and is
widely used as a catalyst, for jewelry, etc.
[< Sp. *plata* silver]

plat·i·tude (plat′ə·t′ŏŏd) *n.* 1 A dull or commonplace statement; an obvious truism. 2
Dullness; triteness. [F, flatness] —plat′i·
tu′di·nous *adj.* —plat′i·tu′di·nous·ly *adv.*
—Syn. 2 banality, flatness, staleness.

plau·si·ble (plô′zə·bəl) *adj.* 1 Seeming likely to
be true, but open to doubt. 2 Superficially
endeavoring or calculated to gain trust: a
*plausible* witness. [< L *plausibilis* deserving
applause] —plau′si·bil′i·ty, plau′si·ble·
ness *n.* —plau′si·bly *adv.*

play (plā) *v.i.* 1 To engage in sport or diversion; amuse oneself. 2 To take part in a
game or game of skill or chance; gamble. 3
To act in a way which is not to be taken seriously. 4 To act in a specified manner: to

play false. 5 To deal carelessly or insincerely: with *with.* 6 To make love sportively.
7 To move quickly or irregularly: lights
*playing* along a wall. 8 To discharge or be
discharged freely or continuously: a fountain *playing* in the square. 9 To perform on
a musical instrument. 10 To give forth musical sounds; sound. 11 To be performed:
*Hamlet* is *playing* tonight. 12 To act on a
stage; perform. —*v.t.* 13 To engage in (a
game, etc.). 14 To imitate in play: to *play*
cowboys. 15 To perform sportively: to *play*
a trick. 16 To oppose in a game or contest.
17 To move or employ (a piece, card, etc.)
in a game. 18 To employ (someone) in a
game as a player. 19 To cause; bring about:
to *play* hob. 20 To perform upon (a musical instrument). 21 To perform or produce,
as a piece of music, a drama, etc. 22 To act
the part of: to *play* the fool. 23 To perform
in: to *play* Chicago. 24 To cause to move
quickly or irregularly: to *play* lights over a
surface. 25 To put into or maintain in action; ply. 26 In games of chance: a To bet. b
To bet on. —play at 1 To take part in. 2 To
do half-heartedly. —play by ear To play (a
musical instrument or composition) without memorization of or reference to written
music. —play down To minimize. —play
into the hands of To act to the advantage
of (a rival or opponent). —play it by ear *Informal* To handle a situation with no prior
planning; improvise. —play it cool *Slang* To
act unconcerned or nonchalant. —play off
1 To oppose against one another. 2 To decide (a tie) by playing one more game. —
play on (or upon) 1 To exploit (another's
hopes, emotions, etc.) 2 To continue: The
band *played on.* —play up *Informal* To emphasize. —play up to *Informal* To curry
favor. —*n.* 1 Activity for diversion, recreation, or sport. 2 A move or turn in a game.
3 The carrying on of a game or sport. 4 The
manner of contending in a game: rough
*play.* 5 Joking; humor; jest. 6 A dramatic
composition; also, a dramatic performance.
7 Action: sword *play.* 8 Light, quick, fitful
movement. 9 Freedom of movement. 10
Free motion of a machine part. 11 Active
operation. 12 Gambling. —make a play for
*Informal* To attempt to win or gain by artful means. [< OE *plegan*]

play·boy (plā′boi′) *n. Informal* A man, usu.
wealthy, whose main interest is the pursuit
of pleasure.

play·ful (plā′fəl) *adj.* 1 Lively and frolicsome.

2 Humorous; joking. —**play′ful·ly** adv. — **play′ful·ness** n.

**play-off** (plā′ôf′, -of′) n. In sports, a decisive game or contest, esp. after a tie.

**play·wright** (plā′rīt′) n. A writer of plays.

**pla·za** (plā′zə, plaz′ə) n. An open square or market place, esp. in a town. [Sp.]

**plea** (plē) n. 1 An act of pleading, or that which is pleaded; an appeal; entreaty. 2 An excuse; pretext or justification. 3 Law a An allegation made by either party in a cause. b In common-law practice, a defendant's answer of fact to the plaintiff's declaration. [< L placere seem right, please]

**plead** (plēd) v. plead·ed (Informal or Regional pled), plead·ing v.i. 1 To make earnest entreaty; implore. 2 Law a To advocate a case in court. b To file a pleading. —v.t. 3 To allege as an excuse or defense: to plead insanity. 4 Law To discuss or maintain (a case) by argument. [< OF plaidier] —**plead′er** n. —**plead′ing·ly** adv. —**Syn.** 1 ask, beg, beseech, entreat, supplicate.

**pleas·ant** (plez′ənt) adj. 1 Giving or promoting pleasure; pleasing; agreeable. 2 Conducive to merriment; gay. [< L placere please] —**pleas′ant·ly** adv. —**pleas′ant·ness** n.

**please** (plēz) v. pleased, pleas·ing v.t. 1 To give pleasure to; gratify. 2 To be the wish or will of: May it please you. —v.i. 3 To give satisfaction or pleasure. 4 To have the will or preference; wish: Go when you please. [< L placere please]

**pleas·ure** (plezh′ər) n. 1 An agreeable sensation or emotion; enjoyment. 2 Sensual gratification. 3 Amusement in general; diversion. 4 One's preference; choice. [< OF plaisir please]

**ple·be·ian** (pli·bē′ən) n. 1 One of the common people of ancient Rome. 2 One of the common people. 3 A vulgar, crude person —adj. 1 Pertaining to the common people. 2 Vulgar; crude. [< L] —**ple·be′ian·ism** n.

**pledge** (plej) v.t. pledged, pledg·ing 1 To give or deposit as security for a loan, etc.; pawn. 2 To bind by or as by a pledge. 3 To promise solemnly, as assistance. 4 To offer (one's word, life, etc.) as a guaranty or forfeit. 5 To drink a toast to. 6 To promise to join (a fraternity). —n. 1 A guaranty for the performance of an act, contract or duty. 2 A solemn promise. 3 The drinking of a health or to good cheer. 4 A pawn of personal property. 5 One who has promised to join a fraternity 6 A token. —**take the pledge** To

make a vow to abstain from alcoholic liquor. [< OF plege security] —**pledg′ee, pledg′er** n.

**plen·i·po·ten·ti·ar·y** (plen′i·pə·ten′shē·er′ē, -shə·rē) adj. Possessing or conferring full powers. —n. pl. ·ar·ies A person, as an ambassador, minister, or envoy, invested with full powers by a government. [< L plenus full + potens powerful]

**plen·te·ous** (plen′tē·əs) adj. 1 Characterized by plenty; amply sufficient. 2 Yielding an abundance. —**plen′te·ous·ly** adv. —**plen′te·ous·ness** n.

**plen·ti·ful** (plen′ti·fəl) adj. Existing in great quantity; abundant. —**plen′ti·ful·ly** adv. —**plen′ti·ful·ness** n. —**Syn.** abounding, ample, bounteous, copious, lavish, plenteous.

**plen·ty** (plen′tē) n. pl. ·ties 1 The state of having an abundance. 2 As much as can be required: plenty of water. —adj. Existing in abundance; plentiful. —adv. Informal In a sufficient degree: The house is plenty large. [< L plenus full]

**pli·a·ble** (plī′ə·bəl) adj. 1 Easily bent or twisted; flexible. 2 Easily persuaded or controlled. —**pli′a·bil′i·ty, pli′a·ble·ness** n. —**pli′a·bly** adv.

**pli·ers** (plī′ərz) n.pl. (often construed as sing.) Small pincers for bending, holding, or cutting. Also pair of pliers.

**plight** (plīt) n. A solemn pledge or promise. —v.t. 1 To pledge (one's word, faith, etc.). 2 To promise, as in marriage; betroth. —**plight one's troth** 1 To pledge one's solemn word. 2 To promise oneself in marriage. [< OE pliht peril] —**plight′er** n.

**plot** (plot) n. 1 A piece or patch of ground set apart. 2 a A chart or diagram, as of a building. b A surveyor's map. 3 A secret plan; conspiracy. 4 The series of incidents forming the plan of action of a novel, play, etc. —v. plot·ted, plot·ting v.t. 1 To make a map, chart, or plan of. 2 To plan for secretly; conspire. 3 To arrange the plot of (a novel, etc.). 4 To represent or position (something), as on a chart, map, or graph. —v.i. 5 To form a plot; conspire. [< OE] —**plot′ter** n.

**plow** (plou) n. 1 An implement for cutting, turning over, stirring, or breaking up the soil. 2 Any implement that operates like a plow: a snowplow. —v.t. 1 To turn up the surface of (land) with a plow. 2 To make or form (a furrow, ridge, etc.) by means of a plow. 3 To furrow or score the surface of. 4 To dig out or remove with a plow: with up or out. 5 To move or cut through (water): to *plow* the waves. —*v.i.* 6 To turn up soil with a plow. 7 To undergo plowing, as land. 8 To advance laboriously; plod. —**plow into** 1 To start work energetically. 2 To collide with. [< OE *plōh*] —**plow′er** *n.*

**pluck** (pluk) *v.t.* 1 To pull out or off; pick: to *pluck* a flower. 2 To pull with force; snatch: with *off, away,* etc. 3 To pull out the feathers, hair, etc., of. 4 To pull and release suddenly. 5 To cause the strings of (a musical instrument) to sound by such action. 6 *Slang* To rob; swindle. —*v.i.* 7 To give a sudden pull; tug: with *at.* —**pluck up** To rouse or summon (one's courage). —*n.* 1 Confidence and spirit in the face of difficulty or danger. 2 A sudden pull; twitch. 3 The act of plucking or state of being plucked. [< OE *pluccian*] —**pluck′er** *n.*

**pluck·y** (pluk′ē) *adj.* **pluck·i·er, pluck·i·est** Showing bravery; courageous. —**pluck′i·ly** *adv.* —**pluck′i·ness** *n.* —Syn. brave, fearless, undaunted, valiant.

**plug** (plug) *n.* 1 Anything, as a piece of wood or a cork, used to stop a hole. 2 A spark plug. 3 A fireplug. 4 *Electr.* A device for inserting in an outlet, etc., so as to complete a circuit or make contact. 5 A flat cake of pressed or twisted tobacco. 6 Any worn-out or useless thing, esp. an old horse. 7 *Slang* A man's high silk hat: **also plug hat.** 8 *Informal* Mention of a product, song, etc., as on a radio or television program; an advertisement. —*v.* **plugged, plug·ging** *v.t.* 1 To stop or close, as a hole, by inserting a plug: often with *up.* 2 To insert as a plug. 3 *Slang* To shoot a bullet into. 4 *Slang* To advertise frequently or insistently. —*v.i.* 5 *Informal* To work doggedly; persevere. 6 To become stopped or closed: with *up.* —**plug in** To insert the plug of (a lamp, etc.) in an electric outlet. [< MDu. *plugge*]

**plum·age** (plōō′mij) *n.* The feathers that cover a bird. [< F *plume* feather]

**plumb** (plum) *n.* 1 A weight hung on a line used to find the exact perpendicular: **also plumb bob.** 2 A nautical sounding lead, a sinker on a fishing line, etc. —**off** (**or out of**) **plumb** Not exactly vertical. —*adj.* 1 Vertical or perpendicular. 2 *Informal* Sheer; complete. —*adv.* 1 In a line perpendicular to the plane of the horizon. 2 *Informal* With exactness; correctly. —*v.t.* 1 To test with a plumb. 2 To make vertical; straighten. 3 To learn the facts about; solve. [< L *plumbum* lead]

**plumb·er** (plum′ər) *n.* One whose work is plumbing.

**plumb·ing** (plum′ing) *n.* 1 The art or trade of installing and maintaining tanks, pipes, etc., as for water, gas and sewage. 2 A system of pipes, ducts, etc. 3 The act of sounding for depth, etc., with a plumb line.

**plume** (plōōm) *n.* 1 A feather, esp. when long and ornamental. 2 A large feather, tuft of feathers, or flowing tuft of hair, worn as an ornament, esp. on a helmet. 3 Something that resembles this: a *plume* of smoke. 4 A prize. —*v.t.* **plumed, plum·ing** 1 To adorn, dress, or furnish with or as with plumes. 2 To smooth or dress (itself or its feathers); preen. —**plume oneself on** (**or upon**) To congratulate oneself on; be proud of. [< L *pluma* small soft feather]

**plun·der** (plun′dər) *v.t.* 1 To rob of goods or property by open violence, as in war. 2 To despoil by robbery or fraud. 3 To take as plunder. —*v.i.* 4 To take plunder; steal. —*n.* 1 That which is taken by plundering; booty. 2 The act of plundering or robbing. 3 *Informal* Personal belongings or goods. 4 Political booty. [< G *plündern*] —**plun′der·age, plun′der·er** *n.* —**plun′der·ous** *adj.*

**plunge** (plunj) *v.* **plunged, plung·ing** *v.t.* 1 To thrust or force suddenly into a penetrable substance. 2 To force into some condition or state: to *plunge* a nation into debt. —*v.i.* 3 To dive, jump, or fall into a fluid, chasm, etc. 4 To move suddenly or with a rush. 5 To move violently forward and downward, as a horse or ship. 6 To descend abruptly or steeply. 7 *Informal* To gamble or speculate heavily and recklessly. —*n.* 1 The act of plunging. 2 A sudden and violent motion, as of a breaking wave. 3 An exceptionally heavy bet or speculation. —**take the** (**a**) **plunge** To begin an uncertain endeavor or enterprise. [< L *plumbum* lead]

**plung·er** (plun′jər) *n.* 1 One who or that which plunges. 2 A heavy or reckless speculator. 3 *Mech.* A part that has a plunging motion. 4 A cuplike device made of rubber and attached to a stick, used to open clogged drains.

**plu·ral** (plōōr′əl) *adj.* 1 Containing, consisting of, or designating more than one. 2 *Gram.* Denoting words or forms that indicate more than one. —*n.* *Gram.* 1 The plural number. 2 A plural form of a word. [< L *pluralis* < *plus* more] —**plu′ral·ly** *adv.*

**plu·ral·i·ty** (plōō·ral′ə·tē) *n. pl.* **·ties** 1 The state of being plural. 2 The greater number; majority. 3 In politics: **a** The excess of the highest number of votes cast for any one candidate over the next highest number. **b** In an election involving more than two candidates, the number of votes cast for any one that exceeds that for any of the others, but does not exceed half of the total number of votes cast.

**plus** (plus) *prep.* 1 Added to or to be added to: Three *plus* two equals five. 2 Increased by: salary *plus* commission. —*adj.* 1 Being or indicating more than zero; positive. 2 Extra; supplemental: *plus* value. 3 *Informal* Denoting a value higher than ordinary in a specified grade: B *plus.* —*n. pl.* **plus·es** 1 The plus sign. 2 An addition; an extra quantity. 3 A positive quantity. 4 *Informal* Something considered advantageous or desirable. [L, more]

**plush** (plush) *n.* A fabric having a pile deeper than that of velvet. —*adj.* 1 Of or made of plush. 2 *Slang* Luxurious: a *plush* apartment house. [< L *pilus* hair] —**plush'i·ness** *n.* —**plush'y** *adj.* (·i·er, ·i·est)

**plu·toc·ra·cy** (plōō·tok'ra·sē) *n. pl.* **·cies** 1 A class that controls the government by its wealth. 2 Government by the wealthy. 3 A state or nation so governed. [< Gk. *ploutos* wealth + *kratein* rule]

**plu·to·crat** (plōō'tə·krat) *n.* 1 One who exercises power by virtue of his wealth. 2 Any very wealthy person. —**plu'to·crat'ic** or **·i·cal** *adj.* —**plu'to·crat'i·cal·ly** *adv.*

**plu·to·ni·um** (plōō·tō'nē·əm) *n.* A radioactive metallic element (symbol Pu), used as a nuclear fuel. [< PⅬᴜᴛᴏ (the planet)]

**ply** (plī) *v.* **plied, ply·ing** *v.t.* To bend, mold, or shape. —*n. pl.* **plies** 1 A web, layer, fold, or thickness, as in a cloth, etc. 2 A strand, turn, or twist of rope, yarn, thread, etc. 3 A bent or bias; inclination. —*adj.* Having (a specified number of) strands, etc.: used in combination: *two-ply.* [< L *plicare* to fold]

**ply·wood** (plī'wŏŏd') *n.* A material composed of a number of thin sheets of wood glued together with the grains of adjacent sheets at right angles.

**pneu·mat·ic** (nʸōō·mat'ik) *adj.* 1 Describing machines that make use of compressed air. 2 Containing air or gas. 3 Pertaining to pneumatics. Also **pneu·mat'i·cal.** —*n.* A tire containing air. [< Gk. *pneuma* breath] —**pneu·mat'i·cal·ly** *adv.*

**pneu·mon·ia** (nʸōō·mōn'yə) *n.* Acute inflammation of the lungs characterized by accumulation of fluid in the alveoli and difficult breathing. [< Gk. *pneumōn* lung] —**pneu·mon·ic** (nʸōō·mon'ik) *adj.*

**poach** (pōch) *v.i.* 1 To trespass on another's property, etc., esp. for the purpose of taking game or fish. 2 To take game or fish unlawfully. 3 To become soft and muddy by being trampled: said of land. —*v.t.* 4 To trespass on. 5 To take (game or fish) unlawfully. 6 To make muddy by trampling. [< OF *pochier* thrust one's fingers into] —**poach'er** *n.*

**pock·et** (pok'it) *n.* 1 A small bag or pouch; esp. one stitched to a garment. 2 A cavity, opening, or receptacle. 3 *Mining* **a** A cavity containing gold or other ore. **b** A small deposit of ore in one spot. 4 One of the pouches in a billiard or pool table. 5 An air pocket. —**in one's pocket** Under one's influence or control. —**line one's pockets** To acquire a lot of money. —*adj.* 1 Small enough to fit into a pocket. 2 Pertaining to, for, or carried in a pocket. —*v.t.* 1 To put into or confine in a pocket. 2 To appropriate as one's own, esp. dishonestly. 3 To enclose as if in a pocket. 4 To accept or endure, as an insult. 5 To conceal or suppress: *Pocket* your pride. [< OF *poque, poche* bag, pouch] —**pock'et·er** *n.* —**Syn.** *v.* 2 embezzle, purloin, steal, take. 5 hide, swallow.

**pock·et·book** (pok'it·bŏŏk') *n.* 1 A woman's purse or handbag. 2 A notebook for the pocket. 3 One's financial resources.

**pod** (pod) *n.* 1 A dehiscent seed vessel containing one or more seeds. 2 A housing for an aircraft part that is mounted outboard. —*v.i.* **pod·ded, pod·ding** 1 To fill out like a pod. 2 To produce pods. [?]

**po·em** (pō'əm) *n.* 1 A composition in verse, either in meter or in free verse, characterized by the imaginative treatment of experience, usu. by the use of language more intensive than ordinary speech, and typically presented with the initial letter of each line capitalized. 2 Any composition in verse. 3 Any composition characterized by beauty of language or thought: a prose *poem.* 4 Any beautiful object or experience. [< Gk. *poiēma,* lit., anything made]

**po·et** (pō'it) *n.* 1 One who writes poems. 2 One esp. endowed with imagination and creativity. [< Gk. *poiētēs*]

**po·et·ic** (pō·et'ik) *adj.* 1 Of or pertaining to poets or poems. 2 Characteristic of or suitable for poetry: *poetic* language. 3 Highly imaginative: a *poetic* nature. 4 Made up of poems. Also **po·et'i·cal.** —**po·et'i·cal·ly** *adv.*

**po·et·ry** (pō'ə·trē, pō'it·rē) *n.* 1 The writings

of a poet; poems. 2 The art of writing poems. 3 Anything resembling poetry in spirit or feeling: Dancing is the *poetry* of motion. 4 Poetic works in general.

**poign·ant** (poin′yənt, poi′nənt) *adj.* 1 Severely painful or acute to the feelings: *poignant* grief. 2 Keenly piercing: *poignant wit.* 3 Sharp or stimulating to the taste; pungent. [< L *pungere* to prick] —**poign′an·cy** *n.* —**poign′ant·ly** *adv.* —**Syn.** 1 agonizing, excruciating, piercing, sharp

**point** (point) *n.* 1 The sharp end of a thing, esp. of anything that tapers. 2 A tool or instrument having a sharp, tapering end. 3 A tapering tract of land extending into water. 4 A distinguishing attribute: Her smile is her best *point.* 5 A physical attribute of an animal, used in judging. 6 The main idea under consideration: the *point* of a story. 7 A particular place or position. 8 A position considered as one of a series: to gain a *point.* 9 A precise degree or grade attained, as in a game. 10 A particular juncture in the course of events: at one *point* during the day. 11 A detail or step: Let us go over this *point* by *point.* 12 Purpose; object: There's no *point* in waiting. 13 For students, a unit of credit. 14 The moment when something is about to take place: He is on the *point* of leaving. 15 NEEDLEPOINT (def. 3). 16 A punctuation mark, esp. a period. 17 *Phonet.* A diacritical mark used to indicate a vowel in a Semitic language. 18 A decimal point. 19 A geometric entity having position as its only inherent property. 20 The attitude assumed by a hunting dog when it finds game. 21 In fencing, a thrust. 22 *Printing* A unit of measure for type, about 1/72 in.: 8-*point* type. 23 One of the 32 divisions of a compass card. 24 A unit of variation in the price of shares, stocks, etc. 25 A fixed place from which distance is reckoned. 26 *Electr.* Any of a set of contacts controlling current flow in a circuit. 27 *Brit. (Usu. pl.)* A tapering section of a railroad track switch. —**at (or on) the point of** On the verge of. —**beside the point** Irrelevant. —**in point** Pertinent. —**in point of** In the matter of; as regards. —**make a point of** To treat as vital or essential. —**see the point** To understand the meaning of a story, joke, etc. —**to the point** Relevant. —*v.t.* 1 To direct or aim, as a finger or weapon. 2 To give force or point to, as a meaning or remark. 3 To shape or sharpen to a point. 4 To punctuate. 5 To mark with points, as decimal fractions:

with *off.* 6 In hunting, to indicate the presence of (game) by standing rigid: said of dogs. —*v.i.* 7 To call attention or indicate direction by extending the finger: usu. with *at* or *to.* 8 To have a specified direction: with *to* or *toward.* 9 To point game. —**point out** To call attention to. [< L *punctus,* pp. of *pungere* to prick]

**poise** (poiz) *v.* **poised, pois·ing** *v.t.* 1 To bring into or hold in balance. 2 To hold; support, as in readiness. —*v.i.* 3 To be balanced or suspended; hover. —*n.* 1 Balance; equilibrium. 2 Equanimity and dignity of manner; composure. 3 Suspense; indecision. [< L *pensare,* intens. of *pendere* weigh]

**poi·son** (poi′zən) *n.* 1 A substance that produces illness or death if swallowed, inhaled, or otherwise introduced into a living organism. 2 Anything that tends to destroy or corrupt. —*v.t.* 1 To kill or injure with poison. 2 To put poison into or on. 3 To affect harmfully. —*adj.* Killing; venomous. [< L *potio* a drink, poisonous draft] —**poi′son·er** *n.*

**poi·son·ous** (poi′zən-əs) *adj.* 1 Containing a poison. 2 Having the effect of a poison; toxic. —**poi′son·ous·ly** *adv.* —**poi′son·ous·ness** *n.*

**pok·er** (pō′kər) *n.* 1 One who or that which pokes. 2 An iron rod for poking a fire.

**pole**[1] (pōl) *n.* 1 Either of the points in which a diameter of a sphere intersects the surface. 2 One of two points where the axis of rotation, as of the earth, meets the surface. 3 *Physics* One of the two points at which opposite physical qualities are concentrated; esp. a point of maximum electric or magnetic force. 4 Either of the ends of any axis. [< Gk. *polos* pivot, pole]

**pole**[2] (pōl) *n.* 1 A long slender piece of wood or metal: a *flagpole.* 2 In linear and surface measure, a rod or a square rod. —*v.* **poled, pol·ing** *v.t.* To propel, as a boat, with a pole. [< L *palus* stake]

**pole·star** (pōl′stär) *n.* 1 POLARIS. 2 That which governs, guides, or directs.

**po·lice** (pə·lēs′) *n.* 1 A body of persons organized to maintain order and enforce law. 2 The whole system of the department of government that maintains and enforces law and order. 3 The regulation of safety, conduct, and public order in a community. 4 The keeping clean of a camp or garrison. —*v.t.* **·liced, ·lic·ing** 1 To protect, regulate, or maintain order with or as with police. 2 To

393

make clean or orderly, as a military camp. [< Gk. *politeia* polity]

**po·lice·man** (pə·lēs′mən) *n. pl.* **·men** (-mən) A member of a police force. **—po·lice′wom′ an** (*pl.* **·wom·en**) *n. Fem.*

**pol·i·cy** (pol′ə·sē) *n. pl.* **·cies** 1 Prudence or sagacity in the conduct of affairs. 2 A course of administrative action. 3 Any system of management. [< Gk. *politeia*]

**pol·ish** (pol′ish) *n.* 1 Smoothness or glossiness of surface. 2 A substance used to produce such a surface. 3 Refinement of manner or style. 4 The process of polishing. *—v.t.* 1 To make smooth or lustrous. 2 To make refined or elegant. *—v.i.* 3 To take a gloss; shine. 4 To become elegant or refined. **—polish off** *Informal* 1 To do or finish quickly. 2 To dispose of. **—polish up** *Informal* To improve. [< L *polire* make smooth] **—pol′ish·er** *n.*

**po·lite** (pə·līt′) *adj.* 1 Exhibiting in manner or speech a considerable regard for others; courteous. 2 Elegant; refined: *polite* society. [< L *politus*, pp. of *polire* to polish] **—po·lite′ly** *adv.* **—po·lite′ness** *n.* **—Syn.** 1 civil, courtly, gracious, well-mannered. 2 cultivated, genteel, polished.

**pol·i·tic** (pol′ə·tik) *adj.* 1 Sagacious and wary in planning; artful. 2 Wisely expedient. 3 Pertaining to the state or its government; political. [< Gk. *politikos* civic] **—pol′i·tic·ly** *adv.*

**po·lit·i·cal** (pə·lit′i·kəl) *adj.* 1 Concerned in the administration of government. 2 Belonging to the science of government. 3 Having an organized system of government. 4 Pertaining to or connected with a party or parties seeking to control government. **—po·lit′i·cal·ly** *adv.*

**pol·i·ti·cian** (pol′ə·tish′ən) *n.* 1 One engaged in politics. 2 One who engages in politics for personal or partisan aims. 3 *Brit.* One skilled in the science of government; a statesman. 4 One holding a political position.

**pol·i·tics** (pol′ə·tiks) *n.* *(construed as sing. or pl.)* 1 The science of government. 2 The administration of political affairs. 3 Political sentiments or beliefs. 4 Political methods or procedures. 5 Participation in political affairs. **—play politics** To scheme for an advantage.

**poll** (pōl) *n.* 1 The head, esp. the top or back of the head. 2 A list of persons, esp. voters. 3 The voting at an election. 4 The number of votes thus cast. 5 *pl.* The place where vot-

ing is done and votes are counted. 6 A survey of public opinion on a given subject. *—v.t.* 1 To receive (a specified number of votes). 2 To register for taxation or voting. 3 To cast at the polls. 4 To interview in a poll. 5 To cut off or trim, as hair, horns, etc. *—v.i.* 6 To vote at the polls. [< MDu. *polle* top of the head] **—poll′er** *n.*

**pol·len** (pol′ən) *n.* The fine yellowish powder borne by the anthers of a flower and consisting of male sex cells. [< L, fine flour]

**poll tax** A tax on a person, as distinguished from that on property, esp. as a prerequisite for voting.

**pol·lut·ant** (pə·lōō′tənt) *n.* Something that pollutes, esp. a harmful chemical or waste substance introduced into the air, water, or soil.

**pol·lute** (pə·lōōt′) *v.t.* **·lut·ed**, **·lut·ing** 1 To make unclean or impure, as by introducing wastes: fumes *polluting* the air. 2 To desecrate; profane. [< L *polluere* make unclean] **—pol·lut′ed·ly** *adv.* **—pol·lut′ed·ness**, **pol·lut′er**, **pol·lu′tion** *n.* **—Syn.** 1 contaminate, foul, befoul. 2 defile.

**pol·troon** (pol·trōōn′) *n.* A mean-spirited coward. [< Ital. *poltrone* cowardly] **—pol·troon′ er·y** *n.*

**pol·y·an·dry** (pol′ē·an′drē) *n.* The condition of having more than one husband at the same time. [< POLY- + Gk. *anēr, andros* a man] **—pol′y·an′drous** *adj.*

**pol·y·eth·y·lene** (pol′ē·eth′ə·lēn) *n.* A thermoplastic resin made by polymerizing ethylene, used widely to make moisture-proof film, containers, insulators, etc.

**po·lyg·a·my** (pə·lig′ə·mē) *n.* The condition of having more than one wife or husband at the same time. [< POLY- + Gk. *gamos* marriage] **—po·lyg′a·mist** *n.* **—po·lyg′a·mous** *adj.* **—po·lyg′a·mous·ly** *adv.*

**pol·y·glot** (pol′i·glot) *adj.* 1 Expressed in several tongues. 2 Speaking several languages. *—n.* A person or book that is polyglot. [< Gk. *polyglōttos*] **—pol·y·glot′tal**, **pol·y·glot′ tic** *adj.*

**pol·y·gon** (pol′i·gon) *n.* A closed plane figure bounded by straight lines. **—po·lyg·o·nal** (pə·lig′ə·nəl), **po·lyg′o·nous** *adj.* **—po·lyg′ o·nal·ly** *adv.*

**pol·y·graph** (pol′i·graf, -gräf) *n.* An instrument for the simultaneous recording of various physiological reactions that are influenced by emotion, as pulse, breathing, perspiration, etc. **—pol′y·graph′ic** or **·i·cal** *adj.*

**pol·yp** (pol′ip) *n.* 1 Any of various coelenterates having a fringe of tentacles at the end of a cylindrical body, as a hydra, sea anemone, etc. 2 An outgrowth arising from mucous membrane, as of the nose, bladder, uterus, or rectum. [< Gk. *poly-* many + *pous* a foot]

**pol·y·un·sat·u·rat·ed** (pol′ə·un·sach′ə·rā′tid) *adj.* Having many double or triple bonds uniting adjacent carbon atoms and forming potential sites for adding hydrogen or various radicals: used esp. of edible oils and fats.

**pome·gran·ate** (pom′gran·it, pum′-) *n.* 1 A fruit with a leathery rind containing many seeds surrounded with juicy, edible pulp. 2 The tropical shrub bearing this fruit. [< L *pomum* apple + *granum*, a grain, seed]

**pomp** (pomp) *n.* 1 Magnificent and majestic display: royal *pomp.* 2 Ostentatious display. [< Gk. *pompē* a parade] —**Syn.** 1 flourish, grandeur, magnificence, splendor. 2 showiness.

**pom·pous** (pom′pəs) *adj.* 1 Marked by assumed stateliness; overbearing. 2 Magnificent; ceremonious or impressive. —**pom·pos·i·ty** (pom·pos′ə·tē), **pom′pous·ness** *n.* —**pom′pous·ly** *adv.*

**pon·der** (pon′dər) *v.t.* 1 To weigh in the mind; consider carefully. —*v.i.* 2 To meditate. [< L *pondus* a weight] —**pon′der·er** *n.* —**Syn.** 1 deliberate, examine. 2 muse, reflect.

**pon·der·ous** (pon′dər·əs) *adj.* 1 Having great weight; bulky. 2 Dull; lumbering. [< L *pondus* a weight] —**pon′der·os·i·ty** (-də·ros′ə·tē), **pon′der·ous·ness** *n.* —**pon′der·ous·ly** *adv.*

**pon·tiff** (pon′tif) *n.* 1 The pope. 2 A bishop. [< L *pontifex* a high priest of ancient Rome.] —**pon·tif′ic** *adj.*

**pon·tif·i·cate** (pon·tif′ə·kit, -kāt) *n.* 1 The office of a pontiff. 2 A pope's term of office. —*v.i.* (-kāt) **·cat·ed, ·cat·ing** To act or speak pompously or dogmatically.

**pon·toon** (pon·tōōn′) *n.* 1 A flat-bottomed boat, airtight cylinder, etc., used in the construction of temporary floating bridges. 2 Either of two floats on the landing gear of a seaplane. [< L *ponto* < *pons* a bridge]

**po·ny** (pō′nē) *n. pl.* **·nies** 1 A horse of any of several small breeds. 2 Anything small of its kind. 3 *Slang* A translation used in the preparation of foreign language lessons. 4 *Informal* A very small glass for alcoholic liquor. —*v.t. & v.i.* **·nied, ·ny·ing** *Slang* 1 To translate (lessons) with the aid of a pony. 2

To pay (money) that is due: with *up.* [< L *pullus* a young animal]

**poo·dle** (pōōd′l) *n.* One of a breed of dogs with long, curly hair, usu. clipped short in a conventional pattern. [G *pudel*]

**pool** (pōōl) *n.* 1 A collective stake in a gambling game. 2 A combination whereby companies or corporations agree to fix rates or prices and divide the collective profits pro rata. 3 Any of various games played on a six-pocket billiard table. 4 A combining of efforts or resources for mutual benefit. 5 The persons forming such a combination. —*v.t.* 1 To combine in a mutual fund or pool. —*v.i.* 2 To form a pool. [< F *poule* a stake, a hen]

**poor** (pōōr) *adj.* 1 Lacking means of comfortable subsistence; needy. 2 Lacking in good qualities. 3 Wanting in strength or spirit; cowardly. 4 Devoid of elegance or refinements. 5 Deserving of pity: the *poor* dog. 6 Devoid of merit; unsatisfactory. [< L *pauper*] —**poor′ly** *adj., adv.* —**poor′ness** *n.* —**Syn.** 1 indigent, penniless, poverty-stricken. 2 deficient. 4 squalid. 5 pitiable, wretched.

**pop** (pop) *v.* **popped, pop·ping** *v.i.* 1 To make a sharp, explosive sound. 2 To burst open with such a sound. 3 To move or go suddenly or quickly: with *in, out,* etc. 4 To protrude; bulge. —*v.t.* 5 To cause to burst or explode, as corn by heating. 6 To thrust or put suddenly: with *in, out,* etc. 7 To fire (a gun, etc.). 8 *Slang* To take (habit-forming or harmful drugs) by mouth or injection: to *pop* pills. —**pop the question** *Informal* To make a proposal of marriage. —*n.* 1 A sharp explosive noise, as of a firearm. 2 A nonintoxicating, variously flavored drink, usu. carbonated. 3 A shot, as in basketball. —*adv.* Like, or with the sound of a pop. [Imit.]

**Pope** (pōp) *n.* The bishop of Rome, the supreme head of the Roman Catholic Church. **Also pope.** [< Gk. *pappas* father]

**pop·u·lace** (pop′yə·lis) *n.* The mass of common people. [< L *populus* people]

**pop·u·lar** (pop′yə·lər) *adj.* 1 Of or carried on by the people at large. 2 Possessing many friends. 3 Widely approved or admired. 4 Suitable for the common people. 5 Prevalent among the people. 6 Suited to the means of the people: *popular* prices. 7 Of folk origin: the *popular* ballad. [< L *populus* the people] —**pop′u·lar·ly** *adv.* —**Syn.** 2 well-liked. 5 common, universal, widespread.

**pop·u·lar·i·ty** (pop′yə·lar′ə·tē) *n.* The condition of possessing the confidence and favor of others.

**pop·u·lar·ize** (pop′yə·lə·rīz′) v.t. ·ized, ·iz·ing To make popular. *Brit. sp.* ·ise′. —**pop′u·lar·i·za′tion, pop′u·lar·iz′er** n.

**pop·u·la·tion** (pop′yə·lā′shən) n. 1 The total group of people or animals of a specified kind in a given area. 2 The number of individuals in such a group. 3 The act or process of populating. 4 The stated experimental base of a statistical study. [< L *populus* the people]

**pop·u·lous** (pop′yə·ləs) adj. Having many inhabitants; thickly settled. —**pop′u·lous·ly** adv. —**pop′u·lous·ness** n.

**porce·lain** (pôrs′lin, pōrs′-, pôr′sə-, pōr′-) n. A white, hard, translucent ceramic ware, usu. glazed, existing in many varieties. [< Ital. *porcellana,* orig. a cowry]

**porch** (pôrch, pōrch) n. 1 A covered structure forming an entrance to a building. 2 A veranda. [< L *porta* a gate]

**por·cu·pine** (pôr′kyə·pīn) n. Any of various rodents having the back and tail covered with long, sharp, defensive spines. [< OF *porc* a hog + *espin* a thorn]

**pore¹** (pôr, pōr) v.i. pored, por·ing 1 To study or read with care and application: with *over.* 2 To meditate; ponder. [ME *pouren*]

**pore²** (pôr, pōr) n. 1 A small natural opening, as a stoma on a leaf or the open end of a sweat gland. 2 A minute hole in any material. [< Gk. *poros*]

**pork** (pôrk, pōrk) n. 1 The flesh of pigs and hogs, used as food. 2 *Slang* Government money, favors, etc., obtained by political patronage. [< L *porcus* a hog]

**po·rous** (pôr′əs, pō′rəs) adj. 1 Having pores. 2 Having many tiny holes. —**po′rous·ly** adv. —**po′rous·ness** n.

**por·poise** (pôr′pəs) n. pl. ·poises or ·poise 1 Any of various small, usu. gregarious, toothed whales with a blunt snout. 2 A dolphin. [< L *porcus* a hog + *piscis* fish]

**port¹** (pôrt, pōrt) n. 1 An opening in the side of a ship, as for a gun, or for the passage of cargo. 2 PORTHOLE. 3 A passageway into or out of a machine or device. [< L *porta* gate]

**port²** (pôrt, pōrt) n. 1 The way in which one bears or carries himself. 2 The position of a rifle when ported. —v.t. 1 *Mil.* To carry, as a weapon, diagonally across the body and sloping to the left shoulder. 2 To carry. [< L *portare* carry]

**port·a·ble** (pôr′tə·bəl, pōr′-) adj. That can be readily carried or moved. [< L *portare* carry] —**port′a·ble·ness, port′a·bil′i·ty** n. —**port′a·bly** adv.

**por·tal** (pôr′təl, pōr′-) n. A passage for gaining entrance; door, esp. one that is grand and imposing. [< L *porta* a gate]

**por·tent** (pôr′tent, pōr′-) n. 1 Anything that warns of a future event; omen. 2 Ominous significance.

**por·ten·tous** (pôr·ten′təs, pōr-) adj. 1 Full of portents of ill; ominous. 2 Amazing; extraordinary. 3 Pretentiously solemn. —**por·ten′tous·ly** adv. —**por·ten′tous·ness** n.

**por·ter** (pôr′tər, pōr′-) n. A keeper of a door or gate. [< L *porta* a gate, a door]

**port·fo·li·o** (pôrt·fō′lē·ō, pōrt-) n. pl. ·li·os 1 A portable case for holding documents, etc. 2 The position or office of a minister of state or member of a government. 3 A list of investments. [< L *portare* carry + *folium* leaf]

**port·hole** (pôrt′hōl′, pōrt′-) n. A small round opening in a ship's side to admit air and light.

**por·ti·co** (pôr′ti·kō, pōr′-) n. pl. ·coes or ·cos An open porch or place for walking with a roof upheld by columns. [< L *porticus* —**por′ti·coed** adj.

**por·tion** (pôr′shən, pōr′-) n. 1 A part of a whole. 2 An allotment; share. 3 The quantity of food served to one person. 4 The part of an estate coming to an heir. 5 A dowry. 6 One's fortune or destiny. —v.t. 1 To divide into shares for distribution: often with *out.* 2 To give a dowry to. [< L *portio*] —**por′tion·er** n. —**por′tion·less** adj. —**Syn.** n. 1 division, piece. 3 serving. 4 inheritance. 6 fate, lot.

**por·trait** (pôr′trit, pōr′-, -trāt) n. 1 A likeness of a person, esp. of the face. 2 A vivid description of something or someone. [< OF *pourtraire* portray] —**por′trait·ist** n.

**por·tray** (pôr·trā′, pōr-) v.t. 1 To represent by drawing, painting, etc. 2 To describe in words. 3 To represent, as in a play. [< L *protrahere* draw forth] —**por·tray′al, por·tray′er** n. —**Syn.** 1 delineate. 2 depict, picture, show. 3 act, perform.

**Por·tu·guese** (pôr′chə·gēz′, -gēs′, pōr′-) n. 1 A citizen or native of Portugal. 2 The language of Portugal. —adj. Of or pertaining to Portugal, its people, or their language.

**pose** (pōz) n. 1 A position of the whole or part of the body, esp. one held for an artist, photographer, etc. 2 A mental attitude assumed for effect. —v. posed, pos·ing v.i. 1 To assume or hold a position, as for a portrait. 2 To affect attitudes. 3 To represent oneself: to *pose* as an expert. —*v.t.* 4 To cause to assume a position, as for a portrait. 5 To put forward for consideration or discussion: to *pose* a difficult question. [< OF *poser* to pose]

**po·si·tion** (pə·zish′ən) *n.* 1 The manner in which a thing is placed. 2 The place in which a thing is located. 3 An advantageous location: to jockey for *position*. 4 Disposition of the parts of the body; posture. 5 The manner of being placed: an awkward *position*. 6 Social standing, esp. if high. 7 A job; employment. 8 Point of view; stand. —*v.t.* To place in a particular or appropriate position. [< L *positus*, pp. of *ponere* to place] —**po·si′tion·al** *adj.*

**pos·i·tive** (poz′ə·tiv) *adj.* 1 That is or may be directly affirmed; sure. 2 Inherent in a thing by and of itself, regardless of its relations to other things; absolute. 3 Openly and plainly expressed; emphatic: a *positive* denial. 4 Confident; self-possessed: a *positive* person. 5 Overly confident; arrogant: a *positive* manner. 6 Incontestable: *positive* proof. 7 Helpful; constructive: *positive* suggestions. 8 Noting one of two opposite directions, qualities, properties, etc., which is taken as primary, or as indicating increase or progression. 9 *Math.* Greater than zero. 10 *Electr.* Having a charge or potential capable of attracting electrons. 11 ELECTROPOSITIVE. 12 Tending to move toward a stimulus: a *positive* tropism. 13 Indicating the presence of a specified condition, disease, or microorganism. 14 Having the lights and shades in their natural relation, as in a photograph. 15 *Gram.* Denoting the simple, uncompared degree of the adjective or adverb. —*n.* 1 That which is positive, as a photograph print, a battery terminal, a quality, a degree, a quantity, etc. 2 *Gram.* a The positive degree of an adjective or adverb. b A word in this degree. [< L *positivus* < *positus* placed] —**pos′i·tive·ly** *adv.* —**pos′i·tive·ness** *n.* —**Syn.** *adj.* 1 actual, existing, real. 3 explicit. 6 indisputable.

**pos·i·tron** (poz′ə·tron) *n.* *Physics* A positively charged particle with a mass equal to that of the electron. [< POSI(TIVE) + (ELEC)TRON]

**pos·sess** (pə·zes′) *v.t.* 1 To have as property; own. 2 To have as a quality, attribute, etc. 3 To exert control over; dominate: his fear *possessed* him. 4 *Archaic* To seize; gain. [< L *possessus*, pp. of *possidere* possess] —**pos·ses′sor** *n.*

**pos·ses·sion** (pə·zesh′ən) *n.* 1 The act or state of possessing or being possessed; ownership or occupancy. 2 A thing possessed or owned. 3 *pl.* Property; belongings. 4 The state of being dominated by an idea, emotion, evil spirit, etc. 5 Self-possession. 6 A territory under the control of a foreign country.

**pos·ses·sive** (pə·zes′iv) *adj.* 1 Pertaining to possession or ownership. 2 Overly desirous of owning or controlling. 3 *Gram.* Designating a case of a noun or pronoun indicating possession. —*n.* *Gram.* 1 The possessive case. 2 A possessive form or construction. —**pos·ses′sive·ly** *adv.* —**pos·ses′sive·ness** *n.* • In English the *possessive* is formed in nouns by adding 's to the singular and irregular plurals: *Larry's* hammer; *men's* minds, and a simple apostrophe to the regular plural and sometimes to singulars and proper names ending in a sibilant: *boys'* games; *Dickens'* (or *Dickens's*) novels. Pronouns have special possessive forms: *my, mine, your, yours, his, her, hers, our, ours, their, theirs, whose.*

**pos·si·bil·i·ty** (pos′ə·bil′ə·tē) *n. pl.* **·ties** 1 The fact of being possible. 2 A possible thing.

**pos·si·ble** (pos′ə·bəl) *adj.* 1 That may be or may become true. 2 That may come about or be done. 3 That may be suitable: a *possible* site for a camp. [< L *posse* be able] —**pos′si·bly** *adv.*

**post**[1] (pōst) *n.* 1 An upright piece of timber or other material used as a support. 2 A line serving to mark the starting or finishing point of a racecourse. —*v.t.* 1 To put up (a poster, etc.) in some public place. 2 To fasten posters upon. 3 To announce by or as by a poster. 4 To publish the name of on a list. 5 To forbid trespassing on (land, etc.) by posting signs. [< L *postis* a door post]

**post**[2] (pōst) *n.* 1 Any fixed place where a soldier or policeman is stationed. 2 A place where troops are garrisoned. 3 The troops occupying a military installation. 4 A local unit of a veterans' organization. 5 An office or employment; position. 6 A trading post, esp. in an undeveloped region. —*v.t.* To assign to a particular position or post. [< L *positum*, pp. neut. of *ponere* to place]

**post**[3] (pōst) *n.* 1 An established system for transporting and delivering letters, packages, and other mail matter. 2 The mail delivered and carried at one time. 3 Formerly, a courier who traveled over a fixed route carrying letters and dispatches. 4 Formerly, any of the series of stations on such a route, furnishing relays of men and horses, and carriages for travelers. —*v.t.* 1 To place in a mailbox; mail. 2 To inform: He *posted* us on the latest news. 3 In bookkeeping, to transfer (items or accounts) to the ledger. —*v.i.* 4 To travel with post horses. 5 To travel with speed; hasten. 6 In horseback riding, to rise from the saddle in rhythm with a horse's trot. —*adv.* Speedily; rapidly. [< L *posita*, pp. fem. of *ponere* to place]

**post·age** (pōs′tij) *n.* The charge levied on mail matter.

**pos·tal** (pōs′təl) *adj.* Pertaining to the mails or to mail service. —*n.* A postal card.

**post·er** (pōs′tər) *n.* A printed sheet for advertising, public information, etc., to be posted on a wall or other surface. —**Syn.** bill, notice, placard, sign.

**pos·te·ri·or** (pos·tir′ē·ər) *adj.* 1 Situated behind or toward the hinder part. 2 Coming after another in a series. —*n. Often pl.* The buttocks. [< L *posterus* following] —**pos·te·ri·or·i·ty** (pos·tir′ē·ôr′ə·tē, -or′ə-) *n.* —**pos·te′ri·or·ly** *adv.*

**pos·ter·i·ty** (pos·ter′ə·tē) *n.* 1 A person's descendants. 2 Succeeding generations, collectively. [< L *posterus* following]

**post·grad·u·ate** (pōst′graj′o͞o·it, -āt) *adj.* Of or pertaining to studies pursued after receiving a first degree; graduate. —*n.* One who pursues or has completed a postgraduate course.

**post·hu·mous** (pos′cho͞o·məs) *adj.* 1 Born after the father's death: said of a child. 2 Published after the author's death, as a book. 3 Arising after a person's death: a *posthumous* reputation. [< L *postumus* latest, last] —**post′hu·mous·ly** *adv.*

**post·mark** (pōst′märk′) *n.* The mark of a post office on mail handled there, serving to cancel stamps, and usu. giving the date and place of mailing. —*v.t.* To stamp with a postmark.

**post·mor·tem** (pōst·môr′təm) *adj.* Occurring, done, or made soon after death. —*n.* AUTOPSY. [L]

**post·paid** (pōst′pād′) *adj.* Having postage prepaid.

**post·pone** (pōst·pōn′) *v.t.* ·poned, ·pon·ing To put off to a future time. [< L *post-* after + *ponere* put] —**post·pone′ment**, **post·pon′er** *n.* —**Syn.** defer, delay, procrastinate.

**post·script** (pōst′skript′) *n.* 1 A supplemental addition to a written or printed document. 2 Something added to a letter after the writer's signature. [< L *postscribere* write after]

**pos·tu·late** (pos′cho·lit) *n.* 1 A basis of argument laid down as well known or too plain to require proof. 2 A proposition assumed as true; an axiom. —*v.t.* (pos′cho·lāt) ·lat·ed, ·lat·ing 1 To claim; demand. 2 To set forth as self-evident or already known. 3 To assume the truth or reality of. [< L *postulare* to demand] —**pos′tu·la′tion**, **pos′tu·la′tor** *n.*

**pos·ture** (pos′chər) *n.* 1 The way in which the body is held; bearing. 2 Situation or condition at a given time; circumstances: the military *posture* of a nation. 3 Frame of mind; attitude. —*v.* ·tured, ·tur·ing *v.t.* 1 To place in a specific posture; pose. —*v.i.* 2 To assume a specific posture. 3 To pose for effect; attitudinize. [< L *positus*, p.p. of *ponere* to place] —**pos′tur·al** *adj.* —**pos′tur·er**, **pos′tur·ist** *n.*

**po·ta·to** (pə·tā′tō) *n. pl.* ·toes 1 A starchy, edible tuber of a plant of the nightshade family. 2 The plant. 3 SWEET POTATO. [< Sp. *patata*]

**po·tent** (pōt′nt) *adj.* 1 Producing marked effects: a *potent* drug. 2 Convincing: a *potent* argument. 3 Having great authority. 4 Able to perform sexual intercourse: said of males. [< L *potens* pr.p. of *posse* be able, have power] —**po′ten·cy** ( *pl.* ·cies), **po′tence** *n.* —**po′tent·ly** *adv.*

**po·ten·tate** (pōt′n·tāt) *n.* One having great power or sway; a sovereign.

**po·ten·tial** (pə·ten′shəl) *adj.* 1 Possible but not actual. 2 Having capacity for existence, but not yet existing. 3 *Physics* Existing by virtue of position: said of energy. 4 *Gram.* Indicating possibility or capability by the use of *can*, *could*, *may*, etc. 5 Having force or power. —*n.* 1 Anything that may be possible. 2 *Gram.* The potential mood. 3 *Physics* The work required to move a body from a point infinitely distant to a given point in a field of force. 4 *Electr.* A difference of electric potential; voltage. [< L *potens* potent] —**po·ten·ti·al·i·ty** (pə·ten′shē·al′ə·tē) ( *pl.* ·ties) *n.* —**po·ten′tial·ly** *adv.*

**po·tion** (pō′shən) *n.* A draft, as of a liquid having medicinal, poisonous, or supposed magical properties. [< L *potare* to drink]

**pot·pour·ri** (pō·po͞o·rē′) *n.* 1 A mixture of dried, sweet-smelling flower petals used to perfume a room. 2 A collection of various things; miscellany. [F. lit., rotten pot]

**pouch** (pouch) *n.* 1 A small bag or sack. 2 *Zool.*

**a** A saclike part for containing or carrying food. **b** MARSUPIUM. —*v.t.* 1 To put in or as in a pouch; pocket. 2 To fashion or arrange in pouchlike form. —*v.i.* 3 To take on a pouchlike shape. [< OF *poche*] —**pouch′y** *adj.* (·i·er, ·i·est)

**poul·try** (pōl′trē) *n.* Domestic fowls, as chickens, ducks, turkeys, and geese. [< OF *poulet* fowl]

**pounce** (pouns) *v.i.* pounced, pounc·ing To swoop, as in seizing prey; with *on*, *upon*, or *at.* —*n.* The act of pouncing. [?] —*Syn.* *n.*, *v.* jump, leap, spring. —**pounc′er** *n.*

**pound¹** (pound) *n.* 1 **a** A unit of avoirdupois weight equal to 0.45359 kilogram or 16 avoirdupois ounces. **b** A unit of troy weight equal to 0.37324 kilogram or 12 troy ounces. 2 The basic monetary unit of the United Kingdom, formerly equal to 20 shillings, but after 1971 equal to 100 pence: **also pound sterling.** 3 The basic monetary unit of various other countries, as Cyprus, Gambia, Ireland, Israel, Lebanon, Libya, Malawi, Malta, Nigeria, Rhodesia, Sudan, Syria, Turkey, and Egypt. [< L *pondus* weight]

**pound²** (pound) *n.* 1 A place, enclosed by authority, in which stray animals are kept. 2 An enclosed shelter for cattle or sheep. 3 A trap for wild animals. —*v.t.* To confine in or as in a pound. [< OE *pund*]

**pour** (pôr, pōr) *v.t.* 1 To cause to flow by gravity in a continuous stream, as water, sand, etc. 2 To emit or utter continuously. —*v.i.* 3 To flow in a continuous stream; gush. 4 To rain heavily. 5 To serve as a hostess at a social tea. 6 To move in great numbers; swarm. —*n.* A pouring or downfall. [ME *pouren*] —**pour′er** *n.* —**pour′ing·ly** *adv.*

**pout** (pout) *n.* One of various freshwater catfishes having a pouting appearance. [< OE *pūte*]

**pov·er·ty** (pov′ər·tē) *n.* 1 The state of being poor; need. 2 Scarcity of something needed. 3 Meagerness; inadequacy: *poverty* of language. [< L *pauper* poor]

**pow·der** (pou′dər) *n.* 1 A mass of fine, free particles of a solid substance. 2 A cosmetic preparation. 3 A medicine in the form of powder. 4 GUNPOWDER. —**take a powder** *Slang* To run off; disappear suddenly. —*v.t.* 1 To pulverize. 2 To sprinkle or cover with or as with powder. —*v.i.* 3 To be reduced to powder. 4 To use powder as a cosmetic. [< L *pulvis, pulveris* dust] —**pow′der·er** *n.* —**pow′der·y** *adj.*

**pow·er** (pou′ər) *n.* 1 Ability to act; potency. 2 Potential capacity. 3 Strength or force. 4 The right, ability, or capacity to exercise control. 5 Any agent that exercises control or dominion: naval *power.* 6 Great or telling force or effect. 7 Any form of energy that can perform work: water *power.* 8 *Physics* The time rate at which energy is transferred, or work is done. 9 *Math.* **a** The product of a number taken a given number of times as a factor. **b** An exponent. 10 *Optics* Magnifying capacity, as of a lens. —**in power** 1 In office. 2 In control. —**the powers that be** Those in control. —*v.t.* 1 To provide with means of propulsion. 2 To force or push, esp. when overcoming resistance: He *powered* his way through for a touchdown. —*v.i.* 3 To force one's way: The truck *powered* through the mud. —*adj.* Operated by a motor or by electricity: *power* tool. [< OF *poeir* be able] —*Syn.* *n.* 1 capacity, efficacy. 3 energy, might. 4 authority, command.

**pow·er·ful** (pou′ər·fəl) *adj.* 1 Possessing great force. 2 Having great intensity or energy. 3 Exercising great authority. 4 Having great effect on the mind; convincing. —*adv.* *Informal* Very; exceedingly. —**pow′er·ful·ly** *adv.*

**prac·ti·ca·ble** (prak′tə·k′·bəl) *adj.* 1 That can be put into practice; feasible. 2 Usable. —**prac′ti·ca·bil′i·ty, prac′ti·ca·ble·ness** *n.* —**prac′ti·ca·bly** *adv.*

**prac·ti·cal** (prak′ti·kəl) *adj.* 1 Pertaining to actual use and experience rather than theory. 2 Trained by practice or experience. 3 Useful. 4 Manifested in practice. [< Gk. *praktikos* fit for doing] —**prac′ti·cal′i·ty** (-kal′ə·tē), prac′ti·cal·ness** *n.*

**prac·tice** (prak′tis) *v.* ·ticed, ·tic·ing *v.t.* 1 To make use of habitually: to *practice* economy. 2 To apply in action: *Practice* what you preach. 3 To work at as a profession: to *practice* law. 4 To do or perform repeatedly in order to acquire skill. —*v.i.* 5 To repeat or rehearse something in order to acquire proficiency. 6 To work at or pursue a profession. —*n.* 1 Any customary action; habit. 2 An established custom or usage. 3 The act or process of executing or accomplishing. 4 The pursuit of a profession; the *practice* of medicine. 5 Frequent and repeated exercise in order to gain skill. 6 The skill so gained: The violinist was out of *practice.* 7 The rules by which legal proceedings are governed. Also **prac′tise**. [< LL *practicus* practical] —**prac′tic·er** *n.* — **Syn.** *v.* 4 drill, exercise, rehearse. • In Britain, *practice* is almost invariably the spelling used for the noun, *practise* for the verb. In the U.S., the noun form is more commonly *practice*, although *practise* is also used; both spellings are widely used as verbs.

**prac·ti·tion·er** (prak·tish′ən·ər) *n.* 1 One who practices an art or profession. 2 A Christian Science healer.

**prai·rie** (prâr′ē) *n.* A level or rolling tract of treeless land covered with coarse grass and generally of rich soil. [< L *pratum* meadow]

**praise** (prāz) *v.t.* **praised, prais·ing** 1 To express approval of; applaud. 2 To express adoration of; glorify (God, etc.). —*n.* The act of praising or the state of being praised; commendation or adoration. —**sing (one's) praises** To praise highly. [< L *pretium* price] —**prais′er** *n.* —**Syn.** *v.* 1 commend, eulogize, extol, laud. *n.* acclaim, applause, eulogy, plaudit.

**prance** (prans, pråns) *v.* **pranced, pranc·ing** *v.i.* 1 To move with high steps, esp. by springing from the hind legs, as a spirited horse. 2 To ride on a prancing horse. 3 To move in an arrogant manner; swagger. 4 To gambol; caper. —*v.t.* 5 To cause to prance. —*n.* The act of prancing. [< Scand.] —**pranc′er** *n.* —**pranc′ing·ly** *adv.*

**prank** (prangk) *n.* A mischievous act; joke. —*v.i.* To play pranks or tricks. [?] —**prank′ish** *adj.* —**prank′ish·ly** *adv.* —**prank′ish·ness, prank′ster** *n.*

**prat·tle** (prat′l) *v.* **·tled, ·tling** *v.i.* 1 To talk like a child; prate. —*v.t.* 2 To utter in a foolish way: to *prattle* secrets. —*n.* 1 Childish speech; babble. 2 Idle or foolish talk. [Freq. of PRATE] —**prat′tler** *n.* —**prat′tling·ly** *adv.*

**pray** (prā) *v.i.* 1 To address prayers to a deity. 2 To make entreaty; beg. —*v.t.* 3 To ask (someone) earnestly; entreat. 4 To ask for by prayers or entreaty. 5 To effect by prayer. [< L *precari* ask, pray]

**prayer** (prâr) *n.* 1 The act of offering reverent petitions to a deity. 2 Any earnest request. 3 *Often pl.* A religious service made up largely of prayer. 4 Something prayed for. 5 A form of words appropriate to prayer. [< L *precari* pray] —**prayer′ful** *adj.* —**prayer′ful·ly** *adv.* —**prayer′ful·ness** *n.*

**preach** (prēch) *v.i.* 1 To deliver a sermon. 2 To give advice or urge a course of action, esp. in a meddlesome or tedious way. —*v.t.* 3 To

advocate or recommend urgently: to *preach* peace. 4 To proclaim; expound upon. 5 To deliver (a sermon, etc.). [< L *prae-* before + *dicare* make known]

**pre·am·ble** (prē′am·bəl) *n.* 1 A statement introductory to and explanatory of what follows, as in a constitution or a contract. 2 A preliminary event or action. [< L *prae-* before + *ambulare* to walk] —**pre·am′bu·lar′y** *adj.*

**pre·car·i·ous** (pri·kâr′ē·əs) *adj.* 1 Subject to uncertainty. 2 Subject or leading to danger; hazardous. [< L *precarius* obtained by prayer] —**pre·car′i·ous·ly** *adv.* —**pre·car′i·ous·ness** *n.* —**Syn.** 1 doubtful. 2 insecure, perilous, risky.

**pre·cau·tion** (pri·kô′shən) *n.* 1 Care taken in advance against danger, etc. 2 A provision made for some emergency. [< L *prae-* before + *cavere* take care] —**pre·cau′tion·al, pre·cau·tion·ar·y** (pri·kô′shən·er′ē) *adj.*

**pre·cede** (pri·sēd′) *v.t.* & *v.i.* **·ced·ed, ·ced·ing** To go before in order, place, rank, time, etc. [< L *prae-* before + *cedere* go]

**prec·e·dence** (pri·sēd′ns, pres′ə·dəns) *n.* 1 The act or right of preceding in place, time, or rank. 2 Higher or superior rank. Also **prec·e′den·cy**.

**prec·e·dent** (pres′ə·dənt) *n.* A case that may serve as an example or model for a future action, procedure, etc. —*adj.* (pri·sēd′nt) Previous; preceding. —**prec·e·den·tial** (pres′ə·den′shəl) *adj.* —**prec′e·dent·ly** *adv.*

**pre·cept** (prē′sept) *n.* A prescribed rule of conduct or action. [< L *prae-* before + *capere* receive, take]

**pre·cinct** (prē′singkt) *n.* 1 A place definitely marked off by fixed lines. 2 A minor territorial or jurisdictional district. 3 An election district. 4 A police subdivision of a city or town. [< LL *praecingere* gird about]

**pre·cious** (presh′əs) *adj.* 1 Highly priced or prized, as for rarity or other value. 2 Beloved; cherished. 3 *Informal* Very considerable. 4 Too refined; fastidious: a *precious* writer. [< L *pretiosus*< *pretium* price] —**pre′cious·ly** *adv.* —**pre′cious·ness** *n.* — **Syn.** 1 costly, priceless, valuable.

**prec·i·pice** (pres′i·pis) *n.* A high, steep place; the brink of a cliff. [< L *praeceps* headlong < *prae-* before + *caput* head]

**pre·cip·i·tate** (pri·sip′ə·tit) *adj.* 1 Rushing down headlong. 2 Lacking due deliberation; hasty. 3 Sudden and brief. —*v.* (pri·sip′ə·tāt) **·tat·ed, ·tat·ing** *v.t.* 1 To hasten the occurrence of. 2 To hurl from or as from a height. 3 *Meteorol.* To cause (water vapor) to condense and fall as a liquid or solid. 4 *Chem.* To separate (a constituent) in solid form, as from a solution. —*v.i.* 5 *Meteorol.* To fall as water or ice. 6 *Chem.* To separate out of solution as a solid. 7 To fall headlong; rush. —*n.* (pri·sip′ə·tit, -tāt) *Chem.* A solid precipitated from a solution. [< L *praeceps* headlong] —pre·cip′i·tate·ly *adv.* —pre·cip′i·tate·ness, pre·cip′i·ta′tor *n.* —pre·cip′i·ta′tive *adj.*

pre·cip·i·ta·tion (pri·sip′ə·tā′shən) *n.* 1 The state of being thrown downward. 2 Headlong or rash haste. 3 A falling, flowing, or rushing down with violence or rapidity. 4 *Chem.* a The process of precipitating any of the constituents of a solution. b PRECIPITATE. 5 *Meteorol.* The depositing of moisture or ice from the atmosphere upon the surface of the earth. 6 Rain, snow, sleet, etc.

pre·cise (pri·sīs′) *adj.* 1 Sharply or clearly determined; accurate. 2 No more and no less than. 3 Scrupulously observant of rule; punctilious. [< L *praecisus,* p.p. of *praecidere* cut off short] —pre·cise′ness *n.*

pre·ci·sion (pri·sizh′ən) *n.* The quality of being precise; accuracy. —pre·ci′sion·ist *n.*

pre·co·cious (pri·kō′shəs) *adj.* 1 Developing before the natural season. 2 Unusually forward or advanced, as a child. [< L *praecox*] —pre·co′cious·ly *adv.* —pre·co′cious·ness, pre·coc′i·ty (-kos′ə·tē) *n.*

pre·con·ceive (prē′kən·sēv′) *v.t.* ·ceived, ·ceiv·ing To form an idea or opinion of beforehand. —pre·con·cep·tion (prē′kən·sep′shən) *n.*

pred·a·to·ry (pred′ə·tôr′ē, -tō′rē) *adj.* 1 Living by preying upon other animals: a *predatory* animal. 2 Characterized by plundering or stealing. [< L *praeda* prey] —pred′a·tor, pred′a·to′ri·ness *n.* —pred′a·to′ri·ly *adv.*

pred·e·ces·sor (pred′ə·ses′ər) *n.* 1 One who goes or has gone before another in a position, office, etc. 2 A thing that has preceded another. 3 An ancestor. [< L *prae-* before + *decedere* retire]

pre·des·ti·na·tion (prē·des′tə·nā′shən) *n.* 1 The act of predestinating; fate. 2 *Theol.* The foreordination of all things by God.

pre·dic·a·ment (pri·dik′ə·mənt) *n.* 1 A trying, embarrassing, or puzzling situation. 2 A specific state, position, or situation. [< LL *praedicamentum* that which is predicated] —Syn. 1 dilemma, fix, plight, strait.

pred·i·cate (pred′i·kāt) *v.* ·cat·ed, ·cat·ing *v.t.*

1 To declare; affirm. 2 To affirm concerning the subject of a proposition. 3 To found or base (an argument, proposition, etc.): with *on* or *upon.* —*v.i.* 4 To make a statement or affirmation. —*adj.* 1 Predicated. 2 *Gram.* Belonging to the predicate. In "Trees are leafy," *leafy* is a predicate adjective; in "He was king," *king* is a predicate noun. —*n.* (pred′i·kit) *Gram.* The word or words in a sentence that express what is affirmed or denied of a subject. In the sentence, "Life is short," "is short" is the predicate. [< L *praedicare* make known] —pred′i·ca′tion *n.* —pred′i·ca′tive *adj.* —pred′i·ca′tive·ly *adv.*

pre·dict (pri·dikt′) *v.t.* 1 To make known beforehand. 2 To assert on the basis of theory, data, or experience but in advance of proof. —*v.i.* 3 To make a prediction. [< L *prae-* before + *dicere* say] —pre·dict′a·ble *adj.* —pre·dict′a·bly *adv.* —pre·dic′tor *n.*

pre·dic·tion (pri·dik′shən) *n.* 1 The act of predicting. 2 The thing predicted; forecast. —pre·dic′tive *adj.* —pre·dic′tive·ly *adv.*

pre·di·lec·tion (pred′ə·lek′shən, prē′də-) *n.* A preference or liking: with *for.* [< L *prae-* before + *diligere* love, choose]

pre·dis·pose (prē′dis·pōz′) *v.t.* ·posed, ·pos·ing To give a tendency to; make susceptible: Exhaustion *predisposes* one to sickness. —pre·dis·po·si·tion (prē′dis·pə·zish′ən) *n.*

pre·dom·i·nate (pri·dom′ə·nāt) *v.i.* ·nat·ed, ·nat·ing 1 To have influence or control: with *over.* 2 To be superior to all others, as in power, height, number, etc. —pre·dom′i·nat′ing·ly *adv.* —pre·dom′i·na′tion *n.*

pre·em·i·nent (prē·em′ə·nənt) *adj.* Supremely eminent; distinguished above all others. —pre·em′i·nent·ly *adv.* —pre·em′i·nence *n.*

pre·empt (prē·empt′) *v.t.* 1 To seize or appropriate beforehand. 2 To occupy (public land) so as to acquire by preemption. —pre·emp′tor *n.*

pre·emp·tion (prē·emp′shən) *n.* 1 The right or act of purchasing before others. 2 Public land obtained by exercising this right. [< L *prae-* before + *emptus,* pp. of *emere* buy] —pre·emp′tive, pre·emp′to·ry (-tər·ē) *adj.*

pre·fab·ri·cate (prē·fab′rə·kāt) *v.t.* ·cat·ed, ·cat·ing 1 To fabricate beforehand. 2 To manufacture in sections that can be rapidly assembled, as a building. —pre·fab′ri·ca′tion *n.*

pref·ace (pref′is) *n.* 1 A brief explanation to the reader at the beginning of a publication. 2 Any introductory speech, writing, etc. —*v.t.* **·aced, ·ac·ing** 1 To introduce or furnish with a preface. 2 To be or serve as a preface for. [< L *prae-* before + *fari* speak]

**pref·a·to·ry** (pref′ə·tôr′ē, -tō′rē) *adj.* Of the nature of a preface; introductory. Also **pref′a·to′ri·al.** —**pref′a·to′ri·ly** *adv.*

**pre·fer** (pri·fûr′) *v.t.* **·ferred, ·fer·ring** 1 To hold in higher regard or esteem; like better. 2 To give priority to. 3 To advance or promote. 4 To offer, as a suit or charge, for consideration or decision before a court. [< L *prae-* before + *ferre* to bear] —**pre·fer′rer** *n.*

**pref·er·a·ble** (pref′ər·ə·bəl) *adj.* To be preferred; more desirable. —**pref′er·a·bil′i·ty, pref′er·a·ble·ness** *n.* —**pref′er·a·bly** *adv.*

**pref·er·ence** (pref′ər·əns) *n.* 1 The choice of one thing or person over another. 2 The state of being preferred. 3 An object of favor or choice. 4 The giving of priority to one person over others; favoritism. 5 The right to a prior choice or claim.

**pre·fer·ment** (pri·fûr′mənt) *n.* 1 The act of promoting or appointing to higher office. 2 A superior post or dignity: said esp. of ecclesiastical rank.

**pre·fix** (prē′fiks) *n.* 1 *Gram.* A syllable affixed to the beginning of a word to modify or alter the meaning, as *non-* in *nonessential* or *post-* in *postwar.* 2 Something placed before, as a title before a name. —*v.t.* (prē·fiks′) To put before or at the beginning. [< L *prae-* before + *figere* to fix] —**pre′fix·al** *adj.* —**pre·fix·ion** (prē·fik′shən) *n.*

**preg·nan·cy** (preg′nən·sē) *n. pl.* **·cies** The condition or a time of being pregnant.

**preg·nant** (preg′nənt) *adj.* 1 Carrying developing offspring in the uterus. 2 Carrying great weight or significance. 3 Fruitful; teeming with ideas. 4 Implying more than is expressed. [< L *praegnans*] —**preg′nant·ly** *adv.*

**pre·his·tor·ic** (prē′his·tôr′ik, -tor′-, prē·is-) *adj.* Of or belonging to a time before that covered by written history. Also **pre′his·tor′i·cal.** —**pre′his·tor′i·cal·ly** *adv.* —**pre′his′to·ry** *n.*

**prej·u·dice** (prej′ŏŏ·dis) *n.* 1 A judgment or opinion formed without due examination of facts, etc. 2 An unreasonable judgment held despite facts to the contrary. 3 Fear of and hatred for other races, religions, etc. 4 Detriment arising from a hasty and unfair judgment. —*v.t.* **·diced, ·dic·ing** 1 To affect or influence with a prejudice; bias. 2 To affect detrimentally by some action or opin-

ion. [< L *prae-* before + *judicium* judgment] —**Syn.** *n.* 1 bias, preconception. 3 bigotry, intolerance, racism.

**prej·u·di·cial** (prej′ŏŏ·dish′əl) *adj.* Having power or tendency to injure. —**prej′u·di′cial·ly** *adv.*

**prel·ate** (prel′it) *n.* A member of a higher order of clergy, as a bishop. [< L *praelatus* set over] —**prel′ate·ship** *n.*

**pre·lim·i·nar·y** (pri·lim′ə·ner′ē) *adj.* Antecedent or introductory to the main discourse, proceedings, or business; prefatory; preparatory. —*n. pl.* **·ries** 1 A preparatory step or procedure. 2 A preliminary examination. [< PRE- + L *limen, liminis* threshold] —**pre·lim′i·nar′i·ly** *adv.*

**prel·ude** (prel′yŏŏd, prāl-, prā′lŏŏd, prē′-) *n.* 1 *Music* a An independent instrumental composition of moderate length. b An opening piece at the start of a church service. c The overture of an opera. d An opening section or movement for a composition. 2 Any introductory or opening performance or event. —*v.* **·ud·ed, ·ud·ing** *v.t.* 1 To introduce with a prelude. 2 To serve as a prelude to. —*v.i.* 3 To serve as a prelude. 4 To provide or play a prelude. [< L *prae-* before + *ludere* to play]

**pre·ma·ture** (prē′mə·chŏŏr′, -t′ŏŏr′) *adj.* Existing, arriving, or done before the proper time; untimely. [< L < *prae-* before + *maturus* ripe] —**pre′ma·ture′ly** *adv.* —**pre′ma·tu′ri·ty, pre′ma·ture′ness** *n.*

**pre·mi·er** (pri·mir′, -myir′, prē′mē·ər, *esp. Brit.* prem′yar) *adj.* 1 First in rank or position; principal. 2 First in order of occurrence; earliest. —*n.* 1 The head of government, esp. a prime minister. 2 In Canada, the prime minister of a province. [F< L *primus* first] —**pre′mi·er·ship** *n.*

**pre·miere** (pri·myâr′, -mir′, -mē·âr′) *adj.* 1 First. 2 Leading; chief: *premiere* ballerina. —*n.* The formal opening of a play, opera, film, ballet, etc. —*v.* **·miered, ·mier·ing** *v.t.* 1 To present publicly for the first time, as a play. —*v.i.* 2 To make one's first public performance. 3 To present a play, opera, etc., publicly for the first time. Also **pre·mière.** [< F *première*]

**prem·ise** (prem′is) *n.* 1 A proposition laid down that serves as a ground for argument or for a conclusion. 2 *Logic* Either of the two propositions in a syllogism from which the conclusion necessarily follows. 3 *pl.* A distinct portion of real estate; land with its appurtenances, as buildings. —*v.* (prem′is, pri·miz′) ·ised, ·is·ing v.t. 1 To state beforehand, as by way of introduction or explanation. —v.i. 2 To make a premise. [< L praemissus, pp. of praemittere send before]

pre·mi·um (prē′mē·əm) n. 1 A reward or prize. 2 A sum offered or given to secure a loan. 3 The rate at which stocks, shares, or money are valued in excess of their nominal value. 4 The amount paid for insurance. 5 An object offered free or at low cost as an inducement to purchasers of certain goods or services. —at a premium Above par; valuable and in demand. [< L prae- before + emere to buy]

pre·mo·ni·tion (prē′mə·nish′ən, prem′ə-) n. 1 A warning of something yet to occur. 2 An instinctive foreboding; presentiment. [< L prae- before + monere warn] —pre·mon·i·to·ry (pri·mon′ə·tôr′ē, -tō′rē) adj. —pre·mon′i·to′ri·ly adv.

pre·oc·cu·py (prē·ok′yə·pī) v.t. ·pied, ·py·ing 1 To engage fully; engross, as the mind. 2 To take possession in advance of another or others. —pre·oc′cu·pan·cy (-pən·sē), pre·oc·cu·pa·tion (prē·ok′yə·pā′shən) n

pre·or·dain (prē′ôr·dān′) v.t. To decide or decree beforehand; foreordain. —pre·or·di·na·tion (prē′ôr·də·nā′shən) n.

prep·a·ra·tion (prep′ə·rā′shən) n. 1 The act, process, or operation of preparing. 2 The fact or state of being prepared; readiness. 3 Something made or prepared, as a compound for a specific purpose; medicinal preparations. 4 Preliminary study, as for college or business.

pre·pare (pri·pâr′) v. ·pared, ·par·ing v.t. 1 To make ready, fit, or qualified. 2 To provide with what is needed; outfit. 3 To bring to a state of completeness. —v.i. 4 To make preparations; get ready. [< L prae- before + parare make ready] —pre·par·ed·ly (pri·pâr′id·lē) adv. —pre·par′er n.

pre·pay (prē·pā′) v.t. ·paid, ·pay·ing To pay or pay for in advance. —pre·pay′ment n.

pre·pon·der·ant (pri·pon′dər·ənt) adj. Having superior force, weight, importance, number, etc. —pre·pon′der·ance, pre·pon′der·an·cy (-ən·sē) n. —pre·pon′der·ant·ly adv.

prep·o·si·tion (prep′ə·zish′ən) n. Gram. 1 A word such as for, from, in, to, with, etc., functioning to indicate certain relations between other words. A preposition is usually placed before its object (whence its name), and together they constitute a prepositional phrase: He sat beside the fire; sick at heart; a man of honor. 2 Any word or construction that functions in a similar manner: He telephoned in reference to (equals about) your letter. [< L prae- before + ponere to place] —prep′o·si′tion·al adj. —prep′o·si′tion·al·ly adv.

pre·pos·sess·ing (prē′pə·zes′ing) adj. Inspiring a favorable opinion from the start. —pre′pos·sess′ing·ly adv.

pre·pos·ter·ous (pri·pos′tər·əs) adj. Contrary to nature, reason, or common sense; ridiculous. [< L praeposterus the last first, inverted] —pre·pos′ter·ous·ly adv. —pre·pos′ter·ous·ness n. —Syn. absurd, foolish, idiotic, irrational, silly.

pre·req·ui·site (prē·rek′wə·zit) adj. Required as necessary to something that follows. —n. Something that is prerequisite.

pre·rog·a·tive (pri·rog′ə·tiv) n. 1 An unquestionable right, esp. a hereditary or official right: the royal prerogative. 2 Any generally recognized privilege. [< L praerogativa right of voting first]

Pres·by·te·ri·an (prez′bə·tir′ē·ən, pres′-) n. 1 One who believes in the government of the church by presbyters. 2 A member of the Presbyterian church. —adj. Of or pertaining to the Presbyterian church. —Pres·′by·te′ri·an·ism n.

pre·scribe (pri·skrīb′) v. ·scribed, ·scrib·ing v.t. 1 To set down as a direction or rule to be followed. 2 To order (a medicine or treatment) as a remedy. —v.i. 3 To lay down laws or rules. 4 To order medical treatment. [< L prae- before + scribere write] —pre·scrib′er n. —Syn. 1 command, designate, enjoin, ordain.

pre·scrip·tion (pri·skrip′shən) n. 1 The act of prescribing, directing, or dictating. 2 That which is prescribed. 3 a A physician's order for a medicine. b The remedy so ordered. —pre·scrip′tive adj. —pre·scrip′tive·ly adv.

pres·ence (prez′əns) n. 1 The state or fact of being present. 2 Vicinity within view or access: He said that in my presence. 3 Something invisible, but sensed, as a ghost. 4 Personal appearance; bearing. 5 Personal qualities collectively. 6 A person of high rank: a royal presence.

pres·ent¹ (prez′ənt) adj. 1 Being in a place or company referred to; being at hand. 2 Now going on; current. 3 Gram. Relating to or signifying what is going on at the time being: the present tense. —n. 1 Present time; now. 2 Gram. a The present tense. b A verb in this tense. —at present Now. —

**by these presents** *Law* By this document. —**for the present** For the time being. [<L *praesens* being in front of or at hand]

**pre·sent²** (pri·zent⁄) *v.t.* 1 To bring into the presence or acquaintance of another. 2 To display. 3 To suggest to the mind: This *presents* a problem. 4 To put forward for consideration or action, as a petition. 5 To make a gift to. 6 To offer formally: to *present* a diploma. 7 To exhibit before the public: to *present* a play. 8 To give or send: to *present* a bill. —**present arms** 1 To hold a gun vertically in front of and close to the body in salute. 2 This salute. 3 The command for a soldier to salute in this way. — *n.* (prez⁄ənt) That which is presented or given. [<L *praesentare* set before<*praesens* present] —**pre·sent⁄er** *n.*

**pre·sent·a·ble** (pri·zen⁄tə·bəl) *adj.* 1 Fit to be offered or bestowed. 2 In suitable condition or attire for company. 3 Fit to be shown or seen. —**pre·sent⁄a·bil⁄i·ty, pre·sent⁄a·ble·ness** *n.* —**pre·sent⁄a·bly** *adv.*

**pres·en·ta·tion** (prez⁄ən·tā⁄shən, prē⁄zən-) *n.* 1 The offering of a gift. 2 That which is bestowed; a present. 3 A formal introduction, esp. to a superior: *presentation* at court. 4 The bringing before the public, as a play. 5 A submitting for consideration: the *presentation* of a plan.

**pre·sen·ti·ment** (pri·zen⁄tə·mənt) *n.* A prophetic sense of something to come; a foreboding. [<L *prae-* before + *sentire* feel]

**pre·serve** (pri·zûrv⁄) *v.* **·served, ·serv·ing** *v.t.* 1 To keep in safety; guard. 2 To keep intact or unimpaired. 3 To prepare (food) for future consumption, as by drying, salting, pickling, canning, etc. 4 To keep from decomposition: to *preserve* a specimen in alcohol. 5 To keep for one's private use. —*v.i.* 6 To make preserves, as of fruit. —*n.* 1 *Usu. pl.* Fruit which has been cooked, usu. with sugar, to prevent its fermenting. 2 A place set apart for one's own private use. 3 An area set aside for the protection of wildlife. [<L *prae-* before + *servare* keep] —**pre·serv⁄a·bil⁄i·ty, pres·er·va·tion** (prez⁄ər·vā⁄shən), **pre·serv⁄er** *n.* —**Syn.** *v.* 1 defend, protect, secure, shield. 2 maintain, uphold.

**pre·side** (pri·zīd⁄) *v.i.* **·sid·ed, ·sid·ing** 1 To be in charge of an assembly, government, etc. 2 To exercise control. [< L *praesidere* sit in front of, protect, guard] —**pre·sid⁄er** *n.*

**pres·i·den·cy** (prez⁄ə·dən·sē) *n. pl.* **·cies** 1 The office, function, or term of office of a pres-

ident. 2 *Often cap.* The office of president of the United States.

**pres·i·dent** (prez⁄ə·dənt) *n.* 1 One who is chosen to preside over an organized body, as a corporation, society, college, etc. 2 *Usu. cap.* The chief executive of a republic, as of the United States. —**pres·i·den·tial** (prez⁄ə·den⁄shəl) *adj.*

**press** (pres) *v.t.* 1 To act upon by weight or pressure. 2 To compress so as to extract the juice. 3 To extract by pressure, as juice. 4 To exert pressure upon so as to smooth or shape. 5 To smooth or shape by heat and pressure, as clothes; iron. 6 To embrace closely; hug. 7 To force or impel; drive. 8 To distress or harass: I am *pressed* for time. 9 To urge persistently; importune. 10 To advocate persistently. 11 To put forward insistently: to *press* a gift on a friend. 12 To urge onward; hasten. —*v.i.* 13 To exert pressure; bear heavily. 14 To advance forcibly or with speed: *Press* on! 15 To press clothes, etc. 16 To crowd; cram. 17 To be urgent or importunate. —*n.* 1 A dense throng. 2 The act of crowding together or of straining forward. 3 Hurry or pressure of affairs. 4 An upright closet for clothes, etc.: a linen *press*. 5 An apparatus or machine by which pressure is applied, as for making wine, cider, etc. 6 Newspapers or periodical literature collectively. 7 The body of persons writing for such publications. 8 The art, process, or business of printing. 9 The place of business in which a printing press is set up. 10 Criticism, comments, news, etc., in newspapers and periodicals. [< L *pressare,* freq. of *premere* to press] —**press⁄er** *n.*

**pres·sure** (presh⁄ər) *n.* 1 The act of pressing, or the state of being pressed. 2 *Physics* A force distributed over a surface, expressed as units of force per unit area. 3 Pressure of a fluid exceeding atmospheric pressure: a hose under *pressure.* 4 An impelling or constraining influence: the *pressure* to conform socially. 5 Exigent demand on one's time or energy: to be under daily *pressure.* —*v.t.* **·sured, ·sur·ing** *Informal* To compel, as by forceful persuasion or influence. —**pres⁄sur·al** *adj.*

**pres·ti·dig·i·ta·tion** (pres⁄tə·dij⁄ə·tā⁄shən) *n.* The art of sleight of hand. [< LL *praestus* nimble + *digitus* finger] —**pres⁄ti·dig⁄i·ta⁄tor** *n.*

**pres·tige** (pres·tēzh⁄, -tēj⁄) *n.* Authority or importance based on past achievements or reputation. [< L *praestigium* illusion]

**pre·sume** (pri·zōōm′) *v.* **·sumed, ·sum·ing** *v.t.* 1 To take upon oneself without permission. 2 To assume to be true until disproved: I *presume* you are right. —*v.i.* 3 To make excessive demands: with *on* or *upon*: He *presumes* on my good nature. [< L *praesumere* take first] —**pre·sum′a·ble** *adj.* —**pre·sum′a·bly, pre·sum·ed·ly** (pri·zōō′mid·lē) *adv.* —**pre·sum′er** *n.*

**pre·sump·tion** (pri·zump′shən) *n.* 1 The act of presuming. 2 Something taken for granted. 3 A reason for presuming; probability. 4 Overweening self-assertion; arrogance.

**pre·sump·tu·ous** (pri·zump′chōō·əs) *adj.* Unduly confident or bold; forward. —**pre·sump′tu·ous·ly** *adv.* —**pre·sump′tu·ous·ness** *n.*

**pre·sup·pose** (prē′sə·pōz′) *v.t.* **·posed, ·pos·ing** 1 To imply or involve as a necessary antecedent condition. 2 To take for granted. —**pre·sup·po·si·tion** (prē′sup·ə·zish′ən) *n.*

**pre·tend** (pri·tend′) *v.t.* 1 To assume or display a false appearance of. 2 To claim or assert falsely. 3 To feign in play; make believe. —*v.i.* 4 To make believe, as in play or for the purpose of deception. 5 To put forward a claim: with *to*. [< L *prae-* before + *tendere* spread out]

**pre·tense** (prē′tens, pri·tens′) *n.* 1 The act of pretending, as in play; a making believe. 2 Something pretended; ruse. 3 The false assumption of a character or condition. 4 A claim to a right or title. 5 A false claim. *Brit. sp.* **pre·tence.** —**Syn.** 2 pretext, wile. 3 affectation, dissimulation, show.

**pre·ten·tious** (pri·ten′shəs) *adj.* 1 Making unwarranted or exaggerated claims to greatness or importance: a *pretentious* person. 2 Showy or ostentatious: a *pretentious* style of living. —**pre·ten′tious·ly** *adv.* —**pre·ten′tious·ness** *n.*

**pre·ter·nat·u·ral** (prē′tər·nach′ər·əl, -rəl) *adj.* 1 Diverging from or exceeding the common order of nature; extraordinary. 2 Supernatural. —**pre′ter·nat′u·ral·ism** *n.* —**pre′ter·nat′u·ral·ly** *adv.*

**pre·text** (prē′tekst) *n.* A fictitious reason given to conceal a real one; a specious excuse or explanation. [< L *prae-* before + *texere* to weave]

**pret·zel** (pret′səl) *n.* A glazed salted biscuit in the form of a loose knot. [< G *Brezel*]

**pre·vail** (pri·vāl′) *v.i.* 1 To gain mastery: with *over* or *against*. 2 To be effective; succeed.

3 To be prevalent. 4 To have general or widespread use or acceptance. —**prevail on** (upon or with) To persuade; influence. [< L *prae-* before + *valere* be strong]

**prev·a·lent** (prev′ə·lənt) *adj.* 1 Predominant. 2 Of wide extent or frequent occurrence. [< L *praevalere* prevail] —**prev′a·lence** *n.* —**prev′a·lent·ly** *adv.*

**pre·var·i·cate** (pri·var′ə·kāt) *v.i.* **·cat·ed, ·cat·ing** To speak or act in a deceptive manner; lie. [< L *praevaricare* walk crookedly] —**pre·var′i·ca′tion, pre·var′i·ca′tor** *n.*

**pre·vent** (pri·vent′) *v.t.* 1 To keep from happening, as by previous measures: to *prevent* accidents. 2 To keep from doing something; hinder. [< L *prae-* before + *venire* come] —**pre·vent′a·ble** or **·i·ble** *adj.* —**pre·vent′a·bil′i·ty** or **·i·bil′i·ty, pre·vent′er** *n.*

**pre·ven·tion** (pri·ven′shən) *n.* 1 The act of preventing. 2 A hindrance; obstruction.

**pre·ven·tive** (pri·ven′tiv) *adj.* Intended or serving to prevent, esp. to ward off a disease. —*n.* That which prevents or hinders, esp. a method of warding off disease. Also **pre·vent·a·tive** (pri·ven′tə·tiv). —**pre·ven′tive·ly** *adv.* —**pre·ven′tive·ness** *n.*

**pre·view** (prē′vyōō′) *n.* 1 A showing, to the public, as of a motion picture, etc., before its formal opening. 2 The showing of scenes from a motion picture or television show in advance of its scheduled presentation as a means of advertisement. —*v.t.* (prē·vyōō′) To view in advance.

**pre·vi·ous** (prē′vē·əs) *adj.* 1 Being or taking place before something else in time or order. 2 *Informal* Acting, occurring, or speaking too soon. —**previous to** Before. [< L *praevius* going before] —**pre′vi·ous·ly** *adv.* —**pre′vi·ous·ness** *n.* —**Syn.** 1 antecedent, former, preceding, prior.

**prey** (prā) *n.* 1 Any animal seized by another for food. 2 Booty; pillage. 3 A person or thing made a victim; a *prey* to swindlers. 4 The act of hunting other animals for food: a bird of *prey*. —*v.i.* 1 To seek or take prey for food. 2 To make a victim of someone, as by cheating. 3 To exert a wearing or harmful influence: to *prey* upon impressionable children. [< L *praeda* booty] —**prey′er** *n.*

**price** (prīs) *n.* 1 The amount of money or goods given or asked in exchange for something. 2 Anything given or done to obtain something. 3 Worth; cost. 4 A reward for the capture or death of. —**beyond price** 1 So valuable that no adequate price can be set. 2 Not able to be bribed. —**set a price on**

one's head **To offer a reward for the capture of a person, dead or alive.** —*v.t.* **priced, pric·ing 1** To ask the price of. **2** To set a price on. —**price out of the market** To charge such high prices for goods that no one will buy them. [< L *pretium*] —**Syn.** *n.* **1** charge, cost, outlay. **3** value.

**price·less** (prīs′lis) *adj.* **1** Beyond price or valuation; invaluable. **2** *Informal* Wonderfully amusing or absurd. —**price′less·ness** *n.*

**prick** (prik) *v.t.* **1** To pierce slightly, as with a sharp point; puncture. **2** To affect with sharp mental pain. **3** To outline or indicate by punctures. **4** To cause to stick up: often with *up*. **5** To urge on; goad. —*v.i.* **6** To have or cause a stinging or piercing sensation. **7** To stick up; point, as a dog's ears. —*n.* **1** A mark or puncture made by pricking. **2** A stinging or prickling sensation. **3** Something sharply pointed, as a thorn. **4** A mental sting or spur: the *prick* of conscience. [< OE *prica* sharp point] —**prick′er** *n.*

**pride** (prīd) *n.* **1** An undue sense of one's own superiority; arrogance; conceit. **2** A proper sense or feeling of personal dignity and worth. **3** That of which one is justly proud. **4** The best part of a group, nation, etc. **5** The best or prime period: in the *pride* of youth. **6** A group or family of lions. —*v.t.* **prid·ed, prid·ing** To take pride in (oneself) for something: with *on* or *upon*. [< OE *prūt* proud] —**pride′ful** *adj.* —**pride′ful·ly** *adv.* —**pride′ful·ness** *n.*

**priest** (prēst) *n.* **1** One consecrated to the service of a divinity, and serving as mediator between the divinity and his worshipers. **2** In the Anglican, Greek, and Roman Catholic churches, a clergyman ranking next below a bishop, and having authority to administer the sacraments. [< L *presbyter* elder] —**priest′hood** *n.*

**priest·ess** (prēs′tis) *n.* A woman or girl who performs sacred rites.

**prim** (prim) *adj.* Affectedly precise and formal; stiffly proper and neat. —*v.t.* **primmed, prim·ming** To fix in a precise or prim manner. [Prob. < OF *prim* first, prime] —**prim′ly** *adv.* —**prim′ness** *n.*

**pri·ma don·na** (prē′mə don′ə, prim′ə) *pl.* **pri·ma don·nas 1** A leading female singer, as in an opera company. **2** *Informal* A temperamental or vain person. [Ital., lit., first lady]

**pri·ma·ry** (prī′mer·ē, -mər·ē) *adj.* **1** First in time or origin; primitive; original. **2** First in a series or sequence. **3** First in degree,

rank, or importance; chief. **4** Constituting the fundamental or original elements of which a whole is comprised; basic; elemental: the *primary* forces of life. **5** Of the first stage of development; elementary: *primary* school. **6** *Electr.* Of or designating the input or input circuit of a transformer or similar device. —*n. pl.* **·ries 1** That which is first in rank, dignity, quality, importance, etc. **2** Any of the primary colors. **3** In the U.S. **a** A meeting in which voters belonging to one political party in an election district nominate candidates for office, choose delegates for a party convention, etc. **b** DIRECT PRIMARY. [< L *primus* first]

**pri·mate** (prī′māt, -mit) *n.* **1** The prelate highest in rank in a nation or province. **2** Any of an order of mammals having five digits with nails on hands and feet, binocular vision, a large brainpan, etc., and including man, apes, monkeys and several monkeylike forms. [< L *primus* first] —**pri·ma·tial** (prī·mā′shəl) *adj.*

**prime** (prīm) *adj.* **1** First in rank, dignity, or importance; chief. **2** First in value or excellence; first-rate. **3** First in time or order; original; primitive; primeval. **4** *Math.* Having no integral factors other than itself and unity, as certain integers. **5** Not derived from anything else; original; first. —*n.* **1** The period succeeding youth and preceding age. **2** The period of full perfection or vigor in anything. **3** The beginning of anything. **4** The best of anything; a *prime* grade. **5** A mark or accent (′) written above and to the right of a letter or figure to indicate feet, minutes of time, minutes of angle, etc. **6** *Music* The interval of unison. —*v.* **primed, prim·ing** *v.t.* **1** To prepare; make ready for some purpose. **2** To put a primer into (a gun, mine, etc.) preparatory to firing. **3** To pour water into (a pump) so as to displace air and promote suction. **4** To cover (a surface) with sizing, a first coat of paint, etc. **5** To supply beforehand with facts, information, etc.: to *prime* a witness. —*v.i.* **6** To carry water along with the steam into the cylinder: said of a steam boiler or engine. **7** To make a person or thing ready or prepared for something. [< L *primus* first] —**prime′ly** *adv.* —**prime′ness** *n.* —**Syn.** *adj.* **1** main, leading, premiere, head, principal, top.

**prim·er** (prim′ər) *n.* **1** An elementary reading

and spelling book. 2 A beginner's textbook in any subject. [< Med. L *primarius* basic]

**pri·me·val** (prī-mē′vəl) *adj.* Of or pertaining to the first ages; primordial. [< L *primus* first + *aevum* age] —**pri·me′val·ly** *adv.*

**prim·i·tive** (prim′ə·tiv) *adj.* 1 Of or belonging to the earliest ages. 2 Of, like, or belonging to an early period or stage of development: *primitive* Christianity. 3 Characteristic of the earliest ages of man, as in style, manner of living, etc.: a *primitive* tribe of Indians in Brazil. 4 Rough, simple, plain, undeveloped, etc.: *primitive* vacation facilities. 5 Basic; primary. —*n.* 1 A primitive person or thing. 2 A work of art created during the very early, often prehistoric, ages of man; also, a work of art imitative of this. 3 A work of art characterized by a naive, childlike simplicity; also, the artist, often untrained, of such a work. 4 A simple, unsophisticated person. [< L *primitivus* < *primus* first] —**prim′i·tive·ly** *adv.* —**prim′i·tive·ness** *n.*

**prince** (prins) *n.* 1 A nonreigning male member of a royal family, esp. the son of a sovereign. 2 A male ruler of a state or principality. 3 One of a high order of nobility. 4 One of the highest rank of the class to which he belongs: a merchant *prince*. [< L *princeps* first, principal]

**prin·ci·pal** (prin′sə·pəl) *adj.* First in rank, character, or importance; chief. —*n.* 1 One who takes a leading part in some action. 2 *Law* a The actor in a crime, or one present aiding and abetting. b The employer of one who acts as an agent. c One primarily liable for whom another has become surety. d The capital or body of an estate. 3 The head officer or teacher of a school. 4 The leading actor or performer. 5 Any person in authority. 6 The amount of money owed or invested, minus the interest charged or accumulated. 7 The face value: the *principal* of a stock. 8 Any of the chief rafters of a roof. [< L *princeps* chief] —**prin′ci·pal·ly** *adv.* —**prin′ci·pal·ship** *n.* —**Syn.** *adj.* 1 main, central, foremost, leading.

**prin·ci·ple** (prin′sə·pəl) *n.* 1 A basic truth, law, force, etc., on which others may be founded: the *principle* of self-government. 2 An essential character or quality of something. 3 A fundamental origin or cause of something. 4 Moral standards or rules of conduct, esp. superior standards or rules: a man of *principle*. 5 In natural phenomena, an established law or mode of action: the *principle* of gravity. 6 The essential mode of operation of something: the *principle* of a digital computer. [<L *principium* a beginning]

**print** (print) *n.* 1 An impression or mark made upon a surface by pressure; imprint. 2 Something having such a mark on it. 3 A device for making such a mark. 4 An impression made by type or plates that have been inked. 5 Type used in printing. 6 Printed matter, as a newspaper. 7 The state of being printed. 8 A photographic reproduction of a work of art. 9 An original picture or design made from an engraved plate, stone, woodblock, etc. 10 A fabric stamped with a design; also, a garment made from such fabric. 11 A positive photographic copy made from a negative. —**in print** Still available at the publisher. —**out of print** No longer available at the publisher, the edition being exhausted. —*v.t.* 1 To mark, as with inked type, a stamp, die, etc. 2 To stamp or impress (a mark, seal, etc.) on or into a surface. 3 To fix as if by impressing: The scene is *printed* on my memory. 4 To produce (a book, newspaper, etc.) by the application of inked type, plates, etc., to paper or similar material. 5 To cause to be put in print; publish: The newspaper *printed* the story. 6 To write in letters similar to those used in print. 7 *Phot.* To produce (a positive picture) by transmitting light through a negative onto a sensitized surface. —*v.i.* 8 To be a printer. 9 To take or give an impression in printing. 10 To form letters similar to printed ones. —**print out** To deliver (information) automatically in printed form, as a computer. [<L *premere* to press]

**pri·or** (prī′ər) *adj.* Preceding in time, order, or importance. —**prior to** Before in time. —*n.* 1 In an abbey, a monastic officer next in rank below an abbot. 2 The man in charge of a priory. [L, earlier; superior]

**pri·or·i·ty** (prī-ôr′ə·tē, -or′-) *n. pl.* **·ties** 1 The condition of being prior; precedence. 2 A preferential rating or right to do, buy, or use something. 3 A certificate giving this right. 4 Something that takes precedence over another thing or things.

**prism** (priz′əm) *n.* 1 *Geom.* A solid whose bases or ends are equal and parallel plane figures, and whose lateral faces are parallelograms. 2 *Optics* An instrument consisting of such a solid, usu. having triangular ends and made of glass or other transparent material. [< Gk. *prisma* something sawed]

**pris·on** (priz′ən) *n.* 1 A public building for the safekeeping of persons in legal custody, as in punishment for having committed a crime; a penitentiary. 2 Any place of confinement. 3 Imprisonment. —*v.t.* IMPRISON. [<L *praehensio* seizure]

**pris·on·er** (priz′ənər, -nər) *n.* 1 One who is confined in a prison. 2 Any person whose liberty is forcibly restrained. 3 A person whose freedom is restricted by some cause or condition: a *prisoner* of ignorance.

**pris·tine** (pris′tēn, -tin, pris·tēn′) *adj.* 1 Of or pertaining to the earliest state or time; primitive. 2 Uncontaminated; pure. [<L. *pristinus* primitive] —**pris′tine·ly** *adv.*

**pri·va·cy** (prī′və·sē; *Brit.*, also priv′ə·sē) *n. pl.* **·cies** 1 The condition of being private; seclusion. 2 Personal matters that are or should be private. 3 Secrecy.

**pri·vate** (prī′vit) *adj.* 1 Removed from public view; secluded. 2 Confidential; secret. 3 That is one's own; personal: a *private* sorrow. 4 Not for the public at large: *private* schools. 5 Not in the public or governmental employ: a *private* citizen. 6 Working or conducted independently of other groups, organizations, etc.: a *private* detective; a *private* practice. —*n.* See GRADE. —**in private** In secret; privately. [<L *privus* single, one's own] —**pri′vate·ly** *adv.* —**pri′vate·ness** *n.*

**pri·va·tion** (prī·vā′shən) *n.* 1 The state of lacking something necessary or desirable. 2 Want of the common comforts or necessities of life. [<L *privare* deprive]

**priv·i·lege** (priv′ə·lij, priv′lij) *n.* 1 A special or peculiar benefit, advantage, right or immunity. 2 A fundamental civil right: the *privilege* of voting. —*v.t.* **·leged, ·leg·ing** To grant a privilege to. [<L *privus* one's own + *lex, legis* law]

**prize** (prīz) *n.* 1 That which is offered or won as an honor and reward for superiority. 2 Anything offered or won in a contest, game of chance, etc. 3 Something desirable, either acquired or to be striven for. —*adj.* 1 Offered or awarded as a prize. 2 Having received a prize. 3 Highly valued or esteemed. —*v.t.* **prized, priz·ing** 1 To value highly. 2 To appraise. [Var. of PRICE]

**prob·a·bil·i·ty** (prob′ə·bil′ə·tē) *n. pl.* **·ties** 1 The state or quality of being probable; likelihood. 2 Something probable. 3 *Stat.* The ratio of the chances favoring an event to the total number of chances for and against it.

**prob·a·ble** (prob′ə·bəl) *adj.* 1 Likely to be true or to happen, but leaving room for doubt. 2 That renders something worthy of belief, but fails to prove: *probable* evidence. [< L *probare* prove, test] —**prob′a·bly** *adv.*

**pro·bate** (prō′bāt) *n.* 1 The act or legal process of proving the genuineness of a document, as a will. 2 The final determination of the genuineness of a will. 3 The authentic copy of a probated will. —*adj.* Of probate or probate court. —*v.t.* **·bat·ed, ·bat·ing** To secure probate of, as a will. [< L *probare* prove]

**pro·ba·tion** (prō·bā′shən) *n.* 1 A trial or period of testing of a person's character, qualifications, etc. 2 A legal procedure allowing a person convicted of an offense to go at large under suspension of sentence, but usu. under the supervision of a probation officer. 3 The status or condition of one undergoing probation; also, the period of probation. —**pro·ba′tion·al, pro·ba′tion·ar′y** *adj.*

**probe** (prōb) *v.* **probed, prob·ing** *v.t.* 1 To explore with a probe. 2 To investigate or examine thoroughly. —*v.i.* 3 To investigate; search. —*n.* 1 *Med.* An instrument for exploring wounds, etc. 2 The act of probing. 3 An examination or exploratory search, esp. an investigation or inquiry into crime, malpractice, etc. 4 A spacecraft designed to explore and collect and transmit data to earth about the upper atmosphere, celestial bodies, or outer space. [< L *probare* prove] —**prob′er** *n.*

**pro·bi·ty** (prō′bə·tē) *n.* Virtue or integrity tested and confirmed; strict honesty. [< L *probus* good, honest]

**prob·lem** (prob′ləm) *n.* 1 A perplexing question presented for solution. 2 A puzzling or difficult circumstance, situation, person, etc. 3 *Math.* Something to be worked out or solved, as by a series of operations. —*adj.* 1 Presenting and dealing with a problem. 2 Being a problem: a *problem* child. [< Gk. *problēma* something thrown forward (for discussion)]

**prob·lem·at·ic** (prob′ləm·at′ik) *adj.* 1 Constituting or involving a problem. 2 Uncertain; questionable; contingent. Also **prob′lem·at′i·cal.** —**prob′lem·at′i·cal·ly** *adv.*

**pro·bos·cis** (prō·bos′is) *n. pl.* **·bos·cis·es** or **·bos·ci·des** (-bos′ə·dēz) 1 An elephant's trunk, or any long flexible snout. 2 A tubular structure used for sucking, sensing, etc., as of certain insects, worms, and mollusks. 3 A human nose: a humorous use. [< Gk. *pro-* before + *boskein* to feed]

**pro·ce·dure** (prə·sē′jər, prō-) *n.* 1 A manner of proceeding or acting. 2 A special course of action. 3 The established methods or forms for the conduct of various proceedings, as in business, legal courts, etc. —**pro·ce′du·ral** *adj.*

**pro·ceed** (prə·sēd′, prō-) *v.i.* 1 To go on or forward. 2 To begin and carry on an action or process. 3 To issue or come, as from some cause, source, or origin: with *from*. 4 *Law* To institute and carry on legal proceedings. [< L *pro-* forward + *cedere* go]

**proc·ess** (pros′es, pros′əs, *esp. Brit.* prō′ses) *n. pl.* **proc·ess·es** (pros′ə·siz, pros′es·əz, pros′ə·sēz′) 1 A course or method of operations in the production of something: a metallurgical *process*. 2 A forward movement or continuous development, as of time, growth, etc. 3 *Law* a Any judicial writ or order. b A writ issued to bring a defendant into court. c The whole course of proceedings in a cause. 4 *Biol.* An accessory outgrowth of an organism. —*adj.* Produced by a special method: *process* cheese. —*v.t.* 1 To treat or prepare by a special method. 2 *Law* a To issue or serve a process on. b To proceed against. [< L *processus* pp. of *procedere* proceed]

**pro·ces·sion** (prə·sesh′ən, prō-) *n.* 1 A line, as of persons or vehicles, moving forward in a formal manner; a parade. 2 A continuous course: the *procession* of the stars. 3 The act of proceeding or issuing forth.

**pro·claim** (prō·klām′, prə-) *v.t.* 1 To announce or make known publicly or officially; declare. 2 To make plain; manifest. 3 To praise; laud. [< L *pro-* before + *clamare* to call] —**pro·claim′er** *n.*

**proc·la·ma·tion** (prok′lə·mā′shən) *n.* 1 The act of proclaiming. 2 That which is proclaimed.

**pro·cliv·i·ty** (prō·kliv′ə·tē) *n. pl.* **·ties** Natural disposition or tendency, esp. toward something not desirable. [< L *proclivus* downward]

**pro·cras·ti·nate** (prō·kras′tə·nāt) *v.* **·nat·ed**, **·nat·ing** *v.i.* 1 To put off taking action until a future time; be dilatory. —*v.t.* 2 To defer or postpone. [< L *pro-* forward + *cras* tomorrow] —**pro·cras′ti·na′tion**, **pro·cras′ti·na′tor** *n.*

**pro·cure** (prō·kyŏor′) *v.* **·cured**, **·cur·ing** *v.t.* 1 To obtain by some effort or means; acquire.

2 To bring about; cause. 3 To obtain for the sexual gratification of others. —*v.i.* 4 To obtain women for prostitution. [< L *procurare* look after] —**pro·cur′a·ble** *adj.* —**pro·cure′ment**, **pro·cur′er** *n.*

**prod·i·gal** (prod′ə·gəl) *adj.* 1 Wastefully extravagant, as of money, time, etc. 2 Yielding in profusion; bountiful. 3 Lavish; profuse. —*n.* One who is wastefully extravagant; a spendthrift. [< L *prodigus* wasteful] —**prod′i·gal′i·ty** (-gal′ə·tē) *n.* —**prod′i·gal·ly** *adv.*

**pro·dig·ious** (prə·dij′əs, prō-) *adj.* 1 Enormous or extraordinary in size, quantity, or degree. 2 Marvelous; amazing. —**pro·dig′ious·ly** *adv.* —**pro·dig′ious·ness** *n.*

**prod·i·gy** (prod′ə·jē) *n. pl.* **·gies** 1 Something extraordinary or awe-inspiring. 2 An exceptionally gifted child. 3 A monstrosity of nature. [< L *prodigium*]

**pro·duce** (prə·d′ōōs′) *v.* **·duced**, **·duc·ing** *v.t.* 1 To bring forth or bear; yield. 2 To bring forth by mental effort; compose, write, etc. 3 To cause to happen or be: His words *produced* a violent reaction. 4 To bring to view; exhibit; show: to *produce* evidence. 5 To manufacture; make. 6 To bring to performance before the public, as a play. 7 To extend or lengthen, as a line. 8 *Econ.* To create (anything with exchangeable value). —*v.i.* 9 To yield or generate an appropriate product or result. —*n.* (prod′ōōs, prō′d′ōōs) That which is produced, esp. farm products collectively. [< L *pro-* forward + *ducere* to lead] —**pro·duc′i·ble** *adj.*

**pro·duc·er** (prə·d′ōō′sər) *n.* 1 One who or that which produces. 2 One who makes things for sale and use. 3 One in charge of the production of a public presentation, as of a play, motion picture, etc.

**prod·uct** (prod′əkt, -ukt) *n.* 1 Anything produced or obtained as a result of some operation or work. 2 *Math.* The result obtained by multiplication. 3 *Chem.* Any substance resulting from chemical change.

**pro·duc·tion** (prə·duk′shən) *n.* 1 The act or process of producing. 2 The amount produced. 3 Something produced, esp. an artistic work, as a play, motion picture, etc. 4 In political economy, a producing of goods or services.

**pro·fane** (prō·fān′, prə-) *v.t.* **·faned**, **·fan·ing** 1 To treat (something sacred) with irreverence or abuse; desecrate. 2 To put to an unworthy or degrading use; debase. —*adj.* 1 Manifesting irreverence or disrespect toward sacred things. 2 Not sacred or religious in theme, content, use, etc.; secular. 3 Not esoteric; ordinary. 4 Vulgar. [< L *pro-* before + *fanum* temple] —**pro·fan·a·to·ry** (prō·fan′ə·tôr′ē, -tō′rē, prə-) *adj.* —**pro·fane′ly** *adv.* —**pro·fan′er** *n.*

**pro·fan·i·ty** (prō·fan′ə·tē, prə-) *n. pl.* **·ties** 1 The state of being profane. 2 Profane speech or action. **Also pro·fane′ness** (-fān′nis).

**pro·fess** (prə·fes′, prō-) *v.t.* 1 To declare openly; avow; affirm. 2 To assert, usu. insincerely; make a pretense of: to *profess* remorse. 3 To declare or affirm faith in. 4 To have as one's profession: to *profess* the law. 5 To receive into a religious order. —*v.i.* 6 To make open declaration; avow; offer public affirmation. 7 To take the vows of a religious order. [< L *professus*, pp. of *profiteri* avow, confess] —**pro·fessed′** *adj.* —**pro·fess′ed·ly** (-fes′id·lē) *adv.*

**pro·fes·sion** (prə·fesh′ən) *n.* 1 An occupation that involves a higher education or its equivalent, and mental rather than manual labor, as law, medicine, teaching, etc. 2 The collective body of those following such an occupation. 3 Any calling or occupation requiring special skills, talents, etc.: the acting *profession.* 4 Any occupation. 5 The act of professing or declaring: *professions* of good will. 6 That which is avowed or professed.

**pro·fes·sion·al** (prə·fesh′ən·əl) *adj.* 1 Connected with, preparing for, engaged in, appropriate, or conforming to a profession: *professional* courtesy; *professional* skill. 2 Performing or doing for pay an activity often engaged in only for pleasure or recreation: a *professional* golfer. 3 Engaged in by performers, players, etc., who are paid: *professional* hockey. 4 Single-minded and zealous, often excessively so: a *professional* do-gooder. —*n.* 1 One who practices any profession or engages in any activity for pay. 2 One who is exceptionally skilled in some activity. —**pro·fes′sion·al·ism′** *n.* —**pro·fes′sion·al·ly** *adv.*

**pro·fes·sor** (prə·fes′ər) *n.* 1 A teacher of the highest grade in a university or college. 2 One who professes skill and offers instruction in some sport or art: a *professor* of gymnastics. 3 One who makes open declaration of his opinions, religious faith, etc. —**pro·fes·so·ri·al** (prō′fə·sôr′ē·əl, -sō′rē-, prof′ə-) *adj.* —**pro′fes·so′ri·al·ly** *adv.* —**pro′fes·so′ri·ate** (-it), **pro·fes′sor·ship** *n.* •

In writing to a college or university professor, one may use either *Professor* or *Prof.* if the name is written in full or if the initials are used with the last name: *Professor Alfred Kern; Prof. C. E. Young.* If only the last name is used, *Professor* is spelled out.

**prof·fer** (prof′ər) *v.t.* To offer for acceptance. —*n.* The act of proffering, or that which is proffered. [< L *pro-* in behalf of + *offerre* to offer] —**prof′fer·er** *n.*

**pro·fi·cient** (prə·fish′ənt) *adj.* Thoroughly competent; skilled; expert. —*n.* An expert. [< L *proficere* make progress, go forward] —**pro·fi′cient·ly** *adv.*

**pro·file** (prō′fīl, *esp. Brit.* prō′fēl) *n.* 1 A human head or face, as viewed from the side; also, a drawing of such a side view. 2 A drawing or view of something in outline or contour. 3 A somewhat brief biographical sketch. 4 Degree of exposure to public attention; public image: The army generals who seized control maintained a very low *profile.* 5 A vertical section of stratified soil or rock. —*v.t.* **·filed,** **·fil·ing** 1 To draw a profile of; outline. 2 To write a profile of. [< Ital. *proffilare* draw in outline]

**prof·it·a·ble** (prof′it·ə·bəl) *adj.* Bringing profit or gain. —**prof·it·a·bil·i·ty** (prof′ə·tə· bil′ə·tē), **prof′it·a·ble·ness** *n.* —**prof′it·a· bly** *adv.* —**Syn.** advantageous, beneficial, desirable, expedient, gainful, lucrative, productive, useful, worthwhile.

**prof·li·gate** (prof′lə·git, -gāt) *adj.* 1 Extremely immoral or dissipated; dissolute. 2 Recklessly extravagant. —*n.* A profligate person. [< L *profligare* strike to the ground, destroy] —**prof′li·gate·ly** *adv.*

**pro·found** (prə·found′, prō-) *adj.* 1 Intellectually deep or exhaustive: *profound* learning. 2 Reaching to, arising from, or affecting the depth of one's being: a *profound* look; *profound* respect. 3 Reaching far below the surface; deep: a *profound* chasm. 4 Complete; total: a *profound* revision of the book. [< L *pro-* very + *fundus* deep] —**pro·found′ly** *adv.* —**pro·found′ness** *n.*

**pro·fuse** (prə·fyōōs′, prō-) *adj.* 1 Giving or given forth lavishly; extravagantly generous. 2 Copious; abundant: *profuse* vegetation. [< L *profusus,* pp. of *profundere* pour forth] —**pro·fuse′ly** *adv.* —**pro·fuse′ness** *n.*

**pro·gen·i·tor** (prō·jen′ə·tər) *n.* 1 A forefather or parent. 2 The originator or source of something. [< L *progignere* beget] —**pro·gen′i·tor·ship′** *n.*

**prog·e·ny** (proj′ə-nē) *n. pl.* **·nies** Offspring; descendants. [< L *progignere* beget]

**prog·no·sis** (prog-nō′sis) *n. pl.* **·ses** (-sēz) A prediction or forecast, esp. as to the future course of a disease. [< Gk. *pro-* before + *gignōskein* know]

**prog·nos·ti·cate** (prog-nos′tə-kāt) *v.t.* **·cat·ed, ·cat·ing** 1 To foretell by present indications. 2 To indicate beforehand; foreshadow. —**prog·nos′ti·ca′tion, prog·nos′ti·ca′tor** *n.* —**prog·nos′ti·ca′tive** (-kā′tiv) *adj.*

**pro·gram** (prō′gram, -grəm) *n.* 1 A printed list giving in order the items, selections, etc., making up an entertainment; also, the selections, etc., collectively. 2 A printed list of the cast of characters, the performers, the acts or scenes, etc., in a play, opera, or the like. 3 A radio or television show. 4 Any prearranged plan or course of proceedings. 5 A sequence of instructions to be executed by a computer in solving a problem, usu. with means for automatically modifying the sequence depending on conditions that arise. *Brit. sp.* **·gramme.** —*v.t.* **·gramed** or **·grammed, ·gram·ing** or **·gram·ming** 1 To arrange a program of or for; to *program* one's day. 2 To schedule (an act, performer, etc.) for a program. 3 To furnish a program for (a computer). 4 To feed (information, instructions, etc.) into a computer. [< LL *programma* public announcement] —**pro·gram·mat·ic** (prō′grə·mat′ik) *adj.* —**pro′gram·er, pro′gram·mer** *n.*

**prog·ress** (prog′res, *esp. Brit.* prō′gres) *n.* 1 A moving forward in space, as toward a destination. 2 Advancement toward something better; improvement. —*v.i.* (prə·gres′) 1 To move forward or onward. 2 To advance toward completion or improvement. [< L *progressus,* pp. of *progredi* go forward]

**pro·gres·sion** (prə·gresh′ən) *n.* 1 The act of progressing. 2 A successive series of events, happenings, etc. 3 *Math.* A sequence of numbers or elements each of which is derived from the preceding by rule. 4 *Music* **a** An advance from one tone or chord to another. **b** A sequence or succession of tones or chords. 5 Course or lapse of time; passage. —**pro·gres′sion·al** *adj.* —**pro·gres′sion·ism** *n.*

**pro·gres·sive** (prə·gres′iv) *adj.* 1 Moving forward in space; advancing. 2 Increasing by successive stages: a *progressive* deterioration. 3 Aiming at or characterized by progress toward something better: a *progressive* country. 4 Favoring or character-ized by reform, new techniques, etc.: a *progressive* party, jazz, etc. 5 Increasing in severity: said of a disease. 6 *Gram.* Designating an aspect of the verb which expresses continuing action: formed with any tense of the auxiliary *be* and the present participle; as, He *is speaking; he had been speaking.* —*n.* One who favors or promotes reforms or changes, as in politics. —**pro·gres′sive·ly** *adv.* —**pro·gres′sive·ness** *n.*

**pro·hib·it** (prō·hib′it, prə-) *v.t.* 1 To forbid, esp. by authority or law; interdict. 2 To prevent or hinder. [< L *prohibere*] —**pro·hi·b′it·er** *n.* —**Syn.** 1 disallow, ban, deny, bar, debar. 2 impede, restrict, constrain, check, block, obstruct.

**pro·hi·bi·tion** (prō′ə·bish′ən) *n.* 1 A prohibiting or being prohibited. 2 A decree or order forbidding anything. 3 *Often cap.* The forbidding of the manufacture, transportation, and sale of alcoholic liquors as beverages. —**pro′hi·bi′tion·ist** *n.*

**pro·hib·i·tive** (prō·hib′ə·tiv, prə-) *adj.* Prohibiting or tending to prohibit. **Also pro·hib′i·to′ry** (-tôr′ē, -tō′rē). —**pro·hib′i·tive·ly** *adv.*

**proj·ect** (proj′ekt) *n.* 1 A course of action; a plan. 2 An organized, usu. rather extensive undertaking: a research *project.* 3 A group of single dwellings or of apartment houses forming a residential complex. —*v.t.* (prə·jekt′) 1 To cause to extend forward or out. 2 To throw forth or forward, as missiles. 3 To cause (an image, shadow, etc.) to fall on a surface. 4 To plan or estimate something in the future: to *project* living expenses. 5 To create or invent in the mind: to *project* an image of one's destiny. 6 To cause (one's voice) to be heard at a distance. 7 To have the ability to communicate (a dramatic role, one's personality, ideas, etc.) effectively, as to an audience. 8 *Psychol.* To ascribe or impute (one's own ideas, feelings, etc.) to another person, group, or object. 9 To make a projection (def. 4) of. —*v.i.* 10 To extend out; protrude. 11 To cause one's voice to be heard at a distance. 12 To communicate effectively, as to an audience. 13 *Psychol.* To impute one's own ideas, feelings, etc., to another person, group, or object. [< L *pro-* before + *jacere* throw]

**pro·jec·tile** (prə·jek′təl, -til) *adj.* 1 Projecting, or impelling forward. 2 Capable of being or intended to be projected or shot forth. —*n.* 1 A body projected or thrown forth by force.

2 A missile for discharge from a gun, cannon, etc.

**pro·jec·tion** (prə·jek′shən) *n.* 1 The act of projecting. 2 That which projects. 3 A prediction or estimation of something in the future based on current information, data, etc. 4 A system of lines drawn on a given fixed plane, as on a map, which represents, point for point, a given terrestrial or celestial surface. 5 *Psychol.* The process or an instance of projecting. 6 The exhibiting of pictures upon a screen. —**pro·jec′tive** *adj.* —**pro·jec′tive·ly** *adv.*

**pro·jec·tor** (prə·jek′tər) *n.* One who or that which projects, esp. an apparatus for throwing images on a screen: a motion-picture *projector.*

**pro·le·tar·i·an** (prō′lə·târ′ē·ən) *adj.* Of the proletariat. —*n.* A member of the proletariat. [< L *proletarius* a Roman citizen of a class that, lacking property, served the state only by having children. < *proles* offspring] —**pro′le·tar′i·an·ism** *n.*

**pro·le·tar·i·at** (prō′lə·târ′ē·ət) *n.* 1 Formerly, the lower classes. 2 The laboring class, esp. industrial wage earners.

**pro·lif·ic** (prō·lif′ik, prə-) *adj.* 1 Producing abundantly, as offspring or fruit. 2 Producing creative or intellectual products abundantly: a *prolific* writer. [< L *proles* offspring + *facere* make] —**pro·lif′i·ca·cy** (-i·kə·sē), **pro·lif′ic·ness** *n.* —**pro·lif′i·cal·ly** *adv.*

**pro·logue** (prō′lôg, -log) *n.* 1 A preface, esp. an introduction, often in verse, spoken or sung by an actor before a play or opera. 2 Any anticipatory act or event. —*v.t.* To introduce with a prologue or preface. Also **pro′log.** [< Gk. *pro-* before + *logos* discourse]

**pro·long** (prə·lông′, -long′) *v.t.* To extend in time or space: continue; lengthen. Also **pro·lon′gate** (-lông′gāt, -long′-). [< L *pro-* forth + *longus* long] —**pro′lon·ga′tion,** **pro·long′ment,** **pro·long′er** *n.*

**prom·e·nade** (prom′ə·nād′, -näd′) *n.* 1 A leisurely walk taken for pleasure. 2 A place for promenading. 3 A concert or ball opened with a formal march. —*v.* **·nad·ed,** **·nad·ing** *v.i.* 1 To take a promenade. —*v.t.* 2 To take a promenade through or along. 3 To take or exhibit on or as on a promenade; parade. [< L *prominare* drive forward] —**prom′e·nad′er** *n.*

**prom·i·nent** (prom′ə·nənt) *adj.* 1 Jutting out; projecting; protuberant. 2 Conspicuous. 3

Very well known; eminent: a *prominent* lawyer. [< L *prominere* to project] —**prom′i·nent·ly** *adv.* —**Syn.** 3 famous, noted, renowned, celebrated, popular, honored, outstanding.

**pro·mis·cu·ous** (prə·mis′kyōō·əs) *adj.* 1 Composed of persons or things confusedly mingled. 2 Indiscriminate; esp., having sexual relations indiscriminately or casually with various persons. 3 Casual; irregular. [< L *promiscuus* mixed] —**pro·mis′cu·ous·ly** *adv.* —**pro·mis′cu·ous·ness** *n.*

**prom·ise** (prom′is) *n.* 1 An assurance given that a specified action will or will not be taken. 2 Reasonable ground for hope or expectation of future excellence, satisfaction, etc. 3 Something promised. —*v.* **·ised,** **·is·ing** *v.t.* 1 To engage or pledge by a promise: He *promised* to do it. 2 To make a promise of (something) to someone. 3 To give reason for expecting. 4 *Informal* To assure (someone) —*v.i.* 5 To make a promise. 6 To give reason for expectation: often with *well* or *fair.* [< L *promissum,* pp. of *promittere* send forward] —**prom′is·er** *n.*

**prom·is·so·ry** (prom′ə·sôr′ē, -sō′rē) *adj.* Containing or of the nature of a promise.

**prom·on·to·ry** (prom′ən·tôr′ē, -tō′rē) *n.* *pl.* **·ries** A high point of land extending into a body of water; headland. [< L *promunturium*]

**pro·mote** (prə·mōt′) *v.t.* **·mot·ed,** **·mot·ing** 1 To contribute to the progress, development, or growth of; further; encourage. 2 To advance to a higher position, grade, or rank. 3 To advocate actively. 4 To publicize (a person, product, event, etc.), as by advertising, public appearances, etc. [< L *pro-* forward + *movere* to move] —**pro·mot′a·ble** *adj.*

**pro·mo·tion** (prə·mō′shən) *n.* 1 Advancement in dignity, rank, grade, etc. 2 Furtherance or development, as of a cause. 3 Anything, as advertising, public appearances, etc., done to publicize a person, product, event, etc. —**pro·mo′tion·al** *adj.*

**prompt** (prompt) *v.t.* 1 To incite to action; instigate. 2 To suggest or inspire (an act, thought, etc.) 3 To remind of what has been forgotten or of what comes next; give a cue to. —*v.i.* 4 To give help or suggestions. —*adj.* 1 Quick to act, respond, etc.; ready. 2 Taking place at the appointed time; punctual. [< L *promptus* brought forth, hence, at hand] —**promp′ti·tude,** **prompt′ness** *n.* —**prompt′ly** *adv.*

**prom·ul·gate** (prom′əl·gāt, prō·mul′gāt) *v.t.*

·gat·ed, ·gat·ing 1 To make known or announce officially, as a law, dogma, etc. 2 To make known or effective over a wide area or extent. [<L *promulgare* make known] — **prom·ul·ga·tion** (prom′əl·gā′shən, prō′-mul-) **prom′ul·gat·or** *n.*

prone (prōn) *adj.* 1 Lying flat, esp. with the face, front, or palm downward; prostrate. 2 Leaning forward or downward. 3 Mentally inclined or predisposed: with *to*. [< L *pronus*] —**prone′ly** *adv.* —**prone′ness** *n.*

pro·noun (prō′noun) *n.* A word used as a substitute for a noun, as *he, she, that.* [< L *pro-* in place of + *nomen* name, noun]

pro·nounce (prə·nouns′) *v.* ·nounced, ·nounc·ing *v.t.* 1 To utter or deliver officially or solemnly; proclaim. 2 To assert; declare, esp. as one's judgment: The judge *pronounced* her guilty. 3 To give utterance to; articulate (words, etc.). 4 To articulate in a prescribed manner: hard to *pronounce* his name. 5 To indicate the sound of (a word) by phonetic symbols. —*v.i.* 6 To make a pronouncement or assertion. 7 To articulate words; speak. [< L *pronuntiare* proclaim < *pro-* forth + *nuntiare* announce] — **pro·nounce′a·ble** *adj.* —**pro·nounc′er** *n.*

pro·nun·ci·a·tion (prə·nun′sē·ā′shən) *n.* The act or manner of pronouncing words.

proof (prōōf) *n.* 1 The act or process of proving; esp., the establishment of a fact by evidence or a truth by other truths. 2 A trial of strength, truth, fact, or excellence, etc.; a test. 3 Evidence and argument sufficient to induce belief. 4 *Law* Anything that serves to convince the mind of the truth or falsity of a fact or proposition. 5 The state or quality of having successfully undergone a proof or test. 6 The standard of strength of alcoholic liquors: see PROOF SPIRIT. 7 *Printing* A printed trial sheet showing the contents or condition of matter in type. 8 In engraving and etching, a trial impression taken from an engraved plate, stone, or block. 9 *Phot.* A trial print from a negative. 10 *Math.* A procedure that shows that a proposition is true. 11 Anything proved true; experience. 12 In philately, an experimental printing of a stamp. —*adj.* 1 Employed in or connected with proving or correcting. 2 Capable of resisting successfully; firm: with *against: proof* against bribes. 3 Of standard alcoholic strength, as liquors. —*v.t.* 1 To make a test or proof of. 2 To protect or make impervious: to *proof* a garment against stains. 3 PROOFREAD. [< L *probare* PROVE]

prop·a·gan·da (prop′ə·gan′də) *n.* 1 Any widespread scheme or effort to spread or promote an idea, opinion, or course of action in order to help or do damage to a cause, person, etc. 2 The ideas, opinions, etc., so spread or promoted: now often used disparagingly because of the deceitful or distorted character of much propaganda. [< NL *(congregatio de) propaganda (fide)* (the congregation for) propagating (the faith)]

prop·a·gate (prop′ə·gāt) *v.* ·gat·ed, ·gat·ing *v.t.* 1 To cause (animals, plants, etc.) to multiply by natural reproduction; breed. 2 To reproduce (itself). 3 To spread abroad or from person to person; disseminate. 4 *Physics* To transmit (a form of energy) through space. —*v.i.* 5 To multiply by natural reproduction; breed. 6 *Physics* To pass or spread through space, as waves, heat, etc. [< L *propago* a slip for transplanting] —**prop′a·ga′tion, prop′a·ga′tor** *n.* —**prop′a·ga′tive** *adj.*

pro·pel (prə·pel′) *v.t.* ·pelled, ·pel·ling To cause to move forward or ahead; drive or urge forward. [< L *pro-* forward + *pellere* drive]

pro·pel·ler (prə·pel′ər) *n.* 1 One who or that which propels. 2 Any device for propelling a craft through water or air; esp., a set of rotating vanes operating like a screw. Also **pro·pel′lor.**

pro·pen·si·ty (prə·pen′sə·tē) *n. pl.* ·ties Natural disposition to or for; tendency. [< L *pro-* forward + *pendere* hang]

prop·er (prop′ər) *adj.* 1 Having special fitness; specially suited; appropriate. 2 Conforming to a standard; correct: the *proper* pronunciation. 3 Seemly; right; fitting: the *proper* outfit. 4 Genteel and respectable, often excessively so. 5 Understood in the most correct or strict sense: usu. following the noun modified: Boston *proper.* 6 Naturally belonging to a person or thing: with *to*: Snow is *proper* to winter. —*n.* Often *cap.* That portion of the breviary or missal containing the prayers and collects suitable to special occasions. [< L *proprius* one's own] — **prop′er·ly** *adv.* —**prop′er·ness** *n.*

prop·er·ty (prop′ər·tē) *n. pl.* ·ties 1 Any object that a person may lawfully acquire and own; any possession, esp. land or real estate. 2 A specific piece of land or real estate. 3 The legal right to the possession, use, and disposal of a thing. 4 An inherent quality or characteristic. **5** In the theater, movies, television, ballet, etc., any portable article, except scenery and costumes, used by the performers while performing. [< L *proprius* one's own]

**proph·e·cy** (prŏf′ə-sē) *n. pl.* **·cies 1** A prediction made under divine influence. **2** Any prediction. [< Gk. *pro-* before + *phanai* speak]

**proph·e·sy** (prŏf′ə-sī) *v.* **·sied, ·sy·ing** *v.t.* **1** To utter or foretell with or as with divine inspiration. **2** To predict (a future event). **3** To point out beforehand. —*v.i.* **4** To speak by divine influence. **5** To foretell the future. [< PROPHECY] —**proph′e·si′er** *n.*

**proph·et** (prŏf′ĭt) *n.* **1** One who delivers divine messages or interprets the divine will. **2** One who foretells the future. **3** A religious leader. **4** An interpreter or spokesman for any cause. —**the Prophet** According to Islam, Mohammed. —**the Prophets** The Old Testament books written by the prophets. [< Gk. *pro-* before + *phanai* speak] —**proph′et·ess** *n. Fem.* —**proph′et·hood** [-hŏŏd] *n.*

**pro·phy·lac·tic** (prō′fə-lak′tĭk, prŏf′ə-) *adj.* Pertaining to prophylaxis. —*n.* **1** A prophylactic medicine or appliance. **2** A condom.

**pro·phy·lax·is** (prō′fə-lak′sĭs, prŏf′ə-) *n.* Preventive treatment for disease. [< Gk. *pro-* before + *phylaxis* a guarding]

**pro·pin·qui·ty** (prō·pĭng′kwə·tē) *n.* **1** Nearness in place or time. **2** Kinship. [< L *propinquus* near]

**pro·pi·ti·ate** (prō·pĭsh′ē·āt) *v.t.* **·at·ed, ·at·ing** To cause to be favorably disposed; appease; conciliate. [< L *propitiare* render favorable, appease] —**pro·pi·ti·a·ble** (prō·pĭsh′ē·ə·bəl), **pro·pi′ti·a′tive,** *adj.* —**pro·pi·ti·a·tion** (prō·pĭsh′ē·ā′shən), **pro·pi′ti·a′tor** *n.* —**Syn.** pacify, placate, mollify, reconcile.

**pro·pi·tious** (prō·pĭsh′əs) *adj.* **1** Kindly disposed; gracious. **2** Attended by favorable circumstances; auspicious. [< L *propitius* favorable] —**pro·pi′tious·ly** *adv.* —**pro·pi′tious·ness** *n.* —**Syn. 2** timely, fortunate, lucky, providential, happy, felicitous.

**pro·por·tion** (prə·pôr′shən, -pōr′-) *n.* **1** Relative magnitude, number, or degree, as existing between parts, a part and a whole, or different things. **2** Balance and harmony; symmetry. **3** A proportionate or proper share. **4** *pl.* Size; dimensions. **5** An equality or identity between ratios. **6** *Math.* An identity or equation involving a pair of fractions,

in the general form $4/2 = 8/4$. —*v.t.* **1** To adjust properly as to relative magnitude, amount, or degree. **2** To form with a harmonious relation of parts. [< L *pro-* before + *portio* a share] —**pro·por′tion·a·ble** *adj.* —**pro·por′tion·a·bly** *adv.* —**pro·por′tion·er** *n.*

**pro·po·sal** (prə·pō′zəl) *n.* **1** An offer proposing something to be accepted or adopted. **2** An offer of marriage. **3** Something proposed.

**pro·pose** (prə·pōz′) *v.* **·posed, ·pos·ing** *v.t.* **1** To put forward for acceptance or consideration. **2** To nominate, as for admission or appointment. **3** To intend; purpose. **4** To suggest the drinking of (a toast or health). —*v.i.* **5** To form or announce a plan or design. **6** To make an offer, as of marriage. [< OF *pro-* forth + *poser* put] —**pro·pos′er** *n.*

**prop·o·si·tion** (prŏp′ə·zĭsh′ən) *n.* **1** A scheme or proposal offered for consideration or acceptance. **2** *Informal* Any matter or person to be dealt with: a tough *proposition.* **3** *Informal* A proposal for illicit sexual intercourse. **4** A subject or statement presented for discussion. **5** *Logic* A statement in which the subject is affirmed or denied by the predicate. **6** *Math.* A statement whose truth is assumed or demonstrated. —*v.t. Informal* To make a proposal to (someone) to have illicit sexual intercourse. —**prop′o·si′tion·al** *adj.* —**prop′o·si′tion·al·ly** *adv.*

**pro·pound** (prə·pound′) *v.t.* To put forward for consideration, solution, etc. [< L *pro·ponere* set forth] —**pro·pound′er** *n.*

**pro·pri·e·tor** (prə·prī′ə·tər) *n.* A person having the exclusive title to anything; owner. —**pro·pri′e·tor·ship′** *n.* —**pro·pri′e·tress** *n. Fem.*

**pro·pri·e·ty** (prə·prī′ə·tē) *n. pl.* **·ties** The character or quality of being proper; esp., accordance with recognized usage, custom, or principles. —**the proprieties** The standards of good social behavior. [< L *proprius* one's own]

**pro·pul·sion** (prə·pul′shən) *n.* **1** A propelling or being propelled. **2** Something that propels. [< L *propulsus,* pp. of *propellere* propel] —**pro·pul′sive** (-sĭv) *adj.*

**pro·sa·ic** (prō·zā′ĭk) *adj.* **1** Unimaginative; commonplace; dull. **2** Of or like prose. [< L *prosa* prose] —**pro·sa′i·cal·ly** *adv.* —**pro·sa′ic·ness** *n.*

**pro·sce·ni·um** (prō·sē′nē·əm) *n. pl.* **·ni·ums** or **·ni·a** (-nē·ə) **1** In a modern theater, that part of the stage between the curtain and the orchestra, sometimes including the curtain and its arch (**proscenium arch**). 2 In the ancient Greek or Roman theater, the stage. [< Gk. *proskēnion* < *pro-* before + *skēnē* a stage, orig. a tent]

**pro·scribe** (prō-skrīb´) *v.t.* **·scribed, ·scrib·ing** 1 To denounce or condemn; prohibit; interdict. 2 To outlaw or banish. 3 In ancient Rome, to publish the name of (one condemned or exiled). [< L *pro-* before + *scribere* write] —**pro·scrib´er, pro·scrip´tion** (-skrip´shən) *n.* —**pro·scrip´tive** *adj.* —**pro·scrip´tive·ly** *adv.*

**prose** (prōz) *n.* 1 Speech or writing as found in ordinary conversation, letters, newspapers, etc. 2 Writing, esp. in literature, distinguished from poetry by the lack of conscious rhyme and usu. by rhythms suggesting ordinary speech or by a presentation in the form of a series of sentences with the initial letters capitalized. 3 Commonplace or tedious talk, style, quality, etc. —*adj.* 1 Of or in prose. 2 Tedious. —*v.t.* & *v.i.* **prosed, pros·ing** To write or speak in prose. [< L *prosa (oratio)* straightforward (discourse)]

**pros·e·cute** (pros´ə-kyōōt) *v.* **·cut·ed, ·cut·ing** *v.t.* 1 To go on with so as to complete; pursue to the end: to *prosecute* an inquiry. 2 To carry on or engage in, as a trade. 3 *Law* **a** To bring suit against for redress of wrong or punishment of crime. **b** To seek to enforce or obtain, as a claim or right, by legal process. —*v.i.* 4 To begin and carry on a legal proceeding. [< L *prosequi* pursue]

**pros·e·cu·tion** (pros´ə-kyōō´shən) *n.* 1 The act or process of prosecuting. 2 *Law* **a** The instituting and carrying forward of a judicial or criminal proceeding. **b** The party instituting and conducting it.

**pros·e·lyte** (pros´ə-līt) *n.* One who has been converted to any opinion, belief, sect, or party. —*v.t.* & *v.i.* **·lyt·ed, ·lyt·ing** PROSELYTIZE. [< Gk. *prosēlytos* a convert to Judaism] —**pros´e·lyt·ism** (-lit´iz-əm, -lə-tiz´əm), **pros´e·lyt·ist** *n.*

**pros·pect** (pros´pekt) *n.* 1 A future probability or something anticipated. 2 *Usu. pl.* Chances, as for success. 3 A scene; an extended view. 4 The direction in which anything faces; an exposure; outlook. 5 A potential buyer, candidate, etc. 6 The act of observing or examining; survey. 7 *Mining* **a** A place having signs of the presence of mineral ore. **b** The sample of mineral obtained by washing a small portion of ore or dirt. —

*v.t.* & *v.i.* To explore (a region) for gold, oil, etc. [< L *pro-* forward + *specere* look]

**pro·spec·tive** (prə-spek´tiv) *adj.* 1 Anticipated; expected. 2 Looking toward the future; anticipatory. —**pro·spec´tive·ly** *adv.*

**pros·pec·tor** (pros´pek-tər) *n.* One who prospects for mineral deposits, oil, etc.

**pro·spec·tus** (prə-spek´təs) *n.* 1 A paper containing information of a proposed literary or business undertaking. 2 A summary; outline. [L, a look-out, prospect]

**pros·per** (pros´pər) *v.i.* 1 To thrive; flourish. —*v.t.* 2 To render prosperous. [< OF < L favorable]

**pros·per·ous** (pros´pər-əs) *adj.* 1 Successful; flourishing. 2 Wealthy; well-to-do. 3 Promising; favorable. [< L *prosper* favorable] —**pros´per·ous·ly** *adv.* —**pros´per·ous·ness** *n.*

**pros·trate** (pros´trāt) *adj.* 1 Lying prone, or with the face to the ground. 2 Brought low in mind or body, as from grief, exhaustion, etc. 3 Lying at the mercy of another; defenseless. 4 *Bot.* Trailing along the ground. —*v.t.* **·trat·ed, ·trat·ing** 1 To bow or cast (oneself) down, as in adoration or pleading. 2 To throw flat; lay on the ground. 3 To overthrow or overcome; reduce to helplessness. [< L *prostratus*, pp. of *prosternere* lay flat] —**pros·tra´tion** *n.*

**pro·tect** (prə-tekt´) *v.t.* 1 To shield or defend from attack, harm, or injury; guard; defend. 2 *Econ.* To assist (domestic industry) by protective tariffs. 3 In commerce, to provide funds to guarantee payment of (a draft, etc.). [< L *pro-* before + *tegere* to cover] —**pro·tec´tive** *adj.* —**pro·tec´tive·ly** *adv.* —**pro·tec´tive·ness, pro·tec´tor** *n.*

**pro·tec·tion** (prə-tek´shən) *n.* 1 The act of protecting or the state of being protected. 2 That which protects: Our dog is a great *protection*. 3 A system aiming to protect the industries of a country, as by imposing duties. 4 A safe-conduct pass. 5 *Slang* Security purchased under threat of violence from racketeers; also, the money so paid.

**pro·té·gé** (prō´tə·zhā, prō·tə·zhā´) *n.* One aided, esp. in promoting a career, by another who is older or more powerful. [F, pp. of *protéger* protect] —**pro´té·gée** *n. Fem.*

**pro·tein** (prō´tēn, -tē·in) *n.* Any of a class of complex nitrogenous compounds found in all living matter and forming an essential part of the diet of animals. —*adj.* Composed of protein.

**pro·test** (prō′test) *n.* 1 An objection, complaint, or declaration of disapproval. 2 A public expression of dissent, esp. if organized. 3 A formal certificate attesting the fact that a note or bill of exchange has not been paid. —*adj.* Of or relating to public protest: *protest* demonstrations. —*v.* (prə·test′) *v.t.* 1 To assert earnestly or positively; state formally, esp. against opposition or doubt. 2 To make a protest against; object to. 3 To declare formally that payment of (a promissory note, etc.) has been duly submitted and refused. —*v.i.* 4 To make solemn affirmation. 5 To make a protest; object. [< L *pro-* forth + *testari* affirm] —**pro·test′er**, **pro·test′or** *n.*

**Prot·es·tant** (prot′is·tənt) *n.* Any Christian who is not a member of the Roman Catholic or Eastern Orthodox Churches. —*adj.* Pertaining to Protestants or Protestantism. —**Prot′es·tant·ism** *n.*

**prot·es·ta·tion** (prot′is·tā′shən, prō′tes-) *n.* 1 The act o protesting. 2 That which is protested. 3 Any protest or objection.

**pro·to·col** (prō′tə·kol) *n.* 1 The preliminary draft of an official document, as a treaty. 2 The preliminary draft or report of the negotiations and conclusions arrived at by a diplomatic conference, having the force of a treaty when ratified. 3 The rules of diplomatic and state etiquette and ceremony. —*v.t.* To write or form protocols. [< LGk. *prō tokollon* the first glued sheet of a papyrus roll]

**pro·ton** (prō′ton) *n.* A stable, positively charged subatomic particle found typically in atomic nuclei, having a charge equal in magnitude to that of an electron and a mass of about $1.672 \times 10^{-24}$ gram. [<Gk. *prōtos* first]

**pro·to·type** (prō′tə·tīp) *n.* A first or original model; an archetype. —**pro′to·typ′al** (-tī′pəl), **pro′to·typ′ic** (-tip′ik), **pro′to·typ′i·cal** *adj.*

**pro·tract** (prō·trakt′, prə-) *v.t.* 1 To extend in time; prolong. 2 In surveying, to draw or map by means of a scale and protractor; plot. 3 *Zool.* To protrude or extend. [< L *protractus*, pp. of *protrahere* extend] —**pro·trac′tion** *n.* —**pro·tract′i·ble**, **pro·trac′tive** *adj.*

**pro·trude** (prō·trōōd′, prə-) *v.t. & v.i.* ·trud·ed, ·trud·ing To push or thrust out; project outward. [< L *pro-* forward + *trudere* thrust] —**pro·tru′dent** *adj.* —**pro·tru′sion** (-trōō′zhən) *n.*

**pro·tu·ber·ance** (prō·t′ōō′bər·əns) *n.* 1 Something that protrudes; a knob; prominence. 2 The state of being protuberant. Also **pro·tu′ber·an·cy.** [< LL *protuberare* bulge out] —**pro·tu′ber·ant** *adj.* —**pro·tu′ber·ant·ly** *adv.*

**proud** (proud) *adj.* 1 Moved by, having, or exhibiting a due sense of pride; self-respecting. 2 Characterized by excessive or immoderate pride. 3 Being a cause of honorable pride: a *proud* occasion. 4 Appreciative of an honor; glad: *proud* of his heritage. 5 High-mettled, as a horse; spirited. [< OE *prūd*] —**proud′ly** *adv.* —Syn. 2 arrogant, haughty, supercilious, disdainful.

**prove** (prōōv) *v.* proved, proved or prov·en (prōō′vən), prov·ing *v.t.* 1 To show to be true or genuine, as by evidence or argument. 2 To determine the quality or genuineness of; test. 3 To establish the authenticity or validity of, as a will. 4 *Math.* To verify the accuracy of by an independent process. 5 *Printing* To take a proof of or from. 6 *Archaic* To learn by experience. —*v.i.* 7 To turn out to be: His hopes *proved* vain. [< L *probare* to test, try] —**prov′a·ble** *adj.* —**prov′er** *n.*

**prov·erb** (prov′ərb) *n.* 1 A terse expression of a popularly accepted piece of wisdom. 2 Something proverbial; a typical example; byword. [< L *pro-* before + *verbum* a word] —Syn. 1 adage, aphorism, maxim, motto, saying, truism.

**pro·ver·bi·al** (prə·vûr′bē·əl) *adj.* 1 Of the nature of or pertaining to a proverb. 2 Generally known or remarked. —**pro·ver′bi·al·ly** *adv.*

**pro·vide** (prə·vīd′) *v.* ·vid·ed, ·vid·ing *v.t.* 1 To acquire for or supply; furnish. 2 To afford; yield: to *provide* pleasure. 3 To set down as a condition; stipulate. —*v.i.* 4 To take measures in advance: with *for* or *against.* 5 To furnish means of subsistence: usu. with *for.* 6 To make a stipulation. [< L *providere* foresee] —**pro·vid′er** *n.*

**prov·i·dence** (prov′ə·dəns) *n.* 1 Often *cap.* The care exercised by nature or God's will over the universe. 2 Care exercised for the future; foresight. [< L *providentia* < *providens*, pr.p. of *providere* foresee]

**prov·i·dent** (prov′ə·dənt) *adj.* 1 Anticipating and preparing for future wants or emergencies; exercising foresight. 2 Economical; thrifty. —**prov′i·dent·ly** *adv.*

**prov·i·den·tial** (prov′ə·den′shəl) *adj.* 1 Resulting from or revealing the action of God's providence. 2 As if caused by divine intervention; wonderful. —**prov′i·den′tial·ly** *adv.*

**prov·ince** (prov′ins) *n.* 1 An administrative division within a country: the *provinces* of Canada. 2 A region or country ruled by the Roman Empire. 3 *pl.* Those regions that lie at a distance from the capital or major cities. 4 A sphere of knowledge or activity: the *province* of chemistry. 5 Proper concern or compass, as of responsibilities or duties: The *province* of the judge is to apply the laws. [< L *provincia* an official duty or charge, a province]

**pro·vin·cial** (prə·vin′shəl) *adj.* 1 Of or characteristic of a province. 2 Confined to a province; rustic. 3 Narrow; unsophisticated; uninformed. —*n.* 1 A native or inhabitant of a province. 2 One who is provincial. —**pro·vin′ci·al′i·ty** (-shē·al′ə·tē) *n.* —**pro·vin′cial·ly** *adv.*

**pro·vi·sion** (prə·vizh′ən) *n.* 1 A measure taken in advance, as against future need. 2 *pl.* Food or a supply of food; victuals. 3 Something provided or prepared in anticipation of need. 4 A stipulation or requirement. —*v.t.* To provide with food or provisions. [< L *provisus,* p.p. of *providere* foresee] —**pro·vi′sion·er** *n.*

**pro·vi·sion·al** (prə·vizh′ən·əl) *adj.* Provided for a present service or temporary necessity: a *provisional* army. Also **pro·vi′sion·ar′y** (-er′ē). —**pro·vi′sion·al·ly** *adv.*

**pro·vi·so** (prə·vi′zō) *n. pl.* **·sos** or **·soes** 1 A conditional stipulation. 2 A clause, as in a contract or statute, limiting, modifying, or rendering conditional its operation. [< Med. L *proviso* (quod) it being provided (that)]

**prov·o·ca·tion** (prov′ə·kā′shən) *n.* 1 The act of provoking. 2 Something that provokes or incites; esp., something that provokes anger or annoyance.

**pro·voc·a·tive** (prə·vok′ə·tiv) *adj.* Serving to provoke or excite; stimulating: a *provocative* theory. —*n.* That which provokes or tends to provoke. —**pro·voc′a·tive·ly** *adv.* —**pro·voc′a·tive·ness** *n.*

**pro·voke** (prə·vōk′) *v.t.* **·voked, ·vok·ing** 1 To stir to anger or resentment; irritate; vex. 2 To arouse or stimulate to some action. 3 To stir up or bring about: to *provoke* a quarrel. [< L *pro-* forth + *vocare* to call]

**prow·ess** (prou′is) *n.* 1 Strength, skill, and courage, esp. in battle. 2 Formidable skill; expertise. [< OF *prou* brave]

**prowl** (proul) *v.t. & v.i.* To roam about stealthily, as in search of prey or plunder. —*n.* The act of prowling. [ME *prollen*] —**prowl′er** *n.*

**prox·im·i·ty** (prok·sim′ə·tē) *n.* The state or fact of being near; nearness. [< L *proximus* nearest]

**prox·y** (prok′sē) *n. pl.* **prox·ies** 1 A person empowered by another to act for him. 2 The means or agency of one so empowered: to vote by *proxy.* 3 The office or right to act for another. 4 A document conferring the authority to act for another. [< L *procurare* procure]

**prude** (prood) *n.* One who displays an exaggerated devotion to modesty and propriety, esp. in sexual matters. [F < *prudefemme* an excellent woman] —**prud′ish** *adj.* —**prud′ish·ly** *adv.* —**prud′ish·ness** *n.*

**pru·dence** (prood′ns) *n.* 1 The exercise of thoughtful care, sound judgment, or discretion; cautious wisdom. 2 Economy; thrift. —**pru·den·tial** (proo·den′shəl) *adj.*

**pru·dent** (prood′nt) *adj.* 1 Habitually careful to avoid errors and to follow the most reasonable or practical course; politic. 2 Exercising sound judgment; wise; judicious. 3 Characterized by discretion; cautious in manner. 4 Frugal; provident. [< L *prudens* knowing, skilled] —**pru′dent·ly** *adv.* —Syn. 1 shrewd. 2 sensible, sagacious, thoughtful. 3 circumspect.

**prud·er·y** (prood′dər·ē) *n. pl.* **·er·ies** 1 Exaggerated devotion to modesty and propriety, esp. in sexual matters. 2 An action characteristic of a prude.

**prune** (proon) *n.* 1 The dried fruit of any of several varieties of plum. 2 *Slang* A stupid or disagreeable person. [< Gk. *prounon* a plum]

**pru·ri·ent** (proor′ē·ənt) *adj.* 1 Tending to excite lustful thoughts or desires; lewd. 2 Characterized by or having lustful thoughts or desires: *prurient* interest. [< L *prurire* itch, long for] —**pru′ri·ence, pru′ri·en·cy** *n.* —**pru′ri·ent·ly** *adv.*

**pry** (prī) *v.t.* **pried, pry·ing** 1 To raise, move, or open by means of a lever. 2 To obtain by effort. —*n.* 1 A lever, as a bar, stick, or beam. 2 Leverage. [< PRIZE[2]]

**psalm** (säm) *n.* A sacred song or lyric, esp. one contained in the Old Testament Book of Psalms; a hymn. [< Gk. *psalmos* a song sung to the harp]

**psalm·ist** (sä′mist) *n.* A composer of psalms. —**the Psalmist** King David, the traditional author of many of the Scriptural psalms.

**pseu·do·nym** (soo′də·nim) *n.* A fictitious

name; pen name. [<Gk. *pseudēs* false + *onyma* a name] —**pseu·don·y·mous** (sōō·don'ə·məs) *adj.* —**pseu·don'y·mous·ly** *adv.* —**pseu·don'y·mous·ness, pseu·do·nym·i·ty** (sōō'də·nim'ə·tē) *n.*

**psy·che** (sī'kē) *n.* 1 The human soul. 2 The mind. [< Gk. *psychē* the soul < *psychein* breathe, blow]

**psy·che·del·ic** (sī'kə·del'ik) *adj.* Causing or having to do with abnormal alterations of consciousness or perception: *psychedelic* drugs. [< Gk. *psychē* soul + *del(os)* manifest + -IC] —**psy'che·del'i·cal·ly** *adv.*

**psy·chi·a·trist** (si·kī'ə·trist) *n.* A medical doctor specializing in the practice of psychiatry.

**psy·chi·a·try** (sī·kī'ə·trē) *n.* The branch of medicine concerned with mental and emotional disorders. [< PSYCH(O)- + Gk. *iatros* healer] —**psy·chi·at·ric** (sī'kē·at'rik) or **·ri·cal** *adj.* —**psy'chi·at'ri·cal·ly** *adv.*

**psy·chic** (sī'kik) *adj.* 1 Of or pertaining to the psyche or mind. 2 Inexplicable with reference to present knowledge or scientific theory: *psychic* phenomena. 3 Sensitive or responsive to phenomena apparently independent of normal sensory stimuli: a *psychic* person. Also **psy'chi·cal.** —*n.* 1 A psychic person. 2 A spiritualistic medium. [< Gk. *psychē* soul] —**psy'chi·cal·ly** *adv.*

**psy·cho·a·nal·y·sis** (sī'kō·ə·nal'ə·sis) *n.* 1 A method of psychotherapeutic treatment developed by Sigmund Freud and others, which seeks to alleviate certain mental and emotional disorders. 2 The theory or practice of such treatment. —**psy'cho·an'a·lyt'ic** (-an'ə·lit'ik) or **·i·cal** *adj.* —**psy'cho·an'a·lyt'i·cal·ly** *adv.*

**psy·cho·an·a·lyze** (sī'kō·an'ə·līz) *v.t.* **·lyzed, ·lyz·ing** To treat by psychoanalysis. *Brit. sp.* **·lyse.**

**psy·cho·log·i·cal** (sī'kə·loj'i·kəl) *adj.* 1 Of or pertaining to psychology. 2 Of or in the mind. 3 Suitable for affecting the mind: the *psychological* moment. Also **psy'cho·log'ic.** —**psy'cho·log'i·cal·ly** *adv.*

**psy·chol·o·gy** (sī·kol'ə·jē) *n.* 1 The science of the mind in any of its aspects. 2 The systematic investigation of human or animal learning, behavior, etc. 3 The pattern of mental processes characteristic of an individual or type.

**psy·cho·neu·ro·sis** (sī'kō·nyŏŏ·rō'sis) *n. pl.* **·ses** (-sēz) NEUROSIS. —**psy'cho·neu·rot'ic** (-rot'ik) *adj., n.*

**psy·cho·sis** (sī·kō'sis) *n. pl.* **·ses** (-sēz) A severe mental disorder marked by disorganization of the personality. [< Gk. *psychōsis* a giving of life]

**psy·cho·so·mat·ic** (sī'kō·sō·mat'ik) *adj.* 1 Of or pertaining to the interrelationships of mind and body, esp. with reference to disease. 2 Designating a physical ailment caused or influenced by emotional stress. [< PSYCHO- + SOMATIC]

**psy·cho·ther·a·py** (sī'kō·ther'ə·pē) *n.* The treatment of certain nervous and mental disorders by psychological techniques such as counseling, psychoanalysis, etc. Also **psy'cho·ther'a·peu'tics** (-ther'ə·pyōō' tiks). —**psy'cho·ther'a·peu'tic** *adj.* —**psy'cho·ther'a·pist** *n.*

**psy·chot·ic** (sī·kot'ik) *n.* One suffering from a psychosis. —*adj.* Of psychosis or a psychotic. —**psy·chot'i·cal·ly** *adv.*

**pto·maine** (tō'mān, tō·mān') *n.* Any of a class of usu. nontoxic compounds derived from decomposing protein. Also **pto'main.** [< Gk. *ptōma* a corpse]

**pub·lic** (pub'lik) *adj.* 1 Of, pertaining to, or affecting the people at large. 2 Of or relating to the community as distinguished from private or personal matters. 3 For the use of or open to all; maintained by or for the community: *public* parks. 4 Well-known; open: a *public* scandal. 5 Occupying an official position. 6 Acting before or for the community: a *public* speaker. —*n.* 1 The people collectively. 2 A group of people sharing some attribute or purpose: the church-going *public.* [< L *publicus*] —**pub'lic·ly** *adv.* —**pub'lic·ness** *n.*

**pub·li·ca·tion** (pub'lə·kā'shən) *n.* 1 The act of publishing. 2 That which is published; any printed work placed on sale or otherwise distributed.

**pub·lic·i·ty** (pub·lis'ə·tē) *n.* 1 The state of being public. 2 Information, news, or promotional material intended to elicit public interest in some person, product, cause, etc.; also the work or business of preparing and releasing such material. 3 The attention or interest of the public.

**pub·li·cize** (pub'lə·sīz) *v.t.* **·cized, ·ciz·ing** To give publicity to; promote. *Brit. sp.* **pub'li·cise.**

**pub·lish** (pub'lish) *v.t.* 1 To print and issue (a book, magazine, etc.) to the public. 2 To make known or announce publicly. 3 To print and issue the work of. —*v.i.* 4 To engage in the business of publishing books, magazines, newspapers, etc. 5 To have one's work printed and issued. [< L *publicare* make public] —**pub·lish·a·ble** *adj.* — Syn. 2 promulgate, proclaim, declare, advertise.

**pud·dle** (pud′l) *n.* 1 A small pool of water or other liquid. 2 A pasty mixture of clay and water. —*v.t.* **·dled, ·dling** 1 To convert (molten pig iron) into wrought iron by melting and stirring in the presence of oxidizing agents. 2 To mix (clay, etc.) with water to obtain a watertight paste. 3 To line, as canal banks, with such a mixture. 4 To make muddy; stir up. [ME < OE *pudd* a ditch] —**pud′dler** *n.*

**pudg·y** (puj′ē) *adj.* **pudg·i·er, pudg·i·est** Short and thick; fat. [< Scot. *pud* belly] —**pudg′i·ly** *adv.* —**pudg′i·ness** *n.*

**pu·er·ile** (pyŏŏ′ər·il, pwer′il, -īl) *adj.* Childish; immature; silly. [< L *puer* boy] —**pu′er·ile·ly** *adv.* —**pu′er·il′i·ty. pu′er·ile·ness** *n.*

**pug·na·cious** (pug·nā′shəs) *adj.* Disposed or inclined to fight; quarrelsome. [< L *pugnus* fist] —**pug·na′cious·ly** *adv.* —**pug·nac·i·ty** (-nas′ə·tē), **pug·na′cious·ness** *n.*

**pull** (pŏŏl) *v.t.* 1 To apply force to so as to cause motion toward or after the person or thing exerting force; drag; tug. 2 To draw or remove from a natural or fixed place: to *pull* a tooth or plug. 3 To give a pull or tug to. 4 To pluck, as a fowl. 5 To draw asunder; tear; rend: with *to pieces, apart,* etc. 6 To strain so as to cause injury: to *pull* a ligament. 7 In sports, to strike (the ball) so as to cause it to curve obliquely from the direction in which the striker faces. 8 *Informal* To put into effect; carry out: to *pull* off a robbery. 9 *Informal* To make a raid on; arrest. 10 *Informal* To draw out so as to use: to *pull* a knife. 11 To make or obtain by impression from type: to *pull* a proof. 12 In boxing, to deliver (a punch, etc.) with less than full strength. 13 In horse-racing, to restrain (a horse) so as to prevent its winning. 14 To operate (an oar) by drawing toward one. —*v.i.* 15 To use force in hauling, dragging, moving, etc. 16 To move: with *out, in, away, ahead,* etc. 17 To drink or inhale deeply. 18 *Informal* To attract attention or customers: an ad that *pulls.* 19 To row. — **pull for** 1 To strive in behalf of. 2 *Informal* To declare one's allegiance to. —**pull oneself together** To regain one's composure. — **pull through** To survive in spite of illness, etc. —**pull up** To come to a halt. —*n.* 1 The act or process of pulling. 2 Something that

is pulled, as a handle. 3 A long swallow or a deep puff. 4 The drawing of an oar in rowing. 5 A steady, continuous effort, as in climbing: a long *pull* to the top. 6 *Informal* Influence, esp. with those in power: political *pull.* 7 An attractive force: the *pull* of gravity. [< OE *pullian* pluck] —**pull′er** *n.*

**pul·let** (pŏŏl′it) *n.* A young hen, usu. less than a year old. [< L *pullus* chicken]

**pul·ley** (pŏŏl′ē) *n.* 1 A wheel or wheels grooved to receive a rope, usu. mounted in a block, used singly to reverse the direction of force applied, as in lifting a weight, and in various combinations to increase force at the expense of distance. 2 A flat or flanged wheel driving, carrying, or being driven by a flat belt, used to transmit power. [< Gk. *polos* a pivot, axis]

**pul·mo·nar·y** (pŏŏl′mə·ner′ē, pul′-) *adj.* 1 Pertaining to or affecting the lungs. 2 Having lunglike organs. 3 Designating the blood vessels carrying blood between the lungs and heart. Also **pul·mon·ic** (pŏŏl·mon′ik, pul-) [< L *pulmo, pulmonis* lung] • See HEART.

**pulp** (pulp) *n.* 1 A moist, soft, slightly cohering mass, as the soft, succulent part of fruit. 2 A mixture of wood fibers or rags, made semifluid and forming the basis from which paper is made. 3 *pl.* Magazines printed on rough, unglazed, wood-pulp paper, and usu. having contents of a sensational nature. 4 Powdered ore mixed with water. 5 The soft tissue of vessels and nerves that fills the central part of a tooth. • See TOOTH. —*v.t.* 1 To reduce to pulp. 2 To remove the pulp from. —*v.i.* 3 To be or become pulp. [< L *pulpa* flesh, pulp] —**pulp′i·ness** *n.* —**pulp′y** *adj.*

**pul·sate** (pul′sāt) *v.i.* **·sat·ed, ·sat·ing** 1 To move or throb with rhythmical impulses, as the pulse or heart. 2 To vibrate; quiver. [< L *pulsare,* freq. of *pellere* beat] —**pul·sa′tion** *n.* —**pul′sa·tive** (-sə-tiv), **pul′sa·to′ry** *adj.*

**pulse** (puls) *n.* 1 The rhythmic pressure in the arteries due to the beating of the heart. 2 Any short, regular throbbing; pulsation. 3 A brief surge of energy, esp. electrical or electromagnetic energy. 4 Feelings and attitudes sensitively perceived as belonging to a group or community; also, an indication of such feelings. —*v.i.* **pulsed, puls·ing** To manifest a pulse; pulsate; throb. [< L *pulsus* p.p. of *pellere* beat]

**pul·ver·ize** (pul′və·rīz) *v.* **·ized, ·iz·ing** *v.t.* 1 To

419

reduce to powder or dust, as by grinding or crushing. 2 To demolish; annihilate. —*v.i.* 3 To become reduced to powder or dust. *Brit. sp.* **·ise.** [< L *pulvis*, *pulveris* a powder, dust] —**pul'ver·iz'a·ble**, **pul'ver·a·ble** (pul'və·rə·bəl) *adj.* —**pul'ver·i·za'tion**, **pul'ver·iz'er** *n.*

**pum·ice** (pum'is) *n.* Porous volcanic lava, used as an abrasive and polisher, esp. when powdered. **Also pumice stone.** —*v.t.* **·iced**, **·ic·ing** To smooth, polish, or clean with pumice. [< L *pumex*] —**pu·mi·ceous** (pyōō·mish'əs) *adj.*

**pump** (pump) *n.* A device using suction or pressure to raise, circulate, exhaust, or compress a liquid or gas. —*v.t.* 1 To raise (a liquid) with a pump. 2 To remove the water, etc., from. 3 To inflate with air by means of a pump. 4 To propel, discharge, force, etc., from or as if from a pump. 5 To cause to operate in the manner of a pump. 6 To question persistently or subtly. 7 To obtain (information) in such a manner. —*v.i.* 8 To work a pump. 9 To raise water or other liquid with a pump. 10 To move up and down like a pump or pump handle. [< MDu. *pompe*] —**pump'er** *n.*

**pump·kin** (pump'kin, pum'-, pung'-) *n.* 1 A coarse trailing vine with gourdlike fruit. 2 Its large, edible, orange-yellow fruit. [< Gk. *pepōn* a melon]

**pun** (pun) *n.* The humorous use of two words having the same or similar sounds but different meanings, or of a word having two more or less incongruous meanings. —*v.i.* **punned**, **pun·ning** To make a pun or puns. [? <Ital. *puntiglio* a fine point]

**punch** (punch) *n.* 1 A tool for perforating or indenting, or for driving an object into a hole. 2 A machine for impressing a design or stamping a die. —*v.t.* To perforate, shape, indent, etc., with a punch. [ME *punchon* puncheon]

**punc·til·i·ous** (pungk·til'ē·əs) *adj.* Very exacting in observing rules or conventions. [< Ital. *puntiglio* small point] —**punc·til'i·ous·ly** *adv.* —**punc·til'i·ous·ness** *n.*

**punc·tu·al** (pungk'chōō·əl) *adj.* 1 Arriving on time; prompt. 2 Habitually exact as to appointed time. 3 Consisting of or confined to a point. [< L *punctus* a point] —**punc'tu·al'i·ty** *n.* —**punc'tu·al·ly** *adv.*

**punc·tu·ate** (pungk'chōō·āt) *v.* **·at·ed**, **·at·ing** *v.t.* 1 To divide or mark with punctuation. 2 To interrupt at intervals. 3 To emphasize.

—*v.i.* 4 To use punctuation. [< L *punctus* a point] —**punc'tu·a'tor** *n.* ·

**punc·tu·a·tion** (pungk'chōō·ā'shən) *n.* 1 The use of points or marks in written or printed matter to aid in the better comprehension of the meaning and grammatical relation of the words. 2 The marks so used.

**punc·ture** (pungk'chər) *v.* **·tured**, **·tur·ing** *v.t.* 1 To pierce with a sharp point. 2 To make by pricking, as a hole. 3 To cause to collapse: to *puncture* a cherished illusion. —*v.i.* 4 To be pierced or punctured. —*n.* 1 A small hole, as one made by piercing. 2 The act of puncturing. [< L *punctus*, p.p. of *pungere* prick]

**pun·gent** (pun'jənt) *adj.* 1 Causing a sharp pricking, stinging, piercing, or acrid sensation. 2 Affecting the mind or feelings so as to cause pain; piercing; sharp. 3 Caustic; keen; cutting: *pungent* sarcasm. 4 Telling; pointed. [< L *pungere* prick] —**pun'gen·cy** *n.* —**pun'gent·ly** *adv.*

**pun·ish** (pun'ish) *v.t.* 1 To subject (a person) to pain, confinement, or other penalty for a crime or fault. 2 To subject the perpetrator of (an offense) to a penalty. 3 To treat roughly; injure; hurt. [< L *punire*] —**pun'ish·a·ble** *adj.* —**pun'ish·a·bil'i·ty**, **pun'ish·er** *n.*

**pun·ish·ment** (pun'ish·mənt) *n.* 1 Penalty imposed, as for a violation of law. 2 Any pain or loss inflicted in response to wrongdoing. 3 The act of punishing. 4 Physical damage or abuse.

**pu·ni·tive** (pyōō'nə·tiv) *adj.* Pertaining to or inflicting punishment. —**pu'ni·tive·ly** *adv.* —**pu'ni·tive·ness** *n.*

**punt[1]** (punt) *v.i.* To gamble or bet in certain card games, esp. against the banker. [< L *punctum* a point]

**punt[2]** (punt) *n.* In football, a kick made by dropping the ball from the hands and kicking it before it strikes the ground. —*v.t.* 1 To propel (a football) with a punt. —*v.i.* 2 In football, to make a punt. [?] —**punt'er** *n.*

**pu·ny** (pyōō'nē) *adj.* **·ni·er**, **·ni·est** Small or inferior, as in power, significance, etc. [< OF *puisne* born afterward] —**pu'ni·ly** *adv.* —**pu'ni·ness** *n.* —**Syn.** slight, minor, unimportant, frail.

**pu·pa** (pyōō'pə) *n. pl.* **·pae** (-pē) or **·pas** A quiescent stage between larva and adult in the metamorphosis of certain insects. [L, a girl, puppet] —**pu'pal** *adj.*

**pu·pil** (pyōō'pəl) *n.* A person under the care of a teacher, as in a school. [< L *pupillus* and *pupilla*, dim. of *pupus* boy and *pupa* girl] —pu′pil·age, pu′pil·lage n. —Syn. student, disciple, scholar, learner.

pup·pet (pup′ĭt) n. 1 A small figure, as of a person or animal, manipulated usu. by the hands, or by pulling strings or wires attached to its jointed parts. 2 A person controlled by the will or whim of another. 3 A doll. —adj. 1 Of puppets. 2 Performing the will of an unseen power; not autonomous: a puppet state or government. [< L pupa a girl, doll, puppet] —pup′pet·ry (-rē) n.

pup·py (pup′ē) n. pl. ·pies A young dog. [< L pupa a girl, doll]

pup tent A small tent providing shelter for one or two people.

pur·chase (pûr′chəs) v.t. ·chased, ·chas·ing 1 To acquire by paying money or its equivalent; buy. 2 To obtain by exertion, sacrifice, flattery, etc. 3 To move, hoist, or hold by a mechanical purchase. —n. 1 The act of purchasing. 2 That which is purchased. 3 A mechanical hold or grip. 4 A device that gives a mechanical advantage, as a tackle or lever. [OF porchacier seek for] —pur′chas·er n. —Syn. 1, 2 get, obtain, procure, secure.

pure (pyōōr) adj. pur·er, pur·est 1 Free from mixture or contact with that which weakens, impairs, or pollutes. 2 Free from adulteration; clear; clean: pure water. 3 Faultless; righteous: pure motives. 4 Chaste; innocent. 5 Concerned with fundamental research, as distinguished from practical application: pure science. 6 Bred from stock having no admixture for many generations. 7 Nothing but; sheer: pure luck. [< L purus clean, pure] —pure′ness n.

pur·ga·to·ry (pûr′gə·tôr′ē, -tō′rē) n. pl. ·ries 1 In Roman Catholic theology, a state or place where the souls of those who have died penitent are made fit for paradise by expiating venial sins. 2 Any place or state of temporary banishment, suffering, or punishment. [< AF < L purgare cleanse] —pur′ga·to′ri·al adj.

purge (pûrj) v. purged, purg·ing v.t. 1 To cleanse of what is impure or extraneous; purify. 2 To remove (impurities, etc.) in cleansing: with away, off, or out. 3 To rid (a group, nation, etc.) of individuals regarded as undesirable. 4 To remove or kill such individuals. 5 To cleanse or rid of sin, fault, or defilement. 6 Med. a To cause evacuation of (the bowels, etc.). b To induce evacuation of the bowels of. —v.i. 7 To become clean or pure. 8 Med. To have or induce evacuation of the bowels. —n. 1 The action of an orga-

nization, esp. a government, in removing from office or positions of power individuals regarded as undesirable. 2 The act of purging. 3 That which purges; a cathartic. [< L purgare cleanse] —pur·ga·tion (pûr·gā′shən), purg′er n.

pu·ri·fy (pyōōr′ə·fī) v. ·fied, ·fy·ing v.t. 1 To make pure or clean; rid of extraneous or noxious matter. 2 To free from sin or defilement. 3 To free of debasing elements. — v.i. 4 To become pure or clean. [< L purus pure + facere make] —pu·rif·i·ca·to·ry (pyōō·rif′ə·kə·tôr′ē, -tō′rē) adj. —pu·ri·fi·ca·tion (pyōōr′ə·fə·kā′shən), pu′ri·fi′er n.

pu·ri·tan (pyōōr′ə·tən) n. One who is unusually or excessively strict regarding adherence to morality or religious practice. — adj. Of or characteristic of puritans. [< LL puritas purity] —pu′ri·tan′ic or ·i·cal adj. —pu′ri·tan′i·cal·ly adv. —pu′ri·tan′i·cal·ness, pu′ri·tan·ism n.

Pu·ri·tan (pyōōr′ə·tən) n. One of a group of English Protestants of the 16th and 17th centuries, many of whom emigrated to the American colonies, who advocated simpler forms of creed and ritual in the Church of England. —adj. Of or relating to the Puritans. —Pu′ri·tan′ic or ·i·cal adj. —Pu′ri·tan·ism n.

pur·lieu (pûr′lōō) n. 1 pl. Outlying districts; outskirts. 2 A place habitually visited; a haunt. 3 pl. Bounds. [< OF puraler go through]

pur·loin (pûr·loin′) v.t. & v.i. To steal; filch. [< AF purloignier remove, put far off] —pur·loin′er n.

pur·ple (pûr′pəl) n. 1 A color of mingled red and blue, between crimson and violet. 2 Cloth or a garment of this color, an emblem of royalty. 3 Royal power or dignity. 4 Preeminence in rank. —adj. 1 Of the color of purple. 2 Imperial; regal. 3 Conspicuously fanciful or ornate: purple prose. —v.t. & v.i. ·pled, ·pling To make or become purple. [< Gk. porphyra purple dye] —pur′plish adj.

pur·port (pər·pôrt′, -pôrt′, pûr′pôrt, -pōrt) v.t. 1 To have or bear as its meaning; signify; imply. 2 To claim or profess (to be), esp. falsely. —n. (pûr′pôrt, -pōrt) 1 That which is conveyed or suggested as the meaning. 2 The substance of a statement, etc., given in other than the exact words. [< L < pro- forth + portare carry] —Syn. n. 1 import, significance. 2 gist, meaning. —pur·port′ed·ly adv.

pur·pose (pûr′pəs) n. 1 An end of effort or action; something to be attained; plan; design; aim. 2 Settled resolution; determination. —on purpose Intentionally. —v.t. & v.i. ·posed, ·pos·ing To intend to do or accomplish; aim. [< OF *porposer*] —pur′pose·less *adj.* —pur′pose·less·ly *adv.* —pur′pose·less·ness *n.*

purse (pûrs) *n.* 1 A small bag or pouch for money. 2 A receptacle carried usu. by women for holding personal articles, as a wallet, cosmetics, etc.; pocketbook. 3 Resources or means; a treasury. 4 A sum of money offered as a prize or gift. —v.t. pursed, purs·ing To contract into wrinkles or folds; pucker. [< Gk. *byrsa* a skin]

pur·su·ance (pər·sōō′əns) *n.* The act of pursuing; a following after or following through: in *pursuance* of the truth.

pur·su·ant (pər·sōō′ənt) *adj.* Pursuing. —pursuant to In accordance with; by reason of.

pur·sue (pər·sōō′) *v.* ·sued, ·su·ing *v.t.* 1 To follow in an attempt to overtake or capture; chase. 2 To seek to attain or gain: to *pursue* fame. 3 To advance along the course of, as a path or plan. 4 To apply one's energies to or have as one's profession. 5 To follow persistently; harass; worry. —v.i. 6 To follow. 7 To continue. [< L *pro-* forth + *sequi* follow] —pur·su′er *n.*

pur·suit (pər·sōōt′) *n.* 1 The act of pursuing. 2 A continued employment, vocation, or preoccupation.

pu·ru·lent (pyōōr′ə·lənt, -yə·lənt) *adj.* Consisting of or secreting pus; suppurating. [< L *pus, puris* pus] —pu′ru·lence or ·len·cy *n.* —pu′ru·lent·ly *adv.*

pur·vey (pər·vā′) *v.t.* & *v.i.* To furnish or provide, as provisions. [< L *providere* foresee] —pur·vey′or *n.*

push (pŏŏsh) *v.t.* 1 To exert force upon or against (an object) for the purpose of moving. 2 To force (one's way), as through a crowd. 3 To develop, advocate, or promote vigorously and persistently: to *push* a new product. 4 To bear hard upon; press: to be *pushed* for time. 5 *Informal* To approach or come close to: He's *pushing* fifty. 6 *Slang* To sell (narcotic or other drugs) illegally. —v.i. 7 To exert pressure against something so as to move it. 8 To move or advance vigorously or persistently. 9 To exert great effort. —n. 1 The act of pushing; a propelling or thrusting pressure. 2 Anything pushed to cause action. 3 Determined activity; energy; drive. 4 A vigorous and persistent advance or ef-

fort. 5 An emergency; exigency. [< L *pulsare* to push, beat] —Syn. *v.* 1 shove, thrust, press, propel, drive.

push·o·ver (pŏŏsh′ō′vər) *n. Slang* 1 Anything that can be done with little or no effort. 2 Someone easily defeated, overcome, outwitted, etc.; one who represents no challenge to one's aims.

pu·sil·lan·i·mous (pyōō′sə·lan′ə·məs) *adj.* Weak or cowardly in spirit; lacking strength of mind or courage. [< L *pusillus* very little + *animus* mind] —pu′sil·la·nim′i·ty (-lə·nim′ə·tē), pu′sil·lan′i·mous·ness *n.* —pu′sil·lan′i·mous·ly *adv.*

pus·tule (pus′chōōl) *n.* 1 A small, circumscribed elevation of the skin with an inflamed base containing pus. 2 Any elevation resembling a pimple or a blister. [< L *pustula*] —pus′tu·lar, pus′tu·lous *adj.*

pu·ta·tive (pyōō′tə·tiv) *adj.* Supposed; reported; reputed. [< L *putare* think] —pu′ta·tive·ly *adv.*

pu·tre·fac·tion (pyōō′trə·fak′shən) *n.* 1 The process of rotting or decomposing, as by bacterial action. 2 The state of being putrefied. —pu′tre·fac′tive *adj.*

pu·tre·fy (pyōō′trə·fī) *v.t.* & *v.i.* ·fied, ·fy·ing To decay or cause to decay; rot. [< L *puter* rotten + *facere* make] —pu′tre·fi′er *n.*

pu·tres·cent (pyōō·tres′ənt) *adj.* 1 Becoming putrid. 2 Pertaining to putrefaction. [< L *putrescere* grow rotten] —pu·tres′cence *n.*

pu·trid (pyōō′trid) *adj.* 1 Being in a state of putrefaction; rotten. 2 Indicating or produced by putrefaction: a *putrid* smell. 3 Corrupt. [< L *putridus*] —pu·trid·i·ty (pyōō′trid′ə·tē), pu′trid·ness *n.*

put·ty (put′ē) *n.* 1 A doughy mixture of clay and linseed oil, used to cement panes in windows, fill cracks, etc. 2 Any substance similar in properties or uses. —v.t. ·tied, ·ty·ing To fill, stop, fasten, etc., with putty. [< OF *potee* calcined tin, lit., a potful] —put′ti·er *n.*

puz·zle (puz′əl) *v.* ·zled, ·zling *v.t.* 1 To confuse or perplex; mystify. 2 To solve by investigation and study, as something perplexing: with *out.* —v.i. 3 To be perplexed or confused. —puzzle over To attempt to understand or solve. —n. 1 Something difficult to understand or explain; an enigma or problem. 2 A device, as a toy, or a problem designed for recreation and requiring ingenuity to solve. 3 The state of being puzzled; perplexity. [?] —puz′zle·ment, puz′zler *n.*

pyg·my (pig′mē) *adj.* Diminutive; dwarfish.

—*n. pl.* ·mies 1 Someone of no importance. 2 A dwarfish person or animal.

py·or·rhe·a (pī′ə·rē′ə) *n.* A discharge of pus; esp., inflammation and pus discharge affecting the gums and tooth sockets. Also py′or·rhoe′a. [< Gk. *pys, pyos* pus + *rheein* flow] —py′or·rhe′al *adj.*

pyr·a·mid (pir′ə·mid) *n.* 1 A solid structure of masonry with a square base and triangular sides meeting in an apex, such as those constructed by the ancient Egyptians as royal tombs. 2 Something having the form of a pyramid. 3 *Geom.* A solid having a polygonal base and triangular sides that meet in a common vertex. —*v.i.* 1 To increase in a series of steps; escalate. 2 To buy or sell stock with paper profits used as margin to finance succeeding transactions. —*v.t.* 3 To increase by steps. 4 To buy and sell (stock) with paper profits used as margin to finance succeeding transactions. [< Gk. *pyramis*] —py·ram·i·dal (pi·ram′ə·dəl, pir′ə·mid′əl), pyr′a·mid′ic or ·i·cal *adj.* —pyr′a·mid′i·cal·ly *adv.*

pyre (pīr) *n.* A heap of combustibles arranged for burning a dead body as a funeral rite. [< Gk. *pyr* a fire]

Py·rex (pī′reks) *n.* A type of heat-resistant glass: a trade name.

py·ro·tech·nics (pī′rə·tek′niks) *n. pl. (construed as sing. in def. 1)* 1 The art of making or using fireworks. 2 A display of fireworks. 3 An ostentatious display, as of oratory; virtuosity. [< PYRO- + Gk. *technē* an art] —py′ro·tech′nic or ·ni·cal *adj.*

py·thon (pī′thon, ·thən) *n.* A large, nonvenomous snake that crushes its prey. [< Gk. *Pythōn* a serpent slain by Apollo]

## Q

quack¹ (kwak) *v.i.* To utter a harsh, croaking cry, as a duck. —*n.* The sound made by a duck, or a similar croaking noise [Imit.]

quack² (kwak) *n.* 1 A pretender to medical knowledge or skill. 2 A charlatan. —*adj.* Of or pertaining to quacks or quackery. —*v.i.* To play the quack. [Short for QUACKSALVER] —quack′ish *adj.* —quack′ish·ly *adv.*

quad·ran·gle (kwod′rang·gəl) *n.* 1 *Geom.* A plane figure having four sides and four angles. 2 An area shaped like a quadrangle, esp. when it is enclosed by buildings. 3 The buildings that enclose such an area. [< L *quattuor* four + *angulus* angle] —quad·ran′gu·lar *adj.*

quad·rant (kwod′rənt) *n.* 1 A quarter part of a circle; also, its circumference, having an arc of 90°. 2 An instrument having a graduated arc of 90°, with a movable radius for measuring angles on it. [< L *quattuor* four] —quad·ran·tal (kwod·ran′təl) *adj.*

quad·ri·lat·er·al (kwod′rə·lat′ər·əl) *adj.* Formed or bounded by four lines; four-sided. —*n.* 1 *Geom.* A polygon of four sides. 2 A space or area defended by four enclosing fortresses. [< QUADRI- + L *latus, lateris* side]

qua·drille (kwə·dril′) *n.* 1 A square dance for four couples. 2 Music for such a dance. [< L *quattuor* four]

quad·roon (kwod·rōōn′) *n.* A person having one Negro and three white grandparents. [< Sp. *cuarto* fourth]

quad·ru·ped (kwod′rōō·ped) *n.* A four-footed animal, esp. a mammal. —*adj.* Having four feet. [< L *quattuor* four + *pes* foot] —quad·ru·pe·dal (kwod·rōō′pə·dəl, kwod′roo·ped′l) *adj.*

quad·ru·ple (kwod·rōō′pəl, -ru′-, kwod′rōō·pəl) *adj.* 1 Four times as great or as many. 2 Having four parts or members. 3 Marked by four beats to the measure. —*n.* A number or sum four times as great as another. —*v.t. & v.i.* ·pled, ·pling To multiply by four. —*adv.* Fourfold. [< L *quadruplus*]

quad·ru·plet (kwod·rōō′plit, -ru′-, kwod′rōō-) *n.* A combination of four objects. 2 One of four offspring born of the same mother at one birth.

quad·ru·pli·cate (kwod·rōō′plə·kit, -kāt) *adj.* 1 FOURFOLD. 2 Raised to the fourth power. —*v.t.* (-kāt) ·cat·ed, ·cat·ing To multiply by four; quadruple. —*n.* The fourth of four like things: to file a *quadruplicate*. —in quadruplicate In four identical copies. —quad·ru′pli·ca′tion *n.*

quail (kwāl) *v.i.* To shrink with fear; lose heart or courage. [ME *quailen*]

quaint (kwānt) *adj.* 1 Pleasingly different, fanciful, or old-fashioned. 2 Unusual; odd; curious. [< L *cognitus* known] —quaint′ly *adv.* —quaint′ness *n.*

Quak·er (kwā′kər) *n.* A member of the Society of Friends: originally a term of derision, and still not used within the society. See SOCIETY OF FRIENDS. [< QUAKE, *v.*; with ref. to their founder's admonition to them to tremble at the word of the Lord] —Quak′er·ish *adj.* —Quak′er·ism′ *n.*

qual·i·fy (kwol′ə·fī) *v.* ·fied, ·fy·ing *v.t.* 1 To make fit or capable, as for an office, occupation, or privilege. 2 To make legally capable, as by the administration of an oath. 3 To limit, restrict, or lessen somewhat: He *qualified* his enthusiasm with a few criticisms. 4 To attribute a quality to; describe; characterize or name. 5 To make less strong or extreme; soften; moderate. 6 To change the strength or flavor of. 7 *Gram.* To modify. —*v.i.* 8 To be or become qualified. [< L *qualis* of such a kind + *facere* make] — **qual′i·fi′a·ble** *adj.* —**qual′i·fi′er** *n.*

**qual·i·ty** (kwŏl′ə·tē) *n. pl.* **·ties** 1 That which makes a being or thing such as it is: a distinguishing element or characteristic: a *quality* of gases. 2 The basic nature or character of something: the *quality* of a summer's day. 3 Excellence: striving for *quality*. 4 Degree of excellence; relative goodness; grade: high *quality* of fabric. 5 A personal attribute, trait or characteristic: a woman with good and bad *qualities*. 6 *Archaic* Social rank: also, persons of rank, collectively. 7 *Music* That which distinguishes one tone from another, aside from pitch or loudiness; timbre. —*adj.* Characterized by or having to do with quality: a *quality* product. [< L *qualis* of such a kind]

**qualm** (kwäm, kwôm) *n.* 1 A twinge of conscience; moral scruple. 2 A sensation of fear or misgiving. 3 A feeling of sickness. [? < OE *cwealm* death] —**qualm′ish, qualm′y** *adj.* —**qualm′ish·ly** *adv.* —**qualm′ish·ness** *n.*

**quan·da·ry** (kwon′dər·ē, -drē) *n. pl.* **·da·ries** A state of hesitation or perplexity; predicament. [?]

**quan·ti·ty** (kwon′tə·tē) *n. pl.* **·ties** 1 A definite or indefinite amount or number. 2 *pl.* Large amounts or numbers: *quantities* of food and drink. 3 That property of a thing which admits of exact measurement and numerical statement. 4 In prosody and phonetics, the relative period of time required to produce a given sound. [< L *quantus* how much, how large]

**quan·tum** (kwon′təm) *n. pl.* **·ta** (-tə) *Physics* A fundamental unit of energy or action as described in the quantum theory. [< L *quantus* how much]

**quar·an·tine** (kwôr′ən·tēn, kwor′-) *n.* 1 A period of time fixed for the isolation and observation of persons, animals, or plants suspected of harboring an infectious disease. 2 A place for such isolation. 3 The isolation of subjects exposed to or infected with a communicable disease. —*v.t.* **·tined,**

**·tin·ing** To retain in quarantine. [< L *quadraginta* forty; a ref. to the original 40-day quarantine]

**quar·rel** (kwôr′əl, kwor′-) *n.* 1 An unfriendly, angry, or violent dispute. 2 A falling out or contention; breach of friendly relations: a lover's *quarrel*. 3 The cause for dispute. —*v.i.* **·reled** or **·relled, ·rel·ing** or **·rel·ling** 1 To engage in a quarrel; dispute; contend; fight: to *quarrel* about money. 2 To break off a mutual friendship; fall out; disagree. 3 To find fault; cavil. [< L *querela* complaint] — **quar′rel·er** or **quar′rel·ler** *n.* —**Syn.** *n.* 1 altercation, bickering, brawl, controversy, feud, fracas, fray. 2 disagreement, fuss, misunderstanding, scene.

**quar·ry** (kwôr′ē, kwor′ē) *n. pl.* **·ries** 1 An animal being hunted down; game; prey. 2 Anything hunted, slaughtered, or eagerly pursued. [< L *corium* hide]

**quart** (kwôrt) *n.* 1 a A U.S. measure of dry capacity equal to 2 pints or 1.10 liters. b A U.S. measure of fluid capacity equal to 2 pints or 0.946 liter. 2 A vessel of such capacity. [< L *quartus* fourth]

**quar·ter** (kwôr′tər) *n.* 1 One of four equal parts of something; a fourth. 2 Fifteen minutes or the fourth of an hour, or the moment with which it begins or ends. 3 A fourth of a year or three months. 4 A limb of a quadruped with the adjacent parts. 5 In the U.S. and Canada, a coin of the value of 25 cents. 6 *Astron.* a The time it takes the moon to make one fourth of its revolution around the earth. b Either of the phases of the moon between new moon and full moon. 7 *Nav.* One of the four principal points of the compass or divisions of the horizon; also, a point or direction of the compass. 8 A person, persons, or place, esp. as a source or origin of something; gossip coming from all *quarters*. 9 A particular division or district, as of a city. 10 *Usu. pl.* Proper or assigned station, position, or place, as of officers and crew on a warship. 11 *pl.* A place of lodging or residence. 12 *Naut.* The part of a vessel's after side, between the aftermost mast and the stern. 13 *Her.* Any of four equal divisions into which a shield is divided, or a figure or device occupying such a division. 14 Mercy shown to a vanquished foe by sparing his life; clemency. 15 One of the four periods into which a game, as football, is divided. —**at close quarters** Close by; at close range. —*adj.* 1 Consisting of a quarter. 2

Equal to a quarter. —*v.t.* 1 To divide into four equal parts. 2 To divide into a number of parts or pieces. 3 To cut the body of (an executed person) into four parts: He was hanged, drawn, and *quartered.* 4 To range from one side to the other of (a field, etc.) while advancing: The dogs *quartered* the field. 5 To furnish with quarters or shelter; lodge, station, or billet. 6 *Her.* a To divide (a shield) into quarters by vertical and horizontal lines. b To bear or arrange (different coats of arms) upon the quarters of a shield or escutcheon. —*v.i.* 7 To be stationed or lodged. 8 To range from side to side of an area, as dogs in hunting. 9 *Naut.* To blow on a ship's quarter: said of the wind. [< L *quartus* fourth]

**quar·ter·ly** (kwôr′tər·lē) *adj.* 1 Containing or being a quarter. 2 Occurring at intervals of three months. —*n. pl.* ·**lies** A publication issued once every three months. —*adv.* 1 Once in a quarter of a year. 2 In or by quarters.

**quar·tet** (kwôr·tet′) *n.* 1 A composition for four voices or instruments. 2 The four persons who render such a composition. 3 Any group of four persons or things. Also **quar·tette′.** [< Ital. *quarto* fourth]

**quar·to** (kwôr′tō) *adj.* Having four leaves or eight pages to the sheet: a *quarto* book. —*n. pl.* ·**tos** 1 The size of a piece of paper obtained by folding a sheet into four leaves. 2 Paper of this size; also, a page of this size. 3 A book made of pages of this size. [< L *(in) quarto* (in) fourth]

**quartz** (kwôrts) *n.* A hard mineral form of silicon dioxide occurring in many varieties, some of which are valued as gems. [< G *Quarz*]

**quash** (kwosh) *v.t. Law* To make void or set aside, as an indictment; annul. [< LL *cassare* to empty]

**qua·si** (kwā′zī, -sī, kwä′zē, -sē) *adj.* More in resemblance than in fact: a *quasi* scholar. [L, as if]

**quat·rain** (kwot′rān, kwot·rān′) *n.* A stanza of four lines. [< F *quatre* four]

**qua·ver** (kwā′vər) *v.i.* 1 To tremble or shake: said usu. of the voice. 2 To produce trills or quavers in singing or in playing a musical instrument. —*v.t.* 3 To utter or sing in a tremulous voice. —*n.* 1 A trembling or shaking, as in the voice. 2 A shake or trill, as in singing. 3 An eighth note. [< ME *cwafian* tremble] —**qua′ver·y** *adj.*

**quay** (kē) *n.* A wharf or artificial landing place where vessels load and unload. [F]

**quean** (kwēn) *n.* A brazen woman; harlot; prostitute. [< OE *cwene* woman]

**queen** (kwēn) *n.* 1 The wife of a king. 2 A female sovereign or monarch. 3 A woman preeminent in a given activity, accomplishment, etc. 4 A place or thing of great beauty, excellence, etc. 5 The most powerful piece in chess, capable of moving any number of squares in a straight or diagonal line. 6 A playing card bearing a conventional picture of a queen in her robes. 7 An egg-producing female in a colony of social insects, as bees, ants, etc. —*v.t.* 1 To make a queen of. —*v.i.* 2 To reign as or play the part of a queen: often with *it.* [< OE *cwēn* woman, queen] —**queen′ly** *adj., adv.* —**queen′li·ness** *n.*

**queer** (kwir) *adj.* 1 Different from the usual; strange; odd. 2 Of questionable character; open to suspicion; mysterious. 3 *Slang* Counterfeit. 4 Mentally unbalanced or eccentric. 5 Queasy or giddy. 6 *Slang* Homosexual: a contemptuous term. —*n. Slang* 1 Counterfeit money. 2 A homosexual, esp. a male homosexual: a contemptuous term. —*v.t. Slang* 1 To jeopardize or spoil. 2 To put into an unfavorable or embarrassing position. [< G *quer* oblique] —**queer′ly** *adv.* —**queer′ness** *n.* —**Syn.** *adj.* 1 bizarre, curious, droll, fantastic, grotesque, peculiar, singular. 2 suspect, suspicious. 4 peculiar, odd, deranged.

**quell** (kwel) *v.t.* 1 To put down or suppress by force; extinguish. 2 To quiet; allay, as pain. [< OE *cwellan* kill] —**quell′er** *n.*

**quench** (kwench) *v.t.* 1 To put out or extinguish, as a fire. 2 To slake or satisfy (thirst). 3 To suppress or repress, as emotions. 4 To cool, as heated iron or steel, by thrusting into water or other liquid. [ME *cwenken*] —**quench′a·ble** *adj.* —**quench′er** *n.*

**quer·u·lous** (kwer′ə·ləs, -yə·ləs) *adj.* 1 Disposed to complain or be fretful; faultfinding. 2 Indicating or expressing a complaint. [< L *queri* complain] —**quer′u·lous·ly** *adv.* —**quer′u·lous·ness** *n.* —**Syn.** 1 carping, captious, disparaging, critical, censorious.

**que·ry** (kwir′ē) *v.t.* ·**ried,** ·**ry·ing** 1 To inquire into; ask about. 2 To ask questions of; interrogate. 3 To express doubt concerning the correctness or truth of, esp., as in printing, by marking with a question mark. —*n. pl.* ·**ries** 1 An inquiry; question. 2 A doubt. 3 A question mark. [< L *quaerere* ask]

**quest** (kwest) *n.* 1 The act of seeking; a looking for something. 2 A search, as an adventure or expedition in medieval romance; also, the person or persons making the search. —*v.i.* To go on a quest. [< L *quaerere* ask, seek] —**quest'er** *n*

**ques·tion** (kwes'chən) *n.* 1 An inquiry, esp. to obtain information, test knowledge, etc. 2 A written or vocal expression of such an inquiry; an interrogative sentence, clause, or expression. 3 A subject of debate or dispute. 4 An issue or problem: It's not a *question* of time. 5 A doubt or uncertainty: There is no *question* of his skill. —**out of the question** Not to be considered as a possibility. —*v.t.* 1 To put a question or questions to; interrogate. 2 To be uncertain of; doubt. 3 To make objection to; challenge; dispute. —*v.i.* 4 To ask a question or questions. [< L *quaerere* ask] —**ques'tion·er** *n.*

**ques·tion·a·ble** (kwes'chən·ə·bəl) *adj.* 1 Open to question; debatable. 2 Dubious or suspect, as regards morality, integrity, respectability, etc.: *questionable* motives. —**ques'tion·a·bil'i·ty, ques'tion·a·ble·ness** *n.* —**ques'tion·a·bly** *adv.*

**queue** (kyoo) *n.* 1 A braid of hair hanging from the back of the head; a pigtail. 2 A line of persons or vehicles waiting in the order of their arrival. —*v.i.* queued, queu·ing To form such a line: usu. with *up.* [< L *cauda* a tail]

**quib·ble** (kwib'əl) *n.* 1 An evasion of a point or question; an equivocation. 2 A minor objection; cavil. —*v.i.* ·bled, ·bling To use quibbles. [< L *quibus,* ablative pl. of *qui* who, which] —**quib'bler** *n.*

**quick** (kwik) *adj.* 1 Done or occurring in a short time; expeditious; brisk; prompt; speedy: a *quick* answer. 2 Characterized by rapidity or readiness of movement or action; nimble; rapid; swift: a *quick* pace. 3 Alert; sensitive; perceptive: a *quick* ear; *quick* wit. 4 Responding readily; excitable; hasty: *quick-tempered.* 5 Lasting only a short time: a *quick* lunch. —*n.* 1 That which has life; those who are alive: chiefly in the phrase **the quick and the dead.** 2 The living flesh; esp., the tender flesh under a nail. 3 The most sensitive feelings: hurt to the *quick.* —*adv.* Quickly; rapidly. [< OE *cwic* alive]

**quick·en** (kwik'ən) *v.t.* 1 To cause to move more rapidly; hasten or accelerate. 2 To

make alive or quick; give or restore life to. 3 To excite or arouse; stimulate: to *quicken* the appetite. —*v.i.* 4 To move or act more quickly. 5 To come or return to life; revive. —**quick'en·er** *n.*

**quick-freeze** (kwik'frēz') *v.t.* -froze, -fro·zen, -freez·ing To preserve by freezing rapidly and storing at a low temperature. —**quick'-fro'zen** *adj.*

**quick·sand** (kwik'sand') *n.* A deep, wet bed of sand subjected to pressure by water below it and usu. incapable of supporting the weight of a person or animal.

**quick·sil·ver** (kwik'sil'vər) *n.* Elemental mercury.

**qui·es·cent** (kwī·es'ənt, kwē-) *adj.* Being in a state of repose or inaction; quiet; still. [< L *quiescere* be quiet] —**qui·es'cence** *n.* —**qui·es'cent·ly** *adv.*

**qui·et** (kwī'ət) *adj.* 1 Being in a state of repose; still; calm; motionless. 2 Free from turmoil, strife, or busyness; tranquil; peaceful. 3 Having or making little or no noise; silent. 4 Gentle or mild, as of disposition. 5 Undisturbed by din or bustle; secluded. 6 Not showy or obtrusive, as dress. —*n.* The condition or quality of being free from motion, disturbance, noise, etc.; peace; calm. —*v.t.* & *v.i.* To make or become quiet: often with *down.* —*adv.* In a quiet or peaceful manner. [< L *quies* rest, repose] —**qui'et·ly** *adv.* —**qui'et·ness** *n.*

**quill** (kwil) *n.* 1 A large, strong, wing or tail feather. 2 The hollow, horny stem of a feather. 3 Something made from this, as a pen or a plectrum. 4 A spine of a porcupine or hedgehog. [ME *quil*]

**quilt** (kwilt) *n.* 1 A bedcover made by stitching together two layers of cloth with a soft padding between them. 2 Any bedcover, esp. if thick. 3 A quilted skirt or other quilted article. —*v.t.* 1 To stitch together (two pieces of material) with a soft substance between. 2 To stitch in ornamental patterns or crossing lines. —*v.i.* 3 To make a quilt or quilted work. [< L *culcita* mattress] —**quilt'work'** *n.*

**qui·nine** (kwī'nīn, *esp. Brit.* kwi·nēn') *n.* 1 A bitter alkaloid obtained from cinchona. 2 A medicinal compound of quinine, used to relieve the symptoms of malaria. [< Sp. *quina* cinchona bark + -INE]

**quin·tes·sence** (kwin·tes'əns) *n.* 1 The essence of anything, esp. in its most pure, concentrated form. 2 The perfect manifestation or embodiment of anything. [< L *quinta essentia* fifth essence] —**quin·tes·sen·tial** (kwin′tə·sen′shəl) *adj.*

**quin·tet** (kwin·tet′) *n.* 1 A musical composition for five voices or instruments. 2 The five performers of such a composition. 3 Any group of five persons or things. Also **quin·tette′**. [< Ital. *quinto* fifth]

**quin·tu·ple** (kwin·t′ōō′pəl, -tup′əl, kwin′t′ōō·pəl) *v.t. & v.i.* **·pled**, **·pling** To multiply by five; make or become five times as large. —*adj.* 1 Consisting of five. 2 Being five times as much or as many. —*n.* A number or an amount five times as great as another. [< L *quintus* fifth + *-plex* -fold]

**quip** (kwip) *n.* 1 A witty or sarcastic remark or retort; gibe. 2 A quibble. 3 An odd, fantastic action or object. —*v.i.* **quipped**, **quip·ping** To make a quip or quips. [< L *quippe* indeed] —**quip′pish** *adj.* —**quip′ster** *n.*

**quit** (kwit) *v.* **quit** or **quit·ted**, **quit·ting** *v.t.* 1 To cease or desist from; discontinue. 2 To give up; renounce; relinquish: to *quit* a job. 3 To go away from; leave. 4 To let go of (something held). 5 To free; release. 6 To discharge; pay back. —*v.i.* 7 To resign from a position, etc. 8 To stop; cease; discontinue. 9 To leave; depart. —*adj.* Released, relieved, or absolved from something, as a duty, obligation, encumbrance, or debt; clear; free; rid. —*n.* The act of quitting. [< L *quies* rest, repose]

**quit·claim** (kwit′klām′) *n. Law* 1 The giving up of a claim, right, title, or interest. 2 An instrument by which one person gives up to another a claim or title to an estate. —*v.t.* To relinquish or give up claim or title to; release from a claim. [< QUIT + CLAIM]

**quite** (kwīt) *adv.* 1 Completely; fully; totally: not *quite* finished. 2 To a great or considerable extent; very: *quite* ill. 3 Positively; really: *quite* certain. [ME, rid of]

**quit·tance** (kwit′ns) *n.* 1 Discharge or release, as from a debt or obligation. 2 A document in evidence of this; receipt. 3 Something given or tendered by way of repayment. [< F *quiter* quit]

**quiv·er** (kwiv′ər) *v.i.* To shake with a slight, tremulous motion; vibrate; tremble. —*n.* The act or fact of quivering; a trembling or shaking. [?< QUAVER]

**quiz** (kwiz) *n. pl.* **quiz·zes** 1 The act of questioning; specifically, a brief oral or written examination. 2 A person given to ridicule or practical jokes. 3 A hoax; practical joke. —*v.t.* **quizzed**, **quiz·zing** 1 To examine by asking questions; question. 2 To make fun of; ridicule. [?] —**quiz′zer** *n.*

**quiz·zi·cal** (kwiz′i·kəl) *adj.* 1 Mocking; teasing. 2 Perplexed; puzzled. 3 Queer; odd. —**quiz′zi·cal·ly** *adv.*

**quon·dam** (kwon′dəm) *adj.* Having been formerly; former. [L]

**Quon·set hut** (kwon′sit) A prefabricated metal structure in the form of half a cylinder resting lengthwise on its flat surface: a trade name.

**quo·rum** (kwôr′əm, kwō′rəm) *n.* The number of members of any deliberative or corporate body that is necessary for the legal transaction of business, usu., a majority. [L, of whom]

**quo·ta** (kwō′tə) *n.* A proportional part or share given to or required from a person, group, etc. [< L *quotus* how great]

**quote** (kwōt) *v.* **quot·ed**, **quot·ing** *v.t.* 1 To repeat or reproduce the words of. 2 To repeat or cite (a rule, author, etc.), as for authority or illustration. 3 In commerce: a To state (a price). b To give the current or market price of. —*v.i.* 4 To make a quotation, as from a book. —*n.* 1 QUOTATION. 2 QUOTATION MARK. [< Med. L *quotare* distinguish by number < L *quot* how many] —**quot′a·bil′i·ty**, **quot′er** *n.* —**quot′a·ble** *adj.*

**quo·tient** (kwō′shənt) *n. Math.* The result obtained by division; a factor by which a given number must be multiplied to produce a given product. [< L *quotiens* how often]

# R

**rab·bi** (rab′ī) *n. pl.* **·bis** 1 A Jew authorized to teach or expound Jewish law. 2 The official head of a Jewish congregation. [< Heb. *rabbi* my master]

**rab·bin·i·cal** (rə·bin′i·kəl) *adj.* Of or pertaining to the rabbis or to their opinions, languages, writings, etc. Also **rab·bin′ic**. —**rab·bin′i·cal·ly** *adv.*

**rab·bit** (rab′it) *n.* 1 Any of numerous small, herbivorous mammals having soft fur, long legs and ears, and a short tail. 2 HARE. 3 The pelt of a rabbit or hare. —*v.i.* To hunt rabbits. [ME *rabette*] —**rab′bit·er** *n.*

**rab·ble** (rab′əl) *n.* A disorderly crowd; mob. —**the rabble** The common people: a contemptuous term. [?]

**rab·id** (rab′id) *adj.* 1 Affected with, arising from, or pertaining to rabies; mad. 2 Unreasonably zealous; fanatical. 3 Furious;

raging. [< L *rabere* be mad] —**ra·bid·i·ty** (rə·bid′ə·tē), **rab′id·ness** *n.* —**rab′id·ly** *adv.*

**rac·coon** (ra·kōōn′) *n.* 1 A North American nocturnal, tree-climbing mammal with a black face mask, long gray-brown fur, and a bushy, black-ringed tail. 2 The fur of this animal. Also **ra·coon′.** [< Algon.]

**race** (rās) *n.* 1 A subdivision of mankind having a relatively constant set of physical traits, such as color of skin and eyes, stature, texture of hair, etc. 2 Any grouping of peoples according to geography, nation, etc. 3 A genealogical or family stock; clan: the *race* of MacGregor. 4 Any class of people having similar activities, interests, etc.: the *race* of lawyers. 5 *Biol.* A group of plants or animals within a species with distinct, inheritable characteristics; a variety. [< Ital. *razza*]

**ra·cism** (rā′siz·əm) *n.* 1 An excessive and irrational belief in the superiority of one's own racial group. 2 A doctrine, program, or practice based on such belief. —**ra′cist** *adj., n.*

**rack** (rak) *n.* 1 Something on which various articles can be hung, stored, or canned. 2 A triangular frame for arranging the balls on a billiard table. 3 *Mech.* A bar having teeth that engage those of a gearwheel or pinion. 4 A machine for stretching or making tense; esp., an instrument of torture which stretches the limbs of victims. 5 Intense mental or physical suffering or its cause. 6 A wrenching or straining, as from a storm. —**on the rack** In great physical or mental pain. —*v.t.* 1 To place or arrange in or on a rack. 2 To torture on the rack. 3 To torment. 4 To strain, as with the effort of thinking: to *rack* one's brains. 5 To raise (rents) excessively. —**rack up** *Informal* To gain or achieve: to *rack up* a good score. [Prob. < MDu. *recken* to stretch] —**rack′er** *n.*

**rack·et** (rak′it) *n.* 1 A bat consisting of an oval, wooden or metal hoop strung with catgut, nylon, etc., and having a handle, used in playing tennis, etc. 2 *pl. (construed as sing.)* A game resembling court tennis, played in a court with four walls: also **rac·quets** (rak′its). [< Ar. *rāha* palm of the hand]

**rack·et·eer** (rak′ə·tir′) *n.* One who gets money or other benefits by fraud, intimidation, or other illegitimate means. —**rack′et·eer′ing** *n.*

**ra·dar** (rā′där) *n. Electronics* A device which detects, locates, and indicates the speed and approximate nature of aircraft, ships, objects, etc., by means of reflected microwaves. [< RA(DIO) D(ETECTING) A(ND) R(ANGING)]

**ra·di·ance** (rā′dē·əns) *n.* The quality or state of being radiant. Also **ra′di·an·cy, ra′di·ant·ness.**

**ra·di·ate** (rā′dē·āt) *v.* **·at·ed, ·at·ing** *v.i.* 1 To emit rays or radiation; be radiant. 2 To issue forth in rays. 3 To spread out from a center, as the spokes of a wheel. —*v.t.* 4 To send out or emit in rays. 5 To spread or show (joy, love, etc.) as if from a center. —*adj.* (·dē·it) Divided or separated into rays; having rays; radiating. [< L *radiare* emit rays] —**ra′di·a′tive** *adj.*

**ra·di·a·tion** (rā′dē·ā′shən) *n.* 1 The act or process of radiating or the state of being radiated. 2 That which is radiated, as energy in the form of particles or waves.

**radiation sickness** Sickness resulting from exposure to X-rays, nuclear explosions, etc.

**ra·di·a·tor** (rā′dē·ā′tər) *n.* 1 That which radiates. 2 A device for distributing heat, partly by radiation, as in heating or cooling systems.

**rad·i·cal** (rad′i·kəl) *adj.* 1 Thoroughgoing; extreme: *radical* measures. 2 Of, pertaining to, or professing policies and practices of extreme change, as in government. 3 Of or pertaining to the root or foundation; essential; basic. —*n.* 1 One who holds radical or extreme convictions. 2 In politics, one who advocates extreme governmental changes. 3 The primitive or underived part of a word; root. 4 *Math.* An indicated root of a number, expression, etc. 5 *Chem.* A group of atoms that act as a unit in a compound and remain together during a chemical reaction. [< L *radix, radicis* root] —**rad′i·cal·ly** *adv.* —**rad′i·cal·ness** *n.*

**ra·di·o** (rā′dē·ō) *n. pl.* **·os** 1 The technology and process of communicating by means of radio waves. 2 A transmitter or receiver used in such communication. 3 The process, business, or industry of producing programs to be communicated in this way. —*adj.* Of, pertaining to, designating, employing, or produced by radiant energy, esp. electromagnetic waves: a *radio* beam. —*v.t. & v.i.* **·di·oed, ·di·o·ing** 1 To transmit (a message, etc.) by radio. 2 To communicate with (someone) by radio. [< RADIO (TELEGRAPHY)]

**ra·di·ol·o·gy** (rā′dē·ol′ə·jē) *n.* That branch of

science concerned with radioactivity, X-rays, etc., esp. in diagnostic and therapeutic applications. —ra·di·o·log·i·cal (rā′dē·ə·loj′i·kəl) or ra′di·o·log′ic adj. —ra′di·ol′o·gist n.

ra·di·om·e·ter (rā′dē·om′ə·tər) n. An instrument for detecting and measuring radiant energy by noting the speed of rotation of blackened disks suspended in a partially evacuated chamber.

radio telescope A sensitive radio receiver designed to receive radio waves from space.

ra·di·um (rā′dē·əm) n. A radioactive metallic element (symbol Ra) found in pitchblende as a disintegration product of uranium. [< L radius ray]

ra·di·us (rā′dē·əs) n. pl. ·di·i (-dē·ī) or ·di·us·es 1 A straight line segment joining the surface of a sphere or circumference of a circle with its center. 2 Anat. The shorter of the two bones of the forearm. 3 Zool. A corresponding bone in the forelimb of other vertebrates. 4 Bot. A ray floret of a composite flower. 5 A raylike part, as a wheel spoke. 6 A circular area or boundary measured by its radius. 7 Sphere, scope, or limit, as of activity. 8 A fixed or circumscribed area or distance of travel. [L, spoke of a wheel, ray]

raf·fle (raf′əl) n. A form of lottery in which a number of people buy chances on an object. —v. ·fled, ·fling v.t. 1 To dispose of by a raffle: often with off. —v.i. 2 To take part in a raffle. [<OF rafle a game of dice] —raf′fler n.

raft (raft, räft) n. 1 A float of logs, planks, etc., fastened together for transportation by water. 2 A flat, often inflatable object, as of rubber, that floats on water. —v.t. 1 To transport on a raft. 2 To form into a raft. —v.i. 3 To travel by or work on a raft. [< ON raptr log] —rafts′man n.

raft·er (raf′tər, räf′-) n. A timber or beam giving form, slope, and support to a roof. [< OE ræfter]

rag (rag) v.t. ragged, rag·ging Slang 1 To tease or irritate. 2 To scold. —n. Brit. A prank. [?]

ra·ga (rä′gə) n. One of a large number of traditional melodic patterns, used by Hindu musicians as the basis for improvisation. [< Skt. rāga (musical) color]

raid (rād) n. 1 A hostile or predatory attack, as by a rapidly moving body of troops. 2 AIR RAID. 3 Any sudden breaking into, invasion, or capture, as by the police. 4 A manipulative attempt to make stock prices fall by concerted selling. —v.t. 1 To make a raid on. —v.i. 2 To participate in a raid. [< OE rād a ride] —raid′er n.

rail (rāl) n. 1 A bar, usu. of wood or metal, resting on supports, as in a fence, at the side of a stairway or roadway, or capping the bulwarks of a ship; a railing. 2 One of a series of parallel bars, of iron or steel, resting upon cross-ties, forming a support and guide for wheels, as of a railway. 3 A railroad: to ship by rail. —v.t. To furnish or shut in with rails; fence. [< L regula ruler]

rail·ler·y (rā′lər·ē) n. pl. ·ler·ies Merry jesting or teasing. [< F raillerie jesting]

rail·road (rāl′rōd′) n. 1 A graded road, having metal rails supported by ties, for the passage of trains or other rolling stock drawn by locomotives. 2 The system of tracks, stations, etc., used in transportation by rail. 3 The corporation or persons owning or operating such a system. —v.t. 1 To transport by railroad. 2 Informal To rush or force with great speed or without deliberation: to railroad a bill through Congress. 3 Slang To cause to be imprisoned on false charges or without fair trial. —v.i. 4 To work on a railroad. —rail′road′er n.

rail·way (rāl′wā′) n. 1 A railroad, esp. one using comparatively light vehicles. 2 Brit. RAILROAD. 3 Any track having rails for wheeled equipment.

rai·ment (rā′mənt) n. Wearing apparel; clothing; garb. [< ARRAY + -MENT]

rain (rān) n. 1 The condensed water vapor of the atmosphere falling in drops. 2 The fall of such drops. 3 A fall or shower of anything in the manner of rain. 4 A rainstorm; shower. 5 pl. The rainy season in a tropical country. —v.i. 1 To fall from the clouds in drops of water. 2 To fall like rain. 3 To send or pour down rain. —v.t. 4 To send down like rain; shower. [< OE regn]

raise (rāz) v. raised, rais·ing v.t. 1 To cause to move upward or to a higher level; lift; elevate. 2 To place erect; set up. 3 To construct or build; erect. 4 To make greater in amount, size, or value: to raise the price of corn. 5 To advance or elevate in rank, estimation, etc. 6 To increase the strength, intensity, or degree of. 7 To breed; grow: to raise chickens or tomatoes. 8 To rear (children, a family, etc.) 9 To cause to be heard: to raise a hue and cry. 10 To cause; occasion, as a smile or laugh. 11 To stir to action or emotion; arouse. 12 To waken; animate or reanimate: to raise the dead. 13 To

obtain or collect, as an army, capital, etc.
14 To bring up for consideration, as a question. 15 To cause to swell or become lighter;
leaven. 16 To put an end to, as a siege. 17
In card games, to bid or bet more than. 18
*Naut.* To cause to appear above the horizon,
as land or a ship, by approaching nearer.
—*v.i.* 19 *Regional* To rise or arise. 20 In card
games, to increase a bid or bet. —**raise
Cain** (or **the devil, the dickens, a rumpus,**
etc.) *Informal* to make a great disturbance;
stir up confusion. —*n.* 1 The act of raising.
2 An increase, as of wages or a bet. [< ON
*reisa* lift, set up]

**rai·sin** (rā′zən) *n.* A grape of a special sort
dried in the sun or in an oven. [< L *racemus*
bunch of grapes]

**rake** (rāk) *n.* A long-handled, toothed implement for drawing together loose material,
making a surface smooth, etc. —*v.* **raked,
rak·ing** *v.t.* 1 To gather together with or as
with a rake. 2 To smooth, clean, or prepare
with a rake. 3 To gather by diligent effort.
4 To search or examine carefully. 5 To direct heavy gunfire along the length of. —*v.i.*
6 To use a rake. 7 To scrape or pass roughly
or violently: with *across, over,* etc. 8 To
make a search. —**rake in** *Informal* To earn
or acquire (money, etc.) in large quantities.
—**rake up** *Informal* To make public or bring
to light: to *rake up* old gossip. [< OE *raca*]

**rak·ish** (rā′kish) *adj.* 1 Dashing; jaunty. 2
*Naut.* Having the masts unusually inclined,
usu. connoting speed. [< RAKE²] —**rak′ish·ly**
*adv.* —**rak′ish·ness** *n.*

**ral·ly** (ral′ē) *v.* **·lied, ·ly·ing** *v.t.* 1 To bring together and restore to effective discipline: to
*rally* fleeing troops. 2 To summon up or revive: to *rally* one's spirits. 3 To bring together for common action. —*v.i.* 4 To return
to effective discipline or action: The enemy
*rallied.* 5 To unite for common action. 6 To
make a partial or complete return to a normal condition. 7 In tennis, badminton, etc.,
to engage in a rally. —*n. pl.* **·lies** 1 An assembly of people, esp. to arouse enthusiasm. 2 A quick recovery or improvement, as
of health, spirits, vigor, etc. 3 A reassembling, as of scattered troops. 4 In tennis,
badminton, etc., an exchange of several
strokes before one side wins the point. 5 A
competition for automobiles that emphasizes driving and navigational skills rather
than speed. [< F *re-* again + *allier* join]

**ram** (ram) *n.* 1 A male sheep. 2 BATTERING-RAM.
3 Any device for forcing or thrusting, as by

heavy blows. 4 A device for raising water by
pressure of its own flow; a hydraulic ram.
—*v.t.* **rammed, ram·ming** 1 To strike with or
as with a ram; dash against. 2 To drive or
force down or into something. 3 To cram;
stuff. [< OE]

**ram·ble** (ram′bəl) *v.i.* **·bled, ·bling** 1 To walk
about freely and aimlessly; roam. 2 To write
or talk aimlessly or without sequence of
ideas. 3 To proceed with turns and twists;
meander. —*n.* 1 The act of rambling. 2 A
meandering path; maze. [?]

**ram·i·fy** (ram′ə·fī) *v.t. & v.i.* **·fied, ·fy·ing** To divide or spread out into or as into branches.
[< L *ramus* branch + *facere* make]

**ra·mose** (rā′mōs, rə·mōs′) *adj.* 1 Branching.
2 Consisting of or having branches. [< L
*ramus* branch]

**ram·page** (ram′pāj) *n.* An outbreak of boisterous or angry agitation or violence. —*v.i.*
(ram·pāj′) **·paged, ·pag·ing** To rush or act
violently; storm; rage [Orig. Scot.,? < RAMP²]

**ram·pant** (ram′pənt) *adj.* 1 Exceeding all
bounds; unrestrained; wild. 2 Widespread;
unchecked, as an erroneous belief. 3
Standing on the hind legs; rearing: said of
a quadruped. 4 *Her.* Standing on the hind
legs, with both forelegs elevated. [< OF *ramper* to climb] —**ram′pan·cy** *n.* —**ram′pant·
ly** *adv.*

**ram·part** (ram′pärt, -pərt) *n.* 1 The embankment surrounding a fort, on which the
parapet is raised. 2 A bulwark or defense.
—*v.t.* To supply with or as with ramparts;
fortify. [< OF *re-* again + *emparer* prepare]

**ranch** (ranch) *n.* 1 An establishment for rearing or grazing cattle, sheep, horses, etc., in
large herds. 2 The buildings, personnel,
and lands connected with it. 3 A large farm.
—*v.i.* To manage or work on a ranch. [< Sp.
*rancho* group eating together, mess] —**ranch′er, ranch′man** *n.*

**ran·cid** (ran′sid) *adj.* Having the bad taste or
smell of spoiled fats. [< L *rancere* be rancid]
—**ran·cid·i·ty** (ran·sid′ə·tē), **ran′cid·ness** *n.*

**ran·cor** (rang′kər) *n.* Bitter and vindictive enmity. *Brit. sp.* **ran·cour.** [< L *rancere* be
rank] —**ran′cor·ous** *adj.* —**ran′cor·ous·ly**
*adv.* —**ran′cor·ous·ness** *n.* —Syn. malice,
spite, hatred, hostility.

**ran·dom** (ran′dəm) *n.* Lack of definite purpose or intention: now chiefly in the phrase
**at random,** without careful thought, planning, intent, etc.; haphazardly. —*adj.* 1
Done or chosen without deliberation or
plan; chance; casual. 2 Chosen, deter-

mined, or varying without pattern, rule, or bias. [< OF *randonner, rander* move rapidly, gallop] —**ran′dom·ly** *adv.* —**ran′dom·ness** *n.*

**range** (rānj) *n.* 1 The area over which anything moves, operates, or is distributed. 2 An extensive tract of land over which cattle, sheep, etc., roam and graze. 3 Extent or scope: the whole *range* of political influence. 4 The extent of variation of anything: the temperature *range*. 5 A line, row, or series, as of mountains. 6 The horizontal distance between a gun and its target. 7 The horizontal distance covered by a projectile. 8 The maximum distance for which an airplane, ship, vehicle, etc., can be fueled. 9 The maximum effective distance, as of a weapon. 10 *Math.* The entire set of possible values of a dependent variable. 11 A place for shooting at a mark: a rifle *range*. 12 A large cooking stove. —*adj.* Of or pertaining to a range. —*v.* **ranged, rang·ing** *v.t.* 1 To place or arrange in definite order, as in rows. 2 To assign to a class, division, or category; classify. 3 To move about or over (a region, etc.), as in exploration. 4 To put (cattle) to graze on a range. 5 To adjust or train, as a telescope or gun. —*v.i.* 6 To move over an area in a thorough, systematic manner. 7 To rove; roam. 8 To occur; extend; be found: forests *ranging* to the east. 9 To vary within specified limits. 10 To lie in the same direction, line, etc. 11 To have a specified range. [< OF *ranger* arrange < *renc* row]

**rang·er** (rān′jər) *n.* 1 One who or that which ranges. 2 One of a group of mounted troops that protect large tracts of country. 3 One of a herd of cattle that feeds on a range. 4 A warden employed in patrolling forest tracts. 5 *Brit.* A government official in charge of a royal forest or park. 6 One of a group of soldiers trained esp. for raiding and close combat.

**rank** (rangk) *n.* 1 A series of objects ranged in a line or row. 2 A degree of official standing: the *rank* of colonel. 3 A line of soldiers side by side in close order. 4 *pl.* An army; also, the common body of soldiers: to rise from the *ranks*. 5 Relative position in a scale; degree; grade: a writer of low *rank.* 6 A social class or stratum: from all *ranks* of life. 7 High degree or position: a lady of *rank.* —*v.t.* 1 To place or arrange in a rank or ranks. 2 To assign to a position or classification. 3 To outrank: Sergeants *rank*

corporals. —*v.i.* 4 To hold a specified place or rank. 5 To have the highest rank or grade. [< OF *ranc, renc*]

**ran·som** (ran′səm) *v.t.* 1 To secure the release of (a person, property, etc.) for a required price, as from captivity or detention. 2 To set free on payment of ransom. —*n.* 1 The price paid to ransom a person or property. 2 Release purchased, as from captivity. [< L *redimere* redeem] —**ran′som·er** *n.*

**rant** (rant) *v.i.* 1 To speak in loud, violent. or extravagant language. —*v.t.* 2 To exclaim or utter in a ranting manner. —*n.* Declamatory and bombastic talk. [< MDu. *ranten*] —**rant′er** *n.* —**rant′ing·ly** *adv.*

**rape** (rāp) *v.* **raped, rap·ing** *v.t.* 1 To commit rape on. 2 To plunder or sack (a city, etc.) —*v.i.* 3 To commit rape. —*n.* 1 The act of a man who has sexual intercourse with a woman against her will or (called **statutory rape**) with a girl below the age of consent. 2 Any unlawful sexual intercourse or sexual connection by force or threat: homosexual *rape* in prison. 3 The plundering or sacking of a city, etc. 4 Any gross violation, assault, or abuse: the *rape* of natural forests. [< L *rapere* seize] —**rap′ist** *n.*

**rap·id** (rap′id) *adj.* 1 Having or done with great speed; swift; fast. 2 Marked or characterized by rapidity. —*n. Usu. pl.* A swift-flowing descent in a river. [< L *rapidus* < *rapere* seize, rush] —**ra·pid′i·ty** (rə·pid′ə·tē), **rap′id·ness** *n.* —**rap′id·ly** *adv.*

**ra·pi·er** (rā′pē·ər, rāp′yər) *n.* 1 A long, pointed, two-edged sword with a large cup hilt, used in dueling, chiefly for thrusting. 2 A shorter straight sword without cutting edge and therefore used for thrusting only. [< F *rapière*]

**rap·port** (rə·pôr′, -pōr′, *Fr.* ra·pōr′) *n.* Harmonious, sympathetic relationship; accord. —**en rapport** (äṅ ra·pōr′) *French* In close accord. [<F *rapporter* refer, bring back]

**rapt** (rapt) *adj.* 1 Carried away with lofty emotion; enraptured; transported. 2 Deeply engrossed or intent. [<L *raptus,* pp. of *rapere* seize]

**rap·ture** (rap′chər) *n.* 1 The state of being rapt or transported; ecstatic joy; ecstasy. 2 An expression of excessive delight. —*v.t.* **·tured, ·tur·ing** To enrapture; transport with ecstasy. —**rap′tur·ous** *adj.* —**rap′tur·ous·ly** *adv.*

**rare** (râr) *adj.* **rar·er, rar·est** Not thoroughly cooked, as roasted or broiled meat retaining its redness and juices. [<OE *hrēre* lightly boiled]

**rar·i·ty** (râr′ə·tē) *n. pl.* **·ties** 1 The quality or state of being rare, uncommon, or infrequent. 2 That which is exceptionally valued because scarce. 3 Thinness; tenuousness.

**ras·cal** (ras′kəl) *n.* 1 An unscrupulous person; scoundrel. 2 A mischievous person; tease; scamp. [<OF *rasque* filth, shavings] —**ras·cal′i·ty** (-kal′ə·tē) *n.* —**ras′cal·ly** *adj. & adv.*

**rash**[1] (rash) *adj.* 1 Acting without due caution or regard of consequences; reckless. 2 Exhibiting recklessness or precipitancy. [ME *rasch*] —**rash′ly** *adv.* —**rash′ness** *n.*

**rash**[2] (rash) *n.* A patch of redness, itchiness, or other usu. temporary skin lesion.

**rasp** (rasp, räsp) *n.* 1 A filelike tool having coarse, pointed projections. 2 The act or sound of rasping. —*v.t.* 1 To scrape with or as with a rasp. 2 To affect unpleasantly; irritate. 3 To utter in a rough voice. —*v.i.* 4 To grate; scrape. 5 To make a harsh, grating sound. [<OF *rasper* to scrape] —**rasp′er** *n.* —**rasp′y** *adj.* (·i·er, ·i·est)

**rasp·ber·ry** (raz′ber′ē, -bar·ē, räz′-) *n. pl.* **·ries** 1 A sweet, edible fruit, composed of drupelets clustered around a fleshy receptacle. 2 Any of a genus of brambles yielding this fruit. 3 *Slang* BRONX CHEER. [Earlier *rasp, raspis* raspberry + BERRY]

**rat** (rat) *n.* 1 Any of a genus of long-tailed rodents of worldwide distribution, larger and more aggressive than the mouse. 2 Any of various similar animals. 3 *Slang* A contemptible person, esp. one who deserts or betrays his associates. 4 A pad over which a woman's hair is combed to give more fullness. —*v.i.* **rat·ted, rat·ting** 1 To hunt rats. 2 *Slang* To desert one's party, companions, etc. 3 *Slang* To betray or inform: with *on*. [< OE *rǣt*]

**rate** (rāt) *n.* 1 The quantity, quality, degree, etc., of a thing in relation to units of something else: a typing *rate* of 50 words per minute. 2 A price or value, esp. the unit cost of a commodity or service: the *rate* for electricity. 3 Rank or class: to be of the first *rate*. 4 A fixed ratio: the *rate* of exchange. 5 *Brit.* A local tax on property. —**at any rate** In any case; anyhow. —*v.* **rat·ed, rat·ing** *v.t.* 1 To estimate the value or worth of; appraise. 2 To place in a certain rank or grade. 3 To consider; regard: He is *rated* as a great statesman. 4 To fix the rate for the

transportation of (goods), as by rail, water, or air. —*v.i.* 5 To have rank, rating, or value. [<L *ratus*, pp. of *reri* reckon] —**rat′er** *n.*

**rat·i·fy** (rat′ə·fī) *v.t.* **·fied, ·fy·ing** To give sanction to, esp. official sanction. [<L *ratus* fixed, reckoned +′*facere* make] —**rat′i·fi·ca′tion, rat′i·fi′er** *n.* —**Syn.** confirm, approve, endorse, validate.

**ra·tio** (rā′shō, -shē·ō) *n. pl.* **·tios** 1 Relation of degree, number, etc., between two similar things; proportion; rate. 2 A fraction or indicated quotient, esp. one used to compare the magnitudes of numbers. [L, computation<*reri* think]

**ra·tion** (rash′ən, rā′shən) *n.* 1 A portion; share. 2 A fixed allowance or portion of food or provisions, as alloted daily to a soldier, etc. 3 *pl.* Food or provisions, as for an army, expedition, etc. —*v.t.* 1 To issue rations to, as an army. 2 To give out or allot in rations. [<L *ratio* computation]

**ra·tion·al** (rash′ən·əl) *adj.* 1 Of, pertaining to, or attained by reasoning. 2 Able to reason; mentally sound; sane. 3 Sensible; judicious. 4 *Math.* a Of or being a rational number. b Denoting an algebraic expression, as $\sqrt{x^2 - y^2}$, containing a radical that can be solved. [<L *ratio* reckoning] —**ra′tion·al′i·ty** (-al′ə·tē) *n.* —**ra′tion·al·ly** *adv.*

**rat·tan** (ra·tan′) *n.* 1 The long, tough, flexible stem of various climbing palms, used in wickerwork, etc. 2 Any of these palms. [< Malay *rotan*]

**rat·tle** (rat′l) *v.* **·tled, ·tling** *v.i.* 1 To make a series of sharp noises in rapid succession. 2 To move or act with such noises. 3 To talk rapidly and foolishly; chatter. —*v.t.* 4 To cause to rattle. 5 To utter or perform rapidly or noisily. 6 *Informal* To confuse; disconcert. —*n.* 1 A series of short, sharp sounds in rapid succession. 2 A plaything, implement, etc., adapted to produce a rattling noise. 3 The series of jointed horny rings in the tail of a rattlesnake, or one of these. 4 Rapid and noisy talk; chatter. 5 A sound caused by the passage of air through mucus in the throat. [< ME *ratelen*]

**rat·tle·snake** (rat′l·snāk′) *n.* Any of various venomous American snakes with a tail ending in a series of horny rings that rattle when the tail is vibrated.

**rau·cous** (rô′kəs) *adj.* 1 Rough in sound; hoarse; harsh. 2 Noisy and rowdy. [< L *raucus*] —**rau′cous·ly** *adv.* —**rau′cous·ness** *n.*

**rav·age** (rav′ij) *v.* **·aged, ·ag·ing** *v.t.* 1 To lay waste, as by pillaging or burning; despoil; ruin. —*v.i.* 2 To wreak havoc; be destructive. —*n.* Violent and destructive action, or its result; ruin. [< F *ravir* ravish] —**rav′ag·er** *n.*

**rave** (rāv) *v.* **raved, rav·ing** *v.i.* 1 To speak wildly or incoherently. 2 To speak with extravagant enthusiasm. 3 To make a wild, roaring sound; rage. —*v.t.* 4 To utter wildly or incoherently. —*n.* 1 The act or state of raving. 2 *Informal* A highly favorable review. —*adj. Informal* Extravagantly enthusiastic: *rave* reviews. [< L *rabere* to rage] —**Syn.** 1 babble, rant, gibber.

**rav·en·ous** (rav′ən·əs) *adj.* 1 Violently hungry; voracious. 2 Extremely eager; greedy; grasping: *ravenous* for praise. [< OF *ravine* rapine] —**rav′en·ous·ly** *adv.* —**rav′en·ous·ness** *n.*

**ra·vine** (rə·vēn′) *n.* A deep gorge or gully, esp. one worn by a flow of water. [F, small gully or torrent]

**rav·ish** (rav′ish) *v.t.* 1 To fill with strong emotion, esp. delight; enrapture. 2 To rape. 3 To carry off by force. —*n.* 1 To seize] —**rav′ish·er, rav′ish·ment** *n.*

**raw** (rô) *adj.* 1 Not changed or prepared by cooking; uncooked. 2 In its original state or condition; not refined, processed, etc.: *raw* wool; *raw* sugar. 3 Having the skin torn or abraded: a *raw* wound. 4 Bleak; chilling: a *raw* wind. 5 Newly done; fresh: *raw* paint; *raw* work. 6 Inexperienced; undisciplined: a *raw* recruit. 7 Vulgar; off-color: a *raw* joke. 8 *Informal* Brutally harsh or unfair: a *raw* deal. —*n.* A sore or abraded spot. —**in the raw** 1 In a raw, unspoiled, or unrefined state. 2 *Informal* Nude. [< OE *hrēaw*] —**raw′ly** *adv.* —**raw′ness** *n.*

**ray** (rā) *n.* 1 A narrow beam of light. 2 Any of several lines radiating from an object. 3 *Geom.* A straight line emerging from a point and extending in one direction only. 4 A slight amount or indication: a *ray* of hope. 5 *Zool.* a A supporting spine of a fish's fin. b Any of numerous parts radiating from a common center, as the arms of a starfish. 6 *Bot.* a RAY FLOWER. b One of the flower stalks of an umbel. 7 *Physics* A stream of particles or waves. —*v.i.* 1 To emit rays; shine. 2 To radiate. —*v.t.* 3 To send forth as rays. 4 To mark with rays or radiating lines. [< L *radius*]

**raze** (rāz) *v.t.* **razed, raz·ing** 1 To tear down; demolish. 2 To scrape or shave off. [< L *rasum,* pp. of *radere* scrape]

**ra·zor** (rā′zər) *n.* A sharp cutting implement used for shaving off the beard or hair. [< OF *raser* to scrape]

**reach** (rēch) *v.t.* 1 To stretch out or forth, as the hand. 2 To present or deliver; hand over. 3 To touch, grasp, or extend as far as: Can you *reach* the top shelf? 4 To arrive at or come to by motion or progress. 5 To achieve communication with; gain access to. 6 To amount to; total. 7 To have an influence on; affect. —*v.i.* 8 To stretch the hand, foot, etc., out or forth. 9 To attempt to touch or obtain something: He *reached* for his wallet. 10 To have extent in space, time, amount, influence, etc.: The ladder *reached* to the ceiling. 11 *Naut.* To sail on a tack with the wind on or forward of the beam. —*n.* 1 The act or power of reaching. 2 The distance one is able to reach, as with the hand, an instrument, or missile. 3 An extent or result attained by thought, influence, etc.; scope; range. 4 An unbroken stretch, as of a stream; a vista or expanse. 5 *Naut.* The sailing, or the distance sailed, by a vessel on one tack. [< OE *rǣcan*] —**reach′er** *n.*

**re·act** (rē·akt′) *v.i.* 1 To act in response, as to a stimulus. 2 To act in a manner contrary to some preceding act. 3 To be affected by a circumstance, influence, act, etc. 4 *Chem.* To undergo chemical change.

**re·ac·tion** (rē·ak′shən) *n.* 1 Any response, as to a stimulus, event, influence, etc. 2 A trend or tendency toward a former state of things; esp., a trend toward an earlier, usu. outmoded social, political, or economic policy or condition. 3 Any change in an organism effected by an agent, as a drug, food, allergen, etc., or an environmental condition, as heat, cold, etc. 4 *Physics* The force exerted on an agent by the body acted upon. 5 Any process involving a change in the composition or structure of an atomic nucleus, as fission, fusion, or radioactive decay. 6 *Chem.* A molecular change undergone by two or more substances in contact. —**re·ac′tion·al** *adj.* —**re·ac′tion·al·ly** *adv.*

**re·ac·tion·ar·y** (rē·ak′shən·er′ē) *adj.* Of, relating to, favoring, or characterized by reaction (def. 2). —*n. pl.* **·ar·ies** One who generally opposes change or liberalism in political or social matters. Also **re·ac′tion·ist.**

**re·ac·tor** (rē·ak′tər) *n.* 1 One who or that which reacts. 2 An assembly of fissionable material, moderator, coolant, shielding, and other accessories, designed to control and utilize the energy released by atomic fission.

**read** (rēd) v. **read** (red), **read·ing** (rē'ding) v.t. 1 To apprehend the meaning of (a book, writing, etc.) by perceiving the form and relation of the printed or written characters. 2 To utter aloud (something printed or written). 3 To understand the significance of as if by reading: to *read* the sky. 4 To apprehend the meaning of something printed or written in (a foreign language). 5 To make a study of: to *read* law. 6 To discover the nature or significance of (a person, character, etc.) by observation or scrutiny. 7 To interpret (something read) in a specified manner. 8 To take as the meaning of something read. 9 To have or exhibit as the wording: The passage *reads* "principal," not "principle." 10 To indicate or register: The meter *reads* zero. 11 To extract (data) from storage: said of a computer or other information-retrieval system. 12 To bring into a specified condition by reading: I *read* her to sleep. —v.i. 13 To apprehend the characters of a book, musical score, etc. 14 To utter aloud the words or contents of a book, etc. 15 To gain information by reading: with *of* or *about*. 16 To learn by means of books; study. 17 To have a specified wording: The contract *reads* as follows. 18 To admit of being read in a specified manner. 19 To give a public reading or recital. —**read between the lines** To perceive or infer what is not expressed or obvious. —**read into** To discern (implicit meanings or implications) in a statement or position. —**read out** To expel from a religious body, political party, etc., by proclamation or concerted action. —**read up** (or **up on**) To learn by reading. —adj. (red) Informed by or acquainted with books or literature: *well-read*. [< OE *rǣdan* advise, read]

**read·y** (red'ē) adj. **read·i·er**, **read·i·est** 1 Prepared for use or action. 2 Prepared in mind; willing. 3 Likely or liable: with *to: ready* to sink. 4 Quick to act, follow, occur, or appear; prompt. 5 Immediately available; convenient; handy. 6 Designating the standard position in which a rifle is held just before aiming. 7 Quick to understand; alert; quick; facile: a *ready* wit. —n. The position in which a rifle is held before aiming. —v.t. **read·ied**, **read·y·ing** To make ready; prepare. [< OE *rǣde, gerǣde*] —**read'i·ly** adv. —**read'i·ness** n.

**re·al** (rē'əl, *Sp.* rä·äl') n. pl. **re·als** or **re·a·les** (rä·ä'läs) 1 A former small silver coin of Spain. 2 pl. **reis** (rās) A former Portuguese and Brazilian coin; one thousandth of a milreis. [Sp., lit., royal]

**real estate** Land, including whatever is made part of or attached to it by man or nature, as trees, houses, etc. —**re'al·es·tate'** adj.

**re·al·i·ty** (rē·al'ə·tē) n. pl. **·ties** 1 The fact, state, or quality of being real, genuine, or true to life. 2 That which is real; an actual thing, situation, or event. 3 *Philos.* The absolute or the ultimate.

**re·al·ly** (rē'ə·lē, rē'lē) adv. 1 In reality; actually. 2 Truly; genuinely: a *really* fine play. —interj. Oh: used to express surprise, doubt, etc.

**realm** (relm) n. 1 A kingdom. 2 Domain; sphere: the *realm* of imagination. [< L *regalis* royal]

**reap** (rēp) v.t. 1 To cut and gather (grain) with a scythe, reaper, etc. 2 To harvest a crop from: to *reap* a field. 3 To obtain as the result of action or effort. —v.i. 4 To harvest grain, etc. 5 To receive a return or result. [< OE *repan*] —**reap'a·ble** adj. —**reap'ing** n.

**rear**[1] (rir) n. 1 The back or hind part. 2 A place or position at the back of or behind anything. 3 That division of a military force which is farthest from the front. —adj. Being in the rear. [< ARREAR]

**rear**[2] (rir) v.t. 1 To place upright; raise. 2 To build; erect. 3 To care for and bring to maturity. 4 To breed or grow. —v.i. 5 To rise upon its hind legs, as a horse. 6 To rise high; tower, as a mountain. [< OE *rǣran* set upright] —**rear'er** n.

**rea·son** (rē'zən) n. 1 A motive or basis for an action, opinion, etc. 2 A statement which explains or accounts for an action, belief, etc. 3 The ability to think logically and rationally. 4 Sound thinking or judgment; common sense. 5 Sanity. —**by reason of** Because of. —**in** (or **within**) **reason** Within reasonable limits or bounds. —**it stands to reason** It is logical. —**with reason** Justifiably. —v.i. 1 To think logically; obtain inferences or conclusions from known or presumed facts. 2 To talk or argue logically. —v.t. 3 To think out carefully and logically; analyze: with *out*. 4 To influence or persuade by means of reason. 5 To argue; debate. [< L *ratio* computation] —**rea'son·er** n.

**re·bate** (rē'bāt, ri·bāt') v.t. **·bat·ed, ·bat·ing** 1 To allow as a deduction. 2 To make a deduction from. —*n.* A deduction from a gross amount; discount: also **re·bate′ment.** [< OF *ràbattre* beat down] —**re′bat·er** *n.*

**re·bel** (ri·bel′) *v.i.* **·belled, ·bel·ling** 1 To resist or fight against any authority, established custom, etc. 2 To react with violent aversion: usu. with *at.* —*n.* (reb′əl) One who rebels. —*adj.* (reb′əl) 1 Rebellious; refractory. 2 Of rebels. [< L *re-* again + *bellare* make war]

**re·bel·lion** (ri·bel′yən) *n.* 1 The act of rebelling. 2 Organized resistance to a government or to any lawful authority.

**re·bel·lious** (ri·bel′yəs) *adj.* 1 Being in a state of rebellion; insubordinate. 2 Of or pertaining to a rebel or rebellion. 3 Resisting control; refractory: a *rebellious* temper. — **re·bel′lious·ly** *adv.* —**re·bel′lious·ness** *n.*

**re·bound** (ri·bound′) *v.i.* 1 To bounce or spring back after or as after hitting something. 2 To recover, as from a difficulty. 3 To reecho. —*v.t.* 4 To cause to rebound. — *n.* (rē′bound′, ri·bound′) 1 A bounding back; recoil. 2 Something that rebounds, as a basketball from a backboard. 3 Reaction after a disappointment: to fall in love on the *rebound.* [< F *re-* back + *bondir* bound]

**re·buff** (ri·buf′) *v.t.* 1 To reject or refuse abruptly or rudely. 2 To drive or beat back; repel. —*n.* 1 A sudden repulse; curt denial. 2 A sudden check; defeat. 3 A beating back. [< Ital. *ribuffare*]

**re·buke** (ri·byōōk′) *v.t.* **·buked, ·buk·ing** To reprove sharply; reprimand. —*n.* A strong expression of disapproval. [< OF *re-* back + *bucher* beat] —**re·buk′er** *n.*

**re·call** (ri·kôl′) *v.t.* 1 To call back; order or summon to return. 2 To summon back in awareness or attention. 3 To recollect; remember. 4 To take back; revoke; countermand. —*n.* (ri·kôl′, rē′kôl′) 1 A calling back. 2 An ability to remember. 3 Revocation, as of an order. 4 A system whereby public officials may be removed from office by popular vote.

**re·cap¹** (rē′kap′, rē·kap′) *v.t.* **·capped, ·cap·ping** 1 To provide (a worn pneumatic tire) with a tread of new rubber. 2 To replace a cap on. —*n.* (rē′kap′) A tire which has been so treated. [< RE- + CAP]

**re·cap²** (rē′kap′) *v.t.* & *v.i.* **·capped, ·cap·ping** RECAPITULATE. —*n.* RECAPITULATION (def. 2).

**re·ca·pit·u·late** (rē′kə·pich′ōō·lāt) *v.t.* & *v.i.* **·lat·ed, ·lat·ing** To restate or review briefly; sum up. [< LL *re-* again + *capitulare* draw up in chapters]

**re·cede** (rē·sēd′) *v.t.* **·ced·ed, ·ced·ing** To cede back; grant or yield to a former owner.

**re·ceipt** (ri·sēt′) *n.* 1 The act or state of receiving anything: to be in *receipt* of good news. 2 *Usu. pl.* That which is received: cash *receipts.* 3 A written acknowledgment of the payment of money, of the delivery of goods, etc. 4 RECIPE. —*v.t.* 1 To give a receipt for the payment of. 2 To write acknowledgment of payment on, as a bill. —*v.i.* 3 To give a receipt, as for money paid. [< L *re-ceptus,* pp. of *recipere* take back, receive]

**re·ceiv·a·ble** (ri·sē′və·bəl) *adj.* 1 Capable of being received; fit to be received, as legal tender. 2 Due to be paid. —*n. pl.* Outstanding accounts listed as business assets.

**re·ceive** (ri·sēv′) *v.* **·ceived, ·ceiv·ing** *v.t.* 1 To take into one's hand or possession (something given, offered, delivered, etc.). 2 To gain knowledge or information of. 3 To take from another by hearing or listening. 4 To bear; support. 5 To experience; meet with: to *receive* abuse. 6 To undergo; suffer: He *received* a wound in his arm. 7 To contain; hold. 8 To allow entrance to; admit; greet. 9 To perceive mentally: to *receive* a bad impression. 10 To regard in a specified way: The play was well *received.* —*v.i.* 11 To be a recipient. 12 To welcome visitors or callers. 13 *Telecom.* To convert incoming signals, as radio waves, into intelligible sounds or shapes, as in a radio or television set. [< L *re-* back + *capere* take]

**re·ceiv·er** (ri·sē′vər) *n.* 1 One who receives; a recipient. 2 An official assigned to receive money due. 3 *Law* A person appointed by a court to take into his custody the property or funds of another pending litigation. 4 One who knowingly buys or receives stolen goods. 5 Something which receives; a receptacle. 6 *Telecom.* An instrument designed to receive electric or electromagnetic signals and process them or transmit them to another stage.

**re·cent** (rē′sənt) *adj.* 1 Of or pertaining to a time not long past. 2 Occurring, formed, or characterized by association with a time not long past; modern; fresh; new. [< L *re-cens*] —**re′cent·ly** *adv.* —**re′cen·cy, re′cent·ness** *n.*

**re·cep·ta·cle** (ri·sep′tə·kəl) *n.* 1 Anything that serves to contain or hold other things. 2 *Bot.* The base on which the parts of a flower grow. 3 An electric outlet. [< L *receptare,* freq. of *recipere* receive]

**re·cep·tion** (ri·sep´shən) *n.* 1 The act of receiving, or the state of being received. 2 A formal social entertainment of guests: a wedding *reception.* 3 The manner of receiving a person or persons: a warm *reception.* 4 *Telecom.* The act or process of receiving or, esp., the quality of reproduction achieved: poor radio *reception.*

**re·cep·tive** (ri·sep´tiv) *adj.* 1 Able or inclined to receive favorably: *receptive* to new ideas. 2 Able to contain or hold. —**re·cep´tive·ly** *adv.* —**re·cep·tiv·i·ty** (rē´sep·tiv´ə·tē), re·cep´tive·ness *n.*

**re·cess** (rē´ses, ri·ses´) *n.* 1 A depression or indentation in any otherwise continuous line or surface, esp. in a wall; niche. 2 A time of cessation from employment or occupation. 3 *Usu. pl.* A quiet and secluded spot; withdrawn or inner place: the *recesses* of the mind. —*v.* (*usu.* ri·ses´) *v.t.* 1 To place in or as in a recess. 2 To make a recess in. 3 To interrupt for a recess. —*v.i.* 4 To take a recess. [< L *recessus*, pp. of *recedere* go back]

**re·ces·sion** (rē´sesh´ən) *n.* The act of ceding back, as to a former owner.

**rec·i·pe** (res´ə·pē) *n.* 1 A list of ingredients and directions for combining them, as in cooking, pharmacy, etc. 2 The means prescribed for attaining an end. [< L, imperative of *recipere* take]

**re·cip·i·ent** (ri·sip´ē·ənt) *adj.* Receiving or ready to receive; receptive. —*n.* One who or that which receives. —**re·cip´i·ence, re·cip´i·en·cy** *n.*

**re·cip·ro·cal** (ri·sip´rə·kəl) *adj.* 1 Done or given by each of two to the other; mutual. 2 Mutually interchangeable. 3 Related or corresponding, but in an inverse manner; opposite. 4 *Gram.* Expressive of mutual relationship or action: *One another* is a *reciprocal* phrase. 5 *Math.* Having a product of 1, as a pair of numbers. —*n.* 1 That which is reciprocal. 2 *Math.* Either of a pair of numbers having 1 as their product. [< L *reciprocus*] —**re·cip´ro·cal·ly** *adv.*

**re·cip·ro·cate** (ri·sip´rə·kāt) *v.* ·cat·ed, ·cat·ing *v.t.* 1 To cause to move backward and forward alternately. 2 To give and receive mutually; interchange. 3 To give, feel, do, etc., in return. —*v.i.* 4 To move backward and forward. 5 To make a return in kind. 6 To give and receive favors, gifts, etc., mutually. [< L *reciprocare* move to and fro] —**re·cip´ro·ca´tion, re·cip´ro·ca´tor** *n.* —**re·cip´ro·**ca´tive, re·cip´ro·ca·to´ry (-kə·tôr´ē, -kə·tō´rē) *adj.*

**rec·i·proc·i·ty** (res´ə·pros´ə·tē) *n.* 1 Reciprocal obligation, action, or relation. 2 A trade relation between two countries by which each makes concessions favoring the importation of the products of the other.

**re·cite** (ri·sīt´) *v.* ·cit·ed, ·cit·ing *v.t.* 1 To declaim or say from memory, esp. formally, as in public or in a class. 2 To tell in particular detail; relate. 3 To enumerate. —*v.i.* 4 To declaim or speak something from memory. 5 To repeat or be examined in a lesson or part of a lesson in class. [< L *re-* again + *citare* cite] —**re·cit´er** *n.*

**reck·less** (rek´lis) *adj.* 1 Foolishly heedless of danger; rash. 2 Careless; irresponsible. [< OE *recceleās*] —**reck´less·ly** *adv.* —**reck´less·ness** *n.*

**reck·on** (rek´ən) *v.t.* 1 To count; compute; calculate. 2 To look upon as being; regard. 3 *Regional* To suppose or guess; expect. —*v.i.* 4 To make computation; count up. 5 To rely or depend: with *on* or *upon.* —**reckon with** 1 To settle accounts with. 2 To take into consideration; consider. [< OE *recenian* explain] —**reck´on·er** *n.*

**re·claim** (ri·klām´) *v.t.* 1 To bring (a swamp, desert, etc.) into a condition to support cultivation or life, as by draining or irrigating. 2 To obtain (a substance) from used or waste products. 3 To cause to reform. —*n.* The act of reclaiming or state of being reclaimed. [< L *re-* against + *clamare* cry out] —**re·claim´a·ble** *adj.* —**re·claim´er, re·claim´ant** *n.*

**rec·la·ma·tion** (rek´lə·mā´shən) *n.* 1 The act of reclaiming. 2 Restoration, as to ownership, usefulness, etc.

**re·cline** (ri·klīn´) *v.t. & v.i.* ·clined, ·clin·ing To assume or cause to assume a recumbent position; lie or lay down or back. [< L *re-* back + *clinare* lean] —**rec·li·na·tion** (rek´lə·nā´shən), re·clin´er *n.*

**rec·luse** (rek´lōōs, ri·klōōs´) *n.* One who lives in solitude and seclusion; hermit. —*adj.* Secluded or retired from the world. [< L *recludere* shut off] —**re·clu´sion** *n.* —**re·clus´sive** *adj.*

**rec·og·nize** (rek´əg·nīz) *v.t.* ·nized, ·niz·ing 1 To perceive as identical with someone or something previously known. 2 To identify or know, as by previous experience or knowledge: I *recognize* the symptoms. 3 To perceive as true; realize: I *recognize* my error. 4 To acknowledge the independence arid validity of, as a newly constituted government. 5 To indicate appreciation or approval of. 6 To regard as valid or genuine: to *recognize* a claim. 7 To give (someone) permission to speak, as in a legislative body. 8 To admit the acquaintance of; greet. [Back formation < RECOGNIZANCE] —rec·og·niz·a·ble (rek'əg·nīz'ə·bəl) *adj.* —rec'og·niz'a·bly *adv.* —rec'og·niz'er *n.* —Syn. 8 acknowledge, admit, allow.

re·coil (rē'koil) *v.t. & v.i.* To coil again.

rec·ol·lect (rek'ə·lekt') *v.t.* 1 To call back to the mind; remember. —*v.i.* 2 To have a recollection of something. [< L *recollectus*, pp. of *recolligere* gather together again]

re·col·lec·tion (rek'ə·lek'shən) *n.* 1 The act or power of recollecting. 2 Something remembered. —rec'ol·lec'tive *adj.* —rec'ol·lec'tive·ly *adv.* —rec'ol·lec'tive·ness *n.*

rec·om·mend (rek'ə·mend') *v.t.* 1 To commend or praise as desirable, worthy, etc. 2 To make attractive or acceptable. 3 To advise; urge. 4 To give in charge; commend. —rec'om·mend'a·ble, rec'om·men'da·to·ry (-də·tôr'ē, -tōr'ē) *adj.* —rec'om·mend'er *n.*

rec·om·men·da·tion (rek'ə·mən·dā'shən, -men-) *n.* 1 The act of recommending. 2 Something that recommends, as a letter or statement.

rec·om·pense (rek'əm·pens) *v.t.* ·pensed, ·pens·ing 1 To give compensation to; pay or repay; reward. 2 To give compensation for, as a loss. —*n.* An equivalent for anything given, done, or suffered; payment; compensation; reward. [< L *re-* again + *compensare* compensate]

rec·on·cile (rek'ən·sīl) *v.t.* ·ciled, ·cil·ing 1 To bring back to friendship after estrangement. 2 To settle or adjust, as a quarrel. 3 To bring to acquiescence, content, or submission. 4 To make or show to be consistent or congruous; harmonize. [< L *re-* again + *conciliare* unite] —rec'on·cile'ment, rec'on·cil'er, rec·on·cil·i·a·tion (rek'ən·sil'ē·ā'shən) *n.* —rec'on·cil'i·a·to·ry (-sil'ē·ə·tôr'ē, -tō'rē) *adj.*

re·con·noi·ter (rē'kə·noi'tər, rek'ə-) *v.t.* 1 To examine or survey, as for military, engineering, or geological purposes. —*v.i.* 2 To make a reconnaissance. *Brit. sp.* ·noi'tre. [< OF *reconoistre*] —re'con·noi'ter·er, re'con·noi'trer *n.*

re·cord (rek'ərd) *n.* 1 An account in written or other permanent form serving as evidence of a fact or event. 2 Something on

which such an account is made, as a monument. 3 Information preserved and handed down: the heaviest rainfall on *record.* 4 The known career or performance of a person, animal, organization, etc. 5 The best listed achievement, as in a competitive sport. 6 *Law* a A written account of an act, statement, or transaction made by an officer acting under authority of law. b An official written account of a judicial or legislative proceeding. 7 A disk or cylinder, grooved so as to reproduce sounds that have been registered on its surface. —go on record To state publically or officially. —off the record Not for quotation or publication. —*adj.* Surpassing any previously recorded achievement or performance of its kind. —re·cord (ri·kôrd') *v.t.* 1 To write down or otherwise inscribe, as for preservation, evidence, etc. 2 To indicate; register. 3 To offer evidence of. 4 To register and make permanently reproducible, as on tape, a phonograph record, etc. —*v.i.* 5 To record something. [< L *recordari* call to mind]

re·cord·er (ri·kôr'dər) *n.* 1 One who records. 2 A magistrate having criminal jurisdiction in a city or borough. 3 A type of flute blown at one end. 4 A device that records, as a tape recorder.

re·cov·er (ri·kuv'ər) *v.t.* 1 To obtain again, as after losing; regain. 2 To make up for; retrieve, as a loss. 3 To restore (oneself) to natural balance, health, etc. 4 To reclaim, as land. 5 *Law* To gain or regain in judicial proceedings. —*v.i.* 6 To regain health, composure, etc. 7 *Law* To succeed in a lawsuit. [< L *recuperare*] —re·cov'er·a·ble *adj.*

re·cov·er·y (ri·kuv'ər·ē) *n. pl.* ·er·ies 1 The act, process, or an instance of recovering. 2 The duration of recovering. 3 Restoration from sickness or from any undesirable or abnormal condition. 4 The extraction of usable substances and materials from byproducts, waste, etc. 5 The retrieval of a flying object, as a balloon, space vehicle, meteorite, etc., after it has fallen to earth.

rec·re·ant (rek'rē·ənt) *adj.* 1 Unfaithful to a cause or pledge; false. 2 Craven; cowardly. —*n.* A cowardly or faithless person; also, a deserter. [< L *re-* back + *credere* believe] —rec're·ance, rec're·an·cy *n.* —rec're·ant·ly *adv.*

rec·re·a·tion (rek'rē·ā'shən) *n.* 1 Refreshment of body or mind, esp. after work; diversion; amusement. 2 Any pleasurable exercise or occupation. —rec're·a'tion·al *adj.*

**re·cruit** (ri·krōōt′) v.t. 1 To enlist (men or women) for service, as in a military organization or a police force. 2 To muster; raise, as an army, by enlistment. 3 To enlist the aid, services, or support of: to recruit new members for a political party. 4 To replenish. —v.i. 5 To enlist new personnel for service, as in an army or other organization. 6 To gain or raise new supplies of anything lost or needed. —n. 1 A newly enlisted person, as a soldier or sailor. 2 Any new adherent of a cause, organization, or the like. [< F recrutte] —re·cruit′er, re·cruit′ment n.

**rec·tan·gle** (rek′tang·gəl) n. A parallelogram with all angles right angles. [< L rectus straight + angulus angle] • See PARALLELOGRAM.

**rec·tan·gu·lar** (rek·tang′gyə·lər) adj. 1 Having right angles. 2 Resembling a rectangle. —rec·tan′gu·lar′i·ty (-lar′ə·tē) n. —rec·tan′gu·lar·ly adv.

**rec·ti·fy** (rek′tə·fī) v.t. ·fied, ·fy·ing 1 To make right; correct; amend. 2 Chem. To refine or purify, as a liquid, by distillation. 3 Electr. To change (an alternating current) into a direct current. 4 To allow for errors or inaccuracies in, as a compass reading. [< L rectus right + facere make] —rec′ti·fi′a·ble adj. —rec′ti·fi·ca′tion (-tə·fə·kā′shən) n.

**rec·ti·tude** (rek′tə·t′ōōd) n. 1 Uprightness in principles and conduct. 2 Correctness of judgment, method, etc. [< L rectus right]

**re·cum·bent** (ri·kum′bənt) adj. 1 Lying down, wholly or partly. 2 Resting; inactive. [< L re- back + cumbere lie] —re·cum′bence, re·cum′ben·cy n. —re·cum′bent·ly adv.

**re·cu·per·ate** (ri·k′ōō′pə·rāt) v. ·at·ed, ·at·ing v.i. 1 To regain health or strength. 2 To recover from loss, as of money. —v.t. 3 To obtain again after loss; recover. 4 To restore to vigor and health. [< L recuperare] —re·cu′per·a′tion, re·cu′per·a′tor n. —re·cu′per·a′tive adj.

**re·cur** (ri·kûr′) v.i. ·curred, ·cur·ring 1 To happen again or repeatedly. 2 To come back or return, as to the memory, in conversation, etc. [< L re- back + currere run]

**re·cur·rent** (ri·kûr′ənt) adj. 1 Happening or appearing again or repeatedly; recurring. 2 Turning back toward the source, as certain arteries and nerves. —re·cur′rence, re·cur′ren·cy n. —re·cur′rent·ly adv.

**re·cy·cle** (rē·sī′kəl) v.t. ·cy·cled, ·cy·cling To reclaim (waste materials, as used newsprint, glass bottles, etc.) by using in the manufacture of new products. —re·cy′cla·ble adj.

**red** (red) adj. red·der, red·dest 1 Having or being of a bright color resembling blood. 2 Of a hue approximating red: red hair. 3 Ultraradical in politics, esp. communistic. —n. 1 One of the primary colors, occurring at the opposite end of the spectrum from violet; the color of fresh human blood. 2 A hue or tint that approximates primary red. 3 Any pigment or dye having or giving this color. 4 A red animal or object. 5 Often cap. An ultraradical or revolutionary in politics, esp. a communist: from the red banner of revolution. —in the red Informal Operating at a loss; owing money. —see red To be very angry. [< OE rēad] —red′dish adj. —red′ly adv. —red′ness n.

**re·deem** (ri·dēm′) v.t. 1 To regain possession of by paying a price. 2 To pay off, as a promissory note. 3 To convert into cash or a premium: to redeem stocks or trading stamps. 4 To set free; ransom. 5 Theol. To rescue from sin and its penalties. 6 To fulfill, as an oath or promise. 7 To make worthwhile. [< L re- back + emere buy] —re·deem′a·ble, re·demp′ti·ble (-demp′tə·bəl) adj.

**re·demp·tion** (ri·demp′shən) n. 1 The act of redeeming, or the state of being redeemed. 2 The recovery of what is mortgaged or pawned. 3 The payment of a debt or obligation, esp. the paying of the value of its notes, warrants, etc., by a government. 4 Deliverance or rescue, as by paying a ransom. —re·demp′tive, re·demp′to·ry adj.

**re·dound** (ri·dound′) v.i. 1 To have an effect or result. 2 To return; reflect. —n. A return by way of consequence; result. [< L redundare to overflow]

**re·dress** (ri·dres′) v.t. 1 To set right or make reparation for, as a wrong, by compensation or by punishment. 2 To make reparation to; compensate. 3 To remedy; correct. —n. (rē′dres, ri·dres′) 1 Satisfaction for wrong done; reparation; amends. 2 A restoration; correction. [< F redresser straighten] —re·dress′er or re·dres′sor n.

**re·duce** (ri·d′ōōs′) v. ·duced, ·duc·ing v.t. 1 To make less in size, amount, number, intensity, etc.; diminish. 2 To bring into a certain system or order; classify. 3 To bring to a lower condition; degrade. 4 To bring to submission; subdue; conquer. 5 To bring to a specified condition or state: with to: to reduce rock to powder; reduced to tears. 6 To thin (paint, etc.) with oil or turpentine. 7 *Math.* To change (an expression) to a more elementary form. 8 *Chem.* a To remove oxygen from (a compound). b To add electrons to (an atom). c To decrease the positive valence of (an atom). 9 *Phot.* To diminish the density of (a photographic negative). —*v.i.* 10 To become less in any way. 11 To decrease one's weight, as by dieting. [< L *re-* back + *ducere* lead] —re·duc′er, re·duc′i·bil′i·ty n. —re·duc′i·ble *adj.* —re·duc′i·bly *adv.*

re·duc·ti·on (ri·duk′shən) n. 1 The act or process of reducing. 2 Something that results from reducing. 3 The amount by which something is reduced. —re·duc′tion·al, re·duc′tive *adj.*

re·dun·dan·cy (ri·dun′dən·sē) n. pl. ·cies 1 The condition or quality of being redundant. 2 Something redundant, esp. unnecessary repetition. 3 Excess; surplus. 4 In information theory, repeated information in a message, used to lessen the probability of error. Also re·dun′dance.

re·dun·dant (ri·dun′dənt) *adj.* 1 Being more than is required; constituting an excess. 2 Unnecessarily repetitive or verbose. [< L *redundare* to overflow] —re·dun′dant·ly *adv.* —**Syn.** 1 superfluous, excessive, inordinate, undue. 2 repetitious, iterative, reiterative, wordy.

reef (rēf) n. 1 A ridge of sand or rocks, or esp. of coral, at or near the surface of the water. 2 A lode, vein, or ledge. [< ON *rif* rib, reef] —reef′y *adj.* • See ATOLL.

reek (rēk) *v.i.* 1 To give off smoke, vapor, etc. 2 To give off a strong, offensive smell. 3 To be pervaded with anything offensive. —*v.t.* 4 To expose to smoke or its action. 5 To give off; emit. [< OE *rēocan*] —reek′er n. —reek′y *adj.* (·i·er, ·i·est)

reel (rēl) n. 1 A rotatory device or frame for winding rope, cord, photographic film, or other flexible substance. 2 Such a device attached to a fishing rod. 3 The length of wire, film, thread, etc., wound on one reel. —*v.t.* 1 To wind on a reel or bobbin, as a line. 2 To draw in by reeling a line: with *in:* to *reel* a fish in. 3 To say, do, etc., easily and fluently: with *off*. [< OE *hrēol*] —reel′a·ble *adj.* —reel′er n.

re·fer (ri·fûr′) *v.* ·ferred, ·fer·ring *v.t.* 1 To direct or send for information or other purpose. 2 To hand over for consideration, settlement, etc. 3 To assign or attribute to a source, cause, group, class, etc. —*v.i.* 4 To

make reference; allude. 5 To turn, as for information, help, or authority. [< L *re-* back + *ferre* bear, carry] —ref·er·a·ble (ref′ər·ə·bəl, ri·fûr′-). re·fer′ra·ble or re·fer′ri·ble *adj.* —re·fer′rer n.

ref·e·ree (ref′ə·rē′) n. 1 A person to whom a thing is referred for judgment or decision. 2 An official who sees that the rules of certain sports events are observed. —*v.t.* & *v.i.* To judge as a referee.

ref·er·ence (ref′ər·əns, ref′rəns) n. 1 The act of referring. 2 An incidental allusion or direction of the attention. 3 A note or other indication in a book, referring to some other book or passage. 4 One who or that which is or may be referred to. 5 A book or other source intended to be referred to for information, as a dictionary. 6 Relation: in *reference* to your inquiry. 7 A person to whom an employer may refer for information about a potential employee. 8 A written statement or testimonial referring to character or dependability. —ref′er·en′tial (-ər·en′shəl) *adj.* —ref′er·en′tial·ly *adv.*

ref·er·en·dum (ref′ə·ren′dəm) n. pl. ·dums or ·da (-də) 1 The submission of a proposed public measure or law, which has been passed upon by a legislature or convention, to a vote of the people for ratification or rejection. 2 The vote itself. [L, gerund of *referre* refer]

re·fill (rē·fil′) *v.t.* & *v.i.* To fill or become filled again. —n. (rē′fil′) Any commodity packaged to fit and fill a container originally containing that commodity. —re·fill′a·ble *adj.*

re·fine (ri·fīn′) *v.* ·fined, ·fin·ing *v.t.* 1 To make fine or pure. 2 To make more elegant, polished, etc. 3 To improve or perfect. —*v.i.* 4 To become fine or pure. 5 To become more polished or cultured. 6 To make fine distinctions; use subtlety in thought or speech. [< RE- + FINE¹, *v.*] —re·fin′er n.

re·flect (ri·flekt′) *v.t.* 1 To turn or throw back, as rays of light, heat, or sound. 2 To produce a symmetrically reversed image of, as a mirror. 3 To cause or bring as a result: with *on:* He *reflects* credit on his teacher. 4 To show or manifest: His writings *reflect* great imagination. —*v.i.* 5 To send back rays, as of light or heat. 6 To return in rays. 7 To give back an image; also, to be mirrored. 8 To think carefully; ponder. 9 To bring blame, discredit, etc.: with *on* or *upon*. [< L *re-* back + *flectere* bend]

re·flec·tion (ri·flek′shən) n. 1 The act of reflecting, or the state of being reflected. 2 *Physics* The throwing off or back (from a surface) of impinging light, heat, sound, or any form of radiant energy. 3 Reflected rays or an image thrown by reflection. 4 Careful, serious thought or consideration. 5 The result of such thought. 6 Censure; discredit; also, a remark or action tending to discredit. **—re·flec′tion·al** *adj.*

**re·flec·tive** (re·flek′tiv) *adj.* 1 Given to reflection or thought; meditative. 2 Of or caused by reflection. 3 That reflects. **—re·flec′tive·ly** *adv.* **—re·flec′tive·ness, re′flec·tiv′i·ty** *n.*

**re·flex** (rē′fleks) *adj.* 1 Turned, bent, directed, or thrown backward. 2 *Physiol.* Of, pertaining to, or produced by an involuntary action or response. **—***n.* 1 Reflection, as of light, or an image produced by reflection. 2 *Physiol.* An involuntary response to a stimulus: also **reflex action.** 3 A habitual or automatic reaction. [< L *reflexus* reflected, pp. of *reflectere* bend back]

**re·form** (ri·fôrm′) *v.t.* 1 To make better by removing abuses, malpractice, etc. 2 To make better morally; persuade or educate from a sinful to a moral life. 3 To put an end to; stop (an abuse, malpractice, etc.). **—***v.i.* 4 To give up sin or error; become better. **—***n.* A correction or improvement of social or personal evils or errors. [< L *re-* again + *formare* to form] **—re·form′a·tive** *adj.* **—re·for′mer** *n.* **—re·form′ist** *adj., n.*

**re-form** (rē′fôrm′) *v.t. & v.i.* To form again. **—re′-for·ma′tion** *n.*

**ref·or·ma·tion** (ref′ər·mā′shən) *n.* 1 The act of reforming. 2 The state of being reformed.

**re·fract** (ri·frakt′) *v.t.* 1 To deflect (a ray) by refraction. 2 *Optics* To determine the degree of refraction of (an eye or lens). [< L *refractus,* pp. of *refringere* turn aside]

**re·frac·tion** (ri·frak′shən) *n. Physics* The change of direction of a ray, as of light or heat, in oblique passage between media of different densities. **—re·frac′tive** *adj.* **—re·frac′tive·ness, re·frac·tiv·i·ty** (rē′frak·tiv′ə·tē), **re·frac′tor** *n.*

**re·frain** (ri·frān′) *v.i.* To hold oneself back. [< L *refrenare* curb] **—re·frain′er** *n.* **—Syn.** abstain, forbear, forgo, renounce.

**re·fresh** (ri·fresh′) *v.t.* 1 To revive (a person), as with food or rest. 2 To make fresh, clean, cool, etc. 3 To stimulate, as the memory. 4 To renew or replenish with or as with new supplies. **—***v.i.* 5 To become fresh again; revive. 6 To take refreshment. **—re·fresh′er** *n.*

**re·fresh·ment** (ri·fresh′mənt) *n.* 1 The act of refreshing, or the state of being refreshed. 2 That which refreshes. 3 *pl.* Food, or food and drink, served as a light meal.

**re·frig·er·ate** (ri·frij′ə·rāt) *v.t.* **·at·ed, ·at·ing** 1 To keep or cause to become cold; cool. 2 To freeze or chill for preservative purposes, as foodstuffs. [< L *re-* thoroughly + *frigerare* to cool] **—re·frig′er·a′tion** *n.* **—re·frig′er·a′tive** *adj., n.* **—re·frig′er·a·to′ry** *adj.*

**re·frig·er·a·tor** (ri·frij′ə·rā′tər) *n.* A box, cabinet, room, railroad car, etc., equipped with a cooling apparatus for preserving the freshness of perishable foods, etc.

**ref·uge** (ref′yōōj) *n.* 1 Shelter or protection, as from danger or distress. 2 A safe place; asylum. 3 Something that brings relief, lessens difficulties, etc. [< L *refugere* to retreat]

**ref·u·gee** (ref′yŏŏ·jē′, ref′yŏŏ·jē′) *n.* One who flees to find refuge in another land or place, as from persecution or political danger.

**re·fuse**[1] (ri·fyōōz′) *v.* **·fused, ·fus·ing** *v.t.* 1 To decline to do, permit, take, or yield. 2 To decline to fulfill the request or desire of (a person). 3 To balk at jumping over (a ditch, hedge, etc.): said of a horse. **—***v.i.* 4 To decline to do, permit, take, or yield something. [< L *refusus,* pp. of *refundere* pour back] **—re·fus′er** *n.*

**ref·use**[2] (ref′yŏŏs) *n.* Anything worthless; rubbish. [< OF *refus* refused]

**re·fute** (ri·fyōōt′) *v.t.* **·fut·ed, ·fut·ing** 1 To prove the incorrectness or falsity of (a statement). 2 To prove (a person) to be in error; confute. [< L *refutare*] **—re·fut′a·ble** *adj.* **—re·fut′a·bly** *adv.* **—ref·u·ta·tion** (ref′yə·tā′shən), **re·fu′tal, re·fut′er** *n.*

**re·gal** (rē′gəl) *adj.* Belonging to or fit for a king; royal, stately, magnificent, etc. [< L *rex, regis* king] **—re·gal·i·ty** (ri·gal′ə·tē) *n.* **—re′gal·ly** *adv.*

**re·gale** (ri·gāl′) *v.* **·galed, ·gal·ing** *v.t.* 1 To give unusual pleasure to; delight. 2 To entertain royally or sumptuously; feast. **—***v.i.* 3 To feast. [< F *régaler*] **—re·gale′ment** *n.*

**re·ga·li·a** (ri·gā′lē·ə, ·gāl′yə) *n. pl.* 1 The insignia and emblems of royalty, as the crown, scepter, etc. 2 The distinctive symbols, insignia, etc., of any society, order, or rank. 3 Fine clothes; fancy trappings.

**re·gard** (ri·gärd′) *v.t.* 1 To look at or observe attentively. 2 To look on or think of in a certain way. 3 To take into account; consider. 4 To have relevance to. **—***v.i.* 5 To pay attention. 6 To gaze or look. **—***n.* 1 A look; gaze. 2 Careful attention; consideration. 3

Respect; esteem. 4 *Usu. pl.* Greetings; good wishes. 5 Reference; relation: with *regard* to your letter. [< OF *regarder* look at]

re·gat·ta (ri·gat′ə, -gä′tə) *n.* A boat race, or a series of such races. [Ital.]

re·gen·cy (rē′jən·sē) *n. pl.* ·cies 1 The government or office of a regent or body of regents. 2 The period during which a regent or body of regents governs. 3 A body of regents. 4 The district under the rule of a regent. Also re′gent·ship.

re·gen·er·ate (ri·jen′ə·rāt) *v.* ·at·ed, ·at·ing *v.t.* 1 To cause moral and spiritual reformation in. 2 To produce or form anew; reestablish; recreate. 3 *Biol.* To replace (a lost organ or tissue) with new growth. —*v.i.* 4 To form anew; be reproduced. 5 To become spiritually regenerate. 6 To effect regeneration. — *adj.* (ri·jen′ər·it) 1 Having new life; restored. 2 Spiritually renewed; regenerated. —re·gen′er·a·cy (-ər·ə·sē), re·gen′er·a′tion, re·gen′er·a′tor *n.*

re·gent (rē′jənt) *n.* 1 One who rules in the name and place of a sovereign. 2 One of various officers having charge of education, as of a university or state. [<L *regens,* pr.p. of *regere* rule]

re·gime (ri·zhēm′) *n.* 1 System of government or administration. 2 A particular government or its duration of rule. 3 A social system. 4 REGIMEN. Also ré·gime (rā·zhēm′). [< F<L *regimen]*

reg·i·men (rej′ə·mən) *n.* A system of diet, exercise, etc., used for therapeutic purposes. [<L *regimen<regere* to rule]

reg·i·ment (rej′ə·mənt) *n.* A military unit larger than a battalion and smaller than a division. —*v.t.* 1 To form into a regiment or regiments; organize. 2 To assign to a regiment. 3 To form into well-defined or specific units or groups; systematize. 4 To make uniform. [<LL *regimentum<L regere* to rule] —reg′i·men′tal *adj.* —reg′i·men·ta′tion *n.*

re·gion (rē′jən) *n.* 1 An indefinite, usu. large portion of territory or space. 2 A specific area or place. 3 A specified area of activity, interest, etc.: the *region* of art. 4 A portion of the body. [<L *regio<regere* to rule]

reg·is·ter (rej′is·tər) *n.* 1 An official record, as of names, events, transactions, etc. 2 The book containing such a record. 3 An item in such a record. 4 Any of various devices for adding or recording: a cash *register.* 5 REGISTRAR. 6 A device for regulating the admission of heated air to a room. 7 *Music* a The range or compass of a voice or instru-

ment. b A series of tones of a particular quality or belonging to a particular portion of the compass of a voice or instrument. 8 *Printing* a Exact correspondence of the lines and margins on the opposite sides of a printed sheet. b Correct imposition of the colors in color printing. —*v.t.* 1 To enter in or as in a register; enroll or record officially. 2 To indicate on a scale. 3 To express or indicate: His face *registered* disapproval. 4 *Printing* To effect exact correspondence or imposition of. 5 To cause (mail) to be recorded, on payment of a fee, so as to insure delivery. —*v.i.* 6 To enter one's name in a register, poll, etc. 7 To have effect; make an impression. 8 *Printing* To be in register. [<L *regestus,* pp. of *regerere* record] —reg·is·tra·ble (rej′is·trə·bəl) *adj.* —reg′is·trant (-trənt) *n.*

reg·is·trar (rej′is·trär) *n.* An authorized keeper of a register or of records, esp. of a college or court.

reg·is·tra·tion (rej′is·trā′shən) *n.* 1 The act of registering, as of voters, students, etc. 2 The number of persons registered. 3 An entry in a register.

re·gret (ri·gret′) *v.t.* ·gret·ted, ·gret·ting 1 To look back upon with a feeling of distress or loss. 2 To feel sorrow or grief concerning. — *n.* 1 Distress of mind in recalling some past event, act, loss, etc. 2 Remorseful sorrow; compunction. 3 *pl.* A polite refusal in response to an invitation. [< OF *regreter]* — re·gret′ter *n.*

re·gret·ful (ri·gret′fəl) *adj.* Feeling, expressive of, or full of regret. —re·gret′ful·ly *adv.* — re·gret′ful·ness *n.* —Syn. sorry, remorseful, contrite, apologetic.

reg·u·lar (reg′yə·lər) *adj.* 1 Made, formed, or arranged according to a rule, standard, or type; symmetrical; normal. 2 Methodical; orderly: *regular* habits. 3 Conforming to a fixed or proper procedure or principle. 4 Customary; habitual: his *regular* breakfast. 5 Officially authorized. 6 Without variation or abnormality: His pulse is *regular.* 7 Thorough; unmitigated: a *regular* bore. 8 *Informal* Pleasant, good, honest, etc.: a *regular* guy. 9 *Gram.* Undergoing the inflection that is normal or most common. 10 *Bot.* Having all similar parts or organs of the same shape and size: said mainly of flowers. 11 *Eccl.* Belonging to a religious order: the *regular* clergy. 12 *Mil.* Pertaining or belonging to the permanent army. 13 In politics, designating, nominated by, or loyal to the official party organization or platform. 14 *Geom.* Having equal sides and angles. 15 *Math.* Controlled or formed by one law or operation throughout. —*n.* 1 A soldier belonging to a permanent or standing army. 2 In sports, a starting member of a team. 3 An habitual customer, patron, etc. 4 A clothing size for those of average height and weight. 5 *Eccl.* A member of a religious order. 6 A person loyal to a certain political party. [< L *regula* rule] —**reg′u·lar′i·ty** *n.* —**reg′u·lar·ly** *adv.*

**reg·u·late** (reg′yə·lāt) *v.t.* **·lat·ed, ·lat·ing** 1 To direct, manage, or control according to certain rules, principles, etc. 2 To adjust according to a standard, degree, etc.: to *regulate* currency. 3 To adjust to accurate operation. 4 To put in order; set right. [< L *regula* a rule<*regere* rule, lead straight] —**reg′u·la′tive, reg′u·la·to′ry** (-lə·tôr′ē, -tō′rē) *adj.*

**reg·u·la·tion** (reg′yə·lā′shən) *n.* 1 The act of regulating, or the state of being regulated. 2 A prescribed rule of conduct or procedure. —*adj.* 1 Required by rule or regulation. 2 Normal; customary.

**reg·u·la·tor** (reg′yə·lā′tər) *n.* 1 One who or that which regulates. 2 A device for regulating the speed of a watch. 3 A contrivance for controlling motion, flow, voltage, etc.

**re·ha·bil·i·tate** (rē′hə·bil′ə·tāt, rē′ə-) *v.t.* **·tat·ed, ·tat·ing** 1 To restore to a former state, capacity, privilege, rank, etc.; reinstate. 2 To restore to health or normal activity. [< Med. L *rehabilitare*] —**re′ha·bil′i·ta′tion** *n.*

**re·hearse** (ri·hûrs′) *v.* **·hearsed, ·hears·ing** *v.t.* 1 To practice privately in preparation for public performance, as a play or song. 2 To instruct or direct (a person) by way of preparation. 3 To say over again; repeat aloud; recite. 4 To give an account of; relate. —*v.i.* 5 To rehearse a play, song, dance, etc. [< OF *reherser* harrow over, repeat] —**re·hears′er** *n.*

**reign** (rān) *n.* 1 Sovereign power or rule; sovereignty. 2 The time or duration of a sovereign's rule. 3 Domination; sway: the *reign* of rationalism. —*v.i.* 1 To hold and exercise sovereign power. 2 To hold sway; prevail: Winter *reigns.* [< L *regnum* rule]

**re·im·burse** (rē′im·bûrs′) *v.t.* **·bursed, ·burs·ing** 1 To pay back (a person) an equivalent for what has been spent or lost; recompense. 2 To pay back; refund. [< RE- + < L

*in-* in + *bursa* purse] —**re′im·burs′a·ble** *adj.* —**re′im·burse′ment** *n.*

**rein** (rān) *n.* 1 *Usu. pl.* A strap attached to each end of a bit to control a horse or other draft animal. 2 Any means of restraint or control. —*v.t.* 1 To guide, check, or halt with or as with reins. —*v.i.* 2 To check or halt a horse by means of reins: with *in* or *up.* [< OF *resne*]

**rein·deer** (rān′dir′) *n.* *pl.* **·deer** A European form of caribou, often domesticated. [< ON *hreinn* reindeer + *dyr* deer]

**re·in·force** (rē′in·fôrs′, -fōrs′) *v.t.* **·forced, ·forc·ing** 1 To give new force or strength to. 2 *Mil.* To strengthen with more troops or ships. 3 To add some strengthening part or material to. 4 To increase the number of. [< RE- + *inforce*, var. of ENFORCE]

**re·in·force·ment** (rē′in·fôrs′mənt, -fōrs′-) *n.* 1 The act of reinforcing. 2 Something that reinforces. 3 *Often pl. Mil.* A fresh body of troops or additional vessels.

**re·in·state** (rē′in·stāt′) *v.t.* **·stat·ed, ·stat·ing** To restore to a former state, position, etc. —**re′in·state′ment** *n.*

**re·it·er·ate** (rē·it′ə·rāt) *v.t.* **·at·ed, ·at·ing** To say or do again and again. [< L *re-* again + *iterare* say] —**re·it′er·a′tion** *n.* —**re·it′er·a′tive** *adj.* —**re·it′er·a′tive·ly** *adv.* —**Syn.** iterate, repeat, retell, recapitulate.

**re·ject** (ri·jekt′) *v.t.* 1 To refuse to accept, recognize, believe, etc. 2 To refuse to grant; deny, as a petition. 3 To refuse (a person) recognition, acceptance, etc. 4 To expel; react against physiologically. 5 To cast away as worthless; discard. —*n.* (rē′jekt) A person or thing that has been rejected. [< L *re-* back + *jacere* to throw] —**re·ject′er** or **re·jec′tor, re·jec′tion** *n.*

**re·joice** (ri·jois′) *v.* **·joiced, ·joic·ing** *v.i.* 1 To feel joyful; be glad. —*v.t.* 2 To fill with joy; gladden. [< L *re-* again + *ex-* thoroughly + *gaudere* be joyous] —**re·joic′er, re·joic′ing** *n.* —**re·joic′ing·ly** *adv.*

**re·join·der** (ri·join′dər) *n.* 1 An answer to a reply. 2 Any reply or retort. [< F *rejoindre* to answer, reply]

**re·ju·ve·nate** (ri·jōō′və·nāt) *v.t.* **·nat·ed, ·nat·ing** To make young; give new vigor or youthfulness to. [< RE- again + L *juventis* young + -ATE] —**re·ju′ve·na′tion** *n.*

**re·late** (ri·lāt′) *v.* **·lat·ed, ·lat·ing** *v.t.* 1 To tell the events or the particulars of; narrate. 2 To bring into connection or relation. —*v.i.* 3 To have relation: with *to.* 4 To have reference; with *to*. [< L *relatus*, pp. of *referre* to carry back] —re·lat′er *n.*

re·la·tion (ri·lā′shən) *n.* 1 The fact or condition of being related or connected: the *relation* between poverty and disease. 2 Connection by blood or marriage; kinship. 3 A person connected by blood or marriage; a relative. 4 Reference; regard; allusion: in *relation* to your request. 5 *pl.* The contacts or dealings between or among individuals, groups, nations, etc.: race *relations;* political *relations.* 6 The act of relating or narrating; also, that which is related or told. —re·la′tion·al *adj.*

rel·a·tive (rel′ə·tiv) *adj.* 1 Having connection; pertinent: an inquiry *relative* to one's health. 2 Resulting from or depending upon a relation to or comparison with something else; comparative: a *relative* truth. 3 Intelligible only in relation to something else; not absolute. 4 *Gram.* Referring to or qualifying an antecedent: a *relative* pronoun. —*n.* 1 One who is related; a kinsman. 2 A relative word or term. —rel′a·tive·ly *adv.* —rel′a·tive·ness *n.*

rel·a·tiv·i·ty (rel′ə·tiv′ə·tē) *n.* 1 The quality or condition of being relative; relativeness. 2 *Philos.* Existence viewed only as an object of, or in relation to, a thinking mind. 3 A condition of dependence or of close relation of one thing on or to another. 4 *Physics* The principle of the interdependence of matter, energy, space, and time, as mathematically formulated by Albert Einstein. The **special theory of relativity** states that the speed of light is the same in all frames of reference and that the same laws of physics hold in all frames of reference that are not accelerated. The **general theory of relativity** extends these principles to accelerated frames of reference and gravitational phenomena.

re·lax (ri·laks′) *v.t.* 1 To make lax or loose; make less tight or firm. 2 To make less stringent or severe, as discipline. 3 To abate; slacken, as efforts. 4 To relieve from strain or effort. —*v.i.* 5 To become lax or loose; loosen. 6 To become less stringent or severe. 7 To rest. 8 To unbend; become less formal. [< L *re-* again + *laxare* loosen] —re·lax′a·ble *adj.* —re′lax·a′tion, re·lax′er *n.*

re·lease (ri·lēs′) *v.t.* ·leased, ·leas·ing 1 To set free; liberate. 2 To deliver from worry, pain, obligation, etc. 3 To free from something that holds, binds, etc. 4 To permit the cir-

culation, sale, performance, etc., of, as a motion picture, phonograph record, or news item. —*n.* 1 The act of releasing or setting free, or the state of being released. 2 A discharge from responsibility or penalty; also, a document authorizing this. 3 *Law* An instrument of conveyance by which one person surrenders and relinquishes all claims or rights to another person. 4 The releasing of something to the public; also, that which is released, as a news item, motion picture, etc. 5 *Mech.* Any catch or device to hold and release something. [< L *relaxare* relax] —re·leas′er *n.*

rel·e·gate (rel′ə·gāt) *v.t.* ·gat·ed, ·gat·ing 1 To send off or consign, as to an obscure position or place. 2 To assign, as to a particular class or sphere. 3 To refer (a matter) to someone for decision, action, etc. 4 To banish; exile. [< L *re-* away, back + *legare* send] —rel′e·ga′tion *n.*

re·lent (ri·lent′) *v.i.* To soften in temper; become more gentle or compassionate. [< L *relentescere* grow soft]

rel·e·vant (rel′ə·vənt) *adj.* Fitting; pertinent; applicable. [< Med. L *relevare* bear upon] —rel′e·vance, rel′e·van·cy *n.* —rel′e·vant·ly *adv.*

re·li·a·ble (ri·lī′ə·bəl) *adj.* That may be relied upon; worthy of confidence. —re·li′a·bil′i·ty, re·li′a·ble·ness *n.* —re·li′a·bly *adv.* —Syn. trustworthy, dependable, loyal, constant.

re·li·ance (ri·lī′əns) *n.* 1 The act of relying. 2 Confidence; trust; dependence. 3 That upon which one relies.

rel·ic (rel′ik) *n.* 1 Some remaining portion or fragment of that which has vanished or is destroyed. 2 A custom, habit, etc., from the past. 3 A keepsake or memento. 4 The body or part of the body of a saint, or any sacred memento. 5 *pl.* A corpse; remains. [< L *reliquiae* remains < *relinquere* leave]

re·lief (ri·lēf′) *n.* 1 The act of relieving, or the state of being relieved. 2 That which relieves. 3 Charitable aid, as money or food. 4 Release, as from a post or duty; also, the person or persons who take over for those released. 5 In architecture and sculpture, the projection of a figure, ornament, etc., from a surface; also, any such figure. 6 In painting, the apparent projection of forms and masses. 7 *Geog.* a The unevenness of land surface, as caused by mountains, hills, etc. b The parts of a map which portray such unevenness.

**re·lieve** (ri·lēv') *v.t.* **·lieved, ·liev·ing** 1 To free wholly or partly from pain, stress, pressure, etc. 2 To lessen or alleviate, as pain or pressure. 3 To give aid or assistance to. 4 To free from obligation, injustice, etc. 5 To release from duty by providing a substitute. 6 To make less monotonous, harsh, or unpleasant; vary. 7 To bring into prominence; display by contrast. [< L *relevare* lift up] —**re·liev'a·ble** *adj.* —**re·liev'er** *n.*

**re·lig·ion** (ri·lij'ən) *n.* 1 A belief in a divine or superhuman power or principle, usu. thought of as the creator of all things. 2 The manifestation of such a belief in worship, ritual, conduct, etc. 3 Any system of religious faith or practice: the Jewish *religion.* 4 The religious or monastic life: to enter *religion.* 5 Anything that elicits devotion, zeal, dedication, etc.: Politics is his *religion.* [< L *religio*]

**re·lig·ious** (ri·lij'əs) *adj.* 1 Feeling and manifesting religion; devout; pious. 2 Of or pertaining to religion: a *religious* teacher. 3 Faithful and strict in performance; conscientious: a *religious* loyalty. 4 Belonging to the monastic life. —*n. pl.* **·ious** A monk or nun. —**re·lig'ious·ly** *adv.* —**re·lig'ious·ness** *n.*

**re·lin·quish** (ri·ling'kwish) *v.t.* 1 To give up; abandon. 2 To renounce: to *relinquish* a claim. 3 To let go (a hold or something held). [< L *re-* back, from + *linquere* leave] —**re·lin'quish·er, re·lin'quish·ment** *n.*

**rel·ish** (rel'ish) *n.* 1 Appetite; appreciation; liking. 2 The flavor, esp. when agreeable, in food and drink. 3 The quality in anything that lends spice or zest: Danger gives *relish* to adventure. 4 A savory food or condiment served with other food to lend it flavor or zest. 5 A hint, trace, or suggestion of some quality or characteristic. —*v.t.* 1 To like; enjoy: to *relish* a dinner or a joke. —*v.i.* 2 To have an agreeable flavor; afford gratification. [< OF *relaisser* leave behind] —**rel'ish·a·ble** *adj.*

**re·luc·tance** (ri·luk'təns) *n.* 1 The state of being reluctant; unwillingness. 2 *Electr.* Capacity for opposing magnetic induction. Also **re·luc'tan·cy.**

**re·luc·tant** (ri·luk'tənt) *adj.* 1 Disinclined; unwilling. 2 Marked by unwillingness. [< L *reluctari* fight back] —**re·luc'tant·ly** *adv.*

**re·ly** (ri·lī') *v.i.* **·lied, ·ly·ing** To place trust or confidence: with *on* or *upon.* [< L *re-* again + *ligare* to bind] —**Syn.** lean, depend, count, bank (all with *on* or *upon*).

**re·main** (ri·mān') *v.i.* 1 To stay or be left behind after the removal, departure, or destruction of other persons or things. 2 To continue in one place, condition, or character. 3 To be left as something to be done, dealt with, etc. 4 To endure or last; abide. [< L *re-* back + *manere* stay, remain]

**re·main·der** (ri·mān'dər) *n.* 1 That which remains; something left over. 2 *Math.* a The result of subtraction; difference. b The difference of the product of the quotient and divisor subtracted from the dividend in division. 3 *Law* An estate in expectancy, but not in actual possession and enjoyment. 4 A copy or copies of a book remaining with a publisher after sales have fallen off or ceased. —*adj.* Left over; remaining. —*v.t.* To sell as a remainder (def. 4).

**re·mand** (ri·mand', -mänd') *v.t.* 1 To order or send back. 2 *Law* a To recommit to custody, as an accused person after a preliminary examination. b To send (a case) back to a lower court. —*n.* The act of remanding or the state of being remanded. [< L *re-* back + *mandare* to order] —**re·mand'ment** *n.*

**re·mark** (ri·märk') *n.* 1 A comment or saying; casual observation. 2 The act of noticing, observing, or perceiving. —*v.t.* 1 To say or write by way of comment. 2 To take particular notice of. —*v.i.* 3 To make remarks: with *on* or *upon.* [< F *re-* again + *marquer* to mark] —**re·mark'er** *n.*

**re·mark·a·ble** (ri·mär'kə·bəl) *adj.* 1 Worthy of special notice. 2 Extraordinary; unusual. —**re·mark'a·ble·ness** *n.* —**re·mark'a·bly** *adv.*

**re·me·di·al** (ri·mē'dē·əl) *adj.* Of the nature of or adapted to be used as a remedy: *remedial* measures. —**re·me'di·al·ly** *adv.*

**rem·e·dy** (rem'ə·dē) *v.t.* **·died, ·dy·ing** 1 To cure or heal, as by medicinal treatment. 2 To make right; repair; correct. 3 To overcome or remove (an evil or defect). —*n. pl.* **·dies** 1 A medicine or remedial treatment. 2 A means of correcting an evil, fault, etc. 3 *Law* A legal mode for enforcing a right or redressing or preventing a wrong. [< L *re-* thoroughly + *mederi* heal, restore]

**re·mem·ber** (ri·mem'bər) *v.t.* 1 To bring back or present again to the mind or memory; recall. 2 To keep in mind carefully, as for a purpose. 3 To bear in mind with affection, respect, awe, etc. 4 To reward (someone) with a gift, legacy, tip, etc. —*v.i.* 5 To bring something back to or keep something in the mind. 6 To have or use one's memory. —**remember (one) to** To inform a person of the regard of: *Remember* me *to* your wife. [< L *re-* again + *memorare* bring to mind] — **re·mem′ber·er** *n.*

**re·mem·brance** (ri·mem′brəns) *n.* 1 The act or power of remembering or the state of being remembered. 2 The period within which one can remember. 3 That which is remembered. 4 A gift, memento, or keepsake. 5 An observance in commemoration.

**re·mind** (ri·mīnd′) *v.t.* To bring to (someone's) mind; cause to remember. —**re·mind′er** *n.* —**re·mind′ful** *adj.*

**re·miss** (ri·mis′) *adj.* Lax or careless in matters requiring attention; negligent. [< L *remittere* send back, slacken] —**re·miss′ness** *n.*

**re·mit** (ri·mit′) *v.* ·mit·ted, ·mit·ting *v.t.* 1 To send, as money in payment for goods; transmit. 2 To refrain from exacting or inflicting, as a penalty. 3 To pardon; forgive. 4 To slacken; relax, as vigilance. 5 To restore; replace. 6 To put off; postpone. 7 *Law* To refer (a legal proceeding) to a lower court for further consideration. —*v.i.* 8 To send money, as in payment. 9 To diminish; abate. [< L *re-* back + *mittere* send] —**re·mit′ter** or **re·mit′tor** *n.*

**re·mit·tance** (ri·mit′ns) *n.* 1 The act of remitting money or credit. 2 That which is remitted, as money.

**rem·nant** (rem′nənt) *n.* 1 That which remains of anything. 2 A piece of cloth, etc., left over after the last cutting. 3 A remaining trace or survival of anything: a *remnant* of faith. 4 A small remaining number or quantity, as of people. —*adj.* Remaining. [< OF *remaindre* remain]

**re·mod·el** (rē·mod′l) *v.t.* ·eled or ·elled, ·el·ing or ·el·ling 1 To model again. 2 To make over or anew.

**re·mon·strance** (ri·mon′strəns) *n.* The act of an instance of remonstrating; protest.

**re·mon·strate** (ri·mon′strāt) *v.* ·strat·ed, ·strat·ing *v.t.* 1 To say or plead in protest or opposition. —*v.i.* 2 To protest; object. [< L *re-* again + *monstrare* show] —**re·mon·stra·tion** (rē′mon·strā′shən, rem′ən-), **re·mon′stra′tor** *n.* —**re·mon′stra·tive** (-strə·tiv) *adj.*

**re·morse** (ri·môrs′) *n.* The keen or hopeless anguish caused by a sense of guilt; distressing self-reproach. [< LL *remorsus* a biting back] —**re·morse′ful** *adj.* —**re·morse′ful·ly** *adv.* —**re·morse′ful·ness** *n.*

**re·mote** (ri·mōt′) *adj.* 1 Located far from a specified place. 2 Removed far from pre-

sent time. 3 Having slight bearing on or connection with: a problem *remote* from our discussion. 4 Distant in relation: a *remote* cousin. 5 Not obvious; faint; slight: a *remote* likeness. 6 Cold; aloof: a *remote* manner. [< L *remotus,* p.p. of *removere* remove] —**re·mote′ly** *adv.* —**re·mote′ness** *n.*

**re·mov·al** (ri·mōō′vəl) *n.* 1 The act of removing or the state of being removed. 2 Dismissal, as from office. 3 Changing of place, esp. of habitation.

**re·move** (ri·mōōv′) *v.* ·moved, ·mov·ing *v.t.* 1 To take or move away from one place to another. 2 To take off. 3 To get rid of; do away with: to *remove* abuses. 4 To kill. 5 To displace or dismiss, as from office. 6 To take out; extract: with *from.* —*v.i.* 7 To change one's place of residence or business. 8 To go away; depart. —*n.* 1 The act of removing. 2 The distance or degree of difference between things: He is only one *remove* from a fool. [< L *re-* again + *movere* move] —**re·mov′er** *n.*

**re·mu·ner·ate** (ri·myōō′nə·rāt) *v.t.* ·at·ed, ·at·ing 1 To pay (a person) for something, as for services, losses, etc. 2 To compensate or reward for (work, diligence, etc.). [< L *remunerari*] —**re·mu′ner·a′tion,** **re·mu′ner·a′tor** *n.* —**re·mu′ner·a·tive** (-nər·ə·tiv, -nə·rā′tiv) *adj.* —**re·mu′ner·a·tive·ly** *adv.*

**rend** (rend) *v.* rent or rend·ed, rend·ing *v.t.* 1 To tear apart forcibly. 2 To pull or remove forcibly: with *away, from, off,* etc. 3 To pass through (the air) violently and noisily. 4 To distress (the heart, etc.), as with grief or despair. —*v.i.* 5 To split; part. [< OE *rendan* tear, cut down] —**rend′er** *n.*

**ren·der** (ren′dər) *v.t.* 1 To give, present, or submit for action, approval, payment, etc. 2 To provide or furnish; give: to *render* aid. 3 To give as due: to *render* obedience. 4 To perform; do: to *render* great service. 5 To give or state formally. 6 To give by way of requital or retribution: to *render* good for evil. 7 To represent or depict, as in music or painting. 8 To cause to be: to *render* someone helpless. 9 To express in another language; translate. 10 To melt and clarify, as lard. 11 To give back; return: often with *back.* 12 To surrender; give up. [< L *reddere* give back] —**ren′der·a·ble** *adj.* —**ren′der·er** *n.*

**ren·dez·vous** (rän′dā·vōō, -də-) *n. pl.* ·vous (-vōōz) 1 An appointed place of meeting. 2 A meeting or an appointment to meet. —*v.t. & v.i.* ·voused (-vōōd), ·vous·ing (-vōō′ing)

To assemble or cause to assemble at a certain place or time. [< F *rendez-vous*, lit., betake yourself]

**ren·di·tion** (ren·dish′ən) *n.* 1 A version or interpretation of a text. 2 A performance or interpretation, as of a musical composition, role, etc. 3 The act of rendering. [< OF *rendre* render]

**ren·e·gade** (ren′ə·gād) *n.* 1 One who abandons a previous loyalty, as to a religion, political party, etc. 2 One who gives up conventional or lawful behavior. —*adj.* Traitorous. [< Sp. *renegar* deny]

**re·new** (ri·n(y)ōō′) *v.t.* 1 To make new or as if new again. 2 To begin again; resume. 3 To repeat: to *renew* an oath. 4 To regain (vigor, strength, etc.). 5 To cause to continue in effect; extend: to *renew* a subscription. 6 To revive; reestablish. 7 To replenish or replace, as provisions. —*v.i.* 8 To become new again. 9 To begin or commence again. [< RE- + NEW] —re·new′a·ble *adj.* —re·new′al, re·new′er *n.* —re·new′ed·ly *adv.*

**re·nounce** (ri·nouns′) *v.t.* ·nounced, ·nounc·ing 1 To give up, esp. by formal statement. 2 To disown; repudiate. [< L *renuntiare* protest against] —re·nounce′ment, re·nounc′er *n.* —Syn. 1 abjure, disavow, disclaim, forswear.

**ren·o·vate** (ren′ə·vāt) *v.t.* ·vat·ed, ·vat·ing 1 To make as good as new, as by repairing, cleaning, etc. 2 To renew; refresh; reinvigorate. [< L *re-* again + *novare* make new] —ren′o·va′tion, ren′o·va′tor *n.*

**rent**[1] (rent) *n.* Compensation, esp. payment in money, made by a tenant to a landlord or owner for the use of property, as land, a house, etc., usu. due at specified intervals. —**for rent** Available in return for a rent. —*v.t.* 1 To obtain the temporary possession and use of in return for paying rent. 2 To grant the temporary use of for a rent. —*v.i.* 3 To be let for rent. [< L *reddita* what is given back or paid] —rent′a·ble *adj.* —rent′er *n.*

**rent**[2] (rent) A *p.t.* & *p.p.* of REND. *n.* 1 A hole or slit made by rending or tearing. 2 A violent separation; schism.

**rent·al** (ren′təl) *n.* 1 An amount paid or due to be paid as rent. 2 The revenue derived from rented property. 3 The act of renting. —*adj.* 1 Of or pertaining to rent. 2 Engaged in the business of renting or supervising rents.

**re·pair** (ri·pâr′) *v.t.* 1 To restore to sound or good condition after damage, injury, decay,

etc. 2 To make up, as a loss; compensate for. —*n.* 1 The act or instance of repairing. 2 Condition after use or after repairing: in good *repair*. [< L *re-* again + *parare* prepare] —re·pair′er *n.*

**rep·a·ra·tion** (rep′ə·rā′shən) *n.* 1 The act of making amends; atonement. 2 That which is done or paid by way of making amends. 3 *pl.* Indemnities paid by defeated countries for acts of war. 4 The act of repairing, or the state of being repaired. —re·par·a·tive (ri·par′ə·tiv) *adj.*

**rep·ar·tee** (rep′är·tē′, -ər-, -tā′) *n.* 1 Conversation marked by quick and witty replies. 2 Skill in such conversation. 3 A witty reply. [< F *re-* again + *partir* depart]

**re·past** (ri·past′, -päst′, rē′past) *n.* Food taken at a meal; a meal. [< LL *repascere* feed again]

**re·peal** (ri·pēl′) *v.t.* To withdraw the authority to effect; rescind; revoke. —*n.* The act of repealing; revocation. [< OF *rapeler* recall] —re·peal′a·ble *adj.* —re·peal′er *n.*

**re·peat** (ri·pēt′) *v.t.* 1 To say again; reiterate. 2 To recite from memory. 3 To say (what another has just said). 4 To tell, as a secret, to another. 5 To do, make, or experience again. —*v.i.* 6 To say or do something again. 7 To vote more than once at the same election. —*n.* 1 The act of repeating. 2 *Music* a A sign indicating that a passage is to be repeated. b A passage meant to be repeated. [< L *repetere* do or say again] —re·peat′a·ble *adj.*

**re·pent** (ri·pent′) *v.i.* 1 To feel remorse or regret, as for something done or undone; be contrite. 2 To change one's mind concerning past action: with *of.* —*v.t.* 3 To feel remorse or regret for (an action, sin, etc.). [< L *re-* again + *poenitere* cause to repent] —re·pent′er *n.*

**re·pen·tance** (ri·pen′təns) *n.* The act of repenting; sorrow for having done wrong. —re·pen′tant *adj.* —re·pen′tant·ly *adv.*

**rep·er·toire** (rep′ər·twär) *n.* 1 A list of works, as of music or drama, that a company or person is prepared to perform. 2 Such works collectively. 3 The aggregate of devices, methods, etc., used in a particular line of activity: the teacher's *repertoire* of visual aids. [< LL *repertorium* inventory]

**rep·e·ti·tion** (rep′ə·tish′ən) *n.* 1 The doing, making, or saying of something again. 2 That which is repeated; a copy. —re·pet·i·tive (ri·pet′ə·tiv) *adj.* —re·pet′i·tive·ly *adv.*

**re·place** (ri·plās′) *v.t.* ·placed, ·plac·ing 1 To

put back in place. 2 To take or fill the place of; supersede. 3 To refund; repay. —re·place/a·ble adj. —re·plac/er n.

re·place·ment (ri·plās/mənt) n. 1 The act of replacing, or the state of being replaced. 2 Something used to replace, as a substitute.

re·plen·ish (ri·plen/ish) v.t. 1 To fill again. 2 To bring back to fullness or completeness, as diminished supplies. [< L re- again + plenus full] —re·plen/ish·er, re·plen/ish·ment n.

re·plete (ri·plēt/) adj. 1 Full to the uttermost. 2 Gorged with food or drink; sated. 3 Abundantly supplied or stocked. [< L repletus, p.p. of replere fill again] —re·ple/tion, re·plete/ness n.

re·ply (ri·plī/) v. ·plied, ·ply·ing v.i. 1 To give an answer. 2 To respond by some act, gesture, etc. 3 To echo. 4 Law To file a pleading in answer to the statement of the defense. —v.t. 5 To say in answer: She replied that she would do it. —n. pl. ·plies Something said, written, or done by way of answer. [< L replicare fold back, make a reply] —re·pli/er n.

re·port (ri·pôrt/, -pōrt/) v.t. 1 To make or give an account of; relate, as information obtained by investigation. 2 To bear back or repeat to another, as an answer. 3 To complain about, esp. to the authorities. 4 To state the result of consideration concerning: The committee reported the bill. —v.i. 5 To make a report. 6 To act as a reporter. 7 To present oneself, as for duty. —n. 1 That which is reported. 2 A formal statement of the result of an investigation. 3 Common talk; rumor. 4 Fame, reputation, or character. 5 A record of the transactions of a deliberative body. 6 An account prepared for publication in the press. 7 An explosive sound: the report of a gun. [< L re- back + portare carry] —re·port/a·ble adj. —Syn. v. 1 describe, record, transcribe. n. 1, 2, 5, 6 account, statement, announcement. 3 gossip, hearsay.

re·port·er (ri·pôr/tər, -pōr/-) n. 1 One who reports. 2 One employed to gather and report news for publication or broadcasting. —rep·or·to·ri·al (rep/ər·tôr/ē·əl, -tō/rē-) adj.

re·pose (ri·pōz/) n. 1 The state of being at rest. 2 Sleep. 3 Freedom from excitement or anxiety; composure. 4 Dignified calmness; serenity; peacefulness. —v. ·posed, ·pos·ing v.t. 1 To lay or place in a position of rest. —v.i. 2 To lie at rest. 3 To lie in death. 4 To

rely; depend: with on, upon, or in. [< LL re- again + pausare to pause] —re· pose/ful adj. —re·pose/ful·ly adv.

re·pos·i·to·ry (ri·poz/ə·tôr/ē, -tō/rē) n. pl. ·ries 1 A place in which goods may be stored; a depository. 2 Anything considered as a place of storage or assembly: a repository of Indian lore. 3 A person to whom a secret is entrusted. [< L repositorium]

rep·re·sent (rep/ri·zent/) v.t. 1 To serve as the symbol, expression, or designation of; symbolize: The dove represents peace. 2 To serve as an example, specimen, type, etc., of; typify: They represent the best in America. 3 To set forth a likeness or image of; depict; portray. 4 To serve as or be the delegate, agent, etc., of, as by legal authority or by election. 5 To act the part of; impersonate. 6 To bring before the mind; present clearly: Goya etchings that represent the horrors of war. 7 To set forth in words, esp. in a forceful and persuasive manner. 8 To describe as being of a specified character or condition: to represent a signature as authentic. [< L re- again + praesentare to present]

rep·re·sen·ta·tion (rep/ri·zen·tā/shən) n. 1 The act of representing, or the state of being represented. 2 A likeness or model. 3 A statement usu. purporting to be descriptive that represents a point of view and is intended to influence judgment. 4 A dramatic performance. 5 Representatives collectively.

rep·re·sen·ta·tive (rep/ri·zen/tə·tiv) adj. 1 Typifying a group or class. 2 Acting or having the power to act as an agent. 3 Made up of representatives. 4 Based on the political principle of representation. 5 Presenting, portraying, or representing. —n. 1 One who or that which is typical of a group or class. 2 One who is authorized as an agent or delegate. 3 Often cap. A member of a legislative body, esp., in the U.S., a member of the lower house of Congress or of a state legislature. —rep/re·sen/ta·tive·ly adv. —rep/re·sen/ta·tive·ness n.

re·press (ri·pres/) v.t. 1 To keep under restraint or control. 2 To block the expression of: to repress a groan. 3 To put down; quell, as a rebellion. [< L repressus, p.p. of reprimere press back] —re·press/er, re·pres/sive·ness n. —re·press/i·ble, re·pres/sive adj. —re·pres/sive·ly adv. —Syn. 1 curb, rein. 2 suppress, hold in.

re·pres·sion (ri·presh/ən) n. 1 The act of repressing, or the condition of being repressed. 2 *Psychoanal.* The exclusion from consciousness of painful desires, memories, etc., and consequent manifestation through the unconscious.

**re·prieve** (ri·prēv′) *v.t.* ·prieved, ·priev·ing 1 To suspend temporarily the execution of a sentence upon. 2 To relieve for a time from suffering or trouble. —*n.* 1 The temporary suspension of a sentence. 2 Temporary relief or cessation of pain; respite. [< F *reprendre* take back]

**rep·ri·mand** (rep′rə·mand) *v.t.* To reprove sharply or formally. —*n.* Severe reproof or formal censure. [< L *reprimendus* to be repressed]

**re·pri·sal** (ri·prī′zəl) *n.* Any action done in retaliation for harm or injuries received, esp. an action involving the use of force and sanctioned by a government or political group. [< OF *reprendre* take back]

**re·proach** (ri·prōch′) *v.t.* To charge with or blame for something wrong; rebuke. —*n.* 1 The act of or an expression of reproaching; censure; reproof. 2 A cause of blame or disgrace. 3 Disgrace; discredit. [< OF *reprochier*] —**re·proach′ful** *adj.* —**re·proach′ful·ly** *adv.* —**re·proach′ful·ness** *n.*

**rep·ro·bate** (rep′rə·bāt) *adj.* 1 Utterly depraved; profligate; corrupt. 2 *Theol.* Abandoned in sin; condemned. —*n.* One who is reprobate. —*v.t.* ·bat·ed, ·bat·ing 1 To disapprove of heartily; condemn. 2 *Theol.* To abandon to damnation. [< LL *reprobare* reprove] —**rep′ro·ba′tion** *n.* —**rep′ro·ba′tive** *adj.*

**re·pro·duce** (rē′prə·d<sup>y</sup>ōōs′) *v.* ·duced, ·duc·ing *v.t.* 1 To make a copy or image of. 2 To bring (offspring) into existence by sexual or asexual generation. 3 To replace (a lost part or organ) by regeneration. 4 To cause the reproduction of (plant life, etc.). 5 To produce again. 6 To recall to the mind; recreate mentally. —*v.i.* 7 To produce offspring. 8 To undergo copying, reproduction, etc. —**re′pro·duc′er** *n.* —**re′pro·duc′i·ble** *adj.*

**re·pro·duc·tion** (rē′prə·duk′shən) *n.* 1 The act or process of reproducing. 2 Any process by which animals or plants give rise to new organisms. 3 Something reproduced, as a photocopy. —**re′pro·duc′tive** *adj.* —**re′pro·duc′tive·ly** *adv.* —**re′pro·duc′tive·ness** *n.*

**re·prove** (ri·prōōv′) *v.t.* ·proved, ·prov·ing 1 To censure, as for a fault; rebuke. 2 To express disapproval of (an act). [< L *re-* again

+ *probare* to test] —**re·prov′er** *n.* —**re·prov′ing·ly** *adv.* —**Syn.** 1 admonish, chasten, chide, reproach, scold.

**rep·tile** (rep′til, -til) *n.* 1 Any of a class of coldblooded, air-breathing vertebrates having a scaly skin, as crocodiles, lizards, snakes, turtles, etc. 2 A groveling, abject person. —*adj.* 1 Of, like, or characteristic of a reptile. 2 Groveling, sly, base, etc. [< L *reptus,* p.p. of *repere* creep] —**rep·til·i·an** (rep·til′ē·ən) *adj., n.*

**re·pub·lic** (ri·pub′lik) *n.* 1 A state in which the sovereignty resides in the people entitled to vote for officers who represent them in governing. 2 This form of government. [< L *res* thing + *publicus* public]

**re·pub·li·can** (ri·pub′li·kən) *adj.* Pertaining to, of the nature of, or suitable for a republic. —*n.* An advocate of a republican form of government. —**re·pub′li·can·ism** *n.*

**re·pu·di·ate** (re·pyōō′dē·āt) *v.t.* ·at·ed, ·at·ing 1 To refuse to accept as valid, true, or authorized; reject. 2 To refuse to acknowledge or pay. 3 To cast off; disown, as a son. [< L *repudium* divorce] —**re·pu′di·a′tion, re·pu′di·a′tor** *n.*

**re·pug·nance** (ri·pug′nəns) *n.* 1 A feeling of strong distaste or aversion. 2 Contradiction; inconsistency.

**re·pug·nant** (ri·pug′nənt) *adj.* 1 Offensive to taste or feeling; exciting aversion. 2 Contradictory; inconsistent. [< L *re* back + *pugnare* to fight] —**re·pug′nant·ly** *adv.*

**re·pulse** (ri·puls′) *v.t.* ·pulsed, ·puls·ing 1 To drive back; repel, as an attacking force. 2 To repel by coldness, discourtesy, etc.; rebuff. 3 To excite disgust in. —*n.* 1 The act of repulsing, or the state of being repulsed. 2 Rejection; refusal. [< L *repulsus,* p.p. of *repellere* repel] —**re·puls′er** *n.*

**re·pul·sion** (ri·pul′shən) *n.* 1 The act of repelling, or the state of being repelled. 2 Aversion; repugnance. 3 *Physics* The mutual action of two bodies that tends to drive them apart.

**re·pul·sive** (ri·pul′siv) *adj.* 1 Exciting strong feelings of dislike or disgust; offensive. 2 Such as to discourage approach; forbidding. 3 Acting to repulse. —**re·pul′sive·ly** *adv.* —**re·pul′sive·ness** *n.*

**rep·u·ta·tion** (rep′yə·tā′shən) *n.* 1 The general estimation in which a person or thing is held by others, either good or bad. 2 High regard or esteem. 3 A particular credit ascribed to a person or thing: a *reputation* for honesty. [< L *reputare* be reputed.]

**re·pute** (ri·pyōōt′) *v.t.* ·put·ed, ·put·ing To regard or consider: usu. in the passive: *reputed* to be clever. —*n.* REPUTATION (defs. 1 & 2). [< L *re-* again + *putare* think, count]

**re·quest** (ri·kwest′) *v.t.* 1 To express a desire for, esp. politely. 2 To ask a favor of. —*n.* 1 The act of requesting; entreaty; petition. 2 That which is requested, as a favor. 3 The state of being requested: in *request.* [< L *requisitus*, p.p. of *requirere* seek again]

**re·qui·em** (rek′wē·əm, rē′kwē-) *n.* 1 *Often cap.* Any musical composition or service for the dead. 2 *Often cap.* A musical setting for such a service. [< L *Requiem* rest, the first word of a Roman Catholic mass for the dead]

**re·quire** (ri·kwīr′) *v.* ·quired, ·quir·ing *v.t.* 1 To have need of; find necessary. 2 To call for, demand: Hunting *requires* patience. 3 To insist upon: to *require* absolute silence. 4 To command; order. —*v.i.* 5 To make a demand or request. [< L *re-* again + *quaerere* ask, seek] —**re·quir′er** *n.*

**re·quire·ment** (ri·kwīr′mənt) *n.* 1 That which is required, as to satisfy a condition; a requisite. 2 A need or necessity.

**req·ui·site** (rek′wə·zit) *adj.* Required by the nature of things or by circumstances; indispensable. —*n.* That which cannot be dispensed with. —**req′ui·site·ly** *adv.* —**req′ui·site·ness** *n.*

**req·ui·si·tion** (rek′wə·zish′ən) *n.* 1 A formal request, as for supplies or equipment. 2 The act of requiring or demanding, as that something be supplied. 3 The state of being required. —*v.t.* To make a requisition for or to.

**re·scind** (ri·sind′) *v.t.* To cancel or make void, as an order or an act. [< L *re-* back + *scindere* to cut] —**re·scind′ment, re·scind′er** *n.*

**res·cue** (res′kyōō) *v.t.* ·cued, ·cu·ing 1 To save or free from danger, captivity, evil, etc. 2 *Law* To take or remove forcibly from the custody of the law. —*n.* The act of rescuing. [< L *re-* again + *excutere* shake off] —**res′cu·er** *n.*

**re·search** (ri·sûrch′, rē′sûrch) *n.* Studious, systematic investigation or inquiry to ascertain, uncover, or assemble facts, used as a basis for conclusions or the formulation of theory. —*v.t.* 1 To do research on or for: to *research* an article. —*v.i.* 2 To do re-

search; investigate. [< F *recherche*] —**re·search′er** *n.*

**re·sem·blance** (ri·zem′bləns) *n.* 1 The quality of similarlity in nature, appearance, etc.; likeness. 2 A point or degree of similarity. 3 That which resembles a person or thing; semblance.

**re·sem·ble** (ri·zem′bəl) *v.t.* ·bled, ·bling To be similar to in appearance, quality, or character. [< OF *re-* again + *sembler* seem]

**re·sent** (ri·zent′) *v.t.* To be indignant at, as an injury or insult. [< L *re-* again + *sentire* feel] —**re·sent′ful** *adj.* —**re·sent′ful·ly** *adv.* —**re·sent′ful·ness** *n.*

**re·sent·ment** (ri·zent′mənt) *n.* Anger and ill will caused by a feeling of injury or mistreatment.

**res·er·va·tion** (rez′ər·vā′shən) *n.* 1 A feeling of doubt or skepticism, expressed or unexpressed. 2 A qualification; condition; limitation. 3 An agreement to hold something back, as a hotel room, restaurant table, etc., for use at a particular time; also, a record of such an agreement. 4 The act of reserving. 5 A tract of public land set aside for some special purpose, as for the use of Indians or for the preservation of wildlife.

**re·serve** (ri·zûrv′) *v.t.* ·served, ·serv·ing. 1 To hold back or set aside for special or future use. 2 To arrange for ahead of time; have set aside for one's use. 3 To hold back or delay the determination or disclosure of: to *reserve* judgment. 4 To keep as one's own; retain: to *reserve* the right to quit. —*n.* 1 Something stored up for future use or set aside for a particular purpose. 2 A restrained quality of character or manner; reluctance to divulge one's feelings, thoughts, etc. 3 *Usu. pl.* a A military force held back from active duty to meet possible emergencies. b Members or units of such a force. 4 A substitute player on an athletic team. 5 Funds held back from investment, as in a bank, to meet regular demands. 6 The act of reserving; stint; qualification: without *reserve.* —**in reserve** Subject to or held for future use when needed. —*adj.* Constituting a reserve: a *reserve* supply. [< L *re-* back + *servare* keep] —**re·serv′er** *n.* —**Syn.** *n.* 2 reticence, diffidence, aloofness, modesty, restraint.

**res·er·voir** (rez′ər·vwär, -vwôr -vôr) *n.* 1 A place where some material is stored for use, esp. a lake, usu. artificial, for collecting and storing water. 2 A receptacle for a fluid. 3 An extra supply; store.

**re·side** (ri·zīd′) v.i. **·sid·ed, ·sid·ing** 1 To dwell for a considerable time; live. 2 To exist as an attribute or quality: with *in.* 3 To be vested: with *in.* [< L *residere* sit back]

**res·i·dence** (rez′ə·dəns) n. 1 The place or the house where one resides. 2 The act of residing. 3 The length of time one resides in a place. 4 The act or fact of residing. 5 The condition of residing in a particular place to perform certain duties or to pursue studies, often for a specified length of time.

**res·i·dent** (rez′ə·dənt) n. 1 One who resides or dwells in a place. 2 A physician engaged in residency. 3 A diplomatic representative residing at a foreign seat of government. — *adj.* 1 Having a residence; residing. 2 Living in a place in connection with one's official work. 3 Not migratory: said of certain birds.

**re·sid·u·al** (ri·zij′ŏŏ·əl) adj. 1 Pertaining to or having the nature of a residue or remainder. 2 Left over from a total, as after subtraction. —n. 1 That which is left over from a total, as after subtraction. 2 *Often pl.* A payment made to a performer for each rerun of taped or filmed TV material in which he or she has appeared. —**re·sid′u·al·ly** adv.

**res·i·due** (rez′ə·dŏō) n. 1 A remainder after a part has been separated or removed. 2 *Chem.* Matter left unaffected after combustion, distillation, evaporation, etc. 3 *Law* That portion of an estate which remains after all charges, debts, and particular bequests have been satisfied. [< L *residuus* remaining]

**re·sign** (ri·zīn′) v.t. 1 To give up, as a position, office, or trust. 2 To relinquish (a privilege, claim, etc.). 3 To give over (oneself, one's mind, etc.), as to fate or domination. —v.i. 4 To resign a position, etc. [< OF < L *re-* back + *signare* to sign] —**re·sign′er** n.

**res·ig·na·tion** (rez′ig·nā′shən) n. 1 The act of resigning. 2 A formal notice of resigning. 3 The quality of being submissive; unresisting acquiescence.

**res·in** (rez′in) n. 1 A solid or semisolid, usu. translucent substance exuded from certain plants, used in varnishes, plastics, etc. 2 Any of various substances resembling this made by chemical synthesis. 3 ROSIN. —v.t. To apply resin to. [< Gk. *rhētinē*] —**res·i·na·ceous** (rez′ə·nā′shəs), **res′in·ous** adj.

**re·sist** (ri·zist′) v.t. 1 To stay the effect of; withstand; hold off: Steel *resists* corrosion. 2 To fight or struggle against; seek to foil or frustrate: to *resist* arrest; to *resist* temptation. —v.i. 3 To offer opposition. [< L *re-* back + *sistere*, causative of *stare* stand] — **re·sist′er, re·sist′i·bil′i·ty** n. —**re·sist′i·ble, re·sis′tive** adj. —**re·sist′i·bly** adv.

**re·sis·tance** (ri·zis′təns) n. 1 The act of resisting. 2 Any force tending to hinder motion. 3 The capacity of an organism to ward off the effects of potentially harmful substances, as toxins. 4 *Electr.* The opposition of a body to the passage through it of an electric current. 5 The underground and guerrilla movement in a conquered country opposing the occupying power. — **re·sis′tant** adj.

**res·o·lute** (rez′ə·lŏōt) adj. Having a fixed purpose; determined. [< L *resolutus*, p.p. of *resolvere* to resolve] —**res′o·lute·ly** adv. — **res′o·lute·ness** n. —Syn. steady, constant, firm, decisive.

**res·o·lu·tion** (rez′ə·lŏō′shən) n. 1 The act of resolving or of reducing to a simpler form. 2 The making of a resolve. 3 The purpose or course resolved upon. 4 Firmness of purpose. 5 An outcome or result that serves to settle a problem, uncertainty, or conflict. 6 A statement expressing the intention or judgment of an assembly or group. 7 *Music* a The conventional replacement of a dissonant tone, chord, etc., by one that is consonant. b The tone or chord replacing the dissonant one. 8 The capacity of a telescope, microscope, etc., to give separate images of objects close together.

**re·solve** (ri·zolv′) v. **·solved, ·solv·ing** v.t. 1 To decide; determine (to do something). 2 To cause to decide or determine. 3 To separate or break down into constituent parts; analyze. 4 To clear away or settle, as a problem, uncertainty, or conflict; explain or solve. 5 To state or decide by vote. 6 *Music* To cause (a dissonant tone, chord, etc.) to undergo resolution. 7 To make distinguishable, as with a telescope or microscope. —v.i. 8 To make up one's mind: with *on* or *upon.* 9 To become separated into constituent parts. 10 *Music* To undergo resolution. —n. 1 Fixity of purpose; determination. 2 Something resolved upon; a decision. 3 A formal expression of the intention or judgment of an assembly or group. [< L *resolvere* loosen again] —**re·solv′a·ble** adj. —**re·solv′er** n.

**res·o·nant** (rez′ə·nənt) adj. 1 Having the quality of prolonging and amplifying sound by reverberation; producing resonance. 2 Resounding; displaying resonance. 3 Full of or characterized by resonance: a *resonant* voice. [< L *resonare* resound, echo] —**res′·o·nant·ly** *adv.*

**re·sort** (rǐ·zôrt′) *v.i.* 1 To go frequently or habitually; repair. 2 To have recourse: with *to*. —*n.* 1 A hotel or other place that provides recreational facilities and sometimes entertainment, esp. for those on vacation. 2 The use of something as a means; a recourse; refuge. 3 A person looked to for help. 4 A place frequented regularly. [< OF *re-* again + *sortir* go out] —**re·sort′er** *n.*

**re·source** (rē′sôrs, -sōrs, -zôrs, -zōrs, rǐ·sôrs′, -sōrs′, -zôrs′, -zōrs′) *n.* 1 *Usu. pl.* That which can be drawn upon as a means of help or support. 2 *Usu. pl.* Natural advantages, esp. of a country, as forests, oil deposits, etc. 3 *pl.* Available wealth or property. 4 Skill or ingenuity in meeting any situation. 5 Any way or method of coping with a difficult situation. [< L *re-* back + *surgere* to rise, surge]

**re·spect** (rǐ·spekt′) *v.t.* 1 To have deferential regard for; esteem. 2 To treat with propriety or consideration. 3 To avoid intruding upon; regard as inviolable. 4 To have reference to; concern. —*n.* 1 A high regard for and appreciation of worth; esteem. 2 Due regard or consideration: *respect* for the law. 3 *pl.* Expressions of consideration; compliments: to pay one's *respects*. 4 The condition of being honored or respected. 5 A specific aspect or detail: In some *respects* the plan is impractical. 6 Reference or relation: usu. with *to*: with *respect* to profits. [< L *respectus*, p.p. of *respicere* look back, consider] —**re·spect′er** *n.*

**re·spect·a·ble** (rǐ·spek′tə·bəl) *adj.* 1 Deserving of respect. 2 Conventionally correct; socially acceptable. 3 Having a good appearance; presentable. 4 Moderate in quality, size, or amount; fair: a *respectable* talent. —**re·spect′a·bil′i·ty, re·spect′a·ble·ness** *n.* —**re·spect′a·bly** *adv.*

**re·spec·tive** (rǐ·spek′tiv) *adj.* Relating separately to each of those under consideration; several.

**res·pi·ra·tion** (res′pə·rā′shən) *n.* 1 The act of inhaling air and expelling it; breathing. 2 The process by which an organism takes in and uses oxygen and gives off carbon dioxide and other waste products. —**re·spir·a·to·ry** (res′pər·ə·tôr′ē, rǐ·spīr′ə·tôr′ē) *adj.*

**res·pi·ra·tor** (res′pə·rā′tər) *n.* 1 A screen, as of fine gauze, worn over the mouth or nose, as a protection against dust, etc. 2 An apparatus for artificial respiration.

**res·pite** (res′pǐt) *n.* 1 Postponement; delay. 2 Temporary relief from labor or effort; an interval of rest. [< Med. L *respectus* delay]

**re·spond** (rǐ·spond′) *v.i.* 1 To give an answer; reply. 2 To act in reply or return. 3 To react favorably: to *respond* to treatment. —*v.t.* 4 To say in answer; reply. [< L *re-* back + *spondere* to pledge] —**re·spond′er** *n.*

**re·spon·dent** (rǐ·spon′dənt) *n.* 1 One who responds or answers. 2 *Law* The party called upon to answer an appeal or petition; a defendant. —**re·spon′dence, re·spon′den·cy** *n.*

**re·sponse** (rǐ·spons′) *n.* 1 Words or acts called forth as a reaction; an answer or reply. 2 *Eccl.* A portion of a church service said or sung by the congregation in reply to the officiating priest. 3 *Biol.* Any reaction resulting from a stimulus. 4 The action of a physical system when energized or disturbed.

**re·spon·si·bil·i·ty** (rǐ·spon′sə·bil′ə·tē) *n. pl.* **·ties** 1 The state of being responsible or accountable. 2 That for which one is responsible; a duty or trust. Also **re·spon′si·ble·ness.**

**re·spon·si·ble** (rǐ·spon′sə·bəl) *adj.* 1 Subject to being called upon to account or answer for something; accountable. 2 Able to discriminate between right and wrong. 3 Able to account or answer for something; able to meet one's obligations. 4 Being the cause: Rain was *responsible* for the delay. —**re·spon′si·bly** *adv.*

**re·spon·sive** (rǐ·spon′siv) *adj.* 1 Constituting a response. 2 Inclined to react with sympathy or understanding. 3 Containing responses. —**re·spon′sive·ly** *adv.* —**re·spon′sive·ness** *n.*

**rest** (rest) *n.* That which remains or is left over. —**the rest** That or those which remain; the remainder; the others. —*v.i.* To be and remain: *Rest* content. [< L *restare* stop, stand]

**res·tau·rant** (res′tə·rənt, -tränt, -tər·ənt) *n.* A place where meals are prepared for sale and served on the premises. [F, lit., restoring]

**res·ti·tu·tion** (res′tə·tʸoo′shən) *n.* 1 The act of restoring something that has been taken away or lost. 2 Restoration or return to a rightful owner. 3 The act of making good for injury or loss. [< L *restituere* restore]

**res·to·ra·tion** (res′tə·rā′shən) *n.* 1 The act of restoring, or the state of being restored. 2 The bringing back to an original or earlier condition, as a work of art or a building;

also, the object so restored. —**the Restora-tion 1** The return of Charles II to the English throne in 1660. **2** The period following his return up to the revolution in 1688.

**re·store** (ri·stôr′, -stōr′) *v.t.* **·stored, ·stor·ing 1** To bring into existence or effect again: to *restore* peace. **2** To bring back to a former or original condition, as a work of art or a building. **3** To put back in a former place or position; reinstate. **4** To bring back to health and vigor. **5** To give back (something lost or taken away); return. [< L *restaurare*] —**re·stor′er** *n.*

**re·strain** (ri·strān′) *v.t.* **1** To hold back from acting, proceeding, or advancing. **2** To restrict or limit. **3** To deprive of liberty, as by placing in a prison. [< L *re*- back + *stringere* draw tight] —**re·strain′ed·ly** (-strān′id·lē) *adv.* —**re·strain′er** *n.*

**re·straint** (ri·strānt′) *n.* **1** The act of restraining, or the state of being restrained. **2** Something that restrains, as a harness or similar device. **3** A restriction on conduct; stricture. **4** Control over the display of one's emotions, opinions, etc.; self-control.

**re·strict** (ri·strikt′) *v.t.* To hold or keep within limits or bounds; confine. [< L *re*- back + *stringere* draw tight]

**re·stric·tion** (ri·strik′shən) *n.* **1** The act of restricting, or the state of being restricted. **2** That which restricts; a limitation or restraint.

**re·sult** (ri·zult′) *n.* **1** The outcome of an action, course, or process. **2** A quantity or value derived by calculation. —*v.i.* **1** To be a result or outcome; follow: with *from.* **2** To have as a consequence; end: with *in.* [< L *resultare* spring back]

**re·sul·tant** (ri·zul′tənt) *adj.* Arising or following as a result. —*n.* **1** That which results; a consequence. **2** *Physics* A vector representing the sum of two or more other vectors.

**re·sume** (ri·zōōm′) *v.* **·sumed, ·sum·ing** *v.t.* **1** To begin again after an interruption. **2** To take or occupy again: *Resume* your places. —*v.i.* **3** To continue after an interruption. [< L *resumere* take up again] —**re·sum′er** *n.*

**rés·u·mé** (rez′ōō·mā, rez′ōō·mā′) *n.* A summary, as of one's employment record, education, etc., used in applying for a new position. **Also res·u·mé′, res·u·me′.** [F]

**re·sump·tion** (ri·zump′shən) *n.* The act of resuming; a beginning again.

**re·tail** (rē′tāl) *n.* The selling of goods in small quantities directly to the consumer. —**at**

retail **1** In small quantities to the consumer. **2** At retail prices. —*adj.* Of, pertaining to, or engaged in the sale of goods at retail. —*adv.* AT RETAIL. —*v.t.* **1** To sell in small quantities directly to the consumer. **2** (ri·tāl′) To repeat, as gossip. —*v.i.* **3** To be sold at retail. [< OF *retailler* cut up] —**re′tail·er** *n.*

**re·tain** (ri·tān′) *v.t.* **1** To keep in one's possession; hold. **2** To maintain in use, practice, etc.: to *retain* one's standards. **3** To keep in a fixed condition or place. **4** To keep in mind; remember. **5** To hire or engage, as an attorney. [< L *re*- back + *tenere* to hold]

**re·tain·er** (ri·tā′nər) *n.* **1** One employed in the service of a person of rank; servant. **2** One who or that which retains.

**re·tal·i·ate** (ri·tal′ē·āt) *v.* **·at·ed, ·at·ing** *v.i.* **1** To return like for like; esp., to repay evil with evil. —*v.t.* **2** To repay (an injury, wrong, etc.) in kind; revenge. [< L *re*- back + *talio* punishment in kind] —**re·tal′i·a′tion** *n.* —**re·tal′i·a′tive, re·tal′i·a·to·ry** *adj.*

**re·tard** (ri·tärd′) *v.t.* **1** To hinder the advance or course of; impede; delay. —*v.i.* **2** To be delayed. —*n.* Delay; retardation. [< L *re*- back + *tardus* slow] —**re′tar·da′tion, re·tar·d′er** *n.* —**re·tard′a·tive** *adj.*

**re·ten·tion** (ri·ten′shən) *n.* **1** The act of retaining, or the state of being retained. **2** The ability to retain data, images, etc., in the mind subject to later recall. **3** *Med.* A retaining within the body of materials normally excreted.

**re·ten·tive** (ri·ten′tiv) *adj.* Having the power or tendency to retain, esp. to retain in the mind: a *retentive* memory. —**re·ten′tive·ly** *adv.* —**re·ten′tive·ness, re·ten·tiv′i·ty** *n.*

**ret·i·cent** (ret′ə·sənt) *adj.* **1** Reluctant to speak or speak freely; habitually silent; reserved. **2** Subdued or restrained; shunning bold statement: *reticent* prose. [< L *re*- again + *tacere* be silent] —**ret′i·cence, ret′i·cen·cy** *n.* —**ret′i·cent·ly** *adv.*

**ret·i·na** (ret′ə·nə, ret′nə) *n.* *pl.* **·nas** or **·nae** (-nē) The light-sensitive membrane lining the back of the eyeball at the distal end of the optic nerve. [< L *rete* net] —**ret′i·nal** *adj.*

**ret·i·nue** (ret′ə·n yōō) *n.* The group of retainers attending a person of rank. [< F *retenir* retain]

**re·tire** (ri·tīr′) *v.* **·tired, ·tir·ing** *v.i.* **1** To withdraw oneself from business, public life, or active service. **2** To go away or withdraw, as for privacy, shelter, or rest. **3** To go to bed. **4** To fall back; retreat. **5** To move back; recede. —*v.t.* **6** To remove from active service.

7 To pay off and withdraw from circulation: to *retire* bonds. 8 To withdraw (troops, etc.) from action. 9 In baseball, to put out, as a batter. [< F *re-* back + *tirer* draw]

**re·tire·ment** (ri·tīr′mənt) *n.* 1 The act of retiring, or the state of being retired. 2 A withdrawal from active engagement in one's occupation or profession, esp. because of age. 3 An age or date at which retirement is planned. 4 A secluded place.

**re·tort** (ri·tôrt′) *v.t.* 1 To direct (a word or deed) back upon the originator. 2 To reply to, as an accusation or argument, by a similar one. 3 To say in reply. —*v.i.* 4 To answer, esp. sharply. 5 To respond to an accusation, etc., in kind. —*n.* A sharp or witty reply that turns back a previously expressed accusation, insult, etc., upon its originator. [<L *retorquere* twist back] — re·tort′er *n.* —**Syn.** *n.* rejoinder, riposte, comeback.

**re·tract** (ri·trakt′) *v.t. & v.i.* 1 To take back (an assertion, accusation, admission, etc.); disavow. 2 To draw back or in, as the claws of a cat. [<F<L *retractare* draw back] —re·tract′a·ble, re·trac′tive *adj.* —re·trac′tion, re·trac′tor *n.*

**re·tread** (rē′tred′) *n.* A tire furnished with a new tread to replace a worn one. —*v.t.* (rē·tred′) To fit or furnish (a tire) with a new tread.

**re·treat** (ri·trēt′) *v.i.* 1 To go back or backward; withdraw. 2 To curve or slope backward. —*n.* 1 The act of retreating or drawing back, as from danger or conflict. 2 The retirement of an armed force from a position of danger. 3 In the armed forces, a signal, as by bugle, for the lowering of the flag at sunset. 4 A place of retirement or security; a refuge. 5 A period of religious contemplation and prayer by a group withdrawn from regular society. [<L *re-* again + *trahere* draw]

**re·trench** (ri·trench′) *v.t.* 1 To cut down or curtail (expenditures). 2 To cut off or away. —*v.i.* 3 To economize. [<MF *re-* back + *trencher* to cut] —re·trench′er, re·trench′ment *n.*

**ret·ri·bu·tion** (ret′rə·byōō′shən) *n.* 1 The impartial infliction of punishment, as for evil done. 2 That which is done or given in requital, as a reward or, esp., a punishment. [<L *re-* back + *tribuere* to pay] —re·trib·u·tive (ri·trib′yə·tiv), re·trib′u·to′ry *adj.* — re·trib′u·tive·ly *adv.*

**re·trieve** (ri·trēv′) *v.* ·trieved, ·triev·ing *v.t.* 1

To get back; regain. 2 To restore; revive, as flagging spirits. 3 To make up for; remedy the consequences of. 4 To call to mind; remember. 5 To locate and provide access to (data) in computer storage. 6 In tennis, etc., to return (a ball, etc.) after a run. 7 To find and bring in (wounded or dead game): said of dogs. —*v.i.* 8 To retrieve game. —*n.* The act of retrieving; recovery. [< OF *re-* again + *trouver* find] —re·triev′a·bil′i·ty *n.* —re·triev′a·ble *adj.*

**re·triev·er** (ri·trē′vər) *n.* 1 Any of various breeds of dog usu. trained to retrieve game. 2 A person who retrieves.

**ret·ro·ac·tive** (ret′rō·ak′tiv, rē′trō-) *adj.* Effective or applicable to a period prior to the time of enactment: a *retroactive* ruling granting wage increases as of last May. —ret′ro·ac′tive·ly *adv.* —ret′ro·ac·tiv′i·ty *n.*

**ret·ro·gress** (ret′rə·gres) *v.i.* To go back to a more primitive or worse condition. [<L *retro-* backward + *gradi* walk] —ret′ro·gres′sion *n.* —ret′ro·gres′sive *adj.*

**ret·ro·rock·et** (ret′rō·rok′it) *n.* An auxiliary rocket that provides a backward thrust, as for reducing speed.

**ret·ro·spect** (ret′rə·spekt) *n.* A looking back on things past. —**in retrospect** In recalling or reviewing the past. [<L *retro-* back + *specere* look] —ret′ro·spec′tion *n.*

**re·turn** (ri·tûrn′) *v.i.* 1 To come or go back, as to or toward a former place or condition. 2 To come back or revert in thought or speech. 3 To revert to a former owner. 4 To answer; respond. —*v.t.* 5 To bring, carry, send, or put back; restore; replace. 6 To give in return, esp. with an equivalent: to *return* a favor. 7 To yield or produce, as a profit. 8 To send back; reflect, as light or sound. 9 To render (a verdict, etc.). 10 In sports, to throw, hit, or carry back (a ball). 11 In card games, to lead (a suit previously led by one's partner). —*n.* 1 The act of bringing back or restoring something to a former place or condition; restoration or replacement. 2 An appearing again; recurrence. 3 Something given or sent back, esp. in kind or as an equivalent; repayment. 4 Something, as an article of merchandise, returned for exchange or reimbursement 5 *Often pl.* Profit or revenue; yield. 6 A response; answer; retort. 7 A formal or official report: a tax *return.* 8 *pl.* A report of the tabulated votes of an election. 9 In sports, the act of returning a ball. —**in return** in repayment; as an equivalent —*adj.* 1 Of or for a return: a *return* ticket. 2 Constituting a return or recurrence: a *return* engagement. 3 Returning. 4 Used for return: a *return* address. [< OF] —**re·turn′er** *n.*

**re·veal** (ri·vēl′) *v.t.* 1 To make known; disclose; divulge. 2 To make visible; expose to view. [< L *revelare* unveil]

**rev·eil·le** (rev′i·lē) *n.* A morning signal by drum or bugle, notifying soldiers or sailors to rise. [< F *reveillez-vous,* imperative of *se reveiller* wake up]

**rev·el** (rev′əl) *v.i.* **·eled** or **·elled, ·el·ing** or **·el·ling** 1 To take delight: with *in:* He *revels* in his freedom. 2 To make merry; engage in boisterous festivities. —*n.* 1 A boisterous festivity; celebration. 2 Merrymaking. [< OF < L *rebellare* to rebel] —**rev′el·er** or **rev′el·ler** *n.*

**rev·e·la·tion** (rev′ə·lā′shən) *n.* 1 The act of revealing. 2 That which is revealed, esp. news of a surprising nature. 3 *Theol.* a The act of revealing divine truth. b That which is so revealed.

**re·venge** (ri·venj′) *n.* 1 The act of returning injury for injury to obtain satisfaction. 2 A means of avenging oneself or others. 3 The desire for vengeance. 4 An opportunity to obtain satisfaction, esp. to make up for a prior defeat, humiliation, etc. —*v.t.* **·venged, ·veng·ing** 1 To inflict punishment, injury, or loss in return for. 2 To take or seek vengeance in behalf of. [MF< L *re-* again + *vindicare* vindicate] —**re·venge′ful** *adj.* —**re·venge′ful·ly** *adv.* —**re·veng′er** *n.*

**rev·e·nue** (rev′ə·nyōō) *n.* 1 Total current income of a government. 2 Income from any property or investment. 3 A source or an item of income. [< F *revenir* to return]

**re·ver·ber·ate** (ri·vûr′bə·rāt) *v.* **·at·ed, ·at·ing** *v.i.* 1 To resound or reecho. 2 To be reflected or repelled. 3 To rebound or recoil. —*v.t.* 4 To echo back (a sound); reecho. 5 To reflect. [< L *reverberare* strike back, cause to rebound < *re-* back + *verberare* to beat] —**re·ver′ber·ant** *adj.* —**re·ver′ber·a′tor** *n.*

**re·vere** (ri·vir′) *v.t.* **·vered, ·ver·ing** To regard with profound respect and awe; venerate. [< L *re-* again and again + *vereri* to fear] —**re·ver′er** *n.*

**rev·er·ence** (rev′ər·əns) *n.* 1 A feeling of profound respect often mingled with awe and affection. 2 An act of respect; an obeisance, as a bow or curtsy. 3 The state of being revered. 4 A reverend person: used as a title. —*v.t.* **·enced, ·enc·ing** To regard with

reverence. —**Syn.** *n.* 1 adoration, awe, homage, honor, veneration.

**rev·er·end** (rev′ər·ənd) *adj.* 1 Worthy of reverence. 2 *Usu. cap.* Being a clergyman: used as a title. 3 Of or pertaining to the clergy. —*n.* A clergyman. • In formal usage, *Reverend* follows *the* and precedes the clergyman's full name or title of address and last name: *the Reverend Donald Smith; the Rev. Mr.* (or *Dr.) Smith.* Less formally, *Reverend* is used as a title of address: *Reverend Smith.* The use of *reverend* as a noun should be avoided, esp. in writing: *The reverend's sermon was much admired.*

**rev·er·ent** (rev′ər·ənt) *adj.* Feeling or expressing reverence. —**rev′er·ent·ly** *adv.*

**rev·er·en·tial** (rev′ə·ren′shəl) *adj.* Proceeding from or expressing reverence. —**rev′er·en′tial·ly** *adv.*

**rev·er·ie** (rev′ər·ē) *n. pl.* **·er·ies** 1 Abstracted musing; daydreaming. 2 DAYDREAM. **Also** re·v′er·y. [< F *rêver* dream]

**re·ver·sal** (ri·vûr′səl) *n.* 1 The act of reversing. 2 A change to an opposite direction or course.

**re·verse** (ri·vûrs′) *adj.* 1 Turned backward; contrary or opposite in direction, order, etc. 2 Having the other side or back in view. 3 Causing backward motion. —*n.* 1 That which is directly opposite or contrary. 2 The back, rear, or secondary side or surface. 3 A change to an opposite position, direction, or state; reversal. 4 A change for the worse; a misfortune. 5 *Mech.* A gear that causes reverse motion. —*v.* **·versed, ·vers·ing** *v.t.* 1 To turn upside down or inside out. 2 To turn in an opposite direction. 3 To transpose; exchange. 4 To change completely or into something opposite: to *reverse* one's stand. 5 To set aside; annul: The higher court *reversed* the decision. 6 To apply (the charges for a telephone call) to the party receiving the call. 7 *Mech.* To cause to have an opposite motion or effect. —*v.i.* 8 To move or turn in the opposite direction. 9 To reverse its action: said of engines, etc. [< L *reversus,* p.p. of *revertere* turn around] —**re·verse′ly** *adv.* —**re·vers′er** *n.*

**re·vers·i·ble** (ri·vûr′sə·bəl) *adj.* 1 Capable of being worn or used with either side open to view, as a fabric, coat, rug, etc. 2 Capable of being reversed, as a chemical reaction. —*n.* A reversible coat, fabric, etc. —**re·vers′i·bil′i·ty** *n.* —**re·vers′i·bly** *adv.*

**re·vert** (ri·vûrt′) *v.i.* 1 To go or turn back to a former place, condition, attitude, topic, etc.

**2** *Biol.* To return to or show characteristics of an earlier, primitive type. [< L *re-* back + *vertere* to turn]

**re·view** (ri·vyōō′) *v.t.* **1** To go over or examine again: to *review* a lesson. **2** To look back upon, as in memory. **3** To study carefully; survey or evaluate: to *review* test scores. **4** To write or make a critical evaluation of, as a new book or film. **5** *Law* To examine (something done or adjudged by a lower court) so as to determine its legality or correctness. —*v.i.* **6** To go over material again. **7** To review books, films, etc. —*n.* **1** An examination or study of something; a retrospective survey. **2** A lesson studied again. **3** A careful study or survey. **4** A critical evaluation, as of a new book or film. **5** A periodical featuring critical reviews. **6** A formal inspection, as of troops. **7** *Law* The process by which the proceedings of a lower court are reexamined by a higher court. [< MF < L *re-* again + *videre* see] —**re·view′a·ble** *adj.* —**re·view′er** *n.*

**re·vile** (ri·vīl′) *v.* **·viled**, **·vil·ing** *v.t.* **1** To assail with abusive language; attack verbally. —*v.i.* **2** To use abusive language. [< OF *reviler* treat as vile] —**re·vile′ment**, **re·vil′er** *n.* — Syn. abuse, vilify, malign, slander, defame.

**re·vise** (ri·vīz′) *v.t.* **·vised**, **·vis·ing** **1** To read over so as to correct errors, make changes, etc. **2** To change; alter: to *revise* one's opinion. —*n.* **1** An instance of revising. **2** A corrected proof after having been revised. [< L *revisere* look back, see again] —**re·vis′er** or **re·vi′sor** *n.*

**re·vi·sion** (ri·vizh′ən) *n.* **1** The act or process of revising. **2** A revised version or edition. —**re·vi′sion·ar′y**, **re·vi′sion·al** *adj.*

**re·viv·al** (ri·vī′vəl) *n.* **1** The act of reviving, or the state of being revived. **2** A restoration or renewal after neglect or obscurity: the *revival* of radio drama. **3** An awakening of interest in religion. **4** A series of often emotional evangelical meetings.

**re·vive** (ri·vīv′) *v.* **·vived**, **·viv·ing** *v.t.* **1** To bring to life or consciousness again. **2** To give new vigor, health, etc., to. **3** To bring back into use or currency, as after a period of neglect or obscurity: to *revive* an old play. **4** To renew in the mind or memory. —*v.i.* **5** To return to consciousness or life. **6** To assume new vigor, health, etc. **7** To come back into use or currency. [< L *revivere* < *re-* again + *vivere* live] —**re·viv′er** *n.*

**re·voke** (ri·vōk′) *v.* **·voked**, **·vok·ing** *v.t.* **1** To annul or make void; rescind. —*v.i.* **2** In card

games, to fail to follow suit when possible and required by the rules. —*n.* In card games, neglect to follow suit. [< L *re-* back + *vocare* call] —**re·vok′er** *n.*

**re·volt** (ri·vōlt′) *n.* **1** An uprising against authority, esp. a government; a rebellion or insurrection. **2** An act of protest or refusal. —*v.i.* **1** To rise in rebellion against constituted authority. **2** To turn away in disgust or abhorrence. —*v.t.* **3** To cause to feel disgust or revulsion; repel. [< L *revolutus*, p.p. of *revolvere* revolve] —**re·volt′er** *n.*

**rev·o·lu·tion** (rev′ə·lōō′shən) *n.* **1** The act or state o revolving. **2** A motion in a closed curve around a center, or a complete or apparent circuit made by a body in such a course. **3** Any turning, winding, or rotation about an axis. **4** A round or cycle of successive events or changes. **5** The period of space or time occupied by a cycle. **6** The overthrow and replacement of a government or political system by those governed. **7** Any extensive or drastic change.

**re·volve** (ri·volv′) *v.* **·volved**, **·volv·ing** *v.i.* **1** To move in a circle or closed path about a center. **2** To rotate. **3** To recur periodically. —*v.t.* **4** To cause to move in a circle or closed path. **5** To cause to rotate. **6** To turn over mentally. [<L *re-* back + *volvere* roll, turn]

**re·volv·er** (ri·vol′vər) *n.* A handgun with a cylinder that revolves to make possible successive discharges without reloading.

**re·vul·sion** (ri·vul′shən) *n.* **1** A sudden change of feeling; a strong reaction. **2** Complete disgust or aversion; loathing. [< L *revulsus*, p.p. of *revellere* pluck away] —**re·vul′sive** *adj.*

**re·ward** (ri·wôrd′) *n.* **1** Something given or done in return, esp. to acknowledge and encourage merit, service, or achievement. **2** Money offered, as for the return of lost goods. —*v.t.* To give a reward to or for; recompense. [< AF *rewarder* look at] —**re·ward′er** *n.*

**rhap·so·dy** (rap′sə·dē) *n. pl.* **·dies** **1** Any rapturous or highly enthusiastic utterance or writing. **2** *Music* An instrumental composition of free form. [< Gk. *rhaptein* stitch together + *ōidē* song] —**rhap·sod′ic** (rap·so-d′ik) or **·i·cal** *adj.* —**rhap·sod′i·cal·ly** *adv.*

**rhet·o·ric** (ret′ə·rik) *n.* **1** Skill in the use of language, as in writing or speech. **2** The pretentious use of language. [< Gk. *rhētorikē* (*technē*) rhetorical (art)]

**rheu·ma·tism** (rōō′mə·tiz′əm) *n.* Any of various painful disorders of the joints. [< Gk. *rheuma* rheum] —**rheu′ma·toid** (-toid) *adj.*

**Rh factor** (är′ăch′) A genetically, transmitted substance in the blood of most individuals (**Rh positive**) and which may cause hemolytic reactions under certain conditions, as during pregnancy, or following transfusions with blood lacking this factor (**Rh negative**). [< RH(ESUS) monkey, the laboratory animal used in discovering this substance]

**rhi·noc·e·ros** (rī·nos′ər·əs) *n. pl.* **·ros·es** or **·ros** Any of various large, herbivorous, three-toed mammals of Africa and Asia, with one or two horns on the snout and a thick hide. [< Gk. *rhis, rhinos* nose + *keras* horn]

**rho·do·den·dron** (rō′də·den′drən) *n.* Any of a genus of usu. evergreen shrubs or small trees with profuse clusters of flowers. [< Gk. *rhodon* rose + *dendron* tree]

**rhu·barb** (rōō′bärb) *n.* 1 Any of a genus of large-leaved perennial herbs. 2 The fleshy stalks of a species of rhubarb used in cooking. 3 *Slang* A heated argument or quarrel. [< Gk. *rha* rhubarb + *barbaron* foreign]

**rhyme** (rīm) *n.* 1 A similarity of sounds of two or more words, esp. at the ends of lines of poetry. 2 A word wholly or partly similar in sound to another word. 3 A poem or verse employing such words, esp. at the ends of lines. 4 Poetry or verse in general. —*v.* **rhymed, rhy·ming** *v.i.* 1 To make rhymes or verses. 2 To be a rhyme. 3 To end in rhymes: said of verses. —*v.t.* 4 To write in rhyme. 5 To use as a rhyme. 6 To cause to be a rhyme or rhymes. [< Gk. *rhythmos* rhythm] —**rhym′er** *n.*

**rhythm** (rith′əm) *n.* 1 Movement or process characterized by the regular or harmonious recurrence of a beat, sound, action, development, etc.: the *rhythm* of the pulse; the *rhythm* of the seasons; the *rhythms* of speech. 2 a The property of music that arises from comparison of the relative duration and accents of sounds. b A particular arrangement of durations and accents: a dance *rhythm*. 3 In literature, drama, etc., a forward-moving or compelling development toward a particular end, effect, etc.: The *rhythm* of the play was all off. 4 In art, the regular or harmonious recurrence of colors, forms, etc. 5 In prosody: a The cadenced flow of sound as determined by the succession of accented and unaccented syllables. b A particular arrangement of

such syllables: iambic *rhythm*. [<Gk. *rhythmos* < *rheein* flow] —**rhyth′mic** or **·mi·cal** *adj.* —**rhyth′mi·cal·ly** *adv.* —**rhyth′mist** *n.*

**rib** (rib) *n.* 1 *Anat.* One of the series of curved bones attached to the spine of most vertebrates, and enclosing the chest cavity. 2 Something, as a structural element, likened to a rib: the *rib* of an umbrella. 3 The curved piece of an arch; also, one of the intersecting arches in vaulting. 4 A curved side timber bending away from the keel in a boat or ship. 5 A raised wale or stripe in cloth or knit goods. 6 A vein or nerve of a leaf or insect's wing. 7 A cut of meat including one or more ribs. 8 A wife: in jocular allusion to the creation of Eve from Adam's rib. *Gen.* 2:22. 9 *Slang* A practical joke. —*v.t.* **ribbed, rib·bing** 1 To make with ridges: to *rib* a piece of knitting. 2 To strengthen by or enclose within ribs. 3 *Slang* To make fun of; tease. [< OE *ribb*]

**rib·ald** (rib′əld) *adj.* Of or indulging in coarse, vulgar language or jokes. —*n.* A ribald person. [< OF *ribauld*] —**Syn.** *adj.* improper, unseemly, gross, obscene, impure.

**rib·ald·ry** (rib′əl·drē) *n. pl.* **·ries** Ribald language or jokes.

**rib·bon** (rib′ən) *n.* 1 A narrow strip of fabric made in a variety of weaves, used as trimming, for tying, etc. 2 Something shaped like or suggesting a ribbon. 3 *pl.* A narrow strip; a shred: torn to *ribbons*. 4 An ink-bearing strip of cloth in a typewriter. 5 A colored strip of cloth worn to signify the ward of a prize, etc. 6 *Mil.* A strip of cloth worn to indicate campaigns served in, medals won, etc. —*v.t.* 1 To ornament with ribbons. 2 To tear into ribbons. [< OF *riban*]

**ri·bo·fla·bo·fla·vin** (rī′bō·flā′vin) *n.* A vitamin of the B complex found in many foods and essential for normal growth.

**rich** (rich) *adj.* 1 Having large possessions, as of money, goods, or lands; wealthy. 2 Abundantly supplied: *with in* or *with*. 3 Yielding abundant returns; plentiful: a *rich* source of oil. 4 Of precious materials, fine workmanship, etc.: *rich* fabrics. 5 Luxuriant; sumptuous. 6 Having many choice ingredients, as butter, cream, etc.: a *rich* dessert. 7 Pleasingly full and resonant: a *rich* tone. 8 Deep; intense: a *rich* color. 9 Very fragrant; pungent: a *rich* perfume. 10 Containing a high percentage of fuel to air: said of fuel mixtures. 11 Abounding in desirable qualities: *rich* soil. 12 *Informal* Very funny:

a *rich* joke. [< OE *rice*] —**rich′ly** *adv.* —**rich′ness** *n.*

**rick·ets** (rik′its) *n. pl. (construed as sing.)* A children's disease in which the bones do not harden normally, usu. due to vitamin D deficiency. [?]

**rid** (rid) *v.t.* **rid** or **rid·ded**, **rid·ding** To free, as from a burden or annoyance: usu. with *of.* —*adj.* Free; clear; quit: with *of*: We are well *rid* of him. [< ON *rythja* clear (land) of trees]

**rid·dance** (rid′ns) *n.* 1 A removal of something undesirable. 2 The state of being rid.

**rid·dle** (rid′l) *v.t.* **·dled**, **·dling** 1 To perforate in numerous places, as with shot. 2 To sift through a coarse sieve. 3 To damage, injure, refute, etc., as if by perforating: to *riddle* a theory. —*n.* A coarse sieve. [< OE *hriddel* sieve] —**rid′dler** *n.*

**ride** (rīd) *v.* **rode** (*Regional* **rid**), **rid·den** (*Regional* **rid**), **rid·ing** *v.i.* 1 To sit on and be borne along by a horse or other animal. 2 To be borne along as if on horseback. 3 To travel or be carried on or in a vehicle or other conveyance. 4 To be supported in moving: The wheel *rides* on a shaft. 5 To float; be borne: The ship *rides* on the waves. 6 To carry a rider, etc., in a specified manner: This car *rides* well. 7 To seem to float in space, as a star. 8 To lie at anchor, as a ship. 9 To overlap or overlie, as broken bones. 10 To depend: with *on*: Everything *rides* on him. 11 To be a bet: with *on*: They let their money *ride* on the filly. 12 *Informal* To continue unchanged: Let it *ride.* —*v.t.* 13 To sit on and control the motion of (a horse, bicycle, etc.). 14 To be borne or supported upon. 15 To overlap or overlie. 16 To travel or traverse (an area, certain distance, etc.) on a horse, in an automobile, etc. 17 To harass or bother oppressively: usu. in the past participle: *ridden* with shame. 18 To accomplish by riding: to *ride* a race. 19 To convey. 20 *Informal* To tease or torment by ridicule, criticisms, etc. 21 To keep somewhat engaged, usu. unnecessarily: to *ride* the brake. —**ride for a fall** To be headed for trouble, failure, etc. —**ride herd on** To control or supervise closely. —**ride out** To survive; endure successfully. —**ride up** To move upward out of place, as clothing. —*n.* 1 An excursion by any means of conveyance. 2 A means of transportation: to ask for a *ride.* 3 A manner of riding: a smooth *ride.* 4 A mechanical contrivance for riding, as at an amusement park. —**take for a ride** *Slang* 1 To remove (a person) to a place with the intent to murder. 2 To cheat; swindle. [< OE *rīdan*] —**rid′a·ble**, **ride′a·ble** *adj.*

**rid·er** (rī′dər) *n.* 1 One who or that which rides. 2 A piece of writing added to a document, contract, etc. 3 An addition to a legislative bill.

**ridge** (rij) *n.* 1 A raised mass of land long in proportion to its width and height. 2 A long, raised or top part of something, as the backbone of an animal, crest of a wave or mountain, ribbed part of a fabric, etc. 3 That part of a roof where the rafters meet the ridgepole. —*v.* **ridged**, **ridg·ing** *v.t.* 1 To mark with ridges. 2 To form into ridges. —*v.i.* 3 To form ridges. [< OE *hrycg* spine, ridge]

**rid·i·cule** (rid′ə·kyool) *n.* Language or actions expressing amused contempt or scorn; derision; mockery. —*v.t.* **·culed**, **·cul·ing** To make fun of; hold up as a laughingstock; deride. [< L *ridiculum* a jest] —**rid′i·cul′er** *n.* —**Syn.** *v.* banter, chaff, jeer, mock, taunt, satirize, scoff.

**ri·dic·u·lous** (ri·dik′yə·ləs) *adj.* 1 Absurdly comical: a *ridiculous* costume. 2 Unworthy of consideration; preposterous. —**ri·dic′u·lous·ly** *adv.* —**ri·dic′u·lous·ness** *n.* —**Syn.** 1 droll, funny, grotesque, laughable. 2 absurd, nonsensical, foolish, stupid, asinine, senseless.

**rife** (rīf) *adj.* 1 Prevalent; widespread. 2 Plentiful; abundant. 3 Containing in abundance: with *with.* [< OE *rīfe*]

**rif·fle** (rif′əl) *n.* 1 A shoal or rocky obstruction lying beneath the surface of a stream and causing a stretch of choppy water. 2 Such a stretch of water. 3 A way of shuffling cards. —*v.t. & v.i.* **·fled**, **·fling** 1 To cause or form a riffle. 2 To shuffle (cards) by bending up adjacent corners of two halves of the pack, and permitting the cards to slip together as they are released. 3 To thumb through (the pages of a book). [?]

**ri·fle** (rī′fəl) *n.* 1 A firearm having spiral grooves on the surface of the bore for imparting rotation to the projectile. 2 Such a weapon fired from the shoulder. 3 *pl.* A body of soldiers equipped with rifles. —*v.t.* **·fled**, **·fling** To cut a spirally grooved bore in (a firearm, etc.). [< OF *rifler* to scratch]

**rift** (rift) *n.* 1 An opening made by splitting; a cleft; fissure. 2 A break in friendly relations. —*v.t. & v.i.* To rive; burst open; split. [< Scand.]

**rig** (rig) *v.t.* **rigged, rig·ging 1** To fit out; equip. **2** *Naut.* **a** To fit, as a ship, with rigging. **b** To fit (sails, stays, etc.) to masts, yards, etc. **3** *Informal* To dress; clothe, esp. in finery: usu. with *out*. **4** To construct hurriedly or by makeshifts: often with *up*. **5** To prepare or arrange for special operation: controls *rigged* for the left hand only. —*n.* **1** The arrangement of sails, spars, etc., on a vessel. **2** *Informal* Dress or costume. **3** Gear, machinery, or equipment: an oil-well *rig*. **4** A carriage and its horse or horses. [< Scand.]

**right** (rit) *adj.* **1** In accordance with some moral, just, or equitable law or standard; virtuous; upright. **2** Conformable to truth or fact; correct; accurate. **3** Proper; fitting; suitable. **4** Most desirable or preferable: to go to the *right* parties. **5** In an orderly or satisfactory state or condition: to put things *right*. **6** Sound; healthy; normal, as in mind or body. **7 a** Designating, being, or closest to that side of the body which is toward the south when one faces the sunrise. **b** Designating a corresponding side of anything. **8** Designating that surface or part of something designed to be worn outward or, when used, to be seen. **9** Politically conservative or reactionary. **10** *Geom.* Formed by lines, segments, or planes perpendicular to a base. —*adv.* **1** According to some moral, just, or equitable law or standard. **2** Correctly; accurately. **3** In a straight line; directly: Go *right* home. **4** Precisely: He stood *right* in the doorway. **5** Suitably; properly: I can't fix it *right*. **6** Completely: burned *right* to the ground. **7** Thoroughly: He felt *right* at home. **8** Immediately: *right* after the storm. **9** Very: used regionally or in certain titles: a *right* nice day; the *Right* Reverend. **10** On or toward the right: to go *right*. —*n.* **1** That which is right, good, just, true, proper, etc. **2** *Often pl.* Any power or privilege to which a person has a moral, legal, or just claim: the *right* to vote. **3** *pl.* A claim or title to, or interest in, anything that is enforceable by law or custom: *rights* to property; fishing *rights*. **4** Something a person feels belongs justly or properly to him: a *right* to leave. **5** The correct or factual report or interpretation of something. **6** The right hand or side of a person or thing. **7** A direction to or a location on the right. **8** Something adapted for right-hand use or position. **9** In boxing: **a** A blow delivered with the right hand. **b** The right hand. **10** *Often cap.* In politics, a conservative or reactionary position, or a party or group advocating such a position, so designated because of the views of the party occupying seats on the right side of the presiding officer in certain European legislative bodies. —**by right** (or **rights**) Justly; properly. —**to rights** *Informal* Into a proper or orderly condition. —*v.t.* **1** To restore to an upright or normal position. **2** To put in order; set right. **3** To make correct or in accord with facts. **4** To make reparation for; redress or avenge: to *right* a wrong. **5** To make reparation to (a person); do justice to. —*v.i.* **6** To regain an upright or normal position. —*interj.* I agree! I understand! —**right on** *Informal* An interjectory phrase expressing enthusiastic agreement or encouragement: also used adjectively: He was *right on* in that speech. [< OE *riht*]

**right·eous** (ri′chəs) *adj.* **1** Morally right and just. **2** Virtuous; blameless: a *righteous* man. **3** Justifiable; defensible: *righteous* anger. [< OE *riht* right + *wis* wise] —**righ·teous·ly** *adv.* —**right′eous·ness** *n.*

**rig·id** (rij′id) *adj.* **1** Resisting change of form; stiff. **2** Rigorous; inflexible; severe; strict. **3** Precise; exact, as reasoning. [< L *rigere* be stiff] —**rig′id·ly** *adv.* —**ri·gid′i·ty, rig′id·ness** *n.*

**rig·ma·role** (rig′mə·rōl, rig′ə·mə-) *n.* Incoherent or uselessly complicated talk, writing, procedures, etc. [Alter. of *ragman roll* catalog, long list]

**rig·or** (rig′ər) *n.* **1** Harshness; strictness; severity, as of opinions, methods, temperament, etc. **2** Severe hardship, discomfort, etc. **3** Inclemency, as of the weather. **4** Exactitude; precision. **5** The condition of being stiff or rigid. *Brit. sp.* **rig′our.** [< L *rigere* be stiff] —**rig′or·is′tic** *adj.*

**rig·or·ous** (rig′ər·əs) *adj.* **1** Marked by or acting with rigor; severe. **2** Rigidly accurate; exact; strict. **3** Extremely difficult, arduous, or demanding. **4** Extremely variable, as weather; inclement. —**rig′or·ous·ly** *adv.* —**rig′or·ous·ness** *n.*

**rile** (ril) *v.t. Informal* **1** To vex; irritate. **2** To roil; make muddy. [Var. of ROIL]

**rim** (rim) *n.* **1** The edge or border of an object, usu. of a circular object. **2** The circumference of a wheel, esp., on an automobile wheel, the detachable, metal band over which the tire is fitted. —*v.t.* **rimmed, rim·ming 1** To provide with or serve as a rim; border. **2** In sports, to roll around the edge of (the basket, cup, etc.) without falling in. [< OE *rima*]

**rind** (rīnd) *n.* The skin or outer coat that may be peeled or taken off, as of fruit, cheese, bacon, plants, etc. [< OE *rind* bark, crust]

**ring**[1] (ring) *n.* 1 Any object, line, or figure having the form of a circle or similar closed curve. 2 A rim or border of something circular. 3 A circular band of precious metal, worn on a finger. 4 Any metal or wooden band used for holding or carrying something: a napkin *ring*. 5 A group of persons or things in a circle. 6 A group of persons engaged in some common, often corrupt activity, business, etc.: a dope *ring*. 7 A place where the bark has been cut away around a branch or tree trunk. 8 A concentric layer of wood formed during a single year's growth in most trees and shrubs: also **annual ring.** 9 An area or arena, usu. circular, for exhibitions, etc.: a circus *ring*. 10 a A square area, usu. bordered with ropes, for boxing or wrestling matches. b The sport of prizefighting: with *the*. 11 Any field of competition or rivalry: He tossed his hat into the *ring*. —*v.* **ringed, ring·ing** *v.t.* 1 To surround with a ring; encircle. 2 To form into a ring or rings. 3 To provide or decorate with a ring or rings. 4 To cut a ring of bark from (a branch or tree); girdle. 5 To put a ring in the nose of (a pig, bull, etc.). 6 To hem in (cattle, etc.) by riding in a circle around them. 7 In certain games, to cast a ring over (a peg or pin). —*v.i.* 8 To form a ring or rings. 9 To move or fly in rings or spirals; circle. [< OE *hring*]

**ring**[2] (ring) *v.* **rang, rung, ring·ing** *v.i.* 1 To give forth a resonant sound, as a bell when struck. 2 To sound loudly or be filled with sound or resonance; reverberate; resound. 3 To cause a bell or bells to sound, as in summoning a servant. 4 To have or suggest, as by sounding, a specified quality: His story *rings* true. 5 To have a continued sensation of ringing or buzzing: My ears *ring*. —*v.t.* 6 To cause to ring, as a bell. 7 To produce, as a sound, by or as by ringing. 8 To announce or proclaim by ringing: to *ring* the hour. 9 To summon, escort, usher, etc., by or as by ringing: with *in* or *out*: to *ring* out the old year. 10 To strike (coins, etc.) on something so as to test their quality. 11 To call on the telephone: often with *up*. —*n.* 1 The sound produced by a bell. 2 A sound suggesting this: the *ring* of laughter. 3 Any loud, reverberating sound. 4 A telephone

call. 5 A sound that is characteristic or indicative: with *of*: His words have the *ring* of truth. [< OE *hringan*] —**Syn.** *v.* 1 clang, resound, peal, toll, chime.

**ring·lead·er** (ring′lē′dər) *n.* A leader of any undertaking, esp. of an unlawful one.

**ring·worm** (ring′wûrm′) *n.* A contagious skin disease caused by certain fungi and marked by itchy lesions that spread ringlike from the site of infection.

**rink** (ringk) *n.* 1 A smooth surface of ice, used for sports, as ice-skating, hockey, curling, etc. 2 A smooth floor, used for roller-skating. 3 A building containing a surface for ice-skating or roller-skating. [< OF *renc* row, rank]

**rinse** (rins) *v.t.* **rinsed, rins·ing** 1 To remove soap, dirt, impurities, etc., from by immersing in or flooding with clear water. 2 To remove (soap, dirt, etc.) in this manner. 3 To wash lightly: often with *out*. 4 To use a rinse on (the hair). —*n.* 1 The act of rinsing. 2 A solution used for coloring the hair. [? < L *recens* recent, fresh] —**rins′er** *n.*

**ri·ot** (rī′ət) *n.* 1 A violent or tumultuous public disturbance by a large number of persons; uproar; tumult. 2 Any boisterous outburst: a *riot* of laughter. 3 A vivid show or display: a *riot* of color. 4 *Informal* An uproariously amusing person, thing, or performance. —**run riot** 1 To act or move wildly and without restraint. 2 To grow profusely, as vines. —*v.i.* 1 To take part in a riot. 2 To live a life of unrestrained revelry. —*v.t.* 3 To spend (time, money, etc.) in riot or revelry. [< OF *riote*] —**ri′ot·er** *n.*

**ri·ot·ous** (rī′ət·əs) *adj.* 1 Of, pertaining to, like, or engaged in a riot. 2 Loud; boisterous. 3 Profligate: *riotous* spending. —**ri′ot·ous·ly** *adv.* —**ri′ot·ous·ness** *n.*

**rip** (rip) *v.* **ripped, rip·ping** *v.t.* 1 To tear or cut apart, often roughly or violently. 2 To tear or cut from something else, often in a rough or violent manner: with *off, away, out,* etc. 3 To saw or split (wood) in the direction of the grain. —*v.i.* 4 To be torn or cut apart; split. 5 *Informal* To rush headlong. —**rip into** *Informal* To attack violently, as with blows or words. —**rip off** *Slang* 1 To steal or steal from. 2 To cheat, swindle, or dupe. —**rip out** *Informal* To utter with vehemence. —*n.* 1 A tear or split. 2 The act of ripping. [< ME *rippen*] —**rip′per** *n.*

**ripe** (rīp) *adj.* **rip·er, rip·est** 1 Grown to maturity and fit for food, as fruit or grain. 2 Brought to a condition for use: *ripe* cheese.

3 Fully developed; matured; also, advanced, as in years. 4 In full readiness to do or try; prepared; ready: *ripe* for mutiny. 5 Resembling ripe fruit; rosy; luscious. 6 Ready for surgical treatment, as an abscess. [< OE *ripe* ready for reaping] —**ripe′ly** *adv.* —**ripe′ness** *n.*

**rip·en** (rī′pən) *v.t.* & *v.i.* To make or become ripe; mature. —**rip′en·er** *n.*

**rip·ple** (rip′əl) *v.* **·pled, ·pling** *v.i.* 1 To become slightly agitated on the surface, as water. 2 To flow with small waves or undulations. 3 To make a sound like water flowing in small waves. —*v.t.* 4 To cause to form ripples. —*n.* 1 A small wave or undulation on the surface of water. 2 Anything suggesting this in appearance. 3 Any sound like that made by rippling. [?] —**rip′pler** *n.* —**rip′pling** *adj.* —**rip′pling·ly** *adv.*

**rise** (rīz) *v.* **rose, ris·en, ris·ing** *v.i.* 1 To move upward; go from a lower to a higher position. 2 To slope gradually upward: The ground *rises* here. 3 To have height or elevation; extend upward: The city *rises* above the plain. 4 To gain elevation in rank, status, fortune, or reputation. 5 To swell up: Dough *rises.* 6 To become greater in force, intensity, height, etc. 7 To become greater in amount, value, etc. 8 To become elated or more optimistic: Their spirits *rose.* 9 To become erect after lying down, sitting, etc.; stand up. 10 To get out of bed. 11 To return to life. 12 To revolt; rebel: The people *rose* against the tyrant. 13 To adjourn: The House passed the bill before *rising.* 14 To appear above the horizon: The sun *rose.* 15 To come to the surface, as a fish after a lure. 16 To have origin; begin. 17 To become perceptible to the mind or senses: The scene *rose* in his mind. 18 To occur; happen. 19 To be able to cope with an emergency, danger, etc.: Will he *rise* to the occasion? —*v.t.* 20 To cause to rise. —**rise above** To prove superior to; show oneself indifferent to. —*n.* 1 A moving or sloping upward; ascent. 2 An elevated place, as a small hill. 3 Appearance above the horizon. 4 The height of a stair step or of a flight of stairs. 5 Advance, as in rank, status, prosperity, etc. 6 Increase, as in price, volume, intensity, etc. 7 An origin, source, or beginning. 8 *Informal* An emotional reaction; a response or retort, esp. in the phrase **get a rise out of** (someone). 9 *Brit.* An increase in salary. [< OE *rīsan*]

**risk** (risk) *n.* 1 A chance of encountering harm or loss; hazard; danger. 2 In insurance: **a** Chance of loss. **b** Degree of exposure to loss or injury. **c** An applicant for an insurance policy considered with regard to the hazard of insuring him. —*v.t.* 1 To expose to a chance of injury or loss; hazard. 2 To incur the risk of. [< Ital. *risicare* to dare] —**risk′er** *n.*

**rite** (rīt) *n.* 1 A solemn ceremony performed in a prescribed manner. 2 The words or acts accompanying such a ceremony. 3 Any formal practice or custom. [< L *ritus*]

**rit·u·al** (rich′ōō·əl) *n.* 1 A prescribed form or method for the performance of a rite. 2 The use or performing of such rites. 3 A book setting forth such a system of rites or observances. 4 Any act, observance, or custom performed somewhat regularly or formally. —*adj.* Of, pertaining to, or consisting of a rite or rites. —**rit′u·al·ly** *adv.*

**ri·val** (rī′vəl) *n.* 1 One who strives to equal or excel another; a competitor. 2 A person or thing equaling or nearly equaling another, in any respect. —*v.t.* **·valed** or **·valled, ·val·ing** or **·val·ling** 1 To strive to equal or excel; compete with. 2 To be the equal of or a match for. —*adj.* Being a rival or rivals; competing. [< L *rivalis*]

**ri·val·ry** (rī′vəl·rē) *n. pl.* **·ries** 1 The act of rivaling. 2 The state of being a rival or rivals; competition.

**riv·er** (riv′ər) *n.* 1 A large, natural stream of water, usu. fed by converging tributaries along its course and discharging into a larger body of water. 2 A large stream of any kind; copious flow. —**sell down the river** To betray; deceive. —**send up the river** *Slang* To send to a penitentiary. [< L *riparius*]

**riv·et** (riv′it) *n.* A metal bolt, having a head on one end, used to join objects, as metal plates, by passing the shank through holes and forming a head by flattening out the plain end. —*v.t.* 1 To fasten with or as with a rivet. 2 To fasten firmly. 3 To engross or attract (the eyes, attention, etc.). [< OF *river* to clench] —**riv′et·er** *n.*

**road** (rōd) *n.* 1 An open way for public passage; a highway. 2 Any course followed in a journey or a project. 3 A railroad. —**on the road** 1 On tour: said of circuses, theatrical companies, athletic teams, etc. 2 Traveling, as a canvasser or salesman. [< OE *rād* a ride, a riding]

**road·block** (rōd′blok′) *n.* 1 An obstruction, as of men or materials, for blocking passage.

as along a road. 2 Any obstacle to progress or advancement.

**roam** (rōm) *v.i.* 1 To move about purposelessly from place to place; wander; rove. —*v.t.* 2 To wander over; range: to *roam* the fields. —*n.* The act of roaming. [ME *romen*] —**roam′er** *n.*

**roar** (rôr, rōr) *v.i.* 1 To utter a deep, prolonged cry, as of rage or distress. 2 To make a loud noise or din, as a cannon. 3 To laugh loudly. 4 To move, proceed, or act noisily. —*v.t.* 5 To utter or express by roaring: The crowd *roared* its disapproval. —*n.* 1 A full, deep, resonant cry. 2 Any loud, prolonged sound, as of wind or waves. 3 Loud, boisterous laughter. [< OE *rārian*] —**roar′er** *n.*

**roast** (rōst) *v.t.* 1 To cook by subjecting to the action of heat, as in an oven or by placing in hot ashes, embers, etc. 2 To heat to an extreme degree. 3 To dry and parch: to *roast* coffee. 4 *Informal* To criticize or ridicule severely. —*v.i.* 5 To roast food in an oven, etc. 6 To be cooked or prepared by this method. 7 To be uncomfortably hot. —*n.* 1 Something prepared for roasting, or that is roasted. 2 A social gathering where food is roasted: a corn *roast.* 3 *Informal* Severe criticism or ridicule. —*adj.* Roasted. [< OHG *rösten*]

**rob** (rob) *v.* **robbed, rob·bing** *v.t.* 1 To seize and carry off the property of by unlawful violence or threat of violence. 2 To deprive (a person) of something belonging, necessary, due, etc.: *robbed* him of his honor. 3 To take something unlawfully from: to *rob* a store. 4 To steal: to *rob* gold. —*v.i.* 5 To commit robbery. [< OHG *roubon*] —**rob′ber** *n.*

**rob·ber·y** (rob′ər·ē) *n. pl.* **·ber·ies** The act of robbing, esp. the taking away of the property of another unlawfully by using force or intimidation.

**robe** (rōb) *n.* 1 A long, loose, flowing, outer garment. 2 *pl.* Such a garment worn as a badge of office or rank. 3 A bathrobe or dressing gown. 4 A blanket or covering: lap *robe.* —*v.* **robed, rob·ing** *v.t.* 1 To put a robe upon; clothe; dress. —*v.i.* 2 To put on robes.

**rob·in** (rob′in) *n.* 1 A large North American thrush with reddish brown breast and underparts. 2 A small European songbird with cheeks and breast yellowish red. [Dim. of *Robert*]

**ro·bot** (rō′bət, ·bot) *n.* 1 A machine designed to resemble a person and perform human tasks. 2 Any mechanical device that per-

forms complex, often humanlike actions automatically or by remote control. 3 A person who lives or works mechanically, without spontaneity, etc. [< Czech *robota* work, compulsory service]

**ro·bust** (rō·bust′, rō′bust) *adj.* 1 Possessing or characterized by great strength or endurance. 2 Requiring strength. 3 Boisterous; rude: *robust* humor. 4 Rich, as in flavor: a *robust* soup. [< L *robur, roboris,* a hard variety of oak, strength] —**ro·bust′ly** *adv.* —**ro·bust′ness** *n.*

**rock¹** (rok) *n.* 1 A large mass of stone or stony matter, often forming a peak or cliff. 2 A piece of stone of any size. 3 *Geol.* Solid mineral matter, such as that forming an essential part of the earth's crust. 4 Any strong, solid person or thing, often acting as a support, refuge, defense, etc. 5 *Slang* A precious gem, esp. a diamond. —**on the rocks** *Informal* 1 In a ruined or disastrous condition. 2 Bankrupt; destitute. 3 Served with ice cubes: said of an alcoholic beverage. —*adj.* Made or composed of rock; hard; stony. [< OF *roque*]

**rock²** (rok) *v.i.* 1 To move backward and forward or from side to side; sway. 2 To sway, reel, or stagger, as from a blow. —*v.t.* 3 To move backward and forward or from side to side, esp. so as to soothe or put to sleep. 4 To cause to sway or reel. —*n.* 1 The act of rocking or a rocking motion. 2 A type of popular music whose origins lie in jazz, country music, and blues, characterized by a strong, persistent rhythm, simple, often repeated melodies, and usu. performed by small, electronically amplified instrumental-singing groups: also **rock and roll, rock-and-roll, rock'n'roll.** [< OE *roccian*]

**rock·er** (rok′ər) *n.* 1 One who or that which rocks. 2 On of the curved pieces on which a rocking chair or a cradle rocks. 2 ROCKING CHAIR.

**rock·et** (rok′it) *n.* 1 a A usu. cylindrical firework, projectile, missile, or other device propelled by the reaction of ejected matter. b An engine that develops thrust by ejecting matter. 2 A vehicle propelled by rockets and designed for space travel. —*v.i. & v.t.* 1 To move or cause to move rapidly, as a rocket. 2 To rise or cause to rise rapidly: Her career *rocketed.* [< Ital. *rocchetta* spool]

**rock·et·ry** (rok′it·rē) *n.* The science and technology of rocket flight, design, and construction.

**ro·dent** (rōd′nt) *n.* Any of an order of gnawing mammals having incisors that grow continually, as a squirrel, beaver, or rat. —*adj.* 1 Gnawing. 2 Pertaining to the rodents. [< L *rodere* gnaw]

**roe**[1] (rō) *n.* A mass of eggs of fish or of certain crustaceans, as lobsters. [< MDu. *roge*]

**roe**[2] (rō) *n.* A small, graceful deer of Europe and w Asia. Also **roe deer.** [< OE *rā*]

**rogue** (rōg) *n.* 1 A dishonest and unprincipled person; scoundrel. 2 One who is innocently mischievous or playful. 3 A dangerous animal separated from the herd: also used adjectively: a *rogue* elephant. —*v.* rogued, ro·guing *v.t.* 1 To practice roguery upon; defraud. —*v.i.* 2 To live or act like a rogue. [?] —Syn. ne'er-do-well, dastard, good-for-nothing, scamp, knave, rascal.

**ro·guish** (rō′gish) *adj.* 1 Playfully mischievous. 2 Knavish; dishonest. —**ro′guish·ly** *adv.* —**ro′guish·ness** *n.*

**role** (rōl) *n.* 1 A part or character taken by an actor. 2 Any assumed office or function. 3 A specific or acceptable pattern of behavior expected from those in a certain social status, profession, etc. Also **rôle.** [< F < Med. L *rotulus* roll of parchment]

**roll** (rōl) *v.i.* 1 To move upon a surface by turning round and round, as a wheel. 2 To move, be moved, travel about, etc., on or as on wheels. 3 To rotate wholly or partially: Her eyes *rolled.* 4 To assume the shape of a ball or cylinder by turning over and over upon itself. 5 To move or appear to move in undulations or swells, as waves or plains. 6 To sway or move from side to side, as a ship. 7 To rotate on a front-to-rear axis, as a projectile. 8 To walk with a swaying motion. 9 To make a sound as of heavy, rolling wheels; rumble: Thunder *rolled* across the sky. 10 To become spread or flat because of pressure applied by a roller, etc. 11 To perform a periodic revolution, as the sun. 12 To move ahead; progress. —*v.t.* 13 To cause to move by turning round and round or turning on an axis: to *roll* a ball; to *roll* a log. 14 To move, push forward, etc., on wheels or rollers. 15 To impel or cause to move onward with a steady, surging motion. 16 To begin to operate: *Roll* the presses. 17 To rotate, as the eyes. 18 To impart a swaying motion to. 19 To spread or make flat by means of a roller. 20 To wrap round and round upon itself. 21 To cause to assume the shape of a ball or cylinder by means of rotation and pressure: to *roll* a cigarette. 22 To wrap or envelop in or as in a covering.

23 To utter with a trilling sound: to *roll* one's r's. 24 To emit in a full and swelling manner, as musical sounds. 25 To beat a roll upon, as a drum. 26 To cast (dice) in the game of craps. 27 *Slang* To rob (a drunk or unconscious person). —**roll back** To cause (prices, wages, etc.) to return to a previous, lower level, as by government order. —**roll in** 1 To arrive, usu. in large amounts: Money *rolled in.* 2 *Informal* To have large amounts of: *rolling in* money. —**roll out** 1 To unroll. 2 *Informal* To get out of (bed, etc.) 3 To flatten by means of rollers. —**roll up** 1 To assume or cause to assume the shape of a ball or cylinder by turning over and over upon itself. 2 To accumulate; amass: to *roll up* large profits. 3 To arrive, as in an automobile. —*n.* 1 The act or an instance of rolling. 2 Anything rolled up. 3 A list of names, a register of items, etc.: an honor *roll.* 4 A long strip of something rolled upon itself: a *roll* of carpet. 5 Any food rolled up in preparation for eating or cooking, esp. small, variously shaped pieces of baked bread dough. 6 A roller. 7 A rolling gait or movement. 8 A rotation on an axis from front to rear, as of an aircraft. 9 A reverberation, as of thunder. 10 A trill. 11 A rapid beating of a drum. 12 An undulation or swell, as of waves or land. 13 *Slang* A wad of paper money; also, money in general. [< L *rota* wheel]

**roll·back** (rōl′bak′) *n.* A return, esp. by government order, to a lower level, as of prices, wages, or rents.

**rol·lick·ing** (rol′ik·ing) *adj.* Carelessly gay and frolicsome. Also **rol′lick·some** -(səm). [< earlier *rollick*, blend of ROMP and FROLIC]

**ro·mance** (rō·mans′, rō′mans) *n.* 1 Adventurous, fascinating, or picturesque nature or appeal: the *romance* of faraway places. 2 A disposition to delight in the mysterious, adventurous, sentimental, etc.: a child of *romance.* 3 A love affair. 4 A long narrative from medieval legend, usu. involving heroes in strange adventures and affairs of love. 5 Any fictitious narrative embodying adventure, love affairs, etc. 6 The class of literature consisting of romances (defs. 4 and 5). 7 An extravagant falsehood. —*v.* (rō·mans′) ·manced, ·manc·ing *v.i.* 1 To tell romances. 2 To think or act in a romantic manner. 3 *Informal* To make love. —*v.t.* 4 *Informal* To make love to; woo. [< OF *romans* a story written in French] —**ro·manc′er** *n.*

**romp** (romp) *v.i.* 1 To play boisterously. 2 To

win easily. —*n.* 1 One, esp. a girl, who romps. 2 Noisy, exciting frolic or play. 3 An easy victory. [Var. of RAMP[2]]

**roof** (rōōf, rŏŏf) *n.* 1 The exterior upper covering of a building. 2 Any top covering, as of the mouth, a car, etc. 3 A house; home. 4 The most elevated part of anything; top; summit. —*v.t.* To cover with or as with a roof. [< OE *hrōf*] —**roof′er** *n.*

**room** (rōōm, rŏŏm) *n.* 1 a A space for occupancy or use enclosed on all sides, as in a building. b The people in a room. 2 Space available or sufficient for some specified purpose: *room* to park. 3 Suitable or warrantable occasion; opportunity: *room* for doubt. 4 *pl.* Lodgings. —*v.i.* To occupy a room; lodge. [< OE *rūm* space]

**roost** (rōōst) *n.* 1 a A perch upon which fowls rest at night. b Any place where birds resort to spend the night. 2 Any temporary resting place. —*v.i.* 1 To sit or perch upon a roost. 2 To come to rest; settle. [< OE *hrōst*]

**roost·er** (rōōs′tər) *n.* The male of the chicken; cock. [< ROOST + -ER[1]]

**root** (rōōt, rŏŏt) *n.* 1 The descending axis of a plant, usu. growing underground, providing support and absorbing moisture from the soil. 2 Any underground growth, as a tuber or bulb. 3 Some rootlike part of an organ or structure: the *root* of a tooth, hair, nerve, etc. • See TOOTH. 4 That from which something derives its origin, growth, life, etc.: Money is the *root* of all evil. 5 *pl.* A mental or emotional attachment to some place or people, as through birth, childhood, etc. 6 The essence or basic part: the *root* of the problem. 7 *Ling.* A word or word part serving as the basic constituent element of a related group of words, as *know* in *unknown, knowledge, knowable*, and *knowingly.* 8 *Math.* A number or element that, taken a specified number of times as a factor, will produce a given number or element. 9 *Music* The principal tone of a chord. —*v.i.* 1 To put forth roots and begin to grow. 2 To be or become firmly fixed or established. —*v.t.* 3 To fix or implant by or as by roots. 4 To pull, dig, or tear up by or as by the roots; extirpate; eradicate: with *up* or *out.* [< OE *rōt*] —**root′y** *adj.*

**rope** (rōp) *n.* 1 An assembly of intertwined strands of fiber, wire, plastic, etc., forming a thick cord. 2 A collection of things plaited or united in a line. 3 A sticky or glutinous filament or thread of something, as of beaten egg yolks. 4 a A cord or halter used in hanging. b Death by hanging. 5 LASSO. —*v.t.* roped, rop·ing 1 To tie or fasten with or as with rope. 2 To enclose, border, or divide with a rope: usu. with *off*: He *roped* off the arena. 3 To catch with a lasso. 4 *Informal* To deceive: with *in.* [< OE *rāp*]

**ro·sa·ry** (rō′zə-rē) *n. pl.* ·ries *Eccl.* 1 A string of beads for keeping count of a series of prayers, used esp. in Roman Catholicism. 2 The prayers. [< LL *rosarium* a rose garden]

**rose** (rōz) *n.* 1 Any of a genus of hardy, erect or climbing shrubs with prickly stems and flowers of pink, red, white, yellow, etc. 2 The flower. 3 Any of various other plants or flowers having a likeness to the true rose. 4 A pinkish or purplish red color. 5 An ornamental knot, as of ribbon or lace; a rosette. 6 A form in which gems, esp. diamonds, are often cut. —*adj.* 1 Of, containing, or used for roses. 2 Of the color rose. 3 Rose-scented. [< L *rosa* < Gk. *rhodon*]

**ro·sette** (rō·zet′) *n.* 1 A painted or sculptured architectural ornament with parts circularly arranged. 2 A ribbon badge shaped like a rose and worn to indicate possession of a certain military decoration. 3 Any flowerlike cluster as of leaves, markings, etc. [F, little rose]

**ros·in** (roz′in) *n.* A hard, usu. amber-colored resin obtained from turpentine. —*v.t.* To apply rosin to. [Var. of RESIN] —**ros′in·y** *adj.*

**ros·ter** (ros′tər) *n.* 1 A list of officers and men enrolled for duty. 2 Any list of names. [< Du. *rooster* list]

**rot** (rot) *v.* rot·ted, rot·ting *v.i.* 1 To undergo decomposition. 2 To fall or pass by decaying: with *away, off*, etc. 3 To become morally rotten. —*v.t.* 4 To cause to decompose; decay. —*n.* 1 The process of rotting or the state of being rotten. 2 Any of various plant and animal diseases characterized by destruction of tissue. 3 *Informal* Nonsense; bosh. —*interj.* Nonsense. [< OE *rotian*]

**ro·ta·ry** (rō′tər·ē) *adj.* 1 Turning on an axis, as a wheel. 2 Having some part that so turns: a *rotary* press. [< L *rota* wheel]

**rotary engine** An engine, as a turbine, in which rotary motion is directly produced without reciprocating parts.

**ro·tate** (rō′tāt, rō·tāt′) *v.t. & v.i.* ·tat·ed, ·tat·ing 1 To turn or cause to turn on or as on its axis. 2 To alternate in a definite order or succession. [< L *rota* wheel] —**ro·tat′a·ble, ro′ta·tive** (-tə-tiv) *adj.* —**ro′ta·tor** *n.*

**ro·ta·tion** (rō·tā′shən) *n.* 1 The act or state of

rotating. 2 Alternation or succession in some fixed order. 3 *Agric.* The practice of planting a field with a series of various crops to preserve the fertility of the field: also *crop rotation.* —ro·ta′tion·al *adj.*

**ROTC, R.O.T.C.** Reserve Officers' Training Corps.

**rote** (rōt) *n.* A routine, mechanical way of doing something. —**by rote** Mechanically; without intelligent attention: to learn *by rote.* [ME]

**ro·tis·se·rie** (rō·tis′ə·rē) *n.* 1 An establishment where meat is roasted and sold. 2 A device for roasting meat by rotating it on a spit before or over a source of heat. [< F *rôtir* to roast]

**ro·tor** (rō′tər) *n.* 1 A rotary part of a machine. 2 *Aeron.* The horizontally rotating airfoil assembly of a helicopter. [Contraction of ROTATOR]

**ro·tund** (rō·tund′) *adj.* 1 Rounded out, spherical, or plump. 2 Full-toned, as a voice or utterance. [< L *rota* wheel] —ro·tun′di·ty, ro·tund′ness *n.* —ro·tund′ly *adv.*

**rouge** (rōōzh) *n.* 1 Any cosmetic used for coloring the cheeks or lips. 2 A red powder, mainly ferric oxide, used in polishing. —*v.* **rouged, roug·ing** *v.t.* & *v.i.* To color with or apply rouge. [< L *rubeus* ruby]

**rough** (ruf) *adj.* 1 Having an uneven surface: a *rough* pavement. 2 Coarse in texture; shaggy: a *rough* tweed. 3 Disordered or ragged: a *rough* shock of hair. 4 Characterized by rude or violent action: *rough* sports. 5 Agitated; stormy: a *rough* passage. 6 Rude; coarse: a *rough* manner. 7 Lacking finish and polish; crude: a *rough* gem. 8 Done or made hastily and without attention to details: a *rough* sketch. 9 *Phonet.* Uttered with an aspiration, or *h* sound. 10 Harsh to the senses: *rough* sounds. 11 Without comforts or conveniences: the *rough* life of the poor. 12 Requiring physical strength: *rough* work. 13 *Informal* Difficult; trying: It's been a *rough* day. —**in the rough** In an unpolished or crude condition. —*n.* 1 Any rough ground. 2 A crude, incomplete, or unpolished object, material, or condition. 3 Any part of a golf course on which tall grass, bushes, etc., grow. 4 *Chiefly Brit.* A rude or violent person; ruffian. —*v.t.* 1 To make rough; roughen. 2 To treat roughly: often with *up.* 3 To make, cut, or sketch roughly: to *rough* in the details of a plan. —*v.i.* 4 To become rough. 5 To behave roughly. —**rough it** To live under or endure

conditions that are hard, rustic, inconvenient, etc. —*adv.* In a rude manner. [< OE *rūh*] —**rough′ly** *adv.* —**rough′ness** *n.* —Syn. *adj.* 3 unkempt. 6 boorish, uncultivated.

**round** (round) *adj.* 1 Having a shape like a ball, ring, or cylinder; spherical, circular, or cylindrical. 2 Semicircular: a *round* arch. 3 Plump. 4 Formed or moving in rotation or a circle: a *round* dance. 5 Approximate to the nearest ten, hundred, thousand, etc., as a number. 6 Pronounced with the lips forming a circle, as the vowel *o.* 7 Full; complete: a *round* dozen. 8 Large; ample; liberal: a good *round* fee. 9 Full in tone or resonance. 10 Free and easy; brisk: a *round* pace. —*n.* 1 Something round, as a globe, ring, or cylinder. 2 *Often pl.* A circular course or range; circuit; beat: to make one's *rounds.* 3 Motion in a circular path. 4 A series of recurrent actions; a routine: the daily *round* of life. 5 An outburst, as of applause. 6 In some sports and games, a division based on action or time. 7 A short canon for several voices. 8 A single shot fired by a weapon or by each of a number of weapons. 9 The ammunition used for such a shot. 10 ROUND DANCE (def. 1). 11 The state of being carved out on all sides: opposed to *relief.* 12 The state or condition of being circular; roundness. 13 A portion of a hind leg of beef, between the rump and lower leg. 14 A rung of a chair or ladder. —**go the rounds** To pass from person to person, as gossip, a rumor, etc. —*v.t.* 1 To make round or plump. 2 *Phonet.* To utter (a vowel) with the lips in a rounded position. 3 To travel or go around; make a circuit of. —*v.i.* 4 To become round or plump. 5 To make a circuit; travel a circular course. 6 To turn around. —**round off** (or **out**) 1 To make or become round. 2 To bring to perfection or completion. —**round up** 1 To collect (cattle, etc.) in a herd, as for driving to market. 2 *Informal* To gather together; assemble. —*adv.* 1 On all sides; in such a manner as to encircle: A crowd gathered *round.* 2 In a circular path, or with a circular motion: The plane circled *round;* The wheel turns *round.* 3 To each of a number, one after the other: provisions enough to go *round.* 4 In circumference: a log three feet *round.* 5 From one position to another; here and there. 6 In the vicinity: to loiter *round.* 7 So as to complete a period of time: Will spring ever come *round* again? 8 In a circuitous or indirect way: Come *round* by way of the shopping center. **9** In the opposite direction: to turn *round*. —*prep.* **1** Enclosing; encircling; a belt *round* his waist. **2** On every side of; surrounding. **3** Toward every side of; about: He peered *round* him. **4** In the vicinity of: farms *round* the town. **5** To all or many parts of: driving friends *round* the city. **6** Here and there in: to look *round* a room. **7** So as to get to the other side of: walking *round* the corner. **8** In a group or mass surrounding: a rich socialite with hangers-on *round* him. [< L *rotundus*] —**round′ness** *n.*

**rouse** (rouz) *v.* **roused, rous·ing** *v.t.* **1** To cause to awaken from slumber, repose, unconsciousness, etc. **2** To excite to vigorous thought or action; stir up. **3** To startle or drive (game) from cover. —*v.i.* **4** To awaken from sleep or unconsciousness. **5** To become active. **6** To start from cover: said of game. —*n.* The act of rousing. [?] —**rous′er** *n.* —**Syn.** *v.* 2 Animate, incite, arouse, stimulate.

**rout** (rout) *v.i.* **1** To turn up the earth with the snout, as swine. **2** To search; rummage. —*v.t.* **3** To dig or turn up with the snout. **4** To disclose to view; turn up as if with the snout: with *out*. **5** To hollow, gouge, or scrape, as with a scoop. **6** To drive or force out. [Var. of ROOT²]

**rou·tine** (roo͞-tēn′) *n.* **1** A detailed method of procedure, prescribed or regularly followed. **2** Anything that has become customary or habitual. —*adj.* **1** Customary; habitual. **2** Uninspired; dull: a *routine* performance. [< F *route* way, road] —**rou·tine′ly** *adv.*

**rove¹** (rōv) *v.* **roved, rov·ing** *v.i.* **1** To go from place to place without any definite destination. —*v.t.* **2** To roam over, through, or about. —*n.* The act of roving or roaming. [? < Du. *rooven* rob] —**Syn.** 1 ramble, roam, wander.

**rove²** (rōv) A *p.t.* & *p.p.* of REEVE¹.

**row** (rō) *n.* An arrangement or series of persons or things in a continued line, as a street lined with buildings on both sides, or a line of seats in a theater. —**a long row to hoe** A hard task or undertaking. —*v.t.* To arrange in a row: with *up*. [< OE *rāw* line]

**row·dy** (rou′dē) *n. pl.* **·dies** One inclined to create disturbances or engage in rows; a rough, quarrelsome person. —*adj.* **·di·er, ·di·est** Rough and loud; disorderly. [?] —**row′di·ly** *adv.* —**row′di·ness, row′dy·ism** *n.* —**row′dy·ish** *adj.*

**roy·al** (roi′əl) *adj.* **1** Of, pertaining to, or being a king, queen, or other sovereign. **2** Of, pertaining to, or under the patronage or authority of a sovereign. **3** Like or suitable for a sovereign. **4** Of superior quality or size: *royal* octavo. —*n.* A small sail or mast next above the topgallant. [< L *regalis* kingly] —**roy′al·ly** *adv.* —**Syn.** *adj.* 3 imperial, kingly, noble, regal, stately.

**roy·al·ty** (roi′əl·tē) *n. pl.* **·ties** **1** The rank, status, or authority of a sovereign. **2** A royal personage; also, royal persons collectively. **3** Royal nature or quality. **4** A share of proceeds paid to a proprietor, author, inventor, etc.

**rub** (rub) *v.* **rubbed, rub·bing** *v.t.* **1** To move or pass over the surface of with pressure and friction. **2** To cause (something) to move or pass with friction. **3** To cause to become frayed, worn, or sore from friction: This collar *rubs* my neck. **4** To clean, shine, dry, etc., by means of pressure and friction, or by means of a substance applied thus. **5** To apply or spread with pressure and friction: to *rub* polish on a table. **6** To force by rubbing: with *in* or *into*: to *rub* oil into wood. **7** To remove or erase by friction: with *off* or *out*. —*v.i.* **8** To move along a surface with friction; scrape. **9** To exert pressure and friction. **10** To become frayed, worn, or sore from friction; chafe. **11** To undergo rubbing or removal by rubbing: with *off*, *out*, etc. —**rub down** To massage. —**rub it in** *Slang* To harp on someone's errors, faults, etc. —**rub out** *Slang* To kill. —**rub the wrong way** To irritate; annoy. —*n.* **1** A subjection to frictional pressure; rubbing: Give it a *rub*. **2** A hindrance or doubt: There's the *rub*. **3** Something that injures the feelings; a sarcasm. [ME *rubben*]

**rub·ber** (rub′ər) *n.* **1** A tough, resilient, elastic material made from the latex of certain tropical plants, or synthesized from coal, petroleum, etc. **2** An article made of this material, as: **a** A rubber overshoe. **b** A condom. **3** One who or that which rubs. —*adj.* Made of rubber. [< RUB] —**rub′ber·y** *adj.*

**rub·bish** (rub′ish) *n.* **1** Waste refuse; garbage; trash. **2** Silly or worthless ideas, talk, etc.; nonsense. [?] —**rub′bish·y** *adj.* —**Syn.** 1 debris, litter. 2 absurdness, foolishness.

**rub·ble** (rub′əl) *n.* **1** Rough, irregular pieces of broken stone, brick, etc. **2** The debris to which buildings of brick, stone, etc., have been reduced by destruction or decay. **3**

Masonry composed of irregular or broken stone: also **rub·ble·work**'.

**ru·by** (rōō'bē) n. pl. **·bies** 1 A translucent gemstone of a deep red color, a variety of corundum. 2 A rich red color like that of a ruby. —adj. Deep red. [< L rubeus red]

**rud·der** (rud'ər) n. 1 Naut. A broad, flat device hinged vertically at the stern of a vessel to direct its course. 2 Anything that guides or directs a course. 3 Aeron. A hinged or pivoted surface, used to turn an aircraft about its vertical axis. [< OE rōthor oar, scull] — **rud'der·less** adj.

**rud·dy** (rud'ē) adj. **·di·er, ·di·est** 1 Red or tinged with red. 2 Having a healthy glow; rosy: a ruddy complexion. [< OE rudig] — **rud'di·ly** adv. —**rud'di·ness** n.

**rude** (rōōd) adj. **rud·er, rud·est** 1 Offensively blunt or uncivil; impolite. 2 Characterized by lack of polish or refinement; uncouth. 3 Unskilfully made or done; crude. 4 Characterized by robust vigor; strong: rude health. 5 Barbarous; savage. 6 Jarring to the ear; harsh; discordant. 7 Lacking skill, training, accuracy, etc. [< L rudis rough] — **rude'ly** adv. —**rude'ness** n. —Syn. 1 discourteous, impertinent. 2 boorish, uncultivated. 5 uncivilized.

**ru·di·ment** (rōō'də·mənt) n. 1 A first step, stage, or condition. 2 That which is undeveloped or partially developed. [< L rudis rough]

**ru·di·men·ta·ry** (rōō'də·men'tər·ē) adj. 1 Introductory; elementary: rudimentary knowledge. 2 Being in an imperfectly developed state; undeveloped. 3 Vestigial. Also **ru'di·men'tal.** —**ru'di·men'ta·ri·ly** adv. —**ru'di·men'ta·ri·ness** n.

**rue** (rōō) v. **rued, ru·ing** v.t. 1 To feel sorrow or remorse for; regret extremely. —v.i. 2 To feel sorrow or remorse. —n. Archaic Sorrowful remembrance; regret. [< OE hrēowan be sorry] —**ru'er** n.

**rue·ful** (rōō'fəl) adj. 1 Feeling or expressing sorrow, regret, or pity. 2 Causing sympathy or pity; pitiable. —**rue'ful·ly** adv. —**rue'ful·ness** n.

**ruff** (ruf) n. 1 A pleated, round, heavily starched collar popular in the 16th century. 2 A natural collar of projecting feathers or hair around the neck of a bird or mammal. 3 The male of a European species of sandpiper, which has a large ruff in the breeding season. [Short for RUFFLE¹] — **ruffed** adj.

**ruf·fi·an** (ruf'ē·ən, ruf'yən) n. A lawless, brutal person. —adj. Lawlessly or recklessly brutal or cruel. [< MF rufian] —**ruf'fi·an·ism** n. —**ruf'fi·an·ly** adj.

**ruf·fle** (ruf'əl) n. 1 A pleated strip; frill, as for trim or ornament. 2 Anything resembling this, as a bird's ruff. 3 A disturbance; discomposure. 4 A ripple. —v. **·fled, ·fling** v.t. 1 To disturb or destroy the smoothness or regularity of: The wind ruffles the lake. 2 To draw into folds or ruffles; gather. 3 To furnish with ruffles. 4 To erect (the feathers) in a ruff, as a bird when frightened. 5 To disturb or irritate; upset. 6 a To riffle (the pages of a book). b To shuffle (cards). —v.i. 7 To be or become rumpled or disordered. 8 To become disturbed or irritated. [ME ruffelen to ruffle]

**rug** (rug) n. 1 A covering for all or part of a floor, made of some heavy, durable fabric, strips of rag, animal skins, etc. 2 A warm covering, as of cloth, fur, etc., for the lap and feet.

**rug·ged** (rug'id) adj. 1 Having a surface that is rough or uneven. 2 Rough; harsh: a rugged life. 3 Furrowed and irregular: rugged features. 4 Lacking polish and refinement. 5 Tempestuous; stormy: rugged weather. 6 Robust; sturdy: rugged health. [< Scand.] —**rug'ged·ly** adv. —**rug'ged·ness** n.

**ru·in** (rōō'in) n. 1 Destruction, downfall, or decay. 2 A person or thing that has decayed, fallen, or been destroyed. 3 Usu. pl. That which remains of something that has decayed or been destroyed: the ruins of Dresden. 4 That which causes destruction, downfall, or decay: Gambling was his ruin. 5 The state of being destroyed, fallen, decayed, etc: to fall into ruin. —v.t. 1 To bring to ruin; destroy. 2 To bring to disgrace or bankruptcy. 3 To deprive of chastity; seduce. —v.i. 4 To fall into ruin. [< L ruere to fall] —**ru'in·er** n. —Syn. n. 1 collapse, devastation, dilapidation. v. 1 demolish, ravage, raze.

**ru·in·ous** (rōō'in·əs) adj. 1 Causing or tending to ruin. 2 Falling to ruin. —**ru'in·ous·ly** adv. —**ru'in·ous·ness** n.

**rule** (rōōl) n. 1 Controlling power, or its possession and exercise; government; reign; also, the period of time during which a ruler or government is in power. 2 A method or principle of action; regular course of procedure: I make early rising my rule. 3 An authoritative direction or regulation about something to do or the way of doing it. 4

The body of directions laid down by or for a religious order: the *rule* of St. Francis. 5 A procedure or formula for solving a given class of mathematical problems. 6 An established usage fixing the form of words: a *rule* for forming the plural. 7 Something in the ordinary course of events or condition of things: In some communities illiteracy is the *rule*. 8 *Law* A judicial decision on some specific question or point of law. 9 A straight-edged instrument for use in measuring, or as a guide in drawing lines; a ruler. 10 *Printing* A strip of type-high metal for printing a rule or line. —as a rule Ordinarily; usually. —v. ruled, rul·ing v.t. 1 To have authority or control over; govern. 2 To influence greatly; dominate. 3 To decide judicially or authoritatively. 4 To restrain; keep in check. 5 To mark lines on, as with a ruler. —v.i. 6 To have authority or control. 7 To form and express a decision: The judge *ruled* on that point. —rule out 1 To eliminate or exclude. 2 To preclude; prevent. [< L *regula* ruler, rule]

**rul·er** (rōō′lər) *n.* 1 One who rules or governs, as a sovereign. 2 A straight-edged strip of wood, metal, etc., used in drawing lines and in measuring.

**rum·ba** (rum′bə, *Sp.* rōōm′bä) *n.* 1 A dance originated by Cuban Negroes. 2 A ballroom dance based on this. 3 Music for such a dance. —v.i. To dance the rumba. [Sp.]

**rum·ble** (rum′bəl) *v.* ·bled, ·bling v.i. 1 To make a low, heavy, rolling sound, as thunder. 2 To move or proceed with such a sound. —v.t. 3 To cause to make a low, heavy, rolling sound. 4 To utter with such a sound. —n. 1 A continuous low, heavy, rolling sound; a muffled roar. 2 A seat or baggage compartment in the rear of an automobile or carriage: also rumble seat. 3 *Slang* A street fight involving a group, usu. deliberately provoked. [< MDu. *rommelen*]

**ru·mi·nate** (rōō′mə·nāt) *v.t. & v.i.* ·nat·ed, ·nat·ing 1 To chew (food previously swallowed and regurgitated) over again; chew (the cud). 2 To meditate or reflect (upon). — ru′mi·nat′ing·ly, ru′mi·na′tive·ly *adv.* — ru′mi·na′tion, ru′mi·na′tor *n.* —Syn. 2 brood, consider, contemplate, muse.

**rum·mage** (rum′ij) *v.* ·maged, ·mag·ing v.t. 1 To search through (a place, box, etc.) by turning over and disarranging the contents; ransack. 2 To find or bring out by searching: with *out* or *up*. —v.i. 3 To make a thorough search. —n. 1 Any act of rummaging, esp., disarranging things by searching thoroughly. 2 Odds and ends. [< MF *arrumer* pack or arrange cargo] —rum′mag·er *n.*

**ru·mor** (rōō′mər) *n.* 1 A story or report circulating without known foundation or authority. 2 Common gossip; hearsay. —v.t. To tell or spread as a rumor; report abroad. *Brit. sp.* ru′mour. [L, noise]

**rump** (rump) *n.* 1 The upper part of the hindquarters of an animal. 2 A cut of beef from this part. 3 The buttocks. 4 A last, often unimportant or undesirable part.

**rum·ple** (rum′pəl) *v.t. & v.i.* ·pled, ·pling To form into creases or folds; wrinkle. —n. An irregular fold or crease; wrinkle. [< MDu. *rumpelen*]

**rum·pus** (rum′pəs) *n. Informal* A usu. noisy disturbance or commotion. [?]

**run** (run) *v.* ran, run, run·ning v.i. 1 To move by rapid steps, faster than walking. 2 To move rapidly; go swiftly. 3 To flee; take flight. 4 To make a brief or rapid journey: We *ran* over to Staten Island last night. 5 To make regular trips: This steamer *runs* between New York and Liverpool. 6 a To take part in a race. b To be a candidate or contestant: to *run* for dogcatcher. 7 To finish a race in a specified position: I *ran* a poor last. 8 To move or pass easily: The rope *runs* through the pulley. 9 To pass or flow rapidly: watching the tide *run* out. 10 To proceed in direction or extent: This road *runs* north. 11 To flow: His nose *runs*. 12 To become liquid and flow, as wax; also, to spread or mingle confusedly, as colors when wet. 13 To move or roam about freely and easily: to *run* around town with friends. 14 To pass into a specified condition: to *run* to seed. 15 To unravel, as a fabric. 16 To give forth a discharge or flow. 17 To leak. 18 To continue or proceed without restraint: The conversation *ran* on and on. 19 To be operative; work: Will the engine *run?* 20 To continue or extend, as in time or space: Our property *runs* down to the sea. 21 To be reported or expressed: The story *runs* as follows. 22 To migrate, as salmon from the sea to spawn. 23 To occur or return to the mind: An idea *ran* through his head. 24 To occur with specified variation of size, quality, etc.: The corn is *running* small this year. 25 To be performed or repeated in continuous succession: The play *ran* for forty nights. 26 To pass or spread, as from mouth to mouth or point to point: rumors *running* wild. **27** To creep or climb, as a vine. —*v.t.* **28** To run or proceed along, as a route or path. **29** To make one's way over, through, or past: to *run* rapids. **30** To perform or accomplish by or as by running: to *run* a race or an errand. **31** To compete against in or as in a race. **32** To become subject to; incur: to *run* the risk of failure. **33** To present and support as a candidate. **34** To hunt or chase, as game. **35** To bring to a specified condition by or as by running: to *run* oneself out of breath. **36** To drive or force: with *out of, off, into, through,* etc. **37** To cause to move, as in some manner or direction: They *ran* the ship into port. **38** To move (the eye, hand, etc.) quickly or lightly: He *ran* his hand over the table. **39** To cause to move, slide, etc., as into a specified position: to *run* up a flag. **40** To transport or convey in a vessel or vehicle. **41** To smuggle. **42** To cause to flow: to *run* water into a pot. **43** To trace back: trying to *run* a bit of gossip to its source. **44** To mold, as from melted metal; found. **45** To sew (cloth) in a continuous line, usu. by taking a number of stitches with the needle at a time. **46** To control the motion or operation of; operate: to *run* an engine. **47** To direct or control; manage. **48** To allow to continue or mount up, as a bill. **49** In games, to make (a number of points, strokes, etc.) successively. **50** To publish in a magazine or newspaper: to *run* an ad. **51** To mark, set down, or trace, as a boundary line. **52** To suffer from (a fever, etc.). —**run across** To meet by chance. —**run down 1** To pursue and overtake, as a fugitive. **2** To strike down while moving. **3** To exhaust or damage, as by abuse or overwork. **4** To speak of disparagingly. —**run for it** To run to avoid something, to escape, seek safety, etc. —**run in 1** To insert; include. **2** *Slang* To arrest and place in confinement. —**run into 1** To meet by chance. **2** To collide with. —**run off 1** To produce on a typewriter, printing press, etc. **2** To decide (a tied race, game, etc.) by the outcome of another, subsequent race, game, etc. —**run out** To be exhausted, as supplies. —**run out of** To exhaust one's supply of. —**run over 1** To ride or drive over; run down. **2** To overflow. **3** To go over, examine, or rehearse. —**run through 1** To squander. **2** To stab or pierce. **3** To rehearse quickly. —**run up** To make hurriedly, as on a sewing machine. —*n.* **1** The act, or an act, of running or going rapidly. **2** A running

pace: to break into a *run.* **3** Flow; movement; sweep: the *run* of the tide. **4** A distance covered by running. **5** A journey or passage, esp. between two points, made by a vessel, train, etc. **6** A rapid journey or excursion: take a *run* into town. **7** A swift stream or brook. **8** A migration of fish, esp. to up-river spawning grounds; also, the fish that so migrate. **9** A grazing or feeding ground for animals: a sheep *run.* **10** The regular trail or path of certain animals: an elephant *run.* **11** The privilege of free use or access: to have the *run* of the place. **12** A runway. **13** *Music* A rapid succession of tones. **14** A series, sequence, or succession. **15** A trend or tendency: the general *run* of the market. **16** A continuous spell (of some condition): a *run* of luck. **17** A surge of demands, as those made upon a bank or treasury to meet its obligations. **18** A period of continuous performance, occurrence, popularity, etc.: a play with a long *run.* **19** Class or type; also, the usual or general class or type. **20** A period of operation of a machine or device: an experimental *run.* **21** The output during such a period. **22** A period during which a liquid is allowed to run. **23** The amount of liquid allowed to flow at one time. **24** A narrow, lengthwise ravel, as in a sheer stocking. **25** An approach to a target made by a bombing plane. **26** In baseball, a score made by a player who completes a circuit of the bases from home plate before three outs are made. **27** An unbroken series of successful shots, strokes, etc., as in billiards. —**in the long run** As the ultimate outcome of any train of circumstances. —**on the run 1** Hastily: to eat *on the run.* **2** Running, running away, or retreating. —*adj.* **1** Made liquid; melted. **2** That has been melted or cast: *run* metal. [< OE *rinnan* to flow]

**rung** (rung) *n.* **1** A round crosspiece of a ladder or chair. **2** A spoke of a wheel. [< OE *hrung* crossbar]

**runt** (runt) *n.* **1** A stunted animal, esp. the smallest of a litter. **2** A small or stunted person. [?] —**runt′i·ness** *n.* —**runt′y** *adj.* (·**i·er,** ·**i·est**)

**rup·ture** (rup′chər) *n.* **1** The act of breaking apart or the state of being broken apart. **2** HERNIA. **3** Breach of peace and agreement between individuals or nations. —*v.t. & v.i.* ·**tured,** ·**tur·ing 1** To break apart. **2** To affect with or suffer a rupture. [< L *ruptus,* p.p. of *rumpere* to break]

**ru·ral** (rŏŏr′əl) *adj.* Of or pertaining to the country, country people, country life, or agriculture. [< L *rus, ruris* country] —**ru′ral·ism, ru′ral·ist, ru′ral·ness** *n.* —**ru′ral·ly** *adv.*

**ruse** (rōōs, rōōz) *n.* An action intended to mislead or deceive; a stratagem; trick. [< F *ruser* dodge, detour]

**rush** (rush) *v.i.* 1 To move or go swiftly, impetuously, forcefully, or violently. 2 To make an attack; charge: with *on* or *upon.* 3 To proceed recklessly or rashly; plunge: with *in* or *into.* 4 To come, go, pass, act, etc. with suddenness or haste: Ideas kept *rushing* to her mind. 5 To advance a football in a running play. —*v.t.* 6 To move, push, drive, etc. with haste, impetuosity, or violence. 7 To do, perform, deliver, etc. hastily or hurriedly: to *rush* one's work. 8 To make a sudden assault upon. 9 *Slang* To seek the favor of with assiduous attentions. 10 To advance (a football) in a running play. —*n.* 1 The act of rushing; a sudden turbulent movement, drive, surge, etc. 2 Frantic activity; haste: the *rush* of business. 3 A sudden pressing demand; a run: a *rush* on foreign bonds. 4 A sudden exigency; urgent pressure: a *rush* of business. 5 A sudden flocking of people, as to some new location. 6 A general contest or scrimmage between students from different classes. 7 In football, an attempt to take the ball through the opposing linemen and toward the goal. 8 *Usu. pl.* In motion pictures, the first film prints of a scene or series of scenes, before editing or selection. —**with a rush** Suddenly and hastily. —*adj.* Requiring urgency or haste: a *rush* order. [< AF *russher* to push] —**rush′er** *n.* —**Syn.** *v.* 1 Dash, hasten, hurry.

**rus·set** (rus′it) *n.* 1 Reddish brown or yellowish brown. 2 A coarse homespun cloth, russet in color, formerly used by country people. 3 A winter apple of russet color. —*adj.* 1 Reddish brown or yellowish brown. 2 Made of russet. [< L *russus* reddish] —**rus′set·y** *adj.*

**rust** (rust) *n.* 1 A reddish or yellow coating on iron or iron alloys due to spontaneous oxidation. 2 A corroded spot or film of oxide on any metal. 3 Any of various parasitic fungi living on higher plants. 4 A plant disease caused by such fungi, which form spots on stems and leaves. 5 Any spot or film resembling rust on metal. 6 Any of several shades of reddish brown. —*v.t. & v.i.* 1 To become or cause to become coated with rust. 2 To contract or cause to contract the plant disease rust. 3 To become or cause to become weakened because of disuse. [< OE *rūst*]

**rus·tic** (rus′tik) *adj.* 1 Of or pertaining to the country; rural. 2 Uncultured; rude; awkward. 3 Unsophisticated; artless. 4 Made of the rough limbs of trees with the bark on them: *rustic* furniture. —*n.* 1 One who lives in the country. 2 An unsophisticated, coarse, or ignorant person, esp. one from a rural area. [< L *rus* country] —**rus′ti·cal·ly** *adv.*

**rus·tle** (rus′əl) *v.t. & v.i.* ·tled, ·tling To move or cause to move with a quick succession of small, light, rubbing sounds, as dry leaves or sheets of paper. —*n.* A rustling sound. [ME *rustelen*] —**rus′tler** *n.* —**rus′tling·ly** *adv.*

**rut** (rut) *n.* 1 A sunken track worn by a wheel, as in a road. 2 A groove, furrow, etc., in which something runs. 3 A settled and tedious routine. —*v.t.* rut·ted, rut·ting To wear or make a rut or ruts in. [? Var. of ROUTE] —**rut′ti·ness** *n.* —**rut′ty** *adj.* (·i·er, ·i· est)

**ruth·less** (rōōth′lis) *adj.* Having no compassion; merciless. —**ruth′less·ly** *adv.* —**ruth′less·ness** *n.*

**rye** (rī) *n.* 1 A hardy, cultivated cereal grass. 2 The seeds of this grass. 3 Flour made from these seeds. 4 Whiskey consisting of a blend of bourbon and neutral spirits: also **rye whiskey.** [< OE *ryge*]

# S

**Sab·bath** (sab′əth) *n.* 1 The seventh day of the week, a day of rest observed in Judaism and some Christian sects; Saturday. 2 The first day of the week as observed as a day of rest by Christians; Sunday. [< Heb. *shā bath* to rest]

**sa·ber** (sā′bər) *n.* A heavy one-edged cavalry sword, often curved. —*v.t.* ·bered or ·bred, ·ber·ing or ·bring To strike, wound, kill, or arm with a saber. Also, and *Brit. sp.*, **sa′bre.** [< MHG *sabel*]

**sa·ble** (sā′bəl) *n.* 1 A N Eurasian species of marten bearing costly fur. 2 The dressed fur of a sable. 3 *pl.* Garments made wholly or partly of this fur. 4 The color black. —*adj.* 1 Black; dark. 2 Made of sable fur. [< Med. L *sabelum*]

**sab·o·tage** (sab′ə·täzh) *n.* 1 A wasting of materials or damage to machinery, tools, etc., by workmen to make management comply with their demands. 2 The destruction of bridges, railroads, supply depots, etc., either by enemy agents or by underground resisters. 3 Any deliberate effort to obstruct plans or aims. —*v.t.* & *v.i.* ·taged, ·tag·ing To engage in, damage, or destroy by sabotage. [F < *saboter* work badly, damage]

**sab·o·teur** (sab′ə·tûr′, *Fr.* sȧ·bô·tœr′) *n.* One who engages in sabotage. [F]

**sac** (sak) *n.* A membranous pouch or cavity, often fluid-filled, in a plant or animal. [< L *saccus*]

**sac·cha·rin** (sak′ər·in) *n.* A sweet compound derived from coal tar, used as a substitute for sugar. [< Gk. *sakcharon* sugar]

**sa·chet** (sa·shā′) *n.* 1 A small bag for perfumed powder, used to scent closets, dresser drawers, etc. 2 The perfumed powder so used. [< L *saccus* a sack]

**sack** (sak) *n.* 1 A large bag for holding heavy articles. 2 Such a bag and its contents: a *sack* of potatoes. 3 A measure or weight of varying amount. 4 A loosely hanging dress without a waistline, often worn without a belt: **also sack dress.** 5 A short, loosely fitting coatlike garment worn by women and children. 6 *Slang* Dismissal, esp. in the phrases **get the sack, give (someone) the sack.** 7 In baseball slang, a base. 8 *Slang* A bed; mattress. —**hit the sack** *Slang* To go to bed; retire for the night. —*v.t.* 1 To put into a sack or sacks. 2 *Slang* To dismiss, as an employee. [< Gk. *sakkos* < Heb. *saq* sackcloth]

**sac·ra·ment** (sak′rə·mənt) *n.* 1 A rite ordained by Christ or by the church as an outward sign of grace, as baptism, confirmation, marriage, etc. 2 *Often cap.* **a** The Eucharist. **b** The consecrated bread and wine of the Eucharist: often with *the*. 3 Any solemn covenant or pledge. 4 Anything considered to have sacred significance. [< L *sacramentum* oath, pledge] —**sac′ra·men′tal** *adj.* —**sac′ra·men′tal·ly** *adv.*

**sa·cred** (sā′krid) *adj.* 1 Dedicated to religious use; hallowed. 2 Pertaining or related to religion: *sacred* books. 3 Consecrated by love or reverence: *sacred* to the memory of his father. 4 Dedicated to a person or purpose: a memorial *sacred* to those killed in battle. 5 Not to be profaned; inviolable: a *sacred* promise. [< L *sacer* holy] —**sa′cred·ly** *adv.* —**sa′cred·ness** *n.*

**sac·ri·fice** (sak′rə·fīs) *n.* 1 The act of making an offering to a deity. 2 That which is sac-

rificed; a victim. 3 A giving up of something cherished or desired. 4 Loss incurred or suffered without return. 5 A reduction of price that leaves little profit or involves loss. 6 In baseball, a hit by which the batter is put out, but the base runner is advanced: **also sacrifice hit.** —*v.* ·ficed, ·fic·ing *v.t.* 1 To give up (something valued) for the sake of something else: to *sacrifice* one's principles for expediency. 2 To sell or part with at a loss. 3 To make an offering, as to a god. 4 In baseball, to advance (one or more runners) by means of a sacrifice. —*v.i.* 5 To make a sacrifice. [< L *sacer* holy + *facere* to make] —**sac′ri·fic′er** *n.* —**sac′ri·fic′ing·ly** *adv.*

**sac·ri·fi·cial** (sak′rə·fish′əl) *adj.* Pertaining to, performing, or of the nature of a sacrifice. —**sac′ri·fi′cial·ly** *adv.*

**sac·ri·lege** (sak′rə·lij) *n.* The act of violating or profaning anything sacred. [< L *sacer* holy + *legere* to plunder]

**sac·ri·le·gious** (sak′rə·lij′əs, -lē′jəs) *adj.* Disrespectful or injurious to sacred persons or things. —**sac′ri·le′gious·ly** *adv.* —**sac′ri·le′gious·ness** *n.* —Syn. blasphemous, godless, impious, irreligious, profane.

**sad** (sad) *adj.* **sad·der, sad·dest** 1 Sorrowful or depressed in spirits; mournful. 2 Causing sorrow or pity; distressing. 3 *Informal* Very bad; awful: a *sad* situation. 4 Dark-hued; somber. [< OE *sæd* sated] —**sad′ly** *adv.* —**sad′ness** *n.* —Syn. 1 dejected, despondent, disconsolate, miserable, unhappy, depressed. 2 deplorable, grievous, lamentable, pitiful.

**sad·den** (sad′n) *v.t.* & *v.i.* To make or become sad.

**sad·dle** (sad′l) *n.* 1 A seat or pad for a rider, as on the back of a horse, bicycle, motorcycle, etc. 2 A padded cushion for a horse's back, as part of a harness or to support a pack, etc. 3 The two hindquarters and part of the backbone of a carcass, as of mutton, venison, etc. 4 Some part or object like or likened to a saddle, as in form or position. —**in the saddle** In a position of control. —*v.t.* ·dled, ·dling 1 To put a saddle on. 2 To load, as with a burden. 3 To place (a burden or responsibility) on a person. [< OE *sadol*]

**sad sack** *Slang* A well-meaning but bungling person, esp. a soldier.

**sa·fa·ri** (sə·fä′rē) *n. pl.* ·ris A hunting expedition or journey, esp. in E Africa. [< Ar. *safara* travel]

**safe** (sāf) *adj.* **saf·er, saf·est 1** Free or freed from danger. **2** Having escaped injury or damage. **3** Not involving risk or loss: a *safe* investment. **4** Not likely to disappoint: It is *safe* to promise. **5** Not likely to cause or do harm or injury: Is this ladder *safe?* **6** No longer in a position to do harm: a burglar *safe* in jail. **7** In baseball, having reached base without being retired. —*n.* **1** A strong iron-and-steel receptacle, usu. fireproof, for protecting valuables. **2** Any place of safe storage. [< L *salvus* whole, healthy] — **safe′ly** *adv.* —**safe′ness** *n.* —**Syn. 1** secure. **2** unharmed, unscathed. **3** dependable, reliable.

**safe·guard** (sāf′gärd′) *n.* **1** One who or that which guards or keeps in safety. **2** A mechanical device designed to prevent accident or injury. —*v.t.* To defend; guard.

**safety match** A match that ignites only if struck on a chemically prepared surface.

**safety pin 1** A pin whose point springs into place within a protecting sheath. • See PIN. **2** A pin which prevents the premature detonation of a hand grenade.

**sag** (sag) *v.* **sagged, sag·ging** *v.i.* **1** To droop from weight or pressure, esp. in the middle. **2** To hang unevenly. **3** To lose firmness; weaken, as from exhaustion, age, etc. **4** To decline, as in price or value. —*v.t.* **5** To cause to sag. —*n.* **1** A sagging. **2** A depressed or sagging place: a *sag* in a roof. [ME *saggen*] —**sag′ging·ly** *adv.*

**sa·ga·cious** (sə·gā′shəs) *adj.* **1** Ready and apt to apprehend and to decide on a course; intelligent. **2** Shrewd and practical. [< L *sagax* wise] —**sa·ga′cious·ly** *adv.* —**sa·ga′cious·ness** *n.* —**Syn. 1** acute, discerning, clear-sighted, keen, perspicacious.

**sage** (sāj) *n.* A venerable man of profound wisdom, experience, and foresight. —*adj.* **1** Characterized by or proceeding from calm, far-seeing wisdom and prudence: a *sage* observation. **2** Profound; learned; wise. [< L *sapere* be wise] —**sage′ly** *adv.* —**sage′ness** *n.*

**sail** (sāl) *n.* **1** *Naut.* A piece of canvas, etc., attached to a mast, spread to catch the wind, and thus to propel a craft through the water. **2** Sails collectively. **3** *pl.* **sail** A sailing vessel or craft. **4** A trip in any watercraft. **5** Anything resembling a sail in form or use, as a windmill arm. —**set sail** To begin a voyage. —**take in sail** To lower the sails of a craft. —**under sail** With sails spread and driven by the wind. —*v.i.* **1** To move across the surface of water by the action of wind or steam. **2** To travel over water in a ship or boat. **3** To begin a voyage. **4** To manage a sailing craft: Can you *sail?* **5** To move, glide, or float in the air; soar. **6** To move along in a stately or dignified manner: She *sailed* by haughtily. **7** *Informal* To pass rapidly. **8** *Informal* To proceed boldly into action: with *in.* —*v.t.* **9** To move or travel across the surface of (a body of water) in a ship or boat. **10** To navigate. —**sail into 1** To begin with energy. **2** To attack violently. [< OE *segl*]

**sail·or** (sā′lər) *n.* **1** An enlisted man in any navy. **2** One whose work is sailing. **3** One who works on a ship. **4** One skilled in sailing. **5** A passenger on a ship or boat, esp. in reference to seasickness: a good *sailor.* **6** A low-crowned, flat-topped hat with a brim. —**sail′or·ly** *adj.*

**saint** (sānt) *n.* **1** A holy or sanctified person. **2** Such a person who has died and been canonized by certain churches, as the Roman Catholic. **3** *Often cap.* A member of any of certain religious sects calling themselves saints. **4** A very patient, unselfish person. —*v.t.* To canonize; venerate as a saint. —*adj.* Holy; canonized. [< L *sanctus* holy, consecrated] —**saint′hood** *n.*

**sake¹** (sāk) *n.* **1** Purpose; motive; end: for the *sake* of peace and quiet. **2** Interest, regard, or consideration: for the *sake* of your children. [< OE *saccu* a (legal) case]

**sa·ke²** (sä′kē) *n.* A Japanese fermented alcoholic liquor made from rice: also **sa′ki.**

**sal·a·ble** (sā′lə·bəl) *adj.* Such as can be sold; marketable. —**sal′a·bil′i·ty, sal′a·ble·ness** *n.* —**sal′a·bly** *adv.*

**sal·ad** (sal′əd) *n.* **1** A dish of vegetables such as lettuce, cucumbers, tomatoes, etc., usu. uncooked and served with a dressing, sometimes mixed with chopped cold meat, fish, hard-boiled eggs, etc. **2** Any green vegetable that can be eaten raw. [< L *salare* to salt]

**sal·a·man·der** (sal′ə·man′dər) *n.* **1** Any of an order of tailed amphibians having a smooth, moist skin. **2** A fabled reptile purportedly able to live in fire. [< L *salamandra*] —**sal′a·man′drine** (-drin) *adj.*

**sal·a·ry** (sal′ər·ē) *n. pl.* **·ries** A periodic payment as compensation for official or professional services. —*v.t.* **·ried, ·ry·ing** To pay or allot a salary to. [< L *salarium* money paid Roman soldiers for their salt]

**sale** (sāl) *n.* **1** The exchange or transfer of

property for money or its equivalent. 2 A selling of merchandise at prices lower than usual. 3 An auction. 4 Opportunity of selling; market: Stocks find no *sale*. 5 *Usu. pl.* The amount sold: last year's *sales*. —for sale Offered or ready for sale. —on sale For sale at bargain rates. [< OE *sala*]

**sales·man** (sālz′mən) *n. pl.* **·men** (-mən) A man hired to sell goods, stock, etc., in a store or by canvassing.

**sa·li·ent** (sā′lē·ənt) *adj.* 1 Standing out prominently: a *salient* feature. 2 Extending outward; projecting: a *salient* angle. 3 Leaping; springing. —*n.* An extension, as of a fortification or a military line protruding toward the enemy. [< L *salire* to leap] —**sa′li·ence,** **sa′li·en·cy** *n.* —**sa′li·ent** (ly *adv.* —Syn. 1 conspicuous, noticeable, significant. 2 jutting.

**sa·line** (sā′lēn, sā′līn) *adj.* Constituting, consisting of, or characteristic of salt; salty. —*n.* 1 A metallic salt, esp. a salt of one of the alkalis or of magnesium. 2 A solution of sodium chloride or other salt. 3 A natural deposit of salt. [< L *sal* salt] —**sa·lin·i·ty** (sə·lin′ə·tē) *n.*

**sa·li·va** (sə·lī′və) *n.* A mixture of mucus and fluid secreted by glands in the cheeks and lower jaw. [L] —**sal·i·var·y** (sal′ə·ver′ē) *adj.*

**sal·low** (sal′ō) *adj.* Of an unhealthy yellowish color or complexion. —*v.t.* To make sallow. [< OE *salo*] —**sal′low·ness** *n.*

**salm·on** (sam′ən) *n.* 1 Any of various anadromous food and game fishes inhabiting cool ocean waters and certain landlocked lakes. 2 The pinkish orange color of the flesh of certain salmon: also **salm′on-pink′.** —*adj.* Having the color salmon: also **salm′on-pink′.** [< L *salmo*]

**sa·lon** (sə·lon′, sal′on, *Fr.* sá·lôn′) *n.* 1 A room in which guests are received; a drawing-room. 2 The periodic gathering of noted persons, under the auspices of some distinguished personage. 3 A hall or gallery used for exhibiting works of art. 4 An establishment devoted to some specific purpose: a beauty *salon*. [< Ital. *sala* a room, hall]

**sa·loon** (sə·lōōn′) *n.* 1 A place where alcoholic drinks are sold; a bar. 2 A large room for public use, as on a passenger ship: a dining *saloon*. [< F *salon* salon] • In the U.S., *saloon* (def. 1) is now used mainly in historical contexts dealing with the American western frontier or as a rough equivalent of *dive* in describing a squalid bar.

**salt** (sôlt) *n.* 1 A white, soluble, crystalline

compound of sodium and chlorine, widely distributed in nature and found in all living organisms: **also table salt, common salt.** 2 *Chem.* Any compound derived from an acid by replacement of all or part of the hydrogen by an electropositive radical or a metal. 3 *pl.* Any of various mineral compounds in common use, as Epsom salts, smelling salts, etc. 4 Piquant humor; dry wit. 5 That which preserves, corrects, or purifies: the *salt* of criticism. 6 A sailor. 7 A saltcellar. —**salt of the earth** A person or persons regarded as being fine, honest, kindly, etc. —**take with a grain of salt** To allow for exaggeration; have doubts about. —**worth one's salt** Worth one's pay or keep; hardworking. —*adj.* 1 Seasoned with salt; salty. 2 Cured or preserved with salt. 3 Containing, or growing or living in or near, salt water. —*v.t.* 1 To season with salt. 2 To preserve or cure with salt. 3 To furnish with salt: to *salt* cattle. 4 To add zest or piquancy to. 5 To add something to so as fraudulently to increase the value: to *salt* a mine with gold. —**salt away** 1 To pack in salt for preserving. 2 *Informal* To store up; save. [< OE *sealt*] —**salt′er** *n.*

**sal·u·ta·tion** (sal′yə·tā′shən) *n.* 1 The act of saluting. 2 Any form of greeting. 3 The opening words of a letter, as *Dear Sir* or *Dear Madam.*

**sa·lu·ta·to·ri·an** (sə·lōō′tə·tôr′ē·ən, -tō′rē-) *n.* In colleges and schools, the graduating student who delivers the salutatory at commencement.

**sa·lu·ta·to·ry** (sə·lōō′tə·tôr′ē, -tō′rē) *n. pl.* **·ries** An opening oration, as at a college commencement. —*adj.* Of or relating to a salutatory address. [< L *salutare* SALUTE]

**sa·lute** (sə·lōōt′) *v.* **·lut·ed,** **·lut·ing** *v.t.* 1 To greet with an expression or sign of welcome, respect, etc.; welcome. 2 To honor in some prescribed way, as by raising the hand to the cap, presenting arms, firing cannon, etc. —*v.i.* 3 To make a salute. —*n.* 1 An act of saluting; a greeting, show of respect, etc. 2 The attitude assumed in giving a military hand salute. [< L *salutare* < *salus* health] —**sa·lut′er** *n.*

**sal·vage** (sal′vij) *v.t.* **·vaged,** **·vag·ing** 1 To save as a ship or its cargo, from wreck, capture etc. 2 To save (material) from something damaged or discarded for reuse: to *salvage* aluminum. —*n.* 1 The saving of a ship cargo, etc., from loss. 2 Any act of saving property. 3 The compensation allowed t persons by whose exertions a vessel, its cargo, or the lives of those sailing on it are saved from loss. **4** That which is saved from a wrecked or abandoned vessel or from or after a fire. **5** Anything saved from destruction. [< OF *salver* to save] —**sal′vag·er** *n.*

**sal·va·tion** (sal·vā′shən) *n.* **1** The process or state of being saved. **2** A person or thing that delivers from evil, danger, or ruin. **3** *Theol.* Deliverance from sin and penalty; redemption. [< LL *salvare* to save]

**salve** (salv) *v.t.* **salved, salv·ing** To save from loss; salvage. [Back formation < SALVAGE]

**sal·vo** (sal′vō) *n. pl.* **·vos** or **·voes 1** A simultaneous discharge of artillery, or of two or more bombs from an aircraft. **2** A sudden discharge or burst: a *salvo* of hail. **3** Tribute; praise. [< Ital. *salva* a salute]

**sam·ple** (sam′pəl) *n.* **1** A portion, part, or piece taken or shown as a representative of the whole. **2** An instance: This is a *sample* of his kindness. —*v.t.* **·pled, ·pling** To test or examine by means of a portion or sample. —*adj.* Serving as a sample: a *sample* dress. [< OF *essample* example]

**san·a·to·ri·um** (san′ə·tôr′ē·əm, -tō′rē-) *n. pl.* **·to·ri·ums** or **·to·ri·a** (-tôr′ē·ə, -tō′rē·ə) An institution for the treatment of chronic disorders, as mental illness, alcoholism, etc. [< LL *sanatorius* healthy]

**sanc·ti·fy** (sangk′tə·fī) *v.t.* **·fied, ·fy·ing 1** To set apart as holy; consecrate. **2** To free of sin; purify. **3** To render sacred or inviolable, as a vow. [< L *sanctus* holy + *facere* to make] —**sanc′ti·fi·ca′tion, sanc′ti·fi′er** *n.*

**sanc·ti·mo·ni·ous** (sangk′tə·mō′nē·əs) *adj.* Making an ostentatious display or a hypocritical pretense of sanctity. —**sanc′ti·mo′ni·ous·ly** *adv.* —**sanc′ti·mo′ni·ous·ness** *n.*

**sanc·tion** (sangk′shən) *v.t.* **1** To approve authoritatively; confirm; ratify. **2** To countenance; allow. —*n.* **1** Final and authoritative confirmation; justification or ratification. **2** A formal decree. **3** A provision for securing conformity to law, as by the enactment of rewards or penalties or both. **4** *pl.* In international law, a coercive measure adopted by several nations to force a nation to obey international law, by limiting trade relations, by military force and blockade, etc. [< L *sanctus*, p.p. of *sancire* make sacred]

**sanc·ti·ty** (sangk′tə·tē) *n. pl.* **·ties 1** The state of being sacred or holy. **2** Saintliness; holiness. **3** Something sacred or holy.

**sanc·tu·ar·y** (sangk′chŏō·er′ē) *n. pl.* **·ar·ies 1** A holy or sacred place, esp. one devoted to the worship of a deity. **2** The most sacred part of a place in a sacred structure; esp. the part of a church where the principal altar is situated. **3** A place of refuge: a wildlife *sanctuary.* **4** Immunity from the law or punishment. [< L *sanctus* holy] —**Syn. 1** church, shrine, temple. **3** preserve, shelter.

**san·dal** (san′dəl) *n.* **1** A foot covering, consisting usu. of a sole only, held to the foot by thongs or straps. **2** A light, openwork slipper. [< Gk. *sandalion*] —**san′daled** *adj.*

**sand·pa·per** (sand′pā′pər) *n.* Strong paper coated with abrasive for smoothing or polishing. —*v.t.* To rub or polish with sandpaper.

**sand·stone** (sand′stōn′) *n.* A rock consisting chiefly of quartz sand cemented with other materials.

**sand·wich** (sand′wich, san′-) *n.* **1** Two or more slices of bread, having between them meat, cheese, etc. **2** Any combination of alternating dissimilar things pressed together. —*v.t.* To place between other persons or things. [< John Montagu, fourth Earl of *Sandwich,* 1718–92]

**sane** (sān) *adj.* **san·er, san·est 1** Mentally sound; not deranged. **2** Proceeding from a sound mind. **3** Sensible; wise. [< L *sanus* whole, healthy] —**sane′ly** *adv.* —**sane′ness** *n.*

**san·guine** (sang′gwin) *adj.* **1** Of buoyant disposition; hopeful. **2** Having the color of blood; ruddy: a *sanguine* complexion. **3** *Obs.* Bloodthirsty; sanguinary. **Also san·guin·e·ous** (sang·gwin′ē·əs). [< L *sanguis* blood] —**san′guine·ly** *adv.* —**san′guine·ness** *n.* —**Syn. 1** ardent, confident, enthusiastic, optimistic. **2** rubicund.

**san·i·tar·i·um** (san′ə·târ′ē·əm) *n. pl.* **·i·ums** or **·i·a** (-ē·ə) **1** A health resort. **2** SANATORIUM. [< L *sanitas* health]

**san·i·tar·y** (san′ə·ter′ē) *adj.* **1** Relating to the preservation of health and prevention of disease: *sanitary* measures. **2** Free from filth; clean; hygienic. —*n. pl.* **·tar·ies** A public toilet. [< L *sanitas* health] —**san′i·tar′i·ly** *adv.*

**san·i·ta·tion** (san′ə·tā′shən) *n.* **1** The science or process of establishing sanitary conditions, esp. as regards public health. **2** The removal of sewage, garbage, etc.

**san·i·ty** (san′ə·tē) *n.* **1** The state of being sane or sound; mental health. **2** Sane moderation or reasonableness. [< L *sanus* healthy] —**Syn.** 1 rationality, saneness. 2 common sense, level-headedness, sensibleness.

**sap**[1] (sap) *n.* 1 The juices of plants, which contain and transport the materials necessary to growth. 2 Any vital fluid; vitality. 3 Sapwood. 4 *Slang* A foolish, stupid, or ineffectual person. [< OE *sæp*]

**sap**[2] (sap) *v.* **sapped, sap·ping** *v.t.* 1 To weaken or destroy gradually and insidiously. 2 To approach or undermine (an enemy fortification) by digging trenches. — *v.i.* 3 To dig a sap or saps. —*n.* A deep, narrow trench dug so as to approach or undermine a fortification. [< MF *sappe* a spade] —**Syn.** *v.* 1 debilitate, disable, enervate, enfeeble.

**sap·phire** (saf′ir) *n.* 1 Any one of the hard, transparent, colored varieties of corundum, esp. a blue variety valued as a gem. 2 Deep blue. —**star sapphire** A sapphire cut without facets, showing six rays on the dome. —*adj.* Deep blue. [< Gk. *sappheiros* a gemstone]

**sar·casm** (sär′kaz·əm) *n.* 1 The use of keenly ironic or scornful remarks. 2 Such a remark. [< Gk. *sarkazein* tear flesh, speak bitterly] —**Syn.** 2 gibe, sneer, taunt.

**sar·cas·tic** (sär·kas′tik) *adj.* 1 Characterized by or of the nature of sarcasm. 2 Taunting. Also **sar·cas′ti·cal.** —**sar·cas′ti·cal·ly** *adv.*

**sar·coph·a·gus** (sär·kof′ə·gəs) *n.* *pl.* **·gi** (-jī) or **·gus·es** 1 A stone coffin or tomb. 2 A large ornamental coffin of marble or other stone placed in a crypt or exposed to view. [< Gk. *sarx* flesh + *phagein* eat]

**sar·don·ic** (sär·don′ik) *adj.* Scornful or derisive; sneering; mocking; cynical. [< Gk. *sardanios* bitter, scornful] —**sar·don′i·cal·ly** *adv.* —**sar·don′i·cism** *n.*

**sash**[1] (sash) *n.* An ornamental band or scarf, worn around the waist or over the shoulder. [< Ar. *shāsh* muslin, turban]

**sash**[2] (sash) *n.* A frame, as of a window, in which glass is set. —*v.t.* To furnish with a sash. [Alter. of CHASSIS, taken as a pl.]

**sate** (sāt) *v.t.* **sat·ed, sat·ing** 1 To satisfy the appetite of. 2 To indulge with too much so as to weary or sicken; satiate. [< OE *sadian*] —**Syn.** 1 gratify. 2 cloy, glut, stuff, surfeit.

**sat·el·lite** (sat′ə·līt) *n.* 1 A body held in orbit about a more massive one; a moon. 2 An artificial body propelled into orbit, esp. around the earth. 3 One who attends upon a person in power. 4 Any obsequious at-

tendant. 5 A small nation dependent on a great power. [< L *satelles* an attendant]

**sa·ti·ate** (sā′shē·āt) *v.t.* **·at·ed, ·at·ing** 1 To satisfy the appetite or desire of; gratify. 2 To fill or gratify excessively; glut. —*adj.* Filled to satiety; satiated. [< L *satis* enough] —**sa′ti·a′tion** *n.*

**sat·in** (sat′ən) *n.* A fabric of silk, rayon, etc., with glossy face and dull back. —*adj.* Of or similar to satin; glossy; smooth. [< OF] —**sat′in·y** *adj.*

**sat·ire** (sat′īr) *n.* 1 The use of sarcasm, irony, or wit in ridiculing and denouncing abuses, follies, customs, etc. 2 A literary work that ridicules in this manner. [< L *satira*]

**sa·tir·i·cal** (sə·tir′i·kəl) *adj.* 1 Given to or characterized by satire: a *satirical* writer. 2 Sarcastic; caustic; biting. Also **sa·tir′ic.** —**sa·tir′i·cal·ly** *adv.* —**sa·tir′i·cal·ness** *n.*

**sat·i·rize** (sat′ə·rīz) *v.t.* **·rized, ·riz·ing** To subject to or criticize in satire. —**sat′i·riz′er** *n.*

**sat·is·fac·tion** (sat′is·fak′shən) *n.* 1 The act of satisfying, or the state of being satisfied. 2 The making of amends, reparation, or payment. 3 That which satisfies; compensation.

**sat·is·fy** (sat′is·fī) *v.* **·fied, ·fy·ing** *v.t.* 1 To supply fully with what is desired, expected, or needed. 2 To please; gratify. 3 To free from doubt or anxiety; convince. 4 To give what is due to. 5 To pay or discharge (a debt, obligation, etc.). 6 To answer sufficiently or convincingly, as a question or objection. 7 To make reparation for; expiate. —*v.i.* 8 To give satisfaction. [< L *satis* enough + *facere* do] —**sat′is·fi′er** *n.* —**sat′is·fy′ing·ly** *adv.*

**sat·u·rate** (sach′ə·rāt) *v.t.* **·rat·ed, ·rat·ing** To soak or imbue thoroughly to the utmost capacity for absorbing or retaining. —*adj.* Saturated. [< L *satur* full] —**sat′u·ra′tor** or **sat′u·rat′er** *n.*

**sat·u·ra·tion** (sach′ə·rā′shən) *n.* 1 A saturating or being saturated. 2 A massive concentration, in any given area, as of advertising, military force, etc., for a specific purpose: often used attributively: *saturation* bombing.

**sat·yr** (sā′tər, sat′ər) *Gk. Myth.* A wanton woodland deity with a man's body and goatlike legs. —*n.* A lascivious man. [< Gk. *satyros*] —**sa·tyr·ic** (sə·tir′ik) or **·i·cal** *adj.*

**sauce** (sôs) *n.* 1 An appetizing, usu. liquid relish for food to improve its taste. 2 A dish of fruit pulp stewed and sweetened: cranberry *sauce.* 3 *Informal* Pert or impudent language. 4 *Slang* Alcoholic liquor. —*v.t.*

**sauced, sauc·ing** 1 To flavor or dress with sauce. 2 *Informal* To be saucy to. [< L *salsus* salted]

**sau·cer** (sô′sər) *n.* 1 A small dish for holding a cup. 2 Any round, shallow thing of similar shape. [< OF *saucer* sauce]

**sau·cy** (sô′sē) *adj.* ·ci·er, ci·est 1 Disrespectful to superiors; impudent. 2 Piquant; sprightly; amusing. —**sau′ci·ly** *adv.* —**sau′ci·ness** *n.*

**sauer·kraut** (sour′krout′) *n.* Shredded and salted cabbage fermented in its own juice. [< G *sauer* sour + *kraut* cabbage]

**saun·ter** (sôn′tər) *v.i.* To walk in a leisurely or lounging way; stroll. —*n.* 1 A slow, aimless manner of walking. 2 An idle stroll. [< ME *santren* muse] —**saun′ter·er** *n.* —**saun′ter·ing·ly** *adv.*

**sau·sage** (sô′sij) *n.* Finely chopped and highly seasoned meat, commonly stuffed into a prepared animal intestine or other casing. [< L *salsus* salted]

**sav·age** (sav′ij) *adj.* 1 Of a wild and untamed nature; not domesticated. 2 Fierce; ferocious. 3 Living in or belonging to the most primitive condition of human society; uncivilized. 4 Remote and wild: *savage* mountain country. —*n.* 1 A primitive or uncivilized human being. 2 A brutal and cruel person. —*v.t.* **sav·aged, sav·a·ging** To beat or maul cruelly. [< L *silva* a wood] —**sav′age·ly** *adv.* —**Syn.** *adj.* 1 undomesticated, feral. 2 brutal, bloodthirsty, barbarous. 3 uncultivated.

**sa·vant** (sə·vänt′, sav′ənt; *Fr.* sà·väṅ′) *n.* A person of exceptional learning. [F < L *sapere* be wise]

**save** (sāv) *v.* **saved, sav·ing** *v.t.* 1 To preserve or rescue from danger, harm, etc. 2 To keep from being spent, expended, or lost. 3 To set aside for future use; accumulate: often with *up.* 4 To treat carefully so as to avoid fatigue, harm, etc.: to *save* one's eyesight. 5 To prevent by timely action: A stitch in time *saves* nine. 6 *Theol.* To deliver from the consequences of sin; redeem. —*v.i.* 7 To be economical. 8 To preserve something from harm, etc. 9 To accumulate money. [< L *salvus* safe] —**sav′er** *n.*

**sav·ior** (sāv′yər) *n.* One who saves. —**the Savior** Jesus Christ. *Brit. sp.* **sav′iour.**

**sa·vor** (sā′vər) *n.* 1 Taste and smell: a *savor* of garlic. 2 Specific or characteristic quality. 3 Relish; zest: The conversation had *savor.* —*v.i.* 1 To have savor; taste or smell: with *of.* 2 To have a specified savor or char-

acter: with *of.* —*v.t.* 3 To give flavor to; season. 4 To taste or enjoy with pleasure; relish. 5 To have the savor or character of. *Brit. sp.* **sa′vour.** [< L *sapere* taste, know] —**sa′vor·er** *n.* —**sa′vor·ous** *adj.*

**saw**[1] (sô) *n.* 1 A cutting tool with pointed teeth arranged continuously along the edge of a blade or disk. 2 A tool or machine having such teeth: a power *saw.* —*v.* **sawed, sawed** or **sawn, saw·ing** *v.t.* 1 To cut or divide with or as with a saw. 2 To shape or fashion with a saw. 3 To make a motion as if sawing: The speaker *saws* the air. —*v.i.* 4 To use a saw. 5 To cut: said of a saw. 6 To be cut with a saw: This wood *saws* easily. [< OE *sagu*] —**saw′er** *n.*

**saw**[2] (sô) *n.* A proverbial or familiar saying; old maxim. [< OE *sagu*]

**say** (sā) *v.* **said, say·ing** *v.t.* 1 To speak. 2 To express in words; tell. 3 To state positively: *Say* which you prefer. 4 To recite; repeat: to *say* one's prayers. 5 To allege: They *say* that he lied. 6 To assume: He is worth, *say,* a million. —*v.i.* 7 To make a statement; speak. —**say nothing of** Without mentioning. —**that is to say** In other words. —*n.* 1 What one has said or has to say: Let him have his *say.* 2 *Informal* Right or turn to speak or choose: Now it is my *say.* —**the say** *Informal* Authority: Who has the *say* in this office? —*interj.* A hail or exclamation to command attention: also *Brit.* **I say!** [< OE *secgan*] —**say′er** *n.* —**Syn.** *v.* 1 articulate, pronounce, utter. 2 declare, affirm. 5 assert.

**say·ing** (sā′ing) *n.* 1 An utterance. 2 A maxim or saw. —**go without saying** To be so evident as to require no explanation.

**scab** (skab) *n.* 1 A crust on a wound or sore. 2 A contagious disease of sheep. 3 Any of certain plant diseases marked by a roughened or warty exterior. 4 A worker who will not join a labor union. 5 A worker who does the job of a person on strike. —*v.i.* **scabbed, scab·bing** 1 To form or become covered with a scab. 2 To act or work as a scab. [< Scand.] —**scab′bi·ly** *adv.* —**scab′bi·ness** *n.* —**scab′by** *adj.* (·i·er, ·i·est)

**scab·bard** (skab′ərd) *n.* A sheath for a weapon, as for a bayonet or a sword. —*v.t.* To sheathe in a scabbard. [< OHG *scar* a sword + *bergan* hide, protect]

**scaf·fold** (skaf′əld, -ōld) *n.* 1 A temporary elevated structure for the suport of workmen, materials, etc., as in constructing, painting, or repairing a building. 2 A platform for the execution of criminals. **3** Any raised platform. —*v.t.* To furnish or support with a scaffold. [< OF *escadafaut*]

**scal·a·wag** (skal′ə·wag) *n.* **1** *Informal* A worthless person; rascal. **2** A Southern white who became a Republican during the Reconstruction period: a contemptuous term. Also **scal′la·wag, scal′ly·wag.** [?]

**scald** (skôld) *v.t.* **1** To burn with hot liquid or steam. **2** To cleanse or treat with boiling water. **3** To heat (a liquid) to a point just short of boiling. **4** To cook in a liquid which is just short of the boiling point. —*v.i.* **5** To be or become scalded. —*n.* **1** A burn due to a hot fluid or steam. **2** Surface injury of plant tissue due to various causes, as exposure to sun, fungi, etc. [< L *ex-* very + *calidus* hot]

**scale** (skāl) *n.* **1** One of the thin, horny, usu. overlapping, protective plates covering most fishes, reptiles, etc. **2** SCALE INSECT. **3** A specialized leaf, as of a pine cone. **4** A flaky coating on metal, as from corrosion, etc. **5** Any thin, scalelike piece, as of skin. —*v.* **scaled, scal·ing** *v.t.* **1** To strip or clear of scale or scales. **2** To form scales on; cover with scales. **3** To take off in layers or scales; pare off. —*v.i.* **4** To come off in layers or scales; peel. **5** To shed scales. **6** To become incrusted with scales. [< OF *escale* a husk] —**scal′er** *n.*

**scal·lop** (skal′əp, skol′-) *n.* **1** Any of various mollusks having a hinged shell with radiating ribs and wavy edge. **2** The edible abductor muscle of certain scallops. **3** A scallop shell. **4** One of a series of semicircular curves along an edge, as for ornament. —*v.t.* **1** To shape the edge of with scallops for ornamentation. **2** To bake (food) in a casserole with a sauce, usu. topped with bread crumbs. [< MF *escalope* shell] —**scal′lop·er** *n.*

**scalp** (skalp) *n.* **1** The skin of the top and back of the skull, usu. covered with hair. **2** A portion of this, cut or torn away as a trophy among certain North American Indians. —*v.t.* **1** To cut or tear the scalp from. **2** *Informal* To buy (tickets) and sell again at prices exceeding the established rate. **3** *Informal* To buy and sell again quickly to make a small profit. —*v.i.* **4** *Informal* To scalp bonds, tickets, etc. [< Scand.] —**scalp′er** *n.*

**scal·pel** (skal′pəl) *n.* A small, sharp, surgical knife. [< L *scalpere* to cut]

**scamp** (skamp) *n.* A confirmed rogue; rascal.

[< obs. *scamp* to roam] —**scamp′ish** *adj.* — **scamp′ish·ness** *n.*

**scam·per** (skam′pər) *v.i.* To run quickly or hastily. —*n.* A hurried flight. [< L *ex* out + *campus* a plain, battlefield] —**scam′per·er** *n.*

**scan** (skan) *v.* **scanned, scan·ning** *v.t.* **1** To examine in detail; scrutinize closely. **2** To pass the eyes over quickly; glance at. **3** To separate (verse) into metrical feet. **4** *Electronics* To cause a beam, as of light, electrons, microwaves, etc., to pass systematically over a surface or through a region. —*v.i.* **5** To scan verse. **6** To conform to metrical rules: said of verse. [<LL *scandere* scan verses] —**scan′ner** *n.*

**scan·dal** (skan′dəl) *n.* **1** A discreditable action or circumstance offensive to public morals or feelings. **2** Injury to reputation. **3** General criticism that injures reputation; malicious gossip. **4** A person whose conduct arouses public censure. [< Gk. *skandalon* a snare] —**Syn.** 2 discredit, disgrace, disrepute. 3 calumny, defamation, slander.

**scan·dal·ize** (skan′dəl·īz) *v.t.* **·ized, ·iz·ing** To shock the moral feelings of; outrage. — **scan′dal·i·za′tion, scan′dal·iz′er** *n.*

**scan·dal·ous** (skan′dəl·əs) *adj.* **1** Causing or being a scandal; disgraceful. **2** Consisting of evil or malicious reports. —**scan′dal·ous·ly** *adv.* —**scan′dal·ous·ness** *n.*

**scant** (skant) *adj.* **1** Meager in measure or quantity. **2** Being just short of the measure specified: a *scant* half-hour; a *scant* five yards. —**scant of** Insufficiently supplied with: to be *scant of* breath from running. — *v.t.* **1** To restrict or limit in supply; stint. **2** To treat briefly or inadequately. —*adv.* Regional Scarcely; barely. [< ON *skammr* short] —**scant′ly** *adv.* —**scant′ness** *n.*

**scape·goat** (skāp′gōt′) *n.* **1** In the Bible, the goat upon whose head Aaron symbolically laid the sins of the people on the day of atonement, after which it was led away into the wilderness. *Lev.* 16. **2** Any person bearing blame for the misdeeds of others. —*v.t.* *Informal* To make a scapegoat of. [< ESCAPE + GOAT]

**scar** (skär) *n.* **1** The mark left after the healing of a lesion. **2** Any lingering sign, as from hardship, misfortune, etc.: the *scars* of poverty. —*v.t.* & *v.i.* **scarred, scar·ring** To mark or become marked with a scar. [< LL *eschara* a scab]

**scarce** (skârs) *adj.* **scarc·er, scarc·est 1** Rare and unusual: *scarce* antiques. **2** Scant; insufficient. **—make oneself scarce** *Informal* To go or stay away. [< OF *eschars* scanty, insufficient] **—scarce′ness** *n.*

**scar·ci·ty** (skâr′sə·tē) *n. pl.* **·ties** 1 Scantiness; insufficiency: a *scarcity* of truffles. 2 Rarity: the *scarcity* of genius.

**scare** (skâr) *v.* **scared, scar·ing** *v.t.* 1 To strike with sudden fear; frighten. 2 To drive or force by frightening: with *off* or *away*. —*v.i.* 3 To take fright; become scared. **—scare up** *Informal* To get together hurriedly; produce: to *scare up* a meal from leftovers. — *n.* A sudden fright; alarm. —*adj. Informal* Intended to provoke alarm or concern: *scare* tactics. [< ON *skiarr* shy] **—scar′er** *n.* **—scar′ing·ly** *adv.* **—Syn.** *v.* 1 alarm, startle, terrify. *n.* fright, panic.

**scarf** (skärf) *n. pl.* **scarfs** 1 In carpentry, a lapped joint made as by notching two timbers at the ends, and bolting them together to form a single piece: also **scarf joint.** 2 The notched end of either of the timbers so cut. —*v.t.* 1 To unite with a scarf joint. 2 To cut a scarf in. [ME]

**scar·let** (skär′lit) *n.* 1 A brilliant red, inclining to orange. 2 Cloth or clothing of a scarlet color. —*adj.* Brilliant red. [< Pers. *saqalāt* a rich, scarlet cloth]

**scat·ter** (skat′ər) *v.t.* 1 To throw about in various places; strew. 2 To disperse; rout. 3 *Physics* To reflect (radiation) in more than one direction. —*v.i.* 4 To separate and go in different directions. —*n.* The act of scattering or the condition of being scattered. [ME *scateren*] **—scat′ter·er** *n.* **—Syn.** *v.* 1 disseminate, sow, spread, sprinkle. 2 drive away.

**scav·en·ger** (skav′in·jər) *n.* 1 Any organism that feeds on refuse, carrion, etc. 2 A person who removes refuse or unwanted things, as a garbage collector or a junkman. [< AF *scawage* inspection]

**scene** (sēn) *n.* 1 A locality and all connected with it, as presented to view; a landscape. 2 The setting for a dramatic action. 3 The place and surroundings of any event, as in literature or art. 4 A division of an act of a play. 5 A specific incident or episode in a play, novel, motion picture, etc.: the ghost *scene* in *Hamlet.* 6 The painted canvas, hangings, etc., for the background for a play. 7 An unseemly display of anger or excited feeling, esp. in public. 8 *Slang* A place or realm of a currently popular activity: the country music *scene.* **—behind the scenes** 1 Out of sight of a theater audience; back-

stage. 2 Privately; in secret. [< Gk. *skēnē* a tent, a stage]

**scen·er·y** (sē′nər·ē) *n. pl.* **·er·ies** 1 The features of a landscape; view. 2 The painted backdrops, etc., used in the theater to represent a setting in a play.

**sce·nic** (sē′nik, sen′ik) *adj.* 1 Of or relating to beautiful natural scenery: a *scenic* spot. 2 In art, representing a situation, action, etc. 3 Relating to stage scenery. **—sce′ni·cal·ly** *adv.*

**scent** (sent) *n.* 1 An odor. 2 The effluvium by which an animal can be tracked. 3 A clue aiding investigation. 4 A fragrant, fluid essence; perfume. 5 The sense of smell. — *v.t.* 1 To perceive by the sense of smell. 2 To form a suspicion of. 3 To cause to be fragrant; perfume. —*v.i.* 4 To hunt by the sense of smell. [< L *sentire* to sense]

**scep·ter** (sep′tər) *n.* 1 A staff or wand carried as the badge of command or sovereignty. 2 Kingly office or power. —*v.t.* To confer the scepter on; invest with royal power. **Also,** *esp. Brit.,* **scep′tre** (-tər). [< Gk. *skēptron* a staff]

**scep·tic** (skep′tik) *n.* SKEPTIC.

**sched·ule** (skej′ool, *Brit.* shed′yool) *n.* 1 A list specifying the details of some matter. 2 A timetable. 3 A detailed and timed plan for the steps in a procedure. —*v.t.* **·uled, ·ul·ing** 1 To place in or on a schedule. 2 To appoint or plan for a specified time or date: He *scheduled* his appearance for five o'clock. [< LL *scedula*]

**scheme** (skēm) *n.* 1 A plan of something to be done; program. 2 An underhand plot: a *scheme* to defraud consumers. 3 A systematic arrangement: a color *scheme.* 4 An outline drawing; diagram. —*v.* **schemed, schem·ing** *v.t.* 1 To make a scheme for; plan. 2 To plan or plot in an underhand manner. —*v.i.* 3 To make schemes; plan. 4 To plot underhandedly. [< Gk. *schēma* a form, plan] **—schem′er** *n.*

**schism** (siz′əm, skiz′əm) *n.* 1 A division of a church into factions because of differences in doctrine. 2 A splitting into antagonistic groups. [< Gk. *schizein* to split]

**schiz·o·phre·ni·a** (skit′sō·frē′nē·ə) *n.* Mental illness characterized in varying degrees by irrational thinking, disturbed emotions, bizarre behavior, etc. [< SCHIZO- + Gk. *phrēn* mind] **—schiz′o·phren′ic** (-fren′ik) *adj., n.*

**schol·ar** (skol′ər) *n.* 1 A person eminent for learning. 2 An authority or specialist in an academic discipline. 3 The holder of a scholarship. 4 One who learns under a teacher; a pupil. [< L *schola* school]

**schol·ar·ly** (skol′ər·lē) *adj.* 1 Of or characteristic of a scholar: a *scholarly* mind. 2 Exhibiting great learning. 3 Devoted to learning. —*adv.* After the manner of a scholar. —**schol′ar·li·ness** *n.* —Syn. *adj.* 2 erudite, intellectual, learned, lettered. 3 bookish, studious.

**scho·las·tic** (skō·las′tik, skə-) *adj.* 1 Pertaining to or characteristic of scholars, education, or schools. 2 Pertaining to or characteristic of the medieval schoolmen. Also **scho·las′ti·cal.** —*n. Often cap.* 1 A schoolman of the Middle ages. 2 An advocate of scholasticism. [< Gk. *scholazein* devote leisure to study] —**scho·las′ti·cal·ly** *adv.*

**school** (skōōl) *n.* 1 An educational institution. 2 The building or group of buildings in which formal instruction is given. 3 A period or session of an educational institution: *School* begins tomorrow. 4 The pupils and teachers in an educational institution. 5 A subdivision of a university devoted to a special branch of higher education: a medical *school.* 6 The training of any branch of the armed services: gunnery *school.* 7 A body of disciples of a teacher or a group of persons whose work shows a common style or influence: a painting of the Flemish *school.* 8 Any sphere or means of instruction: the *school* of hard knocks. 9 A group of people having similar opinions, patterns of behavior, interests, etc.: He belongs to the old *school.* —*v.t.* 1 To instruct in a school; train. 2 To subject to rule or discipline. [< Gk. *scholē* leisure, school]

**schoon·er** (skōō′nər) *n.* 1 A fore-and-aft rigged vessel having originally two masts, but later often three or more. 2 A large beer glass, holding about a pint. [< dial. *scoon* skim on water.]

**sci·ence** (sī′əns) *n.* 1 Knowledge as of facts, phenomena, laws, and proximate causes, gained and verified by exact observation, organized experiment, and analysis. 2 Any of the various branches of such knowledge, as biology, chemistry, physics (**natural sciences**); economics, history, sociology (**social sciences**); agriculture, engineering (**applied sciences**). 3 Any department of knowledge in which the results of investigation have been systematized in the form of hypotheses and general laws subject to verification. 4 Expertness; skill: the *science*

of statesmanship. 5 Originally, knowledge. [< L *scire* know]

**science fiction** Novels and short stories dealing with actual or imaginary scientific developments and their effect on society or individuals. —**sci′ence-fic′tion** *adj.*

**sci·en·tif·ic** (sī′ən·tif′ik) *adj.* 1 Of, pertaining to, discovered by, derived from, or used in science. 2 Agreeing with the rules, principles, or methods of science; systematic. 3 Versed in science or a science. —**sci′en·tif′i·cal·ly** *adv.*

**Sci·en·tist** (sī′ən·tist) *n.* A Christian Scientist.

**sci·on** (sī′ən) *n.* 1 A child or descendant. 2 A bud or shoot from a plant or tree, used in grafting. [< OF *cion*]

**scis·sors** (siz′ərz) *n.pl.* 1 A cutting implement with handles and a pair of blades pivoted face to face: sometimes a **pair of scissors.** 2 *(construed as sing.)* In wrestling, a hold secured by clasping the legs about the body or head of the opponent. [< LL *cisorium* a cutting instrument]

**scle·ro·sis** (sklə·rō′sis) *n.* Abnormal thickening and hardening of tissue. [< Gk. *sklēros* hard] —**scle·ro′sal** *adj.*

**scoff** (skôf, skof) *v.i.* 1 To speak with contempt or derision: often with *at.* —*v.t.* 2 To deride; mock. —*n.* 1 Words or actions of contempt. 2 A person or thing held in contempt. [ME *scof*] —**scoff′er** *n.* —**scoff′ing·ly** *adv.* —Syn. *v.* 1, 2 gibe, jeer, scorn, sneer, taunt.

**soold** (skōld) *v.t.* 1 To find fault with harshly. —*v.i.* 2 To find fault harshly or continuously. —*n.* One who scolds constantly: also **scold′er.** [< ON *skāld* a poet, satirist] —**scold′ing·ly** *adv.*

**sconce** (skons) *n.* An ornamental wall bracket for holding a candle or other light. [< L *abscondere* to hide]

**scoop** (skōōp) *n.* 1 The part of a dredge or steam shovel that lifts earth, sand, coal, etc. 2 A small shovellike implement for flour, sugar, ice cream, etc. 3 An implement for bailing, as water from a boat. 4 A spoon-shaped instrument for using in a cavity: a surgeon's *scoop.* 5 An act of scooping. 6 A scooping motion. 7 The amount scooped at once: a *scoop* of ice cream. 8 *Informal* A news story obtained and published ahead of rival papers. —*v.t.* 1 To take or dip out with a scoop. 2 To hollow out, as with a scoop; excavate. 3 *Informal* To heap up or gather in mass as if in scoopfuls; amass. 4 *Informal* To obtain and publish a news story before (a rival). [< MDu. *schōpe* a vessel for bailing out water] —**scoop′er** *n.*

**scoot** (skōot) *v.i. Informal* To go quickly; dart off. —*n.* The act of scooting. [? < Scand.]

**scope** (skōp) *n.* 1 A range of view or action. 2 Capacity for achievement. 3 End in view; aim. 4 *Informal* A telescope, microscope, oscilloscope, etc. [< Gk. *skopos* a watcher]

**scorch** (skôrch) *v.t.* 1 To change the color, taste, etc., of, by slight burning. 2 To wither or shrivel by heat. 3 To criticize severely. —*v.i.* 4 To become scorched. 5 *Informal* To go at high speed. —*n.* 1 A superficial burn. 2 A mark caused by a slight burn. [ME *scorchen*] —**scorch′ing·ly** *adv.*

**score** (skôr, skōr) *n.* 1 The record of the winning points, counts, runs, etc., in competitive games. 2 A record of indebtedness; bill. 3 *Music* A printed or written copy of a musical composition in which all vocal and instrumental parts are shown on two or more connected staves one above another. 4 A group of 20. 5 *pl.* An indefinite large number. 6 A value assigned to an individual or group response to a test or series of tests, as of intelligence or performance. 7 *Slang* A success, esp. in making a purchase of narcotics. —**to pay off (or settle) old scores** To get even with someone for past wrongs, injuries, etc. —*v.* **scored, scor·ing** *v.t.* 1 To mark with notches, cuts, or lines. 2 To mark with cuts or lines for the purpose of keeping a tally. 3 To delete by means of a line drawn through: with *out.* 4 To make or gain, as points, runs, etc. 5 To count for a score of, as in games: A touchdown *scores* six points. 6 To rate or grade, as an examination paper. 7 *Music* a To orchestrate. b To arrange or adapt for an instrument. 8 *Informal* To criticize severely; scourge. 9 In cooking, to make superficial cuts in (meat, etc.). —*v.i.* 10 To make points, runs, etc., as in a game. 11 To keep score. 12 To make notches, cuts, etc. 13 To achieve a success. 14 *Slang* To purchase marihuana or narcotics. 15 *Slang* To succeed in having sexual intercourse with someone. [< ON *skor* a notch] —**scor′er** *n.*

**scorn** (skôrn) *n.* 1 A feeling of contempt. 2 An object of supreme contempt. —*v.t.* 1 To hold in or treat with contempt; despise. 2 To reject with scorn; spurn. [< OF *escarn*] —**scorn′er, scorn′ful·ness** *n.* —**scorn′ful** *adj.* —**scorn′ful·ly** *adv.* —**Syn.** 1 disdain, scoffing. *v.* 1 contemn, detest.

**scor·pi·on** (skôr′pē·ən) *n.* 1 Any of an order of arachnids with long segmented tails bearing a poisonous sting. 2 In the Bible, a whip or scourge. [< Gk. *skorpios*]

**scoun·drel** (skoun′drəl) *n.* An unscrupulous, dishonest person; villain. —*adj.* Villainous; base. [?] —**scoun′drel·ly** *adj.*

**scour** (skour) *v.t.* 1 To clean or brighten by thorough washing and rubbing. 2 To remove dirt, grease, etc., from; clean. 3 To clear by means of a strong current of water; flush. —*v.i.* 4 To rub something vigorously so as to clean or brighten it. 5 To become bright or clean by rubbing. —*n.* 1 The act of scouring. 2 A cleanser used in scouring. 3 *Usu. pl.* A dysentery affecting cattle. [< OF *escurer*] —**scour′er** *n.* —**Syn.** *v.* 1 polish, scrub. 2 cleanse.

**scourge** (skûrj) *n.* 1 A whip for inflicting suffering or punishment. 2 Any severe punishment. 3 Any means for causing suffering or death: the *scourge* of cholera. —*v.t.* **scourged, scourg·ing** 1 To whip severely; flog. 2 To punish severely; afflict. [< LL *excoriare* flay] —**scourg′er** *n.*

**scow** (skou) *n.* A large boat with a flat bottom and square ends, chiefly used to carry freight, garbage, etc. [< Du. *schouw*]

**scowl** (skoul) *n.* 1 A lowering of the brows, as in anger. 2 Gloomy aspect. —*v.i.* 1 To contract the brows in anger, sullenness, or disapproval. 2 To look threatening; lower. —*v.t.* 3 To affect or express by scowling. [?<Scand.]

**scrab·ble** (skrab′əl) *v.* **·bled, ·bling** *v.i.* 1 To scratch, scrape, or paw. 2 To scribble. 3 To struggle or strive. —*v.t.* 4 To scrible on. 5 To scrape together. —*n.* 1 The act of scrabbling; a moving on hands and feet or knees. 2 A scrambling effort. [< Du. *schrabbelen*] —**scrab′bler** *n.*

**scram·ble** (skram′bəl) *v.* **·bled, ·bling** *v.i.* 1 To move by clambering or crawling. 2 To struggle in a disorderly manner; scuffle. 3 To strive for something in such a manner. —*v.t.* 4 To mix together haphazardly or confusedly. 5 To gather or collect hurriedly or confusedly. 6 To cook (eggs) with the yolks and whites stirred together. 7 *Telecom.* To encode (a message) so that a special decoder is needed to make it intelligible. —*n.* 1 A difficult climb, as over rough terrain. 2 A struggle for possession: a *scramble* for power. [?] —**scram′bler** *n.*

**scrap** (skrap) *n.* 1 A small piece; fragment. 2 A small part of something written. 3 *pl.* Bits of unused food. 4 Old or refuse metal. —*v.t.* **scrapped, scrap·ping** 1 To break up into scrap. 2 To discard. —*adj.* Having the form of scraps: *scrap* metal. [<ON *skrap* scraps] —**Syn.** 1 Bit, chip, segment, shard. 3 leftovers.

**scrape** (skrāp) *v.* **scraped, scrap·ing** *v.t.* 1 To rub, as with something rough or sharp, so as to abrade. 2 To remove an outer layer thus: with *off, away,* etc. 3 To rub (a rough or sharp object) across a surface. 4 To rub roughly across or against (a surface). 5 To dig or form by scratching or scraping. 6 To gather or accumulate with effort or difficulty. —*v.i.* 7 To scrape something. 8 To rub with a grating noise. 9 To make a grating noise. 10 To draw the foot backward along the ground in bowing. 11 To manage or get along with difficulty. 12 To be very or overly economical. —*n.* 1 The act or effect of scraping; also, the noise made by scraping. 2 A difficult situation. 3 A quarrel or fight. 4 A scraping or drawing back of the foot in bowing. [<ON *skrapa*] —**scrap′er** *n.*

**scratch** (skrach) *v.t.* 1 To tear or mark the surface of with something sharp or rough. 2 To scrape or dig with something sharp or rough. 3 To scrape lightly with the nails, etc., as to relieve itching. 4 To rub with a grating sound; scrape. 5 To write or draw awkwardly or hurriedly. 6 To erase or cancel by scratches or marks. 7 To withdraw (an entry) from a competition, race, etc. —*v.i.* 8 To use the nails or claws, as in fighting or digging. 9 To scrape the skin, etc., lightly, as to relieve itching. 10 To make a grating noise. 11 To manage or get along with difficulty. 12 To withdraw from a game, race, etc., —*n.* 1 A mark or incision made on a surface by scratching. 2 A slight flesh wound or cut. 3 The sound of scratching. 4 The line from which contestants start, as in racing. 5 *Slang* Money. —**from scratch** From the beginning; from nothing. —**up to scratch** *Informal* Meeting the standard or requirement. —*adj.* 1 Done by chance; haphazard. 2 Made for hurried notes, figuring, etc.: a *scratch* pad. 3 Chosen hastily and at random: a *scratch* team. [<MDu. *cratsen*] —**scratch′er** *n.*

**scrawl** (skrôl) *v.t. & v.i.* To write hastily or illegibly. —*n.* Irregular or careless writing. [?] —**scrawl′er** *n.*

**scraw·ny** (skrô′nē) *adj.* **·ni·er, ·ni·est** Lean and bony. [?] —**scraw′ni·ness** *n.*

**scream** (skrēm) *v.i.* 1 To utter a prolonged, piercing cry, as of pain, terror, or surprise. 2 To make a piercing sound: the wind *screamed* in the trees. 3 To laugh loudly or immoderately. 4 To use heated, hysterical language. —*v.t.* 5 To utter with a scream. —*n.* 1 A loud, shrill, prolonged cry or sound. 2 *Informal* A hugely entertaining person or thing. [<ON *skraema* to scare] —**scream′ing·ly** *adv.*

**screech** (skrēch) *n.* A shrill, harsh cry; shriek. —*v.i.* 1 To utter with a screech. —*v.i.* 2 To shriek. [<ON *skrēkja*] —**screech′er** *n.* —**screech′y** *adj.* (·i·er, ·i·est)

**screen** (skrēn) *n.* 1 Something that separates or shelters, as a light partition. 2 A coarse or fine metal mesh used for sifting, or as protection: a window *screen.* 3 Something that serves to conceal or protect: a smoke *screen.* 4 A surface, as a canvas or curtain, on which motion pictures and slides may be shown. 5 The surface of a cathode-ray tube, on which television pictures, computer information or graphics, etc., may be viewed. —**the screen** Motion pictures. —*v.t.* 1 To shield or conceal with or as with a screen. 2 To pass through a screen or sieve; sift. 3 To classify or scan for suitability, qualifications, etc.: to *screen* applicants for a job. 4 To project on a motion-picture screen. 5 To photograph (a motion picture); shoot. 6 To adapt (a play, novel, story, etc.) for motion pictures. —*v.i.* 7 To be suitable for representation as a motion picture. [<OF *escren*]

**screw** (skrōō) *n.* 1 A device resembling a nail but having a slotted head and a tapering or cylindrical spiral for driving into wood, metal, plaster, etc., or for insertion into a corresponding threaded part. 2 A cylindrical socket with a spiral groove or thread 3 Anything having the form of a screw. 4 SCREW PRO-PELLER • See RUDDER. 5 A turn of or as of a screw. 6 Pressure; force. 7 *Slang* A prison guard. 8 *Brit. Slang* An old, worn-out, or bad-tempered horse. —**have a screw loose** *Slang* To be mentally deranged, eccentric, etc. —**put the screws on** (or to) *Slang* To exert pressure or force upon. —*v.t.* 1 To tighten, fasten, attach, etc., by a screw or screws. 2 To turn or twist. 3 To force; urge: to *screw* one's courage to the sticking point. 4 To contort, as one's features. 5 To practice oppression or extortion on; defraud. 6 To obtain by extortion. 7 *Slang* To act maliciously toward; harm. —*v.i.* 8 To turn as a screw. 9 To become attached or detached by means of twisting: with *on*, *off*, etc. 10 To twist or wind. 11 To practice oppression or extortion. —**screw up** *Slang* To botch; make a mess of: *He screwed up his career.* [< OF *escroue* nut] —**screw′er** *n.*

**screw·driv·er** (skrōō′drī′vər) *n.* A tool for turning screws.

**scrib·ble** (skrib′əl) *v.* ·**bled**, ·**bling** *v.t.* 1 To write hastily and carelessly. 2 To cover with careless or illegible writing. —*v.i.* 3 To write carelessly or hastily. 4 To make illegible or meaningless marks. —*n.* 1 Hasty, careless writing. 2 Meaningless lines and marks; scrawl. [< L *scribere* write] —**scrib′bler** *n.* —**scrib′bly** *adj.*

**scrim·mage** (skrim′ij) *n.* 1 A rough-and-tumble contest; fracas. 2 In American football, a mass play from the line of scrimmage after the ball has been placed on the ground and snapped back, the play ending when the ball is dead. —**line of scrimmage** In football, the hypothetic line, parallel to the goal lines, on which the ball rests and along which the opposing linemen take position at the start of play. —*v.t.* & *v.i.* ·**maged**, ·**mag·ing** To engage in a scrimmage. [Var. of SKIRMISH]

**scrimp** (skrimp) *v.i.* 1 To be very economical or stingy. —*v.t.* 2 To be overly sparing toward; skimp. 3 To cut too small, narrow, etc. [?] —**scrimp′er** *n.*

**script** (skript) *n.* 1 Handwriting; also, a particular style of handwriting. 2 Printed matter in imitation of handwriting. 3 A manuscript or text. 4 The written text of a play, TV show, etc. [< L *scribere* write]

**scrip·ture** (skrip′chər) *n.* 1 The sacred writings of any people. 2 Any authoritative book or writing. [< L *scribere* write] —**scrip′tur·al** *adj.* —**scrip′tur·al·ly** *adv.*

**scroll** (skrōl) *n.* 1 A roll of parchment, paper, etc., esp. one containing or intended for writing. 2 The writing on such a roll. 3 Anything resembling a parchment roll, as a convoluted ornament or part. —*v.i.* To move one or more lines of copy off the top of a computer screen, so that additional lines may be displayed at the bottom, or vice versa. [< AF *escrowe*]

**scrub¹** (skrub) *v.* **scrubbed**, **scrub·bing** *v.t.* 1 To rub vigorously in washing. 2 To remove (dirt, etc.) by such action. —*v.i.* 3 To rub something vigorously in washing. —*n.* The act of scrubbing. [<MDu. *schrobben*] —**scrub′ber** *n.*

**scrub²** (skrub) *n.* 1 A stunted tree. 2 A tract of stunted trees or shrubs. 3 A domestic animal of inferior breed. 4 A poor, insignificant person. 5 In sports, a player not on the varsity or regular team. 6 A game of baseball contrived hastily by a few players. —*adj.* 1 Undersized or inferior. 2 Consisting of or participated in by untrained players or scrubs: *scrub* team. [Var. of SHRUB]

**scruff** (skruf) *n.* The nape or outer back part of the neck. [Earlier *scuff* < ON *skopt* hair]

**scru·ple** (skrōō′pəl) *n.* 1 Doubt or uncertainty about what one should do. 2 Reluctance arising from conscientious disapproval. 3 An apothecaries' weight of 20 grains. 4 A minute quantity. —*v.t.* & *v.i.* ·**pled**, ·**pling** To hesitate (doing) from considerations of right or wrong. [< L *scrupus* a sharp stone]

**scru·pu·lous** (skrōō′pyə·əs) *adj.* 1 Cautious in action for fear of doing wrong; conscientious. 2 Resulting from the exercise of scruples; careful. —**scru′pu·lous·ly** *adv.* —**scru′pu·los′i·ty** (-los′ə·tē), **scru′pu·lous·ness** *n.* —**Syn.** 1 ethical, honest, upright. 2 exact, precise.

**scru·ti·nize** (skrōō′tə·nīz) *v.t.* ·**nized**, ·**niz·ing** To observe carefully; examine in detail. —**scru′ti·niz′er** *n.* —**scru′ti·niz′ing·ly** *adv.*

**scru·ti·ny** (skrōō′tə·nē) *n. pl.* ·**nies** Close investigation; careful inspection. [< L *scrutari* examine]

**scu·ba** (sk′ōō′bə) *n.* A device worn by a free-swimming diver to provide a supply of air for breathing. [<*s(elf-) c(ontained) u(nder-water) b(reathing) a(pparatus)*]

**scuf·fle** (skuf′əl) *v.i.* ·**fled**, ·**fling** 1 To struggle roughly or confusedly. 2 To drag one's feet; shuffle. —*n.* A disorderly struggle; fracas. [? < Scand.] —**scuf′fler** *n.*

**sculp·tor** (skulp′tər) *n.* A person who sculptures. —**sculp′tress** (-tris) *n. Fem.*

**sculp·ture** (skulp′chər) *n.* 1 The art of fashioning three-dimensional figures, busts, abstract pieces, etc., of stone, wood, clay, bronze, or other material. 2 A piece or group produced by sculpture. —*v.t.* ·**tured**, ·**tur·ing** 1 To fashion, (stone, wood, metal, etc.) into sculpture. 2 To represent or portray by sculpture. 3 To embellish with sculpture. 4 To change (features on the surface of the earth) by erosion. —*v.i.* 5 To work as a sculptor. [< L *sculpere* carve in stone] —**sculp′tur·al** *adj.* —**sculp′tur·al·ly** *adv.*

**scum** (skum) *n.* 1 A layer of impure or extraneous matter on the surface of a liquid. 2

Low, contemptible people. —v. **scummed, scum·ming** v.t. 1 To take scum from; skim. —v.i. 2 To become covered with or form scum. [< MDu. *schuum*] —**scum′mi·ness** n. —**scum′my** adj. (·mi·er, ·mi·est)

**scur·ry** (skûr′ē) v.i. ·ried, ·ry·ing To move or go hurriedly; scamper. —n. pl. ·ries The act or sound of scurrying. [?] —Syn. v. dart, dash, scoot, scuttle.

**scur·vy** (skûr′vē) A disease due to lack of vitamin C, marked by weakness, spotted skin, and bleeding gums. —adj. ·vi·er, ·vi·est Low or contemptible. [< SCURF] —**scur′vi·ly** adv. —**scur′vi·ness** n.

**scut·tle** (skut′l) n. 1 A small opening or hatchway with movable lid or cover, esp. in the roof or wall of a house, or in the deck or side of a ship. 2 The lid closing such an opening. —v.t. ·tled, ·tling 1 To sink (a ship) by making holes below the water line. 2 To wreck or destroy. [< MF *escoutille* a hatchway]

**scythe** (sīth) n. A tool composed of a long curved blade fixed at an angle to a long handle, used for mowing, reaping, etc. — v.t. scythed, scyth·ing To cut with a scythe. [< OE *sithe*]

**sea** (sē) n. 1 The great body of salt water covering most of the earth's surface; the ocean. 2 A large body of salt water partly or wholly enclosed by land: the Adriatic *Sea*. 3 An inland body of water, esp. if salty: the *Sea* of Galilee. 4 The state of the ocean with regard to the course, flow, swell, or turbulence of the waves. 5 A heavy wave or swell. 6 Anything vast or boundless that resembles or suggests the sea. —**at sea** 1 On the ocean. 2 Bewildered. —**follow the sea** To follow the occupation of a sailor. —**put to sea** To sail away from the land [< OE *sœ*]

**sea·far·ing** (sē′fâr′ing) n. 1 The occupation of a sailor. 2 Traveling over the sea. —adj. Of, pertaining to, given to, or engaged in seafaring.

**seal** (sēl) n. 1 An impression made on a letter, document, etc., to prove its authenticity. 2 A wax wafer, piece of paper, etc., bearing such an authenticating impression. 3 A device with a raised or cut initial, word, or design, used to make such an impression. 4 A stamp, ring, etc., bearing such a device. 5 Something used to close or secure a letter, door, lid, wrapper, joint, passage, etc., firmly. 6 Anything that confirms, ratifies, or guarantees; pledge. 7 A sign or indication; token. 8 An ornamental stamp for packages, etc. —v.t. 1 To affix a seal to, as to prove authenticity or prevent tampering. 2 To stamp or otherwise impress a seal upon in order to attest to weight, quality, etc. 3 To fasten or close with a seal: to *seal* a glass jar. 4 To confirm the genuineness or truth of, as a bargain. 5 To establish or settle finally. 6 To secure, set, or fill up, as with plaster. [< L *sigillum* a small picture, seal] —**seal′a·ble** adj. —**seal′er** n.

**seam** (sēm) n. 1 A visible line of junction between parts, as the edges of two pieces of cloth sewn together. • See PINK². 2 A line, ridge, or groove marking joined edges, as of boards. 3 Any similar line, ridge, etc., as that formed by a scar, wrinkle, etc. 4 A thin layer or stratum, as of rock or ore. —v.t. 1 To unite by means of a seam. 2 To mark with a cut, furrow, wrinkle, etc. —v.i. 3 To crack open; become fissured. [< OE *sēam*] —**seam′er** n.

**sea·man** (sē′mən) n. pl. ·men (-mən) 1 An enlisted man in the navy or in the coast guard, graded according to his rank. 2 A mariner; sailor. —**sea′man·like′** (-līk′) adj. —**sea′man·ly** adj., adv.

**seam·stress** (sēm′stris) n. A woman whose occupation is sewing. [< OE *sēam* seam + -ST(E)R + -ESS]

**sear** (sir) v.t. 1 To wither; dry up. 2 To burn the surface of; scorch. 3 To burn or cauterize; brand. 4 To make callous; harden. — v.i. 5 To become withered; dry up. —adj. Dried or blasted; withered. —n. A scar or brand. [< OE *sēar* dry]

**search** (sûrch) v.t. 1 To look through or explore thoroughly in order to find something. 2 To subject (a person) to a search. 3 To examine with close attention; probe. 4 To penetrate or pierce: The wind *searches* my clothes. 5 To learn by examination or investigation: with *out*. —v.i. 6 To make a search. —n. 1 The act of searching. 2 An act of boarding and inspecting a ship in pursuance of the right to search. [< LL *circare* go round, explore] —**search′a·ble** adj. —**search′er** n.

**search·light** (sûrch′līt′) n. 1 An apparatus consisting of a powerful light equipped with a reflector and mounted so that it can be projected in various directions. 2 The light so projected.

**sea·shore** (sē′shôr′, -shōr′) n. Land bordering on the sea.

**sea·sick** (sē′sik′) adj. Suffering from seasickness.

**sea·sick·ness** (sē′sik′nis) *n.* Nausea, dizziness, etc., caused by the motion of a ship at sea.

**sea·son** (sē′zən) *n.* 1 A division of the year as determined by the earth's position with respect to the sun: spring, summer, autumn, and winter. 2 A period of time. 3 A period of special activity or when a specified place is frequented: usu. with *the:* the opera *season;* the Palm Beach *season.* 4 A fit or suitable time. 5 The time of and surrounding a major holiday. —**in season** 1 At a time of availability and fitness, as for eating: Clams are *in season* during the summer. 2 In or at the right time. 3 Able to be killed or taken by permission of the law. 4 Ready to mate or breed: said of animals. —*v.t.* 1 To increase the flavor or zest of (food), as by adding spices, etc. 2 To add zest or piquancy to. 3 To render more suitable for use. 4 To make fit, as by discipline; harden. 5 To mitigate or soften; moderate. —*v.i.* 6 To become seasoned. [< LL *satio* sowing time] —**sea′son·er** *n.*

**sea·son·a·ble** (sē′zən·ə·bəl) *adj.* 1 Being in keeping with the season or circumstances. 2 Done or occurring at the proper or best time. —**sea′son·a·ble·ness** *n.* —**sea′son·a·bly** *adv.* —**Syn.** 1 timely, well-timed. 2 opportune, favorable, propitious, advantageous.

**seat** (sēt) *n.* 1 The thing on which one sits; a chair, bench, stool, etc. 2 That part of a thing upon which one rests in sitting, or upon which an object or another part rests. 3 That part of the person which sustains the weight of the body in sitting; buttocks. 4 That part of a garment which covers the buttocks. 5 The place where anything is situated or established: the *seat* of pain, the *seat* of a government. 6 A place of abode, esp. a large estate. 7 The privilege or right of membership in a legislative body, stock exchange, or the like. 8 The manner of sitting, as on horseback. 9 A surface or part upon which the base of anything rests. —*v.t.* 1 To place on a seat or seats; cause to sit down. 2 To have seats for; furnish with seats: The theater *seats* only 299 people. 3 To put a seat on or in; renew or repair the seat of. 4 To locate, settle, or center: usu. in the passive: The French government is *seated* in Paris. 5 To fix, set firmly, or establish in a certain position, place, etc. [< ON *sǣti*]

**seat belt** A strap or harness that holds a passenger firmly in the seat, as while riding in a car or airplane.

**sea·weed** (sē′wēd′) *n.* Any marine plant or vegetation, esp. any multicellular alga.

**se·cede** (si·sēd′) *v.i.* ·**ced·ed,** ·**ced·ing** To withdraw formally from a union, fellowship, etc., esp. from a political or religious organization. [< L *se-* apart + *cedere* go] —**se·ced′er** *n.*

**se·ces·sion** (si·sesh′ən) *n.* 1 The act of seceding. 2 *Usu. cap. U.S.* The withdrawal of the Southern States from the Union in 1860–61. —**se·ces′sion·al** *adj.* —**se·ces′sion·ism, se·ces′sion·ist** *n.*

**se·clude** (si·klōōd′) *v.t.* ·**clud·ed,** ·**clud·ing** 1 To remove and keep apart from the society of others; isolate. 2 To screen or shut off, as from view. [< L *se-* apart + *claudere* to shut]

**se·clu·sion** (si·klōō′zhən) *n.* 1 The act of secluding, or the state or condition of being secluded; solitude; retirement. 2 A secluded place. —**se·clu′sive** *adj.* —**se·clu′sive·ly** *adv.* —**se·clu′sive·ness** *n.*

**sec·ond¹** (sek′ənd) *n.* 1 A unit of time, 1/60 of a minute. 2 A unit of angular measure, 1/60 of a minute. 3 An instant; moment: Wait a *second.* [< Med. L *seconda (minuta),* lit., second (minute), i.e., the result of the second sexagesimal division]

**sec·ond²** (sek′ənd) *adj.* 1 Next in order, authority, responsibility, etc., after the first. 2 Ranking next below the first or best. 3 Of lesser quality or value; inferior; subordinate. 4 Identical with another or preceding one; other. 5 *Music* Lower in pitch, or rendering a secondary part. —*n.* 1 The one next after the first, as in order, rank, importance, etc. 2 The element of an ordered set that corresponds to the number two. 3 An attendant who supports or aids another, as in a duel. 4 *Often pl.* An article of merchandise of inferior quality. 5 *Music* a The interval between any tone and another a whole step or half step away from or below it. b A subordinate part, instrument, or voice. 6 In parliamentary law, the act or declaration by which a motion is seconded: Do I hear a *second?* 7 *pl. Informal* A second portion of food. —*v.t.* 1 To act as a supporter or assistant of; promote; stimulate; encourage. 2 To support formally, as a motion, resolution, etc. —*adv.* In the second order, place, rank, etc. [< L *secundus* following]

**sec·on·dar·y** (sek′ən·der′ē) *adj.* 1 Of second

rank, grade, or influence; subordinate. 2 Depending on, resulting from, or following what is primary 3 Second in order of occurrence or development. 4 *Electr.* Of or pertaining to the output of a transformer. —*n. pl.* **·dar·ies** 1 One who or that which is secondary or subordinate. 2 *Electr.* A secondary circuit or coil. —**sec′on·dar′i·ly** *adv.*

**sec·ond·hand** (sek′ənd·hand′) *adj.* 1 Previously owned, worn, or used by another; not new. 2 Received from another; not direct from the original source: *secondhand* information. 3 Of, pertaining to, or dealing in merchandise that is not new. —*adv.* Indirectly.

**se·cre·cy** (sē′krə·sē) *n. pl.* **·cies** 1 The condition or quality of being secret; concealment. 2 The character of being secretive.

**se·cret** (sē′krit) *adj.* 1 Kept separate or hidden from view or knowledge, or from all persons except the individuals concerned; unseen. 2 Affording privacy; secluded. 3 Good at keeping secrets; close-mouthed. 4 Unrevealed or unavowed: a *secret* partner. 5 Not revealed to everyone; mysterious; esoteric. —*n.* 1 Something known only by a few people. 2 Something that is not explained or is kept hidden; mystery. 3 An underlying reason; key. —**in secret** In privacy; in a hidden place. [< L *se-* apart + *cernere* to separate] —**se′cret·ly** *adv.*

**sec·re·tar·y** (sek′rə·ter′ē) *n. pl.* **·tar·ies** 1 An employee who deals with correspondence, records, and clerical business for a person, business, committee, etc. 2 An official in a business, club, etc., who has overall responsibility for somewhat similar work. 3 An executive officer presiding over and managing a department of government. 4 A writing desk with a bookcase on top. [< L *secretum* a secret] —**sec′re·tar′i·al** (-târ′-ē-əl) *adj.*

**se·crete** (si·krēt′) *v.t.* **·cret·ed**, **·cret·ing** 1 To remove or keep from observation; conceal; hide. 2 *Biol.* To form and release (an enzyme, hormone, etc.). [Alter. of obs. *secret,* to conceal] —**se·cre′tor** *n.*

**se·cre·tion** (si·krē′shən) *n.* 1 *Biol.* The cellular process by which materials are separated from blood or sap and converted into new substances: the *secretion* of milk, urine, etc. 2 The substance secreted. 3 The act of concealing or hiding.

**sect** (sekt) *n.* 1 A religious denomination, esp. a body of dissenters from an established or older form of faith. 2 Adherents of a particular philosophical system or teacher, esp. a faction of a larger group. [< L *sequi* follow]

**sect.** section; sectional.

**sec·tion** (sek′shən) *n.* 1 The act of cutting; a separating by cutting. 2 A slice or portion separated by or as if by cutting. 3 A separate part or division, as of a book or chapter. 4 A distinct part of a country, community, etc. 5 *U.S.* An area of land one square mile in extent and constituting 1/36 of a township. 6 A portion of a railroad's right of way under the care of a particular crew of men. 7 In a sleeping-car, a space containing two berths. 8 A representation of an object, as if cut by an intersecting plane. —*v.t.* 1 To divide into sections. 2 To shade (a drawing) so as to designate a section or sections. [< L *sectus,* p.p. of *secare* to cut]

**sec·u·lar** (sek′yə·lər) *adj.* 1 Of or pertaining to this world; temporal; worldly. 2 Not controlled by the church; civil; not ecclesiastical. 3 Not concerned with religion; not sacred: *secular* art. 4 Not bound by monastic vows, and not living in a religious community. 5 Of or describing a trend or process continuing for a long, indefinite period of time. —*n.* 1 A member of the clergy who is not bound by monastic vows and who does not live in a religious community. 2 A layman as distinguished from a member of the clergy. [< L *saeculum* generation, age]

**se·cure** (si·kyoŏr′) *adj.* **·cur·er**, **·cur·est** 1 Free from or not likely to be exposed to danger, theft, etc.; safe. 2 Free from fear, apprehension, etc. 3 Confident; certain. 4 In a state or condition that will not break, come unfastened, etc.: Is the door *secure?* 5 Reliable; steady; dependable: a *secure* job. —*v.* **·cured**, **·cur·ing** *v.t.* 1 To make secure; protect. 2 To make firm, tight, or fast; fasten. 3 To make sure or certain; insure; guarantee. 4 To obtain possession of; get. —*v.i.* 5 To stop working: said of a ship's crew. 6 To berth; moor: said of a ship. [< L *se-* without + *cura* care] —**se·cur′a·ble** *adj.* —**se·cure′ly** *adv.* —**se·cure′ness**, **se·cur′-er** *n.*

**se·cur·i·ty** (si·kyoŏr′ə·tē) *n. pl.* **·ties** 1 The state of being secure; freedom from danger, risk, care, poverty, doubt, etc. 2 One who or that which secures or guarantees; surety. 3 *pl.* Written promises or something deposited or pledged for payment of money, as stocks, bonds, etc. 4 Defense or protection against espionage, attack, escape, etc.

5 Measures calculated to provide such defense or protection. 6 An organization or division of one charged with providing for safety and protection.

**se·dan** (si·dan′) *n.* 1 A closed automobile having one compartment, front and rear seats, and two or four doors. 2 A closed chair, for one passenger, carried by two men by means of poles at the sides: also **sedan chair**. [?]

**se·date** (si·dāt′) *adj.* Not disturbed by excitement, passion, etc. [< L *sedare* make calm, settle] —**se·date′ly** *adv.* —**se·date′ness** *n.* —Syn. calm, composed, staid.

**sed·a·tive** (sed′ə·tiv) *adj.* Tending to calm or soothe; esp., acting to allay nervousness or emotional agitation. —*n.* A sedative medicine.

**sed·en·tar·y** (sed′ən·ter′ē) *adj.* 1 Accustomed to sit much or to work in a sitting posture. 2 Characterized by sitting. 3 Remaining in one place; not migratory. 4 Attached or fixed to an object. [< L *sedere* sit] —**sed′en·tar′i·ly** *adv.* —**sed′en·tar′i·ness** *n.*

**sedge** (sej) *n.* Any of a large family of grasslike plants growing in wet ground and usu. having triangular, solid stems and tiny flowers in spikes. [< OE *secg*] —**sedged, sedg′y** *adj.*

**sed·i·ment** (sed′ə·mənt) *n.* 1 Matter that settles to the bottom of a liquid; dregs; lees. 2 *Geol.* Fragmentary material deposited by water, ice, or air. [< L *sedere* sit, settle] —**sed′i·men·ta′tion** *n.*

**se·di·tion** (si·dish′ən) *n.* The incitement and act of resistance to or revolt against lawful authority. [< L *sed-* aside + *itio* a going]

**se·di·tious** (si·dish′əs) *adj.* 1 Of, pertaining to, or having the character of sedition. 2 Inclined to, taking part in, or guilty of sedition. —**se·di′tious·ly** *adv.* —**se·di′tious·ness** *n.*

**se·duce** (si·dōōs′) *v.t.* **·duced, ·duc·ing** 1 To lead astray, as from a proper or right course: *seduced* by quick profits. 2 To entice into wrong, disloyalty, etc.; tempt. 3 To induce to have sexual intercourse. [< L *se-* apart + *ducere* lead] —**se·duc′er** *n.* —**se·duc′i·ble** or **se·duce′a·ble** *adj.*

**se·duc·tive** (si·duk′tiv) *adj.* Tending to seduce. —**se·duc′tive·ly** *adv.* —**se·duc′tive·ness** *n.*

**sed·u·lous** (sej′ōō·ləs) *adj.* 1 Constant in application or attention; assiduous. 2 Diligent; industrious. [< L *se dolo* without

guile] —**sed′u·lous·ly** *adv.* —**sed′u·lous·ness** *n.*

**see¹** (sē) *v.* **saw, seen, see·ing** *v.t.* 1 To perceive with the eyes; gain knowledge or awareness of by means of one's vision. 2 To perceive with the mind; comprehend. 3 To find out or ascertain; inquire about: *See* who is at the door. 4 To have experience or knowledge of; undergo: We have *seen* more peaceful times. 5 To encounter; chance to meet: I *saw* your husband today. 6 To have a meeting or interview with; visit or receive as a guest, visitor, etc.: The doctor will *see* you now. 7 To attend as a spectator; view. 8 To accompany; escort. 9 To take care; be sure: *See* that you do it! 10 In poker, to accept (a bet) or equal the bet of (a player) by betting an equal sum. —*v.i.* 11 To have or exercise the power of sight. 12 To find out; inquire. 13 To understand; comprehend. 14 To think; consider. 15 To take care; be attentive: *See* to your work. 16 To gain certain knowledge, as by awaiting an outcome: We will *see* if you are right. —**see about** 1 To inquire into the facts, causes, etc., of. 2 To take care of; attend to. —**see through** 1 To perceive the real meaning or nature of. 2 To aid or protect, as throughout a period of danger. 3 To finish. [< OE *sēon*]

**see²** (sē) *n.* 1 The official seat from which a bishop exercises jurisdiction. 2 The authority or jurisdiction of a bishop. [< L *sedes* a seat]

**seed** (sēd) *n.* 1 The ovule containing an embryo from which a plant may be reproduced. 2 That from which anything springs; source. 3 Offspring; children. 4 The male fertilizing element; semen; sperm. 5 Any small granular fruit, singly or collectively. —*v.t.* 1 To sow with seed. 2 To sow (seed). 3 To remove the seeds from: to *seed* raisins. 4 To strew (moisture-bearing clouds) with crystals, as of dry ice, silver iodide, etc., in order to initiate precipitation. 5 In sports: a To arrange (the drawing for positions in a tournament, etc.) so that the more skilled competitors meet only in the later events. b To rank (a skilled competitor) thus. —*v.i.* 6 To sow seed. 7 To grow to maturity and produce or shed seed. —**go to seed** 1 To develop and shed seed. 2 To become shabby, useless, etc.; deteriorate. [< OE *sǣd*] —**seed′er** *n.* —**seed′less** *adj.*

**seed·ling** (sēd′ling) *n.* 1 Any plant grown from seed. 2 A very small or young tree or plant.

485

**seed·y** (sē′dē) *adj.* **seed·i·er, seed·i·est 1** Abounding with seeds. **2** Gone to seed. **3** Poor and ragged; shabby. **4** Feeling or looking wretched. —**seed′i·ly** *adv.* —**seed′i·ness** *n.*

**seek** (sēk) *v.* **sought, seek·ing** *v.t.* **1** To go in search of; look for. **2** To strive for; try to get. **3** To endeavor or try: He *seeks* to mislead me. **4** To ask or inquire for; request: to *seek* information. **5** To go to; betake oneself to: to *seek* a warmer climate. —*v.i.* **6** To make a search or inquiry. [< OE *sēcan*] —**seek′er** *n.*

**seem** (sēm) *v.i.* **1** To give the impression of being; appear. **2** To appear to oneself: I *seem* to remember her face. **3** To appear to exist: There *seems* no reason for hesitating. **4** To be evident or apparent: It *seems* to be raining. [< ON *sœma* honor, conform to]

**seep** (sēp) *v.i.* To soak through pores or small openings; ooze. [< OE *sipian* soak] —**seep′y** *adj.*

**seep·age** (sē′pij) *n.* **1** The act or process of seeping; oozing; leakage. **2** The fluid that seeps.

**seer** (sē′ər *for def. 1;* sir *for def. 2*) *n.* **1** One who sees. **2** One who foretells events; a prophet. [< SEE[1] + -ER]

**seethe** (sēth) *v.* **seethed, seeth·ing** *v.i.* **1** To boil. **2** To foam or bubble as if boiling. **3** To be agitated, as by rage. —*v.t.* **4** To soak in liquid; steep. **5** *Archaic* To boil. —*n.* The act or condition of seething. [< OE *sēothan*]

**seg·ment** (seg′mənt) *n.* **1** A part cut off or distinct from the other parts of anything: a section. **2** *Geom.* A part of a line or curve lying between two of its points. —*v.t. & v.i.* To divide into segments. [< L *secare* to cut] —**seg·men·tal** (seg·men′təl) *adj.* —**seg·men′tal·ly** *adv.* —**seg′men·tar·y** (seg′mən·ter′ē) *adj.*

**seg·re·gate** (seg′rə·gāt) *v.* **·gat·ed, ·gat·ing** *v.t.* **1** To place apart from others or the rest; isolate. **2** To cause the separation of (a race, social class, etc.) from the general mass of society or from a larger group. —*v.i.* **3** To separate from a mass and gather about nuclei, as in crystallization. —*adj.* (-git) Separated or set apart from others; segregated [< L *se-* apart + *grex* a flock] —**seg′re·ga′tive** *adj.* —**seg′re·ga′tor** *n.*

**seg·re·ga·tion** (seg′rə·gā′shən) *n.* **1** A segregating or being segregated or process of segregating. **2** The act or policy of separating a race, social class, etc., from the general mass of society or from a larger group.

**seine** (sān) *n.* Any long fishing net, having floats at the top edge and weights at the bottom. —*v.t. & v.i.* **seined, sein·ing** To fish or catch with a seine. [< Gk. *sagēnē* a fishing net]

**seis·mo·graph** (sīz′mə·graf, -gräf, sīs′-) *n.* An instrument for automatically recording the movements of the earth's crust. —**seis′mo·graph′ic** *adj.* —**seis·mog′ra·pher** (sīz·mog′rə·fər, sīs-), **seis·mog′ra·phy** *n.*

**seis·mol·o·gy** (sīz·mol′ə·jē, sīs-) *n.* The science dealing with earthquakes and related phenomena. —**seis·mo·log·ic** (sīz′mə·loj′ik, sīs′-) or **·i·cal** *adj.* —**seis′mo·log′i·cal·ly** *adv.* —**seis·mol′o·gist** *n.*

**seize** (sēz) *v.* **seized, seiz·ing** *v.t.* **1** To take hold of suddenly and forcibly; clutch; grasp. **2** To grasp mentally; understand. **3** To take possession of by authority or right. **4** To take possession of by or as by force. **5** To take prisoner; capture. **6** To act upon with sudden and powerful effect; attack; strike. **7** To take advantage of immediately, as an opportunity. **8** *Naut.* To fasten or bind by turns of cord, line, or small rope; lash. —*v.i.* **9** To take hold or make use: usu. with *on* or *upon*. [< OF *saisir, seisir*] —**seiz′a·ble** *adj.* —**seiz′er** *n.*

**sei·zure** (sē′zhər) *n.* **1** The act of seizing or the state of being seized. **2** A sudden incapacitation, as by disease.

**sel·dom** (sel′dəm) *adv.* At widely separated intervals, as of time or space; infrequently; rarely. —*adj.* Infrequent; rare. [< OE *seldan*]

**se·lect** (si·lekt′) *v.t.* **1** To take in preference to another or others; pick out; choose. —*v.i.* **2** To choose. —*adj.* **1** Chosen in preference to others. **2** Excellent; superior; choice. **3** Exclusive. **4** Very particular in selecting. [< L *se-* apart + *legere* choose] —**se·lect′ness, se·lec′tor** *n.*

**self** (self) *n. pl.* **selves 1** One's own person known or considered as the subject of his own consciousness. **2** The distinct and characteristic individuality or identity of any person or thing. **3** Personal interest or advantage. —*adj.* **1** Being uniform or of the same quality throughout. **2** Of the same kind (as in material, color, etc.,) as something else: a coat with a *self* belt. —*pron.* Myself, yourself, himself, or herself. [< OE]

**self·ish** (sel′fish) *adj.* **1** Motivated by personal needs and desires to the disregard of the welfare or wishes of others. **2** Proceeding from or characterized by undue concern

486

for self. —**self′ish·ly** adv. —**self′ish·ness** n.

**sell** (sel) v. **sold, sell·ing** v.t. 1 To transfer (property) to another for a consideration; dispose of by sale. 2 To deal in; offer for sale. 3 To deliver, surrender, or betray in violation of duty or trust: often with out: to sell one's country. 4 Informal To cause to accept or approve something: They sold him on the scheme. 5 Informal To cause or promote the acceptance, approval, or sale of. 6 Slang To deceive; cheat. —v.i. 7 To engage in selling. 8 To be on sale or be sold. 9 To work as a salesperson. 10 To be popular with buyers, customers, etc. —**sell out** 1 To get rid of (one's goods, etc.) by sale. 2 Informal To betray one's trust, cause, associates, etc. —n. 1 Slang A trick; joke; swindle. 2 An act or instance of selling. [< OE sellan give]

**se·man·tics** (si·man′tiks) n. pl. (construed as sing.) 1 Ling. The study of the meanings of speech forms, esp. of the development and changes in meaning of words and word groups. 2 Logic The study of the relation between signs or symbols and what they signify. —**se·man′ti·cist** n.

**sem·a·phore** (sem′ə·fôr, -fōr) n. An apparatus for giving signals, as with movable arms, disks, flags, or lanterns. —v.t. To send by semaphore. [< Gk. sēma a sign + pherein carry] —**sem′a·phor′ic** (-fôr′ik, -for′ik) or **·i·cal** adj.

**sem·blance** (sem′bləns) n. 1 An outward, sometimes deceptive appearance; look. 2 A representation, likeness, or resemblance. 3 The barest trace; modicum. [< OF sembler seem]

**se·mes·ter** (si·mes′tər) n. Either of the two periods of approximately 18 weeks into which an academic year is divided. [< L sex six + mensis month] —**se·mes′tral** adj.

**sem·i·cir·cle** (sem′i·sûr′kəl, sem′ē-) n. 1 A half-circle; an arc of 180°. 2 Anything formed or arranged in a half-circle. —**sem′i·cir′cu·lar** adj. —**sem′i·cir′cu·lar·ly** adv.

**sem·i·co·lon** (sem′i·kō′lən, sem′ē-) n. A mark (;) of punctuation, indicating a greater degree of separation than the comma but less than the period.

**sem·i·con·duc·tor** (sem′ē·kən·duk′tər, sem′ī-) n. 1 One of a class of crystalline solids, as germanium or silicon, having an electrical conductivity intermediate between conductors and insulators, used in making transistors and related devices. 2 A transistor or related device.

**sem·i·con·scious** (sem′ē·kon′shəs, sem′ī-) adj. Partly conscious; not fully aware or responsive. —**sem′i·con′scious·ly** adv. —**sem′i·con′scious·ness** n.

**sem·i·fi·nal** (sem′ē·fī′nəl, sem′ī-) adj. Next before the final, as in a series of competitions. —n. 1 A semifinal match. 2 A semifinal round. —**sem′i·fi′nal·ist** n.

**sem·i·month·ly** (sem′ē·munth′lē, sem′ī-) adj. Taking place, issued, etc., twice a month. —n. pl. **·lies** A publication issued twice a month. —adv. Twice monthly.

**sen·ate** (sen′it) n. 1 Usu. cap. The upper branch of many national or state legislative bodies, as in the U.S. 2 A legislative body, as at a university; council. 3 A body of distinguished or venerable men often possessing legislative functions. 4 The highest governing body of the ancient Roman state. [< L senatus, lit., a council of old men]

**sen·a·tor** (sen′ə·tər) n. A member of a senate. —**sen′a·to′ri·al** adj. —**sen′a·to′ri·al·ly** adv. —**sen′a·tor·ship′** n.

**send** (send) v. **sent, send·ing** v.t. 1 To cause or enable to go: to send a messenger; to send one's daughter to medical school. 2 To cause to be conveyed; transmit; forward: to send a letter. 3 To cause to issue; emit or discharge, as heat, smoke, etc.: with forth, out, etc. 4 To drive by force; impel. 5 To cause to come, happen, etc.; grant: God send us peace. 6 To bring into a specified state or condition: The decision sent him into a panic. 7 To transmit, as an electric or magnetic signal. 8 Slang To thrill or delight. —v.i. 9 To dispatch an agent, messenger, or message. —**send for** To summon or order by a message or messenger. —**send packing** To dismiss abruptly or roughly. [< OE sendan] —**send′er** n.

**se·nile** (sē′nīl, sen′īl) adj. Of, pertaining to, proceeding from, or characteristic of old age, esp. pertaining to or exhibiting certain mental infirmities often resulting from old age. [< L senex old] —**se′nile·ly** adv. —**se·nil·i·ty** (sə·nil′ə·tē) n.

**sen·ior** (sēn′yər) adj. 1 Older in years; elder; after personal names (usu. abbreviated Sr.), to denote the elder of two related persons of the same name, esp. a father and his son. 2 Longer in service or superior in rank or dignity. 3 Of or pertaining to a senior or seniors. —n. 1 One older in years, longer in office, or more advanced in rank or dignity than another. 2 Any elderly person. 3 A member of a graduating class. [< L *senior* older]

**sen·sa·tion** (sen·sā′shən) *n.* 1 a A mental event due to stimulation of a sense organ, as hearing, taste, etc. b The capacity to respond to such stimulation. 2 A state of mind induced by indeterminate stimuli: a *sensation* of fear. 3 A state of interest or excitement. 4 That which produces such a state of interest or excitement. [< L *sensus* sense]

**sen·sa·tion·al** (sen·sā′shən·əl) *adj.* 1 Of or pertaining to the senses or sensation. 2 Causing excitement; startling; thrilling. 3 Tending to shock, startle, etc., esp. by lurid or melodramatic details, techniques, etc. 4 *Informal* Excellent, great, etc. —**sen·sa′tion·al·ly** *adv.*

**sen·sa·tion·al·ism** (sen·sā′shən·əl·iz′əm) *n.* 1 *Philos.* The theory that all knowledge has a sensory basis. 2 The use of details, techniques, etc., that are intended to shock, or startle, as in literature, motion pictures, etc. —**sen·sa′tion·al·ist** *n.* —**sen·sa′tion·al·is′tic** *adj.*

**sense** (sens) *n.* 1 Any of the faculties of man and animals, specialized to receive and transmit external or internal stimuli, as sound, hunger, etc.; sight, touch, taste, hearing, and smell. 2 A perception or feeling produced by the senses. 3 A special capacity to perceive, appreciate, estimate, etc.: a *sense* of humor. 4 A somewhat vague perception or feeling; a *sense* of danger. 5 Rational perception or discrimination; awareness; realization: a *sense* of wrong. 6 Normal power of mind or understanding: The fellow has no *sense.* 7 That which is in accord with reason and good judgment: to talk *sense.* 8 Signification; meaning. 9 One of several meanings of the same word or phrase. 10 The opinion or judgment, as of a majority: the *sense* of the meeting. —*v.t.* **sensed, sens·ing** 1 To perceive; become aware of. 2 *Informal* To comprehend; understand. [< L *sensus* perception, p.p. of *sentire* feel]

**sen·si·ble** (sen′sə·bəl) *adj.* 1 Possessed of good mental perception; wise. 2 Capable of physical sensation; sensitive: *sensible* to pain. 3 Perceptible through the senses: *sensible* heat. 4 Perceptible to the mind. 5 Emotionally or mentally sensitive; aware. 6 Great enough to be perceived, appreciable.

[< L *sensus*, p.p. of *sentire* feel, perceive] —**sen′si·ble·ness** *n.* —**sen′si·bly** *adv.*

**sen·si·tive** (sen′sə·tiv) *adj.* 1 Of or pertaining to the senses or sensation. 2 Receptive and responsive to sensations. 3 Responding readily to sensations, esp. of a particular kind: a *sensitive* ear. 4 Acutely receptive or responsive to the quality or strength of attitudes, feelings, or relationships. 5 Capable of appreciating aesthetic or intellectual subtleties. 6 Easily irritated; tender: *sensitive* skin. 7 Hurt; sore. 8 Reacting excessively, as to an agent or substance: *sensitive* to insect bites. 9 Apt to take offense on slight provocation; touchy. 10 Capable of indicating very slight changes or differences; delicate: a *sensitive* barometer. 11 Readily fluctuating or tending to fluctuate: a *sensitive* stock market. [<L *sensus* sense] —**sen′si·tive·ly** *adv.* —**sen′si·tive·ness**, **sen′si·tiv′i·ty** *n.*

**sen·su·al** (sen′shŏŏ·əl) *adj.* 1 Of or pertaining to the senses or their gratification; fleshly; carnal. 2 Unduly indulgent to the appetites or senses. 3 Caused by or preoccupied with bodily or sexual pleasure. [< L *sensus* perception] —**sen′su·al·ly** *adv.*

**sen·su·al·i·ty** (sen′shŏŏ·al′ə·tē) *n.* 1 The state of being sensual. 2 Sensual indulgence; lewdness; lasciviousness.

**sen·su·ous** (sen′shŏŏ·əs) *adj.* 1 Of, pertaining or appealing to, or perceived or caused by the senses. 2 Keenly appreciative of or susceptible to the pleasures of sensation. —**sen′su·ous·ly** *adv.* —**sen′su·ous·ness** *n.*

**sen·tence** (sen′təns) *n.* 1 A determination; opinion, esp. one expressed formally. 2 A final judgment, esp. one pronounced by a court. 3 The penalty pronounced upon a convicted person. 4 *Gram.* A word or group of words expressing a complete thought in the form of a declaration, a question, a command, a wish or an exclamation, usu. beginning with a capital letter and concluding with proper end punctuation. —*v.t.* **·tenced, ·tenc·ing** To pass sentence upon; condemn to punishment. [< L *sententia* opinion < *sentire* feel, be of opinion] —**sen′tenc·er** *n.* —**sen·ten·tial** (sen·ten′shəl) *adj.*

**sen·ten·tious** (sen·ten′shəs) *adj.* 1 Saying much in few words; terse; pithy. 2 Habitually using or full of aphoristic language. 3 Habitually using or full of moralistic language. [< L *sententia* opinion] —**sen·ten′tious·ly** *adv.* —**sen·ten′tious·ness** *n.*

**sen·ti·ent** (sen′shē·ənt, -shənt) *adj.* Possessing the powers of feeling or perception. [< L *sentire* feel] —**sen′ti·ence** *n.* —**sen′ti·ent·ly** *adv.*

**sen·ti·ment** (sen′tə·mənt) *n.* 1 Noble, tender, or refined feeling; delicate sensibility, esp. as expressed in a work of art. 2 A complex of opinions and feelings used as a basis for judgment or action. 3 A mental attitude, judgment, or thought often conditioned by feeling more than reason. 4 SENTIMENTALITY. 5 The meaning of something said, as distinguished from its expression. 6 A thought or wish phrased in conventional language, as a toast. [< L *sentire* feel]

**sen·ti·men·tal** (sen′tə·men′təl) *adj.* 1 Of, pertaining to, caused by, having, or showing sentiment. 2 Experiencing, displaying, or given to sentiment in an extravagant or maudlin manner. —**sen′ti·men′tal·ism**, **sen′ti·men′tal·ist** *n.* —**sen′ti·men′tal·ly** *adv.*

**sen·ti·men·tal·i·ty** (sen′tə·men·tal′ə·tē) *n. pl.* **·ties.** 1 The state or quality of being overly sentimental, esp. in a superficial or maudlin way. 2 An expression of this.

**sen·try** (sen′trē) *n. pl.* **·tries** 1 A guard, esp. a soldier placed on guard to see that only authorized persons pass his post and to give warning of approaching danger. 2 The guard kept by a sentry. [? var. of SENTINEL]

**sep·a·ra·ble** (sep′ər·ə·bəl, sep′rə-) *adj.* Capable of being separated or divided. —**sep′a·ra·bil′i·ty**, **sep′a·ra·ble·ness** *n.* —**sep′a·ra·bly** *adv.*

**sep·a·rate** (sep′ə·rāt) *v.* **·rat·ed, ·rat·ing** *v.t.* 1 To set apart; sever; disjoin. 2 To keep apart; divide: The Hudson River *separates* New York from New Jersey. 3 To divide into components, parts, etc. 4 To isolate or obtain from a compound, mixture, etc.: to *separate* the wheat from the chaff. 5 To consider separately; distinguish between. 6 *Law* To part by separation. —*v.i.* 7 To become divided or disconnected; draw apart. 8 To part company; sever an association. 9 To cease living together as man and wife. 10 To break up into component parts, as a mixture. —*adj.* (sep′ər·it, sep′rit) 1 Existing or considered apart from others; distinct; individual. 2 Detached; disunited. 3 Existing independently; not related. —*n.pl.* Garments to be worn in various combinations, as skirts and blouses. [< L *se-* apart + *parare* prepare] —**sep′a·rate·ly** *adv.* —**sep′**

**a·rate·ness**, **sep′a·ra′tor** *n.* —**sep′a·ra′tive** (-rā′tiv, -ə·rə·tiv) *adj.*

**sep·a·ra·tion** (sep′ə·rā′shən) *n.* 1 The act or process of separating. 2 The state of being separated. 3 A gap or dividing line. 4 *Law* Relinquishment of cohabitation between husband and wife by mutual consent.

**sep·ul·cher** (sep′əl·kər) *n.* 1 A burial place; tomb; vault. 2 A receptacle for relics, esp. in an altar slab. —*v.t.* **·chered** or **·chred**, **·cher·ing** or **·chring** To place in a grave; entomb; bury. Also **sep′ul·chre** (-kər). [< L *sepulcrum*]

**se·pul·chral** (si·pul′krəl) *adj.* 1 Of a sepulcher. 2 Dismal in color or aspect. 3 Low or melancholy in sound. —**se·pul′chral·ly** *adv.*

**se·quel** (sē′kwəl) *n.* 1 Something which follows; a continuation; development. 2 A narrative which, though entire in itself, develops from a preceding one. 3 A consequence; result. [< L *sequi* follow]

**se·quence** (sē′kwəns) *n.* 1 The process or fact of following in space, time, or thought; succession or order. 2 Order of succession; arrangement. 3 A number of things following one another, considered collectively; a series. 4 An effect or consequence. 5 A section of motion-picture film presenting a single episode, without time lapses or interruptions. [< L *sequi* follow]

**se·ques·ter** (si·kwes′tər) *v.t.* 1 To place apart; separate. 2 To seclude; withdraw: often used reflexively. 3 *Law* To take (property) into custody until a controversy, claim, etc., is settled. 4 In international law, to confiscate and control (enemy property) by preemption. [< LL *sequestrare* remove, lay aside] —**se·ques′tered** *adj.*

**ser·e·nade** (ser′ə·nād′) *n.* An evening piece, usu. the song of a lover beneath his lady's window. —*v.t. & v.i.* **nad·ed, ·nad·ing** To entertain with a serenade. [< L *serenus* clear, serene] —**ser′e·nad′er** *n.*

**se·rene** (si·rēn′) *adj.* 1 Clear, bright, and fair; cloudless; untroubled. 2 Tranquil; calm; peaceful. 3 *Usu. cap.* Of exalted rank: used chiefly in royal titles: His *Serene* Highness. [< L *serenus*] —**se·rene′ly** *adv.* —**se·ren·i·ty** (si·ren′ə·tē), **se·rene′ness** *n.* —**Syn.** 2 composed, collected, placid.

**serf** (sûrf) *n.* 1 In feudal times, a person attached to the estate on which he lived. 2 Any person in servile subjection. [< L *servus* a slave] —**serf′dom**, **serf′age**, **serf′hood** *n.*

**serge** (sûrj) *n.* 1 A strong twilled woolen fabric woven with a diagonal rib on both sides. 2 A twilled silk or synthetic lining fabric. [< L *serica (lana)* (wool) of the Seres, an eastern Asian people]

**ser·geant** (sär′jənt) *n.* 1 See GRADE. 2 A police officer of rank next below a captain or lieutenant. 3 SERGEANT AT ARMS. [< L *servire* serve] —**ser′gean·cy, ser′geant·cy, ser′geant·ship** *n.*

**sergeant at arms** *pl.* **sergeants at arms** An officer in a legislative body, court, etc. who enforces order.

**se·ri·al** (sîr′ē·əl) *adj.* 1 Of, like, or arranged in a series. 2 Published or presented in a series at regular intervals. 3 Of a serial or serials. 4 Of, pertaining to, or being atonal music consisting of a fixed series of tones based on the twelve-tone chromatic scale. —*n.* 1 A novel or other story regularly presented in successive installments, as in a magazine, on radio or television, or in motion pictures. 2 A periodical. —**se′ri·al·ly** *adv.*

**se·ries** (sîr′ēz) *n. pl.* **se·ries** 1 An arrangement or connected succession of related things placed in space or happening in time one after the other: a *series* of games; a *series* of lakes. 2 *Math.* The indicated sum of any finite set of terms or of an ordered infinite set of terms. 3 *Chem.* A group of related compounds or elements showing an orderly succession of changes in composition or structure. 4 *Electr.* An arrangement of electric devices in which the current flows through each in order. [L < *serere* join]

**se·ri·ous** (sîr′ē·əs) *adj.* 1 Grave and earnest in quality, feeling, or disposition; thoughtful; sober. 2 Being or done in earnest; not jesting or joking. 3 Involving much work, thought, difficulty, etc.: a *serious* problem. 4 Of grave importance; weighty. 5 Attended with considerable danger or loss: a *serious* accident. [< L *serius*] —**se′ri·ous·ly** *adv.* —**se′ri·ous·ness** *n.* —**Syn.** 1 sedate, staid, solemn, grim. 3 complex, complicated, involved, hard, troublesome.

**ser·mon** (sûr′mən) *n.* 1 A discourse, usu. based on a passage or text of the Bible, delivered as part of a church service. 2 Any serious talk or exhortation, as on duty, morals, etc. [< L *sermo* talk] —**ser·mon·ic** (sər·mon′ik) *adj.*

**ser·pent** (sûr′pənt) *n.* 1 A snake, esp. a poisonous or large one. 2 A treacherous person. [< L *serpere* to creep]

**ser·pen·tine** (sûr′pən·tīn, -tēn) *adj.* 1 Of or like a serpent. 2 Winding; zigzag. 3 Subtle; cunning. —*n.* A massive or fibrous, often mottled green or yellow, magnesium silicate.

**se·rum** (sîr′əm) *n. pl.* **se·rums** or **se·ra** (sîr′ə) 1 The fluid constituent of blood. 2 The serum of the blood of an animal which has developed immunity to a specific pathogen. 3 WHEY. 4 Any watery plant or animal secretion. [L, whey]

**ser·vant** (sûr′vənt) *n.* 1 A person employed to assist in domestic matters, sometimes living within the employer's house. 2 A government worker. [< OF *servir* to serve]

**serve** (sûrv) *v.* **served, serv·ing** *v.t.* 1 To work for as a servant. 2 To be of service to; wait on. 3 To promote the interests of; aid; help: to *serve* one's country. 4 To obey and give homage to: to *serve* God. 5 To satisfy the requirements of; suffice for. 6 To perform the duties connected with, as a public office. 7 To go through (a period of enlistment, term of punishment, etc.). 8 To furnish or provide, as with a regular supply. 9 To offer or bring food or drink to (a guest, etc.); wait on at table. 10 To bring and place on the table or distribute among guests, as food or drink. 11 To operate or handle; tend: to *serve* a cannon. 12 To copulate with: said of male animals. 13 In tennis, etc., to put (the ball) in play by hitting it to one's opponent. 14 *Law* a To deliver (a summons or writ) to a person. b To deliver a summons or writ to. 15 *Naut.* To wrap (a rope, stay, etc.), as with wire, cordage, etc., so as to strengthen or protect. —*v.i.* 16 To be a servant. 17 To perform the duties of any employment, office, etc. 18 To go through a term of service, as in the army or navy. 19 To offer or give food or drink, as to guests. 20 To wait on customers. 21 To be suitable or usable, as for a purpose; perform a function. 22 To be favorable, as weather. 23 In tennis, etc., to put the ball in play. —*n.* In tennis, etc.: a The delivering of the ball by striking it toward an opponent. b The turn of one who serves. [< L *servus* a slave]

**ser·vice** (sûr′vis) *n.* 1 The act or occupation of serving. 2 The manner in which one serves or is served. 3 A division of employment, esp. of public or governmental employment: the diplomatic *service*. 4 Any branch of the armed forces. 5 A facility for meeting some public need: electric *service*. 6 Installation, maintenance, and repair provided for the buyer of something. 7 Assistance; aid; benefit: to be of *service*. 8 *Often pl.* A useful result or product of labor which is not a tangible commodity: a doctor's *services*. 9 *Often pl.* A public exercise of worship. 10 A religious or civil ritual: the marriage *service*. 11 The music for a liturgical office or rite. 12 A set of articles for a particular purpose: a tea *service*. 13 *Naut.* The protective wire, cordage, etc., wrapped around a rope. 14 *Law* The legal communication of a writ, process, or summons to a designated person. 15 In animal husbandry, the copulation of a female. —*adj.* 1 Pertaining to or for service. 2 Of, for, or used by servants or tradespeople: a *service* entrance. 3 Of, pertaining to, or belonging to a military service: a *service* flag. 4 For rough or everyday usage. —*v.t.* ·viced, ·vic·ing 1 To maintain or repair: to *service* a car. 2 To supply service to. 3 SERVE (def. 12). [< L *servus* a slave]

ser·vile (sûr′vil, -vil) *adj.* 1 Having the spirit of a slave; slavish; abject. 2 Of, pertaining to, or appropriate for slaves or servants: *servile* employment. [< L *servus* a slave] — ser′vile·ly *adv.* —ser·vil′i·ty, ser′vile·ness *n.* —Syn. 1 obsequious, fawning, groveling, cowering, submissive, cringing.

ser·vi·tude (sûr′və·t′ood) *n.* 1 The condition of a slave; slavery; bondage. 2 Enforced service as a punishment for crime: penal *servitude*. [< L *servus* a slave]

ses·sion (sesh′ən) *n.* 1 The sitting together of a legislative assembly, court, etc., for the transaction of business. 2 A single meeting or series of meetings of an assembly, court, etc. 3 In some schools, a term. 4 Any period of some specified activity: a *session* with the boss. [< L *sessus*, p.p. of *sedere* sit] — ses′sion·al *adj.* —ses′sion·al·ly *adv.*

set (set) *v.* set, set·ting *v.t.* 1 To put in a certain place or position; place. 2 To put into a fixed, firm, or immovable position, condition, or state: to *set* brick; to *set* one's jaw. 3 To bring to a specified condition or state: *Set* your mind at ease; He *set* the barn afire; She has *set* her heart on being a doctor. 4 To restore to proper position for healing, as a broken bone. 5 To place in readiness for use: to *set* a trap. 6 To adjust according to a standard: to *set* a clock. 7 To adjust (an instrument, dial, etc.) to a particular calibration or position. 8 To place

knives, forks, etc., on (a table) for a meal. 9 To bend the teeth of (a saw) to either side alternately. 10 To appoint or establish; prescribe: to *set* boundaries, regulations, fashions, etc. 11 To fix or establish a time for: We *set* our departure for noon. 12 To assign for performance, completion, etc.; to *set* a task. 13 To assign to some specific duty or function; appoint; station: to *set* a guard. 14 To cause to sit. 15 To present or perform so as to be copied or emulated: to *set* the pace. 16 To give a specified direction to: He *set* his course for the Azores. 17 To put in place so as to catch the wind: to *set* the jib. 18 To place in a mounting or frame, as a gem. 19 To stud or adorn with gems: to *set* a crown with rubies. 20 To place (a hen) on eggs to hatch them. 21 To place (eggs) under a fowl or in an incubator for hatching. 22 To place (a price or value): with *by* or *on:* to *set* a price on an outlaw's head. 23 To arrange (hair), as with curlers, lotions, etc. 24 *Printing* a To arrange (type) for printing; compose. b To put into type, as a sentence, manuscript, etc. 25 *Music* To compose music for (words) or write words for (existing music). 26 To describe (a scene) as taking place: to *set* the scene in Monaco. 27 In the theater, to arrange (a stage) so as to depict a scene. 28 In some games, as bridge, to defeat. —*v.i.* 29 To go or pass below the horizon, as the sun. 30 To wane; decline. 31 To sit on eggs, as fowl. 32 To become firm; solidify; congeal. 33 To become fast, as a dye. 34 To begin to move, as on a journey: with *forth, out, off.* etc. 35 To begin: *Set* to work. 36 To have a specified direction; tend. 37 To hang or fit, as clothes. 38 To mend, as a broken bone. 39 *Regional* To sit. 40 *Bot.* To begin development or growth, as a rudimentary fruit. —set against 1 To balance; compare. 2 To make unfriendly to; prejudice against. —set off 1 To put apart by itself. 2 To serve as a contrast or foil for; enhance. 3 To make begin; set in motion. 4 To cause to explode. —set out 1 To display; exhibit. 2 To lay out or plan. 3 To begin a journey. 4 To begin any enterprise. 5 To plant. —set to 1 To start; begin. 2 To start fighting. —set up 1 To place in an upright or high position. 2 To raise. 3 To place in power, authority, etc. 4 a To construct or build. b To put together; assemble. c To found; establish. 5 To provide with the means to start a new business. 6 To cause to be heard: to *set up* a cry. 7 To propose or put forward (a theory, etc.). **8** To cause. **9** To work out a plan for. **10** To claim to be. **11 a** To pay for the drinks, etc., of; treat. **b** To pay for (drinks, etc.). **12** To encourage; exhilarate. —**set upon** To attack; assail. —*adj.* **1** Established by authority or agreement; prescribed; appointed: a *set* time or method. **2** Customary; conventional: a *set* phrase. **3** Deliberately and systematically conceived; formal: a *set* speech. **4** Fixed and motionless; rigid. **5** Firm in consistency. **6** Fixed in opinion or disposition; obstinate. **7** Formed; built; made: deep-*set* eyes. **8** Ready; prepared: to get *set.* —*n.* **1** The act or condition of setting. **2** Permanent change of form, as by bending, pressure, strain, etc. **3** The arrangement, tilt, or hang of a garment, hat, sail, etc. **4** Carriage or bearing: the *set* of his shoulders. **5** The sinking of a heavenly body below the horizon. **6** The direction of a current or wind. **7** A young plant ready for setting out. **8** Inclination of the mind; bent. **9** *Psychol.* A temporary condition assumed by an organism preparing for a particular response or activity. **10** An arrangement of the hair, as by curling. **11** In tennis, a group of games completed when one side wins six games, or, if tied at five games, wins either two more games consecutively or wins a tie breaker. [< OE *settan* cause to sit]

**set·ter** (set′ər) *n.* **1** One who or that which sets. **2** One of a breed of medium-sized, silky-coated dogs trained to indicate the location of game birds while standing rigid.

**set·tle** (set′l) *v.* **·tled, ·tling** *v.t.* **1** To put in order; set to rights; to *settle* affairs. **2** To establish or fix permanently or as if permanently: He *settled* himself on the couch. **3** To calm; quiet: to *settle* one's nerves. **4** To cause (sediment or dregs) to sink to the bottom. **5** To make firm or compact: to *settle* dust or ashes. **6** To make clear or transparent, as by causing sediment or dregs to sink. **7** To make quiet or orderly: One blow *settled* him. **8** To decide or determine finally, as an argument, legal case, etc. **9** To pay, as a debt; satisfy, as a claim. **10** To establish residents or residence in (a country, town, etc.). **11** To establish as residents. **12** To establish in a permanent occupation, home, etc. **13** *Law* To make over or assign (property) by legal act: with *on* or *upon.* —*v.i.* **14** To come to rest. **15** To sink gradually; subside. **16** To become clear by the sinking of sediment. **17** To become more firm by

sinking. **18** To become established or located: The pain *settled* in his arm. **19** To establish one's abode or home. **20** To come to a decision; determine; resolve: with *on, upon,* or *with.* **21** To pay a bill, etc. —**settle down 1** To start living a regular, orderly life, esp. after a period of wandering or irresponsibility. **2** To become quiet or orderly. —*n.* A long, wooden, high-backed bench, usu. with arms and sometimes having a chest from seat to floor. [< OE *setl* a seat]

**set·tle·ment** (set′l·mənt) *n.* **1** The act of settling or the condition of being settled. **2** An area newly colonized. **3** A small, usu. remote village. **4** *Law* **a** The act of assigning property, money, etc., to someone. **b** That which is thus assigned. **5** An agreement or adjustment, as of differences. **6** An urban welfare institution that provides various educational or recreational services to a community or neighborhood: **also settlement house.**

**set·to** (set′tōō′) *n.* A bout at fighting, arguing, etc.

**sev·er** (sev′ər) *v.t.* **1** To put or keep apart; separate. **2** To cut or break into two or more parts. **3** To break off; dissolve, as a relationship. —*v.i.* **4** To come or break apart or into pieces. **5** To go away or apart; separate. [< L *separare* separate] —**sev′er·a·ble** *adj.* —**sev′er·er** *n.*

**sev·er·al** (sev′ər·əl, sev′rəl) *adj.* **1** Being of an indefinite number, more than one or two, yet not large; divers. **2** Considered individually; single; separate. **3** Individually different; various or diverse. [< L *separ* separate]

**sev·er·ance** (sev′ər·əns, sev′rəns) *n.* The act of severing, or the condition of being severed.

**se·vere** (si·vir′) *adj.* **·ver·er, ·ver·est 1** Difficult; trying. **2** Unsparing; harsh; merciless: a *severe* punishment. **3** Conforming to rigid rules; extremely strict or accurate. **4** Serious and austere in disposition or manner; grave. **5** Austerely plain and simple, as in style, design, etc. **6** Causing sharp pain or anguish; extreme: *severe* hardship. —**se·vere′ness** *n.* [< L *severus*] —**se·vere′ly** *adv.*

**sew** (sō) *v.* **sewed, sewed** or **sewn, sew·ing** *v.t.* **1** To make, mend, or fasten with needle and thread. **2** To enclose or secure by sewing. —*v.i.* **3** To work with needle and thread. —**sew up 1** To mend by sewing. **2** *Informal* **a** To achieve absolute control or use of. **b** To

492

make or be totally successful. [< OE *siwan, siowian*]

**sew·age** (sōō'ij) *n.* The waste matter carried off in sewers. [< SEW(ER) + -AGE]

**sew·er** (sōō'ər) *n.* 1 A conduit, usu. laid underground, to carry off drainage and excrement. 2 Any large public drain. [< OF *seuwiere* a channel from a fish pond]

**sew·er·age** (sōō'ər·ij) *n.* 1 A system of sewers. 2 Systematic draining by sewers. 3 SEWAGE.

**sex** (seks) *n.* 1 Either of two divisions, male and female, by which organisms are distinguished with reference to the reproductive functions. 2 Males or females collectively. 3 The character of being male or female. 4 The activity or phenomena of life concerned with sexual desire or reproduction. 5 *Informal* Any act affording sexual gratification, as sexual intercourse. —*adj. Informal* SEXUAL. [< L *sexus*]

**sex·a·ge·nar·i·an** (sek'sə·jə·nâr'ē·ən) *adj.* Sixty years old, or between sixty and seventy. —*n.* A person of this age. [< L *sexageni* sixty each]

**sex appeal** A physical quality or charm which attracts sexual interest.

**sex·ism** (seks'iz·əm) *n.* Prejudice or discrimination against women. [< SEX + -ISM, on analogy with *racism*] —**sex'ist** *n., adj.*

**sex·ol·o·gy** (seks·ol'ə·jē) *n.* The study of human sexual behavior. —**sex·o·log·ic** (sek'sə·loj'ik) or **i·cal** *adj.* —**sex·ol'o·gist** *n.*

**sex·tant** (seks'tənt) *n.* An instrument for measuring the angular distance between two objects, as between a heavenly body and the horizon, used esp. in determining latitude at sea. [< L *sextus* sixth]

**sex·ton** (seks'tən) *n.* An officer of a church having charge of maintenance and also of ringing the bells, overseeing burials, etc. [< Med. L *sacristanus* sacristan]

**sex·u·al** (sek'shōō·əl) *adj.* 1 Of, pertaining to, peculiar to, characteristic of, or affecting sex, the sexes, or the organs or functions of sex. 2 Characterized by or having sex. [< L *sexus* sex] —**sex'u·al'i·ty** (-al'ə·tē) *n.* —**sex'u·al·ly** *adv.*

**sex·y** (sek'sē) *adj.* **sex·i·er, sex·i·est** 1 *Informal* Provocative of sexual desire: a *sexy* dress; a *sexy* woman. 2 *Informal* Concerned in large or excessive degree with sex: a *sexy* novel. 3 *Slang* Interesting, exciting, or stimulating: Crime was the *sexiest* issue of the political campaign.

**shab·by** (shab'ē) *adj.* **·bi·er, ·bi·est** 1 Threadbare, ragged. 2 Characterized by worn or ragged garments. 3 Mean; paltry. [< OE *sceabb* a scab] —**shab'bi·ly** *adv.* —**shab'bi·ness** *n.*

**shack·le** (shak'əl) *n.* 1 A bracelet or fetter for encircling and confining a limb or limbs. 2 *Usu. pl.* Any impediment or restraint. 3 One of various forms of fastenings, as a link for coupling railway cars. —*v.t.* **·led, ·ling** 1 To restrain or confine with shackles; fetter. 2 To keep or restrain from free action or speech. 3 To connect or fasten with a shackle. [< OE *sceacul*] —**shack'ler** *n.*

**shad** (shad) *n. pl.* **shad** Any of various anadromous fish related to the herring. [< OE *sceadd*]

**shade** (shād) *v.* **shad·ed, shad·ing** *v.t.* 1 To screen from light or heat. 2 To make dim with or as with a shadow; darken; 3 To screen or protect with or as with a shadow. 4 To cause to change, pass, blend, or soften, by gradations. 5 a To represent (degrees of shade, colors, etc.) by gradations of light or shading. b To represent varying shades, colors, etc., in (a picture of painting). 6 To make slightly lower, as a price. —*v.i.* 7 To change or vary by degrees. *n.* 1 Relative darkness caused by the interception or partial absence of rays of light. 2 A place having such relative darkness. 3 That part of a drawing, painting, etc. represented as being relatively dark or in shadow. 4 A gradation of darkness or blackness in a color. 5 A minute difference, variation, or degree: *shades* of meaning. 6 A screen or cover that partially or totally shuts off light: a lamp *shade*. 7 A ghost or phantom. 8 *pl. Slang* SUNGLASSES. —**in** (or into) **the shade** 1 In or into a shady place. 2 In or into a condition of inferiority, defeat, obscurity, etc. [< OE *sceadu* a shade]

**shad·ow** (shad'ō) *n.* 1 A comparative darkness within an illuminated area caused by the interception of light by an opaque body. 2 The dark figure or image thus produced on a surface: the *shadow* of a man. 3 The shaded portion of a picture. 4 A mirrored image: to see one's *shadow* in a pool. 5 A phantom, ghost, etc. 6 A faint representation or indication; a symbol: the *shadow* to things to come. 7 A remnant; vestige: *shadows* of his former glory. 8 An insignificant trace or portion: not a *shadow* of evidence. 9 Gloom or a saddening influence. 10 An inseparable companion. 11 One who trails or follows another, as a detective or spy. 12 A slight growth of beard, esp. in the phrase five o'clock shadow. —v.t. 1 To cast a shadow upon; shade. 2 To darken or make gloomy. 3 To represent or foreshow dimly or vaguely: with *forth* or *out*. 4 To follow closely or secretly; spy on. 5 To shade in painting, drawing, etc. —adj. Of or pertaining to a shadow cabinet. [< OE *sceadu* a shade] — **shad′ow·er** n.

**shad·ow·y** (shad′ō-ē) adj. **·ow·ier**, **·ow·i·est** 1 Dark; shady. 2 Vague; dim. 3 Unreal; ghostly. —**shad′ow·i·ness** n.

**shaft** (shaft, shäft) n. 1 The long narrow rod of an arrow, spear, lance, harpoon, etc. 2 An arrow or spear. 3 Something hurled like or having the effect of an arrow or spear: *shafts* of ridicule. 4 A beam of light. 5 A long handle, as of a hammer, ax, etc. 6 *Mech.* A long and usu. cylindrical bar, esp. if rotating and transmitting motion. 7 *Archit.* a The portion of a column between capital and base. b A slender column, as an obelisk. 8 The stem of a feather. 9 The slender portion of a bone or the portion of a hair from root to the end. 10 A tall, narrow building or spire. 11 A narrow, vertical passage, as the entrance to a mine or an opening through a building for an elevator. 12 A conduit for the passage of air, heat, etc. 13 *Slang* Malicious or abusive treatment: with *the*, esp. in the phrases **get the shaft**, **give (someone) the shaft**. —v.t. *Slang* To act maliciously or abusively toward. [< OE *sceaft*]

**shake** (shāk) v. **shook**, **shak·en**, **shak·ing** v.t. 1 To cause to move to and fro or up and down with short, rapid movements. 2 To affect by or as by vigorous action: with *off*, *out*, *from*, etc.: to *shake* out a sail; to *shake* off a tackler. 3 To cause to tremble or quiver; vibrate: The blows *shook* the door. 4 To cause to stagger or totter. 5 To weaken or disturb: to *shake* one's determination. 6 To agitate or rouse; stir: often with *up*. 7 *Informal* To get rid of or away from. 8 To clasp (hands) as a form of greeting, agreement, etc. 9 *Music* TRILL. —v.i. 10 To move to and fro or up and down in short, rapid movements. 11 To be affected by vigorous action: with *off*, *out*, *from*, etc. 12 To tremble or quiver, as from cold or fear. 13 To become unsteady; totter. 14 To clasp hands. 15 *Music* TRILL. —**shake down** 1 To cause to fall by shaking. 2 To cause to settle by shaking. 3 To test or become familiar with (new equipment, etc.). 4 *Slang* To extort money from. —**shake up** 1 To mix or blend by shaking. 2 To agitate or rouse; stir. 3 To jar

or jolt. 4 To effect or cause rather extensive changes or reorganization in. 5 *Slang* To cause to lose one's composure; disconcert. —n. 1 The act or an instance of shaking: a *shake* of the hand. 2 A tight fissure in rock or timber. 3 *pl. Informal* A fit of bodily shaking or trembling: usu. with *the*. 4 MILKSHAKE. 5 *Informal* EARTHQUAKE. 6 *Informal* An instant; jiffy. 7 *Informal* A deal: to get a fair *shake*. 8 *Music* TRILL. —**give (someone or something) the shake** To get away from (someone or something). [< OE *scacan*]

**shak·y** (shā′kē) adj. **shak·i·er**, **shak·i·est** 1 Not firm or solid. 2 Not well founded, thought out, etc.: a *shaky* theory. 3 Not dependable or reliable. 4 Characterized by shaking. 5 Weak; unsound, as in body. — **shak′i·ly** adv. —**shak′i·ness** n.

**shal·lot** (sha·lot′, shal′ət) n. 1 A mild, onionlike vegetable allied to garlic. 2 SCALLION. [< OF *eschalotte*]

**shal·low** (shal′ō) adj. 1 Lacking depth. 2 Not extending far inwards or outwards: a *shallow* room. 3 Lacking intellectual depth; superficial. —n. *Usu. pl.* but construed as sing. or pl. A shallow place in a body of water; shoal. —v.t. & v.i. To make or become shallow. [ME *schalowe*] —**shal′low·ly** adv. — **shal′low·ness** n.

**sham** (sham) adj. False; pretended; counterfeit; mock. —n. 1 A person who shams. 2 A hoax; deception. 3 An imitation; counterfeit. 4 Cheap artificiality or pretension. 5 A decorative cover or the like for use over a household article: a pillow *sham*. —v. **shammed**, **sham·ming** v.t. 1 To counterfeit; feign. —v.i. 2 To make false pretenses; feign something. [? dial. var. of SHAME]

**sham·bles** (sham′bəlz) n. pl. *(usu. construed as sing.)* 1 SLAUGHTERHOUSE. 2 Any place of carnage or execution. 3 A place marked by great destruction, disorder, or confusion. [< OE *scamel* a bench.]

**shame** (shām) n. 1 A painful feeling caused by a sense of guilt, unworthiness, impropriety, etc. 2 Disgrace; humiliation. 3 A person or thing causing disgrace or humiliation. 4 Misfortune; outrage: It's a *shame* they didn't go. —**put to shame** 1 To disgrace; make ashamed. 2 To surpass or eclipse. — v.t. **shamed**, **sham·ing** 1 To cause to feel shame. 2 To bring shame upon; disgrace. 3 To impel by a sense of shame: with *into* or *out of*. [< OE *scamu*]

**shame·ful** (shām′fəl) adj. 1 Bringing shame or disgrace; disgraceful; scandalous. 2 Indecent. —**shame·ful·ly** adv. —**shame·ful·ness** n. —**Syn.** 1 disreputable, dishonorable, ignoble, ignominious, base, despicable, contemptible, deplorable, vile, odious.

**sham·poo** (sham·pōō′) v.t. 1 To lather and wash (the hair and scalp) thoroughly. 2 To cleanse by rubbing. —n. The act or process of shampooing, or a preparation used for it. [< Hind. *châmpnā* to press] —**sham·poo′er** n.

**sham·rock** (sham′rok) n. Any of several plants, with trifoliate leaves, accepted as the national emblem of Ireland, esp. the wood sorrel. [< Irish *seamar* trefoil]

**shang·hai** (shang′hī, shang′hī′) v.t. ·haied, ·hai·ing 1 To drug or render unconscious and kidnap for service aboard a ship. 2 To cause to do something by force or deception. [< *Shanghai*]

**shank** (shangk) n. 1 The leg between the knee and the ankle. 2 The entire leg. 3 A cut of meat from the leg of an animal; the shin. 4 The stem, as of a tobacco pipe, key, anchor, etc. 5 The part of a tool connecting the handle with the working part; shaft. 6 The projecting piece or loop in the back of some buttons by which they are attached. 7 *Printing* The body of a type. 8 The narrow part of a shoe sole in front of the heel. • See SHOE. —**shank of the evening** *Informal* The early part of the evening. [< OE *sceanca*] —**shanked** adj.

**shan·ty** (shan′tē) n. pl. ·ties A small, rickety shack or cabin. [< F (Canadian) *chantier* lumberer's shack]

**shape** (shāp) n. 1 Outward form or contour. 2 Appearance of a body with reference only to its contour; figure. 3 Something that gives or determines shape, as a pattern or mold. 4 An assumed aspect or appearance; guise. 5 A developed or final expression or form: to put an idea into *shape*. 6 Any embodiment or form in which a thing may exist: the *shape* of a novel. 7 A ghost or phantom. 8 *Informal* The condition of a person or thing as regards health, orderliness, etc. —**in shape** In good physical condition or appearance. —**out of shape** In bad physical condition or appearance. —**take shape** To begin to have or assume definite form. —v. shaped, shap·ing v.t. 1 To give shape to; mold; form. 2 To adjust or adapt; modify. 3 To devise; prepare. 4 To give direction or character to: to *shape* one's course of action. 5 To put into or express in words. — v.i. 6 To take shape; develop; form: often

with *up* or *into*. —**shape up** 1 To develop fully or appropriately; work out. 2 *Informal* To do, work, behave, etc., properly. [< OE *gesceap* creation] —**shap′er** n.

**shape·ly** (shāp′lē) adj. ·li·er, ·li·est Having a pleasing shape; well-formed. —**shape′li·ness** n.

**share** (shâr) n. 1 A portion alloted or due to a person or contributed by a person. 2 One of the equal parts into which the capital stock of a company or corporation is divided. 3 An equitable part of something used, done, or divided in common. —v. **shared, shar·ing** v.t. 1 To divide and give out in shares or portions; apportion. 2 To enjoy, use, participate in, endure, etc., in common. —v.i. 3 To have a part; participate: with *in.* 4 To divide something in equal parts: with *out* or *with.* [< OE *scearu*] —**shar′er** n.

**sharp** (shärp) adj. 1 Having a keen edge or an acute point; capable of cutting or piercing. 2 Not rounded; pointed; angular: *sharp* features. 3 Abrupt in change of direction: a *sharp* curve. 4 Distinct; well-defined: a *sharp* contrast. 5 Keen or quick in perception or discernment. 6 Keen or acute, as in seeing or hearing. 7 Shrewd, as in bargaining. 8 Quickly aroused; harsh: a *sharp* temper. 9 Heated; fiery: a *sharp* debate. 10 Vigilant; attentive: a *sharp* watch. 11 Quick; vigorous. 12 Keenly felt: *sharp* hunger pangs. 13 Intense or penetrating in effect; incisive to the point of being unsettling or wounding: a *sharp* look; a *sharp* tongue. 14 Shrill: a *sharp* sound. 15 Having an acid or pungent taste or smell. 16 *Slang* Stylishly dressed or well groomed. 17 *Music* Being above the proper or indicated pitch. —adv. 1 In a sharp manner. 2 Promptly; exactly: at 4 o'clock *sharp.* 3 *Music* Above the proper pitch. —n. 1 *Music* A character (#) used on a natural degree of the staff to make it represent a tone a half-step higher; also, the tone so indicated. 2 A sewing needle of long, slender shape. 3 A cheat; sharper: a *card-sharp.* —v.t. 1 *Music* To raise in pitch, as by a half-step. —v.i. 2 *Music* To sing, play, or sound above the right pitch. [< OE *scearp*] —**sharp′ly** adv. —**sharp′ness** n.

**sharp·en** (shär′pən) v.t. & v.i. To make or become sharp. —**sharp′en·er** n.

**shat·ter** (shat′ər) v.t. 1 To break into pieces suddenly, as by a blow. 2 To break the health or well-being of, as the body or mind. 3 To damage or demolish. —v.i. 4 To break into pieces; burst. —*n. pl.* Shattered pieces or fragments, esp. in the phrase **in shatters.** [ME *schateren* to scatter]

**shave** (shāv) *v.* **shaved, shaved** or **shav·en, shav·ing** *v.t.* 1 To cut hair or beard close to the skin with a razor. —*v.t.* 2 To remove hair or beard from (the face, head, etc.) with a razor. 3 To cut (hair or beard) close to the skin with a razor: often with *off.* 4 To trim closely as if with a razor: to *shave* a lawn. 5 To cut thin slices or pieces from. 6 To touch or scrape in passing; graze; come close to. 7 *Informal* To lower or deduct from (a price, amount, etc.). —*n.* 1 The act or operation of shaving with a razor. 2 A thin slice or piece; shaving. 3 *Informal* The act of barely grazing something. [< OE *scafan*]

**shawl** (shôl) *n.* A wrap, as a square cloth, or large broad scarf, worn over the head or shoulders. [< Pers. *shāl*]

**sheaf** (shēf) *n. pl.* **sheaves** (shēvz) 1 Stalks of cut grain or the like, bound together. 2 Any collection of things, as papers, held together by a band or tie. —*v.t.* To bind in a sheaf; sheave. [< OE *scēaf*]

**shear** (shir) *n.* 1 Either of the blades of a pair of shears. 2 A cutting machine for sheet metal. 3 *Physics* a A deformation of a solid body, equivalent to a sliding over each other of adjacent layers. b A force or system of forces tending to cause this. 4 The act or result of shearing. —*v.* **sheared** (*Archaic* **shore**), **sheared** or **shorn, shear·ing** *v.t.* 1 To cut the hair, fleece, etc., from. 2 To remove by cutting or clipping: to *shear* wool. 3 To deprive; strip, as of power or wealth. 4 To cut or clip with shears or other sharp instrument: to *shear* a cable. —*v.i.* 5 To use shears or other sharp instrument. 6 To slide or break from a shear (def. 3). 7 To proceed by or as by cutting a way: with *through.* [< OE *sceran* to shear] —**shear′er** *n.*

**sheath** (shēth) *n.* 1 An envelope or case, as for a sword; scabbard. 2 *Biol.* Any structure that enfolds or encloses. [< OE *scēth*]

**sheathe** (shēth) *v.t.* **sheathed, sheath·ing** 1 To put into a sheath. 2 To plunge (a sword, etc.) into flesh. 3 To draw in, as claws. 4 To protect or conceal, as by covering: to *sheathe* plasterboard; to *sheathe* one's anger.

**shed** (shed) *v.* **shed, shed·ding** *v.t.* 1 To pour forth in drops; emit, as tears or blood. 2 To cause to pour forth. 3 To send forth or abroad; radiate: to *shed* light on a subject.

4 To throw off without allowing to penetrate, as rain; repel. 5 To cast off by natural process, as hair, skin, a shell, etc. —*v.i.* 6 To cast off or lose hair, skin, etc., by natural process. 7 To fall or drop, as leaves or seed. —*n.* That which sheds, as a sloping surface or watershed. [< OE *scēadan* separate, part]

**sheen** (shēn) *n.* 1 A glistening brightness, as if from reflection. 2 Bright, shining attire. —*v.i.* To shine; gleam; glisten. [< OE *scēne* beautiful] —**sheen′y** *adj.*

**sheep** (shēp) *n. pl.* **sheep** 1 Any of a genus of woolly, medium-sized ruminants, esp. domesticated species grown for their fleece, flesh, and hide. 2 A meek or timid person. [< OE *scēap*]

**sheer** (shir) *adj.* 1 Having no modifying conditions; absolute; utter: *sheer* folly. 2 Exceedingly thin and fine: said of fabrics. 3 Perpendicular; steep: a *sheer* precipice. 4 Pure; pellucid. —*n.* Any very thin fabric used for clothes. —*adv.* 1 Entirely; utterly. 2 Perpendicularly. [ME *schere*] —**sheer′ly** *adv.* —**sheer′ness** *n.*

**sheet** (shēt) *n.* 1 A thin, broad, usu. rectangular piece of any material, as metal, glass, etc. 2 A broad, flat surface or expanse: a *sheet* of flame. 3 A large, usu. rectangular piece of cotton, linen, silk, etc., used as bedding. 4 A usu. rectangular piece of paper, used esp. for writing, printing, etc. 5 *Usu. pl. Printing* A printed signature for a book. 6 *Informal* A newspaper. 7 A sail: a literary use. 8 *Naut.* A rope or chain attached to the lower corner of a sail, used to regulate the angle of the sail to the wind. 9 The large, unseparated block of stamps printed by one impression of a plate. —*v.t.* To cover with, wrap in, or form into a sheet or sheets. —*adj.* Formed or cut into sheets: *sheet* metal. [< OE *scēte* linen cloth]

**sheik** (shēk, shāk) *n.* The chief of an Arab tribe or family. Also **sheikh.** [< Ar. *shakha* grow old] —**sheik′dom, sheikh′dom** *n.*

**shelf** (shelf) *n. pl.* **shelves** (shelvz) 1 A piece of material set horizontally into or against a wall, cabinet, closet, etc., to support articles. 2 The contents of a shelf. 3 Any flat projecting ledge, as of rock. 4 A reef; shoal. [< LG *schelf* set of shelves]

**shell** (shel) *n.* 1 The hard outer covering of a mollusk, lobster, egg, nut, etc. • See OYSTER. 2 Something like a shell in shape or function, as the outer framework of a building, a ship's hull, a hollow pastry or pie crust for filling, etc. **3** A sleeveless blouse or sweater. **4** A very light, long, and narrow racing rowboat. **5** A hollow metallic projectile filled with an explosive or chemical. **6** A metallic or paper cartridge case containing the powder, bullet, or shot for breechloading small arms. **7** Any case used to contain the explosives of fireworks. **8** A reserved or impersonal attitude: to come out of one's *shell.* —*v.t.* **1** To divest of or remove from a shell, husk, or pod. **2** To separate from the cob, as Indian corn. **3** To bombard with shells, as a fort. **4** To cover with shells. — *v.i.* **5** To shed or become freed from the shell or pod. **6** To fall off, as a shell or scale. [< OE *scell* shell] —**shell′er** *n.* —**shell′y** *adj.* (**·i·er, ·i·est**)

**shel·lac** (shə·lak′) *n.* **1** A purified lac in the form of thin flakes, used in varnish, insulators, etc. **2** A varnish made of shellac dissolved in alcohol. —*v.t.* **·lacked, ·lack·ing 1** To cover or varnish with shellac. **2** *Slang* **a** To beat. **b** To defeat utterly. Also **shel·lack′.** [< OE SHELL + LAC[1]]

**shelve** (shelv) *v.* **shelved, shelv·ing** *v.t.* **1** To place on a shelf. **2** To postpone indefinitely; put aside. **3** To retire. **4** To provide or fit with shelves. —*v.i.* **5** To incline gradually.

**shep·herd** (shep′ərd) *n.* **1** A keeper or herder of sheep. **2** Figuratively, a pastor, leader, or guide. —*v.t.* To herd, guide, protect, or direct, as a shepherd. [< OE *scēaphyrde*] —**shep′herd·ess** *n. Fem.*

**sher·bet** (shûr′bit) *n.* **1** A frozen dessert, usu. fruit-flavored, made with water or milk, gelatin, etc. **2** Originally, a Turkish drink, made of fruit juice sweetened and diluted with water. Also **sher′bert** (-bərt). [< Ar. *sharbah* a drink]

**sher·iff** (sher′if) *n.* **1** The chief law-enforcement officer of a county, who executes the mandates of courts, keeps order, etc. **2** In Canada, an official whose job is to enforce minor court orders, such as the eviction of persons for nonpayment of rent. [< OE *scīr-gerēfa* shire reeve] —**sher′iff·dom** *n.*

**shield** (shēld) *n.* **1** A broad piece of defensive armor, commonly carried on the left arm; a large buckler. **2** Anything that protects or defends. **3** Any of various devices that afford protection, as from machinery, electricity, radiation, etc. **4** Anything shaped like a shield, as a policeman's badge, decorative emblem, etc. **5** A heraldic escutcheon. —*v.t.* **1** To protect from danger;

defend; guard. **2** To hide or screen from view. —*v.i.* **3** To act as a shield or safeguard. —**shield′er** *n.*

**shift** (shift) *v.t.* **1** To change or move from one position, arrangement, place, etc., to another. **2** To change for another or others of the same class. —*v.i.* **3** To change position, place, attitude, etc. **4** To manage or get along. **5** To evade; equivocate. —*n.* **1** The act of shifting. **2** A change in position, place, direction, etc. **3** A change in attitude, loyalty, etc. **4** An action or recourse taken in an emergency; expedient. **5** A trick or evasion. **6** GEARSHIFT. **7** A relay of workers or their period of work: the night *shift.* **8** A woman's dress that is not belted or fitted at the waist. **9** *Archaic* A chemise or undergarment. [< OE *sciftan* divide] —**shift′er** *n.*

**shil·ling** (shil′ing) *n.* **1** A current silver coin of Great Britain, equal to five (new) pence or 1/20 of a pound. **2** A former colonial American coin, varying in value from 12 to 16 cents. [< OE *scilling*]

**shim·mer** (shim′ər) *v.i.* To shine faintly; give off or emit a tremulous light; glimmer. —*n.* A tremulous shining or gleaming; glimmer. [< OE *scimerian*] —**shim′mer·y** *adj.*

**shin** (shin) *n.* **1** The front part of the leg below the knee; also, the shinbone. **2** The lower foreleg: a *shin* of beef. —*v.t.* & *v.i.* **shinned, shin·ning** To climb (a pole) by gripping with the hands or arms and the shins or legs: usu. with *up.* [< OE *scinu*]

**shine** (shīn) *v.i.* **shone** or (*esp. for def. 5*) **shined, shin·ing 1** To emit light; beam; glow. **2** To show or be conspicuous. **3** To excel; be preeminent. —*v.t.* **4** To cause to shine. **5** To brighten by rubbing or polishing. —*n.* **1** Radiance; luster; sheen. **2** Fair weather; sunshine. **3** *Informal* A liking or fancy. **4** *Informal* A smart trick or prank. **5** A gloss or polish, as on shoes. [< OE *scīnan*]

**shin·gle** (shing′gəl) *n.* **1** A thin, tapering piece of wood or other material, used in courses to cover roofs. **2** A small signboard bearing the name of a doctor, lawyer, etc., and placed outside his office. **3** A short haircut. —*v.t.* **·gled, ·gling 1** To cover (a roof, building, etc.) with shingles. **2** To cut (the hair) short. [< L *scandula* a shingle] —**shin′gler** *n.*

**ship** (ship) *n.* **1** Any large vessel suitable for deep-water navigation. **2** The crew and officers of such a vessel. **3** An aircraft or spacecraft. —*v.* **shipped, ship·ping** *v.t.* **1** To transport by ship. **2** To send by any means of transportation, as by rail, truck, or air. 3 To hire and receive for service on board a vessel, as sailors. 4 To draw (oars) inside a boat. *Naut.* To receive over the side: to *ship* a wave. —*v.i.* 2 To go on board ship; embark. 7 To enlist as a seaman. [< OE *scip*]

**shirk** (shûrk) *v.t.* 1 To avoid doing (something that should be done). —*v.i.* 2 To avoid work or evade obligation. —*n.* One who shirks: also **shirk′er.** [?]

**shirt** (shûrt) *n.* 1 A garment for the upper part of the body, usu. having a collar and cuffs and buttoning along the front. 2 UNDERSHIRT. **—lose one's shirt** *Slang* To lose everything. [< OE *scyrte* shirt, short garment]

**shiv·er** (shiv′ər) *v.t.* & *v.i.* To break suddenly into fragments; shatter. —*n.* A splinter; silver. [ME *schivere*]

**shoal** (shōl) *n.* A thing or school, as of fish. —*v.i.* To gather in shoals. [< OE *scolu* shoal of fish.]

**shoat** (shōt) *n.* A young hog. [ME *shote*]

**shock**[1] (shok) *n.* 1 A violent collision or concussion; impact; blow. 2 The result of such a collision. 3 A sudden, severe effect on the mind or emotions; jolt: the *shock* of recognition. 4 Something causing such an effect. 5 An acute impairment of vital functions associated with failure of the circulatory system following grave trauma such as burns, poisoning, brain injury, massive bleeding, etc. 6 Involuntary muscular contraction caused by the passage of an electric current through the body. —*v.t.* 1 To disturb the emotions or mind of; horrify; disgust. 2 To subject to an electric shock. 3 To shake by sudden collision; jar. [< OF *choc*] **—shock′er** *n.* **—Syn.** *v.* 1 appall, take aback, surprise, astound.

**shock**[2] (shok) *n.* A number of sheaves of grain, stalks of corn, or the like, stacked for drying upright in a field. —*v.t.* & *v.i.* To gather (grain) into a shock or shocks. [ME *schokke*] **—shock′er** *n.*

**shod·dy** (shod′ē) *n.* *pl.* **·dies** 1 Reclaimed wool obtained by shredding waste materials. 2 Fiber or cloth manufactured of inferior material. 3 Vulgar display; sham. 4 Refuse; waste. —*adj.* **·di·er, ·di·est** 1 Poorly made; inferior. 2 Made of or containing shoddy. 3 Cheaply pretentious; vulgar. 4 Nasty; mean: a *shoddy* remark. [?] **—shod′di·ly** *adv.* **—shod′di·ness** *n.* **—Syn.** *adj.* 1 tawdry, cheap, sloppy, second-rate.

**shoe** (shōō) *n.* 1 An outer covering, usu. of leather, for the human foot. 2 Something resembling a shoe in position or use. 3 A rim or plate of iron to protect the hoof of an animal. 4 The tread or outer covering of a pneumatic tire. 5 A braking device that stops or retards the motion of an object. —*v.t.* **shod** or **shoed, shoe·ing** To furnish with shoes or the like. [< OE *scōh*] **—sho′er** *n.*

**shoe·mak·er** (shōō′mā′kər) *n.* One who makes or repairs shoes. **—shoe′mak′ing** *n.*

**shoot** (shōōt) *v.* **shot, shoot·ing** *v.t.* 1 To hit, wound, or kill with a missile discharged from a weapon. 2 To discharge (a missile or weapon): to *shoot* an arrow or a gun. 3 To send forth, as questions, glances, etc. 4 To pass over or through swiftly: to *shoot* rapids. 5 To photograph or film. 6 To thrust out; dart; flick: with *out:* He *shot* out an arm in gesture. 7 To push into or out of the fastening, as the bolt of a door. 8 To propel, discharge, or dump, as down a chute or from a container. 9 *Slang* To inject (a drug, esp. a narcotic). 10 In games: a To score (a goal, point, total score, etc.). b To play (golf, craps, pool, etc.). c To propel (a basketball, puck, marble, etc.) to attempt a score. d To cast (dice). —*v.i.* 11 To discharge a missile from a firearm, bow, etc. 12 To go off; discharge. 13 To move swiftly; dart. 14 To extend or project. 15 To put forth buds, leaves, etc. 16 To record photographically. 17 In games, to make a play by propelling the ball, puck, etc., in a certain manner. **—shoot at** (or **for**) *Informal* To strive for; seek to attain. **—shoot the works** *Informal* To risk everything. —*n.* 1 A young branch or growth; offshoot. 2 The process of early growth. 3 A narrow passage in a stream; a rapid. 4 An inclined passage down which anything may be shot. 5 The act of shooting; a shot. 6 A shooting match, hunting party, etc. [< OE *scēotan*] **—shoot′er** *n.*

**shop** (shop) *n.* 1 A place where goods and services are sold at retail: also **shoppe.** 2 A place for the carrying on of any skilled work: a machine *shop.* **—talk shop** To discuss one's work. —*v.i.* **shopped, shop·ping** To visit shops or stores to purchase or look at goods. [< OE *sceoppa* booth] **—shop′per** *n.* • *Shoppe* is an archaic spelling but is still used in the names of some establishments to suggest a quaint, old-fashioned character. However, the spelling *shop* has been in use since at least 1600, so it is hardly a novelty.

**shore** (shôr, shōr) *n.* 1 The land adjacent to an ocean, sea, lake, or large river. 2 Land, as distinguished from a body of water. [ME]

**short** (shôrt) *adj.* 1 Having relatively little linear extension; not long. 2 Being below the average stature; not tall. 3 Having relatively little extension in time; brief. 4 Of no great distance: a *short* trip. 5 Less than the usual or standard duration, quantity, extent, etc.: on *short* notice; a *short* letter. 6 Having few items: a *short* list. 7 Not reaching or attaining a goal or requirement: an effort *short* of the mark. 8 Not retentive: a *short* memory. 9 Abrupt in manner; curt. 10 Having an inadequate supply: *short* of cash. 11 Quickly aroused or agitated: a *short* temper. 12 *Phonet.* a Of relatively brief duration. b Describing any vowel sound that contrasts with a long vowel, as the vowel sound in *mat* contrasted with that in *mate*. 13 In finance: a Not having in one's possession when selling, as stocks or commodities. b Describing a sale of stocks or commodities that the seller does not possess but anticipates procuring subsequently at a lower price for delivery as contracted. 14 In English prosody, unaccented. 15 Flaky or crisp: pastry made *short* with lard. —**for short** For brevity and ease of expression: The University of Connecticut is called Uconn *for short.* —**in short** In summary; briefly. —**in short order** Without delay; forthwith; promptly. —*n.* 1 Something short, as a garment, vowel, syllable, etc. 2 *pl.* Short trousers extending to the knee or above the knee. 3 *pl.* A man's undergarment resembling short trousers. 4 SHORT CIRCUIT. 5 SHORT SUBJECT. —*adv.* 1 Abruptly: to stop *short.* 2 In a curt manner. 3 So as to be short of a goal or mark. 4 By means of a short sale. —*v.t. & v.i.* 1 To give (someone) less than the amount due. 2 SHORT-CIRCUIT. [< OE *sceort*] —**short′ness** *n.*

**short·age** (shôr′tij) *n.* An inadequate supply; deficiency.

**short·com·ing** (shôrt′kum′ing) *n.* A defect; imperfection.

**short·en** (shôr′tən) *v.t.* 1 To make short or shorter; reduce; lessen. 2 To make flaky or crisp, as pastry. —*v.i.* 3 To become short or shorter. —**short′en·er** *n.*

**short·hand** (shôrt′hand′) *n.* 1 Any of various systems of recording speech by writing symbols, abbreviations, etc.; stenography. 2 Any method of quick communication. —

*adj.* 1 Written in shorthand. 2 Using shorthand.

**short·stop** (shôrt′stop′) *n.* In baseball, an infielder stationed between second and third bases.

**shot** (shot) *n.* 1 The act of shooting, as a firearm. 2 Something likened to a shot, as a cutting remark. 3 *pl.* **shot** a Any of the lead pellets that comprise ammunition for a shotgun; also, the pellets collectively. b A solid missile, as a ball of iron, fired from a cannon or other gun. 4 A solid metal ball thrown for distance in sports competitions. 5 The range of a projectile. 6 One who shoots; a marksman. 7 A single effort, attempt, or opportunity to do a specific thing: to have a *shot* at getting the job. 8 In certain sports and games, the act or manner of shooting the ball, puck, etc., as in attempting a score. 9 A conjecture; guess. 10 A hypodermic injection, as of a drug, or the dose so administered. 11 An action or scene recorded on film. 12 The taking of a photograph; also, a photograph. 13 A blast, as in mining. —**like a shot** Very quickly. —*adj.* 1 Having a changeable or variegated appearance: purple fabric *shot* with gold. 2 *Informal* Utterly exhausted or ruined; washed-up. [< OE *scot*]

**shoul·der** (shōl′dər) *n.* 1 The part of the trunk between the neck and the arm or forelimb. 2 The joint connecting the arm or forelimb with the body. 3 *pl.* The area of the upper back including both shoulders. 4 The shoulders considered as a support for burdens or the seat of responsibility. 5 The part of a garment designed to cover the shoulder. 6 The forequarter of an animal. 7 Something resembling a shoulder in form, as the broadened part of a bottle below the neck. 8 Either edge of a road or highway. —**straight from the shoulder** *Informal* Candidly; straightforwardly. —*v.t.* 1 To assume as something to be borne: to *shoulder* the blame. 2 To bear upon the shoulders. 3 To push with or as with the shoulder. —*v.i.* 4 To push with the shoulder. —**shoulder arms** To rest a rifle against the shoulder, holding the butt with the hand on the same side. [< OE *sculder* shoulder]

**shout** (shout) *n.* A sudden and loud outcry. —*v.t.* 1 To utter with a shout; say loudly. —*v.i.* 2 To utter a shout; cry out loudly. [ME *shouten*] —**shout′er** *n.*

**shove** (shuv) *v.t. & v.i.* **shoved**, **shov·ing** 1 To push, as along a surface. 2 To press forcibly (against); jostle. **—shove off 1** To push along or away, as a boat. **2** *Informal* To depart. **—n.** The act of pushing or shoving. [< OE *scūfan*] **—shov′er** *n.*

**shov·el** (shuv′əl) *n.* A flattened scoop with a handle, as for digging, lifting earth, rock, etc. **—v.** **·eled** or **·elled, ·el·ing** or **·el·ling** *v.t.* **1** To take up and move or gather with a shovel. **2** To toss hastily or in large quantities as if with a shovel. **3** To clear or clean with a shovel, as a path. **—v.i. 4** To work with a shovel. [< OE *scofl*] **—shov′el·er, shov′el·ler, shov′el·ful** *n.*

**show** (shō) *v.* **showed, shown** or **showed, show·ing** *v.t.* **1** To cause or permit to be seen; present to view. **2** To cause or allow (something) to be understood or known; explain. **3** To make known by behavior or expression; reveal: to *show* emotion. **4** To cause (someone) to understand or see; explain something to. **5** To confer; bestow: to *show* favor. **6** To make evident by the use of logic; prove. **7** To guide; lead, as into a room: Please *show* them in. **8** To enter in a show or exhibition. **—v.i. 9** To become visible or known. **10** To appear; seem. **11** To make one's or its appearance. **12** To give a theatrical performance; appear. **13** In racing, to finish third or better. **—show off** To exhibit proudly; display ostentatiously. **— show up 1** To expose or be exposed, as faults. **2** To be evident or prominent. **3** To make an appearance. **4** *Informal* To be better than. **—n. 1** A presentation, as of a film, television program, or live entertainment, for viewing by spectators. **2** An exhibition, as of merchandise or art. **3** A competition at which certain animals, as dogs, are displayed and judged. **4** Someone or something regarded as a spectacle to be viewed, as in wonder or amusement. **5** An act of showing; display or manifestation: a *show* of strength. **6** Pretense or semblance; also, ostentation: mere *show*. **7** A sign of metal, oil, etc., in a mining or drilling operation. **8** In racing, a finish of third place or better. [< OE *scēawian*] **—show′er** *n.* **—Syn.** *v.* **1** exhibit, manifest, display. **4** convince, teach. *n.* **1** viewing, showing. **5** mark, sign, indication.

**show·er** (shou′ər) *n.* **1** A fall of rain, hail, or sleet, esp. of short duration. **2** A copious fall, as of tears, sparks, or other small objects. **3** A bath in which water is sprayed from an overhead nozzle: also **shower bath**. **4** A party for the giving of gifts, as to a bride.

**—v.t. 1** To sprinkle or wet with or as with showers. **2** To discharge in a shower; pour out. **3** To bestow upon in large numbers; overwhelm: to *shower* her with gifts. **—v.i. 4** To fall as in a shower. **5** To take a shower bath. [< OE *scūr*] **—show′er·y** *adj.*

**show·y** (shō′ē) *adj.* **show·i·er, show·i·est 1** Striking; splendid; brilliant. **2** Brilliant or conspicuous in a superficial or tasteless way; gaudy; meretricious. **—show′i·ly** *adv.* **—show′i·ness** *n.*

**shrap·nel** (shrap′nəl) *n. pl.* **·nel 1** A projectile for use against personnel, containing metal balls and a charge that expels them in mid-air. **2** Shell fragments. [< Henry *Shrapnel*, 1761–1842, British artillery officer]

**shred** (shred) *n.* **1** A long, irregular strip torn or cut off. **2** A fragment; particle. **—v.t. shred·ded** or **shred, shred·ding** To tear or cut into shreds. [< OE *scrēade* cutting] **—shred′der** *n.*

**shrew** (shrōō) *n.* **1** Any of numerous tiny mouselike mammals having a long pointed snout and soft fur. **2** A vexatious or nagging woman. [< OE *scrēawa*] **—shrew′ish** *adj.* **—shrew′ish·ly** *adv.* **—shrew′ish·ness** *n.*

**shrewd** (shrōōd) *adj.* **1** Having keen insight, esp. in practical matters; clever; able. **2** Artful; sly. [< ME *shrew* malicious person] **—shrewd′ly** *adv.* **—shrewd′ness** *n.*

**shriek** (shrēk) *n.* A sharp, shrill cry or scream. **—v.i. 1** To utter a shriek. **—v.t. 2** To utter with a shriek. [< ON *skrœkja*] **— shriek′er** *n.*

**shrill** (shril) *adj.* **1** High-pitched and piercing, as a sound. **2** Emitting a sharp, piercing sound. **3** Harsh and immoderate: *shrill* criticism. **—v.t. 1** To cause to utter a shrill sound. **—v.i. 2** To make a shrill sound. [ME *shrille*] **—shrill′ness** *n.* **—shrill′y** *adv.* **— Syn. 1** penetrating. **3** intemperate, hysterical, bitter.

**shrimp** (shrimp) *n. pl.* **shrimp** or **shrimps 1** any of numerous small, long-tailed crustaceans having ten legs and a fused head and thorax covered with a carapace, esp. various edible marine species. **2** *Informal* A small or insignificant person. [ME *shrimpe*]

**shrine** (shrīn) *n.* **1** A receptacle for sacred relics. **2** A sacred tomb or chapel. **3** A thing or spot made sacred by historic or other association. [< L *scrinium* case]

**shrink** (shringk) *v.* **shrank** or **shrunk, shrunk** or **shrunk·en, shrink·ing** *v.i.* **1** To draw together; contract as from heat, cold, etc. **2** To become less or smaller; diminish.

**3** To draw back, as from disgust or horror; recoil: with *from.* —*v.t.* **4** To cause to shrink, contract, or draw together. —*n.* **1** The act of shrinking. **2** *Slang* A psychiatrist or psychoanalyst. [< OE *scrincan*] —**shrink′a·ble** *adj.* —**shrink′er** *n.*

**shrink·age** (shringk′ij) *n.* **1** The act or process of shrinking; contraction. **2** The amount lost by contraction. **3** Decrease in value; depreciation.

**shriv·el** (shriv′əl) *v.t.* & *v.i.* **·eled** or **·elled,** **·el·ing** or **·el·ling** **1** To contract into wrinkles; shrink and wrinkle. **2** To make or become helpless or impotent; wither. [?]

**shroud** (shroud) *n.* **1** A cloth used to wrap a corpse for burial. **2** Something that envelops or conceals. **3** *Naut.* One of a set of ropes or wires stretched from a masthead to the sides of a ship, serving to strengthen the mast laterally. —*v.t.* **1** To clothe in a shroud. **2** To envelop or conceal; block from view. [< OE *scrūd* a garment]

**shrub** (shrub) *n.* A woody perennial of low stature, usu. with several stems. [< OE *scrybb* brushwood] —**shrub′bi·ness** *n.* —**shrub′by** *adj.* (**·bi·er, ·bi·est**)

**shrub·ber·y** (shrub′ər·ē) *n. pl.* **·ber·ies** A group of shrubs, as in a garden.

**shrug** (shrug) *v.t.* & *v.i.* **shrugged, shrug·ging** To draw up (the shoulders), as in displeasure, doubt, surprise, etc. —*n.* The act of shrugging the shoulders. [?]

**shrunk** (shrungk) *p.t.* & *p.p.* of SHRINK.

**shud·der** (shud′ər) *v.i.* To tremble or shake, as from fright or cold. —*n.* A convulsive shiver, as from horror or fear. [ME *shudren*] —**Syn.** *v.* shiver, quake. *n.* tremor.

**shuf·fle** (shuf′əl) *v.* **·fled, ·fling** *v.t.* **1** To shift about so as to mix up or confuse; disorder. **2** To change the order of by mixing, as cards in a pack. **3** To move (the feet) along with a dragging gait. **4** To change or move from one place to another. —*v.i.* **5** To scrape the feet along. **6** To change position; shift ground. **7** To resort to indirect or deceitful methods; prevaricate. **8** To shuffle cards. —*n.* **1** A dragging of the feet. **2** The act of shuffling, as cards. **3** A deceitful or evasive course; artifice. [< LG *schuffeln*] —**shuf′fler** *n.*

**shun** (shun) *v.t.* **shunned, shun·ning** To keep clear of; avoid. [< OE *scunian*] —**shun′ner** *n.*

**shunt** (shunt) *v.t.* **1** To turn aside. **2** In railroading, to switch, as a train or car, from one track to another. **3** *Electr.* **a** To connect

a shunt in parallel with. **b** To be connected as a shunt for or of. **4** To put off on someone else, as a task. —*v.i.* **5** To move to one side. **6** *Electr.* To be diverted by a shunt: said of current. **7** To move back and forth; shuttle. —*n.* **1** The act of shunting. **2** A railroad switch. **3** *Electr.* A conductor joining two points in a circuit and diverting part of the current. —**shunt′er** *n.*

**shut** (shut) *v.* **shut, shut·ting** *v.t.* **1** To bring into such position as to close an opening. **2** To close (an opening) so as to prevent passage or movement in or out. **3** To close and fasten securely, as with a lock. **4** To keep from entering or leaving: with *out* or *in.* **5** To close, fold, or bring together, as extended parts: to *shut* an umbrella. —*v.i.* **6** To be or become closed or in a closed position. —**shut down 1** To cease from operating, as a factory. **2** To lower; come down close: The fog *shut down.* —**shut off 1** To cause to stop operating: to *shut off* a light. **2** To separate: usu. with *from: shut off* from all companionship. —**shut out** In sports, to keep (an opponent) from scoring during the course of a game. —**shut up 1** *Informal* To stop talking or cause to stop talking. **2** To close all the entrances to, as a house. **3** To imprison; confine. —*adj.* **1** Made fast or closed. **2** *Regional* Freed, as from something disagreeable; rid: with *of.* [< OE *scyttan*]

**shut·ter** (shut′ər) *n.* **1** A hinged screen or cover, as for a window. **2** *Phot.* A mechanism for momentarily admitting light through a camera lens to a film or plate. **3** One who or that which shuts. —*v.t.* To furnish, close, or divide off with shutters.

**shut·tle** (shut′l) *n.* **1** A device used in weaving to carry the weft to and fro between the warp threads. **2** A similar device in a sewing machine. **3** A system of transportation for moving goods or passengers in both directions between two nearby points; also, the vehicle, as a bus, train, or airplane, operating between these points, usu. frequently. —*v.t.* & *v.i.* **·tled, ·tling** To move back and forth frequently or like a shuttle. [< OE *scytel* missile]

**shy** (shī) *adj.* **shy·er, shy·est,** or **shi·er, shi·est** **1** Easily frightened or startled; timid. **2** Uneasy in the company of others; bashful; reserved. **3** Circumspect; watchful; wary. **4** Expressing or suggesting diffidence or reserve: a *shy* look. **5** *Informal* Having less than is called for or expected; short. —*v.t.*

**shied, shy·ing** 1 To start suddenly to one side, as a horse. 2 To draw back, as from doubt or caution: with *off* or *away*. —*n.* A starting aside, as in fear. [< OE *scēoh* timid] —**shy′ly** *adv.* —**shy′ness** *n.*

**sick** (sik) *adj.* 1 Affected with disease; ill; ailing. 2 Of or used by sick persons. 3 Affected by nausea; nauseated. 4 Sickly; weak: a *sick* laugh. 5 Mentally or emotionally upset or ill: *sick* with grief. 6 Disposed to find offensive or wearisome from being surfeited: with *of*: *sick* of hearing transistor radios in public places. [< OE *sēoc*] —**sick′ish** *adj.* —**sick′ish·ly** *adv.* —**sick′ish·ness** *n.*

**sick·le** (sik′əl) *n.* A cutting or reaping implement with a long, curved blade mounted on a short handle. —*v.t.* ·**led,** ·**ling** To cut with a sickle, as grass, hay, etc. [< OE *sicel*]

**side** (sīd) *n.* 1 Any of the boundary lines of a surface or any of the surfaces of a solid: the *side* of a box. 2 A boundary line or surface, distinguished from the top and bottom or front and back. 3 Either of the surfaces of an object of negligible thickness, as a sheet of paper or a coin. 4 The right half or the left half of a human body, esp. of the torso, or of any animal. 5 The space beside someone. 6 A lateral part of a surface or object: the right *side* of a room. 7 The lateral half of a slaughtered animal: a *side* of beef. 8 One of two or more contrasted surfaces, parts, or places: the far *side* of a river. 9 A slope, as of a mountain. 10 An opinion, aspect, or point of view: the conservative *side* of the issue. 11 A group of competitors or partisans of a point of view. 12 Family connection, esp. by descent through one parent: my father's *side.* —**on the side** In addition to the main part or chief activity. —**side by side** 1 Alongside one another. 2 In a spirit of cooperation; together. —**take sides** To give one's support to one of two sides engaged in a dispute. —*adj.* 1 Situated at or on one side. 2 Being from one side: a *side* glance. 3 Incidental: a *side* issue. 4 Being in addition to the main dish: a *side* order. —*v.t.* To provide with a side or sides. —**side with** To range oneself on the side of; support, esp. in a dispute. [< OE]

**sid·ing** (sī′ding) *n.* 1 A railway track by the side of the main track. 2 A material used to cover the side of a frame building, as paneling or shingles.

**siege** (sēj) *n.* 1 The surrounding of a town or fortified place in an effort to seize it, as after a blockade. 2 A steady attempt to win something. 3 A trying time: a *siege* of illness. —*v.t.* **sieged, sieg·ing** BESIEGE. [< L *sedere* sit]

**sieve** (siv) *n.* A utensil or apparatus for sifting, consisting of a frame provided with a bottom of mesh wire. —*v.t.* & *v.i.* **sieved, siev·ing** To sift. [< OE *sife* sieve]

**sift** (sift) *v.t.* 1 To pass through a sieve in order to separate the fine parts from the coarse. 2 To scatter by or as by a sieve. 3 To examine carefully. 4 To separate as if with a sieve; distinguish: to *sift* fact from fiction. —*v.i.* 5 To use a sieve. 6 To fall or pass through or as through a sieve: The light *sifts* through the trees. [< OE *siftan* sift] —**sift′er** *n.*

**sigh** (sī) *v.i.* 1 To draw in and exhale a deep, audible breath, as in expressing sorrow, weariness, pain, or relief. 2 To make a sound suggestive of a sigh, as the wind. 3 To yearn; long: with *for*. —*v.t.* 4 To express with a sigh. —*n.* 1 The act of sighing. 2 A sound of sighing or one suggestive of sighing. [ME *sighen*] —**sigh′er** *n.*

**sight** (sīt) *n.* 1 The act or faculty of seeing; vision. 2 Something seen; an image perceived by the eye; spectacle: an inspiring *sight;* an ugly *sight.* 3 A view; glimpse: to catch *sight* of someone. 4 The range or scope of vision. 5 *Informal* Something remarkable or strange in appearance. 6 *Usu. pl.* A place or thing of particular interest, as to a tourist: seeing the *sights.* 7 A point of view; estimation. 8 Mental perception or awareness: Don't lose *sight* of the facts. 9 A device to assist aiming, as a gun or a leveling instrument. 10 An aim or observation taken with a telescope or other sighting instrument. —**at** (or **on**) **sight** 1 As soon as seen. 2 On presentation for payment. —**out of sight** 1 Beyond range of sight. 2 *Informal* Beyond expectation; too great or too much. 3 *Slang* Extraordinarily good. —*v.t.* 1 To catch sight of; discern with the eyes: to *sight* shore. 2 To look at through a sight, as a telescope; observe. 3 To adjust the sights of, as a gun. 4 To take aim with. —*v.i.* 5 To take aim. 6 To make an observation or sight. —*adj.* 1 Understood or performed on sight without previous familiarity or preparation: *sight* reading of music. 2 Payable when presented: a *sight* draft. [< OE *gesiht*]

**sign** (sīn) *n.* 1 Anything that directs the mind or attention toward something: a *sign* of aging; a *sign* of intelligence. 2 A telltale mark or indication; trace: the first *sign* of spring. 3 A motion or action used to communicate a thought, desire, or command. 4 A symbol; token: black armbands as a *sign* of grief. 5 A conventional written or printed symbol representing a word or relation: $ is a dollar *sign*; = is an equal *sign*. 6 Information, directions, advertising, etc., publicly displayed. 7 A structure on which such information is printed or posted. 8 An occurrence taken to be miraculous and proof of divine commission. 9 One of the twelve equal divisions of the zodiac. —*v.t.* 1 To write one's signature on, esp. in acknowledging or attesting to the validity of a document. 2 To write (one's name). 3 To indicate or represent by a sign. 4 To mark or consecrate with a sign, esp. with a cross. 5 To engage by obtaining the signature of to a contract. 6 To hire (oneself) out for work: often with *on*. —*v.i* 7 To write one's signature. 8 To make signs or signals. — **sign off** To announce the end of a program from a broadcasting station and stop transmission. —**sign up** To enlist, as in a branch of military service. [< L *signum*] —**sign′er** *n*. —Syn. *n*. 2 vestige, evidence, spoor.

**sig·nal** (sig′nəl) *n*. 1 A sign or event agreed upon or understood as a call to action. 2 Any device, sound, gesture, etc., used to convey information or give direction or warning. 3 An event that incites to action or movement: His yawn was our *signal* to leave. 4 *Telecom*. A flow of energy that varies so as to transmit information. —*adj*. 1 Out of the ordinary; notable; distinguished. 2 Used to signal. —*v*. ·**naled** or ·**nalled**, ·**nal·ing** or ·**nal·ling** *v.t.* 1 To inform or notify by signals. 2 To communicate by signals. —*v.i.* 3 To make a signal or signals. [< L *signum* sign] —**sig′nal·er** or **sig′nal·ler** *n*.

**sig·na·ture** (sig′nə·chər) *n*. 1 The name of a person written by himself. 2 The act of signing one's name. 3 Any identifying mark or sign, as a musical theme to signal the beginning and end of a television show. 4 *Printing* a A distinguishing mark or number on the first page of each sheet of pages to be gathered as a guide to the binder. b A printed sheet that when folded and trimmed constitutes a section of a book, as 32 pages. 5 *Music* A symbol or group of symbols at the beginning of a staff, indicating time or key. [< L *signum* sign]

**sig·nif·i·cance** (sig·nif′ə·kəns) *n*. 1 Importance; consequence. 2 That which is signi-

fied or intended to be expressed; meaning. 3 The state or character of being significant. Also **sig·nif′i·can·cy.**

**sig·nif·i·cant** (sig·nif′ə·kənt) *adj*. 1 Having or expressing a meaning; esp., rich in meaning: *significant* details. 2 Important; momentous. —**sig·nif′i·cant·ly** *adv*. —Syn. 1 meaningful, suggestive. 2 weighty, consequential.

**sig·ni·fy** (sig′nə·fi) *v*. ·**fied**, ·**fy·ing** *v.t.* 1 To represent; mean; suggest. 2 To make known by signs or words; express. —*v.i.* 3 To have some meaning or importance; matter. [< L *signum* sign + -FY] —**sig′ni·fi′er** *n*.

**sign·post** (sin′pōst′) *n*. A post bearing a sign.

**si·lage** (sī′lij) *n*. Succulent fodder stored in a silo.

**si·lence** (sī′ləns) *n*. 1 Absence of sound; stillness. 2 Abstinence from speech or from making any sound. 3 Failure to mention; oblivion; secrecy. —*v.t.* ·**lenced**, ·**lenc·ing** 1 To make silent. 2 To stop the activity or expression of; put to rest. —*interj*. Be silent. [< L *silere* be silent]

**si·lent** (sī′lənt) *adj*. 1 Not making any sound or noise; noiseless. 2 Not speaking; mute. 3 Disinclined to talk; taciturn. 4 Present but not audible: *silent* tears. 5 Characterized by the absence of comment: His statement was *silent* on that point. 6 Free from activity, motion, or disturbance. 7 Written but not pronounced, as the *e* in *bake*. 8 Not accompanied by a sound track: a *silent* film. [< L *silere* be silent] —**si′lent·ly** *adv*. —**si′lent·ness** *n*.

**sil·hou·ette** (sil′ŏō·et′) *n*. 1 A profile drawing or portrait having its outline filled in with uniform color, usu. black. 2 The outline of a solid figure. —*v.t.* ·**et·ted**, ·**et·ting** To cause to appear in silhouette; outline. [< Étienne de *Silhouette*, 1709–1767, French minister]

**sil·i·ca** (sil′i·kə) *n*. The dioxide of silicon, occurring pure as quartz and as an important constituent of rocks, sand, and clay. [< L *silex, silicis* flint]

**silk** (silk) *n*. 1 A soft, shiny fiber produced by various insect larvae, as silkworms, to form their cocoons. 2 Cloth or thread made of this fiber. 3 Anything resembling silk, as the fine strands of an ear of corn. 4 *Usu. pl.* A garment of silk, as the uniform of a jockey. —*adj*. Consisting of or like silk; silken. [< OE *seoloc*]

**sill** (sil) *n*. 1 A horizontal member or beam forming the foundation, or part of the foundation, of a structure, as at the bottom of a casing in a building. 2 The horizontal part at the bottom of a door or window frame. [< OE *syll*]

**sil·ly** (sil′ē) *adj.* **·li·er, ·li·est** 1 Showing a lack of ordinary sense or judgment; foolish. 2 Trivial; frivolous. 3 *Informal* Stunned; dazed, as by a blow. —*n. pl.* **·lies** *Informal* A silly person. [< OE *gesǣlig* happy] — **sil′li·ly** or **sil′ly** *adv.* —**sil′li·ness** *n.*

**si·lo** (sī′lō) *n. pl.* **·los** 1 A pit or tower in which fodder is stored. 2 An underground structure for the housing and launching of guided missiles. —*v.t.* **·loed, ·lo·ing** To put or preserve in a silo. [< Gk. *siros* pit for corn]

**silt** (silt) *n.* 1 An earthy sediment consisting of extremely fine particles suspended in and carried by water. 2 A deposit of such sediment. —*v.t. & v.i.* To fill or become filled or choked with silt: usu. with *up*. [ME *sylte*] —**silt·ta·tion** (sil·tā′shən) *n.* —**silt′y** *adj.* (**·i·er, ·i·est**)

**sil·ver** (sil′vər) *n.* 1 A pale gray, lustrous, malleable metallic element (symbol Ag), having great electric and thermal conductivity and forming various photosensitive salts. 2 Silver regarded as a commodity or as a standard of currency. 3 Silver coin considered as money. 4 Articles, as tableware, made of or plated with silver; silverware. 5 A luster or color resembling that of silver. —*adj.* 1 Made of or coated with silver. 2 Resembling silver; having a silvery grey color. 3 Relating to, connected with, or producing silver. 4 Having a soft, clear, bell-like tone. 5 Designating a 25th wedding anniversary. 6 Favoring the use of silver as a monetary standard. —*v.t.* 1 To coat or plate with silver or something resembling silver. —*v.i.* 2 To become silver or white, as with age. [< OE *siolfor*] —**sil′ver·er** *n.* —**sil′ver·ly** *adv.*

**sil·ver·y** (sil′vər·ē) *adj.* 1 Containing silver. 2 Resembling silver, as in luster or hue. 3 Having a soft, clear, bell-like tone. —**sil′ver·i·ness** *n.*

**sim·i·lar** (sim′ə·lər) *adj.* 1 Bearing resemblance to one another or to something else. 2 Having like characteristics, nature, or degree. 3 *Geom.* Shaped alike, but differing in measure. [< L *similis* like] —**sim′i·lar·ly** *adv.*

**sim·i·lar·i·ty** (sim′ə·lar′ə·tē) *n. pl.* **·ties** 1 The quality or state of being similar. 2 A point in which compared objects are similar.

**sim·i·le** (sim′ə·lē) *n.* A figure of speech expressing comparison or likeness by the use of such terms as *like* or *as*. [< L *similis* similar] • See METAPHOR.

**si·mil·i·tude** (si·mil′ə·t′ōōd) *n.* 1 Similarity; correspondence. 2 One who or that which is similar; counterpart. 3 A point of similarity. [< L *similis* like]

**sim·mer** (sim′ər) *v.i.* 1 To boil gently; be or stay at or just below the boiling point. 2 To be on the point of breaking forth, as with rage. —*v.t.* 3 To cook in a liquid at or just below the boiling point. —*n.* The state of simmering. [?]

**sim·per** (sim′pər) *v.i.* 1 To smile in a silly, self-conscious manner; smirk. —*v.t.* 2 To say with a simper. —*n.* A silly, self-conscious smile. —**sim′per·er** *n.* —**sim′per·ing·ly** *adv.*

**sim·ple** (sim′pəl) *adj.* **·pler, ·plest** 1 Easy to comprehend or do: a *simple* problem or task. 2 Not complex or complicated. 3 Without embellishment; plain; unadorned: a *simple* dress. 4 Having nothing added; mere: the *simple* truth. 5 Not luxurious or elaborate: a *simple* meal. 6 Consisting of one thing; single. 7 Free from affectation; artless: a *simple* soul. 8 Weak in intellect; silly or foolish. 9 Of humble rank or condition; ordinary. 10 *Bot.* Not divided: a *simple* leaf. —*n.* 1 One who is foolish or ignorant; simpleton. 2 A medicinal plant. [< L *simplex*] —**sim′ple·ness** *n.* —**Syn.** 4 bare, sheer. 5 frugal, austere. 7 guileless, unsophisticated.

**sim·plic·i·ty** (sim·plis′ə·tē) *n. pl.* **·ties** 1 The state of being simple; freedom from complexity or difficulty. 2 Freedom from ornament or ostentation. 3 Freedom from affectation; artlessness; sincerity. 4 Foolishness; stupidity.

**sim·pli·fy** (sim′plə·fī) *v.t.* **·fied, ·fy·ing** To make more simple or less complex. —**sim′pli·fi·ca′tion, sim′pli·fi′er** *n.*

**sim·u·late** (sim′yə·lāt) *v.t.* **·lat·ed, ·lat·ing** 1 To make a pretense of; imitate, esp. to deceive. 2 To assume or have the appearance or form of, without the reality. [< L *similis* like] —**sim′u·la′tive** *adj.* —**sim′u·la′tor** *n.*

**sim·u·la·tion** (sim′yə·lā′shən) *n.* 1 The act of simulating. 2 Something given the form or function of another, as in order to test or determine capability; model.

**si·mul·ta·ne·ous** (sī′məl·tā′nē·əs, sim′əl-) *adj.* Occurring, done, or existing at the same time. [< L *simul* at the same time] —

si·mul·ta·ne·ous·ly *adv.* —si′mul·ta′ne·ous·ness, si′mul·ta·ne′i·ty (-tə-nē′ə-tē) *n.*

sin (sin) *n.* 1 A transgression against moral or religious law or divine authority, esp. when deliberate. 2 The state of having thus transgressed; wickedness. 3 Any action or condition regarded as morally wrong or deplorable. —*v.* sinned, sin·ning *v.i.* 1 To commit a sin. 2 To do wrong. [< OE *synn*]

sin·cere (sin·sir′) *adj.* ·cer·er, ·cer·est Free from hypocrisy, deceit, or calculation; honest; genuine: a *sincere* friend; *sincere* regrets. [< L *sincerus* uncorrupted] —sin·cere′ly *adv.* —sin·cere′ness *n.*

sin·cer·i·ty (sin·ser′ə·tē) *n.* The state or quality of being sincere; honesty of purpose or character; freedom from hypocrisy.

si·ne·cure (sī′nə·kyŏŏr, sin′ə-) *n.* A position or office providing compensation or other benefits but requiring little or no responsibility or effort. [< L *sine* without + *cura* care]

sin·ew (sin′yōō) *n.* 1 TENDON. 2 Strength or power. 3 *Often pl.* A source of strength. —*v.t.* To strengthen, as with sinews. [< OE *sinu, seonu*] —sinu, seonu] —sin′ew·less *adj.*

sing (sing) *v.* sang or *(now less commonly)* sung, sung, sing·ing *v.i.* 1 To produce musical sounds with the voice. 2 To perform vocal compositions professionally or in a specified manner. 3 To produce melodious sounds, as a bird. 4 To make a continuous, melodious sound suggestive of singing, as a teakettle, the wind, etc. 5 To buzz or hum; ring: My ears are *singing*. 6 To be suitable for singing. 7 To relate or celebrate something in song or verse. 8 To compose poetry. 9 *Slang* To confess the details of a crime, esp. so as to implicate others. 10 To be joyous; rejoice. —*v.t.* 11 To perform (music) vocally. 12 To chant; intone. 13 To bring to a specified condition or place by singing: *Sing* me to sleep. 14 To relate, proclaim, praise, etc., in or as in verse or song. —*n.* *Informal* A singing, esp. by a group. [< OE *singan*] —sing′a·ble *adj.*

singe (sinj) *v.t.* singed, singe·ing 1 To burn slightly. 2 To remove bristles or feathers from by passing through flame. 3 To burn the ends of (hair, etc.). —*n.* A slight or superficial burn; scorch. [< OE *sengan*] —sing′er *n.*

sin·gle (sing′gəl) *adj.* 1 Consisting of only one. 2 With no other or others; solitary; lone; alone. 3 Unmarried; also, pertaining to the unmarried state. 4 Of, pertaining to or involving only one person. 5 Consisting of only one part; simple. 6 Upright; sincere; honest. 7 Designed for use by only one person: a *single* bed. 8 *Bot.* Having only one row of petals, as a flower. —*n.* 1 One who or that which is single. 2 In baseball, a hit by which the batter reaches first base. 3 In cricket, a hit which scores one run. 4 *pl.* In tennis or similar games, a match with only one player on each side. —*v.* ·gled, ·gling *v.t.* 1 To choose or select (one) from others: usually with *out.* —*v.i.* 2 In baseball, to make a single. [< L *singulus*] —sin′gle·ness *n.* —sin′gly *adv.*

sing·song (sing′sông′, -song′) *n.* 1 Monotonous regularity of rhythm and rhyme in verse. 2 Verse characterized by such regularity. 3 A voice, speech tones, etc., characterized by a monotonous rise and fall of pitch. —*adj.* Having a monotonous rhythm or rise and fall of pitch.

sin·gu·lar (sing′gyə·lər) *adj.* 1 Being the only one of its type; unique; separate; individual. 2 Extraordinary; remarkable; uncommon: a *singular* honor. 3 Odd; not customary or usual. 4 *Gram.* Of, pertaining to, or being a word from which denotes one person or thing. —*n.* *Gram.* The singular number, or a word form having this number. —sin′gu·lar·ly *adv.* —sin′gu·lar·ness *n.* —**Syn.** 1 peculiar, distinctive. 3 strange, conspicuous.

sin·is·ter (sin′is·tər) *adj.* 1 Malevolent; evil: a *sinister* expression on the face. 2 Boding or attended with misfortune or disaster; inauspicious. 3 Of, pertaining to, or situated on the left side or hand. 4 *Her.* On the wearer's left, the spectator's right. [L, left, unlucky] —sin′is·ter·ly *adv.* —sin′is·ter·ness *n.*

sink (singk) *v.* sank or sunk, sunk (*Obs.* sunk·en), sink·ing *v.i.* 1 To go beneath the surface or to the bottom, as of water or snow. 2 To go down, esp. slowly or by degrees. 3 To seem to descend, as the sun. 4 To incline downward; slope gradually, as land. 5 To pass into a specified state: to *sink* into a coma. 6 To approach death: He's *sinking* fast. 7 To become less in force, volume, or degree: His voice *sank* to a whisper. 8 To become less in value, price, etc. 9 To decline in quality or condition; retrogress; degenerate: usu. with *into* or *to.* 10 To penetrate or be absorbed: The oil *sank* into the wood. 11 To be impressed or fixed, as in the heart or mind: I think that lesson will *sink* in. —*v.t.* 12 To cause to go beneath the surface or to the bottom: to *sink* a fence post. 13 To cause or allow to fall or drop; lower. 14 To cause to penetrate or be absorbed. 15 To make (a mine shaft, well, etc.) by digging or excavating. 16 To reduce in force, volume, or degree. 17 To debase or degrade. 18 To suppress or hide; restrain. 19 To defeat; ruin. 20 To invest. 21 To invest and subsequently lose. 22 To pay up; liquidate. 23 In certain sports, to cause (a ball or other object) to go through or into a receptacle or hole. —*n.* 1 A basinlike receptacle with a drainpipe and usu. a water supply. 2 A sewer or cesspool. 3 A place where corruption and vice gather or are rampant. 4 A hollow place or depression in a land surface, esp. one in which water collects or disappears by evaporation or percolation. 5 A body or mechanism by which matter or energy is absorbed or dissipated: a heat *sink*. [< OE *sincan*] —**sink′·a·ble** *adj.* —**Syn.** 2 descend, dwindle, diminish, lessen.

**sip** (sip) *v.* **sipped, sip·ping** *v.t.* 1 To imbibe in small quantities. 2 To drink from by sips. 3 To take in; absorb. —*v.i.* 4 To drink in sips. —*n.* 1 A very small amount sipped. 2 The act of sipping. [< OE *sypian* drink in] —**sip·per** *n.*

**si·phon** (sī′fən) *n.* 1 A bent tube for transferring liquids from a higher to a lower level over an intervening barrier. 2 SIPHON BOTTLE. 3 *Zool.* A tubular structure in certain aquatic animals, as the squid, for drawing in or expelling liquids. —*v.t.* 1 To draw off by or cause to pass through or as through a siphon. —*v.i.* 2 To pass through a siphon. [< Gk. *siphōn*] —**si′phon·al** *adj.*

**si·ren** (sī′rən) *n.* 1 *Often cap.* Gk. *Myth.* One of a group of sea nymphs who lured sailors to destruction by their sweet singing. 2 A seductive, enticing woman. 3 A device for producing a series of loud tones, as for a warning, often consisting of a perforated rotating disk or disks through which sharp puffs of steam or compressed air are permitted to escape. —*adj.* Of or pertaining to a siren; seductive; enticing. [< Gk. *seirēn*]

**sir·loin** (sûr′loin) *n.* A cut of meat, esp. of beef, from the upper portion of the loin. [< OF *sur-* above + *longe* loin]

**sir·up** (sir′əp) *n.* SYRUP.

**sis·ter** (sis′tər) *n.* 1 A female person having the same parents as another person. 2 A female of the lower animals having one parent in common with another. 3 a HALF SISTER. b SISTER-IN-LAW. c A foster sister. 4 A woman or girl allied to another or others by race, creed, a common interest, membership in a society, etc. 5 *Eccl.* A member of a sisterhood; nun. 6 *Chiefly Brit.* A head nurse in the ward or clinic of a hospital; also, any nurse. 7 A person or thing having similar characteristics to another. —*adj.* Bearing the relationship of a sister or one suggestive of sisterhood. [< OE *swostor*] —**sis′ter·ly** *adj.*

**sit** (sit) *v.* **sat, sit·ting** *v.i.* 1 To rest on the buttocks or haunches; be seated. 2 To perch or roost, as a bird. 3 To cover eggs so as to give warmth for hatching. 4 To pose, as for a portrait. 5 To be in session; hold a session. 6 To occupy a seat in a deliberative body. 7 To have or exercise judicial authority. 8 To fit or hang: That dress *sits* well. 9 To rest; lie: an obligation that *sat* heavily on her. 10 To be situated or located. 11 BABY-SIT. —*v.t.* 12 To have or keep a seat or a good seat upon: to *sit* a horse. 13 To seat (oneself): *Sit* yourself down. —**sit in** (on) 1 To join; participate: to *sit in on* a game of cards or a business deal. 2 To attend or take part in a discussion or music session. 3 To take part in a sit-in. —**sit on** (or **upon**) 1 To belong to (a jury, commission, etc.) as a member. 2 To hold discussions about or investigate. 3 *Informal* To suppress, squelch, or delay action on or consideration of. —**sit out** 1 To remain until the end of. 2 To sit during or take no part in: They *sat out* a dance. 3 To stay longer than. —**sit up** 1 To assume a sitting position. 2 To maintain an erect posture while seated. 3 To stay up later than usual at night. 4 To be startled or show interest. [< OE *sittan*]

**si·tar** (si·tär′) *n.* A stringed instrument used in Hindu music, somewhat resembling the lute, having a long neck, a resonating gourd or gourds, and a variable number of strings, some of which are plucked, others vibrating sympathetically. [< Hind. *sitār*]

**site** (sit) *n.* 1 A plot of ground used for or considered for some specific purpose. 2 The place, scene, or location of something: the battle *site*. [< L *situs* position]

**sit-in** (sit′in) *n.* 1 SIT-DOWN (def. 2). 2 An organized demonstration in which a protesting group occupies an area prohibited to them, as by taking seats in a restricted restaurant, etc. —**sit′in·ner** *n.*

**sit·u·a·tion** (sich′ōō·ā′shən) *n.* 1 The way in which something is situated, relative to its surroundings; position; location. 2 A locality; site. 3 Condition as modified or determined by circumstances. 4 A salaried post of employment. 5 A combination of circumstances at a specific time; state of affairs. 6 An unusual, difficult, critical, or otherwise significant state of affairs. —**sit′u·a′tion·al** *adj.*

**sixth** (siksth) *adj. & adv.* Next in order after the fifth. —*n.* 1 The element of an ordered set that corresponds to the number six. 2 One of six equal parts. 3 *Music* The interval between a tone and another five steps away in a diatonic scale.

**size** (sīz) *n.* 1 The dimensions of a thing as compared with some standard; physical magnitude or bulk. 2 Considerable amount, dimensions, etc. 3 One of a series of graded measures, as of hats, shoes, etc. 4 *Informal* State of affairs; true situation: That's the *size* of it. —*v.t.* **sized, siz·ing** 1 To arrange or classify according to size. 2 To cut or otherwise make (an article) to a required size. —**size up** *Informal* 1 To form an opinion of. 2 To meet specifications. [< OF *assise* ASSIZE]

**siz·zle** (siz′əl) *v.* **·zled, ·zling** *v.i.* 1 To emit a hissing sound under the action of heat. 2 To seethe with rage, resentment, etc. —*v.t.* 3 To cause to sizzle. —*n.* A hissing sound, as from frying. [Imit.]

**skate** (skāt) *n.* 1 A metal runner attached to a frame, with clamps or straps for fastening it to the sole of a boot or shoe, enabling the wearer to glide over ice. 2 A shoe or boot with such a runner permanently attached. 3 ROLLER SKATE. —*v.i.* **skat·ed, skat·ing** To glide or move over ice or some other smooth surface, on or as on skates. [< Du. *schaats*] —**skat′er** *n.*

**skein** (skān) *n.* 1 A fixed quantity of yarn, thread, silk, wool, etc., wound in a loose coil. 2 Something like this: a *skein* of hair. [< OF *escaigne*]

**skel·e·ton** (skel′ə·tən) *n.* 1 The supporting framework of a vertebrate, composed of bone and cartilage. 2 Any framework constituting the main supporting parts of a structure. 3 A mere sketch or outline of anything. 4 A very thin person or animal. —**skeleton in the closet** A secret source of shame or discredit. —*adj.* Of, pertaining to, or like a skeleton. [< Gk. *skeletos* dried up] —**skel·e·tal** *adj.*

**skep·tic** (skep′tik) *n.* 1 A person characterized by skepticism, esp. in regard to religion. 2 A person who advocates or believes in philosophical skepticism. *Chiefly Brit. sp,* **scep′tic.** [< Gk. *skeptikos* reflective]

**skep·ti·cal** (skep′ti·kəl) *adj.* Of, pertaining to, characteristic of, or marked by skepticism. *Chiefly Brit. sp.* **scep′ti·cal.** —**skep′ti·cal·ly** *adv.* —**skep′ti·cal·ness** *n.*

**sketch** (skech) *n.* 1 A rough or undetailed drawing or design, often done as a preliminary study. 2 A brief plan, description, or outline. 3 A short literary or musical composition. 4 A short scene, play, comical act, etc. —*v.t.* 1 To make a sketch or sketches of. —*v.i.* 2 To make a sketch or sketches. [< Gk. *schedios* impromptu] —**sketch′er** *n.*

**skew·er** (skyōō′ər) *n.* 1 A long pin of wood or metal, used for fastening meat while roasting. 2 Any of various articles of similar shape or use. —*v.t.* To run through or fasten with or as with a skewer. [?]

**ski** (skē, *Brit. also* shē) *n. pl.* **skis** 1 One of a pair of flat, narrow runners of wood, metal, or other material, worn clamped to boots for gliding over snow. 2 WATER SKI. —*v.* **skied, ski·ing** *v.i.* 1 To glide or travel on skis. —*v.t.* 2 To glide or travel over on skis. [Norw.< ON *skidh* snowshoe] —**ski′er** *n.*

**skid** (skid) *n.* 1 A log, plank, etc., often one of a pair, used to support or elevate something or as an incline on which heavy objects can be rolled or slid. 2 A low, movable platform that holds material to be moved, temporarily stored etc. 3 A shoe, drag, etc., used to prevent a wheel from turning. 4 A runner used in place of a wheel in the landing gear of an airplane or helicopter. 5 The act of skidding. —**on the skids** *Slang* Rapidly declining in prestige, power, etc. —*v.* **skid·ded, skid·ding** *v.i.* 1 To slide instead of rolling, as a wheel over a surface. 2 To slide due to loss of traction, as a vehicle. 3 *Aeron.* To slip sideways when turning. —*v.t.* 4 To put, drag, haul, or slide on skids. 5 To brake or hold back with a skid. [?] —**skid′der** *n.*

**skiff** (skif) *n.* 1 A light rowboat. 2 A small, light sailing vessel. [< OHG *scif* ship]

**skill** (skil) *n.* 1 Ability or proficiency in execution or performance. 2 A specific art, craft, trade, or job; also such an art, craft, etc., in which one has a learned competence. [< ON *skil* knowledge]

**skil·let** (skil′it) *n.* A frying pan. [ME *skelet*] • See APPLIANCE.

**skill·ful** (skil′fəl) *adj.* 1 Having skill. 2 Done with or requiring skill. Also **skil′ful.** —**skil′l′ful·ly** *adv.* —**skill′ful·ness** *n.*

**skim** (skim) *v.* **skimmed, skim·ming** *v.t.* 1 To remove floating matter from the surface of (a liquid): to *skim* milk. 2 To remove (floating matter) from the surface of a liquid: to *skim* cream from milk. 3 To cover with a thin film, as of ice. 4 To move lightly and quickly across or over. 5 To cause to bounce and ricochet swiftly and lightly, as a coin across a pond. 6 To read or glance over hastily or superficially. —*v.i.* 7 To move quickly and lightly across or near a surface; glide. 8 To make a hasty and superficial perusal; glance: with *over* or *through*. 9 To become covered with a thin film. —*n.* 1 The act of skimming. 2 That which is skimmed off. 3 A thin layer or coating. — *adj.* Skimmed: *skim* milk. [< OF *escume* scum, foam] —**skim′mer** *n.*

**skimp** (skimp) *v.i.* 1 To provide too little; scrimp. 2 To keep expenses at a minimum. —*v.t.* 3 To do poorly, hastily, or carelessly. 4 To be stingy in providing for. —*adj.* Scant; meager. [?] —**skimp′ing·ly** *adv.*

**skin** (skin) *n.* 1 The membranous outer covering of an animal body. 2 The pelt or hide of an animal. 3 A vessel for holding liquids, made of the skin of an animal. 4 Any outside layer, coat, or covering resembling skin, as fruit rind. —**by the skin of one's teeth** *Informal* Very closely or narrowly; barely. —**get under one's skin** 1 To provoke one. 2 To be a source of excitement, emotion, etc., to one. —**have a thick (thin) skin** To be very insensitive (or sensitive), as to insult, criticism, etc. —**save one's skin** *Informal* To avoid harm or death. —*v.* **skinned, skin·ning** *v.t.* 1 To remove the skin of; peel. 2 To cover with or as with skin. 3 To remove as if taking off skin: to *skin* a dollar from a roll of bills. 4 *Informal* To cheat or swindle. —*v.i.* 5 To become covered with skin. 6 To climb up or down; shin. [< ON *skinn*] —**skin·ner** *n.*

**skin diving** Underwater swimming in which the swimmer is equipped with a breathing apparatus, as a snorkel, goggles, and with various other equipment as foot fins, rubber garments, etc. —**skin diver**

**skin·flint** (skin′flint) *n.* One who tries to get or save money in any possible way. —**Syn.** miser, niggard, scrooge.

**skin·ny** (skin′ē) *adj.* **·ni·er, ·ni·est** 1 Consisting of or like skin. 2 Without sufficient

flesh; too thin. 3 Lacking the normal or desirable quality, quantity, size, etc. —**skin′ni·ly** *adv.* —**skin′ni·ness** *n.*

**skip** (skip) *v.* **skipped, skip·ping** *v.i.* 1 To move with springing steps, esp. by a series of light hops on alternate feet. 2 To be deflected from a surface; ricochet. 3 To pass from one point to another without noticing what lies between. 4 *Informal* To leave or depart hurriedly; flee. 5 To be advanced in school beyond the next grade in order. — *v.t.* 6 To leap lightly over. 7 To cause to ricochet. 8 To pass over or by without notice. 9 *Informal* To leave (a place) hurriedly. 10 To fail to attend a session or sessions of (church, school, etc.) 11 To cause to be advanced in school beyond the next grade in order. —*n.* 1 A light bound or spring, esp. any of a series of light hops on alternate feet. 2 A passing over without notice. [Prob. < Scand.]

**skir·mish** (skûr′mish) *n.* 1 A minor fight or encounter, usu. an incident in a larger conflict. 2 Any unimportant dispute, argument, etc. —*v.i.* To take part in a skirmish. [< OF *eskermir* to fence, fight] —**skir′mish·er** *n.*

**skirt** (skûrt) *n.* 1 That part of a dress, gown, etc., that hangs from the waist down. 2 A separate garment for women or girls that hangs from the waist down. • See PLEAT. 3 Anything that hangs or covers like a skirt: the *skirt* of a dressing table. 4 *Slang* A girl; woman. 5 The margin, border, or outer edge of anything. 6 *pl.* The border, fringe, or edge of a particular area; outskirts. —*v.t.* 1 To lie along or form the edge of; to border. 2 To surround or border: with *with.* 3 To pass around or about, usu. to avoid crossing: to *skirt* the town. —*v.i.* 4 To be on or pass along the edge or border. [< ON *skyrt* shirt]

**skit** (skit) *n.* 1 A short theatrical sketch, usu. humorous or satirical. 2 A short piece of writing, humorous or satirical in tone. [?]

**skit·tish** (skit′ish) *adj.* 1 Easily frightened, as a horse. 2 Very playful or lively. 3 Unreliable; fickle. [ME] —**skit′tish·ly** *adv.* — **skit′tish·ness** *n.*

**skulk** (skulk) *v.i.* 1 To move about furtively or slily; sneak. 2 *Chiefly Brit.* To shirk, evade work or responsibility. —*n.* One who skulks. [< Scand.] —**skulk′er** *n.*

**skull** (skul) *n.* 1 The bony framework of the head of a vertebrate animal; the cranium. 2 The head considered as the seat of intelligence; mind. [< Scand.]

**skunk** (skungk) *n.* 1 A small nocturnal carnivore of North America, usu. black with a white stripe down the back, and ejecting an offensive odor when attacked. 2 *Informal* A low, contemptible person. —*v.t. Slang* To defeat, as in a contest, esp. to defeat so thoroughly as to keep from scoring. [< Algon. *seganku*]

**sky** (skī) *n. pl.* **skies** 1 The blue vault that seems to bend over the earth; the firmament. 2 *Often pl.* The upper atmosphere, esp. in regard to its appearance: cloudy *skies.* 3 The celestial regions; heaven. 4 Climate; weather. —**out of a clear (or blue) sky** Without any warning. —**to the skies** Without reservations: to praise something *to the skies.* —*v.t.* skied or skyed, sky·ing *Informal* 1 To hit, throw, bat, etc., high into the air. 2 To hang, as a picture, etc. at an exhibition, above eye level. [< ON *skȳ* cloud]

**sky·rock·et** (skī′rok′it) *n.* A rocket that is shot high into the air. —*v.t. & v.i.* To rise or cause to rise or ascend steeply, like a skyrocket, as wages, prices, etc.

**sky·scrap·er** (skī′skrā′pər) *n.* A very high building.

**slab** (slab) *n.* 1 A fairly thick, flat piece or slice, as of metal, stone, meat, etc. 2 An outer piece cut from a log. —*v.t.* **slabbed, slab·bing** 1 To saw slabs from, as a log. 2 To form into a slab or slabs. [ME]

**slack**[1] (slak) *adj.* 1 Hanging loosely. 2 Careless; remiss; slovenly; slow. 3 Weak; loose: a *slack* mouth. 4 Lacking activity; not brisk or busy; slow or sluggish: a *slack* season. 5 Listless; limp: a *slack* grip. 6 Flowing sluggishly, as water. —*v.t.* 1 To make slack. 2 To slake, as lime. —*v.i.* 3 To be or become slack. 4 To become less active or less busy: usu. with *off.* —*n.* 1 The part of anything, as a rope, that is slack. 2 A period of inactivity. 3 A cessation of movement, as in a current. —*adv.* In a slack manner. [< OE *slæc*] —**slack′ly** *adv.* —**slack′ness** *n.*

**slack**[2] (slak) *n.* A mixture of coal dust, dirt, and small pieces of coal left after coal has been screened. [ME *sleck*]

**slack·en** (slak′ən) *v.t. & v.i.* To make or become slack.

**slag** (slag) *n.* 1 *Metall.* The fused residue separated in the reduction of ores. 2 Volcanic scoria. —*v.t. & v.i.* **slagged, slag·ging** To form into slag. [< MLG *slagge*] —**slag′gy** *adj.*

**slake** (slāk) *v.* **slaked, slak·ing** *v.i.* 1 To lessen the force of; quench: to *slake* thirst or flames. 2 To mix (an oxide, as lime, etc.)

with water; to hydrate. —*v.i.* 3 To become hydrated; said of lime. [< OE *slacian* retard]

**slam** (slam) *v.* **slammed, slam·ming** *v.t.* 1 To shut with violence and noise. 2 To put, dash, throw, etc., with violence. 3 *Slang* To strike with the fist. 4 *Informal* To criticize severely. —*v.i.* 5 To shut or move with force. —*n.* 1 A closing or striking with a bang; the act or noise of slamming. 2 *Informal* Severe criticism. [? < Scand.]

**slan·der** (slan′dər) *n.* 1 The uttering of false statements or misrepresentations which defame and injure the reputation of another. 2 Such a statement. —*v.t.* 1 To injure by uttering a false statement, etc.; defame. —*v.i.* 2 To utter slander. [< L *scandalum* scandal] —**slan′der·er** *n.* • Popularly, *slander* and *libel* are used synonomously to mean defamation. Legally, however, *slander* refers to oral defamation and *libel* to defamation by any other means, as writing, pictures, effigies, etc.

**slan·der·ous** (slan′dər-əs) *adj.* 1 Uttering slander. 2 Containing or constituting slander. —**slan′der·ous·ly** *adv.* —**slan′der·ous·ness** *n.*

**slang** (slang) *n.* 1 A type of popular language comprised of words and phrases of a vigorous, colorful, or facetious nature, which are invented or derived from the unconventional use of the standard vocabulary. 2 The special vocabulary of a certain class, group, profession, etc.; argot; jargon. [?] —**slang′i·ness** *n.* —**slang′y** *adj.*

**slant** (slant) *v.t.* 1 To give a sloping direction to. 2 To write or edit (news or other literary matter) so as to express a special attitude or appeal to a particular group, interest, etc. —*v.i.* 3 To have or take an oblique or sloping direction. —*adj.* Sloping —*n.* 1 A slanting direction, course, line, etc.; incline. 2 A point of view, esp. one that is personal or peculiar. [< Scand.] —**slant′ing** *adj.* —**slant′ing·ly** *adv.* —**slant′ing·ness** *n.*

**slap** (slap) *n.* 1 A blow delivered with the open hand or with something flat. 2 The sound made by such a blow, or a sound like it. 3 An insult or rebuff. —*v.* **slapped, slap·ping** *v.t.* 1 To strike with the open hand or with something flat. 2 To put, place, throw, etc., violently or carelessly. —*adv.* 1 Suddenly; abruptly. 2 Directly; straight: *slap* into his face. [< LG *slapp*] —**slap′per** *n.*

**slash** (slash) *v.t.* 1 To cut violently with or as with an edged instrument; gash. 2 To strike with a whip; lash; scourge. 3 To slit, as a garment, so as to expose ornamental material or lining in or under the slits. 4 To criticize severely. 5 To reduce sharply, as salaries. —*v.i.* 6 To make a long sweeping stroke with or as with something sharp; cut. —*n.* 1 The act of slashing. 2 The result of slashing; cut; slit; gash. 3 An ornamental slit cut in a garment. 4 An opening in a forest, covered with debris, as from cutting timber. 5 Such debris. [? < OF *esclashier* to break] —**slash'er** *n.*

**slat** (slat) *n.* Any thin, narrow strip of wood or metal; lath. —*v.t.* **slat·ted, slat·ting** To provide or make with slats. [< OF *esclat* splinter, chip]

**slaugh·ter** (slô'tər) *n.* 1 The act of killing, esp. the butchering of animals for market. 2 The wanton or savage killing of one or more human beings, esp. of a great number in battle. —*v.t.* 1 To kill for the market; butcher. 2 To kill wantonly or savagely, esp. in large numbers. [< ON *slátr* butcher's meat] —**slaugh'ter·er** *n.* —**slaugh'ter·ous** *adj.* —**slaugh'ter·ous·ly** *adv.*

**slave** (slāv) *n.* 1 A person who is owned by and completely subject to another; one bound by slavery. 2 A person who is totally subject to some habit, influence, etc. 3 One who labors like a slave; drudge. 4 A machine or device that is controlled by another machine or device. 5 SLAVE ANT. —*v.i.* **slaved, slav·ing** To work like a slave; toil; drudge. [< Med. L *sclavus* Slav]

**slay** (slā) *v.t.* **slew, slain, slay·ing** 1 To kill violently; slaughter. 2 *Informal* To amuse, impress, etc., in an overwhelming way. [< OE *slēan*] —**slay'er** *n.*

**slea·zy** (slē'zē, slā'-) *adj.* ·zi·er, ·zi·est 1 Lacking firmness of texture or substance. 2 Cheap in character or quality; shoddy, shabby, etc.: a *sleazy* novel; a *sleazy* dress. [?] —**slea'zi·ly** *adv.* —**slea'zi·ness** *n.*

**sleek** (slēk) *adj.* 1 Smooth and glossy. 2 Well-groomed or well-fed. 3 Smooth-spoken and polished in behavior, esp. in a specious way. —*v.t.* 1 To make smooth or glossy; polish. 2 To soothe; mollify. [Var. of SLICK] —**sleek'ly** *adv.* —**sleek'ness** *n.*

**sleep** (slēp) *n.* 1 A natural, recurrent physiological state characterized by cessation of voluntary movement and inattention to external stimuli. 2 A period of sleep. 3 Any condition of inactivity or rest. —**last sleep** Death. —*v.* **slept, sleep·ing** *v.i.* 1 To be or fall asleep; slumber. 2 To be in a state resembling sleep. —*v.t.* 3 To rest or repose in: to *sleep* the sleep of the dead. 4 To provide with sleeping quarters; lodge: The hotel can *sleep* a hundred guests. —**sleep away** To pass or spend in sleeping. —**sleep in** To sleep in the house where one works. —**sleep off** To get rid of by sleeping: He *slept off* a headache. —**sleep on** To postpone a decision upon. [< OE *slēp*]

**sleep·er** (slē'pər) *n.* 1 One who or that which sleeps. 2 A railroad sleeping car. 3 A heavy beam resting on or in the ground, as a support for a roadway, rails, etc. 4 *Informal* Someone or something thought to be unpromising that unexpectedly attains value, importance, notoriety, etc.

**sleet** (slēt) *n.* 1 A mixture of snow or hail and rain. 2 Partly frozen rain. 3 A thin coating of ice, as on rails, wires, roads, etc. —*v.i.* To pour or shed sleet. [ME *slete*] —**sleet'y** *adj.*

**sleeve** (slēv) *n.* 1 The part of a garment that serves as a covering for the arm. 2 *Mech.* A tube or tubelike part surrounding another part or into which another part fits. —**up one's sleeve** Hidden but at hand —*v.t.* **sleeved, sleev·ing** To furnish with a sleeve or sleeves. [< OE *slēfe*]

**sleigh** (slā) *n.* A light vehicle with runners, used esp. for transporting people on snow and ice. —*v.i.* To ride or travel in a sleigh. [< Du. *slee*, contraction of *slede* sledge¹] —**sleigh'er** *n.*

**sleight** (slīt) *n.* 1 Deftness; skill; dexterity. 2 Craft; cunning. [< ON *slœgdh* slyness]

**sleight of hand** 1 Skill in performing magical tricks or in juggling. 2 An instance of such skill in performing.

**slen·der** (slen'dər) *adj.* 1 Having a small width or circumference, in proportion to length or height; long and thin. 2 Having a slim figure; attractively slight. 3 Having slight force or foundation. 4 Small or inadequate. [ME *slendre*] —**slen'der·ly** *adv.* —**slen'der·ness** *n.*

**slice** (slīs) *n.* 1 A thin, broad piece cut off from a larger body. 2 A share or portion. 3 Any of various implements with a thin, broad blade, as a spatula. 4 a The course of a ball so hit that it curves in the direction of the dominant hand of the player who propels it. b The ball that follows such a course. —*v.* **sliced, slic·ing** *v.t.* 1 To cut or remove from a larger piece: often with *off, from,* etc. 2 To cut, separate, or divide into parts, shares, or thin, broad pieces. 3 To stir,

510

spread, etc. with a slice. 4 To hit (a ball) so as to produce a slice. —*v.i.* 5 To cut with or as with a knife. 6 To slice a ball, as in golf. [< OHG *slizan* to slit] —slic′er *n.*

slick (slik) *adj.* 1 Smooth, slippery, or sleek. 2 *Informal* Deceptively clever; tricky; smooth. 3 Clever; deft; adept. 4 *Informal* Technically skillful but shallow and insignificant: a *slick* novel. 5 *Slang* Very good, attractive, enjoyable, etc. —*n.* 1 A smooth place on a surface of water, as from oil. 2 A film of oil on the surface of water. 3 *Informal* A magazine printed on glossy paper. —*adv. Slang* In a slick or smooth manner; deftly, cleverly, smoothly, etc. —*v.t.* 1 To make smooth, trim, or glossy. 2 *Informal* To make smart or presentable: often with *up.* [< OE *slīcian* make smooth]

slide (slīd) *v.* slid, slid or slid·den, slid·ing *v.i.* 1 To pass along a surface with a smooth movement. 2 To move smoothly over snow or ice. 3 To move or pass stealthily or imperceptibly. 4 To proceed in a natural way; drift: to let the matter *slide.* 5 To pass or fall gradually (into a specified condition). 6 To slip from a position: The cup *slid* off the saucer. 7 To slip or fall by losing one's equilibrium or foothold. 8 In baseball, to throw oneself along the ground toward a base. —*v.t.* 9 To cause to slide, as over a surface. 10 To move, put, enter, etc., with quietness or dexterity: with *in* or *into.* —*n.* 1 An act of sliding. 2 An inclined plane, channel, etc., on which persons, goods, logs, etc., slide downward to a lower level. 3 A small plate of glass on which a specimen is mounted and examined through a microscope. 4 A small plate of transparent material bearing a single image for projection on a screen. 5 A part or mechanism that slides, as the U-shaped portion of the tubing which is pushed in and out to vary the pitch of a trombone. 6 The slipping of a mass of earth, snow, etc., from a higher to a lower level. 7 The mass that slips down. [< OE *slīdan*] —slid′er *n.*

slide rule A device consisting of a rigid ruler with a central sliding piece, both graduated, used in calculation.

slight (slīt) *adj.* 1 Of small importance or degree: a *slight* illness. 2 Slender in build: a *slight* figure. 3 Frail; fragile: a *slight* structure. —*v.t.* 1 To omit due courtesy toward or respect for: to *slight* a friend. 2 To do carelessly or thoughtlessly; shirk. 3 To treat as trivial or insignificant. —*n.* An act of dis-

courtesy or disrespect. [< ON *slēttr* smooth] —slight′er, slight′ness *n.* —slight′ly *adv.*

slim (slim) *adj.* slim′mer, slim′mest 1 Small in thickness in proportion to height or length. 2 Slight; meager: a *slim* chance of survival. —*v.t.* & *v.i.* slimmed, slim·ming To make or become thin or thinner. [< Du. *slim* bad] —slim′ly *adv.* —slim′ness *n.*

slim·y (slī′mē) *adj.* slim·i·er, slim·i·est 1 Covered with slime. 2 Containing slime. 3 Filthy; foul. —slim′i·ly *adv.* —slim′i·ness *n.*

sling (sling) *n.* 1 A strap or pocket with a string attached to each end, for hurling a stone. 2 One of various devices for holding up an injured arm. 3 A device, as a band or chain, for lifting or moving heavy objects. 4 The act of slinging; a sudden throw. 5 A drink made of sugar, liquor, and water: a gin *sling.* —*v.t.* slung, sling·ing 1 To fling; hurl. 2 To move or hoist, as by a rope or tackle. 3 To suspend loosely in a sling. [? < ON *slyngva* hurl] —sling′er *n.*

slink (slingk) *v.* slunk or slinked, slink·ing *v.i.* To move or go furtively or stealthily. [< OE *slincan*] —slink′ing·ly *adv.* —Syn. creep, steal, sneak, skulk.

slip (slip) *v.* slipped, slip·ping *v.t.* 1 To cause to glide or slide. 2 To put on or off easily, as a loose garment. 3 To convey slyly or secretly. 4 To free oneself or itself from. 5 To unleash, as hounds. 6 To release from its fastening and let run out, as a cable. 7 To dislocate, as a bone. 8 To escape or pass unobserved: It *slipped* my mind. —*v.i.* 9 To slide so as to lose one's footing. 10 To fall into an error. 11 To escape. 12 To move smoothly and easily. 13 To go or come stealthily: often with *off, away,* or *from.* 14 To overlook: to let an opportunity *slip.* —let slip To say without intending to. —slip one over on *Informal* To take advantage of by trickery. —slip up *Informal* To make a mistake. —*n.* 1 A sudden slide. 2 A slight mistake. 3 A narrow space between two wharves. 4 A pier. 5 An inclined plane leading down to the water, on which vessels are repaired or constructed. 6 A woman's undergarment approximately the length of a dress. 7 A pillowcase. 8 A leash containing a device which permits quick release of the dog. 9 Undesired relative motion, as between a wheel and the road; also, the amount of this. —give (someone) the slip To elude (someone). [< MLG *slippen*]

**slip·cov·er** (slĭp′kŭv′ər) *n.* A fitted cloth cover for a piece of furniture, that can be readily removed.

**slip·knot** (slĭp′nŏt′) *n.* 1 A knot so made that it will slip along the rope or cord around which it is formed. 2 A knot easily untied by pulling. **Also slip knot.**

**slip·per** (slĭp′ər) *n.* A low, light shoe into or out of which the foot is easily slipped. —**slip′pered** *adj.*

**slip·per·y** (slĭp′ər·ē) *adj.* ·per·i·er, ·per·i·est 1 Having a surface so smooth that bodies slip or slide easily on it. 2 That evades one's grasp; elusive. 3 Unreliable; tricky. —**slip′per·i·ness** *n.*

**slip·shod** (slĭp′shŏd′) *adj.* 1 Wearing shoes or slippers down at the heels. 2 Slovenly; sloppy. 3 Performed carelessly: *slipshod work.*

**slit** (slĭt) *n.* A relatively straight cut or a long, narrow opening. —*v.t.* **slit, slit·ting** 1 To make a long incision in; slash. 2 To cut lengthwise into strips. 3 To sever. [ME *slitten*] —**slit′ter** *n.*

**sliv·er** (slĭv′ər) *n.* 1 A slender piece, as of wood, cut or torn off lengthwise; a splinter. 2 Corded textile fibers drawn into a fleecy strand. —*v.t. & v.i.* To cut or be split into long thin pieces. [< ME *sliven* to cleave] —**sliv′er·er** *n.*

**sloe** (slō) *n.* 1 A small, plumlike, astringent fruit. 2 The shrub that bears it; the blackthorn. [< OE *slā*]

**slo·gan** (slō′gən) *n.* 1 A catchword or motto adopted by a political party, advertiser, etc. 2 A battle or rallying cry. [< Scot. Gael. *sluagh* army + *gairm* yell]

**slop** (slŏp) *v.* **slopped, slop·ping** *v.i.* 1 To splash or spill. 2 To walk or move through slush. —*v.t.* 3 To cause (a liquid) to spill or splash. 4 To feed (a domestic animal) with slops. —**slop over** 1 To overflow and splash. 2 *Slang* To show too much zeal, emotion, etc. —*n.* 1 Slush or watery mud. 2 An unappetizing liquid or watery food. 3 *pl.* Refuse liquid. 4 *pl.* Waste food or swill. [< ME *sloppe* mud]

**slope** (slōp) *v.* **sloped, slop·ing** *v.i.* 1 To be inclined from the level; slant downward or upward. 2 To go obliquely. —*v.t.* 3 To cause to slope. —*n.* 1 Any slanting surface or line. 2 The degree of inclination of a line or surface from the plane of the horizon. [< OE *aslupan* slip away] —**slop′er, slop′ing·ness** *n.* —**slop′ing·ly** *adv.*

**slop·py** (slŏp′ē) *adj.* ·pi·er, ·pi·est 1 Slushy; splashy; wet. 2 Watery or pulpy. 3 Splashed with liquid or slops. 4 *Informal* Messy; slovenly; careless. 5 *Informal* Maudlin; overly sentimental. —**slop′pi·ly** *adv.* —**slop′pi·ness** *n.*

**slot** (slŏt) *n.* 1 A long narrow groove or opening; slit. 2 A narrow depression cut to receive some corresponding part in a mechanism. 3 *Informal* An opening or position, as in an organization, or a place in a sequence. —*v.t.* **slot·ted, slot·ting** To cut a slot or slots in. [< OF *esclot* the hollow between the breasts]

**sloth** (slōth, slŏth, slôth) *n.* 1 Disinclination to exertion; laziness. 2 Any of several slow-moving, arboreal mammals of South America. [< SLOW]

**sloth·ful** (slōth′fəl, slŏth′-, slôth′-) *adj.* Inclined to or characterized by sloth. —**sloth′ful·ly** *adv.* —**sloth′ful·ness** *n.* —**Syn.** lazy, indolent, sluggish, shiftless.

**slouch** (slouch) *v.i.* 1 To have a downcast or drooping gait, look, or posture. 2 To hang or droop carelessly. —*n.* 1 A drooping movement or appearance caused by depression or carelessness. 2 An awkward or incompetent person. [?] —**slouch′y** *adj.* (·i·er, ·i·est) —**slouch′i·ly** *adv.* —**slouch′i·ness** *n.*

**slough**[1] (slou; slōō *esp. for def.* 2) *n.* 1 A place of deep mud or mire. 2 A stagnant swamp, backwater, etc. 3 A state of great despair or degradation. [< OE *slōh*] —**slough′y** *adj.*

**slough**[2] (slŭf) *n.* 1 Dead tissue separated and thrown off from living tissue. 2 The skin of a serpent that has been or is about to be shed. —*v.t.* 1 To cast off; shed. 2 To discard; shed, as a habit or a growth. —*v.i.* 3 To be cast off. 4 To cast off a slough or tissue. [ME *slouh*] —**slough′y** *adj.*

**slov·en·ly** (slŭv′ən·lē) *adj.* ·li·er, ·li·est Untidy and careless in appearance, work, habits, etc. —*adv.* In a slovenly manner. —**slov′en·li·ness** *n.*

**slow** (slō) *adj.* 1 Taking a long time to move, perform, or occur. 2 Behind the standard time: said of a timepiece. 3 Not hasty: *slow to anger.* 4 Dull in comprehending: a *slow student.* 5 Uninteresting; tedious: a *slow drama.* 6 Denoting a condition of a racetrack that retards the horses' speed. 7 Heating or burning slowly; low: a *slow flame.* 8 Not brisk; slack: *Business is slow.* —*v.t. & v.i.* To make or become slow or slower: often with *up* or *down.* —*adv.* In a slow manner. [< OE *slāw*] —**slow′ly** *adv.* — **slow′ness** *n.*

**sludge** (sluj) *n.* 1 Soft, water-soaked mud. 2 A slush of snow or broken or half-formed ice. 3 Muddy or pasty refuse, sediment, etc. [?] —**sludg′y** *adj.* (·i·er, ·i·est)

**slug** (slug) *n.* 1 A bullet. 2 *Printing* a A strip of type metal between words or letters. b A metal strip bearing a line of type in one piece. 3 Any small chunk of metal; esp., one used in place of a coin in automatic machines.

**slug·gard** (slug′ərd) *n.* A person habitually lazy. —*adj.* Lazy; sluggish. [< SLUG²] —**slu-g′gard·ly** *adv.*

**slug·gish** (slug′ish) *adj.* 1 Having little motion; inactive; torpid. 2 Habitually idle and lazy. —**slug′gish·ly** *adv.* —**slug′gish·ness** *n.*

**sluice** (slōōs) *n.* 1 Any artificial channel for conducting water. 2 A device for controlling the flow of water; a floodgate: also **sluice gate.** 3 The water held back by such a gate. 4 Something through which anything issues or flows. 5 A sloping trough in which gold is washed from sand. —*v.* **sluiced, sluic·ing** *v.t.* 1 To drench or cleanse by a flow of water. 2 To wash in or by a sluice. 3 To draw out or conduct by or through a sluice. 4 To send (logs) down a sluiceway. —*v.i.* 5 To flow out or issue from a sluice. [< L *excludere* shut out]

**slum** (slum) *n.* A squalid, dirty, overcrowded street or section of a city. —*v.i.* **slummed, slum·ming** To visit slums, as for reasons of curiosity. [?] —**slum′mer** *n.*

**slum·ber** (slum′bər) *v.i.* 1 To sleep lightly or quietly. 2 To be inactive; stagnate. —*v.t.* 3 To spend or pass in sleeping. —*n.* Quiet sleep. [< OE *slūma* sleep] —**slum′ber·er** *n.* —**slum′ber·ing·ly** *adv.*

**slump** (slump) *v.i.* 1 To fall or fail suddenly. 2 To stand, walk, or proceed with a stooping posture; slouch. —*n.* 1 The act of slumping. 2 A collapse or decline: a *slump* in the stock market. [Prob. < Scand.]

**slush** (slush) *n.* 1 Soft, sloppy material, as melting snow or soft mud. 2 Greasy material used for lubrication, etc. 3 Sentimental talk or writing. [ME *sloche*] —**slush′y** *adj.*

**slut** (slut) *n.* 1 A slatternly woman. 2 A sexually promiscuous woman; whore. 3 A female dog. [?] —**slut′tish** *adj.* - -**slut′tish·ly** *adv.* —**slut′tish·ness** *n.*

**sly** (slī) *adj.* **sli·er** or **sly·er, sli·est** or **sly·est** 1 Artfully dexterous in doing things secretly. 2 Playfully clever; roguish. 3 Meanly or stealthily clever; crafty. 4 Done with or marked by artful secrecy: a *sly* trick. —**on the sly** In a stealthy way. [< ON *slœgr*] —**sly′ly** *adv.* —**sly′ness** *n.*

**smack** (smak) *n.* 1 A quick, sharp sound, as of the lips when separated rapidly. 2 A noisy kiss. 3 A sounding blow or slap. —*v.t.* 1 To separate (the lips) rapidly. 2 To kiss noisily. 3 To slap. —*v.i.* 4 To make a smacking noise, as in tasting, kissing, striking, etc.; slap. —*adv.* Directly; exactly: also **smack′-dab′** (-dab′). [< MDu. *smack* a blow]

**small** (smôl) *adj.* 1 Not as large as other things of the same kind; little. 2 Being of slight degree, weight, or importance. 3 Ignoble; mean: a *small* nature. 4 Of humble background; poor. 5 Acting or transacting business in a limited way: a *small* shopkeeper. 6 Weak in characteristic properties: *small* beer. 7 Having little body or volume. 8 Not capital: said of letters. —**feel small** To feel humiliated or ashamed. —*adv.* 1 In a low or faint tone: to sing *small*. 2 Into small pieces. 3 In a small way; trivially. —*n.* 1 A small or slender part: the *small* of the back. 2 A small thing or quantity. [< OE *smœl*] —**small′ness** *n.*

**smart** (smärt) *v.i.* 1 To experience a stinging sensation. 2 To cause a stinging sensation. 3 To experience remorse, grief, hurt feelings, etc. —*v.t.* 4 To cause to smart. —*adj.* 1 Quick in thought; clever. 2 Impertinently witty. 3 Harsh; severe: a *smart* slap. 4 Brisk: to go at a *smart* pace. 5 Keen or sharp, as at trade; shrewd. 6 *Informal* or *Regional* Large; considerable: a *smart* crop of wheat. 7 Sprucely dressed. 8 Fashionable; chic. —*n.* 1 An acute stinging sensation, as from a scratch or an irritant. 2 Any mental or emotional suffering. [< OE *smeortan*] —**smart′ly** *adv.* —**smart′ness** *n.*

**smash** (smash) *v.t.* 1 To break in many pieces suddenly. 2 To flatten; crush. 3 To dash or fling violently so as to break in pieces. 4 To strike with a sudden blow. 5 To destroy; ruin. 6 In tennis, to strike (the ball) with a hard, swift, overhand stroke. —*v.i.* 7 To be ruined; fail. 8 To move or be moved with force; collide. —**go to smash** *Informal* To be ruined; fail. —*n.* 1 An instance or sound of smashing. 2 Any disaster or sudden collapse, esp. financial ruin. 3 In tennis, a strong overhand shot. 4 *Informal* An outstanding public success. —*adj.* Outstandingly successful: a *smash* hit. [?] —**smash´er** *n.*

**smat·ter·ing** (smat´ər·ing) *n.* 1 A superficial or fragmentary knowledge. 2 A little bit or a few.

**smear** (smir) *v.t.* 1 To rub or soil with grease, paint, dirt, etc. 2 To spread or apply in a thick layer or coating. 3 To harm the reputation of; slander. 4 *Slang* To defeat utterly. —*v.i.* 5 To become smeared. —*n.* 1 A soiled spot; stain. 2 A specimen, as of blood, tissue cells, etc., spread on a slide for microscopic examination. 3 A slanderous attack. [< OE *smeoru* grease] —**smear´y** *adj.* —**smear´i·ness** *n.*

**smell** (smel) *v.* **smelled** or **smelt, smell·ing** *v.t.* 1 To perceive by means of the nose and its olfactory nerves. 2 To perceive the odor of. 3 To test by odor or smell. 4 To discover or detect, as if by smelling. —*v.i.* 5 To give off a particular odor: to *smell* of roses. 6 To have an unpleasant odor. 7 To give indications of: to *smell* of treason. 8 To use the sense of smell. —*n.* 1 The sense by means of which odors are perceived. 2 That which is smelled; odor. 3 An unpleasant odor. 4 A faint suggestion; hint. 5 An act of smelling. [ME *smellen*] —**smel´ler** *n.* —**smel´ly** *adj.* (**·i·er, ·i·est**) —**Syn.** *n.* 2 aroma, fragrance, scent. 3 reek, stench, stink.

**smelt** (smelt) *v.t. Metall.* 1 To reduce (ores) by fusion in a furnace. 2 To obtain (a metal) from the ore by a process including fusion. —*v.i.* 3 To melt or fuse, as a metal. [< MDu. *smelten* melt]

**smile** (smil) *n.* 1 A pleased or amused expression of the face, formed by curling the corners of the mouth upward. 2 A favorable appearance or aspect: the *smile* of fortune. —*v.* **smiled, smil·ing** *v.i.* 1 To exhibit a smile; appear cheerful. 2 To show approval or favor: often with *upon.* —*v.t.* 3 To express by means of a smile. [<ME *smilen.*] —**smil´er** *n.* —**smil´ing·ly** *adv.*

**smirk** (smûrk) *v.i.* To smile in a self-complacent, affected manner. —*n.* An affected or artificial smile. [<OE *smercian*] —**smirk´er** *n.* —**smirk´ing·ly** *adv.*

**smith** (smith) *n.* 1 One whose work is shaping metals, esp. a blacksmith. 2 A maker: used in combination: *gunsmith; wordsmith.* [<OE]

**smock** (smok) *n.* A loose outer garment worn to protect one's clothes. —*v.t.* To decorate (fabric) with smocking. [< OE *smoc*]

**smog** (smog) *n.* A noxious mist resulting from the action of sunlight on atmospheric pollutants. [<SM(OKE) + (F)OG]

**smoke** (smōk) *n.* 1 The vaporous products of the combustion of an organic compound, as coal, wood, etc., charged with fine particles of carbon or soot. 2 Any system of solid particles dispersed in a gas. 3 The act of or time taken in smoking tobacco. 4 *Informal* A cigarette, cigar, or *pipeful of tobacco.* —*v.* **smoked, smok·ing** *v.i.* 1 To emit or give out smoke. 2 To emit smoke excessively, as a stove or lamp. 3 To inhale and exhale the smoke of tobacco. —*v.t.* 4 To inhale and exhale the smoke of (tobacco, opium, etc.). 5 To use, as a pipe, for this purpose. 6 To treat, cure, or flavor with smoke. 7 To drive away or force out of hiding by or as if by the use of smoke: *smoke* bees; *smoke* out the enemy. 8 To change the color of (glass, etc.) by darkening with smoke. [<OE *smoca*]

**smoke·stack** (smōk´stak´) *n.* An upright pipe through which combustion gases from a furnace are discharged into the air.

**smok·y** (smō´kē) *adj.* **smok·i·er, smok·i·est** 1 Giving forth smoke, esp. excessively or unpleasantly. 2 Containing smoke: *smoky* air. 3 Like or suggestive of smoke: a *smoky* flavor. 4 Discolored by smoke. 5 Smoke-colored. —**smok´i·ly** *adv.* —**smok´i·ness** *n.*

**smol·der** (smōl´dər) *v.i.* 1 To burn showing little smoke and no flame. 2 To show suppressed feeling. 3 To exist in a latent state or inwardly. —*n.* A smoldering fire or thick smoke. *Brit. sp.* **smoul´der.** [ME *smolderen*]

**smooth** (smōōth) *adj.* 1 Having no surface irregularities; continuously even. 2 Free from obstructions, shocks, or jolts. 3 Without lumps; well blended. 4 Free from hair. 5 Flowing or moving evenly and without interruption. 6 Mild-mannered; calm. 7 Suave and flattering, usu. in a deceitful way: a *smooth* talker. 8 Pleasant-tasting; mild: a *smooth* wine. 9 *Phonet.* Having no aspiration. —*adv.* Calmly; evenly. —*v.t.* 1 To make smooth or even on the surface. 2 To free from obstructions. 3 To soften the worst features of: usu. with *over.* 4 To make calm; mollify. —*v.i.* 5 To become smooth. —*n.* 1 The smooth portion or surface of anything. 2 The act of smoothing. [<OE *smōth*] —**smooth´er, smooth´ness** *n.* —**smooth´ly**

*adv.* —**Syn.** *adj.* 1 glossy, polished, sleek. 6 collected, placid, unruffled. *v.* 3 extenuate, palliate. 4 soothe.

**smoth·er** (smuth'ər) *v.t.* 1 To prevent (someone) from breathing. 2 To kill by such means; suffocate. 3 To cover, or cause to smolder, as a fire. 4 To hide or suppress: to *smother* a scandal. 5 To cook in a covered pan or under a blanket of some other substance. —*v.i.* 6 To be covered without vent or air, as a fire. 7 To be hidden or suppressed, as wrath. —*n.* That which smothers, as stifling vapor or dust. [< OE *smorian*] —**smoth'er·er** *n.* —**smoth'er·y** *adj.*

**smudge** (smuj) *v.* **smudged, smudg·ing** *v.t.* 1 To smear; soil. —*v.i.* 2 To be or become smudged. —*n.* 1 A smear; stain. 2 A smoky fire or smoke for driving away insects, preventing frost, etc. [? var. of SMUTCH] —**smudg'i·ly** *adv.* —**smudg'i·ness** *n.* —**smudg'y** *adj.* (·i·er, ·i·est)

**smug** (smug) *adj.* **smug·ger, smug·gest** 1 Self-satisfied or extremely complacent. 2 Trim; neat; spruce. [?<LG *smuk* neat] —**smug'ly** *adv.* —**smug'ness** *n.*

**smug·gle** (smug'əl) *v.* **·gled, ·gling** *v.t.* 1 To take (merchandise) into or out of a country illegally. 2 To bring in or introduce illicitly or secretly. —*v.i.* 3 To engage in or practice smuggling. [<LG *smuggeln*] —**smug'gler** *n.*

**smut** (smut) *n.* 1 The blackening made by soot, smoke, etc. 2 Obscene writing, speech, or illustration. 3 Any of various fungus diseases of plants, characterized by patches of powdery black spores. 4 The parasitic fungus causing such a disease. —*v.t.* & *v.i.* **smut·ted, smut·ting** To make or become smutty. [<LG *schmutt* dirt]

**smut·ty** (smut'ē) *adj.* **·ti·er, ·ti·est** 1 Soiled with smut; stained. 2 Affected by smut: *smutty* corn. 3 Obscene; indecent. —**smut'ti·ly** *adv.* —**smut'ti·ness** *n.* —**Syn.** 1 blackened, dirty. 3 coarse, earthy, suggestive.

**snag** (snag) *n.* 1 A jagged or sharp protuberance, esp. the stumpy base of a branch left in pruning. 2 A snaggletooth. 3 The trunk of a tree fixed in a river, bayou, etc., which presents a danger to navigation. 4 Any hidden obstacle or difficulty. —*v.t.* **snagged, snag·ging** To injure, destroy, or impede by or as by a snag. [<Scand.] —**snag'gy** *adj.*

**snake** (snāk) *n.* 1 Any of a large variety of limbless reptiles having a scaly body, no eyelids, and a specialized swallowing apparatus. 2 A treacherous person. 3 A flexible wire used to clean clogged drains, etc. —*v.* **snaked, snak·ing** *v.t.* *Informal* 1 To drag or pull forcibly; haul, as a log. —*v.i.* 2 To wind or move like a snake. [<OE *snaca*]

**snap** (snap) *v.* **snapped, snap·ping** *v.i.* 1 To make a sharp, quick sound, as of twigs breaking. 2 To break suddenly with a crackling noise. 3 To close, fasten, etc., with a snapping sound. 4 To bite or snatch with a sudden, grasping motion: often with *up* or *at.* 5 To speak sharply: often with *at.* 6 To move or act with sudden, neat gestures: He *snapped* to attention. 7 To give way suddenly, as under mental pressure. —*v.t.* 8 To seize suddenly or eagerly; snatch: often with *up.* 9 To sever with a snapping sound. 10 To cause to make a sharp, quick sound. 11 To close, fasten, etc., with a snapping sound. 12 To take (a photograph). —**snap out of it** *Informal* 1 To recover quickly. 2 To change a mood, attitude, etc., quickly. —*n.* 1 The act of snapping or a sharp, quick sound produced by it. 2 A sudden breaking or release of anything or the sound so produced. 3 Any catch, fastener, etc., that closes or springs into place with a snapping sound. 4 A small, thin, crisp cake, esp. a gingersnap. 5 Brisk energy; zip. 6 A brief spell: said chiefly of cold weather. 7 Any easy task or duty. 8 A snapshot. —*adj.* 1 Made or done suddenly: a *snap* judgment. 2 Fastening with a snap. 3 *Informal* Easy. —*adv.* Briskly; quickly. [<MDu. *snappen* bite at]

**snap·shot** (snap'shot') *n.* A photograph taken with a small, simple camera.

**snare** (snâr) *n.* 1 A device, as a noose, for catching birds or other animals; a trap. 2 Anything that misleads, entangles, etc. —*v.t.* **snared, snar·ing** 1 To catch with a snare; entrap. 2 To capture by trickery; entice. [<ON *snara*] —**snar'er** *n.*

**snarl** (snärl) *n.* A sharp, angry growl. —*v.i.* 1 To growl harshly, as a dog. 2 To speak angrily and resentfully. —*v.t.* 3 To utter or express with a snarl. [<MLG *snarren* to growl] —**snarl'er** *n.* —**snarl'ing·ly** *adv.* —**snarl'y** *adj.*

**snatch** (snach) *v.t.* 1 To seize, take, grasp, etc., suddenly or eagerly. 2 To take or obtain as the opportunity arises: to *snatch* a few hours of sleep. —*v.i.* 3 To attempt to seize swiftly and suddenly: with *at.* —*n.* 1 A hasty grab or grasp: usu. with *at.* 2 A small amount; fragment: *snatches* of a conversation. [ME *snacchen*] —**snatch'er** *n.*

**sneak** (snēk) *v.i.* 1 To move or go in a stealthy manner. 2 To act slyly or with cowardice. — *v.t.* 3 To put, give, move, etc., secretly or stealthily. 4 *Informal* To pilfer. —**sneak out of** To avoid (work, etc.) by sly means. —*n.* 1 One who sneaks; a stealthy, despicable person. 2 *pl. Informal* Sneakers. 3 A stealthy movement. —*adj.* Stealthy; covert: a *sneak* attack. [?] —**sneak′i·ly, sneak′ing·ly** *adv.* —**sneak′i·ness** *n.* —**sneak′y** *adj.* (·i·er, ·i·est)

**sneer** (snir) *n.* 1 A grimace of contempt or scorn. 2 A mean or contemptuous sound, word, etc. —*v.i.* 1 To show contempt or scorn by a sneer. 2 To express contempt in speech, writing, etc. —*v.t.* 3 To utter with a sneer. [ME *sneren*] —**sneer′er** *n.* —**sneer′ing·ly** *adv.* —**Syn.** *v.* 2 gibe, jeer, scoff, taunt.

**sneeze** (snēz) *v.i.* **sneezed, sneez·ing** To drive air forcibly and audibly out of the mouth and nose by a spasmodic involuntary action. —**not to be sneezed at** *Informal* Entitled to consideration; not to be ignored. —*n.* An act of sneezing. [ME *fnesen*] —**sneez′er** *n.*

**snick·er** (snik′ər) *n.* A half-suppressed· or smothered laugh, usu. scornful. —*v.i.* 1 To utter a snicker. —*v.t.* 2 To utter or express with a snicker. [Imit.]

**snide** (snīd) *adj.* **snid·er, snid·est** Malicious; nasty. [?] —**snide′ly** *adv.* —**snide′ness** *n.*

**sniff** (snif) *v.i.* 1 To breathe through the nose in short, quick, audible inhalations. 2 To express contempt, etc., by sniffing: often with *at*. 3 To inhale a scent in sniffs. —*v.t.* 4 To inhale. 5 To smell or attempt to smell with sniffs. 6 To perceive as if by sniffs. —*n.* 1 An act or the sound of sniffing. 2 Something perceived by sniffing; an odor. [ME *sniffen*]

**snip** (snip) *v.* **snipped, snip·ping** *v.t.* 1 To clip, remove, or cut with a short, light stroke or strokes, as of shears: often with *off*. —*v.i.* 2 To cut with small, quick strokes. —*n.* 1 An act of snipping. 2 A small piece snipped off. 3 *Informal* A small or insignificant person. [<Du. *snippen*] —**snip′per** *n.*

**sniv·el** (sniv′əl) *v.i.* ·eled or ·elled, ·el·ing or ·el·ling To cry in a snuffling manner. —*n.* The act of sniveling. [<OE (assumed) *snyflan*] —**sniv′el·er** or **sniv′el·ler** *n.*

**snob** (snob) *n.* 1 One who regards wealth and elevated social position as of paramount importance and who typically seeks to improve his station by associating with the rich or powerful or popular and by avoiding or behaving with condescension to those with whom association is inexpedient. 2 One who affects to be superior, as in taste or learning: an intellectual *snob*. [?] —**snob′ber·y** (*pl.* ·ies), **snob′bish·ness** *n.* —**snob′bish** *adj.* —**snob′bish·ly** *adv.*

**snore** (snôr, snōr) *v.i.* **snored, snor·ing** To breathe with loud, snorting noises while asleep. —*n.* An act or sound of snoring. [Imit.] —**snor′er** *n.*

**snor·kel** (snôr′kəl) *n.* 1 A long ventilating tube capable of extending from a submerged submarine to the surface of the water. 2 A similar device used for underwater breathing. —*v.i.* To swim with a snorkel. [<G *Schnorchel*] —**snor′kel·er** *n.*

**snort** (snôrt) *v.i.* 1 To force the air violently and noisily through the nostrils, as a horse. 2 To express indignation, ridicule, etc., by a snort. —*v.t.* 3 To utter or express by snorting. —*n.* 1 The act or sound of snorting. 2 *Slang* A small drink of liquor. [ME *snorten*] —**snort′er** *n.*

**snout** (snout) *n.* 1 The projecting muzzle of a vertebrate. 2 Some similar anterior prolongation of the head, as that of a gastropod, skate, weevil, etc. 3 A person's nose, esp. a large one. [ME *snute*]

**snow** (snō) *n.* 1 Precipitation in the form of ice crystals formed from water vapor in the air when the temperature is below 32°F., usu. falling in irregular masses or flakes. 2 A fall of snow. 3 Flickering light or dark spots appearing on a television or radar screen. 4 *Slang* Cocaine. —*v.i.* 1 To fall as snow. —*v.t.* 2 To cause to fall as or like snow. 3 *Slang* To overpower with insincere or flattering talk. —**snow in** To close in or obstruct with snow. —**snow under** 1 To cover with snow. 2 *Informal* To overwhelm: *snowed under* with work. [<OE *snāw*]

**snow·ball** (snō′bôl′) *n.* 1 A small round mass of snow to be thrown. 2 A shrub related to honeysuckle, having globular clusters of sterile white flowers: also **snowball bush** or **tree**. —*v.i.* 1 To throw snowballs. 2 To gain in size, importance, etc. —*v.t.* 3 To throw snowballs at.

**snow·plow** (snō′plou′) *n.* Any large, plowlike device for removing snow from roads, railroad tracks, etc.

**snow·shoe** (snō′shōō′) *n.* A device, usu. a network of sinew in a wooden frame, to be fastened on the foot and used to prevent sinking in soft snow when walking. —*v.i.* ·**shoed,** ·**shoe·ing** To walk on snowshoes.

**snub** (snub) *v.t.* **snubbed, snub·bing** 1 To treat with contempt or disdain. 2 To stop or check, as the movement of a rope in running out. —*n.* 1 An act of snubbing; a deliberate slight. 2 A sudden checking, as of a running rope or cable. —*adj.* Short and slightly turned-up: said of the nose. [<ON *snubba*] —**snub′ber** *n.* —**Syn.** *v.* 1 cut, high-hat, ignore, rebuff, slight.

**snuff** (snuf) *v.t.* 1 To draw in (air, etc.) through the nose. 2 To smell; sniff. —*v.i.* 3 To snort; sniff. —*n.* An act of snuffing. [?<MDu. *snuffen*] —**snuf′fi·ness** *n.* —**snuf′fy** *adj.*

**snug** (snug) *adj.* **snug·ger, snug·gest** 1 Comfortable and cozy. 2 Well-built and compact; trim: said of a ship. 3 Fitting closely, as a garment. —*v.* **snugged, snug·ging** —*v.t.* 1 To make snug. —*v.i.* 2 SNUGGLE. — **snug down** To prepare (a vessel) for a storm, as by lashing down movables. [?] — **snug′ly** *adv.* —**snug′ness** *n.*

**snug·gle** (snug′əl) *v.t. & v.i.* ·**gled, ·gling** To nestle; cuddle; often with *up* or *together.* [Freq. of SNUG]

**soak** (sōk) *v.t.* 1 To place in liquid till thoroughly saturated; steep. 2 To wet thoroughly; drench. 3 *Informal* To drink, esp. to excess. 4 *Slang* To charge exorbitantly. — *v.i.* 5 To remain or be placed in liquid till saturated. 6 To penetrate; pass: with *in* or *into.* 7 *Slang* To drink to excess. —**soak up** 1 To take up; absorb. 2 *Informal* To take eagerly into the mind. —*n.* 1 The process or act of soaking, or state of being soaked. 2 Liquid in which something is soaked. 3 *Slang* A hard drinker. [<OE *socian*] — **soak′er** *n.* —**soak′ing·ly** *adv.*

**soap** (sōp) *n.* 1 *Chem.* A metallic salt of a fatty acid. 2 A cleansing agent consisting of a sodium or potassium salt of a fatty acid made by boiling a fat or oil with a lye. 3 *Slang* Money used for bribes. —**no soap** *Slang* It's not possible or acceptable. —*v.t.* To rub or treat with soap. [< OE *sāpe*] — **soap′i·ly** *adv.* —**soap′i·ness** *n.* —**soap′y** *adj.*

**soar** (sôr, sōr) *v.i.* 1 To float aloft through the air on wings, as a bird. 2 To sail or glide through the air. 3 To rise above any usual level: Prices *soared.* —*n.* 1 An act of soaring. 2 A range of upward flight. [<L *ex* out + *aura* breeze, air] —**soar′er** *n.* —**soar′ing·ly** *adv.*

**sob** (sob) *v.* **sobbed, sob·bing** *v.i.* 1 To weep with audible, convulsive catches of the breath. 2 To make a sound like a sob, as the wind. —*v.t.* 3 To utter with sobs. 4 To bring to a specified condition by sobbing: to *sob* oneself to sleep. —*n.* The act or sound of sobbing. [Imit.] —**sob′bing·ly** *adv.*

**so·ber** (sō′bər) *adj.* 1 Moderate in or abstaining from the use of alcoholic beverages. 2 Not drunk. 3 Temperate in action or thought; rational. 4 Not frivolous; straightforward. 5 Solemn; serious: a *sober* expression. 6 Of subdued or modest color. — *v.t.* 1 To make sober. —*v.i.* 2 To become sober, as after intoxication: with *up.* [<L *sobrius*] —**so′ber·ly** *adv.* —**so′ber·ness** *n.* — **Syn.** *n.* 1 abstemious. 3 calm, dispassionate, staid, steady.

**so·bri·e·ty** (sō·brī′ə·tē) *n. pl.* ·**ties** 1 The state or quality of being moderate, serious, or sedate. 2 Abstinence from alcoholic drink.

**soc·cer** (sok′ər) *n.* A form of football in which the ball is propelled toward the opponents' goal by kicking or by striking with the body or head, but never with the hands. [Alter. of *association (football),* original name]

**so·cial** (sō′shəl) *adj.* 1 Of or pertaining to society or its organization: *social* questions. 2 Friendly toward others; sociable. 3 Living in a society: *social* beings. 4 Of or pertaining to public welfare: *social* work. 5 Pertaining to or characteristic of fashionable, wealthy people: the *social* register. 6 Living in communities: *social* ants. 7 Grouping compactly, as individual plants. 8 Partly or wholly covering a large area of land: said of plant species. —*n.* An informal social gathering. [<L *socius* ally]

**so·cial·ism** (sō′shəl·iz′əm) *n.* 1 The theory of public collective ownership or control of the basic means of production, distribution, and exchange, with the avowed aim of operating for use rather than for profit. 2 A political system or party advocating or practicing this theory. —**so′cial·ist** *adj., n.* —**so′cial·is′tic** *adj.*

**social work** Any of various activities for improving community welfare, as services for health, rehabilitation, counseling, recreation, adoptions, etc. Also **social service.** —**social worker**

**so·ci·e·ty** (sə·sī′ə·tē) *n. pl.* ·**ties** 1 A group of people, usu. having geographical boundaries and sharing certain characteristics, as language, culture, etc. 2 The people making up such a group. 3 The fashionable, usu. wealthy portion of a community.

**4** A body of persons associated for a common purpose; an association, club, or fraternity. **5** Association based on friendship or intimacy: to enjoy the *society* of one's neighbors. [< L *socius* a friend]

**so·ci·ol·o·gy** (sō′sē·ol′ə·jē, sō′shē-) *n.* The science dealing with the origin, evolution, and development of human society and its organization, institutions, and functions. —**so′ci·o·log′i·cal** *adj.* —**so′ci·o·log′i·cal·ly** *adv.* —**so′ci·ol′o·gist** *n.*

**sock**[1] (sok) *n.* A short stocking reaching part way to the knee. [<L *soccus* slipper]

**sock**[2] (sok) *Slang v.t.* To strike or hit, esp. with the fist. —*n.* A hard blow. [?]

**sock·et** (sok′it) *n.* A cavity into which a corresponding part fits: an electric light *socket;* the eye *socket.* [<OF *soc* a plowshare]

**sod** (sod) *n.* **1** Grassy surface soil held together by the matted roots of grass and weeds. **2** A piece of such soil. —*v.t.* **sod·ded, sod·ding** To cover with sod. [< MDu. *sode* piece of turf]

**so·da** (sō′də) *n.* **1** Any of several sodium compounds in common use, as sodium bicarbonate, carbonate, hydroxide, etc. **2** SODA WATER **3** A soft drink containing soda water and flavoring and sometimes ice cream. [<Ital. *soda (cenere)* solid (ash)]

**soda water** An effervescent drink consisting of water charged under pressure with carbon dioxide, formerly generated from sodium bicarbonate.

**so·fa** (sō′fə) *n.* A long upholstered couch having a back and arms. [< Ar. *soffah* a part of a floor raised to form a seat]

**soft** (sôft, soft) *adj.* **1** Easily changed in shape by pressure. **2** Easily worked: *soft* wood. **3** Less hard than other things of the same kind: *soft* rock. **4** Smooth and delicate to the touch: *soft* skin. **5** Not loud or harsh: a *soft* voice. **6** Mild; gentle: a *soft* breeze. **7** Not glaring; subdued: *soft* colors. **8** Expressing mildness or sympathy: *soft* words. **9** Easily touched in feeling: a *soft* heart. **10** Out of condition: *soft* muscles. **11** *Informal* Weak-minded: *soft* in the head. **12** *Informal* Overly lenient: a judge *soft* on criminals. **13** Free from mineral salts that form insoluble compounds with soap: said of water. **14** Biodegradable: said of detergents. **15** Regarded as being nonaddicting and less harmful than hard narcotics: said of drugs, esp. marihuana. **16** *Phonet.* Describing *c* and *g* when articulated fricatively as in *cent*

and *gibe.* **17** *Informal* Easy: a *soft* job. —*n.* That which is soft; a soft part or material. —*adv.* **1** Softly. **2** Quietly; gently. —*interj. Archaic* Hush! Stop! [<OE *sōfte*] —**soft′ly** *adv.* —**soft′ness** *n.* —Syn. *adj.* **1** flexible, malleable, pliable. **5** low. **9** compassionate, kind, sympathetic.

**sog·gy** (sog′ē) *adj.* ·**gi·er,** ·**gi·est 1** Saturated with water or moisture; soaked. **2** Heavy and wet: said of pastry. [<dial. E *sog* a swamp, bog] —**sog′gi·ly** *adv.* —**sog′gi·ness** *n.*

**soil**[1] (soil) *n.* **1** Finely divided rock mixed with decayed vegetable or animal matter, constituting the portion of the surface of the earth in which plants grow. **2** Region, land, or country. [<L *solum* a seat, mistaken for *solum* the ground]

**soil**[2] (soil) *v.t.* **1** To make dirty; smudge. **2** To disgrace; defile. —*v.i.* **3** To become dirty. —*n.* A spot or stain. [<L *suculus,* dim. of *sus* a pig]

**so·journ** (sō′jûrn, sō·jûrn′) *v.i.* To stay or live temporarily. —*n.* (sō′jûrn) A temporary residence or short visit. [<OF *sojourner*] —**so′journ·er** *n.*

**sol·ace** (sol′is) *v.t.* ·**aced,** ·**ac·ing 1** To comfort in trouble or grief; console. **2** To alleviate, as grief; soothe. —*n.* **1** Comfort in grief, trouble, or calamity. **2** Anything that supplies such comfort. [<L *solacium*] —**sol′ac·er** *n.* —Syn. *v.* **2** assuage, ease, mitigate. *n.* **1** cheer, consolation.

**so·lar** (sō′lər) *adj.* **1** Of, from, reckoned by, or pertaining to the sun. **2** Using energy from the sun: *solar* heat. [<L *sol* sun]

**solar system** The sun and the bodies that orbit it. • See PLANET.

**sol·der** (sod′ər) *n.* **1** An easily melted alloy used for joining metal parts. **2** Anything that unites or cements. —*v.t.* **1** To unite or repair with solder. **2** To join together; bind. —*v.i.* **3** To work with solder. **4** To be united by or as by solder. [<L *solidus* firm, hard] —**sol′der·er** *n.*

**sol·dier** (sōl′jər) *n.* **1** A person serving in an army. **2** An enlisted man in an army, as distinguished from a commissioned officer. **3** A brave, skillful, or experienced warrior. **4** One who serves a cause loyally. —*v.i.* **1** To be or serve as a soldier. **2** To shirk: to *soldier* on the job. [<LL *solidus*] —**sol′dier·ly** *adj.* —**sol′dier·li·ness** *n.*

**sole**[1] (sōl) *n.* **1** The bottom surface of the foot. **2** The bottom surface of a shoe, boot, etc. **3** The lower part or bottom of anything. —*v.t.*

**soled, sol·ing** To furnish with a new sole, as a shoe. [< L *solea* a sandal]

**sole²** (sōl) *n.* Any of several marine flatfishes allied to the flounders, highly esteemed as food. [< L *solea* sole¹, fish]

**sole³** (sōl) *adj.* 1 Being the only one: a *sole* survivor. 2 Only: His *sole* desire was for sleep. 3 *Law* Unmarried; single. 4 Of or for only one person or group. 5 Acting or accomplished without another. [< L *solus* alone] —**sole′ness** *n.*

**sol·emn** (sol′əm) *adj.* 1 Characterized by majesty, mystery, or power; awe-inspiring. 2 Characterized by ceremonial observances; sacred. 3 Marked by gravity; earnest. [< L *solemnis*] —**sol′emn·ly** *adv.* —**sol′emn·ness** *n.* —**Syn.** 1 impressive. 3 grave, sedate, serious, somber.

**so·lem·ni·ty** (sə·lem′nə·tē) *n. pl.* **·ties** 1 The state or quality of being solemn. 2 A solemn rite or observance.

**sol·em·nize** (sol′əm·nīz) *v.t.* **·nized, ·niz·ing** 1 To perform according to legal or ritual forms: to *solemnize* a marriage. 2 To celebrate with formal ritual. 3 To make solemn, grave, or serious. —**sol′em·ni·za′tion, so·l′em·niz′er** *n.*

**so·lic·it** (sə·lis′it) *v.t.* 1 To ask for earnestly; beg or entreat. 2 To seek to obtain, as by persuasion. 3 To entice (one) to an unlawful or immoral act. —*v.i.* 4 To make a petition. [< L *sollicitare* agitate] —**so·lic′i·ta′tion** *n.*

**so·lic·i·tor** (sə·lis′ə·tər) *n.* 1 A person who solicits money for causes, subscriptions, etc. 2 The chief law officer of a city, town, etc. 3 In England, a lawyer who may appear as an advocate in the lower courts only. —**so·lic′i·tor·ship′** *n.*

**so·lic·i·tous** (sə·lis′ə·təs) *adj.* 1 Full of anxiety or concern. 2 Full of eagerness. —**so·lic′i·tous·ly** *adv.* —**so·lic′i·tous·ness** *n.*

**so·lic·i·tude** (sə·lis′ə·t′ōōd) *n.* 1 The state of being solicitous. 2 That which makes one solicitous.

**sol·id** (sol′id) *adj.* 1 Having a definite shape and volume; resistant to stress; not fluid. 2 Filling the whole of the space occupied by its form; not hollow. 3 Of the same substance throughout: *solid* marble. 4 Three-dimensional. 5 Well-built; firm: a *solid* building. 6 United or unanimous: a *solid* base of support. 7 Financially safe; sound. 8 Continuous; unbroken: a *solid* hour. 9 Written without a hyphen: said of a compound word. 10 Carrying weight or convic-

tion: a *solid* argument. 11 Serious; reliable: a *solid* citizen. 12 *Informal* Being on good terms: They were *solid* with the boss. 13 *Slang* Excellent. 14 *Printing* Having no leads or slugs between the lines; not open. —*n.* 1 A mass of matter that has a definite shape which resists change. 2 A three-dimensional figure or object. [< L *solidus*] —**so·l′id·ly** *adv.* —**so·lid′i·ty** (*pl.* **·ties**), **sol′id·ness** *n.*

**sol·i·dar·i·ty** (sol′ə·dar′ə·tē) *n. pl.* **·ties** Unity of purpose, relations, or interests, as of a race, class, etc.

**so·lid·i·fy** (sə·lid′ə·fī) *v.t. & v.i.* **·fied, ·fy·ing** 1 To make or become solid, hard, firm, or compact. 2 To bring or come together in unity. —**so·lid′i·fi·ca′tion** *n.*

**so·lil·o·quy** (sə·lil′ə·kwē) *n. pl.* **·quies** 1 A talking to oneself. 2 A speech made by an actor while alone on the stage, revealing his thoughts to the audience. [< L *solus* alone + *loqui* to talk]

**sol·i·taire** (sol′ə·târ′) *n.* 1 A diamond or other gem set alone. 2 Any of various card games played by one person. [< L *solitarius* solitary]

**sol·i·tar·y** (sol′ə·ter′ē) *adj.* 1 Living, being, or going alone. 2 Made, done, or passed alone: a *solitary* life. 3 Remote; secluded. 4 Lonesome; lonely. 5 Single; one; sole: Not a *solitary* soul was there —*n.* 1 *pl.* **·tar·ies** One who lives alone; a hermit. 2 *Informal* Solitary confinement in prison, usu. directed as a punishment. [< L *solus* alone] —**sol′i·tar′i·ly** *adv.* —**sol′i·tar′i·ness** *n.*

**sol·i·tude** (sol′ə·t′ōōd) *n.* 1 A being alone; seclusion. 2 Loneliness. 3 A deserted or lonely place. [< L *solus* alone] —**Syn.** 1 privacy, retirement. 2 isolation, lonesomeness.

**so·lo** (sō′lō) *n. pl.* **·los** or **·li** (-lē) 1 A musical composition or passage for a single voice or instrument, with or without accompaniment. 2 Any of several card games, esp. one in which a player plays alone against others. 3 Any performance accomplished alone or without assistance. —*adj.* 1 Performed or composed to be performed as a solo. 2 Done by a single person alone: a *solo* flight. —*v.i.* **·loed, ·lo·ing** To fly an airplane alone, esp. for the first time. [< L *solus* alone] —**so′lo·ist** *n.*

**sol·stice** (sol′stis) *n.* Either of the times of year when the sun is farthest from the celestial equator, either north or south. In the northern hemisphere the **summer sol-**

stice occurs about June 22, the **winter solstice** about December 22. [<L *solstitium*] — **sol·sti·tial** (sol·stish′əl) *adj.*

**sol·u·ble** (sol′yə-bəl) *adj.* 1 Capable of being dissolved. 2 Capable of being solved or explained. [<L *solvere* solve, dissolve] — **sol′u·bil′i·ty, sol′u·ble·ness** *n.* —**sol′u·bly** *adv.*

**so·lu·tion** (sə-lōō′shən) *n.* 1 A homogeneous mixture of varying proportions, formed by dissolving one or more substances, whether solid, liquid, or gaseous, in another substance, usu. liquid but sometimes gaseous or solid. 2 The act or process by which such a mixture is made. 3 The act or process of explaining, settling, or solving a difficulty, problem, or doubt. 4 The answer or explanation reached in such a process. [<L *solutus*, pp. of *solvere* dissolve]

**solve** (solv) *v.t.* **solved, solv·ing** To arrive at or work out the correct solution or the answer to; resolve. [<L *solvere* solve, loosen] — **solv′a·ble** *adj.* —**sol′va·bil′i·ty, sol′ver** *n.*

**sol·vent** (sol′vənt) *adj.* 1 Having means sufficient to pay all debts. 2 Capable of dissolving. —*n.* 1 That which solves. 2 A substance, usu. a liquid, capable of dissolving other substances. [<L *solvere* solve, loosen] —**sol′ven·cy** *n.*

**som·ber** (som′bər) *adj.* 1 Dark; gloomy. 2 Somewhat melancholy; sad. *Brit. sp.* **som′bre.** [<F *sombre*] —**som′ber·ly** *adv.* —**som′ber·ness** *n.* — 1 cloudy, dusky, murky.

**som·er·sault** (sum′ər-sôlt) *n.* An acrobatic roll in which a person turns heels over head. —*v.i.* To perform a somersault. [<OF *sobresault*]

**som·nam·bu·lism** (som-nam′byə-liz′əm) *n.* The act or state of walking during sleep. —**som·nam′bu·lant** (-lənt), **som·nam′bu·lis′tic** *adj.* —**som·nam′bu·list** *n.*

**so·nant** (sō′nənt) *Phonet. adj.* Voiced. —*n.* 1 A voiced speech sound. 2 A syllabic sound. [<L *sonare* resound]

**so·nar** (sō′när) *n.* A system or device for using underwater sound waves for sounding, range finding, detection of submerged objects, communication, etc. [<*so(und) na(vigation and) r(anging)*]

**so·na·ta** (sə-nä′tä) *n. Music* An instrumental composition written in three or four movements. [<Ital. *sonare* to sound]

**song** (sông, song) *n.* 1 The act of singing. 2 Any melodious utterance, as of a bird. 3 A short musical composition for voice. 4 A short poem; a lyric or ballad. 5 Poetry; verse. —**for a song** At a very low price. —**song and dance** *Slang* A long, usu. repetitive statement or explanation, often untrue or not pertinent to the subject under discussion. [<OE]

**song·ster** (sông′stər, song′-) *n.* 1 A person or bird given to singing. 2 A writer of songs. —**song′stress** (-stris) *n. Fem.*

**sonic barrier** *Aeron.* The effects, such as drag and turbulence, that hinder flight at or near the speed of sound.

**so·no·rous** (sə-nôr′əs, -nō′rəs, son′ə-rəs) *adj.* 1 Productive or capable of producing sound vibrations. 2 Loud and full-sounding; resonant. 3 High-sounding: *sonorous* verse. [<L *sonare* resound] —**so·nor·i·ty** (sə-nôr′ə-tē, -nor-, son′ôr′ə-tē), **so·nor′ous·ness** *n.* —**so·no′rous·ly** *adv.*

**soot** (sŏŏt, sōōt) *n.* A black deposit of finely divided carbon from the incomplete combustion of wood, coal, etc. —*v.t.* To soil or cover with soot. [<OE *sōt*] —**soot′i·ness** *n.* — **soot′y** *adj.* (·i·er, ·i·est)

**soothe** (sōōth) *v.* **soothed, sooth·ing** *v.t.* 1 To restore to a quiet or normal state; calm. 2 To mitigate, soften, or relieve, as pain or grief. —*v.i.* 3 To afford relief. [<OE *sōthian* verify] —**sooth′er** *n.* —**sooth′ing·ly** *adv.* — **Syn.** 1 compose, pacify, tranquilize. 2 allay, alleviate, ease.

**sooth·say·er** (sōōth′sā′ər) *n.* A person who claims to be able to foretell events. —**sooth′say′ing** *n.*

**sop.** soprano.

**soph·ist** (sof′ist) *n.* 1 A learned person; thinker. 2 One who argues cleverly and deviously. 3 *Often cap.* A member of a certain school of early Greek philosophy, preceding the Socratic school. 4 *Often cap.* One of the later Greek teachers of philosophy and rhetoric, skilled in subtle disputation. [<Gk. *sophos* wise] —**so·phis′tic** or **·ti·cal** *adj.* — **so·phis′ti·cal·ly** *adv.* —**so·phis′ti·cal·ness** *n.*

**so·phis·ti·cat·ed** (sə-fis′tə-kā′tid) *adj.* 1 Worldly-wise. 2 Of a kind that appeals to the worldly-wise. 3 Very complicated in design, function, etc.: a *sophisticated* machine.

**soph·o·more** (sof′ə-môr, -mōr) *n.* A second-year student in an American high school or college. —*adj.* Of or pertaining to second-year students or studies. [Earlier *sophomer* a dialectician < *sophom*, var. of SOPHISM]

**so·pran·o** (sə-pran′ō, -prä′nō) *n. pl.* **so·pran·os** or **so·pra·ni** (sə-prä′nē) 1 A part or singing voice of the highest range. 2 The music for such a voice. 3 A person having such a voice or singing such a part. —*adj.* Of or pertaining to a soprano voice or part. [<Ital. *sopra* above]

**sor·cer·er** (sôr′sər·ər) *n.* A wizard; magician.

**sor·cer·ess** (sôr′sər·es) *n.* A woman who practices sorcery; witch.

**sor·cer·y** (sôr′sər·ē) *n. pl.* **·cer·ies** Use of supernatural agencies; magic; witchcraft. [<L *sors* fate] —**sor′cer·ous** *adj.* —**sor′cer·ous·ly** *adv.*

**sor·did** (sôr′did) *adj.* 1 Of degraded character; vile; base. 2 Dirty; squalid. 3 Mercenary; selfish. [<L *sordidus* squalid] —**sor′did·ly** *adv.* —**sor·did·ness** *n.*

**sore** (sôr, sōr) *n.* 1 A place on an animal body where the skin or flesh is bruised, broken, or inflamed. 2 Anything that causes pain or trouble. —*adj.* **sor·er**, **sor·est** 1 Having a sore or sores; tender. 2 Pained or distressed. 3 Irritating; distressing. 4 Very great; extreme: in *sore* need of money. 5 *Informal* Offended; angry. —*adv. Archaic* Sorely. [<OE *sār*] —**sore′ness** *n.* —**Syn.** *n.* 1 cut, scrape, wound.

**so·ror·i·ty** (sə·rôr′ə·tē, -ror′-) *n. pl.* **·ties** A women's organization having chapters at colleges, universities, etc. [<L *soror* a sister]

**sor·row** (sor′ō, sôr′ō) *n.* 1 Pain or distress because of loss, injury, misfortune, or grief. 2 An event that causes such pain or distress; affliction. 3 The expression of grief; mourning. —*v.i.* To feel or express sorrow; grieve. [<OE *sorg* care] —**sor′row·er** *n.*

**sor·ry** (sor′ē, sôr′ē) *adj.* **·ri·er**, **·ri·est** 1 Feeling or showing regret or remorse. 2 Affected by sorrow; grieved. 3 Causing sorrow; melancholy. 4 Pitiable or worthless; paltry. [<OE *sārig* < *sār* sore] —**sor′ri·ly** *adv.* —**sor′ri·ness** *n.*

**sort** (sôrt) *n.* 1 A collection of persons or things characterized by similar qualities; a kind. 2 Character; nature. 3 Manner; way; style. 4 A person of a certain type: He's a good *sort.* —**of sorts** Of a poor or unsatisfactory kind: an actor *of sorts.* —**out of sorts** Slightly ill or ill-humored. —**sort of** *Informal* Somewhat. —*v.t.* To arrange or separate into grades, kinds, or sizes; assort. [<L *sors* lot, condition] —**sort′er** *n.*

**sor·tie** (sôr′tē) *n.* 1 A sudden attack by troops from a besieged place. 2 A single trip of an aircraft on a military mission. [<F *sortir* go forth]

**S O S** (es′ō·es′) 1 The international signal of distress in the Morse code (. . . — . . .), used by airplanes, ships, etc. 2 *Informal* Any call for assistance.

**sot** (sot) *n.* A habitual drunkard. [<OE *sott* a fool] —**sot′tish** *adj.* —**sot′tish·ly** *adv.* —**sot′tish·ness** *n.*

**soul** (sōl) *n.* 1 That essence or entity of the human person which is regarded as being immortal, invisible, and the source or origin of spirituality, emotion, volition, etc. 2 The moral or spiritual part of man. 3 Emotional or spiritual force, vitality, depth, etc.: His acting lacks *soul.* 4 The most essential or vital element or quality of something: Justice is the *soul* of law. 5 The leading figure or inspirer of a cause, movement, etc. 6 Embodiment: the *soul* of generosity. 7 A person: Every *soul* trembled at the sight. 8 The disembodied spirit of one who has died. 9 Among U.S. Negroes: **a** The awareness of a black African heritage. **b** A strongly emotional pride and solidarity based on this awareness. **c** The qualities that arouse such feelings, esp. as exemplified in black culture and art. 10 SOUL MUSIC. 11 SOUL FOOD. —*adj.* Of or pertaining to soul (def. 9). [<OE *sāwol*]

**sound** (sound) *n.* 1 Energy in the form of a disturbance, usually periodic, in the pressure and density of a fluid or the elastic strain of a solid, detectable by human organs of hearing when between about 20Hz and 20kHz in frequency. 2 The sensation produced by such energy. 3 Any noise, tone, voice, etc., of a specified quality or source: the *sound* of a door slamming shut. 4 Sounding or hearing distance; earshot: within *sound* of the battle. 5 Significance; implication: The story has a sinister *sound.* 6 Mere noise without significance: full of *sound* and fury. —*v.i.* 1 To give forth a sound or sounds. 2 To give a specified impression; seem: The story *sounds* true. —*v.t.* 3 To cause to give forth sound: to *sound* a bell; also, to give forth the sound of: to *sound* A on the violin. 4 To give a signal or order for or announcement of: to *sound* retreat. 5 To utter audibly; pronounce. 6 To make known or celebrated. 7 To test or examine by sound; auscultate. [<OF *son* <L *sonus*]

**sound barrier** SONIC BARRIER.

**sound track** That portion along the edge of a motion-picture film which carries the sound record.

**soup** (sōōp) *n.* 1 A food made of meat or fish,

vegetables, etc., cooked and served, either whole or puréed, in water, stock, or other liquid. 2 *Slang* A heavy fog. 3 *Slang* Nitroglycerin. —**in the soup** *Slang* In difficulties; in a quandary. —**soup up** *Slang* To supercharge or otherwise modify (an engine) for high speed. [< F *soupe*]

**sour** (sour) *adj.* 1 Sharp, acid, or tart to the taste, like vinegar. 2 Having an acid or rancid taste or smell as the result of fermentation. 3 Of or pertaining to fermentation. 4 Cross; morose: a *sour* smile. 5 Bitterly disenchanted. 6 Bad in quality, performance, etc.: an athlete gone *sour*. 7 Wrong or unpleasant in pitch or tone: a *sour* note. 8 Unpleasant. 9 Acid: said of soil. —*v.t.* & *v.i.* To become or make sour. —*n.* 1 Something sour. 2 A cocktail, made usu. with lemon juice, fruit garnishes, etc.: a whiskey *sour*. [< OE *sūr*] —**sour′ly** *adv.* —**sour′ness** *n.* —**Syn.** 1 dour, acid, bitter, unhappy.

**source** (sôrs, sōrs) *n.* 1 That from which something originates or is derived. 2 A cause or agency: a *source* of joy. 3 The spring or fountain from which a stream of water originates. 4 A person, writing, or agency from which information is obtained. [< L *surgere* to rise]

**south** (south) *n.* 1 The general direction to the right of sunrise. 2 The point of the compass at 180°, directly opposite north. 3 A region or point lying in this direction. —*adj.* 1 Situated in a southern direction relatively to the observer or to any given place or point. 2 Facing south. 3 Belonging to or proceeding from the south. —*v.i.* To turn southward. —*adv.* 1 Toward or at the south. 2 From the south. —**the South** 1 In the U.S., those states lying south of Pennsylvania and the Ohio River and east of the Mississippi. 2 The Confederacy. [< OE *sūth*]

**sou·ve·nir** (sōō′və·nîr′, sōō′və·nîr) *n.* A token of remembrance; memento. [< L *subvenire* come to mind]

**sov·er·eign** (sov′rin, -ə·rən, -ərn, suv′-) *adj.* 1 Exercising or possessing supreme jurisdiction or power. 2 Free; independent; autonomous: a *sovereign* state. 3 Supremely excellent, great, or exalted. 4 Extremely potent or effective: a *sovereign* remedy. 5 Total; unmitigated: *sovereign* hate. 6 Of chief importance, supremacy, etc.: *sovereign* claims. —*n.* 1 One who possesses sovereign authority; a monarch. 2 A body of persons in whom sovereign power is vested. 3 An English gold coin equivalent to one

pound sterling. [< L *super* above] —**sov′er·eign·ly** *adv.*

**so′vi·et** (sō′vē·et, sō′vē·et′, sov′ē-, -ē·it) *n.* 1 In the Soviet Union, any of the elected legislative councils existing at various governmental levels. 2 Any of various similar socialist legislative councils. [< Russ. *sovyet* a council]

**So·vi·et** (sō′vē·et, sō′vē·et′, sov′ē-, -ē·it) *adj.* Of or pertaining to the Union of Soviet Socialist Republics. —*n.pl.* The Soviet people, esp. the officials of the government.

**sow** (sō) *v.* **sowed, sown** or **sowed, sow·ing** *v.t.* 1 To scatter (seed) over land for growth. 2 To scatter seed over (land). 3 To disseminate; implant: to *sow* the seeds of distrust. —*v.i.* 4 To scatter seed. [< OE *sāwan*] —**sow′er** *n.*

**space** (spās) *n.* 1 The three-dimensional expanse that is considered as coextensive with the universe. 2 A limited or measurable distance or area, as that between or within points or objects. 3 A specific area designated for a particular purpose: landing *space*. 4 OUTER SPACE. 5 An interval or period of time. 6 One of the degrees of a musical staff between two lines. 7 *Printing* **a** A blank piece of type metal, used for spacing between lines, characters, etc. **b** The area occupied by such pieces. 8 Reserved accommodations, as on a ship or airliner. —*adj.* Of or pertaining to space, esp. to outer space. —*v.t.* **spaced, spac·ing** 1 To separate by spaces. 2 To divide into spaces. [< L *spatium*] —**space′less** *adj.* —**spac′er** *n.*

**space·craft** (spās′kraft′, -kräft′) *n.* Any vehicle, manned or unmanned, designed for flight in outer space.

**space·ship** (spās′ship′) *n.* Any vehicle designed to travel outside the earth's atmosphere.

**spa·cious** (spā′shəs) *adj.* 1 Of large or ample extent; not cramped or crowded; roomy. 2 Large or great in scale or scope. —**spa′cious·ly** *adv.* —**spa′cious·ness** *n.* —**Syn.** 1 extensive, ample, sizable, capacious, commodious.

**spade**[1] (spād) *n.* An implement used for digging in the ground, heavier than a shovel and having a flatter blade. —**call a spade a spade** 1 To call a thing by its right name. 2 To speak the plain truth. —*v.t.* **spad·ed, spad·ing** To dig or cut with a spade. [< OE *spadu*] —**spade′ful, spad′er** *n.*

**spade**[2] (spād) *n.* 1 A figure, resembling a heart with a triangular handle, on a playing card.

2 A card so marked. 3 *Usu. pl.* The suit of cards so marked. [<Gk. *spathē* broad sword]

**spa·ghet·ti** (spə·get′ē) *n.* 1 A thin, cordlike pasta. 2 Insulated tubing through which bare wire is passed, as in a radio circuit. [<Ital. *spago* a small cord]

**span**[1] (span) *v.t.* **spanned, span·ning** 1 To measure, esp. with the hand with the thumb and little finger extended. 2 To extend in time across: His influence *spanned* two centuries. 3 To extend over or from side to side of: This road *spans* the continent. 4 To provide with something that stretches across or extends over. —*n.* 1 The distance or measure between two points, ends, or extremities: the *span* of an eagle's wing. 2 The space or distance between the supports of an arch, abutments of a bridge, etc. 3 The part that spans such a space or distance: the graceful *spans* of Brooklyn Bridge. 4 A period of time or duration: life *span.* 5 The extreme space over which the hand can be expanded, usu. considered to be nine inches. [<OE *spann* distance]

**span·gle** (spang′gəl) *n.* 1 A small bit of brilliant metal foil, plastic, etc., used for decoration, esp. on theatrical costumes. 2 Any small sparkling object. —*v.* **·gled, ·gling** *v.t.* 1 To adorn with or as with spangles; cause to glitter. —*v.i.* 2 To sparkle as spangles; glitter. [<MDu. *spang* a clasp, brooch] — **span′gly** *adj.*

**span·iel** (span′yəl) *n.* 1 A small or medium-sized dog having large pendulous ears and long silky hair. • See SPRINGER. 2 An obsequious follower. [<OF *espaignol* Spanish (dog)]

**spar**[1] (spär) *n.* 1 *Naut.* A pole for extending a sail, as a mast, yard, or broom. 2 A similar heavy, round beam forming part of a derrick, crane, etc. 3 That part of an airplane wing which supports the ribs. —*v.t.* **sparred, spar·ring** To furnish with spars. [<ON *sparri* a beam]

**spar**[2] (spär) *v.i.* —**sparred, spar·ring** 1 To box, esp. with care and adroitness, as in practice. 2 To bandy words; wrangle. 3 To fight, as cocks, by striking with spurs. —*n.* The act or practice of boxing: also —**spar′ring.** [< L *parare* prepare]

**spar**[3] (spär) *n.* Any of various vitreous, crystalline, easily cleavable, lustrous minerals. [< MDu.]

**spare** (spâr) *v.* **spared, spar·ing** *v.t.* 1 To refrain from injuring, molesting, or killing; treat mercifully. 2 To free or relieve (someone) from (pain, expense, etc.): *Spare* us the sight. 3 To use frugally; refrain from using or exercising. 4 To dispense or dispense with; do without: Can you *spare* a dime? —*v.i.* 5 To be frugal. 6 To be lenient or forgiving. —*adj.* **spar·er, spar·est** 1 That is over and above what is necessary, used, filled, etc.: *spare* time. 2 Held in reserve; additional; extra. 3 Thin; lean. 4 Not abundant or plentiful; scanty. 5 Not elaborate or fussy: a *spare* style of writing. —*n.* 1 A duplicate of something that has been saved for future use. 2 An extra tire usu. carried in or on a vehicle as a replacement in the event of a flat tire: also **spare tire.** 3 In bowling, the act of overturning all the pins with the first two balls; also, the score thus made. [<OE *sparian* to spare] —**spare′ly** *adv.* —**spare′ness, spar′er** *n.*

**spark** (spärk) *n.* 1 An incandescent particle, esp. one thrown off by a fire. 2 Any similar glistening or brilliant point or particle. 3 A small trace or indication: a *spark* of wit. 4 Anything that kindles or animates. 5 *Electr.* The luminous effect of an electric discharge, or the discharge itself. —*v.i.* 1 To give off sparks. 2 In an internal-combustion engine, to have the electric ignition operating. —*v.t.* 3 To activate or cause: The shooting *sparked* a revolution. [<OE *spearca*] — **spark′er** *n.*

**spar·kle** (spär′kəl) *v.i.* **·kled, ·kling** 1 To give off flashes or bright points of light; glitter. 2 To emit sparks. 3 To effervesce, as certain wines, etc. 4 To be brilliant or vivacious. —*n.* 1 A spark; gleam. 2 Brilliance; vivacity. [Freq. of SPARK]

**sparse** (spärs) *adj.* **spars·er, spars·est** Thinly spread or scattered; not dense: a *sparse* crowd. [<L *sparsus*, pp. of *spargere* sprinkle] —**sparse′ly** *adv.* —**sparse′ness, spar·si·ty** (spär′sə·tē) *n.*

**spasm** (spaz′əm) *n.* 1 A sudden, involuntary muscular contraction. 2 Any sudden action or effort. [<Gk. *spasmos* < *spaein* draw, pull]

**spas·mod·ic** (spaz·mod′ik) *adj.* 1 Of the nature of a spasm; intermittent; temporary; transitory. 2 Violent or impulsive. Also **spas·mod′i·cal.** —**spas·mod′i·cal·ly** *adv.*

**spas·tic** (spas′tik) *adj.* Of, pertaining to, or characterized by spasms. —*n.* A person afflicted with cerebral palsy or similar disability. —**spas′ti·cal·ly** *adv.*

**spat·ter** (spat′ər) *v.t.* 1 To scatter in drops or

splashes, as mud or paint. **2** To splash with such drops; bespatter. **3** To defame. —*v.i.* **4** To throw off drops or splashes. **5** To fall in a shower, as raindrops. —*n.* **1** The act of spattering or the condition of being spattered. **2** The mark or soiled place caused by spattering. **3** The sound of spattering. **4** A small amount or number. [?<OE *spatlian* spit out]

**spat·u·la** (spach′ŏŏ·lə) *n.* A knifelike instrument with a dull, flexible, rounded blade, used to spread plaster, cake icing, etc. [L]

**spawn** (spôn) *n.* **1** The eggs of fishes, amphibians, mollusks, etc., esp. in masses. **2** A great number of offspring: usu. derisive. **3** Any large quantity or yield. —*v.i.* **1** To produce spawn; deposit eggs or roe. **2** To come forth as or like spawn. —*v.t.* **3** To produce (spawn). **4** To give rise to; originate. [<L *expandere* expand]

**speak** (spēk) *v.* **spoke** (*Archaic* **spake**), **spo·ken** (*Archaic* **spoke**), **speak·ing** *v.i.* **1** To employ the vocal organs in ordinary speech; utter words. **2** To express or convey ideas, opinions, etc., in or as in speech: Actions *speak* louder than words. **3** To make a speech; deliver an address. **4** To converse. **5** To make a sound; also, to bark, as a dog. —*v.t.* **6** To express or make known in or as in speech. **7** To utter in speech: to *speak* words of love. **8** To use or be capable of using (a language) in conversation. — **so to speak** In a manner of speaking. — **speak for 1** To speak in behalf of; represent officially. **2** To reserve or request: usu. used in the passive voice: Has that appointment been *spoken for*? [< OE *specan*] —**speak′a·ble** *adj.*

**speak·er** (spē′kər) *n.* **1** One who speaks, esp. in public. **2** The presiding officer in a legislative body. **3** LOUDSPEAKER.

**spear** (spir) *n.* **1** A weapon consisting of a pointed head on a long shaft. **2** A similar instrument, barbed and usu. forked, as for spearing fish. **3** A leaf or slender stalk, as of grass. —*v.t.* **1** To pierce or capture with or as with a spear. —*v.i.* **2** To pierce or wound with or as with a spear. **3** To send forth spears, as a plant. [<OE *spere*] — **spear′er** *n.*

**spe·cial** (spesh′əl) *adj.* **1** Out of the ordinary; uncommon; unique; different: a *special* problem. **2** Designed for or assigned to a specific purpose, occasion, etc.: a *special* permit. **3** Memorable; notable: a very *special* occasion. **4** Extra or additional: a *spe-*

*cial* bonus. **5** Intimate; esteemed; beloved: a *special* favorite. —*n.* **1** Something made, detailed for, or appropriated to a specific service, occasion, etc., as a train, newspaper edition, sales item, featured dish, etc. **2** A television show produced and scheduled for a single presentation only. [<L *species* kind, species] —**spe′cial·ly** *adv.* — **Syn.** *adj.* **1** peculiar, particular, distinctive, singular, original, unusual. **3** noteworthy, unforgettable, extraordinary, exceptional, rare.

**spe·cial·ist** (spesh′əl·ist) *n.* A person devoted to one line of study, occupation, or professional work. —**spe′cial·ism** *n.* —**spe′cial·is′tic** *adj.*

**spe·ci·al·i·ty** (spesh′ē·al′ə·tē) *n.* *pl.* **·ties** *Chiefly Brit.* SPECIALTY.

**spe·cial·ty** (spesh′əl·tē) *n.* *pl.* **·ties 1** Something, as a trade, study, activity, etc., in which one specializes. **2** A product or article possessing a special quality, excellence, character, etc.: Fish is the *specialty* of this restaurant. **3** A special mark, quality, or characteristic. **4** The state of being special.

**spe·cie** (spē′shē) *n.* Coined money; coin. —**in specie 1** In coin. **2** In kind. [<L *(in) specie* (in) kind]

**spe·cies** (spē′shēz, -shiz) *n.* *pl.* **·cies 1** A category of animals or plants subordinate to a genus and comprising similar organisms usu. with the capacity of interbreeding only among themselves. **2** A group of individuals or objects having in common certain attributes and designated by a common name. **3** A kind; sort; variety; form. **4** *Eccl.* **a** The visible form of bread or of wine retained by the eucharistic elements after consecration. **b** The consecrated elements of the Eucharist. [L, kind]

**spe·cif·ic** (spi·sif′ik) *adj.* **1** Distinctly and plainly set forth; explicit. **2** Special; definite; particular; distinct: He took no *specific* action. **3** Belonging to or distinguishing a species. **4** Having some distinct medicinal or pathological property: a *specific* germ. **5** Designating a particular property, composition, ratio, or quantity serving to identify a given substance or phenomenon: *specific* gravity. —*n.* **1** Anything adapted to effect a specific result. **2** A medicine affecting a specific condition or pathogen. **3** *Usu. pl.* A particular item or detail. [<L *species* kind + -FIC] —**spe·cif′i·cal·ly** *adv.* —**spec·i·fic·i·ty** (spes′ə·fis′ə·tē) *n.*

**spec·i·fi·ca·tion** (spes′ə·fə·kā′shən) *n.* **1** The

act of specifying. 2 A definite and complete statement, as in a contract; also, one detail in such a statement. 3 In patent law, the detailed description of an invention. 4 *Usu. pl.* A description of dimensions, types of material, capabilities, etc., of a device, building project, etc. 5 A single item in such a description.

**spec·i·men** (spes′ə·mən) *n.* 1 A person or thing regarded as representative of a class. 2 A sample, as of blood, sputum, etc., for laboratory analysis. 3 *Informal* A person of a specified type or character. [<L *specere* look at]

**spe·cious** (spē′shəs) *adj.* Apparently good, right, logical, etc., but actually without merit or foundation: *specious* reasoning. [<L *speciosus* fair] —**spe′cious·ly** *adv.* — **spe′cious·ness** *n.*

**speck** (spek) *n.* 1 A small spot or stain. 2 Any very small thing; particle. —*v.t.* To mark with specks. [<OE *specca*]

**speck·le** (spek′əl) *v.t.* ·led, ·ling To mark with specks. —*n.* A speck.

**specs** (speks) *n. pl. Informal* 1 EYEGLASSES. 2 Specifications. See SPECIFICATION (def. 4).

**spec·ta·cle** (spek′tə·kəl) *n.* 1 A grand or unusual sight or public display, as a pageant, parade, natural phenomenon, etc. 2 An embarrassing or deplorable exhibition. 3 *pl.* EYEGLASSES. [<L *specere* see] —**spec′ta·cled** (-kəld) *adj.*

**spec·tac·u·lar** (spek·tak′yə·lər) *adj.* Of or like a spectacle; unusually wonderfully, exciting, etc. —*n.* Something spectacular, esp. a lavish television production. —**spec·tac′u·lar·ly** *adv.* —**spec·tac′u·lar′i·ty** (-lar′ə·tē) *n.*

**spec·ta·tor** (spek′tā·tər, spek·tā′-) *n.* 1 One who beholds; an eyewitness. 2 One who is present at and views a show, game, spectacle, etc. [<L *spectare* look at]

**spec·ter** (spek′tər) *n.* A phantom; apparition. Also *esp. Brit.* **spec′tre.** [<L *spectrum* vision]

**spec·tral** (spek′trəl) *adj.* 1 Pertaining to a specter; ghostly. 2 Pertaining to a spectrum. —**spec′tral·ly** *adv.*

**spec·tro·scope** (spek′trə·skōp) *n.* An instrument for sorting out into a spectrum the wavelengths in a beam of light or other radiation. —**spec′tro·scop′ic** (-skop′ik) or **·i·cal** *adj.* —**spec′tro·scop′i·cal·ly** *adv.*

**spec·trum** (spek′trəm) *n. pl.* ·tra (-trə) or ·trums 1 The continuous band of colors observed when a beam of white light is dif-

fracted, as by a prism, according to wavelength, ranging from red, the longest visible rays, to violet, the shortest. 2 Any array of radiant energy ordered according to a varying characteristic, as frequency, wavelength, etc. 3 A band of wave frequencies: the radio *spectrum.* 4 A series or range within limits: a wide *spectrum* of activities. [L, a vision]

**spec·u·late** (spek′yə·lāt) *v.i.* ·lat·ed, ·lat·ing 1 To weigh mentally or conjecture; ponder; theorize. 2 To make a risky investment with hope of gain. [<L *speculari* look at, examine] —**spec′u·la′tor** *n.* —**spec′u·la·to′ry** (-lə·tôr′ē, -tō′rē) *adj.* —Syn. 1 guess, presume, surmise, venture, hazard.

**spec·u·la·tion** (spek′yə·lā′shən) *n.* 1 The act of speculating or conjecturing. 2 A theory or conjecture. 3 An investment or business transaction involving risk with hope of large profit.

**speech** (spēch) *n.* 1 The act of speaking; faculty of expressing thought and emotion by spoken words. 2 The power or capability of speaking. 3 That which is spoken; conversation; talk. 4 A public address. 5 A characteristic manner of speaking. 6 A particular language, idiom, or dialect: American *speech.* 7 The study or art of oral communication. [<OE *specan* speak]

**speed** (spēd) *n.* 1 Rapidity of motion; swiftness. 2 Rate of motion: *speed* of light. 3 Rate or rapidity of any action or performance. 4 A transmission gear in a motor vehicle. 5 *Informal* A characteristic interest, life style, etc. 6 *Slang* An amphetamine drug, esp. methamphetamine. 7 *Archaic* Good luck; success: They wished him good *speed.* —*v.* **sped** or **speed·ed**, **speed·ing** *v.i.* 1 To move or go with speed. 2 To exceed the legal driving limit, esp. on highways. —*v.t.* 3 To promote the forward progress of: *speed* a letter. 4 To cause to move or go with speed. 5 To promote the success of. 6 To wish Godspeed to: *Speed* the parting guest. —**speed up** To accelerate in speed or action. —*adj.* Of, pertaining to, or indicating speed. [< OE *spēd* power]

**speed·om·e·ter** (spi·dom′ə·tər) *n.* A device for indicating the speed of a vehicle.

**speed·y** (spē′dē) *adj.* **speed·i·er**, **speed·i·est** 1 Characterized by speed. 2 Without delay. —**speed′i·ly** *adv.* —**speed′i·ness** *n.*

**spell** (spel) *v.* **spelled** or **spelt**, **spell·ing** *v.t.* 1 To pronounce or write the letters of (a word); esp., to do so correctly. 2 To form or be the letters of: C-a-t *spells* cat. 3 To signify; mean. —*v.i.* 4 To form words out of letters, esp. correctly. —**spell out** 1 To read each letter of, usu. with difficulty. 2 To puzzle out and learn. 3 To make explicit and detailed. [< OF *espeler*]

**spend** (spend) *v.* **spent, spend·ing** *v.t.* 1 To pay out or disburse (money). 2 To expend by degrees; use up. 3 To apply or devote, as thought or effort, to some activity, purpose, etc. 4 To pass: to *spend* one's life in jail. 5 To use wastefully; squander. —*v.i.* 6 To pay out or disburse money, etc. [<OE *aspendan*] —**spend′er** *n.*

**spend·thrift** (spend′thrift′) *n.* One who is wastefully lavish of money. —*adj.* Excessively lavish; prodigal.

**sperm** (spûrm) *n.* 1 The male fertilizing fluid; semen. 2 A male reproductive cell; spermatozoon. [<Gk. *sperma* a seed]

**spew** (spyōō) *v.i.* 1 To throw up; vomit. 2 To come or issue forth. —*v.t.* 1 To throw up; vomit. 2 To eject or send forth. —*n.* That which is spewed. [< OE *spīwan*]

**sphere** (sfir) *n.* 1 A round body in which every point on its surface is equidistant from the center; globe. 2 A planet, sun, star, etc. 3 CELESTIAL SPHERE. 4 The apparent outer dome of the sky. 5 The field or place of activity, experience, influence, etc.; scope; province. 6 Social rank or position. —*v.t.* **sphered, spher·ing** 1 To place in or as in a sphere; encircle. 2 To set among the celestial spheres. 3 To make spherical. [<Gk. *sphaira* a ball]

**spher·i·cal** (sfer′i·kəl) *adj.* 1 Shaped like a sphere; globular. 2 Pertaining to a sphere or spheres. Also **spher′ic.** —**spher′i·cal·ly** *adv.* —**spher′i·cal·ness** *n.*

**sphinx** (sfingks) *n. pl.* **sphinx·es** or **sphin·ges** (sfin′jēz) 1 *Egypt. Myth* A wingless monster with a lion's body and the head of a man, a ram, or a hawk. 2 *Gk. Myth. Usu. cap.* A winged monster with a woman's head and breasts and a lion's body, that destroyed those unable to guess her riddle. 3 A mysterious or enigmatical person. [<Gk.]

**spice** (spīs) *n.* 1 An aromatic vegetable substance, as cinnamon, cloves, etc., used for flavoring. 2 Such substances collectively. 3 That which gives zest or adds interest. 4 An aromatic odor; an agreeable perfume. —*v.t.* **spiced, spic·ing** 1 To season with spice. 2 To add zest or piquancy to. [<L *species* kind] —**spic′er** *n.*

**spi·der** (spī′dər) *n.* 1 Any of numerous wingless arachnids capable of spinning silk into webs for the capture of prey. 2 A long-handled iron frying pan, often having legs. 3 Any of various devices with radiating, leg-like projections. [< OE *spithra*] —**spi′der·y** *adj.*

**spike** (spīk) *n.* 1 A very large, thick nail. 2 A slender, pointed piece of metal, as used along the top of an iron fence. 3 A projecting, pointed piece of metal in the soles of shoes to keep the wearer from slipping. 4 A very high, slender heel on a woman's shoe. 5 A straight, unbranched antler, as of a young deer. —*v.t.* **spiked, spik·ing** 1 To fasten with spikes. 2 To set or provide with spikes. 3 To block; put a stop to. 4 To pierce with or impale on a spike. 5 *Informal* To add alcoholic liquor to. [ME] —**spik′er** *n.* —**spik′y** *adj.*

**spill** (spil) *v.* **spilled** or **spilt, spill·ing** *v.t.* 1 To allow or cause to fall or run out or over, as a liquid or a powder. 2 To shed, as blood. 3 *Naut.* To empty (a sail) of wind. 4 *Informal* To cause to fall, as from a horse. 5 *Informal* To divulge; make known, as a secret. —*v.i.* 6 To fall or run out or over: said of liquids, etc. —*n.* 1 The act of spilling. 2 That which is spilled. 3 *Informal* A fall to the ground, as from a horse or vehicle. 4 SPILLWAY. [<OE *spillan* destroy] —**spill′age, spill′er** *n.*

**spin** (spin) *v.* **spun, spin·ning** *v.t.* 1 To draw out and twist into threads; also, to draw out and twist fiber into (threads, yarn, etc.). 2 To make or produce (a web or cocoon) as if by spinning. 3 To tell, as a story or yarn. 4 To protract; prolong, as a story by additional details: with *out.* 5 To cause to whirl rapidly. —*v.i.* 6 To make thread or yarn. 7 To extrude filaments of a viscous substance from the body: said of spiders, etc. 8 To whirl rapidly; rotate. 9 To seem to be whirling, as from dizziness. 10 To move rapidly. —*n.* 1 An act or instance of spinning. 2 A rapid whirling. 3 Any rapid movement or action. 4 A ride, as in an automobile. 5 The uncontrolled, spiral descent of an airplane after a stall. [<OE *spinnan*]

**spin·ach** (spin′ich) *n.* 1 An edible garden plant of the goosefoot family. 2 Its edible leaves. [<Ar. *isbānah*]

**spin·dle** (spin′dəl) *n.* 1 In hand spinning, a notched, tapered rod used to twist into thread the fibers pulled from the distaff. 2 The slender rod in a spinning wheel by the rotation of which the thread is twisted and wound on a spool or bobbin on the same rod. 3 A small rod or pin bearing the bobbin of a spinning machine. 4 A rotating rod, pin, axis, arbor, or shaft, esp. when small and bearing something that rotates: the *spindle* of a lathe. 5 The tapering end of a vehicle axle that enters the hub. 6 A small shaft passing through the lock of a door and bearing the knobs or handles. 7 Any decorative, often tapered rod, used in the back of a chair, etc. 8 A needlelike rod mounted on a weighted base, for impaling bills, checks, etc. —*v.* ·dled, ·dling *v.i.* 1 To grow into a long, slender stalk or body. —*v.t.* 2 To form into or as into a spindle. 3 To provide with a spindle. [<OE *spinel*]

**spine** (spīn) *n.* 1 SPINAL COLUMN. 2 Any of various hard, pointed outgrowths on the bodies of certain animals, as the porcupine and starfish. 3 A thorny projection on the stems of certain plants, as the cactus. 4 The back of a bound book. 5 A projecting eminence or ridge. [<L *spina* spine, thorn]

**spin·ster** (spin'stər) *n.* 1 A woman who has never married, esp. an elderly one. 2 A woman who spins; a spinner. [<SPIN + -STER] —**spin'ster·hood** *n.* —**spin'ster·ish** *adj.*

**spi·ral** (spī'rəl) *adj.* 1 Winding about and constantly receding from or advancing toward a center. 2 Winding and advancing; helical. 3 Winding and rising in a spire, as some springs. 4 Continuously increasing or developing. —*n.* 1 *Geom.* Any plane curve formed by a point that moves around a fixed center at a distance that is always increasing. 2 A curve winding like a screw thread. 3 Something wound as a spiral or having a spiral shape. 4 A continuously developing increase or decrease: price *spirals.* —*v.* ·raled or ·ralled, ·ral·ing or ·ral·ling *v.t.* 1 To cause to take a spiral form or course. —*v.i.* 2 To take a spiral form or course. 3 To increase or decrease continuously or sharply, as prices, costs, etc. [<L *spira* coil] —**spi'ral·ly** *adv.* • The use of the intransitive verb (def. 3) without any accompanying modifier almost always means "to increase," as *Prices spiraled in June.* If "to decrease" is meant, an adverb should be used to prevent ambiguity, as *Prices spiraled downward in June.*

**spire** (spīr) *n.* 1 The tapering or pyramidal roof of a tower; also, a steeple. 2 A slender stalk or blade. 3 The summit or tapering end of anything. —*v.* **spired, spir·ing** *v.i.* 1 To furnish with a spire or spires. —*v.i.* 2 To shoot or point up in or as in a spire. 3 To

put forth a spire or spires; sprout. [< OE *spir* stem] —**spired** *adj.*

**spir·it** (spir'it) *n.* 1 The animating principle of life and energy in man and animals. 2 SOUL (def. 1). 3 That part of a human being characterized by intelligence, emotion, will, etc.; the mind. 4 a A supernatural being without a material body, as an angel, demon, etc. b Such a being regarded as having a certain character, abode, etc.: an evil *spirit.* c A supernatural being regarded as having a visible form, power of speech, etc.; ghost: specter. 5 A state of mind; mood; disposition: low *spirits.* 6 Vivacity, energy, courage, positiveness, etc.: to have *spirit.* 7 A characteristic or prevailing feeling, attitude, motivation, quality, etc.: in the *spirit* of fun; the *spirit* of the Reformation. 8 A person regarded with reference to any specific activity, characteristic, or temper: a blithe *spirit.* 9 True intent or meaning: the *spirit* of the law. 10 Ardent loyalty or devotion: school *spirit.* 11 *pl.* A strong alcoholic liquor or liquid obtained by distillation. 12 *Usu. pl.* A distilled extract: *spirits* of turpentine. 13 *Usu. pl.* A solution of a volatile principle in alcohol; essence: *spirits* of ammonia. —**the Spirit** HOLY GHOST. —*v.t.* 1 To carry off secretly or mysteriously: with *away, off,* etc. 2 To infuse with spirit or animation; inspirit. —*adj.* 1 Of or pertaining to ghosts or disembodied entities. 2 Operated by the burning of alcohol: a *spirit* lamp. [<L *spiritus* breathing, breath of a god]

**spir·i·tu·al** (spir'i·chōō·əl, -ich·əl) *adj.* 1 Of or pertaining to spirit, as distinguished from matter. 2 Of or consisting of spirit; incorporeal. 3 Of, pertaining to, or affecting the highest or purest moral or intellectual qualities of man; not earthly or sensual. 4 Sacred or religious; not lay or temporal. 5 Supernatural. —*n.* 1 Anything pertaining to spirit or to sacred matters. 2 A religious folk song originating among the Negroes of the U.S. —**spir'i·tu·al'i·ty, spir'i·tu·al·ness** *n.* —**spir'i·tu·al·ly** *adv.* 3 otherworldly, unworldly, unearthly, pure, heavenly, angelic.

**spit¹** (spit) *v.* **spat** or **spit, spit·ting** *v.t.* 1 To eject (saliva, blood, etc.) from the mouth. 2 To throw off, eject, or utter by or as if by spitting: often with *out:* to *spit* out an oath. 3 To light, as a fuse. —*v.i.* 4 To eject saliva from the mouth. 5 To make a hissing noise, as an angry cat. 6 To fall in scattered drops or flakes, as rain or snow. —**spit on** *Infor-*

*mal* To treat with contempt. —*n.* 1 Spittle; saliva. 2 An act of spitting or expectorating. 3 A frothy, spitlike secretion of a spittle insect; also, a spittle insect. 4 A light, scattered fall of snow or rain. 5 *Informal* SPITTING IMAGE. [<OE *spittan*] —*spit'ter n.*

**spit²** (spit) *n.* 1 A pointed rod on which meat is skewered and roasted before a fire. 2 A point of low land, or a long, narrow shoal, extending into the water. —*v.t.* **spit·ted**, **spit·ting** To transfix or impale with or as with a spit. [<OE *spitu*]

**spite** (spīt) *n.* 1 Malicious bitterness or resentment, usu. resulting in mean or vicious acts. 2 That which is done in spite. —**in spite of** (or **spite of**) In defiance of; notwithstanding. —*v.t.* **spit·ed**, **spit·ing** To show one's spite toward; vex maliciously; thwart. [Short for DESPITE] —**spite'ful** *adj.* —**spite'ful·ly** *adv.* —**spite'ful·ness** *n.*

**splash** (splash) *v.t.* 1 To dash or spatter (a liquid, etc.) about. 2 To spatter, wet, or soil with a liquid dashed about. 3 To make with splashes: to *splash* one's way. 4 To decorate or mark with or as with splashed colors. 5 To display prominently: His name was *splashed* all over the front page. —*v.i.* 6 To make a splash or splashes. 7 To move, fall, or strike with a splash or splashes. —*n.* 1 The act or noise of splashing liquid. 2 Something splashed, as a spot of liquid. 3 A small area or spot of color, light, etc. 4 A small amount; dash: a *splash* of bitters. 5 A brilliant or ostentatious display. —**make a splash** *Informal* To attract notice or become conspicuous, usu. briefly. [Var. of PLASH] —**splash'er** *n.* —**splash'y** *adj.* (·i·er, ·i·est)

**spleen** (splēn) *n. Anat.* 1 A highly vascular, ductless organ near the stomach of most vertebrates, which modifies, filters, and stores blood. 2 Ill temper; spitefulness: to vent one's *spleen.* [<Gk. *splēn*]

**splen·did** (splen'did) *adj.* 1 Magnificent; imposing. 2 Conspicuously great or illustrious; glorious: a *splendid* achievement. 3 Giving out or reflecting brilliant light; shining. 4 *Informal* Very good; excellent: a *splendid* offer. [<L *splendere* to shine] —**splen'did·ly** *adv.* —**splen'did·ness** *n.* —**Syn.** 1 majestic, dazzling, sublime, superb, grand. 2 outstanding, renowned, celebrated, marvelous.

**splen·dor** (splen'dər) *n.* 1 Exceeding brilliance or brightness. 2 Magnificence; great-

ness; grandeur. *Brit. sp.* ·**dour.** —**splen'dor·ous, splen'drous** *adj.*

**splice** (splīs) *v.t.* **spliced, splic·ing** 1 To unite, as two ropes or parts of a rope, so as to form one continuous piece, by intertwining the strands. 2 To connect, as timbers, by beveling, scarfing, or overlapping at the ends. 3 *Slang* To join in marriage. —*n.* A joining or joint made by splicing. [<MDu. *splissen*] —**splic'er** *n.*

**splint** (splint) *n.* 1 SPLINTER. 2 A thin, flexible strip of split wood used for basket-making, chair bottoms, etc. 3 An appliance for supporting or immobilizing a part of the body. —*v.t.* To confine, support, or brace, as a fractured limb, with or as with splints. [<MDu. *splinte*]

**splin·ter** (splin'tər) *n.* 1 A thin, sharp piece of wood, glass, metal, etc., split or torn off lengthwise; a sliver. 2 SPLINTER GROUP. —*v.t. & v.i.* 1 To split into thin sharp pieces or fragments; shatter; shiver. 2 To separate into smaller groups or factions. [<MDu.] —**splin'ter·y** *adj.*

**split** (split) *v.* **split, split·ting** *v.t.* 1 To separate into two or more parts by or as by force. 2 To break or divide lengthwise or along the grain. 3 To divide or separate: The mountains *split* the state down the middle. 4 To divide and distribute by portions or shares. 5 To divide into groups or factions. 6 To cast (a vote) for candidates of different parties. 7 To act upon as if by splitting or breaking: Thunder *split* the air. —*v.i.* 8 To break apart or divide lengthwise or along the grain. 9 To become divided through disagreement, etc. 10 To share something with others. 11 *Slang* To leave quickly or abruptly. —**split off** 1 To break off by splitting. 2 To separate by or as by splitting. —**split up** 1 To separate into parts and distribute. 2 To cease association; separate. —*n.* 1 The act of splitting. 2 The result of splitting, as a crack, tear, rent, etc. 3 A separation into factions or groups, usu. because of disagreements. 4 A sliver; splinter. 5 A share or portion, as of loot or booty. 6 A small, usu. six-ounce, bottle of wine, soft drink, etc. 7 A wooden strip, as of osier, used in weaving baskets. 8 A confection made of a sliced banana, ice cream, syrup, chopped nuts, and whipped cream. 9 A single thickness of a skin or hide split horizontally. 10 In bowling, the position of two or more pins left standing on such spots that a spare is nearly impossible. 11 An acrobatic trick in which the legs are fully extended to the front and back and at right angles to the body. 12 *Slang* A quick departure. —*adj.* 1 Divided or separated longitudinally or along the grain. 2 Divided, as to agreement, unanimity, etc.: a *split* ballot; a *split* decision. [<MDu. *splitten*] —**split′ter** *n.*

**splurge** (splûrj) *Informal n.* 1 An ostentatious display. 2 An extravagant expenditure. —*v.i.* **splurged, splurg·ing** 1 To show off; be ostentatious. 2 To spend money lavishly or wastefully. [?]

**splut·ter** (splut′ər) *v.i.* 1 To make a series of slight, explosive sounds, or throw off small particles, as meat frying in fat. 2 To speak hastily, confusedly, or incoherently, as from surprise or indignation. —*v.t.* 3 To utter excitedly or confused; sputter. 4 To spatter or bespatter. —*n.* A spluttering noise or utterance. [Blend of SPLASH and SPUTTER] —**splut′ter·er** *n.*

**spoil** (spoil) *v.* **spoiled** or **spoilt, spoil·ing** *v.t.* 1 To impair or destroy the value, usefulness, beauty, enjoyment, etc., of. 2 To weaken or impair the character or personality of, esp. by overindulgence. —*v.i.* 3 To lose normal or useful qualities; specifically, to become tainted or decayed, as food. —*n.* 1 *Usu. pl.* Plunder seized by violence; booty; loot. 2 *Usu. pl.* The jobs in government awarded by a winning political party to its faithful supporters. 3 An object of plunder. 4 Material removed in digging. [<L *spolium* booty] —**spoil′er** *n.* —**Syn.** *v.* 1 damage, injure, harm, mar, mutilate, disfigure, maim, botch, bungle. 2 indulge, humor. 3 decay, decompose, mold, rot, putrefy.

**spoke** (spōk) *n.* 1 One of the members of a wheel which brace the rim by connecting it to the hub. 2 One of the radial handles of a ship's steering wheel. 3 A rung of a ladder. —*v.t.* **spoked, spok·ing** To provide with spokes. [< OE *spāca*]

**spokes·man** (spōks′mən) *n. pl.* ·**men** (-mən) One who speaks in the name and on behalf of another or others. —**spokes′wom′an** (-wŏŏm′ən) *n. Fem.*

**sponge** (spunj) *n.* 1 Any of a phylum of plantlike animals having a fibrous skeleton and growing underwater in large colonies. 2 The light, porous, extremely absorbent skeleton of such animals, used for bathing, cleaning, etc. 3 Any of various absorbent substances or materials used to clean, soak up liquids, etc. 4 Leavened dough. 5 A porous mass of metal, as platinum. 6 *Informal* SPONGER (def. 3). —**throw** (or **toss**) **up** (or **in**) **the sponge** *Informal* To yield; give up; abandon the struggle. —*v.* **sponged, spong·ing** *v.t.* 1 To wipe, wet, or clean with a sponge. 2 To wipe out; expunge; erase. 3 To absorb; suck in, as a sponge does. 4 *Informal* To get by imposing or at another's expense. —*v.i.* 5 To be absorbent. 6 To gather or fish for sponges. 7 *Informal* To be a sponger (def. 3): often with *off* or *on*. [< OE <Gk. *spongos*] —**spong′i·ness** *n.* —**spong′y** *adj.*

**spon·son** (spon′sən) *n.* 1 A curved projection from the hull of a vessel or seaplane, to increase its stability or surface area. 2 A similar protuberance on a ship or tank, for storage purposes or for the training of a gun. 3 An air tank built into the side of a canoe, to improve stability and prevent sinking. [?]

**spon·ta·ne·ous** (spon·tā′nē·əs) *adj.* 1 Acting or arising naturally and without constraint from an inner impulse, prompting, or desire; not planned or contrived. 2 Apparently arising independently without external cause, stimulus, influence, or condition. 3 Produced without human labor; wild; indigenous. [<L *sponte* of free will] —**spon·ta′ne·ous·ly** *adv.* —**spon·ta′ne·ous· ness** *n.*

**spool** (spōōl) *n.* 1 A cylinder having a projecting rim at each end, on which is wound thread, wire, etc., and a hole from one end to the other, as for mounting on a spindle. 2 The quantity of thread, wire, etc., held by a spool. 3 Anything resembling a spool in shape or purpose. —*v.t.* To wind on a spool. [<MLG *spole*]

**spoon** (spōōn) *n.* 1 A utensil having a shallow, generally ovoid bowl and a handle, used in preparing, serving, or eating food. 2 Something resembling a spoon or its bowl. 3 A metallic lure attached to a fishing line: also **spoon bait.** 4 A wooden golf club with lofted face and comparatively short, stiff shaft. —*v.t.* 1 To lift up or out with a spoon. 2 To play or hit (a ball) with a weak shoving or scooping movement. —*v.i.* 3 To spoon a ball. 4 *Informal* To kiss and caress, as lovers. [<OE *spōn* chip]

**spo·rad·ic** (spə·rad′ik) *adj.* 1 Occurring infrequently; occasional. 2 Not widely diffused; occurring in isolated cases: a *sporadic* infection. Also **spo·rad′i·cal.** [<Gk. *sporas* scattered] —**spo·rad′i·cal·ly** *adv.* —**spo-**

**rad′i·cal·ness** n. —Syn. 1 irregular, fitful, spasmodic, intermittent.

**spore** (spôr, spōr) n. 1 The reproductive body in plants that bear no seeds, as bacteria, algae, ferns, etc. 2 A minute body that develops into a new individual; any minute organism; a germ. —v.i. spored, spor·ing To develop spores: said of plants. [<Gk. *spora* seed, sowing] —spo·ra·ceous (spō-rā′shəs, spō-) adj.

**sport** (spôrt, spōrt) n. 1 A diversion; pastime. 2 A particular game or physical activity pursued for diversion, esp. an outdoor or athletic game, as baseball, football, track, tennis, swimming, etc. 3 A spirit of jesting or raillery. 4 An object of derision; a laughingstock; butt. 5 An animal or plant that exhibits sudden variation from the normal type; a mutation. 6 *Informal* A gambler. 7 *Informal* One who lives a fast, gay, or flashy life. 8 A person characterized by his observance of the rules of fair play, or by his ability to get along with others: a good sport. 9 *Archaic* Amorous or sexual play. — v.i. 1 To amuse oneself; play; frolic. 2 To participate in games. 3 To make sport or jest; trifle. 4 To vary suddenly or spontaneously from the normal type; mutate. 5 *Archaic & Regional* To make love, esp. in a trifling manner. —v.t. 6 *Informal* To display or wear ostentatiously. —adj. Of, pertaining to, or fitted for sports; also, appropriate for casual wear: a sport coat: also sports. [Var. of DISPORT] —sport′ful adj. —sport′ful·ly adv.

**spot** (spot) n. 1 A particular place or locality. 2 Any small portion of a surface differing as in color from the rest, as a mark, speck, blotch, etc. 3 A stain or blemish on character; a fault; a reproach. 4 A food fish of the Atlantic coast of the U.S. 5 One of the figures or pips with which a playing card is marked; also, a card having (a certain number of) such marks: the five spot of clubs. 6 *Slang* Paper money having a specified value: a ten spot. 7 *Chiefly Brit.* A portion or bit: a spot of tea. 8 *Informal* Place or allotted time, as on a list, schedule, etc. 9 *Informal* Position, job, or situation. 10 *Informal* SPOTLIGHT. 11 *Slang* NIGHTCLUB. 12 *Informal* A brief commercial or announcement, usu. scheduled between regular radio or television programs. —hit the spot *Slang* To gratify an appetite or need. —in a spot *Slang* In a difficult or embarrassing situation; in trouble. —on the spot 1 At

once; immediately. 2 At the very place of occurrence. 3 *Slang* a In trouble, danger, difficulty, etc. b Accountable for some action, mistake, etc. —v. spot·ted, spot·ting v.t. 1 To mark or soil with spots. 2 To remove spots from. 3 To place or locate in or at a designated spot or spots. 4 To recognize or detect; identify; see. 5 To sully or disgrace, as the reputation of. 6 To schedule or list. 7 To shine a spotlight on. 8 *Informal* To yield (an advantage or handicap) to someone. —v.i. 9 To become marked or soiled with spots. 10 To make a stain or discoloration. —adj. 1 Paid or ready to be paid for at once: spot cash. 2 Ready for instant delivery following sale. 3 Involving cash payment only. 4 Made or selected at random or according to a prearranged plan: a spot check. 5 Broadcast between regular programs: a spot announcement. 6 Televised or broadcast on the spot or from a specific spot. [<LG] —spot′ta·ble adj.

**spouse** (spouz, spous) n. A partner in marriage; one's husband or wife. [<L *sponsus*, pp. of *spondere* to promise, betroth]

**spout** (spout) v.t. 1 To pour out copiously and forcibly, as a liquid under pressure. 2 To speak pompously, somewhat angrily, or at length. —v.i. 3 To cause to pour or shoot forth. 4 To utter pompously, somewhat angrily, or at length. —n. 1 A tube, trough, etc., for the discharge of a liquid. 2 A continuous stream of fluid. [ME *spoute*] — spout′er n.

**sprain** (sprān) n. 1 A violent straining or twisting of the ligaments surrounding a joint. 2 The condition due to such strain. —v.t. To cause a sprain in. [<OF *espreindre* to squeeze]

**sprawl** (sprôl) v.i. 1 To sit or lie with the limbs stretched out ungracefully. 2 To be stretched out ungracefully, as the limbs. 3 To move with awkward motions of the limbs. 4 To spread out in a straggling manner, as handwriting, vines, etc. —v.t. 5 To cause to spread or extend awkwardly or irregularly. —n. 1 The act or position of sprawling. 2 An unplanned or disorderly group, as of houses, spread out over a broad area: urban sprawl. [<OE *sprēawlian* move convulsively] —sprawl′er n.

**spray** (sprā) n. 1 Liquid dispersed in fine particles. 2 An instrument for discharging small particles of liquid; an atomizer. 3 Something like a spray of liquid. —v.t. 1 To disperse (a liquid) in fine particles. 2 To apply spray to. —*v.i.* **3** To send forth or scatter spray. **4** To go forth as spray. [<MDu. *sprayen*] —**spray′er** *n.*

**spread** (spred) *v.* **spread, spread·ing** *v.t.* **1** To open or unfold to full width, extent, etc., as wings, sail, a map, etc. **2** To distribute over a surface, esp. in a thin layer. **3** To cover with something. **4** To force apart or farther apart. **5** To distribute over a period of time or among a group. **6** To make more widely known, active, etc.; promulgate or diffuse: to *spread* a rumor. **7** To set (a table, etc.), as for a meal. **8** To arrange or place on a table, etc., as a meal or feast. **9** To set forth or record in full. —*v.i.* **10** To be extended or expanded; increase in size, width, etc. **11** To be distributed or dispersed, as over a surface or area; scatter. **12** To become more widely known, active, etc. **13** To be forced farther apart; separate. —*n.* **1** The act of spreading. **2** The limit, distance, or extent, of spreading, expansion, etc. **3** A cloth or covering for a table, bed, etc. **4** Something used for spreading: a cheese *spread.* **5** *Informal* A feast or banquet; also, a table with a meal set out on it. **6** A prominent presentation in a periodical. **7** Two pages of a magazine or newspaper facing each other and covered by related material; also, the material itself. —*adj.* Expanded; outstretched. [< OE *spraedan*] —**spread′er** *n.*

**sprig** (sprig) *n.* **1** A shoot or sprout of a plant. **2** An ornament in this form. **3** An heir or offspring of a family, esp. a young man. [ME *sprigge*] —**sprig′ger** *n.*

**spright·ly** (sprīt′lē) *adj.* **·li·er, ·li·est** Full of animation and spirits; vivacious; lively. —*adv.* Spiritedly; briskly; gaily. [<*spright,* var. of SPRITE] —**spright′li·ness** *n.* —**Syn.** *adj.* animated, brisk, bustling, cheerful, nimble, spry, quick.

**spring** (spring) *v.* **sprang** or **sprung, sprung, spring·ing** *v.i.* **1** To move or rise suddenly and rapidly; leap; dart. **2** To move suddenly as by elastic reaction; snap. **3** To happen or occur suddenly or immediately: An angry retort *sprang* to his lips. **4** To work or snap out of place, as a mechanical part. **5** To become warped or bent, as boards. **6** To rise above surrounding objects. **7** To come into being: New towns have *sprung* up. **8** To originate; proceed, as from a source. **9** To develop; grow, as a plant. **10** To be descended: He *springs* from good stock. —*v.t.* **11** To cause to spring or leap. **12** To cause to act, close, open, etc., unexpectedly or

suddenly, as by elastic reaction: to *spring* a trap. **13** To cause to happen, become known, or appear suddenly: to *spring* a surprise. **14** To leap over; vault. **15** To start (game) from cover; flush. **16** To explode (a mine). **17** To warp or bend; split. **18** To cause to snap or work out of place. **19** To force into place, as a beam or bar. **20** To suffer (a leak). **21** *Slang* To obtain the release of (a person) from prison or custody. —*n.* **1** *Mech.* An elastic device that yields under stress, and returns to normal form when the stress is removed. **2** Elastic quality or energy. **3** The act of flying back from a position of tension; recoil. **4** A cause of action; motive. **5** Any source or origin. **6** A flow or fountain, as of water. **7** The act of leaping up or forward suddenly; a jump; bound. **8** The season in which vegetation starts anew; in the north temperate zone, the three months of March, April, and May; in the astronomical year, the period from the vernal equinox to the summer solstice. —*adj.* **1** Of or pertaining to the season of spring. **2** Resilient; acting like or having a spring. **3** Hung on springs. **4** Coming from or housing a spring of water. [<OE *springan*]

**sprin·kle** (spring′kəl) *v.* **·kled, ·kling** *v.t.* **1** To scatter in drops or small particles. **2** To scatter over or upon: *Sprinkle* the top with flour. —*v.i.* **3** To fall or rain in scattered drops. —*n.* **1** The act of sprinkling. **2** A small quantity. **3** A light rain. [ME *sprenkelen*] —**sprin′kler** *n.*

**sprint** (sprint) *n.* **1** The act of sprinting. **2** A short race run at top speed. **3** A brief period, as of speed. —*v.i.* To go or run fast, as in a sprint. [<Scand.] —**sprint′er** *n.*

**sprite** (sprīt) *n.* **1** A fairy, elf, or goblin. **2** A small, elflike person. **3** A ghost. [<L *spiritus*]

**sprock·et** (sprok′it) *n.* **1** A projection, as on the rim of a wheel, for engaging with the links of a chain. **2** A wheel bearing such projections: also **sprocket wheel**. [?]

**sprout** (sprout) *v.i.* **1** To put forth shoots; begin to grow; germinate. **2** To develop or grow rapidly. —*v.t.* **3** To cause to sprout. **4** To remove shoots from. —*n.* **1** A new shoot or bud on a plant. **2** Something like or suggestive of a sprout, as a young person. **3** *pl.* BRUSSELS SPROUTS. [<OE *sprūtan*]

**spruce** (sprōōs) *n.* **1** Any of a genus of evergreen trees of the pine family, having needle-shaped leaves and pendulous cones. 2 The wood of any of these trees. [<Med. L *Prussia* Prussia]

**spry** (sprī) *adj.* **spri·er** or **spry·er, spri·est** or **spry·est** Quick and active; agile. [<Scand.] —**spry′ly** *adv.* —**spry′ness** *n.*

**spume** (spyōōm) *n.* Froth; foam; scum. —*v.i.* **spumed, spum·ing** To foam; froth. [<L *spuma* foam] —**spu′mous, spum′y** *adj.*

**spunk** (spungk) *n.* 1 A slow-burning tinder, as punk. 2 *Informal* Mettle; pluck; courage. [<L *spongia* sponge]

**spur** (spûr) *n.* 1 Any of various pricking or goading instruments worn on the heel of a horseman. 2 Anything that incites or urges; incentive. 3 A part or attachment like a spur, as a steel gaff fastened to a game-cock's leg, a climbing iron used by linemen, etc. 4 A stiff, sharp spine on the legs or wings of certain birds. 5 A crag or ridge extending laterally from a mountain or range. 6 A branch of a railroad, lode, etc. 7 A buttress or other offset from a wall. 8 A brace reinforcing a rafter or post. 9 A tubular extension of a part of a flower, usu. containing the nectar. —**on the spur of the moment** Hastily; impulsively. —**win one's spurs** To gain recognition or reward, esp. for the first time. —*v.* **spurred, spur·ring** *v.t.* 1 To prick or urge with or as with spurs. 2 To furnish with spurs. 3 To injure or gash with the spur, as a gamecock. —*v.i.* 4 To spur one's horse. 5 To hasten; hurry. [<OE *spura*] —**spur′rer** *n.*

**spu·ri·ous** (spyŏŏr′ē·əs) *adj.* 1 Seemingly real or genuine, but actually not; false; counterfeit. 2 Illegitimate, as of birth. [<L *spurius*] —**spu′ri·ous·ly** *adv.* —**spu′ri·ous·ness** *n.*

**spurn** (spûrn) *v.t.* 1 To reject with disdain; scorn. 2 To strike with the foot; kick. —*v.i.* 3 To reject something with disdain. —*n.* The act or an instance of spurning. [<OE *spurnan*] —**spurn′er** *n.*

**spurt** (spûrt) *n.* 1 A sudden gush of liquid. 2 Any sudden, short-lived outbreak, as of anger, energy, etc. —*v.i.* 1 To come out in a jet; gush forth. 2 To make a sudden, forceful effort. —*v.t.* 3 To squirt. [<OE *spryttan* come forth]

**sput·nik** (spŏŏt′nik, sput′-) *n.* An artificial earth satellite, esp. the first, called Sputnik I, launched in October, 1957, by the U.S.S.R. [Russ., lit., fellow traveler]

**sput·ter** (sput′ər) *v.i.* 1 To throw off solid or fluid particles in a series of slight explosions. 2 To speak excitedly and incoher-

ently. 3 To make crackling or popping sounds, as burning wood, frying fat, etc. —*v.t.* 4 To throw off in small particles. 5 To utter excitedly or incoherently —*n.* 1 The act or sound of sputtering; esp. excited talk; jabbering. 2 That which is thrown out in sputtering. [<Du. *sputteren*] —**sput′ter·er** *n.*

**spy** (spī) *n. pl.* **spies** 1 One who is hired to get secret information from or about an enemy, another government, etc.; a secret agent. 2 One who watches another or others secretly. —*v.* **spied, spy·ing** *v.i.* 1 To keep watch closely or secretly; act as a spy. 2 To make careful examination; pry: with *into.* —*v.t.* 3 To observe stealthily and usu. with hostile intent: often with *out.* 4 To catch sight of; see; espy. [<OF *espier* espy]

**spy·glass** (spī′glas′, -gläs′) *n.* A small telescope.

**squab** (skwob) *n.* 1 A young nestling pigeon about four weeks old. 2 A fat, short person. —*adj.* 1 Fat and short; squat. 2 Unfledged or but half-grown. [<Scand.]

**squab·ble** (skwob′əl) *v.t.* **·bled, ·bling** To engage in a petty quarrel; bicker. —*n.* A petty quarrel. [<Scand.] —**squab′bler** *n.*

**squad** (skwod) *n.* 1 A small group of persons organized to do a special job; esp., the smallest tactical unit in the infantry of the U.S. Army. 2 A team: a football *squad.* —*v.t.* **squad·ded, squad·ding** 1 To form into a squad or squads. 2 To assign to a squad. [<L *quattuor* four]

**squad·ron** (skwod′rən) *n.* 1 An assemblage of war vessels smaller than a fleet. 2 A division of a cavalry regiment. 3 The basic unit of the U.S. Air Force, usu. consisting of two or more flights operating as a unit. 4 Any regularly arranged or organized group. —*v.t.* To arrange in a squadron or squadrons. [<Ital. *squadra* squad]

**squal·id** (skwol′id) *adj.* 1 Having a dirty, neglected, or poverty-stricken appearance. 2 Sordid; base. [<L *squalere* be foul] —**squal′id·ly** *adv.* —**squal′id·ness, squa·lid·i·ty** (skwo·lid′ə·tē) *n.* —Syn. 1 foul, filthy, wretched, untidy.

**squall** (skwôl) *n.* A loud, screaming outcry. —*v.i.* To cry loudly; scream; bawl. [<Scand.] —**squall′er** *n.*

**squal·or** (skwol′ər) *n.* The state of being squalid; wretched filth or poverty.

**squan·der** (skwon′dər) *v.t.* To spend (money, time, etc.) wastefully. —*n.* Prodigality; wastefulness. [?] —**squan′der·er** *n.* —**squa-**

n′der·ing·ly *adv.* —**Syn.** *v.* dissipate, waste, lavish, run through, throw away.

**square** (skwâr) *n.* 1 A parallelogram having four equal sides and four right angles. 2 Any object, part, or surface that is square or nearly so, as one of the spaces on a checkerboard. 3 An L- or T-shaped instrument by which to test or lay out right angles. 4 An open area bordered by streets or formed by their intersection. 5 A town or city block; also, the distance between one street and the next. 6 *Math.* The product of a number or element multiplied by itself. 7 *Slang* A person of excessively conventional tastes or habits. —**on the square** 1 At right angles. 2 *Informal* Honest, fair, true, etc.; also, honestly, fairly, truly, etc. —**out of square** Not at right angles; obliquely. —*adj.* **squar·er, squar·est** 1 Having four equal sides and four right angles. 2 Approaching a square or a cube in form: a *square* box. 3 Forming a right angle: a *square* nook. 4 Adapted to forming squares or computing in squares: a *square* measure. 5 Being a square with each side of specified length: two inches *square*. 6 Perfectly adjusted, aligned, balanced, etc. 7 Even; settled: said of debts, etc. 8 Tied, as a score. 9 Honest; fair; just. 10 *Informal* Solid; full; satisfying: a *square* meal. 11 Broad; solid; muscular: a *square* build. 12 *Slang* Excessively conventional or conservative; not sophisticated. 13 *Naut.* At right angles to the mast and keel. —*v.* **squared, squar·ing** *v.t.* 1 To make square. 2 To shape or adjust so as to form a right angle. 3 To mark with or divide into squares. 4 To test for the purpose of adjusting to a straight line, right angle, or plane surface. 5 To bring to a position suggestive of a right angle: *Square* your shoulders. 6 To make satisfactory settlement or adjustment of: to *square* accounts. 7 To make equal, as a game score. 8 To cause to conform; adapt: to *square* one's opinions to the times. 9 To reconcile or set right. 10 *Math.* a To multiply (a number or element) by itself. b To determine the area of. 11 *Slang* To bribe. —*v.i.* 12 To be at right angles. 13 To conform; agree; harmonize: with *with*. —**square away** 1 *Naut.* To set (the yards) at right angles to the keel. 2 To put into good order; make ready. 3 SQUARE OFF. —**square off** To assume a position for attack or defense; prepare to fight. —**square up** To adjust or settle satisfactorily. —*adv.* 1 So as to be square, or at right angles. 2

Honestly; fairly. 3 Directly; firmly. [<OF *esquarre*] —**square′ness, squar′er** *n.* • See PARALLELOGRAM.

**squash** (skwosh) *v.t.* 1 To squeeze or press into a pulp or soft mass; crush. 2 To quell or suppress. 3 *Informal* To silence or humiliate quickly and thoroughly; squelch. —*v.i.* 4 To be smashed or squashed. 5 To make a splashing or sucking sound. —*n.* 1 A crushed mass. 2 The sudden fall of a heavy, soft, or bursting body; also, the sound made by such a fall. 3 The sucking, squelching sound made by walking through ooze or mud. 4 Either of two games played on an indoor court with rackets and a ball. In one (**squash rackets**), a slow rubber ball is used; in the other (**squash tennis**), a livelier, smaller ball. 5 *Brit.* A fruit-flavored beverage. —*adv.* With a squelching, oozy sound. [<L *ex-* thoroughly + *quassare* crush] —**squash′er** *n.*

**squat** (skwot) *v.* **squat·ted** or **squat, squat·ting** *v.i.* 1 To sit on the heels or hams, or with the legs near the body. 2 To crouch or cower down, as to avoid being seen. 3 To settle on a piece of land without title or payment. 4 To settle on government land in accordance with certain government regulations that will eventually give title. —*v.t.* 5 To cause (oneself) to squat. —*adj.* **squat·ter, squat·test** 1 Short and thick. 2 Being in a squatting position. —*n.* A squatting attitude or position. [<OF *esquatir*] —**squat′ter** *n.*

**squaw** (skwô) *n.* An American Indian woman or wife.

**squawk** (skwôk) *v.i.* 1 To utter a shrill, harsh cry, as a parrot. 2 *Slang* To utter loud complaints or protests. —*n.* 1 A shrill, harsh cry. 2 *Slang* A shrill complaint. [imit.] —**squawk′er** *n.*

**squeak** (skwēk) *n.* 1 A thin, sharp, penetrating sound. 2 *Informal* An escape, esp. in the phrase **a narrow** (or **close**) **squeak**. —*v.i.* 1 To make a squeak. 2 *Informal* To let out information; squeal. 3 To succeed or otherwise progress after narrowly averting failure: to *squeak* through. —*v.t.* 4 To utter or effect with a squeak. 5 To cause to squeak. [ < Prob. <Scand.] —**squeak′y** *adj.* (·i·er, ·i·est) —**squeak′i·ly** *adv.* —**squeak′i·ness** *n.*

**squeal** (skwēl) *v.i.* 1 To utter a sharp, shrill, somewhat prolonged cry. 2 *Slang* To turn informer; betray an accomplice or a plot. —*v.t.* 3 To utter with or cause to make a

**squeal.** —*n.* A shrill, prolonged cry, as of a pig. [Imit.] —**squeal′er** *n.*

**squeam·ish** (skwē′mish) *adj.* **1** Easily disgusted or shocked. **2** Overly scrupulous. **3** Nauseated; also, easily nauseated. [<AF *escoymous*] —**squeam′ish·ly** *adv.* —**squeam′ish·ness** *n.*

**squeeze** (skwēz) *v.* **squeezed, squeez·ing** *v.t.* **1** To press hard upon; compress. **2** To extract something from by pressure: to *squeeze* oranges. **3** To get or draw forth by pressure: to *squeeze* juice from apples. **4** To force, push, maneuver, etc., by or as by squeezing: He *squeezed* his car into the narrow space. **5** To oppress, as with burdensome taxes. **6** To exert pressure upon (someone) to act as one desires, as by blackmailing. **7** To embrace; hug. —*v.i.* **8** To apply pressure. **9** To force one's way; push: with *in, through,* etc. **10** To be pressed; yield to pressure. —**squeeze by, through,** etc. *Informal* To avoid failure, defeat, trouble, etc., by the narrowest margin. —*n.* **1** The act or process of squeezing; pressure. **2** A handclasp; also, an embrace; hug. **3** A quantity of something, as juice, extracted or expressed. **4** The state or condition of being squeezed; crush. **5** A time of trouble, scarcity, difficulty, etc. **6** SQUEEZE PLAY. **7** *Informal* Pressure exerted for the extortion of money or favors; also, financial pressure. [< OE *cwēsan* to crush] —**squeez′a·ble** *adj.* —**squeez′er** *n.*

**squelch** (skwelch) *v.t.* **1** To crush; squash. **2** *Informal* To subdue utterly; silence, as with a crushing reply. —*v.i.* **3** To make or move with a splashing or sucking noise. —*n.* **1** A noise, as made when walking in wet boots. **2** A heavy fall or blow. **3** *Informal* A crushing retort or reply. [Imit.] —**squelch′er** *n.*

**squint** (skwint) *v.i.* **1** To look with half-closed eyes, as into bright light. **2** To look with a side glance; look askance. **3** To be cross-eyed. **4** To incline or tend: with *toward,* etc. —*v.t.* **5** To hold (the eyes) half shut, as in glaring light. **6** To cause to squint. —*adj.* **1** Affected with strabismus. **2** Looking obliquely or askance; indirect. —*n.* **1** An affection of the eyes in which their axes are differently directed; strabismus. **2** The act or habit of squinting. [?] —**squint′er** *n.*

**squirm** (skwûrm) *v.i.* **1** To bend and twist the body; wriggle; writhe. **2** To show signs of pain or distress. —*n.* A squirming motion. [?] —**squirm′y** *adj.* (·i·er, ·i·est)

**squir·rel** (skwûr′əl *Brit.* skwir′əl) *n.* **1** Any of

various slender rodents with a long bushy tail, living mainly in trees and feeding chiefly on nuts. The **red squirrel,** the **gray squirrel,** and the **fox squirrel** are North American types. **2** One of various related rodents, as the woodchuck, ground squirrel, etc. **3** The fur of a squirrel. —*v.t.* **squir·reled** or **·relled, squir·rel·ing** or **·rel·ling** To take away and hide (something) for possible use in the future: often with *away.* [< Gk. *skia* shadow + *oura* tail]

**squirt** (skwûrt) *v.i.* **1** To come forth in a thin stream or jet; spurt out. —*v.t.* **2** To eject (water or other liquid) forcibly and in a jet. **3** To wet or bespatter with a squirt or squirts. —*n.* **1** The act of squirting or spurting; also, a jet of liquid squirted forth. **2** A syringe or squirt gun. **3** *Informal* A youngster, esp. a mischievous one. [ME *swirten*] —**squirt′er** *n.*

**stab** (stab) *v.* **stabbed, stab·bing** *v.t.* **1** To pierce with a pointed weapon; wound, as with a dagger. **2** To thrust (a dagger, etc.), as into a body. **3** To penetrate; pierce. —*v.i.* **4** To thrust or wound with or as with a pointed weapon. —*n.* **1** A thrust or wound made with a pointed weapon. **2** A sharp painful or poignant sensation: a *stab* of grief. **3** *Informal* An effort; attempt. [ME *stabbe*] —**stab′ber** *n.*

**sta·bi·lize** (stā′bə·līz) *v.* **·lized, ·liz·ing** *v.t.* **1** To make stable. **2** To keep from fluctuating, as currency: to *stabilize* prices. —*v.i.* **3** To become stable. —**sta′bi·li·za′tion** *n.*

**sta·ble** (stā′bəl) *adj.* **·bler, ·blest** **1** Standing firmly in place; not easily moved, shaken, or overthrown; fixed. **2** Marked by firmness of purpose; steadfast. **3** Having durability or permanence; abiding. **4** Resistant to chemical change. **5** *Physics* Of, having, or exhibiting stability. [< L *stabilis*] —**sta′bly** *adv.* —**sta′ble·ness** *n.*

**stack** (stak) *n.* **1** A large, orderly pile of unthreshed grain, hay, or straw, usu. conical. **2** Any pile or heap of things arranged somewhat neatly or systematically. **3** A group of rifles (usu. three) set upright and supporting one another. **4** *pl.* That part of a library where most of the books are shelved; also, the bookshelves. **5** A chimney; smokestack; also, a collection of such chimneys or flues. **6** *Informal* A great amount; plenty. —*v.t.* **1** To gather or pile up in a stack. **2** To plan or arrange dishonestly beforehand so as to assure a certain result or outcome. **3** To assign (an airplane) to a pattern of designated altitudes while awaiting clearance to land: often with *up*. —**stack up** 1 To total. 2 To compare: often with *against*. [<ON *stakkr*] —**stack′er** *n.*

**sta·di·um** (stā′dē·əm) *n. pl.* **·di·ums**, *for def. 2 ·di·a* (-dē·ə) 1 A large modern structure for sports events, having seats arranged in tiers. 2 In ancient Greece and Rome: **a** A course for footraces, with banked seats for spectators. **b** A measure of length, equaling 606.75 feet. [<Gk. *stadion*, a measure of length]

**staff** (staf) *n. pl.* **staffs**; *also for defs. 1–3* **staves** (stāvz) 1 A stick or piece of wood carried for some special purpose, as an aid in climbing, as a cudgel, or as an emblem of authority. 2 A shaft or pole that forms a support or handle: the *staff* of a flag. 3 A stick used in measuring or testing, as a surveyor's leveling rod. 4 A group of people who function as assistants or advisors to a leader, director, president, etc. 5 A body of persons working together in some specific task, occupation, or enterprise: the hospital *staff*; the editorial *staff*. 6 *Mil.* A body of officers not having command but attached in an executive or advisory capacity to a military unit as assistants to the officer in command. 7 *Music* The five horizontal lines and the spaces between them on which notes are written. —*v.t.* To provide (an office, etc.) with a staff. [<OE *stœf* stick]

**stag** (stag) *n.* 1 The adult male of various deer, esp. the red deer. 2 A castrated bull or boar. 3 A man at a party, dance, etc., who is unaccompanied by a woman. 4 A social gathering for men only. —*adj.* Of or for men only. [<OE *stagga*]

**stage** (stāj) *n.* 1 The platform on which plays, operas, etc., are given. 2 The area on the adjacent sides and in back of this platform, including the wings, backstage, etc. 3 The profession of acting: with *the*. 4 Any of the activities or occupations having to do with the theater or drama: with *the*. 5 Any raised platform or floor, esp. a scaffold for workmen. 6 A horizontal level, section, or story of a building. 7 The scene of, or plan of action for, an event or events. 8 A center of attention. 9 A distinct period or step in some development, progress, or process. 10 A water level: flood stage. 11 A regular stopping place on a journey, esp. a journey by stagecoach. 12 STAGECOACH. 13 The distance traveled between two stopping points; leg. 14 *Electronics* One of a series of modules

through which a signal passes. 15 One of the series of propulsion units used by a rocket vehicle. —*v.t.* **staged**, **stag·ing** 1 To put or exhibit on the stage. 2 To plan, conduct, or carry out: to *stage* a rally. 3 To organize, perform, or carry out so as to appear authentic, legitimate, or spontaneous, when actually not so: The entire incident was *staged* for the press photographers. [<OF *estage*]

**stage·coach** (stāj′kōch′) *n.* A horse-drawn, passenger and mail vehicle having a regular route between towns.

**stag·ger** (stag′ər) *v.i.* 1 To move unsteadily; totter; reel. 2 To become less confident or resolute; waver; hesitate. —*v.t.* 3 To cause to stagger. 4 To affect strongly; overwhelm, as with surprise or grief. 5 To place in alternating rows or groups. 6 To arrange or distribute so as to prevent congestion or confusion: to *stagger* lunch hours. —*n.* The act of staggering. —**the (blind) staggers** Any of various diseases of domestic animals marked by staggering, falling, etc. [<ON *stakra*] —**stag′ger·er** *n.* —**stag′ger·ing·ly** *adv.*

**stag·nant** (stag′nənt) *adj.* 1 Standing still; not flowing: said of water. 2 Foul from long standing. 3 Dull; inert; sluggish. [<L *stagnum* a pool] —**stag′nan·cy** *n.* —**stag′nant·ly** *adv.*

**stag·nate** (stag′nāt) *v.i.* **·nat·ed**, **·nat·ing** To be or become stagnant. —**stag·na′tion** *n.*

**staid** (stād) *adj.* Sedate; sober; serious. [Orig. p.t. and p.p. of STAY[1]] —**staid′ly** *adv.* —**staid′ness** *n.*

**stain** (stān) *n.* 1 A discoloration or spot from foreign matter. 2 A dye or thin pigment used in staining. 3 A moral blemish or taint. —*v.t.* 1 To make a stain upon; discolor; soil. 2 To color with a dye or stain. 3 To bring a moral stain upon; blemish. —*v.i.* 4 To take or impart a stain. [< OF *desteindre* to deprive of color] —**stain′a·ble** *adj.* —**stain′er** *n.*

**stair** (stâr) *n.* 1 A step, or one of a series of steps, for mounting or descending from one level to another. 2 *Usu. pl.* A series of steps. [<OE *stœger*]

**stair·case** (stâr′kās′) *n.* A flight of stairs, complete with the supports, balusters, etc.

**stair·way** (stâr′wā′) *n.* One or more flights of stairs.

**stake** (stāk) *n.* 1 A stick or post, as of wood or metal, sharpened for driving into the ground. 2 A post to which a person is bound to be burned alive; also, death by burning at the stake. 3 A post or stick set upright in the floor of a car or wagon, to confine loose material. 4 *Often pl.* Something wagered or risked, as the money bet on a race. 5 *Often pl.* A prize in a contest. 6 An interest or share, as in an enterprise. 7 GRUBSTAKE. —**at stake** In hazard or jeopardy. —*v.t.* **staked, stak·ing** 1 To fasten or support by means of a stake. 2 To mark the boundaries of with stakes: often with *off* or *out.* 3 *Informal* To wager; risk. 4 *Informal* To supply with money, equipment, etc.; back. [<OE *staca*]

**sta·lac·tite** (stə·lak′tit′, stal′ək-) *n.* 1 An elongated, hanging cone of calcium carbonate formed by slow dripping from the roof of a cave. 2 Any similar formation. [<Gk. *stalaktitos* dripping] —**stal·ac·tit·ic** (stal′ək·tit′ik) or **·i·cal** *adj.*

**sta·lag·mite** (stə·lag′mit′, stal′əg-) *n.* 1 A usu. conical mound deposited on a cave floor by dripping from a stalactite. 2 Any similar formation. [<Gk. *stalagmos* a dripping] —**stal·ag·mit·ic** (stal′əg·mit′ik) or **·i·cal** *adj.* • See STALACTITE.

**stale** (stāl) *adj.* **stal·er, stal·est** 1 Having lost freshness; slightly changed or deteriorated, as air, beer, old bread, etc. 2 Lacking in interest from age or familiarity; trite: a *stale* joke. 3 Lacking effectiveness, energy, spontaneity, etc., from too little or too much activity or practice. —*v.t. & v.i.* **staled, stal·ing** To make or become stale. [?] —**stale′ly** *adv.* —**stale′ness** *n.*

**stalk¹** (stôk) *n.* 1 The stem or axis of a plant. 2 Any support on which an organ is borne, as a pedicel. 3 A supporting part or stem: the *stalk* of a quill. 4 Any stem or main axis, as of a goblet. [ME *stalke*] —**stalked, stalk′less** *adj.*

**stalk²** (stôk) *v.i.* 1 To approach game, etc., stealthily. 2 To walk in a stiff or haughty manner. —*v.t.* 3 To approach (game, etc.) stealthily. 4 To invade or permeate: Famine *stalked* the countryside. —*n.* 1 The act of stalking game. 2 A stalking step or walk. [<OE *bestealcian* move stealthily] —**stalk′er** *n.*

**stall** (stôl) *n.* 1 A compartment in which a horse or bovine animal is confined and fed. 2 A small booth or compartment in a street, market, etc., for the sale or display of small articles. 3 A partially enclosed seat, as in the choir of a cathedral. 4 *Brit.* A seat very near the stage of a theater. 5 A small com-

partment, as for showering. 6 An evasive or delaying action. 7 A condition in which a motor temporarily stops functioning. 8 A condition in which an airplane loses the air speed needed to produce sufficient lift to keep it flying. —*v.t.* 1 To place or keep in a stall. 2 To bring to a standstill; halt the progress of. 3 To stop, usu. unintentionally, the operation or motion of. 4 To put (an airplane) into a stall. 5 To cause to stick fast in mud, snow, etc. —*v.i.* 6 To come to a standstill; stop, esp. unintentionally. 7 To stick fast in mud, snow, etc. 8 To make delays; be evasive: to *stall* for time. 9 To live or be kept in a stall. 10 *Aeron.* To go into a stall. [<OE *steall*]

**stal·lion** (stal′yən) *n.* An uncastrated male horse. [< OHG *stal* stable]

**stal·wart** (stôl′wərt) *adj.* 1 Strong and robust. 2 Resolute; determined. 3 Brave; courageous. —*n.* 1 An uncompromising partisan, as in politics. 2 One who is stalwart. [<OE *stǣl* place + *wierthe* worth] —**stal′wart·ly** *adv.* —**stal′wart·ness** *n.*

**sta·men** (stā′mən) *n. pl.* **sta·mens** or **stam·i·na** (stam′ə·nə) One of the pollen-bearing organs of a flower, consisting of a filament supporting an anther. [L, warp, thread] —**stam·i·nal** (stam′ə·nəl) *adj.*

**stam·i·na** (stam′ə·nə) *n.* Strength and endurance, as in withstanding hardship or difficulty. [L, pl. of *stamen* warp, thread] —**stam′i·nal** *adj.*

**stam·mer** (stam′ər) *v.t. & v.i.* To speak or utter with nervous repetitious or prolongations of a sound or syllable, and involuntary pauses. —*n.* The act or habit of stammering. [<OE *stamerian*] —**stam′mer·er** *n.*

**stamp** (stamp) *v.t.* 1 To strike heavily with the sole of the foot. 2 To bring down (the foot) heavily and noisily. 3 To affect in a specified manner by or as by stamping with the foot: to *stamp* out opposition. 4 To make, form, cut out, etc., with a stamp or die: often with *out:* to *stamp* out a circle from the steel. 5 To imprint or impress with a die, stamp, etc.: to *stamp* the date on a letter. 6 To fix or imprint permanently: The deed was *stamped* on his memory. 7 To characterize; brand: to *stamp* a story false. 8 To affix an official seal, stamp, etc., to. 9 To crush or pulverize, as ore. —*v.i.* 10 To strike the foot heavily on the ground. 11 To walk with heavy, resounding steps. —*n.* 1 The act of stamping. 2 A machine or tool, as a die, that cuts out or shapes a form. 3

An implement or device that imprints a design, character, mark, etc., on something; also, the design, character, mark, etc., so imprinted. 4 A printed device of paper to be attached to something to show that a tax or fee has been paid: a postage *stamp*. 5 TRADING STAMP. 6 A specific impression or effect: the *stamp* of genius. 7 Characteristic quality or form; kind; sort: I dislike men of his *stamp*. [ME *stampen*] —**stamp′er** n.

**stam·pede** (stam·pēd′) n. 1 A sudden starting and rushing off through panic: said primarily of a herd of cattle, horses, etc. 2 Any sudden, impulsive rush or movement of a crowd, as of a mob. 3 A spontaneous mass impulse, trend, or movement, as toward the support of a political candidate. 4 Can. RODEO. —v. ·ped·ed, ·ped·ing v.t. 1 To cause a stampede in. —v.i. 2 To engage in a stampede. [<Am. Sp. *estampar* to stamp] —**stam·ped′er** n.

**stanch** (stanch, stänch) v.t. 1 To stop or check the flow of (blood, tears, etc.). 2 To stop the flow of blood from (a wound). 3 To check or put an end to. —adj. STAUNCH. [< OF *estanchier*° to halt] —**stanch′er** n. • The spelling *stanch* is usu. preferred for the verb in both England and the U.S., and *staunch* for the adjective. Many writers, however, use one or the other spelling for both.

**stan·chion** (stan′shən) n. 1 An upright bar forming a principal support. 2 A device that fits around a cow's neck, used to restrain movement in a stall. —v.t. To provide, restrain, or support with stanchions. [<OF *estanchon*]

**stand** (stand) v. stood, stand·ing v.i. 1 To assume or maintain an erect position on the feet. 2 To be in a vertical position: The oars *stood* in the corner. 3 To measure a specified height when standing: He *stands* six feet. 4 To assume a specified position: to *stand* aside. 5 To be situated; have position or location; lie: The factory *stands* on a hill. 6 To have or be in a specified state, condition, or relation: We *stand* to gain everything by not fighting; He *stood* in fear of his life. 7 To assume an attitude for defense or offense: *Stand* and fight! 8 To maintain one's attitude, opinions, etc.: *Stand* firm. 9 To be or exist in a printed or written form: Photograph the letter just as it *stands*. 10 To remain unimpaired, unchanged, or valid: My decision still *stands*. 11 To collect and remain: Tears *stood* in her eyes. 12 To

be of a specified rank or class: He *stands* third. 13 To stop or pause; halt. 14 *Naut.* To take a direction; steer. 15 *Brit.* To be a candidate, as for election. —v.t. 16 To place upright; set in an erect position. 17 To put up with; endure; tolerate. 18 To be subjected to; undergo: He must *stand* trial. 19 To withstand or endure successfully: to *stand* the test of time. 20 To carry out the duty of: to *stand* watch. 21 *Informal* a To treat: I'll *stand* you to a drink. b To bear the expense of: to *stand* a dinner. —**stand a chance** To have a chance. —**stand by** 1 To stay near and be ready to help or operate. 2 To help; support. 3 To abide by; make good; adhere to. 4 To remain passive, as when help is needed. 5 *Telecom.* To keep tuned in, as for the continuance of an interrupted transmission. —**stand for** 1 To represent; symbolize. 2 To put up with; tolerate. —**stand in for** To act as a substitute for. —**stand off** 1 To keep at a distance. 2 To fail to agree or comply. 3 To put off; evade, as a creditor. —**stand on** 1 To be based on or grounded in; rest. 2 To insist on observance of: to *stand on* ceremony. 3 *Naut.* To keep on the same tack or course. —**stand out** 1 To stick out; project or protrude. 2 To be prominent or conspicuous. 3 To be outstanding, remarkable, etc. 4 To refuse to consent or agree. —**stand pat** 1 In poker, to play one's hand as dealt, without drawing new cards. 2 To resist change. —**stand to reason** To conform to reason. —**stand up** 1 To stand erect. 2 To withstand wear, criticism, analysis, etc. 3 *Slang* To fail, usu. intentionally, to keep an appointment with. —**stand up for** To side with; take the part of. —**stand up to** To confront courageously; face. —n. 1 The act or condition of standing, esp. of halting or stopping, as: a A stopping or halt, as in a retreat, to fight back or resist. b A stop for a performance, made by a theatrical company while on tour; also, the place stopped at. 2 The place or location where one stands or is assigned to stand; position. 3 Any place where something stands: a taxi *stand*. 4 An opinion, attitude, point of view, etc.: to take a *stand*. 5 A structure upon which persons may sit or stand, as: a *Often pl.* A series of raised seats or benches, as at an athletic contest. b A platform: a reviewing *stand*. c A small platform in court from which a witness testifies. 6 A small table. 7 A rack or other structure for holding something: an umbrella *stand*. 8 A stall, counter, or the like where merchandise is displayed or sold. 9 A vertical growth of trees or plants. [<OE *standan*] —**stand′er** *n.*

**stan·dard** (stan′dərd) *n.* 1 A flag, ensign, or banner, used as an emblem of a government, body of men, head of state, etc. 2 A figure or image adopted as an emblem or symbol. 3 Something established and generally accepted as a model, example, or test of excellence, attainment, etc.; criterion. 4 Something established as a measure or reference of weight, extent, quantity, quality, or value. 5 In coinage, the established proportion by weight of pure gold or silver and an alloy. 6 The measurable basis of value in a monetary system. 7 An upright structure, timber, post, etc., used as a support. 8 A musical composition whose popularity has become firmly established over the years. 9 A plant growing on a vigorous, unsupported, upright stem. —*adj.* 1 Having the accuracy or authority of a standard; serving as a gauge or criterion. 2 Of recognized excellence, popularity, reliability, etc.: the *standard* repertoire of symphonies. 3 Not unusual or special in any way; ordinary; typical; regular: *standard* procedure; *standard* equipment. [<OF *estandard* banner]

**stan·za** (stan′zə) *n.* A certain number of lines of verse grouped together and forming a definite division of a poem. [Ital., room, stanza] —**stan·za·ic** (stan·zā′ik) *adj.*

**sta·ple**[1] (stā′pəl) *n.* 1 A principal commodity or product of a country or region. 2 A chief item, element, or main constituent of anything. 3 A product that is constantly sold and used, as sugar or salt. 4 Raw material. 5 The corded or combed fiber of cotton, wool, or flax, with reference to its length. 6 A source of supply; storehouse. —*adj.* 1 Regularly and constantly produced, consumed, or sold. 2 Main; chief. —*v.t.* ·**pled**, ·**pling** To sort or classify according to length, as wool fiber. [<MDu. *stapel* market]

**sta·ple**[2] (stā′pəl) *n.* A U-shaped piece of metal or thin wire, having pointed ends and driven into a surface, as wood or paper, to serve as a fastening. —*v.t.* ·**pled**, ·**pling** To fix or fasten by a staple or staples. [<OE *stapol* post]

**star** (stär) *n.* 1 *Astron.* Any of the numerous celestial objects that emit radiant energy, including visible light, generated by nuclear reactions. 2 Loosely, any of the luminous bodies regularly seen as points of light in the night sky. 3 A conventional figure having five or more radiating points. 4 Something resembling such a figure, as an emblem or device. 5 An asterisk (*). 6 A person of outstanding talent or accomplishment and a quality of personality that attracts wide public interest or attention. 7 A performer who plays the leading role in a play, opera, etc. 8 *Often pl.* Any of the planets or their configuration considered as influencing one's fate. 9 Fortune; destiny. —*v.* **starred**, **star·ring** *v.t.* 1 To set, mark, or adorn with stars. 2 To mark with an asterisk. 3 To present as a star in an entertainment. —*v.i.* 4 To be prominent or brilliant. 5 To play the leading part; be the star. —*adj.* 1 Of or pertaining to a star or stars. 2 Prominent; brilliant: a *star* football player. [<OE *steorra*] —**star′less, star′like** *adj.*

**star·board** (stär′bərd) *n.* The right-hand side of a vessel or aircraft as one faces the front or forward. —*adj.* Of, pertaining to, or on the starboard. —*adv.* Toward the starboard side. —*v.t.* To put, move, or turn (the helm) to the starboard side. [<OE *steorbord* steering side]

**starch** (stärch) *n.* 1 A complex, insoluble carbohydrate produced by photosynthesis and usu. stored in roots, tubers, seeds, etc. 2 A white, powdery substance consisting of purified starch extracted from potatoes, corn, etc. 3 Any starchy foodstuff. 4 A fabric stiffener made of starch suspended in water. 5 A stiff or formal manner. 6 *Informal* Energy; vigor. —*v.t.* To apply starch to; stiffen with or as with starch. [<OE *stearc* stiff]

**stare** (stâr) *v.* **stared, star·ing** *v.i.* 1 To gaze fixedly, usu. with the eyes open wide, as from admiration, fear, or insolence. 2 To be conspicuously or unduly apparent; glare. —*v.t.* 3 To gaze fixedly at. 4 To affect in a specified manner by a stare: to *stare* a person into silence. —**stare down** To gaze back fixedly (at a person) until he turns his eyes away. —**stare one in the face** To be perfectly plain or obvious. —*n.* A steady, fixed gaze. [<OE *starian*] —**star′er** *n.*

**stark** (stärk) *adj.* 1 Deserted; barren; bleak: a *stark* landscape. 2 Severe; difficult: *stark* measures. 3 With little or no ornamentation, color, etc.: a *stark* room. 4 Blunt; grim; pitiless: *stark* reality. 5 Complete; utter: *stark* madness. 6 Stiff or rigid, as in death. 7 Sharp and bare, as of outline. —*adv.* 1 In a stark manner. 2 Completely; utterly: *stark* naked. [<OE *stearc* stiff] —**stark′ly** *adv.* —**stark′ness** *n.*

**star·ling** (stär′ling) *n.* 1 A chubby, gregarious, aggressive bird with iridescent black plumage, introduced from Europe and now common in North America. 2 Any of various related European birds. [<OE *stærling*]

**start** (stärt) *v.i.* 1 To make an involuntary, startled movement, as from fear or surprise. 2 To move suddenly, as with a spring, leap, or bound. 3 To begin an action, undertaking, trip, etc.: They *started* early on their vacation. 4 To become active, operative, etc.: School *starts* in the fall. 5 To be on the team, lineup, etc., that begins a game or contest. 6 To protrude; seem to bulge: His eyes *started* from his head. 7 To be displaced or dislocated; become loose, warped, etc. —*v.t.* 8 To set in motion, activity, etc.: to *start* an engine; to *start* a rumor. 9 To begin; commence: to *start* a lecture. 10 To put on the team, lineup, etc., that begins a game or contest: I'm *starting* the new players today. 11 To set up; establish. 12 To introduce (a subject) or propound (a question). 13 To displace or dislocate; loosen, warp, etc.: The collision *started* the ship's seams. 14 To rouse from cover; cause to take flight; flush, as game. 15 To draw the contents from; tap, as a cask. —**start up** 1 To rise or appear suddenly. 2 To begin; come into being. 3 To begin the operation of (a motor, etc.). —**to start with** In the first place. —*n.* 1 A quick, startled movement or reaction. 2 A temporary or spasmodic action or attempt: by fits and *starts*. 3 A beginning or commencement, as of an action, undertaking, etc. 4 Advantage; lead, as in a race. 5 A place or time of beginning. 6 A loosened place or condition; crack: a *start* in a ship's planking. [ME *sterten* start, leap]

**star·tle** (stär′təl) *v.* ·**tled**, ·**tling** *v.t.* 1 To arouse or excite suddenly; alarm. —*v.i.* 2 To be aroused or excited suddenly; take alarm. —*n.* A sudden fright or shock; a scare. [<OE *steartlian* to kick] —**star′tler** *n.*

**star·va·tion** (stär·vā′shən) *n.* 1 The act of starving. 2 The state of being starved. —*adj.* Insufficient to sustain life or to purchase basic necessities: a *starvation* diet; *starvation* wages.

**starve** (stärv) *v.* **starved**, **starv·ing** *v.i.* 1 To die or perish from lack of food. 2 To suffer from extreme hunger. 3 To suffer from lack or need: to *starve* for friendship. —*v.t.* 4 To

cause to die of hunger. 5 To deprive of food. 6 To bring to a specified condition by starving: to *starve* an enemy into surrender. [<OE *steorfan* die] —**starv′er** *n.*

**state** (stāt) *n.* 1 A mode or condition of being or existing: a *state* of war. 2 A particular physical or chemical stage or condition of something: Ice is the solid *state* of water. 3 Frame of mind: a *state* of utter peace. 4 Any extreme mental condition, as of excitement, nervousness, etc. 5 Social status or position. 6 A grand, ceremonious, or luxurious style of living or doing: to arrive in *state*. 6 A sovereign political community; nation. 7 A political and territorial unit within such a community: the *state* of Maine. —**lie in state** To be placed on public view before burial. —*adj.* 1 Of or pertaining to a state, nation, or government. 2 Intended for use on occasions of ceremony. —*v.t.* **stat·ed**, **stat·ing** 1 To set forth explicitly in speech or writing; declare. 2 To fix; settle: to *state* terms. [<L *status* condition, state < *stare* to stand] —**state′hood** *n.* —Syn. *n.* 1 circumstances. 5 standing. *v.* 1 affirm, assert, aver.

**state·ly** (stāt′lē) *adj.* ·**li·er**, ·**li·est** 1 Dignified; majestic: a *stately* mansion. 2 Slow; measured: a *stately* march. —*adv.* Loftily. —**state′li·ness** *n.* —Syn. 1 imposing, grand, awesome, impressive.

**state·ment** (stāt′mənt) *n.* 1 The act of stating. 2 That which is stated. 3 A summary of assets and liabilities, showing the balance due. 3 A major or dominant idea expressed in the composition of a creative work, as in art, music, or design; motif. 4 The expression of such an idea.

**state·room** (stāt′rōom′, -rōom′) *n.* A small private bedroom on a passenger ship or railroad train.

**states·man** (stāts′mən) *n. pl.* ·**men** (-mən) A person skilled in the science of government and prominent in national and foreign affairs. —**states′man·ly** *adv.* —**states′man·ship** *n.*

**stat·ic** (stat′ik) *adj.* 1 Pertaining to bodies at rest or forces in equilibrium. 2 *Physics* Not involved in or with motion: *static* pressure. 3 *Electr.* Of or caused by stationary electric charges. 4 At rest; not active. 5 Of or pertaining to nonactive elements. 6 Dealing with fixed or stable conditions. **Also stat′i·cal.** —*n. Electronics* Electrical noise, esp. atmospheric, that interferes with radio communications. [<Gk *statikos* causing to stand] —**stat′i·cal·ly** *adv.*

**sta·tion** (stā′shən) *n.* 1 A place where a person or thing usu. stands. 2 The headquarters of some official person or body of men: a police *station.* 3 A starting point or stopping place of a railroad or bus line. 4 A building for the accommodation of passengers or freight, as on a railroad or bus line; depot. 5 Social rank; standing. 6 *Mil.* The place to which an individual, unit, or ship is assigned for duty. 7 The installations of a radio or television broadcasting unit. — *v.t.* To assign to a station; set in position. [<L *stare* to stand]

**sta·tion·ar·y** (stā′shə·ner′ē) *adj.* 1 Remaining in one place. 2 Fixed; not portable. 3 Exhibiting no change of character or condition.

**sta·tion·er·y** (stā′shə·ner′ē) *n.* Paper, pens, pencils, ink, notebooks, and other related goods.

**station wagon** An automotive vehicle with one or more rows of seats behind the front seat and with a hinged tailgate for admitting luggage, etc.

**sta·tis·ti·cal** (stə·tis′tə·kəl) *adj.* 1 Of or pertaining to statistics. 2 Composed of statistics. —**sta·tis′ti·cal·ly** *adv.*

**stat·is·ti·cian** (stat′is·tish′ən) *n.* One skilled in collecting and tabulating statistical data.

**sta·tis·tics** (stə·tis′tiks) *n.pl.* 1 A collection of quantitative data or facts. 2 *(construed as sing.)* The branch of mathematics that deals with the collection and analysis of quantitative data. [<L *status* position, state]

**stat·u·ar·y** (stach′ŏŏ·er′ē) *n. pl.* ·ar·ies Statues collectively. —*adj.* Of or suitable for statues. [<L *statua* statue]

**stat·ue** (stach′ŏŏ) *n.* A three-dimensional representation of a human or animal figure modeled in clay or wax, cast in bronze or plaster, or carved in wood or stone. [<L *status,* pp. of *stare* stand]

**stat·ure** (stach′ər) *n.* 1 The natural height of a body. 2 The height of anything, as a tree. 3 Status or reputation resulting from development or growth: artistic *stature.* [<L *status* condition, state]

**sta·tus** (stā′təs, stat′əs) *n.* 1 State, condition, or relation. 2 Relative position or rank. [<L *stare* to stand]

**stat·ute** (stach′ŏŏt) *n.* 1 *Law* A legislative enactment. 2 An established law or regulation. [<L *statutus,* pp. of *statuere* constitute]

**stave** (stāv) *n.* 1 A curved strip of wood, forming a part of the sides of a barrel, tub, or the like. 2 *Music* A staff. 3 A stanza; verse. 4 A rod, cudgel, or staff. 5 A rung of a rack or ladder. —*v.* **staved** or **stove, stav·ing** *v.t.* 1 To break or make (a hole) by crushing or collision. 2 To furnish with staves. —*v.i.* 3 To be broken in, as a vessel's hull. —**stave off** To ward off: to *stave off* bankruptcy. [< *staves,* pl. of STAFF]

**stay** (stā) *v.i.* 1 To stop; halt: *Stay* where you are. 2 To continue in a specified place or condition: to *stay* home; to *stay* healthy. 3 To remain temporarily as a guest or resident. 4 To tarry: I'll *stay* a few more minutes. 5 *Informal* To have endurance; last. 6 *Informal* To keep pace with a competitor, as in a race. —*v.t.* 7 To bring to a stop; halt. 8 To hinder; delay. 9 To put off; postpone. 10 To satisfy the demands of temporarily; appease: to *stay* the pangs of hunger. 11 To remain for the duration of: to *stay* the night. —*n.* 1 The act or time of staying: a week's *stay* at the beach. 2 A deferment or suspension of judicial proceedings: The court granted a *stay* of sentencing. 3 *Informal* Staying power; endurance. [<L *stare* stand] —**stay′er** *n.*

**stead·fast** (sted′fast′, -fāst′, -fəst) *adj.* 1 Firmly fixed in faith or devotion to duty. 2 Directed fixedly at one point, as the gaze. [<OE *stedefǣst*] —**stead′fast·ly** *adv.* —**stead′fast′ness** *n.*

**stead·y** (sted′ē) *adj.* **stead·i·er, stead·i·est** 1 Stable; not liable to shake or totter: a *steady* ladder. 2 Unfaltering; constant: a *steady* light; *steady* loyalty. 3 Calm; unruffled: *steady* nerves. 4 Free from intemperance and dissipation: *steady* habits. 5 Regular: a *steady* customer. 6 Of a ship, keeping more or less upright in rough seas. —**go steady** *Informal* To date exclusively. — *v.t. & v.i.* **stead·ied, stead·y·ing** To make or become steady. —*interj.* Not so fast; keep calm. —*n. Slang* A sweetheart or constant companion. [< STEAD] —**stead′i·ly** *adv.* — **stead′i·ness** *n.*

**steak** (stāk) *n.* A slice of meat or fish, esp. of beef, usu. broiled or fried. [<ON *steik*]

**steal** (stēl) *v.* **stole, sto·len, steal·ing** *v.t.* 1 To take from another without right or permission. 2 To take or obtain in a subtle manner: He has *stolen* the hearts of the people. 3 In baseball, to reach (another base) without the aid of a hit or error: said of a base runner. —*v.i.* 4 To move quietly and stealthily: to *steal* away in the night. 5 To commit theft. 6 To move secretly or furtively. —*n. Informal* 1 The act of stealing or that which is stolen. 2 Any underhanded financial deal that benefits the originators. 3 A bargain: a *steal* at $3.99. [<OE *stelan*] —**steal′er** *n.* — **Syn.** *v.* 1 filch, pilfer, purloin. 4 skulk, slink.

**stealth** (stelth) *n.* Secret or furtive action, movement, or behavior. [<OE *stelan* steal]

**steam** (stēm) *n.* 1 Water in the form of a gas, esp. above the boiling point of the liquid. 2 The visible mist formed by sudden cooling of hot steam. 3 Any kind of vaporous exhalation. 4 Energy or power derived from hot water vapor under pressure. 5 *Informal* Vigor; force; speed. —**let off steam** To give expression to pent-up emotions or opinions. —*v.i.* 1 To emit steam or vapor. 2 To rise or pass off as steam. 3 To become covered with condensed water vapor: often with *up.* 4 To generate steam. 5 To move or travel by the agency of steam. —*v.t.* 6 To treat with steam, as in softening, cooking, cleaning, etc. —*adj.* 1 Of, driven, or operated by steam. 2 Producing or containing steam: a *steam* boiler; a *steam* pipe. 3 Treated by steam. 4 Using steam: *steam* heat. [<OE *stēam*] —**steam′i·ness** *n.* — **steam′y** *adj.* (·i·er, i·est)

**steam engine** An engine that derives its force from the pressure of hot steam.

**steel** (stēl) *n.* 1 Any of various alloys of iron containing carbon in amounts up to about 2 percent, often with other components that give special properties. 2 Something made of steel, as an implement or weapon. 3 Hardness of character. 4 *Can.* A railway track or line. —*adj.* 1 Made or composed of steel. 2 Adamant; unyielding. —*v.t.* 1 To cover with steel. 2 To make strong; harden: to *steel* one's heart against misery. [<OE *stēl*] —**steel′i·ness** *n.* —**steel′y** *adj.* (·i·er, ·i·est)

**steep** (stēp) *adj.* 1 Sloping sharply; precipitous. 2 *Informal* Exorbitant; high, as a price. —*n.* A cliff; a precipitous place. [<OE *stēap*] —**steep′ly** *adv.* —**steep′ness** *n.* — **Syn.** *adj.* 1 abrupt, high, sharp, sheer.

**stee·ple** (stē′pəl) *n.* A lofty structure rising above the roof of a church, usu. having a spire. [<OE *stēpel*]

**steer** (stir) *v.t.* 1 To direct the course of (a vessel or vehicle). 2 To follow (a course). 3 To direct; guide; control. —*v.i.* 4 To direct the course of a vessel, vehicle, etc. 5 To undergo guiding or steering. 6 To follow a course: to *steer* for land. —**steer clear of** To avoid; keep away from. —*n. Slang* A tip; piece of advice. [<OE *stēoran*] —**steer′er** *n.*

**stel·lar** (stel′ər) *adj.* 1 Of or pertaining to the stars; astral. 2 Chief; principal: a *stellar* role in a play. [<L *stella* star]

**stem¹** (stem) *n.* 1 The main ascending axis of a plant, serving to transport water and nutrients, to hold up the leaves to air and light, etc. 2 A subsidiary stalk supporting a fruit, flower, or leaf. 3 The slender upright support of a goblet, wine glass, vase, etc. 4 In a watch, the small projecting rod used for winding the mainspring. 5 *Music* The line attached to the head of a written musical note. 6 *Ling.* The unchanged element common to all the members of a given inflection. 7 The bow of a boat. —**from stem to stern** 1 From one end of a ship to the other. 2 Throughout; thoroughly. —*v.t.* stemmed, stem·ming To remove the stems of or from. —**stem from** To be descended or derived. [<OE *stemm, stemn*] —**stem′mer** *n.*

**stem²** (stem) *v.t.* stemmed, stem·ming 1 To stop, hold back, or dam up, as a current. 2 To make progress against, as a current, opposing force, etc. [<ON *stemma* stop]

**stench** (stench) *n.* A foul or offensive odor. [<OE *stenc*] —**stench′y** *adj.* —**Syn.** fetidness, miasma, reek, stink.

**sten·cil** (sten′səl) *n.* 1 A thin sheet or plate in which a written text or a pattern is cut through which applied paint or ink penetrates to a surface beneath. 2 Produced by stenciling. —*v.t.* ·ciled or ·cilled, ·cil·ing or ·cil·ling To mark with a stencil. [<OF *estenceler*] —**sten′cil·er** or **sten′cil·ler** *n.*

**ste·nog·ra·pher** (stə·nog′rə·fər) *n.* One who is skilled in shorthand.

**ste·nog·ra·phy** (stə·nog′rə·fē) *n.* 1 The method of rapid writing by the use of contractions or arbitrary symbols; shorthand. 2 The act of using stenography. —**sten·o·graph·ic** (sten′ə·graf′ik) or **i·cal** *adj.* —**sten′o·graph′i·cal·ly** *adv.*

**step** (step) *n.* 1 A change in location or position accomplished by lifting the foot and putting it down in a different place. 2 The distance passed over in making such a motion. 3 Any space easily traversed. 4 A stair or ladder rung. 5 A single action or proceeding regarded as leading to something. 6 A grade or degree: They advanced him a *step.* 7 The sound of a footfall. 8 A footprint; track. 9 *pl.* Progression by walking. 10 A combination of foot movements in dancing.

11 *Music* An interval approximately equal to that between the first two tones of a diatonic scale. —**in step** 1 Walking or dancing evenly with another by taking corresponding steps. 2 Conforming; in agreement. —**out of step** 1 Not in step. 2 Not conforming or agreeing. —**step by step** In slow stages. —**take steps** To adopt measures, as to attain an end. —**watch one's step** To be cautious. —*v.* **stepped, step·ping** *v.i.* 1 To move forward or backward by taking a step or steps. 2 To walk a short distance. 3 To move with measured, dignified, or graceful steps. 4 To move or act quickly or briskly. 5 To pass into a situation, circumstance, etc.: He *stepped* into a fortune. —*v.t.* 6 To take (a pace, stride, etc.). 7 To perform the steps of: to *step* a quadrille. 8 To place or move (the foot) in taking a step. 9 To measure by taking steps: often with *off.* 10 To cut or arrange in steps. —**step down** 1 To decrease gradually. 2 To resign from an office or position; abdicate. —**step in** To begin to take part; intervene. —**step on** (or **upon**) 1 To tread upon. 2 To put the foot on so as to activate, as a brake or treadle. 3 *Informal* To reprove or subdue. —**step on it** *Informal* To hurry; hasten. —**step out** 1 To go outside. 2 *Informal* To go out for fun or entertainment. 3 To step down. 4 To walk with long strides. —**step up** To increase; raise. [<OE *stǣpe*] —**Syn.** *n.* 6 stage, level, position, notch.

**ster·e·o·phon·ic** (ster′ē·ə·fon′ik, stir′-) *adj.* Of, for, or designating a system of sound reproduction in which two independent channels are used so as to present different sounds to each of a listener's ears. —**ster′e·o·phon′i·cal·ly** *adv.*

**ster·e·o·type** (ster′ē·ə·tīp′, stir′-) *n.* 1 A printing plate cast in metal from a matrix molded from a raised surface, as type. 2 Anything made or processed in this way. 3 A conventional or hackneyed expression, custom, or mode of thought. —*v.t.* **·typed, ·typ·ing** 1 To make a stereotype of. 2 To print from stereotypes. 3 To give a fixed or unalterable form to. —**ster′e·o·typ′er, ster′e·o·typ′ist** *n.*

**ster·ile** (ster′əl, *Chiefly Brit.* -īl) *adj.* 1 Having no reproductive power; barren. 2 Lacking productiveness: *sterile* soil. 3 Containing no microorganisms: aseptic: a *sterile* fluid. 4 Lacking vigor or interest; *sterile* prose. 5 Without results; futile: *sterile* hopes. [<L

*sterīlis*] —**ster′ile·ly** *adv.* —**ste·ril·i·ty** (stə·ril′ə·tē), **ster′ile·ness** *n.*

**ster·il·ize** (ster′əl·īz) *v.t.* **·ized, ·iz·ing** 1 To render incapable of reproduction, esp. by surgery. 2 To destroy microorganisms. 3 To make barren. —**ster′i·li·za′tion, ster′il·iz′er** *n.*

**ster·ling** (stûr′ling) *n.* 1 British money. 2 The official standard of fineness for British coins. 3 Sterling silver as used in manufacturing articles, as tableware, etc. 4 Articles made of sterling silver collectively. —*adj.* 1 Made of or payable in sterling: pounds *sterling.* 2 Made of sterling silver. 3 Having great worth; genuine: *sterling* qualities. [<Prob. < OE *steorra* star + -LING]

**stern¹** (stûrn) *adj.* 1 Marked by severity or harshness: a *stern* command. 2 Having an austere disposition: a *stern* judge. 3 Inspiring fear. 4 Resolute: a *stern* resolve. [<OE *styrne*] —**stern′ly** *adv.* —**stern′ness** *n.*

**stern²** (stûrn) *n.* 1 *Naut.* The aft part of a ship, boat, etc. 2 The hindmost part of any object. —*adj.* Situated at or belonging to the stern. [<ON *styra* steer] —**stern′most′** (-mōst′) *adj.*

**ster·oid** (ster′oid) *n.* Any of a large group of structurally similar organic compounds found in plants and animals, including many hormones and the precursors of certain vitamins. [<STER(OL) + -OID]

**steth·o·scope** (steth′ə·skōp) *n.* An apparatus for conducting sounds from the human body to the ears of an examiner. [<Gk. *stēthos* breast + -SCOPE] —**steth′o·scop′ic** (-skop′ik) *adj.* —**steth′o·scop′i·cal·ly** *adv.* —**ste·thos·co·py** (ste·thos′kə·pē) *n.*

**ste·ve·dore** (stē′və·dôr, -dōr) *n.* One whose business is loading or unloading ships. —*v.t. & v.i.* **·dored, ·dor·ing** To load or unload (a vessel or vessels). [<L *stipare* compress, stuff]

**stew** (st‍o͞o) *v.t. & v.i.* 1 To boil slowly and gently. 2 *Informal* To worry. —*n.* 1 Stewed food, esp. a preparation of meat or fish and vegetables cooked by stewing. 2 *Informal* Mental agitation; worry. [<OF *estuver*]

**stew·ard** (st‍o͞o′ərd) *n.* 1 A person entrusted with the management of the affairs of others. 2 A person put in charge of services for a club, ship, railroad train, etc. 3 On shipboard, a person who waits on table and takes care of passengers' staterooms. 4 SHOP STEWARD. [<OE *stī* hall + *weard* ward, keeper] —**stew′ard·ship** *n.*

**stick** (stik) *n.* 1 A stiff shoot or branch cut or broken off from a tree or bush. 2 Any relatively long and thin piece of wood. 3 A piece of wood fashioned for a specific use: a walking *stick*; a hockey *stick*. 4 Anything resembling a stick in form: a *stick* of dynamite. 5 A piece of wood of any size, cut for fuel, lumber, or timber. 6 *Aeron.* The lever of an airplane that controls pitching and rolling. 7 A poke, stab, or thrust with a stick or pointed implement. 8 The state of being stuck together; adhesion. 9 *Informal* A stiff, inert, or dull person. —**the sticks** *Informal* An obscure rural district. —*v.* **stuck, stick·ing** *v.t.* 1 To pierce or penetrate with a pointed object. 2 To stab. 3 To thrust or force, as a sword or pin, into or through something else. 4 To force the end of (a nail, etc.) into something. 5 To fasten

**stiff** (stif) *adj.* 1 Resistant to bending; rigid. 2 Not easily worked or moved: a *stiff* bolt. 3 Moving with difficulty or pain: a *stiff* back. 4 Not natural, graceful, or easy: a *stiff* bow. 5 Taut; tightly drawn: a *stiff* rope. 6 Strong and steady: a *stiff* breeze. 7 Thick; viscous: a *stiff* batter. 8 Harsh; severe: a *stiff* penalty. 9 High; dear: *stiff* prices. 10 Difficult; hard: a *stiff* examination. 11 Stubborn; unyielding: *stiff* resistance. 12 Awkward or noticeably formal; not relaxed or easy; wooden. 13 Strong; potent: a *stiff* drink. 14 Difficult; arduous: a *stiff* climb. —*n. Slang* 1 A corpse. 2 An awkward or unresponsive person. 3 A person; fellow: a working *stiff.* 4 A rough person. [<OE *stif*] —**stiff′ly** *adv.* —**stiff′ness** *n.*

**stiff·en** (stif′ən) *v.t. & v.i.* To make or become stiff or stiffer. —**stiff′en·er** *n.*

**sti·fle** (stī′fəl) *v.* **·fled, ·fling** *v.t.* 1 To kill by stopping respiration; choke. 2 To suppress or repress, as sobs. —*v.i.* 3 To die of suffocation. 4 To experience difficulty in breathing, as in a stuffy room. [ME *stufflen*] —**sti′-fler** *n.* —**sti′fling·ly** *adv.*

**stig·ma** (stig′mə) *n. pl.* **stig·ma·ta** (stig·mă′tə, stig′mə·tə) or *(esp. for def. 2)* **stig·mas** 1 A mark of disgrace. 2 *Bot.* That part of a pistil which receives the pollen. 3 *Biol.* Any spot or small opening. 4 A spot or scar on the skin. 5 *Med.* Any physical sign of diagnostic value. 6 *pl.* The wounds that Christ received at the Crucifixion. [<L, mark, brand] —**stig·mat·ic** (-mat′ik) *adj.* —**Syn.** 1 blemish, blot, stain.

**stig·ma·tize** (stig′mə·tīz) *v.t.* **·tized, ·tiz·ing** 1 To characterize as disgraceful. 2 To mark

with a stigma. *Brit. sp.* **stig′ma·tise.** —**stig′-ma·ti·za′tion, stig′ma·tiz′er** *n.*

**still¹** (stil) *adj.* 1 Being without movement; motionless. 2 Free from disturbance or agitation. 3 Making no sound; silent. 4 Low in sound; hushed. 5 Subdued; soft. 6 Dead; inanimate. 7 Having no effervescence: said of wines. 8 *Phot.* Not capable of showing movement. —*n.* 1 Absence of sound or noise. 2 *Phot.* A still photograph; esp. one taken on a motion-picture set, for advertising purposes. —*adv.* 1 Up to this or that time; yet: He is *still* here. 2 After or in spite of something; nevertheless. 3 In increasing degree; even yet: *still* more. 4 *Archaic* or *Regional* Always; constantly. —*conj.* Nevertheless. —*v.t.* 1 To cause to be still or calm. 2 To silence or hush. 3 To allay, as fears. —*v.i.* 4 To become still. [<OE *stille*] —**stil′l′ness** *n.* —**Syn.** *adj.* 2 peaceful, tranquil, undisturbed. *v.* 1 soothe, tranquilize. 2 quiet.

**still²** (stil) *n.* 1 An apparatus for distilling liquids, esp. alcoholic liquors. 2 DISTILLERY. —*v.t. & v.i.* To distill. [<L *stilla* a drop]

**stilt** (stilt) *n.* 1 One of a pair of slender poles made with a projection above the ground to support the foot in walking. 2 A tall post or pillar used as a support for a dock or building. 3 Any of various shore birds with thin bills and long legs. [ME *stilte*]

**stilt·ed** (stil′tid) *adj.* Excessively formal or stuffy: *stilted* prose. —**stilt′ed·ly** *adv.* —**stilt′ed·ness** *n.*

**stim·u·lant** (stim′yə·lənt) *n.* 1 A drug that stimulates the rate or intensity of vital functions, esp. in the central nervous system. 2 Something that stimulates one to activity.

**stim·u·late** (stim′yə·lāt) *v.* **·lat·ed, ·lat·ing** *v.t.* 1 To rouse to activity; spur. 2 To increase action in by applying some form of stimulus: to *stimulate* the heart. 3 To affect by intoxicants. —*v.i.* 4 To act as a stimulus or stimulant. [< L *stimulus* a goad] —**stim′u·lat′er, stim′u·la′tor, stim′u·la′tion** *n.*

**stim·u·lus** (stim′yə·ləs) *n. pl.* **·li** (-lī, -lē) 1 Anything that rouses to activity, as a stimulant, incentive, etc. 2 Any agent that influences activity in an organism. [<L]

**sting** (sting) *v.* **stung, sting·ing** *v.t.* 1 To pierce or prick painfully: The bee *stung* me. 2 To cause to suffer sharp, smarting pain. 3 To cause to suffer mentally: to be *stung* with remorse. 4 To stimulate or rouse as if with a sting; goad. 5 *Slang* To overcharge. —*v.i.*

6 To have or use a sting, as a bee. 7 To suffer a sharp, smarting pain. 8 To suffer mental distress. —*n.* 1 A sharp offensive or defensive organ, as of a bee, capable of introducing an allergen or a venom into a victim's skin. 2 The act of stinging. 3 A wound made by a sting. 4 The pain caused by such a wound. 5 Any sharp, smarting sensation. 6 A keen stimulus; spur. [<OE *stingan*] —**sting′er** *n.* —**sting′ing·ly** *adv.*

**stin·gy** (stin′jē) *adj.* **·gi·er, ·gi·est** 1 Extremely penurious or miserly. 2 Scantily; meager: a *stingy* portion. [?] —**stin′gi·ly** *adv.* —**sti·n′gi·ness** *n.* —**Syn.** 1 avaricious, niggardly, parsimonious, tight-fisted.

**stink** (stingk) *n.* A strong, foul odor; stench. —*v.* **stank** or **stunk, stunk, stink·ing** *v.i.* 1 To give forth a foul odor. 2 To be extremely offensive or hateful. —*v.t.* 3 To cause to stink. [<OE *stincan*] —**stink′er** *n.* —**stink′ing·ly** *adv.* —**stink′y** *adj.* (**·i·er, ·i·est**)

**stint** (stint) *v.t.* 1 To limit, as in amount. —*v.i.* 2 To be frugal or sparing. —*n.* 1 A task to be performed within a specified time: a weekly *stint*. 2 A bound; restriction. [< OE *styntan* stupefy] —**stint′er** *n.* —**stint′ing·ly** *adv.*

**stip·ple** (stip′əl) *v.t.* **·pled, ·pling** To draw, paint, or engrave with dots. —*n.* 1 In painting, etching, etc., a method of representing light and shade by employing dots instead of lines. 2 The effect resulting from this method. 3 Stippled work. Also **stip′pling**. [<Du. *stip* dot] —**stip′pler** *n.*

**stip·u·late** (stip′yə·lāt) *v.* **·lat·ed, ·lat·ing** *v.t.* 1 To specify as the terms of an agreement, contract, etc. 2 To specify as a requirement for agreement. —*v.i.* 3 To demand something as a requirement or condition. [<L *stipulari* to bargain] —**stip′u·la′tor** *n.* —**stip′u·la·to′ry** (-lə-tôr′ē, -tō′rē) *adj.*

**stip·u·la·tion** (stip′yə·lā′shən) *n.* 1 The act of stipulating. 2 An agreement or contract.

**stir** (stûr) *v.* **stirred, stir·ring** *v.t.* 1 To mix thoroughly by giving a circular motion to, as with a spoon, fork, etc.: to *stir* soup. 2 To cause to move, esp. slightly. 3 To move vigorously; bestir: *Stir* yourself! 4 To rouse, as from sleep, indifference, or inactivity. 5 To incite; provoke: often with *up*. 6 To affect strongly; move with emotion. —*v.i.* 7 To move, esp. slightly: The log wouldn't *stir*. 8 To be active; move about. 9 To take place; happen. 10 To undergo stirring: This molasses *stirs* easily. —*n.* 1 The act of stirring.

2 Movement. 3 Public interest; excitement. 4 A poke; nudge. [<OE *styrian*] —**stir′rer** *n.*

**stir·rup** (stûr′əp, stir′-) *n.* 1 A loop of metal or wood suspended from a saddle to support a horseback rider's foot. 2 A similar device used as a support, as for a beam. [<OE *stigrāp* mounting rope] • See SADDLE.

**stitch** (stich) *n.* 1 A single passage of a threaded needle or other implement through fabric and back again, as in sewing. 2 A single turn of thread or yarn around a needle or other implement, as in knitting or crocheting. 3 Any individual arrangement of a thread or threads used in sewing: a chain *stitch*. 4 A sharp sudden pain. 5 *Informal* A garment: I haven't a *stitch* to wear. —**be in stitches** To be overcome with laughter. —*v.t.* 1 To join together with stitches. 2 To ornament with stitches. —*v.i.* 3 To make stitches; sew. [< OE *stice* prick]

**stock** (stok) *n.* 1 The goods a store or merchant has on hand. 2 A quantity of something acquired or kept for future use: a *stock* of provisions. 3 LIVESTOCK. 4 The original, as a man, race, or language, from which others are descended or derived. 5 A line of familial descent. 6 An ethnic group; race. 7 A related group of plants or animals. 8 A group of related languages; also, a language family. 9 The trunk or main stem of a tree or other plant. 10 a A plant stem from which cuttings are taken for grafting. b A plant stem upon which a graft is made. 11 In finance: a The capital raised by a corporation through the sale of shares that entitle the holder to interest or dividends. b The part of this capital credited to an individual stock holder. c The certificate or certificates indicating this. 12 A fund or debt owed (as by a nation, city, etc.) to individuals who receive a fixed interest rate. 13 The part of a device that functions as a support and to which other parts are attached, as the wooden portion or handle of a firearm, whip, etc. 14 Raw material: paper *stock*. 15 The broth from boiled vegetables, meat, or fish, used in preparing soups, gravies, etc. 16 Something lacking life, feeling, or motion. 17 The group of plays produced by a theatrical company at one theater. 18 A broad, heavily starched band, formerly worn as a cravat. —**in stock** Available for purchase. —**out of stock** Not available; all sold out. —**stock in trade** One's abilities, talents, or resources. —**take**

**stock** 1 To take an inventory. 2 To size up a situation. —**take stock in** *Informal* To have trust or belief in. —**the stocks** 1 A former device for public punishment consisting of a timber frame for confining the ankles, or the ankles and wrists. 2 The timber frame on which a ship or boat is built. —*v.t.* 1 To supply with cattle, as a farm. 2 To supply (a store) with merchandise. 3 To keep for sale: to *stock* avocados. 4 To supply with wildlife: to *stock* a pond. 5 To put aside for future use. 6 To provide with a handle or stock. —*v.i.* 7 To lay in supplies or stock: often with *up.* —*adj.* 1 Kept on hand: a *stock* size. 2 Banal; commonplace: a *stock* phrase. 3 Of or pertaining to the breeding and raising of livestock. 4 Employed in handling or caring for the stock: a *stock* clerk. 5 Of or pertaining to a stock or stocks (def. 9). [<OE *stocc*]

**stock·bro·ker** (stok′brō′kər) *n.* One who buys and sells stocks or securities for others.

**stock car** 1 An automobile, usu. a sedan, modified for racing. 2 A railroad car used for transporting cattle.

**stock company** 1 An incorporated company that issues stock. 2 A theatrical company under one management that presents a series of plays.

**stock exchange** 1 A place where securities are bought and sold. 2 An association of stockbrokers.

**stock·hold·er** (stok′hōl′dər) *n.* One who holds stocks or shares in a company.

**stock·pile** (stok′pīl′) *n.* A storage pile of materials or supplies. Also **stock pile.** —*v.t. & v.i.* ·**piled,** ·**pil·ing** To accumulate a supply or stockpile (of).

**stock·y** (stok′ē) *adj.* **stock·i·er, stock·i·est** Short and stout. —**stock′i·ly** *adv.* —**stock′i·ness** *n.*

**stock·yard** (stok′yärd′) *n.* A large yard with pens, stables, etc., where cattle are kept ready for shipping, slaughter, etc.

**Sto·ic** (stō′ik) *n.* A member of a school of Greek philosophy founded by Zeno about 308 B.C., holding the belief that wisdom lies in being superior to passion, joy, grief, etc. —*adj.* Of or pertaining to the Stoics or Stoicism. [< Gk. *Stoa,* the colonnade at Athens where Zeno taught]

**sto·i·cism** (stō′ə·siz′əm) *n.* Indifference to pleasure or pain.

**stoke** (stōk) *v.t.* **stoked, stok·ing** 1 To supply (a furnace) with fuel. 2 To stir up; intensify.

—*v.i.* 3 To tend a fire. [Back formation < STOKER]

**stole** (stōl) *n.* 1 *Eccl.* A long, narrow band, usu. of decorated silk or linen, worn about the shoulders by priests and bishops. 2 A fur, scarf, or garment resembling a stole, worn by women. [<Gk. *stolē* a garment] —**stoled** *adj.*

**stol·id** (stol′id) *adj.* Expressing no feeling; impassive. [<L *stolidus* dull] —**sto·lid·i·ty** (stə·lid′ə·tē), **stol′id·ness** *n.* —**stol′id·ly** *adv.*

**stom·ach** (stum′ək) *n.* 1 A pouchlike dilation of the alimentary canal, situated in most vertebrates next to the esophagus and serving as one of the principal organs of digestion. 2 Any digestive cavity, as of an invertebrate. 3 The abdomen; belly. 4 Desire for food; appetite. 5 Any desire or inclination. —*v.t.* 1 To put up with; endure. 2 To take into and retain in the stomach; digest. [<Gk. *stomachos*] —**stom′ach·al** *adj.* —**sto·mach·ic** (stō·mak′ik), **sto·mach′i·cal** *adj., n.* • See LIVER.

**stone** (stōn) *n. pl.* **stones** or *for def. 8* **stone** 1 ROCK (def. 3). 2 A small piece of rock, as a pebble. 3 A piece of shaped or hewn rock, as a gravestone. 4 A jewel; gem. 5 Something like a stone in shape or hardness: a *hailstone.* 6 An abnormal, hard concretion in the body. 7 The hard inner part of a drupe. 8 *Brit.* A measure of weight equal to 14 pounds. —**cast the first stone** To be the first to blame (someone). —**leave no stone unturned** To do everything within possibility. —*adj.* 1 Made of stone: a *stone* ax. 2 Made of coarse, hard earthenware: a *stone* bottle. —*v.t.* **stoned, ston·ing** 1 To hurl stones at. 2 To kill by throwing stones at. 3 To remove the stones or pits from. 4 To furnish or line with stone. [<OE *stān*] —**ston′er** *n.*

**stooge** (stōōj) *n.* 1 *Informal* An actor who feeds lines to the principal comedian, acts as a foil for his jokes, etc. 2 Anyone who acts as or is the tool or dupe of another. —*v.i.* **stooged, stoog·ing** To act as a stooge: usu. with *for.* [?]

**stool** (stōōl) *n.* 1 A backless and armless seat intended for one person. 2 A low bench or portable support for the feet or for kneeling. 3 A seat or place used as a toilet. 4 The matter evacuated from the bowels; feces. 5 A stump or root from which suckers or sprouts shoot up. [<OE *stōl*]

**stool pigeon** 1 A living or artificial pigeon

545

used to decoy others into a trap. 2 *Slang* An informer, as for the police.

**stoop**[1] (stōōp) *v.i.* 1 To lean the body forward and down. 2 To stand or walk with the upper part of the body habitually bent forward; slouch. 3 To bend: said of trees, cliffs, etc. 4 To lower or degrade oneself. —*v.t.* 5 To bend (one's head, shoulders, etc.) forward. —*n.* 1 A downward and forward bending of the body. 2 A habitual forward inclination of the head and shoulders. [<OE *stūpian*]

**stoop**[2] (stōōp) *n.* A small porch or platform at the entrance to a house. [<Du. *stoep*]

**stop** (stop) *v.* **stopped, stop·ping** *v.t.* 1 To bring (something in motion) to a halt: to *stop* an automobile. 2 To prevent the doing or completion of: to *stop* a revolution. 3 To prevent (a person) from doing something; restrain. 4 To withhold or cut off, as wages or supplies. 5 To cease doing: *Stop* that! 6 To check, as a flow of blood from a wound. 7 To obstruct (a passage, road, etc.). 8 To fill in or otherwise close, as a hole, cavity, etc. 9 To close (a bottle, barrel, etc.) with a cork, plug, etc. 10 To order a bank not to pay or honor: to *stop* a check. 11 *Music* To press down (a string) or close (a finger hole) to change the pitch of. 12 In boxing, etc., to parry. —*v.i.* 13 To come to a halt; cease progress or motion. 14 To cease doing something. —**stop off** To stop for a brief stay before continuing on a trip. —**stop over** *Informal* To stop briefly, as for a visit or a rest during a journey. —*n.* 1 The act of stopping, or the state of being stopped. 2 That which stops or limits the range or time of a movement; an obstruction. 3 *Music* a The pressing down of a string or the closing of an aperture to change the pitch. b A key, lever, or handle for stopping a string or an aperture. 4 *Music* In an organ, a set of pipes producing tones of the same timbre. 5 a *Brit.* A punctuation mark; a period. b In cables, etc., a period. 6 *Phonet.* a Complete blockage of the breath stream, as with the lips or tongue, followed by a sudden release. b A consonant so produced, as *p, b, t, d, k,* and *g.* —**put a stop to** To end; terminate. [<OE *-stoppian*] —**Syn.** *v.* 2 deter, quash, discontinue.

**stop·per** (stop′ər) *n.* 1 One who or that which stops or brings to a stop. 2 A plug or cork for a container, as a bottle. —*v.t.* To secure or close with a stopper.

**stop·ple** (stop′əl) *n.* A stopper, plug, cork, or

bung. —*v.t.* **·pled, ·pling** To close with or as with a stopple. [<ME *stoppen* stop]

**stor·age** (stôr′ij, stō′rij) *n.* 1 The depositing of articles in a place for their safekeeping. 2 Space for storing goods. 3 A charge for storing. 4 A section of a computer in which data is held for later use; memory.

**storage battery** A connected group of two or more electrolytic cells that can be reversibly charged and discharged.

**store** (stôr, stōr) *v.t.* **stored, stor·ing** 1 To put away for future use. 2 To furnish or supply; provide. 3 To place in a warehouse or other place for safekeeping. —*n.* 1 That which is stored or laid up against future need. 2 *pl.* Supplies, as of food, arms, or clothing. 3 A storehouse; warehouse. 4 A place where merchandise of any kind is kept for sale; a shop. —**in store** Set apart for the future; impending. —**set store by** To value or esteem. [<L *instaurare* restore, erect]

**store·house** (stôr′hous′, stōr′-) *n.* A place in which goods are stored; depository.

**stork** (stôrk) *n.* A large wading bird with a long neck and long legs, related to the herons. [<OE *storc*]

**storm** (stôrm) *n.* 1 A disturbance of the atmosphere that creates strong winds, often with heavy precipitation of rain, snow, dust, etc. 2 Any heavy, prolonged precipitation of snow, rain, etc. 3 Anything similar to a storm: a *storm* of missiles. 4 A violent outburst: a *storm* of applause. 5 A violent and rapid assault. —*v.i.* 1 To blow with violence; rain, snow, hail, etc., heavily. 2 To be very angry; rage. 3 To rush with violence or rage: He *stormed* about the room. —*v.t.* 4 To attack: to *storm* a fort. [<OE]

**storm·y** (stôr′mē) *adj.* **storm·i·er, storm·i·est** 1 Characterized by storms; turbulent. 2 Violent; rough. —**storm′i·ly** —*adv.* —**storm′i·ness** *n.* —**Syn.** 1 blustery, tempestuous. 2 disturbed, passionate, vehement.

**sto·ry** (stôr′ē, stōr′ē) *n. pl.* **·ries** 1 A narrative or recital of an event, or a series of events. 2 A narrative intended to entertain a reader or hearer. 3 An account of the facts relating to a particular person, thing, or incident. 4 A news article in a newspaper or magazine. 5 The material for a news article. 6 An anecdote. 7 *Informal* A lie; falsehood. 8 The series of events in a novel, play, etc. —*v.t.* **·ried, ·ry·ing** 1 *Archaic* To relate as a story. 2 To adorn with designs representing scenes from history, legend, etc. [< L *historia*]

**stout** (stout) *adj.* 1 Fat; thick-set. 2 Firmly built; strong: a *stout* fence. 3 Courageous: a *stout* heart. 4 Stubborn; unyielding: a *stout* denial. —*n.* 1 A stout person. 2 *Usu. pl.* Clothing made for stout or big people. 3 A strong, very dark porter or ale. [<OF *estout* bold, strong] —**stout′ly** *adv.* —**stout′ ness** *n.*

**stove**[1] (stōv) *n.* An apparatus, usu. of metal, in which fuel is consumed for heating or cooking. [<OE *stofa* a heated room]

**stove**[2] (stōv) A *p.t.* & *p.p.* of STAVE.

**stow** (stō) *v.t.* 1 To place or arrange compactly; pack. 2 To fill by packing. —**stow away** 1 To put in a place of safekeeping, hiding, etc. 2 To be a stowaway. [<OE *stōw* a place]

**strafe** (strāf, sträf) *v.t.* **strafed**, **straf·ing** 1 To attack (troops, emplacements, etc.) with machine-gun fire from low-flying airplanes. 2 To bombard or shell heavily. 3 *Slang* To punish. [<G *strafen* punish] —**straf′er** *n.*

**strag·gle** (strag′əl) *v.i.* **·gled**, **·gling** 1 To wander from the road, main body, etc.; stray. 2 To wander aimlessly about; ramble. 3 To occur at irregular intervals. [ME *straglen*] —**strag′gler** *n.* —**strag′gling·ly** *adv.* —**strag′gly** *adj.* (**·i·er**, **·i·est**)

**straight** (strāt) *adj.* 1 Extending uniformly in the same direction without curve or bend. 2 Free from kinks; not curly, as hair. 3 Not stooped; erect. 4 Not deviating from truth, fairness, or honesty. 5 Free from obstruction; uninterrupted. 6 Correctly ordered or arranged. 7 Sold without discount for number or quantity taken. 8 *Informal* Accepting the whole, as of a plan, party, or policy: a *straight* ticket. 9 In poker, consisting of five cards forming a sequence. 10 Having nothing added: *straight* whiskey. 11 *Slang* Conforming to what is accepted as usual, normal, or conventional, esp. according to middle-class standards. 12 *Slang* HETEROSEXUAL. —*n.* 1 A straight part or piece. 2 The part of a racecourse between the winning post and the last turn. 3 In poker, a numerical sequence of five cards. 4 *Slang* A conventional person. 5 *Slang* HETEROSEXUAL. —*adv.* 1 In a straight line or a direct course. 2 Closely in line; correspondingly. 3 At once: Go *straight* to bed. 4 Uprightly: to live *straight*. 5 Correctly: I can't think *straight*. 6 Without restriction or qualification: Tell it *straight*. —**go straight** To reform after hav-

ing led the life of a criminal. —**straight away** or **off** At once; right away. [<OE *streht*, pp. of *streccan* stretch] —**straight′ness** *n.*

**straight·en** (strāt′n) *v.t.* 1 To make straight. —*v.i.* 2 To become straight. —**straighten out** To restore order to; rectify. —**straighten up** 1 To make neat; tidy. 2 To stand in erect posture. 3 To reform. —**straight′en·er** *n.*

**strain** (strān) *v.t.* 1 To pull or draw tight. 2 To exert to the utmost. 3 To injure by overexertion; sprain. 4 To deform in structure or shape as a result of stress. 5 To stretch beyond the true intent, proper limit, etc.: to *strain* a point. 6 To embrace tightly; hug. 7 To pass through a strainer. 8 To remove by filtration. —*v.i.* 9 To make violent efforts; strive. 10 To be or become wrenched or twisted. 13 To filter, trickle, or percolate. —**strain at** 1 To push or pull with violent efforts. 2 To strive for. 3 To scruple or balk at accepting. —*n.* 1 An act of straining or the state of being strained. 2 Any very taxing demand on strength, emotions, etc.: the *strain* of city life. 3 Any violent effort or exertion. 4 The injury resulting from excessive tension or effort. 5 *Physics* The change of shape or structure of a body produced by the action of a stress. [< L *stringere* bind tight]

**strait** (strāt) *n.* 1 *Often pl.* A narrow passage of water connecting two larger bodies of water. 2 Any narrow pass or passage. 3 *Often pl.* Distress; embarrassment: financial *straits*. —*adj. Archaic* 1 Narrow. 2 Strict. [<L *strictus*, p.p. of *stringere* bind tight.] —**strait′ly** *adv.* —**strait′ness** *n.*

**strand**[1] (strand) *n.* A shore or beach, esp. on the ocean. —*v.t.* & *v.i.* 1 To drive or run aground, as a ship. 2 To leave or be left in difficulties or helplessness: *stranded* in a strange city. [<OE]

**strand**[2] (strand) *n.* 1 Any of the fibers, wires, or threads twisted or plaited together to form a rope, cable, cord, etc. 2 A single hair or similar filament. 3 Any of various rope-like objects: a *strand* of pearls. —*v.t.* To break a strand of (a rope). [ME *strond*]

**strange** (strānj) *adj.* **strang·er**, **strang·est** 1 Previously unknown, unseen, or unheard of. 2 Peculiar; out of the ordinary: a *strange* experience. 3 Foreign; alien. 4 Out of place: to feel *strange* in a new school. 5 Inexperienced: *strange* to a new job. [<L *extraneus* foreign] —**strange′ly** *adv.* —**strange′ness** *n.* —**Syn.** 1 unfamiliar. 2 odd, queer, unusual. 4 unaccustomed.

**stran·ger** (strān′jər) *n.* 1 One who is not an acquaintance. 2 An unfamiliar visitor; guest. 3 A foreigner. 4 One unacquainted with something specified: with *to:* a *stranger* to higher mathematics.

**stran·gle** (strang′gəl) *v.* ·gled, ·gling *v.t.* 1 To choke to death; throttle. 2 To repress; suppress. —*v.i.* 3 To suffer or die from strangulation. [<Gk. *strangalaein*] —**stran′gler** *n.*

**stran·gu·late** (strang′gyə·lāt) *v.t.* ·lat·ed, ·lat·ing 1 STRANGLE. 2 *Pathol.* To constrict so as to cut off circulation of the blood. [<L *strangulare*] —**stran′gu·la′tion** *n.*

**strap** (strap) *n.* 1 A long, narrow, and flexible strip of leather, webbing, etc., for binding or fastening things together. 2 A razor strop. 3 Something used as a strap: a shoulder *strap.* —*v.t.* **strapped, strap·ing** 1 To fasten or bind with a strap. 2 To beat with a strap. 3 To sharpen or strop. 4 To embarrass financially. [Var. of STROP]

**strat·a·gem** (strat′ə·jəm) *n.* 1 A maneuver designed to deceive or outwit an enemy. 2 Any device or trick for obtaining advantage. [<Gk. *stratēgēma* piece of generalship] —**Syn.** 2 artifice, deception, ruse, trick.

**strat·e·gist** (strat′ə·jist) *n.* One skilled in strategy.

**strat·e·gy** (strat′ə·jē) *n. pl.* ·gies 1 The science of planning and conducting military campaigns on a broad scale. 2 Any plan based on this. 3 The use of stratagem or artifice, as in business, politics, etc. 4 Skill in management. 5 An ingenious plan or method. [<Gk. *stratēgos* general]

**strat·o·sphere** (strat′ə·sfir) *n. Meteorol.* The portion of the atmosphere beginning at about six miles above the earth, where a more or less uniform temperature prevails. —**strat′o·spher′ic** (-sfer′ik) or ·i·cal *adj.*

**stra·tum** (strā′təm, strat′əm) *n. pl.* ·ta (-tə) or ·tums 1 A natural or artificial layer. 2 *Geol.* A more or less homogeneous layer of rock. 3 A level of society, having similar educational, cultural, and usu. economic backgrounds. [<L *stratus,* p.p. of *sternere* to spread]

**straw** (strô) *n.* 1 A dry stalk of grain. 2 Stems or stalks of grain after being threshed, used for fodder, etc. 3 A mere trifle. 4 A slender tube made of paper, glass, etc., used to suck up a beverage. —**catch (or grab) at a straw** To try anything as a last resort. —**straw in the wind** A sign of the course of future events. —*adj.* 1 Made of or like straw,

as in color. 2 Worthless; sham. [<OE *strēaw* straw]

**straw·ber·ry** (strô′ber′ē, -bər·ē) *n. pl.* ·ries 1 Any of a genus of stemless perennials of the rose family, with trifoliolate leaves, usu. white flowers and slender runners by which it propagates: **also strawberry vine.** 2 Its edible fruit, consisting of a red, fleshy receptacle bearing many achenes. [<STRAW + BERRY]

**stray** (strā) *v.i.* 1 To wander from the proper course; roam. 2 To deviate from right or goodness; go astray. —*adj.* 1 Having strayed; straying: a *stray* dog. 2 Irregular; occasional: He made a few *stray* remarks. —*n.* A domestic animal that has strayed. [<L *extra vagare* wander outside] —**stray′er** *n.*

**streak** (strēk) *n.* 1 A long, narrow mark or stripe: a *streak* of lightning. 2 A trace or characteristic: a *streak* of meanness. 3 A layer or strip: meat with a *streak* of fat and a *streak* of lean. 4 *Informal* A period or interval: a winning *streak.* 5 *Slang* The act or an instance of streaking (*v.* def. 3). —**like a streak** *Informal* As rapidly as possible. —*v.i.* 1 To form a streak or streaks. 2 To move at great speed. 3 *Slang* To appear naked in a public place, usu. briefly and esp. while running, as for a thrill. —*v.t.* 4 To form streaks in or on. 5 *Slang* To appear naked in (a public place), usu. briefly and esp. while running, as for a thrill. [<OE *strica*] —**streak′y** *adj.* (·i·er, ·i·est) —**streak′i·ly** *adv.* —**streak′er, streak′i·ness** *n.*

**stream** (strēm) *n.* 1 A current or flow of water, esp. a small river. 2 Any continuous flow or current: a *stream* of invective. —*v.i.* 1 To pour forth or issue in a stream. 2 To pour forth in a stream: eyes *streaming* with tears. 3 To proceed uninterruptedly, as a crowd. 4 To float with a waving movement, as a flag. 5 To move with a trail of light, as a meteor. 6 To come or arrive in large numbers. [<OE *strēam*] —**Syn.** *n.* 1 A brook, course, creek, rill, rivulet.

**stream·er** (strē′mər) *n.* 1 An object that streams forth, or hangs extended. 2 A long, narrow flag or standard. 3 A stream or shaft of light. 4 A newspaper headline that runs across the whole page.

**stream·line** (strēm′līn′) *n.* 1 A line in a mass of fluid such that each of its tangents coincides with the local velocity of the fluid. 2 Any shape or contour designed to lessen resistance to motion of a solid in a fluid. — *adj.* 1 Designating an uninterrupted flow or drift. 2 Denoting a form or body designed to minimize turbulence in the flow of fluid around it. —*v.t.* ·lined, ·lin·ing 1 To design with a streamline shape. 2 To make more up-to-date, esp. by reorganization.

**stream·lined** (strēm′līnd′) *adj.* 1 STREAMLINE. 2 Improved in efficiency; modernized.

**street** (strēt) *n.* 1 A public way in a city, town, or village. usu. with buildings on one or both sides. 2 Such a public way as set apart for vehicles: Don't play in the *street.* 3 *Informal* The people living on a specific street. —*adj.* 1 Working in the streets: a *street* musician. 2 Opening onto the street: a *street* door. 3 Performed or taking place on the street: *street* crime. 4 Habituated to the ways of life in the streets, esp. in cities: *street* people. [<LL *strata (via)* paved (road)]

**strength** (strength) *n.* 1 The quality or property of being physically strong: the *strength* of a weight lifter. 2 The capacity to sustain the application of force without yielding or breaking. 3 Effectiveness: the *strength* of an argument. 4 Binding force or validity, as of a law. 5 Vigor or force of style: a drama of great *strength.* 6 Available numerical force in a military unit or other organization. 7 Degree of intensity, as of color, light, or sound. 8 Potency, as of a drug, chemical, or liquor; concentration. 9 A support; aid: He is our *strength.* —**on the strength of** Relying on, on the basis of. [<OE *strang* strong] —**Syn.** 1 force, power, vigor. 2 solidity, tenacity, toughness.

**strength·en** (streng′thən) *v.t.* 1 To make strong. 2 To encourage; hearten. —*v.i.* 3 To become or grow strong or stronger. — **strength′en·er** *n.*

**stren·u·ous** (stren′yōō-əs) *adj.* Necessitating or marked by strong effort or exertion. [<L *strenuus*] —**stren′u·ous·ly** *adv.* —**stren′u·ous·ness** *n.*

**strep·to·my·cin** (strep′tō·mī′sin) *n.* A potent antibiotic isolated from a mold. [<Gk. *streptos* twisted + *mykēs* fungus]

**stress** (stres) *n.* 1 Special weight, importance, or significance. 2 Physical or emotional tension. 3 *Mech.* A force tending to deform a body on which it acts. 4 Emphasis. 5 In pronunciation, the relative force with which a sound, syllable, or word is uttered. —*v.t.* 1 To subject to stress. 2 To accent, as a syllable. 3 To give emphasis or weight to.

[<L *strictus,* p.p. of *stringere* draw tight] — **stress′ful** *adj.*

**stretch** (strech) *v.t.* 1 To extend or draw out, as to full length or width. 2 To draw out forcibly, esp. beyond normal or proper limits. 3 To cause to reach, as from one place to another. 4 To put forth, hold out, or extend (the hand, an object, etc.). 5 To tighten, strain, or exert to the utmost: to *stretch* every nerve. 6 To adjust or adapt to meet specific needs, circumstances, etc.: to *stretch* the truth; to *stretch* food. 7 *Slang* To fell with a blow. —*v.i.* 8 To reach or extend from one place to another. 9 To become extended, esp. beyond normal limits. 10 To extend one's body or limbs, as in relaxing. 11 To lie down: usu. with *out.* —*n.* 1 An act of stretching, or the state of being stretched. 2 Extent to which something can be stretched. 3 A continuous extent of space or time: a *stretch* of woodland; a *stretch* of two years. 4 In racing, the straight part of the track. 5 *Slang* A term of imprisonment. —*adj.* Capable of being easily stretched; as clothing: *stretch* socks. [<OE *streccan* stretch] —**stretch′i·ness** *n.* — **stretch′y** *adj.*

**stretch·er** (strech′ər) *n.* 1 Any device for stretching; a shoe *stretcher.* 2 A portable, often webbed frame for carrying the injured, sick, or dead.

**strew** (strōō) *v.t.* strewed, strewed or strewn, strew·ing 1 To spread about at random; sprinkle. 2 To cover with something scattered or sprinkled. 3 To be scattered over (a surface). [<OE *strēawian*]

**strict** (strikt) *adj.* 1 Observing or enforcing rules exactly: a *strict* church. 2 Containing severe rules or provisions; exacting. 3 Harsh; stern: a *strict* teacher. 4 Exactly defined or applied: the *strict* truth. 5 Devout; orthodox: a *strict* Catholic. 6 Absolute: in *strict* confidence. [<L *strictus,* p.p. of *stringere* draw tight] —**strict′ly** *adv.* —**strict′ness** *n.*

**stric·ture** (strik′chər) *n.* 1 Severe criticism. 2 Something that checks or restricts. 3 Closure or narrowing of a duct or passage of the body. [<L *strictus* strict]

**stride** (strīd) *n.* 1 A long and measured step. 2 The space passed over by such a step. — **hit one's stride** To attain one's normal speed. —**make rapid strides** To make quick progress. —**take (something) in one's stride** To do or accept (something) without undue effort or without becoming upset. —

*v.* **strode, strid·den, strid·ing** *v.i.* 1 To walk with long steps, as from haste. —*v.t.* 2 To walk through, along, etc., with long steps. 3 To pass over with a single stride. 4 To straddle; bestride. [<OE *stridan* to stride] — **strid′er** *n.*

**stri·dent** (strīd′nt) *adj.* Having a loud and harsh sound; grating. [<L *stridere* to creak] —**stri′dence, stri′den·cy** *n.* —**stri′dent·ly** *adv.*

**strife** (strīf) *n.* 1 Angry contention; fighting. 2 Any contest or rivalry. 3 The act of striving; strenuous endeavor. [< OF *estriver* strive]

**strike** (strīk) *v.* **struck, struck** (*chiefly Archaic* **strick·en**), **strik·ing** *v.t.* 1 To hit with a blow; deal a blow to. 2 To crash into: The car *struck* the wall. 3 To deal (a blow, etc.). 4 To cause to hit forcibly: He *struck* his hand on the table. 5 To attack; assault. 6 To ignite (a match, etc.) 7 To form by stamping, printing, etc. 8 To announce; sound: The clock *struck* two. 9 To reach: A sound *struck* his ear. 10 To affect suddenly or in a specified manner: He was *struck* speechless. 11 To occur to: An idea *strikes* me. 12 To impress in a specified manner. 13 To attract the attention of: The dress *struck* her fancy. 14 To assume: to *strike* an attitude. 15 To cause to enter deeply or suddenly: to *strike* dismay into one's heart. 16 To lower or haul down, as a sail or a flag. 17 To cease working at in order to compel compliance to a demand, etc. 18 To make and confirm, as a bargain. —*v.i.* 19 To come into violent contact; crash; hit. 20 To deal or aim a blow or blows. 21 To make an assault or attack. 22 To sound from a blow or blows. 23 To be indicated by the sound of blows or strokes: Noon has just *struck.* 24 To ignite. 25 To lower a flag in token of surrender. 26 To take a course; start and proceed: to *strike* for home. 27 To cease work in order to enforce demands, etc. 28 To snatch at or swallow the lure: said of fish. —**strike camp** To take down the tents of a camp. —**strike down** 1 To fell with a blow. 2 To incapacitate completely. —**strike dumb** To astonish; amaze. —**strike home** 1 To deal an effective blow. 2 To have telling effect. —**strike it rich** 1 To find a valuable pocket of ore. 2 To come into wealth or good fortune. —**strike off** 1 To remove or take off by or as by a blow or stroke. 2 To deduct. —**strike oil** 1 To find oil while drilling. 2 *Slang* To meet with unexpected good fortune. —**strike out** 1 To aim a blow or blows.

2 To cross out or erase. 3 To begin; start. 4 In baseball, to put out (the batter) by pitching three strikes. —**strike up** 1 To begin to play, as a band. 2 To start up; begin, as a friendship. —*n.* 1 An act of striking. 2 In baseball, an unsuccessful attempt by the batter to hit the ball. 3 In bowling, the knocking down of all the pins with the first bowl. 4 The quitting of work by a body of workers to secure some demand from management. 5 A new discovery, as of oil or ore. 6 Any unexpected or complete success. 7 The sudden rise and taking of the bait by a fish. —**on strike** Refusing to work in order to secure higher pay, better working conditions, etc. [<OE *strican* stroke, move]

**string** (string) *n.* 1 A slender line, thinner than a cord and thicker than a thread, used for tying parcels, lacing, etc. 2 A cord of catgut, nylon, wire, etc., for musical instruments, bows, tennis rackets, etc. 3 A stringlike formation, as of certain vegetables. 4 A series of things hung on a small cord: a *string* of pearls. 5 A connected series or succession, as of things, acts, or events. 6 A drove or small collection of stock, esp. of saddle horses. 7 *pl.* Stringed instruments, esp., the section of violins, cellos, etc., in a symphony orchestra. 8 In sports, a group of contestants ranked as to skill. 9 *Informal Often pl.* A condition or restriction attached to an offer or gift. —**on a string** Under control or domination. —**pull strings** 1 To control the actions of others, usu. secretly. 2 To influence others to gain an advantage. —*v.* **strung, string·ing** *v.t.* 1 To thread, as beads, on or as on a string. 2 To fit with a string or strings, as a guitar or bow. 3 To bind, fasten, or adorn with a string or strings. 4 To tune the strings of (a musical instrument). 5 To brace; strengthen. 6 To make tense or nervous. 7 To arrange or extend like a string. 8 To remove the strings from (vegetables). —*v.i.* 9 To extend or proceed in a line or series. 10 To form into strings. —**string along** *Slang* 1 To cooperate with. 2 To deceive; cheat. 3 To keep (someone) on tenterhooks. —**string out** *Informal* To protract; prolong: to *string out* an investigation. —**string up** *Informal* To hang. [<OE *streng* string]

**strin·gent** (strin′jənt) *adj.* 1 Rigid; severe, as regulations. 2 Hampered by scarcity of money: said of a market. 3 Convincing; forcible. [<L *stringens,* pr.p of *stringere* draw

tight] —**strin′gen·cy, strin′gent·ness** *n.* —**strin′gent·ly** *adv.*

**strip** (strip) *n.* 1 A narrow piece, comparatively long, as of cloth, wood, etc. 2 A number of stamps attached in a row. 3 A narrow piece of land used as a runway for airplanes. 4 A comic strip. [?]

**stripe** (strīp) *n.* 1 A blow struck with a whip or rod. 2 A weal or welt on the skin caused by such a blow. [Prob. <LG]

**strip·ling** (strip′ling) *n.* A mere youth; a lad. [?]

**strip·tease** (strip′tēz′) *n.* An act, usu. in burlesque, in which a female performer gradually disrobes before an audience. —**strip′teas′er** *n.*

**strive** (strīv) *v.i.* **strove, striv·en** (striv′ən) or **strived, striv·ing** 1 To make earnest effort. 2 To engage in strife; fight; to *strive* against an enemy. [<OF *estriver*] —**striv′er** *n.* — Syn. 1 endeavor, try. 2 contend, struggle.

**strob·o·scope** (strōb′ə·skōp) *n.* An instrument for studying the motion of an object by making the object appear to be stationary, as by periodic instantaneous illumination or observation. [<Gk. *strobos* twirling + -SCOPE] —**strob′o·scop′ic** (-skop′ik) or **·i·cal** *adj.* —**strob·os·co·py** (strō·bos′kə·pē) *n.*

**stroke** (strōk) *n.* 1 The act or movement of striking. 2 One of a series of recurring movements, as of oars, arms in swimming, a piston, etc. 3 A rower who sets the pace for the rest of the crew. 4 A single movement of a pen or pencil. 5 A mark made by such a movement. 6 Any ill effect: a *stroke* of misfortune. 7 APOPLEXY. 8 A sound of a striking mechanism, as of a clock. 9 A sudden or brilliant mental act: a *stroke* of wit. 10 A light caressing movement; a stroking. —**keep stroke** To make strokes simultaneously, as oarsmen. —*v.t.* **stroked, strok·ing** 1 To pass the hand over gently or caressingly. 2 To set the pace for (a rowboat or its crew). [<OE *strācian* strike] —**strok′er** *n.*

**stroll** (strōl) *v.i.* 1 To walk in a leisurely manner; saunter. 2 To go from place to place. — *n.* A leisurely walk. [?]

**strong** (strông, strong) *adj.* 1 Physically powerful; muscular. 2 Healthy; robust: a *strong* constitution. 3 Resolute; courageous. 4 Mentally powerful or vigorous. 5 Especially competent or able: *strong* in mathematics. 6 Abundantly supplied: *strong* in trumps. 7 Solidly made or constituted: *strong* walls. 8 Powerful, as a rival or combatant. 9 Easy

to defend: a *strong* position. 10 In numerical force: an army 20,000 *strong.* 11 Well able to exert influence, authority, etc. 12 Financially sound: a *strong* market. 13 Powerful in effect: *strong* poison. 14 Not diluted or weak: *strong* coffee. 15 Containing much alcohol: a *strong* drink. 16 Powerful in flavor or odor: a *strong* breath. 17 Intense in degree or quality: a *strong* light. 18 Loud and firm: a *strong* voice. 19 Firm; tenacious: a *strong* will. 20 Fervid: a *strong* desire. 21 Cogent; convincing: *strong* evidence. 22 Distinct; marked: a *strong* resemblance. 23 Extreme: *strong* measures. 24 Emphatic: *strong* language. 25 Moving with great force: said of a wind, stream, or tide. 26 *Phonet.* Stressed. 27 *Gram.* Of verbs, indicating changes in tense by means of vowel changes, rather than by inflectional endings, as *drink, drank, drunk.* —*adv.* In a firm, vigorous manner. [<OE] —**strong′ly** *adv.* —**strong′ness** *n.*

**strong-arm** (strông′ärm′, strong′-) *Informal adj.* Using physical or coercive power: *strong-arm* tactics. —*v.t.* 1 To use physical force upon; assault. 2 To coerce; compel.

**stron·ti·um** (stron′chē·əm, -chəm, -tē·əm) *n.* A metallic element (symbol Sr) chemically resembling calcium, used in pyrotechnics. [<*Strontian,* Argyll, Scotland, where first discovered] —**stron′tic** (-tik) *adj.*

**strop** (strop) *n.* A strip of leather on which to sharpen a razor. —*v.t.* **stropped, strop·ping** To sharpen on a strop. [<Gk. *strophos* band]

**struc·ture** (struk′chər) *n.* 1 That which is constructed, as a building. 2 Something based upon or organized according to a plan or design: the political *structure* of a republic. 3 The manner of such organization: a hierarchical *structure.* 4 The arrangement and relationship of the parts of a whole, as organs in a plant or animal, atoms in a molecule, etc. —*v.t.* **·tured, ·tur·ing** 1 To form or organize into a structure; build. 2 To conceive as a structural whole. [<L *structus,* p.p. of *struere* build]

**strug·gle** (strug′əl) *n.* 1 A violent effort or series of efforts. 2 A war; battle. —*v.i.* **·gled, ·gling** 1 To contend with an adversary in physical combat; fight. 2 To strive: to *struggle* against odds. 3 To make one's way by violent efforts: to *struggle* through mud. [ME *strogelen*] —**strug′gler** *n.* —**strug′gling·ly** *adv.*

**strum** (strum) *v.t. & v.i.* **strummed, strum·**

**ming** To play idly or carelessly (on a stringed instrument). —*n.* The act of strumming. [Prob. Imit.] —**strum′mer** *n.*

**strut** (strut) *n.* 1 A proud or pompous step or walk. 2 A supporting piece in a framework, keeping two others from approaching nearer together. —*v.* **strut·ted, strut·ting** *v.t.* 1 To walk pompously and affectedly. — *v.t.* 2 To brace or support with a brace or strut. [<OE *strūtian* be rigid, stand stiffly] —**strut′ter** *n.* —**strut′ting·ly** *adv.*

**strych·nine** (strik′nīn, -nən, -nēn) *n.* A poisonous alkaloid obtained from nux vomica, used in medicine as a stimulant. Also **strych′ni·a** (-nē-ə) [<Gk. *strychnos* nightshade] —**strych′nic** *adj.*

**stub** (stub) *n.* 1 Any short remnant, as of a pencil, candle, cigarette, cigar, or broken tooth. 2 In a checkbook, the short piece on which the amount of a check is recorded and that remains when the check is detached. 3 A tree stump. —*v.t.* **stubbed, stub·bing** 1 To strike, as the toe, against a low obstruction or projection. 2 To clear or remove the stubs or roots from. [<OE *stubb*] —**stub′ber** *n.*

**stub·born** (stub′ərn) *adj.* 1 Inflexible in opinion or intention. 2 Determined to have one's own way. 3 Not easily handled, bent, or overcome. 4 Characterized by perseverance or persistence: *stubborn* fighting. [ME *stoborne*] —**stub′born·ly** *adv.* —**stub′ born·ness** *n.* —**Syn.** 1 opinionated, unyielding. 2 headstrong, obdurate, obstinate.

**stuc·co** (stuk′ō) *n. pl.* **·coes** or **·cos** 1 Any plaster or cement used for the external coating of buildings. 2 Work done in stucco: also **stuc′co·work′.** —*v.t.* **·coed, ·co·ing** To apply stucco to; decorate with stucco. [Ital.] —**stuc′co·er** *n.*

**stud** (stud) *n.* 1 A collection of horses and mares for breeding, riding, hunting, or racing. 2 The place where they are kept. 3 A stallion. —**at stud** Available for breeding purposes: said of male animals. —*adj.* Of or pertaining to a stud. [<OE *stōd*]

**stu·dent** (st′ōōd′nt, -ənt) *n.* 1 A person engaged in a course of study, esp. in an educational institution. 2 One who closely examines or investigates. [<L *studere* be eager, apply oneself, study]

**stu·di·o** (st′ōō′dē·ō) *n. pl.* **·di·os** 1 The workroom of an artist, photographer, etc. 2 A place where motion pictures are filmed. 3 A room or rooms where radio or television programs are broadcast or recorded. 4 A

room or place in which music is recorded. [<L *studere* apply oneself, be diligent]

**stu·di·ous** (st′ōō′dē·əs) *adj.* 1 Given to or fond of study. 2 Considerate; careful; attentive. —**stu′di·ous·ly** *adv.* —**stu′di·ous·ness** *n.*

**stuff** (stuf) *v.t.* 1 To fill completely; pack. 2 To plug. 3 To obstruct or stop up. 4 To fill with padding, as a cushion. 5 To fill (a fowl, roast, etc.) with stuffing. 6 In taxidermy, to fill the skin of (a bird, animal, etc.) with a material preparatory to mounting. 7 To fill too full: cram: He *stuffed* himself with cake. 8 To fill with knowledge, ideas, or attitudes, esp. unsystematically. —*v.i.* 9 To eat to excess. —*n.* 1 The material or matter out of which something is or may be shaped or made. 2 The fundamental element of anything: the *stuff* of genius. 3 *Informal* A specific skill, field of knowledge, etc.: That editor knows her *stuff*. 4 Personal possessions generally. 5 Unspecified material, matter, etc.: They carried away tons of the *stuff*. 6 A miscellaneous collection of things. 7 Nonsense; foolishness. 8 Woven material, esp. of wool. 9 Any textile fabric. [<OF *estoffer* cram] —**stuff′er** *n.*

**stuff·y** (stuf′ē) *adj.* **stuff·i·er, stuff·i·est** 1 Badly ventilated. 2 Filled up so as to impede respiration: a *stuffy* nose. 3 Dull; uninspired: a *stuffy* speech. 4 Strait-laced; stodgy. —**stuff′i·ly** *adv.* —**stuff′i·ness** *n.*

**stum·ble** (stum′bəl) *v.* **·bled, ·bling** *v.i.* 1 To miss one's step in walking or running; trip. 2 To speak or act in a blundering manner: The student *stumbled* through his recitation. 3 To happen upon something by chance: with *across, on, upon*, etc. 4 To do wrong; err. —*v.t.* 5 To cause to stumble. — *n.* The act of stumbling. [ME *stumblen*] —**stum′bler** *n.* —**stum′bling·ly** *adv.*

**stump** (stump) *n.* 1 That portion of the trunk of a tree left standing when the tree is felled. 2 The part of a limb, etc., that remains when the main part has been removed. 3 *pl. Informal* The legs. 4 A place or platform where a political speech is made. 5 A short, thick-set person or animal. 6 A heavy step; a clump. —**take the stump** To electioneer in a political campaign. —**up a stump** In trouble or in a dilemma. —*adj.* 1 Being or resembling a stump. 2 Of or pertaining to political oratory or campaigning: a *stump* speaker. —*v.t.* 1 To reduce to a stump; lop. 2 To remove stumps from (land). 3 To canvass (a district) by making political speeches. 4 *Informal* To bring to a halt by real or fancied obstacles. 5 To stub, as one's toe. —*v.i.* 6 To walk heavily. [<MLG] —**stump′i·ness** *n.* —**stump′y** *adj.*

**stun** (stun) *v.t.* **stunned, stun·ning** 1 To render unconscious or incapable of action. 2 To astonish; astound. 3 To daze or overwhelm. —*n.* The act of stunning or the condition of being stunned. [<OF *estoner*]

**stunt** (stunt) *v.t.* To check the natural development of; dwarf; cramp. —*n.* 1 A check in growth, progress, or development. 2 A stunted animal or person. [<OE, dull, foolish] —**stunt′ed·ness** *n.*

**stu·pe·fac·tion** (stоо̄′pə·fak′shən) *n.* The act of stupefying or state of being stupefied.

**stu·pe·fy** (stоо̄′pə·fī′) *v.t.* **·fied, ·fy·ing** 1 To dull the senses or faculties of; stun. 2 To amaze; astound. [<L *stupere* be stunned + *-FY*] —**stu′pe·fi′er** *n.*

**stu·pen·dous** (stоо̄·pen′dəs) *adj.* 1 Of prodigious size, bulk, or degree. 2 Astonishing; marvelous. [<L *stupere* be stunned] —**stu·pen′dous·ly** *adv.* —**stu·pen′dous·ness** *n.*

**stu·pid** (stоо̄′pid) *adj.* 1 Very slow in understanding; lacking in intelligence; dull-witted. 2 Affected with stupor; stupefied. 3 Dull and profitless; tiresome: to regard rote learning as *stupid.* 4 Resulting from slowness in understanding or a lack of intelligence. 5 *Informal* Annoying; bothersome: This *stupid* nail won't go in straight. [< L *stupidus* struck dumb] —**stu·pid′i·ty** (stоо̄·pid′ə·tē) (*pl.* **·ties**), **stu′pid·ness** *n.* —**stu′pid·ly** *adv.*

**stu·por** (stоо̄′pər) *n.* 1 Abnormal lethargy due to shock, drugs, etc. 2 Extreme intellectual dullness. [<L *stupere* be stunned] —**stu′por·ous** *adj.*

**stur·dy** (stûr′dē) *adj.* **·di·er, ·di·est** 1 Possessing rugged health and strength. 2 Firm and resolute: a *sturdy* defense. [<OF *estourdir* stun, amaze] —**stur′di·ly** *adv.* —**stur′di·ness** *n.* —**Syn.** 1 hardy, lusty, robust, vigorous. 2 determined, unyielding.

**stur·geon** (stûr′jən) *n.* Any of various large edible fishes of northern regions, valued as the source of caviar. [<Med. L *sturio*]

**stut·ter** (stut′ər) *v.t.* & *v.i.* To utter or speak with spasmodic repetition, blocking, and prolongation of sounds and syllables. —*n.* The act or habit of stuttering. [Freq. of ME *stutten* stutter] —**stut′ter·er** *n.* —**stut′ter·ing·ly** *adv.*

**sty¹** (stī) *n. pl.* **sties** 1 A pen for swine. 2 Any filthy habitation. [<OE *sti, stig*]

**sty²** (stī) *n. pl.* **sties** A pustule on the edge of an eyelid. **Also stye.** [<OE *stigan* rise + *ye* eye]

**style** (stīl) *n.* 1 A fashionable manner or appearance: to be in *style.* 2 Fashion: the latest *style* in shirts. 3 A particular fashion in clothing. 4 A distinctive form of expression: a florid *style.* 5 An effective way of expression: His drawings have *style.* 6 Manner: a church in the Romanesque *style* of architecture. 7 A way of living or behaving: Domestic life is not his *style.* 8 A pointed instrument for marking or engraving. 9 An indicator on a dial. 10 *Printing* The typography, spelling, design, etc., used in a given published text. 11 *Bot.* The slender part of a carpel between stigma and ovary. 12 A system of arranging the calendar years so as to average that of the true solar year. Our calendar, adopted in 1752, is called **New Style**, while **Old Style** dates are 13 days earlier. —*v.t.* **styled, styl·ing** 1 To name; give a title to: Richard I was *styled* "the Lion-Hearted." 2 To cause to conform to a specific style: to *style* a manuscript. [<L *stylus* writing instrument] —**styl′er** *n.*

**styl·ish** (stī′lish) *adj.* 1 Having style. 2 Very fashionable. —**styl′ish·ly** *adv.* —**styl′ish·ness** *n.*

**sty·lus** (stī′ləs) *n. pl.* **·lus·es or ·li** (lī) 1 An ancient instrument for writing on wax tablets. 2 A tiny, usu. jewel-tipped needle whose vibrations in tracing the groove in a phonograph record transmit sound. [L]

**suave** (swäv) *adj.* Smooth and pleasant in manner, often superficially so. [<L *suavis* sweet] —**suave′ly** *adv.* —**suave′ness, suav′i·ty** (*pl.* **·ties**) *n.*

**sub·con·scious** (sub·kon′shəs) *adj.* 1 Only dimly conscious; not fully aware. 2 Not attended by full awareness, as an automatic action. —*n.* That portion of mental activity not in the focus of consciousness. —**sub·con′scious·ly** *adv.* —**sub·con′scious·ness** *n.*

**sub·di·vide** (sub′di·vīd′, sub′di·vīd′) *v.t.* & *v.i.* **·vid·ed, ·vid·ing** 1 To divide again. 2 To divide (land) into lots for sale or improvement.

**sub·di·vi·sion** (sub′di·vizh′ən, sub′di·vizh′ən) *n.* 1 Division following upon division. 2 A part, as of land, resulting from subdividing.

**sub·due** (sub·d<sup>y</sup>o͞o′) *v.t.* ·dued, ·du·ing 1 To gain dominion over, as by war or force. 2 To overcome by training, influence, or persuasion. 3 To repress (emotions, impulses, etc.). 4 To reduce the intensity of. [< L *subducere* lead away] —**sub·du′ed·ly** *adv.* —**sub·du′er** *n.* —**Syn.** 1 conquer, subjugate, vanquish. 2 master, tame. 4 lessen, soften.

**sub·ject** (sub′jikt) *adj.* 1 Being under the power of another. 2 Exposed: *subject* to criticism. 3 Having a tendency: *subject* to colds. 4 Conditional upon: *subject* to your consent. —*n.* 1 One who is under the governing power of another, as of a ruler. • See CITIZEN. 2 One who or that which is employed or treated in a specified way, as in an experiment. 3 The theme or topic of a discussion. 4 Something described or depicted in a literary or artistic work. 5 *Gram.* The word, phrase, or clause of a sentence about which something is stated or asked in the predicate. 6 *Music* The melodic phrase on which a composition or a part of it is based. 7 A branch of learning. —*v.t.* (sab·jekt′) 1 To bring under dominion or control; subjugate. 2 To cause to undergo some experience or action. 3 To make liable; expose: His inheritance was *subjected* to heavy taxation. [< L *sub-* under + *jacere* throw] —**sub·jec′tion** *n.*

**sub·or·di·nate** (sa·bôr′da·nit) *adj.* 1 Secondary; minor. 2 Lower in rank. 3 Subject or subservient to another. 4 *Gram.* Used within a sentence as a noun, adjective, or adverb: said of a clause. —*n.* One who or that which is subordinate. —*v.t.* (-nāt) ·nat·ed, ·nat·ing 1 To assign to a lower order or rank. 2 To make subject or subservient. [< L *sub-* under + *ordinare* to order] —**sub·or′di·nate·ly** *adv.* —**sub·or′di·nate·ness, sub·or′di·na′tion** *n.*

**sub·orn** (sa·bôrn′) *v.t.* 1 To bribe (someone) to commit perjury. 2 To incite or instigate to an evil act. [< L *sub-* secretly + *ornare* equip] —**sub·orn′er, sub·or·na·tion** (sub′ôr·nā′shan) *n.*

**sub·poe·na** (sa·pē′na) *n.* A writ requiring a person to appear at court at a specified time and place. —*v.t.* ·naed, ·na·ing To summon by subpoena. **Also sub·pe′na.** [< L *sub-* under + *poena* penalty]

**sub·scribe** (sab·skrīb′) *v.* ·scribed, ·scrib·ing *v.t.* 1 To write, as one's name, at the end of a document; sign. 2 To sign one's name to as an expression of assent. 3 To promise, esp. in writing, to pay or contribute (a sum of money). —*v.i.* 4 To write one's name at the end of a document. 5 To give approval; agree. 6 To promise to contribute money. 7 To pay in advance for a series of periodicals, tickets to performances, etc. with *to*. [< L *sub-* under + *scribere* write] —**sub·scrib′er** *n.*

**sub·scrip·tion** (sab·skrip′shan) *n.* 1 The act of subscribing; confirmation or agreement. 2 That which is subscribed; a signed paper or statement. 3 A signature written at the end of a document. 4 The total subscribed for any purpose. 5 The purchase in advance of a series of periodicals, tickets to performances, etc.

**sub·se·quent** (sub′sa·kwant) *adj.* Following in time, place, or order, or as a result. —**subsequent to** Following; after. [< L *sub-* next below + *sequi* follow] —**sub·se·quence** (sub′sa·kwans), **sub′se·quen·cy, sub′se·quent·ness** *n.* —**sub′se·quent·ly** *adv.*

**sub·ser·vi·ent** (sab·sûr′vē·ant) *adj.* 1 Servile; obsequious; truckling. 2 Adapted to promote some end or purpose, esp. in a subordinate capacity. —*n.* One who or that which subserves. —**sub·ser′vi·ent·ly** *adv.* —**sub·ser′vi·ent·ness, sub·ser′vi·ence, sub·ser′vi·en·cy** *n.*

**sub·side** (sab·sīd′) *v.i.* ·sid·ed, ·sid·ing 1 To sink to a lower level. 2 To become calm or quiet; abate. 3 To sink to the bottom, as sediment; settle. [< L *sub-* under + *sidere* to settle] —**sub·sid·ence** (sab·sīd′ns, sub′sa·dans) *n.* —**Syn.** 1 fall. 2 decrease, diminish, ebb, wane.

**sub·sid·i·ar·y** (sab·sid′ē·er′ē, -sid′a·rē) *adj.* 1 Assisting; supplementary; auxiliary. 2 Of, pertaining to, or in the nature of a subsidy. —*n. pl.* ·ar·ies 1 One who or that which furnishes supplemental aid or supplies. 2 A business enterprise with over half of its assets or stock owned by another company. —**sub·sid·i·ar·i·ly** (sab·sid′ē·er′a·lē) *adv.*

**sub·si·dize** (sub′sa·dīz) *v.t.* ·dized, ·diz·ing 1 To grant a regular allowance or financial aid to. 2 To obtain the assistance of by a subsidy. *Brit. sp.* **sub′si·dise.** —**sub′si·di·za′tion, sub′si·diz′er** *n.*

**sub·si·dy** (sub′sa·dē) *n. pl.* ·dies 1 Financial aid directly granted by government to a person or commercial enterprise whose work is deemed beneficial to the public. 2 Any financial assistance granted by one government to another. [< L *subsidium* auxiliary forces, aid < *subsidere* subside]

**sub·sist** (sab·sist′) *v.i.* 1 To continue to exist.

2 To remain alive; manage to live: to *subsist* on a meatless diet. 3 To continue unchanged; abide. [<L *sub-* under + *sistere* cause to stand] —**sub·sist′er** *n.*

**sub·sis·tence** (səb·sis′təns) *n.* 1 The act of subsisting. 2 That on which or by which one subsists; sustenance; livelihood. [<LL *subsistentia* < *subsistere* SUBSIST] —**sub·sis′tent** *adj.*

**sub·son·ic** (sub·son′ik) *adj.* Designating those sound waves beyond the lower limits of human audibility.

**sub·stance** (sub′stəns) *n.* 1 The material of which anything is made or constituted. 2 The essential meaning of anything said or written. 3 Material possessions; wealth; property. 4 The quality of stability or solidity: an argument lacking *substance*. 5 A distinct but unidentified kind of matter: a gaseous *substance*. 6 Essential components or ideas: The *substance* of the two arguments is the same. —**in substance** 1 Essentially; chiefly. 2 Really; actually. [< L *substare* be present]

**sub·stan·tial** (səb·stan′shəl) *adj.* 1 Solid; strong; firm: a *substantial* bridge. 2 Of real worth and importance: a *substantial* profit. 3 Possessed of wealth or sufficient means. 4 Having real existence; not illusory. 5 Containing or conforming to the essence of a thing: in *substantial* agreement. 6 Ample and nourishing: a *substantial* meal. —**sub·stan′ti·al′i·ty** (-shē·al′ə·tē), **sub·stan′tial·ness** *n.* —**sub·stan′tial·ly** *adv.*

**sub·stan·ti·ate** (səb·stan′shē·āt) *v.t.* **·at·ed, ·at·ing** 1 To establish by evidence; verify. 2 To give form or substance to. [<L *substantia* substance] —**sub·stan′ti·a′tion** —*n.* — **sub·stan′ti·a′tive** *adj.*

**sub·stan·tive** (sub′stən·tiv) *n.* 1 A noun or pronoun. 2 A verbal form, phrase, or clause used in place of a noun. —*adj.* 1 Capable of being used as a noun. 2 Expressive of or denoting existence: The verb "to be" is called the *substantive* verb. 3 Having substance or reality. 4 Being an essential part or constituent. 5 Having distinct individuality. 6 Independent. [<L *substantia* substance] —**sub′stan·ti′val** (sub′stən·tī′vəl) *adj.* —**sub′stan·ti′val·ly**, **sub′stan·tive·ly** *adv.* —**sub′stan·tive·ness** *n.*

**sub·sti·tute** (sub′stə·t′ōōt) *v.* **·tut·ed, ·tut·ing** *v.t.* 1 To put in the place of another person or thing. 2 To take the place of. —*v.i.* 3 To act as a substitute. —*n.* One who or that which takes the place of another. —*adj.* Situated in or taking the place of another: a *substitute* teacher. [<L *sub-* in place of + *statuere* set up]

**sub·sti·tu·tion** (sub′stə·t′ōō′shən) *n.* 1 The act of substituting, or the state of being substituted. 2 A substitute. —**sub′sti·tu′tion·al** *adj.* —**sub′sti·tu′tion·al·ly** *adv.*

**sub·struc·ture** (sub′struk′chər, sub·struk′-) *n.* A structure serving as a foundation. —**sub·struc′tur·al** *adj.*

**sub·ter·fuge** (sub′tər·fyōōj′) *n.* Any plan or trick to escape something unpleasant. [<L *subter-* below, in secret + *fugere* flee, take flight]

**sub·ter·ra·ne·an** (sub′tə·rā′nē·ən) *adj.* 1 Situated or occurring below the surface of the earth. 2 Hidden. **Also sub′ter·ra′ne·ous.** [<L *sub-* under + *terra* earth] —**sub′ter·ra′ne·an·ly, sub′ter·ra′ne·ous·ly** *adv.*

**sub·tile** (sut′l, sub′til) *adj.* 1 Elusive; subtle. 2 Crafty; cunning. [<L *subtilis*] —**sub′tile·ly** *adv.* —**sub′tile·ness, sub·til·i·ty** (sub·til′ə·tē) *n.*

**sub·tle·ty** (sut′l·tē) *n. pl.* **·ties** 1 The state or quality of being subtle. 2 Something that is subtle.

**sub·tract** (səb·trakt′) *v.t. & v.i.* To take away or deduct, as a portion from the whole, or one quantity from another. [<L *sub-* away + *trahere* draw] —**sub·tract′er, sub·trac′tion** *n.* —**sub·trac′tive** *adj.*

**sub·urb** (sub′ûrb) *n.* 1 A district or town adjacent to a city. 2 Outlying districts; environs. —**the suburbs** Residential areas near or within commuting distance of a city. [<L *sub-* near to + *urbs* a city]

**sub·ur·ban** (sə·bûr′bən) *adj.* Of or pertaining to a suburb or its residents.

**sub·ur·ban·ite** (sə·bûr′bən·it) *n.* A resident of a suburb.

**sub·ven·tion** (səb·ven′shən) *n.* A grant of money made, esp. by a government, to an institution, cause, or study; subsidy. [<L *subvenire*] —**sub·ven′tion·ar′y** (-er′ē) *adj.*

**sub·ver·sion** (səb·vûr′shən, -zhən) *n.* 1 The act of subverting; demolition; overthrow. 2 A cause of ruin. —**sub·ver′sion·ar′y** (-er′ē) *adj.*

**sub·ver·sive** (səb·vûr′siv) *adj.* Tending to subvert or overthrow. —*n.* A person regarded as desiring to weaken or overthrow a government, organization, etc. —**sub·ver′sive·ly** *adv.* —**sub·ver′sive·ness** *n.*

**sub·vert** (səb·vûrt′) *v.t.* 1 To overthrow from the very foundation; destroy utterly. 2 To corrupt; undermine the principles or character of. [<L *subvertere* overturn] —**sub·vert′·er** *n.*

**sub·way** (sub′wā) *n.* 1 A passage below the surface of the ground. 2 An underground railroad beneath city streets for local transportation; also, the tunnel through which it runs. 3 UNDERPASS.

**suc·ceed** (sək·sēd′) *v.i.* 1 To accomplish what is attempted or intended. 2 To come next in order or sequence. 3 To come after another into office, ownership, etc. —*v.t.* 4 To be the successor or heir of. 5 To come after in time or sequence; follow. [<L *succedere* go under, follow after] —**suc·ceed′·er** *n.*

**suc·cess** (sək·ses′) *n.* 1 A favorable course or termination of anything attempted. 2 The gaining of position, fame, wealth, etc. 3 A person or thing that is successful. 4 The degree of succeeding: Did you have any *success* in getting an appointment? [<L *succedere* succeed] —**Syn.** 1 achievement, satisfaction. 2 prosperity, eminence, station.

**suc·cess·ful** (sək·ses′fəl) *adj.* 1 Having achieved success. 2 Ending in success: a *successful* venture. —**suc·cess′ful·ly** *adv.* —**suc·cess′ful·ness** *n.*

**suc·ces·sion** (sək·sesh′ən) *n.* 1 The act of following consecutively. 2 A group of things that succeed in order; a series or sequence. 3 The act or right of legally or officially coming into a predecessor's office, possessions, position, etc. 4 A group or hierarchy of persons having the right to succeed. —**in succession** One after another. —**suc·ces′sion·al** *adj.* —**suc·ces′sion·al·ly** *adv.*

**suc·ces·sive** (sək·ses′iv) *adj.* Following in succession; consecutive. —**suc·ces′sive·ly** *adv.* —**suc·ces′sive·ness** *n.*

**suc·ces·sor** (sək·ses′ər) *n.* One who or that which follows in succession; esp. a person who succeeds to an office, position, or property.

**suc·cinct** (sək·singkt′) *adj.* Reduced to a minimum number of words; concise; terse. [<L *sub-* underneath + *cingere* gird] —**suc·cinct′·ly** *adv.* —**suc·cinct′ness** *n.*

**suc·co·tash** (suk′ə·tash) *n.* A dish of corn kernels and beans, usu. lima beans, cooked together. [< L *Algon.*]

**suc·cu·lent** (suk′yə·lənt) *adj.* 1 Juicy; full of juice. 2 *Bot.* Composed of fleshy, juicy tissue: a *succulent* leaf. 3 Absorbing; interesting. —*n.* A succulent plant. [<L *succus* juice] —**suc′cu·lence, suc′cu·len·cy** *n.* —**suc′cu·lent·ly** *adv.*

**suc·cumb** (sə·kum′) *v.i.* 1 To give way; yield, as to force or persuasion. 2 To die. [<L *sub-* underneath + *cumbere* lie]

**such** (such) *adj.* 1 Being the same or similar in kind or quality; of a kind mentioned or indicated: a book *such* as this; screws, bolts, and other *such* items. 2 Indicated but not specified: some *such* place. 3 Extreme in degree, quality, etc.: *such* an uproar. —**such as** As an example or examples of the kind indicated: flowers *such as* dandelions. —*pron.* 1 Such a person or thing or such persons or things. 2 The same as implied or indicated: *Such* was the result. —**as such** As the particular thing or kind it is, regardless of others: People *as such* deserve compassion. —*adv.* 1 So: *such* destructive criticism. 2 Especially; very: She's in *such* good spirits today. [<OE *swelc, swylc*]

**suck** (suk) *v.t.* 1 To draw into the mouth by means of a partial vacuum created by action of the lips and tongue. 2 To draw in or take up by suction. 3 To draw liquid or nourishment from with the mouth: to *suck* an orange or a lollipop. 4 To take and hold in the mouth as if to do this: to *suck* one's thumb. 5 To pull or draw into an association: with *in* or *into:* The lure of quick profits *sucked* him in. —*v.i.* 6 To draw in liquid, air, etc., by suction. 7 To draw in milk from a breast or udder by sucking. 8 To make a sucking sound. —*n.* 1 The act or sound of sucking. 2 That which is sucked. [<OE *sūcan*]

**suc·tion** (suk′shən) *n.* 1 The act or process of sucking. 2 The production of a partial vacuum in a space connected with a fluid or gas under reduced pressure. —*adj.* Creating or operating by suction.

**sud·den** (sud′n) *adj.* 1 Happening quickly and without warning. 2 Causing surprise; unexpected: a *sudden* development. 3 Hurried; hasty; rash. —**all of a sudden** Without warning; suddenly. [<L *subitus*, p.p. of *subire* come or go stealthily] —**sud′den·ly** *adv.* —**sud′den·ness** *n.*

**suds** (sudz) *n. pl.* 1 Soapy water. 2 Froth; foam. 3 *Slang* Beer. [<MDu. *sudde, sudse* a marsh] —**suds′y** *adj.*

**sue** (sōō) *v.* **sued, su·ing** *v.t.* 1 To institute legal proceedings against, as for the redress of some wrong. 2 To prosecute (a legal action). —*v.i.* 3 To institute legal proceedings. 4 To seek to persuade someone by entreaty: with *for:* to *sue* for peace. [<AF *suer* pursue, sue] —**su′er** *n.*

**suede** (swād) *n.* Leather or a fabric having a napped surface. **Also suède.** [<F *gants de Suède* Swedish gloves]

**su·et** (sōō′it) *n.* The white, solid fatty tissue of beef, lamb, etc. [<L *sebum* fat] —**su′et·y** *adj.*

**suf·fer** (suf′ər) *v.i.* 1 To feel pain or distress. 2 To sustain loss, injury, or detriment. 3 To undergo punishment, esp. death. —*v.t.* 4 To have inflicted on one; sustain, as an injury or loss: to *suffer* a fracture of the arm; to *suffer* a business reversal. 5 To undergo; pass through, as change. 6 To bear; endure: He never could *suffer* incompetence. 7 To allow; permit. [<L *sub-* up from under + *ferre* bear] —**suf′fer·a·ble** *adj.* —**suf′fer·a·bly** *adv.* —**suf′fer·er** *n.*

**suf·fi·cien·cy** (sə·fish′ən·sē) *n. pl.* ·**cies** 1 The state of being sufficient. 2 That which is sufficient; esp., adequate means or income.

**suf·fi·cient** (sə·fish′ənt) *adj.* Being all that is needed; adequate; enough. [<L *sufficere* substitute, suffice] —**suf·fi′cient·ly** *adv.* —Syn. ample, satisfactory, fitting.

**suf·fix** (suf′iks) *n.* A letter or letters added to the end of a word or root, forming a new word or functioning as an inflectional element, as *-ful* in faithful and *-ed* in loved. —*v.t.* To add as a suffix. [<L *suffixus*, p.p. of *suffigere* fasten underneath] —**suf′fix·al** *adj.*

**suf·fo·cate** (suf′ə·kāt′) *v.* ·**cat·ed**, ·**cat·ing** *v.t.* 1 To kill by obstructing respiration in any manner. 2 To cause distress in by depriving of an adequate supply or quality of air. 3 To stifle or smother, as a fire. —*v.i.* 4 To die from suffocation. 5 To be distressed by an inadequate supply or quality of air. [<L *sub-* under + *fauces* throat] —**suf′fo·cat·ing·ly** *adv.* —**suf′fo·ca′tion** *n.* —**suf′fo·ca′tive** *adj.*

**suf·frage** (suf′rij) *n.* 1 A vote in support of someone or something. 2 The right or privilege of voting; franchise. 3 Any short intercessory prayer. [<L *suffragium* a vote]

**suf·fuse** (sə·fyōōz′) *v.t.* ·**fused**, ·**fus·ing** To spread over, as with a fluid, light, or color. [<L *suffusus*, p.p. of *suffundere* pour underneath] —**suf·fu′sion** *n.* —**suf·fu′sive** *adj.*

**sug·ar** (shōōg′ər) *n.* 1 A sweet, crystalline foodstuff obtained chiefly from sugar cane and sugar beets; sucrose. 2 Any of a large class of mostly sweet and water-soluble carbohydrates widely distributed in plants and animals, as lactose, glucose, fructose,

etc. —*v.t.* 1 To sweeten, cover, or coat with sugar. 2 To make less distasteful, as by flattery. —*v.i.* 3 To make maple sugar by boiling down maple syrup: usu. with *off.* 4 To form or produce sugar; granulate. [<Ar. *sukkar*] —**sug′ar·less** *adj.*

**sug·gest** (səg·jest′, sə·jest′) *v.t.* 1 To bring or put forward for consideration, action, or approval; propose. 2 To arouse in the mind by association or connection: Gold *suggests* wealth. 3 To give a hint of; intimate: Her gesture *suggested* indifference. [<L *suggerere* carry underneath, suggest] —**sug·gest′er** *n.*

**sug·ges·tion** (səg·jes′chən, sə·jes′-) *n.* 1 The act of suggesting. 2 Something suggested. 3 A hint; trace; touch: a *suggestion* of irony. 4 An association of thoughts or ideas, esp. if based upon incidental or fortuitous similarities rather than upon a logical or rational relationship.

**sug·ges·tive** (səg·jes′tiv, sə-) *adj.* 1 Tending to suggest; stimulating thought or reflection. 2 Suggesting or hinting at something improper or indecent. —**sug·ges′tive·ly** *adv.* —**sug·ges′tive·ness** *n.*

**su·i·cide** (sōō′ə·sīd) *n.* 1 The intentional taking of one's own life. 2 One who takes or tries to take one's own life. 3 Personal or professional ruin brought on by one's own actions. [<L *sui* of oneself + *caedere* kill] —**su·i·ci·dal** (sōō′ə·sīd′l) *adj.* —**su′i·ci·dal·ly** *adv.*

**suit** (sōōt) *n.* 1 A set of garments worn together; esp., a coat and trousers or skirt, made of the same fabric. 2 An outfit or garment for a particular purpose: a bathing *suit.* 3 A group of like things; a set. 4 Any of the four sets of thirteen cards each that make up a deck of cards. 5 A proceeding in a court of law for the recovery of a right or the redress of a wrong. 6 The courting of a woman. —**follow suit** 1 To play a card identical in suit to the card led. 2 To follow an example set by another. —*v.t.* 1 To meet the requirements of or be appropriate to; befit. 2 To please; satisfy. 3 To render appropriate; adapt. 4 To furnish with clothes. —*v.i.* 5 To agree; accord. 6 To be or prove satisfactory. 7 To put on a protective suit or uniform: with *up:* ballplayers *suiting up* before a game. [<OF *sieute* < *sequi* follow]

**suit·a·ble** (sōō′tə·bəl) *adj.* Appropriate; proper; fitting. —**suit′a·bil′i·ty, suit′a·ble·ness** *n.* —**suit′a·bly** *adv.*

**suite** (swēt; *for def. 2, also* sōōt) *n.* 1 A set of

things intended to go or be used together, as a number of connected rooms forming an apartment or leased as a unit in a hotel. 2 A set of matched furniture. 3 A company of attendants; a retinue. 4 *Music* An instrumental composition consisting of a series of short pieces. [<OF *sieute*. See SUIT.]

**suit·or** (sōō′tər) *n.* 1 One who institutes a suit in court. 2 A man who courts a woman. 3 A petitioner.

**sul·fa drug** (sul′fə) Any of various sulfonamide derivatives effective in the treatment of certain bacterial infections.

**sul·fon·a·mide** (sul·fon′ə·mīd, -mid) *n.* Any of a group of organic sulfur compounds containing a univalent amide radical.

**sul·fur** (sul′fər) *n.* 1 An industrially important, abundant nonmetallic element (symbol S), occurring in three allotropic forms and found in both free and combined states. 2 Any of various small yellow butterflies. Also, and for def. 2 always, **sul′phur.** —**sul′fur·y** *adj.*

**sulk** (sulk) *v.i.* To be sullen in mood and tend to shun others. —*n.* A sulky mood or humor. [Back formation < SULKY]

**sul·len** (sul′ən) *adj.* 1 Showing ill-humor, as from dwelling upon a grievance; morose; glum. 2 Depressing; somber: *sullen* clouds. 3 Slow; sluggish. 4 Melancholy; mournful. [<AF *solein* sullen, alone] —**sul′len·ly** *adv.* —**sul′len·ness** *n.* —Syn. 1 gloomy, sad, sulky, moody.

**sul·ly** (sul′ē) *v.* **·lied, ·ly·ing** *v.t.* To mar the brightness or purity of; soil; defile. [<MF *souiller* to soil]

**sul·tan** (sul′tən) *n.* A Muslim ruler. [< Ar. *sultān* a sovereign, dominion]

**sul·try** (sul′trē) *adj.* **·tri·er, ·tri·est** 1 Hot, moist, and still; close: said of weather. 2 Oppressively hot; burning. 3 Inflamed with passion. 4 Expressing or tending to excite sexual interest; sensual. [< obs. *sulter*, var. of SWELTER] —**sul′tri·ly** *adv.* —**sul′tri·ness** *n.*

**sum** (sum) *n.* 1 An amount of money. 2 The result obtained by the addition of numbers or quantities. 3 A problem in arithmetic. 4 The entire quantity, number, or substance; the whole: The *sum* of his effort came to naught. 5 Essence or core; summary: In *sum*, the issue is one of trust; the *sum* of an argument. 6 The highest or furthest point; summit. —*v.* **summed, sum·ming** *v.t.* 1 To present as a summary; recapitulate; summarize: usu. with *up*. 2 To add

into one total: often with *up*. —*v.i.* 3 To give a summary; recapitulate: usu. with *up*. 4 To calculate a sum: often with *up*. [<L *summa (res)* highest (thing)]

**su·mac** (sōō′mak, shōō′-) *n.* 1 Any of a genus of woody plants related to the cashew. 2 A species of sumac with hairy red fruit and compound leaves turning brilliant red in autumn: **also smooth sumac.** 3 The dried and powdered leaves of certain species of sumac, used for tanning and dyeing. Also **su′mach.** [< Ar. *summāq*]

**sum·ma·ry** (sum′ər·ē) *n. pl.* **·ries** A brief account of the substance or essential points of something spoken or written; recapitulation. —*adj.* 1 Giving the substance or essential points; concise. 2 Performed without ceremony or delay; instant: *summary* execution. [<L *summa*. See SUM.] —Syn. *n.* condensation, abridgment, epitome, précis, compendium. —**sum·ma·ri·ly** (sə·mer′ə·lē, sum′ər·ə·lē) *adv.*

**sum·ma·tion** (sum·ā′shən) *n.* 1 The act or operation of obtaining a sum; addition. 2 A sum or total. 3 A summing up of the main points of an argument, as the final speech in behalf of one of the parties in a court trial.

**sum·mer** (sum′ər) *n.* 1 The warmest season of the year, including, in the northern hemisphere, June, July, and August. 2 A year of life. 3 A bright or prosperous period. —*v.i.* 1 To pass the summer. —*v.t.* 2 To keep or care for through the summer. —*adj.* 1 Of, pertaining to, or occurring in summer. 2 Used or intended for use in the summer: a *summer* house. [<OE *sumor, sumer*] —**sum′mer·y** *adj.*

**sum·mit** (sum′it) *n.* 1 The highest part; the top; vertex. 2 The highest degree; maximum. 3 The highest level or office, as of a government or business organization. 4 A meeting of executives of the highest level, as heads of government. —*adj.* Of or involving those at the highest level: a *summit* conference. [<L *summus* highest]

**sum·mon** (sum′ən) *v.t.* 1 To order to come; send for. 2 To call together; cause to convene, as a legislative assembly. 3 To order (a person) to appear in court by a summons. 4 To call forth or into action; arouse: usu. with *up*: to *summon* up courage. 5 To call on for a specific act. [<L *summonere* suggest, hint] —**sum′mon·er** *n.*

**sum·mons** (sum′ənz) *n. pl.* **sum·mons·es** 1 An order or call to attend or act at a particular place or time. 2 *Law* a A notice to a defendant summoning him to appear in court. b A notice to appear in court as a witness or as a juror. [<OF *somondre* summon]

**sump·tu·ous** (sump′chōō·əs) *adj.* 1 Involving or showing lavish expenditure. 2 Luxurious; magnificent. [<L *sumptus* expense] —**sump′tu·ous·ly** *adv.* —**sump′tu·ous·ness** *n.*

**sun** (sun) *n.* 1 The star that is the gravitational center and the main source of energy for the solar system, about 93,000,000 miles distant from the earth, with a diameter of 864,000 miles and a mass 332,000 times that of the earth. 2 Any star, esp. one with a planetary system. 3 The light and heat from the sun; sunshine. 4 Anything brilliant and magnificent; a source of splendor. 5 A day or a year. —*v.* sunned, sun·ning *v.t.* 1 To expose to the light or heat of the sun. —*v.i.* 2 To bask in the sun; sun oneself. [<OE *sunne*]

**sun·beam** (sun′bēm′) *n.* A ray or beam of the sun.

**sun·der** (sun′dər) *v.t. & v.i.* To break apart; sever. [<OE *syndrian*, *sundrian*]

**sun·down** (sun′doun′) *n.* SUNSET (def. 2).

**sun·dries** (sun′drēz) *n. pl.* Various or miscellaneous articles. [< SUNDRY]

**sun·dry** (sun′drē) *adj.* Various; several; miscellaneous. [<OE *syndrig* separate]

**sun·lamp** (sun′lamp′) *n.* An electric lamp radiating ultraviolet rays, used esp. for the therapeutic treatments.

**sun·rise** (sun′rīz′) *n.* 1 The daily first appearance of the sun above the horizon. 2 The time at which the sun rises.

**sun·set** (sun′set′) *n.* 1 The apparent daily descent of the sun below the horizon. 2 The time at which the sun sets. 3 A final period or decline, as of life.

**sun·shine** (sun′shīn′) *n.* 1 The direct light of the sun. 2 The light and warmth of sunlight. 3 Brightness or warmth, as of feeling. —**sun′shin′y** *adj.*

**sun·stroke** (sun′strōk′) *n.* Prostration and fever induced by heat and exposure to the sun. —**sun′struck′** (-struk′) *adj.*

**su·per·a·ble** (sōō′pər·ə·bəl) *adj.* That can be surmounted, overcome, or conquered. [<L *superare* overcome<*super* over] —**su′per·a·bil′i·ty** *n.* —**su′per·a·bly** *adv.*

**su·per·a·bun·dant** (sōō′pər·ə·bun′dənt) *adj.* More than sufficient; excessive. [<LL *superabundare* to superabound] —**su′per·**

**a·bun′dance** *n.* —**su′per·a·bun′dant·ly** *adv.*

**su·per·an·nu·at·ed** (sōō′pər·an′yōō·wāt′id) *adj.* 1 Relieved of active work on account of age; retired. 2 Set aside or discarded as obsolete or too old. [<L *super* beyond + *annus* a year]

**su·perb** (sōō·pûrb′, sōō-) *adj.* 1 Extraordinarily good; excellent: a *superb* wine. 2 Having grand, impressive beauty; majestic: a *superb* cathedral. 3 Luxurious; elegant. [<L *superbus* proud] —**su·perb′ly** *adv.* —**su·perb′ness** *n.*

**su·per·car·go** (sōō′pər·kär′gō) *n. pl.* ·goes or ·gos An officer on board ship in charge of the cargo and its sale and purchase.

**su·per·cil·i·ous** (sōō′pər·sil′ē·əs) *adj.* Haughtily contemptuous; arrogant. [<L *supercilium* eyebrow, pride] —**su′per·cil′i·ous·ly** *adv.* —**su′per·cil′i·ous·ness** *n.*

**su·per·e·go** (sōō′pər·ē′gō, -eg′ō) *n. pl.* ·gos *Psychoanal.* A largely unconscious element of the personality, acting principally as conscience and critic.

**su·per·fi·cial** (sōō′pər·fish′əl) *adj.* 1 Of, lying near, or on the surface: a *superficial* wound. 2 Of or pertaining to only the ordinary and the obvious; not profound; shallow. 3 Hasty; cursory: a *superficial* examination. 4 Apparent only; not real or genuine. [<L *super-* above + *facies* a face] —**su′per·fi′ci·al′i·ty** (-fish′ē·al′ə·tē), **su′per·fi′cial·ness** *n.* —**su′per·fi′cial·ly** *adv.*

**su·per·flu·i·ty** (sōō′pər·flōō′ə·tē) *n. pl.* ·ties 1 The state of being superfluous. 2 That which is superfluous.

**su·per·high·way** (sōō′pər·hī′wā′) *n.* A highway for high-speed traffic, usu. with four or more lanes.

**su·per·in·tend** (sōō′pər·in·tend′) *v.t.* To have the charge and direction of; supervise. [<LL *super-* over + *intendere* direct, aim at] —**su′per·in·ten′dence**, **su′per·in·ten′den·cy** *n.*

**su·per·in·ten·dent** (sōō′pər·in·ten′dənt) *n.* 1 One who has charge of an institution or undertaking; director. 2 One responsible for the maintenance and repair of a building. —*adj.* Superintending.

**su·pe·ri·or** (sə·pir′ē·ər, sōō-) *adj.* 1 Higher in rank, quality, or degree; better or excellent: *superior* vision; *superior* talent. 2 Greater in quantity: a *superior* supply. 3 Higher in relation to other things; upper. 4 *Printing* Set above the line, as 1 in $x^1$. 5 Serenely unaffected or indifferent: with *to*: *superior* to pettiness. 6 Affecting or suggesting an attitude of contemptuous indifference or disdain: *superior* airs. —*n.* 1 One who is superior, as in rank or excellence. 2 The head of an abbey, convent, or monastery. [< L *superus* higher < *super* above] —su·pe·ri·or·i·ty (sə·pir′ē·ôr′ə·tē, -or′-, sōō-) *n.* —su·pe′ri·or·ly *adv.*

su·per·la·tive (sə·pûr′lə·tiv, sōō-) *adj.* 1 Being of the highest degree; most excellent or eminent. 2 *Gram.* Expressing the highest or extreme degree of the quality expressed by the positive degree of an adjective or adverb: "Wisest" is the *superlative* form of "wise." 3 Exaggerated. —*n.* 1 That which is superlative. 2 The highest degree; apex. 3 *Gram.* a The superlative degree. b A form in the superlative degree. [< L *superlatus* excessive < *super-* above + *latus* carried] —su·per′la·tive·ly *adv.* —su·per′la·tive·ness *n.*

su·per·mar·ket (sōō′pər·mär′kit) *n.* A large, chiefly self-service store selling food and household supplies.

su·per·nal (sōō·pûr′nəl) *adj.* 1 Heavenly; celestial. 2 Coming from above or from the sky. [< L *supernus* < *super* over] —su·per′nal·ly *adv.*

su·per·nat·u·ral (sōō′pər·nach′ər·əl, -rəl) *adj.* 1 Existing or occurring through some agency beyond the known forces of nature. 2 Of or concerning phenomena of this kind: *supernatural* tales. 3 Believed to be miraculous or divine. 4 Suggestive of ghosts, demons, or other agents unconstrained by natural law. —*n.* That which is supernatural. [< L *super-* above + *natura* nature] —su′per·nat′u·ral·ism, su′per·nat′u·ral·ness *n.* —su′per·nat′u·ral·ist *adj., n.* —su′per·nat′u·ral·is′tic *adj.* —su′per·nat′u·ral·ly *adv.*

su·per·nu·mer·ar·y (sōō′pər·n′ōō′mə·rer′ē) *adj.* 1 Being beyond a fixed or usual number. 2 Beyond a necessary number; superfluous. —*n. pl.* ·ar·ies 1 A supernumerary person or thing. 2 A stage performer without any speaking part. [< L *super* over + *numerus* a number]

su·per·pow·er (sōō′pər·pou′ər) *n.* One of a few great, dominant nations characterized by superior economic or military strength and by large population.

su·per·scribe (sōō′pər·skrīb′) *v.t.* ·scribed, ·scrib·ing 1 To write or engrave on the outside or on the upper part of. 2 To address,

as a letter. [< L *super-* over + *scribere* write] —su′per·scrip′tion (-skrip′shən) *n.*

su·per·sede (sōō′pər·sēd′) *v.t.* ·sed·ed, ·sed·ing 1 To take the place of, as by reason of superiority or right; replace. 2 To put something in the place of; set aside. [< L *super-* above + *sedere* sit] —su′per·sed′er. su′per·se′dure (-sē′jər) *n.*

su·per·son·ic (sōō′pər·son′ik) *adj.* 1 Of or capable of moving at a speed greater than that of sound. 2 Moving at such a speed. 3 ULTRASONIC. —su′per·son′i·cal·ly *adv.*

su·per·sti·tion (sōō′pər·stish′ən) *n.* 1 An ignorant or irrational belief, often provoked by fear, and based upon assumptions of cause and effect contrary to known scientific facts and principles. 2 Any practice inspired by such belief. 3 Any unreasonable belief or impression. [< L *superstitio* excessive fear of the gods, amazement]

su·per·sti·tious (sōō′pər·stish′əs) *adj.* 1 Disposed to believe in or be influenced by superstitions. 2 Of, based upon, or manifesting superstition. —su′per·sti′tious·ly *adv.* —su′per·sti′tious·ness *n.*

su·per·vene (sōō′pər·vēn′) *v.i.* ·vened, ·ven·ing To follow closely upon something as an extraneous or additional circumstance. [< L *super-* over and above + *venire* come] —su′per·ven′ient (-vēn′yənt) *adj.* —su′per·ven′tion (-ven′shən) *n.*

su·per·vise (sōō′pər·vīz) *v.t.* ·vised, ·vis·ing To have charge of; direct. [< L *super-* over + *videre* see] —Syn. manage, run, oversee, superintend.

su·per·vi·sion (sōō′pər·vizh′ən) *n.* The act or process of supervising; direction, control, or guidance.

su·per·vi·sor (sōō′pər·vī′zər) *n.* 1 One who supervises; a superintendent or manager. 2 In education, an official supervising teachers and responsible for curricula, etc., in a particular subject. —su′per·vi′sor· ship *n.* —su·per·vi·so·ry (sōō′pər·vī′zər·ē) *adj.*

su·pine (sōō·pīn′, sə-) *adj.* 1 Lying on the back, or with the face turned upward. 2 Having no interest or care; listless. [< L *supinus*] —su·pine′ly *adv.* —su·pine′ness *n.*

sup·per (sup′ər) *n.* 1 The last meal of the day; the evening meal. 2 A social event including the serving of supper: a church *supper.* [< OF *soper* sup] —sup′per·less *adj.*

sup·plant (sə·plant′, -plänt′) *v.t.* 1 To take the place of, as of something inferior or out of date; displace. 2 To take the place of (someone) by scheming, treachery, etc. 3 To

560

replace (one thing) with another: to *supplant* naive expectations with realistic goals. [<L *supplantare* trip up] —**sup· plan· ta·tion** (sup′lan·tā′shən), **sup·plant′ er** *n.*

**sup·ple** (sup′əl) *adj.* **sup· pler** (sup′lər, -əl·ər), **sup·plest** 1 Easily bent; flexible; pliant: *supple* leather. 2 Agile or graceful in movement; limber. 3 Yielding readily to the wishes of others; compliant. 4 Servile; obsequious. 5 Quick to respond or adjust, as the mind; adaptable. —*v.t. & v.i.* **·pled**, **·pling** To make or become supple. [<L *supplex*, lit., bending under] —**sup′ple·ly** (sup′əl·ē, sup′lē) or **sup′ply** (sup′lē) *adv.* —**sup′ple·ness** *n.* — Syn. 2 lithe, deft, nimble.

**sup·ple·ment** (sup′lə·mənt) *n.* 1 Something added that supplies a deficiency. 2 An addition to a publication, as a section providing additional information added to a book. —*v.t.* To make additions to; provide for what is lacking in. [<L *supplere*. See SUPPLY.] —**sup·ple·men·tal** (sup′lə·men′təl) *adj.* • Both *supplement* and *complement* refer to something added to make up for a lack of deficiency. *Complement* (not to be confused with *compliment*, an expression of praise) emphasizes the correction or adjustment of something unfinished or imperfect, and often implies a balancing of elements: *The design of the housing project called for low buildings to complement the high-rises.* In the case of *supplement*, the fact of being added is more emphatic, and the expected result is one of improvement rather than completion: *Student teachers supplemented the regular teaching staff, freeing them to give more individual help to slow learners.*

**sup·ple·men·ta·ry** (sup′lə·men′tər·ē, -trē) *adj.* Added as a supplement; additional.

**sup·pli·ant** (sup′lē·ənt) *adj.* Entreating earnestly and humbly. —*n.* One who supplicates. [<L *supplicare* supplicate] —**sup′pli·ant·ly** *adv.* —**sup′pli·ant·ness** *n.*

**sup·pli·cant** (sup′lə·kənt) *n.* One who supplicates. —*adj.* Asking or entreating humbly. [<L *supplicare* supplicate]

**sup·pli·cate** (sup′lə·kāt) *v.* **·cat·ed**, **·cat·ing** *v.t.* 1 To ask for humbly or by earnest prayer. 2 To beg something of; entreat. — *v.i.* 5 To make an earnest request. [<L *sub-* under + *plicare* bend, fold] —**sup′pli·ca′ tion** *n.* —**sup′pli·ca·to′ry** (-kə·tôr′ē, -tō′rē) *adj.*

**sup·ply** (sə·plī′) *v.* **·plied**, **·ply·ing** *v.t.* 1 To make available; provide or furnish: to *supply* electricity to a remote area. 2 To furnish with what is needed: to *supply* an army with weapons. 3 To provide for adequately; satisfy. 4 To make up for; compensate for. 5 To fill (the place of another). —*v.i.* 6 To take the place of another temporarily. —*n. pl.* **·plies** 1 That which is or can be supplied. 2 A store or quantity on hand. 3 *pl.* Accumulated stores, as for an army. 4 The amount of a commodity offered at a given price or available for meeting a demand. 5 The act of supplying. [<L *supplere* < *sub-* from under + *plere* fill] —**sup·pli′er** *n.*

**sup·port** (sə·pôrt′, -pōrt′) *v.t.* 1 To bear the weight of, esp. from underneath; hold in position; keep from falling, sinking, etc. 2 To bear or sustain (weight, etc.). 3 To provide money or necessities for; provide with the means of subsistence. 4 To give approval or assistance to; uphold. 5 To serve to uphold or corroborate; substantiate: His testimony *supports* our position. 6 To endure patiently; tolerate. 7 To provide with the means to endure; keep from collapsing or yielding: Faith *supported* her. 8 To carry on; keep up: to *support* a war. 9 In the theater, etc., to act in a subordinate role to. — *n.* 1 The act of supporting. 2 One who supports. 3 That which supports, as a brace or girdle for the body. [<L *sub-* up from under + *portare* carry] —**sup·port′a·ble** *adj.* —**sup·port′a·bly** *adv.* —Syn. 4 advocate, endorse, help, aid, assist. 5 verify, bear out. 6 bear, suffer. 7 sustain.

**sup·pose** (sə·pōz′) *v.* **·posed**, **·pos·ing** *v.t.* 1 To believe to be true or probable; presume. 2 To assume as true for the sake of argument or illustration. 3 To expect: I am *supposed* to follow. 4 To presuppose; imply: Mercy *supposes* a sense of compassion. — *v.i.* 5 To make a supposition. [<L *supponere* substitute, put under] —**sup·pos′a·ble** *adj.* —**sup·pos′a·bly** *adv.* —**sup·pos′er** *n.*

**sup·po·si·tion** (sup′ə·zish′ən) *n.* 1 Something supposed; a conjecture or hypothesis. 2 The act of supposing. —**sup′po·si′tion·al** *adj.* —**sup′po·si′tion·al·ly** *adv.*

**sup·press** (sə·pres′) *v.t.* 1 To put an end or stop to; crush, as a rebellion. 2 To stop or prohibit the activities of. 3 To withhold from knowledge or publication, as a book, news, etc. 4 To hold back or repress. 5 To stop or check (a hemorrhage, etc.). [<L *suppressus*, p.p. of *supprimere* press down] —**sup·press′er**, **sup·pres′sor** *n.* —**sup·press′i·ble**, **sup·pres′sive** *adj.*

**sup·pres·sion** (sə·presh′ən) *n.* 1 The act of suppressing, or the state of being suppressed. 2 The deliberate exclusion from consciousness of unacceptable ideas, memories, etc.

**su·prem·a·cy** (sə·prem′ə·sē, sŏŏ-) *n. pl.* ·cies 1 The state of being supreme. 2 Supreme power or authority.

**su·preme** (sə·prēm′, sŏŏ-) *adj.* 1 Highest in power or authority; dominant. 2 Highest or greatest, as in degree; utmost: *supreme* devotion. 3 Ultimate; last and greatest. [<L *supremus*, superl. of *superus* < *super* above] —**su·preme′ly** *adv.* —**su·preme′ ness** *n.*

**sur·charge** (sûr′chärj′) *n.* 1 An additional amount charged or imposed. 2 An excessive burden, load, or charge. 3 OVERCHARGE. 4 A new valuation or something additional printed on a postage or revenue stamp. — *v.t.* (sûr·chärj′) ·charged, ·charg·ing 1 OVERCHARGE. 2 To fill or load to excess. 3 To imprint a surcharge on (postage stamps). —**sur·charg′er** *n.*

**sure** (shŏŏr) *adj.* sur·er, sur·est 1 Not subject to uncertainty or doubt; beyond all question; indisputable. 2 Characterized by freedom from doubt or uncertainty; firm: *sure* convictions; a *sure* grasp of his subject. 3 Certain or confident; positive: I was *sure* I had seen her before. 4 Not liable to fail or disappoint; reliable; sound: a *sure* memory. 5 Bound to happen or be: a *sure* winner. 6 *Obs.* Safe; secure. —*adv. Informal* Surely; certainly. —**for sure** Certainly; beyond all question. —**to be sure** Indeed; certainly; quite so. [< L *securus*] —**sure′ness** *n.* — **Syn.** 1 unquestionable, unimpeachable, indubitable. 4 trustworthy, dependable, true.

**sure·ty** (shŏŏr′ə·tē, shŏŏr′tē) *n. pl.* ·ties 1 The state of being sure; certainty. 2 Security against loss or damage. 3 One who assumes the debts, responsibilities, etc., of another; a guarantor. [<L *securus* secure] —**sure′ty·ship** *n.*

**surf** (sûrf) *n.* 1 The swell of the sea that breaks upon a shore. 2 The foam caused by the billows. —*v.i.* To ride the surf on a surfboard; engage in surfing. [?] —**surf′er** *n.*

**sur·face** (sûr′fis) *n.* 1 The outer part or face of an object. 2 That which has area but not thickness. 3 A superficial aspect; external appearance. —*v.* ·faced, ·fac· ing *v.t.* 1 To put a surface on; esp., to make smooth, even, or plain. 2 To cause to rise to the surface, as a submarine. —*v.i.* 3 To rise to the surface. 4 To come to public notice, esp.

something formerly kept secret. [< SUR- + FACE] —**sur′fac·er** *n.*

**surf·board** (sûrf′bôrd′, -bōrd′) *n.* A long, narrow board used in surfing. —*v.i.* SURF. — **surf′board′er** *n.*

**sur·feit** (sûr′fit) *v.t.* 1 To feed or supply to fullness or excess. —*v.i.* 2 To overindulge in food or drink. —*n.* 1 Excess in eating or drinking. 2 The result of such excess; satiety. 3 Any excessive amount: a *surfeit* of praise. [< OF *surfaire* overdo]

**surge** (sûrj) *v.* surged, surg·ing *v.i.* 1 To rise and roll with a powerful, swelling motion, as waves. 2 To be tossed about by waves. 3 To move or go in a powerful, wavelike motion: The mob *surged* through the square. 4 To increase or vary suddenly, as an electric current. —*n.* 1 A large swelling wave; billow. 2 A great swelling or rolling movement, as of waves. 3 *Electr.* A sudden, transient rise in current flow. 4 Any sudden, sharp increase. [< L *surgere*]

**sur·geon** (sûr′jən) *n.* One who practices surgery. [< OF *cirurgie* surgery] —**sur′geon·cy** (-sē) *n.*

**sur·ger·y** (sûr′jər·ē) *n. pl.* ·ger·ies 1 The treatment of disease, injury, etc., by manual and operative means. 2 The branch of medicine concerned with surgical treatment. 3 A place where surgery is performed; an operating room. 4 *Brit.* A physician's office. [< Gk. *cheirourgia* a handicraft < *cheir* the hand + *ergein* to work] —**sur·gi·cal** (sûr′ji·kəl) *adj.* —**sur′gi·cal·ly** *adv.*

**sur·ly** (sûr′lē) *adj.* ·li·er, ·li·est Rude and ill-humored, esp. in response; gruff or insolent. [Earlier *sirly* like a lord < *sir* a lord] — **sur′li·ly** *adv.* —**sur′li·ness** *n.*

**sur·mise** (sər·mīz′) *v.* ·mised, ·mis·ing *v.t. & v.i.* To infer (something) on slight evidence; guess. —*n.* (sər·mīz′, sûr′mīz) A conjecture made on slight evidence; supposition. [< OF *surmettre* accuse < *sur-* upon + *mettre* put] —**Syn.** *v.* suppose, assume, conjecture.

**sur·mount** (sər·mount′) *v.t.* 1 To overcome; prevail over (a difficulty, etc.). 2 To mount to the top or cross to the other side of, as an obstacle. 3 To be or lie over or above. 4 To place something above or on top of; cap. [< L *super-* over + *mons, montis* a hill, mountain]

**sur·pass** (sər·pas′, -päs′) *v.t.* 1 To go beyond or past in degree or amount; exceed or excel. 2 To be beyond the reach or powers of; transcend. —**sur·pass'a·ble** *adj.* —**sur·pass'er** *n.* —**Syn.** 1 eclipse, outdo, outstrip.

**sur·plice** (sûr'plis) *n.* A loose white vestment with full sleeves, worn over the cassock by the clergy and choristers of some churches. [< Med. L *superpellicium (vestimentum)* an overgarment]

**sur·plus** (sûr'plus) *n.* 1 That which remains over and above what is used or required. 2 Assets in excess of liabilities. —*adj.* Being in excess of what is used or needed. [< L *super-* over and above + *plus* more] —**sur'plus·age** (-ij) *n.*

**sur·prise** (sər-prīz', sə-) *v.t.* **·prised**, **·pris·ing** 1 To cause to feel wonder or astonishment, esp. because unusual or unexpected. 2 To come upon suddenly or unexpectedly; take unawares. 3 To attack suddenly and without warning. 4 To lead unawares, as into doing something not intended: with *into.* — *n.* 1 The state of being surprised; astonishment. 2 Something that causes surprise, as a sudden and unexpected event. 3 A sudden attack or capture. [< L *super-* over + *prehendere* take] —**sur·pris'er** *n.*

**sur·ren·der** (sə-ren'dər) *v.t.* 1 To yield possession of or power over to another because of demand or compulsion. 2 To give up or relinquish, esp. in favor of another; resign; abandon. 3 To give (oneself) over to a passion, influence, etc. —*v.i.* 4 To give oneself up, as to an enemy in warfare. —*n.* The act of surrendering. [< OF *surrendre* < *sur-* over + *rendre* give, render]

**sur·rep·ti·tious** (sûr'əp-tish'əs) *adj.* 1 Accomplished by secret or improper means; clandestine. 2 Acting secretly or by stealth. [< L *subreptus*, p.p. of *subripere* steal] —**sur'rep·ti'tious·ly** *adv.* —**sur'rep·ti'tious·ness** *n.*

**sur·ro·gate** (sûr'ə-gāt, -git) *n.* 1 Someone or something taking the place of another; substitute. 2 In some U.S. states, a probate court judge. —*v.t.* (sûr'ə-gāt) **·gat·ed**, **·gat·ing** To put in the place of another; deputize or substitute. [< L *subrogare* < *sub-* in place of another + *rogare* ask]

**sur·round** (sə-round') *v.t.* 1 To extend or place completely around; encircle or enclose. 2 To enclose on all sides so as to cut off communication or retreat. 3 To be or cause something to become a significant part of the environment or experience of: *surrounded* by lies; to *surround* oneself with the best legal talent. —*n. Chiefly Brit.* That

which surrounds, as a border. [< LL *super-* over + *undare* rise in waves]

**sur·tax** (sûr'taks') *n.* An extra or additional tax.

**sur·veil·lance** (sər-vā'ləns, -vāl'yəns) *n.* A careful watching of someone or something, usu. carried on secretly or discreetly; to keep a suspect under *surveillance.* [F< *sur-* over + *veiller* watch] —**sur·veil'lant** *adj.*

**sur·vey** (sər-vā', sûr'vā) *v.t.* 1 To look at in its entirety; view comprehensively, as from a height. 2 To look at carefully and minutely; scrutinize. 3 To determine accurately the area, contour, or boundaries of according to the principles of geometry and trigonometry. 4 To make a survey of. —*v.i.* 5 To survey land. —*n.* (*usu.* sûr'vā) 1 The operation, act, process, or results of surveying land. 2 A systematic inquiry to collect data for analysis, used esp. for the preparation of a comprehensive report or summary. 3 The result of such an inquiry; a comprehensive report. 4 A general or overall view; overview: a *survey* of contemporary theater. [< L *super-* over + *videre* look]

**sur·vey·or** (sər-vā'ər) *n.* One who surveys, esp. one engaged in land surveying.

**sur·viv·al** (sər-vī'vəl) *n.* 1 The act or fact of surviving; a continuation of life or existence. 2 The fact of living or lasting beyond another. 3 One who or that which survives.

**sur·vive** (sər-vīv') *v.* **·vived**, **·viv·ing** 1 *v.i.* To live or continue beyond the death of another, the occurrence of an event, etc.; remain alive or in existence. —*v.t.* 2 To live or exist beyond the death, occurrence, or end of; outlive or outlast. 3 To go on living after or in spite of: to *survive* a flood. [< L *super-* above, beyond + *vivere* live] —**sur·vi'vor, sur·viv'er** *n.*

**sus·cep·ti·ble** (sə-sep'tə-bəl) *adj.* 1 Readily affected; especially subject or vulnerable: with *to:* susceptible to infection; lax supervision *susceptible* to abuse. 2 Capable of being influenced or determined; liable: with *of* or *to:* susceptible of proof. 3 Easily affected in feeling or emotion; sensitive. [< L *suscipere* receive, undertake] —**sus·cep·ti·bil·i·ty** (sə-sep'tə-bil'ə-tē), **sus·cep'ti·ble·ness** *n.* —**sus·cep'ti·bly** *adv.* —**Syn.** 1 unresistant, open. 2 admitting. 3 tender, impressionable.

**sus·pect** (sə-spekt') *v.t.* 1 To think (a person) guilty without evidence or proof. 2 To have distrust of; doubt: to *suspect* one's motives. 3 To have an inkling or suspicion of; think possible. —*v.i.* 4 To have suspicions. —*adj.* (sus′pekt, sə·spekt′) Suspected; exciting suspicion. —*n.* (sus′pekt) A person suspected, esp. of a crime. [< F *suspecter* < L *suspectūs*, p.p. of *suspicere* look under, mistrust] —**sus·pect′er** *n.*

**sus·pend** (sə·spend′) *v.t.* 1 To bar for a time from a privilege or office as a punishment. 2 To cause to cease for a time; interrupt: to *suspend* telephone service. 3 To withhold or defer action on: to *suspend* a sentence. 4 To hang from a support so as to allow free movement. 5 To keep in suspension, as dust particles in the air. —*v.i.* 6 To stop for a time. 7 To fail to meet obligations; stop payment. [< L *sub-* under + *pendere* hang]

**sus·pense** (sə·spens′) *n.* 1 Anxiety caused by an uncertainty, as to the outcome of an event. 2 Excited interest caused by the progressive unfolding of events or information leading to a climax or resolution. 3 The state of being uncertain or indecisive. [< L *suspēnsus*, p.p. of *suspendere* suspend]

**sus·pen·sion** (sə·spen′shən) *n.* 1 The act of suspending, or the state of being suspended. 2 A temporary removal from office or position or withdrawal of privilege. 3 An interruption; cessation: *suspension* of normal procedure. 4 A deferment of action. 5 The state of hanging freely from a support. 6 A dispersion in a liquid or gas of insoluble particles that slowly settle on standing; also, a substance in this condition. 7 *Mech.* A system, as of springs or other absorbent parts, by which the chassis and body of a vehicle is insulated against shocks when moving. 8 a *Music* The prolongation of one or more tones of a chord into the succeeding chord, causing a transient dissonance. b The note so prolonged.

**suspension bridge** A bridge having its roadway suspended from cables supported by towers and anchored at either end.

**sus·pi·cion** (sə·spish′ən) *n.* 1 The act of suspecting; an uncertain but often tenacious feeling or belief in the likelihood of another's guilt, wrongdoing, etc., without evidence or proof. 2 *Informal* A slight amount; trace, as of a flavor. —*v.t. Regional* To suspect. [< L *suspicere*. See SUSPECT.]

**sus·pi·cious** (sə·spish′əs) *adj.* 1 Tending to arouse suspicion; questionable. 2 Having or disposed to have suspicions. 3 Indicating suspicion. —**sus·pi′cious·ly** *adv.* —**sus·pi′cious·ness** *n.*

**sus·tain** (sə·stān′) *v.t.* 1 To keep up or maintain; keep in effect or being. 2 To maintain by providing with food and other necessities. 3 To keep from sinking or falling, esp. by bearing up from below. 4 To endure without succumbing; withstand. 5 To suffer, as a loss or injury; undergo. 6 To uphold or support as being true or just. 7 To prove the truth or correctness of; confirm. [< L *sub-* up from under + *tenere* to hold] —**sus·tain′a·ble** *adj.* —**sus·tain′er, sus·tain′ment** *n.* —**Syn.** 7 corroborate, establish.

**sus·te·nance** (sus′tə·nəns) *n.* 1 The act or process of sustaining; esp., maintenance of life or health; subsistence. 2 That which sustains, as food. 3 Means of support; livelihood.

**su·ture** (soo′chər) *n.* 1 The junction of two edges by or as by sewing. 2 *Anat.* The fusion of two bones at their edges, as in the skull. 3 *Surg.* a The act or operation of joining the edges of an incision, wound, etc. b The thread, wire, or other material used in this operation. —*v.t.* **-tured, ·tur·ing** To unite by means of sutures; sew together. [< L *sutus*, p.p. of *suere* sew] —**su′tur·al** *adj.* —**su′tur·al·ly** *adv.*

**su·ze·rain** (soo′zə·rin, -rān) *n.* 1 A feudal lord. 2 A nation having paramount control over a locally autonomous state. [< L *susum* upwards] —**su′ze·rain·ty** *n.* (*pl.* **·ties**)

**swab** (swob) *n.* 1 A soft, absorbent substance, as of cotton or gauze, usu. secured at the end of a small stick, for applying medication, cleansing a body surface, etc. 2 *Med.* A specimen of mucus, etc., taken for examination with a swab. 3 A mop for cleaning decks, floors, etc. 4 A cylindrical brush for cleaning firearms. 5 *Slang* An oaf; lout. —*v.t.* **swabbed, swab·bing** To clean or apply with a swab. [< MDu. *zwabben* swab] —**swab′ber** *n.*

**swag·ger** (swag′ər) *v.i.* 1 To walk with an air of conspicuous self-satisfaction and usu. of masculine vanity. 2 To behave in a blustering or self-satisfied manner. 3 To boast; brag. —*n.* 1 A swaggering gait or manner. 2 Verve; dash; bravado. —*adj.* Showy or stylish; smart. [< SWAG] —**swag′ger·er** *n.* —**swa·g′ger·ing·ly** *adv.*

**swal·low** (swol′ō) *v.t.* 1 To cause (food, etc.) to pass from the mouth into the stomach by means of muscular action of the esophagus. 2 To take in or engulf in a manner suggestive of this; absorb; envelop: often with *up.* 3 To put up with or endure; submit to, as insults. 4 To refrain from ex-

pressing; suppress: to *swallow* one's pride.
5 To take back: to *swallow* one's words. 6
*Informal* To believe (something improbable
or incredible) to be true. —*v.i.* 7 To perform
the act or the motions of swallowing. —*n.* 1
The act of swallowing. 2 An amount swallowed at once; a mouthful. [< OE *swelgan*
swallow] —**swal′low·er** *n.*

**swamp** (swomp, swômp) *n.* A tract or region
of low land saturated with water; a bog.
Also **swamp′land′** (-land′). —*v.t.* 1 To
drench or submerge with water or other
liquid. 2 To overwhelm with difficulties;
crush; ruin. 3 To sink or fill (a boat) with
water. —*v.i.* 4 To sink in water, etc.; become swamped. [?< LG] —**swamp′y** *adj.* (·i-
er, ·i·est)

**swan** (swon, swŏn) *n.* Any of several large,
web-footed, long-necked birds allied to but
heavier than the goose. [< OE]

**swank** (swangk) *n.* 1 Ostentatious display, as
in taste or manner; swagger. 2 Stylishness;
smartness. —*adj.* 1 Ostentatiously fashionable. 2 Stylish; smart. —*v.i.* *Slang* To
swagger; bluster. [?< MHG *swanken* sway]

**swank·y** (swangk′ē) *adj.* **swank·i·er, swank·
i·est** *Informal* Ostentatiously or extravagantly fashionable. —**swank′i·ly** *adv.* —
**swank′i·ness** *n.*

**swan's-down** (swonz′doun′, swŏnz′-) *n.* 1 The
down of a swan, used for trimming, powder
puffs, etc. 2 Any of various fine, soft fabrics,
usu. with a nap. Also **swans′down′**.

**swarm** (swôrm) *n.* 1 A large number of bees
moving together with a queen to form a
new colony. 2 A hive of bees. 3 A large crowd
or mass, esp. one in apparent overall movement; throng. —*v.i.* 1 To leave the hive in a
swarm: said of bees. 2 To come together,
move, or occur in great numbers: The
crowd *swarmed* out of the stadium; gnats
*swarming* about. 3 To be crowded or overrun; teem: with *with*: *swarming* with
tourists. —*v.t.* 4 To fill with a swarm or
crowd. [< OE *swearm*] —**swarm′er** *n.*

**swarth·y** (swôr′thē) *adj.* **swarth·i·er, swarth·i·
est** Having a dark complexion; tawny. [Var.
of obs. *swarty* < SWART] —**swarth′i·ly** *adv.*
—**swarth′i·ness** *n.*

**swash·buck·ler** (swosh′buk′lər, swôsh′-) *n.*
A swaggering soldier, adventurer, daredevil,
etc. [<SWASH + BUCKLER] —**swash′buck′-
ler·ing** *n.* —**swash′buck′ling** *adj., n.*

**swas·ti·ka** (swos′ti·kə) *n.* 1 A primitive ornament or symbol in the form of a cross with
arms of equal length, bent at the ends at

right angles. 2 Such a figure with the arms
extended clockwise, used as the emblem of
the Nazis. Also **swas′ti·ca.** [< Skt. *sú* good
+ *asti* being < *as* be]

**swath** (swoth, swôth) *n.* 1 A row or line of cut
grass or grain. 2 The space cut by a machine or implement in a single course. 3 A
strip, track, row, etc. —**cut a wide swath** To
make a fine impression. [< OE *swǣth* a
track]

**swathe** (swāth, swàth) *v.t.* **swathed, swath·
ing** 1 To bind or wrap, as in bandages;
swaddle. 2 To envelop; enwrap. —*n.* A bandage for swathing. [< OE *swathian*] —
**swath′er** *n.*

**swear** (swâr) *v.* **swore, sworn, swear·ing** *v.i.*
1 To make a solemn affirmation with an appeal to God or some other deity or to something held sacred. 2 To make a vow. 3 To
use profanity; curse. 4 *Law* To give testimony under oath. —*v.t.* 5 To affirm or assert solemnly by invoking sacred beings or
things. 6 To promise with an oath; vow. 7
To declare or affirm, earnestly or emphatically: I *swear* he's a liar. 8 To take or utter
(an oath). —**swear by** 1 To appeal to by
oath. 2 To have complete confidence in. —
**swear in** To administer a legal oath to. —
**swear off** *Informal* To promise to give up: to
*swear off* drink. —**swear out** To obtain (a
warrant for arrest) by making a statement
under oath. [< OE *swerian*] —**swear′er** *n.*

**sweat** (swet) *v.* **sweat** or **sweat·ed, sweat·ing**
*v.i.* 1 To exude or excrete salty moisture
from the pores of the skin; perspire. 2 To
exude moisture in drops. 3 To gather and
condense moisture in drops on its surface.
4 To pass through pores or interstices in
drops. 5 To ferment, as tobacco leaves. 6 To
come forth, as through a porous surface;
ooze. 7 *Informal* To work hard; toil; drudge.
8 *Informal* To suffer, as from anxiety. —*v.t.*
9 To exude (moisture) from the pores or a
porous surface. 10 To gather or condense
drops of (moisture). 11 To soak or stain with
sweat. 12 To cause to sweat. 13 To cause to
work hard. 14 *Informal* To force (employees)
to work for low wages and under unfavorable conditions. 15 To heat (solder, etc.)
until it melts. 16 To join, as metal objects
with solder. 17 *Metall.* To heat so as to extract an element that is easily fusible; also,
to extract thus. 18 To subject to fermentation, as hides or tobacco. 19 *Slang* To subject to torture or rigorous interrogation to
extract information. —**sweat (something)**

out *Slang* To wait through anxiously; endure. —*n.* 1 Moisture in minute drops on the skin. 2 The act or state of sweating. 3 Hard labor; drudgery. 4 *Informal* Impatience, anxiety, or hurry. [< OE *swǣtan*] —**sweat′i·ly** *adv.* —**sweat′i·ness** *n.* —**sweat′y** *adj.* (**·i·er, ·i·est**)

**sweep** (swēp) *v.* **swept, sweep·ing** *v.t.* 1 To collect or clear away with a broom, brush, etc. 2 To clear or clean with a broom, etc.: to *sweep* a floor. 3 To touch or brush with a motion as of sweeping: to *sweep* the strings of a harp. 4 To pass over swiftly: The searchlight *swept* the sky. 5 To move, carry, bring, etc., with force: The flood *swept* the bridge away. 6 To move over or through with force: The gale *swept* the bay. 7 To drag the bottom of (a body of water, etc.). 8 To win totally or overwhelmingly. —*v.i.* 9 To clean a floor or other surface with a broom, etc. 10 To move or go strongly and evenly: The train *swept* by. 11 To walk with great dignity: She *swept* into the room. 12 To trail, as a skirt. 13 To extend with a long reach or curve: The road *sweeps* along the lake shore on the north. —*n.* 1 The act or result of sweeping. 2 A long stroke or movement: a *sweep* of the hand. 3 The act of clearing out or getting rid of. 4 An unbroken stretch or extent: a *sweep* of beach. 5 A total or overwhelming victory, as in an election. 6 The range, area, or compass reached by sweeping. 7 One who sweeps chimneys, streets, etc. 8 A curving line; flowing contour. 9 A long, heavy oar. 10 A long pole on a pivot, having a bucket suspended from one end, for use in drawing water. 11 *pl.* Sweepings. 12 *pl. Informal* Sweepstakes. [< OE *swāpan*] —**sweep′er** *n.*

**sweet** (swēt) *adj.* 1 Having a flavor like that of sugar, often due to the presence of sugar in some form. 2 Not salted, sour, rancid, or spoiled. 3 Gently pleasing to the senses; agreeable to the taste, smell, etc. 4 Agreeable or delightful to the mind or the emotions. 5 Having gentle, pleasing, and winning qualities. 6 Sound; rich; productive: said of soil. —*n.* 1 The quality of being sweet; sweetness. 2 Something sweet, agreeable, or pleasing. 3 *Usu. pl.* Confections, preserves, candy, etc. 4 A beloved person. 5 *Brit.* DESSERT. [< OE *swēte*] —**sweet′ly** *adv.* —**sweet′ness** *n.*

**sweet·en** (swēt′n) *v.t.* 1 To make sweet or sweeter. 2 To make more endurable; allevi-

ate; lighten. 3 To make pleasant or gratifying. —**sweet′en·er** *n.*

**sweet·heart** (swēt′härt′) *n.* 1 Darling: a term of endearment. 2 A lover.

**sweet pea** A climbing leguminous plant cultivated for its fragrant, varicolored flowers.

**sweet potato** 1 A perennial tropical vine of the morning-glory family, with a fleshy tuberous root. 2 The sweet yellow or orange root, eaten as a vegetable.

**swell** (swel) *v.* **swelled, swelled** or **swol·len, swell·ing** *v.i.* 1 To increase in size or volume, as by inflation with air or by absorption of moisture. 2 To increase in amount, degree, force, intensity, etc. 3 To rise above the usual or surrounding level, surface, etc. 4 To rise in waves or swells, as the sea. 5 To bulge. 6 *Informal* To become puffed up with pride. —*v.t.* 7 To cause to increase in size or volume. 8 To cause to increase in amount, degree, force, intensity, etc. 9 To cause to bulge. 10 To puff with pride. —*n.* 1 The act, process, or effect of swelling; expansion. 2 A long continuous wave without a crest. 3 A rise of, or undulation in, the land. 4 Any bulge or protuberance. 5 *Music* A crescendo and diminuendo in succession; also, the signs (< >) indicating it. 6 A device by which the loudness of an organ may be varied. 7 *Informal* A person who is very fashionable, elegant, or social. —*adj.* 1 *Informal* Very fashionable, elegant, or social. 2 *Slang* Very fine; first-rate; excellent. [< OE *swellan*] —**Syn.** *v.* 1 bulge, dilate, distend, enlarge, expand.

**swel·ter** (swel′tər) *v.i.* 1 To perspire or suffer from oppressive heat. —*v.t.* 2 To cause to swelter. —*n.* A sweltering condition; oppressive heat. [< OE *sweltan* die] —**swel′ter·ing·ly** *adv.*

**swerve** (swûrv) *v.t.* & *v.i.* **swerved, swerv·ing** To turn or cause to turn aside from a course; deflect. —*n.* The act of swerving; a sudden turning aside. [< OE *sweorfan* file or grind away]

**swift** (swift) *n.* Any of various swallowlike birds with extraordinary powers of flight, as the chimney swift. [< SWIFT¹]

**swig** (swig) *n. Informal* A great gulp; deep draft. —*v.t.* & *v.i.* **swigged, swig·ging** *Informal* To take swigs (of). [?]

**swill** (swil) *v.t.* 1 To drink greedily or to excess. 2 To drench, as with water; rinse; wash. 3 To fill with, as drink. —*v.i.* 4 To drink greedily or to excess. —*n.* 1 Semiliquid food for domestic animals, as the mixture of edible refuse and liquid fed to pigs. 2 Garbage. 3 Unappetizing food. 4 A great gulp; swig. [<OE *swillan* to wash]

**swim** (swim) *v.* **swam** (*Regional* **swum**), **swum, swim·ming** *v.i.* 1 To move through water by working the legs, arms, fins, etc. 2 To float. 3 To move with a smooth or flowing motion. 4 To be flooded. —*v.t.* 5 To cross or traverse by swimming. 6 To cause to swim. —*n.* 1 The action or pastime of swimming. 2 The distance swum or to be swum. 3 The air bladder of a fish: also **swim bladder, swimming bladder.** —**in the swim** Active in current affairs, esp. those involved with fashion, socializing, etc. [< OE *swimman*] —**swim′mer** *n.*

**swin·dle** (swin′dəl) *v.* **·dled, ·dling** *v.t.* 1 To cheat; defraud. 2 To obtain by such means. —*v.i.* 3 To practice fraud. —*n.* The act or process of swindling. [< G *schwindeln* cheat] —**swin′dler** *n.* —**Syn.** *v.* 1 deceive, dupe, rook.

**swine** (swin) *n. pl.* **swine** 1 A pig or hog: usu. used collectively. 2 A low, greedy, or vicious person. [< OE *swin*] —**swin′ish** *adj.* —**swin′ish·ly** *adv.* —**swin′ish·ness** *n.*

**swing** (swing) *v.* **swung, swing·ing** *v.i.* 1 To move to and fro or backward and forward rhythmically, as something suspended. 2 To ride in a swing. 3 To move with an even, swaying motion. 4 To turn; pivot: We *swung* around and went home. 5 To be suspended; hang. 6 *Informal* To be executed by hanging. 7 *Slang* To be very up-to-date and sophisticated, esp. in one's amusements and pleasures. 8 *Informal* To sing or play with or to have a compelling, usu. jazzlike rhythm. 9 *Slang* To be sexually promiscuous. —*v.t.* 10 To cause to move to and fro or backward and forward. 11 To brandish; flourish: to *swing* an ax. 12 To cause to turn on or as on a pivot or central point. 13 To lift, hoist, or hang: They *swung* the mast into place. 14 *Informal* To bring to a successful conclusion: to *swing* a deal. 15 *Informal* To sing or play in the style of swing (*n.*, def. 8). —*n.* 1 The action process, or manner of swinging. 2 A free swaying motion. 3 A contrivance of hanging ropes with a seat on which a person may move to and fro through the air. 4 Freedom of action. 5 The arc or range of something that swings. 6 A swinging blow or stroke. 7 A trip or tour: a *swing* through the west. 8 A type of jazz music played by big bands, achieving its effect by lively, compelling rhythms, contrapuntal styles, and arranged ensemble playing: also **swing music.** —**in full swing** In full and lively operation. [< OE *swingan* scourge, beat up]

**swipe** (swip) *v.* **swiped, swip·ing** —*v.t.* 1 *Informal* To strike with a sweeping motion. 2 *Slang* To steal; snatch. —*v.i.* 3 To hit with a sweeping motion. —*n. Informal* A hard blow. [Var. of SWEEP]

**swirl** (swurl) *v.t. & v.i.* To move or cause to move along in irregular eddies; whirl. —*n.* 1 A whirling along, as in an eddy. 2 A curl or twist; spiral. [ME *swyrl*] —**swirl′y** *adj.*

**switch** (swich) *n.* 1 A small flexible rod, twig, or whip. 2 A tress of false hair, worn by women in building a coiffure. 3 A mechanism for shifting a railway train from one track to another. 4 The act or operation of switching, shifting, or changing. 5 The tuft of hair at the end of the tail in certain animals, as a cow. 6 *Electr.* A device used to start or stop a flow of current. 7 A blow with or as with a switch. —*v.t.* 1 To whip or lash. 2 To move, jerk, or whisk suddenly or sharply. 3 To turn aside or divert; shift. 4 To exchange: They *switched* plates. 5 To shift, as a railroad car, to another track. 6 *Electr.* To connect or disconnect with a switch. —*v.i.* 7 To turn aside; change; shift. 8 To swing back and forth or from side to side. 9 To shift from one track to another. [?] —**switch′er** *n.*

**switch·board** (swich′bôrd′, -bôrd′) *n.* A panel bearing switches or controls for several electric circuits, as a telephone exchange.

**swiv·el** (swiv′əl) *n.* 1 A coupling or pivot that permits parts, as of a mechanism, to rotate independently. 2 Anything that turns on a pin or headed bolt. 3 A cannon that swings on a pivot: also **swivel gun.** —*v.* **·eled** or **·elled, ·el·ing** or **·el·ling** *v.t.* 1 To turn on or as on a swivel. 2 To provide with or secure by a swivel. —*v.i.* 3 To turn or swing on or as on a swivel. [< OE *swifan* revolve]

**swoon** (swoon) *v.i.* To faint. —*n.* A fainting fit. [< OE *swōgan* suffocate]

**swoop** (swoop) *v.i.* 1 To drop or descend suddenly, as a bird pouncing on its prey. —*v.t.* 2 To take or seize suddenly; snatch. —*n.* The act of swooping. [< OE *swāpan* sweep]

**swop** (swop) *n. & v.* **swopped, swop·ping** SWAP.

**sword** (sôrd, sōrd) *n.* A weapon consisting of a long blade fixed in a hilt. —**at swords′ points** Very unfriendly; hostile. —**cross swords** 1 To quarrel; argue. 2 To fight. —**put to the sword** To kill with a sword. —**the**

567

**sword** 1 Military power. 2 War. [< OE *swe-ord*]

**sword·fish** (sôrd′fish′, sōrd′-) *n. pl.* **·fish** or **·fish·es** A large fish of the open sea having the upper jaw elongated into a swordlike process.

**syc·a·more** (sik′ə-môr, -mōr) *n.* 1 A medium-sized tree of Syria and Egypt allied to the fig. 2 Any of various plane trees widely distributed in North America. 3 An ornamental maple tree: also **sycamore maple**. [< Gk. *sykon* a fig + *moron* a mulberry]

**syc·o·phant** (sik′ə-fənt, -fant) *n.* A servile flatterer; toady. [< Gk. *sykon* fig + *phainein* to show] —**syc′o·phan·cy** (-sē) (*pl.* **·cies**) *n.* — **syc′o·phan′tic** (-fan′tik), **syc′o·phan′ti·cal** *adj.* —**syc′o·phan′ti·cal·ly** *adv.*

**syl·lab·i·fy** (si·lab′ə-fī) *v.t.* **·fied, ·fy·ing** To form or divide into syllables. —**syl·lab′i·fi·ca′tion** *n.*

**syl·la·ble** (sil′ə-bəl) *n.* 1 *Phonet.* A word or part of a word uttered in a single vocal impulse. 2 A part of a written or printed word corresponding to the spoken division. 3 The least detail or mention: Please don't repeat a *syllable* of what you've heard here. —*v.* **·bled, ·bling** *v.t.* 1 To pronounce the syllables of. —*v.i.* 2 To pronounce syllables. [< Gk. *syn-* together + *lambanein* take]

**sylph** (silf) *n.* 1 A being, mortal but without a soul, living in and on the air. 2 A slender, graceful young woman or girl. [< NL *sylphus*]

**syl·van** (sil′vən) *adj.* 1 Of, pertaining to, or located in a forest or woods. 2 Composed of or abounding in trees or woods. —*n.* A person or animal living in or frequenting forests or woods. [< L *silva* a wood]

**sym·bol** (sim′bəl) *n.* 1 Something chosen to stand for or represent something else, as an object used to typify a quality, idea, etc.: The lily is a *symbol* of purity. 2 A character, mark, abbreviation, letter, etc., that represents something else. —*v.t.* **sym·boled** or **·bolled, sym·bol·ing** or **·bol·ling** SYMBOLIZE. [< Gk. *syn-* together + *ballein* throw]

**sym·bol·ic** (sim·bol′ik) *adj.* 1 Of, pertaining to, or expressed by a symbol. 2 Used as a symbol: with *of.* 3 Characterized by or involving the use of symbols or symbolism: *symbolic* poetry. Also **sym·bol′i·cal.** — **sym·bol′i·cal·ly** *adv.* —**sym·bol′i·cal·ness** *n.*

**sym·bol·ism** (sim′bəl-iz′əm) *n.* 1 The use of symbols to represent things; the act or art of investing things with a symbolic mean-ing. 2 A system of symbols or symbolical representation. 3 Symbolic meaning or character.

**sym·bol·ize** (sim′bəl-īz) *v.* **·ized, ·iz·ing** *v.t.* 1 To be a symbol of; represent symbolically; typify. 2 To represent by a symbol or symbols. 3 To treat as symbolic or figurative. — *v.i.* 4 To use symbols. *Brit. sp.* **sym′bol·ise.** —**sym′bol·i·za′tion, sym′bol·i·zer** *n.*

**sym·me·try** (sim′ə-trē) *n. pl.* **·tries** 1 Corresponding arrangement or balancing of the parts or elements of a whole in respect to size, shape, and position on opposite sides of an axis or center. 2 The element of beauty and harmony in nature or art that results from such arrangement and balancing. 3 *Math.* An arrangement of points in a system such that the system appears unchanged after certain partial rotations. [< Gk. *syn-* together + *metron* a measure] —**sym·met′ric** (si·met′rik), **sym·met′ri·cal** *adj.* —**sym·met′ri·cal·ly** *adv.* —**sym·met′ri·cal·ness** *n.*

**sym·pa·thet·ic** (sim′pə-thet′ik) *adj.* 1 Pertaining to, expressing, or proceeding from sympathy. 2 Having a compassionate feeling for others; sympathizing. 3 Being in accord or harmony; congenial. 4 Of, proceeding from, or characterized by empathy. 5 Referring to sounds produced by responsive vibrations. Also **sym′pa·thet′i·cal.** — **sym′pa·thet′i·cal·ly** *adv.*

**sym·pa·thize** (sim′pə-thīz) *v.i.* **·thized, ·thiz·ing** 1 To experience or understand the sentiments or ideas of another. 2 To feel or express compassion, as for another's sorrow or affliction: with *with.* 3 To be in harmony or agreement. *Brit. sp.* **sym′pa·thise.** — **sym′pa·thiz′er** *n.* —**sym′pa·thiz′ing·ly** *adv.*

**sym·pa·thy** (sim′pə-thē) *n. pl.* **·thies** 1 The fact or condition of an agreement in feeling: The *sympathy* between husband and wife was remarkable. 2 A feeling of compassion for another's sufferings. 3 Agreement or accord: to be in *sympathy* with an objective. 4 Support; loyalty; approval: trying to enlist my *sympathies.* [< Gk. *syn-* together + *pathos* a feeling, passion] —**Syn.** 1 affinity, concord. 2 commiseration, condolence, pity.

**sym·pho·ny** (sim′fə-nē) *n. pl.* **·nies** 1 A harmonious or agreeable mingling of sounds. 2 Any harmony or agreeable blending, as of color. 3 A composition for orchestra, consisting usu. of four extensive movements.

4 SYMPHONY ORCHESTRA. [< Gk. *syn-* together + *phōnē* a sound] —sym·phon·ic (sim·fon'ik) *adj.* —sym·phon'i·cal·ly *adv.*

sym·po·si·um (sim·pō'zē·əm) *n. pl.* ·si·ums, ·si·a (-zē·ə) 1 A meeting for discussion of a particular subject or subjects. 2 A collection of comments, opinions, essays, etc. on the same subject. [< Gk. *syn-* together + *posis* drinking] —sym·po'si·ac (-ak) *adj.*

symp·tom (simp'təm) *n.* 1 An organic or functional condition indicating the presence of disease, esp. when regarded as an aid in diagnosis. 2 A sign or indication that serves to point out the existence of something else: *symptoms* of civil unrest. [< Gk. *syn-* together + *piptein* fall] —symp'to·mat'ic (-tə·mat'ik), symp'to·mat'i·cal *adj.* —symp'to·mat'i·cal·ly *adv.* —Syn. 2 earmark, mark, signal, token.

syn·a·gogue (sin'ə·gog, -gog) *n.* 1 A place of meeting for Jewish worship and religious instruction. 2 A Jewish congregation or assemblage for religious instruction and observances. Also syn'a·gog. [< Gk. *synagōgē* an assembly]

syn·chro·nize (sing'krə·nīz, sin'-) *v.* ·nized, ·niz·ing *v.i.* 1 To occur at the same time; coincide. 2 To move or operate in unison. —*v.t.* 3 To cause to operate synchronously: to *synchronize* watches. 4 To cause (the appropriate sound of a motion picture) to coincide with the action. 5 To assign the same date or period to; make contemporaneous. [< SYNCHRONOUS] —syn'chro·niz'er *n.*

syn·co·pate (sing'kə·pāt, sin'-) *v.t.* ·pat·ed, ·pat·ing 1 To contract, as a word, by syncope. 2 *Music* To treat or modify (a rhythm, melody, etc.) by syncopation. [< LL *syncope* *syncope*]

syn·co·pa·tion (sing'kə·pā'shən, sin'-) *n.* 1 The act of syncopating or state of being syncopated; also, that which is syncopated. 2 *Music* The suppression of an expected rhythmic accent by the continuation of an unaccented tone that begins just before it. 3 Any music featuring syncopation, as ragtime, jazz, etc. 4 Syncope of a word, or an example of it.

syn·di·cate (sin'də·kit) *n.* 1 An association of individuals united to negotiate some business or to engage in some enterprise, often one requiring large capital. 2 An association for purchasing feature articles, etc., and selling them again to a number of periodicals, as newspapers, for simultaneous publication. 3 The office or jurisdiction of a syn-

dic; also, a body of syndics. —*v.t.* (-kāt) ·cat·ed, ·cat·ing 1 To combine into or manage by a syndicate. 2 To sell for publication in many newspapers or magazines. [< F *syndic* syndic] —syn'di·ca'tion, syn'di·ca'tor *n.*

syn·drome (sin'drōm) *n.* 1 The aggregate of symptoms and signs characteristic of a specific disease or condition. 2 A group of traits regarded as being characteristic of a certain type, condition, etc. [< Gk. *syn-* together + *dramein* run] —syn·drom·ic (sin·drom'ik) *adj.*

syn·od (sin'əd, -od) *n.* 1 An ecclesiastical council. 2 Any assembly, council, etc. [< Gk. < *syn-* together + *hodos* a way]

syn·o·nym (sin'ə·nim) *n.* 1 A word having the same or almost the same meaning as some other or others in the same language. 2 A word used in metonymy to substitute for another. [< Gk. *syn-* together + *onyma* a name] —syn'o·nym'ic, syn'o·nym'i·cal *adj.* —syn'o·nym'i·ty *n.*

sy·non·y·mous (si·non'ə·məs) *adj.* Being equivalent or similar to meaning. —sy·non'y·mous·ly *adv.*

sy·nop·sis (si·nop'sis) *n. pl.* ·ses (-sēz) A general view or condensation, as of a story, book, etc.; summary. [< Gk. *syn-* together + *opsis* a view] —Syn. abridgment, abstract, digest, précis.

syn·tax (sin'taks) *n.* 1 The arrangement and interrelationship of words in grammatical constructions. 2 The branch of grammar which deals with this. [< Gk. *syn-* together + *tassein* arrange] —syn·tac·tic (sin·tak'tik), syn·tac'ti·cal *adj.* —syn·tac'ti·cal·ly *adv.*

syn·the·sis (sin'thə·sis) *n. pl.* ·ses (-sēz) 1 The assembling of separate or subordinate parts into a new form. 2 The complex whole resulting from this. 3 *Chem.* The building up of a compound by the direct union of its elements or of simpler compounds. [< Gk. *syn-* together + *tithenai* to place] —syn'the·sist *n.*

syn·thet·ic (sin·thet'ik) *adj.* 1 Of, pertaining to, or using synthesis. 2 Produced artificially by chemical synthesis 3 Artificial; spurious. Also syn·thet'i·cal. —*n.* Anything produced by synthesis, esp. by chemical synthesis, as a material. [< Gk. *syn-* together + *tithenai* to place] —syn·thet'i·cal·ly *adv.*

syph·i·lis (sif'ə·lis) *n.* An infectious, chronic, venereal disease caused by a spirochete transmissible by direct contact or congenitally. [< *Syphilus*, a shepherd in a 16th-century Latin poem who had the disease] —**syph·i·lit·ic** (sif′ə·lit′ik) *adj.*, *n.*

**syr·inge** (si·rinj′, sir′inj) *n.* 1 An instrument used to remove fluids from or inject fluids into body cavities. 2 HYPODERMIC SYRINGE. —*v.t.* ·**inged**, ·**ing·ing** To spray, cleanse, inject, etc. with a syringe. [< Gk. *syrinx* a pipe]

**sys·tem** (sis′təm) *n.* 1 A group or arrangement of parts, facts, phenomena, etc., that relate to or interact with each other in such a way as to form a whole: the solar *system*; the nervous *system*. 2 Any orderly group of logically related facts, principles, beliefs, etc.: the democratic *system*. 3 An orderly method, plan, or procedure: a betting *system* that really works. 4 A method of classification, organization, arrangement, etc.: books classified according to the Dewey decimal *system*. 5 The body, considered as a functional whole. —**the system** The dominant political, economic, and social institutions and their leaders, regarded as resistant to change or to effective influence. [< Gk. *systēma* an organized whole]

**sys·tem·at·ic** (sis′tə·mat′ik) *adj.* 1 Of, pertaining to, or characterized by system or classification. 2 Acting by or carried out with system or method; methodical. 3 Forming or based on a system. Also **sys·′tem·at′i·cal.** —**sys′tem·at′i·cal·ly** *adv.* — **Syn.** 2 orderly, organized, procedural, routine. 3 organizational, bureaucratic.

**sys·tem·a·tize** (sis′tə·mə·tīz′) *v.t.* ·**tized**, ·**tiz·ing** To make into a system; organize methodically. Also **sys′tem·ize.** *Brit. sp.* **sys′tem·a·tise′.** —**sys′tem·a·ti·za′tion, sys′tem·i·za′tion** *n.* —**sys′tem·a·tiz′er, sys′tem·iz′er** *n.*

**sys·to·le** (sis′tə·lē) *n.* 1 The rhythmic contraction of the heart, esp. of the ventricles, that impels the blood outward. 2 The shortening of a syllable that is naturally or by position long. [< Gk. *syn-* together + *stellein* send] —**sys·tol·ic** (sis·tol′ik) *adj.*

# T

**tab·er·nac·le** (tab′ər·nak′əl) *n.* 1 A tent or similar temporary structure. 2 *Usu. cap.* In the Old Testament, the portable sanctuary used by the Israelites in the wilderness. 3 *Usu. cap.* The Jewish temple. 4 Any house of worship, esp. one of large size. 5 The

human body as the dwelling place of the soul. 6 The ornamental receptacle for the consecrated eucharistic elements. [< L *taberna* shed] —**tab·er·nac·u·lar** (tab′ər·nak′yə·lər) *adj.*

**ta·ble** (tā′bəl) *n.* 1 An article of furniture with a flat top, usu. fixed on legs. 2 Such a table on which food is set for a meal. 3 The food served at a meal. 4 The persons present at a meal. 5 A gaming table, as for roulette. 6 A collection of related numbers, values, signs, or items of any kind, arranged for ease of reference or comparison, often in parallel columns. 7 A compact listing: *table* of contents. 8 A tableland; plateau. 9 Any flat horizontal rock, surface, etc. 10 A tablet or slab bearing an inscription. —**the Tables** Laws inscribed on tablets, as the Ten Commandments. —**turn the tables** To reverse a situation. —*v.t.* ·**bled**, ·**bling** 1 To place on a table. 2 To postpone discussion of (a resolution, bill, etc.). [< L *tabula* board]

**tab·leau** (tab′lō, ta·blō′) *n. pl.* ·**leaux** (-lōz) or ·**leaus** (-lōz) 1 Any picture or picturesque representation. 2 A scene reminiscent of a picture, usu. presented by persons motionless on a stage. [F, lit., small table]

**ta·ble d'hôte** (tab′əl dōt′, tä′bəl) *pl.* **ta·bles d'hote** (tab′əlz dōt′, tä′bəlz) A complete meal of several specified courses, served in a restaurant at a fixed price. [F, lit., table of the host]

**tab·let** (tab′lit) *n.* 1 A small, flat or nearly flat piece of some prepared substance, as a drug. 2 A pad, as of writing paper or note paper. 3 A small flat surface designed for or containing an inscription or design. 4 A thin leaf or sheet of ivory, wood, etc., for writing, painting, or drawing. 5 A set of such leaves joined together at one end. [< OF *tablete*, lit., small table]

**tab·loid** (tab′loid) *n.* A newspaper, usu. one half the size of an ordinary newspaper, in which the news is presented concisely, often sensationally, and with many pictures. —*adj.* Compact; concise. [< TABL(ET) + -OID]

**ta·boo** (tə·bōō′, ta-) *n. pl.* ·**boos** 1 A religious or social prohibition against touching or mentioning someone or something or doing something because such persons or things are considered sacred, dangerous, etc. 2 The practice of such prohibitions. 3 Any restriction or ban based on custom or convention. —*adj.* Restricted, prohibited, or excluded by taboo, custom, or convention.

—*v.t.* 1 To place under taboo. 2 To avoid as taboo. Also **ta·bu′**. [< Tongan]

**tab·u·lar** (tab′yə-lər) *adj.* 1 Of, pertaining to, or arranged in a table or list. 2 Computed from or with a mathematical table. 3 Having a flat surface. —**tab′u·lar·ly** *adv.*

**tab·u·late** (tab′yə-lāt) *v.t.* ·lat·ed, ·lat·ing To arrange in a table or list. —*adj.* Having a flat surface or surfaces; broad and flat. —**tab′u·la′tion, tab′u·la′tor** *n.*

**tac·it** (tas′it) *adj.* 1 Existing, inferred, or implied without being directly stated. 2 Not spoken; silent. 3 Emitting no sound. [< L *tacitus,* pp. of *tacere* be silent] —**tac′it·ly** *adv.*

**tac·i·turn** (tas′ə-tûrn) *adj.* Habitually silent or reserved. [< L *tacitus.* See TACIT.] —**tac·i·tur·ni·ty** (tas′ə-tûr′nə-tē) *n.* —**tac′i·turn·ly** *adv.* —**Syn.** uncommunicative, reticent.

**tack** (tak) *n.* 1 A small sharp-pointed nail, usu. with a relatively broad, flat head. 2 *Naut.* a A rope which holds down the lower outer corner of some sails. b The corner so held. c The direction in which a vessel sails when sailing closehauled, considered in relation to the position of its sails. d A change in a ship's direction made by a change in the position of its sails. 3 A policy or course of action. 4 A temporary fastening, as any of various stitches in sewing. —*v.t.* 1 To fasten or attach with tacks. 2 To secure temporarily, as with long stitches. 3 To attach as supplementary; append. 4 *Naut.* a To change the course of (a vessel) by turning into the wind. b To navigate (a vessel) to windward by making a series of tacks. —*v.i.* 5 *Naut.* a To tack a vessel. b To sail to windward by a series of tacks. 6 To change one's course of action. 7 ZIGZAG. [< OF *tache* a nail] —**tack′er** *n.*

**tack·le** (tak′əl) *n.* 1 A rope and pulley or combination of ropes and pulleys, used for hoisting or moving objects. 2 The rigging of a ship. 3 The equipment used in any work or sport; gear. 4 The act of tackling. 5 In football, either of two linemen stationed between the guard and end. —*v.t.* ·led, ·ling 1 To fasten with or as if with tackle. 2 To harness (a horse). 3 To undertake to master, accomplish, or solve: *tackle* a problem. 4 To seize suddenly and forcefully. 5 In football, to seize and stop (an opponent carrying the ball). [< MLG *taken* seize] —**tack′ler** *n.*

**tact** (takt) *n.* 1 A quick or intuitive appreciation of what is fit, proper, or right; facility

in saying or doing the proper thing. 2 A delicate sense of discrimination, esp. in aesthetics. [< L *tactus* sense of touch, pp. of *tangere* touch]

**tac·tics** (tak′tiks) *n.pl.* 1 (*construed as sing.*) The science and art of handling troops in securing military and naval objectives. 2 Any adroit maneuvering to gain an end. [< Gk. *taktikos* suitable for arranging]

**tad·pole** (tad′pōl) *n.* The aquatic larva of an amphibian, as a frog or toad, having gills and a tail. [< ME *tadde* toad + *pol* head, poll]

**taf·fe·ta** (taf′ə·tə) *n.* A fine, glossy, somewhat stiff fabric woven of silk, rayon, nylon, etc. —*adj.* Made of or resembling taffeta. [< Pers. *tāftah*]

**taf·fy** (taf′ē) *n.* *pl.* **taf·fies** 1 A chewy confection made usu. of brown sugar or molasses, boiled down, and pulled until it cools. 2 *Informal* Flattery; blarney. [?]

**tag** (tag) *n.* A children's game in which a player, called "it," chases other players until he touches one of them, that person in turn becoming the one who must pursue another. —*v.t.* **tagged, tag·ging** To overtake and touch, as in the game of tag. [?]

**tail** (tāl) *n.* 1 The rear end of an animal's body, esp. when prolonged to form a flexible appendage. 2 Anything similar in appearance, as a pigtail. 3 *Astron.* The luminous cloud extending from a comet. 4 The hind, back, or inferior portion of anything. 5 *Often pl. Informal* The reverse side of a coin. 6 A body of persons in single file. 7 A group of attendants; retinue. 8 *Aeron.* A system of airfoils placed some distance to the rear of the main bearing surfaces of an airplane. 9 *pl. Informal* A man's full-dress suit; also, a swallow-tailed coat. 10 *Informal* A person, as a detective, who follows another in surveillance. 11 *Informal* A trail or course, as one taken by a fugitive. —*v.t.* 1 To furnish with a tail. 2 To cut off the tail of. 3 To be the tail or end of. 4 To join (one thing) to the end of another. 5 To insert and fasten by one end. 6 *Informal* To follow secretly and stealthily; shadow. —*v.i.* 7 To form or be part of a tail. 8 *Informal* To follow close behind. 9 To diminish gradually: with *off.* —*adj.* 1 Rearmost; hindmost: the *tail* end. 2 Coming from behind: a *tail* wind. [< OE *tǽgl*]

**tai·lor** (tā′lər) *n.* One who makes or repairs garments. —*v.i.* 1 To do a tailor's work. —*v.t.* 2 To fit with garments. 3 To make, work at, or style by tailoring. 4 To form or adapt to meet certain needs or conditions. [< LL *taliare* split, cut] —**tai′lor·ing** *n.*

**taint** (tānt) *v.t.* 1 To affect with decay or contamination. 2 To render morally corrupt. —*v.i.* 3 To be or become tainted. —*n.* A cause or result of contamination or corruption. [< OF *teint*, pp. of *teindre* to tinge, color]

**take** (tāk) *v.* **took, tak·en, tak·ing** *v.t.* 1 To lay hold of; grasp. 2 To get possession of; seize; capture; catch. 3 To gain, capture, or win, as in a game or in competition. 4 To choose; select. 5 To buy. 6 To rent or hire; lease. 7 To subscribe to, as a periodical. 8 To assume occupancy of: to *take* a chair. 9 To assume the responsibilities of: to *take* office. 10 To accept into some relation to oneself: He *took* a wife. 11 To assume as a symbol or badge: to *take* the veil. 12 To subject oneself to: to *take* a vow. 13 To remove or carry off: with *away.* 14 To steal. 15 To remove by death. 16 To subtract or deduct. 17 To be subjected to; undergo: to *take* a beating. 18 To submit to; accept passively: to *take* an insult. 19 To become affected with; contract: He *took* cold. 20 To affect: The fever *took* him at dawn. 21 To captivate; charm or delight: The dress *took* her fancy. 22 To react to: How did she *take* the news? 23 To undertake to deal with; contend with; handle: to *take* an examination. 24 To consider; deem: I *take* him for an honest man. 25 To understand; comprehend: I couldn't *take* the meaning of her remarks. 26 To hit: The blow *took* him on the forehead. 27 *Informal* To aim or direct: He *took* a shot at the target. 28 To carry with one: *Take* your umbrella! 29 To lead: This road *takes* you to town. 30 To escort. 31 To receive into the body, as by eating, inhaling, etc.: *Take* a deep breath. 32 To accept or assume as if due or granted: to *take* credit. 33 To require: it *takes* courage. 34 To let in; admit; accommodate: The car *takes* only six people. 35 To occupy oneself in; enjoy: to *take* a nap. 36 To perform, as an action: to *take* a stride. 37 To confront and get over: The horse *took* the hurdle. 38 To avail oneself of (an opportunity, etc.). 39 To put into effect; adopt: to *take* measures. 40 To use up or consume: The piano *takes* too much space. 41 To make use of; apply: to *take* pains. 42 To travel by means of: to *take* a train. 43 To seek: to *take* cover. 44 To ascertain by measuring, computing, etc.: to *take* a census. 45 To obtain or derive from some source. 46 To write down or copy: to *take* notes. 47 To

obtain (a likeness or representation of) by photographing. 48 To conceive or feel: She *took* a dislike to him. 49 *Slang* To cheat; deceive. 50 *Gram.* To require by construction or usage: The verb *takes* a direct object. —*v.i.* 51 To get possession. 52 To engage; catch, as mechanical parts. 53 To begin to grow; germinate. 54 To have the intended effect: The vaccination *took.* 55 To gain favor, as a play. 56 To detract: with *from.* 57 To become (ill or sick). —**take after** 1 To resemble. 2 To follow in pursuit. —**take amiss** To be offended by. —**take back** To retract. —**take down** 1 To humble. 2 To write down. —**take for** To consider to be. —**take in** 1 To admit; receive. 2 To lessen in size or scope. 3 To include; embrace. 4 To understand. 5 To cheat or deceive. 6 To visit. —**take it** To endure hardship, abuse, etc. —**take off** 1 To mimic; burlesque. 2 To rise from a surface, esp. to begin a flight, as an airplane or rocket. 3 To leave; depart. 4 To begin: often used to refer to that point in an economic venture when growth becomes a self-generating and self-sustaining process. —**take on** 1 To hire; employ. 2 To undertake to deal with. 3 *Informal* To exhibit violent emotion. —**take over** To assume control of (a business, nation, etc.) —**take place** To happen. —**take to** 1 To become fond of. 2 *Informal* To adopt a way of doing, using, etc.: He has *taken* to walking to work. 3 To flee: to *take* to the hills. —**take up** 1 To make smaller or less; shorten or tighten. 2 To pay, as a note or mortgage. 3 To accept as stipulated: to *take up* an option. 4 To begin or begin again. 5 To occupy, engage, or consume, as space or time. 6 To develop an interest in or devotion to: to *take up* a cause. —**take up with** *Informal* To become friendly with; associate with. —*n.* 1 The act of taking or that which is taken. 2 *Slang* An amount of money received; receipts; profit. 3 A quantity collected at one time: the *take* of fish. 4 An uninterrupted run of the camera in photographing a movie or television scene. 5 A scene so photographed. 6 The process of making a sound recording. 7 A recording made in a single recording session. [< OE *tacan* < ON *taka*] —**tak′er** *n.* • See BRING.

**take-home pay** (tāk′hōm′) Net wages after tax and other deductions.

**tale** (tāl) *n.* 1 A story that is told or written; a narrative of real or fictitious events. 2 An idle or malicious piece of gossip. 3 A lie. 4

*Archaic.* A tally or amount; total. [< OE *talu* speech, narrative]

**tal·ent** (tal′ənt) *n.* 1 *pl.* A person's natural abilities. 2 A particular aptitude for some special work, artistic endeavor, etc. 3 A person, or people collectively with skill or ability. 4 Any of various ancient weights and denominations of money, used in ancient Greece, Rome, and the Middle East. [< L *talentum*, a sum of money] —**tal′ent·ed** *adj.*

**tales·man** (tālz′mən) *n. pl.* ·**men** (-mən) One summoned to fill a vacancy in a jury when the regular panel has become deficient in number. [< ML *tales (de circumstantibus)* such (of the bystanders) + MAN]

**talk** (tôk) *v.i.* 1 To express or exchange thoughts in audible words; speak or converse. 2 To communicate by means other than speech: to *talk* with one's fingers. 3 To chatter. 4 To confer; consult. 5 To gossip. 6 To make sounds suggestive of speech. 7 *Informal* To give information; inform. —*v.t.* 8 To express in words; utter. 9 To converse in: to *talk* Spanish. 10 To discuss: to *talk* business. 11 To bring to a specified condition or state by talking: to *talk* one into doing something. —**talk back** To answer impudently. —**talk down** To silence by talking. —**talk down to** To speak to patronizingly —**talk shop** To talk about one's work. —*n.* 1 The act of talking; conversation; speech. 2 A speech, either formal or informal. 3 Report; rumor: *talk* of war. 4 A subject of conversation. 5 A conference or discussion. 6 Mere words; empty conversation, discussion, etc. 7 A special kind of speech; lingo: baseball *talk.* 8 Sounds suggestive of speech, as made by a bird or animal. [Prob. < OE *talian* reckon, tell]

**talk·a·tive** (tô′kə·tiv) *adj.* Given to or fond of much talking. —**talk′a·tive·ly** *adv.* —**talk′a·tive·ness** *n.* —**Syn.** garrulous, loquacious, voluble, windy.

**tall** (tôl) *adj.* 1 Having more than average height; high. 2 Having a specified height: five feet tall. 3 *Informal* Extravagant; boastful; exaggerated: a *tall* story. 4 Large; extensive: a *tall* order. —*adv. Informal* Proudly: to walk *tall.* [< OE *getæl* swift, prompt] —**tall′ish** *adj.* —**tall′ness** *n.*

**tal·low** (tal′ō) *n.* Solid, rendered animal fats, as of beef or mutton, used for making candles, soaps, etc. —*v.t.* To smear with tallow. [< MLG *talg, talch*] —**tal′low·y** *adj.*

**tal·ly** (tal′ē) *n. pl.* ·**lies** 1 A piece of wood on which notches or scores are cut as marks

of number. 2 A score or mark. 3 A reckoning; account. 4 A counterpart; duplicate. 5 A mark indicative of number. 6 A label; tag. —*v.* ·**lied,** ·**ly·ing** *v.t.* 1 To score on a tally; mark. 2 To reckon; count; often with *up.* 3 To register, as points in a game; score. 4 To cause to correspond. —*v.i.* 5 To make a tally. 6 To agree precisely: His story *tallies* with yours. 7 To keep score. 8 To score, as in a game. [< L *talea* rod, cutting] —**tal′li·er** *n.*

**tal·on** (tal′ən) *n.* 1 The claw of a bird or other animal, esp. a bird of prey. 2 A human finger or hand thought of as resembling a claw. [< L *talus* heel] —**tal′oned** *adj.*

**tam·bou·rine** (tam′bə·rēn′) *n.* A musical instrument like the head of a drum, with metal disks in the rim, played by striking it with the hand. [F, lit., small tambour]

**tame** (tām) *adj.* **tam·er, tam·est** 1 Having lost its native wildness; domesticated. 2 Docile; tractable; subdued; submissive. 3 Lacking in spirit; uninteresting; dull. —*v.t.* **tamed, tam·ing** 1.To make tame; domesticate. 2 To bring into subjection or obedience. 3 To tone down; soften. [< OE *tam*] —**tam′a·bie** or **tame′a·ble** *adj.* —**tame′ly** *adv.* —**tame′ness, tam′er** *n.*

**tamp** (tamp) *v.t.* 1 To force down or pack closer by repeated blows. 2 In blasting, to pack matter around a charge in order to increase the explosive effect. [Back formation <TAMPION] —**tam′per** *n.*

**tam·per** (tam′pər) *v.i.* 1 To meddle; interfere: usu. with *with.* 2 To make changes, esp. so as to damage, falsify, etc.: with *with.* 3 To use secret or improper measures, as bribery. [Var. of TEMPER] —**tam′per·er** *n.*

**tan** (tan) *v.* **tanned, tan·ning** *v.t.* 1 To convert into leather, as hides or skins, by treating with tannin. 2 To darken, as the skin, by exposure to sunlight. 3 *Informal.* To thrash; flog. —*v.i.* 4 To become tanned. —*n.* 1 TANBARK. 2 TANNIN. 3 A yellowish brown color tinged with red. 4 A dark coloring of the skin, resulting from exposure to the sun. —*adj.* 1 Of the color tan. 2 Of, pertaining to, or used for tanning. [< Med. L *tanum* tanbark]

**tang** (tang) *n.* 1 A sharp, penetrating taste, flavor or odor. 2 Any distinctive quality or flavor. 3 A trace or hint. 4 A slender shank or tongue projecting from the end of a sword blade, chisel, etc., for fitting into a handle, hilt, etc. [< ON *tongi* a point] —**tang′y** *adj.* (·**i·er, ·i·est**)

**tan·gent** (tan′jənt) *adj.* 1 *Geom.* Coinciding at a point or along a line without intersection, as a curve and line, surface and plane, etc. 2 Touching; in contact. —*n.* 1 *Geom.* A line tangent to a curve at any point. 2 *Trig.* A function of an angle, equal to the quotient of its sine divided by its cosine. 3 A sharp change in course or direction. —**fly** (or **go**) **off on a tangent** *Informal* To make a sharp or sudden change, as in a course of action or train of thought. [< L *tangere* to touch] —**tan·gen·cy** (tan′jən·sē) *n.*

**tan·ger·ine** (tan′jə·rēn′, tan′jə·rēn′) *n.* 1 A variety of orange with a loose skin and easily separated segments. 2 A burnt orange color like that of the tangerine. [< *Tangier,* a city in Morocco]

**tan·gi·ble** (tan′jə·bəl) *adj.* 1 Perceptible by touch. 2 Not elusive or unreal; objective; concrete: *tangible* evidence. 3 Having value that can be appraised. —*n. pl.* Things having value that can be appraised. [< L *tangere* to touch] —**tan′gi·bil′i·ty, tan′gi·ble·ness** *n.* —**tan′gi·bly** *adv.*

**tan·gle** (tang′gəl) *v.* ·**gled,** ·**gling** *v.t.* 1 To twist in a confused and not readily separable mass. 2 To ensnare as in a tangle; trap; enmesh. 3 To involve in such a way as to confuse, obstruct, etc. —*v.i.* 4 To be or become entangled. —**tangle with** *Informal* To become involved or fight with. —*n.* 1 A confused intertwining, as of threads or hairs; a snarl. 2 State of confusion or complication. 3 A state of bewilderment. [Prob. < Scand.] —**tan′gler** *n.*

**tank** (tangk) *n.* 1 A large vessel, basin, or receptacle for holding a fluid. 2 A natural or artificial pool or pond. 3 An armored combat vehicle that rides on treads and has mounted guns. 4 *Slang* A jail cell, esp. one for receiving prisoners. —*v.t.* To place or store in a tank. [< Pg. *estanque*]

**tank·er** (tangk′ər) *n.* 1 A cargo ship for the transport of oil or other liquids. 2 A cargo plane used to carry gasoline and to refuel other planes in flight.

**tan·nin** (tan′in) *n.* A yellowish, astringent substance extracted from tanbark, gallnut, etc., used in dyeing, tanning, etc. Also **tannic acid.** [< F *tanin* < *tanner* to tan]

**tan·ta·lize** (tan′tə·līz′) *v.t.* ·**lized,** ·**liz·ing** To tease or torment by promising or showing something desirable and then denying access to it. *Brit. sp.* ·**lise′.** [< TANTALUS] —**tan′ta·li·za′tion, tan′ta·liz′er** *n.* —**tan′ta·liz′ing·ly** *adv.*

**tan·ta·mount** (tan′tə·mount) *adj.* Equivalent: with *to.* [< L *tantus* as much + OF *amonter* to amount]

**tap**[1] (tap) *n.* 1 A spout through which liquid is drawn, as from a cask. 2 FAUCET. 3 A plug or stopper to close an opening, as in a cask. 4 Liquor drawn from a tap, esp. of a particular quality or brew. 5 A tool for cutting internal screw threads. 6 A point of connection for an electrical circuit. 7 The act or an instance of wiretapping. —**on tap** 1 Contained in a cask; ready for tapping: beer *on tap.* 2 *Informal* Available; ready. —*v.t.* **tapped, tap·ping** 1 To provide with a tap or spigot. 2 To pierce or open so as to draw liquid from. 3 To draw (liquid) from a container, body cavity, etc. 4 To make connection with: to *tap* a gas main. 5 To draw upon; utilize: to *tap* new sources of energy. 6 To make connection with secretly: to *tap* a telephone wire. 7 To make an internal screw thread in with a tap. [< OE *tæppa*]

**tap**[2] (tap) *v.* **tapped, tap·ping** *v.t.* 1 To touch or strike gently. 2 To strike gently with. 3 To make or produce by tapping. 4 To apply a tap to (a shoe) —*v.i.* 5 To strike a light blow or blows, as with the finger tip. 6 To walk with a light, tapping sound. 7 TAP-DANCE. —*n.* 1 The act or sound of striking gently. 2 Leather, metal, etc., affixed to a shoe sole or heel, for repair or tap-dancing. 3 *pl.* A military signal sounded on a trumpet or drum for the extinguishing of all lights in soldiers' quarters. [< OF *taper*]

**tape deck** An assembly of magnetic head, tape reels, and drive for tape recording and playback.

**tape measure** A tape marked in inches, feet, etc., for measuring. Also **tape·line** (tāp′līn) *n.*

**ta·per** (tā′pər) *n.* 1 A slender candle. 2 A long wax-coated wick used to light candles, lamps, etc. 3 A weak light. 4 A gradual diminution of size in an elongated object; also, any tapering object, as a cone. 5 Any gradual decrease. —*v.t. & v.i.* 1 To make or become smaller or thinner toward one end. 2 To lessen gradually: with *off.* —*adj.* Growing smaller toward one end. [< OE]

**tape recorder** An electromagnetic apparatus which can record sound on magnetic tape and play it back.

**tap·es·try** (tap′is·trē) *n. pl.* ·**tries** 1 A heavy woven textile with a pictorial design, used for hangings, upholstery, etc. 2 Something like this, as in complexity of design. —*v.t.*

·tried, ·try·ing 1 To hang or adorn with tapestry. 2 To depict or weave in a tapestry. [< Gk. *tapētion*, dim. of *tapēs* rug]

**tape·worm** (tāp′wûrm′) *n.* Any of various long flatworms parasitic in the intestines of man and various animals.

**tap·i·o·ca** (tap′ē·ō′kə) *n.* A starchy, granular foodstuff obtained from cassava, used in puddings, as a thickener for soups, etc. [< Tupi *tipioca*]

**tar**[1] (tär) *n.* A dark, usu. pungent, viscid mixture of hydrocarbons obtained by the dry distillation of wood, coal, etc. —*v.t.* **tarred, tar·ring** To cover with or as with tar. —**tar and feather** To smear with tar and then cover with feathers as a punishment. —*adj.* Made of, derived from, or resembling tar. [< OE *teru*]

**tar**[2] (tär) *n. Informal* A sailor. [Short for TARPAULIN]

**ta·ran·tu·la** (tə·ran′chŏŏ·lə, -tə·lə) *n. pl.* ·las or ·lae (-lē) 1 A large, hairy, venomous spider of s Europe. 2 Any of various large, hairy American spiders capable of inflicting a painful but not dangerous bite. [< *Taranto,* Italy]

**tar·dy** (tär′dē) *adj.* ·di·er, ·di·est 1 Not coming, happening, etc., at the scheduled or proper time. 2 Moving, acting, etc., at a slow pace. [< L *tardus* slow] —**tar′di·ly** *adv.* —**tar′di·ness** *n.* —Syn. 1 late, dilatory, overdue, delayed. 2 slow, sluggish, leisurely, torpid.

**tar·get** (tär′git) *n.* 1 An object presenting a usu. marked surface that is to be aimed and shot at, as in archery practice. 2 Anything that is shot at. 3 One who or that which is made an object of ridicule, criticism, etc.; butt. 4 A goal; objective. 5 A small round shield. —*v.t.* 1 To make a target of. 2 To establish as a goal. [< OF *targe* shield] —**tar′get·a·ble** *adj.*

**tar·iff** (tar′if) *n.* 1 A schedule of government-imposed duties to be paid for the importation or exportation of goods. 2 A duty of this kind, or its rate. 3 Any schedule of charges, prices, etc. —*v.t.* 1 To make a list of duties on. 2 To fix a price or tariff on. [< Ar. *ta′rif* information]

**tar·nish** (tär′nish) *v.t.* 1 To dim the luster of. 2 To sully, mar, debase, etc. —*v.i.* 3 To become tarnished. —*n.* 1 The condition of being tarnished; stain, blemish, loss of luster, etc. 2 The thin discolored film on the surface of tarnished metal. [< OF *ternir*] —**tar′nish·a·ble** *adj.*

**tar·pau·lin** (tär·pô′lin, tär′pə-) *n.* A water-

proof material, esp. canvas, used as a covering for exposed objects. [? < TAR[1] + *palling,* pr.p. of PALL[1]]

**tar·ry** (tar′ē) *v.* ·ried, ·ry·ing *v.i.* 1 To put off going or coming; linger. 2 To remain in the same place; stay. 3 To wait. —*v.t.* 4 *Archaic* To wait for. [< L *tardare* to delay]

**tart** (tärt) *n.* 1 A small open pastry shell filled with fruit, jelly, custard, etc. 2 *Slang* A girl or woman of loose morality. [< OF *tarte*]

**tar·tar** (tär′tər) *n.* 1 A hard deposit of potassium tartrate that forms in wine casks. 2 A yellowish incrustation on teeth, chiefly calcium phosphate. [< Med. Gk. *tartaron*] —**tar·tar′e·ous** *adj.*

**task** (task, täsk) *n.* 1 A piece of work, esp. one imposed by authority or required by duty or necessity. 2 Any unpleasant or difficult assignment; burden. —**take to task** To reprove; lecture. —*v.t.* 1 To assign a task to. 2 To burden. [< L *taxare* appraise]

**task force** 1 A military unit specially trained to execute a specific mission. 2 Any group assigned to handle a specific task.

**tas·sel** (tas′əl) *n.* 1 A tuft of loosely hanging threads or cords used as an ornament for curtains, cushions, etc. 2 Something resembling a tassel, as the inflorescence on Indian corn. —*v.* ·seled or ·selled, ·sel·ing or ·sel·ling *v.t.* 1 To provide or adorn with tassels. 2 To form in a tassel or tassels. —*v.i.* 3 To put forth tassels, as Indian corn. [< OF, clasp]

**taste** (tāst) *v.* tast·ed, tast·ing *v.t.* 1 To perceive the flavor of (something) by taking into the mouth or touching with the tongue. 2 To eat or drink a little of. 3 To recognize by the sense of taste. 4 To experience. —*v.i.* 5 To recognize a flavor by the sense of taste. 6 To take a small quantity into the mouth: usu. with *of.* 7 To have experience or enjoyment: with *of: taste* of great sorrow. 8 To have a specified flavor when in the mouth: Sugar *tastes* sweet. —*n.* 1 The sensation associated with stimulation of the taste buds by foods or other substances. 2 The quality thus perceived; flavor. 3 A small quantity tasted. 4 A slight experience; sample. 5 Special fondness and aptitude; inclination: a *taste* for music. 6 Appreciation of the beautiful in nature, art, and literature. 7 Style or form with respect to the rules of propriety or etiquette. 8 Individual preference or liking. 9 The act of tasting. [< L *taxare* touch, handle, appraise]

**tast·er** (tās′tər) *n.* 1 One who tastes, esp. to

test the quality of something. **2** A device for testing or sampling, as the small, shallow, metal vessel used in testing wines.

**tat·tle** (tat′l) *v.* **·tled, ·tling** *v.i.* **1** To talk idly; chatter. **2** To tell secrets, plans, etc.; gossip. —*v.t.* **3** To reveal by gossiping. —*n.* Idle talk or gossip. [< MDu. *tatelen*] —**tat′tler** *n.*

**tat·too** (ta·tōō′) *n. pl.* **·toos** **1** A continuous beating or drumming. **2** A signal by drum or bugle to soldiers to repair to quarters. —*v.t. & v.i.* **·tooed, ·too·ing** To beat or rap on (a drum, etc.). [< Du. < *tap* tap, faucet + *toe* shut]

**taunt** (tônt) *n.* A sarcastic, biting remark; insult; jibe. —*v.t.* **1** To reproach or challenge with sarcastic or contemptuous words. **2** To provoke with taunts. [? < OF *tanter* provoke] —**taunt′er** *n.* —**taunt′ing·ly** *adv.*

**taut** (tôt) *adj.* **1** Stretched tight. **2** In proper shape; trim; tidy. **3** Tense; tight: *taut* muscles. [? < OE *togian*, to pull, tow] —**taut′ly** *adv.* —**taut′ness** *n.*

**tav·ern** (tav′ərn) *n.* **1** An inn. **2** A place licensed to sell liquor, beer, etc., to be drunk on the premises. [< OF < L *taberna* hut, booth]

**taw·dry** (tô′drē) *adj.* **·dri·er, ·dri·est** Pretentiously showy without taste or quality. [< *St. Audrey*, designating a cheap type of lace sold at St. Audrey's Fair at Ely, England] —**taw′dri·ly** *adv.* —**taw′dri·ness** *n.* —**Syn.** cheap, gaudy, meretricious, flashy.

**taw·ny** (tô′nē) *adj.* **·ni·er, ·ni·est** Tan-colored; brownish yellow. —*n.* The color tan or brownish yellow. [< OF *tanner* to tan] —**taw′ni·ness** *n.*

**tax** (taks) *n.* **1** A compulsory contribution levied upon persons, property, or business for the support of government. **2** A heavy demand, as on one's powers or resources; a burden. —*v.t.* **1** To impose a tax on. **2** To settle or fix (amounts) chargeable in any judicial matter. **3** To impose a burden upon; task. **4** To charge; blame: usu. with *with*. [< L *taxare* estimate, appraise]

**tax·i** (tak′sē) *n. pl.* **tax·is** or **tax·ies** TAXICAB. —*v.* **tax·ied, tax·i·ing** or **tax·y·ing** *v.i.* **1** To ride in a taxicab. **2** To move along the ground or on the surface of the water, as an airplane before taking off or after landing. —*v.t.* **3** To cause (an airplane) to taxi.

**tax·i·cab** (tak′sē·kab′) *n.* A passenger vehicle, usu. fitted with a taximeter, available for hire. [< TAXIMETER + CAB]

**tax·i·der·my** (tak′sə·dûr′mē) *n.* The art of stuffing and mounting the skins of dead animals to simulate their appearance when alive. [< Gk. *taxis* arrangement + *derma* skin] —**tax′i·der′mal, tax′i·der′mic** *adj.* —**tax′i·der′mist** *n.*

**tea** (tē) *n.* **1** An evergreen Asian plant having white flowers. **2** The prepared leaves of this plant, or an infusion of them used as a beverage. **3** A similar potable infusion of plant leaves or animal extract: beef *tea*. **4** *Brit.* A light evening or afternoon meal. **5** A social gathering at which tea is served. **6** *Slang* MARIHUANA. [< dial. Chinese *t'e*]

**teach** (tēch) *v.* **taught, teach·ing** *v.t.* **1** To give instruction to: *teach* a class. **2** To give instruction in: *teach* French. **3** To train by example, practice, or exercise. —*v.i.* **4** To act as a teacher; impart knowledge or skill. [< OE *tēcan*] —**teach′a·bil′i·ty, teach′a·ble·ness** *n.* —**teach′a·ble** *adj.*

**teach·er** (tē′chər) *n.* One who teaches, esp. as an occupation.

**team** (tēm) *n.* **1** Two or more beasts of burden harnessed together. **2** A group of people working or playing together as a unit, esp. a group forming one side in a contest. —*v.t.* **1** To convey with a team. **2** To harness together in a team. —*v.i.* **3** To drive a team. **4** To form or work as a team: to *team* up. [< OE *tēam* offspring, team]

**tear¹** (târ) *v.* **tore, torn, tear·ing** *v.t.* **1** To pull apart, as cloth; rip. **2** To make by tearing: *tear* a hole in. **3** To injure or lacerate. **4** To divide or disrupt: a party *torn* by dissension. **5** To distress or torment: The sight *tore* his heart. —*v.i.* **6** To become torn or rent. **7** To move with haste and energy. —**tear down** **1** To demolish, as a building. **2** To take apart, as a machine for repair. **3** *Informal* To attack or abuse verbally. —**tear into** To attack violently or with impetuous haste. —*n.* **1** The act of tearing. **2** A fissure made by tearing. **3** *Slang* A spree; frolic. **4** A rushing motion. **5** A violent outburst, as of anger. [< OE *teran*]

**tear²** (tir) *n.* **1** A drop of the saline liquid that normally lubricates the eyeball and in weeping flows from the eyes. **2** Something resembling this. **3** *pl.* Sorrow. **4** *pl.* The act of weeping: to burst into *tears*. —*v.i.* To fill with tears. [< OE *tēar*] —**tear′less, tear′y** *adj.*

**tease** (tēz) *v.* **teased, teas·ing** *v.t.* **1** To annoy or harass; pester. **2** To raise the nap, as with teasels. **3** To coax or beg. **4** To comb or card, as wool or flax. **5** To comb (hair) in such a way as to form fluffy layers. —*v.i.* **6**

To annoy a person in a facetious or petty way. —*n.* 1 One who teases. 2 The act of teasing or the state of being teased. [< OE *tǣsan* tease, pluck apart] —**teas′er** *n.* —**teas′ing·ly** *adv.*

**tech·ni·cal** (tek′ni·kəl) *adj.* 1 Of or pertaining to some particular art, science, or trade, esp. to the practical arts or applied sciences. 2 Of, characteristic of, used or skilled in a particular art, science, profession, etc. 3 Of, in, or exhibiting technique. 4 According to an accepted body of rules and regulations: a *technical* defeat. [< Gk. *technē* art] —**tech′ni·cal·ly** (-kə·lē, -klē) *adv.* —**tech′ni·cal·ness** *n.*

**tech·ni·cal·i·ty** (tek′ni·kal′ə·tē) *n. pl.* ·**ties** 1 The state or quality of being technical. 2 A technical point peculiar to some art, trade, etc. 3 A petty, formal, or highly specialized distinction or detail.

**tech·nique** (tek·nēk′) *n.* 1 The way in which an artist, craftsman, scientist, etc., handles technical details or uses basic skills. 2 The degree of excellence in doing these things. 3 Any method of accomplishing something. [< Gk. *technikos* technical]

**tech·nol·o·gy** (tek·nol′ə·jē) *n.* 1 The sum total of the technical means employed to meet the material needs of a society. 2 Applied science. 3 The technical terms used in a science, art, etc. [< Gk. *technē* skill + -LOGY] —**tech′no·log′ic** or ·**i·cal** *adj.* —**tech′no·log′i·cal·ly** *adv.* —**tech·nol′o·gist** *n.*

**te·di·ous** (tē′dē·əs) *adj.* Fatiguing or boring, as because of lack of interest or repetitiousness. [< L *taedium* tedium] —**te′di·ous·ly** *adv.* —**te′di·ous·ness** *n.*

**tee** (tē) *n.* 1 A little peg or cone-shaped mound on which a golf ball is placed in making the first play to a hole. 2 In golf, the area from which a player makes his first stroke at the beginning of play for each hole. —*v.t. & v.i.* ·**teed, tee·ing** To place (the ball) on the tee before striking it. —**tee off** 1 To strike (a golf ball) in starting play. 2 To begin. 3 *Slang* To make angry or resentful. [?]

**teem** (tēm) *v.i.* To be full to overflowing; abound. [< OE *tīeman*]

**teen·age** (tēn′āj′) *adj.* Of, being in, or related to the years from 13 to 19 inclusive. —**teeu′ag′er** *n.*

**tee·to·tal·er** (tē·tōt′l·ər) *n.* One who abstains totally from alcoholic beverages. Also **tee·to′tal·ist, tee·to′tal·ler.**

**tel·e·cast** (tel′ə·kast, -käst) *v.t. & v.i.* ·**cast** or ·**cast·ed, ·cast·ing** To broadcast by televi-

sion. —*n.* A program broadcast by television.

**tel·e·com·mu·ni·ca·tion** (tel′ə·kə·myōō′nə·kā′shən) *n.* The technology of communicating at a distance, as in radio, television, telegraphy, etc. Also **tel′e·com·mu′ni·ca′tions** (*construed as sing.* or *pl.*).

**tel·e·gram** (tel′ə·gram) *n.* A message sent by telegraph.

**tel·e·graph** (tel′ə·graf, -gräf) *n.* Any of various devices, systems, or processes for transmitting messages to a distance, esp. by means of coded electric impulses conducted by wire. —*v.t.* 1 To send (a message) by telegraph. 2 To communicate with by telegraph. —*v.i.* 3 To transmit a message by telegraph. —**te·leg·ra·pher** (tə·leg′rə·fər) *n.*

**te·lem·e·ter** (tel′ə·mē′tər, tə·lem′ə·tər) *n.* An apparatus for indicating or measuring various quantities and for transmitting the data to a distant point. —*v.i. & v.t.* To transmit by telemeter. —**te·lem′e·try** *n.*

**te·lep·a·thy** (tə·lep′ə·thē) *n.* The supposed communication of one mind with another by other than normal sensory means. —**tel·e·path·ic** (tel′ə·path′ik) *adj.* —**tel′e·path′i·cal·ly** *adv.* —**tel′e·pa·thist** *n.*

**tel·e·phone** (tel′ə·fōn) *n.* An instrument for reproducing sound or speech at a distant point, using electric impulses transmitted by wire. —*v.* ·**phoned, ·phon·ing** —*v.t.* 1 To send by telephone, as a message. 2 To communicate with by telephone. —*v.i.* 3 To communicate by telephone. —**tel′e·phon′ic** (-fon′ik) *adj.* —**tel′e·phon′i·cal·ly** *adv.*

**tel·e·pho·to** (tel′ə·fō′tō) *adj.* 1 Denoting a system of lenses which produces a large image of a distant object in a camera. 2 Of, pertaining to, or being telephotography.

**Tel·e·prompt·er** (tel′e·promp′tər) *n.* A prompting device for television whereby a magnified script, unseen by the audience, is unrolled for a speaker or performer, line by line: a trade name.

**tel·e·scope** (tel′ə·skōp) *n.* An optical instrument for enlarging the image of a distant object. —*v.* ·**scoped, ·scop·ing** *v.t.* 1 To put together so that one part fits into another. 2 To shorten, condense, or compress. —*v.i.* 3 To slide or be forced one into another, as the cylindrical tubes of a collapsible telescope or railroad cars in a collision.

**tel·e·thon** (tel′ə·thon) *n.* A long telecast, usu. to raise funds for a charity. [< TELE- + (MARA)THON]

**tel·e·vi·sion** (tel′ə·vizh′ən) *n.* 1 An optical and electric system for continuous transmission of visual images and sound that may be instantaneously received at a distance. 2 The technology of television transmission. 3 A television receiving set. 4 Television as an industry, an art form, or a medium of communications. 5 A show transmitted by television: to watch *television.*

**tell** (tel) *v.* told, tell·ing *v.t.* 1 To relate in detail; narrate, as a story. 2 To make known by speech or writing; express in words; communicate; utter; say. 3 To divulge; reveal; disclose: to *tell* secrets. 4 To decide; ascertain: I cannot *tell* who is to blame. 5 To distinguish; recognize: to *tell* right from wrong. 6 To command; direct; order: I *told* him to go home. 7 To let know; report to; inform. 8 To state or assure emphatically: It's cold out, I *tell* you! 9 To count; enumerate: to *tell* one's beads. —*v.i.* 10 To give an account or description: usu. with *of.* 11 To serve as indication or evidence: with *of*: Their rags *told* of their poverty. 12 To produce a marked effect: Every blow *told.* — **tell off** 1 To count and set apart. 2 *Informal* To reprimand severely. —**tell on** 1 To wear out; tire; exhaust. 2 *Informal* To tattle on; inform against. [< OE *tellan*] —**Syn.** 1 recount, recite. 2 state, aver. 4 discriminate.

**tem·per** (tem′pər) *n.* 1 A fit of anger; rage. 2 A tendency to become easily angered. 3 State of mind or feeling; mood. 4 TEMPERAMENT (def. 1). 5 Equanimity; self-control: now only in the phrases lose (or keep) one's temper. 6 The hardness and strength of a metal, esp. when produced by heat treatment. 7 Something used to temper a substance or mixture. —*v.t.* 1 To moderate or make suitable, as by adding another quality; free from excess; mitigate: to *temper* justice with mercy. 2 To bring to the proper consistency, texture, etc., by moistening and working: to *temper* clay. 3 To bring (metal) to a required hardness and elasticity by controlled heating and cooling. 4 To make experienced; toughen, as by difficulties, hardships, etc. 5 *Music* To tune (an instrument) by temperament. —*v.i.* 6 To be or become tempered. [< L *temperare* combine in due proportion] —**tem′per·a·bil′i·ty** *n.* —**tem′per·a·ble** *adj.*

**tem·per·a·ment** (tem′pər·ə·mənt, -prə-) *n.* 1 The characteristic nature or disposition of a person. 2 A nature or disposition that is exceedingly dramatic, excitable, moody,

etc. 3 *Music* The tuning of an instrument of fixed intonation to a slightly modified chromatic scale so that it is in tune for all keys. [< L *temperamentum* proper mixture]

**tem·per·ance** (tem′pər·əns) *n.* 1 Habitual moderation and self-control, esp. in the indulgence of any appetite. 2 The principle and practice of moderation or total abstinence from intoxicants. —*adj.* Of, relating to, practicing, or promoting total abstinence from intoxicants. [< L *temperare* mix in due proportions]

**tem·per·ate** (tem′pər·it, tem′prət) *adj.* 1 Characterized by moderation or the absence of extremes; not excessive. 2 Calm; restrained; self-controlled. 3 Observing moderation or self-control, esp. in the use of intoxicating liquors. 4 Moderate as regards temperature; mild. [< L *temperare* mix in due proportions] —**tem′per·ate·ly** *adv.* —**tem′per·ate·ness** *n.*

**tem·per·a·ture** (tem′pər·ə·chər, -prə-) *n.* 1 The degree of heat in the atmosphere as measured on a thermometer. 2 The degree or intensity of heat in a living body; also, the excess of this above the normal. 3 The intensity of heat or cold in any substance. [< L *temperatura* due measure]

**tem·pes·tu·ous** (tem·pes′chŏŏ-əs) *adj.* Stormy; turbulent; violent. —**tem·pes′tu·ous·ly** *adv.* —**tem·pes′tu·ous·ness** *n.*

**tem·ple** (tem′pəl) *n.* The region on each side of the head above the cheek bone. [< L *tempus* temple]

**tem·po·ral** (tem′pər·əl) *adj.* 1 Of or pertaining to the present as opposed to a future life. 2 Worldly; material, as opposed to spiritual. 3 Ephemeral; transitory, as opposed to eternal. 4 Of or relating to time. 5 *Gram.* Of, pertaining to, or denoting time: *temporal* conjunctions. [< L *tempus, temporis* time] — **tem·po·ral·i·ty** (tem′pə·ral′ə·tē), **tem′po·ral·ness** *n.* —**tem′po·ral·ly** *adv.*

**tem·po·rar·y** (tem′pə·rer′ē) *adj.* Lasting, to be used, etc., for a time only; not permanent. [< L *tempus, temporis* time] —**tem′po·rar′i·ly** *adv.* —**tem′po·rar′i·ness** *n.*

**tem·po·rize** (tem′pə·rīz) *v.i.* ·rized, ·riz·ing 1 To act evasively so as to gain time or put off commitment. 2 To comply with or yield to the situation, circumstances, etc.; compromise. [< L *tempus, temporis* time] —**tem′po·ri·za′tion**, **tem′po·riz′er** *n.* —**tem′po·riz′ing·ly** *adv.*

**ten·a·ble** (ten′ə·bəl) *adj.* Capable of being

held, maintained, or defended. [< L *tenere* to hold] —**ten′a·bil′i·ty, ten′a·ble·ness** *n.* —**ten′a·bly** *adv.*

**te·na·cious** (ti·nā′shəs) *adj.* 1 Having great cohesiveness; tough. 2 Adhesive; sticky. 3 Stubborn; obstinate; persistent. 4 Strongly retentive: a *tenacious* memory. [< L *tenax* holding fast] —**te·na′cious·ly** *adv.* —**te·na′cious·ness, te·nac·i·ty** (tə·nas′ə·tē) *n.*

**ten·ant** (ten′ənt) *n.* 1 A person who rents a house, land, etc., for his own use. 2 One who holds or possesses lands or property by any kind of title. 3 A dweller in any place; an occupant. —*v.t.* 1 To hold as tenant; occupy. —*v.i.* 2 To be a tenant. [< F *tenir* to hold] —**ten′ant·a·ble** *adj.*

**tend** (tend) *v.i.* 1 To have an aptitude, tendency, or disposition; incline. 2 To lead or conduce: Education *tends* to refinement. 3 To go in a certain direction. [< L *tendere* extend, tend]

**ten·den·cy** (ten′dən·sē) *n. pl.* ·**cies** 1 Inclination; propensity; bent: a *tendency* to lie. 2 A movement or course toward some purpose, end, or result. 3 The purpose or trend of a speech or story. [< L *tendere* extend, tend] —**Syn.** 1 aptitude, proclivity, disposition, leaning, predilection.

**ten·der** (ten′dər) *adj.* 1 Easily crushed, bruised, broken, etc.; delicate; fragile. 2 Easily chewed or cut: said of food. 3 Physically weak; not strong or hardy. 4 Youthful and delicate; not strengthened by maturity: a *tender* age. 5 Characterized by gentleness, care, consideration, etc.: a *tender* respect for the aged. 6 Kind; affectionate; loving: a *tender* father. 7 Sensitive to impressions, feelings, etc.: a *tender* conscience. 8 Sensitive to pain, discomfort, roughness, etc.: a *tender* skin. 9 Of delicate quality: a *tender* color. 10 Capable of arousing sensitive feelings; touching: *tender* memories. 11 Requiring deft or delicate treatment; ticklish; touchy: a *tender* subject. —*v.t.* To make tender; soften. [< L *tener*] —**ten′der·ly** *adv.* —**ten′der·ness** *n.*

**ten·der·foot** (ten′dər·fŏŏt′) *n. pl.* ·**feet** (-fēt′) or ·**foots** 1 A newcomer, esp. to a rough or unsettled region. 2 Any inexperienced person or beginner. 3 A Boy Scout in the beginning group. —*adj.* Inexperienced.

**ten·der·loin** (ten′dər·loin′) *n.* 1 The tender part of the loin of beef, pork, etc., that lies parallel to the backbone. 2 *Often cap.* A city district noted for its high incidence of crime, corruption, and police leniency.

**ten·don** (ten′dən) *n.* One of the bands of tough, fibrous tissue attaching a voluntary muscle to a bone. [< Gk. *tenōn* a sinew < *tenein* stretch] —**ten′di·nous** *adj.*

**ten·dril** (ten′dril) *n.* One of the slender, threadlike, usu. coiling organs serving to attach a climbing plant to a supporting surface. [< OF *tendron* sprout] —**ten′driled** or **ten′drilled, ten′dril·ous** *adj.*

**ten·e·ment** (ten′ə·mənt) *n.* 1 A room, or set of rooms, designed for one family; apartment; flat. 2 TENEMENT HOUSE. 3 *Law* Anything, as land, houses, offices, franchises, etc., held of another by tenure. [< LL *tenementum* tenure < L *tenere* to hold] —**ten′e·men′ta·ry** (-men′tər·ē), **ten′e·men′tal** (-men′təl) *adj.*

**ten·et** (ten′it, tē′nit) *n.* A principle, dogma, or doctrine, esp. one held by a group or profession. [L, he holds]

**ten·nis** (ten′is) *n.* 1 A game in which two opposing players or pairs of players strike a ball with rackets over a low net on a court (**tennis court**), as of clay or synthetic materials, usu. outdoors. 2 An old form of tennis played in an interior space: also **court tennis.** [< AF *tenetz* take, receive, imperative of *tenir* hold]

**ten·on** (ten′ən) *n.* A projection on the end of a timber, etc., for inserting into a mortise to form a joint. —*v.t.* 1 To form a tenon on. 2 To join by a mortise and tenon. [< OF *tenir* to hold] • See MORTISE.

**ten·or** (ten′ər) *n.* 1 General intent or purport; substance: the *tenor* of the speech. 2 General course or tendency: the even *tenor* of their ways. 3 General character or nature. 4 A man's voice singing higher than a baritone and lower than an alto; also, a singer having, or a part to be sung by, such a voice. —*adj.* 1 Of or pertaining to a tenor. 2 Having a range of or similar to a tenor voice. [< L, a course < *tenere* to hold]

**tense** (tens) *adj.* **tens·er, tens·est** 1 Stretched tight; taut. 2 Under mental or nervous strain; apprehensive. 3 *Phonet.* Pronounced with the tongue and its muscles taut, as (ē) and (ōō). —*v.t.* & *v.i.* **tensed, tens·ing** To make or become tense. [< L *tensus*, pp. of *tendere* to stretch] —**tense′ly** *adv.* —**tense′ness** *n.* —**Syn.** 2 anxious, nervous, restless, jittery, restive, fidgety.

**ten·sion** (ten′shən) *n.* 1 The act of stretching or the condition of being stretched tight; tautness. 2 Mental or nervous strain or anxiety. 3 Any strained relation, as between governments. 4 *Physics* a A stress that tends to lengthen a body. b The condition of a body when acted on by such stress. 5 A device to regulate the tightness or tautness of something, esp. the thread in a sewing machine. 6 A condition of balance or symmetry produced by opposing elements, as in an artistic work. 7 Electric potential. —ten′sion·al *adj.*

tent (tent) *n.* A shelter of canvas or the like, supported by poles and fastened by cords to pegs (called tent pegs) driven into the ground. —*v.t.* 1 To cover with or as with a tent. —*v.i.* 2 To pitch a tent; camp out. [< L *tendere* stretch]

ten·ta·cle (ten′tə·kəl) *n.* 1 *Zool.* Any of various long, slender, flexible appendages of animals, esp. invertebrates, functioning as organs of touch, motion, etc. • See SEA ANEMONE. 2 *Bot.* A sensitive hair, as on the leaves of some plants. [< L *tentare* to touch, try] —ten·tac′u·lar (ten·tak′yə·lər) *adj.*

ten·ta·tive (ten′tə·tiv) *adj.* 1 Not definite or final; subject to change. 2 Somewhat uncertain or timid: a *tentative* glance. [< L *tentatus*, pp. of *tentare* to try, probe] —ten′ta·tive·ly *adv.* —ten′ta·tive·ness *n.*

ten·u·ous (ten′yōō·əs) *adj.* 1 Without much substance; slight; weak: *tenuous* arguments. 2 Thin; slender. 3 Having slight density; rare. [< L *tenuis* thin] —ten′u·ous·ly *adv.* —ten′u·ous·ness, ten·u·i·ty (te·nyōō′ə·tē, tə-) *n.*

ten·ure (ten′yər) *n.* 1 The act, right, length of time, or manner of holding something, as land, elected office, or a position. 2 The permanent status of a teacher, civil servant, etc., after fulfilling certain requirements. [< L *tenere* to hold] —ten′ured, ten·u·ri·al (ten·yŏŏr′ē·əl) *adj.* —ten·u′ri·al·ly *adv.*

te·pee (tē′pē) *n.* A conical tent of the North American Plains Indians, usu. covered with skins.

tep·id (tep′id) *adj.* 1 Moderately warm, as a liquid. 2 Not enthusiastic. [< L *tepere* be lukewarm] —te·pid·i·ty (tə·pid′ə·tē), tep′id·ness *n.* —tep′id·ly *adv.*

term (tûrm) *n.* 1 A word or expression used to designate some definite thing in a science, profession, art, etc.: a medical *term*. 2 *Often pl.* Any word or expression conveying some conception or thought: a *term* of reproach; to speak in general *terms*. 3 *pl.* The conditions or stipulations according to which something is to be done or acceded

to: the *terms* of a contract; peace *terms*. 4 *pl.* Mutual relations; footing: usu. preceded by *on* or *upon*: to be on friendly *terms*. 5 *Math.* a The numerator or denominator of a fraction. b One of the units of an algebraic expression that are connected by the plus and minus signs. 6 *Logic* a In a proposition, either of the two parts, the subject and predicate, which are joined by a copula. b Any of the three elements of a syllogism. 7 A fixed or definite period of time, esp. of duration: a *term* of office. —*v.t.* 8 A school semester or quarter. 9 End; conclusion. 10 *Law* a One of the prescribed periods of the year during which a court may hold a session. b A specific extent of time during which an estate may be held. c A space of time allowed a debtor to meet his obligation. 11 *Med.* The time for the normal termination of a pregnancy. —in terms of With respect to; as relating to. —*v.t.* To designate by means of a term; name or call. [< L *terminus* a limit]

ter·mi·nal (tûr′mə·nəl) *adj.* 1 Situated at or forming the end, limit, or boundary of something: a *terminal* bus station. 2 Situated or occurring at the end of a series or period of time; final: a *terminal* experiment. 3 At, undergoing, or causing the termination of life: *terminal* cancer; a *terminal* patient. 4 Of or occurring regularly in or at the end of a term or period of time: *terminal* payments. 5 Borne at the end of a stem or branch. —*n.* 1 A terminating point or part; termination; end. 2 a Either end of a railroad line, bus line, airline, etc. b A passenger or freight station located at these end points. c Any large passenger or freight station serving an area of considerable size. 3 a A point in an electric circuit at which it is usual to make or break a connection. b A connector designed to facilitate this. 4 An electronic device by means of which a user may communicate with a computer, usually including a cathode-ray tube, a keyboard, and a printer. [< L *terminus* boundary] —ter′mi·nal·ly *adv.*

ter·mi·nate (tûr′mə·nāt) *v.* ·nat·ed, ·nat·ing *v.t.* 1 To put an end or stop to. 2 To form the conclusion of; finish. 3 To bound or limit. —*v.i.* 4 To have an end; come to an end. [< L *terminus* a limit] —ter′mi·na′tive *adj.*

ter·mi·na·tion (tûr′mə·nā′shən) *n.* 1 The act of terminating or the condition of being terminated. 2 That which bounds or limits in time or space; close; end. 3 Outcome; result; conclusion. 4 The final letters or syllable of a word; a suffix. —ter′mi·na′tion·al adj.

ter·mi·nol·o·gy (tûr′mə·nol′ə·jē) n. pl. ·gies The technical terms relating to a particular subject, as a science, art, trade, etc. [< L terminus a limit + -LOGY] —ter′mi·no·log′i·cal (-nə·loj′i·kəl) adj. —ter′mi·no·log′i·cal·ly adv.

ter·mi·nus (tûr′mə·nəs) n. pl. ·nus·es or ·ni (-nī, -nē) 1 The final point or goal; end; terminal. 2 Either end of a railroad or bus line, airline, etc.; also, a town or station located at either end [L]

ter·race (ter′is) n. 1 A raised level space, as of lawn, usu. with sloping sides; also, such levels collectively. 2 A raised street supporting a row of houses; also, the houses occupying such a street. 3 A flat roof, esp. of an Oriental or Spanish house. 4 An open, paved area connected to a house, apartment, or building, usu. with places for seating, plantings, etc. 5 A balcony. 6 A park-like area extending down the middle of a wide street or boulevard. 7 A relatively narrow step in the face of a steep natural slope. —v.t. ·raced, ·rac·ing To form into or provide with a terrace or terraces. [< L terra earth]

ter·ra cot·ta (ter′ə kot′ə) 1 A hard, kiln-burnt clay, reddish brown and usu. unglazed, used for pottery, sculpture, etc. 2 A statue made of this clay. 3 A brownish red color. [Ital., lit, cooked earth]

Ter·ra·my·cin (ter′ə·mī′sin) n. An antibiotic effective against a wide variety of pathogenic organisms: a trade name.

ter·rar·i·um (te·râr′ē·əm) n. pl. ·rar·i·ums or ·rar·i·a (-râr′ē·ə) 1 A glass enclosure for growing a collection of small plants. 2 A vivarium for small land animals. [< L terra earth + -arium, on analogy with aquarium]

ter·res·tri·al (tə·res′trē·əl) adj. 1 Belonging to the planet earth. 2 Pertaining to land or earth. 3 Living on or growing in earth. 4 Belonging to or consisting of land, as distinct from water, air, etc. 5 Worldly; mundane. —n. An inhabitant of the earth. [< L terra land] —ter·res′tri·al·ly adv.

ter·ri·ble (ter′ə·bəl) adj. 1 Causing extreme fear, dread, or terror. 2 Severe; extreme: a terrible headache. 3 Awesome: a terrible burden of guilt. 4 Very bad; dreadful; awful: a terrible play. [< L terribilis < terrere terrify] —ter′ri·ble·ness n. —ter′ri·bly adv.

ter·ri·er (ter′ē·ər) n. Any of several breeds of

small, active, wiry dogs, formerly used to hunt burrowing animals. [<L terrarius pertaining to earth]

ter·rif·ic (tə·rif′ik) adj. 1 Arousing great terror or fear; frightening. 2 Informal a Very great; extraordinary; tremendous. b Unusually good; excellent. —ter·rif′i·cal·ly adv.

ter·ri·fy (ter′ə·fī) v.t. ·fied, ·fy·ing To fill with terror; frighten severely. [<L terrere frighten + -FY]

ter·ri·to·ri·al (ter′ə·tôr′ē·əl, -tō′rē-) adj. 1 Of or pertaining to a territory or territories. 2 Of, restricted to, or under the jurisdiction of a particular territory, region, or district. 3 Often cap. Organized or intended primarily for home defense: the British Territorial Army. —ter′ri·to′ri·al·ism′, ter′ri·to′ri·al·ist n. —ter′ri·to′ri·al·ly adv.

ter·ri·to·ry (ter′ə·tôr′ē, -tō′rē) n. pl. ·ries 1 The domain over which a nation, state, etc., exercises jurisdiction. 2 Any considerable tract of land; a region; district. 3 A region having a certain degree of self-government, but not having the status of a state or province. 4 A special sphere or province of activity, knowledge, etc. 5 A specific area used by or assigned to a person, group, etc.: a salesman's territory. [<L terra earth]

ter·ror (ter′ər) n. 1 Overwhelming fear. 2 A person or thing that causes extreme fear. 3 Informal A difficult or annoying person, esp. a child. 4 TERRORISM. [<L terrere frighten]

ter·ror·ism (ter′ə·riz′əm) n. The act or practice of terrorizing, esp. by violence committed for political purposes, as by a government seeking to intimidate a populace or by revolutionaries seeking to overthrow a government, compel the release of prisoners, etc. —ter′ror·ist n. —ter′ror·is′tic adj.

ter·ror·ize (ter′ə·rīz) v.t. ·ized, ·iz·ing 1 To reduce to a state of terror; terrify. 2 To coerce or intimidate through terrorism. —ter′ror·i·za′tion, ter′ror·iz′er n.

terse (tûrs) adj. ters·er, ters·est Short and to the point; succinct. [< L tersus, pp. of tergere rub off, rub down] —terse′ly adv. —terse′ness n. —Syn. brief, concise, pithy, curt, laconic.

test (test) v.t. 1 To subject to an examination or proof; try. —v.i. 2 To undergo or give an examination or test: usu. with for: to test for accuracy. 3 To receive a rating as a result of testing: The alcohol tested 75 percent. —n. 1 An examination or observation to find out the real nature of something or to prove or disprove its value or validity. 2 A method or technique employed to do this. 3 A criterion or standard of judgment or evaluation. 4 An undergoing of or subjection to certain conditions that disclose the character, quality, nature, etc., of a person or thing: a *test* of will. 5 A series of questions, problems, etc., intended to measure knowledge, aptitudes, intelligence, etc. 6 *Chem.* a A reaction by means of which a compound or ingredient may be identified. b Its agent or the result. [< L *testum* an earthen vessel < *testa* potsherd, shell] —test′a·ble *adj.* —test′er *n.*

**tes·ta·ment** (tes′tə·mənt) *n.* 1 The written declaration of one's last will: now usu. in the phrase last will and testament. 2 A statement testifying to some belief or conviction; credo. 3 Proof; evidence: a *testament* to their courage. 4 In Biblical use, a covenant; dispensation. [< L *testari* testify] —tes′ta·men′tal, tes′ta·men′ta·ry (-men′tər·ē) *adj.*

**tes·ti·fy** (tes′tə·fī) *v.* ·fied, ·fy·ing *v.i.* 1 To make solemn declaration of truth or fact. 2 *Law* To give testimony; bear witness. 3 To serve as evidence or indication. —*v.t.* 4 To bear witness to; affirm. 5 *Law* To state or declare on oath or affirmation. 6 To be evidence or indication of. 7 To make known publicly; declare. [< L *testis* witness + -FY] —tes′ti·fi·ca′tion, tes′ti·fi′er *n.*

**tes·ti·mo·ni·al** (tes′tə·mō′nē·əl) *n.* 1 A statement, often a letter, recommending the character, value, etc., of a person or thing. 2 An act, statement, event, etc., that gives public acknowledgment of esteem or appreciation. —*adj.* Pertaining to or constituting testimony or a testimonial.

**tes·ti·mo·ny** (tes′tə·mō′nē) *n. pl.* ·nies 1 An oral statement of a witness under oath in a court, usu. made in answer to questioning by a lawyer or judge. 2 Any public acknowledgment or declaration, as of a religious experience. 3 Proof of something; evidence. [< L *testimonium* < *testis* a witness]

**tes·ty** (tes′tē) *adj.* ·ti·er, ·ti·est Irritable; touchy. [< AF *testif* heady < OF *teste* head] —tes′ti·ly *adv.* —tes′ti·ness *n.* —Syn. irascible, peevish, petulant, querulous, snappish, crabby, grouchy.

**tet·a·nus** (tet′ə·nəs) *n.* An acute and often fatal infectious bacterial disease marked by spasmodic contraction of voluntary muscles, esp. the muscles of the jaw. [<

Gk. *tetanos* spasm < *teinein* to stretch] —te·tan·ic (ti·tan′ik) *adj.*

**tête-à-tête** (tāt′ə·tāt′, *Fr.* tet·à·tet′) *adj.* Confidential, as between two persons. —*n.* 1 A confidential chat between two persons. 2 An S-shaped sofa on which two persons may face each other. —*adv.* In private or personal talk. [F, lit., head to head]

**teth·er** (teth′ər) *n.* 1 Something used to check or confine, as a rope for fastening an animal. 2 The limit of one's powers or field of action. —at the end of one's tether At the extreme limit of one's resources, patience, etc. [< Scand.]

**tet·ra·he·dron** (tet′rə·hē′drən) *n. pl.* ·drons or ·dra (-drə) A solid bounded by four plane triangular faces. [< Gk. *tetra-* four + *hedra* base] —tet′ra·he′dral *adj.*

**Teu·ton** (t′ōōt′n) *n.* 1 One of an ancient German tribe that dwelt in Jutland north of the Elbe, appearing in history as Teu·to·nes (t′ōō′tə·nēz). 2 One belonging to any of the Teutonic peoples, esp. a German.

**Teu·ton·ic** (t′ōō·ton′ik) *adj.* 1 Of or pertaining to the Teutons. 2 Of or pertaining to Germany or the Germans. 3 Of or pertaining to the peoples of northern Europe, including the English, Scandinavians, Dutch, etc. — Teu·ton′i·cal·ly *adv.*

**text** (tekst) *n.* 1 The actual or original words of an author or speaker, as distinguished from notes, commentary, illustrations, etc. 2 Any of the written or printed versions or editions of a piece of writing. 3 The main body of written or printed matter of a book or a single page, as distinguished from notes, indexes, illustrations, etc. 4 The words of a song, opera, etc. 5 A verse of Scripture, esp. when cited as the basis of a sermon. 6 Any subject of discourse; a topic; theme. 7 One of several styles of letters or types. 8 TEXTBOOK. [< L *textus* fabric, structure < *texere* to weave]

**tex·tile** (teks′tīl, -til) *adj.* 1 Pertaining to weaving or woven fabrics. 2 Such as may be woven; manufactured by weaving. —*n.* 1 A fabric, esp. if woven or knitted; cloth. 2 Material, as a fiber, yarn, etc., capable of being woven. [< L *textus* fabric. See TEXT.]

**tex·ture** (teks′chər) *n.* 1 The arrangement or characteristics of the threads, etc., of a fabric: a tweed having a rough *texture*. 2 The arrangement or characteristics of the constituent elements of anything, esp. as regards surface appearance or tactile qualities: the *texture* of bread. 3 The overall or characteristic structure, form, or interrelatedness of parts of a work of art, music, literature, etc.: the tightly-knit *texture* of his poems. 4 The basic nature or structure of something: the *texture* of rural life. [< L *textus* fabric. See TEXT.] —**tex′tur·al** *adj.* —**tex′tur·al·ly** *adv.*

**thank** (thangk) *v.t.* 1 To express gratitude to; give thanks to. 2 To hold responsible; blame: often used ironically: We have him to *thank* for this mess. —**thank you** An expression of gratitude or in acknowledgment of a service rendered. [< OE *thancian*]

**thank·ful** (thangk′fəl) *adj.* Feeling or manifesting thanks or gratitude; grateful. —**thank′ful·ly** *adv.* —**thank′ful·ness** *n.*

**thanks·giv·ing** (thangks′giv′ing) *n.* 1 The act of giving thanks. 2 A manner of expressing thanks, as a prayer, public celebration, etc.

**thaw** (thô) *v.i.* 1 To melt or dissolve, as snow or ice. 2 To lose the effects of coldness or of having been frozen: often with *out*. 3 To rise in temperature so as to melt ice and snow: said of weather: It *thawed* last night. 4 To become less aloof, unsociable, rigid in opinions, etc. —*v.t.* 5 To cause to thaw. —*n.* 1 The act of thawing. 2 Warmth of weather such as melts things frozen. 3 A becoming less aloof, unsociable, etc. [< OE *thāwian*] —**thaw′er** *n.*

**the·a·ter** (thē′ə·tər) *n.* 1 A structure for the indoor or outdoor presentation of plays, operas, motion pictures, etc. 2 A place resembling such a structure, used for lectures, surgical demonstrations, etc. 3 The theatrical world and everything relating to it, esp.: a The legitimate stage, as distinguished from motion pictures, television, etc. b The works written for or the arts connected with the theater. 4 Theatrical effectiveness: The play was not good *theater*. 5 Any place that is the scene of events or action: a *theater* of war operations. Also **the′a·tre**. [<Gk. *theatron* < *theasthai* behold]

**theft** (theft) *n.* 1 The act or an instance of stealing; larceny. 2 That which is stolen. [< OE *thēoft*]

**the·ism** (thē′iz·əm) *n.* 1 Belief in a god or gods. 2 Belief in a personal God as creator and supreme ruler of the universe. [< Gk. *theos* god] —**the′ist** *n.* —**the·is′tic** or **·ti·cal** *adj.* —**the·is′ti·cal·ly** *adv.*

**theme** (thēm) *n.* 1 A main subject or topic, as of a poem, novel, play, speech, etc. 2 A short essay, often written as an exercise. 3

In a musical composition, a melodic, harmonic, or rhythmic subject or phrase, usu. developed with variations. 4 THEME SONG. [< Gk. *thema*] —**the·mat′ic** (-mat′ik) or **·i·cal** *adj.* —**the·mat′i·cal·ly** *adv.*

**thence** (thens) *adv.* 1 From that place. 2 From the circumstance, fact, or cause; therefore. 3 From that time; after that time. [<OE *thanon* from there]

**thence·forth** (thens′fôrth′, -fôrth′) *adv.* From that time on; thereafter. Also **thence′for′ward** (-fôr′wərd), **thence′for′wards**.

**the·oc·ra·cy** (thē·ok′rə·sē) *n. pl.* **·cies** 1 A state, polity, or group of people that claims a deity as its ruler. 2 Government by a priestly class claiming to have divine authority, as in the Papacy. [<Gk. *theos* god + *kratein* rule] —**the·o·crat** (thē′ə·krat) *n.* —**the·o·crat·ic** (thē′ə·krat′ik) or **·i·cal** *adj.* —**the′o·crat′i·cal·ly** *adv.*

**the·o·lo·gi·an** (thē′ə·lō′jən) *n.* One versed in theology.

**the·ol·o·gy** (thē·ol′ə·jē) *n. pl.* **·gies** 1 The study of God, his attributes, and his relationship with man and the universe, esp. such studies as set forth by a specific church, religious group, or theologian. 2 The study of religion and religious doctrine, culminating in a synthesis or philosophy of religion. [<Gk. *theos* god + *logos* discourse]

**the·o·rem** (thē′ər·əm, thir′əm) *n.* 1 A proposition demonstrably true or so universally acknowledged as such as to become part of a general theory. 2 *Math.* A proposition to be proved or which has been proved. [<Gk. *theōrēma* sight, theory] —**the·o·re·mat·ic** (thē′ər·ə·mat′ik) *adj.*

**the·o·ret·i·cal** (thē′ə·ret′i·kəl) *adj.* 1 Of, relating to, or consisting of theory. 2 Existing only in theory; not applied; speculative; hypothetical. 3 Addicted to theorizing. Also **the′o·ret′ic**. —**the′o·ret′i·cal·ly** *adv.*

**the·o·rize** (thē′ə·rīz) *v.i.* **·rized, ·riz·ing** To form or express theories; speculate. —**the′o·ri·za′tion**, **the′o·riz′er** *n.*

**the·o·ry** (thē′ər·ē, thir′ē) *n. pl.* **·ries** 1 A plan, scheme, or procedure used or to be used as a basis or technique for doing something. 2 A merely speculative or an ideal circumstance, principle, mode of action, etc.: often with *in*: In *theory*, the plan worked. 3 A body of fundamental or abstract principles underlying a science, art, etc.: a *theory* of modern architecture. 4 A proposed explanation or hypothesis designed to account for any phenomenon. 5 Loosely, mere speculation, conjecture, or guesswork. [<Gk. *theōría* view, speculation]

the·os·o·phy (thē·os′ə·fē) *n.* 1 Any of several religious or philosophical systems claiming to have mystical insight into the nature of God and the universe. 2 *Usu. cap.* The religious system of a modern religious sect (**Theosophical Society**) that is strongly Buddhist or Brahmanic in character and claims to have and to be able to teach such mystical insights. [<Gk. *theos* god + *sophos* wise] —the·o·soph·ic (thē′ə·sof′ik) or ·i·cal *adj.* —the′o·soph′i·cal·ly *adv.* —the·os′o·phist *n.*

ther·a·peu·tic (ther′ə·pyōō′tik) *adj.* 1 Having healing qualities; curative. 2 Pertaining to therapeutics. Also ther′a·peu′ti·cal. [<Gk. *therapeuein* serve, take care of] —ther′a·peu′ti·cal·ly *adv.*

ther·a·peu·tics (ther′ə·pyōō′tiks) *n.pl. (construed as sing.)* The branch of medicine that treats of remedies for disease. —ther′a·peu′tist *n.*

ther·a·py (ther′ə·pē) *n. pl.* ·pies 1 The treatment of disease or any bodily disorder or injury by drugs, physical exercise, etc. 2 PSYCHOTHERAPY. [<Gk. *therapeuein* take care of] —ther′a·pist *n.*

ther·mal (thûr′məl) *adj.* 1 Of, coming from, or having hot springs. 2 Of, relating to, or caused by heat. 3 Hot or warm: a *thermal* draft. 4 Aiding to conserve body heat: *thermal* fabrics. Also ther′mic. —*n.* A rising current of warm air in the atmosphere. [<Gk. *thermē* heat]

ther·mom·e·ter (thər·mom′ə·tər) *n.* An instrument for measuring temperature, often consisting of a tube with a bulb containing a liquid which expands or contracts so that its height in the tube is proportional to the temperature. —ther·mo·met·ric (thûr′mō·met′rik) or ·ri·cal *adj.* —ther′mo·met′ri·cal·ly *adv.*

ther·mo·nu·cle·ar (thûr′mō·n′ōō′klē·ər) *adj. Physics* Pertaining to or characterized by reactions involving the fusion of light atomic nuclei subjected to very high temperatures.

ther·mo·stat (thûr′mə·stat) *n.* An automatic control device used to maintain a desired temperature. [<THERMO- + Gk. *statos* standing] —ther′mo·stat′ic *adj.* —ther′mo·stat′i·cal·ly *adv.*

the·sau·rus (thi·sôr′əs) *n. pl.* ·sau·ri (-sôr′ī) or sau′rus·es 1 A book containing words and their synonyms grouped together. 2 A book

containing words or facts dealing with a specific subject or field. [<Gk. *thēsauros* treasure]

the·sis (thē′sis) *n. pl.* ·ses (-sēz) 1 A proposition, esp. a formal proposition advanced and defended by argumentation. 2 A formal treatise on a particular subject, esp. a dissertation presented by a candidate for an advanced academic degree. 3 a *Logic* An affirmative proposition. b An unproved premise or postulate, as opposed to a hypothesis. [<Gk., a placing, proposition]

thi·a·mine (thī′ə·min, -mēn) *n.* Vitamin B₁, a compound found in cereal grains, liver, egg yolk, etc., and also made synthetically. Also thi′a·min (-min). [<THI(O)- + -AMINE]

thick (thik) *adj.* 1 Relatively large in depth or extent from one surface to its opposite; not thin. 2 Having a specified dimension of this kind, whether great or small: an inch *thick*. 3 Having the constituent or specified elements growing, packed, arranged, etc., close together: a field *thick* with daisies. 4 Viscous in consistency: a *thick* sauce. 5 Heavy; dense: a *thick* fog. 6 Foggy, hazy, smoky, etc. 7 Very dark; impenetrable: a *thick* gloom. 8 Indistinct; muffled; guttural, as speech. 9 Very noticeable; decided: a *thick* German accent. 10 *Informal* Dull; stupid. 11 *Informal* Very friendly; intimate. 12 *Informal* Going beyond what is tolerable; excessive. —*adv.* In a thick manner. —*n.* The thickest or most intense time or place of anything: the *thick* of the fight. [< OE *thicce*] —thick′ish *adj.* —thick′ly *adv.* —thick′ness *n.*

thick·en (thik′ən) *v.t. & v.i.* 1 To make or become thick or thicker. 2 To make or become more intricate or intense: The plot *thickens*. —thick′en·er *n.*

thief (thēf) *n. pl.* thieves (thēvz) One who takes something belonging to another, esp. secretly. [<OE *thēof*]

thiev·er·y (thē′vər·ē) *n. pl.* ·er·ies The practice or act of thieving; theft; also, an instance of thieving. —thiev′ish *adj.* —thiev′ish·ly *adv.* —thiev′ish·ness *n.*

thigh (thī) *n.* 1 The human leg between the hip and the knee. 2 The corresponding portion in other animals. [< OE *thēoh*]

thim·ble (thim′bəl) *n.* 1 In sewing, a pitted cover worn to protect the finger that pushes the needle. 2 Any similar device, esp. a ring on a rope to prevent chafing. [< OE *thȳmel* < *thūma* thumb]

thin (thin) *adj.* thin·ner, thin·nest 1 Having

opposite surfaces relatively close to each other; being of little depth or width; not thick. 2 Lean and slender of figure. 3 Having the component parts or particles scattered or diffused; rarefied: a *thin* gas. 4 Not large or abundant, as in number: a *thin* audience. 5 Lacking thickness of consistency: a *thin* sauce. 6 Not dense or heavy: a *thin* fog. 7 Having little intensity or richness: a *thin* red. 8 Having little volume or resonance; shrill, as a voice. 9 Of a loose or light texture: *thin* clothing. 10 Insufficient; flimsy: a *thin* excuse. 11 Lacking essential ingredients or qualities: *thin* blood. 12 Meager; scant: *thin* hair. 13 Lacking vigor, force, substance, complexity, etc.; superficial; slight: *thin* humor. —*adv.* In a thin way: Slice the sausage *thin*. —*v.t. & v.i.* thinned, thin·ning To make or become thin or thinner. [<OE *thynne*] —thin′ly *adv.* —thin′ness *n.*

thing (thing) *n.* 1 That which exists or is conceived to exist as a separate entity: all the *things* in the world. 2 That which is designated, as contrasted with the word or symbol used to denote it. 3 A matter or circumstance: *Things* have changed. 4 An act, deed, event, etc.: That was a shameless *thing* to do. 5 A procedure or step, as in an ordered course or process: the first *thing* to do. 6 An item, particular, detail, etc.: each *thing* on the schedule. 7 A statement or expression; utterance: to say the right *thing*. 8 An idea; opinion; notion: Stop putting *things* in her head. 9 A quality; attribute; characteristic: Kindness is a precious *thing*. 10 An inanimate object. 11 An object that is not or cannot be described or particularized: What kind of *thing* is that? 12 A person, regarded in terms of pity, affection, or contempt: that poor *thing*. 13 *pl.* Possessions; belongings: to pack one's *things*. 14 *pl.* Clothes; esp. outer garments. 15 A piece of clothing, as a dress: not a *thing* to wear. 16 A piece of literature, art, music, etc.: He read a few *things* by Byron. 17 The proper or befitting act or result: with *the*: That was not the *thing* to do. 18 The important point, attitude, etc.: with *the*: The *thing* one learns from travel is how to combat fatigue. 19 *Informal* A point; issue; case: He always makes a big *thing* out of dividing up the bill. 20 *Informal* A strong liking, disliking, fear, attraction, etc.: to have a *thing* for tall girls. 21 *Law* A subject or property or dominion, as distinguished from a

person. —do one's (own) thing *Slang* To express oneself by doing what one wants to do or can do well or is in the habit of doing. [<OE, thing, cause, assembly]

think (thingk) *v.* thought (thôt), think·ing *v.t.* 1 To produce or form in the mind; conceive mentally: to *think* evil thoughts. 2 To examine in the mind; meditate upon, or determine by reasoning: to *think* a plan through. 3 To believe; consider: I *think* him guilty. 4 To expect; anticipate: They did not *think* to meet us. 5 To bring to mind; remember; recollect: I cannot *think* what he said. 6 To have the mind preoccupied by: to *think* business morning, noon, and night. 7 To intend; purpose: Do they *think* to rob me? —*v.i.* 8 To use the mind or intellect in exercising judgment, forming ideas, etc.; engage in rational thought; reason. 9 To have a particular opinion, sentiment, or feeling: I don't *think* so. —think of (or about) 1 To bring to mind; remember; recollect. 2 To conceive in the mind; invent; imagine. 3 To have a specified opinion or attitude toward; regard. 4 To be considerate of; have regard for. —think over To reflect upon; ponder. —think up To devise, arrive at, or invent by thinking. —*n. Informal* The act of thinking. [<OE *thencan*] —think′er *n.*

thirst (thûrst) *n.* 1 Discomfort or distress due to a need for water. 2 A craving or taste for any specified liquid: a *thirst* for alcohol. 3 Any longing or craving: a *thirst* for glory. —*v.i.* 1 To feel thirst; be thirsty. 2 To have an eager desire or craving. [<OE *thurst*] —thirst′er *n.*

thirst·y (thûrs′tē) *adj.* thirst·i·er, thirst·i·est 1 Affected with thirst. 2 Lacking moisture; arid; parched. 3 Eagerly desirous. 4 *Informal* Causing thirst. [<OE *thurstig*] —thirst′i·ly *adv.* —thirst′i·ness *n.*

this·tle (this′əl) *n.* Any of various prickly plants with cylindrical or globular heads of composite flowers. [<OE *thistel*] —this′tly *adj.*

thith·er (thith′ər, thith′-) *adv.* To that place; in that direction. —*adj.* Situated or being on the other side; more distant. [< OE *thider*]

thong (thông, thong) *n.* 1 A narrow strip, usu. of leather, as for fastening. 2 A lash of a whip. [<OE *thwang* thong]

tho·rax (thôr′aks, thō′raks) *n. pl.* tho·rax·es or tho·ra·ces (thôr′ə·sēz, thō′rə-) 1 The part of the body between the neck and the abdomen, enclosed by the ribs. 2 The middle segment between the head and abdomen of an insect. • See INSECT. [<Gk. *thōrax*] —**tho·rac·ic** (thô·ras'ik) *adj.*

**tho·ri·um** (thôr'ē·əm, thō'rē-) *n.* A rare, radioactive, metallic element (symbol Th), used as a fuel in certain nuclear reactors. [< THOR] —**tho'ric** *adj.*

**thorn** (thôrn) *n.* 1 A sharp, rigid outgrowth from a plant stem. 2 Any of various thorn-bearing shrubs or trees. 3 A cause of discomfort, pain, or annoyance. 4 The name of the Old English rune þ, equivalent to *th*, as in *thorn*, from which it derives its name. — *v.t.* To pierce or prick with a thorn. [<OE] —**thorn'less** *adj.*

**thor·ough** (thûr'ō, thûr'ə) *adj.* 1 Complete; exhaustive: a *thorough* search. 2 Attentive to details and accuracy; painstaking: a *thorough* worker. 3 Completely (such and such); through and through: a *thorough* nincompoop. [Emphatic var. of THROUGH] —**thor'ough·ly** *adv.* —**thor'ough·ness** *n.* — **Syn.** 1 comprehensive, sweeping, out-and-out, total. 2 exact, precise, meticulous, careful, conscientious. 3 absolute, downright, utter, unmitigated, perfect.

**thor·ough·bred** (thûr'ə·bred') *adj.* 1 Bred from pure stock; pedigreed. 2 Possessing or showing excellence, as in training, education, manners, culture, etc.; first-rate. —*n.* 1 A thoroughbred animal. 2 A person of culture and good breeding.

**thor·ough·fare** (thûr'ō·fâr', thûr'ə-) *n.* 1 A much frequented road or street through which the public have unobstructed passage. 2 A passage: now chiefly in the phrase **no thoroughfare**. [<OE *thurh* through + *faru* going]

**though** (thō) *conj.* 1 Notwithstanding the fact that; although: *Though* he was sleepy, he stayed awake. 2 Granting that; even if: *Though* she may win, she will have lost her popularity. 3 And yet; still; however: I am well, *though* I do not feel very strong. — *adv.* Notwithstanding; nevertheless: It's not a good play, but I like it *though.* [< ON *thō*]

**thought¹** (thôt) *n.* 1 The act or process of thinking. 2 The product of thinking, as an idea, concept, judgment, opinion, or the like. 3 Intellectual activity of a specific kind, time, place, etc.: Greek *thought.* 4 Consideration; attention; heed: Give the plan some *thought.* 5 Intention; plan; design: All *thought* of returning was abandoned. 6 Expectation; anticipation: He had no *thought* of finding her there. 7 A trifle; a small

amount: Be a *thought* more cautious. [<THOUGHT²]

**thought·ful** (thôt'fəl) *adj.* 1 Full of thought; meditative. 2 Showing, characterized by, or promoting thought. 3 Attentive; careful, esp. manifesting regard for others; considerate. —**thought'ful·ly** *adv.* —**thought'ful·ness** *n.*

**thou·sand** (thou'zənd) *n.* 1 The product of ten times a hundred. 2 *Usu. pl.* An indefinitely large number. —*adj.* Consisting of a hundred times ten. [<OE *thūsend*] —**thou'sand·fold'** (-fōld') *adj., adv.*

**thrall** (thrôl) *n.* 1 A person in bondage; a slave; serf. 2 One controlled by a passion or vice. 3 Slavery. [<ON *thrǣl*]

**thrall·dom** (thrôl'dəm) *n.* 1 The state of being a thrall. 2 Any sort of bondage or servitude. Also **thral'dom.**

**thrash** (thrash) *v.t.* 1 To thresh, as grain. 2 To beat as if with a flail; flog; whip. 3 To move or swing with flailing, violent motions. 4 To defeat utterly. —*v.i.* 5 To move or swing about with flailing, violent motions. 6 To make one's way by thrashing. —**thrash out** (or **over**) To discuss fully and usu. come to a conclusion. —*n.* The act of thrashing. [Dial. var. of THRESH]

**thread** (thred) *n.* 1 A very slender cord or line composed of two or more filaments, as of flax, cotton, silk, nylon, etc., twisted together. 2 A filament of metal, glass, etc. 3 A fine beam: a *thread* of light. 4 Something that runs a continuous course through a series or whole: the *thread* of his discourse. 5 *Mech.* The helical ridge of a screw. —*v.t.* 1 To pass a thread through the eye of: to *thread* a needle. 2 To string on a thread, as beads. 3 To cut a thread on or in, as a screw. 4 To make one's way through or over: to *thread* a maze. 5 To make (one's way) carefully. —*v.i.* 6 To make one's way carefully. 7 To fall from a fork or spoon in a fine thread: said of boiling syrup. [<OE *thrǣd*] —**thread'er** *n.*

**thread·bare** (thred'bâr') *adj.* 1 Worn so that the threads show, as a rug or garment. 2 Clad in worn garments. 3 Commonplace; hackneyed. —**thread'bare'ness** *n.* —**Syn.** 2 shabby. 3 common, stale, stereotyped, trite.

**threat** (thret) *n.* 1 A declaration of an intention to inflict injury or pain. 2 Any menace or danger. [< OE *threat* crowd, oppression]

**threat·en** (thret'n) *v.t.* 1 To utter threats against. 2 To be menacing or dangerous to.

3 To portend (something unpleasant or dangerous). 4 To utter threats of (injury, vengeance, etc.). —*v.i.* 5 To utter threats. 6 To have a menacing aspect; lower. —**threat′en·er** *n.* —**threat′en·ing·ly** *adv.*

**thresh** (thresh) *v.t.* 1 To beat stalks of (ripened grain) with a flail so as to separate the grain from the husks. —*v.i.* 2 To thresh grain. 3 To move or thrash about. —**thresh out** To discuss fully and to a conclusion. —**thresh over** To discuss over and over. [<OE *therscan*]

**thresh·er** (thresh′ər) *n.* 1 One who or that which threshes, esp. a machine for threshing. 2 A large shark having an extremely long tail: also **thresher shark.**

**thresh·old** (thresh′ōld, -hōld) *n.* 1 The plank, timber, or stone lying under the door of a building; doorsill. 2 The entering point or beginning of anything: the *threshold* of the 20th century. 3 The minimum degree of stimulation necessary to produce a response or to be perceived. [< OE *therscold*]

**thrice** (thrīs) *adv.* 1 Three times. 2 Fully; extremely. [<OE *thriwa* thrice]

**thrift** (thrift) *n.* Care and wisdom in the management of one's resources; frugality. [<ON] —**thrift′less** *adj.* —**thrift′less·ly** *adv.* —**thrift′less·ness** *n.*

**thrift·y** (thrif′tē) *adj.* **thrift·i·er, thrift·i·est** 1 Displaying thrift or good management; frugal. 2 Prosperous; thriving. —**thrift′i·ly** *adv.* —**thrift′i·ness** *n.* —**Syn.** 1 economical, provident, prudent, saving.

**thrill** (thril) *v.t.* 1 To cause to feel a great or tingling excitement. —*v.i.* 2 To feel a sudden wave of emotion. 3 To vibrate or tremble; quiver. —*n.* 1 A feeling of excitement. 2 A thrilling quality. 3 A pulsation; quiver. [<OE *thyrlian* pierce] —**thrill′ing·ly** *adv.*

**thrive** (thrīv) *v.i.* **throve** (thrōv) or **thrived, thrived** or **thriven** (thriv′ən), **thriv·ing** 1 To prosper; be successful. 2 To flourish. [<ON *thrīfast* reflexive of *thrīfa* grasp] —**thriv′er** *n.* —**thriv′ing·ly** *adv.*

**throat** (thrōt) *n.* 1 The front part of the neck. 2 The passage extending from the back of the mouth and containing the epiglottis, larynx, trachea, and pharynx. 3 Any narrow passage resembling a throat. —**jump down one's throat** To scold or criticize with sudden violence. —**lump in the throat** A feeling of tightness in the throat, as from strong emotion. —**stick in one's throat** To be difficult or painful to say. [<OE *throte*]

**throb** (throb) *v.i.* **throbbed, throb·bing** 1 To pulsate rhythmically, as the heart. 2 To feel or show emotion by trembling. —*n.* 1 The act or state of throbbing. 2 A pulsation, esp. one caused by excitement or emotion. [imit.] —**throb′ber** *n.*

**throe** (thrō) *n.* 1 A violent pang or pain. 2 *pl.* The pains of death or childbirth. 3 Any agonized or agonizing activity. [<OE *thrawe*]

**throm·bo·sis** (throm·bō′sis) *n.* The formation of a blood clot inside the heart or a blood vessel. [<Gk. *thrombos* clot] —**throm·bot′ic** (-bot′ik) *adj.*

**throne** (thrōn) *n.* 1 The chair occupied by a king, pope, etc., on state occasions. 2 The rank or authority of a king, queen, etc. —*v.t. & v.i.* **throned, thron·ing** To enthrone; exalt. [<Gk. *thronos* seat]

**throng** (thrông, throng) *n.* 1 A closely crowded multitude. 2 Any numerous collection. —*v.t.* 1 To crowd into and occupy fully; jam. 2 To crowd upon. —*v.i.* 3 To collect or move in a throng. [<OE *gethrang*] —**Syn.** *n.* 1 crowd, host, jam, mass, press.

**throt·tle** (throt′l) *n.* 1 A valve controlling the supply of fuel or steam to the cylinders of an engine: also **throttle valve.** 2 The lever which operates the throttle valve: also **throttle lever.** —*v.t.* **-tled, ·tling** 1 To strangle, choke, or suffocate. 2 To silence, stop, or suppress. 3 To reduce or shut off the flow of (steam or fuel to the cylinders of an engine). 4 To reduce the speed of by means of a throttle. —*v.i.* 5 To suffocate; choke. [Dim. of ME *throte* throat] —**throt′tler** *n.*

**through** (thrōō) *prep.* 1 From end to end, side to side, or limit to limit of; into at one side, end, or point, and out of at another. 2 Covering, entering, or penetrating all parts of; throughout. 3 From the first to the last of: *through* the day. 4 Here and there upon or in. 5 By way of: He departed *through* the door. 6 By the instrumentality or aid of. 7 Having reached the end of: He got *through* his examinations. —*adv.* 1 From one end, side, surface, etc., to or beyond another. 2 From beginning to end. 3 To a termination or conclusion: to pull *through.* 4 Completely; entirely: He is wet *through.* —**through and through** Thoroughly; completely. —*adj.* 1 Going to its destination without stops: a *through* train. 2 Usable or valid for an entire trip: a *through* ticket. 3 Extending from one side or surface to another. 4 Allowing unobstructed or direct

**throw** (thrō) *v.* **threw** (thrōo), **thrown**, **throw·ing** *v.t.* 1 To propel through the air by means of a sudden straightening or whirling of the arm. 2 To propel or hurl. 3 To put hastily or carelessly: He *threw* a coat over his shoulders. 4 To direct or project (light, shadow, a glance, etc.). 5 To bring to a specified condition or state: to, *throw* the enemy into a panic. 6 To cause to fall: The horse *threw* its rider. 7 In wrestling, to force the shoulders of (an opponent) to the ground. 8 To cast (dice). 9 To make (a specified cast) with dice. 10 To shed; lose: The horse *threw* a shoe. 11 *Informal* To lose purposely, as a race. 12 To move, as a lever or switch. 13 *Slang* To give (a party, etc.). 14 In ceramics, to shape on a potter's wheel. —*v.i* 15 To cast or fling something. —**throw away** 1 To cast off; discard. 2 To squander. —**throw cold water on** To discourage. —**throw off** 1 To reject; spurn. 2 To rid oneself of. 3 To do or utter in an offhand manner. 4 To emit; discharge. 5 To confuse; mislead. 6 To elude (a pursuer). —**throw oneself at** To strive to gain the affection or love of. —**throw oneself into** To take part in vigorously. —**throw oneself on** (or **upon**) To rely on utterly. —**throw open** 1 To open suddenly, as a door. 2 To free from restrictions or obstacles. —**throw out** 1 To emit. 2 To discard; reject. 3 To utter as if accidentally: to *throw out* hints. 4 In baseball, to retire (a runner) by throwing the ball to the base toward which he is advancing. —**throw over** 1 To overturn. 2 To jilt. —**throw together** To put together carelessly. —**throw up** 1 To vomit. 2 To erect hastily. 3 To give up. 4 *Informal* To mention (something) repeatedly and reproachfully; taunt. —*n.* 1 An act of throwing. 2 The distance over which a missile may be thrown: a long *throw.* 3 A cast of dice, or the resulting number. 4 A scarf or other light covering. 5 In wrestling, a flooring of one's opponent so that both his shoulders touch the mat simultaneously for ten seconds. [<OE *thrāwan* to turn, twist, curl] —**throw′er** *n.* —**Syn.** *v.* 1 fling, heave, hurl, pitch.

**thrum** (thrum) *v.* **thrummed**, **thrum·ming** *v.t.* 1 To play on (a stringed instrument), esp. idly; strum. 2 To drum on monotonously with the fingers. —*v.i.* 3 To strum a stringed instrument. —*n.* The sound made by thrumming. [Prob. imit.]

**thrush** (thrush) *n.* Any of many species of migratory songbirds, usu. having long wings and spotted under parts, as the **hermit thrush**, the **wood thrush**, the robin, and the bluebird. [<OE *thrysce*]

**thrust** (thrust) *v.* **thrust**, **thrust·ing** *v.t.* 1 To push or shove with force. 2 To pierce with a sudden forward motion, as with a sword. 3 To interpose. —*v.i.* 4 To make a sudden push or thrust. 5 To force oneself on or ahead: to *thrust* through a crowd. —*n.* 1 A sudden and forcible push, esp. with a pointed weapon. 2 A vigorous attack; sharp onset. 3 A force that drives or propels. 4 Salient force or meaning: the *thrust* of his remarks. [<ON *thrýsta*] —**thrust′er** *n.* —**Syn.** *v.* 1 lunge. 2 stab, stick. *n.* 4 import, intention, significance, sense, gist.

**thud** (thud) *n.* 1 A dull, heavy sound. 2 A blow causing such a sound; a thump. —*v.i.* **thud·ded, thud·ding** To strike or fall with a thud. [<OE *thyddan* strike, thrust, press]

**thug** (thug) *n.* 1 Formerly, one of an organization of religious assassins in India. 2 Any assassin or ruffian. [<Skt. *sthaga* swindler]

**thumb** (thum) *n.* 1 The short, thick digit of the human hand. 2 A similar part in certain animals. 3 The division in a glove or mitten that covers the thumb. —**all thumbs** Clumsy with the hands. —**thumbs down** A signal of negation or disapproval. —**thumbs up** A signal of approval. —**under one's thumb** Under one's influence or power. —*v.t.* 1 To rub, soil, or wear with the thumb in handling. 2 To handle clumsily. 3 To run through the pages of (a book, etc.) rapidly. —**thumb a ride** To get a ride by signaling with the thumb. [<OE *thūma*]

**thump** (thump) *n.* 1 A blow with a blunt or heavy object. 2 The sound made by such a blow; a thud. —*v.t.* 1 To beat or strike so as to make a heavy thud or thuds. 2 *Informal* To beat or defeat severely. —*v.i.* 3 To strike with a thump. 4 To pound or throb, as the heart. [Imit.] —**thump′er** *n.*

**thun·der** (thun′dər) *n.* 1 The sound that accompanies lightning, caused by the explosive effect of the electric discharge. 2 Any loud noise resembling thunder. 3 A vehement or powerful utterance. —**steal one's thunder** To undermine the effectiveness of an opponent by anticipating his next move, argument, etc. —*v.i.* 1 To give forth peals of thunder: It is *thundering.* 2 To make a noise like thunder. 3 To utter vehement denunciations. —*v.t.* 4 To utter or express with a noise like thunder: The cannon *thundered* defiance. [<OE *thunor*] —**thun·der·er** *n.*

**thun·der·clap** (thun′dər·klap′) *n.* 1 A sharp, violent detonation of thunder. 2 Anything violent or sudden.

**thun·der·struck** (thun′dər·struk′) *adj.* Amazed, astonished, or confounded. Also **thun′der·strick′en** (-strik′ən).

**thwack** (thwak) *v.t.* To strike heavily with something flat; whack. —*n.* A blow with something flat. [Prob. imit.] —**thwack′er** *n.*

**thyme** (tim) *n.* 1 Any of various small shrubby plants of the mint family, having aromatic leaves. 2 The dried leaves of certain thyme plants, used for seasoning in cookery. [<Gk. *thymon*] —**thy·mic** (-mik), **thym′y** *adj.*

**thy·roid** (thī′roid) *adj.* 1 Of or pertaining to the cartilage of the larynx which forms the Adam's apple. 2 Of, pertaining to, or describing a large ductless gland situated near the larynx on each side of the trachea and secreting thyroxin. —*n.* 1 The thyroid cartilage. 2 The thyroid gland. [<Gk. *thyreoeidēs* shield-shaped]

**ti·a·ra** (tē·âr′ə, -är′ə) *n.* 1 The pope's triple crown. 2 The upright headdress worn by the ancient Persian kings. 3 A jeweled head ornament or coronet worn by women on very formal or state occasions. [Gk., Persian headdress]

**tick** (tik) *n.* 1 A light recurring sound made by a watch, clock, etc. 2 *Informal* The time elapsing between two ticks of a clock; an instant. 3 A mark, as a dot or dash, used in checking off something. —*v.i.* 1 To sound a tick or ticks. —*v.t.* 2 To mark or check with ticks. [Prob. imit.]

**tick·et** (tik′it) *n.* 1 A printed card showing that the holder is entitled to something, as transportation in a public vehicle, admission to a theater, etc. 2 A label or tag: a price *ticket*. 3 A list of candidates of a single party on a ballot: the Democratic *ticket*. 4 *Informal* A court summons for a traffic violation, usu. involving a fine. —*v.t.* 1 To fix a ticket to; label. 2 To furnish with a ticket. [<OF *estiquette*]

**tick·le** (tik′əl) *v.* **·led**, **·ling** *v.t.* 1 To excite the nerves of by touching or scratching on some sensitive spot, producing a sensation resulting in spasmodic laughter or twitching. 2 To please: Compliments *tickle* our vanity. 3 To amuse or entertain; delight. 4 To move, stir, or get by tickling. —*v.i.* 5 To have a tingling sensation: My foot *tickles*. 6

To be ticklish. —*n.* 1 The sensation produced by tickling. 2 The touch or action producing such sensation. [ME *tikelen*]

**tick·lish** (tik′lish) *adj.* 1 Sensitive to tickling. 2 Liable to be upset. 3 Easily offended; sensitive. 4 Requiring tact in handling; delicate: a *ticklish* situation. —**tick′lish·ly** *adv.* —**tick′lish·ness** *n.*

**tid·bit** (tid′bit′) *n.* A choice bit, as of food. [<dial. E *tid* a small object + BIT¹]

**tide** (tid) *n.* 1 The periodic rise and fall of the surface of the ocean caused by the gravitational attraction of moon and sun. 2 Anything that comes like the tide at flood. 3 The natural drift or tendency of events. 4 A current; stream: the *tide* of public feeling. 5 Season; time: *Eastertide*. —**turn the tide** To reverse a condition completely. —*v.i.* **tid·ed, tid·ing** To ebb and flow like the tide. —**tide over** 1 To give or act as temporary help, as in a difficulty. 2 To surmount. [<OE *tid* a period, season]

**ti·dings** (tī′dingz) *n.pl.* (*sometimes construed as sing.*) Information; news. [<OE *tidung*]

**ti·dy** (tī′dē) *adj.* **·di·er, ·di·est** 1 Neat in appearance; orderly: a *tidy* desk. 2 Keeping things in order: a *tidy* housekeeper. 3 *Informal* Moderately large: a *tidy* sum. 4 *Informal* Fairly good. —*v.t.* & *v.i.* **ti·died, ti·dy·ing** To put (things) in order. —*n.pl.* **·dies** An antimacassar. [<OE *tid* time] —**ti′di·ly** *adv.* —**ti′di·ness** *n.* —Syn. *adj.* 1 shipshape, spruce, trim, well-kept.

**tie** (tī) *v.* **tied, ty·ing** *v.t.* 1 To fasten with cord, rope, etc., the ends of which are then knotted. 2 To draw the parts of together by a cord fastened with a knot: to *tie* one's shoes. 3 To form (a knot). 4 To form a knot in, as string. 5 To fasten, or join in any way. 6 To restrict; bind. 7 **a** To equal (a competitor) in score or achievement. **b** To equal (a competitor's score). 8 *Informal* To unite in marriage. 9 *Music* To unite by a tie. —*v.i.* 10 To make a tie or connection. 11 To make the same score; be equal. —**tie down** To hinder; restrict. —**tie up** 1 To fasten with rope, string, etc. 2 To wrap, as with paper, and fasten with string, cord, etc. 3 To moor (a vessel). 4 To block; hinder. 5 To be previously committed, so as to be unavailable: His money is *tied up* in real estate. —*n.* 1 A flexible bond or fastening secured by drawing the ends into a knot or loop. 2 Any bond or obligation. 3 In a contest, a draw; also, the point at which this occurs. 4 Something that is tied or intended for tying, as a shoelace, necktie, etc. 5 *Engin.* A structural member fastening parts together. 6 *Music* A curved line joining two notes of the same pitch to make them represent one tone. 7 One of a set of timbers laid crosswise on the ground as supports for railroad tracks. 8 *pl.* Low shoes with laces. [<OE *tigan* bind] — **ti´er** *n.*

**tier** (tir) *n.* A rank or row in a series of things placed one above another. —*v.t. & v.i.* To place or rise in tiers. [<OF, a sequence]

**tiff** (tif) *n.* A slight quarrel; a spat. —*v.i.* To be in or have a tiff. [?]

**ti·ger** (tī´gər) *n.* 1 A large carnivorous feline of Asia, with black stripes on a tawny body. 2 A fiercely determined, spirited, or energetic person or quality. [<Gk. *tigris*] —**ti´gress** *n. Fem.* —**ti´ger·ish, ti´grish** *adj.*

**tight** (tīt) *adj.* 1 Impervious to fluids; not leaky: often used in combination: *watertight.* 2 Firmly fixed or fastened in place; secure. 3 Fully stretched; taut: *tight* as a drum. 4 Strict; stringent: a *tight* schedule. 5 Fitting closely; esp. too closely: *tight* shoes. 6 *Informal* Difficult to cope with; troublesome: a *tight* spot. 7 *Informal* Stingy. 8 *Slang* Intoxicated. 9 Evenly matched: said of a race or contest. 10 Difficult to obtain because of scarcity or financial restrictions: said of money or of commodities. —*adv.* 1 Firmly; securely: Hold on *tight.* 2 With much constriction: The dress fits too *tight.* —**sit tight** To remain firm in one's position or opinion. [?<ON *thēttr* dense] —**tight´ly** *adv.* —**tight´ness** *n.*

**tight·en** (tīt´n) *v.t. & v.i.* To make or become tight or tighter. —**tight´en·er** *n.*

**tile** (tīl) *n.* 1 A thin piece of baked clay, stone, etc., used for covering roofs, floors, etc., and as an ornament. 2 A thin piece of linoleum, plastic, cork, etc., for covering walls and floors. 3 A short earthenware pipe, as used in forming sewers. 4 Tiles collectively; tiling. 5 Any of the pieces in the game of mah jong. —*v.t.* **tiled, til·ing** To cover with tiles. [<L *tegula* < *tegere* to cover] —**til´er** *n.*

**till** (til) *n.* 1 A money drawer behind the counter of a store. 2 The money in such a drawer; also, available cash. 3 Formerly, a drawer for holding valuables. [ME *tillen*]

**till·age** (til´ij) *n.* 1 The cultivation of land. 2 The state of being tilled. 3 Land that has been tilled. 4 Crops growing on such land. [<TILL + -AGE]

**till·er** (til´ər) *n.* 1 A lever to turn a rudder. 2 A

means of guidance. [<Med. L *telartum* a weaver's beam]

**tilt** (tilt) *v.t.* 1 To cause to rise at one end or side; slant. 2 To aim or thrust, as a lance. 3 To charge or overthrow in a tilt or joust. —*v.i.* 4 To incline at an angle; lean. 5 To contend with the lance; joust. 6 To argue; debate. —*n.* 1 A slant or slope. 2 The act of tilting something. 3 A medieval sport in which mounted knights, charging with lances, endeavored to unseat each other. 4 A quarrel or dispute. 5 *Can.* In certain provinces, a seesaw. —**at full tilt** At full speed. [ME *tylten* be overthrown, totter] —**tilt´er** *n.*

**tim·ber** (tim´bər) *n.* 1 Wood suitable for building or constructing things. 2 Growing or standing trees; forests. 3 A single piece of squared wood prepared for use or already in use. 4 Any principal beam in a ship. —*v.t.* To provide or shore with timber. [<OE] —**tim´ber·er** *n.*

**tim·bre** (tam´bər, tim´-; *Fr.* taṅ´br´) *n.* The distinctive quality of sound, produced chiefly by overtones, that characterizes or identifies a singing voice, a musical instrument, or a voiced speech sound. [F <L *tympanum* a kettledrum]

**time** (tīm) *n.* 1 The general idea, relation, or fact of continuous or successive existence; the past, present, and future. 2 A definite moment, hour, period, etc.: The *time* is 3:30. 3 Epoch; era: the *time* of the Vikings. 4 The portion of duration allotted to some specific happening, condition, etc. 5 Leisure: He has no *time* to play golf. 6 Experience on a specific occasion: to have a good *time.* 7 A point in duration; occasion: Your *time* has come! 8 A period considered as having some quality of its own: *Times* are hard. 9 A system of reckoning or measuring duration: daylight-saving *time.* 10 A case of recurrence or repetition: three *times* a day. 11 *Music* The division of a musical composition into measures; meter. 12 Period during which work has been or remains to be done; also, the amount of pay due one: *time* and a half for overtime. 13 Rate of movement, as in dancing, marching, etc.; tempo. 14 Fit or proper occasion: This is no *time* to quibble. —**against time** As quickly as possible so as to finish within the allotted time. —**at the same time** 1 At the same moment. 2 Despite that; nevertheless. —**at times** Now and then. —**behind the times** Out-of-date; passé. —**for the**

**time being** For the present time. —**from time to time** Now and then; occasionally. —**in good time** 1 Soon. 2 At the right time. —**in time** 1 While time permits or lasts. 2 Ultimately. —**keep time** 1 To indicate time correctly, as a clock. 2 To make regular or rhythmic movements in unison with another or others. 3 To render a musical composition in proper time or rhythm. 4 To make a record of the number of hours worked by an employee. —**on time** 1 Promptly. 2 Paid for, or to be paid for, later or in installments. —**time after time** Again and again. —*adj.* 1 Of or pertaining to time. 2 Devised so as to operate, explode, etc., at a specified time: a *time* bomb, *time* lock. 3 Payable at, or to be paid for at, a future date. —*v.t.* **timed, tim·ing** 1 To record the speed or duration of: to *time* a race. 2 To cause to correspond in time: They *timed* their steps to the music. 3 To arrange the time or occasion for: He *timed* his arrival for five o'clock. 4 To mark the rhythm or measure of. [< OE *timal*]

**time·keep·er** (tīm′kē′pər) *n.* 1 One who or that which keeps time. 2 TIMEPIECE.

**time·ta·ble** (tīm′tā′bəl) *n.* A schedule showing the times at which trains, boats, airplanes, buses, etc., arrive and depart.

**tim·id** (tim′id) *adj.* 1 Easily frightened; fearful. 2 Lacking self-confidence. [< L *timere* to fear] —**ti·mid·i·ty** (ti·mid′ə·tē), **tim′id·ness** *n.* —**tim′id·ly** *adv.* —**Syn.** 2 retiring, shrinking, shy, timorous.

**tim·or·ous** (tim′ər·əs) *adj.* Fearful and anxious; timid. [< L *timor* fear] —**tim′or·ous·ly** *adv.* —**tim′or·ous·ness** *n.*

**tin** (tin) *n.* 1 A soft, silvery white, corrosion-resistant metallic element (symbol Sn) usu. found combined with oxygen; used in making alloys. 2 Tin plate. 3 *Chiefly Brit.* A can, as of preserved food. —*v.t.* **tinned, tin·ning** 1 To coat or cover with tin, solder, or tin plate. 2 *Chiefly Brit.* To pack or preserve (food) in cans. —*adj.* Made of tin. [< OE]

**tinc·ture** (tingk′chər) *n.* 1 A medicinal solution, usu. in alcohol. 2 A tinge of color; tint. 3 A slight trace. [< *tinctura* a dyeing]

**tin·der** (tin′dər) *n.* Any dry, readily combustible substance that will ignite on contact with a spark. [< OE *tynder*] —**tin′der·y** *adj.*

**tine** (tīn) *n.* A spike or prong, as of a fork or of an antler. [< OE *tind*] —**tined** *adj.*

**tin·foil** (tin′foil′) *n.* 1 Tin or an alloy of tin made into very thin sheets. 2 A similar sheeting made of rolled aluminum, commonly used as wrapping material.

**tinge** (tinj) *v.t.* **tinged, ting·ing** or **ting·ing** 1 To imbue with a faint trace of color. 2 To impart a slight trace of a quality to. —*n.* 1 A faint trace of added color. 2 A slight trace, as of a quality. [< L *tingere* to dye] —**Syn.** *n.* 1, 2 dash, hint, soupçon, tincture, touch.

**tin·gle** (ting′gəl) *v.* **·gled, ·gling** *v.i.* 1 To experience a prickly, stringing sensation. 2 To cause such a sensation. 3 To jingle; tinkle. —*v.t.* 4 To cause to tingle. —*n.* 1 A prickly, stinging sensation. 2 A jingle or tinkling. [Appar. var. of TINKLE] —**tin′gler** *n.* —**tin′gly** *adj.*

**tink·er** (tingk′ər) *n.* 1 A mender of pots and pans, etc. 2 A clumsy workman; a botcher. 3 Work done hastily and carelessly. —*v.i.* 1 To work as a tinker. 2 To work in a clumsy, makeshift fashion. 3 To potter; fuss. —*v.t.* 4 To mend as a tinker. 5 To repair clumsily or inexpertly. [Var. of earlier *tinekere* a worker in tin]

**tin·kle** (ting′kəl) *v.* **·kled, ·kling** *v.i.* 1 To produce slight, sharp, metallic sounds, as a small bell. —*v.t.* 2 To cause to tinkle. 3 To summon or signal by a tinkling. —*n.* A sharp, clear, tinkling sound. [Imit.] —**tin′kly** (·kli·er, ·kli·est) *adj.*

**tin·sel** (tin′səl) *n.* 1 Very thin glittering bits of metal or plastic used for display and ornament. 2 Anything sparkling and showy, but with little real worth. —*adj.* 1 Made or covered with tinsel. 2 Like tinsel; superficially brilliant. —*v.t.* **·seled** or **·selled, ·sel·ing** or **·sel·ling** 1 To adorn or decorate with or as with tinsel. 2 To give a false attractiveness to. [< L *scintilla* a spark]

**tint** (tint) *n.* 1 A variety of color; tinge: red with a blue *tint.* 2 A gradation of a color made by dilution with white. 3 A pale or delicate color. 4 In engraving, uniform shading produced by parallel lines or hatching. —*v.t.* To give a tint to. [< L *tinctus* a dyeing] —**tint′er** *n.*

**ti·ny** (tī′nē) *adj.* **·ni·er, ·ni·est** Very small; minute. [< obs. *tine* a small amount, bit] —**ti′ni·ness** *n.*

**tip¹** (tip) *n.* A slanting position; a tilt. —*v.* **tipped, tip·ping** *v.t.* 1 To cause to lean; tilt. 2 To put at an angle: to *tip* one's hat. 3 To overturn or upset: often with *over.* —*v.i.* 4 To become tilted; slant. 5 To overturn; topple: with *over.* [ME *tipen* overturn] —**tip′per** *n.*

**tip²** (tip) *v.t.* **tipped, tip·ping** 1 To strike lightly;

tap. 2 In baseball, to strike (the ball) a light, glancing blow. —*n.* A tap; light blow. [Prob. < LG *tippe*]

**tip³** (tip) *n.* 1 A small gift of money for services rendered. 2 A helpful hint. 3 A piece of confidential information: a *tip* on a horse race. —*v.* **tipped, tip·ping** *v.t.* 1 To give a small gratuity to. 2 *Informal* To give secret information to, as in betting, etc. —*v.i.* 3 To give gratuities. —**tip off** *Informal* 1 To give secret information to. 2 To warn. [? < TIP²] —**tip′per** *n.*

**tip⁴** (tip) *n.* 1 The point or extremity of anything tapering; the *tip* of the tongue. 2 A piece made to form the end of something, as a nozzle, ferrule, etc. 3 The uppermost part; top: the *tip* of a flagpole. —*v.t.* **tipped, tip·ping** 1 To furnish with a tip. 2 To form the tip of. 3 To cover or adorn the tip of. [Prob. < MDu., a point]

**tip·ple** (tip′əl) *v.t. & v.i.* **·pled, ·pling** To drink (alcoholic beverages) frequently and habitually. —*n.* Liquor consumed in tippling. [< earlier *tipler* bartender]

**tip·sy** (tip′sē) *adj.* **·si·er, ·si·est** 1 Mildly intoxicated. 2 Shaky; unsteady. [< TIP¹] —**tip′si·ly** *adv.* —**tip′si·ness** *n.*

**tip·toe** (tip′tō′, -tō′) *n.* The tip of a toe, or the tips of all the toes. —**on tiptoe** 1 On one's tiptoes. 2 Expectantly; eagerly. 3 Stealthily; quietly. —*v.i.* **toed, toe·ing** To walk on tiptoe; go stealthily or quietly. —*adv.* On tiptoe.

**ti·rade** (tī′rād, tī·rād′) *n.* A prolonged declamatory outpouring, as of censure. [< Ital. *tirata* a volley]

**tire¹** (tīr) *v.* **tired, tir·ing** *v.t.* 1 To reduce the strength of, as by exertion. 2 To reduce the interest or patience of, as with monotony. —*v.i.* 3 To become weary or exhausted. 4 To lose patience, interest, etc. —**tire of** To become bored or impatient with. —**tire out** To weary completely. [< OE *tīorian*] —**Syn.** 1 exhaust, fag, fatigue, wear out, weary.

**tire²** (tīr) *n.* 1 A band or hoop surrounding the rim of a wheel. 2 A tough, flexible tube, usu. of inflated rubber, set around the rims of the wheels of automobiles, bicycles, etc. —*v.t.* **tired, tir·ing** To put a tire on. *Brit. sp.* **tyre.** [Prob. < obs. *tire* to attire]

**tire·some** (tīr′səm) *adj.* Tending to tire, or causing one to tire; tedious. —**tire′some·ly** *adv.* —**tire′some·ness** *n.*

**tis·sue** (tish′ōō) *n.* 1 Any light or gauzy textile fabric. 2 *Biol.* An aggregate of cells and intercellular material having a particular function: nerve *tissue.* 3 A network; chain: a *tissue* of lies. 4 TISSUE PAPER. 5 A disposable square of soft absorbent paper for use as a handkerchief, etc. [< OF *tistre* to weave]

**tithe** (tīth) *n.* 1 One tenth. 2 *Usu. pl.* A tax of one tenth part of yearly income arising from lands and from the personal industry of the inhabitants, for the support of the clergy and the church. 3 A small part. 4 Loosely, any tax or levy. —*v.t.* **tithed, tith·ing** 1 To give or pay a tithe, or tenth part of. 2 To tax with tithes. [< OE *tēotha, tēogotha* a tenth] —**tith′er** *n.*

**ti·tle** (tīt′l) *n.* 1 The name of a book, play, motion picture, song, etc. 2 A title page, as of a book. 3 A descriptive name; epithet. 4 a An appellation showing rank, office, profession, station in life, etc. b In some countries, a designation of nobility or one conferred for unusual distinction. 5 In some sports, championship: to win the *title.* 6 *Law* a The legal right to own property. b Legal evidence of such a right. c A document setting forth such evidence. —*v.t.* **·tled, ·tling** To give a name to; entitle. [< L *titulus* a label, inscription]

**tit·ter** (tit′ər) *v.i.* To laugh in a suppressed way. —*n.* The act of tittering. [Imit.] —**tit′ter·er** *n.* —**tit′ter·ing·ly** *adv.* —**Syn.** *v.* chuckle, giggle, snicker, snigger, snort.

**toad** (tōd) *n.* 1 Any of various tailless, jumping, insectivorous amphibians resembling the frog but usu. having a warty skin and resorting to water only to breed. 2 A contemptible or loathsome person. [< OE *tādige*]

**toad·y** (tō′dē) *n. pl.* **toad·ies** An obsequious flatterer; a sycophant. —*v.t. & v.i.* **toad·ied, toad·y·ing** To act the toady (to). [< earlier *toad-eater,* a charlatan's attendant who pretended to eat toads] —**toad′y·ism** *n.*

**toast¹** (tōst) *v.t.* 1 To brown the outside of (a piece of bread, etc.) by heating in an oven, toaster, etc. 2 To warm thoroughly. —*v.i.* 3 To become warm or toasted. —*n.* Toasted bread. [< L *tostus* parch, roast]

**toast²** (tōst) *n.* 1 The act of drinking to someone's health or to some thing. 2 The person or thing thus named. —*v.t. & v.i.* To drink a toast or toasts (to). [< TOAST¹, from a custom of flavoring a drink with a spiced piece of toast] —**toast′er** *n.*

**toast·mas·ter** (tōst′mas′tər, -mäs′tər) *n.* A person who, at public dinners, announces the toasts, calls upon the speakers, etc.

**to·bac·co** (tə·bak′ō) *n. pl.* **·cos** or **·coes** 1 Any of various plants of the nightshade family, with large sticky leaves and yellow, white, or purple flowers. 2 The leaves of several of these plants, processed for smoking, chewing, etc. 3 The various products prepared from tobacco leaves, as cigarettes, cigars, etc. [< Sp. *tabaco*]

**to·bog·gan** (tə·bog′ən) *n.* A long sledlike vehicle without runners, consisting of thin boards curved upward in front. —*v.i.* 1 To coast on a toboggan. 2 To descend swiftly: Wheat prices *tobogganed*. [< Algon.] —**to·bog′gan·er, to·bog′gan·ist** *n.*

**toc·sin** (tok′sin) *n.* 1 A signal sounded on a bell; alarm. 2 An alarm bell. [< Prov. *tocar* to strike, touch + *senh* a bell]

**to·day** (tə·dā′) *adv.* 1 On or during this present day. 2 At the present time. —*n.* The present day or age. Also **to·day′**. [< OE *tō* to + *daeg* day]

**tod·dle** (tod′l) *v.i.* **·dled, ·dling** To walk unsteadily with short steps, as a little child. —*n.* The act of toddling. —**tod′dler** *n.*

**toe** (tō) *n.* 1 One of the five digits of the foot. 2 The forward part of the foot. 3 That portion of a shoe, boot, sock, etc., that covers or corresponds to the toes. 4 Anything resembling a toe in contour, function, position, etc. —**on one's toes** Alert. —**tread on (someone's) toes** To trespass on (someone's) feelings, prejudices, etc. —*v.* **toed, toe·ing** *v.t.* 1 To touch or kick with the toes. 2 To furnish with a toe. 3 To drive (a nail or spike) obliquely. 4 To attach by nails driven thus. —*v.i.* 5 To stand or walk with the toes pointing in a specified direction: to *toe* out. —**toe the mark (or line)** 1 To touch a certain line with the toes preparatory to starting a race. 2 To conform to a discipline or a standard. [< OE *tā*]

**to·geth·er** (tŏŏ·geth′ər, tə-) *adv.* 1 In company: We were sitting *together*. 2 In or into one group, mass, unit, etc.: They put the jigsaw puzzle *together*. 3 Into contact with each other: Glue these two pieces *together*. 4 Simultaneously: Let's sing it *together*. 5 With one another; mutually: They discussed it *together*. 6 In agreement or harmony: The tie and shirt go well *together*. 7 Considered collectively: He has more courage than all of us *together*. 8 Without cessation: He talked for hours *together*. —**get it all together** *Slang* To achieve a positive outlook on life; free oneself from anxiety. —**together with** Along with. [< OE *tōgædere*]

**toil** (toil) *n.* 1 Fatiguing work; labor. 2 Any work accomplished by great labor. —*v.i.* 1 To work strenuously and tiringly. 2 To make one's way laboriously: to *toil* up a hill. —*v.t.* 3 To accomplish with great effort: to *toil* one's way. [< L *tudiculare* stir about] —**toil′er** *n.* —**Syn.** *v.* 1 drudge, labor, slave, travail.

**toi·let** (toi′lit) *n.* 1 A fixture in the shape of a bowl, used for urination and defecation and equipped with a device for flushing and discharging with water. 2 A room containing such a fixture or fixtures. 3 PRIVY. 4 The act or process of bathing, grooming, and dressing oneself. 5 Formerly, a woman's attire or costume: also **toi·lette** (twa·let′). —*adj.* Used in dressing or grooming: *toilet* articles. [< F *toilette* orig. a cloth dressing gown, dim. of *toile* cloth]

**to·ken** (tō′kən) *n.* 1 A visible sign; indication: This gift is a *token* of my affection. 2 Some tangible proof or evidence of one's identity, authority, etc. 3 A keepsake; souvenir. 4 A characteristic mark or feature. 5 A piece of metal issued as currency and having a face value greater than its actual value: a bus *token*. —**by the same token** Moreover; furthermore. —**in token of** As a sign or evidence of. —*adj.* 1 Having only the appearance of; nominal; minimal: *token* resistance; *token* integration. 2 Partial or very small: a *token* payment. [< OE *tācen*]

**tol·er·a·ble** (tol′ər·ə·bəl) *adj.* 1 Endurable; bearable. 2 Fairly good: *tolerable* health. [< L *tolerare* endure] —**tol′er·a·ble·ness** *n.* —**tol′er·a·bly** *adv.*

**tol·er·ance** (tol′ər·əns) *n.* 1 The character, state, or quality of being tolerant. 2 Freedom from prejudice; openmindedness. 3 The act of enduring, or the capacity for endurance. 4 An allowance for variations from specified measure, as of machine parts. 5 *Med.* Ability to withstand large or increasing amounts of a specified substance or stimulus.

**tol·er·ant** (tol′ər·ənt) *adj.* 1 Of a long-suffering disposition. 2 Indulgent; liberal. 3 *Med.* Resistant to the effects of a specific substance or stimulus. [< L *tolerare* endure] —**tol′er·ant·ly** *adv.*

**tol·er·ate** (tol′ə·rāt) *v.t.* **·at·ed, ·at·ing** 1 To allow without opposition. 2 To concede, as the right to opinions or participation. 3 To bear or be capable of bearing. 4 *Med.* To be tolerant. [< L *tolerare* endure] —**tol′er·a′tive** *adj.* —**tol′er·a′tion, tol′er·a′tor** *n.* —**Syn.** 1 permit. 3 endure, sustain.

**toll** (tōl) *v.t.* 1 To sound (a church bell) slowly and at regular intervals. 2 To announce (a death, funeral, etc.) by tolling a church bell. 3 To call or summon by tolling. —*v.i.* 4 To sound slowly and at regular intervals. —*n.* 1 The act of tolling. 2 The sound of a bell rung slowly and regularly. [ME *tollen*] — **toll′er** *n.*

**toll·gate** (tōl′gāt′) *n.* A gate at the entrance to a bridge, or on a road, at which toll is paid.

**tom·a·hawk** (tom′ə·hôk) *n.* An ax used as a tool and as a war weapon by the Algonquian Indians. —*v.t.* To strike or kill with a tomahawk. [< Algon.]

**to·ma·to** (tə·mā′tō, -mä′-) *n. pl.* **·toes** 1 The pulpy edible berry, yellow or red when ripe, of a tropical American plant related to the potato, used as a vegetable. 2 The plant itself. 3 *Slang* An attractive girl or woman. [< Nah. *tomatl*]

**tomb** (tōōm) *n.* 1 A burial place; grave. 2 A tombstone or monument. —**the tomb** Death. —*v.t.* To entomb; bury. [< Gk. *tymbos* a mound]

**tom·boy** (tom′boi′) *n.* A young girl who behaves like a lively, active boy. [< TOM + BOY] —**tom′boy′ish** *adj.* —**tom′boy′ish·ness** *n.*

**tomb·stone** (tōōm′stōn′) *n.* A stone, usu. inscribed, marking a place of burial.

**to·mor·row** (tə·môr′ō, -mor′ō) *adv.* On or for the next day after today. —*n.* The next day after today. **Also to·mor′row.** [< OE *tō* to + *morgen* morning, morrow]

**tone** (tōn) *n.* 1 A vocal or musical sound; also, the quality of such a sound. 2 *Music* **a** A sound having a definite pitch, loudness, and timbre. **b** WHOLE STEP. 3 A predominating disposition; mood. 4 Characteristic tendency; quality: a want of moral *tone*. 5 Style or elegance: The party had *tone*. 6 Vocal inflection: a *tone* of pity. 7 The acoustical pitch, or change in pitch, of a phrase or sentence: A question is indicated by a rising *tone*. 8 The effect of light, shade, and color as combined in a picture. 9 A shade of a particular color: a deep *tone* of yellow. 10 Tonicity. —*v.* **toned, ton·ing** *v.t.* 1 To give tone to; modify in tone. 2 INTONE. —*v.i.* 3 To assume a certain tone or hue. 4 To blend or harmonize, as in tone or shade. —**tone down** 1 To subdue the tone of. 2 To moderate in quality or tone. —**tone up** 1 To raise in quality or strength. 2 To elevate in pitch. 3 To gain in vitality. [< Gk. *tonos* a pitch of voice, a stretching] —**ton′er** *n.*

**tongs** (tôngz, tongz) *n. pl.* (sometimes construed as sing.) An implement for grasping, holding, or lifting objects, consisting usu. of a pair of pivoted levers. **Also pair of tongs.** [< OE *tange*]

**tongue** (tung) *n.* 1 A muscular organ attached to the floor of the mouth of most vertebrates, important in masticating and tasting food, and in man as an organ of speech. • SEE MOUTH. 2 A similar organ in various insects, etc. 3 An animal's tongue, as of beef, prepared as food. 4 The power of speech: Have you lost your *tongue*? 5 Manner or style of speaking: a smooth *tongue*. 6 Utterance; talk. 7 A language or dialect. 8 Anything resembling a tongue in appearance, shape, or function. 9 A slender projection of land. 10 A long narrow bay or inlet. 11 A jet of flame. 12 A strip of leather for closing the gap in front of a laced shoe. • SEE SHOE. 13 The free or vibrating end of a reed in a wind instrument. 14 The clapper of a bell. 15 The harnessing pole of a horse-drawn vehicle. 16 The projecting edge of a tongue-and-groove joint. —**hold one's tongue** To keep silent. —**on the tip of one's tongue** On the verge of being remembered or uttered. —**with tongue in cheek** Facetiously, insincerely, or ironically. —*v.* **tongued, tongu·ing** *v.t.* 1 To use the tongue to attack or separate (notes) in playing a wind instrument. 2 To touch or lap with the tongue. 3 In carpentry: **a** To cut a tongue on (a board). **b** To join by a tongue-and-groove joint. —*v.i.* 4 To use the tongue to attack or separate notes in playing a wind instrument. 5 To extend as a tongue. [< OE *tunge*]

**ton·ic** (ton′ik) *adj.* 1 Having power to invigorate or build up; bracing. 2 Pertaining to tone or tones; in music, of the principal tone of a scale or tonal system. 3 *Physiol.* Of or pertaining to tension, esp. muscular tension. 4 *Pathol.* Rigid; unrelaxing: *tonic* spasm. 5 Of or pertaining to musical intonations or modulations of words, sentences, etc. 6 *Phonet.* Accented or stressed. —*n.* 1 *Med.* A medicine that promotes physical well-being. 2 Whatever imparts vigor or tone. 3 The basic tone of a key or tonal system. [< Gk. *tonos* sound, tone]

**to·night** (tə·nīt′) *adv.* In or during the present or coming night. —*n.* The night that follows this day; also, the present night. **Also to-night′.** [< OE *tō* to + *niht* night]

**ton·nage** (tun′ij) *n.* 1 Weight, as expressed in tons. 2 Capacity, as of a vessel or vessels, expressed in tons. 3 A tax levied at a given rate per ton. [< OF *tonne* a ton, tun]

**ton·sil** (ton′səl) *n.* Either of two oval lymphoid organs situated on either side of the passage from the mouth to the pharynx. [< L *tonsillae* tonsils] —**ton′sil·lar, ton′sil·ar** *adj.* • SEE MOUTH.

**ton·sil·lec·to·my** (ton′sə·lek′tə·mē) *n. pl.* **·mies** Removal of the tonsils by surgery.

**ton·sil·li·tis** (ton′sə·lī′tis) *n.* Inflammation of the tonsils. —**ton′sil·lit′ic** (-lit′ik) *adj.*

**ton·sure** (ton′shər) *n.* 1 The shaving of the head, or of the crown of the head, as of a priest or monk. 2 That part of a priest's or monk's head left bare by shaving. —*v.t.* **·sured, ·sur·ing** To shave the head of. [< L *tonsura* a shearing]

**tool** (tōōl) *n.* 1 A simple implement, as a hammer, saw, spade, chisel, etc., used in work. 2 A power-driven apparatus used for cutting, shaping, boring, etc. 3 The active part of such an apparatus. 4 *Often pl.* Something necessary to the performance of a profession, vocation, etc.: Paints and brushes are an artist's *tools*. 5 A person used to carry out the designs of another or others, esp. when such designs are unethical or unlawful. —*v.t.* 1 To shape or work with a tool. 2 To provide, as a factory, with machinery and tools. 3 In bookbinding, to ornament or impress designs upon with a tool. —*v.i.* 4 To work with a tool. 5 *Informal* To drive or travel in a vehicle: usu. with *along*. 6 To install, as in a factory, equipment, tools, etc; usu. with *up*. [< OE *tōl*] —**tool′er** *n.* —Syn. *n.* 1 appliance, device, instrument, utensil. 5 dupe, stooge.

**toot** (tōōt) *v.i.* 1 To blow a horn, whistle, etc., with short blasts. 2 To give forth a short blast. —*v.t.* 3 To sound (a horn, etc.) with short blasts. 4 To sound (a blast, etc.). —*n.* 1 A short blast on a horn, whistle, etc. 2 *Slang* A drinking spree. [? < MLG *tūten*] —**toot′er** *n.*

**tooth·ache** (tōōth′āk′) *n.* Pain in a tooth or in the nearby area.

**top** (top) *n.* 1 The uppermost or highest part: the *top* of a hill. 2 The higher or upper surface: the *top* of a bureau. 3 A lid or cover: a bottle *top*. 4 The roof of a vehicle, as an automobile. 5 The crown of the head. 6 *pl.* The aboveground part of a root vegetable. 7 The highest degree of reach: at the *top* of one's voice. 8 The most prominent place or rank: at the *top* of one's profession. 9 One who is highest in rank: the *top* of one's class. 10

The choicest or best part: the *top* of the crop. 11 The upper part of a shoe or boot. —**blow one's top** *Slang* To break out in a rage. —**from top to toe.** 1 From head to foot. 2 Completely. —**on top** 1 Successful. 2 With success; victoriously. —**over the top** Over the upper edge of a trench so as to attack. —*adj.* 1 Of or pertaining to the top. 2 Forming or comprising the top. 3 Most important; chief: *top* authors. 4 Greatest in amount or degree: *top* prices; *top* speed. —*v.* **topped, top·ping** *v.t.* 1 To remove the top of; prune: to *top* a tree. 2 To provide with a top, cap, etc. 3 To form the top of. 4 To reach the top of; surmount: to *top* a wave. 5 To surpass or exceed: Can you *top* this? 6 In golf, tennis, etc., to hit the upper part of (the ball) in making a stroke. —*v.i.* 7 To top someone or something. —**top off** To complete, esp. with a finishing touch. [< OE]

**to·paz** (tō′paz) *n.* 1 A yellow or brownish yellow crystalline mineral, valued as a gemstone. 2 A yellow sapphire. 3 A yellow variety of quartz resembling topaz. [< Gk. *topazos*]

**top·flight** (top′flit′) *adj. Informal* Of the highest quality; outstanding; superior.

**top·ic** (top′ik) *n.* 1 A subject treated of in speech or writing. 2 A theme for discussion. 3 A subdivision of an outline or a treatise. [< L *Topica*, title of a work by Aristotle] —Syn. 1 issue, matter, point, question.

**top·i·cal** (top′i·kəl) *adj.* 1 Of or belonging to a place or spot; local. 2 Of or relating to matters of present or local interest; limited in relevance to a time or place. 3 Of or pertaining to a topic. 4 *Med.* Pertaining to a restricted area of the body. —**top′i·cal·ly** *adv.*

**top·most** (top′mōst′) *adj.* Being at the very top.

**to·pog·ra·phy** (tə·pog′rə·fē) *n. pl.* **·phies** 1 The art of representing on a map or chart the physical features of a place, as mountains, lakes, canals, usu. with indications of elevation. 2 The physical features of a region. 3 Topographic surveying. [< Gk. *topos* place + -GRAPHY] —**to·pog′ra·pher** *n.* —**top·o·graph·ic** (top′ə·graf′ik) or **·i·cal** *adj.* —**top′o·graph′i·cal·ly** *adv.*

**top·ple** (top′əl) *v.* **·pled, ·pling** *v.i.* 1 To fall, top foremost, by or as if by its own weight. 2 To seem to be about to fall; totter. —*v.t.* 3 To cause to totter or fall. 4 To cause to collapse; overthrow: to *topple* a government. [Freq. of TOP, *v.*]

**torch** (tôrch) *n.* 1 A stick of wood or some material dipped in tallow or oil and set ablaze at the end to provide a light that can be carried about. 2 Anything that illuminates or brightens. 3 A portable device giving off an intensely hot flame and used for burning off paint, melting solder, etc. 4 *Brit.* A flashlight. [< OF *torche*]

**tor·ment** (tôr′ment, -mənt) *n.* 1 Intense bodily pain or mental anguish. 2 A source of pain or anguish, or a persistent annoyance. 3 The inflicting of torture. —*v.t.* (tôr·ment′) 1 To subject to intense or persistent physical or mental pain; make miserable. 2 To harass or vex. 3 To disturb; agitate; stir up. [< L *tormentum* a rack] —**tor·men′tor, tor·men′ter** *n.* —**Syn.** *n.* 1 agony, torture, suffering, misery.

**tor·na·do** (tôr·nā′dō) *n. pl.* **·does** or **·dos** 1 A whirling wind of exceptional force and violence, accompanied by a funnel-shaped cloud marking the narrow path of greatest destruction. 2 Any hurricane or violent windstorm. [Alter. of Sp. *tronada* a thunderstorm < *tronar* to thunder] —**tor·nad′ic** (-nad′ik) *adj.*

**tor·pe·do** (tôr·pē′dō) *n. pl.* **·does** 1 A self-propelled, tubeshaped underwater missile with an explosive warhead. 2 Any of various devices containing an explosive, as a submarine mine. —*v.t.* **·doed, ·do·ing** 1 To damage or sink (a vessel) with a torpedo. 2 *Informal* To destroy utterly; demolish: Publicity could *torpedo* the agreement. 3 ELECTRIC RAY. [L, stiffness, numbness < *torpere* be numb]

**tor·pid** (tôr′pid) *adj.* 1 Having lost sensibility or power of motion, partially or wholly, as a hibernating animal; dormant; numb. 2 Slow to act or respond; sluggish. 3 Apathetic; spiritless; dull. [< L *torpidus* < *torpere* be numb] —**tor·pid′i·ty** (tôr·pid′ə·tē), **tor′pid·ness** *n.* —**tor′pid·ly** *adv.*

**tor·por** (tôr′pər) *n.* 1 Complete or partial loss of sensibility or power of motion; stupor. 2 Apathy; listlessness; dullness. [< L *torpere* be numb] —**tor·po·rif·ic** (tôr′pə·rif′ik) *adj.*

**tor·rent** (tôr′ənt, tor′-) *n.* 1 A stream of liquid, esp. water, flowing rapidly and turbulently. 2 Any violent or tumultuous flow; a gush: a *torrent* of abuse. [< L *torrens*, lit., boiling, burning, pr.p. of *torrere* parch]

**tor·rid** (tôr′id, tor′-) *adj.* 1 Parched or hot from exposure to heat, esp. of the sun. 2 Intensely hot and dry; scorching. 3 Passionate. [< L *torridus* < *torrere* parch] —**tor·rid·i·ty** (tô·rid′ə·tē, to-), **tor′rid·ness** *n.* —**tor′rid·ly** *adv.*

**tor·sion** (tôr′shən) *n.* 1 The act of twisting, or the state of being twisted. 2 *Mech.* Deformation or stress caused by twisting. [< L *tortus*, p.p. of *torquere* twist] —**tor′sion·al** *adj.* —**tor′sion·al·ly** *adv.*

**tor·so** (tôr′sō) *n. pl.* **·sos** or **·si** (-sē) 1 The trunk of a human body. 2 The part of a sculptured human figure corresponding to the trunk, esp. when the head and limbs are missing. [Ital., a stalk, trunk of a body]

**tor·toise** (tôr′təs) *n.* A turtle, esp. one living on land. [< Med. L. *tortuca*]

**tor·tu·ous** (tôr′chōō·əs) *adj.* 1 Abounding in bends, twists, or turns; winding. 2 Not straightforward; devious: *tortuous* logic. [< L *tortus* twisted. See TORSION.] —**tor′tu·ous·ly** *adv.* —**tor′tu·ous·ness** *n.*

**toss** (tôs, tos) *v.t.* 1 To throw, pitch, or fling about: *tossed* in a small boat on the open sea. 2 To throw or cast upward or toward another: to *toss* a ball. 3 To throw, esp. casually or indifferently: to *toss* clothes on a chair. 4 To remove from abruptly or violently: with *out*: He was *tossed* out of a job. 5 To throw (a coin) in the air to decide a question by comparing the side facing up, upon landing, with a previous call. 6 To lift with a quick motion, as the head. 7 To insert or interject casually or carelessly: to *toss* in impressive but irrelevant statistics. 8 To utter, write, or do easily or in an offhand manner: with *off*. 9 To bandy about, as something discussed. 10 To turn over and mix the contents of: to *toss* a salad. 11 To make restless; agitate. 12 To drink at one draft: often with *off*. —*v.i.* 13 To be moved or thrown about, as a ship in a storm. 14 To roll about restlessly or from side to side, as in sleep. 15 To go quickly or angrily, as with a toss of the head. 16 To toss a coin. —*n.* 1 The act of tossing, as a throw or pitch. 2 A quick movement, as of the head. 3 The state of being tossed. 4 TOSS-UP (def. 1). [Prob. < Scand.] —**toss′er** *n.* —**Syn.** *v.* 2 flip, flick, hurl. 12 quaff, swallow, gulp.

**tot** (tot) *v.* **tot·ted, tot·ting** *Informal v.t.* 1 To add; total: with *up*. —*v.i.* 2 To add. [Short for TOTAL]

**to·tal·i·tar·i·an** (tō·tal′ə·târ′ē·ən) *adj.* 1 Designating or characteristic of a government controlled exclusively by one party or faction that suppresses political dissent by force or intimidation and whose power to control the economic, social, and intellectual life of the individual is virtually unlimited. 2 Tyrannical; despotic. —n. An adherent of totalitarian government. —to·tal′i·tar′i·an·ism n.

tot·ter (tot′ər) v.i. 1 To shake or waver, as if about to fall; be unsteady. 2 To walk unsteadily. —n. An unsteady or wobbly manner of walking. [Prob. < Scand.] —tot′ter·er n. —tot′ter·ing·ly adv. —tot′ter·y adj.

touch (tuch) v.t. 1 To place the hand, finger, or other body part in contact with; perceive by feeling. 2 To be or come in contact with. 3 To bring into contact with something else. 4 To hit or strike lightly; tap. 5 To lay the hand or hands on: Please don't *touch* the paintings. 6 To border on; adjoin. 7 To come to; reach: The temperature *touched* 90°. 8 To rival or equal: As a salesman, nobody could *touch* him. 9 To color slightly: The sun *touched* the clouds with gold. 10 To affect the emotions of, esp. so as to feel compassion or gratitude; move: She was *touched* by their concern for her health. 11 To hurt the feelings of. 12 To relate to; concern; affect: The war *touches* us all. 13 To have to do with, use, or partake of: He never *touches* anything stronger than ginger ale. 14 To affect injuriously; taint: vegetables *touched* by frost. 15 *Slang* To borrow money from. —v.i. 16 To touch someone or something. 17 To come into or be in contact. —touch at To stop briefly at (a port or place) in the course of a journey or voyage. —touch down To land after flights. —touch off 1 To cause to explode; detonate; fire. 2 To provoke or initiate, esp. a violent reaction. —touch on (or upon) 1 To relate to; concern: That *touches on* another question. 2 To treat or discuss briefly or in passing. —touch up To add finishing touches or corrections to, as a work of art or writing. —n. 1 The act or fact of touching; a coming into contact, as a tap. 2 The sense stimulated by touching; the tactile sense by which a surface or its characteristics, as of pressure or texture, may be perceived. 3 A sensation conveyed by touching: a silky *touch*. 4 Communication or contact: Let's keep in *touch*. 5 A distinctive manner or style, as of an artist, author, or craftsman: a master's *touch*. 6 Delicate sensitivity, appreciation, or understanding: a fine *touch* for collecting rare china. 7 Any slight or delicate detail that helps to finish or perfect something, as a work of art or writing: to apply the finishing *touches*. 8 A trace; hint: a *touch* of irony. 9 A slight attack; twinge: a *touch* of rheumatism. 10 A small quantity; dash: a *touch* of perfume. 11 The resistance to motion offered by the keys of a piano, typewriter, etc. 12 The manner in which something is struck or touched, as the keys of a piano. 13 *Slang* Borrowed money, or a request to borrow money. 14 *Slang* A person from whom money may be borrowed, esp. easily: a soft *touch*. [< OF *tochier*] —touch′a·ble adj. —touch′er n.

tough (tuf) adj. 1 Capable of bearing tension or strain without breaking, esp. because strong in texture or composition. 2 Difficult to cut or chew. 3 Strong in body or mind, esp. in resisting or enduring stress. 4 Requiring determined or intense effort; difficult: a *tough* assignment. 5 Resolute; unyielding; inflexible: a *tough* stand in the negotiations. 6 Severe; harsh: a *tough* punishment. 7 Given to or characterized by violence or rowdyism: a *tough* neighborhood. 8 *Informal* Unfortunate; regrettable. 9 *Slang* Great; fine. —n. A ruffian; rowdy. —v.t. *Informal* To manage to get through; endure: often with *out*: to *tough out* a recession. [< OE *tōh*] —tough′ly adv. —tough′ness n. —Syn. 5 uncompromising, stubborn, militant.

tour (toŏr) n. 1 An excursion or journey, as for sightseeing. 2 A trip, usu. over a planned course, as to conduct business, present theatrical performances, etc. 3 A set period of time, as of service in a particular place; turn or shift. 4 A brief survey; circuit: a *tour* of the grounds. —v.t. 1 To make a tour of; travel. 2 To present on a tour: to *tour* a play. —v.i. 3 To go on a tour. [< OF *tor* a turn < L L *tornus* a lathe]

tour·ist (toŏr′ist) n. One who makes a tour or a pleasure trip. —adj. Of or suitable for tourists. —tour′ist·y adj.

tour·na·ment (tûr′nə·mənt, toŏr′-) n. 1 A series of competitive sports events or games for prizes or cash awards and often for a championship: a golf or bridge *tournament*. 2 In medieval times, a pageant in which two opposing parties of men in armor contended on horseback with blunted weapons, esp. lances. [< OF < *torneier* to tourney]

tour·ney (tûr′nē, toŏr′-) v.i. To take part in a tournament. —n. TOURNAMENT. [< OF *torneier*]

**tou·sle** (tou′zəl) *v.t.* **·sled**, **·sling** To disarrange or dishevel; rumple. —*n.* A tousled mass, esp. of hair. [Freq. of ME *tousen*]

**tout** (tout) *Informal* *v.i.* **1** To solicit patronage, customers, votes, etc. **2** To sell information, as to a bettor, about horses entered in a race. —*v.t.* **3** To solicit; importune. **4** To praise highly or proclaim: *touted* as the world's fastest human. **5** To sell information concerning (a race horse). —*n.* **1** One who touts. **2** One who solicits business. [<OE *tōtian*, *tȳtan* peep, look out]

**tow**¹ (tō) *n.* A short, coarse hemp or flax fiber prepared for spinning. [Prob. < OE *tōw-spinning*]

**tow**² (tō) *v.t.* To pull or drag, as by a rope or chain. —*n.* **1** The act of towing, or the state of being towed. **2** That which is towed, as a barge. **3** TOWLINE. —**in tow** **1** In the condition of being towed. **2** Drawn along as if being towed: a film star with her fans *in tow*. **3** Under one's protection or care: took the orphan *in tow*. [< OE *togian*]

**tow·el** (toul, tou′əl) *n.* A cloth or paper for drying anything by wiping. —*v.t.* **·eled** or **·elled**, **·el·ing** or **·el·ling** To wipe or dry with a towel. [< OF *toaille*]

**tow·er** (tou′ər) *n.* **1** A structure very tall in proportion to its other dimensions, and either standing alone or forming part of a building. **2** A place of security or defense; citadel. **3** Someone or something likened to a tower in strength or command. —*v.i.* To rise or stand like a tower; extend to a great height. [< L *turris*]

**tow·line** (tō′līn′) *n.* A line, rope, or chain used in towing.

**town** (toun) *n.* **1** Any collection of dwellings and other buildings larger than a village and smaller than a city. **2** A closely settled urban district, as contrasted with less populated or suburban areas or with the open country. **3** A city of any size. **4** The inhabitants or voters of a town. **5** TOWNSHIP. **6** Those residents of a town who are not associated educationally or administratively with a college or university situated in the town: *town* and gown. —**go to town** *Slang* To work or proceed with dispatch; get busy. —**on the town** *Slang* On a round of bars, nightclubs, etc., in the city in search of diversion or excitement. —**paint the town red** *Slang* To go on a spree; carouse. —*adj.* Of, situated in, or for a town. [< OE *tūn*, *tuun* an enclosure, group of houses]

**town·ship** (toun′ship) *n.* **1** In the U.S. and Canada, a territorial subdivision of a county with certain corporate powers of municipal government for local purposes. **2** In New England, a local political unit governed by a town meeting.

**tox·ic** (tok′sik) *adj.* **1** Poisonous. **2** Due to or caused by poison or a toxin. [< Gk. *toxicon (pharmakon)* (a poison) for arrows < *toxon* a bow] —**tox′i·cal·ly** *adv.* —**tox·ic′i·ty** (-sis′ə-tē) *n.*

**tox·in** (tok′sin) *n.* **1** Any of various poisonous compounds produced by living organisms and acting as causative agents in many diseases. **2** Any toxic matter generated in living or dead organisms. [< TOX(IC) + -IN]

**toy** (toi) *n.* **1** Something designed or serving as a plaything for children. **2** Something trifling or unimportant. **3** An ornament; trinket. **4** A small animal, esp. one of a breed characterized by small size. —*v.i.* **1** To act or consider something without seriousness or conviction; trifle: to *toy* with an idea. **2** To use someone or something for one's amusement. **3** To act flirtatiously. —*adj.* **1** Designed as a toy. **2** Resembling a toy; esp., of miniature size: a *toy* dog. [Prob. < ME *toye* flirtation, sport] —**toy′er** *n.*

**trace** (trās) *n.* **1** A vestige or mark left by some past event or by a person or thing no longer present. **2** An imprint or mark indicating the passage of a person or thing, as a footprint, etc. **3** A path or trail beaten down by men or animals. **4** A barely detectable quantity, quality, or characteristic. **5** A lightly drawn line; something traced. —*v.* **traced**, **trac·ing** *v.t.* **1** To follow the tracks or trail of. **2** To follow the course or development of, esp. by investigation of a series of events. **3** To find out or determine by investigation. **4** To follow (tracks, a course of development, etc.). **5** To draw; sketch. **6** To copy (a drawing, etc.) on a superimposed transparent sheet. **7** To form (letters, etc.) painstakingly. —*v.i.* **8** To have its origin; go back in time. **9** To follow a track, course of development, etc. [< OF *tracier* to trace] —**trace′a·bil′i·ty**, **trace′a·ble·ness** *n.* —**trace′a·ble** *adj.* —**trace′a·bly** *adv.* —*Syn.* **1** remnant, sign, aftermath, token, clue.

**trac·er·y** (trā′sər·ē) *n. pl.* **·er·ies** **1** Ornamental stonework formed of branching lines, as in a Gothic window. **2** Any delicate ornamentation resembling this.

**track** (trak) *n.* **1** A mark or trail left by the passage of anything, as a series of footprints. **2** A path or way marked or worn out by the repeated passage of people, animals, or vehicles. 3 Any course or path, esp. one describing movement: the *track* of a missile or a comet. 4 A pair of parallel rails, usu. including the ties, that guide the wheels of a train, trolley, etc. 5 A usu. elliptical course for racing. 6 A sport in which footraces of various distances are held on a track. 7 TRACK AND FIELD. 8 A sequence of events; a succession of ideas. 9 Awareness of the progress or sequence; count; record: to lose *track* of an old friend; to keep *track* of expenses. 10 An endless metal belt, usu. one of a pair, by means of which certain vehicles are capable of moving over soft, slippery, or uneven surfaces. 11 The distance between the front or rear wheels of a vehicle, usu. measured from the center of the treads. 12 SOUND TRACK. 13 In education, any of two or more classes covering the same course of study, in which students are placed according to their preparation and ability. —**in one's tracks** Right where one is; on the spot. —**make tracks** *Informal* To run away in haste; hurry. —**on** (or **off**) **the track** Keeping in view (or losing sight of) the subject or objective. —*v.t.* 1 To follow the tracks of; trail. 2 To discover or apprehend by following up marks, clues, or other evidence: with *down:* to *track* down a suspect; to *track* down a shipment of contaminated canned food. 3 To observe or plot the course of (an aircraft, spacecraft, etc.). 4 To make tracks upon or with: to *track* mud into a house. 5 To go through or traverse, as on foot: to *track* the wilderness. 6 To furnish with rails or tracks. —*v.i.* 7 To measure a certain distance between front or rear wheels. 8 To run in the same track or groove; be in alignment. 9 To leave tracks. —*adj.* Pertaining to or performed on a track, esp. a track for racing: *track* events. [< OF *trac*] —**track′er** *n.* —**track′less** *adj.*

**tract** (trakt) *n.* A short treatise or pamphlet, as on religion or morals. [< L *tractatus* a handling]

**tract·a·ble** (trak′tə·bəl) *adj.* 1 Easily led or controlled; docile. 2 Readily worked or handled; malleable. [< L *tractare* handle, freq. of *trahere* draw] —**tract′a·bly** *adv.* —**tract′a·ble·ness, tract′a·bil′i·ty** *n.* —**Syn.** 1 manageable, compliant, mild, submissive.

**trac·tion** (trak′shən) *n.* 1 The act of drawing, as by motive power over a surface. 2 The state of being pulled or drawn: to place a fractured limb in *traction.* 3 The power em-

ployed in pulling or drawing. 4 Adhesive or rolling friction, as of tires on a road. [< L *tractus.* See TRACT¹.] —**trac′tion·al, trac·tive** (trak′tiv) *adj.*

**trac·tor** (trak′tər) *n.* 1 A powerful, self-propelled vehicle used to pull farm machinery. 2 An automotive vehicle with a driver's cab, used to haul trailers, etc. 3 An airplane with the propeller or propellers situated in front of the lifting surfaces. [<L *tractus.* See TRACT¹.]

**trade** (trād) *n.* 1 A business or occupation. 2 A skilled or specialized line of work, as a craft. 3 The people or companies engaged in a particular business. 4 The buying and selling or exchange of commodities; also, an instance of such commerce. 5 A firm's customers. 6 An exchange of personal articles; swap. 7 Any exchange of things or people having negotiable value: a baseball *trade.* 8 *Usu. pl.* TRADE WIND. —*adj.* 1 Of or pertaining to a trade. 2 Used by or intended for the members of a particular trade: a *trade* journal. —*v.t.* **trad·ed, trad·ing** 1 To give in exchange for something else. 2 To barter or exchange. —*v.i.* 3 To engage in commerce or in business transactions. 4 To make an exchange. 5 *Informal* To do one's shopping: with *at:* to *trade* at a store. —**trade in** To give in exchange as payment or part payment. —**trade off** To match or correlate, as incompatible elements or objectives, in the process of reaching a solution or compromise. —**trade on** To take advantage of. [< MLG, a track] —**trad′er** *n.*

**trade·mark** (trād′märk′) *n.* 1 A name, symbol, design, device, or word used by a merchant or manufacturer to identify his product and distinguish it from that of others. 2 Any distinctive or characteristic feature. —*v.t.* 1 To label with a trademark. 2 To register and bring under legal protection as a trademark.

**trade union** LABOR UNION. **Also trades union.** —**trade unionism** —**trade unionist**

**tra·di·tion** (trə·dish′ən) *n.* 1 The transmission of knowledge, opinions, customs, practices, etc., from generation to generation, esp. by word of mouth and by example. 2 The body of beliefs and usages so transmitted; also, any particular story, belief, or usage of this kind. 3 A custom so long continued that it has almost the force of a law. [< L *traditus,* p.p. of *tradere* deliver] —**tra·di′tion·al** *adj.* —**tra·di′tion·al·ly** *adv.*

**traf·fic** (traf′ik) *n.* 1 The passing of pedestrians, vehicles, aircraft, messages, etc., in a limited space or between certain points. 2 The people, vehicles, messages, etc., so moving. 3 The business of buying and selling commodities; trade. 4 Unlawful or improper trade: *traffic* in stolen goods. 5 The people or freight transported by a carrier, as a railroad. 6 The business of transportation. 7 Communication or contact; connection. —*v.i.* ·ficked, ·fick·ing 1 To engage in buying and selling illegally: with *in*: to *traffic* in narcotic drugs. 2 To have dealings: with *with*. [< MF < Ital. *traffico*] —traf′fick·er *n*.

tra·ge·di·an (trə·jē′dē·ən) *n*. 1 An actor of tragedy. 2 A writer of tragedies.

trag·e·dy (traj′ə·dē) *n. pl.* ·dies 1 A form of drama in which the protagonist comes to disaster, as through a flaw in character, and in which the ending is usu. marked by sorrow or pity. 2 A play, film, etc., of this kind. 3 Any tragic or disastrous incident or series of incidents. 4 *Informal* A misfortune. [< Gk. *tragōidia*]

trag·ic (traj′ik) *adj.* 1 Of or having the nature of tragedy. 2 Appropriate to or suggestive of tragedy: a *tragic* manner. 3 Causing or likely to cause suffering, sorrow, or death: a *tragic* accident. [< Gk. *tragikos* pertaining to tragedy] —trag′i·cal·ly *adv.*

trail (trāl) *v.t.* 1 To draw along lightly over a surface. 2 To drag or draw after: to *trail* oars; to *trail* an injured leg. 3 To follow the track of; trace: to *trail* game. 4 To be or come along behind. 5 To follow behind, as in pursuit or to keep under surveillance: to *trail* a suspect. —*v.i.* 6 To hang or extend loosely so as to drag over a surface. 7 To grow extensively and usu. irregularly along the ground or over rocks, etc. 8 To be or come along behind. 9 To move or walk heavily or ponderously; trudge. 10 To lag behind: to *trail* by 30,000 votes; to *trail* in the development of auto safety standards. 11 To flow or extend, as in a stream. —*n.* 1 The track left by something that has moved or been drawn or dragged over a surface. 2 The track, scent, etc., indicating the passage of someone or something. 3 The path worn by persons or by animals, esp. through a wilderness. 4 Something that trails or is trailed behind, as the train of a dress or the track of a meteor. 5 A sequence of results or conditions following after something: left a *trail* of broken hearts. [< AF *trailler* haul, tow a boat]

trail·er (trā′lər) *n*. 1 One who or that which trails. 2 A vehicle drawn by a cab or tractor having motive power. 3 A vehicle usu. drawn by an automobile or truck and equipped to serve as living quarters. 4 PRE-VIEW (def. 2).

train (trān) *n*. 1 A series of connected railway cars, often drawn by a locomotive. 2 Anything drawn along behind, as a trailing part of a skirt. 3 A line or group of followers; retinue. 4 A moving line of people, animals, vehicles, etc.; procession. 5 A series, succession, or set of connected things; sequence: a *train* of thought. 6 Something, as a period of time or set of circumstances, following after something else; aftermath: The argument left bitter feelings in its *train*. 7 *Mech.* A series of parts acting on each other, as for transmitting motion. —*v.t.* 1 To bring to a desired standard by careful instruction; esp., to guide in morals or manners. 2 To make skillful or proficient: to *train* soldiers. 3 To make obedient to orders or capable of performing tricks, as an animal. 4 To lead into taking a particular course; develop into a fixed shape: to *train* a plant on a trellis; to *train* the hair to lie flat. 5 To put or point in an exact direction; aim: to *train* a rifle or a gaze on someone. —*v.i.* 6 To undergo a course of training. [< OF *trahiner* to draw] —train′a·ble *adj.* —train′er *n*. —Syn. *v.* 1 educate, instruct, rear, bring up, mold.

trait (trāt) *n*. A distinguishing feature or quality, as of character. [< L *tractus* a drawing out < *trahere* draw]

trai·tor (trā′tər) *n*. 1 One who commits treason. 2 One who betrays a trust or acts deceitfully and disloyally. [< L *tradere* betray] —trai′tress (-tris) *n. Fem.*

tra·jec·to·ry (trə·jek′tər·ē) *n. pl.* ·ries The path described by an object or body moving in space, as of a comet or a bullet. [< L *trajectus*, p. p. of *trajicere* throw over]

tram·mel (tram′əl) *n*. 1 Usu. *pl.* That which limits freedom or activity; hindrance. 2 A fetter or shackle, esp. one used in teaching a horse to amble. 3 An instrument for drawing ellipses. 4 An adjustable hook used to suspend cooking pots from a fireplace crane. 5 A net formed of three layers, the central one of finer mesh, to trap fish passing through either of the others: also **trammel net**. —*v.t.* ·meled or ·melled, ·mel·ing or ·mel·ling 1 To hinder or obstruct; restrict. 2 To entangle in or as in a snare; imprison. [< LL *tremaculum* net < L *tri-* three + *macula* a mesh] —**tram′mel·er** or **tram′mel·ler** *n.*

**tramp** (tramp) *v.i.* 1 To walk or wander about, esp. as a tramp or hobo. 2 To walk heavily or firmly. —*v.t.* 3 To walk or wander through. 4 To walk on heavily; trample. — *n.* 1 One who travels from place to place, usu. on foot and destitute and dependent on charity for a living. 2 The sound of heavy marching or walking. 3 A long stroll; hike. 4 A steam vessel that goes from port to port picking up freight wherever it can: also **tramp steamer.** 5 *Slang* A sexually promiscuous woman. [ME *trampen*] —**tramp′er** *n.* —**Syn.** *n.* 1 vagrant, vagabond, hobo, bum.

**tram·ple** (tram′pəl) *v.* **·pled,** **·pling** *v.t.* 1 To tread heavily, esp. so as to crush. 2 To injure or encroach upon someone or something by or as by tramping: with *on:* to *trample* on someone's rights. —*v.t.* 3 To tread heavily or ruthlessly on. —*n.* The sound of treading under foot. [< ME *trampen* tramp] —**tram′pler** *n.*

**trance** (trans, träns) *n.* 1 A state in which one appears to be unable to act consciously, as though hypnotized or governed by a supernatural force. 2 A dreamlike or sleepy state, as that induced by hypnosis. 3 A state of profound concentration marked by lack of awareness of one's surroundings; deep abstraction. [< OF *transir* pass, die]

**tran·quil** (trang′kwil) *adj.* 1 Free from agitation or disturbance; calm: a *tranquil* mood. 2 Quiet and motionless: a *tranquil* scene. [< L *tranquillus* quiet] —**tran′quil·ly** *adv.* — **tran′quil·ness** *n.* —**Syn.** 1 relaxed, serene. 2 placid.

**tran·quil·ize** (trang′kwəl·īz) *v.t.* & *v.i.* **·ized, ·iz·ing** To make or become tranquil, esp. by using a drug. Also **tran′quil·lize.** *Brit. sp.* **·lise.** —**tran′quil·i·za′tion** *n.*

**tran·quil·iz·er** (trang′kwəl·ī′zər) *n.* 1 One who or that which tranquilizes. 2 Any of various drugs that calm mental agitation without impairing consciousness. Also **tran′quil·liz′er.**

**tran·quil·li·ty** (trang·kwil′ə·tē) *n.* The state of being tranquil; peacefulness; quiet. Also **tran·quil′i·ty.**

**trans·act** (trans·akt′, tranz-) *v.t.* 1 To carry through; accomplish; do. —*v.i.* 2 To do business. [< L *transactus,* p.p. of *transigere* drive through, accomplish] —**trans·ac′tor** *n.*

**trans·ac·tion** (trans·ak′shən, tranz-) *n.* 1 The

act or process of transacting. 2 Something transacted; esp., a business deal. 3 *pl.* Published reports, as of a society. —**trans·ac′tion·al** *adj.*

**tran·scend** (tran·send′) *v.t.* 1 To go or pass beyond the limits of: knowledge that *transcends* reason. 2 To rise above in excellence or degree. —*v.i.* 3 To be surpassing; excel. [< L *trans-* beyond, over + *scandere* to climb]

**tran·scen·dent** (tran·sen′dənt) *adj.* 1 TRANSCENDENTAL (def. 1). 2 *Theol.* Existing apart from and above the material universe: said of God. [< L *transcendere* transcend] — **tran·scen′dence, tran·scen′den·cy** *n.* — **tran·scen′dent·ly** *adv.*

**tran·scen·den·tal** (tran′sen·den′təl) *adj.* 1 Rising above or going beyond ordinary limits; surpassing. 2 Beyond natural experience; supernatural. 3 Of or pertaining to transcendentalism. —**tran′scen·den′tal·ly** *adv.*

**tran·scribe** (tran·skrīb′) *v.t.* **·scribed, ·scrib·ing** 1 To write over again; copy from an original. 2 To make a record of in handwriting or typewriting, as of something spoken. 3 To translate (shorthand notes, etc.) into standard written form. 4 To make a recording of for use in a later broadcast. 5 To adapt (a musical composition) for a change of instrument or voice. [< L *trans-* over + *scribere* write] —**tran·scrib′er** *n.*

**tran·script** (tran′skript) *n.* 1 Something transcribed, as from a stenographer's notes. 2 Any copy, esp., an official copy of a student's academic record. [< L *transcribere* transcribe]

**tran·scrip·tion** (tran·skrip′shən) *n.* 1 The act of transcribing. 2 Something transcribed; a copy; transcript. 3 A recording made for a later broadcast. 4 *Music* The adaptation of a composition for a different instrument or voice. —**tran·scrip′tion·al** *adj.*

**tran·sept** (tran′sept) *n.* A projecting part of a cruciform church crossing at right angles to the longer part and situated between the nave and choir; also, its projecting ends. [< L *transversus* transverse + *septum* an enclosure] —**tran·sep′tal** *adj.*

**trans·fer** (trans·fûr′, trans′fər) *v.* **·ferred, ·fer·ring** *v.t.* 1 To carry, or cause to pass, from one person, place, etc., to another. 2 To make over possession of to another. 3 To convey (a drawing) from one surface to another. —*v.i.* 4 To transfer oneself. 5 To be transferred. 6 To change from one vehicle or line to another. —*n.* (trans′fər) 1 The act of transferring, or the state of being transferred. 2 That which is transferred, as a design conveyed from one surface to another. 3 A place, method, or means of transfer. 4 A ticket entitling a passenger on one vehicle to ride on another. 5 A delivery of title or property from one person to another. 6 A person transferred from one organization or position to another. [< L *trans*- across + *ferre* carry] —**trans·fer′a·bil′i·ty, trans·fer′ ence, trans·fer′rer** *n.* —**trans·fer′a·ble, trans·fer′ra·ble** *adj.*

**trans·fig·ur·a·tion** (trans′fig·yə·rā′shən) *n.* A change in shape or appearance. —the **Transfiguration** 1 The supernatural transformation of Christ on the mount. 2 A festival commemorating this, August 6.

**trans·fig·ure** (trans·fig′yər) *v.t.* **·ured, ·ur·ing** 1 To change the outward form or appearance of. 2 To make glorious. [< L *trans*- across + *figura* shape] —**trans·fig′ure·ment** *n.*

**trans·fix** (trans·fiks′) *v.t.* 1 To pierce through, as with a pointed implement; impale. 2 To fix in place by impaling. 3 To make motionless, as with horror, amazement, etc. [< L *trans*- through, across + *figere* fasten] — **trans·fix′ion** (-fik′shən) *n.*

**trans·form** (trans·fôrm′) *v.t.* 1 To change the form or appearance of. 2 To change the nature or character of; convert. 3 *Electr.* To subject to the action of a transformer. —*v.i.* 4 To be or become changed in form or character. [< L *trans*- over + *forma* a form] — **trans·form′a·ble, trans·form′a·tive** *adj.*

**trans·for·ma·tion** (trans′fər·mā′shən) *n.* 1 The act of transforming or the state of being transformed. 2 *Ling.* Any of the systematic processes by which grammatical sentences of a language may be derived from underlying constructions. —**trans′for·ma′tion·al** *adj.*

**trans·fuse** (trans·fyōōz′) *v.t.* **·fused, ·fus·ing** 1 To cause to flow or pass from one person or thing to another. 2 *Med.* **a** To transfer (blood, plasma, etc.) from one person or animal to another. **b** To give a transfusion to. 3 To pass into; permeate. [< L *transfusus*, p.p. of *transfundere*] —**trans·fus′er** *n.* —**trans·fus′i·ble, trans·fu·sive** (trans·fyōō′siv) *adj.*

**trans·fu·sion** (trans·fyōō′zhən) *n.* 1 The act or an instance of transfusing. 2 *Med.* The introduction of a fluid, as saline solution, blood, blood plasma, etc., into the blood stream.

**trans·gress** (trans·gres′, tranz-) *v.t.* 1 To disregard and go beyond the bounds of, as a divine or traditional law; violate. 2 To pass beyond or over (limits); exceed. —*v.i.* 3 To break a law; sin. [< L *transgressus*, p.p. of *transgredi* step across] —**trans·gres′sor** *n.*

**trans·gres·sion** (trans·gresh′ən, tranz-) *n.* The act or an instance of transgressing, esp. a sin.

**tran·sient** (tran′shənt, tranch′ənt, tranz′ ē·ənt) *adj.* 1 Occurring or existing only for a time; not permanent; transitory. 2 Brief; fleeting; momentary. 3 Residing or staying in a place temporarily: a large *transient* population. —*n.* One who or that which is transient, esp. a temporary resident. [< L *transirego* across] —**tran′sience, tran′sien· cy** *n.* —**tran′sient·ly** *adv.* —**Syn.** 1 temporary, passing. 2 ephemeral, fugitive, evanescent. 3 casual.

**tran·sis·tor** (tran·zis′tər, -sis′-) *n. Electronics* 1 A semi-conductor device having three terminals and the property that the current between one pair of them is a function of the current between another pair. 2 A transistorized radio. [< TRANS(FER) (RES)ISTOR]

**tran·sit** (tran′sit, -zit) *n.* 1 The act of passing over or through; passage. 2 The process of change; transition. 3 The act of carrying across or through; conveyance. 4 Transportation, esp. for carrying large numbers of people, as in a city: public *transit.* 5 *Astron.* **a** The passage of one celestial body over the disk of another. **b** The passage of a celestial body across the meridian. 6 A surveying instrument resembling a theodolite. [< L *transire* go across]

**tran·si·tion** (tran·sish′ən, tranz-) *n.* 1 Passage from one place, condition, or stage to another; change. 2 Something, as a period of time or a situation, that leads from one stage or period to another. 3 *Music* A passage or modulation connecting sections of a composition. —**tran·si′tion·al** *adj.* —**tran· si′tion·al·ly** *adv.*

**tran·si·tive** (tran′sə·tiv) *adj.* 1 *Gram.* Having, requiring, or completed by a direct object: said of a verb. 2 Of or pertaining to transition. —*n. Gram.* A transitive verb. [< L *transitus* transit] —**tran′si·tive·ly** *adv.* —**tran′ si·tive·ness, tran′si·tiv′i·ty** *n.*

**tran·si·to·ry** (tran′sə·tôr′ē, -tō′rē) *adj.* 1 Existing for a short time only; soon extinguished or annulled. 2 Brief; ephemeral. — **tran′si·to′ri·ly** *adv.* —**tran′si·to′ri·ness** *n.*

**trans·late** (trans·lāt′, tranz-, trans′lāt, tranz′-)

*v.* ·lat·ed, ·lat·ing *v.t.* 1 To change into another language. 2 To change from one form, condition, or place to another. 3 To explain in other words; interpret. 4 *Mech.* To change the position of in space, esp. without rotation. —*v.i.* 5 To change the words of one language into those of another, esp. as an occupation. 6 To admit of translation. [< L *translatus,* lit., carried across] —**trans·lat′a·ble** *adj.* —**trans·la′tor** *n.*

**trans·la·tion** (trans·lā′shən, tranz-) *n.* 1 The act of translating, or the state of being translated. 2 Something translated; esp., a reproduction of a work in a language different from the original. 3 *Mech.* Motion in which all the parts of a body follow identical courses. —**trans·la′tion·al** *adj.*

**trans·lu·cent** (trans·lōō′sənt, tranz-) *adj.* Allowing the passage of light, but not permitting a clear view of any object. [< L *trans-* through, across + *lucere* to shine] —**trans·lu′cence, trans·lu′cen·cy** *n.* —**trans·lu′cent·ly** *adv.*

**trans·mit** (trans·mit′, tranz-) *v.t.* ·mit·ted, ·mit·ting 1 To send from one place or person to another; convey. 2 To pass on (a gene, a virus, etc.) from one organism to another. 3 To cause (light, sound, etc.) to pass through space or a medium. 4 To send out, as by means of radio waves. 5 To serve as a medium of passage for; conduct: Iron *transmits* heat. 6 *Mech.* To convey (force, motion, etc.) from one part or mechanism to another. [< L *trans-* across + *mittere* send] —**trans·mit′ta·ble** *adj.* —**trans·mit′tal, trans·mit′tance** *n.*

**trans·mute** (trans·myōōt′, tranz-) *v.t.* ·mut·ed, ·mut·ing To change in nature or form. Also **trans·mu′tate.** [< L *trans-* across + *mutare* to change] —**trans·mut′a·ble** *adj.* —**trans·mut′a·bil′i·ty, trans·mut′a·ble·ness, trans·mut′er** *n.* —**trans·mut′a·bly** *adv.*

**tran·som** (tran′səm) *n.* 1 A horizontal piece framed across an opening; a lintel. 2 A small window above and often hinged to such a bar, usu. situated above a door. 3 The horizontal crossbar of a gallows or cross. [< L *transtrum* a crossbeam] —**tran′somed** *adj.*

**trans·par·en·cy** (trans·pâr′ən·sē, -par′-) *n. pl.* ·cies 1 The state or quality of being transparent. 2 Something whose transmission of light defines an image, esp. a piece of photographic film, often mounted as a slide and viewed by projecting its image on a screen or other surface.

**trans·par·ent** (trans·pâr′ənt, -par′-) *adj.* 1 Allowing the passage of light and of clear views of objects beyond. 2 Having a texture fine enough to be seen through; diaphanous. 3 Easy to understand. 4 Without guile; frank; candid. 5 Easily detected; obvious: a *transparent* lie. [< L *trans-* across + *parere* appear, be visible] —**trans·par′ent·ly** *adv.* —**trans·par′ence, trans·par′ent·ness** *n.*

**tran·spire** (trans·pīr′) *v.* ·spired, ·spir·ing *v.t.* 1 To give off through permeable tissues, as of the skin and lungs or of leaf surfaces. —*v.i.* 2 To be emitted, as through the skin; be exhaled, as moisture or odors. 3 To become known. 4 To happen; occur. [< L *trans-* across, through + *spirare* breathe] • An accepted meaning of *transpire* is to become known or leak out: *It transpired that he had died penniless.* The word is more commonly used today, however, with the sense of "to happen"; *We shall never know what transpired at that meeting.* The latter usage still strikes the more traditionally inclined as improper or ignorant. That judgment may be unduly harsh, but as a matter of style the usage is almost always inelegant and often pretentious.

**trans·plant** (trans·plant′) *v.t.* 1 To remove and plant in another place. 2 To remove and settle for residence in another place. 3 *Surg.* To transfer (an organ or tissue) from its original site to another part of the body or to another individual. —*v.i.* 4 To admit of being transplanted. —*n.* (trans′plant′) 1 That which is transplanted, as a seedling or an organ of the body. 2 The act of transplanting. —**trans′plan·ta′tion, trans·plan·t′er** *n.*

**trans·port** (trans·pôrt′, -pōrt′) *v.t.* 1 To carry or convey from one place to another. 2 To carry away with emotion, as with delight; enchant. 3 To banish to another country. —*n.* (trans′pôrt, -pōrt) 1 The act or a means of transporting; transportation. 2 A state of emotional rapture; intense delight. 3 A ship, train, truck, etc., used to transport troops, supplies, etc. 4 A system of transportation. 5 A deported convict. [< L *trans-* across + *portare* carry] —**trans·port′a·bil′i·ty, trans·port′er** *n.* —**trans·port′able** *adj.*

**trans·por·ta·tion** (trans′pər·tā′shən) *n.* 1 The act of transporting. 2 A means of transporting or traveling. 3 The conveying of passengers or freight, esp. as an industry. 4

Money, a pass, etc., used for being transported.

**trans·pose** (trans-pōz′) *v.t.* ·posed, ·pos·ing 1 To reverse the order or change the place of: to *transpose* two numerals or a word in a sentence. 2 *Math.* To transfer (a term) from one side of an algebraic equation to the other with reversed sign. 3 *Music* To write or play in a different key. [< L *trans-* over + OF *poser* put] —**trans·pos′a·ble** *adj.* —**trans·po′sal**, **trans·pos′er**, **trans·po·si·tion** (trans′pə-zish′ən) *n.*

**trans·sex·u·al** (trans-sek′shōō-əl, -sek′shəl) *n.* A person who is genetically and physically of one sex but who identifies psychologically with the other and may seek treatment by surgery or with hormones to bring the physical sexual characteristics into conformity with the psychological preference. —*adj.* Of, for, or characteristic of transsexuals. —**trans·sex′u·al·ism** *n.*

**trans·verse** (trans-vûrs′, tranz-) *adj.* Lying or being across or from side to side. —*n.* (*also* trans′vûrs, tranz′-) That which is transverse. [< L *transversus* lying across] —**trans·verse′ly** *adv.*

**trans·ves·tite** (trans-ves′tīt, tranz-) *n.* One who wears the clothes of the opposite sex. [< L *trans-* over + *vestire* to clothe + -ITE] —**trans·ves′tism**, **trans·ves′ti·tism** (-ves′tə-tiz′əm) *n.*

**trap** (trap) *n.* 1 A device for catching game or other animals, as a pitfall or a baited contrivance set to spring shut on being slightly jarred or moved. 2 A devious plan or trick by which a person may be caught or taken unawares. 3 A device for hurling clay pigeons into the air, used in trapshooting. 4 Any of various devices that collect residual material or that form a seal to stop a return flow of noxious gas, etc., as a water-filled U- or S-bend in a pipe. 5 In golf, an obstacle or hazard: a sand *trap.* 6 TRAPDOOR. 7 A light, two-wheeled carriage suspended by springs. 8 *pl.* Percussion instruments, as drums, cymbals, etc. 8 *Slang* The mouth. —*v.* **trapped**, **trap·ping** *v.t.* 1 To catch in or as if in a trap. 2 To provide with a trap. 3 To stop or hold by the formation of a seal. 4 To catch (a ball) just as or after it strikes the ground. —*v.i.* To set traps for game; be a trapper. [< OE *træppe*]

**tra·peze** (tra-pēz′, trə-) *n.* A short swinging bar suspended by two ropes, for gymnastic exercises and acrobatic stunts. [< NL *trapezium* a trapezium]

**trap·e·zoid** (trap′ə-zoid′) *n. Geom.* 1 A quadrilateral of which two sides are parallel. 2 *Brit.* TRAPEZIUM (def. 1). [< Gk. *trapeza* a table + *eidos* a form] —**trap′e·zoi′dal** *adj.*

**trash** (trash) *n.* 1 Worthless or waste matter; rubbish. 2 That which is broken or lopped off, as twigs and branches. 3 Foolish or idle talk. 4 Anything worthless, shoddy, or without merit: literary *trash.* 5 A person regarded as worthless or of no account. —*v.t.* & *v.i. Slang* To wreck or destroy (something) purposefully but often indiscriminately as an expression of alienation or rebellion. [?] —**trash′i·ness** *n.* —**trash′y** (·i·er, ·i·est) *adj.*

**trau·ma** (trou′mə, trô′-) *n. pl.* ·mas or ·ma·ta (-mə·tə) 1 Any physical injury resulting from force. 2 A severe emotional shock having a deep effect upon the personality. [< Gk., a wound] —**trau·mat·ic** (trou·mat′ik, trô-) *adj.* —**trau·mat′i·cal·ly** *adv.*

**trav·el** (trav′əl) *v.* **trav·eled** or ·**elled**, **trav·el·ing** or ·**el·ling** *v.i.* 1 To go from one place to another or from place to place; make a journey or tour. 2 To proceed; advance. 3 To go about from place to place as a traveling salesman. 4 *Informal* To move with speed. 5 Tō pass or be transmitted, as light, sound, etc. 6 *Mech.* To move in a fixed path, as a machine part. 7 In basketball, to commit the infraction of failing to dribble while moving with the ball. —*v.t.* 8 To move or journey across or through: traverse. —*n.* 1 The act of traveling. 2 *Often pl.* A journey or tour, usu. extensive. 3 Passage to, over, or past a certain place. 4 Distance traveled, as by a machine part. [< OF *travailler* to travail]

**tra·verse** (trə-vûrs′, tra-) *v.* ·**ersed**, ·**ers·ing** *v.t.* 1 to pass over, across, or through. 2 To move back and forth over or along. 3 To examine carefully; scrutinize. 4 To oppose; thwart. 5 *Law* To make denial of. —*v.i.* 6 To move back and forth. 7 To move across; cross. —**trav·erse** (trav′ərs) *n.* 1 Something that traverses, as a crosspiece of a machine or structure. 2 Something serving as a screen or barrier. 3 The act of traversing or denying; a denial. —*adj.* (trav′ərs) Lying or being across; transverse. [< L *transversus* transverse] —**tra·vers′a·ble** *adj.* —**tra·vers′al**, **tra·vers′er** *n.*

**trav·es·ty** (trav′is·tē) *n. pl.* ·**ties** 1 A grotesque imitation, as of a lofty subject; burlesque. 2 A distorted or absurd rendering or example, as if in mockery: a *travesty* of justice.

—*v.t.* ·**tied**, ·**ty·ing** To make a travesty of; burlesque; parody. [< Ital. *travestire* to disguise]

**trawl** (trôl) *n.* **1** A large net for towing on the bottom of the ocean by a fishing boat. **2** A stout fishing line, anchored and buoyed, from which many lines bearing baited hooks may be secured. —*v.i.* **1** To fish with a trawl. —*v.t.* **2** To drag, as a net, to catch fish. [?]

**tray** (trā) *n.* **1** A flat, shallow utensil with raised edges, used to hold or carry several or a number of articles, as dishes. **2** A tray and the articles on it. **3** A shallow, topless box serving as a compartment, as in a tool or sewing box. [< OE *trēg* a wooden board] —**tray′ful** (-fŏŏl′) *n.*

**treach·er·ous** (trech′ər·əs) *adj.* **1** Likely to betray allegiance or confidence; untrustworthy. **2** Of the nature of treachery; perfidious. **3** Apparently safe or secure, but in fact dangerous or unreliable: *treacherous* footing. —**treach′er·ous·ly** *adv.* —**treach′er·ous·ness** *n.*

**tread** (tred) *v.* **trod**, **trod·den** or **trod**, **tread·ing** *v.t.* **1** To step or walk on, over, along, etc. **2** To press with the feet; trample. **3** To crush or oppress harshly. **4** To accomplish in walking or in dancing: to *tread* a measure. **5** To copulate with: said of male birds. —*v.i.* **6** To place the foot down; walk. **7** To press the ground or anything beneath the feet: usu. with *on.* —**tread water** In swimming, to keep the body erect and the head above water by moving the feet and arms. —*n.* **1** The act, manner, or sound of treading; a walking or stepping. **2** The part of a wheel or automobile tire that comes into contact with the road or rails. **3** The impression made by a foot, a tire, etc. **4** The horizontal part of a step in a stairway. [< OE *tredan*] —**tread′er** *n.*

**tread·le** (tred′l) *n.* A lever operated by the foot, usu. to cause rotary motion. —*v.i.* ·**led**, ·**ling** To work a treadle. [< OE *tredel* < *tredan* tread] • See POTTER'S WHEEL.

**trea·son** (trē′zən) *n.* **1** Betrayal, treachery, or breach of allegiance toward a sovereign or government. **2** A breach of faith; treachery. [< L *traditio* a betrayal, delivery] —**trea′son·ous** *adj.* —**trea′son·ous·ly** *adv.*

**treas·ure** (trezh′ər) *n.* **1** Riches accumulated or possessed, as a store of precious metals, jewels, or money. **2** Someone or something very precious. —*v.t.* ·**ured**, ·**ur·ing** **1** To set a high value upon; prize. **2** To lay up in store; accumulate. [< L *thesaurus*] —**Syn.** *v.* **1** cherish, esteem, value, venerate. **2** hoard.

**treas·ur·er** (trezh′ər·ər) *n.* **1** An officer authorized to receive, care for, and disburse revenues, as of a government, business corporation, or society. **2** A similar custodian of the funds of a society or a corporation.

**treas·ur·y** (trezh′ər·ē) *n. pl.* ·**ur·ies 1** A place of receipt and disbursement of public revenue or private funds. **2** The revenue or funds. **3** The place where a treasure is stored. **4** A department of government concerned with finances, the issuance of money, etc. [< OF *tresor* treasure]

**treat** (trēt) *v.t.* **1** To conduct oneself toward (a person, animal, etc.) in a specified manner. **2** To look upon or regard in a specified manner: They *treat* it as a childhood prank. **3** To give medical or surgical attention to. **4** To deal with in writing or speaking. **5** To depict or express artistically in a specified style. **6** To pay for the entertainment, food, or drink of. —*v.i.* **7** To deal with a subject in writing or speaking: usu. with *of.* **8** To carry on negotiations; negotiate. **9** To pay for another's entertainment. —*n.* **1** Something that gives unusual pleasure. **2** Entertainment of any kind furnished gratuitously to another. **3** *Informal* One's turn to pay for refreshment or entertainment. [< OF *tretier*, *traitier*] —**treat′er** *n.*

**trea·tise** (trē′tis) *n.* A formal, systematic, written exposition of a serious subject: a *treatise* on labor relations. [< OF *traitier*]

**trea·ty** (trē′tē) *n. pl.* ·**ties** A formal agreement or compact between two or more nations. [< OF *traitié*, p.p. of *traitier* treat]

**treb·le** (treb′əl) *v.t. & v.i.* ·**led**, ·**ling** To multiply by three; triple. —*adj.* **1** Threefold. **2** *Music* **a** Of the highest range. **b** Soprano. —*n.* **1 a** *Music* A part or instrument of the highest range. **b** A soprano singer. **2** High, piping sound. [< L *triplus* triple] —**treb′ly** *adv.*

**tree** (trē) *n.* **1** A woody perennial plant having a distinct trunk with branches and foliage at some distance above the ground. **2** Any shrub or plant with a treelike shape or dimensions. **3** Something whose outline resembles the spreading branches of a tree, as a diagram: a genealogical *tree.* **4** A timber, post, or piece of wood used for a particular purpose. —*v.t.* **treed**, **tree·ing 1** To force to climb or take refuge in a tree: to *tree* an opossum. 2 *Informal* To get the advantage of; corner. [< OE *trēow*]

**tre·foil** (trē'foil) *n.* 1 Any of various plants having three-fold leaves, as clover. 2 An architectural ornament having the form of a three-lobed leaf. [< L *trifolium*]

**trel·lis** (trel'is) *n.* A grating or lattice, often of wood, used as a screen or a support for vines, etc. —*v.t.* 1 To interlace so as to form a trellis. 2 To furnish with or fasten on a trellis. [< L *trilix* of three threads]

**trem·ble** (trem'bəl) *v.i.* ·**bled**, ·**bling** 1 To shake involuntarily, as with fear or weakness. 2 To move slightly or vibrate, as from some jarring force: The building *trembled*. 3 To feel anxiety or fear. 4 To quaver, as the voice. —*n.* The act or state of trembling. [< LL *tremulus* tremulous] —**trem'bler** *n.* — **trem'bling·ly** *adv.* —**trem'bly** *adj.* —**Syn.** *v.* 2 quiver, shake, totter, quake.

**tre·men·dous** (tri·men'dəs) *adj.* 1 Extraordinarily large or extensive; enormous; great. 2 Causing astonishment by its magnitude, force, etc.; awe-inspiring. 3 *Informal* Wonderful; marvelous. [< L *tremendus* to be trembled at] —**tre·men'dous·ly** *adv.* — **tre·men'dous·ness** *n.*

**trem·or** (trem'ər, trē'mər) *n.* 1 A quick, vibratory movement; a shaking. 2 Any involuntary quivering or trembling, as of a muscle. 3 A state of agitation or excitement, as in anticipation of something. [< OF *tremour* fear, a trembling]

**trem·u·lous** (trem'yə·ləs) *adj.* 1 Characterized or affected by trembling: *tremulous* speech. 2 Showing timidity and irresolution. 3 Characterized by mental excitement. Also **trem'u·lant**. [< L *tremulus*] —**trem'u·lous·ly** *adv.* —**trem'u·lous·ness** *n.*

**trench** (trench) *n.* 1 A long narrow ditch, esp. one lined with a parapet of the excavated earth, to protect troops. 2 A long, narrow region much deeper than the adjacent surfaces, as along the ocean floor. —*v.t.* 1 To dig a trench or trenches in. 2 To fortify with trenches. 3 To cut deep furrows in. —*v.i.* 4 To cut or dig trenches. 5 To cut; carve. 6 To encroach. [< OF *trenchier* to cut] —**trench'er** *n.*

**trench·ant** (tren'chənt) *adj.* 1 Clear, vigorous, and effective: a *grenchant* rebuttal. 2 Cutting, as sarcasm; biting. 3 Incisive; sharp; keen: *trenchant* wit. 4 *Archaic* Cutting deeply and quickly: a *trenchant* sword. [< OF *trenchier*]

**trend** (trend) *n.* 1 A prevailing or probable tendency; predominant or likely course or direction; drift: a *trend* toward smaller families; investment *trends*; to study *trends* in education. 2 A popular preference or inclination: fashion *trends*. 3 The general course or direction, as of a coast; bent. — *v.i.* 1 To have or follow a general course or direction. 2 To exhibit a tendency; move: wheat prices *trending* upward. [< OE *trendan* to roll]

**tre·pan** (tri·pan') *n.* 1 An early form of the trephine. 2 A large rock-boring tool —*v.t.* ·**panned**, ·**pan·ning** To use a trepan upon. [< Gk. *trypanon* a borer]

**trep·i·da·tion** (trep'ə·dā'shən) *n.* 1 Tremulous agitation caused by fear; apprehension. 2 *Archaic* An involuntary trembling; tremor. [<L *trepidare* hurry, be alarmed]

**tres·pass** (tres'pəs, -pas') *v.i.* 1 To violate the personal or property rights of another; esp., to go unlawfully onto another's land. 2 To go beyond the bounds of what is right or proper; transgress. 3 To intrude; encroach: to *trespass* on one's privacy. —*n.* 1 *Law* a Any act accompanied by actual or implied force in violation of another's person, property, or rights. b An action for injuries sustained because of this. 2 Any transgression of law or moral duty. 3 An intrusion; encroachment. [<Med. L *trans-* across, beyond + *passare* to pass] —**tres'pass·er** *n.*

**tress** (tres) *n.* 1 A lock or curl of human hair. 2 *pl.* The hair of a woman or girl, esp. when long and worn loose [< OF *tresce*] —**tressed** (trest) *adj.*

**tres·tle** (tres'əl) *n.* 1 A beam or bar braced by two pairs of divergent legs, used to support tables, platforms, etc. 2 A braced framework functioning like a bridge in supporting a roadway or railway over a short span. [< L *transtrum* crossbeam]

**tri·ad** (trī'ad) *n.* 1 A group of three persons or things. 2 *Music* A chord of three tones, esp. a tone with its third and fifth. [< Gk. *trias<treis* three] —**tri·ad'ic** *adj.*, *n.*

**tri·al** (trī'əl, trīl) *n.* 1 The examination in a court of law, often before a jury, of the facts of a case in order to determine its disposition. 2 The act of testing or proving by experience or use. 3 The state of being tried or tested. 4 An experience, person, or thing that puts strength, patience, or faith to the test. 5 An attempt or effort to do something. 6 Hardship; difficulty: the *trials* of poverty. —**on trial** In the process of being tried or tested. —**trial and error** The trying of one thing after another until something succeeds. —*adj.* 1 Of or pertaining to a trial or trials. 2 Made or used in the course of trying or testing. [<AF<*trier* to try] —**Syn.** *n.* 2 examination, experiment. 5 endeavor. 6 misfortune, trouble.

**tri·an·gle** (trī′ang′gəl) *n.* 1 *Geom.* A figure, esp. a plane figure, bounded by three sides, and having three angles. 2 Something resembling such a figure in shape. 3 A situation involving three persons: the eternal *triangle.* 4 *Music* A percussion instrument consisting of a resonant metal bar bent into a triangle and sounded by striking with a small metal rod. [< L *tri-* three + *angulus* an angle]

**tri·an·gu·lar** (trī·ang′gyə·lər) *adj.* 1 Pertaining to, like, or bounded by a triangle. 2 Concerned with or pertaining to three things, parties, or persons. —**tri·an′gu·lar′i·ty** (-lar′ə·tē) *n.* —**tri·an′gu·lar·ly** *adv.*

**tribe** (trīb) *n.* 1 A group of people, under one chief or ruler, united by common ancestry, language, and culture. 2 In ancient Israel, any of the 12 divisions of the Hebrews. 3 In ancient Rome, any of the three clans making up the Roman people. 4 A number of persons of any class or profession taken together: often contemptuous. 5 *Biol.* a A group of closely related genera. b Any group of plants or animals. [< L *tribus*] —**tri′bal** *adj.* —**tri′bal·ly** *adv.*

**trib·u·la·tion** (trib′yə·lā′shən) *n.* 1 A condition of distress; suffering. 2 The cause of such distress. [< L *tribulare* thrash] —**Syn.** 1 misery, oppression, sorrow, trouble.

**tri·bu·nal** (trī·byōō′nəl, tri-) *n.* 1 A court of justice. 2 Any judicial body, as a board of arbitrators. 3 The seat set apart for judges, magistrates, etc. [< L *tribunus* tribune]

**trib·u·tar·y** (trib′yə·ter′ē) *adj.* 1 Supplying a larger body, as a stream flowing into a river. 2 Paying tribute. —*n. pl.* **·tar·ies** 1 A stream flowing into a larger one. 2 A person or state paying tribute. [< L *tributarius.* See TRIBUTE.]

**trib·ute** (trib′yōōt) *n.* 1 Money or other valuables paid by one state to another as the price of peace and protection, or by virtue of some treaty. 2 Any obligatory payment, as a tax. 3 Anything given that is due to worth, affection, or duty: a *tribute* of praise. [< L *tributum,* neut. p.p. of *tribuere* pay, allot]

**trick** (trik) *n.* 1 A deception; a petty artifice. 2 A malicious or annoying act: a dirty *trick.* 3 A practical joke; prank. 4 A particular char-

acteristic; trait: a *trick* of tapping her foot. 5 A peculiar skill or knack. 6 A feat of jugglery. 7 In card games, the whole number of cards played in one round. 8 A turn or spell of duty. 9 *Informal* A child or young girl. —**do** (or **turn**) **the trick** *Slang* To produce the desired result. —*v.t.* 1 To deceive or cheat; delude. —*v.i.* 2 To practice trickery or deception. [< OF *trichier* cheat] —**trick′er** *n.* —**Syn.** *n.* 1 ruse, stratagem, subterfuge, device.

**trick·le** (trik′əl) *v.* **·led,** **·ling** *v.i.* 1 To flow or run drop by drop or in a very thin stream. 2 To move, come, go, etc., bit by bit. —*v.t.* 3 To cause to trickle. —*n.* 1 The act or state of trickling. 2 A thin stream. [ME *triklen*]

**tri·col·or** (trī′kul′ər) *adj.* Having or characterized by three colors: also **tri′col′ored.** —*n.* The French national flag. *Brit. sp.* **tri′col′our.**

**tri·cy·cle** (trī′sik·əl) *n.* A three-wheeled vehicle worked by pedals, esp. one used by children.

**tri·dent** (trīd′nt) *n.* A three-pronged implement or weapon, the emblem of Neptune (Poseidon). —*adj.* Having three teeth or prongs: also **tri·den·tate** (trī·den′tāt), **tri·den′tat·ed.** [< L *tri-* three + *dens* a tooth]

**tri·en·ni·al** (trī·en′ē·əl) *adj.* 1 Taking place every third year. 2 Lasting three years. —*n.* 1 A ceremony celebrated every three years. 2 A plant lasting three years. [< L *tri-* three + *annus* year] —**tri·en′ni·al·ly** *adv.*

**tri·fle** (trī′fəl) *v.* **·fled,** **·fling** *v.i.* 1 To treat or speak of something as of no value or importance: with *with.* 2 To play; toy. —*v.t.* 3 To spend (time, money, etc.) idly and purposelessly: He *trifled* away his entire fortune. —*n.* 1 Anything of very little value or importance. 2 A dessert, popular in England, made of layers of macaroons or ladyfingers with sugared fruit, custard, and meringue or whipped cream. 3 A small amount: It costs only a *trifle.* —**a trifle** slightly; to a small extent: a *trifle* short. [< OF *truffer* deceive, jeer at] —**tri′fler** *n.*

**trig·ger** (trig′ər) *n.* 1 A lever of a gun activating the firing mechanism when moved by a finger. • See REVOLVER. 2 Any one of various devices designed to activate other devices or systems. —**quick on the trigger** 1 Quick to shoot a gun. 2 Quick-witted; alert. —*v.t. Informal* To cause or set off (an action). [< Du. *trekken* pull, tug at]

**trig·o·nom·e·try** (trig′ə·nom′ə·trē) *n.* The branch of mathematics based on the use of trigonometric functions, as in studying the relations of the sides and angles of triangles. [< Gk. *trigōnon* a triangle + *metron* measure] —**trig·o·no·met·ric** (trig′ə·nə·met′rik) or **·ri·cal** *adj.* —**trig′o·no·met′ri·cal·ly** *adv.*

**trill** (tril) *v.t.* 1 To sing or play in a quavering or tremulous tone. 2 *Phonet.* To articulate with a trill. —*v.i.* 3 To utter a quavering or tremulous sound. 4 *Music* To execute a trill. —*n.* 1 A tremulous utterance of successive tones, as of certain insects or birds; a warble. 2 *Music* A quick alternation of two notes either a tone or a semitone apart. 3 *Phonet.* A rapid vibration of a speech organ, as of the tip of the tongue. 4 A consonant or word so uttered. [< Ital. *trillare*] —**trill′er** *n.*

**tril·lion** (tril′yən) *n. & adj.* See NUMBER. [< MF *tri-* three + *million* million] —**tril′lionth** *adj., n.*

**trim** (trim) *v.* **trimmed, trim·ming** *v.t.* 1 To make neat by clipping, pruning, etc. 2 To remove by cutting: usu. with *off* or *away.* 3 To put ornaments on; decorate. 4 In carpentry, to smooth; dress. 5 *Informal* a To chide; rebuke. b To punish. c To defeat. 6 *Naut.* a To adjust (sails or yards) for sailing. b To cause (a ship) to sit well in the water by adjusting cargo, ballast, etc. 7 To bring (an airplane) to stable flight by adjusting controls. —*v.i.* 8 *Naut.* a To be or remain in equilibrium. b To adjust sails or yards for sailing. 9 To act so as to appear to favor opposing sides in a controversy. —*n.* 1 State of adjustment or preparation; fitting condition. 2 Good physical condition: in *trim* to play tennis. 3 *Naut.* Fitness for sailing. 4 *Naut.* Actual or comparative degree of immersion. 5 The moldings, etc., as about the doors of a building. 6 Ornament, as on a dress; trimming. 7 The attitude of an aircraft in flight. —*adj.* **trim·mer, trim·mest** Having a smart appearance; spruce. —*adv.* In a trim manner: also **trim′ly.** [< OE *trymman* arrange, strengthen] —**trim′ness** *n.* —Syn. *v.* 1 cut, lop. 2 pare. 3 adorn, garnish.

**tri·ni·tro·tol·u·ene** (trī·nī′trō·tol′yōō·ēn) *n.* An explosive made by treating toluene with nitric acid. Also **tri·ni′tro·tol′u·ol** (-yōō·ōl, -ol). [< TRI- + NITRO- + TOLUENE]

**Trin·i·ty** (trin′ə·tē) *n.* In Christian theology, the union in one divine nature of Father, Son, and Holy Spirit.

**trin·ket** (tring′kit) *n.* 1 Any small ornament,

as of jewelry. 2 A trifle; trivial object. [< AF *trenquet*]

**tri·o** (trē′ō) *n. pl.* **tri·os** 1 Any three things grouped or associated together. 2 *Music* a A composition for three performers. b A group of three musicians who perform trios. [< Ital. *tre* three]

**trip** (trip) *n.* 1 A journey; excursion. 2 A misstep or stumble. 3 An active, nimble step or movement. 4 A catch or similar device for starting or stopping a movement, as in a mechanism. 5 A sudden catch of the legs or feet to make a person fall. 6 A blunder; mistake. 7 *Slang* a The hallucinations and other sensations experienced by a person taking a psychedelic drug. b Any intense, usu. personal experience. —*v.* **tripped, trip·ping** *v.i.* 1 To stumble. 2 To move quickly and lightly. 3 To make an error. 4 To run past the nicks or dents of the ratchet escape wheel of a timepiece. 5 *Slang* To experience the effects of a psychedelic drug: often with *out.* —*v.t.* 6 To cause to stumble or make a mistake: often with *up.* 7 To perform (a dance) lightly. 8 *Mech.* To activate by releasing a catch, trigger, etc. —**trip it** To dance. [< OF *treper, triper* leap, trample] —**Syn.** *n.* 1 jaunt, tour, sojourn, voyage.

**trip·ham·mer** (trip′ham′ər) *n.* A heavy power hammer that is raised mechanically and allowed to drop by a tripping action.

**trip·le** (trip′əl) *v.* **·led, ·ling** *v.t.* 1 To make threefold in number or quantity. —*v.i.* 2 To be or become three times as many or as large. 3 In baseball, to make a triple. —*adj.* 1 Consisting of three things united. 2 Multiplied by three; thrice said or done. —*n.* 1 A set or group of three. 2 In baseball, a fair hit that enables the batter to reach third base without the help of an error. [< Gk. *triploos* threefold] —**trip′ly** *adv.*

**trip·let** (trip′lit) *n.* 1 A group of three of a kind. 2 Any of three children born at one birth. 3 *Music* A group of three notes that divide the time usu. taken by two. [< TRIPLE]

**trip·li·cate** (trip′lə·kit) *adj.* Threefold; made in three copies. —*n.* One of three precisely similar things. —in triplicate In three identical copies. —*v.t.* (-kāt) **·cat·ed, ·cat·ing** To make three times; triple. [< L *triplicare* to triple] —**trip′li·cate·ly** *adv.* —**trip′li·ca′tion** *n.*

**tri·pod** (trī′pod) *n.* A three-legged frame or stand, as for supporting a camera, etc. [< Gk. *tri-* three + *pous* foot] —**trip·o·dal** (trip′ə·dəl), **tri·pod·ic** (tri·pod′ik) *adj.*

**tri·sect** (trī·sekt′) *v.t.* To divide into three parts, esp., as in geometry, into three equal parts. [< TRI- + L *sectus,* p.p. of *secare* to cut] —**tri·sec′tion** (-sek′shən), **tri·sec′tor** *n.*

**trite** (trīt) *adj.* **trit·er, trit·est** Made commonplace or hackneyed by frequent repetition. [< L *tritus,* p.p. of *terere* to rub] —**trite′ly** *adv.* —**trite′ness** *n.* —**Syn.** stale, stereotyped, threadbare, cliché, shopworn, tired, stock.

**trit·i·um** (trit′ē-əm, trish′ē-əm) *n.* The radioactive hydrogen isotope of atomic mass 3, having a half-life of 12.5 years. [< Gk. *tritos* third]

**tri·umph** (trī′əmf) *v.i.* **1** To win a victory. **2** To be successful. **3** To rejoice over a victory; exult. —*n.* **1** A victory or conquest: a *triumph* of will power. **2** An important success: the *triumphs* of modern medicine. **3** Exultation over a victory. **4** In ancient Rome, a pageant welcoming a victorious general. [< Gk. *thriambos* a processional hymn to Dionysus] —**tri·um·phal** (trī·um′fəl) *adj.* —**tri·um′phal·ly** *adv.* —**tri′umph·er** *n.*

**tri·um·phant** (trī·um′fənt) *adj.* **1** Exultant for or as for victory. **2** Crowned with victory; victorious. —**tri·um′phant·ly** *adv.*

**triv·i·al** (triv′ē-əl) *adj.* **1** Of little value or importance; insignificant. **2** *Archaic* Ordinary; commonplace. [< L *trivialis* of the crossroads, commonplace] —**triv′i·al·ism** *n.* —**triv′i·al·ly** *adv.* —**Syn.** 1 slight, mean, paltry, inconsiderable, piddling.

**tro·chee** (trō′kē) *n.* In prosody, a foot comprising a long and short syllable (‾ ˘), or an accented syllable followed by an unaccented one. [< Gk. *trochaios (pous)* a running (foot) < *trechein* to run] —**tro·cha·ic** (trō·kā′ik) *adj.*

**troll** (trōl) *v.t.* **1** To sing in succession, as in a round. **2** To sing in a full, hearty manner. **3** To fish for with a moving lure, as from a moving boat. —*v.i.* **4** To roll; turn. **5** To sing a tune, etc., in a full, hearty manner. **6** To fish with a moving lure. —*n.* **1** A song taken up at intervals by several voices; round. **2** A rolling movement or motion. **3** In fishing, a spoon or other lure. [?] —**troll′er** *n.*

**trol·ley** (trol′ē) *n. pl.* **·leys** **1** A device that rolls or slides along an electric conductor to carry current to an electric vehicle. **2** A trolley car; also, a system of trolley cars. **3** A small truck or car suspended from an overhead track and used to convey material, as in a factory, mine, etc. —*v.t. & v.i.* To convey or travel by trolley. [< TROLL[1]]

**trolley car** A car arranged with a trolley and motor for use on an electric railway.

**trom·bone** (trom·bōn′, trom′bōn) *n.* A brass wind instrument of the trumpet family in the tenor range, usu. equipped with a slide for changing pitch. [< Ital. *tromba* a trumpet] —**trom·bon′ist** *n.*

**troop** (trōōp) *n.* **1** A gathering of people. **2** A flock or herd, as of animals. **3** A unit of cavalry having 60 to 100 men and corresponding to a company in other military branches. **4** *pl.* Soldiers. **5** A unit of Boy Scouts or Girl Scouts. —*v.i.* **1** To move along as a group: shoppers *trooping* through a store. **2** To go: to *troop* across the street. —*v.t.* **3** To form into troops. [< LL *troppus* a flock] —**Syn.** 1 company, crowd, multitude, throng.

**tro·phy** (trō′fē) *n. pl.* **·phies** **1** Anything taken from an enemy and displayed or treasured in proof of victory. **2** A prize representing victory or achievement: a tennis *trophy.* **3** An animal skin, mounted head, etc., kept to show skill in hunting. **4** Any memento. [< Gk. *tropē* a defeat, turning] —**tro′phied** *adj.*

**trop·ic** (trop′ik) *n.* **1** *Geog.* Either of two parallels of latitude, the *tropic of Cancer* at 23° 27′ north of the equator and the *tropic of Capricorn* 23° 27′ south of the equator, between which lies the torrid zone. **2** *Astron.* Either of two corresponding parallels in the celestial sphere similarly named, and respectively 23° 27′ north or south from the celestial equator. **3** *pl.* The regions in the torrid zone. —*adj.* Of or pertaining to the tropics; tropical. [< Gk. *tropikos (kyklos)* the tropical (circle), pertaining to the turning of the sun at the solstice.]

**trop·i·cal** (trop′i·kəl) *adj.* **1** Of, pertaining to, or characteristic of the tropics. **2** Of the nature of a trope or metaphor. —**trop′i·cal·ly** *adv.*

**trop·o·sphere** (trōp′ə·sfir, trop′-) *n. Meteorol.* The region of the atmosphere extending from six to twelve miles above the earth's surface, characterized by decreasing temperature with increasing altitude. [< Gk. *tropos* a turning + SPHERE]

**trot** (trot) *n.* **1** The gait of a quadruped, in which each diagonal pair of legs is moved alternately. **2** The sound of this gait. **3** A slow running gait of a person. **4** A little child. **5** *Informal* A literal translation of a foreign-language text, used by students, often dishonestly. —**the trots** *Slang* Diarrhea. —*v.* **trot·ted, trot·ting** *v.i.* 1 To go at a trot. 2 To go quickly; hurry. —*v.t.* 3 To cause to trot. 4 To ride at a trotting gait. — **trot out** *Informal* To bring forth for inspection, approval, etc. [< OHG *trottôn* to tread]

**troth** (trôth, trŏth) *n.* 1 Good faith; fidelity. 2 The act of pledging fidelity. 3 Truth; verity. —**plight one's troth** To promise to marry or be faithful to. [< OE *trēowth* truth]

**trou·ble** (trub′əl) *n.* 1 The state of being distressed or worried. 2 A person, circumstance, or event that occasions difficulty or perplexity. 3 A condition of difficulty: to be in *trouble* at school; money *troubles*. 4 A disease or ailment: heart *trouble*. 5 Bother; effort: They took the *trouble* to drive me home. 6 Agitation; unrest: *trouble* in the streets. —*v.* **·led, ·ling** *v.t.* 1 To distress; worry. 2 To stir up or roil, as water. 3 To inconvenience. 4 To annoy. 5 To cause physical pain or discomfort to. —*v.i.* 6 To take pains; bother. [< OF *turbler* to trouble] — **troub′ler** *n.*

**trou·ble-shoot·er** (trub′əl·shōō′tər) *n.* 1 A skilled workman able to analyze and repair breakdowns in machinery, electronic equipment, etc. 2 A person assigned to eliminate sources of difficulty or to mediate disputes, esp. in diplomacy and politics. — **troub′le-shoot′ing** *n.*

**trou·ble·some** (trub′əl·səm) *adj.* 1 Causing trouble; trying. 2 Difficult: a *troublesome* task. —**troub′le·some·ly** *adv.* —**troub′le·some·ness** *n.* —**Syn.** 1 burdensome, disturbing, galling, harassing.

**trough** (trôf, trof) *n.* 1 A long, narrow receptacle for food or water for animals. 2 A similarly shaped receptacle, as for mixing dough. 3 A long, narrow depression, as between waves. 4 A gutter for rain water fixed under the eaves of a building. 5 *Meteorol.* An elongated region of relatively low atmospheric pressure. [< OE *trog*]

**trounce** (trouns) *v.t.* **trounced, trounc·ing** 1 To beat or thrash severely; punish. 2 *Informal* To defeat. [?]

**troupe** (trōōp) *n.* A company of actors or other performers. —*v.i.* **trouped, troup·ing** To travel as one of a company of actors or entertainers. [< OF *trope* troop]

**trou·sers** (trou′zərz) *n. pl.* A two-legged garment, covering the body from the waist to the ankles or knees. [Blend of obs. *trouse* breeches and DRAWERS]

**trous·seau** (trōō′sō, trōō-sō′) *n. pl.* **·seaux** (-sōz, -sōz′) or **·seaus** A bride's outfit, esp. of clothing. [F < OF, dim. of *trousse* a packed collection of things]

**trout** (trout) *n.* Any of various fishes of the salmon family found mostly in fresh waters and esteemed as a game and food fish. [< OE *trūht*]

**trow·el** (trou′əl, troul) *n.* 1 A flat-bladed, sometimes pointed implement, used by masons, plasterers, and molders. 2 A small concave scoop with a handle, used in digging about small plants. —*v.t.* **·eled** or **·elled, ·el·ing** or **·el·ling** To apply, smooth, or dig with a trowel. [< L *trulla*, dim. of *trua* a stirring spoon] —**trow′el·er** or **trow′el·ler** *n.*

**troy weight** A system of weights in which 12 ounces or 5,760 grains equal a pound, and the grain is identical with the avoirdupois grain. • See MEASURE.

**tru·ant** (trōō′ənt) *n.* 1 A pupil who stays away from school without leave. 2 A person who shirks responsibilities or work. —**play truant.** 1 To be absent from school without leave. 2 To shirk responsibilities or work. —*adj.* 1 Being truant; idle. 2 Relating to or characterizing a truant. [< OF, a vagabond] —**tru·an·cy** (trōō′ən·sē) *n.* (*pl.* **·cies**)

**truce** (trōōs) *n.* 1 An agreement for a temporary suspension of hostilities; an armistice. 2 A temporary stopping, as from pain, etc.; respite. [<OE *truwa* faith, a promise]

**truck** (truk) *n.* 1 Any of several types of strongly built motor vehicles designed to transport heavy loads, bulky articles, freight, etc. 2 A two-wheeled barrowlike vehicle for moving barrels, boxes, etc., by hand. 3 A small wheeled vehicle used for moving baggage, goods, etc. 4 A disk at the upper extremity of a mast or flagpole through which the halyards of signals are run. 5 A small wheel. —*v.t.* 1 To carry on a truck. —*v.i.* 2 To carry goods on a truck. 3 To drive a truck. [< Gk. *trochos* a wheel]

**truck·le** (truk′əl) *v.* **·led, ·ling** *v.i.* 1 To yield or submit weakly: with *to*. 2 To move on rollers or casters. —*v.t.* 3 To cause to move on rollers or casters. —*n.* A small wheel. [< L *trochlea* system of pulleys] —**truck′ler** *n.*

**truc·u·lent** (truk′yə·lənt) *adj.* Of savage character; cruel; ferocious. [< L *trux, trucis* fierce] —**truc·u·lence** (truk′yə·ləns), **truc′u·len·cy** *n.* —**truc′u·lent·ly** *adv.* —**Syn.** barbarous, brutal, fierce, ruthless, vicious.

**true** (trōō) *adj.* **tru·er, tru·est** 1 Faithful to fact or reality. 2 Being real; genuine, not counterfeit: *true* gold. 3 Faithful to friends, promises, or principles; loyal. 4 Exact: a *true* copy. 5 Accurate, as in shape, or position: a *true* fit. 6 Faithful to the requirements of law or justice; legitimate: the *true* king. 7 Faithful to truth; honest: a *true* man. 8 Faithful to the promise or predicted event: a *true* sign. 9 *Biol.* Possessing all the attributes of its class: a *true* root. 10 *Music* Exactly in tune. —**come true** To turn out as hoped for or imagined. —*n.* The state or quality of being true; also, something that is true: usu. with *the.* —**in** (or **out of**) **true** In (or not in) line of adjustment. —*adv.* 1 In truth; truly. 2 Within proper tolerances: The wheel runs *true.* —*v.t.* **trued, tru·ing** To bring to conformity with a standard or requirement: to *true* a frame. [< OE *trēowe*] —**true′ness** *n.*

**truf·fle** (truf′əl, troo′fəl) *n.* Any of various fleshy underground edible fungi regarded as a delicacy. [< OF *truffe*]

**tru·ism** (troo′iz·əm) *n.* An obvious or self-evident truth; a platitude.

**tru·ly** (troo′lē) *adv.* 1 In conformity with fact. 2 With accuracy. 3 With loyalty.

**trump** (trump) *n.* 1 In various card games, a card of the suit selected to rank above all others temporarily. 2 The suit thus determined. 3 *Informal* A fine, reliable person. —*v.t.* 1 To take (another card) with a trump. 2 To surpass; excel; beat. —*v.i.* 3 To play a trump. —**trump up** To invent for a fraudulent purpose. [Alter. of TRIUMPH]

**trump·er·y** (trum′pər·ē) *n. pl.* **·er·ies** 1 Worthless finery. 2 Rubbish; nonsense. —*adj.* Having a showy appearance, but valueless. [< OF *tromper* to cheat]

**trum·pet** (trum′pit) *n.* 1 A soprano brass wind instrument with a flaring bell and a long metal tube. 2 Something resembling a trumpet in form. 3 A tube for collecting and conducting sounds to the ear; an ear trumpet. 4 A loud penetrating sound like that of a trumpet. —*v.i.* 1 To sound or publish abroad. —*v.i.* 2 To blow a trumpet. 3 To give forth a sound as if from a trumpet, as an elephant. [< OF *trompette*]

**trun·cheon** (trun′chən) *n.* 1 A short, heavy stick, esp. a policeman's club. 2 Any baton of office or authority. —*v.t.* To beat as with a truncheon; cudgel. [< OF *tronchon* a stump]

**trun·dle** (trun′dəl) *n.* 1 A small broad wheel, as of a caster. 2 The act, motion, or sound

of trundling. 3 TRUNDLE BED. —*v.* **·dled, ·dling** *v.t.* 1 To propel by rolling along: to *trundle* a wheelbarrow. 2 To haul or carry in a wheeled vehicle. —*v.i.* 3 To move ahead by revolving. 4 To progress on wheels. [< OE *trendel* a circle] —**trun′dler** *n.*

**trundle bed** A bed with very low frame resting upon casters, so that it may be rolled under another bed.

**trunk** (trungk) *n.* 1 The main stem or stock of a tree. 2 An animal or human body, apart from the head and limbs; the torso. 3 The thorax of an insect. 4 The main stem of a nerve, blood vessel, or lymphatic. 5 A main line of communication or transportation, as the circuit connecting two telephone exchanges. 6 A proboscis, as of an elephant. 7 A large box or case used for packing and carrying clothes or other articles. 8 *pl.* Very short, close-fitting trousers worn by swimmers, athletes, etc. 9 *Archit.* The shaft of a column. 10 A compartment in an automobile, opposite the end housing the motor, for carrying luggage, tools, etc. —*adj.* Being or belonging to a trunk or main body: a *trunk* railroad. [< L *truncus* stem, trunk]

**truss** (trus) *n.* 1 A supporting framework, as for a roof or bridge. 2 A bandage or support for a hernia. 3 A bundle or package. 4 *Naut.* A heavy iron piece by which a lower yard is attached to a mast. —*v.t.* 1 To tie or bind; fasten: often with *up.* 2 To support or brace (a roof, bridge, etc.) with trusses. 3 To fasten the wings of (a fowl) before cooking. [< OF *trousser, trusser* pack up, bundle] —**truss′er** *n.*

**trust** (trust) *n.* 1 A reliance on the integrity, veracity, or reliability of a person or thing. 2 Something committed to one's care for use or safekeeping. 3 The state or position of one who has received an important charge. 4 Confident expectation; hope. 5 In commerce, credit. 6 *Law* **a** The confidence reposed in a person to whom the legal title to property is conveyed for the benefit of another. **b** The property or thing held in trust. **c** The relation subsisting between the holder and the property so held. 7 A combination of business firms formed to control production and prices of some commodity. —**in trust** In the charge or care of another or others. —**on trust** 1 On credit. 2 Without investigating: to accept a statement *on trust.* —*v.t.* 1 To rely upon. 2 To commit to the care of another; entrust. 3 To commit something to the care of: with *with.*

**4** To allow to do something without fear of the consequences. **5** To expect; hope. **6** To believe. **7** To allow business credit to. —*v.i.* **8** To place trust or confidence; rely: with *in.* **9** To allow business credit. —trust to To depend upon; confide in. —*adj.* Held in trust: *trust* property. [< ON *traust,* lit., firmness] —trust′er *n.* —Syn. *n.* 1 confidence, credence, faith.

**trus·tee** (trus·tē′) *n.* **1** One who is entrusted with the property of another. **2** One of a body of persons, often elective, who hold and manage the affairs of a company or institution.

**truth** (trōōth) *n. pl.* **truths** (trōō*th*z, trōōths) **1** The state or character of being true. **2** That which is true. **3** Conformity to fact or reality. **4** The quality of being true; fidelity; constancy. —in truth Indeed; in fact. [< OE *treowe* true]

**try** (trī) *v.* **tried, try·ing** *v.t.* **1** To make an attempt to do or accomplish. **2** To make experimental use or application of: to *try* a new pen. **3** To subject to a test; put to proof. **4** To put severe strain upon; tax: to *try* one's patience. **5** To subject to trouble or tribulation. **6** To extract by rendering or melting; refine. **7** *Law* To determine the guilt or innocence of by judicial trial. —*v.i.* **8** To make an attempt; put forth effort. **9** To make an examination or test. —try on To put on (a garment) to test it for fit or appearance. —try out **1** To attempt to qualify: He *tried out* for the team. **2** To test the result or effect of. —*n. pl.* tries The act of trying; trial. [< OF *trier* sift, pick out] —tri′er *n.* • try and, try to These constructions are both standard in modern English: *Try and meet me at six; Try to finish your work on time.* However, *try to* is usu. preferable in precise, formal writing.

**tryst** (trist, trīst) *n.* **1** An appointment to meet at a specified time or place. **2** The meeting place agreed upon. **3** The meeting so agreed upon. [< OF *triste, tristre* an appointed station in hunting]

**T-shirt** (tē′shûrt′) *n.* A knitted cotton undershirt with short sleeves.

**tu·ba** (t′ōō′bə) *n. pl.* **·bas** or **·bae** (-bē) A large bass instrument of the tuba family. [< L, a war trumpet]

**tube** (t′ōōb) *n.* **1** A long hollow cylindrical body of metal, glass, rubber, etc., generally used to convey or hold a liquid or gas. **2** Any device having a tube or tubelike part, as a telescope. *Biol.* Any elongated hollow part

or organ. **4** A subway or subway tunnel. **5** An electron tube. **6** A collapsible metal or plastic cylinder for containing paints, toothpaste, glue, and the like. —the tube *Slang* Television. —*v.t.* tubed, tub·ing **1** To fit or furnish with a tube. **2** To make tubular. [< L *tubus*] —tu′bal adj.

**tu·ber** (t′ōō′bər) *n.* **1** A short, thickened portion of an underground stem, as a potato. **2** A tubercle. [L, a swelling]

**tu·ber·cu·lo·sis** (t′ōō·bûr′kyə·lō′sis) *n.* A communicable disease caused by the tubercle bacillus and characterized by tubercles in the lungs or other organs or tissues of the body. —tu·ber′cu·lous (t′ōō·bûr′kyə-ləs) *adj.*

**tuck** (tuk) *v.t.* **1** To thrust or press in the ends or edges of: to *tuck* in a blanket. **2** To wrap or cover snugly. **3** To thrust or press into a close place; cram. **4** To make tucks in, by folding and stitching. —*v.i.* **5** To contract; draw together. **6** To make tucks. —*n.* **1** A fold sewed into a garment. **2** Any inserted or folded thing. **3** A position in diving in which the knees are bent and the upper legs pressed against the chest. [< OE *tūcian* ill-treat, lit., tug]

**Tues·day** (t′ōōz′dē, -dā) *n.* The third day of the week. [< OE *tīwesdǣg* day of Tiw, a god of war]

**tug** (tug) *v.* **tugged, tug·ging** *v.t.* **1** To pull at with effort; strain at. **2** To pull or drag with effort. **3** To tow with a tugboat. —*v.i.* **4** To pull strenuously: to *tug* at an oar. **5** To strive; struggle. —*n.* **1** A violent pull. **2** A strenuous contest. **3** A tugboat. **4** A trace of a harness. [< OE *tēon* tow] —tug′ger *n.* — Syn. *n.* 2 draw, haul, heave, lug.

**tu·i·tion** (t′ōō·ish′ən) *n.* **1** The act or business of teaching. **2** The charge or payment for instruction. [< L *tuitio* a guard, guardianship] —tu·i′tion·al, tu·i′tion·ar′y (-er′ē) *adj.*

**tu·lip** (t′ōō′lip) *n.* **1** Any of numerous bulbous plants of the lily family, bearing variously colored cup-shaped flowers. **2** A bulb or flower of this plant. [< Turkish *tuliband* turban]

**tum·ble** (tum′bəl) *v.* **·bled, ·bling** *v.i.* **1** To roll or toss about. **2** To perform acrobatic feats, as somersaults, etc. **3** To fall violently or awkwardly. **4** To move in a careless or headlong manner; stumble. **5** *Informal* To understand; comprehend: with *to.* —*v.t.* **6** To toss carelessly; cause to fall. **7** To throw into disorder; rumple. —*n.* **1** The act of tumbling; a fall. 2 A state of disorder or confusion. [< OE *tumbian* fall, leap]

**tu·mid** (t$\overline{oo}$′mid) *adj.* 1 Swollen; enlarged, protuberant. 2 Inflated or pompous. [< L *tumidus* < *tumere* swell] —**tu·mid′i·ty, tu′mid·ness** *n.*

**tu·mor** (t$\overline{oo}$′mər) *n.* A local swelling on or in the body, esp. from growth of tissue having no physiological function. *Brit. sp.* **tu′mour.** [< L *tumere* to swell] —**tu′mor·ous** *adj.*

**tu·mult** (t$\overline{oo}$′mult) *n.* 1 The commotion, disturbance, or agitation of a multitude; an uproar. 2 Any violent commotion. 3 Mental or emotional agitation. [< L *tumultus* < *tumere* swell] —**Syn.** ferment, hubbub, racket, turbulence.

**tu·mul·tu·ous** (t$\overline{oo}$·mul′ch$\overline{oo}$·əs) *adj.* 1 Characterized by tumult; disorderly; violent. 2 Greatly agitated or disturbed. 3 Stormy; tempestuous. —**tu·mul′tu·ous·ly** *adv.* —**tu·mul′tu·ous·ness** *n.*

**tune** (t$\overline{oo}$n) *n.* 1 A coherent succession of musical tones; a melody or air. 2 Correct musical pitch or key. 3 Fine adjustment: the *tune* of an engine. 4 State of mind; humor: He will change his *tune.* 5 Concord; agreement: to be out of *tune* with the times. —**sing a difficult tune** To assume a different style or attitude. —**to the tune of** *Informal* To the amount of: *to the tune of* ten dollars. —*v.* **tuned, tun·ing** *v.t.* 1 To put into tune; adjust precisely. 2 To adapt to a particular tone, expression, or mood. 3 To bring into harmony or accord. —*v.i.* 4 To be in harmony. —**tune in** 1 To adjust a radio or television receiver to (a station, program, etc.) 2 *Slang* To become or cause to become aware, knowing, or sophisticated. —**tune out** 1 To adjust a radio or television receiver to exclude (interference, a station, etc.). 2 *Slang* To turn one's interest or attention away from. —**tune up** 1 To bring (musical instruments) to a common pitch. 2 To adjust (a machine, engine, etc.) to proper working order. [< ME *tone* tone] —**tun′er** *n.*

**tung·sten** (tung′stən) *n.* A hard, heavy metallic element (symbol W), having a high melting point, used to make filaments for electric lamps and various alloys. [Sw. < *tung* weighty + *sten* stone]

**tu·nic** (t$\overline{oo}$′nik) *n.* 1 Among the ancient Greeks and Romans, a loose body garment, with or without sleeves, reaching to the knees. 2 A modern outer garment gathered at the waist, as a short overskirt or a blouse. 3 A short coat worn as part of a uniform. 4 *Biol.* A mantle of tissue covering an organism or a part: also **tu′ni·ca** (-kə) [< L *tunica*]

**tun·nel** (tun′əl) *n.* 1 An underground passageway or gallery, as for a railway or roadway. 2 Any similar passageway under or through something. 3 A burrow. —*v.* **·neled** or **·nelled, ·nel·ling** or **·nel·ling** *v.t.* 1 To make a tunnel or similar passage through or under. 2 To proceed by digging or as if by digging a tunnel. —*v.i.* 3 To make a tunnel. [< OF *tonne* a cask] —**tun′nel·er** or **tun′nel·ier** *n.*

**tur·ban** (tûr′bən) *n.* 1 A head covering consisting of a sash or shawl, twisted about the head or about a cap, worn by men in the Orient. 2 Any similar headdress. [< Pers. *dulband* < *dul* a turn + *band* a band] —**tur′baned** (-bənd) *adj.*

**tur·bid** (tûr′bid) *adj.* 1 Muddy or opaque: a *turbid* stream. 2 Dense; heavy: *turbid* clouds of smoke. 3 Confused; disturbed. [< L *turbidus* < *turbare* to trouble] —**tur′bid·ly** *adv.* —**tur′bid·ness, tur·bid·i·ty** (tûr·bid′ə·tē) *n.* • **turbid, turgid** Because these words sound alike, they are often confused: *Turbid* usu. refers to water, smoke, etc., so filled with sediment or particles as to be opaque. *Turgid* means abnormally swollen or inflated.

**tur·bine** (tûr′bin, -bīn) *n.* An engine consisting of one or more rotary units, mounted on a shaft and provided with a series of vanes, actuated by steam, water, gas, or other fluid under pressure. [< L *turbo* a whirlwind, top]

**tur·bo·jet** (tûr′bō·jet′) *n. Aeron.* A jet engine that uses a gas turbine to drive the air compressor.

**tur·bu·lent** (tûr′byə·lənt) *adj.* 1 Violently disturbed or agitated: a *turbulent* sea. 2 Inclined to rebel; insubordinate. 3 Having a tendency to disturb. [< L *turbulentus* full of disturbance] —**tur′bu·lence, tur′bu·len·cy** *n.* —**tur′bu·lent·ly** *adv.* —**Syn.** 1 stormy, tumultuous, wild. 2 obstreperous, unruly.

**tu·reen** (t$\overline{oo}$·rēn′) *n.* A large, deep, covered dish, as for soup. [< F *terrine*]

**turf** (tûrf) *n. pl.* **turfs** (*Archaic* **turves**) 1 A mass of grass and its matted roots. 2 A plot of grass. 3 Peat. 4 *Slang* **a** A home territory, esp. that of a youthful street gang, defended against invasion by rival gangs. **b** Any place regarded possessively as the center of one's activity or interest: Philadelphia is his home *turf.* —**the turf 1** A racecourse. **2** Horse racing. —*v.t.* To cover with turf; sod. [< OE]

**tur·gid** (tûr′jid) *adj.* **1** Unnaturally distended; swollen. **2** Using high-flown language; bombastic: *turgid* prose. [< L *turgere* swell] — **tur·gid·i·ty** (tər·jid′ə·tē), **tur′gid·ness** *n.* — **tur′gid·ly** *adv.* • See TURBID.

**tur·key** (tûr′kē) *n. pl.* **·keys 1** A large North American bird related to the pheasant, having the head naked and a spreading tail. **2** The edible flesh of this bird. **3** *Slang* A play or a motion picture that fails. [From mistaken identification with a guinea fowl originating in *Turkey*]

**tur·moil** (tûr′moil) *n.* Confused motion; disturbance; tumult. [?]

**turn** (tûrn) *v.t.* **1** To cause to rotate, as about an axis. **2** To change the position of, as by rotating: to *turn* a trunk on its side. **3** To move so that the upper side becomes the under: to *turn* a page. **4** To reverse the arrangement or order of; cause to be upside down. **5** To ponder: often with *over.* **6** To sprain or strain: to *turn* one's ankle in running. **7** To make sick or disgusted: The sight *turns* my stomach. **8** To shape in a lathe. **9** To give rounded or curved form to. **10** To give graceful or finished form to: to *turn* a phrase. **11** To perform by revolving: to *turn* cartwheels. **12** To bend, curve, fold, or twist. **13** To bend or blunt (the edge of a knife, etc.). **14** To change or transform: to *turn* water into wine. **15** To translate: to *turn* French into English. **16** To exchange for an equivalent: to *turn* stocks into cash. **17** To cause to become as specified: The sight *turned* him sick. **18** To make sour or rancid; ferment or curdle. **19** To change the direction of. **20** To change the direction or focus of (thought, attention, etc.). **21** To deflect or divert: to *turn* a blow. **22** To repel: to *turn* a charge. **23** To go around: to *turn* a corner. **24** To pass or go beyond: to *turn* twenty-one. **25** To compel to go; drive: to *turn* a beggar from one's door. —*v.i.* **26** To rotate; revolve. **27** To move completely or partially on or as if on an axis: He *turned* and ran. **28** To change position, as in bed. **29** To take a new direction: We *turned* north. **30** To reverse position; become inverted. **31** To reverse direction or flow: The tide has *turned.* **32** To change the direction of one's thought, attention, etc.: Let us *turn* to the next problem. **33** To depend; hinge: with *on* or *upon.* **34** To be affected with giddiness; whirl, as the head. **35** To become upset, as the stomach. **36** To change attitude, sympathy, or allegiance: to *turn* on one's neighbors. **37** To become transformed; change: The water *turned* into ice. **38** To become as specified: His hair *turned* gray. **39** To change color: said esp. of leaves. **40** To become sour or fermented, as milk or wine. —**turn against** To become or cause to become opposed or hostile to. —**turn down 1** To diminish the flow, volume, etc., of: *Turn down* the gas. **2** *Informal.* **a** To reject or refuse, as a proposal, or request. **b** To refuse the request, proposal, etc., of. —**turn in 1** To fold or double. **2** To bend or incline inward. **3** To deliver; hand over. **4** *Informal* To go to bed. —**turn off 1** To stop the operation, flow, etc., of. **2** To leave the direct road; make a turn. **3** To deflect or divert. **4** *Slang* To cause (a person) to lose interest in or liking for. —**turn on 1** To set in operation, flow, etc.: to *turn* on an engine. **2** *Slang* To experience the effects of taking a psychedelic drug. **3** *Slang* To arrange for (someone) to take such a drug. **4** *Slang* To evoke in (someone) a profound or rapt response. —**turn out 1** To turn inside out. **2** To eject or expel. **3** To bend or incline outward. **4** To produce or make. **5** To come or go out: to *turn out* for a meeting. **6** To prove (to be). **7** To equip or fit; dress. **8** *Informal* To get out of bed. —**turn over 1** To change the position of. **2** To upset; overturn. **3** To hand over; transfer. **4** To do business to the amount of. **5** To invest and get back (capital). —**turn to 1** To set to work. **2** To seek aid from. **3** To refer or apply to. —**turn up 1** To fold the under side upward. **2** To incline upward. **3** To find or be found: to *turn up* new evidence. **4** To increase the flow, volume, etc., of. **5** To arrive. —*n.* **1** The act of turning, or the state of being turned. **2** A change to another direction or position: a *turn* of the tide. **3** A deflection from a course; a bend. **4** The point at which a change takes place: a *turn* for the better. **5** A rotation or revolution: the *turn* of a crank. **6** A regular time or chance in some sequence of action: It's his *turn* at bat. **7** Characteristic form or style. **8** Disposition; tendency: a humorous *turn.* **9** A deed: an ill *turn.* **10** A walk or drive: a *turn* in the park. **11** A round in a skein or coil. **12** *Music* An ornament in which the main tone alternates with the seconds above and below. **13** *Informal* A spell of dizziness or nervousness: The explosion gave me quite a turn. 14 A variation or difference in type or kind. 15 A short theatrical act. 16 A twist, as of a rope, around a tree or post. 17 A business transaction. —at every turn On every occasion; constantly. —by turns 1 In alternation or sequence: also turn by turn. 2 At intervals. —in turn One after another. —out of turn Not in proper order or sequence. —to a turn Just right: meat browned to a turn. —take turns To act, play, etc. in proper order. [< L tornare turn in a lathe < turnus a lathe] —turn′er n.

turn·buck·le (tûrn′buk′əl) n. Mech. A threaded coupling that receives a threaded rod at each end so that it may be turned to regulate the distance between them.

tur·nip (tûr′nip) n. 1 The fleshy, yellow or white edible root of certain plants related to cabbage. 2 Any of these plants. [< Earlier turnepe]

turn·out (tûrn′out′) n. 1 A turning out. 2 An assemblage of persons, as at a meeting: a good turnout. 3 A quantity produced; output. 4 Array; equipment; outfit. 5 A railroad siding. 6 A carriage or wagon with its horses and equipage.

turn·o·ver (tûrn′ō′vər) n. 1 An upset. 2 A change or revolution: a turnover in affairs. 3 A tart made by covering half of a circular crust with fruit, jelly, etc., and turning the other half over on top. 4 The amount of money taken in and paid out in a business within a given period. 5 The selling out and restocking of goods, as in a store. 6 The rate at which persons hired within a given period are replaced by others; also, the number of persons hired. —adj. Turning over, or capable of being turned over.

turn·pike (tûrn′pīk′) n. 1 A road on which there are, or formerly were, tollgates: also turnpike road. 2 TOLLGATE. [ME turnpyke a spiked road barrier <TURN, v. + PIKE[1]]

turn·stile (tûrn′stīl′) n. A kind of gate consisting of a vertical post and horizontal arms which by revolving permit persons to pass.

turn·ta·ble (tûrn′tā′bəl) n. 1 A rotating platform, usu. circular, on which to turn a locomotive or other vehicle around. 2 The revolving disk of a phonograph on which records are played.

tur·pen·tine (tûr′pən·tīn) n. 1 A resinous, oily liquid obtained from any of several coniferous trees. 2 The colorless essential oil (oil of turpentine) formed when turpentine is

distilled, widely used in industry, medicine, and in mixing paints. —v.t. ·tined, ·tin·ing To treat or saturate with turpentine. [< L terebinthus a Mediterranean tree]

tur·pi·tude (tûr′pə·t′ood) n. Inherent baseness; depravity. [< L turpis vile] —Syn. corruption, degeneracy, vileness, wickedness.

tur·quoise (tûr′koiz, -kwoiz) n. 1 A blue or blue-green stone, esteemed as a gemstone when highly polished. 2 A light, greenish blue: also turquoise blue. —adj. Light, greenish blue. [< MF (pierre) turquoise Turkish (stone)]

tur·ret (tûr′it) n. 1 A small projecting tower, usu. at the corner of a building. 2 Mil. A rotating armed structure containing guns and gunners, forming part of a warship or tank. 3 A structure for a gunner on a combat airplane, usu. enclosed in transparent plastic material. [<OF tor tower] —tu·r′ret·ed adj.

tusk (tusk) n. A long, projecting tooth, as in the boar, walrus, or elephant. —v.t. To use the tusks to gore, root up, etc. [< OE tūx]

tus·sle (tus′əl) v.t. & v.i. ·sled, ·sling 1 To scuffle or struggle. 2 To argue. —n. 1 A scuffle or struggle. 2 An argument. [Var. of TOUSLE]

tus·sock (tus′ək) n. 1 A tuft or clump of grass or sedge. 2 A tuft, as of hair or feathers. [?] —tus′sock·y adj.

tu·te·lage (t′oo′tə·lij) n. 1 The state of being under the care of a tutor or guardian. 2 The act or office of a guardian. 3 The act of tutoring; instruction. [< L tutela a watching, guardianship]

tu·te·lar·y (t′oo′tə·ler′ē) adj. 1 Watching over; protecting. 2 Of or pertaining to a guardian. Also tu′te·lar. —n. pl. ·ar·ies A guardian spirit, divinity, etc.

tu·tor (t′oo′tər) n. 1 A private teacher. 2 A college teacher who gives individual instruction. 3 Brit. A college official entrusted with the tutelage and care of undergraduates assigned to him. —v.t. 1 To act as tutor to; train. 2 To treat sternly; discipline. —v.i. 3 To do the work of a tutor. 4 To be tutored or instructed. [< L, a watcher, guardian]

tux·e·do (tuk·sē′dō) n. pl. ·dos 1 A man's semiformal dinner or evening jacket without tails. 2 The suit of which the jacket is a part. Also Tux·e′do. [< Tuxedo Park, N.Y.]

twad·dle (twod′l) v.t. & v.i. ·dled, ·dling To talk foolishly and pretentiously. —n. Pretentious, silly talk. [?] —twad′dler n.

**twain** (twān) *adj. & n. Archaic* Two. [< OE *twēgen* two]

**twang** (twang) *v.t. & v.i.* **twanged, twang·ing** 1 To make or cause to make a sharp, vibrant sound. 2 To utter or speak with a harsh, nasal sound. —*n.* 1 A sharp, vibrating sound. 2 A sharp, nasal sound of the voice. 3 A sound resembling these. [Imit.] —**twang'y** *adj.* (·i·er, ·i·est)

**tweak** (twēk) *v.t.* To pinch and twist sharply. —*n.* A twisting pinch. [< OE *twiccan* twitch]

**tweed** (twēd) *n.* 1 A woolen fabric often woven in two or more colors to effect a check or plaid pattern. 2 *pl.* Clothes made of tweed. [< Scot. *tweel*, var. of TWILL]

**tweet·er** (twē'tər) *n.* A loudspeaker specially designed to reproduce only high-frequency sounds.

**tweez·ers** (twē'zərz) *n.pl. (construed as sing. or pl.)* Small pincers for picking up or extracting tiny objects. **Also pair of tweezers.** [< F *étui* a small case]

**twelfth** (twelfth) *adj. & adv.* Next in order after the 11th. —*n.* 1 The element of an ordered set that corresponds to the number 12. 2 One of 12 equal parts. [< OE *twelfta*]

**twice** (twis) *adv.* 1 Two times. 2 In double measure; doubly. [< OE *twiga*]

**twig** (twig) *n.* A small shoot or branch of a woody plant. [< OE *twigge*]

**twi·light** (twī'līt') *n.* 1 The light diffused over the sky after sunset and before sunrise. 2 The period during which this light prevails. 3 Any faint light; shade. 4 An obscure condition following the waning of past glory, achievements, etc. —*adj.* Pertaining or peculiar to twilight. [< OE < *twa* two + LIGHT]

**twill** (twil) *n.* 1 Cloth woven in such a way as to produce diagonal, parallel ribs or lines. 2 The pattern formed by such weaving. —*v.t.* To weave (cloth) with a twill. [< OE *twili* a twilled fabric]

**twin** (twin) *n.* 1 Either of two young produced at the same birth. 2 Either of two persons or things greatly alike. —**the Twins** GEMINI. —*adj.* 1 Being a twin or twins: *twin* boys. 2 Being one of a pair of similar and closely related people or things. —*v.* **twinned, twin·ning** *v.i.* 1 To bring forth twins. 2 To be matched or equal. —*v.t.* 3 To bring forth as twins. 4 To couple; match. [< OE *twinn, getwinn*]

**twine** (twīn) *v.* **twined, twin·ing** *v.t.* 1 To twist together, as threads. 2 To form by such twisting. 3 To coil or wrap about something. 4 To encircle by winding or wreathing. —*v.i.*

5 To interlace. 6 To proceed in a winding course; meander. —*n.* 1 A string composed of two or more strands twisted together. 2 The act of twining or entwining. 3 A thing produced by twining. [< OE *twin* a twisted double thread < *twa* two] —**twin'er** *n.* —**twin'ing·ly** *adv.*

**twinge** (twinj) *v.t. & v.i.* **twinged, twing·ing** To affect with or suffer a sudden pain. —*n.* 1 A sharp, darting, local pain. 2 A mental pang. [< OE *twengan* pinch] —**Syn.** *n.* 1 ache, cramp, throe.

**twin·kle** (twing'kəl) *v.* ·**kled, ·kling** *v.i.* 1 To shine with fitful, intermittent gleams. 2 To be bright, as with amusement: Her eyes *twinkled.* 3 To wink or blink. 4 To move rapidly to and fro; flicker: *twinkling* feet. —*v.t.* 5 To cause to twinkle. 6 To emit (light) in fitful, intermittent gleams. —*n.* 1 A tremulous gleam of light; glimmer. 2 A quick or repeated movement of the eyelids. 3 An instant; a twinkling. [< OE *twinclian*] —**twin'kler** *n.*

**twirl** (twûrl) *v.t. & v.i.* 1 To whirl or rotate rapidly. 2 To twist or curl. 3 In baseball, to pitch. —*n.* 1 A whirling motion. 2 A curl; twist; coil. [?] —**twirl'er** *n.*

**twist** (twist) *v.t.* 1 To wind (strands, etc.) around each other. 2 To form by such winding: to *twist* thread. 3 To give a spiral shape to. 4 To deform or distort, esp. by means of torque. 5 To distort the meaning of. 6 To confuse; perplex. 7 To wreathe, twine, or wrap. 8 To cause to revolve or rotate. 9 To impart spin to (a ball) so that it moves in a curve. —*v.i.* 10 To become twisted. 11 To move in a winding course. 12 To squirm; writhe. —*n.* 1 The act, manner, or result of twisting. 2 The state of being twisted. 3 *Physics* A torsional strain. 4 A curve; turn; bend. 5 A wrench; strain, as of a joint or limb. 6 A peculiar inclination or attitude: a mind with a criminal *twist.* 7 An unexpected turn or development. 8 A variant or novel approach or method: a mystery novel with a new *twist.* 9 Thread or cord made of tightly twisted or braided strands. 10 A twisted roll of bread. 11 A spin given to a ball by a certain stroke or throw. [< OE · *twist* a rope]

**twitch** (twich) *v.t.* 1 To pull sharply; pluck with a jerky movement. —*v.i.* 2 To move with a quick, spasmodic jerk, as a muscle. —*n.* 1 A sudden involuntary contraction of a muscle. 2 A sudden jerk or pull. [ME *twicchen*]

**twit·ter** (twit′ər) *v.i.* 1 To utter a series of light chirping or tremulous notes, as a bird. 2 To titter. 3 To be excited. —*v.t.* 4 To utter or express with a twitter. —*n.* 1 A succession of light, tremulous sounds. 2 A state of excitement. [Imit.]

**type** (tīp) *n.* 1 A class or group having traits and characteristics in common: an old *type* of car. 2 A standard or model. 3 The characteristic plan, form, style, etc., of a given class or group. 4 A person, animal, or object embodying the characteristics of a class or group. 5 *Printing* a A piece or block of metal or of wood bearing, usu. in relief, a letter or character for use in printing. b Such pieces collectively. 6 Typewritten or printed letters and numerals. 7 The characteristic device on either side of a medal or coin. —*v.* **typed, typ·ing** *v.t.* 1 To represent; typify. 2 To determine the type of; identify: to *type* a blood sample. 3 TYPEWRITE. 4 To prefigure. —*v.i.* 5 TYPEWRITE. [< Gk. *typos* an impression, figure, type]

**type·set·ter** (tīp′set′ər) *n.* 1 One who sets type. 2 A machine for setting type. —**type′set′ting** *adj.*, *n.*

**type·writ·er** (tīp′rī′tər) *n.* 1 A keyboard machine for producing characters, as letters, numbers, etc., that have the appearance of printer's type. 2 A typist.

**typhoid fever** A serious infectious disease caused by a bacillus transmitted in contaminated water or food and characterized by high fever, severe intestinal disturbances, and prostration.

**ty·phoon** (tī·fōōn′) *n.* A violent tropical storm, occurring in the w Pacific. [< Chin. *tai feng*, lit., big wind]

**ty·phus** (tī′fəs) *n.* Any of a group of contagious rickettsial diseases marked by high fever, a rash, nervous and mental disorders, and extreme prostration. [< Gk. *typhos* smoke, a stupor] —**ty′phous** *adj.*

**typ·i·cal** (tip′i·kəl) *adj.* 1 Having the nature or character of a type: a *typical* schoolboy. 2 Characteristic or representative of a group, class, etc.: *typical* middle-class values. [< Gk. *typos* TYPE] —**typ′i·cal·ly** *adv.* —**typ′i·cal·ness** *n.*

**typ·i·fy** (tip′ə·fī) *v.t.* **·fied, ·fy·ing** 1 To represent by a type. 2 To serve as a characteristic example of. —**typ′i·fi·ca′tion** (-fə·kā′shən) *n.* —**typ′i·fi′er** *n.*

**typ·ist** (tī′pist) *n.* 1 One who uses a typewriter. 2 A person whose work is operating a typewriter.

**ty·pog·ra·pher** (tī·pog′rə·fər) *n.* An expert in typography, esp. a printer or compositor.

**ty·po·graph·i·cal** (tī′pə·graf′i·kəl) *adj.* Of or pertaining to printing. Also **ty′po·graph′ic.** —**ty′po·graph′i·cal·ly** *adv.*

**ty·pog·ra·phy** (tī·pog′rə·fē) *n.* 1 The arrangement, style, and appearance of printed matter. 2 The act or art of composing and printing from types.

**ty·ran·ni·cal** (ti·ran′i·kəl, tī-) *adj.* Of or like a tyrant; despotic; arbitrary. Also **ty·ran′nic.** —**ty·ran′ni·cal·ly** *adv.* —**ty·ran′ni·cal·ness** *n.*

**tyr·an·nize** (tir′ə·nīz) *v.* **·nized, ·niz·ing** *v.i.* 1 To exercise power cruelly or unjustly. 2 To rule as a tyrant; have absolute power. —*v.t.* 3 To treat tyrannically; domineer. —**tyr′an·niz′er** *n.*

**tyr·an·nous** (tir′ə·nəs) *adj.* Despotic; tyrannical. —**tyr′an·nous·ly** *adv.* —**tyr′an·nous·ness** *n.*

**tyr·an·ny** (tir′ə·nē) *n. pl.* **·nies** 1 The office, power, or jurisdiction of a tyrant. 2 A government or ruler having absolute power; despot or despotism. 3 Power used in a cruel or oppressive manner. 4 Harsh rigor; severity. 5 A tyrannical act. [< L *tyrannus* a tyrant]

**ty·rant** (tī′rənt) *n.* 1 One who rules oppressively or cruelly; a despot. 2 Any person who exercises power or authority in a harsh, cruel manner. [< Gk. *tyrannos* a master, a usurper]

**ty·ro** (tī′rō) *n. pl.* **·ros** One who is beginning to learn or study something; novice. [< L *tiro* a recruit]

# U

**u·biq·ui·tous** (yōō·bik′wə·təs) *adj.* Existing, or seeming to exist, everywhere at once; omnipresent. —**u·biq′ui·tous·ly** *adv.* —**u·biq′ui·tous·ness** *n.*

**u·biq·ui·ty** (yōō·bik′wə·tē) *n.* The state of being or seeming to be everywhere at the same time; omnipresence, real or seeming. [< L *ubique* everywhere]

**ud·der** (ud′ər) *n.* A large, pendulous, milk-secreting gland having nipples or teats for the suckling of offspring, as in cows. [< OE *ūder*]

**ug·ly** (ug′lē) *adj.* **·li·er, ·li·est** 1 Distasteful in appearance; unsightly. 2 Distasteful to any of the senses. 3 Morally revolting or repulsive. 4 Bad in character or consequences, as a rumor or a wound. 5 Ill-tempered;

quarrelsome. 6 Portending storms; threatening. [< ON *uggligr* dreadful < *uggr* fear] — **ug′li·ly** *adv.* —**ug′li·ness** *n.* —**Syn.** 1 homely, ill-looking, unlovely, unseemly. 2 repulsive, repellent, repugnant, revolting, abhorrent, disgusting. 5 ill-humored, irascible, irritable, testy, querulous.

**u·kase** (yōō·kās′, -kāz′, yōō′kās, ōō·kōz′) *n.* 1 In imperial Russia, an edict or decree of the czar. 2 Any official decree. [<Russ. *ukaz*]

**u·ku·le·le** (yōō′kə·lā′lē; *Hawaiian* ōō′kōō·lā′lā) *n.* A small, guitarlike musical instrument having four strings. [Hawaiian <*uku* insect + *lele* jump; from the movements of the fingers in playing]

**ul·cer** (ul′sər) *n.* 1 An open sore on skin or mucous membrane with disintegration of tissue. 2 Any evil or corrupt condition or vice. [< L *ulcus, ulceris*] —**ul′cer·ous** *adj.* —**ul′cer·ous·ly** *adv.*

**ul·cer·ate** (ul′sə·rāt) *v.t.* & *v.i.* **·at·ed, ·at·ing** To make or become ulcerous. —**ul′cer·a′tion** *n.* —**ul′cer·a′tive** *adj.*

**ul·ti·mate** (ul′tə·mit) *adj.* 1 Beyond which there is no other; maximum, greatest, utmost, etc. 2 Last; final, as of a series. 3 Most distant or remote; farthest. 4 Not susceptible of further analysis; elementary; primary. —*n.* The best, latest, most fundamental, etc., of something. [< L *ultimus* farthest, last, superl. of *ulter* beyond] —**ul′ti·mate·ness** *n.*

**ul·ti·ma·tum** (ul′tə·mā′təm, -mä′-) *n. pl.* **·tums** or **·ta** (-tə) A final statement of terms, demands, or conditions, the rejection of which usu. results in a breaking off of all negotiations, a resorting to force, etc. [<L *ultimus* last, ultimate]

**ul·tra·high frequency** (ul′trə·hī′) Any wave frequency between 300 and 3,000 megahertz.

**ul·tra·ma·rine** (ul′trə·mə·rēn′) *n.* 1 A deep purplish blue pigment. 2 The color of ultramarine. —*adj.* Beyond or across the sea. [<L *ultra* beyond + *mare* sea]

**ul·tra·son·ic** (ul′trə·son′ik) *adj.* Pertaining to or designating sound waves having a frequency above the limits of audibility.

**ul·tra·vi·o·let** (ul′trə·vī′ə·lit) *adj.* Having wavelengths shorter than those of visible violet light and longer than those of X-rays.

**um·ber** (um′bər) *n.* 1 A chestnut- to liverbrown iron oxide earth, used as a pigment. 2 The color of umber, either in its natural state (**raw umber**), or heated, so as to produce a reddish brown (**burnt umber**). —*adj.* 1 Of or pertaining to umber. 2 Of the color of umber. —*v.t.* To color with umber. [<F (*terre d′*)*ombre*<Ital. *ombra*<L *umbra* shade, shadow]

**um·brage** (um′brij) *n.* 1 A feeling of anger or resentment, esp. in the phrase **take umbrage,** to have such feelings. 2 That which gives shade, as a leafy tree. 3 Shade or shadow. [<L *umbraticus* shady<*umbra* shade] —**um·bra′geous** (-brā′jəs) *adj.* —**um·bra′geous·ly** *adv.*

**um·brel·la** (um·brel′ə) *n.* 1 A light portable canopy on a folding frame, carried as a protection against sun or rain. 2 A usu. radial formation of military aircraft, used as a protective screen for operations on the ground or on water. 3 Something serving as a cover or shield, or as a means of linking together various things under a common name or sponsor: the expanding *umbrella* of nuclear power. [< L *umbella* parasol, dim. of *umbra* shadow]

**um·pire** (um′pīr) *n.* 1 A person called upon to settle a disagreement or dispute. 2 In various games, as baseball, a person chosen to enforce the rules of the game and to settle disputed points. —*v.t.* & *v.i.* **·pired, ·pir·ing** To act as umpire (of or in). [Alter. of ME *noumpere*]

**un·af·fect·ed** (un′ə·fek′tid) *adj.* 1 Not showing affectation; natural; sincere. 2 Not influenced or changed. —**un′af·fect′ed·ly** *adv.* —**un′af·fect′ed·ness** *n.*

**u·nan·i·mous** (yōō·nan′ə·məs) *adj.* 1 Sharing the same views or sentiments. 2 Showing or resulting from the assent of all concerned: the *unanimous* voice of the jury. [< L *unus* one + *animus* mind] —**u·na·nim·i·ty** (yōō′nə·nim′ə·tē) *n.* —**u·nan′i·mous·ly** *adv.*

**un·as·sum·ing** (un′ə·sōō′ming) *adj.* Not pretentious; modest. —**un′as·sum′ing·ly** *adv.*

**un·bal·anced** (un·bal′ənst) *adj.* 1 Not in a state of equilibrium. 2 In bookkeeping, not adjusted so as to balance. 3 Lacking mental balance; unsound; erratic.

**un·bear·a·ble** (un·bâr′ə·bəl) *adj.* Not to be borne; intolerable; insufferable. —**un′bear′a·bly** *adv.*

**un·be·com·ing** (un′bi·kum′ing) *adj.* 1 Not becoming or appropriate, as a dress. 2 Not fitting or decorous; improper. —**un′be·com′ing·ly** *adv.* —**un′be·com′ing·ness** *n.*

**un·bend** (un·bend′) *v.* **·bent, ·bend·ing** *v.t.* 1 To relax, as from exertion or formality. 2 To straighten (something bent or curved). 3 To relax, as a bow, from tension. 4 *Naut.* To loose or detach, as a rope or sail. —v.i. 5 To become free of restraint or formality; relax. 6 To become straight or nearly straight again.

**un·bi·ased** (un·bī'əst) *adj.* Having no bias; not prejudiced; impartial. **Also un·bi' assed.** —**un·bi'ased·ly** *adv.* —**un·bi'ased·ness** *n.*

**un·bound·ed** (un·boun'did) *adj.* 1 Having no bounds or limits; boundless. 2 Going beyond bounds; unrestrained. —**un·bound'ed·ly** *adv.* —**un·bound'ed·ness** *n.*

**un·bro·ken** (un·brō'kən) *adj.* 1 Not broken; whole; entire. 2 Not violated: an *unbroken* promise. 3 Uninterrupted; continuous. 4 Not tamed or trained. 5 Not bettered or surpassed. 6 Not disarranged or thrown out of order.

**un·can·ny** (un·kan'ē) *adj.* 1 Weird; unnatural; eerie. 2 So good as to seem almost supernatural in origin: *uncanny* accuracy. —**un·can'ni·ly** *adv.* —**un·can'ni·ness** *n.*

**un·civ·i·lized** (un·siv'ə·līzd) *adj.* 1 Not civilized; barbarous. 2 Uncouth; rude; gross. 3 Remote from civilization. —**Syn.** 1 savage, brutish, brutal, ferocious. 2 crude, cross, boorish, churlish, vulgar, coarse.

**un·cle** (ung'kəl) *n.* 1 The brother of one's father or mother. 2 The husband of one's aunt. 3 *Informal* An elderly man; used in direct address. 4 *Slang* A pawnbroker. [< L *avunculus* a mother's brother]

**un·clean** (un·klēn') *adj.* 1 Not clean; foul. 2 Morally impure. 3 Ceremonially impure. —**un·clean'ness** *n.*

**un·com·mon** (un·kom'ən) *adj.* 1 Not usual or common. 2 Strange; remarkable. —**un·com'mon·ly** *adv.* —**un·com'mon·ness** *n.*

**un·com·pro·mis·ing** (un·kom'prə·mī'zing) *adj.* Making or admitting of no compromise; inflexible; strict. —**un·com'pro·mis'ing·ly** *adv.* —**Syn.** resolute, steadfast, firm, indomitable, inexorable, tenacious, obstinate.

**un·con·di·tion·al** (un'kən·dish'ən·əl) *adj.* Limited by no conditions; absolute. —**un'con·di'tion·al·ly** *adv.*

**un·con·scion·a·ble** (un·kon'shən·ə·bəl) *adj.* 1 Unbelievably bad, wrong, inequitable, etc.: an *unconscionable* error. 2 Wholly unscrupulous. —**un·con'scion·a·ble·ness** *n.* —**un·con'scion·a·bly** *adv.*

**un·con·scious** (un·kon'shəs) *adj.* 1 Temporarily deprived of consciousness. 2 Not cognizant; unaware: with *of: unconscious* of his charm. 3 Not produced or accompanied

by conscious effort; not intended or known: an *unconscious* pun. 4 Not endowed with consciousness or a mind. 5 Of or having to do with the unconscious. —*n.* That area of the psyche which is not in the immediate field of awareness and whose content may become manifest through dreams, morbid fears and compulsions, etc.: with *the.* —**un·con'scious·ly** *adv.* —**un·con'scious·ness** *n.*

**un·con·sti·tu·tion·al** (un'kon·sti·t<del></del>ō'shən·əl) *adj.* Contrary to or violating the precepts of a constitution. —**un'con·sti·tu'tion·al'i·ty** *n.* —**un·con'sti·tu'tion·al·ly** *adv.*

**un·con·ven·tion·al** (un'kən·ven'shən·əl) *adj.* Not adhering to conventional rules, practices, etc.; informal; free. —**un'con·ven'tion·al'i·ty** *n.* —**un'con·ven'tion·al·ly** *adv.*

**un·couth** (un·kōōth') *adj.* 1 Marked by awkwardness or oddity; outlandish. 2 Coarse, boorish, or unrefined, as in manner or speech. [< OE *uncūth* unknown] —**un·couth'ly** *adv.* —**un·couth'ness** *n.*

**un·cov·er** (un·kuv'ər) *v.t.* 1 To remove a covering from. 2 To make known; disclose. —*v.i.* 3 To remove a covering. 4 To raise or remove the hat, as in token of respect.

**unc·tion** (ungk'shən) *n.* 1 The act of anointing, as for religious or medicinal purposes. 2 A substance used in anointing, as oil. 3 Anything that soothes or palliates. 4 A quality of speech, esp. in religious discourse, that awakens or is intended to awaken deep sympathetic feeling. 5 Excessive or affected sincerity or sympathy in speech or manner. [< L *unctio* < *ungere* anoint]

**unc·tu·ous** (ungk'chōō·əs) *adj.* 1 Like an unguent; greasy. 2 Greasy or soapy to the touch, as certain minerals. 3 Characterized by excessive or affected sincerity, sympathy, concern, etc. 4 Unduly smooth or suave in speech or manner. 5 Having plasticity, as clay. [< L *unctum* ointment, orig. neut. p.p. of *ungere* anoint] —**unc'tu·ous·ly** *adv.* —**unc'tu·ous·ness**, **unc'tu·os'i·ty** (-chōō·os'ə·tē) *n.*

**un·daunt·ed** (un·dôn'tid, -dän'-) *adj.* Not daunted; fearless; intrepid. —**un·daunt'ed·ly** *adv.* —**un·daunt'ed·ness** *n.*

**un·de·cid·ed** (un'di·sī'did) *adj.* 1 Not having the mind made up; irresolute. 2 Not decided upon or determined. —**un'de·cid'ed·ly** *adv.*

**un·der·bid** (un'dər·bid') *v.t.* **·bid**, **·bid·ding** 1 To bid lower than, as in a competition. 2 In bridge, to fail to bid the full value of (a hand). —**un′der·bid′der** n.

**un·der·clothes** (un′dər·klōz′, -klōth z′) n.pl. UNDERWEAR. **Also un′der·cloth′ing.**

**un·der·cur·rent** (un′dər·kûr′ənt) n. 1 A current, as of water or air, below another or below the surface. 2 A hidden drift or tendency, as of popular sentiments.

**un·der·es·ti·mate** (un′dər·es′tə·māt) v.t. ·mat·ed, ·mat·ing To put too low an estimate or valuation upon (things or people). —n. (-mit) An estimate below the just value, expense, opinion, etc. —**un′der·es′ti·ma′tion** n.

**un·der·ex·pose** (un′dər·ik·spōz′) v.t. ·posed, ·pos·ing Phot. To expose (a film) to less light than is required for a clear image. —**un′der·ex·po′sure** (-spō′zhər) n.

**un·der·gar·ment** (un′dər·gär′mənt) n. A garment to be worn beneath outer garments.

**un·der·go** (un′dər·gō′) v.t. ·went, ·gone, ·go·ing 1 To be subjected to; have experience of; suffer. 2 To bear up under; endure.

**un·der·grad·u·ate** (un′dər·graj′ōō-it) n. A student of a university or college who has not taken the bachelor's degree. —adj. Of, being, or for an undergraduate.

**un·der·ground** (un′dər·ground′) adj. 1 Situated, done, or operated beneath the surface of the ground. 2 Done in secret; clandestine. 3 Of, relating to, or characterized by the underground (defs. 3 and 4), their works, actions, etc. —n. 1 That which is beneath the surface of the ground, as a passage or space. 2 Brit. SUBWAY. 3 A group secretly organized to resist or oppose those in control of a government or country: usu. with the. 4 An avant-garde movement in art, cinema, journalism, etc., generally considered to be in opposition to conventional culture or society and whose works are usu. experimental, erotic, or radical in style, content, or purpose: usu. with the. —adv. (un′dər·ground′) 1 Beneath the surface of the ground. 2 In or into hiding, secrecy, etc.

**un·der·hand·ed** (un′dər·han′did) adj. & adv. UNDERHAND. —**un′der·hand′ed·ly** adv. —**un′der·hand′ed·ness** n.

**un·der·lie** (un′dər·lī′) v.t. ·lay, ·lain, ·ly·ing 1 To lie below or under. 2 To be the basis or reason for: What motives underlie his refusal to go? 3 To constitute a first or prior claim or lien over.

**un·der·line** (un′dər·līn′) v.t. ·lined, ·lin·ing 1 To mark with a line underneath; under-

score. 2 To emphasize. —n. A line underneath a word or passage, as for emphasis.

**un·der·ling** (un′dər·ling) n. A subordinate; inferior.

**un·der·mine** (un′dər·mīn′, un′dər·mīn) v.t. ·mined, ·min·ing 1 To excavate beneath; dig a mine or passage under. 2 To weaken by wearing away at the base. 3 To weaken or impair secretly, insidiously, or by degrees.

**un·der·pin·ning** (un′dər·pin′ing) n. 1 Material or framework used to support a wall or building from below. 2 Often pl. Something used or functioning as a basis or foundation: the underpinnings of guilt in our society.

**un·der·rate** (un′dər·rāt′) v.t. ·rat·ed, ·rat·ing To rate too low; underestimate.

**un·der·score** (un′dər·skôr′, -skōr′) v.t. · scored, ·scor·ing To draw a line below, as for emphasis; underline. —n. (un′dər·skôr′, -skōr′) A line drawn beneath a word, etc., as for emphasis.

**un·der·sell** (un′dər·sel′) v.t. ·sold, ·sell·ing 1 To sell at a lower price than. 2 To present or promote, as a point of view or commodity, in an understated manner.

**un·der·shirt** (un′dər·shûrt′) n. A collarless undergarment, usu. without sleeves, worn beneath a shirt.

**un·der·signed** (un′dər·sīnd′) n. The person or persons who have signed their names at the end of a document, letter, etc.

**un·der·stand** (un′dər·stand′) v. ·stood, ·stand·ing v.t. 1 To come to know the meaning or import of. 2 To perceive the nature or character of: I do not understand her. 3 To have comprehension or mastery of: Do you understand German? 4 To be aware of; realize: She understands her position. 5 To have been told; believe: I understand that she went home. 6 To take or interpret: How am I to understand that remark? 7 To accept as a condition or stipulation: It is understood that the tenant will provide his own heat. —v.i. 8 To have understanding; comprehend. 9 To grasp the meaning, significance, etc., of something. 10 To believe or assume something to be the case. 11 To have a sympathetic attitude or tolerance toward something. [< OE under- under + standan stand] —**un′der·stand′a·ble** adj. —**un′der·stand′a·bly** adv.

**un·der·stand·ing** (un′dər·stan′ding) n. 1 An intellectual grasp of something; comprehension. 2 The power or capacity to think, acquire and retain knowledge, interpret experience, etc.; intelligence. 3 An agreement or settlement of differences. 4 An informal or confidential compact or agreement. 5 An individual viewpoint, interpretation, or opinion. 6 A sympathetic comprehension of or tolerance for the feelings, actions, attitudes, etc., of others. —*adj.* Possessing or characterized by comprehension, compassion, etc. —**un′der·stand′ing·ly** *adv.*

**un·der·stud·y** (un′dər·stud′ē) *v.t. & v.i.* **·stud·ied**, **·stud·y·ing** 1 To study (a part) in order to be able, if necessary, to substitute for the actor playing it. 2 To act as an understudy to (another actor). —*n. pl.* **·stud·ies** 1 An actor or actress who can substitute for another actor in a given role. 2 A person prepared to perform the work or fill the position of another.

**un·der·take** (un′dər·tāk′) *v.t.* **·took**, **·tak·en**, **·tak·ing** 1 To take upon oneself; agree or attempt to do. 2 To contract to do; pledge oneself to. 3 To guarantee or promise. 4 To take under charge or guidance.

**un·der·tak·er** (un′dər·tā′kər *for def. 1;* un′dər·tā′kər *for def. 2*) *n.* 1 One who undertakes any work or enterprise; esp. a contractor. 2 One whose business it is to prepare a dead person for burial and to conduct funerals.

**un·der·tak·ing** (un′dər·tā′king, *esp. for def. 3;* un′dər·tā′king) *n.* 1 The act of one who undertakes any task or enterprise. 2 The thing undertaken; an enterprise; task. 3 The business of an undertaker (def. 2). 4 An engagement, promise, or guarantee.

**un·der·tone** (un′dər·tōn′) *n.* 1 A low or subdued tone, esp. a vocal tone, as a whisper. 2 A subdued color, esp. one with other colors imposed on it. 3 A meaning, suggestion, quality, etc., that is implied but not expressed.

**un·der·tow** (un′dər·tō′) *n.* A flow of water beneath and in a direction opposite to the surface current, esp. such a flow moving seaward beneath surf.

**un·der·val·ue** (un′dər·val′yōō) *v.t.* **·ued**, **·u·ing** 1 To value or rate below the real worth. 2 To regard or esteem as of little worth. —**un′der·val′u·a′tion** *n.*

**un·der·wear** (un′dər·wâr′) *n.* Garments worn underneath the ordinary outer garments.

**un·der·write** (un′dər·rīt′) *v.* **·wrote**, **·writ·ten**, **·writ·ing** *v.t.* 1 To write beneath or sign something, as a document. 2 To agree or subscribe to, esp. to agree to pay for (an enterprise, etc.). 3 In insurance: a To sign

one's name to (an insurance policy), thereby assuming liability for certain designated losses or damage. b To insure. c To assume (a risk or a liability for a certain sum) by way of insurance. 4 To engage to buy, at a determined price and time, all or part of the stock in (a new enterprise or company) that is not subscribed for by the public. —*v.i.* 5 To act as an underwriter; esp., to issue a policy of insurance.

**un·der·writ·er** (un′dər·rī′tər) *n.* 1 A person or company in the insurance business; also, an insurance employee who determines the risks involved, the amount of the premiums, etc., for a specific applicant or policy. 2 One who underwrites something.

**un·do** (un·dōō′) *v.t.* **·did**, **·done**, **·do·ing** 1 To cause to be as if never done; reverse, annul, or cancel. 2 To loosen or untie. 3 To unfasten and open. 4 To bring to ruin; destroy. 5 To disturb emotionally. [< OE *undōn*] —**un·do′er** *n.*

**un·dress** (un·dres′) *v.t.* 1 To divest of clothes; strip. 2 To remove the dressing or bandages from, as a wound. 3 To divest of special attire; disrobe. —*v.i.* 4 To remove one's clothing. —*n.* 1 The state of being nude or in only partial attire, as in undergarments, dressing robe, etc. 2 The military or naval uniform worn by officers when not in full dress.

**un·due** (un·dōō′) *adj.* 1 Excessive; immoderate. 2 Not justified by law; illegal. 3 Not yet due, as a bill. 4 Not appropriate; improper.

**un·du·late** (un′dyə·lāt, -jə-) *v.* **·lat·ed**, **·lat·ing** *v.t.* 1 To cause to move like a wave or in waves. 2 To give a wavy appearance or surface to. —*v.i.* 3 To move like a wave or waves. 4 To have a wavy form or appearance. —*adj.* (-lit, -lāt) Having a wavelike appearance, surface, or markings: also **un′du·lat′ed.** [< L *unda* wave]

**un·du·ly** (un·dōō′lē) *adv.* 1 Excessively. 2 Improperly; unjustly.

**un·dy·ing** (un·dī′ing) *adj.* Immortal; eternal.

**un·eas·y** (un·ē′zē) *adj.* **·eas·i·er**, **·eas·i·est** 1 Deprived of ease; disturbed; unquiet. 2 Not comfortable; causing discomfort. 3 Showing embarrassment or constraint; strained. 4 Not stable or secure; precarious: an *uneasy* peace. —**un·eas′i·ly** *adv.* —**un·eas′i·ness** *n.*

**un·e·qual** (un·ē′kwəl) *adj.* 1 Not equal in size, importance, weight, ability, duration, etc. 2 Inadequate; insufficient: with *to.* 3 Not balanced or uniform; variable; irregular. 4 Involving poorly matched competitors or contestants: an *unequal* contest. —**un·e′qual·ly** *adv.*

**un·e·qualed** (un·ē′kwəld) *adj.* Not equaled or matched; unrivaled. Also **un·e′qualled.**

**un·e·quiv·o·cal** (un′i·kwiv′ə·kəl) *adj.* Understandable in only one way; not ambiguous; clear. —**un′e·quiv′o·cal·ly** *adv.* —**un′e·quiv′o·cal·ness** *n.*

**un·err·ing** (un·ûr′ing, -er′-) *adj.* 1 Making no mistakes. 2 Certain; accurate; infallible. —**un·err′ing·ly** *adv.*

**un·e·ven** (un·ē′vən) *adj.* 1 Not even, smooth, or level; rough. 2 Not straight, parallel, or perfectly horizontal. 3 Not equal or even, as in length, width, etc. 4 Not balanced or matched equally. 5 Not uniform; variable; fluctuating. 6 Not fair or just. 7 Not divisible by two without remainder; odd: said of numbers. —**un·e′ven·ly** *adv.* —**un·e′ven·ness** *n.*

**un·fail·ing** (un·fā′ling) *adj.* 1 Giving or constituting a supply that never fails; inexhaustible: an *unfailing* spring. 2 Always fulfilling requirements or expectation. 3 Sure; infallible. —**un·fail′ing·ly** *adv.* —**un·fail′ing·ness** *n.*

**un·fair** (un·fâr′) *adj.* 1 Marked by injustice, deception, or bias; not fair. 2 Not honest or ethical in business affairs. —**un·fair′ly** *adv.* —**un·fair′ness** *n.*

**un·fast·en** (un·fas′ən, -fäs′-) *v.t.* To untie or undo; loosen or open.

**un·feel·ing** (un·fē′ling) *adj.* 1 Not sympathetic; hard; callous. 2 Having no feeling or sensation. —**un·feel′ing·ly** *adv.* —**un·feel′ing·ness** *n.*

**un·feigned** (un·fānd′) *adj.* Not feigned; sincere; genuine. —**un·feign′ed·ly** (-fān′id·lē) *adv.*

**un·flag·ging** (un·flag′ing) *adj.* Not diminishing or failing; tireless. —**un·flag′ging·ly** *adv.*

**un·flinch·ing** (un·flin′ching) *adj.* Done without shrinking; steadfast. —**un·flinch′ing·ly** *adv.*

**un·fold** (un·fōld′) *v.t.* 1 To open or spread out (something folded). 2 To unwrap. 3 To reveal or make clear, as by explaining or disclosing gradually. 4 To develop. —*v.i.* 5 To become opened; expand. 6 To become manifest or develop fully.

**un·for·tu·nate** (un·fôr′chə·nit) *adj.* 1 Not fortunate or lucky. 2 Causing, attended by, or resulting from misfortune; disastrous. 3 Not suitable or proper; bad; regrettable: an

*unfortunate* thing to say. —*n.* One who is unfortunate. —**un·for′tu·nate·ly** *adv.* —**un·for′tu·nate·ness.** *n.*

**un·found·ed** (un·foun′did) *adj.* 1 Not based on fact; groundless; baseless. 2 Not established.

**un·furl** (un·fûrl′) *v.t.* & *v.i.* 1 To unroll, as a flag; spread out. 2 To unfold. —**un·furled′** *adj.*

**un·gain·ly** (un·gān′lē) *adj.* 1 Awkward; clumsy. 2 Not attractive. —**un·gain′li·ness** *n.*

**un·gov·ern·a·ble** (un·guv′ər·nə·bəl) *adj.* That cannot be governed; wild; unruly. —**un·gov′ern·a·bly** *adv.*

**un·guard·ed** (un·gär′did) *adj.* 1 Having no guard; unprotected. 2 Thoughtless; careless. 3 Without guile; direct; open. —**un·guard′ed·ly** *adv.*

**un·guent** (ung′gwənt) *n.* An ointment or salve. [< L *unguere* anoint] —**un′guen·tar′y** (-gwən·ter′ē) *adj.*

**un·hand** (un·hand′) *v.t.* To remove one's hand from; release from the hand or hands; let go.

**un·heard** (un·hûrd′) *adj.* 1 Not perceived by the ear. 2 Not granted a hearing. 3 Obscure; unknown.

**un·heard-of** (un·hûrd′uv′, -ov′) *adj.* 1 Not known of before; unknown or unprecedented. 2 Outrageous; unbelievable.

**u·ni·corn** (yōō′nə·kôrn′) *n.* A mythical, horselike animal with one horn growing from the middle of its forehead. [< L *unicornis* one-horned]

**u·ni·form** (yōō′nə·fôrm′) *adj.* 1 Being always the same or alike; not varying: *uniform* temperature. 2 Having the same form, color, character, etc. as others: a line of *uniform* battleships. 3 Being the same throughout in appearance, color, surface, etc.: a *uniform* texture. 4 Consistent in effect, action, etc.: a *uniform* law for all drivers. —*n.* A distinctive dress or suit worn, esp. when on duty, by members of the same organization, service, etc., as soldiers, sailors, postmen, etc. —*v.t.* To put into or clothe with a uniform. [< L *unus* one + *forma* form] —**u′ni·form·ly** *adv.*

**u·ni·form·i·ty** (yōō′nə·fôr′mə·tē) *n. pl.* **·ties** 1 The state or quality of being uniform. 2 An instance of it.

**u·ni·fy** (yōō′nə·fī) *v.t.* **·fied, ·fy·ing** To cause to be one; make uniform; unite. [< L *unus* one + *facere* make] —**u′ni·fi·ca′tion** (-fə·kā′shən), **u′ni·fi′er** *n.*

**u·ni·lat·er·al** (yōō'nə·lat'ər·əl) *adj.* 1 Of, relating to, or affecting one side only; one-sided. 2 Made, undertaken, done, or signed by only one of two or more people or parties. 3 Growing on or turning toward one side only. —**u'ni·lat'er·al·ism** *n.* —**u'ni·lat'er·al·ly** *adv.*

**un·im·peach·a·ble** (un'im·pē'chə·bəl) *adj.* Not impeachable; beyond question as regards truth, honesty, etc.; faultless; blameless. —**un'im·peach'a·bly** *adv.*

**un·ion** (yōōn'yən) *n.* 1 The act or an instance of uniting two or more things into one, as: **a** A political joining together, as of states or nations. **b** Marriage; wedlock. 2 The condition of being united or joined; junction. 3 Something formed by uniting or combining parts, as: **a** A confederation, coalition, or league, as of nations, states, or individuals. **b** LABOR UNION. 4 A device for joining mechanical parts, esp. a coupling device for pipes or rods. 5 A college or university organization that provides facilities for recreation, meetings, light meals, etc.: **also student union.** 6 A device emblematic of union used in a flag or ensign, as the blue field with white stars in the flag of the U.S. —*adj.* Of, being, or relating to a union. —**the Union** The United States of America. [< L *unus* one]

**u·nique** (yōō·nēk') *adj.* 1 Being the only one of its kind; single; sole. 2 Being without equal; unparalleled. 3 Very unusual or remarkable; exceptional, extraordinary, etc. [< L *unicus* < *unus* one] —**u·nique'ly** *adv.* —**u·nique'ness** *n.*

**u·ni·sex** (yōō'nə·seks') *Informal adj.* For, appropriate to, or having characteristics of both sexes: *unisex* fashions. —*n.* The embodiment or integration of qualities, characteristics, etc., of both sexes, as in appearance, clothes, or activities.

**u·ni·son** (yōō'nə·sən, -zən) *n.* 1 A condition of perfect agreement and accord; harmony. 2 *Music* **a** The interval between tones of identical pitch. **b** The simultaneous sounding of the same tones by two or more parts. —**in unison** 1 So that identical tones are sounded simultaneously by two or more parts. 2 So that identical words or sounds are uttered simultaneously. 3 In perfect agreement. [<L *unisonus* having a single sound]

**u·nit** (yōō'nit) *n.* 1 A predetermined quantity, as of time, length, work, value, etc., used as a standard of measurement or compar-ison. 2 A fixed amount of work or classroom hours used in calculating a scholastic degree. 3 The quantity, as of a drug or antigen, required to produce a given effect or result. 4 A person or group considered both singly and as a constituent part of a whole: a military *unit.* 5 Something, as a mechanical part or device, having a specific function and serving as part of a whole: the electrical *unit* of a percolator. 6 *Math.* A quantity whose measure is represented by the number 1. —*adj.* Of or being a unit: the *unit* value of an article of merchandise. [Short for UNITY]

**U·ni·tar·i·an** (yōō'nə·târ'ē·ən) *n.* A member of a Protestant denomination which rejects the doctrine of the Trinity, but accepts the ethical teachings of Jesus and emphasizes complete freedom of religious opinion and the independence of each local congregation. —*adj.* Pertaining to the Unitarians, or to their teachings. —**U'ni·tar'i·an·ism** *n.*

**u·nite** (yōō·nīt') *v.* **u·nit·ed, u·nit·ing** *v.t.* 1 To join together so as to form a whole; combine. 2 To bring into close connection, as by legal, physical, marital, social, or other ties: to be *united* in marriage; allies *united* by a common interest. 3 To have or possess in combination: to *unite* courage with wisdom. 4 To cause to adhere; combine. —*v.i.* 5 To become or be merged into one; be consolidated by or as if by adhering. 6 To join together for action. [< L *unus* one]

**u·ni·ty** (yōō'nə·tē) *n. pl.* **·ties** 1 The state or quality of being one or united; oneness. 2 The product or result of being one or united. 3 Singleness of purpose or action. 4 A state of mutual understanding. 5 The quality or fact of being a whole through the unification of separate or individual parts. 6 In a literary or artistic production, a combination of parts that exhibits a prevailing oneness of purpose, thought, spirit, and style; also, the cohesive or harmonious effect so produced. 7 *Math.* **a** The number one. **b** The element of a number system that leaves any number unchanged under multiplication. [< L *unus* one]

**u·ni·ver·sal** (yōō'nə·vûr'səl) *adj.* 1 Prevalent or common everywhere or among all things or persons. 2 Of, applicable to, for, or including all things, persons, cases, etc., without exception. 3 Accomplished or interested in a vast variety of subjects, activities, etc.: Leonardo da Vinci was a *universal* genius. 4 Adapted or adaptable to a great variety of uses, shapes, etc. 5 *Logic* Including or designating all the members of a class. —*n.* 1 *Logic* A universal proposition. 2 Any general or universal notion or idea. 3 A behavioral trait common to all men or cultures. —u′ni·ver′sal·ly *adv.* —u′ni·ver′sal·ism, u′ni·ver′sal·ness *n.*

u·ni·ver·sal·i·ty (yōō′nə·vər·sal′ə·tē) *n.* 1 The quality, condition, or an instance of being universal. 2 Limitlessness, as of range, occurrence, etc.

u·ni·verse (yōō′nə·vûrs) *n.* 1 The aggregate of all existing things; the whole creation embracing all celestial bodies and all of space; the cosmos. 2 In restricted sense, the earth. 3 Something regarded as being a universe in its comprehensiveness, as a field of thought or activity. [< L *universus* turned, combined into one < *unus* one + *versus*, p.p. of *vertere* turn]

u·ni·ver·si·ty (yōō′nə·vûr′sə·tē) *n. pl.* ·ties 1 An educational institution for higher instruction, usu., in the U.S., an institution that includes an undergraduate college or colleges and professional schools granting advanced degrees in law, medicine, the sciences, academic subjects, etc. 2 The buildings, grounds, etc., of a university. 3 The students, faculty, and administration of a university.

un·just (un·just′) *adj.* Not legitimate, fair, or just; wrongful. —un·just′ly *adv.*

un·kempt (un·kempt′) *adj.* 1 Not combed: said of hair. 2 Not neat or tidy. 3 Without polish; rough. [< UN-¹ + *kempt* combed, p.p. of *kemb*, dial. var. of COMB]

un·kind (un·kīnd′) *adj.* Lacking kindness; unsympathetic; harsh; cruel. —un·kind′ly *adj.* (·li·er, ·li·est) & *adv.* —un·kind′li·ness, un·kind′ness *n.*

un·learn (un·lûrn′) *v.t.* ·learned or ·learnt, ·learn·ing 1 To dismiss from the mind (something learned); forget. 2 To attempt to abandon the habit of.

un·learn·ed (un·lûr′nid) *adj.* 1 Not possessed of or characterized by learning; illiterate; ignorant. 2 Characterized by lack of knowledge, professional skill, etc. 3 (un·lûrnd′) Not acquired by learning or study.

un·let·tered (un·let′ərd) *adj.* Not educated; not lettered; illiterate.

un·like (un·līk′) *adj.* Having little or no resemblance; different. —*prep.* 1 Not like; different from. 2 Not characteristic of: It's *unlike* her to complain. —un·like′ness *n.*

un·like·ly (un·līk′lē) *adj.* 1 Improbable. 2 Not

inviting or promising success. —*adv.* Improbably. —un·like′li·hood, un·like′li·ness *n.*

un·lim·it·ed (un·lim′it·id) *adj.* 1 Having no limits in space, number, or time. 2 Not restricted or limited.

un·man (un·man′) *v.t.* ·manned, ·man·ning 1 To cause to lose courage; dishearten. 2 To deprive of manly qualities; make weak or timid. 3 To castrate; emasculate.

un·nerve (un·nûrv′) *v.t.* ·nerved, ·nerv·ing 1 To deprive of strength, firmness, courage, etc. 2 To make nervous.

un·par·al·leled (un·par′ə·leld) *adj.* Without parallel; unmatched; unprecedented.

un·prec·e·dent·ed (un·pres′ə·den′tid) *adj.* Being without precedent; preceded by no similar case; novel.

un·prej·u·diced (un·prej′ōō·dist) *adj.* 1 Free from prejudice or bias; impartial. 2 Not impaired, as a right.

un·qual·i·fied (un·kwol′ə·fīd) *adj.* 1 Being without the proper qualifications; unfit. 2 Without limitation or restrictions; absolute: *unqualified* approval.

un·rav·el (un·rav′əl) *v.* ·eled or ·elled, ·el·ing or ·el·ling *v.t.* 1 To separate the threads of, as a tangled skein or knitted article. 2 To unfold; explain, as a mystery or a plot. —*v.i.* 3 To become unraveled.

un·re·mit·ting (un′ri·mit′ing) *adj.* Incessant; not stopping or relaxing. —un′re·mit′t·ing·ly *adv.* —un′re·mit′ting·ness *n.*

un·rest (un′rest′, un·rest′) *n.* 1 Restlessness, esp. of the mind. 2 Angry dissatisfaction, bordering on revolt.

un·scathed (un·skāthd′) *adj.* Not injured.

un·seem·ly (un·sēm′lē) *adj.* ·li·er, ·li·est Unbecoming, indecent, unattractive, or inappropriate. —*adv.* In an unseemly fashion. —un·seem′li·ness *n.*

un·set·tle (un·set′l) *v.* ·tled, ·tling *v.t.* 1 To move from a fixed or settled condition. 2 To confuse, upset, or disturb. —*v.i.* 3 To become unsettled. —un·set′tling·ly *adv.*

un·sheathe (un·shēth′) *v.t.* ·sheathed, ·sheath·ing To take from or as from a scabbard or sheath; bare.

un·sight·ly (un·sīt′lē) *adj.* ·li·er, ·li·est Offensive to the sight; ugly. —un·sight′li·ness *n.*

un·so·phis·ti·cat·ed (un′sə·fis′tə·kā′tid) *adj.* 1 Showing inexperience or naïveté; artless. 2 Genuine; pure. 3 Not complicated; simple. —un′so·phis′ti·cat′ed·ly *adv.* —un′so·phis′ti·cat′ed·ness, un′so·phis′ti·ca′tion *n.*

**un·speak·a·ble** (un·spē′kə·bəl) *adj.* 1 That cannot be expressed; unutterable: *unspeakable* joy. 2 Extremely bad or objectionable: an *unspeakable* crime. —**un·speak′a·ble·ness** *n.* —**un·speak′a·bly** *adv.*

**un·til** (un·til′) *prep.* 1 Up to the time of; till: We will wait *until* midnight. 2 Before: used with a negative: The music doesn't begin *until* nine. —*conj.* 1 To the time when: *until* I die. 2 To the place or degree that: Walk east *until* you reach the river. 3 Before: with a negative: He couldn't leave *until* the car came for him. [< ME *und-* up to, as far as + TILL] • See TILL².

**un·veil** (un·vāl′) *v.t.* 1 To remove the veil or covering from; disclose to view; reveal. —*v.i.* 2 To remove one's veil; reveal oneself.

**un·wont·ed** (un·wôn′tid, -won′-) *adj.* Not ordinary or customary; unusual; uncommon. —**un·wont′ed·ly** *adv.* —**un·wont′ed·ness** *n.*

**up·braid** (up·brād′) *v.t.* To reproach for some wrongdoing; scold. [< OE *up-* up + *bregdan* weave; twist] —**up·braid′er** *adj.* —**up·braid′ing·ly** *adv.* —**Syn.** admonish, chastise, rebuke, reprimand.

**up·heav·al** (up·hē′vəl) *n.* 1 The act of upheaving, or the state of being upheaved. 2 A violent change or disturbance, as of the established social order.

**up·hold** (up·hōld′) *v.t.* **·held**, **·hold·ing** 1 To hold up; keep from falling or sinking. 2 To raise; lift up. 3 To aid, encourage, sustain, or confirm. —**up·hold′er** *n.*

**up·hol·ster** (up·hōl′stər) *v.t.* To fit, as furniture, with coverings, cushioning, springs, etc. [ult. < ME *upholder* tradesman] —**up·hol′ster·er** *n.*

**up·lift** (up·lift′) *v.t.* 1 To lift up, or raise aloft; elevate. 2 To put on a higher plane, mentally, morally, culturally, or socially. —*n.* (up′lift′) 1 The act of lifting up raising. 2 An elevation to a higher mental, spiritual, moral, or social plane. 3 A social movement aiming to improve, esp. morally or culturally. 4 A brassiere designed to lift and support the breasts. —**up·lift′er** *n.*

**up·per·most** (up′ər·mōst′) *adj.* Highest in place, rank, authority, importance, etc.; foremost. —*adv.* In the highest place, rank, importance, etc.

**up·right** (up′rīt′) *adj.* 1 Being in a vertical position; erect. 2 Righteous; just. —*n.* 1 The state of being upright: a post out of *upright.* 2 Something having an upright position, as a vertical timber. 3 An upright piano. 4 In a football, a goal post. —*adv.* In an upright position; vertically. [< OE *up-* up + *rīht* right] —**up′right′ly** *adv.* —**up′right′ness** *n.*

**up·ris·ing** (up′rī′zing) *n.* 1 The act of rising up; esp., a revolt or insurrection. 2 An ascent; upward slope; acclivity.

**up·roar** (up′rôr′, -rōr′) *n.* 1 A state of confusion, disturbance, excitement, tumult, etc. 2 A loud, boisterous noise; din. [< Du. *op-* up + *roeren* stir]

**up·roar·i·ous** (up·rôr′ē·əs, -rō′rē-) *adj.* 1 Accompanied by or making uproar. 2 Very loud and boisterous. 3 Provoking loud laughter. —**up·roar′i·ous·ly** *adv.* —**up·roar′ous·ness** *n.*

**up·root** (up·rōōt′, -rōōt′) *v.t.* 1 To tear up by the roots. 2 To destroy utterly; eradicate. —**up·root′er** *n.*

**up·set** (up·set′) *v.* **·set**, **·set·ting** *v.t.* 1 To overturn. 2 To throw into confusion or disorder. 3 To disconcert, derange, or disquiet. 4 To defeat (an opponent favored to win): The amateur team *upset* the professionals. —*v.i.* 5 To become overturned. —*adj.* (also up′set′) 1 Overturned. 2 Physically ill or mentally disturbed. —*n.* (up′set′) 1 The act of overturning. 2 A physical or emotional disorder. 3 A defeat of an opponent favored to win. —**up·set′ter** *n.*

**up·shot** (up′shot′) *n.* The outcome; result.

**up·stairs** (up′stārz′) *adj.* Of or on an upper story. —*n.* The part of a building above the ground floor; an upper story or stories. —*adv.* To or on an upper story.

**up·start** (up′stärt′) *n.* A person who has suddenly risen from a humble position to one of consequence; esp., such a person who behaves in a way that is presumptuous, arrogant, etc.

**up·ward** (up′wərd) *adv.* 1 In or toward a higher place, position, or part. 2 Toward a source or interior part. 3 In the upper parts. 4 To or toward a higher, greater, or better condition. Also up′wards. —**upward of** or **upwards of** Higher than or in excess of. —*adj.* Turned, directed toward, or located in a higher place. —**up′ward·ly** *adv.*

**u·ra·ni·um** (yŏŏ·rā′nē·əm) *n.* A heavy, radioactive, metallic element (symbol U), found only in combination and in association with radium, used in the generation of atomic energy. [< URANUS]

**U·ra·nus** (yŏŏ′ə·nəs, yŏŏr·ā′nəs) *Gk. Myth.* The son and husband of Gaea (Earth) and father of the Titans, Furies, and Cyclopes. —*n.* The planet of the solar system seventh in distance from the sun. • See PLANET. —U·ra′ni·an adj.

ur·ban (ûr′bən) adj. 1 Of, pertaining to, characteristic of, constituting, or including a city. 2 Living or located in a city or cities. [See URBANE.]

ur·bane (ûr·bān′) adj. Characterized by or having refinement, esp. in manner; polite; courteous; suave. [< L urbs, urbis a city] —ur·bane′ly adv. —ur·bane′ness n.

ur·ban·i·ty (ûr·băn′ə·tē) n. pl. ·ties 1 The character or quality of being urbane. 2 pl. Urbane acts or behavior; courtesies, amenities, etc.

ur·chin (ûr′chin) n. 1 A roguish, mischievous child. 2 A ragged street child. 3 HEDGEHOG. 4 SEA URCHIN. [< L ericius hedgehog]

urge (ûrj) v. urged, urg·ing v.t. 1 To drive or force forward. 2 To plead with or entreat earnestly: He urged them to accept the plan. 3 To advocate earnestly: to urge reform. 4 To move or force to some course or action. —v.i. 5 To present or press arguments, claims, etc. 6 To exert an impelling or prompting force. —n. 1 A strong impulse to perform a certain act. 2 The act of urging. [< L urgere to drive, urge] —Syn. v. 1 impel, press. 2 exhort, importune.

ur·gen·cy (ûr′jən·sē) n. pl. ·cies 1 The quality of being urgent; insistence: the urgency of her plea. 2 Something urgent: to prepare for any possible urgencies.

ur·gent (ûr′jənt) adj. 1 Requiring prompt attention; pressing; imperative. 2 Eagerly importunate or insistent. [< L urgere drive] —ur′gent·ly adv.

u·ri·nate (yŏŏr′ə·nāt) v.i. ·nat·ed, ·nat·ing To void or pass urine. —u′ri·na′tion n.

u·rine (yŏŏr′in) n. A usu. fluid substance secreted by the kidneys of vertebrates and some invertebrates and containing nitrogenous and saline wastes. [< L urina]

urn (ûrn) n. 1 A vase, usu. having a foot or pedestal, variously used as a receptacle for the ashes of the dead, or ornament, etc. 2 A vase-shaped receptacle having a faucet, designed to make and serve tea, coffee, etc. [< L urna]

us·a·ble (yŏŏ′zə·bəl) adj. 1 Capable of being used. 2 That can be used conveniently. Also use′a·ble. —us′a·ble·ness n. —us′a·bly adv.

us·age (yŏŏ′sij, -zij) n. 1 The act or manner of using; treatment. 2 Customary or habitual practice; custom; habit. 3 The accepted and established way of using words, speech patterns, etc.

use (yŏŏz) v. used, us·ing v.t. 1 To put into service: to use a hammer. 2 To borrow; avail oneself of: May I use your pen? 3 To put into practice or employ habitually: to use diligence in business. 4 To conduct oneself toward; treat: to use one badly. 5 To partake of: He does not use tobacco. 6 To take advantage of; exploit: to use one's friends. 7 To expend, exhaust, or consume: usu. with up. —v.i. 8 To be accustomed: used in the past tense with an infinitive: We used to go to the theater regularly. —n. (yŏŏs) 1 The act of using, or the state of being used. 2 Function: He has lost the use of his legs. 3 Way or manner of using: to make good use of one's time. 4 Habitual practice or employment; custom; usage. 5 The ability or right to use, or the privilege of using. 6 Advantage; benefit; usefulness. 7 The purpose for which something is used. 8 Law The benefit or profit of property to which legal title is vested in another in trust for the beneficiary. —have no use for 1 To have no need of. 2 To have dislike or contempt for. —in use Being used or occupied. —make use of To have occasion to use; use. —put to use To utilize; employ. [< L usus, pp. of uti to use] —us′er n.

use·ful (yŏŏs′fəl) adj. Capable of being used; serviceable; helpful. —use′ful·ly adv. —use′ful·ness n.

u·su·al (yŏŏ′zhŏŏ·əl) adj. Such as occurs in the ordinary course of events; customary; common. [< L usus use] —u′su·al·ly adv. —u′su·al·ness n. —Syn. everyday, general, ordinary, prevalent.

u·surp (yŏŏ·sûrp′, -zûrp′) v.t. To seize and hold (an office, rights, powers, etc.) without right or legal authority; take possession of by force. [< L usurpare make use of, usurp]

u·sur·pa·tion (yŏŏ′sər·pā′shən, -zər-) n. The act of usurping, esp. the unlawful seizure of sovereign power.

u·su·ry (yŏŏ′zhər·ē) n. pl. ·ries 1 The act or practice of lending money and charging interest that is excessive or unlawfully high. 2 Interest that is excessive or unlawfully high. [<L usura < usus, pp. of uti to use]

u·ten·sil (yŏŏ·ten′səl) n. A vessel, tool, implement, etc., serving a useful purpose, esp. for domestic or farming use. [<L utensilis fit for use]

u·til·i·ty (yŏŏ·til′ə·tē) n. pl. ·ties 1 Fitness for some desirable, practical purpose; usefulness. 2 Fitness to supply the needs of people. 3 Something useful. 4 A public service, as a telephone system, gas, water, etc. 5 A company that provides such a service. [< L *utilis* useful < *uti* use]

**u·til·ize** (yōō′təl·īz) *v.t.* **·ized, ·iz·ing** To make use of. *Brit. sp.* **u′til·ise.** **—u′til·i·za′tion, u′til·iz′er** *n.*

**U·to·pi·a** (yōō·tō′pē·ə) *n.* An imaginary island described as the seat of a perfect social and political life in the book by Sir Thomas More, published in 1516. [< Gk. *ou* not + *topos* a place] **—U·to′pi·an** *adj., n.*

**ut·ter**[1] (ut′ər) *v.t.* **1** To say, express, give out, or send forth, as in words or sounds. **2** To put in circulation; esp., to deliver or offer (something forged or counterfeit). [< ME *out* say, speak out] **—ut′ter·er** *n.*

**ut·ter**[2] (ut′ər) *adj.* **1** Complete; absolute; total: *utter* mistery. **2** Unqualified; final: an *utter* denial. [< OE *ūttra,* orig. compar. of *ūt* out] **—ut′ter·ly** *adv.*

**ut·ter·ance** (ut′ər·əns) *n.* **1** The act of uttering. **2** A manner of speaking. **3** A thing uttered.

**u·vu·la** (yōō′vyə·lə) *n. pl.* **·las** or **·lae** (-lē) The pendent fleshy portion of the soft palate in the back of the mouth. [LL, dim. of *uva* grape] • See MOUTH.

# V

**va·cant** (vā′kənt) *adj.* **1** Containing or holding nothing; empty. **2** Not lived in or occupied. **3** Not being used; free: a *vacant* hour. **4** Being or appearing without intelligence: a *vacant* stare. **5** Having no incumbent, officer, or possessor. [< L *vacans* pr.p. of *vacare* be empty] **—va′cant·ly** *adv.* **—va′cant·ness** *n.* **—Syn.** 1 blank, void. 4 vapid, dull, vacuous, witless, obtuse, blank.

**va·cate** (vā′kāt′, vā·kāt′) *v.* **·cat·ed, ·cat·ing** *v.t.* **1** To make vacant, as a dwelling, position, etc. **2** To set aside; annul. **—v.i.** **3** To leave an office, dwelling, place, etc. **4** *Informal* To go away; leave. [< L *vacare* be empty]

**va·ca·tion** (vā·kā′shən) *n.* A time set aside from work, study, etc., for recreation or rest; a holiday. **—v.i.** To take a vacation. [See VACATE. **—va·ca′tion·er, va·ca′tion·ist** *n.*

**vac·ci·nate** (vak′sə·nāt) *v.* **·nat·ed, ·nat·ing** *v.t.* **1** To inoculate with a vaccine as a preventive or therapeutic measure; esp., to inoculate against smallpox. **—v.i.** **2** To perform the act of vaccination. **—vac′ci·na′tor** *n.*

**vac·cine** (vak·sēn′, vak′sēn) *n.* **1** The virus of cowpox, as prepared for inoculation to produce immunity to smallpox. **2** Any modified virus or bacterium used to give immunity against a specific disease. [< L *vaccinus* pertaining to a cow] **—vac′ci·nal** (-sə·nəl) *adj.*

**vac·il·late** (vas′ə·lāt) *v.i.* **·lat·ed, ·lat·ing** **1** To move one way and the other; waver. **2** To waver in mind; be irresolute. [< L *vacillare* waver] **—vac′il·la′tion** *n.* **—vac′il·la·to′ry** (-ə·lə·tô′rē, -tō′rē) *adj.* **—Syn.** 1 fluctuate, oscillate, sway.

**vac·u·um** (vak′yōō·əm, -yōōm) *n. pl.* **·u·ums** or **·u·a** (-yōō·ə) **1** *Physics* A space devoid, or nearly devoid, of matter. **2** A reduction of the pressure in a space below atmospheric pressure. **3** A void; an empty feeling. **4** *Informal* A vacuum cleaner. **—v.t. & v.i.** *Informal* To clean with a vacuum cleaner. [L, neut. of *vacuus* empty]

**vacuum cleaner** A machine for cleaning floors, carpets, etc., by means of suction.

**vacuum tube** *Electronics* An electron tube containing a negligible amount of gas.

**vag·a·bond** (vag′ə·bond) *n.* **1** One who wanders from place to place without visible means of support; a tramp. **2** A shiftless, irresponsible person. **—adj.** **1** Wandering; nomadic. **2** Having no definite residence; irresponsible. **3** Driven to and fro; aimless. [< L *vagus* wandering] **—vag′a·bond′age, vag′a·bond′ism** *n.*

**va·gar·y** (vā′gə·rē, və·gâr′ē) *n. pl.* **·gar·ies** A wild fancy; extravagant notion. [< L *vagari* wander]

**va·grant** (vā′grənt) *n.* A person who wanders from place to place without a settled home or job and who exists usu. by begging or stealing; a tramp. **—adj.** **1** Wandering about aimlessly; wayward. **2** Pertaining to or characteristic of a vagrant. [< OF *wacrer* to walk, wander] **—va′grant·ly** *adv.* **—va′grant·ness** *n.*

**vague** (vāg) *adj.* **vagu·er, vagu·est** **1** Lacking definiteness; not clearly stated: *vague* rumors; *vague* promises. **2** Indistinct; hard to perceive: *vague* shapes in the fog. **3** Not thinking or expressing oneself clearly. [< L *vagus* wandering] **—vague′ly** *adv.* **—vague′ness** *n.*

**vain** (vān) *adj.* **1** Having or showing excessive pride in oneself; conceited. **2** Unproductive; useless: *vain* efforts. **3** Without substantial foundation; unreal. **—in vain 1** To no purpose; without effect. **2** Irreverently: to take the Lord's name *in vain.* [< L *vanus* empty]

—**vain′ly** *adv.* —**vain′ness** *n.* —**Syn.** 1 Boastful, egotistical, narcissistic.

**vain·glo·ry** (vān′glôr′ē, -glôr-, vān·glôr′ē) *n.* 1 Excessive or groundless vanity; boastfulness. 2 Empty, showy pomp. [< Med. L *vana gloria* empty pomp, show] —**vain·glo′ri·ous** *adj.* —**vain·glo′ri·ous·ly** *adv.* —**vain·glo′ri·ous·ness** *n.*

**val·ance** (val′əns, vā′ləns) *n.* 1 A drapery hanging from the tester of a bedstead. 2 A short, full drapery across the top of a window. [Prob. < OF *avaler* descend] —**val′anced** *adj.* • See CANOPY.

**val·e·dic·tion** (val′ə·dik′shən) *n.* 1 A bidding farewell. 2 VALEDICTORY. [< L *valedicere* say farewell]

**val·e·dic·to·ry** (val′ə·dik′tər·ē) *adj.* Pertaining to a leave-taking. —*n. pl.* **·ries** A parting address, as by a member (ordinarily the first in rank) of a graduating class.

**val·en·tine** (val′ən·tīn) *n.* 1 A card or small gift sent as a token of affection on Valentine's Day. 2 A sweetheart.

**val·et** (val′it, val′ā, val·ā′) *n.* 1 A man's personal servant. 2 A manservant in a hotel who cleans and presses clothes. —*v.t. & v.i.* To act as a valet. [F < OF *vaslet, varlet,* dim. of *vasal* vassal]

**val·iant** (val′yənt) *adj.* 1 Strong and intrepid; powerful and courageous. 2 Performed with valor; heroic. [< OF *valoir* be strong] —**val′iant·ly** *adv.* —**val′i·an·cy** or **val′i·ance, val′iant·ness** *n.*

**val·id** (val′id) *adj.* 1 Based on facts or evidence; sound: a *valid* argument. 2 Legally binding: a *valid* will. [< L *validus* powerful] —**val′id·ly** *adv.* —**va·lid·i·ty** (və·lid′ə·tē), **val′id·ness** *n.*

**va·lise** (və·lēs′) *n.* A traveling bag; suitcase. [< Ital. *valigia*]

**val·ley** (val′ē) *n.* 1 A long, wide area drained by a large river system: the Hudson *valley.* 2 Low land lying between mountains or hills. 3 Any hollow or depression shaped like a valley. [< L *vallis*]

**val·or** (val′ər) *n.* Marked courage; personal heroism; bravery. *Brit. sp.* **val′our.** [< L *valere* be strong] —**val′or·ous** *adj.* —**val′or·ous·ly** *adv.* —**val′or·ous·ness** *n.*

**val·u·a·ble** (val′yōo·ə·bəl, val′yə·bəl) *adj.* 1 Having financial worth, price, or value. 2 Very costly. 3 Worthy; estimable: a *valuable* friend. —*n. Usu. pl.* An article of value, as a piece of jewelry. —**val′u·a·ble·ness** *n.* —**val′u·a·bly** *adv.*

**val·ue** (val′yōo) *n.* 1 The desirability or worth of a thing; merit: the *value* of self-discipline. 2 Something regarded as desirable, worthy, or right, as a belief or ideal. 3 Worth in money; market price. 4 A bargain. 5 Purchasing power: a decline in the *value* of the dollar. 6 Exact meaning: the *value* of a word. 7 *Music* The relative length of a tone. 8 *Math.* The number assigned to or represented by a symbol or expression. 9 In art, the relative lightness or darkness of a color. 10 The relation, as of light and shade, of one part to another in a work of art. —*v.t.* **·ued, ·u·ing** 1 To assess; appraise. 2 To regard highly; prize. 3 To place a relative estimate of value upon: to *value* health above all else. [< L *valere*] —**val′u·er** *n.*

**valve** (valv) *n.* 1 *Mech.* Any device used to block, direct, or otherwise control motion of a fluid. 2 *Anat.* A membranous structure inside a vessel or other organ, allowing fluid to flow in one direction only. 3 *Zool.* One of the parts of a shell, as of a clam, etc. 4 *Bot.* One of the parts into which a seed capsule splits. —*v.t.* **valved, valv·ing** To control the flow of by means of a valve. [< L *valva* leaf of a door]

**vam·pire** (vam′pīr) *n.* 1 In folklore, a reanimated corpse that rises from its grave at night to suck the blood of persons who are asleep. 2 A person who preys upon those of the opposite sex; esp. a woman who degrades or impoverishes her lover. 3 A bat of tropical America that drinks the blood of mammals: also **vampire bat.** 4 An insect- or fruit-eating bat mistakenly thought to suck blood: also **false vampire.** [< Slavic] —**vam′pir·ism** *n.*

**van** (van) *n.* 1 A large covered wagon or truck for transporting furniture, household goods, etc. 2 *Brit.* A closed railway car for luggage, etc. [Short for CARAVAN]

**van·dal** (van′dəl) *n.* One who engages in vandalism. [< VANDAL]

**van·dal·ism** (van′dəl·iz′əm) *n.* Willful destruction or defacement of public or private property.

**vane** (vān) *n.* 1 A thin plate, pivoted on a vertical rod, to indicate the direction of the wind; a weathercock. 2 An arm or blade, as of a windmill, propeller, projectile, turbine, etc. 3 The web, or flat portion, of a feather. [< OE *fana* a flag] —**vaned** (vānd) *adj.*

**van·guard** (van′gärd) *n.* 1 The forward part of an advancing army. 2 The foremost position in a movement, trend, etc. 3 The leaders of a movement, trend, etc. [< OF *avant* before + *garde* guard]

**va·nil·la** (və·nil′ə) *n.* 1 Any of a genus of tall climbing orchids of tropical America. 2 The long seed capsule of one species: also **vanilla bean.** 3 A flavoring extracted from these capsules or made synthetically. [< Sp. *vaina* sheath, pod] —**va·nil′lic** *adj.*

**van·ish** (van′ish) *v.i.* 1 To disappear; fade away. 2 To pass out of existence. [< L *evanescere* fade away] —**van′ish·er** *n.*

**van·i·ty** (van′ə·tē) *n. pl.* ·**ties** 1 Excessive pride in one's talents, looks, possessions, etc. 2 Worthlessness; futility. 3 Something that is worthless or futile. 4 A low table with an attached mirror, for use while dressing the hair or putting on makeup. 5 VANITY CASE. [< L *vanus* empty, vain]

**van·quish** (vang′kwish, van′-) *v.t.* 1 To defeat in battle; conquer. 2 To suppress or overcome (a feeling): to *vanquish* fear. 3 To defeat in any encounter. [< L *vincere*] —**van′quish·er van′quish·ment** *n.* —Syn. 1 beat, overcome, overpower, overwhelm, upset.

**van·tage** (van′tij) *n.* 1 Superiority, as over a competitor; advantage. 2 A position, place, situation, etc., that gives superiority or an advantage. [< OF *advantage* advantage]

**vap·id** (vap′id, vā′pəd) *adj.* 1 Having lost sparkle and flavor. 2 Flat; insipid. [< L *vapidus* insipid] —**va·pid·i·ty** (və·pid′ə·tē), **vap′id·ness** *n.* —**vap′id·ly** *adv.*

**va·por** (vā′pər) *n.* 1 Moisture in the air; esp. visible floating moisture, as light mist. 2 Any cloudy substance in the air, as smoke. 3 The gaseous phase of any substance. 4 Something that is fleeting and unsubstantial. 5 A remedial agent applied by inhalation. —**the vapors** *Archaic* Depression of spirits. —*v.t.* 1 VAPORIZE. —*v.i.* 2 To emit vapor. 3 To pass off in vapor; evaporate. *Brit. sp.* **va′pour.** [< L *vapor* steam] —**va′por·er** *n.*

**va·por·ize** (vā′pə·rīz) *v.t. & v.i.* ·**ized,** ·**iz·ing** To convert or be converted into vapor. —**va′por·er** *n.*

**va·por·ize** (vā′pə·rīz) *v.t. & v.i.* ·**ized,** ·**iz·ing** To convert or be converted into vapor. —**va′por·i·za′tion** *n.*

**var·i·a·ble** (vâr′ē·ə·bəl, var′-) *adj.* 1 Having the capacity of varying; alterable. 2 Having a tendency to change; not constant. 3 Having no definite value as regards quantity. 4 *Biol.* Prone to deviate from a type. —*n.* 1 That which is liable to change. 2 *Math.* a A

quantity that may be equal to any one of a specified set of numbers. b A symbol representing such a quantity. 3 A shifting wind. —**var′i·a·bil′i·ty, var′i·a·ble·ness** *n.* —**var′i·a·bly** *adv.* —Syn. *adj.* 2 fluctuating, unstable, unsteady, wavering.

**var·i·ance** (vâr′ē·əns, var′-) *n.* 1 The act of varying or the state of being varied. 2 Discrepancy; difference. 3 A dispute; quarrel. 4 A license or official permission to do something contrary to official regulations. —**at variance** Not in agreement; disagreeing.

**var·i·ant** (vâr′ē·ənt, var′-) *adj.* 1 Varying; differing, esp. differing from a standard or type. 2 *Archaic* Variable; changeable. —*n.* 1 A person or thing that differs from another in form only. 2 One of several different spellings, pronunciations, or forms of the same word.

**var·i·a·tion** (vâr′ē·ā′shən, var′-) *n.* 1 The act or process of varying; modification. 2 The extent to which a thing varies. 3 A thing changed in form from others of the same type. 4 *Music* A repetition of a theme or melody with changes in key, rhythm, harmony, etc. 5 *Biol.* Deviation from the typical structure or function. —**var′i·a′tion·al** *adj.*

**var·i·e·gate** (vâr′ē·ə·gāt′, var′-) *v.t.* ·**gat·ed,** ·**gat·ing** 1 To mark with different colors; dapple; streak. 2 To make varied; diversify. —*adj.* VARIEGATED. [< L *varius* various + *agere* to drive, do] —**var′i·e·ga′tion** *n.*

**va·ri·e·ty** (və·rī′ə·tē) *n. pl.* ·**ties** 1 Absence of sameness or monotony; diversity; variation; difference. 2 Sort; kind: a sweet *variety* of pickle. 3 A collection of diverse kinds; assortment: a *variety* of flowers. 4 A subdivision of a species. 5 Vaudeville: also **variety show.** [< L *varius* various]

**va·ri·o·la** (ver′ē·ō′lə, və·rī′ə·lə) *n.* SMALLPOX. [< L *varius* speckled] —**va·ri′o·lar** *adj.*

**var·nish** (vär′nish) *n.* 1 A solution of certain gums or resins in alcohol, linseed oil, etc., used to produce a shining, transparent coat on a surface. 2 The glossy, hard finish made by this solution when dry. 3 Any substance or finish resembling varnish. 4 Outward show; deceptive appearance. —*v.t.* 1 To cover with varnish. 2 To give a glossy appearance to. 3 To hide by a deceptive appearance; gloss over. [< Med. L *vernicium*, a kind of resin] —**var′nish·er** *n.*

**var·y** (vâr′ē, var′-) *v.* **var·ied, var·y·ing** *v.t.* 1 To change the form, nature, substance, etc., of; modify. 2 To cause to be different from one another. 3 To diversify. 4 *Music* To systematically alter (a melody or other thematic element). —*v.i.* 5 To become changed in form, substance, etc. 6 To differ. 7 To deviate; depart: with *from.* 8 To alternate. 9 *Math.* To be subject to change. 10 *Biol.* To show variation. [< L *varius* various, diverse] —var′y·ing·ly *adv.*

**vase** (vās, vāz, väz) *n.* An urnlike vessel used as an ornament or for holding flowers. [<L *vas* vessel]

**va·sec·to·my** (va·sek′ta·mē) *n. pl.* ·to·mies Surgical removal of a portion of the vas deferens, thus producing sterilization by preventing semen from reaching the seminal vesicles. [< VAS(O)- + -ECTOMY]

**Vas·e·line** (vas′a·lēn, vas·a·lēn′) *n.* PETROLATUM: a trade name.

**vas·sal** (vas′al) *n.* 1 In feudalism, a man who held land from a superior lord to whom he rendered, in return, military or other service. 2 A person who is in a position that is subordinate, lowly, servile, slavish, etc. — *adj.* Of or pertaining to a vassal. [< LL *vassus* a servant]

**vast** (vast, väst) *adj.* 1 Of great extent; immense: a *vast* desert. 2 Very great in number, quantity, or amount. 3 Very great in degree, intensity, or importance. [<L, waste, empty, vast] —vast′ly *adv.* —vast′ness *n.* —Syn. 1,2 enormous, extensive, huge, tremendous.

**vat** (vat) *n.* A large vessel, tub, or cistern, esp. for holding liquids during some process, as heating, fermenting, etc. —*v.t.* vat·ted, vat·ting To treat in a vat. [< OE *fæt*]

**vault** (vôlt) *n.* 1 An arched roof or ceiling, usu. of masonry. 2 Any vaultlike covering, as the sky. An arched passage or room. 4 An underground room or compartment for storage. 5 A place for keeping valuables: bank *vault.* 6 A burial chamber. —*v.t.* 1 To cover with or as with a vault. 2 To construct in the form of a vault. [< OF *volte, vaute*]

**vaunt** (vônt, vänt) *v.i.* 1 To boast. —*v.t.* 2 To boast of. —*n.* A brag or boast. [<LL *vanitare* brag<L *vanus* empty, vain]

**veal** (vēl) *n.* 1 A calf, esp. one grown or suitable for food. 2 The flesh of a calf as food. [<L *vitellus,* dim. of *vitulus* calf]

**veep** (vēp) *n. Slang* A vice president, esp. the vice president of the U.S. [< *V.P.,* abbr. of vice president]

**veer** (vir) *v.i.* 1 To shift or turn in position or direction: The wind *veered* to the east. 2 To

shift from one opinion, belief, etc., to another. —*v.t.* 3 To change the direction of. —*n.* A change in direction. [<F *virer* to turn]

**veg·e·ta·ble** (vej′a·ta·bal, vej′ta-) *n.* 1 A plant, esp. one cultivated for food. 2 The edible part of a plant, raw or cooked. 3 *Informal* A person who is mindless, apathetic, or passive. —*adj.* 1 Pertaining to plants, as distinct from animals: the *vegetable* kingdom. 2 Derived from, of the nature of, or resembling plants. 3 Made from or pertaining to edible vegetables: *vegetable* soup. 4 *Informal* Showing little mental activity; apathetic, passive, etc. [<L *vegetus* vigorous, lively<*vegere* be lively]

**veg·e·tar·i·an** (vej′a·târ′ē·an) *n.* A person whose diet is made up of vegetables, fruits, grain, nuts, and sometimes animal products, as milk, eggs, etc. —*adj.* 1 Pertaining to or advocating the eating of only vegetable foods. 2 Made up exclusively of vegetables, fruits, grain, etc. —veg′e·tar′i·an·ism *n.*

**veg·e·tate** (vej′a·tāt) *v.i.* ·tat·ed, ·tat·ing 1 To grow, as a plant. 2 To live in a monotonous, passive way.

**veg·e·ta·tion** (vej′a·tā′shan) *n.* 1 The process or condition of vegetating. 2 Plant life in the aggregate.

**ve·he·ment** (vē′a·mant) *adj.* 1 Arising from or marked by strong feeling or passing. 2 Acting with great force; violent. [< L *vehemens,* -*entis* impetuous, rash] —ve′he·mence, ve′he·men·cy *n.* —ve′he·ment·ly *adv.* —Syn. 1 Ardent, fervent, zealous, fierce. 2 energetic, forceful, intense, powerful.

**ve·hi·cle** (vē′a·kal, vē′hi-) *n.* 1 Any device for carrying or transporting persons or things, as a car, spacecraft, etc. 2 A neutral medium for administering a medicine, etc. 3 The medium with which pigments are mixed in painting. 4 Any means by which thoughts or ideas are transmitted or communicated. [<L *vehiculum*<*vehere* to carry, ride] —ve·hic·u·lar (vi·hik′ya·lar) *adj.*

**veil** (vāl) *n.* 1 A piece of thin and light fabric, worn over the face or head for concealment, protection, or ornament. 2 A piece of cloth, as a curtain, that covers, conceals, etc. 3 Anything that conceals or covers. —take the veil To become a nun. —*v.t.* 1 To cover with a veil. 2 To conceal, cover, hide, disguise, etc. [<L *velum* piece of cloth, sail]

**vein** (vān) *n.* 1 Any of the tubular vessels that convey blood to the heart. 2 One of the radiating supports of an insect's wing. 3 One of the slender vascular bundles that form the framework of a leaf. 4 LODE. 5 A long, irregular, colored streak, as in wood, marble, etc. 6 A distinctive tendency or disposition. —*v.t.* 1 To furnish or fill with veins. 2 To streak or ornament with veins. 3 To extend over or throughout as veins. [< L *vena* blood vessel

**vel·lum** (vel′əm) *n.* 1 Fine parchment made from the skins of calves; used for expensive binding, printing, etc. 2 A manuscript written on vellum. 3 Paper or cloth made to resemble vellum. [< OF *veel, viel* calf]

**ve·loc·i·pede** (və·los′ə·pēd) *n.* 1 An early form of bicycle or tricycle. 2 A child's tricycle. [< L *velox* swift + -PEDE]

**ve·loc·i·ty** (və·los′ə·tē) *n. pl.* **·ties** 1 Quickness of motion; speed; swiftness. 2 *Physics* A vector representing the rate of change of position of a body. [< L *velox* swift]

**vel·vet** (vel′vit) *n.* 1 A fabric of silk, rayon, nylon, etc., having on one side a short, smooth pile. 2 Something resembling velvet. 3 *Slang* Unexpected profit or gain. —*adj.* 1 Made of velvet. 2 Smooth and soft to the touch like velvet. [Ult. < L *villus* shaggy hair] —**vel′vet·y** *adj.*

**ve·nal** (vē′nəl) *adj.* 1 Capable of being corrupted or bribed. 2 Characterized by corruption or bribery. [< L *venum* sale] —**ve·nal·i·ty** (vē·nal′ə·tē) *n.* —**ve′nal·ly** *adv.*

**vend** (vend) *v.t.* 1 To sell, as by peddling. 2 To sell by means of a vending machine. 3 To give expression to in public —*v.i.* 4 To sell merchandise. [< L *vendere*] —**Syn.** *v.t.* 1 dispense, hawk, market, peddle.

**ven·dor** (ven′dər) *n.* 1 One who vends; seller. 2 VENDING MACHINE. Also **vender.**

**ve·neer** (və·nir′) *n.* 1 A thin layer, as of choice wood, upon a cheaper surface. 2 Mere surface or outside show: a *veneer* of politeness. —*v.t.* 1 To cover (a surface) with veneers. 2 To conceal, as something disagreeable or coarse, with an attractive and deceptive surface. [< G *furnieren* inlay < F *fournir* furnish] —**ve·neer′er** *n.*

**ven·er·a·ble** (ven′ər·ə·bəl) *adj.* Meriting or commanding veneration because of dignity, age, religious or historical associations, etc. [< L *venerari* revere] —**ven′er·a·bil′i·ty, ve·n′er·a·ble·ness** *n.* —**ven′er·a·bly** *adv.*

**ven·er·ate** (ven′ə·rāt) *v.t.* **·at·ed, ·at·ing** To regard with respect and deference; revere. [< L *venerari* revere]

**ven·er·a·tion** (ven′ə·rā′shən) *n.* 1 Profound respect combined with awe. 2 The act of worshiping; worship.

**venereal disease** Any of several diseases transmitted by sexual intercourse, as syphilis, gonorrhea, etc.

**Venetian blind** A flexible window screen having movable, overlapping slats so fastened on webbing or tape as to exclude or admit light.

**ven·geance** (ven′jəns) *n.* The infliction of a deserved penalty; retributive punishment. —**with a vengeance** 1 With great force or violence. 2 Extremely; to an unusual extent. [< L *vindicare* defend, avenge]

**venge·ful** (venj′fəl) *adj.* Seeking to inflict vengeance; vindictive. —**venge′ful·ly** *adv.* —**venge′ful·ness** *n.*

**ve·ni·al** (vē′nē·əl, vēn′yəl) *adj.* So slight or trivial as to be overlooked, as a fault. [< L *venia* forgiveness, mercy] —**ve′ni·al′i·ty** (-al′ə·tē), **ve′ni·al·ness** *n.* —**ve′ni·al·ly** *adv.* —**Syn.** excusable, forgivable, pardonable.

**ven·i·son** (ven′ə·zən, -sən) *n.* The flesh of a wild animal, esp. a deer, used for food. [< L *venari* to hunt]

**ven·om** (ven′əm) *n.* 1 The poison secreted by certain reptiles, insects, etc., which is transferred to a victim by a bite or sting. 2 Ill will; spite. [< L *venenum* poison] —**Syn.** 2 hate, malice, rancor, spitefulness.

**ve·nous** (vē′nəs) *adj.* 1 Of, pertaining to, contained, or carried in a vein or veins. 2 Designating the blood carried by the veins back to the heart and lungs. 3 Marked with or having veins: also **ve′nose.** [< L *vena* vein] —**ve′nous·ly** *adv.* —**ve·nos·i·ty** (vē·nos′ə·tē, və-), **ve′nous·ness** *n.*

**vent** (vent) *n.* 1 An outlet; means of escape. 2 An opening for the passage of liquids, gases, etc. 3 A slit in a garment, as a coat. 4 *Zool.* An opening through which wastes are eliminated. —**give vent to** To utter or express: to *give vent* to one's anger. —*v.t.* 1 To give expression to. 2 To permit to escape at a vent, as a gas. 3 To make a vent in. [< OF < *fendre* cleave < L *findere* split]

**ven·ti·late** (ven′tə·lāt) *v.t.* **·lat·ed, ·lat·ing** 1 To produce a free circulation of air in, as by means of open windows, doors, etc. 2 To provide with a vent. 3 To expose to examination and discussion. 4 To oxygenate, as blood. [< L *ventus* wind] —**ven′ti·la′tion** *n.* —**ven′ti·la′tive** *adj.*

**ven·ti·la·tor** (ven′tə·lā′tər) *n.* 1 One who or that which ventilates. 2 A device or opening for replacing stale air with fresh air.

**ven·tri·cle** (ven′trə·kəl) *n.* Any cavity in the body, esp. either of the two lower chambers of the heart, from which blood is forced into the arteries. [< L *venter, ventris* belly] — **ven·tric·u·lar** (-trĭk′yə-lər) *adj.* • See heart.

**ven·tril·o·quism** (ven-trĭl′ə-kwĭz′əm) *n.* The art of speaking in such a way that the sound seems to come from some source other than the person speaking. Also **ven·tril′o·quy** [< L *venter* belly + *loqui* speak] —**ven·tri·lo·qui·al** (ven′trə-lō′kwē-əl), **ven·tril′o·quis′tic** *adj.* —**ven′tri·lo′qui·al·ly** *adv.* —**ven·tril′o·quist** *n.* —**ven·tril′o·quize′** (-kwĭz) (·quized, ·qui·zing) *v.i. & v.t.*

**ven·ture** (ven′chər) *v.* ·tured, ·tur·ing *v.t.* 1 To expose to chance or risk; stake. 2 To run the risk of. 3 To express at the risk of denial or refutation: to *venture* a suggestion. 4 To place or send on a chance, as in a speculative investment. —*v.i.* 5 To take risk in going, coming, etc.: to *venture* into deep water. —*n.* 1 A risk; hazard. 2 An undertaking attended with risk. 3 That which is ventured, esp. property risk. —**at a venture** At random; haphazardly. [Alter. of ADVENTURE] —**ven′tur·er** *n.*

**ven·ture·some** (ven′chər·səm) *adj.* 1 Bold; daring. 2 Involving hazard; risky. —**ven′ture·some·ly** *adv.* —**ven′ture·some·ness** *n.*

**ven·tur·ous** (ven′chər·əs) *adj.* 1 Adventurous; bold. 2 Hazardous; risky; dangerous. —**ven′tur·ous·ly** *adv.* —**ven′tur·ous·ness** *n.*

**Ve·nus** (vē′nəs) *Rom. Myth.* The goddess of love and beauty. —*n.* 1 A beautiful woman. 2 The planet of the solar system second in distance from the sun. • See PLANET.

**ve·ra·cious** (və-rā′shəs) *adj.* 1 Speaking the truth; truthful. 2 True; accurate. [< L *verus* true] —**ve·ra′cious·ly** *adv.* —**ve·ra′cious·ness** *n.*

**ve·rac·i·ty** (və-răs′ə-tē) *n. pl.* ·ties 1 Honesty; truthfulness. 2 Accuracy; trueness. 3 That which is true; truth. [< L *verax*] —**Syn.** 1 candor, frankness, integrity.

**ve·ran·da** (və-răn′də) *n.* An open porch, usu. roofed, along one or more sides of a building. Also **ve·ran′dah.** [< Pg. *varanda* railing, balustrade]

**verb** (vûrb) *n. Gram.* 1 One of a class of words which express existence, action, or occurrence, or that function as a copula or an auxiliary. 2 Any word or construction functioning similarly. [< L *verbum* word]

**ver·bal** (vûr′bəl) *adj.* 1 Of, in, or pertaining to words: a *verbal* contract; a *verbal* image. 2 Of, pertaining to, or concerned with words rather than the ideas they convey. 3 Word

for word; verbatim; literal: a *verbal* translation. 4 *Gram.* **a** Partaking of the nature of or derived from a verb: a *verbal* noun. **b** Used to form verbs: a *verbal* prefix. 5 *Informal* Adept at using words, as in choice or range of vocabulary: She's very *verbal* for her age. —*n. Gram.* A noun directly derived from a verb, in English often having the form of the present participle, as, "There shall be *weeping* and *wailing* and *gnashing* of teeth"; also, an infinitive used as a noun, as, "*To err* is human": also *verbal noun.* [< L *verbum* word] —**ver′bal·ly** *adv.* • See oral.

**ver·bi·age** (vûr′bē-ĭj) *n.* 1 Use of too many words. 2 Manner of verbal expression. [< F *verbe* word]

**ver·bose** (vər·bōs′) *adj.* Using or containing an unnecessary number of words; wordy. [< L *verbum* word] —**ver·bose′ly** *adv.* —**ver·bose′ness, ver·bos′i·ty** (-bŏs′ə-tē) *n.* — Syn. garrulous, long-winded, prolix.

**ver·dant** (vûr′dənt) *adj.* 1 Green with vegetation; fresh. 2 Immature in experience. [< F *verdoyer* grow green] —**ver′dan·cy** *n.* —**ver′dant·ly** *adv.*

**ver·dict** (vûr′dĭkt) *n.* 1 The decision of a jury in an action. 2 A conclusion expressed; an opinion. [< L *vere dictum* truly said]

**ver·di·gris** (vûr′də·grēs, -grĭs, -grē) *n.* 1 A green or greenish blue acetate of copper obtained by treating copper with acetic acid. 2 The blue-green crust formed by corrosion of copper, bronze, or brass in air, sea water, etc. [< OF *vert de Grece*, lit., green of Greece]

**ver·dure** (vûr′jər) *n.* 1 The fresh greenness of growing vegetation. 2 Green vegetation. [< F *verd* green]

**verge** (vûrj) *n.* 1 The extreme edge; brink: on the *verge* of bankruptcy. 2 A bounding or enclosing line surrounding something. — *v.i.* verged, verg·ing 1 To be contiguous or adjacent. 2 To form the limit or verge. [< L *virga* twig]

**ver·i·fi·ca·tion** (ver′ə·fə·kā′shən) *n.* 1 The act of verifying, or the state of being verified. 2 A proof or confirmation, as by examination. —**ver′i·fi·ca′tive** *adj.*

**ver·i·fy** (ver′ə·fī) *v.t.* ·fied, ·fy·ing 1 To prove to be true or accurate; confirm. 2 To test the accuracy or truth of. 3 *Law* To affirm under oath. [< L *verus* true + *facere* make] —**ver′i·fi′er** *n.* —**Syn.** 1 authenticate, corroborate, substantiate. 2 ascertain.

**ver·i·si·mil·i·tude** (ver′ə·sĭ·mĭl′ə·t(y)ood) *n.* 1

Appearance of truth; likelihood. 2 That which resembles truth. [< L *verisimilitudo*]

**ver·i·ta·ble** (ver′ə·tə·bəl) *adj.* Genuine; true; real. [< F *vérité* truth] —**ver′i·ta·ble·ness** *n.* —**ver′i·ta·bly** *adv.*

**ver·i·ty** (ver′ə·tē) *n. pl.* ·**ties** 1 Truth; correctness. 2 A true statement; a fact. [< L *veritas* truth < *verus* true]

**ver·mi·cel·li** (vûr′nɪə·chel′ē, -sel′ē) *n.* A food paste made into slender wormlike cords thinner than spaghetti. [Ital., lit., little worms]

**ver·mi·fuge** (vûr′mə·fyōōj′) *n.* Any remedy that destroys intestinal worms. [< L *vermis* a worm + *fugare* expel]

**ver·mil·ion** (vər·mil′yən) *n.* 1 A brilliant, durable red pigment obtained from cinnabar or made synthetically. 2 An intense orange-red color. —*adj.* Of a bright orange-red color. —*v.t.* To color with vermilion. [< OF *vermeil*]

**ver·min** (vûr′min) *n. pl.* ·**min** 1 Noxious small animals or parasitic insects, as lice, worms, mice, etc. 2 *Brit.* Certain animals injurious to game, as weasels, owls, etc. 3 A repulsive person or persons. [< L *vermis* a worm] —**ver′min·ous** *adj.* —**ver′min·ous·ly** *adv.* —**ver′min·ous·ness** *n.*

**ver·nac·u·lar** (vər·nak′yə·lər) *n.* 1 The native language of a locality. 2 The common daily speech of any people. 3 The specialized vocabulary of a profession or trade. 4 An idiomatic word or phrase. —*adj.* 1 Belonging to one's native land; indigenous: said of a language, idiom, etc. 2 Using the colloquial native tongue: *vernacular* poets. 3 Written in the language indigenous to a people: a *vernacular* translation of the Bible. [< L *vernaculus* domestic, native] —**ver·nac′u·lar·ly** *adv.*

**ver·nal** (vûr′nəl) *adj.* 1 Belonging to, appearing in, or appropriate to spring. 2 Youthful; fresh. [< L *vernus* belonging to spring] —**ver′nal·ly** *adv.*

**ver·sa·tile** (vûr′sə·til, -tīl) *adj.* 1 Having many aptitudes or talents. 2 Having many uses: a *versatile* fabric. 3 Movable in more than one direction, as the toe of a bird. 4 *Bot.* Turning about so freely on the support to which it is attached: said of an anther. [< L *versare*, freq. of *vertere* turn] —**ver′sa·tile·ly** *adv.* —**ver′sa·til′i·ty** (-til′ə·tē) *n.*

**verse** (vûrs) *n.* 1 A single line of a poem. 2 A group of lines in a poem; stanza. 3 Metrical composition as distinguished from prose; poetry. 4 A specified type of metrical composition: iambic *verse*. 5 One of the short divisions of a chapter of the Bible. [< L *versus* a turning, a verse]

**versed** (vûrst) *adj.* Having ready skill and knowledge; proficient. [< L *versari* occupy oneself] —**Syn.** experienced, practiced, seasoned, skillful.

**ver·si·fy** (vûr′sə·fī) *v.* ·**fied**, ·**fy·ing** *v.t.* 1 To turn prose into verse. 2 To narrate or treat in verse. —*v.i.* 3 To write poetry. —**ver·si·fi·ca·tion** (vûr′sə·fə·kā′shən), **ver′si·fi′er** *n.*

**ver·sion** (vûr′zhən, -shən) *n.* 1 A translation or rendition from one language into another. 2 A description of an event, occurrence, etc., from a personal viewpoint. [< Med. L *versio* a turning < L *vertere* to turn] —**ver′sion·al** *adj.*

**vers li·bre** (ver lē′br′) *French* Free verse. —**vers li·brist** (lē′brist).

**ver·te·bra** (vûr′tə·brə) *n. pl.* ·**brae** (-brē, -brā) or ·**bras** Any of the individual bones of the spinal column. [L, a joint, vertebra < *vertere* to turn] —**ver′te·bral** *adj.*

**ver·te·brate** (vûr′tə·brit, -brāt) *adj.* 1 Having a backbone or spinal column. 2 Pertaining to or characteristic of vertebrates. 3 Pertaining to, having, or composed of vertebrae. —*n.* Any of a division of animals characterized by a spinal column, as fishes, birds, and mammals. [< L *vertebratus* jointed] —**ver′te·brat′ed** *adj.*

**ver·ti·cal** (vûr′ti·kəl) *adj.* 1 Perpendicular; upright. 2 Of or pertaining to the vertex. 3 Occupying a position directly overhead; at the highest point. 4 Of or pertaining to a business concern that undertakes a process from raw material to consumer: a *vertical* trust. —*n.* 1 A vertical line, plane, or circle. 2 An upright beam or rod in a truss. —**ver′ti·cal′i·ty** (-kal′ə·tē), **ver′ti·cal·ness** *n.* —**ver′ti·cal·ly** *adv.*

**ver·ti·go** (vûr′tə·gō′) *n. pl.* ·**goes** or **ver·tig·i·nes** (vər·tij′ə·nēz) A disorder in which a person or his surroundings seem to whirl about in such a way as to make the person dizzy and usu. sick. [L, lit., a turning around]

**ves·sel** (ves′əl) *n.* 1 A hollow receptacle capable of holding a liquid, as a pot, tub, pitcher, etc. 2 A ship or large boat. 3 Any of several aircraft. 4 *Biol.* A duct or canal for containing or transporting a fluid. [< L *vas* a vessel]

**ves·ti·bule** (ves′tə·byōōl) *n.* 1 A small antechamber leading into a building or another room. 2 An enclosed passage from one railway passenger car to another. 3 *Anat.* Any cavity leading to another cavity: the *vestibule* of the ear. —*v.t.* ·**buled,** ·**bul·ing** To provide with a vestibule or vestibules. [< L *vestibulum* an entrance hall] —**ves·tib′u·lar** (-tib′yə-lər) *adj.*

**ves·tige** (ves′tij) *n.* 1 A trace of something absent, lost, or gone. 2 *Biol.* A remnant of an organ that is no longer functional. [< F < L *vestigium* a footprint] —**Syn.** 1 hint, remnant, tinge, touch.

**vest·ment** (vest′mənt) *n.* 1 An article of clothing. 2 Any of several ritual garments of the clergy. [< L *vestire* clothe] —**vest·ment·al** (vest·men′təl) *adj.*

**vet·er·an** (vet′ər·ən, vet′rən) *n.* 1 An experienced soldier or an ex-soldier. 2 A member of the armed forces who has been in active service. 3 A person with long experience in an occupation, calling, etc. —*adj.* 1 Having had long experience or practice. 2 Of, pertaining to, or for veterans. [< L *vetus, veteris* old]

**vet·er·i·nar·i·an** (vet′ər·ə·nâr′ē·ən, vet′rə-) *n.* A practitioner of medical and surgical treatment of animals.

**vet·er·i·nar·y** (vet′ər·ə·ner′ē, vet′rə-) *adj.* Of, pertaining to, or designating the science or practice of preventing, curing, or alleviating the diseases and injuries of animals, esp. domestic animals. —*n. pl.* ·**nar·ies** VETERINARIAN. [< L *veterinarius* pertaining to beasts of burden < *veterina* beasts of burden]

**ve·to** (vē′tō) *v.t.* ·**toed,** ·**to·ing** 1 To refuse approval of (a bill passed by a legislative body). 2 To forbid or refuse to consent to. —*n. pl.* ·**toes** 1 The right of one branch of government to cancel, prohibit, postpone, etc., the projects of another branch; esp., the right of a chief executive, as the president or a governor, to refuse to approve a legislative enactment by withholding his signature. 2 A message giving the reasons of a chief executive for refusing to approve a bill. 3 The exercise of the right to veto. 4 Any authoritative prohibition. [< L, I forbid] —**ve′to·er** *n.*

**vex** (veks) *v.t.* 1 To annoy by petty irritations. 2 To trouble or afflict. 3 To baffle, puzzle, or confuse. [< L *vexare* to shake] —**vex·ed·ly** (vek′sid·lē) *adv.* —**vex′ed·ness, vex′er** *n.* —**Syn.** 1 chagrin, irritate, pester, pique.

**vi·a** (vī′ə, vē′ə) *prep.* 1 By way of; by a route passing through. 2 By means of. [< L *via* a way]

**vi·a·duct** (vī′ə·dukt) *n.* A bridgelike structure,

esp. a large one of arched masonry, to carry a road or railroad over a valley, section of a city, etc. [< L *via* a way + (AQUE)DUCT]

**vi·al** (vī′əl) *n.* A small bottle, usu. of glass, for medicines and other liquids. [< Gk. *phialē* a shallow cup]

**vi·and** (vī′ənd) *n.* 1 An article of food, esp. meat. 2 *pl.* Provisions; food. [< OF *viande*]

**vi·brate** (vī′brāt) *v.* ·**brat·ed,** ·**brat·ing** *v.i.* 1 To move back and forth, as a pendulum. 2 To move back and forth rapidly. 3 To resound: The note *vibrates* on the ear. 4 To be emotionally moved. —*v.t.* 5 To cause to move back and forth. 6 To cause to quiver. 7 To send forth (sound, etc.) by vibration. [< L *vibrare* to shake]

**vi·bra·tion** (vī·brā′shən) *n.* 1 The act of vibrating; oscillation. 2 *Physics* **a** A periodic, back-and-forth motion of a particle or body. **b** Any physical process characterized by cyclic changes in a variable, as wave motion. **c** A single cycle of such a process. 3 *pl. Slang* One's emotional response to an aura felt to surround a person or thing, esp. when considered in or out of harmony with oneself. —**vi·bra′tion·al** *adj.*

**vi·bra·to·ry** (vī′brə·tôr′ē, -tō′rē) *adj.* 1 Pertaining to, causing, or characterized by vibration. 2 That vibrates or is capable of vibration.

**vi·car·i·ous** (vī·kâr′ē·əs, vī-) *adj.* 1 Suffered or done in place of another: a *vicarious* sacrifice. 2 Felt through identifying with another's experience: *vicarious* pleasure in his wife's talent. 3 Filling the office of or acting for another. 4 Delegated: *vicarious* authority. [< L *vicarius*] —**vi·car′i·ous·ly** *adv.* —**vi·car′i·ous·ness** *n.*

**vice** (vīs) *n.* 1 Moral depravity; evil. 2 An immoral action, trait, etc. 3 A habitual, usu. trivial, failing or defect; shortcoming. [<L *vitium* a fault] —**Syn.** 1 corruption, dissoluteness, profligacy.

**vice·ge·rent** (vis·jir′ənt) *n.* One duly authorized to exercise the powers of another; a deputy. —*adj.* Acting in the place of another. [<L VICE + *gerere* carry, manage] —**vice·ge′ren·cy** (-sē) *n.* (*pl.* ·**cies**)

**vice·roy** (vīs′roi) *n.* One who rules a country, colony, or province by the authority of his sovereign. [< VICE- + F *roi* a king] —**vice·roy′al** (-roi′əl) *adj.* —**vice′roy·al·ty** (*pl.* ·**ties**), **vice′roy·ship′** *n.*

**vi·ce ver·sa** (vī′sē, vûr′sə, vī′sə vûr′sə, vīs′ vûr′sə) With the relation of terms being reversed; conversely. [L]

**vi·cin·i·ty** (vi·sin′ə·tē) n. pl. ·ties 1 A region adjacent or near; neighborhood. 2 Nearness; proximity. [<L vicinus nearby]

**vi·cious** (vish′əs) adj. 1 Corrupt in conduct or habits; depraved; immoral. 2 Of the nature of vice: vicious acts. 3 Unruly or dangerous, as an animal: a vicious dog. 4 Marked by evil intent; malicious; spiteful: a vicious lie. 5 Worthless or invalidated because defective; full of errors or faults: vicious arguments. 6 Informal Unusually severe or punishing: a vicious blow. 7 Informal Savage; heinous: a vicious crime. [<OF<L vittiosus<vittium a fault] —vi′cious·ly adv. —vi′cious·ness n.

**vi·cis·si·tude** (vi·sis′ə·t′ōōd) n. 1 Usu. pl. Irregular changes or variations, as of conditions or fortune: the vicissitudes of life. 2 A change or alteration; also, the condition or quality of being changeable. [<L vicis a turn, change] —vi·cis·si·tu·di·nary (və·sis′ə·t′ōō/də·ner′ē), vi·cis′si·tu′di·nous adj.

**vic·tim** (vik′tim) n. 1 A person injured or killed by circumstances beyond his control: a victim of a flood. 2 A sufferer from any diseased condition: a victim of arthritis. 3 One who is swindled; a dupe. 4 A living creature killed as a sacrifice to a deity. [< L victima a beast for sacrifice]

**vic·tim·ize** (vik′tim·iz) v.t. ·ized, ·iz·ing 1 To make a victim of; cause suffering to. 2 To cheat; dupe: victimized by loan sharks. —vic·tim·i·za·tion (vik′tə·mə·zā′shən) n. —vic′tim·iz′er n.

**vic·tor** (vik′tər) n. One who wins any struggle or contest. —adj. Victorious: the victor nation. [<L victus, p.p. of vincere conquer]

**vic·to·ri·ous** (vik·tôr′ē·əs, -tō′rē-) adj. 1 Having won victory; triumphant. 2 Characterized by or relating to victory. —vic·to′ri·ous·ly adv. —vic·to′ri·ous·ness n.

**vic·to·ry** (vik′tər·ē) n. pl. ·ries 1 The overcoming of an enemy or adversary; triumph, as in war. 2 An overcoming of any difficulty or obstacle, considered as an achievement earned through effort. [< L victor victor]

**vict·ual** (vit′l) n. 1 Food fit for consumption by man. 2 pl. Food prepared for consumption. 3 pl. A supply of food; provisions. [< L victualis of food<victus food]

**vid·e·o** (vid′ē·ō) adj. 1 Of or pertaining to television, esp. to the picture. 2 Producing a signal convertible into a television picture: a video recording —n. 1 Television image or the electric signal corresponding to it. 2 Videotape. [L, I see]

**vie** (vi) v. vied, vy·ing v.i To put forth effort to excel or outdo others. [<MF envier invite, challenge] —vi′er n.

**view** (vyōō) n. 1 The act of seeing or examining; survey; examination; inspection. 2 Range of vision. 3 Something seen: a view of the harbor. 4 A representation of a scene, esp. a landscape. 5 Something regarded as the object of action; purpose. 6 Opinion; judgment; belief: What are your views on this subject? 7 The immediate or forseeable future: no end in view. —in view of In consideration of. —on view Set up for public inspection. —with a view to With the aim or purpose of. —v.t. 1 To look at; behold. 2 To scrutinize; examine. 3 To survey mentally; consider. 4 To regard in a certain way. [< OF veoir see < L videre]

**vig·il** (vij′əl) n. 1 An act or period of keeping awake. 2 An act or period of keeping watch. 3 Eccl. a The eve of a holy day. b pl. Religious devotions on such an eve. [< L vigil awake]

**vig·i·lance** (vij′ə·ləns) n. The quality of being vigilant; alertness to threat or danger.

**vig·i·lant** (vij′ə·lənt) adj. Alert to danger; wary. [< L vigilare keep awake < vigil awake] —vig′i·lant·ly adv. —Syn. cautious, circumspect, heedful, watchful.

**vi·gnette** (vin·yet′) n. 1 A short, subtly wrought picture in words; sketch. 2 A decorative design before the title page of a book, at the end or beginning of a chapter, etc. 3 An engraving, photograph, etc., that shades off gradually into the background. —v.t. ·gnet·ted, ·gnet·ting To finish, as an engraving or photograph, in the manner of a vignette. [< F vigne a vine]

**vig·or** (vig′ər) n. 1 Active bodily or mental strength; energy. 2 Vital or natural growth, as in a healthy plant. 3 Intensity or force. 4 Legal force; validity. Brit. sp. vig′our. [< L < vigere be lively, thrive]

**vile** (vil) adj. vil·er, vil·est 1 Morally base; corrupt. 2 Disgusting; loathsome. 3 Very bad: vile food. [< L vilis cheap] —vile′ly adv. —vile′ness n.

**vil·i·fy** (vil′ə·fi) v.t. ·fied, ·fy·ing To speak of abusively or slanderously; defame. [< L vilis cheap + facere make] —vil′i·fi·ca′tion (-fə·kā′shən), vil′i·fi′er n. —Syn. denigrate, malign, revile, traduce.

**vil·la** (vil′ə) n. A house, usu. large and imposing, in the country or suburbs or at the seashore. [L, a country house, farm]

**vil·lage** (vil′ij) n. 1 A collection of houses in a rural district, smaller than a town but larger than a hamlet. **2** Such a settlement incorporated as a municipality. **3** The inhabitants of a village, collectively. [< L *villaticus* pertaining to a villa < *villa* a villa]

**vil·lain** (vil′ən) *n.* **1** One who has committed crimes or evil deeds; scoundrel: now often used humorously. **2** A character in a novel, play, etc., who is the opponent of the hero. **3** VILLEIN. [< OF *vilain* a farm servant]

**vim** (vim) *n.* Force or vigor; energy; spirit. [L, accusative of *vis* power]

**vin·di·cate** (vin′də·kāt) *v.t.* ·cat·ed, ·cat·ing **1** To clear of accusation, censure, suspicion, etc. **2** To defend or maintain, as a right or claim, against challenge or attack and show to be just, right, and reasonable. **3** To provide justification for; justify. [< L *vindicare* avenge, claim] —**vin·di·ca·tive** (vin·dik′ə·tiv, vin′də·kā′tiv), **vin′di·ca·to′ry** (-kə·tôr′ē, -tō′rē) *adj.* —**vin′di·ca′tor** *n.*

**vin·di·ca·tion** (vin′də·kā′shən) *n.* **1** The act of vindicating, or the state of being vindicated. **2** A justification; defense.

**vin·dic·tive** (vin·dik′tiv) *adj.* Having or characterized by a vengeful spirit. [< L *vindicta* a revenge] —**vin·dic′tive·ly** *adv.* —**vin·dic′tive·ness** *n.* —**Syn.** retaliatory, revengeful, spiteful.

**vine** (vīn) *n.* **1** Any climbing plant. **2** The flexible stem of such a plant. **3** GRAPEVINE (def. 1). [< L *vinum* wine]

**vin·e·gar** (vin′ə·gər) *n.* **1** A variously flavored solution of acetic acid obtained by the fermentation of cider, wine, etc., and used as a condiment and preservative. **2** Acerbity, as of speech. [< OF *vin* wine + *aigre* sour] —**vin′e·gar·y** *adj.*

**vi·nous** (vī′nəs) *adj.* **1** Pertaining to, characteristic of, or having the qualities of wine. **2** Caused by, affected by, or addicted to wine. [< L *vinum* wine] —**vi·nos·i·ty** (vī·nos′ə·tē) *n.*

**vin·tage** (vin′tij) *n.* **1** The yield of grapes or wine from a vineyard or wine-growing district for one season. **2** The harvesting of a vineyard and the making of wine; also, the season when these things are done. **3** Wine, esp. fine wine of a particular region and year. **4** The year or the region in which a particular wine is produced. **5** *Informal* The type or kind current at a particular time: a joke of ancient *vintage.* —*adj.* Of a fine vintage: *vintage* wines. [< OF *vendage* < L *vinum* wine + *demere* remove]

**vi·nyl** (vī′nəl) *n.* An organic radical derived from ethylene and entering into the composition of numerous plastics. [< L *vinum* wine + -YL

**vi·o·late** (vī′ə·lāt) *v.t.* ·lat·ed, ·lat·ing **1** To break or infringe, as a law, oath, agreement, etc. **2** To profane, as a holy place. **3** To break in on; interfere with: to *violate* one's privacy. **4** To ravish; rape. **5** To offend or treat contemptuously: to *violate* a person's beliefs. [< L *violare* use violence <*vis* force] —**vi′o·la′tion**, **vi′o·la′tor** *n.* —**vi′o·la′tive** *adj.* —**Syn. 2** desecrate, pollute. **3** disturb; interrupt.

**vi·o·lence** (vī′ə·ləns) *n.* **1** Physical force exercised to injure, damage, or destroy. **2** An instance of such exercise of physical force; an injurious or destructive act. **3** Intensity; severity; force: the *violence* of a tornado. **4** Injury or damage, as by irreverence, distortion, or alteration: editing that did *violence* to the original text.

**vi·o·lent** (vī′ə·lənt) *adj.* **1** Proceeding from or marked by great physical force or activity. **2** Caused by or exhibiting intense emotional or mental excitement; passionate: a *violent* rabble-rouser. **3** Characterized by intensity of any kind: *violent* heat. **4** Marked by the unjust or illegal exercise of force: to take *violent* measures. **5** Resulting from external force or injury; unnatural: a *violent* death. [< L *violentus* < *vis* force] —**vi′o·lent·ly** *adv.*

**vi·o·let** (vī′ə·lit) *n.* **1** Any of a widely distributed genus of perennial herbs, bearing irregular flowers usu. of a bluish purple color. **2** Any of several plants having violet-colored flowers. **3** A bluish purple color. —*adj.* Bluish purple. [< L *viola*]

**vi·o·lin** (vī′ə·lin′) *n.* **1** A musical instrument having four strings and a sounding box of wood, and played by means of a bow. **2** A violinist, esp. in an orchestra. [< Ital. *viola* a viola]

**vi·o·lon·cel·lo** (vī′ə·lən·chel′ō, vē′ə-) *n. pl.* ·los CELLO. [< Ital. *violone* a bass viol, aug. of *viola*] —**vi′o·lon·cel′list** *n.*

**VIP, V.I.P.** *Informal* very important person.

**vi·ra·go** (vi·rä′gō, -rā′-, vi-) *n. pl.* ·goes or ·gos A loud, ill-tempered woman; shrew; scold. [L, manlike woman]

**vir·gin** (vûr′jin) *n.* **1** A person, esp. a young woman, who has never had sexual intercourse. **2** A maiden or unmarried woman. —*adj.* **1** Being a virgin. **2** Consisting of virgins: a *virgin* band. **3** Pertaining or suited to a virgin; chaste; maidenly. **4** Uncorrupted; pure; clean: *virgin* whiteness. **5** Not hitherto used, touched, tilled, or worked upon: *virgin* forest. 6 Not previously processed or manufactured; new: *virgin* wool. 7 Occurring for the first time; initial: a *virgin* effort. [< L *virgo* a maiden]

**vir·ile** (vir′əl, īl) *adj.* 1 Having the characteristics of manhood. 2 Having the vigor or strength of manhood. 3 Able to procreate. [< L *vir* a man] —**vi·ril·i·ty** (və·ril′ə·tē) *n.*

**vi·rol·o·gy** (və·rol′ə·jē, vī-) *n.* The study of viruses, esp. in relation to disease. —**vi·rol′o·gist** *n.*

**vir·tu·al** (vûr′chōō·əl) *adj.* Being so in essence or effect, but not in form or fact. [< Med. L *virtualis* < L *virtus* strength] —**vir′tu·al′i·ty** (-al′ə·tē) *n.* —**vir′tu·al·ly** *adv.*

**vir·tue** (vûr′chōō) *n.* 1 General moral excellence; uprightness; goodness. 2 A particular moral excellence. 3 Any admirable quality or merit: Patience is a *virtue*. 4 Sexual purity; chastity. 5 Efficacy; potency, as of a medicine. —**by** (or **in**) **virtue of** By or through the force or authority of. —**make a virtue of necessity** To do willingly what one has to do anyhow. [< L *virtus* strength, bravery <*vir* man] —**Syn.** 1 integrity, rectitude, righteousness, worthiness.

**vir·u·lent** (vir′ə·lənt) *adj.* 1 Extremely harmful; noxious; deadly. 2 Severe and rapid in its progress: said of a disease. 3 Very infectious: said of a pathogenic microorganism. 4 Full of bitter hatred; hostile. [< L *virulentus* full of poison <*virus* a poison] —**vir′u·lence**, **vir′u·len·cy** *n.* —**vir′u·lent·ly** *adv.*

**vi·rus** (vī′rəs) *n.* 1 Any of a class of ultramicroscopic filter-passing pathogens capable of reproduction only within specific living cells. 2 Venom, as of a snake. 3 Any evil influence: the *virus* of greed. [L, poison, slime]

**vi·sa** (vē′zə) *n.* An official endorsement on a passport certifying that it has been examined and that the bearer may enter or pass through the country which has granted the endorsement. —*v.t.* **·saed**, **·sa·ing** 1 To put a visa on. 2 To give a visa to. [F< L < p.p. of *videre* see]

**vis·age** (viz′ij) *n.* 1 The face. 2 Appearance; aspect; look. [< L *visus* a look] —**vis′aged** *adj.*

**vis·cer·a** (vis′ər·ə) *n.pl. sing.* **vis·cus** (vis′kəs) 1 The internal organs of the body, as the stomach, lungs, heart, etc. 2 Commonly, the intestines. [L, pl. of *viscus* an internal organ]

**vis·cos·i·ty** (vis·kos′ə·tē) *n. pl.* **·ties** 1 The property of fluids by which they offer re-

sistance to flow or to change in the arrangement of their molecules. 2 The measure of this property.

**vis·count** (vī′kount) *n.* A nobleman ranking below an earl or count and above a baron. [< OF *visconte*] —**vis′count·cy**, **vis′count·ship**, **vis′count·y** *n.*

**vis·cous** (vis′kəs) *adj.* 1 Greatly resistant to flow; of high viscosity. 2 VISCID. [< L *viscum* birdlime] —**vis′cous·ly** *adv.* —**vis′cous·ness** *n.*

**vise** (vīs) *n.* A clamping device, usu. of two jaws made to be closed together with a screw, lever, or the like, for grasping and holding a piece of work. —*v.t.* **vised**, **vis·ing** To hold, force, or squeeze in or as in a vise. [< OF *vis* a screw <L *vitis* vine]

**vis·i·bil·i·ty** (viz′ə·bil′ə·tē) *n. pl.* **·ties** 1 The fact, condition, or degree of being visible. 2 *Meteorol.* The clearness of the atmosphere in terms of the distance at which objects can be seen distinctly.

**vis·i·ble** (viz′ə·bəl) *adj.* 1 Capable of being seen. 2 That can be perceived mentally; evident. [< L *visus*, p.p. of *videre* see] —**vis′i·ble·ness** *n.* —**vis′i·bly** *adv.* —**Syn.** 1 perceptible. 2 clear, distinct, obvious, plain.

**vi·sion** (vizh′ən) *n.* 1 The act or power of seeing; sense of sight. 2 That which is seen. 3 A beautiful person, landscape, etc. 4 A mental representation of external objects or scenes, as in sleep. 5 A conception in the imagination; mental image: *visions* of power and wealth. 6 The ability to perceive, discern, and anticipate; foresight; imagination. —*v.t.* To see in or as in a vision. [< L *visus*, p.p. of *videre* see] —**vi′sion·al** *adj.* —**vi′sion·al·ly** *adv.*

**vis·it** (viz′it) *v.t.* 1 To go or come to see (a person) from friendship, courtesy, on business, etc. 2 To go or come to (a place, etc.), as for transacting business or for touring: to *visit* the Louvre. 3 To be a guest of; stay with temporarily: I *visited* them for several days. 4 To come upon or afflict. 5 To inflict upon. —*v.i.* 6 To pay a visit; call. 7 To stay with someone temporarily. 8 *Informal* To converse; chat. —*n.* 1 The act of visiting a person, place, or thing. 2 A social call or short stay. 3 *Informal* A friendly chat. 4 An official call, as for inspection, medical examination, etc. [< L *visare* < *visus*, p.p. of *videre* see]

**vis·i·ta·tion** (viz′ə·tā′shən) *n.* 1 The act of visiting; esp., an official inspection, examination, etc. 2 A dispensation of punishment or reward, as by God. —**the Visitation** 1 The visit of the Virgin Mary to her cousin, Elizabeth. *Luke* 1:39–56. 2 A church feast, observed on July 2, commemorating this event. —**vis′i·ta′tion·al** *adj.*

**vis·i·tor** (viz′ə·tər) *n.* One who visits; guest.

**vi·sor** (vi′zər) *n.* 1 A projecting piece on a cap shielding the eyes. 2 In armor, the front piece of a helmet which protected the upper part of the face and could be raised or lowered. 3 A movable device over the inside of the windshield of a car, serving to reduce glare. [< OF *vis* face] —**vi′sored** (-zərd) *adj.*

**vis·ta** (vis′tə) *n.* 1 A view, esp. one seen through a long, narrow space, as along an avenue, between rows of trees, etc. 2 The space itself. 3 A mental view embracing a series of events. [Ital., sight <L *videre* see] —**vis′taed** (vis′təd) *adj.*

**vis·u·al** (vizh′oo·əl) *adj.* 1 Of or pertaining to the sense of sight. 2 Perceptible by sight; visible. 3 Done or perceived by sight only. 4 Instructing through the sense of sight: *visual* aids. [< L *visus* a sight < *videre* see] —**vis′u·al·ly** *adv.*

**vi·tal** (vīt′l) *adj.* 1 Of or pertaining to life. 2 Essential to or supporting life. 3 Affecting life in a destructive way; fatal: a *vital* wound. 4 Of the utmost importance or interest. 5 Full of life; vigorous; energetic; dynamic. —*n.pl.* 1 The organs necessary to life, as the brain, heart, etc. 2 The necessary parts of anything. [< L *vitalis* < *vita* life] —**vi′tal·ly** *adv.*

**vi·tal·i·ty** (vī·tal′ə·tē) *n.* 1 The power to live and develop. 2 Power of continuing in force or effect. 3 Physical or mental energy; vigor; strength.

**vi·ta·min** (vī′tə·min) *n.* Any of a group of organic substances whose presence in the diet in minute quantities is essential for the maintenance of specific physiological functions. [< L *vita* life + AMINE] —**vi′ta·min′ic** *adj.*

**vi·ti·ate** (vish′ē·āt) *v.t.* ·at·ed, ·at·ing 1 To impair the use or value of; spoil. 2 To debase or corrupt. 3 To render weak, ineffective, legally invalid, etc.: Fraud *vitiates* a contract. [< L *vitium* a fault] —**vi′ti·a′tion, vi′ti·a′tor** *n.*

**vit·re·ous** (vit′rē·əs) *adj.* 1 Of, pertaining to, or like glass; glassy. 2 Obtained from glass. 3 Of or pertaining to the vitreous humor. [< L *vitrum* glass] —**vit′re·os′i·ty** (-os′ə·tē), **vit′re·ous·ness** *n.*

**vit·ri·fy** (vit′rə·fī) *v.t. & v.i.* ·fied, ·fy·ing To change into glass or a vitreous substance;

make or become vitreous. [< L *vitrum* glass + *facere* make] —**vit′ri·fac′tion** (-fak′shən), **vit′ri·fi·ca′tion** *n.*

**vi·tu·per·ate** (vī·t′ŏŏ′pə·rāt, vi-) *v.t.* ·at·ed, ·at·ing To find fault with abusively; rail at; berate; scold. [< L *vituperare* blame, scold < *vitium* a fault + *parare* prepare] —**vi·tu′per·a′tion, vi·tu′per·a′tor** *n.* —**vi·tu′per·a′tive** *adj.* —**vi·tu′per·a′tive·ly** *adv.*

**vi·va·cious** (vi·vā′shəs, vī-) *adj.* Full of life and spirits; lively; active. [< L *vivax* < *vivere* live] —**vi·va′cious·ly** *adv.* —**vi·va′cious·ness** *n.* —**Syn.** animated, brisk, cheerful, sparkling, spirited.

**viv·id** (viv′id) *adj.* 1 Having an appearance of vigorous life; lively; spirited. 2 Very strong; intense: said of colors. 3 Producing or suggesting lifelike images. 4 Producing a sharp impression on the senses: a *vivid* description. [< L *vividus* lively < *vivere* to live] —**viv′id·ly** *adv.* —**viv′id·ness** *n.*

**viv·i·sec·tion** (viv′ə·sek′shən) *n.* Cutting, dissection, or other operation on a living animal, esp. in experiments designed to promote knowledge of physiological and pathological processes. [< L *vivus* living, alive + *sectio* a cutting] —**viv′i·sec′tion·al** *adj.* —**viv′i·sec′tion·ist** *n., adj.*

**vix·en** (vik′sən) *n.* 1 A female fox. 2 A turbulent, quarrelsome woman; shrew. [< ME *fixen* a she-fox] —**vix′en·ish** *adj.* —**vix′en·ly** *adj., adv.*

**viz, viz.** namely (L *videlicet*).

**vo·cab·u·lar·y** (vō·kab′yə·ler′ē) *n. pl.* ·lar·ies 1 A list of words or of words and phrases, esp. one arranged in alphabetical order and defined or translated; a lexicon; glossary. 2 All the words of a language. 3 All the words used or understood by a particular person, class, profession, etc. 4 The range of expression at a person's disposal, esp. in art. [< L *vocabulum*. See VOCABLE.]

**vo·cal** (vō′kəl) *adj.* 1 Of or pertaining to the voice or the production of the voice. 2 Having voice; able to speak or utter sounds: *vocal* creatures. 3 Composed for, uttered by, or performed by the voice: a *vocal* score. 4 Full of voices or sounds; resounding: The air was *vocal* with their cries. 5 Freely expressing oneself in speech: the *vocal* segment of the populace. [< L *vocalis* speaking, sounding] —**vo·cal·i·ty** (vō·kal′ə·tē), **vo′cal·ness** *n.* —**vo′cal·ly** *adv.*

**vo·ca·tion** (vō·kā′shən) *n.* 1 A stated or regular occupation. 2 A call to, or fitness for, a certain career. 3 The work or profession for which one has or believes one has a special fitness. [< L *vocare* to call] —**vo·ca'tion·al** *adj.* —**vo·ca'tion·al·ly** *adv.*

**vo·cif·er·ous** (vō·sif'ər·əs) *adj.* Making or characterized by a loud outcry; noisy; clamorous. —**vo·cif'er·ous·ly** *adv.* —**vo·cif'er·ous·ness** *n.*

**vogue** (vōg) *n.* 1 Fashion or style. 2 Popular favor; popularity. [F, fashion, orig., rowing] —**vogu'ish** *adj.*

**voice** (vois) *n.* 1 The sound produced by the vocal organs of a vertebrate, esp. by a human being in speaking, singing, etc. 2 The quality or character of such sound: a melodious *voice.* 3 The power or ability to make such a sound: to lose one's *voice.* 4 Something suggesting the sound of vocal utterance: the *voice* of the wind. 5 Expressed opinion, choice, etc. 6 The right to express an opinion, choice, etc. 7 A person or agency by which the thought, wish, or purpose of another is expressed: This journal is the *voice* of the teaching profession. 8 Expression: to give *voice* to one's ideals. 9 *Phonet.* The sound produced by vibration of the vocal cords, as heard in the utterance of vowels and certain consonants, as *b, d,* and *z.* 10 A singer: Caruso was a great *voice.* 11 In a musical composition, a part for a singer or an instrument. 12 *Gram.* A form of a verb which indicates whether its subject is active or passive. —**in voice** Having the voice in good condition for singing and speaking. —**lift up one's voice** 1 To shout or sing loudly. 2 To protest. —**with one voice** With one accord; unanimously. —*v.t.* **voiced, voic·ing** 1 To put into speech; give expression to; utter. 2 *Music* To regulate the tones of, as the pipes of an organ. 3 *Phonet.* To utter with voice. [< L *vox, vocis*] • When the subject of a verb performs the action, the verb is in the active voice: *My aunt baked a chocolate cake; Her father gave her a bicycle.* When the subject of a verb is acted upon, the verb is in the passive voice: *The chocolate cake was baked by my aunt; She was given a bicycle by her father.*

**void** (void) *adj.* 1 Containing nothing; without content; empty. 2 Having no legal force or validity; not binding. 3 Producing no effect; useless. —**void of** Lacking; without. —*n.* 1 An empty space; vacuum. 2 The quality or condition of feeling empty, lonely, lost, etc. —*v.t.* 1 To make void or of no effect; annul. 2 To empty or remove (contents); evacuate.

—*v.i.* 3 To eliminate waste from the body; urinate or defecate. [< L *vacuus* empty] —**void'er, void'ness** *n.* —**void'ly** *adv.*

**vol·a·tile** (vol'ə·til; *chiefly Brit.* -til) *adj.* 1 Evaporating rapidly; capable of being vaporized. 2 Inconstant; changeable. 3 Transient; fleeting. [< L *volatilis* < *volare* fly] —**vol'a·tile·ness, vol·a·til·i·ty** (vol'ə·til'ə·tē) *n.*

**vol·can·ic** (vol·kan'ik) *adj.* 1 Of, pertaining to, produced by, or characterized by a volcano or volcanoes. 2 Like a volcano; explosive; violent. —**vol·can'i·cal·ly** *adv.* —**vol·can·ic·i·ty** (vol'kə·nis'ə·tē) *n.*

**vol·ca·no** (vol·kā'nō) *n. pl.* **·noes** or **·nos.** *Geol.* An opening in the earth's surface from which hot matter is or has been ejected, often surrounded by a hill or mountain of ejected material. [< L *Vulcanus* Vulcan]

**vo·li·tion** (və·lish'ən) *n.* 1 The act of willing; exercise of the will. 2 The power of willing; willpower. [< L *velle* to will] —**vo·li'tion·al, vo·li'tion·ar·y** (-ən·er·ē), **vol·i·tive** (vol'ə·tiv) *adj.* —**vo·li'tion·al·ly** *adv.*

**vol·ley** (vol'ē) *n.* 1 A simultaneous discharge of many guns. 2 A discharge of many bullets, stones, arrows, etc. 3 Any discharge of many things at once: a *volley* of oaths. 4 In tennis, the flight of the ball before it touches the ground; also, a return of the ball before it touches the ground. —*v.t.* & *v.i.* **·leyed, ·ley·ing** 1 To discharge or be discharged in a volley. 2 In tennis, to return (the ball) without allowing it to touch the ground. [< MF *voler* to fly] —**vol'ley·er** *n.*

**volt** (vōlt) *n.* A unit equal to the difference of electric potential which, when steadily applied to a conductor whose resistance is one ohm, will produce a current of one ampere. [< A. *Volta,* 1745–1827, Italian physicist]

**vol·u·ble** (vol'yə·bəl) *adj.* Having a flow of words or fluency in speaking; talkative. [< L *volubilis* easily turned < *voluus,* p.p. of *volvere* to turn] —**vol'u·bil'i·ty** (vol'yə·bil'ə·tē), **vol'u·ble·ness** *n.* —**vol'u·bly** *adv.*

**vol·ume** (vol'yōōm, -yəm) *n.* 1 A collection of sheets of paper bound together; a book. 2 A book that is part of a set. 3 A quantity or amount: a large *volume* of sales. 4 A measure of quantity in terms of space occupied, as cubic inch, cubic centimeter, liter, pint, etc. 5 *Acoustics* Fullness or quantity of sound or tone. —**speak volumes** To be full of meaning; express a great deal. [< L *volumen* a roll, scroll] —**vol'umed** *adj.*

**vo·lu·mi·nous** (və·lōō′mə·nəs) *adj.* 1 Consisting of or capable of filling volumes: a *voluminous* correspondence. 2 Writing or speaking much. 3 Having great volume or bulk; large. [< L *volumen* a roll] —**vo·lu·mi·nos·i·ty** (və·lōō′mə·nos′ə·tē), **vo·lu′mi·nous·ness** *n.* —**vo·lu′mi·nous·ly** *adv.*

**vol·un·tar·y** (vol′ən·ter′ē) *adj.* 1 Done, made, or given by one's own free will or choice: a *voluntary* contribution. 2 Endowed with or exercising will or free choice. 3 Acting without constraint: a *voluntary* donor. 4 Subject to or directed by the will, as a muscle or movement. 5 Intentional; volitional: *voluntary* manslaughter. —*n. pl.* **·tar·ies** 1 Voluntary action or work. 2 A solo, usu. on the organ, often improvised, played before, during, or after a church service. [< L *voluntas* will] —**vol·un·tar·i·ly** (vol′ən·ter′ə·lē, vol′ən·ter′-) *adv.* —**vol′un·tar′i·ness** *n.*

**vol·un·teer** (vol′ən·tir′) *n.* 1 One who enters into any service of his own free will. 2 One who voluntarily enters military service. —*adj.* 1 Of, pertaining to, or composed of volunteers; voluntary. 2 Serving as a volunteer. —*v.i.* 1 To offer or give voluntarily: to *volunteer* one's services. —*v.i.* 2 To enter or offer to enter into some service or undertaking of one's free will. [< OF *voluntaire* voluntary]

**vo·lup·tu·ar·y** (və·lup′chōō·er′ē) *n. pl.* **·ar·ies** One addicted to luxury and sensual indulgence. [< L *voluptas* pleasure] —**Syn.** hedonist, sensualist, sybarite.

**vo·lup·tu·ous** (və·lup′chōō·əs) *adj.* 1 Pertaining to, inclining to, producing, or produced by sensuous or sensual gratification. 2 Devoted to the enjoyment of pleasures or luxuries. 3 Suggesting the satisfaction of sensual desire. [< L *voluptas* pleasure] —**vo·lup′tu·ous·ly** *adv.* —**vo·lup′tu·ous·ness** *n.*

**vom·it** (vom′it) *v.i.* 1 To disgorge the contents of the stomach; throw up. 2 To issue with violence from any hollow place; be ejected. —*v.t.* 3 To disgorge (the contents of the stomach). 4 To discharge or send forth copiously or forcibly: The volcano *vomited* smoke. —*n.* 1 The act of vomiting. 2 Matter ejected from the stomach in vomiting. [< L *vomere*] —**vom′it·er** *n.*

**vo·ra·cious** (vô·rā′shəs, vō-, və-) *adj.* 1 Eating with greediness; ravenous. 2 Very eager, as in some desire; insatiable. 3 Immoderate: a *voracious* appetite. [< L *vorax* < *vorare* devour] —**vo·ra′cious·ly** *adv.* —**vo·rac·i·ty** (-ras′ə·tē), **vo·ra′cious·ness** *n.*

**vor·tex** (vôr′teks) *n. pl.* **·tex·es** or **·ti·ces** (-tə·sēz) 1 A mass of rotating or whirling fluid, esp. one spiraling in toward a center; a whirlpool or whirlwind. 2 Something resembling a vortex, as an activity or situation from which it is difficult to escape. [< L, var. of *vertex* top, point] —**vor′ti·cal** (-ti·kəl) *adj.* —**vor′ti·cal·ly** *adv.*

**vo·ta·ry** (vō′tər·ē) *n. pl.* **·ries** 1 One who is bound by vows, as a nun or priest. 2 One devoted to some particular worship, pursuit, study, etc. Also **vo′ta·rist.** —*adj.* 1 Of, pertaining to, or like a vow. 2 Consecrated by a vow. [< L *votus,* p.p. of *vovere* vow]

**vote** (vōt) *n.* 1 A formal expression of choice or opinion, as in electing officers, passing resolutions, etc. 2 That by which such choice or opinion is expressed, as the ballot, a show of hands, etc. 3 The number of ballots cast, hands raised, etc., to indicate such choice or opinion. 4 The votes of a specified group; also, the group itself. 5 The right to vote. 6 A voter. —*v.* **vot·ed, vot·ing** *v.t.* 1 To enact or determine by vote. 2 To cast one's vote for: to *vote* the Democratic ticket. 3 To elect or defeat by vote. 4 *Informal* To declare by general agreement: to *vote* a concert a success. —*v.i.* 5 To cast one's vote. —**vote down** To defeat or suppress by voting against. —**vote in** To elect. [< L *votum* a vow, wish, orig. p.p. neut. of *vovere* vow]

**vouch** (vouch) *v.i.* 1 To give one's own assurance or guarantee: with *for:* I will *vouch* for their honesty. 2 To serve as assurance or proof: with *for:* The evidence *vouches* for his innocence. —*v.t.* 3 To bear witness to; attest or affirm. 4 To cite as support or justification, as a precedent, authority, etc. 5 To uphold by satisfactory proof or evidence; substantiate. [< L *vocare* call < *vox, vocis* a voice]

**vouch·er** (vou′chər) *n.* 1 A document that serves to vouch for the truth of something, or attest an alleged act, esp. the expenditure or receipt of money. 2 One who vouches for another: a witness.

**vow** (vou) *n.* 1 A solemn promise, as to God or a god. 2 A pledge of faithfulness: marriage *vows.* 3 A solemn and emphatic affirmation. —**take vows** To enter a religious order. —*v.t.* 1 To promise solemnly. 2 To declare with assurance or solemnity. 3 To make a solemn promise or threat to do, inflict, etc. —*v.i.* 4 To make a vow. [< L *votum.* See VOTE.] —**vow′er** *n.*

**vow·el** (vou′əl, voul) *n.* 1 *Phonet.* A voiced speech sound produced by the relatively unimpeded passage of air through the mouth. 2 A letter indicating such a sound, as *a, e, i, o,* or *u.* —*adj.* Of or pertaining to a vowel or vowels. [< L *vocalis (littera)* vocal (letter)]

**voy·age** (voi′ij) *n.* 1 A journey by water, esp. by sea. 2 Any journey, as one by aircraft. —*v.* ·**aged,** ·**ag·ing** *v.i.* 1 To make a voyage; travel. —*v.t.* 2 To traverse. [< L *viaticum*] — **voy′ag·er** *n.* —**Syn.** *n.* 1 crossing, cruise, sail, trip.

**vo·yeur** (vwä·yûr′) *n.* One who is sexually gratified by looking at sexual objects or acts. [< F *voir* see] —**vo·yeur′ism** *n.*

**vul·can·ize** (vul′kən·īz) *v.t. & v.i.* ·**ized,** ·**iz·ing** To heat (natural rubber) with sulfur in order to increase strength and elasticity. [< Vul-CAN] —**vul′can·i·za′tion, vul′can·iz′er** *n.*

**vul·gar** (vul′gər) *adj.* 1 Lacking good manners, taste, etc.; coarse; unrefined. 2 Offensive or obscene in expression: a *vulgar* usage. 3 Of or pertaining to the common people; general; popular. 4 Written in or translated into the common language or dialect; vernacular. [< L *vulgus* the common people] —**vul′gar·ly** *adv.* —**Syn.** 1 boorish, crude, tasteless. 2 indecent, taboo. 3 ordinary, plebeian.

**vul·gar·i·ty** (vul·gar′ə·tē) *n. pl.* ·**ties** 1 The state, quality, or character of being vulgar. 2 Something vulgar, as an act or expression.

**vul·ner·a·ble** (vul′nər·ə·bəl) *adj.* 1 That may be wounded; capable of being hurt. 2 Open to attack; assailable. 3 In contract bridge, having won one game of a rubber, and therefore subject to doubled penalties if contract is not fulfilled. [< L *vulnerare* to wound < *vulnus* a wound] —**vul′ner·a·bil′i·ty, vul′ner·a·ble·ness** *n.* —**vul′ner·a·bly** *adv.*

**vul·ture** (vul′chər) *n.* 1 Any of various large birds related to hawks and falcons, having a naked head and dark plumage, and feeding on carrion. 2 Something or someone that preys upon others. [< L *vultur*] —**vul′tur·ous** *adj.*

# W

**wad·dle** (wod′l) *v.i.* ·**dled,** ·**dling** 1 To walk with short steps, swaying from side to side. 2 To move clumsily; totter. —*n.* A clumsy rocking walk, like that of a duck. [Freq. of WADE] —**wad′dler** *n.* —**wad′dly** *adj.*

**wade** (wād) *v.* **wad·ed, wad·ing** *v.i.* 1 To walk through water or any substance more resistant than air, as mud, sand, etc. 2 To proceed slowly or laboriously: to *wade* through a lengthy book. —*v.t.* 3 To pass or cross, as a river, by walking on the bottom; walk through; ford. —**wade in** (or **into**) *Informal* To attack or begin energetically or vigorously. —*n.* An act of wading. [< OE *wadan* go]

**wa·fer** (wā′fər) *n.* 1 A very thin crisp biscuit, cooky, or cracker; also, a small disk of candy. 2 *Eccl.* A small flat disk of unleavened bread, used in the Eucharist in some churches. 3 A thin hardened disk of dried paste, gelatin, etc., used for sealing letters, attaching papers, or receiving the impression of a seal. —*v.t.* To attach, seal, or fasten with a wafer. [< AF *wafre* < MLG *wafel*]

**waf·fle**[1] (wof′əl, wô′fəl) *n.* A batter cake, crisper than a pancake, baked in a waffle iron. [< Du. *wafel* a wafer]

**waf·fle**[2] (wof′əl, wô′fəl) *v.i.* ·**fled,** ·**fling** 1 *Chiefly Brit. Informal* To speak or write nonsense. 2 *Informal* To avoid giving a direct answer; hedge. —*n.* *Chiefly Brit. Informal* Nonsense; twaddle. [< obs. *woff, waff* to yelp]

**waft** (waft, wäft) *v.t.* 1 To carry or bear gently or lightly over air or water; float. 2 To convey as if on air or water. —*v.i.* 3 To float, as on the wind. 4 To blow gently, as a breeze. —*n.* 1 The act of one who or that which wafts. 2 A breath or current of air. 3 A passing sound or odor. 4 A waving motion. [< Du. *wachten* to guard] —**waft′er** *n.*

**wag** (wag) *v.* **wagged, wag·ging** *v.t.* 1 To cause to move lightly and quickly from side to side or up and down, as a dog's tail. 2 To move (the tongue) in talking. —*v.i.* 3 To move lightly and quickly from side to side or up and down. 4 To move busily in animated talk or gossip: said of the tongue. —*n.* 1 The act or motion of wagging: a *wag* of the head. 2 A droll or humorous person; wit. [Prob. < Scand.]

**wage** (wāj) *n.* 1 *Often pl.* Payment for service rendered, esp. such payment calculated by the hour, day, or week, or for a certain amount of work. 2 *Usu. pl. (construed as sing. or pl.)* Reward: the *wages* of sin. —*v.t.* **waged, wag·ing** To engage in and maintain vigorously; carry on: to *wage* war. [< AF *wagier* pledge] —**Syn.** *n.* 1 compensation, earnings, pay, remuneration.

**wa·ger** (wā′jər) *v.t. & v.i.* To bet. —*n.* 1 A bet.

2 The thing bet on. [< AF *wagier*] **—wa′ger·er** *n*

**wag·on** (wăg′ən) *n.* 1 Any of various four-wheeled, usu. horse-drawn vehicles for carrying heavy loads. 2 A child's open, four-wheeled cart, pulled and steered by a long handle. 3 PATROL WAGON. 4 STATION WAGON. 5 *Brit.* A railway freight car. 6 A stand on wheels or casters for serving food or drink: a tea *wagon*. **—on** (or **off**) **the** (water) **wagon** *Informal* Abstaining (or no longer abstaining) from alcoholic beverages. **—fix** (someone's) **wagon** *Slang* To even scores with; get revenge on. **—v.t.** To carry or transport in a wagon. *Brit. sp.* **wag′gon.** [<Du. *wagen*]

**waif** (wāf) *n.* 1 A homeless, neglected person, esp. a child. 2 A stray animal. [Prob. < Scand.]

**wail** (wāl) *v.i.* 1 To grieve with mournful cries; lament. 2 To make a mournful, crying sound, as the wind. **—v.t.** 3 To mourn; lament. 4 To cry out in sorrow. **—n.** 1 A prolonged, high-pitched sound of lamentation. 2 Any mournful sound, as of the wind. [< ON *vei* woe] **—wail′er** *n.* **—wail′ful** *adj.* **—wail′ful·ly, wail′ing·ly** *adv.*

**wain·scot** (wān′skət, -skŏt, -skōt) *n.* 1 A facing for inner walls, usu. of paneled wood. 2 The lower part of an inner wall, when finished with material different from the rest of the wall. **—v.t.** ·**scot·ed** or ·**scot·ted,** ·**scot·ing** or **scot·ting** To face or panel with wainscot. [< MLG *wagen* a wagon + *schot* a wooden partition]

**waist** (wāst) *n.* 1 The part of the body between the lower ribs and the hips. 2 The middle part of any object, esp. if narrower than the ends: the *waist* of a violin. 3 That part of a woman's dress covering the body from the waistline to the shoulders. 4 BLOUSE. 5 WAISTLINE (def. 2). [ME *wast*]

**wait** (wāt) *v.i.* 1 To stay in expectation, as of an anticipated action or event: with *for, until,* etc. 2 To be or remain in readiness. 3 To remain temporarily neglected or undone. 4 To perform duties of personal service; esp. to act as a waiter or waitress. **—v.t.** 5 To stay or remain in expectation of: to *wait* one's turn. 6 *Informal* To put off or postpone: Don't *wait* breakfast for me. **—wait on** (or **upon**) 1 To act as a clerk or attendant to. 2 To go to see; visit. 3 To attend as a result or consequence. **—wait up** 1 To delay going to bed in anticipation of someone's arrival or of something happening. 2 *Informal* To stop until someone catches up.

**—n.** The act of waiting, or the time spent in waiting; delay. **—lie in wait** To remain hidden in order to make a surprise attack. [< AF *waitier*] **—Syn.** *v.* 1 abide, linger, remain, tarry.

**waive** (wāv) *v.t.* **waived, waiv·ing** 1 To give up or relinquish a claim to. 2 To refrain from insisting upon or taking advantage of; forgo. 3 To put off; postpone; delay. [< OF *gaiver* abandon]

**waiv·er** (wā′vər) *n. Law* 1 The voluntary relinquishment of a right, privilege, or advantage. 2 The instrument which evidences such relinquishment. [< AF *weyver* abandon, waive]

**wake** (wāk) *v.* **woke** or **waked, waked** (*Regional* **wok·en**), **wak·ing** *v.i.* 1 To emerge from sleep: often with *up.* 2 To be or remain awake. 3 To become aware or alert. 4 *Regional* To keep watch at night; esp., to hold a wake. **—v.t.** 5 To rouse from sleep or slumber; awake: often with *up.* 6 To rouse or stir up; excite. 7 To make aware; alert. 8 *Regional* To hold a wake over. **—n.** A vigil, esp. a watch over the body of a dead person through the night, just before the burial. [Fusion of OE *wacan* awaken and *wacian* be awake]

**wake·ful** (wāk′fəl) *adj.* 1 Not sleeping or sleepy. 2 Watchful; alert. 3 Sleepless; restless: a *wakeful* time. **—wake′ful·ly** *adv.* **—wake′ful·ness** *n.* **—Syn.** 1 awake. 2 cautious, vigilant, wary.

**wak·en** (wā′kən) *v.t.* 1 To rouse from sleep; awake. 2 To rouse or urge to alertness or activity. **—v.i.** 3 To cease sleeping; wake up. [< OE *wacnian*] **—wak′en·er** *n.*

**walk** (wôk) *v.i.* 1 To advance on foot in such a manner that one part of a foot is always on the ground, or, in quadrupeds, that two or more feet are always on the ground. 2 To go on foot for exercise or amusement. 3 To move in a manner suggestive of walking, as certain inanimate objects. 4 To act or live in some manner: to *walk* in peace. 5 In baseball, to advance to first base after being pitched four balls. **—v.t.** 6 To pass through, over, or across at a walk: to *walk* the floor. 7 To lead, ride, or drive at a walk: to *walk* a horse. 8 To force or help to walk. 9 To accompany on a walk: I'll *walk* you to school. 10 To bring to a specified condition by walking. 11 To cause to move with a motion resembling a walk: to *walk* a trunk on its corners. 12 In baseball, to allow to advance to first base by pitching four balls. **—**

**walk away from** 1 To outrun or outdo (someone). 2 To sustain little or no injury in an accident. —**walk off** 1 To depart, esp. abruptly. 2 To get rid of (fat, etc.) by walking. —**walk off with** 1 To win, esp. with little difficulty. 2 To steal. —**walk out** *Informal* 1 To go out on strike. 2 To depart suddenly. —**walk out on** *Informal* To forsake; desert. —**walk over** 1 To defeat easily. 2 To treat with contempt. —*n.* 1 The act of walking, as for enjoyment. 2 Manner of walking; gait. 3 A place prepared for walking, as a sidewalk. 4 The distance covered or time spent in walking. 5 A piece of ground set apart for the feeding and exercise of domestic animals. 6 In baseball, the act of walking a batter; also, a being walked. —**walk of life** One's social or financial status. [< OE *wealcan* roll, toss] —**walk′er** *n.* —**Syn.** *v.* 1 saunter, step, stride, tread.

**walk·ie-talk·ie** (wô′kē-tô′kē) *n.* A portable radio transmitting and receiving set.

**walking papers** *Informal* Notice of dismissal from employment, office, etc.

**wall** (wôl) *n.* 1 A continuous structure designed to enclose an area, to be the surrounding exterior of a building, or to be a partition between rooms or halls. 2 A fence of stone or brickwork, surrounding or separating yards, fields, etc. 3 *Usu. pl.* A barrier or rampart constructed for defense. 4 A sea wall; levee. 5 A barrier enclosing a cavity, vessel, or receptacle: the *wall* of the abdomen. 6 Something suggestive of a wall: a *wall* of bayonets. —**drive (push or thrust) to the wall** To force (one) to an extremity; crush. —**drive (or send) up the wall** *Informal* To make extremely nervous, tense, etc. —*v.t.* 1 To provide, surround, protect, etc., with or as with a wall or walls. 2 To fill or block with a wall: often with *up.* —*adj.* 1 Of or pertaining to a wall. 2 Hanging from, growing on, or built into a wall. [< OE *weall* < L *vallum* a rampart]

**wal·let** (wol′it) *n.* A small, usu. folding case, as of leather, for holding paper money, cards, etc., and sometimes change, carried in a pocket or purse. [ME *walet*]

**wal·lop** (wol′əp) *Informal v.t.* 1 To beat soundly; thrash. 2 To hit with a hard blow. —*n.* A hard blow. [< AF *waloper*] —**wal′lop·er** *n.*

**wal·low** (wol′ō) *v.i.* 1 To roll about, as in mud, snow, etc. 2 To move with a heavy, rolling motion, as a ship in a storm. 3 To indulge oneself wantonly: to *wallow* in sensuality.

—*n.* 1 The act of wallowing. 2 A depression or hollow made by wallowing. [< OE *wealwian*] —**wal′low·er** *n.*

**wal·nut** (wôl′nut′, -nət) *n.* 1 Any of various deciduous trees cultivated as ornamental shade trees and valued for their timber and their edible nuts. 2 The wood or nut of any of these trees. 3 The shagbark or its nut. 4 The color of the wood of any of these trees, esp. of the black walnut, a very dark brown: also **walnut brown.** [< OE *wealh* foreign + *hnutu* a nut]

**wal·rus** (wôl′rəs, wol′-) *n.* A very large, seal-like mammal of arctic seas, with flexible hind limbs, projecting tusklike canines in the upper jaw, a bushy, bristly mustache on the muzzle, and a very tough hide. —*adj.* 1 Belonging or pertaining to a walrus. 2 Designating a type of bushy mustache drooping at the ends. [< Scand.]

**waltz** (wôlts) *n.* 1 A dance to music in triple time. 2 Music for or in the style of such a dance. —*v.i.* 1 To dance a waltz. 2 To move quickly: She *waltzed* out of the room. —*v.t.* 3 To cause to waltz. —*adj.* Pertaining to the waltz. [< G *walzen* to waltz, roll] —**waltz′er** *n.*

**wan** (won) *adj.* **wan·ner, wan·nest** 1 Pale, as from sickness; careworn. 2 Faint; feeble: a *wan* smile. [< OE *wann* dark, gloomy] —**wan′ly** *adv.* —**wan′ness** *n.* —**Syn.** 1 ashen, livid, pallid. 2 weak.

**wand** (wond) *n.* 1 A slender, flexible rod waved by a magician. 2 Any rod symbolizing authority, as a scepter. 3 A musician's baton. [< ON *vöndr*]

**wan·der** (won′dər) *v.i.* 1 To travel about without destination or purpose; roam. 2 To go casually or by an indirect route; stroll. 3 To twist or meander. 4 To stray. 5 To deviate in conduct or opinion; go astray. 6 To be delirious. —*v.t.* 7 To wander through or across. [< OE *wandrian*] —**wan′der·er** *n.* —**wan′der·ing·ly** *adv.* —**Syn.** 1 range, rove.

**wane** (wān) *v.i.* **waned, wan·ing** 1 To diminish in size and brilliance. 2 To decline or decrease gradually. 3 To draw to an end. —*n.* 1 A waning or decreasing. 2 The period of such decrease. —**on the wane** Decreasing; declining. [< OE *wanian* lessen]

**want** (wont, wônt) *v.t.* 1 To feel a desire or wish for. 2 To wish; desire: used with the infinitive: to *want* to help. 3 To be deficient in, esp. to a required or customary extent. 4 To desire to see, speak to, arrest, etc.: He *wants* you on the phone; *wanted* by the police. 5 *Chiefly Brit.* To need; require. —*v.i.* 6 To have need: usu. with *for.* 7 To be needy or destitute. —*n.* 1 Lack; scarcity; shortage. 2 Poverty; destitution. 3 Something lacking; a need or craving. [Prob. < ON *vanta* be lacking] —**want′er** *n.* —**Syn.** *n.* 1 dearth, deficiency, insufficiency. 2 indigence, privation.

**wan·ton** (won′tən) *adj.* 1 Licentious; lewd; lustful. 2 Heartless or unjust; malicious: *wanton* savagery. 3 Unprovoked; senseless: a *wanton* murder. 4 Extravagant; unrestrained: *wanton* speech. 5 Not bound or tied; loose: *wanton* curls. 6 Capricious; frolicsome. —*v.i.* 1 To act in a wanton manner; be wanton. —*v.t.* 2 To waste or squander carelessly. —*n.* A lewd or licentious person. [< OE *wan* deficient + *tēon* bring up, educate] —**wan′ton·ly** *adv.* —**wan′ton·ness** *n.*

**war** (wôr) *n.* 1 Armed strife or conflict between nations or states, or between different parties in the same nation. 2 Any act or state of conflict, struggle, or strife: a *war* against poverty. 3 Military science or strategy. —*v.i.* **warred, war·ring** 1 To wage war; fight or take part in a war. 2 To be in any state of active opposition. —*adj.* Of, pertaining to, used in, or resulting from war. [< OHG *werra* strife, confusion]

**war·ble** (wôr′bəl) *v.* **·bled, ·bling** *v.t.* 1 To sing (something) with trills and runs or with tremulous vibrations. —*v.i.* 2 To sing with trills, etc. 3 To make a liquid, murmuring sound, as a stream. 4 YODEL. —*n.* The act or sound of warbling. [< OF *werble* a warble]

**ward** (wôrd) *n.* 1 In a hospital: **a** A large room for six or more patients. **b** A division for specific illnesses or groups of patients: the children's *ward.* 2 A division of a city for administrative or electoral purposes. 3 *Law* A person, as a minor, who is in the charge of a guardian or court. 4 The act of guarding or the state of being guarded. 5 A division or subdivision of a prison. 6 Any means of defense or protection. —*v.t.* To repel or turn aside, as a thrust or blow: usu. with *off.* [< OE *weardian* to watch, guard]

**war·den** (wôr′dən) *n.* 1 A supervisor or custodian of something: a game *warden;* prison *warden.* 2 *Brit.* The head of certain colleges. 3 CHURCHWARDEN (def 1). [< AF *wardein*] —**war′den·ry** (*pl.* **·ries**), **war′den·ship** *n.*

**ward·robe** (wôrd′rōb′) *n.* 1 A large upright

cabinet for wearing apparel. 2 All the garments belonging to any one person. 3 The clothes for a particular season: a spring *wardrobe.* 4 The costumes of a theater, theatrical troupe, motion-picture company, etc.; also, the place where such costumes are kept. [< AF *warder* keep + *robe* a robe]

**ware** (wâr) *n.* 1 Articles of the same class: used collectively in compounds: *glassware.* 2 *pl.* Articles for sale; merchandise. 3 Pottery; earthenware. [< OE *waru*]

**ware·house** (wâr′hous′) *n.* 1 A storehouse for goods or merchandise. 2 *Chiefly Brit.* A large wholesale shop. —*v.t.* **·housed** (-houzd′), **·hous·ing** (-hou′zing) To place or store in a warehouse.

**war·head** (wôr′hed′) *n.* The chamber in the nose of a bomb, guided missile, etc., containing an explosive, incendiary, or chemical charge.

**warm** (wôrm) *adj.* 1 Moderately hot; having heat somewhat greater than temperate: *warm* water; a *warm* climate. 2 Imparting heat: a *warm* fire. 3 Imparting or preserving warmth: a *warm* coat. 4 Having the natural temperature of most living persons or animals: *warm* blood. 5 Heated, as from exertion. 6 Ardent; enthusiastic; fervent: *warm* interest. 7 Lively; agitated: a *warm* argument. 8 Cordial; friendly: a *warm* welcome. 9 Amorous; loving: a *warm* glance. 10 Excitable; fiery: a *warm* temper. 11 Having predominating tones of red or yellow. 12 Recently made; fresh: a *warm* trail. 13 Near to finding a hidden object or fact, as in certain games. 14 *Informal* Uncomfortable by reason of annoyances or danger: They made the town *warm* for him. —*v.t.* 1 To make warm. 2 To make ardent or enthusiastic; interest. 3 To fill with kindly feeling. —*v.i.* 4 To become warm. 5 To become ardent or enthusiastic: often with *up* or *to.* 6 To become kindly disposed or friendly: with *to* or *toward.* —**warm up** 1 To warm. 2 To exercise the body, voice, etc., as before a game or performance. 3 To run an engine, etc., in order to attain correct operating temperature. —*n. Informal* A warming or being warm. [< OE *wearm*] —**warm′er, warm′ness** *n.* —**warm′ly** *adv.*

**warn** (wôrn) *v.t.* 1 To make aware of possible harm; caution. 2 To advise; counsel. 3 To give notice in advance. 4 To notify (a person) to go or stay away. —*v.i.* 5 To give warning. [< OE *wearnian*] —**warn′er** *n.*

**warp** (wôrp) *v.t.* 1 To turn or twist out of

shape, as by shrinkage or heat. 2 To corrupt; pervert: a mind *warped* by bigotry. 3 *Naut.* To move (a vessel) by hauling on a rope or line fastened to something stationary. —*v.i.* 4 To become turned or twisted out of shape, as wood in drying. 5 To deviate from a correct or proper course: go astray. 6 *Naut.* To move by means of ropes fastened to a pier, anchor, etc. —*n.* 1 The state of being warped, twisted out of shape, or biased. 2 The threads that run the long way of a fabric, crossing the woof. 3 *Naut.* A rope or line used for warping. [< OE *weorpan* to throw] —**warp′er** *n.*

**war·rant** (wôr′ənt, wor′-) *n.* 1 *Law* A judicial writ or order authorizing arrest, search, seizure, etc. 2 Something which assures or attests; guarantee. 3 That which gives authority for some course or act; sanction; justification. 4 A certificate of appointment given to a naval or military warrant officer. 5 A document giving a certain authority, esp. for the receipt or payment of money. —*v.t.* 1 To assure or guarantee the quality, accuracy, certainty, or sufficiency of: to *warrant* a title to property. 2 To guarantee the character or fidelity of; pledge oneself for. 3 To guarantee against injury, loss, etc. 4 To be sufficient grounds for; justify. 5 To give legal authority or power to; authorize. 6 *Informal* To say confidently; feel sure. [< AF *warant*] —**war′rant·er** *n.*

**war·ran·ty** (wôr′ən·tē, wor′-) *n.* *pl.* **·ties** 1 *Law* A guarantee by the seller of property, a product, etc., that whatever is sold is or shall be as represented. 2 An official authorization or warrant. [< AF *warant* a warrant]

**war·ren** (wôr′ən, wor′-) *n.* 1 A place where rabbits live and breed. 2 Any building or area overcrowded with people. [< AF *warenne* a game park, a rabbit warren]

**war·ri·or** (wôr′ē·ər, wôr′yər, wor′-) *n.* A man engaged in or experienced in warfare or conflict.

**wart** (wôrt) *n.* 1 A small, usu. hard, benign excrescence on the skin, caused by a virus. 2 Any of various natural protuberances on certain plants and animals. [< OE *wearte*] —**wart′y** *adj.* (·i·er, ·i·est)

**war·y** (wâr′ē) *adj.* **war·i·er, war·i·est** 1 Carefully watching and guarding. 2 Shrewd; wily. [< OE *wǣr*] —**war′i·ly** *adv.* —**war′i·ness** *n.*

**wash** (wosh, wôsh) *v.t.* 1 To cleanse with water or other liquid, as by immersing, scrubbing, etc. 2 To wet or cover with water or other liquid. 3 To flow against or over: a beach *washed* by the ocean. 4 To remove or carry by the use or action of water: with *away, off, out,* etc. 5 To form or wear by erosion. 6 To purify, as gas, by passing through a liquid. 7 To coat with a thin layer of color. 8 To cover with a thin coat of metal. 9 *Mining* a To subject (gravel, earth, etc.) to the action of water so as to separate the ore, etc. b To separate (ore, etc.) thus. —*v.i.* 10 To wash oneself. 11 To wash clothes, etc., in water or other liquid. 12 To withstand the effects of washing: That calico will *wash.* 13 *Informal* To undergo testing successfully: That story won't *wash.* 14 To flow with a lapping sound, as waves. 15 To be carried away or removed by the use or action of water: with *away, off, out,* etc. 16 To be eroded by the action of water. —**wash out** Slang To fail and be dropped from a course, esp. in military flight training. —*n.* 1 The act or an instance of washing. 2 A number of articles, as of clothing, set apart for washing. 3 Liquid or semiliquid refuse; swill. 4 Any preparation used in washing or coating, as a mouthwash. 5 A paint, as water color, spread lightly on a surface. 6 The breaking of a body of water upon the shore, or the sound made by this. 7 Erosion of soil or earth by the action of running water. 8 Material collected and deposited by water, as along a river bank. 9 Agitation or turbulence in water or air caused by something passing through it. 10 An area washed by a sea or river; a marsh; bog. 11 In the w U.S., the dry bed of a stream. —*adj.* Washable without injury: *wash* fabrics. [< OE *wascan*]

**wash·er** (wosh′ər, wô′shər) *n.* 1 One who washes. 2 *Mech.* A small, flat, perforated disk of metal, rubber, etc., used to make a nut or joint tight. 3 WASHING MACHINE.

**wash·out** (wosh′out′, wôsh′-) *n.* 1 A considerable erosion of earth by the action of water; also, the excavation thus made. 2 *Slang* A hopeless or total failure.

**wasp** (wosp, wôsp) *n.* Any of numerous insects related to bees, having membranous wings, biting mouth parts, and effective stings, and including both social and solitary species. [< OE *wæsp*]

**wasp·ish** (wos′pish, wôs′-) *adj.* 1 Of or like a wasp. 2 Irritable; bad-tempered. —**wasp′ish·ly** *adv.* —**wasp′ish·ness** *n.*

**waste** (wāst) *v.* **wast·ed, wast·ing** *v.t.* 1 To use

or expend thoughtlessly; squander. 2 To make weak or feeble. 3 To use up; consume. 4 To fail to use or take advantage of, as an opportunity. 5 To lay waste; devastate. 6 *Slang* To kill; destroy. —*v.i.* 7 To lose strength, vigor, or bulk: often with *away*. 8 To diminish or dwindle gradually. 9 To pass gradually: said of time. —*n.* 1 Thoughtless or unnecessary expenditure, consumption, etc. 2 Failure to benefit or gain from something, as an opportunity. 3 A desolate or devastated place or region; wilderness; desert. 4 A continuous, gradual wearing away of strength, vigor, or substance. 5 Something discarded or rejected as worthless or unneeded, esp. tangled spun cotton thread. 6 Something that escapes without being used, as steam. 7 Garbage; rubbish; trash. 8 Something excreted from the body, as urine or excrement. —**lay waste** To destroy or devastate. —*adj.* 1 Cast aside as worthless; discarded. 2 Excreted from the body. 3 Not cultivated or inhabited; wild; barren. 4 Superfluous: *waste* energy. 5 Containing or conveying waste products. [< L *vastare* lay waste] —**wast′er** *n.* —Syn. *v.* 1 dissipate. 2 debilitate, enfeeble.

**watch** (woch, wôch) *v.i.* 1 To look attentively; observe closely. 2 To be on the alert. 3 To wait expectantly for something: with *for*. 4 To do duty as a guard or sentinel. 5 To keep vigil. —*v.t.* 6 To look at attentively; observe. 7 To keep informed concerning. 8 To be alert for; to *watch* one's opportunity. 9 To keep watch over; guard. —**watch out** To be careful. —*n.* 1 Close and continuous attention; careful observation. 2 Service as a guard or sentry. 3 The period of time during which a guard is on duty. 4 The person or persons set to guard or watch. 5 A small, portable timepiece worn on the wrist or carried in a pocket. 6 A vigil or wake. 7 *Naut.* a A spell of duty on board ship, usu. four hours. b The division of a crew on duty during such a period. [< OE *wœccan*] —**watch′er** *n.*

**watch·ful** (woch′fəl, wôch′-) *adj.* Watching carefully; vigilant; alert. —**watch′ful·ly** *adv.* —**watch′ful·ness** *n.*

**watch·word** (woch′wûrd′, wôch′-) *n.* 1 PASSWORD. 2 A slogan or maxim.

**wa·ter** (wô′tər, wot′ər) *n.* 1 The colorless liquid that covers over 70 percent of the earth's surface, is capable of wetting and dissolving many different substances, and is an essential constituent of all organisms.

2 A chemical compound of hydrogen and oxygen which occurs as a solid, a liquid, or a vapor, depending upon its temperature. 3 *Often pl.* Any body of water, as a lake, river, or a sea. 4 Any liquid or liquid secretion of the body, as perspiration, tears, urine, etc. 5 Any preparation of water holding a substance in solution: mineral *water*. 6 An undulating sheen given to certain fabrics, as silk, etc. 7 In commerce and finance, stock issued without an increase of assets or earning power to back it. —**above water** Out of danger, debt, etc.; secure. —**hold water** To be logical, valid, or dependable. —**like water** Freely; prodigally. —**of the first water** Of the finest quality. —*v.t.* 1 To provide (land, plants, etc.) with water, as by sprinkling or irrigating. 2 To provide with water for drinking. 3 To dilute or weaken with water: often with *down*. 4 To give an undulating sheen to the surface of (silk, linen, etc.). 5 To enlarge the number of shares of (a stock company) without increasing the company assets in proportion. —*v.i.* 6 To secrete or discharge water, tears, etc. 7 To fill with saliva, as the mouth, from desire for food. 8 To drink water. [< OE *wœter*] —**wa′ter·er** *n.*

**wa·ter·col·or** (wô′tər·kul′ər, wot′ər-) *n.* 1 A pigment or coloring matter prepared for painting with water as the medium. 2 A picture or painting done in watercolors. Also **water color.** —*adj.* Of or painted with watercolors.

**wa·ter·fall** (wô′tər·fôl′, wot′ər-) *n.* A fall of water over a precipice.

**wa·ter·line** (wô′tər·lin′, wot′ər-) *n.* 1 *Naut.* a A line on the hull of a ship which shows where the water surface reaches. b Short, horizontal lines on a ship's hull which correspond with the surface of the water when the ship is unloaded, partly loaded, or fully loaded. 2 Any line or mark showing to what level water has risen.

**wa·ter·logged** (wô′tər·lôgd′, -logd′, wot′ər-) *adj.* 1 So saturated or filled with water as to be unmanageable and barely able to float, as a ship, etc. 2 Soaked with water.

**wa·ter·mark** (wô′tər·märk′, wot′ər-) *n.* 1 WATERLINE (def. 2). 2 A mark or design made in paper by pressure while the paper is still in a pulpy state; also, the metal pattern which produces these markings. —*v.t.* 1 To impress (paper) with a watermark. 2 To impress (a mark or design) as a watermark.

**wa·ter·proof** (wô′tər·prōof′, wot′ər-) *adj.* 1 WA-

TERTIGHT. **2** Coated with some substance, as rubber, which prevents the passage of water. —*n.* **1** Waterproof fabric. **2** *Brit.* A raincoat or other waterproof garment. —*v.t.* To render waterproof.

**wa·ter·shed** (wô′tər·shed′, wot′ər-) *n.* **1** A ridge of high land that divides two areas drained by different river systems. **2** The whole region from which a river receives its supply of water. **3** A decisive turning point affecting outlook, actions, etc.

**wa·ter·ski** (wô′tər·skē′, wot′ər-) *v.i.* **-skied, -ski·ing** To glide over water on skilike runners (**water skis**) while being towed by a motorboat. —**wa′ter·ski′er** *n.*

**wa·ter·tight** (wô′tər·tīt′, wot′ər-) *adj.* **1** So closely made that water cannot enter or leak through. **2** That cannot be misunderstood, found illegal or in error, etc.: a *watertight* contract. —**wat′er·tight′ness** *n.*

**watt** (wot) *n.* A unit of power equivalent to one joule per second, or about 1/746 of a horsepower. [< J. *Watt*, 1736–1819, Scottish engineer]

**wave** (wāv) *v.* **waved, wav·ing** *v.i.* **1** To move freely back and forth or up and down, as a flag in the wind. **2** To signal by moving something back and forth or up and down. **3** To have an undulating shape or form: Her hair *waves*. —*v.t.* **4** To cause to wave: to *wave* a banner. **5** To flourish, as a weapon. **6** To give a wavy appearance to or form into waves: to *wave* one's hair. **7** To signal by waving something: He *waved* me aside. **8** To express by waving somthing; to *wave* farewell. —*n.* **1** A ridge or undulation moving on the surface of a liquid. **2** A similar undulation on a freely moving surface: *waves* in the tall grass. **3** A curve or curl in the hair. **4** A curved pattern or shape, as on watered silk. **5** A back-and-forth or up-and-down motion, as with the hand. **6** A more or less prolonged meterological condition: a heat *wave*. **7** An upsurge of something: a crime *wave*; a *wave* of emotion. **8** A surging movement, as of a mass or group: a *wave* of refugees. **9** *Usu. pl.* A large body of water. **10** *Physics* A periodic disturbance propagated through a medium, characterized by a function of time that defines its frequency, amplitude, phase, and velocity. [< OE *wafian*] —**wav′r** *n.*

**wa·ver** (wā′vər) *v.i.* **1** To move one way and the other; flutter. **2** To be uncertain; vacillate. **3** To show signs of falling back or giving way; falter. **4** To flicker; gleam. —*n.* A wa-vering. [< OE *wafian* to wave] —**wa′ver·er** —*n.* —**wa′ver·ing·ly** *adv.* —Syn. **1** oscillate, quiver, shake. **2** hesitate.

**wax** (waks) *n.* **1** BEESWAX. **2** Any of various pliable plant and animal substances that are insoluble in water, that burn in air, or otherwise resemble beeswax. **3** A solid mineral substance resembling wax, as paraffin. **4** SEALING WAX. **5** A waxlike commercial product, used for polishing furniture, floors, etc. —*v.t.* To coat or polish with wax. —*adj.* Made of or pertaining to wax. [< OE *weax*]

**way** (wā) *n.* **1** Direction; route: Which *way* is the city? **2** A path, course, road, etc., leading from one place to another. **3** Space or room to advance or work: Make *way* for the king. **4** Distance in general: a little *way* off. **5** Direction in general: Look the other *way*. **6** Passage from one place to another: on our *way* to Europe. **7** A customary or habitual manner or style of acting or being: Do it her *way*. **8** A plan of action; procedure; method: In what *way* will you accomplish this? **9** Respect; point; particular: He erred in two *ways*. **10** A course of life or experience: the *way* of sin. **11** Desire; wish: to get one's *way*. **12** *Informal* State or condition: to be in a bad *way*. **13** The range of one's experience or observation: An accident threw it in his *way*. **14** *Informal* Neighborhood or locality: out our *way*. **15** *Naut.* **a** Forward motion; headway. **b** *pl.* A tilted framework of timbers upon which a ship slides when launched. —**by the way** In passing; incidentally. —**by way of 1** With the object or purpose of; to serve as: *by way of* introduction. **2** Through; via. —**give way (to) 1** To yield or submit. **2** To collapse. —**go out of one's (or the) way** To inconvenience oneself. —**in the way** In a position that impedes or hinders. —**out of the way 1** In a position so as not to hinder or impede. **2** Out of the usual or convenient location or route. **3** Unusual. **4** Improper; wrong: Has he done anything *out of the way*? —**under way** In motion; making progress. —*adv. Informal* All the distance to: He went *way* to Denver. [< OE *weg*]

**way·far·er** (wā′fâr′ər) *n.* One who travels, esp. on foot. —**way′far′ing** *n.*, *adj.*

**way·lay** (wā′lā′) *v.t.* **-laid, -lay·ing 1** To lie in ambush for and attack. **2** To accost on the way. —**way′lay′er** *n.*

**way·side** (wā′sīd′) *adj.* Pertaining to or near the side of a road. —*n.* The side or edge of the road or highway.

**way·ward** (wā′wərd) *adj.* 1 Willful; head-strong. 2 Not predictable; erratic. [< ME *awei* away + -WARD] —**way′ward·ly** *adv.* —**way′ward·ness** *n.* —**Syn.** 1 disobedient, perverse, refractory, stubborn. 2 capricious.

**weak** (wēk) *adj.* 1 Lacking in physical strength, energy, or vigor; feeble. 2 Incapable of resisting stress or supporting weight: a *weak* wall. 3 Lacking in strength of will or stability of character. 4 Not effective, forceful, or convincing: *weak* reasoning. 5 Lacking in power, intensity, etc.: a *weak* voice. 6 Lacking a specified component or components in the usual or proper amount: *weak* tea. 7 Lacking the power or ability to function properly: a *weak* heart. 8 Lacking mental or intellectual capability. 9 Lacking skill, experience, etc.: a *weak* player. 10 Lacking in power, influence, or authority: a *weak* state. 11 Deficient in some specified thing or quality: *weak* in languages. 12 *Gram.* Denoting a verb in English or other Germanic languages that forms its past tense and past participle by adding *d* or *t* rather than by vowel changes. 13 *Phonet.* Unstressed; unaccented, as a syllable or sound. 14 In prosody, indicating a verse ending in which the accent falls on a word or syllable otherwise without stress. 15 Characterized by declining prices: said of the stock market. [< ON *veikr*] —**Syn.** 1 slight, puny, enfeebled, frail.

**weak·en** (wē′kən) *v.t. & v.i.* To make or become weak or weaker. —**weak′en·er** *n.* —**Syn.** debilitate, enervate, enfeeble, sap.

**wealth** (welth) *n.* 1 A large amount of money or property; riches. 2 The state of being rich. 3 Great abundance of anything: a *wealth* of learning. 4 *Econ.* a All material objects which have economic utility. b All property possessing a monetary value. [ME *welthe < wele* weal]

**wean** (wēn) *v.t.* 1 To transfer (the young of any mammal) from dependence on its mother's milk to another form of nourishment. 2 To free from usu. undesirable habits or associations: usu. with *from.* [< OE *wenian* accustom] —**wean′er** *n.*

**weap·on** (wep′ən) *n.* 1 Any implement of war or combat, as a sword, gun, etc. 2 Any means that may be used against an adversary. 3 Any defensive organ or part of an animal or plant, as a claw, tooth, thorn, etc. [< OE *wǣpen*] —**weap′on·ry** (-rē) *n.*

**wear** (wâr) *v.* **wore, worn, wear·ing** *v.t.* 1 To have on the person as a garment, ornament, etc. 2 To have on the person habitually: He *wears* a derby. 3 To have in one's aspect; exhibit: He *wears* a scowl. 4 To have as a characteristic: She *wears* her hair short. 5 To display or fly: A ship *wears* its colors. 6 To impair or consume by use or constant action. 7 To cause by scraping, rubbing, etc.: to *wear* a hole in a coat. 8 To bring to a specified condition by wear: to *wear* a sleeve to tatters. 9 To exhaust; weary. —*v.i.* 10 To be impaired or diminished gradually by use, rubbing, etc. 11 To withstand the effects of use, handling, etc.: These shoes *wear* well. 12 To remain sound or interesting over a period of time: a friendship that *wore* well. 13 To become as specified from use or attrition: His patience is *wearing* thin. 14 To pass gradually: with *on* or *away.* 15 To have an unpleasant or exhausting effect. —**wear down** 1 To make or become less through friction, use, etc. 2 To tire out; exhaust. 3 To overcome the resistance of by constant pressure, harassment, etc. —**wear off** To diminish gradually. —**wear out** 1 To make or become worthless by use. 2 To waste or use up gradually. 3 To tire or exhaust. —*n.* 1 The act of wearing, or the state of being worn. 2 Material or articles of dress to be worn: often in combination: *footwear, underwear.* 3 Vogue; fashion. 4 Destruction or impairment from use or time. 5 Capacity to resist use or time; durability. —**wear and tear** Loss or damage from use over a period of time. [< OE *werian*] —**wear′er** *n.*

**wea·ry** (wir′ē) *adj.* **·ri·er, ·ri·est** 1 Worn out; tired; fatigued. 2 Discontented or bored: usu. with *of: weary* of life. 3 Indicating or characteristic of fatigue: a *weary* sigh. 4 Causing fatigue; wearisome. —*v.t. & v.i.* **·ried, ·ry·ing** To make or become weary. [< OE *wērig*] —**wea′ri·ly** *adv.* —**wea′ri·ness** *n.*

**wea·sel** (wē′zəl) *n.* 1 Any of certain small, slender, usu. nocturnal carnivorous mammals. 2 A sly or treacherous person. —*v.i.* **·seled, ·sel·ing** *Informal* 1 To fail to fulfill a promise, etc.; renege: with *out.* 2 To speak ambiguously; equivocate. [< OE *wesle*]

**weath·er** (weth′ər) *n.* 1 The general atmospheric condition, as regards temperature, moisture, winds, or related phenomena. 2 Unpleasant atmospheric conditions. —**keep one's weather eye open** *Informal* To be alert. —**under the weather** *Informal* 1 Ailing; ill. 2 Suffering from a hangover. 3

Drunk. —*v.t.* 1 To expose to the action of the weather. 2 To discolor, crumble, or otherwise affect by action of the weather. 3 To pass through and survive, as a crisis. 4 *Naut.* To pass to windward of: to *weather* Cape Fear. —*v.i.* 5 To undergo changes from exposure to the weather. 6 To resist the action of the weather. —*adj.* Facing the wind. [< OE *weder*]

**weave** (wēv) *v.* **wove** or *esp. for defs.* 7, 8, & 11 **weaved, woven** or *esp. for defs.* 7, 8, & 11 **weaved, weaving** *v.t.* 1 To make (a fabric) by interlacing threads or yarns, esp. on a loom. 2 To interlace (threads or yarns) into a fabric. 3 To form by interlacing strands, strips, twigs, etc.: to *weave* a basket. 4 To produce by combining details or elements: to *weave* a story. 5 To twist or introduce into: to *weave* ribbons through one's hair. 6 To spin (a web). 7 To make by going from one side to another: to *weave* one's way through a crowd. 8 To direct (a car, etc.) in this manner. —*v.i.* 9 To make cloth, etc., by weaving. 10 To become woven or interlaced. 11 To make one's way by moving from one side to another. —*n.* A particular method, style, or pattern of weaving. [< OE *wefan*]

**web** (web) *n.* 1 Fabric being woven on a loom. 2 The network of delicate threads spun by a spider or by certain insect larvae. 3 An artfully contrived trap or snare. 4 Any complex network of interwoven parts, elements, etc.: a *web* of lies; a *web* of highways. 5 *Zool.* A membrane connecting the digits, as in aquatic birds, frogs, etc. 6 The vane of a feather. 7 *Anat.* A membrane or tissue. 8 A plate or sheet, as of metal, connecting the ribs, frames, etc., of a structure. 9 *Archit.* The part of a ribbed vault between the ribs. 10 A large roll of paper, as for use in a web press. —*v.t.* **webbed, webbing** 1 To provide with a web. 2 To cover or surround with a web; entangle. [< OE]

**webbed** (webd) *adj.* 1 Having a web. 2 Having the digits united by a membrane.

**web-foot** (web′fŏŏt′) *n.* 1 A foot with webbed toes. 2 A bird or animal having such feet. —**web′-foot′ed** *adj.*

**wed** (wed) *v.* **wed-ded, wed-ded** or **wed, wed-ding** *v.t.* 1 To take as one's husband or wife; marry. 2 To join in wedlock. 3 To unite or join closely: He is *wedded* to his job. —*v.i.* 4 To take a husband or wife; marry. [< OE *weddian* to pledge]

**wed-ding** (wed′ing) *n.* 1 The ceremony of a

marriage. 2 The anniversary of a marriage: golden *wedding*. [< OE *weddian* to pledge]

**wedge** (wej) *n.* 1 A V-shaped piece of metal, wood, etc., used for splitting wood, raising weights, etc. 2 Anything in the form of a wedge. 3 Any action which facilitates policy, entrance, intrusion, etc. 4 An iron golf club with the face at an angle for lofting the ball. —*v.* **wedged, wedg-ing** *v.t.* 1 To force apart with a wedge. 2 To fix in place with a wedge. 3 To crowd or squeeze (something). —*v.i.* 4 To force oneself or itself in like a wedge. [< OE *wecg*]

**wed-lock** (wed′lok) *n.* The state of being married. [< OE *wedd* a pledge + -*lāc*, suffix of nouns of action]

**Wednes-day** (wenz′dē, -dā) *n.* The fourth day of the week. [< OE *Wōdnesdǣg* day of Woden]

**weed** (wēd) *n.* 1 Any unwanted or unsightly plant, esp. one that hinders the growth of cultivated plants. 2 *Informal* a Tobacco. b A cigarette or cigar. c Marihuana; also, a marihuana cigarette. 3 A thin, ungainly person. —*v.t.* 1 To pull up and remove weeds from. 2 To remove (a weed): often with *out.* 3 To remove (anything regarded as harmful or undesirable): with *out.* 4 To rid of anything harmful or undesirable. —*v.i.* 5 To remove weeds, etc. [< OE *wēod*] —**weed′er** *n.*

**week** (wēk) *n.* 1 A period of seven successive days, esp. one beginning with Sunday. 2 The period within a week devoted to work: a 35-hour *week.* —**week in, week out** Every week. [< OE *wicu, wice*]

**week-ly** (wēk′lē) *adj.* 1 Of, pertaining to, or lasting a week. 2 Done or occurring once a week. 3 Reckoned by the week. —*adv.* 1 Once a week. 2 Every week. —*n. pl.* ·**lies** A publication issued once a week.

**weep** (wēp) *v.* **wept, weep-ing** *v.i.* 1 To manifest grief or other strong emotion by shedding tears. 2 To mourn; lament: with *for.* 3 To give out or shed liquid in drops. —*v.t.* 4 To weep for; mourn. 5 To shed (tears, or drops of other liquid). —*n.* 1 The act of weeping, or a fit of tears. 2 An exhudation of liquid; moisture. [< OE *wēpan*] —**weep′-er** *n.* —**Syn.** *v.* 1 cry, sob. 2 bewail, grieve.

**wee-vil** (wē′vəl) *n.* Any of numerous small beetles with elongated snoutlike heads, often having larvae destructive to cotton, grain, fruit, etc. [< OE *wifel* a beetle] —**wee′vil·y, wee′vil·ly** *adj.*

**weigh** (wā) *v.t.* 1 To determine the weight of. 2 To balance or hold in the hand so as to estimate weight. 3 To measure (a quantity or quantities of something) according to weight: with *out.* 4 To consider or evaluate carefully: to *weigh* one's words. 5 To raise or hoist: now only in the phrase **weigh anchor.** —*v.i.* 6 To have a specified weight: She *weighs* ninety pounds. 7 To have influence or importance: The girl's testimony *weighed* heavily with the jury. 8 To be burdensome or oppressive: with *on* or *upon:* What *weighs* on your mind? 9 *Naut.* a To raise anchor. b To begin to sail. —**weigh down** 1 To press or force down by weight or heaviness. 2 To burden or oppress. —**weigh in** To be weighed before a fight or other athletic contest. [< OE *wegan* weigh, carry, lift] —**weigh′er** *n.*

**weight** (wāt) *n.* 1 The quality of having heaviness. 2 The measure of this quality, expressed indefinitely or in standard units: its *weight* is ten pounds. 3 A piece of something, usu. metal, used as a standard unit in weighing: a three-pound *weight.* 4 Any unit of heaviness, as a pound, ounce, etc.; also, a system of such units. 5 *Physics* The force of gravity exerted on any object, equal to the mass of the object multiplied by its acceleration due to gravity. 6 Any mass weighing a definite amount: a four-pound *weight* of flour. 7 Any object having heaviness and used to balance things, exert downward force, etc., as a paperweight, a counterbalance in a machine, a dumbbell for exercising, etc. 8 Burden; pressure: the *weight* of responsibility. 9 Influence; importance; consequence: the great *weight* of this decision. 10 The larger or most valuable part: the *weight* of the data is negative. 11 The comparative heaviness of clothes, as appropriate to the season: summer *weight.* —**carry weight** To be important, significant, influential, etc. —**pull one's weight** To do one's share. —**throw one's weight around** *Informal* To use one's importance or influence in an overbearing or improper manner. —*v.t.* 1 To add weight to; make heavy. 2 To oppress or burden. 3 To adulterate or treat (fabrics or other merchandise) with cheap foreign substances. [< OE *wiht, gewiht*]

**weight·less** (wāt′lis) *adj.* 1 Having little or no heaviness. 2 Subject to little or no gravitational force. —**weight′less·ly** *adv.* —**weigh-t′less·ness** *n.*

**weird** (wird) *adj.* 1 Manifesting or concerned with the supernatural; unearthly; un-

canny. 2 Odd; bizarre; fantastic. [< OE *wyrd* fate] —**weird′ly** *adv.* —**weird′ness** *n.*

**wel·come** (wel′kəm) *adj.* 1 Admitted or received gladly and cordially. 2 Producing satisfaction or pleasure; pleasing: *welcome* tidings. 3 Made free to use or enjoy: She is *welcome* to our car. —*n.* The act of bidding or making welcome; a hearty greeting. —**wear out one's welcome** To come so often or to linger so long as no longer to be welcome. —*v.t.* **·comed, ·com·ing** 1 To greet gladly or hospitably. 2 To receive with pleasure: to *welcome* advice. [< OE *wilcuma*] —**wel′come·ly** *adv.* —**wel′come·ness, wel′com·er** *n.*

**weld** (weld) *v.t.* 1 To unite, as two pieces of metal, by the application of heat along the area of contact. 2 To bring into close association or connection. —*v.i.* 3 To be welded or capable of being welded. —*n.* The joining of pieces of metal by welding; also, the closed joint so formed. [Alter. of WELL[1]] —**weld′a·ble** *adj.* —**weld′er** *n.*

**wel·fare** (wel′fâr) *n.* 1 The condition of being happy, healthy, prosperous, etc.; well-being. 2 WELFARE WORK. 3 Money given to those in need; relief. —**on welfare** Receiving welfare (def. 3) from the government. [< ME *wel* well + *fare* a going]

**well[1]** (wel) *n.* 1 A hole or shaft sunk into the earth to obtain a fluid, as water, oil, or natural gas. 2 A place where water issues naturally from the ground. 3 A source of continued supply; fount: a *well* of learning. 4 A depression, cavity, or vessel used to hold or collect a liquid: an *inkwell.* 5 A deep vertical opening descending through floors of a building, as for light, ventilation, stairs, etc. —*v.i.* 1 To pour forth or flow up, as water in a spring. —*v.t.* 2 To gush: Her eyes *welled* tears. [< OE *weallan* boil, bubble up]

**well[2]** (wel) *adv.* **bet·ter, best** 1 Satisfactorily; favorably: Everything goes *well.* 2 In a good or correct manner; expertly: to dance *well.* 3 Suitably; with propriety: I cannot *well* remain here. 4 Agreeably or luxuriously: He lives *well.* 5 Intimately: How *well* do you know him? 6 To a considerable extent or degree: *well* along in years. 7 Completely; thoroughly; fully: *well* aware. 8 Far: He lagged *well* behind us. 9 Kindly; graciously: to speak *well* of someone. —**as well** 1 Also; in addition. 2 With equal effect or consequence: He might just as *well* have sold it. —**as well as** 1 As satisfactorily as. 2 To the same degree as. 3 In addition to. —*adj.* 1 Suitable, fortunate, right, etc.: It is *well* you called first. 2 In good health. 3 Prosperous; comfortable. —*interj.* An exclamation used to express surprise, expectation, indignation, etc., or to preface a remark. [< OE *wel*] —**Syn.** *adv.* 2 excellently. 3 befittingly, properly. 4 comfortably. • *Well* often appears in combination with participles to form modifiers. When used after a verb such as *be, seem,* etc., such a modifier is written as two words: to be *well satisfied*. When placed before a noun, it must be hyphenated: a *well-kept* secret.

**well-bred** (wel'bred') *adj.* 1 Well brought up; polite. 2 Of good or pure stock: said of animals.

**well-fa·vored** (wel'fa'vərd) *adj.* Of attractive appearance; comely; handsome.

**well-nigh** (wel'nī') *adv.* Very nearly; almost.

**well-off** (wel'ôf', -of') *adj.* 1 In comfortable circumstances; comely. 2 Fortunate.

**well-to-do** (wel'tə-dōō') *adj.* In prosperous or wealthy circumstances; affluent.

**well-wish·er** (wel'wish'ər) *n.* One who wishes well, as to another. —**well'-wish'ing** *adj., n.*

**Welsh** (welsh, welch) *adj.* Pertaining to Wales, its people, or their language. —*n.* 1 The people of Wales. 2 The Celtic language of Wales.

**welt** (welt) *n.* 1 A raised mark on the skin, resulting from a blow or lashing; wale. 2 A strip of material, covered cord, etc., applied to a seam to cover or strengthen it. 3 In shoemaking, a strip of leather set into the seam between the edges of the upper and the outer sole. —*v.t.* 1 To sew a welt on or in; decorate with a welt. 2 *Informal* To flog severely, so as to raise welts. [ME *welte*]

**wel·ter** (wel'tər) *v.i.* 1 To roll about; wallow. 2 To lie or be soaked in some fluid, as blood. —*n.* 1 A rolling movement, as of waves. 2 A turmoil; commotion. [< MDu. *welteren*]

**wend** (wend) *v.* **wend·ed** (*Archaic* went), **wend·ing** *v.t.* 1 To go on (one's way); proceed. —*v.i.* 2 *Archaic* To proceed; go. [< OE *wendan*]

**west** (west) *n.* 1 The general direction in which the sun appears at sunset. 2 The point of the compass at 270°, directly opposite east. 3 Any region lying in this direction. —**the West** 1 The countries lying west of Asia and Asia Minor, including Europe and the Western Hemisphere; the Occident. 2 In the U.S.: a Formerly, the region west of the Allegheny Mountains. b The region west of

the Mississippi, esp. the NW part of this region. 3 The noncommunist countries of Europe and the Western Hemisphere. —*adj.* 1 To, toward, facing, or in the west; western. 2 Coming from the west: the *west* wind. —*adv.* In or toward the west; in a westerly direction. [< OE]

**wet** (wet) *adj.* **wet·ter, wet·test** 1 Moistened, saturated, or covered with water or other liquid. 2 Marked by showers or by heavy rainfall; rainy. 3 Not yet dry: *wet* varnish. 4 Permitting the manufacture and sale of alcoholic beverages: a *wet* county. 5 Preserved or bottled in a liquid. —**all wet** *Slang* Quite wrong; mistaken. —*n.* 1 Water; moisture; wetness. 2 Showery or rainy weather. 3 *Informal* One opposed to prohibition. —*v.t. & v.i.* **wet** or **wet·ted, wet·ting** To make or become wet. [< OE *wǣt*] —**wet'ly** *adv.* —**wet'ness, wet'ter** *n.* —**Syn.** *v.* dampen, moisten, soak.

**wet·back** (wet'bak') *n. Informal* A Mexican who enters the U.S. illegally, esp. by swimming or wading across the Rio Grande.

**whale** (hwāl) *n.* 1 Any of various very large, air-breathing marine mammals of fishlike form. 2 *Informal* Something extremely good or large: a *whale* of a party. —*v.i.* **whaled, whal·ing** To engage in the hunting of whales. [< OE *hwæl*]

**whale·bone** (hwāl'bōn') *n.* 1 The horny, pliable substance hanging in plates from the upper jaw of certain whales. 2 A strip of whalebone, used in stiffening corsets, etc.

**whal·er** (hwā'lər) *n.* A person or a ship engaged in whaling.

**whal·ing** (hwā'ling) *n.* The industry of capturing whales. —*adj. Slang* Huge; whopping.

**wharf** (wôrf) *n. pl.* **wharves** (wôrvz) or **wharfs** 1 A structure of masonry or timber erected on the shore of a harbor, river, etc., alongside which vessels may lie to load or unload cargo, passengers, etc. 2 Any pier or dock. —*v.t.* 1 To moor to a wharf. 2 To deposit or store on a wharf. [< OE *hwearf* a dam]

**what·not** (hwot'not', hwut'-) *n.* An ornamental set of shelves for holding bric-a-brac, etc.

**wheal** (hwēl) *n.* A small raised area or pimple on the skin. [Alter. of WALE]

**wheat** (hwēt) *n.* 1 Any of a genus of cereal grasses, esp. cultivated species yielding spikes of edible grain. 2 Grains of these species collectively, constituting a staple food usu. ground into flour.

**whee·dle** (ʰwēd′l) *v.* **·dled, ·dling** *v.t.* **1** To persuade or try to persuade by flattery, cajolery, etc.; coax. **2** To obtain by cajoling or coaxing. —*v.i.* **3** To use flattery or cajolery. [?] —**whee′dler** *n.* —**whee′dling·ly** *adv.*

**wheel** (ʰwēl) *n.* **1** A solid disk or a circular rim connected to a hub by spokes or rays capable of rotating on a central axis and used to facilitate movement, as in vehicles, or to act with a rotary motion, as in machines. **2** Anything resembling or suggestive of a wheel. **3** An instrument or device having a wheel or wheels as its distinctive characteristic, as a steering wheel, a potter's wheel, a water wheel, etc. **4** *Informal* A bicycle. **5** An old instrument of torture or execution, consisting of a wheel to which the limbs of the victim were tied and then stretched or broken. **6** A turning or rotating movement; revolution. **7** *Usu. pl.* That which imparts or directs motion or controls activity: the *wheels* of democracy. **8** *Slang* A person of influence or authority: **also big wheel. 9** *pl. Slang* An automobile. —**at (or behind) the wheel 1** Steering a motor vehicle, motor boat, etc. **2** In charge or in control. —*v.t.* **1** To move or convey on wheels. **2** To cause to turn on or as on an axis; pivot or revolve. **3** To perform with a circular movement. **4** To provide with a wheel or wheels. —*v.i.* **5** To turn on or as on an axis; pivot. **6** To change one's course of action, attitudes, opinions, etc.: often with *about*. **7** To move in a circular or spiral course. **8** To move on wheels. —**wheel and deal** *Slang* To act freely, aggressively, and often unscrupulously, as in the arrangement of a business or political deal. [< OE *hwēol*]

**wheeze** (ʰwēz) *v.t. & v.i.* **wheezed, wheez·ing** To breathe or utter with a husky, whistling sound. —*n.* **1** A wheezing sound. **2** *Informal* A trite joke. [Prob. < ON *hvǣsa* hiss] —**wheez′er, wheez′i·ness** *n.* —**wheez′i·ly, wheez′ing·ly** *adv.* —**wheez′y** *adj.* (·i·er, ·i·est)

**whelp** (ʰwelp) *n.* **1** One of the young of a dog, wolf, lion, or certain other carnivores. **2** A dog. **3** A worthless young fellow. —*v.t. & v.i.* To give birth (to): said of certain carnivores. [< OE *hwelp*]

**whence** (ʰwens) *adv.* From what place or source: *Whence* does he come? —*conj.* From what or out of which place, source, or cause: asked *whence* these sounds arise. [< OE *hwanne* when]

**where·a·bouts** (ʰwâr′ə·bouts′) *adv.* Near or at what place; about where. —*n.pl. (construed as sing. or pl.)* The place in which a person or thing is.

**where·as** (ʰwâr′az′) *conj.* **1** Since the facts are such as they are; seeing that: often used in the preamble of a resolution, etc. **2** While on the contrary; when in truth. —*n. pl.* **·as·es** A clause or item beginning with the word "whereas."

**wher·e·er** (ʰwâr·âr′) *adj. & conj.* WHEREVER.

**where·fore** (ʰwâr′fôr′, -fōr′) *adv. Archaic* For what reason; why: *Wherefore* didst thou doubt? —*conj.* **1** For which. **2** THEREFORE. —*n.* The cause; reason: the whys and *wherefores.* [< WHERE + FOR]

**where·with·al** (ʰwâr′with·ôl′, -with-) *n.* The necessary means or resources, esp. money: used with *the.*

**whet** (ʰwet) *v.t.* **whet·ed, whet·ting 1** To sharpen, as a knife, by friction. **2** To make more keen or eager; excite; stimulate, as the appetite. —*n.* **1** The act of whetting. **2** Something that whets. [< OE *hwettan*] —**whet′ter** *n.*

**wheth·er** (ʰweth′ər) *conj.* **1** If it be the case that: Tell us *whether* you are going or not. **2** In case; if: *whether* he lived or died, we never heard. **3** Either: He came in first, *whether* by luck or plan. —**whether or no** Regardless; in any case. [< OE *hwǣther*]

**whet·stone** (ʰwet′stōn′) *n.* A fine-grained stone for whetting knives, axes, etc.

**whey** (ʰwā) *n.* A clear liquid that separates from the curd when milk is curdled, as in making cheese. [< OE *hwǣg*] —**whey′ey, whey′ish** *adj.*

**which** (ʰwich) *pron.* **1** What specific one or ones: *Which* are for sale? **2** The specific one or ones that: I know *which* I bought. **3** The thing, animal, or event designated earlier: used restrictively or nonrestrictively: The flood *which* wiped us out was last year; That car, *which* is not old, no longer runs. **4** *Archaic* The person or persons designated earlier: "Our Father, *which* art in heaven," **5** WHICHEVER: Use *which* you find most convenient. **6** A thing, situation, or fact that: He decided to go, *which* was lucky. —*adj.* **1** What specific one or ones: *Which* play did you see? **2** WHICHEVER: Take *which* one you want. **3** Being the one or ones designated earlier: The clock struck one, at *which* point he left. • See WHO. [< OE *hwelc, hwilc*]

**which·ev·er** (ʰwich′ev′ər) *pron. & adj.* **1** Any one (of two or of several): Select *whichever* (ring) you want. 2 No matter which: *Whichever* (song) you choose, sing it well. Also **which'so·ev'er.**

**whiff** ('wĭf) *n.* 1 A slight gust or puff of air. 2 A gust or puff of odor: a *whiff* of onions. 3 A sudden expulsion of breath or smoke from the mouth; a puff. —*v.t.* 1 To drive or blow with a whiff or puff. 2 To smoke, as a pipe. —*v.i.* 3 To blow or move in whiffs or puffs. 4 To exhale or inhale whiffs. [Imit.] —**whiff'er** *n.*

**while** ('wīl) *n.* A period of time: a brief *while.* —**between whiles** From time to time. —**the while** At the same time. —**worth (one's) while** Worth one's time, labor, trouble, etc. —*conj.* 1 During the time that. 2 At the same time that; although: *While* he found fault, he also praised. 3 Whereas: This man is short, *while* that one is tall. —*v.t.* whiled, whil·ing To cause to pass pleasantly: usu. with *away*: to *while* away the time. [< OE *hwīl*]

**whim** ('wĭm) *n.* A sudden, capricious idea, notion, or desire; fancy. [Short for earlier *whim·wham* a trifle]

**whim·per** ('wĭm'pər) *v.i.* 1 To cry with plaintive broken sounds. —*v.t.* 2 To utter with or as if with a whimper. —*n.* A low, broken, whining cry. [Imit.] —**whim'per·er** *n.* —**whim'per·ing·ly** *adv.*

**whim·si·cal** ('wĭm'zĭ·kəl) *adj.* 1 Capricious; fanciful; unpredictable. 2 Odd; fantastic; quaint. —**whim·si·cal'i·ty** (-kal'ə·tē) (*pl.* ·ties), **whim'si·cal·ness** *n.* —**whim'si·cal·ly** *adv.*

**whim·sy** ('wĭm'zē) *n. pl.* ·sies 1 A whim; caprice. 2 Humor that is somewhat odd, fanciful, or quaint. Also **whim'sey.** [Prob. related to WHIM]

**whine** ('wīn) *v.* whined, whin·ing *v.i.* 1 To utter a high, plaintive, nasal sound expressive of grief or distress. 2 To complain in a fretful or childish way. 3 To make a steady, high-pitched sound, as a machine. —*v.t.* 4 To utter with a whine. —*n.* The act or sound of whining. [< OE *hwīnan* whiz] —**whin'er** *n.* —**whin'ing·ly** *adv.* —**whin'y** *adj.*

**whin·ny** ('wĭn'ē) *v.* ·nied, ·ny·ing *v.i.* 1 To neigh, esp. in a low or gentle way. —*v.t.* 2 To express with a whinny. —*n. pl.* ·nies A low, gentle neigh. [< WHINE]

**whip** ('wĭp) *v.* whipped, whip·ping *v.t.* 1 To strike with a lash, rod, strap, etc. 2 To punish by striking thus; flog. 3 To drive or urge with lashes or blows: with *on, up, off,* etc. 4

To strike in the manner of a whip: The wind *whipped* the trees. 5 To beat, as eggs or cream, to a froth. 6 To seize, move, jerk, throw, etc., with a sudden motion: with *away, in, off, out,* etc. 7 In fishing, to make repeated casts upon the surface of (a stream, etc.). 8 To wrap or bind about something. 9 To sew, as a flat seam, with a loose overcast or overhand stitch. 10 *Informal* To defeat; overcome, as in a contest. —*v.i.* 11 To go, move, or turn suddenly and quickly: with *away, in, off, out,* etc. 12 To thrash about in the manner of a whip: pennants *whipping* in the wind. 13 In fishing, to make repeated casts with rod and line. —**whip up** 1 To excite; arouse. 2 *Informal* To prepare quickly, as a meal. —*n.* 1 An instrument consisting of a lash attached to a handle, used for discipline or punishment. 2 A whipping or thrashing motion. 3 A member of a legislative body, as congress or parliament, appointed unofficially to enforce discipline, attendance, etc.: also **party whip.** 4 A dessert containing whipped cream or beaten egg whites, flavoring, sometimes fruit, etc. [ME *wippen*] —**Syn.** *v.* 1 Beat, scourge, switch, thrash.

**whip·cord** ('wĭp'kôrd') *n.* 1 A strong, hard-twisted cord, used in making whiplashes. 2 A twill fabric with a pronounced diagonal rib.

**whip hand** 1 The hand in which a person holds the whip while driving. 2 A position or means of advantage.

**whip·poor·will** ('wĭp'ər·wĭl) *n.* A small nocturnal bird, allied to the goatsuckers, common in E North America. [Imit.]

**whir** ('wûr) *v.t. & v.i.* whirred, whir·ring To fly or move with a buzzing sound. —*n.* 1 A whizzing, swishing sound. 2 Confusion; bustle. Also **whirr.** [Prob. < Scand.]

**whirl** ('wûrl) *v.i.* 1 To turn or revolve rapidly, as about a center. 2 To turn away or aside quickly. 3 To move or go swiftly. 4 To have a sensation of spinning: My head *whirls.* —*v.t.* 5 To cause to turn or revolve rapidly. 6 To carry or bear along with a revolving motion. —*n.* 1 A swift rotating or revolving motion. 2 Something whirling. 3 A state of confusion. 4 A round of activities, social events, etc. 5 *Informal* A short drive. 6 *Informal* A try. [Prob. < ON *hvirfla* revolve] —**whirl'er** *n.*

**whirl·i·gig** ('wûr'lə·gĭg') *n.* 1 Any toy that spins. 2 A merry-go-round. 3 Anything that moves in a cycle. 4 A whirling motion. 5

Any of certain water beetles that move on the water in swift circles: also **whirligig beetle.** [< WHIRL + GIG]

**whirl·pool** (hwûrl′pool′) n. 1 An eddy or vortex where water moves in a rapid whirling motion, as from the meeting of two currents. 2 Anything resembling a whirlpool, esp. in movement.

**whirl·wind** (hwûrl′wind′) n. 1 A forward-moving column of air, with a rapid circular and upward spiral motion. 2 Anything resembling a whirlwind in movement, energy, or violence. —adj. Extremely swift or impetuous: a whirlwind courtship.

**whisk** (hwisk) v.t. 1 To brush or sweep off lightly: often with away or off. 2 To cause to move with a quick sweeping motion. 3 To beat with a quick movement, as eggs, cream, etc. —v.i. 4 To move quickly and lightly. —n. 1 A light sweeping or whipping movement. 2 A little bunch of straw, feathers, etc. for brushing. 3 A culinary instrument of wire loops for whipping (cream, etc.). [Prob. < Scand.]

**whisk·er** (hwis′kər) n. 1 pl. The hair of a man's beard, esp. the hair that grows on the cheeks. 2 A hair from the whiskers. 3 One of the long, bristly hairs near the mouth of some animals, as the cat, mouse, etc. [< WHISK] —whisk′ered, whisk′er·y adj.

**whis·key** (hwis′kē) n. pl. ·keys or ·kies 1 An alcoholic liquor obtained by the distillation of a fermented mash of grain, as rye, corn, barley, or wheat. 2 A drink of whiskey. —adj. Pertaining to or made of whiskey. Also **whis′key.** [< Ir. uisce beathadh, lit., water of life] • In the U.S. and Ireland, whiskey is usu. spelled with an e. Scotch and Canadian whisky, however, are traditionally spelled without the e.

**whis·per** (hwis′pər) n. 1 An act or instance of breathy speech with little or no vibration of the vocal chords. 2 An utterance made with such speech. 3 A secret communication; hint; insinuation. 4 Any low, rustling sound. —v.i. 1 To speak in a low, breathy way with little or no vibration of the vocal chords. 2 To talk cautiously or furtively; plot or gossip. 3 To make a low, rustling sound, as leaves. —v.t. 4 To utter in a whisper. 5 To speak to in a whisper. [< OE hwisprian] —whis′per·er n. —whis′per·ing·ly adv. —whis′per·y adj.

**whis·tle** (hwis′əl) v. ·tled, ·tling v.i. 1 To make a sound by sending the breath through the teeth or through puckered lips. 2 To make

a sharp, shrill sound by forcing air, steam, etc., through a small opening. 3 To make a similar sound by swift passage through the air, as bullets, the wind, etc. 4 To make a shrill cry, as certain animals or birds. 5 To blow or sound a whistle. —v.t. 6 To produce (a tune) by whistling. 7 To call, manage, or direct by whistling. —n. 1 An instrument for making whistling sounds: a train whistle; a toy whistle. 2 A whistling sound. 3 The act of whistling. —wet one's whistle Slang To take a drink. [< OE hwistlian a shrill pipe] —whis′tler n.

**whit** (hwit) n. The smallest particle; speck: usu. with a negative: not a whit abashed. [< OE (ǣnig) wiht a little amount] —Syn. bit, grain, iota, jot, shred.

**white** (hwit) adj. whit·er, whit·est 1 Having the color produced by reflection of all the rays of the solar spectrum, as the color of pure snow. 2 Light or comparatively light in color: white wine. 3 Bloodless; ashen: white with rage. 4 Very fair; blond. 5 Silvery or gray, as with age. 6 Snowy. 7 Wearing white clothing: white nuns. 8 Not malicious or harmful: a white lie. 9 Innocent; pure. 10 Unmarked by ink or print; blank. 11 Having a light-colored skin; Caucasian. 12 Of, pertaining to, or controlled by Caucasians: the white power structure. 13 Informal Fair; straightforward; honest. 14 Music Of, pertaining to, or being a tonal quality having accuracy of pitch but lacking resonance, color, and warmth. —n. 1 A white color. 2 The state or condition of being white; whiteness. 3 The white or light-colored part of something; esp., the albumen of an egg, or the white part of the eyeball. 4 Anything that is white or nearly white, as cloth, white wine, etc. 5 pl. A white uniform or outfit: the summer whites of the Navy. 6 A Caucasian. —v.t. whit·ed, whit·ing To make white; whiten. [< OE hwit] —white′ly adv. —white′ness n.

**white·fish** (hwit′fish′) n. pl. ·fish or ·fish·es 1 Any of various silvery North American food fishes, living mostly in lakes. 2 Any of various other whitish or silvery fishes.

**whit·en** (hwit′n) v.t. & v.i. To make or become white or nearly white. —whit′en·er n. —Syn. blanch, bleach.

**white·wash** (hwit′wosh′, -wôsh′) n. 1 A mixture of slaked lime and water used for whitening walls, etc. 2 A suppressing or hiding of faults and defects. 3 Informal A defeat in which the loser fails to score. —v.t. 1 To coat with whitewash. 2 To gloss over; hide. 3 *Informal* In games or sports, to defeat without allowing one's opponent to score. —**white'wash'er** *n.*

**whith·er** (**ʰwith'**ər) *adv. Archaic* To what place, condition, end, etc.: *Whither* are we bound? —*conj.* 1 To which place, condition, end, etc.: the village *whither* we went. 2 To whatever place, condition, end, etc.: Go *whither* you will. [< OE *hwider*]

**whit·tle** (**ʰwit'l**) *v.* **·tled, ·tling** *v.t.* 1 To cut or shave bits from (wood, a stick, etc.). 2 To make or shape by whittling. 3 To reduce or wear away a little at a time: with *down, off, away,* etc. —*v.i.* 4 To whittle wood. [< OE *thwitan* to cut] —**whit'tler** *n.* —**Syn.** *v.* 1 carve, trim, pare.

**whiz** (**ʰwiz**) *v.* **whizzed, whiz·zing** *v.i.* 1 To make a hissing and humming sound while passing rapidly through the air. 2 To move or pass with such a sound. —*v.t.* 3 To cause to whiz. —*n.* 1 The sound made by whizzing. 2 *Slang* Any person or thing of extraordinary excellence or ability. Also **whizz.** [Imit.] —**whiz'zer** *n.* —**whiz'zing·ly** *adv.*

**whole** (**hōl**) *adj.* 1 Containing all the parts necessary to make up a total; entire; complete. 2 Not broken, injured, defective, etc.; sound; intact. 3 Being the full amount, number, duration, etc.: He failed the *whole* class. 4 In or having regained sound health; hale. 5 Having the same parents: a *whole* brother. 6 *Math.* Integral; not mixed or fractional. —**as a whole** Altogether. —**on the whole** Taking all into consideration; in general. —*n.* 1 All the parts or elements making up a thing. 2 A complete unity or system. [< OE *hāl*] —**whole'ness** *n.*

**whole·sale** (**hōl'sāl'**) *n.* The sale of goods in large bulk or quantity, usu. for resale by retailers. —*adj.* 1 Pertaining to or engaged in such selling. 2 Made or done on a large scale or indiscriminately: *wholesale* murder. —*adv.* 1 In bulk or quantity. 2 Extensively or indiscriminately. —*v.t.* & *v.i.* **·saled, ·sal·ing** To sell (something) in large quantity, usu. for resale by retailers. [< ME *by hole sale* in large quantities] —**whole'sal·er** *n.*

**whole·some** (**hōl'səm**) *adj.* 1 Tending to promote health: *wholesome* air or food. 2 Tending to promote mental or moral well-being: a *wholesome* play. 3 Healthy: *wholesome* red cheeks. [< WHOLE + -SOME] —**whole'some·ly** *adv.* —**whole'some·ness** *n.*

**whol·ly** (**hō'lē,** **hōl'lē**) *adv.* 1 Completely; totally. 2 Exclusively; only.

**whoop** (**hōōp,** **ʰwōōp,** **ʰwŏŏp**) *v.i.* 1 To utter loud cries, as of excitement, rage, or exultation. 2 To hoot, as an owl. 3 To make a loud, gasping intake of breath. —*v.t.* 4 To utter with a whoop or whoops. 5 To call, urge, chase, etc., with whoops. —**whoop it** (or **things**) **up** *Slang* 1 To celebrate in a noisy, riotous manner. 2 To arouse enthusiasm. —*n.* 1 A shout of excitement, joy, derision, etc. 2 A loud, convulsive intake of breath. 3 An owl's hoot. [Imit.]

**whooping cough** A contagious respiratory disease of bacterial origin chiefly affecting children, marked in later stages by violent coughing.

**whop·per** (**ʰwop'**ər) *n. Informal.* 1 Something large or remarkable. 2 An outrageous falsehood.

**whorl** (**ʰwûrl,** **ʰwôrl**) *n.* 1 The flywheel of a spindle. 2 *Bot.* A set of leaves, etc., distributed in a circle around a stem. 3 *Zool.* A turn of a spiral shell. 4 Any of the convoluted ridges of a fingerprint. [? < WHIRL] —**whorled** *adj.*

**wick** (**wik**) *n.* A strand of loosely twisted or woven fibers, as in a candle or lamp, acting by capillary attraction to convey fuel to a flame. [< OE *wēoca*] —**wick'ing** *n.*

**wick·ed** (**wik'id**) *adj.* 1 Evil; depraved. 2 Mischievous; roguish. 3 Troublesome; painful: a *wicked* headache. [< OE *wicca* a wizard] —**wick'ed·ly** *adv.* —**wick'ed·ness** *n.* —**Syn.** 1 malevolent, sinful, wrong. 2 devilish.

**wick·er** (**wik'**ər) *adj.* Made of twigs, osiers, etc. —*n.* 1 A pliant young shoot or rod; twig; osier. 2 WICKERWORK. [Prob. < Scand.]

**wick·et** (**wik'it**) *n.* 1 A small door or gate often within a larger entrance. 2 A small opening in a door. 3 A small sluicegate at the end of a millrace. 4 In cricket: **a** Either of two arrangements of three upright rods set near together. **b** The level playing space between these. **c** A player's turn at bat. 5 In croquet, an arch, usu. of wire, through which one must hit the ball. [< AF *wiket*]

**wide** (**wīd**) *adj.* **wid·er, wid·est** 1 Having relatively great extent between sides. 2 Extended far in every direction; spacious: a *wide* expanse. 3 Having a specified degree of width: an inch *wide.* 4 Distant from the desired or proper point, issue, etc.: *wide* of the mark. 5 Having great scope, range, inclusiveness, etc.: a *wide* variety. 6 Loose; ample; roomy: *wide* trousers. 7 Fully open;

expanded or extended: *wide* eyes. **8** *Phonet.* Formed with a relatively relaxed tongue and jaw: said of certain vowels. —*n.* In cricket, a ball bowled so as not to be within the batsman's reach. —*adv.* **1** To a great distance; extensively. **2** Far from the mark, issue, etc. **3** To the greatest extent; fully open. [< OE *wid*] —**wide′ly** *adv.* —**wide′ness** *n.* —**Syn.** *adj.* **2** ample, broad, extensive, vast.

**wide·an·gle lens** (wīd′ang′gəl) A type of camera lens designed to permit an angle of view wider than that of the ordinary lens.

**wid·en** (wīd′n) *v.t. & v.i.* To make or become wide or wider. —**wid′en·er** *n.*

**wid·ow** (wid′ō) *n.* **1** A woman who has lost her husband by death and has not remarried. **2** In some card games, an additional hand dealt to the table. **3** *Printing* A short line of type ending a paragraph at the top of a page or column; also, such a line at the end of any paragraph. —*v.t.* To make a widow of. [< OE *widewe*]

**wid·ow·er** (wid′ō·ər) *n.* A man who has lost his wife by death and has not remarried.

**width** (width) *n.* **1** Dimension or measurement of an object taken from side to side, or at right angles to the length. **2** Something that has width: a *width* of cloth. [< WIDE]

**wield** (wēld) *v.t.* **1** To use or handle, as a weapon or instrument. **2** To exercise (authority, power, influence, etc.). [Fusion of OE *wealdan* to cause and OE *wildan* to rule] —**wield′er** *n.*

**wife** (wīf) *n. pl.* **wives** (wīvz) **1** A woman joined to a man in lawful wedlock. **2** *Archaic* A woman: now used in combination or in certain phrases: *housewife*, old *wives'* tales. — **take to wife** To marry (a woman). [< OE *wīf*] —**wife′dom, wife′hood** *n.*

**wig** (wig) *n.* A covering of real or artificial hair for the head. —*v.t.* **wigged, wig·ging 1** To furnish with a wig or wigs. **2** *Brit. Informal* To berate or scold. [Short for PERIWIG]

**wig·gle** (wig′əl) *v.t. & v.i.* **·gled, ·gling** To move or cause to move quickly from side to side; wriggle. —*n.* The act of wiggling. [< MLG *wiggelen*] —**wig′gly** *adj.* (**·gli·er, ·gli·est**)

**wig·wag** (wig′wag′) *v.t. & v.i.* **·wagged, ·wag·ging 1** To move briskly back and forth; wag. **2** To send (a message) by hand flags, torches, etc. —*n.* **1** The act of wigwagging. **2** A message sent by wigwagging. [< dial. E *wig* wiggle + WAG¹] —**wig′wag′ger** *n.*

**wig·wam** (wig′wom, -wôm) *n.* A dwelling or lodge of certain North American Indians,

commonly a rounded or conical framework of poles covered with bark, rush matting, or hides. [< Algon.]

**wild** (wīld) *adj.* **1** Living or growing in a natural state; not tamed, domesticated, or cultivated: *wild* animals; *wild* flowers. **2** Being in the natural state without civilized inhabitants or cultivation: *wild* prairies. **3** Uncivilized; primitive: the *wild* men of Borneo. **4** Undisciplined; unruly. **5** Morally dissolute; profligate. **6** Violent; turbulent: a *wild* night. **7** Reckless; imprudent: a *wild* speculation. **8** Unusually odd or strange; extravagant; bizarre: a *wild* imagination. **9** Eager and excited: *wild* with delight. **10** Frenzied; crazed: *wild* with fury. **11** Disorderly; disarranged: a *wild* mop of hair. **12** Far from the mark aimed at; erratic: a *wild* pitch. **13** In some card games, having its value arbitrarily determined by the dealer or holder. **14** *Slang* Terrific; great: The party was *wild.* **15** *Slang* Showy; jazzy: a *wild* necktie. —*n. Often pl.* An uninhabited or uncultivated place; wilderness: the *wilds* of Africa. —**the wild 1** The wilderness. **2** The free, natural, wild life. —*adv.* In a wild manner: to run *wild.* [< OE *wilde*] —**wild′ly** *adv.* —**wild′ness** *n.* —**Syn.** *adj.* **3** barbarous, savage. **7** irresponsible, rash. **8** fantastic.

**wil·der·ness** (wil′dər·nis) *n.* **1** An uncultivated, uninhabited, or barren region. **2** A multitudinous and confusing collection of persons or things. [< OE *wilder* a wild beast + -NESS]

**wile** (wīl) *n.* **1** An act or a means of cunning deception. **2** Any trick or artifice. —*v.t.* **wiled, wil·ing** To lure, beguile, or mislead. —**wile away** To pass (time) pleasantly. [< OE *wil*] —**Syn.** *n.* **2** machination, maneuver, ruse, stratagem.

**will** (wil) *n.* **1** The power to make conscious, deliberate choices or to control what one does. **2** The act or experience of exercising this power. **3** A specific desire, purpose, choice, etc.: the *will* of the people. **4** Strong determination or purpose: the *will* to succeed. **5** Self-control. **6** Attitude or inclination toward others: ill *will.* **7** *Law* The legal declaration of a person's intentions as to the disposition of his estate after his death. —**at will** As one pleases. —**with a will** Energetically. —*v.* **willed, will·ing** *v.t.* **1** To decide upon; choose. **2** To resolve upon as an action or course. **3** *Law* To bequeath by a will. **4** To control, as a hypnotized person, by the exercise of will. **5** To decree: The king *wills* it. —*v.i.* **6** To wish; desire: as you *will.* [< OE *willa*]

**will·ful** (wil′fəl) *adj.* **1** Deliberate; intentional: *willful* disregard of the law. **2** Stubborn; headstrong: a *willful* child. —**will′ful·ly** *adv.* —**will′ful·ness** *n.*

**wil·low** (wil′ō) *n.* **1** Any of a large genus of shrubs and trees having usu. narrow leaves and flexible shoots often used in basketry. **2** The wood of a willow. **3** *Informal* Something made of willow wood, as a cricket bat. —*adj.* Made of willow wood. [< OE *wilige, welig*] • See WEEPING WILLOW.

**wilt** (wilt) *v.i.* **1** To lose freshness; droop or become limp. **2** To lose energy and vitality; become faint or languid. **3** To lose courage or spirit. —*v.t.* **4** To cause to wilt. —*n.* **1** The act of wilting or the state of being wilted. **2** A plant disease that causes wilting. [Prob. dial. var. of obs. *welk*]

**wi·ly** (wī′lē) *adj.* **·li·er, ·li·est** Full of or characterized by wiles; sly; cunning. —**wi′li·ly** *adv.* —**wi′li·ness** *n.*

**win** (win) *v.* **won, won, win·ning** *v.i.* **1** To gain a victory; be victorious in a contest, endeavor, etc. **2** To succeed in reaching or attaining a specified end or condition: get: often with *across, over, through,* etc. —*v.t.* **3** To be successful in; gain victory in: to *win* an argument. **4** To gain in competition or contest: to *win* the blue ribbon. **5** To gain by effort, persistence, etc.: to *win* fame. **6** To influence so as to obtain the good will or favor of: often with *over.* **7** To secure the love of; gain in marriage. **8** To succeed in reaching: to *win* the harbor. —**win out** Informal To succeed; triumph. —*n. Informal* A victory; success. [< OE *winnan* contend, labor] —**Syn.** *v.* **5** achieve, attain, earn, secure.

**wince** (wins) *v.i.* **winced, winc·ing** To shrink back; flinch. —*n.* The act of wincing. [< AF *wenchier*] —**winc′er** *n.*

**winch** (winch) *n.* **1** A windlass, particularly one turned by a crank and used for hoisting. **2** A crank with a handle for transmitting motion. [< OE *wince*] —**winch′er** *n.*

**wind¹** (wind) *n.* **1** Any movement of air, esp. a natural horizontal movement. **2** Any powerful or destructive movement of air, as a tornado. **3** The direction from which a wind blows. **4** Air pervaded by a scent, as in hunting. **5** The power of breathing; breath: He lost his *wind.* **6** Idle chatter. **7** Bragging; vanity; conceit. **8** *pl.* The wind instruments of an orchestra; also, the players of these instruments. **9** The gaseous product of indigestion; flatulence. —**break wind** To expel gas through the anus. —**get wind of** To receive a hint or intimation of. —**how the wind blows (or lies, etc.)** What is taking place, being decided, etc. —**in the teeth of the wind** Directly against the wind: also **in the wind's eye.** —**in the wind** Impending; afoot. —*v.t.* **1** To follow by scent; to catch a scent of on the wind. **2** To exhaust the breath of, as by racing. **3** To allow to recover breath by resting. **4** To expose to the wind, as in ventilating. [< OE] —**Syn.** *n.* **1** blast, breeze, gale, gust, zephyr.

**wind²** (wind, wind) *v.t.* **wind·ed or wound, wind·ing 1** To blow, as a horn; sound. **2** To give (a call or signal), as with a horn. [< WIND¹; infl. by WIND²]

**wind·fall** (wind′fôl′) *n.* **1** Something, as ripening fruit, brought down by the wind. **2** A piece of unexpected good fortune.

**wind·lass** (wind′ləs) *n.* Any of several devices for hoisting or hauling, esp. one consisting of a drum turned by means of a crank so that the hoisting rope winds on the drum. [< ON *vinda* wind + *āss* a beam]

**win·dow** (win′dō) *n.* **1** An opening in the wall of a building, etc., to admit light or air, usu. capable of being opened and closed, and including casements or sashes fitted with glass. **2** A windowpane or the sash or framework that encloses it. **3** Anything resembling or suggesting a window, as a transparent patch in certain envelopes. —*v.t.* To provide with a window or windows. [< ON *vindr* wind + *auga* an eye]

**wind·pipe** (wind′pīp′) *n.* TRACHEA.

**wind·row** (wind′rō′) *n.* **1** A long row of hay or grain raked together preparatory to building into cocks. **2** A line of dust, surf, leaves, etc. swept together by wind. —*v.t.* To rake or shape into a windrow. —**wind′row′er** *n.*

**wind·shield** (wind′shēld′) *n.* A transparent screen, as of glass, across and above the dashboard of motor vehicles, power boats, etc., providing protection from the wind.

**wind·ward** (wind′wərd) *adj.* **1** Of or toward the direction from which the wind blows. **2** Being on the side exposed to the wind. —*n.* The direction from which the wind blows. —*adv.* In the direction from which the wind blows.

**wind·y** (win′dē) *adj.* **wind·i·er, wind·i·est 1** Of or abounding in wind; stormy; tempestuous: *windy* weather. **2** Exposed to the wind.

3 Suggestive of wind; boisterous; violent. 4 Flatulent. 5 Boastful, talkative, or pompous. 6 Idle; empty: *windy* talk. —**wind′·i·ly** *adv.* —**wind′i·ness** *n.*

**wing** (wing) *n.* 1 An organ of flight; esp. one of a pair of appendages of a bird or bat, adapted for flight. 2 An analogous organ in insects and some other animals. 3 Anything resembling or suggestive of a wing in form or function. 4 *Aeron.* The (or one of the) main supporting surface(s) of an airplane. 5 *Bot.* Any thin, winglike expansion of certain stems, seeds, etc. 6 A vane, as of a windmill. 7 Anything regarded as conferring the swift motion or rapture of flight: on *wings* of song. 8 Flight by or as by wings. 9 *Archit.* A part attached to a side, esp. a projection or extension of a building on the side of the main portion. 10 An annex or separate section of a large building: the surgical *wing* of a hospital. 11 Either of two sides, unseen by the audience, of a proscenium stage; also, a piece of scenery for the side of a stage. 12 Either of two sidepieces on the back of an armchair. 13 A side section of something that shuts or folds, as a screen. 14 A tactical and administrative unit of the U.S. Air Force, larger than a group. 15 *Mil.* Either division of a military force on either side of the center. 16 An analogous formation in certain outdoor games, as hockey or football. 17 Either of two extremist groups or factions in a political organization: the left *wing*. 18 A subsidiary group of a parent organization. 19 *Slang* An arm, esp., in baseball, a pitching or throwing arm. 20 *pl.* The insignia worn by certain qualified aircraft pilots, navigators, etc. —**on** (or **upon**) **the wing** 1 In flight. 2 Departing; also, journeying. —**take wing** To fly away. —**under one's wing** Under one's protection. —*v.t.* 1 To pass over or through in flight. 2 To accomplish by flying: the eagle *winged* its way. 3 To enable to fly. 4 To cause to go swiftly; speed. 5 To transport by flight. 6 To provide with wings for flight. 7 To supply with a side body or part. 8 To wound (a bird) in a wing. 9 To disable by a minor wound. —*v.i.* 10 To fly; soar. —**wing it** *Slang* To act, do, arrange, etc., without advance preparation; improvise. [< ON *vǣngr*]

**wink** (wingk) *v.i.* 1 To close and open the eye or eyelids quickly. 2 To draw the eyelids of one eye together, as in making a sign. 3 To emit fitful gleams; twinkle. —*v.t.* 4 To close and open (the eye or eyelids) quickly. 5 To move, force, etc., by winking: with *away, off,* etc. 6 To signify or express by winking. —**wink at** To pretend not to see. —*n.* 1 The act of winking. 2 The time necessary for a wink. 3 A twinkle. 4 A hint conveyed by winking. 5 A brief bit (of sleep): I had a *wink* after lunch. —**forty winks** A short nap. [< OE *wincian* close the eyes]

**win·ning** (win′ing) *adj.* 1 Successful in achievement, esp. in competition. 2 Capable of charming; attractive; winsome. —*n.* 1 The act of one who wins. 2 *Usu. pl.* That which is won, as money in gambling. —**win′ning·ly** *adv.* —**win′ning·ness** *n.*

**win·now** (win′ō) *v.t.* 1 To separate (grain, etc.) from the chaff. 2 To blow away (the chaff) thus. 3 To separate (what is valuable) or to eliminate (what is valueless): to *winnow* out the good or the bad. 4 To blow upon; cause to flutter. 5 To beat or fan (the air) with the wings. 6 To scatter by blowing; disperse. —*v.i.* 7 To separate grain from chaff. 8 To fly; flap. —*n.* 1 Any device used in winnowing grain. 2 The act of winnowing. [< OE *windwian* < *wind* the wind] —**win′now·er** *n.*

**win·some** (win′sǝm) *adj.* Charming; attractive. [< OE *wyn* joy] —**win′some·ly** *adv.* —**win′some·ness** *n.* —**Syn.** amiable, appealing, engaging, pleasant, winning.

**win·ter** (win′tǝr) *n.* 1 The coldest season of the year, extending from the end of autumn to the beginning of spring. 2 A time marked by lack of life, warmth, and cheer. 3 A year as including the winter season: a man of ninety *winters.* —*v.i.* 1 To pass the winter. —*v.t.* 2 To care for, feed, or protect during the winter: to *winter* plants. —*adj.* Pertaining to, suitable for, or characteristic of winter. [< OE] —**win′ter·er** *n.*

**win·ter·green** (win′tǝr·grēn) *n.* 1 A small evergreen plant bearing aromatic oval leaves, white, bell-shaped flowers and edible red berries. 2 A colorless, volatile oil extracted from the leaves of this plant or made synthetically, used as a flavor.

**win·ter·ize** (win′tǝ·rīz) *v.t.* **·ized, ·iz·ing** To prepare or put in condition for winter, as a motor vehicle, etc.

**win·try** (win′trē) *adj.* **·tri·er, ·tri·est** Of or like winter; cold, bleak, cheerless, etc. **Also win′ter·y** (-tǝr·ē). —**win′tri·ly** *adv.* —**win′tri·ness** *n.*

**wipe** (wīp) *v.t.* **wiped, wip·ing** 1 To subject to slight friction or rubbing, usu. with some soft, absorbent material. 2 To remove by rubbing lightly: usu. with *away* or *off*. 3 To move or draw for the purpose of wiping: He *wiped* his hand across his brow. 4 To apply by wiping. —**wipe out** 1 To kill or murder. 2 To destroy utterly; annihilate. 3 In surfing, to be overturned by a wave. —*n.* The act of wiping. [< OE *wipian*] —**wip′er** *n.*

**wire** (wīr) *n.* 1 A slender rod, strand, or thread of metal. 2 Something made of wire, as a fence, a cord to conduct an electric current, etc. 3 WIREWORK. 4 A telephone or telegraph cable. 5 The telegraph system as a means of communication. 6 TELEGRAM. 7 The screen of a paper-making machine. 8 A line marking the finish of a race. —**get (in) under the wire** To conclude or achieve something at the very last moment. —**pull wires** *Informal* To use secret or private sources of influence to attain something. —*v.* **wired**, **wir·ing** *v.t.* 1 To fasten or bind with wire. 2 To furnish or equip with wiring. 3 To telegraph: to *wire* an order. 4 To place on wire, as beads. —*v.i.* 5 To telegraph. [< OE *wir*] —**wir′er** *n.*

**wire·less** (wīr′lis) *adj.* 1 Without wire or wires; having no wires. 2 *Brit.* Radio. —*n.* 1 The wireless telegraph or telephone system, or a message transmitted by either. 2 *Brit.* Radio. —*v.t. & v.i. Brit.* To communicate (with) by radio.

**Wire·pho·to** (wīr′fō′tō) *n. pl.* **·tos** An apparatus and method for transmitting and receiving photographs by wire: a trade name.

**wire·tap** (wīr′tap′) *n.* 1 A device used to make a connection with a telephone or telegraph wire to listen to or record the message transmitted. 2 The act of wiretapping. —*v.* **·tapped**, **·tap·ping** *v.t.* 1 To connect a wiretap to. 2 To monitor by the use of a wiretap. —*v.i.* 3 To use a wiretap. —**wire′tap′per** *n.*

**wir·y** (wīr′ē) *adj.* **wir·i·er**, **wir·i·est** 1 Lean, but tough and sinewy: said of persons. 2 Like wire; stiff; bristly. —**wir′i·ly** *adv.* —**wir′i·ness** *n.*

**wis·dom** (wiz′dəm) *n.* 1 The ability to discern what is true or right and to make sound judgments based on such discernment. 2 Insight or intuition. 3 COMMON SENSE. 4 A high degree of knowledge; learning. 5 An accumulated body of knowledge, as in philosophy, science, etc. [< OE *wis* wise] —**Syn.** 1 sapience, sagacity. 4 enlightenment, erudition.

**wisdom tooth** The last tooth on either side of the upper and lower jaws in man. —**cut one's wisdom teeth** To acquire mature judgment. • See TOOTH.

**wise** (wīz) *adj.* **wis·er**, **wis·est** 1 Having or showing wisdom (def. 1). 2 Having or showing insight, intuition, common sense, or knowledge. 3 Shrewd; calculating; cunning. 4 *Informal* Aware of: *wise* to his motives. 5 *Slang* Arrogant; fresh: a *wise* guy. —**get wise** *Slang* 1 To learn the true facts about. 2 To become arrogant or fresh. —**wise up** *Slang* To make or become aware, informed, or sophisticated. [< OE *wīs*] —**wise′ly** *adv.* —**wise′ness** *n.*

**wish** (wish) *n.* 1 A desire or longing, usu. for some definite thing. 2 An expression of such a desire; petition. 3 Something wished for. —*v.t.* 1 To have a desire or longing for; want: We *wish* to be sure. 2 To desire a specified condition or state for (a person or thing): I *wish* this day were over. 3 To invoke upon or for someone: I *wished* him good luck. 4 To bid: to *wish* someone good morning. 5 To request, command, or entreat: I *wish* you would stop yelling. —*v.i.* 6 To have or feel a desire; yearn; long: usu. with *for*: to *wish* for a friend's return. 7 To make or express a wish. —**wish on** *Informal* To impose (something unpleasant or unwanted) on a person. [< OE *wȳscan*] —**wish′er** *n.*

**wisp** (wisp) *n.* 1 A small bunch, as of hay, straw, or hair. 2 A small bit; a mere indication: a *wisp* of vapor. 3 A slight, delicate thing: a *wisp* of a child. 4 WILL-O'-THE-WISP. [ME *wisp*, *wips*] —**wisp′y** *adj.* (**·i·er**, **·i·est**)

**wis·te·ri·a** (wis·tir′ē·ə, -târ′-) *n.* Any of a genus of woody twining shrubs of the bean family, with pinnate leaves, elongated pods, and showy clusters of blue, purple, or white flowers. Also **wis·tar·i·a** (wis·târ′ē·ə). [< C. *Wistar*, 1761–1818, U.S. anatomist]

**wist·ful** (wist′fəl) *adj.* 1 Wishful; yearning. 2 Musing; pensive. [Appar. < *obs. wistly* intently] —**wist′ful·ly** *adv.* —**wist′ful·ness** *n.*

**wit** (wit) *n.* 1 The power of perceiving, reasoning, knowing, etc.; intelligence. 2 *pl.* **a** The mental faculties: to use one's *wits*. **b** Such faculties in relation to their state of balance: out of one's *wits*. 3 Practical intelligence; common sense. 4 The ability to perceive unexpected analogies or incongruities and to express them in an amusing or epigrammatic manner. 5 The ability to make jokes, amusing remarks, etc. 6 A person with wit (defs. 4 & 5). 7 Speech or writing characterized by wit (defs. 4 & 5). —**at one's**

**wits' end** At the limit of one's devices and resources. —**live by one's wits** To make a living by using one's practical intelligence and resourcefulness, often in unscrupulous or fraudulent ways. [< OE]

**witch** (wich) n. 1 A woman who practices sorcery or has supernatural powers, esp. to work evil. 2 An ugly old woman; a hag. 3 A bewitching or fascinating woman or girl. — v.t. 1 To work an evil spell upon; effect by witchcraft. 2 To fascinate or charm. —v.i. 3 DOWSE². [< OE wicce a witch, fem. of wicca a wizard]

**witch·craft** (wich′kraft′, -kräft′) n. 1 Black magic; sorcery. 2 Extraordinary influence or fascination.

**witch·er·y** (wich′ər·ē) n. pl. ·er·ies 1 Witchcraft; black magic; sorcery. 2 Power to charm; fascination

**with·draw** (with·drô′, with-) v. ·drew, ·drawn, ·draw·ing v.t. 1 To draw or take away; remove. 2 To take back, as an assertion or a promise. 3 To keep from use, sale, etc. — v.i. 4 To draw back; retreat. 5 To remove oneself; leave, as from an activity.

**with·er** (with′ər) v.i. 1 To become limp or dry, as a plant when deprived of moisture. 2 To waste, as flesh. —v.t. 3 To cause to become limp or dry. 4 To abash, as by a scornful glance. [ME widren] —Syn. 1 shrink, shrivel. 4 confuse, shame.

**with·hold** (with·hōld′, with-) v. ·held, ·hold·ing v.t. 1 To hold back; restrain. 2 To refuse to grant, permit, etc. 3 To deduct (taxes, etc.) from a salary before payment. —v.i. 4 To refrain. —**with·hold′er** n.

**with·stand** (with·stand′, with-) v. ·stood, ·stand·ing v.t. & v.i. To resist, oppose, or endure, esp. successfully. [< OE with-against + standan stand]

**wit·ness** (wit′nis) n. 1 A person who has seen or knows something and is therefore competent to give evidence concerning it. 2 That which serves as or furnishes evidence or proof. 3 Law a One who has knowledge of facts relating to a given cause and is subpoenaed to testify. b A person who has signed his name to a legal document in order that he may testify to its authenticity. 4 Evidence; testimony. —**bear witness** 1 To give evidence; testify. 2 To be evidence. —v.t. 1 To see or know by personal experience. 2 To furnish or serve as evidence of. 3 To give testimony to. 4 To be the site or scene of: This spot has witnessed many heinous crimes. 5 Law To see the execution of (an instrument) and subscribe to its authenticity. —v.i. 6 To give evidence; testify. [< OE witnes knowledge, testimony] —**wit′ness·er** n.

**wit·ti·cism** (wit′ə·siz′əm) n. A witty or clever remark. [< WITTY]

**wit·ty** (wit′ē) adj. ·ti·er, ·ti·est Having, displaying, or full of wit. [< OE wittig wise] —**wit′ti·ly** adv. ·-**wit′ti·ness** n.

**wiz·ard** (wiz′ərd) n. 1 A magician or sorcerer. 2 Informal A very skillful or clever person. —adj. Of or pertaining to wizards. [< OE wīs wise]

**wiz·ened** (wiz′ənd) adj. Shriveled; dried up. [< OE wisnian, dry up, wither]

**woe** (wō) n. 1 Overwhelming sorrow; grief. 2 Heavy affliction or calamity; disaster; suffering. —interj. Alas! [< OE wā misery]

**woe·be·gone** (wō′bi·gôn′, -gon′) adj. Having or exhibiting woe; mournful; sorrowful. —Syn. dejected, depressed, lugubrious, melancholy.

**woe·ful** (wō′fəl) adj. 1 Accompanied by or causing woe; direful. 2 Expressive of sorrow; doleful. 3 Paltry; miserable; mean; sorry. —**woe′ful·ly** adv. —**woe′ful·ness** n.

**wolf** (woolf) n. pl. **wolves** (woolvz) 1 Any of various wild, carnivorous mammals related to the dog. 2 Any ravenous, cruel, or rapacious person. 3 Slang A man who zealously and aggressively pursues women. —**cry wolf** To give a false alarm. —**keep the wolf from the door** To avert want or starvation. —v.t. To devour ravenously: often with down. [< OE wulf]

**wom·an** (woom′ən) n. pl. **wom·en** (wim′in) 1 An adult human female. 2 The female part of the human race; women collectively. 3 Womanly character; femininity: usu. with the. 4 A female attendant or servant. 5 A paramour or mistress. 6 Informal A wife. — adj. 1 Of or characteristic of women. 2 Female: a woman lawyer. [< OE wīf a wife + mann a human being] • See LADY.

**wom·an·hood** (woom′ən·hood) n. 1 The state of a woman or of womankind. 2 Women collectively.

**wom·an·ly** (woom′ən·lē) adj. Having the qualities natural, suited, or becoming to a woman; feminine. —**wom′an·li·ness** n.

**won·der** (wun′dər) n. 1 A feeling of mingled surprise, admiration, and astonishment. 2 One who or that which causes wonder. — v.t. 1 To have a feeling of curiosity or doubt in regard to. —v.i. 2 To be affected or filled with wonder; marvel. 3 To be curious or doubtful. —*adj.* Spectacularly successful: a *wonder* drug. [< OE *wundor*] —**won′der·er** *n.* —**won′der·ing·ly** *adv.*

**won·der·ful** (wun′dər·fəl) *adj.* 1 Of a nature to excite wonder; astonishing. 2 Very good; excellent. —**won′der·ful·ly** *adv.* —**won′der·ful·ness** *n.*

**won·drous** (wun′drəs) *adj.* Wonderful; marvelous. —*adv.* Surprisingly. —**won′drous·ly** *adv.* —**won′drous·ness** *n.*

**wont** (wônt, wōnt) *adj.* Accustomed: He is *wont* to eat late. —*n.* Ordinary manner of doing or acting; habit. [< OE *gewunod*, p.p. of *gewunian* be accustomed]

**won′t** (wōnt) Contraction of *will not.*

**wont·ed** (wun′tid, wōn′-) *adj.* 1 Commonly used or done; habitual. 2 Habituated; accustomed. —**wont′ed·ness** *n.*

**woo** (wōō) *v.t.* 1 To make love to, esp. so as to marry. 2 To entreat earnestly; beg. 3 To seek. —*v.i.* 4 To pay court; make love. [< OE *wōgian*] —**woo′er** *n.*

**wood** (wōōd) *n.* 1 The hard, fibrous material between the pith and bark of a tree or shrub. 2 Trees or shrubs cut for use, as for building, fuel, etc. 3 *Usu. pl.* A large, dense growth of trees; forest. 4 Something made of wood, as a woodwind or certain golf clubs having a wooden head. —*adj.* 1 Made of wood; wooden. 2 Made for burning wood: a wood stove. 3 Living or growing in woods. —*v.t.* 1 To furnish with wood for fuel. 2 To plant with trees. —*v.i.* 3 To take on a supply of wood. [< OE *widu, wiodu*]

**wood·cut** (wōōd′kut′) *n.* 1 A block of wood engraved, as with a design, for making prints. 2 A print made from such a block.

**wood·ed** (wōōd′id) *adj.* Abounding with trees.

**wood·en** (wōōd′n) *adj.* 1 Made of wood. 2 Stiff; awkward. 3 Dull; stupid. —**wood′en·ly** *adv.* —**wood′en·ness** *n.*

**wood·peck·er** (wōōd′pek′ər) *n.* Any of a large family of birds having stiff tail feathers, strong claws, and a sharp bill for drilling holes in trees in search of wood-boring insects.

**wood·y** (wōōd′ē) *adj.* **wood·i·er, wood·i·est** 1 Made of or containing wood. 2 Resembling wood. 3 Wooded; abounding with trees. —**wood′i·ness** *n.*

**woof** (wōōf, wōōf) *n.* 1 The threads that are carried back and forth across the warp in a loom. 2 The texture of a fabric. [< OE *ōwef*]

**woof·er** (wōōf′ər) *n.* A loudspeaker designed to reproduce sounds of low frequency. [< WOOF² + -er]

**wool** (wōōl) *n.* 1 The soft, durable fiber obtained from the fleece of sheep and some allied animals, as goats, alpacas, etc. 2 Yarn or fabric made of such fibers. 3 Garments made of wool. 4 Something resembling or likened to wool. —**pull the wool over one's eyes** To delude or deceive one. —*adj.* Made of or pertaining to wool or woolen material. [< OE *wull*]

**wool·en** (wōōl′ən) *adj.* 1 Of or pertaining to wool. 2 Made of wool. —*n. Usu. pl.* Cloth or clothing made of wool. Also **wool′len.**

**wool·gath·er·ing** (wōōl′gath′ər·ing) *n.* Idle daydreaming; absent-mindedness. —**wool′gath′er·er** *n.*

**word** (wûrd) *n.* 1 A speech sound or combination of sounds which has come to signify and communicate a particular idea or thought, and which functions as the smallest meaningful unit of a language when used in isolation. 2 The letters or characters that stand for such a language unit. 3 *Usu. pl.* Speech; talk: hard to put into *words.* 4 A brief remark or comment. 5 A communication or message: Send him *word.* 6 A command, signal, or direction: Give the *word* to start. 7 A promise: a man of his *word.* 8 Rumor, gossip, or news: What's the latest *word*? 9 A watchword or password. 10 *pl.* The text of a song: *words* and music. 11 *pl.* Language used in anger, rebuke, etc.: They had *words.* —**in a word** In short; briefly. —**eat one's words** To retract what one has said. —**mince words** To be evasive or overly delicate in what one says. —**take one at his word** To believe literally in what another has said and act or respond accordingly. —**word for word** In exactly the same words; verbatim. —*v.t.* To express in a word or words; phrase. —**the Word** 1 LOGOS (def. 2). 2 GOSPEL (def. 1). 3 The Scriptures; the Bible. [< OE]

**word·ing** (wûr′ding) *n.* The style or arrangement of words; diction; phraseology.

**word·y** (wûr′dē) *adj.* **word·i·er, word·i·est** 1 Expressed in many or too many words; verbose. 2 Of or pertaining to words; verbal. —**word′i·ly** *adv.* —**word′i·ness** *n.* —**Syn.** 1 long-winded, prolix, roundabout, redundant.

**work** (wûrk) *n.* 1 Continued physical or mental exertion or activity directed to some purpose or end; labor; toil. 2 Employment; job: to be out of *work.* 3 One's profession, occupation, business, trade, etc.: What is your *work?* 4 The place where one is employed or occupied professionally: She is at *work.* 5 An undertaking or task, often a part of one's job or occupation: to take *work* home; also,.the amount of this that is accomplished or required: a day's *work.* 6 *pl.* A place where something is made, undertaken, etc.: often used in combination: the *oilworks.* 7 The material used or processed in manufacturing something. 8 Something that has been made, created, accomplished, etc., esp.: a An engineering structure, as a bridge. b A feat or deed: remembered for her good *works.* c Needlework or embroidery. d A product of the mind and imagination: the *works* of Beethoven. 9 Manner, quality, or style of doing something; workmanship. 10 *pl.* Running gear or machinery: the *works* of a watch. 11 The action of natural forces or the result of such action: the *work* of a storm. 12 *Physics* A transfer of energy between physical systems. —the works *Slang* 1 Everything belonging, available, etc. 2 Drastic or vicious treatment: to give someone *the works.* —shoot the works *Slang* 1 To risk everything. 2 To make a final, supreme effort. —*v.* worked (*Archaic* wrought), working *v.i.* 1 To perform work; labor; toil. 2 To be employed in some trade or business. 3 To perform a function; operate: The machine *works* well. 4 To prove effective or influential: His stratagem *worked.* 5 To move or progress gradually or with difficulty: He *worked* up in his profession. 6 To become,as specified, as by gradual motion: The bolts *worked* loose. 7 To move from nervousness or agitation: His features *worked* with anger. 8 To undergo kneading, hammering, etc.; be shaped: Copper *works* easily. 9 To ferment. —*v.t.* 10 To cause or bring about: to *work* a miracle. 11 To direct the operation of: to *work* a machine. 12 To make or shape by toil or skill. 13 To prepare, as by manipulating, hammering, etc.: to *work* dough. 14 To decorate, as with embroidery or inlaid work. 15 To cause to be productive, as by toil: to *work* a mine. 16 To cause to do work: He *works* his employees too hard. 17 To cause to be as specified, usu. with effort: We *worked* the timber into position. 18 To make or achieve by effort: to *work* one's passage on a ship. 19 To carry on some activity in (an area, etc.): cover: to *work* a sales territory. 20 To solve, as a problem in arithmetic. 21 To cause to move from nervousness or excitement: to *work* one's jaws. 22 To excite;

provoke: He *worked* himself into a passion. 23 To influence or manage, as by insidious means; lead. 24 To cause to ferment. 25 *Informal* To practice trickery upon; cheat; swindle. 26 *Informal* To make use of for one's own purposes; use. —work in To insert or be inserted. —work off To get rid of, as extra flesh by exercise. —work on (or upon) 1 To try to influence or persuade. 2 To influence or affect. —work out 1 To make its way out or through. 2 To effect by work or effort; accomplish. 3 To exhaust, as a mine. 4 To discharge, as a debt, by labor rather than by payment of money. 5 To develop; form, as a plan. 6 To solve. 7 a To prove effective or successful. b To result as specified. 8 To exercise, train, etc. —work over 1 To repeat. 2 *Slang* To treat harshly or cruelly; beat up, torture, etc. —work up 1 To excite; rouse, as rage or a person to rage. 2 To form or shape by working; develop: to *work up* a new advertising campaign. 3 To make one's or its way. 4 To cause or bring about. [< OE *weorc*]

work·er (wûk′kər) *n.* 1 One who or that which performs work. 2 A social insect, as a bee, ant, etc., that is sexually sterile and performs work for the colony. 3 A member of the working class.

world (wûrld) *n.* 1 The earth. 2 The universe. 3 Any celestial body: Are there other inhabited *worlds?* 4 *Often cap.* A part of the earth: the *Old World.* 5 A specific time or period in history: the ancient *world.* 6 A division of existing or created things belonging to the earth; the animal *world.* 7 The human inhabitants of the earth; mankind. 8 A definite class of people having certain interests or activities in common: the scientific *world.* 9 Secular or worldly aims, pleasures, etc., as distinguished from religious or spiritual ones; also, those people who pursue such aims or pleasures. 10 Individual conditions or circumstances of a person's life: His *world* has changed. 11 A large quantity or amount: a *world* of trouble. —come into the world To be born. —for all the world 1 In every respect. 2 For any reason. —on top of the world *Informal* Elated. —out of this world *Informal* Exceptionally fine; wonderful. [< OE *weorold*]

worm (wûrm) *n.* 1 *Zool.* Any of numerous limbless, elongated, soft-bodied invertebrate animals, including flatworms, roundworms, and annelids. 2 Any small animal resembling a worm, as a caterpillar, maggot, snake, shipworm, etc. 3 Something which suggests the inner, hidden gnawings of a worm: the *worm* of remorse. 4 A despicable or despised person. 5 Something conceived to be like a worm, as the thread of a screw. 6 *pl.* Any disorder due to parasitic worms in the intestines, etc. —*v.t.* 1 To move, proceed, insinuate, etc. (oneself or itself) in a wormlike manner: to *worm* one's way. 2 To draw forth by artful means, as a secret: with *out.* 3 To rid of intestinal worms. —*v.i.* 4 To move or progress slowly and stealthily. [< OE *wyrm*] —**worm′i·ness** *n.* —**worm′ y** *adj.* (·i·er, ·i·est)

**worm·wood** (wûrm′wŏŏd′) *n.* 1 Any of various European herbs or small shrubs related to the sagebrush, esp. a species yielding a bitter oil used in making absinthe. 2 Something that embitters or is unpleasant. [< OE *wermōd*]

**wor·ry** (wûr′ē) *v.* ·ried, ·ry·ing *v.i.* 1 To be uneasy in the mind; feel anxiety. 2 To manage despite trials or difficulties; struggle: with *along* or *through.* —*v.t.* 3 To cause to feel uneasy in the mind; trouble. 4 To bother; pester. 5 To bite, pull at, or shake with the teeth. —*n. pl.* ·ries 1 A state of anxiety or uneasiness. 2 Something causing such a state. [< OE *wrygan* strangle] —**wor′ri·er, wor′ri·ment** *n.*

**worse** (wûrs) Comparative of BAD and ILL. —*adj.* 1 Bad or ill in a great degree; inferior. 2 Physically ill in a greater degree. 3 Less favorable, as to conditions, circumstances, etc. 4 More evil, corrupt, etc. —*n.* Someone or something worse. —*adv.* 1 In a worse manner, way, etc. 2 With greater intensity, severity, etc. [< OE *wyrsa*]

**wor·ship** (wûr′ship) *n.* 1 Adoration, homage, etc., given to a deity. 2 The rituals, prayers, etc., expressing such adoration or homage. 3 Excessive or ardent admiration or love. 4 The object of such love or admiration. 5 *Chiefly Brit.* A title of honor in addressing certain persons of station. —*v.* ·shiped or ·shipped, ·ship·ing or ·ship·ping *v.t.* 1 To pay an act of worship to; venerate. 2 To have intense or exaggerated admiration or love for. —*v.i.* 3 To perform acts or have sentiments of worship. [< OE *weorthscipe* < *weorth* worthy] —**wor′ship·er, wor′ship· per** *n.* —Syn. *v.* 1 exalt, praise. 2 adore, dote on, idolize.

**worst** (wûrst) Superlative of BAD and ILL. —*adj.* 1 Bad or ill in the highest degree. 2 Least favorable, as to conditions, circumstances, etc. 3 Most evil, corrupt, etc. —**in the worst way** *Informal* Very much. —*n.*

Someone or something that is worst. —**at worst** Under the worst possible circumstances or conditions. —**get the worst of it** To be defeated or put at a disadvantage. —*adv.* 1 To the greatest or most extreme degree. 2 To the greatest or most extreme degree of inferiority, badness, etc. —*v.t.* To defeat; vanquish. [< OE *wyrsta*]

**wors·ted** (wŏŏs′tid, wûr′stid) *n.* 1 Woolen yarn spun from long staple, with fibers combed parallel and twisted hard. 2 A tightly woven fabric made from such yarn. —*adj.* Consisting of or made from such yarn. [< *Worsted,* former name of a parish in Norfolk, England]

**worth** (wûrth) *n.* 1 Value or excellence of any kind. 2 The market value of something. 3 The amount of something obtainable at a specific sum: two cents' *worth* of candy. 4 Wealth. —*adj.* 1 Equal in value (to); exchangable (for). 2 Deserving (of): not *worth* going. 3 Having wealth or possessions to the value of: He is *worth* a million. —**for all it is worth** To the utmost. —**for all one is worth** With every effort possible. [< OE *weorth*]

**wor·thy** (wûr′thē) *adj.* ·thi·er, ·thi·est 1 Possessing valuable or useful qualities. 2 Having such qualities as to deserve or merit some specified thing: *worthy* of the honor. —*n. pl.* ·thies A person of eminent worth: sometimes used humorously. —**wor′thi·ly** *adv.* —**wor′thi·ness** *n.*

**wound** (wŏŏnd) *n.* 1 A hurt or injury, esp. one in which the skin is torn, cut, etc. 2 A cutting or scraping injury to a tree or plant. 3 Any cause of pain or grief, as to the feelings, honor, etc. —*v.t. & v.i.* 1 To inflict a wound or wounds (upon). 2 To injure the feelings or pride of. [< OE *wund*] —Syn. *v.* 2 affront, hurt, offend, pique.

**wran·gle** (rang′gəl) *v.* ·gled, ·gling *v.i.* 1 To argue noisily and angrily. —*v.t.* 2 To argue; debate. 3 To get by stubborn arguing. 4 To herd or round up, as livestock. —*n.* An angry dispute. [ME *wranglen*] —**wran′gler** *n.*

**wrap** (rap) *v.* wrapped or wrapt, wrap·ping *v.t.* 1 To surround and cover by something folded or wound about. 2 To fold or wind (a covering) about something. 3 To surround so as to blot out or conceal: a mountain *wrapped* in clouds. 4 To fold or wind. —*v.i.* 5 To be or become twined, coiled, etc.: with *about, around,* etc. —**wrap up** 1 To cover with paper, etc. 2 To put on warm garments. 3 *Informal* To conclude or finish. —**wrapped up in** Involved or absorbed in:

*wrapped up in* his music. —*n.* 1 A garment folded about a person. 2 *pl.* Outer garments collectively. 3 A blanket. —**keep under wraps** To keep secret. [ME *wrappen*]

**wrap·per** (rap′ər) *n.* 1 A paper enclosing a newspaper, magazine, or similar packet for mailing or otherwise. 2 A woman's dressing gown. 3 One who or that which wraps.

**wrath** (rath, räth; *Brit.* rôth) *n.* 1 Violent rage, anger, or fury. 2 An act done in violent rage. [< OE *wrǣth* wroth]

**wreak** (rēk) *v.t.* 1 To inflict or exact, as vengeance. 2 To give free expression to, as a feeling or passion. [< OE *wrecan* drive, avenge]

**wreath** (rēth) *n. pl.* **wreaths** (rēthz, rēths) 1 A band, as of flowers or leaves, commonly circular, as for a crown, decoration, etc. 2 Any curled or spiral band, as of smoke, snow, etc. [< OE *writha*] —**wreath·y** (rē′thē, -thē) *adj.*

**wreathe** (rēth) *v.* **wreathed**, **wreath·ing** *v.t.* 1 To form into a wreath, as by twisting or twining. 2 To adorn or encircle with or as with wreaths. 3 To envelop; cover: His face was *wreathed* in smiles. —*v.i.* 4 To take the form of a wreath. 5 To twist, turn, or coil, as masses of cloud.

**wreck** (rek) *v.t.* 1 To cause the destruction of, as by a collision. 2 To bring ruin, damage, or destruction upon. 3 To tear down, as a building; dismantle. —*v.i.* 4 To suffer destruction; be ruined. 5 To engage in wrecking, as for plunder or salvage. —*n.* 1 The act of wrecking, or the condition of being wrecked. 2 That which has been wrecked or ruined by accident, collision, etc. 3 The broken remnants or remains of something wrecked. 4 SHIPWRECK. 5 The ruined, usu. stranded hulk of a ship that has been wrecked. 6 A person who is ill or under great strain. [< AF *wrec* < Scand.]

**wreck·age** (rek′ij) *n.* 1 The act of wrecking, or the condition of being wrecked. 2 Broken remnants or fragments from a wreck.

**wren** (ren) *n.* 1 Any of numerous small, active, usu. brown birds having short rounded wings and tail and a thin, curved bill. 2 Any one of numerous similar birds. [< OE *wrenna*]

**wrench** (rench) *n.* 1 A violent twist. 2 A sprain or violent twist or pull in a part of the body. 3 A sudden surge of emotion, as of sorrow, pity, etc. 4 Any of various gripping tools for turning or twisting bolts, nuts, pipes, etc. —*v.t.* 1 To twist violently; turn suddenly by force. 2 To twist forcibly so as to cause

strain or injury; sprain. 3 To cause to suffer. 4 To twist from the proper meaning, intent, or use. —*v.i.* 5 To give a twist or wrench [< OE *wrencan* to wrench]

**wrest** (rest) *v.t.* 1 To pull or force away by violent twisting or wringing; wrench. 2 To turn from the true meaning, intent, etc.; distort. 3 To seize forcibly. 4 To gain or extract by great effort. —*n.* 1 An act of wresting. 2 A key for tuning a piano, harp, etc. [< OE *wrǣstan*] —**wrest′er** *n.*

**wres·tle** (res′əl) *v.* **·tled**, **·tling** *v.i.* 1 To engage in wrestling. 2 To struggle, as for mastery; contend. —*v.t.* 3 To contend with (someone) in wrestling. 4 To throw (a calf) and hold it down for branding. —*n.* 1 The act or an instance of wrestling. 2 A hard struggle. [< OE *wrǣstlian*] —**wres′tler** *n.*

**wretch** (rech) *n.* 1 A vile or contemptible person. 2 A miserable or unhappy person. [< OE *wrecca* an outcast]

**wretch·ed** (rech′id) *adj.* 1 Sunk in dejection; profoundly unhappy. 2 Causing or characterized by misery, poverty, etc. 3 Unsatisfactory in ability or quality. 4 Despicable; contemptible. —**wretch′ed·ly** *adv.* —**wretch′ed·ness** *n.* —Syn. 1 distressed, miserable. 3 bad, paltry, worthless.

**wrig·gle** (rig′əl) *v.* **·gled**, **·gling** *v.i.* 1 To twist in a sinuous manner; squirm; writhe. 2 To proceed as by twisting or crawling. 3 To make one's way by evasive or indirect means. —*v.t.* 4 To cause to wriggle. 5 To make (one's way, etc.) by evasive or sly means. —*n.* The act or motion of one who or that which wriggles. [<MLG *wriggeln*] —**wrig′gly** *adj.*

**wring** (ring) *v.* **wrung**, **wring·ing** *v.t.* 1 To squeeze or compress by twisting. 2 To squeeze or press out, as water, by twisting. 3 To acquire by forcible means. 4 To distress: Her plight *wrung* their hearts. 5 To twist violently: to *wring* his neck. —*v.i.* 6 To writhe or squirm with great effort. —*n.* A twisting or wringing. [< OE *wringan*]

**wrin·kle** (ring′kəl) *n.* 1 A small ridge, as on a smooth surface; a crease; fold. 2 A small fold or crease in the skin, usu. produced by age or by excessive exposure to the elements. —*v.* **·kled**, **·kling** *v.t.* 1 To make wrinkles in. —*v.i.* 2 To become wrinkled. [< OE *wrincle*] —**wrin′kly** *adj.*

**wrist** (rist) *n.* 1 The part of the arm that lies between the hand and the forearm; the carpus. 2 The part of a glove or garment that covers the wrist. [< OE]

**writ** (rit) *n.* 1 *Law* A written order, issued by

a court, and commanding the person to do or not to do some act. **2** That which is written: now chiefly in the phrase *Holy Writ,* the Bible. [< OE *writan* write]

**writhe** (rīth) *v.* **writhed, writh·ing** *v.t.* **1** To cause to twist or be distorted. —*v.i.* **2** To twist or distort the body, face, or limbs, as in pain. **3** To undergo suffering, as from embarrassment, sorrow, etc. —*n.* An act of writhing. [< OE *writhan*] —**writh′er** *n.*

**wrong** (rông) *adj.* **1** Not correct; mistaken. **2** Not appropriate: the *wrong* shoes for hiking. **3** Not morally or legally right. **4** Not in accordance with the correct or standard method: the *wrong* way to bake. **5** Not working or operating properly: What is *wrong* with the furnace? **6** Not meant to be seen, used, etc.: the *wrong* side of the fabric. **7** Not intended: a *wrong* turn. —**go wrong 1** To behave immorally. **2** To turn out badly; fail. **3** To take a wrong direction, etc. —*adv.* In a wrong direction, place, or manner; erroneously. —*n.* **1** That which is morally or socially wrong or unacceptable. **2** An injury or injustice. —**in the wrong** In error; wrong. —*v.t.* **1** To violate the rights of; inflict injury or injustice upon. **2** To impute evil to unjustly: You *wrong* him. **3** To seduce (a woman). **4** To treat dishonorably. [<Scand.] —**wrong′er, wrong′ness** *n.* —**wrong′ly** *adv.*

**wrong·ful** (rông′fəl) *adj.* **1** Characterized by wrong or injustice; injurious; unjust. **2** Unlawful; illegal. —**wrong′ful·ly** *adv.* —**wrong′ful·ness** *n.*

**wry** (rī) *adj.* **wri·er, wri·est 1** Bent to one side or out of position; contorted; askew. **2** Made by twisting or distorting the features: a *wry* smile. **3** Distorted or warped, as in interpretation or meaning. **4** Somewhat perverse or ironic: *wry* humor. —*v.t.* **wried, wry·ing** To twist; contort. [< OE *wrigian* move, tend] —**wry′ly** *adv.* —**wry′ness** *n.*

## X

**xe·rog·ra·phy** (zi·rog′rə·fē) *n.* A method of copying by which a colored powder is distributed by the action of light on an electrically charged plate to form a negative, which is then transferred thermally to a paper or other surface. [< Gk. *xēros* dry + -GRAPHY] —**xe·ro·graph·ic** (zir′ə·graf′ik) *adj.*

**Xmas** (kris′məs, eks′məs) *n.* CHRISTMAS. [< X, abbr. for *Christ* < Gk. X, chi, the first letter of *Christos* Christ + -MAS(s)]

**X-ray** (eks′rā′) *n.* **1** An electromagnetic radiation having a wavelength shorter than that of ultraviolet light and longer than that of a gamma ray. **2** A photograph made with X-rays. —*adj.* Of, made by, or producing X-rays. —*v.t.* **1** To examine, diagnose, or treat with X-rays. —*v.i.* **2** To use X-rays. **Also X ray.**

**xy·lo·phone** (zī′lə·fōn′) *n.* A musical instrument consisting of an array of wooden bars graduated in length to produce a scale, played by striking the bars with two small mallets. [< Gk. *xylon* wood + *phōnē* sound] —**xy′lo·phon′ist** *n.*

## Y

**yacht** (yot) *n.* Any of various relatively small sailing or motor-driven ships built or fitted for private pleasure excursions or racing. —*v.i.* To cruise, race, or sail in a yacht. [< Du. *jaghte,* short for *jaghtschip* a pursuit ship]

**yam** (yam) *n.* **1** The fleshy, edible, tuberous root of any of a genus of climbing tropical plants. **2** Any of the plants growing this root. **3** A variety of sweet potato. [< Pg. *inhame* < a native w African name]

**Yan·kee** (yang′kē) *n.* **1** A native or citizen of the U.S. **2** A native or inhabitant of the northern U.S. **3** A native or inhabitant of New England. —*adj.* Of, like, or characteristic of Yankees. [?] —**Yan′kee·dom, Yan′kee·ism** *n.*

**yard¹** (yärd) *n.* **1** A unit of length equal to 3 feet or 0.914 meter. **2** A long, slender spar set crosswise on a mast and used to support sails. [< OE *gierd* rod, yard measure]

**yard²** (yärd) *n.* **1** A plot of ground enclosed or set apart, as for some specific purpose: often in combination: *barnyard.* **2** The ground or lawn belonging and adjacent to a house, college, university, etc. **3** An enclosure used for building, selling, storing, etc.: often in combination: *shipyard; stockyard.* **4** An enclosure or piece of ground usu. adjacent to a railroad station, used for making up trains and for storage. —*v.t.* To put or collect into or as into a yard. [< OE *geard* an enclosure]

**yard·stick** (yärd′stik′) *n.* **1** A graduated measuring stick a yard in length. **2** Any measure or standard of comparison; criterion.

**yarn** (yärn) *n.* **1** Any spun fiber, as cotton, wool, or nylon, prepared for use in weaving, knitting, or crocheting. **2** *Informal* A tale of adventure, often of doubtful truth. —*v.i. Informal* To tell a yarn or yarns. [< OE *gearn*]

**yawn** (yôn) *v.i.* 1 To open the mouth wide, usu. involuntarily, with a full inhalation, as the result of drowsiness, boredom, etc. 2 To stand wide open: A chasm *yawned* below. —*v.t.* 3 To express or utter with a yawn. —*n.* 1 An act of yawning. 2 A wide opening. [< OE *geonian*] —**yawn′er** *n.*

**yea** (yā) *adv.* 1 Yes: used in voting orally. 2 *Archaic* Not only so, but more so. 3 *Archaic* In reality; verily: a form of introduction in a sentence. —*n.* 1 An affirmative vote. 2 One who casts such a vote. [< OE *gēa*]

**year** (yir) *n.* 1 The period of time in which the earth completes a revolution around the sun: about 365 days, 5 hours, 49 minutes, and, in the Gregorian calendar, divided into 12 months beginning January 1 and ending December 31. 2 Any period of 12 months. 3 The period of time during which a planet revolves around the sun. 4 Any part of a year devoted to some activity: the school *year.* 5 *pl.* Any extended or past period of time: the *years* before automobiles. 6 *pl.* Length or time of life; age: active for his *years.* [< OE *gēar*]

**year·ling** (yir′ling) *n.* An animal between one and two years old. —*adj.* Being a year old.

**year·ly** (yir′lē) *adj.* 1 Of a year. 2 Occurring once a year; annual. 3 Continuing for a year: a *yearly* subscription. —*adv.* Once a year; annually.

**yearn** (yûrn) *v.i.* 1 To desire something earnestly; long: with *for.* 2 To be deeply moved; feel sympathy. [< OE *giernan*] —**yearn′er** *n.* —**Syn.** 1 wish, want, covet, hunger, crave, pine for.

**yearn·ing** (yûr′ning) *n.* A strong emotion of longing or desire, esp. with tenderness.

**yeast** (yēst) *n.* 1 Any of various single-celled fungi that produce ethyl alcohol and carbon dioxide in the process of fermenting carbohydrates. 2 A commercial preparation of certain yeasts, usu. in dry powdery form, used to leaven bread, make beer, etc. 3 Froth or spume. 4 Something causing mental or moral ferment. —*v.i.* To foam; froth. [< OE *gist*]

**yell** (yel) *v.t. & v.i.* 1 To shout; scream. 2 To cheer. —*n.* 1 A sharp, loud cry, as of pain, terror, etc. 2 A rhythmic shout by a group, as in cheering an athletic team. [< OE *giellan*] —**yell′er** *n.*

**yel·low** (yel′ō) *adj.* 1 Of the color yellow. 2 Changed to a sallow color by age, sickness,

etc.: a paper *yellow* with age. 3 Having a yellowish or light brown complexion. 4 Cheaply or offensively sensational: said of newspapers: *yellow* journalism. 5 *Informal* Cowardly; mean; dishonorable. —*n.* 1 The color of ripe lemons or, in the spectrum, the color between green and orange. 2 Any pigment or dyestuff having such a color. 3 The yolk of an egg. —*v.t. & v.i.* To make or become yellow. [< OE *geolu*] —**yel′low·ly** *adv.* —**yel′low·ness** *n.*

**yelp** (yelp) *v.i.* To utter a sharp or shrill cry. —*v.t.* To express by a yelp or yelps. —*n.* A sharp, shrill cry, as of a dog in distress. [< OE *gielpan* boast] —**yelp′er** *n.*

**yen**[1] (yen) *Informal n.* An ardent longing or desire. —*v.i.* yenned, yen·ning To yearn; long. [< Chin., opium]

**yen**[2] (yen) *n.* The basic monetary unit of Japan.

**yeo·man** (yō′mən) *n. pl.* ·men (-mən) 1 A petty officer in the U.S. Navy or Coast Guard who performs clerical duties. 2 *Brit.* A farmer, esp. one who cultivates his own farm. 3 YEOMAN OF THE GUARD. 4 *Brit.* One of the attendants of a nobleman or of royalty. [? < OE *geong* young + *mann* a man]

**yes·ter·day** (yes′tər-dē, -dā′) *n.* 1 The day preceding today. 2 The near past. —*adv.* 1 On the day last past. 2 At a recent time. [< OE *geostran* yesterday + *dœg* day]

**yew** (yōō) *n.* 1 Any of a genus of evergreen trees and shrubs, with narrow, flat, dark green, poisonous leaves and red berrylike cones containing a single seed. 2 The hard, tough wood of the yew. [< OE *ēow, īw*]

**yield** (yēld) *v.t.* 1 To give forth by a natural process, or as a result of labor or cultivation: The field will *yield* a good crop. 2 To give in return, as for investment; furnish: The bonds *yield* five percent interest. 3 To give up, as to superior power; surrender; relinquish: often with *up*: to *yield* oneself up to one's enemies. 4 To give up one's possession of: to *yield* the right of way. —*v.i.* 5 To provide a return; produce; bear. 6 To give up; submit; surrender. 7 To give way, as to pressure or force. 8 To assent or comply, as under compulsion; consent: We *yielded* to their persuasion. 9 To give place, as through inferiority or weakness: with *to*: We will *yield* to them in nothing. —*n.* The amount yielded; product; result, as of cultivation, investment, etc. [< OE *gieldan* pay] —**yield′er** *n.*

**yo·del** (yōd′l) *v.t. & v.i.* ·deled or ·delled, ·del·ing or ·del·ling To sing by changing the voice quickly from its low register to a falsetto and back. —*n.* Something yodeled, as a melody or refrain. Also **yo′dle.** [< G *jodeln,* lit., utter the syllable *jo*] —**yo′del·er, yo′del·ler, yo′dler** *n.*

**yoke** (yōk) *n.* **1** A curved frame used for coupling draft animals, as oxen, usu. having a bow at each end to receive the neck of the animal. **2** Any of many similar contrivances, as a frame worn on the shoulder to balance pails of milk. **3** A pair of animals joined by a yoke. **4** Something that binds or connects; tie; bond: the *yoke* of marriage. **5** Any of various parts or pieces that connect or hold two things together. **6** Servitude; bondage. **7** A fitted part of a garment designed to support a plaited or gathered part, as at the hips or shoulders. —*v.* **yoked, yok·ing** *v.t.* **1** To attach by means of a yoke, as draft animals. **2** To join with or as with a yoke. —*v.i.* **3** To be joined or linked; unite. [< OE *geoc*]

**yolk** (yōk, yōlk) *n.* **1** The yellow portion of an egg. **2** An oily exudation in unprocessed sheep's wool. [< OE *geolu* yellow] —**yolk′y** *adj.*

**yon** (yon) *adj. & adv.* Archaic & Regional YONDER. [< OE *geon*]

**yon·der** (yon′dər) *adj.* Being at a distance indicated or known. —*adv.* In that place; there. [< OE *geond,* yond]

**yore** (yôr, yōr) *n.* Time long past: in days of *yore.* [< OE *geara* formerly]

**young** (yung) *adj.* **young·er** (yung′gər), **young·est** (yung′gist) **1** Being in the early period of life or growth; not old. **2** Not having progressed or developed far; newly formed: The day was *young.* **3** Pertaining to youth or early life. **4** Full of vigor or freshness. **5** Inexperienced; immature. **6** Denoting the younger of two persons having the same name or title; junior. **7** Geol. Having the characteristics of an early stage in the geological cycle: said of a river or of certain land forms. —*n.* **1** Young persons as a group. **2** Offspring, esp. of animals. —**with young** Pregnant. [< OE *geong*] —**young′ness** *n.* — **Syn. 1** lively, strong, active, spirited. **5** raw, green, unseasoned, uninitiated.

**youth** (yōōth) *n. pl.* **youths** (yōōths, yōōt͟hz) **1** The state or condition of being young. **2** The period when one is young; that part of life between childhood and adulthood. **3** The early period of being or development, as of a movement. **4** A young person, esp.

a young man. **5** Young people as a group: the nation's *youth.* [< OE *geoguth*]

**Yule** (yōōl) *n.* Christmas or Christmas time. [< OE *geōl*]

**yule log** Formerly, a large log, place on the hearth as the foundation of the traditional Christmas Eve fire.

# Z

**za·ny** (zā′nē) *adj.* **·ni·er, ·ni·est** Absurdly funny; ludicrous. —*n. pl.* **·nies 1** In old comic plays, a clown who absurdly mimics the other performers. **2** Any ludicrous comic or buffoon. **3** A simpleton; fool. [< Ital. *zanni*] —**za′ni·ly** *adv.* —**za′ni·ness** *n.*

**zeal** (zēl) *n.* Ardor, as for a cause; fervor. [< Gk. *zēlos*] —**Syn.** enthusiasm, eagerness, devotion, passion, verve, spirit, heart.

**zeal·ot** (zel′ət) *n.* One who is zealous, esp. to an immoderate degree; partisan, fanatic, etc. —**zeal′ot·ry** *n.*

**zeal·ous** (zel′əs) *adj.* Filled with, marked by, or showing zeal; enthusiastic. —**zeal′ ous· ly** *adv.* —**zeal′ous·ness** *n.*

**ze·bra** (zē′brə, Brit. & Can. zeb′rə) *n.* Any of various African ponylike mammals having a whitish body with dark stripes. [Pg.] — **ze′brine** (-brēn, -brin), **ze′broid** (-broid) *adj.*

**ze·nith** (zē′nith) *n.* **1** The point of the celestial sphere that is exactly overhead. **2** The highest or culminating point; summit; acme. [< Ar. *samt (ar-rās)* the path (over the head)]

**zeph·yr** (zef′ər) *n.* **1** The west wind. **2** Any soft, gentle wind. **3** Worsted or woolen yarn of very light weight: also **zephyr worsted.** [< Gk. *zephyros*]

**ze·ro** (zir′ō, zē′rō) *n. pl.* **ze·ros** or **ze·roes 1** The numeral or symbol 0; a cipher. **2** *Math.* The element of a number system that leaves any element unchanged under addition, esp. a real number $0$ such that $a + 0 = 0 + a = a$ for any real number $a$. **3** The point on a scale, as of a thermometer, from which measures are counted. **4** The temperature registered at the zero mark on a thermometer. **5** Nothing. **6** The lowest point: Our hopes dropped to *zero.* —*v.t.* **ze·roed, ze·ro·ing** To adjust (instruments) to an arbitrary zero point for synchronized readings. —**zero in 1** To move or bring into a desired position, as an airplane. **2** To adjust the sight of (a gun) or direct (ammunition) toward (a target). —**zero in on 1** To direct gunfire, bombs, etc. toward (a specific target). **2** To concentrate or focus one's energy, attention, efforts, etc., on. —*adj.* 1 Of, at, or being zero. 2 That limits vertical visibility to 50 feet or less: said of a cloud ceiling. 3 That limits horizontal visibility to 165 feet or less: said of conditions on the ground. [< Ar. *ṣifr*] In popular usage the symbol for zero (0) is often rendered orally as (ō), as if it were the letter O.

**zest** (zest) *n.* 1 Agreeable excitement and keen enjoyment. 2 A quality that imparts such excitement. 3 Any piquant flavoring. [< F *zeste* lemon or orange peel] —**zest′ful, zest′y** *adj.* (·i·er, ·i·est) —**zest′ful·ly** *adv.* —**zest′ful·ness** *n.* —**Syn.** 1 Delight, gusto, relish, pleasure, gratification, savor, thrill, kick.

**zig·zag** (zig′zag) *n.* 1 One of a series of sharp turns or angles. 2 A path or pattern characterized by such turns or angles going from side to side. —*adj.* Having a series of zigzags. —*adv.* In a zigzag manner. —*v.t.* & *v.i.* ·**zagged**, ·**zag·ging** To move in zigzags. [< G *zickzack*]

**zinc** (zingk) *n.* A bluish white metallic element (symbol Zn) occurring mostly in combination, extensively used in alloys, as bronze and brass, for galvanizing, and in electric batteries. —*v.t.* **zinced** or **zincked, zinc·ing** or **zinck·ing** To coat or cover with zinc; galvanize. [< G *zink*] —**zinc′ic** (-ik), **zinc′ous** (-əs), **zinck′y, zinc′y, zink′y** *adj.*

**zip-code** (zip′kōd′) *v.t.* ·**cod·ed**, ·**cod·ing** *Sometimes cap.* To provide (mail) with a zip code.

**zith·er** (zith′ər, zith′-) *n.* A stringed instrument having a flat sounding board and 30 to 40 strings that are played by plucking. Also **zith′ern** (-ərn). [< Gk. *kithara*]

**zo·di·ac** (zō′dē·ak) *n.* 1 An imaginary belt encircling the heavens and extending about 8° on each side of the ecliptic, within which are the orbits of the moon, sun, and larger planets. It is divided into twelve parts, called **signs of the zodiac**, which formerly corresponded to twelve constellations. 2 Any complete circuit; round. [< Gk. *(kyklos) zōdiakos* (circle) of animals] —**zo·di·a·cal** (zō·dī′ə·kəl) *adj.*

**zone** (zōn) *n.* 1 One of five divisions of the earth's surface, bounded by parallels of latitude and named for the prevailing climate. These are the **torrid zone**, extending on each side of the equator 23° 27′; the **temperate** or **variable zones**, included between the parallels 23° 27′ and 66° 33′ on both sides of the equator; and the **frigid zones**, within the parallels 66° 33′ and the poles. 2 *Ecol.* A belt or area delimited from others

by the character of its plant or animal life, its climate, geological formations, etc. 3 A region, area, belt, etc., distinguished or set off by some special characteristic: a demilitarized *zone;* a residential *zone;* a no-parking *zone.* 4 An area, usu. circular, within which a uniform rate is charged for delivery of goods, telephone calls, etc. 5 In the U.S. postal system: a Any of the areas within which a uniform rate is charged for parcel post. b Any of the numbered postal districts in a city. 6 *Geom.* A portion of the surface of a sphere enclosed between two parallel planes. —*v.t.* **zoned, zon·ing** 1 To divide into zones; esp., to divide (a city, etc.) into zones which are restricted as to types of construction and activity, as residential, industrial, etc. 2 To encircle with a zone or belt. 3 To mark with or as with zones or stripes. [< Gk. *zōnē* a girdle] —**zoned** *adj.*

**zoo** (zōō) *n. pl.* **zoos** A park or place where wild animals are kept for exhibition. [Short for *zoological garden*]

**zoo-** *combining form* Animal: *zoology.* [< Gk. *zōion* an animal]

**zo·o·log·i·cal** (zō′ə·loj′i·kəl) *adj.* 1 Of, pertaining to, or occupied with zoology. 2 Relating to or characteristic of animals. Also **zo′o·log′ic.** —**zo′o·log′i·cal·ly** *adv.*

**zo·ol·o·gy** (zō·ol′ə·jē) *n.* 1 The science that treats of animals with reference to their structure, functions, development, nomenclature, and classification. 2 The animal life of a particular area. 3 A scientific treatise on animals. [< ZOO- + -LOGY] —**zo·ol′o·gist** *n.*

**zoom** (zōōm) *v.i.* 1 To make a low-pitched but loud humming or buzzing sound, esp. when related to speed: The cars *zoomed* down the road. 2 To climb sharply upward, as an airplane. 3 To rise sharply, as prices. 4 To move a motion picture or TV camera rapidly or adjust the focus, as with a zoom lens, to make an image appear to come very close or become more distant: often with *in* or *out.* —*v.t.* 5 To cause to zoom. —*n.* The act of zooming. [Imit.]

**zuc·chi·ni** (zōō·kē′nē) *n.* An elongated summer squash having a thin green skin. [< Ital. *zucca* a gourd, squash]

**zy·mol·o·gy** (zī·mol′ə·jē) *n.* The science of fermentation. [< Gk. *zymē* leaven + -LOGY] —**zy·mo·log·ic** (zī′mə·loj′ik) or ·**i·cal** *adj.* —**zy·mol′o·gist** *n.*

**zy·mot·ic** (zī·mot′ik) *adj.* Of, pertaining to, or caused by fermentation. [< Gk. *zymōtikos*]